CW01085350

Eboracum

You are holding a reproduction of an original work that is in the public domain in the United States of America, and possibly other countries.You may freely copy and distribute this work as no entity (individual or corporate) has a copyright on the body of the work.This book may contain prior copyright references, and library stamps (as most of these works were scanned from library copies).These have been scanned and retained as part of the historical artifact.

This book may have occasional imperfections such as missing or blurred pages, poor pictures, errant marks, etc. that were either part of the original artifact, or were introduced by the scanning process. We believe this work is culturally important, and despite the imperfections, have elected to bring it back into print as part of our continuing commitment to the preservation of printed works worldwide. We appreciate your understanding of the imperfections in the preservation process, and hope you enjoy this valuable book.

EBORACUM:

OR THE

HISTORY

AND

ANTIQUITIES

OF THE

CITY of *YORK*,

From its ORIGINAL to the PRESENT TIMES.

Together with the

History of the CATHEDRAL CHURCH,

AND THE

LIVES of the ARCHBISHOPS of that SEE,

From the first Introduction of CHRISTIANITY into the Northern Parts of this ISLAND, to the present State and Condition of that MAGNIFICENT FABRICK.

Collected from Authentick Manuscripts, Publick Records, Ancient Chronicles, and Modern Historians.

And illustrated with COPPER PLATES.

In Two BOOKS.

ASTOR LIBRARY NEW-YORK

By *FRANCIS DRAKE*, of the CITY of *YORK*, Gent.
F. R. S. and Member of the SOCIETY of *Antiquaries* in *London*.

Nec manet ut fuerat, nec formam servat eandem,
Sed tamen ipsa eadem est. OVID. MET. Lib. XV.

LONDON,
Printed by WILLIAM BOWYER for the AUTHOR. MDCCXXXVI.

L4

H46.4

TO THE

RIGHT HONOURABLE

Sir *RICHARD BOYLE*,

Earl of BURLINGTON,

Earl of Corke, Viſcount Dungarvon and Kynalmachy in *Ireland*,

Baron *Clifford* of *Londesburgh*,

AND

Knight of the moſt noble Order of the GARTER.

My LORD,

THE author of this work preſents it to your patronage, as to a perſon every way qualified for an addreſs of this nature. For, where ſhould the hiſtory of an ancient

ancient *Roman* city, in *Britain*, find greater favour, or meet with a better reception, than from a nobleman, whoſe particular genius, almoſt, ſpeaks him of *Roman* extraction?

DEDICATIONS, my Lord, are in our days ſo commonly proſtituted to venal purpoſes, that, they look more like humble petitions for charity than proper addreſſes. Beſides, the patron's genius or taſte is rarely conſulted in this ſort of application.—— I hope I am free from any imputation of that kind. The ſtrong relation, and attachment, your Lordſhip bears to the noble ſubject I have choſen, calls loudly for this publick declaration of it.

THE illuſtrious name of CLIFFORD, the blood of which noble houſe now runs in your veins, for many ages, has been familiar to *York*. Nor, is the name of BOYLE a ſtranger to our records; your Lordſhip's great grandfather, the then earl of *Burlington*, having done this city an extraordinary honour in bearing the office of its recorder. —— Beſides, I can with pleaſure ſay, the places of your Lordſhip's *Engliſh* titles make no ſmall figure in this very hiſtory; having been, indubitably, one of them a *Roman port*; and, the other, your paternal and favourite ſeat, a *Roman ſtation* in our neighbourhood.

FOR

For yourſelf, beſides the title of governour of *York*, and its peculiar diſtrict the *Ainſty*, which you have born; you have ſtill a much nearer affinity to it, by accepting of a *diploma* for a free citizen in that body. And, when I mention the noble edifice, deſigned and finiſhed under your particular care and direction, not to ſpeak of your generous and liberal donations to it, I muſt farther ſay that it will be a laſting monument of the great regard and value you pay to this ancient city. For *York*, by your means, is now poſſeſſed of a ſtructure, in a truer and nobler taſte of architecture, than, in all probability, the *Roman* Eboracum could ever boaſt of. Your Lordſhip's great knowledge in this art, ſoars up to the *Auguſtan* age and ſtyle; and, that *Pretorian* palace, once in old Eboracum, made ever memorable for the reſidence and deaths of two *Roman* emperors, and, in all likelihood, for the birth of a third, muſt, if now ſtanding, have given place to your *Egyptian* hall in our preſent *York*.

Your Lordſhip's taſte in hiſtory and antiquities, as well as in the liberal arts and ſciences, is too well known to need any comment. And, when I inform the world that I have your permiſſion to addreſs this work to you, I dare ſay that I ſhall readily be believed. You did me the honour to ſee and approve of my firſt

a draught,

draught, or ſcheme of this great work. A noble deſign, though drawn by your Lordſhip, may be ill executed. Yet, howſoever mean this performance may be found, the ſubject it treats of muſt be allowed worthy the patronage of the *Earl of* BURLINGTON.

MY LORD,

YOUR other ſhining characteriſticks in life are now before me. But, to the preſent age it would be ſaying nothing to tell what every one is acquainted with. And, ſhould I pretend to ſpeak to futurity, your own pencil, and the works proceeding from it, will leave nobler proofs of your exalted genius than my poor pen can draw. Yet, give me leave to ſpeak to you, as the poet did of old, to another truly noble patron, *Dii tibi divitias dederint*, and, what is, by far, the greater bleſſing, ARTEM FRUENDI. For, if the right uſe of riches conſiſts in the exerciſe of all moral, ſocial, and beneficent virtues to our fellow creatures, both equal and inferiour to us in fortune; if, along with titles, honours, and eſtates, we meet with humanity, good nature, and affability to all mankind; and if we find riches laid out in a delicacy of taſte, ſuperiour to any thing ſeen before in this Iſland; then, we may, ſurely, pronounce the perſon ſo bleſſed, every way *qualified to enjoy them*.

THAT

DEDICATION.

THAT your Lordship may long continue, what you now really are, a singular ornament to this country, is the hearty and sincere wish of

My LORD,

Your Lordship's

Most obedient, and

Most obliged

Humble Servant,

London, August 1,
1736.

FRANCIS DRAKE.

	l.	*s.*	*d.*
THE Number of Sheets proposed for this WORK was 125, besides Copper Plates, at two Guineas,	2	2	0
The Work being encreased to 200 Sheets and a half, the additional 75 Sheets and a half at 2 *d. per* Sheet, according to the Proposals, amount to —— ——	0	12	7
Total for each Book in small Paper	2	14	7

The Price of the large is double the small Paper.

N.B. The Author, notwithstanding the Expence he has been at in engraving a much greater Number of Copper Plates than was at first proposed, is willing to reduce the Price to two Guineas and a half for the small Paper, and five Guineas for the large, to his SUBSCRIBERS.

THE
PREFACE.

A Preface to a book is so fashionable and so particular an ornament to it, that without one, or at least an introduction, the work would look like a new built house, to which the architect had made no entrance. But, though this, many times necessary exordium, *to a book, must, according to its title, precede the contents of it; yet it is generally the last thing the author puts his hand to, of the whole performance. I own that I am sorry I can no way avoid such a preamble; there being many and strong reasons to urge me to it; else I should, willingly, beg to be excused; the itch of scribbling, with me, having been sufficiently abated by what I have already gone through. Besides, as I declare, I hardly, myself, ever read a preface in my life, I can scarcely expect that any other person should ever take the pains to read mine. Yet, as there may be several that wait for and will take more notice of this preceding than of its consequential part, to such I address myself; and shall declare the reasons, just mentioned, in as brief a manner as the nature of the subject will bear, or the pen of a tired writer will necessarily induce him to.*

First, I think it proper to give some account to the publick what were the motives that put me upon writing on a subject so very foreign to the profession I was brought up in; but those being somewhat unaccountable, I shall not waste much time in the disquisition. I shall only say, that, being bred a surgeon, and, possibly, allowed some share of knowledge in my profession, yet History *and* Antiquity *were always, from a child, my chiefest tast; nor could I stifle a* genius, *which as I take it was born with me, without being a kind of a* Felo de se, *which I should not care to be guilty of. I take it, there are now, almost, as many books published on the cure of the body as there are of the soul; and the practice of the former, both externally and internally, is made so evident and clear, by them, to the meanest capacity, that in reading a common* Dispensatory *only, we may imagine that no body has occasion to dye; and we are now every day assured, in publick* Advertisements, *that the blind shall see, the deaf hear, the dumb talk, and the lame throw away their crutches by the slightest and most insignificant applications and remedies. In an age like this, when art is brought to such a perfection as even to work miracles upon nature, I should be highly presumptuous to pretend to exceed. Besides, I am rather a sceptick in the matter, and have so much of the* Antiquarian *in me that I cannot help thinking that the art of physick was as well known, except in one or two specificks, two thousand years ago as it is now; and that the divine* Hippocrates *saw as far into a diseased human system, and knew as well how to restore it, as the clearest sighted physician of this age. And, should I put pen to paper for my life, in my own way, I am sensible I could not outdo what has been wrote many centuries since by* Celsus, Fallopius, *the two* Fabritii, &c. *on the chyrurgical art, and what the last age has produced on that noble and salutary subject.*

Under a diffidence like this, and, as I said, being naturally inclined to it, I have turned my skill a quite different way; and have endeavoured to revive the memory of a decayed city, at present the second in Britain, *but of old the first, and in antiquity, the glory of the whole* Island. *How I have succeeded, the following voluminous tract will shew; I judge, if I know any thing more particular than the rest of mankind, it is on this subject and in this way. The many unexpected lights which I have met with, in such a dark and intricate passage, deserve laying open to the publick; and I only wish that my ability was greater that I might expose them as*

 they

they ought to be. My acquaintance and correspondents all know me to be communicative enough, both in epistolary and common conversation; having been ever of the same mind with old Persius, *in this, that*

Scire tuum nihil est, nisi te scire hoc sciat alter.

Having premised thus much, I think it further proper to say something on the nature of the subject I have chosen, and to point out who they were who have gone before me in this tract, and from whom my collections have been any ways bettered or enriched. I apprehend the history of any very remarkable ancient city, or peculiar county in Britain, *is enough to exercise the genius of the ablest historian or antiquary. And yet I am well aware that the history of any particular place, or local history, meets with no such encouragement from the world as the more general historians are honoured with. We have an instance before our eyes of an history of* England *taking a prodigious run; and making its way, at no small expence to the buyers, almost, into every family in the kingdom. And, will in time be as much engrafted there, made familiar, and had in as great regard as the old family* Bible. *Whilst such an history as mine is must lag behind, be raised by the heavy method of* subscription, *thrust into the press and dragged through it by all the force and strength that the author, or his friends, can apply to the engine. This discouragement from the publick does not in the least abate in me a value for local histories. We all know that the history of a hero or warrior, of a statesman, and sometimes, even, of a private person is frequently full of uncommon events or accidents; though deduced down in no longer a series than the short course of human life. By how much more therefore must the history of such a city as this exceed in matter, could we, as in the former case, as clearly discern it through a series of so many revolutions of things and persons in the course of so many ages? And yet, after all, I must own that to a person who is not a tolerable master of general history, this particular one will be found to have less salt, be tastless to him, or unintelligible.*

Mr Camden. *To mention the writers who have gone before me on this subject, I shall here take notice of few or none, in a general way, but, that honour to our country, the great Mr.* Camden. *And, indeed, the city of* York *is much indebted to the memory of that able historian and antiquary for the clear and succinct account he has left us of it. As he seems pleased with the subject, so he has done it a great deal of justice; and, considering the extensiveness of his whole design,* York *has as great a share in his work as* London *itself; which I am sure is no small compliment to our city. His learned translator and continuator, the present bishop of* London, *says, that he has little to add to so particular an account as the historian has given; and only wishes "that this ancient and noble city may yet receive a clearer lustre from a "manuscript history of its antiquities wrote by sir* Thomas Widdrington, *sometime "recorder of* York, *which upon some disgust he prohibited the publication of." The learned writer adds, that the original manuscript is now in the* Fairfax *family. What other general historians I have been indebted to, are all mentioned in the body of the work, as the several quotations are made from them.*

Sir Thomas Widdrington. *And now, since sir* Thomas Widdrington*'s name is on the carpet, I must first own my obligations to that gentleman, who was the first, that I know of, who undertook to write in a particular way the history of this city. The great and strange scenes of life sir* Thomas *run through is not so much my province to write of; who will, may meet with some account of this gentleman in* Anthony Wood*'s* Atheniæ Oxonienses, *and in a late octavo book published under the title of the life and death of* Oliver Cromwell. *This writer in all probability began to make his collections for his history in king* Charles *the first's time, when he was recorder of* York. *For in a speech to that monarch, at his coming to the city, in the year 1639, he pays a strained compliment to the king of* its being more honoured by his having been duke of *York,* than by the residence and deaths of emperors*, *which shews that he had then read something of the antiquities of it. The civil wars intervening, in which our author could not be unconcerned, his history seems only to be finished in the* Halcyon *days, for his party, that ensued. And it must be after the* Restoration *that he sent the city word he intended to print and dedicate his elaborate performance to them. I presume he sent them al-*

* See the speech, p. 136.

print

ſo a copy of what he intended to ſay to the magiſtracy, whom he propoſed to addreſs it to; elſe the anſwer, which is ſmart enough, could not have retorted ſo ſtrongly upon it. This rebuff, we are told, was the reaſon, though he did not, as ſir* Walter Rawleigh *is ſaid to do, burn his manuſcript, that a prohibition was laid upon his deſcendants ever to publiſh it. I cannot atteſt the truth of this, which, if ſo, in all probability might be found in his will, now in the prerogative-office of* Canterbury; *but the circumſtance is not ſo material to me as to occaſion the trouble of a ſearch for it. Sir* Thomas *had married a ſiſter of lord* Thomas Fairfax, *and left behind him four daughters, all well beſtowed in marriage to as many conſiderable families in this kingdom. By which former alliance and the great reſpect he bore to the lord* Fairfax, *it is very poſſible that he gave or left the original manuſcript to that noble lord. Two copies of which are, as I am informed, one of them in the* Fairfax *of* Menſton *family; and the other in that of* Shaftoe *of the biſhoprick of* Durham; *which laſt had married one of ſir* Thomas Widdrington's *daughters. I ſay, I am informed, becauſe I never could get a ſight of either copy; though I once took great pains to procure the favour. That in the* Fairfax *family being kept* ſub ſigillo; *as biſhop* Nicholſon *rightly expreſſes it in his* Engliſh *hiſtorical library. I was leſs anxious about the matter, when, by the indulgence of the city, an order was made to ſuffer me to inſpect their records, and copy what I pleaſed for my book. By this means another copy of this noted manuſcript of ſir* Thomas's *fell into my hands. How, or when, the city procured it, I cannot ſay; but I know it to be a true one, though the ignorance of the tranſcriber, in the* Latin *tongue, ſuffered him to make ſeveral miſtakes in copying that language. How I came to be certain that this is a true copy was by an accident that I never expected to meet with, and is this. The reverend Dr.* Vernon *of St.* George's Bloomſbury *hearing of my deſign, ſince I came to* London, *informed Mr.* Gyles *the bookſeller, one of the perſons mentioned in my propoſals to take in ſubſcriptions for me, of a manuſcript in the hands of ſir* Robert Smyth *of* Bury *in* Suffolk, *Bart. which he ſaid related to the hiſtory and antiquities of* York. *I was ſurprized at this, when it was told me; thinking I had then ſeen every thing of that kind which it was poſſible for me to get at. Upon application to the doctor he was ſo good as to procure me the loan of the manuſcript; but I was much more ſurprized to find it ſir* Thomas Widdrington's *work; and what is yet more extraordinary, I dare aver that this is the very* original *which he himſelf intended for the preſs. The reaſon which makes me ſo poſitive in it, is, that though this manuſcript was wrote by ſome* amanuenſis, *yet it is interlined and noted in the margin by his own hand in many places; ſeveral things, and thoſe expreſſions chiefly which bore any thing hard upon the church or monarchy, are ſtruck out and expunged. Of which I could give from the manuſcript many inſtances were it neceſſary to do it. At the head of an* appendix *to the book is this note on the margin,* I purpoſe not to add this appendix to the book when it is printed; in regard the appendix is imperfect. *There are other references and notes put in by the author, which ſhew, moſt evidently, that this was the very book which he himſelf dreſſed up and put the laſt hand to for the preſs. On the title page of the copy in the city's cuſtody is a remark made that the author did expunge ſeveral things from his manuſcript, as the reader will ſee at* p. lxxxiv. *of my* appendix, *where I have cauſed the title, his dedication, and the city's anſwer to be all printed together. And there it is ſaid to be in the poſſeſſion of the lord* Fairfax. *If this was* Thomas *lord* Fairfax, *his effects, library, &c. were all ſold and diſperſed at his death; ſo that this manuſcript might come, at laſt, into the hands of ſo diligent a collector as the late Mr.* Richardſon *apothecary in* London. *Sir* Robert Smyth *bought it at Mr.* Oſborn's *ſale of that gentleman's library, about a year or two ago; which is all the intelligence I could learn about it.*

After what I have thought neceſſary here to ſay, it may eaſily be believed that I have had all the aſſiſtance which the hiſtory of this city wrote by ſir Thomas Widdrington *could give me. It is true, I have not followed his method, becauſe I did not approve of it; for which reaſon what I have thought fit to extract from him lyes mixed and interſperſed with mine, and others, throughout the whole performance. But I am poſitive that I have not made uſe of one quotation from this work without a ſir* T. W. *to it; either in the body of my work, or in a marginal note.*

* See the dedication and anſwer at page lxxxiv. and lxxxv of the *appendix*

Sir

Sir Thomas, as I have said, finished his history about the year 1659, or 60; as by several things in his book may be shewn; particularly his mentioning Mrs. Middleton's hospital in Skeldergate, which was built and endowed the same years. This gentleman had been then a long while recorder of the city; by which means he had liberty to inspect the records and extract what he wanted for his use. This, with his own skill in his profession, in which I have heard he was very eminent, made him very capable to write the law part of his history; and indeed it is that part I am the most indebted to him for. Though what I have given on that head is not all, nor near all, taken from his collections. Sir Thomas was returned and sat in the Long Parliament for the town of Berwick; but in that memorable Convention, which put the staff of the protectorship into Cromwell's hands, and would, if he had desired it, have set the crown on his head, he served for the city of York. He was chosen speaker of this meeting, and in a most solemn and religious form, and with a set speech to the purpose, invested his highness with his robes and honours. It was at this time that, being in great power and favour, he might have done much more profitable things for the city than writing a history of it. Yet I do not find any thing attempted by him in that way. This must disgust his fellow citizens, and they seemed only to wait a fair opportunity to tell him as much of it. In the first parliament at the Restoration sir Thomas was again returned for this city; but I suppose his interest here sunk very soon after, for he lost his seat the next, and threw up his recordership the same year, viz. 1661. It was about this time, no doubt, that the letter was sent him relating to the publication of his book; which, though anonymous, he must needs know from whence it came, and by whose direction it was wrote. The sting in the tail of it sufficiently shews their resentment against him; by pointing out to him their wants, which he must have been acquainted with, and, probably, might have remedied in the height of his power.

Thus much I have thought fit to say relating to sir Thomas Widdrington and his manuscript history of York. I could not well say less on a predecessor of such uncommon merit and eminence. And I should have been thought very lame and defective, in my own account, if I could not have assured the publick, in this manner, that the original, or a true copy of that manuscript, had passed my hands. What remains, is only to recommend it to the present proprietors of the other copies that they would print it; since one of them has been offered to sale, and since no injunction from the author obliges them now to the contrary. The world would then judge whether what I have alledged in this matter is true or not; and whether I have not done justice in this work to the memory of sir Thomas Widdrington.

Mr. Dodsworth.

During the time the former author was compiling his particular history of York, the most industrious Mr. Dodsworth was collecting and transcribing his many voluminous tracts, of ecclesiastical and monastical antiquities, which now enrich the Bodleyan library at Oxford. One volume of these collections he designed should be called Monasticon Boreale *; being particularly intended for York, and the old Northumbrian division. At the publication of Mr. Dodsworth's transcripts, sir William Dugdale altered this method; but they stand so in his own manuscripts at Oxford. I just mention this indefatigable collector, because I have been indebted to him for many useful instruments in my ecclesiastical part, and so must every historian else, that pretends to write on this subject, or a more general account of the church or diocese of York. Besides, Mr. Dodsworth was almost a native of this city, being born in our neighbourhood †; and his father was register to our ecclesiastical courts. Nor must the famous Tower be forgot in which that great magazine of antiquities was deposited; and from which he had just made his transcripts when the tower and they were blown up by the rebel Scots and made one heap of ruins.

Christopher Hildyard, Esq;

The next which falls in my way (to mention small things with great) is Christopher Hildyard Esq; of an ancient family in this county, recorder of Heddon, and steward of St. Mary's court at York. This gentleman, more out of zeal to the subject, and to assist a more general historian, than any ostentation of his own, pub-

* Catal. libror. MSS. in Anglia, &c. 4119. vol. VII, VIII, IX. Oxon.

† The Account he gives of himself in the aforesaid manuscripts is this: "Roger Dodsworth born July 24, 1585. "at Newton Grange in the parish of St. Oswald in Rydale in the house of Ralph Sandwith Esq; father of Elenor wife to "Mat. Dodsworth Esq, my father." Catal. ut supra 5032 ex vol XCIX. This Newton-Grange near Helmsley Yorkshire is now bought and annexed to the great lordship of Helmsley, being part of the possessions of Thomas Duncombe Esq;

lished

lished a pretty exact catalogue of our mayors and sheriffs from anno 1273 *to* 1664 *. *In this are some historical remarks interspersed, but very thinly; his preface containing more of the antiquities of* York *than his whole book. The late industrious Mr.* Torre, *whom I shall enlarge upon in the sequel, copied this printed book, as he has done several more, which he thought scarce, and with some additions of his own, taken from* Camden *and others; it precedes his ecclesiastical account of the city of* York, *in that volume of his manuscripts which contain them. A copy of this, or the original transcript, was given by the collector, or otherways fell into hands of the late Mr.* Francis Hildyard *bookseller; who dressed it up for the press, with a pompous title page, and, too injudiciously, put Mr.* Torre's *name to it. It were to be wished Mr.* Hildyard *had informed the publick, that this was only a copy of his name-sake's printed book, since he must know it, and only a few extracts added by Mr.* Torre; *it would have prevented some peevish advertisements,* pro *and* con, *betwixt the son of our great collector and the bookseller. How this necessary preface came to be omitted in the book I know not; Mr.* Hildyard, *for the course of many years, bore a very fair character in his business; and I cannot suspect him to have done it with any design; especially, when such a declaration would rather have cleared up than obstructed the matter on all sides. By this mistake I am obliged to say, in order to vindicate the memory of a person to whose labours this work of mine is so greatly indebted, that a* lean † catalogue *as bishop* Nicholson, *justly calls it, of our mayors, and sheriffs,* &c. *published long ago by another hand, is crept into the world again under the title of the* ANTIQUITIES OF YORK CITY, *&c. with the name of* JAMES TORRE, *gent. as author prefixed to it* ‡.

Following the course of this last book has led me out of my road, and I must go back to give an account of an author, some of whose collections, intended for a history of York, *have also accidentally fallen into my hands. This was* Henry Keep *author of the* Monumenta Westmonasteriensia ‖; *who had taken some pains to collect materials, also, for a history of this church and city. What occasioned this stranger to come down to* York, *for this purpose I know not. But, probably, it was to get money by it, though his design with us went further than* a bundle of epitaphs *as his* Westminster-book *is rightly called. Some account of this writer may be met with in* Anthony Wood, *and in bishop* Nicholson. *It seems he turned* Papist *in king* James *the second's time, and falling to decay soon after the* Revolution, *his intended history of* York *was never finished. The former part of his work, fairly transcribed for the press, is in the* Museum *of* Roger Gale, *esq; who kindly lent it me. The papers from which his second part was to have been composed, were in the possession of* Thomas Adams, *esq; late recorder of* York, *and they were put into my hands for this use. This author was writing his account of* York *about the year* 1684; *the assistance I have had from him, has been but small; having met with much better authorities; except in the* Heraldic *way, in which he seems to have been very particular, in his description of the arms in the painted windows of the several churches in* York. HENRY KEEP.

But in all the branches which compose the ecclesiastical part of this work, I have been the most obliged to the laborious performances of Mr. James Torre, *gent. a person of uncommon application in this way. As I have been so particularly befriended by them, I can do no less than publish some account of that gentleman, and his writings, especially since no one has ever yet attempted to do his memory that justice it deserves.*

The name and family of TORRE, *or* de Turre, *who bear for their arms,* sable, *a tower embattled* argent, *was originally of* Warwickshire; *but since the time of king* Henry IV. *have lived chiefly in the isle of* Haxholm, *in the county of* Lincoln. *Mr.* Torre's *father, whose name was* Gregory, *in the time of the* civil-wars *bore arms in the* royal cause; *for which act of loyalty his estate was sequestered by the rebels, and he was obliged to compound for it at* Goldsmith's-hall, *and pay such a fine as those plunderers thought fit to set upon it.* In May 1660, *this gentleman de-* Mr. JAMES TORRE.

* *Quarto*, *York*, printed for *Stephen Bulkley*, 1664.
† *Nicholson's* English hist. library fol. edit. p. 27.
‡ *Octavo*, YORK, printed by G. WHITE for FRANCIS HILDYARD, *&c.* 1719.
‖ *Octavo*, *London*, 1682.

parted this life, and was buried at Haxey, com. Lincoln; *he had married* Anne *daughter and heir to* John Farre *of* Epworth, *esq; by whom he had* James Torre, *our author, who succeeded him in his inheritance at* Haxey, Burnham, Epworth *and* Belton. April 30, 1649, *this* James *was baptized; and having acquired a sufficient stock of school learning, was sent to* Cambridge, *and entered in* Magdalene-college *in that* university. *He staid there about two years and a half, and afterwards was admitted into the society of the students of the* Inner-temple London. *In all probability, his natural inclinations were not to the law, for I do not find that he was ever called to the* bar; *and having married two wives he settled chiefly at* York, *and bent his genius, intirely, to the study of ecclesiastical antiquities and of family descents. The former of which he followed with that prodigious application and exactness, as, perhaps, never any man before or since could equal. And in the latter he has been no less assiduous; for going upon the plan of and copying sir* William Dugdale's baronage, *he has corrected, in many places, and infinitely exceeded that admired author.*

One of his manuscript volumes, relating to church affairs, bears this title,
Antiquities ecclesiastical of the city of YORK, concerning,

Churches { parochial. / conventual. / chapels. / hospitals. / gilds. } And in them { chantries / and / interments.

Also churches { parochial / and / conventual.

Within the archdeaconry of the *West-riding*. Collected out of publick records and registers. *A. D.* 1691.

It appears by two notes the author has placed in the margin of this title page, that he began to transcribe from his papers, and to methodize them, for the former part, September 4. 1691, *and finished it* October 27, *the same year. And, for the latter on* March 15, 1691, *and compleated it* June 9, 1692. *A prodigious work, when I inform the reader, that this volume contains no less than one thousand two hundred and fifty five columns,* in folio; *mostly close writ, and in a very small, but legible hand. There is, likewise, a compleat Index to the whole. The other archdeaconries of the diocese are treated in the same manner in two more volumes; and there is, also, one more of peculiars belonging to the church or see. This, almost, invaluable treasure to them was given to the dean and chapter's library, by the executors to the last will of the late archbishop* Sharp. *No doubt the worthy sons of that very eminent prelate imagined they had an unquestionable right to make this present. I shall not enter further into this affair, which by the good archbishop's death, and other persons concerned, is now rendered inscrutable; yet this I may venture to say, that there never was a* quantum meruit *paid to the author's relict, or his heir, for them.*

These books are an Index, *or a key, to all the records of the archbishops, deans and chapters, and all other offices belonging to the church or see of* York. *By which means, for instance, in one particular, a person in search for the patronage of any living, in their district, has at one view, the exact separate dates of years and days of institution, a list of the several incumbents to it, their patrons, when and how vacated, with the authorities for all, as high as the archiepiscopal registers do run. His authorities, in particular marks, are explained at the beginning of the volume. And here I must take notice, that our fund of this sort of antiquity at* York *is much nobler, and runs higher than the registers of the see of* Canterbury, *by near one hundred years. Their's beginning only at archbishop* Rayner, *who sat in that chair about the year* 1307; *whereas ours begins with archbishop* Walter Grey, *who entered upon his dignity in the year* 1216. *I shall not take upon me to give any farther detail of what is contained in these invaluable volumes; the reader may observe in the course of this work of what great use they have been to me in a particular way; and they would be the same, or more in proportion, to any historian that shall hereafter attempt a general account of the whole diocese. They have saved me an infinite deal of trouble; and indeed what my profession would not have allowed me time for such an avocation from it, nor my inclination strong as it is, to these kinds of studies, have suffered me to apply myself to such a laborious performance. My book therefore, in church matters, is only a key or index to some part of Mr.* Torre's *collections; as his are to the records themselves; for I have quoted his manuscript, and not his authorities in the greatest part of what I extracted from him. I own I had a great inclination to have completed his catalogues of rectors, vicars,* &c. *which I have made use of, and brought them down to the present incumbents; but, upon enquiry, I found it impracticable. The later archiepiscopal registers are not yet given into the office; and where they are, they are* far out of my reach. *I must farther inform the publick, that these manuscript volumes of Mr.* Torre's, *relating to church history, are not kept in the publick library of the* Dean *and* Chapter; *but,* sub sigillo, *in the register's office. For this reason I esteem it a much greater favour, which the present dean granted me, in having the volume I wanted to my own house; and to keep it my own time, until I had drawn out and transcribed, at my leisure, what I thought proper for my purpose. A favour, I say, so extraordinary, that I can do no less than make him this publick acknowledgment of it.*

Nor was Mr. Torre's *studies and application intirely applied to church history; he was besides an excellent master of* Heraldry *and* Genealogy. *In both which he shines to some purpose in five manuscript volumes, in folio, which are now in the possession of his son* Nicholas Torre *of* Snydall, *near* Pontefract, *esquire. The title to these books is this,* English Nobility and Gentry, or supplemental collections to sir *William Dugdale's* baronage; carrying on the genealogical descents and historical remarks of families therein contained. By *James Torre.*

In this great work the author has transcribed all Dugdale's *baronage throughout; corrected it in many places, added many historical remarks, and enriched it with the genealogies of many families of lesser note, and especially of the northern gentry. The whole illustrated with the coats armorial and different quarterings of the several families prettily tricked out with his pen; to all which is added a copious* Index. *It is great pity, since the world is expecting a new edition of the Baronage, that this manuscript is not printed and published instead of it. It would stamp a very great additional value on sir* William Dugdale's *performance; would eternize both the names of* Dugdale *and* Torre, *and be a very great honour to this country.*

There are besides in his son's custody, and in that of the dean and chapter, several smaller manuscript volumes of collections from which he extracted his larger works. In these the prodigious application of the author is demonstrated; who hardly ever let a scarce printed book pass his hands without transcribing all or most of it. Such a close and constant attention to this kind of work made me suppose, because Mr. Torre *died at a middle age, that it had hurt his constitution. But, upon enquiry, I am informed, that it did not seem in the least to impair his health; and on the contrary, that he was always a hearty robust man, and died of a fever.*

Great part of this information I have had from my honest friend and old acquaintance Nicholas Torre, *esq; the author's only son and successor; from some memoirs of the family drawn up by his father. He had married two wives; by the latter of which,* Anna, *the daughter of* Nicholas Lister *of* Rigton com. Ebor. *gent. he had this son* Nicholas, *and one daughter. He purchased the estate of* Snydall, anno 1699; *and died there* July 31. *the same year, and was buried in his parish church of* Normanton. *Over whom, in order to conclude, my account of this eminent benefactor to my work, is the following epitaph.*

Hic situs est *Jacobus Torre* de *Snidall*
Generosus.
Qui prisca fide, antiquis moribus, vetusta
Scientia ornatus,
De ecclesia de republica optime meruit.
Res ab ultimo antiquitatis aevo repetitas
Scrutatus est,
Tenebrisque situque obsitas in lucem proferens
Aeternum sui nominis exegit monumentum.
Diem obiit pridie calendas *Augustas*
Anno post salutem datam 1699.
Aetatis suae 49.
Beatus sibi, desideratus omnibus.

Some

Sir William Dugdale. *Some matters relating to the history of the church of* York, *were published, as there declared, from sir* William Dugdale's *papers, at the end of his history of St.* Paul's; anno 1716, folio. *Bishop* Nicholson *had seen the manuscript before it was printed, and says of it* that there is no such appearance of records as the reader may expect to find in it. *What this prelate has asserted is literally true, for I could find very little of any thing to my purpose in the whole performance.*

Mr. Samuel Gale. *But, on the contrary, what has served greatly to enrich the ecclesiastical part of this work are the collections of Mr.* Samuel Gale. *That gentleman had once a design of publishing something on this subject himself; and from his father's papers, the worthy dean of* York *of that name, and his own industry he had made a considerable progress in it. Being called from an attention on these matters to a publick employ, his design, of course, dropped with it. By which means the world is frustrated from seeing a more noble performance than I am able to give. Upon my application to this gentleman for some intelligence he very readily put all his papers into my hands; told me that he could not now think of publishing them himself; and wished they might be of any use or service to my intended performance. What use they have been to me the reader may find in the course of the church account; where, especially in the* Appendix, *are many things printed from these papers, and some, I think, of great value.*

Mr. Hopkinson. *I have now run through a list of my predecessors, and particular benefactors, in the literal way, to this work. Except, I inform the reader, that the law-part of it relating, chiefly, to the several courts of this city, their customs, by-laws,* &c. *was taken from a copy of part of Mr.* Hopkinson's *collections; who was* clerk of the peace *to the* West-riding *of this county, about the year* 1670. *This gentleman was a very industrious searcher into antiquities; and left behind him several volumes of collections, in manuscript, relating to the affairs of this county, in several branches. Some of these manuscripts I believe, are embezled; but what are remaining of them are now in a fair way of preservation; being lately given to the library of that eminent physician, and very worthy gentleman, Dr.* Richardson *of* North-Byerley *in this county.*

Dr. N. I. *Before I dismiss this head, I must also take notice, lest the reader should think me quite ignorant of the matter, that I have heard much of several voluminous tracts relating to the county and city of* York; *but never could get an opportunity to inspect them. I was less anxious about this, when I read bishop* Nicholson's *smart reflection * on this collector's monstrous performance; and was, also, informed by eye-witnesses, that the manuscripts are wrote in such an awkward* Arabick *scrall as to be scarce legible. Some few years since a proposal was made, on a sufficient subscription, to have these volumes, amounting, in folio, to above forty in number, placed in the library belonging to the cathedral of* York. *They might then, possibly, have been of some use to me, or any future historian. As they are, they are of no use at all; nor, in all probability, ever will be; it being as equally impossible as impracticable to pass such a heap of matter through the press without much sifting and cleansing of it.*

Mr. T. G. *The last thing which I shall mention is to inform the publick, that I have seen and read a small octavo printed tract, the title page of which bears this inscription,* The antient and modern history of the famous city of York; and in a particular manner of its magnificent cathedral, commonly called York-Minster, &c. The whole diligently collected by *T. G.* York, printed at the printing-office in Coffee-yard, M.DCC.XXX. *I have nothing to say to this work, but to assure my cotemporary historian, that I have stoln little or nothing from his laborious performance; wherein Mr.* T. G. *as author, printer, and publisher of the work himself, endeavouring to get a livelihood for his family, deserves commendation for his industry.*

What of course occurs to me next, is to give thanks to those gentlemen who have lent me manuscripts, perused, corrected, or any ways added to any part of this work. Which, with those I have already mentioned, are the reverend Mr. Barnard, *master of the free-school at* Leeds; Roger Gale, *esq;* Bryan Fairfax, *esq; the reverend Dr.* Langwith; John Anstis, *sen. esq;* Brown Willis, *esq; and the reve-*

* *Nicholson's* English hist. library p. 27.

rend

rend Mr. Creyk. *To the first of these gentlemen the whole performance is, in some measure, owing. He it was that principally encouraged me to undertake it; lent me several very scarce historians out of his own collection; and, upon perusing some part of the manuscript, gave it as his judgment, that I needed not despair of success. Whether he was right or no, the world must now judge; but it was no small encouragement to me to proceed, when I had the approbation of a person whose great learning and parts are very well known in our neighbourhood. Consciousness of inability in an author is a necessary ingredient to cool and temper a too forward presumption, and I had enough of it. I had no other living guide to help or conduct me through the various scenes and mazes which I must necessarily tread till I came to* London. *And, there, indeed, whatever was the occasion of the journey, or howsoever the author might suffer by the accident, the book lost nothing; but, on the contrary, was considerably enriched, corrected and amended by it. The rest I have been obliged to in some or all of the several ways that I have mentioned; and, especially to Dr.* Langwith *and Mr.* Anstis, *as the reader may find sufficient proof of in the* Appendix. *I think it, also, proper here to mention Mr.* George Reynoldson, *an honest and industrious citizen of* York. *From whose collections and observations I had many useful hints given me, relating to the decayed trade and navigation of the city; and the probable means to revive both. Nor must I forget the gentlemen keepers of the several offices of records which I have had occasion to consult both in* London *and* York. *Amongst the former, my very ingenious friend and brother antiquary,* George Holms, *esq, deputy-keeper of the records in the* Tower *of* London, *I have been most particularly obliged to.——— From all these authors, gentlemen, and offices, I have collected many materials for this work; the difficulty, only, lay in judging what to chuse and what to reject. By which means the subject grew upon me to a monstrous bulk; so that what I imagined at first would turn out into a folio of a moderate size, is now swelled into two. And should I still go on to collect, more matter would still occur; for I can, well, say with the poet,*

——— multum coeli post terga relictum est;
Ante oculos plus est ———

Next, I return thanks to my subscribers in general; but especially to those who chiefly promoted the subscription; amongst whom, I must beg leave to mention John Hylton *of* Hylton-castle, *in the county of* Northumberland, *esquire. Who, though a stranger, in some measure, to* York, *yet, in regard to the performance, respect to the author, or his known humanity to all mankind, took great pains to sollicite the subscription, and bear off that* dead weight *from my own shoulders. I am the more obliged to this gentleman and several others, in that, I here declare, I never did, or could ask one subscription for the book myself. I know this may be called* pride *in me as well as* modesty. *But, whatever it was, it restrained me from standing the shock of a refusal. For an author offering his own proposals to any gentleman, does no less than offer himself to his judgment, whether he be equal to the performance or not; and I own I never could bring myself to stand in such an uneasy posture before any stranger; or, scarce, before a friend. Lastly, as in duty bound, I return my most hearty thanks to those of the nobility and gentry, of both sexes, as well as to the clergy, who have honoured me with their names, as contributors to the several plates which adorn this book. Amongst whom, also, I cannot avoid mentioning, in a particular manner, the right honourable the lord* Petre; *to whose generosity, and promoting the subscription to the utmost of his power, the author of this work owes the highest obligation.*

What remains is now to give some further account of the work and the purport of it; which will conclude all I have to say on the matter.

In this, I shall not, with a late extraordinary historian, make a solemn asseveration, that there are neither lyes nor mistakes in my book. For the former, I believe I can safely assert, that there are fewer in it than in that admirable chronicler *of his own times. But, as to mistakes, I freely admit there may be a thousand in the work; though I have taken all imaginable pains to avoid them; having copyed, or wrote, almost every individual thing in the whole book, even to the* Index, *with my own hand. Notwithstanding this care, many, gross, errors of the pen or press may have happened; and, which, in a work of this nature, it is* *impossible to shew. There are millions of mistakes made in the so much justly celebrated* Monasticon Anglicanum; *some few instances of which I have given in the* Appendix *. *Nor is the famous translation of the* Britannia *without some errors; and those not inconsiderable; which are crept even into the last edition of that most noble and most extraordinary performance. All which have happened, not from any want of care in the compilers, but from trusting to transcribers; who, either through ignorance or negligence, mistook the originals they copied from.*

As I allow of many mistakes in those matters, so I, also, shall not take upon me to defend the style, or manner of expression, throughout this whole performance. I will not say that many sentences may not be picked out of it, and proved to my face to be neither English *nor sense. To judge rightly of such a work as this, is not to take a particular chapter, page, sentence or word, and criticise with severity upon that which I shall never defend; no more than I will a mistake of a figure, or a misnomer, in the* Index. *But, let the reader consider the weight and bulk of the whole work; and the long series of time and things through which I have been obliged to carry it; and then he will not wonder at my making some slips by the way. Nevertheless, I must caution the reader not to judge too hastily; but, when he meets with a mistake or a blunder in the book, to turn to the* Appendix; *and there see if it does not stand corrected, either by my learned annotators or my self.*

If I have, also, by some lightnesses, here and there interspersed, deviated from the strict gravity of an historian, I ask pardon of my censurers for it. My intimates all know that Mercury *was a more predominant planet at my birth than* Saturn. *And, I confess I never thought an historian ought to be dull because his subject was so. Many a dull story has been set in an agreeable light, in common conversation, by the manner, only, of telling it; as, on the contrary, many a good one has been spoiled. And, it would be very ill natured in the gravest* Cynick *to quarrel with a companion, in a long tiresome journey, for his being, now and then, a little too ludicrous or merry in the way. I pretend to be neither a* Livy *nor a* Tacitus *in reciting state affairs; nor an* Usher *or a* Stillingfleet *in church matters. What I knew I have put down in, what I think, a proper manner; and if I have larded some lean passages, I hope they will not relish the worse for it, with a* courteous reader.

There may be, also, some particular families, who may fancy themselves struck at, in the account I have given of their ancestors; whether prelates or otherwise. To these I declare that I have no such intention; but I cannot make a bishop of a better family, put better blood in his veins, or ascribe better actions to his life, than history or records will allow him. An historian, or biographer, that dares not speak truth, or, cringingly sculks behind it, is not worthy of the name. So that what I have said, any where, on this head I hope will not be imputed to any satyrical strokes on the living; or any, purposely, false representations of the dead.

But, after all, what I am the most diffident in, and think my self the least capable of writing, is the church history of this see. It may be urged against me as a piece of boldness and audacity, that I, a layman, *with only a moderate share of* school learning, *should enter upon such subjects as the* deepest divines, *and ablest scholars, have been puzzled with. It is for this reason, no doubt, and a mean opinion of what any layman can produce on this subject, that I have found so little encouragement from the body of the clergy in general; and from those of our own church in particular. And, it was a sensible concern and discouragement to me, when our present most reverend and most worthy* Metropolitan, *not only refused, upon my repeated application to him, to accept of the dedication of the church account, but even to subscribe to the book. I say, it must proceed from a contempt of any layman's productions on this head. Else, without doubt, every prelate would be glad to encourage an historian who is about to publish a large account of his church and predecessors. Especially, when it is natural to suppose that they earnestly desire to scan over their predecessor's actions; with a view, worthy of the sacred function, of imitating the best; and avoiding the rocks and precipices, there described, on which some of them have, unhappily, split; or, dangerously, hurt their sacred characters. On the same footing I must put the ill success I have had with*

* See p. lxxxii. and lxxxiii.

the

the present reverend Dean *and* Chapter *of* York; *except in the great favour which I have already acknowledged, and some few subscriptions from them. It seems as if most of this body, also, despised a layman's attempt on a subject, which, I own, indeed, is more in their way, more suitable to their dignities in the church, and more adapted to the manner of their education and studies. For I will not suppose that party-prejudice can any ways affect men of their sanctity and morals. Yet, let these consider, that all the historians I have hitherto had occasion to mention in this preface, were laymen; excepting* Usher *and* Stillingfleet. *And, since the practice of old, of registring, along with the affairs of their church or monastery, the more publick transactions of this kingdom, has been long since disused and out of practice; they must be beholden to some layman, who will take the trouble off their hands, and do this necessary piece of drudgery for them. It is for want of proper encouragement, I say, that the outside views of our most noble cathedral are contracted into the compass I have caused them to be engraven in. I considered, in order to save some part of the great expence, that the external part of the fabrick, had been frequently exhibited, at large, by several hands. And, to do justice to the internal views, which were never before taken, those of the outside which I have given, I imagined sufficient for my purpose. —— Thus much I think proper to declare, since my subscribers ought to be made acquainted with the true reason why any thing bears a mean aspect in this performance. And, when they consider how few of the reverend body have graced the plates of the inside views of the church, with their names and titles, they will not be surprised when they come to look without.*

And now, to make an end of this tedious discourse, which, like the book itself, has spun out to a greater length than I, principally, designed it; I shall only say, that I neither desire nor expect to have another edition of it pass my hands. I am too conscious of this performance; and all I can hope for, is, that it may, in futuro, *be sought after, enquired into, and made use of as a plan, or groundwork, on which some abler hand may build a stronger and a more noble structure. As such, I present it to the present age, and leave it to posterity.*

London, *Aug.* 1,
1736.

A LIST

A
L I S T
OF THE
SUBSCRIBERS.

N. B. *The author proposed to the subscribers to send in with their names their family coats and places of abode; in order, as he then imagined, to have all their arms engraved. But, not one in fifty having taken any notice of this, he supposes the matter indifferent to the majority of the subscribers; and therefore he has omitted doing a thing which would have given himself an infinite deal of more trouble, retarded the publication of the work, and, upon second thoughts, have been of no manner of signification to it.*

This mark * *stands for the* royal paper.

A.

* *THE right honourable the earl of* Anglesey.
* *The right honourable the earl of* Aylesford.
* *The honourable* Bertram Ashburnham, *esq;*
The honourable Richard Arundel, *esq; surveyor of his majesty's works.*
* *The honourable* John Aislabie, *esq;*
Sir Robert Abdy, *bart.*
Sir Joseph Ayloffe, *bart.*
John Anstis, *esq; garter principal king at arms.*
John Audley, *LL. D. chancellor of the diocese of* York.
George Aldridge, *M. D.*
Robert Andrews, *esq;*
Henry Atkinson, *esq;*
Joseph Athrop, *esq;*
Thomas Archer, *esq;*
William Aislabie, *esq;*
William Archer, *esq;*
The reverend Mr. Andrews, *fellow of* Magdalen *college*, Oxon.
The reverend Mr. Aislabie, *rector of* Birkin.
The reverend Mr. Allot *vicar of* South-Kirkby.
Adam Askew, *M. B. of* Newcastle.
Mr. Ashenden *surgeon in* Durham.
Mr. Ascough *of* York.
Mr. Tho. Agar *in* York.
Mr. George Atkinson *of* York.
* *The* Antiquarian *Society*, London.
The Antiquarian *Society at* Peterborough.
The Antiquarian *Society at* Spalding *in* Lincolnshire.
The Office of Arms *in* London.

B.

* *The right honourable the earl of* Burlington, *two copies.*
* *The right honourable the countess of* Burlington.
* *The right honourable the countess dowager of* Burlington.
* *The right honourable the lord* Bruce.
The right honourable the lady Bingley.
The right honourable the lady Jane Boyle.
The honourable John Berkeley, *esq;*
Sir George Beaumont, *bart.*
Sir John Bland, *bart.*
Hugh Bethel, *esq;*
* Charles Bathurst, *esq;*
Philip Byerley, *esq;*
* George Bowes, *esq;*
Robert Buck, *esq;*
William Burton, *esq;*
Dr. Burton *of* Wakefield.
John Boucherett, *esq;*

Thomas

Thomas Bramfton, *efq*;
Thomas Sclater Bacon, *efq*;
* Walter Calverley Blacket, *efq*;
Lewis Barlow, *efq*;
Richard Backwell, *efq*;
* John Bright, *efq*;
Thomas Bright, *efq*;
* *Mrs*. Anne Bright.
John Bufland, *efq*;
Thomas Booth, *efq*;
Henry Bradfhaw, *efq*;
William Brigham, *efq*;
Richard Bagfhaw, *efq*;
Richard Braithwait, *efq*;
Mark Braithwait, *LL. D.*
The reverend Mr. Benfon, *M. A. vicar of* Ledfham.
The reverend Mr. Barnard, *mafter of the free-fchool at* Leeds.
The reverend Mr. Buck, *rector of* Marfton.
The reverend Mr. Bradley, *canon refidentiary of the cathedral church of* York.
The reverend Mr. H. Breary, *rector of* Boxworth, *com.* Cant.
The reverend Mr. Bradley, *vicar of* Warthill.
The reverend Mr. Blake, *rector of* Goldfborough.
The reverend Mr. Bourn, *vicar of St.* Mary's, Caftlegate, York.
Mrs. Elizabeth Bateman.
* *Mr.* Samuel Booth, *fteward to the duke of* Montague.
Mr. John Bofvile, Cheapfide, London.
Mr. Bolton, *merchant in* Newcaftle.
Mr. Beckwith *of* York.
Mr. Stephen Beverley *of* York.
Mr. Roger Bridgewater *of* York.
Mr. Birbeck, *jun. of* York.
Mr. Bowyer, *printer in* White-fryars, London.

C.

His grace the lord archbifhop of Canterbury.
The right honourable the earl of Carlifle.
* *The right honourable the earl of* Cholmondeley.
The right honourable the earl of Carnwath.
* *The right honourable the lord* Craven.
The right honourable the lord Colerain.
* *The right honourable the lady baronefs* Clifford.
The right honourable Samuel Clarke, *lord-mayor of* York.
* *The honourable* Edward Coke, *efq*;
The honourable George Compton, *efq*;
Sir William Carew, *bart.*
Sir John Hind Cotton, *bart.*
Sir Walter Calverley, *bart.*
Sir Francis Clavering, *bart.*
Sir Nathanael Curzon, *bart.*
Mr. Juftice Commins, *one of the judges of the common pleas.*
* William Conolly, *efq*;
Leonard Childers, *efq*;
William Cowper, *efq*;
Hugh Cholmley, *efq*;
Robert Chapell, *efq*;
William Cradock, *efq*;
Edward Clerke, *efq*;
Edward Collingwood, *efq*;
John Cook, *efq*;
Samuel Chetham, *efq*;
James Chetham, *efq*;
Thomas Cartwright, *efq*;
William Craven, *efq*;
George Chafin, *efq*;
Langford Collin, *efq*;
* Edward Chaloner, *efq*;
Richard Crowle, *efq*;
Haworth Currer, *efq*;
William Chefelden, *efq*; *ferjeant furgeon to the queen.*
The reverend Richard Cayley, *B. D. fellow of St.* John's college, Cambridge.
The reverend Dr. Crofs, *mafter of* Catherine hall, *and prebendary of* York.
* *The reverend Mr.* Creyk. *Two copies.*
The reverend Mr. Carte.
The reverend Mr. Cook, *rector of* Stoxley *and prebendary of* York.
Dr. Cook *of* Ripon.
William Clinch *of* York, *M. D.*
Captain Cockayne.
Mrs. Cuttler *of* Hayton.
Mr. William Cookfon, *alderman of* Leeds.
* *Mr.* John Chaloner *of* Gifbrough.
Mr. Charles Cotton, *merchant in* London.
Mr. John Chippendale *of* York.
Mr. Thomas Carr *of* York.
Mr. James Cook, *jun. of* Yarum.
Mr. Croxton *of* Manchefter.
Mr. John Cole *of* Bafinghall-ftreet, London.
Mr. James Carpenter *of* York.

D.

* *The right honourable the earl of* Derby.
* *The right honourable the earl of* Donnegal.
The right honourable the earl of Delorrain.
The right honourable the lord vifcount Downe.
The honourable John Dawney, *efq*;
The honourable Chriftopher Dawney, *efq*;
Sir Edward Defbouverie, *bart.*
* *Sir* Francis Henry Drake, *bart.*
* *The reverend fir* John Dolben, *bart.*
Sir Charles Dalton, *knt. gentleman ufher of the black-rod.*
* Thomas Duncombe, *efq*;
* William Drake, *efq*; *of* Shardelois, *com.* Bucks.
* William Drake, *efq*; *of* Barnoldfwickcotes, *com.* Ebor.
Daniel Draper, *efq*;
John Difney, *efq*;
Ely Dyfon, *efq*;
* Peter Delme, *efq*;
* John Delme, *efq*;
William Dobfon, *efq*; *alderman of* York.
The reverend Dr. Deering, *dean of* Ripon, *prebendary of* York, *and archdeacon of the* Eaft-riding.

The reverend Mr. Dunn, *prebendary of* York.
The reverend Mr. Ramsden Dodsworth, *chaplain to his grace the duke of* Somerset, *and fellow of* Jesus College, Cambridge.
* *The reverend* John Drake, *B. D. rector of* Smeeton, *vicar of* Pontefract, *and prebendary of* York.
* *The reverend* Samuel Drake, *S. T. P. rector of* Treeton, *and of* Holm Spalding-moor.
The reverend Mr. Thomas Drake, *rector of* Norham *in* Northumberland.
The reverend Mr. Nathan Drake, *minor canon of the cathedral church of* Lincoln.
The reverend Mr. Samuel Drake, *minor canon of the same.*
The reverend Mr. Joseph Drake, *rector of* Burleigh.
The reverend Mr. Francis Drake *of* East-Hardwick.
The reverend Mr. William Drake *of* Hatfield.
Captain William Drake.
Mrs. Dubois.
Mr. Thomas Drake *of* Halyfax.
Mr. Jeremy Drake *of* Halyfax.
Mr. Thomas Dawson *of* York.
Mr. John Dawson *of* York.
Mr. Bryan Dawson *of* York.
Mr. Humphrey Duncalf, *merchant in* London.
* *Mr.* Dawes, *surgeon in* York.
Mr. Jerome Denton *of the pipe-office*, Gray's-inn.
Mr. Richard Dicken *of* York-street, Covent-garden.

E.

Sir John Evelyn, *bart.*
Thomas Empson, *esq;*
Anthony Eyres, *esq;*
Dr. Eyres *of* Doncaster.
George Escrick, *esq; alderman of* York.
* *The reverend Mr.* Elsley, *prebendary of* York.
The reverend Mr. Elmsal, *rector of* Thornhill.
The reverend Mr. Emmerson.
* *Mrs.* Mary Edwards.
Mr. George Errington, London.

F.

The right honourable the earl of Fitz Walter.
* *The right honourable the lord viscount* Fauconberg.
The reverend and honourable Edward Finch, *canon-residentiary of* York.
The honourable Charles Fairfax *of* Gilling, *esq;*
The honourable John Finch, *esq;*
The honourable Mrs. Finch.
* *Sir* William Foulis, *bart.*
* George Fox, *esq;*
The honourable Mrs. Fox.
Thomas Fairfax *of* Newton, *esq;*
* Bryan Fairfax, *esq; one of the honourable commissioners of the customs.*
Thomas Fothergill, *esq;*
Cuthbert Fenwick, *esq;*
Robert Fenwick, *esq;*
Basil Forcer, *esq;*
Charles Frederic, *esq;*
Francis Fawkes, *sen. esq;*
Thomas Fawkes, *esq;*
Samuel Foster, *esq;*
John Fountain, *esq;*
Thomas Frewen, *esq;*
The reverend Dr. Felton, *rector of* Barwick *in* Elmet.
Antonio Dominico Ferrari, *LL. D.*
* *Mr.* Marmaduke Fothergill *of* York.
Miss Fothergill.
Mr. Freak, *surgeon in* London.
Mr. Thomas Fetherston *of* York.
Mr. Frye, *painter in* London.

G.

* *The right honourable the lord* Gower.
The right honourable the lord viscount Galway.
The honourable William Leveson Gower, *esq;*
* *The honourable Mrs.* Graham.
Sir Edward Gascoign, *bart.*
Sir Robert Grosvenor, *bart.*
Sir Reginald Graham, *bart.*
* Richard Graham, *esq;*
* Roger Gale, *esq;*
Henry Grey, *esq;*
Edward Gibbon, *esq;*
John Goodricke, *esq;*
Thomas Gyll, *esq;*
Smithson Green, *esq;*
The reverend Dr. Goodwin, *rector of* Tankersley, *and prebendary of* York.
The reverend Dr. Gouge, *rector of* Gilling, *and prebendary of* York.
Dr. Gaugy *of* Peterborough.
Mr. Samuel Gale.
Mr. Roger Gathome.
Mr. Henry Grice *of* York.
Mr. John Gill *of* York.
Mr. Gosling, *bookseller in* Fleet-street.
Mr. Gyles, *bookseller in* Holbourn.
Mr. Darcy Godard, *surgeon.*
Mr. Richard Gowland, *druggist*, London.
Mr. John Gowland, *apothecary*, London.

H.

* *The right honourable the earl of* Hartford.
The honourable George Hamilton, *esq;*
The right honourable the lady Henrietta Herbert.
* *The right honourable the lady* Elizabeth Hastings.
The right honourable the lady Mary Hastings.
Sir William Halford, *bart.*
Sir Walter Hawksworth, *bart.*
* Thomas Hesketh, *esq;*
Sir Rowland Hill, *bart.*
* John Hylton, *esq;*

John

John Hutton, *esq*;
Stephen Holms, *esq*;
* Robert Humpheys, *esq*;
Alexander Hales, *esq*;
* Richard Honeywood, *esq*;
George Holms, *esq*; *deputy keeper of the records in the tower of* London.
Thomas Hardcastle *of* Gray's-inn, *esq*;
Mr. John Hilileigh *of* York.
Mr. Hall, *surgeon in* Manchester.
Mr. Hildyard, *bookseller in* York.
Mr. Joseph Harley *of* Stockton.
Mr. Hunter *of* Manchester.
Mr. Haslegrave, *surgeon in* York.
Mr. Holland, *painter in* London.
Mr. John Hodson, *cabinet-maker*, London.

I.

The right honourable the lord viscount Irwin.
The honourable captain Charles Ingram.
Sir Justinian Isham, *bart.*
Stephen Theodore Janssen, *esq*;
Peter Johnson, *esq*;
* James Joye, *esq*;
Lewis Jones, *M. D.*
The reverend Mr. Jones.
Mr. Jubb, *deputy register to the archbishop of* York.

K.

* *Sir* John Lister Kaye, *bart. representative in parliament, and alderman of the city of* York.
The reverend Richard Kershaw, *D. D. rector of* Ripley.
The reverend Mr. Knight, *succentor canon. of the church of* York.
Jasper Kinsman, *esq*;
William Kent, *esq*; *architect, master carpenter to his majesty*.
Mr. Knowlton *of* Londesburgh.

L.

* *His grace the duke of* Leeds.
* *The right honourable the earl of* Litchfield.
The right reverend Edmund, *lord bishop of* London.
The right honourable the lord Langdale.
* *The right honourable the lord* Lovel.
The honourable Fitzroy Henry Lee, *esq*;
The honourable Heneage Legge, *esq*;
* *Lady* Liddel.
* Thomas Lister, *esq*;
Henry Lambton, *esq*;
William Levinz, *jun. esq*;
John Lambe, *esq*;
Darcy Lever, *esq*;
* Thomas Lupton, *esq*;
Smart Lethuillier, *esq*;
Richard Langley, *esq*;
Peter Leigh, *jun. esq*;
* *Colonel* Lascelles.
* *The reverend* Thomas Lamplugh, *M. A. canon-residentiary of the church of* York.
The reverend Henry Laybourne, *M. A. rector of* Coleorton *in* Leicestershire.
The reverend Francis Lascelles, *A. M. of* Pontefract.
The reverend Dr. Langwith, *rector of* Petworth *in* Suffex, *and prebendary of* Chichester.
The reverend Dr. Legh, *vicar of* Halifax, *and prebendary of* York.
Signeur Giacomo Leoni, *architect. Two books.*
Mr. Richard Lawson, *merchant in* York.
Captain Lamprere *of the Tower.*
Mr. Thomas Lascelles *of* University college, Oxon.
Shepherd Lynam, *esq*; *peruke-maker in* Covent-garden.

M.

* *His grace the duke of* Marlborough.
* *The right honourable the earl of* Malton. *Six copies.*
The right honourable the earl of Mountrath.
Sir Oswald Mosley, *bart.*
* *Sir* William Milner, *bart.*
Sir Paul Methuen, *knight of the* Bath.
John Myddelton, *esq*;
Bacon Morrit, *esq*;
* William Metcalf, *esq*;
The reverend Dr. Mangey, *prebendary of* Durham.
The reverend Mr. Marsden, *archdeacon of* Nottingham.
* *Dr.* Mead.
Dr. Middleton Massey.
* *Mr.* John Marsden *of* York.
Mr. Richard Marsh *of* York.
Mr. Roger Metcalf, *surgeon in* London.
The library at Manchester college.
Mr. Thomas Micklethwaite, *alderman of* Leeds.
Mr. Thomas Mason *of* York.
Mr. Thomas Matthews *of* York.
Mr. Macmoran, *merchant in* London.
Captain Nicholas Masterson *of* York.
Captain Macro *of the guards.*
Mr. Thomas Martin *of* Palsgrave *in* Suffolk.
Mr. Samuel Morris *of* Iron-monger's-hall, London.
Miss Morrice *of* York.
Mr. Mancklyn, *bookseller in* York.
Mr. Christopher Mitchell *of* York.
Mr. Maitland *author of the Antiquities of* London.

N.

* *His grace the duke of* Norfolk.
* *The right honourable the lord* North *and* Guilford.
The right honourable the countess dowager of Nottingham.
The right honourable the lady North *and* Guilford.
The reverend Mr. Cavendish Nevill.
Charles Newby, *esq*;
Mr. John Napier *of* York.

O.

* *The right honourable the earl of* Oxford.
The right honourable the earl of Orkney.
William Osbaldeston, *esq*;
The reverend Richard Osbaldeston, *S. T. P. dean of* York.

P.

* *The right honourable the lord* Petre.
The right honourable the lady Petre.
German Pole, *esq*;
Robert Pigot, *esq*;
Thomas Pigot, *esq*;
Thomas Pullein, *esq*;
Thomas Plampion, *esq*;
Henry William Portman, *esq*;
Prescot Pepper, *esq*;
Richard Price, *esq*;
* James Pennyman, *esq*;
Nathanael Paylor, *esq*;
Armstead Parker, *esq*;
Thomas Patten, *esq*;
The reverend Mr. Penny *of* Ashton-under-line.
Mr. Robert Fairfax Pawson *of* York.
Mr. William Pawson, *merchant at* Oporto.
Mr. John Pawson, *merchant in* Newcastle.
Mr. Plant, *proctor at* York.
Mr. Christopher Peak *of* York.
* *Mrs.* Parker *of* York.
Mr. Thomas Pickering *of* Westminster.

R.

* *His grace the duke of* Rutland.
* *Sir* Thomas Robinson, *bart. one of the honourable commissioners of excise.*
Sir John Rhodes, *bart.*
Gregory Rhodes, *esq*;
Cuthbert Routh, *esq*;
Matthew Ridley, *esq*;
John Reed, *esq*;
* Thomas Strangeways Robinson, *esq*;
John Rudd, *esq*;
* Richard Rawlinson, *esq*; *LL.D. et F.R.S.*
Matthew Robinson, *esq*;
Lancelot Rollelton, *esq*;
Edward Rooks, *esq*;
The reverend Mr. Ray, *prebendary of* Ripon.
* *The reverend Mr.* Remmington *of* Garraby.
The reverend William Richardson, *D. D. master of* Emanuel college, Cambridge.
The reverend Mr. Henry Richardson.
Dr. Richardson *of* North Byerley.
Mr. John Richardson *of* York.
Mr. George Reynoldson *of* York.
Mr. George Rhodes *of* York.
Mr. Edward Ridsdale *of* Ripon.
John Rogers, *M. D. of* Leeds.
Mr. John Raper *of* York.
The society of Ringers *at* York.

S.

* *The right honourable the earl of* Strafford.
* *The right honourable the earl of* Shaftsbury.
The right honourable the earl of Scarborough.
The right honourable the lord Noel Somerset.
Sir Thomas Sanders Seabright, *bart.*
Sir William St. Quintin, *bart.*
* *Sir* Henry Slingsby, *bart.*
Sir William Strickland, *bart.*
* *Sir* Hans Sloane, *bart.*
Sir John Swinburn, *bart.*
* *Sir* Hugh Smithson, *bart.*
* *Sir* Miles Stapylton, *bart.*
Sir Philip Sydenham, *bart.*
Sir William Stapleton, *bart.*
Sir George Savile, *bart.*
Sir Robert Smyth, *bart.*
Sir Edward Smith, *bart.*
* Richard Shuttleworth, *esq*;
Matthew Chitty St. Quintin, *esq*;
Charles Slingsby, *esq*;
Nicholas Shuttleworth, *esq*;
Philip Southcote, *esq*;
Samuel Savile, *esq*;
Bryan Stapylton, *esq*;
* Thomas Scawen, *esq*;
William Spencer *of* Bramley-grange, *esq*;
William Spencer *of* Cannon-hall, *esq*;
Henry Simpson, *esq*;
Henry Stratford, *esq*;
Matthew Smales, *esq*;
Richard Sterne, *esq*;
John Stanhope, *esq*;
William Simpson, *esq*;
Thomas Selby, *esq*;
John Smith, *esq*;
Gervase Scrope, *esq*;
William Shippen, *esq*;
Edward Smith, *esq*;
Brownlow Sherrard, *esq*;
John Sawbridge, *esq*;
William Sheppherd, *esq*;
Samuel Swire, *esq*;
Philip Saltmarsh, *esq*;
The reverend Mr. Stephens, *archdeacon of* Exeter *and prebendary of* York.
The reverend Dr. Stukely.
The reverend Mr. Sississon.
The reverend Dr. Sharp, *archdeacon of* Northumberland, *&c.*
The reverend Mr. Steer, *rector of* Ecclesfield, *and prebendary of* York.
The reverend Mr. William Smith.
The reverend Mr. Serenius *of* Sweden.
The reverend Mr. Sympson *of* Babworth, *com.* Nott.
Mr. John Shaw *of* York.
Mr. Smith, *surgeon in* Coventry.
Mr. John Swale, *bookseller in* Leeds.
Mr. Sellers *of* York.
Mr. George Skelton *of* York.
Mr. Nicholas Sugar *of* York.

Mr.

Mr. Thomas Smith *of* York.
Mr. William Stephenson *of* York.
Mr. Richard Stockton *of* York.
Mr. David Saunders *of* York.
Mr. Sutton *of* Stockton.
Mr. John Stephenson.
Mrs. Sarah Stephenson.
Sign. F. Slater, *history painter.*
Mr. James Swan *of* Fulham.
Mr. John Strangewayes *of* York.
Mr. Josephus Sympson, *engraver*, London.
Mr. Strahan, *bookseller in* Cornhill.

T.

* *The right honourable the earl of* Thanet.
Sir George Tempest, *bart.*
* Edward Thompson, *esq; representative in parliament for the city of* York.
* John Twisleton, *esq;*
John Tempest, *esq;*
Richard Townley, *esq;*
Stephen Tempest, *esq;*
Bartholomew Tate, *esq;*
Nicholas Torre, *esq;*
Arthur Trevor, *esq;*
Leonard Thompson, *esq;*
Stephen Thompson, *esq;*
Cholmley Turner, *esq;*
* William Turner *of* Stainsby, *esq;*
William Thornton, *esq;*
The reverend Dr. Trimnel, *precentor of the church at* Lincoln.
The reverend John Taylour, *LL. D.*
Mr. John Thomlinson *of* York.
Mr. Thomas Thursby, *surgeon in* Newcastle.

V.

The honourable Henry Vane, *esq;*
George Venables Vernon, *esq;*
William Vavasour, *esq;*
The reverend Dr. Vernon, *rector of S.* George's Bloomsbury.
Mrs. Vavasour *of* York.
Mrs. Ann Unet, *bookseller at* Wolverhampton.

W.

* *The right honourable the earl of* Winchelsea *and* Nottingham.
* *The honourable* Thomas Willoughby, *esq;*
The honourable Mrs. Willoughby.
The honourable Rothwell Willoughby, *esq;*
The honourable Henry Willoughby, *esq;*
The honourable Montague Wortley, *esq;*
Sir William Wyndham, *bart.*
Sir Francis Whichcote, *bart.*
Sir John Webb, *bart.*
* *The lady* Wentworth *of* Howsam.
William Wickham, *esq;*
William Woodyeare, *esq;*
Patience Warde, *esq;*
Pleasaunce Watson, *esq;*
* James West, *esq;*
Brown Willis, *esq;*
George Wright, *esq;*
William Wrightson, *esq;*
Henry Witham, *esq;*
Godfrey Wentworth, *esq;*
Matthew Wentworth, *esq;*
* Richard Walwyn, *esq;*
Andrew Wilkinson, *esq;*
* John Wilkinson, *esq;*
Thomas Wright, *esq;*
John Wood, *esq;*
Thomas Wilson, *esq;*
* Watkin Williams Wynne, *esq;*
Charles Stourton Walmsley, *esq;*
George Wright, *esq;*
Henry Walton, *esq;*
* *Dr.* Wintringham *of* York.
Mr. Clifton Wintringham.
Dr. Wilsford *of* Pontefract.
Major White *of the Tower.*
Captain Wad. Windham.
The reverend Mr. Wakefield, *rector of* Sezay *and prebendary of* Ripon.
The reverend Mr. Wickham, *rector of* Guiseley.
The reverend Mr. Weatherhed *of* Bolton-abbey.
Mr. John Willberfoss, *merchant in* Gainsborough.
Mr. Thomas Wilson *of* Leeds.
Mr. William Watson *of* Sheffield.
Mr. Woodhouse *of* York.
Mr. Henry Waite *of* York.
Mr. William Watkinson *of* York.
Mr. Watson *of* Stockton.
Mr. John Wilmer *of* York.
Mr. Wilcockson *of* Manchester.
Mr. William Webber *of* Exeter.
Mr. Williamson, *bookseller in* Holborn.
Mess. Ward *and* Chandler, *booksellers at* Scarborough, York *and* London. *One large and four small.*

Y.

John Yorke, *esq;*
Thomas Yarborough, *esq;*
The reverend Mr. Younge, *rector of* Cattwick *in* Holderness.
The City of York *fifty pounds.*

THE

CONTENTS.

BOOK I.

BOOK II.

APPENDIX.

APPENDIX.

ERRATUM. Book II. Chap. II. p. 519. ſect. 2.

For, *The whole pavement is a brick floor*, read, *The whole pavement is* on *a brick floor*, &c. Page 4. Note *(i)* for *Sir H. Spelman's notes on* Tacitus, r. *Sir H. Savile's*.

The number and order of placing the looſe prints.

In the APPENDIX.

EBORACUM:

I,

EBORACUM:

OR, THE

HISTORY

AND

ANTIQUITIES

OF THE

CITY of *YORK*.

BOOK I.

CHAP. I.

YORK, *its different names and etymologies; with the obscure history of it to the coming of the* ROMANS *into* BRITAIN.

EBORACUM, or *York*, the Metropolis of ЄBORΛCΣLIRIΛ, or *Yorkshire*, situate at the confluence of the rivers *Ouse* and *Foss*, placed near the centre of the island, in the richest, pleasantest, and most extensive valley in *Britain*, if not in all *Europe*, draws its original from the earliest ages. And wrapt in such obscurity is the etymology of its name, that to me it seems much too high for human comprehension; and, I may justly say, that CAPUT INTER NVBILA CONDIT.

The etymology of the name of *York*, encompassed with such difficulties and uncertainties, must however be an evident token of the great antiquity of the place; and if not as old, yet near coeval with *London*, whose derivation is as little understood. As indeed the title of our whole island *Britain*, if the story of *Brute* and his *Trojans* be deny'd, is lost in numberless conjectures. (*a*) *Stow*, in his Survey of *London*, has made no scruple to deduce the

(*a*) As *Rome* the chief city of the world, to glorify itself, drew her original from Gods, Goddesses; and Demi-Gods by the *Trojan* progeny; so this famous city of *London*, for greater glory, and in emulation of *Rome*, deriveth itself from the very same original. *Stowe's* Survey of *London*, 1 *ed. A.* 1599. Sir *Thomas Elliot* and Dr. *Charles Leigh* have stretch'd farther in ascribing the name of *Neomagus* to the city of *Chester*, from *Magus* the son of *Samothes* son of *Japhet* its founder. *Leigh's* Nat. Hist. of *Lancashire*, *Cheshire*, &c.

original

original of that city from Gods, Goddesses, and Demi-Gods. I am not so bold an historian as he, tho' I have the same reason to do it to ours; yet I shall not stick to give what is related in the *British Historian* concerning our city's antiquity; with this reserve in the enquiry, not to obtrude any thing in evidence without its witness, submitting the truth of the facts to better judgments. And, with the author of a MS now before me, (*b*) shall think it much more congruous to right reason and ingenuity, to conclude with a sceptical consideration, in this nice affair, rather than a peremptory resolution.

The credit of the writer of the *British History* may be disputed by those who intend a general account of the Island; but, in a particular way, I should be much to blame to call that fable and romance, which redounds so mightily to the honour of my subject; and no author I have yet met with, in my judgment, has so far refuted old *Geofry*'s testimony, that it shou'd be wholly rejected by a *Modern Historian* (*c*).

Geofry of *Monmouth*, I say, is the sole evidence that can be produced, as an author, to vindicate this chronology; the rest of the historians, which mention the same, are only so many echoers or copyers of that original. To begin then,

Brutus and his wandring *Trojans* having conquer'd *Albion*, built a City on the river *Thames*, and gave it the name of *Troja Nova*; this name of *Troja Nova* came afterwards by corruption, says my author, to be called *Troy Novant*, and since chang'd into *Ludstown* or *London*. The historian places this epoch at the time when the sons of *Hector*, after the expulsion of *Antenor*, reign'd in *Troy*; when *Eli* the High Priest govern'd in *Judea*; and when *Silvius Æneas*, the son of *Æneas* and uncle to *Brutus* the third King of the *Latins*, rul'd in *Italy*. If this be true, then *London* first raised its head about the year, from the
A. M. 2860. world's creation, two thousand eight hundred and sixty; or eleven hundred and six years be-
Ante C. 1106. fore the birth of *Christ*.

The historian, in the sequel of his wondrous account, goes on and tells us, that *Ebraucus*, the son of *Mempricius* the third King from *Brute*, did build a city north of *Humber*, which from his own name he called *Kaer-ebrauc*, that is, the city of *Ebraucus*; about the time that
A. M. 2983. *David* reign'd in *Judea*, *Sylvius Latinus* in *Italy*, and that *Gad*, *Nathan*, and *Asaph*, prophe-
Ante C. 983. fied in *Israel*, which *Epoch* falls near *A. M.* 2983, or *ante Christum* 983.

We are told, by the aforesaid author, that this King *Ebraucus* built two more cities; one call'd (*d*) *Aclud* towards *Albania*, and the town of *Mount* (*e*) *Agned*, which is at this time, says he, call'd the *Castle of Maidens* or *the Mountain of Sorrow*. That he reign'd sixty years, and by twenty wives had twenty sons and thirty daughters, whom he has thought fit to give us the names of; that he was the first after *Brute* who went with a navy into *Gaul*, and returned victorious; and lastly, in an extream old age he died, and was buried at *Kaer-ebrauc*. Thus much for King *Ebrauc*, and whether he built our city? or whether indeed there was ever such a King? I leave to judgment on the testimony above; if the last be granted, the other may easily be allowed a consequence.

In the appellation of the *British Kaer-ebrauc*, we are to find out the *Roman EBORACVM*, which Sir *T. W.* strives to do after this manner; some learned men, says he, by writing the second *Latin* vowel with an apostrophe for speaking of it short, the *Italians* by inadvertency have changed it into the fourth, and for *Eberacum* write *Eboracum*, as for *Edouardus*, they now write *Edwardus*; for which reason *Civitas Ebrauci* is now called *Civitas Eborauci*; and the learned *John Cajus* says (*f*), that the name is changed from *Evoracum* to *Eborum*.

My author goes on and says, "he cannot conceal what he had from a noble person, "which he was pleased in modesty only to term a conjecture; it appears by *Cæsar* and "*Tacitus*, that several colonies of the *Gauls* seated themselves, as in other countries, so in "*Spain*; from whence again being disturbed by the *Romans*, *Carthaginians*, and other nati-"ons, they were forced to seek new habitations, and might either first seize on the western part "of middle *England*; or, from *Ireland*, that place not sufficing for them, empty themselves "hither; giving the name of *Eboracum* to *York*, from *Ebora* a town in *Portugal*, for *Ebura* "in *Andalusia*; the former of which is to this day call'd *Evora*, to which if you add *c*, be-"ing in the antient *Gaulogists* a diminutive, you have *Eborac*, the last syllable (*um*) being "a *latin* termination. This is also *Buchanan*'s opinion.

"If you will have it more immediately derived from *Gaul*, or *Gallia Belgica*, you have "then the *Eburones*, a people that inhabited about *Liege* in the time of *Cæsar*; who, possi-"bly transplanted hither, might give it the name of *Eburac*, or little *York*. There are "also the *Eburaci* or *Ebroici*, for it is read both ways, in *Gallia Celtica*, whose chief city "*Eboraicum* favours exceedingly the etymology of *York*; and it may very well argue a "transplanting of the natives hither.

Thus far the learned Knight; on the other hand *Verstegan* in his book of the restitution of decayed intelligence, says, "that the antient *Britons* call'd the city of *York*, *Caer-efroc*: "our ancestors **Eborwic, Everwic** and **Eberwic**; which by vulgar Abbreviation might

(*b*) Sir *Thomas Withrington*'s MS history of *York*.

(*c*) The verity of *Geofry*'s history has been excellently well vindicated by Mr. *Aaron Thompson*, in the preface to an *English* edition of that author, *London* printed 1718.

(*d*) By some said to be *Bremham Castle* on the river *Eden* near *Carlisle*, by others, *Aldburgh*.

(*e*) *Edenborough*.

(*f*) *J. Cajus in Ant. Acad. Cant.*

" come to Boric or Woric, and so lastly to *York*. Eber or Ever is in the old *Saxon* " wild boar, tho' this latter name be *English* also : Wic is a refuge or retreat, and it may " be it had of our anceſtors that appellation, as being the refuge or retreat from the wild " boars, which heretofore might have been in the *Foreſt of Galtres (g)*, which is within a mile " of that city ; and the more like it is, for that there yet remains a toll call'd Guyde Lawe, " which is paid for Cattle at *Bowdam-Bar*, a gate of the city ſo call'd, and was firſt paid " for the payment of guides which conducted them, belike, to ſave them from this cruel " beaſt through the ſaid foreſt.

That there were wild boars as well as wolves in this iſland formerly, I ſuppoſe will not be denyed ; and no foreſt could better harbour theſe creatures, than this famous wood, called in antient authors CALETERIVM NEMVS ; whoſe extent, if we may give credit to an hiſtorian, ſtretched north-weſt from the city *(h)* twenty miles. It may here be taken notice of, in order to ſtrengthen *Verſtegan*'s conjecture, that there is a village at the extremity of the foreſt, north from *Bowdam-Bar*, and in the road to it, call'd *Tollerton*, which probably was the place that travellers took their guides from, and paid one part of their toll or tax for it. That there is another village on the foreſt, about a mile from the city, named *Huntington* ; which no doubt took its name from the hunting of wild beaſts in thoſe days. And laſtly, it is farther obſervable, that there is over the north door of the weſt end of the cathedral, pointing to the gate and foreſt aforeſaid, in a ſort of *Baſſo relievo*, the figures of a wild boar purſu'd by one winding a hunter's horn ; ſurrounded with a pack of hounds, whilſt the boar is ſlain by a man armed with a ſhield and lance. In this hieroglyphical deſcription, the builders of this famous edifice might probably allude to the name of Ebor, as mention'd by *Verſtegan*. *(i)* Our late *Leeds* antiquary is of this author's opinion, and ſays, that the preſent name of *York* may be eaſily enough deduced from the *Saxon* Eoꝼeꞃƿic ; the initials of which were no doubt in thoſe ages pronounced as Yo. This is yet continued in ſome parts of the north, where eode is pronounced yode. I my ſelf, adds he, have been told upon the road, that *ſike a yan yode that way*. The ꝼ, continues our etymologiſt, was omitted for ſoftneſs in pronunciation, as alſo ƿ ; and he had of the monies of King *Edward* the Confeſſor, whereon for EOFER is writ EOR (YOR) to which add the laſt letter C (now converted into K) and you have the modern name YORC or YORK.

Others believe that the name of this city is derived from nothing more than the river *Eure* it ſtands upon: and then the ſignification of the word amounts to no more than a town or city ſtanding or placed upon *Eure*. Thus the *Eberanci*, a people of *France*, ſat down by the river *Eure* near *Eureux* in *Normandy*, and from thence contracted their name. This is the opinion of that great antiquary *Camden* ; and if the point be cleared, that the river *Ouſe* was formerly call'd *Eure* as low as *York*, we need look no further for our etymology.

John Leland, that great magazine of antiquity, to whoſe collections the ableſt *Engliſh* antiquaries have been ſo particularly obliged, eſteems the river *Ouſe* to be one of the Rivers of *Iſis*. *(k)* " The river *Ouſe*, ſays he, ariſes in the fartheſt part of the province of *Richmond*, at a " place call'd *Cotterhill* or *Cotterend* ; it paſſes through divers places, and comes at laſt to " *Burrough-Bridge*, and there is call'd ISVRIVM, the name of *Iſis* being prepoſed to " *Eure*. *Ptolemy*, adds my author, ſpeaking of the cities of the BRIGANTES, mentions " this of ISVRIVM, and ſo does *Antoninus* in his itinerary ; but this city came to nothing when the *Danes* deſtroyed all *England* with fire and ſword. *Nunc ſeges eſt & villa* " *ruſtica ubi* ISVRIVM *fuit*. Here the plowman frequently finds reliques of old walls " and *Roman* coyn ; the name of the place is now called *Aldborough*, as much as to ſay " *old town*. Now here lies the difficulty, adds he, for the inhabitants hereabouts ſay " that *Ouſe* a little below *Burrough-bridge* doth receive the name of *Eure*, which ſeems " not very probable, ſince ISVRIVM antiently, as may be collected from the very " word, doth carry the names of both the rivers ; and leſſer rivers do many times give " name to greater, as appears in the *Thames*, as well as this ; ſo the river a little after " it is paſt *Burrough-bridge* by the people affecting brevity, wholly leaving out *Eure* have " taken up the firſt part of the name and call it *Iſis* vulgarly *Ouſe*. And if a man, purſues he, ſhall fully conſider the name Eurewic, which by contraction is *York*, he will " underſtand that it hath taken the name from Iſurewic, retaining the firſt letter, and " caſting away the ſecond and changing the third into *O*, as Iorewic or Yorewic which " is ſoon thrown into *York*.

(l) This great antiquary in another part of his works is ſtill more explicit in this affair, which I ſhall beg leave to give the reader in his own words as follows ; *ſunt qui ſuſpicentur*,

(g) Boars at this day, ſays Lawyer *Hildyard*, who is very fond of this opinion, are call'd in *Yorkſhire*, *Gautes*. *Hild.* Ant. *York* 1664.

(h) Conſtat igitur quod Nemus Caleterinum, *quod anglice* Galtres *dicitur, attingit pene* Eborum, *& inde verſus Zephyrum extenditur juxta* Aldburgh, *in longum ſpatio* xx *milliarium, cujus nemoris plurima pars hodie ſuccſis arbuſculis ad culturam redigitur.* *Palichron.* R. Higdeni.

(i) Thoreſby's *Ducat. Leod. in appendice.*

(k) J. Leland in Com. Cant.

(l) J. Leland in *Geneth.* Ed. primi.

neo

nec temere, illud flumen, quod urbem alluit ISVRIVM, olim dictum fuisse ab Iside & Uro *superius confluentibus. Ise fluvius a saxonibns Ouse dicitur, argumento sunt* Ouseford, *id est, Isidis vadum*; Ouseburn, *id est, Isidis aqua. Si hæc conjectura valet, ut certè plurimum valere videtur,* ISVROVICVM *aptum, elegans, rotundum etiam urbi nomen erat.*

The justly celebrated Mr. *Camden* has taken thro' his works all imaginable pains to destroy the credit of the *British* historian; and old *Geofry* is represented by him, as a dreamer of dreams, and seer of visions; for which reason he is not a little fond of this opinion, which makes the derivation of our city's name to be entirely *Roman*; and says the name of the *British* King *Ebrauc* was coin'd out of EBORACVM. *(m)* He lays it down as an uncontestable truth, that the *Eure* at *Burrough-bridge* has gained the name of *Ouse*, from a little petty rivulet which runs into it at *Ouseburn*, a village so called, to which it hath given the name and robbed the river *Eure* of it. *(n)* The reader may easily find that *Camden* comes into *Leland*'s opinion in this; I will not say that he borrowed it of him without mentioning his author; a right reverend *Prelate* in his *English* editions of that book, having sufficiently vindicated him from any such aspersion; but it is certain *Leland* was positive in this affair before *Camden* was born; and in another part of his works, giving a description of the river *Nid*, he says it runs into *Eure*, corruptly there call'd *Ouse*, at *Nun monkton (o)*.

It is not impossible but this may be the true definition of *York*, and its latin *(p)* EBVRACVM or EBORACVM, as it is spelt both ways in the itinerary ascribed to the emperour *Antoninus*. It is true, the name has nothing derivative from either *Latin* or *Greek* in it; nor indeed is the name of any *Roman* station in *Britain* to be well construed that way; yet whetheir EBVRACVM and the *Saxon (q)* Eupe-pic Yupe-pic, *&c.* are not more sensibly derived from a station or town on the river *Eure* or *Yure* than from *Kaer-Ebrauc* I leave to the readers judgment. If the *Welch*, or *Cambro Britons* as they are called, are allowed to have yet retained the language of the primary inhabitants of this island, which all their historians wou'd have us to believe; it would have been a strong testimony of *Geofry*'s verity for them to have called *York* after his manner at this day. *Humphry Lhuyd*, their learned antiquary, in mentioning the *Brigantine* towns that are in *Ptolemy*'s geography, says, *(r)* EBORACVM is well known to be the very same city that the *Britons* call *Caer-Effroc*, the *Anglo Saxons* Euppyck and is now contracted into *York*. Of the rest, adds he, it is uncertain. But *Caer-Effroc* and *Ebrauc* are somewhat different in sound.

Our late antiquary Mr. *Baxter (s)* conjectures that the *Roman* EBVRACVM is derived from the *British* Eur, vel Ebr, which answers to the *Greek* Ὑδωρ; thence, he says, the adjective is formed Evraüc, *aquosum*, watery; and the *British* name to this city Caer-Evrauc, *aquosa civitas*, a watery city. This grave author goes on somewhat pleasantly, and says that the *Latin* word *ebrius*, drunk, signifies no more than *bene madidus*, well moistened. The neighbouring river, he adds, is called *Eura*, or *Ebura*; of which very name there is another river in *France*, as well as a people called *Eburones*, &c. The watery situation, this author speaks of, will fit us well enough; but I am not so learned in the *British* language, as either to confirm or contradict his assertion. Indeed, after all, I am of opinion with *Buchanan* in this, that the original of words depends not on the notions of the wiser sort, but on the pleasure of the vulgar, who for the most part are rude and unpolished; and therefore anxiously to enquire after their judgments is a piece of needless curiosity; and if you should find out what they mean, it would not be worth your labour *(t)*.

Thus having given the opinions of the learned upon this intricate affair, it must be left to every ones thoughts to frame out of them his own conjecture. I must next do that justice to *York*, which *Stow* and his editor *Stripe* have not scrupled to do for *London*; which is, to transcribe out of our aforecited *British* historian, what memorables he has noted relating to us, and do that honour to the city which he and his numberless followers have attested the verity of; but in this I shall not pretend to adjust the different chronologies.

The copyers of our author in his *British* history I find have prettily enlarged upon his scheme as often as occasion served. So *Ebraucus*, the ever renowned founder of *Kaer-Ebrauc*, is said by them to have built a temple to *Diana* in his city; and sat there as first *Arch-flamen*. And, he had such a respect for the city he had planted, that after a long and prosperous reign over the *Britons*, he chose to die and order'd his body to be buried in it *(u)*. As was his son and successor *Brutus* sirnamed *Greenshield*, by the same authority; but to these particulars *Geofry* himself is silent.

(m) Camden's remains.
(n) Britannia.
(o) Lelandi collectanea.
(p) Iter ab EBORACO LONDINIUM in *Blandiniano* [ed.] Iter ab VBVRACO: & in *Neopolitano*, ab EBVRACO. *Longoliani Blandinianam* lectionem praeferunt, & EBVRACO corrigunt. *Hieron. Surit.* not. in *Anton.* itin. ed. *Gale.*

(q) Ea-upe-pic. i. e. castrum ad, vel secus, aquam URE. *Somner's Saxon* dictionary.
(r) Humph. Lhuyd frag. *Brit.* descriptio.
(s) Baxter's glossarium antiquitat. *Brit.* vide EBORACVM.
(t) Buchani hist. *Scotiae.*
(u) Fabian and *Stow*, &c.

Some

Some time after the death of the former, the *British* writer tells us that two brothers *Belinus* and *Brennus* jointly ruled in *Britain*. But falling at variance, *(w) Brennus* was driven out of the kingdom. He fought aid of the kings of *Denmark* and *Norway*; the former went with him in perſon, and the latter aſſiſted him with troops; and landing in *Northumberland*, he ſent his brother word that if he did not comply with his demands he would deſtroy him and the whole iſland from ſea to ſea. *Belinus* upon this marches againſt him, with the flower of the kingdom in his army, and found his brother drawn up in a wood called *Calater (x)* ready to receive him. The fight was bloody and long, becauſe, ſays my author, the braveſt men were engaged on both ſides, and ſo great was the ſlaughter, that the wounded fell on heaps, like ſtanding corn cut down by the reapers. At laſt the *Britons* prevailed, and *Brennus* was forced back to his ſhips with the loſs of twenty thouſand men.

In this battle *Guilthdacus*, king of *Denmark*, is ſaid to be taken priſoner; and the victor *Belinus* called a council at *(y) York* to know how to diſpoſe of him. All the nobles of the kingdom being aſſembled at the aforeſaid city, it was agreed that the king ſhould be ſet at liberty, on condition to hold his crown of the king of *Britain*; and likewiſe to pay him an *(z)* annual tribute. Oaths and hoſtages being taken on this occaſion, the *Daniſh* monarch was releaſed from priſon; and returned into his own countrey.

The next we find, in *Monmouth*'s hiſtory, wherein our ſubject is any way concerned, is a *Britiſh* prince called *Archigallus (a)* or *Artogal*, who was diſpoſſeſſed by his nobles of crown and dignity, for ſeveral indirect practices, and his brother *Elidurus* put up in his ſtead. A very remarkable ſtory occurs here, which, true or falſe, will claim a place in our hiſtory.

Artogal being depoſed, as has been ſaid, and his brother advanced to the crown, wandered about a fugitive and outlaw; and having travelled over ſeveral kingdoms in hopes to procure aid to recover his loſt dominions, finding none, and being no longer able to bear the poverty to which he was reduced, returned back to *Britain*, with only ten men, in his company, with a deſign to repair to thoſe who were formerly his friends. *Elidure*, who had been five years in poſſeſſion of the kingdom, as he happened to be hunting one day in the wood call'd *Calaterium*, in the wildeſt part of this vaſt foreſt, got ſight of his unhappy brother, and forgetting all injuries ran to him and affectionately embraced him. As he had long ſecretly lamented his brother's misfortunes, he took this opportunity to endeavour to remedy them. He conveyed him privately to the city *Aclud*, where he hid him in his bed-chamber. He there feigned himſelf ſick, and ſent meſſengers over the whole kingdom, to ſignify to all his prime nobility, that they ſhould come to viſit him. Accordingly, when they were all met together, at the city where he lay, he gave orders that they ſhould come into his chamber ſoftly and without noiſe; his pretence for this was, that, ſhould they all croud in together, their talk would be a diſturbance to his head. The nobles in obedience to his commands, and without the leaſt ſuſpicion of any deſign, entered his houſe one after another. But *Elidure* had given charge to his ſervants, who were ſet ready for the purpoſe, to take each of them as they entered, and cut off their heads, unleſs they would again ſubmit themſelves to *Artogal* his brother. Thus did he with every one of them apart, and compelled them through fear to be reconciled to *Artogal*. The agreement being ratifyed, *Elidure* conducted his brother to *York*, where he took the crown off his own head and ſet it on his brothers; which rare example produced as wonderful an effect, for *Artogal*, after his reſtoration, we are told, proved a moſt excellent governour, and after a mild reign of ten years, he died, was buried at *York*, and *Elidurus* again ſucceeded him.

In the following reigns of more than thirty ſucceſſors to this laſt prince, the *Britiſh* hiſtory is ſilent to any thing but their names, and ſome of their characters; to the landing of *Caeſar* in *Britain*. From which *aera* we tread more certain ſteps, and by the aſſiſtance of the beſt hiſtorical guides the world has produced, it is hoped, I may be able to ſet my ſubject in a clearer light. For whoſo will frown at *Monmouth*'s ſtory and call it all dream and fiction; will however pay ſome regard to the teſtimony of a *Tacitus*, a *Dion*, or an *Herodian*.

(w) This *Brennus*, our author would have us believe, was the ſame perſon who led the army of the confederate *Gauls*, and took and burnt *Rome* in the dictatorſhip of *Camillus*.

(x) Galtres foreſt juxta *Ebor*.

(y) Intra *Eboracum*. *Gal. Mon.* It is remarkable that *Geofry* never calls *York Kaer-Ebrauck*, but once throughout his whole work.

(z) Fabian and *Hollingſhead* have thought fit to aſſign the ſum of 1000*l*. for this Tribute; but I do not find the original mentions it.

(a) Fabian and *Stow*, in their chronicles, mention *Rivallus*, *Gurguſtius* his ſon, *Iago* or *Lago* and *Kimmacus*, all Kings of *Britain*, and all before *Artogal*, to be buried at *Kaerbrauc*. But ſince *Geofry* is ſilent, this muſt be an improvement on his ſcheme.

It will not be amifs, to conclude this head, to prefent the reader, at one view, with a lift of the different names this city has had, with the different authorities for them; and firft,

EBORACVM.	*Multis teftibus.*
Εβόρακον.	Ptolemeus *in opere Geograph.* Ufher *de primord.*
Ευόρακον.	Ptol. *in canon. aftronomicis.*
Βριγάντιον.	Ptol. *in magna fyntaxi lib.* 2. Ufher *de prim.*
CIVITAS BRIGANTIVM.	Tacitus *in vita Agricolae.*
(*b*) VBVRACVM & EBVRACVM.	*In itin.* Antonini.
KAER-EBRAVC. / CAIR-BRAVC.	Gal. Mon. Nennius *in cat. Urbium Brit. ed.* Gale. Hen. Hunt. Alph. Bever. Harrifon, &c.
CAIR-EFFROC.	*By the Britons at this day.* Ufher *de prim.* Verftegan. Humph. Llhuyd.
EVOR-ƿIC. / EVER-ƿIC. / EOFER-ƿIC. / EOFOR-ƿIC. / EFER-ƿIC.	*Saxonice.*
EOFOR-ƿIC-CEASTER. / CEASTER *fimplice.*	Somner. & Chron. Saxon. *ad ann.* 685, 763, 780. &c.
VRDWIC.	Leland.
ISVROVICVM.	Leland.
VROVICVM.	Ortelius. Harrifon.
EBORACA.	Girald Cambrenfis.
ALTERA ROMA. / VICTORIA.	Harrifon's *defcription of Britain.*
SEXTA.	Selden's *titles of honour.*
Civitas Eborum & Eurvic.	Lib. Domefday.
Euorwic. / Euerwyke. / Eoforwiic. / Yeuorwiic. / Urewiic. / Yurewiic.	Knighton. Hen. Hunt. R. Hoveden. Record. *in cuftodia civium Ebor. cum aliis.*

Hodie YORKE *vel* YORK.

(*b*) *Veteres faepiffime U pro O utuntur; & vice verfa.*

CHAP.

CHAP. II.

Contains the ſtate of the city under the Roman *government in* Britain.

AS the original of this ancient city is ſo much obſcured that nothing but conjectural hints can be given of it, ſo likewiſe the affairs of the whole iſland want the ſame illuſtration; and we are no more in the dark than our neighbours, till the times that the *Romans* thought fit to give us their firſt viſit. This deſcent happened on the *Kentiſh* ſhore, and as *Caeſar* never penetrated ſo far north as *York*, it cannot be expected that any account of our city can be found in that noble hiſtorian. Indeed, what he does relate concerning the cities or towns, which he ſaw in *Britain*, is not much for their credit; *(a) the inhabitants*, ſays he, *knew nothing of building with ſtone*; *but called that a town, which had a thick intangled wood, defended with a ditch and bank about it.* The ſame kind of fortification the *Iriſh* call to this day *A Faſtneſs*. If we were a city at *Caeſar*'s landing, there is no room to doubt but that this muſt have been our ſtate; and the famous *Caleterium nemus*, or the foreſt mentioned before, might have ſerved for great part of its fortification.

I ſhall not carry off my readers with any particularities relating to the *Romans* firſt or ſecond landing in *Britain*; nor any other of their affairs in this iſland, any more than what I think conſonant to my deſign. That the *Britons* called this place KAER, *(b)* or city, before the *Romans* came, I preſume will hardly be denied. Our former teſtimony, old *Monmouth* writes that *Caſſibelaun*, king of the *Trinobantes*, as *Caeſar* himſelf ſtyles him, general of the united forces of the iſland, after making a peace with the *Romans*, retired to *York*, died and was buried there, *(c)*. The *(d) Brigantes*, as the more northern inhabitants of *Britain* were called, certainly muſt have had their fortreſſes, and muſt have been very formidable in thoſe days. Elſe an attack upon them by *Petilius Cerialis* the *Roman* lieutenant, as related by *Tacitus*, would not have ſtruck the whole iſland with a general terror. It is true, they had been reduced ſome time before by *Oſtorius*; but in this revolt, they had taken care to fortify themſelves in ſuch a manner, and were ſuch a numerous hardy race of people, that they were thought unconquerable by their countrymen. I ſhall not take upon me to tranſlate CIVITAS BRIGANTVM, as here mentioned by *Tacitus*, into *York*; I am aware that the beſt commentators on that author agree that, *Civitas* ought to be underſtood as a country or diſtrict quite through his work. It is indeed a word of great latitude; and ſince I ſhall have occaſion to mention it in another quotation, from a *Roman* hiſtorian, where it muſt be allowed me that it abſolutely ſignifies the city it ſelf, I think proper here to diſcuſs a little this ſignificant term. A. C. LXXVI.

Urbs, *civitas*, and *oppidum*, were words which the *Romans* made uſe of to denote cities and towns of greater reſort and more immediate command in the empire. The firſt was always ſingularly applied to the great city it ſelf, and never to any other place. *Oppidum* chiefly regarded a mercantile ſituation, from its derivative *opes*; whence always *oppidum Londinii*. But *civitas* is by much more extenſive than either of them, and does not only denote a city, but a place, people, conſtitution, cuſtom, laws, religion, and every thing annexed to its juriſdiction within the whole province. The word is taken from *civis* and *civilis*; which are the ſame as the *Greek* πολίτης and πολιτικός. And may be underſtood as a city or country, inhabited by a ſet of people, bound by laws and cuſtoms to one another. *(e) Omnis civitas* HELVETIAE *in quatuor pagos diviſa eſt*, ſays *Caeſar*, *Switzerland* is divided into four cantons. And *Aulus Gellius* writes *(f) civitas & pro loco, & pro oppido, & pro jure quoque omnium, & pro hominum multitudine dicitur*. So though *Rome* was ſtyled *urbs*, *per eminentiam*, yet *Athens* and even *Conſtantinople*, by claſſical authority, claim but the title of *oppida*, reſpecting the buildings only; for it never includes the people, as *urbs* ſometimes does, and *civitas* always.

The diſputable paſſage in *Tacitus*, which I here contend about is this, *(g) & terrorem ſtatim intulit* PETILIVS CERIALIS, BRIGANTVM CIVITATEM, *quae numeroſiſſima provinciae totius perhibetur, aggreſſus; multa praelia, & aliquando non incruenta, magnamque* BRIGANTVM *partem aut victoria amplexus aut bello.* Sir *H. Savile* tranſlates the former part of this ſentence thus, the general ſtruck the *Britons* with the greateſt terror, when he durſt

(a) Caeſaris Com.

(b) De nomine Caer *vide* Uſher *de primord.* p. 71. The *Britiſh Caer* and the *Saxons Cheſter* were ſynonymous. See *Kennet*'s parochial antiq. p. 688.

(c) In urbe Eboraco *ſepultus.* Gal. Mon.

(d) BRIGANTES, whence derived. Conſult *Camden*, *Buchan*, *Baxter*, &c.

(e) Caeſ. Com. l. i. c. xii.

(f) Auli Gel. l. xviii. c. vii

(g) In vita Agricolae.

make

make an assault upon the *city of the Brigantines*, which was then esteemed the most populous of the whole province. A late *(h)* translator gives it this turn, struck them at once with general terrors, by attacking the *community* of the *Brigantes*, *&c.* now whether of these are in the right I leave it to the learned to determine. If the former, we may with great assurance set it down for the city of *York*.

But a *British* fortress is not worth our further contending for; it seems to be much more honour to us to derive our original from the *Romans* themselves. In all probability this was the case; for *York* being placed near the centre of the island, and in a spatious and fruitful valley; naturally strong in its situation, and having a communication with the safest bays and harbours on the *German* ocean; their geography and policy might teach them that this was the properest place to build and fortify. *Alcuin*, a native of this city, and who lived near a thousand years agoe, is of this opinion; and has left us this testimony of it,

> *Hanc* Romana *manus muris, & turribus, altam*
> *Fundavit primo*———
> *Ut fieret ducibus secura potentia regni;*
> *Et decus imperii, terrorque hostilibus armis.*

> This city, first, by *Roman* hand was form'd,
> With lofty towers, and high built walls adorn'd.
> It gave their leaders a secure repose;
> Honour to th' empire, terror to their foes.

The authority of an historian of so antient a date is almost equal to a *Roman* one; and without doubt, the traditional account of the origine of this city, in his time, was such as he has related. Besides, the situation of *York* is very agreeable to the site of antient *Rome*. For *(i) Sigonius* writes that *Fabius* left a picture of *Rome*, in form of a *bow*, of which the river *Tyber* was the *string*. Whoever surveys the ichnography of *York*, in the sequel, will find
Circa A. C. it answer this description very justly. And what is on the west side the river *Ouse* with us,
LXXXX. seems to agree also with the old *Transtyberim* of *Rome*. It is probable to me that this city was first planted and fortified by *Agricola*; whose conquests in the island stretched beyond *York*; and that great general might build here a fortress, to guard the frontiers after his return. What seems to add to the probability of this, is, that when the emperour *Hadrian* came into *Britain*, to inspect into and overlook the guards and garrisons of the island; and
A. to endeavour the conquest of Caledonia; he was dissuaded from the attempt by some old
CXXIV. soldiers of *Agricola*'s that he met with at *York*. They represented that part of the island to be not worth his conquest; the war more laborious than honourable; and should his undertaking be crown'd with success, that it wou'd procure no great advantage to the empire. These veterans had had their share of the *Caledonian* expedition under *Agricola*; and did not care to engage the emperour in a new attempt. He took however their advice, and rather chose to throw up a long rampart of earth to secure this country from the invasions of the more northern *Britons*, than adventure his reputation and army in so hazardous an enterprise *(k)*.

The ablest modern historians all agree that *Hadrian* brought into *Britain* with him in this expedition, the sixth legion; styled Legio Sexta Victrix. At his departure this legion was stationed at *York*; not only to keep the native *Britons* in subjection, but also to be in readiness, with the other auxiliaries, to oppose the northern invaders; in case they should attempt to overthrow his rampart. We can trace this legion in this particular station for the space of 300 years and upwards. Such a considerable body of men being inhabitants of this city for so long a time, and having leave to marry among the natives, which they most commonly did, might make a *York-man* proud of his descent. For says *Camden*, in his refutation of the *British* historians, if the *English* are so fond of deducing their original from the *Trojans*, they may draw it a better way than from *Brute*, *viz.* from the *Romans*; who certainly sprung from the *Trojans* and we from them. *(l)* Yet the sequel of this history will much abate our pride in this particular, and too truly shew, that had we an ocean of *Roman* blood amongst us formerly, there is sufficient occasion to believe that the last drop has been drained from us long ago.

It is not improper here to let the reader understand, from the best authorities, of what number of men a *Roman* legion consisted. As also the civil and military government of them during their residence with us; but this will fall apter under another head of this work. *(m)* And a particular disquisition on the sixth and ninth legions may be met with in the sequel of this.

(h) Gordon's Tacitus.
(i) Car. Sigonius *historia de reg.* Italiae.
(k) Britanniam *petiit, in qua multa correxit, murumque per octaginta millia passuum primus duxit qui* Barbaros Romanosque *divideret. Vit.* Hadriani *inter script. aug.*
(l) Camden's remains.
(m) See Chap. vi.

To pursue the course of my annals. The emperor *Hadrian* having reduced *Britain* to obedience and planted guards and garrisons where he thought convenient, returned to *Rome*; where he soon after struck coin, with this inscription on the reverse, RESTITVTOR BRITANNIAE *(n)*. I come next to shew what figure our city bore in the reigns of his successors.

About the time of the date in the margin, this city was one of the greatest if not the A.
most considerable station in the province. By the itinerary ascribed to *Antoninus*, which I CL.
shall have occasion to treat more largely on in the sequel, EBORACVM, or EBVRACVM, occurs in all its northern journeys, and frequently with the addition of LEGIO VI. VICTRIX *(o)*. This adjunct, so particular to our city, denotes it of high authority in the province at this time; but whether the itinerary belongs to this *Antonine*, or any other emperour of that name, I shall examine in the sequel.

Under the government of MARCVS AVRELIVS, LVCIVS, a *British* king, is said to have embraced *christianity*. And, if we are not too partial to our country, he is also said to have been the first crowned head in the world that declared for that religion. As I intend to treat on our ecclesiastical affairs under another head, the mention of this monarch has small signification here, unless I suppose him living under the *Roman* protection in this city; for though the *British* historian tells us that he died at *Gloucester*, and was there interred, yet the same authority assures us, that his father *Coilus* lived, died, and was buried at *York (p)*. In the death of this *Lucius*, the wonderful line of *Brute* failed, after they had continued, says an historian, kings of this island 1300 years; and it opening a door for many claims, the nation fell into a bloody civil war for the space of 15 years *(q)*.

In the reign of COMMODVS the *Caledonians* took up arms, and cut in pieces the *Roman* army, commanded by an unexperienced general, and ravaged the country in a terrible manner as far as *York (r)*. The whole province was in danger to be over-run, had not the emperor immediately sent over *Marcellus Ulpius*, who in a small time put an end to this A.
seeming dangerous war, and drove those restless spirits to their strong holds again. At his CLXXX.
return to *York*, he set about to discipline the *Roman* army, and bring it to its antient strictness. For he had observed that these commotions and inroads of the *Caledonians*, were chiefly owing to an entire neglect of good discipline amongst his men. This severity the army took so ill, having been long used to an unbridled licence, that though *Marcellus* got safe to *Rome*, his successor *Pertinax*, following his steps with the same rigour and military discipline, had like to have lost his life in a mutiny of the *ninth legion*. In all probability this mutiny was at *York*; for that the ninth legion was there in station, as well as the sixth, will appear by what follows. But,

We come now to an history of more than bare probabilities and surmises in the life of that illustrious emperor SEVERVS. This great man, in the thirteenth year of his reign, undertook an expedition into *Britain*, though he was at that time somewhat aged and clogged with infirmities. The banished *Britons* had been so bold, *(s)* say their historians, as to advance so far, in their conquests, as to besiege *York*; under *Fulgenius*, or *Sulgenius*, a *Scithian* general; whom they had drawn over to their aid, in order to drive the *Romans* from all their conquests in the island. Suppose this so far true, or not, it is certain, by *Roman* authority, that VIRIVS LVPVS, then *Propraetor* in *Britain*, was hard put to it to defend himself; for *Herodian* tells us, that he wrote to the emperor "informing him of the insurrections and inroads of the *Barbarians*, and the havock they made far and near, and begging either a greater force, or that the Emperor would come over in person." This last was granted; *Severus*, attended with his two sons *Caracalla* and *Geta*, his whole court, A.
and a numerous army, arrived in *Britain*, in the year 207, say some chronologers; but, I CCVII.
find the particular time is disputed by others. vel
CCVIII.

(t) The invaders, being apprised of this great armament against them, thought fit to retire north of *Hadrian*'s wall, where they feared no enemy, and watch another opportunity. But the emperor was fully determined to destroy this nest of hornets, which had given his predecessors so much trouble; and he no sooner found that they were retired to their fastnesses, than he prepared to follow them. When every thing was got ready for the expedition, he marched from *York* with his son *Caracalla*, but left *Geta* in that station to administer justice till his return. With this young prince he joined in commission ÆMILIVS PAVLVS PAPINIANVS, that oracle of the law, as he is justly styled, as an aid and assistant to him, in order to direct his steps, and fortify his youthful levity. *Severus* was 60 years of age when he undertook this expedition, very infirm, and crippled with the gout *(u)*, insomuch that he was carried against the *Caledonians* in an horse-litter. But being a man of invincible spirit, he despised the danger, and bravely overcame it. He penetrated to the extremity of the island, subduing those fierce and barbarous nations, hitherto unconquered. But knowing that he could not keep them in subjection, without a strong army

(n) *Mediobarbj* imp. Rom num. p. 177.
(o) Itin *Antonini*.
(p) *Geofry Mon.*
(q) *Languett*'s Chronicle.
(r) See *Rapine*'s hist. of *England*. *Dion. Cass.*
(s) *Geof Mon. Johan Fordun* hist *Scotiae* inter script. v. ed *Gale*.
(t) *Dion. Cassius, Herodian*
(u) *Senex et pedibus aeger*. Spartian *in vita* Severi, *inter script. rei aug.*

upon the spot; he took hostages of them, and chose rather to build a stone wall, of above eighty miles in length, and of great strength, in the place where his predecessor *Hadrian* had thrown up his rampart of earth. *Severus* is said by *Dion*, to have lost 50000 men in this expedition, not slain by the enemy, but starved, killed and drowned, in cutting down woods, draining of bogs, and the like.

The credit of the *British* historian here falls to the ground, when set in opposition to the *Roman* writers. *Geofry* says, that *Fulgenius* being beaten by *Severus*, at his landing, fled into *Scythia*, where he got together a mighty army, and returned into *Britain*. That he besieged *York*, whilst the emperor was in it; and in a battle before the city *Severus* was slain, and *Fulgenius* mortally wounded. *John Fordun*, the antient chronicler of *Scotland*, writes much the same; but *Bede*, an antienter historian than either of them, follows the *Roman* account, which no doubt is the truest.

Severus left his son *Caracalla* in the north, to inspect the building of the wall, and returned to *York*. Here he took upon himself, and stamped upon his coin the title of BRITANICVS MAXIMVS (*x*), as conqueror of the whole island. He lived more than three years in the *Praetorian* palace of this city; for *Herodian* writes, that some years after his first coming to it, he and his son *Caracalla* sat in the *Praetorium*, and gave judgment, even in very common cases, as in that of *Sicilia*, about the recovery of right of possession of slaves or servants. This rescript or law is still preserved in the *Code*, to the great glory and renown of this city, as *Burton* rightly expresses it, dated from thence, with the names of the consuls of that year; nor can I forbear to publish it, adds that author, as the *gallantest monument of antiquity*, which it hath (*y*).

Cod. l. 3 tit. 32. de rei vindicatione.

ETIAM per alienum servum bona fide possessum ex re ejus qui eum possidet, vel ex operis servi adquiri dominium vel obligationem placuit. Quare si tu quoque bona fide possidisti eundem servum, et ex nummis tuis mancipia eo tempore comparuit, potes secundum juris formam uti defensionibus tuis. Mancipium autem alienum mala fide possidenti nil potest acquirere, sed qui tenet non tantum ipsum sed etiam operas ejus, nec non ancillarum partus et animalium foetus reddere cogitur.

A. CCXI.

P. P. III. NON. MAII. EBORACI FAVSTINO ET RVFO COSS.

If *Burton*, in a general account which he wrote of the island, could think it necessary to publish this whole edict or law, I suppose I may easily be forgiven, who am obliged to be as particular as possible in the course of these annals. The reader may observe, that there is nothing in the rescript itself to my purpose; but the sanction and date are of such great moment in this affair, that it claims a thorough discussion.

P. P. is understood by *Ursatus* to denote *posuit praefectus* (*z*); by which it appears, that *Caesar* enacted, and the *praefect* or judge of the court enrolled and gave a sanction to it. Who this *Civilian* was, has been already taken notice of, but will require greater hereafter. The date runs from the third of the nones of *May*, or *May* 4, *Faustinus* and *Rufus* then consuls. (*a*) Some of our chronologers, especially *Isaacson*, make this to fall *anno ab urbe cond.* 963. or *anno Dom.* 210. Sir *Henry Savile anno* 211. *Severus* is said to have died *pridie non. Februarii*, or *Feb.* 5, *anno Dom.* 212; so that according to this calculation the emperor must have lived in *Britain* near two or three. Our city claims the honour of his residence in it most of this time; for we can trace him no where, but either on his more northern expedition, or at EBORACVM.

It was at, or about, this period of time, that our city shone in full lustre; *Britannici orbis* ROMA ALTERA, PALATIVM *Curiae*, and PRAETORIVM *Caesaris* (*b*) are titles it might justly lay claim to. The prodigious concourse of tributary kings, foreign ambassadors, &c. which almost crowded the courts of the sovereigns of the world, when the *Roman* empire was at or near its prime, must bring it to the height of sublunary grandeur. And this without mentioning the emperor's own magnificence, his numerous retinue, the noblemen of *Rome*, or the officers of the army, which must all necessarily attend him.

The reader will excuse me if I dwell longer on this pleasing subject than the course of these annals may seem to allow of: for, before I bring this great man to his end, I must premise whatever remarkables I find recorded concerning him, whilst he lived in this city.

In this emperor's days, and before, no doubt, the temple of BELLONA stood here. This Goddess of war the heathens feigned to be the sister or wife of *Mars*. *Camden* says, "it was looked upon as a great presage of the emperor's death; that at his entrance into "the city, and willing to do sacrifice to the Gods, he was met and misled by an ignorant "*Augur*, to the temple of *Bellona*, &c." *Spartian*, from whom our antiquary quotes, in accounting for the many presages and bodements which seemed to foretel the death of

(*x*) *Mediobarb.* imp. *Rom.* num. p. 279.
(*y*) *Burton*'s itin. *Antonini.*
(*z*) *Sertorius Ursatus* de notis *Romanorum.*
(*a*) Anno ab v. cond. MCCCCLXIII. *i. e.* A. D. CCXI. *Marcus Acilius Faustinus C. Caesonius Macer Rufianus Coss.* call'd so in Sir *H. Savile*'s Chron. but *Faustinus* and *Rufus* in Chron. *Aur. Cassiodor.*
(*b*) *Alcuin. Ebor. Lelandi* Coll. t. vi.

Severus,

Severus, hath this remarkable passage, which I shall give in his own words (*c*) *et in* CIVITATEM *veniens, quum rem divinam vellet facere, primum ad* BELLONAE TEMPLUM *ductus est errore Aruspicis rustici; deinde hostiae furvae sunt applicitae, quod cum esset aspernatus, atque ad* PALATIUM *se reciperet, negligentia ministrorum, nigrae hostiae usque ad limen* domus PALATINAE *sequutae sunt*; which may be rendered into *English* thus: At his coming into the city, being desirous to give thanks to the gods, he was led by an ignorant soothsayer to the temple of *Bellona*; presently black sacrifices were ordered, which when rejected, and the emperor went on to his *palace*, by the negligence of his attendants these dark offerings followed him even to the door of the *imperial palace*.

To consider this quotation, from our *Roman* author, thoroughly, which is so expressive in our favour and tends so much to the glory of our city, I should begin with CIVITAS. But that word has been sufficiently discussed before; and I shall only say here of it, that, as in this sentence it must mean *the city itself*, so by giving it no adjunct, which the author thought there was not any occasion for, it indisputably proves this city to be the head of the province in these days.

That the *temple* of BELLONA stood here is also evident from the foregoing passage; a temple built no where but in *Rome* it self, or in the principal cities of the empire. For here it served, as in the great city, to denounce war from a pillar before it. *Bellona* is called the goddess of war; before whose temple, as a *Roman* author writes, stood a little pillar, called the martial pillar, from whence a spear was thrown when war was declared against an enemy (*d*). The best account that can be now met with of this *martial* temple *Ovid* gives us, who is very exact as to its situation and use. His words are these,

Hac sacrata die Tusco BELLONA *duello*
Dicitur . . . .
Prospicit à tergo summum brevis area Circum,
Est ubi non parvae parva Columna *notae*;
Hinc solet hasta manu belli praenuntia, mitti;
In regem & gentes cum placet arma capi. Fasti lib. vi.

Thus imitated,
Behind the *Circus* is a temple seen,
(Sacred to thee, *Bellona*, warlike queen,)
In whose short court, behold! a pillar rise
Of great remark, though of the smallest size;
For hence the spear projected does presage
'Gainst kings and nations war and hostile rage.

The cirque here mentioned was the *circus Flaminius*, which antiently lay near the *porta Carmentalis*, (*e*) without the city; so that this temple stood betwixt the cirque and the gate, upon a publick highway; that of *Janus*, or the temple of peace, being close to it. In the *area*, or *piazza*'s, of *Bellona*'s temple was a small marble pillar erected; I suppose it called *parva*, in comparison to the many stupendous pillars of an enormous size which once adorned that famous city. From this pillar, as the poet indicates, was a spear cast, it is said by the *Consul*, when war was declared against a nation. Whatever was done at *Rome* in regard of this ceremony, the same we may presume was executed at *York*; for the temple must serve for the same purpose in one place as the other. Now, in order to fix on a situation, in or about our city, where it may be supposed this temple once stood, it will be proper to examine more closely where the site of it was in *Rome*.

(*f*) *Donatus* has proved by many quotations, of unquestionable authority, that the *circus Flaminius* was without the city; and *Ovid* above acquaints us that this temple was on the back of the cirque, and only separated by a narrow court, where the martial pillar stood. It was here they used to give audience to foreign ambassadors, says *Publius Victor*, when they would not admit them into the city (*g*). And it was here also, they entertained their generals, after their return from performing some signal service abroad (*h*). Lastly, *Vitruvius* is very expressive about it, when he says that the temple of war was built *out of the city*, lest it should stir up amongst the citizens any civil dissensions (*i*). By all

(*c*) *AElius Spartianus in Severo*, inter scriptores hist. Aug.

(*d*) Bellona, *dicebatur dea bellorum, ante cujus templum erat columnella, quae bellica vocabatur, supra quam hastam jaciebat cum bellum indicebatur.* Sextus Pompeius. Vide notas in usum Delph.

(*e*) *Portae urbis quae jam non extant antiquiss. quatuor; inter quas tertia, vocatur* Carmentalis, *& aliis nominibus* Tarpeia, *&* Scelerata, *&* Veientana, *&, ut ex* Plinio *conjici potest*, lib. viii. Ratumena. Justus Lipsius *ant.* Roman. *descript.*

(*f*) Roma *vetus ac recens &c. auctore* Alex. *Donato.* Romae 1639. *Et in collectione* Graevii v. 3.

(*g*) *Tertium senatulum memorat citra aedem* Bellonae, *in* circo Flaminio, *ubi dabatur senatus legatis quos in urbem admittere nolebant.* Pub. Victor. *Senatus* Marcello *ad aedem* Bellonae *datus est, postulavit, ut triumphanti urbem inire liceret.* Livius.

(*h*) P. Scipioni, *senatu extra urbem dato in aede* Bellonae.

(*i*) *Templum* Martis *extra urbem collocatur, ne sit inter cives belligera dissentio.* Vitruvius.

which authorities it plainly proves, that this temple was erected out of one of the gates at *Rome*, and we must suppose that it had the same situation at *York*.

By considering the last quotation from *Spartian*, with one antecedent from the same author, it will appear that the entrance into the city, there mentioned, was after *Severus* his northern expedition; and his giving directions for the building of his mighty wall. So consequently it must be the second time, at least, that he had visited it. The words of *Spartian* are these, *post murum aut vallum missum in* Britannia, *quùm ad proximam mansionem rediret, non solum victor, sed etiam in aeternum* pace fundata. The *proxima marsio* here has by some historians been interpreted *York*; but neither the sence, nor the distance nor the dignity of expression will allow of it. It was only a proper house, or station, that the emperor rested at in his return to the city, and it was here he met the first bad omen, a *negro*, which *Spartian* relates *(k)*. The next ill fortune was when he arrived at the city it self; *& in* civitatem *veniens, &c.* as has been before recited. It was here he stumbled upon the most unlucky adventure that could have happened to a superstitious heathen, just returning from what he thought an entire conquest. Inclining to do sacrifice to the gods for his victory, he was carried by an ignorant country priest, unawares, to the temple of war, which stood without the gates, and in all probability was the first they came at. Surprized, when he saw black sacrifices preparing, the emblems of war, when he dreamed of nothing but eternal peace, he turned from them and went on to his palace. But as ill luck still would have it, these black cattle, kept in that temple for sacrifices to the goddess of war, by the negligence of his retinue, followed the emperor even to the door of the imperial palace. These black omens, with the words the black fellow spoke to him, *Spartian* supposes were sure tokens of the approaching dissolution of the great *Severus*.

Now, if we consider the road the emperor must take to come at the city from the north, it can be supposed to be no other than the grand military way, mentioned in the first and second journey in *Antonine's* itinerary. This brings him down to ISVRIVM, **Aldburgh**; from which station the *Roman* road to *York* came to **Aldwark**-*ferry*; then went through the forest to **Beningburgh**; as I shall have occasion to shew in the sequel, and entered the city at our *Bootham-bar*. This old gate, though it does not at present exhibit so certain a proof of *Roman* architecture as *Michlegate-bar*, another gate of the city, yet the many massy stones, of the *gritt kind*, with which it is built up, sufficiently shew its antiquity. Besides, the *Roman* tower near it, and the *Roman* burial place without it, are evident proofs that this part of the town was very considerable in those days.

Without this gate then must our temple have antiently stood; but to fix upon a particular place is impossible at this day. *Donatus* has given us a sketch of a draught how he supposed this temple was situated at *Rome*; which I have caused to be copied for the reader's greater satisfaction. By comparing this plan, to which he has put a compass, it will appear to stand north west from the gate aforementioned. And if any one will consider the plan of our city at the same time, given in the sequel, the temple of *Bellona* with us, he will find must have been near where the abby of St. *Maries*, or the *mannor*, now stands. The gate, the city walls, and the river have a very near similitude to one another. Lastly, where could a temple dedicated to the goddess of war more properly stand, than facing northward, against the boldest, most dangerous, and, at length, the only enemies they had in this island?

See plate viii. fig. i.

What is meant by the *aruspex rusticus*, or country wizzard, as *Burton* calls him, as also the reason why black sacrifices were thought ominous by the *Romans*, may be seen in that author. It being somewhat foreign to my subject to treat of them here. I shall leave this temple therefore, with a remark, that this unlucky omen of *Spartian's* has been however fortunate to us in having given occasion for that historian to mention *Bellona's* temple as once standing in *Eboracum*. And it is also an undeniable argument that there were several more temples, or places of heathen worship, erected there in those days.

The PALATIVM, or DOMVS PALATINA, of the *Roman* emperor's, here spoken of, deserves also a particular regard. The imperial palace at *Rome* being seated on the *Mons Palatinus*, that and all their royal houses in the empire, took name from thence *(l)*. The palace at *York*, has here two expressive names to denote its grandeur; and we may reasonably suppose that it was reedified or rather first built for this emperor's reception. That it must have been very magnificent, appears from the words immediately following, *limen domus Palatinae, &c.* in the preceding quotation, which are *sunt per plurimas civitates opera ejus insignia*, there are several of his grand buildings in many other cities of the empire.

(k) Volvens animo quid ominis sibi occurreret, AEthiops quidam, a numero militari, clarae inter scurras famae, & celebratorum semper jocorum, cum corona à cupressu facta, eidem occurrit. Quem quùm ille iratus removeri ab oculis praecepisset, & coloris ejus tactus omine & corona, dixisse ille dicitur joci causa,
Totum fuisti, totum vicisti, jam deus esto victor. Spartian. *in* Severo.

(l) Imperatoris aedes Palatium *nominatur, non quod ita aliquando decretum sit, sed quod in* Palatino Augustus Caesar *habitabat; ibique* praetorium *ejus erat, ac domus ejus ab eo monte, propterea quod ibi* Romulus *habitabat, multum splendoris accepit. Ideoque etiam si alibi imperator domicilium suum habuit, tamen id quoque* palatii *nomen obtinet.* Dion. Cass. lib. 53.

The *officia palatina*, or royal courts and appartments, which were included within the palace, were very extensive and large; among which was the PRAETORIVM *(m)*, or judgment hall, as our *English* bibles translate the word. The baths must also have had a great share in the building. The ground which this imperial palace may be supposed to have stood on, in our city, extends as I take it from *Christ-church* down through all the houses and gardens on the east side of *Gothram-gate* and St. *Andrew-gate*, through the *Bedern* to Aldwark. Which last name still retains some memorial of it. *Christ Church* is called in all ancient charters ecclesia sancte trinitatis in CVRIA REGIS, *Saxonice*, coning gapth, or king's *yard*. *Constantine* the great, as we shall find hereafter, is said to have been born in BEDERNA *Civitatis* EBORACI; and *Constantius* his father to be laid in the new demolished church of St. *Helen* on the wall in *Aldwark*. *Guthram* or *Gothram* was the name of a *Danish* king, or general, who was *(n)* governour here after their conquests; and probably gave his name to the street contiguous to the regal palace. That the *Saxons* and *Danes* made use of the *Roman* buildings for their chief habitations, in other places as well as this, will appear in the sequel.

But to return to our annals.

Severus was now drawing near his end, his former robust constitution being quite broken with deseases, and his firm mind at length giving way to the cares of empire. The dissoluteness he observed in his eldest son was likewise a great grief to him; and must give a shock to his constitution. This young prince discovered an inhuman nature very early; which, joined with his vast ambition to be sole ruler, made him more than once attempt the life of him that begot him. It was in this city however that the great and warlike *Severus* met his fate, with that intrepidity as became so great a soldier. It was here that he chiefly resided for some years after his coming into the island; it was here that he triumphed for one of the greatest conquests the *Romans* ever gained, and which, with the building of the wall *Spartian* expressly calls the greatest glories of his reign. Old age and chronical distempers did not advance upon him so fast, but that he might, after he had settled *Britain*, have ended his days in *Rome*, had he chose it. But this seems to have been his favourite place; and his chusing to die here, when he had all the cities of the empire to go to, if he pleased, will be a lasting honour to EBORACVM.

(o) A little before the death of *Severus* the *Caledonians* again took up arms; and attacked the *Roman* garrisons on the frontiers. This put the emperor into such a fury that he lost all patience, and, believing *Britain* could not be safe till the whole race of these people were destroyed, he sent out his legions with positive orders to put man woman and child to the sword. These orders were given them at *York*, and were expressed in two *Greek* verses, which carry this bloody meaning,

Let none escape you; spread the slaughter wide;
Let not the womb the unborn infant hide
From slaughters cruel hand.

But scarce were they begun to be put in execution when the emperor found his own death approaching.

A truly great man is not fully known, says the philosopher, till you see his latter end; and here this admirable heathen finished the course of a glorious life by as exemplary a death. *Dion* relates of him that, lying on his death-bed, to his latest gasp of breath, he busied himself and counsellors with settling the empire on as sure a basis as possible. His last words of advice to his sons whom he left joint emperors, were nervous and noble. "I leave you, my *Antonines*, *(p)* a firm and steady government if you will follow my steps, "and prove what you ought to be; but weak and tottering if otherways." "Do every "thing that conduces to each others good."——Cherish the soldiery and then you may "despise the rest of Mankind."——"A disturbed, and every where distracted, repub-"lick I found it; but to you I leave it firm and quiet:——*even to the Britons*." Then turning to his friends he shewed the philosopher in these words, "I have been all;——and "yet am now no better for it." Alluding to his rise from a low beginning through all the stations of life. Then calling for the urn which was to contain his ashes, after the *Ossilegium* or burning of his body, and looking steadily upon it. "Thou shalt hold, says he, "what the whole world could not contain." His last words were, "is there "any thing else, my friends, that I can do for you?" thus gallantly dying, says an

(m) For the form, extent, &c. of the *Roman* PRAETORIVM, see *Justus Lipsius in antiquitat.* Roman. *descriptione*.

(n) See the annals *A.* 899.

(o) Dion & Herodian *in Severo*.

(p) *Antonine* was then a darling name of the *Romans*; and for that reason *Severus* had given it to both his sons. But the eldest proved such a sad wretch, that the senate made a law that the name should never be made use of for the future.

author, I shall use the poets words on *Achilles* to *Severus*, who as far surpassed that feigned hero as true history does romance *(q)*.

> ———*de tam magno restat* Achille
> *Nescio quid, parvam quod vix bene compleat urnam:*
> *At vivit totum, quae gloria compleat orbem.*
>
> What's left of great *Severus* scarce will fill
> The smallest urn. Whose glory, when alive,
> Thro' the whole world diffus'd the fullest lustre.

As his whole life, so did his death, and even his funeral obsequies, altogether, contribute to render the name of this great prince immortal. The last were solemniz'd at a small distance from the city; and have left such a testimonial as will make the place famous to all posterity. We are told that the body of this martial emperor, was brought out in a military manner by the soldiers; that it was habited in a soldier's dress, and laid on a most magnificent pile, erected for that purpose, to burn him on. His sons first put the lighted torch to it, and when the flames ascended, the pile was honoured with the *peridrome*, decursion or riding round it by the young princes, his chief officers and soldiers *(r)*. This kind of *Roman* funeral ceremony is elegantly described by *Virgil*.

> *Ter circum accensos, cincti fulgentibus armis*
> *Decurrêre rogos; ter moestum funeris ignem*
> *Lustravere in equis.*
>
> Then thrice around the burning piles they run
> Clad in bright armour. Thrice the mournful flame
> They encompassed on horseback.

After the body of the emperor was consumed in the flames, his ashes were collected, and, with sweet odours, put into a porphyrite urn. This was carried to *Rome* and deposited in the *Capitol*, in the monument of the *Antonines*. He had afterwards the extraordinary ceremony of the *Apotheosis*, or deification, conferred upon him by the senate and people.

But that the memory of him might last in *Britain* as long as the world, his grateful army with infinite labour, raised three large hills in the very place where his funeral rites were performed. Which hills after so many ages being washed with rains, and often plowed are still very apparent, but must have been much higher than they are at present. *Suetonius* tells us, that the soldiers in *Germany* raised an honorary tomb to the memory of *Drusus*, though his body had been carried to *Rome* and deposited in the *Campus Martius (s)*. Such kind of *Tumuli*, or *Cumuli*, sepulchral hills, were raised by the *Romans* at vast trouble and expence, over their men of highest note, in order to eternize their memories. No sort of monument, of which they had several, can possibly subsist longer; for nothing but an earthquake can destroy them. *Seneca* speaks of them in this manner, *caetera sunt quae per constructionem lapidum, & marmoreas moles, &* terrenos tumulos *in magnam eductos celsitudinem constant.*

It has been objected to me that these hills seem to be natural ones, and indeed the plough has contributed very much to that appearance of them. But we have undoubted testimony, both history and tradition, to assure us that they have born the name of *Severus*'s *hills* for many ages. Mr. *Camden* quotes *Radulphus Niger* for saying they were in his time called the Severes *(t)*. *Radulph de diceto*, an earlier historian than the former, following the *British* story, writes thus, *sed eo tandem a Pictis perempto requiescit Eboraci, in monte qui ab eo* Severs-ho *vocatus est (u)*. But *Severus* being slain by the *Picts* at *York*, was buried in a hill called from him Severs-ho. The learned primate, in his chronology, tells us that the corps of this emperor was laid on the funeral pile, in a place which, to this very day, retains the name of Severs-hill *(x)*. From all which testimonies, and the constant tradition of the inhabitants of *York*, we have no room to doubt but that these hills were raised for the reason aforesaid.

That there are three of these hills is likewise no objection, for I take them to have been raised all at the same time in memory of the dead emperor, and in honour of the two living ones, his sons and successors. I need say no more to prove this custom to have been a very common one amongst the *Romans*, as it was also used by the *pagan Britons*, *Saxons* and *Danes*. The *Goths*, or *Ang. Saxons*, made their tombs very like the *Roman tumuli*, from

(q) Burton's Ant. itin from *Ovid*. Metam.

(r) *Dion Cassius. Herodian* in *Severo*.

(s) *Suetonius* in *Claudio*.

(t) *Radulphus Niger* lived in *H.* the thirds reign, *A.* 1250, says *Hollingshead*; but *Nicholson* places him *A.* 1217, and *R. de diceto* before him. Hist. library.

(u) Rad. de diceto. *inter xv. script. ed.* Gale.

(x) *Corpus ejus rogo est impositum in loco qui ad hunc usque diem* Severs-hill, *sive* Severi *collis nomen retulit.* Usher's *primord. eccl.* Britan.

which

J. Haynes delin. W. H. Toms sculp.

The honourable Thomas Willoughby of Birdsal Esq.r presents this plate of these venerable monuments of Roman grandeur to this work. 1736.

which word came the *French tombeaux*. Numbers of these sepulchral hills, by the country people called **Barroughs** (*y*), are to be met with in this island; especially upon our *Wolds*, where there are many of them of different magnitudes according to the quality of the officer entomb'd. The lowest was not buried without the soldiers under his command, each laying a turf upon his grave. And the S. T. T. L. in some of their monumental inscriptions, or *sit tibi terra levis, may this earth lay light*, plainly alludes to this custom. It cannot be wondered then that these *tumuli* of ours are of such an extraordinary bulk, when there went the power of the whole *Roman* army, then in *Britain*, as well as the natives to raise them. They seem to have been raised from a flat superficies, and the place whence this vast quantity of earth was dug is now a small village, at the foot of the hills, called *Holegate*. I shall take leave of these venerable remains of *Roman* grandeur with presenting the curious with a view of them.

But it may now be asked what certain testimony have we that *Severus* did actually die at *York*? To prove it I shall only mention the authority of two *Roman* writers which will put the matter out of dispute. *Eutropius* gives it us in these words——*decessit* EBORACI (Severus) *admodum senex, imperii anno* xviii, *mense* iv; *& divus appellatus est* (*z*). And *Spartian* now expresly names the place, *periit* EBORACI, *in* Britannia, *subactis gentibus quae* Britanniae *videbantur infestae, anno imperii* xviii, *morbo gravissimo extinctus, jam senex* (*a*). To deny this evidence is to say abruptly that EBORACVM is not *York*; which however disputable other stations may be in *Britain*, the learned men of all ages, since the time of the *Romans*, have unanimously concurred in.

Dion Cassius, the consular historian, who lived a few years after *Severus*, has left us a story of the empress *Julia*; known in the *Roman* coins by the name of *Julia Domna*. The story has been translated and retailed by several modern authors, but as I apprehend the subject of it was transacted at *York*, where the court then was, it cannot be amiss to insert it here.

It was the custom of the ancient *Britons*, to live promiscuously, to make use of one anothers wives, and bring up their children in common (*b*). Which inordinacy, as it was contrary to *Roman* laws, *Severus* endeavoured to restrain; for even his own soldiers gave too much into the practice of it. *Dion* says he made several edicts against adulterers *&c*; by which many were brought upon their trials and punished for it (*c*). I can affirm upon my own knowledge, adds my author, having in my consulship seen it on our records, that above three thousand offenders, in this kind, have been libelled against at one time. But when few persons could be met with that would perform the executive part of the laws with vigour, the emperor began to be more remiss in prosecutions of this nature. The empress *Julia*, persues my author, rallied a *British* lady the wife of *Argentocoxus* a *Caledonian* prince, probably a prisoner, or an hostage, at *York*, with the licentiousness of her country women, for committing such open obscenities with their men. The bold *Briton* answered her with great vivacity, *I think, madam, we have much the advantage of you* Roman *ladies in this particular, and satisfy our natural inclinations with much better grace; for we, in open daylight, admit the noble and the brave to our embraces; but you in darkness and dungeons make use of your most degenerate slaves.* A cutting reply to one their own historians do not stick to brand with the infamy of it (*d*).

The aforesaid author has given us this emperor's daily course of life, in the last years of it, in this manner, " he came, says he, early to, and constantly sat in the judgment hall " till noon; after which he rode out as long as he was able. At his return from this exercise he bathed, then dined, either alone or with his sons; but so luxuriously and plentifully, as constantly threw him into a sound sleep after dinner. When he awaked he walked about some time, and diverted himself with a *Greek* or *Latin* author. In the evening he bathed again, and after supped with his domesticks and familiars; for no other guests were admitted; except at some set times, when he would treat his whole court, at supper, very magnificently."

I shall conclude my account of this great *Roman*, with a description of his person and character of his parts, *&c.* drawn from the same historian as the former. " He was, says he, of a gross habit of body, but yet very strong and robust; except when weakened with the gout which he suffered much from. He had an excellent and piercing judgment; in the study of the liberal arts he had been wonderfully diligent, which rendered his speech and counsel both eloquent and persuasive. To his friends most grateful and always mindful to do them good; but to his enemies implacable. Diligent in the execution of business; but when dispatched no one ever heard him speak of it again. Greedy enough of money; which he took all methods to get together, except

(*y*) *Barroughs* comes from the A. S. Beape or Beopȝ tumulus, collis, *&c.* whence our word to *bury* is derived. *Somner's Saxon* dict.

(*z*) Eutropii *hist.* Roman. *vide notas variorum in* Eutrop & S. Havercampi.

(*a*) *Historiae* August. *cum notis* Isaaci Casaubon & *alior.*

(*b*) *Utuntur communibus uxoribus liberosque omnes alunt.* Tacitus.

(*c*) *Licet & ipsa adulteriis famosa.* Dio Xiphilin. Juliam *famosam adulteriis.* Spartian.

(*d*) Several laws are extant in the *code* made by *Papinian, contra moechos*; probably at *York*, though none of them are dated as the former.

that

"that he never put any one to death in the attaining of it. He erected many *new palaces* "and *temples*, and repaired several old ones; two, especially, to *Bacchus* and *Hercules* he "built very magnificently. And though his expences in these and other matters were ve-"ry great, yet, at his death, he left in gold many thousands behind him: And also, as "much corn to the city of *Rome*, as would serve it seven years *(e)*." This is a great character for a heathen, and what few of our *Christian* princes have attained to. The blackest crime that any historian can lay to his charge, is, that he raised the *fifth persecution* against the *Christians*.

A. CCXI. vel CCXII. *Severus* being dead, the government devolved upon his two sons CARACALLA and GETA; and the court still continuing at EBORACVM, the course of this history must necessarily attend it. The eldest of these princes, *Bassianus*, who was surnamed *Caracalla*, from the short coats he gave to the soldiers, I have taken notice on to have as bad a natural disposition, as it was possible for one man to be possessed of. He has made it his boast, *that he never learned to do good*; and indeed the whole course of his life sufficiently shews it. His father left the world not without suspicion of foul play from him, as *Dion* hints; but, be that as it would, it is certain he had been tampering with the emperor's physicians to destroy him. For, the first that tasted of his cruelty were those, whom he instantly put to death, for not obeying his orders in it *(f)*. The greatest weakness the father ever betrayed, was his partiality or blindness to this incorrigible son. And he can never be excused for being the cause of the death of the younger, says *Dion*, and having in some measure delivered him over to his brother, who he might foresee would put him to death *(g)*.

(h) *Geta* was of a different temper from his brother, and was very grateful to the senate and citizens; he had also a powerful party, even in the army. *Caracalla* aspiring to be sole emperor, had resolved upon his brother's death: But to come at the fratricide with more ease and safety to himself, upon a slight pretence of a mutiny, he caused 20000 of the soldiery, whom he suspected to be in his brother's interest, to be put to the sword. This done, it was no great difficulty to get the rest to proclaim *Geta* an enemy to his country; who, upon hearing of it, fled for protection to his mother *Julia*. But, alas! it was all in vain, the inhuman butcher followed his bloody purpose, and with his own hands pierced the unhappy prince's heart, even in the arms of her who who gave him life *(i)*.

Caracalla had still another obstacle to surmount before he could make himself easy in his government, and that was the taking off his father's faithful friend and counsellor *Papinian*. This eminent civilian, whom I have before mentioned, was the greatest ornament, not only of EBORACVM, but of the whole island of *Britain*. *Camden* quotes from *Forcatulus*, a *French* antiquary *(k)*, that the tribunal at *York* was exceeding happy, in that it heard *Papinian* the oracle of right and law. *Cujacius*, almost as great a name as the former, gives *Papinian* this high character, *that he was the most eminent of all civilians that either ever were in the world, or ever would be; whom no one in the science of the law, could ever yet outdo, nor can he be equalled in it in any future times (l)*. *Papinian* studied under *Scaevola*, was master of requests, treasurer, and captain of the guards to *Severus*; and by the emperor's second marriage nearly related to him. The exactness and perfections which are in his writings, says a modern author *(m)*, and the great abundance of them, would induce one to think, that he exceeded the ordinary course of life; but yet it is agreed, on all hands, that he was not eight and thirty when he was taken off by a violent death; which, adds my author, cannot be imputed to any other cause than his own virtue, and the cruelty of him that commanded it. Nor was *Papinian* alone in the *Praetorium*, several other great names *(n)* occur in history as counsellers or coadjutors to him in it. Amongst these were *Ulpianus* and *Paulus*, the next two learned men of that age, and who are supposed to be *Papinian*'s successors in the tribunal. To these great men, but more especially to the first, did *Severus*, on his death-bed, leave the guardianship of his sons, and the whole affairs of the empire. For it is not to be supposed, that so wise a prince would trust them to the care of any absent tutor, who could not receive instructions and directions about them from his own mouth.

It will be somewhat derogatory to the honour of my subject, to take pains to prove, that the murder of these two eminent persons, *Geta* and *Papinian*, was perpetrated at *York*. But good and bad must be recorded. I am well aware, that two very great authorities, *Dio* and *Herodian*, both write, that *Geta* was slain at *Rome*, in the palace, and almost in the bo-

(e) This last sentence is from *Spartian*.

(f) *Herodian*.

(g) *Xiphiline* from *Dio*.

(h) *Nihil inter fratres simile*. Spartianus. *apud exercitum carissimus erat, praesertim quod facie patri simillimus esset*. Dio.

(i) *Ac jam tum ex collo ejus pendebat, adhaerebatque ipsius pectori atque uberibus, occidit lamentantem clamantemque in haec verba*, Mater, mater, genetrix, genetrix fer opem, occidor, &c. Xiphilin. *a* Dione.

(k) Steph. Forcat *de* Gallor. *philos. et im.*

(l) *Primus omnium jurisconsultorum qui fuerunt vel futuri sunt; quem nemo unquam juris scientia superavit, nec in posterum aequare poterit*. Cujacius.

(m) Duck *de jure civili*.

(n) There are 25 more names of persons as auditors to *Papinian*, and Counsellors to *Severus* at *York*. See *Isaacson*'s chronology from *Lamprid.* *Func. Helvet.* &c.

som

ſom of his mother. Yet I muſt be of opinion, with a very learned antiquary, (*o*) that our city was the ſcene of this black impiety; and I ſhall give his and my own reaſons for it.

It is agreed by all that *Geta* was aſſaſſinated firſt; and *Papinian*, for refuſing to make an oration in favour of the murderer, and telling him, *that it was much eaſier to commit a crime of this nature, than excuſe it*, fell by the hands of a common executioner; his head being ſtruck off with an axe (*p*) and not by a ſword. I ſhall beg leave to quote a *Roman* hiſtorian (*q*) here, in his own words, who, I take it, writes much to our purpoſe, *quae victoria*, meaning *Geta*'s murder, Papiniani *exitio foedior facta, ut ſane putant memoriae curioſi; quippe quem ferunt illo tempore* Baſſiani *ſcrinia curaviſſe, monitumque uti mos eſt*, deſtinando Romam *quam celerrime componeret, dolore* Getae *dixiſſe* haudquaquam pari facilitate velari parricidium qua fieret. *Idcirco morte affectum*. By which words, ſays *Burton*, they, out of whom *Victor* took them, did not only believe that the murder of *Geta*, but this brave ſaying uttered by *Papinian*, happen'd both before *Caracalla*'s return to *Rome*, and conſequently at *York*. *Deſtinando* ROMAM, the learned *Caſaubon* maintains the reading of, and ſays it plainly ſhews it (*r*). A paſſage in *Spartian* makes this yet plainer, (*s*) *denique niſi querelis de* Geta *editis, et animis militum delinitis, enormibus etiam ſtipendiis datis*, Romam Baſſianus redire non potuit. Theſe mutinies and diſorders in the army could proceed from nothing ſo much as *Geta*'s murder; for though *Caracalla* had got them to proclaim his brother an enemy to his country, yet they were not aware of his bloody intent upon it. *Eutropius* writes, that immediately upon his being proclaimed, as above, he was ſlain (*t*). And *Ignatius* has left *Caracalla* this character, *that he was no leſs diſobedient to his father* Severus, *whilſt alive, than wicked to his brother* Geta, *whom after his father's death he inſtantly ſlew* (*u*). After all, ſays *Burton*, how can I think that he, who more than once attempted his father's life, and that too in the preſence of his victorious army, ſhould ſpare his brother, but for an hour, eſpecially having gained thoſe military men ſo much to his ſide, as to proclaim *Geta*, both an enemy to him and the common-wealth, immediately on his father's death. That we had a *Palatium*, or *domus* PALATINA is evident, and that the empreſs *Julia* was in *Britain*, *Herodian* ſeems to hint, but *Dio* puts it paſt doubt, by the above recited ſtory of her. The eraſement of *Geta*'s name out of ſeveral inſcriptions, found in *Britain*, ſeems to have been done by the other's orders before he left the iſland (*x*). All which authorities too plainly prove, that *Geta*'s and *Papinian*'s murders, and probably *Caracalla*'s inceſtuous marriage with his father's wife, were all of them perpetrated in EBORACVM. I ſhall conclude with the ſenſe of *Spartian*, who ſumming up the good emperors that had left bad ſons and ſucceſſors, leaves this monſter of mankind this character, "How happy would it have been to the empire, if *Severus* had not begot *Baſſianus*? who, under pretence of plots againſt himſelf, and with a patricidial lye, immediately murdered his innocent brother. Who married his mother-in-law, nay rather his mother, in whoſe very boſom he had ſlain her ſon *Geta*. And who deſtroyed *Papinian*, that *aſylum* of the law, and learned repoſitory of it, becauſe he would not excuſe his brother's murder (*y*).

The imperial court having reſided at EBORACVM, from *Severus* his firſt coming to it, to *Caracalla*'s return to *Rome*, muſt, as I have noted, give a luſtre to my ſubject, and make its glory ſhine equal, if not ſuperior to the moſt renowned cities, except *Rome* and *Conſtantinople*, in the empire. From *Severus* his excellent government and his ſon's leaving the iſland, for near the ſpace of an age, we hear no more of our city; and indeed but lightly of the affairs of *Britain* in general. Thoſe antient depredators the *Picts* and *Scots* were ſo humbled and cooped in by the emperor's conduct, and his prodigious wall, that he had built and garriſon'd againſt them, that it required much time for them to ſurmount thoſe difficulties. In the mean while the gallant ſixth legion continued in their old quarters at *York*; and though not in war were certainly not in a ſtate of indolency. The many noble high-roads, the veſtiges of which are in many places ſtill very extant, make it obvious, that neither they nor their fellow-ſoldiers in other legions, in the times of profoundeſt peace, wanted employment. The peaceable age, the iſland enjoyed after *Severus*, is thought by moſt hiſtorians to be the time the *Roman* ſoldiers were employed by their commanders, in caſting up high-ways, making of brick, cutting down woods, and draining of bogs. That this work was extremely neceſſary, for the more effectual enſlaving a free people; by deſtroying their *faſtneſſes*, and the quicker march of troops and military engines, from place to place, as occaſion required; may be evinced by modern practice in the art of war. The noble high-roads from town to town, in *Flanders*, ſhew, that *Lewis* XIV. of *France* under-

A. CCXI. vel CCXII.

(*o*) See *Burton*'s *Ant.* Itin.

(*p*) *Securi percuſſus*. Spartian.

(*q*) Sextus Aurelius Victor.

(*r*) Iſaaci Caſaubon. *notae in ſcript. Aug.*

(*s*) Spartian, *vel* Jul. Capitol. *in vita* Getae.

(*t*) *Nam* Geta *hoſtis publicus judicatus*, confeſtim *periit*, Eutropius.

(*u*) Severo *patri adhuc viventi, contumax, nec minus in fratrem* Getam *impius, quem patre mortuo* ſtatim *occiderat*. Joh. Bap. Ignatius.

(*x*) See *Gibſon*'s *Camden*. *Horſley*'s *Britannia*, *Rom.* *Muſgrave*'s *Geta Britannicus*, &c. on this Head.

(*y*) *Quod* Severo Septimio, *ſi* Baſſianum *non genuiſſet?* *qui* ſtatim *inſimulantem fratrem, inſidiarum contra ſe cogitatarum, patricidiali etiam figmento interemit. Qui novercam, matrem quinimo, in cujus ſinu* Getam *filium ejus, occiderat, uxorem duxit. Qui* Papinianum, *juris aſylum et doctrinae legalis theſaurum, quod parricidium excuſare noluiſſet, occidit.* AElius Spartianus *in vita* Getae.

ftood the maxim thoroughly. And the later conduct of our prefent governours, in refpect to the highlands of *Scotland*, does fufficiently fhew us, that this part of *Roman* military difcipline is not forgotten.

The *Latin* writers, particularly *Ammianus*, call thefe high ways *aggeres itinerarii*, *actus publici*, *viae ftratae*, &c. I fhall not take upon me, nor is it to my purpofe, to write exprefsly on all the *Roman* roads in *Britain*. That fubject has been largely and excellently well treated by our learned antiquary, his judicious continuator, the late Mr. *Horfley*, and others. But I cannot here avoid taking notice of thefe, which, from feveral different parts and ftations, do all centre at EBORACVM; and the rather becaufe it will ferve to fill up a very great chafm in my annals.

(z) A modern author, in his defcription of *Italy*, makes this obfervation on the *Roman* roads in that country, " Of all the antique monuments I have hitherto feen, fays he, there " is nothing in my opinion deferves fo much to be admired as thefe famous roads. The " buildings, that are preferved, have been expofed to few accidents; and, all things being " well confidered, it is rather matter of aftonifhment that edifices, fo exceedingly folid, were " fo foon ruined, than to fee them ftill remaining. But that an innumerable number of " paffengers, horfes and carriages, fhould perpetually tread on a pavement, for fo many " ages, and yet fuch confiderable pieces of it fhould ftill be found entire, is a thing " which feems almoft incredible.

It is not to be expected, that we fhould meet with fuch noble remains of high-roads round *York*, as are yet apparent on the *Appian* and *Flaminian* ways in *Italy*. Thofe roads to the great city were, no doubt, laid with wonderful care and coft; befides, the drynefs of that climate and foil, when compared with ours, muft make a great difference, as to the finking or turning up of the *agger* which compofed them. But we can, however, make a boaft of feveral remarkable veftiges in this kind of *Roman* induftry, which are to be feen at this day in our neighbourhood. Which roads, as I hinted before, tending all from different fea-ports and ftations, and pointing directly at the city itfelf, muft make it more confiderable than any writer, either antient or modern, that I have feen, has yet attempted. And I have the vanity to fay, that the difcovery of fome of thefe roads is folely owing to my felf.

The *itinerary* afcribed to *Antoninus pius*, and which has long born his name, feems rather to have been made in the time of *Severus*; and his fon *Antoninus Caracalla* took the honour of it. In this I follow the opinion of our great antiquary, Mr. *Burton*, *Horfley*, and others. I take it to have been no more than what our modern military men would call a fettled *rout*, for the march of troops from ftation to ftation, as occafion required, quite over the province. The diftances are here exactly put down, from an actual furvey; and each ftationary officer, having a copy, might at one view have a juft idea of the *Roman* ports, forts and towns in *Britain*. He might alfo, by the emperor or his lieutenant's commands, march his men upon any defign, with great celerity and fafety; when his quarters, or ftations, were thus depicted, and the roads made excellently good, to and from them all. This furvey muft have been a work of fome years, and not a hafty progrefs through the province; and therefore, it cannot properly be allowed to have any other director than that able and moft experienced foldier *Severus*.

It is eafy to fee, that EBORACVM is the principal in all thefe *itinera*, or routs. And, as at *Rome* there was a gilded pillar fet up at the head of the *Forum*, in *umbilico urbis (a)*, by the order of *Auguftus*; from whence the menfuration of the roads quite through *Italy* were taken; fo it is more than barely probable that a pillar of this kind, whether gilt or not, is out of queftion, was erected by *Severus*, to ferve for the fame purpofe through *Britain*, at EBORACVM. If our modern antiquaries will not allow me this pofition, they muft however acknowledge, that *York* is, at this day, the only point from whence they can with certainty fix any *Roman* ftation in the north of *England*. *Tacitus* calls this pillar at *Rome*, *milliarium aureum*, and fays it ftood near the temple of *Saturn*; whence the phrafe, *ad tertium*, *quartum*, *quintum ab urbe lapidem*. So the poet,

Intervalla viae feffis praeftare videtur,
Qui notat infcriptus millia crebra lapis.

The weary'd traveller knows the diftant way,
Where the mark'd ftones the num'rous miles difplay.

(z) *Miffon*'s Voyage to *Italy*. He writes, that under the upper Pavement is another lay of very maffy ftones placed on a bed of fand, which ferves for the foundation of this pavement, and hinders it from finking. Bifhop *Burnet* tells us, that thefe caufeways in *Italy* were twelve foot broad, all made of huge ftones, moft of them blue; that they are generally a foot and half large on all fides. And, admiring the ftrength of the work, he adds, that it has lafted above 1800 years, yet in moft places it is for feveral miles together as entire as when it was firft made. *Letter* 4.

(a) *Suetonius*. *Dio*. Mr. *Laffels* writes, that this pillar was ftanding in *Rome* in his time. *Laffels*'s voyage to *Italy*.

Some

Some of these milliary pillars, or milestones, found in the north of *England*, are preserved and given in Mr. *Horsley's Brit. Romana*; and I have seen several on the *Roman* roads leading to this city, but the inscription worn off.

The termination of all the *Roman* high roads, by *Ulpian's* authority, was either at the Sea, some great river, or city. This position will be made most evident by what I am going to shew. The grand military way, which divides *England* in length, runs from the port RITVPAE, now *Richborough* in *Kent*, *usque ad lineam valli*; to the limit of the *Roman* wall, in *Northumberland*, and beyond it. It came down to that known station DANVM, *Doncaster*. From whence it stretches northward over *Scawsby-lees* to *Barnsdale*. It is easily traced on to *Hardwick*, *Tanshelf*, *Pontefract-park*, and *Castleford*. Whether *Pontefract* or this last named place bids the fairest for the *Roman* LEGIOLIVM, may be the subject of another work I intend for the press as soon as this is finished. For my part, I give my vote for *Pontefract* or *Tanshelf*, rather than *Castleford*; and I have the opinion of our great antiquary, *J. Leland*, on my side. At *Castleford* it passes the river *Air*, then over *Peckfield*, runs very apparently to *Aberford*; at the north-end of which town is the vestige of a *Roman* camp. On *Bramham-moor* it is in many places exceedingly perfect; *Leland* writes, *that in all his travels he never saw so noble and perfect a* Roman *road as this; which shews*, adds he, *that there went more than ordinary care and labour in the making of it* (*b*). The *stratum* is still so firm and good, that, in travelling over it, we may say with the poet, in a description of another such road in the west of *England*,

(*c*) Now o'er true *Roman* way our horses sound;
Graevius would kneel, and kiss the sacred ground.

That the reader may have an idea of what appearance these venerable remains of *Roman* art and industry make at this day, I have bestowed a draught of it.

From *Bramham-moor* this grand road points directly for *Tadcaster*, the old CALCARIA; which it enters opposite to the site of the castle. But the ford over which the north road went, was at St. *Helen's-ford*, a little higher on the river *Wherse*. From which it begins again; and though on this side of the river the country is marshy and deep, so that there appear but faint traces of it, yet the course of the road is called **Rudgate**, *quasi Roadgate*, by the country people at this day. We follow it over the river *Nid* to *Whixley*, where it is very apparent. The out-buildings of which village are almost wholly built of the peebles dug out of it. From *Whixley* the road is easily traced to *Aldburgh*, the known ISVRIVM of the *Romans*, and so on; for I shall follow it no further, it not being consonant to my design.

What I observe from hence, is, that in all the journeys in the *Itinerary*, from south to north, as for instance, in the second, *a vallo usque ad portam* RVTVPIS, the two extream points of the province, EBORACVM is always put down as in the road. The preceding course evidently shews, that it is not so; and consequently it can only be placed there as a station not to be omitted in the journey. Mr. *Burton* writes, that these skips, as he is pleased to call them, are frequently taken out of the way; yet he allows it is never done but to pay a visit to some more than ordinary station; where the emperor, *propraetor*, or legate, turn'd aside for business; as to hold courts of justice, enlist more soldiers, or confirm the old ones. And here, he adds, that *York* was the only place in the north, appointed for the meeting of this officer. Mr. *Horsley*, more properly, calls these turns out of the road, *angles*, which the military way makes to any place of importance. For instance, **Watling-street**, called so, as he supposes, from its winding turns, comes from *Richborough* to *London*; from thence runs to *Chester*, and there crossing again, makes directly for *York*.

There is another *Roman* road comes out of *Lancashire* from that noted station MANCVNIVM, *Manchester*, by CAMBODVNVM near *Almonbury*, or *Almry* in this county, and falls into the grand military way near *Aberforth*. This may yet be traced, but is not very visible. It is the road taken in the second *Iter*. But from COCCIVM, *Ribchester*, in *Lancashire*, is one still very obvious. Mr. *Warburton*, who traced this road, and has delineated it in his map of this county, says its stone pavement is yet in many places very firm, being eight yards broad. It comes to *Gisburn*, crosses *Ramwald's-moor* to that known station OLICANA, *Ilkley*; from thence to ADELOCVM, which our *Leeds* antiquary has, with probability enough, placed at *Addle*, and strikes into the road for *York* with the former. It is very plain that these two high-ways were directed to the city it self, because when they wanted to go more northward, there is another *Roman* road from *Skipton*, cross *Knares-burgh* forest to *Aldburgh*, which is many miles nearer to the grand north road.

Upon the river (*d*) *Wharfe*, and full on the great military way, stood the *Roman* CALCARIA, now *Tadcaster*; which place, as it was the next station to *York*, it comes within my CALCARIA, *Tadcaster*.

(*b*) *Leland's* itin. v. 5.
(*c*) *Gay's* epistle to Lord *Burlington*.
(*d*) Supposed to be the *Roman* VERBEIA. *Skinner* defines it in this manner, **Wherf** *seu* **Wharf** *in com.* Ebor. *Fluvius A. S.* Guerf *forte an a C. Br.* Guer *vel* Guern; *quod* rapidum *notat*; *et est sane valde rapidus. Vel a* **Belg. Werbel**, *vortex*, **Werbelen** *circumvertere, circumgyrare.* Etym. dict

limit

limit to treat of. The learned *Camden*, with whom his continuator agrees, was most certainly right in deriving this towns name from *Calx* lime, or *Calcaria*, lime-kilns. To his authority there is *Tertullian de carne christi*, who mentions *Calcaria ad Carbonariam*. *Ammianus Mar.* does the same. And *Ulpian* acquaints us that to these *Calcaria* offending persons were condemned, as to the gallies in *France* at this time; whence in the *Code* we meet with the *Calcarienses*. It must be granted that the *Romans* had occasion for vast quantities of lime to spend in their buildings at *York*. For which reason a settlement was thought proper to be established here to take care that this valuable commodity should be duly manufactured and burned; and that slaves and offenders should be kept strictly to it. There is no part of the country that does still yield this kind of stone so plentifully as this place; from whence it may be conveyed to *York*, either by water or land, with ease. The *Saxons* and *Normans* in their churches and fortifications with us, no doubt, made use of the same convenience. The builders of our majestick cathedral were much encouraged to proceed in it, when the stone for the work and lime were got within a mile of one another. And to this day it is so plentifully dug up here, as to supply not only our city, but the whole country round it.

But I must not omit what a late antiquary *(e)* has published in relation to the etymology of *Calcaria*. It is a great guess indeed, but whether a probable one I shall leave to the readers conjecture. "May not the derivation of this name, says he, come from the "trade of making spurs there? *Ripon* has been famous in our time, and the best spurs were "said to come from thence. If there was a town upon the *Wherse*, which in the *Romans* "time dealt in this manufacture it might, adds he, be transferred to *Ripon* on the others "being razed."

(f) Some other late authorities have also displaced CALCARIA from its old station at *Tadcaster*, and have carried it a mile further up the river to a village called *Newton-kime (g)*. They are not without their reasons for this stretch, the town no doubt must have been formerly of an unusual length, whence the *Saxon* name Langbyrig, **Langburgh** was aptly given to it. But the remains of antiquity which Mr. *Camden* saw, all of which are still evident at *Tadcaster*, must make us hold to his notion, notwithstanding the seeming probability of the later. That antiquary observed the marks of a trench quite round the old town; takes notice of the platform of an antient castle; out of the ruins of which, adds he, not many years ago, a bridge was made over the *Wharfe*. That it measures just nine *Italian* miles from *York*; the exact number put down in the itinerary. That a hill a small distance from it is still called **Kelk-bar**; which retains somewhat of its ancient name. And lastly, that a great number of *Roman* coins have been found in the fields about it.

For all which reasons I give my vote, with the late Mr. *Horsley*, for fixing their CALCARIA at our *Tadcaster*. For though the hill called **Kelk-bar**, is nearer *Newton* than *Tadcaster*; and there have been found several *Roman* coins and other curiosities in *Newton-water-field*, it is no argument that the station should be built in this place, rather than the former. I do not deny but that the out-buildings, or suburbs of this town, might stretch along the road, almost as far as this ford over the river. They might have been the habitations of these dealers in lime, or *Calcarienses*, from whence the town took its name. The *Langbrough-pennys*, as the country people still call the *Roman* coins that are found in these fields, give us an idea of a long street of houses this way. **Kelk-bar** is full in this road, and opposite to a place called *Smawes (h)*, where are some, not despisable remains of antiquity, and an innumerable quantity of very old lime-pits on the north side of the hill. Besides I take this ancient name **Kelk-bar**, if it mean any thing, to signify a bar, or gate, in this street leading to *Calcaria*. The situation seems to allow of such an outwork from the town.

But, if I may be allowed a conjecture of my own, here will two stations rise up near together; an *itinerarian*, and a *notitial* one; as may be seen in the sequel; and then, the dispute is easily settled betwixt them. The three fords on this river will be a means to help us to account for it.

What is most to my purpose here, is the site of CALCARIA, or *Tadcaster* it self; which by being placed full on the road to *York*, was certainly a fortress designed for the security or a key to the city on that side; as DERVENTIO, a station on the river *Derwent*, was on the other. Whatever some late antiquaries have advanced; I am as certain, as a man can be in this matter, that the *Roman* road, from *Tadcaster* to *York*, took the same rout then as now. The objection of *Tadcaster* moor being unpassable, without a stone causeway being built over it, is nothing against us; for I take it this causeway has for its foundation the old *Roman* one; which is the occasion of its present strength and firmness; and any one that

(e) *Salmons* Survey &c.

(f) *Gibson's Camden* from Mr. *Fairfaxes* notes &c.

(g) called so from being formerly in the possession of the barons *de kime*. Though it has since long been in the ancient family of *Fairfax*. *Tho. Fairfax* Esq; the present possessor.

(h) *Smawes* is one of the most agreeable situations in all this country. It belongs at present to *Thomas Lister* of *Gisburn-park*, Esq; I could never understand what *Smawes* signifies.

carefully

A view of part of the Roman *road on* Bramham-moor, *leading towards* Tadcaster.

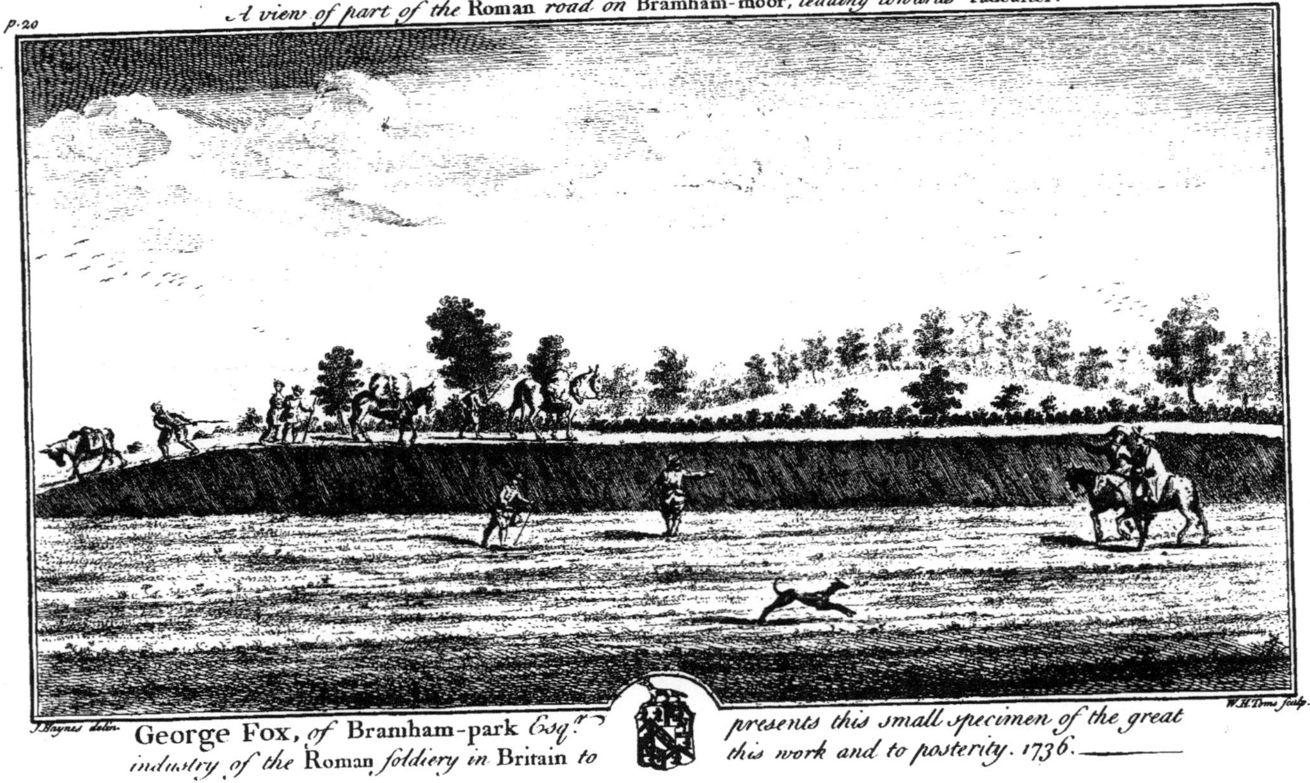

J. Haynes delin. W. H. Toms sculp.

George Fox, *of* Bramham-park *Esq.r* presents this small specimen of the great industry of the Roman soldiery in Britain to this work and to posterity. 1736.

LIBRARY
N.Y.

carefully observes it will be of my opinion. From this moor the rood went to *Street-houses*; which name and place bears evident testimony of it. The *(i) Saxon* Sꞇꞃeꞇ or Sꞇꞃeꞇe, apparently comes from the latin *stratum*, which in *Pliny* signifies a *street*, or a *paved high-road*. All the *Roman* roads being firmly paved with stone occasioned this name to them. Where-ever we meet with a road called a *street*, by the country people, or any town or village said to lie upon the *street*, for instance *Aithwick on the street* by *Doncaster*, we may surely judge that a *Roman* road was at or near it. There are several more instances of this kind which I shall have occasion to mention in the sequel; which makes me so particular in this. The length of time, the wetness of the situation and the very great number of carriages and passengers that have travelled this road for many ages, have in this place tore the *agger* up to the very foundations. Stones, of a monstrous bulk and weight, lie here in the way, which are certainly adventitious, and have been brought hither, by infinite labour, to make the foundation of the road firm and solid. We meet with several more such where the ground is any where cut deep by carriages nearer the city. A little further than *Street-houses* is a place called *Four-mile-hill*, being the half way betwixt *York* and *Tadcaster*. It is a little rising on the side of the road which I take to have been a *tumulus*; it being the constant custom of the *Romans* to make their funeral monuments near their highways, or some publick place. Whence *siste viator* and *abi viator* was proper for their inscriptions; but very absurd to be taken from them and put on a monument in the inside of a church; of which we have too many instances in these days.

From hence the road runs to a village, vulgarly called *Ringhouses*, but anciently **Dreng-houses**. Our late *Leeds* antiquary *(k)* says the right name of this place is **Dreng-howe**, or **Howes**; and quotes his authorities for it. He supposes the *Romans* had upon this road what the *Saxons* call a *howe* or *howes*, little hills, round which they had their diverting exercises. There are no hills about this place at present to justify his assertion; for which reason he has drawn in the little hill above mentioned to support it. A huge and massy stone coffin and lid was of late years dug up near this place; and now lies in the street, which is most certainly *Roman*. From hence the road leads to the city it self, and enters it at *Micklegate-bar*; where is still a noble *Roman* arch, which I shall have occasion to treat more particularly on in the sequel.

The destruction of CALCARIA, as well as other stations in the north, may be imputed to the merciless fury of the *Danes*, who destroyed all here before them with fire and sword. It is remarkable that this place was in some repute in *Beda*'s time, and that it was then called *Calca-cester*. That author gives an account of a religious woman whom he calls *Heina*, who being the first that took the sacred habit of a nun upon her in those parts, retired, says he, to the city of *Calcaria*, by the *English* called *Calca-cester*; where she built a house for her dwelling *(l)*. From whence might come *Talca-cester*, and so, more corruptly, *Tadcaster*.

St. *Helen's-ford*, takes its name from a chapel dedicated to St. *Helen*, the mother of *Constantine* the great, which stood in *Leland*'s time *(m)* on the east banks of the river. Here is still St. *Helen's* well. *Tadcaster* has sometimes been called in ancient writers *Helecestre (n)*; not from St. *Helen*, but, as I suppose, by a wrong translation of *Calx* lime into the *Saxon* Hele, the heele of the foot, which it also signifies. *Helagh* a village in the *Ainsty* still retains the sound of it. Our learned dean *Gale* was of opinion this ford might take its name from the goddess NEHALENNIA, the patroness of *Chalk-workers*; and thence might be called *Nahalen's-ford*, corruptly *Helen's-ford (o)*. But this *etymon* seems to be a little too far stretched; and *Leland*'s chapel, before mentioned, has a much nearer signification to it. This place is fordable most part of the summer, and was no doubt more so before the mill and damm was built at *Tadcaster*. Our *Saxon* ancestors made use of the *Roman* roads and built wooden bridges for their greater convenience in passing the rivers. The sills or piles of such a bridge, in this place, do yet appear at low water. But when the north road came to be turned, and stone bridges were built at *Wetherby*, *Washford*, and *Burrough-bridge* over the rivers *Wharfe*, *Nid* and *Eure*, this old road was quite neglected, and the bridge suffered to fall.

The neighbouring *Roman* stations to *York* being all concerned in this account of the roads leading to the city, they come within my sphere to treat on as well as the last. And in order to it I shall transcribe the first *iter*, or rout, which is put down in the *itinerary*, from the *Suritan* edition, published by our learned dean *Gale* as follows. The *English* names to

(i) Stratum, vicus, via, platea. Vide Somner's *dict. Saxon. Stratum,* is the very word made use of by Ven. *Bede* to denote a *Roman* road quite through his work.

(k) Thoresby's *ducat.* Leod. 130.

(l) Heina, *religiosa* Christi *famula, quae prima foeminarum fertur in provincia* Nordanhymbrorum *propositum vestemque sanctimonialis habitus, consecrante* AEdano *episcopo, suscepisse; secessit ad civitatem* Calcariam, *quae a gente* Anglorum, Kalcacestir *appellatur. Ibique mansionem sibi instituit.* Beda, *ed.* Smith.

(m) Lelandi *itin.*

(n) MON Ang. 1. 399. *Calx pedis, in eadem lingua Tab unde hodierna dictio* Tahdcaster *inserta litera d euphoniae gratia.* Gale's *itin* p 45.

(o) Artem Calcariam olim in Britanniis *coluisse testantur inscriptiones apud* Reinesium, p 190. *harum unam pono*

DEAE NEHALENNIAE OB
MERCES RITE CONSERVA-
TAS M. SECVND SILVANVS
Negotiator NEGOTTOR CRETARIVS
BRITANNICIANVS
V. S. L. M. *Itin.* Ant. Gale.

the ſtations are here diverſified according to the opinions of the authors that have wrote on them.

A limite, i. e. *a vallo* PRAETORIVM *uſque*, M. P. CLVI.		The firſt rout, from the limits, that is, from the *Roman* wall to *Praetorium* is 156 miles.
A BREMENIO CORSTOPITUM	M. P. XX.	*Brampton*, Camd. *Riechester*, *Corbridge*, Horſley.
VINDAMORA. . . .	M. P. IX.	*Walls-end*, Camd. *Ebchester*, Horſley.
VINOVIA.	M. P. XIX.	*Binchester*, Burton, Horſley, Gale, &c.
CATARACTONI. : .	M. P. XXII.	*Catarick*, Camd. Horſley, &c.
ISVRIVM. . . .	M. P. XXIV.	*Aldburgh*, Camden, Horſley, &c.
EBORACVM. LEG. VI. VICTRIX.	M. P. XVII.	*YORK*.
DERVENTIONE. . .	M. P. VII.	*Aldby*, Camden. On the *Derwent*, Horſley, *Stanfordburgh*, Drake.
DELGOVITIA. : :	M. P. XIII.	*Godmondham*, *Weighton*, Camden. &c. *Londesburgh*, Drake.
PRAETORIVM. : :	M. P. XXV.	*Patrington*, Camden, &c. *Hebberstow-fields*, or *Broughton* in *Lincolnſhire*, Horſley. A moveable encampment, or *Spurnhead*. Drake.

From the limits of the *Roman* empire in *Britain* to this *Praetorium*, which I ſuppoſe was a camp ſomewhere on the eaſtern ſea coaſt of our country, is ſet down at the diſtance of one hundred and fifty ſix *Italian* miles. Which agrees very well with our preſent computed ones. I look upon this rout to have been put down primarily, take it backwards or forwards, as a convenient paſſage for auxiliary troops to land and march to the confines; or return from thence and reimbark for *Italy*, or any other part of the empire. In both which it was neceſſary to call at *York* to take orders from the emperor, or the *propraetor* in his abſence. The adjunct of *legio ſexta victrix* to *Eboracum*, as well as *legio viceſ. vict.* to DEVA, *Cheſter*, in the next *iter* ſhews plainly that this ſurvey was drawn after the model of *Ptolemy*'s, who mentions both thoſe ſtations in like manner. From whence this could ſerve for no other uſe than as a map or directory of the country, as I have before hinted, and for a memorial of the ſtations of thoſe two *important legions*.

For a further explanation of this affair I ſhall beg leave to tranſcribe from *Ptolemy*'s geographical deſcription of *Britain* his account of the *Brigantine* towns, as they were ſituated in his time. It is here to be noted, that though *Ptolemy* puts down none but the chief; and though ours be the laſt of eight in his order of naming them, yet they are there geographically placed according to their ſituations, not dignities.

" Again, ſouth from the *Elgovae* and the *Otadeni*, and reaching from ſea to ſea, are the BRIGANTES; whoſe towns are

" *Epiacum*,
" *Vinnovium*.
" *Cataractonium*.
" *Calatum*.
" ISVRIVM.
" *Rigodunum*.
" *Olicana*.
" EBORACVM.
LEGIO SEXTA VICTRIX.
Λεγιὼν Ζ. Νικηφόρειος,
" CAMVNLODVNVM.

" Beſides theſe about the SINVS PORTVOSVS, or the well-havened bay, are the " PARISI; and the town PETVARIA."

The principal ſtations that concern my deſign, are put in *Roman* capitals, in this and the former abſtract, the reſt are far too diſtant for it. I ſhall begin then with ISVRIVM, which being the neareſt ſtation to us on the north road, and having been a very remarkable *Roman* town deſerves a particular diſquiſition.

ISVRIVM *Aldburgh.*

ISVRIVM, called alſo in the itinerary ISVBRIGANTVM, which is no more than a contraction from ISVRIVM BRIGANTVM, is derived by *Leland*, from the rivers ISIS and EVRVS; but by *Camden* from the laſt only. Mr. *Burton* has a learned diſſertation on the name of ISIS given to rivers; of which *Leland* writes that there are no leſs than three in this iſland; but I am afraid it would not be thought ſignificant enough here to inſert it. The river *Ure*, ſtill running under this Town, gives us a proper derivation of its name. Mr. *Baxter* (p) ſuppoſes this place to have been originally a *britiſh* city, and

(p) *Caput hoc erat* Brigantum Britannici *generis*, *ſicuti* & Eburacum, Romanorum. *Gloſs. Ant.* Brit.

ſome

p. 22

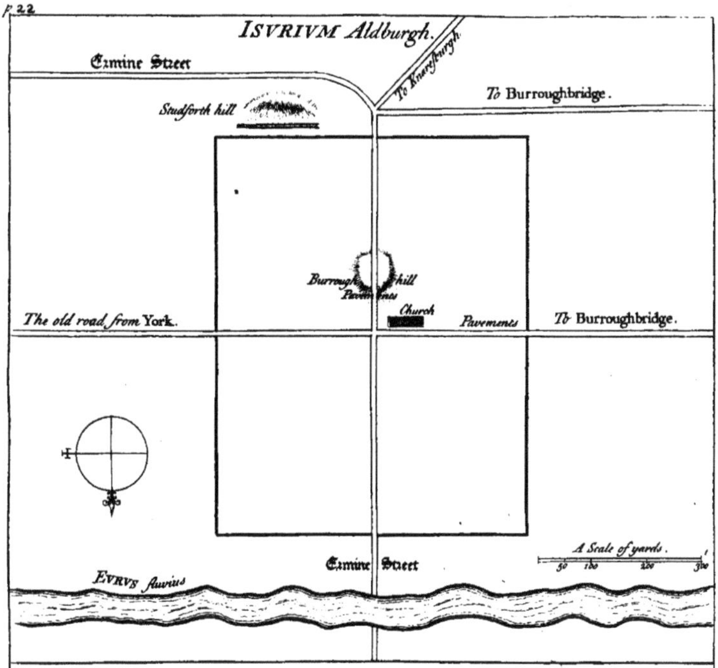

ISVRIVM Aldburgh.
Ermine Street
To Knaresburgh.
To Burroughbridge.
Studforth hill
Burrough hill
Pavements
Church
The old road from York.
Pavements
To Burroughbridge.
A Scale of yards.
50
100
200
300
Ermine Street
EVRVS fluvius

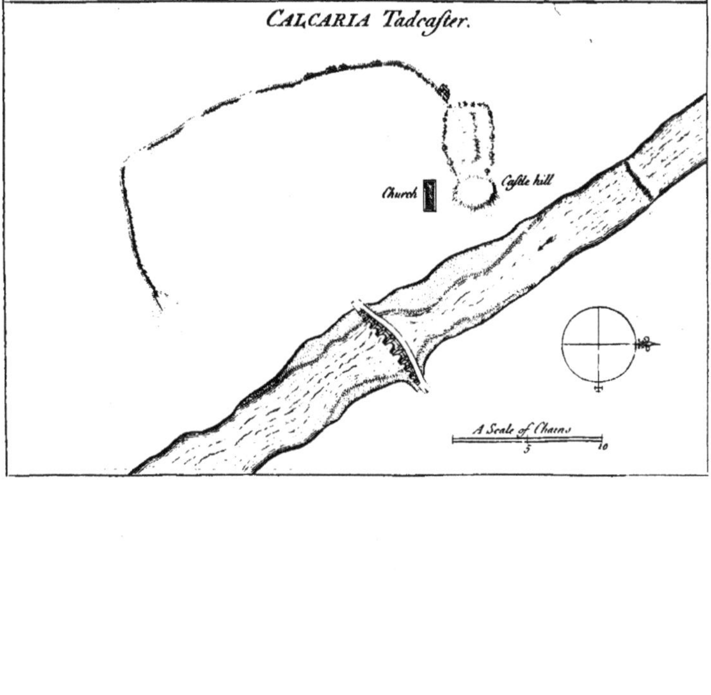

CALCARIA Tadcaster.
Castle hill
Church
A Scale of Chains
5
10

ſome call it the capital of the *Brigantine* people. Our *monkiſh* writers, who follow *Monmouth*'s ſtory, are of this opinion; and confidently enough affirm *(q)* that this place was the city *Aclud*, or *Alclud* mentioned above. But in truth, it is nothing leſs; the name and walls and ſeveral other teſtimonies ſhew plainly that this town was of *Roman* extraction; and that it was plac'd on this river, and on the grand road to *York*, as another advance guard to ſecure that important place on this ſide. The name of *Iſu-Brigantum* it might get to diſtinguiſh it from ſome other of the ſame appellation in the province.. There is no doubt to be made but that there were ſeveral *Roman* towns and ſtations, in the iſland, whoſe names we never heard of.

This ſtation was firſt aſſigned to *Aldburg*, near *Burrough-bridge*, by *J. Leland*, and *William Harriſon*; then *Camden*, *Burton*, *Gale*, *Horſley*, &c. have ſufficiently confirmed it. The diſtance of *Iſurium* from *York*, is put down in the firſt *iter*, at fourteen miles, but in the reſt at ſeventeen. Which laſt is rather too much, unleſs there were two ways of going to it from the city. The *milliarium*, or *mille paſſus*, of the *Romans* was called ſo from its conſiſting of one thouſand paces; each containing five *Roman* feet, ſomewhat leſs than ours. So, as it is computed, that four of their miles make only one *French* league, then four *French* leagues from *York* to *Aldburgh*, which I believe twelve *Yorkſhire* miles may be allowed to meaſure to, will fix the diſtance at ſixteen *Italian* miles that it exactly ſtands at. The copiers of the itinerary, may well be allowed a mile or two, over or under, in their numerals *(r)*. But was the diſtance from *York* unaſcertained, yet the preſent name of the place, the ſite of it, and the many undeniable teſtimonies which have been for many ages and are ſtill found and dug up here, will prove beyond contradiction, that the now poor *Engliſh* village of *Aldburgh* had once the honour to be the *Roman* town ISVRIVM. As I ſhall have frequent occaſion to mention this *Saxon* word, or termination, *Burgh*, in the ſequel, it will not be improper here to give the ſence of our etymologiſts upon it.

What with us is called *Brough*, *Borough*, *Bury*, &c. is taken from the *Saxon* Buɼɡ, Buɼɡe, or Býɼiɡ, which the learned *Somner* interprets *urbs*, *(s) civitas*, *arx*, *caſtrum*, *burgus*, *municipium*; a city, a fort, a fortreſs, a tower, a caſtle, a borough, a free-borough, a city, or town incorporate. *Eſt enim locus munitus ad ſalutem hominum.* It ſignifies, adds that author, any fortified place for the ſafety of mankind. In this laſt ſence it ſeems to hit our purpoſe beſt; it is notoriouſly known that the *Saxons* made uſe of and poſſeſſed the deſerted *Roman* ſtations and palaces, and kept up their fortifications till they were beat out of them by the *Danes*, who burnt and deſtroyed many of thoſe fortreſſes to the ground. *Burgh* then was a common appellation for ſuch a ſanctuary; but the name becoming at laſt too common, without an adjunct, by way of diſtinction it was given; as to *Canterbury*, St. *Edmond's-bury*, *Saliſbury*, &c. *Jed-burgh*, *Aldburgh*, *New-burgh*, *Londeſburgh*, &c. Nay the city of *London* it ſelf was ſometimes called by our *Saxon* Anceſtors, Lonꝺon-býɼiɡ, and Lonꝺenbuɼɡe *(t)*. In later times when they fortified any place, by building a wall about it, it was uſual for them to call it *Burgh*. Of which we have an inſtance in *Peterborough*; whoſe more ancient name, we find, was *Medeſhamſtede*; until *Kenulph* the abbot, *anno* 963, thought fit to erect a wall round the monaſtery, and then he gave it the title of *Burgh (u)*.

The term, or termination, *Cheſter*, or *Caſter*, is alſo of great ſignificancy in finding out the more remarkable *Roman* ſtations in *Britain*. The *Saxon* ceaſtɼe, ſays Dr. *Gibſon*, bears a plain alluſion to the *Roman (x) caſtrum*; and was no doubt given to thoſe places where ſuch *caſtra*, or walled fortifications, were found.

For this reaſon the city of *York* is, in ſeveral places of the *(y) Saxon* annals, called ſimply, Ceaſtɼe, as well as Eoꝼoɼpic-Ceaſtɼe; which honour the city of *Cheſter*, as a noted *Roman* ſtation, keeps to this day. The capital city of the *Northumbrian* kingdom, in the *heptarchy*, needed no other adjunct to diſtinguiſh it; and probably it would now have been called ſo, if the *Roman* name EBORACVM, which venerable *Bede* gives it quite through his work, had not in ſome meaſure ſtuck to it, though ſtrangely corrupted in the *Saxon* dialect. Having premiſed thus much, I return to *Aldburgh*.

The antiquaries who have wrote on this place come next under conſideration; and I believe it will not be unacceptable to the reader to give him *J. Leland*'s account of it in his own words *(z)*.

(q) R. Higden's *policbron*, &c.

(r) In a late edition of the *itineraria veterum* Romanorum, *curante* Petro Weſſelingio *cum ſuis notis*. Amſteladami MDCCXXXV.

ISVRIVM.

EBVRACM. LEG. VI. VICTRIX. M.P. XVII.

Nota. In Blandiniano M. P. XIIII. & *in ſequenti itin.* M. P. XVII. *qui numerus rectè bujus itineris manſionum ſummam conficit. In* Neapolitano M. P. XVII. & *in libris* Longolianis XIIII. & XII. *corrigitur*; & *ſequenti itinere* M. P. XVII *ab* Iſurio Eboracum *adponuntur*.

(s) See *Somner's Saxon* dict. *Skinner's* etym. *ibid.* & *Gibſon*'s *regulae generales de nominibus locorum. Chron. Saxon. in appendice.*

(t) Chron. Saxon. *vide indicem.*

(u) Hic [Kenulphus] *primus extruxit murum circa monaſterium, actum indidit ei nomen* Burgh, *quod antea appellatus* Medeſhamſtede. *Chron.* Saxon. *verſione latin.* p. 120.

(x) Regulae general. ut antea.

(y) See the table of names.

(z) Lelandi *itin.* v. viii.

" Aldburge

"Aldburge is about a quarter of a mile from Burrough-brigge. This was in the Romans "time a great citte on Wathlyng-street called ISVRIA BRIGANTVM and was wallid, "whereof I saw *vestigia quaedam sed tenuia.*

"The cumpace of it hath been by estimation a mile. It is now a small village, and hathe "a paroch chirch, where lie buried two or three knights of the Aldburges, Syr Guilielm "and Syr Richard de Aldburg; whose name yet remains ther, but now men of mean "landes.

"Ther be now large feelds fruitful of corne in the very places where the houses of the "towne was; and in these feelds yerely be founde many coines of silver and brasse of the "*Romain* stampe.

"Ther also have been found sepulchres, *aquae ductus*, *tessallata pavimenta*, &c.

"Ther is a hille on the side of the feeld, where the old toune was, caulid Stothart as "if it had bene the kepe of a castelle.

Mr. *Camden* writes of this place, according to the translation of his learned continuator, in this manner *(a)*.

"Here is a village which carries antiquity in its very name; being called Caldborough, "or Aldborough, that is to say an old borough. There is now little or no signs remain-"ing of a city; the plot thereof being converted into arable and pasture grounds, so that "the evidence of history itself would be suspected in testifying this to be the old *Isurium*, "if the name of the river *Ure*, the *Roman* coins continually digged up here, and the di-"stance betwixt it and *York*, according to *Antoninus*, were not convincing and undeni-"able."

The bishop proceeds in this account, and in being a little more particular, as he says, on the remains of antiquity they have met with in this place, he gives the substance of a letter he had from the reverend Mr. *Morris*, minister of that town, in these words, "here "are some fragments of aqueducts, cut in great stones and covered with *Roman* tile. In the "late civil wars, as they were digging a cellar, they met with a sort of vault, leading, as "'tis said, to the river. If of *Roman* work, for it has not yet met with any one curious e-"nough to search it, it might probably be a repository for the dead. The coins, gene-"rally of brass, but some few of silver, are mostly of *Constantine* and *Carausius*. There "are too of *Maximian*, *Dioclesian*, *Valerian*, *Severus*, *Pertinax*, *Aurelius*, and of other "emperors; as also of *Faustina* and *Julia*. They meet with little *Roman* heads of brass; "and have formerly also found coined pieces of gold, with chains of the same metal, but "none of late. About two years ago were found four *signet* polished stones; three where-"of were *cornelians*. The first had a horse upon it, and a stump of laurel shooting out "five branches. The second a *Roman* sitting with a sacrificing dish in one hand and "resting the other on a spear. The third a *Roman*, if not *Pallas*, with a spear in one "hand, wearing a helmet, with a shield on the back, or on the other arm, and under "that something like a quiver hanging to the knee. The fourth of a purple colour, "has a *Roman* head like *Severus* or *Antonine*, Several pavements have been found about "a foot under ground; compassed about with stones about an inch square; but with-"in are little stones of a quarter that bigness, wrought into knots and flowers after "the *Mosaick fashion*. No altars are met with, but pieces of urns and old glass are com-"mon. In the vestry wall of the church is placed a figure of *Pan*, or *Silvanus*, in one "rough stone nyched.

Mr. *Morris*, from whom the learned bishop had this account, was a divine of great honour and integrity, and was vicar of *Aldburgh* above forty years. Since his time several great curiosities have been discovered at this place; particularly, about four years ago, in digging the foundation of a house here, a *mosaick* pavement *(b)* was laid open of singular figure and beauty. It is now about two foot from the level of the street, and is an oblong square of about six, though there was more of it than they could take into the house. This pavement is well preserved, and shewn by an old woman, who keeps the house, to strangers. It is somewhat remarkable, that the name of this poor old creature is *Aldburgh*, probably the last of that family, which *Leland* mentions, and who were once lords of this town.

See the plate Fig. 1.

Fig. 2.

At the door of this cottage I was shewn another tessellated pavement of a different form from the other; and though not above two or three yards from it, is a foot nearer the surface of the street. We bared as much of it as to take the figure; the former was composed of white and black squares, with a border of red; but the stones of this were lesser squares, and were white, yellow, red, and blue. Not long since more pavements of this kind were discovered on a hill called the *Burrough hill*. Here was likewise the foundation walls of a considerable building laid open. Two bases of pillars of some regular order. Large stones, of the grit kind, with joints for cramping. Sacrificing vessels. Flews, or hollow square pipes for conveyance of smoke or warm air. Bones and

Fig. 3, 4.

(a) Gibson's Camden 1st ed

(b) *Mosaick* work came originally from *Greece*; but 'tis plain that it had been used in *Italy* for near two thousand years. *Vitruvius*, who lived in the time of *Augustus*, speaks of it under the term of *opus sectile*, *pavimenta sectilia*, *opera musaea*, & *musiva*. It was also called *tessalatum*.

The right hon.ble Robert James *Lord* Petre, *Baron of* Writtle, *a great encourager of*
of this work, has by this plate preserved these remains of Roman *antiquity.* 1736.

horns of beasts, mostly stags. An ivory needle, and a copper *Roman* style, or *pin*. From all which we may reasonably suppose, that a temple was formerly built in this place. I am informed his grace the duke of *Newcastle*, the present lord of *Aldburgh*, has ordered a house to be built over the pavements, to secure them from the weather. But lest this should not prove so, and these fine remains of *Roman* ingenuity should wholly perish, I have caused them to be drawn, as exactly as possible, and do here present the reader with a view of them.

The antient walls of this town, which are yet easily traced, measure to 2500 yards in circumference, somewhat more than a mile and an half round. The form is near square. About a hundred paces from the south wall is the hill called *Stodhart*, or *Studforth*, which *Leland* speaks of. It is a kind of a semicircle, which shape would tempt one to believe it had been a theatre. A neighbouring minister does imagine that the present name of this hill is derived from the *Latin Stadium*, which signifies a plot of ground for champions or combatants, to perform their exercises in. *Suetonius* tells us, that a very noble one was built for *Domitian* at *Rome*(c). But whether this conjecture is probable, I leave to the reader's judgment. I take it to have been an out-fort or work for the greater security of the town on this side; the great military way coming close by it.

But now I mention the road, I am persuaded that the present post-road was not the *Roman* way from *Aldburgh* to *York*. And though the traces of another be very imperfect at this day, the country hereabouts having a deep moist soil, so that the *agger* of it is wholly sunk; yet we may reasonably suppose, that there was once a different communication betwixt these two important stations. There are two roads yet obvious that direct to this place, which I have mentioned before; the one is the grand military way that runs from *Tadcaster*; the other comes out of *Lancashire* to *Skipton*; from thence I have traced it my self to *Bolton-bridge*, and to *Blueburgh-houses*, over *Knaresburgh-forest* to the town; near the bridge of which is a very fine piece of it entire. From thence it went in a direct line to *Aldburgh*. But there are no such visible remains of the road we are seeking for; tradition indeed points us out what the inhabitants of this place call to this day the old way to *York*, to lye south-east, and brings us to a ford over the river *Ouse*, now **Aldwark-ferry**. This name denotes some antient *Roman* work or fortress to have formerly stood here, as a guard to the river which is often fordable at this place; and it is very probable the road to *York* led this way. From whence it might strike in a direct line over the forest of *Galtres*, by *Benningburgh*(d), to the city. This was the opinion of the late Mr. *Morris*; and I have seen a letter to him from that great antiquary dean *Gale*, to confirm it. These roads, the walls of *Isurium*, and what other things I have treated on, relating to that station, will be better understood by the annexed plan or ichnography of it, or the map of the vale and county of *York*, in which the *Roman* roads to this place the city, &c. are all delineated.

It is impossible to be at *Aldburgh* and not take notice of *Burrough-bridge*, which has sprung up out of the ruins of the former. For a monkish (e) writer tells us, it continued in great splendour till it was burned by the *Danes*, who almost set all *England* in a flame about the year 766. *Burrough-bridge* may be plainly seen to have been built from the old *Isurium*, whose very walls yielded such a quantity of flint pebbles, as has not only paved the streets of both these towns, but has served for all their out-buildings, as yards, stables, &c.

Tradition tells us that the antient bridge over the river *Ure* lay at the foot of *Aldburgh*; and they have this authority to confirm it. Some lands that lye in their fields, and stretch to the river-side, are called **Brig-gates**. Besides, I am told a great beam of solid oak was taken up not many years ago out of the river here, which had been part of this bridge; and was so hard and black as to serve to inlay the canopy of their present pulpit in the church. When our ancestors thought fit to alter the road and build a bridge about half a mile above the old one, a town immediately sprung up with it, whose name includes no more than a borough or town at a bridge. This is at present a fine stone-bridge, but there must have been a wooden one, also here, in the reign of *Ed.* II. for we are told, by our historians, that in a battle here, where *Thomas* earl of *Lancaster* was taken prisoner, *Humphrey de Bohun*, earl of *Hereford*, was slain upon the bridge by a soldier, who struck him into the belly with a spear from under it (f).

But our principal business at *Burrough-bridge* is to take particular notice of the *pyramids* in its neighbourhood, which are wonders indeed; and which I propose to shew are of *Roman* extraction, and are all solid stones. These stupendous monuments of antiquity have long borne the name of the *devil's arrows*, and a ridiculous traditional story is told of them by the country people hereabouts. They probably had this name given them in the times of ignorance and monkery; when any thing beyond their comprehension was ascribed to mi-

(c) *Studio ad tempus extructo*. Suet. *in* Dom. Dr. *Stukeley* observes, that most amphitheatres abroad are placed without the cities, for wholesomeness, and upon elevated ground, for the benefit of the air, and perflation; a thing, he says, much recommended by *Vitruvius*, *Stukeley*'s iter curiosum.

(d) *Benningburgh* seems to be derived from Bung a fortified town and Bene prayer; this place having been antiently given to some religious houses in *York*, to pray for the souls of the donors. See St. *Mary's* abbey, St. *Leonard's* hospital. &c.

(e) *Rad. Higden*, polichron

(f) *Vide annal. sub anno* 1321.

racle or witchcraft. So you have the *devil's quoites* in *Oxfordshire*, the *devil's causway* in *Lancashire*, &c. " Dr. *Plot*, says the learned bishop *Gibson (g)*, is of opinion, they were a " *British* work, erected in memory of some battle fought there, or *British* deities, agree- " ing with Dr. *Stillingfleet*, grounding upon the custom of the *Phenicians* and *Greeks*; who, " say they, were nations undoubtedly acquainted with *Britain*, before the arrival of the " *Romans*, and who set up unpolished stones, instead of images, to the honour of their " gods." How far the two nations, here mentioned, were acquainted with the mechanical powers, I know not; but I am persuaded the poor *Britons* were not only destitute of tools to hew such blocks of stone out of the quarry, for such I take them to be, but, also, utterly incapable to bring them away, and erect them in this place.

If we suppose them set up as *Pagan deities*, it does not disprove that they might be erected by the *Romans* in honour of some of their gods. The *Egyptians*, from whom the *Romans* copied many idolatrous superstitions, we are told by *Herodotus*, erected pyramids, which were thought by them to be a symbol of human life. The beginning whereof is represented by the bottom, and the end by the *apex*, or top; on which account it was, they used to erect them on sepulchres. *Herodian* testifies, that *Heliogabalus*, which is the *Baal* of the *Tyrians*, was worshipped in a great stone, round at bottom, and ending in a cone, to signify the nature of fire. In the like figure, *Tacitus* reports, that *Venus Paphia* was worshipped; which is, says a *(b)* learned author, the moon, *Astarte*, the wife of *Baal*, he supposes, for the *Cyprian* superstition is likely to come from the *Tyrians*. He adds, I find also, that *Lapis* has been a surname of *Jupiter*; *Jupiter Lapis*.

These stones are placed near the meeting of four *Roman* high roads; the first from *Catarict*, the second from *Ickley* by *Knaresburgh*, the third from *Castleford* over St. *Helen's-ford* near *Tadcaster*; and the fourth comes hither from *York*.

That profound antiquary, dean *Gale*, was of opinion, that these pyramids were *Roman*; and that they were their *Hermae* or *Mercurys (i)*; because placed on the greatest military way they had in *Britain*. This would be a strong argument, that our road was the *Ermine-street*; and no weak confirmation of Mr. *Selden's* notion, who derives that word from the *Saxon* Irmunpull. I am told, that Dr. *Gale* ascended to the top of one or more of these stones, to see if there was not a cavity to place a head in, as was usual in the *Roman Mercurys*; but nothing of that nature was found upon them. That they are rude, and shew no signs of *Roman* elegance, in their make, is not significant. It is well known they affected a rudeness often, where something, of what the *French* call the *marveilleux*, concurred. I take the famous *Stonehenge* to be a kind of *Roman* monument of inimitable structure. But it is a much easier matter to suppose our obelisks *Roman*, than to prove for what reason they were erected; they seem to me to be either sepulchral monuments, or trophies of some victory; of this last opinion was *J. Leland*, who, in his travels to these parts, has given us this description of them *(k)*.

" A little withoute the toune of *Burrough-bridge*, on the west part of **Watling-street**, standith four great main stones, wrought above *in conum*, by mennes handes.

" They be set in three several feldes at this tyme; one of them standith in a several feld, " a good stonecast from the other, and is bigger and higher than the rest. I esteem it to " be the waite of five waine load or mo.

" Inscription could I finde none yn thes stones; and yf ther were, it might be woren " out; for they be sore woren and scalid with wether.

" I take them to be *trophaea a* Romanis *posita* yn the side of **Wathelyng-street**, as " yn a place much occupyed in yorneying, and so much yn fyght."

Another dispute which has long been amongst our antiquaries, though I think with very small reason, is the nature of these stones, and whether they are not a composition. Mr. *Camden* broached this notion first, and supposes them to be a compound of sand, lime and small pebbles cemented together. Without doubt, as Dr. *Lister* observes *(l)*, the bulk of the stones surprised him; as not thinking it possible for the art of man to contrive to set them up. When, if he had considered what trifles these are, compared with the least obelisks at *Rome*, some of which were brought by water from *Egypt*, the wonder would have vanished, and he might have concluded, that nothing of this nature was too hard for *Roman* ingenuity. The pyramids are truly of the most common sort of stone we have in the north of *England*, called the *coarse rag-stone*, or *miln-stone grit*. A large rock of which stone, and from which probably these obelisks were taken, is at *Plumpton*, within five miles of them. And if Mr. *Camden* also supposed, that there was no *English* rock big enough to yield natural stones of that magnitude, he might have known that a little above *Ickly*, another *Roman* station, within sixteen miles of *Burrough-bridge*, there is one solid bed of this sort of stone, whose perpendicular depth only will yield obelisks at least thirty foot long. If they were a composition, it must be allowed more wonderful than the other opinion; for

(g) Add. to *Camden's* last edition.
(b) *Cowley's* notes on his *Davideis*, book 2.
(i) *Gale's* itin. *Ant.*
(k) *Lelandi* itin. v. 8.
(l) Philosoph. transactions, v. 3. *Lowthorp's* abridg.

I have

8

I have by me a piece of an obelisk, and a piece of the rock, at *Plumpton*; and it is impossible to tell the difference.

I here observe further, along with our famous Dr. *Lister (m)*, that almost all the monuments of the *Romans* with us are of this sort of stone, as appears by what remains in the antient gates of *York*, and the great quantity of it that is wrought up in most of our churches; and is still daily dug out of foundations. It is well known by what we see of *Roman* industry, at this distance from them, that their whole study was to build so as, if possible, to last to perpetuity. For this reason the grand architect *Vitruvius* lays it down for a rule in building of houses, temples, &c. that materials of all kinds should be got ready three years beforehand. And at the same time recommends building with this sort of stone or brick, as the only preservative in case of fire; for they will equally stand it like a crucible, when most other kind of stone, and even marble itself, will fly, with heat, into a thousand pieces. The beauty of a building lyes in the proportion; not in the whiteness of its stone; and the *Romans* would have laughed at the foppery, if I may so call it, of several in our age, who send so many miles, at vast expence, for stone to build with, only for the sake of its colour.

Another qualification that the grit-stone has, is, that it is scarce to be impaired by time or weather. Our naturalists observe, that it gains rather than loses, by the particles in the air adhering to its rough coat. For this reason, and the former, all their palaces, temples, &c. with us, were certainly built of it, and every where else in the island where they could get it; almost all their monumental inscriptions, found in the north, were cut in one kind or other of it. Their *sarcophagi*, or stone coffins, were entirely grit. Nay their statues were of the same, which Dr. *Lister* gives an undeniable instance of, a vast *Roman* head, perhaps, says he, of one of their emperors, was dug out of the foundations of some houses in *Castlegate, York*. It had a neck or square pedestal of one solid stone, with the point of the square to the eye; and was, adds he, of as coarse a grit as that of the obelisks abovementioned. I have to add, from the aforesaid author, that he also saw a large pedestal, which had been the base of some mighty pillar, of this coarse rag, found in his time at *York*. So the two bases, discovered lately at *Aldburgh*, and which are now to be seen there, are directly of this kind of stone.

It may be thought folly in me to say, that in my walks about this city, when I cast my eye upon any of this stone, it strikes me with an awful reverence of the once *Roman* state and grandeur. And I cannot but observe here, that as the churches of *Aldburgh*, *Burroughbridge*, *Myton*, and *Ouseburn*, have store of this grit; some of it with the evident marks of fire upon it, wrought up in the walls of them, which could come from no place but the old ISVRIVM; so the like kind of stone, some in mighty blocks, which the churches, gates and walls of *York* are full of, does most assuredly evince us, whose work they were originally of; what masons and architects had the first cutting and erecting of them; and at the same time gives us a faint far distant view of the ruins of those two eminent stations.

But to return to the obelisks. What sort of mechanism they used to draw these monstrous stones, is not so easy to account for. Dr. *Huntington*, in his account of the pyramids of *Egypt*, in whose composition are many stupendous blocks of marble, has endeavoured to give some notion of the mechanical powers that were used in erecting them. A very ingenious gentlemen, well versed in this kind of knowledge, has told me, that these great stones of ours might have been moved hither upon rollers. But this must have required infinite labour and pains, besides time. And how must all these be multiplied, when, instead of six or sixteen miles from the quarry, they got one of these stones to *Rudston* near *Burlington*, at least forty miles from any quarry of this sort of stone; and over a very uneven country besides?

The number of these obelisks, at *Burrough-bridge*, was four; but the least of them fell by chance, or was pulled down; part of which stone now makes a foot-bridge over a small brook near the town. There is a place marked in the plate, where this stone pillar stood; and the height of it, according to Dr. *Gale*, was 21 foot. The three remaining stand, near in a line, about a stone's cast from one another. In the year 1709, Mr. *Morris*, whom I have mentioned before, caused the ground about the middlemost of these obelisks to be opened nine foot wide. "At first a good soil was found about a foot deep, and then a course "of stones, rough and of several kinds, but most were large cobbles, (pebbles) laid in a "bed of coarse grit and clay; and so for four or five courses underneath one another, round "about the pyramid in all probability, to keep it upright; nevertheless, they all seem to "encline a little to the south-east. Under the stones was a very strong clay, so hard "that the spade could not affect it. This was near two yards deep from the surface of "the earth, and a little lower was the bottom of the stone resting upon the clay, and was "flat. As much of the stone as was within ground is a little thicker than what appears "above, and has the marks of a *first dressing* upon it; that is, it has been *taxata, non per-*

(m) Ab. philosoph transact. v. 3.

"*dolata,*

" *dolata, ferro.* The entire height of this stone, is thirty foot six inches from the " bottom" (*n*).

The foundations of these stones being laid with the same clay and pebble as the walls of *Aldburgh*, is another convincing proof of their being *Roman*, as well as the marks of the chissel upon them, beneath ground, assure us that they are no compositions, but natural stones. After such a long disputation on these wonders, it will not be improper for me to exhibit a view of them. They are taken by scale, by which the height and other dimensions are shewn. The furrows on the top of each are supposed by some to have been worn by rain and weather; but it is my opinion they were cut so at first, in order to carry off the wet. The landscape shews their situation and the place where the fourth stone formerly stood.

Having now said what I can on these obelisks, I shall return to *Aldburgh*. And notwithstanding the testimonies of all the eminent antiquaries I have cited, with its own most convincing proofs of a *Roman* station, a late writer (*o*), in his *survey of England*, has thought fit to place *Isurium* at *Ripon*. This assertion can mean nothing but novelty, there being not one convincing argument to prove it. For though that author has been sagacious enough in some other discoveries in *Britain*; yet when he asserts this, and with the like arbitrariness has carried LEGIOLIVM to *Doncaster*, I must beg leave to dissent from him in both.

That I may omit nothing that has been said by the learned, on the subject of this station and obelisks, I shall subjoin a transcript of a letter sent by Mr. *Morris* to the bishop of *London*, before the publication of his last edition of *Camden*. The copy, under his own hand, was found in his study, after his death, and communicated to me by the reverend Mr. *Prance* of *Easingwold*. The substance of it is given by the learned bishop in the edition aforesaid; but as it will compleat all that can now be said on this subject, so I beg leave to give it in the author's own words. I hope it may prove an incitement to the successors of that curious person, to imitate him in recording every thing which may hereafter be discovered in a place so fruitful of *Roman analects*.

" Reverend Dr. *Gibson*, *Aldburgh, Julii ult.* 1708.

" I Am informed, by the very industrious antiquary Mr. *Thoresby*, of your desire to put " forth another edition of *Camden*, which will be very grateful to all lovers of that " kind of useful learning; wherein I heartily wish you good success: But being a little con- " cerned in your last edition, by the publishing a letter of mine, writ to the very learned " Dr. *Tancred Robinson*, concerning this place, which I intended not for the publick, in " that loose style I writ it, as to a friend; without that regard I should have done, if I " had expected that honour from you. This, Sir, and Mr. *Thoresby*'s invitation, joined " with a desire of serving you, gives you the trouble of my second thoughts. Wherein, " if you find any thing useful, please to give it a dress suitable to your own, both in style " and method.

" That the pyramids of *Burrough-bridge* are natural, appears very fully from some seams, " as taken from its bed, near *Knaresborough*, or at *Plumpton-tower*, built of stone of the " same grit; from whence stones of a much larger proportion might be raised. We have " much of the same kind in our old buildings; doubtless, coming from the same quarry, " distant about five miles. That these were erected, as Mr. *Camden* conjectures, for tro- " phies, may seem probable; if we refer to the tradition held, that *Severus*, dying at *York*, " left the empire to his two sons, *Caracalla* and *Geta*, which was acceptable to the em- " press, and approved of by the soldiers, but not to the two brothers; but they were re- " conciled by the mediation of the empress and a sister (*p*). In memory whereof, four " stones were erected, but three only now remain; for one was taken down the last centu- " ry. That the *Britons* had the art of cementing grit, and of carriage of such stupendous " weighty stones, I have received no cause to believe. Neither can I subscribe to the " opinion of the most learned Dr. *Stillingfleet*, that the *Romans* or *Grecians* had such prodi- " gious representatives for their little gods at their gates to receive their libations.

" *Isurium Brigantium* is now a small country village, containing within the old *Roman* " walls, as appeared by a late survey, sixty acres. Almost a direct square, upon a de- " clining hill towards the river *Ure* on the north side. **Roadgate**, leading to the old *Ca- " taractonium*, went through it to *Millby* over an old wooden bridge. The way through " the meadows may yet be traced, and bears the name of **Briggates**, near half a mile east " of the present bridge. The old *walls* were about four yards thick, founded on large peb- " bles, laid on a bed of blue clay, now wholly covered with earth, but laid open by such " as want stones for building; where they have some large coarse stones of red sandy grit, " taken from a rock of the same in the town. To the clay, *viz.* the foundation, in several

(*n*) *Hearn*'s notes on *Leland*'s itinerary. Mr. *Morris*, in his letter to Mr. *Hearn*, does not tell him, that he thrust in a quantity of king *William*'s halfpence under this stone, and some of queen *Anne*'s medals, which, if ever they be found, in future ages, will cause a wonder almost equal to the Stone itself.

(*o*) *N. Salmon.*

(*p*) This traditional account is still fresh in the mouths of the country people hereabouts; though how they came by the story is impossible to know.

places

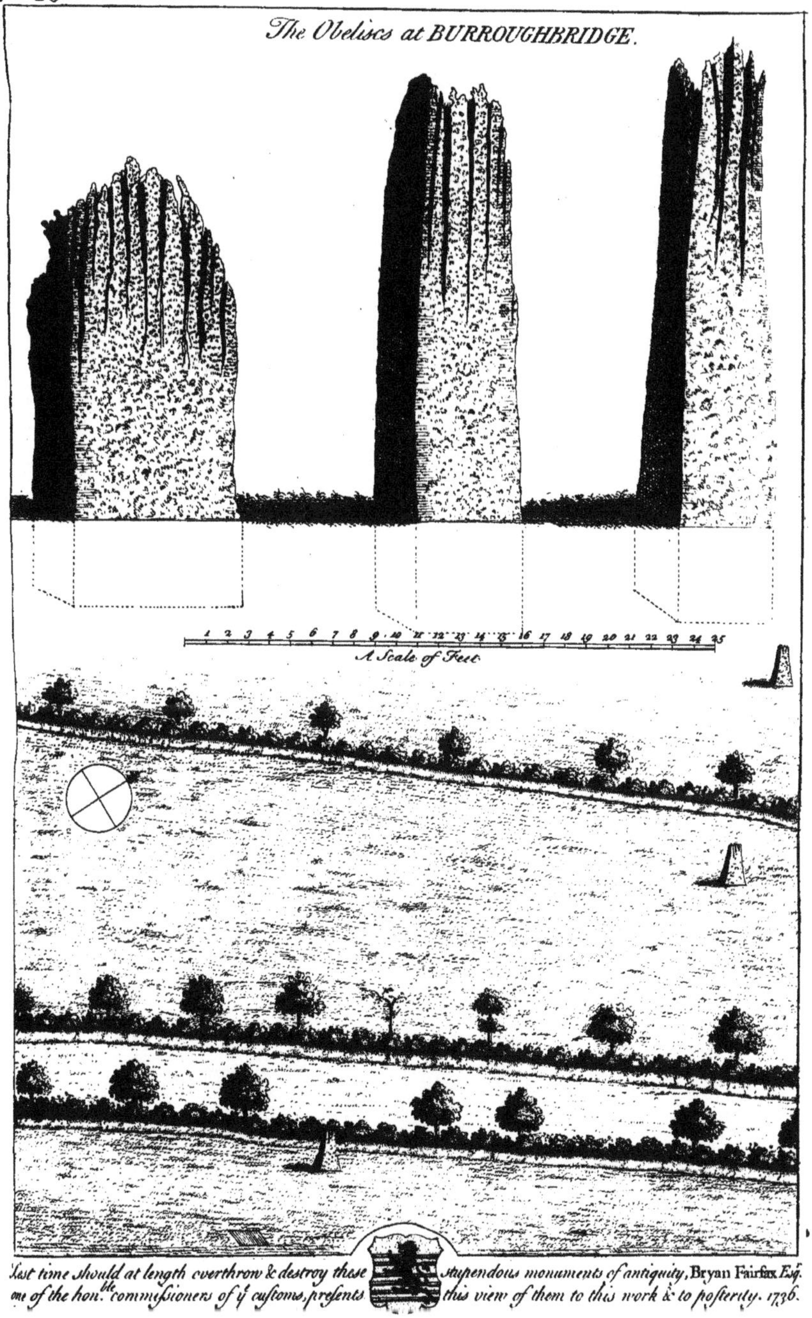

The Obeliscs at BURROUGHBRIDGE.

Lest time should at length overthrow & destroy these stupendous monuments of antiquity, Bryan Fairfax Esq. one of the hon.ble commissioners of y.e customs, presents this view of them to this work & to posterity. 1736.

" places is four or five yards deep. The soil is all of a black earth from whence the tradi-
" tion may be allowed of, that it was burnt by the *Danes*, when *York* was almost destroyed
" by them. And this also appears frequently, upon opening the ground bones are found
" half burned, with other black ashes, which appears not unlike a vein of black earth
" covered with a lighter colour. That it was a *Roman* colony the author well proves from
" the coins frequently found, not many elder than *Claudius*, yet some of *Augustus Caesar*;
" and so down to the *Antonines*, with *Carausius*; two of the thirty tyrants, *viz. Posthumus*
" and *Tetricus*; also *Caradicus* and *Alectus*; but *Constantines* are most abounding. Several
" vessels of red earth, broken, wrought with knots, flowers, heads, as one with that of
" *Jupiter Ammon*; others with birds or beasts, and some with *Capricorns* upon them.
" One little *lamp* of earth entire (*q*), and large pieces of *Roman* glass were found *anno* 1707.
" Within thirty years last past, in the circuit of the old walls, have been found about
" twenty little *polished signet stones* of diverse kinds and cuts. One of *Jupiter Ammon's*
" head. A second with an eagle with a civic crown in its bill. A third found about *March*
" last of which I give you the impression, *viz.* a winged victory crowning a trophy. In
" the catalogue of broken pots, I should have noted one to you of a *Cothon* or *poculum la-*
" *conicum*; which the soldiers used in marching to clear water by passing into several con-
" cavities therein made. Also a *British* axe, and several other things, which perhaps will
" be given you by some more learned pens; to whom I did my self the honour to present
" them as a foundation for a more noble collection. If I can be further serviceable pray
" command,

GOOD DOCTOR,

Your most humble servant

EDWARD MORRIS.

In my return from *Aldburgh* to *York* I take the *Roman* road I have mentioned over *Ald-wark-ferry*. Some vestiges of it may be observed in the villages leading to this place, particularly a great quantity of the pebble in their buildings which formed in all probability, the *strata* of the road. But from the *Ferry* to *York* the *agger* is quite sunk; and though it has been sought for with care, by several antiquaries as well as my self, not the least footstep is remaining. Yet since it is agreed to by all that the old road must have gone this way; I here observe that it is the fourth considerable *Roman* high way I have mentioned to lead particularly to the city it self.

To take a just survey of the *Roman* roads which direct from the *Humber*, and the several ports of the *German* ocean, to *York*, I must necessarily mention *Lincoln*. LINDVM, or *Lincoln*, bears so many evident tokens of being a considerable *Roman* station, both in history, and the remains of antiquity which it does yet exhibit, that it is pity some able pen does not undertake a particular account of it. There were two remarkable high roads which led from LINDVM to EBORACVM; the first is still very evident, cross the heath, and is easily traced on to a town called *Wintringham*, on the great river *Humber*. The other is more a land passage, and comes from *Lincoln*, through *Littlebrough* on the *Trent* and so to *Rossington-bridge*, where it meets the *Ermine-street*, which leads to *Doncaster*, and so on. It is true this is not so particular a road for my purpose as the former; because the *Ermine-street* directs for any station north of *Lincoln* as well as *York*. Yet the communication betwixt these two stations, cross the *Humber*, might frequently be prevented by winter, or stress of weather; and therefore it was absolutely necessary to have a more convenient passage, though not a nearer, to come intirely by land.

The *Roman* road from *Lincoln* to the river *Humber* I have said comes down to old *Wintringham* on one side of the river; whose opposite has a town called *Brough* on the *Yorkshire* coast; this still continues to be the constant landing place for the ferry. The military way, on this side, most certainly began again here, and continued to DELGOVITIA; for 'tis not possible to suppose that they would lay so fine a road down to the *Humber*, if they had not frequent passages over it; and a way to proceed on for *York*, when they were got to the other side. But the traces of this road are faint; and the next station must be our only guide, which as it lies in a direct line for *York*, and has been remarkable in our neighbourhood, I cannot pass it by without notice. For at this last named station, wherever it will chance to fall, must have been a conjunction of two grand roads; that from PRAETORIVM, and this other from *Lincoln*; which is a circumstance that argues it a place of consequence in those days.

In *Ptolemy's* geographical sea chart of the *German* ocean, where he describes the promontorys, bays, and rivers on the *British* coasts, his ABVS AESTVARIVM is agreed

(*q*) This lamp is now in the possession of the reverend Mr. *Prance*; who has several other curiosities of the like nature found at *Aldburgh*. He presented me with a piece of *white brick* with M. M. part of a broken inscription, stamped upon it. This might stand for *Magister militum*. The *Romans* had a way to bake *white brick*, exceeding hard; an art I believe, now not known.

by all to be our great river *Humber*. As his OCELLVM PROMONTORIVM, next it northward, muſt have been *Spurnhead*. On this river Mr. *Camden*, for the ſake of etymology, or ſound, and the diſtance from *Delgovitia*, has found out *Patrington*, in *Holderneſs*, to be the PRAETORIVM of *Antonine*'s itinerary. So the PETVARIA of *Ptolemy*, which that writer mentions, as the chief town of the PARISI, a people inhabiting this part of the country, Mr. *Horſley* and ſome others, has placed at *Brough*. I beg leave to diſſent from both.

PRAETORIVM. If the copiers of *Antonine's* itinerary may be depended on, this name has a ſignification very different from any of the whole catalogue of *Roman* ſtations in *Britain*. It is purely *latin*, derived from the *Greek*, and will bear a great variety of interpretations *(r)*. If it mean any thing in this *iter*, it can never be a town or ſtation, but rather an occaſional encampment ſome where on theſe eaſtern ſea coaſts. In this ſence the learned continuator of *Camden*, tranſlates it from *Lipſius*; and ſuch indeed it ſeems to have been at the time this journey or ſurvey was made; but where, is now impoſſible to determine. Theſe coaſts have, even in the memory of man, ſuffered greatly from the ſea; and poſſibly this camp, or ſtation, may have been long ſince ſwallowed up by it *(s)*.

I have given the authority of *Ulpian*, and indeed the itinerary it ſelf confirms it, that the *Roman* military ways were always laid to ſome principal ſtation, or ſome ſea port. Mr. *Horſley* then muſt be greatly miſled to carry this ſtation croſs the *Humber*, and drop it betwixt that river and *Lincoln*. For, after all, if we allow an eaſy miſtake or two in the tranſcribers of the itinerary, which is very allowable in a thing handed down to us, through ſo many ages, and through ſuch viciſſitudes of times, this PRAETORIVM of *Antoninus* will mean no other than the PROMONTORIVM of *Ptolemy*. The one ſeeming to be making a ſea chart, in which he is very exact; and the other is full as circumſtantial in the placing the inland forts and ſtations on the military ways in *Britain*.

To the name of *Promontorium* in *Ptolemy*, is joined *Ocellum*; which is the diminutive from *oculus*, a *little eye*. This agrees well with the ſite of the place; and no doubt, in the time of the *Romans*, a watch-tower was built here, not only to overlook the mouth of the *Humber*, but as a guard to theſe coaſts. The preſent name of *Spurnhead*, called in our old *Engliſh* Chronicles **Spurenhead**, is certainly derived from the *Saxon* verb Spẏɲıan or Spẏɲıᵹean *exquirere*, *ſcrutari*, *explorare*, &c. *(t)* to look out, watch, or explore. So remarkable a point of land as this was, might ſerve for the ſame purpoſe in their time as well as the former. Here was alſo formerly, a remarkable ſea port town, called *Ravenſburgh*, well known in our hiſtorians for two deſcents made at it by our *H.* IV. and *E.* IV. but it is now almoſt ſwallowed up. I ſhall not diſcant upon the name of this town, which carries an indelible mark of antiquity along with it; but leave this uncertain path with ſaying that if the miſtake I have mentioned be allowed me, as alſo another in the numerals, of xxxv miles from DELGOVITIA inſtead of xxv, this diſputed ſtation will drop at *Raveneſburgh (u)*.

PETVARIA. *Brough*, or *Burgh*, by our modern antiquaries has likewiſe had the honour to be put down for *Ptolemy's* PETVARIA; but with as little reaſon as the former. That it ſeems to bid fair for being a *Roman* fortreſs, on this ſide *Humber*, both on account of the military way from *Lincoln*, and its own name, which I have elſewhere defined, is no argument to prove that PETVARIA belongs to it. The *Romans*, no doubt, had many ſtations and fortreſſes in the iſland, the names of which are not handed down to us, by any accounts whatſoever. *Ptolemy* tells us that *about the ſure-haven'd-bay* lived the people called PARISI; and that there alſo was the town PETVARIA. Mr. *Baxter* reads this PECVARIA; and if his definition of PARISI be right, which is, that it comes from *paſturage* or *Shepherds*; then PECVARIA is a notable and apt name for the chief town of thoſe people. It is remarkable that the country many miles circumjacent to *Burlington-bay*, is ſtill much inhabited by ſhepherds; but where to fix the *Roman* town here ſpoken of is the difficulty. *Pocklington*, *Driffield*, or *Beverley* bid the faireſt for it, in my opinion; the former has Mr. *Baxter*'s option; that learned man deriving it from the *Greek* ΠΟΚΟΣ, which is, ſays he, the *latin vellus*, a *fleece of wool*; from whence *Pecus* is eaſily deduced. *Driffield* is a town of great antiquity, *Alfred* one of our *Northumbrian* kings lies buried in it; beſides here are many *barrows* or *tumuli* about it. And *Beverley* has the votes of ſome on this account; near which a few years ago, was diſcovered, in a field, a curious *Roman* teſſelated pavement; which is a ſtronger argument in its behalf than either of the former.

DELGOVITIA. *Londeſburgh.* DELGOVITIA has been hitherto agreed to by all to be our *Wighton* or *Weighton*; Mr. *Camden* has learnedly defined that word to come from the *Britiſh Delgwe*, which ſignifies, ſays he, the ſtatues, or images, of heathen Gods. And he ſeems to make no doubt but that this place was dedicated to idol worſhip even in the times of the *Britons*. *Weighton* is not without its derivative from the ſame cauſe; **Weightelberg** in *Germany* is noted by

(r) *Praetorium* is a word of great latitude in the *Roman* tongue; and ſometimes only ſignifies a *country houſe*, or *villa*. *Tacit & Sueton.*

(s) There are ſeveral towns mentioned to have been once on theſe coaſts, in *Camden*, &c. which are now wholly ſwallowed up.

(t) See *Somner's Saxon* dict.

(u) This town's name ſeems to be derived from the *Saxon* verb Repan or Reuan *remigare* to row. Repanbuɲᵹ a proper name for a ſea port.

Conrad

8

Conrad Celtes, says Dr. *Gale*, as a remarkable town of the *Druids* in those parts. Whatever it was in the times of the *Britons*, it is certain that under the idolatry of our *Saxon* ancestors, this town had a near neighbour to it, called by venerable *Bede* **Godmundingaham**. Which is interpreted *deorum septa*; but whether the name has any reference to the other, I shall not determine. In the *anonymous chorography* of *Britain*, this station is called DEVOVICIA, corruptly no doubt for DELGOVICIA; from whence if we take VIC, and add the *Saxon* termination ton, there is something in the sound of *Wighton*, probably, derived from the old word; especially when we consider that the *Saxon u* and *w* were sounded alike. And this is all that can be said for it.

For *Weighton* has discovered no marks of antiquity to denote it a station, and except the distance in the itinerary there is no other proof of it. Something like a *tumulus*, indeed appears at the west end of the town, as Mr. *Horsley* observed, in the road to *York*. But if the name of this place had any reference to idol worship, as Mr. *Camden* has defined, its near neighbour *Godmondham* has a much clearer title to it; being called by venerable *Bede* expresly *locus idolorum*, or a place of idols. In the ecclesiastical part of this work the reader will find the reason why our author has occasion to mention it. But he was strangely out in his chorography, when he describes the situation of it to be *not far from York*, and *near* the river *Derwent*; for 'tis eight miles from the latter and sixteen from the former. Mr. *Burton* indeed has handsomly excused the venerable author for this mistake in distance; he says, that *Bede* living a close monastick life in his cell, must write of places that he never saw, nor consequently could judge of. It was natural however, for him to describe the site of this idol temple from the nearest and most remarkable things to it, in the country, which certainly were *York* and the river *Derwent*. Besides, he adds, that the term *non longe ab* EBORACO, not far from *York*, may be allowed for this distance, when some other great historians have made use of the same expression, particularly *Herodian*, for a distance of a thousand miles (*x*).

But the present name of *Godmondham* is so little altered from what the venerable monk writes it, that there is no doubt to be made but it is the very same place he speaks of. Mr. *Burton* seems to lay a stress on the *quondam idolorum locus*, and says it may allude as well to *Roman* idols as *Saxon*. But this is too far strained, and we may justly enough conclude that this was a temple neither of *Roman* structure nor worship, but a place dedicated to the *Saxon* idolatry; such a one as is described in *Verstegan*, enclosed with a *hedge* instead of a *wall*.

Yet, because I would not differ from my learned predecessors in this kind of knowledge, and remove DELGOVITIA from *Weighton* and *Godmondham*, without just grounds; I took an exact survey of both the places. At the former, as I said, is nothing to be observed; but at the other on the east side of the village, is a pretty large spot of ground, so uneven and full of hills and holes, that it look'd exceedingly like a ruin, covered by time with earth and turf. I was shewn this place by my lord *Burlington*, the present lord of the mannor of *Godmondham*, who gave me leave to dig it where, and when I pleased. I took an opportunity and set some men at work on several parts of it; who dug pretty deep, but it turned out to be nothing but chalk-pits, or lime, which last has and may still be got here in great plenty; and very probably was here burnt when wood was more common in this country than it is now. The site of the *pagan temple*, in *Godmondham*, in all probability, was on the very same spot of ground the church now stands. The ground will well allow of it, being a fine sloping dry hill. It is notorious to all that our *christian* ancestors, both here and in other parts of the world, took care to abolish, and even erase paganism wherever they could. To that end when a heathen temple was demolished, a *christian* church was built in the very same place. History gives us many instances of this in our own island; but at *Rome* the case is still evident; where several of the very temples themselves which anciently served for the old *Roman* superstition, have been consecrated and converted into *christian-churches*, and are at this day used as such (*y*).

Since then *Godmondham* can have no share in a *Roman* station, I have the same opinion of *Weighton*, and we must look for our DELGOVITIA elsewhere. Our great antiquary seems here also to have spun his etymology too fine, by searching the *British* language for the derivation of this *Roman* name. But whatever can be strained out of *Delgovitia*, I am sure *Weighton* or *Wighton*, can furnish nothing for an antiquary to build a *Roman* station on. The word is entirely *Saxon*; and is plainly derived from Ƿeᵹ, or (*z*) Ƿæᵹ, *via*, *stratum*, a road or street; or from the verb Ƿeᵹan *ire*, *transire*, to travel or journey through; the termination ton is obvious to all. So the *Belgick* or *High-dutch*, **Wech**, **Wegh**, **Weghe**, are the same as our *way* and signify the very same thing. *Weghton* stands at the conjuncture of several great roads, which now meet at this town, and ran from thence over *Kexby-bridge* to *York*. But that the *Roman* military ways, both from PRAETORIVM and from LINDVM, took a different course to the city, I shall shew in the sequel. The old road

(*x*) See *Burton's* itinerary, p. 63.

(*y*) *Fabricius* gives us a list of near sixty heathen temples which are now coverted into churches. *Georgii Fabricii Roma antiqua & moderna; in cap. de templis gentilium in templa diverum mutatis.*

(*z*) See *Somner's Saxon* and *Skinner's* etymo. dict.

being

being turned this way, a new town ſprung up, which took its name from the occaſion of altering it.

Beſides the *Saxon* termination tun is one of the commoneſt they had; and ſometimes was made the local name of a family, as *Edwardſton*, *Alfredſton*, *Johnſton*, &c. Thus *Verſtegan* rhimes it,

In Ford, in Ham, in Ley, and Tun,
The moſt of engliſh ſirnames run.

But if we are to look out for a *Roman* ſtation, in any part of our iſland, we ſhall always find that the name or termination, of *Burgh* or *Cheſter*, will lead us the ſooneſt to it. Where then can we fix DELGOVITIA better than at *Londeſburgh*, in the neigbourhood of *Weighton*; and will anſwer as well to the calculated miles in the itinerary? For, allowing that the *Roman* road from *York*, this way, came by *Standford-bridge*, which I hope to prove in the ſequel, twenty *Italian* miles (*a*) will be near the exact diſtance betwixt the city and *Londeſburgh*.

But to take from the reader any notion that he may conceive that this difference in me, from our former great antiquaries in this matter, proceeds from an affectation, of ſaying ſomething new on the ſubject; or a deſire of paying a ſtrained compliment to the noble lord, my patron, whoſe *Yorkſhire* ſeat *Londeſburgh* is; I ſhall beg leave to give the ſubſtance of two letters, which I received in anſwer to ſome queries, from Mr. *Knowlton* the noble lord's chief gardiner at that place; a ſenſible, intelligent and a moſt creditable perſon. It is remarked that the road from *Brough* to *Londeſburgh* park pail, is in a continued ſtreight line; that it was formerly, and is ſtill by ſome elderly people called Humber-ſtreet; that the *ſtratum* of the road may be traced, under hedges, &c. croſs one of the canals in the park, which being lately made, occaſioned the accident of finding of it. It is compoſed of materials very ſcarce in that country, and lies buried under a fine ſoil about fifteen inches; and it was with great difficulty that the workmen could dig through the *agger*. The curioſity of finding ſuch a road in ſuch an uncommon place, led my correſpondent to trace it on both ſides of the canals up the hills; and he can now, he ſays, ſhew it at any time, with ſpades, one way pointing directly to the aforeſaid Humber-ſtreet; the other up the park again, through that part called the *Lawn*, butting up againſt hedges, trees, &c. clear to the *Wolds*; where it pointed either to *Wartyr*, or *Nunburham*, but which he had not then leiſure to trace. The *Malton* and *York* roads lying that way.

There can be no clearer proof than this, that the *Roman* military way, on the eaſt ſide of the *Humber*, from *Brough*, took this rout for *York*; and that *Londeſburg* was the ſtation on it we are ſeeking after, is, I think, as certain. The name is plainly derived from a Burgh, or fortreſs, on land; to diſtinguiſh it from *Brough*, or Burgh, on the water (*b*). The *Saxon* Lond is well known, whence Englonde, &c. and that there is no found of the *Roman* name, in this word, is not ſignificant; becauſe the *Saxons* retained few or none of their appellations, and the title Burgh, as I have elſewhere taken notice of, is ſufficient to teſtify that it was a place of note before their time. But to give yet a ſtronger evidence in this caſe, there have been found at *Londeſburgh* ſeveral *Roman* coins, of the middle and leſſer braſs. A great many repoſitories for their dead have been diſcovered in digging in and about the town, park, gardens, and even under the hall. The bones were found to lie in pure clean chalk, ſeven eight or more bodies together, ſide by ſide, very freſh and entire, though in ſome places not above twenty or twenty two inches deep from the ſurface. The cuſtom of burying their dead in chalk or rock, where ſtone coffins were not to be had, is very obvious. Laſtly if the *Roman* DELGOVITIA is to be defined from the *Britiſh*, then Delw. *idolorum*, and Koeth *Silva*, as our preſent *Britons* interpret it, a *wood of idols*, will agree with *Londeſburgh*, as well as any other place thereabouts; no ſoil being more productive of wood in all that country.

Londeſburgh was one of the ſeats of the truly ancient family of *Clifford* for ſeveral ages. Sir *Francis Clifford* of *Londeſburgh* was high ſheriff of this county *anno* 1600; as divers of his anceſtors had been before him. This gentleman ſucceeded his brother *George* in the honours and earldom of *Cumberland*. He was father to *Henry* the fifth and laſt earl of that family, whoſe ſole daughter was married to the earl of *Cork*, from whom is deſcended *Richard*, now earl of *Burlington*, &c. baron *Clifford* of *Londeſburgh*.

DERVENTIO. *Standford-burgh.*

From *Delgovitia*, the next ſtation in the road to *York*, mentioned in the itinerary, is DERVENTIO; which is put down as ſeven miles diſtant from the city. There is no ſtation in the whole which had perplexed our antiquaries, before *Camden*, more than this. *Talbot* and *Humphry Lhuyd*, with their followers, notwithſtanding the irreconcilable diſtance, had fixed it at *Derby*. *William Harriſon*, in both his editions of the itinerary, with

EBORACVM.
DERVENTIONE. M. P. VII.
DELGOVITIA. M. P. XIII. (*a*)
Nota In Blandiniano *exemplari & libris* Longolianis Delgovitia M. P. XIII. *& in* Neopolitano M. P. XII. *Itin.* Weſſelingii.

(*b*) In all ancient writings it is thus ſpelt; even in *Doomſday book* mention is made of ſome lands belonging to *Thomas*, then archbiſhop of *York*, lying in Godmandham and Londenesburgh.

ſome

something more of judgment, had placed it at *Tadcaster*. And even Mr. *Camden* owns he might have sought for it long enough, was he not pointed to look for it at *Aldby*, on the *Derwent*; by that polite and accurate scholar, as he is pleased to call him, Mr. *Robert Marshall* of *Tadcaster*.

But notwithstanding the name of *Aldby*, which signifies, says our antiquary, *habitatio antiqua*, an old habitation; the distance from *York*, and the *vestiges* of an *ancient castle* next the river, all concur to strengthen his opinion, yet I must beg leave, with Mr. *Horsley* to dissent from it. I have hinted before that the *Romans* built no bridges over rivers, but took special care to guard the fords. Now, there is no place on the *Derwent* fordable, that I know of, from *Malton* down to the river *Ouse*, but at a village, vulgarly called *Standford bridge*. The *Saxon* chronicle mentions this place under the name of Stængforden-brycge; but *Higden* in his *Polychronicon*, more properly calls it **Stain-forth-burgg**; which is easily interpreted a stony ford, or passage, over a river at a town. To put ford and bridge together is downright nonsence; *Ferry-bridge* is ill enough, but not so bad as the former.

It is possible it might get this alteration in the name, from *Pons belli* or *Battle-bridge*, which the *Normans* called it soon after the *conquest*; from a famous and decisive battle that was fought here, betwixt *Harold* the *English*, and *Harold Harfager* the *Norwegian* king. A particular account of which I shall give in the sequel. The passage over the river here is rocky, and was easily fordable in low water, especially before the miln was built above it. The village lies on both sides the river, and is large enough to admit of a station; of which the east bank is not without some vestiges.

From *Londesburgh* to this ford, the *Roman* road must have passed to *Pocklington*; which town is not unobserved by antiquaries, as I have already shewn. From whence the line directs you on the north side of *Barnby-moor* towards *Stainfordburgh*. Mr. *Horsley* thought he observed a ridge on *Barnaby-moor* pointing this way; but this road having been now long disused, the ground moorish, enclosed and plowed, it is impossible to trace it. On the upper part of this moor, next *Barnby-town*, Dr. *Lister* perceived the marks of a *Roman* pottery, near which were scattered pieces of *urns*, *slag* and *cinders* (c). It was here placed no doubt, for the convenience of the fine sand to mix with the clay, and which the ground here discovers in great abundance. It is to be observed that the present road to *York* goes through this bed of sand, cinders, &c. but the *Roman* way lies, as I suppose, a little on the right hand of it.

DERVENTIO then must be now our *Standford-bridge*, or *Burgh*; at which place a detachment of the *Roman* army was constantly kept as a guard to the city on that side, all the while the *Romans* were in possession of it. We have notice of this from the time the itinerary was made to the declension of the empire in *Britain*. For in the *notitia*, or survey made of the western empire, about that time, it is put down,

Sub dispositione viri spectabilis ducis Britanniarum
Praefectus numeri Derventionensis. DERVENTIONE.

The name *Derventio* seems to be taken from the river on which this station was placed; a thing not strange, says Mr. *Burton*, to either *Greeks* or *Romans*; and may be frequently taken notice of in old chorographical descriptions. One of our ablest antiquaries (d) deduces the name of this river from the *British Deur-guent*, which says he signifies *white water*. And indeed, I have observed that it turns of a whey-colour upon any sudden rains. There is a more plausible definition of this word in *Leland*, that *Deir-went* is no more than *Deirorum flumen*, the river of the country of *Deira*; now our *East-riding* (e). But as this seeming easy etymology is *Saxon*, it must fall to the ground; and it is more probable that the district here spoken of took its name from the river; than the river from the country. Mr. *Baxter* (f) has a hint for us, which if allowed, will not only give the just etymology of this word, but does also point us to the station. The *Kentish Derventio*, which is called at this day **Darent**, has a town on it, says he, called **Dartford**, or a ford to *Derventio*. Suppose then the *British* name of this river to be *Deir*, *went* may signifie *trajectus*, a ford or passage over it, from whence it is easily *latinized* into DERVENTIO. It is worth observing here that the names of all, or most of, the *Roman* stations in *Britain*, cannot any ways be derived from the *Latin* or *Greek* tongues; they must therefore claim their etymology from the *British*.

If it be objected, there have been no discoveries of *Roman* coins altars, monuments, &c. found at *Stainford-burgh*, to denote it a *Roman* station; the same may be said of *Aldby*. Which name, though Mr. *Camden* says it bears an indelible mark of antiquity, yet the *Saxon* termination *by*, which he himself translates only *habitatio*, a house, or dwelling, cannot mean a town; as *burg* always does. But, not to strip this place wholly of the honour our great antiquary has done it, I really take it to have been a *Roman* palace, or man-

(c) *Ab. philos. trans.* v. 3.
(d) Humph. Lhuyd's *descript.* Britan.
(e) Lelandi *Coll. in vita S.* Johannis Bever.
(f) *Baxter's* glossary.

ſion; moſt probably built for the *praefect*, or commander in chief, of the detachment aforeſaid, to reſide in. The nearneſs to *Stanford-burgh*, being but a ſhort mile, will allow of this conjecture; and this might probably be the palace, which *Bede* writes, that the *Saxon* king *Edwin* reſided in, when he had like to have been aſſaſſinated; as the reader will find in the ſequel.

But to return to our ford; the road leads from it in a direct line for *York*, of which there are ſome veſtiges of the *agger*, here and there remaining; beſides a village called *Gate-Helmſley* or *Street-Helmſley*, which is full upon it. Mr. *Horſley* writes that it is evident and univerſally agreed that the military way muſt have gone out from *York* towards the eaſt or ſouth-eaſt; but it is ſtrange, adds he, that neither tradition, nor remains, nor other evidences, have hitherto been ſufficient to aſcertain the particular tract of it. That gentleman, in his general ſurvey of *Britain*, could not be ſo particular in his enquiries, as I have been, relating to this affair; and being led from *Barnby-moor* to *Kexby*, he quite loſt the ſcent of his military way, except in the point which I have mentioned, that he made on the moor aforeſaid. Beſides to conclude this matter and bring us home, I have found in ancient hiſtory that a ſtreet in the ſuburbs of this city, out of *Walm-gate-bar*, and through which the road muſt paſs to *York*, was anciently called **Watlingate**; which is a further evidence in our favour.

SINVS PORTVOSVS. *Burlington Bay.* We muſt now retire back again to the ſea coaſt; and we find that the next remarkable bay, in *Ptolemy*, is called GABRANTVICORVM εὐλίμενος κόλπος, *ſinus portuoſus*, *vel ſalutaris*; which muſt certainly be our *Burlington-bay*. A village upon it is now called *Sureby*, *quaſi Sure-bay*, and is an exact tranſlation of *Ptolemy*'s *Greek* appellation. That which is ſafe and free from danger, ſays *Camden*, was by the *Britons* and *Gauls*, called *Seur*; which is yet retained in the *Engliſh* tongue. Nor has it its name for nothing, being eſteemed the largeſt and ſafeſt bay on theſe coaſts. The name of GABRANTVICI, given to the people inhabiting about this bay, I ſhall not take upon me to etymologize; having, I doubt, trode too much already in thoſe obſcure and uncertain paths. Who will, may conſult Mr. *Camden* and *Baxter* upon it; if it came from *goats*, 'tis probable the people, more into the country, were called PARISI, *ſhepherds*, and theſe *goat-herds*; which is all I ſhall ſay about it *(g)*.

From this famous bay the *Roman* ridge is ſtill very apparent, for many miles, over the wolds, directing in a ſtreight line for *York*. The country people call it the **Dykes** *(h)*; it is now ſcarce any high road at all to near *Sledmere*. At this laſt mentioned village the ridge wholly diſappears; for which reaſon Mr. *Warburton* in his ſurvey of this county has drawn it on to *Frydaythorpe* as the neareſt way to *York*. I do not deny but that there might run an occaſional road this way to *Stainford-burgh*, as the neareſt cut to the city; though no traces of it at all appear at this day. But there was another remarkable ſtation in this diſtrict, which though not mentioned in *Antonine*'s itinerary, yet it is plain enough pointed out to us in *Ptolemy*'s geography. This is CAMVLODVNVM, which by the name, ſituation, and tract of the road to it, can be no where ſo well placed as at *Malton*. It would

CAMVLODVNVM. *Malton.* be very erroneous to ſuppoſe that the CAMBODVNVM, in the itinerary, and this were the ſame; the rout in the *iter* fixes that in a different part of the county. But *Ptolemy* from *York*, is plainly drawing up to deſcribe the ſea coaſts, and *well-havened bays*; and therefore mentions this ſtation as in the road to it. From *Sledmere* then our road points to *Malton*; and, though not by far ſo viſible as before, yet the *ſtratum* is eaſily traced on the wolds, by *Wharram en le ſtreet*, as it is called, to *Setterington-brow*; from whence it run, no doubt, to *Malton*. The affinity in the name is another ſtrong proof of this aſſertion; *Malton* is the very ſame as *Maldune*, ton and *dune* are ſynonymous; nor can it admit of any other interpretation. It being ridiculous to derive it from *Malton*, a *town of Malt*, when there is ſuch evident reaſon to deduce it from the *Roman* appellation.

Cambodvnvm and Camvlodvnvm are two different ſtations, though the affinity of their names have cretaed ſeveral miſtakes about them. In ſome copies of the itinerary the laſt named ſtation is put down at ſeventeen miles from *York*; an agreeable diſtance for *Malton*. But then it has been miſtaken for the former; which lies in the ſecond *iter* in the road to *Mancheſter*; and in all probability was the name of the grand camp now to be ſeen on the hill near *Almonbury*. Camvlodvnvm by its adjunct LEG. VI. VIC. is rightly ſuppoſed by Dr. *Gale*, to be a ſummer ſtation for that legion; but *Malton* bids much fairer for that honour than the other, on ſeveral accounts. For no perſon, that was not obliged to it, would either winter or ſummer on the other.

But to make this ſtation ſtill more conſiderable we muſt retire back to the ſea coaſts and take notice of two more bays convenient for landing in them. Theſe are *Filey-bay* and *Scarburgh*; which though not put down in *Ptolemy*'s general tables of the whole *Roman* empire, could not have been omitted in a particular geographical account of *Britain*. The art of ſailing was in their time at a very low ebb, and it is not to be ſuppoſed that when

(g) Mr. *Baxter* has alſo defined *Burlington* in this manner; Burlinton, *nonnullis vitioſe* Brelington, *ibridâ dicatur compoſitione pro* Bückar-lin, *quod* Caper *eſt* ad marinum [illegible] *Quid aſſertius?*

(h) D[illegible]e, [illegible] *dic.* Danice, *diige*, *dige*. Belg. [illegible], Agger, [illegible], vallum, *&c. vide dict. etym.* Skinner.

the

the *Romans* set sail, or rather rowed from the *Belgick* or *Gaulick* coast for *Britain*, that they could be sure of their landing place on the other side. These two considerable bays then must have been occasionally made use of by them; and though no military road does, seemingly, lead from them to *Malton*; yet we are not without some light testimonies to prove it. From *Filey* to *Flotmanby*, the seat of my late worthy friend *Robert Buck* Esq; from whom I had this information, the road is vulgarly called the *street*; and in his grounds, on this road, is the vestige of a fortress, most probably *Roman*, now called **Castle-hill**. From hence the *street* runs to *Spittal*, where it meets the *Scarburgh* road. Whoever surveys the way from *Scarburgh* by *Seamour*, to this last named place, with an antiquary's eye, will find several traces of *Roman* work on it. Particularly I aver it is very visible on both sides the bridge betwixt *Seamour* and *Spittal*, which is over a rivulet that runs from the vast carrs in this place. The quantity of large *blew pebble*, the nature of that stone, which I shall have occasion to speak of hereafter, and the particular manner of jointing, sufficiently indicate it to be *Roman*; and was there no other testimony in the whole road but this, I should vote in its favour. The road is evidently forced through these carrs, which were otherways unpassable, and seems to have required *Roman* industry and labour to perfect it. Besides, this is the direct way from *Burlington-bay* to *Whitby*, two noted *Roman* ports; and I must believe that there was a communication by land betwixt them. The *Comites litoris* SAXONICI or guardians of these sea coasts against the invasions of the *Saxons*, as mentioned in the NOTITIA, could not have defended them without such a juncture. And I make no doubt, but some more visible testimonies of it remain on this road, though I never had leisure enough to search it.

What is more to my purpose is, to deduce our *Roman* way from the port of *Scarburgh* to *Spittal*; which last name comes from an **Hospital**, which our *christian saxon* ancestors usually built at the conjunction of several roads, for the relief and entertainment of poor distressed travellers. Here, I presume, it met the *Filey* road, and ran with it in a direct line for *Malton*. I own, there are no sort of remains now apparent to confirm this; and except the name of the street, with my own conjecture, I have no further reasons to urge about it. The *Roman* vicinary, or occasional roads, were not raised with that care and pains as their grand military ways; for which reason we are not to expect to meet with them at this day.

S

The next considerable port, on the *British* coasts, is the DVNVM SINVS of *Ptolemy*, which our antiquaries have fixed at *Whitby*. In *Bede* this place is called **Streneshall**, from the *Saxon* Streoneshealk, whose several etymologies I shall not trouble my self with (*i*). Mr. *Horsley* has here made an egregious mistake, by placing DVNVM at the mouth of the river *Teise*, and has taken no notice at all of this remarkable sea port. **Dunsley**, now a village on this bay, bears yet some testimony of the antient name; but, what makes it more considerable, is a *Roman* road which runs from it, for many miles over these vast moors and morasses towards *York*. This extraordinary road, not now made use of, is called, by the country people, **Wade's Causey**; and they tell a ridiculous traditional story of *Wade's wife and her cow* (*k*), as the reason of the making of it. It is worth observing, however, that this name suits well with Mr. *Camden*'s *Saxon* duke *Wada*; who, he says, lived at a castle on these coasts, and probably in the abandoned *Roman* fortress or station. It is believed, adds he, that this *Saxon* prince was a gyant; and they shew you his tomb, which are two stones about seven foot high a-piece, and set up at twelve foot distance, called now **Wade's grave**. It is odd, Mr. *Camden* got no intelligence of the *causway*, as well as the grave, when he was upon the spot. But these stones, I take it, are *Roman tumuli* of the nature of those at *Burrough-bridge*.

S DVNVM SINUS. *Whitby-port.*

I had my first intelligence of this road, and a camp upon it, from *Thomas Robinson* of *Pickering*, Esq; a gentleman well versed in this kind of learning. My curiosity led me to see it; and coming to the top of a steep hill, the vestiges of the camp were easily discernable. At the foot of the hill began the road or causway, very plain; and I had not gone a hundred paces on it, but I met with a *mile-stone* of the *grit kind*, a sort not known in this country. It was placed in the midst of the causway, but so miserably worn, either by sheep or cattle rubbing against it, or the weather, that I missed of the inscription, which, I own, I ran with great eagerness to find. The causway is just twelve foot broad, paved with a flint pebble, some of them very large, and in many places it is as firm as it was the first day. A thing the more strange, in that not only the distance of time may be considered, but the total neglect of repairs, and the boggy rotten moors it goes over. In some places the *agger* is above three foot raised from the surface. The country people curse it often, for being almost wholly hid in the ling, it frequently overturns their carts laden with turf, as they happen to drive cross it.

(*i*) See *Camden*, *Gibson*, *Baxter*, &c.

(*k*) The story is, that *Wade* had a cow, which his wife was obliged to milk at a great distance, on these moors; for her better convenience he made this causway, and she helped him by bringing great quantities of stones in her apron; but the strings breaking once with the weight, as well they might, a huge heap (about twenty cart load) is shewn that dropped from her. The rib of this monstrous cow is still kept in *Moult-grave castle*.

It

It was great pleasure to me to trace this wonderful road, especially when I soon found out, that it pointed to the bay aforesaid. I lost it sometimes by the interposition of valleys, rivulets, or the exceeding great quantity of ling growing on these moors. I had then nothing to do but to observe the line, and riding crossways, my horse's feet, through the ling, informed me when I was upon it. In short, I traced it several miles, and could have been pleased to have gone on with it to the sea-side, but my time would not allow me. However, I prevailed upon Mr. *Robinson* to send his servant and a very intelligent person of *Pickering* along with him, and they not only made it fairly out to *Dunsley*, but brought me a sketch of the country it went through with them. From which I have pricked it out in the map, as the reader will find at the end of this account.

We now return back to our camp, which is an extraordinary situation indeed; and was, no doubt, placed here as a guard to this important road, which led clear through it. The form of it I have given in the annexed draught; and though not so regular as several that I have seen, the shape of the hill not admitting of it, was certainly a *Roman* fortification. The half moons, which form some of the entrances into it, are exactly like those of some *Roman* camps in Mr. *Horsley*'s *Britannia (l)*. And here are a number of *tumuli* of several sizes about it. It is not possible to suppose, by the extream bleakness of the situation, that this camp could be garrisoned all the year. Nor, indeed, was there reason to fear any invasion in the winter. The soldiers had barracks built in it for their lodgings; the vestiges of which do appear in many places. The ditches of this camp are on some sides now above three yards deep perpendicular. *Cropton-Castle*, so called, a large circular mount, seemingly artificial, and within a quarter of a mile of this camp, deserves also an antiquary's notice.

From the camp the road disappears towards *York*, the *agger* being either sunk or removed by the country people for their buildings. But taking the line, as exactly as I could, for the city, I went down the hill to *Thornton-Risebrow*, and had some information from a clergyman, of a kind of a camp at a village called vulgarly **Barf**; but corruptly, no doubt, from **Burgh**. Going to view this place, I was agreeably surprised to fall upon my long lost road again; and here plainly appeared also a small intrenchment on it; from whence, as I have elsewhere hinted, the *Saxon* name *Burgh* might come. The road is discernable enough, in places, to *Newsam-bridge* over the river *Rye*; not far from which is a *mile-stone* of *grit* yet standing. On the other side of the river the *Stratum*, or part of it, appears very plain, being composed of large blue pebble, some of a tun weight; and directs us to a village called *Aimanderby*. *Barton on the street*, and *Appleton on the street*, lye a little on the side of the road; these villages were so called, no doubt, to distinguish them from some others of the same name in the county. I was once of opinion, that the road went from hence, as the line to *York* directed, somewhere through lord *Carlisle*'s park, and might enter the *Malton* road to *York* at *Spittalbeck*. But, considering the nearness of CAMVLODVNVM, I am persuaded it could not have missed this station; and therefore I have directed the road to *Malton*, where I take that station to have been. I could find no footsteps of it from *Aimerby* town-end, in the line to *York*, though I searched diligently for it; and consequently the road must run to *Malton*, which is very little out of the way.

V

This is another particular proof that the *Roman* CAMOLODVM was our *Malton*, which stood at the conjunction of three or four roads from the eastern sea-ports; and having the river *Derwent*, here fordable, for its defence, served as another key to the city on this side. I know there is some dispute, whether *new* or *old Malton* has the greater claim to this honour. They are both upon the river, a short mile from one another. The epithet *old* gives it for the latter; but then it stands more out of the line, and has no shew of antiquity about it; except the ruins of a dissolved monastery, now converted into a parish-church. The other town has the remains of an antient fortification, which stands like a bulwark against the river; *antiqua arce insigne*, says *Baxter*, who imagines it, from *Ptolemy*, to have been a camp or fortress belonging to the sixth legion then stationed at *York*. The convenience of the site, and the strength of the old foundation, tempted, no doubt, our more modern ancestors to build a castle upon it, which formerly was in the possession, says *Camden*, of the noble family of *Vescy* in this county. It came afterwards to be the chief seat of the lords *Eure* or *Evers*; and is at present possess'd by, and gives title to, *Thomas* earl of *Malton*; to whose generous encouragement the author of this work owes great obligation.

From *Malton*, I take it, the *Roman* road led to *York* the same way it does now; and though, in such a *via trita*, there are few footsteps of it remaining, yet to a curious and observant person some of them are obvious enough. Especially to those who are as well acquainted with the *Roman* pavement on the moors, the nature of the stone they used in it, and the setting or jointing of them, as my self. I can point out several pieces of it pretty entire; and in some places the exact breadth of the *stratum* may be measured; which corresponds, to an inch, with the pavement I have mentioned. This road run up to the city almost due west; and entered it, very probably, where it does now, at, or about, *Monk-*

(l) See p. 44. *Britannia Rom.*

A Roman Camp on the moors near Pickering.

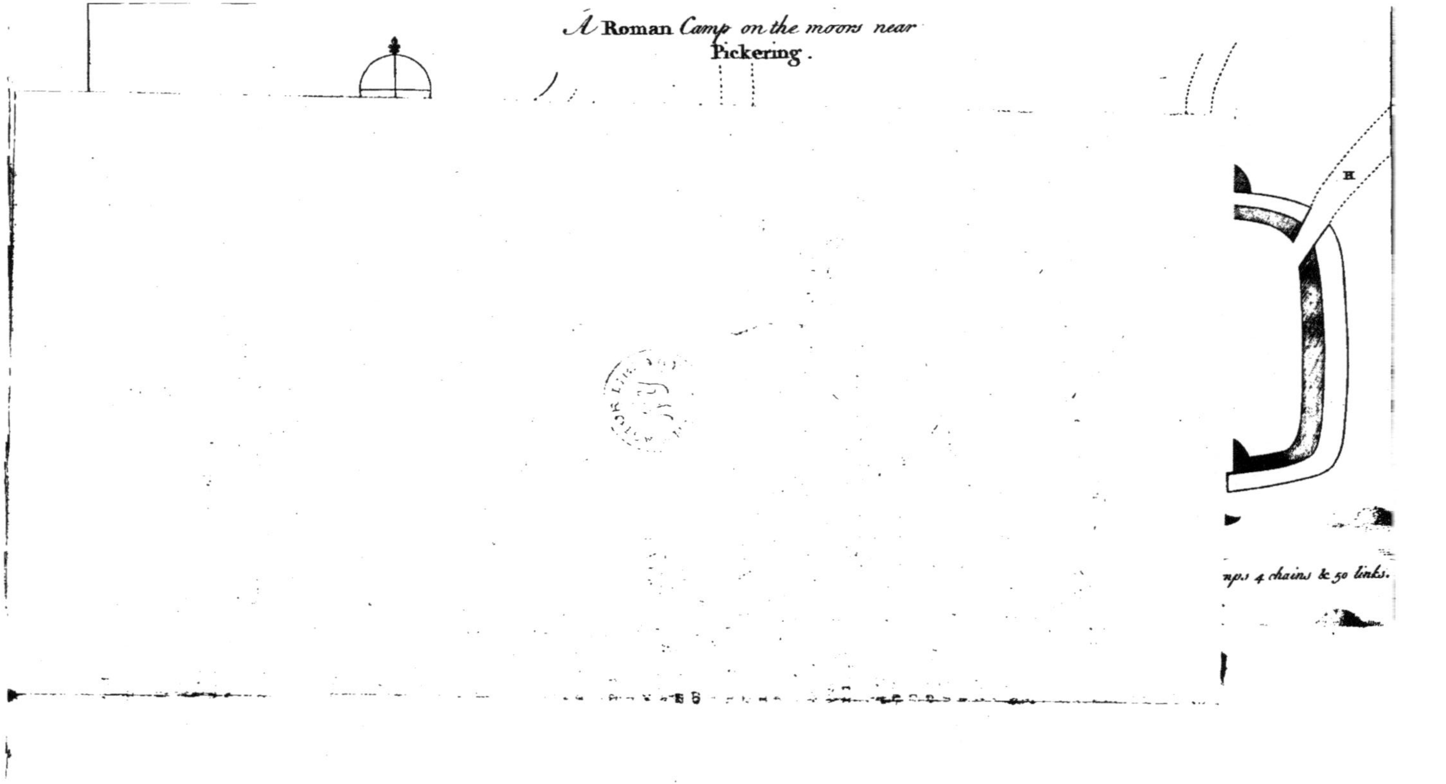

[illegible] *xtum* may be meafured;
ponds, to an inch, with the pavement I have mentioned. This road run up
moft due weft; and entered it, very probably, where it does now, at, or

(*l*) See p. 44. *Britannia Rom.*

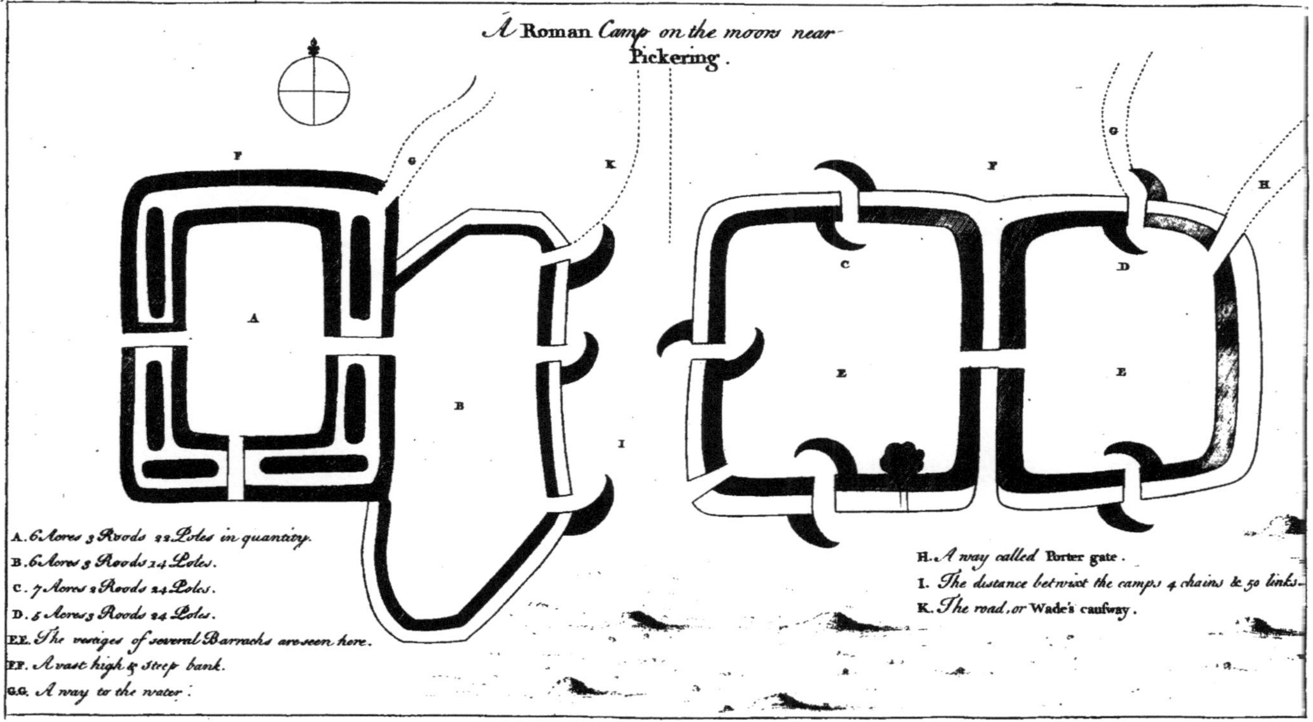

Thomas Strangewayes Robinson of Pickering Esqr. as an encouragement to the author of this work contributes this plate. 1736.

bar. In dean *Gale*'s time, a firm ftone caufway was difcovered at eight foot deep, between (m) *Monk-gate* and the bridge, on the north fide the prefent ftreet, which poffibly might be part of the termination of our road. The frequent deftructions of our city having laid thefe, as well as other matters, deep in the ruins or rubbifh of it.

Having now almoft run round the city, and tired my reader as well as my felf, I fhould purfue the courfe of my annals, did not another road prefent it felf, which, whether *Roman* or not, I fhall leave to better judgment. There is a remarkable eftuary, or bay, not taken notice of in *Ptolemy*, more northward than the laft, which is the mouth of the river *Teife* or *Tees*. This bay, or what you will call it, muft have been occafionally made ufe of, as well as fome others, on this coaft; and therefore we might prefume to meet with a road from it to the city. *Cleveland* is a very bad place to expect now to find it in; nor do I remember to have taken notice of any fhew of it over *Hambleton-hills*, which are in the line to *York* from the bay. But I obferved fomewhat very like a *Roman ftratum* in the lane betwixt *Coxwold* and *Newburgh*; which laft-named place might have been an entrenchment on it. *Newburgh*, called *Novus Burgus* by *Leland*, plainly indicates, that it fprung from the ruins of fome old **Burgh**, or town, in this place. Up the hill, by lord *Falconberg*'s park-wall, a good deal of it is obvious; particularly, oppofite to the extream corner of this wall, is a piece of it, ten yards out of the prefent road, and almoft under the hedge, very frefh and apparent. I muft obferve, that this pavement is of the fame kind of pebble and manner of laying, as thofe I have already defcribed; and that it is here fet upon a dry fandy hill, a place none but the *Romans* would have laid a ftreet over. For good and bad with them were paved alike. I traced the veftiges, or the ftones of it, farther in the lane as far as *Creyke*; which place, though I can deduce nothing from its name, feems to bid fair for a *Roman* fortrefs upon this road. *Creyke*, *Crek*, or Cpeac, was a royal *villa*, or palace, in the time of the *Saxons*, and was given as early as the year 685, by *Egfrid* the *Northumbrian* king, with three miles of land in circumference, to St. *Cuthbert*, then bifhop of *Lindisfarn* or *Holy-ifland*. And there is this reafon affigned for it, *that* Cuthbert *going or returning to and from* York, *might have a houfe there to reft himfelf at* (n). If we would go the readieft way to *Holy-ifland*, from *York*, it is certain this is the road; and taking fhipping at the *Teefe* mouth, the journey by land is very much fhortened. From whence we may conjecture, that this *Roman* road, as I take it to be, was then good, and made ufe of in St. *Cuthbert*'s time to that purpofe. Befides, the *Romans* had a further convenience in this road, which was a much nearer cut for them from *York* to the wall or frontiers; and by croffing the *Teefe-mouth* only, they faved many miles in the march, from the grand military way by *Aldburgh*, and fo on.

Creyke-caftle, now a ruin, is fituated upon a hill the fitteft for a *caftrum exploratorum* of any in the large vale of *York*; for it has a great command of the country quite round. But though I met with fome probable traces of a *Roman* road up to this place, yet I was not able to difcover the leaft remains of it from hence to *York*. The vaft and fpatious foreft of **Galtres**, began almoft at the foot of this hill, the ground of which being loofe and watery, has long fince fwallowed up the *agger* of this road. But, as the way from *Creyke* to *York* is now in a ftreight line, we may conjecture the old road did follow the fame tract, and enter the city near or at its prefent gate, or bar on this fide.

I have now finifhed my furvey of the *Roman* roads leading to our antient EBORACVM; I hope I fhall not be thought to deviate from my fubject in treating of them and our neighbouring ftations. The importance of any city or town, is beft judged by the number of roads leading to and from it; and if, at the diftance of fo many ages, we can find fuch evident traces of them at this day, it muft not only be matter of wonder and furprife, but greatly help to aggrandize my fubject. The *Romans*, I may fay, were the firft that opened this country, by making high-roads over places before unpaffible; but then they planted fufficient guards upon them, at proper diftances, that thefe conveniences they made only for their own ufe, fhould not ferve either the native *Britons*, or any foreign invader, to diflodge them. That the reader may at one view have a juft idea of all thefe roads, I have fubjoined a map of the large and fpatious vale of *York*, with the ports and bays on the eaftern fea-coafts. In this the *Roman* high-ways, up to the city, are delineated; it is to be obferved that the lines are drawn where the *agger* or *ftratum* is now vifible, and the dots or pricks where we may well fuppofe the roads directed, though the *agger* which compofed them be now quite funk or removed.

Befides thefe land-roads which lead to EBORACVM from fo many different ftations and fea-ports, by means of the river it ftood upon, the communication, by water, was open to the *German* ocean; and confequently veffels might arrive there from any port in the empire; nor was there a fhip then in ufe, but might be moored under the very walls of the city. I confefs, I was always at a lofs to confider and make out which way that vaft armament they kept garrifoned on the wall, the other northern ftations, and in the city it felf, were

(m) E MS *Gale*.

(n) *Rex* Ecfrid *villam fuam de* Crek, *et tria in circuitu milliaria; dedit* S. Cuthberto, *ut haberet* Ebor. *iens vel inde rediens manfionem, ubi requiefcere poffet.* Lel. *Coll.* 2. 369.

supplied with corn as well as other provisions, unless it was imported to them from abroad. But I find they had a more noble contrivance, more suitable to the genius and industry of the *Roman* people; and by it they made the southern and more cultivated parts of the island supply the northern with ease and convenience. I was agreeably let into this discovery by a letter I received since this work was put to the press, from the reverend Dr. *Stukeley*, the ingenious author of the *Itinerarium Curiosum, &c.* I shall give it the reader at length, and am glad it came time enough to be inserted in a proper place of the work, since I am sure it will prove a very great ornament to my subject.

SIR,

"SEeing you engaged in the antiquities of *York*, I was willing to contribute somewhat toward your laudable design; the more so, because it must be from this country that we deduce the origin of that famous city; which considerable particularity might, by reason of distance, very easily escape your observation. The proposition will seem unintelligible till I have explained my self. If we enquire why the *Romans* built the city of *York*, and why in the very place? it must be answered, by considering that famous work of theirs in *Lincolnshire*, which we call the **Car-dike**.

"Such was the admirable genius of that great people, raised up by divine providence to civilize mankind for the introduction of the gospel: Such their dexterity in arts of peace and government, that they were only equalled therein by their own military discipline. It is well said in *Sulpiciæ satyra*,

——duo sunt quibus extulit ingens
Roma *caput, virtus belli & sapientia pacis* (o).

"I have often admired this great instance, the **Car-dike**, though it is little taken notice of. Since the account of it in my *Itinerarium*, pag. 7. I have had frequent opportunities of observing it, and it would be (I doubt not) of singular use to an *engineer*, to trace its whole length from *Peterborough* to *Lincoln*, and to observe their method of carrying on the level; of combating, as usual to them, with earth and water, passing plains and rivers, avoiding elevations, guarding against land-floods and the like. My purpose at present shall only be to give you a general account of that noble work, and of the great commodities resulting therefrom, which will sufficiently evince its relationship to your city of *York*.

"The *Romans* were infinitely delighted with the fertility and temperature of this island, as is evident from the very great number of cities and roads with which they have adorned it, like a choice garden plot. Their great care was to fence the beautiful part of it against the horrors of the north. This was the work, from time to time, of several emperors, by walls, trenches, *castella*, and a continual guard of soldiers upon those frontiers. With this view it was, that the city of *York* was built and made the residence of the emperors, as it is the highest part up the river *Ouse*, to which the navigation extends, and by means of our **Car-dike** was furnished with corn from the more southern parts of the island. The *Romans* permitted nothing to chance which they could possibly avoid; the carriage by sea was dangerous and uncertain, so they contrived this admirable method of an inland navigation, more safe, certain and expeditious; it was made at least so early as *Antoninus*'s time, perhaps in *Nero*'s.

"The *Romans* began this notable projection upon the *Northamptonshire* river, the *Nyne*; an open country abounding with tillage. The cut commences just below *Peterborough-minster*. A fair silver coin of *Antoninus* was lately found upon the bank, and given to me. Reverse COS. III. DES. IIII. A military figure standing. It belongs to the year of the city 895. Many *Roman* coyns are found about the *minster*; and I doubt not, but the scite of it was a *Roman castrum* walled about, and many granaries built there, for conservation and guard of the corn, by our *Saxon* ancestors called the **burgh**, till from St. *Peter*'s monastery it took its present name, being a place of great trade in *Roman* times, there were many buildings by the river beside the *castrum*. Those ruins the *Saxons* called **Medeshamstede**, not knowing the *Roman* name, signifying the remains of houses on the meadow.

"Three miles higher up the river is *Castor*, another *castrum* of the *Romans* for a further guard in these parts; and over against it upon the river, *Chesterton*, where between the river and the *London* road, is the ancient city DVROBRIVIS, now plowed over. Thirtieth of *August* 1731, I conducted Mr. *Roger Gale* hither, and we surveyed it together; it is called *Castlefield*. The great *Hermenstreet* road goes through it: There was a bridge over the river; they took up the piers lately, when they made the river navigable. I believe this city originally was one of the forts built by

(o) To raise *Rome*'s mighty head went two great parts,
In *war* their *valour*, and in *peace* their *arts*.

A. Plau-

" *A. Plautius* in his first conquests here: Infinite numbers of coins found in this place: I " have a fair silver *Hadrian* reverse COS. III. This city was walled about, and had a " very broad ditch: Plenty of *Roman* fragments gathered off by the plowmen with which " they mend the highways: At *Allerton* hard by, so called corruptly from *Aldwalton* " and *Aldwarkton*, were formerly *Roman* buildings: So at *Stanground* and *Horsey bridge*: " Great care was taken for security of the river hereabouts, where the artificial chanel " began.

" To *Peterborough*, as a center, came all the corn of *Northamptonshire* by the river *Nyne*; " all the corn of *Huntingtonshire* by *Chateris*, and across *Whitlesea mere*; and of *Bedfordshire* " by the several rivers that run to *Huntington* by St. *Neots*: and of *Cambridgshire* intirely by " the old *Ouse*, across St. *Audreys* causey. *Grantchester* seems to have been a granary to " receive the corn of that country, and to send it down the river. *Cambridge* at that time " was a *Roman* town, upon the *Roman* road, passing from DUROSIPONTE, at *Godmanchester* by *Gogmagog-hills* into *Essex*: By the *Ouse* at *Thetford*, which is the SITOMAGUS of " the *Romans* upon the *Iknil-street* road, came in the corn from great part of *Suffolk* and " *Norfolk*: So that hither arrived the united product of six large counties fruitful in " corn.

" As the **Cardike** advances on the edge of the high grounds below *Peterborough*, it runs " through the town of *Peakirk*, between the church and St. *Pega's* chapel, then across the " rector's garden and so to *East Deeping*. Here the river *Welland* from *Stamford* brings in " the corn of *Rutland* and parts circumjacent. At *Cates-bridge* it meets the old *hermen-street* road: At *Wilsthorp*, hard by, many *Roman* coins are found. They call the *Roman* " road here **Kings-gate**: The **Cardike** runs between the church and the rectory house of " *Thurlby*; and so proceeds all the way upon the western edge of the fen. At *Nocton* the " seat of my learned friend and patron Sir *Richard Ellys* it bounds his park, by the ruins " of the priory. It enters the river *Witham* at *Washenburgh* below *Lincoln*, where, I suppose, was a great sluice into the river, as at its head at *Peterborough*. I observe here " at *Stamford* they call the beginning of an artificial cut from the river, the **Washes**.

" All the corn of *Linconshire* came in by this artificial channel and the river of *Witham*. " From *Lincoln* they continued the cut upon fenny low grounds into the river *Trent*: This " is called the **Foss-dike**: Here the *Roman* name of *fossa* is preserved. Bishop *Atwater* " began to cleanse this river, but died before compleated. *Hoveden* mentions the scouring " it by king *Henry* I. In the time of *Domesday-book*, the king's *monetarii* at *Nottingham* are " said, in the days of *Edward confessor*, to have the care of the river *Trent* and of the " **Foss-dike** and of the navigation therein; and of *the road to York*, and might amerce any " one for defaults: As it is recited by the great *Camden* in *Nottinghamshire*.

" By means of the *Trent*, they brought in the corn of all *Nottinghamshire*. I have a " discourse by me, which I wrote three years ago, wherein I show that *Newark* was a " *Roman* town: That it is in reality the famous *Sidnacester*, the ancient episcopal see of the " *Saxons*, so much sought after by antiquaries. I show that its *Roman* name was ELTABONA, that good part of the castle there, is the remains of a *Roman* granary made for " the reception of corn, for the very purpose we are upon. From the *Trent*, the navigation of the corn-boats was continued across the *Humber* into the river *Ouse*: There they " took the advantage of the tides, which carried them up to *York*.

" When I was there in the year 1725, I observed the *vestigia* of the *Roman* dock or " station of the boats, now overgrown with sedge and moor, where the river which has " the name of *Foss*, enters the *Ouse*: Thereabouts, no doubt, were the *Roman* granaries " to lay up the corn in, for the use of the armies: I leave the further enquiry to your curiosity and diligence: Hence appears the general grandeur of the design, the use of it " and the execution, the happy union of art and nature, whereby so vast a tract of land " in the more southern part of the province supplied the wants of the northern; where a " great body of soldiers must necessarily be kept up, in time of peace, to guard the walls " and *praetentures*; but more so in times of war, which was very frequently the case with " the *Picts* or old *Britons*: This well became the wisdom and magnanimity of the *Romans*, " and we enjoy the fruits of it to this day: for with their eagles the swifter glad tidings " of the gospel flew hither; with their bright arms that peaceful and more powerful light, " visited our northern regions and conquered farther than their swords.

" Here we see the origin of the city of *York*, honoured with the *imperial palace*: From " hence all the northern garrisons received their support; And those barren countries, by " a very easy conveyance partook of the plenty of the south: It seems to me that the *Romans* made forts upon this navigation at about five miles distance, all along, for the " security of it, against the GIRVII who inhabited the fens, and others: Thus from DUROBRIVIS to *Peterborough* is five *Roman* miles, from thence to *Waldram-hall* five miles: " To *Cate-bridge* upon the river *Glen* is five miles, near *Wilsthorp* where they find much " *Roman* coin: Five miles further was the *Roman* town at *Stanfield*: Then *Billing-borough*, " *Garwick*, *Walcote*, *Washenborough*, *Lincoln*, *Torksey*, which was a *Roman* city: Then upon " the *Trent* AGELOCUM, *Ganesborongh*, *Waltrith* which we may call TRAJECTUS AD " VALLUM, *Buringham*, *Flixborough*, *Alkborough* AQUAE: Upon the *Ouse* is ARMINEXA " *Armin*,

" *Armin*, *Hemmingborough*, *Acaster*, and the like, which may well amuse those that have " leisure and curiosity to enquire after them.

" The name of **Cardike** is *british*, Caeirs *palus*.

WILLIAM STUKELEY.

Stamford 21 *June* 1735.

This ingenious letter requires little comment; being explanatory enough in it self; and to enlarge upon it is the work of one that shall publish a new edition of *Camden*, the *Britannia Romana*, or the *Roman* history of the whole island. But yet I must not let it pass without some few additional remarks on this grand subject.

And first, I must beg leave to dissent from the reverend Dr. in the proposition he has laid down that the origine of our famous city must be deduced from this great cut in *Lincolnshire*. I am of opinion that the direct contrary is to be believed, and that the grand canal he writes of owes its original to EBORACVM. We must suppose that our city was built and fortified long before this cut was made; and that this prodigious undertaking, the work of an age, though carried on by *Roman* arts and industry, was not begun till the island from the *wall* southward was intirely subjected to them. This was by no means so till *Severus* his coming into *Britain*, as has been shewn; who having cooped in the *Picts* and *Scots* by the mighty ramparts he built against them, fell upon this noble expedient of furnishing the garrisons that were stationed on the wall with proper and never failing provisions. This great general would not leave the island until this grand design was at least set on foot; and it is highly probable his stay at *York*, till he died, was to see it carried on with vigour. The peaceable age the island enjoyed after this emperor's death was the properest time the *Romans* ever had to finish a work of this nature in. The builder of the wall must have been the projector of this other great scheme; the keeping and maintaining that vast armament upon it, by a safe and sure way, was a thought worthy of the head and conduct of the great *Severus*.

From the extraordinary care and pains the *Romans* bestowed in making the great cuts aforesaid, we must be assured that their receptacles at *York*, both on land and water, were proportionably large, to contain the prodigious quantity of corn, that was brought, and the vast number of boats necessary for the conveyance of it to the city. The river *Ouse* was by no means large enough, nor safe enough, for the purpose; by reason of the great landfloods which often come impetuously down it. They had recourse then to a more noble undertaking; which was to cut another river, and bring down as much water as they wanted from the country above them. This is what we call the *Foss*, whose very name still retains the memory of its original. Its source is no higher, up the country, than six or seven miles north of the city; and by making this cut many conveniences accrued. For it was not only a considerable drain to the great forest of *Galtres* on that side; which before must have been a perfect bog by its flatness; but it would also add to the fortification of the city; and, at the same time serve to fill up a large bason, or reservoir, necessary for the reception, and laying up in safety, of the number of boats employed in this navigation.

Whoever will take a survey of the *Foss* at *York*, or consider it in the print or plan of the city, which I have given in the sequel; will surely be of opinion that this *Foss* was no other than an artificial conveyance for their vessels to pass and repass to and from this part of the town. The great dam head which is thrown cross the *Foss*, at the *Castle milns*, seems by its present strength to have been the antient flood-gates, or stoppage to the water on that side. Through this sluice the vessels were let into the water, which did formerly not only surround the castle and tower, but made a very considerable bason besides. But the grand dock, or reservoir of water, lay still higher in the city; and extended probably over all that morass called now the *Foss island*; from *Foss-bridge* to *Layrthorp-bridge*. This island is far from being firm land at present; and no doubt is collected since the time of the *Romans*. For it was certainly navigable for fishing-boats down as low as the time of *Ed.* III. and was then called *stagnum regis de Foss*. This will appear by several grants and inquisitions, taken at that time relating to this fishery, which will be recited when I come to treat on this particular place in the sequel. The king's claim to this water and the fishery of it was then of a great extent, for it reached from the *Castle milns*, then also called the *king's milns*, up as high as the abbot of St. *Mary's milns*, which formerly stood on the *Foss* above *Earsley-bridge*, in the road to *Huntington*.

This prodigious collection of water, which now has no less than five bridges laid over different parts of it to come at the city by, was no doubt a great security to it on that side. But the main dock, I take it, was principally, where the island is at present. In this noble bason some hundreds of vessels, such as they then used, might lie in the utmost safety. From the east there came in, or rather was drawn into it, another stream, called also the *Foss*. And as the tides from the river *Ouse* had likewise a communication with it, there could be no fear of wanting water either winter or summer. Thus did *Roman* arts and ingenuity

ity abundantly make up what nature had denied to the situation of EBORACVM. For though the river *Ouse* was then navigable, and was so several ages after, for any ship then used at sea; yet the narrowness of the river would not allow room for such a number of vessels to lie together as must necessarily meet on this occasion. *Flaccus Albinus*, or *Alcuinus*, a native of *York*, an author of great authority, and ancient testimony, it being near one thousand years since he lived, writes thus of his city,

> *Hanc Romana manus muris & turribus altam*
> *Fundavit primo*———
> *Ut foret* EMPORIVM *terrae commune marisque*———
>
> To be the common *mart* of earth and sea.

And *William* of *Malmsbury* speaking of the magnificence of *York*, before it was destroyed by the conqueror, has these words, EBORACVM, *urbs ampla & metropolis est, elegantiae* Romanae *praeferens indicium; a duabus partibus* Husae *fluminis edificata.* Includit in medio sinu sui naves a *Germania*, & *Hibernia* venientes. Now though the river *Ouse* is here named, yet it is rather to shew the extent of the buildings of the city than that the Ships here mentioned lay in it. *Sinus* by our best dictionaries, is rendered a *large bay*, in respect to shipping, or a place of safety *(p)*; and to me this passage seems rather to point at the grand bason aforesaid, than any place above or below bridge, on the river *Ouse*.

Besides, we are well acquainted, both by tradition, history, and our own records, that very able merchants, who have been magistrates of this city, and at the same time mayors of the staple, of *Calais*, lived all along the side of the *Foss*, from *Castlegate* up to *Peaseholm-green*; and no doubt had their warehouses upon it. The *Merchants-hall* at *York*, a fine old spacious building, stands upon this navigation. The company of merchants is still called the *old Hans company*; which derives its name from being free of the *Hans*-towns, or the great trading towns in the east. This hall was their bourse or exchange; and was no doubt built where it is for their more frequent and convenient meeting in it. At the extremity of this grand bason, beyond *Layethorp-bridge*, is a place at this day called *Jewbury*, *quasi* **Jewburgh**; which certainly was the district allowed those mercantile people to live in, *extra muros*; and where they might also have the advantage of this navigation. Lastly, I have been told by living witnesses that in their time had been dug up *broken planks of boats*, *iron rings*, and *anchors* near *Layethorp-bridge*; which does most evidently shew that the navigation from the *Ouse* reached at least so high as to this part of the city.

It does not appear any where that I know of when this navigation was disused; it is probable they were choaked out of it by degrees. A work done by a *Roman* arm must require great strength to keep up and sustain it. And the bason in time filling up, would soon become firm land, if the stoppage at the water milns below was taken away. But what a noble piece of water must here anciently have been? A bason, or dock, of more than a mile in circumference. What a sight it was to see it filled with *Roman* Ships, galleys, boats for pleasure and use. And that very place which is now the disgrace of *York* by being in summer time little better than a *stinking morass*, was then one of the greatest ornaments old EBORACVM.

The place where the castle of *York* now stands, in all probability, was, in the time of the *Romans*, the grand magazine or repository, for the corn aforesaid. There being space enough within its *area*, for such a purpose. The *Foss* washing the walls, and anciently drawn round both *castle* and *tower*, added a great strength to its natural situation. It was an easy matter here for boats to unload, and then go up further into the dock to lie there till another occasion.

Just below the castle the *Foss* is called **Foss-dike**, and **Browney**, or **Brown ea-dike**; to its entrance into the *Ouse*. The former part of this last name seems to be compounded of an old *English* adjective, and a *Norman* substantive *(q)*. The A. S. Bpun, *fuscus*, brown and *eau*, water; a proper appellation for the liquid that runs through it; being chiefly drawn from moors and morasses above the city. **Dike** is here expressive enough; and having the same termination at *York* that the grand canal has in the counties through which the Dr. has traced it, most evidently proves both to be artificial conveyances. The *Saxon* Dic *(r)* is as plainly deduced from the verb to dig, as the *Latin fossa a fodiendo*. And, though in several places these words are alternately used, and sometimes put together, to denote a *Roman* cut, high road, dry ditch, or bank; yet, wet or dry, no place in *Britain* can claim either of these appellations from a natural cause.

(p) *Sinus pro securitate & praesidio est*, R. Steph. *thesaur. L. L.*

(q) By a second letter from the Dr I am informed that a town upon this cut, near *Bourn* in *Lincolnshire*, is called *Dikea D.ke-ea*, that is, dike water.

(r) Dic dice. *Vallum, fossa*, a **trench**, a **ditch**, a **dike**, a **mote**. *Limes ille de quo in* Chron. Saxon. *ad ann.* 905, *mentio facta fortasse*, **Foss-dike**, *agros* Catabrigiensem & Suffolciensem *qui disterminat.* Somner *dict.* Saxon.

M I shall

4

I shall take leave of this head, until I come to the particular chapter which treats of the ancient navigation of the river *Ouse*, with observing that the reverend Dr. omits that this water carriage extended as far up the river as *Aldburgh*, the old ISVRIVM upon the *Eure*; which is the very extremity of it. To this antient *Roman* station, corn and other provisions, were no doubt conveyed by water from their grand magazine at *York*. From whence by land carriages it was conducted up the *Hermen-street* to serve all the garrisons on the wall, and in the more northern stations from *Aldburgh*. The *castra*, or *castella*, for the guard of the river above *York*, were in all probability placed at the same distance the reverend Dr. mentions; and then they will fall out to have been built anciently at *Beningburgh*; *Aldwark-ferry* and *Aldburgh*. At about five miles distance, by water, from each other.

What the Dr. observes that *car* is derived from the *British Coeurs*, *palus*; he needed not to have gone so far for his etymology; *car*, and *cars* being as common words as any we have in the north to express low watry grounds; though it is somewhat strange that Dr. *Skinner has omitted it.*

And now to pursue the course of my annals. I must put the reader in mind that the emperor *Severus* being dead and his son returned to *Rome*, the *Roman* historians inform us of no wars or commotions, in *Britain*, for near the space of a century from that period. At length it happened that, under the reign of the emperor *Dioclesian*, there were six general officers rebelled; amongst whom *Carausius (s)* who was sent by the emperor, with a fleet, to guard the *Belgick* coasts, took an opportunity to slip over into *Britain*, and got himself proclaimed emperor at *York*. This *Carausius*, according to *Eutropius*, was originally a *Britan*, but of mean and obscure parentage. The *Scotch* historians mention him, though they differ from the *Latin* as to chronology, and say, that to secure himself in *Britain*, he entered into a fast league with the *Picts* and *Scots*; by whose assistance he overcame *Quintus Bassianus*, a *Roman* lieutenant, who was sent over by *Dioclesian* to dispossess and destroy him *(t)*.

After which, say they, *Carausius* got himself proclaimed king of *Britain* at *York*. They add that he retained two thousand *Picts* and *Scots* for his life-guard; and gave up all the lands from *Hadrian*'s wall to the city of *York*, to the kings of those countries, as their patrimony for ever; and as a reward to them for this service.

How far this testimony may be depended upon I shall not determine; but that *Carausius* called himself *Caesar*, and was resident in *Britain*, the many coins of his stamp, found no where but in this island do sufficiently testify. Our city, and especially *Aldburgh*, have turn'd out several; and at the last mentioned place the coins of this emperor are as frequent-
A. CCXCVII. ly found as of most others. In all probability he was slain by his friend *Allectus* at *York*, or in these parts; who immediately after took on him the same authority, as his coins do bear witness; which are equally common amongst us. *Allectus* bore sway here till *Constantius*, surnamed *Chlorus*, was made emperor, who coming over into *Britain* slew *Allectus* and reduced the province to its former obedience. This tyrant, we are told, was also of *Plebian* race; and had been originally a smith; for the soldier, who killed him, told him, for the greater ignominy sake, that *it was with a sword of his own making*.

Constantius had married a *British* lady called *Helena*; the daughter of *Gallius*, *Colius*, or *Coel* one of our island kings. Authors clash violently in opinion relating to the character of this lady; some allowing her to be no better than a common prostitute *(u)*; whilst others, especially those of the *Romish* persuasion, crie her up as a *saint*, and set her at the head of the *calendar*. Mr. *Bale* no favourer of saints, or superstition, has dressed our *Helen* up in the greatest ornaments, both of mind and body, that ever the best of her sex was possessed of *(x)*.

The marriage of *Constantius*, with the princess *Helena*, must have happened several years before his last mentioned expedition into *Britain*; for *Constantine*, the issue of it, was above thirty years old at his father's death. The *panegyrist (y)*, whom I shall have great occasion to quote in the sequel, in his oration to that emperor, tells him that he was begot in the *very flower and pride of his father's youth*; which time, upon casting backwards, will fall to be in the distractions of *Britain*, under the usurpations of the thirty tyrants; or, *anno christi*, 272. The learned cardinal *Baronius*, a foreigner, and who had no occasion to compliment *Britain* with the honour of being the birth place of *Constantine* the great, makes this expedition of *Constantius* into the province, to happen *anno christi* 274 *(z)*. It was then, he says, that *Constantius*, sirnamed *Chlorus*, only a *Patrician*, or senator of *Rome*, yet of imperial lineage and related to the late emperor *Claudius (a)*, was sent first into *Britain*; to the end that he might contain that nation, frequently accustomed to revolts, in their duty and allegiance to the emperor. Here is a contradiction amongst some of our chronologers of a year or two; but that does not much alter the case. *Aurelian* was then emperor,

(s) *Victor Diac.*
(t) *Hollingshead's Scotch* chron. *Hector Boetius. Buchanan.*
(u) *Milton*, &c.
(x) Baleus *de script.* Britan.
(y) Eumenius *inter panegyr. veteres.*
(z) Baronii *ann. ad an.* 306. *Sect.* 16.
(a) *Post duos familiae tuae tertius imperator.* Panegyr. *ad* Const. Nº IX.

and

and *Constantius*, a young and bold commander, was employed by him to reduce this province; which, as well as other parts of the empire, was at last effected. He was at that time made *propraetcr (c)*, and lived several years in the island; for being of a graceful personage *(d)*, says my authority, and of a bold and enterprising genius, he was the fittest to bear rule in so turbulent a province. That the emperor *Aurelian* did send aid into *Britain*, needs no other testimony than the *Mauri Aureliani*, stationed, in the *Notitia*, much further north than *York*; and who certainly derived their name from that emperor.

There is no part of *Roman* history, relating to their transactions in *Britain*, so dark as at this period; that is, towards the latter end of the third century. And it is no wonder, the empire was then torn and divided into many shares; civil dissensions continually disturbing of it; all which happened so much nearer home, that *Britain*, a remote province, was little taken notice of in the histories of those times. For this cause it is, that we cannot trace *Constantius* at EBORACUM, whilst he was only *propraetor* or lieutenant of *Britain*: but there is all the reason in the world to believe, that he made this place his chief residence, whilst he was deputy, since he certainly did so when he was principal.

Our chronologers make this last expedition of *Constantius* into *Britain*, to fall in the year three hundred and five; and two years after he is said to have died in this city *(e)*. A. CCCV. *Eusebius*, in his life of the son, is very particular in describing the last moments of the father. *Constantine*, who had been left as a pledge of his father's fidelity with his collegues *Dioclesian* and *Galerius* at *Rome*; having great reason to suspect they meant him no good, escaped from thence, and with wonderful celerity and cunning in his flight *(f)* came and presented himself to his father at *York*. The sight of his eldest and best beloved son, whom he had long wished for, but never hoped to see, so revived the dying emperor, that raising himself in bed, and embracing him closely, he gave thanks to the gods for this great unexpected favour; affirming, that now death was no terror to him, since he had seen his son, and could leave his yet unaccomplished actions to be performed by him. Then gently lying down, he disposed of his affairs to his own mind; and taking leave of his children of both sexes, who, says my authority, like a choir stood and encompassed him lying in the *imperial palace (g) and royal bed*; and having delivered over to the hands of the eldest, as natural reason required, the imperial dominion, he expired.

We have here another instance of an imperial palace at EBORACUM, which two of the greatest and most admired pagan emperors, the *Roman* state ever saw, lived and died in. A. CCCVII. JULII XXV. It is true *Eusebius* does not expresly mention, that *York* was the place where *Constantius* breathed his last; but other authorities, particularly St. *Jerome*, and *Eutropius*, a heathen writer of that age, confirm it. *Obiit in* BRITANNIA EBORACI *principatus autem tertio decimo (h) et inter divos relatus est.* He died at *York* in *Britain*, in the thirteenth year of his reign, and is inrolled amongst the gods.

If then *Constantius* died at *York*, there must his funeral obsequies be solemnized; and, as we have reason to believe, his ashes entombed; as also, the ceremony of the *apotheosis*, or deification, conferred upon him. *Eusebius* writes, that his son and successor, *Constantine* the great, was immediately, upon his father's death, saluted emperor, and was invested with the purple robe in his father's own palace *(i)*. After which the dead emperor's funeral rites were performed with the utmost magnificence; an infinite number of people assisting, who with dances, songs, and loud acclamations, congratulated his ascension to the gods *(k)*.

Rome, in the height of all her grandeur and magnificence, had not a more glorious show to exhibit than the *apotheosis*, or deification, of their emperors. It is here we want an *Herodian* to give us the ceremony of the funeral and *apotheosis* of *Constantius*, as particularly as that author has described those of *Severus*. But that the reader may have some notion of this uncommon piece of *Roman* pageantry, I shall beg leave, from *Herodian* to give a description of it. I make no doubt, that this ceremony was performed alike at *York* as at *Rome*, with this difference only, that at *Rome* an ivory image of *Severus* was substituted, but at *York* it was doneon the real body of *Constantius*.

"The image of the dead emperor, being exquisitely carved to resemble a sick person, "was laid on an ivory best-stead, ready furnished, in the porch of his palace. The prin- "ces and senators sat all on the left side of the bed, clad in black habits, whilst their ladies, "in white robes, sat on the other; the physicians diligently attending. When seven days "were ended, as if he was then just dead, the image was taken up by the prime nobility

(c) *Zosimus* l. 6. et not. *Joseph. Scaliger* in *Eusebium* anno 273.

(d) *Eurip.* apud *Porphyr.*

(e) *Ducange* in famil. aug. *Bizant.* writes, that he died here, *July* 25, *anno Christi* 307.

(f) He is said to have hamstringed all the post-horses he made use of to prevent a pursuit.

(g) *In* palatio *et in* regio cubili *jacens*—— Eusebius *versione* Vilesii *in vita* Constantini.

(h) Principatus anno tertio decimo. *Notae, falsum est, si enim annos quibus Caesaris potestatem exercuit conjungas cum annis quibus* Augustum *imperium obtinuit, annos* xv. *invenies; quippe creatus est* Caesar *an. ab urbe cond.* 1043; *P. C.* 291; *deinde* Augustus *factus anno U. C.* 1056, *P. C.* 304. *decessit biennio post et tribus mensibus.* Eutrop. *not. varior. et S.* Havercampi.

(i) *Paterna ornatus purpura*——paternis aedibus, *idem.*

(k) The panegyrist to *Constantine*, whom I shall quote fuller in the sequel, expresses this deification in these words, *Vere enim profecto illi superum templa patuerunt, receptusque est consessu coelitum,* Jove ipso dextram porrigente. *Panegyr. veteres,* n. v.

"with

4

" with the bed, and carried into the *forum*, where all the *praetorian* youths and noble vir-
" gins encompassed it, singing most doleful hymns and dirges. From thence the image, *&c.*
" was removed to the *field of Mars*, where a frame of timber was erected, four square, of
" a very great compass and height, the gradations still ascending pyramidically to the top,
" richly adorned with gold and purple ornaments, and statues of great art and price. On
" the second of these ascents was placed the imperial bed and image, with a prodigious
" quantity of odorifick gums and perfumes. The young nobility rid round the pile in a
" kind of dance, whilst others represented great kings and princes in their chariots. His
" successor first put fire to the frame, and, after him, the people, on all sides, did the
" like. When all was in a blaze, an eagle, secretly enclosed within, was let fly out of
" the top of the pile, the multitude following its flight with shouts and prayers; supposing,
" that therewith the emperor was mounted into heaven.

Except the flight of the eagle, the peculiar symbol of their deification, this piece of pompous pageantry had been executed on the body of *Severus*, at *York*, where he died. The custom afterwards was to strike coin on the occasion, where an eagle was always represented on the reverse. The medals, or coin, struck upon the *apotheosis* of *Constantius*, which are mentioned by several authors, and are common enough in the cabinets of the curious, have the head of the emperor, *velatum et laureatum*; the inscription DIVO CONSTANTIO PIO; reverse, an altar, with an eagle on each side of it, holding a label in their beaks betwixt them, inscribed, MEMORIA FELIX. This was the last ceremony of its kind, that was performed in the *Roman* state; and probably for the greater honour to this excellent prince, two eagles were let fly from his pile, instead of one which was the custom before. *Eusebius*, a *christian* writer of that age, has left *Constantius* this great character.

(*l*) " A while after, the emperor *Constantius*, a man agreeable in every point of life,
" who was remarkable for his clemency to his subjects, and singular benevolence to those
" of our persuasion, leaving his eldest son emperor in his stead, was snatched away by
" death. He was, by *Pagan* custom, enrolled amongst the gods, *and had all the honours,*
" *which had ever been paid at their funerals, bestowed upon him.* He was the most be-
" nign and merciful of all princes; and of all the emperors up to our time, he, alone,
" led a life suitable to his great dignity. Lastly, as in other things, he was human
" and beneficent to all; so towards us he behaved with great moderation, and kept the true
" worshippers of God, who lived under his government, free from harm or danger; nei-
" ther destroying our churches, or suffering any thing to molest us. For which God so
" blessed him, that this excellent father left a more excellent son, the heir of his well ac-
" quired empire.

Constantius being dead, and his funeral obsequies being solemnized at *York*; we come next to enquire where his ashes were deposited. None of the historians, I have mentioned, take notice of this circumstance; but since they are, at the same time, silent as to their being removed from hence, we may justly conclude, that where the tree fell, there it was ordered to lye. I am aware that *Matthew* of *Westminster (m)* mentions a place in *Wales*, where, he says, the tomb of *Constantius* was found; but the old monk seems to doat in this story, and there is no other authority, that I know of, to confirm it. Our great antiquary, *Camden*, has given some light to this affair, and perfectly secured to us the honour of this emperor's sepulchre, if you do not believe that the *lamp* which he was credibly informed, when at *York*, was found *burning* in a *vaulted tomb*, within a *little chapel*, soon after the *reformation*, was any more than an *ignis fatuus*. (*n*) The intelligence about the *lamp*, our author says, *he had from several understanding men in the city, who told him, that the vault was found under ground, in a place where constant fame had ever reported the ashes of* Constantius *to be laid.* Though *Camden* mentions not the particular place where this wonderful monument was discovered; yet since no age can produce an interval where churches and other consecrated places were so narrowly searched, and so severely plundered, as this I have mentioned, this ancient sepulchre might then be broke up, and pryed into for an imaginary treasure; which the most barbarous *pagan* nations, who had so often taken and sacked *York*, since the death of *Constantius*, had never presumed to do.

To add a little more confidence to this story, from *Camden*, I must say, that *tradition* still informs us, that the sepulchre he speaks of, was found in the parish church of St. *Helen* on the walls, which once stood in **Aldwark**. This church was demolished at the union of them in this city; and it is not impossible, but that *Constantine* the great, when converted to *christianity*, might order a church or chapel to be erected over his father's ashes, which was dedicated, perhaps after his time, to his mother. For since he must have a sepulchre somewhere amongst us, I know no place, in or about the city, more likely for it to have stood in than this.

But the story of the *burning lamp* will require a little further disquisition. Our antiquary has in some measure given us a receipt out of *Lazius*, for this wonderful composition; a fiction, I doubt, he too readily credited. I am aware of several great and venerable names,

(*l*) Eusebii *eccles. hist. sect.* iv.
(*m*) *In* Westmin. *in anno* 1283.
(*n*) *Gibson's Camden*, see *York.*

such

ſuch as *Plutarch*, *Pliny*, *Ludovicus Vives*, *Baptiſta Porta*, *Licetus*, *Pancirollus*, St. *Auſtin*, *&c.* that give teſtimony of the truth of this; from whom we learn, that the ancients had a method *to diſſolve gold into a fatty ſubſtance that would burn for ages.* But, with ſubmiſſion to theſe great authorities, I ſhall ſooner concur in opinion with that eminent antiquary, of our own days, *Monfaucon*; who ſays, it is impoſſible that there ever was, or could be, ſuch lamps in the world. Our natural philoſophy, as well as our natural reaſon, teaches, that no fire can ſubſiſt without air; but this unaccountable flame is ſaid to be extinguiſhed by it. We read in the *Roman* hiſtories, and other accounts of the ancients, that there was at *Rome*, in the temple of the goddeſs *Veſta*, a perpetual fire; as alſo, in the temple of *Minerva* at *Athens*, and of *Apollo* at *Delphi*. But this was ſo far from an everlaſting flame, in our ſenſe, that it ſubſiſted no longer than whilſt it was ſupplied at each place; that is, by the *veſtal virgins* at *Rome*, and at *Athens*, and by the *widows* at *Delphi*. For it went out in the time of the civil wars at *Rome*, and of *Mithridates* at *Athens*; and at *Delphi* it failed, when the *Meeds* deſtroyed that temple. Of this ſort was that fire which our ſacred ſcripture tells us that *God* appointed *Moſes*, *the fire ſhall always burn upon my altar, which the prieſt ſhall always keep lighted, putting under wood day by day.* And *Pancirollus* tells us, in the caſe of ſepulchral lamps, that it was uſual for the nobility at *Rome*, when they made their wills, to take ſpecial care that they might have a lamp burning in their ſepulchers; but then they uſually manumized one or more of their ſlaves, on condition of being watchful in feeding and preſerving the flame. A trouble that might well have been ſpared were *perpetual lamps* to be had.

I know I dwell too long on this juſtly exploded notion, for which I aſk pardon, though our credulous *Wilkins (o)* as well as *Camden*, comes fully into the belief of it. And if it be ſtill thought ſo by ſome, who are fond of the *marvellous*, it muſt, at the ſame time, be owned, that this rare invention will be, *in aeternum*, put amongſt the *artes perditae* of the ancients. But to conclude this head, that there never were ſuch things as everlaſting lamps, I ſay, is no argument that the tomb of *Conſtantius* might not have been found in this city at the time before mentioned. Something extraordinary muſt have been diſcovered to give occaſion for the report; and the ſtory of the burning lamp, like that ſaid to be found in the tomb of *Tullia*, *Cicero*'s daughter, might be feigned to give the greater authority to the conjecture.

Upon the demiſe of the laſt emperor, the army and people of *Rome*, who were then in this city, immediately proclaimed *Conſtantine*, his eldeſt ſon, his ſucceſſor. The imperial purple was put on him by the ſoldiery; which, we are told, he accepted of with ſome reluctancy; nay even to mount his horſe, and *ride away* from the army, who purſued him with the *robe of royalty (p)*; and to accept of it *with tears*. The ſurpriſe of his father's death, and this new offered dignity, might ſtagger the young prince's mind at firſt; but, being perſuaded by his friends, the princes of the empire; particularly, ſays an hiſtorian *(q)* by *Erocus*, a *German* king, who then was in the court at *York*, he at laſt accepted of this high command.

The inauguration of this great monarch, which muſt have happened in our city, as likewiſe a ſtrong claim we have to the drawing his firſt breath in it, will render it ever famous to poſterity. And though this laſt be ſomewhat more dubious than the former, yet the honour is ſo great, that the argument requires a more than ordinary diſquiſition, which I ſhall attempt in the ſequel.

The pomp and ceremony of receiving the imperial purple at a time when the *Roman* power extended over moſt of the then known world, and had either their tributary kings in perſon, their hoſtages, or their ambaſſadors, conſtantly reſident with them, muſt add a prodigious luſtre to EBORACUM; and gives me reaſon to call it here once again ALTERA ROMA. I can meet with no hiſtorian that has been particular enough to deſcribe the inveſtiture of this auguſt emperor in the colours it deſerves. We are told, however, that the *Britiſh* ſoldiers in *Roman* pay, ſaluted their countryman *Conſtantine* emperor at *York*, and preſented him with a *tufa*, or golden ball, as a ſymbol of his ſovereignty over the iſland of *Britain*. This emblem he was much taken with; and, upon his converſion to *chriſtianity*, he placed a croſs upon it, and had it carried before him in all proceſſions whatſoever. It is, ſince this emperor's time, become the uſual ſign of majeſty, and uſurped, I will not ſay improperly, ſays an author *(r)*, by all other *chriſtian* princes, and reckoned amongſt their *regalia*. When, by its firſt acceptation by *Conſtantine*, it evidently ſhews, that he took this globe as a ſymbol only, of his being lord of the iſland of *Britain*. Our *Saxon*

(o) *Wilkins*'s mechan. powers.

(p) *Imperator tranſitum facturus in coelum vidit quem relinquebat haeredem. Illico enim atque ille terris fuerat exemptus*, univerſus in te conſedit exercitus, *te omnium mentes oculique ſignarunt; et quanquam tua ad* ſeniores principes *de ſumma reip. quid fieri placeret retuliſſes, praevenerunt tamen ſtudio, quod illi mox judicio probaverunt.* Purpuram *ſtatim tibi, cum primus copiam tui fecit egreſſus* milites, *utilitate publicae magis quam tuis affectibus ſervientes*, injecere lacrymanti, *neque enim fas erat diutius flere* principem conſecratum. *Diceris etiam, imperator invicte, ardorem te depoſcentis exercitus fugere conatus*, equum calcaribus incitaſſe; *quod quidem, ut verum audias*, adoleſcentiae errore *faciebas*, *&c.* Eumenii *panegyr. ad* Conſt. *mag.*

(q) Victor *in epitom.* Caeſar.

(r) *Churchill*'s divi *Britan.*

monarchs,

monarchs, when they became universal lords, assumed this emblem of unlimited royalty, but with them it was a globe of feathers, called, after the *British* name, þuuf; *Bede* mentions this ensign to have been carried before *Edwin* the great, *&c.* A bunch of feathers, as appears in the time of *Richard* II. in a grant of Sir *Gervase de Clifton* to *Robert de Bevercotes*, was called *une tuffe de plume* (*s*). And a tuft of feathers, with us at this day, still retains the old *British* and *Saxon* appellation.

The birth of *Constantine* the great, according to a very learned chronologer (*t*), happened in the year of *Christ* two hundred and seventy two. His words are, Constantinus *magnus hoc anno in* Britannia *natus, patre* Constantio *et matre* Helena. I have hinted before, that it was, in all probability, when *Constantius* was legate in *Britain*, under the emperor *Aurelian*; and the whole number of the years of *Constantine*'s life confirm this chronology. But I find, that not only the express place where this great man was born, but even the country is disputed. For the latter, three very eminent writers (*u*), as ever any age produced, have put the affair out of contradiction; and if so, what particular place in *Britain* can bid fairer for it than Eboracum?

The proofs that the learned authors, whose names I have given in the notes, bring to shew their assertion just, are too copious, and too foreign for my purpose, excepting the quotations from the *panegyrist*, whose oration to *Constantine*, supposed to be made at his accession, and consequently at *York*, is very remarkable. The historians of this age are so lame and defective, as to give us few hints of the road we are to pursue; but this orator is particular enough, and illustrates several dark passages which could not have been made clear without him. I have to add, that his authority is unquestionable by all, but *Milton*; whose own testimony, in history, is not looked upon to be near so valid as the other (*x*). The oration is said to be made by one *Eumenius*, a *Gaul*; and if we were sure, that it was spoke in this city, on this great occasion, the whole, though long enough, could not be thought impertinent to my subject. But as it is, there are several remarkable passages in the speech which do require particular notice.

The *exordium* of this harangue turns chiefly on the nobility of *Constantine*'s birth, and the undoubted right he had to the empire by succession. In displaying his eloquence, the panegyrist tells him of his noble extraction, in very strong terms, which by no means suits with the character some authors give of his mother (*y*). The passages which seem to make it evident, that this emperor was born in *Britain*, I shall beg leave to give in the orator's own words and expression. The first is taken from an oration made to *Constantine* and *Maximian* by an uncertain orator (*z*), who expatiating on the great honour and benefits done to *Britain*, by him and his father, has this remarkable expression.

Liberavit ille Britannias *servitute, tu enim nobiles illic* oriendo *fecisti.* This obvious passage has been objected against by some eminent criticks; but the learned *Italian Patarol*, who has published the last and best edition of these orations, with an *Italian* version, has given us a note upon it, by which it appears, that the great cardinal and this author were of the same opinion (*a*). In the oration made to *Constantine* alone, by *Eumenius*, he speaks thus,

O fortunata et nunc *omnibus beatior terris* Britannia, *quae* Constantinum Caesarem prima *vidisti! merito te omnibus coeli et soli bonis natura donavit; in qua nec rigor est nimius hiemis, nec ardor aestatis, in qua segetum tanta foecunditas, ut muneribus utriusque sufficiat, et* Cereris *et* Liberi, *in qua nemora sine immanibus bestiis, terra sine serpentibus noxiis; contra pecorum mitium innumerabilis multitudo lacte distenta, et onusta velleribus, certè quod propter vitam diligitur, longissimae dies, et nullae sine aliqua luce noctes, dum illa littorum extrema planities non attollit umbras, noctisque metam, coeli et siderum transit aspectus; ut* sol *ipse qui nobis videtur occidere ibi appareat praeterire.* Di boni! quid hoc est, quod semper ex aliquo supremo fine mundi nova deum numina universo orbi colenda descendunt? *Sic* Mercurius *a* Nilo *se cujus fluminis origo nescitur; sic* Liber *ab* Indis *prope consciis solis orientis deos se gentibus ostendere praesentes. Secretiora sunt profecto mediterraneis loca vicina coelo,* et inde proprius a diis mittitur imperator ubi terra finitur.

In this description, though the whole island is named, yet the particular *vale of* York seems to be in the orator's eye, in describing the fertility, riches, and pleasantness of the country. It must be allowed me, that he speaks of the more northern parts of the island; and in this high flown complement, stretched too far indeed, the panegyrist can allude to nothing less than the country where *Constantine* was born. The objectors against this passage alledge, that it does not mean that the emperor was born in *Britain*, but that *Britain*

(*s*) *Smith*'s notes on *Bede*.

(*t*) Chron. *Abrahami Bucholt*.

(*u*) Baronii cardinal. annal. *tom* 3. *ad an.* 306, Sect. 16.

Usher de primord. eccles. *Britan.* c. 8. et epist. illic ad *Gul. Camd.*

Joh. Selden ad *Justum Lipsium*, *&c.*

(*x*) See *Milton*'s preface to his introduction to *Eng.* history.

(*y*) *Inter omnes inquam participes majestatis tuae hoc habes*, Constantine, *praecipuum, quod imperator es*, tantaque est nobilitas originis tuae, *ut nihil tibi addiderat honoris imperium; nec possit* fortuna numini tuo *imputare quod tuum est; omisso ambitu et suffragatione.* Panegyr. vet. ix. A fine argument for the hereditary right of princes.

(*z*) *Incerti panegyr.* Maxim. & Constantino, n. v.

(*a*) Oriendo. *Insultat acriter* Livineius *illis qui* Constantinum *in* Brit. *natum dicunt Ejusdem opinionis fuisse* Lipsium *videre est in ipsius opere de* magnitud. Romana, lib. 4 c. ii. *et fusius in notis ad eundem locum Uni autem fere nituntur isti* Julii Fermici *testimonio, ipsum apud* Tarsum *genitum affirmantis. Alii non apud* Tarsum *sed apud* Naissum Daciae *oppidum; inter quos vide* Ruperti observat in Besold. *Quicquid sit, tamen communissima scriptorum opinione non recedendum mihi videtur, ut uni tantùm aut alteri adhaereatur.* Laurent Patarol. *Notae in panegyr orationes veterum: ed.* 2.

saw

saw him first *Caesar*. But this is easily confuted; for though *Constantine* was certainly declared emperor by the army at *York*, immediately upon his father's death, as the former quotations shew; yet it was when he got into *Gaul*, that the senate and people of *Rome* confirmed the election, and gave him the title of *Caesar*.

The last passage, which I shall quote from these authorities, comes yet closer to the matter.

(*b*) SACRUM ISTUD PALATIUM, *non* candidatus *imperii*, *sed* designatus *intrasti*; confestimque te illi paterni lares successorem videre legitimum. *Neque enim erat dubium quin ei competeret haereditas, quem primum imperatori filium fata tribuissent. Te enim tantum ille, & imperator in terris, & in coelo deus, in primo aetatis suae flore generavit, toto adhuc corpore vigens, illa praeditus alacritate & fortitudine, quam bella plurima, praecipue campi* Vindonis *idonei testes declararunt. Inde est quod tanta ex illo in te formae similitudo transivit, ut signata natura vultibus tuis impressa videatur.*

It cannot be denied that the palace here spoken of must have been at EBORACUM; that *sacred palace*, made so illustrious and ever memorable, for the residence and deaths of two *Roman* emperors; and in all probability, for the birth and inauguration of a third. I may be thought perhaps too partial in applying the first part of this paragraph to my subject, but in my sence the Orator seems to speak thus to *Constantine* in it, *viz. Thou didst enter that* sacred palace, *where thy father lay expiring*, and where thou drewst thy first breath, not as a candidate, but born *to the empire. And no sooner did those* paternal houshould gods *behold thee, but they instantly acknowledged thee thy father's lawful successor. For what doubt cou'd there be who should succeed to the empire, but he whom they knew was the emperor's eldest son. Thou, whom thy father, once lord of the earth, and now a god in heaven, begot in the flower of his age* (*c*); *his body yet nervous and strong; endued with that alacrity and fortitude, which many wars especially that of the* Vindonian *camp gave sufficient proof of. Whence it was that the likeness of thy father's person so passed into thee, that his natural impress is clearly seen in thy countenance.*

To me this passage, I say, seems to make it most evident that the palace, here spoken of, was *Constantine*'s birth place; the orator could not have introduced it with any other design. The term *istud palatium, that very or yonder palace*, points plainly at it; and seems as if the oration had been made to the emperor, at the head of his army, in some field within view of the city and palace. Nor could the houshold gods, or *Lares*, be supposed to know him for the eldest son unless he had been born amongst them. Those petty deities of the *Romans* had no more knowledge ascribed to them, than belonged to the family they presided in (*d*). In short the reason, as I take it, that the orator was not clearer in this particular, might be the repudiation of *Constantine*'s mother, which his father, for reasons of state, had been forced to submit to. The emperor having several sons by his latter wife, the orator took care to lay a great stress on the legitimacy of *Constantine*, throughout the whole paragraph; but seems purposely to avoid mentioning his mother, as a point too tender to touch on.

But that his birth was at *York*, directly, and not elsewhere, says Mr. *Burton*, (*e*) though we have no express proof of it, amongst the ancients, that he knew of; yet the authority seems to be drawn from them, which the embassadors of *England* made use of in the hearing of the learned world; both at the council of *Constance*, as also at *Basil*. At the former (*f*), there being a contest about precedency between the *French* and *English* embassadors, the *English* had these words, *domus regalis* Angliae *sanctam* Helenam, *cum suo filio* Constantino *magno imperatore*, *nato in* urbe regia EBORACENSI, *educere comperta est. It is well known that the royal house of* England *produced* S. HELEN, *with her son, the emperor*, CONSTANTINE the great; born in the imperial city EBORACUM. The *English* again, at *Basil* (*g*) opposing the precedency of *Castile*, speak thus, CONSTANTINUM *illum magnum, qui primus imperator* christianus *licentiam dedit per universum orbem ecclesias constituere; immensa ad hoc conferent bona*; PETERNAE *natum in* EBORACENSI civitate. CONSTANTINE *the great, the first* christian *emperor, who gave leave to build churches through the universe, to the immense benefit of it; was born at* PETERNE *in the city of* YORK. *Peterne* is corrupted from *Bedbern*, now a college of vicars choral belonging to the cathedral; but what tradition does assure us was anciently part of the *imperial palace* at *York* (*h*).

These are all the quotations, ancient and modern, that I have yet met with to secure to us the honour of the birth of this most illustrious emperor. I shall not perplex my self more about it, but leave the matter to better judgments to determine. I shall conclude however, with this assertion, that if the birth of *Constantine* cannot be clearly made out, *York* has more to say for it than any other city in the world.

The *Britons* remained in quiet during the long reign of *Constantine*, according to the *Latin* historians,

(*b*) *Eumenii* panegyr. N°. IX.

(*c*) When he was about twenty four years old, says *Patarol*.

(*d*) In the palace of the emperor *Domitian* there was only one boy assigned to take care of the *Lares* in his chamber. *Suetonius*.

(*e*) *Burton*'s *Anton.* itinerary.

(*f*) *A. D.* 1414.

(*g*) *A D.* 1431.

(*h*) See *Bedbern* in the account of the city.

A. C. CCCXXV. historians, but the *Scotch* chroniclers (*i*) remark that in his twentieth year, that is *A. C.* CCCXXV. *Octavius* king of the *Britons* rebelled; but was soon vanquished by *Traberus*, the *Roman* lieutenant, and forced to fly to *Fincomark*, king of *Scotland*, for aid. The *Roman* general demanded the rebel, as he called him, of the *Scotch* king; and he refusing, a war ensued, wherein the *Romans* are said to be worsted; their general flying to *York*, durst not stand a siege, but abandoned the city to the enemy; who caused *Octavius* to be crowned there king of all *Britain*; the city and country, as the said testimony asserts, expressing great joy on the occasion. But after this we are told that *Octavius* seeking to dispossess the *Scots* and *Picts* from that part of the country, allotted to them by *Carausius*, as is before mentioned, called a council at *York*, in order to find out a method for it; but the *Scotch* king hearing of this came suddenly upon *Octavius* and forced him to fly into *Norway*, &c.

Constantine the great, for the better government of his vast and extensive dominions, divided the whole into four *praefectures*, viz. *Italy*, *Gaul*, the *East* and *Illyria*; which contained under them fourteen large diocesses or provinces. *Britain*, of the fourteen, was subject to the praefect of *Gaul*; and this province was again subdivided by the emperor, into three parts, or principalities, *viz.* BRITANNIA PRIMA, or the country south of the *Thames*, the capital station probably *London*; BRITANNIA SECVNDA, was *Wales*, the capital perhaps *Isca*, or *Caer-leon*; and MAXIMA, or FLAVIA CAESARIENSIS, the capital city most certainly *York* (*k*).

It is easy to see by this division, that the greatest part of the island had *York* for its *metropolis*. But I can go further, and make it probable that the supream command of all the province of *Britain* proceeded from hence (*l*). For though the *Roman* garrisons on the sea coasts had their commanders called *comites litoris Saxonici*; yet those, with all the inland guards and garrisons, were subject to the DVX BRITANNIARVM; the emperors immediate representative. That the principal residence of this supream military officer was always at *York*, in the *praetorian palace* there, will appear in the sequel. The title of MAXIMA, or FLAVIA, CAESARIENSIS, given to this particular district of *Britain*, in all probability alludes to the capitals being the emperor's birth-place, to his accession there, or, parhaps, to both. FLAVIVS or FLAVIA, was his father's, mother's, and his own *praenomen*; and, consequently whatever country the emperor thought fit to bestow it on, must have a particular allusion, along with CAESARIENSIS, to himself and family.

More of the acts of this great emperor are foreign to my purpose; he not only deserted *York*, and *Britain*, but even *Europe*; removing the seat of the empire from *Rome* to *Byzan-*
A. C. *tium*, or *Constantinople*. To the support of which he had drawn great numbers of *British* sol-
CCCXXXVII diers over with him. *Constantine* the great, died *A. C.* CCCXXXVII; but from the removing of the imperial seat from *Rome*, we may date the declension of the *Roman* power in *Britain*, and the subversion of our EBORACVM. From the death of *Constantine* the *Romans* held their sway in *Britain* for about a century. The *Latin* writers of that age are very sparing in their accounts of the affairs of this island. Two or three commotions at the most, are recorded, but they are not to my purpose. Yet that the *sixth legion* continued in their old quarters at *York*, to their final desertion of the island, appears from the NOTITIA IMPERII, or general survey of the empire; which our best historians agree was taken but a small time before that period.

A short space, also, before the date of the NOTITIA, it seems there were only a DVX
A. C. BRITANNIARVM, and a *Comes tractus maritimi*, which is the same as the *Comes littoris*
CCC LXXV. *Saxonici* aforementioned, as commanders in *Britain*. For, under *Valentian*, *Nectardus* was count of the maritime marches, as they then called him; and *Buchobaudes* first, and then *Theodosius* were dukes of *Britain* (*m*). This duke, or general, had under his command in the province, according to the account made out by the NOTITIA, fourteen thousand foot, and nine hundred horse; which, when reckoned with those of the other commanders, made in all nineteen thousand two hundred foot, and one thousand seven hundred horse. These were the whole number of forces the *Romans* kept in the island, for guards and garrisons, in the time of profoundest peace; as well to awe the *Britons*, ever prone to revolt, as to defend this much esteemed province of theirs from any foreign invasion. It is pretty remarkable, that our present governours and legislators have copied this part of *Roman* policy, by keeping up, at this day, near the same number of forces, called a *standing army*; in order to protect our *liberties* and *properties*; secure us from *home-bred divisions*, and *foreign invasions*. But to the purpose.

I have shewn our city at the summit of its glory and magnificence; but we must now descend apace; and, from being the *residence of the lords of the universe*, from that glorious prospect, sink at once to the most profound abiss of human misery. It is some happiness that I have none but a general account to give of this great revolution and dreadful cala-

(*i*) *Joh. Fordun. Hist. Boetius. Hollingshead's Scotch* chronicle.

(*k*) See *Selden*'s titles of honour.

(*l*) *Merito contendunt viri docti hanc* [*civitatem*] *hujusce insulae fuisse metropolim; cujus rei argumentum inde capio, quod tempore* Constantini *magni videam tractum illum in quo sedet* EBVRACVM *dici* Britanniam primam. Itin. Gale. 20.

(*m*) *Ammian. Marcell.* See also *Selden*'s titles of honour.

mity

mity that befall the *Britons* after being deserted by the *Romans*. Their historians are now for ever dumb, and the little that can be collected of these bloody times, is chiefly from old *Gildas*, a *British* writer; who seems to tremble in the bare description of the miseries of his country.

But to take leave of our *Roman* lords and masters, with that decency they deserve, it will not be improper to let the unlearned reader understand, what number of officers and private men a *Roman* legion consisted of. Next to shew the precedence of the sixth; which will best be understood by an abstract of the guards and garrisons, from the NOTITIA, under the command of the *vir spectabilis*, as he is there styled, DVX BRITANNIARVM: And lastly to give an account what *Roman* marks of antiquity, devouring time, with the assistance of fire and sword, ignorance and superstition, has not yet been able to erase from amongst us.

"(*i*) The *Roman* legions were generally divided into footmen and horsemen; the number not certain, but changed according to the difference of times and alterations of states. A legion under the first emperors consisted of about six thousand foot and six hundred horse. The first officer of the legion was called *legatus legionis*; who had charge both of horse and foot under the lieutenant general of the army, or governor of the province, for the emperors. Which lieutenant, or governour, is commonly called, in *Roman* history, *propraetor*, as the governor of the senate and people was called *praeconsul*.

"The inferior officers of the army were the centurions, ensign-bearers, &c.

"The footmen of the legion were equally divided into ten cohorts or companies; whereof each one had a superintendant officer.

"The six hundred horse in the legion were divided into ten troops called *Turmae*; every troop containing three decuries, or thirty horse, over whom were placed officers called *decurions*; each having a charge of ten horse. The chief officer of the troops was called *praefectus turmae*.

"The additions of the numbers, I. II. VI. &c. were given to the legions at their first raising; and the style VICTRIX was bestowed on those who distinguished themselves by some more than ordinary action in war, which sirname was ever afterwards appropriated to them, as to the sixth legion at *York*."

By this account, and what is subsequent, it appears that a whole legion to the number of six or seven thousand, horse and foot, were constantly quartered, or more properly station'd, at *York* all the time the *Romans* were masters of *Britain*. The several extraordinary proofs for the residence of the *sixth* legion at *York* are indisputable; and the last age has been so fortunate, as to find as convincing an argument that it was also the station for the *ninth*. It will not here be amiss to give a short account of both.

The *legions*, *cohorts*, and *Numbers* of the *Roman* army in *Britain*, had their fixed stations; to which after every accidental expedition, they always returned. Here their families remained in their absence. Here they erected their altars, temples, &c. which were also repaired by the same *legions*, &c. successively; for they were as the same body, or society, and had one common sepulture. There is not a legion mentioned in any of the writers of the *Augustan* story more remarkable than the sixth. Its station at *York* being easily traced for the space of three hundred years, and upwards; which was almost the whole time that they were masters of this province. It was first brought out of *Germany* into *Britain* by the emperor *Hadrian*; and says *Camden*, after it had served him in his more northern expedition, was left as a garrison in *York* (*k*). Here we find it expresly stationed in *Ptolemy's* geographical tables of the empire; who mentions none but the sixth legion at *York*, and the twentieth at *Chester*, to be in the province at that time. In *Antonine's itinerary*, we meet with it again, and it occurs with *York* in all the northern journeys. In *Roman* authors frequent accounts of this legion are inserted; and though the particular name of their station is not assigned, yet 'tis sufficiently hinted at; as in this passage of (*l*) *Dio*, where he tells us that there were two fixt legions in the empire, the one placed in *lower Britain*, called the *conquering legion*; the other in *Judea*, styled the *iron one*, or *Ferratensis*. This province, 'tis supposed, was divided by *Severus* into *higher* and *lower Britain*; and that *York* was the chief station in the latter is not to be doubted. Nor were the *Roman* poets wholly silent, in assigning due praises, and pointing us to the residence of this legion. *Claudian*, in giving an account of the legions that were sent to serve *Stilicho* against *Alarick* king of the *Goths*, which happened two hundred years after *Dio's* time, has these lines,

LEGIO VI. VICTRIX.

Circa A. CXX.

Venit & extremis Legio *praetenta* Britannis,
Quae Scoto *dat fraena truci*, *ferroque notatas*
Perlegit exanimes Picto *moriente figuras* (*m*).

Scoto Hyberno, *Scoto-Britanno*, Dr. *Gale*.

Then from the borders of the *British* lands
Came the bold legion, which the *Scot* commands;
Wh' admire the figur'd *Picts*, when dying by their hands.

(*i*) Sir *H. Spelman's* notes on *Tacitus*.
(*k*) *Brit.* see *York*. We are indebted to an inscription for the account of this legion's passing out of *Germany* into *Britain*. Dr. *Gale* has given it us in his *itin. Ant.* p. 47.
(*l*) *Dion. Cass* hist *Rom.* l. 55.
(*m*) Claudian *de bell. Getico*.

O If

If I could take time, in the courfe of fo long a ftory, to be very particular in the defcription of every thing in my way, the fublime hiftory of our fixth legion would run through many pages. And though it muft be allowed that the account of this legion, whilft in *Britain*, is chiefly owing to an infcription found amongft us; yet they are a noble and undoubted authority *(n)*. Mr. *Horfley* obferves that he does not find the name of this legion mentioned in any infcription in the fouthern parts of the ifland. It is to this laft named author that I muft refer the reader for further fatisfaction on this head; I fhall only add that for the tried courage and conftancy of our legion they had not only the firname of *victrix*, but *pia*, *fidelis*, given them. *Severus* himfelf, in an oration made to his army, beftowed great encomiums on their knowledge and fervice in the affairs of the ifland; and for their fidelity, he faid he believed, if there was occafion, *that they would venture naked through the fire for his fake* (o). That this legion continued in their old quarters till the declenfion of the empire, appears from the *Notitia Imperii* taken about that time; and we have reafon to think that they were the laft of the *Roman* forces that were withdrawn from *Britain*. So that from their fettlement, by *Hadrian*, to this laft named period, will take in the fpace of about three hundred and twenty, or thirty, years.

LEGIO NONA. The ninth legion came over into *Britain* under the emperor *Claudius*; the foot of it had the misfortune to be cut in pieces by the forces of the queen *Boadicea*. It was afterwards recruited from *Germany*, fays *Tacitus* (p); but it fuffered again in a fierce attack of the *Caledonians* when *Julius Agricola* was *prepraetor* and legate here. After this no manner of account can be met with of it in any hiftorian; and it was quite dead to the learned world till two infcriptions found in our city revived it. The account when and where thefe two remarkable monuments of antiquity were met with, will fall beft in the fequel.

It is the opinion of Mr. *Horfley*, and his notion feems to be right, that this legion was incorporated into the fixth. He gives a quotation from *Dio* to prove that the *Romans* fometimes broke their legions and incorporated one into another. But in the lift that confular hiftorian gives of the names of the legions which were in the empire in his days, the ninth is not fo much as mentioned. Which makes it probable that it had been broke, perhaps by *Severus*, and the foldiers that compofed it thrown into the fixth; from whence their ftyle *victrix* might be borrowed by the other; for it does not appear that they ever had that honourable appellation before. In the infcription of the *fignifer*, or enfign-bearer to this legion, it is ftyled plain LEGIO VIIII, *legio nona*; but this officer might die before his regiment was broke. The *brick* however gives us the adjunct VIC; but I leave a further explanation of them to the draughts, and what follows on that head.

The Notitia has been publifhed in *England*, firft by Mr. *Selden*, then by Dr. *Gale*, and laftly by Mr. *Horfley* (q). They have all endeavoured from Mr. *Camden*, later antiquaries, and their own conjectures, to affix the prefent *Englifh* names of towns to the ancient *Roman* ftations. In what I fhall chufe to tranfcribe from this admired record, I fhall follow Mr. *Horfley*'s verfion; that author as he ftood on others fhoulders, and having taken more than ordinary pains to afcertain the ftations, *ad lineam valli*, and the north of *England*, where he lived, is more to my purpofe. But I fhall leave it to the reader to confult the book it felf for the arguments he ufes on that occafion.

The Notitia, in *L'abbe*'s edition, begins firft with the Vicarivs Britanniarvm, next the Comes littoris Saxonici, then the Comes Britanniae, and laftly the Dvx Britanniarvm. It is plain by the lift of the officers and diftricts put under the vicar general of *Britain*, that the whole province was fubject to this civil magiftrate in all legiflative affairs. Dr. *Stillingfleet* has placed this dignatary in his tribunal at *London*; for no reafon that I know of; that ftation being not fo much as mentioned in the Notitia; or even hinted at in all the account. For this caufe I have given the vicar-generals court and officers as actually refident with us at *York*. For where fhould a fucceffor of the great *Papinian* fit to execute judgment, but in the fame Praetorivm, and on the fame tribunal, that he did? Befides, 'tis further obfervable, that the confular governors of the diftrict called *Maxima Caefarienfis*, by *Conftantine* the great, begin the account; and this precedency evidently fhews it to have been the principal part, as well as its capital the principal city, in the province.

But what does more immediately concern my fubject, and will admit of no difpute, is the refidence of the Dvx, general, or military commander, in *Britain*. That the reader may fee what preheminence and dignity our city bore in this Notitia imperii, I have thought fit to draw out the account of the guards and garrifons that were ftationed in the north under the command, as the title directs, of this great general. The firft garrifon put down, was that of a whole legion; and though no place be mentioned for its ftation, yet it moft evidently appears from *Ptolemy*, the *Itinerary*, and many other proofs, that Eboracvm was always the ftated quarters of this legion. The blank left here then is a fingular honour done to the capital, and the refidence of the great officers in it. For there

(n) *Horfley's Britannia Romana*. See *Weftmorland* N° vi, and viii. &c.

(o) *In oratione ad legatos & praefectos in* Britannia; *apud* Dion. *hift*. Rom. l. 38.

(p) Annal lib. xiv.

(q) *Selden*'s titles of honour. *Inter xv. fcriptores, edit.* Gale. Horfley's Britannia Romana.

was

was no need to name a place so notoriously known to be the head of the province. Mr. *Horsley* has taken notice that the forces, said to be quartered at the following stations, were all certainly auxiliaries to the sixth legion. And, by inspecting his map of the island, it will appear that they lie round about *York*; which, adds he, was a very proper situation if upon any occasion it should have been necessary to call them together.

Now follows part of a copy of this grand record.

Ex NOTITIA *dignitatum imperii* ROMANI *circa tempora* ARCADII & HONORII.

Circa A.C. CCCC.

Sub dispositione viri spectabilis VICARII BRITANNIARVM.

Consulares,

MAXIMAE CAESARIENSIS,
VALENTIAE.

Praesides,

BRITANNIAE PRIMAE,
BRITANNIAE SECVNDAE,
FLAVIAE CAESARIENSIS.

Officium autem habet idem vir spectabilis VICARIVS *hoc modo,* PRINCIPEM *de schola* Agentium *in rebus ex* Ducenariis.

Cornicularium.
Numerarios *duos.*
Commentariensem.
Ab Actis.
Curam Epistolarum.
Adjutorem.
Subadjuvas.
Exceptores.
Singulares & reliquos officiales.

From the NOTITIA or general account of the *Roman* empire taken about the time of the emperors *Arcadius* and *Honorius*.

Under the government of the honourable the *vicar general* of *Britain, Consular* governors of those parts of *Britain* called *Maxima Caesariensis* & *Valentia.*

Presidial governors of those parts called *Britannia prima, Britannia secunda,* & *Flavia Caesariensis.*

The same honourable *Vicar* has his court composed in the following manner,

1. A principal officer of the *agents,* chosen out of the *Ducenarii* or under officers.
2. A principal *clerk,* or *secretary.*
3. Two chief *accountants* or *auditors.*
4. A *Master* of the *prisons.*
5. A publick *notary.*
6. A *secretary* for dispatches.
7. An *assistant* or *surrogate.*
8 Under *assistants.*
9. *Clerks* of the *appeals.*

Serjeants and other inferior officers.

Sub dispositione viri spectabilis DVCIS BRITANNIARVM.

1. PRAEFECTVS LEGIONIS SEXTAE.
2. *Praefectus equitum* Dalmatarum — — PRAESIDIO.
3. *Praefectus equitum* Chrispianorum — — DANO.
4. *Praefectus equitum* Catafractoriorum — — MORBIO.
5. *Praefectus numeri* Barcariorum Tigritensium — — ARBEIA.
6. *Praefectus numeri* Nerviorum Dictensium — — DICTI.
7. *Praefectus numeri* Vigilum — — CONCANGIOS.
8. *Praefectus numeri* Exploratorum — — LAVATRES. *alias* RT
9. *Praefectus numeri* Directorum veterum — — VENERIS.

10. *Prae-*

4

10. *Praefectus numeri* Defensorum. — — BRABONIACO.
11. *Praefectus numeri* Solensium — — MAGLOVAE.
12. *Praefectus numeri* Pacensium — — MAGIS.
13. *Praefectus numeri* LONGOVICARIORUM — LONGOVICO.
14. *Praefectus numeri* DERVENTIONENSIS — DERVENTIONE.

Item per lineam Valli.

1. *Tribunus cohortis quartae* Lergorum — SEGEDVNO.
2. *Tribunus cohortis* Cornoviorum — — PONTE AELII.
3. *Praefectus alae primae* Afcorum — — CONDERCO.
4. *Tribunus cohortis primae* Frixagorum — VINDOBALA.
5. *Praefectus alae* Savinianae — — HVNNO.
6. *Praefectus alae secundae* Aftorum — — CILVRNO.
7. *Tribunus cohortis primae* Batavorum — PROCOLITIA.
8. *Tribunus cohortis primae* Tungrorum — BORCOVICO.
9. *Tribunus cohortis quartae* Gallorum — VINDOLANA.
10 *Tribunus cohortis primae* Aftorum — AESICA.
11 *Tribunus cohortis secundae* Dalmatarum MAGNIS.
12. *Tribunus cohortis primae* AEliae Dacorum — AMBOGLANNA.
13. *Praefectus alae* Petrianae — — PETRIANIA.
14. *Praefectus numeri* Maurorum Aurelianorum — ABALLABA.
15. *Tribunus cohortis secundae* Lergorum — CONGAVATAE.
16. *Tribunus cohortis primae* Hispanorum — AXELODVNO.
17. *Tribunus cohortis secundae* Thracum — GABROSENTI.
18. *Tribunus cohortis primae* AEliae Classicae — TVNNOCELLO.
19. *Tribunus cohortis primae* Morinorum — GLANNIBANTA.
20. *Tribunus cohortis tertiae* Nerviorum — ALIONE.
21. *Cuneus* Armaturarum — — BREMETENRACO.
22. *Praefectus alae primae* Herculane — OLENACO.
23. *Tribunus cohortis sextae* Nerviorum — VIROSIDO.

Under the government of the honourable the Duke of *Britain*.

1. The Prefect of the *sixth Legion*.
2. The Prefect of the *Dalmatian horse* stationed at — *Broughton Lincolnshire*.
3. The Prefect of the *Christian horse* at — *Doncaster*.
4. The Prefect of a body of *Cuirasiers* at — *Templeburgh*.
5. The Prefect of a detatchment of the *Barcarii Tigrisienses* at — *Moresby*.
6. The Prefect of a detachment of the *Nervii* called *Dictenses* at — *Amblesside*.
7. The Prefect of a detachment of soldiers for the *watch* at — *Kendal*.
8. The Prefect of a detachment of *Scouts* at — *Bowes*.
9. The Prefect of a detachment styled *Directores* at — *Burgh*.
10. The Prefect of a detachment called *Defensores* at — *Overburgh*.
11. The Prefect of a detachment of the *Solenses* at — *Greta-bridge*.
12. The Prefect of a detachment of the *Pacenses* at — *Pierce-bridge*.
13. The Prefect of a detachment of LONGOVICORII at — *Langburg* near *Tadcaster*.
14. The Prefect of a detachment styled DERVENTIONENSIS at — STAINFORD-*burgh*.

Also along the line of the Wall.

1. *The Tribune of the fourth cohort of the* Lergi at — *Cousin's house Northumb.*
2. The Tribune of a cohort of the *Cornavii* at — *Newcastle*.
3. The Prefect of the first wing of the *Asti* at — *Benwel-hill*.
4. The Tribune of the first cohort of the *Frixagi* at — *Rutchester*.
5. The Prefect of the wing called *Saviniana* at — *Halton Chesters*.
6. The Prefect of the second wing of the *Asti* at — *Walwick Chesters*.
7. The Tribune of the first cohort of the *Batavi* at — *Carraw-burgh*.
8. The Tribune of the first cohort of the *Tungri* at — *House steads*.
9. The Tribune of the fourth cohort of the *Gauls* at — *Little Chesters*.
10. The Tribune of the first cohort of the *Asti* at — *Great Chesters*.
11. The Tribune of the second cohort of the *Dalmatians* at — *Carvoran*.
12. The Tribune of the first cohort of *Dacians* called *Aelia* at — *Burdeswald*.
13. The Prefect of the wing called *Petriana* at — *Cambeck-fort*.
14. The Prefect of a detachment of *Moors* styled *Aureliani* at — *Watch-Cross*.
15. The Tribune of the second cohort of the *Lergi* at — *Stanwicks*.
16. The Tribune of the first cohort of *Spaniards* at — *Burgh*.
17. The Tribune of the second cohort of *Thracians* at — *Drumburgh*.
18. The Tribune of the first marine cohort styled *Aelia* at — *Bowness*.

19. The

19. The Tribune of the first cohort of the *Morini* at — *Lanchester*.
20. The Tribune of the third cohort of the *Nervii* at — *Whitley Castle*.
21. A body of men in armour at *old Penreth*, or *Brampton*
22. The Prefect of the first wing called *Herculea* at —— *Old Carlisle*. Or
23. The Tribune of the sixth cohort of the *Nervii* — *Elenburgh*.

Officium autem habet idem vir spectabilis Dux *hoc modo*,

1. Principem *ex officiis magistrorum militum praesentalium alternis annis*.
2. Commentariensem *utrumque*
3. Numerarios *ex utrisque officiis omni anno*.
4. Adjutorem.
5. Subadjuvam.
6. Regerendarium.
7. Exceptores.
8. *Singulares & reliquos familiares*.

The same honourable *Duke* has his court made up of the following *officers*.

1. A *principal officer* from the courts of the generals of the soldiers in ordinary attendance; changed yearly.
2. *Masters of the prisons* from both.
3. *Auditors* yearly, from both courts.
4. An *Adjutant*.
5. A *Subadjutant*.
6. A *register*.
7. *Clerks of appeals*.
8. *Serjeants* and other officers.

It appears by this abstract of the *Notitia* that the *Romans*, at the last of their stay in the island, had drawn down all their forces from the west, and south-west, to defend the northern borders against the *Picts* and *Scots*. This great armament was chiefly stationed along the line of the wall; of which there were no less than twenty three cohorts, *&c.* placed to guard it. And allowing Sir *H. Spelman*'s calculation of the number of a legion to be just, that a cohort consisted of six hundred foot; that number multiplied by twenty three, makes thirteen thousand eight hundred; a vast body of men for that purpose. By inspecting Mr. *Horsley*'s map, and his draughts of this prodigious *vallum*, it will appear that the garrisons on it were placed as thick as they could well stand; and must have been sufficient, both in number and strength, to stop any attempts of the *Barbarians* against them.

The rest of the forces in the abstract, consisting of a whole legion, and thirteen several detatchments, of horse and foot, were stationed at *York*, and other places circumjacent to the capital; that as Mr. *Horsley* justly observes, they might, upon any emergency, be easily drawn together. The proper stations of these troops may well be supposed to have lain on the grand military ways, our eastern sea coasts, and the fords of the greater rivers in the north of *England*. Their high roads were made for the more easy and quicker march of their own forces; but were blocked up in order to impede an enemy. Our sea-coasts, on the *German* ocean, must also have had their guards and garrisons somewhere disposed upon them; for sure it was as necessary to take care to prevent any invasions of the *Saxons* on this shoar as the more southerly coasts of the island. The fords were likewise diligently to be watched; for by being masters of those, they had the country in a total subjection; and could well defend it against any foreign attempt, or inbred commotion. To this end these politick lords built no stone bridges in *Britain*; else, no doubt but some remains of such works would appear with us, at this day, as well as in other parts of the empire. We may however, presume that they had occasional wooden bridges, made portable, such as our modern military men call *pontons*; which they could throw over any river in their march, when swelled too high for fording, and afterwards take away with them. Some account of such bridges is given in *Dio*; which *Severus* carried with him from *York*, in his expedition against the *Caledonians*.

Having premised thus much, I am satisfied that a judicious antiquary, upon an exact survey, will draw in some of the *Notitial* stations to a nearer distance from *York*, than they have been hitherto placed. Mr. *Horsley* supposes the forces, which are here mentioned, were all auxiliaries to the sixth legion; and consequently we may infer that they were posted, at proper places, as advance guards to the city; of which that legion was the grand garrison. For instance,

All our antiquaries, from Mr. *Camden*, have sought out a town called LONGVS VICVS, the station of a detachment of *Longovicorii*, by an affinity in the translation of the name. For which reason *Lanchester* in the north, and the city of *Lancaster*, bidding the fairest for the interpretation, they have each had their turns in that honour. But, if I may be allowed a conjecture, we need not ramble so far to seek this station; and it will most evidently turn out to have been a town formerly seated on the river *Wharfe*, betwixt *Tadcaster* and *Wetherby*, called **Langburgh**. The name of this town, though long since destroyed, is still fresh in the mouths of the country people; who call the *Roman* coins, frequently found in the fields hereabouts, **Langbrough-pennys**. And if we are in search for a translation of LONGVS VICVS, where can we meet with an apter? Tradition, I take it, is as certain as any history, where the etymologies of names answer so well as in those now before us. Besides, this town was placed full on the great military way, from north to south, at an easy ford over the *Wharfe*, and seems to correspond with the next garrison mentioned in the account to it, on the other side *York*, DERVENTIO; which is proved to have been placed on the ford over the river *Derwent*. The *Saxon* termination *burgh* has been so often taken notice of, that it is needless to say any more of it here.

There are three fords over this sometime rapid river *Wharfe*, which the *Romans*, no doubt, were acquainted with, and took great care to guard. These, at no great distance from one another, are at *Tadcaster*, St. *Helen's-ford*, and *Wetherby*. The first was the immediate key to the city itself, and on which CALCARIA was built as a proper guard to it. The others, I presume, were under the care of the *Longovicorii*, in the *notitia*; whose station stretching along the river by *Newton*, which town's name plainly hints at an elder brother, had its title from its length. That this place is not mentioned in the *itinerary*, is no rule why it might not have been a station, even at that time. The rout there coming always from the north, by *York*, to *Tadcaster*, and so on, our *Langburgh* does not happen to fall in any of the journeys.

There is a vicinary road, on *Bramham-moor*, yet very apparent, but which was never taken notice of by any that I know of. It is most certainly *Roman*, by its dimensions and manner of paving, agreeable to all that I have yet seen of this sort, although the quantity of *agger* does not raise it any thing like the other grand military way on the same moor. It comes from the ford at *Wetherby* up to *Bramham*; I traced it fairly from thence, over the moor, to *Bramham-moor-house*, as it is called; the house stands full upon it; from which it goes directly on for *Tadcaster*, and falls into the grand road, where the two lanes meet, about a quarter of a mile from the town. This road makes part of a circle from *Wetherby* to *Tadcaster*, and *Bramham* is placed in the midst of the line. Might I be allowed another supposition, though at a much wider distance than the former, I would call this place the BRABONIACVM, in the *notitia*, the station of a body of soldiers styled *defensores*, defenders, probably, or protectors of these passes. It is true the place has discovered no other antique tokens that I know of, but the road I have mentioned, and the seeming affinity in the name; yet the situation of it adds a probability to the conjecture. For as this road must have been originally designed for a communication betwixt the two fords of *Wetherby* and *Tadcaster*, including St. *Helen's-ford*, it seems to be a proper station for an advanced guard to them all. The vestiges of a *Roman* camp at (r) *Aberford*, still visible, is another argument of their vigilance, in regard of these important passes on the greatest military way in the island.

Mr. *Horsley* imagines the PRAESIDIVM in the *notitia* is the same with PRAETORIVM in the *itinerary*, if so, it must, as I have hinted, lye somewhere on our eastern coast: And it is somewhat strange, however, that no more stations are marked out for that quarter. I, perhaps, have been too bold already in my former conjectures, and therefore shall not presume to make any more alterations in the *English* names assigned to the *notitial* stations, by men of much deeper reach in antiquity than my self. Besides, it is too foreign to my subject; I shall therefore wave the matter, and pass on to the next head that I proposed to treat on, before I concluded this chapter.

To give an account of the several remains of antiquity which have been found taken taken notice of, or are still preserved amongst us. I shall range them in the order of time that they were discovered.

Our celebrated antiquary was the first that led the way; for though there must have been, in all ages since the *Romans* left us, many of their memorials found in this city, yet the barbarous or superstitious ignorance of those times, either destroyed or defaced them. It may seem strange, after what has been said before, that there is not at this day many nobler testimonies of *Roman* grandeur to be seen amongst us. That we shew no ruins of *temples*, *amphitheatres*, *palaces*, *publick baths*, &c. whose edifices must once have made EBORACVM shine as bright almost as *Rome* it self. The wonder will cease in any one who reads the sequel of this story; such terrible burnings and devastations; such horrid destruction of every thing, sacred or profane, will be found in it; that, it is rather matter of surprize, how it was possible this mutilated city could ever so much as raise its head from those heaps of ashes and ruins, it has so often and so deeply been overwhelmed and buried in. For,

(r) *Aber* in the *British* is *Ostium*. *Baxter*. A place called **Castle-cary** is at *Aberford*, which some have thought bears an allusion to the old CALCARIA.

though

though the temple of *Bellona* be long ſince removed from *York*, yet, in the reſt of the inteſtine troubles of *England*, this city has had ſo great a ſhare, has ſeen it ſelf ſo often the ſeat of war, that the altar of the fire-eyed goddeſs might have ſmoked with human gore for ſeveral ages, after it, and the temples were eraſed from their firſt Foundations.

To our *chriſtian* anceſtors, the *Anglo-Saxons* and *Normans*, we likewiſe owe the defacing or demoliſhing of almoſt every *Roman* altar, or votive monument that were diſcovered in their time. Being zealots in their perſuaſion, and utterly ignorant of their great uſe in hiſtory, they took care to eradicate all marks of *paganiſm* wherever they found them. For their own conveniency they were obliged to make uſe of the ruins of the *Roman* buildings in *York*, to erect their churches with; yet it is evident, that whenever they met with an inſcription, like the *Turks* at preſent in *Greece*, they either buried it in the foundation, turned it into the wall, broke or utterly obliterated it. Several inſtances of this I have ſeen and obſerved; and I am perſuaded, that whenever thoſe churches fall, or are pulled down to be rebuilt, many now buried *Roman* monuments and inſcriptions will ſee the light. It is to be hoped ſucceeding ages will have more veneration for theſe marks of antiquity than the latter. All we have now to exhibit, is what the laſt century has turned out; and it is a ſatisfaction to me to think, that time may yet produce materials for ſome abler pen to raiſe this ſubject to the height it deſerves.

I have ſaid that Mr. *Camden* was the firſt who took notice of any *Roman* antiquities or inſcriptions in *York*. That author, after giving us the reading of the reverſe of ſome of the emperor *Severus*'s coins, which I ſhall have occaſion to mention in the ſequel, tells us of a memorable inſcription, which, he ſays, he ſaw in *the houſe of a certain alderman of that city*. In his own and continuator's *Britannia*, it is publiſhed in this manner:

M. VEREC. DIOGENES IIIIII. VIR
COL. EBOR. IDEMQ. MORT. CIVES
BITVRIX. HAEC SIBI VIVVS FECIT.

Our antiquary does not give us the reading of this inſcription, nor inform us what it was upon; how nor where it was found. Mr. *Burton*, in his commentary, has aimed at the reading of it. The faults of the *quadrator* or ſtone-cutter, being amended, ſays that author, as *ibidemque* for *idemque*, and *civis* for *cives*, the inſcription is eaſily read, and ſignifies no more than that *Marcus Verecundus Diogenes*, a native of *Bury*, in *Gaſcoigny*, overſeer of the highways to the *colony* at *York*, died there; who, while alive, made this monument for himſelf.

Dr. *Gale*, on the *itinerary*, has there given us a draught of this monument, which had been ſo little regarded at *York*, that in his time he found it at *Hull*, where it then ſerved as a trough for watering horſes at a publick inn. The learned Dean calls it *theca*, which properly ſignifies any hollow cheſt or other convenience for putting things in. He has likewiſe added four letters more to the inſcription which he ſaw upon the ſtone, but which are omitted by *Camden*. The letters are C V B V S, and the dean reads them *clariſſimus vir bene vivens*.

Mr. *Horſley* took the pains to ſearch out this venerable monument of antiquity. He found it ſtill at *Hull*, but removed to another place, miſerably broken and defaced. It has certainly been *ſepulchral*, and was deſigned as a repoſitory of urns for a whole family; the chief of which family having taken care to provide it in his lifetime, as the inſcription teſtifies. There have been ſome of theſe *thecae* found lately in the *Roman* burial-place without *Bootham-bar*, but no inſcriptions on them. I have ſeen there likewiſe, graves for urns, ſquare ſpots in the earth, the bottom covered with white ſand on which the urns were placed, inverted, three, four, or more together. By the letters and numerals on the ſtone, it appears plainly, that *Burton* was miſtaken in his reading of them. IIIIII. VIR has ſix numerals, and therefore he muſt be the *ſextumvir* of the *Roman* colony at *York*. But who this officer was, whether civil or military, is not ſo eaſy to determine. *Urſatus, in notis Romanorum*, has at leaſt twenty different interpretations of this ſingle abbreviation. That the *Romans* had their *duumvir*, *triumvir*, and ſo to *decemvir*, is apparently known, which were all civil officers; and ſo, by the colony immediately following this title, our *ſevir* ſeems to have been one of the ſame order in the civil government. The forecited author has a reading ſomething parallel to this, VI. VIR. SEN. ET AVG. C. DD. which he interprets, *ſextumvir ſeniorum et auguſtalis coloniae dedicavit*, the CVBVS mentioned by dean *Gale*, and ſaid to be upon the ſtone, is likewiſe confirmed by Mr. *Horſley*, though it is ſtrange Mr. *Camden* ſhould miſs it. But that author obſerves, that our antiquary uſed frequently to omit ſuch letters as were doubtful or unintelligible to him, though even yet ſufficiently viſible. The quotations *Horſley* draws from *Pliny* and *Strabo*, ſettle his reading of CVBVS beyond contradiction. For if the *Bituriges* were alſo called *cubi*, as thoſe writers teſtify, it can bear no other. The interpretation of the whole inſcription then is this, that *Marcus Verecundus Diogenes*, a *ſevir*, or magiſtrate, in the colony at *York*, died there; he was originally a native or citizen of *Bourdeaux* in *France*; he made this repoſitory for his family's urns

in

in his lifetime, and his relations took care to put his name, office, and place of extraction, on it, after his death.

The remains of this monument is still at *Hull*, in the place and condition Mr. *Horsley* describes it. I had once a thought to have got it convey'd back to *York*, from a town that has no more reference than regard to antiquity; but upon sight, it seems not at present worth the trouble. All I can do then to preserve the memory of an inscription, PLATE VIII. Fig. 2. which is the only one that I ever saw or heard of, wherein the name of EBOR is particularly put in it, is to present the reader with Mr. *Horsley*'s draught of it. The size of the chest is very large, being six foot long, and near three deep, and is of miln-stone-grit; the chasm, through which the pricked letters are carried, shews what is wanting of them at this time.

The next remarkable *Roman* monument was found under-ground, in digging the foundation for a house on *Bishop-hill* the elder, in the year 1638. It was presented to king *Charles* I. when at *York*, 1639, by the then Sir *Ferdinando Fairfax*, and was kept at the *mannor*. Afterwards Sir *Thomas Widdrington* got it to his house in *Lendal-street*; from whence it was conveyed to the new house lord *Thomas Fairfax* built on *Bishophill*, where it remained to the desertion of that house by his son-in-law the duke of *Buckingham*. From that time neither dean *Gale*, Mr. *Horsley*, nor my self, have been able to get the least intelligence where it was carried to. Dr. *Martin Lister*, our celebrated physician, phylosopher, and antiquary, saw it at the duke's house, and gave this account of it to the *royal society* (s). He said it was a small but elegant *altar*, with figures in *basso relievo*, of sacrificing instruments, &c. on the sides of it. He adds, that it suffered an unlucky accident by the stupid ignorance of the masons, who were ordered, by the late lord *Fairfax*, to place it upon a pedestal in the court of his house at *York*. He further observes, that this altar is the only instance he ever met with, of the *Romans* making use of any other stone than *grit* for them. And yet he adds, that this is not of the common lime-stone, or what is usually called free-stone, but of a certain sort brought from the quarries about *Malton*; because of the *lapides judiaci* to be seen in the texture of it. It is pity the Dr. did not preserve the form of the altar as well as the inscription, since he commends it so much for its elegant sculpture. But, since that seems irretrievable, the reader must be content with the dedication, which, though printed several times, I have been favoured with the most exact copy of it yet published; taken from the original by *Bryan Fairfax* Esq; and sent me by his son *Bryan Fairfax* Esq; now one of the honourable commissioners of the customs.

PLATE VIII. Fig. 3. The inscription has the fewest abbreviations in it that I ever met with; and except the last line, is obvious to any one that understands the *latin* tongue. This bears several readings; Mr. *Horsley* gives it *aram sacra faciendo noncupavit dedicavit*. Mr. *Ward*, in his annotations, published in the *Britannia Romana*, takes it to mean *aram sacram factam nomine communi dedicavit*. For my part, I prefer *Ursatus* his notes, who for certain had seen the like on other altars abroad, and he reads it, *numini conservatori dedicatam, vel dari jussit*. The *English* version of the whole is this, To the great and mighty *Jupiter*, and to all gods and goddesses, houshold and peculiar gods, *Publius Aelius Marcianus*, prefect of a cohort, for the preservation of his own health, and that of his family, dedicated this altar to the great preserver.

(t) Dr. *Lister* took notice of another remarkable inscription which he found in the south wall of the church of *All-Saints* in *North-street*, an account of which he likewise sent up to the society. The letters, says the Dr. though a little defaced, are exceeding fairly cut, beyond any thing of that kind that he had yet seen in *England*. The inscription, adds he, has a figure of a naked woman on the left side of it, and is undoubtedly a monument of conjugal affection. But the attempts, both by the Dr. and Mr. *Horsley* to read it, are frivolous; there being nothing to be understood from it, except the last word, which is very plain and apparent, CONIVGI. The stone is put up in the wall of the church so close to a large buttress; that I imagined half of the inscription was hid by it; and therefore I got a workman to make a tryal, in order to lay it all open: But upon search we found the stone was broke off in the midst, to make way for the buttress to enter the wall, and bind it the firmer. I refer the reader for a further explication of this fragment to the draught of it, taken as it appears at present.

(u) Dr. *Gale* gives us another imperfect inscription, which, in his time, was built up in a wall, without *Mickle-gate-bar*, near the *Mount*. It is now lost, so that I have taken it Fig. 5. from the dean's authority, but have no more to say of it, than that this seems also to have been sepulchral; MINNA being the name of the person deceased, the name occurs in *Gruter* (x).

We are indebted to Dr. *Lister* likewise, for a curious observation he made of the basis of a multangular tower, and some length of a wall, whose manner of building, with brick and stone, does evidently shew it to be *Roman*. The description the Dr. made of it to the *royal society*, I shall chuse to give in his own words, as follows.

(s) *Ab. philos. transact.* v. 3.
(t) *Ab. philos. trans.* v. 3.
(u) *Anton.* iter *Britan.*
(x) p. CIↃXXIV. n. 5.

(y) " Care

plate VIII. p. 56.

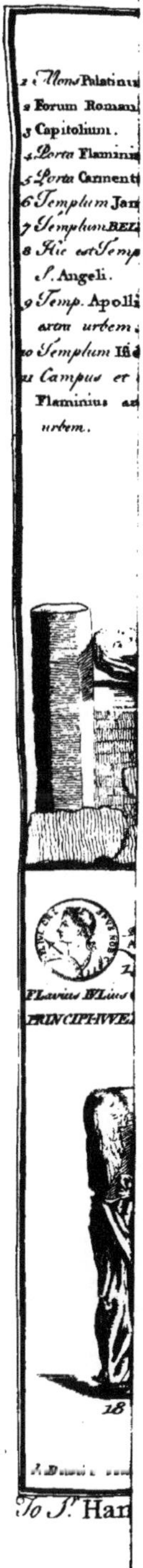

To S.r Han

NY

A Roman *tower and wall in* York.

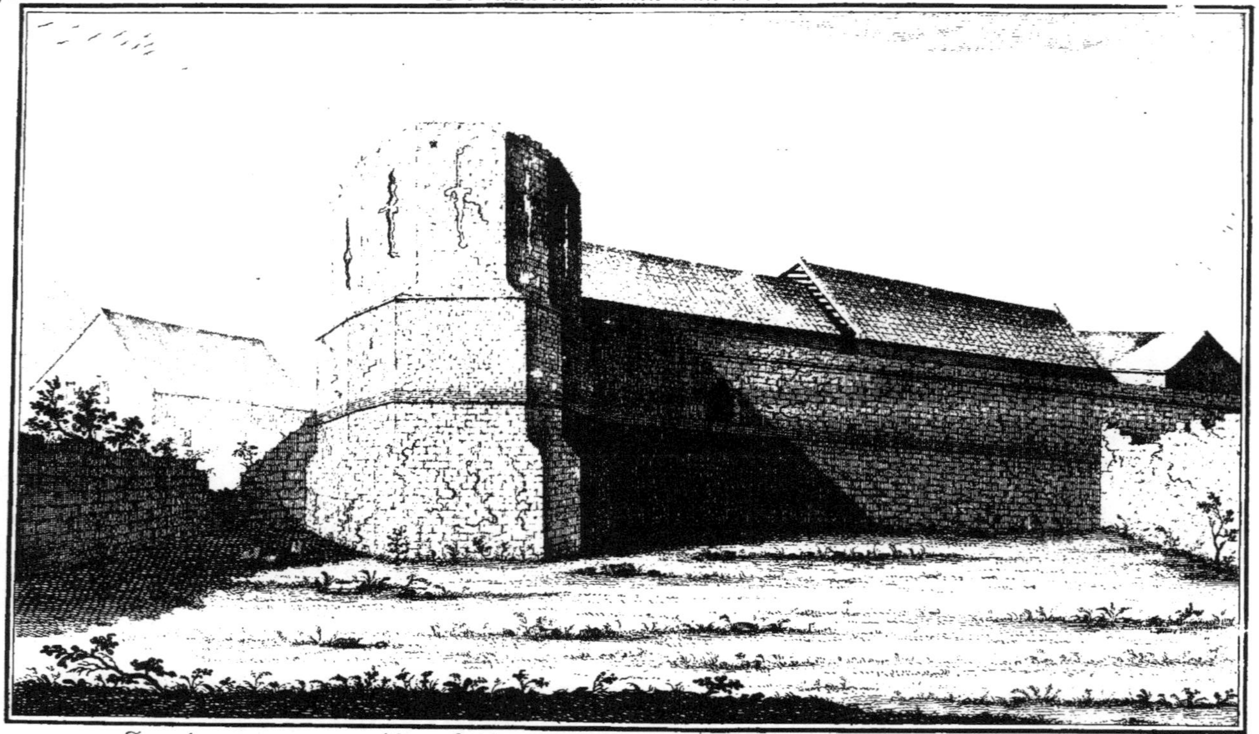

In order to preserve an idea of this antient Roman *fortification,* Benjamin Langwith *D.D. Rector of* Petworth *in* Suffex, *a native of* York, *contributes this plate. 1736.*

(*y*) " Carefully viewing the antiquities of *York*, the dwelling of at least two of the " *Roman* emperors, *Severus* and *Constantius*, I found a part of a wall yet standing, which " is undoubtedly of that time. It is the south wall of the *Mint-yard*, formerly the hospi- " tal of St. *Laurence* (*z*); it consists of a multangular tower, which did lead to *Bootham-* " *bar*, and about ——— of a wall, which ran the length of *Coning-street*, as he who shall " attentively view it on both sides may discern.

" The out-side to the river is faced with a very small *saxum quadratum* of about four inches " thick, and laid in levels like our modern brick-work; but the length of the stones is " not observed, but are as they fell out in hewing. From the foundation twenty courses " of these small squared stones are laid, and over them five courses of *Roman* brick. " These bricks are laid some length-ways, some end-ways in the wall, and were called *la-* " *teres diatoni*; after these five courses of brick, other twenty two courses of small square " stones, as before described, are laid, which raise the wall ——— feet higher, and then " five more courses of the same *Roman* bricks are laid; beyond which the wall is imper- " fect, and cap'd with modern building. Note, that in all this height there is no case- " ment or loophole, but one entire and uniform wall, from which we may infer, that the " wall was built some courses higher, after the same order. The bricks were to be as tho- " roughs, or, as it were, so many new foundations, to that which was to be superstruct- " ed, and to bind the two sides together firmly; for the wall it self is only faced with small " square stone, and the middle thereof filled with mortar and pebble.

" These bricks are about seventeen inches long of our measure, about eleven inches " broad, and two and an half thick. This, having caused several to be carefully measur- " ed, I give in round numbers, and do find them to agree very well with the *Roman* foot, " which the learned antiquary *Graves* has left us, viz. of its being about half an inch less " than ours. They seem to have shrunk in the baking more in the breadth than in the " length, which is but reasonable, because of its easier yielding that way; and so for the " same reason more in thickness; for we suppose them to have been designed in the mold " for three *Roman* inches. This demonstrates *Pliny*'s measures to be true, where he says, " *genera laterum tria, didoron, quo utimur longum sesquipede, latum pede*; and not those of " *Vitruvius* where they are extant; the copy of *Vitruvius*, where it describes the *Didoron* " and its measures, being vitious. And indeed all I have yet seen with us in *England*, are " of *Pliny*'s measure, as at *Leicester* in the *Roman* ruin there, called the *Jews-wall*, and at " St. *Albans*, as I remember, as well as with us at *York*.

" I shall only add this remark, that proportion and uniformity, even in the minutest " parts of building, is to be plainly observed, as this miserable ruin of *Roman* workman- " ship shews. In our *Gothick* buildings there is a total neglect of measure and proportion " of the courses, as though that was not much material to the beauty of the whole; " whereas, indeed, in nature's works, it is from the symmetry of the very grain whence a- " rises much of the beauty.

I have to remark upon this very particular description of the Doctor's, that the stones of the wall are not of the grit-kind, but of the common free-stone; there being no occasion to fear fire in an exterior part of a fortification. Next, that the building of the tower is the same on the inside of it, as on the out, and has a communication with *Bootham-bar*, under the *vallum* or rampart that hides it that way. The foundation of this tower is of a singular shape and strength, the angle it commands requiring the latter in an extraordinary degree. And the form of it comes the nearest a circle that any such building can admit of. The wall that runs from it S. E. makes a streight line, and, no doubt, anciently went along the east side of *Conyng-street*, as far as the *Foss* (*a*). The foundations of all the houses in the line, discovering the marks of it. I saw a piece of it laid open in *Lendal*, about twenty or thirty yards below the *Mint-yard* gates, which happened by an accident of digging a drain. But the cement, that composed this fragment, was so exceeding hard, that the workmen had much ado to lower it to their level; in their way they threw up a small *denarius* or two, but they were obliterated. What this very high wall and particular fortification, without any *vallum*, and on this side the river, could serve for, I cannot conjecture. The reader is presented with a view of this piece of antiquity, as it appears at this day, in the annexed plate.

Since the time of Dr. *Lister*, a stone, with an inscription on it, was discovered in digging a cellar in *Conyng-street* in the line of the *Roman* wall aforesaid. The stone is of *grit*, the letters large, and is now up in the back-yard-wall of Mrs. *Crumpton*'s house, below the *Black-swan*-inn in that street. Our countryman, and late diligent antiquary Mr. *Thoresby* of *Leeds*, gave the *royal society* an account of it in these words:

(*b*) " The *Roman* monument, lately discovered at *York*, was found not far from the *Ro-* PLATE VIII. " *man* wall and multangular tower, which Dr. *Lister* has given so curious a description Fig. 6.

(*y*) Abridg. of philosoph. transact. v. 5.

(*z*) A mistake it is S. *Leonard's*

(*a*) See the plan of the city, where a line is drawn from this tower along *Conyng-street* and *Castlegate* to the *Foss*. I take it to make an interiour fortification to the city. *Clifford*'s tower, whose mount is certainly *Roman*, commands one end of it.

(*b*) Abridg. of philosoph. transf. v. 5.

" of. This monument, dedicated to the *genius*, or tutelar deity of the place, is not of
" the courſe rag that the generality of the *Roman* altars are, but of a finer grit like that at
" my lord *Fairfax*'s houſe in *York*. It is twenty one inches long and eleven broad; and is
" inſcribed Genio loci feliciter; there was a larger ſtone found with it, but without
" any inſcription; nor is there upon either of them the repreſentation of a ſerpent or a
" young viſage; by both which the ancients ſometimes deſcribed theſe dii topici. If
" the name had been added, it would have gratified the curioſity of ſome of our *neſteric*
" antiquaries. But they muſt yet acquieſce, for ought I know, in their old dvi, who is
" ſaid to be the tutelar deity of the city of the *Brigantes*.

" The author of this votive monument ſeems to have the ſame ſuperſtitious veneration
" for the *genius* of *York*, as thoſe at *Rome* had for theirs, whoſe name they were prohibited
" to mention or enquire after. Hence it is, that upon their coins the name of this deity
" is never expreſſed, but in a more popular manner by Genivs P. R. or Pop. Rom.

The dedication of this votive tablet, for altar its ſhape will not admit of, is moſt certainly a great compliment paid to our city; and *Rome* it ſelf could not have had a greater in
its fulleſt glory. It is well known that the ſuperſtitious *Romans* believed a good and a
bad *genius* did attend both perſons, cities, and countries; hence *Virgil* at *Aeneas* his entrance
into *Italy*,

> —————————geniumque loci primamque deorum
> *Tellurem, &c.*

Genio Pop. Rom. in coins is common quite through the *Pagan* empire; nor is there wanting many inſtances in *Gruter, Camden, Monfaucon,* and *Horſley,* of altars, and other monuments, dedicated to the *genii* of perſons, places, *&c.* *(c).* But yet I never met with an
inſcription of this ſort, with ſo remarkable an adjunct, as *feliciter* to it. It ſeems they
thought the tutelar deity of Eboracvm was happily placed by being guardian of the imperial city of *Britain*, and gave this teſtimony of their veneration of it. Genio loci feliciter [*regnanti*] or ſome ſuch word, ſeems to be the ſence of the inſcription; and it can
hardly bear any harſher conſtruction.

Concerning the god Dvi, which Mr. *Thoreſby* mentions, there is a remarkable inſcription, on an altar, given us both in *Camden* and *Gruter*, relating to that deity. Mr. *Camden* ſays it was found near *Gretland*, on the *Calder*, in the weſt riding of *Yorkſhire*; and he ſaw
it at the ſeat of Sir *John Savile* Kt. Mr. *Horſley* found it lying in the church-yard of *Conyng-
ton*, and took an exact draught of both ſides of the altar, with their inſcriptions. It may
be ſeen in his *Britan. Rom.* fig. xviii, *Yorkſhire.* The reading of it is thus, Dvi civitatis brigantvm, *et numinibus Auguſtorum,* Titus Aurelius Aurelianus *dedicat pro ſe et
ſuis.* On the reverſe is Antonino *tertium et* Geta *conſulibus.*

Whether this Dvi be the name of the deity, omitted in the former inſcription; or Civitas Brigantvm, expreſsly means the city, the province, or both, I ſhall not determine. The word *civitas*, I have before explained; Mr. *Camden* ſeems poſitive, that this
Dvi was the peculiar and *local genius* of the *city it ſelf.* By the beſt conjecture that can be
made of the date on the reverſe of the altar, it was erected *A. C.* ccviii, when *Severus* and
his two ſons were at *York*; and the inſcription appears to be a high compliment paid, by
ſome commander, to the three emperors, and to the *tutelar genius* of the place they then
York, reſided in.

As the heathens had their good *genii*, ſo likewiſe their evil ones are traditionally handed
down to us; by thoſe many idle ſtories of local ghoſts which the common people do ſtill
believe haunt cities, towns and family ſeats, famous for their antiquities and decays. Of
this ſort are the apparitions at *Verulam, Silcheſter, Reculver,* and *Rocheſter*; the Demon
of *Tedworth*, the black-dog of *Wincheſter*, the Padfoot of *Pontefrete*, and the 𝕭𝕒𝕣𝕘𝕦𝕖𝕱 of
York, &c.

But the greateſt and moſt remarkable diſcovery that we have yet made, happened about
the year 1686. The honour of being the firſt obſervator of this, as well as the next, is due
to the memory of our northern antiquary, Mr. *Thoreſby.* He ſent an account of them to
the *royal ſociety*, which was afterwards publiſhed in their tranſactions. The aforeſaid writer
has been a little more explicit about theſe venerable reliques in his *Ducatus Leod:* And I
ſhall make uſe of his own words from thence.

(d) " The ſepulchral monument of the ſtandard-bearer to the ninth legion was dug up
" in *Trinity-gardens*, near *Micklegate, York*; and was happily reſcued by *Bryan Fairfax* Eſq
" from the brutiſh workmen, who had broke it in the midſt, and were going to make uſe
" of it for two throughs, as they call them, to bind a wall; but by that worthy gentle-
" man's direction it was walled upright with the inſcription and effigies to the front, and
" is ſince removed to the gardens of Sir *Henry Goodrick* at *Ribſton.*— The brick had been
" ſeveral times made uſe of, with broken ſtones and brick-bats, by Mr. *Smith* in making

(c) Genii, Lares, et Penates, are frequently uſed by the (d) *Thoreſby*'s ducat. *Leodiſenſis.* p. 320.
Romans, as ſynonimous terms. *Vide Monfaucon,* v.1.

" molds

" molds for casting bells. Upon my enquiry after inscriptions in that ancient city, he " recollected himself, that he had seen some old letters, but thought the brick was lost, " though upon search we found the piece, which is inscribed LEGIO IX. VIC. This is also " an argument of the peace those parts enjoyed at that time, which I take to be the lat- " ter end of *Severus* his reign; making of bricks, casting up highways, being the usual " employment for soldiers at such vacancies. Fig. 7.

I forbear giving our old gentleman's reading of the first inscription, as well as his historical account of it; because I think Mr. *Horsley*, perhaps by standing on the other's shoulders, has done it much better. From his work then I extract the following account,

" (*e*) This very curious and remarkable inscription was first discovered in *Trinity-yard* " in *Micklegate*, and is now at *Ribston* near *Wetherby*, being carefully preserved, under cover " in a garden belonging to Sir *Henry Goodrick*, who knows how to set a just value on this " curious piece of antiquity. It has been communicated to the publick by Mr. *Thoresby*, " in the *philosophical transactions*; and from thence it has been inserted in the late edition of " *Camden*'s *Britannia*, but ill represented as to the shape and cut of the letters. Dr. *Gale*, " in his edition of *Antonini itinerarium*, has done it more justice; for the letters are well " cut, strong and clear, and all of them yet very legible; particularly the LEGIO VIIII, " at the end of the fourth line is distinct and certain, which is the great curiosity of the in- " scription. The principal difficulty, in respect to the reading, is in the beginning of " the second line. Mr. *Thoresby*, who gives us no part of the inscription but the last line " and this, would have it to be *lubens voluit*, which is neither agreeable to the letters them- " selves, or the situation of them, nor at all consistent with the obvious sense of the rest " of the inscription. Upon sight of the original, I was soon convinced these letters were " L VOLTF, the last three L T F being all connected together; and they must I think " be read *Lucii voltinia* [*tribu*] *filius*; so that it expresses the father's tribe, though the son " was of *Vienna* in *Gaul*, which was a famous *Roman* colony. *Provincia Viennensis* was one " of the seventeen provinces of *Gaul*, which were under the *praefectus praetorio Galliarum*. " This *tribus voltinia* is likewise mentioned upon another inscription (*f*) in *Cumberland*. " It may seem strange perhaps, that the F for *filius* should be joined in the same character " that includes two letters of the preceding words; but we have an instance of the like " kind on another inscription at great *Salkild* in *Cumberland*, where the same cypher in- " cludes two letters belonging to two different words (*g*). The flourish annexed to the foot " of the first N in the third line, is somewhat peculiar, but very distinct. The word *Ru-* " *finus* occurs in another of our inscriptions (*h*). The rest has no diffiulty; and as for the " *legio nona*, I have given a full account of it in the history of the *Roman* legions in *Bri-* " *tain*. The figure of this *signifer* is placed above the inscription with his *vexillum* in one " hand, or the *signum* of a *cohort* according to Mr. *Ward*, whose conjecture I shall add, " and a thing like a basket in the other. There is somewhat of much the same appea- " rance in the hand of a soldier upon a funeral stone at *Skirway* in *Scotland*. This may " possibly represent the vessel for holding or measuring of corn, which was part of a *Ro-* " *man* soldier's pay." What our author adds from Mr. *Ward* is this:

" I am inclined to think, what the image holds in his right hand is the ensign of a *co-* " *hort* or *manipulus*. It seems very possible, from a passage in *Caesar*, that every *cohort* " had its particular ensign; his words are these (*i*), *quartae cohortis omnibus fere centurioni-* " *bus occisis, signifero interfecto, signo amisso, &c.* Now in all the legionary coins of *Mark* " *Anthony*, the eagle is placed between two such ensigns as this image holds in his right " hand. As the eagle therefore was the standard of the whole legion, one would be led " to think, these were designed to represent the ensigns of the *cohorts*, as next in or- " der. But since some very learned men have thought them rather the ensigns of the " *manipuli*, I would leave every one to judge of them as he pleases. What the image " holds in his left hand, I take to be the *vexillum* of a century. The form of the *vexil-* " *lum* seems, I think, to favour this opinion; for it was four-square, as appears by a " draught of it given above (*k*).

I have nothing to add after this particular description of the monument, by these great antiquaries, but to present the reader with a draught of it. It was taken by scale, so that the height of the whole, the figure, and the letters, may be measured. By comparing this with Mr. *Horsley*'s a sensible difference will appear; but whether the drawer or engraver was in fault I know not. I stood over my workman whilst mine was taken; and the monument is exactly as I have represented it. This curious piece of antiquity remains still under cover, in the gardens at *Ribston*; but I could wish that the possessor would return it back to *York*, to be reposited in some safe place, as a lasting monument of its ancient glory. PLATE VIII. Fig 8.

(*e*) *Horsley*'s *Brit. Rom.* f. viii. *Yorkshire*, p. 308.
(*f*) N° LXIII.
(*g*) N° LI.
(*h*) N° XCVI. *Northumberland*.
(*i*) *De bello* Gallico, l. II. c. 15.
(*k*) *Northumberland*, N° LX.

Such

Such a curious observer as Dr. *Lister*, and the other antiquaries I have mentioned were, one would imagine could not let a noble *Roman arch*, yet standing in a principal gate of the city, escape their notice. And yet I do not find that any of them have made the least mention of it. The arch I speak of, is, the chief in *Micklegate-bar* by the port-cullis; which being wholly built of *Milnstone-grit*, and a true segment of a circle, I always considered it as *Roman*; but my small skill in architecture would not let me absolutely call it so, till much better authority confirmed my notion. When I had the honour a year or two ago, to walk about the city with lord *Burlington*, to shew his lordship the poor remains of antiquity we can now boast of; I was much pleased that I had an opportunity to ask the opinion of a person whose peculiar taste and skill in all branches of architecture has rendred his lordship the admiration of the present age. Accordingly I brought him under the arch, and desired his opinion of it; his lordship having considered it a little, said pleasantly this must be a *Roman* arch or else built since *Inigo Jones*'s time. The improbability of the latter is apparent enough. In short his lordship assured me that it was a *Roman* arch and of the *Tuscan* order. The arch is a *triplit*, and supports a massy pile of *Gothick* turrets, *&c.* which no doubt has been frequently renewed upon it, since the strong foundation was built by those admirable architects the *Romans*. It seems yet to bid defiance to time; though probably erected fifteen hundred years ago; and when its foundations come to be razed some ages hence, some stone perhaps in the building will be found to bear an inscription sufficient to denote its antiquity; and be another testimony of the glory of the once famous EBORACVM. As it is at this day I present the reader with a view of it; there is here and there a stone of another kind put in, where the old ones have failed; but that does not alter the symetry and proportion of the arch. The gate faces the grand road to CALCARIA or *Tadcaster*; and is placed near the center of the *vallum* and wall which fortifies this part of the city. At a good bow-shot from it is a place called the *mount*; which is said to have been thrown up in our late civil wars; but to me it seems of much greater antiquity; and I take it to have been an outwork, or *Roman* fortress, erected for the greater security of this *land side* of the city, as I may so call it. Whoever will take a view of the antient LINDVM, *Lincoln*, drawn out by that diligent and intelligent antiquary Dr. *Stukeley*, will find such an outwork as this but much larger to have been made, *extra muros* of that famous city *(l)*.

There has nothing else in my time, of stone or sculpture, been discovered worth notice; some miserable remains of the latter excepted. These I have collected from different parts of the city, where they are stuck up in old walls, or lie neglected in courts or gardens. On the church yard wall of St. *Laurence*, *extra Walmgate*, lie two very antient statues, prostrate; but whether *Roman* or *Saxon*, *Pagan* or *Christian*, since better antiquaries than my self have been puzzled, I shall not determine *(m)*. I submit them to the reader; the things they hold in their hands, are also represented, as well as they may be, by them. But the head which is stuck in the wall underneath these statues is certainly *Roman*, both from the gritt and sculpture that its age demonstrates. In *Trinity-yard Micklegate* is a base, which has two feet of a statue upon it; and on it has been a large inscription; but *heu dolor!* obliterated; as I take it, not by time, but malice, or ignorance, or the mistaken foolish zeal of our *christian* ancestors. The rest, such as they are, I submit to the reader's judgment.

PLATE VIII. Fig. 9. Fig. 10. Fig. 2. 12.

The last thing which I shall take notice of, in relation to the *Romans*, is the quantity of their *coins*, *signets*, *fibulae*, *urns*, *sarcophagi*, *&c.* which have been found with us. As to the *coins*, though no doubt every age, since their time, has discovered many; yet an accident in the last has thrown out more than could be seen without it. This has happened by the quantity of ground dug up for gardens, in and about the city of late years; but then, though several by this means are found, yet we may presume many more are destroyed by it. The loads of manure which the gardiners use, to enrich the soil to their purpose, has by its nitrous quality, perfectly dissolved all those, which time had any way eroded before-hand.

Whatever has been discovered in *York*, of these curiosities, both of late years and anciently, are now so dispersed, that it is not possible to give any particular account of them. Indeed I never heard of any exceeding rare that were found; being mostly of the *bass empire*; and, amongst those, *Geta*'s coins are with us, the commonest of any. About four years ago a *gold Chrispus* was taken up, in a garden, next to the house of *William Metcalf* Esq; in *Bootham*. The coin is well preserved, and being placed amongst the *rarissimi* by the collectors, I have thought fit to exhibit a draught of it in the next plate. It is at present in the possession of *Bryan Fairfax*, Esq; to whom the author of this work presented it.

PLATE VIII. Fig. 13.

But what lends a greater lustre to our subject are the coins of the emperor *Severus*, which *Camden* speaks of; and which are inscribed on the reverse, adds that author, COL. EBO-

(l) Stukely's *itin. curiosum.* See the plan of *York* for the *Mount*.

(m) Dr. *Gale* supposed them to be the statues of a *Roman* senator and his lady; but I am not of that opinion by the form of the beard on one.

P. 60.

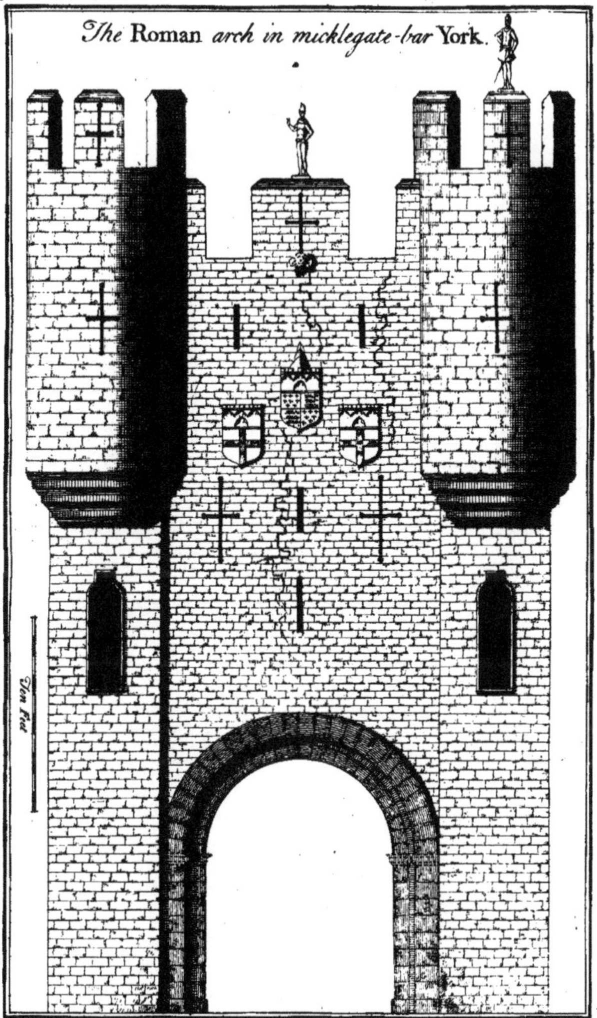

J. Haynes delin. W. H. Toms Sculp.

William Drake of Barnoldswick-cotes Esq;, in regard to this extraordinary monument of Roman architecture in Britain, & in respect to his relation, y author of this history, presents this plate. 1736

RACVM LEGIO VI. VICTRIX (*n*). He does not name his authority for this assertion, nor does he say that he ever saw the coin. But in dean *Gale*'s itinerary *Goltzius* is quoted in the margin as the author from whence Mr. *Camden* might take it; and it is very probable he did so. That learned *German* antiquary in his *Thesaurus rei antiquariae*, C. xviii. *coloniarum, municipiorumque* Romanorum *nomina & epitheta*, p. 239, gives the reading of the reverse of one of the emperor *Severus* his coins as Mr. *Camden* has expressed it. But it is a pity he did not at the same time publish a drawing of this curious coin, as also of the preceding one of *Geta*'s, whose reverse was as he writes COL. DIVANA LEG. XX. VIC. in honour of that legion stationed at *Chester*. It would not only have been a very particular and extraordinary memorial of those two important stations, but a great illustration to the whole *Roman* history of *Britain*. Nothing being more expressive, in that sence than inscriptions on coins, medals, and stones. I am aware that the single authority of *Goltzius* is only to this point; and also that it is, and has been disputed by our modern antiquaries; that neither *Mediobarbus*, nor Monsieur *Vaillant* in his colony coins, makes any mention of any such stamp; yet that does not argue, but their elder brother in antiquity, might have seen coins which never might fall into their hands. Besides, it is at present acknowledged that the authority of *Goltzius* is every day gaining strength; by a number of curious coins, only mentioned by him, and which have lately been brought to light. Upon the whole, it is not my business to dispute this matter at all; and I am only sorry I cannot exhibite a drawing of this remarkable coin, for I am very sure it would have given a very great lustre to my subject.

When I mention *Mediobarbus* and *Vaillant*, I must take notice that the coins struck in honour of *Severus*, *Caracalla* and *Geta*, which have on their reverse VICTORIAE BRITANNICAE, & CONCORDIA AVGVSTORVM, as quoted in those authors, were, in all probability, struck at *York*. For the former was stamped in honour of his *Caledonian* expedition, after his return to our city; as the latter bare testimony of the reconcilement he supposed he made a little before his death, betwixt his sons. So the title of BRITANNICVS MAXIMVS, which he certainly assumed at *York*, as lord of the whole island of *Britain*; and struck upon his coins; can no where be supposed to have its original stamp better than in the same city where he triumphed for the greatest glory of his reign. It is not to be imagined but that the mint attended the imperial court; for no sooner was a great action performed, but the whole empire was made acquainted with it, by some signal reverse struck immediately upon the current coin.

Nor have we a less claim to those medals coined in honour of the deification of the emperor *Constantius Chlorus*; and the inauguration of his son *Constantine the great*. The ceremony of both these remarkable events, having been performed, as I have elsewhere shewn, at EBORACVM. But, as there appears nothing inscribed on all these coins to support this notion, at least that I have seen, I shall leave it as a conjectural hint only; for neither the inscriptions on the *head*, *reverse*, or *exergue*, of any of them, bear any testimony of their being struck at EBORACVM.

Signets, or Seals, of different sorts, both what the *Italians* call *Cameos* and *Intaglios*, have most certainly been found in or about our city, in every age since the time of the *Romans*; but how lost again or dispersed is uncertain. Two or three have fallen into my hands lately discovered; all of which I think curious enough, not only to exhibit a drawing of, but to give a short dissertation upon them.

The first was discovered in the *Mannor-garden*; and had an unlucky stroke of the spade Fig. 14.
cross it when it was dug up. It is a *Beryl* on which is engraven, as I think, a *Pallas*; the spear, shield, snake, &c, denoting that goddess. But what makes this stone more remarkable is, that it has been set and made use of for a private seal or device, for a person who probably found it two or three hundred years ago. *Sigillum meum apposui* is a necessary appendix to all ancient deeds, grants, &c; before signing, as well as sealing, was used. The nobility had seals with the impress of their different bearings upon them; but the commonality made use of any device they thought proper to invent for that purpose. If persons had no proper seals of their own, they generally procured the affixing of some more authentick seal; as in the form of several charters,

—— *Quia sigillum meum penitus est incognitum ideo sigillum* —— *apponi procuravi.*

This then must have been a curious seal for the person inscribed on the verge of it; and by calling it *secretum*, the private seal, he seemed to place greater confidence in this than his publick one. The name of the man *R. Richard* or *Robert de Sepesheved*, probably some monk of the abby, is *Sheepshead*. Hevet is head in the more modern *English*, so Gatey-hevet, *Gates-head*, Great-hevet, *Great-head*, &c; are other surnames of that sort.

The next seal is cut on another *Beryl*, but of a different and more extraordinary impress Fig. 15.
than the former. It is a ludicrous representation, in hierogliphicks, of the warm love, to call it no worse, that *Otho*, before he was emperor, had for *Poppaea Sabina*; the lady whom

(*n*) *Britannia.* See *York*; this is one of the arguments to prove EBORACVM a colony as well as a *Municipium* by *Camden*. See also chap. vi. of this work, on this head.

R *Nero*

4

Nero took from him, married, and afterwards killed with a kick on the belly; when she was with child by the monster. The story of *Otho*'s amours with *Poppaea* is related very fully in *Tacitus, ann.* 13, in *Suetonius, in vitâ Othonis*; and also in *Plutarch, vitâ Galbae*. By these authorities it appears that there was a sham marriage trumped up betwixt the two lovers, in order to prevent *Nero*'s taking her from *Otho*; the *Romans* holding it highly unlawful to take another mans wife from him. But this did not hinder the tyrant from committing the rape; and 'tis matter of wonder that he let *Otho* escape with his life; which he did, though he sent him *propraetor*, into a very remote province; a kind of an honourable banishment; whilst *Nero* enjoyed the lady, and at length dispatched her in the manner as has been related.

This satyrical representation has the figure of a *Priapus*; dressed out with all the emblems of lust imaginable. It has a cock's head with the mouth open; the body of a *penis* on which is planted *Cupid*'s wings; the tail of a goat, and satyrs legs; the thighs of which plainly represent the *testes*. This strange creature is offering a bright flaming torch, or a dart, upon an altar with one of his feet. The inscription on the verge OTHO POP SABI and underneath F C, thus read, *Otho Poppaeae Sabinae facem conjugalem* [*offert.*] or some such other word; the verb being oftner understood then expressed in longer *Roman* inscriptions than this.

I must here acknowledge that I was led into the story and reading of this seal, by that excellent antiquary *Roger Gale* Esq; by whose sagacious judgment, in these matters, many dark and obscure inscriptions have been brought to light. It is well known what regard the superstitious *Romans*, especially their ladies, paid to the *virile member*. *Priapus* the god of the gardens as he is called, was furnished with one of an enormous size; which the good matrons, in their *orgia*, worshipped with uncommon veneration. The *Romans* had this god and the custom of worshipping him from the *Ægyptians* and *Greeks*. Diodorus Siculus *narrat* Priapi *ritus originem duxisse a phallo, quem consecratum ab* Iside Ægyptii *solemni pompa in* Osiridis *festis diebus circumferebant.*

Origo.

Cum Typhon Osyridem *fratrem* Ægypti *regem membratim concidisset*, Isis, *mortui vidua, membra conquisivit anxiè*; *&* verpam *forte repertam consecravit.* Roma *antiq. & modern.*

But though the ladies had this god in such reverence, the men we find by *Horace* made a jest of it; where he makes the statue say,

Olim truncus eram ficulnus, inutile lignum,
Cum faber incertus, scamnum faceretne Priapum,
Maluit esse Deum. *Hor.* Sat.

Imitated.

Once I was common wood, a shapeless log,
Thrown out a pissing post for every dog.
The workman stood considering, with his tool,
Whether to make a god or a joint-stool; At length he chose a god.

Mounfaucon has a short dissertation on the *Roman Priapus*, which the good father has wrapped up in the *Latin* tongue, that none but learned readers should understand it.

I shall follow his example, for modesty sake, and give a quotation or two from him in his own words. The reader may observe from hence that the cock's head and comb, *crista galli* was a common hieroglyphick of lust amongst the *Romans*.

(*o*) *Monstrosas alias profanorum impurorumque hominum imagines oculis castis subjicere non licet*; *quamvis illae magno numero in musaeis variis compareant. Una ex imaginibus, a clarissimo viro* Cauceo *publicatis, pretomen exhibet hominis cui vultus loco phallus apponitur, seu ithyphallus*, coronaque galli gallinacei cristae similis, *cum inscriptione graeca*, σωτὴρ κόσμου, servator mundi.

Spurcissimus alius & infami τῶν αἰδοίων ἐγέρσει *execrandus, qui* galli gallinacei cristam barbamque habet, *ac marsupium manu tenet, ideo Mercurius* Priapus *potest dici.*

The seal was found somewhere in *Conyng-street*, and it was presented me by Mr. *Beckwith* the jeweler, *York*. I have caused the drawing of it to be taken just as big again as the stone really is for better observation.

Fig. 16, 17. The next is a gem that I bought in our city of a person in whose family he said it had been above forty years; and it was always reported to him to be found in it, but where he could not inform me. The stone is a beautiful large *onyx*, with the poetical representation of *Bellerophon*, *Pegasus*, and *Chimaera* cut upon it.

Upon shewing this antique seal to Mr. *Gale*, he told me he could produce a drawing of the very same *intaglio* published in a book of antique gems, coins, *&c.* in the *elector Palatine*'s cabinet. Accordingly he fetched the book and they exactly agreed in the figures; the difference only, this being cut on an *Onyx*, the other on a *Sardonyx* and is somewhat larger (*p*).

(*o*) *Antiquitates de Monfaucon.* Tom. I.

(*p*) *Gemmae & numismata in thesauro* Palatino *illustrat. & authore* L. Begero, *serenis elector.* Palat. *Antiquario & Biblioth.* Heidelbergae. MDCLXXXV.

The

The story of *Bellerophon* and *Chimaera* is very well known by the *connoiseurs* in classical learning. The monster is represented to have

> *Caudaque serpentis, caputque leonae.*
> A lyonesse's head and serpent's tail.

Again,

> *Qui fieri potuit triplici cum corpore & unâ*
> *Primo* leo, *postremo* draco, *medio ipsa* Chimaera,
> *Ore foras acrem flaret de corpore flammam.*
>
> Who moves its triple body join'd in one;
> A lyon's head, behind a dragon shewn,
> *Chimera* does usurp the middle space;
> And flames of fire come darting from its face.

The plate represents both.

About two years ago was found in *Walmgate*, *York*, I think in digging a cellar, the little image represented, in the plate.

It is certainly an image of *Chronus tempus*, or *Saturn*; but whether *Roman* or no is uncertain. Though a particular elegance in it, as well as the mixed metal it is cast with, denotes it of *Roman* workmanship. If so, this image has in all probability been one of their *Penates* or household-gods. A hollowness within seems to shew as if it had been set upon a prop for chamber worship. But I leave the figures as drawn in both views to the reader's judgement. Fig. 18, 91.

By an accident of opening a large piece of ground to dig clay for bricks, betwixt *Bootham* and *Clifton*, on the left hand, at about half a quarter of a mile distance from the city, have been disclosed and thrown up several of their *Sarcophagi*, or stone coffins; and a great quantity of urns, of different colours, sizes and shapes. The law of the twelve tables expresly says *hominem mortuum in urbe, ne sepelito neve urito*, which ordained that the dead, and the rites belonging to them, should be removed to some distance from the city. This law, which they likewise had from the *Greeks*, the *Athenians* were strict in; but we are told the *Romans* frequently dispensed with it. What was then practised at *Rome*, we may believe was the same at *York*; and indeed, I never heard of any urns being found within, though many hundreds, I may say, have been discovered without the city. *Stone-coffins*, indeed, have been frequently dug up, and some monuments discovered; as LVCIVS DVCCIVS, *&c*; but no urns that I ever heard of. It is natural to suppose that they lighted their funeral piles *extra urbem*; and we are told by *Herodian* that the CAMPVS MARTIS was the common place for such solemnities. This place which was formerly an open field, is now the principal part of new *Rome*; and if the reader will re-examine the draught of *Romulus*'s wall, and the *campus martis* without it, which I have given from *Donatus*, he will find that it exactly corresponds with our burial place at *York*. *Clifton fields* have not been enclosed a century; and were formerly open enough to have been the CAMPVS MARTIVS to EBORACVM. There is a plain *tumulus*, beyond the brickhilns, on which a wind miln has been placed; and no doubt if the ground was to be opened that way several more buried remains would be discovered. The gate which leads to this grand repository of their dead, is called *Bootham-bar*; which name, our learned dean *Gale* observed, might be deduced from the *British* word *Boeth*, which signifies *burning*; as a gate out of which the *Romans* used to burn their dead. I shall not contradict this etymology, it is apt enough, and did not another bid much fairer for it, which I must mention in the sequel, it would do us a great deal of honour. But be that as it may, the place I have described, was most certainly, in their time, a common place of interment on this side the city; though by what follows, it will appear that in others parts, *extra muros*, urns, *&c.* have been discovered; which shews that if the like accident of digging should happen elsewhere, the same curiosities might be found, though perhaps not in such quantities.

What has been remarked by Dr. *Lister*, Mr. *Thoresby*, *&c.* and sent up to the *Royal Society*, concerning these sepulchral repositories of the ancients, shall be given in their own words; which with some further discoveries and observations of my own, will dismiss the whole affair.

And first the learned Dr.

" *(q)* Here are found at *York*, in the road or *Roman* street, out of *Micklegate*, and " likewise by the river side where the *Brick-kilns* now are, urns of three different tempers, " *viz.* 1. Urns of a *blewish gray colour*, having a great quantity of coarse sand wrought in " with the clay. 2. Others of the same colour having either a very fine sand mixed with " it full of *mica*, or cat silver, or made of clay naturally sandy. 3. *Red urns* of fine clay, " with little or no sand in it. These last are quite throughout of a red colour like fine

(q) Ab. of the phyl tranf. v. 3.

" bole.

" bole. Also many of these red pots are elegantly adorned with figures in *basso relievo*; " and usually the workman's name, which, I think, others have mistaken for the person's " name buried there, upon the bottom or cover as IANARIVS, and such like; but that " very name I have seen upon several pots both here and at *Aldburgh*; after all, these are " glazed inside and out with a kind of varnish of a bright coral colour.

" The composition of the first kind of pots did first give me occasion to discover the " places where they were made. The one about the midway betwixt *Wilberfoss* and *Barnby* " *on the moor*, six miles from *York*, in the sand hills or rising ground where now the *warren* " is; where I have found scattered widely up and down, broken pieces of urns, slag and " cinders. The other is on the *sand hills*, at *Santon* near *Brigg* in *Lincolnshire*.

I shall omit what the Dr. observes further on these sort of urns, and give Mr. *Toresby*'s account who followed him.

" (*r*) I have added to my *Roman* curiosities two entire urns, both of the *blewish gray* " colour, of different forms, with some of the burnt bones in them; the lesser of them is " almost in the form of the *Roman simpulum* or *guttus*, and by the narrowness of the neck " seems rather to have been a kind of *lacrimatory*, or vessel for some kind of liquid mat- " ter rather than ashes. I have likewise part of an *aquaeduct*, which is turned in form of " a screw on the inside, has a narrow neck at one end to put into the open end of the " next, and several of these each a foot long and four inches broad were found thus placed " in the *Roman* burial place at *York*, by the river side out of *Bootham-bar*, which was in- " disputably the place the *Romans* made use of for that end, as appears by the great num- " ber of urns frequently there found when they dig the clay for bricks. And that it " continued the place of their sepulture, after that custom of burning, introduced in the " tyrannous dictatorship of *Sylla*, was abolished, is evident by a remarkable *Hypogaeum*, " without any urns in it, discovered last winter, 1696; it was large enough to contain " two or three corpses, and was paved with brick nigh two inches thick, eight in breadth " and length being equilaterally square; upon which was a second pavement of the same " *Roman* brick, to cover the seams of the lower, and prevent the working up of vermin. " But those that covered the vault were the most remarkable that I ever saw, being about " two foot square, and of a proportionable thickness." Again,

" (*s*) I have procured part of the bottom, which consisted of several such pieces, for " the convenience of baking, of an old *Roman* coffin, which was lately dug up in their " burying place out of *Bootham-bar* at *York*. 'Tis of the red clay, but not so fine as the " urns, having a greater quantity of course sand wrought up in the clay. As to the " form, which is entire as it was at first moulded, it is fourteen inches and a half long " and eleven broad, at the narrow end, and nigh twelve and a half at the broader; this " was the lowest part for the feet, and the rest were proportionably broader till it came " to the shoulder; it is an inch thick besides the ledges, which are one broad and two " thick, and extend from the bottom of either side to within three inches of the top, " where it is wholly flat and somewhat thinner for the next to lie upon it; which several " parts were thus joined together by some pin I presume, for at the end of each tile is a " hole that would receive a common slate pin. These edges are wrought a little hollow, " I suppose to receive the sides, and at the feet are two contrary notches to fasten the end " piece. This bottom, I should conclude to have consisted chiefly of eight such parts, " from a like character 8 imprest upon the clay by the *Sandapilarius*'s finger before its baking, " but that I somewhat doubt whether numeral figures be of that antiquity in these *European* " parts. I got also some scars of broken urns dug up in Mr. *Giles*'s garden, which are " of the finest clay that I have ever seen, with which was found a *Roman Shuttle*, about " three inches and a half long but not one broad in the very middle; the hollow for the " *licium* being but one fourth of an inch in the broadest part, shews that it was for silk " or very fine linen.

At the same place the aforesaid author gives this account of another discovery. " They " have lately found a very remarkable *lead coffin*, which was about seven foot long, was " enclosed in a prodigious strong one made of oak planks about two inches and a half thick, " which, besides the rivettings, were tacked together with *braggs* or great iron nails: " the nails were four inches long, the heads not die-wise as the large nails now are, but " perfectly flat and an inch broad. Many of them are almost consumed with rust, and " so is the outside of the planks, but the heart of the oak is firm and the lead fresh and " pliable; whereas one found a year ago, 1701, is brittle and almost wholly consumed, " having no planks to guard it. The bones are light and entire, though probably enter- " red 1500 years ago, for it is above so many centuries since that custom of burning gave " place to that more natural one of interring the dead; which according to *Monsieur Mu-* " *ret* was re-introduced by the *Antonines*. I have a thigh bone which is wonderfully light, " and the lower-jaw which was furnished with all its teeth. The *double coffins* were so heavy " that they were forced to drag them out of the dormitory with a team of oxen.

(*r*) Ab. of the phyl. trans. v 3.

(*s*) *Idem.* v. 5. ed. *Jones*.

" (*t*) An

p.65

CAPVT EX Aere ELEGANTISSIMVM

EBORACO REPERTVM

HODIE IN MVSÆO ROGERI GALE ARM: S.R.L.P.R.

An° Dn: MDCCXXXVI. G: Vertue del: & Sculp.

(*t*) " An anonymous writer to the *R. Society* says, there was lately found at the *brick-kilns* " without *Bootham-bar*, an old earthen vessel which is preserv'd in the *musaeum Ashmoleum* " at *Oxford*. It is by some supposed to be an *urn*, by others a *flower pot*; the clay is of " the colour of *Halifax* clay when burnt. The potters part is well perform'd, the face " being boss'd from within with a finger, when upon the wheel, and some strokes of " red paint about the curls of the head and eye-brows, and two red threads about the neck. " On the backside of the vessel a leaf is drawn in red, which is still very fresh, but no " glazing neither upon the clay nor red colour; the face upon the vessel is as large as " that of a middle siz'd woman.

Some other kinds of *urns*, &c. were found at *York*, and had a place in our *Leeds* antiquaries *musaeum*. These he has thought fit to give us the *icones* of; and from his plate, to omit nothing that may illustrate my subject, I have added them to mine.

Roman curiosities found at *York*, and were in Mr. *Thoresby*'s *musaeum*.

The *Roman* brick. LEG. IX. VIC.

Fig. 21. A *Roman Key*, made in the form of a ring to wear upon the finger; found at the *Brick-kilns* out of *Bootham-bar*. PLATE VIII
22. A *Fibula vestiaria* found at the same place.
23. A *Roman Bracelet*, of copper wreathed, found in the *Hypogaeum* already described, *York*, being eight inches in circumference.
24. A bead of earth curiously wrought.
25. Another of blue glass with white snakes of that sort called *adder beads*; or *druids* amulets.
26. Another curiosity enamelled white, red, and dark blue. All these found at the place aforesaid.
27. A sepulchral urn containing near a gallon.
28. Another near a quart.
29. A small one full of the ashes of a child.
30. A small red urn.
31. One of blue.
32. Another of a different form.
33. One of those commonly called *Lacrimatorys*.
34. One of white clay.
35. A red pottle containing half a *congius*.
36. Part of a vessel that seems to have been a *Patera*.
37. One of the parts of a *Roman aqueduct*.
All discovered near the *brick-kilns* aforesaid.

There are more curiosities, I am told, preserved in the *Ashmolean musaeum* at *Oxford*, which were found at *York* in the aforesaid burial place, as amulets, bracelets, &c. but I have not had an opportunity to get drawings of them.

But amongst the many *Roman* curiosities found at *York*, and yet preserved; there are none deserves a place in this work better, than this antique head; which I here exhibit a draught of; as large as the original. It was found in digging a cellar in the *Mannor*, or the ruins of the abbey of St. *Mary's York*, about twenty years ago. It was given to and is preserved by *Roger Gale*, Esq; that gentleman supposes it a *Lucretia*; there being no goddess in all their theology to ascribe it to. For the rest I refer to the plate; which was drawn and engraven by that very ingenious artist, in this kind of sculpture, Mr. *Vertue*; member of the society of antiquaries, *London*. The plate was generously bestowed upon this work by Mr. *Gale*; as a lasting memorial of *Roman* elegance and ingenuity.

Since the accounts hitherto published, there has nothing very remarkable turn'd up in this *Roman* repository of their dead; but urns, and pieces of urns, are, when they dig, still daily discovered. Entire urns, either by their own brittleness, or the labourer's carelesness, are seldom preserved; but any one that pleases may in half an hours time gather a large quantity of fragments. Amongst which, I have pick'd up several pieces of a fine black colour, which adds a fourth sort of urns to Dr. *Lister*'s observation. A *Roman* grave for urns, the floor covered with white sand, two *Sarcophagi*, or stone coffins, were lately discovered; in which last the bones were found very light and dry, but entire. The custom of burning their dead, by the *Romans*, is said to have ceased under the empire of the *Antonines*. But we have good authority to believe that it did not wholly cease amongst them till the empire became *christian* (*u*). And though this expensive and troublesome manner of performing their sepulchral rites was *religiously* observed by the *Greeks* and *Romans*, yet it was then held in abhorrence by several other nations. It seems to have been the peculiar care of the ancients to invent proper methods to preserve human bodies; or, at least some part of them, as long as the world. We all know how readily every part of us un-

(*t*) *Idem* v. 5. edit. *Jones*.

(*u*) Joh Kirkmannus *de funeribus* Romanorum, &c

dergoes a change after death, and will come to a total diffolution; the bones not excepted, unlefs prevented by art. What care and pains muft the *Egyptians* have taken to preferve their *Ptolemys*, *&c.* fome thoufands of years, in the manner as they are found at this day? The *Romans*, tis true, confumed the body, but by the calcination of the bones belonging to it, fome identical part of the man might be preferved to all eternity. Thofe burnt afhes, if carefully preferved, can undergo no other change; and powder'd and mixed up properly, they make the ftrongeft cement that is poffible to be compofed. When the cuftom of burning intermitted, the care of preferving the remains of their friends and relations ftill continued; for then they took care to bury their bodies in huge (x) ftone coffins, of the gritt kind; which by its porofity, would let the liquid part filtre through, and at the fame time preferve the folid. Or they dug graves out of a folid rock or chalk, large enough fometimes for the interment of a family; of which. fort I have feen at *Lincoln* and *Londefburgh*; or elfe built fuch fepulchers for the prefervation of their dead, where the rock was a wanting, as are defcribed above, by Mr. *Thorefby*, to have been found in our *Roman* burial place at *York*. And there is no doubt but when the reft of this ground comes to be laid open, feveral more *Roman* fepultures will be difcovered in it.

Nor, as I hinted before, was this laft mentioned place the only one about our city where urns and ftone coffins are found. For in feveral other parts, where they have had occafion to dig deep, they have been difcovered. Particularly, a few years ago was dug up near the *mount*, out of *Mickle-gate-bar*, a *glafs* and a *leaden* urn, the only one of that fort that I ever heard of. The glafs urn was broke into two or three pieces, but thofe I got and preferved; it was coated on the infide with a fort of a blueifh filver colour, like that of a looking-glafs; and is what our philofophers call the *electrum* of the ancients. The leaden one was immediately fold, by the workmen who found it, to a plummer; whofe ignorance fuffered him to beat it together, and melt it down, before I was informed of the accident. A ftupidity very common, but unpardonable by an antiquary.

And now, having conducted this brave race of men to their graves; I cannot leave them at a fuller period. And, indeed, it was not long after their deferting *Britain*, that the fometime dreadful *Roman* name and arm, which, for many ages, had fpread terror and conqueft through the then known world, was torn in pieces, loft, funk, and buried in an abyfs, never to rife again. Rome is ftill in *Italy*, and Eboracvm is *York*; but alas! how mutilated from both their former ftates may be eafily conjectured. I fhall beg leave conclude this head with two lines of an old poet, in a reflection of his on the deftruction of *Carthage*;

> (y) *Et querimur, genus infelix! humano labore*
> *Membra aevo, cum regno palam moriantur, & urbes.*

> Unhappy men! to mourn our lives fhort date,
> When *cities*, *realms* and *empires* fhare our fate.

(x) *Mounfaucon* has a learned differtation of the *Roman* Sarcophagi, and places of fepulture. See t. 5.

(y) Jacob Sannazar. *de partu virg.*

CHAP.

CHAP. III.

The state of the city from the Romans *leaving the island to the calling over the* Saxons; *and quite through the* Heptarchy, *&c. to the* Norman *conquest.*

AFter a course of near five hundred years, the *Romans* left the island, if we reckon from *Caesar*'s first attempt on it; or about four hundred from the conquest by *Claudius*. In the reign of *Theodosius jun.* the *Roman* empire sunk so fast, that *Britain* was totally neglected; the last lieutenant *AEtius*, who had been sent over to defend them from their old invaders, at his departure advised the *Britons to stand to their arms; be upon their guard themselves, and for the future provide for their own safety; for they must never more expect any succours from them, who had their hands full enough of troubles nearer home.* A. CCCCXXX.

And now, says an old *British* historian (a), the *Scots* and *Picts* with greater confidence than ever, *like flies and vermin in the heat of summer*, issued out of their narrow holes and caves, and immediately seized on all the country as far as the wall; which without resistance they made themselves masters of. In the mean time the guards on the wall, instead of preparing to receive their enemies with vigour and courage, like idle spectators stood trembling on it; and suffered themselves to be pulled down with hooks from the top of it. It was not long before their enemies had undermined and broken those mighty ramparts the *Romans* had built for their defence; and then like an irresistible torrent rushed in and bore down all before them. The poor dispirited *Britons* were driven like sheep, and slaughtered without mercy. In this dreadful calamity they call aloud on their old friends to help and support them; and in a most moving letter sent to *AEtius* governour of *Gaul*, they cry (b), *we know not which way to turn us, the Barbarians drive us to the sea, and the sea back to the Barbarians.* Thus *of two kinds of death always present before our eyes, one or other must be our choice, either to be swallowed up by the waves or butchered by the sword.*

There is a very good reason to be given for this dispiritedness of the *Britons* at this juncture. The *Romans* had drained the country of their ablest men; and the rest which staid, they never would suffer to bear arms; out of a politick view, whilst they were amongst them. How is it possible, then, without discipline and without arms, but their courage must also forsake them? yet we shall find these dastardly creatures recover their spirits, and treat their enemies in another manner shortly.

In this general calamity our city must have had a mighty share fall to its lot. It had been always a place from whence the *Barbarians* received their strongest repulses; a *station* which the *Romans* chose to plant part of the flower of their army in; as a garrison to curb and restrain the inroads of these depredators; and therefore must inevitably feel their fiercest vengeance. But we are here in dumb sorrow, and lost in the general confusion. In this calamity the *British* princes assembled, and in council with the other great men of the island, it was determined that since they were to expect no succour from the *Roman* arm, to call in the *Saxon*; which at that time held the highest repute for strength and valour; in order to stem this torrent of their merciless enemies, who had now well nigh over-run the whole island. They can never be blamed for this resolution, the exigencies of their affairs required it; nor would the consequence have been any ways to their disadvantage, had not *Vortigern*, their inconsiderate king, instead of giving the *Saxons* the stipulated pay, and sending them home again after they had done their work, allowed them a settlement in the island.

From this fatal epocha, and *Vortegern*'s sottish marriage with the *Saxon* general's daughter, we may date the beginning of the utter destruction of the *British* name and people. For though several of their kings, contended, inch by inch, for the preservation of their country from these rapacious foreigners; yet they having found a much better part of the world than they left, made all the efforts imaginable to possess themselves of it. And after all the vigorous struggles for liberty, and after a most resolute defence of their country, the *Britons* were forced at last to give up all, to the very people they had called in to defend it.

The description which old *Gildas* gives of the strength of the island, when the *Romans* left it, is very great; for he says it was fortified with twenty eight cities, besides many castles, fortresses, towers, gates and other buildings. A list of the *British* names of these

(a) *Gildas.*

(b) AETIO III CON. *gemitus* Britannorum, *post pauca querentes inquiunt, repellunt nos* Barbari *ad mare*, —*repellit ad* Barbaros. *Inter haec oriuntur duo genera funerum aut jugulamur aut mergimur.* Gildae *sapient. hist*, ed. Gale *inter script.* Ang. xv.

cities, as they are ſet down by *Nennius*, *H. Huntingdon*, *&c.* may not be amiſs in this place; becauſe, in this account, ours has the preeminence of the whole *(c)*.

(d) Nomina urbium Britannicarum *ex* Nennio, Henrico Huntingdon, Alfred. Beverlacenſi, *& aliis collectaneis.*

De nobilibus civitatibus Britonum. *Erat autem* Britannia *quondam civitatibus viginti & octo nobiliſſimis inſignita, praeter caſtella innumera, quæ & ipſa muris, turribus, portis ac ſeris erant inſtructa firmiſſimis.*

Civitatum quoque nomina haec erant Britanicè.

Kair-Ebranc, i. e. —	EBORACUM.	Kair-Dorm. —	*Dormceaſtria.*
Kair-Chent —	*Cantuaria.*	Kair-Loichoit —	*Lincolnia.*
Kair-Gorangen —	*Wigornia.*	Kair-Mardin —	*Caermarthen.*
Kair-Lundune —	*Londonia.*	Kair-Guorcon —	
Kair-Legion —	*Leiceſtria.*	Kair-Cucerat	
Kair-Collen —	*Coleceſtria.*	Kair-Guortigern	
Kair-Glou —	*Glouceſtria.*	Kair-Urnac	
Kair-Cei —	*Ciceſtria.*	Kair-Meguaid	
Kair-Briſtou —	*Briſtol.*	Kair-Peris —	*Portceſtre.*
Kair-Cerin —	*Cerinceſtria.*	Kair-Drayton	
Kair-Guent —	*Winceſtria.*	Kair-Celemion	
Kair-Graunt —	*Cantabrigia.*	Kair-Licelid	
Kair-Leon —	*Carliel.*	Kair-Legion * —	* *In qua fuit Archiep. temp.* Briton. *ſed nunc deſtructa; ubi* Uſca *cadit in* Sabrinam.
Kair Dauri —	*Dorceſtria.*	Kair-Mercipit	

A. CCCCL. Now to our annals. It was not long after the *Britons* had called over the *Saxons*, that they felt the ſting of the ſnake which they had taken into their boſom. The *Picts* and *Scots* had perfectly ſubdued all the country north of *Humber*; ſo that our city lay as it were buried in its own ruins ſo deep, that I ſhould not know where to find it, had not the *Scotch* hiſtorians lent me ſome light; who are very particular in the deſcription of their countrymens conqueſts, as they are pleaſed to call them, at this time.

Hengiſt the *Saxon* general, upon his arrival in *Britain* with his army, immediately marched againſt the enemy, and near unto *York*, ſays my authorities *(e)*, a bloody battle was fought, wherein the *Saxons* had the better, ſlew a great number of the *Picts* and *Scots*, took from them the city of *York* and all the country on this ſide the river *Teeſe*. The blow was ſo great, that had the *Saxon* general followed it, the war would quickly have been at an end; but this leader of *auxiliary troops*, was too wiſe and politick to act in that manner; for not willing, ſays *H. Boetius*, to drive the *Scots* and *Picts* quite home again; which was to knock the war on the head all at once; he choſe rather to withdraw his army to the city of *York*, where he ſtaid ſome time to refreſh, as he pretended, his wearied troops.

Soon after this when the deluded *Britons* began to ſmell out the *Saxons* deſign, and had ſent for *Aurelius Ambroſius* from *Armorica*, to defend them from this undreamt-of danger; the ſubtle *Hengiſt* privately ſent down his ſon *Occa*, in order to ſecure all the northern fortreſſes, but eſpecially *York (f)*. The ſon obeyed the father's inſtructions, and at *York* feigned accuſations againſt many of the nobility, gentry and principal inhabitants of the city and country, that they had a deſign to betray their own country into the hands of the enemies they had juſt got rid off; and, upon this ſtrange pretence, put many of them to death, ſome ſecretly, others openly, as actually convicted of the treaſons laid to their charge.

This villanous affair was reſented as it deſerved. The *Britons*, rouzed from their lethargy, and having an able and an experienced general of their own natural royal ſtock at their head, *Vortimer* the ſon of *Vortigern*, before the arrival of *Ambroſius*, fell upon the *Saxons*, and defeated them in four ſeveral battles. This leader ſlew ſuch numbers of them, that, had they not ſprung up like *Hydra*'s heads, and poured in freſh ſupplies from their inexhauſtible ſprings in *Germany*, their total expulſion muſt have been inevitable.

Under the conduct of their victorious king, *Aurelius Ambroſius*, *Hengiſt* the *Saxon* general met his fate; being ſlain at *Conyngſburg*, according to *G. Mon.* after a moſt obſtinate and bloody battle. His two ſons *Occa*, or *Octa*, and *Eoſa* fled with the ſhattered remains of their army more northward; the former to *York*, and *Eoſa* to the city of *Aclud*; *Aldburgh*.

Aurelius quickly perſued them and coming before *York* ſummoned *Octa* to ſurrender *(g)*. The young prince, terrified no doubt by his father's fate, conſulted with his friends ſome

(c) In the other *Britiſh* catalogues *Kaer Ebrauc* is only the fourth in number, but it always preceeds *Kaer Lundune*; which, in *Nennius* his own catalogue, comes but in as the twentieth. *Vide* Nennium, *inter* xv. ſcript. ed *Gale*.

(d) *Inter* ſcript. xx ed. *Gale*.

(e) *Hollingſhead*'s Scotch chron. *Buchani hiſt.*

(f) Scotch chron.

(g) G. *Mon.* R. *Higden*. Polichron.

time

time whether he should stand a siege or not? at length determining to try the victor's clemency, he came out of the city with his principal captains, carrying, each a chain in his hand, and dust upon his head, and presented himself to the king with this address; *my Gods are vanquished, and I doubt not but the sovereign power is in your God; who has compell'd so many noble persons to come before you in this suppliant manner; be pleased therefore to accept of us and this chain; if you do not think us fit objects of your clemency, we here present our selves ready to be fettered, and are willing to undergo any punishment you shall judge us worthy of.* *Aurelius*, who had equally the character of a merciful as well as a valiant prince, could not hear this without being moved; and being touched with compassion at the spectacle, after advising with his counsellors what to do with them, at the instigation of a *Bishop*, says *Geofry*, he granted free pardon to them all. The other brother encouraged by *Octa*'s success, came to *York*, surrendred himself in like manner, and met with the same reception. Nay more, this generous victor assigned them the country bordering on *Scotland* for residence, and made a firm league and alliance with them. A. CCCCLXVI.

If it was consonant to my design to stop to make reflexions, I should undoubtely censure the extraordinary clemency of the *British* king to the most barbarous and dangerous foes he had in the world. To have banished them and all their brood, would now be judged ill policy, because they so well knew the way back; but to suffer the vipers to stay and nest in the land is an act of clemency beyond credit; did not more writers, than *he of Monmouth*, as *Milton* always styles him, attest the truth of it. The consequence will shew the bad effects of this too charitable proceeding.

(*h*) His pagan enemies being now subdued, *Aurelius* summoned all the princes and nobility of the whole kingdom to *York*. At this general council he gave orders to them for the speedy restauration of the church and its worship; which the heathenish *Saxons* had every where suppressed and destroyed. He himself undertook to rebuild the *metropolitical church* at *York*; with all those in the province; but of this in its destined place.

(*i*) *Uther* or *Uter*, to whom *Geofry*, has given the terrible sirname of *Pendragon*, succeeded his Brother *Ambrosius* in the kingdom. In the very beginning of this king's reign *Octa* and *Eosa* began to shew their gratitude for former favours. Taking hold of the opportunity, they revolted, and according to their barbarous inclinations, wasted and spoiled the country as far as *York*; which they invested. It was not long before the *British* king came to its relief, where under the very walls, after an obstinate resistance, *Uter* discomfited their whole army and took both the brothers prisoners. A. CCCCLXXXX.

(*k*) The next that comes upon the *British* stage, and bids the fairest for immortality, is the victorious *Arthur*; who, if the chroniclers of those times deceive us not, fought twelve battles with the *Saxons*, successful in all. *Geofry* has larded the reign of this king with many uncommon fictions of knight-errantry; but certainly he was, says *William of Malmsbury*, a prince more worthy to be dignified by true history than romance, for he was the only prop and chief support of his country.

Arthur was crowned *king of Britain* at eighteen years of age. The *Saxons* took the advantage of his youth to make another attempt upon *Britain*; the two princes *Octa* and *Eosa*, having escap'd out of prison, fled home, returned with a strong force, and had again made themselves masters of the northern parts of the kingdom, which they divided into two parts, the more southern was called *Deira*, and the north *Bernicia*. *Arthur* had attacked them and defeated them in several battles, and so far pushed his conquests that *Octa* finding himself distressed, committed the south to *Baldulphus* and *Colgrin*, the two sons of *Ella*, the founder of the two kingdoms aforesaid, and reserved *Bernicia* to himself in order to defend it against the continual attacks of the more northern invaders. *Colgrin* lost a great battle to *Arthur*, which put him under the necessity of shutting himself up in *York*, whilst the *British* king immediately marched to besiege him. *Baldolph* inform'd of his brother's loss and flight, set forward to relieve him with a body of six thousand men; for at the time of the last battle he was upon the sea coast waiting the arrival of *Childric*, another *Saxon* general, from *Germany*. *Baldolph* was now within ten miles of *York*, and his purpose was to make a speedy march in the night time and fall upon them unawares. But *Arthur*, having intelligence of the design, sent out a detachment of six hundred horse and three thousand foot, under the command of *Codor* duke of *Cornwal* to meet him the same night. *Codor* happening to fall into the same road, along which the enemy was passing, made a sudden assault upon them, which intirely defeated the *Saxons* and put them to flight. A. DXVI.

Baldolph was excessively grieved at this disappointment in the relief intended his brother, and began to think of some other stratagem to gain access to him; in which if he could but succeed, he thought they might concert measures together for their mutual safeties. Since he had no other way for it; he shaved his head and beard, and put on the habit of a *jester* with a harp in his hand. In this disguise he walked up and down in the trenches without suspicion, playing all the while upon his instrument like a common harper. By little and

(*h*) G. Mon.
(*i*) G. Mon. Polichron. &c.
(*k*) Nennius, &c.

little he advanced nearer the walls of the city, from whence being at length discovered by the centinels, he was drawn up in the night time, and conducted to his brother. This unexpected, but much desired, interview caused a great many tender embraces betwixt them; before they began to consider what stratagems to make use of for their escape. But all seemed desperate, for *Arthur* pushed the siege on vigorously, hoping to take the town before the arrival of the *Saxon* general, whom he knew was bringing a fresh supply from *Germany*. At last, when they were on the point of surrendring, came news that *Childric*, was landed and had defeated *Codor* whom *Arthur* had sent to hinder his descent, and was marching towards *York*, with an army of brave soldiers, which he had brought over in no less than six hundred transports. Upon this a council of war was called, and *Arthur* was advised to raise the siege and retire to *London*, for fear of hazarding a battle, in the winter time, with so potent and numerous an enemy.

A. DXX.

But the next summer, after the bloody battle on *Badon hills*, said by the *Scotch* historians (*l*) to be our *Blake a more*, where *Arthur* gained a decisive victory and slew ninety thousand of the enemy; the city of *York* was delivered up to him as soon as ever he approached it. This battle says *Gildas* happened forty four years after the *Saxons* first arrival in *Britain*, wherein all the *Saxon* generals were slain and their army entirely cut to pieces.

This was the second siege of *York* remarkable for any opposition; for, though after the *Romans* leaving the island it had been taken by the *Picts* and *Scots*, and then taken from them again by the *Saxons*; yet in neither case was there much struggle about it. In the former, the general consternation was so great amongst the poor deserted *Britons* that no resistance could be expected from them; and in the latter, the fame of the *Saxons* valour so terrified these northern plunderers, especially after experiencing a litle of it, that it was all they could do to get back, with precipitation enough to their own country.

I can't help giving the reader a notable reflection of *Mon. Rapin Thoyras* on the conduct of the *Britons* at this juncture. "When one reflects, says he, on the weakness and dispi-
"ritedness of the *Britons* before the arrival of *Hengist*, one cannot but be surprized at their
"being able to withstand the *Saxons* in the first war, and which lasted so long. These very
"*Britons* who after the departure of the *Romans* dared not to look the *Picts* and *Scots* in
"the face, successfully defended themselves against both *Saxons* and *Picts*. A long war
"teaches, at length, the most unwarlike nation the use of their arms, and very frequently
"puts them in condition to repair in the end the losses they sustained in the beginning. Had
"the *Saxons* invaded *Britain* with a numerous army, in all appearance, they would have
"conquered the whole in a very little time; but sending over a small number of forces at a
"time, they spun the war out to a great length, and by that means taught the *Britons* a
"trade the *Romans* had done all they could to make them forget. But,

I now proceed. *Arthur*, after the defeat of the *Saxons*, made an expedition into *Scotland*, in order to destroy that country from end to end, as the seat of ancient enmity against *South Britain*. This we are told, he would certainly have effected, but the interposition of some *Bishops* prevented him. It seems, the *Scots* had just then received the *Gospel*, and it was represented to *Arthur* that a *christian* ought not, on any pretence whatsoever, to spill the blood of his brethren. A maxim rarely, or never, followed since.

(*m*) *Arthur* after this expedition against the *Scots* retired to *York*; where he first set himself to regulate the affairs of the *church* again miserably rent and torn by the *Pagan Saxons*. *Sampson* or *Sanxo* the *Archbishop* had been expelled, the churches and altars all demolished, or else profaned with heathen ceremonies. He called an Assembly of the clergy and people, and appointed *Pyramus* his chaplain *metropolitan* of that see. The churches which lay level with the ground he caused to be rebuilt, and, what was the chiefest ornament, saw them fill'd with assemblies of devout persons, says my author, of different sexes. The nobility also, which was driven out of the city by the disturbances of the *Saxons*, he restored to their former honours and habitations.

A. DXXI. (*n*) At this time did this great monarch, his clergy, all his nobility and soldiers, keep their *christmas* in *York*. The first festival of that kind ever held in *Britain*; and which all those ever since have in some measure taken their model from. *Buchanan* and Sir *Thomas Withrington* severely censure *Arthur*'s conduct in the extravagant solemnization of this festival.

The sence of the former is this, "*Arthur* took up his residence at *York*, for his winter
"quarters, whither they resorted to him the prime persons of the neighbourhood and spent
"the latter end of *December* in mirth, jollity, drinking and the vices that are too often
"the consequence of them; so that the representations of the old heathenish feasts dedicated
"to *Saturn* were here again revived. But the number of days they lasted were doubled;
"and amongst the wealthier sort trebled; during which time they counted it almost a sin
"to treat of any serious matter. Gifts are sent mutually from and to one another; fre-
"quent invitations pass betwixt friends, and domestick offenders are not punished. Our
"countrymen call this feast *Julitide*, substituting the name of *Julius Caesar* for that of *Sa-*

(*l*) *Scotch* chron. *Buchanan*.
(*m*) *G. Mon.*
(*n*) *Scotch* chron.

"*turn*

" *turn*. The vulgar are yet persuaded that the nativity of *Christ* is then celebrated, but " mistakenly, for 'tis plain they imitate the lasciviousness of the *Bacchanalians*, rather than " the memory of *Christ*, then as they say, born.

Thus far *Buchanan*. It is easy to see on what principles this sarcastical description of the celebration of *Christmas* is founded. His *Jule-tide*, however, is false quoted; *Yule-tide* is the word, as *Christmas* is, at this day, called in *Scotland*, and as we in the north term *Christmas eve*. As for his derivation, he might with equal justice, I believe, have drawn it from *Claudius*, as *Julius Caesar*. It is true, that no word whatever has puzzled the antiquaries more than *Yule*; some deriving it from the (*o*) *Latin* words *exulo*, *ululo*, *jubilo*, or the *Heb. Haleluia*. In the *Saxon* tongue it is called Iehul, in the *Danish Uledag*. Mrs. *Elstob*, the celebrated translator of the *Saxon* homily (*p*), says the best antiquaries derive it from the word Ol *Ale*; which was much us'd, says she, in their festivities and merry meetings (*q*). Ol or *Ale*, adds the learned lady, did not only signify the liquor they made use of, but gave denomination to their greatest festivals, as this Iehol or *Yule* at *midwinter*; as it is plainly to be seen in that custom of *Whitsun-Ale* at the other great festival of *midsummer*. Bp. *Stillingfleet* has observed that this word seems to come from the *Gothick* Iole, which in that language signifies to *make merry* (*r*). *Bede* tells us, indeed, that the last day of the year was observed amongst the heathen *Saxons* with great solemnity; illuminating, at that time, their houses with fire and candles, as an emblem of the return of the *sun* and the lengthening of days. And Bp. *Stillingfleet* confirms this, by observing that in the old Runick *Fasti*, a wheel was used to denote this festival. But what had the *Saxons* to do with *Julius* for a *god*? no such deity being ever known in their *Theology*. *Buchanan* and our Sir *Thomas* here jump in opinions, but both may be easily derived from what *Hector Boetius* has recorded of *Arthur*, who says, *that he and his knights having recovered* York *from the* Scots *and* Picts, *kept there such a grand christmas, that afterwards fighting again with the* Saxons, *the soldiers were found so weakened with intemperance and superfluity, that their arrows could hardly pierce the* Saxons *furred doublets*; *being able before to strike through their iron armour*.

Arthur, after all his conquests, had the misfortune to be slain in a rebellion of his own subjects, and by the hands of his own nephew. From whose death, dissensions arising amongst the *British* Princes, the *Saxons* so far prevailed as to gain an entire conquest over all; driving the miserable remains of the *Britons* that would not submit to their *Yoke*, to seek shelter in the *Cambrian* mountains; where their posterity, according to *Welch* history, have ever since remained.

Our *Saxon* conquerours divided the territories of the plundered *Britons* into seven shares, which since is styled the *Heptarchy*; over each presiding a king. But I cannot omit taking notice here, for the better comprehending the sequel, that, though the land was in this manner divided into seven several kingdoms, and each of their kings had a sovereign command within his own limits, yet one of them ever seemed to be superior to the rest; and that prince, who had the greatest power or success in his wars, was always esteemed the head, and called the *king of Englishmen* (*s*).

(*t*) In the division, the kingdom of the *Northumbers*, which is more immediately my concern, because its capital was *York*, contained all that part of the island from the *Humber* mouth to *S. Johnston* in *Scotland*, say some, though others, only to the *Fryth* of *Edenborough*. This country, I have before noted, was divided by *Octa* the son of *Hengist* into two parts, *Deira* and *Bernicia*, over both which did *Ida* reign, a lineal descendant, according to the *Saxon* genealogy, from their famous god *Woden*, and whom *Malmsbury* styles *nobilissimus aetate & viribus integer*. *Ida* left two sons, to whom he divided his dominions and gave *Deira* to *Ella*, whose kingdom took in all from the *Humber* to the *Tyne*; and *Bernicia* to *Adda*, his other son, which contained all northward from that boundary. Of all the kingdoms of the *Saxons* this of *Deira* was of the shortest continuance, it began by a division of the whole *Northumbrian* district between the sons of *Ida*, and was again united under *Oswin* ninety one years after *Ella* (*u*). A DXLVII.

York was, at this period, the capital of *Deira* only; but the district was large and took in all *Yorkshire*, *Lancashire*, *Durham*, *Westmorland*, *Cumberland* and some part of *Northumberland* at first; though since, the country betwixt the *German* ocean, the *Humber* and the river *Derwent*, now the *Eastriding*, bore that appellation. The last named river, most certainly, retains some part of the ancient name, *Deir-went*, being no more than *Dierae vel Deirorum flumen*; and lower or hollow *Diera*, which lies betwixt the sea and the *Humber*, in respect to the higher country, and because it extends itself like a *nose* or neck of land, the inhabitants have added the *French* word *Nesse*; which, together makes Hol-dier-ness (*x*).

(*o*) *Skinner*'s ety. dict.

(*p*) Mrs. *Elstob*'s Sax. homily.

(*q*) *Christmas* was antiently known at *York* by the name of Iool-girth-ol. See the Sheriffs riding chap. vi.

(*r*) *Stillingfleet*'s orig. sac.

(*s*) *Bede*.

(*t*) *Anno ab incarnatione* 547, *post mortem* Hengisti 60, *ducatus* Northumbrensis *in regnum mutatus est*. *Regnavit ibi primus* IDA *haud dubie nobillissimus aetate, & viribus integer*. Gul. Malmsf.

(*u*) *Harrison*'s diss. of *Britain*.

(*x*) *Antiquitus sola illa patria quae introclusa mari orient*. Deirwenta & Humbra Deira *vocabatur*; *nunc vero* Eastridingia. Deirent *flumen i. e.* Deirae *vel* Deirorum *flumen notorie vocatur*. *Cava* Diera, *respectu altioris, inter mare &* Humbram, *& quia extenditur instar nasi, additur ab incolis haec syllaba* Nesse *& dicitur vulgariter* Hol-dier-ness. Leland. Coll. *vita* S. Joh. Beverlaci.

The

A. DCXVII. The firſt of the *Saxon* kings that comes in my way is *Edwin* king of *Deira*, afterwards ſole monarch of *Engliſhmen*, and juſtly ſtyled Edwin the Great. This king being converted to chriſtianity by a miracle, *Bede* and the other monks are very laviſh in his praiſes. Our eccleſiaſtical hiſtory will take in moſt of this monarch's life; and except ſome few paſſages, I refer wholly thither. *Edwin* had by wonderful providence, eſcaped divers ſnares laid for his life; had ſurmounted many difficulties; and, by conqueſt over his neighbour princes, had not only joined *Bernicia*, to *Deira*, but was alſo declared grand monarch of the *Anglo-Saxons*. That his reſidence was at *York* will not be diſputed by thoſe that read venerable *Bede*'s ſtory of his converſion; and it was here he made thoſe ſalutary laws, which were ſo well obſerved, that the ſame author tells you, in his time a *weak woman might have travelled with a new born babe over the whole iſland without the leaſt moleſtation.*

In this time of profound peace, which the iſland enjoyed during *Edwin*'s adminiſtration, great happineſs muſt occur. Strong were the ſtruggles amongſt the *Saxon* princes for ſuperiority; for no ſooner, were they maſters of the booty, but like robbers, they fell out about dividing the ſpoil. For two hundred and fifty years and upwards few of them died in their beds; and *England* was all that time, except this ſmall interval of *Edwin*'s, one continued ſcene of blood and war and miſery. So great was the power and virtue of this monarch that *William* of *Malmſbury* gives him this high character (y), not only ſays he, *the* Engliſh, Scots *and* Picts, *but, even the* Orcades *and all the* Britiſh *iſlands dreaded his arms and adored his grandeur. No publick thief nor houſe-breaker was found in his time, the adulterer was a ſtranger, and the ſpoiler of other mens goods afar off. His glory ſhines, even to our own age, with ſplendour. Bede* ſays, his magnificence was ſo great, that he had not only in battle, the enſigns proper to war born before him, but in times of peace, in his progreſs through the cities and great towns of his kingdoms, or when ever he appeared in publick, that kind of ſtandard by the *Britains* called Tufa, and the *Saxons* (z) Thuuf, the mark of ſovereignty over the iſland, was carried before him with great ſolemnity.

But neither *Edwin's* power nor his piety could ſave him from the ſtroke ſo fatal to the *Saxon* princes in thoſe days. He had many ſecret enemies who maligned his greatneſs; but yet dreaded his power too much to dare to ſhew it openly. One of theſe invidious opponents whom *Bede* calls *Quichelm* king of the *Weſt-Saxons* had ſuborn'd a ruffian to murder *Edwin*; which the villain undertook to do in the midſt of his guards. The accident happening in our neighbourhood muſt not eſcape our notice.

A. DCXXVI. *Edwin* had a ſummer retreat, ſeven miles from *York*, formerly a *Roman* ſtation called *Derventio*; ſtanding, ſays *V. Bede, juxta amnem* Doroventionem *ubi tunc erat* villa *regalis. Edwin* was at this place when the aſſaſſin arrived, and begged audience of the king, who readily granted it (a). Pretending ſecret buſineſs, he took *Edwin* a little aſide from his guards, and ſlyly drawing a two-edged poiſoned weapon (b), which he had brought for ſurer work, he attempted the murder with ſuch reſolution, that he wounded the king through the very body of one of his guards; who by chance ſaw the villain's deſign, and had only time to throw himſelf betwixt to intercept the ſtroke. The name of this, properly called, life-guard man, whom *Bede* has handed to poſterity was *Lilla*; and the aſſaſſin's reſolution was ſuch, that he was not cut in pieces before he had ſlain another knight of the guard called *Forther*. But

A. DCXXXIII. *Edwin*'s peaceable reign of ſeventeen years now drew to a fatal period, for he was ſlain in a moſt bloody battle at a place ſince called (c) *Heavenfield*, by *Penda* the pagan king of *Mercia*, who had joined with *Cadwallo* the now only *Britiſh* king of *Wales*, in order to deſtroy him. This victory is reported to be more cruel than any in the monuments of hiſtory; for whilſt *Penda* endeavoured to root out the *Chriſtians*, and *Cadwallo* the *Saxons*, their fury was ſo great that it ſpared neither ſex nor age (d). The head of *Edwin* was buried in St. *Gregory*'s porch in his own church at *York*; but his body in the monaſtery at *Whitby*.

The kingdom of *Northumberland*, and its capital *York*, was ravaged in a terrible manner, after the loſs of this battle with their king. And though the *Northumbrians* choſe *Oſrick* and *Anfrid*, the neareſt relations of *Edwin*, kings, one of *Deira*, the other of *Bernicia*; his only ſon having been ſlain with his father; yet they could not put a ſtop to the victors; for we are told that *Oſrick* venturing raſhly to beſiege *Cadwallo* in *York*, with an army of undiſciplined troops, the *Welſh* king diſdaining to be thus braved, ſallied out and attacked him ſo briſkly in his trenches, that he put his army to the rout, and left him dead on the

(y) Angli, Scoti, Picti. *ſed & inſulae* Orcadum *&* Meneveniarum, *qui nunc* Angleſei, i. e. Anglorum *inſulas dicimus, & arma ejus metuerunt & poteſtatem adorarunt. Nullus tunc praedo publicus, nullus latro domeſticus, inſidiator conjugalis pudoris procul, expilator alienae haereditatis exul. Magnum id in ejus laudibus & noſtra aetate ſplendidum.* Gul. Malmſ.

(z) The globe of feathers mentioned before.

(a) Sax. annals.

(b) *Sica biceps toxicata,* Bede. *Sica genus armorum eſt, ſimile vidubli,* i. e. *viſudubii. Sica etoit une petite epee courbee en forme de* Faux, *comme le portoient les* Thraces. Monſieur *Daciers* notes on *Horace*, and the word *Sicarius.*

(c) Called ſo no doubt by the number of chriſtians ſlain there. Since corrupted to *Hatfield* a village nigh *Doncaſter. Dicitur autem quod* Hatfeld *rubeo undique nobilium cruore fumabat; ibi namque mirabilis & inopinata fortiſſimorum ſtrages facta eſt.* Brompton.

(d) *Buch.*

ſpot.

ſpot. *Anfrid* the other brother met the ſame fate by the ſame hand. The reigns of theſe two kings were of ſo ſhort a continuance, beſides their lives being branded with *apoſtacy*, that the *monkiſh* hiſtorians have for the moſt part omitted them. V. *Bede* ſays, that for their apoſtacy from the *chriſtian religion* they had the juſt judgment of *God* inflicted upon them. *Oſrick*, ſays he, and his whole army, penn'd in the *ſuburbs of their own city*, were miſerably ſlain; and *Anfrid* unadviſedly coming to *Cadwallo* at *York* with only twelve perſons in his retinue, in order to treat of peace, was by this outragious tyrant cruelly put to death in that city. A. DCXXXIV.

Oſwald, the ſucceſſor and brother of *Anfrid* revenged his death upon *Cadwallo*; for coming unexpectedly upon him from *Scotland* with a very ſmall army, but great in the faith of *Chriſt*, ſays *Bede*, at *Denniſburn* in *Northumberland*, obtained a deciſive victory over him, deſtroying both the *Britiſh* king and all his army. *Oſwald* after this was ſole monarch over the *Northumbers*: the many religious acts he did in our city, claim another place; and I have nothing to add here but his great character from *Bede*, who ſays, *in his time the whole iſland flouriſhed both in peace and plenty, and acknowledged their ſubjection to him. All the nations of* BRITAIN *who ſpoke four different languages, that is to ſay, the* BRITONS, RED-SHANKS, SCOTS *and* ENGLISHMEN *were wholly ſubject to him. And yet being advanced to ſuch an exalted greatneſs, he was, what is wonderful to ſpeak of,* adds my author, *humble to all, gracious to the poor, and bountiful to ſtrangers.*

That this great monarch's ſeat of reſidence was at *York*, is fully proved in our church hiſtory; but neither his religion, nor his innate goodneſs could protect him from the fate of *Edwin*, and the two *apoſtates* his predeceſſors: for we read that *Penda* king of *Mercia*, the *Chriſtians* old *antagoniſt*, declared war againſt *Oſwald*, met him at a place called (e) *Maſerfield*, and in a bloody battle ſlew him. The cruelty of this monſter extended beyond death, for he ordered *Oſwald*'s body, in a barbarous and brutiſh manner, to be torn in pieces by wild horſes. A. DXLII.

I ſhall not trouble the reader with the lives of the *Northumbrian* kings in the *Heptarchy*, any more than ſuits my purpoſe; thoſe melancholy times have been excellently well treated on by other hands, and it is not my deſign to give a general hiſtory of *Britain*, but a particular one of the city of *York*. Whoever undertakes to write on theſe northern wars ſhould mind what *Hoveden* ſays, who, ſpeaking of the *Northumbrian* people, *ſingulorum autem bellorum geſta et modos et fines ad plenum determinare, nimiſtas prolixitatis neceſſario prohibet. Gens enim* ANGLORUM *dura naturaliter erat, et ſuperba et bellis inteſtinis inceſſanter attrita.*

There is nothing remarkable from the date I have inſerted to the reign of *Egbert*, the firſt univerſal *Saxon* monarch, who kept his ſway and delivered it down to his ſucceſſors; except that our city continued the *metropolis* of the northern kingdom, and uſually ran the ſame fate with its governours. A ſhort account of the ſucceſſion of theſe, fighting and praying, monarchs, may not be improper to give, becauſe it continues the thread of our hiſtory, and I ſhall beg leave to take them from the firſt.

* A compleat ſucceſſion of the *Northumbrian* kings in the *Heptarchy*.

A. C.	BERNICIA.	*A. C.*	DEIRA.
DXLVII.	*Ida*, the ſon of *Eoppa*, reigned twelve years, and had both the kingdoms.		
DLIX.	*Adda*, or *Odda*, his ſon five years.	DLIX.	*Ella*, another ſon, thirty years.
DLXIV.	*Clappa* ſeven years.		
DLXXI.	*Theodwulf* one year.		
DLXXII.	*Freothwulf* ſeven years.		
DLXXIX.	*Theodoric* ſeven years.		
DLXXXVIII.	*AEthelric* two years.		
	Theſe two laſt were the ſons of *Ida*, and reign'd in this province whilſt *Ella* continued king of *Deira*. *AEthelric*, on the death of *Ella*, had both the kingdoms and reigned five years.	DLXXXIX.	*Edwin* ſon of the ſame, was in a ſhort time expulſed by *Athelfrid* king of *Bernicia*, who ſubjected both the kingdoms, and reign'd fourteen years, till *Edwin* was reſtor'd.

(e) From this overthrow called *Oſwalſtree*, in *Shropſhire*.

* *N. B.* This chronological table is taken out of *Tyrrel*'s hiſtory of *England*, and publiſhed in *Latin* at the end of Dr. *Hick*'s *theſaurus linguarum ſepten.* I here alter ſome of his dates, and the reader may obſerve, in his ſucceſſion of *Daniſh* rulers, that the courſe of my annals contradicts their poſitions in ſome places.

A. C.

DLXXXXIII. *AEthelfrid* reigned twenty four years, and was in possession of both the kingdoms.

DCXVII. *Edwin* the son of *Ella* seventeen years, had likewise both kingdoms, but being slain, his empire was divided into two, for at that time reign'd in

A. C.	Bernicia.	*A. C.*	Deira.
DCXXXIV.	*Osric* the son of *Alfred* one year.	DCXXXIV.	*Eanfred* the son of the late king *Ethelred*.

Both slain in one year.

DCXXXIV. *Oswald* the brother of *Eanfred* reigned nine years in both provinces, being slain.

DCXLII.	*Oswyn* the brother of *Oswald* reigned nine years in *Bernicia*.	*A. C.* DCXLIV.	*Oswin* the son of *Osric* in *Deira* had a seven years reign, and was then slain by

DCLI. *Oswyn*, lately mentioned, who entered upon both the kingdoms, which from that time continued united. He reigned twenty eight years, then

DCLXX. *Egfrid*, his lawful son, reign'd fifteen years. Slain.

DCLXXXV. *Alfred*, bastard, son to *Oswyn* nineteen years; buried at *Driffield*. After him

DCCIV. *Oswed* his son, a child of eight years old; *Stow* says after he had reigned eleven years he was murthered; but *Brompton* writes, that he was unfortunately slain in a battle by his kinsman

DCCXV. *Kenred*, who ruled *Northumberland* two years; then

DCCXVII. *Osric*, his brother, who reigned eleven years, and elected for his successor

DCCXXVIII. *Ceolwulph* the kinsman of *Kenred*. Venerable *Bede* wrote his history in this king's reign, and dedicated it to him. This monarch turned monk, and to him succeeded, after eight years,

DCCXXXVI. *Egbert*, cousin-germain to *Ceolwulph*, who reigned peaceably twenty years, then turned monk; which, I find, was much in fashion in those days, amongst the rest of the *Saxon* monarchs in the *heptarchy*. Then came

(*f*)

DCCLVI. *Oswald*, slain by his subjects in the first year of his reign.

DCCLVII. *Ethelwald*, surnamed *Mollo*, usurped; but after eleven years he was murthered by

DCCLXVIII. *Alred*, who, says *Hoveden*, was driven out of his capital city (*g*) Everwic, in *Easter-week*, after he had reigned eleven years; and the *Northumbrians* chose

DCCLXXIX. *Edelred*, the son of *Mollo*, who was also in the fifth year of his reign deprived, and

DCCLXXXIV. *Athelwold* proclaimed king; who after eleven years was slain by

DCCLXXXXVI. *Osred*, who succeeded, but he was driven out by his nobles the same year, or taken, says *Milton*, and forcibly shaven a monk at *York*.

Alred or *Athelred* again restored, and after four years was miserably slain. From which time the kingdom of *Northumberland* was sorely shaken with civil wars for forty years together; during which time there ruled, without the title of king, as some write,

Eardulf; but the *Saxon* chronicle says, that he was consecrated king at *York*, *May* 4, 795, by *Eanbald* archbishop, *Ethelbert*, *Higbald*, and *Badewulf*, bishops. *

Alfwold.

Eandred.

Etheldred.

Readulph. This last, says *Stow*, was slain at *York* with

DCCCXL. *Osbert* king, removed by

Ella, the usurper, both these kings were slain at *York* by the *Danes*.

DCCCLXVI. *Egbert*, sole monarch of the *English*, driven out by the *Danes*, who gave the kingdom of *Northumberland* to their countryman

Rigsidge; he ruled it eleven years, then another *Egbert*, a *Saxon*, was made king by them.

DCCCLXXII. *Egbert*, who dying, the *Danes* and *Northumbrians* were without a king till

Guthrum or *Guthred*, a poor slave, was elected, to whom the *Brigantes* were subjected for eleven years, till

(*f*) *Anno* DCCXLI *igni incensum est* Eboracum. Chron. *Saxon*. 55.

(*g*) Chron. *Saxon*. DCCLXXIV.

* Idem p. 66.

Alfred

A. C.	
DCCCLXXXXIV.	*Alfred* the great, drove the *Danes* in *England* to the last extremity; and made them chuse in *Northumberland* another,
DCCCCII.	*Rigsidge* for king, who being slain,
DCCCCIII.	*Reginald* and *Nigel*, both *Danes*, reigned together, and had the whole kingdom after *Alfred*'s death. *Nigel* being slain,
DCCCCXIV.	*Sitbrick*, his brother, took his share. After him these *Danes* succeeded, *viz.*
DCCCCXIX.	*Ingauld.*
DCCCCXXVI.	*Guthford.*
DCCCCXLIV.	*Anlaf*, the last of the *Northumbrian* kings in the *heptarchy*.

The succession of the *Danish* kings after their victory over *Osbert* and *Ella* in *Northumberland*, was first, *Haldene*, says *H. Huntington*, then *Guthrum*, after followed *Nigellus*, and *Sitbrick*, and *Riginald*, and *Anlaff*. The *Danes*, adds the aforesaid author, reigned very confusedly; now only one king, then two, and some times many, till *Edred* king of *West-sex* conquer'd this kingdom, and perfectly dissolv'd the heptarchical monarchy.

A. DCCC.

About the year 800, the *Saxon heptarchy* drawing to a period, the spring of an entire monarchy began to shew itself, says *Speed*, and the glory of the *English* men, more clearly, to arise. For though they had weakened each other in their almost continual wars, yet was their power strong in the possession of the whole, and the overborn *Britons* disregarded. *Egbert*, King of the *West-Saxons*, had perfectly subdued his brother kings, and gained an universal sovereignty over all; yet such is the instability of human affairs, that when he thought himself the greatest and happiest, he had the mortification to see a new enemy start up, which, after continual invasions, never desisted till they had gained an entire conquest over these conquerors. Thus those *Saxons*, who, by blood and violence had made themselves lords of other mens rights, were repaid in their own coin, and with equal destruction forced to give up their conquests to another invader. The source and spring of these attempts are attributed to two causes, one of which concerns in an especial manner the subject of my history, and therefore must be particularly related.

(*b*) The *Danes* were a fierce, hardy and warlike people, next neighbours to the *Saxons* in their own country, and had long envied their happiness in the possession of the greatest and wealthiest island in the then known world. Encouraged to hope for success, by the continual division amongst the *Saxon* rulers, they had several times made descents upon the island, but were always driven back with loss. In the reign of this *Egbert* they drew together all their forces; and as they were, at that time, the best sailors in the world, they fitted out a mighty fleet, with a numerous land army on board; encouraged doubly by the extraordinary revolution which had just happened in *England*, and the expectation of a general revolt in their favour, as soon as they should land in the northern parts. This design proved abortive, they made a descent, 'tis true, in the year 794, and burnt the monastery of *Lindisfarn*, or *Holy-Island*; but, finding the natives not to stir as they expected, they went off again with a great booty. No ways discouraged at this, they made several other attempts in other parts of the island, and at length prevailed; for, having gotten a taste, they never desisted, till they had intirely dispossessed the *Saxons* of it.

It was this *black storm from the north*, which our *Alcuin* prophetically speaks on, in a letter to *Egelbert* or *Egbert* King of *Northumberland*, in these words, (*i*) *What can be the meaning*, says he, *of that shower of blood which, in* Lent, *we saw at* York, *the* metropolis of the kingdom, *near St.* Peter's *church, descending with great horrour from the roof of the north part of the house, in a clear day? may not one imagine that this presages destruction and blood to us from that quarter?* This letter was wrote from *France* to *Egbert*, near fifty years before the first *Danish* invasion, *A. C.* 740, and whether we believe the prodigy, or that this man was a prophet; it is certain the event fulfilled the prediction, for never was blood more cruelly spilt than in this war; nor no part of *England* felt it so sensibly as the city of *York*.

A. DCCCLXVII.

(*k*) In the year 867, the *Northumbrians* had revolted from *Ethelred* sole monarch of *England*, and chose for their king one *Osbert* or *Osbrightus*. This *Osbert*, says *Rapin*, (*l*) kept his court and residence at *York*. Returning one day from hunting, the king had a mind to refresh himself at the house of a certain *earl*, named *Bruern-Bocard*, guardian of the sea-coasts, against the irruptions of the *Danes*. The earl happening to be from home, his *lady*, to whose charming beauty was joined the most engaging behaviour, adds our *Frenchman*, entertained her sovereign with the respect due to his quality. *Osbert* quite overcome with the sight of so much beauty, resolved, let the consequence be what it would, to satisfy

(*b*) *Daniel*'s history of *England*.

(*i*) *Quid significat pluvia sanguinis quae quadragesimali tempore* Euboraca *civitate in ecclesia beati* Petri *principis apostolorum, quae caput est totius regni, vidimus de borealibus domus sereno aere de summitate minaciter cadere tecti? Nonne potest putari a borealibus poenas sanguinis venire super populum, quod in hoc facto nuper ingruenti super domum dei incepisse videri potest.* Ex epist. *Albini* ad *Ethelredum* regem *Northumbrorum*, et ejus nobiles. *Lelandi* coll.

(*k*) Vide *chron.* Saxon. *hoc anno.*

(*l*) *Rapin*'s history of *England*.

tisfy his passion without delay. Accordingly on pretence of having some matters of importance to communicate to her in the earl's absence, he led her insensibly into a private room; where, after several attempts to bring her to comply by fair means, he fell at length to downright force. Entreaties, tears, cries, reproaches, were ineffectual to put a stop to his raging passion; and his servants, who knew their master's design, and had served him no doubt, on the like occasions before, took care no interruption should be given. After the commission of this infamous deed, he left the countess in such excess of grief and vexation, that it was not possible for her to hide the cause from her husband. So outragious an affront is never to be forgiven. Though *Osbert* was king, and earl *Bruern* his subject, he resented so highly this injury, that he resolved not to stick at any means to be revenged (*m*). *Bruern* being nobly born, and very powerful in kindred, soon called together the heads of them in consultation; and giving them to understand the base usage of the king, he told them, he positively resolved at any rate to be revenged. His relations and friends came readily into his measures, and went along with him to *York*. When the King saw the earl, he in a very obliging manner called him to him. But the earl, backed with his troop of friends, immediately gave a bold defiance to *Osbert*, and all homage, faith, lands, or whatever else he held of, or ought him, from that time gave up; saying, that for the future he never more would obey so scandalous a master. And without more delay he and his friends retired.

How well he kept his resolution will appear too plain in the sequel. *Bruern* had great interest with the *Northumbrians*, and this base action of *Osbert*'s, was naturally apt to alienate the minds of his subjects from him. Accordingly, by the management of this earl, the *Beruicians* in a little time revolted, and looking upon *Osbert* as unworthy to govern, they elected another king called *Ella* into the throne, with a resolution to support him in it. Thus, says *Rapin*, the old divisions which seemed to be quite laid asleep, were set on foot again, and *Northumberland* once more divided betwixt two kings, and two factions, who, continually aiming at one another's destruction, were but too successful in their endeavours.

A civil war was the fatal consequence of this division. The two kings did what they could to decide the controversy by arms, but the equality of their forces prevented the scale from turning on either side, and they both kept their ground. Earl *Bruern* was heartily in *Ella*'s interest, and one would think his revenge might have been satisfied in dispossessing *Osbert* of half of his dominions; but it was by no means compleat whilst he saw him on the throne of *Deira*. And therefore, since it would be, as he rightly judged, a difficult matter to carry it any further without a foreign aid, his rash and inconsiderate passion hurried him to a fatal resolution, and he immediately sailed for *Denmark*, in order to beg an assistance, which was but too readily granted him. He represented to the king (*n*) the present distracted state of the *Northumbrian* kingdom, and let him see that, if he would make use of the opportunity, he might with ease become master of it.

(*o*) The king of *Denmark* readily came into an enterprize, which his ambition and revenge spurred him on to. His revenge was on account of *Lothbrocb*, a *Danish* general, the father of *Hinguar* and *Hubba*, who being driven, by accident, on the coast of *Norfolk* in a small fishing-boat, was taken and sentenced, as he had been informed, to be thrown into a ditch full of serpents, where he miserably perished. Concerting measures therefore with *Bruern*, the *Danish* king got ready a mighty fleet against the spring, and constituted the two brothers *Hinguar* and *Hubba* his generals. They entered the *Humber* with this fleet, which was so great, that it spread a terror all over *England*; *Bruern* was their conductor, and as the *Northumbrians* were wholly ignorant of the design, they were in no readiness to dispute their landing. They soon became masters of the northern shore, and having burnt and destroyed the towns and inhabitants on the *Holderness* coast, they marched directly towards *York*, where *Osbert* was drawing an army together to oppose them.

In this great extremity *Osbert* applied to *Ella*, though his enemy, for his assistance, who willingly agreed to drop his private quarrel and join forces against the common enemy; accordingly he proceeded with all possible expedition to bring a powerful reinforcement. If *Osbert* could have brought himself to have staid at *York*, says *Rapin*, till *Ella*'s arrival, he would doubtless have embarrassed the *Danish* generals, who by that means would have been forced to oppose their enemies in two places at once. But his great courage would not let him go so safe a way to work. Perhaps it was with regret that he saw himself constrained to have recourse to his mortal foe for aid, or it may be, he feared some treachery. However, this adds my author, he sallied out of *York*, and attacked the *Danes* so vigorously, that they had much a do to stand the shock, and were very near being put in disorder. But their obstinate resistance having at length slackened the ardour of their enemies, they pushed

(*m*) *Brompton*.

(*n*) *Rapin* calls him *Ivar* or *Hinguar*; but *Brompton Codrinus*.

(*o*) *Ivar* says *Rapin* very readily came into an enterprise, which the desire of revenge, as well as his ambition spurred him on to; *Regnerus* his father having been taken prisoner in *England*, was thrown into a ditch full of serpents, where he miserably perished. This whole sentence, with submission to that great historian, is a mistake, as the consequence will shew.

them

them in their turn, and compelled them, at last, to retire without any order into the city. *Osbert* desperately vexed to see the victory snatched out of his hands when he thought himself sure of it, used all his endeavours to rally his broken troops again; but was slain in the retreat with abundance of his men.

This victory opened the gates of *York* to the *Danes*, who entered the city in order to refresh themselves, says *Rapin*, whilst *Ella* was advancing in hopes of repairing the loss *Osbert* had suffered by his too great haste. *Hinguar* having just triumphed over one of the kings, and not believing the other to be more formidable, spared him some trouble by going to meet him. This battle was no less fatal to the *English*, *Ella* lost his life, and his army was entirely routed. Some say this prince, adds my author, was not slain in battle, but taken prisoner; and *Hinguar* ordered him to be flayed alive, in revenge, for his father's murther.

Rapin has been the author chiefly from whence I have copied the history of the last memorable event; whom I have chose to follow as well for his diction as matter. But from what authority he claims I know not, for four antient and creditable writers of *English* history give almost a different account of this whole transaction; except in the case of the *rape*, which is recorded by *Brompton*. I have taken the liberty also to alter some of his proper names, as I found them miscalled; and as to his last conjecture, that *Ella* was taken prisoner, and used in that barbarous manner by *Hinguar*, in revenge for his father's murther, it would have been a great mistake if he had asserted it, for it was *Edmund* king of the *East-Angles* was the supposed murtherer, and paid dearly for it afterwards; being tied to a tree and shot to death, by the *Danes* with arrows. The spring of this great revolution in the *Northumbrian* kingdom, and after in all *England*, with the consequences of it to our city, I shall beg leave to give from the authorities in the notes *(p)*.

Brompton writes that *Lothbroch*, *(q)* the father of *Hinguar* and *Hubba*, being fishing and fowling in a small boat, singly on some of the *Danish* coasts, was driven by a sudden tempest out to sea, and after a dangerous passage, was thrown ashore in his boat on the *Northfolk* coast in *England*. He had no creature with him but his hawk and his dog; and being found was presented to *Edmund* king of the *East-Angles*. *Edmund* was taken with his graceful presence, and, hearing his story, he took him into his court; where *Lothbroch*, being a true sportsman, was associated with *Bern*, the king's huntsman, and partook with him in all those diversions.

It was not long before he shewed his dexterity in all kinds of rural sports to be much superior to the huntsman's, and was mightily in the king's favour for it. This *Bern* grew uneasy at it, and resolving to get rid of so troublesome a rival, he took an opportunity to draw *Lothbroch* aside into a thicket, where the villain slew him, and hid the body. The next day the king enquiring for *Lothbroch*, was told by *Bern*, that he lost him in the woods, and had not seen him since. Some days passed when *Lothbroch*'s dog, half starved, came to the palace, and being fed goes away again. Doing thus several times, the king's servants took notice of it, and following the dog were brought to the sight of the dead body. *Bern* was charged with the murder, tried, and found guilty of it; the sentence the king passed on him was to put him into *Lothbroch*'s boat, and, without tackling, sails or provisions, to commit him to the mercy of the seas. The boat, as if it knew its way back, was thrown upon the *Danish* coast, where *Bern* being apprehended as an *Englishman*, and carried to the king, he informed him of *Lothbroch*; and in a malitious lye told him, that *Edmund*, on his landing, had ordered him to be immediately thrown into a ditch full of serpents.

This accident happening before the *Saxon* nobleman's arrival in order to draw the *Danish* king to invade *Northumberland*, in revenge for the ravishing of his wife by *Osbert*, made the *Dane* more ready to embrace it. Getting together a mighty fleet, they set sail and entered the *Humber* with safety; and landing their forces as near *York* as they could, they marched directly to it, and took it with much ease; the walls of the city, says *(r)* an historian, being in a weak condition at that time, occasioned by the former *Saxon* wars. *Osbert* and *Ella* having, upon this occasion, joined their forces, marched to attack the *Danes* even in the city itself; where a cruel fight ensued in the very midst on it. The two kings having beat down the walls, fell upon the *Danes* with such fury, that they made a prodigious slaughter of them, and drove them to the last extremity. Their despair at this time occasioned their victory, say my authors, for pressing in their turn, the *Saxons* lost ground, and their two kings happening to be slain, the victory entirely fell to the *Danes*. In this conflict the city was wholly destroyed by the enraged barbarians, and in it, not only all the inhabitants, but all those who upon the news of the invasion, fought refuge there, miserably perished. The battle, says *R. Hoveden*, was fought on the 21st day of *March*, A.
A. D. 867. *Asser Menevensis* describes this dreadful calamity in this manner. *(s)* By DCCCLXVII.

(p) Brompton, H. Hunt. S. Dunelm. Asser. Men. R. Hoveden.

(q) Lothbroch, Anglice, Leatherbreech. This story is given by the translator of *Rapin*.

(r) Non enim tunc adbuc illa civitas firmos et stabilitos muros illis temporibus habebat. Asser. Meneven.

(s) Pueros, senes, cum junioribus in plateis civitatis obviam factos jugulat, scil. Hinguar, *et matronalem seu*

the generals cruel orders they knocked down and cut the throats of all the boys, young and old men that they met in the streets of the city. Matrons and virgins were ravished at pleasure. The husband and wife either dead or dying, were tossed together. The infant, snatched from its mother's breast, was carried to the threshold, and there left butchered at its parent's door, to make the general outcry more hideous.

Brompton differs somewhat from the other historians in the description of this battle, and says that *Ella* was not slain with *Osbert*; but was so little concerned, that having been hunting the day after the battle was fought, as he sat at dinner, he chanced to say, *we have had great luck to take four deer and six fawns to day*, to which words an express, that was just arrived, answered, *my lord if you have had such luck to day, and gained so much, you yesterday lost an hundred times more; for the* Danes *have taken the city of* York, *and slain* Osbert, *and are just entering your dominions to do the like to you. Ella* at this starting up, collected his forces, and marched towards *York* with great expedition. The *Danes* were aware of his coming, and met him to the utter destruction of him and his. The place where the battle was fought, *non longe ab* Eboraco, says my author, is called to this day *Ella's-croft*, *(t)* that is, *Ella*'s overthrow.

The *Danes* having reduced the kingdom of *Northumberland* to their obedience, and put an end to the *Saxon* rule there, after it had continued in their possessions near three hundred years, *Hinguar* gave the command of it to his brother *Hubba*, and constituted him at the same time governour of *York*. The two brothers then pushed their conquests southward, where I shall not follow them, but observe that *Hubba* made one *(u) Godram* or *Guthurn*, a *Danish* officer his deputy to act in his absence, and left a garrison under him in the city. There is a street in *York* which still retains the name of this captain, called **Godram** or **Guthram-gate**; which also tradition tells us comes from a *Danish* general's residing in it; and as it lies near where the old *royal palace* once stood, it is not improbable that this was the true derivation. But if any one quarrel with the etymology, let him produce an apter, from any other language, if he can.

A. DCCCLXX. But the *Danes* were not willing to trust the government of the *Northumbrian* kingdom under any other form than kingly; accordingly at their return to *York*, from their southern conquest, the two brothers *Hinguar* and *Hubba* constituted one *Egbert* a *Saxon*, but one entirely devoted to their service, king of *Northumberland*. At this time, says Sir *John Spelman*, (x) the *Danish* generals, with their whole army, resided at *York*, where they indulged themselves in all kinds of violence, and barbarous treatment of the people. The blood of men, women, and children was daily shed to make them sport; corn and other provisions, more damaged then consumed, says my author, they rioted in for above a year together.

Egbert was soon deprived of his sovereignty, and one *Rigsidge*, or *Ricsisius*, a *Dane* had the government conferred upon him; but he being murthered by the populace at *York*, according to *Simeon* of *Durham*, *Egbert* was again restored. This held not long neither, for the *Danes* still advancing in power, and having no dread of the natives, the large and rich kingdom of *Northumberland* was cantoned out amongst their own officers. For we find in the reign of *Edward* the elder, three kings of *Danish* race possessed it. *Sitbrick*

A. DCCCLXXVII. and *Nigell* his brother reigned beyond the *Tyne*, and *Reginald* had the city of *York* with all the country betwixt the rivers *Tine* and *Humber*. These kings were at last compelled to submit to the arms of the victorious *Athelstane*, the successor of the last named *Edward*, and doing homage, were permitted to keep their possessions. *Sitbrick*, one of them, had his daughter in marriage, on condition he would turn *Christian*.

A. DCCCCXXVI. This calm lasted for a very small time, for *Sitbrick* dying the first year of his marriage, *(y)* his sons *Godfrey* and *Anlaff*, offended that their *pagan gods* were neglected, by means of their father's last wife, stirred up the *Northumbrian Danes* to rebel; which attempt brought *Athelstane* upon them so suddenly, that the two sons of *Sitbrick*, with *Reginald* had much ado to escape falling into his hands at *York*. The city he took, and with it all *Northumberland* submitted, except the castle of *York*; which being then prodigiously strong, and well manned with *Danish* soldiers, held out a long time. For we are told that, *Godfrid* made an attempt upon *York*, by means of his friends in the garrison, but did not succeed in it. What end made *(z) Reginald* I know not; but the two brothers *Godfrey* and *Anlaff*, having been disappointed in their last attempt, fled one into *Scotland*, and the other into *Ireland*, in order to gain aid to try their fortunes once again. They succeeded so well,

virginalem pudicitiam ludibrio tradendam mandat. Maritus cum conjuge aut mortuus aut moribundus jacebat; in limine infans raptus a matris uberibus ut major esset ejulatus, trucidabatur coram maternis obtutibus.

(t) There is no place, in or near the city, that I can fix this name upon, except it be corrupted to *Ling-croft*, near *Foulford*. It is certain there is no *ling* growing on it, nor probably ever was, the soil being a dry sand cannot naturally produce that plant. *Ling* does certainly here import another meaning, for Dr. *Skinner* says it is a word *quod qualitatem notat, et pertinere aut spectare ad aliquem est*. *Skinner's* etym. dict.

(u) This *Guthrum* turned Christian, and when baptized, *Alfred* the Great was his godfather; who gave him the country of *East-Anglia*, which he governed, or rather spoiled for twelve years *Holl.* chron.

(x) Spelman in vita *Alfredi* Magni.

(y) Rapin.

(z) The *Saxon* chronicle says that *A.* DCCCCXXIV. king *Reginald* wone the city of *York* by assault, *expugnavit* Eboracum. *Gibson's Sax.* chron.

that

8

that they drew along with them a vast multitude of *Irish*, *Scotch*, and even *Welsh* soldiers, with their respective kings at the head of them; who all had reason to fear the growing greatness of *Athelstane*. Entering the *Humber* with a fleet of six hundred sail, whilst *Athelstane* was carrying the war on in *Scotland*, they landed their forces and marched to *York* before the king had any intelligence of the matter. They soon raised the siege of the castle, which *Athelstane* had turned into a blockade; but durst not attempt to take the city, hearing that *Athelstane* was on his march against them. As a battle was to be fought, and trusting in their numbers, they went from *York* to meet him, and at **Brunanburg**, since called *Bromford*, in *Northumberland*, a most bloody engagement ensued, where *Athelstane* gained a compleat victory, and slew *Constantine* king of *Scotland*, five petty kings of *Ireland* and *Wales*, twelve general officers, and destroyed their whole army.

Athelstane at his return to *York* from this victory, razed the *(a)* castle to the ground, A. DCCCCXXXVII.
lest it should be any more a nursery of rebellion; and being now sole monarch of *England*, he conferred those honours on the churches of *St. John* of *Beverley*, and *St. Wilfrid* at *Ripon*, which the *monkish* histories are so full of. Our own historians stick not to say, that this victory made him king of the whole island; but *Buchanan* here stickles for his country, and seems to sneer at the credulity of the *English*, who are so *wise* as to believe it. *Athelstane*, however, died in perfect tranquillity, and left his whole dominions to *Edmund* the eldest of the legitimate sons of *Edward*, surnamed *the Elder*, himself dying without issue *(b)*.

This prince was very young at his coming to the crown, which encouraged the *Northum-* A. DCCCCXL.
bers, ever prone to rebel, to hope for a revolution in their favour. They sent to invite *Anlaff* from *Ireland*, whither he had the good luck to escape to from the last battle, to come over and head them. But *Anlaff* wisely knowing that an invasion without strong assistance from some foreign power, would be of no service, set himself about once more to obtain it. He found means to draw over *Olaus* king of *Norway* to his interest, with a large promise of money if he succeeded. With the troops and shipping that this king furnished him with, he once more entered the north, and coming before *York*, the gates were immediately opened to him, by means of the good understanding he had with the principal inhabitants, who were then most or all of them *Danish* in that city. *(c)* The example of the *metropolis* was soon followed by several other towns in that district, whose garrisons were either drove out or cut in pieces by the inhabitants; and thus got *Anlaff* entire possession of all *Northumberland*; and, not content, was stretching his conquest farther and attacked *Mercia*.

Edmund, the *English* king, though not above seventeen or eighteen years old, was not backward in his preparations, to stop the progress of this bold invader. Having raised an army, he met *Anlaff* at *Chester*, where an obstinate battle was fought, but with such equality, that neither side could brag of victory. Resolving to try it out next day, a peace was concluded by the mediation of *Odo* and *Wolstan*, the two archbishops of *Canterbury* and *York*; who laboured all night to obtain it. By this treaty *Edmund* was obliged to give up all the country, north of the *Roman* highway, which divides *England* into two equal parts, to *Anlaff*. This concession of *Edmund*'s was highly dishonourable, but the two bishops prevailed on him to accept it; and thus got *Anlaff* a larger share of *Britain* than his father *Sithrich* ever possessed.

But his glory was short lived, for the *Northumbrians*, vexed at a tax he had imposed on them, in order to pay off the great subsidy due to the king of *Norway* for his aid and assistance, revolted again. The antient kingdom of *Bernicia* first shewed the way, by sending for *Reginald*, son to his brother *Godfrid*, and crowning him king at *York*. Once more a civil war was preparing to break out betwixt the uncle and nephew; the *English* king might have laid hold of this opportunity to have destroyed them both; but he did no more than come with a great army and frighten them at once into peace and *christianity*. A treaty was begun and concluded at *York*, wherein it was stipulated, that *Reginald* should keep the crown he had got, and *Edmund* obliged them both to swear fealty to him, as also to turn *Christians*. The king himself stood godfather to *Reginald*, who had been baptized at his confirmation; and to *Anlaff* at the font; the ceremony was performed by *Wolstan*, then archbishop of this see, in his cathedral *(d)*.

A religion and peace, imposed upon them by compulsion, lasted them not long; and it A. DCCCCXLIV.
was a very small time before they took up arms and broke the latter; which shews the former was no tye to them. *Edmund* was sudden in his coming against them, and marched so quick that he surprized them before they could draw a sufficient number of forces ready to oppose him. In short they both fled the island, and the *Danes* being thus deserted by their leaders, had nothing to do but to fling down their arms and submit to the king's mercy. This they obtained of him, and *Edmund* took no other revenge on them than to cause their principal to swear allegiance to him, which they did; however he joined their

(a) Athelstanus *interea* Castrum, *quod olim* Dani *in* Eboraco *obfirmaverant, ad solum diruit, ne esset quod se tutari posset perfidia.* Gul. Meldunensis.

(b) Speed.

(c) Rapin.

(d) Sim. Dun. Hen. Hunt.

whole

whole country to his own government, without the admittance of any secondary, or viceroy, to rule there under him (*e*).

A. Dccccxlvi. Thus was the *Saxon* king *Edmund* re-instated into the sovereignty of all *England*; but, being taken off in the flower of his age, by an unhappy accident, *Edred* his brother succeded him. It was now, again, the turbulent spirit of the *Northumbrian Danes* began to shew it self, imagining that this king wanted, with the years, the experience of his brother (*f*). But they found themselves mistaken, for *Edred* was not inferiour to the former king, either in courage or conduct; and in this first affair he sufficiently shewed it. For he made such expedition in marching against them, that he got into the heart of their country, before the *Danes* could think that he knew their design. Catched so at unawares, they had nothing to do but to submit to the conqueror's mercy; which like that of his brother's was soon come at; a fine, no ways considerable, was all he imposed, they promising with oaths and protestations to be for ever obedient and peaceable. But it was not in their nature to keep this promise, and *Edred* had hardly got back into *West-sex* before they sent over for their old friend *Anlaff*, who had again fled to *Ireland*. He made such haste to obey their summons, and by their assistance, after his arrival, pushed on his conquest so fast, that he was master of *York* and all the north, before *Edred* could come to oppose him; and when he did come, he found it impossible to dislodge him.

A. DCCCCL. In spight of all that *Edred* could do, *Anlaff* continued king of *Northumberland* four years after his last restauration (*g*). But his tyrannical temper, or their mutability, occasioned another revolt; and *Anlaff* was expelled, and one *Eric* was chose by them in his room. This brought on another civil war; *Anlaff* had yet a party, and the two factions endeavouring to destroy one another, gave *Edred* an opportunity that he well knew how to improve. He marched directly into the north which was all in confusion, for the *Northumbrians* had taken no measure to resist him; so eager they were to seek each others destruction. At *Edred*'s coming *Eric* fled into *Scotland*, leaving his people once more to the *Saxon* king's mercy, who had threatned to destroy their whole country with fire and sword from end to end. He began to put his threats in execution by burning the town and monastery of *Ripon*; but being shocked enough with that, the good king desisted from any further mischief to them, and suffered himself to be so far amused with their solemn oaths and protestations, which they were no ways sparing on to appease his just anger, that his generous disposition not only forgave them their trespasses, but he recalled *Eric* out of *Scotland* to *York*, replaced him on the throne, and, without imposing any tribute, took only his oath of allegiance.

It is amazing to think that a person of *Edred*'s high character in history, for wisdom and conduct, should suffer himself to be diverted so far from his first intention, by any thing these faithless people could say or do to him. Numberless examples of their sincerity in keeping the most solemn oaths and protestations, to himself and predecessors, might have taught him that nothing but the sword, exercised in the sharpest manner, could give him security of these parts of his kingdom. But, the *christian religion* which teaches *to forgive our enemies, and to do good to those that hate and despitefully use us*, was so warmly placed in the breast of this good king, as well as in some others of his race, that to shed the blood even of pagan *Danes* was held unlawful. A few christnings usually disarmed their fiercest anger; and to stand *godfather* at the baptism of a pagan prince, was looked upon to be more glorious than the conquering his kingdom. Nay so far did their *zeal* stretch, that they seemed to invite martyrdom at the hands of these heathens when overcome by them; as in the case of St. *Edmund*, who might have escaped from his cruel enemy *Hinguar*, if he had not been actuated by this principle. A stedfast adherence to the *Christian* religion when it comes even to a fiery tryal, is highly commendable; and one dying martyr converts more than a thousand living preachers. But to avoid such a fate as much as possible, in an honest way, is surely consonant to the law of nature, and I am ignorant of any passage in the law of *God* that puts us upon it. So also the destruction of our own species in war, is, most certainly, cruel and barbarous in the execution, but yet to slay is to save in some cases; and *Edred*'s ill-timed mercy here with the *Danes*, as that before in *Aurelius Ambrosius* with the *Saxons*, when he might have extirpated the whole generation of his enemies from his own country, with all the justice in the world, proved the loss of thousands of his own subjects lives and the kingdom also.

To give *Edred* a speedy instance what wonderful effects his clemency had wrought on their minds, after he had settled matters to his own, and, seemingly, to their contents, he took leave of them, and marched southward with his army, in a careless and disorderly manner. Not dreaming of danger, nor keeping any guard against a people he had just then so prodigiously obliged. The *Danes*, taking notice of his negligence and disorderly march, sallied out of *York* in great numbers after him; and overtaking him at *Castleford*, (*h*) set upon his rear with such fury and resolution, that had not the king's valour, con-

(*e*) *Speed*.
(*f*) *Rapin*.
(*g*) *Rapin*, *Speed*.

(*h*) *Lelandi* coll. it appears by this rout of the army that they followed the *Roman* roads in those days.

duct,

duct and management, in this nice juncture, been very extraordinary, he and all his army must infallibly have been cut to pieces. Enraged at this black piece of ingratitude, he once more ordered his standard to be turned against them. His *christian* virtues of mercy, pity, *&c.* this last attempt had quite struck out of his breast; and instead thereof came anger, fury and revenge; with which he advanced to the gates of *York*, in order to make dreadful examples of these miscreants to all posterity. At his coming to the city, they beheld him ready to take vengeance of them, and they not able to make the least resistance. In this extremity they had recourse to their old subtlety, but being sensible their oaths and protestations would go for nothing with the king, they very humbly implored his pardon on what terms he would be pleased to give it. And to convince the king they were now in earnest, they solemnly renounced *Eric*, and put him to death; along with *Amac*, the son of *Anlaff*, whom they charged with being the principal movers in this treachery. Then, says old *Simeon* of *Durham*, *regis injurias honoribus, detrimenta muneribus expleverunt; ejusque offensam pecunia non modica placaverunt. Edred* was pacified by these means, he spared their lives, but took deep vengeance on their purses; and also took from them the very power to rebel again, by placing strong *English* garrisons in their chiefest towns and fortresses; he likewise dissolved their monarchical government, and turned the antient kingdom of *Northumberland* into a *province*. What became of *Anlaff*, the last king, I know not; it is probable he died abroad; no author making any mention of him after *Edred*'s last expedition into the north. We now drop from a *kingdom* to an *earldom*, as *Edred* thought fit to alter the government; the first *earl* thereof, by his own appointment, was one *Osulph*, an *Anglo-Saxon* or *Englishman*.

A. DCCCCLI.

The alteration made in the government produced a very good effect; for the turbulent and rebellious spirit of the *Northumbrian-Danes* was so continually awed by *English* governours and *English* garrisons, that during the almost constant wars betwixt the *Saxon* and *Danish* kings, for near an age after this, the northern parts kept quiet. And *York* continued with its *earls*, as *Edred* left it, till the division of the kingdom into *shires*, and the *vicecomes* took place of the real one.

A. MX.

The *Scotch* historians, however, write, *(l)* that the total conquest over the *Saxons* by the *Danes* was gained in a victory near our city; by *Swain* king of *Denmark*, against *(m) Egelred* king of *England*. The *Danes* had pitched their tents on the banks of the river *Ouse* not far from *York*, where *Egelred* with an army, strengthened with a number of *Scots*, marched to attack them. *Swain* sent an *herald* to warn the *Scots* from fighting, having some obligation to their king; but they refusing, a bloody battle ensued, in which the *English* and *Scots* were worsted, great numbers slain, and an entire victory left to the *Danes*. *Egelred* himself, with some few others got a boat, and passing over the river *Ouse*, fled streight into *Normandy*, leaving his crown and kingdom to the conqueror.

We now come to a succession of the *earls*, or *Comites Northumbriae*, who had their residence in *York* as well as the kings; and had, under subjection to the universal monarch of *England*, the same authority. We are told that *Edred* first commissioned

(n) Osulph, who in the succeeding reign of *Edgar* had

Oslac for a partner in the government. *Osulph* took the more northern parts; and *Oslac* had *York*, and the confines of the province on that side, committed to his care. To these succeeded in the whole

Waltheof, usually called the elder; whose son

Utbred, or *Uctbred* came after him; then

Hircus, or *Yricus*, made earl of *Northumberland* by king *Canute*.

Eadulph, surnamed *Cutel* or *Cudel*; to whom succeeded

Aldred, who being slain,

Eadulph, the second, his brother, enjoyed it; to all these, historians have affixed no dates; nor any particulars relating to their respective governments; till this earl was slain by

A. C.

MLIV. *Siward*; then succeeded

MLV. *Tosty*; brother to *Harold* king of *England*. Slain at *Stanfordburgh*; lastly came

MLXV. *Morchar*; which deduces the earls of *Northumberland* to the *Norman* conquest. An historical account of the three last is much to my purpose.

Siward earl of *Northumberland* was the most valiant man of his time, and of such uncommon fortitude and might, that the *Danes*, says *William* of *Malmsbury*, surnamed him *(o)* **Digera**, that is, *the great*. *Brompton* says, he was almost of a gigantick stature; and tells an odd story, that his father *Bern was born of a young lady in* Denmark, *whom a bear met accidentally in a wood and ravished.* The offspring of this extraordinary copulation

(l) Holl. Scotch chron. *H. Boet.*
(m) The *English* historians call him *Ethelred.*
(n) Sim. Dunelm.
(o) **Digera**, *Danice, magnus.* **Alexander digera**, i. e. *Alexander magnus.* Jacob. Serenii *diction.* Ang. Suethic. Lat.

had the ears of his father given him to ſhew his breed *(p)*. This *Siward* was ſent by king *Edward* the confeſſor, with an army of ten thouſand *Engliſh* ſoldiers into *Scotland*, to aid *Malcolm* againſt the tyrant *Macbeth*; him he ſlew and ſet *Malcolm* on the throne of *Scotland*. His only ſon was ſlain in this expedition, which when the earl was told of, he ſternly aſked, *whether he had received his death's wound before or behind?* being told before, *it is well*, anſwers he, *I rejoice that my ſon was thought worthy of ſo honourable a death (q)*.

A MLV. *Siward* fell ill of the flux at *York*, and being brought to the laſt extremity by that filthy diſeaſe, the warrior cried out, *(r) Oh what a ſhame is it for me, who have eſcaped death in ſo many dangerous battles, to die like a beaſt at laſt. Put me on my impenetrable coat of mail*, adds he, *gird on my ſword, place on my helmet, give me my ſhield in my right hand, and my (s) golden battle-ax in my left; thus as a valiant ſoldier I have lived, even ſo I will die.* His friends obeyed him, which was no ſooner done then he expired; and was buried in the *cloiſter of his own monaſtery at* York *(t)*

Siward left a ſon, born after the loſs of the former; but he being in the cradle *(u)* at his father's death, *Toſty* or *Toſto*, ſecond ſon to earl *Goodwin*, chief miniſter of ſtate to *Edward* the confeſſor, found means to procure this opulent *earldom* to himſelf. A man of the vileſt character, in every point of life, that I have yet met with. *Toſto* ruled over the *Northumbrians* with great cruelty and barbarity; impoſing numberleſs taxations on them for the ſpace of ten years together. It was a long time for their ſtubborn ſpirits to bear ſuch treatment; at length being provoked, at his cauſing certain noblemen of that country to be *(x)* murthered, in his own chamber, at *York*; when he had allured them thither on pretence of eaſing their grievances. As alſo another more ſcandalous affair of making minced-meat of his brother *Harold*'s ſervants; their hearts were ſo much ſet againſt him, that they roſe with one accord in order to rid themſelves, and the world, of ſuch a monſter. The *Northumbrians* came upon *Toſto* ſo ſuddenly, that he narrowly eſcaped their fury; and had juſt time to fly from *York* with his wife and children to the ſea-coaſt; from
A. MLXV. whence he found means to be conveyed into *Flanders*, and came no more into *England* during the *confeſſor's* reign. Miſſing of their chief aim, the revolters took all the revenge they could on what he had left behind him. They ſpoiled and plundered his palace, broke open his exchequer, took and converted whatever money was there to their own uſe, drowned two hundred of his ſervants in the river *Ouſe*, as *Simeon* ſays, *extra muros civitatis*; and whatever horſes, armour, or houſholdſtuff was in or about the palace was all carried off *(z)*. Beſides all this, they obſtinately refuſed to lay down their arms, till the king ſhould appoint another governor, whom they promiſed punctually to obey.

At the news of this inſurrection, *Harold* the brother of *Toſto* was ſent to reduce them; but he having had a ſmart taſte of his brother's cruelty, eaſily gave into the juſtneſs of their complaints *(a)*. Eſpecially when they told him plainly, *that they being freemen born and bred out of bondage, would not ſuffer any cruel ruler to lord it over them, being taught by their anceſtors, either to live in liberty, or die in the defence of it (b)*. Upon which at their own requeſt, and by the king's conſent, he aſſigned them one *Morchard* or *Morcharus* for their governor.

Toſto was now an exile in *Flanders*, but no ſooner did he hear of king *Edward*'s death, and his brother's ſeizing the crown, than he prepared to invade him. He muſtered a few forces and ſhipping, with which he landed on the *Lincolnſhire* coaſt; but *Morchar* the new earl defeated him, and ſent him to ſea again. After this misfortune he ſailed into *Scotland*, in hopes to ſtir up *Malcolm* the *Scotch* king to invade *England*; but that prince diſdaining his cauſe, he was obliged to put to ſea again, where he purpoſed to land ſomewhere on the *Engliſh* coaſt, and once more to try his fortune. At ſea he met with a ſtorm which drove him into *Norway*, and here he accidentally ſtumbled, ſays *Rapin*, on what he had been ſeeking for ſo induſtriouſly.

(c) Harold Harfager king of *Norway* had juſt then ſubdued ſome of the iſles called *Orcades* belonging to *Scotland*, and was fitting out a fleet more numerous in order to extend his conqueſts. *Toſto* being informed of this prince's deſigns, went directly to him, pretending he was come on purpoſe to propoſe a more noble undertaking. He repreſented to him that a favourable opportunity offered to conquer *England*, if he would but turn his arms that

(p) Brompton.

(q) Quere, Whether this ſpeech, and unconcern for the death of an only ſon, did not favour very much of the *grandfather?*

(r) Higdeni Polichron.

(s) Securis aureus, or the golden battle-ax, was formerly a mark of ſovereignty.

(t) A. 1055. *Sirenuus dux* Northanhimbrorum Siwardus Eboraci *deceſſit, et in monaſterio* Galmanho, *quod ipſe conſtruxerat ſepultus eſt.* Hoveden.

(u) Parvulus erat in cuneis jacens. Polichron.

(x) The names of two of them were *Gamel* the ſon of *Ornus*, and *Ulſus* the ſon of *Delphinus*. S. *Dun.*

(z) Chron. *Sax.*

(a) Toſto upon a quarrel with his brother went down to his country-houſe and ſlew all his ſervants, who were preparing an entertainment for the king's coming down there. After which he chopped them in pieces, and caſt into this hogſhead of wine a leg, into that barrel of cyder an arm, into this veſſel of ale a head, and ſo beſtowed all the dead carcaſſes into what other hogſheads of wine, mead, *&c.* that he could come at in the houſe. *H. Hunt. M West.*

(b) Knighton.

(c) Rapin, Speed.

way.

way. The better to perſuade him to it, he told him there were in *England* two powerful factions, the one for prince *Edgar*, the other for the duke of *Normandy*; and therefore the *Engliſh* arms being thus divided, he would find it no hard matter to ſubdue all. Adding, that he himſelf had a ſtrong party in *Northumberland*, which would much forward the buſineſs. In fine, he brought him to believe that the king his brother was extremely odious to the *Engliſh*, and would certainly be deſerted by them, as ſoon as they ſhould find in *England* a foreign army ſtrong enough to ſupport them. *Harfager*, greedy of fame, and already devouring in his imagination ſo glorious a prize, wanted little ſollicitation to draw him to it.

The king of *Norway* and *Toſto* having got all things in readineſs for their intended invaſion, ſet ſail for *England* with a fleet of near ſix hundred ſail, ſays *Simeon* of *Durham*; ſome call them five hundred great ſhips, others only two hundred, whilſt others have raiſed them to a thouſand, ſays *Milton*. With this mighty fleet they entered the (*e*) *Humber* and brought their ſhips againſt the ſtream of the river *Ouſe*, as far as **Rickall** or **Rich-hall** within ſix miles of *York*. Here they landed and moored their veſſels. It is certain ſo vaſt and numerous a fleet, containing ſuch a great number of land-forces on board, could come no nearer *York*; and it is wonderful at this time a day how they could advance ſo high. Having landed their forces, they marched directly againſt *York*, which, ſays *Simeon* they took by ſtorm, after a ſore conflict with *Morchar* the governour, and *Edwin* earl of *Cheſter*, his brother, who had haſtily raiſed a few forces to intercept them (*f*). This defeat happened on the eve of St. *Mathew*, *A.* 1066, at **Foulford**, a village a mile ſouth-eaſt of the city, where, ſays *H. Huntington*, the place of battle is yet ſhewn. The laſt named author, with others, alledge that the city was not taken by ſtorm, but the two generals being worſted, and their ſmall army being either drowned in the river *Ouſe* or cut in pieces, the city ſurrendered on terms; the inhabitants wholly unprovided for a ſiege, choſe rather to try the victor's clemency, than expoſe themſelves to certain ruin.

A. MLXVI.

Harold king of *England* was no ways backward in his preparations, to ſtop the progreſs of this dangerous invaſion; but brought down to *York* a puiſſant army, immediately after the enemy had taken it. At his approach they withdrew their forces from the city, taking with them five hundred hoſtages of the principal inhabitants, whom they ſent under a ſtrong guard on board their ſhips, and left, ſays *Milton*, one hundred and fifty of their own in it. They entrenched themſelves in ſo extraordinary a manner, that it ſeemed a thing impoſſible to diſlodge them. For they had the river *Derwent* in their front, and on their right-hand, not fordable, with only a wooden bridge to paſs over by; their left was flanked by the river *Ouſe*; where lay their navy ready to retire to in caſe of neceſſity; and their backs ſecured by the *German* ocean. In this ſituation they thought themſelves ſafe from any human force diſlodging of them. But *Harold*, notwithſtanding the great diſadvantage, was reſolved to attack them in their trenches; and the event ſhews that nothing can be too hard for valour joined with conduct. The fight began by day break, and the attempt ſo deſperate to paſs the bridge, that one ſingle *Norwegian*, for which our hiſtorians have juſtly made his fame immortal, ſtopped the paſſage to all *Harold*'s army for three hours together; and ſlew forty of his men with his own hand. At laſt this hardy fellow being ſlain, by a dart flung at him, ſay ſome, or, as others (*g*) write, by one in a boat, who got under the bridge and thruſt him into the body with a ſpear, the *Norwegians* gave way, diſmayed with the loſs of their champion, and retiring to their trenches, ſuffered all *Harold*'s army to paſs the river. The extraordinary valour of this hero that ſtopped the bridge, will hardly be credited by poſterity, ſays *William* of *Malmſbury*; for ſtanding in the midſt of it, he ſuffered none to paſs over, and ſlew all that attempted it, or came within his reach (*h*). Being deſired to yield himſelf up to the *Engliſh* king with large promiſes of reward, adequate to ſuch mighty ſtrength and valour, he ſternly ſmiled at the proffer, and deſpiſed both it and the weakneſs of thoſe that let one ſingle man reſiſt them all (*i*).

The champion being ſlain, as I ſaid, and the *Engliſh* army paſſed the bridge, *Harold* drew up his men, and attacked the enemies trenches ſword in hand, where a moſt bloody and obſtinate fight enſued. The aforementioned hiſtorian writes, that there had never been ſeen in *England* an engagement betwixt two ſuch armies, each containing ſixty thouſand men; *pugna ingens*, adds he, *utriſque gentibus extrema nitentibus*. This battle laſted from ſeven in the morning till three in the afternoon, with all the fury imaginable; no quarter being either aſked or received during this dreadful conflict. The victory fell to *Harold* the *Engliſh* king; the king of *Norway* and *Toſto* were ſlain, with the deſtruction of almoſt their whole army. For of five or ſix hundred ſhips that brought them to *England*, twenty ſerved to carry back the miſerable remains that were ſpared from ſlaughter; which the

A. MLXVI.

(*e*) Humbram *ingrediuntur et per* Ouſe *fluviolum*, *pene ad* Eboracum, *omnes puppes advehuntur.* Ingulphus.

(*f*) Chron *Saxon*.

(*g*) *H. Hunt M. Weſt* and *Knighton* write, *donec unus* Anglus *naviculam ingreſſus ipſum* Noricum *per foramina pontis lancea perfodiſſet.*

(*h*) *Gul. Malmſ.*

(*i*) It ſeems by this that there was no bridge over the *Derwent* at *Kexby* when this battle was fought; elſe *Harold* might have paſſed over his army at that place, and have attacked them in flank, being only two miles below the other.

victor

victor suffered to depart with *Olaus*, the king of *Norway*'s son, and *Paul* earl of *Orkney*; who had escaped the battle by being set to guard the ships. *Harold* however made them deliver up their hostages safe, the citizens of *York*, and take a solemn oath never to disturb his dominions again.

The king of *England* shewed great magnanimity in this battle, and, if we may credit our writers, *(k)* slew the *Norwegian* king with his own hand. *Tosto* his brother, being sought for amongst the dead bodies, was at length found; but so mangled, that had not a remarkable wart betwixt his shoulders discovered him, he might have served to fill a pit with the commonest soldiers (*l*). He was carried to *York*, and there, ignominiously enough, says my authority, interred. The booty which was found in the camp was so great, that *Aimund Bemensis* writes, they took so much gold, that twelve young men could hardly bear it on their shoulders (*m*). This account, since no historian of our own confirms it, I must beg leave to dissent from; unless we suppose that the city of *York* had afforded them in plunder such a vast treasure. For it is not to be imagined, that after fitting out so great a fleet, so much superfluous gold should be brought along with them. However it is agreed on all hands, that the spoil was great, which *Harold*, contrary to true policy, his natural temper, which was esteemed generous, and the common custom of those times, kept to his own private use; and did not reward the soldiers as he ought to have done, after such a signal proof of their courage and bravery. This conduct is looked upon by our historians to be one reason the soldiers did not exert themselves so heartily in his cause, in the succeeding battle with the duke of *Normandy*.

A. MLXVI. This battle was fought within six miles of *York*, eastward, at a place now called (*n*) *Stanfordbridge*, on the 23[d] day of *September*, *A.* 1066. The *Saxon* chronicle calls this place Stœnᵹ-ꝼoꞃꝺeꞃ-bꞃẏcᵹe, *Higden* in his *Polychronicon* **Stein-forth-burgg**; but after the conquest the village had the name of *Pons-belli*, or *Battle-bridge*, given it, to perpetuate the memory of this great overthrow. However it now retains its antient name, and no remembrance of the fight, except a piece of ground on the left-hand of the bridge called **Battle-flatts** at this day. In the plowing this ground have been, of late years, found pieces of old swords, and a very small sort of horse-shoes, which could only fit an ass, or the least breed of northern horses. I must not forget that the inhabitants of this village have a custom, at an annual feast, to make pies in the form of a *swill*, or *swine-tub*; which, tradition says, was made use on by the man that struck the *Norwegian* under the bridge instead of a boat. This may be true, for the river being but very lately made navigable up here on the *Derwent*, a boat was not easily to be had to perform the exploit in. The bridge also continued to be a wooden one, till falling greatly to decay it was taken down, and a new one begun and finished, about a hundred yards below the old one, at the county charge, *A.* 1727. But to our history.

Harold's great joy for the gaining of this signal victory was of a very short date; returning to *York* that night, he gave orders for solemn feasts and rejoicings to be begun the next day with all the magnificence imaginable (*o*). Our city may be well supposed to have a real share in the general joy, as not only being relieved from foreign fetters, but secured from the just fears of *Tosto*; who, no doubt, would have taken ample vengeance on his enemies, as soon as his conquest was compleat. But *Harold* had scarce begun his triumphs, when a messenger arrived from the south, who told him, as he sat in this city in great state, at a magnificent entertainment, that duke *William* was landed with a mighty army at *Pevensey* near *Hastings* in *Sussex*.

The obstinate battle at *Stanfordburgh*, where *Harold* must have lost a great many of his choice men, as well as the distaste his soldiers took at him, for not dividing the spoils, are reasons given, as I said, for his ill-fortune in *Sussex*. For here his whole army was cut in pieces, and himself shot into the brains with an arrow, left his crown and kingdom to the conqueror; who shortly after took possession of both. This fight and tragical event happened only nine days after the former victory; and gives us a smart instance of the extream mutability of all human affairs.

I have now brought this chapter to its period; to recapitulate what has been said in the briefest manner, I am sure would seem tedious. It has been small satisfaction to me, in this nice scrutiny, to endeavour to put things together so as to make them appear tolerable; and I am afraid it will be much less to the reader, unless he be so much a master of *English* history, as to know how difficult a matter it is, even in a general way, to set off these affairs in pleasing colours, and yet stick to the originals. The writers of these dark ages, we have now passed through, Sir *William Temple* styles *poor, jejune, and obscure guides not worth the minding*. But herein I differ from his opinion; for let their style and composure be never so mean, the historical facts may be true; and it would be as ridiculous in us to quarrel with these, when we can have no other assistance, as for a man to send back a guide, who came to meet him with a *lanthorn* in a dark night, because he did not bring him a *torch*.

(*k*) *Fabian*'s chron. from *Guido*.
(*l*) *Gul. Malmſ.*
(*m*) *Cambden*.
(*n*) This name has lead some of our modern historians to fix this battle at *Stanford* in *Lincolnshire*.
(*o*) *Gul. Malmſ.*

It is very true the *monkish* historians are so stuffed with visions, miracles, and their own monastical affairs, that for the first two no kind of *popish* legend can outdo them; and for the latter it takes up three parts in four, almost of their whole performance *(p)*. But still they are our only directors; the only men of that age, who had either learning or curiosity enough to enquire into and hand down to posterity, in a style and diction suitable to the times they lived in, the memorable events that happened in their own or forefather's days. I am told it is still the custom in the monasteries abroad, to keep one of their order particularly to be the *historiographer*, both of the publick as well as their own private affairs; and can we blame them for being circumstantial enough in the latter? no surely, *proximus sum egomet mihi.* How happily, says the author of the life of Mr. *Somner*, would it spread the glory of the *English* church and nation if among divines, addicted to these studies, some one were preferred to a dignity in every collegiate church on condition, to employ his talent in the history and antiquities of that body, of which he was a grateful and an useful member. Monsieur *Rapin Thoyras*, the late celebrated *English* historian is no friend to the monks; but, on the contrary, slips no opportunity to lash them, and says, that they could never find in their hearts to let any extraordinary event take place without ascribing it to some supernatural cause, by way of miracle. But I would ask that gentleman, were he alive, to whom was he obliged for materials in composing that fine part of his history, the ecclesiastical and civil affairs of *England*, during the *Saxon* government, but to the monks? And as it is natural for every man to praise the bridge he goes over, though a mean one, so it can never seem well in any author to fall upon his only guides, and abuse them for telling him now and then a diverting story by the way. The only guides I call them, for excepting *Roger de Hoveden*, or *Howden*, our countryman, who was a layman, the priests and other ecclesiasticks were the sole chroniclers of the last and some succeeding ages from this period. The common sort of laity were entirely ignorant and illiterate; and by what they have left us relating to the affairs of their country, it is very probable, few of the nobility were bred up to the use of any other thing than the sword.

I beg pardon for this digression; and to conclude this head I shall only take leave to put the reader in mind, that our city was reduced by *Edred* the *West-Saxon* from being, as *Alcuin* styles it, *caput totius regni*, i. e. *Northanhumbrorum*, to be only the capital of an earldom. This state it remained in to *Edward* the confessor's days; in whose time it suffered a much greater revolution. For though it is said, that *(q) Alfred* the great first divided *England* into counties, **Shires**, or *shrievealties*, and appointed a chief officer to govern each, called a **Shire-reve**, or *sheriff*, instead of the earl or *comes*; yet I cannot find that this was done in the north till the time above mentioned. And now the capital of the *Roman* province in *Britain*, the *Saxon* kingdom, and the earldom of *Northumberland*, which last antiently contained all from the *German* to the *Irish* sea in breadth, and from the *Humber* to the *Tweed* in length, was split into six or seven distinct *shires* or counties; with each a city or chief town at the head of it. So that *York*, from the command of the whole, was now, in civil affairs, only metropolis of somewhat the largest share; called, in *Domesday-book*, **Eurewicscire**; in which lot it has continued ever since, and in all human probability ever will do.

Shire comes from Scyran, *Sax.* to divide; and this large *Saxon* district was then split in this manner, says *R. Hoveden*,

Eberwickscire.
Richmundescire.
Loncastrescire.
Coplande, since called the *bishoprick* of *Durham*.
Westmerlonde.
Northumbrelonde.
Cumbrelonde.

(p) In a blank page of *Eadmer's* history in our church library are these lines, wrote by an old hand, but a true *protestant* one no doubt.

Quanta antiquati reverentia debita, si non
Redderet insulsos fabula multa libros?
Fiala nigro calamo fiat inanis pagina dele,
Et totum poteris dicere deinde bonum.
Ecce, deinde tenebris; lege nunc, concedo, sed illud
Pagina jam facta est quod fuit ante liber.

R. Godfrey. 1634.

In *English* by the same hand thus:

How greats the honour due to eld,
Were not their books with fables filled?
Those old wives tales and fryers dreams
Wipe out, and then commend their themes.
'Tis done, now read, I yield, but look
Here's but a page which was a book.

[illegible]

(q) *Spelman* in vita *Alfredi* mag.

CHAP. IV.

The historical annals of the city continued from the Norman *conquest, to the uniting of the two houses of* York *and* Lancaster.

A. MLXVI. WHAT has preceded this period of time, has been a series of uncommon events and turns of fate, which our city has suffered during the *Saxon*, *Danish*, and other foreign invasions. Fire and sword in the hands of the most inhuman barbarians, have so often subverted its walls and bulwarks, that I have been forced to seek for it, as it were, in its own dust and rubbish. One might imagine that after such an extrordinary revolution in favour of the duke of *Normandy*, who knew as well how to make the best of a victory as to gain one, our harrassed city might have enjoyed that calm, which the rest of the kingdom had from the conqueror's first acts of clemency. But, so much to the contrary, I shall shew under the reign of this *christian* tyrant, its destruction and desolation surpassed whatever had been done to it before by the most wicked *pagan* princes.

No sooner was the duke of *Normandy*, thoroughly, established on the *English* throne, than he shewed the principles laid down by *Matchiavel*, some ages after, to be his sole rule and guide *(a)*. That able politician teaches the prince who conquers a kingdom, to destroy and root out as much as possible the antient nobility of it; and reduce the commonality to as low an ebb of beggary and misery as they can possibly live under. *Keep them poor, and keep them honest.* This maxim the conqueror stuck close to, and soon let the poor *English* understand that he would rule them with a rod of iron; and since he never expected them to love him, he resolved they should have cause enough to fear him. His title to the crown was by the longest sword, and he well employed the sharpest in the sustaining of it. It is somewhat amazing that after one has read the history of his reign given by the best historians, we should find in the last age so great a man as Sir *William Temple* arise, and write a panegyrical account of his life and actions. A *true Briton* must startle at the bare mention of such a tyrant, who without any right, or colour of right, first invaded, possessed, and afterwards maintained that possession, by the most horrid acts of cruelty imaginable. History does not want numberless instances of this; and if an alteration of the antient *English* laws, customs, fashions, manner of living, language, writing, and, in short, every thing but religion, can be called a *thorough revolution*, here it is beyond contradicton exemplified. But I shall confine myself to what our city and country about it felt from him; which, I believe, without mentioning aught else, will make the name of such a *conqueror* odious to all posterity.

A. MLXVIII. *York* had still earl *Morchar* for its governour, *William* had not yet changed any thing so far north; he and his brother *Edwin* earl of *Chester*, could not bear to see their country so miserably enslaved, and therefore resolved, if possible, to throw off the yoke; for they soon found, by *William*'s proceedings, that the greatest slavery was hastening down to them. As these *Saxon* lords had a very great interest in the kingdom, they quickly raised forces, which were augmented by *Blethwin* king of *Wales* their nephew. The conqueror's policy made him fear that this revolt would be general, if he did not nip it in the bud; he therefore hastened down into the north, but not so fast but he took time to fortify the castle at *Warwick*, and gave orders for the building a new one at *Notingham*, by way of securing a safe retreat in case of the worst *(b)*. From thence he proceeded either to fight the rebels or to besiege *York*, which had sided with them. At the beginning of this insurrection *William* had displaced *Morchar* from his government, and made one *Robert* a *Norman*, for his cruel and austere nature, earl of *Northumberland*. This man he sent down to *Durham*, some time before he came himself, with a guard of seven hundred, others say nine hundred, *Normans* to exercise what cruelty he pleased, provided he kept those turbulent spirits in subjection *(c)*. The stout *Northumbrians* could not bear this usage, but arming privately, they came upon this new made governour in the night, at his quarters in *Durham*, and with fire and sword destroyed both him and his *Normans* to a man. The sword drawn it was not to be sheathed again in haste. Earl *Gospatrick* their commander, and *Edgar Atheling* their lawful prince, who was come to them out of *Scotland*, where he had fled for protection from *William*'s conquering sword, immediately marched at the head of the *Northumbrians* towards *York*. Here they were received by *Morchar*, *Edwin*, and the citizens of *York*, with all the joy and triumph they could possibly testify on this occasion *(d)*. But this lasted a very small time; for *William* came on apace; and the generals being as yet in no condition to with-

(a) Matchiavel's prince.
(b) S. Dunel.
(c) Wal. Hemingford canon of *Gisburgh.*
(d) Annales Waverlacenses.

ſtand his numerous army, conſulted whether they ſhould fly the country, or yield themſelves up to the conqueror's mercy. The laſt was agreed on, and having taken care to ſend back prince *Edgar* into *Scotland*, they voluntarily ſubmitted themſelves to the victor's clemency. This method was right, ſays *Rapin*, for how cruel ſoever *William* was in his nature, he had policy enough, adds he, to pardon theſe earls at this time, with a view to reclaim the *Engliſh*, and give them a better opinion of his merciful temper. The inhabitants of *York* had the ſame political mercy extended to them; for when they ſaw how well the generals were treated, and knew at the ſame time they were in no condition to ſtand a ſiege, they came out of the city to meet the conqueror, delivered him the keys with great ſubmiſſion, and were ſeemingly received into favour. This gained them a remiſſion of corporal puniſhment, but they were obliged to pay a large fine; and moreover had the mortification to ſee *two caſtles* fortifyed in the city, and ſtrongly garriſoned with *Norman* ſoldiers (*e*).

William's mercy was ſoon found to be a copy of his countenance; for at the ſame time that he pardoned ſome, he not only puniſhed others who were leſs guilty; but he impriſoned ſeveral who had no hand at all in the revolt. This gave occaſion to the leaders to look about them, and put them in mind what they were to expect as ſoon as opportunity would permit. The three earls *Morchar*, *Edwin*, and *Goſpatrick*, fled into *Scotland* to *Malcolm* the *Scotch* king; who very generouſly gave them his protection. *Malcolm* had lately married *Margaret* the eldeſt ſiſter to prince *Edgar*; from which conjunction a long race of *Scotiſh* kings, and ſince of *Great Britain* are lineally deſcended. The *Norman*, ſays *Buchanan*, puſt up with the good ſucceſs of his affairs, ſent an herald into *Scotland* to demand *Edgar Atheling* (*f*), and the *Engliſh* lords; but *Malcolm* looking upon it as a cruel and faithleſs thing to deliver up his ſuppliant gueſt and kinſman, and one, adds my author, *againſt whom his very enemics could object no crime*, to his mortal foe to be put to death, reſolved to protect him, and ſuffer any thing rather than do it. He well knew that *William* would be ſpeedily with him for this refuſal, and conſequently was not ſlow to provide for his reception.

A conſiderable league was now formed againſt the conqueror (*g*); *Edwin* and *Morchar* were ſent into *Denmark*, who perſuaded king *Swain* that it would be an eaſy matter to conquer *England* at this juncture; and the *Daniſh* king came readily into the propoſal. Being aſſured of a powerful army of *Engliſh* and *Scotch* to join the forces he ſhould ſend over, he diſpatched away *Oſbern* his brother, the two ſons of *Harold*, a biſhop, called *Chriſtiern*, earl *Turkyl*, or *Turketyl*; with two hundred and fifty *tall ſhips*, which all entered the *Humber* in ſafety. At their landing they were immediately joined by the *Engliſh* malecontents, and the *Scotch* auxiliaries; which, when united together, compoſed a formidable army, ſufficient to have ſhaken *William*'s crown, had they all acted as they ought to have done. It is certain the news of this alarm ſo ſtruck him, that he thought proper to ſend his wife and children into *Normandy*, as a better place of ſecurity; before he undertook to lay this ſtorm, which looked ſo black upon him from the *north*.

Oſbern the *Daniſh* general, at the head of the confederate army, marched directly towards *York* (*h*), where, we may imagine, they were not unwelcome to the citizens. The *Norman* garriſon in the caſtles were reſolved to hold out to the laſt extremity, not doubting but their king would ſpeedily come to their aſſiſtance. Making all things ready for a ſiege, the *Normans* ſet fire to ſome houſes in the ſuburbs, on that ſide of the city, leſt they ſhould ſerve the enemy to fill up the ditches of their fortifications. This fire ſpreading by an accidental wind, further than it was deſigned, burned down great part of the city, and with it the cathedral church; where that famous library, which *Alcuin* writes of, placed there by archbiſhop *Egbert*, about the year 800, to the unſpeakable loſs of learning, was entirely conſumed in the flames. Divine vengeance, ſays *Hoveden*, ſoon repayed them this injury; for the *Danes* taking the advantage of this confuſion, which the fire muſt neceſſarily occaſion, entered the city without oppoſition; and then the confederates dividing their forces attacked both the caſtles at the ſame time; the *Danes* one, and the *Engliſh* and *Scotch* the other. This charge was made ſo vigorouſly on both ſides, that they beat down all before them, and entered the caſtles ſword in hand. A miſerable ſlaughter enſued, for all the *Norman* garriſon was cut in pieces, and every one elſe that was in them, except, ſay our hiſtorians, (*i*) *William Mallet* then high-ſheriff of the county, his wife and two children, *Gilbert de Gaunt* and a few others.

(*e*) *Rex autem* Willielmus Snotingham *venit ubi caſtello firmato* Eboracum *perrexit, ibidemque* duobus Caſtellis *firmatis quingenos* milites *in eis poſuit.* Hoveden. *Hoc anno, ſcil.* 1068, *rex firmavit unum caſtrum apud* Snotingham & duo *apud* Eboracum. Bromp. Duobus caſtellis, &c. Sim. Dunel.

(*f*) Atheling, *ab* A. S. Æðeling, *quo nomine regius filius, regni haeres, princeps juventutis olim appellabatur, ab* Æðel *nobilis,* q. d. *Nobilium primarius, omnino ut in* Graeco Romano *imperio nobiliſſimus.* Skinner. *dict. etymol.*

(*g*) *S. Dunel.*

(*h*) *R. Hoveden.*

(*i*) This *William Mallet* or *Malet* came in with the conqueror, and was with him at the famous battle of *Haſtings*. In the 3d year of the conqueror's reign he was conſtituted *high-ſheriff* of *Yorkſhire*. *Dugdale's* baron.

This

A. MLXIX. This conflict happened in our city *September* 19, 1069. The number of the slain is variously reported by historians *(k)*, but is much superiour to the garrison, which *Hoveden*, &c. write, *William* left in the castles to keep the city in awe, which was no more than five hundred men. Here they all agree were slain three thousand *Normans* at least, and *William* of *Newburgh* writes that *conniventia civium plusquam quatuor millia* Normannorum *trucidantur*; *Camden* speaks of decimating the prisoners they had taken afterwards. Now how five hundred could grow up to five thousand imperceptibly, I cannot conjecture, unless that the editors of these antient gentry, or the authors themselves, have omitted a numeral in the first account. For five hundred men can never be called a sufficient garrison to man two castles, and keep a city and country in subjection, that heartily detested the *Norman* in person as well as government; and which he was not unacquainted with.

The *Danish* general, by consent of all, made *Waltheof*, the son of the valiant *Siward*, before spoken of, governor of the city; with a stout garrison of *English* and *Scotch* soldiers under him. After which the *Danes* retired and entrenched themselves in a convenient place, betwixt the *Humber* and the *Trent*; waiting the coming of the *Norman* king *(l)*.

William was not slack in his proceedings against them, for when he heard of the destruction of the *Norman* garrison at *York*, he spurred on to take vengeance with all the fury imaginable. It was now, says *Rapin*, that he had opportunity to put forth his natural temper, he was often heard to say in his march to the north, *that by God's splendour*, his usual oath, *he would not leave a soul of them alive*; and he began to put his threats in execution, as soon as ever he arrived in the country, with great punctuality.

At his coming before the city he summoned the governour with terrible menaces of fire and sword, if he refused, to surrender. *Waltheof* set at nought his threats, for being well garrisoned, and excellently well furnished with all necessaries for a siege, and moreover satisfied of assistance from the *Danish* army, he sent him a brave defiance. *William* saw plainly these obstacles were invincible, and that he could never reduce the city at such a disadvantage; neither durst he attack the *Danes* in their entrenchments, the two armies were so posted to succour one another. In this exigency he had recourse to policy, and tried how far the dint of money would operate on the *Danish* general. The affair succeeded *(m)* beyond his expectation, for the faithless *Dane* made a secret compact with *William*, receiving a round sum of money in hand, and leave to plunder the sea coasts at his going off, he promised to depart as soon as the spring would permit him. *Osbern* kept his word, embarked his forces, and basely left his allies to the mercy of the *Normans*; for which, say historians, he was severely punished by his brother at his return.

This desertion of the *Danes* caused the utmost consternation amongst the citizens and garrison of *York*. They had now nothing but their own valour to trust to; but being encouraged by the bravery of their governour, who was the foremost in all dangers for their defence, they were resolved to sell their lives at as dear a rate, to the conqueror, as possible.

A. MLXX. *William* now eased of his fears from the *Danes*, pushed on the siege with double vigour, and with his engines made a large breach in the walls. Through this he attempted to take the city by storm, and made a fierce attack upon it, but was repulsed by the garrison with great loss. The governour himself, says *William* of *Malmsbury*, a man of prodigious might and strength, stood single in the breach, and cut off the heads of several *Normans*, that attempted to enter it, with his own hands. How long this famous siege lasted, no one historian I have yet met with is so particular as to mention. I can however compute it to be about six months; for from the 17th of *September*, the day the castles were taken by the *Danes*, &c. to *Osbern*'s going back, which was in the spring, and the city's holding out somewhat longer, it may be said that *William* sat down before it about *Michaelmas*, and the surrender happened about *Lady-day*. This opposition makes it evident, that had the *Danes* kept faithful, *William* must have divided his forces; and then, in all probability, the city had never fallen into his hands. *Leland* has given us a copy of an act of state which the conqueror did when he laid before this city; which was a grant to his nephew *Alain* earl of *Britany*, afterwards of *Richmond*, of all the lands of *Edwin* earl of *Chester*, who was then in *York* against him. The style of which donation, as well for brevity as strength, is very remarkable; and is an instance that large estates were formerly conveyed in very few words. I offer it to our modern lawyers as a *specimen*.

> **Ego** Gulielmus, **cognomine Bastardus, do et concedo tibi** Alano, **nepoti meo,** Britanie **comiti, et heredibus tuis in perpetuum, omnes illas villas et terras, que nuper fuerunt comitis** Edwini **in** Eboraſcria; **cum feodis militum, et ecclesiis, et aliis libertatibus et consuetudinibus, ita libere et honorifice sicut idem** Edwinus **ea tenuit.**
>
> **Dat. in obsidione coram civitate** Eboraci.

(k) S. Dunel. R. Hoveden, W. Malmsbury, W. Newburgh.

(l) H. Hunt.

(m) R. Hoveden.

This

ASTOR LIBRARY
NY

Ego Willms cognoie Bastard9 Rex Anglie do t
ocedo tibi Nepoti meo Alano Britannie Comiti
i heredib, tuis imppm omes villas t tras. que
nup fuerut Comitis Edwini in Eborasshi
ra cu feodis Militu t ecclis t aliis libtat
t osuetudib; ita libe t honorifice sicut ide
Edwin' ea tenuit. Dat in obsidione coram
Ciuitate Ebor.

This absolute confiscation of the large estate and possessions, no less than near two hundred manors and townships, as appears by the conqueror's survey, then of right belonging to an ancient *Saxon* earl, was a taste of his cruelty; and was sufficient to let the besieged know what mercy the rest of them was to expect when he should have them in his power. But as this arbitrary grant is very particular, as to the form of them at that time; and is besides a singular testimony of this famous siege, the annexed plate, which is printed in Mr. *Gale*'s survey of *Richmondshire*, and which, by that gentleman's favour, I have procured, will give the reader a better idea of the conqueror and his chief officers, then with him at the siege, than I can pretend to. And serve to hand down yet to posterity an action very memorable in its kind, though attended with the utter destruction of a noble earl and all his family.

William of *Malmsbury* mentions a battle which the conqueror gained against a powerful army sent to the relief of the city. These I presume were *Scots* and *Northumbrians*, for the *Danes* had deserted before that time. It seems by it that this last struggle for liberty was very great in the north, and all possible efforts made to shake off the *Norman* yoke; nor was this attempt made to raise the siege easily frustrated; the aforesaid author tells us that the battle was terrible and bloody; nor did he gain the victory without a very considerable loss of his own men (*n*).

Earl *Waltheof*, the governour, rendered also the siege of the city exceeding difficult, merely by his courage and conduct, insomuch that *William* almost dispaired of going through with it. But being now freed from the fears of any other enemy, he drew down the whole strength of the kingdom against it, and beleaguered it quite round; resolving to starve them into a compliance, since force would not prevail. I must here observe that his army must be very numerous to surround this city, and begirt it so close that no provision could be thrown into it. In the last civil war fifty thousand men, the number of the *English* and *Scotch* forces that besieged *York*, were insufficient; and could not wholly prevent it. However this method took, and famine began to rage so violently within the walls, that it obliged the besieged to try the victor's clemency. *William* greatly desirous to surmount this difficulty, stuck at neither oaths nor promises to obtain it; the articles (*o*) of surrender were as honourable as possible, considering the circumstances the city was in; nay after the surrender, he seemed so charmed with the valour and conduct of the governour, which he A. MDLXX.
had personally beheld in the siege, that he gave him afterwards in marriage his niece, *Judeth*, daughter to the countess of *Albemarl*; and first made him earl of *Northampton* and *Huntington*; and afterwards earl of *Northumberland*.

Whatever favours *William* conferred upon the governour, it is certain the city felt none of them. And so great was the difference in this case, as renders the earl's character but very suspicious. To make the best of it, it can only be said, that, when the governour saw the affair desperate, he made the most advantageous terms he could for himself, as well as the city. *William*'s profound policy obliged him to keep faith with a man as *Waltheof* in his interest at that time, but he trusted him no farther than he could see him; and in a small time let him both see and feel his error, for he took off his head on account of a conspiracy which *Waltheof* himself first informed him of (*p*).

Thus fell the last of the *Saxon* earls of *Northumberland*, with the honour of being the first nobleman that ever was beheaded in *England*. *Morchar* and *Edwin* not caring to trust the conqueror's mercy, found means to escape out of the city before the surrender; but being hunted from place to place by this insatiable blood-hound, the two brothers at last met the same fate, and had the misfortune to be both murthered in a mutiny of their own men. Prince *Edgar* likewise escaped into *Scotland* (*q*).

Whatever articles the governour had stipulated for in the surrender in behalf of the city and citizens, they were little regarded by the conqueror. *Malmsbury* says, that he looked upon this place as the only nest of rebellion in the kingdom; he supposed them abettors in the destruction of the *Norman* garrison, and therefore they were to feel his fiercest vengeance. He razed the city to the ground, and with it fell (*r*) all the principal nobility and gentry, and most of the other inhabitants; the few that were saved, were forced to purchase their lives with such large fines, that they were reduced to the utmost penury to discharge them. The *English* and *Scotch* garrison, notwithstanding the articles, all perished; and thus, says my author, was this noble city wasted by famine, fire and sword, to the very roots. Nor did his implacable malice stop here, but, lest the country should be capable of supporting the city in this dreadful calamity, he laid all waste betwixt *York* and *Durham*; destroyed or drove out the inhabitants, and made the country so desolate, that for nine years after neither plow nor spade was put into the ground. If any of the wretched people escaped the sword, they were but reserved for a much worse fate, being forced for

(*n*) Urbem metropolim, *quam* Angli *cum* Danis *et* Scotis obstinate *tenebant, in deditionem accepit*; civibus longe inedia consumptis. *Maximum quoque hostium numerum, qui obsessis in auxilium convenerant, ingenti et gravi praelio fudit; non incruenta sibi victoria multos suorum amittens.* Gul. Malm.

(*o*) *M. Paris.*

(*p*) *R. Hoveden.*

(*q*) *Ingulphus.*

(*r*) *Et tunc quidem cum civitate omnis nobilitas popularis emarcuit, falce belli demessa* Gul. Malm.

sustenance through famine to eat dogs, cats, horses, and even human flesh, to preserve their miserable lives. Thus was our city, and even our whole country, so wholly wasted and destroyed, except the lands belonging to St. *John* of *Beverley*, (s) which the tyrant thought fit to spare, that my own words can neither come up to the description, or if they did, would they find the least belief in the recital. Hear then the historians, who wrote the nearest these times, in their own phrase and diction.

And first, *William* the librarian of *Malmsbury* (t), who, though a *Norman*, has not excused his countryman the conqueror; but has done him ample justice, as the following quotation will testify.

EBORACUM urbs *ampla et* metropolis *est, elegantiae* Romanae *praeferens inditium, a duabus partibus* Husae *fluminis aedificata. Includit in medio sinus sui naves a* Germania *et* Hibernia *venientes. Furori aquilonalium gentium prima semper obnoxia, barbaricos* Danorum *motus, toto tempore quo dominati sunt in* Anglia, *excepit et ingemuit. Ultima peste sub* Gulielmo *rege concidit, qui urbanis iratus, quod* Danis *adventantibus receptui et consultui fuissent, prius inedia, mox flammâ civitatem confecit. Regionis etiam totius vicos et agros corrumpi, fructus vel fruges igne vel aquâ labefactare jussit. Ita provincia quondam fertilis, nervi praeda, incendio, sanguine succisi. Humus per sexaginta milliaria omnifariam inculta, nudum omnium solum ad hoc usque tempus. Urbes olim praeclaras, turres proceritate sua in coelum minantes, agros laetos pascuis, irriguos fluviis, siquis modo vidit peregrinus, ingemit; si vetus agricola, non agnoscit.*

What *Simeon* of *Durham*, *Roger Hoveden*, *William* of *Newburgh*, *Knighton*, &c. write of this tragedy, may be all comprehended in old *Simeon's* (u) words.

Normannis Angliam *vastantibus in* Northimbria, *et in quibusdam aliis provinciis anno praecedenti, praesenti et subsequenti fere per totam* ANGLIAM, *sed maxime per* NORTHYMBRAM *et per contiguas illi provincias adeo fames praevaluit, ut homines humanas, equinas, caninas, et catinas carnes, et quicquid usus abhorret, cogente inedia, comederent. Alii vero in servitutem perpetuam sese venderent, dummodo qualitercunque miserabilem vitam sustentarent, alii vero extra patriam profecturi in exilium, medio itinere deficientes animas emiserunt. Erat horror ad intuendum per domos, plateas et itinera cadavera dissolvi, et tabescentia putredine cum foetore horrendo scaturire vermibus. Neque enim supererat qui ea humo cooperiret, omnibus vel extinctis gladio vel fame, vel propter famem paternum solum relinquentibus. Interea ita terra cultore destituta, lata ubique solitudo patebat per novem annos. Inter* Eboracum *et* Dunelmum *nusquam villa inhabitata, bestiarum tantum et latronum latibula, magna itinerantium fuere timori.*

I believe I may venture to say that no history whatever can parallel these accounts; nor was there ever a tyrant in the *christian* or *pagan* world, that exercised his power so much to the destruction of his fellow creatures, before or since. A farther account of this great devastation may not be unacceptable to the reader in old *English* rhymical verse; taken out of *Peter Langtoft's* chronicle published by Mr. *Hearn*.

Now William *has sojourned and slayne alle his enmys,*
And to þe southe is turned, als king þot wan þe pris.
Tidings cam him fulle stout, þat a grete oste and stark,
With Harold *and with* Knoute, *þe king's sonnes of* Denmark,
Were aryved in Humbere, *and an earl* Turkylle,
With foulk withouten numbere þe Norreis *selle þam tille,*
Comen to þe earl Edgar, *with all þos of his kinde,*
Sir Walthof *he is thar, þo with that he met finde*
Marlswain Turkyl *son, ond* Swayne *a doughty knyght;*
Of Scotlande Gospatrick, *with þam at all his myght.*
The Normans *in the southe, were in soe grete affray,*
Of kastells and of tounes, they com oute alle day.
To York ran ilk a man, to rescet in that toune,
That no Danes *man þe walles to breke doune.*
Sir William Mellet *was warden of þe cuntres,*
Sibrigh *þe gaunt was set with to kepe þe pees.*
Thise tuo brought tydyng, þei were comen by þat coste
Therfore William *þe king, did turne agayn his hoste,*
And swore a grete othe, þat he suld never spare
Neiþer lithe nor lose, Northeren *whut so þei were.*
William *turned agayn, and held what he had sworn,*
All mad he wasteyn, pasture, medow and korne.
And slough both fader and sonne, women lete þei gon
Hors and houndes þei ete, unciþis skaped non.

(s) He had sent a commander and a party out to destroy this country too, but the officer chanced to fall from his horse in his march thither, and break his neck in such manner, that his face was turned quite backward, when it was told to the king, he believed it an omen sent from S. *John* to warn him to spare his territories, and therefore desisted from spoiling those parts. *Knighton.*

(t) *Gul. Malm.* vix. temp. *R. Step.*

(u) *Sim. Dun.* vix. A. 1164.

Now

Now dwellis William *efte, full bare was money wone,*
Of gode men er non lefte, but flayn er ilk one.
Grete fin did William, *þat fwilk wo did werk,*
Soe grete vengeance he nam, of men of holy kirk,
That did no wem till him, ne no trefpafs,
Fro York *unto* Durham, *no wonyng ftede was,*
Nien yere, fayes my buke, lafted fo grete forrowe,
The bifhop clerkes tuke, þar lyves for two borrowe.

The fubject is too melancholy to dwell any longer upon, or trouble the reader with any more proofs to make good my affertion. I fhall only fay, that the ufage *William* gave our city is felt yet; having never fince his time fhewed half the fplendour that it did before, and humanly fpeaking never will again. The city of *London*, though now fo overgrown and mighty, was not to be compared to the capital city of the *Northumbrian* kingdom in thofe days; **Ye fhaul underftaund,** fays *J. Hardynge*, *(x)* **that in thofe dayes the cyte of** London **had much building from** Ludgate **towarde** Weftminfter, **and litle or non wher the chefe or harte of the cyte ys now, except that in diverfe places ftoode houfyng, but they ftoode oute of ordere. So many townes or cytes as** York, Canterbury, **and diverfe othere in** Englande, **paffed** London **for buyldyng in thofe dayes. But after the conquefte it increafed and fhortly aftere paffed all otheres.** *Johannes Severianus*, fpeaking of *York*, and the troubles in the *heptarchy*, has thofe words *(y)*, *praefatum vero oppidum in id virium et temeritatis temporis proceffu excrevit, ut urbibus antiquis audeat fe conferre.* For though we have often feen it fuffer grievoufly under the *Saxon*, *Danifh*, and other invafions; yet it always returned, in any recefs, to its former greatnefs. *William*'s barbarity ftruck at the very roots of it, and his malice went fo far as to eraze as much as poffible, all the noble remains of antiquity it could then produce; for, fays *Leland (z)*, *haec clades deturpavit, aut potius penitus abrafit, quicquid erat monumentorum aut antiquae nobilitatis a* Romanis *relictae* Eboraci. And *Malmfbury* writes, as if he faw this defolation, *in aliquibus tamen parietum ruinis, qui femiruti remanfere videas mira* Romanorum *artificia*. What wonder then that we have fo few *Roman* antiquities to produce? The fuburbs of the city, before the conqueft, according to *Leland (a)*, extended to the towns a mile round it, *conftans fama eft aliquot villas effe uno ab* Eboraco *milliario, ubi, ante tempora* Gulielmi nothi, *termini erant fuburbanarum aedium*. To conclude this whole affair, the author of the *Polychronicon* writes, *(b)* that *York feemed as fair as the city of* Rome, *before it was burnt by* William *the conqueror*; and what was juftly enough by *William Harrifon* ftyled *Altera Roma, from the beauty and fine buildings of it (c)*, and by *Alcuin Caput totius regni*, at this period was nothing but a heap of ruins. A. MLXXII.

Quis, talia fando,
Temperet a lacrimis?

We have now a gap of time which is impoffible to fill up with any materials to the purpofe. Our city lay dead, as it were, after *William*'s cruel ufage near an age; for few figns of life can I meet with in hiftory about it. The contefts betwixt the two metropolitical archbifhops excepted, which concern another part of this work. However we may imagine it had crept out of its rubbifh in king *Stephen*'s time, and had once more reared its head, when another unhappy accident befel it. A cafual fire burft out, and burnt down the cathedral church, St. *Mary's (d)* abby, St. *Leonard*'s hofpital, with thirty nine parifh churches in the city, and *Trinity* church in the fuburbs. Mr. *Camden* writes that the famous library in the cathedral, mentioned above, was deftroyed by this fire; but *R. Hoveden* dates its deftruction more juftly, from the former conflagration. The hand of fate was ftill heavy upon us, and this repeated blow was fenfibly felt by the inhabitants; who were reduced fo low by it, that their churches, efpecially the cathedral, lay a long time in rubbifh for want of means to re-erect them. In *Stephen*'s time, befides the bloody wars that occupied his whole reign, *England* may be faid to be all in a flame; there being no lefs than twenty cities and chief towns cafually burnt in a very fhort fpace; amongft which ours had the misfortune to be the greateft fufferer. A. MCXXXVII. A MCXXXVIII.

David king of *Scotland* knowing the nation was divided into two great parties, and a bloody civil war begun betwixt *Maud* the emprefs and *Stephen*; took this opportunity to enter *England* with a powerful army, *(e)* and fending his horfe abroad into the country commanded them to wafte and fpoil all before them. In the mean time he purpofed to befiege *York*, which if he could have taken, he determined to have made a frontier town on it againft *Stephen* and his adherents. Wherefore calling in his horfe, he marched towards the city, and fat down before it.

In the mean time archbifhop *Thurftan*, whom *Stephen* had made lieutenant governour of the north, called together the nobility and gentry of the counties, and thofe adjoining to the

(x) J. Hardynge *floruit temp.* Hen. V.
(y) *Leland*'s coll.
(z) *Ibid.* coll.
(a) *Ibid.* coll.
(b) *R. Higdeni* polychron.
(c) Defcription of *Brit.*
(d) *Stow*, &c.
(e) *Hollingfhed.*

the city of *York*; whose names I find thus recorded by *Richard*, prior of *Hexham* (*f*), *William* (*g*) *de Albemarl*; *Walter de Gant*, *Robert de Brus*, *Roger de Mowbray*, *Walter Espec*, *Ilbert de Lacy*, *William de Percy*, *Rich. de Curcy*, *William Fossard*, and *Robert de Stouteville*, all antient barons of this county, with *William Peverel* and *Geofrey Halsaline* of Notinghamshire, and *Robert de Ferrers* of Darbyshire. These barons inraged to see their country so miserably wasted by the *Scotch*, raised forces, and being encouraged by an oration the archbishop made to them, marched against the enemy with great bravery. The king of *Scotland* did not wait their coming, but drew his army from before *York*, and retired northward with some precipitation. The *English* lords came up with him at Northalerton, where a terrible battle was fought, and where the *Scots* were entirely routed, and ten thousand of their men slain upon the spot. This battle is called by historians *bellum standardi*, or the battle of the standard; whence, says the prior, *Hugo de Rotavogina*, archdeacon of of York, at that time, wrote the following distich on the ensign erected in the field of battle,

> *Dicitur a stando standardum, quod stetit illic*
> *Militiae probitas vincere sive mori.*

> *Standard from stand this fight we aptly call.*
> Our men here stood to conquer or to fall.

And now, instead of terrible wars, fire, famine, murders, and desolations, which I have been all along obliged to stick to in these historical annals for many ages last past; the tables are turned to give an account of parliaments, conventions, coronations, royal marriages and interviews, which our city has been honoured with, in some succeeding years from this period. Blood and fire will for a time be strangers, except in some matters of much less moment, to my subject; and must give way to a more pleasant recital of the pomps and ceremonies of our former *English* monarchs, displayed in our antient city, on several occasions. This will require the skill of both the politician and courtier, to set them forth in the colours they deserve; for want of which abilities, I must be obliged to wave a great many flourishes naturally arising in my way; and the reader must be content with a plain relation of matter of fact, as I find it delivered by original historians.

Our city continued in a state of profound peace for some ages after this; for though the *Scotch* wars were violent enough in some of the succeeding reigns, yet they were to the northward of us, and never reached York, but once, as shall be shewn in its proper place. The miseries of the foregoing ages, and the happiness of this, in relation to our city, is sung by a *Scotch* poet and historian in these lines (*h*).

> *Visito quam felix* Ebraucus *condidit urbem,*
> Petro *se debet pontificalis apex.*
> *Civibus haec toties viduata, novisque repleta,*
> *Diruta prospexit maenia saepe sua.*
> *Quid manus hostilis queat est experta frequenter.*
> *Sed quid? nunc pacis otia longa fovent.*

Thus englished in my lord of *London*'s edition of *Camden*.

> There happy *Ebrank*'s lofty towers appear,
> Who owe their mitre to St. *Peter*'s care.
> How oft in dust the hapless town hath lain?
> How oft its walls have changed? how oft its men?
> How oft the rage of sword and fire has mourn'd?
> But now long joy and lasting peace's return'd.

Another *Scotch* poet has likewise sung our praises in the following verses (*i*).

> *Praesidet extremis* Artoae *finibus orae*
> *Urbs vetus, in veteri facta subinde nova;*
> Romanis *aquilis quondam ducibusque superba,*
> *Quam post barbaricae diripuere manus.*
> Pictus *atrox*, Scotus, Danus, Normannus *et* Anglus,
> *Fulmina in hanc martis detonuere sui.*
> *Post diras rerum clades, totque aspera fata,*
> *Blandius aspirans aura serena subit.*
> Londinum *caput est et regni urbs prima* Britanni,
> Eboracum a *prima jure secunda venit.*

(*f*) *Richard Hagust.*.

(*g*) Made the first earl of *York* by *Stephen*. Chron. *Saxon*. p. 241.

(*h*) *Alexander Necham, Camden.*

(*i*) *John Johnson* of *Aberdeen*, *Camden*.

O'er

O'er the last borders of the northern land
York's antient towers, though oft made new, command.
Of *Rome*'s great princes once the lofty seat,
'Till barbarous foes o'erwhelm'd the sinking state.
The *Picts*, the *Scots*, the *Danes* and *Normans*, here,
Discharg'd the loudest thunders of the war.
But this once ceas'd, and every storm o'erblown,
A happier gale refresh'd the rising town.
Let *London* still the just precedence claim,
York ever shall be proud to be the next in fame.

One of the first *parliaments* (*i*) mentioned in history, by that name, was held in **York** about the year 1160, in the reign of *Henry* the second. At this *convention*, as *Buchanan* calls it, *Malcholm* the *Scotch* king was summoned to appear, to answer to such articles as were to be alledged against him by *Henry*. The chief article was, that *Malcholm*, when he attended the *English* king in his wars in *France*, betrayed all their counsels to the enemy. The *Scotch* king, by many substantial reasons, overthrew this allegation; but he could not prevent the sentence passing on him, which I suppose was the reason of his being summoned; that was, to lose all the lands he held of *Henry* in *England*, and to do homage also for his kingdom of *Scotland* for himself and successors. For doing the last, which was what *Henry* chiefly aimed at, he relinquished **Northumberland** of the former part of the sentence to him. This condescension of their king, the *Scotch* nobility highly resented, and, at his return, were with great difficulty brought to forgive him. A. MCLX.

This *parliament*, or convention of the estates, was not the same as now, the house of commons not being of so old a date; but composed of the *barons* and *bishops*, and other great men of the land, whom the king pleased to call together on any extraordinary occasion. It is the first however, that I can find, that was ever held in this city, or perhaps in *England*; *Rapin*'s *Saxon Witten-gemot* was a thing not known in the *Northumbrian* kingdom of the *heptarchy*; at least, it has not fallen in my way to describe it. The grand affair which made *Henry* collect his nobles at this time, is a business of such consequence to the succeeding *Scotch* wars, that I think it proper, for the reader's better information, to beg leave to explain it.

Ever since the *Saxon* government in *England* became universal, and the power of the nation united, the *English* kings had looked on *Scotland* with an avaritious eye; and took all the opportunities they could to gain an entire conquest over that part of the island. Some of the *Scotch* kings held the three counties of **Northumberland, Cumberland,** and **Huntingdonshire**, as a fealty from the crown of *England*; for which they did homage to the king of *England* at his accession; or when he pleased to call for it. But this was not all the *English* kings aimed at; the sovereignty of *Scotland* was the chief claim; and the ground of a perpetual quarrel betwixt them. Nor did the kings of *England* ever miss an opportunity, when the *Scotch* affairs were at a low ebb, to make their kings submit to perform that ceremony, or run the hazard of a declaration of war against them. It was on this account that *Henry* II. summoned *Malcholm* to *York*, before himself and barons, to answer to a feigned accusation, where he was terrified into a compliance; for which he lost the hearts of his nobility, who were always, strictly, tenacious of their antient rights and privileges.

In the year 1171, this *Henry* called another convention of the barons and bishops of the realm at *York*, before whom he cited *William* the successor of *Malcholm* to appear and do homage to him for the whole kingdom of *Scotland* (*k*). This *William* had before been taken prisoner and ransomed at *York* for the sum of four thousand pound. *William* durst do no other than obey the summons, and accordingly set out from *Scotland*, with *David* his brother, and appeared before the king and parliament at *York*; where his homage was taken in the most submissive and binding manner possible. *Knighton* says, that *William* with the consent of all his peers and prelates did homage to *Henry* for the kingdom of *Scotland*; he likewise signed letters patents binding himself and all his successors, and all the subjects of *Scotland* to do homage and fealty, with all faithfulness, whenever the kings of *England* should require it. In token of which subjection, the *Scottish* king offered and deposited upon the altar of St. *Peter*, in the cathedral church at *York*, his (*l*) *breast-plate*, *spear* and *saddle*; which, adds my author, remain there at this day. The peers of *Scotland*, now humble enough, took an oath, binding them and their heirs, that if at any time their king should go off from his faith and break this agreement, they would rise with one accord and compel him to stick close to the same. A. MCLXXI.

This was the most abject submission that ever the *Scotch* gave to the *English* nation. *Buchanan* himself, who is mighty apt to slip or gild over the transactions of his countrymen,

(*i*) *H. Bost.*
(*k*) *Scotch* chron.
(*l*) Capellum, lanceam *et* sellam *super altare beati* PETRI EBOR. *obtulit, quae in eadem ecclesia usque ad hodiernam diem remanent, et servantur.* Knighton. *inter x script.* In a claim of king *Edward* I. to his rights in *Scotland* sent to the pope, mention is made of these pledges of *Scotch* subjection then kept in the cathedral church of *York*; but they are long since lost. *Ryley*'s placit. parl. 596. in append.

when he thinks them any ways derogatory to the honour of the *Scotch* name, does not deny the fact above; but seems to bewail the miseries of their nation, who were then reduced to such extremities, that they had no other way left to redeem their *good king*, as he calls him, and save themselves from certain ruin.

In the succeeding reign of *Richard* king of *England*, and at his coronation, an accident happened of singular concern to our city, and attended with such consequences as history can scarce parallel. A particular account of which, taken chiefly from *William* of
A. MCLXXXIX. *Newburgh*, and *Walter Hemingford* canon of *Gisburgh*, both *Yorkshire* monks, who are naturally led to be copious in relating the transactions of their own county cannot be unacceptable to the reader.

The *Jews* were a people first introduced into *England* by *William* the conqueror; a tribe of these must have placed themselves at *York* soon after; where, by trade, they were grown so immensely rich, that they were found to be worth the plundering both by prince and people, as oft as they could form an excuse for that purpose. The fear they constantly lived under made them take all opportunities by rich presents, &c. to ingratiate themselves with the reigning prince, that they might securely live under his protection. Which favour was sometimes hard to gain; so zealously affected to the *christian* religion were our former *English* kings, that they could not bear an open avowed enemy to it to live amongst them. The naturalizing of this people, and making them *free denisons* of *England*, was reserved for a later age to enact. *Richard* the first was as zealous a *Christian* as ever sat on the *English* throne; and as bitter an enemy to its opponents. Notwithstanding which the *Jews* were undisturbed, but abhorring their religion, and, as my authority speaks, doubting some sorcery, or other finister end from them, he strictly commanded, that, at his coronation, no *Jews*, whatever, should appear, either at church or at dinner.

(*m*) Some of the richest and principal men of the *Jews* in the kingdom, were summoned from all parts, where they resided, by their brethren in *London*, to come up to the coronation, and present some very rich gift to the new king, in order to procure his friendship towards them, for confirming the privileges and liberties granted them by his predecessors. The chief of the *Jews* at *York* were two very rich and wealthy merchants, and very great usurers, called *Benedict* and *Jocenus* (*n*). These went from hence to *London* with a pompous retinue in order to meet their brethren, and attend the coronation. Notwithstanding the king's injunction, many of the *Jews* had the curiosity to mix with the croud, in order to see the ceremony; where being discovered by the guards, they were beat and abused, and some few slain. The people, who watched all opportunities to plunder their houses, took it presently for granted, that the king had given orders they should all be destroyed. Possessed with this notion, a general massacre began in *London*; where the *Jews* were murdered, their houses plundered, and burnt to the ground with their wives and children in them. The king ordered immediately a proclamation to stop these proceedings on the severest penalties; but, for all that, the example of the metropolis, was followed by divers other places in the realm, as at *Norwich*, *Lynn*, *Stamford*, but especially at *York*; where, say my authors, the cruel commands of the fiercest tyrant, the rigour of the severest laws, could never have so far exceeded the bounds of reason and humanity, as to tolerate such a proceeding.

Benedict and *Jocenus*, our *Jews* of *York*, it seems, had the curiosity to go amongst the rest to see the ceremony; *Benedict* was grievously bruised and wounded in the conflict, and being dragged into a (*o*) church, was there forced to renounce *Judaism* and be baptized. The next day when the tumult was ceased he was brought before the king, who demanded of him whether he was a *Christian* or no? *Benedict* answered, that he had been forced into baptism, but that he continued a *Jew* in his heart, and ever should do; that he chose much rather to suffer death at his hands, since the severe usage he had undergone the day before informed him, that he could not long survive it. At which words being driven from the king's presence he was restored to the *Jews*; but the miserable man soon after expired.

Jocenus his companion had the good fortune to escape the fray in *London*; but where he thought himself the safest, he met with a much worse fate at *York*. The king soon after going on his voyage to the holy land, had left orders with the lord chancellor to protect the *Jews*, and punish severely all that should offend them. But this was little regarded at *York*, for a conspiracy was formed against them by several of the city and county; men thirsting for blood, say my authorities, who wanted but an opportunity to put their cruel designs in execution. A considerable part of the city took fire in a very boisterous night, by accident as was supposed, but rather imagined to be done on purpose, that the citizens being busy in extinguishing the flames might not obstruct their barbarous intentions. In this interval the conspirators broke into the house of *Benedict* slain at *London*; which being prodigiously strong, his wife, children and friends had made a sanctuary of, as dreading some commotion. But, this being overcome by engines prepared for that purpose, they entered and

(*m*) *Gul. Newburgiensis* hist. *Walter. Hemingford* inter xx script. ed. *Gale*.

(*n*) *Thomas Wykes*, more probably, calls him *Josias*. Chron. *Thom. Wykes*, inter xx script.

(*o*) *Baptizatus est a* Wilielmo *priore S.* Mariae Eboraci *in ecclesia S.* Innocent. & *vocatus est* Wilielmus. R. Hoveden.

murdered

murdered the whole family, gutted the houſe, and afterwards ſet fire to it, and burnt it down to the ground. An alarm of this kind ſtruck all the *Jews* at *York* with the utmoſt terror; but *Jocenus* eſpecially dreaded their fury ſo much, that he got leave of the governor to convey all his vaſt bulk of wealth into the *caſtle*; as if it had belonged to the king, or was under his protection. In a very few days theſe night robbers and plunderers, with greater force and fury, returned and attacked the houſe of *Jocenus*; which though ſtrongly fortified with conſiderable towers, underwent the ſame fate with the former; except that the *Jew* preſaging the evil, had withdrawn himſelf, wife and children into the caſtle. His example was followed by all the reſt of the *Jews* in the city; leaving few or none, nor any of their goods, behind them. The robbers being enrag'd at the loſs of ſo much plunder, which they had already devoured in their minds; threw off all diſguiſe or any fear of magiſtrates or laws, and not being content with the deſtruction of their houſes, flew like madmen on ſome *Jews*, that were left out of the caſtle, and either forced them to be baptized or ſuffer immediate death. Whilſt this was acting in the city, the multitude of *Jews* that had taken ſanctuary in the caſtle, ſeemed to be perfectly ſecured from the malice of their enemies. But it happened that the governor coming out of the caſtle upon ſome buſineſs of his own, when he would have returned was prevented by the *Jews*; who feared leaſt in this time he might have made ſome agreement with their enemies to deliver them up. The governor went immediately to the (p) high ſheriff of the county, who was then in *York* negotiating the king's affairs, and told him that the *Jews*, under pretence of begging protection in the caſtle, had fraudulently ſhut him out of it. The high ſheriff was angry to the laſt degree; which was ſtill inflamed by thoſe near him, who wiſhed the *Jews* no good, by ſaying that it was the higheſt indignity to the perſon of the king himſelf, to have one of the moſt conſiderable fortreſſes in the kingdom ſiezed by theſe miſcreants. He inſtantly ordered out the writ of *poſſe comitatus* to raiſe the country to beſiege the caſtle. *Excurrit irrevocabile verbum*, ſays *Hemingford*, and now was ſhewn the zeal, adds he, of the *chriſtian* populace; for an innumerable company of armed men, as well from the city as county, roſe at once and begirt the fortreſs round. When the high ſheriff ſaw this, he began to repent of his too haſty order; and would fain have recalled his writ; but, to thoſe incenſed people, whatever he could ſay or do, by authority or reaſon, was to no purpoſe. The better or wiſer ſort of the citizens, aware of the king's diſpleaſure, cautiouſly avoided theſe extravagant proceedings. A great many of the clergy however were in it; and amongſt them a certain friar, agitated by a furious miſtaken zeal, was violent in the buſineſs. The caſtle was fiercely aſſail'd for ſeveral days together, and no one was bolder in all attempts than this canon hermit of the *Praemonſtratenſian* order, as my authors ſtyle him; for clad in a (q) white veſture he was every where diligent, and crying out with a loud voice *that the enemies of Chriſt ſhould be deſtroyed*, by his own labour and boldneſs he greatly encouraged the reſt of the beſiegers. But being too ſtrenuous in his endeavours in fixing the battering engines againſt the walls, he came ſo near them that a large ſtone put an end to his zeal, by daſhing out his brains.

The *Jews* being driven to great diſtreſs, held a council amongſt themſelves what was to be done; they had offered a mighty ſum of mony only to eſcape with their lives, but it was rejected (r). When a certain *rabbin*, or doctor of their law, who was come from foreign parts to teach and inſtruct the *Jews*, ſtood up amongſt them and ſaid, (s) *Men of* Iſrael, *our God, whoſe laws I have preſcribed to you, commands that we ſhould at any time dye for our law; and behold, now death looks us in the face, and we have but to chuſe whether we ſhould lead a baſe and ſcandalous life, or take the beſt method to come at a gallant and glorious death. If we fall into the hands of our enemies, at their own will and pleaſure we muſt dye; but our creator when he gave us life, did alſo enjoin us that with our own hands, and of our own accord, we ſhould devoutly reſtore it to him again, rather than wait on the cruelty of any enemy. This many of our brethren in many great tribulations have bravely performed; they knew how to do it, and the moſt decent manner of execution is pointed out to us.* Many of the *Jews* embraced the dreadful counſel of the *rabbin*; but the reſt thought his advice much too harſh and would not conſent. The elder perceiving this ſaid, *thoſe that this good and pious courſe diſpleaſes, let them ſeparate and be cut off from the holy congregation; we for the ſake of our paternal law deſpiſe the love of tranſitory life.* Several withdrew upon this, and rather choſe to try the victor's clemency, than follow the *rabbin's* advice. Before they begun to execute the horrid ſentence, the elder commanded that all their rich houſhold goods, ſtuff and garments, ſhould be publickly burnt. Nay even their plate, which would not ſuffer by the fire, was by an artful and malicious method ſtrangely damnified; leſt the enemy ſhould be enriched by their ſpoils. This done, and fire put to all the towers of the caſtle, whilſt their companions who had choſen life looked ſullenly on, each man prepared for the ſlaughter. Being told by their elder that thoſe who bore the ſteddieſt minds, ſhould firſt cut the throats of their wives and children, the celebrated *Jocenus* began the execution by doing that barbarous act on his own wife; whom our hiſtorians call *Anna*, and five children. The example was ſpeedily follow-

(p) The high ſheriff of this county 1 *Rich.* I. was *Randul. de Glanvile.*

(q) Probably the habit of his order, that being white. Vid. *Dug.* mon.

(r) *Hoveden.*

(s) *M. Paris.*

ed

ed by the rest of the masters of families; and afterwards the *rabbin* cut the throat of *Jocenus* himself, as a point of honour he chose to do him above the rest. In short, the whole crew of miserable men, who had thus voluntarily given themselves up to destruction, slew themselves or one another; and amongst the rest fell their impious adviser (*t*).

In the mean time the fire that had been put to the castle raged much; which those poor *Jews* who had chosen life endeavoured as much as possible to quell. At day-break the besiegers thronged, as usual, to assault the fortress; when the wretched remains of the massacre within stood upon the walls, and in a most lamentable manner declared the horrid *catastrophe* of their brethren. They threw their dead bodies over the wall, to convince them of it; and in a most suppliant and moving manner, begged mercy, with an assurance of all of them turning *christians*. But the heads and ringleaders of these merciless bloodhounds, of whom one *Richard*, says my author, called for his beastiality *mala bestia*, was the chief, took no compassion on their sufferings. However, feigning a concern, the *Jews* let them into the castle; which was no sooner done than they slew every one of those poor creatures, who, add my authorities, to the last cried out for baptism. The worthy exploit performed, the heroes ran strait to the cathedral church, where the bonds the *christians* were bound to the *Jews* in for money were deposited; and violently broke open the chests, took and burnt all the writings in the midst of the church, and thus set themselves and many more free from their avaritious usury. And after all each man went his way, the soldiers to their colours, and the commons to their houses, in as much joy and triumph, as if they had done the gallantest and most meritorious action.

This massacre happened at *York* on the eleventh day of *March A.* $11\frac{89}{90}$. For certain, it was the bonds in the church, and the plunder they expected to find in their houses, more than a zeal for the *christian* religion, provoked these miscreants to commit such an inhuman massacre. For such indeed was their procurement, though the *Jews* performed the executive part mostly themselves. *William* of *Newburgh* writes, that there were five hundred men took sanctuary in the castle, besides women and children; if so, this slaughter must be very considerable; and it cannot be computed that less than one thousand or fifteen hundred persons were destroyed.

A. MCLXXXX. But we must now see what vengeance king *Richard* took on his rapacious subjects, for committing such lawless and unprecedented robberies. The king himself was then engaged in the holy war; but before he left *England*, he not only put forth the proclamation aforesaid in favour of the *Jews*, but gave them his word and honour they should no more be disturbed. When the news of this bloody affair at *York* reached him in the *Holy Land*, he was in a vehement passion, that his commands should be so far slighted; and sent orders to the bishop of *Ely*, his chancellor and regent, to go down in person to *York*, and execute strict justice without favour or affection on all offenders. The bishop, a man of fierce nature and proud, set out with a strong body of troops, and came to the city; but the chief authors of the riot having notice of his coming, were fled into *Scotland*. The citizens he examined with great strictness; they denied the having the least hand in it, nor were they aiding or assisting the rioters in any degree; which they offered undeniably to prove. They said the whole affair was transacted by the inhabitants of the neighbouring towns; who came upon them in such multitudes of armed men, that they were not able, either by force or advice, to prevent the consequence. This excuse did not wholly satisfy the bishop, for he laid a very large fine on the city, and made each man pay his proportion before he left the place. Hearing that this was done by a precept from the high sheriff, he removed both him and the governour of the castle from their places, and committed them to prison; he gave the government of the county to his brother *Osbert de Longcamp* (*u*). He built or repaired a castle in the old fortification which king *William Rufus* had formerly strengthened. The commonalty of the city he did not molest, since their ringleaders were gone off; but the soldiers who were concerned in the fray he caused to be punished and turned out of the service. And after having taken an hundred hostages of the city, as bondsmen to answer for the good behaviour of the rest, and to the charge of being guilty of the death of the *Jews* before the king, he departed. Thus, says *Hemingford*, the bishop rather sought to satisfy his own avaritious temper by mulcts, fines, *&c.* than do the justice he ought to have done; for not one man, adds he, either then or since, was executed for the villainy (*x*).

(*t*) An instance somewhat parallel to this of *Jewish* fortitude, is in *Josephus*; who writes, that he and forty of his brethren hid themselves in a cave, but being found out by the *Romans*, *Vespasian* offered them quarter which they all refused. *Josephus* advised them to cast lots one after another for their lives, and he upon whom the lot fell was to be killed by the next man, thus every man to take his fortune round. The advice was followed and executed so far, that *Josephus* himself by great chance and one other *Jew*, were all that were left alive, whom he persuaded to surrender to the *Romans*. But this he [illegible] contrary to *Jewish* law and custom, to fall alive into their enemy's hands. *L'Estrange's Josephus.*

(*u*) *Deinde idem cancellarius tradidit* Osberto de Longo Campo *fratri suo comitatum* Eboracensem *in custodia, et praecipit firmare castellum in* veteri castellaria *quod rex* Willielmus Rufus *ibi construxerat.* Hoveden.

(*x*) One *Richard Malebisse*, probably of the *Acaster* family, paid ccc marks for his pardon, *&c*, on account of being concerned in the slaughter of the *Jews* at *York*, 6 *Rich.* I. Again xx marks to have his land restored which was seized on that occasion. *Madox*'s excheq. 300.

This

This prelate's haughty pride may be shewn also by another instance; *(y)* for being angry at the clergy of the metropolitan church of *York*, for not receiving him with the honours due to an apostolical legate, with procession, *&c.* he laid the whole church under an interdict; and kept it on till such time as the bells of the cathedral were taken down to the ground, and the canons, vicars and other ecclesiasticks came in an humble manner and made submission at his feet.

Notwithstanding this terrible destruction of the *Jews*, the city was supplied with a new colony of them; who under the protection of our kings grew rich, and lived here in great splendour and magnificence. That they continued inhabitants of this city to their total expulsion (z) by *Edward* I. and that they carried on their old trade of usury here, is evident from a grant of that king to one *William Latimer* of some houses in *Conyng-street*, belonging, as is expressed, to an exiled *Jew*, which I have caused to be placed in the appendix *(a)* along with some of their ancient mortgages. The names of two places in and about the city still retain the memory of them.

A. MCXCIX.

In the reign of king *John* the *Scotch* had recovered their spirits, and a war was likely to break out betwixt the two nations *(b)*. But *John*, having work enough cut out for him in *France* and at home, proposed a mediation of this affair. And a meeting betwixt the two kings and their nobles was at *York* *(c)*. Here it was agreed that *Richard* and *Henry*, sons to *John*, should in the space of nine years marry *Margaret* and *Isabell*, daughters to *William*, *&c.* For the confirmation of which nine noblemen of *Scotland* were delivered to the *English* king.

In this assembly at *York* king *William* surrendered into the hands of king *John* the lands of **Cumberland, Huntingtonshire** and **Northumberland**; to the intent that he should assign them again to his son prince *Alexander*. Which prince was to do homage for the same, according to the manner and custom in that case provided; for a recognition that those districts were held of the kings of *England*, as superiour lords of the same.

The reader must excuse the history of a miraculous cure, which I cannot well omit, done by the *Scotch* king at this meeting at *York* *(d)*. Here the *royal touch* was in an especial manner exemplify'd, and shewn to be of great efficacy in the kings of *Scotland*, as immediate descendants from *Edward* the confessor. The kings of *England*, at least *John*, I find did not pretend to have this sanative quality in those days. The chronicle says, that "during the abode of these two kings at *York*, there was brought unto them a child of singular beauty, "son and heir to a gentleman of great possessions in those parts. The child was grievously "afflicted with sundry diseases, for one of its eyes was consumed and lost through an issue "which it had of corrupt and filthy humours; one of his hands was dried up; one of his "feet was so taken that he had no use of it; and his tongue likewise that he could not "speak. The physicians who saw him thus troubled with contrary infirmities deemed him "incurable. Neverthelefs king *William* making a cross on him restored him immediately "to health." The chronicler adds this observation, "that it was believed by many that "this was done by miracle, through the power of almighty *God*, that the vertue of so *god*-"*ly* a prince might be notified to the World."

A. MCCXVI.

During the intestine troubles of *England*, betwixt king *John* and his barons, our city is not mentioned; the more southern parts being only affected. Except that in the last year of this king the northern barons having recovered some strength from their last overthrow, came and laid siege to *York* *(e)*. But receiving a thousand marks from the inhabitants, they granted truce to them till the octaves of *Pentecost*.

A. MCCXX.

In the reign of *John*'s successor *Henry* III *(f)*, the civil broils being in some measure appeased, that king, willing to have a strict alliance with *Scotland* in order to be the better able to cope with his factious barons, came to a convention at *York*. Where on St. *Barnabas* day, the king of *Scots* swore before *Pandulph*, the *popes* legate, to take *Joan Henry*'s sister to wife, and in three days after solemnly married her. This was the lady whom the *Scotch* in derision called *Joan Makepeace*. A name not in vain, says *Buchanan*, for from that time there was a strict alliance betwixt the two kings as long as they lived. I find in the *Foedera* two acts of state dated at this time at *York* under these titles,

(g) De sorore regis Alexandro *regi* Scotiae *tradend. in uxor. Dat. apud* Eborum *in praesentia domini* Pandulphi Norwicensis *electi, domini papae camerarii & apost. sedis legati, 15 die mensis* Junii *anno regni nostri quarto, A. D.* 1220.

De maritagio regis Scotiae Alexandri *cum sorore regis* Angliae *dat. apud* Ebor. *die predict.*

As likewise the jointure which *Alexander* made to his queen *Joan* under this title.

De dote concessa a rege Scotiae *sponsae suae* Johannae *sorori regis* Angliae *dat. apud* Eborum *ut supra. (h)*

(y) R. Hoveden.

(z) The *Jews* were all banish'd the realm *A.* 1290. 18 *Edw.* I. the number of them expulsed at this time was fifteen thousand and sixty persons, to whom the king only allowed what ready money they had to carry with them; and the king amassed great riches by the sale of their houses and goods. *Holl.* chron. *Stowe.*

(b) Scotch chron. *M. Paris.*

(c) The citizens of *York* were fined c. pounds for not coming to meet the king when he came to the city, *&c.* *Maddox*'s excheq. p. 392.

(d) Hollingshed's Scotch chron.

(e) Stowe.

(f) Hen. III. *reg. A.* 4.

(g) Rymer's Foedera.

(h) Omnium querelarum inter Angliae *et* Scotiae *reges finalis concordia; coram* Othone cardinali legato *apud* E-

A. MCCXXX. In the fourteenth year of the reign of *Henry* III. we find that prince at *York* (*i*); where he kept his *Christmas* in a most magnificent manner. He had invited his brother *Alexander* king of *Scotland* to meet him. At this Festival was present, besides the two kings, *Otho* the cardinal legate, the archbishops, bishops and other spiritual ecclesiasticks, with the earls, barons, and general officers of the kingdom, and the king's whole houshold. The king of *England* with great prodigality bestowed upon his brother many magnificent presents, says *M. Paris*, as fine horses, rings, jewels, precious stones, with various other gifts. The two kings dined together in publick three days successively in the most splendid manner, and celebrated the festival with all imaginable pleasure and satisfaction. On the fourth day they parted.

But this interview was nothing in comparison to another which happened at *York*, *A.* 1251. betwixt the aforesaid *Henry* of *England* and *Alexander* III, son of the former king of *Scotland*. This was so extraordinary a meeting which our city was then honoured with, that I shall beg leave to be very particular in the description of it; from the monk of St. *Alban*'s history, who was contemporary and the annalist of *Henry* the third's reign.

A. MCCLI. In the year of our lord 1251, the thirty fifth of king *Henry* III, came that monarch to *York* in order to marry his daughter, just then marriageable, to *Alexander* the young king of *Scotland*; and to see the ceremony performed with that grandeur and magnificence, that the nuptials betwixt two such extraordinary personages deserved. There came also from each kingdom a multitude of clergy and laity, in order to see this great wedding; for the report of it had spread far and near. Along with the king and queen of *England* came all the peers of the realm, whose names, says my author, are too tedious to mention. With the king of *Scotland* came his mother the queen dowager of *Scotland*, who on this occasion was sent for from *France*. She was of the house of *Coucy*, and brought along with her divers of the *French* nobility, which, with the *Scotch* that accompanied their king, made a grand appearance. When they were all got to *York*, those who came with the king of *Scots*, were carefully lodged together in one street.

But it happened that some of the *English* noblemens servants, which were called marshals, whilst they were providing lodgings for their masters, fell out about them; and first fought it at fists, then with clubs, and lastly with swords. In which fray several were grievously wounded and one slain outright. The officers which the king of *England* had with him, who were grave and modest men, so bestirred themselves that they appeased this tumult, and made peace both amongst the servants and their masters. The archbishop's officers also, lest the scarcity of lodgings should occasion any more such bickerings, took care to settle every man according to his quality in as good a manner as the hurry would permit of.

On *Christmas* day *Henry* conferred the honour of knighthood on *Alexander* the *Scotch* king, and twenty other young noblemen of his retinue. He arrayed them all in most sumptuous and elegant habits suitable to the occasion. On the next day the king of *Scots* was married to the daughter of the king of *England* by the archbishop in the cathedral; but to prevent the ill consequence which might happen from such multitudes pressing to see the solemnity, the ceremony was secretly and unexpectedly, done very early in the morning. Here was such a mixture of nations such crouds of *English*, *French* and *Scotch* nobility, such an incredible number of officers of war dressed in effeminate habits, priding themselves in silk and sattin ornaments, that if, adds the old monk, I should describe to the full the wanton vanities of the age, it would occasion a weariness, as well as admiration, in the ears of the auditors. More than one thousand military commanders (*l*) **queintly**, vulgarly speaking, clad in silk vestures appeared at the nuptials on the part of the king of *England*; and the next day throwing them by, attended in quite new attire. The king of *Scots* was waited upon by sixty knights, and a great number of gentlemen, richly habited and adorned; which made a most gallant appearance.

At this meeting the king of *Scotland* did homage to the king of *England* for some lands he held of him in *Lothian*. But when king *Henry* urged him to do the same for the whole realm of *Scotland*, as several of the *Scottish* king's predecessors had done to *Henry*'s, *Alexander* answered, *that he came thither peaceably to do honour to the king of* England, *and by his consent to marry his daughter, in order to knit a stronger friendship between them. That he could not answer such a difficult question, which he had not besides consulted his peers and counsellors about.* *Henry* when he heard this prudent reply of the young monarch's, whatever might be his real sentiments, dissembled so far, as not to obstruct or darken the glory of this great festival by any more discourse about it.

The earl marshal of *England*, according to an ancient custom, demanded the king of *Scotland*'s palfry as his fee for his knighthood. But he was also answered, *that the king of* Scotland *would not suffer such an exaction; for that if he had liked it, he might have had that*

boracum, *cum multis testibus. A.* 1242. *Rymer's Fœdera.* Tom. I. p 400.

(*i*) *M. Paris.*

(*k*) *M. Paris.*

(*l*) *Cointise. M. P.* rendered *queintly* in the glossary. *Milites vestitu serico, ut vulgariter loquamur*, cointises. *Sane* cointise Gallis *est elegantia*, Coint, *nitidus*, & *nos* queint *eadem significatione retinemus.* Gloss. in hist. M. P.

honour from some other prince, or one of his own nobility; but out of respect and reverence to so great a king as his neighbour and father in law was, he rather chose to have it from his hands than any other. Thus, says *Paris*, by *Henry*'s commands all other controversies ceased. An instance of this young king's humanity and good nature is also apparent by this; being informed that the lord *Lovel* had been expell'd the court for bribery, he was solicited to reinstate him in the king's favour. He took a fit opportunity and fell down on his knees before *Henry*, and would not be persuaded to rise till the king had promised to grant him his request. This was to pardon *Lovel*, which was done, and he was afterwards made lord treasurer.

The two kings spent the *Christmas* jovially; in which, adds *Matthew*, if I was fully to explain the great abundance and diversity of victuals, the various changes of rich attire, the mirth and jollity of the guests, with the quantity of strong liquor they drank, those that were not eye-witnesses would never credit the recital. To give one instance as an example for all; the archbishop himself spent upon his royal guests and their company, at one entertainment, and at the first course, sixty fat oxen. Sometimes they eat with him, and at other times with king *Henry*; and whatever this transitory world could afford was exhibited in great abundance. The archbishop, like a northern prince, shewed the greatest hospitality to all. He entertained the whole company several times, and in all cases of necessity lent his helping hand for their better accommodation; as in the care of the strangers lodgings, providing provender and pasturage for their horses; in fuel for fires, and gifts of money he satisfied all their wants; insomuch that this meeting, for his master's honour, cost him four thousand marks. Which was all sown, adds the monk, on a barren soil, and never rose to his profit: It did however this service, that by this magnificence he added to his usual character, and stopped the mouths of all invidious slanderers.

The nuptial solemnities ended, with the entertainments, the king of *Scotland* begged leave to depart into his own kingdom with his beautiful bride. On whom waited sir *Robert Norrice* knight, Marshal of the king's house, sir *Stephen Bausan*, as also the lady *Maud*, widow of lord *William Cantalupe*; with several others.

I shall now proceed from this marriage to the rest of the memorable events that have happened in our city; subjoining for the reader's better information, and for the connection of the facts, that the sudden deaths of this young king and queen of *Scotland*, with those of a son and daughter, their whole stock of children, follow'd so quick, as to make a continuation of mourning, says *Buchanan*, in that kingdom. And reason enough for it; the royal line failing by this mortality, opened a door for so many titles to enter and make their claim, as tore the whole nation to pieces. In the competition, *Baliol* and *Bruce* were the most remarkable claimants; the *English* kings knew how to make their advantage of this division, and did not a little foment the disturbance, by siding with each of these rivals, for sovereignty, as they saw occasion. The war was bloody on all sides, during the reigns of the three *Edwards* of *England*, and brings our city much in question in the continuance; and since nothing remarkable is met with on the civil affairs of the city, during the rest of *Henry* the third's reign, I come next to give an account of what happened in the time of his ever famous son and successor.

After *Easter* king *Edward* going into *Scotland* staid some time at *York*, where the famous MCCXCI.
welchman Rice ap Meredith, before taken in *Wales*, was brought, tried for high treason and condemned. *(m)* He was drawn through the city to the gallows, and there hanged and quartered.

An. 1298. *Edward* I. summoned a parliament to meet at *York* *(n)*; and in an especial manner MCCXCVIII
required his mutinous barons to attend it on the day after St. *Hilary*, without excuse or delay; accounting them rebels that disobeyed. Accordingly came at the summons the earls of *Warren* and *Gloucester*; the earls *Marshal*, *Hereford* and *Arundele*; *Guy* son to the earl of *Warwick*, in his father's room. Of barons, the lord *Henry Piercy*, the lord *John Wake*, the lord *Segrave*, with many more nobles too tedious to mention. These being assembled, the king's confirmation of *Magna Charta* and *Charta de Foresta* were read. After which the bishop of *Carlisle*, in *pontificalibus*, pronounced a heavy curse against all those that went about to break the same. And because the *Scottish* lords appeared not, according to summons, it was agreed that the whole *English* army should rendezvous at *York* in *April* following; and a general muster to be then and there taken of it. At this parliament the commons of the realm granted the king the ninth penny of their goods *(o)*; the archbishop of *Canterbury*, with the clergy of his province, the tenth penny, and the archbishop of *York* and his clergy a fifth.

It was now that a flame broke out, which burnt with violence for near a century in the continuance of these *Scottish* wars. According to the last summons, the army under the command of the earl of *Surrey*, whom the king had made general in his absence, met at *York*. The *Scotch* lords not yet coming in, though they were again summoned to do it, the army march'd on to *Newcastle*, from thence to *Roxburgh*, which the *Scots* had besieged. King *Edward* having finished his business in *Flanders*, hastened over to *England*, and removed

(m) *Stowe*. (n) *Speed*. (o) *Daniel*.

moved the courts of juſtice to *York*. Here he ſummoned another parliament, as alſo the *Scotch* nobility to meet at it; which they not obeying, he iſſued out his commiſſion of array, ordering all his ſubjects to meet him in arms at *Roxburgh* on St. *John baptiſt* day next enſuing, which they accordingly did. What followed was the battle of *Foukirk*, a fatal day to the *Scotch*; and which occaſioned ſoon after the conqueſt of the whole kingdom (*p*).

A. MCCXCIX. The king held another parliament at *York*, *A.* 1299. From whence he proceeded as ſoon as the ſpring would give him leave to purſue his laſt victory in *Scotland* (*q*).

MCCCVI. In the year 1306, after the total reduction of *North-Britain*, king *Edward* came to *York*, where he ſtaid ſome time, and from thence went to *London*. The courts of king's-bench and exchequer, after they had continued ſeven years in this city, were now removed back again. Theſe courts of juſtice, ſays an hiſtorian (*r*), were brought from *London* to *York*, that the king and his council might be near one another and *Scotland*, to provide better for the conqueſt or defence of that kingdom (*s*).

A. MCCCVII. *Anno* 1307, being the laſt of the life of this great king, he ended his days in the midſt of his conqueſts at *Burgh upon Sands* in *Northumberland*, and was buried at *Weſtminſter*. He was ſucceeded by his ſon

Edward II, in whoſe time affairs took a different turn. For this king having nothing of the ſpirit or conduct of his father, either at the council board or in the field, ſuffered not only all *Scotland* to be regained from him, but likewiſe had the mortification to ſee a *Scotch* army brave him in his own dominions as far as *York*.

A. MCCCXI. In the fourth year of his reign he kept his *Chriſtmas* at *York*; where *Piers Gaveſton* and his followers, who had been baniſhed from him by his father, came to him and was received, ſays my author, as a gift from heaven (*t*). As if he foreſaw an invaſion, he now cauſed the walls of the city to be ſtrongly fortified, and put in a poſture of defence; which proved very neceſſary to be done.

A. MCCCXIV. In the eighth year of his reign after the fatal battle of *Bannockburn*, in which the *Scotch* hiſtorians (*u*) ſay we loſt fifty thouſand men ſlain upon the ſpot, the king himſelf, narrowly eſcaping, fled to *York*; not thinking himſelf ſafe till he got thither. Here he called a great council of the *Engliſh* nobles, that were ſpared from ſlaughter, to conſult what methods he might take to reſtore his ſhattered army, and revenge himſelf on *Robert Bruce*. But they could not find any expedient for it at that time, nor of ſome years after did they ſtir, notwithſtanding the many provocations the *Scotch* gave them.

A. MCCCXIX. King *Edward* being informed that *Robert* king of *Scotland* was gone into *Ireland*, and carried over with him the flower of his army, thought this a fit opportunity to revenge his former loſſes (*x*). Accordingly he came down to *York* in order to raiſe an army, but found that city and country ſo thinly ſtocked with inhabitants, that he was obliged to draw from the ſouthern and weſtern parts of the kingdom to compleat his forces.

October 15, the ſame year, the clerks of the exchequer, by the king's order, ſet out for *York*, with the book called *Doomſday*, and other records; which, with proviſion, laded twenty one carts (*y*). The judges of the king's-bench came alſo, and ſat and did buſineſs in that city for the ſpace of ſix months (*z*).

Edward having gotten together an army, ſet out from *York* to beſiege *Berwick*, but he was ſcarcely got thither (*a*) when *Thomas Randolph* earl of *Murray*, the *Scotch* general, paſſed the river *Solway*, and marched another way into *England*; where he waſted all with fire and ſword till he came to the very gates of *York*; and had like to have taken the queen before ſhe could get into the city (*b*). The city however he did not attempt to beſiege, but burnt and deſtroyed the ſuburbs, which done he drew off his men and marched back towards his own country (*c*).

The (*d*) archbiſhop of *York*, a reverend grave old divine, but a young ſoldier, more for the indignity of the affront, ſays the *Scotch* hiſtorian (*e*), than any hopes of ſucceſs, took up arms, and aſſembled ſuch forces as he could raiſe; compoſed of clergymen, monks, canons and other ſpiritual men of the church; with a confuſed heap of huſbandmen, labourers, artificers, tradeſmen, in all to the number of ten thouſand. Theſe able ſoldiers had as experienced commanders, the archbiſhop and biſhop of *Ely*, lord-chancellor, being the leaders of theſe warlike troops; much fitter to pray for the ſucceſs of a battle than to fight it (*f*). This formidable army, breathing nothing but revenge, followed the *Scotch*, but they did not follow the proverb, *to build a bridge for a flying enemy*, and overtook them at *Myton* upon *Swale*, about eleven miles from *York*. The *Scotch* army finding themſelves purſued, drew upon the other ſide of the river in battallia. Then they ſet fire to ſome hay-ſtacks

(*p*) There were ſlain at this battle of the *Scotch* twenty thouſand. *N. Trivet*. Forty thouſand, *M. Weſt*. Thirty thouſand, *Knighton*. Sixty thouſand, *T. Wykes*.

(*q*) *Knighton*.

(*r*) Chron. *T. Wykes*.

(*s*) *Maddox*, in his book of the exchequer, gives the records of this matter, p. 553. They were kept in the caſtle of *York*. *Ryley's placita parl.* 225.

(*t*) *Stow*.

(*u*) *Buchanan*.

(*x*) Ibid.

(*y*) *Stow*.

(*z*) The precepts for this removal of the courts is in *Ryley*. p. 564. dated *Ebor*. 28 *Maii anno reg*. 12.

(*a*) *Buchanan*.

(*b*) *Daniel*.

(*c*) *Walſingham*.

(*d*) *Will. de Melton*.

(*e*) *Buchanan*.

(*f*) *Hollingſhed*,

which

which were upon the place; the smoak of which driving with a brisk wind in the faces of the *English*, as they passed the river, so blinded them that they could not see the enemy; who came down in good order upon them, and without any great resistance entirely routed them. There were slain and drowned of the *English* above two thousand, some say, four thousand, the rest with their generals made great haste back to the city. In this conflict fell *Nicholas Flemming*, then mayor of *York*, who had headed up his citizens to the battle; there were taken prisoners Sir *John de Pabeham*, Knt. lord *William Ayrmine*, and several others. Here was such a fall of the priesthood, that the *English*, says *Buchanan*, called this fight, for a long time after, the *white battle*.

This battle was fought *October* 12, 1319. The archbishop had business enough to fill up vacancies in the church at his return. But in an especial manner, he shewed his gratitude to the mayor, his body was honourably buried in the parish church of S. *Wilfrid*, and an indulgence granted of forty days relaxation of sin to all parishioners thereof (*g*), who being truly contrite, penitent and confessed, should say for his soul the lord's prayer, and the salutation of the blessed virgin. For him also in the same church was a chauntry founded (*g*).

King *Edward* hearing of this overthrow, as he lay before *Berwick*, raised the siege and retired to *York*.

Whatever were the misfortunes in the reign of this king, they were chiefly owing to the civil dissensions in *England*, betwixt this *Edward* and his uncle *Thomas* earl of *Lancaster*, with other great lords of the realm; which gave the *Scotch* such extraordinary advantage over the *English* at that time. For had this king been followed with the same zeal his father was, he might not only have stemmed the tide, but, perhaps, have had it in his power to have turned it against his foreign enemies (*h*). We must allow this to be a reason sufficient to account for most or all of his miscarriages, as those who will consult the history of those times may find. After various disputes and several bloody battles betwixt the king and his barons, he at length entirely subdued them. For at the battle of *Burrough-bridge*, *Thomas* earl of *Lancaster* was taken prisoner by *Andrew de Harclay*; *Humphrey de Bohun* earl of *Hereford* slain, and their whole army cut in pieces. With the earl was taken many more barons who were all brought to *York* to the king. The barons were tried by judges appointed for that purpose, condemned and sentenced to be hanged and quartered; and by the instigation of the *Spencers*, says *Knighton*, the sentence was executed upon several of them in different parts of the kingdom. *John* lord *Clifford*, *Roger* lord *Moubraye*, Sir *Joceline D'eivill* suffered at *York*. The earl of *Lancaster*, out of regard to his blood and near alliance to the king, was sentenced to be beheaded; which was executed upon him before his own castle at *Pontfrete*. *Andrew de Harelay* for this great piece of service was made earl of *Carlisle*; but he did not enjoy his new dignity long, for hatching an invasion with the *Scotch*, he was seized at *Carlisle*, tried, condemned and executed; and one of his quarters placed upon the bridge at *York* (*i*). A. MCCCXXI.

The next year, about ascension-day, king *Edward* called another (*k*) *parliament* at *York*; wherein he exerted the regal power to some purpose. The whole decree which had been passed at *London* against his favourites the *Spencers* was thoroughly examined and entirely disannulled, and the *Spencers* restored to all their lands and offices. The lord *Hugh Spencer* the father, was made earl of *Winchester*; the lord *Andrew Harclay*, as I mentioned before, earl of *Carlisle*. In this parliament was also disinherited all that had bore arms against the king, and sided with the barons. Here also the king made *Robert Baldock*, a man very ill beloved, lord chancellor; and lastly the king's eldest son *Edward* was, with great solemnity, made prince of *Wales* and duke of *Aquitain*. At this *parliament*, the king caused all the ordinances made by the barons, to be examined by men skilled in the laws; and such as were thought necessary to be established, he commanded should be called **statutes**. A great subsidy was now granted to the king by the temporality; and the clergy of the province of *Canterbury* gave five pence out of every mark; those of this province four pence. A. MCCCXXII.

With this supply *Edward* raised so great an army, that he thought nothing could resist it, and marched into *Scotland*. But his ill-fortune still pursued him, for meeting with no forage to support his troops, which had been purposely destroyed, he was obliged to retire into *England*. *Robert* the *Scotch* king, perceiving this, watched his motions so narrowly, that he surprized him at dinner, some say, in *Byland* abby, about fourteen miles from *York*, and falling upon his forces unawares, they were easily routed and put to flight (*m*). The *Scots* took several prisoners, amongst whom was *John* earl of *Richmond*, and the king himself narrowly escaped, by the goodness of his horse, to the city of *York*.

Here he staid some months, kept his *Christmas*, and diverted the chagrin his last overthrow had given him by all the amusements he could compass.

(*f*) Mr. *Torre*.
(*g*) See S. *Wilfrid* in *Blakestreet*.
(*h*) *Hollinshed*.
(*i*) *Dug. Bar.*
(*k*) An act of state is in *Foedera* with this title, *de parliamento nuper apud* Ripon *summonito, apud* Ebor. *tenend. teste rege apud* Ebor. 4 *die Novembris* 1322.
(*l*) *Speed*.
(*m*) *Buchanan*.

In ſhort, the whole life of this unfortunate prince was almoſt a continued ſeries of ill accidents; yet he was a prince, ſays *Daniel*, rather weak than wicked, and whatever exorbitancies he might commit, he was out-done by his people, adds he, in the rough and ſcandalous uſage he received from them moſt of his reign. And being at laſt depoſed by his queen and ſon, he was barbarouſly murdered in his impriſonmeut in *Berkly-caſtle*. Which is one inſtance of king *Charles* I. remarkable annotation, *that there is but a ſmall ſtep betwixt the priſons and graves of princes.*

A. MCCCXXVII. *Edward* III. was crowned king of *England* at fourteen years of age. In the very firſt year of his reign the *Scots* entered *England* with two powerful armies, under the conduct of two famous generals *Thomas Randolph* and *James Douglaſs*. Theſe were ſent, ſays *Buchanan*, with twenty thouſand gallant light horſe, but no foot, by king *Robert*, and penetrated as far as *Stanhope-park* in *Wiredale*. This, when the young king was appriſed of, he ordered a general rendezvous of the whole army at *York*; in order to put a ſtop to theſe bold invaders. The *Scotch* had then ſo mean an opinion of the *Engliſh* valour, occaſioned by their many victories in the laſt reign, that they derided them in the moſt ſcurrilous manner; and got this diſtich put up over the church-door of St. *Peter*'s, oppoſite to **Staingate**, ſays my author, in *York*, when the king was in the city (*n*).

Long beards hartleſs, painted hoods witleſs,
Gay coats graceleſs, makes England **thriftleſs.**

This taunt was thrown at the *Engliſh* in thoſe days, ſay our hiſtorians, as well upon account of their puſillanimity, as their dreſs and length of beard; but it was not long before theſe deriders of *Engliſh* manhood were called to ſo ſtrict an account, that the ſmart of it was felt for ſome ages after. And even yet the name of *Edward* III. as well as the *firſt*, ſounds dreadful in the ears of a *Scotchman*.

Whilſt the king lay at *York*, preparing for this expedition againſt the *Scotch*, there came to his aid *John* lord *Beaumont* of *Hainault*, ſaid to be one of the moſt gallant knights then in the world. *Froiſart* has given us the names of divers other knights and commanders that accompanied this lord, which, with his own retinue, made up five hundred men. *Knighton* ſays, the number of all the foreigners, that came to gain honour under this hopeful young king, amounted to two thouſand. The king aſſigned lodgings to moſt of theſe ſtrangers in the ſuburbs; but to lord *John* himſelf (*o*) he allotted an *abby of white monks* in the city for the reſidence of him and his attendants. The king with the queen-mother lodged in the (*p*) *monaſtery* belonging to the *fryers minors*, which muſt have been a ſtately building in thoſe days, for, we are told, they each kept court apart in it. The king's was very magnificent in order to do honour to the ſtrangers; and ſuch care was taken that proviſions of all kinds was both plentiful and cheap. The city and country, ſays my authority, were rich and flouriſhed in abundance. For full ſix weeks did the king lie here with an army of ſixty thouſand men about him, yet all that time the price of proviſions was nothing raiſed, but every thing was ſold as reaſonable, as it was before. There was plenty of *Rheniſh*, *Gaſcoign* and *Anjovan* wines, ſays my author; with pullein, wild fowl, and other proviſion, of that kind, at moderate rates. Hay, oats, *&c.* were daily brought to the ſtrangers lodgings for their uſe; ſo that they had great reaſon to be well ſatisfied with their entertainment.

But this proſperity had liked to have proved very fatal to them; for preſuming much on the king's favour and protection, they carried themſelves with all imaginable haughtineſs towards his ſubjects. The *Engliſh* reſented this uſage, as they ought, and a contention begun which ended not without much blood-ſhed on both ſides.

On *trinity* ſunday, the king, for the ſake of theſe ſtrange lords, held a ſolemn and magnificent feaſt at the friary aforeſaid (*r*). To his uſual attendance of five hundred knights, he then added fifty more; and the queen, his mother, had in her retinue ſixty ladies of the greateſt rank and beauty in the kingdom. There was that day, ſays my author, a moſt ſplendid entertainment, and a truly royal ſhew of whatever was choice and excellent. At night there was a moſt gallant ball; but whilſt the lords and ladies were in the midſt of their diverſions, a ſtrange and hideous noiſe interrupted them, and alarmed the whole court. It ſeems the ſervants and pages of theſe foreign auxiliaries, had by their inſolence ſo exaſperated the minds of ſome *Engliſh* archers (*s*), who lodged with them in the ſuburbs, that a great fray began amongſt them. This diſcord, once ſet on foot, continually encreaſed, new abettors ſucceſſively coming in on each ſide till near three thouſand of the archers being gathered together, many of the *Hainaulters* were ſlain; and the reſt flying were fain to enter their lodgings and fortify themſelves as well as they could againſt the fury of their enemies. Moſt part of the knights their commanders were at court; but on the firſt noiſe of the fray they haſtened to their lodgings to defend themſelves

(*n*) *Hollinſhed*. &c.
(*o*) *Froiſart*.
(*p*) *La maiſon de freres mineurs*. Froiſart.
(*q*) *Froiſart* calls it *Vin d'Auſſois*; which his annotator ſuppoſes to be wine of *Alſace ſur le Rhine*.
(*r*) *Froiſart*.
(*s*) *Knighton*.

and their people. Some part of the city was fired in the hurly burly, many of the *Hainaulters* were ſlain and more hurt; but at laſt by the authority of the king, and earneſt endeavours of the queen mother, who had a great affection for the foreigners, the archers thirſt of blood was ſtayed and the quarel ceaſed for that time (*t*). But that very night the ſtrangers, not ſo much thinking of ſleep as revenge, being now headed by their commanders, aroſe privately, and joining together ſet upon the archers of *Lincolnſhire* and *Northamptonſhire*, for the men of each county were marſhalled and quartered by themſelves, and ſlew three hundred of them. In the morning they certainly had paid dear for this deſperate action, for a body of ſix thouſand *Engliſh* ſoldiers had combined together to kill them every man either within doors or without as they could come at them; but that the king took care to protect his foreigners, by ſetting ſtrong guards about their lodgings, and diſplacing the archers from their former quarters. However the ſtrangers were ſo uneaſy that they ſcarce durſt ſleep; but kept good watch, their horſes ready ſaddled and their arms at hand for a month together after this; ſo well they knew it behooved them, ſays *Joſhua Barnes* (*u*), to look about them after ſuch an egregious affront to the common ſoldiery of *England*. Of the *Engliſh* ſlain in this conflict, there were (*x*) eighty *Lincolnſhire* men buried under one ſtone in the church-yard belonging to the now demoliſhed church of S. *Clement* in *Foſſgate*.

King *Edward* had lain at *York*, with his vaſt army, for three weeks, when the *Scotch* ambaſſadors arrived there in order to treat of peace. And when in three weeks more no terms of accommodation could be agreed on betwixt the two contending powers, the ambaſſadors returned, and the king gave command that in a week's time every man ſhould be ready to march againſt the enemy. That ſuch, to whom the care was committed, ſhould find and provide carts, waggons, &c. for the carriage of tents, pavillions, and other warlike preparations proper for the expedition. This done, at the day appointed, the king and all his barons with their whole army began their march from *York*; all gallantly armed with trumpets ſounding, and banners waving in the wind. *J. Barnes* has collected the names of many nobles who was with the king at *York*, and attended him in this expedition, which would be too tedious for me to mention. But I cannot omit taking notice, that the foreign troops, both in their march, and in their quarters, were placed immediately next the king's own guards, as well to ſecure them from the archers, who ſtill meditated revenge, as to do them the greater honour; and let the whole army know that whoever ſought their damage would at the ſame time highly treſpaſs upon the king himſelf.

In the *Foedera* I find a mandate from the king for putting the city of *York* into a poſture of defence, which I ſhall beg leave to tranſlate as follows:

(*y*) *The king to his wel-beloved the mayor and bayliffs of his city of* York, *greeting.*

SINCE *the* Scotch, *our enemies and rebels, have thought fit to enter our kingdom in an hoſtile manner near* Carliſle, *with all their power, as we are certainly informed; and kill, burn, deſtroy and act other miſchiefs as far as they are able. We have drawn down our army in order, by God's aſſiſtance to reſtrain their malice, and to that end turn our ſteps towards that country and thoſe enemies.*

We, conſidering our aforeſaid city of York, *eſpecially whilſt* Iſbell *queen of* England *our moſt dear mother, our brother and ſiſters (z) abide in the ſame, to be more ſafely kept and guarded; leaſt any ſudden danger from our enemy's approach ſhould happen to the ſaid city; or fear or fright to our mother, brother and ſiſters, which God avert, for want of ſufficient munition and guard.*

We ſtrictly command and charge you, upon your faiths and allegiance, and on the forfeiture of every thing you can forfeit to us, immediately at ſight of theſe preſents, without excuſe or delay, to inſpect and overlook all your walls, ditches and towers, and the ammunition proper for the defence of the ſaid city; taking with you ſuch of our faithful ſervants as will be choſen for this purpoſe; and to take ſuch order for its defence, that no danger can happen to the city by neglect of ſuch ſafeguards.

And we by theſe preſents, give you full power and authority to diſtrain and compell all and ſingular owners of houſes or rents in the ſaid city, or merchants or ſtrangers inhabiting the ſame, by the ſeizure of their bodies or goods, to be aiding towards the ſecurity of the walls, bulwarks or towers; as you in your diſcretion ſhall think fit to ordain, for the making other uſeful and neceſſary works about it. Puniſhing all thoſe that are found to contradict or rebel againſt this order by impriſonment, or what other methods you think fit.

Study therefore to uſe ſuch diligence in the execution of the premiſſes, that we may find it in the effect of your works; and that we may have no occaſion from your negligence, ſhould danger happen, to take ſevere notice of you.

Dated at *Durham*, *July* 15, *A.* 1327, By the KING.

(*t*) *Froiſart.*

(*u*) *J. Barnes's Edw.* III.

(*x*) **The Henauders and the Engliſhmen faute by chaunce on Trinite Sundaye at York, where eighty Lincolnſhire men were ſleyne and buried under a ſtone in S. Clement chirch trod in Foſſgate,** Leland coll. **out of a chronique in Peter college Library.**

(*y*) *Rymer's Foedera ſub A.* 1327.

(*z*) Prince *John* of *Eltham*, and the princeſſes *Joan* and *Eleanor*. See *Speed's* chron.

This

This special mandate sensibly shews that the king and his counsel were in great fear of the *Scots* at that time; least whilst he was hunting them more northward they should slip him and attempt something upon *York*, as they had done in the former reign. I shall follow *Edward* no farther in this expedition, than just to hint that the *Scotch* army was at length overtaken, and being cooped up by the *English* in *Stanhope* park for fifteen days, were almost famish'd, and upon the point of surrendring; when, by the treachery of lord *Mortimer*, as is said, they slipped through *Edward*'s fingers, and shewed that they were really what *Buchanan* calls them, *light horsemen*, by an expeditious march into their own country. The young king, sadly chagrined at the missing his prey, when it was already in his net, returned back to *York*, and went from thence to *London*.

Lord *John* of *Hainault* was bounteously rewarded by the king notwithstanding the disappointment, and honourably sent back into his own country. The next year he returned with his niece *Philippa* daughter to *William* earl of *Hainault* his brother; and with a great retinue conducted her to *York*, where the court then was, in order for her marriage with the king of *England* in that city.

Before I enter upon a description of the ceremony of this grand affair, it will be necessary to premise somewhat relating to this princess, who is spoke of by all historians as the most celebrated beauty of the age she lived in. *Philippa* was the youngest daughter to *William* earl of *Hainault* and *Holland*, and *Jane de Valois*; she was, says *J. Barnes*, a most beautiful lovely creature, the mirror of her sex, and was then scarce fourteen years old. The persons sent about this treaty of marriage were Dr. *Roger Northborough*, bishop of *Litchfield* and *Coventry*, two knights bannerets, and two other gentlemen learned in the laws. These persons had commission to treat with the earl, and chuse a wife for their king out of his five daughters. The ambassadors, attended with an honourable equipage, came to *Valenciennes* the chief city of *Hainault*; the earl *William* and his countess received them very gladly, and entertain'd them with great splendour and magnificence. Upon a set day the earl brought out his five daughters before them, to take their choice of; at the sight of so much beauty and delicate Shapes, they all stood amazed, not knowing to which to give the preference. Till the piercing eye of the bishop, says my author, observing with good heed the lady *Philippa to be the best built about the hips, and of a good sanguine complexion, agreeing with the king's*; he secretly advised his colleagues that she was the lady, amongst them all, most likely by her sweet disposition, to please the king their master, and also to bring forth a numerous and hopeful progeny. This observation in a bishop, says Mr. *Hearne (a)*, whose order was not then allowed to marry, gave occasion of much mirth to the rest. However the judgment prevailed, and madam *Philippa*, though the youngest of the ladies, was pitched upon for their queen.

This story of the penetrating bishop, and given by a grave divine, I thought not improper to introduce the following marriage. Nor was the prelate wrong in his prolifick notion of the lady, for she bore king *Edward* seven sons and three daughters, almost in the space of as many years.

MCCCXXVIII. The king kept his *Christmas* at *York*, *A.* 1328, in great state and magnificence; and before the solemnity of the festival was ended, lord *John* of *Hainault* arrived with his beautiful niece and a very numerous attendance. They were received by the young and amorous king, whose blood had been sufficiently fired by his ambassadors description, with all the pomp and ceremony so great a monarch could possibly shew on this extraordinary occasion. All the justs, tournaments, triumphs, plays and pastimes then in use were exhibited, in order to testify his joy, and do the greater honour to his charming bride.

On the twenty fourth of *January*, being *Sunday*, the eve of St. *Paul*'s conversion, the marriage was publickly solemnized in the cathedral; at which solemnity the most reverend Dr. *William Melton*, archbishop of *York*, and the right reverend Dr. *John Hotham*, bishop of *Ely*, sang the mass. Upon these happy nuptials the whole kingdom teemed with joy, and the court at *York* expressed it in a more than ordinary manner; for there were nothing, says *Froisart*, but justs and tournaments in the day time, maskings, revels, and interludes with songs and dances in the evenings; along with continual feasting for three weeks together.

During this great concourse at *York*, the *Hainaulters* still bearing malice in their hearts, set fire to and almost consumed a whole parish in the suburbs of the city, by reason of a difference raised betwixt the inhabitants and them. The cause was no mean one, for the strangers had made bold to ravish several of the others wives, daughters and maid servants. The *suburbians* scandalized at such outragious proceedings challenged the *Hainaulters* to fight them; and a select company of each well armed, one *Wednesday* before sun rising, *dormiente tota civitate*, says my authority *(b)*, met in a street called **Watlingate** and fought their quarrel fairly out. In this conflict were slain and drowned in the river *Ouse* of the *Hainaulters* 527, besides those who were mortally wounded and died soon after. Of the *English* fell likewise 242.

(a) *Hearn*'s glossary to *Peter Langtoft*'s chronicle. (b) *Leland*'s coll.

This

a

This account I look to be true, notwithstanding that I have no other testimony than the *collectanea* to support it. The contest in the preceding year was still green in their memories, and such a fresh provocation would easily stir up a resentment. The affair might be so hushed up, out of respect to the queen's countrymen, that few historians of that age could come to the knowledge of it, and there is no circumstance in the relation which can make it be taken for the tumult before mentioned. It is certain these foreigners behaved very insolently and saucily to the *English* at both times of their coming to *York*; which our ancient *British* spirit could ill bear, without endeavouring to retaliate the affront. The former contest shews a just resentment of injuries in the *English* in general; and the latter is an evident proof, to our present citizens, of the spirit and valour of their ancestors.

King *Edward* summoned a *parliament* to meet at *York*. Where the king's special affairs that should have been done at it, were frustrated by the squabbles which happened betwixt the two archbishops about the bearing their crosses in each other's province (*d*). A. MCCCXXXII.

The king in his march to *Scotland* staid and kept his *Christmas* at *York*. From thence he proceeded on his journey; and having pretty well adjusted matters with king *Baliol*, he returned to this city to hold a *parliament* which had been summoned to meet here on the day before St. *Peter in cathedra*, being *Feb.* 21, 1334 (*e*). A. MCCCXXXIV.

Joshua Barnes has collected all the statutes, and other transactions done and agreed to at this session of *parliament*, which lasted from the date above to *May* 15. But as I am careful not to swell my subject with what is unnecessary, I shall omit them. At this meeting of the king, lords and commons of *England*, *John Baliol* king of *Scotland* was to have done particular homage to *Edward* for holding that kingdom; but his affairs were then at so low an ebb that he durst not trust himself for fear of being seized by the *Scotch* lords in the journey. So he sent the lords *Beaumont* and *Montacute* to *York*, to excuse him to *Edward*.

During the wars in *France* in which *Edward*, and his ever renowned son the *black prince*, wone such signal victories, *David Bruce*, *Baliol*'s competitor, undertook to invade *England*, which was then left to the sole governance of the queen. *David* made himself sure of conquest, and resolved to destroy the towns and countrey with fire and sword till he came to *York*; where he only expected opposition. Four towns excepted, *viz. Hexham*, *Corbridge*, *Durham* and *Darlington*, which he was advised to spare, and keep as store-houses for his army's subsistance. With this resolution he entered *England*, and meeting none to oppose him, dealt his fire and sword about unmercifully, and really penetrated so far that some of his army came so near *York* as to burn part of the suburbs; but after retired to their main body. *Philippa*, our ever famous queen was then in *York*; and though a woman, shewed in this case such courage and conduct, as was worthy the *wife* and *mother* of such a *husband* and *son* (*g*). She got what forces she could together at *York*, and from thence marched in person with them against the enemy. The *Scots*, not expecting such a visit, were drawn to battle at a place called *Nevill's-cross* near *Durham*; and after an obstinate resistance were wholly routed; fifteen thousand of their men left dead upon the spot, and their king himself taken prisoner (*h*). The archbishop of *York*, *William de la Zouch*, commanded the second corps of the *English* army, and behaved very gallantly in the fight. A. MCCCXLVI.

After the battle the victorious queen returned to *York* with great joy and triumph; where soon after king *David* was delivered to her by *John Coplande* (who took him prisoner) with much ceremony (*i*). The queen staid in the city till she had seen it strongly fortified; and then, leaving the lords *Percy* and *Nevill* to the governance of the north, she returned to *London* carrying her royal prisoner along with her to present to her husband (*k*).

The rest of *Edward* the third's glorious reign being chiefly employed in the wars of *France*, is therefore foreign to my purpose; I shall only say that *William* of *Hatfield* the second son of *Edward*, by his queen *Philippa* died young, and was buried in our cathedral (*l*). And *Edmund Langley* the fifth son was, in the reign of his successor, made the first duke of *York*.

Richard the second began his reign *A.* 1377. in the course of which were no feats of war concerning us; but in civil affairs, by the king's especial grace and favour, divers honours, privileges and immunities were granted us, which the chapter of the charters, &c. will recite at large. A. MCCCLXXVII.

A. 1385. I find this king at *York* in an expedition he made against the *Scots*; which was only memorable for the death of the lord *Ralph Stafford*, eldest son to the earl of *Stafford*, who was slain in the fields near *Bishopthorp* by sir *John Holland* the king's half brother (*m*). But the occasion of the quarrel, and the king's resentment, are matters inserted at large in *Stow* and *Hollingshead*, and therefore unnecessary here. A. MCCCLXXXV.

A. 1389. came king *Richard* to *York*, says *Knighton*, in order to accommodate some differences which had arisen betwixt the archbishop, the dean and chapter, and the mayor and A. MCCCLXXXIX.

(*d*) *J. Barnes.*
(*e*) *Act. pub.*
(*f*) *J. Barnes.*
(*g*) *Froissart.*
(*h*) *Hollingshead, Oct.* 17, 1347.
(*i*) *Hollingshead.*

(*k*) *A.* 1348. began a great mortality in the city of *York*, which continued to spread with great violence from *Ascension-day* to the feast of *S. James* the apostle, says *Stubbs.*, *Act. Pont. Ebor.*
(*l*) *Speed.*
(*m*) *Knighton.*

commonality of the city. The affair was of great consequence, but the king by excellent management perfectly settled it *(n)*; and, as my authority speaks, was so favourable to the citizens as to grant them almost all they desired of him. It was at this time that our own records speak king *Richard* took his Sword from his side and gave it to be born before *William de Selby* as first *lord mayor* of *York*.

A. MCCCXC. *A.* 1390. A contagious distemper began in these northern parts, and swept out of *York* in a very small time eleven hundred persons *(o)*. But in the next year the same kind of pestilence, I suppose, broke out with greater violence, all over *England*, and, as my authorities testify, there died in the city of *York* only, *eleven thousand* in a short space.

A. MCCCXCII. The courts of *King's-bench* and *Chancery* were removed from *London* to *York*, at the instigation of *Thomas Arundel* then archbishop of *York*, and lord chancellor of *England*. This was designed for the benefit of the city, but they did only remain here from *Midsummer* to *Christmas* and then returned. In this year king *Richard* presented the first mace to the city to be born before the lord mayor thereof. And,

A. MCCCXCVI In the nineteenth year of his reign he appointed two sheriffs instead of three bailiffs, which made it a county of it self. Which, with several privileges and large immunities, recited in the charter granted by this king to the city and citizens of *York*, prove that he paid an extraordinary regard to it.

Nor were the inhabitants unmindful of these royal concessions and great benefactions, but took the first opportunity to testify their loyalty and gratitude to *Richard*, even after his deposition and murder. This, though it cost them dear, yet, deserves a perpetual memorial, because the effort they made proceeded purely from the principles above.

The subject of the deposition of this prince, and his most execrable murder, is a theam so melancholy that I am glad our city, and consequently my pen, has nothing to do with it. It cannot be denied by a reader of *English* history, that the natives of this island are prone to rebel, fond of novelty and change, and, without ever considering the consequence, follow the cry that is set up, and pursue it with eagerness. This they have often done till tired, out of breath, and lost in numberless mazes and uncertainties, they begin to consider at last, and would then fain tread back again those steps they have taken; which contrary motion, is always attended with so much danger and difficulty, that many thousands have perished in the attempt.

Facilis descensus Averni;
Sed revocare gradum, &c.

A. MCCCXCIX. For instance, *Henry* the fourth having, by the assistance of his friends, the male-contents of *England*, deposed his lawful sovereign, mounted his throne, and imprisoned him in *Pontfrete* castle, where he was, soon after, most inhumanly put to death; found it irksome to owe so high an obligation to his subjects. And they, by whose help he had acquired that grandeur, had so high a notion of their services in this affair, that if he had shared his crown and crown-lands amongst them, it would not have satisfied all their cravings. He grew uneasy at seeing so many mouths gaping about him which he was obliged to fill; and they grew jealous of him and even of one another. Discontents from hence quickly arose in their minds, which were for some time smothered and kept down by the help of that court virtue, hypocrisy; but at last it broke out with all the fire and flame, that their pent-up malice could enforce. These terrible, inborn, contentions lasted for near an age together, with some intermission; and did so weaken and shatter this kingdom, that our own historians all agree, were not our ancient enemies the *French* and *Scotch*, either busy in the like work themselves, or carelesly supine at home, this nation must certainly have fallen a prey to the first invader. I shall enlarge no farther about the battles and events, which this first rebellion produced, than is consistent with my design; nor in the continuance of the civil war betwixt the houses of *York* and *Lancaster*, will I step out of my bounds, except to *Towton*, whose bloody and ever memorable field, called by some **York Field**, being in the neighbourhood of us, deserves a very particular description.

A. MCCCCV. *Henry Peircy*, earl of *Northumberland*, the chief instrument of king *Henry's* exaltation, having lost his brother and son slain at the battle of *Shrewsbury (p)*; the archbishop of *York*, *Richard Scroop*, whose brother the king had beheaded, and *Thomas Mowbray* earl marshal, who had likewise lost his father, who died an exile in *Venice*, all mortal enemies to *Henry*, conspired his ruin. The lords *Falconberge*, *Bardolf*, *Hastings*, and many others did join in this conspiracy. The order they took was to meet all at a time and at an appointed place, which was *York*; and the earl of *Northumberland* to take the supreme command of their united forces. The archbishop's impatience broke the neck of this well laid design, for being retired from court to his see, together with the earl marshal, he thought to facilitate the enterprise by giving the cause a sanction of religious justice. And having framed several articles against the king, and sent copies of them into other counties, he caused them to be

(n) *Causa igitur hujusmodi cum luculento consilio ad plenum regaliter discisa, reddidit rex civibus, quasi in omnibus, votum suum.* Knyghton.

(o) *Stowe. Hollingshed.*

(p) *Biondi.*

fixed

fixed upon the church doors of his own city and diocese. This was to invite the people to take arms in order to reform abuses introduced by the ill management of the present government. The archbishop was of an amiable countenance, of great learning and virtue, and having till this present lead a blameless life he was far from being suspected for any evil intentions; so that when he was pleased to declare his mind to the people in a sermon which he preached to them in his cathedral, full twenty thousand men suddenly rose and came to his standard at *York*; which standard was painted with the five wounds of our *Saviour (q)*.

This diligence was unseasonable both for the archbishop and his confederates *(r)*; for *Henry*, by this means, having early notice of their intentions had levied thirty thousand fighting men, and sent them, under the conduct of the earl of *Westmoreland (s)*, and his own son *John (t)*, against these northern malecontents. At their coming to *York* the earl found the archbishop encamped in a place just out of the city, on the forest of **Galtres**, so advantageously, that he did not think fit to attack him, though the archbishop was much inferior in forces; but encamped his army right over against the other. And now the earl changing the lion's skin for the fox's, and following the *French* adage *à defaut de la force il faut employer le ruse*, sent the archbishop word *that he wondered a man of his profession, should be found in such a posture; since he could not shew any reason why he should arm the king's people contrary to the king's peace.* To which the archbishop mildly answered, *that he was so far from infringing the king's peace, that all which he did tended to the preservation of it.* Upon this, entering into the merits of the cause on either side, a treaty was begun, and the articles of grievances shewn; which for the earl's better satisfaction the archbishop thought fit to send him by a gentleman of his own. The earl, though he was determined what to do in the case, seemed to rest satisfied with the justness of them; but said *that a business of this high nature being in question, it was requisite they should meet together and treat thereof, which might easily be done, each of them bringing a like number of men betwixt the two camps (u).* There is no net, says the polite *(x) Italian* from whom I quote, so secure as that which is spread in commendation of him who is to be deceived. For the good archbishop, measuring other mens consciences by his own, hearing his actions applauded by one he thought his enemy, was confident he could bring the earl over to his interest, and therefore made no difficulty to give him the meeting; and, which is more, brought the earl marshal, reluctant enough, along with him. For he, being of a deeper reach in politicks, long withstood it. At this meeting, with equal numbers betwixt the two camps, *Westmoreland*, after some short discourse, seemed perfectly satisfied, and professed *that in so just a cause, he himself would fight to the last of his life.* The generals then shook hands in sight of both armies; wine was called for, and drank about in token of friendship and mutual love. And now the earl said to the archbishop, *that their differences being ended in a joint consent, it was not expedient to detain any longer so many people, with so much inconvenience to themselves, from their houses and shops; but that being suddenly disbanded, it was but reason they should together with them enjoy the fruits of the established reconciliation.* The archbishop believed the earl, and his people him, who immediately broke up their camp and returned to the city; joyful enough, no doubt, to avoid a battle, and go back to their shops, from which they were most of them taken. The bowls of wine in the mean time went briskly round; whilst the earls party, scattered at first, imperceptibly gathering one by one together, grew to such a multitude, that he, having now no cause of fear, arrested the archbishop of high-treason upon the spot; as also the earl marshal. Notwithstanding this he plighted his faith to them that they should not suffer in their lives; but meeting the king at *Pontfrete* as he was hastening to *York*, he brought back with him the prisoners, who, says *Biondi*, much commiserated and bemoaned, were adjudged to dye and were forthwith beheaded.

There fell along with the archbishop and earl marshal sir *John Lamplugh*, sir *Robert Plumpton*, with several others. The earl's body was by the king's permission, says *Walsingham*, suffered to be buried in the cathedral. But his head, fixed upon a stake, stood long on the walls of the city exposed to heat, wind and rain. Which, when the king at length granted should be buried with the body, was found, says my author, neither fallen, nor wasted, nor scarcely discoloured, but kept the same comliness which it had when living *(y)*.

I shall not stop to make any reflections on the course of this event, the story speaks itself. What else is particular in the strange tryal and barbarous execution of the archbishop will be found in his life.

And now *Henry* took ample vengeance on the citizens of *York* for siding with their archbishop; for first I find in the publick acts a mandate directed to two of his captains, I suppose, immediately to sieze the city's liberties to this purport,

(q) Tho. Walsingham.

(r) Hollingshed.

(s) Ralph Nevill earl of *Westmoreland.*

(t) John earl of *Lancaster*; afterwards duke of *Bedford.*

(u) This whole coutroversy is elegantly described in *Shakespear's* historical play of *Henry* IV.

(x) Sir *Francis Biondi* knight, an *Italian* and gentleman of the bed-chamber to king *Charles* I. wrote an elegant history, as bishop *Nicholson* justly calls it, in his own language of the civil wars betwixt the houses of *York* and *Lancaster*; translated into *English* by *Henry* earl of *Monmouth.* This book deserves a more modern translation.

(y) Caput in nullo fluxum, in nullo marcidum, nec penitus decoloratum, sed eundem praetulisse decorem, quem vivens obtinuerat. T. Walsingham.

(z) The

(z) *The king to his chosen and faithful servants* John Stanley *and* Roger Leeche, *greeting.*

KNOW ye that for certain special causes, intimately, concerning us and the state of our kingdom of England, *we do assign you, together or separately, to our city of* York *together with all and singular liberties, franchises, and privileges to the citizens of the said city, by our progenitors or predecessors sometime kings of* England, *or our self, before this time granted and confirmed, to take and seize into our hands; and the said city thus taken and seized, till further orders from us, in our name to keep and govern.*

And therefore we command you, or either of you, diligently to take heed to the premises, and that you should do and execute them in the manner aforesaid.

Also we command all and singular high sheriffs, mayors, bayliffs and their officers, and all other our faithful subjects, as well within liberties as without, by the tenour of these presents strictly to aid and assist you, or either of you, in the execution of the premises, being helpful, advising and obedient to you as they ought.

In testimony of which, &c.

Witness the king at his castle of **Pountfrete** *the third day of* June, *A.* 1405, *in the sixth year of his reign.*

By the KING.

This severe mandate from *Henry* fell like a clap of thunder on our city, and was sent before him as a taste of what they were to expect at his arrival (*a*). What followed were tryals, executions, pains, penalties and grievous fines, which he imposed and exacted with great rigour on all the citizens who had followed the archbishop (*b*). After which he marched northward against the earl of *Northumberland*, who hearing of the fate of his confederates had retired to his government of *Berwick*. But *Henry* not thinking it politick to leave so many vexed spirits behind him, who might expect worse treatment at his return, by the advice of his council sent back a general pardon, dated from *Ripon* (*c*), and directed to the high-sheriffs of several counties, for all the archbishop's adherents; amongst those our city received the same favour; which, though thinned in its inhabitants, and stripped of its treasure, yet was now reinstated to its former privileges.

A. MCCCCVIII King *Henry* made *York* another visit on much the some errand as before; for we are told that after the discomfiture of the earl of *Northumberland*'s forces, by Sir *Thomas Rokesby*, high sheriff of *Yorkshire*, on *Bramham-Moor*, where the old earl was slain (*d*); the king came to *York*, where what he had left undone before was now compleated in the executions and confiscations of several citizens, though I do not find they had aided the earl in his enterprise. Amongst those that suffered death was the abbot of *Hales*, who being taken in armour at the battle was here executed. The earl of *Northumberland*, the chief instrument in deposing *Richard* and raising up this *Henry*, after having the misfortune to live to see most of his family cut off before him, he, the stock and root of the name of *Piercy*, was miserably slain at this battle (*e*). His head, covered with silver hairs, being put upon a stake, was carried, in a kind of mock procession, through all the towns to *London*, and then placed on the bridge, where, says my author, it long stood as a *monument of divine justice* (*f*).

I have gone through all that I can find in our chronicles, relating to our city, in *Henry* the fourth's reign. Except I should take notice that in the second year of it, at his return out of *Scotland*, he came to *York*, and saw a duel, or martial combat, by challenge fought there betwixt two foreign and two *English* knights, in which the latter prevailed. One of the *English*, Sir *John Cornwall*, so pleased the king by his valour shewn in the combat, that he gave him his sister the widow of *John* earl of *Holland* and *Huntingdon* to wife (*g*).

A. MCCCCXII. *Henry* V. began his short, but glorious reign, which may also be called a politick one; for by amusing his people in carrying on a prosperous war in *France*, he kept them from prying into his title at home. Our chronicles produce very little to my purpose during his time; but our city's old registers gives a mandate from this king to the lord-mayor of *York* (*h*), to sieze and confiscate the estate and effects of *Thomas* lord *Scrope* of *Massam*, beheaded for high-treason at *Southampton* in the first year of his reign. His head came along with the mandate, and was ordered in the same to be placed on the top of **Pickel-lyth-bar**. This lord *Scrope* was lord treasurer of *England*, and had married *Joan* duchess dowager of *York*. After the mandate is an inventory of goods, plate, &c. delivered by indenture to the said duchess as part of her husband's effects; the whole I have thought curious enough to place in the *appendix*. The earl of *Cambridge*, who had married the heiress of the house of *York*, with Sir *Thomas Grey*, was beheaded at the same time with lord *Scrope*. And this, says *Rapin*, was the first spark of that fire, which almost consumed, in process of time, the two houses of *Lancaster* and *York*. Most of our historians are so busy in attending this monarch in his *French* wars, that a progress he made to *York* has

(z) Act pub. tom. VII.
(a) *Hollinshed.*
(b) *Brondi.*
(c) Act. pub.
(d) *Stow.*
(e) *Dug. Bar.*
(f) *Hollinshed.*
(g) *Speed.*
(h) Regis. ant. super pontem *Usae.*

escaped their notice. *Walsingham* writes that *Anno* 1421, the ninth of *Henry* V. after the coronation of *Catherine* of *France* at *Westminster*, the king and queen made a progress through the kingdom to *York*. From thence they went to visit the shrine of St. *John* of *Beverly*. It was at *York* that the news came to him of the death of the duke of *Clarence* his brother, slain in *France*. There had been a strong report that the tomb of St. *John* of *Beverly* sweat blood all the day that the famous battle of *Agincourt* was fought. And it being imputed to the merits of that saint, that this great victory was gained; *Henry*, a zealous catholick prince, thought it his duty to make a pilgrimage to the shrine. And this is all that I can learn of this great monarch's transactions at *York*; or in these parts.

But we come now to a scene of misery indeed, such as this kingdom never felt, either before or since; and it ought to be every *Englishman*'s hearty prayer, that it never may again. All the foreign invasions this nation had suffered never spilt half so much blood at a time as this most unnatural intestine war. The whole kingdom was divided into two fierce parties or factions, and such an implacable fury and revenge reigned in their breasts, that nothing but the utter extirpation of one could satiate this extravagant thirst of blood. In the space of thirty six years twelve set battles were fought within this kingdom, by natives only; and above fourscore princes of the blood royal of *England* fell by each other's swords (*i*). And it is worthy observation, says Sir *John Habington*, that in this long and cruel conflict betwixt the two houses, never any stranger of name was present at our battles; as if we had disdained, adds he, to conquer or perish by other weapons than our own.

Henry VI. the very reverse of his father, was fitter for a monastick than a regal life. His weak and unsteady hand, made feebler by the murder of his uncle *Humphry* duke of *Glocester*, was by no means fit to guide the helm of government in so turbulent a season. The house of *York* laid hold of this opportunity to assert their title to the throne; and wading through a sea of blood at length obtained it. It is not my purpose to describe these melancholy times at length; who will may read them elegantly treated on by Sir *Francis Biondi*, an *Italian* writer, who must shew the least partiality to either house; and therefore what relates to my subject is chiefly copied from that author. A.

After the battle of *Wakefield*, where *Richard* duke of *York* met his fate; his head, which MCCCCLX. had boldly aspired to a golden diadem, was crowned with paper, in dirision, put on a long pole, and placed on the top of *Micklegate-bar*, with his face to the city; as *Shakespear* makes the haughty queen *Margaret*, opprobriously, speak that

York *may overlook the town of* York.

For company, with the duke's were likewise placed the heads of *Richard* earl of *Salisbury*, Sir *Richard Limbrick*, Sir *Ralph Stanley*, *John Harrow*, captain *Hanson*, &c. all taken prisoners at the aforesaid battle and beheaded at *Pontfrete* (*k*).

But this success of the *red rose* party lasted not long; for, upon the death of his father, *Edward* earl of *March* waved the title of duke of *York*, and got himself, almost every where, proclaimed king of *England*. After which came on the most remarkable bloody battle ever fought, perhaps, in the whole world. It was truly the *Pharsalia* of this nation, and deserves a pen equal to *Lucan*'s to describe it.

Edward, after the death of his father, being received for king, and as such proclaimed, immediately left *London* (*l*). The condition of his affairs being such, as would not suffer him idly to enjoy that dignity, the duration of which could not be hoped for but by the utter ruin of his adversary. He easily gathered together a great army, for being a prince, says *Hollingshead*, highly favoured of the people for liberality, clemency, upright dealing and extraordinary courage, each man made an offer to him of all he had; so that his forces were very soon forty nine thousand strong; with which he encamped at *Pontfrete*; himself residing in the castle and his army round him. It was then thought proper to send the lord *Fitzwater*, with a detachment, to guard the pass at *Ferrybridge*; to prevent any sudden surprise from the enemy.

Henry, his queen and their army lay in, and about, *York*; to the number, as most account, of sixty thousand fighting men. The command of this army was given to the duke of *Somerset*, the earl of *Northumberland*, and the lord *Clifford*; all mortal enemies to the house of *York*, and whose fathers had all perished in this unhappy quarrel at the battle of St. *Alban*'s. These generals set forward from *York* with their forces, leaving *Henry*, his queen and son in the city, as in a place, says my author, of greatest security to their persons. Understanding that *Edward* had gained and guarded the pass at *Ferrybridge*, they made a halt, and sent the lord *Clifford* with a body of light horse to dislodge them. *Clifford* made such haste, that, setting upon the bridge by break of day, he easily won it, the guards being all asleep, and not dreaming of an enemy so near them. The lord *Fitzwater* awaked by the noise, supposing it to arise from some tumult amongst his own men, jumped out of bed, and unarmed, with only a battle-ax in his hand, went to appease them. But, too late aware of his mistake, he was there slain, together with the bastard of *Salisbury*,

(*i*) *Daniel, Kennet*'s hist. of *England*.
(*k*) *Hollingshed*.
(*l*) *Biondi*.

A MCCCCLXI. brother to the famous earl of *Warwick*. This young gentleman's death did ſo much grieve the ſaid earl, as well as the unhappy ſucceſs of this firſt encounter, which he thought might diſmay the army, that riding full ſpeed to *Edward* to inform him of this croſs event, he lighted off horſeback and thruſt his ſword into the horſe's belly, ſaying at the ſame time, *fly who will fly, I will not fly; here will I ſtay with as many as will keep me company*; and kiſſing the croſs on the hilt of his ſword, by way of vow, put it up again. *Edward* who did very much reſent this misfortune; not that it was of ſo great conſequence in itſelf, but that it being the firſt encounter an ill omen might be drawn from it; made proclamation that it ſhould be lawful for any man that had not a mind to fight to depart; he promiſed large recompences to thoſe that would tarry, but death to thoſe who ſtaid and after fled, with reward and double pay to thoſe that ſhould kill them. No man accepted ſo ignominious a leave, but all choſe rather to die then declare themſelves ſuch baſe cowards. The lord *Clifford*'s ſucceſs was in the mean time of no long continuance; for the lord *Falconberg* had paſſed the river *Aire* at *Caſtleford*, three miles above *Ferrybridge*, accompanied with Sir *Walter Blount* and *Robert Horn*, with an intention to ſurprize him; whereof *Clifford* being appriſed drew off his men and retired in great haſte to the main body. In this retreat he fell in unawares with a party, and having his helmet off, either for heat or pain, was ſhot into the throat with an arrow, as ſome ſay, without a head, and inſtantly fell down dead. A fate too good for ſuch a monſter, who, in cool blood, had ſome time before murdered an innocent child of ten years old, the earl of *Rutland*, *Edward*'s youngeſt brother; whoſe moving interceſſion for mercy from him, might have extorted compaſſion from the rougeſt barbarian.

When this conflict was over *Edward*'s whole army marched to meet the enemy, and in the fields betwixt *Towton* and *Saxton*, two miles weſt of *Tadcaſter*, found them drawn up ready to receive them. The number of forces on the *Yorkiſt*'s ſide was then forty thouſand ſix hundred and ſixty men; the other exceeded, being full ſixty thouſand. The right wing of *Edward*'s army was commanded by the earl of *Warwick*; the left by the lord *Falconberg*; in the abſence of the duke of *Norfolk* who was ſick; the main body was led by *Edward* himſelf, and the rearguard committed to the care of Sir *John Venloe*, and Sir *John Denham* two valiant commanders. The *Lancaſtrian* generals I have mentioned. Before the battle joined, *Edward* commanded that this dreadful proclamation ſhould be made betwixt the two armies, that no priſoner ſhould be taken but all, indifferently, put to the ſword; which was anſwered by the like proclamation from the other ſide. *Edward* did not do this out of cruelty, ſay hiſtorians, but that his army, being much inferiour in numbers, might not be incumbered with priſoners.

And now on the 29th of *March*, being *Palm-ſunday*, early in the morning the fight began; firſt with a flight of arrows from *Henry*'s men; which by reaſon of a ſhower of ſnow which blew with the wind full in their faces when they ſhot, were of no execution, but all dropped ſhort of their mark. This when *Falconberg* perceived, he ordered his men to ſhoot one flight, then to retire back three paces and ſtand; which they did, till the *Lancaſtrians* had emptied their quivers in vain. The *Yorkiſts* then advanced upon them, and, not only ſent their own arrows, which, aided by the wind, came full againſt them, but alſo picked up the ſhort arrows of the enemy in their march and returned them to their maſters. All hiſtorians agree, that this conduct of *Falconberg*'s was a great help to the victory. The earl of *Northumberland* and Sir *Andrew Trolop*, who lead the vanguard, ſeeing this diſadvantage, puſhed their men as faſt as poſſible to handyblows. And now began a battle indeed, each man ſtood his ground till ſlain or knocked down, and then another took his place. The proclamation for not giving quarter ſeemed to be needleſs, the extream hatred betwixt the two parties called for nothing but blood and death. Ten hours this direful conflict laſted in ſuſpence, and victory fluctuated from ſide to ſide, till at length it ſettled in the houſe of *York*; in a great meaſure owing to their king and leader. *Edward* was an eye-witneſs of his ſoldier's valour, and they of his *captain*-like courage; a fight which rather made them chuſe to die, than not to imitate him. In ſhort, the *Lancaſtrians* gave way and fled towards *York*, but ſeeking, in a tumultuary manner, to gain the bridge at *Tadcaſter*, ſo many of them fell into the rivulet *Cock*, as quite filled it up, and the *Yorkiſts* went over their backs to purſue their brethren. This rivulet, and the river *Wharfe*, into which it hereabouts empties itſelf, were died with blood; and there is no wonder in this, if the number which hiſtorians give of the ſlain is to be credited. Thirty ſix thouſand ſeven hundred and ſeventy ſix *Engliſhmen*, here fell a ſacrifice for their father's tranſgreſſions; and the wounds they died on being made by arrows, battle-axes or ſwords, would bleed plentifully (*m*). The blood of the ſlain, ſays an hiſtorian, lay caked with the ſnow, which at that time covered the face of the ground, and afterwards, diſſolving with it, ran down, in moſt horrible manner, the furrows and ditches of the fields, for two or three miles together (*n*). Not one man, except the earl of *Devonſhire*, was taken priſoner, and

(*m*) Sir *J Habb Edw.* IV.

(*n*) *Occiſorum nempe cruor cum nive jam commixtus, qui totam tunc temporis operiebat terrae ſuperficiem, poſtmodum uſque duo vel tria milsaria cum nive reſoluta per ſulcos et lacunas horribiliter decurrit.* Hiſt. croy. cont. Fire-arms were in uſe before this battle, but I do not find that any were made uſe on at it.

he

he feemed to be faved when they were weary with killing. The dukes of *Somerfet* and *Exeter* fled the field, and brought the fatal news to *Henry*, and his queen at *York*; whom with all fpeed they perfuaded to fly with them into *Scotland*. Nor was their hafte in vain, for victorious *Edward* was clofe at their heels, and they had fcarce left the city before he entered it in hopes to furprife them.

Miffing of his principal aim, the firft thing *Edward* did was to take down his father's head along with the others that had been placed on the bar, and had them buried with their bodies; and then caufed *Thomas Courtney* earl of *Devon*, the earl of *Kyme*, Sir *William Hill*, Sir *Thomas Foulford* to be beheaded and fet their heads in the fame place *(p)*. The names of the nobility which fell in the battle are thus recorded by *Stowe*, *Henry Piercy* earl of *Northumberland*, the earl of *Shrewfbury*, *John* lord *Clifford*, the lord *Beaumont*, *John* lord *Nevill*, the lord *Willoughby*, *Leonard* lord *Wells*, the lord *Roos*, the lord *Scales*, the lord *Grey*, *Ranulph* lord *Dacres*, the lord *Fitzhugh*, the lord *Molineux*, lord *Henry Beckingham*. Of knights, two baftard fons of *Henry Holland* duke of *Exeter*, Sir *Richard Piercy*, Sir *John Heyton*, Sir *Gervafe Clifton*, Sir *Edmund Hamis*, Sir *Thomas Crakenthorpe*, Sir *William Haryll*, Sir *John Ormonde*, Sir *Andrew Trolop*, Sir *Roger Molyne*, Sir *Radulph Pigote*, Sir *Henry Narbohew*, Sir *David Trolope*, Sir *John Burton*, whom *Stowe* calls captain of *York*, I fuppofe he means governour, with many other knights too tedious to mention.

The flain were buried in five great pits yet appearing, adds *Stowe*, in the field by north *Saxton* church; but, fays he, Mr. *Hungate* caufed them to be removed from thence, and to be buried in the church-yard of *Saxton*; where the lord *Dacres* has a mean tomb erected to his memory.

This tomb is a flat marble ftone, now much broken and defaced; but round it may ftill be read this imperfect infcription,

> **Hic jacet Ranulphus Ds. de Dakre et ———— Miles et occifus erat in bello principe Henrico VI° Anno Dom. M,CCCC,LXI. XXIX die Martii videlicet dominica die palmarum. Cujus anime propitietur Deus. Amen.**

The pits which *Stow* fpeaks of could not contain one hundred part of the flain, but they muft have been buried in feveral other places of the field, and indeed the plowfhare oft difcovers their miferable remains in almoft every part of them. At *Towton* king *Richard* the third began a great chapel, as *Leland* fays *(o)*, over the bodies of the *Yorkifts* flain in that battle who were buried there; which he intended to have endowed as a chantry chapel, but lived not to fee it finifhed. His fucceffor, we may fuppofe, had no inclination to carry the work on, and now no remains of the building appears, nor any memorial of it, fave a piece of ground on the north fide of the village called **Chapel-garth**. It may not be unacceptable to the reader to add that, about a year or two ago, two gentlemen and my felf had the curiofity to go and fee a frefh grave opened in thefe fields. Where amongft vaft quantities of bones, we found fome arrow piles, pieces of broken fwords, and five very frefh groat pieces of *Henry* the fourth, fifth, and fixth's coin. Thefe laid, near all together, clofe to a thigh bone, which made us conjecture that they had not time to ftrip the dead before they toffed them into the pit. I fhall now take leave of this famous battle with thefe lines out of the *Anglorum proelia*.

> *(p) Moerentes hodie, quoties profcindit arator*
> *Arva propinqua locis, dentale revellere terrâ*
> *Semifepulta virûm fulcis cerealibus offa.*
> *Moefto execrantur planctu civile duellum,*
> *Quo periere hominum plus centum milia caefa,*
> *Nobile* Tadcaftrum *clades accepta coegit*
> *Millibus enectis ter denis nomen habere.*

> As often as the plowman turns the fields,
> Half buried human bones the foil ftill yields;
> The dire remains of horrid civil ftrife;
> An hundred thoufand men bereft of life
> This quarrel claims; and *Tadcafter* may boaft
> That thirty thoufand in her fields were loft.

The battle of *Towton* proved decifive in favour of the houfe of *York*; for *Henry* having loft all his army, and moft of his chief friends being flain, made hafte into *Scotland*. There that unfortunate prince was obliged to fue, in the humbleft manner, for protection from his mercilefs enemies, and freely gave up the important town of *Berwick* to the *Scotch* king for his fubfiftence; whilft *Edward*, having quieted all the northern parts, returned to *London*, where *June* 28, 1461, he was with all poffible pomp and magnificence crowned king of *England*, &c. at *Weftminfter*.

(o) Sir *John Multon*'s father, fays *Leland*, laid the firft ftone of it. *Itin.* Q. Sir *John Melton*; that family long flourifhed in this county?

(p) *Hollingfhead.*

A. MCCCCLXIV. *An.* 1464, king *Edward* came to *York*, accompanied with his brethren, and moſt of the nobility the realm; bringing along with him a mighty army againſt the *Scotch*, *French* and *Northumbrians*, who had taken arms in *Henry*'s favour. At *Hexam* the armies met, and a ſore battle was fought betwixt them, but the victory fell to *Edward*. *Henry*, ſays *Hollingſhead*, ſhewed himſelf here an excellent horſeman, for he rid ſo faſt that none could overtake him. His equipage, however, and ſeveral of his ſervants fell into the enemy's hands. In the former was found the royal cap called **Abacot** being garniſhed with two rich crowns; with which *Edward* was again crowned, *May* 4, with great ſolemnity at *York*. Lord *George* and ſir *Humphry Nevil* now loſt their heads in this city; with twenty five more perſons executed, all taken priſoners in the laſt battle.

It is an eaſy matter to gueſs what part our city took during all theſe inteſtine troubles, and whoſe cauſe the citizens favoured moſt, when I mention a record of an extraordinary grant from this king to them, which I met with in the tower of *London*. The patent is dated at *York*, *June* 10, *An. Reg.* 4, 1464, and expreſſes the king's great concern for the ſufferings and hardſhips the city had undergone during theſe wars, inſomuch as to be almoſt reduced to the loweſt degree of poverty, *in extremam paupertatis abiſſum*, by them. In conſideration of which he not only relinquiſhes the uſual farm of the city, but aſſigns them an annual rent of 40 *l.* to be paid them out of his cuſtoms in the port of *Hull* for twelve years to come. The whole record is ſo ſingular that it muſt find a place in the *appendix* (*q*).

For ſome years after this did *Edward*, with little diſturbance, keep poſſeſſion of the crown; but at length the ſcales turned, and he who had driven *Henry* into exile, was obliged to ſhare the ſame fortune himſelf, and ſeek protection in a foreign country. This was wholly owing to the deſertion of the famous earl of *Warwick* from him and his family's intereſt. The earl being diſgraced in an embaſſy to *France* by *Edward*, who had privately married a lady in *England*, whilſt *Warwick* was publickly treating of a marriage for him with the *French* king's ſiſter in *France*, took it ſo heinouſly that he not only went over to *Henry*'s cauſe himſelf, but he likewiſe perſuaded his two brothers the marquis *Montacute* and lord *George*, the one lord preſident, the other archbiſhop of *York*, to take the ſame courſe. The ſprings and motives of this next revolution, being ſet on foot in our city, requires a particular diſquiſition.

The earl's two brothers had a conſultation with him at *Calais*, of which town he was governor; and there it was agreed that they two ſhould ſtir up ſome commotion in the north, whilſt he ſhould land in the ſouth; and they took this method to put their deſign in execution. There was in our city an hoſpital dedicated to S. *Leonard*, where, ſays my author (*r*), by an ancient inſtitution the poor was fed, and the diſeaſed healed. The intention was ſo laudable, that there was no owner of ground in all that county that did not contribute, at the time of harveſt, ſomewhat to the maintenance of it. This contribution at firſt was voluntary, but after, by uſe, became a cuſtom; and they had proper officers to collect it for the ſervice of the hoſpital. The two malecontent lords cauſed a report to be ſpread in the country, that the hoſpital having ſufficient revenues of its own, had no need of this contribution of corn; which only went to enrich the provoſt and prieſts, and was of no benefit to the poor. It was no hard matter to bring the people to believe this, eſpecially ſince it was their intereſt; and the news quickly ſpreading from one mouth to another, the collectors were not only denied their uſual alotments, but inſulted and wounded in the execution of their offices. The populace being enraged that they ſhould ſo long bear this exaction, as they thought it, reſolved to revenge themſelves upon the hoſpital, and even the city itſelf. About fifteen thouſand of them aſſembled and marched towards *York*; the inhabitants of the city were in great conſternation at the news, not knowing whether they ſhould keep within the walls, or ſally forth to give them battle before their numbers increaſed. The marquis eaſed them of this fear; for making a ſmall draught of ſome choice men, he fell upon them unexpectedly in the night, even under the city walls, overthrew them, killed and took priſoners great numbers, amongſt whom was their leader *Robert Holdern*; whoſe head he cauſed to be ſtruck off before one of the city gates. This was a piece of policy in the marquis, which, like all the reſt of his future conduct, was unaccountable. To have joined theſe men, thus raiſed, ſeemed the faireſt way to execute their deſigns againſt *Edward*; and there can be no reaſon given for his deſtroying of them, but that by this action he might gain more confidence with the king, in order to work his downfall the ſurer.

However this, the rebels were only quelled not quaſhed; for upon the death of their leader, the eldeſt ſons of the lord *Fitzhugh*, and *Nevil* lord *Latimer*, both of them young men, to give the better grace to their enterpriſe, were choſen to command them. Theſe two young gentlemen were nigh relations to the earl of *Warwick*, the one his nephew and the other couſin german, but yet in this affair they were ſubordinate to the direction of an elder commander, Sir *John Conniers*, whom my author ſtyles one of the vallianteſt men of thoſe parts. Thus headed, the rebels would have gone again to *York*, but wanting artillery to batter the walls, they boldly ſet forward ſouthward; and the wheel thus ſet on motion ne-

(*q*) Several orders, grants, &c. are in the *Foedera*, dated at *York*; which proves that the king ſtaid near a month here, after the battle, to ſettle affairs.

(*r*) *Brend.* *Hall*'s chron.

ver

ver stopped, till *Edward* was cast from the top to the bottom of it. Taken prisoner by the earl of *Warwick* he was committed to the care and custody of the archbishop of *York*, who placed him in the castle of *Middleham*. Where being too slackly guarded, he soon found means to make his escape, and fled beyond seas, for protection, to his aunt the duchess of *Burgundy*.

Henry was now once again re-instated in his kingly dignity, by that great *setter up and puller down of kings*, Warwick, and changed a prison for a throne. But his evil fate suffered him not to enjoy it long; for *Edward*, having influenced the duke of *Burgundy* to lend him an aid of men and money, set sail and landed at *Ravenspurg*, a town which formerly stood on the outmost promontory of the *Holderness* coast of *Yorkshire*, with two thousand soldiers besides mariners. The first thing he did was to send out some light horse to descry the country and found the affections of the inhabitants; who finding them very averse to his title, and perfectly easy under *Henry*, he artfully changed his note, and gave out that he now utterly disclaimed his regal title, and came only to gain his patrimonial estate of *York*; under obedience to *Henry*. This politick step had its effect, every one admired his moderation, and thought it the highest injustice to keep him from his dukedom. But *Warwick*, though he heard all this, believed nothing of it, and sent strict orders to *York* not to admit him; with the like charge to other places. To his brother the marquis, who lay then with a great army at *Pontfrete*, he gave command to march immediately and fight him; which however the marquiss neglected. *Edward* in the mean time was advancing towards *York*, proclaiming every where *Henry* king, and styling himself, only, Duke of *York*. Coming near the city he was met on the road by two (*x*) *Aldermen*, who were sent to acquaint him *that the city could not receive him, but that they were obliged to do him all possible mischief if he came that way.* He answered them, *that he came not to fight against the king, nor any ways to molest him, acknowledging him to be his sovereign lord; but he thought he might very well enter into the duchy of* YORK, *his antient patrimony; hoping, that as there were none could justly inhibit him this, so they least of any, being the natural subjects of his house, from whence they had at all times received all manner of grace and favour.* The aldermen returned with this answer, and, *Edward* following softly after, in an instant the citizens minds were changed; those who were got upon the walls to defend them against him, now came down to be his guides and conductors, and to keep him from being injured by any one (*y*). Two of the citizens, by name *Robert Clifford* and *Thomas Burgh*, were sent out to assure him that he might safely advance, for no man would hinder his admittance into the city. The magistrates, however, used more precaution, for at his coming to the gates, and addressing himself to them with his usual affability, stiling them at every word, says my author, *your worships*, they told him they would readily admit him if he would swear to two things; first, to preserve the city's liberties, next, to be obedient and faithful to all *Henry*'s commands. This oath, however bitter the potion was, he scrupled not to swallow, religion in princes ever giving way to their interest, and a priest being there ready for the purpose, it was given him at the city gates with much solemnity. Nay in his entrance he rode directly to the cathedral, and there in a more solemn manner confirmed it at the altar. This wilful perjury, historians remark, though the due punishment of it was witheld from *Edward* himself, yet fell in full measure on his children. Sir *Richard Baker* indeed excuses this action and says, that *Edward* IV. swore at the gates of *York* that he came only to seek his *own inheritance*; meaning the *kingdom*, and not his *dukedom*; by which, adds that historian, he was not forsworn (*z*). A. 1471.

Hall in his chronicle gives the conference that *Edward* held with the citizens of *York* under the walls, in these words.

" My lord mayor and you worshipful aldermen, for each of you is so, (and then as a good nomenclator had many of their names) " I come not to demand the kingdom which " I did for some years enjoy, but was driven out of it by the fury and rashness of the earl " of *Warwick* and others; I am much fatisfied that such a pinnacle is not the safest station, " I am resolved from henceforth to stand upon lower ground. I found the crown clogged " with so many cares that I deem it not worth the taking up again. I shall not disturb king " *Henry* in that, I only desire my own town and my proper inheritance, derived to me " from my ancestors the dukes of *York*, and I have good cause to hope that you the lord- " mayor, worshipful aldermen, and citizens will aid me in this. This noble city is in all " our names, you the lord-mayor, aldermen, sheriffs, and citizens of *York*, and I by my " right duke of *York*; this is all the favour I desire, that you and I may have the same " place inserted in our names which is **York**."

The lord-mayor answered,

" Most noble duke, for other style you seem not to require, or if you should can we " acknowledge; we are very sensible what bloody conflicts have been for the crown, which " have been the ball of contention between the *red rose* and the *white*; I name the *red rose*

(*x*) *Hollingshead* says it was *Thomas Conniers*, then recorder of *York*, who met *Edward* in this manner; but I meet with no such name in the catalogue of recorders.

(*y*) *Hollingshead*.

(*z*) *Baker*'s chron.

A. 1471. " first, because that is in the present possession, and if you sir duke should set on foot the " claim of the *white rose* we know not what mischief might follow; sure we are we should if " we admit you be blamed by king *Henry*, and by that make-king the earl of *Warwick* " whom you mention. Therefore in few words this is our resolution, that unless you will " swear not to make any pretension to the crown, nor disturb the king in the government, " and not to prejudice the rights and privileges of this city, we will not admit you to en-" ter into this place.

But no sooner had *Edward* got possession of the city, than he immediately assumed his regal title; and having cajoled *their worships* into the loan of a round sum of money, he left a sufficient garrison in it, and marched southward. The marquis *Montacute* was all this time asleep, one would think, at *Pontfrete*, and never once opposed him in his passage. *Edward* not caring to come with his small army into his teeth at *Ferrybridge*, pass'd over the river *Aire* at *Castleford*, only two or three miles higher, without the least resistance. This conduct of the marquis might make one suspect that he secretly favoured *Edward's* cause; and yet the battle of *Barnet*, fought soon after, where he and his brother *Warwick* lost their lives, evinces the contrary. *Edward* having gained this conquest, and sent *Henry* once more to the tower, where the butcher *Richard* took care to secure him from any more elopements, reigned peaceably to the end of his days.

There is but one accident more regarding us in the remaining part of this king's reign, which though no history mentions, one of our old (*a*) registers tells us, that (*b*) *Edward* on the 20th day of *September*, 1478, made a progress into the north accompanied with a very numerous suit of dukes, marquisses, earls and barons, and a great croud of other courtiers. He was met in his journey by all the gentry and publick officers of these parts, and amongst the rest by (*c*) *John Ferriby* then lord-mayor of *York*, who, accompanied with many of the richest citizens, went as far as *Wentbridge* to meet him, and escorted him to *Pontfrete*. Upon the mayor's taking his leave, the king assured him that he intended to visit his loving subjects the citizens of *York*. In a week's time the king with all his nobles came to the city; he was met at some distance by the lord-mayor, aldermen and commonality on horse-back; and by the rest of the better sort of citizens on horseback or on foot, who conducted the king with loud acclamations into the city. He made the city a present of a sum of money as is apparent, says the register, in the city's book of that year, but the particular sum is here, either by time or wilfulness, obliterated. The king staid a few days in *York*, and then set forward for *London*.

On the 9th day of *April*, 1483. died *Edward* IV; his brother *Richard*, whom he had left protector and guardian over the young king and realm, was then in *York* (*d*); and here had a solemn funeral *requiem* performed in the cathedral for the repose of his brother's soul. It was here also that the duke of *Buckingham* sent a trusty servant, one *Percival*, says *Hall*, to instill those notions of ambition into him, which afterwards proved of such dire effect to his nephews as well as himself.

But it is plain that *Richard* had laid his schemes for obtaining the crown even before his brother's death; and some of his evil machinations, affecting our city in particular, I shall beg leave to give them, as a taste of those times, from an old record not yet delivered down in print by any historian that I know of (*e*).

By a deposition taken the 14th of *February*, 1482, it appears that his projects were working in our city, the substance of which is as follows,

(*f*) " Memorandum that the 14th day of *February*, in the twenty second year of king " *Edward* IV. came afore (*g*) *John Marshall* lieutenant, *Robert Rede Gyrdewler*, unto the " council chamber with odyr persons with him; and then and there shewyd, how that *Wil-*" *liam Welles* carpenter should report, that the last day of *January* last past, sytyng at the " *Ale* at *Eden Berys Gotherymgate*, that one askyd and said emong the fellishhip sityng at " *Ale*, syrs whome shall we have to our mair this yere? whereunto answered and said " *Stephen Hodgson*, syrs methyng, and it please the commons, I wodd we had master " *Wrangwish*, for he is the mair that my lord of *Gloucester* will do for, &c."

The whole deposition is too long to insert, but it is obvious by this part of it, that there were some underhand dealings in the city in *Richard's* favour, as the consequence will shew; and I take notice that this *Thomas Wrangwish* was made mayor the year after, and assisted at *Richard's* coronation in *York*.

Soon after his brother's death *Richard* began to shew himself more openly; and by taking from about his nephews their surest friends, the queen their mother, and her brethren, made way for his own ambition. At this time he thought it his interest to cajole the whole kingdom with kind letters, fair speeches and promises, in order to bring them the more readily over to countenance his designs. *York* and the northern parts were his strongest

(*a*) Ex regist. in custod. civium *Ebor*.
(*b*) The registrarian gives the king this pompous title, *illustrissimus, ac uti fama omnium fert metuendissimus, ac christianissimus* Edwardus *rex*, &c.
(*c*) *A*. 1478, *John Firriby* mayor, cat. of mayors. *Nobilis hujusce almae urbis ea vice major*. Regist. *Ebor*.
(*d*) *Hollingshead*.
(*e*) In the chamber on *Ousebridge*.
(*f*) Ex chart. in custod. com. *Ebor*.
(*g*) Deputy mayor, I suppose, for he had been lord-mayor two years before Cat. of mayors.

attach-

attachment, and in order to make the city more in his interest, a remarkable letter was sent from him and delivered in great form to the lord-mayor, by *Thomas Brackenbury*, one of his creatures, which I shall give from the manuscript, as far as it is legible, *verbatim*. A. 1483.

(b) " *The duke of* Gloucester, *brother and uncle of kings protectour and desensour, grett chamberleyne, constable, and lord high admiral of* England.

" Right trusty and well beloved, wee grett you wele. Wheras by your letter of supplica- " tion to us, delivered by our servant *John Brackenbury*, wee understaund that by reason " of your great charges that yee have had and susteined, as well in the defence of this realm " against the *Scottes* as otherways, your worshipful citty remains greatly unpaid for, and " the which yee desire us to be gud mover unto the king's grace, for any ease of such " charges as yee yerely bere and pay unto his grace's-highness. Wee let you wott that " for such great matter and buisnesses, and wee now have to doe for the wele and useful- " ness of the realme, we as yet ne can have convenient leisure to accomplish this your be- " sinefs, but be assured that for your kind and lufyng disposition to us at all tymes shewed, " which wee never can forgett, wee in all gudly haste shall so endeavour for your ease in " this behalf as that . . . . yee shall veryly understand we be your especial gud and " lufyng lord, as our said friend shall shew you; to whome it wod lyke you hym to give " further credence to, and for your diligent service which he hath done to our singular " plesure unto us at this time, we pray you to give unto him laud and thanks, and God " keep you.

" Given under our signet at the tower of *London* this 8th day of *June*.

Superscribed.

" *To our trusty and well-beloved the mair, aldermen, sheriffs and commonality of the city* " *of* York."

This letter was artfully contrived to curry favour with the citizens of *York*, at a very critical juncture; and it was soon followed by another of a different nature which the same record gives in these words.

" Memorandum the 15th of *June* in the first yere of the reign of *Edward* V. *Richard* " *Ratcliff*, Knt. delivered to *John Newton* mair a letter from the duke of *Gloucestre*, the " tenour of which ensueth.

(i) " *The duc of* Gloucestre, *brother and uncle of kinges protectour, desensour, gret chamberleyne,* " *constable, and admiral of* England.

" Right trusty and well beloved, wee greet you well. And as you love the wele of us, " and the wele and surety of your own self, we heartily pray you to come up unto us " to *London*, in all the diligence ye can possible, after the sight hereof, with as many as " ye can make defensibly arrayed, there to aid and assist us against the queen, her bloody " adherents, and affinity, which have entended, and dayly do entend, to murder and ut- " terly destroy us, and our cousyn the duc of *Buckingham*, and the old royal blood of this " realm; and as is now openly known by their subtle and dampnable wais forecasted the " same, and also the final destruction and disherison of you, and all odyr the enheritors and " men of honour, as well of the north parts as odyr countrees, that belongen unto us, as " our trusty servant this bearer shall more at large shew you, to whom we pray you to " give credence, and as ever we may do for you in tym comyng, fail not but haste you to " us.

" Given under our signet at *London* the 10th of *June*.

The reader may observe that this letter is dated but two days after the former, so that the protector's danger came very suddenly upon him, if he did not know it when he wrote the first; but his fallacy and policy is now easily seen through (k). Sir *Richard Radcliff*, had brought the queen's relations down to *Pontefract-castle* and imprisoned them, from whence he came to *York* and delivered this letter to the mayor, and my manuscript says, that it was agreed betwixt them, that such forces as the city could raise, of such a sudden, should be on the *Wednesday* night next at *Pontfrete*, where the earl of *Northumberland* waited for them to conduct them and others to *London*. I find the proclamation for raising them in these words,

(l) " *Forma proclamat. factae in civit.* 19 *die mensis* Junii *anno regni regis* Edwardi *quinti* " *primo.* Sequitur in his verbis.

" *Richard* brother and unkill of kinges, duc of *Gloucestre*, protectour, defendour, gret " chamberleyne, constabill and admirall of *England*, straitly charge and command " all manner of men, in their best defensible array, incontenent after this proclamation " made, do rise and come up to *London* to his highness in company of his cousyne the earl

(b) Ex libro chart. in custod. com. *Ebor*.
(i) Ex eodem.
(k) Ex eodem.
(l) Ex eodem.

" of

A. 1483. " of *Northumberland*, the lord *Nevil*, and odyr men of worship by his highness appointed, " there to aid and assist him to the subdewing, correcting and punnishing the quene, her " blode, and odyr hyr adherents, which hath intended and dayly doth intend to murthur " and utterly destroy his royal person, his cousyne the duc of *Buckingham*, and odyr of " old royal blode of this realm; as alsoe the nobillmen of their companys; and as it is no- " tably known by many subtill and dampnabill wais forecasted the same, and also the final " destruction and disheryson of them, and of all others the inheritors and men of honour, " as well of these north parts, as of other cuntrees that belongen them. And therefore in " all diligence prepare yourself, and come up as yee love your honour, weles and suretys, " and the suretys of yourself and the commonweil of this realm."

What effect this proclamation produced history informs us, which, though not much to the credit of my fellow citizens, must be given. It is true that *George Buck*, Esq; who has wrote a panegyrical account of this king's reign, calls them *four thousand gentlemen of the north* who came up to assist at *Richard*'s coronation (*m*). *Hall* and *Grafton* say there were five thousand, but speak opprobriously of our countrymen, *evil apparelled and worse harnessed*, say they, *which when mustered were the contempt of the beholders*. (*n*) *Fabian* who lived at this time, and probably saw this armament, being a *Londonner*, has left this account of them. Richard, **not daring to trust the** Londoners, **for fear of the queenes blood, and others of which he had jelousye, he sent for a strenth of men out of the north. The which came shortly to** London **a little before his coronation, and mustered in the** Morefeelds **well upon four thousand men in their best jacks and rusty salletts; with a few in white harnesse, but not burnished to the sale; and shortly after his coronation were countermaunded home with sufficient rewards for their travaile.**

Richard having got possession of the crown of *England*, his nephews imprisoned, and their relations executed at *Pontfrete*; made a progress into the north as far as *York*, in order for a second coronation in that city. This place he seemed, if the hypocrite could ever be sincere, to pay an extraordinary regard to, though, according to *Rapin*, his pretence of going down now was to minister justice every where; nor could he help executing some of his northern soldiers, who in their march back from *London* had committed great outrages. *Richard* made his progress by *Windsor*, *Oxford*, *Coventry* to *Nottingham*; during this, the execrable murder of the two young princes was perpetrated in the tower; a fact so horrid that every tongue must falter, and every hand tremble that either speaks or writes of it. From *Nottingham* I find a letter in the same record, wrote by his secretary to stir up a zeal in the citizens of *York*, towards his better reception there. The letter is an original indeed, and proves the secretary worthy of the master.

(*o*) " *To the gude masters the mair, recorder, and aldermen, and sheriffs of the cite of* " York.

" I recommend me unto you as heartyly as I can. Thanked be *Jesu* the king's grace is " in good health, as is likewise the queenes grace, and in all their progress have byn " worshipfully resceyved with pageants and odyr, &c. And his lords and judges in every " place sittyng determinyng the compleyntes of pore folkes with due punicion of offenders " against his lawes. The cause I writ to you now is, for so much as I veryly know the " king's mind and entire affection that his grace beareth towards you and your worshipful " cite, for manifold your kind and lovyn desynings to his grace, shewed heretofore, which " his grace will never forget, and intendeth therefore soe to doe unto you, that all the " kings that ever reigned bestowed upon you did they never soe much; doubt not hereof " ne make ne manner of petition or desire of any thing by his highness to you to be " graunted. But this I advise you, as laudably as your wisdom can imagin, to receive " him and the queen at their coming, dispose you to do as well with pageants with such " gude speeches, as can gudely, this short warning considered, be devised and under such " form as master *Lancaster* of the king's councell this brynger shall sumwhat advertise you " of my mind in that behalf; as in hangyng the streetes through which the king's grace " shall come with clothes of arras, tappestre work and other; for there comen many " sothern lords and men of worship with them, which will mark greatly your resayving " thar graces. Me neded not thus to advise you, howbeit many things I shew you thus " of good heart, and for the singular zele and love which I beer to you and your cite afore " all other. Ye shall well know, that I shall not forbere calling on his grace for your " weles, ne remember it as master *Lancaster* shall shew you which in part heard the king's " grace speak hereon, to whom touching the premisses it may like you . . . . . " in haste the 23d day of *August* at *Nottingham*, with the hand of your friend and lover,

John Kendale, secretary."

(*m*) *Kennet*'s Hist. of *England*.
(*n*) *Robert Fabian* ended his chronicle the last of *Richard* III. he was sheriff of *London* anno 1494.
(*o*) Ex libro chart. supradict.

This

2

This letter needs no comment; it muſt produce an extraordinary emulation in our citizens to outvy other places, and even one another in the pomp and ceremony of the king's reception; but I cannot meet with a particular account of it in our records. Mr. *Buck*, whom I have quoted before, ſays, that *Richard* coming to the goodly and antient city of *York*, the ſcope and goal of his progreſs, he was received with all poſſible honour and feſtivity. And now all things are preparing for the coronation, in order for which the king ſent from *York*, on the laſt day of *Auguſt*, to *Piers Courteis* keeper of his wardrobe this order following (*p*), A 1483.

" *By the KING.*

" WE wol and charge you to deliver to the bryngers hereof for us the parcells following. That is to ſay, one doublett of purple ſattin lined with *Holland* cloth, and enterlined with buſke. One doublett of tawney ſattin, lined in likewiſe. Two ſhort gowns of crymſyn cloth of gold; the one with drippis, and the other with netts, lined with green velvet. One cloak with a cape of velvet ingrayned; the bow lined with black velvet. One ſtomacher of purple ſattin, and one ſtomacher of tawney ſattin. One gown of green velvet lined with tawney ſattin. One yard and three quarters courſe of ſike (ſilk) medled with gold, and as much black corſe of ſilk for our ſpurs. Two yards and half and three nayles of white cloth of gold, for a crynelze for a borde. Five yards of black velvet for the lining of a gown of green ſattin. One plakard made of part of the ſaid two yards; and one half and two nayles of white cloth of gold lined with buckram. Three pair of ſpurrs, ſhort all gilt; two pair of ſpurs long white parcell gilt. Two yards of black buckram for amending of the lining of diverſe trappers. One banner of ſarſanet of our lady; one banner of the trinity; one banner of St. *George*; one banner of St. *Edward*; one of St. *Cutbert*; one of our own arms, all ſarcenet. Three coats of arms beaten with fine gold for owr own perſon. Five coat armors for heralds lined with buckram. Forty trumpet banners of ſarcenett. Seven hundred and forty penſills of buckram; three hundred and fifty penſills of tarter. Four ſtandards of ſarcenett with boars. Thirteen thouſand quinyſans of fuſtian with boars. And theſe our letters, *&c.*"

How this cargo of extraordinary garniture was uſed is not ſo particularly known; but we may ſuppoſe that the coronation was performed with great magnificence. *Hall* indeed tells us, (*q*) that *Richard* was received at *York* with great pomp and triumph, by the citizens. That at the day of his coronation, which by proclamation he had invited the whole country to come to, the clergy of the church in their richeſt copes, and with a reverend ceremony went about the ſtreets in proceſſion. After whom followed the king with his crown and ſceptre, apparelled in his ſurcoat robe royal, accompanied with a great number of the nobility of the realm. Then followed queen *Anne* his wife, crowned likewiſe, leading in her left hand prince *Edward* her ſon, having on his head a demy crown appointed for the degree of a prince. In this manner they marched to the cathedral, where archbiſhop *Rotboram* ſet the crown on *Richard*'s head in the chapter-houſe (*r*). On the ſame day was *Edward* his ſon, a youth of ten years of age, inveſted with the principality of *Wales* by a golden rod and a coronet of gold, and other enſigns. The king now knighted *Gaufridus de Saſiola* ambaſſador from the queen of *Spain*, being preſent at this ſolemnity, by putting a collar of gold about his neck, and ſtriking three times upon his ſhoulders with his ſword; and by other marks of honour, according to the *Engliſh* cuſtom, with agreeable words added (*s*). In teſtimony whereof, the king gave him his letters patents dated at his court at *York*. He alſo here knighted *Richard*, ſurnamed of *Gloceſter* (*t*), his *baſtard ſon*; and many gentlemen of theſe parts. The lords ſpiritual and temporal of the realm were preſent on this ſolemn occaſion; and indeed it was a day of great ſtate, ſays *Polidore Vergil*, there being then three princes in *York* wearing crowns, the king, the queen, and prince of *Wales*. And now followed tilts and tournaments, maſques, revels and ſtage-plays, with other triumphant ſports, with feaſting to the utmoſt prodigality. In which was ſquandered away all that treaſure, which his glorious brother had for many years been collecting with great ſkill and induſtry; and being left by his laſt will to the diſpoſition of his executors, was ſnatched up by *Richard* at his intruſion into the kingdom, ſays my authority, which runs contemporary with theſe times, and waſted in this manner (*u*).

(*p*) *Kennet*'s notes on *G. Buck*, Eſq;

(*q*) *Hall*'s chron.

(*r*) *September* 8, 1483.

(*s*) *Kennet* on *Buck*.

(*t*) This *Richard* of *Glouceſter*, baſtard ſon to king *Richard*, who is no where elſe, that I know of, mentioned by hiſtorians, nor is his mother taken notice of at all, has a very odd account given of the courſe of life, he was driven to take after his father was ſlain. It is ſaid he found himſelf apprentice to a bricklayer, and actually worked at that trade for ſeveral years. Till at length being found out, a gentleman took pity of him, and ſuffered him to build a houſe in his park, in which he lived and died. The ſtory at length is given in the reverend Mr. *Peck*'s *deſiderata curioſa* v. 2. Some better memorials of it may be had from the right honourable the earl of *Winchelſea*; in whoſe noble park of *Eaſtwell* in *Kent*, this *Richard Plantagenet*, as the pariſh regiſter calls him, reſided and ended his days.

(*u*) *Non deerant tunc theſauri ulli quibus tam elevatae mentis ſuae propoſitum adimpleret; cum ea quae glorioſiſſimus rex* Edwardus *frater ſuus, ſummo ingenio, ſummaque induſtria multis ante annis collegerat, quaeque ad complimentum ſuae ultimae voluntatis ſuorum executorum diſpoſitioni commiſſerat, iſte quam primum de ſua intruſione in regnum cogitavit, omnia diripuit.* Hiſt Croy. cont.

A. 1483. Before *Richard* left *York* he did not forget the promise, made by him and his secretary to the city and citizens, for old services and new; and willing to do some extraordinary bounty to them, I find this, imperfect, memorial of it.

" *Memorandum*, That the xvii[th] day of the month of *September* in the first yere of the " reign of king *Richard* the third, *John Newton* then being mair of the cite of *York*, our " said sovereign lord the king, of his most special gude grace, remembring the gude service " that the said cite hath don to his gude grace . . . . made to " defray and fitt in the yorney made in the same yere to *Edenburg* and . . . . . . " . . . . to *London* to the coronation of his gude " grace; callid afore his gude grace the said day to the chapter house of the cathedral church " of S. *Peter* in *York*, the said mair, his bredyr the aldermen, and mong other the commons " of the said cite, and then and there our said sovereign lord openly rehersed the said service " to his gude grace don, and also the dekay and the great poverty of the said cite, of his " most special gude grace without any petition or asking of any thing by the said mair " or any odyr, our said sovereign lord only of his abundant grace most graciously and ha- " bundantly granted and gave in relief of the said cite in esyng of the **Tolls, Murage, Bu-** " **cher-pennys** and **Skaitgild** of the said cite yerely xxiii *l.* xi *s.* ii *d.* for evyr, that is to say " for the murage xx *l.* and the residue to the sheriffs, so that from thence forward it shold " be lefull to every person coming to the said cite with their guds and cattell, and them " freely to sell in the same without any thing gratifying . . . . or paying for toll or " murage of any of the said guds; and his grace . . . . most graciously " granted to the mair and commonality of the said cite yerely xl *l.* for ever, to the behoof " of the commonality and chamber of the said cite; and yerely to the mair for the tyme be- " ing, as his chief serjeant at ayrms, xii *d.* of the day, that is to say by the yere xviii *l.* vi *s.* (y)

It is a true though a homely proverb, that *it is an ill wind brings no body profit*. *Richard*'s munificence to our city at this time, whether it proceeded from gratitude or policy, was a truly royal gift: I never found him, amongst all his other vices, taxed with covetousness; and he had many reasons, both on his own and family's account to induce him even to do more for a city, which had always signalized itself in the interest of his house. Every one that is acquainted with *English* history must know, that there is hardly any part of it so dark as the short reign of this king. The *Lancastrian* party, which destroyed and succeeded him, took care to suppress his vertues, and to paint his vices in the most glaring colours. A countryman of ours has endeavoured to vindicate his memory from the load of black calumnies thrown upon it; but in this I think the herald has far overshot his mark. However, what opinion our citizens of *York* had of king *Richard* at that time, will best appear by their own records; in which they took care to register every particular letter and message they received from him. And as his fate drew nigh they endeavoured to shew their loyalty, or their gratitude, to this prince in the best manner they were able. Some more letters which were sent to the mayor and citizens when the commotions begun, as likewise their daily orders in council, about the state of affairs, to the king's death and after, may not be unacceptable to the reader in a literal extract from the city's registers as follows (z):

Very soon after *Richard* had been crowned at *York*, the duke of *Buckingham* took up arms against him; of which insurrection the king sent notice to the citizens of *York*. A memorial of it I find entered in the records as follows:

" *Mem.* 13 *Oct.* 1 *Rich.* III. *John Otyr* yeoman of the crown brought the following letter " to the lord-maior, aldermen, sheriffs, and comunality.

" *By the* KING.

" TRusty and right wel-beloved, we grete ye wele, and let ye wit that the duke of *Bucking-* " *ham* traiterously is turned upon us, contrary to the dute of his legeance, and en- " tendeth the utter distruction of us, you, and all other our true subgietts that have taken " our part; whose traiterous entent we with God's grace entend briefly to resist and

(x) Ex chart. supra dict.

(y) To give the reader a better notion of the value of these royal gifts take this *computus* from the *Chronicon pretiosum* of bishop *Fleetwood*, of what price corn bore, in the south of *England*, *An.* 1463. just twenty years before this.

		l.	*s.*	*d.*
A 1463. at *London*	wheat was by the quarter	00	02	00
	barley *per* quarter	00	01	10
	pease the quarter	00	03	04
	oats the quarter	00	01	02

		l.	*s.*	*d.*
At *Norfolk* the same year,	wheat *per* quarter	00	01	08
	barley ———	00	01	00
	malt ———	00	01	08
	oats, Mr. *Stow*,	00	01	00

So that the value of one shilling, even in the time of the civil wars, bought one quarter of barley or oats, which makes the donation very considerable.

(z) These registers are to be found according to the date of the year in the chamber on *Ouse-bridge*. What register the following is chiefly collected from, is marked *ab anno* 1479. *ad* 1485. *R.* but it is imperfect towards the end.

" subdue

" subdue. We desire and pray you in our hearty wise that yee will send unto us as ma- A. 1483.
" ny men defensibly arraied on horseback as ye may godely make to our town of *Leicestre*
" the 21 day of this present month withouten fail, as ye will tendre our honner and your
" own wele, and wee shall so see you paid for your reward and charges as yee shall hold yee
" wele content. Geving further credence to our trusty pursuivant this berer.

" Geven under our signet at our cite of *Lincoln* the *xith* day of *October*.

Superscribed,

" *To our trusty and right well beloved the maire, aldermen, sheriffs and communalitie of the* " *citie of* York.

A proclamation under the privy seal dated at *Lincoln October* 15, declaring the duke of *Buckingham* a traitor, was proclaimed at *York October* 16, says the record; but the distance makes it seem scarce possible. A. 1483.

In the same records I find another letter dated *April* the xi[th], which must be in the year 1484, when the tide was beginning to turn against king *Richard*, giving an account of the number of lyes, as he expresses himself, and contumelious speeches which were then spread abroad against him. Requiring the magistrates of this city to suppress all such slanders, and to take up the spreaders of it. The letter is a very particular one; and shews the depth of policy in this king's reign more than any thing that I have yet seen published of it. I shall give this, also, *verbatim*.

" TRusty and welbeloved, we grete you wele. And where it is soe that diverse sedi- " tious and evil disposed personnes, both in our citie of *London* and elswhere, with- " in this our realme, enforce themselfs daily to sowe sede of noise and disclaindre agaynest " our persone, and agenst many of the lords and estates of our land to abuse the multitude " of our subgetts and alter there mynds from us, if they could by any meane atteyne to that " there mischevous entent and purpose; some by setting up of billes, some by message and " sending furth of false and abhominable langage and lyes; some by bold and presumptu- " ous opene spech, wherthewyth the innocent people, whiche wold live in rest and peas, " and truly undre our obbeissance as they oght to do, being gretely abused, and oft tymes " put in daungeres of there lives landes and goods, as ofte as they folowe the stepps and de- " vises of the said seditious and mischevous persones, to our hevynesse and pitie. For re- " medy wherof, and to thentent the truth openlye declared shuld represse all suche false and " contrived inventions, we now of late called before us the maire and aldermen of our ci- " tie of *London*, togidder with the moost sadde and disgrete persones of the same citie in " grete numbre, being present many of the lords spiritual and temporal of our land, and the " substance of all our housholde, to whom we largely shewed our true entent and mynde " in all suche thinges which the saide noise and disclandre renne upon, in such wise as we " doubt not all wel disposed persones were and be therwith right wele content. Where we " alsoe at the same tyme gafe straitly in charge as well to the said maire as to all other our " officers, servants and faithfull subgettes, wheresoere they be, that from hensfurth as ofte as " they find any persone speking of us, or any other lord or estate of this our land, otherwayes, " then is according to honour, trouth and the peas and ritefullnesse of this our realme, or " telling of tales and tidings wherby the people might be stirred to commotions and unlaw- " full assembles, or any strife and debate arise between lord and lord, or us and any of the " lords and estates of this our land, they take and arrest the same persone unto the tyme he " have broght furth hyme or them of whom he understode that that is spoken, and so pro- " ceding from oon to other unto the tyme the furst auctor and maker of the said seditious " speche and langage be taken and punyshed according to his deserts. And that whosoever " furst finde any seditious bills set up in any place he take it downe and without reding or " shewing the same to any other persone bring it forthwith unto us or some of the lords or " other of our counsaill. All which charges and commandements, soo by us taken and geven " by our mouthe to our citie of *London*, we notifie unto you by these our letters to thentent " that ye shewe the same within all the places of your jurisdiction, and see there the due exe- " cution of the same from tyme to tyme. As ye woll eschewe our grevous indignation, and " answere unto us at your extreme perill.

" Given under our signet at our citie of *London* the xi[th] day of *April*.

" *By the* KING.

Superscribed,

" *To our trusty and wel-beloved the maire and his brethre of the citye of* York.

Richard's short reign drawing still nearer a period, and his tragical end approaching, I find an order of council, entered in the register of those times, of the date and in the manner following:

" Veneris

A. 1485.

July 8. " Veneris *post festum S.* Thome Martyris, *viz.* viii° *die* Julii *an. reg. regis* R. III. *tertio.*

" *Nicholaus Lancastre,* Mr.
" *Thomas Wrangwiche.*
" *Willielmus Snawsell.*
" *Johannus Tong.*
" *Willielmus Chymney.*
" *Thomas Fynch.* Vic.
xxiv.
" *Thomas Ellay.*
" *Willhelmus Spence.*
" *Willielmus Tayte.*
" *Ricardus Clerk.*
" *Johannes Hay.*
" *Willielmus White.*
" *Milo Grenebank.*

Wer assembled in the counsail chambre within the *Guild-hall* of this citie, where and when it was thought by the counsail that such bill of proclamation as was then shewed by the maire, delivered unto hym on the king's behalve by the sheref of the shire to be proclamed thrugh out the citie, should be shewed unto the serchers of evere craft within this citie, which shall have in commaundement by the maire that evere man of any craft within this citie forsaid, being franchest, be redie defensibly arrayed to attend upon the mayre of this citie and his brethre for the savegard of the same, to the king's behove or otherwayes at his commaundment.

August 16. " Martis *post festum assumpt.* beate Marie Virg. *viz.* xvi *die* Augusti *an. reg. regis* R. III. *tertio.*

" *Nicholaus Lancastre* Mr.
" *Willielmus Snawsell,*
" *Johannes Tong,* } *de* xii.
" *Willielmus Chymney,*
" *Johannes Gylliot,*
" *Thomas Fynche,* } Vic.
" *Thomas Cator,*
" *Willielmus Spense,*
" *Willielmus Tayte,*
" *Ricardus Clercke,* } *de* xxiv
" *Johannes Hay,*
" *Willielmus White,*
" *Ricardus Hardsang,*

Wer assembled in the counsail chambre upon *Ouse brig,* where and when it was determyned by the same that *John Spon* sergeant to the Mase shuld ride to *Nottingham* to the king's grace to understaund his plesure in sending up any of his subgettes within this citie to his said grace, for the subduing of his enemies lately arrived in the partes of *Wales* or otherwise to be dispofed at his most high plesure. Also it was determyned that all such aldermen and other of the counsail as was sojournyng, for the plage that reigneth, without the citie shuld be sent for to give their best advises in such things as concerned the wele and savegard of the said citie, and all othyr inhabitauts of the same. —— Also that every warden of this citie serche the inhabitants within his ward that they have sufficient wapens and armes for their
" defence of the wall of this citie. — Also that ther shall proclamations be maide thrugh out
" this citie that evere man fraunchest within this citie be redie, in the most defensible araye,
" to attend upon the maire for the welfare of this citie within an owres warnyng on payne
" of imprisonment."

August 19. " Veneris *post fest. assumpt. &c. viz.* xix *die* Augusti *an. ut supra.*

" *Nicholaus Lancastre,* Mr.
" *&c.* N° 17.

Wer assembled in the counsail chambre, wher and when it was determined upon the report of *John Nicholson,* who was comen home from the king's grace fro **Beskwood** that
" iv c. men of the citie defensibly arrayed, *John Hastings* gentleman to the mace being cap-
" tayn, shuld in all hast possible depart towards the king's grace for the subduyng of his e-
" nemyes forsaid. Wherupon eche parish in the citie was sessed as it appeareth hereafter.
" And that eche sougior shuld have x *s.* for x days, being furth xii *d.* by day. — And also
" that the counsail shuld meet at ii of the clock at afternone, the same day at the *Geld-hall*
" ther to poynt such personnes as shuld take wages and there to receve the same."

August 23. " Martis *vigil. S.* Bartholomei, *viz.* xxiii° *die* Augusti *an. &c. vacat. regal. potest.*

" *Nicholaus Lancastre,* Mr.
" *&c.* N° 15.

Wer assembled in the counsail chambre, wher and when it was shewed by diverse personnes, especially by *John Spon* sent unto the **feld of Redemore** to bring tydings from the
" same to the citie that king *Richard* late *lawfully* reigning over us was thrugh grete treason
" of the duc of *Northfolk,* and many othyr that turned agenst hym, with many othyr lords
" and nobilitie of thes north partes, was *pitiously slane and murdred* to the grete hevyness of
" this citie, the names of whom followeth herafter.

" Wherfore it was determyned for so much as it was that the erle of *Northumberland*
" was comen to *Wressel* that a lettre shuld be conveyed unto the said erle, beseching hym to
" give unto them his best advise how to dispose them at this *wofull season,* both to his ho-
" nor and worship, and well and prouffit of this citie. The tenor wherof followeth :

" Right potent and right noble our moost honorable especial and singular good lord in
" our moost humble wise we recommend us unto your good lordship, loving almightie god
" of your home enduryng at this wooful season, beseching your good lordship to be towards
" us

" us and this citie as ye have ben hertofore right good and tendre lord, and so to advertise A. 1485.
" us at this tyme as may be to the honor of your lordship as well and prouffit of us and
" sauffegard of this said citie, wherunto we shall applye us both with bodie and goods, and
" to owe unto your lordship our faithful and true Further we beseech your
" lordship to geve full faith and credence unto our servant *John Nicholson* the berer hereof in
" such things as he shall shewe unto your lordship of our behalve; and the blessed trini-
" ty, *&c.*

" Yours, *&c.*

" *Maire, aldermen, sheriffs,* xxiv *of the counsail of the*
" *citie of* York *with thole communaltie of the same.*

To, &c. *the erle of* Northumberland.

" Mercurii *festum S.* Bartholomei, *viz.* xxiiii° *die* Augusti, *Anno &c. Vacat regalis potestas.*

" *Nicholaus Lancastre*, M^r^. Wer assembled in the counsail chambre wher and when it
" *&c.* N° 13. was determined that the maire with his brethre shuld attend
and mete sir *Henry Percey* at ii. o' the clok at afternone, at
" the miln in the strete without *Walmgate-bar*, ther to understand how they shall be disposed
" enent the king's grace *Henry* the sevent, so proclamed and crowned at the feld of *Rede-*
" *more*.

" Also it was determined that oon sir *Roger Cotam* knight unto the said kings grace, now
" comen to this citie to proclame the said king *Henry*, shuld be presented with ii. and
" ii. gallons of wyne at the chambre cost.

" Also *John Nicholson* which was sent to *Wressell* to the erle of *Northumberland* with wri-
" ting, appered in the counsail chambre, and shewed how it was shewed unto hym by sir
" *Henry Percy* being ther, that the said erle was with the king at *Leicestre* for the well of
" himself and this citie, and that the said sir *Henry* wold be at the milne without the bar as
" above. Wherfore it was determined to meet with hyme ther.

" Also the same day forsomuch as the forsaid sir *Roger Cotam* durst not for fere of deth
" come thrugh the citie to speake with the maire and his brethre, it was thought that they
" shuld goo unto him, wherupon the maire and his brethre went unto the sign of the boore
" and ther they speak with the said knight, which shewed unto them that the king named
" and proclamed *Henry* the vii. grete them well, and wold be unto them and this citie as
" good and gratiouse soveraign lord as any of his noble progenitors was before. With o-
" thyr words of comforth. Wherof the maire and his brethre thankes him moch and soo
" departed.

" Also it was determined that such sogiers as went furth of this citie having wages for x.
" dayes, xii *d.* by the day, and was furth but iiii dayes and a half, shuld have wages for vi.
" dayes and no more, and the residue of the money to be repaid to the chamberlaynes to
" pay to such parishes as paid the same.

" Jovis *post fest. S.* Bartholomei, *viz.* xxv° *die Augusti A. dom.* M.CCCC.LXXXV.

" *Nicholaus Lancastre*, M^r^. Wer assembled in the counsail chambre, wher and when
" *&c.* N° 11. it was determined that *William Wells*, *William Chimney*,
Robert Hawk aldermen, *William Tayte* and *John Hay* of the
" xxiv, shall ride unto the kings grace *Henry* the vii. in the name of th'ole bodie of this
" citie, beseching his grace to be good and gracious lord unto this citie as othyr his noble
" progenitours hath ben tofore, and to confirme of his most habundant grace all such fran-
" chises, liberties, fees and freedoms as hath ben granted to the said citie hertofore by his
" said noble progenitours; and that ther be several letters made as well to the erle of
" *Northumberland* as the lord *Stanelay* for the good speed of the premisses. Also that the
" said aldermen and ii. of the xxiiii. be accompanyed with xv. yomen and horses, and have
" gownes of **must devilles**, and ther gownes of othyr color convenient for them. And
" that *Alexander Dauson* chamberlayn, ride with the same personnes and bere all costs pro-
" vided of the chambre.

" Also, that ther shal be a proclamacion mad thrugh out this citie, which proclamacion
" was delivered unto the mayre and his brethre by one of the kings herolds called *Wyndsore*
" in the counsail chambre, having upon hym a cote armor of the armes of *England* and
" *Fraunce*; which herold shewed unto the mayre by mouthe, that the kings grace grete
" hym and his bredre wele, and would be as good and gracious lord unto this citie as any
" of his progenitours were before him, with othyr moch wordes of comforth, wherfore
" he desired hym on the kings behalve to make a proclamacion after the tenor that folow-
" eth.

A. 1485.

Copia proclamationis Henrici *regis Ang.* VII.

" *HENRY* by the grace of God, king of *England*, and of *Fraunce*, prince of *Wales*, " and lord of *Irland* strictly charges and commaundeth upon peyne of deth, that no " manner of man robbe nor spoyle na manner of commons comyng from the feld; but suf- " fre theme to passe home to ther cuntrees and dwelling places with their horses and har- " nesse. And morover that noo manner of man take upon hym to goe to noo gentilmanz " place neither in the cuntree nor within cities nor borows, nor pike no quarells for old or " for new matters, but kepe the kings peace upon payne of hanging, &c. And morover " if ther be any man affered to be robbed and spoyled of his goods, let hym come to master " *Richard Borow*, the king's sergeant here, and he shall have a warrant for his bodie and " his goods, unto the tyme the kings pleasure be knowne. — And morover the king asser- " tayneth you, that *Richard* duc of *Gloucestre*, late callid king *Richard*, was slayne at a " place called *Sandeford*, within the shyre of *Leicestre*, and brought dede of the feld unto the " towne of *Leicestre*, and ther was laide oppenly that every man might se and luke upon " him. And also ther was slayne uppon the same feld *John* late duc of *Northfolk*, *John* late " erle of *Lincoln*, *Thomas* late erle of *Surrey*, *Fraunceys* vicount *Lovell*, sir *Walter Deveres*, " lord *Ferreres*, *Richard Ratcliff* knight, *Robert Brachenbury* knight, with many othyr " knights, squires, and gentilmen, **of whose soules God have mercy.**

" After which proclamation made, the said mayre and his brethre comyng to the cham- " bre agayn, determined that the said harold for his message and comforthable words shuld " have in reward of the chambre vi. marks iiii. aungells.

" *Copie of a letter directed to the erle of* Northumberland *for the good spede forsaid.*

" RIGHT potent and right noble our moost especial and singular good lord in our moost " humble wise we recommend us unto your good lordship, loving almighty God of " your prosprouse lif the which *Jesu* continue in felicity both ghostly and bodily, thanking " your good lordship of your tendre luff and favor which your lordship ever hath borne to- " wards us and this citie, whom we beseeche you continue and in especial at this season, in " the which we know right wele your lordship unto us is moost necessarye. And wheras " we send up unto the kings grace iii. of our aldermen and othyr of our counsail chambre to " beseche his grace to accept us benignely unto his grace, graunting unto us and this citie all " all such fraunchises, liberties, freedoms, and annual fees, with all othyr commodities and " prouffitts unto the same belonging and graciously graunted by all othyr his moost noble " progenitours; we beseche your good lordship in the good furtherance and spede herof to " shew unto our said brethre your noble advise how to labor to the said kings grace for the " same; and we shall ever pray for the state of you right potent and right noble our moost " especial and singular good lord in felicitie ever to endure.

" From *York* the xxvi[ta] day of *August*.

" *Your orators and servants, the mayre, aldermen*
" *and sheruffs, and* xxiv *of the counsail of the citie*
" *of* York, *with th'ole communalitie of the same.*

" Sabbati, *viz.* xxvii° *die* Augusti *Anno regni regis* Henrici *septimi primo incipien.*

" *Nicholaus Lancastre*, M[r]. " &c. N°. 5.

Wer assembled in the counsail chambre, when and wher oon *Robert Rawdon* gentilman, sergeant unto the kings grace personally appered and gave unto the maire and the " counsail a commandement and warrant under the kings signet and signe manual to him " direct to attache *Robert* bishop of *Bath* (a), and sir *Richard Ratcliff* knight, and to bring " them personaly unto his highnesse and to sease into his hands all their goods, moveable, " and immoveable, as it appereth more at large in the warrant, wherof the tenor wherof " followeth herafter. Wherupon the said *Rawdon* instantly desired the said maire and she- " riffs on the kings behalve as his true liege men and subgetts that in thexecution of his " said warrant they wold geve ther attendaunce, aid and assistence. Wherin after som con- " sultation upon the same, for so moch as the said bishop was attached tofore by oon he- " rold *Wyndsore* and *Robert Borow* gentilman, the kings servants, and broght unto the citie " and lay within the fraunchesse and liberty of the same, and was *sore crased by reason of his* " *trouble and carying*, the maire taking with hym the above written of the counsail of the " chambre, the said *Rawdon* and *Rob. Borow*, instantly prepared to go to the said bishop to " master *Neleson* place, to speke with him; being come unto hym unto the said place,

(a) *Robert Stillington.*

" shuld

" wher and when it was appointed of the consent of the said *Rawdon*, that the said bishop A. 1485.
" shuld continue still within the said citie for iv. or v. days for his ease and rest. The tenor
" of the warrant foloweth:

" *HENRY*, by the grace of God, king of *England*, and of *Fraunce*, and lord of *Irland*,
" to our trusty and wel-beloved *Robert Rawdon* gentleman, greting. For as moch
" as *Robert* bishop of *Bath* and sir *Richard Ratcliff* knight, adherents and assistents to our
" grete enemy *Richard* late duc of *Gloucestre*, to his aide and assistance, have by deverse
" ways offended agenst the crowne to us of right appurteyneyng, we will and charge you
" and by this our warrant commit and geve you power to attache the said bishop and knight,
" and them personaly bring unto us, and to sease into our hands all such goods, moveables
" and immoveables as the xxiid day of *August* the first year of our reigne appurteyned and
" belonged unto them whersoever they be found, as well in places privileged as ellefwhere,
" and the same soo seased to put into such suerte and savegard as ye will answer to us for
" them at all tymes. Chargyng morover, and strictly commaundyng all our true subgettes
" and legemen that to thexecution herof they geve you attendaunce, aide, and assistence,
" without doeing of any thyng that shall be prejudicial to the premisses, as they will a-
" voyde our grievious displeasure and answer unto us at their peril.

" Geven undre our signet at our towne of *Leicestre* the xxiiid day of *August*, the first
" yere of our reign.

" *Per signet. et sigillum manuale*

FOX.

" Lune, *viz. penult. die* Augusti, *anno reg. regis* Henrici *primo*.

" *Nicholaus Lancaster*, Mr. " &c. No. 9. Wer assembled in the counsail chambre, where and when it was determined, that the gates and posturnes of the citie shuld be shut evere night at ix of the clock, and opened
" at morowning at iiij: And that iiij men of every warde be warned to watch at evere gate
" evere night for the safegard of the citie, and the inhabitants of the same. Also ther was
" a lettre direct from the kings grace unto the maire and his brethre charging them by the
" same to geve ther assistence and aide in such matters as appereth in the said letters,
" wherof the tenor followeth:

" *By the KING.*

" TRusty and welbeloved we grete you wele, and late you wit that for diverse causes us
" touching, we send unto your partes our trusty and welbeloved servant sir *John*
" *Halewell* knight, wherfore we woll and pray you, and upon that on your liegeance in-
" stantly charge and command you, that in all such matters as the said sir *John* shall shew
" unto you on our behalve yee geve your assistence and aide, and that yee ne faile therof
" as yee will deserve of us our especial thankes.

" Geven undre our signet at our towne of *Leycestre*, the xxiii day of *August*.

Superscribed,

" *To our trusty and welbeloved the maire, aldermen and sherriffs of our citie of York.*

" Sabbati, *viz.* iiij *die* Septembris *regni regis* Henrici VII. *primo*.

" *Nicholaus Lancastre*, Mr. " &c. No. 16. Wer assembled in the counsail chambre within the *Guild-hall*, when and where it was shewed by *Thomas Wrang-wishe*, *William Welles*, *William Chymney*, aldermen, *Willi-*
" *am Tate* and *John Hay* of the xxiv late sent unto the king for the well of this citie, that
" the said kings grace accept them in the name of tholl bodie of this citie, graciously unto
" his highnesse graunting that the said citie shuld be holdein of the same, and that the inha-
" bitants and citizens of the said citie shall have and enjoy all and all manner of fraunchisses,
" liberties, freedoms, graunts, issues and prouffits unto them belonging in as large and am-
" ple manner and forme, with better, as any of his noble progenitours had graunted to the
" said citie at any tyme hertofore. The which premisses was shewed by the mouth of the
" said *Thomas Wrangwishe*, not only unto the mayre and the counsail, but also incontinent-
" ly to the commons assembled the said day in the *Guild hall* forsaid. After which the maire
" taking with hym all above written entered the chambre agayn, where after due thanks ge-
" ven unto the said *Thomas Wrangwishe* and his felows for ther grete labor and comfortable
" tidings, it was determined that *William Welles* and *William Chymney* shuld towards ther
" horsehyre have in reward xx *s.* and either of the xxiv. v *s.* And on this ——— *desunt caetera*.

These

8

A. 1485. These sketches of history, long buried in silence, I bring to light, as a tast of those times rendred dark enough by the writers of the *Lancastrian* party. Here is subject sufficient for an historian to expatiate largely upon, and to such I leave it; the growing bulk of this work not suffering me to enter into it. Let the times then speak for themselves. It is plain that *Richard*, represented as a monster of mankind by most, was not so esteemed in his life time in these northern parts. And had the earl of *Northumberland* staid and raised forces here, he might have struck *Henry*'s new acquired diadem into the hazzard. Wanting that nobleman's personal appearance amongst them, our city had nothing to do, but with the rest of the kingdom, to submit to the conqueror. His policy taught him to shew great acts of clemency at his entrance into government; though he must know, that neither his title, nor his family, were recognized, or respected, in these northern parts of the kingdom.

The first thing the victor did, after his conquest near *Bosworth*, was to send immediately for the princess *Elizabeth*, the heiress of the house of *York*; whom he had sworn to marry before his invasion. This princess had been sent by *Richard*, a kind of a prisoner, to *Sherrif-hutton castle* in our neighbourhood; as a place of great strength and security. It is said the uncle intended to marry his niece himself, to prevent any other from doing it. The messenger made use of by *Henry* on this important occasion seems to be sir *John Halewell*, mentioned in one of the warrants; the *secret commission* he was entrusted with pointing at no less. The princess was conducted publickly up to *London*, and a numerous suit of nobility met and attended her. But there was another of royal blood, in the same castle, whom *Henry*'s jealousy would not allow such pageantry to. This was no less a person than *Edward Plantagenet*, earl of *Warwick*, only son to *George* duke of *Clarence* the late king *Richard*'s elder brother; just then fifteen years of age. This branch of a royal stock was born to be unhappy; if the knowledge of his birth-right, which was kept industriously from him, as well as every part of education had not made him thoughtless about it. To whose care and custody *Richard* had entrusted these two particulars I know not; the castle was then in possession of the *Nevil*'s but this is another great instance of the trust he had in the northern, rather than the southern, parts of the kingdom. We are told that *Henry* dispatched away sir *Robert Willoughby*, the day after the battle, to take the prince from his keepers, and convey him privately to the tower of *London*. It was not long after that this innocent youth shared the same fate with his cousins, *Edward* V. and his brother; the difference only, that the former execrable deed is said to have been acted in the dead of the night, and *Henry* with as much justice, caused his head to be struck off in open day-light. In this prince the royal line of the *Plantagenet*'s failed. Monsieur *Rapin Thoyras*, an historian apparently opposite to an hereditary title to the crown of *England*, writes thus, however, of this unfortunate prince; "A prince, says he, who was the sole relict of the male "issue of *Edward* the third, which had been so numerous, but was almost entirely destroyed "by the late civil wars. The last of the *Angavin* or *Plantagenet* race, which had been in "possession of the crown of *England*, *from father to son*, during the space of three hundred "and thirty years."

The princess *Elizabeth* was presently married to *Henry*; but he always seemed to scorn the title he had with her, and was the first king of *England* that chose, rather, to make his claim to the crown *de facto* than *de jure*. (a) It was three years before he would have her crowned according to his oath; and, *it is very true*, says the great lord *Verulam*, *that* Henry *shewed himself no very indulgent husband to the lady* Elizabeth, *though she was beautiful, gentle and fruitful, and but then nineteen years of age. His aversion to the house of* York, continues that author, *was so predominant in him, that it found place not only in his wars and councils, but in his chamber, and even in his bed.*

I now conclude this chapter, being a series of four hundred and twenty years; and shall hasten to our historical annals in the reigns of this *Henry* and his successors.

(a) Bacon's Henry the seventh.

CHAP.

CHAP. V.

A continuation of the historical annals of the city, from this period to the present times.

HENRY VII, called the *English Solomon*, having mounted the throne, kept possession A. 1486. of it all his life; with that strength of judgment and policy, as might deserve in some measure that high title. However, the partisans of the house of *York*, could not bear that a prince of the other family should reign over them; notwithstanding the specious title he drew from the queen might very well serve to gild over his own. Several commotions were raised, in which, those that concerned *Lambert Symnel*, and *Perkin Warbeck*, were not inconsiderable; and gave him no small trouble to compose. The northern counties, and, especially the city of *York*, preserved their respect to the family which bore that title; and seemed to watch all opportunities to testify their loyalty to it. In the second year of his reign, in a progress *Henry* made into the north, in order to nip an insurrection in the bud which was then on foot in this country, he came to *York*; where before he had A. 1488. sent a great multitude of unarmed men, that he might rather seem to pacify than exasperate his adversaries. This piece of policy had like to have proved fatal to him; for, says the history of *Croyland*, he had certainly been taken by them, whilst he was devoutly solemnizing of St. *George*'s day in that city; had not the earl of *Northumberland* been more prudent in coming to his rescue. *Henry* seized upon some of the principal movers of this disturbance, and presently caused them to be hanged upon a gibbet at *York*. After which, adds my authority, the king returned in peace to the south (*a*).

(*b*) This insurrection had been countenanced by the lord *Lovel*, the two *Staffords*, and afterwards headed by the earl of *Lincoln*, who had landed with *Lambert Symnel* from *Ireland* with forces. They came directly to *York*, after the king had left it, in hopes to be powerfully reinforced in these parts; not doing the city or country any harm, that their mock-king might gain a greater character, and seem tender of his subjects lives. But finding the country not to come in as they expected, they went incontinent to meet the king and fight him with the numbers they had. What followed was the battle of *Stoke*, where *Henry* got the victory; and the counterfeit *Plantagenet* taken prisoner was made a turnspit in the palace; in which post he behaved himself so handsomely, that, after some years, he was raised to be one of the king's falconers.

The parliament had granted certain subsidies to defray the expence of an army sent in- A. 1489. to *Britany*; this was to be levied by a tax on land through *England*; which was readily paid by all the counties, except *Yorkshire* and the bishoprick of *Durham* (*c*). The two last, says lord *Verulam*, openly and resolutely refused to pay it; not out of necessity, but by reason of the old humour of these countries, where the memory of king *Richard* was so strong, adds the noble lord, *that it laid like lees in the bottom of mens hearts, and, if the vessels were once stirred, it would rise.* The commissioners appointed for the gathering this tax, were amazed at this great rub in their way, and applied to the earl of *Northumberland* for his advice and aid in this affair. The earl forthwith wrote to court about it, and received answer from the king, that, peremptorily, he would not abate one penny. Because, since it was a tax granted by parliament, if he did, it might encourage other counties to hope for an abatement; and he would never allow the people to disannul the authority of a parliament, in which their votes were included. Upon this advice the earl summoned all the nobility and gentry to *York*, and speaking to them in that imperious language the king had sent him; the words suiting, says my author, his natural disposition, it did not only irritate them to a great degree, but imagining the words to be as much the earl's own as the king's, and that he had been the chief adviser in laying this tax, they rose and assayled his house, and slew him with many of his servants (*d*). The sword thus drawn, they threw away the scabbard, and chose for their leader Sir *John Egremond*, whom lord *Bacon* calls a factious person, and one who had a long time born an ill mind towards the king. To him they added a fellow of mean degree, called *John a Chambre*, who bore much sway amongst the common people, and was a perfect *boute-feu*. With these commanders they entered into open rebellion, giving out in flat terms that they would march against king *Henry* and fight for their *liberties* and their *properties*.

(*a*) Hist. *Croy.* contin.
(*b*) *Bacon's Henry* VII.
(*c*) *Biondi.*
(*d*) *Dug.* baronage.
(*e*) This earl was buried at *Beverley*, where he had a stately monument, but now much defaced. The destruction of this earl so soon after the revolution in favour of *Henry*, was probably in revenge for his deserting the house of *York*; who had restored him to those honours forfeited by his father at *Towton*.

A. 1489. When the king heard of this new insurrection, being a fever that almost took him every year, after his manner, he seemed little troubled therewith. He sent *Thomas* earl of *Surrey*, whom he had a little before released out of the tower, and pardoned, with a competent power against the rebels. The earl met and fought with the principal band of them, defeated them and took *John a Chambre*, their firebrand prisoner; with several others. The rest fled to *York*, but upon the generals approach, they durst not abide a siege, but ran out of the city some one way and some another. *Egremond* got into *Flanders*, where he was protected by *Margaret* duchess of *Burgundy*, sister to *Edward* IV. and *Henry*'s mortal enemy. *John a Chambre* was executed in great state at *York*; for he was hanged on a gibbet raised a stage higher, in the midst of a square gallows, as a traitor *paramount*; and a number of his men, that were his chief accomplices, were hanged, upon the lower story, round about him (*f*).

The king though he made use of the earl of *Surrey* for a general, yet followed after himself, and though he heard of the victory, yet he came on as far as *York*, in order, says my author, to pacify and settle that city and county. From whence he returned to *London*, leaving the earl of *Surrey* his lieutenant in these northern parts, and Sir *Richard Tunstal* his principal commissioner to levy the subsidy; of which he did not remit one *denier* (*g*).

This strictness in *Henry* so dampt the spirits of the northern malecontents, that, whatever they might think of his title, they never more offered to disturb him; and even in the rebellion occasioned by *Perkin Warbeck*'s claim, the sham duke of *York*, our chronicles make no mention of any insurrection in these parts in his favour.

I suppose them quiet, submissive, and very good subjects, during the rest of this king's reign, and as a testimony of the loyalty of the city of *York*, I find, in our own records, an account of the reception of *Margaret*, *Henry*'s eldest daughter into the city, in her journey for *Scotland*; in order to consummate a marriage, which had been solemnized by proxy, betwixt this princess and *James* IV. king of *Scotland*, some time before in *London*. Which I shall give in its own words and orthography.

A. 1541. (*h*) "On *Saturday* the 14th of *July* in the year of our lord 1503, Sir *John Gylliot* merchant knight of the *Bath* being then lord-mayor of the city of *York*, and *John Ellis* and "*Thomas Braikes* sheriffs, *Margaret* the king's eldest daughter, and wife of *James* the fourth "king of *Scotland* came to *York*; accompanied with many lords, ladies, knyghtes, and "esquyers, and gentlemen, to the number of five hundreth persons, being met by the she"riffs in crymsyn gownes, attended by one hundreth persons on horseback in one clothing, "at the midst of *Tadcaster-bridge*, who, with humble salutations, welcomed her majesty in"to the libertys of the said city, and so bare their white wands before her until she came "at *Micklegate-bar*; and ther the lord-mayor, cloathed in fine crymsin sattin engrayned, "having a collar of gold of his majestys livery about his neck, being on horseback his sad"dle of fine crymsin velvet, and the trappis of the same, with gilt bullion, his footmen "apparelled in green sattin, with the armes of the city and his own armes, accompanyed "with the recorder and aldermen in scarlet together on horseback, their sadles being co"vered with fine cloth bordered with black velvet, and their trappis of the same with gilt "bullion, the twenty four in their red gownes on foot, with the tradesmen and com"moners honestly cloathed, standing on the north-side of the bar, made low obeysance "unto her grace, who with all her company was most nobly and richly apparelled, and so "came near unto her chayr upon the palfreys covered with cloth of gold, who causing the "palfreys to stand still, the lord-mayor said, *most noble and excellent princess, I and my bre*"*thren with all the commonality of this city, in our most heartiest wise, welcometh your noble* "*grace, with all those the other nobles that attend upon you*; *at which words she inclined herself* "*towards the lord mayor, and thanked him, his brethren, and all the rest of the city*; and then "it was ordered by the lord treasurer that the lord-mayor should ride next before her "chayr, betwixt two serjeants at armes, to bear the mace to her lodgings.

"On the morrow, about nine a clock in the forenoon, the lord-mayor, recorder, alder"men, and twenty-four and chamberlaynes, went into the bishop's pallace, and ther pre"sented her with a goodly standing silver piece with a cover, well over-gilt, and an hun"dreth angells of gold in the same; amounting to the summe of eighty three poundes six "shillings and eight pence; for which she heartily thanked him, his brethren, and all "the body of the city, and so went forward towards the minster, the lord archbishop and "other bishops and nobles going before her in order, the lord-mayor bearing the mace be"twixt two serjeants at armes next before her; and after mass was done returned back to "the pallace to dinner, the lord-mayor bearing the mace as aforesaid, untill she came to her "chamber, and ther took his leave till monday morning.

"On monday morning about twelve of the clock her grace took her chayre to go on "her voyage that night to *Newburgh*; and then every science stood in order from the "*Minstergates* to *Boutham-bar*, the lord mayor and his brethren riding in like order as they "did at her coming, the sheriffs bearing their rods rode forth at the said bar before her

(*f*) Lord *Bacon*. *Stowe*'s chron.
(*g*) Lord *Bacon*.

(*h*) From a register on *Ousebridge*.

"untill

"untill they came at *Mawdlyn* chappel, and there the lord-mayor, making a long oration, "took his leave, whereupon ſhe heartily thanked his lordſhip and the reſt, and ſaid, *my* "*lord-mayor, your bretbren, and all the whole city of* York, *I ſhall evermore endeavour to love* "*you and this city all the dayes of my life.* And ſo departed on her journey." A. 1503.

This teſtimony of loyalty in our citizens at this time was not merely political, my lord *Bacon* ſays, the joy this princeſſe's marriage occaſioned was exceeding great all over the kingdom; and, *might be attributed*, adds the noble hiſtorian, *to a ſecret inſtinct or inſpiring, which many times runneth not only in the hearts of princes, but in the pulſe and veins of the people, touching the happineſs thereby to enſue in time to come.* By it he means the union of the two kingdoms, accompliſhed in the perſon of *James* VI. this queen's grandſon. But this paſſage is repreſented, by a late hiſtorian, as one of lord *Verulam*'s partial ſtrokes in favour of king *James*.

Henry VII. died without any more occurrences to furniſh our annals with. He was ſucceeded by his only ſon *Henry*, who was crowned king of *England* at *Weſtminſter*, at the age of ſixteen years by the title of *Henry* VIII. A. 1509.

The life of this prince, in whom the two claims of *York* and *Lancaſter* were indiſputably conjoined, is excellently well wrote by the lord *Herbert* in particular; and by ſeveral others in the general hiſtory of *England*. It is a remarkable one indeed, and too plainly makes appear, that he inherited, along with the titles, all the vices of his anceſtors of both houſes put together; without the leaſt allay of any of their virtues.

September 9. was fought the famous battle of *Flodden*, in which *James* the fourth of *Scotland*, king *Henry*'s brother-in-law, was killed, and his army entirely routed. The earl of *Surrey* commanded the *Engliſh* army, being lord lieutenant of the north, in *Henry*'s abſence who was then at the ſiege of *Tournay* in *France*. The earl had drawn together to oppoſe the *Scots* twenty ſix thouſand men, I mention this becauſe I find in an old record that five hundred ſoldiers were raiſed by the lord lieutenant's warrant in the city and ainſty for that purpoſe. The body of the *Scotch* king, ſlain in that fight, was brought to *York*, expoſed to publick view; and kept there by the earl till the king's return from *France*, and then carried and preſented to him at *Richmond* (*i*). A. 1513.

Many years now paſſed without any materials for our hiſtory; but about the year 1536. the innovations in religion cauſed ſeveral inſurrections and commotions in *England*, eſpecially in the northern parts; amongſt which a conſpiracy was carried on by the lord *Darcy*, *Robert Aſk*, Eſq; Sir *Robert Conſtable*, Sir *John Bulmer* and his wife, Sir *Thomas Piercy*, brother to the earl of *Northumberland*, Sir *Stephen Hamilton*, *Nicholas Tempeſt*, *William Lumley*, Eſqrs. Theſe men at the head of forty thouſand *prieſts*, *peaſants* and *labourers*, declared by their proclamation, ſolemnly made, that this their riſing and commotion, ſhould extend no farther than only to the maintenance and defence of the faith of *Chriſt*, and deliverance of *holy church* ſore decayed and oppreſſed; and alſo for the furtherance as well of private as publick matters in the realm, in regard to the welfare of the king's poor ſubjects (*k*).

This inſurrection was ſtyled, by the ring-leaders of it, the **pilgrimage of grace**; and under that ſpecious pretence they kept together ſome time, and committed ſeveral outrages. The king ſent an army againſt them with a proclamation for a general pardon; which had that effect as to diſperſe the crowd, and the heads of the revolters were taken. Moſt of them, with the abbots of *Fountains*, *Jervaux* and *Rivaulx*, the prior of *Burlington*, were executed at *Tyburn*. Sir *Robert Conſtable* was hanged in chains over *Beverley-gate* at *Hull*; and *Robert Aſk*, who was the principal of them all, had the ſame ſuſpenſion on a tower, I ſuppoſe *Clifford*'s tower, at *York*. A. 1537.

Several inſurrections ſucceeded this in the north; it ſeems they took the change in religion much worſe then in the ſouthern parts of the kingdom, and made ſeveral ſmart ſtruggles againſt it. All being at length pretty quiet, the king thought it policy to go a progreſs amongſt them and receive their ſubmiſſion in perſon.

(*l*) In the month of *Auguſt* king *Henry* began his progreſs to the city of *York*; where in a rebellion this very year Sir *John Nevil* knight, and ten perſons more were taken and executed. The king paſſed through *Lincolnſhire*, where was made to him humble ſubmiſſion by the temporality, confeſſing their faults and thanking him for his pardon. The town of *Stamford* preſented him with twenty pounds; the city of *Lincoln* forty pounds; *Boſton* fifty pounds; that part of the county called *Lindſey* gave three hundred pounds; and *Keſtern*, with the church at *Lincoln*, fifty pounds more. At his entrance into *Yorkſhire* he was met by two hundred gentlemen of the ſame county, in velvet coats and ſuitable accoutrements; with four thouſand tall yeomen, ſay my authors, and ſervants well horſed. A. 1541.

(*i*) The body of this great king, who died valiantly fighting, was by king *Henry*'s orders firſt carried to the *Charter-houſe*, from thence to *Sheen*, a monaſtery in *Surrey*; where, ſays *Stowe*, it remained for a time in what order I am not certain. But ſince the diſſolution of the abbies in the reign of *Edward* VI. *Henry Grey* then du\c of *Su ff.lk* keeping houſe there, I have been ſhewed, adds he, the ſame body as was affirmed, lapped in lead, thrown into an old waſte room, amongſt old timber, ſtone, lead, and other rubbiſh. *Stowe*. A ſtrange monument of human inſtability.

(*k*) *Hollingſhead*'s chron.

(*l*) Idem *Stowe*, &c.

Theſe

A. 1541. These on their knees made submission to his majesty by the mouth of Sir *Robert Bowes*, and presented him with nine hundred pounds. On *Barnesdale* the archbishop of *York*, with three hundred of his clergy and more, met the king, and making a like submission, gave him six hundred pounds. From thence this great king, gallantly attended, came to the city of *York*, were he was as magnificently received as the city's present condition could shew. All due submission made, the lord-mayor presented his majesty with one hundred pounds; as did the mayors of *Newcastle* and *Hull* who came to *York* to meet him. It was at this time and in this city, says *Speed*, that *Henry* had proposed a meeting betwixt the king of *Scots* and him, in order to settle a firm peace betwixt the two kingdoms. Which meeting, though at first agreed to, yet, was afterwards withstood by the *Scotch* nobility, misdoubting *Henry*'s sincerity. He stayed in *York* twelve days, from thence he went to *Hull*; and so crossing the *Humber*, returned through *Lincolnshire* into the south.

A 1546. Died *Henry* VIII. with the terrible character of neither *sparing man in his anger*, nor *woman in his lust* throughout his whole reign. The occurrences of it as to civil affairs, as may may be noted, have been very little to my purpose; but, in church history, a great deal of extraordinary matter falls in my way which I leave to more proper places. His only son succeeded him by the name of *Edward* the sixth, being then just nine years old.

A. 1548. (n) In the second year of this king's reign a small insurrection began in these parts at *Seamour* near *Scarborough*. The principal raisers of this sedition were very inconsiderable fellows to have their names remembered in history. *William Ambler* of *East-Haslerton*, yeoman, *Thomas Dale* parish-clerk of *Seamour*, and one *Stevenson* of the same, rose upon the old topick of reforming abuses crept into religion, and set the beacon on fire at *Staxton* in the night, and so gathered together a rude rout to the number of three thousand. A party of this rabble, says my author, went to Mr. *White*'s house and took him and *Clapton* his wife's brother, one (o) *Savage* a merchant of *York*, and *Berry* a servant to Sir *Walter Mildmay*, out of their beds, and carried them upon the wolds near *Seamour*, and there murdered them, and left their bodies stark naked for the crows to feed on. The lord president sent out a detachment against them from *York*, and a general pardon to all that would immediately submit; most of them dispersed upon this, but *Ambler* and the abovenamed rebels refused the mercy. They were soon taken, brought to *York*, and executed *September* 21, 1549. Along with whom suffered *Henry Barton*, *John Dale*, *Robert Wright*, *William Peacock*, *Wetherell* and *Buttery*, all busy stirrers in this sedition.

A. 1551. On the 15th of *April* began that terrible contagious distemper the *sweating sickness* in *England*. A disease never heard of before nor since in the whole world. To be a little particular in the account of this strange contagion, whose effects were severely felt in our city, and because it may very well serve to fill up a large gap in our annals, I presume may not be unacceptable to the reader.

(p) This plague first shewed itself at *Shrewsbury*, in *April* aforesaid, but had not ceased in the north of *England* till the end of *September* following. It broke out in *London* in *July*, and was so violent that in the very first week in swept off eight hundred persons. People in the best state of health, as indeed is usual in other contagions, were the most liable to be seized by it; and at first was certain death to them in twenty four hours time. This sudden and severe attack did so terrify people of all sorts, that those who could any ways afford it left the kingdom upon it. But, what is almost incredible, the contagion followed them, and them only; for at *Antwerp* and several other towns in *Flanders*, where the *English* had retired to, and were mixed with divers other nations, not one but they were infected with it. The manner of its first seizing a person was with a sudden chilness, then succeeded a violent sweat, which upon the admission of the least cold immediately the chilness came on and death. Sleep at first was mortal in it, for they usually swooned away, or else died upon waking, if they slept but half a quarter of an hour. *Stowe* instances the quick fatality of this disease by seven housholders, who all supped chearfully together over night, but before eight the next morning six of them were dead. Few that were taken with full stomachs escaped. No physical regimen did any service; except keeping moderately close, with some air and a little warm drink, as posset-drink or the like, for thirty hours together, and then the danger was past, if you did not go too suddenly into the cold. This disease going clear through the kingdom, and affecting none but our natives abroad made the nation begin to repent and give alms, and remember *God*, says *Hollingshead*; from whom that plague might well seem to be sent; but as the contagion in time ceased, so our devotion soon after decayed. How many died in this city of this strange distemper is not remarked; but we are told, in Mr. *Hildyard*'s collections, that this year there was a great plague in *York*.

The young king *Edward* was taken ill of a violent cold in *January*, which ended in a consumption, whereof he died on the 6th of *July* following; in the sixteenth year of his age, and in the seventh year of his reign. He was succeeded by

(n) *Stowe*'s chron.

(o) I take this man to be *Richard Savage*, who was sheriff of *York anno* 1540. Vid. cat.

(p) *Hollingshead*, *Stowe*.

Mary

Mary the eldest daughter of king *Henry* VIII. by *Catherine* of *Spain*. In the short reign of this queen I have nothing to my purpose to be inserted here. Our historians have shewn her a woman of bloody and cruel disposition, but our city bears no manner of testimony of it; for not one execution either for treason or religion was performed in it during her administration; at least, the copious Mr. *Fox* is silent as to any such matter. A. 1553.

(*q*) A brother historian of mine has fetched a *king of Muscovy*, as he styles him, to *York*. I confess it a little surprized me, because I thought the late *Czar Peter*, had been the very first of his family, that ever ventured out of his own country, at least so long and so hazardous a voyage. But upon search into Mr. *Stowe*'s annals I find the *man* has been taken for the *master*. A. 1557.

Anno 1556, says *Stowe*, an ambassador from the high and mighty *Evan Vasiliwisch* emperor of all *Russia*, &c. by name *Osep Napea* was sent to the famous and excellent princes *Philip* and *Mary*, king and queen of *England*, with presents in order to establish a commerce betwixt the two nations. It seems the ship where the ambassador was, being driven from the rest by stress of weather, was tossed upon the seas four months; and at length was shipwrecked on the coast of *Scotland*; his *Russian* excellency and some few others only saved. As soon as it was known in *London* the fate of their ship, and that the ambassador was in safety, the merchants procured letters from queen *Mary* to the queen *dowager* of *Scotland*, for his kind entertainment there and safe conduct up to *London*. In his journey from north to south he came to *York*, where a strange sight he must be, being the first of his country ever seen in *England*.

Queen *Mary* died and was succeeded by *Elizabeth*, another daughter of king *Henry* by *Anna Bullein*. A. 1558.

(*r*) A bold conspiracy was set on foot by *Thomas Piercy*, earl of *Northumberland* and others against this queen. The rebellion began in the north, and was afterwards strengthned by the coming in of *Charles Nevil* earl of *Westmorland* with others. Their design was to have seized the earl of *Sussex* the queen's lieutenant of the north, at the house he then lived in, I suppose the archbishop's palace, in *Cawood*; but, being prevented, the affair was let drop to another opportunity. Soon after the earl of *Northumberland*'s designs being known at court, he was sent for by special messengers to appear there. These had well nigh surprised him in his bed at his manor of *Topliff*, but by a stratagem he escaped. After this the two earls threw off all disguise, raised forces, and published their intentions, which were no less, than to restore the *catholick religion*, and to advance *Mary* queen of *Scots* to the *English* throne. In the heat of this zeal they hastened to *Durham* with their army; and forthwith went to the cathedral, where they tore and destroyed all the bibles, communion books, &c. that they could meet with. The same night they marched to *Branspeth*; the next day to *Darlington*; where, says *Hollingshead*, a contemporary, and bitter enemy to them, they *lewdly heard mass, and besprinkled all their army with holy water*. Their forces increasing they marched from thence to *Richmond*, then to *Ripon*, where they again had mass said in the cathedral. It was here, to give the greater sanction to their cause, that they had a cross with a banner, painted with the five wounds of our saviour, born before them. Their standard-bearer was one *Richard Norton*; whom *Speed* and *Hollingshead* call *old Norton*. The same night they marched on to *Burroughbridge*, and the next day to *Wetherby*; on which day at night a party of them entered *Tadcaster*, and took two hundred footmen, chasing their leaders who were conducting them to the earl of *Sussex* at *York*. The day following the rebels mustered on *Clifford-moor*, where their numbers amounted to sixteen hundred horse and four thousand foot. With these forces their intention was to march directly to besiege *York*; but judging themselves, I suppose, yet too weak, they altered their rout and retired back into the *bishoprick* of *Durham*, in order to lay siege to *Bernard-castle*. This castle, though fiercely assailed, was valiantly defended against their whole army, the space of eleven days, by Sir *George Bowes*, and *Robert Bowes* his brother. Being greatly distressed, Sir *George* capitulated and delivered the castle to them on composition, to march out with bag and baggage, armour, munition, &c. which he and his garrison forthwith did towards *York*. A. 1569.

At this city the earl of *Sussex* was drawing forces together in order to quash this rebellion; and having raised five thousand effective men, the lord lieutenant accompanied with the earl of *Rutland* his lieutenant, the lord *Hunsden* general of the horse, *William* lord *Evers* who had the command of the rear, Sir *Ralph Sadler* treasurer, all marched from *York* on *Sunday December* 11, in order to fight the rebels. On the 12th they halted at *Sezay*, and Sir *George Bowes* from *Bernard's-castle* meeting them, the lord president made him marshal of the army. From hence they marched to *Northallerton*, *Smeeton*, *Croft-bridge*, and so on to *Aukland*; at whose, so near, approach the rebells thought fit to retire to *Hexham*. Their stay there was not long, for upon a report that the queen had another great army marching towards them under the command of the earl of *Warwick* and lord *Clinton*, the two earls, their generals, found it was dangerous to stay, and therefore fled into *Scotland*,

(*q*) Lawyer *Hildyard*'s antiq. of *York*.

(*r*) *Speed*'s chron.

A. 1569. leaving their miserable army to shift for themselves; who being thus deserted by their leaders dispersed several ways, but were almost all killed or taken by the queen's army and the country people. Of those that were taken were executed at *Durham* to the number of sixty six, constables and such fellows, for I find none of any note here except an alderman named *Struther*, and a priest called parson *Plumtree*. Sir *George Bowes* had it now in his power to glut his revenge, which he did to the purpose; my author (*s*) says, he had it from himself, that he caused some of them to be executed in every market town, and every publick place, from *Newcastle* to *Wetherby*; a country sixty miles long, and forty broad, which must needs destroy great numbers of these wretches.]

A. 1570. On *Good-Friday*, *March* 27, *Simon Digby* of *Askew*, *John Fulthorpe* of *Iselbeck* in this county, esqrs. *Robert Pennyman* of *Stoxley*, *Thomas Bishop*, the younger, of *Pocklington* gentlemen, were drawn from the castle of *York* to the place of execution, called **Knaresmire**, and there hanged, headed and quartered. Their four heads were set up on the four principal gates of the city, with four of their quarters. The other quarters were set up in diverse places in the country (*t*).

The two earls being fled into *Scotland*, the earl of *Westmorland* found means soon after to get into *Flanders*, where, according to *Speed*'s charitable insinuation, he died miserably eaten up with the *pox*. The other unfortunate nobleman, having been forced to live sculking some time amongst the *robbing borderers*, was at length found out and betrayed by a person he had very much obliged in like circumstances, the earl of *Moreton* (*u*) then vice-roy of *Scotland*, who delivered him to the lord *Hunsdon* governour of *Berwick*, and being brought to *York*, having been before attainted by parliament, he was on the 22d of *August* beheaded on a scaffold set up for that purpose in the *Pavement*; his head was set on a high poll on
A. 1572. *Micklegate-bar* (*x*); but his body was buried in *Crux-church* by two of his servants; where he now lies without any memorial. He died, says *Speed*, *avowing the pope's supremacy, denying subjection to the queen, affirming the land to be in a schism, and her obedient subjects no better than hereticks.*

This was the last open attempt made to restore the *Roman* catholick religion in this kingdom; which might have given *Elizabeth* much more trouble to quell, had the conspiracy been strengthned by the promised aid from *Rome*. But wanting the sinews of war, money, *an hundred thousand pounds from the apostolical chamber*; religion itself was too weak for the overthrow of so mighty a queen; established in the throne of her ancestors, and held there, by the deepest policy in herself, as well as the more general inclinations of her subjects.

A. 1602. She finished the course of a long, prosperous and truly glorious reign, without any more occurrences in it for my purpose. And died at her manor of *Richmond* on *Thursday* (*y*) *March* 22, after a reign of forty four years, five months, and odd days.

Immediately, upon *Elizabeth*'s demise, *James* VI. king of *Scotland*, son to the late queen *Mary* of that kingdom, and grandson to that princess, whom we received with so much honour and respect in this city some years before, was proclaimed king of *England*, &c. in *London*. But notwithstanding the speedy and publick notice given of the queen's death, together with the proclamation of the immediate and undoubted lawfull successor to the *English* crown and kingdom, says the continuator of *Stowe*'s annals, yet the news of it reached not the city of *York*, only one hundred and fifty miles distant, untill *Sunday March* 27. Neither, adds my author, did the lord-mayor and aldermen of *York* give full credit to the report then; though they had received it from the lord *Burleigh*, then lord president of the council in the north and lord lieutenant of *Yorkshire*. *Robert Water* lord-mayor of *York*, with the aldermen his brethren, had prepared themselves to have made proclamation in their chief market-place of the death of the queen, and the present right of king *James* to the succession that *Sunday* morning, yet such was their doubt of the truth of the report that they stopped proceedings, till they had sent the recorder with *Thomas Herbert* and *Robert Askwith* aldermen to the lord president to know what certainty his lordship had of it. The lord president answered them that he had no other intelligence, but only from a secret friend at court, whom he believed. But whilst they were thus in the house of the lord president, a gentleman of his own arrived, with a packet of letters from the nobility and privy counsellors, declaring the queen's death, and the proclamation of the king by them and the lord-mayor of *London*. Then instantly the lord-mayor of *York* and his brethren having received the proclamation in print, proclaimed the king of *Scots* their true and lawful king; that is to say, *James by the grace of God king of* England, Scotland, France, *and* Ireland, *defender*, &c. in all the publick places of the city with all duty, love, integrity and joyful acclamations.

(*s*) *Stowe*.

(*t*) Idem.

(*u*) This was, says *Dugdale*, in order to curry favour with *Elizabeth*, that she might deliver to him *Mary* queen of *Scots*, then prisoner in *England*. *Dug. Bar.*

(*x*) Where it continued for two years, but was afterwards stoln from thence.

(*y*) This day of the week was fatal to king *Henry* VIII, and all his posterity; himself, his son *Edward*, his daughters *Mary*, and *Elizabeth*, having made *Thursday* remarkable by their *exits* on it. *Stowe.*

Maſter *Edmund Howes*, the continuator of *Stowe*'s hiſtory, ſeems, by the particularity of this affair, which I have taken from him, to have been either a native or an inhabitant of this city, or one, at leaſt, that paid a great regard to the affairs of it. The reader will the more readily come into my conjecture, when he ſees the account this author gives of king *James*'s reception into *York*, in his firſt progreſs from *Edinborough* to *London*; which I ſhall beg leave to give in his own words. A. 1603.

" On the fifteenth of *April* his majeſty ſet forwards from *Durham* towards *Yorke*, his " traine ſtill increaſing, by the numbers of gentlemen from the ſouth parts, that came to " offer him fealty: whoſe love although he greatly tendered, yet did their multitudes ſo " oppreſs the country, and made proviſion ſo dear, that he was fain to publiſh an inhibi- " tion againſt the inordinate and daily acceſs of the people coming, that many were ſtopped " in their way.

" The high ſheriffe of *Yorkſhire* very well accompanied attended his majeſty to maſter " *Inglebyes* beſide *Topcliffe*; being about ſixteen miles from *Walworth*, where the king had " lain the night before; who with all joy and humility received his majeſty, and he reſted " there that night.

" The lord-mayor and aldermen of *Yorke*, upon certayne knowledge of the king's jour- " ney into *England*, with all diligence conſulted what was fitteſt to be done for the receiving " and entertayning ſo mighty and gracious a ſoveraygne as well within the city, as at the " outmoſt bounds and limits thereof: as alſo what further ſervice or duteous reſpect they " ought to ſhew his majeſty uppon ſo good and memorable occaſion as now was offered " unto them: and thereupon they ſent *Robert Aſkwith* alderman unto *Newcaſtle*, and there " in the behalfe of the lord-mayor and citizens of *Yorke*, to make tender of their zealous " love and dutie, for the which his majeſtie gave them heartie thankes.

" And uppon *Saturday* the 16th of *April*, *John Robinſon* and *George Buck* ſheriffes of " *Yorke*, with their white roddes, being accompanyed with an hundreth cittizens, and three- " ſcore other eſquiers, gentlemen and others, the moſt ſubſtantial perſons; being all well " mounted, they received the king at the eaſt-end of *Skip-bridge*, which was the utmoſt " boundes of the libertyes of the cittie of *Yorke*; and there kneeling, the ſheriffes delivered " their white roddes unto the king with acknowledgement of their love and allegiance unto " his majeſtie, for the which the king, with cheerfull countenance, thanked them and gave " them their roddes agayne; the which they carried all the way up-right in their handes " ryding all the way next before the ſergeants at armes.

" And before the king came to the cittie, his majeſtie had ſent Syr *Thomas Challenor* to " the lord-major and aldermen, to knowe who formerlie had borne the ſworde before the " kinges of *England* at their coming to *Yorke*; and to whome of right that office for that " tyme appertayned; becauſe it had been anciently performed by the earles of *Cumberland*; " as hereditary to that houſe, but was now chalenged by the lord *preſident* of the north for " the time being as proper to his place: but uppon due ſearch and examination it was " agreed, that the honour to bear the ſworde before the king in *Yorke*, belonged unto *George* " earl of *Cumberland*, who all the while the king was in *Yorke* bare the ſworde, for ſo the " king willed, and for that purpoſe ſent Syr *Thomas Challener* agayne to the lord-mayor, " and the lord-major bare the great mace of the cittie going alwayes on the lefte hande of " the earle.

" And when the king came to the cittie, which was well prepared to give his highneſs " and his royal trayne entertainement, then the lord-major with the twelve aldermen in " their ſcarlett robes, and the foure and twenty in crimoſin gownes, accompanyed with " many others of the graveſt menne, met the king at *Micklegate-bar*, his majeſty going " betweene the duke of *Linneox* and the lord *Hume*, and when the king came near to the " ſcaffold where the lord-major with the recorder, the twelve aldermen and the foure and " twentie all kneeling, the lord-major ſaid, *moſt high and mightie prince, I and my bretbren* " *do moſt heartilie wellcome your majeſtie to your highneſs cittie, and in token of our duties, I de-* " *liver unto your majeſtie all my authoritie of this your highneſs cittie*, and then roſe uppe and " kiſſed the ſword and delivered it into the kinges hand, and the king gave it to the duke " of *Linneox*, who according to the kinges appoyntment delivered it unto the earle of " *Cumberland* to beare it before his majeſtie.

" The lord-major alſo delivered up the keyes of the cittie, the which the lord *Hume* " received and carried them to the manor: and when the recorder had ended his grave ora- " tion in behalfe of the cittie, then the lord-major, as the king commanded, tooke horſe " and bare the cittie mace ryding on the lefte hande of the earle of *Cumberland*, who bare " the ſword of the cittie, and ſo attended his majeſtie to St. *Peter*'s church, and was there " royaly received by the deanes, prebends, and the whole quyer of ſinging menne of that " cathedral church in their richeſt coapes. At the entrance into the church, the deane " made a learned oration in *Latine*, which ended the king aſcended the quyer: the canapa " was ſupported by ſix lords, and was placed in a throne prepared for his majeſtie, and " during divine ſervice there came three ſergeantes at armes with their maces preſſing to " ſtand by the throne; but the earl of *Cumberland* put them downe, ſaying, that place for " that tyme belonged to him and the lord-major, and not to them.

" Divine

A. 1603. "Divine service being ended, the king returned in the same royal manner he came: the "canapa being carryed over him unto the mannor of St. *Maryes*, where the lord *Burleigh* "and councel gave their attendance, and received his majestie, where doctor *Bennet* having "ended his eloquent oration, the king went into his chamber, the sworde and mace being "there borne by the earle and lord-mayor, who left the sworde and mace there that "night; and when the lord-major was to depart, the lord *Hume* delivered him agayne the "keyes of the cittie.

"The next day being *Sunday* the 17th of *April*, 1603, the lord-major with the re-"corder, the aldermen and sheriffes, and the twentie foure with all their chiefe officers, "and the preacher of the cittie and towne-clerk, in very comely order went unto the "manor; of whome so soon as the king hadde knowledge of their comming, willed that "so many of them as the roome would permitte should come into the privie chamber, "where the lord-major presented his majestie with a fayre cuppe, with a cover of silver "and gilt, weighing seventie and three ounces, and in the same two hundreth angells of "gold: and the lord-major sayde, *most high and mightie prince, I and my brethren and all* "*the whole communaltie of this your highnesse cittie, present unto your most excellent majestie this* "*cuppe and golde, in token of the dutifull affection wee beare your highnesse in our heartes, most* "*humblie beseeching your highnesse favourable acceptaunce thereof, and your most gracious favour* "*to this your highnesse cittie of* Yorke; the which his majestie gratiously accepted and saide "unto them, *God will bless you the better, for your good will towards your king*. The lord-"major humbly besought the king to dine with him uppon the next *Tuesdaie*: the king "answered, he should ride thence before that tyme, but he would break his fast with him "in the next morning.

"This *Sundaie* the king went to the minster and heard a sermon made by the deane (z), "who was byshoppe of *Limericke* in *Ireland*, the lord-major, aldermen and sheriffes, and "foure and twenty attended upon the king, the earle still bearing the sword, the lord-"major the mace, and the sheriffs bearing up their roddes, as well within the church, "as in the streets, marching before the king unto the mannor; the next daye being *Mon-"daie*, at nine a clock the lord-major came to the mannor, being accompanyed and at-"tended by the recorder, the aldermen, and foure and twentie and others, and attended "there: and at tenne of the clock the king, with his royal traine, went to the lord-ma-"jor's house and there dined; after dinner the king walked to the deanes-house, and was "there entertained with a banquette; at the deanerie the king took horse, and passed "through the cittie forth at *Micklegate* towards *Grimstone*, the house of sir *Edward Stan-"hope*, the earle of *Cumberlande* and the lord-major beareing the sword and mace before "the king untill they came unto the house of St. *Kathren*, at which place the earl said "*is it your majesties pleasure that I deliver the sword agayne unto my lord-maior, for he* "*is now at the utmost partes of the liberties of this cittie*, then the king willed the earle "to deliver the major his sworde againe: then the major alighted from his horse and kneel-"ing, tooke his leave of the king, and the king pulling off his glove, tooke the major "by the hande and gave him thankes, and so rode towards *Grimstone*, being attended by "the shrieffes to the midell of *Tadcaster-bridge*, being the utmost boundes of their liber-"ties. The next day the lord-major, according as he was commanded by a nobleman, "came the next morning unto the court at *Grimstone*, accompanyed with the recorder and "foure of his brethren, *viz. W. Robinson, James Birkbie, William Greenburie*, and *Robert* "*Askwith*, and certain chiefe officers of the cittie, and when his majestie understood of "their comming, he willed that the major with master *Robinson* and master *Birkbie* should "be brought up into his bed-chamber, and the king said, *my lord-major, our meaning* "*was to have bestowed a knighthood upon you in your own house, but the companie, being so* "*great we rather thought it good to have you here*, and then his majestie knighted the lord-"major (a), for which honour the lord-major gave his majestie most humble and heartie "thankes and returned.

This was the first reception king *James* met with in the city of *York* from the citizens; and it was here also, that all the lords of the council did attend his majesty; and all preparation was made that he might appear, says an historian, in that northern metropolis like a king of *England*, and take that state on him which was not known in *Scotland* (b). The king seemed so much pleased with the duty and honours paid him by the lord mayor and citizens, that at dinner with them he expressed himself much in favour of the city, seemed concerned that their river was in so bad a condition, and said *it should be made more navigable*; *and that he himself would come and be a burgess among them* (c).

We come next to the queen's reception into *York*, in her journey to *London* from *Edenborough*; the same annalist, I have before quoted, writes thus of this affair:

"The queen, says he, being in all respects prepared, accompanyed, and attended as was "meet for soe greate a princesse, being likewise accompanyed with her two eldeste chil-"deren, that is to say, prince *Harry* and the lady *Elizabeth*, they made a happy journey from

(z) Dr. *Thornborough*.
(a) Sir *Robert Water*.
(b) Hist. of the court of king *James* I.
(c) *Hildyard's* ant. of *York*.

"*Scotland*

" *Scotland* to *England*, and were in all places wheresoever they arrived most joyfully received " and entertained in as loving, duteous and honourable a manner as all cities, townes, and " particularly knyghtes and gentlemen had formerlie done to the kinges most excellent ma- " jestie; which for brevities sake I here omit. And for a tast for all will only speak briefly " of their coming to the cittie of *Yorke*, where the lord mayor, aldermen and cittizens, at- " tending their coming at the outmost boundes of their liberties, with all magnificence " brought the queen, the prince, and the lady *Elizabeth* unto the cittie of *York* the 11th of " *June*: where they reposed themselves certain daies, in which space the cittie spared not " for any coste to give them royal entertainment, and presented them with several giftes as " true signes of their zealous love and duty: the queen came thither on *Whitsun* eve, and " upon *Wednesday* following, the queen with the prince the lady *Elizabeth* rode from *York* " to *Grimstone*, *&c*.

The presents that were bestowed on this occasion, I find in an old Manuscript *(d)*, were first, a large silver cup with a cover double gilt weighing forty eight ounces to the queen, with fourscore angells of gold included in it. To the prince was presented a silver cup with a cover double gilt weight twenty ounces, and twenty pounds in gold. And lastly to the princess *Elizabeth* a purse of twenty angells of gold.

The same year a great pestilence began in *London*, of which died in twelve months 30578 persons.

The next year *London* was intirely free from this plague, but the rest of the kingdom suffered extreamly by it; and at *York* died of it to the number of 3512 persons. A number would make a great gap in its present inhabitants. The markets were all cried down; the lord president's courts adjourned to *Ripon* and *Durham*; many of the citizens left their houses. The infected were sent to *Hob-more* and *Horsefair*, where booths were erected for them of boards. The minster and minster-yard were close shut up *(e)*. This is the last contagion this city has been visited with. *Et avertat Deus in aeternum.* A. 1604.

A most unhappy and melancholy accident fell out in an honourable and ancient family of this county, which because I bear a great regard for a very worthy descendant of that house, I omit the particulars. The miserable actor of it stood mute at his tryal in *York*, and was therefore adjudged to be pressed to death, which was accordingly executed on him *Aug.* 5. the same year at the castle of *York*. A. 1605.

About *Martinmass* began an extream frost; the river *Ouze* was wholly frozen up, so hard that you might have passed with cart and carriage as well as upon firm ground. Many sports were practised on the ice; as shooting at eleven score, says my ancient *(f)* authority, bowling, playing at football, cudgels, *&c*. And a horse-race was run from the tower at S. *Mary-gate-end*, along and under the great arch of the bridge, to the *Crain* at *Skelder-gate* postern. A. 1607.

(g) December 3. the honourable sir *John Sheffield*, with his brothers sir *Edmond* and Mr. *Philip Sheffield*, sons to the lord *Sheffield* lord president of the north, in passing *Whitgift* ferry, were drowned with all their servants, and none of their bodies ever found. A. 1614.

(h) On the 16th of *January* the same year it began to snow and freeze, and so by intervals snowing without any thaw till the 7th of *March* following; at which time was such a heavy snow upon the earth as was not remembered by any man then living. It pleased God that at the thaw fell very little rain, nevertheless the flood was so great, that the *Ouze* ran down *Northstreet* and *Skeldergate* with such violence as to force all the inhabitants of those streets to leave their houses. This inundation chanced to happen in the assize week, *John Armitage* esquire, being then high-sheriff of *Yorkshire*. Business was hereby much obstructed; at *Ouse bridge* end were four boats continually employed in carrying people cross the river; the like in *Walmgate* cross the *Foss*. Ten days this inundation continued at the height and many bridges were driven down by it in the country, and much land overflown. After this storm, says my manuscript, followed such fair and dry weather, that in *April* the ground was as dusty as in any time of summer. This drought continued till the 20th of *August* following without any rain at all; and made such a scarcity of *hay*, *beans* and *barley*, that the former was sold at *York* for 30*s.* and 40*s.* a wayne load; and at *Leeds* for four pounds.

On the 10th of *August* came king *James* to *York*, in his progress towards *Scotland*, accompanied with many earls, barons, knights, esquires, both *Scotch* and *English (i)*. The sheriffs of the city, clad in their scarlet gowns, attended with one hundred young citizens on horseback in suitable habits, met the king on *Tadcaster* bridge, and carried their white rods before him till they came at *Micklegate-bar*. Here the lord-mayor, aldermen, and twenty four with many other citizens, standing on the north-side within the rails, did welcome his majesty to his city of *York*. The lord-mayor on his knees presented the sword with all the keys of the gates and posterns, and likewise presented a standing cup with a cover of silver double gilt, which cost 30*l.* 5*s.* 7*d*; a purse of 3*l.* price, with one hundred double sovereigns in it; and, adds my authority, made a very *worthy* and *witty speech* at the delivery of A. 1617.

(d) *Ex MS. penes me.*
(e) *Ex eodem.*
(f) *Ex eodem.*
(g) *Ex eodem.*
(h) *Ex eodem.*
(i) *Ex eodem MS.*

A. 1617. each particular to the king. After him serjeant *Hutton*, recorder, made a long oration; which ended, the king delivered the city's sword to the earl of *Cumberland*, the city's *chief captain*, as he is here called, who carried it, and the lord-mayor the mace before his majesty. On the top of *Ouse-bridge* another speech was made to the king by one *Sands Percvine*, a *London* poet, concerning the cutting of the river, and making it more navigable. From thence his majesty rode to the minster, where he heard divine service, and so to the manor where he kept his court.

The next day he dined with the lord *Sheffield*, lord president, at sir *George Young*'s house in the minster yard, where he lay during the king's abode at the manor. After dinner and banquet, he made eight knights, walked into the cathedral, viewed the chapter-house and church, which he much commended for its elegant workmanship.

The day after his majesty rode in his coach through the city with all his train to *Bishopsthorp* where he dined with *Toby Mathew* archbishop.

On the 13th being *Sunday*, his majesty went to the cathedral, where the archbishop preached a learned sermon before him. After sermon ended he touched about seventy persons for the *King's-evil*. This day he dined with the lord-mayor with his whole court; after dinner he knighted *(k)* the lord-mayor and serjeant *(l) Hutton* the recorder.

On *Monday* the king rode to *Sheriff-hutton* Park.

On *Tuesday August* 15. Dr. *Hodgson* chancellor of the church and chaplain to his majesty preached before him at the manor. After sermon the king took coach in the manor-yard, where the lord-mayor, aldermen, and sheriffs took their leaves of his majesty, who went that night to *Ripon*.

My manuscript informs me, that at this time the city was charged with 117*l.* in fees to the king's officers.

A. 1625. Died king *James*, and was succeeded by *Charles* his second son, the eldest, *Henry*, dying before the father.

We now enter upon a busy reign indeed, unfortunate, in all respects, both to prince and people. The prince's prerogative and the people's rights here clashed so furiously, that in the end they were both lost in anarchy and confusion. Tyranny and aiming at absolute power, the topicks the malecontents threw against king *Charles*'s government, was by the just judgment of *God*, in the person of *Cromwell*, sufficiently retorted.

What share our city bore, in these home-bred divisions, is very considerable; and since not handed down, so distinctly as it ought, by any historian, I have taken pains to collect from manuscripts, records, and histories, what I found worthy notice; and shall beg leave to be very particular in the recital. The reader will find that our city's loyalty was, in an especial manner, exemplified to its injured sovereign, quite through these dreadful scenes of blood and misery; and deserves a more lasting memorial than my pen can bestow upon it; my endeavour as much as possible is, without partiality, to let the times speak for themselves.

A. 1633. King *Charles* in a peaceable progress for *Scotland* came to *York*, *May* 24. He was met on *Tadcaster-bridge* by the sheriffs with six score liveries, and conducted by them to the city. The lord-mayor, recorder and aldermen, standing within *Micklegate-bar*, on a scaffold erected for that purpose, saluted the king at his entrance, and the lord-mayor on his knees delivered up the keys of the city in a blue silk string, as also the sword and mace, and delivered himself in the following manner *(m)*.

Most high and mighty monarch,

"Our most gracious and ever renowned sovereign, whose person is the image of the glo-
"rious *God*, whose courses are paths of piety and religion, whose wisdom and goodness is
"the peaceable government of this your common-wealth; ever happy be the day of your
"birth, and thrice happy be the day that brings your gracious majesty hither to this your
"ancient and famous city of *York*; whose royal presence as it does abundantly satisfy our
"expectations, so doth it fill the hearts of us your humble subjects and citizens, with
"such overflowing of consolations, as that our tongues would become unfit messengers of
"our hearts, should they endeavour to express them.

"And, in humble testimony of our obedience, we render unto you all power with the
"sword of justice, that it hath pleased your gracious majesty and noble progenitors to have
"honoured the government of this your ancient city withal; rejoicing to return unto you,
"what we have received from you, accounting it our greatest happiness to live under the
"command of him, who is the light of his subjects eyes, the glory and admiration of the
"known world.

"And with the sword, in further testimony of our faith and obedience, we also present
"unto you this mace, with the keys of our city-gates, acknowledging and well assuring our

(k) Sir *Robert Askwith*.
(l) Sir *Richard Hutton* afterwards judge *Hutton*.
(m) *Ex MS.* This harangue from a person who was afterwards a member of that parliament which voted the king's destruction, is a testimony of the great sincerity of the *puritan party*.

" ſelves never to be ſo happy as when we are under your gracious government and pro- A. 1633.
" tection; whoſe ingreſs and ſtaying here with us we humbly deſire may be delightful and " happy unto your further progreſs, and return may be proſperous and ſucceſsful.

" And that it may be ſo, let all true hearted ſubjects ever pray, *vivat rex*, *God* bleſs " king *Charles*, *Amen*, *Amen*.

The recorder of *York*, when the lord-mayor had ended his harangue, addreſs'd himſelf, on his knees, to the king as follows:

(*n*) " *Moſt gracious ſovereign*,

" Your faithful and obedient ſubjects the mayor and commonality of this city, in all " humble manner preſent themſelves and their bounden ſervices to your ſacred majeſty, " which according to precedent cuſtom they humbly preſent by me though every way unfit " to ſpeak in your royal preſence; and therefore I humbly beg your majeſty's favourable " excuſe of my imperfections, and that you will be graciouſly pleaſed to licence me a few " words on the behalf of this your city, which is the metropolitan of theſe parts, ſcituate " towards the middle of this iſland, and equally diſtanced between your two regal cities of " the ſame.

" This city, *dread ſovereign lord*, for antiquity is not inferiour to any other of this realm; " in former time it hath been beautified by the reſidence and courts, of ſome *Roman* empe- " rours, and afterwards of divers kings; enrich'd by trade, and by thoſe means was grea- " ter and more populous than now it is; for of later times trading here decreas'd and that " principally by reaſon of ſome hindrance in the river and the greatneſs of ſhips now in " uſe; for which nevertheleſs this river, by your royal aſſiſtance, might be made ſervicea- " ble; and untill that be done, there is noe hope that this citty will attain its former ſplen- " dour and greatneſs.

" In the mean time we are much ſupported by other means from your royal majeſty, as " by an eminent ſeat of juſtice here continued before the lord preſident and council, to the " great eaſe and benefit of us and all other your ſubjects in theſe parts. Likewiſe of your " munificent charter for confirmation of our ancient liberties with ample addition of divers " more.

" And now that we have an opportune time by your gracious preſence we render to your " excellent majeſty our humbleſt thankfulneſs for theſe royal favours, and together, with " them for all other benefits which we enjoy by your majeſty's religious and juſt govern- " ment, in regard whereof may be truly ſaid of your majeſty in your own perſon as was " ſome time ſaid of the wiſe king, that there is *ſapientia Dei in rege ad faciendam juſti-* " *tiam*.

" But, moſt eſpecially, when we conſider the happy and admired peace wherein we live, " whilſt other nations are full of the miſeries of warrs, as if this ſingular bleſſing was appro- " priated to your majeſty alone, and ſoe derived to us your ſubjects, then we want words " ſufficiently to expreſs our thankfullneſs for ſuch protection; but in your majeſty's own pi- " ous words doe acknowledge that you reign, *Chriſto auſpice*; and we heartily pray almigh- " ty *God* that your ſacred majeſty may long and proſperouſly reign over us, and that your " throne may be eſtabliſhed on you and yours to the world's end with increaſe of all honour " and felicity. *Amen*.

The recorder having ended his oration the king ordered the ſword, mace and keys to be delivered back to the lord-mayor, who mounted on horſeback, being clad in a ſcarlet gown faced with rich furr and carried the mace (*o*) before his majeſty; four footmen in black velvet attending him. The aldermen richly decked and horſed made up the ceremony, riding before the king to the manor.

The next day the king dined with the lord mayor at his houſe in the *pavement* and knighted (*p*) him and the recorder (*q*). The day after he dined with the archbiſhop, and knighted his ſon; and the day following took coach at the manor for *Scotland* (*r*).

King *Charles* was moſt ſumptuouſly entertained in the city at this time; and Mr. *Eachard* remarks two things on that head, firſt, that the good will and loyalty of this, and ſome other corporations, was in a very noble manner ſhewn to their king; as alſo that at this time feaſting to exceſs was introduced into *England*; which, ſays he, has ever ſince been carried on to the great damage of many eſtates and more manners in the kingdom.

The *Scots* having thought fit to rebel, the king came down to *York* in an expedition a- A. 1639. *March* 30.
gainſt them. He was accompanied with moſt of the nobility and general officers of the kingdom. He was met by the ſheriffs at *Tadcaſter* as uſual, and by them conducted to *Mickle-*

(*n*) *Ex eodem MS.*

(*o*) There being none preſent who had right to bear the ſword, I ſuppoſe it carried as in the next ſolemnity.

(*p*) Sir *William Allenſon.*

(*q*) Sir *William Belt.*

(*r*) The preſents at this time were a large ſilver cup and cover, and a purſe of gold to the value of 100 *l.* or more. *MS.*

gate-bar;

A. 1639. *gate-bar*; where the lord-mayor, recorder, aldermen, *&c.* attended him. After delivering up the ſword, mace, and keys, by the lord-mayor, and returning them by the king; the recorder, *Thomas Widdrington* eſquire, addreſſed himſelf to his majeſty, on his knees, as follows (*s*):

" *Moſt gratious and dread ſovereign,*

" Be gratiouſly pleaſed to pardon this ſtay that we the leaſt and meaneſt motes in the fir-" mament of your majeſty's government, ſhould thus dare to cauſe you, our bright and " glorious ſun, to ſtand. Give us leave who are the members of this ancient and decayed " city, to make known unto your majeſty, even our ſun it ſelf, where the ſun now ſtands,

" in the city of *York*;

" which now like an ill drawn picture needs a name; a place ſoe unlike itſelf, that I may " may venture to ſay *Niobe* was never ſoe unlike *Niobe*, never old man ſo unlike himſelf be-" ing young, as is the city of *York* ſoe unlike the city of *York*: heretofore an imperial city, " the place of the life and death of the emperour *Conſtantius Chlorus*, in whoſe grave a burn-" ing lamp was found many centuries of years after. The place honoured with the birth of " *Conſtantine* the great; and with the moſt noble library of *Egbert*.

" I might goe further, but this were only to ſhew or rather ſpeak of antient tombs.

" This city was afterwards twice burned, ſoe that the very aſhes of theſe antiquitys are " not to be found; and if later ſcarrs had not defaced our former glory, what was it truly " in effect of what we now enjoy?

" The births, lives and deaths of Emperours are not ſoe much for the honour of *York*, " as that king *Charles* was once duke of *York*; your very royal aſpect ſurmounts our for-" mer glory, and ſcatters our later clouds.

" It is more honour to us that king *Charles* has given a new life, nativity and being, " by a moſt benign and liberal charter, then that *Conſtantine* the great had his firſt being " here. And as for the lamp found in the grave of *Chlorus*, your majeſty maintains a lamp " of juſtice in this city, which burns more clearly than that of *Chlorus*, and ſhines into five " ſeveral countys, at which each ſubject may light a torch; by the brightneſs whereof he " may ſee his own right, and find and taſt ſome of that ſweet and wholſom manna, here at " his own door, which drops from the influence of your majeſty's moſt juſt and gracious " government. Soe that if the library of *Egbert* was now extant amongſt us, that very idea " of eloquence, which the moſt ſkilfull orator could extract out of it, would not be able to " expreſs what we owe to your majeſty; there being not any acknowledgments anſwerable " to our obligations. For beſides all this,

" The beams and lightnings of thoſe eminent vertues, ſublime gifts and illuminations, " wherewith you are endowed, doe caſt ſoe forcible reflections upon the eyes of all men, " that you fill not only this city, this kingdom, but the whole univerſe with ſplendour. " You have eſtabliſhed your throne on two columns of diamond, piety and juſtice; the one " gives you to *God*, the other gives men to you, and all your ſubjects are moſt happy in " both.

" For our ſelves, *moſt gratious king*, your majeſty's humbleſt and meaneſt ſubjects, obe-" dience the beſt of ſacrifices is the only ſacrifice which we have to offer to your moſt ſacred " majeſty. Yet vouchſafe to believe, *moſt mighty king*, that even our works, ſuch as " they are, ſhall not reſemble thoſe ſacrifices whereout the heart is plucked, and where of all " the head nothing is left but the tongue; our ſacrifices are thoſe of our hearts not of our " tongues.

" *The memory of king* Charles *ſhall ever be ſacred unto us as long as there remains an altar,* " *or that oblation is offered on earth. The moſt devout and fervent prayres of your majeſty's dayly* " *votarys the poor citizens of* York *are, and ever ſhall be, that the ſcepter of king* Charles *may* " *like* Aaron's *rod budd and bloſſom and be an eternal teſtimony againſt all rebells; and our moſt* " *cheerfull and unanimous acclamations are that king* Charles *may long live and triumphantly* " *reign; and that this kingdom may never want a king* Charles *over it.*

This oration ended the lord-mayor mounted on horſeback with his brethren, their horſes in rich furniture; four footmen attending the mayor clad in black velvet with the city's arms, embroidered before and behind them. The lord-mayor carried the mace before the king, and the common ſword-bearer the ſword, but not with the point erect. In this order they marched through the city to the palace.

The country being now up in arms, the trained bands of the city and *Ainſty*, clad in buff-coats, ſcarlet breeches with ſilver lace, ruſſet boots, black caps and feathers to the number of ſix hundred men, ſtood drawn up on the out-ſide *Micklegate-bar*, to receive the king at his entrance, and gave him a handſome volly. And when the king was got to the *manor* they drew up in *Biſhop's-fields*, over againſt it, and performed an exerciſe, where the muſketeers diſcharged four times. On *Sunday*, when the king went to the cathedral, theſe men of arms ſtood rank and file in the minſter-yard for his majeſty to paſs through them.

(*s*) *Ex MS.*

Their whole behaviour soe pleased the king, that he ordered a sum of mony to be distributed amongst them, and gave them thanks in person *(r)*. A. 1639.

On *Sunday* in the afternoon, the king held a council at the manor on the *Scotch* affairs; and as this was the rendezvous of the whole army that was to march against those rebells, the king's time was chiefly taken up with reviewing his troops, which were quartered in the city and the neighbouring market towns.

Upon *Thursday* before *Easter* the king kept his Maunday *(s)* in the cathedral; where the bishop of *Ely* washed the feet of thirty nine poor aged men, in warm water, and dried them with a linnen cloth. Afterwards the bishop of *Winchester* washed them over again in white wine, wiped and kissed them. The king gave to every one of the poor men, a gown, of very good cloth, a holland shirt, new stockings and shoes. Also in one leathern purse every one had twenty pence in money given him, and in another purse thirty nine single pennies being the just age of the king. Lastly each man had a wooden scale full of wine given him, scale and all, a joule of salt fish and a joule of salmon, with a six-penny loaf of bread. This ceremony, says my authority, was performed in the south isle of the minster. Near where the bells hang *(t)*. April 11.

Upon *Good-Friday* the king touched *(u)* for the king's-evil in the minster two hundred persons. Upon *Easter-Sunday* the king received the sacrament at the cathedral. On *Monday* he ordered seventy pound to be given to each of the four wards of the city; to be distributed amongst poor widows. On *Tuesday* and *Wednesday* he touched each day an hundred persons for the evil. At his leisure hours, his usual diversion, during his stay in *York*, was to play at a game called the *Balloon*.

Before the king left *York*, he and his whole court were nobly treated by the lord-mayor *(x)*, whom his majesty knighted, and *Thomas Widderington*, esquire recorder. The florid harangue this last named gentleman made the king at his entrance, is printed in *Rushworth*; except the last paragraph, which containing some warmer expressions of loyalty than are usual to meet with, and by no means suiting his future conduct, the orator, though he spoke them, thought them not fit for the press. I do not object against the strange bombast stile in his speech, because I know it was agreeable to the age he lived in; but his, almost fulsome, flattery, which was that of the *tongue* and not of the *heart*, is an instance, what small regard princes ought to pay to publick speeches, as well as publick addresses. A late ingenious author *(y)* observes, *that kings should not be affected by any oration of this kind; but only regard it as a vain ceremony which they are obliged to suffer, and to which they ought to give little attention.*

To proceed; king *Charles*, after he had staid near a month in *York*, took his journey with his nobility and all his army towards *Scotland*. At his approach the *Scots* submitted, laid down their arms and swore obedience to their sovereign. But the very next year, when the king had disbanded his forces, and thought all quiet; the *Scottish* army under the command of *Al. Lesley*, earl of *Leven*, and the marquis of *Montross* entered *England* in defiance of the most solemn oaths, says Mr. *Eachard*, contrary to their allegiance to their natural king, and in direct opposition to his antient rights and authority over them. This bold attempt put the whole kingdom in an uproar; the *Militia* was raised, and a strong press for soldiers was in all places. Through *York* marched several bodies of light horse, under the command of the earl of *Northumberland*, lord *Conway*, sir *John Digby*, and other leaders as they could collect their forces. These were strong enough to have driven the *Scotch* home again, but by the scandalous neglect of the lord *Conway*, the king's general, they were suffered, after a slight skirmish, to possess themselves of all *Northumberland*, and the

(Margin: April 29. — A. 1640.)

(r) *Ex MS.*

(s) *Ex eodem.* Maunday Thursday *Dies Jovis diem passionis immediatè praecedens.* Minshaw *dictum putat quasi dies* mandati, *quo sc. die Christus eucharistam instituit, et magnum illud mandatum discipulis reliquit, sc. in sacramento illo commemorandi.* Spelman *longè melius deflectit a Fr. G.* Mande, *sportula; quia sc. illo die, rex pauperibus quibus pedes lavat, uberiores eleemosynas distribuit.* Skinner *dict. etym.*

(t) In an old writing given me by my worthy friend the reverend Mr. *Creyk*, I find this more particular account of the ceremony of *Maunday* at *York*, &c.

" *Thursday* before *Easter* 1639.

" The *Maundy* given in *York-minster* for the king by " the bishop of *Winchester* in manner as followeth, to " thirty nine poor men sitting along one by another.

" *First*, the right foot of every of them washed in cold " water by the bishop's pantler, and six pence a piece gi- " ven them in money: *Secondly*, washed again in claret " wyne lukewarme by the bishop's chaplain: *Lastly*, washt " againe and dryed by the bishop himselfe and kist every " tyme.

" 2. To each of them three ells of course holland for a " shirt.

" 3. To each of them a cloth gowne of gray freese.

" 4. To each of them one pair of shoes.

" 5. To each of them a wooden dubler whereon was " a jowle of *old ling*, a jowle of *Salmond*, six *red herrings* " and two loaves of *bread*.

" 6. To each of them a little purse wherin was xx*s*. " in money; and so many single pennies as the king was " years of age, being thirty nine.

" 7. To every of them a little scale of *claret* wyne " which they drank off, and so after a few prayers read the " ceremony ended, and the poor men carried away all " that was given them.

" During the tyme the king touched those that had " the disease called the *evill*, were read these words:

" *They shall lay their hands upon the sick, and they shall " recover.*

" During the tyme the king put about every of their " necks an angel of gold with a white ribben, were read " these words:

" *That light was the true light which lighteth every " man which cometh into the world.*

(u) *Ex eodem.*

(x) Sir *Roger Jaques.*

(y) Voltair *Hist. de* Car. XII. *Roi de* Suede.

A. 1640. bishoprick of *Durham* to the skirts of *Yorkshire*. All which they taxed at eight hundred and fifty pound *per diem*, and loudly threatned that they would be in *York* ere long.

August 23. To put a stop to this bold invasion, the king set out from *London* and came to *York* in three days; accompanied with the lord marquis of *Hamilton* and the duke of *Lenox*; he was received in *York* with the usual gifts, speeches, and ceremonies, which the hurry of the times will not allow me to enlarge upon.

From *York* the king published a proclamation in which he declared, "that he had endeavoured to appease the rebellious courses of his subjects in *Scotland*, who under pretence "of religion had thought to shake off his regal government, and did now take arms and "invade the kingdom of *England*: and therefore he declared that those who had already "entered, or should presume in a warlike manner to enter any part of *England* should be "adjudged and were thereby denounced rebels and traytors against his majesty. However, he added, if they would yet acknowledge their former crimes, crave pardon and "yield obedience for the time to come, he tendered them his gracious pardon, they returning home and demeaning themselves like loyal subjects for the future (z)."

This proclamation had no effect upon the rebels, but they continued in the country they had taken possession of, and abundantly satisfied with what they never hoped to enjoy made no haste to advance their new conquests (a).

On the 31st of *August*, the king, for his greater security at *York*, rode about the city accompanied with the marquis of *Hamilton*, several general officers, some aldermen and citizens, and with pickaxes, spades and shovels marked out several intrenchments and fortifications (b).

September 1, the king and his council had advice that the *Scots* did not come forward but remained at *Newcastle*; the next day the king dispatched Mr. *John Bellasise* second son to the lord *Falconberg*, with a command, that upon their allegiance, they should not stir any further till a treaty was begun.

September 4, came a petition to the king from the *Scots* thus directed:

To the KING's most excellent majesty.

The humble petition of your commissioners of the late parliament, and others of his majesty's most loyal subjects of the kingdom of Scotland.

(c) The substance of which is as follows, "that whereas by many sufferings they were "constrained for relief, and obtaining their humble and just desires to come into *England*; "where they had lived upon their own means, victuals and goods brought along with "them, neither troubling the peace of the kingdom, nor hurting any of his majesty's subjects, till they were constrained to use violence aginst those who opposed their peaceable "passage at *Newburn* upon *Tyne*; who have brought their own blood upon their own "heads. For preventing the like or greater opposition, and that they might come to his "majesty's presence, for obtaining from his justice and goodness full satisfaction to their "demands; they, his majesty's most humble and loyal subjects, do persist in that most "humble and submissive way of petitioning, which neither good success nor bad shall make "them desist from humbly entreating that his majesty, in the depth of his royal wisdom, "would consider their pressing grievances, and with the consent of the *English* parliament "would settle a firm and durable peace against all invasions both from sea and land.

"That they might with chearfulness pay his majesty, their native king, all duty and "obedience against the many and great evils at this time threatening both kingdoms, which "makes all his majesty's good subjects tremble to think on, and which they unanimously "pray God to avert that his majesty's throne may be established in righteousness."

To which his majesty gave this answer by his secretary.

At the court at York, September 5, 1640.

"His majesty has seen and considered the within written petition, and is graciously "pleased to return this answer by me, that he finds it in such general terms, that till you "express the particulars of your desires, his majesty can give no direct answer thereunto: "wherefore his majesty requireth that you would set down the particulars of your demands "with expedition; he having been always ready to redress the grievances of his people. "And for the more mature deliberation of the weighty affairs, his majesty hath already "given out summons for the meeting of the peers of this kingdom in the city of *York*, the "24th day of this month, that with the advice of the peers you may receive such answer "to your petition, as shall most tend to his honour, and the peace and welfare of his dominions. And in the mean time, if peace be that you so much desire as you pretend; "he expects, and by this his majesty commands that you advance no further with your army "into these parts, which is the only means that is left for the present to preserve peace

(z) Eachard.
(a) Lord Clarendon.
(b) Ex MS.
(c) Rushworth's coll. *sub hoc anno*

"between

"between the two nations, and to bring these unhappy differences into a reformation, A. 1640.
"which none is more desirous of then his most sacred majesty.

"*Lanericke.*"

The king in this exigency of his affairs, at this time, resolved upon an expedient, which my lord *Clarendon* calls a new invention not before heard of, or so old that it had not been practised for some hundred of years, which was to call a great council of all the peers of *England* to meet and attend his majesty at *York*. The ground and intention of this particular summons was never known, but, adds the noble historian, it probably was the result of troubled and afflicted thoughts, since no other way occurred. Howsoever that, such a resolution was taken, and writs immediately issued under the great seal to all peers to attend his majesty at *York* within twenty days; and preparations were made to receive them accordingly.

Whoever will look back into these annals will find, that, in the former *Scotch* wars, many consultations of this kind were held in this very city, on any sudden invasion, where the commons were not concerned. *Anno* 1298, *Edward* I. summoned all the peers of the realm, exclusive of the commons, to meet at *York* on an extraordinary occasion. In his son's unfortunate reign there were many more; and indeed all those meetings at *York*, which are termed parliaments during the *Scotch* wars, were no other then a great council of the *bishops*, *abbots* and *barons* of the realm, hastily convened by the king's writ, and if any of the commons had the honour to be called amongst them, it was by the same authority, and not by any election of the people. Affairs were much too pressing to wait such dilatory methods, as at this time, when the enemy had entered into the country, plundered and spoiled the inhabitants, and, notwithstanding their specious pretences in the petition, continued to exact the eight hundred and fifty pound a day with great rigour.

This affair however at this time made a great noise, and was blown up with great zeal by the king's enemies into a report, that the king intended to lay aside one of the three estates of the nation; when in truth it was no more than, as my lord *Clarendon* expresses it, an expedient for the purpose since no other way occurred. The form of the writ itself may be matched with many of the same kind in the *Foedera Ang.* and since it respects my subject in two particulars, I shall give it as follows,

(*d*) REX *reverendissimo in* Christo *patri consiliario nostro* WILLIELMO *eadem gratia* CANTUAR. *archiepiscopo, totius* ANGLIAE *primati et metropolitano, salutem. Quia, super quibusdam arduis et urgentissimis negotiis nos & regni nostri statum coronaeque nostrae jura specialiter concernentibus, vobiscum et cum aliis praelatis magnatibus et proceribus ipsius regni apud civitatem nostram* EBORACI, *die jovis* 24 *die instantis mensis* Septembris, *colloquium habere volumus et tractatum, Vobis, in fide et dilectione quibus nobis tenemini, firmiter injungimus et mandamus, quod, cessante excusatione quacunque, dictis die et loco personaliter interstitis nobiscum et cum praelatis magnatibus et proceribus praedictis super dict. negotiis tractaturi, vestrumque consilium impensuri; et hoc sicut nos et honorem nostrum ac tranquillitatem regni nostri juriumque nostrorum praedict. diligitis nullatenus omittatis.*

Teste meipso apud EBORACUM *septimo die* Septembris, 1640.

Per ipsum REGEM.

(*e*) The same day the writs went out, came into *York* sir *Jacob Astley* with the king's whole army, making now about twelve thousand foot and three thousand horse. These forces were encamped half in *Clifton-fields*, and half in *Bishop-fields*; on both sides the river *Ouse*, and a bridge of boats conjoined them. There came into *York* at this time fifty odd pieces of ordnance great and small, six score and twelve waggons loaden with powder, match and shot, with several other carriages full of pickaxes, spades and shovels, all from the king's magazine at *Hull*. Many of the cannon were planted before the camp, where several ramparts and bulwarks were thrown up. The rest of the cannon and carriages stood in the *Almonry-yard*. There was a court of guard kept at every bar and every postern in the city, day and night, for the space of nine weeks; for notwithstanding the open pretences of the *Scotch*, the king had been secretly informed that they intended to surprise him in *York*; and therefore it behoved him to make these preparations to receive them. The army lay incamped in the manner aforesaid from the 1st of *September* till near *Martinmas*, and then, by reason of the cold weather, they were disposed of to the neighbouring towns andvillages.

Many were the petitions that came to the king at this time from all parts for him to call a parliament; some of them, especially that from the city of *London*, then remarkably disloyal, *presumptive enough*.

September 10, the king called the *Yorkshire* gentry together, and propounded to them the payment of the trained bands for two months; which proposition they took into present consideration; being also much satisfied that his majesty had summoned a great council of his peers to meet at *York*.

(*d*) *Rushworth's* coll.

(*e*) *Ex MS.*

On

A. 1640. On the next day they returned answer to this effect, that the petitioners have consulted together concerning the payment of the trained bands for two months, and have agreed upon doing the same, to which purpose they will use their utmost endeavours; humbly beseeching his majesty to consider, out of his royal wisdom how to compose the differences with the *Scots*, that the country may enjoy peace again, and not run more into danger; and do most humbly beseech his majesty to think of *summoning a parliament*, the only way to confirm a peace betwixt both kingdoms.

Mr. *Rushworth* here makes this remark, that the *Yorkshire* gentry desired the lord *Strafford* to present this petition to his majesty; which he inclined to do leaving out those words of advice to the king to call a parliament, *for that he knew it was the king's full purpose to do it*; but, adds he, the *Yorkshire* gentlemens hearts, and the voice of the whole kingdom being fervent for a parliament, they were unwilling to leave out these words of summoning a parliament, therefore they delivered their petition themselves; which was well taken by his majesty.

Two petitions were presented to the king from the poor distressed inhabitants of the county of *Northumberland* and bishoprick of *Durham*, complaining grievously of the intolerable hardships imposed upon them by the *Scotch*; "that besides the sum of six hundred "and fifty pound a day, they demand a great proportion of hay and straw, by means of "which their cattle, if any should be left them, were in danger of being starved. They "had none but *God* and his majesty to fly for relief to; in this unexpected calamity, humbly "beseeching the king to take pity of their miseries, *&c*."

September 24, the great assembly of peers met in the deanery, the hall of which was richly hung with tapistry for that purpose; the king's chair of state was placed upon the half pace of the stairs, at the upper end of the hall, from whence his majesty delivered himself in the following speech to them.

"*My lords*,

"UPON sudden invasions, where the danger was near and instant, it hath been the "custom of my predecessors to assemble the great council of the peers, and "by their advice and assistance to give a timely remedy to such evils, which could not "admit a delay so long as must of necessity be allowed for the assembling of a parlia-"ment.

"This being our condition at this time, and an army of rebels lodged within this king-"dom, I thought it most fit to conform myself to the practice of my predecessors in like "cases; that with your advice and assistance, we might justly proceed to the chastisement "of these insolencies and securing of my good subjects.

"In the first place I must let you know that I desire nothing more than to be rightly "understood of my people; and to that end I have of myself resolved to call a parliament; "having already given order to the lord keeper to issue the writs instantly, so that the "parliament may be assembled by the 3d of *November* next. Whither if my subjects bring "those good affections, which become them, towards me, it shall not fail on my part to "make it a happy meeting. In the mean time there are two points wherein I shall desire "your advice, which indeed are the chief end of your meeting.

"First, what answer to give to the petition of the rebels, and in what manner to treat "with them. Of which that you may give a sure judgment I have ordered that your lord-"ships shall be clearly and fully informed of the state of the whole business; and "upon what reason the advices which my privy-council unanimously gave me were "grounded.

"The second is, how my army shall be kept on foot and maintained until the supplies "from a parliament may be had. For so long as the *Scotch* army remains in *England*, I think "no man will council me to disband mine; for that would be an unspeakable loss to all "this part of the kingdom, by subjecting them to the greedy appetite of the rebels, besides "the unspeakable dishonour that would thereby fall upon this nation."

I shall not trouble the reader with the debates at this first days meeting; which he may so readily meet with in *Rushworth*, *Clarendon* and *Eachard*. I shall only say, that when the *Scotch* petition came to be read, who, says the noble historian, knew their time, and had always given the king, how rough and undutiful soever their actions were, as good and as submissive words as can be imagined; this petition, *full of as much submission as a victory itself could produce*, as was urged by some lords, could not but beget a treaty; and accordingly sixteen peers (*f*) were nominated for it. These commissioners, that they might breed no jealousy in the *Scotch*, were chosen out of the party that hated the lord *Strafford*, and even the king himself, as their future conduct sufficiently attested. *York* was the place mentioned by the king for the treaty, which the *Scots* would not consent to; giving for

(*f*) Earl of *Hertford*.	Earl of *Warwick*.	Viscount *Mandevile*.	Lord *Pawlet*.
Earl of *Bedford*.	Earl of *Bristol*.	Lord *Wharton*.	Lord *Howard*.
Earl of *Essex*.	Earl of *Holland*.	Lord *Pagget*.	Lord *Savile*.
Earl of *Salisbury*.	Earl of *Berkshire*.	Lord *Brook*.	Lord *Dunsmore*.

reason

reason that it was not a place secure, since their great enemy the earl of *Strafford* commanded there in chief; so *Ripon* was nominated by them, and agreed to by the king. An. 1640.

The treaty being opened, the great council of peers continued to meet, and took into consideration the king's second proposition, concerning the keeping up and paying the forces, and being acquainted by the lord *Strafford*, that it would take two hundred thousand pound to support them, it was resolved that the sum should be borrowed of the city of *London*; and a letter from the lords was prepared and sent accordingly.

In one of the day's debates *Edward* lord *Herbert*, commonly called the black lord *Herbert*, unsatisfied with the demands of the *Scotch* commissioners, which was no less than forty thousand pound a month, advised the king to fortify *York*, and refuse it; the reasons he gave in his speech are as follows, from *Rushworth*,

" First, that *Newcastle* being taken, it was necessary to fortify *York*; there being no other " considerable place betwixt the *Scots* and *London*, which might detain their army from ad- " vancing forwards.

" Secondly, that reasons of state having admitted fortification of our most inland towns " against weapons used in former times; it may as well admit fortification against the " weapons used in these times.

" Thirdly, that towns have been always averse to wars and tumults, as subsisting by " the peaceable ways of trade and traffick. Insomuch that when either great persons for " their private interests, or the commons for their grievances have taken arms, towns- " men have been noted ever to continue in their accustomed loyalty and devotion.

" Fourthly, that this agreeth with the custom of all other countries, there being no town " any where he knew in *Christendom*, of the greatness of *York*, that hath not its bastions " and bulwarks.

" As for the charges, the citizens of *York* might undertake that by his majesty's permis- " sion; for since it is a maxim of war, that every town may fortify its circumference, with- " in the space of two months, the expences cannot be great.

" And for the manner of doing it, nothing else is needful, but that at the distance of " every twenty five score paces round about the town, the walls should be thrown down, " and certain bastions or bulwarks of earth be erected by the advice of some good en- " gineer.

" For the performing whereof every townsman might give his helping hand, digging " and casting up earth, only where the said engineer should appoint. And for ordnance, " ammunition and a magazine, the townsmen, likewise for their security, might be at the " charge thereof in these dangerous times; it being better to employ some money so to " prevent the taking of the town, than to run the hazard of being in that estate in which " *Newcastle-men* now are. I could add something concerning an antient law or custom " called *murage*, by which money was raised for fortifying of inland towns; but because I " know not of what validity this law or custom is at this time, I shall refer the further con- " sideration thereof to the learned in our antiquities.

" I shall conclude therefore, with your majesty's good favour, for the fortifying of " *York*, as assuring myself that if for want of such fortification it fall into the *Scotchmen's* " *hands*, they will quickly fortify it as they have already done *Newcastle*.

This lord spoke also very warmly against the treaty carrying on at *Ripon*, said many smart things against it, and the *Scotch* exorbitant demand, and concluded his whole speech with this sensible paragraph.

" That if his majesty would try whether they meant really a treaty or an invasion, the " commissioners should move for disbanding the armies on both sides, all things else re- " maining in the state they now were, until the treaty were ended; howsoever the forty " thousand pound *monthly* should be kept rather for paying the king's army and reinforcing " it, if need were, than any other way whatsoever.

I cannot forbear taking notice, that whilst the king was at *York* this time, and the treaty subsisting, the brave marquis of *Montross*, one of the *Scotch* generals, observing the scandalous proceedings at the treaty, was so touched with the reflection of espousing so bad a cause, that he wrote a dutiful and submissive letter to the king, offering to support him with his life and fortune. A copy of this letter, to shew what sort of people the king had about him, was immediately sent back to *Lesly*, the other general, who challenged the marquis *with holding correspondence with the enemy*; the marquis undauntedly owned it, and asked, *who it was that durst reckon the king an enemy?* Which bravery of his so quashed the charge, that they durst not proceed against him in a judicial manner (*f*).

From the 24th of *September* to the 18th of *October* following, did the king and his great council of peers continue to sit as usual. The commissioners from time to time repaired to *York*, to let them know how they proceeded, which all ended in nothing; for the commissioners being of the same principles, as to religion and politicks, with the rebels they treated with, cared not how much the king's affairs were embarrassed, and therefore chose rather to persuade the king to remove the treaty to *London*, and subject the country still to pay the

(*f*) *Eachard's* hist. of *England*, &c.

A. 1640. contribution of 850 *l.* a day till all was concluded on; rather than suffer the earl of *Strafford* to dislodge them which he had already begun to do by defeating three or four of their regiments which advanced too far during the treaty. And shewed the country that there was a better way to get rid of this rebellious rout, their cruel oppressors, than long spun treaties and fruitless negotiations.

Thus did the king and his lords remove from thence to *London*, without concluding any thing with the *Scotch* but a cessation; in order to meet the parliament. A parliament, whom none can blame the king for being slow in calling, who considers the consequences. For they were no sooner got together but they were seen to be his most implacable enemies; and never left their persecutions, till they had made the first and second estates of the nation yield up all to the third.

A. 1641. For proof of this, their first attempts were to weaken the king's councils, by taking from his side, these Bulwarks of his and the church's prerogatives, archbishop *Laud*, and *Thomas* earl of *Strafford*. And to begin with the earl they voted down the *council court* of this city which had stood near an age in *York*; and was no doubt of great advantage to it, whatever it might be to the rest of the kingdom. The earl of *Strafford* was the last president and judge of this court, and had a more ample commission than any before him. I shall be more particular in this when I come to treat of the *abby* and *manor*, the house where the presidents resided in *York*.

And now began the heats that had been kindled by ill-designing men betwixt the king and his parliament to threaten an irruption. *November* 20. this year the king came to *York* accompanied with the prince of *Wales*, the *palsgrave* of the *Rhine*, the duke of *Lenox*, the marquis of *Hambleton*, and several other nobles. He was received in the city with the usual formalities; the next day he dined with the lord-mayor and knighted him *(g)*, and *Robert Berwick* esquire, recorder. This was in a progress the king was making to *Scotland*, where he had summoned a parliament in order to try their tempers towards him; being well assured he could not find them worse disposed than those he had left at *Westminster*.

A. 164½. At the king's return to *London* matters growing every day worse betwixt him and his parliament, and loudly threatning a rupture, the king thought fit, says lord *Clarendon*, to put a former design in execution, which was to remove himself and court to *York*; as a place, adds he, of good reception and convenience for those that were willing to attend him. Accordingly the king, prince *Charles*, the prince elector and other nobles with some hazard to his own person, but more to his attendants, set out from *London*, and *March* 18. came to *York*. Here it was, says *Eachard*, that the king began to breath fresh air, and he soon found himself more at ease, and in a condition more safe and eligible than before. Most persons of quality of this great county, and of those adjacent, resorted to him, and many persons of condition from *London*, and the southern parts; who had not the courage to attend upon him at *Whitehall*, or near the parliament; some out of a sense of duty and gratitude, and others out of indignation at the parliament's proceedings, came to *York*; so that in a short time the court appeared with some lustre, and our city may be truly called to this persecuted king *a city of refuge*.

To welcome his majesty into these parts he was presented soon after his arrival at *York* with this petition; subscribed by great numbers of the *Yorkshire* nobility and gentry, ministers and freeholders assembled at the assizes held in this city at that time. The petition runs in these words, in *Rushworth*:

" *Most humbly sheweth*,

" THAT, although the piercing anguish of our souls, proceeding from the general distraction of this kingdom, be eased by the comfort of your majesty's royal presence and gracious confidence in the affections of this county, which hath filled our hearts with hopes, and our tongues with joy; yet the fellow-feeling of our passionate sorrows, and heart-breaking apprehensions which overwhelms the other parts of this afflicted kingdom, doe inforce us (after the humble tender of our lives and fortunes, for the safety and assurance of your majesty's royal person, crown, honour and estate, just prerogative and sovereignty, in any capacity wherein we may serve your majesty according to the laws) to follow that sacrifice of bounden duty, with our earnest prayers and petitions, which shall not cry in your princely ears for help to almost ruined *Ireland*, nor implore your majesty's concurrence for the propagation of the protestant religion, and suppression of popery, since your majesty's gracious declaration of your self in those particulars, render it an unpardonable crime to desire further assurance or addition to your majesty's own words sacred before God and man. But emboldened by your royal resolution, declared to take away not only the just fears, but alsoe the jealousys of your loyal subjects, and enforced by that infallible oracle of truth that a kingdom divided cannot stand, we, from the centre of every one of our hearts, most earnestly supplicate that your majesty, (being most interested in the flourishing state and union of your dominions, and by long experience in government, best acquainted with prevention of dangers, and remedy of evils) will be graciously

(g) Sir *Christopher Croft*, knight, lord-mayor 1641. *Ex MS.*

" pleased

" pleased to declare such fit means and expedients, as may take away all distances and mis- A. 1642.
" understandings betwixt your majesty and your great council; to whom we will also ad-
" dress ourselves for such endeavours on their parts as may beget in your majesty a confi-
" dence in their counsels, and that blessed union soe necessary to this perplexed kingdom,
" and most desired by us and all your majesty's loving and faithful subjects.

" *And your petitioners shall ever pray for your majesty's long and prosperous reign*, &c.

Upon the delivery of this petition his majesty immediately returned them this answer,

" *Master sheriffe and gentlemen*,

" I Believe you expect not a present and particular answer to your petition, because it is " new to me; only in general I must tell you, that I see by it that I am not deceived " in the confidence I have in the affections of this county to my person and state, and I as- " sure you that I will not deceive your confidence, which at this time you have declared in " your petition to have in me; and I am glad to see that it is not upon mistaken grounds as " other petitions have been to me since I came to this place; concerning which let me ob- " serve unto you, that my answers were to clear those mistakings; for I never did go about " to punish or discourage them from petitioning to me in an humble way, though the sub- " ject did not agree with my sense; albeit within the memory of man people have been dis- " couraged and threatened to be punished for petitions.

" I observe that your petition is soe modest, that it doth not mention any particular for " your own good; which indeed I expected, as knowing that in some particulars I have " great reason to do; and therfore, that you may not fare the worse for your modesty, I will " put you in mind of three particulars, which I conceive to be for the good of this county.

" The first is concerning your trained bands, to reduce them to a lesser number, for " which I profess to stand engaged by promise to you, which I had performed long since, " if I had been put in mind of it; and now I tell you shew me but the way, and, when " you shall think fit, I shall instantly reduce them to that number which I promised you " two years agoe.

" The second is, that which is owing to this county for billet money; the truth is that " for the present I cannot repay it; only I will say this, that if all the water had come to " the right mill, upon my word, you had been long agoe satisfied in this particular. And " soe I leave to your discretions which way you will advise, and assist me to comply with " your engagements in this point.

" The third, that for which I was petitioned as I came up the last year, both by the lord- " mayor and aldermen of this city, and likewise by diverse others of this county, as I went " southward, and that is concerning the court of *York*. And first let me tell you, that as " yet I know noe legal dissolution of it, for hitherto formally there has nothing come to me, " either directly or indirectly, for the taking of it away, therefore I may say, it is rather " shaken in pieces than dissolved. Now my desire is, in complyance to what I answered last " year unto the several petitions delivered to me on this subject, that you would consult " and agree among yourselves in what manner you would have the court established most to " your own contentments, and to the good of all these northern parts, in such a legal way " as that it may not justly be accepted again, and I assure you, on the word of an honest " man, that you shall not blame me, if you have not full satisfaction in it.

" Within a day or two yee shall have a particular answer to your petition, which shall be " such a one as I am confident will give you good satisfaction, and put you into such a way " as I hope may produce good effects for the good of all this kingdom.

In two days his majesty's secretary of state delivered to the *Yorkshire* gentry this answer *April* 7. to their petition.

" IN the first place his majesty is glad to see that what you say concerning the relief of his " distressed subjects in *Ireland*, and the propagation of the true religion amongst us a- " gainst superstition of popery, is only to shew your confidence in his princely word, where- " in he again hath commanded me to assure you, that he will neither deceive your trust nor " wrong himself soe much, as not to be very punctual in performance of the engagements he " hath already made concerning those particulars, which besides the performance of his word, " which he holds most dear to him, his own inclinations naturally induce him unto.

" Now concerning the prayer of your petition his majesty doth gratiously interpret, that " your desiring him to declare such fit means and expedients as may take away all distance " and misunderstandings betwixt his majesty and his great council, is noe otherways then to " have the more authentick ground, and the better direction which way to carry yourselves " in your addresses to the parliament for that effect. And therefore his majesty assures you " that not only the best, (but as he conceives) the sole way for this good understanding be- " twixt his majesty and his parliament (which he assures you that he no less desires then " yourselves) is, that the parliament will take his majesty's message of the 20th of *January* " last into consideration speedily, seriously and effectually; and that the *militia* of this king- " dom

4

A 1642. " dom may be settled by act of parliament, according to his majesty's explanation of his answer concerning the militia, which he made in the answer returned to both houses upon " the petition presented to him the 25th of *March* last. And therefore his majesty desires " you to take those answers and that message into your serious consideration, and thereupon to " proceed (according to the intimation in your petition) in your addresses to the parliament, " as you shall judge fittest for the good of this kingdom; and the expressions of your duty " and affection to his majesty's person and state.

" At the court at *York*, *April* 7, 1642.

Signed

OLIVER NICHOLAS.

The king gave orders for his majesty's printers to set up their presses, which was done in the house, formerly S. *William*'s college, but then sir *Henry Jenkins*'s, in the minster-yard; in order to begin a paper war; which was briskly carried on by both parties till they entered upon a real one.

April 7. the king kept his maunday in the cathedral, where the bishop of *Winchester*, lord almoner, performed the usual ceremonies. The same day *James* duke of *York* came to this city, where the day following the king kept the festival of St. *George* in great state; and the young duke of *York* was made knight companion of the garter, in the chapter-house, with the utmost magnificence.

And now came on the grand affair of *Hull*; one of the chief reasons that the king came down into the north, is owned both by lord *Clarendon* and *Eachard*, was to seize upon the vast magazine in that town; which at that time far surpassed the collection of warlike stores in the tower of *London*. The possession of this would have been of infinite service to the king's affairs, and probably have prevented a rupture. The parliament might dread falling out with a king so well provided to return their injuries; on the contrary it may be affirmed that this step of the parliament's denying the king entrance into one of his own towns, was an overtact no better than *high-treason*: Since there was no law then in being that countenanced, in the least, such a proceeding, but many a one against it; so they, with their governour, the actor of this famous exploit, were answerable for all the bloodshed occasioned by it.

I shall not trouble the reader with the particulars of an affair, so very well known; I shall only say, that the king, after his repulse by sir *John Hotham*, laid that night at *Beverly*. And the next day returned to *York*, full of trouble and indignation for this high affront, which he foresaw would produce infinite mischiefs.

A petition and a message, however, falls in my way, which I cannot omit; the petition was delivered to his majesty at *York* upon his arrival there, by a great number of the gentlemen of that county, concerning the magazine at *Hull*, before his majesty went thither. And the message is from the king himself to the parliament, with a relation of his motives of going, and treatment there, and a demand of justice against sir *John Hotham* for his refusal. In these words[b]:

" *To the KING's most excellent majesty.*

(b) " *The humble petition of the gentry and commons of the county of* York.

Most royal sovereign,

" ENcouraged by your majesty's many testimonies of your gracious goodness to us and our county, which we can never sufficiently acknowledge; we in all duty and loyalty of heart, address our selves to your sacred majesty, beseeching you to cast your eyes " and thoughts upon the safety of your own person, and your princely issue, and this " whole county; a great means of which we conceive doth consist in the arms and ammunition at *Hull*, placed there by your princely care and charge, and since upon general " apprehensions of dangers from foreign parts represented to your majesty, thought fit as " yet to be continued; we for our parts, conceiving our selves to be still in danger, do " most humbly beseech your majesty that you will be pleas'd to take such course and order that your magazine may still there remain, for the better securing of these and the " northern parts: and the rather, because we think fit, that that part of the kingdom " should be best provided where your sacred person doth reside. *Your person being like* " DAVID'*s*, *the light of* ISRAEL, *and more worth than ten thousand of us*,

Who shall daily pray, &c.

" *His majesty's message sent to the parliament* April 24, 1642, *concerning Sir* John Hotham'*s* " *refusal to give his majesty entrance into* Hull.

" HIS majesty having received the petition inclosed from most of the chief gentlemen " near about *York*, desiring the stay of his majesty's arms and munition in his ma-

(b) These two are taken out of a pamphlet imprinted at *London* by *Tho. Faucett* 1642.

gazine

"gazine at *Hull*; for the safety, not only of his majesty's person and children, but like- A. 1642.
"wise of all these northern parts; the manifold rumours of great dangers inducing them
"to make their said supplication, thought it most fit to go himself in person to his town
"of *Hull*, to view his arms and munition there, that thereupon he might give directions
"what part thereof might be necessary to remain there, for the security and satisfaction of
"his northern subjects, and what part thereof might be spared for *Ireland*, the arming of
"his majesty's *Scotch* subjects that are to go there, or to replenish his chiefest magazine in
"the tower of *London*. Where being come upon the 23^d^ of this instant *April*, much con-
"trary to his expectation, he found all the gates shut upon him, and the bridges drawn
"up, by the express command of sir *John Hotham*, who for the present commands a gar-
"rison there, and from the walls flatly denied his majesty entrance into his said town, the
"reason of which denial was as strange to his majesty as the thing itself, it being that he
"could not admit his majesty without breach of trust to his parliament, which did the more
"incense his majesty's anger against him, for that he most seditiously and traiterously would
"have put his disobedience upon his majesty's parliament; which his majesty being willing to
"clear, demanded of him if he had the impudence to averr that the parliament had directed
"him to deny his majesty entrance, and that if he had any such order that he should shew
"it in writing, for otherways his majesty could not believe it, which he could no ways
"produce, but malitiously made that false interpretation, according to his own inferences,
"confessing that he had no such positive order, which his majesty was ever confident of.
"But his majesty not willing to take so much pains in vain, offered to come into that his
"town only with twenty horse, finding that the main of his pretence lay, that his majesty's
"train was able to command the garrison; notwithstanding his majesty was so desirous to
"go thither in a private way that he gave warning thereof but overnight, which he re-
"fusing, but by way of condition, which his majesty thought much below him, held it
"most necessary to declare him a traytor, unless, upon better thoughts, he should yield
"obedience, which he doubly deserved, as well for refusing entrance to his natural so-
"vereign, as by laying the reason thereof groundlessly and malitiously upon his parlia-
"ment.

"One circumstance his majesty cannot forget, that his son the duke of *York*, and his
"nephew the prince *elector* having gone thither the day before, sir *John Hotham* delayed
"the letting them out to his majesty till after some consultation.

"Hereupon his majesty has thought it expedient to demand justice of his parliament
"against the said sir *John Hotham*, to be exemplarily inflicted on him according to the
"laws, and the rather because his majesty would give them a fit occasion to free themselves
"of this imputation by him so injuriously cast upon them, to the end that his majesty may
"have the easier way for chastising so high a disobedience."

All the answer the parliament thought fit to give to this message was this, printed in their votes, and is extant in *Rushworth*.

"*Resolved upon the question. Die Jovis* 28 April. 1642.

"That sir *John Hotham* knight, according to this relation, hath done nothing but in
"obedience to the command of both houses of parliament.

"*Resolved*, &c. That this declaring of sir *John Hotham* traitor, being a member of the
"house of commons, is a high breach of the privilege of parliament.

"*Resolved*, &c. That this declaring of sir *John Hotham* traitor, without due process of
"law, is against the liberty of the subject, and against the law of the land."

To this they added a declaration at large; wherein they vindicated their proceedings, insisted upon publick rights, and boldly asserted that they had done nothing contrary to his majesty's royal sovereignty in the town, or his legal propriety in the magazine. This smart declaration was sent and delivered to the king at *York*, by the lord *Howard* of *Escrick*, the lord *Fairfax*, sir *Hugh Cholmley*, sir *Philip Stapleton*, and sir *Henry Cholmley*. These gentlemen, besides this commission, were charged by the parliament with another, which was to reside at *York*, to be spies upon the king and his actions. This last commission, though the king well knew it, as well by their saucy behaviour to him, as otherways, says *Echard*, yet his affairs were then at so low an ebb, that he durst not commit them to prison, nor expel them the city; nor even inhibit them the court; so they continued in *York* above a month, in perfect defiance of him and his authority.

On the other hand the nobility and gentry of the county of *York*, looked upon the affair of *Hull* to be an open declaration of war; as in truth, says my authority, it could be construed no other, for no set of people in the whole world, durst have done so barefaced an injury to their sovereign, if they were not resolved to go further, and in a petition to his majesty at his return, they expressed a mighty sense and passion on his majesty's behalf, and offered *to raise the power of the country and take the town by force*. It may well be thought that one of king *Charles*'s evil *genii* presided over his councils

P p when

A. 1642. when he rejected that proposal; but he, as a foreign historian justly observes, *never went to extreams, till he had made trial of several useless precautions (i).*

Many were the declarations, messages, resolutions, petitions which passed betwixt the king and his parliament and others, whilst he resided at *York*, which I have seen and perused in printed copies of those times, or in *Rushworth*; to give them at full would swell this work to an enormous size, for barely to mention them all is too much. The good king was amusing himself at *York* in employing his tongue with speeches, and his pen with remonstrances, whilst the parliament was laying in stores of money, ammunition, &c. and so strongly reinforced the garrison at *Hull*, that sir *John Hotham* was in no fear of an assault; but was in a better condition to attack and take *York*, than the king *Hull*.

May 4. The king published an answer to the declaration, votes and order of assistance of both houses of parliament concerning the magazine at *Hull*, which ends thus:

We conclude with master Pyms **own words**, *if the prerogative of the king overwhelm the liberty of the people, it will be turned to tyranny; if liberty undermine the prerogative it will grow into anarchy*, **and so we may say into confusion.**

His majesty had sent out a summons to the *Yorkshire* gentry to meet him at the city of *York*, on the 12th of this month, and accordingly they being assembled together, to the number of four thousand, says my manuscript, his majesty spoke to them as follows *(k)*.

May 12. " *Gentlemen,*

" I Have cause of adding, not altering, what I meant to say to you; when I gave out " the summons for this day's appearance I little thought of these messengers or " of such a message as they brought, the which (because it confirms me in what I intend " to speak, and that I desire you should be truly informed of all passages between me and " the parliament) you shall hear read, first my answer to the declaration of both houses con- " cerning *Hull*. The answer of the parliament to my two messages concerning *Hull*; to- " gether with my reply to the same, and my message to both houses, declaring the rea- " sons why I refused to pass the bill concerning the *militia*.

All which being read, his majesty proceeded,

" I will make no paraphrases upon what you have heard, it more befitting a lawyer than " a king; only this observation, since treason is countenanced so near me, it is time to look " to my safety. I avow it is part of my wonder that men (whom I thought heretofore " discreet and moderate) should have undertaken this employment; and that since they " came (I having delivered them the answer you have heard, and commanded them to " return personally with it to the parliament) should have flatly disobeyed in pretence " of the parliaments commands. My end in telling you this is to warn you of them; " for since these men have brought me such a message, and disobeyed so lawful a com- " mand, I will not say what their intent of staying here is, only I bid you take heed not " knowing what doctrine of disobedience they may preach to you under colour of obey- " ing the parliament. Hitherto I have found and kept you quiet, the enjoying of which " was a chief cause of my coming hither, (tumults and disorders having made me leave " the south) and not to make this a seat of war, as malice would (but I hope in vain) make " you believe. Now if disturbances come, I know who I have reason to suspect.

" To be short, you see that my magazine is going to be taken from me, (being my " own proper goods) directly against my will. The *militia* (against law and my consent) " is going to be put in execution; and lastly, sir *John Hotham*'s treason is countenanced. " All this considered, none can blame me to apprehend dangers; therefore I have thought " fit upon these real grounds to tell you that I am resolved to have a guard (the parlia- " ment having had one all this while upon imaginary jealousies) only to secure my person. " In which I desire your concurrence and assistance, and that I may be able to protect you, " the laws and the true protestant profession from any affront or injury that may be offered; " which I mean to maintain myself without charge to the country, intending not longer " to keep them on foot, then I shall be secured of just apprehensions, by having satisfac- " tion in the particulars aforementioned."

This speech was taken into consideration by two different parties; the *republicans* of the county met the high sheriff at the dean's house, and subscribed an answer to his majesty's propositions, wherein " they desired his majesty to throw himself intirely upon his parlia- " ment, of whose loyal care and affection to his majesty's honour and safety they were most " confident. That the gentlemen who were lately employed to attend his majesty from both " houses, were men of quality and estates in this county, and trusted to serve in that most " honourable assembly. They humbly craved leave to express their confidence in their un- " stained loyalty and affection to his majesty, as his majesty may securely admit their at- " tendance to negotiate their imployments, until they be recalled by the parliament. And " for their fidelity they did all engage themselves to his majesty, and were most assured,

(i) *Pere* d'Orleance *hist. de revolut. d'Ang.*

(k) This speech was printed at *York*, by *Robert Barker*, printer to the king's most excellent majesty, and by the assigns of *John Bill*. 1642.

" that

" that his royal person would be secure in the general fidelity of his subjects in this county " without any extraordinary guard (*l*)." A. 1642.

At the head of the subscribers to this answer was sir *Thomas Fairfax*; it was delivered to the king by the *high sheriff*, and by whom his majesty returned this short answer. May 12.

His majesty expects the like affection from you, that he doth from the other gentlemen; and that he hath the same confidence in you that he hath in them.

But the loyal party, being much more numerous, convened themselves, and agreed upon the following declaration:

" WE the knights and gentlemen whose names are subscribed do unanimously present " this our answer to your majesty's propositions concerning the raising of a guard " of horse, for the security and defence of your sacred person.

" To which proposition as we conceive our selves bound by allegiance do willingly con- " curr. For that purpose humbly desiring that the aforesaid may be raised by legal au- " thority: and likewise that it may consist of persons unquestionable in their religion, and " gentlemen."

The substance of his majesty's answer to this.

His majesty gave them thanks, for it appeared as a satisfactory answer, and in it they had shewed great circumspection and wisdom, by chusing such whose loyalty could not be questioned, and by excluding recusants, and all suspected to be disaffected.

Immediately upon this two hundred young gentlemen, of this county, voluntarily listed themselves into a troop; under the command of the prince of *Wales*; whose lieutenant-colonel was sir *Francis Wortley*. His majesty had also a regiment of seven hundred foot of the trained bands commanded by sir *Robert Strickland*. This small armament the king constantly caused to be paid every *Saturday* at his own charge, when he had little more than would defray the expences of his own table, which was kept with all the parsimony imaginable; the prince and duke not having tables apart, as was usual, but eating at his majesty's. The court was kept at this time at old sir *Arthur Ingram*'s house in the minster-yard, and not in the manor (*m*).

For the favour and affection shewn him by the *Yorkshire* gentry, his majesty directed the following letter to them.

" *To our right trusty and well beloved the gentry of* York, *and others of this our county of* " York, *whom it doth or may concern* (*n*). May 16.

" WE have with great contentment considered your dutiful and affectionate answer to " our proposition concerning the unsufferable affront we received at *Hull*. We " have not been deceived in that confidence we have had in your affection, wherefore we " desire you to assure the rest of your countrymen, who through negligence were omitted " to be summoned, that we shall never abuse your love by any power wherewith *God* shall " enable us, to the least violation of the least of your liberties, or the diminution of those " immunities which we have granted you, this parliament, though they be beyond the acts " of most, if not all, our predecessors. Being resolved with a constant and firm resolution " to have the law of this land duly observed, and shall endeavour, only, so to preserve " our just royal rights as may enable us to protect our kingdom and people, according to " the antient honours of the kings of *England*; and according to the trust which by the " law of *God* and this land is put into the crown; being sufficiently warned by the late " affront at *Hull* not to transfer the same out of our power. Concerning which affront " we will take some time to advise which way we may usefully imploy your affections; in " the mean time we shall take it well from all such as shall personally attend us, so fol- " lowed and provided, as they shall think fit for the better safety of our person, because " we know not what sudden violence or affront may be offered to us, having lately re- " ceived such an actual testimony of rebellious intentions as sir *John Hotham* hath expressed " at *Hull*. Being thus secured by your affections and assistance, we promise you our pro- " tection from any contrary power whatever, and that you shall not be molested for your " humble and modest petition, as of late you have been threatned.

" Given at our court at *York*, *May* 16, 1642.

The small army in the north, raised for defence of the king's person, made a great noise in the south, and the parliament laid hold of the occasion to declare that the king was levying forces to subdue them. And now came out thundering pamphlets to instil fears and jealousies into the people; one of which lies now before me published by their own authority, with this dreadful title:

(*l*) From a pamphlet published by authority of parl. *Lond* 1642. The high sheriff of the county this year was sir *Richard Hutton* of *Goldsburgh*, knight.

(*m*) *Ex MS.*

(*n*) Printed at *York* by the king's printers, 1642.

" Hor-

A. 1642. " Horrible news from *York*, *Hull*, and *Newcastle*; concerning the king's majesty's intent to " take up arms against the parliament.

" With his majesty's threatnings to imprison the lord *Fairfax*, sir *Philip Stapleton*, and " the rest of the committee appointed by the parliament to sit at *York*. And the joint " votes of both houses concerning the same.

" Also the lord *Stamford*'s report to the parliament concerning the danger of *Hull*; and " his majesty's resolutions to take up arms.

Imprim. Jo. Brown, *cler. parl.*

This blow was occasioned by a letter sent from the before named gentlemen, the parliament's committee at *York*, to the speaker of the house of commons, together with a copy of the king's last speech to the gentry of *Yorkshire*, and the different resolutions upon it. This letter because it gives a particular account of the transactions at this meeting, and because it betrays them to be what the king really took them for, *viz. spies* upon his actions, I shall give, *verbatim*, as follows *(o)*:

" *S I R*,

" IN our last letter we gave you an account of our first and second waiting on the king. " We writ to you then that his majesty commanded us to attend him yesterday, being " *Thursday*, to hear what he said to the gentlemen; which a little before the meeting he " seconded by a particular message. Being come thither his majesty caused the several " messages between him and the parliament mentioned in this enclosed printed paper to " be read.

" This was done with much humming and applause of the king's messages, by some " persons who had placed themselves near about where the king stood; but when any " thing from the parliament came to be read, with so much hissing and reviling the par- " liament, that though in respect and duty to the king's person, we could not resent it as " otherways we should have done, yet we have since expostulated and complained of it to " his majesty. Some were so bold as to say openly, that *the parliament-men should set* " *their houses in order, for many of them should shortly have their heads off*. One of which, as " since we are credibly informed, was one *Hurst* a servant to one master *William Crofts*. In " this which was said by the king, you will see what reason we had to vindicate ourselves, " and therefore we immediately repaired to the dean's house with all the other gentlemen, " and there we took notice of the rough usage we had received; we told them that it was " neither indiscretion nor disobedience in us, (as his majesty was pleased to call it) to de- " liver the parliament's message, or to stay here though commanded to the contrary; since " we conceived no man needed to be satisfied in so clear a case as this; that every mem- " ber of each house ought to obey their commands when they were pleased to imploy " them. But since his majesty thought fit to bid them take heed of us, not knowing what " doctrine of disobedience we might preach to them, we appealed to every man, whether " we had in word or deed, in publick or in private, done any thing that became not ho- " nest men, and persons employed from the parliament. That we had communicated " our instructions to his majesty, being that we would avow all our actions, and that we " were confident it would not be said, we had trangressed them. This was very well " taken and justified by the country. Yesterday there came divers thousands of free- " holders to this city, though none but the gentry were summoned, but receiving a com- " mand from the king not to come to court, they forbore and staid in the castle-yard, " yet sent this petition *(p)* inclosed from his majesty, and received the answer annexed " thereunto. There was likewise a committee of twelve gentlemen appointed yester- " night to consider of drawing up an answer to the king's proposition concerning a " guard. But nothing could be done then, because it was past three a clock before the " gentlemen were admitted to the king. This morning the freeholders assembled " again in the castle-yard, and there they made this protestation enclosed, of their right " of voting in what concerneth the peace of the country, as having their interest " therein.

" When we all met this morning at the dean's house, we who are your committees re- " ceived this message by sir *Edward Stanhope*, that he came from his majesty to command " us, that we should depart from this meeting, and if we did stay, his majesty would " judge us guilty of that he spoke on yesterday, which was *tampering*. Notwithstand- " ing which command we read the fourth article of our instructions to the whole compa- " ny, that being pertinent to the business we were then upon, and desired them to con-

(o) From a pamphlet printed at *London*, 1642, by authority. This letter is also in *Rushworth, sub hoc anno.* Soon after came out a pamphlet titled, " more news from " *Hull*; or a most happy and fortunate prevention of a " most hellish and divelish plot, occasioned by some un- " quiet and discontented spirits against the town of *Hull*, " endeavouring to command their admittance by casting " balls of wild fire into the town, which by policy and " entreaty, they could not obtain" *London* printed for *R. Cooper*. 1642.

(p) The petition, answer, and protestation I have, but thought them too long to insert. The freeholders were only nettled that they were left out of the summons, and therefore joined with the disaffected at this time.

sider,

" sider, whether the parliament had not expressed therein such a care of the king's safety, A. 1642.
" that there would be little need of guards. We told them we had a good right of being " there as freeholders of the county; but that in obedience to the king we would depart " for this time; but whensoever there should be occasion for our being there, in pursuance " of our instructions and commands from the parliament, we should be ready. The whole " company expressed great satisfaction, and desired a copy of that instruction, which we " gave them. We were the more willing at that time to go from thence, because we should " not only give obedience to the king's command, which otherways he would have said " we constantly disobeyed, but because the committee of twelve appointed yesternight were " then to withdraw, so that there was nothing for the present for us to do. We imme- " diately went to the king and besought him, that since we were continually so discounte- " nanced by him in the face of our country, that he would be pleased to let us know in " particular, wherein we had given the occasion, for we otherways conceived we were de- " prived of that liberty, which was our due in respect of that interest we had here. His " majesty was pleased to tell us, that if we would lay aside that condition of committees " from the parliament, he would not hinder us to be there as gentlemen of the country; " we humbly replied that we could not lay that down; nor could we be absent from any " meeting where our presence was required for the service as committees from the parlia- " ment, to which his majesty said, that indeed he thought we could not lay it down, nei- " ther was it reasonable that we should have votes and be in a double capacity.

" The committee hath been together most part of this day; but, not agreeing, six of " them have drawn up this answer enclosed, which they have communicated to the gentle- " men and freeholders. The greater part of the gentlemen and all the freeholders have " agreed to and subscribed it. The other six have concluded upon this other answer, con- " senting to a guard of horse, but this we do not hear they have gotten many names to, " nor can we get a copy of those names as yet, though these be very few, yet whether " they can bring in any horse or no we cannot yet judge. The king has received both " these resolutions, which with his answers to them you have likewise here enclosed. His " majesty had declared himself yesterday that he would raise the regiment which was sir " *Robert Strickland*'s for his foot guard; but he hath now laid aside that resolution. The " freeholders of the county are now newly summoned, to attend his majesty about a " week hence, the three ridings on three several days, but for what service we do not " know.

" Sir you have here a large narative of the passages at this meeting, what dangers this " poor country lies under, we humbly refer it to you to judge, not taking upon us to de- " liver any opinion. The business lasted so long that it hindred us from giving a more " speedy account. Sir, this is what at this time is sent from

Your assured friends and servants

York, 13 *Maii* 1642.

FER. FAIRFAX.
HU. CHOLMLEY.
PHILIP STAPLETON.
HE. CHOLMLEY.

I shall trouble the reader with no comment on this long letter, though in many places the sense of it lies open for a smart one; if he thinks as I do, he will wonder at the king's patience under all these insults to keep his hands off these actors; and the parliament was so sensible that their worthy committee deserved imprisonment that they thought fit to pass this order against it.

" That whosoever should offer to attach and imprison any members of both the " houses employed in their service, it should be held as a high breach of the priviledges " of parliaments."

I have met with a speech said to be spoken by sir *Philip Stapleton*, one of these gentlemen of the committee, to the king at *York*; but whether genuine or not is disputable, from the oddness of the style, some of it being in rhyme or verse. I chose to give it however, in this place, though I take it to be a *firebrand* thrown out at *London* against the king and his court at *York*, without any foundation for it; because the assembly here mentioned was not held till *June* 3, which was after this speech was said to have been spoke, and was actually printed.

" *A renowned speech spoken to the KING's most excellent majesty at the last great assembly " of the gentry and commonality of* Yorkshire, *by that most judicious gentleman sir* Philip " Stapleton.

" *Most gracious sovereign,*

" LET not me incur your majesty's displeasure, if I that am one of the poorest of your " subjects presume to speake some few words unto *my lord the king.*

A. 1642. "According to your majesties command, we the gentry and commonality of *Yorkshire*, "are here met to know your majesties pleasure, and knowing to fullfill what we with "honour may performe, or with loyalty execute: nor have we brought with us the least "thought of such a feare, since 'twere disloyalty in the highest degree to think a prince so "gratious, from whom we have received such large expressions of royal love and favour, "should command any thing not suitable to law and to our consciences; far be it from us "to think it, only let me take licence to tell what some men mutter, as touching your "majesties demands to have a guard of horse and foot to waite upon your majestie.

"First, that the malignant party hath counselled your majestie to take this course; and "under this pretence to gain a power of horse and foote which should be imployed against "the parliament.

"We hope much better, nor can we give just credit to such vain reports, yet should we "with our persons and estates purchase a ruine to ourselves and kingdome, it would be a "sad reward for all our service.

"Oh my dread lord,

"Let but your serious judgment call to mind what sad disasters homebred strife doth "breed in private families, and if in them, what mischief in a kingdome that is divided in-"to as many factions as there is counties. The church, the state, the court, the city, "and the county too full of dissention; let your majesty call to mind the hellish plots the "*papists* dayly layd to ruine and destroy your royal father; could they hate him, and "yet love you so deare? believe it not my lord; their flattering tongues and their dis-"sembling traines are inwardly all poyson; *their oyly councels seeme to quench this fire, but* "*with that oyle they do your fall conspire*: cast back your eye to *Yorke* and *Lancaster*, how "many nobles lost their noble lives, how many subjects paid their lives as tributes to their "then doubtfull king? How was this kingdom wasted and destroyed? *And in the end when* "*warre did cease to frown, he lost a kingdome to obtain a crown.*

"Besides, great king, admit a guard was raised as is intended (depending on your royal "wisdome in the use of them) what could such forces do against a kingdome? what can "rawe soldiers do against those thousands of expert soldiers which have taken oathe to "defend your royal majesty, and the high court of parliament? But if your majesty shall "put your self in opposition, and raise forces against your loyal and obedient subjects, "they ought in laws of nature, both human and divine, to defend and make resistance; "and should this come to pass, which God forbid, tillage and trade must cease; foreign "commerce and traffique must have an end; and hostility must be the practice of this "kingdome, both to defend your sacred majesty from your domestick enemies the *papists* "(which but assembled by your gracious licence would soon declare themselves your own "and kingdomes greatest enemies) and to secure the kingdom from the invasion of foreign "enemies, that dayly watch advantage to get a footing in this fruitfull isle, and to sup-"press the gospell; and it is greatly to be feared, that by their grand incendiarys here they "are the chiefest authors of these great distractions.

"I fear I have displeased your majesty; if so, I crave your gracious pardon. It is my "true love and zealous loyaltie to your sacred majesty, and this my native kingdome that "makes me bold to press your majesty; beside the interest and assurance I have of the "fidelity of that great councell, whereof by the favour of my country I was chosen a mem-"ber; which trust I will till death faithfully discharge, both to your sacred majesty, and "this my country.

"Spoken *May* 28, and printed *June* 2, 1642. *London* by *J. Horton*.

May 17. About this time the king gave notice to the lord-keeper at *London* to issue forth writs for the adjournment of the next *term* to *York*; but this was obstructed by a vote of the house.

May 20. Came the *Portugal* ambassador to *York*; and what added exceedingly to the king's satisfaction, sir *Edward Littleton* lord keeper of the *great seal*, by an excellent management, brought off that important mark of sovereignty, as well as himself, safe to his master.

Many of the peers now left their seats in parliament, and came to pay their duty to the king at *York*. A list of which noblemen as it was then printed at *London*, with a design to blacken them, is as follows,

The lord *keeper*.	Earl of *Clare*.	Lord *Longavile*.
Duke of *Richmond*.	Earl of *Westmorland*.	Lord *Rich*.
Marquis of *Hartford*.	Earl of *Monmouth*.	Lord *Andover*.
Marquis of *Hamilton*.	Earl of *Lindsey*.	Lord *Faulkonbridge*.
Earl of *Cumberland*.	Earl of *Newcastle*.	Lord *Lovelace*.
Earl of *Bath*.	Earl of *Dover*.	Lord *Paulet*.
Earl of *Southampton*.	Earl of *Carnarvan*.	Lord *Newark*.
Earl of *Dorset*.	Earl of *Newport*.	Lord *Coventry*.
Earl of *Salisbury*.	Earl of *Thanett*.	Lord *Savile*.
Earl of *Northampton*.	Lord *Moubray*.	Lord *Dunsmore*.
Earl of *Devonshire*.	Lord *Strange*.	Lord *Seymour*.
Earl of *Carlisle*.	Lord *Willoughby*.	Lord *Capell*.

The

I

The parliament presented a *(q)* petition to his majesty at *York* concerning the disbanding of his guard; intimating, "that under colour of raising a guard (which considering the fi- " delity and care of his parliament there can be no use for) his majesty hath commanded " troops both of horse and foot to assemble at *York*, and which is a just cause of great jea- " lousy and danger to the whole kingdom. A 1642. May 23.

" They therefore humbly beseech his majesty to disband all such forces, and rely for his " security, as his predecessors had done, on the affections of his people. Otherways they " should hold themselves bound in duty towards *God*, and the trust reposed in them by the " people, to imploy their care and utmost power to secure the parliament, and preserve " the peace and quiet of the kingdom.

Along with their petition they sent his majesty three resolutions of parliament, *viz.*

Die Veneris Maii 20, 1642.

" *Resolved upon the question,*

" *First*, That it appears that the king (seduced by wicked council) intends to make war " against the parliament, who, in all their consultations and actions, have proposed no o- " ther end unto themselves but the care of his kingdoms, and the performance of all duty " and loyalty to his person.

" *Secondly*, That whensoever the king maketh war upon the parliament, it is a breach of " the trust reposed in him by his people, and contrary to his oath, and tending to the dis- " solution of this government.

" *Thirdly*, That whosoever shall serve or assist him in such wars, are traitors by the fun- " damental laws of this kingdom, and have been so adjudged by two acts of parliament *(r)*, " and ought to suffer as traitors *(s)*.

His majesty's answer.

" WE cannot but extreamly wonder that the causeless jealousys concerning us, raised and " fomented by a malignant party in this kingdom, which desire nothing more " than to snatch themselves particular advantages out of a general combustion, (which means " of advantage shall never be administred to them by our fault or seeking) should not only " be able to seduce a weak party in this our kingdom, but seem to find so much counte- " nance even from both houses, as that our raising of a guard (without further design than " for the safety of our person, an action soe legal in manner, soe peaceable upon causes soe " evident and necessary) should not only be looked upon and petitioned against by them, as " a causeless jealousy, but declared to be the raising of a war against them, contrary to our " former professions of our care of religion and law. And we noe less wonder that this " action of ours should be said (in a very large expression) to be apprehended by the inha- " bitants of this country, as an affrightment and disturbance to our people; having been as " well received here, as it is every where to be justify'd; and (we speak now of the general " not of a few seduced particulars) assisted and sped by this country, with that loyal affe- " ction and alacrity as is a most excellent example set to the rest of the kingdom, of care of " our safety upon all occasions, and shall never be forgotten by us, nor we hope by our po- " sterity; but shall ever be paid to them in that which the proper expression of a prince's " gratitude, and perpetual vigilant care to govern them justly, and to preserve the only rule " by which they can be governed, the law of the land. And we are confident, that if you " were yourselves eye-witnesses, you would soe see the contrary, as to give little present " thanks, and hereafter little credit to your informers: And if you have noe better intelli- " gence of the inclinations of the rest of the kingdom, certainly the minds of our people " (which to some ends and purposes you represent) are but ill represented unto you.

" Have you soe many months together not contented your selves to rely for security (as " your predecessours have done upon the affection of the people, but by your own single " authority raised to your selves a *guard*, and that sometimes of noe ordinary numbers, and " in no ordinary way) and could not all those pikes and protestations, that army on one " side and that navy on the other, perswade us to command you to disband your forces, " and to content yourselves with your ordinary (that is with noe) guard, and work in us an " opinion, that you appeared to levy war against us, or had any further design: And is it " possible that the same persons should be soe apt to suspect and condemn us who have been " soe unapt in the same matter (upon much more ground) to tax or suspect them? This is " our case, notwithstanding the care and fidelity of our parliament, our fort is kept by arm- " ed men against us, our proper goods first detained from us, and then, contrary to our " command, by strong hand offered to be carried away (in which at once all our property " as a private person, all our authority as a king are wrested from us) and yet for us to se- " cure ourselves in a legal way, that sir *John Hotham* may not by the same forces, or by more

(q) Out of a quarto book published at *London* 1643. intituled, *An exact collection of all remonstrances, declarations, votes, orders, ordinancys, proclamations, petitions, messages, answers, and other remarkable passages between the king's most excellent majesty and his high court of parliament, from* December 1641. *to* March 1643.

(r) 11 *Rich.* II. 1 *Hen.* IV.

(s) These votes and some old acts of parliament taken out of the records of the tower were ordered to be printed. *Jo. Brown cleric. parliamentorum.* Collection, &c.

" raised,

A. 1642. "raised, by pretence of the same authority, (for they say he dayly raiseth some, and we know "it noe new thing in him to pretend orders he cannot shew) continue the war that he hath "levied against us, and as well imprison our person as detain our goods, and as well shut "us up in *York*, as shut us out of *Hull*, is said to be esteemed a cause of great jealousy to "the parliament, a raising war against them, and of danger to the whole kingdom. While "these injuries and indignities offered to us are countenanced by them who ought to be most "forward in our vindication and their punishment, in observation of their oaths and of the "trust reposed in them by the people, and to avoid the dissolution of the present govern-"ment. Upon which case the whole world is to judge; whether we had not reason not "wholy to rely upon the care and fidelity of our parliament (being soe strangely blinded by "malignant spirits as not to perceive our injurys) but to take some care of our own person, "and in order to that to make use of that authority, which the laws declare to be in us; "and whether this parliament, with such a threatning conclusion, accompanied with more "threatning votes, gives us not cause rather to increase than diminish our guard; especially "since we saw before the petition a printed paper dated *May* 17, underwritten *Hen. Elsing* "*Cler. D. Com.* commanding, in the name of both lords and commons, the sheriffs of all "our countys, to raise the power of all those countys, to suppress such of our subjects, "as by any of our commands shall be drawn together, and put, as that paper calls "it, in a posture of war; charging our officers and subjects to assist them in the per-"formance thereof at their perills. For though we cannot suspect that this paper "(or any bare votes not grounded upon law or reason, or quotations of repealed sta-"tutes) should have any ill influence upon our good people, who know their dutys too "well, not to know that to take up arms against those who upon a legal command (that is "ours) come together to a most legal end (that is our security and preservation) were to "levy war against us, and who appear in this county (and we are confident they are soe "throughout the kingdom) noe less satisfied with the legality, conveniency, and necessity "of these our guards, and noe less sensible of the indignitys and dangers (which makes it "necessary) then we ourself: Yet if that paper be really the act of both houses, we can-"not but look upon it as the highest of scorns and indignitys; first to issue commands of "force against us, and after those have appeared useless, to offer, by petition, to perswade "us to that which that force should have effected.

"We conclude this answer to your petition with our counsel to you, that you join with "us in exacting satisfaction for that unparallelled, and yet unpunished, action of sir *John Ho-"tham*'s; and that you command our fort and goods to be returned to our own hands; "that you lay down all pretences (under pretence of necessity or declaring what is law) to "make laws without us, and, by consequence, put a cypher upon us; that you declare ef-"fectually against tumults, and call in such pamphlets, (punishing the authors and pub-"lishers of them) as seditiously endeavour to disable us from protecting our people by "weakning (by false aspersions and new false doctrines) our authority with them, and their "confidence in us. The particulars of which tumults and pamphlets, we would long since "have taken care that our learned council should have been enabled to give in evidence, "if, upon our former offer, we had received any return of encouragement from you in it. "And if you doe this, you then (and hardly till then) will perswade the world that you "have discharged your duty to God, the trust reposed in you by the people, and the fun-"damental laws and constitutions of the kingdom, and imployed your care and utmost "power to secure the parliament (for we are still a part of the parliament, and shall be till "this well-founded monarchy be turned to a democracy) and to preserve the peace and quiet "of the kingdom. Which together with the defence of the protestant profession, the laws "of the land, and our own just prerogative (as a part of, and a defence to those laws) "have been the main end which in our consultations and actions we proposed to ourself.

This message of the king's to the parliament, was followed by a proclamation, forbidding all his majesty's subjects belonging to the trained bands or militia of this kingdom, to rise, march, muster or exercise by virtue of any order or ordinance of one or both houses of parliament, without consent or warrant from his majesty upon pain of punishment according to the law.

Dated at the court at York *the* 27th *day of* May 1642.

In answer to this came out two orders from the parliament, the one directed to all high sheriffs, justices of the peace, and other officers within one hundred and fifty miles of the city of *York*, to take special care to stop all arms and ammunition carrying towards *York*, and the apprehending of all persons going with the same. The other in particular to the high-sheriff, justices of the peace &c. of the county of *Lancaster*, requiring them upon the penalty of being declared disturbers of the peace of the kingdom to suppress the raising and coming together of any soldiers horse or foot by warrant, commission, or order from his majesty, &c.

The county of *Lancaster* shewed their attachment to his majesty's interest by a very remarkable petition: for that time, presented to the king on the last of *May* by the high-sheriff of that county and divers other gentlemen of quality. Subscribed by sixty four knights,

knights and esquires, fifty five divines, seven hundred and forty gentlemen, and of freeholders and others above seven thousand. This petition because it manifestly shews that all his majesty's subjects were not then infatuated with notions of reformation in church and state, I shall beg leave to give at large; with the king's answer (*t*). A. 164½.

" *To the sacred majesty of our most gratious sovereign lord* CHARLES; *by the grace of God, of* England, Scotland, France *and* Ireland, *king, defender of the faith,* &c.

" *The humble petition, and gratulation, of divers of his majesty's faithful subjects of the true protestant religion, within the county palatine of* Lancaster.

" *Most gratious sovereign,*

" THE most real and convincing testimonys of your princely care, for the advancement " of God's true religion in your majesty's realms, and the common good of all " your subjects, could doe noe less than draw from us (who have hitherto in these stirring " times sat still) this humble acknowledgement of our due and necessary thanks.

" We, with the inmost and choicest thoughts of our souls, doe esteem and prize your ma" jesty's most righteous intentions of governing your liege people according to the wholsome " laws of this kingdom, a thing with such earnestness avowed by your majesty, whereunto " we yield that hearty credence which is due to soe religious and righteous a prince. We " doe also with all humility and thankfulness, acknowledge your manifold and evident ma" nifestations to the world that you affect not an arbitrary government, but the common " prosperity and happiness of all your loyal subjects, by your readiness to join with your " parliament in a speedy raising of forces, for a timely suppression of that odious rebellion " in *Ireland*; by your late proclamation, for the putting in due execution the laws against " *papists*; by your most gratious condescending to the desires of your great council, in sign" ing the bills for triennial parliaments; for relinquishing your title of imposing upon mer" chandize, and power of pressing soldiers; for the taking away of the star-chamber and " high commission courts; for the regulating of the council table; as alsoe the bills for the " forests and stannery courts; with other most necessary acts. Moreover we are confident " and well assured of your majesty's zeal for the advancement of the true protestant religion, " and with inexpressible joy doe understand your most christian and pious resolution, for " the preservation of those powerful encouragements of industry, learning and piety, " the means and honour of the ministry, for the maintenance and encouragement of our " our church-government, and solemn liturgy of the church, of long continued and general " approbation of the most pious and learned of this nation, and of other countrys; com" posed according to the primitive pattern, by our blessed martyrs and other religious and " learned men. As alsoe your gratious pleasure that all abuses of church and state, shall be " reformed according to the modell of queen *Elizabeth*'s days, of ever blessed and famous " memory; by the one you have weakned the hopes of the sacrilegious devourers of the " churche's patrimony, (if there be any such) and by the other at once provided against all " popish impietys and idolatrys, and alsoe against the growing danger of anabaptists, " brownists, and other novellists; all which piety, love, and justice we beseech God to re" turn into your royal bosom. But yet, *most gratious sovereign*, there is one thing that sads " our hearts, and hinders the perfection of our happiness, which is the distance and misun" derstanding between your majesty and your parliament; whereby the hearts of your " subjects are filled with fears and jealousys, justice neglected, sacred ordinancys profaned, " and trading impaired, to the impoverishing of many of your liege people: For the re" moval whereof, we cannot find out any lawfull means without your majesty's assistance " and direction.

" Wherefore we humbly beseech your most excellent majesty to continue your most chri" stian and pious resolution, of ruling your people according to the laws of the land, and " maintaining of the same; of being a zealous defender of the established doctrine, liturgy, " and government of the church, from heresy, libertinism and profaneness; an advancer of " learning, piety and religion; an encourager of painfull orthodox preachers; and what" soever your parliament shall offer to your royal view, conducing to this blessed end, the " common good, and tranquility of your subjects, to be pleased to condescend unto and " gratiously confirm. And withal to declare unto us some expedient way, how we may " make a dutifull adress unto your parliament for the taking away of those differences and " impediments, which stay the happy proceedings of that most honourable assembly, where" of your majesty is the head, (which once removed, we doubt not but you will speedily " be as near your parliament in person as in affection, that there may be a blessed harmony " between your highness and that great council) and we shall with all alacrity observe the " same, humbly tendering our lives and fortunes for the preservation of your royal person, " crown and dignity, according to our bounden duty and allegiance; and heartily praying " for your majesty's long and prosperous reign over us.

(*t*) *York*, printed by the king's printers, 1643.

A. 1642.

At the court at York, June 6, 1642.

" HIS majesty has commanded me to give you this answer to your petition :
" That he is very glad to find such real acknowledgments of those great graces " which he hath bountifully bestowed upon this his kingdom of *England* in the time of this " parliament; and likewise it is a great contentment to him to find soe many true sons of " the church of *England*, as by your expressions in the said petition doth plainly appear to " him; assuring you that he shall not yield in his zeal and constancy, neither to queen *Eliza-* " *beth*, nor to his father of ever blessed memory, both against popish superstition on the " one side, and schismatical innovation and confusion on the other. In the last place, as he " doth take it in very good part, your desire of a good understanding between his majesty " and his two houses of parliament, soe likewise he cannot but much commend the way that " you take therein. And as for your directions, if you will but seriously consider his ma- " jesty's just and necessary desires, expressed in his answers and declarations since his coming " to *York*, your zeal and knowledge will not need more particular instructions to make " such addresses to both houses of parliament as the times require, and befitting such loyal " and true affected subjects to your king and country, as this petition expresseth you to " be.

O. NICHOLAS.

This and several other such addresses from other parts of the kingdom, must chear the king's heart in the midst of his afflictions by the ill treatment he had from the parliament, and let him see that his subjects were not yet soe blinded but they could perceive their interest in keeping and sustaining a king of his excellent principles and qualifications on the throne of his ancestors.

On the 27th of *May* last the king had issued out a proclamation requiring all ministers, freeholders, farmers, and substantial copy-holders, to assemble and meet together on *Heworth-Moor* near the city of *York*, on *Friday* the third of *June* following. Accordingly at the day appointed, a vast multitude of them appeared, to the number of seventy thousand, some say one hundred thousand, and waited his majesty's appearance. *(u)* About eleven o' clock the king came to the moor accompany'd with a great number of lords and knights of great quality. His majesty had appointed eight hundred foot compleatly armed to guard his person. The prince alsoe led a troop of horse consisting of one hundred and fifty knights, with esquiers, and gentlemen, which with servants, all armed, made another troop.

As soon as his majesty came near the moore, the people saluted him with three loud huzza's; and being come to them, and as much silence made as possible, his majesty made a speech, which, because it is printed at large in my lord *Clarendon* I shall omit. The speech ended, the king rode round the moor with a prodigious croud following him, with loud acclamations of *God bless the king (x)*. And having surveyed all the field he returned to his palace attended by great part of the said company; who seeing him safe within his court gates, another loud huzza left him.

About this time came down to *York* to the king, the humble petition and advice of the parliament, with nineteen propositions annexed; all which, with their answer by his majesty, are in the noble historian, and therefore needless here.

His majesty thought fit to make a declaration to all the lords attending him at *York*, and to others of his majesty's privy council there in these words *(y)*:

CHARLES, R.

" WE doe declare that we will not require nor exact any obedience from you, but shall " be warranted by the known law of the land; as we doe expect that you shall not " yield to any commands not legally grounded or imposed by any other.

" And we doe further declare that we will defend every one of you, and all such as shall " refuse any such commands, whether they proceed from votes and orders of both houses, or " any other way from all dangers and hazards whatsoever.

" And we doe further declare, that we will defend the true protestant religion, established " by the law of the land, the lawfull liberties of the subjects of *England*, and just priviledges " of all the three estates of parliament; and shall require noe further obedience from you, " then as accordingly we shall perform the same.

" And we doe declare, that we will not, as is falsly pretended, engage you or any of you " in any war against the parliament, except it be for our necessary defence and safety against " such as doe insolently invade or attempt against us or such as shall adhere to us.

York 13 *Junii* 1642.

(u) Out of a pamphlet printed at *London* 1642, by authority of parliament.

(x) *Ex MS.*

(y) From the collection of publick acts.

Upon

I

A. 1642.

Upon which the lords entered into the following engagement:

" WE doe engage our selves not to obey any orders or commands whatsoever, not " warranted by the known laws of the land.

" We doe engage our selves to defend your majesty's person, crown and dignity, toge-" ther with your majesty's just and legal prerogative against all persons and power whatso-" ever.

" We will defend the true protestant religion established by the law of the land; the law-" full libertys of the subjects of *England*, and just privileges of your majesty and both your " houses of parliament.

" And lastly, we engage our selves not to obey any rule, order, or ordinance whatsoever " concerning the *militia*, that hath not the royal assent.

York, June 13, 1642. Subscribed by

Lord *Keeper*, lord duke of *Richmond*, lord marquis of *Hereford*, earl of *Lindsey*, earl of *Cumberland*, earl of *Huntingdon*, earl of *Bath*, earl of *Southampton*, earl of *Dorset*, earl of *Salisbury*, earl of *Northampton*, earl of *Devonshire*, earl of *Cambridge*, earl of *Bristol*, earl of *Westmorland*, earl of *Barkeshire*, earl of *Monmouth*, earl of *Rivers*, earl of *Newcastle*, earl of *Dover*, earl of *Carnarvon*, earl of *Newport*, lord *Mowbray* and *Matravers*, lord *Willoughby* of *Eresby*, lord *Rich*, lord *Charles Howard* of *Charlton*, lord *Newark*, lord *Paget*, lord *Chandos*, lord *Faulconbridge*, lord *Paulet*, lord *Lovelace*, lord *Savile*, lord *Coventry*, lord *Mohun*, lord *Dunsmore*, lord *Seymour*, lord *Gray* of *Ruthin*, lord *Capell*, lord *Falkland*, Mr. *Comptroller*, Mr. Secretary *Nicholas*, Mr. *Chancellour of the Exchequer*, lord chief justice *Banks*.

In all forty lords, besides the great officers.

By this it appears that the court at *York* was exceeding splendid at this time, nor were the king's affairs so desperate though the parliament had seized upon his revenues and magazine, but that by the help of these loyal noblemen he might raise head against them. Many of these noble lords lost their lives in his service, and more their estates; which the pen of their fellow sufferer, in these troubles, has recorded; and painted their characters in such lively colours, that latest posterity may have a strong idea of their unshaken loyalty and unblemished worth.

Two days after the date of the former act his majesty thought proper to publish a solemn protestation, wherein *he takes God to witness that he always did abhor the thoughts of making war upon his parliament, and requires the nobility and council upon the place to declare whether they have not been witnesses of his frequent and earnest declarations and professions for peace. Whether they see any colour of preparations or councils that might reasonably beget a belief of any such design. And whether they be not fully perswaded that he hath no such intention; but that all his endeavours tend to the firm and constant settlement of the true protestant religion, the just privileges of parliament, the liberty of the subject, the law, peace, and prosperity of this kingdom.*

To which declarations the noble lords, *&c.* subjoined the following:

" WE whose names are underwritten in obedience to his majesty's desire, and out of " the duty which we owe to his majesty's honour, and to truth, being here upon " the place and witnesses of his majesty's frequent and earnest declarations and professions of " his abhorring all designs of making war upon his parliament, and not seeing any colour of " preparations or councils that might reasonably create the belief of any such design; do " profess before God, and testify to all the world, that we are fully perswaded that his ma-" jesty hath noe such intention, but that all his endeavours tend to the firm and constant set-" tlement of the true protestant religion, the just privileges of parliament, the liberty of the " subject, the law, peace, and prosperity of this kingdom."

York, June 15, 1642. Subscribed as before.

Can any man venture to say, after reading these declarations, that the king was not forced into a war with his parliament? Or that he begun the fray? If the solemn asseveration of a prince is disputed, who I may safely assert had more true religion in him than most, or all of his successors put together; yet, the testimonies of so many noble patriots who stood up in his justification, at a time when 'twas not possible that either interest or awe should sway them to it, will be a lasting monument of his majesty's peaceable intentions.

The question was then, and has been since, who struck the first blow? Or begun the first acts of hostility? The answer is at hand, and a very peremptory one, the *parliament*. For an undeniable proof of this assertion besides the unsufferable affront of sir *John Hotham*'s shutting the king out of his own town, and the parliaments vindication of the action, the following petition, that I have now before me, subscribed and consented to, as the paper witnesses, by all the nobility of *Yorkshire*, forty baronets and knights, many esquires, and o-

ther

A 1642. ther persons of distinction, will put the matter out of dispute to any but a subscriber to that heap of infamous scandal published by Mr. *Oldmixon*.

(z) *To the right honourable the lords and commons assembled in parliament.*

The humble petition and remonstrance of the nobility and gentry of the county of York.

Sheweth,

" THAT this county is extreamly perplexed, by reason of the publick acts of hostility " committed by sir *John Hotbam*, and the garrison at *Hull*, to the great disturbance " of the peace of this county, threatning no less then the ruin and destruction of it. That " the first putting a garrison into that town, was pretended to be to defend it against the " *papists* at home, and the invasion of *foreign enemys*. Since that time the gates have been " shut against our gratious sovereign, and entrance denied to his own royal person, several " persons have been thrown out of the town, and expelled from their own freeholds, and " personal estates, and some part of the country is drowned by sir *John Hotbam* to the utter " ruin of many familys. *Sallies* have been made with *armed men*, who have *burned* and " *plundered* houses, and murthered their fellow subjects, (when we were confident of a cessa- " tion) with all the circumstances of *rage* and *cruelty*, which uses to be contracted by a *long* " *and bloody war*. After all this, his majesty (who keeps his residence here with all the " demonstrations of care and affection towards us) gratiously forbears to lay any siege to that " place, and hath declared to us, that, by noe act of his, this county shall be made a seat " of war; and yet by the new supply of soldiers taken into *Hull*, and the late actions there " (which we conceive to be manifestly against the oaths of supremacy and allegiance, the " petition of right, and the late protestation) we have cause to fear that some violence is in- " tended both against our persons and our fortunes.

" The premisses considered, we cannot but be infinitely jealous, that sir *John Hotbam* " cannot derive his authority to commit such *barbarous acts of hostility* from the two houses of " parliament, from whom we expect all the effects of happy peace and preservation of our " laws and libertys.

" We humbly desire therefore to know, whether these *outrages* are done by your autho- " rity, and whether this *country* must be *subject* to that *garrison*, that we may thereupon pro- " vide in such a manner for our *safetys*, that these *injurys*, *violences*, *and oppressions*, be noe " longer imposed upon us by our *fellow subjects*; that we may be all lyable to the known " laws of the land, to which we are born, and which is the only security and evidence we " have for our lives and fortunes.

This petition hath several particular instances of sir *John Hotbam*'s depredations annexed to it, which for brevity sake I omit. It was not long after that this unhappy gentleman either touched in conscience for the unlawfulness and undutifulness of his action to the king, or not so highly regarded and rewarded as the important and leading piece of service might justly challenge from the parliament; the queen being also newly arrived in these parts, who by a stratagem of lord *Digby*'s had dealt with sir *John* about the matter, he began to falter in the firmness he had professed for the parliament. This being guess'd at by some strict observers of him, as he was not reserved enough in a thing of that consequence, a party was made against him in his own garison, and he too late endeavouring to have secured *Hull* for the king, was in the bustle knocked down in the streets, secured with his son and both sent up prisoners to the tower; where not long after they were brought to tryal and executed. The eye of providence here is very visible, and the fulfilling of a dreadful imprecation which sir *John* wished might fall on him and his, if he was not a loyal subject to his majesty, when the king stood at the gates of *Hull*, is very obvious; for now see both father and son adjudged by their *fellow-members*, and condemn'd by their own beloved *martial law*, for intending to deliver up *Hull* to his majesty; which, if it had been done at first, would not only have saved their own lives, but, probably, many thousands of their fellow subjects.

But to proceed to the rest of king *Charles*'s publick acts whilst he kept his court at *York*, I shall beg leave only to transcribe the titles and dates of them as they occurred; for though they deserve a more particular mention, yet the nature of my subject will not admit of it. And first,

(a) " His majesty's answer to the petition of the lords and commons in parliament, pre- " sented to his majesty at *York*, *June* 17, 1642.

" By the king. A proclamation forbidding all levys of forces without his majesty's ex- " press pleasure, signified under his great seal, and all contributions or assistance to any " such levy. Given at the court at *York*, *June* 18, in the eighteenth year of our " reign. 1642.

" By the king. A proclamation to inform all our loving subjects of the lawfulness of " our commissions of array issued into the several countys of the realm of *England* and domi-

(z) Imprinted at *York* by the king's printers, 1642. From the printed copy, *penes me*.

(a) From the collection of publick acts, &c.

" nion

"nion of *Wales*; and of the use of them: and commanding them to obey our commis- A. 1642.
"sioners therein named in the execution of their said commissions. Given at our court at
"*York, June* 20, *an. reg.* 18, 1642.

"A copy of a warrant from the king's most excellent majesty, directed unto the high
"sheriff of the county of *York*, for summoning of all gentlemen and others, being pro-
"testants, who are charged with horses for his majesty's service, or have listed themselves,
"to attend personally for his majesty's security to make their appearance at *York* on *Thurs-*
"*day* the 7th of *July*, 1642.

"Dated at *York, June* 30, 1642. *June* 30.

"His majesty's answer to the declaration of both houses of parliament concerning the
"commission of array. Dated *York, July* 1, 1642.

"The king's majesty's charge sent to all the judges of *England* to be published in their *July* 4.
"respective circuits by his majesty's special command. *Given at our court at* YORK, *July* 4,
"1642.

"By the king. A proclamation against the forcible seizing and removing any the ma-
"gazine or ammunition of any county. And concerning the execution of the militia within
"this kingdom. Dated *York, July* 4, 1642.

"By the king. A proclamation forbidding all relieving or succouring the town of *King-*
"*ston* upon *Hull* against his majesty. Dated *York die predict.*

"His majesty's message to both houses of parliament, *July* 11, with the proclamation
"ensuing.

"By the king. A proclamation declaring our purpose to go in our royal person to
"*Hull*; and the true occasion and end thereof."

And now, the winds blowing high, the flame that had long laid smothered broke out to the purpose; the parliament had passed votes for raising an army, naming a general, *&c.* and the king, after making a short expedition to *Nottingham* and *Leicester*, returned to *York*, where he had summoned the *Yorkshire* gentry to attend him.

Accordingly *August* 4, the heads of the county attended his majesty at *York*; where this unfortunate prince took his last leave of them in a pathetick and moving speech; which because it will be a lasting testimony of the county's and city's loyalty to their injured sovereign, I shall beg leave to give *verbatim*; and the rather because it is wholly omitted by my lord *Clarendon*, *Eachard*, and every other historian of those times that I have seen, except the compiler of the collections before quoted. *August* 4.

"*Gentlemen*,

"WHEN I directed that summons should be sent out for your meeting here this day, "my principal end was that I might give you thanks for the great forwardness "and expressions you have made of your affections to me since I came into this county; "and to assure you that as the whole kingdom hath great reason to value you exceedingly "for it, so I shall be very unsatisfied, till I have found some way to fix a mark of favour "and estimation upon this county, and this people, which may tell posterity how good "subjects you have been, and how much gentlemen; and I am confident the memory of "it will grow up with my sons too in a just acknowledgment. This was the most I in-"tended to say to you, but there is an unquiet spirit abroad, which every day throws in "new accidents to disturb and confound the publick peace. How I was driven from "*London*, when I chose *this place* for my safety, is so notorious that all men know it, who "know any thing; with what strange violences and indignities I have been pursued since "I came hither, needs no other evidence than sir *John Hotham*'s behaviour at *Hull*; who "is now arrived to that insolence, that he will not suffer his treason to be confined longer "within the walls, but makes sallies out of the town upon his fellow-subjects, drowns "their lands, burns and plunders their houses, murthers, and with unheard of cruelties; "torments their persons; and this with so much delight, that he would not have the pa-"tience to wait what answer should be sent to my just demands, though in that respect I "engaged myself to forbear to use any violence, and kept my word; but chose the "night before that came (as if he well knew what answer I was to receive) to act those "outrages.

"You see the sad effects of fears and jealousies, the miseries they have produced; no "man can tell you the least good they have brought forth, or the least evil they have pre-"vented. What inconvenience my presence hath been here, what disturbance it hath "brought upon the publick, or grievance upon any private person, yourselves are best "judges. And whatever scandal some men have been pleased to cast upon the *cavaliers* "(which they intend shall reach all my retinue, and by degrees shall involve all gentle-"men) I am confident there hath not been any eminent disorder or damage befallen any "man, by any person of my train, or under my protection.

"I am sure my directions have been very strict in that point, and if they had not been "observed, I think I should have heard of it by nearer complaints then from *London*, I "pray God the same care may be taken there: I am sure it hath not been. Now to give

A. 1642. "you the fulleſt teſtimony of my affection to you and the peace of this county, and to "ſhew you that no provocation ſhall provoke me to make this place to be a ſeat of war, "I have for your ſakes, paſſed over the conſiderations of honour; and notwithſtanding the "reproaches every day laid on me, laid no ſiege to that place, that they may not have the "leaſt pretence of doing you miſchief, but reſolve by God's help to recover *Hull* ſome "other way; for that I will ever ſit down under ſo bold and inexcuſable a treaſon, no ho- "neſt man can imagine. But it ſeems other men are not of my mind, but reſolve to make "a war at your own doors, whatſoever you do or I ſuffer. To what purpoſe elſe is their "new general armed with an authority to kill and deſtroy all my good ſubjects; their le- "vies of horſe and foot, ſome whereof are on their march towards you with cannon "mounted; and the ſending ſo many new ſoldiers into *Hull*, when there is no approach "made towards it, but to ſally out and commit rapine, and, by degrees, to pour out an "army upon you. In this I muſt aſk your advice what you would do for your ſelves, "and what you would have me do for you? you ſee how I am ſtript of my navy at ſea, "which is imployed againſt me; of my forts and towns at land, which are filled with "armed men to deſtroy me; my money and proviſions of my houſe taken from me, and "all my good ſubjects forbid and threatned if they come near me, that I may by famine "or ſolitarineſs be compelled to yield to the moſt diſhonourable propoſitions, and to put "myſelf and children into the hands of a few malignant perſons, who have entered into a "combination to deſtroy us; and all this done under pretence of a truſt repoſed by the "people. How far you are from committing any ſuch truſt, moſt of the perſons truſted "by you, and your own expreſſions of duty to me, hath manifeſted to all the world; and "how far the whole kingdom is from avowing ſuch a truſt, hath already in a great mea- "ſure, and I doubt not will more every day appear, by the profeſſions of every county; "for I am wholly caſt upon the affections of my people, and have no hope but in the "bleſſing and aſſiſtance of God, the juſtneſs of my cauſe, and the love of my ſubjects "to recover what is taken from me and them; for I may juſtly ſay they are equal loſers "with me.

"Gentlemen, I deſire you to conſider what courſe is to be taken for your own ſecurity "from the excurſions from *Hull*, and the violence which threatens you from thence; I "will aſſiſt you any way you propoſe. Next I deſire you out of the publick proviſion, or "your private ſtore, to furniſh me with ſuch a number of arms, muſquets and corſlets, as "you may conveniently ſpare, which I do promiſe to ſee fully repaid to you. Theſe arms "I deſire may be ſpeedily delivered to the cuſtody of my lord-mayor of *York* for my uſe, "principally from thoſe parts, which by reaſon of their diſtance from *Hull* are leaſt ſubject "to the fear of violence from thence.

"And whoſoever ſhall ſo furniſh me ſhall be excuſed from their attendance and ſervice "at muſters, till their arms ſhall be reſtored; which may well be ſooner than I can pro- "miſe or you expect. I deſire nothing of you but what is neceſſary to be done for the "preſervation of God's true religion, the laws of the land, the liberty of the ſubject, "and the very being of this kingdom of *England*; for it is too evident all theſe are at "ſtake.

"For the compleating my ſon's regiment for the guard of my perſon, under the com- "mand of my lord of *Cumberland*, I refer it wholly to yourſelves who have already ex- "preſſed ſuch forwardneſs in it."

A few more acts of ſtate occurred, e're his majeſty left *York*, which I ſhall curſorily mention, in order as they happened, till I come to the laſt; which being a very memorable proclamation, and the firſt of that kind wherein his majeſty ſhewed himſelf reſolved to fight, and bearing date from hence muſt find a place in our annals.

"By the king. A proclamation for the ſuppreſſing of the preſent rebellion, under the "command of *Robert* earl of *Eſſex:* and the gracious offer of his majeſty's free pardon "to him, and all ſuch of his adherents, as ſhall within ſix days after the date hereof "lay down their arms. *Given at our court at* York *the ninth day of* Auguſt, 1642, "*an. reg.* 18.

"By the king. A proclamation declaring his majeſty's expreſs command, that no po- "piſh recuſant, nor any other, who ſhall refuſe to take the oaths of allegiance and ſu- "premacy ſhall ſerve him in his army, and that the ſoldiery commit no rapines upon the "people, but be fitly provided of neceſſaries for their money. At the court of *York*, "*Auguſt* 10, 1642.

"His majeſty's declaration to all his loving ſubjects concerning the proceedings of this "preſent parliament. *York, Auguſt* 12.

"His majeſty's meſſage to the houſe of commons from the court at *York, Auguſt* 12, "1642.

By

A. 1642.

By the KING.

WHereas divers persons bearing an inward hatred and malice against our person, and government, and ambitious of rule, and places of preferment and command, have raised an army and are now trayterously and rebelliously, (though under the specious pretence of our royal name and authority, and of the defence of our person and parliament) marching in battle array, against us their leige lord and soveraign, contrary to their duty and allegiance, whereby the common peace is likely to be wholly destroyed, and this flourishing kingdom in danger to perish under the miseries of a civil war, if the malice and rage of these persons be not instantly resisted. And as we do and must relie on almighty God (the protector and defender of his anointed) to defend us and our good people against the malice and pernicious designs of these men tending to the utter ruin of our person, the true protestant religion, the laws established, the property and liberty of the subject, and the very being of parliaments; so we doubt not but our good people will in this necessity contribute unto us, with all alacrity and cheerfulness, their assistance in their persons, servants, and money, for the suppressing of the same rebellion. And herein we cannot but with much contentment of heart acknowledge the love and affection of our subjects of our county of York, and divers other counties, in their free and ready assistance of us, which we shall never forget, and our posterity will, as we hope, ever remember for their good.

Nevertheless, in this our extream necessity, though we have been most unwilling, we are inforced for our most just and necessary defence, again to call and invite them and all other of our subjects of the true protestant religion, reciding on the north side of Trent, or within twenty miles southward thereof, whose hearts God almighty shall touch with a true sence and apprehension of our sufferings, and the ill use which the contrivers and fomenters of this rebellion, have made of our clemency and desire of peace, that according to their allegiance, and as they tender the safety of our person, the property of their estates. their just libertys, the true protestant religion, and privileges of parliament, and indeed the very being of parliaments, they attend our person upon Monday the two and twentieth of this instant August at our town of Nottingham, where and when we intend to erect our standard-royal, in our just and necessary defence; and whence we resolve to advance forward for the suppression of the said rebellion, and the protection of our good subjects amongst them, from the burthen of the slavery and insolence under which they cannot but groan till they be relieved by us.

And we likewise call and invite all our subjects of the true protestant religion, in the remoter parts of this our kingdom, to whom notice of this our proclamation cannot so soon arrive, that with all speed possible, as they tender the fornamed considerations, they attend our person in such place as we shall then happen to encamp. And such of our said subjects, as shall come unto us (either to our said town of Nottingham, or to any other place where we shall encamp) armed and arrayed with horse, pistols, muskets, pikes, corslets, horses for dragoons, or other fitting arms and furniture we shall take them into our pay; such of them excepted who shall be willing as voluntiers to serve us in this our necessity without pay.) And whosoever shall in this our danger and necessity, supply us either by guift, or loan of money, or plate, for this our necessary defence (wherein they are alsoe soe nearly concerned) we shall as soon as God shall enable us, repay whatsoever is lent, and upon all occasions remember, and reward these our good subjects, according to the measure of their love and affections to us and their country.

Given at our court at *York* the twelfth day of *August* in the eighteenth year of our reign, 1642.

God save the KING.

After a stay of five months king *Charles* left the city of *York* in order to erect the standard royal at *Nottingham*. Mr. *Eachard* says, it would have been much more for the king's service, if the standard had been first erected at *York*; as having most of the northern counties at his devotion. And it had been so, but that the northern gentry persuaded the king that the people's fears were very great, that their country should be made a seat of war; judging wrongly that the war would be no where but with the king's army. But, after some recollection, when the time of the king's departure drew near, they considered that the garrison of *Hull* would be a thorn in their sides; that there were several persons of quality and interest, in the country, disaffected to his majesty's service; that a member *(b)* of the house of commons had declared in a speech concerning *York*, *that there was a mark set upon that place*; therefore they desired his majesty to constitute the earl of *Cumberland* supream commander of the country in all military affairs; and appoint sir *Thomas Glemham* to stay with them and command those forces the earl should think necessary to raise for their defence. In both which his majesty readily gratified them.

Two of the principal instruments the parliament made use of to carry on this unnatural war in these parts, lived in this county, and one in our neighbourhood; which were *Ferdinando* lord *Fairfax* of *Denton*, and his son sir *Thomas Fairfax* of *Nunappleton*. The father

(b) Mr. *Hollis*.

has

A. 1642. has already been mentioned as a warm man against the court by bringing the parliaments message to the king about *Hull*; and the son very early began to shew his hatred to the royal cause, if we may believe his own words in the short memorial of his life.

These two gentlemen were, almost, the only persons of any considerable quality in the county, who were not well disposed to his majesty, and who were, says *Eachard*, influenced by two or three others of inferiour rank. The king had once resolved to have taken them all prisoners before he left *York*, which had probably prevented the mischiefs that ensued, but was persuaded from it by the gentlemen of the country, who alledged that such an unpopular act would prove their ruin; exposing them to the fury of the disaffected party, who would rather encrease than be weakned by it. So tender and careful, says the historian, were men to persuade his majesty from any thing that carried not the full face of the law with it, vainly imagining *the mildest physick most proper for such violent outragious distempers.*

September 2. Upon the king's departure, the lord-mayor summoned all the citizens, *&c.* to the *Guild-hall*, where the commission of *Henry* earl of *Cumberland* was read; and according to the tenure of it, the city was immediately ordered to be put in a posture of defence, and ordnance mounted on the gates *(c)*.

And now a cruel and bloody war began, which I shall persue no farther than the boundaries of the city will allow me, and in that district shall be very careful to let no memorable event on either side escape particular notice; few historians having thought fit to transmit our affairs to posterity.

At the first setting out, the gentlemen of both parties were so cautious of involving this county in a war, that a treaty was set on foot, and fourteen articles agreed on betwixt them; by, and with, the consent of the right honourable *Henry* earl of *Cumberland*, lord lieutenant general of all his majesty's forces in the county of *York*, and *Ferdinando* lord *Fairfax*. These articles *(d)* comprehended a suspension of all military actions and preparations in this county on both sides, which are too long to insert; but they were agreed to at *Rodwell*, *September* 29, 1642, and signed by *Henry Bellasyse*, *William Savile*, *Edward Osborne*, *John Ramsden*, *Ingram Hopton*, and *Francis Nevile* on the king's party; and *Thomas Fairfax*, *Thomas Maleverer*, *William Lister*, *William White*, *John Farrar*, and *John Stockdale* of the other party.

This amicable treaty and agreement was but of small effect; and as I find subsisted no longer than the parliamentarians thought themselves strong enough to cope with the king's party in these parts. *(d)* A declaration of the earl of *Cumberland*'s published about this time makes this appear too plain, wherein he tells the publick, "that it had been his own "and his majesty's peculiar care to remove the cloud of war from this county which had "hung dreadfully over their heads for some time. That since his majesty's departure, he "had applied himself by all the ways and means which human reason could dictate, to "procure a timely remedy for these bleeding wounds. Therefore at the treaty of *Rodwell*, "with some gentlemen of this county, whose affection to peace and unity, though differing "in opinion, he thought himself most confident, sundry articles were agreed upon, all "wholly tending to a real settlement of peace amongst them. For the attaining of which, "he willingly let pass the manifest advantages, which he had over the opposers of peace "in this county, and judging the affections of others by his own, quitted all considera-"tions but such as might purchase amity amongst them. Nay, when it lay in his power "to have forced or destroyed them, that nothing might be wanting to oblige them, he "set at liberty several prisoners, some of good quality, upon their word and faith to re-"turn if the treaty was not concluded. Notwithstanding all this, adds the earl, with-"out the least breach on our side, as soon as they were free from danger, contrary to "their *hands*, *faith*, and *protestations*, they have wholly broken that agreement, so solemn-"ly concluded; and by a specious offer of peace, prepared themselves for war, and opened "a breach which must now most inevitably overwhelm this distressed country." The noble earl after enumerating many scandalous enormities, murders, and cruelties committed by the parliamentarians, concludes thus, *however though we perish in this work we shall rest satisfied, that we have preserved our faith and honour untainted; and yet we hope by God's blessing upon our just endeavours, to repress the enemies of his majesty's peace, and to conserve ourselves and this country to the glory of God, the service of our king, and mutual comfort of one another.*

The war now was entered into briskly on both sides, but the rebels had much the better of the earl. Sir *Thomas Fairfax* and capt *Hotham* son to the governor of *Hull*, had advanced so far against *York*, as to fortify *Tadcaster* and *Wetherby*; and had twice repulsed sir *Thomas Glemham* in two furious assaults he had made upon their forces in the last mentioned town.

(c) Ex MS.

(d) From a copy printed at *York*.

(e) Entituled the declaration of the right honourable *Henry* earl of *Cumberland* lord lieutenant general of all his majesty's forces in *Yorkshire*. And of the nobility and gentry and others his majesty's subjects, now assembled at *York*, for his majesty's service and the defence of this city and county. Printed at *York* by *Stephen Bulkley*, 1642. by special command.

This

This made the *Yorkshire* gentry send to desire the earl of *Newcastle* to come to their aid; who had levied considerable forces in the north, and he accordingly made a speedy march to the city. A. 1642.

November 30, came the earl to *York* with an army of six thousand horse and foot, and ten pieces of Ordnance. They were received with great joy by the citizens, but especially, says a manuscript of that time, by sir *Edward Osborn* and sir *Marmaduke Langdale*, the agents for the rest of the gentlemen on that side of the question in these parts.

At the earl of *Newcastle*'s arrival, the earl of *Cumberland*, being of too peaceable a disposition for the spirits of the *Yorkshire* gentry, says sir *Thomas Fairfax* (*e*), resigned his commission to him; who staid no longer in *York*, than three days to refresh his men, when he marched out from thence with four thousand horse and foot and seven pieces of ordnance, in order to attack the enemy's entrenchments at *Tadcaster*. At the same time the lord general sent his lieutenant general, the earl of *Newport*, to *Wetherby* with two thousand men, and commission as soon as that place was taken to come and assist him by falling upon their backs at *Tadcaster*.

The lord general made his attack upon the enemy's works about eleven o' clock in the forenoon; the enemy had in their trenches two thousand men, as my manuscript speaks, though sir *Thomas* says only seven hundred, which is scarce possible; they reserved their shot till the royalists came very near them, and then disposed of it to so good purpose, that they were forced to retire and shelter themselves behind the hedges. The fight continued from the time aforesaid till four or five in the afternoon with cannon and musket without intermission. Lord *Ferdinando* in his letter to the parliament, about this action, writes that, besides cannon, at least forty thousand musket shot was discharged on both sides in this conflict (*f*). Captain *Hotham* at the beginning of the fight wrote a letter to the earl of *Newport*, signed *Will. Newcastle*, and sent it by a running foot-boy to tell him that though his commission was to come and assist him, yet he might now spare his pains, and stay till he sent him orders the next morning (*g*). This sham letter had the desired effect, for though *Wetherby* was relinquish'd to the parliament's forces before noon, yet the earl on the receipt of it stopped his proceedings and waited for further orders. *Newport*'s not coming up was a great discouragement to the lord general and his forces, who nevertheless continued the attack with great bravery till five in the afternoon; when their powder and match being spent, they were obliged to desist till he had sent for a supply from *York*; intending to renew the assault next morning. But in the night lord *Fairfax* drew off his men to *Selby* and *Cawood*; and left the earl free possession of the place. There were slain on both sides about three hundred; but none of note except one captain *Lister*, whom sir *Thomas* calls a great loss, being a *discreet man*. The father styles him a *valiant and gallant gentleman*, and says he was shot in the head by a musket bullet (*h*). Thus by the mercy of God, adds sir *Thomas*, were a few delivered from an army who in their thoughts had swallowed us up.

After this, *Sheffield*, *Wakefield*, *Leeds*, *Hallifax*, and *Bradford*, and several other towns and garrisons, against the king, were in six week's space, by the valour and conduct of the lord general, reduced to his majesty's subjection. But by the various chance of war lost and won again, sometimes by one party, and sometimes by another; and *Yorkshire*, spite of all precaution, was for some years a scene of blood and misery.

But, to keep within my limits, our city was the lord general's chief quarters for him and often for his whole army; and so full was it usually of soldiers, that my manuscript informs me that five hundred were billetted, on free quarter sometimes, in one parish that had but forty houses in it. This must be for disaffection; but it was a miserable time, scarce a night happened without quarrels, blood and murder among the men, which the vigilancy of the governor sir *Thomas Glemham* could by no means prevent; and he himself was several times in danger to be slain, in endeavouring to appease these contentious mutinies. At this time also all the goals in the city were full of prisoners, and some other places made use of for that occasion; at one time three hundred and eighty prisoners in the castle; in *Davy-hall* one hundred, in *Merchant's-hall* one hundred and eight; who by close confinement, want of victuals, *&c.* were put into raging fevers; in which unhappy condition several of these wretches became their own executioners.

About this time a pamphlet was published at *York* by the lord general, intituled, *a declaration of his excellency the earl of* Newcastle, *in answer to the aspersions cast upon him by the lord* Fairfax *in his warrant bearing date* Feb. 2, 1642. *Printed at* York *by* Stephen Bulkly *by special command.*

(*e*) *Fairfax*'s memoirs.

(*f*) Collection of publick acts.

(*g*) *Ex MS.*

(*h*) I find in *Thoresby*'s *Ducatus Leod* a remarkable instance of filial affection relating to this gentleman, as follows: "*William Lister* esquire, slain at *Tadcaster* in the "civil wars. His son passing through that place many "years after, had the curiosity to enquire where his fa-"ther was buried; and finding the sexton digging in the "choir, he shewed him a skull just dug up, which he a-"verred to be his father's. The skull upon handling was "found to have a bullet in it; which testimony of "the truth of the sexton's words so struck the son, that "he sickened at the sight of it, and died soon after." —— Their estate, at *Thornton* in *Craven*, is now in the possession of my very worthy friend sir *John Lister Kaye* baronet, and may it be so *per plurimos annos*.

A. 1642. In this the earl, in a very handsome manner, and nervous style, answers all the objections, or rather scandalous and opprobrious aspersions, which the lord *Fairfax* had thrown on him; as having raised an army of *papists*, and with those had invaded, robbed and plundered this county; killing and destroying religious protestant subjects; imprisoning and banishing God's holy ministers. All which the earl endeavours to wipe off. This declaration, with the answer to it again by the lord *Fairfax*, are extant in *Rushworth*; and were they not too prolix should find a place in these annals; for, in my opinion, nothing could give a juster notion of each party's pretensions to honour, honesty, and the justice of their cause, than may be found in them. And I believe the reader will say, when he has read them, that their pens and swords carried equal sharpness; the former having as little remorse in destroying each other's characters, as the latter their persons.

(*i*) *Feb.* 22. came the joyful news to *York* of the queen's majesty's safe arrival and landing at *Bridlington-key*. Her majesty had embarked on board the *princess-royal* of *Great-Britain*, *Feb.* 16. at *Helvoet-sluice*; under the convoy of seven *Dutch* men of war, commanded by admiral *Van Trump*; on the 20th they cast anchor in *Bridlington-bay*; and on the 22d she landed, as soon as the lord general arrived, who came with a strong body of troops to guard her person. Her majesty brought along with her thirty six pieces of brass and two of iron ordnance, with small arms for ten thousand men. I need not here mention the insolence of *Batten* the parliament's vice-admiral, who missing of his prey at sea, *Feb.* 24. came into the bay with four men of war and a pinnace; in the night time he drew up his ships, as near the key as possible, and discharged above one hundred great shot, cross bars and twelve pounders, all of them aimed at the house where the queen lay. Some of these shot making way through her very chamber, she was forced out of her bed to take shelter behind a bank in the fields. This barbarous usage sufficiently shews what she might have expected had they met her majesty at sea.

On the 7th of *March* the queen lay at *Malton*; and the next day entered *York*, with three coaches, escorted by the lord general, with eight troops of horse and fifteen companies of foot. She was met on *Heworth Moor* by the lord-mayor, aldermen, *&c.* and great multitudes of citizens with all possible, and I believe unfeigned, demonstrations of joy; the noble supply she brought to the king challenging no less.

March 9. came the ammunition to *York*; loading for five hundred carts; which stores with three mortar-pieces were laid up in the common-hall. At this time the city was every where strongly fortified, and above twenty cannon, great and small, were planted about it. Two cannon were planted upon *old Bayle*, one at the *Fryers*, two sling pieces, and one small drake in three or four barks which cross'd the river in a breast near the *Crane-house*; two at *Micklegate-bar*, two at *Monk-bar*; two at *Walmgate-bar*; out of which last was a strong bulwark erected. At several lanes ends, within the city, were ditches and banks made and cast up, with hogsheads filled with earth for barricadoes. By the general's orders the magistrates were to find eight hundred men to work daily at the repairs of the walls, and securing the ditches of the city; and they had likewise eight hundred more out of the county to help them. This must be a vast expence and fall heavy upon every particular inhabitant; when besides, adds the writer of a manuscript, each citizen paid two pounds a month, that maintained a man in arms, towards provision for the army. And if their own servants bore not their arms, it cost five shillings a week for one to bear them. Add to this six shillings a month for firing at the several guards in the city, with two, three or four soldiers billeted upon free billet in a house, and it will make their case very deplorable.

A. 1643. The earl of *Montross*, who will be ever famous in history, having deserted the covenanter's cause came with the lord *Ogilvy* and one hundred and twenty horse, and presented himself to the queen at *York*. He informed her majesty with the covenanters preparations to invade *England*, and that they would in a very little time bring a great army into it. The marquis of *Hamilton* came also hither to salute the queen, and by his arts refuted *Montross*'s assertions, and prayed her majesty to give no credit to one *so vain and young*, which she unhappily inclined to. Sir *Hugh Cholmley*, governor of *Scarborough-castle*, with three hundred men came in to the queen at *York*, returning to his obedience to his sovereign. The two *Hothams* seemed also to attempt it, but unforutnately. So dangerous rebellion is, says my authority, that it often ruins those that would return to their duty again.

The queen staid eight weeks in *York* as some write, but by a (*k*) printed paper now before me, it appears she resided near three months in this city. The paper bears this title; *To the queen's most excellent majesty, the humble petition of the nobility and gentry of the county of* York; and is thus worded,

“ *Most gratious queen,*

“ WE the nobility and gentry of the county of *York* having always found your maje-“ sty's most gratious and constant affection and assistance to restore the peace of the “ kingdom in general, and of this county in particular (for which we shall never be want-

(*i*) *Ex MS.*

(*k*) Printed at *York* for *Stephen Bulkly*, *A.* 1643.

“ ing

X

"ing in our loyal endeavours and service to your sacred majesty) do in all humility and in A. 1643.
"the behalf of all his majesty's well affected subjects in this county, crave of your majesty, "that now in our greatest and most pressing necessities, your majesty will gratiously continue "to contribute your care and protection to us and these northern parts. And we, seriously "considering the great benefit to his majesty's affairs, that all helps be applied to the settling "these northern countys in peace, and that the rebels in this and other neighbouring countys "are of more consideration and danger than formerly, and that if a disaffected party in the "kingdom of *Scotland* should invade these parts (which we know is now earnestly endeavoured "by some ill instruments, and fearing the lessening of our forces here will be a great advantage "to them therein) before the rebels of this county be reduced, the work will be of as great "danger to us and the whole kingdom as can be imagined. We do therefore most hum- "bly crave that we may receive comfort and encouragement by assurance from your majesty, "that you will not in your sacred person depart, or carry any forces from us, until it please "God the peace of this county be in a more recovering and settled condition; which will "be a gratious expression of your majesty's wisdom and tender care of these northern parts, "and have a greater impression on the hearts of such forces as being to wait on your ma- "jesty's sacred person may leave their natural countrys, kindred and friends, in a more "hopeful and happy way of security. And we doe most heartily make our protestations "to your majesty, that in this our desire of your majesty's stay with us, we are exceeding- "ly moved by the apprehension we have of great hazard to your majesties person, in your "journey to the king, it being certain the rebels southward have disposed their forces dan- "gerously, and we doubt, purposely, to hinder your majesty's passage.

"And our royal soveraign's, and your majesty's safety and honour, is the greatest earth- "ly blessing we can enjoy, for which we shall willingly engage our dearest lives and "fortunes.

Dated *June* 1, 1643. *And ever pray*, &c.

Notwithstanding this, and the just apprehension the queen might have of being impeded *June* 6.
in her passage, she resolutely set forward from *York* to meet the king; guarded by a strong body of horse and foot under the conduct of the valiant earl of *Newcastle*. The general safely conveyed her majesty to the king, for which piece of excellent conduct, as well as other his most eminent services, his majesty created him a *marquis*.

I must not omit that, whilst the queen staid in *York*, there was a remarkable instance of her majesty's generosity and good nature extended to the prisoners of war in this city. For being told of their miserable condition, and that their wounds would not heal unless fresh victuals were allow'd them, she out of her own private purse sent them twenty pounds; besides ordering them a great quantity of provisions, and getting an order also from the general that each prisoner should have three pence a day allowed for his maintenance. This note I take from a manuscript of those times now before me, and may be credited, because the anonymous writer of it shews himself, in many places, apparently against the king and royal cause. And, considering the barbarous usage the queen had lately met with at *Burlington*, is an uncontestable proof of a kind and generous disposition.

A. 1644. proved a busy year both in this city and the neighbourhood. Sir *Thomas Glem-* A. 1644.
ham was still governor of *York*, and colonel *Thwaites* deputy governor, both under the command of the brave marquis of *Newcastle*, the lord general. Sir *Thomas Fairfax*, having gained a considerable victory at *Selby* against the king's forces, thought of nothing now but bringing the city to accept such terms as he should be pleased to give it. Accordingly he sent to *Lesly* the *Scotch* general, who had just then entered *England* with a great army, to meet and with their united forces undertake the siege of *York*. These forces, however, *April* 19.
were not thought sufficient to invest the city; for being spacious, the north side continued open, and the marquis having four or five thousand horse in it, by the help of a bridge over the river, could transport them to either side, and fall upon any quarter he saw divided from the rest. It was therefore thought fit that the earl of *Manchester* with his army, out of the associated countys, should advance to the others assistance. Accordingly the earl came up, and he in person, with about six hundred foot and one hundred horse, and twelve field pieces, were placed and quartered near *Bootham-bar*, and on that north side towards *Clifton* (*l*).

The city was now closely beleaguered by an army, consisting in all, of forty thousand men, under the command of the three afore-mentioned generals. What had been done before *Manchester* came up, was only a kind of blockade, and some slight skirmishes; but now, being begirt much closer than before, several batteries were erected against the city, particularly one on a hill near *Walmgate-bar*, where four pieces of cannon played almost incessantly on the tower, castle, and town. Nor were they idle from within, but in one day bestowed above one hundred great shot from their several platforms on the besieger's works (*m*).

The besieged having fired the suburbs in most parts about the city, and drawn their peo-

(*l*) *Rushworth*. (*m*) *Ex MS.*

ple

A. 1644. ple into the town, the besiegers endeavoured to quench it, and preserve the houses for their shelter. Hereupon several hot skirmishes ensued. *Manchester's* forces fell on near *Walmgate-bar*, and took S. *Nicholas* church; but were soon obliged to retire; the *Scots* also about *Micklegate-bar* took and brought off a booty of cattle which were conveying to the city. The besieged made several gallant sallies, but were still beat back with like courage. Every day, says *Rushworth*, produced some notable action; he seems to lament they were not journalized by any hand that he ever saw; which makes him less particular in the description of this than many less remarkable sieges in the war.

All the hopes the loyal party in the city had to be rescued from their enemies, was in prince *Rupert*; who after he had raised the siege of *Newark* with great loss to the parliament, made what haste he could to do the like for *York*. In the mean time the lord general thought fit to amuse the commanders of the rebels, with specious shews of treating about the rendition of the city; and sent a letter dated *June* 8, to the earl of *Leven* in these words:

(n) My Lord,

I Cannot but admire that your Lordship has soe near beleaguered this city on all sides, made batterys against it, and soe near approached to it, without signifying what your intentions are, and what you desire or expect, which is contrary to the rules of all military discipline and customs of war; therefore I have thought fit to remonstrate thus much to your Lordship, to the end that your lordship may signify your intentions and resolutions therein, and receive ours. And soe I remain, my Lord,

York, June 8, 1644. Your lordship's humble servant,

WILL. NEWCASTLE.

Directed to his excellency the earl of *Leven*.

To which *Lesly* returned this answer:

(o) My Lord,

AT this distance I shall not dispute with your lordship points of military discipline, nor the practice of captains in such cases; yet to give your lordship satisfaction in that your letter desires from me, your lordship may take notice that I have drawn my forces before this city, with intention to reduce it to the obedience of king *and* parliament. *Whereunto if your lordship shall speedily conform, it may save the effusion of much innocent blood, whereof I wish your lordship to be noe less sparing than I am. Who rests*

From *Fowforth*, *June* 8, 1644. Your lordship's most humble servant,

To his excellency the lord marquis of *Newcastle*. *LEVEN.*

The lord *Fairfax* and afterwards the earl of *Manchester* received letters from the marquis to the same effect, and finding that he was willing to treat about the rendition, the three generals met on the ninth of *June* in the night, and expressed their readiness to enter into it. General *Lesly* named for commissioners the earl of *Lindsay* and the lord *Humbee*; the lord *Fairfax* named sir *William Fairfax* and colonel *White*; and the earl of *Manchester* named colonel *Russel* and colonel *Hammond*; but withal signified to the marquis, that they were unwilling to yield to a cessation from hostilities in any part but the place appointed for treaty. The marquis after two days delay sent the generals this answer:

(p) My Lords,

I Have received your lordships letter, with the names of the commissioners appointed by your lordships; but since your lordships have declared in your letter to allow a cessation of arms only on that side of the town during the time of the treaty, I find it not fit for me to incline to it on those conditions; and had returned your lordships this answer long before this time, if some weighty matters had not retarded my affairs in that particular. I am, my Lords,

York, June 11, 1644. Your Lordships most humble servant,

WILL. NEWCASTLE.

The next day the three generals sent the following summons directed to the marquis:

(q) *WE the generals of the army raised for the king and parliament, and now employed in this expedition against* York, *that no further effusion of blood be occasioned, and that the city of* York *and inhabitants may be preserved from ruin, doe hereby require your lordship to surrender the said City to us, in the name and for the use of the* king *and* parliament, *within the space of*

(n) *Rushworth.*
(o) *Idem.*
(p) *Idem.*
(q) *Idem.*

twenty

twenty four hours after the receipt thereof; which if you refuse to doe, the inconveniencys insuing upon your refusal, must be required at your lordship's hands; seeing our intentions are not for blood or destruction of towns, cities or countries, unless all other means being used we be necessitated thereunto; which shall be contrary to the minds and hearts of, my Lord, A. 1644.

June 12, 1644. Your excellency's most humble servants,

LEVEN. MANCHESTER. FAIRFAX.

The marquis's answer the following day directed to all the three generals ran thus:

(r) My LORDS,

I Have received a letter from your lordships, dated yesterday, about four a clock this afternoon; wherein I am required to surrender the city to your lordships in twenty four hours after the receipt; but I know your lordships are too full of honour to expect the surrendring the city upon a command, and upon so short an advertisement to me, who have the king's commission to keep it; and where there are so many generous persons, and men of honour, quality and fortune, concerned in it. But, truly, I conceive this said demand high enough to have been exacted from the meanest governor of any of his majesty's garisons, and your lordships may be pleased to know, that I expect propositions to proceed from your lordships, as becomes persons of honour to give and receive from one another. If your lordships therefore think fit to propound honourable and reasonable terms, and agree upon a general cessation from all acts of hostility during the time of the treaty, then your Lordships may receive such satisfaction therein as may be expected from persons of honour, and such as desire to avoid the effusion of christian blood, or destruction of cities, towns and countries, as any whatever; yet will not spare their own lives rather than to live in the least stain of dishonour. And so desiring your lordships resolutions. I remain

Your lordship's most humble servant,

York, June 13, 1644. *WILL. NEWCASTLE.*

June 14, the generals yielded to a compleat cessation during the treaty; and thereupon the commissioners meeting; those for the city offered the following propositions *(s)*.

"I. That the city should be rendered in twenty days if no relief come.

"II. That the marquiss with all his officers and soldiers shall depart with colours flying, "drums beating, match lighted, with their arms, *&c.* to be conveyed where they please, "and not to be forced to march above eight miles a day: and that they have liberty to stay "forty days for settling or conveying to other places such goods as they shall not be able to "carry with them.

"III. That no oath, *&c.* be administered to any of them, farther than is warranted by "the known laws. And that the gentry have liberty to go to their own houses, and be "protected from violence, and not questioned for what they have done. And that the "townsmen may enjoy all privileges as before, and not questioned for what they have done; "and that the garrison placed here be only *Yorkshire* men.

"IV. That all the churches be kept from profanation: That divine service be perform-"ed therein as formerly: That the revenues belong to the officers as it has done; that the "prebendaries continue in their prebends according to the laws, and that oll other ecclesia-"stical persons have liberty to depart and serve God and enjoy their estates without distur-"bance.

"V. *Lastly,* That hostages be given and that *Clifford*'s tower (the chief fort in the city) "be kept by the king's party till the articles are performed."

Rushworth says, that the besieger's commissioners expressed great dislike at the haughtiness of these propositions, and after long debate upon them, three of the chief were sent by the rest to lay them before the generals. In about two hours they returned, and brought a paper with them in which were these: *(viz.)* That *York* with all the arms *&c.* in and about the same, be delivered up for the use of the king and parliament on the conditions following:

"I. That the soldiers go to their own homes, and carry with them their clothes and mo-"ney (not exceeding fourteen days pay) and have safe conduct, promising hereafter not to "take arms against the parliament or protestant religion.

"II. That the ordinary inhabitants be protected from violence, and have the same free "trade as others under protection of king and parliament; and that none be quartered here "except those appointed for the garrison.

"III. That the officers have liberty to go to their own homes with swords and horses, "and to carry their apparel and money not exceeding one months pay: And any officer re-"commended by the marquis shall have a pass to go beyond sea, promising not to serve a-"gainst the parliament and protestant religion.

"IV. That the gentry and other inhabitants of the county now residing at *York*, may "go to their own homes, and be protected from violence. A positive answer to be returned "to these propositions by three a-clock to morrow afternoon.

(r) Rushworth. *(s) Ex MS.*

A. 1644. These conditions so widely different from the other were resented as they ought by the commissioners for the city; who, says *Rushworth*, *were so far from accepting of them that they refused to carry a copy of them to the marquis.* But next morning *Lesley* sent one by a drum, to which the marquis returned the following answer:

My Lord,

I Have perused the conditions and demands your lordship sent, but when I considered the many professions and demands made to avoid the effusion of christian blood, I did admire to see such propositions from your lordships, conceiving this not the way to it, for I cannot suppose that your lordships do imagine that persons of honour can condescend to any of these propositions, and so remain, my lord,

York, June 15, 1644. Your lordship's most humble servant,

WILLIAM NEWCASTLE.

Upon the receipt of this letter the cessation expired, and the three generals renewed their assaults upon the city, on all sides, with double vigour. *Manchester's* forces had undermined St. *Mary's* tower at the north-east corner of the *Manor*, and colonel *Crayford*, a *Scotchman*, who commanded that quarter, sprung the mine, which took effect, quite demolished the tower, and buried a great many men and women in the ruins. After this he attempted to storm the city with his forces, having made another breach in the wall by cannon lower down in *Marygate*, which entring they scaled two or three other walls, and took possession of the *Manor*. This happened to be *Trinity-Sunday*, when most of the commanders for the city were at the cathedral, the violent blow, occasioned by springing the mine, sufficiently alarmed them, and each man ran to his post to watch the consequence. In the mean time a party of the garrison went out by a private sally port in the city walls, entered the *Manor* and cut off the only way the enemy had to retreat. Upon which a smart rencounter ensued, the rebels stood the conflict some time in the bowling-green, but fifty of them being killed, the rest, being about two hundred and fifty, threw down their arms and submitted. On the garrison's side were slain sir *Philip Byron* and colonel *Huddlestone*, with Mr. *Samuel Brearey*, the captain of a company of two hundred and fifty volunteer citizens, being an alderman's son of this city.

From this time to *Monday*, *June* 24, no extraordinary accident happened; but small skirmishes and cannon playing to and from the city continued both night and day. On the 24th of *June* aforesaid, about four in the morning a commanded party of about six hundred sallied out from *Monkbar*, and furiously assaulted the earl of *Manchester's* quarters, but after a sharp conflict were driven back with loss (*u*).

The siege continued with all possible vigour, and several bold attempts were made by the besiegers, whose attacks were as bravely repulsed by the besieged. The very women in the city, as my manuscript speaks, underwent great danger and fatigue in doing all that laid in their power, and as far as modesty would permit, put on manly courage for the defence of it. (*x*) The line of circumvallation now cut off all dealings with the country, which made fresh provisions sell at a high rate. Mutton sold at sixteen shillings *per* quarter. Beef at four shillings a stone. A pig at seven shillings. A hen at four shillings. Eggs at three pence a piece. Fresh butter was two shillings and eight pence a pound, and oatmeal at two shillings and eight pence a peck: Yet being so long apprized of the siege, such a quantity of salt provisions and grain was laid in by the lord general, that there was no scarcity of either; and all sorts of liquors were plentiful enough.

June 30, towards evening, the generals of the parliament forces had notice that prince *Rupert*, with an army of twenty thousand men, was advancing, and would quarter that night at *Knaresborough* and *Burrough-bridge*, within twelve miles of *York*. Whereupon, not thinking themselves able to fight him and continue the siege, they resolved to rise. Accordingly *July* 1, they drew off from their trenches without loss, and marched to a great moor, four or five miles distant call *Marston-moor*, and there drew up expecting the prince would make that his way to *York*. But his highness caused only a party of horse to face the enemy at *Skipbridge*, where they might secure their retreat over the *Ouse* at *Nunmonkton*; and keeping the rest of his army on that side left them that night in the forest of *Galtres*; whilst he with about two hundred horse rode on to the city.

At *York* the prince must needs be a most welcome guest, and had he not hurried his affairs too precipitately, might, not only, have relieved the city, but established the royal cause on a basis too strong for rebellion to shake. Upon calling a council of war the marquis delivered his opinion to the prince, that he should not yet attempt any thing upon the enemy, for he had certain intelligence of some discontent among the generals, and that they were resolved to divide. Besides he expected in two days colonel *Clavering* with above three thousand men from the north, and two thousand drawn out of several garrisons (*y*). This reinforcement actually came at the time appointed, though it was then too

(*t*) *Rushworth.*
(*u*) *Ex MS.*
(*x*) Lawyer *Hilyard's* preface to his antiquities of *York*.
(*y*) *Newcastle's* life by the dutchess.

late. Nor was the marquis out in his notions of the divisions in the enemy's councils. A. 1644.
For general *Fairfax* himself writes, that colonel *Crayford*, who sprung the mine and made the assault, without orders, would certainly have been called to a strict account for it, had not the *triumviral government*, as he is pleased to term it, made his case more easy to evade punishment (z). Sir *Thomas* adds, that a division arose in council about tarrying to fight the prince there, or to retreat in order to gain time and place of more advantage. Which last the *Scotch* prevailed for, and they accordingly broke up and marched towards *Tadcaster*, lieutenant general *Cromwell*, *Lesley* and himself having the charge of bringing up the rear.

Notwithstanding this the prince had not the good fortune to listen to the marquis's advice; but alledging that he had a letter from his majesty, then at *Oxford*, with a positive and absolute command to fight the enemy, he thought it his duty to obey it. To which the marquis replied, that *he was ready and willing to obey the prince in all things, no otherways than if his majesty was there in person himself.* And though several of his friends advised the marquis not to engage in battle, because the command, as they said, was taken from him; yet that noble lord answered, *that happen what would he would not shun the fight; having no other ambition then to live and die a faithful subject to his majesty* (a).

Whether the prince had such a command from the king, or his own rashness urged him to fight is uncertain. However on *Tuesday July* 2, he marched out of *York* with his whole army, and his van consisting of five thousand horse came up with the rebels before they had drawn their forces out of the moor. Upon this their whole army made a stand, and drew back both foot and carriages with all speed, they finding that the prince was resolved to fight them. Both parties were now busy in drawing up their men, and the parliamentarians, finding the prince had possessed himself of great part of the moor, were obliged to range theirs in a large field of rye at *Marston* town end, where their pioneers made way to extend their wings. This being a rising ground the prince sent a party to dislodge them, but they were driven back, and that cornfield possessed by the enemy. Their right wing was placed just by *Marston* town side, the town on their right hand fronting the east; and as their foot and horse came up, they formed their batalia and left wing, endeavouring to gain as much to the left as they could; so that at last their army fronted to the moor from *Marston* to *Topwith*, being a mile and a half in length. The number of the parliament's forces were somewhat more than the king's according to sir *Thomas* (b). Their right wing of horse was commanded by him, consisting of eighty troops, being his own and part of the *Scotch* horse. The main batalia by his father lord *Ferdinando*, who also commanded the foot towards the right wing, consisting of all his own infantry, and two brigades of *Scots* for a reserve. Towards the left general *Lesley* commanded with the rest of the *Scotish* forces; two brigades of the earl of *Manchester's* with six regiments of *Scots* and one of *Manchester's* brigades for a reserve. The left wing was lead on by the earl of *Manchester* and his lieutenant general *Cromwell*, consisting of the earl's whole cavalry, and three regiments of the *Scotish* horse, under major general *Lesley*, making in all about seventy troops.

This disposition took up a great deal of the day, but prince *Rupert* was as late as they before he had fully drawn up his forces. Part of his foot and horse lay on the north side of the river *Ouse*, and had to come over *Poppleton* ferry; which, however, happened to be fordable at that time (c). It was betwixt two or three a clock in the afternoon before both armies were formed for the battle. The prince had, with the forces drawn out of the city, in all in the field, about fourteen thousand foot and nine thousand horse, and twenty five pieces of ordnance. His highness himself led on the right wing of horse, which had in it twelve divisions consisting of an hundred troops, which might be five thousand men. The left wing of horse was commanded by sir *Charles Lucas* and colonel *Hurry*; but who commanded the main body, whether general *Goring*, major general *Porter*, or general *Tilyard* is uncertain. Nor do I find what particular charge the marquis had this day, though it is certain he was engaged very valiantly in the battle. The prince's army extended in front somewhat longer than the enemy's, and therefore on their left hand to secure the flank, they placed the *Scotish* dragoons, under the command of colonel *Frizle*. The field word given by the prince was *God and the king*; the others, *God with us*.

About three a clock the great ordnance began to play on both sides, but without doing any considerable damage or execution. About five there was a general silence, both sides expecting who should begin the charge first, for there was a small ditch and a bank betwixt the two armies, which though they had drawn up within musquet-shot of one another, must incommode the party that passed it, and lay them more open to their enemy. In this posture and dreadful dilemma, they continued some time, insomuch that every one concluded there would be no action that night, but about seven in the evening, *Whitlock* says seven next morning, the parliament's generals were resolved to fall on, and the signal

(z) Sir *T. Fairfax's* memoirs.
(a) Marquis's life.
(b) *Fair.* mem.
(c) *Ex MS.*

being

A. 1644. being given, the earl of *Manchester*'s foot and the *Scots* of the main body advancing in a running march, ſoon made their way over the ditch and gave a ſmart charge.

The front diviſions of horſe mutually charged, the reſpective oppoſite right and left wings meeting. The firſt diviſion of prince *Rupert*'s advanced, and with them his highneſs in perſon charged *Cromwell*'s diviſion of three hundred horſe, in which he was alſo in perſon and very hard put to it being charged by the prince's braveſt men both in front and flank, and ſtood at ſword's point a pretty while hacking one another. But at laſt *Cromwell* broke through, and at the ſame time the reſt of his horſe of that wing, and major general *Leſley*'s regiments had wholly broken all that right wing of the prince's, and were in chace of them beyond their left wing; the earl of *Mancheſter*'s foot on the right hand of them went on by their ſide, almoſt as faſt as they, diſperſing and cutting down the prince's foot. It was at this time that the marquis of *Newcaſtle*'s own regiment, called *White-coats* from their cloathing, conſiſting of a thouſand ſtout *Northumbrians*, being deſerted by the horſe, yet ſcorning either to fly or aſk quarter, were cut in pieces by the enemy, all bravely falling in rank and file as they had ſtood. The reſt of this wing which eſcaped killing, or being taken priſoners, fled in confuſion towards *York*.

But the prince's left wing lead by colonel *Hurry*, had better ſucceſs, and did as much to the parliament's right. For though ſir *Thomas Fairfax* and colonel *Lambert* with five or ſix troops charged through them, and went to their own left wing, the reſt of his troops were defeated, and the lord *Fairfax*'s brigade being furiouſly aſſaulted, and at the ſame time diſordered by ſome of ſir *Thomas*'s new raiſed regiments, who wheeled about; and being cloſely perſued, fled back upon them and the reſerve of *Scotiſh* foot, and broke them wholly, treading many underfoot; ſo that their right wing and great part of their main body were routed, and fled out of the field ſeveral miles towards *Tadcaſter* and *Cawood*, giving out that all was loſt. The three generals, *Mancheſter*, *Leven*, and *Fairfax* thought ſo too, and were haſtning out of the field, when the victory they deſpaired of, unexpectedly, fell into their hands.

For whilſt the royaliſts were, too eagerly, purſuing the chace, and juſt ſiezing on their enemies carriages, &c. *Cromwell* with his regiment, and ſir *Thomas Fairfax* having rallied ſome of his horſe and *Mancheſter*'s foot, came back from the chace of the prince's right wing, and perceiving their friends in the mean time thus worſted advanced in good order to a ſecond charge with all the prince's horſe and foot that had thus diſordered their main battle and right wing, who ſeeing their approach gave over the purſuit and prepared to receive them. Both ſides being not a little ſurprized to ſee they muſt fight it over again for that victory which they thought they had already gained. However the royaliſts marched with great reſolution down the cornfield, the face of the battle being exactly counterchanged, for now the king's forces ſtood on the ſame ground, and with the ſame front that the parliament's right wing before ſtood to receive their charge, and the parliament's forces in the ſame ground and with the ſame front which the king's did when the fight began.

The battle thus renewed grew deſperate and bloody; but, in fine, after the utmoſt efforts of ſtrength and courage on either ſide for three hours, victory wholly inclined to the parliament's forces; who, before ten a clock had cleared the field, and not only recovered their own ordnance, but took all the princes train of artillery and followed the chace with great ſlaughter within a mile of *York*.

The number of the ſlain on both ſides is ſaid to be eight thouſand; though authors vary much in this as well as other particulars. The countrymen who were commanded to bury the bodies gave out, that they interred four thouſand one hundred and fifty (*n*). It is generally believed that the prince loſt at leaſt three thouſand men, the parliamentarians would not own to above three hundred being ſlain on their ſide; which is incredible from the circumſtances of the fight.

Cromwell, though the author of *Hollis*'s memoirs taxes him with cowardice, and ſays he withdrew very ſoon from the fight for a ſlight wound in the neck, is by moſt writers allowed to be the main inſtrument in gaining this victory. His known courage joined with coolneſs reſtored the day, which was infallibly loſt by prince *Rupert*'s wanting that laſt neceſſary qualification in a general. Sir *Thomas Fairfax* alſo carried himſelf with great bravery, he tells us that he muſt ever remember the goodneſs of God to him that day, for having charged through the enemy, and his men going after the purſuit, he ſtopped to return to his other troops, when unexpectedly he fell into the midſt of the enemy's horſe alone; but taking the ſignal out of his hat, he paſt through them again as one of their own commanders. He adds, that he eſcaped the dangers of that field with only a cut in his cheek given him at the firſt charge, and his horſe ſhot under him in the ſecond. The other generals are ſaid to have all fled the field; and *Leven* after a flight of ten miles was taken by a conſtable.

The principal perſons ſlain on the prince's ſide were ſir *William Wentworth*, ſir *William Lambton*, ſir *William Langdale*, ſir *Thomas Metham*, colonel *Eury* and colonel *Slingſby*.

(*n*) The graves are yet to be ſeen on the moor near *Wilſtrop-wood*.

Priſoners

Priſoners of note were ſir *Charles Lucas* lieutenant general to the marquis of *Newcaſtle*'s horſe, major general *Porter*, major general *Tilyard*, and the lord *Goring*'s ſon, with near a hundred other officers, fifteen hundred common ſoldiers, (*Whitlock*, three thouſand priſoners in all) twenty five pieces of ordnance; one hundred and thirty barrels of powder, ſeveral thouſand arms, and was computed near a hundred colours. For which though there was a proclamation made to bring them to the generals, yet the ſoldiers had already torn to pieces moſt of them, delighting to wear the ſhreds in their hats (*d*). A. 1644.

Of the parliamentarians none of note were ſlain except captain *Micklethwait* and major *Fairfax*, who died of his wounds at *York*; as did alſo *Charles Fairfax* ſon to the general, and was buried at *Marſton*. Some hiſtorians mention a *Scotch* lord *Diddup* to be ſlain here; which when it was told the king that a lord of that name was killed on the parliament's ſide, his majeſty ſaid *he did not remember ſuch a lord in* Scotland, to which was replied, *it might very well be, ſince that lord had forgot there was ſuch a king in* England.

On the king's party every gentleman, volunteer, &c. ſerved in this battle with uncommon bravery; and charged with all the reſolution that could be expected from men; that prince *Rupert* ſaid, at his return to *York*, *I am ſure my men fought well, and know no reaſon for our rout but this, becauſe the devil did help his ſervants.* The prince himſelf narrowly eſcaped to the city by the goodneſs of his horſe.

To add to the misfortunes of this day, the very next proved a worſe ſtroke to the king's affairs; for the brave marquis of *Newcaſtle*, and his friends, being diſcontented at the prince's conduct, tired and diſcouraged to the laſt degree, reſolved to leave the land. This reſolution was in ſome meaſure copied by the prince, for almoſt at the ſame inſtant they ſent meſſages to one another that they intended to leave this city and country; the prince ſaid he would march that very morning away with his horſe, and as many foot as he had left towards the ſouth, and the marquis that he would that inſtant repair to the ſea-coaſt and tranſport himſelf beyond ſeas. Both which, to the ſurprize of friends and enemies, they immediately performed; the prince drew out what forces he could rally twelve miles north of *York* waiting the coming up of colonel *Clavering*, and then marched into *Lancaſhire*. The marquis conducted by one troop of horſe went to *Scarborough*, where two ſhips being ready to ſail for *Hamborough*, he imbarked himſelf and company therein, which were his two ſons, *Charles* viſcount *Mansfield*, and lord *Henry Cavendiſh*, his brother ſir *Charles Cavendiſh*, Dr. *Bramhall* biſhop of *Londonderry*, the lord *Falconberg*, the lord *Widdrington*, the earl of *Ethyne*, the lord *Carnwath*, colonel *Carnaby*, colonel *Baſſet*, colonel *Mazin*, ſir *William Vavaſour*, ſir *Francis Mackworth*, and about eighty more, who in four days all arrived ſafe at *Hamborough*. The marquis came no more into *England* till the wonderful reſtoration of king *Charles* II, ſixteen years after.

This ſtrange deſertion of the city of *York* and northern parts proved of the utmoſt diſſervice to the king's affairs; for had they ſtaid in the city, they might in time have wearied out and waſted thoſe enemies they now left it to the mercy of. Diſſenſions amongſt the northern generals of the parliament's ſide, were very conſiderable both before and after the battle. The *Scots*, according to their cuſtom, wanted to be marching home with their booty, and they had another reaſon, for the marquis of *Montroſs* had already lighted a flame in their country which the parliament at *Edenborough* could not extinguiſh. Then ſuch quantities of proviſions had been thrown into the town, that they had little ſtomach to the renewing of the ſiege, till the certain intelligence of the king's two generals abrupt and final departure ſo far reconciled them, that where nothing elſe could, they, after two days, returned to their poſts before the city, which was now left to the ſole diſcretion of the governour ſir *Thomas Glembam*, and beleaguered ſtraiter than ever.

They ſummoned the city to ſurrender on mercy, to which ſir *Thomas Glembam* and the lord-mayor anſwered, *that they could not yield on any ſuch terms*, ſo the beſiegers went on vigorouſly with their attacks againſt it. And *July* 11, having made their approaches almoſt up to the very walls, and prepared ſcaling ladders, &c. for a general aſſault, the beſieged beat a parley and deſired a treaty; whereupon ſir *William Conſtable* and colonel *Lambert* were ſent into the city to conclude it. *July* 5.

And *July* 15, that gallant gentleman the governour having done as much as man could do in defence of the city, after a ſiege of eighteen weeks, in which he had valiantly withſtood twenty two ſtorms, four countermines, and ſlain four or five thouſand of the enemy before it; having but a ſmall garriſon, moſt of their artillery drawn out and loſt at *Marſton-moor*, little or no warlike ammunition left, and laſtly deſerted by their beſt and braveſt men, thought fit to ſurrender up the city on the following articles (*e*).

(*d*) Some of the colours ſent up to the parliament by captain *Stewart* were theſe: prince *Rupert*'s ſtandard with the arms of the *Palatine*, near five yards long and broad, with a red croſs in the midſt. A black cornet with a black and yellow fringe, and a ſword brandiſhed from the clouds with this motto, *terribilis ut acies ordinata.* A willow-green with the portraiture of a man holding in one hand a knot, in the other a ſword with this, *who ſhall untie it.* Another coloured with a face and this motto, *aut mors aut vita decora.* A yellow cornet in its middle, a lyon couchant, and behind him a maſtiff ſeeming to ſnatch at him, and a label from his mouth written *Kimbolton*; at his feet little beagles, and before their mouths written, *Pym*, *Pym*, *Pym*: and out of the lion's mouth theſe words proceeding, *quouſque tandem abutere patientia noſtra. Ruſhworth.*

(*e*) *Ex MS.*

 " I. That

A. 1644. " I. That sir *Thomas Glemham* as governour of the city of *York*, shall surrender and de- " liver up the same, with the forts, tower, cannon, ammunition and furniture of war be- " longing thereunto on the 16th of *July* instant, at eleven a clock in the forenoon to the " three generals, or to whom they shall appoint for the use of the king and parliament in " the manner and upon the conditions following;

" II. That all the officers shall march forth the city with their arms, drums beating, co- " lours flying, match lighted, bullet in mouth, bag and baggage.

" III. That they shall have a convoy that no injury be done them in their march to " *Skipton*.

" IV. That sick and maimed soldiers shall not be hindered from going after their re- " coveries.

" V. That all soldiers wives and children may have liberty to go to their husbands " and fathers to their own homes and estates, and to enjoy them peaceably under con- " tribution.

" VI. That no soldier shall be enticed away.

" VII. That the citizens and inhabitants may enjoy all their privileges which formerly " they did at the beginning of these troubles, and may have freedom of trade both by " sea and land, paying such duties and customs as all other cities under obedience of par- " liament.

" VIII. That if any garrison be placed in the city, two parts in three shall be *Yorkshire-* " *men*, no free quarter shall be put upon any without his own consent, and the armies " shall not enter the city before the governour and lord-mayor be acquainted.

" IX. That in all charges the citizens, resiants and inhabitants shall bear only such part " with the county at large as was formerly in all other assessments.

" X. That all citizens, gentlemen, resiants, sojourners, and every other person within " the city, shall, if they please, have free liberty to remove themselves, family, and goods, " and to dispose thereof and their estates at their pleasures, according to the law of the land, " either to live at their own homes or elsewhere, and to enjoy their goods and estates with- " out molestation, and to have protection and safeguard for that purpose; so that they " may rest quietly at their abodes, and travel safely and freely about their occasions. And " for their better removal may have letters of safe conduct, and be furnished with horses " and carriages at reasonable rates.

" XI. That all gentlemen and others that have goods within the city, and are absent " themselves may have free liberty to take, carry away, and dispose of them as in the fore- " going articles.

" XII. That neither churches nor other buildings shall be defaced, nor any plunderings, " nor taking of any man's person, nor any part of his estate suffered; and that justice shall " be administred within the city by the magistrates according to law, who shall be assisted " therein, if need require, by the garrison.

" XIII. That all persons whose dwellings are in the city, though now absent, may en- " joy the benefit of these articles as if they were present.

Signed

FERD. FAIRFAX. MANCHESTER.
ADAM HEPBORNE. (f) *THO. GLEMHAM.*
Lord *HUMBEE.*
WILL. CONSTABLE.

These extraordinary concessions granted to people, driven to the utmost despair, may shew posterity how eager they were to be possessed of the city; their own divisions making it impracticable for them to lie long before it. On these terms the city, together with its forts, towers, five and thirty pieces of ordnance, three thousand arms, five barrels of powder and other ammunition, were yielded up to the enemy by sir *Thomas Glemham*, with the consent of the lord-mayor and magistrates of the place.

And *July* 16, the forces marched out being about a thousand, besides sick and wounded, the besiegers being drawn up on both sides the way out of *Micklegate-bar* for near a mile, that the besieged might march through them. Then the three generals went into the city in procession, directly to the minster church, says *Rushworth*, where a psalm was sung and thanks returned to God by master *Robert Douglass* chaplain to the earl of *Leven*. And *Thursday* after was appointed a day of thanksgiving to be solemnly kept by the whole army.

Some writers have taxed the generals with a breach of their articles by suffering their soldiers to plunder, &c. But if we may believe *Rushworth*, it was only this, that some

(f) Sir *Thomas Glemham* afterwards held *Carlisle* nine weeks for the king, against pestilence, famine and the power of *Scotland*; and delivered it upon good terms. He was also governour of *Oxford*, which he surrendered by the king's orders to general *Fairfax*. Being arrested in *London*, contrary to the *Oxford* articles, he was some time kept prisoner in the fleet, from whence he found means to pass into *Holland*, where soon after this worthy gentleman died. His brother Dr. *Glemham* was after the restauration, made bishop of St. *Asaph*. *Lloyd's* memoirs of loyalists.

troopers

troopers of *Manchester*'s army took away from the king's forces, as they were marching, cloaths, plate, and money, contrary to articles. Upon which the generals expressed themselves much offended; and, adds he, *Manchester* published a declaration, that if any trooper concerned in the plunder would in two days bring to his captain what he had taken, he should be forgiven, if not; they should suffer death according to the articles of war published by the earl of *Essex*. A. 1644.

Immediately after the rendition of the city, the three armies thought fit to separate; being heartily tired of one another's company. The *Scotch* marched northward, the earl of *Manchester* into *Lincolnshire*, and the lord *Fairfax* remained at *York*, being constituted governour of it by the parliament. Where he and his son were to take in all the garrisons that still held out for the king in this county; which in a small time after were wholly brought under subjection.

In one of their excursions, in order to reduce the castle of *Helmsley*, sir *Thomas Fairfax* received a dangerous shot in the shoulder. Being brought back to *York*, he laid there some time so ill of his wound that his life was despaired of. Upon his recovery he was voted by the parliament commander in chief of all their forces; and did that signal service for them as to reduce the king's affairs to the lowest ebb of fortune; of which none could more heartily repent, if we may believe his own memoirs, then the *hero* himself.

Upon the taking of the city, the new made governour displaced sir *Edmund Cooper* from the office of lord-mayor, which he had held four years, when few durst undertake it, with all the testimony of loyalty and courage a good subject could pay to his sovereign. *Thomas Hoyle* alderman, one of the city's representatives in parliament, was for a contrary reason put into the place (*g*). The governour also procured *John Geldart*, *Stephen Watson*, *Thomas Dickenson*, *Robert Horner*, *Leonard Thomson*, and *Simon Coulton*, to be chosen aldermen for their eminent disaffection to the king; in the places of sir *Robert Belt*, sir *Roger Jaques*, *Robert Hemsworth*, *William Scot*, and *John Myers* displaced, and even disfranchised for their loyalty to their sovereign; which deserves a more lasting memorial than I am afraid my pen can give them.

The city walls much shattered in the time of the siege were by order of the governour and lord-mayor put into repair. And the same year, *January* 1, though it ought to be buried in eternal oblivion, came the great convoy to *York*, commanded by major general *Skippon*, with the two hundred thousand pound, *the price of blood*; which money was paid to the *Scots* at the *common-hall* of this city. At their coming in all the artillery about the city was discharged (*h*). A. 1645.

A petition from the inhabitants of the county and city of *York* and of the northern parts of the kingdom of *England* was presented to the parliament, to lay a foundation for an university at *York*, which I shall give in another part of this work. The whole kingdom being now, almost under subjection to the parliament, and having no more enemies to fear, this city was dismantled of its garrison, *Clifford's* tower only excepted, of which the lord-mayor was constituted governour and so continued several years. A. 1647.

January 30, *Charles* I. king of *Great Britain* was murdered upon a scaffold, before his own palace, in open daylight; by a set of men whom an act of parliament brands with the name of *miscreants, who were as far from being true protestants as they were true subjects*. The first crowned head in the world that ever was taken off by such barefaced villany, and the only king that ever died in that barefaced manner for religion. The noble historian, Mr. *Eachard* and others, have taken care to paint this horrid proceeding in the colours it deserves. I shall only say, that even *Oldmixon* himself, who writes with equal malice and equal truth against the family of the *Stewarts*, as *Woolston* against the miracles of *our Saviour*, dares not once go about to excuse it. A. 1648.

The same year in *March* came down judge *Thorp* to *York*, to hold the *Lent* assize; where in an elaborate charge to the grand jury, he endeavoured to justify the murder of the king, and to vindicate the parliament in all their proceedings. In order to make the change from the king's name in forms of law, which it had ever ran in, to the commons of *England*, acceptable to the people, he has raked up all the invidious and scandalous invectives against kings and monarchy, which the most celebrated republicans to his time had ever wrote. The speech was printed at *York*. At this assize was a great goal delivery, twenty three were condemned, sixteen men and seven women, all executed save two. One of the women was condemned for crucifying her mother, and offering a calf and a cock for a burnt sacrifice. The husband of the woman was hanged for having a hand in the fact; another taste of the strange enthusiastick flights of those times.

August 23, were executed at *Tyburn* near *York*, colonel *John Morrice* and lieutenant *Blackburn*. The former was governour of *Pontfrete* castle, which he had with extream pains taken and with extream hardships kept. The latter was one of that *gallant party* which was sent out of the castle in that memorable expedition to *Doncaster*; and the very man that killed *Rainsborough*. After the rendition of the castle they were both taken as A. 1649.

(*g*) Lawyer *Hilyard*'s ant. of *York*.
(*h*) *Ex MS.*
(*i*) *Lloyd*'s mem.

they

A. 1649. they were endeavouring to get abroad, and brought prisoners to *York*. They had once an opportunity to make their escapes, and one of them had slid down the castle walls by a rope; which his partner endeavouring to do after him, by haste or inadvertency, fell and broke his leg. This misfortune cost them both their lives, for the colonel would not leave his unhappy companion; but out of a noble spirit of generosity staid by him till they were retaken. After twenty two weeks imprisonment they were sentenced to die by judge *Thorp* and *Puleston*, who were purposely sent down to try them; and both testified at their deaths that steady loyalty which had made their lives so remarkable.

But since we are upon executions, and to divert the reader from these melancholly reflections, I cannot omit giving an account of an odd accident which happened this year to an *alderman* of *York*, and one of our *burgesses* in that infamous long parliament, who upon the same day of the month of *January*, and as near as possible at the same hour of the day, on which the *royal martyr* suffered the year before, took occasion to do that justice on himself which the times denied him, by hanging himself at his house in *Westminster*. This man, though not considerable enough to be one of the king's judges, or even named a commissioner, was one that went in with them in all their villanies; and whether remorse or madness, as some would please to have it, caused him to act the deed is left to the reader's conjecture. Upon this accident the wits of those times bestowed the following elogy (*k*).

" *On the happy memory of alderman* Hoyl *of* York, *that hanged himself* January 30, 1649.

" All hail fair fruit! may every crabtree bear
" Such blossoms, and so lovely every year.
" Call ye me this a slip? marry 'tis well,
" *Zacheus* slip'd to *heaven*, the thief to *hell:*
" But if the *saints* thus give 's the slip, 'tis need
" To look about us to preserve the breed.
" Th' are of the running game, and thus to post
" In nooses, blanks the reckoning with their host.
" But hark you, sir, if haste can grant the time,
" See you the danger yet what 'tis to climb
" In king's prerogatives? things beyond just,
" When law seems brib'd to doom them, must be truss'd.
" But oh! I smell your plot strong thro' your hose,
" 'Twas but to cheat the hangman of your cloaths;
" Else your more active hands had fairly staid
" The leisure of a psalm: *Judas* has pray'd.
" Yet let me ask one question, why alone?
" One member of a corporation?
" But I perceive the knack; old women say,
" And be't approv'd, *each dog shall have his day.*
" Hence sweep the almanack, *Lilly* make room.
" And blanks enough for the *new saints* to come (*l*).
" All in *red letters*, as their faults have been
" *Scarlet*, so limn their universe of sin.
" And to their children's credits and their wives,
" Be it still said they leap fair for their lives, &c."

Cromwell the renowned protector of these realms has little share in these annals, though a very considerable one in the annals of *England*. I cannot learn he was ever at *York*, except after the battle of *Marston-moor* with the generals. And another time I find this memorial of him (*m*).

A. 1650. *July* 4, came general *Cromwell* to *York*, in an expedition made into *Scotland*, at which time all the artillery of the tower were discharged. The next day he dined with the lord-mayor, and the following set forward for *Scotland*. To compliment his excellency, and to shew their zeal for the cause, our magistrates now thought fit to take down the king's arms at *Micklegate* and *Bootham-bars*, through both which he must needs pass in his journey, and put up the state's arms in their stead.

This is all I can meet with during the commonwealth and *Cromwell*'s usurpation; after whose death affairs began to wheel about. Divisions and distractions daily encreased amongst the rulers, and every honest man saw plainly there was no other way to settle the kingdom on its sure and *antient basis*, but calling in their *lawful king*.

It must be allowed that the first person of quality that stirred in these parts, and seemed to point at a *restauration* was the lord *Fairfax*. He had kept a secret correspondence with

(*k*) *Rump*, or a collection of songs and poems by the most eminent wits from *an.* 1639 to *an.* 1667. *London* printed 1662.

(*l*) This accident really had a place in the almanacks for some years after the *Restauration*.

(*m*) *Ex MS.*

general

general *Monk* for some time, and had promised to raise forces. in consort with sir *George Booth*, and fall upon *Lambert*'s rear, who was stationed at *Newcastle*, in order to put a stop, one way or other, to *Monk*'s proceedings. By which action, says an author (*n*), his lordship was likely to recover the honour, in pursuing that army, which, when he was formerly their general, he had lost by leading it. Lord *Fairfax*'s preparations were, it seems, discovered too soon; and the general having a tender concern for him and his party, who had so gallantly declared for *Monk*; and knowing how unequal they were to deal with *Lambert*'s army, he resolved to hasten to their relief; and to that end marched his forces immediately over the *Tweed*. A 1659.

Lambert's army deserting him on *Monk*'s approach, the general came to *Newcastle*, where he halted three days. From thence he reached *York*, by easy marches, having received intelligence before that lord *Fairfax* had summoned the city, and was actually in possession of it. On *January* 11, 1659/60, general *Monk* made his entrance into *York*; I myself have been told by an ancient magistrate of our city (*o*), who is since dead at a very advanced age, that he remembered very well the general's marching into it at the head of his army. He said he rode on a gallant *white horse*, betwixt two *presbyterian teachers*, to whom he seemed to pay great regard. This circumstance is a testimony of the deep dissimulation the general was obliged to keep at that time. In his march through the country, and even in the city itself, the general had the inward pleasure to find almost every one of his own mind. For though the men, that met him in crowds, durst not shew their inclinations by any thing but loud huzzas for fear of the army; yet the women were more open in their loyalty; and several of them were heard to say, as the general passed by them in cavalcade, *ah* MONK, *God bless thee, we hope thou has a king in thy belly.*

At this city the general staid five days; one of which being *Sunday*, he went to the cathedral and heard a sermon preached by Mr. *Bowles*, chaplain and chief councellor to the lord *Fairfax*. He had much business to do in the city during his stay in it; for here, by his own authority, he fell to modelling his army; and disposed of such forces as had belonged to *Lambert*. *Lambert*'s own regiment he gave to colonel *Bethell*, as a reward of his service in joining with lord *Fairfax*. Major *Smithson* had *Lilburn*'s regiment given him; that officer having brought it off from *Lambert*, to the lord *Fairfax* and his party. This lord visited the general frequently, and had much secret discourse with him. One day they dined together privately in the general's own chamber, whilst the principal officers and others were treated and entertained at a publick table by his chaplain deputed for that purpose. The chaplain here mentioned was Dr. *Price*; who afterwards wrote and published *the mystery and method of his majesty's* HAPPY RESTAURATION; *being privy to all the secret passages and particularities* as the title of the book expresses it, *of that* GLORIOUS REVOLUTION (*p*). It is from this author that I extract the following remarkable story. It seems that the night of that day on which the lord *Fairfax* and the general dined privately together, Mr. *Bowles* was sent by his lordship to confer with the general; and they were in close conference together till after midnight. For about that time Dr. *Price* entering the chamber to go to prayers, as usual, he found him and *Bowles* in very private discourse; the general ordering him to go out for a while, but not to bed. After *Bowles* was gone, he called the doctor to him, commanding his servants to stay without. He took him close to him and said, *what do you think? Mr. Bowles has pressed me very hard to stay here, and declare for the king; assuring me that I shall have great assistance.* The doctor started at the boldness of the proposition, and asked the general whether he had made *Bowles* any such promise. *No truly*, cried he, *I have not*, or, *I have not yet*. The doctor found he was much perplexed in his thoughts, as he himself was; 'till after a little pause the doctor recovered himself and spoke to this effect, that after the famous *Gustavus* king of *Sweden* was killed in *Germany*, his effigies in wax, with his queen's and childrens, was carried up and down to be shewn for a sight; the spectators were entertained with the story of his life, in which the doctor remembered this passage, that when this king entered *Germany*, he said, *that if his shirt knew what he intended to do, he would pull it off and burn it.* The doctor's application of it to the general was designed to entreat him to sleep between *York* and the walls of *London*; and when he came within them, then to open his eyes and consider what he had to do. This advice the doctor backed with such other reasons as he thought most prevalent.

Nor was it the general only that was strongly sollicited to declare for the king at *York*, some of his officers were also set upon and promised great rewards for so doing. One of whom was so modest as only to demand to be made *lord high chancellor of* ENGLAND for that service. This circumstance, my author says, sir *Edward Hide* told the general after the king came in, and he to him.

By this it appears that it was a moot point whether the general had not actually proclaimed *Charles* II. king of *England*, &c. at *York*. But at last determining to carry on his dissimulation with that *rascally rump* at *Westminster* a little further, and having received orders from them to march up to *London*, in requital of their kindness, he publickly caned one of his

(*n*) The life of general *Monk* published from the original MS of Dr. *Skinner* by *W. Webster*, 8° *London* 1725.

(*o*) Ald. *Hutton*.

(*p*) *London*, for *John Vade*. 1680.

A. 1659. officers for saying *this* Monk *will at last bring in* Charles Stewart. Commanding his other officers to do the like to those under their command that should so offend.

One of these days the general paid a visit to the lord *Fairfax* at his country-seat at *Nun-Appleton*; where he and his officers were magnificently entertained at dinner. The same night he returned again to his quarters at *York*. Hitherto the general had marched about one hundred miles in length, from *Coldstream* to *York*, with his army, by his own sole authority and discretion; but here it was, as I said before, that he received orders from that *rag of government* at *Westminster*, to keep on his way to *London*. It seems they had taken no satisfaction at the lord *Fairfax*'s rising in *Yorkshire*; though, says my author, he had prefaced his actions with the *authority of parliament*; being very well assured that he had other designs in it beyond their safety. Nor could they be pleased with general *Monk*'s stay in that country, where he might probably receive other impressions than those, they hoped, he had brought out of *Scotland* with him. Besides the union of two such persons against them, esteemed the best generals in the nation, might have given them another kind of disturbance than what they had received from *Fleetwood* or *Lambert*. They had suffered him to advance so far, that now they could not decently command him back to *Scotland*, without some disobligation to the general and disgust to his army; nor were they sure of their own forces in *London*; and therefore, though much against their stomachs, they were constrained to authorise general *Monk*'s advance thither, rather than leave him any longer in *Yorkshire*.

Upon receiving his orders, by auditor *Tompson*, to remove all umbrage and apprehension from his worthy masters above, he resolved to reduce his army; and from *York* he sent back major *Morgan* into *Scotland* with two regiments of horse and foot. The general had used the best means in his power to secure that nation before he left it; yet not well assured of the busy humour of the *Scots*, he thought it his best way to send *Morgan* back; in order to keep together a considerable reserve, in case the general should have need, or have lost a battle in *England*. At *York*, also, he left another regiment under the command of colonel *Fairfax*; who being a native of this county, and very well allied and esteemed amongst them, say the same authorities, was the most proper person to be entrusted with the care of the city, and the safety of the county. And now having reduced his army to just four thousand foot and eighteen hundred horse, a number seemingly insignificant to attempt a *revolution* with, he marched out of *York*, *Jan.* 16. and went in two days to *Mansfield* in *Nottinghamshire*.

Here I shall leave him. Success attended all the general's motions; and providence singled him out to be the happy instrument to restore the *king*, and *royal family*, to the throne of their *ancestors*; the *church* of *England* to its revenues and discipline; and the *laws* of the *land* to their ancient course and chanel; from which they had been *so long and so shamefully perverted*.

A. 1660. *York* may be supposed to taste a little of those joys which bishop *Burnet* says the whole nation was drunk and mad with on this memorable occasion for three years together (*q*). The loyal citizens in it had suffered extreamly from the rigid governnment of their magistrates imposed upon them after the rendition. Sir *Edmond Cooper* and the rest of the aldermen displaced had sunk under their misfortunes, and were all dead, save one, before the happy restoration. But when it was publickly known that this change was agreed upon, and a proclamation sent down for that purpose, *Charles* II. was proclaimed king of *Great-Britain*, *&c*, at *York* in the following manner.

May 11. The lord-mayor, aldermen, and twenty four, on horseback in their proper habits, preceded the cavalcade; next followed the chamberlains and common-council-men on foot in their gowns. These were attended by more than a thousand citizens under arms, and lastly came a troop of country gentlemen, near three hundred, with lord *Thomas Fairfax* at their head, who all rode with their swords drawn and hats upon their swords points. When the proclamation was read at the usual places, the bells rung, the cannon played from the tower, and the soldiers gave several vollies of shot. At night were tar-barrels, bonfires, illuminations, *&c*: with the greatest expressions of joy that could possibly be testified on that happy deliverance. And on

29. The king's birth-day, and the day of his publick entrance into the city of *London*, the loyalty of our citizens was in a more especial manner expressed. For, says my author, an eye-witness, the effigies of the late tyrant and usurper *Oliver Cromwell* cloathed in a pinked satten suit, with that, adds he, of that base miscreant and unjust judge *John Bradshaw* habited in a judges robe, as likewise the hellish *scotch* covenant, and the late state's arms, which were erected in the common-hall, were all on the same day hung upon a gallows set up for that purpose in the *pavement*; and at last put into three tar barrels and burnt, together with the gallows, in the presence of one thousand citizens in arms, and a multitude of other spectators.

A. 1663. Was an insurrection in *Yorkshire*, the leaders of which were all conventicle preachers, and old parliament soldiers. Their pretences for this rebellion were, to redeem themselves from the excise and all subsidies; to re-establish a gospel magistracy and ministry; to restore the

(*q*) *Burnet*'s history of his own times. (*r*) *Hildyard*'s antiq. of *York*, 1664.

long

long parliament and to reform all orders and degrees of men especially the lawyers and clergy. In order to this they printed a declaration, or, according to *Eachard*, a call to rebellion, beginning with these words: *If there be any city, town or county in the three nations that will begin this righteous and glorious work, &c.* according to which a great number of them appeared in arms at *Farnley-wood* in *Yorkshire*. A. 1663.

But the time and place of rendezvous being known, a body of regular troops with some of the county militia was sent against them; who seized upon several and prevented the execution of their design. A commission was sent down to *York* in the depth of winter to try the principal leaders of them, and *Thomas Oats*, *Samuel Ellis*, *John Nettleton*, sen. *John Nettleton*, jun. *Robert Scot*, *William Tolson*, *John Forster*, *Robert Olroyd*, *John Askwith*, *Peregrine Corney*, *John Snowden*, *John Smith*, *William Ash*, *John Errington*, *Robert Atkins*, *William Cotton*, *George Denham*, *Henry Watson*, *Richard Wilson*, *Ralph Rymer* and *Charles Carre*, were condemned and executed, most of them at *York*, and three at *Leeds*. Several of these hot-headed zealots behaved very insolently upon their tryals. *Corney* had the assurance to tell the judge, *that in such a cause he valued his life no more than he did his handkerchief.* Two of these enthusiastical wretches were quartered, and their quarters set up upon the several gates of the city. Four of their heads were set upon *Micklegate-bar*; three at *Bootham-bar*; one at *Walmgate-bar*, and three over the castle gates. These were the last persons that I can find, except some popish priests, that were executed for high treason in our city.

Saturday Aug. 5. came *James* duke of *York* and his duchess to this city, and were met on *Tadcaster-bridge* by the sheriffs, and at *Micklegate-bar* by the lord-mayor, aldermen, *&c.* in their formalities on horseback, the chamberlains and common-council on foot. *Richard Etherington* esquire, deputy-recorder, made a speech to his highness, which being ended, they were entertained at alderman *Bawtry*'s house, and afterwards conducted to the lord *Irwin*'s in the *Minster-yard*. This progress was made by the duke and duchess when the plague raged high in *London* and some more southern parts. His royal highness staid near two months at *York*. I find that on *Saturday September* 23. he left the city and took a post chaise to go to the king and parliament then assembled at *Oxford*. On *Tuesday* following the duchess set forward; both of them expressing their sense of the great civilities, honours and respects which the lord-mayor, aldermen, sheriffs, and the whole city shewed to them during their residence in this place. A. 1666.

When the popish plots, bills of exclusion, *&c.* ran high against the duke, he chose to retire from court, and on the 6th of *November* this year came to *York* in his journey to *Edinburgh* with his duchess. At this time his highness was not received with all the formalities above, and the lord-mayor and aldermen thought fit only to attend him in his presence-chamber at Mr. *George Aislaby*'s house in the *minster-yard*, where Mr. *Pricket*, deputy-recorder, made this short but pithy harangue to him (s). A. 1679.

"YOUR royal highness is very welcome to this ancient and loyal city, which glories "more in her known loyalty, and in your highness's title of being duke of *York*, than "in the birth and residence of emperors; wherewith she has formerly been honoured. Our "lives and estates are all devoted to his majesty's service, under whose religious and peace-"able government, we account our selves happy; and we heartily wish prosperity to "his majesty, your royal highness, and the whole royal family."

Notwithstanding the warm expressions of loyalty which this speech testifies, the not receiving the duke with that ceremony which was requisite by the magistrates, (though the sheriffs of the city had done their duty and had rode to *Tadcaster* to meet his highness as usual) was resented at court; and occasioned the following reprimand in a letter from the secretary of state; which, as our records give it, is as follows,

" *My lord mayor and gentlemen,* *Whitehall, Nov.* 11, 1679.

"THE king being given to understand that you did not receive his royal highness, "upon his late coming to the city, with that respect which was due to him, and in "the manner heretofore accustomed; his majesty commands me to signify to you, that as "he was much surprised by this your proceeding, so he cannot but express to you his dissa-"tisfaction at it. And therefore his majesty bids me let you know, that it is his express "pleasure that whensoever his royal highness shall come again to *York*, you do not fail to "attend and receive him in the like manner as he was received there some years ago; and "as his majesty has reason to expect *his brother* should be by all good subjects in your "station.

My lord mayor and gentlemen,
Your most humble servant,
SUNDERLAND.

Superscribed,
" *For his majesty's special service, to the lord mayor* "*and aldermen of the city of* York.

(s) Ex MS. (t) Ex MS.

The

A. 1684. The slight put upon the king's brother, and immediate heir to the crown, gained the city no good will at court, and the magistracy at that time being noted for disaffection, they fell so far under the king's displeasure, that a *Quo Warranto* was granted against them by king *Charles* II. in the last year of his reign, to shew cause how they came to usurp to themselves such and such liberties, *&c.* Their charter being also called for to be perused, was detained by the ministry, nor was it renewed to them in this king's reign. The proceedings in this matter will fall apter under another head of this work; and I shall only say here, that king *James* the second succeeding his brother in the throne, notwithstanding any distaste he might have taken at the citizens of *York*, upon their humble petition to him, granted them a new, full and extensive charter; in which indeed care was taken to remove, by name, several magistrates and common-council-men, whom he suspected not to be in his interest, from their offices. The government of the city was also taken from the lord-mayor, and given to sir *John Reresby*, baronet, soon after representative in *parliament*, also, for the city of *York*.

A. 1685. The king at this time having called a *parliament*, the candidates for the city were sir *John Reresby*, sir *Metcalf Robinson*, baronets, and *Toby Jenkins* and *James Moyser*, esquires. The struggle was great, and I find by an entry in the city's books that the two former being chosen, the other in resentment caused five aldermen, who were much in the elected members interest, to be represented at court as disaffected to the government. Their names were *Ramsden*, *Elcock*, *Herbert*, *Edward Thompson* and *Waller*; all the said aldermen, except *Herbert*, with some of the common-council, represented as disloyal in like manner, were seized on by an order of king and council *June* 29, and sent prisoners to *Hull*; where they remained till the 25th of *July* following. When, the duke of *Monmouth*'s rebellion being quashed, they were released; and, notwithstanding the new charter was not yet come down, they took their places in their own court as usual.

At the summer assizes the year before, I find that the lord chief justice *Jefferys* came down to *York*, as one of the judges of assize for this circuit, and the mayor and aldermen being advised to wait upon him to know his majesty's pleasure concerning the city in the state it was, accordingly did; and, as the entry in the city's books declares, after a speech made to him by Mr. *Pricket*, the city's council, his lordship expressed himself to this effect, *That the king expected nothing but the government of the city to be at his dispose; and if the mayor would call a court and common-council, and make a petition to his majesty under the common seal to the effect proposed, he would take care to get it presented, and doubted not of a gracious answer in a week's time. In the mean while all things should stand in* statu quo. A petition was accordingly drawn up, and presented to the lord chief justice; who approved of it and sent it up to the king. And, in the second week of the assizes, being invited to dinner at the city's charge, he was treated at the lord mayor's house, and then and there the lord chief justice declared he had received an account, *that his majesty was well pleased with the city's petition, and assured them that they should have a new charter, with that proviso or reservation only of having the nomination and approbation of the magistrates and persons in office therein.*

A. 1685. But, as I said before, the renewal of their charter by this king was prevented by his death, which happened *Feb.* 6, 168¾. And *James* the Second was the king who granted our city the last charter it has had; an abstract of which may be met with in the following chapter. Great was the joy the citizens testified on that occasion; an account of which was sent up to *London* and printed in the *Gazette*, from which authority I give it.

London-Gazette, anno 1685. N° 2060.

"*York*, *Aug.* 8. This evening was brought hither his majesty's most royal charter to this "city by sir *Henry Thompson* of *Castlegate* and Mr. *Scot*; being met at some distance from "hence by a great many horse and foot, to the number of near five thousand, and received "at the gate of the city by the lord-mayor, aldermen, and common-council in their formalities; who passed from thence, amidst the continued acclamations of the people, with "drums beating and trumpets sounding, to the lord-mayor's house; where the whole company drank their majesty's healths. The streets were filled with bonfires, the musick "played, the bells rung, and nothing was omitted that might on this occasion express the "duty and loyalty of the inhabitants of this city."

A. 1688. Our city continued to shew their loyalty and gratitude to this unfortunate king; and on every publick occasion took care to address his majesty with the warmest expressions of love and duty to his person and government. Particularly, I find entered in the city's books of that year, that *June* 18, 1688, upon the news brought to the city that the queen was delivered of a young prince, the lord-mayor, *Thomas Raynes*, aldermen, sheriffs, four and twenty and common-council, did with a full consent agree that the lord-mayor should go to *London*, to address the king upon the joyful news of the prince's birth, and that sir *Henry Thompson*, sir *Stephen Thompson* knights, and alderman *Shackleton*, with Mr. sheriff *Bell* and Mr. *Thomas Thompson*, should accompany the said lord-mayor to court on this occasion. Ordered also, at the same time, that the said lord-mayor, aldermen, and twenty four should have two gallons of wine to drink the kings, queens and young prince's healths; and the commons four gallons, for the like purpose, all at the publick expence. The address itself

itself is either through carelessness or willfulness lost from the city's books; but, upon search into the *Gazettes* of that year, which I have been favoured with the loan of, I find this very address entered in these words: A. 1688.

London-Gazette. N°. 2368. From *Thursday July* 26. to *Monday July* 30. 1688.

To the king's most excellent majesty.

" *May it please your majesty,*

" THE mayor, aldermen, and commons of your majesty's ancient and loyal city of " *York* were transported with joy at the birth of the young prince; and after they " had made what demonstrations they could at home of their rejoicing, thought it their duty " to send, and have sent, some of the principal members of their body to congratulate your " majesty for so great and extraordinary a blessing both to your majesty and your subjects. " The great God, who hath at sundry times miraculously preserved your majesty, both at " sea and land, hath at this time enlarged his blessings to your majesty and your people " by giving us a royal prince; who, we pray, may long live to inherit the virtues and " crown of his ancestors; and that there may never want one of your royal family to sway " the scepter of these kingdoms; for the support and maintenance whereof we are, and " shall always be, ready to sacrifice our lives and fortunes. And that the God of heaven " would be graciously pleased to shower down his blessings upon your majesty, your royal " consort, the young prince, and the whole royal family is the hearty prayer of us,

Your majesty's most dutiful, obedient and loyal subjects, &c.

" Which address his majesty received very graciously.

It was not long after this when the tide beginning to turn against king *James*, the affections and declarations of his people took also the same bent. But as the springs and motions of this *great revolution* are so dark and intricate to find out, that many people have been crushed to death in endeavouring of it; and being, also, somewhat foreign to my purpose, I shall here chuse to conclude my *annals. Tu sapiens finire memento,* said a brother historian of mine upon somewhat a like occasion. There, likewise, have been no royal visits paid to our city from any succeeding crowned heads, or any of their family, from the date above. And nothing of publick transactions, except the several proclamations for peace or war, and of the several monarchs, having happened here worthy notice, I cannot find a fitter period to put an end to this long discourse. But, in order to preserve the character of an impartial historian, which I have all along endeavoured to do through the whole course of these annals, I shall conclude them with a copy of another address of a different nature from the former, though not much different in date, and from the self-same people.

" *To the high and mighty prince* William Henry *prince of* Orange.

" *The humble address of the lord-mayor and commonalty of the city of* York.

" WE the lord mayor and commonalty of the city of *York*, being deeply sensible of " God almighty's great blessing upon this nation in inclining your princely heart " to hazard your self and fortune for the rescuing the protestant religion, laws and liberties " of this kingdom, out of the hands of those who have sacrificed them all to their boundless " malice; do render our due and humble thanks to your highness for so transcendent a bene- " fit to the nation, whereof your highness (next under God) hath apparently been the sole " instrument. And as we have been the earliest of those (who were not under the imme- " diate protection of your highness's army) that have shewed our selves and joined with the " earl of *Danby* and others of your highness's friends in so glorious a design, so we (as ear- " ly as our distance from your highness can admit) do most humbly and heartily congratu- " late your happy success, and promise still to stand by your highness in defence of the pro- " testant religion and the laws of the kingdom to the utmost peril of our lives and fortunes; " wishing to your highness length of days and an happy issue, and increase of honour pro- " portionable to your great worth, and that all your enterprizes may be crowned with " success.

" In testimony whereof we have hereunto put our common seal the fourteenth day " of *December, anno domini* 1688.

CHAP. VI.

The government of the city during the times of Romans, Saxons, Danes *and* Normans; *with the present government by a lord-mayor, aldermen, sheriffs,* &c. *The ancient and present navigation of the river* Ouse. *Of the gilds, crafts, trades and fraternities, franchises, liberties, charters, gifts and donations, privileges granted to the community of the city; with their by-laws, ancient customs, fairs, markets,* &c.

I Shall not take upon me to describe what form of government the *Britons* used in their cities, before the *Romans* conquered them; nor, indeed, does their chief historiographer *Geffry Mon.* how particular he may be in other matters of less moment, ever touch upon this. It was the custom in the primary ages of the world, when a more civilized had conquered a more barbarous race of men, to persuade them, or drive them, into cities, towns and communities; in order to cultivate a better understanding of human nature amongst them, and wear off that savage disposition, which they necessarily must have acquired under a more loose and neglected discipline. The (*a*) author of the life of *Alexander the great* tells us, that he built, through all his conquests, at least, seventy cities; and had them peopled with the natives of the countries, where masters of sciences were placed to teach and instruct them. This course, according to the *stoick*, was taken long before *Alexander*, by *Theseus*, when he undertook the government of the *Athenian* republick; and laid the foundation of the most civilized and most learned body of men the sun ever saw.

> ——— *ingenuas didicisse fideliter artes,*
> *Emollit mores, nec sinit esse feros,*

says *Ovid*; and to this day the *Portuguese*, and *Spaniards*, endeavour, by drawing them into cities and towns, to wear off the natural rough behaviour, and restrain the savage lives of the *Brazilians*, and other *Americans*.

Thus if it be disputed that the *Romans* found us a city, it can never be denied that they made us one; and, probably, with the same politick view as above. The poor *Britons* were utter strangers to men and manners, and took their first lessons from the *Romans* with a very froward disposition. Unwilling to leave their ancient barbarous customs, they frequently rebelled against their masters, who were forced to rule them with a rod of iron, and break them as they would the wildest and fiercest horse. Nay, so ingrafted was this natural principle of savage liberty in them, that some who have had more than ordinary care taken of their education, and been carried children to *Rome* for that purpose, have at their return divested themselves of their reason, as well as cloths, and run naked into the mountains, to starve amongst their few unconquered countrymen (*b*). Like the *Hottentots* of *Africa*, who have thrown off the finest garments, and left the choicest diet, to besmear their bodies with stinking grease, and fall to gnawing, again, of dirty guts and garbage (*c*).

The fierce untameable disposition of the *Britons*, made it absolutely necessary to keep them in great awe; which could not be done but by a settled body of regular troops in the island, and the strictest military discipline. A *Roman colony* was therefore thought proper to be settled at Eboracum. That it was a *Colony*, and not a *Municipium*, is indisputably evident from Mr. *Camden*'s *Roman* coin, and funeral inscription mentioned before; it is here therefore necessary to explain those two models of *Roman* government.

A *colony* was always drawn out of the city of *Rome* itself, when they wanted supplies; whereas a *municipium* were natives of some conquered country, made free and enjoying the same privileges with the citizens of *Rome* within their own district. This was the state of Verulamium, called since by the *Britons Caer Municipii*, and some others in this province (*d*), who either had this favour granted them, or else the free use of their own constitutions. Our learned antiquary, *Camden*, says, that it was not strange for a *colony* to be changed into a *municipium* at the request of the inhabitants; yet Eboracum never was, and probably, for this reason, not because the native inhabitants could not obtain such a favour, which cannot be supposed; but, that it being the settled station of a large army of *Roman*

(*a*) *Q. Curtius.*
(*b*) *Langborn* ant. *Albion.*
(*c*) Hist. of the *Cape of Good Hope.*
(*d*) *Nennius. H Hunt.*

soldiers,

soldiers, they must be governed after the military manner. There were under the *Roman* discipline two sorts of *colonies*, the one civil drawn out from amongst the *Togati* or *gowned citizens* of *Rome*, as well as the mixed sort of people; the other *military*, taken out of *legions* and *cohorts*, when they were past service; and settled in cities, towns or elsewhere, as a reward for their blood spent in the service of the commonwealth. The former of these became many times free boroughs, *municipia*, in the empire, but the latter never so; it being thought derogatory that such as had born arms should admit of an inferior and less glorious condition; much less, says the learned *Burton* (e), when a whole legion had, by the beneficence and large indulgence of successive emperors, sat down any where, as here at EBORACVM.

Notwithstanding what has been said, I take this city to have been governed by both the civil and military Laws; and therefore *Victor* is not so much in the wrong, as *Camden* would make him, when he says, speaking of the death of the emperor *Severus*, *neque multo post* BRITANIAE municipio, *cui* EBORACI *nomen*, *morbo extinctus est* (f). That the civil law and power was executed in it in those days, I suppose no body will deny that has read the former part of this work. That here was the PRAETORIVM, tribunal or chief place of judicature which once gave law to the whole empire; and where the emperor himself sometime sat in person, is indisputable. What greater title can any city in the world, except *Rome*, claim for being a *municipium* as well as a *colony*, and the enjoying every other privilege that could be granted (g)? Besides *Papinian*, the judge advocate of this high court at *York*, *Ulpian*, *Paulus*, *&c.* were successors to him in the tribunal, after the execrable murder of the former (h); and no doubt it continued in the same state, though in a lesser degree sometimes, till the declension of the empire.

Thus I may venture to say that, under the *Roman* government in this island, our city was a perfect model of the great city itself, and it was no vanity, in some old authors (i), to call it ALTERA ROMA. For, indeed, it was *Rome*, in little, having the same lineaments and proportions, though in a lesser compass; composed of the same magistrates; ruled by the same laws; governed by a like civil and military power as the parent city was; and, consequently, must, in every respect, be its *true picture in miniature*.

How *Rome* was governed by her *priests*, *civil magistrates*, *praetors*, *&c.* with the military power of legions and cohorts, although it might not be improper here to treat on, yet I am unwilling to swell this book to too great a bulk by filling it with other mens works. I shall beg the reader's excuse therefore, if it be judged a neglect; the learned world have been sufficiently instructed in these matters by abler pens than mine, and I am not sorry the thread of this discourse will not suffer me to break into it.

So much has been wrote already concerning the state of our city after the departure of the *Romans*, to the conquest of the island by the *Saxons*, that I shall not need to recapitulate. Such an effusion of blood, so many murders, and such a general devastation ensued, that no account can be given of a government so distracted and torn by civil dissensions, as well as foreign invasions. Nor, indeed, when the *Saxons* became entire lords and masters, and had divided the land into seven shares, can any thing be gathered from historians, about the civil government of a city; when all controversies, both publick and private, seem to have been decided by the sword. It is true when *Edwin the great* had subdued his neighbour kings, and was recognized first *sole monarch of Englishmen*, we are told by *Bede* (k) that he enacted such wholsome laws, and caused them to be so strictly observed, that *a weak woman might have walked over all the island, with her newborn babe, without let or impediment. York*, the capital city of the *Northumbrian* kingdom, was *Edwin*'s chief seat of residence, and we may believe it tasted, not a little, of the mildness of the times. But *Edwin*'s reign was short, and fierce wars again succeeding, sometimes betwixt *Saxons* and *Saxons*, at other times betwixt *Saxons* and *Danes*, our city and the kingdom of *Northumberland* was governed by a succession of tyrants, as each could cut the throat of his competitor; till *Edred*, who became another universal monarch, changed the government from a kingdom to an earldom, and made one *Osulph*, an *Englishman*, first earl of *Northumberland*.

The jurisdiction of this earl was near equal to the former kings; he was called by the *Saxons* Ealdorman, *Ealderman*, which was antiently an appellation annexed to a place of great trust and honour, though now transferred to officers of less note. The *Latin* word for this name was *Comes*, and when *Alfred the great* divided the kingdom into counties and shires, he appointed *justiciarii*, and *vicecomites*, through them, to govern instead of the *Ealdermen*, or earls of them (l). Thus the Scýpegemot, which was a court kept twice a

(e) *Ant.* itin.

(f) *Sextus Aurelius Victor* in *Severo*.

(g) To strengthen this argument, some editions of *Antoninus*'s itin. have EBVRACVM MPM. VI. VICTR. M.P.XVII. which is read *Eburacum municipium sextae Victricis, mill. pass.* XVII. Itin. *Gale*.

(h) *Duck de jure civ.*

(i) *Alcuin. Ebor. Harrison*'s description of *Britain*.

(k) —— *tanta autem eo tempore pax in* Britania, *quaquaversum imperium regis* AEDWINI *pervenerat, fuisse perhibetur, ut sicut usque hodie in proverbio dicitur; etiam si mulier una cum recens nato parvulo vellet totam perambulare insulam a mari ad mare, nullo se laedente valeret.* Ven. Bedae hist.

(l) *Selden*.

year,

year, as the *sheriff's turn* is at this day, was held first by the *bishop* of the diocess and the *ealderman*, and afterwards by the *bishop* and *sheriff*, where both the ecclesiastical and temporal laws were together, given in charge to the county (*m*).

As it was with the county so it must be with the city, for I can find no account of any separate jurisdiction, nor any officers of its own, except military ones, as governours, *&c.* till an age or two after this. The conqueror was very sparing in granting charters and privileges to any city or town in this kingdom; and the city of *York* might well be farthest from expecting any such favours from him. Old *Fabian* writes, that in this *William*'s days, there was almost no *Englishman* that bore any office of honour or rule. **Howbeit**, adds he, **some deale he favoured the citee of** London, **and graunted unto the citezens the first charter that ever they had, the which is written in the** Saxon **tonge, and seled with green waxe, and expressed in eight or nyne lines** (*n*).

Notwithstanding this, neither *Fabian*, who is very particular in the affairs of *London*, nor yet Mr. *Stowe*, mention any mayor, or even bayliffs to govern that city till the first of
A. 1190. *Richard* I, when, by that king's especial favour, at his coronation, two bayliffs were appointed and continued annually to be chosen out of the body of the commons, till the tenth of king *John*; who at their earnest suit, says *Fabian*, granted them licence, by his letters
A. 1209 patents, to chuse a mayor and two sheriffs, instead of bayliffs; which has ever since continued to be the practice in that city.

The titles of **Portreve** and **Burghreve** the *Saxons* bestowed upon the *counts* of cities, or great towns; so **Marchgreve**, whence the *French* marquis, count of the frontiers; **Landgreve**, count of provinces, and our **Shirereve**, from **Grave** or **Greve**, a count or chief officer, in each district (*o*). Old *Fabian* mentions **Portgreve** to be the name of the governour of the city of *London* before, and after, the conquest. *Stowe* has given us the proper names of some of them, as in a grant from *Edward* the confessor directed in these words: Edward **king greeteth** Alfward **B. and** Wolfgrave **my Portgreve, and all the burgesses in** London. So that grant of the conquerors was directed to W. **bishop and** Godfry **portgreve**, &c. (*p*). From whence I conclude that this *portreve* was the same within the city as the **shirereve** without, and acted equally in consort with the bishop of the place.

But what I infer from all this, is, that the governour of our city must have had the same appellation as the chief magistrate of *London*, though we are not so happy as to find out any records to vouch it. The dreadful fire and devastation, which happened at the conquest, not only destroyed the records of the metropolitan church but those of the city also. And *anno* 1137, another fire, but casual, consumed the whole city, and in it all that was saved from the former; so that nothing, so antient, can be expected from that quarter. History, however, is not altogether silent in our cause, but gives us the name of a mayor of *York*, higher than the dates of either the mayors, or even bayliffs, of the city of *London*. King *Stephen*, at his rebuilding of St. *Peter*'s hospital, and endowing it with his threaves of corn, commanded *Nigel*, then mayor of *York*, to deliver up a place in the city, near the west wall, to receive the poor and lame in. This is mentioned by *Stowe* in his chronicle, as well as others; and though the year is not taken notice of, yet *Stephen* dying *anno* 1153, must make it, at least, forty years before *Richard* I. gave bayliffs to the city of *London*; or sixty years before their first mayor.

From this *Nigel* to the first of *Edward* I, *anno* 1273, nor register-books, nor histories, mention the names of mayors and bayliffs of this city; I mean those registers belonging to the city; but, in an old leiger-book of the famous abby of *Fountains*, which I have been favoured with the loan of, I have recovered the names of some mayors and several bayliffs before the date above; which have been witnesses to grants of houses, *&c.* antiently bestowed on that monastery, within the city of *York*. For though we are assured by some grants of king *John* and *Henry* III, inscribed *majori et civibus* Ebor; that there were mayors and bayliffs in the city, in those kings reigns, yet none of their names occurred, till this venerable relict of antiquity not only discovered some of our antient senators to us, before unknown, but also several dignitaries of the cathedral. Copies of all such grants as refer to these, as well as other, affairs in the city, may be seen in the *appendix*. There are also other antient testimonies of mayors and bayliffs belonging to this city, before the date above mentioned, all which I have entered in the catalogue as the reader may observe.

Having proved that the city of *York* was very antiently governed by a *mayor* and *bayliffs*, I shall next shew the change to a *lord-mayor* and two *sheriffs*; which, with a *recorder*, twelve *aldermen*, *twenty-four*, as they are called, assistants, seventy two *common-council-men*, with eight *chamberlains*, compose the body that governs the city of *York* at this day. The etymology of whose several names I shall just touch upon, and first of the word *mayor*.

Mayor. The word *mayor*, or *major*: which the *Cambro-Britons* call MAER; the *Low Dutch* and *Germans* **Meyer**, all signify the same as the *Latin Praetor* (*q*). *Verstegan* has given a good de-

(*m*) *Omni comitatu, bis quotannis conventus agitor, cui quidam illius dioecesis* episcopus & senator *interfunto; quorum alter jura divina, humana alter populum edocerto.* Dudg. *orig. jud.*

(*n*) *Fabian*'s chron.

(*o*) *Selden*'s tit. of hon.

(*p*) *Stowe*'s survey of *London*.

(*q*) *Skinner*'s etym. dict.

finition

finition of this word, not in deriving it from the *Latin major*, as some erroneously have done, but from the old *English* word meier, *powerful*, *able*; from the verb *may possum*. In *Juvenal* the word *potestas* is made use on in the same sense with the *Italian podestia*, and the *French maire du palais*, *praefectus praetorio*, or *praetor*. *Davis*, another etymologist, derives it from the *Welch* or *British* MAER, *praetor*, and this from MIROR, *custos*, a keeper, or governour. I profess myself to know nothing of the *Welch* language, but this derivation sounds well; though I take it to be no more than an old *French* word introduced by the *Norman*, who did as much as he could to drive out the *Saxon* language. *Mair de palais* was, in old time, the principal officer of the crown in *France*, and steward of the king's house, which since has been called the *Seneschal de France*; so the *Mair de Village*, in old *French*, is the judge thereof. But whether this word has any affinity to the *Gaullic* language, and consequently to the *British*, I shall not determine.

The mayor of *York*, by antient prescription, assumes the title of *lord* in all writing or speaking to him; which honour peculiar only to the nobility, bishops, judges, and the highest officers of the realm, was bestowed on our chief magistrate by king *Richard* II. That monarch after granting the citizens a new and a most extensive charter, of privileges, *anno* 1389, 12 *reg.* at his coming to the city that year, took his *sword from his side* and gave it to *William de Selby*, then mayor, to be born before him and his successors. Which sword, by the express words of the charter, or any other sword they pleased, was to be born before them with the *point erected*, except in the king's presence, within the precincts of their liberties, *in perpetuum* (r). From this emblem (s) of justice we deduce our title of *lord-mayor*; he being by it constituted the king's more immediate *vicegerent* than before. *Anno* 1393, the same king presented *Robert Savage*, then lord-mayor, with a large gilt mace, to be born likewise before him and his successors; as also a cap of maintenance to the sword bearer. These truly royal gifts to the chief magistrate of *York*, made him equal if not exceed the mayor of *London* in those days; for it does not appear, either in *Fabian* or *Stowe*, when the title of *lord* was assumed by that officer. *Lord-mayor.*

The office of *lord-mayor* of *York* is a place of great trust and honour; and, if used in its full extent, he is very near an absolute governour within his district. No persons, of what quality soever, living or residing within the liberties, but must obey his mandate, or summons, on any complaint exhibited against them. He is the king's *lieutenant* in his absence; nor does he give place, or drop his ensigns of authority to any but the *king's own person*, or the *presumptive heir* to the crown; at whose appearance he is, only, dispossessed, and carries the mace himself before his majesty. The *judge of assize* sits on his right-hand in the courts of justice; himself keeping the chair. At the sessions of peace he is supream; being always a justice of peace, and one of the *quorum*. In council he has a casting voice; and in full senate no act nor law can be made without his concurrence. He never stirs abroad, in private, but in his habit, and an officer attending; but on publick occasions, such as swearing days, proclamations of kings, proclaiming of peace or war, &c. he is habited in *scarlet* with a rich mantle of *crimson silk*, and a massy *gold chain*, the ensigns of authority before him, his brethren, the twenty-four, and common council, in their proper habits, attending. A handsome revenue, consisting, chiefly, of the toll of all corn coming to market, * which he enters upon every 24th of *February*, is allowed him for the maintenance of an hospitable table. At which, formerly, all strangers and others were every day made welcome, but of late years that custom was abated to twice a week; and, by a later regulation, to as often as the *lord-mayor* pleases to invite company to dine with him. Which has rendered the office much more easy to be born; as also much less chargeable. A noble house has been lately built for the lord-mayors and his family's residence, which has all suitable furniture belonging to it. So that, in short, we want nothing but a *coach of state*, to make our chief magistrate appear with the same dignity with his brother of *London*. *His office and state.*

Whosoever shall offer to strike, or otherways abuse, the lord-mayor, during his office, with an intent either to affront or mischief him, are severely fined, imprisoned or punished, according to the degree of the crime. Two remarkable instances of this kind are upon record, which I shall give. *Striking lord-mayor.*

(t) *Anno* 1618, one *Charles Coulson*, a taylor, being in drink, came to *Thomas Agar*, then lord-mayor, and gave him a stab with a knife three inches deep in the left breast; but the wound proved not mortal. However the said *Coulson* was adjudged to be strongly fettered

(r) *Ex charta* Ebor.

(s) This very sword is still reserved and carried before the lord-mayors of *York* on some principal days; it being the last of four belonging to that magistrate, but valued above them all in commemoration of this royal favour.

* All toll of corn, &c. in this city, is for the use of the mayor and citizens; but is farmed to the lord-mayor by the commonality at an easy or small rent, for the ease of the charge of his office of mayoralty. It is accordingly collected to his use by officers of his own appointment, and at his own charge. *January* 15, 1677. the commons considering the lord-mayor's respect in inviting them to dinner on the swearing day, which had been discontinued, and some unusual charges incident to his office, they presented him, and all future lord-mayors with an abatement of ten pound *per annum*, out of the *toll rent* reducing it to twenty nobles.

(t) *Ex regist.* Ebor.

with iron; to be imprisoned for seven years; then to pay one hundred pound, or else to lie in jail for life. Moreover, at every quarter sessions, during the seven years, he should be carried through the city on horse-back, with his face to the horse's tail, and a paper on his forehead denoting his crime; and that on every of the said days he should stand some hours in the pillory. Which was performed accordingly.

(*u*) *Anno* 1664, sir *Miles Stapleton* of *Wigbill*, being also disordered with liquor, came to the house of *Edward Elwick* then lord-mayor, ond struck at him with his cane. For which affront being indicted the next sessions, he did personally appear at the bar of the common hall, and there before the lord-mayor and court confessed the indictment, acknowledged the heinousness of the crime, professed his sorrow for it, and humbly submitted himself to the censure of the honourable bench; who, at the earnest intercession of his friends, only fined him *five hundred pounds*.

This great officer is annually chosen; it being impolitick to trust so much power in one man's hand too long; and it is observable that it is sometimes parted with reluctancy; so bewitching a thing is power, to some kind of people, though joined to a great deal of trouble and small profit. Antiently, however, this office was continued in one man for several years together. In the reign of *Edward* III, *Nicholas Langton* was mayor for thirteen years successively; but this happening in the height of the *Scottish* wars, I suppose it was not thought advisable to change magistrates in such an important place as this city must be at that time. This man held the office, with an *interregnum* of three years, for seventeen years together, the longest of any in the catalogue (*w*); and his son *John Langton*, who was knighted by *Edward* III, was eight times mayor successively. But the citizens finding it inconvenient to let the power lie so long in one hand, *anno* 1394. came to a consultation, and made an order about it, that from henceforth no lord-mayor should stand above one year, till the twelve, being able, should bear office after him. This order was soon disregarded, for sir *William Frost*, knighted by *Richard* II, was lord-mayor *anno* 1397, and in ten years after was seven times in that office. However, after him and one more, the former order seems to take place again, for we find little or no variation from it down to the present times; except that in the last civil war, sir *Edmund Cooper* was three times lord-mayor, by king *Charles's* own appointment.

These officers following have all diet at the lord-mayor's house, during his mayoralty, and are his reputed servants, *viz.* a *chaplain*, who is usually the minister of the parish, a *town* or *common clerk*, with his man or men, two *esquires*, *viz.* the *sword* and *mace-bearer*, *four officers* at *mace*, formerly six; a *porter*, a *cook*, with his man or men, a *baker*, &c.

If the lord-mayor be married, his wife is dignified by her husband's title, and is called *my lady*; and although the husband parts with both honour and title at the same time, yet by the courtesy of *York*, and in favour to that sex, her *ladyship* still enjoys hers; by no other right that I know of than that of an old *rhiming proverb*, still amongst us, which is this,

He is a lord for a year and a day;
* But she is a lady for ever and ay.

Bailiff. The title of *bailiff*, though it is now by prostituting of it to a pack of fellows become an odious name; yet formerly was bestowed on none but the chief magistrates of a city or corporation; of which last some retain it to this day. This also is originally a *French* word from *Franco-gaulick Bailli*, which signifies a patron, or master of an houshold; or else from *bail* a tutor, guardian or keeper. So the *Italian*, *baglio*, *nutritius*, that is, the cherisher or protector of a city or province, and all from the *Latin bajulus*, which though it classically means a *porter* (*x*), yet, in the later writers, *bajulus* is sometimes used for a pedagogue, a monitor, a merchant, a bailiff. *Anno* 1397, this office was laid down in this city; and instead of *three bayliffs*, were substituted *two sheriffs*; by which it became a *city* and *county* of itself (*y*).

The next in dignity to the lord-mayor I take to be the *sheriffs*, as places, *durante termino*, of much greater trust and authority than any of the subsequent officers of the city; but as they usually come in after the *recorder* and *aldermen*, I shall so place them.

Recorder. The *recorder's* seat therefore must be at the elbow of the lord-mayor; whose name, like the former, is *French* from the *Latin recordari*. This officer must be *causidicus*, a barrister at law; whose office is to be an assistant or coadjutor to the mayor and bench. To be their mouth or publick orator, not only in haranguing princes and crowned heads, when they do us the honour of a visit, but in directing juries, summing up evidences, and the like. To take great care that the city's privileges are no ways infringed; to see that *meum* and *tuum* be honestly regained when lost. To see that justice be inflicted on rogues, whores, thieves and vagrants; according to the several acts of parliament made for that purpose; and, lastly, to be careful, as his name directs, that the antient *records*, *charters*, &c, be-

(*u*) *Ex eodem.*
(*w*) See cat. of mayors, &c.
* There were one, or two, old epitaphs in the cathedral, which gave this title to the wife of one that had been lord-mayor; which see.
(*x*) Vide *Spelman's* glossar. *Skinner*, &c.
(*y*) 20 *Rich.* II.

longing

longing to the city be preserved; as well as to see that all *new acts*, *by-laws*, &c. be duly registered and transmitted to posterity.

The word *alderman* though now appropriated to citizens and townsmen of a corporation, was antiently a title of very high degree; witness this epitaph found on a tomb in *Ramsey* monastery. *Aldermen.*

(z) Hic requiescit Ailwinus, inclyti regis Edgari
cognatus, totius Angliae aldermannus, et
hujus sacri coenobii miraculose fundator.

The term, as I have elsewhere noted, comes either from the *English Saxon* Eld, which signifies an old man; from Eldor, or Ealdor, older, Eld old age, or Eldor, an elderly man, prince or senior; so that Elderman signifies as much as a princely senator. Our *Saxon* ancestors, following the examples of the *Romans*, turned names of eldership or age, into titles of dignity; for they had their *senator*, *patricius*, *pater conscriptus*, and the like; as well as we our *elders*, *aldermen*, &c. But yet it is not easy to determine when this title dropt from being *alderman* of all *England*, or a province, to be only *alderman* of a corporation (a). About an age after the conquest I find mention made of some magistrates of this city, but not with this title; for, amongst the witnesses to an old grant to *Fountain's-abbey*, *Hugo de Seleby* is styled *major civitatis* Eboraci, and *Thomas de Graunt* is called *praepositus ejusdem villae*. In another, *Nicholas Orger* is mayor, and the former *Hugo de Seleby* is set down as a witness, *cum aliis civibus et* praepositis *Ebor*. Now the best translation of *praepositus* is *provost*, a *French* title; but if any one will say that it is *Latin* for an *alderman*, they have my leave. I shall only add that the title *alderman* being laid down at the conquest, for the introduction of the *Norman* names of officers, it lay neglected, till a proper *English* appellation being wanted for a magistrate of this nature, this old *Saxon* name was taken up, fitted well, has continued ever since to be a mark of that dignity; and in all probability ever will do.

This magistrate has little business when he is not mayor; he continues a justice of peace, and if a senior is one of the *quorum*. But, though he is always duly summoned to attend the sessions, council chamber, and every election of mayor, aldermen, sheriffs, common councilmen, *&c.* yet he is not obliged to appear, if any other material business of his own intervene. If a lord-mayor is called abroad, he substitutes one of these aldermen *Deputy mayor.* for his deputy, who acts in full power till his return, and is as much *dominus fac totum* as he whom he represents in all things, except signing notes for money.

The title of *sheriff* I have defined before to come from the *Saxon* Scire, and Greve, *comes*, *praefectus*, *exactor*, an earl, prefect, or he whose business it was to gather the prince's revenue. This is another *Saxon* name for an officer, which the *Normans* could not well alter, there being no word, in their language, so expressive of the place. For though *shire* was changed into *county*, or *comté*, by them; yet, in *law French*, the king's writs were directed to the **schrieve**, or *sheriff*, of the place. The *Latin vice-comes*, which is, plainly, an officer substituted in the earl's stead, is since become an hereditary title of honour being the *French viscount*. The sheriff's officers and duties I shall give in the sequel. *Sheriff.*

Chamberlain lies the next in my road to define; which word we have from the *Teutonic* *Chamberlain.* **kammerling**, the *French chambellan*, the *Italian cambellano*, all a corruption of the *Latin camerarius*; which is used a little barbarously for *cubicularius*; but what relation these words have to this office, in particular, I am to learn. In *France*, *Flanders*, *Germany*, and some other foreign parts, this title is rightly used for an officer or officers, who are in the nature of *treasurers*, or receivers, of the publick stock; and dispose and lay up the same in several rooms and chambers; where they likewise keep their courts and give their attendance. It is not improbable but this has antiently been their office in this city; as in some measure appears by their accounts in the old registers; but being always very young tradesmen that come into this office in this city, it has not been thought proper to trust them with the publick money and goods; and, except the principal, who has the title and honour of being the lord-mayor's chamberlain, they are chose rather to pay their money than receive any.

This office is no doubt, of antient date; and as I said they are now chosen out of the body of the younger tradesmen, who are in a thriving condition. As a feather to the place, the title *master*, or *Mr.* is always prefixed to their names, in speaking or writing to them, ever after. In *London*, they are so well bred as to give this appellation of Mr. to a *porter*, or a *cobler*; but in *York*, when any one is called so that has not passed this office, or is of so mean an account as not to be thought worthy of it, *Mr. quoth 'a, pray who was lord-mayor when he was chamberlain?* an opprobrious question often used in this city by the vulgar.

After the election of these eight subaltern, as I may call them, officers, they take place according to the trade or company they are of. In *anno* 1607, a great difference arose

(a) *Leland's* coll.

(a) One *Thomas de Everwyck* paid a fine to the king for being admitted *alderman* of the *gild* of *merchants* in that city. *Maddox's* exchequer.

about the precedence, whether an alderman's son, made a chamberlain, should take place of a merchant? After much debate the former carried it; and for the future it was agreed that the chamberlain who was the son of an alderman, out of respect to the high office his father had born, should have the precedence of the *merchant*.

Bridge-masters To these chamberlains were formerly added, as assistants, two *bridge-masters*; which office is of very antient date, and was very necessary, before stone-bridges were so much in use, to take care of the repairs of timber ones (*b*). These continued in office till the first of *Charles* I. when they were laid down; and a citizen in fee was appointed to collect the city's rents; now called the *city steward*.

Having now gone through the etymologies of the names, and touched upon some of the offices of our governours, I shall next proceed to discribe the other parts which constitute the civil power of the city of *York*; which by the charters, privileges and indulgencies of several kings is at this day no other than a little *commonwealth*.

The twenty four. Besides the officers already mentioned, the city has an additional number of men to the body of governours, who, having passed the office of sheriff, are sworn into the privy-council; and, with the lord-mayor and aldermen, compose an higher house. These citizens are commonly called by the name of the *twenty four*; though they may be more or less than that number. They are usually summoned, and sit in consult, with the chief magistrates, on any business relating to the city, and have votes in every election of officers, &c. equal with an alderman; except in that of a lord-mayor, aldermen and sheriffs.

The common-council. The last, though not the meanest, nor the least in authority, are a body of men drawn from the lower class of citizens to the number of seventy two, and are called the *common-council men* of the city. They were first called in to the legislature by a charter of king *Henry* VIII. and then were appointed to be chosen two out of each of the thirteen companies following, *viz. merchants, mercers, drapers, grocers, apothecaries, goldsmiths, dyers, skinners, barbers, fishmongers, taylors, vintners, pinners* and *glasiers*. With one from each of the fifteen lower companies hereafter named, *viz. hosiers, inholders, vestment-makers, wax-chandlers, brewers, weavers, walkers, ironmongers, sadlers, masons, bakers, butchers, glovers, pewterers* and *armorers*. And then also the *eldest searcher* of every of the said crafts, together with the common council aforesaid, had voices in all *elections* of mayor, aldermen and sheriffs.

But now, according to a later regulation and grants confirmed by the charter of king *Charles* II, they are chosen from and distinguished into four wards respecting the four principal gates of the city, *viz. Micklegate-ward, Bootham, Monk*, and *Walmgate-wards*. They are *eighteen* in number in each ward, whose *senior* presides in his own, but have a general *foreman* or *speaker*, for the whole body. This is a direct *house of commons*; with this difference only that they are in no danger of betraying their trust by either *bribes* or *pensions*. And, to speak the truth of the present members that compose this *lower class* of the corporation, there are amongst them, to my knowledge, men of as much publick spirit, and who have the real interest of the city as much at heart, as any magistrate whatever. Like as in the legislature of the whole kingdom, so in this *epitome* of it our corporation, no act can be passed but what has the consent of the three estates. This body acting as the *commons*, the aldermen and twenty four are a sort of *house of lords*; and all under the direction of the *supream governour* the lord mayor.

And now, having gone through with the several orders and degrees of magistrates in this city, I shall in the next place inform the reader with the customs, manner, and time of electing them into their respective offices; and first of the

LORD-MAYOR.

Election of the lord-mayor. This prime officer is annually chosen out of the number of aldermen, who are not impeded by age or sickness; who have not been twice mayor of the city; or born that office within six years last past; and are thought to be every way qualified to undertake the duty. Upon St. *Maurice*'s day, *January* 15, unless it be *Sunday*, and then it is deferred to the day following, the lord-mayor, recorder, aldermen, sheriffs, and privy-council, in their scarlet gownes, with the chamberlains and common-council, in their black, meet at the gild, or common, hall about nine a clock in the morning. Here, having the doors

1 *Feb.* 25 *Eliz.* 1982.

(*b*) Thomas Spragon *de civitate* Ebor. sadler, Rowlandus Fawcet *de eadem civitate* taylor, Johannes Sym *de eadem civitate* joyner, *recogn. se debere dominae reginae* } CC *l.*

The condition of this recognizance is such, that if the above bounden *Thomas Spragon* one of the bridge-masters of *Ousebridge* and *Fossbridge* do truly account, pay, and deliver over all such rents, sums of money, emplements, and other things belonging to this corporation, as shall come to his hands during his office, that is to say, all the said rents and sums of money to the hands of the chamberlains of the said city, of which rents and sums 30*l.* is to be paid at *Midsummer* next, and the residue on St. *Thomas*'s eve; and all the said emplements and other things by indenture to the hands of their next successors bridge-masters of the said city for the time being, within six days next after they be sworne; then this present recognizance to be utterly void, frustrate and of none effect, or else the same to remain and abide in full strength and vertue. *City records.*

closed

closed, the common-council on their oaths, present to the lord-mayor and court of aldermen a note, with the names of three aldermen, one which is pitched upon by the said court, and he is immediately seated next the chair; from that time to the day of his swearing into the office, he is styled *lord elect*. After this the bench retire into an inner apartment to refresh themselves; from whence passing through the hall, where the commons stand bare to receive them, they all conduct the *lord elect* to his own house; where usually is a noble collation prepared for them. The lord elect had formerly one esquire and two officers of those belonging to the lord-mayor to attend on him, who were dyeted upon him.

When the day for swearing the lord elect is come, being St. *Blaze*, *Feb.* 3. *Sunday* or not, the lord elect goes to the present lord mayor's house, and from thence, attended with the said lord-mayor, recorder, aldermen and privy council in their scarlet habits, with the chamberlains, and common-council in black gowns, walk in procession to *Ouse-bridge*. There in the council-chamber, they take an account of all the plate, jewels, houshold-stuff, and other perquisites, belonging to the lord-mayors for the time being. From thence they march in the same order to the common hall, where the lord elect takes the state oaths, and the usual oaths for the welfare of the city, the sword-bearer on his knees holding the book. After the oaths are taken, the said sword-bearer divests the old lord-mayor of his gold chain, and puts it on the neck of the new, which ends the ceremony. The company then wait upon their new magistrate to his own house, where he gives them a very splendid entertainment, anciently called the **venison-feast**, because it chiefly used to consist of that kind of food, but this has been long disused, venison being now much scarcer than formerly. The feast being ended, all the aforesaid company, except the new lord-mayor, return with the late lord, and wait upon him to his house, the officers and city musick attending; where they are again regaled with a banquet, wine, *&c.* after which the company pay their respects and conclude the solemnity with the day.

The form of electing a lord-mayor is now proceeded in as it was prescribed to the citizens by the charter of K. *Hen.* VIII. But more anciently it was otherways; and being chosen then by the whole body of the citizens without any form, day, or order, the elections were usually tumultuous, and attended with dangerous consequences. Insomuch that the royal authority has frequently interposed, and constituted a mayor by a *mandamus*. I find that in the forty ninth year of *Hen.* VI. the parliament had this affair of electing a mayor at *York* under consideration; and made an act to prescribe a rule for that purpose. But civil dissensions being then very high, the citizens could not agree about their chief magistrate, and a *mandamus* was sent by the king to appoint *William Holbeck* mayor for that year *(c)*. In the beginning of the reign of *Edward* IV, that king by letters patents *(d)* constituted a form for this election; which was that the searchers of every craft should summon the masters of trades to the *Guild-hall* of the city, on the day of St. *Maure*, *viz.* 15th day of *January*, and there to elect and nominate two honest and able aldermen of the said city, of which neither of them had been twice mayor before, nor bore that office of five years last past. The names thus taken by the recorder, senior sheriff, and town clerk, were carried up by them to the upper house, which officers afterwards took the suffrages of that court privately, and he of the two sent up on whom the most votes fell was to be mayor for the succeeding year from the feast of St. *Blaze*, *&c.* But this order not answering the purpose, in the thirteenth year of the same king other letters patents were granted *(e)*, whereby the searchers of each craft were ordered to summon all the citizens, yearly, on the feast of St. *Blaze*, *Feb.* 3. to the *Guildhall*, where they were to elect *one* able alderman of the said city, who had not been mayor for three years last past, to be then mayor of the said city, from the feast of St. *Julian* the virgin, *viz.* the 16th of the same month, for one whole year following. And that they should in a peaceable and quiet manner present the name of the mayor so chosen, in writing, to the mayor then in being. Which said mayor so chosen on the said feast of St. *Julian*, about ten o'clock in the forenoon, in the said *Guildhall*, before all the citizens, was to take the usual oath, and that doing he was actually mayor of the said city. Then the aldermen and citizens there present were to swear to be attending and assisting to the said mayor in his office, and that they would support and maintain him, during the time of his mayoralty, in all and singular things conducing to the honour, wellfare, and prosperity of the said city. A mayor dying in his office, or otherways removed, another alderman to be chosen in the same manner, upon a general summons, for the remaining part of the year.

When a man of the law offers himself to be *recorder* of the city of *York*, the whole body of the corporation have a right of voting at his election *(f)*. This is a place of honour more than profit, his fee being only twenty marks a year and robes accustomed. By an ordinance of the city made *Jan.* 8, 1581. *William Robinson* mayor, whosoever shall be recorder of this city, shall be only so during the pleasure of the lord-mayor and his brethren; and he to make the most part of his dwelling within the city. But since by the charter of *Char.* II. this officer, when chosen, is to have the approbation of the king, and so the place runs for life. Sir *T. W.* has taken pains to draw out a list of his predecessors to his time, which I

Election of recorder.

(c) *p.* 49. *H.* 6. *m.* 8.
(d) *p.* 4. *E.* 4 *p.* 2. *m.* 20. *et Fœd.* Ang. *Tom.* xi. *p.* 529.
(e) *p.* 13 *E* 4. *p.* 2. *m.* 16.

(f) This was determined *an.* 1701. when *Marmaduke Pricket* esquire, was elected recorder, that the commons had an equal right of voting in this election with the bench.

ſhall give in their proper place, deduced down to the preſent. Each recorder at his admiſſion takes the following oath:

His oath. " You ſhall ſwear that you, during the time that you ſhall be recorder of the city of " *York*, ſhall truly and indifferently give your beſt counſel unto the lord-mayor of this city, " the aldermen, ſheriffs, and all other of the common-council of the ſaid city, that now are " and hereafter ſhall be, and to every of them in all caſes and matters concerning the ſaid ci- " ty, and ſhall come unto the ſaid council of the ſaid city, when as you ſhall be required to " do the ſame, by my lord-mayor or his lieutenant, having ſufficient warning given unto " you, (except that you ſhall be letted by ſickneſs, or ſome other ſpecial cauſe,) and that " you ſhall not be abſent from the ſaid city except it ſhall be for reaſonable cauſes. So help " you God and holy dame and by the whole contents of this book.

City council. Beſides the *recorder*, this city by their charter hath another learned council aſſigned to the lord-mayor, aldermen, *&c.* called the *city-council*; a juſtice of peace by his place, and one of the *quorum*. The ancient manner of his election, with the reaſon thereof, you have in *Bernard Wilkinſon's caſe*, who was elected city council *June* 11. *an. reg. Eliz.* 10. 1568. The preſent *city council* is ſir *Richard Winn*, knight, ſerjeant at law.

Election of an alderman. An *alderman* is elected, in a vacancy, from the body of the more ſubſtantial citizens, ſuch as have ſerved the office of ſheriff or fined for it. The method is thus, at a general meeting of the corporation, the commoners ſend up the names of three citizens to the bench, who are called *lights* for aldermen; out of theſe they elect one. The word *light* is plainly deduced from the *Teutonick* Lieght, *clarus*, *lucidus*, which ſignifies a citizen eſteemed worthy of this honour by the ſplendor of his fortune, or his other ſhining qualities. I know no corporation in *England* that makes uſe of this word in this ſenſe, though the reader, I hope, will allow that the term is ſignificant. The firſt vacancy after a new alderman is elected, he is generally complimented with the high office of lord-mayor (*f*).

Of ſheriffs. The *ſheriffs* are choſen, in the ſame manner as the aldermen, on St. *Matthew*'s day, *Sept.* 21. annually. With this difference only, that the commons now ſend up four *lights*, out of which the bench chuſe two. If at the ſame time they are ſworn, then the lord-mayor, bench and privy council have on their ſcarlet habits, and the other their black ones, otherwiſe not, as ſometimes it happens, for they enter not into office till *Michaelmas* day, *September* 29, in the afternoon.

A *ſheriff* being choſen and through obſtinacy, ſelf-wilfulneſs, or any other unlawful impediment, refuſing to ſtand, he is not only fined, but is ſometimes eſteemed as ſheriff notwithſtanding his removal from the city with his houſe and family, and hath been obliged to account to the king for his fee-farm as if he had really executed that office. This was the caſe of *John Smith* who was elected ſheriff 18 *Hen.* VIII. and was ſo elected for five years together, but refuſing to ſtand, withdrew himſelf and family to *Skipton* in *Craven*; nevertheleſs at his death his executors became liable to account to the king for his fee-farm from the time of his election, and paid it accordingly.

Death. If a ſheriff dye in his office, the ſame order is obſerved as in caſe of the lord-mayor's death, and another is choſen in his ſtead. With this difference that the lord mayors hold not only the remaining part of the year to which they are choſen, but likewiſe the year following, as has happened in ſeveral inſtances; but the ſheriff continues only that part of the year which his predeceſſor wanted to ſupply, and then goes out without further charge, as much qualified to all the privileges of the city as if he had ſtood the whole year.

Fine for ſheriffs. Thoſe who fined for the office of ſheriff paid formerly no more than fifty pound, but of late years it has been uſually ſeventy pound. Every ſheriff about a month after his election takes an oath of ſecrecy in the council chamber, and then is admitted to be one of the privy council. At which ſolemnity the lord-mayor, aldermen, recorder and ſheriffs, with the reſt of the council, drink wine out of a bowl, ſilver-gilt; which is called the *black bowl*. A veſſel the commoners of *York* have an utter averſion to.

Their office. The ſheriffs of the city of *York* have a double function, *miniſterial* and *judicial*. By the firſt they execute all *proceſſes* and precepts of the courts of law, and make returns of the ſame. And by the next they have authority to hold ſeveral courts of diſtinct nature, which I ſhall give in the ſequel. They collect all publick profits, cuſtoms and taxes of the city and county of the ſame, and all fines, diſtreſſes and amerciaments. The ſheriff is chief gaoler, and has charge of all priſoners for debt, or miſdemeanors. They view and inſpect all weights, meaſures *&c.* viſit the markets, ride the fairs, and are anſwerable to the king's exchequer for all iſſues and profits ariſing from the office. Their attendance uſed formerly to be very grand, when they appeared on a publick occaſion, having four ſerjeants at mace, and each of them ſix or more livery men with halberts to attend them; for the neglect of which they have been fined in the mayor's court. This has been thought ſuperfluous, for now two ſerjeants are ſufficient; which with a bailiff, a gaoler, *&c.* make up their retinue at this time; except on their riding day, which ceremony claims another place.

Sheriff's oath. " *Sirs*, Ye ſhall ſwear, and either of you ſhall ſwear, that ye well and truly ſhall ſerve

(*g*) When a citizen is choſen alderman, and refuſes to ſtand, he is uſually fined at the diſcretion of the ſame court. In the year 1489 one *Thomas Scotton* was fined forty pound for not taking on him this office. And *an.* 1624. one *Edward Calvert* was fined and paid three hundred pound for exemption from this office. *City records.*

" the king in the office of the sheriffs of the city of *York*, and the profit of the king ye shall " do in all things that pertains to you after your wit and power, and his rights. As much " as pertaineth to the crown, ye shall truly keep, nor ye shall not assent unto no distres- " sing nor unto no concealment of right to the king or his crown, be it in lands or in " rents, or in franchises, or suits councelled or withdrawn, ye shall do your true power for " to let it, and if ye may not let it ye shall shew it to the king or to some of the council, of " which ye shall be certain that they shall shew it to the king. And the duty of the king " neither for gift nor favour respect there where ye shall well without right great grievance " of the debt make levy of them. And that ye shall truly, and by way of right treat the " people of your bailiwicks, and to each one do right as well to the poore and to the rich; " as that that pertaineth to you to do; and neither for gift, nor for promise, nor for favour, " nor for hate, ye shall do no wrong to no man, and other mens rights ye shall not disturb, " and that ye shall truly acquit the people of what ye shall receive of them as to duties of " the king. And ye shall take nothing by the which the king may lose, or by the which " right may be disturbed, or the duties of the king delayed, and that ye shall truly make " return and truly serve the writs of the king at your coming and at your power. And ye " shall take no bailiff into your service but for whom ye will answer, and that ye shall make " your bailiffs take such an oath as pertaineth unto them, and that ye shall receive nor take " no writ by you, nor by none other but such as shall be lawfully sealed. And that ye shall " take such serjeants into your service for this year, that was serjeants within the space of " three years next before past; and that the service of our sovereign lord the king that is " due for the city with the weapontage of **Ancitty**, ye shall truly pay at the terms assigned " therefore. And ye shall save the city without damage or hurt, and all the franchises, li- " berties, usages and accustoms, statutes and ordinances of the same ye shall save and main- " tain; and ye shall make no return, no impannel in plea of land, rents or tenements to be " holden afore the mayor and sheriffs without the oversight and advice of the mayor. So help " you God, *&c.*

Upon the day of the election of a lord-mayor, *viz. January* 15, the old *chamberlains* present to the lord-mayor, aldermen, and twenty four, *sixteen* fit and able citizens to the best of their judgments, out of which number, though I find they are not strictly tied to it, the magistrates usually chuse *eight* to succeed in that office. In which election after the eight chamberlains are chosen by the house, before they be published to the whole court, the lord-mayor hath the power of putting out one of the said eight, and nominating another in his place, who is called the lord-mayor's chamberlain. And if it happen that the chamberlain which the lord-mayor so chuses, and the first and chiefest of the other chamberlains be both of one occupation, it is then at the will and pleasure of the lord mayor to chuse whether of the two shall be first and chiefest chamberlain. Every chamberlain pays to the common chamber for the honour of his office, at his election, **twenty nobles**, or six pound six shillings and eight pence, and is ever after reputed a gentleman by it. *Of chamberlains.*

If a chamberlain upon his election refuse to hold the office, he is usually fined at the discretion of the court. *Anno* 1489, sir *John Gylliot* mayor, one *John Dodson* was fined forty pound for not taking on him the office of chamberlain. *Fine for refusing.*

The chamberlains of the city of *York* are very considerable in point of power; for no man can set up shop or occupy any trade, without being sworn before one or more of them and the lord-mayor, who is accordingly enrolled in their book, which is a book of record. *Power.*

The office of the chamberlains of the city of *York* was to collect and gather the city's rents, and all other perquisites and profits; and have an officer in fee assigned for theirs and the city's receiver, who pays the same to the said chamberlains, for which they account to the city. They have also care of all plate, jewels, bonds, and other charitable bequests belonging to the whole commonality of the city; and have formerly used to account from the feast of St. *Maurice*, but of later time from the feast of St. *Blaiz*, the day of swearing the lord-mayor. *Office of old*

It will not be improper here to take notice, that some or all of these offices and employments having been thought to be very chargeable, troublesome, and uneasy to the bearers of them, many of the richer and better sort of citizens have, heretofore, sought to avoid them; and by applying with money to his majesty's predecessors have procured letters patents under the broad seal of *England* to exempt them for ever from these offices. The city by these means began to abate much of its glory and splendour, when their magistrates being of the vulgar and common sort, by consequence became more contemptible and less regarded. This being taken notice on by the gentry residing in the city, county and parts adjacent, they unanimously joined in a petition to a parliament (*b*) held at *Westminster* 29 *Henry* VI, and made their complaints of the danger and ill consequences of such exemptions. Wherefore the king, with the consent of the lords and commons in that parliament assembled, **for the good and welfare of his antient city**, enacted that all such letters patents should be revoked, and a penalty laid on all those who should procure the like for the future. This penalty was no less than forty pound, whereof one half was to go to the *A.* 1450.

(*b*) *Ex rot. parl.*

king

king, and the other moiety to the common chamber, to be recovered by an action of debt. By means of this statute, an effectual stop was put to this dangerous evil, and the magistrates were chosen out of the body of the more substantial citizens as formerly.

Election of common-council men. I have before taken notice, that the *common-council* of the city of *York* consists of seventy two citizens, chosen out of the four wards of the city, eighteen for each ward. When any of these dye, or are removed, the rest present upon their oaths to the lord-mayor and aldermen, three able and fit citizens, out of which the bench chuse one. This office is of a different nature from the before mentioned, for here strong interest has been made to get into a body, where a citizen of any merit, though never so well qualified for sheriff, &c. lies hid for some years, and is exempt from the office only because his brethren will not put him up. This, with some other privileges joined to it, makes this office very desirable; and it was lately no small expence in *rummers* and *drams* for the candidate to attain to it. But, to the just praise of the present worthy members that compose that body, who, regarding their own constitutions, in respect of the destructive practice abovesaid, as also, and more especially, the *constitution of the city*, which was in danger of being shocked by country gentlemen's interfering in such elections as party inclined them to, have made a binding order amongst themselves, that if any citizen or other does so much as ask a vote of this kind from any of the body, or for any office that they have votes in, he shall not be elected. A custom worthy of imitation at the election of all knights, citizens, and burgesses throughout the kingdom. For which reason they have no more to do in their own elections, when a vacancy happens, than for that ward to nominate six, out of which number the whole body of common council send up three to the bench, who chuse one.

Authority. The *common-council* represents the whole comonality of the city; and are at all times to be attending upon the lord-mayor and aldermen, when duly summoned, to advise and consult the publick weal and good of the city (*i*). They have an authority that in some cases the mayor and aldermen cannot act without them. As in all elections of magistrates into offices, and exemptions from offices. In letting or disposing of the city's revenues. And formerly in taverning and letting of wine-licences; and all other acts and things which pass the common seal; in making of by-laws, wherein every citizen, either by himself or his representative, gives his consent.

Coroners. There are in this city three other officers called *coroners*, who have been used to be chosen by the bench, twenty four and commoners. One for the river *Ouse*, another for *Foss*, and a third for the district between those rivers. Their offices are so well known that I need not mention them. But this is remarkable, that the county court, as it is called of the city, cannot be held without the presence of the sheriffs and one of these coroners.

Constables. The office of a *constable* is also very well known; there are two petty constables elected, by the bench and privy-council, for each parish annually. To conclude this dry account,

There are besides the city's steward, or husband, other places in the city which run for life, or *durante bene placito*, as *town-clerk*, *city surgeon*, *sword* and *mace bearer*, *coal-measurers*, *serjeants*, *bayliffs* and *beedals*. These offices are some of them bestowed by the votes of the whole corporation, but most by the bench and privy council only. The *town-clerk* is elected by the whole and his name sent up to the king for approbation. A place of the great trust as well as profit the city has to give.

Lord high steward. Besides all these offices, within the city, it will not be improper here to take notice of one of considerable note without; and which it has been usual to compliment some nobleman with, as the city's advocate and recommender of their requests and affairs to the king. This office is called the *lord high steward* of the city of *York*; but is not of great antiquity, nor has not, I am afraid, been of great use to it. The first nobleman that I can find upon the books that bore this office was *George Villars* duke of *Buckingham*, who was so constituted under the seal of the commonality, *anno* 1673. But he falling into disgrace at court, and retiring into *Yorkshire*, the city then unanimously chose his grace the duke of *Richmond* into that office. This happened *anno* 1683; and I have seen some letters from the duchess of *Portsmouth*, entered in the books, to thank the city for the great honour they had done her son, and to assure them, that every thing in his or her power should be done for the service and welfare of the city. The last high steward that I find upon record was the right honourable *Thomas* earl of *Danby*, so constituted *December* 4, 1688; and was the person who carried and presented the city's address to his highness the prince of *Orange*, as is before mentioned.

Having now gone through the several officers and offices in and out of the city, there should also be somewhat more said of the *port* and *dignity* of the *lord-mayor* of *York*, and the aldermen his brethren, in regard of *place* and *precedence*, as well in the king's own presence, as out of it. The reader may observe in the annals that I have given some testimony, from antient history, that the *lord-mayor* of *York* always carried the city's *mace* before the kings of *England*, at their entrance and during their stay in the city; as the king's chief serjeant at arms. The bearing of the city's *sword* at the same time, has been for many ages hereditary in the noble house of *Clifford*, as the city's chief captain, so

(*i*) *Ex chart.* Hen. VIII.

called.

called. At other times the enſigns of authority are carried before the *lord-mayor* by the proper officers aſſigned for them; the *point* of the *ſword*, in all places, and before all perſons whatſoever, *erected*. This laſt honour is by the expreſs words of the charter of *Richard* II; and though it has been diſputed by the *lord preſidents* of the north, particularly by the lord *Sheffield*, yet in a tryal relating to the mayor's having his ſword born with the point erect in his preſence, in the earl marſhal's court, the *lord preſident* was caſt, and judgment given for the *lord-mayor* againſt him. The *dean* and *chapter* of *York* have alſo taken great ſcandal at the mayor's enſigns of authority being carried into the *cathedral* without any abaſement. And have many times endeavoured to get an order from the crown to humble them. This has been ſometimes effected; and as low as the reign of king *Charles* I, *anno reg.* 13. I find a mandate from that prince to the *lord-mayor* of *York*, that *he ſhall not uſe the enſigns of his authority within the cathedral church*, &c. Copies of the records of all theſe matters, as alſo a copy of a decree for precedency of place betwixt the magiſtrates of the city and the officers of the *ſpiritual court*, adjudged 18 *Henry* VIII. with ſome other matters of the ſame nature the reader may meet with in their proper place of the *appendix*.

I come next to give an account of the ſeveral courts of law and juſtice kept in it, of which the ſheriff's courts I take to be the principal, and theſe are diſtinguiſhed into three; the firſt called the

Sheriff's turn, enquiring into all criminal offences againſt the common law, not prohibited by any ſtatutes. The next called the

County court, wherein they hear and determine all civil cauſes under forty ſhillings. The third is their

Court of common pleas, wherein is determined any cauſe whatſoever, tryable at common law.

SHERIFF's TURN.

The court of *ſheriff's turn*, incident to that office, is kept twice a year, a month after *Eaſter* and *Michaelmas*. The ſheriffs do by cuſtom keep this court at a place called the *Butts*, at *Dringhouſe's* town end, in the weapontack of the ancity. *Court of ſheriff's turn.*

The oath of the inqueſt and the articles which were wont to be enquired into in this court are theſe (*k*) (*l*).

"This hear yee the ſheriffs, that I ſhall truly inquire and truly preſent all the points "and articles that belong to the enquiry of the ſheriff's turn, the king's council, and my "fellows and my own. —I ſhall truly keep council ſo help me God, and the day of "doome. *Oath of the inqueſt.*

"And when they have made their oath in the form rehearſed, then the recorder, or the "under ſheriff ſhall rehearſe to them theſe articles ſeverally as they follow.

"Firſt, yee ſhall enquire if yee know any man or any woman that hath imagined the "king's death. *Articles.*

"Alſo if any man be forſworn the king's londe, and is come again into the lond, and "hath no charter of pardon.

"Alſo yee ſhall enquire of falſe money-makers, and falſe money-clippers, whether it "be gold or ſilver, nobles, half pennys of gold, farthings of gold, roundgars of gold, "waſhers of gold, groats, pennyes or two pennyes, halfpennyes or farthings, of their re-"ceaters, and all falſe money *uſeleſs*.

"Alſo of robbers and of rovers by night or by day, and of their receaters, whether "the theft be leſs or more, as of an ox or a cow, a pot or a panne, gold or ſilver, and all "other things that are of great value.

"Alſo of milchers, as of capons, or hens, &c. of wool, a broad cloth, a towel, or "other things of little value.

"Alſo of houſe breakers and ſneck drawers.

"Alſo of them that ſleeps of the day and wakes of the night, and is well clad and fed, "and hath of the beſt victuals that comes to the towne, and hath neither rent to live upon, "nor craft, nor ſcience.

"Alſo of them that lyeth in waite to beat men, or to ſlay men, or elſe for to rob men "by night or by day.

"Alſo of affrayes and blood that has not been corrected before this time; and of waſe "and ſtraye.

"Alſo of thoſe that by any ſubtletye or engines withdraw any doves from any man's "dove-coat.

"Alſo of all thoſe that by netts, or by any ſuttlety, ſetts in the ſtream of *Ouſe*, by "cauſe of the which, the toll of the bowe of the bridge is loſt or hindered.

"Alſo of all thoſe that bring any good to the city, that ought to be towled of, and "ſo withdrawe the towle.

(*k*) Vide *Crompton*'s juriſdiction of courts, fol. 231.

(*l*) All or moſt of theſe extracts following are taken from a manuſcript which is in my hands, the collector unknown; but I believe they are all faithfully and judiciouſly made, by what I have had leiſure to examine of them.

" Also if any franchist man of this city, have couloured any other man's goods that " ought to be towled, because of which coulouring the towle is withdrawne.

" Also of any baker of this citty, if they bake good bread and of good moulter, and if " the bread hold good weight according to the statutes thereupon made.

" Also if they have sufficient bread to sell, and in whose default it is that they have not " enough to serve the people.

" Also yee shall enquire of all manner of forestallers by water and by land, by night or " by day, either flesh, or fish, or poultry, or any manner of cornstallers, because of the " which the fuel and victual is scarcer or more dear then it should be. Warne such fore- " stallers, warne them, *&c.*

" Also of brewers of the citty if they sell after the assize, and by true measure in- " sealed.

" Also of the common of the citty, that is made several, whether the commoners of " the citty should have common for all the time of the yeare, or for any season of the " yeare.

" Also of the common lanes of the citty and the suburbs that are enclosed either by " hedge, or yate, or door in hindring the commoners.

" Also of them that on nights watche under other men's windows to escrye their coun- " cell or their privety.

" Also of them that hath been sworn at the sheriff's turne, or before justices of peace, " and hath escryed the king's councell, their fellowes, or their owne.

" Also of rape of women, whether they be wives, maids, or widdowes, and of those " that were helpers thereto.

" Also of all manner of treasure that hath been found within ground, whether it be gold, " silver, or jewells, pearle or pretious stones, and in whose keeping it is in.

" Also of them that are common dice-players, and with false dice deceiveth people.

" Also of them that make any assemblyes or riots by night or by day against the " kinges peace, or any disturbance to the lett of the execution of the common lawe.

" Also of cookes and regraters that sells any charchaused meat, or any unwholsome meat " for man's body.

" When the twelve men have heard the articles before rehearsed unto them, the con- " stables that are present shall be charged by oathe they have made to the citty, for to " commune and speake together of the articles aforesaid, and if they know any man defect " in any of them, they shall send two of the constables to the inquest and informe them " of the defaults.

" When the inquest has communed of all this matter and they will fine any man, they " shall give their verdict up to the sheriffs ensealed with their seales."

The COUNTY COURT.

The county court. (*m*) " The sheriffs of *Yorke* shall have their *county court* in the same form as other she- " riffs of *England* ought to have, with all the freedome that belonges thereto. And the " county court shall be holden on the *Monday*, and so it shall be holden from month to " month without end.

" If a county court falls on **Yole-day**, or any feast in the year it shall be holden, not- " withstanding the high feast, the same day that the court falls upon. The county court " may not be holden without the presence of one of the sheriffs and one of the coroners.

Custom. " At the county court before the coroners, exigents shall be called from court to court, " to the time that they be out-lawed.

" By force of the exigent no man ought to be arrest, but every man that's in the exigent " may yield them to the sheriffs to be outlawed, either in the county or else out of the " county, and when he is yielden to the sheriffs, then the sheriffs may put him in prison, " or take a fine and sufficient main-prize and sufficient men bounden for them, that he that " is in the exigent shall keepe his day, before the justice, at the day of the exigent re- " turnable.

" At the county-court before the sheriffs and coroners shall be holden, pleas of " that are called *replegiarum* in this forme, that if a distress be taken of any man for farme " or other cause, he that owes the distress that is taken shall come at the county court and " enter a plaint of *replegiarum* against him that tooke the distress, and the plantiffe shall " find **burrows**, that if so be that the law deem that the distress be lawfully taken, then " for to inn the distress againe, or else the price; and this surety made a precept shall be " directed to one of the serjeants of the sheriffs for to deliver the distress to him that owes " the distress, *&c.*

" The sheriffs and coroners may receive at the county appeale of robery and appeale of " man's death, whether that be for the wife of him that is dead, or for the heire of him

(*m*) From the same manuscript.

" that

"that is dead; which appeale may be made at any court within the yeare and the day, after the time the deed is done.

"If appeale be made at the county court it availes not, unlesse that the person that shall be appealed be imprisoned at the time of the appeale making.

"If a man make appeale at the county, him it behoves to be at the court in proper person to make his appeale, and he must find borrowes at the same county to pursue his appeale, and he shall give his appeale written at his owne perill, and he shall have day to the next county to pursue his appeale; and if the plantiffe faile at any court of his appearance in proper person the appeale is abated.

"If a man make appeale and be nonsuite in his appeale, he shall never be received to make appeale after.

"If a man be slaine or murdered the heire may make no appeale, living the wife of him that is dead.

"If the wife begin not her appeale within twelve months and a day after the death of her husband, she shall never after be received to make appeale.

"If a man be slain and have no wife, his heir shall be admitted to make appeale within the twelve months and a day, and if he begin the appeale but two dayes or the yeare be past, it is as availing as he had begun it at the beginning of the yeare.

"If a wife have begun to make appeale of her husband dead, and dye within the year, the heire, notwithstanding her appeale abated, may begin a new appeal.

"There shall no woman make appeale but of her husband's death.

"There shall none of the blood make appeale but the next heir of blood, that should have the heritage by law after the death of him that is slaine.

The court of COMMON PLEAS.

(*n*) "The sheriffs of the city of *York* do keep a court of record within the same city by prescription and custom, where they hold pleas of debt for any sum whatsoever. *Court of common pleas.*

"They have their court both of men of the city and of strangers, but in several degrees. The court between franchised men of the city shall be three days in the week and no more, *i. e. Tuesday*, *Thursday*, and *Saturday*, but if the one of the partys be a stranger and infranchised, then the court shall be every day except *Sunday* for the ease of the stranger at the will of the sheriffs.

The style of the court.

"*Cur' cit' Ebor. tent' ibm die martis prox' p. festm scti Mich. anno R. Henrici quinti p. conqu' &c. nono coram Johe Austinmore & Thome Aton vic' cit' p'dict'.* *Style,*

"*Cur' cit' p'dict' tent' ibm die Jovis prox' p' fest' scti Mich. anno supradict' cora' ejsdm vic' &c.* *or title.*

"This manner of title of the court shall be throughout all the year from court day to court day.

"The sheriffs shall have their courts with all the amerciaments thereto belonging, and if a man enter any plainte in the court, for what cause soever it be, if he be nonsuite in his plainte, he shall pay four pence to the sheriffs: and if there be two plaintiffs or more in one plainte and nonsuite, they shall all pay but four pence for the nonsuite. *Amerciaments.*

"Also what serjeant or constable do any office, whether the partys are accorded or not, the constable or serjeant shall enter thereof a plaint, and the sheriff shall have the amerciament of four pence. And if the constable or serjeant conceal the same and enter it not, he shall make a fine to the sheriff for the concealment.

"Also if a plaint be entered against any man, and the defendant be called in the court and come not, he shall be amerced for the default four pence; and if a man be essoined and make default after the essoin, he shall be amerced for the default eight pence.

"If a man make default and be amerced in a plaint four pence, though he make never so many defaultes afterwards in the same plea, he shall no more be amercied.

"If a man be summoned by a plaint of debt, and grant the debtor any other plaint, grant the action of the plaintiffe, the sheriffs for that grant shall have four pence of the defendant for the amerciament.

"If the defendant put him in the mercie, in what plaint soever it be, the sheriffs shall have amerciaments of the defendant.

"If the defendant fail of his law he shall be amercied four pence.

"If the defendant grant parcel of the debt and wager his law of the residue and perform his law, the sheriffs shall have double amerciaments, *i. e.* four pence of the plaintiff, because his plaint was more than was due to him, and four pence of the defendant for granting of the debt as in parcel.

"If a man be impleaded by a plaint of debt, and the defendant drive the debt and will be tryed by twelve men, then if it be found that the defendant owe parcel of the debt,

(*n*) From the same manuscript.

but

4

" but not all, the sheriffs shall have double amerciaments, that is, one of the plaint and another of the defendant.

" If a man take a plaint against another, and the defendant take exception to the plaint, as for to say he has a wrong name, or else taking his plaint against one man where he should have taken it against two men, or else taken it in one kind where he should have taken it in another kind, and the plaint be abated by any such exception, then the sheriff shall have amerciament of the plaintiff.

" If a man take a plaint against another, and the defendant dye, or the plaintiff either, the plaint is abated, but then the sheriff shall have no amerciament; for it is the doing of God, and not the default of the party.

" If a strange arrest be made of any good and prized by the default, shall pay amerciament, and in every action wherein the defendant wageth his law and performeth it.

Summons and essoigns. " If so be that a franchised man do summon another, him behoves to be summoned ever before the night against the court on the morrow.

" Then the defendant may have a delay and avisement of his answer, and ask day reasonable, that is to say eight days avisement, and the plaintiff and the defendant shall have day to that day se'ennight; and that day se'nnight the defendant may be essoined, which essoyn is called essoign after day reasonable; and upon essoign day shall be given by the court to the foresaid to the day se'night, and at that day se'night may prefer his law that he owes no penny to the plaintiff in that manner that he tells; and upon that the defendant shall have day of his law to that day se'nnight, which essoigne is called *essoigne unde lex*, or essoigned of his law, and upon that essoigne day shall be given to the defendant to make his law to that day se'nnight, and if the defendant fail of his law he shall be condemned in the debt, and if he perform his law the plaintiff shall take nought by his plaint, but in the mercy, *&c.*

" If so be that a man prefer law, and the summ that he asketh be beneath a mark, the defendant shall have day to perform his law with five persons and himself the sixth and no more; and if the summ pass a mark, then the defendant shall have day with eleven persons and himself the twelfth.

" A man unfranchised or another stranger shall not have day reasonable; and if there be two franchist men or three and one defendant stranger the process shall be continued as all were strangers, *&c.*

" In all causes where a stranger is essoigned against a franchist man the day shall be given to that day se'nnight.

" In all causes where a man unfranchised is essoyned he shall have his day till on the morn and no longer.

" If a franchist man implead another by an action of debt, or withold it on account, and the defendant say that he owes no debt, or else witholds not the thing that is asked again him, or else denys the cause of action on account, and that he will be tryed by twelve men, then the next court that the partys beforesaid are pleaded to an inquest, the defendant may be essoined, and he shall have day to that day se'nnight, and this essoign is called essoign *unde jur'*, or else an essoign after an inquest joined, and if the defendant keep not his day that he hath by his essoign, then the inquest shall be awarded by his default.

Adjournments. " If an inquest be sworn and may not accord during the time the sheriffs sits in the court, then the inquest shall be taken in a chamber till three in the afternoon, or what hour the sheriffs will assign to the partys; and in the mean time the court shall be adjourned to the inquest be passed; and if the inquest were not accorded of all the night, then the said court lasts at all times till the inquest be passed, and the attorneys in the mean time may not absent them without leave of the sheriffs for fear that they loose not their plaints, and when the inquest is passed then the court shall be adjourned, and not before.

Court-days. " The court-day next before St. *Thomas's* day before Yole, if a franchist man be essoined against another the day shall be given by that essoign to the next court-day after St. *Hillary* day, and in the same wise the same day shall be given by day reasonable; and when the court is done it shall be adjourned betwixt franchist men to the next court after St. *Hillary* day, in the same wise if a franchist man wage his law he shall have the same day to make his law.

" The court-day the *Tuesday* next after *Palm-sunday* shall be adjoined, and the parties shall have day till *Tuesday* next after *Low-sunday*; and the likewise the court-day the *Thursday* next before *Whit-sunday*, shall be adjourned to the *Tuesday* next after *Trinity-Sunday*; and these courts are called the courts of long adjournments.

Form of distraining. " If a man be distrained to answer in any plea in this court, the serjeants shall bring sufficient distress to the court, such as will most disease him and the titteft (*o*) will gar him answer; and if he come not, the distress shall abide in the court, and he shall be

(*o*) This is broad *Yorkshire*; and means *the soonest will cause him to answer.*

" new

" new diſtreined from court-day to court-day to the time that he appears either in proper " perſon or by attourney; then the diſtreſs ſhall be delivered again to the party that " owns it.

" If a man ſhall be deſtrayned and make default, he ſhall looſe no iſſue by the cuſtom " of the citty.

" If a man ſhall be deſtrayned, and the ſerjeant return that he hath no good to be de- " ſtrayned by, then the court ſhall award a *capias*, directed to the ſerjeant, to take the de- " fendant to anſwer to the plaintiff in the plea.

" If an inqueſt be ſummoned between partyes and partyes, and the inqueſt make de- " fault, then the jurors of the inqueſt ſhall be diſtrained by their goods ſeveral, from court- " day to court-day, till they appear, and they ſhall not have their diſtreſs again till " twelve appear; but they ſhall looſe no iſſues by the cuſtom of the city.

" If a man be arreſted by a plaint of treſſpaſs and find **burrowes**, and the defendant make " default, both he and his **burrowes** ſeverally ſhall be eſtrayned till the defendant appear to " anſwer the palintiff; and when the defendant appears to the plaint, both he and his " **burrowes** ſhall have their diſtreſs again.

" If a man be condemned on a plaint of debt, execution ſhall be made in this manner " and forme, *viz.* the ſerjeants ſhall bring into the court as mickle good of the defendants " to be prayſed as the ſumm and the damages amounts unto; and when it is brought in- " to the court, two prayſers ſhall be ſworne in the court on a booke, to prayſe it truly " what it is worth between chapman and chapman, and themſelves will give for it, and " the party refuſe it, and when it is prayſed the prayſing ſhall be entered on record, and " that good that is prayſed ſhall abide after eight days in the court, and at the eight days " end, the plaintiff may come into the court and aſk the deliverance of the good as they " are prayſed, and then the ſerjeant ſhall be charged to warn him that owes the goods to " make gree to the party, or elſe the goods ſhall be delivered to the plaintiff at the next " court after; and at the next court after if the ſerjeant record that the party that owes " the goods is warned as it is before ſaid, then the goods ſhall be delivered to the plain- " tiff by the court; and if the ſumm after the apprizing be not ſo much as the ſumm that " is recovered, then execution ſhall be made of the remnant, as before is rehearſed, to " the time that the plaintiff have full of all the ſumm with the damages that is reco- " vered, and if the ſumm after the apprizing be more than the ſumm that is recover- " ed, then the plaintiff ſhall pay to the defendant the ſurplaſſage into the court, or the " time that he have deliverance out of the court of the good that is apprayſed.

" If good be prayſed for execution, as before is ſaid, to the greater price than its worth, " then the plaintiff at the eight days end may come into court, and ſhew this matter to " the court, and refuſe the goods, and pray that the apprayſers have the good as they " have prayſed it, and that he may have execution for the ſumm that he has recovered of " the goods of the prizers, and then the ſerjeants ſhall be charged to warn the prizers to " be at the next court to hear what they can anſwer to the matter; and if the ſerjeants " return in the court that the prizers are warned in the form beforeſaid, and come not " to the court, the execution ſhall be made of the prizers goods, and the aforeſaid good " that is prayſed ſhall be delivered to the prayſers by the cuſtome of the city.

" If execution be awarded for a ſumm to raiſe of any manner of goods, and the ſerjeant " return that the defendant hath no goods for to put in execution, then a *capias* ſhall be " awarded by the court to the ſerjeant to take the body of the defendant, and when he " is taken by that *capias*, he ſhall abide in priſon till the plaintiff be made gree of his " ſumm, *&c.*

" If a man be eſtrayned by his goods to anſwer, or any manner of inqueſt to appear, " or the goods of any man is taken for execution, or a ſtranger arreſt is made of any " man of his good, if another man will come to the court and ſay that there where ſuch a " man is diſtrayned by pott or by pan, or by any other goods, *&c.* he that is deſtrayned " of that good the day of the taking of that diſtreſs, it was not his goods that was di- " ſtreyned, but it was his that comes to claim it without fraud or guile, and that he will " own with five hands and himſelf the ſixth hand, he ſhall be admitted to owne it in all " the caſe aforeſaid, and it ſhall be delivered to him, and the court ſhall diſcharge the di- " ſtreſs, *&c.*

" And this ſhall be the oath of him that will owne the good, *This heare yee the ſheriffs, " that this good that is arreſted as the good of ſuch a man, the day of the arreſt the aforeſaid good " was my property, and not the good of him as whoſe good it was arreſted; and this appropria- " tion is not done by fraud nor guile, in the diſturbance of the execution of the common law, nor " in deceipt of man.*

" If a ſtrange arreſt be made of certain goods, and the party defendant make default, the " plaintiff may aſk the good to be prayſed, and from its being prayſed, it ſhall lye four " dayes after in the court, and at four dayes end the plaintiff may aſk livery of the good, " and it ſhall be delivered; but or it be delivered, the plaintiff ſhall find ſurety in the " court, that is to ſay two ſufficient men bound in law for the good, or the value after it "is prized, if the defendant come within twelve months and a day, and can prove law-"fully that he owes not the summ that is asked by the plaintiff.

"Also if good be praysed and lye in the court eight dayes, and after eight dayes by the "summ that is praysed be delivered to the plaintiff for execution, then a third man comes "too late for to owne it.

"Also if a strange arrest be made of certain goods and praysed, and after four dayes "delivered to the plaintiff, then a third man comes too late to owne the goods, *&c.*

"If a strange arrest be made of certain good and praysed, by default this good shall "pay the amerciament.

Fines to the sheriffs.

Fines. "If a man be arrested by a plaint of debt and proffer *maine pernors* for to have him at "the next court, the sheriff shall have a fine or mainprize of him that is arrested, for ease "that he comes not in prison. If he that is arrested abide in prison till the next court, "then if he find *maine pernors* he shall pay no fine.

"If a man be arrested by a plaint on the statute of labourers he shall be brought to "prison, or else delivered to the sheriffs, and if the sheriffs have him to mainprize, or in "baile to the next court, the sheriffs shall have a fine or a mainprize, and for that fine "they are in jeopardy for to loose to the king forty pound, and five pound to the partye; "and after the first court if he proffer *mainpernors*, he shall be letten to mainprize without "any fine making.

"If the defendant in a plaint upon the statute of labourers be content that he depart out "of his service by the verdict of twelve men, he that is convict for the contempt against "the statute shall make a fine.

"If a man put forth an obligation, or any other deed sealed, and that be denyed, "and by a verdict of twelve men it be found to be his deed, then he that denyeth the "deed, for his falsehood, shall goe to prisson, or else he shall make fine to the she-"riffs.

"In the same manner againward, if a man put forth an obligation, or a deed ensealed "and it be denyed, and by verdict of twelve men it be proved that he sealed it not, or "else the deed to be found false, then he that put forth the false deed into court shall "goe to prisson, or make fine to the sheriffs, and the deed shall be cancelled and damp-"ned, *&c.*

"If a man be convict by a plaint of tresspass by a verdict of twelve men, and it be "found that the tresspass be done by force and arms, then the defendant shall make fine "for the force and arms, but if he be found guilty of the tresspass only, then he shall "make no fine.

Affrayes and bloodwites. "The sheriffs of this citty shall have *affrayes* and *bloodwites* made in the citty in form "that followeth, if any affraye or bloodwite be presented to the sheriffs by any serjeant "or constable, and they that made the affraye or bloodwite be arrested and come before "the sheriffs, and be arraigned thereof, if he grant the affraye or bloodwite, and put him "in the king's grace and the sheriffs, then he shall pay for the bloodwite a noble, and for "the affray forty pence at the will of the sheriffs. But if he deny the affraye or bloodwite, "and say that he will be declared by his neighbours, he shall find then two burrowes, "or four, at the will of the sheriffs to abide an inquest in this matter, and if he be found "guilty, then the sheriffs need not forgive him a penny thereof, but sett it at more if "themselves like.

Assize of bread. "The *assize of bread* belongs to the sheriffs with all the proffit that appertains there-"unto, and the assize shall be taken in form that follows, that is to say, the sheriffs what "time of the year, harvest or other, they think proper, shall goe to the mayor and say, "that on the morrow they purpose to take the assize of bread. Then on the morrow the "sheriffs shall send their four serjeants into all the city, and every one shall have a por-"ter with him and a sack, to the hucksters also, if they like, and to take of all manner "of bread to bring to the court, both wastell, simmell, halfe penny loafe, and farthing "loafe, wholsome bread and horse-bread to bring to the court, and that all the bread thus "taken by serjeants shall be laid on the counter to be weighed in the court; and when "the court is begun, then the mayor shall come to the court and sitt with the sheriffs in the "**toll-boothe** for to take the assizes, and for to weigh bread, and or the bread be weighed, "the mayor and the sheriffs shall take an inquest when the court is most full of honest per-"sons present, and when the inquest is charged their charge shall be this, —— to enquire "truly how the market went the last market day, before the taking of this assize, and "then they shall enquire of their prices, first of the highest price, of the middle and lowest "price, and they shall have information by the three markett keepers if they will; and when "the inquest has given their verdict up to the mayor and sheriffs with the prices middle "and lowest, then shall the assize be taken, and the bread in every degree shall be weighed "by the weights that are ordained therefore, and what every loafe, wastell, simmell, *&c.* "ought to weigh shall be declared by the register and the sheriffs clerke. When the bread "is weighed and the weight accord with the size, then every baker shall have his own "bread

" bread again without loſs, and in caſe the bread weigh leſs than it ought to do, then the " backſters ſhall be amerced, and the amerciament ſhall be to the ſheriffs; and if ſo be " the loaſe or waſtell weigh leſs then it ought to do beneath eleven ounces, then the ſhe- " riffs ſhall have of him that baked it a reaſonable amerciament, and if the loafe or waſtell " weigh leſs than it ought to do by eleven ounces or more, then he ſhall have judgement " to go to the pillory at the will of the ſheriffs, and the fine belongs to the ſheriffs.

GOAL and GOAL-FEES.

" The ſheriffs have the keeping of the goal in the city, and there ſhall be no more " goals in the city but thoſe that they and their officers ſhall keep; and of every man that " is arreſted and entreth the goal the ſheriff ſhall have four pence, if he ſtep but once with- " in the door and come out again; and if he abide there ſeven years or more, he ſhall pay " but four pence for his goal-fee. *Goal-fees.*

" If the mayor ſett any man in the goal for things that belong to the mayoralty, he that " is ſett in the goal at his going out ſhall pay no goal-fees.

" In diverſe caſes a man ſhall pay goal-fees if he comes not therein, as if a man be ar- " reſted by a *capias*, by the commandment of the king, he that is arreſted, if he never come " in priſſon ſhall pay four pence for his fee.

" Alſo he that is arreſted by a precept of peace ſhall pay goal-fees if he never come " therein.

" Alſo he thats arreſted by a plaint of debt ſhall pay goal-fees though he never come " therein.

" Alſo he thats arreſted by a *capias* awarded out of the ſheriffs court, if the ſerjeant re- " turn a *nihil*, ſhall pay goal-fee if he come not in perſon.

" Alſo if a man be arreſted by the ſtatute of labourers, or by an indictment of felony, " or on a plaint of treſſpaſs, though he find burrowes, he ſhall pay goal-fee.

A table of fees and duties which are allowed to be paid to the goaler of Ouze-bridge *by priſoners which ſhall be committed or remaine in his cuſtody; being paſſed and approved on by the right bonourable the lord-mayor and others juſtices of the peace, at the general quarter ſeſſions holden for the city of* York, *the laſt day of* July, *anno dom.* 1672.

	s.	d.
" When any foreigner or ſtranger ſhall be brought to the ſaid goal, at his en- " trance ſhall pay for his garniſh not above	2	0
" For his dyett, if he do not remain in goal above three days, his lodging to " included	4	0
" If he ſtay in goal above three days, then for his dyett and lodging for one " week, and ſo for every week after, ſo long as he continues in goal	8	0
" And if after the firſt week of his coming to priſon he think fit to provide " himſelf of dyett, then to pay the goaler for his lodging *per* night	0	4
" For his fees to the goaler at his releaſing	2	4
" To the turnkey	0	4
" And for a freeman at his entrance to the goal, if he intend to remain in the " high-houſe, to pay for his garniſh not above	1	0
" For his fee at his enlargement	0	4
" To the turnkey	0	4
" And as to dyett and lodging as a foreigner.		
" If any perſon be impriſoned in the goalers cuſtody upon a *capias ad ſatisfaciendum* out of any of the courts at *Weſtminſter*, to pay not above two pence a " pound for eaſe of his irons.		
" If any priſoner deſire to go into the citty about his neceſſary buſineſs, and " the goaler ſhall ſuffer him to go with a keeper, he ſhall pay his keeper for his " attendance, ſo as he exceed not three hours	0	4
" If any perſon be committed in open court of aſſizes or ſeſſions, and diſcharged " before, or upon adjournment of the court, then to pay the goaler only two " ſhillings and no more, unleſs he deſire one to attend him till he go into the " citty to procure baile, or do ſome buſineſs therein, then to pay his keeper	4	0
" If any perſon be committ upon ſuſpition of treaſon or fellony, and con- " victed for the ſame, and be reprieved or plead his pardon, he ſhall pay to the " goaler for his fee at his enlargement	9	6

" And its further ordered that every perſon or perſons of what degree, ſtation or con- " dition whatſoever, he or they be or ſhall be, being or remaining a priſſoner within the " ſaid goale, that ſhall uſe any unlawfull ſwearing, railing, reaſoning, or other undecent " conference of any matters whatſoever at any time or times, that every ſuch perſon or " perſons ſo offending ſhall forfeitt for every ſuch default twelve pence, to be levied and " to be beſtowed upon the poor men in the low priſſon; or elſe every ſuch perſon ſo

" offending

"offending to be put into the said low prisson, at the discretion of the keeper or his "deputys.

"And its further ordered that every person or persons that shall goe astray without the "said goale, not having the licence or consent of their keeper or his deputys, shall for"feit for every such default twelve pence, to be levied for the use of the poor men in the "low goal, or else every such person so offending shall suffer as above.

Sheriffs officers

"The officers belonging to the sheriffs courts are first their,

"*Deputys* or *undersheriffs*, each of them one, who are men of the law, and chosen by "themselves.

"A *protbonator*, who is also clerk of the peace, and keeper of the sheriffs office and "records of the court.

"Four *attourneys*, four *serjeants* at *mace* to execute writs and precepts; two *bayliffs* of the "weapontack of the **Ancitty**, and a *goaler* or *keeper* of the prisons.

SHERIFFS RIDING.

Sheriffs riding. "The sheriffs by the custom of the citty do ride to several parts in the same every year, "betwixt *Michaelmas* and *midwinter*, that is **Yole**, and there to make proclamation in "the form following.

Proclamation. "O yes, *&c.* we command in our liege lord's behalf the king of *England* whom God "save and keep, that the peace of the king be well kept and maintained within this city, "and the suburbs thereof by night and by day with all manner of men, both gentle and "simple, in pain that falls thereon.

"Also we command that no man walk armed within the city by night or by day, ex"cept the officers assigned for keeping the peace, on pain of forfeiting his armour and his "body to prison.

"Also we command that the bakers of the city bake good bread, and of good boulter, "and sell after the assize, *&c.* and that no baker nor no huckster put to sale any manner "of bread, unless that it be sealed with a seal delivered from the sheriffs.

"Also we command that the brewers of the city brew good ale, and wholsome for mans "body, and sell after the assize, and by measure ensealed.

"Also that no manner of man pass out of the citty by night or by day to encounter any "manner of victual coming to the city to sell, neither by water nor by land, to lett to come "to the market, upon paine ordained therefore.

"Also that corn brought to the market be *pursuand*, i. e. as good beneath in the sack as "above, upon forfeiture of the same corn and his body to prison.

"Also that corn thats once brought into the market to sell, be not led out of the mar"ket for to keep from market-day to market-day, without licence of the sheriff or his "deputys, upon pain that falls thereupon.

"Also we command that no manner of man walk in the city nor in the suburbs by "night without light before him, *i. e.* from **Pasche** to *Michaelmas* after ten of the clock, "and from *Michaelmas* to **Pasche** after nine of the clock.

"Also we command that no ostler harbour any strange man no longer than a night "and a day, unless he do the sheriffs to witt, and if he do the contrary he shall answer "for his deeds.

"Also we command that no foreign victualer bring any victuals to the city for to sell, "whether that it be flesh, or fish, or poultry, that he bring it to the market-stead li"mitted therefore in the city, and not sell it or it come there, upon pain that falls there"upon.

"Also we command that the lanes and streets of the citty be cleansed of all manner of "nuisance, *i. e.* of stocks, of stones, of middings, and of all manner of filth, on the paine "that falls thereupon.

"Also we command that no manner of men make no insurrection, congregation, or "assembly within the city or suburbs in disturbance of the peace; nor in letting of the "execution of the common-law, upon paine of punishment, and all that he may forfeit "to the king.

"Also that no *common woman* walk in the street without a **ray-hood** (*p*) **on her head and "a wand in her hand.**

This proclamation I have given at length as it was antiently used in the city, what is *Ceremony of riding.* used now is much abridged. The ceremony of riding, one of the greatest shews the city of *York*, does exhibit, is performed on this manner, the riding day of the sheriffs is usually on *Wednesday*, eight days after *Martinmas*; but they are not strictly tied to that day, any day betwixt *Martinmas* and **Yole**, that is *Christmas*, may serve for the ceremony. It is then they appear on horseback, apparelled in their black gowns and velvet tippits, their horses in suitable furniture, each sheriff having a white wand in his hand, a badge of his

(*p*) A radiated, or striped, hood I, suppose.

"office

2

office, and a servant to lead his horse, who also carries a gilded truncheon. Their serjeants at mace, attorneys and other officers of their courts, on horseback in their gowns riding before them. These are preceeded by the city's waites, or musicians, in their scarlet liveries and silver badges playing all the way through the streets. One of these waites wearing on his head a red pinked or tattered ragged cap, a badge of so great antiquity, the rise or original of it cannot be found out. Then follows a great concourse of country gentlemen, citizens, &c. on horseback, who are invited to do this honour to and afterwards dine with them, and though they dine separately I have seen near four hundred people at one entertainment. In this equipage and manner, with the sheriffs waiters distinguished by cockades in their hats, who are usually their friends now, but formerly were their servants in livery cloaks, they first ride up *Micklegate* into the yard of the priory of the *Trinity* (q), where one of the serjeants at mace makes proclamation as has been given. Then they ride through the principal streets of the city, making the same proclamation at the corners of the streets on the west side *Ousebridge*. After that at the corner of *Castlegate* and *Ousegate*; then at the corner of *Coneystreet* and *Stonegate* over against the *Common-hall*; then again at the south gate of the *Minster*. After that they ride unto St. *Marygate* tower without *Bootham-bar*, making the same proclamation there. Then returning they ride through the streets of *Petergate*, *Colliergate*, *Fossgate*, over *Fossbridge* into *Walmgate*, where the proclamation is again made; and lastly they return into the market-place in the *Pavement*; where the same ceremony being repeated, the sheriffs depart to their own houses, and after to their house of entertainment; which is usually at one of the publick halls in the city.

(r) "The sheriffs of the city of *York* have antiently used on St. *Thomas's* day the apostle "before **Yoole**, at toll of the bell to come to *Allhallows* kirk in the *Pavement*, and there to "hear a mass of St. *Thomas* at the high quiere, and to offer at the mass; and when mass "was done to make proclamation at the pillory of the **Yoole-girthol**, in the form that follows by their serjeant, &c. *An antient custom.*

"We command that the peace of our lord the king be well keeped and mayntayned "by night and by day, &c. *prout solebat in proclamatione praedict' vicecomitum in eorum "equitatione.*

"Alsso that all manner of **whores, thieves, dice-players**, and all other **unthrifty folk** "be wellcome to the towne, whether they come late or early, at the reverence of the **high "feaste of Yoole**, till the twelve dayes be passed.

"The proclamation made in form aforesaid, the fower serjeants shall go and ride, whither they will, and one of them shall have a **horne of brass** of the **toll-boothe**, and the "other three serjeants shall have each of them a **horne**, and so go forth to the fower barrs "of the citty and blow the **youle-girthe**; and the sheriffs for that day use to goe together, "they and their wives, and their officers, at the reverence of the high feast of **Yoole**, at "their proper costs, &c.

Having now gone through the several courts, &c. of the sheriffs, I come next to give an account of those courts in the city where the lord-mayor presides, and first of the court of *Lord-mayors courts*

GUILD-HALL.

(s) "This court is a very antient court of record, and is always held in **Guild-hall** before the lord-mayor and sheriffs of *York* for the time being, for all pleas, real, mixed, "and personal; and when any matter is to be argued or tried in this court, Mr. *recorder* "sits as judge with the lord-mayor and sheriffs, and gives rules and judgements therein. *Court of Guild-hall.*

HUSTING.

"This court is the same with that called the court of *Hustings* in *Guild-hall*, *London*, "as appears by *Fleta*, l. 2. in the chap. *de differentiis curiarum, &c. habet rex curiam suam, "&c. et in civitatibus et burgis, et in bustingis* London, Lincoln, Winton, *et* Eborum; *et "alibi in libertatibus, &c.* cap. 48. *habet rex curiam suam in civitatibus burgis & locis, exeunt "sicut in bustingis* London, Lincoln, Winton, Eborum, *et apud Shepii ubi barones et cives "recordum habent, &c.* so that neither the name nor court is appropriated singly to *Lon-"don* (t). *or busting.*

"This court must be held on *Monday* every week, the title of the court by an antient "regifter-book in the councel-chamber on *Ousebridge* is as followeth:

"*Placita cur' Ebor' tent' ibm coram majore et balivis civ'* EBOR' *die lune prox' ante fest' "S. Augustini anno regni regis R. ii. post conquest' sexto* (u). And again, *Title.*

"*Curia dom' regis civ' sue praedict' tent' ibid' apud* **Guildhaldam** *pred' secund' consuetudinem "et libert' pred' &c. coram prefatis majore et balivis die lune prox' ante festum convers.* S. Pauli "*anno regni regis predict', &c.* (x).

(q) The riding of the sheriffs into this priory, and into *Bootham*, formerly the jurisdiction of the abbot of St. *Mary's*, must have commenced a custom since the reformation; and seems to be a taking possession of those two, before privileged, places.

(r) *Ex antiquo regist.* Ebor.

(s) From the same manuscript as before.

(t) Vide *Stowe's* annals p. 769. *Cook's* inst. pt. 4. fol. 247, &c.

(u) Lib. 5. fol. 136.

(x) *Lib.* 4. *fol.* 137. *temp. reg.* E. III.

"In this court deeds may be enrolled, recoveries may be passed, wills may be proved; "replevins, writts of error, writts of right, patents, writts of wast, writts of partition and "writts of dower may be determined for any matters within the city of *York*, and liberties "thereof.

Inrolments of deeds. "The method for inrolling of deeds is thus; first the partys that sealed the deed must "go before the lord mayor, or the recorder and one alderman, and acknowledge it to "be their act and deed, and if a wife be a party she is examined by them whether it was "done freely by her and without compulsion, and then his lordship, *&c.* sets his or their "hands in testimony thereof. Then the deed must be delivered to the clerk of the en-"rollments, who will at the court next following cause proclamation to be made, if any "person can say any thing why the said deed shall not be enrolled, and then proceeds to "enroll the same.

"A deed enrolled in this court of *Guild-hall* in *York* is accounted as good as a fine in "common law; for that it barrs the wife from claiming her dower.

Wills. "When a will is to be proved in the court of *Guild-hall*, the witnesses thereto must be "sworn at some court at *Guild-hall*, and if their evidence be full, the clerk of the inrollments "will enter it upon record, which is the best way of proving wills touching estates in the "city of *York* and libertys thereof, *&c.*

Replevying of goods. "When any person would replevy goods in *York* he must go to the prothonitor, or clerk "of the court, and give in the particulars, and security to restore the goods or the value, "in case upon a tryal it shall appear the same did not belong unto him. And then the "clerk will give a warrant to one of the sheriffs officers to cause the goods to be appraysed, "and to deliver them to the plaintiff. After the appraysment made, and the goods de-"livered, the officer must make return thereof to the clerk, *&c.* who will immediately "thereupon certify the record thereof into this court, where the same must be decided. And "if issue shall be joined to try in whom the property of the goods was when the same "were taken, a jury must be summoned to try the issue, *&c.*

The lord-mayor's court, or court of mayor and aldermen.

Lord-mayors court. "This court is a court of record, and ought to be held at the chamber of the *Guild-"hall*; the recorder of the city of *York* for the time being is judge of this court; but the "mayor and aldermen do sit as judges with him. This court is held by custom, and all "proceedings are saidto be before the mayor and aldermen.

Court of law and equity. "This court is a court both of law and equity, for there are proceedings at law by "action and arrest of the body, as also by attachments of the defendant's goods.

"It is also a court of chancery or equity held before the lord-mayor, wherein they do "proceed by *English* bill, answer replication and rejoinder, much like the proceedings in "the high court of chancery, and is held every day in the week if the lord-mayor please "to sit.

A custom. "The custom of the city is and has been time out of mind, that when a man is implead-"ed before the sheriffs, the mayor, upon the suggestion of the defendant, may send for "the partys, and for the record, and examine the partys upon their pleas; and if it be "found upon examination that the plaintiff is satisfied, that of so much he may barr him, "but not after judgment.

Correction of offences. "In this court the mayor, aldermen, and sheriffs redress and correct all offences against "the customs and ordinancies of the city, and justify victualers and people of all mysterys "and occupations, and treat and ordain for the general good of the city, and do right to "all that repair to it.

Determine of pleas. "Here they determine pleas of debt, and other actions personal, betwixt merchant and "merchant, to whomsoever will complain, as does at large appear in the register-book in "the councel-chamber on *Ousebridge*, marked A, fol. 333.

"In this high court of mayor and aldermen are also many other courts included. As "first,

Court of orphans. "*A court for orphans*, which court is usually kept monthly at the will of the mayor, "for the use of the poor of the city, and for binding of apprentices, granting weekly "allowances to poor and needy citizens, and providing for fatherless children, poor wi-"dows, *&c.*

Court of common-council. "*A court of common-council*, in this court they make constitutions and laws for the ad-"vancement of trade and traffick, and for the better government of the city, and for the "better execution of the laws and statutes of the realm, or *pro bono publico*, so as these "constitutions and laws be not contrary to the laws and statutes of the realm. And these "acts being made by the said mayor, aldermen and common-councel do bind within the city "of *York*, and the libertys thereof. They of the commonality do give their consent by hold-"ing up of their hands. The lord-mayor, aldermen, sheriffs, common-councel-men, re-"corder, city councel, water-bayliffs, *&c.* are elected into their several offices by this court.

Court of ward-mote. "*A court of ward-mote*, which resembles country leets, every ward being as a hundred, "and the parishes as towns; and in every ward there is an inquest of twelve or more sworn "every year to enquire of and present nusances and other offences, by not paving of the "streets and lanes of the city and suburbs.

"A court

"*A court of hall-mote*, this is derived from **hall** and **mote**, which is as much as to say *Of hall-mote.*
"*hall-court*; *conventus civium in aulam publicam.* Every company of crafts have a hall
"wherein they keep their court, which was antiently called the **hall-mote** or **folke-**
"**mote**.

"*A court of chamberlains*, in this court all indentures of apprentices are and ought to be *Of chamberlains.*
"enrolled; and the lord-mayor and chamberlains are judges of all complaints here, either
"of the master against the servant or servant against the master, and punisheth the of-
"fender at their discretions. In this court are made free all apprentices; a man may be
"made free of the city of *York* three several ways;

1. By *service*, as in case of apprenticeship. *Freedom of the city.*

"2. By *birthright*, being the son of a freeman, and that is called freedom by his father's
"copy.

"3. By *redemption*, by order of the court of mayor and aldermen.

"*A court of coroner*, the mayor is coroner within the city, and this court is holden be- *Of coroners.*
"fore him, or the sheriffs, or their deputys, *&c.*

"*A court of escheator*, the lord-mayor is also escheator within the said city, and this court *Of escheator.*
"is holden before him or his deputies, *&c.* This court having been dependant upon the
"*court of wards* is now along with it out of date.

I shall here give the reader an odd custom antiently held in this city, which I translate out of the record, of a release and forgiveness of a son for his father's death to the person that occasioned it before the mayor and court of aldermen; we must suppose the death accidental, the tenour of the record runs thus:

(y) *Memorandum*, that on *Monday* the 27th day of *February*, *anno dom.* 1390, and in the fourteenth year of the reign of king *Richard* II, were assembled in the council-chamber on *Ousebridge*, *Robert Savage* then mayor, *John de Hovedin*, *John de Doncaster* bayliffs, with *John de Rippon*, *Robert del Gare*, *Robert Warde*, *John de Bolton*, *William de Rumlay*, *Hugh Straunge* and other creditable persons, amongst whom personally appeared *Ralph del See* the son of *Richard del See* of *York*. Whilst these were treating and talking, a certain man called *Robert de Ellerbeck* mercer, came into the aforesaid chamber before the mayor, bayliffs and other honest citizens, with naked feet and head uncovered; who kneeling down and prostrating himself before the said *Ralph del See* besought him humbly in these words, weeping, *I beseech thee* Ralph, *for the love of our lord* Jesus Christ, *who redeemed mankind by his pretious blood on the cross, that thou wilt pardon and remit to me the death of* Richard del See *thy father*. At which words the aforesaid mayor, bayliffs and other citizens together, intreated the said *Ralph*, that for the love of God he would forgive the said *Robert de Ellerbeck* the death of *Richard* his father. Which same *Ralph*, being moved to pity, turning himself to the said *Robert*, weeping, said, *in reverence to God, and at the entreaty of these worthy men, and for the sake of the soul of the said* Richard, *I remit and release to thee for ever the death of the said* Richard del See *my father*. *An antient custom.*

The court of conservator of the water and river of Ouse.

(z) "The lord-mayor, aldermen, and recorder for the time being, four, three or two *Court of conservation of the river Ouse.*
"of them, of whom the lord-mayor and recorder always to be, have the conservation and
"be justices to oversee and keep the waters and great rivers of *Ouse*, *Humber*, *Wharfe*, *Der-*
"*went*, *Are*, *Dun*, as well in the county of *York* and *Lincoln*, and in the county of the
"city of *York*, that is the river of *Wharf*, from the water and river of *Ouse* unto the town
"and bridge of *Tadcaster*, *Derwent* unto the town and bridge of *Sutton*. *Are* unto the
"town and pool of the milns at *Knottingley*. *Dun* to the town and milns of *Doncaster*, to
"correct and amend the defect thereof, and to the due execution of the statutes made for
"the like purposes, according to the strength, form, and effects of the same, as well by
"their overseeing, advisements, and directions, as by inquisition to be taken thereupon,
"within the liberties and without if at any time it shall be needful, and to hear and deter-
"mine upon the premisses according to the law and custom of the realm. They are also to
"foresee the streams, milnes, stankes, pales, piles and kiddals made before the time of
"*Edward* the son of king *Henry*; and those which shall be found too high or strait, to
"correct, pull down and mend according to the form, force and effect of the aforesaid
"statutes, and according to the law and custom aforesaid; and have authority to punish
"such as use unlawful nets, or other unlawful engins in fishing, or that take fish under size
"or unseasonably. And to do and execute all other things singular in the waters and ri-
"vers aforesaid, within the marks and limits aforesaid, as the mayor and citizens of the
"city of *London* have used or ought to do in the water and river of *Thames*. *Vide chart.*
"Ed. IV. *anno regni* 2. *et anno dom.* 1462.

"The court is held before the lord-mayor at such times as he shall appoint and direct,
"within the respective countys near adjacent to the said city of *York*.

"Acts of parliament for the conservation of the river of *Ouse*, and other great rivers.

(y) *Ex reg. lit. A. fol.* 144.

(z) From the same manuscript as before.

"The

2

Acts of parliament. "The waters of *Humber*, *Ouse*, *Trent*, *Dunn*, *Are*, *Wharfe*, *Derwent*, &c. shall be in "defence for taking salmons, *&c.* And there shall be assigned overseers of this statute, *&c.* "*Westminster c.* 47. 13 *Ed.* I.

"The statute 13 *Edward* I. confirmed joining to the same, *&c.* In the waters of *Thames*, "*Humber*, *Ouse*, and other waters of the realm, there shall be assigned and sworn good "and sufficient conservators of the statute as in the statute of *Westminster*, *ut supra.*

"For default of good conservators, *&c.* it is accorded, *&c.* that the justices of the peace "in the countys of *England* shall be conservators of the statute in the countys where they "be justices, *&c.* And that they, and every of them, at all times shall survey the offences "and defaults attempted against the statutes aforesaid; and shall survey and search all the "wears in such rivers, *&c.* 17 *Rich.* II. *c.* 9.

"The chancellour of *England* shall have power to grant commissions to enquire, redress "and amend all defaults in rivers, and annoyances of the passage of boats in the waters, "according to the purport and tenour of the statutes. 3 *Hen.* VI. *c.* 5.

"An act was made for amending of the rivers *Ouse* and *Humber*, and pulling down "and avoyding of fishgarths, piles, stakes and other things set in the said river, *&c.* "23 *Hen.* VIII. *c.* 18.

"An act made against casting into any channel or river, flowing or running to any "port-town or to any city, *&c.* any ballast, rubbish, gravel, or any other wreck or filth "but only on the land above the full sea, *&c.* penalty five pound. 34 *Hen.* VIII. *c.* 9.

"It is ordained that the lord admiral of *England*, the mayor of the city of *London* for "the time being, and all and every person and persons, bodys politick and corporate which "by grant, and other lawful ways and means, have or ought to have any conservation or "preservation of any rivers, streams or waters, or punishment and correction of offences "committed in them, shall have full power and authority to enquire of offences done with"in his or their lawful rule, government, jurisdiction and conservation, *&c.* saving to eve"ry person and persons, bodys politick and corporate all such right, title, interest, claim, "privilege, conservation, enquiry and punishment as they lawfully have and enjoy, or of "right ought to have and enjoy by any manner of means, *&c.* 1 *Eliz. c.* 16. (*a*)

Jurisdiction of London *over the river of* Thames. "The city of *London* have jurisdiction over the river of *Thames* in point of right, "*&c.* (*b*).

"1. By prescription.
"2. By allowance in *eyre.*
"3. By antient charters.
"4. By acts of parliament.
"5. By inquisition.
"6. By decrees upon hearing *coram rege* "*ipso in camera stellata.*
"7. By letters patents.
"8. By proclamations.
"9. By report of the king's councel.
"10. By *quo warranto.*

Secondly in point of usage.

"1. By ordinances antient.
"2. By punishment of offenders.
"3. By writts and precepts.
"4. By accounts for charges of searchers.
"5. By commission.
"6. By continual claim ever since 37 *Hen*"*ry* VIII, when the lord admiral first "interrupted their authority below *Lon*"*don-bridge.*

Lord-mayor of York's *jurisdiction in* Ouse. "In all or most of these abovementioned respects the mayor and commonality of the "city of *York*, do challenge the like jurisdiction in the river *Ouse*, &c. The lord-mayor "always bearing the style and title of *conservator* or overseer thereof. First in point of "right, as

1. By prescription. "That the city of *York* always had the election of a *water-bayliff*, who was used to be "sworn yearly in common hall on St. *Blaze* day, well and truly to execute his office as "other officers of the city are.

"In the book of the register of *Robert Hall* (*c*) you may find this office of water-bay"liff, and that the

"*Water-bayliff* shall at the command of the lord-mayor go down at the common cost "and pursue the **wears** and **fishgarths** in the water of *Ouse*, and bounders within the king's "commission, *&c.*

"The bounders of the river are as antient as the bounders of the franchises of the city, "and the mayor and bayliffs have used always to make arrests and executions in the said "water of *Ouse* (*d*).

2. By acts of parliament. "See 23 *Henry* VIII. *c.* 18. for amending of the river of *Ouse*, and several other acts of "parliament as before mentioned, which see at large in the book of acts.

3. By inquisition. "The mayor and aldermen have always had the power of correcting and amending the "abuses of the river, and doing execution upon the statutes made for that purpose, by inqui"sition or otherways at their discretion.

(*a*) *Rastal's* statutes, c. 17. fol. 180.
(*b*) *Stowe's* survey of *London*, fol. 18. 20.
(*c*) 33 *Henry* VIII.
(*d*) See register-book, council chamber, let. A. fol. 314.

"In

"In the regifter-book, councel-chamber, letter A (*e*) you have recorded a command 4. *By decrees.*
"from the king againft the admiralty, upon a difference betwixt the admiralty and the ci-
"ty, as to the jurifdiction of the river of *Oufe*, &c.

"By letters pattents of king *Edward* IV, in the fecond year of his reign (*f*), which 5. *By letters patent.*
"grants and confirms the overfight of water and river of *Oufe*, &c. to the mayor, aldermen,
"recorder, *&c.*

"In point of ufage.

"The city of *York* have always from time to time made ordinancys for better regulating 6. *By antient ordinancies.*
"the fifhery and fifhermen, and other matters in the river of *Oufe*, and punifhing offenders
"upon information, or therways.

"In the regifter-book letter A as before (*g*), it is recorded, that in the fourteenth year 7. *By writs and precepts.*
"of king *Richard* II, the fheriffs of the city of *York* did execution of a judgement out
"of the fheriffs court upon a fhip and goods upon the river of *Oufe*, &c.

"In the feveral regifter-books of the city, from time to time, will appear the accounts 8. *By accounts.*
"and charges of the lord-mayor and chamberlains view of the river of *Oufe*; and for the
"taking away of hindrances to navigation.

"The mayor has always ufed to grant commiffions and licences for fifhing within the 9. *By commiffion.*
"river of *Oufe*; of which may be found many prefidents amongft the records of the
"city.

"The city's claim will appear by the lord-mayor and chamberlains frequent going down 10. *By a continual claim.*
"the faid river of *Oufe*, to claim the royalty thereof for fifhing in the fame; and by the
"feveral orders of the mayor and aldermen for the fame; of which many prefidents are in
"the regifter-books of the city.

"*The office of a water-bayliff is* *Water-bayliff.*

"To prefent fuch as caft **rammell**, *dung* or *filth*, into *Oufe*; penalty fix fhillings and eight
"pence, the bayliff one half and the common chamber the other.

"To prefent all fuch perfons as put any four footed cattle into **moats** contrary to the fta-
"tutes of the city; and he to have one moiety of the amerciaments, and the other moiety
"to the ufe of the common chamber.

"The water-bayliff fhall at the command of the lord-mayor go down at the common
"coft to purfue the wears and fifhgarths within the water of *Oufe*, and bounders within the
"king's commiffion.

"The water-bayliff to have the proffit of all abufes, and have power to prefent any
"that deliver merchandize in any other place or places contrary to the ordinancys of the
"city; and he to have the moiety of the amerciaments. 33 *Henry* VIII, *July* 8, *Robert*
"*Hall*, mayor.

Sir *T. W.* has proved that the river *Oufe* was, of very antient times, navigable up to "*Burrough-bridge*; and that *Edmund* earl of *Cornwall* laid claim to the right of that river by vertue of being lord of the manors of *Knarefborough* and *Burrough-bridge*. And he by vertue of that gave leave to the hofpital of St. *Leonard York* to bring their victuals, goods, *&c.* from *Burrough-bridge* down the faid river cuftom free; as appears by his *charter*, which fir *T.* has given at length.

Afterwards he finds *in quodam rotulo affife an.* 7 Ed. I. *coram* Willielmo de Sakam *com.* Ebor. that the king fent his writ to the juftices, *&c.* here, upon the complaint of the mayor and citizens of *York*, that *Richard* king of *Allemaine*, who was earl of *Cornwall*, deceafed, did levy fome new cuftoms and took new tolls of the paffengers which carried their wares by the rivers of **Use** and **Yure** to *Burrough-bridge* and York; and for that he hindred the faid citizens and others from their *free pifcary* in the faid rivers; the king fent his writ to the faid juftices and others to know from what time his faid uncle deceafed, and *Edward* earl of *Cornwall* his fon had continued the faid ufurpations, *&c.*

The faid mayor faid that the faid *Richard*, &c. did take of the paffengers, *&c.*

"*Edward* earl of *Cornwall* prayed aid of the king becaufe, that king *Henry*, father of "the king that now is, did give unto the faid *Richard* the manors of *Knarefborough* and "*Burrough-bridge*, and faith that thefe rivers are part of the faid manors; and the earl "produced another writ of the king directed to the former juftices in thefe words, *wee* "*have thought fit to give you this premunition as well for the prefervation of our right, as for* "*the exhibition of juftice to others, as of right ought to be done.* And becaufe it feemed to "the juftices that this writ did not fuperfede their proceedings, according to the tenour of "the former writ, and that it appears to be the pleafure of the king, out of thefe words "in the latter writt *pro exhibitione juftitie*, to be a command to proceed, and therefore they "did preceed to take inqueft upon the articles contained in the faid writts, whether thefe "rivers be part of the manors aforefaid.

"And *Walter de Falconbergh*, *Marmaduke de Tweng*, *John de Bellew*, *William de Roffe*, "*Simon le Coneftable*, *Ralph Fitz-William*, *William de Ryther*, *William de Hartlington*, *Wil-*

(*e*) Regifter book, council chamber, letter A, fol. 141.
(*f*) 2 *Ed.* IV. p. 1. m. 9.
(*g*) Letter A, fol. 141.

"*liam de Holtby*, *William Lovell*, *Francis le Teyes*, *Amand de Fue*, *John de Bulmer*, *Adam* " *de Seton*, *William Fitz-Thomas*, *Adam de Marewell*, *Robert Holme*, *Henry* the son of *Conan*, " *Roger de Burton*, *John* the son of *Michael*, *William de Hastthorpe*, *Nicholas Maliverer*, " *Richard de Waxand*, *Geofry de Hewick*, *Robert de Buleford*, *Hawlake de Hanlakenby*, all " of them knights, did say upon their oaths, that the said rivers of Use and Yure are not " of the appurtenances of the said mannor of *Burrough-bridge* nor *Oldborough*, nor ever " were; and they further said that the said rivers, time whereof the memory of man was " not to the contrary, were free and common; and that all people were free to fish there, " and to take passage of the same for all carriages of merchandize and necessarys between " the walls of the city of *York* and *Burrough-briggs*, until the said *Richard* did usurpe to " himself the said waters to hold as his own. And thereupon the justices gave judgement, " that the said rivers as the king had commanded be for ever after free to all people for " fishing, and for the carriage of their victuals, merchandize, and other goods by battels " and ships, between the city aforesaid and *Burrough-bridge*, without giving any thing " therefore, and without any impediment. An inhibition was given on the king's be- " half that no man then after should be hindred from fishing, or carriages in or upon the " said rivers.

" Sir *Thomas* remarks two things in this,

" 1. That it appeareth by it that the justice of those times run against so great a person " as the earl of *Cornwall*.

" 2. That very eminent persons did then serve upon jurys; these being all of them " knights.

" The cittizens of *York* did in those days carry their merchandize up the river of Ouse, " *usque ad veterem pontem*, which is Aldbrough, *ad pontem burgi*, which is *Burrough-bridge*; " and very antient men do say, that this last named place did actually belong to the city " of *York*, before they were deprived of it by the earl of *Cornwall*.

There are two or three more passages in the manuscript of sir *T. W.* to prove the privilege of the citizens up the river; but what I have mentioned is sufficient for my purpose.

Next come the *charters* of the city of *York*, granted by diverse kings, under consideration. And here I have chose only to make abstracts from those charters wherein any remarkable additional privileges, or alterations, have been made and granted to the citizens. Except the two first, which are of that antiquity and unquestionable authority, being now upon the rolls amongst the records in the tower of *London*, that I have caused the former granted by king *John*, to be engraven from the very character it now stands in; and to give a transcript at length of the other in its own language. The reader may observe that both these charters recite three before them of a much older date, one of *Richard* I. another of *Henry* II. and one as old as *Henry* I. great grandfather to *John*; which last king died *anno* 1135, just six hundred years ago. I shall not take upon me to compare dates with any other city's charters; but, I believe that *London* itself cannot shew, *upon record*, any such testimony of royal favours and indulgences, of the same antiquity with the following. The reader may observe that *John*'s charter is dated *anno reg*. 1. which was *anno* 1199, at *York*. This was at the time that monarch came down here, to meet *William* king of *Scotland* in this city; as has been recited in the annals.

Confirmatio

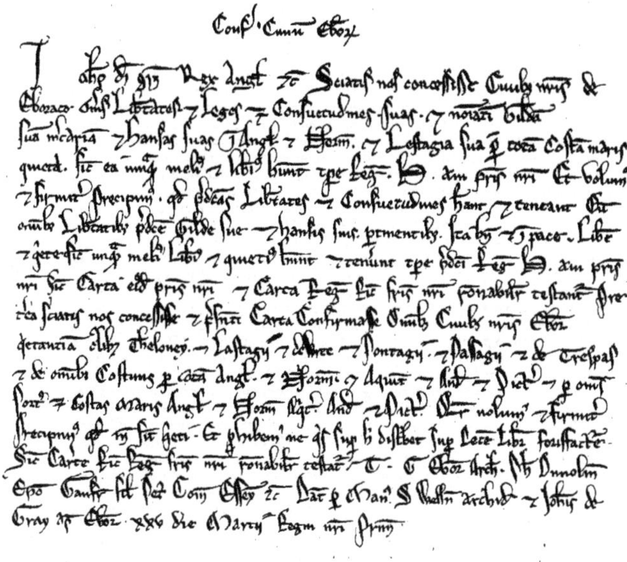

Confirmatio [cartarum] civium EBORACI.

(*b*) JOHANNES *dei gratia rex* ANGLIE, *&c. Sciatis nos concessisse civibus nostris de* EBORACO *omnes libertates, et leges, et consuetudines suas; et nominatim* Gildam *suam* mercariam, *et* Hansas *suas in* Anglia *et* Normannia; *et* lastagia *sua per totam costam maris quieta; sicut unquam melius et liberius habuerunt tempore regis* HENRICI *avi patris nostri. Et volumus et firmiter precipimus quod predictas libertates et consuetudines habeant et teneant, cum omnibus libertatibus predicte* Gilde *sue et* Hansis *suis pertinentibus, ita bene et in pace, libere et quiete, sicut unquam melius, liberius et quietius habuerunt et tenuerunt tempore predicti regis* HENRICI *patris nostri; sicut carta ejusdem patris nostri, et carta regis* RICARDI *fratris nostri rationabiliter testantur.* Praeterea *sciatis nos concessisse, et praesenti carta confirmasse, omnibus civibus* EBORACI *quietanciam cujuslibet* thelonii, *et* lastagii, *et de* **wrecc**, pontagii, passagii, *et de* **tresspass**, *et de omnibus* costumis *per totam* ANGLIAM, *et* NORMANNIAM, *et* AQUITANIAM, *et* ANDEGAVIAM, *et* PICTAVIAM, *et per omnes portus et costas maris* ANGLIAE, *et* NORMANNIAE, *et* AQUITANIAE, *et* ANDEGAVIAE, *et* PICTAVIAE. Quare *volumus et firmiter precipimus quod inde sint quieti, et probibemus ne quis super haec disturbet super decem librarum forisfactura, sicut carta* RICHARDI *regis fratris nostri rationabiliter testatur. Testibus* Galfrido Eboracensis *archiepiscopo*, Gaufrido filio Petri *comite* Essexiae, *et aliis.* Data *per manum S.* Wellensis *archidiaconi et* Johannis de Gray, *apud* EBORACUM, XXV *die* Martii, *anno regni nostri* primo.

(*b*) 1 J. *p.* 2. *n.* 135.

Charta

Charta regis Henrici III. concessa civibus *Ebor.*

(i) REX *archiep.* &c. *salutem.* Inspeximus *cartam* Ricardi *quondam regis* Anglie *avunculi mei, in qua continetur quod idem rex concessit et confirmavit civibus nost.* Ebor. *quietantiam cujuslibet* thelonii, lastagii, *et de* **wreck**, pontagii, *et* passagii, *et de* tresspass, *et de omnibus customis per totam* Angliam, Normanniam, Aquitaniam, Andegaviam, *et* Pictaviam; *et per omnes portas et costas maris* Angliae, Normanniae, Andegaviae, Aquitaniae, *et* Pictaviae; *et quod iidem* **Namia** (k) *capiant de debitis suis, et se defendant ab omnibus appellationibus per juramenta* xxxvi. *hominum civitatis, nisi quae appellatio fuit de corpore regis.* Inspeximus *etiam chartam dom.* Johannis *regis patris nostri continentem quod idem rex concessit et confirmavit eis villam* Ebor. *cum omnibus pertinentiis, et libertatibus suis, sicut eas unquam melius et liberius habuerunt, et cum omnibus rebus ad firmam ejusdem ville pertinentibus, habend. et tenend. eis et haeredibus suis de ipso rege et haeredibus suis pro* centum et sexaginta libris *eidem regi annuatim solvendis ad scaccarium suum scilicet medietatem ad festum S.* Michaelis, *et alteram medietatem ad* Pascham, *bene et in pace, libere et quiete, et integre, cum omnibus libertatibus et consuetudinibus ad firmam ejusdem ville pertinentibus.* Confirmavit *etiam idem* Johannes *rex pater noster per cartam suam quam inspeximus omnes libertates leges et consuetudines suas, et nominatim* Gildam *suam mercatoriam et* Hansas *suas in* Anglia, *et* Normannia, *et* lastagia *sua per totam costam maris, quieta sicut dicti cives ea unquam melius et liberius habuerunt tempore regis* Henrici *avi praedict.* Johannis, *patris nost. et tempore regis* Henrici *avi nostri; et quod predictas leges et consuetudines habeant et teneant, cum omnibus libertatibus praedicte* Gilde *sue et* Hansis *suis pertinentibus, ita bene et in pace, libere, et quiete, sicut unquam melius, liberius et quietius, habuerunt et tenuerunt temp. predict. regis* Henrici *avi patris predict.* Johannis *patris nost. sicut carta patris ejusdem patris nost. et carta regis* Richardi, *avunculi nost. rationabiliter testantur.* Preterea, *idem* Johannes *rex pater noster concessit et confirmavit per eandem cartam suam eisdem civibus quietantiam cujuslibet* thelonii, lastagii, *et de* **wrec**, pontagii, *et* passagii, *et de* **tresspass**, *et de omnibus customis per totam* Ang. Norman. Aquit. And. *et* Pict. *et per omnes portus et costas maris* Ang. Norm. Aquit. And. *et* Pict. *et quod nullus super hoc eos disturbet super* decem librarum forisfactura, *sicut carta regis* Richardi *avunculi nost. rationabiliter testatur.* Nos *autem praedicti concessiones, leges, usus, consuetudines, libertates, et quietanciam, ratas habentes et gratas eas pro nobis et heredibus nost. concedimus et confirmamus sicut eis hucusque usi sunt, infra villam et extra, sicut carte supradict. rationabiliter testantur.* Adjicientes *pro nobis et heredibus nost. quod iidem cives in suburbiis civit. nost.* Ebor, *de* **expealtatione** (l) *canum suorum ibidem in perpetuum sint quieti, et quod iidem cives reddant nobis singul. annis ad scaccar. nost. firmam suam, terminis statutis et consuetis, per manum suam propriam; et quod reddant nobis et hered nost. et respondeant ad scaccar. nost. de summonitionibus ejusdem scaccar. ipsos cives contingentibus, similiter per manum suam propriam; tamen ita quod nullus* vicecomes, *aut alius* balivus *nost. prout ipsos cives in aliquo se intermittat, infra libertatem predicte civitatis de firma et summonitionibus ante dictis. His testibus* Guydone de Lezingnan, Willielmo de Valentia *fratribus nostris,* Johanne Mounsell *preposito* Beverlay, *magistro* Willmo de Kylkenny *archid.* Covent. Bertramo de Criol, Gilberto de Segrave, Rogero de Thurkelby, Edwardo de Westm. Barthol. Pethe. Johanne Gubaud, Nicholao de S. Mauro, Radulpho de Bukepuz, Johanne de Geres, *et aliis.*

Data per manum nost. apud West. xxvi *die* Feb.

Abstracts from the several charters *granted to the city of* York *by divers kings.*

City's charters. King Henry I. grants several liberties.

Richard I. grants to the citizens of *York* to be quit of all manner of **toll, lastage** and of **wreck, pontage, passage,** and of **tresspass,** and of all customs throughout the realm of *England*, dutchy of *Normandy*, &c. And that the same citizens may take distresses for their debts. And that they may defend themselves from all appeals by the oaths of thirty six men of the city, except any be appealed of the body of the king.

And that no man do disturb them on the forfeiture of ten pound.

King John confirms to the said citizens all their *liberties*, *laws*, and *customs*, and namely their **gild** of the merchants, and *hanses* in *England* and *Normandy*, &c. and their **lastages** throughout all the coasts of the sea, to be quit as they had them in the time of king *Henry* his great grand-father, *&c.* And that they be quit of all manner of *toll*, &c. And that no man do disturb them upon *pain* of ten pound. And by a later charter settles the farm of the city at a *hundred and sixty pound per annum.*

(i) *Cart.* 36 H. III. *m.* 19.

(k) Namia from the A. S Nœme, *captio, captura,* a distress, or seizure. See *Somner's Saxon* dict. *Spelman's* glossary, *&c.*

(l) By the antient forest laws of *England*, all persons whatsoever that let any great dogs run loose in the king's forests, without first cutting out the balls of their fore-feet, or pairing their nails, paid three shillings fine to the king. *Blount's* law dictionary. The forest of *Galtres* being so near to *York* occasioned many forfeitures of this kind which this charter releases.

King

King HENRY III. confirms, by *inspeximus*, the charters of his uncle king *Richard*, and his father king *John*; and further grants that the citizens inhabiting the suburbs be quit of **expeditating**, or cutting the feet of their dogs. And settles the payments of the usual farm of the city, *&c*. *City's charters.*

By a later charter, the same king further grants, that none of the citizens shall sue, or be sued, before any of the justices without the city, for lands or tenements which they hold within the liberty of the city, but before the mayor and bayliffs, *&c*.

And that the said citizens be not convict by any foreigners upon any appeals, rights, injuries, trespasses, faults surmises, or demands done unto them, or to be done, but only by their fellow citizens, except the matter touch the commonality, *&c*.

And that the citizens do not answer of any land or tenement being within the liberty of the city, or of any trespass done in the said liberty before any of our justices of assize at *York*, in any other place then in their *Guildhall*, &c.

And that that may have and hold the city, with all things belonging to the same, with all laws, liberties and customs of their lands, or tenements, within the city and without, with all other laws, liberties, uses, customs, within the said city, and without; which hitherto they reasonably have used.

That they, or their goods, being found in any place of our kingdom, or dominion, be not arrested for any debt, of the which they have not been sureties, or principal debtors, *&c*.

And the said citizens with one or two of their fellow-citizens, bringing hereupon the letters patents of their commonality, may require their court and liberty as well before us as our justices of the bench, and other justices, bayliffs, or ministers whatsoever. And the same to have of all persons, matters and complaints of the which it doth appertain to them to have their court by the aforesaid charter.

And that the citizens be free of **murage, pannage, passage, scavage, stalage, warnage, terrage, pickage** and **kevage** throughout our whole realm, *&c*.

And that they by reason of lands or tenements in the city and suburbs (being or by occasion of any trespass done in the said city and suburbs of the same) should not be put in any assizes, juries or inquisitions, without the city to be taken, *&c*.

And that no marshals, justices of us or our heirs coming to *York*, in the time of their being there shall not make delivery of any persons forth of the houses or lodgings in the said city and suburbs, against the will of those whose houses and lodgings they be, but only to the same our justices, and in their circuits, *&c*.

And all that dwell in the city and suburbs of the same, occupying merchandize, and willing to enjoy the liberties of the said citizens in **tallages**, contributions and other common charges happening unto the whole commonality, *&c*.

And that they in the presence of us and of our heirs, have and exercise for ever the assize of *bread* and *ale*, and assay of *measures* and *weights*, and all other things belonging to the office of the market, *&c*.

And that the *clerk* of the *market*, and other ministers of us and our heirs, do not enter the said city, or suburbs of the same, for any things which do pertain unto the said office of the market in the same to be done, *&c*.

And also that all profits thereupon coming be always to the said citizens, their heirs and successors, for the help of the farm of the said city, *&c*.

And albeit they have not hitherto used any of these liberties aforesaid in any case happening, notwithstanding, the said citizens, their heirs and successors, may fully enjoy and use the said liberties and quittances, and every one of them, from henceforth without occasion of impediment of us or our heirs, *&c*.

And that the mayor and bayliffs of the said city, for the time being, shall have *cognizance* of all *pleas* of *trespass*, *covenants* and *contracts*, whatsoever, within the city and suburbs of the same; as well chancing in the presence of us, as in the absence of us and our heirs, except only the *king's house*, &c.

King *Richard* II, grants licence to the mayor and citizens of the city of *York*, their heirs and successors, to purchase lands, tenements and rents to the value of one hundred pound by the year, holden of us in **burgage**, within the city and suburbs, for the support of the bridges of *Ouse* and *Foss*; and the same to be certified into *chancery*, that it may be done without damage of us or of others.

And that they have *cognizance* of all *pleas* of *assize* of **novel disseisin**, and **mort d'ancestre** of all manner of *lands* and *tenements* within the said city, and suburbs of the same, as well before our justices of either bench, justices of assize, justices of eyer, as other justices and ministers of our heirs, *&c*. to be holden and kept before the mayor and bayliffs in the *Guild-hall*.

And that the keepers of the peace and justices assigned to hear and determine felonies, *&c*. in the three ridings within the county of *York*, or in any places of the same, do not intermeddle within our city, or the suburbs or the liberties of the same, *&c*.

City's charters. And that the mayor and twelve aldermen of our city and their fucceffors, or four, three or two of them with the faid mayor, have full correction, punifhing, hearing and determining all things and matters, as well of all manner of *felonies*, *trefpaffes*, *mifprifons*, and *extortions*, as of all other *caufes* and *quarrels* whatfoever, happening within the city, *&c.*

And granted and licenfed the mayor and citizens, that they might make *piles* and *pillars* of *ftone* in the river of *Fofs*, for the fpace of a hundred foot, of *affize*, more, and beyond, the fpace that the bridge doth at this prefent contain.

And that the city of *York*, with the fuburbs and precincts of the fame, according to the limits and bounds, which now be and are contained within the body of the county of *York*, be from henceforth clearly feparated and exempted from the faid county, in all things as well by land as by water, and that the faid city of *York*, and fuburbs of the fame, and precincts be from henceforth a county by itfelf, and be called for ever the *county of the city of* York.

And that every mayor of the faid city, for the time being, as foon as he fhall be chofen mayor, fhall be our *efcheator* in the city, fuburbs and precincts of the fame, *&c.*

And that the faid citizens and commonality inftead of their three bayliffs fhall have two *fheriffs*, &c. and fhall chufe every year of themfelves two fit perfons for their *fheriffs* in the faid city, fuburbs and precincts of the fame. The which *fheriffs* forthwith after their election in due manner, fhall take their oaths in due form before the mayor, whofe names fhall be fent yearly for ever under the common feal of the city unto our exchequer, *&c.*

And that the faid *fheriffs* of the city may hold their county-court, on *Monday*, from month to month, *&c.*

And that the faid *efcheator* and *fheriffs* of the city of *York* for the time being, make up their profits and accounts every year before the treafurer and barons of the exchequer, by fufficient attornies, of the fame exchequer and fheriffs for the fame purpofe appointed, by letters under the common feal of the faid city, *&c.*

And that the mayor, fheriffs, and aldermen, with the commonality of our city, their heirs and fucceffors for ever have the *forfeiture* of *victuals*, by the laws however to be forfeited, *viz. bread*, *wine*, *ale*, and all other things that do not pertain unto *merchandize.*

And that the mayor of the city and his fucceffors fhall have their *fword* (without our prefence) carried before them, *with the point upwards*, in prefence, as well of other noblemen and lords of our realm, of *England*, which do touch us near by kindred, as of all others whatfoever, *&c.*

And that the ferjeants of the maces of the mayor and fheriffs of the city of *York*, and their fucceffors, fhall have their *maces gilt*, or of *filver*, and garnifhed with the fign of our arms, *&c.*

And that the *ftewards* and *marfhals* of our *houfe*, or *clerk* of the *market* of our *houfe*, or of our heirs, from henceforth, neither in the prefence of us, nor in the abfence of us, or our heirs, do not *enter* nor *fit* within the *liberties* of the faid city, nor *exercife* their *office* there, nor *enquire* of any thing done, or to be done, within the faid liberty, nor do in any wife *intermeddle* themfelves, *&c.*

And that the *coroners* of the city, and their fucceffors, may *exercife* their *office*, as well in the *prefence* of us and our heirs, as in the *abfence* of us and our heirs; like as they have ufed from the time which the memory of man is not, *&c.*

And that the *citizens* be *not bound* to intend or obey any precepts or commandments of our *conftables*, *marfhals*, or *admirals* of *England*, or the *keepers* of the marches towards *Scotland*, or any of our *officers* or *minifters*, &c. except of our great and privy-feal, *&c.* except, alfo, the *commandments* of our *juftices* according to the form of the ftatutes, *&c.*

And that *no foreign merchant*, not being *free* of the *city*, fhall *fell* any merchandize to any other merchant not being free in the faid city; neither fhall any foreign merchant buy any merchandize within the liberty of the faid city of any foreigner merchant; always provided that againft rebels, and our enemies of *Scotland*, to refift, *&c.*

That the hundred, or wapontack of the **Ancitty**, with the appurtenances in our county of our faid city of *York*, be annexed and united to be parcel of the faid county, and that the faid fuburbs of the city, precincts, hundred, or weapontack, and every one of them with their appurtenances, and every thing that is contained in them, and every of them, (except our caftle of *York*, its *towers* and *ditches* pertaining to the caftle of *York*) be of the county of the faid city of *York*, as well by land as by water; and that all *bayliffs* of **frechiges** within the faid county of the city of *York*, be attendant and obedient only to the precepts and commands of the fheriffs of the county of the city of *York*, and to no other fheriffs.

And that the mayor and citizens aforefaid and their fucceffors have all *goods* and *chattels* of *felons*, *fugitives*, *out-laws*, *waifes*, and *condemned felons of themfelves*, *deodands*, *convicts*, *efcheats*, *profits* and *revenues* of the fame, *&c.*

And that the faid mayor and citizens to have for ever all and fingular *cuftoms* aforefaid, of *things* to be *fold*, coming to our aforefaid city, without any account to be made thereon to us or our heirs or fucceffors, to be levied and gathered for the *clofure* and *fupportation* of the *walls* of the city, *&c.* (except always the church of *York*, archbifhop, dean and chapter of the fame) with all profits, privileges, *&c.*

And

And that the said mayor and aldermen, and also the recorder of the said city for the time being, four, three or two of them, of whom the mayor and recorder always to be two, for ever be our *justices* to *oversee* and *keep* our waters, and great rivers, of *Ouse*, *Humber*, *Wherse*, *Derwent*, *Aire* and *Dunn*, as well within our county of *York* and *Lincoln*, as in the county of our city of *York*, &c. City's charter.

He further grants to the mayor and citizens, or mayor and commonality of the city of *York*, and to their successors for ever, to hold *two fairs* or markets every year at the said city, *&c.*

One the *Monday* next after the *feast* of the *ascension of our Lord*, and by five days immediately following, *&c.* The other on the feast of St. *Luke* the evangelist, and by five days immediately following. With all *liberties*, *priviledges*, and *free customs*, and other *profits*, *advantages* and *commodities* to the same *fairs* appertaining, *&c.*

HENRY VIII, by his *charter* dated the 18th of *July* in the ninth year of his reign, *anno* 1518, grants to the citizens of *York* a *common-council*, to assist and counsel the mayor, aldermen and sheriffs; with the manner of their election, out of the several *crafts* of the city. That is to say,

Two out of each of the thirteen *crafts* of *merchants*, *mercers*, *drapers*, *grocers*, *apothecaries*, *goldsmiths*, *dyers*, *skinners*, *barbers*, *fishmongers*, *taylors*, *vintners*, *pinners* and *glaziers*. And one out of each of the fifteen *lower crafts*, viz. *hosiers*, *inholders*, *vestment-makers*, *waxchandlers*, *bowers*, *weavers*, *walkers*, *ironmongers*, *sadlers*, *masons*, *bakers*, *butchers*, *glovers*, *pewterers* and *armorers*.

And every of the said *thirteen crafts*, and of the said *fifteen*, upon their assembly yearly, on the *Monday* after the feast of St. *James* the apostle, shall severally chuse discreet and able persons to be *searchers* of their own *craft* for the year following; that is to say, *merchants* and *mercers* four, *taylors* four, *weavers* four, *bakers* three, *barbers* three, and every other of the said thirteen and fifteen crafts shall name two, and likewise the next day present the same persons to the mayor, aldermen and sheriffs to be sworn to use and exercise all things belonging to their office for the commonweal of the city.

And that the said *common-council*, and the *eldest searcher* of every of the said *crafts*, shall in peaceable manner assemble before the mayor, aldermen and sheriffs, in the *Guild-hall* yearly on St. *Mathew's* day, and there make solemn oath to make and chuse *four* of the most able and discreet persons of the city, such as have not been mayor nor sheriffs, and that the said aldermen and sheriffs by their oaths and voices shall immediately the same day, or they depart, chuse and take *two* of the same *four* to be *sheriffs*, from the feast of St. *Michael* the *archangel* next following, for the year next ensuing, and swear them in their office as in time past.

And when any *alderman* of the city shall *die*, *leave*, or *depart* from his *office*, that the said *common-council* and *eldest searcher* of every the *thirteen* and *fifteen crafts* shall assemble themselves before the mayor, aldermen, and sheriffs for the time being in the *Guild-hall* at a certain day, by the same mayor to be assigned, and then and there make solemn oath to name and chuse *three* of the most grave discreet and able citizens to be *aldermen*; and that the mayor, aldermen and sheriffs by their oaths and voices shall the same day, e'er they depart, chuse and take *one* of the same *three* to be *alderman*, and shall swear him and put him in place of the *alderman* deceased or departed.

And that all the persons of the *common-conncil*, and the eldest in office of every of the said searchers, *&c.* shall assemble themselves yearly before the mayor, aldermen and sheriffs in the *Gild-hall* the 15th day of *January*, and make solemn oath to name and chuse *three* of the most grave, discreet and able persons of the *aldermen*, such as have not been twice *mayor*, nor *mayor* within *six years* next before, and that the mayor, aldermen, and sheriffs, upon their oaths and by their voices, in form before rehearsed, before they depart shall chuse and take one of the *three* to be *mayor* from the feast of St. *Blaze* following, for the year ensuing.

And that no other citizens, other then the *common-council*, and the said *searchers*, shall be *present* at any election of sheriffs, aldermen or mayor of the city, or shall have voices in the election of any of them.

King *Henry* VIII, by his charter of *fee-farm*, granted in the twenty eighth of his reign, *acquitteth* the city of *York* of the payment of forty pound, parcel of the hundred pound *annuity*, to the king.

Queen ELIZABETH by her *charter*, bearing date the 20th of *June*, in the thirty second year of her reign, *anno* 1590, grants to the mayor, aldermen and commonality of the city of *York*, to keep a *fair* within the city and suburbs yearly for ever, to begin every second *Thursday* yearly, betwixt the day called *Palmsunday* and the birth of our Lord *Jesus Christ*, and grants to the said mayor and commonalty to take a *toll* of the goods sold in the said *fair* as followeth,

For

City's charters.

	s.	d.
For every *horse*, or *gelding*, to be bought	o	1
For every *mare* and *foal*	o	1
For a *mare* only	o	1
For an *ox*, or *cow* with *calf*, or without	o	o $\frac{1}{2}$
For two *heifers* of two years old or within	o	o $\frac{1}{2}$
For every ten *sheep*	o	o $\frac{1}{2}$
For five *ewe sheep* with *lambs*	o	o $\frac{1}{2}$
For every ten *lambs*	o	o $\frac{1}{4}$

And further grants, that for *prevention of fire*, there shall be only as many *malt-kilns* hereafter in the city of *York* as the mayor, aldermen and sheriffs, for the time being, or hereafter shall be, or the major part of them assembled, shall think fit; in such convenient places as to them shall seem meet to approve of. And to make ordinances for the rule and good government of *malt-kilns*, and to remove and ordain such number as to them seemeth meet.

And such as have been *sheriffs* to have a *vote* in the ordering of *malt-kilns*; and have power to impose *penaltys*, *amerciaments*, and *imprisonments*, at their discretion for disobedience to their orders. And this power to be good notwithstanding any statute or ordinance to the contrary, &c.

King Chrales II. confirms all former grants whatsoever; and further grants to the said mayor and commonality, that *neither* our *treasurer*, *chancellor*, *barons* of the *exchequer*, *attorney* or *sollicitor-general* do *persecute* or cause to be *persecuted* any *writ* or summons of *quo warranto*, or any other *writs* or *processes* whatsoever against the said mayor and commonality of the city or their successors, for any causes, matters, things or offences by them done, claimed, used, exercised or usurped before the day of the date of these presents.

The mayor to be the king's *escheator*.

The mayor to be *clerk of the market*, and no other clerk of the market to intermeddle, &c.

Grants felon's goods to the city, &c.

Appoints the mayor, recorder and aldermen to be *justices of the peace*; as also the *city's council*, provided they do not exceed the number of two at one time. *Five* of these justices to hold sessions. The mayor, recorder, senior alderman and city's council to be of the *quorum*. And three of the *quorum* to be *present* at a *goal-delivery*, &c.

Coroners to make returns of *inquisitions*, &c.

That no citizen, sheriff, or other officer within the city shall be put to any *recognition*, *jury*, or *inquisition* without, &c. *causes* of the *crown*, excepted, &c.

That the repairs of the *walls*, *bridges*, and *king's staith* be upon the commonality, and the money to be raised by a *tax* upon the inhabitants, &c. on refusal, to levy by *distress* and *sale* of goods, &c.

That the *common-council* of the city do from henceforth consist of *seventy two persons*; and that upon the death, removal or recession of any common-council man, a *new one* shall be elected within the space of *fifteen days* after such death, &c.

Election of *sheriffs*, &c. upon the death of any sheriff another to be elected within *three days*, &c.

Election of *aldermen*, &c. as before.

Election of mayor, &c. If the mayor die within his year another to be elected within *three days*, &c.

Aldermen, and such as have been sheriffs of the city to be constantly *resident* in it, with their families; upon absence from it above the space of sixty days in any one whole year without the licence of the whole commonality, to pay *scot* and *lot*, and all other taxes and assessments; and furthermore every alderman who shall so absent himself shall forfeit five shillings a day above the sixty; and every person that hath been sheriff two shillings and six-pence, &c.

In case the mayor be infirm, one of the oldest aldermen is to execute the office, &c.

The mayor, aldermen, citizens, and burgesses, their officers and ministers whatsoever, shall hold such places in *parliaments*, &c. as their *predecessors* have used, &c.

The mayor, recorder, and other officers to take the *oaths* of allegiance and supremacy.

A recorder, or common clerk, to be hereafter elected, is not to be admitted without the *approbation* of the *king*, though chosen by the whole commonality, &c.

Witness myself at *Westminster*, the 3d day of *June*, in the sixteenth year of our reign.

HOWARD.

King James II. by his *charter*, bearing date, *June* 29, *anno* 1685, grants and confirms as follows,

The

2

The citizens by the name of mayor and commonality shall hold and enjoy, as heretofore by divers other names they have holden and enjoyed, divers *liberties*, *privileges*, *franchises*, &c. *City's charter.*

Confirms the *charter* of king *Charles* II, and all things in that charter contained, not *altered* by these presents.

Confirms all other *charters* heretofore granted to the mayors, commonality or their predecessors, *&c.* And all their customs, prescriptions, liberties, and franchises. And all their messuages, lands, tenements and fairs, *&c.* as the citizens have used and enjoyed by any name or names of incorporation whatsoever, or by any *charter* or *charters* heretofore granted by any of his majesty's predecessors, *&c.*

And to hold the said franchises and privileges of the king, his heirs and successors, paying to the king, *&c.* such rents and services as hath been accustomed.

He ordains *John Thompson*, esquire, to be mayor, *Richard* earl of *Burlington* and *Cork* to be recorder, *George Pricket* esquire deputy recorder, and of council of the city, and appoints the aldermen and sheriffs, the twenty-four, the common-council men, *&c.*

The common-council to consist of *seventy two persons*, as it formerly hath done and now doth.

Election of the mayor, aldermen, sheriffs and common-council men shall be made in such manner as is directed by the *charter* of king *Charles* II; *except* in this, that at the election of sheriffs, the mayor, aldermen, *&c.* shall have *seven* days allowed to chuse two persons out of the *four*, that shall be presented to them by the commons.

The mayor, recorder, and deputy recorder, city council, aldermen, sheriffs, twenty-four, town-clerk and common council may for just cause be *removed* in such manner as their predecessors might have been.

Power given to *George Pricket* to swear the present mayor.

Power given to *John Thompson* mayor to swear all the other officers named in this *charter.*

When the mayor, recorder, city-council, town-clerk, or any of the aldermen, sheriffs, or common-council men shall happen to die, or be removed, new ones shall be chosen in their places in such manner as hath been used for *twenty years* last past, before the making of this charter.

Provided that the king may, at any time, by an order of privy-council, made and put under the seal of the privy-council, *remove* the mayor, recorder, or any other officer, above named, *from his office*; and they shall thereby, *ipso facto*, be removed without any further process.

The mayor to be *escheator.*

The mayor to be *clerk* of the *market.*

Confirms the grants of felon's goods, and of fugitives, out-lawed and condemned persons; and all such forfeitures and amerciaments before the mayor and aldermen.

The mayor, recorder, deputy recorder, city-council and aldermen to be *justices* of the *peace.*

Three justices of the peace have power to deliver the *goal.*

Quorum, the mayor, recorder, deputy recorder, city's-council, the two eldest aldermen then present in court or any three of them.

The mayor may make a *deputy* in case of sicknefs or necessary absence out of the city.

The recorder may make a *deputy.*

The deputy-mayor may do all things to the office of mayor belonging. As may the deputy-recorder to that office. He to be sworn before the mayor duly to execute his office.

Licence to the mayor and commonality to purchase lands, in *mort-main* to the value of two hundred pound *per annum*, above what they now have and possess.

A saving to the church of *York*, and to the archbishop, dean and chapter, all their franchises and privileges, rights and customs.

Mayor and commonality to have no greater power to grant *wine licences* than they had before the making of this *charter.*

Dated *July* 29. in the first year of his reign.

Guildford. *c.* I.

per breve de privat. sigil.

PIGOTT.

ROBERT WALLER lord-mayor.

March 19, 1683.

* It was agreed by the mayor, aldermen, sheriffs and twenty-four, that an appearance should be given to the writ of *quo warranto* brought against the city to know by what authority they use and enjoy several privileges and immunities; and that the seal of the commonality be put to such attorneys as shall appear on the corporation's behalf; but the commons being called up to advise in the point, desired further time to consider of it, which was granted.

* From the register or city book of that year.

March 21, 1683.

Sir *Henry Thompson* knight at this present court (giving his consent at the last court for appearance upon a *quo warranto* brought against this city) doth hereby retract his said opinion therein, and is also very sorry for the same, and alderman *Constable*, Mr. *Moseley* and Mr. *Shackleton* do protest the same together with the said sir *Henry Thompson*.

Then the commons being called for, forty four appeared, and upon taking their votes in the chamber, one by one, there were thirteen for appearing, and thirty that no appearance should be given to the *quo warranto* mentioned in the order of the last court; whereupon the court broke up.

R. WALLER lord-mayor, *JOHN THOMPSON*, lord elect.

Jan. 15, 1684.

Be it remembered that in regard the commons refused to give an appearance to the *quo warranto*, as before is mentioned, the king's attorney general had judgment for seizure of the liberties, privileges and franchises of the city into the king's hands in *Easter* or *Trinity* term. 36 *Car.* II.

And so things stood until king *James* II, by proclamation dated *October* 17, 1688, entitled *a proclamation for restoring corporations to their antient charters, liberties, rights and franchises*, by which proclamation all corporations against whom no judgments on *quo warrantos* were entered, and whose surrenders were not enrolled or recorded were immediately restored; but such corporations against whom judgments were entered on the *quo warrantos* and surrenders enrolled, (amongst which last this city was one) the judgments were to be vacated and surrenders cancelled; and his majesty upon application did require the lord-chancellor, attorney and sollicitor general, without fees, to prepare new charters, *&c.* pursuant to the proclamation; to which this court employed one Mr. *Ralph Grainge* of *London* to procure the judgment on the *quo warranto* to be vacated, and the surrender cancelled which were against this city, which he did in a little time; the charge of which cost him out of purse thirty six pound six shillings and eight pence, and the court sent him fifty pound, which was thirteen pound thirteen shillings and four pence for his pains.

November 9, a writ of restitution was sent down out of the king's-bench, the form of which is as follows,

A translation of a copy of a writ to the sheriffs of the city of York, *for restoring the corporation all their liberties and privileges, after a seizure into the king's hands, upon a judgment entered upon a* quo warranto *brought against the city*, an. reg. *Car.* II. 36.

JAMES II. *&c.* to the sheriffs of the city of *York* greeting. Whereas in *Hillary term*, in the thirty fifth and thirty sixth years of the reign of the late king, a certain information was exhibited in his majesty's court of king's-bench, by sir *Robert Sawyer* knight then attorney-general, against the mayor and commonality of the city of *York*, for that they by the space of one month then last past, and more, without any warrant or royal grant, had used within the said city, and the liberties, limits and precincts of the same, these liberties, privileges and franchises following, *viz.* to be of themselves one body corporate and politick in deed and name, by the name of mayor and commonality of the city of *York*, and by the same name to plead and be impleaded, to answer and to be answered, and also to have sheriffs of the said city and county of the same city, and to name and chuse of themselves two persons to be sheriffs to execute and return all writs, bills and precepts for the administration and execution of justice, and to do and execute all other things belonging to the office of sheriffs without any commission or letters patents obtained from the king, and also that the mayor, recorder and such aldermen as had been mayors should be justices of the peace, and hold sessions of peace, and hear and determine pleas of the crown of their own authority, without any commission or authority granted by the king; and also whereas the said mayor and commonality were summoned to appear in the court of king's-bench, in *Easter* term then next following, to answer the premisses, at which term the then sheriffs of the city did return, that they had summoned the said mayor and commonality to appear as aforesaid to answer by what warrant they claimed and used the same liberties, privileges and franchises, and whereas the said mayor and commonality did not appear but made default, whereupon it was adjudged by the court that the said liberties, privileges and franchises, should be seized into the king's hands till further order; and whereas afterwards in *Michaelmas* term, in the fourth year of his present majesty's reign, the said mayor and commonality, by *Simon Harcourt* their attorney, having heard the said information and judgment, prayed that they might be restored to their said liberties, privileges and franchises; it was therefore considered by the court that the said mayor and commonality should be restored to the said liberties, *&c.* and the king's hands from thence amoved. Therefore we command you, that the said liberties, privileges and franchises, so as aforesaid according to the form of the said judgment seized into our hands, and the profits of the same to our use detained, to the said mayor and commonality without delay you cause to be restored at your peril, and certify how this our precept is executed fifteen days after *Martinmas*, and have there this writ.

Dated at *Westminster October* 30, *an. reg. nost.* 4.

ROB. WRIGHT.

At the court at Whitehall *November* 2, 1688, *present the King's most excellent majesty in council.*

HIS majesty being gratiously pleased that the city of *York*, and the mayor and citizens thereof be restored according to his majesty's gratious proclamation, to their antient charters, rights and franchises, notwithstanding the judgments and proceedings against them in an information in the nature of a *quo warranto* in the court of king's bench; his majesty in council is this day gratiously pleased to order, according to the power to him reserved in the late charters, patents and grants, and it is hereby ordered that all mayors, sheriffs, recorders, aldermen, town-clerks, common-council men, and all other officers and members of the said city of *York*, constituted, named, appointed or elected by virtue of any charter, patent or grant, since the year 1679, from the late king or his majesty; and all and every person and persons, having or claiming any office or place by the same, be removed, displaced and discharged, and they are hereby removed, displaced and discharged accordingly.

PHIL. MUSGRAVE.

A particular of *patents* and *charters* granted to the citizens of *York*, and are now amongst the records in the tower of *London*.

Chart. 1 Joh. *p.* 2. *m.* 16. *n.* 135.

Eborum. *civibus libert. gild. mercat. hansas in* Ang. *et* Normannia, *&c.*

Eborum *cart. divers.*

Cart. 36 H. III. *m.* 19.	*Cart.* 5 E. II. *n.* 23.
Cart. 10 E. II. *n.* 46.	*Cart.* 1 E. III. *n.* 30.
Cart. 2 R. II. *n.* 2.	*Cart.* 15 R. II. *n.* 14.
Cart. 19 R. II. *n.* 1.	*Cart.* 1 H. IV. *p.* 1. *m.* 9
Cart. 2 H. V. *p.* 1. *n.* 10.	*Cart.* H. VI. *n.* 8.

Esch. 31 H. III. *n.* 40.

Eborum. *civitas goala regis de foresta quis ipsam de jure reparare debet. Pro* David Lardiner.

Pat. 10 E. I. *n.* 2.

Eborum. *pro civibus majoritate vill. et libertat. restitutis.*

Pat. 11 E. I. *m.* 13.

Eborum. *pro civibus de villis reddit. ex Wapentack de* Anesty *commiss. eisdem,* &c.

Pat. 10 E. II. *p.* 1. *m.* 13.

Eborum. *pro civibus,* &c. *acquit. pro firm. confirm. cart.* &c.

Pat. 16 E. II. *p.* 1. *m.* 8.

Eborum. *pro majore de reparatione murorum.*

Pat. 4 E. III. *p.* 2. *m.* 20.

Pat. parl. 4 E. III. *apud* Winton. *n.* 90.

Eborum. *civitas de toll. et custom. colligend. de hominibus de* Kingston *et* Ravensere.

Pat. 8 E. III. *p.* 2. *m.* 30. *Et esch.* 33 E. III. *n.* 75.

Eborum. *record. placit. inter abbatem* S. Mariae *et cives pro privilegiis.*

Pat. 24 E. III. *p.* 2. *m.* 29.

Eborum. Boutham *in suburb. ibidem commissio ad audiend. controversias inter abbatem beatae* Mariae *et cives.*

Cart. 25 E. III. *m.* 34.

Eborum. *major de platea de* Botham *et libertat. suis restituend.*

Claus. 6 H. IV. *m.* 3.

Eborum. *quod cives quieti sint de thelon. panag. picag. pontag.* &c. *per totum reg.*

Pat. 7 H. IV. *p.* 2. *m.* 29. *et* 30.

Eborum. *pro civibus et communitate civitatis omnes libertates,* &c. *restitut.*

Inquis. 8 H. IV. *n.* 13.

Eborum. *major,* &c. *de tres messuag. concess. ad inveniend. capellan. in capella super pontem de* Foss.

Pat. 9 H. IV. *p.* 1. *m.* 32.

Eborum. *licentia perquirend.* C l. *terrae ad sustentionem pontium de* Ouse, Foss, *&c.*

Pat. 23 H. VI. *p.* 2. *m.* 1.

Eborum. *vicecomit. de potestate concess. eis et success. conferend. officium clerici vic. civitatis de anno in annum.*

Pat. 27 H. VI. *p.* 1. *m.* 14.

Eborum. *de annexatione hundredi de* Aynstey *communit. civitat.*

Pat.

Cart. 27 H. VI. *n.* 64.

Eborum. *de feria ibidem tenend. per sex dies post Pentecost.*

Pat. 49 H. VI. *m.* 8.

Eborum. *pro electione majoris civitatis.*

Pat. 2 E. IV. *p.* 2. *m.* 19.

Eborum. *major,* &c. *de potestate super videndi ripas aquar. de* Ouse, Humber, Derwent, *&c. et de jurisdict. infra bund. de* Aynsty.

Pat. 2 E. IV. *p.* 2. *m.* 9.

Eborum. *pro majore et civibus.*

Pat. 4 E. IV. *p.* 1. *m.* 9.

Eborum. *pro majore,* &c. XL *l. per an. concess.* &c.

Pat. 4 E. IV. *p.* 2. *m.* 20.

Eborum. *licentia eligend. in majorem et forma prescripta (m).*

Acts and ordinances. *Several* ordinances, *commonly called* **by-laws**, *made by the mayor and commonality for the good government of the city of* York.

Franchised men. *September* 27, in the ninth year of queen *Elizabeth*, 1567, an ordinance was made that franchised men absenting themselves from the city, to have no benefit of their freedom and liberties.

Court's award. *December* 18, 1650. a good order was made for regulating of the court of mayor, aldermen, and sheriffs, that a foreigner should stand to the award of the court, and that a freeman should engage by words to stand to the order of the said court, and to pay costs and damages if awarded against him, *&c.*

ALLEN STAVELY mayor.

Feb. 11. 10 *Hen.* VIII.

Free of one occupation free of all. It was agreed that all franchised men being free of one occupation shall henceforth be free of all occupations, *&c.* And it is also agreed that it shall be lawful from henceforth for every franchised man to take as many apprentices, servants and journeymen, as he pleases; any law or ordinance before this time made to the contrary notwithstanding, *&c.*

Quarrels. If any maintain any quarrel whereby the city's liberties are endangered, he shall be disfranchised. *Vide regist. of occupations, let.* A, *fol.* 338.

THOMAS HARRISON mayor.

May 20, 1575.

City's offices given to freemen. It was agreed that whensoever hereafter it shall chance any office belonging to the gift of this corporation become void, or shall be to be granted, that then every such office shall be from time to time given to a free citizen of this city, if he be able to execute the same before any stranger or foreigner whatsoever, *&c.*

THOMAS HARRISON mayor.

Decem. 16, 1575.

Against foreigners retailing. It was ordered by these presents, that if any citizen of this city shall suffer or allow any foreigner or stranger to sell by retail any wares or goods brought to this market, or within this city, to be sold in other place, save only in the full and open market, that then every such citizen doing or suffering the same, shall forfeit ten pounds to the common chamber *toties quoties.*

THOMAS APPLEYARD, mayor.

March 6, *an. reg. regin. Eliz.* 1584.

Malt. An ordinance was made that all free citizens that have or keep kilns shall enter into bond with sureties, that they shall not make, nor cause to be made, any malt for any strangers, but only for the free citizens of the city, without consent of the lord-mayor for the time being, *&c.*

March 7. 12 *Eliz.* an. 1570.

Corn by water. It was agreed that no manner of person, freeman or stranger, bringing any manner of grain to this city by water, shall be permitted to take up the same or any part before he hath a ticket from the lord-mayor, licensing him to take up the same; or else to sell the same at such prices as the lord-mayor shall appoint.

JOHN GRAVES mayor.

June 4. 20 *Eliz.*

A freeman not to be sued in foreign courts. An ordinance was made that no citizen or citizens of this city shall sue or implead any other citizen or citizens of the same in any court or courts, other than such as are holden within this city, by vertue of the queen's majesty's charter, or other of the laws and customs of this city, for any matter or cause by which he or they may have remedy, or recover in any of the courts holden within this city, by vertue of the said charter, or the custom and

(m) Charters, patents, *&c.* of a later date are to be met with in the chapel of *Rolls*; but as the city's own registers are very particular and full in these matters, I thought it unnecessary to give a list of them here.

lawful

lawful usage of the same city, upon pain of every one so offending to forfeit and pay to the city's use, for every such offence, forty shillings, *&c.*

This order was again confirmed *March* 12, 1666, adding thereto another ordinance as followeth.

Item, Whereas upon a good and reasonable consideration it hath been of long time used within this city, that if any freeman of the same being debtor be at the suit and request of his creditor called before the lord-mayor in the council-chamber upon *Ousebridge*; and there upon sufficient proof or confession of the said debt before the said mayor, do faithfully promise to pay or content his said creditor for his said debt at days then limitted and agreed upon, and the same being entered before the said mayor, if the said debtor shall after that make default of his said payment contrary to his said promise, he shall thereupon at the discretion of the said mayor be committed to ward, unto such time that he hath satisfied the party for his debt. And that no freeman presume to sue another in any foreign court, upon pain of loosing his franchise as well as pay the forty shillings fine as above. *A freeman debtor.*

Item, For the more speedy recovery to be from henceforth had by the creditors against their debtors in the queen's majesty's court before the sheriffs on *Ouse-bridge* by due order of law, it is ordained and agreed, that every plaintiff upon their plaint entered shall first of all cause the defendant, be he freeman or foreigner, to be arrested, and thereupon to find sureties if he can, or else the arrest to be executed according to the custom, saving always that the said plaintiff or defendant shall pay no more fee in such arrest, but only two pence to be taken of the plaintiff being a franchised man. *Recovery of debts.*

Capias ad respondendum *out of the sheriffs court* Jan. 11, an. reg. regin. *Eliz.* 14. 1572.

Assembled in the council-chamber upon *Ouse-bridge* the day and year abovesaid, when and where an order made the second time of the mayoralty of *W. W.* was now openly read to his presence as hereafter. *Capias ad respondend.*

It was ordered upon a *capias ad respondendum* against a freeman forth of the sheriffs court, the defendant shall find sureties or he be delivered to answer the debt, if the plaintiff do recover, and that upon such recovery execution shall pass as well to the sureties as against the party. Whereupon the order was fully confirmed and allowed; and further it is agreed, that if the defendant or defendants do not appear upon such *capias* to be sued against him, and the serjeants return upon the said *capias, non est inventus*, &c. *et quod fugitivus est*, then if the defendant or defendants within twenty eight days next after the return of the said *capias* do not appear by himself or by his or their attorney in the said court, to make answer to the said action, and put in a good surety to answer the debt and damages if it shall be recovered against him, that then the defendant or defendants after the said days ended shall be forthwith disfranchised by the lord-mayor, upon complaint made by the plaintiff to the lord-mayor for the time being, and then the party plaintiff shall be at his liberty to sue every such defendant or defendants as foreigners in any other court.

Whereas divers persons have complained and found themselves grieved and delayed by their debtors, by reason they would not appear and answer after returns, and summons and distringas, and after *capias* against them, neither could be found by the serjeants by means of their secret and cunning absence, for reformation whereof divers orders have been made, which do seem uncertain, for that no time is therein limitted when the serjeants shall make return of their *capias ad respond.* for explanation and reformation whereof it is now ordered by these presents, that if the *capias ad respondendum* shall be against any freeman in the hands of any serjeant for the space of twenty eight days and not executed, or during that term he shall not appear and put in sureties into the court, according to the true meaning of the former orders, then and after when the serjeants shall be required by the plaintiff his attorney, and he shall return his *capias non est inventus*, and the defendant is fugitive, upon which return the defendant against whom such return shall be made, being called in open court, and not appearing nor putting in pledges, *ipso facto*, shall be sued and used as a foreigner, and in that court upon the said plaint the party shall have process against goods and body to answer the action, or else at the election of the plaintiff he shall thenceforth be at liberty to sue every such defendant where he will as against a foreigner.

March 19, 4 *Edward* VI. 1550, this was ordered to be proclaimed, *Corn-market.*

That all those that bring any corn to the city to be sold shall sell the same corn in the market-place of the said city, and in no common street nor within no house, upon pain of every one of them that doth the contrary, and he or they hereafter at any time shall pay a fine to the common chamber of this city, after the quantity of the trespass in that behalf.

Nor to sell in the market place before the corn bell hanging in the market-place of the *Pavement* of this city, be rung at ten a clock, *&c.*

Item that no franchised man of this city do take upon him or them from henceforth to set any stall within any market-place of this city, but that they shall sell their wares only within their shops; and whoso that doth contrary to this proclamation shall pay to the common-chamber for every such offence six shillings and eight pence. This proclamation was made the day and year above said, *Peter Robinson* mayor. *Stalls in the market-place.*

Acts and ordinances. Foreign buying and selling Also that no person or persons which are common sellers of woolen cloth, or linnen cloth, or of any other manner of wares at any time after this present proclamation, shall put to sale any of their cloth or wares to any stranger or strangers within this city, which is commonly called *foreign (m) bought and foreign sold*, against the antient grants, statutes and ordinances of this city; and by reason of such buying and selling the said cloth, and all other merchandize foreign bought and foreign sold within this city, is to be taken and seized to the use of the common chamber of this city. Provided that this proclamation shall not in any wise extend to the hurt and damage of any person or persons that hereafter shall bring to this city woolen cloth or linnen cloth of their own proper making to sell, being but for a small quantity of substance, but that it be lawful for all such person or persons at all times hereafter when they shall repair and come to the said city with any woolen cloth, &c. that they shall forthwith resort and go to the *Thursday market* of the said city, and there to put their said cloth to sale, without any penalty, forfeiture or contradiction in that behalf.

Hawking of wares. And if any person or persons go hawking about this city with their cloth or any other wares, or sell contrary to the antient custom and ordinances of the said city, that they shall pay to the common chamber of this city for every such offence three shillings and four pence, so often times as they or any of them do contrary to this proclamation in selling the said cloth or other wares.

An ordinance of general sessions of the peace for the city of York *July* 10, *an. regni reg.* Jac. 12.

Foreigners. WHereas several unfreemen do drive trades within this city to the prejudice of those that are freemen, it is therefore ordered that when the goods of any unfreeman by them sold to foreigners can be seized, if the owners or pretended owners of such goods shall bring any action for such seizure, &c. the charge of such suit to be born by the chamberlains of the city.

KITCHINGMAN, cler' pacis ibid.

December 18, 1656.

Injunction in the sheriffs court. It is ordered by this court that upon any bill being exhibited for stay of any cause depending in the sheriffs court, if any injunction be awarded, the same shall be served on the plaintiff in the sheriffs court, or his attorney or attorney's known servant some time before the day of tryal; and that the plaintiff in the sheriffs court may proceed to tryal without any motion in that behalf, and to judgment in the said cause if this court shall so expresly think fit notwithstanding any such injunction that shall stay execution therein till the defendant answer to the said bill, and further order be made by this court to dissolve that injunction. And whereas divers times strangers who live without the jurisdiction of this court, do exhibit bills in equity to be relieved in equity against suits commenced against them in the sheriffs court, which being granted, and much time spent in hearing and ordering the same, yet the said plaintiff knowing that the process in this court cannot reach them to compel them to observe the same, refuse to obey the order, unless it be agreeable to their own minds, or to pay costs in case any be ordered against them, it is therefore ordered by this court that before any bill be signed in this court for any foreigner, the plaintiff of that bill shall become bound to the clerk of this court with two sufficient sureties in twenty pound, to stand to such order as this court shall set down in that suit, and pay such costs as shall be awarded against him or them in case any such be. And that every freeman exhibiting his bill in this court, shall bring with him a sufficient person that by his word shall engage that the plaintiff shall abide and perform the order of the court made therein.

Lord-mayor's court.

ROBERT HEMSWORTH mayor.

December 14, 1631.

Order for leases. It is ordered from henceforth for ever hereafter, that no lease for any lands or tenements whatsoever belonging to this corporation shall be letten to any person or persons whatsoever, until the leases of the same lands or tenements be within three years of expiration. And that the same may be more carefully performed, it is further ordered, that every three years there shall be some indifferent persons appointed by this court to inspect all the lands and leases belonging to this corporation.

Ale-houses. It is also agreed and so ordered, that hereafter no person or persons shall be licensed to keep any alehouse within this city or suburbs thereof by any of the justices of peace within the same, except it be openly by the lord-mayor for the time being and aldermen assembled in this court, or at a general quarter sessions, &c.

February 6. 6 *Ed.* VI. 1552.

Badgers. Ordered that all foreign badgers coming to this city shall be stayed to buy any grain in

(m) Dyer mentions this custom in the city of *York*, and calls it a good prescription; but says that the king by letters patents cannot give such a power to them. Dyer's reports, p. 279. lord Cook v. 8. fol. 125. in the case of the city of *London* mentions this of *York*.

the market before one of the clock afternoon, so that the freemen of the city may be first served. *Acts and ordinances.*

ALLEN STAVELEY mayor.

March 10. 10 *Hen.* VIII.

It is agreed that the searchers of no occupation within this city, suburbs and liberties of the same shall have the correction and punishment of the defaults done and commenced, concerning all the said occupations or any of them, but that the same defaults hereafter shall be punished and redressed only by the mayor for the time being and his brethren, and half of the forfeiture of the said defaults shall remain to the weal of the said city, and the other half to such occupation as the case shall require. *Searchers of occupations.*

Also that every ship or boat of all strangers coming to the stayth shall pay one time of the year to the chamberlains of the city for the time being, for every such ship and boat four pence for the ringage.

ROBERT BROOK mayor.

Feb. 7, 1581.

It is agreed that all strangers and others, such as have been freemen and do not keep scot nor lot within this city, nor do pay to the poor of this city, shall pay toll for all such corn as they shall bring to this city. *Toll.*

And it is ordered that all persons, whatsoever they be, which shall at any time hereafter bring any malt or any other corn to this city, sold or to be sold to any person or persons being not free citizens of the same, shall pay toll for the same, &c.

October 16. 5 *Ed.* VI. 1551.

Toll dishes for the corn market sixteen to contain a peck. *Lib. O. fol.* 55. *Toll dishes.*

May 7. 16 *Eliz.* 1554.

Ordered that none of the inhabitants of *Huntington* shall have any dung or manure from within this city, suburbs or liberties of the same, nor any citizen shall suffer the said inhabitants of *Huntington*, or their servants, or any of them, to carry and bear away any of the said dung or manure upon pain of every default three shillings and four pence. *Huntington no dung nor manure.*

This ordinance was made because the inhabitants of *Huntington* impounded divers cattle of free citizens of this city as they were going to the common of *Stockton*.

November 5, 1660.

Order for cleansing the streets every *Saturday*, and the constables to present defaults every *Monday* morning to the lord-mayor upon pain of ten shillings. *Cleansing streets.*

July 7, 1649.

Ordered that the common measurers should have four pence a last from freemen, and six pence from foreigners, and four pence for every weigh of salt. *Measurers and*

November 14, 1640.

That there be three measurers and twenty four porters chosen, and that there be eight porters for every measurer. *porters.*

In pious times. *September* 9, 1649.

Ordered that from henceforth the pageant masters, searchers of the several companies of this city, and all such as shall be admitted free brethren of any of the said companies, do henceforth forbear to make any publick feasts, or brotherhood dinners or suppers, the same appearing to have been much to the prejudice and undoing of divers young tradesmen, &c. *Order against publick feasts.*

December 1. 13 *Eliz.* 1571.

Ordered and agreed that the common Waites of this city, for divers good causes and considerations, shall from henceforth use and keep their morning watch with their instruments accustomed every day in the week except only sundays, and in the time of *Christmas* only; any custom or usage heretofore had and used amongst them or others before them to the contrary notwithstanding. *City waites.*

May 10, 1580.

An order for carrying forth filthy tubs and other filth forth of the city, on pain of three shillings and four pence, &c. *Filth.*

February 21, 1584.

The duty of coalwainers coming through *Micklegate-bar*, let to the wardens of the ward for eighteen pound yearly paid to the chamber; and they sufficiently to repair the causeway yearly from *Micklegate-bar* to the watering place beyond St. *James*'s chapel, upon their own charges on pain of forty shillings to the corporation. *Coalwains.*

December 27, 1565.

It is now ordered that no man licensed by order of the statute and bringing any kind of grain to this city to be sold, shall take up any part thereof unto such time the citizens be served thereof, every of them as they shall need, unto such time as the fourth part of such grain *Corn brought to the city.*

grain so brought at least be sold at the lord-mayor's price for the time being, upon pain to every of them that shall offend contrary to this order, to forfeit their licence.

July 4, 1576.

House of correction.

Boats lying at the staith.

An order for setting the poor of this city on work, and St. *George's* house to be the house of correction for the poor of this city.

Oysters two pence, salt three pence, merchandize four pence, fuel five pence, fuel turfs six pence, fuel wood *dit. Vide mariners ordinary.*

Several customs, prescriptions, and antient usuages in the city, from sir T. W. *&c.*

Customs and prescriptions.

The customs or **gelds** of this city are mentioned, in general, in the book of **Domesday** in the *exchequer*; and are confirmed by several charters of the kings of *England* to the city.

There is a custom in this city that the husband may give his lands, which are of his own purchase, to his wife during the coverture between them: as well as to any other person (*p*). And this saith the book was adjudged a good custom.

Here is also a custom that if the wife do not claim her right within a year and a day after the death of her husband, she shall be barred; and a woman was barred in a *cui in vita* upon this custom (*q*).

The custom of the province of *York* is likewise in the city, that after debts and funeral expences paid, the wife shall have the third part of her husband's goods, *&c.*

Lands are deviseable in *York* by custom, 29 *Edward* III. fol. 27. in the case of *Thomas Sipse* of this city for lands here, the defendant pleaded a devise by will; and it is admitted by the court and parties that the lands are devisable by custom.

Civitas Ebor. 32. it appears in a long plea in *Tr.* 20 *Edward* III, that *William Savage* and five other, the children of *Jordan Savage*, by vertue of a bequest by the will of the said *Jordan* did recover according to the custom of the city aforesaid, (*r*) *&c.*

(*s*) The city of *York* is held of the king in free burgage and without mesne, and all the lands, tenements and services within the city and suburbs, as well in *reversion* as in *demesne* are deviseable by the usage of the said city; and the citizens may devise them, and they may also devise a new rent out of the same tenements in such manner as they shall think best.

And all the testaments by which any lands are devised may be enrolled in the *Guild-hall* on record, at pursuit of any who may take advantage by the said testaments; and these testaments shall be brought in, or caused to come, before the mayor and aldermen in full court, and there the said testament shall be published by the serjeant, and there proved by two honest men of mature years, who shall be sworn and examined severally of all the circumstances of the said testament, and of the estate of the testator, and of his seal; and if the proofs be found good and agreeing, then shall the testament be enrolled in the records of *Guild-hall*, and the fee shall be paid for the enrollment. And no noncupative testament or other testament may be of record, unless the seal of the testator be put to the same; but the testaments which are found good and true are effectual, notwithstanding that they be not enrolled of record.

By antient custom of this city, the citizens or ministers of the same ought not to be obedient to any commandment or to any seal but to the commandments and seal of the king immediately. And no minister of the king, or other, ought to make session or any execution within the said city, nor within the franchise of the same, by land or water, but only the ministers of the city.

By antient custom also the liberties, privileges and other customs of the city use to be recorded, and declared by mouth, without being put or sent elsewhere in writing.

The constables, serjeants, and other officers of this city, of antient time, have used to carry to the **kid-coat**, and there imprison trespasses going in the night against the peace. Men and women of religion, *chaplains*, found in the night time in suspitious places with any woman, and to carry them before the ordinary to be punished according to the law of **holy kirke**.

The prisoners that are arrested within the city, and are committed to prison at the suit of the party, and after sent by writ to the exchequer, or in other place of the king with their causes; the same prisoners after they are delivered into the king's court ought to be sent back to the city, to answer to the parties and expect their deliverance there.

If any house in this city be on fire, so that the flame of the fire be seen without the house, the master of the house shall pay to the bayliff of the city ten pound; because he had no more care of his fire, by which the people of the king are frighted.

Aug. 20. *Eliz. reg. an.* 25. 1583.

It is ordered that from henceforth no **head-beggars** shall be chosen, and from *Christmas* next *John Geldart*, *Thomas Todd* and *William Curtus* now **head-beggars**, shall not have any wages of cloathing of the common chamber, but only their weekly stipends gathered of the money assessed for the relief of the poor.

(*p*) *An.* 12 H. III. *prescript.* 61.

(*q*) *An.* 12 H. III. *prescript.* 62.

(*r*) *Tr.* 20 E. III *coram rege.*

(*s*) Out of the records on *Ouse-bridge.*

Because

Becauſe that antient cuſtoms are treated on in this chapter, I am here tempted to give the reader the following, which was once uſed in this city; though the traditional ſtory of its riſe has ſuch a mixture of truth and fiction, that it may ſeem ridiculous in me to do it. I copied it from a manuſcript that fell into my hands of no very old date, for the reader may obſerve, that this was wrote ſince the *Reformation*, and not above threeſcore years from the diſuſing of the ceremony. The fryery of St. *Peter*, I take it, was what was afterwards called St. *Leonard*'s hoſpital, of much older date than the conqueſt; but I ſhall comment no more upon it.

" *The antient cuſtom of riding on St.* Thomas'*s* day, *the original thereof and diſcontinuance*, &c.

" WILLIAM the conquerour in the third year of his reign (on St. *Thomas*'s day) laid " ſiege to the city of *York*, but finding himſelf inable, either by policy or ſtrength, " to gain it, raiſed the ſiege; which he had no ſooner done, but by accident he met with two " fryers at a place called *Skelton* not far from *York*, who being examined, told him they be- " longed to a poor fryery of St. *Peter* in *York*, and had been to ſeek reliefe for their fellows " and themſelves againſt *Chriſtmas*; the one having a wallet full of victualls and a ſhoulder " of mutton in his hand, with two great cakes hanging about his neck; the other have- " ing bottles of ale, with proviſions likewiſe of beife and mutton in his wallett.

" The king knowing their poverty and condition thought they might be ſerviceable to " him towards the attaining *York*, wherefore (being accompanied with ſir *George Fothergill* " general of the field, a *Norman* born) he gave them money, and withall a promiſe, that " if they would lett him and his ſoldiers into their priory at a time appointed, he would not " only rebuild their priory, but indowe it likewiſe with large revenues and ample privileges. " The fryers eaſily conſented, and the conqueror as ſoon ſent back his army, which that " night, according to agreement, were let into the fryery by the two fryers, by which they " immediately made themſelves maſters of all *York*; after which ſir *Robert Clifford*, who " was governour thereof, was ſo far from being blamed by the conqueror, for his ſtout de- " fence made the preceeding days, that he was highly eſteemed and rewarded for his va- " lour, being created lord *Clifford* and there knighted, with the four magiſtrates then " in office, *viz. Howngate*, *Talbott* (who after came to be lord *Talbott*) *Laſſells* and *Er-* " *ringham*.

" The arms of the city of *York*, at that time, was argent a croſs gules, *viz.* St. *George*'s " *croſs*. The conqueror charged the croſs with five lyons paſſant gardant *or*, in memory " of the five worthy captains magiſtrates, who governed the city ſo well, that he after- " wards made ſir *Robert Clifford* governour thereof, and the other four to aid him in coun- " ſell. And the better to keep the city in obedience he built *two caſtles*, and double moated " them about.

" And to ſhew the confidence and truſt that he putt in theſe old, but new made, officers " by him, he offered them freely to aſk whatſoever they would of him before he went and " he would grant their requeſt; wherefore they (abominating the treachery of the two fry- " ers to their eternal infamy) deſired, that on St. *Thomas*'s day for ever, they might have a " fryer of the pryory of St. *Peter*'s to ride through the city on horſe-back, with his face " to the horſes tayle, and that in his hand inſtead of a bridle, he ſhould have a rope, and " in the other a ſhoulder of mutton, with one cake hanging on his back and another on " his breaſt, with his face painted like a *Jew*, and the youths of the city to ride with him, " and to cry and ſhout **youl, youl**, with the officers of the city rideing before and makeing " proclamation, that on this day the city was betrayed; and their requeſt was granted them. " Which cuſtom continued till the diſſolution of the ſaid fryery; and afterwards in imita- " tion of the ſame, the young men and artizans of the city on the aforeſaid St. *Thomas*'s " day, uſed to dreſs up one of their own companions like the fryer, and called him **youl**; " which cuſtom continued till within this threeſcore years, there being many now living " which can teſtify the ſame, but upon what occaſion ſince diſcontinued I cannot learn: " This being done in memory of betraying the city by the ſaid fryers to *William* the " conqueror.

FAIRS and MARKETS in the city of YORK.

There are ſeveral great fairs kept yearly within this city and the ſuburbs thereof, to the great benefit not only of the citizens, but of the country in general. Three fairs are held without *Bootham-bar*, within the ſuburbs, on the north ſide of the city, on a plot of ground called by the name of *horſe-fair*, for all ſorts of cattle three times in the year, *viz.* on *Whit-ſun-Monday* (*t*), St. *Peter*'s *day* and on *Lammas-day*.

Theſe two fairs are under the order and governance of the ſheriffs of the city; who do by cuſtom ride into the ſaid fairs in their ſcarlet gowns, attended with their ſerjeants at mace, and, formerly with, their livery men, one of which ſerjeants makes always procla- mation in the ſaid fairs as follows. Whitſun-Monday *and* St. Peter's *fairs.*

(*t*) *Cart. pro feria tenend. in civitat.* Ebor. *per ſex dies poſt feſt.* Pentecoſt, *Cart.* 27 H. VI. *n.* 64. *Turre* Lond.

Proclamation. The ſheriffs of the city in his majeſty's name do ſtrictly charge and command, that all and every perſon or perſons whatſoever that do buy or exchange any horſes, geldings, mares, colts or filleys in this fair, ſhall enter the ſame in a book kept for that purpoſe at a booth, at the eaſt end of the fair, by one appointed by the ſaid ſheriffs, noting down the name, ſurname and dwelling places of the buyers and ſellers, and the price of the goods bought and ſold, and ſuch other things as are appointed by the ſtatute in that caſe made and provided; upon pain and peril that ſhall fall thereon, *&c.* *God ſave the king.*

Lammas *fair.* This fair is called the *biſhop's fair*, becauſe the archbiſhop hath the rule and juriſdiction thereof, and begins at the toll of the bell at St. *Michael's* church, *Ouſe-bridge* end, at three of the clock in the afternoon, the day before *Lammas* day. At which time the ſheriffs of the city give up their authority in the city to the lord archbiſhop of *York*, his bayliff or ſubſtitute, in the ſheriffs court on *Ouſebridge* by delivering to him their white-rods. At the end of the fair which is at three of the clock in the afternoon, the day after *Lammas* day, after the knoll of the ſaid St. *Michael's* bell, the biſhop's bayliff redelivers to the ſheriffs of *York* their white rods, and therewith their juriſdictions. According to antient cuſtom a collation or treat is given at ſome tavern in the city by both parties, at the giving up and taking again their authorities.

During this fair, from three a clock on the laſt of *July* till the ſame hour on the ſecond of *Auguſt*, the ſheriffs authority of arreſting any perſon is ſuſpended within the city and ſuburbs. The archbiſhop's bayliff or ſubſtitute hath the only power of executing any judicial proceſs at that time.

Pypowder court. The archbiſhop keeps a court of **pypowder** (*u*) at this fair, and a jury is impannelled out of the town of *Wiſtow*, a town within the biſhop's liberty, for determining all differences of ſuch as complain unto them of matters happening within the ſaid fair.

He alſo receives a toll at the ſeveral gates of the city of all cattle coming to the ſaid fair; and again of all cattle ſold going out of the fair; as likewiſe of all ſmall wares both in *Thurſday market* and *Pavement*, and of every horſepack, wallet, mawnd, baſket, or other thing brought in at any gate of the city which is of the value of twelve pence. The ſtated tolls are theſe.

	d.
For every beaſt coming to be ſold ——— ——— ———	1
For every led horſe, mare or gelding ——— ——— ———	2
For every twenty ſheep ——— ——— ——— ———	4
For every horſepack of wares ——— ——— ——— ———	4
For a load of hay to be ſold ——— ——— ——— ———	4
For every other thing to be ſold in any wallet, maund, baſket, cloth-bag, or portmantua to the value of twelve pence ——— ——— ———	1

With the like toll of all and every of the ſaid goods ſold paid by the buyer at his carrying it out of the ſaid fair, *&c.*

There are ſeveral other fairs kept within the city yearly for all ſorts of cattle in the ſtreets of *Walmgate*, *Foſſgate*, *Colliergate* and *Petergate*, which are *Palmſunday* fair, the *Forthnight fairs*, *All-ſouls*, *Martinmas* and *Candlemas fairs*.

Palm-ſunday *fair.* *Palmſunday* fair is always held on *Thurſday* before *Palm-ſunday* from whence the forthnight fairs follow.

Forthnight. *fairs.* Theſe fairs are held by charter from queen *Elizabeth*, dated *June* 30, in the thirty ſecond year of her reign, and begin the ſecond *Thurſday* yearly for ever betwixt *Palm-ſunday* and *Chriſtmas*. The tolls taken at theſe fairs are given in the abſtract of the charters.

All-ſouls *fair.* This fair for cattle is always kept in *Walmgate*, *Foſſgate*, &c. the ſecond day of *November* yearly.

Martinmas *fair.* This fair for cattle is always kept in the ſtreets aforeſaid on the tenth and eleventh of *November*. And on the ſame days in the market-place on the *Pavement* is kept the *ſtatutes* for hiring all ſorts of houſhold ſervants, both men and women. At which fair there is always great plenty of ſuch ſervants to be hired.

Candlemas *fair.* This fair is held as above in *Walmgate*, *Foſſgate*, &c. and is yearly kept on the *Thurſday* and *Friday* before *Candlemas* day for all ſorts of cattle. By charter dated *an. reg. regis* Caroli I. 7.

St. Luke's *fair.* This fair is always kept in *Micklegate* on St. *Luke's* day for all ſorts of ſmall wares. It is commonly called *diſh fair* from the great quantity of wooden diſhes, ladles, *&c.* brought to it. *An antient cuſtom.* There is an old cuſtom uſed at this fair of bearing a wooden ladle in a ſling on two ſtangs about it, carried by four ſturdy labourers, and each labourer, was formerly, ſupported by another. This without doubt is a ridicule on the meanneſs of the wares brought

(*u*) **Pypowders**, *potius* **piepowders** *court, tribunal tumultuarium, quo ſine formulis legis lites in nundinis contingentes deciduntur.* à T. G. Pied, *pes, et* poudre, *pulvis*; *ſeu* poudré, *pulverizatus*, q. d. *curia pedis pulverizati, quia advenarum cauſa ſtatim, nec dum deterſo calceis pulvere, cognoſcuntur. Judex hujuſmodi curiae forte poſſit appellari judex* pedanius *ſeu* pedarius. Skinner *etym. dict.*

to

to this fair, small benefit accruing to the labourers at it. Held by charter *Jan.* 25. *an. reg. regis* H. VII. 17. *

St. *Luke*'s day is also known in *York* by the name of whip-dog-day, from a strange custom that school-boys use here of whipping all the dogs that are seen in the streets that day. Whence this uncommon persecution took its rise is uncertain; yet though it is certainly very old, I am not of opinion with some that it is as antient as the *Romans*. The tradition that I have heard of its origin seems very probable, that in times of popery, a priest celebrating mass at this festival in some church in *York*, unfortunately dropped the *pax* after consecration; which was snatched up suddenly and swallowed by a dog that laid under the altar table. The profanation of this high mystery occasioned the death of the dog, and a persecution begun and has since continued, on this day, to be severely carried on against his whole tribe in our city. *Another.*

MARKETS.

There are several places within the city where markets are kept, but the principal are called *Thursday market* and the *Pavement*. The description of the places will come under another head, and I shall hear only mention the days they fall on, &c.

In the *Pavement* is kept a market three times a week, *Tuesdays*, *Thursdays*, and *Saturdays*; which is abundantly furnished with all sorts of grain, and vast variety of edibles, of which *wild fowl* is not the least. This last article is so plentiful that I believe, for a constancy, no market in *England* can produce the like, either for quantity, variety, or cheapness. Pavement *market.*

The stand for wheat always ranges on the north side of the *Pavement* market, the rye opposite. The place for pease, beans and oats is in *Coppergate*; and the barley market in upper *Ousegate*, all contiguous. The poulterers vend their wares at the *cross*. *Corn stands for sale.*

The toll of this market is of corn only; and from every sack-load of corn, be it either two or three bushels, is taken two dishfuls for toll. Sixteen of these dishes are to contain a peck, as appears by an ordinance mentioned before. *Toll of corn.*

No corn to be carried out of this market till the toll be gathered, and that the toll-bell be rung. This bell is hung in the turret of the new cross, and is usually rung at eleven o' clock. After which the market is free.

(*x*) *Flesh* market is weekly kept every *Saturday* in *Thursday market-place*, to which the country butchers have free resort. There is also in the common *shambles* and other butcher's shops of free citizens an open market kept every day; whereby this city is as well supplied with all sorts of shambles-meat as most markets in *England*.

Sea fish market is kept every *Wednesday* and *Friday* upon *Foss-bridge*, betwixt grate and grate, for panniermen free of the city; where convenient stalls have been lately erected for them. For panniermen not free of the city, the market is kept in *Walmgate* at the east end of *Foss-bridge*.

Several good ordinances have been made for the regulation of this market, which may be seen in the fishmonger's ordinary; one of which is this, no pannierman whatsoever is allowed to carry any fish out of this market before the citizens of this city be first served, til the market bell be rung. After which every person is free to carry his fish to any other market where he pleases.

The nearness of *York* to the *German* ocean and eastern sea-ports, causes this market to be exceedingly well stocked with sea-fish of most kinds. From whence it is bought up again and exported into the more inland parts by foreign panniermen; there being much more of this valuable blessing brought to the city than can be consumed in it. However it were to be wished that the abovementioned ordinance was more strictly kept, then I am afraid it now is, for the benefit of the citizens in general.

Fresh fish market is appointed to be held at a place known by the name of *Salter-greeses* upon the east end of *Ouse-bridge*, where all kinds of fresh fish took in the rivers *Ouse* and *Humber* are exposed to sale. Salmon caught in these rivers are accounted exceeding good; but when the season will not permit this kind of fish to be carried to *London*, the several fisheries on the *Derwent* and the *Tease* pour it in upon us very plentifully. Here are smelts too, which, at their season, are oft took in such numbers as to be cried about the streets in wheel-barrows, at three half pence a score. Oysters from the *Lincolnshire* and *Norfolk* coasts are here sold.

An order for this fish shambles is in the book of occupations, letter A, fol. 177.

In the fishmongers ordinary is an order that all strangers fisher-boats are to fasten their boats beneath the *Stayth*, with their fish in the water of *Ouse*, annenst Church-lane-end, and to sell their fish upon *Ouse-bridge* end in the place accustomed, and to sell the same betwixt seven and eleven a clock forenoon. *An ordinance.*

* This, and another fair, was granted by a patent of *Henry* VII. as is there expressed, *in consideratione magni et notabilis feodi firmae civitatis. Prima pars pat.* 17 H. VII. Rolls.

(*x*) Every *Christmas* even, *Easter* even and *Whitsun* even, the lord-mayor, aldermen and sheriffs have used to walk into the markets, and take notice of the measures of salt, oatmeal, and such like things. And if any shambles meat be rotten, or otherwise unwholsome, it is openly burnt in *Thursday-market*; and the butcher, or who offered such corrupted meat to sale severely fined. An admirable law to prevent sickness and diseases.

Butter *market.* Is in *Micklegate*, and there kept on *Tuesdays*, *Thursdays* and *Saturdays*, but not prohibited any day in the week, for the benefit of the merchants of this city.

This market is only for firkin butter, a merchandize of the staple to be exported, sold in gross to free merchants of the city, and not to be bought or sold by any until it be brought to the standard of the said market, and there tried and examined, and after marked by the officer thereunto appointed by the lord-mayor for the time being. Who hath for the marking and weighing of every firkin a halfpenny. There is a searcher also appointed by the cheesemongers in *London*, who has an allowance from them of so much *per* firkin. The export of this commodity from the city itself, amounting to near sixty thousand firkins a year, is a great argument of the fertility of the soil about us.

Linnen *market.* This market was formerly kept in *Thursday market-place* every *Friday* weekly, for all sorts of linnen cloth, and of linnen yarn. The yarn is duly searched by the wardens of the company of linnen-weavers that it be true tale from the reel, and well spun thread. The linnen cloth likewise ought to be searched and sealed by the said searchers of linnen-weavers, before the same be sold, for prevention of battling, liming, chalking, or any other deceitful thickning of the same by bleachers or others, contrary to the statute in that case provided. Which, says my authority, if well observed, would be a great improvement to that manufacture in this city.

Upon a complaint to the lord-mayor by the country-websters, an order was made *Feb.* 23. 1592, *Robert Askwith* mayor, as follows,

An ordinance. It is agreed that the said market shall be kept in the said market-place, called *Thursday market-place*, and not in any house or houses. And that the same shall not begin before one of the clock in the afternoon upon the *Friday* weekly. And that none resorting to the said market shall buy or sell there before the said hour, nor in any other place upon pain of the thing bought and sold. And that a standard of a true yard wand shall be set upon the market cross there, and that the inhabitants thereabouts shall be commanded not to suffer any to buy or sell in the houses any of the said cloth brought to the said market, upon pain of such fines as shall be thought meet. And proclamation shall be made in the said market-place to the effect aforesaid, two or three several market days. And that no yard wand shall there be used but such as shall be marked and burned with a burn in that behalf to be made, and agreeable to the said standard, *&c.*

Proclamation was made of the several articles accordingly, and an officer appointed by the mayor and aldermen for the execution of the premisses, and one moiety of the forfeitures allowed for seizure and presentments, *&c.*

Leather *market.* This market for all sorts of tanned leather, both of hides and calf-skins, is kept on *Thursday* every week in the *Thursday market-place* in this city; and the said leather to be searched and sealed there by the searchers of the several companies of cordwainers and curriers in this city, before the same be sold, as well upon the penalties of the ordinancies and by-laws of the city and companies, as of the statutes in that case provided.

Wool *market.* This market is kept on *Peasholm-green*; and was first established *anno* 1707, *Robert Benson* esquire, afterwards lord *Bingley*, lord-mayor. They have a convenient shed built for them where the wool is weighed.

Herb *market.* Used to be kept close under the church in *Ousegate*; but, *anno* 1729, the city built and fitted up a neat little square, adjoining to the church-yard, where there is a pump in the midst, and stalls for the herb-women quite round. Pulse, roots and all sorts of garden-stuff are here daily sold as they come in season. And it is remarkable that, of late years, this city is so much improved in this way, that our little square is an epitome of *Covent-garden. Sic parvis*, &c.

The fee-farm rent of the city of York *as it antiently stood, and is at present accountable for.*

Fee farm. The fee-farm of the city as by the charter of king *John* was in his reign one hundred and sixty pound *per annum.*

How paid may be found in a register-book in the council-chamber, letter Y, fol. 157. Again in letter B, fol. 149.

Out of the aforesaid farm king *Richard* II, by his charter dated *April* 24, *anno reg.* 20. 1394. grants to the mayor and citizens one hundred pounds *per annum* for the support of the bridges of *Foss* and *Ouse*.

In the register-book of the city in the council-chamber on *Ousebridge*, *John Norman* lord-mayor, *anno reg. regis* H. VIII, 16. 1534. the title of the book engraven on brass, is recorded this order following.

September 5. 28 *H.* VIII. *fol.* 13.

That the sheriffs of the city are to pay the fee-farm, and to receive the profits of the shrievalty accustomed. An account of the fee-farm as then paid runs thus,

To

	l.	s.	d.
To the earl of *Rutland*	40	00	00
Parcel of the *Ainsty* to the dean and chapels of St. *Thomas* and St. *Stephen* at *Westminster*	05	14	07
Paid to the lord *Darcy* for the king's river of *Foss*	9	2	06
For the king's goal in *Davy-hall*	7	12	01
For proffers in the king's exchequer	48	00	00
For fees accustomed	07	00	00
For the *Ainsty* yearly paid to sir *Richard Range* knight, for the term of his life	12	00	00
Paid to the lord-mayor's two gentlemen or esquires	02	13	04
Paid to the chamberlains of the city with the reason for it	00	03	09
	92	06	03

And further the sheriffs are discharged from paying forty eight pound which they usually paid to the city; and acquitted of the payment of forty pound parcel of the hundred pound annuity to the king by charter of fee-farm. 28 *H.* VIII. *idem fol.* 13.

The sheriffs to be accountable in the exchequer of the fee-farm of the city and bailywick of the *Ainsty*, and to have the profits and commodities thereof. Register book letter Y, fol. 337. *March* 19. 4 *Ed.* VI. 1550. A commission granted for levying the fee-farm. Some more particulars relating to the farm of *York* may be seen in *Maddox*'s *firma burgi*, p. 176 (y).

Gifts and charitable legacies given to the city of York; *from a manuscript*, 1681.

Gifts and legacies.

	l.	s.	d.
Nicholas Girlington to be lent according to his will in the register-book in the council-chamber	40	00	00
William Drew to be lent	80	00	00
Sir *Martin Bowes* for charitable uses	60	00	00
Thomas Smith to be lent	05	00	00
Dame *Catherine Constable* to be lent	40	00	00
Robert Askwith to be lent	20	00	00
James Cotterill to be lent according to his will	100	00	00
Richard North to be lent to the poor citizens of *All-saints* on the *Pavement* and St. *Margaret*'s parish	20	00	00
Sir *Thomas White* alderman of *London*, devised out of his charitable gift to the city of *Bristol* one hundred and four pounds to be brought to the merchant taylors hall yearly on *Bartholomew* day. One hundred pounds to be lent for ten years space to four poor young men of the city of *York*, freemen and inhabitants being clothiers. The four pounds overplus to be employed about the charges and pains. Beginning at *York anno* 1577, and so successively again at *York* every twenty three years; whereof this city hath now received eight successive payments, *viz.* 1577, 1600, 1623, 1646, 1669, 1682, 1705, 1728, in all	800	00	00
Christopher Turner to be lent	20	00	00
And seven pound yearly out of a house in *Stonegate*, to six poor widows			
Robert Brook alderman to be lent	10	00	00
Lady *Herbert* to the poor in *Walmgate*, *Crux* parish to be first preferred	20	00	00
Lady *Askwith* to six poor citizens, to be lent by five marks a piece St. *Dionis* parish to be first preferred	20	00	00
Francis Agar tanner to be lent	30	00	00
Jane Young to be lent	40	00	00
John Burley to be lent to four three or two young freemen of this city at the rate of six pound *per annum*, from time to time for ever, and the increase to be distributed yearly amongst the prisoners of the lower goal in *York castle*	100	00	00
Thomas Harrison alderman to be lent	30	00	00
Fabian Farley, late officer, to be lent	30	00	00
Sir *Robert Walter* alderman, to be lent to fifteen poor citizens by five marks a piece. Haberdashers and feltmakers to be first preferred	50	00	00
Richard Binns gent. to be lent	50	00	00
William Hawly, sometime town-clerk, to be lent according to his will	20	00	00
George Buck gent. to be lent	20	00	00
William Robinson to be lent	80	00	00
William Weddall of *London*, born in this city, to be lent according to his will	100	00	00

(y) There are several instances upon record in the tower of *London*, and elsewhere, of this city's being seized into the king's hands for neglect of paying this farm. See also *Maddox*'s exchequer.

Gifts and legacies.

More	100	00	00
William Hart, pastor of the *English* church at *Emden*, late inhabitant of this city, to be lent to twenty poor men, by five pound a man two years *gratis*, poorest and most religious to be preferred; and if any of his kindred inhabit in the city regard to be had to their preferment	100	00	00
More to be lent by ten pound a man, for two years *gratis*	200	00	00
Richard Scot esquire, to the relief of the poor	20	00	00
Christopher Topham to be disposed of according to his will	50	00	00
Lady *Moseley* to be lent according to her will	20	00	00
Sir *Robert Walter* alderman to pay ten pound yearly to a preaching minister in *Cruxchurch*	120	00	00
Thomas Agar alderman, to be employed to set the poor on work	100	00	00
Alderman *Brearey* to be lent by forty pound a man yearly	150	00	00
William Dale to be lent	20	00	00
Richard Brewster to be lent	30	00	00
Sir *William Allenson* for setting the poor on work	40	00	00
Henry Thompson alderman, for binding apprentices	80	00	00
And forty pound more to be given by ten pound each ward	40	00	00
John Beares alderman for the relief of the poor	100	00	00
Robert Bucknam gent. for the relief of the poor	100	00	00

Stephen Watson, sometime alderman of this city, gave to the mayor and aldermen four pound *per annum*, out of a house, for the preferring a scholar to *Cambridge*.

Plate belonging to the city of York, 1681, *with the names of the donors.*

Plate, &c.

	oz.
One silver bowl given by *Christopher Moltby* with his name engraven thereon *poize*	14 ½
One silver bowl given by the lady *Harrison*	20
One silver bowl double gilt with a cover, *poize* twelve ounces, given by *William Tankard* esquire, and a silver wine bowl with a cover gilt, *poize* sixteen ounces, given by *Thomas Appleyard*, changed into three wine bowls *poize*	28
One great salt renewed in *anno* 1678	59
Six silver trencher salts	14
One gold chain given by sir *Robert Walter* knight, sometime alderman, *poize*	19 ½
One large silver beer-bowl given by *Jo. Vaux* alderman	16
Two silver flagons given by *Thomas Herbert* sheriff	123 ½
One great silver cann the gift of sir *Thomas Witherington* serjeant at law, recorder *poize*	48
Two silver canns, and two silver goblets parcel gilt, the gift of *Leonard Besson* alderman *poize*	93
One bason and ewer, the gift of *James Hutchenson* alderman	102
One silver sugar box and spoon given by sir *Wiliam Allenson* knight	47
One silver cann *poize*	17
Twenty trencher plates the gift of Mrs. *Anne Middleton* *poize*	283
One dozen of silver spoons the gift of sir *John Hewley* knight	26
One silver tobacco-box the gift of *Richard Etherington* esquire	11 ½
One gold chain, worn by the lady mayoress, given by Mr. *Marmaduke Rawden* late of *London*	16
One gold bowl given by the same gent.	261
One silver chamber-pot by the same	50
One pair of silver candlesticks the gift of alderman *Tyreman*	32
Two silver tankards parcel gilt the gift of alderman *Bawtrey*	128
Six silver tumblers the gift of Mr. *Mark Brearey*	25 ½
One silver tankard the gift of Mrs. *Hodgson* midwife	25
One silver candlestick the gift of Mrs. *Bowes*	40
One large bowl double gilt, with a cover, the gift of *John Turner* serjeant at law sometime recorder of *York*	150

A silver standish the gift of Mr. *Peter Dawson*.

There are likewise belonging to the lord-mayor, during his office, *four swords and two maces*.

Swords and maces.

The *first* of the swords and the largest was the gift of the emperor *Sigismund*, father-in-law to king *Richard* II; it is seldom born but on *Christmas-day* and St. *Maurice*.

Another given by king *Richard* II. from his own side, from whence the title of lord accrued to our chief magistrate. This is the least sword amongst them, but the greatest in value for the reason above.

A *third* is that of sir *Martin Bowes*, lord-mayor of *London*, which is the most beautiful, and is born every *Sunday* and other principal days before the lord-mayor.

The

The *fourth* was formerly made uſe on every time the lord-mayor went abroad or ſtirred from home.

The *maces* are both very large, ſilver gilt and richly adorned, the biggeſt of the two is carried on *Sundays*; the leſſer at all other times.

The ſword-bearer hath a *hat of maintenance*, which he wears only on *Chriſtmas* day, St. *Maurice*'s day, and on the high days of ſolemnity. This hat he puts off to no perſon whatſoever; and ſits with it on all the time during divine ſervice at the cathedral, or elſewhere.

The yearly revenues of the city, with the expences and fees of the common-chamber, as it appeared by the chamberlains accounts taken in the year 1681.

The chamberlains this year charged themſelves with the receipt of monies for the uſe of the common-chamber of the city, as follows,

	l.	*s.*	*d.*
For rents and farms according to an inventory or parchment roll	500	00	00
For caſual receipts — — — — —	341	03	04
For fines at ſeſſions and wardmote courts — — —	12	18	04
For exonerations of offices of chamberlains — — —	53	06	08
For the rent of a houſe in *Midlam*			
For alderman *Watſon*'s gift — — — — — —	06	08	00
Total receipts	1048	03	00

The ſaid chamberlains paid out the ſame year, 1681, for the uſe of the common-chamber of the city of *York* in diſcharge of their accounts as follows,

For fees of the common-chamber 143 *l.* 16 *s.* 8 *d.*

	l.	*s.*	*d.*
To the lord-mayor his fee — — — — —	50	00	00
To the town-clerk for his fee — — — —	20	00	00
To the ſword-bearer his fee — — — —	08	18	00
To the mace-bearer his fee — — — — —	08	16	08
To the four ſerjeants at mace, each 4 *l.* 13 *s.* 4 *d.* *per annum* is	18	15	04
To the city's cook for his fee — — — —	13	06	08
To the city baker his fee — — — —	04	00	00
To the porter his fee — — — — —	04	00	00
To the city's clerk for paper, parchment, *&c.* — —	02	00	00
To the keeper of the common-hall — — — —	00	13	04
To the recorder for his fee — — — — —	13	06	08
	143	16	08
For rents reſolute, *&c.* — — — — — —	09	00	00
For the city's chirurgeon — — — — — —	05	00	00
For expences neceſſary — — — — — — —	556	14	04 $\frac{1}{2}$
For expences in building and repairs — — —	219	05	01 $\frac{1}{2}$
For ſir *Martin Bowes* his gift — — — — —	03	00	00
For *Weddal*'s gift — — — — —	06	00	00
For *Peacock*'s gift — — — — —	06	13	04
For alderman *Vaux*'s his gift — — — — —	15	00	00
For expences of the audit yearly allowed 40 *s.* and 30 *s.* to the chamberlains for yearly expences — — —	03	10	00
For a *Cambridge* ſcholar according to aldermen *Watſon*'s gift —	06	08	00
Total payment	969	07	06

I ſhall now draw this tedious chapter to a concluſion, by giving ſome account, as the title of it directs, of the ſeveral *gilds*, *crafts*, *trades* and *fraternities*, which, have been antiently and are at preſent in this city. The religious gilds and fraternities will fall apter in another part; when I come to deſcribe the places where they were held in *York*. The trades and crafts of the city, which are diſtinguiſhed by having publick halls for their ſeparate meetings, may expect an account of them in the general ſurvey. What I ſhall chuſe to do here is to give a ſhort account of thoſe companies of an higher order in the city at preſent, and a general liſt of all the trades that were occupied in *York* about a hundred years ago. But if the reader be curious to know what occupations were more antiently carried on in this city, he may be ſatisfied by peruſing the account of **corpus Chriſti play**; which was formerly acted every year in *York*, and to which every ſeparate trade from the higheſt to the loweſt, were obliged to fit out a **pageant**. This piece of religious ſolemnity I have extracted from the city's regiſters, and ſhall place in the *appendix*.

There are three *companies*, or *gilds*, in the city of *York*, whoſe officers are exempt from the juriſdiction of the lord-mayor; the maſters and ſearchers of all other companies being ſworn

ſworn before him. The companies here are not as in *London*, all ſeparate and diſtinct trades, though they aſſume a ſeveral coat of arms, as if they were ſo many different companies. For inſtance,

The *merchants, grocers, mercers* (z) and *apothecaries* make but one corporation in *York*, by having one governour, a deputy-governour, two aſſiſtants and a ſecretary. Yet they bear each a diſtinct coat of arms, as ſeveral trades.

So likewiſe the *drapers*, and *merchant-taylors*, are incorporated into one company; have a maſter and ſearchers, but bear diſtinct arms.

The *linnen-weavers*, an occupation now not much in uſe in the city, are a company of themſelves, who likewiſe have a maſter and ſearchers.

Theſe three *fraternities* are the only trades whoſe officers are exempt from taking their oaths in the mayor's court; holding their privileges by *charter*.

An account of the ſeveral trades within the city of York, *and what every trade pays yearly to the ſaid city for the repair of their* **Pote-hall**, *called* **St. Anthony's-gild**, taken *anno* 1623.

Trades.	*s.*	*d.*	*Trades.*	*s.*	*d.*
Merchants and Mercers	5	0	Tanners	4	0
Drapers	4	0	Cordwainers	2	0
Goldſmiths	2	0	Fiſhmongers	1	0
Dyers	1	0	Carpenters	2	0
Haberdaſhers	1	0	Bladeſmiths	1	8
Vintners	2	0	Pewterers	1	4
Sadlers	2	0	Glovers	1	6
Bakers	3	0	Armorers	1	0
Butchers	4	0	Inholders	4	0
Waxchandlers	0	8	Milners	3	4
Marriners	0	8	Coopers	1	4
Braſiers	1	0	Skinners	1	6
Barbers	0	8	Glaſiers	1	0
Embroiderers	0	4	Shearmen	0	6
Girdlers	1	4	Spurriers	0	6
Blackſmiths	0	8	Lockſmiths	0	4
Pannyer-men	1	4	Cookes	1	0
Bricklayers	1	4	Painters	0	8
Parchment-makers	2	0	Founderers	1	0
Linnen-weavers	1	2	Coverlet-weavers	1	8
Pinners	0	6	Ropers	1	0
Curriers	0	8	Porters	1	0
Coblers	1	0	Labourers	0	8
Silk-weavers	1	4	Muſicians	1	0
Tallow-chandlers	0	8			

(z) Mercers Ebor. *Incorporat. per nomen gubernator. Mercator. adventur.* 23 El. *pars* 4. *f.* 5. Rolls.

CHAP.

CHAP. VII.

The ancient and present state of the city of YORK, *in respect to its situation, trade, navigation of the river* OUSE, *number of inhabitants, manufactures, price of provisions,* &c. *An exact survey of the city and suburbs, with their antient and present boundaries. The etymology of the names of several streets, lanes, barrs,* &c. *The streets, lanes, allies, courts, gates, market-places, crosses, bridges, prisons, halls, currents, and rivers. The parish churches; their value in the king's books, ancient and present patronage, lists of the several incumbents, with their respective inscriptions, epitaphs, coats of arms,* &c. *The monasteries, hospitals, maisondieus, demolished churches and chapels, which stood here before the* REFORMATION, *are traced up, as far as possible, to their original structures and endowments.*

THE wisdom of our ancestors is very eminent and remarkable in their choice of the situation of this antient city, both for strength, richness, fertility of the country about it, and salubrity of air. As to the first, the antient *Britons* gave it the name of *Caer*, even in the time of the *Romans*, if not before their landing here, which does to this day in the *British*, or *Welsh*, tongue signify a fortified place. *Caer*, says their antiquary (*a*), is derived from the verb *cau*, to shut up, or inclose; and any trench or bank of an old camp is now so called in *Wales*. From whence, adds he, those places of *Britain*, which had been walled by the *Romans*, the old *English*, however that came to pass, turned every *Caer* of theirs into Ceaster; which came afterwards to Cister, Cester, and Chester. But, with submission to this *British* etymologist, the *Saxon Chester*, &c. seems

(*a*) See *Caer* in *Lhuyd's* adversaria, *Baxter*.

rather to be deduced from the *Roman castrum* than the former. I have elsewhere taken notice that *York* is frequently called Ceaster, simply, by the *Anglo-Saxons*, as well as Eoferwic Ceaster; and this is sufficient to shew that our city had this name, *ab origine*, given it by the natives, from its walls, enclosures, or fortifications. Whoever considers the situation of *York*, in the annexed plan, must allow that nature gives great strength to it. But, when assisted by *Roman* arts and industry, must have rendered the city impregnable in those days. The east part of the city, which in their days seems to have been their strongest and greatest security, is flanked on the west and east by two rivers, meeting in a point south. On the north was an impenetrable forest; to these were added strong high walls and bulwarks, *muris et turribus altam*, says *Alcuin*, especially that wall which antiently ran from the *Roman* tower, already described, parallel with the *Ouse* to the *Foss*. The foundations of this wall have been discovered in digging of drains and cellars along *Lendal*, *Conyngstreet*, and up as far as the *Castlehill*; and I have ventured to draw a line in the plan to shew the course of it. By means of this wall, which the present remains of it demonstrate that it was built up to a prodigious height, and the rivers; this part of the town must be rendered impregnable; and was sufficient to baffle any attack that could then be made against it. The west side of the city, which as I have hinted resembles the *Transtyberim* of *Rome*, was also as strongly fortified by them as the site of it would allow. For from almost a flat superficies such large and noble old ramparts are thrown up, and ditches made, as few cities in *Europe* can boast of. In all probability this also was a *Roman* work; the *Roman* arch yet standing in *Micklegatebar* sufficiently proves that the gate stood where it now does in their days. And there is a work without it called now the *Mount*, whose traces evidently shew it to have been a strong out-work, or castle, raised on both sides the grand road, the better to defend this entrance to the city. I shall be more particular on these matters when I come to describe the things themselves; and shall just take notice that *York*, from the time of the *Romans* and *Saxons*, and even down as low as our later *Scotish* wars, was always esteemed the bulwark of the north, and was the chief guard to *Britain* against those northern invaders. Mr. *Camden*'s description of our city, in his days falls next in my way: "*York*, says our great antiquary (*b*), is the second city in *England*, the "first in this part of the island, and is a great strength and ornament to the north. It is, "adds he, both pleasant, large and strong, adorned with fine buildings, both publick and "private; populous, rich, *&c*. The river *Ure*, which now takes the name of *Ouse*, runs "gently from north to south quite through this city, and divides it into two parts, which "are joined by a noble stone-bridge. The west part of the city is no less populous, lies in "a square form, enclosed partly by stately walls and partly by the river, and has but one "way to it, namely by *Mickle-bar*. The east part is larger, where the buildings stand "thick and the streets are narrow, is shaped like a lentil, and strongly walled; on the south-"east it is defended by a *Foss*, or ditch, very deep and muddy, which runs by obscure "ways into the very heart of the city, and gliding close by the castle-walls, a little farther "falls into the *Ouse*.

As to the great strength which this author gives to our fortifications, though our walls were then reputed strong, and long after his time stood a vigorous siege, against a very formidable army, yet the art of war has, of late years, been so much improved, that they are now of small use; and would be of as little service against a modern attack, as the ramparts they stand on. I have been told, however, by one of the ablest engineers (*c*) in the present age, upon a view, that *York*, by the flatness of its situation, and the great command of water about it, is capable of receiving as strong a fortification as most of the towns in *Flanders*. But then the extent of its walls would demand a very large garrison to sustain it. So much for its strength. Next,

The advantage of its situation, in regard to the fertility of the country about it, is evident; but will be much more so to those who shall carefully survey the map I have before inserted of the richest, and most extensive valley in *Britain*. Whose compass, though some hundreds of miles, is called by antient historians **the Vale of York**. Should I pretend to describe the vast quantities of all kinds of provisions, necessary for the preservation, and even the luxury of human life, which is produced in this district, my subject would swell to a much greater size than I care to treat on. The populousness of the country, and the weekly and even dayly provisions brought out of it to the city, are tokens demonstrative to all of a happy situation in regard to those most essential points of life.

Lastly, as to the salubrity of its air and wholsomeness of the place, we have no less to boast of than the former. Our *geographers* have placed this city in the latitude of fifty four degrees, some odd minutes; no bad situation as to that point. And I have been told that the winters at *Paris*, and several other parts of *France*, are much severer than with us. But our great advantage is, that, being placed at such a distance from the sea, on every side, we are not annoyed with the unwholsome vapours of it. And yet, so near, that the more mild, salubrious breezes of both the eastern, southern and even western seas are wafted over us; which with the natural air of the country round about us, and the advantage of two

(*b*) Camden's *Britannia*. Gibson.

(*c*) Col. *Lascells*, engineer, in chief, to the army.

York, *from* Severus's *hills*.

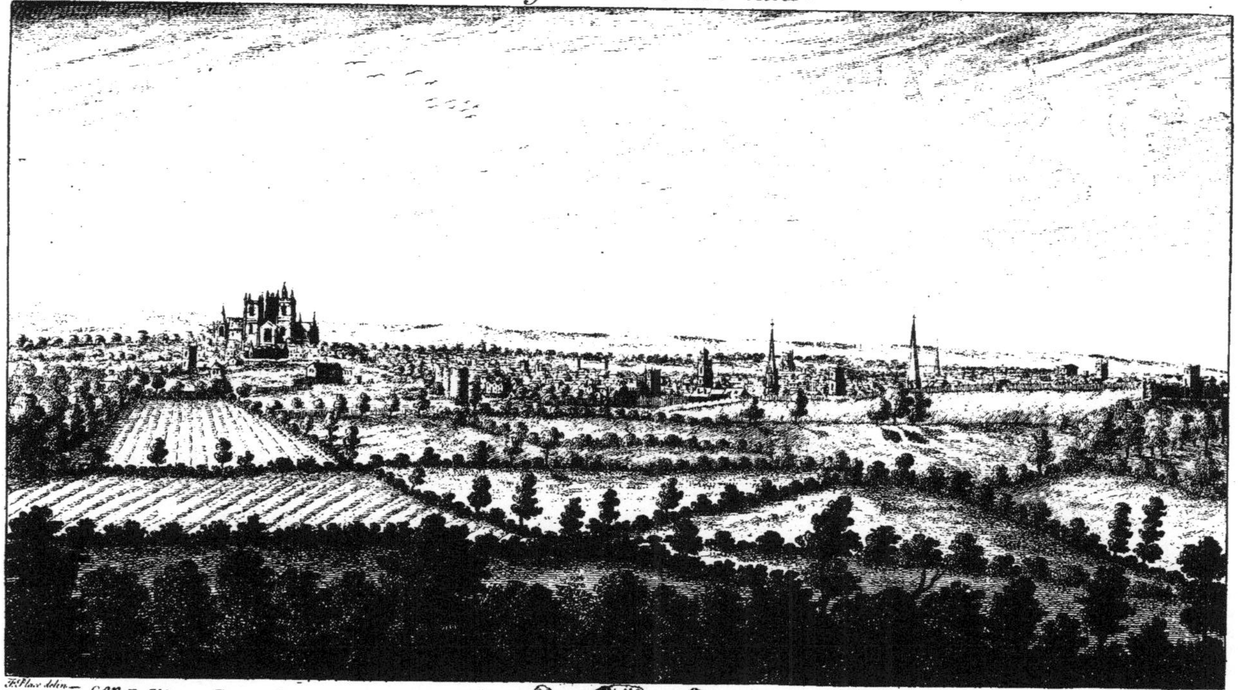

F. Place delin. — W. H. Toms sculp.

Sr Miles Stapylton *of* Myton *Bar.^t* *knight of the shire for the county of* York, *in regard to the honour of the City in general, & in respect to the author of this work in particular, contributes this plate. 1736.*

THE ACTON LIBRARY

considerable rivers, which as drains carry off all superfluous moisture from us, render the situation of *York* as healthful as art and nature can contrive it. Experience, against which lies no appeal, makes good my assertion; for though the flatness of the city and country about it, may make the air to be suspected for unwholsome; yet, it is well known, we have no distempers, which the physicians call *endemick*, attend our climate; but on the contrary, even diseased people, especially *consumptive*, are known to be much supported by the mildness of it. The natural soil of this city is found to be mostly a *morass*; except the west part, and that fine sandy bank which runs along the east side of the river. But it has been sufficiently raised above the mosses, by its several ruins and devastations; and you cannot dig any where, almost, but you meet with burnt earth, cinders, and stone pavements buried very deep in the ground. Along *Petergate*, and near the cathedral, you dig a yard or two deep in chippings of stone, before you come at any soil; which must have been laid there from the vast quantities of that stuff left by the workmen, at the several buildings and reparations of the *Minster*. But what is matter of great surprize, is, that the labourers in digging deep for cellars, about the heart of the city, have met frequently with a large quantity of pure quicksilver; which yet glided from them so fast that they were not able to save any. I should not have given credit to this, had I not heard it attested by persons of undoubted veracity; particularly from my worthy friend Mr. *John Tomlinson*; who assured me that the same accident happened in digging the cellars of the new house he built at the corner of *Collier-gate* and St. *Saviour-gate*. How this mineral, or what you will call it, comes to be found in this soil, I shall leave to the *naturalists* to determine.

I now proceed to give an account of the ancient and present state of trade in this city, which as it was formerly one of its most vital parts, so when it is in danger to be lopped off, or any ways maimed, the whole constitution must suffer by it. It is but a melancholy prospect, to the present inhabitants of this once opulent city, to see their water and trade every day decreasing, finding out and settling in new places and chanels. Nor will it be a more agreeable view to let them see backwards, and shew them the riches and grandeur of their predecessors, which when compared with their own state must make them seem mean and insignificant. I shall therefore just cursorily run over this last article, to shew my fellow citizens the reasons of this strange desertion of trade and water, and point out some probable means to regain it. In this I hope not to be thought tedious; I write for the information of posterity; I shew them the failings of their ancestors; and if I only thought I could influence either our present magistrates, or their successors, to be sollicitous in regaining, what probably is not yet too far gone from us, the recompence of it would far exceed my labour.

That *York* was formerly the chief *emporium*, place of trade, or mart-town in the north of *England* is certain. The advantage of its situation in so fruitful a valley, and on the then *only navigable river* in the county, rendring it exceedingly commodious for the import and export of all the necessaries for life or luxury. Our *Alcuin* (*d*), if he does not flatter his native place too much, gives it great preheminence in the then trading world, and styles it

——————— *Emporium terrae commune marisque.*

The common mart of sea and land. This author who wrote near a thousand years ago has left us this fine description of its trade, riches, and noble situation in his days.

Esset ab extremo venientibus hospita portu
Navibus oceano, longo sua prora remulco,
Navita qua properans ut sistat ab aequore fessus.
(*e*) *Hanc piscosa suis undis interluit* USA,
Florigeros ripis praetendens undique campos.
Collibus et silvis tellus hinc inde decora,
Nobilibusque locis habitatio pulchra, salubris,
Fertilitate sui multos habitura colonos.
Quo variis populis et regnis undique lecti
Spe lucri veniunt, quaerentes divite terra
Divitias, sedem sibimet, lucrumque laremque, &c.

Thus imitated.

From the most distant lands ships did arrive,
And safe in *port* lay there, tow'd up to shore.
Where, after hardships of a toilsome voyage,
The sailor finds a safe retreat from sea.
By flow'ry meads, on each side of its banks,
The *Ouse*, well stored with fish, runs through the town.
With hills and woods the country, finely grac'd,

(*d*) Alcuin. Ebor. *de pontif.* Ebor. (*e*) *Scil.* urbem.

Adorn'd

Adorn'd with noble seats, an healthful soil,
By its fertility invites the carls
T' inhabit,———
Hither for gain, from various foreign parts,
Come various people; seeking opulence,
And a secure abode in wealthy land.

This was the state of our city under the *Saxon* government in this island, and as it was then the *capital* of the *Northumbrian* kingdom, by far the greatest and most powerful in the *Heptarchy*, so must it flourish in riches and trade beyond even *London* itself in those days. What devastation besel us at the conquest, I have elsewhere sufficiently treated of; *William* of *Malmsbury*, in his description of the city, before that thunder-clap fell on us, calls *York (f) a great and a metropolitan city*, and says that *ships trading both from* Germany *and* Ireland *lay then in the heart of it.* If ships could come from these two countries, it is evident that there might, and did, arrive others; and perhaps, as *Alcuin* writes, from all the trading nations then in the world.

(g) About the year 1186, and fifty years after the terrible fire in king *Stephen*'s time, this city so raised its head as to bear half proportion to *London*. For we are told that king *Henry* II. having imposed a tax on his subjects, under pretence to raise money for the *holy war*, he took this method to levy it. He caused a choice to be made of the richest men in all the cities in *England*, for instance in *London* two hundred, in *York* one hundred, and according to this proportion in all the rest. All these at a certain time and place were to appear before him, from whom he exacted the tenth part of all their moveables, by the estimation of credible men who knew their worth; and such as refused he imprisoned till they paid the sum required.

That the city of *York* was very remarkable for trade some ages ago, is evident from the charter of king *John*; who only confirms to the *gild of merchants* all those privileges themselves or their hanses, or colonies, settled in other parts of *England* and *Normandy*, had before his time enjoyed. And, indeed, I find that as high as king *Stephen* these merchants were of great account; for one *Thomas de Eurwic* paid a fine to the king for being made, as is expressed by the record, *alderman of the gild of merchants in Eurwic (h)*. *Hansa*, latinized, is derived from the *German* hansa, or the *Belgick* hans, which is, says *Skinner*, cities or companies, associated or confederated; so the *hans towns*, in *Germany* still retain the old name. Nor is it yet quite lost in *York*, for in this very company of merchants still kept up in the city, those of these old hans are esteemed a degree before any of the rest.

(i) I have taken notice in the annals of this work, that a multitude of *Jews* inhabited here after the conquest; a people who did then, and do still, entirely subsist on trade. And, as they were a sort of *wandring merchants*, would never sit down in a place not convenient for their purpose. And, notwithstanding the fatal *(k)* destruction of them, a new colony came and settled here; where, under the protection of our kings they lived in great splendour and magnificence; so *Joceus* I find the name of an eminent *Jew* at *York* the third of *John*. These *anti-christian* foreigners, whenever the crown wanted money, were mulct and fined at pleasure. *M. Paris* writes that one *Aaron* a *Jew* of *York* told him, that the king, *Henry* III. had squeezed from him, alone, at several times, *(l)* four marks of gold and four thousand of silver, a vast sum of money in those days; and a great instance of the wealth of this merchant that could bear such extraordinary drawbacks. That they staid here till their final expulsion, grew exceeding rich, and that they had houses in the city more like princes palaces than subjects dwellings, as sir *T. W.* writes, can be owing to nothing but their thriving so well by trade in it.

In Mr. *Maddox*'s book of the *exchequer* several records are mentioned where the *Jews* of *York*, their wives, children, and lands, were seized on by a precept directed to the high sheriff for neglecting to pay their share to the king's tallage; in the time of *Richard* I. king *John* and *Henry* III. the tallage for the whole city sometimes amounted to cccc marks in

(f) Eboracum *urbs ampla et metropolis* ——— *includit in medio sinu sui naves a* Germania *et* Hybernia *venientes*. Gul. Malmf. *in prol. pont*. Ebor.

(g) Vide annales sub hoc anno. M. Paris. *Daniel*'s hist. of *England*.

(h) Thomas de Eurwic *filius* Uliveti *debet* i *fugat. ut sit* aldermannus *in* gilda *mercat. de* Eurwic. *Rot*. Pipe *an*. 5 Stephani *reg*.

(i) Vide annales 1189, 90.

(k) Since the press passed over the account of the massacre of the *Jews* at *York*, I have met with some fines in the *Pipe-rolls* taken for that offence.

Ric. Malebisse *r. comp. de* xx *m. pro rehabenda terra sua usque ad adventum dom. regis que saisita fuit in manu regis propter occisionem* Judeorum Ebor. *et ut ipse et* Walterus de Carlton *et* Ric. de Kukeneia *armigeri ejus habeant pacem regis usque ad adventum regis*. *Rot*. Pipe 4 R. I.

Cives Ebor. *red. comp. de* x *mar. pro habendis obsidibus suis qui fuerunt Norhant. propter occisionem* Judeorum. *Rot*. Pipe 5 R. I.

Henricus de Fishergata *debet* c *marc. pro habenda pace sua de interfectione* Judeorum Ebor.

Rob. de Seleby *r. c. de* xx *marc. pro eodem*.

Ric. de Tanga *r. c. de* l *mar. pro eodem*.

Tom. de Bretegata *deb.* c *s. pro eodem*.

And. de Magenebi *r. c. de* l *mar. pro eodem*.

Walt. de Bellouago *r. c. de* x *mar. pro eodem*.

Rot. Pipe 6 R. I.

(l) A mark of gold weighed eight ounces; and as *Cowell* states it out of *Stow*, it came to the value of xvi *l* xiii *s*. iv *d* but this is uncertain. *Selden*'s notes on his *Janus Ang*.

those days. The fifth of *Stephen* an aid of lx pound was paid to the king by *Turgis*, *et quietus est*, for the city. The eighteenth of *Edward* I, and *aid* of cccl marks was paid by the citizens of *York* to the subsidy raised for that king's expedition into *Wales*. p. 418, 425, *&c.*

The many wastings and burnings of this antient city, both accidental and designed, must have often reduced it to a heap of rubbish; and probably, at this day it would have been no better a village than *Aldborough*, had not its situation on a river capable of restoring it again by trade, occasioned a rise, as sudden, almost, as the fall thereof.

But all this is no more than barely asserting, the reader will expect some farther proofs; and of which not only our antient historians, but even our *parliamentary* records bear testimony.

That the free and open navigation of the river from the *Humber* up to the city, was a great encouragement to trade, is most certain. Free and open it must have been antiently, and a strong flow of tide run up it; else such ships as *Malmsbury* speaks on, which then did navigate the *German* and *Irish* seas, could never get up to unlade their burdens, and lie in the heart of the city. In the *Danish* invasions, their fleets, sometimes consisting of five or six hundred sail, came very high up the *Ouse*, before they landed. *Anno* 1066, a vast fleet of ships, with sixty thousand land forces on board, came up the *Humber* and *Ouse* as far as *Rickal*, where they moored their vessels; consisting, as some say, of five hundred, others a thousand ships or transports. *(m) Ingulphus*, an antient and approved historian, says that the *Danes* entered the *Humber* with their navy, and brought all their ships up the river *Ouse*, almost as far as *York*. *Rickal* the place of their landing, mentioned by several authors, is a village within six miles of the city. This invasion happened the year the conqueror came in; and two years after we are told that two hundred and forty *tall ships* came up the *Humber* and *Ouse*, with an army of *Danish* soldiers to the aid and assistance of the northern revolters.

By these instances we may learn what state and condition the flow of the tide was up the river *Ouse* in those days. For allowing that these transports were ships of small burden, yet the stowage of so many men, horses, armour and other implements of war in them, must make them draw deep water, and it may well seem a thing impossible to bring up such a number of ships or transports to *Rickal* at this day.

That the trade of the city was proportionably great and met with encouragement from successive princes and *parliaments* we have also sufficient evidence. *Anno reg.* 27 Ed. III. the **staple of wool**, which had before been kept at *Bridges* in *Flanders*, by act of parliament was fixed at *York*; and some other places in *England*. The act calls it the **staple for wool, leather, woolfells and lead** *(n)*.

In this king's reign, amongst other his conquests, the important town of *Calais* fell into his hands; and in the fourteenth of his successor the **staple** for the export trade of the whole kingdom was fixed at that place. This was a body corporate governed by a mayor, two constables, *&c.* had a common seal, and continued in great affluence of trade and riches, till the town was unfortunately lost in the reign of queen *Mary*. That the merchants of *York* had a considerable share in this **staple**, and were many of them members of this corporation, appears in the catalogue of our senators; where *anno* 1442, *John Thrush* a great merchant, who dwelt in *Hungate* in this city, is styled *mayor of the* **staple** *of* **Calais**, as also **treasurour** there. *Anno* 1449, *William Holbeck* mayor of *York*, is called merchant of this **staple**. And *anno* 1466, sir *Richard York*, one of the guests at archbishop *Nevil*'s great feast, is there called mayor of the **staple** of **Calais** that year, and was sheriff of this city at the same time. Several conveyances I have seen, in our own and other records, of merchandizes and money left by will, belonging to the citizens of *York*; who were merchants of this **staple**.

That a woollen manufacture was held here to the days of *Henry* VIII. and after, to the great advantage of this city, appears by an act of parliament procured in that king's reign, entitled **the assize of coverletts**. The preamble of which act, being very expressive in our favour, I shall beg leave to transcribe.

(o) **Whereas the city of** York, **being one of the antientest and greatest citties within the realme of** England, **before this tyme hath been mayntayned and upholden by divers and sundry handicraftes there used, and most principally by making and weaving of coverlets and coverings for beds, and thereby a great number of the inhabitants and people of the said city and suburbs thereof and other places within the county of** York **have been daily set on work in spinning, dying, carding, and weaving of the said coverletts**, &c.

This act which contains a full power for the sole making and vending of the said commodity from *York*, continues still in force. But though this branch of trade must have been

(m) Humbram *ingrediuntur*, *et per* Ouse *fluviolum*, *fere ad* Eboracum, *omnes puppes advehuntur*. Ingulphus.

(n) Stat. at large. In the time of *H.* II. and *H.* III. The weavers of *York* paid a very considerable yearly farm for their privileges. *Maddox*'s excheq. p. 233. Ebor. *textores ibidem inquis. ampla de forinsecis textoribus contra formam ordinat. et concess. nuper per regem* R. II. *fact. et ordinat. inquis.* 2 H. IV. *n.* 21. *De textoribus et tinctor.* Ebor. *ordin. Claus.* 2 Hen. III. *m.* 16. &c.

(o) Stat. at large.

and would be still very beneficial, I do not believe that there is one coverlet wrought in the city of *York*, in a twelve month, at this day.

About ten years before this last mentioned act was obtained, the city being jealous that several encroachments made on the river might in time quite ruin their navigation; the lord-mayor, aldermen and common-council entered into a petition to *parliament*, setting forth, *that several persons inhabiting on the banks of the* river, *had presumed upon pretended liberties to place in the same diverse* stakes, piles, fishgarths, *and* other engines, *to the great damage and hindrance of the free passage and hindrance of many* ships, keyles, coggs, *and* boats *with* goods *and* merchandize *from the river* Humber *to this city, endangering the lives of the persons and loss of the vessels which come up. Greatly tending to the utter impoverishing and destruction of the said city, which heretofore chiefly subsisted by* trade, *and a free passage up the said* river, *&c.* (*p*).

This petition being taken into consideration, an act passed, that the fish-garths and other incumbrances of the river should be immediately pulled up and taken away. Commissioners were appointed to see it done, with a power to levy *forty pounds a month* on any persons who suffered their works to stand after the publication of this act.

Here are two or three more remarkables to be taken notice of by this act, first that the city did not petition to have their river made more navigable, but only to take away some obstructions from it. By which it is evident that in those days, the tides were strong enough to bring the vessels then used in trade up to the city itself. Next I find the town of *Hull* was equally concerned with the city of *York*, and had an equal share in the commission to see the passage made clear as above. And this also shews that though *Hull* has long enjoyed a separate interest, and grown up from a *small fisher-town* (*q*) to a place of great trade and wealth, by the interception of those merchandizes that used to come on to *York*; yet formerly they had a joint interest, and *Hull* was no more than a port convenient for ships to put into, which were of too great burthen to navigate the river *Ouse*, there to unload and send up the goods in proper vessels to *York*. Several agreements are on our records made betwixt the mayor and citizens of *York*, and the mayor and burgesses of *Hull*; all of which, especially one as old as 1451, sufficiently proves my assertion (*r*).

That the tunnage and customs of *Hull, Ravenser*, and some other towns on the *Humber*, was farmed and paid by the citizens of *York* antiently, will appear by a record of a complaint made by the city to the king and parliament fourth of *Edward* III. against the inhabitants of those towns for non-payment of those duties. The record, in French, is printed at length in *Ryley's placita parliamentaria*; p. 646. and a *distringas* was granted upon it.

From the time of obtaining the abovesaid act of coverlets to the coming of king *James* I. in his primary progress from *Scotland*, to this city, being the space of fifty years, we hear no more of our trade, though it must have been ebbing from us all that time. The art of navigation and ship-building being both enlarged, trade was carried on chiefly where ships of great burthen could get up. This happened about the latter end of queen *Elizabeth's* days; and that great voyages were undertaken before, in ships of small freight, is evident from that in which the great sir *Francis Drake* sailed round the world in; which was but a ship of one hundred tonn burthen, called the *Pellican* (*s*).

King *James*, as I said, coming first out of *Scotland* had his eye upon *York*, as a city very conveniently placed betwixt the two kingdoms. And it is more than probable by his laying out so much money in repairing the *manor*, or palace, at *York*, that he intended to reside here very often. His compliment to the lord-mayor that he liked the city so well *that he would come and be a burgess among them*; and that he desired *to have the river amended and made more navigable*, are words which sufficiently express his design. And though *London*, with the southern parts of the kingdom, had those alurements which made him alter his mind; yet there is no doubt, but that he would have encouraged any proposal from the city for amending their navigation, if the parliament had been petitioned for that purpose in his time. Yet such was the supineness, negligence, or rather stupidity of the magistrates of those days, that they sat still and saw their state every day decreasing without once offering to redress it.

It is true, that in the beginning of the reign of king *Charles* I. sir *Robert Berwick*, then recorder of *York*, in a speech made to that king at his entrance into the city, takes notice of the great decay of trade then; and tells his majesty (*t*), *that though this city was formerly enriched with trade and far greater and more populous then it now is; yet of later times trading here decreased, and that principally by reason of some hindrance in the river, and the greatness of ships now in use. For which*, adds he, *nevertheless this river by your royal assistance might be made serviceable, and until that be done there is no hope that this city will attain its former splendour and greatness.*

(*p*) Statutes at large.

(*q*) *Leland* says, that the towne of *Kingston* was in the time of *Edward* III. but a meane fisher-towne, and longyd as a member to *Hassele*, village a two or three mile upper on the *Humber*. *Leland*'s itin.

(*r*) Articles of agreement betwixt *John Daile* mayor of *Hull* and *Richard Warter* mayor of *York*. Regist. book f. 157.

(*s*) *Drake's* voyages.

(*t*) *Vide annal. sub anno*, 1633.

About

About this time the great cut for draining the levels below *Doncaster* was made. A noble canal, and first undertaken by one *Cornelius Vermeydan* a *Dutchman*; but afterwards compleated by his executors. It is a strait channel of near five miles in length, and near a hundred yards broad at high water; it empties itself into the *Ouse* at a village called *Gool*. This cut was originally designed for a drain to such lands in the levels, whose water could not any other way be so conveniently carried off. But for their own safety, as well as by a remonstrance from the city of *York*, they built a sluice and flood-gates at the mouth of it to stop the tide from taking that course. In the year 1668, or thereabouts, by a violent land flood, this work blew up, and was never since repaired, as there are still living witnesses can testify. The land owners in those parts have been ever since at great expence to stem the tide which flows impetuously in, and daily undermines their works. And though, by direction of the *court* of *sewers*, the mouth of this drain was ordered to be kept at twenty five yards in breadth; yet it is now increased to fifty yards; and is still increasing to the great danger of the country, whose lands for many miles are so many feet lower than the surface of high water; the tide rising here fifteen foot at each flow, that it threatens distruction to the whole country adjoining.

What detriment this has been by the absorbing the tide which used to run more freely up the river *Ouse*, is but too apparent; and will be more so to our successors if not prevented. This vast canal to the *Ouse* is, comparatively speaking, what *Dagenham* breach was to the *Thames*, and from a drain, as it was originally designed, is now turned into a *free river*, and made the passage for navigating into the river *Dunn*. But I shall go on with my history.

During the usurpation, our city had shewn their loyalty in so exemplary a manner to king *Charles*, that they could expect no favours from his murderers; though they were represented in parliament by two stiff fanaticks sir *William Allenson* and *Thomas Hoyl*. *Anno* 1656, sir *Thomas Widdrington*, recorder of this city, was chose speaker of the house of commons. I mention this, because, though that gentleman was a person in high trust at that time, and had the city so much at heart as to write a history of it, yet I do not find that he used his interest at all towards getting an act for amending the navigation of their river, or bettering their trade. It was this the city justly resented, and when sir *Thomas* offered to dedicate his book to them, they in their answer to his letter with some warmth told him, that if he had employed his power in the articles above, towards the relief of their present distrest condition, it would have been of much more advantage to the city, and satisfaction to them, than shewing them the grandeur, wealth and honour of their predecessors; or to that purpose. This taunt sir *Thomas* took so ill, that he put an entire stop to the publication of his book for it; and left a prohibition to his successors that it should never be printed. However, during the rump administration, whether by sir *Thomas*'s procurement or not I know not, a short act was obtained for *mending of the river* Ouse, as it is called, which was to take place the third of *February* 1658, and end on the same day 1659. I have seen a table of rates laid on by the magistrates as a tax on all imports and exports to that purpose. But, as their power was so short lived, little good could come of it.

During the succeeding reigns of king *Charles* II. and king *James*, the city seems to have been wholly taken up with defending and getting their charters renewed and enlarged. The magistrates then in office had some way or other faln grievously under the displeasure of the ministry in king *Charles*'s reign, which occasioned a writ of *quo warranto* against them, and a seizure of the city's liberties, *&c.* into the king's hands, *anno reg.* C. II. 36. which were restored by his successor. Nothing relating to navigation was done all this time; nor till the year 1699; when a petition was sent up to *parliament* praying leave to bring in a bill to make the river *Ouse* navigable; and a bill was brought in accordingly, once read and ordered a second reading. But an end being put to that session the bill was dropt, and *Henry Thompson* esquire lord-mayor, dying soon after, who was the chief promoter of that bill, it was prosecuted no farther.

But I must not forget to register a noble proposal that was made to the city, about the latter end of king *Charles*'s reign, by the then duke of *Bolton*; commonly, but very erroneously, called the *mad-duke of Bolton*. This nobleman proposed to the city, as I have heard, to get an act of parliament at his own charge, for cutting a new river, or canal, from *Blacktoft*, on the *Humber*, in a direct line for *York*. An actual survey was taken, the charge of the ground the cut was to be made through computed; which was not very considerable; moors and morasses, such as *Wallingfen* being the most of it, the whole distance measuring only nineteen miles and a half from the *Humber* to *Waterfoulford*, where it would first enter the *Ouse*. The duke expected a settled rate to be put upon all goods and merchandize coming to *York*, and for ever paid to him and his heirs, as interest for the almost immense sum that he should expend on this occasion. What broke off this treaty I know not, but whatever was the reason of it, it was greatly unfortunate to the city; for if it had been done, such a flow of tide must necessarily have come up, that we now should have had the pleasure of seeing ships of two or three hundred tons burthen lying at *Ousebridge*. That the duke was in earnest, appears from a map he caused to be taken of the whole design,

ſign, which he preſented to the city; and it is now kept in a *tin-caſe* amongſt the records on *Ouſebridge*. A plan of this propoſed cut may be ſeen in the annexed print of the river.

But the credit of laying a ſure foundation for the regaining of our water and trade was preſerved for our own times; and what praiſes muſt ever be paid to the memory of our preſent citizens, magiſtrates and their repreſentatives in parliament, if the act procured in the twelfth of king *George* I, effectually reſtores us thoſe valuable bleſſings. It is true we have murmurers amongſt us, that do not ſtick to ſay, that by it we have loaded ourſelves with new and unneceſſary taxes; that we have more water than trade already; that every branch of trade that ever was, or ever could be expected to be ſettled at *York*, is irrecoverably loſt, and fixed in other places. To this it is anſwered, that the impoſt on goods and merchandize, coming up the river is ſo light, that it is ſcarce felt by the inhabitants; and yet produces a fund ſufficient, in time, to compleat the deſign. That, when we have more water, more trade will certainly follow it; for as our ſituation is not changed, ſo when the navigation of the river is always open, the cheapneſs of the country will undoubtedly invite traders in moſt matters to reſide here as formerly.

I ſhall not take upon me to give the particulars of this late act, the act itſelf being eaſily come at; but, by it is given a full power to make what cuts we pleaſe croſs the land from the *Humber* to *York*; in order to ſhorten the diſtance, and gain more tide. The method to go upon to avoid an exceſſive charge, and yet bring water enough that veſſels which draw, at leaſt, five foot, might paſs to and from the city in the drieſt ſeaſons, and at the loweſt neap tides, was taken into conſideration. Mr. *Perry*, that ſtopped up *Dagenham* breach, and was afterwards employed by the late *Czar*, in ſeveral extraordinary undertakings of this kind, was ſent for. That gentleman, upon a ſurvey of the river, gave his opinion, that *ſluices* and *floodgates*, made and ſet at proper diſtances, was the moſt likely method to overcome the ſhallows, and navigate the *Ouſe* to *York*. This was not approved on; but Mr. *Palmer*'s ſcheme, an engineer of our own growth, as I may call him, was thought more feaſible. This was by contracting the river in ſuch places as required it, that is by obliging it, at low water, to run into a channel of ninety foot broad, which was before above two hundred. By this contracting of it, 'twas hoped that the river itſelf in time would wear a deeper channel; the bottom being a moveable ſand, where it was firſt tried, *viz.* at *Walltig*; which in ſome part has anſwered there, though not ſo fully in the ſhallows nearer home. The bed of the river near the city being found to be compoſed of rubbiſh, broken bricks and tiles, which have been thrown into it, perhaps for ſome ages paſt, and formed a bottom ſo hard as not to be removed by thoſe means.

But all this affair of contracting ſeems to tend to little purpoſe, for unleſs ſuch cuts are made as will bring us better tides, we cannot without dams expect a conſtant navigation up to *York*. I mean ſuch dams as were propoſed by Mr. *Perry* to be made below the city. Whoever takes a view of the map of the river *Ouſe*, which I have cauſed to be drawn, muſt obſerve a great many angles in its courſe, all, or ſome of which cut off, muſt, by making the diſtance nearer, bring up a ſtronger flow of tide to the city. That this may be better comprehended I ſubjoin the following table.

Cuts at ſeveral places.	*Their length.* Yards.		*Preſent courſe.* Yards.		*Difference ſaved.* Yards.	
From *Saltmarſh* to *Skelton* — —	2000		8800		6800	
Over the ſand at *Ayre*'s mouth —	440		1420		880	
The old courſe of *Ouſe* — —	300		4840		4540	
At *Wheel-hall* — — —	450		1760		1310	
From *Kelfield-clough* to four hundred yards above *Wharf* mouth —	1120		3520		2400	
	4310		20240		15930	
	Miles.	*Yards.*	*Miles.*	*Yards.*	*Miles.*	*Yards.*
	2	790	11	880	9	90

The diſtance from *Cawood* to *York* by water is ſomewhat more than nine miles, where the tide uſually riſes ſix or ſeven foot; then it is plain, by this table, that if theſe cuts were made, that we ſhould have at *York* near as good tides as they now have at *Cawoood*; beſides the advantage of taking in great part of that tide which runs up the *Dutch cut*.

The act which empowers the citizens of *York* to make theſe neceſſary preparations for bettering their navigation, was obtained at the expence of *Edward Thompſon* eſquire, one of their repreſentatives in parliament. And a late amendment of it was got, wherein the the duties are better regulated, at the expence of the city. In perſuance of this benefit is expended already four or five thouſand pound in ſtraitning the river, without making one cut; though now it is ſaid that affair is warmly talked on.

Before I diſmiſs this head, I muſt beg leave to take notice that was the navigation made compleat up to *York*, it would be further neceſſary, and it would beſides be an infinite advantage both to city and country, if the rivers were made navigable up the *Nid*, as high as as it could be carried, up the *Swale* to *Morton-bridge*, and up the *Eure* to *Ripon*, and higher. A small expence would execute this affair; and whoever takes a view of the map of the *vale of York*, and knows the richness of the country into which these rivers extend, will easily guess at the advantage. *Lead* in abundance, *flax*, *butter*, *cheese*, *hams*, *tallow*, *hose* for the *army*, *timber* for the *navy*, &c. would come down in great plenty; and be exchanged here for what commodities they are really in want of in those parts.

To conclude, I would not have our present citizens dispair of seeing a revival of trade in *York*; what has been may be again. We are not without instances of many families, yet in being, who must deduce their present fulness from this source. Whoever will look back into our catalogue of senators, and consider the names of them for about an age last past, will find that many of them raised estates by trade; some to so great a bulk as to give place to very few *London* merchants. The country within a few miles round us gives proof of this; nor need I do more than mention the names of *Agar*, *Robinson*, *Brearey*, *Belt*, *Croft*, *Hewley*, *Allenson*, *Jaques* of *Elvington*, *Brook* of *Ellenthorp*, *Metcalf* and *Thompson* to confirm it.

I come next to consider the state of the city, in regard to its number of inhabitants, both antiently and now; their manufactures, method of living, price of provisions, *&c.*

I shall not take upon me to carry the reader so far back as the *Saxon Heptarchy*; under which our city was the capital of the *Northumbrian* kingdom, by far the largest district of them all. Nor do I pretend to give the state and number of its inhabitants in those days, which must have been very considerable both for number and quality, in a place where the regal power always presided. If the (u) quotation in *Leland*'s *collectanea* may be depended on, this city was much too strait for its inhabitants in the times before the conquest; when he says that the *suburbs* were so large as to extend to the villages a mile round it. Whatever it was then, it is certain the blow it received from the conqueror crushed it extreamly; nor has it ever since raised its head (x) to the port it bore before that thorough devastation. A general destruction must have fallen on the rest of the inhabitants when the priests themselves were not spared; for we are told that *Thomas*, made archbishop by *William*, at his coming down to his see found his clergy so scattered, that few or none could be got to perform the sacred service in the cathedral. We find, however, in the space of about fifteen years after this, that our desolated city had begun to creep once more out of its rubbish, and make a tolerable figure. In the book called Domesday, or the general survey of *England*, which was begun to be taken in the sixteenth of the conqueror, and finished, as the book itself testifies, in the twentieth, we have this account of the state of *York* in those days; which I translate in part as follows.

In the city of York *in the time of king* Edward *the confessor, besides the shire of the archbishop, were six shires (y); one of these is wasted in castles.*

In the five shires were one thousand four hundred and eighteen dwelling houses. The archbishop has yet a third part of one of these shires. In these no other person hath custom but the citizens, except Marleswain *in one house which is beneath the castle, and the canons where they inhabit, and except the four judges, to whom the king hath given this gift by patent for the term of their lives.*

But the archbishop in his own shire has all manner of custom.

Of all the aforesaid houses are now inhabited, in the hands of the king paying custom, four hundred and nine great and small; and four hundred houses not inhabited which pay, the better sort, one penny, the others less; and five hundred and forty five so desolate that they pay nothing; and a hundred and forty five which the (z) French *inhabit.*

St. Cuthbert *has one house, which he has always had, as many say, free from all custom; but the citizens say that it was not so in the time of king* Edward, *but as one of their houses, except when the provost had his habitation there with his canons*, &c.

The earl of Moreton *hath here sixteen houses, and two stalls in the shambles, with the church of St.* Crux.

Nigellus de Moneville *hath one house, belonging to a certain* mint-master.

In the shire of the archbishop, in the time of king Edward, *were two hundred dwelling houses; now about one hundred are inhabited great and small, besides the archbishop's palace and the canons houses. In this shire the archbishop hath the same power which the king hath in his shires.*

In the geld of the city are fourscore and four carucats of land, each of which is geldable as much as one house in the city, and in the works of the king they are as with the citizens, &c.

The earl hath nothing in the church manors, nor the king in the manors of the earl, besides what belongs to christianity which is under the archbishop.

In all the lands belonging to St. Peter *of* York, *St.* John, *St.* Cuthbert, *St.* Wilfrid *and St.* Trinity's, *neither the king, nor the earl, nor any other person hath any custom. The king*

(u) *Constans fama est aliquot villas esse uno ab* Eboraco *milliario, ubi ante tempora* Gulielmi Nothi *termini erant suburbanarum aedium.* Leland. *coll. v.* 4. *p* 36.

(x) *Vide an sub an.* 1066.

(y) Shire from Scypan, *Sax.* to divide. This abstract is printed in *Latin inter* xv *script hist.* Ang. *ed.* Gale. But the whole abstract from this grand record, relating to *York* and the places adjacent, may be seen in the appendix.

(z) Francigene. *vid. ext. ab orig. in appendice.*

has

4

has three highways *by* land, *and a* fourth *by* water (*a*). *In theſe, all forfeitures go to the king and earl, wherever theſe roads ſtretch, either through the lands of the king, the archbiſhop, or the earl.*

Peace given under the king's hand, or his ſignet, if it be broken, amend is made to the king by xii *hundreds, each hundred* viii l.

Peace by the earl given and broken by any one, amend is made to the earl by vi *hundreds, each* viii l.

If any perſon be exiled according to law none but the king can pardon him. But if the earl or high ſheriff baniſh any one, they may recal him and pardon him if they pleaſe.

Only thoſe Thanes *pay relief for their lands to the king who are poſſeſſed of more than ſix manors. The relief is* viii l.

But if he hath only ſix manors, or leſs, he pays to the earl for relief four marks of ſilver.

The citizens of York *pay no relief.*

By this account the reader may obſerve, that before the conqueſt, in the time of *Edward* the confeſſor, this city was divided into ſeven ſhires or diviſions; in five of which are ſaid to be one thouſand four hundred and eighteen manſion houſes inhabited. In the ſhire of the archbiſhop were two hundred more. And for that ſhire which was waſted for the caſtles, if we ſuppoſe as many houſes to have ſtood in it as to make up all two thouſand, we may make a tolerable gueſs at the number of inhabitants in thoſe days. For allowing, as ſir *William Petty* (*b*) computes, five perſons to one houſe, and ten thouſand will appear to have dwelt within the walls of the city at that time. And if we, alſo, allow the ſuburbs to have been of the extent that *Leland* mentions, we may reaſonably ſuppoſe above as many more inhabitants to have reſided in them. The great deſolation that the conqueror brought upon our city is, however, very remarkable by this, for of two thouſand inhabited houſes in it before his time, there were, when this ſurvey was taken, only ſix hundred and fifty; one hundred and forty five of which are ſaid to be inhabited by a colony of *French*, which the *Norman* had probably planted in the houſes of the *Engliſh* he had deſtroyed. The reſt of this grand record being too copious for this chapter, I ſhall beg leave to place it all together in the *appendix*. A curioſity of that exactneſs, that value and authenticknеſs, that not a word of it can, or ought to be, omitted in this work.

It was not long after this that our city muſt have recovered a great ſhare of its former popularity; for if we may be allowed to gueſs at the number of the inhabitants by the number of pariſh churches, hiſtory informs us, that *anno* 1147, in king *Stephen*'s time, a dreadful fire conſumed thirty nine of them, beſides the cathedral and other religious houſes in the city. The number of inhabitants muſt be proportionably great, nor do we want another dreadful teſtimony of it, if our chronicles ſpeak true, when they tell us that in the reign of *Richard* II. *anno* 1390, a raging peſtilence, which then over-ran the kingdom, ſwept out of the city of *York* only, eleven thouſand perſons.

Since the number of pariſh churches muſt be allowed to be an undeniable inſtance of the populouſneſs of any city or town, I think it neceſſary to give the reader a general view of all that I could ever find to have ſtood in the city of *York*. In which liſt I ſhall put down the yearly value of thirty nine of them, as they were given in upon oath to the king's commiſſioners, for levying a ſubſidy granted by parliament of two ſhillings *per* pound on all ſpirituals and temporals in the realm, *temp. Hen.* V. for carrying on the *French* war. To theſe I ſhall ſubjoin a liſt of all the chapels, hoſpitals, *maiſon-dieus*, &c. and conclude with the abbies, monaſteries and other religious houſes; which when all were ſtanding muſt have made a great glare in this city. Nor can it be denied that our fore-fathers had much more piety than their ſucceſſors, unleſs it be proved that there is as much religion in pulling down churches, as erecting of them.

A general liſt of all the PARISH CHURCHES *that were ſtanding in the city and ſuburbs of* York *in the time of* Henry *the fifth, with their yearly value* (*c*).

	l.	*s.*	*d.*
1. *Allhallows* in the *Pavement*, *valet per an.* — —	ix		
2. *Allhallows* near *Fiſhergate* — — — —	i		
3. *Allhallows* in *North-ſtreet* — — — —	viii		
4. *Allhallows* in *Peaſeholm* — — — —	iii		
5. St. *Andrew's* — — — — —	iii	vi	viii
6. St. *Clement's* in *Foſs-gate* — — — — —	i		

(*a*) Sir *T. W.* ſuppoſes this to be *Lendall*, but I take it to be the whole courſe of the river. The other high roads mentioned, muſt be the old *Roman* roads, or ſtreets, leading to the city.

(*b*) *Political arithmetick.*

(*c*) *Ex regiſtro in Cam. ſup. pontem Uſæ.*

Some of theſe, if they were given in at full value, may be ſaid to be very ſmall ſtipends for parochial prieſts; but the chantries made them amends, as well as ſeveral other benefactions not known in our days. Yet it is to be noted that according to the value of money then and now, as the author of the *Chronicon Pretioſum* remarks that five pound in *Henry* the ſixth's days was equal to and would have bought as many neceſſaries of life as thirty pound will do now, it alters the caſe, and makes ſome of theſe livings very conſiderable.

	l.	s.	d.
7. St. *Cuthbert*'s in *Peaseholm*	ii		
8. St. *Crux*, or *Holy-cross*	ix		
9. *Christ Church*, alias St. *Trinity's*	viii		
10. St. *Dyonis*	vii		
11. St. *Hellen* on the Wall	ii		
12. St. *Hellen* out of *Fisher-gate*	i		
13. St. *Hellen* in *Stone-gate*	vi		
14. St. *Edward*	i	vi	viii
15. St. *Gregory*'s	ii		
16. S. *Giles*.			
17. St. *George* at *Bean-hills*	iv		
18. St. *George* in *Fisher-gate*.			
19. St. *John de la Pyke*	iv		
20. St. *John* in *Hungate*	i		
21. St. *John* Evangelist at *Ouse-bridge* end	viii		
22. St. *Laurence*	ix		
23. St. *Mary* without *Lathorp* postern	ii		
24. St. *Mary Bishop-hill*, sen.	x		
25. St. *Mary Bishop-hill*, jun.	vi		
26. St. *Mary* in *Castle-gate*	vi		
27. St. *Margaret*'s	vii		
28. St. *Martin* in *Micklegate*	vi		
29. St. *Martin* in *Conyng-street*	x		
30. St. *Maurice*	ii		
31. St. *Michael de Belfray*	xii		
32. St. *Michael* in *Spurrier-gate*	x		
33. St. *Nicholas* by *Micklegate-bar*	vi		
34. St. *Nicholas* without *Walm-gate*	v		
35. St. *Olave* in *Mary-gate*	xxiv		
36. St. *Peter* in the Willows	i		
37. St. *Peter* the little	vii		
38. St. *Saviour*'s	viii		
39. St. *Sampson*'s	viii		
40. St. *Trinity*'s, *Gothram-gate*	iv	xiii	iv
41. St. *Wilfrid*'s, *Blake-street*	v		

To these may be added,

* St. *Benedict* in Patrick-Pool, St. *Stephen*, a church mentioned in *Dug. Mon. Ang.* vol. I. p. 385. S. *Bridget*, *Mon. Ang.* vol. I. p. 564. said to be in Pucclegata. St. *Michael*, *extra Walmgate*. Mr. *Torre*.

CHAPELS before the dissolution of them, temp. Hen. VIII. *in the city and suburbs.*

1. (*d*) St. *Ann*'s at *Foss-bridge*.
2. St. *Ann*'s at *Horse-fair*.
3. St. *Trinity*'s in the *Bedern*.
4. St. *Christopher*'s.
5. St. *Christopher*'s at the *Guild-hall*.
6. St. *Catherine*'s in *Haver-lane*.
7. Bishop's chapel in the fields near *Clementhorp*.
8. St. *George*'s chapel, betwixt *Foss* and *Ouse*.
9. St. *James*'s without *Micklegate*.
10. St. *Mary*'s chapel in St. *Mary*'s abbey.
11. St. *Mary*'s chapel at the *White-fryars*.
12. St. *Mary*'s chapel in St. *Mary-gate*.
13. St. *Mary Magdalene*'s near *Burton-stone*.
14. St. *Stephen* in the *Minster*.
15. St. *Sepulchre*'s near the *Minster*.
16. St. *Trinity*'s chapel at the *Merchant's-hall*.
17. St. *William*'s chapel on *Ouse-bridge*.

HOSPITALS, &c. *before the reformation.*

1. The hospital of our *Lady*, *Horse-fair*.
2. The hospital of St. *John* and our *Lady* in *Foss-gate*.

* The vacant place where this church once stood, butted and bounded, was granted to *W.* archbishop by king E. III, for the use of the vicars choral. See the appen.

(*d*) *Ex MS.*

These being all chantry chapels fell at the suppression, and are all extinct except two, one belonging to the vicars choral in the *Beddern*; and the chapel at *Merchant's* hall still kept up by that company.

3. The

3. The hospital of St. *Leonard*; now the *Mint-yard.*
4. The hospital of St. *Anthony* in *Peaseholm.*
5. The hospital of St. *Nicholas*, without *Walm-gate.*
6. The hospital of St. *Thomas* without *Micklegate-bar.*
7. The hospital belonging to the *Merchant's-hall.*
8. The hospital of St. *Catharine* besides St. *Nicholas* church.
9. The hospital or *Maison Dieu* of the Shoe-makers near *Walmgate-bar.*
10. The hospital or *Maison Dieu* on *Ouse-bridge.*
11. The hospital or *Maison-Dieu* at the *Taylor's-hall.*
12. The spital of St. *Loy* at *Monk-bridge* end.
13. The spital of St. *Catharine* without *Micklegate-bar.*
14. The spital of . . in *Fisher-gate* besides St. *Helens.*
15. The house of St. *Anthony* in *Pease-holm.*
16. The house of St. *Anthony* in *Gilly-gate.*

ABBEYS, PRIORIES, MONASTERIES and other RELIGIOUS HOUSES formerly in York.

1. The abbey of St. *Mary's. Black-fryars, or Benedictines.*
2. The abbey, or monastery, of St. *Augustine. Austin-fryars.*
3. The abbey, or monastery, of the *Franciscans*, or *fryars minors. Grey fryars.*
4. The priory of the holy *Trinity. Benedictines.*
5. The monastery of the fryars *Carmelites. White-fryars.*
6. The college of St. *William.*
7. The priory of St. *Andrew. Gilbertines.*
8. The monastery of *nuns* at *Clementhorp. Benedictines.*
9. The monastery of the *fryars preachers. Dominicans.*

Whoever considers the foregoing catalogue, must allow our city to have been as remarkable for churches and houses of religion formerly as most in the kingdom. I shall be more particular about them when I come to the places where they once stood. It cannot be denied that after the dissolution of the religious houses here, as well as in other places, by king *Henry* VIII. with the chantries, chapels, hospitals and other houses for the sustenance of the poor, that this famous and then flourishing City did not receive a terrible shock by the tearing up of those foundations. Notwithstanding the politick institution of the new council erected for the northern parts, which was in some measure designed to put a stop to a depopulation then really expected to be the consequence. I know I shall be censured as arguing like a downright *papist* in this, but since it is matter of fact, I value not the imputation; for king *Henry* was scarce cold in his grave when this became but too remarkable. Of forty two parish churches, three or four famous abbeys, two priories, a nunnery, and a religious college, with seventeen private chapels, and eighteen hospitals, which had reigned here in great plenty and abundance for some ages, there was not so much left, in these depredations, as to sustain and keep up little more than half the number of parish churches, two or three of the hospitals, and a chapel or two at most. Dr. *Heylin* (e) says, "Monasteries and "religious houses may be reckoned as so many excrescences upon the body of the church; "exempt, for the most part, from the episcopal jurisdiction, wholly depending on the "pope, and such as might be taken away without any derogation to the church's power "or patrimony. That bishops being more essential to the constitution of the same, "*Henry* VIII. encreased their number; the wealthier monasteries he turned into episcopal "sees. Where he found a prior and convent he changed it into a corporation of secular "priests, consisting of a dean and prebendaries; and to every new episcopal see he added "a dean and chapter, and to every such cathedral a competent number of choir men and "other offices all liberally endowed and provided for." This account indeed carries the face of a real reformation along with it; but whatever was done in this method in the rest of the kingdom, we have no instances at *York* to verify the doctor's assertion; for no sooner was the word given here, *sic volo sic jubeo*, but down fell the monasteries, the hospitals, chapels and priories in this city, and with them, for company, I suppose, fell eighteen parish churches; the materials and revenues of all converted to secular uses. It is shocking to think how far these depredations were carried, for not content with what they could find above ground, they dug open vaults and graves, in search for imaginary treasure; toss'd the bones out of stone coffins, and made use of them for hog-troughs, whilst the tops went to the covering of some old wall; of which many a one about this city does yet bear testimony. A piece of such inhumanity as I believe the most savage nation in the world would not have been guilty on. For the lucre of half a pound of brass they would deface the most memorable inscription. And carried their zeal so far against *mass-books, rituals, missals* and the like, that with them were destroyed many of our ancient *english historians*. In short, we should not have had one of those venerable remains of our forefather's actions,

(e) *Heylin's* history of the reformation.

perhaps,

perhaps, at this day left us, if an act of parliament in the beginning of Queen *Elizabeth* had not put a stop to these violent proceedings.

In this manner was the *Reformation* carried on in the north of *England*; wherein the power given was abused in such sort, that it is a shame to think, that our most excellent church should have its origine deduced, or its restauration take date, from such execrable times. What an alteration was made in the face of things at *York*, may be guessed by the number of fine buildings which then lay in ruin; but that was not the greatest evil, for by turning out the lazars, sick and old people out of hospitals, priests and nuns out of religious houses, to starve or beg their bread, the number of poor and helpless objects must have multiplied exceedingly in the city, and made their case very deplorable. That this *Reformation* went so far here as, almost, to put a stop to all religion; that trade and merchandize suffer'd extreamly by it; that the city and suburbs were, in a manner, depopulated; needs no other confirmation than that of a preamble of an act of parliament which was obtained for the relief of the inhabitants in the very first year of king *Edward* the sixth. Which undeniable authority being an evident proof of what I have before asserted, I shall beg leave to give in its own words as follows:

(*f*) **Whereas in the ancient city of York, and suburbs of the same, are many parish churches, which heretofore, the same being well inhabited, and replenished with people, were good and honest livings for learned incumbents, by reason of the privy tithes of the rich merchants, and of the offerings of a multitude, which livings be now so much decayed by the ruin and decay of the said city, and of the trade of merchandize there, that the revenues and proffits of diverse of the same benefices are at this present not above the clear yearly value of six and twenty shillings and eight pence, soe that a great sort of them are not a competent and honest living for a good curate, yea and no person will take the cure, but of necessity as some chauntry priest or els some late religious person being a stipendary, taken and appointed to the said cure and benefice, which for the most part are unlearned and very ignorant persons not able to doe any part of their dutys. By reason whereof the said city is not only replenished with blind guides and pastors, as alsoe the people much kept in ignorance as well of their dutys towards God as alsoe towards the king's majesty and commonwealth of this realm, and to the great danger of their souls.**

In consideration whereof, and for the better relief and order of the said city, &c.

The whole act is too long to insert here, and though most of the churches were pulled down, according to the tenure of it, yet the statute was not put in full execution till the twenty eighth of *Elizabeth*; when the lord archbishop, as ordinary, the lord-mayor and six aldermen, as justices, met by virtue of this statute, and agreed that these parishes following should be united and joined to others, which was performed accordingly.

(*g*) St. *Peter* the little to *Allhallows* in the *Pavement*.

St. *Hellen* on the wall
St. *Mary* without *Lathorp* postern
Allhallows in *Peaseholm* } to St. *Cuthbert*.

St. *George* at *Beanhils* to St. *Dyonis*.

St. *Hellen* out of *Fisher-gate*
Allhallows within it } to St. *Lawrence*.

St. *Clement's* to St. *Mary* the elder *Bishop-hill*.

St. *Peter* in the Willows to St. *Margaret's*.

St. *Gregory's* to St. *Martin's* in *Micklegate*.

St. *Edward* to St. *Nicholas* without *Walmgate-bar*.

St. *Giles* in *Gilly-gate* to St. *Olave*.

St. *John* in *Hungate*
St. *Andrew* } to St. *Saviours*.

St. *John del Pyke* to St. *Trinity's* in *Gutbram-gate*.

St. *Nicholas* to St. *Trinity's* in *Mickle-gate*.

St. *Wilfrid* to St. *Michael de Belfrays*.

St. *Hellen's* church in *Stone-gate* was also demolished, but was rebuilt, as will be shewn in the sequel.

To make some amends for the great devastation which befel our city in this age, the court of the lord president of the north was erected in it. It was first set up by king *Henry* VIII. *anno* 1537, and the twenty eighth year of his reign. *Thomas* duke of *Norfolk* first lord president. I shall be more particular in giving the nature of this commission in the chapter designed for it; but as the power of this court was to hear and determine all causes on the north side *Trent*, the great concourse of people that must necessarily resort to *York* on this occasion, must have been an extraordinary advantage to the city. I shall not take upon me to dispute whether it was any advantage to the rest of the kingdom, or whether the royal prerogative was not stretched too far in the erecting of such a court; it was most certainly very beneficial to the city in particular, nor was it ever so far legally dissolved as to have the sanction of the three estates for abolishing of it. After the restau-

(*f*) *Stat. an. reg. Ed.* VI. 1°.

(*g*) *Ex* original. in *Cam. sup. pont.* Usae cist. 1°.

restauration of king *Charles* II, several petitions were presented to the king and council for re-erecting of this court, by the gentlemen of this county, assembled at quarter sessions and assizes. Nor were the citizens backward in petitioning for what they knew so much to their interest, but without effect; for the king and council were afraid of stirring into this affair, and lord chancellor *Clarendon* would by no means promote it, having himself been a great stickler against it, as several of his speeches extant in *Rushworth* do testify. The petition from the city for the re-establishing this court signed by the mayor and aldermen, citizens, *&c.* is so much to my present purpose that I beg leave to give it as follows;

To the KING's most excellent majesty.

(*h*) The humble petition of the mayor, aldermen, and other inhabitants of the city of *York* and county of the same.

Humbly sheweth,

THAT the petitioners though wasted by the late troubles forget their miseries when your sacred majesty their dread sovereign returned to reign over them in mercy and justice, not doubting but to find your majesty gratiously inclined to restore their just and vital liberties which the late times had robbed them of.

That of all other their sufferings, they are most deeply sensible of the suspension of the late court of presidency of the north, erected and continued under your royal predecessors for above one hundred years past, whereby your petitioners and their ancestors were refreshed with the streams of justice flowing down to their doors by a speedy and easy administration of it. Which was many times promised by our late sovereign your royal father of ever blessed memory to be restored, in confidence whereof, your majesty's supplicants by their petition for reasons therein mentioned, signed by the several grand juries for the northern counties above twelve months since, humbly addressed themselves to your majesty for the re-establishing the said court, so much conducing to the ease, benefit and security of these parts; which petition your majesty was gratiously pleased not only to refer but to recommend to your house then sitting, and a committee was appointed to consider and report their opinions, who report that the said court was only suspended, and that against the benefit of the county.

That the other weighty affairs of the parliament did not suffer them to proceed in re-establishing the same, so that your petitioners ought to be dashed to the utter dejection of their spirits, but that in their present extremities they have recourse unto your majesty's grace and goodness.

Therefore they humbly pray in regard the said court is not taken away, but the proceedings there only suspended, that it may gratiously please your sacred majesty, out of your princely wisdom, to appoint a president and court, that they may be restored to their former ease and plenty, and the peace and safety of the country provided for by the wonted care of the presidents, that, as formerly, justice may flow down like a stream from your majesty, the fountain of justice, upon the heads of your petitioners.

signed

HENRY THOMPSON, mayor, *&c.*

It must be allowed that our city had somewhat more than a limb lopped off by the dissolution of this court, and therefore they could not be blamed for petitioning so warmly for its re-establishment. Their trade was then every day decreasing, and they were ready to grasp at any advantages to save themselves from utter ruin. It is well known that what has raised the city of *London* to such a mighty overgrown bulk, was not trade alone; no, if it had not been aggrandized by other means the city walls and antient suburbs might now have been sufficient to contain the inhabitants. The almost constant *residence* of the *royal family* in their neigbourhood, the *courts of justice*, *frequent parliaments*, and, what is above them all, the *three grand companies*, must necessarily engage a vast concourse of people to attend them; all of which especially the last, have greatly conduced to swell it to the enormous size we see it at this day.

In the year 1652, or thereabouts, I find that a petition was preferred to the then parliament by the northern gentry and inhabitants, for making *York* an university. (*i*) *Rushworth* from whom I copied this petition mentions not a word how it was received. It is more than probable that it was not taken any notice of, for at that time they were beginning to discourage learning, and were so far from thinking it necessary to begin a foundation of a new university, that the two old ones were thought too burthensome and too injurious to the spiritual notions the sectaries were then about to introduce. The petition itself being extraordinary, and no where else to be met with than in the aforesaid author, claims a place in this work.

(*h*) *Ex cop. in cam, sup. pont.* Use.

(*i*) *Rushworth's* collect. v. 5.

To

To the honourable the lords and commons assembled in parliament.

The humble petition of the inhabitants of the county and city of *York*, and of the northern parts of the kingdom of *England*,

Sheweth,

THE earnest and humble desires of the said petitioners, that by the justice, wisdom and favour of this high and honourable court, there may be liberty granted, and some means allowed and appointed for laying the foundation of an university, college or colleges within the city of YORK, *for the education of scholars in arts, tongues and all other learning, that may render them fit for the discharge of the ministerial function in the church of God; to the glory, honour, and advantage of these parts of the kingdom; in which desire, that your petitioners may not seem rash and unreasonable, they offer these ensuing considerations.*

First, *that howsoever the kingdom enjoys the benefit and blessing of two most famous universities, which as they are so, we still hope they shall continue the glory of* Europe, *yet we humbly conceive that they are not commensurable to the largeness and necessity of the kingdom, which appeareth by the deplorable want of a learned and faithful ministry in very many congregations, which, for want of scholars or choice of schools, are betrayed to the ignorance of illiterate men, through whom the sad proverb is fulfilled upon us, the* blind lead the blind, and both fall into the ditch.

Secondly, *as we the inhabitants of the northern parts of this kingdom find our share in this common want and calamity to be very great, insomuch that we have been looked upon as a rude and barbarous people, in respect of those parts which by reason of their vicinity to the universities, have more fully partaked of their light and influence, so we cannot but be importunate in this request; in which if we may prevail we hope it will be a special means of washing from us the stain of rudeness and incivility, and rendring of us to the honour of God and this kingdom, not so much inferiour to others in religion and conversation.*

Thirdly, *We humbly declare that many of us who would gladly offer our children to the service of the church of God, in the work of the ministry, and should hope to accomplish our desires, if a cheaper and more convenient way of education, in point of distance, was allowed us; but we cannot fulfil our wishes in that behalf in regard to the distance and dearness of the southern universities, whose charge we are by continual impoverishments rendered daily more unable to bear.*

Fourthly, *We cannot but apprehend it very necessary not only to the good of these parts, but to the peace and happiness of the whole kingdom, that all possible care be had of reforming the northern parts, now abounding with popery, superstition, and profaneness, the fruits of ignorance; that they may not remain a seminary or nursery of men fit to be instruments of any irreligious or unreasonable design for the overthrow of religion and liberty, which reformation cannot be expected without a learned and painful ministry, which we almost despair of being supplied with from the south, whither we send many scholars, but find* vestigia pauca retrorsum, *and those for the most part such as others have refused.*

Fifthly, *We humbly represent* YORK *as the fittest place for such a work in regard of its healthful situation, cheapness of victual and fuel, (which however by the late and present pressures upon the country now grown dearer, we hope shall recover the former rate and plenty, if God shall vouchsafe us the blessing of peace) some good degree of civility, the convenient distance of it from the other universities and the borders of the kingdom, the advantage of a library, which is there already, and convenient building for such an use.*

Upon these considerations your petitioners humbly desire that the foundation of so good a work, though the revenues of the archbishoprick, dean, dean and chapter, be disposed of to other publick uses, this high and honourable court would be pleased to allow and appoint that place which is commonly called the Bedon, *now a college of vicars choral and singing men, with the maintenance belonging to that corporation, as also what other revenues they in their favour shall think fit. And we doubt not but by the blessing of God, the diligence and bounty of men, well affected to religion and learning, this work may be brought to such perfection as may tend very much to the honour of God, the happiness and advantage, not only of these northern parts, but of the whole kingdom.*

This petition needs no farther comment, than to say that had it been complied with, and the place and revenue appointed according as it requests, it probably might have given rise to a northern university at *York*; which all that know it must agree to be incomparably well situated for that purpose. But to proceed, I shall next enquire what encouragement has been given by our magistrates to the establishing manufactures of any kind in *York*, whereby the poor of the city, now a great burthen to it, might be rendered useful to the community.

And here I am sorry to have occasion to say that those very grants and concessions, which the beneficence of succeeding monarchs have conferred upon this city, by charters, patents, &c. and which no doubt were originally designed for the good and service of it, should have almost proved its ruin. Our magistrates have been too tenacious of their privileges,

vileges, and have for many years last past, by vertue of their charters, as it were locked themselves up from the world, and wholly prevented any foreigner from settling any manufacture amongst ahem; unless under such restrictions as they were not likely to accept of. The paying a large sum of money for their freedoms, with the troublesome and chargeable offices they must after undertake, would deter any person of an enterprising genius, in regard of manufacture, from coming to reside at *York*. I have been told, how true I know not, but it is probable that when the *French* protestants came over, a colony of them was offered to be settled in this city, which the wisdom and foresight of our then magistrates prevented. I have somewhat better authority for another remarkable instance of their steady adherence to their charter laws, which was that the late famous Mr. *Clayton* of *Leverpool*, who raised the *tobacco trade* in that town to the greatest height it ever was at, in his first beginning of business offered to settle at *York*; if the citizens would let him and his followers in, without tying them all down to their usual restrictions. This story came from the late archbishop *Dawes*, who had it from Mr. *Clayton* himself, when he was bishop of *Chester*. Of what infinite service these two establishments would have been to the city at this day I shall leave to the readers judgment.

Of late years, *viz.* 1708, a small number of publick spirited citizens made a joint stock, with the concurrence of the then lord-mayor, and set up a woolen manufacture for working in the *Coventry* and *Norwich* manner, all sorts of stuffs, calimancoes, camlets, &c. This was actually set on foot and carried on for a few years, and the poor employed in spinning, &c. but it all came to nothing; and chiefly, as I have been informed, by the small number of foreigners the city would admit on this occasion; and they also being men of no substance.

But the magistrates and citizens of *York* have it in their power, by a joint concurrence, to lay the foundation of an establishment of this kind, which would be of infinite service to them all. It is well known that there is a great deal of excellent land lies round the city, over which the poor freemen of each ward have a particular stray for their cattle from *Michaelmas* to *Lady-day*. This was originally designed for the good of the poorest sort of citizens, which it really does not effect; for alas, they are not possest of any cattle for that purpose. It is only a midling sort as I may call them which reap the benefit of this stray, which, if it was taken from them, would be no real damage, but make them mind their shops the better, and not depend upon getting a livelihood by lending horses, &c. But what a noble foundation would here be for erecting a workhouse, and providing a stock of hemp, flax, &c. for setting the poor on work? The advantage such a large parcel of choice land would gain by taking off the stray, would be a fund of some thousands a year for that purpose. And, if the magistrates would at the same time soften the rigour of their charter, and invite some handicrafts to come and reside amongst them, I doubt not but in a few years the populousness of this city would be again restored, the poor tax laid aside, and no wretch so miserable as to be obliged to gain a living by begging in the streets.

This project is not new; it has been often attempted to procure an act of parliament to this purpose; and a year or two ago a petition from the city was presented to the house, praying leave to bring in a bill to that end. But an unhappy division arising amongst the citizens about it, it was thought proper to drop the design, and prosecute it no farther. Till this desireable point is gained, there is small hope that any thriving manufacture will be carried on amongst us; but the citizens left, as they have been for several years last past, to live upon one another. For I may safely say that, except some few wine merchants, the export of butter, and some small trifles not worth mentioning, there is no other trade carried on in the city of *York* at this day.

What has been, and is, the chief support of the city, at present, is the resort to and residence of several country gentlemen with their families in it. These have found, by experience, that living at *York* is so much cheaper than *London*, that it is even less expensive than living at their own houses in the country. The great variety of provisions, with which our markets abound, makes it very easy to furnish out an elegant table at a moderate rate. And it is true yet what *Fuller* said of us in his time, *that an ordinary at* York *would make a feast in* London (*k*). Besides our city is very well qualified for the education of their children, especially females, in all the necessary accomplishments belonging to that sex. The diversions which have been of late years set on foot, and are now briskly carried on every winter in the city, are another great inducement to bring company to it. About twenty years ago a weekly assembly was begun here, where gentlemen and ladies met every *Monday* night to dance, play at cards, and amuse themselves with the other innocent diversions of the place. It was first set up at the *Manor*, was several years kept in the lord *Irwin*'s house in the *Minster* yard, and is now continued in the room built on purpose for it in the new buildings. Two or three years ago a musick assembly was began in *York*, and is contined every *Friday* night, in the same room, where a set of choice hands and voices are procured to divert the company each winter. To these are added a company of stage-players, who by subscription, act twice a week, and are al-

(*k*) *Fuller*'s worthies.

lowed

lowed to be the best strollers in the kingdom. All these diversions are had at a most moderate expence, *Monday* assembly being half a crown, musick a crown, and plays were fifteen shillings, which added together makes but one pound two shillings and six pence, the whole charge of a quarter of a year's polite entertainment in *York*.

Twice in the year the assizes, or general goal delivery for the city and county of *York*, are held here. On which occasion, besides the men of business, did formerly resort a great number of our northern gentry to partake of the diversions that were usually set up in the city for that time. Of late years this is altered; and the grand meeting of the nobility and gentry of the north, and other parts of *England*, is now at *York* in or about the month of *August*; drawn thither by the hopes of being agreeably entertained, for a week, in horse-racing, balls, assemblies, *&c.* It is surprising to think to what a height this spirit of horse-racing is now arrived in this kingdom; when there is scarce a village so mean that has not a bit of plate raised once a year for this purpose. *York* and its neighbourhood have been long famous for this kind of diversion; for *Camden* mentions a yearly horse-race to be run on the forest of *Galtres*, where the prize for the horse that won was a little golden bell (*l*). From whence, no doubt, comes the proverb *to bear away the bell.* It is hardly credible, says the antiquary, what great resort of people there is at these races from all parts, and what great wagers are laid upon the horses. But that celebrated author would have been amazed indeed could he possibly have seen one meeting at *York*, or *Newmarket*, on this occasion, in these days. Where the attraction of this, at the best but barbarous diversion, not only draws in the country people in vast crowds, but the gentry, nay even the clergy and prime nobility are mixed amongst them. *Stars*, *ribbons* and *garters* here loose their lustre strangely, when the noble peer is dressed like his groom. But, to make amends for that, view them at night and their splendour returns; and here it is that *York* shines indeed, when, by the light of several elegant lustres, a concourse of four or five hundred of both sexes, out of the best families in the kingdom, are met together. In short the politeness of the gentlemen, the richness of the dress, and remarkable beauty of the ladies, and, of late, the magnificence of the room they meet in, cannot be equalled, throughout, in any part of *Europe*.

These races were first set up *anno* 1709, when a collection was made through the city for purchasing five plates to be run for. *Anno* 1713, the king's gold cup, since changed into one hundred guineas, and given annually to several counties, was procured to be at *York*; where it has ever since continued to be the first plate, and run for on the first day of the week. *Clifton-ings* was for several years the place of trial; but upon a misunderstanding with the owner of that ground, or great part of it, the race was altered; and *Knavesmire*, a common of pasture belonging to the city, was pitched upon for that purpose. It is judged to be the best race in *England* for seeing the diversion; the form of it being a horse-shoe, the company in the midst, can never loose sight of the racers. This diversion, whatever disservice it may do to the country people, by causing them to spend or lose that money that should go to the support of their families, farms, or payment of their rents, is certainly of great benefit to the city and citizens, by being the occasion that some thousands of pounds are annually spent in it in a week's time. Lodgings for that week are usually let at a guinea a room.

The *royal court*, high *court* of *parliament*, the *court* of the *lord president* of the north, have been long strangers to this city; and we have no hopes of a restauration to us of any of them. Mr. *Lochart*, in his memoirs of the *Scotch* nation before the union, affirms that their commissioners insisted strongly that parliaments should be held in *York*; as a place fitly situated for that purpose. I shall not enquire what made the *Scotch* recede from this demand, so much to their own ease and advantage; the giving up of this article, and several others, being too tender points to treat on; but I must say that if it is found to be no inconvenience to them, it was a great misfortune to *York* to lose it. Since then, I say, that no hopes appears of the aforesaid advantages ever being retrieved to us, our races and the residence of the gentry amongst us, in our present decay of trade, seems to be the chief support of the city. Our magistrates take great care that families of this sort should be encouraged to live here; by allowing of all innocent diversions, and making of publick walks for their entertainment, *&c.* Nay the *Roman Catholick* gentry have great liberties allowed them in *York*; which, with the cheapness of the place, has drawn many families of good repute to inhabit with us. Our streets are kept clean, and lighted with lamps, every night in the winter season; and so regular are the inhabitants, to their hours of rest, that it is rare to meet any person, after ten or eleven at night, walking in them. We now reckon forty two gentlemen's coaches, twenty two hackney coaches, and twenty two hackney chairs, to be in full exercise in the city; and it will be no vanity in me to say, that though other cities and towns in the kingdom run far beyond us in trade, and the hurry of business, yet, there is no place, out of *London*, so polite and elegant to live in as the *city of* York.

The native inhabitants of *York* are a civil sort of people; courteous enough to strangers, when they are acquainted a little, but shy enough before. The common people are very

(*l*) Britannia. The bell was tied on the forehead of the horse that won, who was led about in triumph.

well made and proportioned; crookedneſs, either in men or women, is a rarity amongſt them. The women are remarkably handſome; it being taken notice of by ſtrangers that they obſerve more pretty faces in *York* than in any other place. The better ſort of tradeſmen live well in their houſes, whether they verify the proverb when they die or no. There being few of them that do not ſit down to as good a dinner, at their uſual hour twelve a clock, as a very top merchant in *London* would provide for his family. Feaſting to exceſs with one another is ſtrongly in uſe at *York*, and indeed all over the north of *England*, but here they have many ſtrange cuſtoms to provoke it. It is for this reaſon and their conſtantly living upon ſolid meat that few of the inhabitants are long lived in *York*; there are not many inſtances of people living to an extream old age in it, notwithſtanding the natural healthfulneſs of the ſituation. The common people ſpeak *Engliſh* very ill; and have a ſtrange affected pronunciation of ſome words, as *hooſe*, *mooſe*, *coo*, for *houſe*, *mouſe*, *cow* and ſo on. But whatever they do in ſoftning the ſound of theſe words they are equally broad in the pronunciation of others. Dr. *Hickes*, in his *Theſaurus linguarum ſepten.* has given us a ſpecimen of the *Engliſh* language as it was wrote and ſpoke about the year 1395; this I ſhall beg leave to copy, becauſe our city and their way of ſpeaking at that time is mentioned in it. If they ſpoke or wrote worſe than this ſpecimen, it was bad indeed, but that they did not I ſhall make appear by a proclamation for the price of victual in *York*, about the ſame time as the former date, which I have extracted out of one of the city's regiſters. And firſt the doctor.

(*m*) All the longage of the Northumbers and eſpecialiſch at York is ſoe ſcharp ſlitting and frotting and unſchape, that we ſoutherne men may that longage unethe underſtonde. I trowe that is becauſe that they beeth nyh to ſtraunge men and nations that ſpeketh ſtraungeliche, and alſoe becauſe the kynges of Engelond wonheth alway far from that cuntrey, &c.

Proclamation for price of victayll yn Thurdſday market. Anno reg. R. II. xvi. 1393.

For als mykill als proclamation ofte tymes has been made here, als it ys the cuſtome of this cite, that pultre, wildefoule, and other vytayll that is broght hider to be ſalde, be ſalde in thys maner, that ys for to ſay, &c. And that vytaylls that are noght enfraunchess, from the tyme that they come within the precincte, and wythyn thys foreſayd fraunchese that thay bryng yt hider holy to this the kynges marketh here to be ſalde at the price that ys aforeſayd, and that none of the foreſayd vytayll be withdrawn nauther into ſhoppe, ne houſe, ne elſewhere, bot playnly into this marketh, here to be ſalde to every man that will buy it, opon the price abovenſayd, o payn of forfeiture of the ſame vytayll, and on the peril that falls thar opon, And that none be ſoe hardy as to by no manner of vytayll beforeſayd, before tyme that ſex by ſtryken open the common bell at Ouſebrygg, opon the payn abovenmentioned. And that cukes and regratours keep thayr tyme of byynge, als thayre conſtitutions and governance of thys cite wyll, open payn that falls therefore, they knawe that wele ynogh, that ys to ſay that na cuke be hymſelf, na nane other, by na fleſh, fyſh, na other manner of vytayll, fra evereſang ryng at ſent Mychell kyrk at Uſebryghend, unto the morn that ſtryke at the Mynſter, bot unto the value of xviii d. for dyners for travelyng men. And that na cuke by na manner of vytayll in na place, bot in the market that ys ordeyned tharfore.

I leave theſe two ſpecimens of our antient *Engliſh* tongue to the reader's judgment; for my part, I think the latter more intelligible than the former. I ſhall only obſerve on this head, that as our common people ſpeak bad enough, it muſt at the ſame time be allowed, that the better ſort talk the *Engliſh* language in perfection at *York*. Without the affected tone and mincing ſpeech of the ſouthern people, as well as the broad open accent, and twang, of the more northern.

To gueſs at the number of the preſent inhabitants of *York* I ſhall ſubjoin the following table of births and burials that have happened in it for ſeven years paſt. This is extracted carefully from the ſeveral pariſh regiſters, and I leave it to poſterity to copy after and purſue the method.

BIRTHS and BURIALS in the city of YORK *and ſuburbs, from the* 5th *of* Auguſt 1728, *till the* 5th *of* Auguſt, 1735.

	Births.	*Burials.*
The cathedral		7
1. *All ſaints Pavement*	123	218
2. *Allhallows North-ſtreet*	101	111
3. St. *Crux*	132	159
4. St. *Cuthbert's*	55	80
5. St. *Dennis*	92	106
6. St. *Helen's*	113	122

(*m*) Hickeſii *Theſaurus linguar. ſepten.* t. 2.

	Births.	Burials.
7. St. *John's*	136	173
8. St. *Laurence*	60	77
9. St. *Martin's Conyng-street*	73	110
10. St. *Michael le Belfrey*	310	327
11. St. *Michael Spurrier-gate*	198	216
12. St. *Mary's Castle-gate*	150	221
13. St. *Martin's Mickle-gate*	92	117
14. St. *Mary Bishop-hill* elder	103	117
15. St. *Mary Bishop-hill* younger	57	73
16. St. *Maurice*	55	158
17. St. *Margaret's*	118	147
18. St. *Olave's*	147	181
19. St. *Saviour's*	70	103
20. St. *Sampson's*	188	228
21. *Christ Church*	140	119
22. *Trinity Godram-gate*	143	144
23. *Trinity Mickle-gate*	129	152
Total	2785	3466

The proclamation for the price of victuals puts me in mind of the last article I proposed to treat on before I begun my survey, which was to give some account of the stated price of provisions antiently in this city; and what our markets produce and sell for, in every article of that kind, at this day. The reader will better comprehend this by the following tables, the first of which was the stated price of provisions in *York*, in the time of *Richard* II. when the king and all his court were here; and consequently it must be allowed to be dearer than ordinary. The other is the present value, where I must observe, that notwithstanding the great plenty of some years last past, in corn and other articles, yet it is well known that our markets are risen considerably of late years, especially since the fatal 1721, from which date our landlords began to raise their rents, and their tenants the produce. The difference of the value of money in *Richard* the second's time and now, I leave to the readers judgment.

(*n*) These ordinances for the price of victuals were proclaimed by the advice and consent of our lord the king's justices, as well of one bench as the other, with the barons of the exchequer, when a full court was at *York*, in the sixteenth year of the reign of king *Richard* II. in manner following; *Price of provisions.*

	1393.		*The same provisions sold in the markets at York in the years.* 1732.			1735.			
	s.	*d.*	*l.*	*s.*	*d.*	*l.*	*s.*	*d.*	
Good bread, made according to the assize, wheaten and of good boulter, four loaves for		i							
Of another sort two loaves, good weight, for		i							
Item, Beer well brewed, good and strong according to the assize, the best sort *per* gallon		i *ob.*	00	02	00	00	02	00	
Another sort *per* gallon		i	00	01	00	00	01	00	*Eight quarts per gallon.*
A third sort two gallons for		i	00	00	06	00	00	06	
Item, Claret wine, *vyn vermeil*, *per* gallon		viii	00	08	00	00	08	00	*Red port.*
All sorts of white wine *per* gallon		vi	00	06	08	00	06	08	*White port.*
And that no person sell wine or beer without the known measure on pain, *&c.* And that none presume to sell mixed or corrupted wines.									
Butchers how they shall sell.									
For a carcase of choice beef, *beauf sovereign*	xx	iv	10	10	00	09	10	00	
For a carcase of the next sort	xiv		08	00	00	07	00	00	
For a carcase of *Scotch* beast, *sovereign*	xii		04	04	00	03	10	00	
A *Scotch* cow	x		03	00	00	02	15	00	
And the other *Scotch* cattle, as well oxen as cows, according as they appear.									
For a carcase of mutton, the best,		xx	01	10	00	01	02	00	
For a worser sort		xvi	01	00	00	00	15	00	
For a carcase of veal, the best	ii	vi	01	06	00	01	01	00	
Another sort	i	vi	01	00	00	00	15	00	
For a lamb		viii	00	12	00	00	08	00	

(*n*) *Ex registro in cam. sup. pont.* Use. *Gallice.*

For

	1393.		*The same provisions sold in the markets at* York *in the years* 1732.			1735.		
	s.	*d.*	*l.*	*s.*	*d.*	*l.*	*s.*	*d.*
For a hog, or pork, the best — —	iii	iv	02	10	00	01	15	00
For another sort — —	iii		02	00	00	01	01	00
In poultry.								
For a capon, the best — —		iv	00	02	00	00	01	09
For a second sort — — —		iii	00	01	06	00	01	01
For a hen — — — —		i *ob.*	00	00	10	00	00	07
For a pullet — — — —		i	00	00	08	00	00	06
For a pig, the best, — — —		v	00	02	00	00	02	00
Another — — — —		iv	00	01	06	00	01	06
For a fat goose — — — —		iv	00	02	00	00	02	00
Item, For a fresh salmon, the largest and best	ii		00	10	00	00	10	00
The other according to their quantities.								
Item, In an inn a horse at hay and straw by night		i *ob.*	00	00	06	00	00	06
And when oats are sold in the market at eleven pence *per* quarter, then in the inn *per* bushel — —		iv	00	02	08	00	02	08
In the old *English* proclamation aforesaid the prices of wild fowl, &c. are given as follows,								
For a pig — — —		iv	00	02	00	00	02	00
For twelve pidgeons — —		iii	00	01	06	00	01	03
For a partridge — — —		ii	00	00	08	00	00	08
For a plover — — —		i *ob.*	00	00	06	00	00	06
For a woodcock — — —		i *ob.*	00	00	10	00	00	09
For a teal — — —		i *ob.*	00	00	09	00	00	09
For twelve field-fares — — —		ii	00	01	06	00	01	06
For twelve larks — — —		i *ob.*	00	00	06	00	00	06
For a wild duck — — —		iv	00	01	06	00	01	06

The assize of wine taken before the mayor and bayliffs in the Guild-hall *by a jury of twelve citizens* anno reg. regis *R.* II. xvi° *who say upon their oaths that,*

French wine.

	French claret.		*Per hogsh.*					
The best new red wine of *Gascoign* at the port of *Kingston* upon *Hull* sells *per* pipe at	xii *marks.*		44	00	00	44	00	00
A second sort — — —	x *marks.*		36	00	00	36	00	00
A third sort — — —	viii *marks.*		30	00	00	30	00	00

Upon which proclamation was made that a gallon of new choice wine of *Gascoigny* should be sold for eight pence a gallon and no dearer, upon the penalty that would ensue.

Boundaries. The antient and present boundaries of the city are the next things which I propose to give; the liberties one way, indeed, stretch to a great extent, since the *weapontack* of the *Ainsty* were added to it. But that district demands a particular chapter, and I shall here only subjoin an account of the city's jurisdiction in regard to its other privileges.

Antient BOUNDS of the city of YORK *taken* anno reg. regis *H.* V. 1.

From the river *Ouse* on the west which is to **Fleet-bridge** against the **Tygel-house** in the *Bishop's-fields*, extending by one ditch there as far as the bridge to the end of *Holgate* town. Thence as far as the outgang in the moor called **Phorkys** moor. Thence beyond **Knaresmires** as far as **Haydale** cross in the way which leads to **Bishopthorpe.** Thence beyond the water of *Ouse* as far as the cross standing against the **Greendikes** in the way leading to *Fulford.* Thence from the river *Ouse* on the north, *viz.* from the bridge in **Le fleting,** which is called *Little-ing*, so extending by the **Dike** and a **Meere** against the **Spittle well,** by the way as far as the abbot of St. *Maries* miln. And thence as far as the **Magdalene Spyttal,** in the high way which leads to *Clyfton.* And so as far as the **Miln** of **John de Roucliff.** And thence as far as the *Watergate* in the outgang upon the moor. And so by the *Meere* as far as the *White stane cross* upon *Astill briggs.* Thence beyond the water of *Fosse* against the water-milns of the abbot of St. *Maries*, extending to the cross upon *Heworth* moor. Upon which moor is a common of pasture, for all the citizens of *York*, in those crosts beyond the **Kennyndykes.** *Item*, From the cross upon *Heworth* moor as far as the **Theef-brigg,** and so extending as far as the cross against the brigge, from beyond St. *Nicholas*

p. 244.

d humble servant Francis Drake. 1736.

THE ASTOR

cholas miln, in the high way leading to *Kexby*. And from that croſs as far as the croſs in the **Greendykes**, and the gallows of St. *Leonard*. Thence to the wooden croſs in the way which leads to **Fulford** againſt **Algarthſike**, and ſo extending as far as the ſpring called **Hawkes well** directly to the water of *Ouſe*; where the citizens of *York* have a common of paſture.

Another boundary taken anno regni reg. *H.* VI. 23.

From the river *Ouſe* on the north as far as a certain bridge in the **Futzing**, called in *Engliſh* **little-ing**; and ſo extending by a *ditch* and a *moor*, againſt the **Spittal-well**, by a way near the *mill* of the abbot of St. *Mary*'s of *York*; and from thence to **Paulyn-ſpittal**, in the highway which leads from the city of *York* to *Clyfton*. And ſo to the mill late of *John Rocliff*, but now of the heirs of ſir *William Ingleby* knight. And from thence by the way to the gallows of the abbot of St. *Mary*'s aforeſaid. And there was antiently a watergate in the outgang which leads to the foreſt of **Galtres** to a certain woodbridge there. And ſo by the moor to **White-ſtain-croſs** upon **Aſtill-briggs**. And ſo by the great ſtone as far as the river of *Foſſe*, deſcending all along by the river on the weſt ſide to the water-mills of the aforeſaid abbot. And from thence beyond the river of *Foſſe* over againſt the ſaid mills on the ſouth extending to a certain place where a croſs of wood ſtands upon *Heworth moor*, overagainſt the way which leads to *Stockton*. And from thence againſt a ſtone-croſs at the weſt end of the town of *Heworth* to **Theef-brigg** as far as the **ſtreet**. And ſo by the way as far as the croſs in the way which leads to *Oſbaldwycke*. And ſo prooeeding in the highway which leads to *Kexby*, overagainſt the bridge beyond the mill of St. *Nicholas*. And ſo returning from the ſaid croſs againſt the ſaid mill by the way leading to the **Greendykes** over againſt the cloſe of the hoſpital of St. *Nicholas* aforeſaid. And from thence to a croſs in the **Greendikes** over againſt the **gallows** of St. *Leonard*. And thence beyond **Tylmyre**, by a certain way leading to the wooden croſs in the way which leads to *Fulford*, againſt **Hall-garthſyke**; and and ſo extending directly to the river of *Ouſe*; and beyond *Ouſe* as far as a certain croſs called **Haydale-croſs** in the way leading from the city of *York* to *Biſhopthorp*. And from thence directly beyond the fields called the **Nun-fields** croſſing **Knareſmire**, to beyond the gallows there ſtanding on the ſouth ſide, as far as the outgang leading to the moor which is called **Horkyſ-moor**; and from thence by a certain rivulet as far as the bridge at *Holgate town* end, deſcending thence by a ditch there on the weſt to **Fleet-briggs**, in *Biſhop-fields*, on the weſt ſide of the river *Ouſe*.

This laſt boundary was rode and agreed unto *anno* 1637, upon a difference then compromiſed betwixt the city and the dean and chapter of *York*, ſays ſir *T. W.* with which, adds he, I was then acquainted. More antient boundaries than theſe may be found in the regiſter books of the city, letter Y, fol. 7: letter B, fol. 185, *&c.*

Before I enter the gates, it will be neceſſary to take a view of the *ſuburbs*, which are no SUBURBS. ways conſiderable at preſent, but have been, if the author in *Leland*'s *collectanea* may be quoted, of prodigious extent; inſomuch as to reach to ſeveral villages now at a miles diſtance from the city. It is certain that they were of much greater extent than at preſent, even before the late civil wars. Sir *T. W.* ſays they amounted to a ſixth part of the city, wherein were many pariſh churches, many fair and ſubſtantial houſes, adds he, but all theſe were conſumed to aſhes with fire *anno* 1644. I have been informed, by good authority, that there was one continued ſtreet of houſes on both ſides from *Micklegate-bar* to the *Mount*; as alſo another uniform ſtreet from *Bootham-bar* to *Cliſton*; likewiſe a long courſe of houſes out of *Walmgate*, which are now moſt of them vaniſhed. I have met with the names of ſeveral ſtreets ſaid to lie *in ſuburbio civitatis* Ebor. now loſt. In the beginning of the reign of *Edward* III. an army of ſixty thouſand men lay at *York* for ſix weeks together, and great part of this vaſt body, according to *Froiſart* (*o*), were quartered in the ſuburbs of the city. All this is evidence enough to prove their great extent, but as I mentioned the ſiege of the city in 1644, entirely reduced it all to aſhes, except a few houſes out of *Micklegate* which were preſerved from deſtruction by the royal fort. Since that time, of carrying on a reformation by fire and ſword, the ſuburbs has in ſome meaſure raiſed itſelf, which I ſhall now haſten to deſcribe along with the pariſh churches, monaſteries, hoſpitals, *&c.* which were antiently, or are at preſent, to be ſeen in it.

(*p*) Out of *Micklegate-bar* runs a fair broad ſtreet well paved on both ſides, which was, this year carried on in a farther pavement for coaches, carriages, *&c.* beyond the *Mount*. The *Mount* I take to have been a *Roman* work; and antiently ſerved for an exteriour for- MOUNT. tification to the city on this ſide, as I have elſewhere noted. In the late civil wars it alſo was made uſe of as an *outwork*; and commanded the road from *Tadcaſter* to the city. On the eaſt ſide this ſtood formerly the chapel of St. *James*, remarkable for being the place ST. JAMES's from which the archbiſhops of *York* begun their walk on foot to the cathedral, at their in- CHAPEL. thronization; the cloth which was ſpread all the way for that purpoſe being afterwards given to the poor (*q*). This being a chantry chapel it fell at the ſuppreſſion. The laſt part of

(*o*) *Vide annales ſub hoc anno.*

(*p*) *Leland* ſays there was a foundation of an hoſpital hard without the very ſide of *Micklegate*, of the erecting of ſyr *Richard* of *York*, mair of *York*, but it was never finiſhed. *Lel. itin.*

(*q*) The dean and chapter met the archbiſhop here

SUBURBS. *The* SPITAL *of St.* CATHERINE.

the foundation of this chapel was razed in this year in making the broad causway already mentioned. The **spital**, or hospital, of St. *Catherine* is on the right hand near the mount; as there are, or have been, several under this denomination about the city, I shall beg leave to explain this for all. **Spital**, or **spittle**, is contracted from hospital; and was an house of entertainment for poor travellers or pilgrims, who could not afford to pay for lodgings in the town. They were therefore usually placed, *extra muros*, on the side of the high road; and this was a *Xenodochium* of that kind. It is kept up and repaired from time to time at the city's expence for an habitation for a few poor widows, but is now hardly worth mentioning on account of its charity. But,

The HOSPITAL *of St.* THOMAS.

The hospital of St. *Thomas*, out of *Micklegate*, was of a nobler foundation; and is a large stone building, yet standing; bounded on the west by a lane antiently called *Beggargatelane*, and fronting to the high street near the bar on the north. Here was the **gild**, or fraternity of *Corpus Christi*; first instituted *November* 6, the thirty seventh of *Henry* VI. In Mr. *Dodsworth*'s collection in the *Bodleian* library v. 129, fol. 148. is this account of this **gild** (*r*).

For a master and six priests called the keepers of the said gild. Which master and keepers be yerely removeable with the octabes of the feast of Corpus Christi, *and have for themseves no allowance nor fees. Neverthelefs they are bound to keep a solempne procession, the sacrament being in a shryne born in the same through the city of* York, *yerely the* Fryday *after* Corpus Christi *day, and the day after to have a solempne mass and dirige to pray for the prosperity of brothers and sisters lyving, and the souls departed; and to keep yearly ten poor folks having every of them towards their lyvings by yere* iii *l.* vi *s.* viii *d. And furth.r they do find eight beds for poor people being strangers, and one poor woman to keep the said beds by the yere* xiii *s.* iv *d. And since the incorporation of the sayd guyld, ther is purchased by well disposed people and given thereto* xii *l.* xv *s.* iv *d.* per annum, *for the yerely keeping of certain obits, and one priest to pray for the souls abovesaid, and other charges by the year* x *l.* xiv *s. And so it appeareth that the charges thereof yerely doth extend above the revenues of the certainty* lv *l.* x *s. and above reparations and other charges which is yerely born by the charity of the brethren and systers of the sayd guyld. Further the said guild was never charged with the payments of first fruits and tenths.* Valet de claro xi *l.* viii *s.* ii *d.*

I have seen and perused the book of the antient statutes of this fraternity, with an inventary of the jewels, riches, ornaments, &c. belonging to the shrine of *Corpus Christi*. To these is added an exact register of all the masters and keepers of this **gild**, with the names of all the brethren and sisters that were admitted of it, taken annually from the year 1408, to 1546. By this it appears that though this **gild** was only incorporated by letters patents bearing date *Novem.* 6. 37 *H.* VI. yet it was begun in the city some years before; as appears by the title of their statutes, *viz. Liber ordinationis fraternitatis corporis Christi fundat. in* Ebor. *per capellanos et alias honestas personas, tam seculares quam regulares, quorum nomina infra specialiter intitulat. incept. anno dom.* M.CCCC.VIII.

It appears by this register that this religious institution was very popular, some hundreds of persons every year being admitted to the fraternity. The ceremony of *Corpus Christi* play, which they were obliged annually to perform, must have been in its time one of the most extraordinary entertainments the city could exhibit; and would necessarily draw a great concourse of people out of the country to see it. Every trade in the city from the highest to the lowest, were obliged to furnish out a pageant at their own expence on this occasion. The history of the old and new testament was the subject they went upon; and each trade represented some particular part, and spoke some verses on the occasion. Many are the orders and ordinancies in the city's registers about the better regulation of this religious ceremony; which was first instituted, I find, by pope *Urban* IV, about the year 1250, and was to be celebrated each year on the *Thursday* after *Trinity sunday*. For the reader's satisfaction I have placed the manner how it was performed here in the *appendix*; and that it was a piece of religious pageantry much esteemed in *York*, is evident from this, that it was acted till the twenty sixth year of queen *Elizabeth* in this city (*s*).

(*t*) *Anno* 1481, *September* 18. there was an indulgence of forty days granted to all, who should contribute their charity towards the relief and sustentation of the fraternity, or guild, of *Corpus Christi*, ordained and founded in the city of *York*. Or for the souls of the said brethren and sisters should say with a devout mind the lord's prayer, and the angel's salutation. Or else yearly with the like devotion visit personally the city on *Corpus Christi* day, or within eight days after; when in great procession the glorious body of our Lord is honourably placed on the shrine and carried about.

in their formalities, whom after they had sprinkled with holy water and thurifyed, he then put off his shoes and so proceeded thence barefoot to the minster, being attended by the clergy and people. Mr. *Torre*.

(*r*) This extract from *Dodsworth* is printed in the first of the additional volumes to the *Monasticon*. Amongst the records in the *tower* are many charters and grants relating to this fraternity. It appears by these that this **gild** was much older than *Henry* VI. For by *pat*. 45. E. III. *p.* 1. *m.* 31. this **gild** was converted into an hospital, when fourteen messuages, seven shops, and xxxii *s.* rent in the city and suburbs were confirmed to it. See also *pat.* 20 *Ric.* II. *p* 2 *m.* 21.

(*s*) City records, see the *appendix*. See also their seal in the print of antient seals belonging to religious houses in *York*.

(*t*) *Ex MS.* Torre, *p.* 204.

This fraternity, ſubſiſting chiefly on the annual charity collected at the proceſſion, and having little lands, it ſtood till the third of *Edward* VI. when an order was made that the lord-mayor, for the time being, ſhould be choſen yearly maſter of the ſaid hoſpital, and the poor folks and beds were to be maintained, found and uſed in the hoſpital, as before time had been accuſtomed *(u)*. SUBURBS.

September 29, 1583. an order of council was made, that Mr. *recorder* (*William Hilyard* eſquire) Mr. *Aſkwith* and Mr. *Robinſon* aldermen, and Mr. *Belt* with proper attornies ſhould go to *Nayburn* and take poſſeſſion of the lands there, and in *Stainforth-bridge* and *Butter-cram* belonging to St. *Thomas*'s hoſpital, and parcel of the late **gild** of **Corpus Chriſti**, according to a deed made by *William Marſh* of *London* eſquire and *Walter Plummer* citizen and *merchant-taylor* of *London* to the ſaid *recorder*, *Aſkwith* and *Belt*, with a letter of attorney in the ſame deed.

I find alſo that in the year 1598, the land rents received by the city belonging to this hoſpital amounted to xxxiii *l.* vi *s.* ii *d.* *(x)*

There is in this hoſpital bed-rooms for twenty four poor people, and ſo many has ſome time been therein; but now, ſays my authority, this year 1683, there are but ten poor widows and no more *(y)*.

There are a few, remarkably, good houſes out of this gate; the beſt is a large, old, brick building near this hoſpital, which has bore, for ſome years laſt paſt, the name of the *Nunnery*. This occaſioned ſome diſaſter to it at the *Revolution*; but was really then, as now, no more than a boarding ſchool for young ladies of *Roman* catholick families, without being enjoined any other reſtrictions than common. The ſite, the gardens, and agreeable walks beyond it, making it very convenient for that purpoſe. NUNNERY.

But in the fields to the ſouth eaſt of this, down a lane called *Beggargate-lane*, near *Skeldergate* poſtern, ſtood once a real nunnery of *Benedictines*, dedicated to St. *Clement* the pope; part of the ruins of the church are yet ſtanding. *The* NUNNERY *of St.* CLEMENT.

It appears by records that *Thurſtan* archbiſhop of *York*, in the reign of king *Henry* I. *anno* 1145, granted to God, St. *Clement*, and to the nuns there, ſerving God, in pure and perpetual alms, the place wherein this monaſtery with other buildings of the ſaid nuns were erected. Together with two carucats of land in the ſuburbs of *York*; twenty ſhillings annual rent iſſuing out of his fair in *York*, *&c.* This was confirmed by the dean and chapter of *York*.

(z) Anno 1284, *Nicholas Poteman* of *Clementhorp*, ſon of *Adam*, granted unto *Agnes* prioreſs of St. *Clements*, and to the nuns there for a *corody* in the ſaid houſe, two meſſuages in **Clementhorpe**, with a toft and a croft, and half an acre of land.

Likewiſe *Bartholomew*, the chaplain, gave to God and the church of St. *Clements* and the nuns thereof, one meſſuage in **Clementhorpe**, rendring yearly to the archbiſhop the rent of three ſhillings, two hens and one pair of white gloves.

(a) Alſo *Gilbert Fitz-Nigel* gave to them all that meadow which lies beneath the nunnery; rendring *per annum* twelve ſhillings. *Mon.* Ang. 1. p. 511.

And *Hugh Murdac* archdeacon of *Cleaveland*, granted to God and the nuns of St. *Clement*, the moiety of his land in *Clementhorp*, which lies under their garden towards **Uſe**, which he held of the fee of the archbiſhop.

William Maleſours granted to them his land with all the buildings upon Bychehill.

John de Gothelande chaplain, gave to the prioreſs and nuns of St. *Clement*'s eight ſhillings annual rent out of two ſhops in **Staynegate**.

Alſo *Maude* late wife of *Thomas Carpenter de Aldburgh*, granted to them all her land in **Laythorpe**, extending from the king's highway as far as the ditch; rendring **haſgable** to the king.

Thurſtan archbiſhop of *York* gave to them one oxgang of land in **Rawode**, alſo the ſervice of *William de Mala-opera*, and ſix ſhillings and eight pence annual rent. *Mon.* Ang. 1. p. 510.

Thomas Maleſours granted to them ſix oxgang of land in **Grimſton**, together with the manſion houſe of that lordſhip. *idem.*

And *Walter de Rydal* and *Eda* his wife gave them two oxgang of land more in **Grimſton**. *idem* 511.

Alice de Stavely granted to theſe nuns the advowſon and appropriation of the church of **Orton**, and two oxgang of land there. *idem.*

William Foſſard jun. gave them all his land in **Munkhate**. *idem.*

And *Thomas Maleſours* gave them all his land **Munkeaid**, extending in length from **Wite-welle** to **Poter-welle** with common of paſture.

Alſo *Thomas Maleſours* gave them one oxgang of land in **Pileſford**.

(u) Ex regiſt Ebor. A. 1549.

(x) Ex MS. penes me.

(y) In the drawer numb. 4. council chamber, *Ouſe-bridge*, are copies of grants of ſeveral gardens belonging to St. *Thomas*'s hoſpital in *Beggargate*.

(x) *Ex chart. orig.*

(a) Now called *Nun-ings.* *N. B.* All theſe charters, or grants, which are not marked to be extracted from the *Monaſticon*, are taken from the *originals* themſelves, yet preſerved in *York*.

Thurſtan

SUBURBS. *Thurstan* archbishop gave them five shillings out of the tithe of his miln in **Monkton** in **Rypon**. *Mon.* Ang. 1. p. 511.

Ralph de Amundevile granted to this nunnery half a mark in silver out of his miln at *Preston* in *Craven*. *idem.*

Archbishop *Thurstan* gave them one acre of land in **Otley**, with the tithe of a certain miln there. *idem* 510.

Thurstan archbishop gave them six perches of land in **Hudewelle**, lying in **Buthehill**, to build them a house for to lodge in; and three shillings rent out of a certain miln, the tithes of another miln, likewise four other milns there. *idem.*

Alexander de Rieval gave them forty acres of land in the territory of **Baxton**, and ten shillings yearly rent. *idem.*

Anno dom. 1304, *Henry Lacy* earl of *Lincoln* granted to the prioress and nuns hereof, six perches of moor-ground in **Ingle-mor-marsh** *juxta* **Swynfleet**.

And *William de Percy* gave them other six perches of moor in **Ingle-mor**.

On the ides of *November* 1269, *W. Giffard* archbishop of *York* granted to these nuns of St. *Clement*'s the appropriation of the church of **Thorp** *super* **Use**, and ordained a vicaridge out of the same *(b)*.

Nicholas Poteman of *Clementhorp* gave them the fourth part of an oxgang in **Thorp-Mallebys**, containing six acres.

Archbishop *Thurstan* gave them the tithes of an orchard and two milns in **Wilton**. *Mon.* Ang. p. 510.

Peter Percy grants to these nuns a spot of ground opposite to their gate. In the additional volumes to the *Monasticon.*

Nicholas the son of *Ernisius ad barram de Walmgate*, also gives lands, *&c.* in **Walmgate.**

All these grants were confirmed by king *Edward* III. in the first year of his reign at *York*. *Cart.* 1 *Ed.* III. *n.* 44. *Mon.* Ang. 511.

Anno 1192, *Geofry* archbishop of *York* gave this monastery of St. *Clement*'s to the abbey of *Godestow*; but the nuns here, who had from their foundation been always in their own choice, refused to obey the order, and appealed to the pope; *(c)* and *Alicia*, then prioress, went to *Rome* for that purpose. Notwithstanding which, the archbishop, setting at nought the appeal, excommunicated the whole sisterhood.

A CATALOGUE of some of the PRIORESSES of St. CLEMENT's.

An.	Prioressæ.	Vacat.	Autoritat.
1192.	*Alicia.*		
1280.	*Agnes de Wyten.*		Steven's *Mon. v.* 2. *p.* 217.
1315.	Dom^na *Constantia Basy* Monialis domus.		*Mr.* Torre.
1316.	Dom^na *Agnes de Methley.*	*per cession.*	*idem.*
	Dom^na *Alicia Lakenham.*	*per mort.*	*idem.*
1396.	Dom^na *Beatrix de Remington.* Monialis domus.		*idem.*
	Dom^na *Margareta de Holtby.*	*per resig.*	*idem.*
	Dom^na *Margareta de la Ryver.*	*per mort.*	*idem.*
1489.	Dom^na *Isabella de Lancastre.*		*idem.*
1515.	Dom^na *Margareta Carre* Monialis domus.	*per mort.*	*idem.*
1516.	Dom^na *Margareta Franklayne* Monialis domus.		*idem.*

Value at the suppression 55 *l.* 11 *s.* 11 *d.* *Dug.*

(d) Mr. *Willis* mentions *Isabel Ward* as the last prioress, who surrendring up the nunnery to king *Henry* VIII. had a pension of six pound thirteen shillings and four pence *per annum* allowed her. Parish church. The church belonging to this nunnery was very antiently parochial; and was together with the inhabitants and parishioners appropriated to the prioress and convent of the house of St. *Clement juxta* Ebor. To which priory *July* 12, 1464. licence was granted to translate the feast of dedication of the said parish church from the feast day of St. *William* yearly, unto the *Sunday* next after the feast of St. *Peter* and St. *Paul*; because the parishioners of this church, of both sexes, were wont to run to the cathedral in great numbers in the feast of St. *William*, and leave their said parish church on that day empty. This church continued to be parochial, till *anno* 1585, it was by authority of the statute made by the first of *Edward* VI. united to St. *Mary*'s *Bishop-hill* the elder, along with its parish of *Middlethorp*, &c.

CLEMENT-THORPE. It appears by these grants and the name of the place, **Thorpe**, commonly called **Clement-Thorpe**, that here was a considerable village formerly; but now, except the miser-

(b) *Ex MS.* Torre, *f.* 27.
(c) Lelandi *coll.* 3. *p.* 320. *Chron.* Benedict. *abb. ed.* Hearne. *p.* 732.
(d) *Willis* on abbies.

able

2

THE ASTOR LIBRARY
NY

p. 249.

P. Monamy delin.

S.r John Lister Kaye

for t

SUBURBS. 1730.

rable ruin of the church, there are not above two houses. In making the works for rendring the river *Ouse* more navigable, a large foundation of *Ashler* stone was dug out of the banks, which had probably been a *key* or *staith*, belonging to this nunnery. These stones, being often seen at low water, have been mistaken for the foundations of a bridge here; which the ground on the other side gives no such testimony of.

LONG WALK.

There being nothing remarkable in the suburbs on the north of *Micklegate-bar*, I shall pass the river at the ferry out of *Skeldergate* postern, where I have the pleasure to land on the opposite side at a fine walk made a year or two ago at the expence of the city. It runs parallel with the river on a piece of ground called St. *George's* close; and doubtless did belong to the chapel of that name which stands near it. It is now in the city's hands, and is of singular use to the good women of the town for drying linen, &c. The city from this side makes so handsome a view that I chose to present the reader with a print of it. This walk, so much conducing to the entertainment and health of the gentry and citizens in fine weather, was principally obtained, planted and laid out, under the care of that worthy zealous citizen, and commoner, Mr. *John Marsden* apothecary.

ST. GEORGE'S CHAPEL.

Contiguous to this piece of ground stood St. *George's* chapel, and *Castle-milns*. The chapel of St. *George* betwixt *Foss* and *Ouse*, was endowed with one messuage and one acre of land in *Standford*, late *William Baston's*. In *Cart. anno* 19 *Ric.* II. *m.* 7. and *Esch. anno* 46 *Ed.* III. *num.* 65. is an inquisition of certain lands and rents belonging to this chapel, *Esch. anno* 30. *Ed.* III. *num.* 68. whether a piece of land called the **Holm** lying betwixt the castle and the river *Ouse* do belong to the said chapel or the city (*e*). The foundations of this chapel, which now support a dwelling house, are very strong; the frequent inundations of the rivers requiring it. Being put upon the foot of a *chantry chapel*, it was suppress'd with the rest. Here was a **Gild**, brotherhood, or fraternity, established, called the *fellowship of St.* George; for I find by *Pat.* 25 *Hen.* VI. *p.* 2. *m.* 7. licence was given for the founding of it.

CASTLE MILNS.

Of the water-mills here sir *T. W.* writes thus, *before the building of the mills which are now called the castle mills, which is not many years since as I have heard, the place where the mills are was a fair green, and the only passage from* Fishergate *postern to the castle, and it was formerly a place used for shooting, bowling and other recreations, and although now, only occasioned by the dam, it seems a great foss, yet it is often dry in the summer time.*

How this account agrees with the present appearance of this ground, I leave to any one that views it. The dam-heads that stop the water for the use of the milns, seem by their strength and manner of building, to have been much older than sir *T.* writes of. For my part I believe there have been milns here some hundreds of years, and sir *Thomas* himself in his next paragraph partly proves it.

(*f*) *In the fourth of* Edw. I. *it is found by inquisition that the templars had a miln near the castle of* York, *which after belonged to the kings of* England. In the reign of *Edw.* II. these milns were let by lease for forty marks a year, which argues them of considerable value (*g*).

In an old grant, *sans date*, in the register of the abby of *Fountains*, the ground is described to lye betwixt the castle milns on one hand, and the ground belonging to this abby on the other. And though this grant be without date, nor can I assign one to it by the witnesses names, yet its being set at the head of their possessions in *York*, makes me judge it to be of great antiquity.

These milns were granted from the crown, but when I know not, and came at last to be settled upon an hospital in *Heslington*; built and endowed by sir *Thomas Hesketh*; the foundation deed is amongst the city's records on *Ouse-bridge*.

ST. ANDREW'S PRIORY.

In the road to *Fulforth* from hence, in a place now called *Stone-wall-close*, stood once the priory of St. *Andrew*; founded, *an.* 1202, by *Hugh Murdac*; who granted and confirmed, in perpetual alms, to God and to the twelve canons, of the order of *Sempringham*, serving God, at St. *Andrews* in *Fisher-gate Ebor.* the church of the same place, with lands adjacent. Also the rent of twenty one marks issuing out of certain houses in *York*. And twenty six marks for the rent of eleven marks and five shillings. Likewise the lands at **Thorp**, and **Gudemadam** (*h*).

Adam Albus gave them twelve shillings rent out of his land in the parish of St. **Laurence** in **Walmgate** westward (*i*).

On the feast of St. *Laurence*, *an. Dom.* 1202. the dean and chapter of *York*, by their deed, granted to the prior and convent of St. *Andrews*, the rent of the two carucats of land in the town of **Cave**, which belonged to their *common*; in exchange for certain lands lying before the west door of the *minster* in *York**.

(*e*) Sir *T. W. commissio ad inquirend. Pat.* 32. *Ed.* III. *p.* 1. *m.* 24. *dorso.*

(*f*) *Inter record. in thesaur. recept. scaccar. in custodia commissionariorum & camerariorum ibidem.*

(*g*) *Molendina regis subtus castrum concess.* Nichol. L. *pro term.* 6. *annor. redd. inde per ann.* xl. *marcas. Fin.* 17 *Ed.* III. *m.* 2.

(*h*) Ebor. *Prior* S. Andreae *de* ii *tostis.* i *molend.* xv *bovat.* xvi *acras &* i. *rodum terrae,* ii *carruc. prati &* vi *s. reddit. in* **Kyrkby in Clyveland, Dromondby, Stokesle, Buskbe,** *& quorum de Jo. de* Eure. *Pat.* 5. *Ed.* III. *p.* 1. *m.* 5. Ebor. *Monast.* S. Andreae *ibidem de ordine* **Sempingham** *pro libert. &c. carta ampla. Pat.* 3 *Ed.* IV. *p.* 3. *m.* 14.

(*i*) *Ex charta origin.*

* *Mon. Ang.* Vol. II. f. 808.

This

SUBURBS. This priory of St. *Andrew* had given it one carucate and two oxgangs of land in [illegible] which were held by the rent of thirteen pence.

(k) The site of this priory, as *Leland* remarks is right against the nunnery of St. *Clement*; which has given rise for a ridiculous notion that there was a subterraneous passage and communication betwixt them. But these idle stories are common to many other such places. The order of *Sempringham* was that of St. *Gilbert*, and this priory was surrendred the 28th of *November* 1538, by the prior and three monks only, says *Heylin*; but the surrender runs in general terms, *by the consent of the whole brotherhood*, as the rest of them do *(l)*. The value at the dissolution was 47 *l.* 14 *s.* 3 *d.* ½ *Dugdale*, 57 *l.* 5 *l.* 9 *d.* *Speed*. See the Seal.

CHURCH of St. ELENE *extra muros.* The street, as well within the old gate as without, is called *Fisher-gate*. And near the further wind-mill where some stone coffins have been lately dug, stood once the parish church of St. Elens or St. *Hellen*. This was an ancient rectory in the patronage of the prior and convent of St. *Trinity* in *York*; from the first foundation of that monastery. Mr. *Torre* has given us a catalogue of the rectors of this church, as also some testamentary burials; which I shall omit. This church was united to St. *Laurence*, *anno* 1585.

ALL-SAINTS FISHER-GATE. Here was another church, *extra muros*, this was called the parish church of *All-Saints* in *Fisher-gate*; but where it stood I know not. It was a very ancient rectory, so old as to be given by king *William Rufus* to the abbess and convent of *Whitby*; upon condition that the monks there should pray for him and his heirs *(m)*.

May 5, 1431. *Robert Wederfell* Cap. made his testament proved *May* 27, 1431, whereby he gave his soul to God almighty St. *Mary* and *All-Saints*. And his body to be buried in the church of *All-Saints* in *Fisher-gate* without the city walls of *York*.

ASSIS-HALL. Higher up in these suburbs, nearer *Walmgate-bar*, stands a dwelling-house which is called now **Assis-hall**. This name gives reason to suppose that here was a building formerly in which the itinerant judges held their *assizes*, before they were admitted into the castle. Tradition also informs us, that they lodged in the priory of St. *Andrew* aforesaid during their stay. Sir *T. W.* is wholy silent as to this, nor can I get any further light into it, the writings which the present possessor has to shew makes mention of no such thing; but they, indeed, are modern *(n)*.

We come now to a street leading from *Walmgate-bar*, which is fair and broad, and is the road to *Hull*, *Burlington*, &c. I find that the ancient name of this street was called **Mat-lingate** *(o)*, which bears a plain allusion to a *Roman* road. And here it must be that those roads begun, which lead to the *Humber*, and some of the ports on the *German* ocean. At the end of this street, which has lately been paved with a noble broad causeway, by the care of *John Stainworth*, esq; then lord-mayor, and which a stone pillar there bears testimony of, was situated the

S. NICHOLAS HOSPITAL and CHURCH. *Hospital*, and parish church of St. *Nicholas*. The church was parochial, an ancient rectory, and had *Grimstone*, &c. in its district. The pile was quite ruined in the siege of *York*, *anno* 1644, and never rebuilt. It has been a noble structure as appears by part of the tower yet standing; and the ancient porch of it, which is now put up in St. *Margaret's* church in *Walmgate*. The three bells belonging to this church were taken down by the soldiers in the aforementioned siege in order to cast into cannon; but the lord *Fairfax* prevented it. They were since, viz. 1653, hung up in St. *John's* church, *Ouse-bridge* end, being the largest there.

The hospital to whom this church was appurtenant was of royal foundation, though it is not so mentioned in *Dugdale*; being of the patronage of the kings of *England*.

(p) *July* 4, 1303. *William de Grenefeld*, lord high chancellor of *England*, in a royal visitation, ordained certain orders and statutes for the well governance of this house; which consisted of a select number of both sexes. These being to be met with in the *Monasticon* *(q)*, and in the *English* abridgment, are unnecessary here, nor shall I mention more than what sir *T. W.* remarks, that *anno* 3 *Ed. I. Escheat.* there is an inquisition of a carucate of land granted to them by *Maud* the empress, upon this condition; that the brethren of the said hospital, for ever, should find to all lepers, which should come to the said hospital in the vigils of the apostles *Peter* and *Paul*, these victuals, that is to say, *Bread* with *Butter*, *Salmon*, *Cheese*.

Where the learned knight got his bread and butter, &c. from, I know not; I took the pains to extract the inquisition from the records in the tower, and there is no mention made of any such thing. The reader will find it at large in the *appendix*.

Valued at the suppression at 29 *l.* 1 *s.* 4 *d.* *Dugd.*

(k) The present possessor of the ground is the reverend Mr. *Fairfax*.

(l) Johannes Leppington, *prior domus sive prioratus* S. Andreae *apost. prope muros civitatis* Ebor. *in com. ejusdem, & conventus, unanimi assensu & consensu, &c. redd. in manum regis dictam domum, &c. Dat. in domo nostra capitulari vicesimo octavo die mensis Novembris anno regni regis* Hen. VIII. 30. *Claus.* 30 Hen. VIII. *pars* 4. *num* 70.

(m) *Mon. Ang.* vol. I. 75. MS. *Torre*, f. 493.

(n) *Temp.* Car. I. it is called in these writings the *Ace house*, in *Foulforth* liberty, with a circumflex, or note of abbreviation, over it. *C. Baldock*, *York*, the present possessor.

(o) Lelandi *coll. Vide annal. sub anno* 1328.

(p) *Exhibit. in visit. istius hospital. per* Wm. de Grenefeld *summum cancellar.* Angliae *recit. est quod fundas erat per praedecessores* Ed. *primi. Confirm. ampla ordin. statut. cart. libertat. et donat. Pat.* 21 Ric. II. *p.* 1. *m.* 31. *in turre* London.

(q) *Mon. Ang.* vol. II. f. 470.

Near

z

Near the ruin of this ancient pile lyes a grave-stone, on the marble of which a priest is delineated in his vestment, with the chalice, and round it this inscription, SUBURBS.

(r) ICY GIST SIR RICHARD DA GRIMSTON IADYS DE STILYNGFLETE PARSON DIEU LUI FAIT MERCY ET PARDON. AMEN. ✠

In turning over the rubbish of the old building this year, for the reparation of the road near it, was found a white grave-stone with this inscription, in the cleanest, deepest black letter I ever met with,

Orate pro anima Johanne Warym sororis istius Hospitalis que obiit xv. die mensis Julii A. Dom. MCCCCLXXXIII. cujus anime propicietur Deus. Amen.

(s) The parish church of St. *Edward* stood a little above the former on the other side of the street. This was also an ancient rectory, of which the archbishops of *York* were patrons, and so continued till 1585, when by the act of union this parish was united to St. *Nicholas.* Mr. *Torre* has given a list of the incumbents of St. *Edward*, with some testamentary burials which I omit to come to a church yet standing, which is the CHURCH of St. EDWARD.

Parish church of St. *Laurence*. This was anciently a rectory appropriated to the common of the dean and chapter of *York*; and esteemed as one of their great farms. And so together with *Fairburn* was usually demised to one of the canons residentiary of the cathedral church at the annual rent of thirty marks. In which this church of St. *Laurence* was valued at 9*l.* 13*s.* 4*d.* At this rent it has since been leased for term of years CHURCH of St. LAURENCE.

November 11. 26 *Eliz.* to *Thomas Harrison.*

March 27. 18 *Jac.* to sir *Rand. Crew:*

November 11. 7 *Car.* I. to *Thomas Hesketh* esq;

(t) A Vicarage was here ordained, and the vicar was endowed with the whole alterage, paying out of it to the chapter of *York* twenty shillings *per an.* And all the residue of the church the canon residentiary had for the rent of twenty marks.

The church of St. *Michael* without *Walmgate-bar* was united to this of St. *Laurence*, *Oct.* 10, 1365. And all and singular the tythes arising out of the places within the same parish with the oblations of the inhabitants thereof, were entirely granted to the vicars of St. *Laurence*, and their successors for ever; paying the annual pension of xiii *s.* iv *d.* to the prior and convent of **Kyrkham** in recompence of the substraction of those tythes and oblations. CHURCH of St. MICHAEL

(u) *John* bishop of *Bath*, and *William* bishop of *Lincoln*, arbitrators between the dean and chapter of *York*, proprietors of this church, on the one part, and the master and brethren of St. *Leonard*'s hospital on the other part, awarded and decreed the tythes of corn and hay growing upon the lands and meadows belonging to the said hospital in **Heslington**, within the parish of St. *Laurence*, perpetually for the future; notwithstanding they were in the proper hands and culture of the said master and brethren, and at their own costs and expences tilled and managed. Dated *London May* 12, 1439.

A decree or arbitrament was made by the archbishop, that the vicar hereof, by reason of the endowment of his vicarage, shall always receive those tythes and oblations arising out of a certain place called **Grene-dykes**, whether within the limits of St. *Mary*, and the chapelries of St. *Olave* and *Fulford*, as the abbot and convent of St. *Mary*'s alledge, or within the precincts of this church of St. *Laurence*, as *Richard* the vicar thereof asserteth of right to belong to him. dat. *Ebor.* *Jan.* 23, 1457.

Anno dom. 1585, *Edwin* archbishop of *York*, with the mayor, recorder and aldermen of that city, according to the statute of the first of *Edward* VI. united and annexed unto this parish church of St. *Laurence*, the churches of St. *Elene* in *Fishergate*, *Allsaints ibidem*, together with the parishoners of them both. Saving to respective patrons their former right of presenting to those churches.

		l.	*s.*	*d.*
The Vicarage of St. *Laurence* is valued in the king's books	first fruits —	05	10	00
	tenths ——	00	11	00

(r) Here lyes sir *Richard de Grimstone* formerly of *Stillingfleet* parson, God grant him mercy and pardon. *Amen.*

(s) South of this hospital is a round hill, known by the name of *Lamel-hill*, on which a wind-mill has stood, from whence it must have took its name. *Lamel-hill* being no more than *Le meul*, the miln-hill, called so by the *Normans.* I take this hill, as several others round the city, to have been originally raised for *Roman tumuli*; though they afterwards served to plant these kinds of mills upon.

(t) MS. *Torre*, f. 323.

(u) *Carta in custodia clerici vestibulis* Ebor. *cum litera* T. *Torre*, f. 394.

A close

SUBURBS.

A close CATALOGUE *of the* VICARS *of St.* LAURENCE.

Temp. instit. Anno	*Vicarii eccl.*	*Patroni.*	*Vacat.*
1316	Dom. *Rog. de Messington.*	*Decani & Capituli*	
1549	*Nich. de Wartyr.*	Ebor. *ejus*	*per mort.*
	Steph. de Burton.	*fermarii.*	*per resig.*
1350	*Haldenus de Driffield.*		*per mort.*
1351	*John de Wylingham.*		*per resig.*
1358	*Tho. de Folkerthorp.*		
	John de Helperby.		
1428	*Will. Newbald*, cap.		*per mort.*
1430	*John Carter*, cap.		*per resig.*
1431	*Rich. Hawkesworth.*		*per mort.*
1465	*Will. Warde*, cap.		*per resig.*
1474	*Will. Barton*, presb.		*per resig.*
1487	*John North*, presb.		*per resig.*
1488	*Richard Taylor*, presb.		*per resig.*
1490	*Will. Barton*, presb.		*per resig.*
1492	*Will. Clarkson*, presb.		*per mort.*
1509	*Rob. Foster*, presb.		*per resig.*
1509	*John Bucktrout*, presb.		*per resig.*
1510	*Tho. Ovington*, presb.		*per resig.*
1515	*Rich. Horby*, presb.	*Cap.* Ebor.	*per resig.*
1516	*Tho Barton*, cap.	*Dec. & Cap.*	*per mort.*
1523	*John Bentley*, presb.	*fermarii*	*per resig.*
1528	*Will. Todd*, cap.	*eorundem.*	*per mort.*
1531	*Rad. Moore*, cap.		*per mort.*
1549	*Will. Bayles*, cler.		*per mort.*
1558	*Tho. Forster*, cler.	*Cap.* Ebor.	
	Jac. Johnson, presb.	*Dec. & Cap.*	*per mort.*
1586	*John Pattyn*, cler.		*per resig.*
1599	*Tho. Hingeston*, vic. chor.		*per mort.*
1613	*Henry Brinkwell.*		*per mort.*
1619	*John Allen*, M. A.		*per mort.*
1630	*William Smith*, cler.		*per cession*
1631	*Rich. Johnson*, cler.		*per resig.*
1632	*Will. Smith*, cler.		*per cession*
1638	*Tho. Hudson.*		
1661	*Tho. Tonge*, cler.		
	George Tiplin, cler.		*per mort.*
1679	*Will. York*, A. M.		

Wartyr's *chantry in this church* anno domini 1346.

Nicholas Wartyr, perpetual vicar of this church, to the praise and honour of God, St. *Mary*, St. *Laurence*, and all saints, and for the health of his own soul, and for the souls of Mr. *Rich. de Cestria*, *John de Messington*, *Walter de Yarewell* and *John Benge*, cap. gave and granted to God, St. *Mary*, St. *Laurence* and to sir *John de Burtonstather*, chaplain, and his successors perpetually celebrating divine service for the souls aforesaid. And for saying daily *placebo*, *dirige*, with commendation of the dead, *&c.* four messuages in *Walmgate* of the annual value of five marks, according to the king's licence by him obtained. Also the moiety of that house or messuage for the chaplain's habitation, which by licence of the dean and chapter he hath at his own proper costs built on the south-side of the church-yard of St. *Laurence*. So as the vicar for the time being shall have the other moiety for his habitation also.

And willed that after his own decease, the vicar of this church do present a fit priest hereunto to the dean and chapter to be instituted within seven days from the time of notice of any vacation.

Lastly, That the said chaplains his successors do find and sustain for their daily celebrations a chalice, books, vestments and other ornaments necessary, and shall receive from the hands of the vicar *gratis* bread, wine and candles. All which were confirmed by the chapter of *York*, *July* 27, 1346. Val. at the diss. 1 *l.* 11 *s.* 8 *d.*

After follows a close catalogue of the several chaplains to this chantry which I omit. As also the testamentary burials.

This church of St. *Laurence* was near destroyed in the siege, and lay in ruins, like its neighbour, till the year 1669, when it was begun to be re-edified, and is at this day in very good repair. The church hath but one isle, but a handsome large window at the east end, in which is put a coat of arms *arg.* on a bend *sab.* three garbs *or*, crest a garb *or*, banded *az.* Motto CEST LA SEVL VERTVE QVI DONNE LA NOBLESSE. *Hesketh. H. Giles depinx.*

Monumental INTERMENTS.

In the chancel by the communion table on a white stone is this inscription:

Here lyeth the body of Walter Bethel, *fourth son of sir* Walter Bethel, *of* Alne, *knight, and* Mary *the daughter of sir* Henry Slingsby *of* Red-house, *who died the 1st of* Novem. 1686. *aged* 70.

Over the same hangeth on the wall this Escutcheon: Impaled, 1. *argent*, on a chevron between three boars heads trunk'd *sable* a martlet, *argent. Bethel.* 2. Barry of eight pieces *or* and *gules. Poyntz.*

Near the former lyes another white ftone on which is this infcription: SUBURBS.

M. S.

Under this ftone refteth in hope of a joyful refurrection the body of Thomas Hefketh *of* Hefling-ton, *efq; the fon of* Thomas Hefketh *efq;* *and* Jane *his wife, who both lye buried here, he was married to* Mary *the daughter of fir* Walter Bethell *of* Alne, *knight, who here lyes interred. And by her had iffue fix fons and one daughter, five of which are not. His fecond wife was* Mary *the daughter of* Thomas Condon *efq; of* Willarby, *who in teftimony of her affection to her dear husband hath placed this.* Hesketh 1653.

He dyed 5th *of* Feb. anno Dom. 1653. Ætatis fuæ 43.

Reader, wouldeft thou know what goodnefs lyeth here,
Go to the neighbouring town and read it there.
Though things in water writ away do glide,
Yet there in watry characters abide
His memory, and here writ, vertues look
Surer in tears, than ink; in eyes than book.

On another white ftone by the eaft:

Here lyeth the body of Margaret *the daughter of* Thomas Hefketh, *efq; who dyed the* 8th *day of* July 1680. Hesketh 1680.

In the midft of the nave is an old white ftone infcribed,

Hic jacet Dom. Richardus Imyn cujus animæ propitietur Deus. Amen. Imyn.

Mrs. *Yarbrough*, late wife to colonel *Yarbrough* of *Heflington* has an infcription here to this purpofe:

——— *She bore twelve children to her husband, and dyed in child-bed* anno 1718. æt. 42. *She was a woman excellent in all the duties of life, whether we regard her as a chriftian, a parent, or a friend; of whom the world was not worthy.*

Before I take leave of this church, I muft take notice that there are fome very large ftones of the gritt kind wrought up in the wall of it. As alfo at a corner of the fteeple is the reprefentation of St. *Lawrence* on a gridiron rudely cut. But what is moft remarkable are two antique ftatues which lye on the church-yard wall to the ftreet in priefts habits, but whether *chriftian* or *pagan* is a doubt. I cannot think them elegant enough for *Roman*, but they deferve the fculptor's notice, and I leave them to the reader's conjecture*. By thefe venerable pieces of antiquity lye alfo feveral covers for ftone coffins, which now ferve to cover the wall; and near it one of thefe facred repofitories for the dead; which the owners bones have been long fince removed from, and at prefent it has the honour to ferve for a trough to the neighbouring well.

(x) M. *Torre* has found out another church which antiently ftood in thefe fuburbs; of which he gives this account,

The parifh church of St. *Michael extra Walmgate* was an antient rectory, appropriated to the prior and convent of **Kirkham.** Which on the 10th of *October*, 1365, in regard it was of fo mean a value that all the rents, iffues and profits thereof were not fufficient to fupport the third part belonging to the maintenance of one prieft, was, by *John* archbifhop of *York*, with confent of his chapter and parties who had intereft therein; perpetually conjoined and united to the parifh church of St. *Lawrence*, to which it was contiguous. And the parifhoners thereof decreed to be one and the fame with thofe of St. *Laurence*, which thereby was declared their true mother church. And that all tithes and oblations arifing out of places within this parifh of St. *Michael*, and from the inhabitants thereof fhall entirely be received by the vicars of St. *Laurence*, faving all rights archiepifcopal and archidiaconal due from the faid inhabitants and places within the faid parifh of St. *Michael*. *November* 12, 1365, confirmed by the chapter of *York*. CHURCH of St. MICHAEL *extra muros.*

Leaving the fuburbs on this fide I keep by the river *Fofs* and come to a (y) village on the other antiently called **Layrethorpe**. This being the extremity of the foreft of **Galtres** next the city bears a tafte of the antient hunting on that foreft in its name; **Leer**, or **Layre**, fay *Skinner* and *Goldman*, being, in old *Englifh*, a hunting term for a place where deer ufually retired to, after feeding to repofe themfelves. LAYRE-THORPE.

The parifh church of St. *Mary* ftood formerly in *Layrethorp*, valued, *temp. Hen.* V. at two pound *per an.* Mr. *Torre* finds nothing memorable relating to this church, fave that it was with its parifh united to St. *Cuthbert* within the walls, *an.* 28 *Eliz.* St. MARY LAYRE-THORPE.

Croffing the *Fofs* here, the firft piece of ground that lies next it is now called *Jewbury*. This place, by the name, feems to have been a **burgh**, or diftrict, anciently inhabited by thefe people. It lies upon the north weft fide of the river *Fofs*; and by means of that ca- JEWBURY.

* See plate N°. 9.

(x) MS. *Torre*, f. 415. I have not met with an account of this church in any other author.

(y) Robert de Bylton & Thomas de Redenefs *de Ebor. capel. concefferunt abbati & conventui de* Rieval, *& fucceforibus fuis fex meffuagios cum curtelagiis quæ jacent juxta pontem de* **Layrethorp-brigge. Ebor.** *ex chart. orig.*

SUBURB. nal, their goods and merchandize might formerly have been conveyed to them. There is another conjecture, which indeed seems more probable, that it was called *Jewbury* from being a place assigned to the *Jews* for the burial of their dead; and probably where those *Jews* were interred that slew themselves in the castle. We are told by *Hoveden*, that *anno* 1177. our *Henry* II. granted licence to the *Jews* to have a burial place *without the walls of every city in* England; when before they were obliged to carry all their dead to bury at *London*. As there is a street within the city which bears some affinity to these people in its name, I shall have occasion to mention them again. This place is now converted into gardens, *&c.*

MONKGATE. (z) *Monkgate*, is a fair broad street, well paved and pretty well built, leading from the bar to the bridge. The spittal of St. *Loy*, another house for the entertainment of poor strangers, or pilgrims, stood on the east side the bridge. From whence *Monkgate*, and *Monkbar*, have contracted their names I cannot learn, I know no religious house to have stood this way whence it could be derived. All the land and houses on the north side this street was antiently dean and chapter's land, *de terra Ulphi*, and is leased from them at this time. On the south side is an hospital, of a late foundation, called alderman *Agar*'s hospital, but inconsiderable.

Church *of St.* MAURICE. The parish church of St. *Maurice*, is at the head of this street, and is said to stand in **Monkgate**, and **Newbigging**. It antiently appertained to the two prebends of **Frydaythorpe** and **Fenton**; till *Walter Grey* archbishop by the consent of his chapter, united the medieties into one entire rectory, which he assigned unto the prebend of **Fenton**, with all appurtenancies belonging. And in recompence to the prebend of **Frydaythorpe** granted him the rents and services of the prebend of **Fenton** lying in **Newbigging-streete**, and **Monkgate** *(a)*.

Anno 1240, at the petition of *Sewale de Bevil* prebendary of **Fenton**, *Walter* archbishop of *York*, with the consent of the chapter, ordained that the vicar of this church of St. *Maurice* should receive *nomine vicarie omnes obventiones et decimas ipsius ecclesie, solvendo inde annuatim capitulo quatuor marcas sterlingorum ad festa* Pent. *et* S. Martini. *Et quod custodia vicarie cum vacaverit penes canonicum remaneat presentand. viros ydoneos decano et capitulo ad instituend. Et dicte prebende canonicus ab omnimodarum decimarum prestatione, et qualibet consuetudine parochiali sit immunis et semper liber. Et cum canonicus confert ad onera* Ebor. *ecclef. revelanda, vel si aliquod aliud onus ipsi canonico ratione prebende immineat, vicarius hujus ecclesie de S.* Mauritio *et vicarius de* Fenton *in parte duodecima ipsum juvabunt (b).*

This church of St. *Maurice* together with all its separate members, rights and appurtenances was by *Edwyn* archbishop of *York*, the mayor, *&c.* united and annexed to the parish church of St. *Trinity* in *Gothramgate*; according to the statute. Notwithstanding which it is still kept up, and divine service celebrated there, the only instance of this kind in or about the city.

Mr. *Torre* is short in his catalogue of the vicars of this church.

An.	Vicarii.	Patroni.	Vacat.
1521.	Dom. *Robertus Marven.*	*Decan. et capit.*	*per resig.*
1530.	*Henry Carbott*, L. L. D.	*Prebend. de* Fenton.	*per resig.*
1533.	*William Haland* presb.	*idem.*	*per mort.*
1537.	*Miles Esham.*	*idem.*	

Monumental INSCRIPTIONS *in this church.*

Here resteth the body of Leonard Wilberfoss *alderman, late lord-mayor of this city, who died the* 5th *of* January, an. dom. 1691, *in the sixty first year of his age.*

Others are of *Thomas Lutton* of *Knapton* esquire, who died *September* 15, 1719. Of *Arabella* his wife *March* 14, 1711. Of captain *Thomas Harrison* of *Holthy*, *August* ult. 1720. *Richard Man* merchant, *February* 6, 1712. *Charles Man* gent. *October* 16, 1723. *Edward Waddington*, gent. *October* 26, 1690. *Thomas Wilberfoss* attorney at law, *March* 28, 1682. Mr. *Oswald Langwith* clerk of the vestry and library keeper to the cathedral 1723, *&c.*

BARKER-HILL. LORD-MAYOR'S WALK. Opposite to this church runs a street now called *Barker-hill*, antiently called **Parlot-hill**, and probably it had not its name for nothing; *Lovelane* being contiguous to it *(c)*. On the other side of the bar is a place called the *lord-mayor's walk*. This is a long broad walk, which was planted with elms on both sides, *anno* 1718; and is capable of being made a sort of *mall*; was the high road diverted which runs through it.

I shall close the account of this part of the suburbs with an extract from Mr. *Dodsworth*'s coll. of the antient boundary of this parish of St. *Maurice* taken from an old manuscript. *Memorandum that in the yere* M.CCC.LXX. *the boundes of St.* **Maurice** *parishe was troble sore, and they were seene in the mynstere. That is to say from the* **Monkbar** *bulbing fro the* **Calwing towre** *to the* **Goyselayne**; *fro the* **Goyselayne** *to the kinges sewere in the* **Paynely craftes**, *to the dyke end at the abbots mills to the midest of* **Fosse**, *downe midest of* **Fosse** *to* **Monkbrigg**, *fro the*

(z) On the north side this street some years ago was found a stone causeway at eight foot deep. Dean *Gale*.

(a) *Ex MS.* Torre *f.* 35.

(b) *Ibid. f.* 36.

(c) Beyond this stood formerly a place called **Bettrebas**, opposite, it is said to *merchant-taylors* within the walls, but I can give no further account of it.

Monk

Monk brigg *to the* **Laycrthorpe towne,** *fro the* **Laycrthorpe towre** *to the* **Monkbar.** *This beyng the boundes certenly. Witness hereof* **Simon Sheresman** *kyrkemastere the same tyme, dwellyng besyde the* **Coyselayns** *at the same tyme* (*d*).

SUBURBS.

Down a narrow lane, the boundary of the lands of *Ulphus* on that side, lies a large piece of ground called, antiently, **Paynelycrofts**, though now it has corruptly got the name of the *Croves*. This was undoubtedly a large enclosure from the forest, and divided into so many crofts or closes, part of the hedges yet standing shewing it. That this vast forest reached up to the very walls of the city on this side, appears from a perambulation made the twenty eighth of *Edward* I. entitled *Perambulatio forestae dom. regis de* Galtres. *Incipit ad pedem muri civitatis* Ebor. *&c.* This piece of choice ground lies common from *Michaelmas* to *Lady-day*; as many hundred acres more do the same, round the city.

CROVES.

On the north of these crofts is a piece of ground called **Horse-fair**, in which some of the annual fairs before described are kept. But what makes it more remarkable is that a large hospital stood here, which was founded and dedicated to St. *Mary Magdalene*, by *Robert de Pykering* dean of *York*, *anno* 1330. It was afterwards confirmed by *William de Melton* archbishop; who further ordained,

ST. MARY MAGDALENE's hospital.

(*e*) That there shall be therein one perpetual chaplain for the master; whose presentation shall belong to the said *Robert de Pykerings* for his life, and to his heirs after his decease. That the said master and his successors, being assisted with two more chaplains, shall daily celebrate divine service therein for the souls of *Walter* late archbishop, the said *Robert de Pykerings*, and *William* his brother, *&c.* And shall competently sustain those two chaplains with victuals and cloathing, and pay to each twenty shillings *per annum*. And also to sustain with meat, drink and cloathing, other six old lame priests not able to minister, allowing to every one twelve pence a week.

And for the competent maintenance of all the said chaplains and master, the archbishop appropriated to them the church of *Stillingfleet* and to this hospital for ever. Assigning a due portion for a vicar to be instituted therein, at the presentation of the master and brethren hereof.

Mr. *Torre* has subjoined a close list of the masters of this hospital, from the foundation to the suppression, which I shall omit; and only take notice that at the dissolution *Thomas Marser* was found incumbent.

	l.	*s.*	*d.*
(*f*) Their goods were valued at — — — —	02	12	01
Their plate eight ounces and three quarters — —	01	15	00
Lands — — — — — —	23	10	08
The close and orchard belonging to the said hospital	01	06	08
The parsonage of *Stillingflete* appropriated to the said hospital *per an.*	38	04	08

ult. Aprilis anno dom. 1557.

This hospital of St. *Mary's* in *Bootham*, against the city walls, commonly called **le Horse-fayre**, together with all its possessions, was annexed according to due form of law, to the dean and chapter of *York*. Whereupon *Nicholas Wotton* dean, with the consent of the chapter, granted unto *Thomas Luither* priest, a brother and fellow of this hospital, at the time of the making the said union, the annual rent of four pound thirteen shillings and four pence, upon condition that he should never after claim any right, title or demand in the premises by reason or pretence of the said fraternity. And,

The aforesaid dean and chapter, according to the tenour of a grant from *Philip* and *Mary* king and queen of *England*, who had made a resumption of the lands belonging to the hospital, founded a *grammar-school*; and perpetually endowed the master therewith, to be from time to time by them presented. The school is still subsisting in *York*; and, like the colleges in both universities, do in their prayers remember their founders, *Philip* and *Mary*; whose grant to the dean and chapter is so particular in the recital of the many scandalous practices in the disposing of lands given to pious uses, after the *Reformation*, that I think proper to insert it at large in the *appendix* (*g*).

(*h*) *Roger Dallison*, chanter of the cathedral church of *Lincoln*, granted to the dean and chapter of *York* an annuity of four pound, issuing out of the manor of **Hartleholm**, *com. Lincoln*, for them to apply the same to the use of a grammar-school, which was appropriated to this. vii° *Eliz. reg.*

Gillygate, is a street which lies near this, so called from a parish church which antiently stood in it, dedicated to St. *Giles*. This church was of small value, insomuch as to be under one pound *per an. temp. Hen.* V, and not put down in the list I have given. Mr. *Torre* finds nothing memorable about it; and only remarks that this church, together with all its members was united to St. *Olave*, twenty eight *Eliz.* One testamentary burial, *viz.* *William*

GILLYGATE church of St. GILES.

(*d*) *Dod's* coll. v. 115. f. 20.

(*e*) *Ex MS.* Torre. *Hosp. beatae* Mariae *Mag. in* Bootham *juxta civit.* Ebor. *fundat per* Rob. de Pickering *decanum, et pro ecclesia de* **Stivelingfleet** *appropriand. littera regis ad* Papam. *rot.* Rom. *an.* 14 Ed. II. *m.* 3. *Turre* Lond.

(*f*) *Dodsworth's* coll. v. 129. f. 147.

(*g*) *Ex MS. penes me.*

(*h*) *Ex MS* Torre. See St. *Andrew's* church.

Suburbs. *liam Albon* chaplain, late of *Gillygate Ebor.* made his teſtament, proved *November* 17, 1447. whereby he gave his ſoul to God almighty, St. *Mary* and *Allſaints*, and his body to be buried in this church of St. *Egidius* the abbot. There have been ſome diſputes betwixt the mayor and commonality and the inhabitants of this ſtreet, in relation to paving the king's high ways through it, &c. I have met with an antient copy of the caſe, learnedly drawn up, but by whom I know not, which will find a place in the *appendix*.

At the end of this ſtreet, next the *Horſefair*, ſtood once a ſmall religious houſe called the ſpital of St. *Anthony in Gillygate*.

Bootham. *Bootham* hath been time out of mind part of the ſuburbs of the city of *York*. It is the king's ſtreet (*i*) and extended in length from *Bootham-bar* to a *wooden gate*, at the farther end of that ſtreet, which antiently was called **Galmhawlith**; where the officers of the city uſed to ſtand to take and receive the toll and cuſtoms. The breadth of it is from an antient ſtone wall, which encloſeth a court there, called **Earles-burgh**, where the monaſtery of St. *Mary* was afterwards ſeated, to a ditch called **Renyngsdyke**, which encloſeth the ſuburbs on the other ſide. Within which bounds there is a ſtreet called *Gillygate*, and another ſtreet which is called the *Horſefair*, where the mayor and bayliffs do every year hold their chief fairs belonging to the city.

Bootham, muſt certainly have taken its name from a hamlet of booths, erected here, at certain times, by the abbot of St. *Mary's*, where he kept a fair in free burgage. This muſt have been a great grievance to the citizens, and was the occaſion of many diſputes betwixt the monks and them, which often ended with blood-ſhed. In a chartel wrote by a monk of this abby, are ſeveral notes taken of theſe frays; particularly, that (*k*) *anno* 1262, a wicked action was committed by the citizens, ſays he, in the monaſtery of St. *Mary*, which occaſioned great ſlaughter and plundering. In the year 1266, the ſame author ſays that a peace was concluded betwixt the abbot and the citizens in relation to this affair; but it held not long, for the abbot taking this opportunity to build a ſtrong wall from the river *Ouſe* to *Bootham-bar*, as a defence to his monaſtery, the fair was again opened, and the old bickerings renewed. They continued in this manner doing all poſſible miſchief to one another, till archbiſhop *Thoreſby*, ſcandalized at ſuch enormities, brought the abbot to agree with the mayor, aldermen and commonality, and to ſettle the bounds of each juriſdiction. This accord was made by indenture dated at *York*, *January* 16, 1353. wherein is ſpecified that all that part within great *Bootham*, extending the length of the whole ſtreet, except the portal, walls and St. *Marygate* abutting on the ſame ſtreet, with the houſes, tenements and dwellings, although built by the abbot and convent, overagainſt St. *Mary's* tower, be of the juriſdiction of the mayor and commonality of the city of *York*, them, their heirs, and ſucceſſors for ever. As alſo all other parts and places which are not expreſly mentioned to belong to the ſaid abbot and convent. The original indenture is now amongſt the city records, and a tranſlation of it from the old *French*. I ſhall give in the particular chapter of the abbey (*l*).

An antient claim of the citizens to this diſtrict is given in theſe words,

1. The citizens ſay that the ſtreet of **Bootham** is ſuburbs of the city of **York**; and all the tenements of the ſame are **geldable** to the king; and the tenements there are **geldable**, and are held of the king by **husgabal**, and they be deviſeable by will, and they are in all things of the ſame condition and cuſtom as other tenements of the ſaid city, and they pay no relief.

2. That in the ſaid ſtreet of **Bootham** there was never any *market*, *fair*, *tumbril*, *pillory*, or another thing which belongeth to a free burrough levied; but all things belonging to a market, or to cuſtom, or toll, were taken and done by the mayor and bayliffs as within the ſuburbs of the city.

3. The ſtreet of **Bootham** doth begin from the great gate of the city which is called **Bootham-bar**, and goes to an outergate which antiently was called **Galmhawlith**, and to the ditch of the ſaid ſuburbs which is called **Renyng-dykes**.

4. In all the **Eyres** of the juſtices, time out of mind, as well the pleas of the crown as other pleas of **Bootham**, have been pleaded within the city, as a ſuburb thereof. And the ſame have been preſented and terminated by twelve men, and by the coroners of the city.

5. And whereas the citizens have by their charters of the king's progenitors, and by confirmation of the king himſelf, that the *dogs* in the ſuburbs of the ſaid city ſhould not be **expediated**. In the ſuburbs of **Bootham**, which is within the foreſt of **Galtres** that reaches to the great gate of **Bootham-bar**, by vertue of that liberty, the *dogs* have not been expediated.

(*i*) This appears, ſays ſir *T. W.* out of the antient coucher books of the city.

(*k*) *Anno* 1262 *impetus factus a civibus* Ebor. *in monaſterium S.* Mariae *unde magna caedes et depredatio.* Lel. *coll. v.* 111. *p.* 52.

(*l*) This was firſt done by commiſſion under the great ſeal made to *William de Thoreſby* archbiſhop of *York* and lord chancellor of *England*, as appears by *pat.* 24 *Ed.* III. *p.* 2 *m.* 29. *dorſo*. And in the mean time till the agreement was made, the king did grant a commiſſion in the nature of a ſequeſtration for *Bootham* unto ſir *William Tallboys* and ſir *Robert Roſs* of *Ingmanthorp*, reciting that out of the fullneſs of his kingly power he had taken the ſame into his own hands. This commiſſion bears date *July* 24. 24 *Edw.* III. Sir *T. W.*

6. In the book of **Doomesday**, wherein all the **villes** and **burghs** in *England* are named here is no mention of **Bootham**. SUBURBS.

7. Antiently upon the river **Ouse**, between the king's street of **Bootham** and the river aforesaid, there was an antient street inclosed with a ditch, and doth yet appear, which in *English* was called **Earles-burgh**. And it was of old time the land of *Allan* earl of **Richmond**; who gave that street to *Stephen de Lastingham* abbot; within the bounds of which street **Bootham**, or any part of it, is not contained.

8. If **Bootham** was the **burgh** of the abbot, he should rather be called the abbot of **Bootham**, than the abbot of **York**.

9. By the law of the land no man ought to have a free *burgh*, *market*, or *fair*, unless it be distant from the neighbouring *boroughs* and *markets* at least six miles. And if a borough so near as this was tolerated, the king would lose all his contributions, fines, amerciaments, escheats, and other aids to the disherison of the king, and subversion of the city.

(*m*) By an inquisition taken before *M. Pateshull*, and his companions justices itinerant at *York*, in the third year of king *Henry*, son of king *John*, it is found that the said abbot did challenge to himself liberties, as well within the city as without, in the suburbs of the same; and the seisin of the said abbot was enquired of by twenty four knights, and no seisin was found in him of the liberties within **Bootham**.

In the same inquisition it is contained that *Walter Daniel*, a serjeant of the liberty of the abbot, was appealed of the death of his wife, by *William Shyftlyng*, brother of the wife; and the abbot did demand his liberty but he could not have it, and a *duel* was joined between them, and *Walter* was vanquished in the field and hanged, and his goods and chattels forfeited to the king. After this the men of the abbot came and took the body, and interred it in the garden of the abbot, which he claims to be within the precinct that he calls his free borough of **Bootham**. The abbot was hereof convict and put in the king's mercy, and the bayliffs of the king digged up the body and hanged it again in an iron chain.

In the *iter* of the justices itinerant at *York*, in the eight year of king *Edward* son to king *Henry*, it will be found that the abbot of St. *Mary*'s had no right, claim or liberty in **Bootham**, nor challenged any.

In the book of **Doomes-day** it is contained that no man hath custom, as *burgess*, except *Merleswain* in one house which is within the castle, and except the canons wheresoever they dwell.

William of the abbey, and *William* of *Sutton*, *Trussey*, *Lawrence*, *Benchard* and *Laurence* of *Bootham*, dwelling in **Bootham** were heretofore bayliffs of the city of **York**.

On the north side of *Bootham*, the dean and chapter of *York*, claim a jurisdiction, as part of their territories, *de terra* ULPHI; and this last year their coroner executed a writ of inquiry on the body of a woman that was found dead in that part, without molestation from the city.

On the south side, from the abbey gate to St. *Mary*'s tower, the houses are all in the county, being built in the ditch or graft of the abbey-wall. These buildings are of late standing, the oldest of them being but erected by a grant from king *James* I. of part of this waste to build on.

The name of *Bootham* or *Boutham* the learned dean *Gale* has derived from the old *British* language. (*n*) BOETH, *in Brit. lingua significat* exustum; TRE-BOOTH, *exustum oppidulum*, *Saxonica dictio* ham *locus*. By which he conjectures it was the place, at or near which the *Romans* burned their dead. I am perswaded that great antiquary was led into this mistake, by the quantity of *urns*, *sarcophagi*, &c. which were first begun to be discovered in his time by the digging clay for bricks in the neighbourhood of this place. The name can bear no other etymology than I have given, *viz.* *Bootham*, a hamlet of booths, for the fair before mentioned. But Galmanhð, the name of the old wooden gate which was antiently set at the end of this street opposite to St. *Mary*'s tower, is a word of much harder interpretation. That there was a monastery here before the conquest appears from *R. Hoveden*; and that it bore the same name as this gate. *Strenuus dux* Sewardus *decessit* Eboraci *et monasterio* Galmanho *sepultus est*. *Leland* has extracted this remark out of a book wrote by a monk of the abbey of St. *Mary*. *Anno Dom.* 1266, *inceptus est a* Simone *abbate petrinus murus circuiens abbatiam S.* Mariae Ebor. *incipiens ab ecclesia S.* Olavi, *et tendens versus portam civitatis ejusdem quae vocatur* Galmanhlith, [*nunc Boothambar.*] In a letter from Mr. *Hearne*, *the publisher of* Leland, and many other select pieces of antiquity, I have this explanation of this strange word. " In the *collectanea* this word is printed *Galmanlith*, with an *h* over " the *l* to shew that the true reading is *Galmanhith*, the first letter being put over the " other by *Leland* himself. *Hith* is a common word from the *Anglo-Saxon* hyð *portus*, so " **Queenhithe**, *portus regalis*. *Ho* has the same signification. Mr. *Burton*'s [*nunc Bootham*-" *bar*] put in crochets in *Leland*, is the modern name and explains the old one (*o*)." In

(*m*) *Ex MS* sir *T. W.* Ebor *major ibid. de placeo de* **Bootham** *et libertat. suis sibi restituend. Claus.* 29 *Ed.* III. *m.* 24.

(*n*) *Ex MS mihi dat. per* Samuelem Gale arm. *decani filium.*

(*o*) Mr. *Somner* is as much at a loss about the etymology of this word; what he says upon it I shall give as follows. " Galmanho *monasterii nomen est a* Siwardo " *illustri* Northumbrensium *duce, in quo etiam moriens* " *sepeliebatur*. Chron. Sax. Abbingdon *ad ann.* 1055.

Suburbs. another letter which I was favoured with from Mr. *Serenius*, the author of the *dictionarium Anglo-Swethico-Latinum*, I have this account, "your *Galmanhith* I can make nothing of in "the *Gothick* literature. It is true *gald*, aut *gall* signifies *infoecundus*, *vel sterilis*; *Heid locus* "*incultus*, *tesqua vel sylva*. If it agrees with the situation, it is as probable as any thing; "but I know not what to make of the middle syllable;" the reader may observe that I have spared no pains to come at a true definition of this old word, but to little purpose; and all I can draw from the sense of both those gentlemen's opinions is, that this port probably took its name from being a gate to which the vast forest of **Galtres** antiently extended; the toll (*p*) called *guyd-law* was taken at it, which was first granted for the payment of guides, that conducted men and cattle through the said forest; as well to direct them their way, as to protect them from wild beasts and robbers, with both which this immense wilderness must have been abundantly stocked. Besides the word **Galtres** itself is most naturally deduced from the *British cal a tre*, (*q*) which signifies *nemus ad urbem*; the forest extending, as an antient perambulation of it witnesses, which the reader may find in the *appendix*, up to the very walls of the city on this side. I shall take leave of this outer gate and *Bootham*, with observing that the sheriffs of the city do now annually ride in procession to the very spot where it formerly stood; and I wonder how the abbot of St. *Mary*'s could claim any privilege in a place that was thus fenced off, by the city, as an exteriour fortification.

Magdalene's chapel. I have noted before that an uniform street once extended from *Bootham-bar* to a place called *Burton-stone*, where a stone cross formerly stood; the extent of the city's liberties on this side. Close by this, east, stood formerly a chapel dedicated to St. *Mary Magdalen*, with a spital called *Magdalen*'s **spital**; but no remains of either do now appear.

Ingram's hospital. Higher up in this street on the south west side stands an hospital, founded *anno* 1640, by sir *Arthur Ingram* sen. of the city of *York* knight, who by his will, then made, whereof his son sir *Arthur* was sole executor, appointed lands of the yearly value of fifty pound to be ensured to the hospital which he had lately built in *Bootham* for the maintenance of ten poor widows, *viz.* for every one of them five pound a piece yearly; and a new gown every two years for every of them. Also twenty nobles yearly for some honest and able man for reading prayers in the said house, to be assured for ever out of such lands as his said son and heir shall think fit. Willing, that he and his heirs shall from time to time for ever have the placing, naming, and chusing of such poor widows as shall be there placed. and of the person and persons who shall from time to time read prayers in the said house (*r*).

(*s*) This hospital suffered much by fire at the siege of *York*, *anno* 1644, it is since repaired, but not so handsome as it was at first. The badge of these widows is a silver cock gilt, the crest of the family; which, when any of them die, goes to the next old woman that is put in her stead.

Mary-gate Nearer the city still, on the same side stands a handsome *cockpit* by a beautiful *bowling-green*. And not far from hence goes off a street, due west, called St. *Marygate*, which leads down to the river *Ouse*, and the great gate of the old abbey; this street was more antiently called **Earlesburgh**.

The church *of St.* Olave. The parish church of St. *Olave*, a *Danish* king and martyr, stands in this street; and is of the oldest date in history, except the cathedral, of any church in the city. I shall take notice once for all that in the account of parish churches, *Somner*, *Spelman* and *Kennet* are at a loss, and fairly own that their originals are not to be come at. For though they were certainly first begun by the *Anglo-Saxons*, yet the *Normans* are said to have first built them of stone. Yet if we may credit *Bede* (*t*) the *Saxons* were no strangers to stone buildings, even as early as *Edwin*'s time; for, he says, that king, by the instruction of *Paulinus*, took care to build a nobler and larger church, of *stone*, in the place where his wooden one was erected before. *Siward* the valiant earl of *Northumberland* is said to have founded a monastery in this place to the honour of St. *Olave*, where he was buried *anno* 1055. It was afterwards part of earl *Morcar*'s possessions, which the conqueror gave to his nephew *Alain* earl of *Britain*, afterwards of *Richmond*. By this it appears to be the mother of St. *Mary*'s monastery, and *Stephen* (*u*) the first abbot tells us, that earl *Alain*, their founder, gave the chutch of St. *Olave* and four acres of land to build offices on for the monks to dwell in; where they were kindly invited by the said earl to make that church and place their residence. By an inquisition taken, *temp. Hen.* V. for a subsidy granted by parliament on all spirituals and temporals, this church is above double the value of yearly revenue to any within or without the city. I can assign no reason for it, but that the neighbourhood of this famous and once opulent monastery might be an occasion of its former richness,

"*Loci nomen unde petendum diu anceps fui*; *post longam autem investigationem rem a* Johanne Bromptono *abbate* "Jornalensi *sic explicatam tandem reperi.* —— "*Sepultus* "*est in monasterio S.* Mariae *apud* Eborum *in claustro.*" *Script.* x. *col.* 946. But the explanation of the term is by no means made out by this quotation.

(*p*) *Verstegan* of decayed intelligence. p. 137.

(*q*) For *cal a* see *Baxter* under the words *calagum*, *calaxa*, *caledonia*, and for *tre* see *Lluyd*'s *adversaria* at the end of *Baxter*, p. 271. I am indebted to the reverend Dr. *Langwith* for this etymology.

(*r*) *MS.* Torre *p.* 362.

(*s*) *Ex MS penes me.*

(*t*) *Curavit, docente eodem* Paulino, *majorem usque in loco et augustiorem* de lapide *fabricare basilicam.* Bede *l.* xiv.

(*u*) *E libro* Stephani primi abbatis *S.* Mariae Ebor.

as

as well as the fall of that remarkable place the reason of its present poverty. It was accounted as a chapel dependant on the abbey, and its being parochial could not save it from being miserably plundered at the dissolution. Being grown old and ruinous, and greatly shattered in its fabrick by a platform of guns which played from the roof in the siege against the enemy, the parish no ways able to bear the charge of the reparation, a brief was granted and collected, by which assistance, the church was in a manner quite pulled down, some few years ago, and rebuilt in the good order it now stands in. SUBURBS.

The inside of the church is supported by two rows of elegant pillars which divides it into three isles. It has a handsome square steeple with three tuneable bells in it. Monumental inscriptions, as they were taken by the industrious Mr. *Dodsworth anno* 1618, whose original manuscript is faln into my hands were then as follows, but now they are most, or all, of them defaced.

Epitaphs *in* St. OLAVE's.

✠ Hic jacet Robertus Aldby sadler cujus anime propitietur Deus. Amen. Aldby.

Here lyeth the corps of William Drew, sometyme (x) sheriffe of this cittye of York, who dyed to God's mercy the vii day of October, MDLXXXV. Drew 1585.

✠ Hic jacet Johannes Colit (y) quondam vicecomes istius civitatis qui obiit viii die mensis junii anno dom. MCCCCLXXXVII. cujus, &c. Colit. 1487.

✠ Hic jacet Thomas Oudebarow carpentarius cujus anime, &c. amen. Oudebarow.

✠ Hic jacet John de Spawlainge quondam civis Ebor. et Alicia uxor ejus quorum animabus propitietur Deus, qui obiit anno dom. MCCCXCIII. Spawlainge. 1393.

Quis tumulus sonat ut levis concentibus aura, Farley. 1570.
Angelicusve tenens haec loca sacra chorus?
Farlei *monumenta vides; hic siste, viator;*
Ille fuit nostri maxima cura chori.
Quis inopum melius causas oraverit unquam?
Auxilium multis lingua diserta tulit.
Non servus nummis, flavo corruptus et auro,
Civilis doctor juris, et ille pius.
Hoc Farlee, *tibi virtute et arte parasti*
Ut coeli teneas aurea tecta senex.
Anna *soror, cur fles? cur quaeris* Anna *maritum?*
Non obiit, vivit. Nunc satis, hospes, abi.
Qui obiit decimo die Septembris anno Dom. 1570.

Here lyeth the bodye of Joan (z) Farley wife of Fabian Farley, and daughter of John Proctor of Lankland haull, who dyed the age of eighty and sixteen years. 1602. Joan Farley. 1602.

✠ Orate pro anima fratris Ricardi Kendall monachi istius m. Kendall.

For the love of Jesu
Pray for the soule of George Slun-howe. Slunhowe.

✠ Orate pro anima Willielmi Bryggys qui obiit xiii die Junii an. dom. MCCCCXC cujus, &c. amen. Bryggys. 1490.

199 M ta Taylor quorum animabus propitietur Deus.

✠ Hic jacet Henricus Fleminge cujus; &c. amen. Fleminge.

On Williams Sawle
God have mercy.

✠ Orate pro anima Laurentii Idle. Idle.

Willielmus Vendor Agnetis Vendor. Vendor.

✠ Orate pro anima Isabelle Sparry cujus anime propitietur Deus. Amen. Sparry.

Thus far from *Dodsworth.*

Here lyeth the bodyes interred of the right honourable Henry Darcy *esquire, third son of the right honourable* Conyers *lord* Darcy, Meynill *and* Conyers, *who departed this life the* 28th *day of* April, 1662. anno aetatis suae 57. Darcy. 1662.

And Mary Darcy *his wife, daughter and heiress of* William Scrope *of* Heighley-hall *esquire, who departed this life* April 17, 1667. *Who had issue ten children. Now they both rest in* Christ, *waiting for the resurrection of the dead.* Mary Darcy. 1667.

(x) He was sheriff, 1556.
(y) I cannot find this name in the catalogue.
(z) Her husband gave forty pound to the brigg to lend to poor men of the city of xii*d.* ith pound. *Dodsworth.*

Upon

SUBURBS. Upon a pillar hung a wooden frame, on which was depicted this bearing:
Impaling, 1. *Azure*, three cinquefoils and semi de croslets. *Darcy*.
2. *Azure* a bend *or*. *Scrope*.

(*a*) *Anno* 1684, two large tables or atchievements of arms were up in this church, for the family of the *Wentworths*. The one *Sable*, a chevron between three leopards heads *or*, *Wentworth*. Impaling ermine two pyles in point sable, by the name of *Holles*; which was here placed to remember the lady *Arabella* daughter of *John Holles* earl of *Clare*, and second wife to that loyal and noble patriot *Thomas* lord *Wentworth*, baron of *Raby*, after viscount *Wentworth* and earl of *Strafford*; who, says the author of a manuscript I quote from, lost his life through the prevailing power of a most malicious and unreasonable faction.

Wentworth. Holles.

The other table was also to commemorate the lady *Margaret* his first wife, daughter of *Francis* earl of *Cumberland*, who was buried in this church *anno* 1629. *viz.* quarterly of six, three and three. 1. *Sable*, a chevron betwixt three leopards heads *or*. 2. *Argent*, a cross double potent throughout *sable*. 3. *Argent* a cross pattée *sable*. 4. *Argent* on a pale *sable* a congers head coped *or*. 5. *Gules* a saltire *Argent*. 6. *Gules* a fesse of five fusils *or*. All ensigned with a viscount's coronet, and supported by a gryphin rampant *argent* armed *or*, and a lyon rampant *argent*, motto EN DIEV EST TOVT.

Wentworth. Clifford.

It will not be amiss to take notice that the lord president of the north, who resided in the neighbouring abby or manor, had a seat built for him in this church, which he usually went to for divine service.

Lady Milbank 1689. *Here lyeth buried the body of the lady* Faith Milbank *wife to Mr.* Thomas Metcalf, *who died the last day of* April 1689, *in the* 33^d^ *year of her age.*

Over this is an atchievement with the arms of *Metcalf*, *Green*, *&c.*

I must not omit a copartment put up in this church in memory of the late *William Thornton* joyner and architect; since by the ablest judges in the former kind of work, he was look'd upon as the best artist in *England*; and, for architecture, his reparation of *Beverley-minster*, ought to give him a lasting memorial. He died much regretted *Sept.* 23, 1721.

In the church-yard are several inscriptions, but none of them remarkable save this, which a kind husband has bestowed to the memory of his bed-fellow, and the following;

Megson. 1718. *Here lyes the body of* Mary Megson *wife to* Francis Megson, *who departed this life* Feb. 15, 1718.

Under this stone lyes vertue great and good,
As was well known amongst her neighbourhood;
Whose life was charity to her power,
Which God requites her now for evermore.
Under this stone, crammed in a hole, does lye
The best of wives that ever man laid by. Finis.

Mosley 1732. *Hic situs est Reverendus* Thomas Mosley, *A. M. Rector de* Skelton, *Vicarius de* Overton, *& hujus Ecclesiæ Curatus, &c. Pastor fuit fidus & assiduus, non minus privatis monitis quam publicis in concionibus, ad veram Pietatem sibi commissos dirigens, adhortans.*

Ita totus Minister Jesu Christi, *ut omnes agnoscerent Virum vere primitivum, & huic muneri dum partes daret præcipuas, Conjugis, Parentis, Vicini, & Hominis, officia haud neglexit; sed omnium tale se præstitit exemplar, quale imitari neminem pudeat, nunquam poenitebit. Obiit* 26 Nov. *an. Dom.* 1732. *æt.* 69.

Juxta sita est Bridgeta, *uxor ejus; cui pulchra Forma, conjugalis Amor, domestica Cura, semper charam, semper amabilem præbuit; ut illâ Privatus, quasi sui dimidio, vix duos menses manserit superstes. Obiit illa* 29 Sept. *an. Dom.* 1732. *æt.* 59.

Harvey 1733. *Hic jacet* Dan. Harvey, *stirpe* Gallus, *idemque probus. Sculptor, Architector etiam peritus. Ingenio acer, integer Amicitiae; quam sibi citius aliis beneficus. Abi, viator, sequi reminiscere. Obiit undecimo die* Decembris, *A. D.* 1733. *ætatis* 50.

The church of St. *Olave's*, at the dissolution, fell to the king; but is now in the gift of sir *William Robinson*, baronet.

This being a chapel dependant on the abby Mr. *Torre* has not met with a catalogue of its incumbents.

			l.	s.	d.
Valuation in the king's books.	First fruits	——— ———	06	08	04
	Procurations	——— ———	00	13	04

I have now finished my circuit round the city, and I think have omitted nothing memorable in the suburbs, except the abby of St. *Mary's*, which commands a particular chapter. And except I say that at the bottom of this street on the west side a lane leading to **Almry-garth**, of which hereafter, is a *charity school* for girls now kept; which was first set on foot for twenty poor girls, *an.* 1705, to be lodged, fed, taught and cloathed. Of all which donations and bequests the reader may find the particulars in the *appendix*. On the other side this lane, some few years ago, was erected a *glass-house*, which wrought glass for some time; but the gentleman, whose publick spirit engaged him to this undertaking, being thoroughly

Charity-school for girls. *Glass-house.*

(*a*) E *MS. penes* Roger. Gale, *arm.*

employed

I

employed in a buſineſs of a much nobler nature, he could not attend theſe *Salamanders* as they ought, who are known to be egregious cheats without good looking after; for which reaſon the matter was let drop; the houſe pulled down; and the project left open for ſome perſon of more leiſure to purſue it.

I come now to deſcribe the city itſelf, but firſt its encloſure or fortification muſt be taken notice of. The city of *York* is in circumference two miles and almoſt three quarters, which is thus meaſured (*b*):

From the *Red Tower* to *Walm-gate bar*	60	pearches.
From thence to *Fiſher-gate poſtern*	99	
From thence to *Caſtle-gate poſtern*	58	
Thence to *Skelder-gate poſtern*	84	
Thence to *Mickle-gate bar*	136	
From thence to *North-ſtreet poſtern*	140	
Thence to *Bootham-bar*	86	
Thence to *Monk-bar*	116	
From thence to *Laythorpe poſtern*	66	
From thence to the *Red Tower* again	80	

Total 875 pearches.

That is 2 miles 5 furlongs and 96 yards.

There are four principal gates or bars for entrance into the city, and five poſterns, which are theſe:

Micklegate-bar to the South-weſt.
Bootham-bar — North-weſt.
Monk-bar — North-eaſt.
Walm-gate bar — South-eaſt.
North-ſtreet poſtern.
Skelder-gate poſtern.
Caſtle-gate poſtern.
Fiſher-gate poſtern.
Layretborp poſtern.

To theſe ſir *T. W.* adds *Lendal poſtern.*
And I may add —— *Long-walk poſtern*, lately erected.

BRIDGES in the CITY and SUBURBS.

Ouſe-bridge, five arches.
Foſs-bridge, two arches.
Layretborp-bridge, five arches.
Monk-bridge, three arches.
Caſtlegate-bridge, one arch.

John Leland's account of the city's fortifications, as they appeared in his days, I ſhall chuſe to give in his own words:

(*c*) **The towne of** York **ſtandith by weſt and eſt of** Ouſe **river running through it, but that part that lyeth by eſt is twice as gret in building as the other.**

Thus goeth the waul from the ripe of Ouſe **of the eſt part of the cite of** Yorke.

Fyrſt a grete towre with a chein of yron to caſt over the Owſe, **then another towre and ſoe to** Bowdam-gate. **From** Bowdam-gate, **or bar, to** Goodram-gate, **or bar, x towres. Thens four towres to** Laythorpe, **a poſtern-gate, and ſoe by the ſpace of a two ſlite ſhotts the blind and deep water of** Foſſe, **cumming out of the foreſt of** Galtres, **defendeth this part of the cite without waules. Then to** Waumgate **three towres and thens to** Fiſher-gate, **ſtoppid up ſins the communes burnid it yn the tyme of K.** Henry VII.

Thens to the ripe of Foſſe **have three towres and yn the three a poſtern and thens over** Foſſe **by a bridge to the caſtelle.**

The weſt parte of the cyte is thus yncloſed, firſt a turrit and ſoe the waul runnith over the ſide of the dungeon of the caſtelle **on the weſt ſide of** Ouſe **right agayn the** caſtelle **on the eſt ripe. The plotte of this** caſtelle **is now called** Ould Baile, **and the area and ditches of it doe manifeſtly appeare. Betwixt the beginnyng of the firſt parte of this weſt waulle and** Mickle-gate **be ix towres; and betwixt it and the ripe agayn of** Ouſe **be xi towres; and at this xi towers be a poſtern-gate, and the towre of it is right agayn the eſt towre to draw over the chein on** Ouſe **betwixt them.**

It is not eaſy to determine in what year or under what reign our preſent city walls were erected. But I find that in the beginning of the reign of *Henry* III. a patent was granted for taking certain tolls in *ſpecie* of goods, &c. coming to be ſold at *York*, for a certain time there ſpecified, towards the ſupport of the walls and fortifications of the city. The title of the grant is *De villa* Ebor. *claudenda*, and it begins *rex majori & probis hominibus* Ebor. which CITY-WALLS.

(*b*) Survey'd *Feb.* 1664 *per John Maine*, *Ex MS.* The city of *London* within the walls, is very little bigger, being only three miles in circumference, containing four hundred and forty eight acres.

(*c*) *Lelandi itin* vol. I. His itinerary was firſt begun *anno* 1538, at the command of *Henry* VIII.

4

is another proof of the city's being governed by a mayor up to this time. The patent, with a *mandamus* to the dean and chapter of *York (d)*, at the ſame time, charging them that they do not hinder their men from paying theſe tolls, will fall in their proper places in the *appendix*. But it is probable theſe walls were rebuilt in *Edward* the firſt's time; when the *Scotiſh* war began; for then it was abſolutely neceſſary to put this city in a very good poſture of defence. In the progreſs of that war, in his ſon's reign, the *Scots* made ſuch inroads into the country, as to penetrate as far as the very gates of *York*, though they durſt not attempt a ſiege. In *Edward* the third's reign, I have given a mandate, from the *Fœdera*, for putting (*e*) this city in better repair as to its fortifications, with the method how the charge of it was to be born. That the walls were tenable againſt the *conqueror* is alſo taken notice on in the annals; nor muſt I forget here to mention that there is evident teſtimony that this city was ſtrongly walled, as well in the times of the *Saxon* and *Daniſh* wars, as in the time of the *Roman* government in *Britain*. It appears in later times that ſir *William Todd* merchant was a great benefactor to the reparations of theſe walls; two inſcriptions near old *Fiſhergate-bar*, ſtill in being denoting as much. The one is this, under a piece of indifferent ſculpture of a ſenator in his robes, and a woman kneeling by him, **A. Dom. M.CCCC.LXXXVII. ſir William Tod mair jou-ates ſome tyme was ſchyriffe did this coſt himſelfe.** Near this, on a table under the city's arms, is **A° Domini M.CCCC.LXXXVII. ſir William Tod knight L... Mayre this wal was mayde in his dayes lx yerdys.** This ſenator's name is alſo on a ſtone on the platform on the ſouth-ſide *Micklegate-bar*. After the ſiege of *York* 1644, the walls ſtood in great need of repairs; accordingly the next year they were begun by them that were then maſters here, but were three years in perfecting; for *Walmgate-bar*, which ſuffered the moſt from a terrible battery upon *Lamel-hill*, and being undermined in the ſiege, was repaired as appears from an inſcription under the city's arms over the outward gate, *viz. an.* 1648. *Anno* 1666. the walls of the city were repaired betwixt *Monk-bar* and *Laythorp-poſtern*; as alſo near *Bootham-bar* 1669, at the charge of the city. *Anno* 1673, the walls betwixt *Walmgate-bar* and the *Red-tower* were taken down and repaired. In this watry ſituation the walls run all upon arches as they do in other places which want that ſupport. But what adds moſt to the ornament, if not to the ſtrength of the city, are the reparations of the walls from *North-ſtreet* to *Skelder-gate* poſterns; and again from *Fiſher-gate* poſtern to *Walmgate-bar*. Theſe were of late years levelled upon the plat-form, paved with brick, and made commodious for walking on for near a mile together; having an agreeable proſpect of both town and country from them. This makes it to be wiſhed that the ramparts on the inſide were no where leaſed out for private gardens; for then, where the rivers would permit, a walk of this kind, like that on the walls of *Cheſter*, might be carried quite round the city.

The city is divided within its walls into four diſtricts or *wards*; which take their names from the four great gates of the city; *viz. Micklegate-ward*, *Bootham-ward*, *Monk-ward* and *Walmgate-ward*.

Micklegate-ward is in the ſouth-weſt part of the city; and is incompaſſed by the city's wall and the river *Ouſe* together. This ward contains ſix pariſhes, *viz. Biſhop-hill* the elder, and younger; *Trinity*'s, St. *Martin*'s, St. *John*'s and *All-Saints*.

Bootham-ward, takes the north-weſt angle, and has three pariſhes in its diſtrict, *viz. Belfray's*, St. *Ellen*'s and St. *Martin*'s.

Monk-ward, lyes on the north-eaſt of the city, and contains five pariſhes; that is to ſay, *Trinity's*, St. *Cuthbert's*, St. *Saviour's*, *Chriſt*'s pariſh, and St. *Sampſon's*.

Walmgate-ward is ſouth-eaſt; and has ſeven pariſhes, *viz.* St. *Margaret's*, St. *Dyonis*, St. *George*, *Crux* pariſh, *Allhallows*, St. *Mary*'s and St. *Michael*'s. Theſe diviſions take up the whole city within its walls; except the *cloſe* of the cathedral, which will fall in another place.

Before I begin to particularize the ſeveral ſtreets, lanes, &c. that compoſe theſe ſeveral wards, I ſhall take notice that the word *(g)* **Gate** is not with us, as in the ſouth, taken for a port, or ſtraight entrance into any city, town, &c. but for an open paſſage, ſtreet or lane; being uſed as an adjunct, as *Caſtle-gate*, *Spurrier-gate*, *Collier-gate*, and the like. We have few places called ſtreets in *York*, and the great gates or entrances to the city are called **Barrs** *(h)*. I meet with a number of names aſſigned to ſtreets or lanes in this city in old records, or elſewhere, which are now changed into others, or the ſtreets quite loſt, as **Vertergate, Kerregate, Hattergate, Hammerton-lane, Bretegate, Frere-lane, Thruſgate, Benlay-lane, Ratten-row cum les tofts, Litelgate-ſtreet, Loningate, Glover-lane,** &c. But I haſten to the ſurvey of thoſe that are now in being.

(d) By another *mandamus* from king *Edw.* II. the dean and chapter of *York* are ſtrictly commanded not to hinder the gathering the ſettled **tallage**, or tax, for the repairs and fortifications of the city walls and ditches, which they had preſumed to do. *Vide append. clauſ.* 14 *Ed.* II. *m.* 12. *dorſo.*

(e) Vide annal. ſub an. 1329.

(f) An. 148?, ſir *William Tode* mayor.

(g) **Gate**, via, *q. d.* iter, tranſitus. Belg **Gat.** Teut. **Gaſſe.** *Dad.* **Gade**, Platea, vicus, *omnia ab A. S.* **Gan.** ire. Skinner *& dict.*

(h) **Barre**, a Belg. **Barre**, Repagulum, Vectis. Franco-Gaul. Barre & Barreau, *vectis & cancelli tribunalis*. Datur a Cam. Br Barre, *vectis noſtrae, credo, originis. Idem*

1

(b) Mickle-

(*i*) *Micklegate*, called alſo **Mickellyth**, has its name no doubt from the length and ſpaciouſ- MICKLE-
neſs of it; and is a ſtreet which leads from the bar to the bridge. The port or entrance GATE WARD.
to it is a noble one indeed, and ſtill bears a teſtimony of that antiquity which few in the kingdom can boaſt of. It is adorned with lofty turrets and handſomely embattled; over the arch aloft hangs a large ſhield with the arms of *England* and *France* painted and gilt; on each ſide two leſſer, with the arms of the city on them. It appears by a record in the *Pipe-office* that one *Benedict Fitz-Engelram* gave half a mark for licence to build a certain houſe upon this bar, and ſix pence annual rent for having it hereditary, (*k*) the eighth of *Richard* I. But this does not aſcertain the age of the preſent ſtructure. Yet I obſerve the *flower de luces* in the royal arms are not confined to the number three; which puts it out of doubt that they were placed there before *Henry* the fifth's time; who was the firſt that gave that particular number in his bearing. The bar is ſtrengthened by an outer gate which had a maſſy iron chain went croſs it, then a port-cullis, and laſtly a mighty ſtrong double wooden gate, which is cloſed in every night at the uſual hours. It has the character altogether, as to antient fortification, to be as noble and auguſt a port as moſt in *Europe*. The inſide was renewed and beautified *anno* 1716, *R. Townes* lord-mayor, as appears by an inſcription upon it. For the reſt I refer to the print of the gate itſelf in the foregoing ſheets.

Having entered this gate, the firſt thing that offers itſelf to an antiquary's obſervation, Priory *of St.*
is an antient gateway, that ſtands on the right hand this ſpacious ſtreet. This was the por- TRINITY.
tal to the priory of St. *Trinity*, which ſtood in the gardens beyond it. Benedictins.

The priory of St. *Trinity* was a cell to that of *marmontier*, or *majus monaſterium*, in *Tourain* in *France*; founded by *Ralph Paganel*, who, in the conqueror's time, having a certain church in *York*, given him, in fee, built to the honour of St. *Trinity*, heretofore ſtored with canons and eccleſiaſtical ornaments, and endowed with predial rents, but now deſtroyed by *William* at the rendition of the city; this *Ralph* deſigning to reſtore the ſervice of God therein, granted the ſame to the abbey of S. *Martin*, *majoris monaſterii in France*; and to the monks thereof, for a perpetual poſſeſſion; and to be of their ordering and viſitation for ever (*l*).

And for the due ſuſtentation of theſe monks he granted them the church of St. **Trinity** *Revenues.*
itſelf, together with three crofts appertaining, lying on the weſt ſide of the city. Likewiſe the church of St. **Elene** within the ſaid city, with the toft of one deacon adjacent. Alſo the churches of **Allſaints** in **North-ſtreet**, and St. **Bridget** in **Muclegate**. And the chapel of St. **James** without the bar. And in

Yorkſhire, he gave the church of St. **John** of **Adele**, with one carucate of land. The tithes of **Ardington**, the mediety of the town, with the hall tithes there. Alſo one carucate of land in **Bardeby**. The church of **Barton** in **Rydale**, and two parts of his demeſn tithes. The mediety of the church of **Cramburn**. The town of **Drax**, with one piſcary, with the tithes of the other piſcaries. Two carucats of land in **Drengſhireſes**. The tithes of **Fademore** and the hall tythes there. Half a bovate of land in **Hampole**. Fourteen bowates in **Heſleſey**. The church of **Hoton** in **Bilaham**, and the hall tithes thereof, with two parts of the demeſne tithes. The cell (*m*) of **Hedley**, and chapel of **Holbeck**. The church of **Ledes** with the hall-tithes, and half a carucate of land; as alſo two other carucats, and two bovates of land there. The church of **Monkton** and one carucate and half of land there. The church of **Newton** with the hall tithes, and two parts of the tithes demeſne of *Radulph de Rolli*. Two parts of the demeſne tithes of **Newton ſuper Ouſe**. Two bovates of land in **Secroft**. One bovate in **Sipeleer**. Two bovates of land in **Sniterton**. (*n*) The whole town of **Stratton** and tithes thereof, and tithes nf **Strattonhaul**. The church of St. **Elene** of **Terneſco**, and two parts of the demeſne tithes there. (*o*) Four bovates of land in **Huſburn**; alſo enthorning in the wood of **Rye**.

In **Lincolnſhire**, (*p*) the ſaid *Ralph de Paganel* gave them the church of **Barton**, and two parts of the demeſne tithes. In **Eſſeby** two parts of the demeſne tithes of *Simon Tochett*. The church of **Erneham** with its glebe land and tithes, and two parts of the demeſne tithes; and two parts of the tithes of **Aſcelyne-hall**. The town of **Conigeſthorpe**. The churches of **Raſyn** and **Rochbury**. Two parts of the demeſne tithes of *Simon Tochett* in **Scaleberie**. And two parts of the tithe demeſne of *Ralph de Rolli* in **Tanleſby**.

(*i*) **Mickle** *ab* Ang. Sax. Micl, Micel, Teut. *vet.* **Mikil**, Dan. **Megil**, *Magnus*, &c. **Lythe** is not ſo eaſy to account for; Lið, *Saxonice*, is *lenis*, *mollis*, &c. ſo alſo it ſignifies, as a ſubſtantive, *articulus*, *artus*, *nervus*; Fingner Lið *extremum digiti*, the tip of the finger, *Luke* 16. 24. But whether this ſtreet is called ſo from being at the extremity of the town I ſhall not ſay. See *Somner's Saxon* dict.

(*k*) Benedictus *filius* Engelranni *deb. dim m. pro habenda licentia aedificandi quandam domum ſuper portam de* **Mikel-lythe** *in civitate* Eboraci; *et pro annual. redditu* vi*d. et pro habenda praefata domo hereditarie. Rot.* Pipe 8 R. I.

(*l*) *Mon. Ang. v.* 1 *f.* 564. By the conqueror's ſurvey this *Ralph Paganel*, who came in with him, held at that time ten lordſhips in *com. Devon.* five in *com Suffolk*, fifteen in *com. Lincoln*, and fifteen *com Ebor. Dug. Bar.* In the conqueror's time he was high ſheriff of *Yorkſhire. Lel.* col. *Hutton-painell*, *Newport-painel* and ſeveral other towns ſtill bear the name of this family.

(*m*) *Mon. Ang. v.* 1. *f.* 565.

(*n*) *Ex originali.*

(*o*) *Mon. Ang.* 564.

(*p*) *Idem.*

Rad.

MICKLE-GATE WARD. (q) *Rad. Parmantarius* granted to God and the church of St. Trinity, and to the monks *majoris monasterii*, all his land appertaining to two oxgang of land in Gereford. Also *Adam de Preston* granted to them all his land in Gereford nigh Lowes rode. And *Robert* son of *Jordan de Buggethorpe* gave them all his land pertaining to four oxgang of land in Gereford. *Heraldus*, son of *Ralph*, gave to them one oxgang of land in Mickelfeld. And *Adam Fitz-Pater* granted to God and St. *Trinity* ten acres of his meadow in Smethdale. (r) By a patent of *Edward* III. this priory had an ample confirmation of all its possessions and privileges.

This being an *alien priory*, the priors thereof were always preferred by the abbots *de majori monasterio* in *Normandy*; the proper patrons. It was found, by inquisition taken the twenty fourth of *Edward* I. at *York*, that the heirs of the founder claimed no right in the temporals of this priory, upon the death of any prior, but only to place a porter to see that the goods of the priory be not stoln during the vacation. And that when a prior should be deputed by the abbot of *Marmontier*, he might take possession of the priory without any contradiction.

For which reason the priors being neither admitted nor confirmed by the archbishop of the province, says Mr. *Torre*, they are not within his register; therefore a catalogue cannot be given of them.

Anno 30 of *Henry* VIII. this priory of *Holy Trinity Ebor.* was surrendred up by the prior and ten priests. (s) Valued at the dissolution at cxcvi*l.* xi*s.* x*d.* *Dug.* See their seal.

In the *compendium compertorum*, by Dr. *Legh* and Dr. *Clayton*, in their visitation of religious houses by command of *Henry* VIII. these crimes and superstitions are charged upon this fellowship.

(t) *S.* TRIN. EBOR.

Sodom. Ric. Speyte *prior*. Johannes Killingbeck, Willielmus Graine, Oliverus Warde, Ricardus Stubbas, Ricardus Prisshowes, *per vol. pol.*

Incont. Ric. Stubbes, *cum sex pueris et tot feminis.*

Superst. Rob. Parker, Bryanus Braye *petunt exuere habitum religiosum.*

Hic in veneratione habent zonam cujusdam olim prioris hujus domus, parturientibus, ut creditur, salutif.

Nelefon's chantry *in this church.* The chantry of *Thomas Nelefon* in the church of St. *Nicolas*, alias St. *Trinity*'s, was founded and ordained for one chaplain, for ever to celebrate at the altar of St. *Thomas the martyr*, in this conventual church or priory, for the good estate of himself while he lives, and after his decease for his soul and for the soul of *Catherine* his wife. He willed the same to be called by this special name of

(u) **The chantry of Thomas Nelefon.**

And moreover willed and ordained that every chaplain of the same chantry, shall every week celebrate for their said souls three masses, *viz.*

1. *De spiritu sancto.* 2. *De officiis mortuorum.* 3. *De sancta cruce.* And at the end of each mass, immediately after the ending of St. *John*'s gospel, shall make (*sua retroversa*) and say for their said souls *de profundis*, together with the collect *fidelium Deus*, &c. Also that every day they say for the souls aforesaid *placebo, dirige*, with accustomary prayers.

(x) For the sustentation of this chantry a rent was charged coming out of the manor of Connysthorpe, the priory's possession of iii*l.* vi*s.* viii*d.* and xl*l.* *per annum* allowance for the priests meat and drink; which was paid by the king's majesty *Henry* VIII, from the late suppressed house of St. *Trinity*'s. *Valet de claro* iv*l.* xix*s.*

This church is now of small compass, but has been abundantly larger, as appears by the building. The steeple of it being exceeding ruinous was blown down, *anno* 1651, and rebuilt again at the charge of the parish, but not in the same place the former stood. The living is of small value now, and is in the king's gift, five pound *per annum*, besides the parsonage house standing in the east corner of the church-yard, built *an.* 1639, by Mr. *H. Rogers* minister thereof. To this was united, *an.* 1585, the parish of St. *Nicolas* according to the statute.

Monumental INSCRIPTIONS.

Mern 1503. (y) **Orate pro anima domini Roberti Mern capellani gilde corporis Christi an. dom.** 1503. **cujus anime, &c.**

Flos. ✠ **Hic jacet Walterus Flos.**

On a copartment.

Danby 1695. *Epitaphium in obitum* Annae *uxoris* Christopheri Danby *armigeri, quae sanctissima vita emisit animam beatam* xi *die Novembris* MDCXCV *anno aet. suae* 63.

(q) *Omn. ex chart. orig.*
(r) *Pat.* 30 Ed. III. *pars* 1. *m.* 14. *Vide append.*
(s) *Burnet*'s hist. refor.
(t) *Idem.*
(u) MS. *Torre* p. 788.
(x) *Steven's* add. vol. 1.
(y) These two from Mr. *Dodsworth* taken *an.* 1618.

MICKLE-GATE WARD.

Atropos haud valui tamen hanc abscindere vitam,
Tanta intexta fuit vis pietate sua.
Addidit ipse mihi Deus sua stamina vires:
Mortua nunc vivit, non moritura Deo.

Hocce monumentum exsculptum impensis Abstrupi Danby *militis in piam defunctae suae matris memoriam, erecta fuit in hac basilica* XV. *die Jan.* MDCXVI.

On another copartment.

John Green *of* Horsefield *gentleman who died the* 17th *of Aug.* 1708. *in the forty fourth year of his age. Erected by his brother Mr.* William Green. 1729. Green. 1708.

On a brass plate.

He lies the body of Elias Micklethwait *alderman, once lord mayor of this city, who deceased* an. 1638. Micklethwait. 1638.

None else remarkable.

The circuit of the ground, belonging to the site of this priory, is of great extent, being bounded by the street on one side, a lane called *Trinity lane* to the east, where are two good houses built by Mrs. *Dawson* and *Hillary* wine merchants, the city walls on the west, and its own wall on the south. It is now called *Trinity-gardens*, the ground belonging to the family of the *Goodricks* of *Ribston*.

Behind these gardens in the south east corner of the city is a place of great antiquity; so old as seems to mock any search that can be made for its original. It is called in the antientest deeds and histories, that I have yet met with, *vetus ballium*, or **old baile**; which, according to the etymology of the word, can come from nothing sooner than the *Norman baile*, a prison or place of security, or from *baile* an officer who has the jurisdiction over a prison. It took this name probably after the conquest, when the *French* language was substituted, in all places, instead of the *English*; and for that very reason I take it to have been a castle or fortress before that time. It is said by several authors, which I have quoted in the annals, that *William* the conqueror built two castles at *York*, for the better security of both city and country about it. But, if I may be allowed a conjecture, I suppose that he built one castle from the foundation, and repaired the old one; for that there was a fortress here in the time of the *Saxons*, where king *Athelstane* besieged and blocked up the *Danes*, has also been shewn in the annals. *Leland*, and after him *Camden*, are positive that this is the platform of an antient castle, as the former's description of the city walls and bulwarks does plainly shew. And, indeed, whoever carefully views it at this day, must be of the same opinion, especially when he is told that the ramparts, when dug into, are full of foundation stones, as I myself have observed. There is a passage in *R. Hoveden* which says that when the bishop of *Ely*, lord chancellor and regent of *England*, came down to punish the citizens for their barbarous massacre of the Jews, he delivered the high sheriff over to the custody of his brother *Osbert de Longchamp*, and then began to repair the castle in *veteri castellaria*, which king *William* had rebuilt. (z) There is no doubt but by this *vetus castellum* is meant our *old baile*; and this I think is sufficient to prove it a very antient fortress. OLD BAILE.

How it came, from a state fortress, to be the archbishop's prison I know not; yet such it was, and not a palace for them as some have supposed; it being absurd to think they had two palaces in the same town. The site of *old baile*, and the district extending towards *Ousebridge*, is still called *Bishophill*; and in our old registers in the accounts of the constableries of the city, and their proper officers, I find this left for the nomination of the archbishop, *viz. anno* 1380, *vetus ballium in custodia archiepiscopi* Ebor. I am as much at a loss to find when the church gave it up to the civil magistrate, for such it is at this day, without any leasehold that I know of. *Anno* 1326, 1 *Ed.* III. a dispute arose betwixt the citizens (*a*) and *William de Melton* then archbishop, which of them were obliged to repair the walls round this place. The cause was heard before *Isabel* the queen-mother, at that time resident in the archiepiscopal palace at *York*, in council, where *Nicholas Langton*, then mayor of the city alledged, that this district was the express jurisdiction of the archbishop exempt from the city, and therefore he ought to keep up the fortifications of it. The archbishop pleaded that it stood within the ditches (*infra fossatas civitatis*) and therefore belonged to those that repaired the rest. Upon hearing it was given against the archbishop, who was obliged to repair these walls; and this is the reason of that passage in *Stubbs*'s life of this prelate, taken notice of by *Camden* and others, *viz. locum in* Eboraco, *qui dicitur vetus* **ballium**, *primo spissis et longis* xvii *pedum tabulis, secundo lapideo muro fortiter includebat.* The former account, which I have seen in an old register of the city, explains the latter, and gives us to understand, that it was only the city walls, round this place, which the archbishop repaired.

I have nothing further to add about this ruined antiquated castle, or what you will call it

(z) R. Hoveden *sub an.* 1189-90.

(a) *Ex registro* Ebor.

MICKLE-GATE WARD. it, but that the *area* ufed formerly (*b*) to be a place open for fports and recreations, but is now enclofed and leafed out by the city at fix pounds *per annum*. The mount which *Camden* mentions to have been raifed for a tower to be built on, exactly correfponds to the citadel on the other fide of the river. I hope it will not be thought trivial to inform pofterity, alfo, that this mount, the pleafanteft place for profpect about the city, was planted with trees, *anno* 1726, by the late Mr. *Henry Pawfon* merchant then leaffee of the ground; becaufe in time, they muft be a particular ornament to the city, and it may ferve to fatisfy fome people's curiofity, *in futuro*, to know when they were put down there.

SKELDER-GATE. At the foot of *old baile* lies **Skeldergate**, a long narrow ftreet running parallel with the river as far as the bridge. It has a pofterngate at the fouth end of it leading to *Bifhopthorpe*, and was widened of late years for coaches and carriages to pafs through, in compliment I fuppofe to the archbifhop who now comes always this way into the city. This ftreet derives its name from the *Dutch* (*c*) word **keller, keldar**, a cellar; where, when trade flourifhed in *York*, in another manner than it does now, many merchants cellars or warehoufes were kept. But it has fmall title to that name at this time, except from the noble vaults built in it by the late Mr. *Pawfon* wine merchant; whofe father and grandfather were of the fame bufinefs, lived in this ftreet, and were all of them in their times, the chief traders, in that way, in the city. Betwixt thefe vaults and the poftern is a publick *crane* for weighing goods out of fhips, lighters, and other veffels; the property of the city, who put in an officer, and fettle *crane-dues*.

MIDDLETON's hofpital. There is an hofpital erected on the weft fide this ftreet, of the foundation of Mrs. *Anne Middleton*, relict of *Peter Middleton* gent. who was one of the fheriffs of this city, *anno* 1618. It was built and endowed *anno* 1659, for the maintenance and lodging of twenty poor widows of freemen, each widow to have four pounds *per annum*, the difpofition and nomination of whom was left to the mayor, aldermen, and commonality of the city. For the erecting and endowment of this hofpital the faid *Anne Middleton* gave by her will two thoufand pound; but fome confiderable part being loft in ill hands, the widows are now reduced to three pound *per annum* each; which is all they receive at prefent. The hofpital is a fquare brick building round an inner court, the rooms or cells are all on the ground floor, the doors of which, number one to twenty, open all into one paffage. Over the front door is placed the effigies, in ftone, of the foundrefs, with an infcription on each fide, giving an account of this and other her charitable gifts; but lately under an appearance of cleaning it the letters are moft of them filled up with lime, and the infcription illegible. On the back of this hofpital is a fquare garden, where every widow has a proportion allowed for her particular ufe.

Church *of St.* MARY the elder. Turning the corner of this hofpital up a lane called *Kirk-lane* ftands the parifh church of St. *Mary Bifhophill the elder*, to diftinguifh it from a fifter church of the fame name near it. This was a rectory (*d*) of medieties, one whereof belonged, antiently, to the prior and convent of *Helagh-park*, afterwards the *Meringtons*, *Nevils* and the crown; and the other to the families of the *Percys*, *Vavafours* and lord *Scropes* of *Bolton*. *Anno* 1585, the parifh church of St. *Clements*, without *Skeldergate* poftern, was united to this church according to the ftatute of the firft of *Edward* VI.

The two medieties were of equal value in the king's book, *viz.*

	l.	*s.*	*d.*
Firft fruits —	05	06	08
Tenths —	00	10	00
Procur. *Scrope*'s med.	00	06	08

A clofe CATALOGUE of the RECTORS of the PRIORS mediety.

Temp. inftit. Anno.	*Rectores.*	*Patroni.*	Vacat.
1293	*Dom.* Rob. de Ebor.	*Prior et conventus de* Parco-Helagh.	
	Tho. de Hutton, *prefb.*		*per refig.*
1349	John de Parys, *cap.*		*per mort.*
1367	Rob. Sauvage, *prefb.*	Will. de Morington.	*per mort.*
1369	Ric. de Ilyklap, *prefb.*	Kath. *relict.* Will. *praed,*	*per mort.*
1436	Ric. Hamerton.	*Dom^na* Johanna *comitiffa* Weftmorland.	*per mort.*
1464	Joh. Johnfon, *cap.*	Ric. *com. de* Warwick.	*per refig.*
1478	Will. Grendale, *cap.*	*Idem.*	*per mort.*
1490	Chrift. Plummer, *L. B.*	Hen. VII. *rex.*	*per refig.*
1496	John Gibfon, *prefb.*	*Idem.*	*per mort.*

(*b*) Camden. *Clauf. an.* 1 Ed. III. *p.* 2. *m.* 17. *dorfo*, there was a queftion moved before the king's council between the archbifhop and the mayor and commonality of *York*, which of them fhould have the cuftody of a place called the **old bail** againft the affaults of enemies. The difpute of this matter, very imperfect in the city's regifter, is given in the *appendix*.

(*c*) **Keller, Keldar**, *Belg. Cella vinaria, penaria feu promptuaria a lat. cellarium et cella*, a cave or vault. *Skinner.*

(*d*) *Ex MS.* Torre *f.* 713.

Temp.

I

Temp. instit. Anno	*Rectores.*	*Patroni.*	*Vacat.*
1515	Willam Idle, *presb.*	Hen. VIII. *rex.*	*per resig.*
1532	John Bene, *presb.*	*Idem.*	
	John Pulleyne.	*Idem.*	*per resig.*
1574	Christ. Ashburn.	Eliz. *reg.*	*per resig.*
1580	John Grinshawe.	*Eadem.*	*per mort.*
1605	Tho. Longhor, *cap.*	Jac. *rex.*	*per cession.*
1607	Ric. Whittington, *cap.*	*Idem.*	*per cession.*
1613	Will. Bolton, *cap.*	*Idem.*	

The same of the lord SCROPE'*s mediety.*

Temp. instit. Anno	*Rectores.*	*Patroni.*	*Vacat.*
1267	John de Chesterfield, *cl.*	*Dom.* Agnes de Percy.	
1267	Rob. de Herlington.	*Dom.* Rob. *de* Plompton, *mil.*	
1271	Will. Sampson, *cler.*	Joh. le Vavasour, *miles.*	
1280	Symon de Chaterton.	*Idem.*	
1313	Galf. de Boulton, *cap.*	*Dom.* Hen. le Scrope, *miles.*	*per resig.*
1333	John de Eston, *presb.*	*Idem.*	*per mort.*
1349	Ric. de Manfield, *cap.*	*Dom.* Ric. le Scrope *miles, dom. de* Bolton.	
	Dom. Joh. de Lunde.	*Idem.*	*per mort.*
1398	Hen. del Cotes, *presb.*	*Idem.*	*per mort.*
1407	Joh de Cheshant.	*Tutor* Ric. le Scrope.	*per mort.*
1412	Rob. de Morton.	*Dom.* Ric. le Scrope *Dom.* de Bolton.	*per resig.*
1416	Will. Sharrowe, *presb.*	*Idem.*	*per resig.*
1416	Will. Hackford, *presb.*	*Idem.*	*per mort.*
1443	Joh. Midelton, *cler.*	Hen. *Dom.* le Scrope.	*per resig.*
1447	Rob. Slake, *cap.*	Will. Chessever *et* Marg. *soror Dom.* le Scrope.	*per resig.*
1449	Joh. Melote, *cap.*	*Idem.*	*per resig.*
1450	Rob. Cartwright, *presb.*	*Idem.*	*per resig.*
1451	Henry Cliffe, *presb.*	*Idem.*	*per mort.*
1485	Reginald Swayle.	Joh. *Dom.* le Scrope.	*per mort.*
1500	Hen. Richardson.	Hen. *dom.* le Scrope *de* Bolton.	*per resig.*
1505	Ric. Petonse, *presb.*	*Idem.*	*per resig.*
1507	Sim. Hedrington, *presb.*	*Idem.*	*per resig.*
1511	Rob. Thornton, *presb.*	*Idem.*	*per mort.*
1514	Tho. Johnson, *presb.*	*Idem.*	*per resig.*
1517	*Dom.* George Bradridge.	*Idem.*	*per mort.*
1518	Rog. Ashby, *presb.*	*Idem.*	*per mort.*
1522	Rob. Newton, *presb.*	*Idem.*	
	George Dryver, *cler.*	J. G. L. D. *assig. dom.* Scrope.	*per mort.*
1589	Joh. Grymshawe, *cler.*	*Idem.*	*per mort.*
1605	Joh. Sceller, *cler.*	*Idem.*	
1614	Hen. Rogers, *cler.*	*Assign.*	*per mort.*
1622	Hen. Procter, *cler.*	Car. I.	
1668	Will. Stainforth, *cler.*	Tho. *com.* Rivers *jure cober.* T. *dom.* le Scrope.	

Basy'*s chantry.*

There was a chantry the 12th of *May*, 1319, founded, in this church of St. *Mary Bishophill* the elder, at the altar of St. *Katherine* virgin, in the chapel thereunto annexed, by *Roger Basy* some time citizen of *York*; to pray for the soul of the founder, &c. *Valet de claro* 40*l.*

Mr. *Torre*'s chantry priests omitted.

Basy'*s second chantry.*

(e) Founded by *Elizabeth Basy*, *April* 4, 1403. to pray, &c. at the aforesaid altar of St. *Katherine* in this church; and to pay thirteen poor people yearly on St. *Lucy*'s day, which was the day of her burial, thirteen pence each; having an annual rent out of the moiety of the manor of **Bilbrough** *(f) in com.* Ebor. *Valet de claro* 6 *l.* 5 *s.* 9 *d.*

The fabrick of this church discovers a great quantity of mill-stone grit to be wrought up in the walls of it. The church being run much to ruin, the parishioners built a handsome square steeple of brick, *anno* 1659, and repaired the roof of it, &c. The

(e) The original of this chantry is in the chamber of records in the council-room, *Ousebridge*, drawer 5. Value from *Dods. coll. ambo.*

(f) Seven pound rent *per annum* out of the manor of *Bilburg. ut patet per. pat.* 4 *Hen.* IV, *p.* 1. *m.* 2.

inside

MICKLE-GATE WARD. inside is divided into two isles by one row of pillars: monumental inscriptions in it are these,

Northeby. L. M. 1416. ✠ Hic jacet Magareta mater Johannis Northebye civis cujus anime propicietur Deus. Amen.

Westbe. 1486. ✠ Hic jacet Matilda Westbe quondam uxor Willielmi Westbe qui obiit xiii die mensis Augusti an. dom. MCCCCLXXXVI. cujus anime, &c. Amen.

Curtas. 1657. John Curtas *departed this life* October 13. *an.*
Deborah *his wife* 1657.

Mitchell. 1682. *Here lieth the body of* Thomas Mitchell *son of* Robert Mitchell *of* Hooke, *who departed this life* November 23, 1682.

Wilton. 1425. Hic jacet Thomas Wilton quondam et Elena uxor ejus qui obiit quinto die mensis Novembris anno dom MCCCC XXV, cujus, &c.

Pawson. 1677. *Here lieth the body of* John Pawson *merchant, who departed this life the* 4th *of* August, 1677.

Cook. 1642. John Cook *departed this life* December 17, 1642.

Later epitaphs, which are remarkable, are these,
A copartment.

ARMS.

Gules a chevron between three lions paws erected and erased *or.*

On an escutcheon of pretence.
Argent, a fess in chief, three mullets *sable,* the middlemost pierced of the field.

In memory of Elias Pawson *esquire. He was an alderman of this city, and lord-mayor in the year* 1704. *He died the* 5th *of* January, 1715. *aged forty four years. His surviving issue by his wife* Mary *the daughter of Mr.* William Dyneley *of this city, was three sons* Henry, William *and* John, *and three daughters* Mary, Sarah *and* Dorothy. —— *His said wife died* June 2, 1728. *aged* 58 *years.*

Grave stones.

Here lyeth the body of Elias *son of* Elias Pawson *merchant, who died the* 12th *of* August, *anno dom.* 1700. *aged* 2 *years* 9 *months.*

Also the body of Alice *his daughter, who was born the* 3d *of* July, 1702. *and died the same day.*

Also the body of Elias *his son who died the* 30th *of* November, 1705. *aged* 4 *years,* 5 *months and* 7 *days.*

Also the body of his son Dyneley, *aged* 19 *days.*

Also the body of his daughter Elizabeth, *who was born the* 12 *of* September, 1696. *and died the* 19th *of* October, 1708.

Also the body of his son Thomas, *who died the* 11th *of* November, *aged* 3 *years.*

Also the body of the said Elias Pawson *esquire, who died the* 5th *of* January, 1715. *aged* 44 *years.*

Also the body of Mary *his wife, who died the* 2d *of* June, 1728. *aged* 58 *years.*

Another grave stone.

Here was buried the body of Mr. Henry Pawson *of this city merchant, who died* January 24, 1730. *aged* 35 *years and* 4 *months.*

Also the bodies of

Elias *his son, who died* July 21, 1722. *aged* 1 *week.*
Martin *his son, who died* May 29, 1724, *aged* 1 *week.*
Elias *his son, who died* July 1, 1725, *aged* 2 *years.*
Catherine *his daughter, who died* November 26, 1730. *aged* 3 *years and* 6 *months.*

On a copartment north of the altar arms impaled:

1. *Gules,* a chevron entre three lions paws erected and erased *or.* *Pawson.*
2. *Argent,* three bars gemels *gules,* over all a lion rampant *sable.* *Fairfax.*

HENRY PAWSON,

Pawson. 1735 Sheriff 1723. *Son of* ELIAS, *and grandson of* HENRY PAWSON *merchants and citizens of* YORK;
A worthy son of a most worthy father; whose civilities, hospitalities, and charities, not only this parish, this city, but the whole country were sensibly acquainted with.
Their justice and integrity ran parallel with their trade; extensive in all.
Nor will it be presumption to add, that as this truly antient city never enrolled a worthier magistrate than the father, so could it never boast a citizen of a more human and gentlemanlike disposition than the son.

He
a

He married Catherine *the daughter of* Robert Fairfax *of* Steeton *esquire, by whom he had six children; of which the eldest and youngest sons,* Robert *and* Henry, *only, survived him. He died* January 24, 1730; *aged* 35 *years.* MICKLE-GATE WARD.

Names and arms in the windows remarked by Mr. *Dodsworth*; in the choir window,

Orate pro anima domini Roberti Savage.
Orate pro dom. Johanne Mansfeld.

In the same window two coats, *viz.*
Six eagles heads erazed *or.*
Three suns *or.*

In the north choir, called *Fairfax-chapel*, because it was the seat and burial place of that family, when they lived in this parish, is a copartment put against the wall without inscription, but set about with these arms, *viz.*

Argent, three bars gemels *gules*, over all a lion rampant *sable*. *Fairfax.*
Fairfax as before; impaling
Azure, three crescents *or*. *Ryther.*
Then *Fairfax* quartering
Argent, on a fess *sable*, between three flower de lyces *gules*, three besants. *Thwaites.*

A copartment for Mrs. *Mary Fairfax* daughter to *Henry* lord *Fairfax* of *Denton*, who died *September* 24, 1716. Arms in a lozenge. *Fairfax.*

Other inscriptions in the church and church-yard are upon *Ralph Yoward* gentleman, *John Ratcliff*, *Henry Dungworth*, *William Richardson*, *Robert Wilson*, *William Ramsden*, *Alexander Harrison*, *Robert Winn* and his son *John*, &c.

A piece of ground opposite to this church, south, is the *quakers burial place*; in which are some tombs, and some inscriptions, but none remarkable.

North of this church, but in the parish, stands the *skeleton* of a large mansion house, known by the name of *Buckingham-house*. It was built by *Thomas* lord *Fairfax*, (g) and after his death came to *Villars* duke of *Buckingham*, who married his daughter and heiress. When that great, but unfortunate, nobleman was banished the court, and had run his vast estate into difficulties, he chose to retire down to *York*. Here he lived for some time, and, according to his natural gaiety of temper, set all those diversions on foot, in which his whole life, hitherto, had been spent. The miserable circumstances that great man died in, in this country, this his house seems ever since to have mourned; the title to the ground it stands on, as well as the large and spacious gardens beyond it, having had so many equal claimants, that the house is daily dropping away, and is at present in a sad ruinous condition. I am told that *Thomas Fairfax* of *Newton* esquire, has now got over the difficulties and querks in law, and come into a good title of it; if so, it may again raise its head. For it is great pity this fine situation, by far the best in the town, with a noble ascent to it out of *Skeldergate*, and gardens extending to the ramparts of the city walls behind, should not fall into some persons hands, who would alter its present condition, and render it both useful to themselves, and an ornament to the publick. Here is an out shot from this house which I am told was built for the duke's laboratory in chymistry. Which mystery he expended vast sums of money in; and if he did not find out the philosopher's stone by it, it is certain he knew a way of dissolving, or evaporating, gold and other metals, quicker than any other man of that age; or since, except in the person of another noble duke, lately dead, of as exalted a *genius* as the former. BUCKINGHAM house.

Higher up, on *Bishophil*, and near adjoining to the back of the priory of St. *Trinity*, stands a parish church called St. *Mary's*, *Bishophill*, *the younger*.

This church was esteemed one of the great farms belonging to the dean and chapter of *York*; and by them usually demised, with the advowson of the vicarage, to one of the canons residentiary at the rent of sixty marks *per annum*, being called the farm of Copmanthorpe. The town of Copmanthorpe belongs to this church and parish of St. *Mary*, the dean and chapter having the tythe corn and hay thereof; usually let to farm at the rent of 16 *l. per ann.* The town of Over-popilton belongs to this parish also (h). ST. MARY'S younger.

Feb. 21. *an.* 1449. an arbitration was made between the dean and chapter and the abbot and convent of St. *Mary's York*, that this church of St. *Mary* Bishophill should receive the tythes of certain faggots, and *Astelwode*, in the Wood called Suthwode, against Over-popilton (i).

The vicar of this church hath for his portion the oblation of his parishioners, mortuaries and personal tythes, also the tythes of orchards and nurseries, and increase of cattle, for which he shall cause the church and chapel *honestly* to be served, and pay yearly to the far-

(g) It appears by several antient deeds that I have seen in the custody of *Bryan Fairfax* esquire, that the site of this house in *Skeldergate*, and the gardens on *Bishophil*, was purchased from several hands by *Thwaites*; from whom it came to the *Fairfax's* by a marriage of the heiress of that family, *temp. Hen.* VIII.

(h) *Ex* MS. Torre *f.* 697.

(i) *Idem*; *sed notand in custodia cleri vest.* Ebor *cum lit'* G.

MICKLE-GATEWARD. mer of the chapter of *York* 20*s*. All the residue the canon residentiary hath for forty mark (*k*).

				l.	*s.*	*d.*
Valor. in the king's books.	First fruits			10	00	00
	Tenths			00	10	00
	Subsidies			00	06	08

(*l*) *A close CATALOGUE of the VICARS of St.* MARY BISHOP-HILL NOVA.

Temp. instit. Anno	*Vicarii eccl.*	*Patroni.*	*Vacat.*
1317	Tho. de Middleton, *cap.*	*Firmar. decan. & cap.* Ebor.	
1320	Joh. Brown, *presb.*	*Idem.*	
1336	Hugo de Acclom, *presb.*		
	Hugo de Saundby.		*per resig.*
1349	Hugo de Thornton, *cap.*		
	Walter Midelham.		*per mort.*
1361	Gal. Poynings, *presb.*		*per resig*
1364	W. de Copmanthorpe.		*per resig.*
1365	Tho. de Lincolne.		*per resig.*
1369	Ric. de Appelby.		*per mort.*
1370	Will. de Thorle.		
	Will. Burton.		*per mort.*
1407	Joh. de Akum, *S. T. B.*	*Cap.* Ebor.	*per resig.*
1410	Ric. Erghes, *presb.*		*per mort.*
1415	Will. King, *cap.*	*Iidem.*	*per mort.*
1415	Will. Baumberg, *cap.*	*Firmarii cap.*	
	Will. Burton.		*per mort.*
1417	Will. Baumberg.		*per resig.*
1425	Tho. Euphame, *cap.*	*Cap.* Ebor.	*per resig.*
1441	Tho. Deighton, *cap.*	*Firmarii cap.*	*per mort.*
1451	Joh. Evenwode, *cap.*	*Idem.*	*per resig.*
1470	Will. Brand, *decret. B.*		*per resig.*
1472	Thomas Betson, *presb.*	*Firmarii decani et capituli* Ebor.	*per resig.*
1475	Rob. Danby, *cap.*		*per mort.*
1480	John Mirflete, *cap.*		
	Joh. Ripley, *presb.*		*per mort.*
1504	Joh. Collyns, *presb.*		*per mort.*
1522	Tho. Marser, *cap.*		*per resig.*
1531	Rob. Hill, *presb.*		*per mort.*
1541	Rob. Necham, *presb.*	*Assignati decani et capituli.*	
	Tho. Laut, *presb.*		*per mort.*
1557	Will. Dakyns, *cl.*	*Decani et capituli.*	*per mort.*
1558	Will. Hayton, *cler.*	*Iidem, &c.*	*per mort.*
1558	Rob. Norham, *cler.*		*per mort.*
1573	Ed. Swayne, *cler.*		
	John Whitgift, *cler.*		*per mort.*
1620	Marm. Gibbons, *cler.*		*per mort.*
1632	Ric. Johnson, *cler.*		*per mort.*
1638	Hen. Mace, *cler.*		*remov.*
1662	Will. Preston, *cler.*		*per mort.*
1670	Ric. Procter, *cler. M. A.*	*Archiepiscopus per lapsum.*	

This church stands at the confluence of three lanes, *viz. Trinity-lane*, *Bishop-hill* and *Fetter-lane* (*m*). It is a large church but not handsome, the steeple being the largest square tower of any parish-church in town. The north-side of this fabrick is almost wholly built with large and massy stones of the grit, on some of which may be traced the moldings of the regular orders. Ancient epitaphs preserved by Mr. *Dodsworth* are these:

Demlo. ✠ **Orate pro animabus Willielmi Demlo et Matilde et Johanne uxor. ejus.**

Printer 1597. **Here lyeth the body of Robert Printer late of Over-popilton yeoman, who deceased Feb. xviii. in xl. yere of reign of our sovereign lady queen Elizabeth A. D. 1597.**

Crostby 1383. ✠ **Orate pro animabus Willielmi Crostby nuper de Ebor. Cartwright et Johanne et Margarete uxor. ejus, qui quidem Willielmus obiit die Decembris A. D. MCCCCLXXXIII.**

(*k*) *Ex MS.* Torre, *f.* 697.
(*l*) *Ex MS.* Torre, *f.* 698.
(*m*) I have met with the name of a street here called **Seynte Mary-gate**, *juxta* **Bishop-hill**, but I know not where to place it.

✠ **Orate**

✠ Orate pro animabus Briani Middleton armigeri et christiane uroris ejus, qui quidem Brianus obiit vi. die mensis Januarii An. Dom. M.CCCC nonagesimo secundo quorum animabus propitietur deus. Amen. MICKLE-GATE WARD Middleton 1492.

On the same stone are these arms in brass:

1. Fretty on a canton a crescent; impaled with three greyhounds courfant. *Middleton* and *Maliverer*.
2. *Middleton* again.
3. *Middleton* impaled with a lyon rampant.

✠ Orate pro anima Johannis Topham, qui obiit vi. die mensis Januarii An. Dom. MCCCCLXXXII, cujus, &c. Topham, 1482.

ARMS in the church windows 1684 (*n*).

Azure, three suns or stars with divers rays. S. *Wilfrid* (Mr. *Torre*.)
York See. *Gules*, two keys in saltire, *argent*, in chief a crown imperial *or*.
Gules, six doves heads erased, *or*.
Quarterly, 1. *Or*, a cross *vert*. 2. *Argent*, on a chief, *gules*, two mullets pierced, *or*. 3. *Argent*, a bend ingrayl. *sable*. 4. Barry of six, *gules* and *ermine*. 5. *Or*, a cross *vert*. 6. *Argent*, three chevrons brased in base, *sable*. Mr. *Torre* calls these the arms of *Hussy*.

The only remarkable modern monument is north of the altar:

Hic jacet Maria Procter Thomae Procter *pharmacopolae chariſſima conjux, bis binis foecunda liberis relictis, virtutibus foecundior.* Proctor 1698.

Castae si que mentis alia et pudicae,
A qua quod sanctius intaminatae
Discant, vel ipsae virgines.
Lingua nec minus parca nec prodiga:
Et, quae raro convenire solent,
Et placidi oris et sinceri cordis;
Digna meliore monumento,
Hujusque degeneris aevi memoria
Et imitatione digniſſima
In coelum ascendit.
Aug. 23. *anno Dom.* 1698.
Aetatis 44.

In the church-yard is a tombstone sacred to the memory of a young maid, who was accidentally drowned *Dec.* 24, 1696, with these lines inscribed, said to be penned by her lover, which I readily believe:

Nigh to the river Ouse, *in* York'*s fair city,*
Unto this pretty maid death shew'd no pity;
As soon as she'd her pail with water fill'd,
Came sudden death and life like water spill'd.

From hence down a lane, called St. *Martyn's-lane*, we come to the parish church of St. *Martin*, which stands in *Micklegate*. CHURCH of St. MARTIN.

This church was an ancient rectory belonging to the patronage of the barons *Trusbutt*, then to the priory of *Wartyr*, after to the lords *Scrope* of *Massam*. *Anno* 1585, the church of St. *Gregory*, with all its members, was united to this church of St. *Martin*, and the parish thereof, according to the statute 1 *Edw.* I.

		l.	*s.*	*d.*
The rectory of St. *Martin* is thus valued in the king's books.	First fruits	06	13	00
	Or, —	02	12	00
	Tenths —	00	05	02½
	Procurations	00	06	08

(*o*) *A close CATALOGUE of the RECTORS of St.* MARTYN'*s*.

Temp. instit. Anno	*Rectores eccl.*	*Patroni.*	*Vacat.*
1230	*Dom.* Joh. Trusbutt, *cap.*	*Dom*ª. Elena Trusbutt.	
1306	Wal. de Scampston.	*Prior. et convent. de* Wartyr.	
1323	Rob. de Scampston.	*Iidem.*	
1349	Joh. Freman, *presb.*	*Iidem.*	*per mort.*
1357	Tho. de Bretby, *cap*	*Iidem.*	*per resig.*
	Rob. de Ferriby, *presb.*	*Iidem, &c.*	*per resig.*

(*n*) Ex MS. Rog. Gale, *arm.* (*o*) Ex MS. Torre, *f.* 645.

Temp.

2

MICKLE-GATE-WARD.

Temp. instit. Anno	*Restores eccl.*	*Patroni.*	*Vacat.*
1362	Rob. de Nafferton.	*Prior. et convent. de* Wartyr.	
	Joh. de Sharfe, *presb.*		*per mort.*
1369	Rob. de Ferriby, *presb.*		*per mort.*
1372	Rob. de le More, *presb.*		*per mort.*
	Joh. Westowe, *presb.*		*per mort.*
1407	Tho. Cliff, *cler.*	Hen. *dom. le* Scrope *de* Massam.	*per resig.*
1408	Joh. Newark, *cap.*	*Idem.*	*per resig.*
1410	Rob. Bryan, *presb.*	*Idem.*	*per resig.*
1426	Will. Fethyan, *presb.*	Joh. *dom.* Scrope.	*per mort.*
1429	Will. Caleys, *presb.*	*Idem.*	*per resig.*
1430	Nic. Bew, *presb.*	*Idem.*	*per resig.*
1437	Will. Eary, *cap.*	*Idem.*	*per resig.*
1458	(p) Joh. Burton, *cap.*	*Idem.*	*per mort.*
1476	Tho. Breston, *M. A.*	Ric. *dux* Glocest.	
	John Harte, *presb.*		*per mort.*
1519	Rob. Jackson, *presb.*	*Sept. cohered. Gals. dom. le* Scrope.	
	Rowland Helme.		*per mort.*
1556	Jac. Forlton, *cler.*	Rob. Roos *de* Ingmanthorp.	
	Hen. More, *cler.*		*per resig.*
1573	Jac. Frost *vel* Stocke, *cap.*	Will. Tankarder.	*per mort.*
1586	Arthur Hatfeld, *cap.*	Tho. Tankerder.	*per mort.*
1604	Joseph Maskwell, *cap.*	*Idem.*	*per mort.*
1614	Philip Nisbit, *cler.*	*Idem.*	*per cession.*
1617	Joh. Bramhall, *cap.*	*Idem.*	*per cession.*
1618	Joh. Hunlup, *cap.*	*Idem.*	*per resign.*
1619	Marm. Gibbons, *cap.*	Rob. Lupton, *not. pub.*	*per mort.*
1633	Joh. Bichall.	Thomas Hoyle, Hen. Barker.	*per mort.*
1641	Joh. Rawlinson, *c. M. A.*	Edvardus *visc.* Mandevile.	*per mort.*
1662	Toby Conyers, *cap.*	Tho. Dickenson, B. D. R. H. R. N, *&c.*	*per mort.*
1687	Sam. Coyne, *cler.*	Bryan Dawson, Ric. Clomley, Rad. Bell.	*per mort.*
1692	—— Mompesson, *cap.*	*Archiepiscopus per lapsum.*	

This church, sometimes called St. *Martyn cum Gregory*, is a handsome structure. The steeple of it being very ruinous, was taken down to the foundation and rebuilt at the charge of the parish; the first stone of it laid *July* 16, 1677. *Anno.* 1565, *John Been* lord-mayor gave one hundred marks to buy three tuneable bells for this church. And in the year 1680. a new clock and dyal was put up in the steeple at the proper cost and charge of *Sarah Bawtry* of this parish; widow to alderman *Bawtry*.

Mr. *Dodsworth*'s ancient epitaphs in this church are these:

Burton 1475. ✠ **Hic jacet dominus Willielmus Burton baccalaureus in artibus quondam rector istius ecclesie, qui obiit iiii die Martii An. Dom. M.CCCC.LXXV. cujus anime propitietur Deus. Amen.**

Gascoign 1486. ✠ **Orate pro anima Ricardi Gascoyne Vintener, qui obiit vicesimo quarto die mensis Octobris anno Domini Millesimo CCCC octogesimo sexto, cujus anime propitietur Deus. Amen.**

Cattal. 1450. ✠ **Hic jacet dominus Henricus Cattall, quondam capellanus hujus cantarie, qui obiit iiii die Februarii An. Dom. M.CCCC.L. cujus, &c. Amen.**

Person 1490. Vic. Ebor. 1477. ✠ **Orate pro anima Nicholai Person quondam civis et vicecomitis istius civitatis, et pro animabus Alicie et Chialy uxorum ejusdem qui obiit vicesimo die Aprilis Anno Dom. M.CCCC.LXXXX.**

In the west window:

(q) Quarterly, 1. *Argent*, a manch, *gules*. 2. *Argent*, a bend, *gules*.
Quarterly, 1. *Gascoign*. 2. *Gules*, a lyon rampant, *argent*.

In the chancel a copartment:

Carter 1686. Lord mayor 1681. *Near this place lyes the body of* Thomas Carter, *alderman, and late lord-mayor of this city, who departed this life* November 6, 1686. *aged* 52 *years. And also* Sarah *his wife, who departed this life the* 15th *of* April, *An.* 1708. *aged* 58 *years. She was one of the daughters of* John Pierson *of* Lowthorpe, *esq; She had issue by her said husband five sons and seven daughters, nine of which lye interred in this church. Three daughters survived her, the eldest married*

(p) Will Burton. *Vide epitaph. sequent.*

(q) This is a parish where many families of good account, especially in merchandize, have always resided, and therefore I am surprised to find so few epitaphs in Mr. *Dodsworth*'s MS. but these since his time sufficiently fill up the space.

William

William Tancred, *esq*; *of* Arden *in this county*; *and* Frances *married* Richard Colvile *esq*; *of* Newton *in the isle of* Ely; *who erected this monument in memory of her dear parents. The other surviving daughter married* Rich. Pierson *of* Lowthorp *in this county.* MICKLE-GATE WARD.

On the ground, an inscription over the above alderman:

Here lyeth the body of Thomas Bawtry, *once lord-mayor of this city, who died* Nov. 5, 1673. Bawtry 1673. Lord-mayor 1670.

Hic jacet corpus Jehochuae Earnshaw *hujus civitatis nuper praefectus, qui obiit quarto die* Decembris *annoque Domini* 1693. Earnshaw 1693. Lord-mayor 1692.

Quod sibi quisque serit praesentis tempore vitae,
Id sibi messis erit cum dicitur, ite, venite.

Here lieth the body of sir Gilbert Metcalf, *knight, late alderman, and sometime lord-mayor of this city, who departed this life* Jan. 28. *in the* 41st *year of his age, and in the year of our Lord* 1698. Metcalf 1698. Lord-mayor 1695.

Here lyeth the body of William Ramsden, *once lord-mayor of this city, who died the* 10th *of* August 1699, *in the* 75th *year of his age.* Ramsden 1699. Lord-mayor 1675.

In the body of the church:

Sub hoc tumulo conduntur cineres reverendi viri Samuelis Coyne, *S. T. B. filii* Gulielmi Coyne *de* Bolton Percy, *nepotis* Gul. Coyne *de* Overton, *in hoc agro* Ebor. *ministri*; *qui postquam per decennium coll.* Sidn. Suffex. *apud* Cantabrigiam *fuisset socius ecclesiae hujus rector evasit. In linguis doctis, philosophiâ, mathematicâ, medicinâ, theologiâ singulari instructus peritiâ, unde ad utrumque illud officium paratus accessit, et feliciter adornavit; eum amici semper reperêre fidum, constantem, & eorum res prompto animo procurantem, eximia et sibi peculiari morum suavitate et candore demerebatur omnes; qui et eum adhuc chariorem habuerunt ob insignem modestiam ac humilitatem minime fucatam. Filiolis observantiae et pietatis erat exemplar vivum, qui summoperè studuit ne matri amantissimae vel in minimo displiceret. Munus quod incumbebat pastorale indefessâ curâ et diligentiâ administravit: quem aliorum utilitati sic invigilantem, et doctrinâ sanâ et innocentiâ vitae commisso gregi praeeuntem, mors non inopinata, (utpote quam ipse integra fruens valetudine, prope instar praesagiisse videtur) sed immatura tamen corripuit* xiv. *die Martii A. D.* M.DC.XC. *aet.* 37. *Beatus ille servus quem cum venerit Dom. ejus inveniet sic facientem.* Coyne 1690.

Hic jacet corpus Susannae Bielby *uxor* Gulielmi Bielby *de* Micklethwait-grange *arm. obiit* 18. *die* Octobris *A. D.* 1664. Bielby 1664.

M. S.

Richardus Perrot, *coll.* Sidn. *apud* Cantab. *socius S. T. B. et* Eboraci *deinde concionator pientissimus. Hic tandem requievit anno salutis* 1670. *aet. suae* 42. Perrot 1670.

Dorothy Perrot, the mother of this *Richard*; *John Perrot*, and lastly alderman *Perrot*, are also commemorated on the same stone.

Here rests the remains of Mrs. Frances Bathurst, *wife of* Charles Bathurst *esq*; *of* Clints, *daughter and heir of* Thomas Potter, *esq*; *and grand-daughter of* Edward Langsdale, *M. D. She left issue* Charles, Mary, Jane *and* Frances. *She was a person of excellent accomplishments both of body and mind, and adorned the several stations of life she went through; and after a long and severe tryal chearfully resigned her breath in hopes of a blessed resurrection,* Jan. 24, A. D. 1724. *aetatis suae* 42. Bathurst 1724.

Here are likewise other modern inscriptions over the late rector Mr. *Blower* and his wife; Mrs. *Garforth*, *Dawson*, *Sharpe*, *Somner*, *Sowray*, two more *Perrots*, *&c.* which the copiousness of this chapter will not allow me to insert.

ARMS in the windows of this church 1682.

Azure, a bend *or*, and a file of five labels *argent*.
Or, a bend *azure*. *Scrope* of *Masham*.
Gules, a cross varry; impaling, *or* three chevrons *sable*.
Barry of six *or* and *gules*; over all a bend *azure*.
A fess dancettee, on the stone work without south. *Vavasour*.

I now come to the north-side of *Mickle-gate*, and near the bar stood formerly a church dedicated to St. *Nicholas*, which was an ancient vicarage in the patronage of the prior and convent of St. *Trinity*, *A.* 1455. *Maii* 1. the appropriation of the church and altar (r) of St. *Nicholas* was obtained by the prior of St. *Trinity* to be served by any secular priest or chaplain at their pleasure. By the statute of 1 *Edw.* VI. this church was united to the church and parish of St. *Trinity*, though before it made but one and the same vicarage. And such I shall leave it. St. NICHOLAS *Church.*

Toft-green, called anciently **les toftes**, was an open place up to the walls, where formerly was a weekly market kept every *Friday* for live cattle; as I find by an ordinance in the city's records dated *A.* 1457, for all oxen, cows, hogs and other animals for sustentation TOFT-GREEN.

(r) MS. *Torre*, f. 865.

MICKLE-GATEWARD. of mankind to be sold there, and no where els in the city, suburbs or precincts of the same. This has been long disused, and the place now is partly inclosed (s).

TANNER-ROW. GREGORY-LANE. *St* GREGORY'S *church*. From this goes a street called *Tanner-row*, from the people of that trade residing much in it, their tan-pits being on the back of it; it opens into *Mickle-gate* by a lane, called formerly *Gregory-lane*, where once stood the parish church of St. *Gregory*. This was an ancient rectory belonging to the patronage of the prior and convent of St. *Trinity*. And was united to the parish of St. *Martin* in *Micklegate*, with the other churches.

HEWLEY'S *hospital*. *The monastery of the* FRYARS PREACHERS. Lower down in *Tanner-row* stands a neat but small hospital founded *anno* . by the lady *Hewley*, relict of sir *John Hewley*, of *Bell-hall*, some time member for this city. This lady died a *presbyterian*, and the hospital was designed for ten old women of that persuasion, who have ten shillings paid them every first *Monday* in the month, and coals allowed. But anciently the site of this place, and the ground beyond it was put to another religious use; for on the back of this hospital is a large spot of ground, belonging to it, called the *Fryars-gardens*; in which did anciently stand the monastery of the *Fryars preachers* of *York*. This house was of royal foundation as appears by the confirmation of their charters by king *Edward* IV; which proves by *inspeximus* that the site of their monastery was granted them by king *Henry* III. It recites, that this king bestowed on them his chapel of St. *Mary Magdalene*, standing in a place called **Kingestoftes**, and the ground about it exactly described by butments and boundaries, to reach to the city walls one way, and the *king's-street* the other, for them to build upon, *&c*. This charter was dated at *Westminster* the eighth of *March* in the twelfth year of his reign, or *anno* 1228. By another charter of *inspeximus*, granted by the same king, he gives to this priory another piece of ground, near the walls of the city, to enclose for the enlargement of their site; as also gives leave to dig another well for one that was made in it, *&c*. Dated at *York Sept*. 3, in the fifty second year of his reign, or *anno* 1268. King *Edward* I grants them three toftes with their appurtenances towards the enlargement of their situation; the statute of *Mortmain* notwithstanding. Dated at *Langley Feb*. 18, in the twenty-sixth year of his reign, or *anno dom*. 1298. The same king by another charter grants them another piece of ground, as is expressed, contiguous to the court of their monastery towards the water of *Ouse*; for the enlargement of the said court. Dated at *Stamford May* 1. in the 28th year of his reign, or *an. Dom*. 1300. King *Edward* II. in the eighth year of his reign, grants these monks, for the sake of his soul, and those of his ancesters and heirs, two perches of land and a half in breadth contiguous to their site, of the king's measure, *viz*. twenty foot to a perch, and fifteen perches in length of that vacant space called **Kinges-toftes**; to inclose and keep to their use for ever. And because there is a well in the same for publick use, he gives them leave to dig another well at their proper costs in some convenient place for the common use of the men of the city. Dated at *Westminster*, *Nov*. 15, *anno* 1315. All these former grants, by *inspeximus*, were confirmed to this fryery by king *Richard* II; and because some part of their inclosure was broke down, without due process of law, he gives the fryers leave to rebuild and re-inclose, and to hold it for them and their successors for ever. Dated at *Westminster*, *Nov*. 24, in the fifth year of his reign or *Anno* 1382. *Lastly*, king *Edw*. IV. grants and confirms all the recited charters to this monastery and all and singular places and lands therein contained to them and their successors for ever. Witness the king at *York*, *June* 21, in the fourth year of his reign or *anno* 1464.

I have been more particular in the account of this monastery, because there is none to be met with of it, either in the *Monasticon*, or in *Speed*'s collection, or in any other that I have seen, but in these records. What else relates to them as the record of *Henry* the third's original grant to the fryers of this order in *York*; and his mandate to the mayor and bayliffs to deliver the aforesaid places up to them for their use the reader may find in the *appendix*. Being of the order of *mendicants*, or begging fryars, they had no lands but the site of their house. The site of this ancient monastery is now a spacious garden; at present occupied by Mr. *Tilford*, a worthy citizen, and whose knowledge in the mystery of gardening renders him of credit to his profession; being one of the first that brought our northern gentry into the method of planting and raising all kinds of forest trees, for use and ornament.

ALL-SAINTS North-street. The church of *All-saints* in *North-street* comes next in my way to describe, which is an ancient rectory belonging formerly to the patronage of the priory of St. *Trinity* aforesaid. Which was granted to it *temp. Will*. I. and was confirmed thereunto by the Bull of Pope *Alexander* II (t).

			l.	s.	d.
This rectory is thus valued in the king's books.	First fruits	——	04	07	06
	Tenths	——	00	08	09½
	Procurations	——	00	06	08

(s) This was also called **Pageant-green**, I suppose from the fraternity of *Corp. Christi* drawing up here in order for the religious cavalcade round the city.

(t) Mr. *Torre*, f. 601.

A close

I

A CATALOGUE of the RECTORS of ALL-SAINTS, North-street.

Temp. instit. Anno	*Rectores eccl.*	*Patroni.*	*Vacat.*
1241	Lan.' de Ragenhill.	*Prior et convent. S.* Trinit. Ebor.	
1245	—— de Bello homine.	*Archiepiscopus per lapsum.*	
1280	Joh. de Parlington.	*Archiepiscopus per lapsum.*	
1293	Nic. de Gloucestre.		
1299	Hamo de Alverton, *acolitus.*		
1301	Joh. de Redmild, *acolitus.*	*Archiepiscopus per lapsum.*	
1033	Gilb. de Semere, *presb.*		*per mort.*
1349	Rob. Aldingham.	Edvardus III. *rex.*	*per resig.*
1352	Joh. Tanfeld, *presb.*		
1355	Joh. de Clone.	Edvardus III. *rex.*	*per resig.*
1359	Wil. Wrelton, *cap.*	*Idem.*	*per mort.*
1376	Rob. de Aplegarth.	*Idem.*	*per resig.*
1398	Adam de Litchfield.		*per mort.*
1403	Joh. de Whitwell.	*Prior et convent. predict.*	*per resig.*
1406	Wil. Ryall; *presb.*	*Iidem.*	*per resig.*
1410	Joh. Fowler, *presb.*	*Iidem.*	*per mort.*
1413	Jac. Baguley, *cap.*	*Iidem.*	*per mort.*
1440	Tho. Fawren, *cap.*	*Iidem.*	*per mort.*
1472	Tho. Lawrence.	*Iidem.*	*per resig.*
1480	Hen. Hudson.	*Iidem.*	*per resig.*
1483	Rob. Hay, *cap.*	*Iidem.*	*per resig.*
1486	Ric. Smalys, *cap.*	*Iidem.*	*per mort.*
1490	Tho. Warwyck.	*Iidem.*	
	Joh. Hogard, *presb.*	*Iidem.*	*per resig.*
1506	Will. Atkinson.	*Iidem.*	*per resig.*
1507	Tho. Mason, *cap.*	*Iidem.*	
	Tho. Fryston, *cap.*	*Iidem.*	*per mort.*
1511	Rob. Day, *presb.*	*Iidem.*	*per mort.*
1512	Ric. Oliver, *presb.*	*Iidem.*	*per mort.*
1535	Hen. Joye, *S. T. B.*	*Iidem.*	*per resig.*
	Rob. Morres, *presb.*	*Iidem.*	*per resig.*
1549	Rob. Morres, *presb.*	Edvardus VI. *rex.*	
1554	Chris. Ascheton.	Maria *rex.*	*per mort.*
1573	Sym. Blunt, *cl.*	Eliz. *reg.*	*per resig.*
1577	Georg. Cawood, *cler.*	*Eadem.*	*per mort.*
1593	Joh. Stoddert, *cler.*	*Eadem.*	*per resig.*
1627	Rad. Vincent, *cler.*	Carolus I. *rex.*	*per mort.*
1674	Jac. Hickson, *M. A.*	Carolus II. *rex.*	*per cession.*
1688	Joh. Bradley, *cler.*	Jacobus II. *rex.*	

There were many chantries and *obits* belonging to this parish church; no less than eight original grants of them are amongst the records on *Ouse-bridge (u)*. Two taken notice on by *Torre* are these *(x)*:

John Benge, chaplain, founded a chantry in this church at the altar of St. *Mary* the virgin, to pray for the soul of the said *John* and *Hugh Benges* and their ancestors.

Anno 1407, there was another chantry founded in this church at the altar of St. *Thomas* the martyr, for the soul of *William Vesey* of *York* mercer. Who by his testament, *July* 28, 1407, bequeathed one messuage in *Micklegate*, and one hundred pound sterling out of his goods for the founding thereof.

(y) There was another chantry founded within this church by *Allen Hammerton* some time of the said city merchant, *William Skelton* late citizen of *York*, *John Catton* of the same, and *Emetta* his wife; yearly value 4 *l (z)*.

Another by *Adam del Bank*, littester, yearly value 5 *l.* 6 *s.* 8 *d.*

(u) Drawer, N°. 5.

(x) MS. p. 615.

(y) Dodsworth's collections.

(z) Sir *T. W.* gives this memorial of the chantries in this church, to one five messuages *Pat. anno* 11 *Hen.* IV. *pars* 1. *m.* 7. another of five marks, *p. an.* 9 *Ed.* II. *pars* 2. *m.* 9. Another, *John Benges*, *p. an.* 18. *Ed.* II. *pars* 1. *m.* 20. Another, *p. an.* 7. *Ric.* II. *pars* I. *m.* 22. and *p. an.* 2 *Hen.* IV. *pars.* 3. *m.* 6. At the altar of St. *Peter* in this church, a messuage called Stanbow, *p. an.* 2 *Hen* IV. *pars* 3. *m.* 6. and *p an.* 19 *Ric.* II. *pars* 1. *m.* 26.

This

MICKLE-GATE WARD. This church is a handsome structure supported within by two rows of pillars which makes three large and spacious isles. The painted glass in the windows being better preserved than in any parish church in town. It has a noble spire steeple neatly wrought up from the foundation to its *apex*. The south wall is very ancient being built up of grit, some *Roman* brick, and pebble; in it is the broken *Roman* inscription mentioned before. Monumental inscriptions are these *(a)*:

South quire.

Askwith 1609. *Here lyeth the bodies of* Thomas Askwith *and* Anne *his wife, late of this city of* Yorke, *and some time one of the sheriffs of the same citye. Which* Thomas *was borne at* Potgrange, *who in the* LXXI *year of his age, and the* XXIX *day of* August 1609. *departed this life, leaving behind him two sons and one daughter, viz.* Christopher *and* Alice, *whom he had by* Ursula Sandwich *daughter to* Robert Sandwich *of this citye bower; and* Thomas *whom he had by the same* Anne, *and daughter to* Robert Elderker *of* Thoulthorpe *gent. being in their time for good hospitality, and other laudable parts, a credit and ornament to this citye.*

Arms, *Sable* on a fess *or*, between three asses passant a crescent *gules*.

Stocton, *Lord-mayor* 1446. Colynson, *Lord-mayor* 1457. ✠ **Hic jacet Johannes de Wardell** —— and on a plate fixed about the same stone. **Orate specialiter pro animabus Willielmi Stocton et Roberti Colynson quondam majorum civitatis Ebor. et Isabellae uxoris eorundem, quorum animabus propitietur Deus. Amen.**

Atkinson 1642. *Sheriff* 1627. *Here lyeth buried the bodye of* Thomas Atkinson, *tanner, who was sometime sheriff of this citye of* Yorke, *who departed this life the thirtieth day of* April, A. D. 1642, *and was then aged* 71. *Who said often upon his death-bed, although I shall dye, yet I trust my life is hid with Christ in God, for when Christ who is my life shall appear then shall I alsoe appeare with him in glory.*

Paci dum valui, volui dum Christe volebas,
Mortuus et vivus cum moriorque tuus.

Clerke 1482. ✠ **Orate quilibet specialiter pro animabus Thome Clerke quondam clerici civitatis Ebor. et totius communitatis; et Margarete uxoris ejus, qui obierunt xvi diebus Februarii et Martii A. D. MCCCCLXXXII. quorum animabus prop. Deus. Amen.**

In the chancel. Arms, a water-budget in chief three roundels, impaling a chevron between three trees erased. Under the same,

Hic requiescit
JOSUA WITTON,

Witton 1674. *Qui ad annum aetatis sexagesimum pietate et cultus assiduitate adeo sacrarum literarum scientia non vulgari doctus, largitate et continua beneficentia egenis, morum innocua jucunditate omnibus charum se praebuit.*

Ab hac vita ad meliorem commigravit A. D. 1674. *die Junii* 1mo.

Stodart 1599. **Here lyeth the body of Johan late wife of John Stodart clerke parson of this rectory, daughter of Clement Skelton of Hanwyk-field-hall in Cumberland esq; and serjeant of Gillesland, and deputy warden of Carliel-castle under the right honourable William lord Dacres. Who in her life-time was religious, and so making a godly and charitable end at the age of xlii years, was buried the xix of February in the yeare of the reign of queen Elizabeth xlii. A. D.** 1599.

At the head also is written,

John Stodart clerke, parson of this rectory, inducted here of March 1593.

Yllyugwyke. ✠ **Hic jacent Thomas de Yllyngwyke quondam civis Ebor. et Juliana uxor ejusdem, quorum animabus prop. Deus. Amen.**

North-isle.

Londisdal, 1487. ✠ **Orate pro anima Willielmi Londisdall de Ebor. tanner et pro animabus Elene et Alicie uxorum ejus . . . . . . A. D. MCCCCLXXX septimo.**

South-isle.

Killingholme. ✠ **Orate pro animabus Richardi Killingholme et Johanne et Margarete uxorum ejus.**

In the nave.

Graie. *Lord-mayor* 1367. ✠ **Hic jacent Willielmus Graie quondam major civitatis Ebor. et Katherina uxor ejus quorum an. &c.**

COATS of ARMS, &c. *in the windows*, &c. *of this church.*

On a wooden knot over the chancel roof is depicted:

Ermine, on a bend *sable*, three boars heads couped *argent*.

In the north isle window by the door by the portrait of *Blackburn*, in armour kneeling, is this escutcheon:

(a) Ex MS. Torre.

Crest

Gules, a lion rampant checky *ermine* and *ſable* crowned *or*. MICKLE-GATE WARD.

Creſt a lion *paſſant*, checky *ermine* and *ſable*.

In the north choir ſide window are the pictures of *Nich. Blackburn* and his wife at prayer. His armour with ſpurs on his heels, with a ſhield of his arms upon his breaſt, and another over his head *(ut ſupra)* and a ſcroll iſſuing out of his mouth,

Dat venie munus nobis rex.

She with her back towards him holding a prayer-book in her hand wherein is written,

Domine ſalva me a peries et
a peccatis . . . meum.

Under both is inſcribed,

Orate pro animabus Nicholai Blakburne ſen. quondam majoris civitatis Ebor. et Margarete uxoris ejus. Blakburne. *Lord-mayor* 1429.

In the next light of the ſame windows are drawn the portraitures of *Nicholas Blackburn* jun. and his wife kneeling together, ſhe holding a book open in her hands, whereon is wrote, *Sheriff* 1435.

Domine in furore tuo neque in ira
. . . . . . me . . tua . .

ARMS. A lion rampant *(ut ſupra)* with a mullet for difference.

In the eaſt end window of the north choir,

Barry, of ſix *or* and *gules*, over all a bend *azure*.

In the weſt window of the ſouth iſle,

Argent, a bend *azure*.

York fee, impaling *gules*, two bars dancette *ermine*. *Harſnet* (*b*).

Modern epitaphs on Mr. *Matthew Briſtol* rector, who died 1712, on *Lakin*, *Pennyman*, *Raiſin*, *Etty*, &c. are omitted; on this laſt an ingenious architect, who died 1709, are theſe lines,

His art was great, his induſtry no leſs,
What one projected, th' other brought to paſs.

But whoſe art it was that put the arms of the antient family of *Atton*, or *de Etton*, on this ſtone I ſhall not ſay (*c*).

In *North-ſtreet*, called ſo from its ſituation, lying parallel with the river, are ſeveral exceeding ſtrong water walls, which have, no doubt, been the outworks of ſeveral large buildings and ware-houſes, belonging to merchants formerly inhabiting in this ſtreet. Sir *T. W.* ſuppoſes them to have belonged to the *Jews* when they were in *York*, *who had houſes*, ſays *William of Newburgh*, *in the city more like princes palaces than ſubjects dwellings.* There is nothing elſe particular till we come to the laſt publick building undeſcribed, on this ſide the river, which is the NORTH-STREET.

Pariſh church of St. *John* the evangeliſt, commonly called St. *John*'s at *Ouſe-bridge* end. This church belongs to the dean and chapter of *York*, being accounted one of their greater farms, and rented at twelve pound *per annum*. ST. JOHN'S Ouſe-bridge *end.*

Mr. *Torre* has omitted a catalogue of the curates of this church, but has given us the following account of three chantries erected here.

(*d*) *Shupton* or *Briggenhall*'s chantry at the altar of St. *John baptiſt*.

In feſto S. Martini *in hyeme ah. dom.* 1321.

Whereas *John de Shupton*, grandfather to *Richard Briggenhall*, late merchant of *York*, whoſe heir the ſaid *Richard* is, being ſon of *Catherine* daughter of the ſaid *John de Shupton*, had by his charter, then dated at *York*, ordained a certain chantry at the altar of St. *John baptiſt* in this church, and given thereunto ſix marks annual rent out of the city: now on the 10th of *October*, 1400. the ſaid *Richard Briggenhall*, by the king's licence obtained, granted all his lands, and tenements with all thoſe his edifices againſt the church-yard hereof, unto *John de Grafton* chaplain and his ſucceſſors for ever; that he and they might celebrate for his ſoul in the ſame church at mattins, veſpers, and other canonical hours, *placebo dirige*, &c. (*e*) Shupton. *Bayliff* 1297.

(*b*) *Anno* 1630. *Samuel Harſnet*, archbiſhop of *York*, gave to this church one large ſilver bowl with a cover, with his arms engraven.

(*c*) *Robert Savage*, lord-mayor, 1393. unto whom king *Richard* II. gave the firſt mace to be born before him, by his will gave his body to be buried before St. *Nicolas* altar in this church, where the body of *William Savage*, his father, was interred. Teſt. burial. *Torre*.

(*d*) *MS. f.* 631.

(*e*) *P. an.* 12 *Ed.* II. *p.* 2. *m.* 25.

Mickle-gate ward.

*Watel*y's chantry.

There was another chantry founded in this church at the altar of St. *Katherine* the virgin, for the soul of *Richard Wately*, &c. The original licence from *Edward* II. for the founding this chantry is amongst the records on *Ouse-bridge (f)*.

Toller's chantry.

There was another chantry founded in this church by *Richard Toller*, at the altar of St. *Mary* the virgin, late merchant of *York*, to pray for his soul, *&c.*

In the additional volume to the *Monast.* from *Dodsworth's coll.* this chantry is said to be founded by *Richard Toller* or *Tollier*, ancestor of *Edmund Sandford* esquire and *Isabel* his wife, 13 *Martii* 1320. Value at the diss. 1 *l.* 16 *s. per annum.*

York's chantry (*g*).

Founded by sir *Richard York* knight, at the altar of our lady in this church, to pray, *&c.* and help divine service in the said church, value *per annum* 8 *l.* 15 *s.* 4 *d.*

Antient MONUMENTS, INSCRIPTIONS, &c. from Mr. Dodsworth, Torre, *&c.*

Chancel.

Beckwith 1599. *Lord-mayor* 1597. *Here lyeth the body of* Christopher Beckwith *esquire, some tyme lord-major of this city, who deceased* xxiii^d *day of* July, 1599.

Arms a chevron inter three hinds heads couped; quartered with a lion rampant.

Mosley 1624. *Lord-mayor* 1590, 1602. *Here lyeth buried the body of Mr.* Thomas Mosley *late alderman of this cittie, who died the year of his age* 85, *in the year of our saviour* 1624, *after he had been twice lord-mayor. Together with the bodys of his eldest daughter* Mary, *and of* Elizabeth, *his second daughter, and of* Thomas Scot *his grandchild; made at the cost of* Jane *his wife.*

Arms, *sable*, a fess *or*, between three trefoiles sliped *ermine*. *Mosley.*

On another plate upon the same stone.

Moseley 1640. *Here lyeth the body of that worthy and well affected gentlewoman Mrs.* Elizabeth Moseley *widow, some time wife to* John Moseley *of this city esquire, one of the daughters and coheirs of* Thomas Trigott *of* Southkirkby *esquire. She departed this life* anno 1640, *the* 50 *year of her age.*

She gave in her life time to this church of St. John's 40 *l.* per an. *for ever, towards the maintenance of a preaching minister. By which pious work being dead, she yet speaketh.*

ARMS. *Mosley, ut supra.*
A chevron inter three cross crosslets *fitchy. Trigott.*

Memoriae

Mosley 1624. Johannis Mosley *patricii* Thomae Moslei *senatoris filii et haeredis, qui obiit an. dom.* 1624. *Aetat. suae* 44 *non sine plurimorum civium moerore suorumque luctu.*
Pos. Iana. Mater.

Hall 1677. Sarah Hall *daughter of* Charles Hall *merchant was here buried the* 1st *of* December, 1677.

Hall 1678. Samuel Hall *son of* Charles Hall *merchant was here buried the* 19th *of* May, 1678.

South choir.

Wright 1637. *An epitaph on the death of* James Wright *baker, one of the commons of this citye, who died the* 27th *of* March, 1637. *aet. suae* 76.

Look reader as thou passes by,
Underneath this stone does lye
A citizen of great respect,
As free from vice as from defect.
Civilitye and temperance,
Frugalitye and governance,
Were th' epithets that spoke him blest,
And gained him love amongst the best.
Religiously he liv'd and dy'd,
And now we hope in heaven does bide.

(*f*) Drawer 4. (*g*) *Dodsworth*'s coll.

COATS

COATS of ARMS in the church.

In the north choir on knots under the wooden roof is depicted,

Azure, a saltire *argent*. *York*. Impaling *gules*, three greyhounds in pale cursant *argent*. *Maliverer*.

York single, *ut supra*.

Argent, three bars wavy *azure*, on a chief *gules*, a lion passant gardant *argent*. *Merchants of the staple*.

In the north east choir window was,

A man in armour kneeling on his breast, his coat of arms, *viz. azure*, a saltire *argent*; behind him five sons.

On the other side of the window two women kneeling, one of them having on her gown, *gules*, three greyhounds cursant *argent*, impaled with *azure*, a saltire *argent*; behind them four daughters kneeling; under this inscription.

Orate pro anima Ricardi Yorke militis bis majoris civitatis Ebor. ac per . . . . majoris Stapuli Callisie et pro animabus Johanne et Johanne uxorum, ac etiam pro omnibus liberis et benefactoribus suis, qui . . . . die mensis Aprilis anno domini M CCCC VIII. Yorke. *Lord-mayor* 1469, 1482.

Under all these were four men and their wives kneeling, which Mr. *Dodsworth* supposes might be the daughters of sir *Richard* with their husbands. But by the foregoing it appears that some of these men were founders of chantries in this church. Over their heads (*b*).

Ricardus Brikenale et Catherina uxor ejus.
Johannes Randeman et Johanna uxor ejus.
Ricardus Toller et Isabella uxor ejus.
Emanuel de Grafton et Agnes uxor ejus.

In the north window of the same choir.

Orate pro animabus . . . Stockton mercer et Alicie ux. ejus.
Orate pro animabus . . . Syrby spycer et Elizabethe ux. ejus.

Over the former east window were eight escutcheons on a row, supported by as many angels, *viz.*

1. *Argent*, three bars wavy *azure*, on a chief *gules*, a lion of *England*. **Merchants of the staple.**
2. *Argent*, three bugle horns stringed *sable*.
3. *Argent*, a gryphonse greant *sable*, thereon a mullet difference *or*, impaling *argent*, on a pale *sable*, a pike's or lucy's head, couped erect *or*. *Gascoyne*.
4. *Azure*, a saltire *argent*. *York*.
5. *York* as before, impaling *gules*, three greyhounds currant in pale barways *argent*. *Maliverer*.
6. *York* as before, impaling *azure*, crusilly and three cinqfoils *argent*. *Darcy*.
7. *York* as before impaling, on a chevron ingrailed inter three calfs passant *argent*, three mullets *sable*.
8. *York city*.

The steeple of this church was blown down *anno* 1551, and was never since rebuilt; a ring of six tuneable bells are in a small turret, the three largest of which were brought from St. *Nicolas* church, *extra Walmgate*, and hung up here *anno* 1653.

I have now gone through with the remarkables on this side the river *Ouse*, and should come next to the bridge; but before I go further I beg leave to take notice of some handsome houses belonging to private families, as well as publick inns in this part of the city.

Mr. *Camden* commends *York* for a city *neatly built*, and I am certain there was not in his time one brick building in it. The beauty and firmness of this last, compared with the antient timber structures, is infinitely before them. There were no brick buildings in *England* before the reign of *Henry* VII, except chimnies; and what were afterwards built were chiefly in monasteries, or some few palaces for kings and noblemen. It was long after this before any such thing was at *York*; which must be a great detriment to the town, our streets being but narrow, and these buildings projecting very much at the top; insomuch that in some streets they now almost meet on each side. This renders the place closer, and fire must have been very terrible to the inhabitants. Many of these timber buildings are yet standing in *Micklegate*, which have been thought sumptuous at the erection of them; the

(*b*) This is as the window was in Mr. *Dodsworth*'s time (1617) since which it is much defaced. There is an antient marble tomb between the chancel and north choir which is supposed to be that of sir *Richard Yorke*, but it is robbed of its arms, &c. There are some modern monumental inscriptions here as of *Bains*, *Benson*, sir *Stephen Thompson* knight, *Hooper* which I cannot insert.

carved

Mickle-gate ward. carved work at the portals and the corners expressing no less. These were formerly the houses of many eminent merchants, and a gentleman of my acquaintance, yet in being, has told me that he remembers this street to be near full of them. What this street is remarkable for at this day, are the new built houses of *Henry Thompson* esquire, and Mr. alderman *Thompson*, over against St. *John*'s church. Sir *Darcy Dawe*'s near St. *Martin*'s. The house of *Charles Bathurst* esquire, *Gregory-lane* end, and the house lately inhabited by *Hugh Cholmley* esquire near the bar; though there are several other very good new houses in it. Here are likewise two inns of good resort, the *Falcon* and the *Minster*. In *Skelder-gate*, except the ruins of the duke's palace, is nothing worth notice, but one good house inhabited by the widow of the late Mr. *Pawson* and Dr. *Breary*'s. Here is also an old accustomed inn at the sign of the *elephant*. And thus I take leave of *Mickle-gate ward*.

Ouse-bridge.

We now come to *Ouse-bridge*, which, as Mr. *Camden* remarks, is a noble one indeed consisting of five arches; the middlemost *(i)* arch of which is eighty one feet or twenty seven yards wide from the first spring of the arch, and seventeen high, and was esteemed, formerly, one of the largest in *Europe*. The reason this arch was carried on to this extraordinary dimension, was to prevent the like accident from happening which chanced to overturn the old bridge *anno* 1564. When by *(k)* a sharp frost, great snow and a sudden thaw, the water rose to a vast height, and the prodigious weight of the ice and flood drove down two arches of the bridge, by which twelve houses were overthrown, and twelve persons drowned. The bridge continued unrepaired some time, till a proper sum could be levied; and then it was rebuilt in the manner it now stands. Towards which work I find that one Mrs. *Hall*, relict of alderman *Hall*, gave one hundred pound; and the city bestowed a brass plate, which was fixed on the north side of the bridge, with this inscription to her memory, now lost.

William Watson lord mayor an. dom. 1566. } **Lady Jane Hall lo! here the works of faith does shew,**
By giving a hundred pound this bridge for to renew.

This is the history of the new bridge, but of what antiquity the old one was I cannot learn. Stone bridges were not in use till long after the conqueror's time in this kingdom. *London-bridge* was no more than a timber one till *anno* 1176, it was begun to be built with stone, and, as *Stow (l)* says, was thirty three years in finishing; which argues them mean artists at such kind of work in those days. *Anno* 1154, when *William* archbishop of *York* made his first entrance into the city, this bridge being crowded with the multitudes that came to meet him, the timber *(m)* gave way, says my authority, that it was then built with, and all fell into the river; but by the prayers of the archbishop not one of the company perished. Stone bridges coming soon after in use, our seems to take its date from about the year 1235, for I find *(n)* that *Walter Gray*, then archbishop, granted a brief for the rebuilding of *Ouse-bridge*, most probably, of stone, by charitable contributions. *Anno* 1268, I read an account of the origin of a chapel on *(o) Ouse-bridge*, in the *collectanea*, when there was a peace and agreement made with *John Comyn*, a *Scotch* nobleman, and the citizens of *York* (*mediantibus regibus* Angliae *et* Scotiae) for a fray which had happened upon the bridge, and wherein several of *John Comyn*'s servants had been slain. The said lord was to receive three hundred pound, and the citizens were obliged to build a chapel on the place where the slaughter was made, and to find two priests to celebrate for the souls of the slain for ever.

St. William's *chapel.*

How long they continued to pray for the souls of these *Scots*, or whether this is not the chapel which was dedicated to St. *William* I know not. But such a one there was at the reformation in use on this bridge, in which I find mention of these chantries.

One of the foundation of *Richard Towler* and *Isabel* his wife. The original of which is now amongst the records on the bridge.

	l.	*s.*	*d.*
Another of *Helewis de Wistoo* widow of *Robert de Wistoo* citizen of *York*.			
Value at the suppression ——— ———	04	13	04

A third founded by *John de Newton* and *Rauff Marr*, executors of the testaments of sir *Roger de Marr* priest *ad altare S.* Eligii *in capel. S.* Willielmi *sup. pontem* Use.

	l.	*s.*	*d.*
Value at the suppression ——— ——— ———	01	16	05

The chantry of *John Fourbour* at the same altar. The originals of all these grants have not wandered far from the place where they were first intended for, being amongst the records on the bridge *(p)*.

(i) The bridge of the *Rialto* at *Venice*, three parts of a circle, is ninety five foot from one end to the other, on the level of the canal; supposed by this to be near twenty four foot high.

(k) Law *Hildyard*'s ant.

(l) Survey of *London*.

(m) Brompton *inter x script. rupta est lignei pontis compago.* See the life of St. *William*.

(n) *Ex rotul.* Wal. Grey *an. pont.* xviii.

(o) *Coll.* Lelandi *ab annal. mon. beatae* Mariae Ebor.

(p) Drawers numb. 5, 6.

The

I

THE ASTOR LIBRARY
NY

The right honourable S^r. John Leveson Gower Bar^t. Baron Gower of Stittenham, the paternal Seat of that truly antient family in the neighbourhood of York, to encourage this work bestows this plate. 1736.

EXCHANGE. The chapel being a neat and convenient building was after the *Reformation*, converted into a *burse*, or *exchange*, where merchants of the city usually met every morning to transact business. But upon the great decay of trade, here, this was disused.

COUNCIL-CHAMBER. COURTS. On the bridge also stands the great *council-chamber* of the city, near which the records are kept. The *exchequer* and *sheriffs-courts* are also here. Beneath these is the prison for felons, belonging to the city; commonly called the **Kidcote**. And opposite is the goal for debtors; which has lately been built as appears by an inscription, at the equal expence of *city* and *ainsty*, *anno* 1724. The old prison (*q*) on this side was erected *anno* 1575, at **PRISONS.** which time another arch was added to the bridge by way of support to it; but being become exceeding ruinous it was taken down and rebuilt; and, considering the straitness of the place it stands on, is as commodious and convenient as most goals in *England*.

Leland in his *itin.* says that *Ouse-bridge* had in his time six arches in it. That there was on it a *chapel*, a *town-hall*, a *gild*, and an *hospital*; the two last I can find no other account of. For the sustentation of the bridges of *Ouse* and *Foss*, king *Richard* II, by charter grants power to the mayor and citizens to purchase lands to the value of one hundred pound a year, *&c.* as appears by the charter (*r*). I shall take leave of this bridge with presenting the reader with the view of it.

OUSE river. The river *Ouse* comes next under my pen. The name of *Ouse*, which this river taketh before it comes to *York*, I have elsewhere touched upon; and quoted both *Leland* and *Camden* for my authorities. But to me it is absurd to think, that the little paltry brook at *Ouseburn* should change the name of a noble river; and it is much more probable to suppose that the town and brook took their names from the river, than it from them. This river, as it has been very ingeniously hinted to me by the reverend Dr. *Langwith*, seems to have had two antient *British* names given it, *Uys* and *Eur*. Both which signify no more than water in general (*s*); so that the river went by one name or the other, according as the terms *Uys* or *Eur* prevailed. In some places, as particularly about *Aldburgh*, it seems to have gone by both names, from whence we have the compound ISURIUM. Nor is EBURACUM, as we find it frequently spelled in *Roman* authors, without a great relish of the latter. The *Saxon Ouse* seems plainly to be corrupted from the *Roman* ISIS; as this is deduced from the *British Uys*, being more agreeable to the *idiom* of that language. So that I see no manner of reason, with *Camden*, to make the little brook at *Ouseburn* the parent of this name; since both *Isis* and *Eurus* have been alternately used, antiently, for the whole course of the river; though since custom has confined the former word to this lower part of the stream. The source and progress of this river was first described by *Leland*, and copied by *William Harrison*, without naming his author; with some additions, I shall give the reader it in their words.

The *Isis*, or *Ure*, riseth in the farthest parts of all *Richmondshire*, amongst the *Cotterine* **Ure.** hills, in a moss towards the west, fourteen miles beyond *Middleham*; from thence it runneth in a small stream, and taketh in the *Cover* out of *Coverdale* by *Ulsway-bridge*, to *Hol-* **Cover.** *beck*, *Hardraw*, *Hawshouse*, *Butterside*, *Ask-bridge*; thence to *Askarth*, where there is a wonderful cascade of a very great fall, through *Wanless-park* under *Wenslaw-bridge*, built two hundred years since, says my author, by *Alwin* parson of *Wenslaw*, to *Newpark*, *Spennithorn*, *Danby*, *Jervaulxs-abbey*, *Clifton* and *Masham*. At *Masham* it receiveth the *Burn*; **Burn.** from thence the *Ure* runneth to *Tanfield*, *Newton-hall*, *North-bridge*, *Ripon*. Beyond this it taketh in the *Skell*, who run together to *Hewick-bridge*, *Rocliff*, *Thorp*, *Burrough-bridge*, **Skell.** *Aldborough*, ISUROVICUM, and soon after meeteth the *Swale*. These run to *Aldwark-* **Swale.** *ferry*, taking in *Ouseburn* water from the south-east, and here the *Ure* changes into *Ouse*. **Ouseburn.** From thence by *Linton* upon *Ouse*, *Newton* upon *Ouse*, to *Nun-Monkton* where the *Nid* joins it. **Nid.** Thence to *Redhouse*, *Overton*, nether *Poppleton*, *Clifton* and YORK. At *York* it receiveth the *Foss*, and so goes on to *Water-Foulford*, *Bishop-thorp*, *Naburn*, *Acaster-Malbis*, *Acaster-* **Foss.** *Selby*, *Stillingfleet*, not far from which it receives the *Wharf*. Thence to *Cawood*, *Kellfleet*, **Wharf.** *Barlby*, *Selby*, *Turmanhall*, *Langrick*, where it meeteth the *Derwent*, *Booth*, *Airmin*, where **Derwent.** the *Air* joins it. From thence to *Hook*, *Skelton*, *Sandhall*, *Gole*, where it meets the *Dun* **Air.** at the *Dutch* cut, *Swinfleet*, *Redness*, *Saltmarch*, *Whitgift*, *Ousefleet*, *Blacktoft*, *Foxfleet*, where **Dun.** it lastly receiveth the *Trent*; and running from thence to *Bromefleet*, loseth it self and name **Trent.** in the mighty river HUMBER. **Humber.**

The source of the *Ouse* lying up in the northwest hills, and the taking in of so many different streams to its own, renders it very liable to inundations; some of which have been exceeding great, and frequently when we have had no rains at all at *York*. *Anno* 1263, it is recorded that the river *Ouse* flowed to so great a height as to run over the end of the bridge, where the four streets meet (*t*). *Anno* 1689, which is yet in the memory of some living, a mighty flood came down, which meeting with spring tides at the same time

(*q*) Lawyer *Hildyard*'s ant.

(*r*) *Iterum licent. concessa ad inquis.* c *l. terre in perpet. sustentat. pontium de* Ouse *et* Foss, *et alior. et capellan. celebrant, in capellis edif. super pontes predictos. Pat.* 9 Hen. IV. *p.* 1. *m.* 32.

(*s*) See *Baxter*'s gloss. *Brit.* p. 119. and *Lluyd's adversaria*, p. 265.

(*t*) *Usque ad quadrivium.* Tho. Stubbs *lib. pont.* Ebor. *inter x script.*

flowed as high as the former, and did an incredible damage to the country. The mark of the height of the water at this last flood was put upon a wooden board, by some curious person, on the wall at the bottom of the first *Water-lane*, with the day and year it happened upon. This was the highest flow of water we have had in the memory of man, for though in *January*, 1732, the river rose in one night's time near three yards perpendicular; filled the street at the west end of the bridge, and had liked to have drowned the poor prisoners in the low goal, yet it was observed not to reach the mark aforesaid by eleven inches. From this mark to the lowest ebb, in the dryest summer, that ever I observed, by exact mensuration was twenty four foot four inches perpendicular.

October 22, 1689.

The flow of the tide up to the bridge is not now so good as formerly. By a manuscript that I have seen, I learn that in *August*, 1643, the spring tides at *Ouse-bridge* did rise to the height of five foot, a thing almost incredible to the present age. Indeed I have been told, by an ingenious person, that he has observed it to rise four foot, which is extraordinary enough, the common course being only two foot, or two foot and a half; which is a vast disproportion from those mighty flows which are oft sent us from *Burrough-bridge*, &c.

The Eager *in the* Ouse.

I shall leave the river *Ouse*, with taking notice that there is frequently a strange flow, or back current of water, in it, not ruled by the tides, called the **Eager**. This makes a mighty noise at its approach, insomuch as to be heard at some miles distance; and, if it was not well known, would cause a great deal of terror to the country about it. The cause of this preternatural current I shall leave to the naturalists to determine. The word **Eager** is derived, according to Dr. *Langwith*, who has sent me his thoughts upon it, from the *Saxon* Eᵹor *aestus marinus*. Which, as he adds, is further explained in Dr. *Hickes*'s *voces poeticae*, at the end of *Benson*'s dictionary. But, with submission to this learned gentleman, the word seems more naturally to be deduced from the *Saxon* Eᵹor which *Somner* renders *ferus*, *atrox*, *vehemens*, fierce, raging, and vehement, the manner of its coming up being plainly expressed by this name.

At the east end of *Ouse-bridge* is a place that must not be omitted in this work; it is a hole which many believe to run under ground, arched as far as the *Minster*; but for what reason I never could learn. Indeed I never had an opportunity to examine into it myself, and I had less curiosity to do it, after I found amongst the city records, this remark on it,

Salter-greces.

(u) **Salt-hole-greces lefte open for mending the arches on Ousebrigg.**

Walmgate ward. Stayth.

At the foot of *Ouse-bridge* on the east side the river is a convenient *key* or *wharf*, commonly called the *king's stayth*; strongly walled and paved, for lading and unlading of goods and merchandize. I believe it true what a person of good repute has told me, though some perhaps may not, that about twenty years agoe, he came upon this *Stayth*, at noon time a day, and saw neither boat nor ship, great or little upon the river, no manner of goods upon the key, nor man, woman, nor child near it. A melancholly sight indeed, but I hope neither he nor any one else will ever see it again. Business of this kind seems to mend apace in *York*; we have now ships belonging to the city which carry goods and merchandize to several parts. And many vessels of other kinds are daily sailing to and fro in the river.

Topham's *Stayth*.

On the other side is a *Stayth* called alderman *Topham*'s *Stayth*; erected *anno* 1660, *Christopher Topham* mayor, in which he had such a hand as to occasion its being called after his name. It has had several reparations since, as, *anno* 1676, and enlarged 1678, *&c.*

All the religious houses that laid towards the river had keys, or landing places, of their own on it. There was a very fine one at the abbey of St. *Mary*. Lower down another for the hospital of St. *Leonard*; called in antient writings **St. Leonards Lendings**, or landing; where a new one was of very late years erected, but for what use I know not.

The monastery of the Fryers minors.

I shall here take notice of a once famous monastery, which stood in this city, belonging to the brethren of the order of St. *Francis*, or *fryers minors*. The situation of which, whether on the west or east side of the river *Ouse*, I confess I cannot find out; though I have traced it with very great diligence and circumspection. The records that I have met with relating to this religious house, in the tower of *London* and elsewhere, have not pointed me to its site: though neither those nor history are silent as to several royal grants and testifications of the antient magnificence of this building. We are informed by historians that this monastery was usually the residence of our former *English* kings when they came to *York*; and that it was noble and spacious we are assured by *Froisart* *(x)*, who tells us that *Edward* III. and his mother both lodged in it, when the fray happened betwixt the *English* soldiers and the strangers; as related in the annals of this work. We find by this historian, that the building was so convenient, that each of these royal guests, though attended with a numerous suit of quality, kept court *apart* in it; which must argue it a structure of very great extent and magnificence. By a patent of *Richard* II. this affair of its being

(u) *Salte-hole-greces* is plainly derived from a *hole for salt near a pair of stairs*; *greces* being stairs in old *French*, whence our *degrees* from *Lat. gradus*.

(x) *Ils tint un grande cour en le maison de* Freres mineurs, *où le roy et madame se mere étoient habergez, et tenoient leur* tinel *chacun par lui; le roy de ses chevaliers et le roign de ses dames.* Froisart. *Tinel*, in old *French*, signifies housholdry, or train.

made

made use of for a regal palace is confirmed. That king strictly prohibits any persons from carrying of filth, or laying of dunghills, *&c.* in the lanes, or passages, leading to this monastery; where, as the patent expresses, he himself, as well as his grandfather used to inhabit. Also butchers, and other persons, are by the same prohibited from casting into, or washing in, the river *Ouse*, any entrails of beasts, or other nastynesses, to the prejudice or nusance of this monastery. This last plainly proves that the site of it was somewhere on the banks of the river; and in a patent of *Edward* II, being a grant to them to purchase some houses contiguous to their monastery, for the enlargement of their courts, those houses and places are said to extend *from the middle gate of the said monastery, near the chancel of their church, on the back, as far as a lane called* **Hertergate**, *and so descending towards the water of* **Ouse** *to the west.* Hence we might suppose that our monastery lay on the east side of the river; but then again as *Hertergate* is a place unknown at this day, and I have seen other letters patents granted to them as high as *Henry* III, which seem to contradict the former notion, I am as uncertain as ever. That prince, in his fifty third year, gives licence to the *friers-minors* of *York* to inclose a *certain ditch, within the king's domain, but contiguous to their area by the east, lying betwixt the said area, or court, and* **Baill-bridge**, *for the enlargement of their said court. That they were to inclose this ditch with an earthen wall twelve feet high; and the place to serve for preaching in; so as they might make it fit for all persons coming to hear them to pass and repass at pleasure. That they might keep up this place, so inclosed, for ever; unless that by disturbance of the peace, or open war, or any other reason, it was thought necessary to open that ditch for the defence of the castle of* York. If the *pons-ballii*, or **Baill-bridge** here mentioned be supposed to allude to our present **Old-baill**, the case is clear that the site of this house must have been some where on *Bishophill* or in *Skelder-gate*, but as I am very uncertain, as to that point, I shall trouble my self no further about it. WALM-GATE WARD.

There are two more evidences, on record, that that this monastery once stood in our city, and one of them again puts us cross the river to seek it. King *Edward* I, gives licence to this brotherhood to inclose a *certain lane which extends itself from the* King's-street, *in length and breadth, as far as the lane which goes towards the milns near the castle.* There can be no mills but windmills near **Old-baill**; and if we suppose them the watermills near the other castle, as I have proved them very antient, I know no place near them on the *Ouse*, capable of such a situation, but what was taken up by other monasteries.

The last evidence is from our own records, which is a copy of letters patents directed to the guardian and brethren of this monastery from the same king about settling the privileges of a sanctuary they pretended had been violated by the the citizens, *&c.* copies of all these matters, at length, the reader may meet with, in their proper places in the *appendix.*

In this monastery was a conventual church dedicated to St. *Mary*; Mr. *Torre* has given us, in his manuscript, f. 875, several testamentary burials in it. In the additional volumes to the *Monasticon* the order of *Friers-minors*, in *England*, is said to have been divided into seven custodies or wardenships; of which the monastery belonging to them at *York* was one of the chief. This had under its jurisdiction the monasteries of

Doncaster,	*Lincoln*,
Boston,	*Beverley*,
Scardeburgh,	*Grimsby*, in *Lincolnshire*.

In the same additional volumes it is hinted that the friars of this order, called also *grey-friars*, or *predicants*, were the first that suffered persecution for openly opposing king *Henry*'s second marriage with *Anne Bolleyn*. Their monasteries were immediately suppressed, their persons imprisonned, or barbarously used. But by the inrollment of the surrender of their monastery to the king, it appears that it was taken at *York* only in the thirtieth year, when many others fell with them. Bishop *Burnet* writes that *November* 27, 30 *Hen.* VIII. this house of the *Franciscan-friars* in *York*, was surrendred into the king's hands by the guardian fifteen friars and five novices. By the inrollment in the *chapel of the rolls*, *William Vavasour*, doctor of divinity, prior, or guardian of the *Friars-minors*, *within the walls* of the city of *York*, with the unanimous consent, *&c.* of the whole convent, did give, grant, restore, *&c.* to which deed the common seal (*y*) of the monastery was put; and it was dated in the *chapter-house*, belonging to the said monastery, as above. This instrument, though varying little from other surrenders of like nature, I have given at length in the *appendix* to shew the form of them. The order itself was one of the four *mendicants*, and had no possessions in *England* besides the site of their houses; though abroad, I am told, they are in great affluence of riches; and bear a port in their monasteries, churches *&c.* equal to any of the rest.

Below the *King's staith*, is a place of that kind of stone work called *Friars walls*; which is a long raised walk built, or rebuilt *anno* 1659, with a brick wall towards the water. At the end of this walk is a handsome iron palisade gate, in a stone arch, erected as an inscription shews *anno* 1732, *Jonas Thompson* lord-mayor. This leads to the long walk al- FRIARS-WALLS.

(*y*) See their seal amongst the rest. *Claus.* 30 Hen. VIII. *pars* 5.

ready

2

WALM-GATE WARD.

ready described. But the name of *fryars walls*, leads us to look for a monastery which stood near this place, and *Leland* has pointed it out plainly in these words: (z) *The* Augustine-fryars *were betwixt the tower on* Ouse-ripe *and* Ouse-bridge. By which the building must have extended over all or most of the gardens, betwixt these walls and *Castle-gate postern-lane.* The ancient stone wall of the monastery towards the river, is still standing, supported by mighty strong buttresses; where there is an old gate-way walled up.

The monastery of St. Augustine.

Mr *Torre* (a) has proved by several testamentary burials that there was a conventual church belonging to this monastery of St. *Augustine* at *York*. (b) *Speed*, in his catalogue of religious houses, mentions it to be founded by a lord *Scrope*; but when, or of what value, omitted. Nor is it mentioned at all in the *Monasticon*. Dr. *Heylin* (c) has put down the yearly value of the lands of this monastery at 180 *l.* which is very considerable; but no further did I ever meet with of them, except a record in the tower of *London*, of 20 *s.* annual rent granted to them by one *Thomas de Twenge* clerk issuing out of his lands and tenements in **Kotte**, com. *Ebor.* to help them, as the deed witnesses, to find *bread* and *wine* for *holy offices, &c.* Licence given for this donation by king *Edward* III. at *Callis*, *anno reg.* 21.

The same king in the twenty seventh year of his reign gives licence to *William de Hadon* and *William de Haktborp*, clerks, to bestow upon these fryars one messuage contiguous to their house for the enlargement of the same. Copies of these grants may be found in the *appendix*. In one of the testamentary burials of Mr. *Torre*, *Joan Trollop*, *an.* 1441, leaves her body to be buried in the conventual church of the fryars *Eremites* of St. *Augustine* in *York*. The term of *Eremites* to this order is what I have not before met with; the *fryers minors* were styled *Eremitae*, *i. e. Eremi incolae* (d). The (e) **Eremites**, or **Hermits**, in the north were corruptly called **Cremitts**; and there is an annual rent paid out of some houses in *Stone-gate*, called **Cremitt-Money** at this day, which undoubtedly belonged to a religious house of these orders; for some of the poorer sort of monks being called *hermits*, an *hermitage* and an *hospital* had one and the same signification. I have nothing more to say about this religious house, but that *November* 28. 30 *Hen.* VIII. it was surrendred into the king's hands by the prior and six fryars. (f) *John Aske* was then prior, or guardian of it, and the surrender is dated in their *chapter-house* as above.

WATER-LANES.

QUAKER'S MEETING.

There are three lanes leading from *Castle-gate* to the *Stayth*, called now *first*, *second*, *and far water-lanes*; though anciently the first was called *Carr-gate* and the next *Thrush-lane*. In the third, or *far Water-lane*, stands the *quaker's meeting-place*; first built here *anno* 1673, when this set of people increased in this city. Having before as a Manuscript informs me kept their meetings at one *Edward Nightingale's*, a rich grocer in *Upper Ouse-gate*; the most eminent man of that persuasion then in *York*. I cannot leave the *Stayth* without taking notice that the late alderman *Cornwall*, a brewer, built a very handsome house on it.

CASTLE-GATE.

ST. MARY'S *Church*.

Castle-gate, or the street leading to the *castle* of *York*, has a church in it with a beautiful and lofty spire, and is called in ancient writings *ecclesia sanctae* Marie *ad* portam Castri. This was an ancient rectory of medieties, the one belonging to the patronage of the lords *Percy*, earls of *Northumberland*, and the other to the prior and convent of *Kirkham*. Mr. *Torre* has given a catalogue of the rectors of both medieties, but since I find they were united about the year 1400, and became solely in the *Percy's* gift; I presume one will be thought sufficient (g).

This whole rectory is valued thus in the king's books.

		l.	*s.*	*d.*
First fruits	——	02	08	06½
Tenths	——	00	04	10
Procurations	—	00	06	08

A CATALOGUE of the RECTORS of St. MARY'S CASTLE-GATE.

Temp. instit. Anno	*Rectores eccl.*	*Patroni.*	*Vacat.*
1267	Rad. de Ver, *cler.*	*Dom*[a] Agnes *relict. dom.* Ric. de Percy.	
1281	Rog. le Porter, *cap.*	*Eadem.*	
1288	Elias de Richmond.	*Eadem.*	
1302	Joh. de Toppelyve, *subdec.*	Hen. de Percy, *mil.*	
	Simon de Stow.	*Idem.*	*per resig.*
1350	Rob. de Nafferton, *cap.*	*Idem.*	*per resig.*
1362	Rob. de Ferriby, *presb.*	*Idem.*	*per resig.*
1364	Rob. de Kernetby, *cap.*	*Dom.* Idonea de Percy. *Vid.*	*per resig.*
1365	Adam de Ebor.	*Eadem.*	*per resig.*

(z) *Leland's* itin. vol. V.
(a) *Ex MS.* Torre, *f.* 877.
(b) *Speed's* chron.
(c) *Heylin's* hist. reform,
(d) In the library of *Trinity-college* in *Dublin* is a MS. with this title, *Catalogus bibliothecae ordinis fratrum* eremitarum S. August. *in* Eboraco, 1372. *Fratre* Willielmo de Staynton *tunc existente priore.* Wanley *cat. MSS. in* Ang. *et Hybern.* 285, 145.
(e) See *Thoresby's Ducat. Leod.* p 90.
(f) *Burnet's* hist. reform. *Claus.* 30 Hen. VIII. *par.* 5. N° 67
(g) *MS.* Torre, *f.* 363.

Temp.

I

WALM-GATE WARD.

Temp. instit. Anno	Rectores eccl.	Patroni.	Vacat.
1365	Nich. de Cave, *presb.*	*Dom^a.* Idonea de Percy. *Vid.*	*per resig.*
1369	Hen. de Pykeryng, *presb.*	Hen. Percy *mil. dom.* Percy.	*per resig.*
1372	Joh. de Pykering, *presb.*	*Idem.*	
	Nich. de Cave, *presb.*	*Idem.*	*per resig.*
1383	Joh. de Herle, *presb.*	*Idem.* *Com.* Northumb.	
	Tho. de Scardeburg.		*per mort.*
1422	Joh. de Forton *alias* Easingwald, *presb.*	*Idem.*	*per mort.*
1427	Rob. Bedale, *presb.*	*Idem.*	*per resig.*
1429	Will. Gould, *presb.*	*Idem.*	
	Fra. Nicolas Wartre, Dromor. *episcopus.*		*per mort.*
1453	Joh. Leake, *presb.*	Hen. Percy. *com.* Northumb.	
1464	Joh. Garnet, *cap.*	Georgius *dux* Clarentiae.	*per mort.*
1492	Will. Thompson, *decr. B.*	*Feofatores* Hen. *com.* Northumb.	*per mort.*
1502	David John *dec. B.*	Hen. *com.* Northumbr.	*per resig.*
1506	Will. Mason, *presb.*	*Idem.*	*per mort.*
1518	Will. Batty, *presb.*	*Idem.*	*per resig.*
1521	Chris. Wilson, *presb.*	*Idem.*	*per resig.*
1535	Rob. Ashbie, *cap.*	*Idem.*	
1586	Fran. Harpar, *cler.*	Elizabetha *reg.*	*per mort.*
1595	Jac. Graynger, *cler.*	*Eadem.*	*per mort.*
1624	Joh. Wilson, *cler.*	Jacobus *rex.*	*per mort.*
1639	Joh. Peryns, *cler.* *M. A.*	Carolus I. *rex.*	*per mort.*
1688	Joh. Bradley, *cler.*	Jacobus II. *rex.*	

Norfolk's *chantry in this church.*

Die dom^ca in festo conversionis S. Pauli, *anno* 1320.

Thomas son of *Nicolas de Norfolk*, granted to *God* and St. *Mary* and *All-saints*, and to sir ——— *Middelton* chaplain, and his successors daily celebrating divine service at mattins, vespers, and other canonical hours, together with *placebo* and *dirige*, in this church of St. *Mary* in *Castle-gate* at the altar of St. *Thomas* the martyr, for the souls of his father *Nicholas*, *Elene* his mother, *Mauds* his two wives, of sir *John de Malbys*, knight, and dame *Agnes* his wife, and sir *William Malbys*, *Edmund Mauncell* and *Stephen de Hamerton*, *&c.* five mark yearly rent issuing out of all the lands of his inheritance in the town and territory of *Naburn*, to be paid at pent. and mart. by equal portions. *l. s. d.*

(*h*) *Valet de claro* — — — 03 00 00

Gray's *chantry.*

There was another chantry founded in this church of St. *Mary Castle-gate*, in the chapel of St. *John Baptist* and St. *John* the *Evangelist*, for the soul of *William Gray*, or *Graa* of *York*, authorised by king *Rich.* II. *Maii* 12, 1403. *l. s. d.*

(*i*) *Valet de claro* — — — — 02 13 08

Holm's *chantry.*

(*k*) A third was founded by *Thomas Howem* or *Holm*, some time merchant in *York*, licenced by *Richard* II. as appears by his grant dated *Oct.* 7. *an. reg.* 7. to celebrate mass at the altar of the said church, to keep a stall in the choir, to sing and say divine service on *Sundays* and holidays, and to pray, *&c.* *l. s. d.*

Valet de claro. — — — — 04 06 10

Percy's *chantry.*

Mr. *Torre* gives a fourth, which he says was founded in this church at the altar of St. *Mary* the virgin, to pray for the souls of *Henry Bolton*, *&c.* (*l*)

Monumental INSCRIPTIONS from Dodsworth, Torre, *&c.*

✠ Orate pro anima Domini Johannis Garnet quondam rectoris istius ecclesie qui obiit vicesimo die mensis Maii Millesimo CCCCLXXXX. cujus anime propitietur deus. Amen. Garnet 1490.

(*h*) *Pat. anno* 13 Ed. II. *m.* 30.

(*i*) *Dodsworth*'s coll. in the add. vol. to the *Monast.*

There is an original charter of a chantry founded by one *Emma Gra* in this church, city records, *drawer* 5, which I suppose may be this. Rents of lands belonging to this chantry lying as is expressed in **Thrusslane** and **Copper-gate.**

(*k*) *Dodsworth*'s coll. and *pat.* 50 Ed. III. *p.* 2. *m.* 27.

(*l*) *Ex MS.* Torre, *f.* 374.

WALM-GATE WARD. Gray, *Mayor* 1367.

On a very fair tomb with the portraits of a man and his wife is this broken inscription:

✠ Hic jacent Willielmus Gray et Johanna uxor ejus . . . .
credo quod redemptor meus vivit et in novissima die . . . .
. . . . Amen.

The inscription on this tomb, which is still standing in the south choir of the church, Mr. *Torre* could not read; but it appears by the foregoing from *Dodsworth*'s manuscript, that it is the tomb of *William Gray*, who had a chantry founded for him in this church. Arms, on a bend between two cottizes three griffons passant; on the stone twice.

ROGER OVERTON PRAI FOR HIS SOVLE.

In the chancel.

Stillingbec, 1403.

✠ Orate pro anima Johannis Stillingbec, qui obiit vii. die mensis Julii anno Domini M.CCCC.III. cujus anime propitietur Deus. Amen.

Blackburn.

✠ Johannes Blackburn civis et mercator Ebor . . . . . et Katherina uxor ejus.

ARMS. *Or*, a lyon rampant *b.* *Percy.*
. . . . A fess between three mullets, in stone on the steeple and porch.
Argent, on a bend cottised *azure*, three garbs *or*, with a file of three points of the first.
Arms of *England*.
Barry of six *gules* and *argent*.

There are other inscriptions on the following names: *Weightman*, *Wilson*, *Sweeton*, *Marshall*, *Jackson*, *Chapman*, *Archbutt*. Also of *Thomas Barker* of *Ottley* esq; sir *Henry Thompson*, knight, once lord-mayor, who died *Aug.* 26, 1692. Some children of sir *James Bradshaw* of *Risby*. Three copartments, one for *Lewis West*, esquire; another to *Rich. Sauray*, batchelor of physick; the third for *William Mason*, presbyter.

Mr. *Thoresby* had a copper plate in his possession which was found in making a grave in this church, and which, he says, had been covertly conveyed and fastened on the inside of the coffin of a popish priest who was executed for the plot 1680 (*m*). The plate had this inscription on it:

R. D. Thomas Thweng *de* Heworth *collegii* Anglo-Duaceni *sacerdos*, *post* 15. *annos in* Anglicana *missione transactos* Eboraci *condemnatus*, *martyrio affectus est* Oct. *die* 23. *anno Dom.* 1680. *Duobus falsis testibus ob crimen* conspirationis *tunc temporis* catholicis *malitiosè impositum*.

The family of *Thweng*, of *Heworth*, is very ancient in our neighbourhood.

CASTLE *of* YORK.

At the end of this street stands the famous castle of *York*; situated at the confluence of the rivers *Ouse* and *Foss*; the later of which has been drawn in a deep mote quite round it; and made it inaccessible but by two draw-bridges. The larger of these lead to the ancient great gate from the county, the piles and foundations of which I saw lately dug up; the other to a postern-gate from the city. This has been a year ago rebuilt in a handsomer manner, and is at present the only entrance to the castle; except I mention a small postern near the *milns*.

That there was a castle in *York* long before the conqueror's time, I have proved in the (*n*) annals; which I take to have been in the place already described called **Old Bayle**. This therefore, I believe, was built a *solo*, but probably on a *Roman* foundation, by *William* I. and made so strong in order to keep the citizens and *Northumbrians* in awe; and to preserve his garrisons better than they were in the former. It continued to be in his successors hands, the kings of *England*, and was the constant residence of the *high sheriffs* of the county, during their sheriffalty, for some ages after. Several accounts are to be met with in the *pipe-rolls* which the high-sheriffs gave in, from time to time, for the reparations, &c. of this castle (*o*). And, as by these means, these officers have a near affinity to the city, a general list of them, as high as they can be traced, will be given in the succeeding chapter.

Whilst the castle was in the king's hands, it was the store-house and magazine for his revenues in the north. Here was, heretofore, a constable of this castle for that purpose; for I find, says sir *T. W.* in an assize of *Hen.* III. mention made of the fees and customs belonging to this office (*p*). By the 13th of *Rich.* II. *cap.* 15. it is enacted, that the king's castles, which are severed from the counties shall be rejoined to them. From whence, I suppose, the assizes for the county of *York* were always held in the castle; which hath reference to all the three ridings of the county, but yet it stands in none of them; neither is it within the liberties of the city, though it be always assessed, and bears charges with the parish of St. *Mary*'s *Castle-gate*.

(*m*) *Thoresby's Ducat. Leod.* in *appendix*.

(*n*) *Vide annales sub. an.* 939.

(*o*) Henricus de Bada *vic. red. comp. in attractis faciendi. ad operationes castri de* Ebor. cc. *marcas per breve regis. Et in eodem castro firmando* cc. *marcas per breve regis. Et in custodibus operationum castri* cc. *marcas, per breve regis. Rot.* Pipe, 30 Hen. III.

(*p*) *In assiz. in com.* Ebor. *crast.* Mich. 35 Hen. III.

(*q*) Fal-

K.

To ... unty of **YORK**, *in the Year 1728, this plate is*
mo...

A. *The courts of Justice.*
B. *The chapel end.*
C. *The Grand-jury house.*

J. Haine... *J. Basire Sculp.*

THE ASTOR LIBRARY

(q) Falling to decay, it was repaired, or rebuilt, in *Richard* the third's time. But *Leland* found it in a ruinous condition, *the area of this castle*, says that antiquary, *is no very grete quantitie, ther be five ruinous tours in it.* That part of the castle, which remained of the old foundation in sir *T. W*'s time, appeared to be only the gate-house to the old building, by the proportion of the gates yet shewing themselves, says sir *T.* on the east side towards *Fisher-gate* postern; where the great door is walled up, and where the main building of the castle was, as is manifest, adds he, by the foundations of walls all over the said place, if it be tryed with spade or hack. CASTLE of YORK.

The present structure of the courts (r) of justice where the assizes are kept, were erected *anno* 1673, at the charge of the county, *John Ramsden* of *Byron* esq; then high-sheriff. The ancient towers of the castle, which, after it was dismantled of a garrison, became a county prison for felons, debtors, *&c.* being by age rendered exceeding ruinous, and a most miserable goal, was wholly taken down, and the present most magnificent structure erected in its stead, *anno* 1701. A building so noble and compleat as exceeds all others, of its kind, in *Britain*; perhaps in *Europe*. In the left wing is a handsome chapel, neatly and beautifully adorned with suitable furniture. The whole pile was carried on by a tax of 3 *d. per* pound, on all lands, *&c.* within the county; pursuant to an act of parliament obtained for that purpose. By these means a very great sum was collected, but whether all laid out or not, I find is yet disputable.

The justices of peace for this county have of late years taken great care that this goal should be as neat and convenient within, as it is noble without; by allowing of straw for the felons, and raising their beds which before used to be upon the ground. They have likewise caused an infirmary to be built, for the sick to be carried to out of the common prison; allowed a yearly salary to a surgeon to attend them, and have repaired the castle walls quite round. In the reparations, they have quite taken away the arch of the ancient grand entrance, which used to be out of the county into the castle, over a draw-bridge; and I can only now tell posterity, that the gate was exactly opposite to *Fisher-gate* postern; or rather the horse steps near the mill. A circumstance not regardable by any but a true antiquary *.

(s) There were anciently two chapels in or near this castle; in *pat. anno* 19 *Ric.* II. *par.* 2. *m.* 34. there was granted 6 *s.* 8 *d.* rent out of tenements in **Sand hutton** to the king's chapel without the castle. Many lands were holden by special tenures, relating to the custody and safe-guard of the castle.

In a book of tenures kept in the first remembrancer's office in the exchequer, the title of which book is this: *Iste liber compositus et compilatus fuit de diversis inquisitionibus ex officio captis temp. regis* Edvardi *filii regis* Henrici, *&c.*

Com. Ebor. The castle of *York* is worth by year x *s.* (t)

Robertus Belistarius doth hold, by serjeantry, four acres and a half in **Gevedale** by the service of one *Ballister*.

John de Watingham holds, by serjeanty, four carucates of land by the same service, and is worth by the year six mark.

John le Poer holds five carucates and an half of land by the service of an *archer* in the castle of *York*, and it is worth by year x *s.*

Docket homo Camerary holds lands in the city of *York*, which belong to the custody of the gate of the castle, and it is worth by year i *s.*

David le Lardiner holds one serjeanty; and he is keeper of the *Goal* of the *Forest*, and selzer of the cattle which are taken for the king's debts.

Richard the son of *Vide* of **Aslakeby** holds two carucates of land by the service of fitting the king's *trimerium* (u) and it is worth by the year xl *s.*

John de Cawood holds two carucates of land in **Cawood**, by the serjeanty of keeping the forest between *Ouse* and *Derwent*, but the value unknown.

Robert de Gevedale and *Thomas de Gevedale* doe hold all **Gevedale**, by *ballistery* to the castle of *York*.

(x) *Anketine Salvayne*, knight, did hold the day of his death, four tofts and four oxgangs and a half of land in **North Dalton** of the king, *in capite*, as of his crown, by homage and the sixth part of a certain serjeanty; which entire serjeanty is held of the king *in capite* by the service of finding one man with bow and arrows in the castle of *York*, at his own charge for forty days if there be war in the county of *York*; and paying to the king in his exchequer by the hands of the sheriff of *Yorkshire* xv *s.* at *Easter* and *Michaelmas*.

(y) *John le Archer* held the day of his death one messuage and four acres of land in **Papam** of the king *in capite*, by the service of a seventh part of a certain serjeanty, which entire

(q) Camden. Lelandi *itin. incept. an.* 1538.

(r) Called anciently **Moot-hall. Mote** or **Moot** *ab A* S. MOT or GEMOT *convertus* GEMOTHEAL *nobis*, the **Moot-hall.** *Hinc* **Mote-bell** *quae exponitur campana quâ conventus publicus indicitur. Skinner* ety. dict.

(s) *Ex MS.* sir *T. W.*

(t) F. 688. *et* 689. 90.

* Ebor. *portae castri serjeantia ibidem ad quem custodia pertinet et de valore ejusdem per an.* Esch. 55 Hen. III. No. 45.

(u) I cannot find the signification of this word, unless it mean a *triple tower*.

(x) *Esch. anno* 25 Ed. III. No. 57.

(y) *Esch. anno* 2 Ed. III. No. 46.

serjeanty

4

ſerjeanty is held of the king *in capite*, by finding one man with *bow* and *arrows* in the caſtle of *York*, as before.

(z) *William* the ſon of *Cicely de Stavely*, of **North Givendale**, held the day of his death certain lands in that town and in **Eaſt Givendale**, of the king *in capite*, by the ſervice of a ninth part of a certain ſerjeanty, which entire ſerjeanty is held of the kind by the ſervice as above.

(a) *Agnes de Gevendale* at the day of her death held one meſſuage and land in **Eaſt Given-dale** of the king *in capite*, to find, with her fellows, one *baliſter* within a certain tower in the caſtle of *York*, for the ſafe cuſtody of the caſtle for forty days in time of war.

Queen *Elizabeth* by her charter dated *December* 2, in the fifteenth year of her reign, 1573, grants to *Peter Pennant*, alias *Piers Pennant*, the keeping of the goal and the office of kee-per of the caſtle of *York*, and the graſs within the precinċts of the caſtle; with all houſes, cellars, barns, ſtables, gardens and ditches, within the precinċts of the ſame; and the keeping of all priſoners and perſons by the mandate of the preſident and vice-preſident of the council, with the fees pertaining to the office; and after the death of *Pieres Pennant* it was granted to *Anthony Benni*, the king's footman, to be executed by his ſufficient deputy, *&c.*

Whereas in *York-caſtle* there was a goal, the cuſtody whereof the keeper of the caſtle claimed; but the ſheriff of the county took out the priſoners, and the caſtle keeper com-plained, but had no remedy; for that the goal is the ſheriff's, and he is to anſwer for eſcapes. *Anderſon*, vol. I. fol. 345. p. 320.

CASTLE-PREACHERS. 16 *Jan.* 10 *Car.* I. 1634.

Phineas Hodſon, D. D. chancellor of *York*, granted to *John Scott*, dean, *George Stan-hope*, D. D. *Henry Wickham*, D. D. canons reſidentiaries of the ſaid church, their heirs and aſſigns for ever, one annual rent or ſum of thirty pounds, iſſuing out of one meſſuage ſi-tuate in *Bempton*, alias *Benton*, upon the *Woulds*; alſo out of the chapel of *Benton* and *New-ſam*, and out of all manner of tythes, ſheaves of corn and grain, hay, wool, lamb, hemp, calf, and all manner of tythes whatſoever, ſmall and great, to them belonging, *&c.*

It being agreed and covenanted between the ſaid *John Scot*, *&c.* and ſuch perſon or per-ſons who ſhall have the ſaid rent, that they ſhall yearly, after the feaſt of St. *Martin*, biſhop, next coming, pay the ſum of 25 *l.* parcel of the ſaid 30 *l*, half-yearly, within twenty ſix days, *&c.* to ſuch miniſter, or preacher of God's word, as ſhall be nominated and appoin-ted by the ſaid *Phineas* Hodſon, during his life, to preach weekly in the caſtle to the priſo-ners there for the time being through the year; except only aſſize-weeks, and times of in-fećtion.

And the other 5 *l.* out of the ſaid yearly rent of the 30 *l*. ſhall be yearly paid, and weekly diſtributed by 2 *s.* 6 *d. per* week in bread, amongſt the poor, upon the ſermon days, to ſuch of them as ſhall be preſent.

And after the ſaid *Phineas* his death, then the dean and chapter of *York* ſhall appoint and nominate the preacher to the ſaid priſoners in the caſtle for ever, *&c. Torre, f.* 863.

This ſtipend is augmented by the county to 40 *l. per ann.*

The *area* of this caſtle of no great quantity, as *Leland* ſays, is very conſiderable for a priſon; the walls being about 1100 yards in circumference, and the priſoners having the li-berty of walking in it, makes their confinement, within theſe walls, leſs irkſome and more wholeſome. There is a well of excellent water in it, by the houſe where the *grand-jury* meet; which houſe was built the ſame year as the oppoſite courts of juſtice; and are con-joined by a walk, well paved with ſtone, made a year or two ago. I muſt not forget to mention another walk, on the back of the caſtle, next the *Foſſe*, which yet retains the name of ſir *Harry Slingſby's walk*; ſaid to be made by that unfortunate gentleman in his confine-ment in this caſtle. From whence he was removed to *London*, tried, condemned and be-headed by a pack of rebels for his ſteady loyalty to his injured ſovereign. I take leave of the caſtle with preſenting the reader a view of it.

Within ſome paces of the gate, cloſe to the bridge, is erećted (b) the city's arms, at the extent of their liberties; where the city's ſheriffs ſtand to receive the judges of aſſize, and conduċt them to the *common hall* when they come the circuit. It was not immaterial that this mark of diſtinguiſhing the city's liberties from the county's was here ſet up. I find the high-ſheriffs have often laid claim to that part of the ſtreet called *Caſtle-bill*; and have made arreſts thereon. A remarkable inſtance that I have met with in the city's oldeſt regiſter is as follows: (c) *Anno regni regis* Hen. V. *ult.* 1422, *Henry Preſton* lord-mayor was informed that ſir *Hatnatheus Mauleverer*, then high-ſheriff of the county, had come, in his proper perſon, to the houſe of one *William Haſebam*, dwelling on *Caſtle-bill* in this city, and had arreſted one *Agnes Farand*, otherwiſe named *Agnes Bercoats*, commonly known to be the

(z) Eborum, *Eſch. anno* 29 Ed. III. Nº. 48. and *Eſch. anno* 3 Ed. II. Adam de Stavely.
(a) *Eſc. anno* 51 Ed. III. Nº. 13.

(b) Erected on both ſides *anno* 1679. Richard Shaw, mayor.
(c) *Ex regiſtro f.* 64. *ſub hoc anno.*

THE ASTOR LIBRARY NY

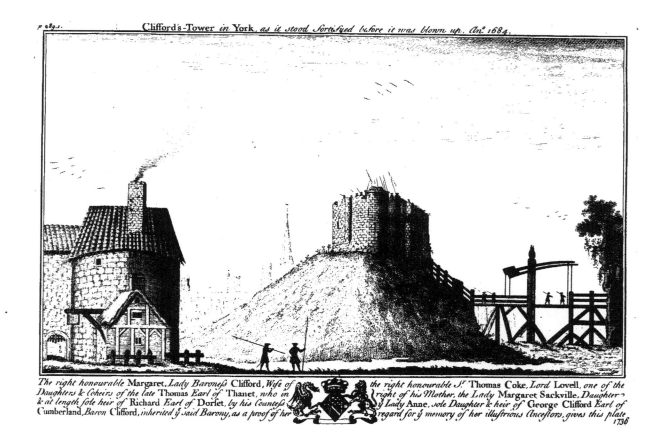

p 289.1.

Clifford's-Tower in York, as it stood fortified before it was blown up. An^o. 1684.

The right honourable Margaret, Lady Baroness Clifford, Wife of the right honourable S^r. Thomas Coke, Lord Lovell, one of the Daughters & Coheirs of the late Thomas Earl of Thanet, who in right of his Mother, the Lady Margaret Sackville, Daughter & at length sole heir of Richard Earl of Dorset, by his Countess y^e Lady Anne, sole Daughter & heir of George Clifford Earl of Cumberland, Baron Clifford, inherited y^e said Barony, as a proof of her regard for y^e memory of her illustrious Ancestors, gives this plate 1736

A perspective view of the inside ruins of Clifford's Tower.

W.H. Toms delin. et sculp. 1735.

The right hon.ble S.r Thomas Coke *Lord* Lovell, *Knight of the most honourable order of the* Bath, *for an encouragement to the author of this work, bestows this plate. 1736.*

PRUDENS QUI PATIENS

(d) concubine of the rector of Wath; and had carried her prisoner into the castle. The mayor, much grieved at this presumption, sent messengers to the high-sheriff, to acquaint him that he had done contrary to the liberties and privileges of the city, in arresting *Agnes* in the said place, and required him to deliver her up. The high sheriff answered peremptorily that he would not, but would detain her prisoner till he had certified the king and council of the fact. However, as the record adds, sir *William Harrington*, lately high sheriff, an honourable person, and a friend to both parties, hearing of it, being then in the castle, sent the mayor word that if he would come down on the morrow to the monastery of the *Augustine fryars*, he would bring them together and try to make a good end of this matter. At this meeting the whole affair was talked over betwixt them, the result of which was the high-sheriff gave up the lady, and commanded her to be conveyed to the place from whence she was taken.

Adjoining to the castle is an high mount, thrown up by prodigious labour, on which stands a tower of somewhat a round form, called *Clifford's tower*. This place has long born that name, and if we may believe tradition, ever since it was built by the *conqueror*; one of that family being made the first governor of it. Sir *T. W.* says, from the authority of *(e) Walter Strickland* esq; whom he calls an excellent antiquary that the lords *Cliffords* have very anciently been called **Castlekyns, Wardens** or **Keepers** of this tower. But whether it be from hence, that the family claim a right of carrying the city's sword before the king in *York*, I know not. I have noted somewhat relating to that honour in the annals of this work, *temp. Jac.* I. what sir *Thomas* has left concerning it, who has been very particular in drawing up the claim, shall be given in the *appendix*. CLIFFORD'S *Tower.*

(f) Leland, in his description of the castle of *York*, says *the arx is al in ruine: And the roote of the hille that it standith on is environid with an arme dervid out of Fosse-water.* It continued in a ruinous condition till the grand rebellion begun, and when the city was ordered to be fortified, this place was looked upon as proper for that purpose. By the direction of *Henry* then *(g)* earl of *Cumberland*, lord lieutenant of the northern parts, and governor of *York*, this tower was repaired; a considerable additional square building put to it, on that side next the castle, on which over the gate, in stone work, is placed the royal arms and those of the *Cliffords*, *viz.* chequée and a fess, ensigned with an earl's coronet, supported by two wiverns with this motto DESORMAIS.

The tower being repaired and strengthened with fortifications, a draw-bridge, deep moat, and pallisadoes; on the top of it was made a platform, on which some pieces of cannon were mounted; two demy culverins and a saker, with a garison appointed to defend it. Sir *Francis Cob* colonel, was made governor of it; who with his lieutenant colonel, major and captains, had their lodgings there during the siege of the city, *an.* 1644. After the rendition of the city to the parliament's generals, it was all dismantled of its garrison except this tower; of which *Thomas Dickenson*, then lord-mayor, a man remarkable for his eminent disloyalty, was made governor. It continued in the hands of his successors, as governors, till the year 1683, when sir *John Reresby* was made governor of it by king *Charles* II. *Anno* 1684, on the festival of St. *George*, about ten at night, the magazine took fire, blew up, and the tower made a shell of; as it continues at this day. Whether this was done accidentally or on purpose is disputable; it was observed that the officers and soldiers of the garrison had removed all their best things before, and I have been told that it was a common toast in the city to drink to the *demolishing of the minced pye*; nor was there one man killed by the accident.

This mount exactly corresponds with much such another on the west side of the river in *Old-Bayle*, which I have described. By the extraordinary labour that must have been applied to the raising this mount, I can judge it to have been effected by no less than a *Roman* power. The conqueror might build the present structure, the inside of which exhibiting a regularity, very uncommon in a *Gothick* building, I have given a print of it. Within this tower was a deep well, now choaked up, said to have been a spring of excellent water. Here was also a dungeon, so dark as not to take in the least ray of light. The property of the tower, mount, ditches, and exterior fortifications is now in private hands, and held by a grant from *James* I. to *Babington* and *Duffield*, amongst several other lands granted to them in and about the city of *York*. The words of the grant are *(h) totam illam peciam terrae nostram scituat. jacent. et existent. in civit. nost.* Ebor. *vocat.* CLIFFORD'S TOWER; but whether the building passed by this grant, or whether the crown did not always reserve the fortifications; is a question proper to be discussed; since by the tower's falling into private hands, it is threatned with an entire erazement, which will be a great blemish to the city; this venerable pile, though a ruin, being a considerable ornament to it. I present the reader with a view of the tower, as it stood fortified *anno* 1680, with its draw bridge or entrance from the castle. What it is at present may be seen in a former plate of the city.

(d) *Concubina rectoris de* Wath.
(e) Of *Boynton*, MS. sir *T. W.*
(f) *Lelandi* itin. Vol. 5.
(g) *MS. penes me.*
(h) *Pat. anno reg. regis* Jac. I. 1ar1.

WALM-GATE WARD. CASTLE-GATE *postern-lane.* I now return into the city by a lane, called *Castlegate postern-lane*; from its leading down to a postern gate of that name. This entrance into the city was also widned for carriages, *&c. an.* 1672, by sir *Henry Thompson*, lord-mayor, his habitation being upon *Castle-hill*, and his country-house at *Escrig*, making it convenient for him so to do. The lane is not remarkable, but for the gardens that go from it down to the river, which was the site of the monastery of the *Augustine* fryars. On *Castle-hill* are some good houses and gardens on both sides the street. Contiguous to the church-yard stands an hospital erected by the former sir *Henry Thompson*, knight, for six poor freemen, whom the lord-mayor and aldermen for the time being have the nomination of. THOMPSON's *hospital.*

COPPER-GATE. At the other end of *Castle-gate* is *Copper-gate*; which has nothing remarkable in its name, or street; except I mention a great inn over against the church-yard called the *White-horse-inn*. NESS-GATE. *Ness-gate* a little street from *Ness Nasus*, a nose or neck of land. OUSE-GATES *High and low Ouse-gate* are streets which lead to the river *Ouse*.

SPURRIER-GATE. *Spurrier-gate* is opposite, and took its name from the *Spurriers*, which were a great craft formerly, when our warriors wore spurs of a most extraordinary length and thickness. In Mr. *Thoresby*'s *Musaeum* at *Leeds*, were many sorts of antique spurs, and some of them, which I saw, were six inches from the heel to the rowel. At the corner of this street and *Low Ouse-gate* stands

S. MICHAEL's *church.* The parish church of St. *Michael*, which is a very ancient rectory, and was given by king *William* the conqueror to the abbey of St. *Mary*'s *York*. And until the dissolution belonged to the patronage of that religious house; which received out of it the annual pension of 36 *s.* (i)

The rectory of St. *Michael* is thus valued in the king's books.

		l.	*s.*	*d.*
	First fruits	08	12	01
	Procurations	00	18	02½
	Subsidies	00	14	00

A CATALOGUE of the RECTORS of St. MICHAEL OUSE-BRIDGE.

Temp. instit. Anno	*Rectores eccl.*	*Patroni.*	*Vacat.*
1255	Reyner. de Schypton, *cl.*	*Abbas et conv.* B. Mar. Ebor.	
1268	Will. de Candelby, *cler.*	*Iidem.*	
1269	Rob. de Sexdecem-vallibus, *presb.*	*Iidem.*	
1288	Rod. de Ponthorpe, *cl. per sequest. tenuit.*	*Iidem.*	
1288	Joh. de Dalton, *subd.*	*Iidem.*	
1305	Will. de Butterwyke, *pr.*	*Iidem.*	
1310	Joh. de Ayremine, *a col.*	*Iidem.*	
1316	Walt. de Yarewell.	*Iidem.*	*per resig*
1326	Ric. Wetherby, *presb.*	*Iidem.*	*per resig.*
1339	Gilb. de Yarewell, *cap.*	*Iidem.*	
	Joh. de Kylpin, *cap.*	*Iidem.*	*per resig.*
1349	Joh. de Tyverington, *pr.*	*Iidem.*	
	Joh. de Burton, *presb.*	*Iidem.*	*per resig.*
1362	Joh. Heriz, *presb.*	*Iidem.*	
	Rad. de Setterington, *pr.*	*Iidem.*	*per mort.*
1403	Tho. de Watton, *presb.*	*Iidem.*	*per resig.*
1404	Rob. Applegarth, *cap.*	*Iidem.*	
1409	Tho. Grenewode, *pr. L.D.*	*Iidem.*	
	Ric. Staynton, *presb.*	*Iidem.*	*per mort.*
1442	Rob. Tarre, *presb.*	*Iidem.*	*per resig.*
1448	Rob. Stillington, *LL.D.*	*Iidem.*	*per resig.*
1450	Will. Langton, *L. B.*	*Iidem.*	*per mort.*
1466	Joh. Lancaster, *L. D.*	*Iidem.*	*per resig.*
1471	Tho. Tewson, *cap.*	*Iidem.*	*per mort.*
1500	Joh. Rutter, *cap.*	*Iidem.*	*per mort.*
1502	Joh. Hedingham, *cap.*	*Iidem.*	*per resig.*
1506	Arthur Wood, *presb.*	*Iidem.*	*per resig.*
1509	Hen. Beston, *cap.*	*Iidem.*	*per mort.*
1522	Joh. Marshall, *L. B.*	*Assign. ab. et convent.*	*per resig.*
1531	Nic. Atkynson, *presb.*	*Iidem.*	*per mort.*
1548	Rad. Whyttling, *presb.*	*Assign. ab. et convent.*	

Salley's *chantry.*

An. 1336. *Rob. de Salley* citizen of *York*, by licence built certain houses on that part of this church-yard of St. *Michael* between the lane called *ad aquam de Use* and this church. And out of the rents appointed for the sustentation of one chaplain perpetually to celebrate at the altar of St. *Mary* in this church for the souls of *John de Rickal* chaplain, and of him the said *Rob. de Salley* and *Maud* his wife. And further to say dayly *placebo, dirige*, with commendation and full service of the dead, and to be assistant at mattins and vespers on *Sundays* celebrated in this church. To celebrate our lady's mass with note on festivals, and without note on other days.

Which chaplain shall be presented by the parishioners of this church within eight days of any vacation, and shall honestly keep the chalice, books, priest's vestments and other ornaments of the chantry; and perpetually find one lamp to burn before the said altar day and night. (k)

	l.	*s.*	*d.*
Yearly value	01	19	04

(i) Ex MS. Torre, *f.* 341.

(k) *Dodsworth* and *Torre*.

Temp.
I

WALM-GATE WARD.

Temp. instit. Anno.	*Rectores eccl.*	*Patroni.*	*Vacat.*
1554	Ric. Blanchard, *cler.*	Phil. *et* Mar. *rex. et reg.*	*per mort.*
1576	Hen. Fisher, *cler.*	Eliz. *reg.*	
1599	Jac. Grainger, *cler.*	*Eadem.*	*per resig.*
1617	Milo White, *presb.*	Jac. *rex.*	
1662	Josias Hunter, *cler.*	Car. II. *rex.*	

Monumental INSCRIPTIONS (*l*).

Quisquis eris qui nunc transis istum prope bustum, Wilson, *Lord-mayor* 1513.
Nullatenus . . . . . funde precesque mane;
Wilson Willielmus glebis jacet hic coopertus,
Vir probus, expertus, sit summo principe certus.

✠ **Hic jacet Alanus Hammerton nuper civis et mercator Ebor. et Isabella uxor ejus, qui quidem Alanus obiit xx die Feb. A. Dom. M. CCCC. V. quorum, &c.** Hammerton 1405.

✠ **Orate pro anima Nicholai Vicars quondam vicecomitis civitatis Ebor. qui obiit xxvi. die mensis Januarii A. Dom. M.CCCC.LXXXVIII.** Vicars 1488.

✠ **Orate pro anima Thome Vicar quondam mercator. istius civitatis Ebor. qui obiit xxviii. die mensis Septem. A. Dom. M.CCCC.XIX.** Vicar 1419.

✠ **Orate pro anima Magistri Willielmi Langton quondam rectoris istius ecc. qui obiit xiii. die mensis Augusti A. Dom. M.CCCC.LXIII.** Langton 1463

✠ **Hic jacet Robert Johnson Grocer quondam major istius civitatis Ebor. qui obiit vii. die mensis Feb. A. Dom. MCCCCLXXXVII. cujus, &c.** Johnson 1497 *Lord-mayor* 1497.

✠ **Orate pro animabus Willielmi Hancok olim istius civitatis Eboraci Apothecarii, qui obiit sexto die mensis Julii A. Dom. M.CCCC.LXXXV. et Elene uxoris sue, que obiit quarto die mensis Augusti A. Dom. M.CCCCLXX. quorum, &c.** Hancok 1485.

✠ **Hic jacent Oliverus Midelton . . . . quondam Vicecomes civitatis Ebor. et Matilda et Johanna uxores ejusdem, qui quidem Oliverus obiit xiv die Jan. A. Dom.** 1504. Midelton 1504.

Here lyeth interred the bodies of Mr. Geffrey Urin, *once sheriff of* Lincoln, *who departed this life the 15th day of* Jan. An. Dom. 1656. *And also the body of Mrs.* Jane Urin *his wife, she departed this life the 10th day of* March, A. D. 1664. *aged* 94. Urin 1656. Urin 1656.

Also Mr. Thomas Maylor, *citizen and merchant of* Yorke, *who departed this life the 16th of* Decemb. A. D. 1676. *Son-in-law to the parties aforesaid.* Aetat. suae 56. Maylor 1676.

Hic jacet Willielmus Lee *sen. almae curiae* Ebor. *procurator generalis, qui obiit* 3° *die* Feb. *A. D.* 1641. *annoque aetat. suae* 45. Lee 1641.

Paris Lee *filius* Gulielmi *et* Margarettae Lee, *hinc non a longinquo repositi curiae* Ebor. *consistorialis nunc procurator unus hoc tumulo jacet sepultus obiit* 6° *die* Feb. *A. D.* 1643. *aetat.* 35. Lee 1643.
Aeternitatis et gloriae candidatus.

Here lyeth the body of Francis Jackson *of* Leeds, *alderman, who departed this life* Aug. 13, 1644. Jackson 1644.

Gulielmus Turbut *arm. dum vixit doctissimus et fidelissimus* Eboracensis *consistorii registrarius modernus, et dilectissimae custodiae spiritus sancti animam hujus sepulchrum marmoreum et proprium corpus tradit, et in pace tuto requiescant, usque ad futuram gloriam repeterentur, ob.* Nov. 16, 1648. *aetat. suae* 74. Turbut 1648.

Here lieth the body of William Shawe *batchelor, late of this city merchant, son of Mr.* Thomas Shawe *late recorder of* Aldingham, *in* Furnese, *in* Lancashire, *who departed this life the* 18th *day of* July *in the year of our Lord* 1681, *being aged* 40 *years; and by his last will gave one hundred pound to the poor of this parish for ever.* Shawe 1681.
This for a memorandum of his name,
Whose virtue yet surviving, let his fame.

Here lyeth the body of Samuel Mancklyn *gent. son of* George Mancklyn *formerly lord-mayor of the city of* Yorke, *who married* Margaret *eldest daughter of* Henry Harrison *of* Holtby *esquire (second son of sir* Thomas Harrison *of* Copgrave*) by whom he had issue one only daughter named* Isabel. *He departed this life* May 18, 1687. Mancklyn 1687.

Here lyeth the body of George Mancklyns *alderman, and some time lord-mayor of this citye, aged* 74 *years, and dyed* 27th *of* December 1683. Mancklyns 1683. *Lord-mayor* 1666.
Also the lady Isabel *his wife, aged* 66, *and died the* 20th *of* November 1680.

✠ **Orate pro anima Richardi Savage quondam vicecom. civit. Ebor. et Alicie uxor. ejusdem, qui obiit xxiii die Aug. an. Dom.** 1544. **quorum animabus, &c.** Savage 1544. *Sheriff* 1540.

Modern inscriptions carry the names of *Williamson*, *Wood*, *Whitehead*, *Stevenson*, *Mitchell*, *Murgetroyd*, *Haerton*, *Geldart*, *Darley*, *Day*, &c.

(*l*) *Ex MSS.* Dodsworth *et* Torre.

I can-

WALM-GATE WARD. I cannot take leave of this church without obferving that the weft end of it is almoft wholly built of the *grit ftone*, of which here are fome blocks of an extraordinary fize; amongft them is an altar ftone, but the infcription defaced. A lane from *Spurrier-gate* goes

ST. MICHAEL'S LANE. half round this church and opens into low *Oufe-gate*, the houfes near the corner have been formerly built on the church-yard, as is obfervable by the quantity of bones dug up in their foundations. This I took no notice of in the corner-houfe, which was pulled down and rebuilt laft year, and thereby the turn made more commodious for coaches, *&c.*

PETER-LANE LITTLE. From upper *Oufe-gate* through two lanes, or allies, one called *Pope's-head alley*, we are brought into another lane called *Peter-lane-little*; which took its name from a church which formerly ftood on the eaft fide of it dedicated to St. *Peter*; for diftinction fake called *ecclefia S.* Petri *parva*, or S. **Peters le littel.**

Church of St. PETER LE LITTLE. (*m*) The parifh church of St. *Peter le little* was an antient rectory belonging to the patronage of the prior and convent of *Durham*. But, *anno* 1585, it having been fome time before demolifhed, was, together with its parifh and all its members, united and annexed to the church of *All faints* in the *Pavement*. There were formerly four chantries belonging to this church.

Akum'*s chantry.*

The firft was founded *anno* 1348, by *John de Akum* citizen of *York*, at the altar of St. *Mary*; and granted two meffuages and fix pound annual rent in the city to a chaplain celebrating for ever, *&c.*

Akum'*s fecond chantry.*

There was another chantry founded in this church *anno* 1358, by *Robert de Swetmouth* and *John de Akum* executors to the former *John*, at the altar of St. *John baptift*, at the requeft of the abbot and convent of *Byland*, for the fouls of the faid *John de Akum* deceafed, *Elene* his wife, and of *Robert* and *Alice* his father and mother.

Setterington's *chantry.*

A third was founded *anno* 1352, by *Stephen de Setterington* of *York* tanner, who granted three meffuages and two pound one fhilling and eight pence annual rent in the city unto *Richard Pape* chaplain and his fucceffors, for celebrating divine fervice at the altar of St. *Mary* in this church of St. *Peter the little*, for his own foul, and the foul of *Agnes* his wife, *&c.*

	l.	s.	d.
Yearly value — — — —	04	18	04 ½

Swetmouth'*s chantry.*

Anno 1352, *Robert Swetmouth* chap. and *William Swetmouth* tanner of *York*, granted unto *John de Gotheland* cap. and his fucceffors for ever celebrating at the altar of St. *Margaret* the virgin in this church, for the fouls, *&c.* two meffuages in **Jubergate**, &c.

	l.	s.	d.
Yearly value — — — — —	03	18	00

PAVEMENT. *Pavement*, whether this was fo called from being the firft or laft paved ftreet in the city, I cannot determine. It has bore that name fome hundred of years; yet I cannot find this place made ufe of for a market, by any regulation in the old regifters of the city. It is but of late years fince the crofs was erected in it, and there was none here before. Bifhop *Morton*, born in this ftreet had a defign to have erected a crofs in it, in his time; but the owner of fome houfes he was about to purchafe, would not fell them. The crofs which ftands here now, was built at the fole expence of Mr. *Marmaduke Rawden*, merchant in *London*, a native of this city; who, amongft other fpecial benefactions, erected this fabrick. Being a fquare with a dome, afcended into by a pair of winding ftairs, and fupported by twelve pillars of the *Ionick* order, but ill executed. *Anno* 1671, to enlarge the market-place, fome houfes were bought and pulled down, which ftood betwixt the church and the crofs. And archbifhop *Stern* gave leave, alfo to take off a good piece of the church-yard, to the north, for the fame purpofe. Whatfoever it was formerly it is now the market for all forts of grain, wild fowl, poultry ware, butter, *&c.* The herb market is in *Oufegate* above it already defcribed.

ALLHALLOWS PAVEMENT. The church of *Allhallows* in the *Pavement*, may more properly be faid to ftand in upper *Oufe-gate*, and in an old grant to the abbey of *Fountains*, which I have feen, the rector of this church, as witnefs, is called (*n*) *rector ecclefie omnium fanctorum in* Ufegata. The northfide of this church is almoft wholly built out of the ruins of EBORACUM; but the tower or fteeple is fo exquifite a piece of *Gothick* architecture, that I have thought fit to fubjoin a perfpective view of it, along with the crofs. The fteeple at the top is finifhed lanthorn wife; and tradition tells us, that antiently a large lamp hung in it, which was lighted in the night time, as a mark for travellers to aim at, in their paffage over the immenfe foreft of *Galtres* to the city (*o*). There is ftill the hook, or pully, on which the lamp hung, in the fteeple. The whole pile narrowly efcaped being confumed with fire, *anno* 1694, when moft of the buildings oppofite to it in *Oufe-gate* were laid in afhes. This was the occafion of fo many handfome ftructures being erected in their ftead in this ftreet.

(*m*) Ex MS. Torre, *f.* 233. Chantries *Dodf.* and *Torre.*
(*n*) *Ex or. regiftro* Fontanenfi.
(*o*) The fame was done by a lanthorn on the top of *Bow-fteeple*, before the fire of *London*, for burning of lights, to give direction to the weary travellers, and to market people, that came from the northern parts to *London*. *Bagford*'s letter to *Hearn*, coll. v. 1.

The 2

The Church and Gothick Steeple *of* Allhallows *in the* Pavement; *with the* Market Crofs *before it*

4 F

WALM-GATE WARD.

The church is an antient rectory, belonging, before the conquest, to the prior and convent of *Durham*. In the book of *Domesday*, it is said, *habet episcopus* Dunelmensis, *ex dono regis, ecclesiam omnium sanctorum, et quae ad eam pertinent in* Ebor. In continued in the patronage of the aforesaid convent to the *Reformation*; when it came to the crown.

		l.	*s.*	*d.*
Value in the king's books.	First fruits — —	03	13	04
	Tenths — —	00	07	04
	Procurations — —	00	06	08

(p) *A CATALOGUE of the RECTORS of the church of* ALL-SAINTS *in the* Pavement.

Temp. instit. Anno	*Rectores eccl.*	*Patroni.*	*Vacat.*
1238	Gilb. de Barton, *cler.*	*Prior, et conv. Dun.*	
1281	Petrus de Kellaw, *subd.*	*Iidem.*	
1283	Alan. de Birland, *presb.*	*Iidem.*	
1301	Tho. Gonwer, *presb.*	*Iidem.*	*per resig.*
1337	Joh. de Pykerings, *cap.*	*Iidem.*	*per resig.*
1344	Hen. de Rayton, *cap.*	*Iidem.*	
	Joh. de Lunde, *presb.*	*Iidem.*	*per mort.*
1406	Joh. Southe, *cap.*	*Iidem.*	
	Joh. Wightman, *cap.*	*Iidem.*	*per resig.*
1408	Tho. Crakaa.	*Iidem.*	*per resig.*
1409	Joh. Wyles, *presb.*	*Iidem.*	*per resig.*
1420	Joh. Bolton, *presb.*	*Iidem.*	*per resig.*
1424	Will. Bramley, *presb.*	*Iidem.*	*per resig.*
1430	Joh. Wendesly, *cler.*	*Iidem.*	
	Will. Nessingwych.	*Iidem.*	*per resig.*
1453	Ed. Mynskyp, *presb.*	*Iidem.*	*per resig.*
1466	Joh. Topliff, *L. B. arch. cap.*	*Iidem.*	*per resig.*
1489	Will. D. G. *epis.* Dromorensis, *viz.* Will. Egremond.	*Iidem.*	*per mort.*
1502	Phil. Metcalf, *dec. doc.*	*Iidem.*	*per resig.*
1509	Georg. Richardson, *presb.*	*Iidem.*	*per resig.*
	Georg. Wilson, *cler.*	*Iidem.*	*per mort.*
1544	Rob. Craggs, *cler.*	Hen. VIII. *rex.*	*depriv.*
1554	Will. Pecock, *cler.*	Maria *regin.*	*per mort.*
1576	Joh. Hunter, *cler.*	Eliz. *regin.*	
1594	Will. Storre, *cler.*	*Eadem.*	*per cession.*
1606	Will. Coxen, *cler.*	Jac. *rex.*	*per mort.*
1631	Hen. Ayscough, *cl. M.A.*	Car. I. *rex.*	*per mort.*
1662	Joshua Stopford, *cl.*	Car. II. *rex.*	*per mort.*
1675	Christ. Jackson, *cler.*	*Idem.*	

Ampleford's *chantry.*

(q) *Robert de Ampleford* citizen of *York* having obtained the king's licence to authorize, *&c.* assigned one messuage in the city of *York* to the dean and chapter of the cathedral church, for to find a perpetual chaplain daily to celebrate divine services in this church of *All-saints* in *Ouse-gate*, alias *Pavement*, for his soul and the soul of *Margaret* his wife, *&c.* Whereupon *Alexander* archbishop of *York*, ordained that the said dean and chapter shall pay yearly five pound thirteen shillings and four pence; quarterly to such chaplain and his successors, *&c.* celebrating, *&c.* The presentation to belong to the said *Robert* for life, and after to the dean and chapter; to present within a month of notice of a vacancy. (r) Dated *Jan.* 24, 1378.

	l.	*s.*	*d.*
Valet de claro	04	17	10 ¼

Besides an obit of five shillings.

Acaster's *chantry.*

(s) There was another chantry founded in this church by *Isolda Acaster*, at the altar of St. *Thomas* the martyr, for the soul of *John de Acaster* her husband, *&c.* Foundation deed dated *penult. die* Ap. 1386.

Valet de claro 04 19 10

(t) The chantry at the altars of St. *John baptist* and St. *Katherine*, in this church, was founded by *William Pomfrett*, and other parishioners, *July* 8, 1485, to pray, *&c.*

	l.	*s.*	*d.*
Valet de claro — — —	02	06	02

(u) Belton's *chantry.*

4 *Julii anno* 1347.

Henry de Belton late citizen of *York*, having at his own proper cost built a chantry at the east end of the church of *All-saints* in *Ouse-gate*, settled thereupon certain houses, against the church, of the yearly value of eight marks of silver and upwards, for the finding of one chaplain perpetually to celebrate divine service at the altar of St. *Mary* the virgin, for the souls of the said *Henry* and *Margaret* his wife, of his father and mother, and sir *Thomas de Cawoode*, &c. *Valor incert.*

(p) *MS.* Torre *f.* 183.
(q) *Idem. f.* 184.
(r) *Dodf.* coll.
(s) *Idem et* Torre. I find this chantry was augmented by sir *John Gylliot* knight of the bath. City's records, drawer numb. 5.
(t) *Dodf.* and *Torre.*
(u) Torre, *pat.* 31 Ed. III. *p.* 2. *m.* 1.

There

(*x*) There was another chantry founded in this church at the altar of St. *Mary* the vir- WALM-
gin, for the ſouls of *Thomas de Alverthorp*, *Robert Haget*, *Elene* his wife, *&c.* *Valor* GATE WARD.
incert.

(*y*) Bolingbroke'*s chantry.*

Founded in this church by *Stephen Bolingbroke*, and other pariſhioners to pray, *&c.*

	l.	*s.*	*d.*
Valet de claro	03	18	03
Goods	00	17	01 ½
Plate	01	15	00

Monumental INSCRIPTIONS *from Mr.* Dodſworth, Torre, *&c.*

✠ Hic jacent Thomas Beverley quondam major iſtius civitatis ac mercator ſtapule ville Beverley
cales, qui obiit undecimo die menſis Auguſti anno Dom. MCCCCLXXX. et Domina 1480.
Alicia uxor ejus, que quidem Alicia obiit . . . die menſ. . . . . . . quorum *Lord-mayor*
animabus propitietur Deus, Amen. 1460.

Hic jacet Robertus Brooke *civis et aldermannus civitatis* Eborum, *bis qui majoratum civitatis* Brooke 1599.
cum laude geſſit. Et Johanna *vel* Jana *uxor ejus, inſimul* 37 *circiter annos vixerunt, vir et* *Lord-mayor*
femina boni, uxor et maritus optimi; liberos habuerunt ſexdecim, undecim reliquerunt; non mali 1582, 1595.
ut liberi nunc ſunt, omnes forſitan bonos; ille aetatis ſuae 68 *fideliter expiravit anno Dom.*
1599, *illa aetatis ſuae* . . .

Reader live well, mourn not thy ſins too late,
There is no way to heaven but through this gate.

✠ Orate pro anima Johannis Gylliot grammatice magiſtri, olim parſone in eccleſia col- Gylliot 1484.
legiata ſancti Johannis Beverlaci hic jacentis qui obiit xix die menſis Julii anno Dom.
MCCCCLXXXIIII cujus anime propitietur Deus.

✠ Hic jacet Johannes Crathorn armiger qui obiit xi die menſis Martii anno Dom. Crathorn
MCCCCLXIV, cujus anime, &c. 1464.

✠ Orate pro animabus Thome Santon quondam majoris hujus civitatis, et Beatricis et Santon
Johanne uxor. ejus, quibus animabus propitietur Deus. Amen. *Lord-mayor*
1414.

Mary *and* Margery *loved like* Martha *and* Mary, *they were religious and virtuous mothers of* Trew 1600.
many children, daughters to Andrew Trew *alderman, ſometyme mayor of this citty, both of*
them married in one ſummer in this grave an. Dom. 1600. *aetat.* 37, 36. *They are not dead,*
but ſleep.

✠ Orate pro anima Thome Gare quondam majoris iſtius civitatis, et Katherine uxoris Gare 1445.
ſuae, obiit vero predictus Thomas an. Dom. MCCCCXXXXV. quibus animabus prop. *Lord-mayor*
Deus. Amen. 1434.

Hic jacet Johannes Thornton nuper draper Ebor. et Katherina uxor ejus juxta ſepulchrum Thornton
Willielmi Pontfracte ſocii eorum tumulati. *Bayliff* 1385.

Hic jacet Johannes Feriby bina vice major hujus civitatis, qui in officio majoris deceſſit Feriby 1491.
xv menſis Maii anno Domini milleſimo quadringenteſimo LXXXX primo et Millicent *Lord mayor*
uxor ejus que obiit octavo die menſis Novembris an. Dom. Milleſimo CCCCLXX, quo- 1478, 1491.
rum animabus propitietur Deus, Amen.

Here lyeth the bodie of one Elizabeth late wief of William Fenay, and daughter of Mr. Fenay 1608
Francis Bunny parſon of Riton and prebendary of Durham. Who in her life time
lived to the lord, and in her death dyed in the lord the xxv day of April, an. 1608.

(*z*) Quod jacet hic ſtratum ſub ſaxo corpus humatum,
Vertitur in cineres quod fuit ante cibis. Gyliot 1484.
Hinc recolas qui laude vales et corpore flores, *Lord-mayor*
Et quod eris ſapiens vilis et egra lues. 1464, 1474.
Aurum quid mortis valeat vinclis reſolutis,
Perpendat quivis vir puer et juvenis.
Fama percelebris GYLIOT fuit iſte JOHANNES,
Bis majoratus geſſit honoris onus.
Hic populum ſtuduit placida perfundere pace,
Urbis quaſi murus civibus alter erat.

Venerabilis vir iſte viceſimo quarto die menſis ſept. deceſſit A. D. MCCCCLXXXIII
cujus anime propitietur Deus. Amen.

(*x*) *Torre.* Of five marks rent granted by the executors of *Tho. Alwrthorp. Pat. an.* 4 Ed. II *pars* 1. *m.* 4. ſir *T. W.*

(*y*) *Dodſ.* and *Torre.*

(*z*) This remarkable epitaph was thus legible in Mr *Dodſworth*'s time; Mr. *Torre* gives ſome fragments of it, but it is now almoſt wholly obliterated.

WALMGATE WARD.

Hic dormit secum chara sua sponsa JOHANNA
Que proles quinas protulit ecce sibi.
Nomina sunt horum Johannes, Ales, et Agnes,
Katherina, Johanna.

Acaster 1379 *Lord mayor* 1361, 1362, 1364, 1379. ✠ Hic jacet Johannes de Acaster quondam major Eborum qui obiit A. D. MCCCLXXIX in die sancti Bricii, et Isolda ux, . que obiit . . . die . A. D. MCCC . quorum animabus propitietur Deus. Amen.

ARMS. On a chevron three acorns (a).

✠ Orate pro anima Agnetis de Braumflete.

Bridesal. ✠ Hic jacet Robertus Bridesale et Matilda uxor ejus quilibet orans pro eis habebit D. C.

Welles. ✠ Orate pro anima Ricardi Welles quondam chandelar Ebor. et Avicie ux. ejus ac liberorum eorundem.

Bromflete 1458 *Sheriff* 1458. ✠ Orate pro anima Thome Bromflete quondam vicecomitis civitatis Eborum, ac Alitie uxoris sue qui quidem Thomas obiit vii die mensis Octobris A. D. MCCCCLVIII quorum animarum, &c. Amen.

Ne sis ingratus, sta, lege, funde precatus
Ut sim mundatus, precibus rogo terge reatus,
Creditur insana mens hic cupiens sibi vana
Vota hinc emana, pro me prece quotidiana,
Vana petunt vanis . . . . callida canis,
Sicque coadjutans votis ego quotidianis,
Sic pater ut valeant . . . bonitate recrescant,.
Lector et ut maneant celis dic ave ut requiescant.

Ampilford. *Bayliff* 1360. ✠ Hic jacet Robertus de Ampilford quondam civis Ebor. et Magdalena uxor ejus quorum anime in pace requiescant.

Todd. *Lord-mayor* 1487. ✠ Orate pro animabus Willielmi Todd quondam vic. hujus civitatis et Agnetis ux. sue ui quidem Willielmus obiit . . . die . . . . . A. D. MCCCC . . . et, dict. Agnes obiit ult. die Augusti A. D. MCCCCLXXII. quorum animabus, &c. Amen.

Fenwick 1421. Hic jacent Willielmus Fenwick civis Ebor. et Margaretta uxor ejus qui obierunt diebus xxv et xxvi mensis Septembris A. D. MCCCCXXI.

Harwood 1615 An epitaph upon the death of Mr. *Richard Harwood* a reverend preacher, who deceased 28 *Mar.* 1615.

Conception of our Saviour was the day
Took Harwood *unto heaven from earth away.*
Christ *in man's flesh, and* Harwood *in* Christ's *glory,*
Have made me write this epicedial story.
Noah's *faithfulness,* Abraham's *obedience,*
Phineas's *strong zeal,* Job's *prais'd innocence.*
St. Jerome's *love,* Chrisostome's *diligence,*
Augustine's *labour and experience,*
Lye buried with Harwood *in this tomb,*
And shall rest with him to the day of dombe.
Let the world cease lament, O glorious gaines,
The earth his corps yet heaven his soul contaynes.
Mortalis cum sis ne irriseris mortuum.

Aiscough 1638 *Aetatem quae superavit ingenio ingenium indole, et pietate quae tenella adbuc matronali a deo emicuit prudentia, et gravitate ut a senibus senem crederes natam, non puella* Elizabetha Aiscough *(indignissimi istius ecclesiae parochi) filia jacet hic beatam praestolans resurrectionem animulae meae in choro* τετελεσμένων *laetabundae tandem tibi corpus languoribus absumptum gloriosum reddetur atque immortale . . Quousque Dom.* Jesu.
Febre petechiali correpta occubuit tertio Martii MDCXXXVIII. *cum jam primam aetatis suae pene explevisset septimana.*

Saluta lector, et, lactantis exemplo,
Disce numen venerari maturius.

More modern epitaphs are not remarkable. There be two atchievements one for Mr. *Thomas Teasman* gent. who died 1689, the other for Mr. *Christopher Birbeck*, a very eminent surgeon in this city, and the author's instructor in that art; who died and was buried in this

(a) Mr. *Torre* calls them covered cups, but they are more probably *acorns* from the *rebus*.

church,

church, *anno* 1717. An inſcription againſt a pillar for *Emanuel Juſtice* eſquire, ſometime lord-mayor, who died 1717. Another for Mr. *Thomlinſon an.* 1709. WALM-GATE WARD.

ARMS in the windows, &c. 1684.

In the window at the ſteeple end,
Impaled, 1. *Gules*, on a bend *argent*, three birds *ſable*. 2. Out.
Cut at the head of a ſtall, north choir,
Percy with his quarterings.
On two wooden knots under the roof in the nave,
Azure a chevron *ſable* inter three bulls heads gaboſhed *gules*.
Azure, a chevron inter three mullets pierced in chief and an annulet in baſe *ſable*.
York city.
Old York ſee.
Merchants of the ſtaple.

The pariſh church dedicated to St. *Crux*, or *Holy-Croſs*, called vulgarly **Crouſe-church**, comes next in our way. It is ſituated at the foot of the *Shambles* or *Butcher-row*, and has a handſome new ſteeple of brick coined with ſtone. The foundation of this ſteeple was laid *April* 1, 1697, and finiſhed at the charge of the pariſh, with ſome other contributions, amongſt which our late excellent archbiſhop *Sharp*, according to his wonted benevolence, bore a handſome part. St. CRUX.

(*b*) The church of St. *Crux* was given by *Nigell Foſſard*, lord of *Doncaſter*, to the abbey of St. *Mary's York*; and payed the annual penſion of twenty ſhillings to that religious houſe.

September 6, *anno* 1424, a commiſſion was directed to *William*, biſhop of *Dromore*, to dedicate this pariſh church; ſo that the preſent ſtructure ſeems to be of that age.

	l.	*s.*	*d.*
The rectory of St. *Crux* is thus valued in the king's books	07	06	08
Firſt fruits — — — —	00	13	08
Tenths — — —	00	06	08
Procurations — — — —	00	12	00
Subſidies — — — —			

A CATALOGUE of the RECTORS of St. CRUX.

Temp. inſtit. Anno	*Rectores.*	*Patroni.*	*Vacat.*
1275	Robertus de Graunt.	*Abbas et conv. beat.* Mar. Eb.	
1301	Rob. de Uſegat, *preſb.*		
1317	Joh. de Pykeryngs, *ſubd.*	*Iidem.*	
	Tho. de Eſcryg, *preſb.*	*Iidem.*	*per reſig.*
1326	Will. de Pykeryngs.	*Iidem.*	
	Joh. Cookyngs, *preſb.*	*Iidem.*	*per reſig.*
1349	Nicol. de Markfeld, *cl.*	*Iidem.*	*per reſig.*
1350	Walt. de Bridlington, *c.*	*Iidem.*	*per reſig.*
1352	Walt. de Heddon, *cap.*	*Iidem.*	
	Rob. Wycliff, *cap.*	*Iidem.*	*per reſig.*
1379	Jo. de Clone, *preſb.*	*Iidem.*	
	Rob. de Ede, *preſb.*	*Iidem.*	*per mort.*
1394	Tho. Teſdale, *cler.*	*Iidem.*	*per mort.*
1420	Ric. Arnale, *preſb.*	*Iidem.*	*per reſig.*
1429	Ric. Tone, *decret. doc.*	*Iidem.*	*per reſig.*
1432	Rad. Louth, *preſb.*	*Iidem.*	
	Pet. de Fryſton, *preſb.*	*Iidem.*	
1449	Will. Middleton, *cler.*	*Iidem.*	*per mort.*
1452	Tho. Bently, *cler.*	*Iidem.*	*per mort.*
1489	Joh. Curwen, *cl. M. A.*	*Iidem.*	*per reſig.*
1489	Chriſt. Panel, *dec. B.*	*Iidem.*	*per mort.*
1516	Will. Marten, *preſb.*	*Iidem.*	*per mort.*
1540	Dionis Hickilton, *preſb.*	Hen. VIII. *rex.*	*per mort.*
1579	Edward Bowling, *cler.*	Eliz. *regina.*	*per reſig.*
1584	Will. Cockſon, *cler.*	*Eadem.*	*per reſig.*
1594	Thomas Word, *cler.*	*Eadem.*	*per reſig.*
1599	Hen. Hayle, *cler.*	*Eadem.*	
1603	Will. Thompſon, *cl. M. A.*	Jac. *rex.*	*per mort.*
1661	Matthew Biggs, *cler.*	Car. II. *rex.*	*per reſig.*
1671	Chriſt. Jackſon, *cl. M. A.*	*Idem.*	

Nayron's *chantry in this church.*

(*c*) Founded by *Adam de Nayron* who left by his will certain tenements for the maintenance of a prieſt perpetually to celebrate for his ſoul, &c. at the altar of St. *Mary the virgin*. The patronage in the mayor and commonality of *York*.

	l.	*s.*	*d.*
Yearly value	01	19	00

Meek's *chantry.*

(*d*) Founded in this church *anno* 1322, by *Robert Meek* mayor of the city, *anno* 1310, to pray, &c. at the altar of St. *Mary the virgin*.

	marks.
Annual rent	6

Bearden's *chantry.*

(*e*) Founded in this church of St. *Crux* at the altar of our *lady*, and St. *Thomas the martyr*, for the ſouls of *John Bearden*, &c.

	l.	*s.*	*d.*
Valet de claro	01	19	04

This belonged to the patronage of the *Gaſcoigns* of *Gawthorpe* knights; and was founded the tenth of *Henry* IV.

(*b*) MS. Torre *f.* 189.
(*c*) MS. *Torre* and *Dodſ.*
(*d*) *Iidem pat.* 10 Ed. II. *p.* 1. *m.* 24. ſir *T. W.*
(*e*) *Torre* and *Dodſworth.*

WALMGATE WARD.

Durant's *chantry*.

(*f*) Founded in the church of *Holy Cross* by *Thomas Durant*, citizen and merchant at the altar of our *Lady* and *All-saints*, to pray, *&c.*

	l.	s.	d.
Yearly value — — — — —	03	08	00
Another founded here by *Thomas Durant* jun. dedicated to St. *John baptist*.	l.	s.	d.
Value — — — — — —	01	06	11

Monumental INSCRIPTIONS which are, or were, in this church from, Dodsworth, Torre, *&c.*

Robinson 1606. *Here lieth entombed* Elizabeth Robinson *wief to* John Robinson *seconde son to* William Robinson *the younger of this citty marchante, who departed this lief the* 8 *of* Aug. 1606.

Against the wall, south of the altar, is a tomb with the effigies of a man, his wife and three children prostrate,

ARMS on the top. *Argent* on a chevron ingrailed inter three chess-rooks *sable*, as many crescents *or*.

Watter 1612. *Lord-mayor* 1591, 1603. *Here lyeth the true portraitures of sir* Robert Watter *knight, alderman and twice lord-mayor of this city. A father to the poore, a friend to the comynalty of this citty, and a good benefactor to this church, who dyed* May 12, 1612. *And of his wief* Margarett *deceased* March 30, 1608. *And of their three children.*

Labor with faith in tyme, using justice well,
Through mercy getts fame, in peace and rest to dwell.

Lightelampe 1485. *Sheriff* 1471. Lyon. ✠ **Orate pro anima Johannis Lightelampe merc. quondam vicecomitis istius civitatis qu. obiit xx. . . . die mensis Novembris anno Domini MCCCCLXXXV, cujus, &c.**

Subjacet hoc lapide Leo Willielmus vocitatus
Et carnis putride mansura morte citatus.
Qui legit hec pro me pater . . . supplica pro me,
Et jungantur ade, Deus ut me liberet abi.

Wrangwys. *Lord-mayor* 1476, 1484. **Here liggs Thomas Wrangwys and Alison his wief, and Alison Wrangwys her daughter Of whose soules Jesu have mercy.**

Shaw 1537. *Lord-mayor* 1510. ✠ **Hic jacent Johannes Shaw olim major civitatis Ebor. et Agnes uxor ejus; qui Johannes obiit duodecimo die Februarii, A. D. millesimo quingentesimo tricesimo septimo.**

Waythen 1421. ✠ **Orate pro anima Elene nuper ux. Johannis Waythen mercatoris, que obiit xv Aprilis A. D. MCCCCXXI, cujus, &c.**

Greenfeld 1487. ✠ **Orate pro animabus . . . . Johannis Greenfeld presbyteri parochialis istius ecclesie et . . . . dem Dom. Johannes obiit xviii die mensis Junii A. D. MCCCCLXXXVII, quorum animabus prop. &c.**

Lambe 1484. *Lord-mayor* 1475. ✠ **Hic jacet Willielmus Lambe quondam major istius civitatis, qui obiit xxix die mensis Junii A. D. MCCCCLXXXIV, cujus, &c.**

Askwith 1597 *Lord-mayor.* 1580, 1593. *Here lyeth the body of* Robert Askwith *late alderman and twice lord-mayor of this citty, borne at* Potgrange, *who dyed the* lxvii *yere of his age, and on the* xviii *day of* August, 1597, *leaving behind him four sons and two daughters*, viz. Robert, Elizabeth, Katherine, Thomas, George *and* Philip. *Being in his life tyme for good hospitality, and other laudable parts, a credit and ornament to this citty.*

Boulington 1408 **Hic jacet Johannes Bowlington, qui obiit xii die Martii A. D. millesimo quadringentesimo octagesimo, cujus, &c.**

Impaling three coats, 1. *Argent* and *sable* entre two mullets in chief and crescent in base all counterchanged. *Alexander*. 2. Par pale barry and *gules*, three lions rampant *argent*. *Herbert*. 3. *Azure*, three gryphons heads erazed *or*. *Cuttler*.

Under these arms,

Posteritati sacrum.

Herbert 1681. *Heic sitae sunt reliquiae* Thomae Herbert, *e nobili et antiqua* Herbertorum *de* Colebrook *in agro* Monumethensi *familia oriundi. Cui ineunte aetate, tam intensus peregrinandi fuit ardor, ut itineris sui in celebriores* Africae, Asiae-majoris *partes, praecipue* Persiae, orientalis Indiae, *insularumque adjacentium, an. Dom.* M DC XXVI, *suscepit. Observationes selectissimas in lucem edidit, quas matura aetate perpolivit. Qui per totum vitae dimensum, ob morum elegantiam, vitaeque probitatem perspicuus, historiarum et penitioris antiquitatis indagator sedulus. Queis in accurata gentis* Hibernianae *historia, ex archivis regiis, authenticis cartis, aliisque indubitatis antiquitatis monumentis manu propria exaratis, et armorum, sigillorum, et tumulorum*

(*f*) *Dodf.* the originals of both in the council-chamber, drawer 4.

ectypis, graphice delineatis, specimen eximium perhibuit. Serenissimo regi Carolo Martyri, *per binos et ultimos vitae tristissimae annos, ab intimis cubiculis, servus exstitit fidelis; rerumque dicti regis, infesta solitudine, gestarum commentariola contexuit, exinde per illustrissimum nunc regem* Carolum II. *in gradum baronetti merito evectus est.* Luciam *filiam* Gualteri Alexander *equitis aurati in uxorem primam duxit, quae fatis cessit A. D.* MDCLXXI. *Ex hac* Philippum, Henricum, *paterni honoris haeredem superstitem,* Montgomerum, Thomam, Gulielmum, *ap.* Thomam, *filiasque quatuor suscepit* Teresiam, Alexandro Bradfield *de* Hanslap *in agro* Buck. *nuptam,* Elizabetham, Roberto Phaire *de* Rostblon *in* Hibernia, Luciam *imprimis* Johanni *de* Clapham *in com.* Surry, *deinde* Gulielmo Herbert *de* Caldecut *in* agro Monumethensi; *et* Annam *provectiori aetate defunctam. Postea cum* Elizabetha *filia* Gervasii Cutler *de* Stainburgh *in com.* Ebor. *equitis aurati modo superstitem, secundas inivit nuptias, ex qua* Elizabetham *trimestrem* Feb. xxi, *A. D.* M DCLXXIII. *extinctam genuit. Tam celebris et charissimi mariti moestissima vidua, ut amoris sui, et virtutum tam insignis viri longaevum praeberet testimonium,* WALM-GATE WARD.

Hocce monumentum. LLM. *posuit.*

Ab hac luce pientissime emigravit 1 *die* Martii *A. D.* M DCLXXXI. *Aetat. suae.* LXXVI.

ARMS, quartering nine coats. 1. Par pale *azure* and *gules*, three lions rampant *argent*, crescent for difference, within a border gobony *or* and *gules*. *Herbert*. 2. *Gules*, two bends *or* and *argent*. 3. *Gules*, a fess of five lozenges *or*. 4. *Argent*, on a cross *gules*, five mullets *or*. 5. *Ermine*, a bend *gules*. 6. . . . . 7. *Argent*, a lion rampant *sable*. 8. *Argent*, three crescents *gules*. 9. . . . . .

An epitaph upon the worshipful Thomas Herbert *esquire late lord-mayor of this city, descended from the most antient and worthy family of the* Herberts *of* Colebrook *in* Monmouthshire, *he died* April 14, 1614. Herbert 1614. Lord-mayor 1604.

See here earth turned to earth . . . .
Who 'ere beholds this wofull monument,
He's here interred whom worth, fame, love,
Might have preserved if stern death would relent;
But he gave place to fates imperious doom,
God takes the best whilst worse supply their room.

It seems this city bore him for herself,
Espousing him to be her turtle dove,
For he for her forgot friends, health and pelf;
York *more he loved then he himself did love.*
And now the widowed city for her dove,
Writes these sad verses on his mourning . . .

He that sustained me in my greatest need,
When wastful plague my people did devour,
And at the best like fearful sheep did feed,
Where 'ere they might their scattered troops secure;
He that kept watch when shepherds were asleep,
He that kept me, his mother, earth doth keep.

He whose white hand would touch no filthy bribe,
Nor make good laws the sword of private ire,
He that adorned the honour of his tribe,
He whom I graced as I did his sire;
He that did feed the poor, the rich advise,
Balmed in my tears, spiced in my love here lyes.

And yet he lyes not here, his better part
Is shrin'd above, his fame lives in the mouth
Of worthy'st men, his love shines in their heart,
His acts examples are for springing youth.
His death, oh stay! that words' a living death,
He died but once, that once, still stops his breath.

How foolish are those painters which devise
The picture of pale death without his eyes;
Death is not blind, but eagle-eyed doth spy
The brightest star that moved in our sky.
His direful arrows never fly at rove,
But hit the choicest plants in all our grove:
Thus gratious Herbert *falls, with whom doth lye*
Entomb'd, religion, wisdom, gravity;
Three things which in one man we seldom see
Were joined in him, wit, wealth and honesty;
On glory vain, or base pelf he never stood,
But left his ease to do his city good.

WALM-GATE WARD.

In arts, arms, numbers, curious was his witt,
Our genius cannot reach the height of it.
No marvel then if York, *still to be just,*
Having nought left of him but sacred dust,
With floods of tears wash o're his sacred hearse,
And on his tombe ingrave this mournful verse,
Long and much honour'd Herbert *here doth sleep,*
Muse say no more, —— *the reader needs must weep.*
Abiit non obiit.
York *bad my birth, from* Brittans, *comes my race,*
The Netherlands *and* France *my youth did guide,*
The citye's rule I took at th' heaviest case.
Two wives five children my dear love have try'd,
Baptized here, here laid with sire and wife,
With brothers, parents, I expect a life.

Herbert 1611. Lord-mayor 1573. *Here under expecting a glorious resurrection are buried the bodys of* Christopher Herbert *esquire, eldest son to sir* Richard Herbert *of* Colebrooke *in* Wales, *which said* Christopher Herbert, *was lord-mayor of this city, and died* 1611; *and with him his beloved lady* Elizabeth *daughter of Mr.* Hemsworth, *who died anno* 1613. *And with them their son* Thomas Herbert *esquire late lord-mayor of this city, he died* April 14, 1614. *And by him are entombed his two virtuous wives,* Mary *daughter of* Thomas Harrison *esquire, who died* August 1604. *And also* Alice *daughter of* Peter Newarke *esquire, she died* 1627. *As also* John *and* Richard Herbert *gent. brothers of the said* Thomas *are here buried.* Christopher Herbert *esquire eldest son of* Thomas, *who died* May 3, 1626, *with* Henry, William *and* Thomas, *his brethren, and* Jane *and* Elizabeth *his two children infants; which said* Christopher *has issue by* Jane, *daughter of Mr.* Heroyd *of* Folkerthorpe *gent.* Thomas Herbert *esquire and* Alice *now living (g).*

Herbert 1667. *Near this is buried* Henry *the son of* Henry Herbert *esquire, eldest son of sir* Thomas Herbert *bart. who married* Anne *daughter of sir* Thomas Harrison *knight, and dame* Margaret *his wife, daughter of the right honourable sir* Conyers Darcy *knight, lord* Darcy *of* Conyers, *who died* 31st *day of* January, A. D. 1667. 27 *days old.*
Fuissem quasi non essem; ex utero translatus in tumulum. Job. x. 19.

Herbert 1674. *Here under is interred* Elizabeth Herbert *daughter of sir* Thomas Herbert *bart. and of* Elizabeth *his wife, daughter of sir* Gervas Cutler *knight, and the lady* Magdalene Egerton *daughter of the right honourable* John *earl of* Bridgewater, *and the lady* Frances Stanly *his wife, daughter and coheir of the right noble lord* Ferdinando *earl of* Derby, *which* Elizabeth *departed this life* Feb. 21, *A. D.* 1674.

Wyman 1411. Lord-mayor 1407, 1408, 1409. **Orate pro animabus Henrici Wyman quondam majoris civit. Ebor. et Agnetis uxoris sue filie Johannis Larden, qui Henricus obiit v die Aug. A. D. MCCCCXI. et Agnes obiit xxii die Sept. A. D. MCCCCXIII quorum animabus prop. Deus.**

CHRISTOPHERUS HAWLEY,

Hawley 1671. *Generosus civis* Eboracensis *per* 50 *annos aut eo circiter feliciter vixit, tandem sept. die* Augusti *anno salutis* 1671. *devixit; et sub hoc marmoreo monumento, cura amantissimae simul et moerentissimae conjugis, constructo placide quievit.*

Atkinson 1682 *Here lyeth the body of* Richard Atkinson *of* Widdington *in the county of* York, *esq; councellor at law, late member of the honourable society of* Grey's-Inn. *Who departed this life,* Feb. 6, 1682.

Rawden 1626 *Here lyeth the body of* Laurence Rawden, *late of this city alderman, who departed this life in the* 58th *year of his age,* July 5, 1626. *Also the body of* Margery *his wife, by whom he had three sons and two daughters,* Roger, Robert, Marmaduke, Elizabeth *and* Mary. *She deceased,* Apr. 17, 1644. *Also the body of* Elizabeth *her grand-child, daughter to sir* Roger Jaques *knight; who deceased in the* 20th *year of her age,* Oct. 20, 1651.

Jennings 1624 *Hic jacet* Petrus Jennings, *A. M. filius natu minimus* Petri Jennings *de* Selden, *gent. obiit* 4° *die* Martii 1624. *aetat. suae* 24. *cujus memoriae dicatur hoc tetrastichon.*
Nomine Petrus *erat* Petrum *fiat undique fide*
Dixeris usque Deo Petri Petronius *(h) iste.*
Claviger est coeli Petrus, Petronius *ergo*
Ingreditur superas Petro *reserante tabernas.*

Jackson 1701. *Nigh this place lies interred the remains of the reverend Mr.* Christopher Jackson, *A. M. rector of this church thirty three years; and of* All-Saints *in the Pavement twenty five; and preben-*

(g) This honourable and antient family of the *Herberts* of *York* is now extinct, at least dead in law; the last baronet of it, sir *Harry Herbert*, having been charitably maintained by *John Bright* esquire of *Badsworth* for many years, at last died there. His title, without estate descending to another brother a low tradesman at *Newcastle*

(h) Petronius *quasi* Petri *filius.*

dary of the cathedral of St. Peter's three; nescius conjugii. *In mind clear and comprehensive; in study laborious and improving; in preaching learned and edifying; in opinion orthodox and peaceable; in life pious and exemplary; in conversation pleasant and harmless; in temperance severe and regular; in charity prudent and extensive; besides his many acts of private charity, he repaired or rather rebuilt the parsonage house; and gave five guineas towards the re-building of the steeple of this church: He gave also two hundred pound, in his life-time, to the lord-mayor and aldermen of this city, in consideration of which they are to pay to two poor decayed tradesmen five pound a piece yearly, for ever.* Obiit an. salut. 1701. ætat. vero 63. WALM-GATE WARD.

Hoc monumentum gratitudinis ergo posuit haec civitas. *John Peckit*, lord-mayor 1702.

Here are some other modern Inscriptions, one on a copartment for *Rob. Bellwood*, serjeant at law, *obiit* 1694; on *Brerewood, Bigland, Chadderton, Pawson, Nowell, Eskrick, Perrit, &c.* I must not omit to take notice, that the body of *Henry* earl of *Northumberland*, beheaded in the *Pavement anno* 1572, was buried in this church, without any memorial. An exact terrier or just account of the revenues, *&c.* of this rectory of St. *Crux*; as also of the united parishes of *All-Saints, Pavement*, and St. *Peter the little*, as they were delivered in *an.* 1716, at the primary visitation of *William* lord archbishop of *York*, by the late incumbent Mr. *Noble*, are come into my hands; but are too long to insert.

The church of St. *Crux* is bounded on the north by a thorough-fare, which goes from the *Shambles* into *Collier-gate*; on the south by *Hosier-lane*, whose name is obvious, on the north by *Foss-gate*, a street chiefly made use of for the sea-fish market, and leads to *Foss-bridge*. HOSIER-LANE.

On the west side this street, near the river, stands the *Merchant's-hall*, or *Gilda Mercatorum* in *York*. It is a noble old room, supported by two rows of strong oak pillars; it has been lately much beautified and sashed, by the care of the present company, and has in it divers pictures of several eminent merchants of the city, late benefactors to that community. FOSS-GATE. MERCHANTS HALL.

But what makes this place more remarkable is the site of an ancient hospital, which was founded here, *anno* 1373, by *John (i) de Rowcliff*, dedicated to *Christ* and the blessed virgin. The said *John* had letters patents from king *Richard* II. dated, *ut supra*, to purchase lands worth ten pound *per ann.* for the sustentation of a priest or master, and for the brethren and sisters of the same. The said priest was to pray for the said king, the founder, and all christian souls; was to pay weekly to thirteen poor folks, and two poor scholars, constantly residing in the hospital every of them four pence of silver. But by reason the founder purchased only in his life-time one house and 26*s.* rent, and no other person since having purchased any other lands, therefore, says my authority, the governors and keepers of the mystery of merchants of the city of *York*, incorporated *July* 12, 8 *Hen.* VI. and authorized by the said incorporation to purchase lands to the value of 10*l. per ann.* and to find a priest out of the profits of the same, did enter into the said lands given to the said hospital, and of the profits and other lands did give yearly to a priest to sing continually in the said hospital, over and besides all charges, vi*l.* TRINITY-HOSPITAL.

(k) The master of this hospital was to be a clergyman of good fame and discretion, and was to have for his whole maintenance the sum of x. marks *per ann.* And if the revenues increase upon his management he is to get another chaplain to assist him, who for his pains was to have vi. marks *per ann.* and both of them to say daily suffrages for the dead, and celebrate masses for the health and good estate of the king's highness, the said *John de Rowcliff*, the mayor of the city, and official of the court of *York* for the time being; and should every week say the penitential psalms with the litany.

Furthermore it was ordained, that there should be in the said hospital continually, thirteen poor and impotent persons maintained, and two poor clerks teaching school, to be at the assumption and election of the *warden*, who shall pay to each of them 4*d.* a week.

	l.	*s.*	*d.*
At the dissolution the goods of this hospital were in value ——	01	06	00
Plate —— —— —— ——	06	10	02½
Valet. per ann. —— —— ——	06	13	04

(l) The chapel belonging to this hospital was built about the year 1411; for I find that *Henry* archbishop granted special licence dated *Aug.* 7, 1411, to the master hereof to celebrate divine service in the *new chapel*, and upon the *new altar* therein erected, at the costs of certain citizens. Also to hallow the bread and water on the *Sundays*, and the same so hallowed to administer to the poor weak and infirm people of the said hospital for ever.

(m) This hospital was dissolved *an.* 3 *Edw.* 6. and the stipend of the priest, as also the lands, granted for maintaining of *obits*, lights, and lamps here, was by act of parliament given to the king. But the hospital and chapel are still kept up by the fellowship of the *merchant-adventurers* of this city; and ten poor widows maintained, under the government and oversight of the governors and wardens thereof.

The chapel is neat and lightsome; beautified and repair'd with double rows of seats one

(i) *Dodsworth* and *Torre*.
(k) *Mon. Ang.* vol. III. f. 99.
(l) *Torre*.
(m) *Ex MS. penes me*.

WALM-GATE WARD. above another on both sides the chapel, done at the costs of the merchant's fellowship, *an.* 1667.

BENEFACTORS to this HOSPITAL, &c.

(n) *Nicholas Warthill, an.* 1396, gave to the poor of this hospital a tenement in *Bootham*, valued at 16 *s. per ann.*

Agnes de Touthorpe gave to the master and brethren of this *guild, an.* 1398, an house in the parish of St. *Peter le little*, to pay to every poor person of the hospital every *Lady-day* 5 *d.*

William Hart, by his will, dated *Jan.* 14, 1632, gave this hospital 300 *l.* to be lent to the fellowship of merchants; and the increase thereof to be paid to the poor folk of the hospital. Which, formerly produced 18 *l. per annum*; the distribution of which was 2 *s.* 8 *d.* a month to each poor widow, N°. 10. —— —— —— —— 16 00 00
To the reader of the hospital —— —— —— 02 00 00

Mr. *William Breary*, by his will dated 1637, gave to the corporation of merchants 25 *l.* to be lent; the increase thereof to be paid to the poor of the hospital for ever, at the discretion of the governors and wardens.

Thomas Herbert, by his will, gave to the fellowship of merchants 30 *s.* for a sermon yearly before the company. The preacher to have 20 *s.* and 10 *s.* to be given to the poor of the hospital every *Michaelmas* court yearly.

Sir *Henry Thompson*, knight and alderman, governor of the fellowship of the merchants *an.* 1669, gave 90 *l.* to be lent at interest for ever; the consideration thereof paid by the wardens to an able minister for preaching three sermons in this chapel upon three quarter court days, *viz. Christmas-court, Lady-day*, and *Midsummer* courts for ever.

Allowed by the fellowship of merchants by an order of their court, made in the year 1619, to the poor of the hospital 5 *s.* every quarter, yearly. This order renewed and confirmed in 1642. adding to be paid to the said poor 1 *s.* 6 *d.* a piece, every *Christmas, Easter* and *Pentecost.* This was again augmented by an order of court made *June* 27, 1681, to 2 *s.* a piece, to be paid by the wardens as above. More granted to the poor of the said hospital by several orders of merchant's court, the one half of all forfeitures for absences at courts and sermons, which some years proves more, some less; which the wardens pay them on making up their accounts.

The ancient register book of the revenues, &c. of this hospital is still in the custody of the merchants adventurers, in their evidence chest in the hall, and mentions these particulars:

Nomina fratrum et sororum hosp. cum statut. ejusdem, f. 1.
Evidentia de terris et tenement. hospit. f. 16. to *f.* 42.
Carta mutationis Gilde in hosp. f. 136.
Carta Ed. III. Ric. II. *et* Hen. VI. *pro gubernatore et* 2 *cust. f.* 133. *f.* 41. *f.* 138.
Litera Johannis Pickering *regi et consilio, f.* 176.
—— *Abbati Fontinensi* —— *idem.*
Advocatio hosp. et alia instrumenta, f. 140, 148, &c.
De terris mercatorum, f. 153.

ARMS over the gate, to the street:

Argent, three bars wavy *azure*, on a chief gules a lyon of *England. Merchants of the staple.*

Two ancient coats that were in one of the windows 1684.

Or, a chevron between three chaplets *sable.*

Argent, a chevron gules between two mullets of six points in chief, a text T in base *sable.*

FOSS-BRIDGE. *Foss-bridge* is next, built of stone of three arches, though one of them is buried on the east side, under which runs the river *Foss*, whose source and conjunction with the *Ouse*, is

FOSS-RIVER. thus described in the *Collectanea* (o). FOSSA, *amnis piger, inter stagnantis aquae collectae ex pluvia et terrae uligine, originem habet ultra castellum* Huttonicum, *terminatque fines* Calaterii *nemoris; tandem serpens prope castellum* Ebor. *in alveum* Usae *fluit.* The river *Foss* arises in the forest, somewhat above *Sherrif-button*, and creeping along enters the city, washes the castle walls, and somewhat further loses itself in the *Ouse.* We have a strong tradition that this river was anciently navigable up as far as *Layrthorp-bridge*; where pieces of *boats* and *anchors* have been found. If so, it must have been for lighters, and other flat-bottomed vessels, to carry goods and merchandize, to the merchants residing in this part of the town. Of which we have the names of several who formerly dwelt in *Foss-gate, Hun-gate*, and *Pease-holm-green* on the banks of this canal. I have elsewhere taken sufficient notice of this, so I have the less to say of it here. But then either the castle milns must have been away, or locks made at them for this conveyance, which last is not to be supposed, because locks are a modern invention. Sir *T. W.* here again asserts, *that these mills are not very ancient, and that before the building of them, the place where they stand was a fair green, and a passage from* Fisher-gate postern *to the castle, and used for fishing, bowling, and other recrea-*

(n) *Ex MS. penes me.*

(o) *Coll.* Lelandi, *tom.* iv.

tions,

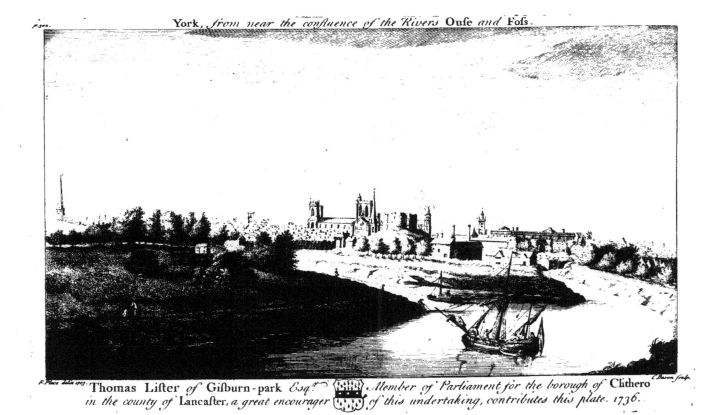

York, *from near the confluence of the Rivers* Ouse *and* Fos.

F. Place delin 1703. C. Baron sculp.

Thomas Lister *of* Gisburn-park *Esq.r* *Member of Parliament for the borough of* Clithero *in the county of* Lancaster, *a great encourager of this undertaking, contributes this plate.* 1736.

THE ASTOR LIBRARY
N.Y.

tions. But this does not seem to appear, but rather the contrary, from what I shall transcribe out of the aforesaid author relating to the claim of fishing on the said river *(p)*. WALM-GATE WARD.

" *Inq*. 30 Edv. III. *coram reg*. Ebor. *rot*. 11. it appears by inquisition of that date that " divers had fished *in stagno dom. regis de* Fose, at divers times, and had made *porcariam*, a " hogsty, upon the bank aforesaid to the prejudice of the fish. *Igitur capiantur*, &c.

" I find that in the time of *Edw*. II. upon the complaint of *Oliver Sandbus*, to whom the " custody of the fish-pond was committed by the king, that he pretended he was hindred " from taking the profits of the lands belonging to the fish-pond, and that others challenge " a right of fishing therein. Upon which a writ was granted, the substance of which was " to enquire, survey and certify the accustomed bounds of the fish-pond, and what other " profits belong thereto *(q)*. This was done by twenty four knights, and other good men " of the city of *York*; by virtue of this an inquisition was taken at *York* on *Saturday* next " after the octaves of St. *Martin* by the oaths of *Thomas de Bolton*, *Thomas Rivers*, *William Wyvill*, *Geofry Upsal*, *John Minors*, *William Darrel*, *Alexander Percy*, *Richard Goldsbrough*, *Henry Hartington*, *Hugh Pickworth*, *Richard Davering*, *John Fleeming*, *Thomas* " *Sheffield*, and *John Nevill*, knights, and others. The justices and jurors did view the " Fish-pond, and found that one head thereof extended to the king's mills, under the castle " of *York*, towards the south; and towards the north and east the fish-pond is divided into " two arms, whereof that towards the north extends itself to the water mill of the abbot of " St. *Mary's York*; and the other arm towards the east extends itself to a certain wooden " cross, anciently scituated at the end of the said arm, between the land of the prebendary " of *Tong*, and the land of the hospital of St. *Nicolas* near *York*. And the old accustomed " bounds of the said fish-pond are so much as the water of the said fish-pond occupies, so " that the water be in the channel within the banks every where, in *English* **Brinks**; and " that the king hath not any ground of his own without the banks aforesaid, or near the " arms aforesaid or profit, unless it be as much as the fisher of the said fish-pond can mow " of the grass and rushes, one of his feet being in a *ship* (boat) and the other foot without " upon the ground of the bank, with a little scythe in his hand in summer-time, the water " being in the channel within the banks every where as aforesaid."

By this old inquisition it plainly appears that the castle mills stood then where they do now; that the extent of those arms, which makes the island of *Foss*, exactly corresponds with their present situation; the abbots mill was at *Earsley-bridge*; and lastly the pieces of boats and anchors, said to be found here, seem to be no more than some remains belonging formerly to the fishermen that occupied this stream.

By the records above, and several others that I have seen, it also appears that this fishery on the *Foss*, belonging then to the crown, was anciently of great account. In the reign of *Edw*. I. upon the supplication of *Nicolas de Meignill*, that he had been at great expence in the repairs of the banks of this water during the time of his sheriffalty a writ of an enquiry was sent out, and these jury-men impannelled to give in their verdict upon it; *Hugo del Wald*, *Hugo de Richale*, *William Presflay*, *John de Maunby*, *William del Gayle*, *William de Myton*, *William Bator*, *Hugo Salwayn*, *William de Thornerby*, *Steph. de Haton*, *Rob. Chychelet*, *Roger de Duggerthorp*, *Henry de le Croyce*, *John Fox de Angram*, *Wyats de Apylton*, *Ralph Cork*, *William Fitz Ralph* and *Henry Fossard*, jun. who say upon their oaths that the same is true.

Several orders for making proclamations have been issued out from the crown for prohibiting under very severe penalties any persons from throwing into this great Fish-pond any dung or excrements of beasts, or other nastinesses; or from laying of them upon the banks of the said river; particularly one in the reign of *Henry* IV, which prohibits such things to the prejudice of the royal fishery under the penalty of 100*l*. for each offence *(r)*.

In the reign of *Hen*. VI. *anno* 8. a complaint was made to *Humphrey* duke of *Gloucester*, lord protector, and *Thomas Longle*, bishop of *Durham*, then lord chancellor, both at that time in *York*, that many roots of seggs, and other weeds, with mud and other rubbish gathered together did annually increase and destroy great numbers of fish in this vivary. And that if the same was not remedied, the whole would in time be destroyed. Therefore the said protector and chancellor sent for the mayor, &c. to enquire into the occasion of it, &c. The whole proceeding upon this matter is too long to insert, but the record of it may be found in the register-book of the city; *lit. B. fol*. lx.

This fishery in the water of *Foss*, there called **Foss-dyke**, was granted to the archbishop for the term of twenty one years, 18 *Hen*. VII *(s)*. But afterwards the whole river of *Foss*, and fishery at *York*, was granted from the crown to the *Nevils* lords of *Sheriff-hutton*; from whence it came to the *Ingrams*, and is at present in the right of the lord viscount *Irwin*. There is no doubt but if this stream was made navigable for small vessels up to, or near, its

(p) *Ex MS*. sir *T.W*.

(q) The patent bears date at *Skipton* in *Craven*, *Oct*. 20. 17 *Ed*. II. The writs and inquisition are amongst the records of the tower, *Inquis*. 17 Ed. II. N°. 192.

(r) *Ne quis civis aut alius projiciat fimos, exitus, intestina sordida, foetida et alias corruptiones in aquam regiam de* Foss, *vel super ripas ejusdem ponat, in destructionem aquae predictae et infectionem piscium regiorum in eadem aqua sub poena centum librarum ad opus regium solvend*. &c. *claus*. 9 H. IV. *m*. 36.

(s) 18 Hen. VII. *pars* 2da. *f*. 268. *Rolls*.

source,

4

WALM-GATE WARD. source, it would be of great service both to city and country. Vast quantities of corn, butter, calves, *&c.* might be sent down it to *York*, and manure, lime, *&c.* returned. The roads on this side of the city being very bad, especially in winter time. I shall take leave of this stream with observing, that it is now, but has been more so, a great defence to the city, by making it unpassable to it except by three bridges on that side it runs on; yet were the mills taken away the benefit would be much greater, by making the stream navigable as I have hinted; by the drainage of a great quantity of ground which now lies under it, and by ridding the city of a nusance, which arises in the summer time from the noisome vapours of so great a collection of stagnating water confined in this place.

By the charter of *Richard* II. the king gave licence to the mayor and commonality of *York*, to purchase lands to the yearly value of 100 *l.* for the sustentation and support of the bridges of *Ouse* and *Foss*. *Foss-bridge* was built in the reign of *Henry* IV, I mean the present structure, for I find a grant the 4th of that king, to the mayor and citizens, for taking a toll of all victuals, *&c.* brought to the market that way, for five years from the date thereof, for the rebuilding of the said bridge *(t)*.

The chapel of St. Anne. *(u)* About the same time was a chapel erected on it, wherein, on 14 *Novemb.* 1424, licence was granted to celebrate divine service. This chapel was dedicated to St. *Anne*, sometimes called St. *Agnes*, and had in it before the dissolution three chantries of considerable value.

(x) The first founded by *Robert Howme*, sen. citizen and merchant *(y)* at the altar of St. *Anne* in this chapel, yearly value 6 *l.* 13 *s.* 3 *d.*

The next by *Alain Hammerton* of the yearly value of 5 *l.* 5 *s.*

(z) A third was founded by *Nicolas Blackburn*, alderman, *Jan.* 6, 1424. for a priest to sing for his soul, *&c.* between the hours of eleven and twelve before noon; but afterwards altered by the advice of the parochians there, as well for their commodity, as for travelling people to betwixt four and five in the morning. Goods and plate valued at 2 *l.* 19 *s.* 8 *d.* Rents 4 *l.* 16 *s.* 4 *d.* A yearly *obit* 6 *s.* 8 *d.*

The wooden piles that supported this chapel were on the north side the bridge, part of which I saw drawn out last year, when, by an order of sewers, the *Foss* was ordered to be scowered up to *Monk-bridge*. *Camden* mentions this bridge as so crowded with houses that he knew not when he was on it. Since his time those have been pulled down, and the water laid open to view on both sides; only *anno* 1728, as appears by an inscription, some fish-stalls were erected on the south-side of it.

WILSON's *hospital.* At the foot of the bridge, east, stands an hospital and school-house founded and endowed, *anno* 1717, by Mrs. *Dorothy Wilson*, an old maid of this parish. Who left lands lying in the townships of *Skipwith* and *Nun-Monkton* for the maintenance of ten women, each of them to have a room to herself, and ten shillings a month allowed her. Also a school for twenty boys, with a salary of 20 *l.* a year to a master for teaching the boys, and reading prayers twice a day to them and the women. New cloathing for the boys once a year. The lands are vested in seven trustees, citizens of *York*, but there is a remarkable clause in this settlement, that *if any one of these should be made an alderman of this city, he should cease to be trustee.*

WALM-GATE *Walmgate* or **Weambgate** called so, as some fondly conjecture, from the wombs or bellies of beasts; carried formerly there to be dressed into tripe, bowstrings, *&c.* is a long, handsome, broad street extending from the bridge to the bar. It has bore that name these five hundred years, as appears by a grant of some houses in it to the nunnery at *Clementhorp*, which I have given, *(temp. Walt. Grey archiepisc.)* but in my opinion this name is a corruption from *Wallingate*; where the *Roman* road begun from *York* to *Lincoln*, and to some of the eastern sea-ports. The street out of the bar was anciently called so; and in an old record, quoted in *Maddox's Firma Burgi*, I find this street, within, spelled **Walingate**; and, after all, it is absurd to think that so spacious a street as this is, should owe its name to so filthy an original as the former etymology alludes to. The reverend Dr. *Langwith* has sent me a very ingenious conjecture about the etymology of the strange name of this street; he says it may be deduced from the *A. S.* Ƿeall, lim, *caementum*, mortar, lime, *&c.* with which the gate or houses of this street being anciently built, or covered, the name of it might come. He adds, that our forefathers, as well as the old *Celtae* in *Germany*, were fond of this covering. And that the *Romans* often built walls of mortar alone; which remain at this day as hard as any stone, a specimen of which work is still to be seen at *Winchester*.

At the bottom of this street is the *Fish-shambles* already described; and higher up stands

S. DYONIS, Walm-gate. A parish church dedicated to St. *Dyonis*, or *Dennis*, the *French* patron; which is an ancient rectory, formerly belonging to the patronage of the hospital of St. *Leonard's York*.

(t) *Pat.* 4 Hen. IV. *part* 1. *m* 22. *de pontagio.*

(u) MS. *Torre*, f. 745.

(x) The original grants of these three chantries are amongst the records on *Ouse-bridge*. *Box num.* 2.

(y) *Dodsworth* and *Torre*. *Inquis.* 8 Hen. IV. *num.* 13. *Torre* Lond.

(z) This *Nicolas Blackburn*, having very dissolute children, says *Leland*, left all his estate, which was very great, to pious uses. *Lel. itin.* He was buried in *All-saints North-street*.

A CA-

(a) *A CATALOGUE of the RECTORS of St.* DYONIS.

Temp. instit. Anno	*Rectores eccl.*	*Patroni.*	*Vacat.*
1269	Martyn de Grymestone, *presb.*	*Magist. et frat. hospitalis S.* Leonardi, Ebor.	*per mort.*
	Johannes		
1326	Philip Winferton, *cler.*	*Iidem.*	
1330	Joh. de Busceby, *cler.*	*Iidem.*	*per mort.*
1349	Simon de Braylock, *cler.*	*Iidem.*	*per mort.*
1349	Tho. de Boutham, *cap.*	*Iidem.*	*per resig.*
1352	Joh. Luke, *cap.*	*Iidem.*	*per resig.*
1362	Elyas de Thoresby, *cap.*	*Iidem.*	*per resig.*
1367	Roger de Wilughby, *pr.*	*Iidem.*	*per resig.*
1370	Joh. de Ulsby, *presb.*	*Iidem.*	*per resig.*
1371	Tho. de Middelton, *pr.*	*Iidem.*	*per resig.*
1372	Rob. Marrays, *presb.*	*Iidem.*	
	Will. Yrelande, *presb.*	*Iidem.*	*per mort.*
1399	Joh. Suthwell, *L. B.*	*Iidem.*	*per resig.*
1416	Will. Browne, *presb.*	*Iidem.*	*per resig.*
1417	Will. Pelleson.	*Iidem.*	*per resig.*
1421	Ric. Kynsman, *subdec.*	*Iidem.*	
	Ric. de Wetwang.	*Iidem.*	*per resig.*
1454	Tho. Benny, *presb.*	*Iidem.*	*per resig.*
1471	Will. Wilkynson, *presb.*	*Iidem.*	*per mort.*
1489	Will. Leycestre, *dec. B.*	*Iidem.*	*per mort.*
1502	Joh. Parker, *L. B.*	*Iidem.*	*per resig.*
1507	Christ. Cuteler, *presb.*	*Iidem.*	*per resig.*
1512	Will. Wyle, *presb.*	*Iidem.*	*per mort.*
1521	Will. Bukburrowe, *cap.*	*Iidem.*	*per mort.*
1544	Ed. Smythe, *cler.*	*Assignati eorundem.*	*per mort.*
1546	Rob. Hall, *cler.*	Hen. VIII. *rex.*	*per mort.*
1569	Will. Prest, *cler.*	Elizabetha *reg.*	
1586	Percival Hutchenson, *cl.*	*Eadem.*	
1603	Gabriel Squire, *cler.*	*Dom.* Will. Cornwallis, *mil.*	*per mort.*
1612	Hen. Rogers, *cler.*	Jacobus *rex.*	*per resig.*
1614	Tho. Browne, *cl. M. A.*	*Assign. dom.* Ric. Fermour, *mil.*	*per resig.*
1615	Joh. Thompson, *cler.*	Jacobus *rex.*	
1620	George Lyddal, *cler.*	*Dom.* Guido Palmes, *mil. et duo alii.*	*per mort.*
1660	Joh. Dugdale, *cl. M. A.*	Carolus II. *rex.*	*per mort.*
1667	George Tilpin, *cl. M. A.*	W. Palmes, *armig.*	

(b) *Monumental INSCRIPTIONS in this church.*

✠ **Orate pro anima Petri Eshe nuper vicecomitis hujus civitatis, qui obiit 11° die Julii A. D. 1551.** Eshe 1551. *Vic.* 1546.

Here lyethe buryed the body of William Holmes late alderman of the cittye of Yorke, sometyme mayor of the same; vice-admiral betweene Humber and Tyne; and the steward of St. Mary Abbay landes; collector for Newburgh; and borne in this cittye, who dyed the 8. of Sept. 1558. Leaving behind him lady Margaret his wife, and had issue by her six sons and seven daughters; unto whome God grant a joyfull resurrection. Holmes 1558. *Lord-mayor* 1546.

Jacet hic Dorothea *uxor* Roberti Hughes *quondam de* Uxbridge, *in com.* Middlesex, *armig*, *filia* Johannis Redman, *quae ab antiqua illa* Redmannorum *familia de* Turre-harwood *traxit originem. Vitam, viator, si exploratam velis, lapis non sufficit; sic contractam, preces et lachrymae. Fuerat una cujus ab infantia nobile consortium mores produxerat non vulgares, cujus ut creverat annorum series, sic vera floruit pietas et sincera fides cum virtute, donec gravis aetate et dolore victa coelum quod toties invocasset vivens possidebat, moriens corpus relinquens hic et exemplum. Annos vixerat* 66. Hughes.

ARMS to this monument:

Gules, a lyon rampant regardant *argent*, crowned *or*. *Hughes*. Impaling *Gules*, three cushions ermine tasseled *or*. *Redman*.

(a) *Ex* MS. Torre, *f.* 461.

(b) *Persona eccl. S.* Dyoniss. *in* Walm-gate *de* 1. *mesuag. dat sibi et successoribus suis per* W. de Redness, *confirm per pat* 16 Ed. II. *p.* 2. *m.* 3.

Walm-gate ward. Lockley 1682. *Hic requiescat in spe resurrectionis* Gulielmus Lockley *artium magister, hujus ecclesiae rector, qui obiit secundo die Sept. A. D.* 1682. *aetat. suae* 34.

Fugget 1515. ✠ Hic jacet corpus Ricardi Fuggett de civitate Ebor. Fish . . . . qui obiit xv die . . . . A. D. M.CCCC.XV. cujus anime propitietur Deus. Amen.

Warde 1405. Bay. 1380. ✠ Hic jacet Robertus Warde quondam civis et mercator Ebor. qui obiit . . . die mensis . . . . An. Dom. M.CCCC.V. cujus anime, &c.

Bellman 1668. *Hic jacet* Lewis Bellman; *cum de se quatuor natis amatis, amans vixit, quid aliud vis? Id satis quod res angusta domi artem suam perosus et solus tamen artis suae artifex ingeniosus. Obiit* Nov. 19, 1668. *aetat. suae* 55.

Wilson 1688. *Hic requiescit in spe resurrectionis* Tho. Wilson *gen. qui obiit vicesimo die* Sept. *A. D.* 1688.

A handsome copartment to the memory of Mrs. *Dorothy Wilson*, foundress of the hospital aforesaid, who died *Nov.* 3, 1717. On which day is an anniversary sermon preached.

ARMS in the windows, 1684.

Chequè, or and *azure*, a fess *gules. Clifford.*

Chequè, or and *azure*, on a chief *gules*, three ostrich feathers in plume issuing therefrom of the first. *Drax.* Quartering, bendy lozengy *argent* and *gules*, a file of three *azure.*

On several parts of the stone work without the church are these arms, *viz.*

A saltire. *Nevil.* Impaling *France* and *England* quarterly within a border. *Holland.*

On a saltire two annulets braced. *Nevil.*

A lyon rampant. *Percy.* Quartering three lucies or pyke-fish hauriant. *Lucy.* Under which there has been an inscription, but not at present legible, except the year M.CCCC.XXIX.

In the north choir of this church is a large blue marble, which has had two effigies on it, and an inscription round in brass, but now quite erazed. Under which, it is said, lyes the
1461. body of *Henry* earl of *Northumberland*; probably him that was slain (*c*) at *Towton-field* on the *Lancastrian* side. In the book of drawings, epitaphs, &c. left the office of arms by sir *William Dugdale* and there kept, is the portraicure of several of this family kneeling, taken from the glass windows of this choir, but now wholly lost. It was in reality their parish church in *York*; for opposite to it north, stood once the *palace* of the earls of *Nor-*
1455. *thumberland*; for I find that in the 33^d^ of *Henry* VI. *Henry* earl of *Northumberland* father to the former, being slain at the battle of St. *Albans*, was found to be possessed amongst other things, of a certain house in Walm-gate, in the parish of St. Dyonis, within the city of York, called Percys-inne (*d*). But to return to the church.

The church is a handsome pile of building with a neat spire steeple in the midst of it, which was shot through in the time of the siege of *York*; a few years since it was almost twisted off by a flash of lightning, which also did great damage to the rest of the church; but the whole is now in good repair, the painted glass in the windows of it being well preserved. *Anno* 1585, the church of St. *George* in *Fisher-gate*, with the parish thereof was united to this church of St. *Dyonis*, according to the statute.

		l.	*s.*	*d.*
The rectory of St. *Dyonis* is thus valued in the king's books.	First fruits	02	10	01½
	Tenths	00	05	01
	Procurations	00	06	08

I find no chantries in this church.

Neut-gate lane. Fisher-gate. *The church of St. George.* From *Walm-gate* there runs a lane south, now called *Neut-gate-lane*, which leads to an old bar called *Fisher-gate-bar*. Which has been walled up ever since it was burnt in an insurrection in *Henry* the seventh's time (*e*). Near the postern adjoining stands the shell of a once parish church dedicated to St. *George*, the patron of *England*, which was united as before. This was an ancient (*f*) rectory belonging formerly to the patronage of the *Palmes* of *Naburn*, which town is in this parish; and where many of that family are interred. It afterwards came to the patronage of the *Malbyes* of *Acaster*, till *temp. Ric.* II. it was appropriated to the nunnery of *Monkton*. The inhabitants of *Nayburn*, a village two miles off, still bury their dead here. An inscription upon a tomb-stone in the church-yard runs thus:

Armstrong 1721. *Here lyeth the body of* Thomas Armstrong *of* Nayburn, *who departed this life* Oct. 29, 1721. *being forty four years of age. Also here lye the bodies of his children, born to him of his wife* Margaret, Catherine, Isabella, Thomas, John *and* George. *And now says* Margaret,

Sleep on blest creature in thy urn,
My sighs and tears cannot awake thee;
I will but stay until my turn
And then, oh then! I'll overtake thee.

(*c*) *Vide annal. sub. anno* 1461.

(*d*) *Dugd. Bar.* vol. I. In the ground on which this house stood, which is now a garden, not long ago, was found by a workman digging amongst the rubbish, one arm of a gold cup, so heavy as to be sold for 50*l.* as I have been credibly informed.

(*e*) This gate, says *Leland*, was burnt in *Henry* the seventh's tyme by the commons of *Yorkshire*, who took the cittye and would have beheaded sir *Richard Yorke*, lord-mayor; and has ever since been blocked up. *Lelandi itin.*

(*f*) *Ex MS.* Torre.

There

THE ASTOR LIBRARY N.Y.

A Window in the parish church of S.t Dyonis-Walmgate, York,
p 307. *taken from thence about the year 1590. but now almost defaced.*

The right honourable Algernon *Baron* Percy *son and heir apparent to his Grace* Charles Seymour *Duke of* Somerset, *Earl of* Hartford, *Viscount* Beauchamp *of* Hache, *Baron* Seymour *of* Troubridge *by* Elizabeth *his late Duchesse the daughter & afterwards sole heiresse of* Jocelin Percy, *late Earl of* Northumberland, *Baron* Percy &c. *presents this antient representation of some of his illustrious ancestors to this work* 1736.

There was one chantry founded in this church of St. *George*, at the altar of St. *Mary*, for the soul of *Nicolas* son of *Hugh de Sutton*. WALM-GATE WARD.

This must formerly have been a very populous part of the city; for I find mention made of two more parish churches which anciently stood here, one dedicated to St. *Andrew*, said to stand beyond *Foss*, in *Fisher-gate*, which was an ancient rectory belonging to the patronage of the priory of *Newburgh*, and given to that house at first by *Roger* lord *Mowbray* (g). St. ANDREW, Fisher-gate.

The other was the parish church of St. *Peter in the willows*, which stood at the upper end of *Long-close* near *Walm-gate bar*. This was an ancient rectory belonging to the patronage of the prior and convent of *Kirkham*; but at the union of churches in *York* it was let drop, and the parish united to St. *Margaret's*. There was a perpetual chantry founded in this church of St. *Peter en les willows*, at the altar of St. *Mary* the virgin; but by whom, or of what value uncertain (h). St. PETER en les willows.

The parish church of St. *Margaret* stands on the north side of *Walm-gate*, somewhat backwards, and was with that of St. *Mary*, which also stood in this street, conjoined into one rectory, belonging to the patronage of the hospital of St. *Peter* or St. *Leonard* in *York*. Whereunto they were given by *Walter Fagenulf*, *temp.* Hen. I (i). St. MARGARET.

The rectory of St. *Margaret's* is thus valued in the king's books. First fruits 02 18 01
Tenths 00 05 09¼

A CATALOGUE of the RECTORS of St. MARGARET's.

Temp. instit. Anno	*Rectores eccl.*	*Patroni.*	*Vacat.*
1219	Geof. de Britonis, *cap. ad ecc. S.* Mariae *vel* Bowes.	*Magister et frat. hosp. St.* Leonardi, Ebor.	
1308	Joh. de Haxeby, *presb. ad utrasq; eccl.*	*Idem.*	*per mort.*

(g) *Mon. Ang.* vol. II. p. 192. *Mr.* Torre. Hugo *filius* Baldurici *habet ecclesiam S.* Andree *quam emit* . . . . *e libro* Doomesday. Sir *T. W. eccl. S.* Andree *que est ultra* Fossam *in* Fischer-gata. *Mon. Ang.* vol. II. p. 192.
(h) *Idem. Pat. an.* 19 Ric. II. *pars* 2. *m.* 20. Sir *T. W.*
(i) *Idem.* f. 437. *Mon. Ang* vol. I. f. 394.

WALM-GATE WARD.

Temp. instit. Anno	*Rectores eccl.*	*Patroni.*	*Vacat.*
1342	Will. de Heffaye, *cap. ad utrasque.*	*Mag. et frat. hosp. S.* Leon. Ebor.	*per mort.*
1349	Joh. Darlington, *cap. ad utrasque.*	*Iidem.*	*per resig.*
1352	Adam de Darlington, *cap. ad utrasque.*	*Iidem.*	*per resig.*
1360	Rob. Sleights, *cap. ad utrasque.*	*Iidem.*	*per resig.*
1361	Walt. de Mafferton, *cap. ad utrasque.*	*Iidem.*	*per resig.*
1392	Rob. de Pocklinton, *ad eccl. S. Margaretae.*	*Iidem.*	
	Ric. Erghes, *presb.*	*Iidem.*	*per resig.*
1410	Joh. de Akam, *S. T. B.*	*Iidem.*	*per resig.*
1412	Joh. Popylton, *presb.*	*Iidem.*	*per resig.*
1415	Joh. Briftowe, *cler.*	*Iidem.*	*per resig.*
1419	Will. Newton, *presb.*	*Iidem.*	*per resig.*
1425	Joh. Apylton, *presb.*	*Iidem.*	*per mort.*
1425	Joh. Warthill, *presb.*	*Iidem.*	*per resig.*
1442	Rob. Slake, *presb.*	*Iidem.*	*per resig.*
1442	Joh. Roos, *cap.*	*Iidem.*	
	Joh. Shipton, *presb.*	*Iidem.*	*per resig.*
1460	Will. Ben, *dec. doc.*	*Iidem.*	*per mort.*
1476	Hen. Wyatt, *presb.*	*Iidem.*	*per mort.*
1514	Will. Bukbarrow, *presb.*	*Iidem.*	*per resig.*
1521	Jac. Barker, *presb.*	*Iidem.*	*per mort.*
1533	Geor. Cook.	*Iidem.*	*per mort.*
1550	Joh. Walker, *cler. ad hanc et ad ecc. S. Petri en les willows.*	Edvardus VI. *rex.*	
1557	Ric. Morton, *cler.*	Maria *reg.*	*per mort.*
1578	Tho. Dawfon, *cler.*	Elizabetha *reg.*	*per mort.*
1591	Georg. Thompfon, *cler.*	*Eadem.*	*per mort.*
1615	Georg. Lyddal, *cler.*	Jacobus *rex.*	*per mort.*
1660	Joh. Dugdale, *cler.*	Carolus II. *rex.*	*per mort.*
1669	Georg. Tylpin, *cler.*	*Idem.*	

Monumental *INSCRIPTIONS* only thefe:

Manars. ✠ **Orate pro anima Agnetis Manars, que obiit sept. die Januarii an. Dom. M.CCCC . . . cujus anime, &c.**

She was a good benefactrefs, fays my author, and gave all the lands belonging to the church *(k)*.

In an east window:

Erghes. **Orate pro anima Ricardi Erghes rectoris istius ecclesie.**

Clerk. ✠ **Hic jacet Ricardus Clerk, quondam Tanner Ebor. qui obiit xxiii° die mensis Oct. A. D. . . . .**

No modern ones worth notice; nor do I find any chantries belonging to this church. The fteeple of it fell down about the year 1672, and broke down the roof of the church, which for want of ability in the parifh lay fome time in ruin. But, *an.* 1684, it was begun to be repaired and finifhed at the charge of the parifh; with fome contributions from the archbifhop, and other pioufly difpofed perfons. This church has one of the moft extraordinary porches, or entrances, I ever obferved; it is fuch an elaborate piece of *Gothick* fculpture and architecture, that I have thought fit to fubjoin a draught of it. Though I am told, it did not belong originally to this church, but was brought from the diffolved hofpital of St. *Nicolas, extra muros*, and put up here.

Walm-gate bar, called fo from the ftreet which leads to it, is built in the fame manner as the other, towards the foundation are fome large blocks of grit, but the arches, &c. are modern. This gate received great damage in the fiege 1644, being near beat down by the rebels; it was likewife undermined, for which it ftood in need of reparation, which was done 1648, as appears by an infcription on the outer gate. *Leland* fays *(l)* that he was told that *Walm-gate bar* was built when *Fifher-gate* was difufed; but he feems to doubt it, and indeed there is no reafon to believe it.

Returning back I take notice of an hofpital founded of late years by one *Perceval Winterfkelf*, fheriff 1705, but inconfiderable.

There was alfo formerly a *Maifon Dieu*, or fmall hofpital, founded and maintained by the company of fhoe-makers in this ftreet.

(k) *Dodfworth's* epitaphs. *MS penes me.*

(l) *Lelands itin.*

In

The Church porch of S.t Margaret in York.

The reverend Samuel Drake, *D.D. Rector of* Treeton, *and of* Holm Spalding-moor, *presents this view of this very antient piece of* Gothick *architecture to this work.* 1736.

THE ASTOR LIBRARY
NY

In *Neut* or *Nowt gate lane* already mentioned, called so from leading to the *Swine-market*, the ancient *Fisher-gate*, is an hospital founded by sir *Robert Watter* knight, some time lord-mayor of this city; who by his will proved *June* 15, 1612, appointed that an hospital should be erected out of his houses in *Nowt-gate*, *York*, which should be for the perpetual maintenance of ten persons. And to consist of a master, governor or reader, who should have 3 *l. per annum* for his stipend, and of certain brethren and sisters, to every of which 40*s. per annum* should be allowed. And that the said rent of 24*l. per annum* should issue out of his lordship of *Cundale* (*n*). Near this is the hall belonging to the company of Haberdashers of this city; which was built by the aforesaid knight for his brethren to assemble in. In an old wall hereabouts is a statue of a knight templar; on his shield a cross *patonce*, with a bar. *Latimer*.

Sir R. WATTER'*s hospital.*

HABERDASHER'S-HALL

I have now gone through with my description of all the remarkables in *Walm-gate ward*, I come next, over *Foss-bridge* again, into *Monk ward*, only taking notice by the way of a small parish church dedicated to St. *Clement*; which stood somewhat backward, betwixt *Foss-gate* and *Hun-gate*. This church was but of a small valuation being put down, *temp. Hen.* V. at 1 *l. per annum*. It is missed by Mr. *Torre*, nor was it subsisting at the union of churches in this city. I have therefore no more to say of it, but what is before taken notice of in the annals, that eighty *Lincolnshire* men, slain in the fray betwixt the *English* and *Hainaulters*, *anno* 1 *Ed.* III, were buried in one hole in the church-yard belonging to this parish. (*o*).

MONK WARD

Church of ST. CLEMENT.

On the same side, higher up, stood formerly the house or convent belonging to the *Fryars Carmelites*, or *Fratres de Monte Carmeli* in *York*, who had a chapel or church there dedicated to the honour of our lady St. *Mary*. The religious order of the *Fryars Carmelites* was one of the four orders of *Mendicants*, or begging fryars; taking both its name and origin from *Carmel*, a mountain in *Syria*; formerly inhabited by the prophets *Elias* and *Elisha*, and by the children of the prophets; from whom this order pretends to come in an uninterrupted succession. The method in which they pretend to make out their antiquity has something in it, says my author (*p*), too ridiculous to be rehearsed. Some amongst them pretend they are nephews to *J. C.* Others go farther and make *Pythagoras* a *Carmelite*; and and the ancient *Druids* regular branches of their order.

Monastery of the FRIARS CARMELITES.

The site of their monastery in *York* is particularly expressed in a charter of confirmation granted to them by king *Edward* I, in the 28th year of his reign, or *anno* 1300, dated at *York*. It appears here, by *inspeximus*, that *William de Vescy* gave them the first piece of ground to build on, and bestowed upon them all his land, messuages and tenements, that he had in a street, or lane, called **le Benetlegh**; extending in length and breadth towards the water of **Fosse** to the south, and from a street, or lane, called **le Perks**, towards the *King's-street* called **Fosse-gate**, to the west. In the reign of *Rich*. II. *Henry de Percy* lord of *Spofford* had leave of the king to grant to these fryars a piece of ground to the west contiguous to their house, sixty foot long and sixty broad, for the enlargement of their monastery. This piece of ground, but of somewhat larger extent, *viz*. one hundred feet long and one hundred broad, was granted to them afterwards by *John Berden* and *John Braythwait*, to the same use as the former. Confirmed by king *Rich*. II. at *York*, in the 16th year of his reign, or *anno* 1393.

Before this, *viz. anno reg. regis* Ed. II. 8°. or *anno* 1314. that king then at *York*, bestowed a messuage and yards upon the prior and brethren of this order situate in the street of **Perks** as the record testifies (though no such name of a street is known to us at present) which he had of the gift of *Galfrid de Saint Quintin*, contiguous to their house, for the enlargement of it. The same king, by another grant, dated a day after the former, gives leave to these fryars to build a *key*, **kaya**, or *wharf*, on his **vivary of the Fosse**, in their own land, and within their close: And so builded to keep to them and their successors for ever. And moreover that they should have a *boat* on his said *vivary* to fetch *stone*, *wood*, *underwood*, or other necessaries, as well under **Fosse-bridge**, as from any other place on the said *vivary*, or fish-pool, to their *key* so built, for the use of the said monastery. The same king in the 9th and 10th years of his reign, grants to these fryars, by two deeds dated at *York* and *Lincoln*, all those houses with their appurtenances in **Fosse-gate**, which he had of the gift of *Thomas* the son of *William le Aguiler* of *York*, and *Cicily* his wife. Also all that land with appurtenances in the same city, extending in length and breadth, as the writing witnesses, which he had by gift from *Abel de Richale* of *York*. To have and to hold &c. for ever, for the enlargement of their monastery.

These are all the testimonies I have met with relating to the site of this monastery of the *Fryars Carmelites* in *York*. By which it appears that it stood betwixt *Foss-gate* and *Hun-gate*; and in a place, now a garden, belonging to my worthy friend Mr. *John Tomlinson* of *York*, late alderman *Hutton*'s, I saw some of the foundation stones of this ancient building dug up a few years ago. The extent of their house, courts, &c. must stretch from the lane still

(*n*) Ex *MS*. Torre.
(*o*) *Leland*. coll.
(*p*) See *Chamber*'s dictionary.

4 K called

MONKWARD called *Stainbow*, down through all these gardens, as the records testify, to the river *Fofs*, which argues the site of this monastery to have been noble, large, and spacious.

That I may omit nothing relating to this fryary that I have found, I shall give what Mr. *Torre* has collected from the church records regarding them. There being no notice taken of this monastery, in *York*, in the *Monasticon*; nor in *Speed*'s catalogue of religious houses. The records I extracted the above account from, may be seen at length in the *appendix*; and this, I think, is sufficient to preserve the memory of this order in *York* from wholly perishing in oblivion. For *November* 27, 30 *Hen.* VIII. or *anno* 1539, this house of the *fryars Carmelites* in *York* was surrender'd into the king's hands by the prior, *Simon Clarkson*, nine brothers and three novices *(p)*.

April 1, 1304, a commission was issued out to dedicate the church-yard of this fryary, in that place where these fryars then inhabited; within the limits of the parish church of St. *Saviours*. And *May* 24, 1340, a decree was made betwixt the rector of St. *Crux* on the one part, and the pryor and brethren of the *Carmelites* on the other, about the celebration of divine service in a certain oratory in *Foss-gate*, erected on the gate of the said priory. That there be thenceforth no service therein celebrated, no bell tolled, bread or water hallowed, nor be administred by any clerk or lay person. And that those religious receive no more oblations there, and that our lady's image, then in that oratory set up, be absolutely removed *(q)*.

Jan. 1, 1320, *William* archbishop of *York* made this ordination between *John Pykering*, rector of the church of St. *Crux*, and the prior and brethren of the order of St. *Mary de Monte Carmeli*, about certain tythes, houses and possessions belonging to that church, by reason of those places which the said prior and brethren had inhabited, or did acquire in the said parish; the same containing nineteen feet in breadth from the inner part of *Foss-gate*, ... and of the latter part seventeen foot *per Staynebow*, *viz.* that the said prior and brethren and their successors shall be free and quit for ever from payment of those tythes, oblations, and obventions, saving the right of the said parish church, for them and others of burial amongst them. And in satisfaction of damage done to the said church in this respect, the said prior and brethren shall give and pay yearly for ever to the said rector, *nomine ecclesie sue*, the portion due to the vicar out of the profits of the said church *(r)*.

STAINBOW-LANE. WHIPMA-WHOPMA-GATE. *Stainbow-lane*, is a narrow thorough-fare leading from *Foss-gate* into *Hun-gate*; above this is a small street, which has the odd name of *Whipma-Whopmagate* given it for what reason I shall not determine. In it is the east end of *Crux* church, and an inn called the *George*; here is also every *Saturday* a market kept for old shoes and boots by the company of *translators*.

COLLIER-GATE. *St.* SAVIOUR-GATE. *Collier-gate* needs no explanation, at the lower end of it begins a street called St. *Saviour-gate*, from a church of that name standing in it. The upper part of this street was, anciently, called **Ket-manger-gate**; **Ket** is a northern word for carrion, but why it took this name in disrespect to the other *Manger-gates*, which I shall speak of in the sequel, I know not. Here is a stone in the wall of Mr. *Tomlinson*'s house which bears this inscription:

Heir stoud the image of Yorke and
remand in the yere of our Lord God
A. M. CC. I. unto the common hall
in the tyme of the mairalty of
John Stockdale.

The image of *York* is supposed to be that of king *Ebrank*, our *British* founder; and here tradition tells you, was the first stone laid of his city. This image is said to have been of wood, but what is become of it I know not, for that taken down at the common-hall for the building of the lord-mayor's house can by no means be supposed to be this, as I shall shew in its proper place.

St. SAVIOUR'S *church*. The parish church of St. *Saviour's* called in old writings *ecclesia sancti salvatoris in Marisco*, this ground being all gained from the marsh, is a neat building, and has some thing in its outside so modern, as would tempt me to believe it has been rebuilt out of the ruins of the monastery once adjoining. It has a handsome tower steeple with a large wooden cross on the top of it. This church is an antient rectory belonging to the patronage of the abbot and convent of St. *Mary*'s *York*; given them at first by king *William* the conqueror, and paid an annual pension of ten shillings to that religious house *(s)*.

(p) Clauf. 30 Hen. VIII. *pars* 5, *num.* 67. *Rolls chap.* The site of this priory was granted to one *Ambrose Beckwith* 35 *Hen.* VIII. *eadem.*

(q) E registro Zouch, *p.* 49.

(r) Ex MS. Torre, *f.* 878.

(s) Mon. Ang. vol. I. fol. 390, 392. MS. *Torre*, f. 545. The three bells belonging to this church were taken out of St. *William*'s chapel, *Ouse-bridge*, and given to this church 1583.

A CA-

MONK WARD

A CATALOGUE of the RECTORS of St. SAVIOURS.

Temp. instit. Anno	*Rectores eccl.*	*Patroni.*	*Vacat.*
1250	Will. Luvell, *cler.*	*Abbas et conv.* B. Mar. Ebor.	
1308	Adam de Spiriden, *diac.*	*Iidem.*	
	Will. de Wolferton.	*Iidem.*	*per mort.*
1349	Joh. de Nesse, *cler.*	*Iidem.*	
1394	Adam Wigan, *cler.*	*Iidem.*	*per mort.*
1433	Joh. Arnal, *dec. Dr.*	*Iidem.*	*per mort.*
1446	Ric. Tone, *dec. Dr.*	*Iidem.*	
	Joh. Bellamy, *presb.*	*Iidem.*	*per mort.*
1452	Will. Tankersley. *cler.*	*Iidem.*	*per resig.*
1453	Peter Percy, *cler.*	*Iidem.*	*per resig.*
1459	Rob. Simpson, *cap.*	*Iidem.*	*per resig.*
1460	Will. Gysburn, *L L. B.*	*Iidem.*	*per resig.*
1463	Rog. Barton, *presb.*	*Iidem.*	
	Thomas Laton, *presb.*	*Iidem.*	*per mort.*
1480	Will. Smythe, *cap.*	*Iidem.*	*per resig.*
1481	Ric. Nicholson, *cap.*	*Iidem.*	*per resig.*
1485	Rob. Wright, *cap.*	*Iidem.*	*per mort.*
1506	Tho. Young, *presb.*	*Iidem.*	*per mort.*
1507	Will. Sherburn, *cap.*	*Iidem.*	*per mort.*
1513	Ric. Berwyck, *presb.*	*Iidem.*	*per resig.*
1538	Ric. Roundale, *presb.*	*Assign. ab. et convent.*	*per mort.* *per mort*
1550	Tho. Lather, *cler.*	*Iidem.*	
1567	Joh. Richardson, *cler.*	Eliz. *regin.*	*per resig.*
1591	Will. Cockson, *cler.*	*Eadem.*	*per mort.*
1631	Joh. Whittaker, *M. A.*	Car. I. *rex.*	
1665	Anth. Wright, *cler.*	Car. I. *rex.*	

There were no less than seven chantries belonging to this church, all of them of considerable value, the first

(*t*) Was a very antient chantry founded at the altar of St. *Mary* in this church, for the soul of *Robert Verdenell.*

(*u*) There was another chantry founded in this church at the altar of St. *John the evangelist*, for the souls of *John de Hathelsey* and *Emma* his wife. *May* 18, 1468, this chantry was united to another chantry in the same church, founded for the souls of *William Burton* and *Ivetta* his wife, at the altar of St. *James the apostle* and St. *Lawrence.*

	l.	*s.*	*d.*
Yearly value	06	05	06

(*x*) *William Burton* of *York* mercer, founded another chantry in this church at the altar of St. *Anne*, mother of our lady St. *Mary*, for his soul and the soul of *Ivetta* his wife.

	l.	*s.*	*d.*
Yearly value	06	00	10

(*y*) There was another chantry founded in this church at the altar of St. *Thomas the martyr*, for the soul of *Adam de Spiriden.*

	l.	*s.*	*d.*
Yearly value ——— ——— ———	04	01	00

(*z*) A chantry called *Richard Watters* chantry, in the parish church of St. *Saviours* in the **Parische** of the foundation of the said *Richard.*

	l.	*s.*	*d.*
Yearly value ——— ——— ———	06	00	00

(*a*) A chantry founded by *William Frost* alderman and *Isabella* his wife, within the said said church. A 1399.

	l.	*s.*	*d.*
Yearly value ——— ——— ———	10	09	11

(*b*) A chantry founded by *William Gilliot.*

	l.	*s.*	*d.*
Value ——— — — — —	05	00	00

(*c*) Besides these chantries there was also a **gild**, or fraternity, of St. *Martin* in this church, which was founded by letters patents from *Henry* VI.

Monumental INSCRIPTIONS.

✠ HIC IACET ROBERTUS VERDENELL CUIUS ANIMAE PROPITIETUR DEUS. Verdenell.

✠ **Orate pro animabus** Rogeri de Moreton **quondam majoris civitatis Ebor. qui obiit v die mensis Junii anno Dom. MCCCC LXXXII. Et Isabelle uxoris sue que obiit vi die mensis Martii anno Dom. millesimo quadragentesimo xii, quorum animabus propitietur Deus.** Moreton 1382 *Lord-mayor* 1373.

✠ **Orate pro anima Roberti de Duffeld.**

✠ **Et pro anima Helene uxoris ejus.**

✠ **PRAY FOR ION. RAYWYKE.**

(*t*) *Ex MS.* Torre.
(*u*) *Idem et* Dods.
(*x*) *Iidem.*
(*y*) *Iidem.*
(*z*) *Dods.* coll. *pat. anno* 6 Ed IV. *pars* 1 *m* 9. sir *T. W*
(*a*) *Dods.*
(*b*) *Idem. Persona eccl. S.* Salvat, *de* iiii *s redd. in* **Hun**gate *concedend. pro lampad. mauntenand. inq.* 11 Hen. IV. *n.* 19. *Turre* Lond.
(*c*) *Pat.* 24 Hen. VI. *p.* 2. *m.* 20.

Modern

2

MONK WARD

Modern inſcriptions are on ſir *Henry Hewley* knight, who died 1697, and his lady 1710. *William Andrews*, *Richard Booth*, and *Chryſtopher Tyrrel*.

The boundaries of this pariſh taken from an antient writing ſtill kept under the cuſtody of the church wardens is a very curious thing, and I preſent the reader with a copy of it, taken *literatim* from the original.

Memorand. That thys ys the bounder of thys peryſhing of ſeynt Sayveyour, **mayde and ſet furthe in the yere of owre Lord God one thouſande three hundreth threeſcore and twoo, in the ſix and thurte yere of the reigne of owre ſovereign lorde** Edwarde **thyrde after the conqueſte.**

Furſt that from olde Yorke **and ſo goynge furth the ſtreet unto one lane calle** Spenlayne, **which layne ledeth from the ſtreet of St.** Savyour-gate, **unto a common ſewer bak warde co-mynge from** Goodrome-gate, **and one other ſewer comynge in it lyeing on the north ſide of** ſeynt Savyeyour-gayt, **aforeſayde, and boundyng unto S.** Andrew-gate, **and from thence unto the ſouth ſide of one** Maſindeu, **ſtandyng in S.** Andrew-gate **aforeſaid, and ſo on further to** Aldwarke, **and from** Aldwarke **aforeſaid to** ſeynt Antons, **and the** ſeynt Antons **is of** ſeynt Saveyours **peryſh, and from thence goinge over** Peaſeholme-grene **unto one layne northe of the** holy pri ſtes, **and ſo goyng of the northe ſyde of one houſe called** Gramary-hall, **and ſo on furth to** Hungate, **and from** Hungate **aforſayd unto the lady Freres, which freres ar of the ſayde paryſhe of** ſeynte Seyveyours **with theire lybertyes, and thence to our** ladies chapell **belongynge to the ſayde Freres, and thence to one** Mayſyndeu **ſtandyng of the north ſyde of one layne called** Standbowlayne, **whiche** Mayſyndeu **hath booth men and women in the ſame, and is of two peryſhyngs, the men is of** Crux **peryſhe, and the women of the peryſhe of** ſeynt Saveyours **aforeſaid, and ſo from the ſaide** Mayſyndeu **unto one houſe belongyng to** Crux **church peryſhe, and the ſayde houſe is allſo of** ſeynt Saveyours **peryſhe, which outermoſte poſt of the ſayde houſe ſtandith even on the weſte parte with** olde Yorke, **and from thence to** Heworth **which has ſix fyer houſes there with the tyeth of twelf organg of lande belongyng unto the ſayde peryſhe church of** ſeynt Sayveyoures.

Anno 1585, the pariſhes of St. *John* in *Hungate* and St. *Andrew* in St. *Andrewgate* were united to this pariſh of St. *Saviours*, according the form of the ſtatute in that caſe ordained.

The rectory of St. *Saviour's* is valued in the king's books	*l.*	*s.*	*d.*
Firſt fruits — — — — —	05	06	08
Tenths — — — — —	00	10	08
Procurations — — — — —	00	06	08

St *Saviour-gate* is one of the neateſt and beſt built ſtreets in the city, the houſes moſt of them new, amongſt which one belonging to *Thomas Fothergill* eſquire, and another, facing the ſtreet at the eaſt end, the property of *Thomas Duncombe* of *Duncombe park* eſquire are the chief. At this end alſo ſtands a pile of building, erected about thirty or forty years ago, as a meeting-houſe for diſſenters of the *preſbyterian* perſwaſion. In digging the foundations of ſome houſes on the north of this ſtreet, I am told, great quantities of horns of ſeveral kinds of beaſts were thrown out; which makes me conjecture that a *Roman* temple ſtood here, being in the neighbourhood of the imperial palace.

HUNGATE.

Hungate goes down to *Foſſe* ſide from St. *Saviours-gate*, but the name of it I cannot tell what to make of; *Hungry-gate* is a poor conjecture, which though it will ſuit the place well enough now, yet formerly there were ſeveral merchants of great account lived here. I muſt alſo take notice that the antient family of the *Hungates* in this county, ſeem to derive their name from hence.

St. JOHN'S *church.*

The pariſh church of St. *John baptiſt* ſtood here, in a place, eaſt of the ſtreet, now gardens; but after the demolition it was long called St. *John's green (d)*. There is not the leaſt remains of the church now ſtanding; which was formerly appropriated to the revenues of the dean and chapter of *York*, and accounted one of their great farms, valued at ſix pound *per annum*. It was united to St. *Saviour's*.

There was a chantry in this church founded by *Richard Ruſſel* citizen and merchant; afterwards augmented by *John Thirſk* a great merchant, alſo mayor of the *ſtaple of* Calais; who both lived in this ſtreet, and were both buried in this church.

	l.	*s.*	*d.*
Yearly value — — — — —	06	00	04

POUND-LANE. HAVER-LANE.

Two lanes leading from *Hungate*, one called *Pound-lane* which runs to a piece of ground called *Poundgarth*, called ſo from being upon the royal fiſhery of *Foſs*; the other is *Haverlane*, with gardens on both ſides leads to *Peaſeholme-green*. The great quantity of ſtone walling about theſe gardens, &c. pleads ſtrongly for many antient buildings to have been hereabouts; and there is no ſmall quantity of grit wrought up in the wall at the bottom of *Hungate* going to *Foſs*. The place called *Holy-prieſts*, I take to have ſtood ſome where in theſe gardens, and probably near a fine well of a round figure of ſtone, called at this day *holy prieſts well*. The hall belonging to the company of ſhoemakers in this city ſtands in *Hungate*.

Peaſeholme-green plainly enough ſpeaks its own name, *holm* is an *Anglo-Saxon* word for a

(*d*) See Mr. *Speed's* plan of the city in his map of the county.

ſmall

2

small island, or any watery situation, which this is; and has been gained from the river *Foss*, first for gardens, and next for buildings. MONK WARD

In the square, as I may call it, though a meanly built one, stood once the parish church of *Allhallows*; some small remains of the wall still marking out the place. The church of *All-saints* (*d*) in *Peseholme*, *Havergate*, all in *Marisco*, was an antient rectory belonging to the patronage of several private families, as the *Nevils*, *Grants*, *Salvayns*, *Langtons*, &c. Amongst the records of the city on *Ouse-bridge*, I met with a very antient writing, which is an exemplification of the right of patronage to this church; it has the old common seal of the city appendant, and is addressed, as I take it, to *Gerard* archbishop, who died *anno* 1109; but being without date I leave it to the reader's conjecture, whether it belongs to him or some of the *Wiliams* his successors? The form of the letters are strong and fine, corresponding with the most antient in *Maddox*'s *formulae*. ALL-SAINTS PEASEHOLM.

Venerabili patri Domino G. *Dei gratia* Eboracensi *archiepiscopo, et* Anglie *primati, humiles filii sui cives* Ebor. *salutem, et debitum, cum omni reverentia, obsequium. Excellentie vestre notificetur quod ecclesia omnium sanctorum in* Marisco *in fundo* Radulfi Nuuel (*e*) *et antecessorum suorum sita est. Scimus etiam pro certo quod antecessores sui a prima fundatione ejusdem ecclesie eam donaverunt, et quod advocatio totius prefate ecclesie ad eundem* Radulfum *pertinet, tam jure haereditario quam ex dono predecessoris sui, qui eam dare potuit. Hujus rei veritatem sub communi sigillo civitatis nostre testificamus. Valeat semper in Christo sanctitas vestra* (*f*).

Near a postern-gate, called *Layrethorpe-postern*, which lead to a village of that name, *extra pontem*, stands the parish church of St. *Cuthbert*; a neat structure, of a much newer aspect than many of the other churches in town. It is a rectory antiently appropriated to the priory of St. *Trinity* in *York*. This was a parish church at the conquest, and then in the patronage of the truly antient family of the *Percy*'s; in the book of *Domesday* it is thus mentioned, *in* Eboraco *civitate ecclesia sancti* Cuthberti, *advocatio* Willielmi de Percy *ab* Hugone *comite*, &c. (*g*). St. CUTHBERT PEASEHOLM.

(*h*) *A CATALOGUE of the* RECTORS *of St.* CUTHBERT.

Temp. instit. Anno.	*Rectores eccl.*	*Patroni.*	*Vacat.*
1239	Ric. de Heton, *cap.*	*Prior et conventus S.* Trin. Ebor.	
1288	Fr. Reynerus. . . .	*Iidem.*	
1307	Rob. de Neuby, *acolitus.*	*Iidem.*	*per resig.*
1316	Symon de Relford, *presb.*	*Iidem.*	
1324	Hugo de Brounfeld, *cl.*	*Iidem.*	*per resig*
1361	Walter de Thorpe, *cap.*	*Iidem.*	*per mort.*
1362	Nic. *fil.* Will. Bayntings de Swanland.	*Iidem.*	
	Joh. Moubray, *presb.*	*Iidem.*	*per mort.*
1399	Hen. de Ravenswath, *pr.*	*Iidem.*	*per resig.*
1401	Joh. Clyveland, *presb.*	*Iidem.*	
1402	Joh. Cave, *presb.*	*Iidem.*	*per mort.*
1406	Rob. de Lyncolne, *presb.*	*Iidem.*	*per mort.*
1428	Joh. Undewall, *presb.*	*Iidem.*	
	Joh. Bempton, *presb.*	*Iidem.*	*per mort.*
1446	Will. Clareburgh, *presb.*	*Iidem.*	*per mort.*
1451	Tho. Coly, *presb.*	*Iidem.*	*per resig.*
1451	Will. Lavorock, *presb.*	*Iidem.*	*per resig.*
1454	Joh. Smythe, *presb.*	*Iidem.*	
1455	Joh. Coke, *presb.*	*Archiepiscopus per lap.*	*per resig.*
1457	Fr. Tho. Richmond, *S. T. D. frat. minor.*	*Prior et convent.*	
1467	Joh. Alcocks, *cap.*	*Iidem.*	
	Anth. Jocson, *cler.*	*Iidem.*	*per resig.*
1585	Tho. Corney, *cler.*	Elizabetha *reg.*	*per resig.*
1631	Mat. Staynton, *cler.*	Car. I. *rex.*	
	Will. Dutton, *cler.*	*Idem.*	*per mort.*
1644	Tho. Morgate, *cler.*	*Idem.*	*per mort.*
1661	Tobie Newcombe, *cler.*	Car. II. *rex.*	*per mort.*
1670	Will. Loe, *cler.*	*Idem.*	

(*d*) Ex *MS.* Torre.
(*e*) *Sic in MS.*
(*f*) See the Seal amongst the others.
(*g*) *Ex MS.* sir T. *W.* See the abstract in the *appendix.*
(*h*) *Ex MS.* Torre *f.* 505.

MONK WARD

Monumental INSCRIPTIONS in this church.

Bowes 13 . *Lord-mayor* 1428. ✠ **Orate pro animabus Will. Bowes senior. quondam majoris civitatis Ebor. qui obiit . die mensis . . . an. dom. MCCCC . . . et Isabelle uxor. sue, que obiit xxv die mensis Julii An. Dom. MCCCC.XXXV. quorum animabus propitietur Deus. Amen.**

Daniel 1670. **Here lyeth the body of** Ingleby Daniel, **the son of lieutenant** Daniel, **who died the x of** November, 1670.

ARMS. *Argent*, a pale lozengee *sable*. *Daniel.*

Hungate 1619 *Here lyeth the corps of* Robert Hungate *esquire, councellour at law; who by his last will founded a school at* Shereburn, com. Ebor. *and gave thirty pound yearly to the master, and twenty marks to the usher. And founded there an hospital of twenty four orphans to have every one five pound yearly to continue for ever; and was a benefactor to this parish; and gave every thirde yeare thirty pound to a preaching minister, to preach once every sabbath, and to catechize once in the week-day in this church. And the like sum to preach and catechize in* Sandhutton *church and* Saxton *church, to continue for thirty five yeares after his death, who dyed* July 25, 1619. *And this thirty pound is to be paid by* Henry Darley *esquire, who married* Margery Hungate *niece of the said* Robert, *who was executrix of the said* Robert. *And this stone was layed in remembrance of the said* Robert *at the cost of the said* Henry Darley.

ARMS. A chevron engrailed inter three hounds *sejant*. *Hungate.*

Hungate 1614 *Here lyeth the body of* Edmund Hungate *gent. fourth son of* William Hungate *late of* Saxton *in the county of* Yorke *esquire, which* Edmund *married* Jane *the daughter of* Richard Bell *gent. late of this parish; and by her had only one daughter named* Katherine, *and dyed upon* Friday *the* 23d *day of* December *anno Dom.* 1641.

ARMS. *Hungate.* Impaling, a fess *ermine*, double cottised inter three martlets. *Bell.*

Bell 1639. *Here lyeth interred the body of* Richard Bell *esquire counsellour at law, late of this parish, who married two wives, the one* Anne *daughter of* John Atkinson *gent. late of this city, by whom he had only one daughter named* Mary, *who dyed very younge; the other* Katherine *yet livinge, who was the late wife and relict of* John Payler *esquire, he departed this life the* 7th *day of* October, 1639.

Watkinson 1666,

Anniculus vix ultra
properavi, lector,
ac tu festinas.
Henricus Watkinson.
H. F.
An. Dom.
1666.

Memoriae sacrum

Watkinson 1712. *Venerabilis et egregii viri* Hen. Watkinson *L. L. D. qui officio cancellariatu archiepiscopatus* Ebor. *summa cum fidelitate et honore per* XXXIX *annos functus, hic bonis omnibus desideratissimus in pace requiescit. Obiit octo kal.* Maii *anno salutis* CIↃ DCCXII *aet. suae* LXXXIV.

H. S. E.

Watkinson 1696. Christopherus Watkinson *armiger,* Henrici *L. L. D. cancel. dios.* Ebor. *filius. Parentum deliciae et dolor, amicorum voluptas et desiderium; candore amici, vitaeque innocentia, peritia legum praesentis patriae, et aeternae, Vixit hominibus, decessit Deo gratus. Frustra triennium pthisis obsedit illius inexpugnabilem patientiam, qui sana valetudine didicerat mori. Quod erat mortale fere vivus deposuit, nec beatis sedibus erat anima minus parata quam matura deo. Coelo fruebatur* 3 *die* Octobris, *A. D.* 1696. *aet. suae* 30.

Desideratissimo filio moestissimi posuerunt parentes
H. E. W.

ARMS in the windows, 1684.

France semy and *England* quarterly. *Edward* III.

France semy and *England* quarterly, a file of five labels par pale *ermine* and *azure*, each of the three last charged with as many flower de lices *or*. *J. Plantagenet* duke of *Bedford*.

France semy and *England* quarterly within a border *argent*. *Humphrey* duke of *Glocester*.

Gules, a saltire *argent*. *Nevil.*

Or, a lion rampant *azure*, quarterly *gules*, three lucies hauriant *argent*. *Percy* and *Lucy*.

Merchants of the **staple**.

Argent, on a chief *sable*, three flowers de lices *erm*. . . . .

Azure, a cross patonce *or*.

Or,

Or, on a bend *sable*, three mullets *arg*. . . . MONK WARD.

York city.

Argent, a cross *gules*. St. *George*.

Cheque *or* and *azure*, a border *gules*, charged with eight lioncels passant gardant of the first, over all a canton *ermine*. *J. Dreux com. Richmondiae.*

Sir *Martin Bowes* lord-mayor of *London*, 1545, gave to the mayor and commonality of this city six hundred pound, they paying one pound six shillings *per annum* on *Martinmas day*, to be distributed in bread to the poor of this parish; also five shillings to the clerk, and five groats a piece to the churchwardens for distributing the bread; four shillings also to the minister for a homily on that day, and six shillings to six aldermen, each of them twelve pence for their trouble, in seeing this his bequest performed. In compliment to this sir *Martin Bowes*, a native of *York*, and a considerable benefactor to the city, the lord-mayor and aldermen, every *Martinmas day*, have used to walk in procession to this church, to hear a sermon; after which they go to the altar, where the lord-mayor, aldermen, the sword and mace bearers do each of them lay down a penny, and take up twelve pence, which they give to the poor.

Anno 1385, 28 *Eliz.* according to a special act of parliament 1 *Edward* VI. this church of St. *Cuthbert* had united to it the parish churches of

St. Helene, *super muros*, *in* Aldwark,

St. Mary *extra* Layerthorp,

All saints *in* Peaseholm.

Together with all their respective parishes.

	l.	s.	d.
The first fruits of it in the king's books — —	00	13	08

This church is endowed with the tithe and glebelands in *Hewerth*, worth forty pound *per annum* (i).

Mr. *Torre* finds that there was a gild or fraternity erected in *Peaseholm* in the parish of St. *Cuthbert*; and licence was given to the brethren and sisters thereof to cause divine service to be celebrated by one chaplain *submissa voce*. *St.* MARY *and St.* MARTIN's *gild.*

And *Jan.* 28, 1452, a commission issued out to *John* bishop, of *Philipi*, to consecrate the chapel of the said fraternity or gild of St. *Mary* and *Martin* the confessor, and the principal altar in the same newly built within the said parish church of St. *Cuthbert*.

The hospital of St. *Anthony* was founded about two hundred years ago, says *Leland* (k), by a knight of *Yorkshire* called *John Langton*, though, adds he, some say he was mayor of *York* (l). The same author puts this down as one of the remarkable places of the city in his time; but gives no account of its value, nor is it mentioned in the *Monasticon*. After the dissolution I find it belonged to a gild or fraternity of a master and eight keepers, commonly called **Tanton pigs**; who gave a great feast every three years, I suppose out of the revenues of the old hospital. But, 1625, this feast was discontinued and the said fellowship dissolved. *St.* ANTHONY's *hall.*

The legendary story of St. *Anthony* of *Padua* and his pig, is represented in one of the windows of the church of St. *Saviour's*. The brethren of this house used to go a begging in the city and elsewhere, for they were *mendicants*, and used to be well rewarded for St. *Anthony*'s sake. But if they were not relieved every time with a very full alms, they grumbled, said their prayers backwards, and told the people that St. *Anthony* would plague them for it. There is an inflammatory cutaneous disease, well known, at present, by the name of St. *Anthony's fire*; this the brethren made the people believe the saint would inflict upon them if they disobliged him; or could cure them of it by his merits. In time they had such an ascendancy here, and the patron of this hospital was held in so high esteem, that when any persons sow pigged, one was set apart, and fed as fat as they could, to give to St. **Antony's freres**; that they might not be tormented with this fiery disease. Thence came the proverb, **As fat as an Antony pig** (m).

Anno 1646, the whole building was re-edifyed, and the city made it a place for the imprisonment and correction of lesser criminals. Here also the lower classes of trades and occupations in *York*, who have no particular halls to meet in, have each a distinct table assigned them. There is a noble antient room belonging to this house, eighty one foot by twenty seven, and at least forty high to the roof, being an admirable frame work of massy timber; this room some time since served very commodiously for a *playhouse*. *House of correction.*

Thursday, *June* 14, 1705, was begun and opened a school for forty poor boys in this hall, to be lodged, cloathed, fed and taught. The lodging room was prepared with beds, bedding, &c. the kitchens and other necessary rooms was prepared and furnished with all proper goods and utensils at the expence and charge of the corporation. The fund for cloathing, feeding and teaching the boys was laid and begun by a voluntary subscription of the clergy, gentry and citizens; which amounted at the first opening of the school to one hundred *Charity school*

(i) *MS* Torre *f.* 890.

(k) Lelandi *itin.*

(l) This *John Langton* was nine times mayor of *York*; the last time *anno* 1363.

(m) *Ex MS* sir *T. W. Bulinger* hosp. Dr. *Beard.*

MONK WARD. dred and ninety pounds *per annum*. Their stock has been since increased by several legacies and donations; which, with a list of the original subscribers, I shall place in the *appendix*; with the number of boys put out apprentices to sailors, husbandmen, and several sorts of trades, since the first institution of this school to the present year.

Anno 1707, a wool market was set up in this *green*, and some poor widows who had lodgings in St. *Anthony's* hall were removed to St. *Thomas's*; the place opened for laying of wool and making a guard room for the soldiery. I have now done with the present state of *Peaseholm-green*, and shall say no more of it as to its ancient condition, except mentioning what *Leland* notes in his short survey of this city, that the noble family of the *Bigots*, or *Bigod*, of *Settrington*, had a fine house just within *Layrethorpe-gate*, and by it was an hospital of their foundation; but, adds he, the present Sir *Francis Bigot* let both the hospital and his house all run to ruin (*n*).

QUEEN'S-STREET. From hence we go up a street, sometimes, called *Queen's-street*, where *Philip Saltmarsh*, esq; descended from a very ancient family in this county (*o*), has a handsome house and gardens. The house late alderman *Redman's*, but much enlarged by his son, deserves notice, and is close to *Taylor-hall-lane*. This lane carries you to *Merchant-taylor's hall*, a large and handsome structure; which serves, both for the meeting of that company, and lately for the acting of stage plays in. The company have lately erected a small hospital near this hall for four poor brothers or sisters. But anciently here was a gild called the gild, or fraternity of the mystery of *taylors* in *York*; it was instituted for the honour of God and St. *John Baptist*, by a patent of the 31st of *Henry* VI, which founds this gild; and gives them leave to buy lands to the value of c *s. per annum*, for the sustentation of a chaplain, and the poor brothers and sisters of it. The patent is large, and recites the reason of this foundation, with other matters too copious for me to insert (*p*).

MERCHANT-TAYLOR'S HALL.

HOSPITAL GILD.

ST. ANDREW-GATE. *Church.* St. *Andrew-gate* faces this lane, which street takes its name from the parish church of St. *Andrew*, which formerly was in it. This church was appropriated to the revenues of the the dean and chapter of *York*, being esteemed one of their great farms; at 2 *s.* rent *per annum*. It was united, as has been said, to S. *Saviour's*. The fabrick is yet standing, and has had the honour to have been converted into a stable at one end, and a brothell at the other. However, since that, it has lately been fitted up, and now serves for a nobler purpose, being made use of for a school-house to the foundation of *Philip* and *Mary*, already mentioned to have been anciently in *Horse-fair*.

School-house.

SPENNY-LANE. From this street runs a lane called *Spenny-lane* into St. *Saviour-gate*.

ALDWARK. *Aldwark*, carries an indelible mark of antiquity in its name. Wherever our ancestors the *Saxons* bestowed the appellation eald, *old*, it must certainly allude to something before their time. *Aldwark* I take to denote a *Roman* building, as much as *Aldborough* a *Roman* station. In another part of this work, I have placed the imperial palace of the *Roman* emperors, when resident in this city, to begin from *Christ-church* and terminate here. A parish church dedicated to St. *Helene* the mother of *Constantine the great* once stood here, in a place, now a garden, next the walls.

St. HELEN'S *church.* (*q*) The church of St. *Helene*, or *Elene*, in *Aldwark*, or **Wyzkestyke**, was anciently a rectory of medieties, and the patronage thereof belonged to the *Graunts*, *Salvaynes* and *Langtons*. The two last presented by turns, till the *Langtons* had the sole presentation to it by the name of a mediety. *An*. 1585, it was united to S. *Cuthbert*. In this church, 'tis said, was found the sepulcher of *Constantius Chlorus*, with a lamp burning in it; of which I have elsewhere treated.

GOTHERAM-GATE. *Goodramgate*, or rather *Guthrumgate*, very probably, took its name from *Guthrum* a *danish* general; who after their invasion and conquest was made governor of the city and the northern parts; and lived, I suppose, in the regal palace contiguous to it. He is also, in ancient historians, called *Gurmond*; and I have met with the name of this street in records to be **Guthermundgate** (*r*); which is compounded of both his names, and is an undeniable evidence of the justness of this etymology.

MONK-BAR. *Monk-bar* stands at one end of this street, a handsome port, with a good quantity of large grit stones in the foundation to denote it ancient, as well as the arms of old *France* quartered with *England* on the battlements without. This gate was formerly made use of for a prison for freemen. Here are two large inns near it, the *minster*, and the *red-lyon*.

UGGLE-FORTH. *Uggle-forth*, comes from the close of *York*, or *Minster-yard*, into *Gothram-gate*. The name seems to derive itself from *Anglo-Saxon* Oʒelic, *deformis*, ugly, and Foꞃð, or *Teut.* **Furth**, *vadum*, a passage; but why it got this appellation I know not. The street is little, but there are now few in the city better built. But I have received a more noble derivation of this, also, strange name of a street from Dr. *Langwith*; who imagines it might come from the *British*, *uchel*, high, and *porth*, pronounced *forth*, a gate; some grand entrance having been anciently this way into the close; the regal palace being near it.

(*n*) *Lelandi* itin.

(*o*) *Saltmarsh*, or *de Salso Marisco*. *Petrus de Salso Marisco* was high sheriff of this county 6 *Edw*. III.

(*p*) *Pat*. 31 Hen. VI. *p*. 2. *m*. 11.

(*q*) *Ex MS*. Torre.

(*r*) Amongst some old records in the custody of *Bryan Fairfax*, esq;

Beddnre, a

Beddern, anciently a college belonging to the vicars choral, is also contiguous to *Gotbram gate*; but this claims another place. MONK WARD. BEDDERN.

The church of St. *Trinity* in *Gotheram-gate* is an ancient rectory, formerly consisting of two medieties; the patronage of the one belonging to the prior and convent of *Durham*; and the other to the archbishops of *York*. *Church of St.* TRINITY.

But, *temp. Hen.* III. *Thomas*, prior, with the consent of the convent of *Durham*, considering that the one mediety without the other was not sufficient for the maintenance of the incumbent, determined, at the special instance of *Walter* archbishop of *York*, to have the same consolidated. Whereupon they transferred all the right they had in one mediety to the free disposal of the said archbishop to be by him disposed of to pious uses, as he should think good. After which both medieties were converted into one rectory, at the sole collation of the archbishops of *York* and their successors.

The churches of St. *Maurice* in *Monk gate*, and St. *John del Pyke*, were united to St. *Trinity, Gotheram-gate, anno* 1585.

		l.	*s.*	*d.*
Thus valued in the king's books.	First fruits ——— ———	04	07	06
	Tenths ——— ———	00	08	09
	Procurations ——— ———	00	06	02

(*s*) *A CATALOGUE of the RECTORS of this church.*

Temp. instit. Anno	*Rectores eccl.*	*Patroni.*	*Vacat.*
1236	Gilbertus, *capell.*	*Archiep.* Ebor. *Prior, et conv.* Dunelm.	
1275	Tho. Cokerell, *presb.*	*Archiep.* Ebor.	
1280	Rob. de Holtham, *presb.*	*Idem.*	
1289	Hugo de Wyleby, *presb.*	*Idem.*	
1293	Will. de Kirketon, *presb.*	*Idem.*	
1330	Joh. de Castleford, *cap.*	*Idem.*	
	Joh. de Scorthingwell.	*Iidem.*	*per resig.*
1339	Rob. de Rishton.	*Iidem.*	
1341	Will. de Skipwith, *cler.*	*Iidem.*	*per mort.*
1349	Tho. Folkerthorpe, *cap.*	*Iidem.*	*per resig.*
	Will. de Allerton.	*Iidem.*	*per mort.*
1361	Joh. de Grantham.	*Iidem.*	*per resig.*
1362	Elyas de Thoresby.	*Iidem.*	*per resig.*
1362	Joh. Luke.	*Iidem.*	
	Nic. de Cave, *presb.*	*Iidem.*	*per mort.*
1400	Will. Pharon : *episc.*	*Iidem.*	*per mort.*
1411	Tho. Wyotte, *presb.*	*Iidem.*	*per resig.*
1420	Joh. Bryan, *cler.*	*Iidem.*	*per resig.*
1423	Joh. Burnell, *subdec.*	*Iidem.*	
	Joh. . . . Philip : *episc.*	*Iidem.*	*per resig.*
1453	Will. Laverock, *cap.*	*Iidem.*	
	Joh. Walker.	*Iidem.*	*per mort.*
1481	Rob. Hikson, *presb.*	*Iidem.*	*per resig.*
1493	Tho. Smythe, *presb.*	*Iidem.*	
1509	Nic. Robinson, *presb.*	*Iidem.*	
1512	Rob. Thomlinson.	*Iidem.*	
	Joh. Holme, *presb.*	*Iidem.*	*per mort.*
1546	. . . .	*Iidem.*	*per mort.*
1569	Joh. Myton, *cler.*	Eliz. *reg. sede vac.*	*per mort.*
1586	Hugo Hicks, *cler.*	*Archiep.* Ebor.	*per mort.*
1605	Will. Sadler, *cler.*	*Iidem.*	
	Christ. Hutchenson, *cler.*	*Iidem.*	*per depriv.*
1688	Arthur Scott, *S. T. B.*	*Iidem.*	*per resig.*
1635	Will. Smith, *cler. M. A.*	*Iidem.*	

There were formerly three chantries belonging to this church

Wandesford's *chantry.*

(*t*) The first founded by *Elyas de Wandesford*, cler. who having obtained the king's licence to authorize, *&c.* gave two messuages in *York* to a certain chaplain, and his successors for ever, to celebrate divine service daily at the altar of St. *Nicolas* in this church; for his own soul, and the souls of all faithful deceased. The presentation was in the mayor and commonalty of *York*.

	l.	*s.*	*d.*
Value at the dissolution ———	01	04	00

Langtoft's *chantry.*

(*u*) *William de Langtoft*, vicar choral of the cathedral church of *York*, having obtained the archbishop's licence, *anno* 1315, erected certain edifices on the south side of this church-yard of St. *Trinity*, in length twenty feet, and sixteen or more in breadth, where no corps was heretofore buried; and leaving sufficient room in the residue of the church-yard for burials, he applied the rents thereof to the finding of a perpetual chantry of St. *Mary*; and ordained that the chaplain admitted thereto should be collated by the archbishop and his successors, patrons of this church; and to be one in priest's orders. Yielding his presence every day at *mattins* and *vespers* celebrated in this church; and also at our lady's mass, with *notes*, celebrated every sabbath-day continually. He shall also say daily the *placebo* and *dirige*, together with the commen-

(*s*) *Ex MS.* Torre, *fol.* 1. Guliel. *archiep.* Ebor. *dedit monachis S.* Cuthberti Dunelm. *eccles. S.* Trinitatis *in civit.* Ebor. Lel. *coll. tom.* I. *p.* 385.

(*t*) *Ex MS.* Torre *et* Dodsworth. *Pat.* 2 Ed. III. *m.* 26. The original of this chantry is amongst our records, *drawer* 5.

(*u*) *Iidem autores.*

MONKWARD dation and service of the dead, for the souls of all faithful deceased. And shall besides support the buildings of the same chantry, and repair and rebuild the same as need shall require.

					l. s. d.
Yearly value	——	——	——	——	01 12 00

(x) Howm's *chantry.*

Robert Howm, merchant of *York*, by his will bearing date and proved *ult. Sept.* 1396. appointed that his executors should pay into the hands of the dean and chapter of *York* four hundred pounds, for them to ordain, within one years space after his death, a perpetual chantry for one priest daily to celebrate at the altar of our lady in the cathedral church of *York*, to pray for his soul and the souls of his two wives *Margaret* and *Katherine*. And to pay him the salary of twelve marks *per ann.* And furthermore willed, that if the said dean and chapter did not perform the conditions within the limited time, that then his executors might employ the said money to the founding of a chantry for him in the said cathedral, or any other church at their discretion. Who according to the power lodged in them, upon failure of the dean and chapter, it seems, founded the said chantry for him at the altar of St. *James* the apostle in this church.

					l. s. d.
Yearly value	——	——	——	——	03 02 04

Monumental INSCRIPTIONS.

Quos deus conjunxit concede
Ut in coelis congaudeant.

Dalton 1605. *Here lyeth buried* Theophane Dalton, *who was one of the daughters of* John Brooke *of* Killingholme *in the county of* Lincoln, *esquire, and was the dearly beloved wife of* William Dalton *of the city of* York, *esq; and had issue by him two sons,* Thomas *and* John Dalton, *and three daughters,* viz. Anne, Mary, *and* Katherine, *of whom she died in child-bed. She was much lamented of all, for she was charitable and wise; and so she lived godly, and dyed happily the* 18th *of* February 1605. aet. suae 34.

Dauby 1458. *Lord-mayor* 1452. ✠ **Orate pro anima Thome Dauby quondam majoris civitatis Ebor. qui obiit tertio die mensis Maii A. Dom. M.CCCC.LVIII. Et Matilde uxoris ejus, que obiit quarto die Januarii A. Dom. MCCCC.LII. quorum animabus propitietur Deus. Amen.**

Youle. *Bayl.* 1367. ✠ **Hic jacet Johannes Youle quondam civis et mercator Ebor. cujus anime propitietur Deus. Amen.**

Richardson 1679. *Lord-mayor* 1671.

WILLIAM RICHARDSON,
Alderman, late lord-mayor of York *resteth under.*
Here lyeth loyalty and love,
The choicest graces sent from above.
One who was pious, prudent, just,
The poor man's friend, in sacred dust.
If in this life perfection be,
Ask for the man, lo! this is he.
Ob. 28 Aug. 1679.

Elyot 1689. *Here lyes, in hope of a joyful resurrection, the body of* Lyonel Elyot, *youngest son of* Thomas Elyot *esq; groom of the bed-chamber to king* Charles II. *who departed this life the* 25th *of* May 1689, aetat. suae 25.

Loe 1678. *Hic jacet corpus* Willielmi Loe *artium liberalium, liberaeque scholae quae est inter septum cathedrale nuper magistri; hujus ecclesiae necnon illius, quae sancti* Cuthberti *memoria dicata est, rectoris. Obiit* 16. *die Junii A. D.* 1678.

Dennis 1678. *In memoriam sacram domini* Ricardi Dennis *almae curiae consistorialis* Eborum *procuratoris; pars cujus terreno sub hoc monumento recumbit, a morte in vitam donec adventi Domini extremum judicium non revocanda. Obiit* 24. *die* Decembris, *an. Dom.* 1678.

Billingham 1703. *Here lyes the body of* Henry Billingham *esq; of* Whitwell *of the hill; who died* June 15, 1703, *aged* 83.

Anderton 1666. *Here lyeth the body of* Richard Anderton, *late surgeon of the city of* York, *who died* July 1, 1666, *aged* 59.

INSCRIPTIONS and ARMS which are or were in the windows of this church.

Thorpe. ✠ **Orate pro animabus Willielmi Thorpe et Isabelle uxoris sue, et omnium liberorum suorum, necnon omnium benefactorum.**

Egremond ✠ **Orate pro anima domini Willielmi Egremond civis Ebor.**

✠ **Orate pro animabus Johannis Billar . . . . uxoris sue, ac omnium liberorum suorum, necnon omnium benefactorum.**

(x) Four original deeds belonging to this chantry are in *drawer* 4, *Ouse-bridge.*

Argent

Argent, a chevron *sable inter* three mullets *or*. MONK WARD.

Old *York* See; impaling quarterly first and fourth, *gules*, a garb within a border ingrayled *or*. *Kempe*, archbishop.

England. *Gules* three water budgets *argent*. *Rosse*.

Quarterly, *gules* and *or*, in the first gules a mullet of six points pierced *argent*. *Vere*.

Gules, a lyon rampant *argent*. *Mowbray*.

Or, a lyon rampant, *azure*. *Percy*.

Paly of six *or* and *gules*.

Gules, a cross patonce *or*. *Latimer*.

A chevron between three chaplets is cut in stone against one of the south pillars.

(*y*) Mrs. *Jane Wright* by her will dated *December* 21, 1675. gave unto this parish of *Gotheram-gate* the sum of one thousand pound, to purchase lands, the rents thereof to be employed as follows:

The whole or part in placing or putting forth so many poor boys and girls born and inhabiting in the said parish to be apprentices, as the minister, church-wardens and vestry men of the said parish shall think fit. *Mrs. Wright's charity.*

And if the whole rents shall not be laid out in placing boys and girls, then the residue yearly be employed towards the relief of poor widows or house-keepers inhabiting in the said parish, and for and towards helping such of the poor boys and girls whose apprenticeship shall be expired, to set up their trades, or in all, or every, or any of the said charitable ways as the said minister and churchwardens, *&c.* shall yearly find cause for, *&c.* but not in any other manner whatsoever. Provided that if the minister, church-wardens, *&c.* neglect to employ the rents to the uses aforesaid, that then the lands go to the governors of *Christ's hospital* in *London*; to the use of the poor children therein.

She also gave the residue and remainder of all her leases, debts and estate whatsoever, her debts and funeral charges being first paid and deducted, unto *Samuel Mansfield* and *Isaac Stevens* to be by them with the advice and consent of the minister and church-wardens of this parish disbursed and laid out in the purchase of lands and tenements for the like charity, uses and ends, as the lands and tenements to be purchased with the 1000*l*; and appointed them sole executors. By which last clause of the will, the minister and church-wardens of the parish of St. *Trinity*, *Gotheram-gate*, obtained for the uses aforesaid, a house in *Gotheram-gate*, yielding seven pounds *per annum*, and about five hundred and fifty pounds in money, all charges deducted, over and above the one thousand pounds before bequeathed; all which is laid out by the minister and church-wardens of the parish of *Gotheram-gate* in the purchase of lands in *Rufforth* and *Poppleton* yielding yearly for the uses aforesaid, the sum of and is annually disposed of by agreement, with the advice of learned counsel in the law, as followeth:

Two third parts thereof to the inhabitants of the parish of St. *Trinity's Gotheram-gate*, and one third part to the united parish inhabitants of St. *John del Pyke*.

I shall take leave of this church with observing, that it bears on its outside many marks of great antiquity, store of grit being wrought up in its walls; some of which does but too plainly shew the extream heat of that general conflagration in *York*, which *temp. reg. Steph.* burnt down thirty six parish churches along with the cathedral.

On the top of *Gutheram-gate* lies *Peter-gate*; which is also got to by a thorough-fare from the church-yard before mentioned. *Peter-gate* takes its name from its neighbourhood to the cathedral, it is a long street extending from *Bootham-bar* to *Christ-church*, and is divided into high, and low *Peter-gate*. There are several good houses in this street, but none remarkable save one built a few years since by Mr. *John Shaw*, an eminent proctor of the court at *York*. It stands about the midst of the street, on the east side, somewhat backwards; and where this house and fine gardens now extend was before a great old inn, called the *Talbot*; one of the most ancient timber buildings that was then in the city. At the upper end of high *Peter-gate* stands PETER-GATE *high and low.*

Christ-church, now so called, but in all ancient writings it is styled *ecclesia S. Trinitatis in aula, vel curia, regis*, in old *English* **Saint Trinityes in Conyng-garthe.** This title plainly denotes, that the old courts of the imperial, or regal, palace, at *York*, reached to this place. There is a house in the neighbourhood of this church, which, in the time of our forefathers, was called **Duke-gild-hall**; the king's house at *York* was heretofore called *manerium suum de Toft* (*z*), in after years it had the former name, and is in many ancient records styled *aula regis*. The *Roman* imperial palace was made the residence of the *Saxon* and *Danish* kings of *Northumberland*; then of the earls, till the conquest; for *Tosti* earl of *Northumberland*, *temp. reg.* Ed. *conf.* had his palace at *York* plundered and burnt by the enraged populace (*a*). After the conquest it became the possession of our *English* kings, but as their residence was seldom at *York*, we may imagine the building to have been very much neglected. From them it probably came to the dukes of *York*, as *Duke-gild-hall* may very well seem to imply (*b*). CHRIST-CHURCH. KING'S COURT.

(*y*) *Ex MS. penes me.* A copy of the will.

(*z*) *Ex MS.* sir *T.W.*

(*a*) *Vide annales sub an.* 1066.

(*b*) The house at present is in the possession of the ci-

The

4

MONKWARD

The church of St. *Trinity*, *in curia regis*, was an ancient rectory belonging some time to the patronage of the family of the *Basyes*, and afterwards came to the lords *Nevil* earls of *Westmoreland*; and was given by *Ralph* earl of *Westmoreland Jul. ult. anno* 1414, to his new founded hospital at *Well*. This *Ralph* procured of *Henry* archbishop of *York* the appropriation of **Christys chyrche in Conyngs-yard**, to the master, brethren and sisters of his hospital. And in recompence of the damage done to his cathedral church thereby, he restored out of the fruits hereof to himself and successors archbishops, the annual pension of thirteen shillings and four pence, and to his dean and chapter ten shillings, payable by the said hospital at *Martinmas* and *Pentecost*; and also three shillings and four pence *per annum*, by them to be distributed amongst the poor of this parish.

And furthermore ordained, that there be in the same a perpetual secular vicar to serve the cure thereof, who shall be presentable by the said earl, during his life, and by the master, brethren, and sisters of the said hospital after his decease, paying to the said vicar quarterly twelve marks *per annum*. And shall bear all ordinary and extraordinary charges whatsoever, which shall be incumbent on the church, whereof the vicar shall be totally free, excepting the charge of finding *straw in winter, and green rushes in summer* for strewing the church, according to the common use of churches (c).

A CATALOGUE of the RECTORS of CHRIST-CHURCH.

Temp. instit. Anno	*Rectores eccl.*	*Patroni.*	*Vacat.*
1308	Joh. Lutterell, *cler.*	*Dom.* Gualt. Lutterel, *mil.*	
1310	Hen. de Hotham, *cler.*	Raynerus Basey.	*per mort.*
1343	Petr. de Langton, *diac.*	Hamo Basey.	*per mort.*
1349	Nich. de Burton, *cler.*	Katherina Basey, *Vid.*	*per mort.*
1371	Joh. de Kirketon, *cler.*	Ric. Basey.	*per mort.*
1412	Joh. Kippax, *presb.*	Rad. *com.* Westmorland.	
	Vicarii ecclesiae.		
1414	Joh. de Berwykes, *presb.*	*Magist. et frat. hosp. de* Welle.	*per resig.*
1425	Joh. Heryng, *presb.*	*Iidem.*	*per mort.*
1453	Joh. Biker, *presb.*	*Iidem.*	*per mort.*
1482	Tho. Metcalfe, *cap.*	*Iidem.*	*per mort.*
1508	Tho. Smythe, *presb.*	*Iidem.*	*per mort.*
1523	Tho. Threplande, *presb.*	*Iidem.*	*per mort.*
1529	Tho. Taylier, *presb.*	*Iidem.*	*per mort.*
1535	Joh. Stapleton, *presb.*	*Iidem.*	*per mort.*
1550	Joh. Baitman, *cler.*	*Iidem.*	*per mort.*
1569	Rob. Burland, *presb.*	Ric. Smerthwait.	*per mort.*
1575	Hen. Fisher, *cler.*	*Magist. et frat. hosp. de* Welle.	*per resig.*
1576	Joh. Motte, *cler.*	*Iidem.*	
1577	Joh. Preston, *cler.*	*Eorundem assignati.*	*per mort.*
1631	Tim. Jackson, *cler.*	*Magist. et frat. hosp. de* Welle.	*per mort.*
1635	Elyas Hutchenson, *cler.*	*Iidem.*	*per resig.*
1638	Tho. Calvert, *cler. A. M.*	*Iidem.*	

Royston's *chantry.*

(d) There was a chantry founded in this church of St. *Trinity in curia regis* at the altar of St. *James* the apostle, for the souls of *Roger de Royston* and *Dionysia* his wife.

Barnby's *chantry.*

Anno 1378. (e) *John Ferriby* and *John de Broddesworth*, feoffees to *Richard de Barnby*, citizen of *York*, assigned certain lands to the dean and chapter and their successors for the finding of a fit chaplain to celebrate daily, *&c.* in the church of St. *Trinity* in *curia regis*, for the souls of *Richard de Barnby*, *Alice* his wife, *&c.* at the altar of St. *Peter* and St. *Paul*. Which was accordingly ordained, with one *obit*, and two wax candles to burn upon his tomb on the day of the celebration of it. Confirmed *Jan.* 10, 1378.

	l.	*s.*	*d.*
Value at the dissolution — — — —	06	00	00

ty. In some old deeds I have met with the name of a place called **le mercerie** to have been in *Peter-gate*; *tres shoppe en le* **mercerie**, *jacentes super corncrium de* Glover-lane. It seems by this to have been a place then occupied by the mercers.

(c) *Ex MS.* Torre, *fol.* 105.

(d) *Ex MS.* Torre. *Pat.* 14. Ed. II. *m.* 30. *Turre* Lond.

(e) *Ex eodem et* Dods.

Langton

MONK WARD

Langton's *chantry.*

(f) There was another chantry founded in this church at the altar of St. *Mary the virgin*, by the executors of *John*, son of *Nicholas Langton.*

	l.	s.	d.
Yearly value ——— ——— ———	05	17	04

Percy's chantry.

(g) There was another chantry founded in this church at the altar of St. *Thomas the martyr*, by some of the family of the *Percy*'s, earls of *Northumberland*, for they were patrons of it.

Monumental INSCRIPTIONS.

✠ **Hic jacet Johannes Towthorpe quondam vicecomes hujus civitatis, et Margaretta uxor ejus, qui quidem Johannes obiit xxii die mensis Nov. A D. M. CCCC. LXXXI. Willielmus Towthorpe et Isabella uxor sua, quorum animabus propitietur Deus. Amen.** Towthorpe 1481. *Sheriff* 1467.

✠ **Orate pro anima Henrici Brother, qui obiit** 20 **die mensis Julii A. D.** 1505. **cujus anime, &c.** Brother 1505.

Hic jacet Thomas Rogerson, *vir pius, probus, misericors, et in arte sua peritissimus, scriba communis hujus civitatis et clericus de statutis mercatoriis . . . . dominis suis fidelissimus, et huic parochiae benefactor.* Rogerson.

✠ **Hic jacet Robertus Gaunt civis et mercator Eborum et Agnes uxor ejus et Margaretta filia eorundem, qui Robertus obiit xii die mensis martii A. D. M. CCCC. VII. quorum animabus, &c.** Gaunt 1407.

✠ **Orate pro anima magistri Thome Jameson, quondam majoris istius civitatis Eborum, qui obiit xx die mensis Aprilis A. D. M. CCCCC. XXVII.** Jameson 1527 *Lord mayor* 1504

✠ **Orate pro anima Willielmi Ormshede quondam majoris istius civitatis Eborum, qui obiit xxii die mensis Septembris A. D. M. CCCC. XXXVII. et pro animabus Elene, Johanne et Agnetis uxorum ejus Pro quibus omnibus dicatur** PATER NOSTER **et** AVE MARIA **ut eis propitietur Deus in secula infinita. Amen.** Ormshede 1437 *Lord-mayor* 1425.

✠ **Orate pro anima Thome Cowper carnificis.** Cowper.

✠ **Hic jacet Thomas Kyrke mercer nuper major civitatis Ebor. qui obiit ix die mensis Aprilis A. D. M. CCCC. XLII. et Alicia uxor ejus, quae obiit xii die mensis . . . A. D. M CCCC XXIV quorum, &c.** Kyrke 1442. *Lord-mayor* 1441.

✠ **Hic jacet John Bolton carpentarius.** Bolton.

Here lyeth the body of Mr. Timothy Squire *woollendraper, late sheriff of this city, who was born 27th of* March, 1617, *and departed this life the 8th of* October, 1666. Squire 1666. *Sheriff* 1663.

Here also lyeth the body of Mr. Timothy Squire *late of this city merchant, son of the abovenamed Mr.* Timothy Squire, *who departed this life* June 15, 1682. Squire 1682.

Hodie mihi cras tibi.
Hic jacet Henricus Tireman *de civitate* Ebor. *major.*
Vir integer vitae, scelerisque purus,
Dei servus, fidelis regis subditus, verus ecclesiae
Anglicanae *filius, filiorum pater paternus.*
Pacis aeque ac charitatis alumnus.
Omnibus amicus.
Obiit decimo nono die Decembris 1672. *aet. suae* 68.

Tireman 1672 *Lord mayor* 1668.

Franciscus Elcock
Hujus civitatis nuper praetor dignissimus;
Vir certe (si quis alius) probus et pius;
Hoc sub lapide justorum resurrectionem expectat.
Ob. 26 Oct. 1686. *Aet. suae* 65.

Elcock 1686. *Lord-mayor* 1677.

	l.	s.	d.
Value in the king's books.			
First fruits ——— ——— ——— ———	05	06	08

Near *Christ church* are the *shambles, great* and *little,* called antiently **High manger gate**, and **Low mangergate** *(i)*; at the end of the little shambles is *butchers-hall*; and at the lower end of the great one, over against *Crux church*, is a noted *tavern*, long known by the name of the *Globe tavern.* SHAMBLES *great and little.*

(f) Idem. The original of this is amongst the city's records, broad box numb. 6.

(g) Torre.

(h) Torre and *Dodf*

(i) From the *French* word *manger* to eat.

MONK WARD JUBBER-GATE.

Jubber-gate, or rather **Joubret-gate**, as I have seen it in an old record, carries some memorial of the *Jews* residing formerly in this street. Tradition tells us that their *synagogue* was here, and, indeed, the north side of the street shews a great deal of old walling, which might belong to some such building. Of these peoples residence in *York*, I have said sufficiently in the annals. The learned Dr. *Langwith* has sent me two very ingenious conjectural hints concerning a different etymology of this name. The first is that *Jubber-gate* might come from *Jubbar (k)*, which he takes to have been an old *Celtic* word, and is still preserved in the *Irish*, and signifies a *yew-tree*; whence this street may deduce its name from some venerable old plant of that kind, as other places have done from oaks, ashes, *&c.*

His next conjecture is from an inscription in *Camden* DVI CI. BRIG. *Dui civitatis brigantum*. What *Dui* was in one dialect of the antient *British*, in another is *Jui*, and in another *Jou*; probably the same with the *Jovis* or *Jupiter* of the *Romans*. He adds if this Jov *brigantum* had a temple here it probably may have been the original of its name. **Joubret-gate**, I myself have seen it wrote to distinguish it from another street called antiently **Bret-gate** in this city *(l)*. But where it was is uncertain; unless the lower end of this street called now *Low-Jubbergate* express it. The word *Bret* I am tempted to derive from the *Saxon* Bretene *Britain*; so Bret-lond, *i. e.* Breoton-land, *Britannorum terra*, says *Somner* *. If this be allowed, the learned doctor's etymology is plainly made out, and this street must deduce its name from a temple dedicated to the god of the *Brigantes*, or *Britons*, aforesaid.

NEWGATE.

Jubber-gate, I say is divided into high and low; at the upper end of which runs a lane towards the *shambles* called *Newgate-street*, where is the remains of an old prison, which I take to have been for offenders within the precincts of the *court*; for I find no account of its being a chapel, as some would have it. The *vicars-choral* had a house, said to stand over against the church-yard of St. *Sampson*'s, where they antiently lived together, and kept hospitality in their common hall. But whether this was any part of that building I am uncertain.

PATRICK-POOL. SWINEGATE.

Swine-gate old, called antiently **Patrick's pool**; *pool* from the *Latin palus* is a place of stagnating water, but whether this was formerly so, and dedicated to this *Irish* patron, as they used to devote all springs and wells to some or other saint, I cannot determine. In this street is a place now called **Bennet's-rents**; in which very antiently stood a church dedicated to St. *Benedict*. But this church being suffered to fall, the place where it was built was in *Edward* III. time no better than a heap of dunghills. *W. de Melton* archbishop got a grant from that king to rebuild this vacant place, with houses, to be let for the use of the *vicars choral* of the cathedral. *John Thoresby* archbishop got this grant confirmed, and built upon the ground to the purpose above. The buttings and boundings are thus particularly expressed in the grant. *(m)* **Bennet-place** in **Patrick pool** antiently dedicated to God, in which the church of St. *Benedict* was situated, but now put to prophane uses and full of dunghils, contains in length towards **Thuresday-marketh** one hundred and fourteen feet, towards **Stayne-gate** twenty four feet; and in breadth towards **Peter-gate** eighty eight feet, and towards **Swynegate** forty feet. At the upper end of this street runs off another into *Peter-gate*, called *Girdler-gate* from the trade; near which, also, betwixt this and an arrow lane, called *Silver street*, stands now,

BENNET RENTS.

GIRDLER-GATE.

Church of St. SAMPSON.

The parish church of St. *Sampson*, by some called *Sanxo*, said to have been archbishop or bishop of *York* in the times of the *Britains*; whose image in stone is still up on the west side of the steeple *in pontificalibus*. This church was an antient rectory at first belonging to the patronage of the archdeacons of *Richmond*, till in the reign of king *Edward* III. it came to the crown. *Richard* II. his successor *anno* 1393, granted the advowson of this church of St. *Sampson* to the *vicars choral* of the cathedral church to be united and appropriated to their college; in regard they had undertaken to celebrate in this church an anniversary *obit*, for him the said king and his royal consort queen *Anne*. And also propounded to sing daily, after the end of the *completory*, one *antiphony* with the collect of St. *John baptist* before the altar of the said saint for ever.

And in recompence of the damage the cathedral church sustained by reason of such appropriation, the archbishop reserved to himself and successors the annual pension of six shillings and eight pence, and twenty shillings more to the chapter of *York* payable out of the fruits thereof by the vicars at *Pentecost* and *Martinmas*.

It was also ordained that the said vicars and their successors shall sustain all burdens incumbent on the same church, which were liable for the rector to bear; and shall at all times provide a fit secular chaplain or priest to serve the cure thereof and administer sacraments therein, and him they shall maintain at their proper costs, and from time to time at their free will and pleasure remove *(n)*.

		l. s. d.
First fruits of this church	——— ———	05 00 00

(k) See *Jubbar* in *Luyd's Irish* ety. dictionary.

(l) In some grants to the abbey of *Fountains* of houses in these streets. *Vid. append.*

* See *Somner's Saxon* dict.

(m) *Pat.* 33 Ed. III. *p.* 2. *m* 6 *turre* London.

(n) *Ex MS.* Torre, *f.* 259.

A CA-

MONKWARD

A CATALOGUE of the RECTORS of St. SAMPSON's.

Temp. instit. Anno	Rectores.	Patroni.	Vacat.
1227	Hamo, *clericus*	*Archidiac.* Rich.	
1275	Adam de Borde, *cler. et eodem temp.* Will. de Ocham.	*Prior et convent. de* Pontfrete.	
1281	Rad. de Thurverton, *presb.*	*Archidiac.* Rich.	
1311	Joh. Browne, *diac.*	*Procura. archiac.* Rich.	
1332	Joh. Bovemfount de Otteley, *presb.*	*Archiepiscopus per laps.*	*per resig.*
1334	Adam de Hocton, *cap.*	Ed. III. *rex.*	*per mort.*
1349	Rob. de Hacthorpe, *cler.*	*Idem.*	*per resig.*
1350	Ric. de Welles, *cler.*	*Idem.*	*per resig.*
1359	Joh. de Shireburn.	*Idem.*	*per resig.*
1379	Joh. Byrsall, *diac.*	Ric. II. *rex.*	*per resig.*
1383	Joh. Byrne *vel del* Brynne, *presb.*	*Idem.*	

Botoner's *chantry.*

(*o*) *Anno* 1336, *Hugh de Botoner* chaplain, obtained the archbishop's licence to build certain houses on the side of the church-yard of St. *Sampson's* against the way called **le Netbgate**, and gave the rents thereof for the sustentation of a certain chaplain in priests orders, celebrating daily at this church at the altar of St. *Mary the virgin* in St. *Benedict*'s choir, for his own soul and the souls of *Robert* and *Isabel* his father and mother, *&c.* And also to celebrate, with the assistance of other clerks, S. *Mary*'s mass with note, on all principal and double festivals, and her mass *de die* without note, *&c.*

	l.	*s.*	*d.*
Yearly value	02	10	04

Kar's *chantry,*

(*p*) *Anno* 1489, *Thomas Sampson* clerk executor of the last will of *John Kar*, late alderman of this city, gave out of the testator's goods the value of eight marks and three shillings to *John Wyntringham* chaplain, and his successor, celebrating at the altar of St. *Nicolas* in this church, for the souls of the said *John Kar* and *Johanna* his wife, and *Thomas* and *Isabel* his parents, *&c,*

	l.	*s.*	*d.*
Yearly value	04	11	03

Burton's *chantry.*

Anno 1379, *John de Waltham* cannon of *York*, and *William Lovell* rector of the church of *Osbaldwykes*, having obtained the king's licence to authorize four messuages in **Patrick-pool**, and **Bennet-place**, together with certain dwelling houses by the church-yard of St. *Sampson's*, granted the same to a certain chaplain perpetually celebrating at the altar of St. *Mary the virgin*, for the souls of *Nicholas de Burton* and *John de Burton* his father and *Elene* his mother.

(*q*) *Alexander* archbishop, amongst other ordinations, ordained that the chaplain of this chantry shall annually celebrate the *obit* of the said *Nicholas* and *John* in this church on every feast day of St. *Nicholas* for ever. Paying two pence to every of the eight priests in this church celebrating thereat; and two pence to the parish clerk for tolling the bell, with four pence to the bellman of the city, *&c.* and also to find two wax candles to burn on St. *Nicholas* his tomb, whilst the said mass is celebrating.

Ancient monumental inscriptions are all defaced in this church, nor are there any modern worth notice but this,

Hic requiescit in spe futurae resurrectionis Gulielmus Richardson, *pietatis, tam privatae quam publicae, amator sincerus; nec non caritatis exemplar assiduum. Cujus anima in coelum migravit die* Decembris 29. *an. Dom.* 1680. Richardson 1680.

ARMS in the windows.

Gules, two keys in saltire argent. St. *Peter.*

Or, seven mascals conjoined three, three, and one, *gules.* St. *William.*

Azure, a bend *or*, a file of three *argent.* *Scrope* of *Massam.*

Sable, three pickaxes *argent.* *Pigot.*

From *Patrick-pool*, through a lane called *Hornpot-lane* we come to a handsome square, were it but all well built, called *Thursday-market*; anciently the chief market in the city; the THURSDAY-MARKET.

(*o*) Ex MSS. Dodf. & Torre.
(*p*) *Iidem.*
(*q*) Torre. *confirmat canturiae fundat. pat.* 11 Ed. III. *p.* 1. *m.* 28 *turre* Lond.

An

MONK WARD

old crofs of which ftood near the midft of it. How long the country butchers have had the privilege to bring and expofe their meat to fale on *Saturdays* in this place, I fhall not fay, but formerly this market was on *Thurfdays*, as appears from feveral proclamations for regulating the price of victuals, which our regifters will fhew.

CROSS. *Anno* 1705, was finifhed a beautiful and ufeful ftructure, for the fhelter of market-people in bad weather, which now ftands on the weft fide of this fquare; in the place where the ancient **toll-booth** of the city was erected; to which did pertain the toll of the market, and it was the guide to all other markets in the city. The *horn of brafs* was kept here, mentioned before. The old crofs was of ftone, fet upon an afcent of five fteps, round which was a pent-houfe fupported by eight wooden pillars; upon one of which was fixed an iron yard wand the ftandard of the market. It ftood in the midft of the fquare.

SILVER-STREET. FINCKLE-STREET. FEASE-GATE. This fquare has four lanes or ftreets at its four corners, which have anciently had pofts and chains acrofs them, to ftop the market people for gathering of toll, &c. *Silver-ftreet, Finkcle-ftreet, Feafe-gate* and *Davy-gate*. The two firft have nothing remarkable. *Feafe-gate* probably took its name from the old *Englifh* **feafe**, or **feag**, *flagellare*, to beat with rods. As the ftreet they ufed to whip offenders through, and fo round the market. Or from an image dedicated to St. *Faith*, in old *French* S. *Fe*, fet up here; upon which fuppofition it ought to be written *Fees-gate*. This laft is Dr. *Langwith*'s conjecture.

DAVY-GATE. But *Davygate*, called in old writings **Davygate Lardiner**, is of much more confequence, and takes its name from **Davy**, or **Lardiner-hall**, which antiently ftood in it. Being part of the poffeffions of *David le Lardiner*; and held by grand ferjeanty of the king, *in capite*, as feveral records teftify, fome of which take as follows,

(*r*) Charta *Stephani* regis *Angliae* facta *Johanni Lardiner* et *David* filio fuo, irrotulatur in his verbis.

STEPHANUS *rex* Ang. *archiepifcopo* Eboraci *comitibus baronibus et vicecomitibus, miniftris et omnibus fidelibus fuis* Francie *et* Anglie *de* Eborafchyra, *falutem. Sciatis me reddidiffe et conceffiffe* Johanni de Lardinario *modo de* Eboraco *et* David *filio fuo terram fuam totam quam tenet de me in foccagio, cum minifterio fuo de* Lardinario, *et liberatione fua, et omnes terras fuas quocunque eas teneat, ficut tenuit die quo rex* Henricus *fuit vivus et mortuus. Quare volo et prae-*

(*r*) *Ex MS.* fir *T. W.* *ex quodam MS. in capella beat.* Willielmi *fuper pontem ufae refervato, cujus titulus eft,* Liber diverforum memorand. civit. Ebor. tangent. de rebus actis temp. *Ed* III. et *Ric.* II. *f.* 89.

cipio

cipio quod bene et in pace, et libere et quiete, teneat in boscis et in planis, et in pratis et pasturis, MONKWARD
et aquis et molendis, in mariscis, et viis et semitis, et in omnibus aliis locis cum **thol, them, saca, socha, infangtheof,** *et cum omnibus consuetudinibus et libertatibus suis, cum quibus unquam liberius tenuit tempore regis* Henrici.

T. R. de Vere *et* Rob. *filio* Richardo *apud* Nottingham.

Amongst the records of the treasury in the receipt of the exchequer remaining there in the custody of the treasurer and chamberlains, *viz.* in the pleas of assize in the county of *York*, the morrow after the feast of St. *Michael* before *Silvester* bishop of *Carlisle*, *Roger de Thurkleby*, and their companions, justices itinerant in the thirty fifth and the beginning of the thirty sixth year of *Henry* II. I find, says sir *T. W.* that the king gave command to those justices to enquire by jury what liberties the ancestors of *David le Lardiner* had used in the city of *York*, and how and what liberties the said *David* claimeth by the charters of any of the king's predecessors. Thereupon *David* came in and said that it did belong to the **serjeanty** which he holds in *York* to receive of every baker who sells bread there every *Saturday* an half penny loaf, or an half penny. And of every brewer of ale there, that sells any ale, a gallon flagon of the best ale, or the value of it. And of every shamble where flesh is sold, and of every one that sells flesh there, a pennyworth of flesh, or a penny every week. And of every carrier of fish at *Foss-bridge*, four pennyworth of fish, or four pence, as the same was bought at the sea upon their words. And of every summage of horse carrying fish, a pennyworth of fish or a penny. And . . . . of all measures of corn by which corn is sold in the city. And to make all distresses for the kings debts in the city; and for every distress to have four pence. And lastly to provide the king's *larder*, as well with *venison* as with *tame beasts*.

And the jurors found this that the ancestors of *David le Lardiner* had used these liberties following,

1. To make the larder of the king.
2. To keep the prisoners of the forest.
3. To have the measure of the king for corn; and to sell the king's corn.
4. That they had daily out of the king's purse five pence; and for these his ancestors had charters.
5. Sometimes they used this liberty to take every *Saturday* from every window of the bakers where bread was set to sale a loaf or an halfpenny. Of every brewer of ale a gallon of ale or an halfpenny. Of every butcher's window a pennyworth of flesh or a penny. Of every cart load of fish sold at *Foss-bridge* four pennyworth of fish, as they were bought at the sea side; and of every horse load of fish, a pennyworth or a penny.
6. That they used to make distresses of the king's debts, and to take four pence for every distress, and that they were **alderman of Minstrells.**

The ancestors of *David le Lardiner* have used these liberties in the time of king *Henry*, grandfather to the king which now is, and in the time of king *Richard* till they were hindred; and they used all these liberties in the name of the **serjeanty**, which they held of the king. The record was sent to the king.

These liberties and privileges, great as they were, must have been very irksome to the city and citizens, and to get them taken away was the occasion of the former inquisition; but they were confirmed to the family of the *Lardiners*, till the thirty eighth of *Henry* III. when a fine was levied at *Westminster*, before the king's justices, between *David le Lardiner* plaintiff, and *John de Selby* mayor, and the citizens of *York* deforciants; by which the said *David* did remit and release to the mayor and citizens all his right in the above articles, except the keeper of the king's goal and larder, for the sum of twenty marks paid him by the said mayor and citizens. This deed was dated at *York*, *ult. April.* 37 *Hen.* III. son of king *John*, wherein *David* promises, that if the mayor and citizens will chyrograph the deed in the king's courts, he will be willing to do it; and he swore *tactis sacro sanctis* to observe it. Witness *Rob. de Sandford*, the king's clerk, *Rob. de Creping (t)* then sheriff of *Yorkshire*, *Adam de Everingham*, *Rob. de Stapleton*, *William de Boteball*, *Gerard Salwayn*, *John de Roundely*, *William de Kirton*, *Sim·n de Halton*, *John de Hammerton*, *Alain de Catberton*, *Simon de Lilling*, *William de Hagget*, *Robert Guerrier*, knights, and others.

By an inquisition taken the fifty fifth of *Henry* III, the jurors say upon their oaths that *David Lardinarius* held the day he died a messuage in the city of *York*, of the yearly rent . . . . . . which received by the hands of the bayliffs of *York*, &c. And that *Thomas Bustard* paid unto him yearly seven shillings for his land in *Bustardthorp*. And the said *David* held also a certain land which is called *Corsteburn*, and was worth by year six shillings and eight pence, and that he held all the premisses of the king *in capite*, by the service of the custody of the *king's goal of the forest*, and by performing the *lardery* of the king, and finding of *salt* at his own charge. He was to have *crura superiora*, and the *loins* of the *deer*, and to make sale for the king's debts, upon summons out of the exchequer, and upon every sale he was to have a fee of two shillings and six pence.

(q) Or *Cripling*, see the list of sheriffs. *Ebor. civit. Gaola regis de foresta ibidem quis ipsum de jure reparare debet. pro* David Lardiner *custod. ejusdem. Esch.* 31 Hen. III. *m.* 4.

MONKWARD. Sir *Tho. Widderington* has taken great pains to collect the records relating to the privileges of this *Davyhall*, but they are too copious to insert, and at present needless, because the city have lately made a purchase of this place, with all its liberties, *&c.* and joined it to the rest. It was for several ages a great incumbrance, standing in the heart of the city, yet neither the mayor, *&c.* or sheriffs could arrest or take fines therein, nor disturb any unfreeman from executing his occupation in it. From the *Lardiners*, it came to several families by marriage of heiresses, who held the place and privileges *per sergeantiam* Lardinarii *dom. regis et custodiam goalae forestae de* Galtres. By marriage of one of the heiresses of *Thwaites*, it came into the *Fairfax* family; and our author, being a relation of that antient house, has drawn up and left us this pedigree, which I give in his manner. Premising first that amongst the pleas of *quo warranto temp. Ed. II. David Lardiner*, saith that, *Proavus Proavi venit in Angliam cum Gulielmo conquestore.*

Lardiner. DAVID LARDINARIUS *regis* Guliel. *primi*

JOHANNES LADINARIUS *temp. reg.* Steph.

DAVID *filius* Joh. Lardinarii

THOMAS *fil.* David *ob.* 2 H. III.

DAVID *fil.* Tho. Lardinarii = BEATRIX *uxor* David.

DAVID *filius* David Lardiner.

PHILIPPUS *filius* David = MATILDA *filia* Johannis le Spicer *majoris* Eborum.

Leke. RADULPHUS LEKE . . de Leke = MARGARETA *filia primogenita* Phil. Lardiner.

Thornton. ROBERTUS THORNTON = ALICIA *filia et sola haeres* Rad. Leke.

Thwaites. JOHANNES THWAITES *de* Thwaites = JOHANNA *filia et sola haeres, sorore mortua*, Rob. Thornton.

THOMAS THWAITES = ALICIA *filia et haeres* Tho. de le Hay.

JOHANNES THWAITES = AGNES *uxor prima.*
ANNA KNEVETT *uxor secunda ob. seis. de man. de* Davy-hall. 32 Hen. VIII.

THOMAS THWAITES *ob. in vita patris.* = EMOTA *filia et haeres* Nicolai Middilton.

Fairfax JOHANNES THWAITES *ob. infans.* WILLIEL. FAIRFAX *de* Steton *miles* = ISABELLA *filia* Thomae *et haeres* Johannis Thwaites.

TAOMAS FAIRFAX *miles* = DOROTHEA *filia* Georgii Gale *arm.*

THOMAS *dominus* Fairfax = ELLENA *filia* Rob. Ask, *arm.*

FERDINANDUS *dom* Fairfax. = MARIA *filia* Edmundi *com.* Mulgrave.

THOMAS *dom.* Fairfax = ANNA *filia et cohaeres* Horatii Vere *baron. de* Tilbury.

CONYNG-STREET. *Cony-street* is at the north end of *Spurrier-gate*, and begins at a channel running into the first *Soyl-lane* and reaches to the gate leading to the *common-hall*. This street has been sometimes called *New Cony-street* to distinguish it from *Old Cony-street*, which is beyond it, now *Lendall.*

Lendall. I need not tell my readers that **Conyng** is *Saxon* for a king, and, indeed, this street deserves the title of *King-street*, if not for the largest, yet for being the best built in the city. BOOTHAM WARD.

St. MARTIN's church.

The parish church of St. *Martin* the bishop, stands here which was a parochial church before the conquest; for in the book of *Doomsday* it is said *Gospatrick habet ecclesiam sancti* Martini *in* Conyng-strete. Since that this church was reckoned amongst the great farms belonging to the common of the dean and chapter of *York*, who *anno* 1331, constituted *William de Langtoft* vicar of the perpetual vicarage thereof, assigning to him and his successors the mansion house by the church for his habitation. Further granting them for their sustentation, and for finding certain priests to administer therein, twenty marks *per annum* sterling, payable, by the hands of their chamberlain, at *Pentecost* and *Martinmas.*

Likewise they granted him and his successors the fruits and obventions of the churches of St. *Andrew*, St. *Stephen*, and St. *John* in *Hungate* and the mediety of the church of St. *Elene* in **Werkdyke**. Besides they granted to him these following churches as depending on this of St. *Martin*'s, *viz.*

The church of St. *Michael de Berefride.*
S. *John ad pontem Use.*
S. *Mary* in *Layrethorpe.*

All which were usually granted to the vicar of this church of St. *Martin*'s, upon his institution thereunto, as chappels dependant on it (*r*).

	l.	*s.*	*d.*
First fruits of this vicaridge — — —	06	13	04
Tenths — — — — — —	00	08	00

A CATALOGUE of the VICARS of St. MARTIN's CONYNG-STREET.

Temp. instit. Anno.	*Vicarii eccl.*	*Patroni.*	*Vacat.*
1331	Will. de Langtoft, *presb.*	*Dec. et cap.* Ebor.	
1331	Tho. de Ludham.	*Iidem.*	*per mort.*
1349	Rad. de Drayton, *presb.*	*Iidem.*	*per mort.*
1359	Rob. de Ferriby, *presb.*	*Iidem.*	*per resig.*
1370	Hugo de Saxton, *presb.*	*Iidem.*	*per resig.*
1385	Rob. de Otteley, *cap.*	*Iidem.*	*per mort.*
1420	Rob. de Apylton, *cap.*	*Iidem.*	*per mort.*
1425	Rob. de Semer, *presb.*	*Iidem.*	*per mort.*
1442	Tho Ellerbeck, *cap.*	*Iidem.*	
	Joh. Herte, *L. B.*	*Iidem.*	*per resig.*
1487	Will. Cooke, *dec. B.*	*Iidem.*	*per resig.*
1499	Will. Burdclever, *presb.*	*Iidem.*	*per mort.*
1506	Will. Savage, *dec. B.*	*Iidem.*	*per resig.*
1508	Tho. Barker, *prior de* Novoburgo.	*Iidem.*	*per resig.*
1509	Rob. Wright.	*Iidem.*	
	Ric. Hornby, *presb.*	*Iidem.*	*per resig.*
1515	Tho. Ovington, *cap.*	*Iidem.*	*per mort.*
1550	Tho Nelson, *cap.*	*Iidem.*	
	Ric. Foxe, *cler.*	*Iidem.*	*per mort.*
1557	Will. Dakyns, *cler.*	*Iidem.*	
	Tho. Grayson.	*Iidem.*	*per mort.*
1578	Jac. Foxgale, *cler.*	*Idiem.*	*per mort.*
1614	Tho. Haynes, *cler.*	*Iidem.*	*per mort.*
1620	Joh. Johnson, *M. A.*	*Iidem.*	*per mort.*
1634	W. Smythe, *M. A. succ. vic.*	*Iidem.*	*per resig.*
1635	Arthur Scott, *cler. S.T.B.*	*Iidem.*	*per mort.*
1640	Will. Smyth, *M. A. succ.*		*per mort.*
1661	Matt. Bigg, *cler.*	*Iidem.*	*per mort.*
1666 / 1667	Joshua Stopford, *cler. M. A.*	*Archiepiscopus per laps.*	
1675	Will. Staynforth, *cler. M. A.*	*Dec. et cap.*	

Ludham's *chantry.*

(*s*) *Anno* 1335, upon an inquisition taken that it would not be damage to the cathedral church of *York*, nor to the dean and chapter appropriators of this church of St. *Martin*, they granted special licence to *Thomas de Ludham* vicar of the same, to erect certain houses on the north side of the church, and in the church-yard, *viz.* eighteen foot in breadth from St. *Martin*'s-*lane* towards the church, and one hundred feet in length from the *King-street* towards the *vicaridge-house*; also a certain part of the church-yard at the end of our lady's chapel. Applying the rents of these edifices for the maintenance of a certain chaplain perpetually to celebrate at the altar of St. *Mary*, with full service of the dead, *placebo*, &c. together with these three collects, *omnipotens sempiterne Deus*, &c. *cui nunquam sine spe*, &c. *quaesumus domine miserere*, &c. for the souls of the said *Thomas*, and of *Elias* and *Agnes*, his father and mother. The chaplain to uphold all these buildings with necessary repairs, upon pain of deprivation. All these were confirmed by the king's letters patent, *June* 16, the third of *Edw.* III. dated at *Pykering*. Dean and chapter patrons.

Cezevauz's *chantry.*

Mr. *Torre* mentions another chantry to be founded in this church at the altar of St. *Mary*, for the soul of *Elene*, late wife of *Nicolas Cezevauz* citizen of *York* deceased. No vuluation of these in *Dodsworth.*

(*r*) *MS.* Torre *f.* 317.

(*s*) *Ibid. p. an.* 9 Ed. III. *pars* 1. *m.* 9.

Monumental

BOOTHAM-WARD.

Monumental INSCRIPTIONS, (*t*)

Payler 1595. *Here lyeth the body of* William Payler *esquier, the queen's majestyes atturney in the north partes, who had by* Anne *his wief twelve children,* viz. *five sonnes and seven daughters, who lived till the age of* 65 *yeres, and then departed this mortal lief in the yere of our Lord* 1595.

Beseby 1563. *Here lyeth* Reynold Beseby *esquier, batchelor of law, and vice-admiral in the north partes, who dyed the* 13*th of* June an. M CCCCC LXIII.

On a board near the altar escutcheoned with this charge,
Argent, a fess inter two colts passant *sable.*

Colthurst 1588. *Here lyeth buried* Thomas Colthurst *of* York *gent. who had to wief* Katherine *daughter to* Richard Audlye *of the same citye gent. which* Thomas Colthurst *deceased* xviii *of* June, *in the yere of our Lord God* 1588.

Maye 1596. Lord-mayor 1586. *Here lyeth* Henry Maye *lord-major of this cittye in the* xxviii *yere of the reigne of our most gracious queen* Elizabeth, *who departed this life* July 1, 1596.

Clavering 1670. *Here lyeth Mrs.* Jane Clavering *daughter to sir* John Clavering *of* Caliley, *in the county of* Northumberland *knight. She died* Novem. 2, *in the year of our Lord* 1670.

Rigden 1690. *Here lyeth the body of Mr.* John Rigden *of this city merchant, who departed this life* March 2, 1690.

Heayes 1690. *Here lyeth interred the body of Mr.* Thomas Heayes *of* . . altsall *in the county of* Stafford, *who departed this life* Novem. 22, 1690.

A monument with two busts, a man and woman on the top, this escutcheon of arms impaled,
1. *Argent,* a chevron inter three garbs *gules. Sheffield.* 2. *Gules,* six flower de luces *argent.* a border *ermine. Darnley.*

Sheffield 1633 *Dominus* Gulielmus Sheffield *miles monumentum hoc suis sumptibus poni hic curavit. Non in vanam gloriam, sed tam in monitionem propriae mortalitatis futurae, quam in memoriam praeteritae chariss. conjugis dominae* Elizabethae Johannis Darnley *de* Kylhurst *in agro* Ebor. *filiae et cohaeredis.*

Obiit illa anno {Christi. 1633. / *Aet.* 55.} Jul. 31.

Hexasticon legitime Iambicum.

v — v — v — v — v — v.

Praeivit aut sequitur omnis hanc homo.
Legis stupesque? quin movere protinus
Cupiditatibus tuis in statim mori,
Deoque te dicare. Sic diu vel hic
Eris, modo bonum stat: quod optimum,
Fruere mortuus beatudine.

A copartment, arms impaled brass,
1. A chevron inter three lions heads erazed, on a chief a spread eagle. *Brown.* 2. A dolphin embowed, on a chief three saltires humette. *Francklyn.*

Brown 1654. Gulielmus Brown *armiger omni literarum genere instructus, juris praecipue consultissimus, qui obiit* 6 *die* Aprilis *an. Dom.* 1654, *aetat. suae* 42. *Uxorem habuit* Franciscam *filiam* Henrici Frankland *de* Aldwark *in com.* Ebor. *militis, quae duos filios totidemque filias peperit.* Francisca *natu maxima jam sola superstes, et haeres, nupta* Johanni Reresby *de* Thriburgh *in dicto com. bart. charae memoriae patris, et ejus virtutum, hoc impar dicavit monumentum. Vicesi. secundo die* Julii *anno* 1681.

Arms at the bottom impaled,
1. *Gules,* on a bend *argent,* three croslets patonce *sable. Reresby.* 2. As the first escutcheon.

Savile 1650. *Hic jacet corpus* Hugonis Savile *de* Welburne *in com.* Ebor. *generosi; qui obiit quarto die* Oct. *anno* 1650.

M. S.
Valentini Nalson, *A. M.*

Nalson 1722. *Hujus ecclesiae pastoris vere evangelici; cathedralis chori succentoris sacrae musices peritissimi, et* Riponensis *ecclesiae canonici. Parentes habuit* Johannem Nalson, *LL. D. et* Aliciam *ortam ex equestri familia* Peytonorum *de* Doddington *in* Eliensi *insula; imbuit sacra fide bonis*

(*t*) Ex MS. Dodf. Torre, &c.

literis

literis instruxit collegium divi Johannis *apud* Cantabrigienses.
Quam exim..us fuit pietatis praedicator
Testantur conciones, quas christiano orbi
Moriens legavit.

At suavissimus, heu! vocis flexus, actioque in concionando perquam decora, non actione neque voce alterius exprimenda, cum ipso perierunt iii *cal.* Martii *anno salutis* M DCC XXII. *Aetatis* XL.

What other inscriptions are here must be omitted. *Horsefield*, a copartment north, *Hesletine*, *Howard*, *Yates*, *Walker*, *Williamson*, *Harrington*, *Girdler*, *Cromwel*, *Banks*, *Barker*, and *Boyes*, &c.

ARMS and antient INSCRIPTIONS which are or were in the windows of this church.

✠ **Orate pro animabus Johannis Kyrkeby et Johanne uxoris sue et pro animabus liberorum suorum.** Kyrkeby.

✠ **Orate pro animabus Alain Hyll. Willielmi Bolton et Agnetis** . . . . . . Hyll Bolton.

In the steeple window wrote about the borders **R. S.**

✠ **Orate pro anima Domini Roberti Semer quondam ministri istius ecclesie et camerarii capelli Ebor. qui** . . . . **et edificavit hoc opus iv die mensis Octobris an. Dom. MCCCCXXXVII. cujus anime propitietur Deus.** Semer 1437.

ARMS. *England.* *York* see. *York* city. *North.*
Argent, a cross *gules*, in the dexter canton a sword erect of the last. *London* city.
Or, three chevrons *gules*. *Clare.*
Or, an eagle displayed *vert*. *Monthermer.*
Or, seven mascals conjoined *gules*, three, three and one. St. *William.*
Azure; on a bend inter six leopards heads *or*, three water budgets *sable.*
Gules, three mullets *argent.*
Azure, a bend *or*, and a file of three *argent*. *Scrope* of *Massham.* *South.*
Or, a buck's head within a border ingrailed, a martlet difference.
Argent, on a bend *sable*, three bezzants.

Anno 1668, a new clock, with a dial, which projects into the street, was set up in this church, at the charge of the parishoners; which since has had several reparations. The church has a handsome tower steeple to the west, and lately an addition of five bells, which now makes the peal to run on eight. The charge of this bore by the parish; with some other contributions.

The *gild*, or *common-hall*, stands in this parish, at the north end of the street; a noble structure, being ninety six by forty three, and supported by two rows of oak pillars, very massive and lofty; though each is cut out of one single tree. *Gild* comes from the *Anglo-Saxon* Gild, *fraternitas*, or *sodalitium*; and here was formerly two brotherhoods of that kind in this place. It appears by an antient writing, that I have seen amongst the city records, that the present *Gild-hall* was built by the mayor and commonality, and the master and brethren of the **Gild** of St. *Christopher*, 24 *Hen.* VI. or *an.* 1446 (*u*). COMMON-HALL.

This gild was founded by one *Robert Dalbey*, or *Dalby*, and other citizens, *temp.* Ric. II. as appears by his letters patents, dated at *York*, *Martii* 12 *anno regni* 19, made to the said *Robert* and citizens, to erect and make the said gild or fraternity. *Gilds of St.* CHRISTOPHER *and* St GEORGE.

After this, another brotherhood called the **Gild** of St. *George* was added to the former, as appears by letters patents from king *Henry* VI. dated at *Westminster anno reg.* 25. to *William Craven* and other citizens; by which authorities the said gilds were not only erected but they had power to purchase lands and tenements lying in the said city, or elsewhere, to the yearly value of . . . . And by the said authority they made and erected divers ordinances for the disposition of their revenues and profits, with other monies that shall accrue unto them to the maintenance of their *common-hall*, called the **Gild-hall** of the city of *York*, and to the repairing and maintaining of certain *brigdes* and *highways* in and about the city, and lastly to the relief of divers poor people in and about the same.

	l.	*s.*	*d.*
The revenues of these were valued at the dissolution at — —	16	15	08

King *Edward* VI. by letters patents dated *Aug.* 4. *anno reg.* 3°. granted to the mayor and commonality of the city of *York*, and their successors, both these dissolved fellowships of St. *Christopher* and St. *George*, &c. with all and singular messuages, tenements, houses in the city of *York* and the suburbs of the same, and in *Stamford-briggs*, *Hemyngburgh*, *Whenby* and *Skarborough* in the county of *York*; except the bells and lead coverings in the said premises, and except the advowson of churches and jury patron. belonging to them (*x*).

(*u*) *Dodsw.* coll. fol. *T W.* says that this common-hall was heretofore part of the possessions of the prior and convent of *Durham*. *Ex MS.*

(*x*) From the city records *Rolls* chap. 7. p. 3 *Ed* VI. for the sum of 212 *l.* 4 *s.* 8 *d.*

BOOTHAM WARD.

The *common-hall* is the court of justice, it has two rooms adjoining for the grand and petty juries to consult in; one of them being neatly wainscotted is the place where the lord-mayor daily resorts to, to hear the complaints of the city *(y)*. Two courts, the *crown* and *nisi prius* are here also for the judges of assize, and formerly the court of the lord president of the north was held in it. The window over the lord-mayor's court, which of late has been handsomely rebuilt, is adorned with the city's arms, sword, mace, and cap of maintenance in fine painted glass; the work of *Edmund Gyles* of this city, the last artist of that kind in these parts; and whose art died with him. On the north side of the hall is hung up a plan of the city, surveyed 1693, by *Benedict Horsley* citizen. At the east end is a table of the principal benefactors to the charity-school.

LORD-MAYOR'S HOUSE.

The chapel of the Gild of St. *Christopher* stood to the street, almost facing *Stone-gate*; which was turned into a dwelling house, and long continued so, till *anno* 1726. it was pulled down, with another adjoining, in order to build the present mansion-house for our lord-mayors. This is a neat convenient building and grand enough; every way furnished for use and entertainment; but those of our magistrates who have proper houses of their own seldom remove hither. I cannot forbear to mention that this house has had the honour to be a precedent for the city of *London* to copy after, though we shall not pretend to compare with them in size and dimensions when their house is erected. What it is the reader will best judge of by the following draughts.

Haec maenia surgunt—in honorem civium Eboracensium 1726. Samuele Clarke Majore.

In a nitch in the old chapel wall, facing *Stone-gate*, stood a statue, which sir *T. W.* supposes was set up as the image or patron of the city; it is, says he, in the form of a *goodly or big woman; anciently the statues of city's used to be set out in a feminine form. It has a mural crown of its head embattled.* Thus adds our author, *Libera*, or the goddess *Tellus*, was set forth,

> *Murali caput summum cinxere corona,*
> *Eximiis munita locis quod sustinet urbeis.* Lucret. *lib.* 2.

Sir *T.* has pursued this fine thought thus far without the least foundation for it; the statue is not of a woman or goddess, but of a king in gilt armour, with a crown imperial on his head, instead of a mural one. The imperial crown shews that it was erected in honour of some of our kings, from *Henry* VI. who was the first that took that mark of distinction; but for whom I know not. It cannot be the image of olde Yorke, mentioned before, because that image was of wood; but it deserves no further disquisition *(z)*.

In *Conyng-street*, besides a number of well built houses, stand the three principal inns of the

(y) An inscription over the fire place, *Cameratum et ornatum fuit hoc conclave sumptibus* Johannis Hewley *militis* 1672 Richardo Shaw *majore*.

(z) This statue is now in a room at the *Gild-hall*.

J Haynes delin. T Harris sculp

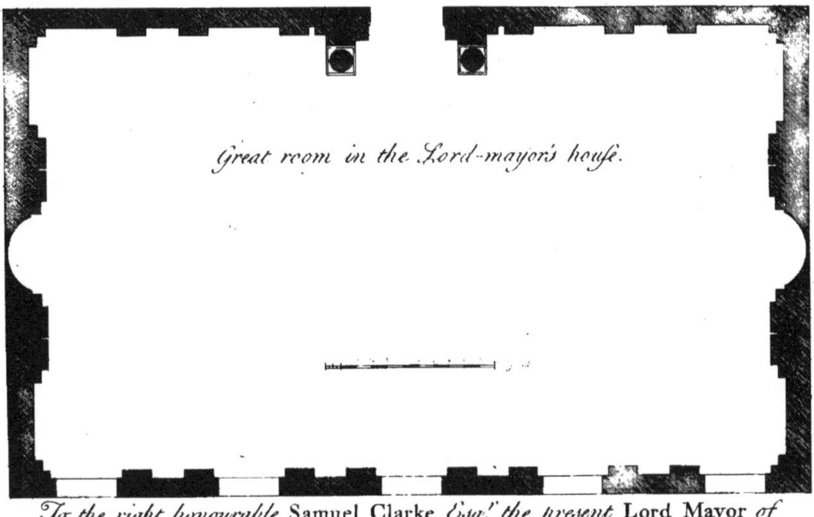

Great room in the Lord-mayor's house.

To the right honourable Samuel Clarke *Esq.r the present* Lord Mayor *of* York, *the author of this work inscribes this plate. 1736.*

THE ASTOR LIBRARY NY

the city, *viz.* the *George*, *Blackswan*, and *Three Crowns.* I mention these inns to shew the power our magistrates exercised formerly, for I find an order in one of the city's registers runs thus, BOOTHAM WARD.

Council-chamber Ouse brige, Wednesday, April 27, 37 Hen. VI. 1459.

(a) It is ordained, that from this day forward no aliens coming from foreign parts shall be lodged within the said city, liberties, or suburbs thereof, but only in the inn of the mayor and commonality, at the sign of the **Bull** in **Conyng-street**; *except otherways licensed by the mayor for the time being. Upon the penalty of forty shillings to be forfeited for the use of the community, by him or them who shall hold any inn, or do contrary to this order for the future.*

From *Conyng-street* runs three lanes to the river, which are chiefly for laying in soil, *&c.* to be conveyed off by boats. The names of two of them are St. *Martin's-lane*, and *Common-hall-lane.*

Lendal-street, more anciently, *old Conyng-street*, lies parallel with the river, it is supposed to have taken its name from a *Stayth*, or *landing place* there, as *land all.* I rather think it is derived from the adjoining hospital of St. *Leonard*, as *Leonard's-hill*, corruptly *Lendell* or *Lendall.* LENDAL-STREET. Every religious house in the city, which stood near the river, had a *Stayth* on it for their convenience, and as this was antiently called **St. Leonardes Lendyngs**, or landings, I leave the reader to guess from whence the derivation comes. From the water side to the great gate of the hospital, still visible in the wall, is a steep ascent which might be called St. *Leonard's hill.*

In *Lendal*, as it is now called, is nothing remarkable, save that the street is broad, airy and well built. In it are two very good houses, the one is in two (*b*) handsome tenements, lately built by alderman *Baines*, the other opposite, on the east side was erected some few years ago, in the old church ward of St. *Wilfrid*, by that *able physician* Dr. *Wintringham.* The situation of this house is somewhat backwards from the street, with two rows of trees before it, which makes it the pleasantest, as indeed, it is in itself one of the best built houses in the city. This building, as it rose by giving health to numbers within this city and country, so may its wholsome situation add length of days to the founder, and after prove, as his printed works will do, a lasting monument of his fame.

The *great water tower* on this side the river, from whence an iron chain went over to the opposite side, was, after the fortifications were slighted, converted into a warehouse for goods. WATER-WORKS. After that, *anno* 1682, it was made use of for fixing an engine in, to force water through wooden pipes into every street of the city, to the great convenience of the inhabitants. Here is a stayth built of late years, the stone taken out of the *abbey*, but being too high, it is of no service, except in a flood. Sir *T. W.* mentions a postern to have been here, which he calls *Lendal postern*, at present it is only a foot way, on sufferance, into the abbey. I chuse here to present the reader with two fine views, backwards and forwards, of the river and city on this side; done by that eminent artist the late Mr. *Fran. Place.*

Fran. Place gen. Ebor. delin. et sculp.

(*a*) *Ex antiquiss. registro f.* 42.

(*b*) One of them now inhabited by Sir *W. Wentworth* bart.

The

Fran Place gen. Ebor. delin et sculp.

ST. LEONARD'S HOSPITAL.

The hospital of St. *Leonard* was one of the antientest, as well as noblest, foundations of that kind in *Britain*. *Anno* 936, *Athelstane*, our famous *Saxon* monarch, being on his expedition to *Scotland*, in his way thither, visited three religious places. *Beverley*, *York*, and *Durham*; where he requested the benefit of their devout prayers on his behalf; promising that if he succeeded well therein he would abundantly recompence them for the same.

Returning with a happy victory over *Constantine* the *Scotch* king, which was gained near *Dunbar* in *Scotland*, he came to *York*, and in the cathedral church there offered his hearty thanks to God and St. *Peter*. Observing, in the same church, certain men of a sanctified life, and honest conversation, called then *Coledei*, who relieved many poor people out of the little they had to live upon, therefore that they might better be enabled to sustain the said poor, keep hospitality, and exercise other works of piety, *anno* 936, he granted to God and St. *Peter*, and the said *Coledei*, and to their successors for ever, *one* **thrave** *of* **corn** *out of every carucate of land, or every plowgoing, in the bishoprick of* York; which to this day is called **Peter corn**. For by grant of the inhabitants, within that district, the king had to him and his successors the said thraves for destroying of *wolves*; which in those days, so exceedingly wasted the country, that they almost devoured the tame beasts of the villages thereabouts; but by these means those ravenous creatures were totally destroyed.

These *Coledei* being thus possessed of the said **thraves**, and a piece of waste ground which the king also gave them, began to found for themselves a certain hospital in the city of *York*; and they elected one of them to preside over the rest, for the better government and preservation of their rights and possessions (*c*).

They continued thus till the conquest; when *William* confirmed the said **thraves** to them. But his successor *William Rufus* was a much greater benefactor, for he translated the site of the hospital into the *royal place* where it now stands; as appears by many houses then being on it, which in times past belonged to the king's use. He likewise built a little church therein, and caused it to be dedicated to St. *Peter*; which name this hospital bore to the last, as their common seal testifies; **Sigillum hospitalis sancti Petri Eboraci** (*d*).

King *Henry* I. granted to them the enlargement of the close, wherein their house is situate, as far as the river *Ouse*; when he shall recover the same from the monks of St. *Mary*. He also confirmed to this hospital all the lands which either he himself, or *Eustace Fitz-John*, *Lambert de Fossgate*, or other of the king's men and burgesses had formerly given

(*c*) Mon. Ang v 2. f. 367.

(*d*) Ibid. 367, 368. Vide sigillum.

there-

2

thereunto, within or without the **burgh**; especially the land in **Usegate**, which *John Lardinarius* had conferred on them. He freed them from **gelds, customs**, and granted to it the liberties of **Sac, Soc, Tol, Theme**, and **Infangtheof**. As a more especial mark of his favour, this king took to himself the name of a brother and warden of this hospital; *frater enim et custos ejusdem domus Dei sum.* BOOTHAM WARD.

King *Stephen* rebuilt this hospital in a more magnificent manner, and dedicated it to the honour of St. *Leonard*; and it has ever since been called *hospitalis S.* Leonardi. This king confirmed the **threaves**, which were, as is here expressed, *all the oats which had been used to be gathered betwixt the river of* TRENT *and* SCOTLAND, *for finding the king's bounds; which was twenty fair sheaves of corn of each plowland by the year, and appointed the dean and canons of the cathedral church to gather them for the relief of the said hospital.* He likewise caused **Nigel**, mayor of **York**, to deliver up a certain place, by the **west wall** of the city, to receive the poor and lame in (e).

All these privileges and possessions were confirmed by *Henry* II. and king *John*; which last ratified them by his charter, and further granted to this hospital, *timber* for their buildings, *wood* for their fires, with *grass* and pasturage for their cattle, through his whole forest of *Yorkshire* (f).

The hospital continued in these possessions which were confirmed and much inlarged by several succeeding monarchs, and piously disposed noblemen and others, to the reign of *Edward* I. when that king, upon return of a writ of *ad quod damnum*, granted to the master and brethren of this hospital, liberty to take down the wall of the said hospital which extended from **Blake-street** to **Botham-barr**, and to set up a new wall for enlarging the court of the said hospital, and so inclosed to hold the same to the master and successors for ever, dated *Apr.* 2. 27 *Ed.* I. (g).

It would take up too much time to enumerate all the confirmations, privileges, charters, &c. that belonged to this once famous hospital; which had all the function of an *act of parliament* the second of *Henry* VI. to confirm them (h). Sir *T. W.* is very prolix upon this head, being then in possession of the coucher book belonging to the hospital, which is since reposited in the *Cotton library*. What the scope of my design will suffer me to add, is only an account of some rules of the house, with the particular number of people that were maintained therein; as also to give some abstracts of donations to them, taken from the originals, which are not printed in the *Monast.* nor elsewhere.

(i) *Anno* 1294, *Walter Langton* master of St. *Leonard*'s hospital made certain orders for the brothers and sisters of it to this effect. That every learned chaplain should have a seat and a desk in the cloister, and all be present at *mattins* and other hours. That at least four brothers, besides the priest, should assist at the mass of the blessed virgin, and after having said all their masses to be at their chairs in the cloister at prayers. How they should behave themselves in the choir, that one should read at their meals; that in summer they should sleep a little after dinner and then read; that after supper they should go to the church and give thanks, and say *complin*, &c. that silence should be observed in the cloister, rectory and dormitory; that if any one happened to be incontinent, disobedient, or hold any thing of his own, to be denied *christian* burial. That the lay brothers should not go beyond the door of the nave of the church, except in processions, That the sisters should have a convenient place for them in the church; and that neither any of them nor the lay brothers go out of the bounds of the church without leave. (k) The master had nothing to himself but reliefs, perquisites of courts, and alterages, which he might dispose of in small gifts for his own honour, and the honour of the house, as he should see expedient. He was to deliver the common seal of the house, to the keeping of two brethren, under his own seal. They were not subject to any visitor, but the king or his deputies; though the hospital was in the collation of the dean and chapter of *York*.

The number that were constantly maintained in this hospital, besides those that were relieved by them elsewhere, were

A master — —	1	
Brethren — —	13	
Secular priests —	4	
Sisters — —	8	
Choristers — —	30	90
Schoolmasters —	2	
Beadmen — —	26	
Servitors — —	6	

(e) Lelandi *coll.* Stowe's *chron.*]

(f) *Mon. Ang. f.* 393. *v.* 1. *cart.* 1 Joh. *n.* 31. King *Henry* VI. granted to this hospital to be quit of toll, tallage, passage, &c. *Ex chart. orig. dat. anno reg.* 18,

(g) *Ex MS.* Torre *f.* 858.

(h) *Rot. parl.* 2 Hen. VI. *n.* 37. *Galliae.*

(i) Sir *T. W.*

(k) *Torre.*

BOOTHAM WARD.

POSSESSIONS from the original grants to this hospital.

(*m*) *Walter de Nafferton* cap. and *Walter de Eoftn*, by the king's licence granted unto *Thomas Brembre* master of St. *Leonard*'s hospital, and the brethren and sisters of the same, eight messuages and one acre and half of land, nine shillings and four pence annual rent in the city of *York*; whereof two messuages were in Petergate, three in Glovergate, two in the street called Patrick-pool, one in Duse-gate, and the said acre and half in *Walm-gate*, dated 33 *Ed.* III. 1359.

William the son of *Pagan de Coleby*, confirmed to this hospital his land in Use-gate, which his father had given to it.

William the physician, son of *Martyn* of *York*, granted to it for the augmentation of one chaplain to celebrate divine service in the new infirmary in the same hospital, all his land in *York*, lying in the corner betwixt Conyng-street and Staine-gate.

William, son of *Wikamar* of Askellebi, confirmed to it all the donations which his father gave, *viz.* a mansion house and edifices in Askellebi; six acres of land and common of pasture in the same town; and two acres of land at Leming-bridge; and five acres of land of the gift of his aunt *Adelize*, &c.

Rob. de Stutevile granted to it half a carucate of land in Parva Aton.

Peter de Ardington granted to it one oxgang of land in the field of Ardington; and pasture for twenty head of cattle, forty sheep, ten goats, ten swine, and five horses.

Elias de Heton granted to it two oxgangs of land in Kyrke-askric in Wandeslaydale.

Emma daughter to *Gikel de Alverton*, granted to it all the ninth garbs of her land in Baggeby; besides twenty acres of land on the south side of Perdeberdesyke in a certain essart (*quodam essarto*) against Baggeby.

William Charles lord of *Briggenhale* granted to it the advowson of the church of Briggenhale.

John son of *Hasculf de Bobes* granted to it one piece of land in Bobes, under the ditch upon Rinemud, as much as belongs to two oxgang of land. And another piece of land of other two oxgangs.

William son of *Geofrey de Skagergile* granted to it two oxgangs of land in the territory of Bobes.

John son of *Asculf de Bobes* granted to it half a carucate of land in Bobes, and the church of Bobes, together with one messuage and another carucate of land.

Thomas son of *Hasculf de Bobes* granted to it the whole part pertaining to two oxgangs of land against Langsale in the territory of Bobes.

John son of *Hasculf de Bobes* granted to it nine acres of land in one culture upon Baldriches-butts.

Eatrede daughter of *Waldese* granted to this hospital of St. *Peter*'s two oxgangs of land in Blenrebeloch.

William son of *Henry de Beningburgh* confirmed to it all that his father and grandfather had given it in the territory of Beningburg, *viz.* a toft and a virgult, and three other measures of land with their crofts, and all the land of Middermine and Adenberge.

Henry son of *William*, son of *Warine*, confirmed to it the lands and meadows which his father had before given, *viz.* one toft and croft, and thirty acres of land in Beningburc.

Masry de Ferlington granted to it all the part of his land lying between the river which runs from Lockleker unto the borders of Beningburc.

William son of *Henry de Beningburc* confirmed to it two oxgangs of land which his father had given in Beningburc.

Agnes de Boythorpe granted to it all the part of her land which is contained between the river which runs from Yskelekar to the precincts of Beningburc.

The fourth of *Henry* VII. *Will. Foster* and *Isabel* his wife granted to it three messuages and five oxgangs of land in Beningburg.

Ralph de Bolrun granted to it one messuage and four acres of land in Bolrun.

Solomon de Brettona granted to it the moiety of one oxgang of land in Bretton.

Serlo son of *Gervase de Brettona* granted thereunto one oxgang of land, with one toft and croft in Bretton eastward.

Roger son of *Eudo de Magna Burton* granted to it two acres and a half of land in Magna Burton,

William son of *Wibumar de Askelbie* confirmed to it the donation which his father made of one carucate of land in Crosseby. *Rob.* son of *Wilbumar* the same.

Thomas de Camera granted to it half a carucate of land in the territory of Coupmanthorpe.

Wiliam son of *Roger de Ketilbergh* granted to it two oxgangs of land in the territory of Canteley.

(*m*) *Omnes ex chart. original.* There are many patents, grants, *&c.* mrde to this hospital in the archives of the tower of *London*, which with the rest would make a volume by themselves.

Richard

(*o*) *Richard Cruer* granted to it one oxgang of land in Kalveton in Rydale. BOOTHAM WARD.

William de Argenton granted to it two oxgangs of land with a toft and croft in Catton.

Nigel de Molbray granted to it thirty two acres of meadow in Cave, together with *Swain* ſon of *Dune de* Tresch, with his toft and croft and two oxgangs of land.

Alanus de Katherton confirmed to it all the land, *viz.* two oxgangs his anceſtors had given thereto in Katherton.

Euſtace de Stutevile granted to it four oxgangs of land in the territory of Rawthorne.

Erniſe ſon of *Accus*, mintmaſter, *monetarius Ebor.* granted to it two oxgangs of land with his capital meſſuage, and two tofts and crofts in N. Dalton.

Walter Patric and *Synthia* his mother granted to it four acres of land in Dehihaim.

William ſon of *Botilda* granted to it one toft and half an acre of land in Cletona *ſuper* Derwent; and a place in Derwent for a fiſhgarth.

William ſon of *Elias de Ergthorn* granted thereunto two oxgangs of land in Ergthorne.

Geofry Furnells granted to it two oxgangs of land in Ainderby.

Richard Souden ſon of *Henry* granted to it one garb out of a carucate of land in Enderby.

Walter de Aberford and his wife *Iſabel*, daughter of *Philip de Gayteſthorpe*, releaſed to it all their right in two oxgangs of land in Gayteſthorp which the ſaid hoſpital had of the gift of *Godfrey de Overton.*

Richard ſon of *Walter de Grimeſton* granted to it one oxgang of land, and one toft in Grimeſton.

Hugh Barber granted to it the mediety of Hales in Grexbroc.

Sir *John* a knights ſon of *Fulk*, [*Johannes miles filius* Fulconis] gave to it half a carucate of land in Gaithill

Gamel ſon of *Liulf de Batheleia* gave to it all his land in Gamel-rode.

Richard Salſarius granted thereunto one toft in the town of Hunds maynebi, containing four acres, and ſix acres of arable land in the territories of the ſame.

John ſon of *Geofry de How* releaſed to it all his right in the manor town and territory of How, as well as in demeſne as ſervices. And ratified his father *Geofry*'s donation of the ſame.

Geofry ſon of *Robert de How* granted to it two oxgangs of land with a toft and croft in How.

Geofrey ſon of *Geofry de Maugnebie* releaſed to it all the right he had in three oxgangs of land with tofts and crofts in How.

Robert ſon of *William de Horneby* granted to it two oxgangs of land in Horneby.

Bertram ſon of *Ralph de Horneby* granted all the part of his land at Hovere-winning, and his two oxgangs of land in the territory of Horneby.

Thomas ſon of *Lawrence de Horneby* granted to it half a carucate of land in the territory of Horneby; and alſo paſture for one hundred ſheep, *&c.*

Hanco de Holeim granted to it all his land in Hedona.

William ſon of *Pagan de Colebie* granted to this hoſpital of St. *Peter*'s one carucate of land in Heworth; that he and his heirs might participate of the benefits of that houſe both in life and death, *&c.*

Temp. Hen. III. There was an agreement made betwixt the maſter and brethren of this hoſpital of St. *Peter*'s on the one part, and the maſter and brethren of the hoſpital of *Jeruſalem* of the other, touching common of paſture in the fields of Huntington, *&c.* from *Martinmaſs* yearly; excepting their draught oxen which were to paſture there before that time.

Thomas ſon of *William de Thurſtanland* granted to it half an oxgang of land in Hulebram.

Thomas de Hoby granted to it eight acres of land in Stodfeld in the territory of Hoby.

Thomas de Jernwic granted to this hoſpital one oxgang of land in the fields of Jernwic.

Hugh ſon of *Thomas de Jernwic*, granted thereunto two oxgangs of land in Gernewic.

Thomas de Jarnewic granted alſo to it eight acres and a half of land, and one toft in his demeſne in the town and fields of Jarnwic.

Erniſe ſon of *William Darrel* granted to it two oxgangs of land in Kirkehale.

Siliarius de monaſteriis granted to it one oxgang of land with a toft and croft in the town of Kertelington.

Robert ſon of *Geofrey de Pykehale* granted to it one oxgang of land in Kertlington with a toft and a croft.

Liſiardus de Maſters granted to it two oxgangs of land in Kertlington.

William ſon of *Robert de Stayneley* granted two oxgangs of land in Kertlington.

Robert de Perceio granted thereunto one carucate of land in Kerendeby; with common of paſture in the field and marſh.

(*o*) *Ex chart. orig. omnes.*

BOOTHAM WARD.

(*p*) *William* ſon of *Robert de Perceio* confirmed to it one carucate of land in **Kerendeby**; and two parts of a culture in **Buchelbedaile**.

William de Lelay granted to it two oxgangs of land in **Lelay**.

Hugh de Lelay granted eight acres of land in the field of **Lelay**.

Michael late chaplain of the hoſpital granted to it ſix acres of land, and an annual rents out of his miln at **Lede**, called **Hartwarthmilne**, of ſix ſhillings and eight pence.

Walter de Mathum granted to it one toft and eight acres of land in **Lokinton**.

Adam de Knapton granted all **Micklemore**.

Richard de Holthorpe granted to it all his land in **Newton**, between the river which runs from **Ighelecker** unto the diviſions of **Beningburgh**.

Juliana de Plaize wife of *Hugh de Gernewic* granted to it one oxgang of land in the territory of **Newton** *ſuper* **Ouſe**.

John ſon of *William de Ocketon* confirmed one oxgang of land in **Ocheton**, with a toft and a croft which *Robert* his grandfather had given it, as alſo five acres of land there.

Lovel de Richmond granted to it two oxgangs of land in **Pichala**, and one toft.

Geofrey ſon of *Salvayn* granted three acres of land in the territory of **Pikala**, in a culture called **Cinsfurland**.

Hugo de Ravensfeld and *Edith* his wife granted ſeven acres of land, with a manſion in **Ravensfeld**.

Jordain Rattus de Elleſham granted all his land and eſſart in **Ramesholm**.

Turgis ſon of *Mauger de Swintune* granted a houſe, toft and croft in **Rugmore**.

Peter ſon of *John Bengrant* gave to it a toft and croft, and nine acres of land in **Kilſtone**.

William ſon of *Roger Barbot* granted to it all his land in **Ringwode**.

Geofrey *de Rughford* granted twenty acres of land in **Rughford**, *viz*, fifteen acres in **Kildeſykeflat**, and five againſt **Molehawe**.

Richard ſon of *Thomas de Middleton* granted three oxgangs of land in the town of **Ulveſton**.

Akarius de Stainford granted to it one toft and four acres of land, and half an acre of meadow in **Warf**.

Robert ſon of *William de Horneby* granted all his miln in **Waleburn**.

William de St. Eligio and *Emma* his wife granted to it the mediety of all **Woodhouſe**, which gave the feefarm rent of half a mark.

Rolph de Woodhouſe granted the other mediety of **Woodhouſe**.

Robert Mauluvil and *Johanna* his wife and *Sarah* her ſiſter releaſed to it all their right in one toft and croft, and twenty acres of land and meadow, with a paſture for twenty ſheep nine oxen and cows and one horſe in **Wrelch Helwell**.

Adam a clerk ſon of *Copſius de Cateriz* granted to it twenty acres of land in the territory of **Withewell**.

William de Yrebi granted to it forty acres of land beneath **Wynadsfell** in **Kendale**:

Beſides theſe they had the benefit of ſeveral *obits* of conſiderable value, which I ſhall not inſert the particulars of, having been too prolix in this affair already (*q*).

Theſe poſſeſſions, with thoſe that are given in the *Monaſticon*, and their large tribute of corn, which was ſtrictly gathered through the northern counties, muſt make the yearly revenues of this hoſpital very conſiderable. And yet the whole, beſides the ſheaves, which I ſuppoſe dropped of themſelves at the diſſolution, was given in at no more than the annual rent of 362 *l.* 11 *s.* 1 *d.* $\frac{1}{2}$ *Dudg. Speed.*

Thomas Magnus maſter of this hoſpital, with the unanimous conſent of the whole brotherhood, ſurrendered it into the king's hands. This ſurrender is dated in their *chapter-houſe Dec.* 1, in the thirty firſt year of the reign of *Henry* VIII. And *memorandum* that the day and year above written, the ſaid maſter and brethren came before *Richard Layton* and *Thomas Leigh*, two clerks of the king's chancery, in the chapter-houſe belonging to the hoſpital of **Seynt Leonards**, and there acknowledged the inſtrument of ſurrender, and all and ſingular in it contained to be juſt. *Clauſ.* 31 Hen. VIII. *p.* 4. *n.* 18.

This *Thomas Magnus* had other preferments beſtowed upon him; as appears by his epitaph in the church of *Sezay*, in this county, of which he died rector, as follows,

Here lyeth Mr. Thomas Magnus archdeacon of theſt riding of the metropolitan church of Yorke, and parſon of this church, who died xxviii Aug. an. Dom. M D L.

Arms in a window there for him, *anno* 1641.

Bendy of ſix *vert* and *gules*, a feſs *or*, charged with a lyon paſſant entre two cinque foils of the ſecond (*r*).

(*p*) *Ex orig omnes.*

(*q*) *Orig. obituum in camerâ ſup.* pontem Uſae *cum ſigill. append. ciſt. n.* 4.

(*r*) Theſe arms ſhew *Thomas* a gentleman; though there is a ſtrange traditional ſtory of him, at *Newark*, where he founded a ſchool, *&c.* that he was a foundling child, and accidentally taken up on the road by ſome *Yorkſhire* clothiers, who had him baptized, and agreed to bear the charge of keeping and educating him amongſt them; for which reaſon he got the name of *Thomas Amang-us*; after changed into *Magnus*.

(*s*) *Anno Dom.* 1544, the king granted the firſt and next advowſon of this hoſpital of St. *Leonard*'s, then ſaid to be in the tenour of *Thomas Magnus*, to ſir *Arthur Darcy* and ſir *Thomas Clifford* knights, and *John Bolles* gent. their executors and aſſigns. After the diſſolution our archbiſhops erected their *mint* in this place, from whence it was called *Mint-yard*; a name it retains at this day. Paſſing through ſeveral hands, the property of the ground came to *George* lord *Savile*, viſcount *Hallifax*; who *anno* 1675, ſold it to the mayor and commonality for eight hundred pound. It is certainly the intereſt of the city to buy up as many of theſe privileged places as they can, but this eſpecially; for being a large and convenient ſite, there was an attempt made to have erected a mart in it, *an.* 1637; but upon a writ *ad quod damnum*, brought by the city, againſt it, the affair was cruſhed (*t*). The ſite of this antient hoſpital is now converted, and let out to leaſe by the commonality, for the building of ſeveral good houſes with gardens, woodyards, ſtables, *&c.* though ſome part of the old building ſtill remains to view, particularly their cloiſters; by which we may gueſs at the magnificence of the reſt. This, at one end of the yard, is now a ſtable, at the other it is put to ſomewhat a better uſe, being converted into *wine-vaults*; at preſent occupied by Mr. *Richard Lawſon* wine merchant. Sir *T. W.* laments the fall of this and ſeveral hoſpitals in this city in theſe words, *there were formerly many hoſpitals in this city, and ſuch hath been the fate and injury of time upon the city itſelf, that moſt of the inhabitants may ſtand in need of the benefit of an hoſpital; but it is to be lamented that the number of hoſpitals is decreaſed amongſt us, ſince the number of poor in the city is ſo much increaſed as to be but too ſenſibly felt at this day* (*u*).

BOOTHAM WARD. MINT-YARD.

The foreſaid authority informs me that there is a ſtreet in this city which was antiently called **Footleſs-lane**, in the pariſh of St. *Wilfrid*; wherein ſtands an houſe, ſays ſir *Thomas*, which did belong to *Walter Strickland* of *Boynton* eſquire. This ſtreet is over againſt the gate of the hoſpital of St. *Leonard*, where, adds he, the maſter of St. *Leonard*'s uſed to keep diſeaſed people before they were in ſome meaſure helped of their infirmities, for fear of infection. This I take to be the lane which leads down to the river; where Mr. *Gee*'s houſe now ſtands. FOOTLESS-LANE.

The ſtreet which comes up by another old gate of the hoſpital, over which is the ancient figure of St. *Peter* or St. *Leonard*, and is the only entrance into the *Mint-yard*, is called by ſome *Finkle*, or *Frinkle-ſtreet*; but wrong, for this I take to be the real *Lendell*, or **Leonards-hill**, mentioned before. I muſt not omit a publick inn here, of great reſort, though without a ſign; good wine, with good uſage, needs no inviting buſh; the houſe is kept by Mr. *George Gibſon*, and his ſtables, ſufficient for two hundred horſes, or more, are in the *Mint-yard*. At the upper end of the ſtreet, within the cloſe of the old hoſpital, ſir *William Robinſon* bart. ſometime member for the city, has built a handſome houſe; whoſe portal is adorned with the city's arms, as holding the ground by leaſe from the commonality; being within the cloſe of St. *Leonard's* hoſpital. Oppoſite to this houſe is, FINCKLE-STREET.

Blakeſtreet, or rather (*x*) **Bleake-ſtrete**, from its lying almoſt open to the northwinds. In this ſtreet ſtood formerly a pariſh church dedicated to St. *Wilfrid*, which was an antient rectory; being mentioned, amongſt the churches that were in *York*, before the conqueſt, in the book of *Doomſday*. This church was given by *Richard* ſon of *Fin* to the abbey of St. *Mary*'s *York*; which religious houſe had the patronage, and received out of it the annual penſion of half a mark, payable by the rector. At the union of churches this pariſh was united to *Bellfrays*; but with this particular reſtriction, *that if ever the pariſhioners think fit to rebuild their church, the pariſh ſhould remain as before.* But this is never likely to be, for by what means I know not, the ſite of the church and church yard is now built with dwelling houſes, or turned into gardens. Towards *Blake-ſtreet*, where the church ſtood, the late major *Wyvil* built a fine houſe; and Dr. *Wintringham*'s houſe ſtands in the church yard; in digging the foundations of the latter ſeveral cart loads of human bones were thrown up. BLAKE-STREET. *Church of St.* WILFRID.

Flemyng's *chantry.*

There was a very remarkable chantry founded in this church of St. *Wilfrid* at the altar of St. *Mary*, for the ſoul of *Nicholas Flemyng* mayor of *York*, who was ſlain at the battle of *Myton* by the *Scots*, *anno* 1319, and here buried. Value unknown. *Lord-mayor* 1311, 1312, 1313, 1314, 1315, 1316, 1319.

Anno 1320, 11 *kal. Sept.* an indulgence was granted of forty days relaxation of ſins to all the pariſhioners thereof, who, being truly penitent, contrite and confeſſed, ſhould in a faithful mind ſay for his ſoul the Lord's prayer and the ſalutation of the bleſſed virgin.

October 21, nine days after the battle, I find that *Elena*, widow to the mayor, took her ſolemn oath of chaſtity from the ſacred hands of *William de Melton* archbiſhop of *York*, within the chapel of his manor of *Thorpe* (*y*).

In this ſtreet, whilſt I am writing, is now a building, and pretty near finiſhed (*z*), a ASSEMBLY-ROOMS.

(*s*) *Ex MS.* Torre.
(*t*) *Ex MS. penes me.*
(*u*) *Ex MS.* ſir *T. W.*
(*x*) **Bleak-wind**, *ventus algidus, ſic dictus, quia intenſum frigus pallidos homines efficit. Alludit Gr.* Βληχρὸς, *debilis, imbecillis.* Skinner.

(*y*) *Ex MS.* Torre.
(*z*) The whole is now finiſhed and the rooms finely illuminated with luſtres of an extraordinary ſize and magnificence; the largeſt of which, with many other ornaments, as chimney pieces, *&c.* were the gifts of the noble architect of the building.

4

Bootham ward. magnificent *assembly-room*, for the gentry of the city to meet in throughout the year, and for the entertainment of the nobility, gentry, *&c.* who usually honour our horseraces with their presence. The room is an antique *Egyptian hall*, but the dimensions and grandeur of the building will be best understood by the adjoining plan, section, and upright of it. The design was first set on foot by a set of publick spirited gentlemen, for the most part resident in the city, who put out proposals for raising the sum of first three then four thousand pound, for the carrying on and erecting this useful and ornamental structure. The subscription met with great encouragement from the nobility and gentry of the county, and several other parts of the kingdom; and though the expence has over-run the first or second proposals; yet no gentleman can be uneasy, when at the small bequest of twenty five pound he is a proprietor in one of the finest rooms in *Europe*. The design was taken by that truly *English* Vitruvius, Richard earl of Burlington from Palladio; who gives the plan, but tells you that it never was executed out of *Egypt*. Our noble lord finding that the ground the gentlemen had bought would accept of this grand design, somewhat altered in its dimensions from *Palladio*, threw it in, and added the common assembly room, *&c.* on one side, and the offices on the other, as further conveniences. The first encouragers of a work of this nature, so much for the credit of both city and countrey, ought to have their names handed down to posterity. I have for that purpose caused the proposals, an abstract of the purchase deeds of the ground, the names of the first chosen stewards to the building, with an exact list of the subscribers to be all placed in the *appendix* (*a*). Before the building of these rooms the street ran up near parallel with the great house facing it; but the proprietors have lately purchased all the houses from the new building to the end of the street; and by pulling them all down a handsome *area* is now made before it. Towards which good work, a thing much wanted in several other parts of the city, the lord-mayor and commonalty gave fifty pounds.

Through a lane, called *Lop*, *Lob* or *Loup-lane*, which last seems to come from the *Belgick* **Loopen** *currere*; or from an image of St. *Loup*, or *Lupus*, who with his companion S. *German* was formerly highly reverenced here for putting a stop to the *Pelagian* heresy, we come from *Blake-street* into *Peter-gate*; at the north end of which stands *Bootham-bar*. The structure of this port is very ancient, being almost wholly built of the *gritt*, but wanting that symmetry so very conspicuous in the arch in *Mickle-gate bar*, it is certainly *Gothick*, though built of *Roman* materials. The inside was rebuilt with free stone *anno* 1719.

In *Petergate*, on the old wall of the *close* of *York*, stands the parish church of St. *Michael de Berefrido*, or **le Belfray**. It can derive this name from nothing but standing near the *turris campanifera*, or *Bellfray* of the cathedral, to distinguish it from the other St. *Michael*.

St. Michael Belfrays. This church is accounted parcel of the ancient possessions of the dean and chapter of *York*; and *anno* 1194, was confirmed to them by the apostolical authority of pope *Celestine* III. It was as an appendant to the vicarage of St. *Martyn's Conyng-street*, and anciently granted with it by the dean and chapter. This church is called a rectory, or parochial church, appendant to the revenues of the dean and chapter, by whom it is usually demised to the incumbent at the rent of ten pounds *per annum*, and sometimes under.

There is no succession of incumbents to this church, in regard they were not canonically instituted thereto; it being no rectory presentative, collative, or donative, but usually let to farm to him that serves the cure. The fabrick being become exceeding ruinous, the whole was taken down and rebuilt in the manner it stands in at this day. The pile is supported within by two rows of light *Gothick* pillars of excellent architecture, and the inscriptions which were in the windows, according to Mr. *Dodsworth*, prove it to have been erected *anno* 1535, and to have been ten years in building. The altar-piece composed of four pillars of the *Corinthian* order, with the entablature, arms of *England*, *&c.* all of oak, was set up *anno* 1714, at the charge of the parish. At the same time was a thorough regulation of all the pews in the church, and it was also wainscotted about. The organ, the only one belonging to any parish church in town, came from the *popish* chapel in the manor; but was first had from the church of *Durham*, as the arms upon it do show. In the organ-loft were lately erected seats for the charity boys, who constantly come to hear divine service in this church on *Sundays*. Under the windows on the north side of the church, outwardly, betwixt the buttresses, are the arms of St. *William*, archbishop *Zouch*, St. *Peter*, the sees of *York* and *London*, four several times over in stone.

Mr. *Dodsworth* has preserved the ancient epitaphs, and the inscriptions which were in the windows in his time, as follows:

Feasamb 1587. Peter Feasamb *esquier, her majestyes attorney before her highness, and her council in these north partes, languishing in sickness, as pleased our gratious God, the* 14th *of* February 1587, *did willingly yield his immortal soule into the hands of his redeemer* Christ, *and did leave his mortal*

(*a*) I must not omit that a latin inscription was done in brass and rivetted into the first stone of the building which was laid with great solemnity by the lord-mayor, *&c.* *March* the 1*st*, 1730, under the north east corner, a copy of which I have, but I hope the original will lye buried for many ages.

body

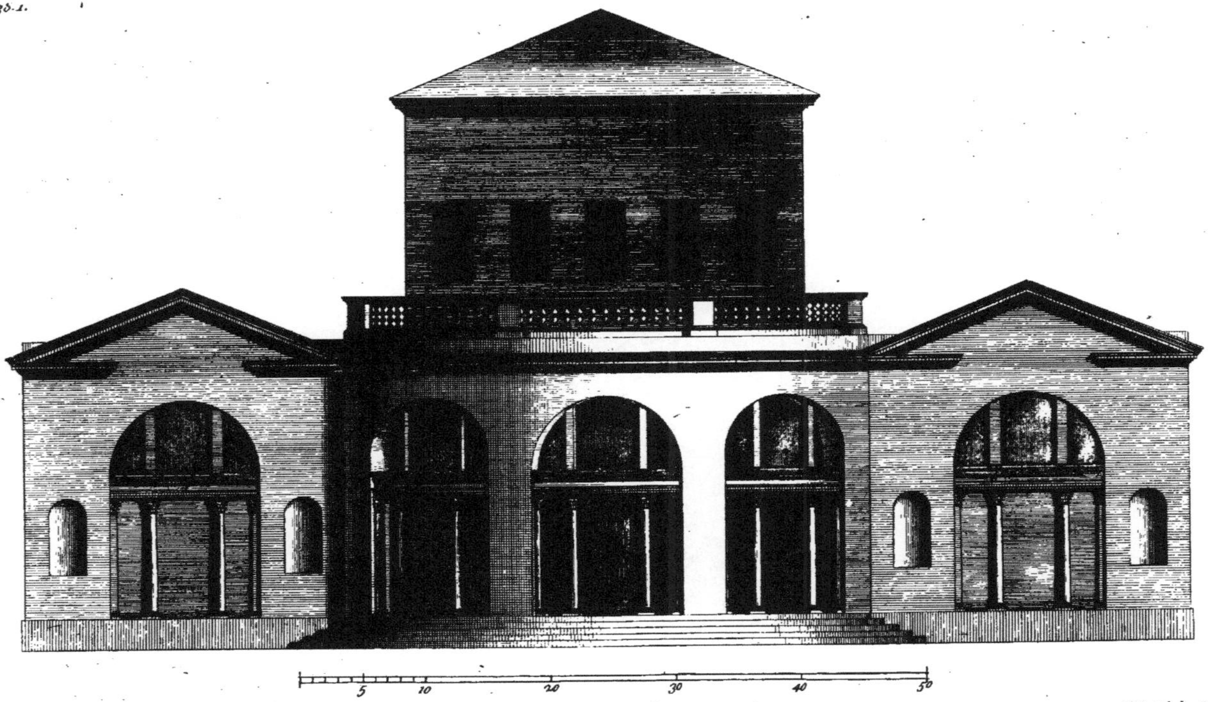

Burlington Arch.

Ædes Concentûs Eboracensis.

P. Fodrinier sculp.

ASTOR LIBRARY NY

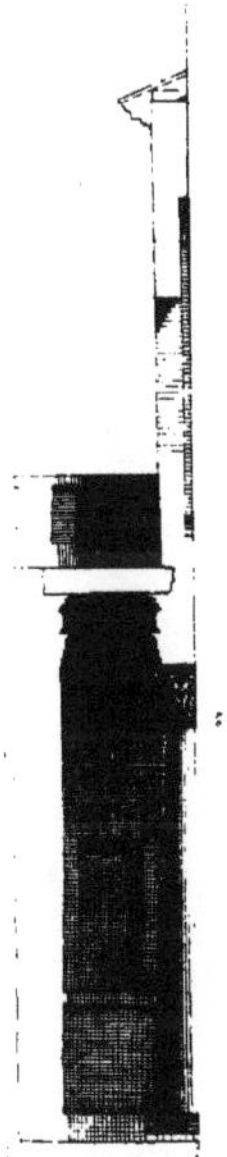

THE ASTOR LIBRARY NY

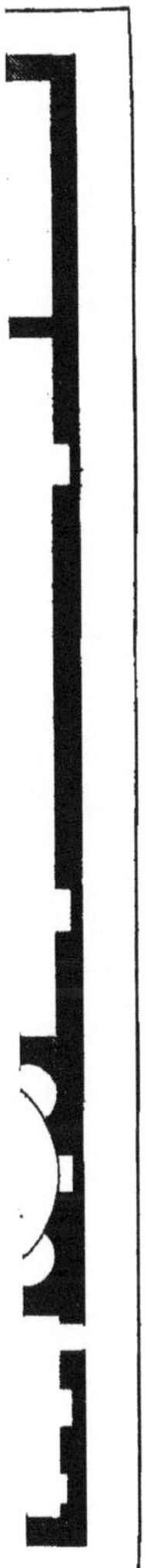

et

Burlington Arch

p 338.3.

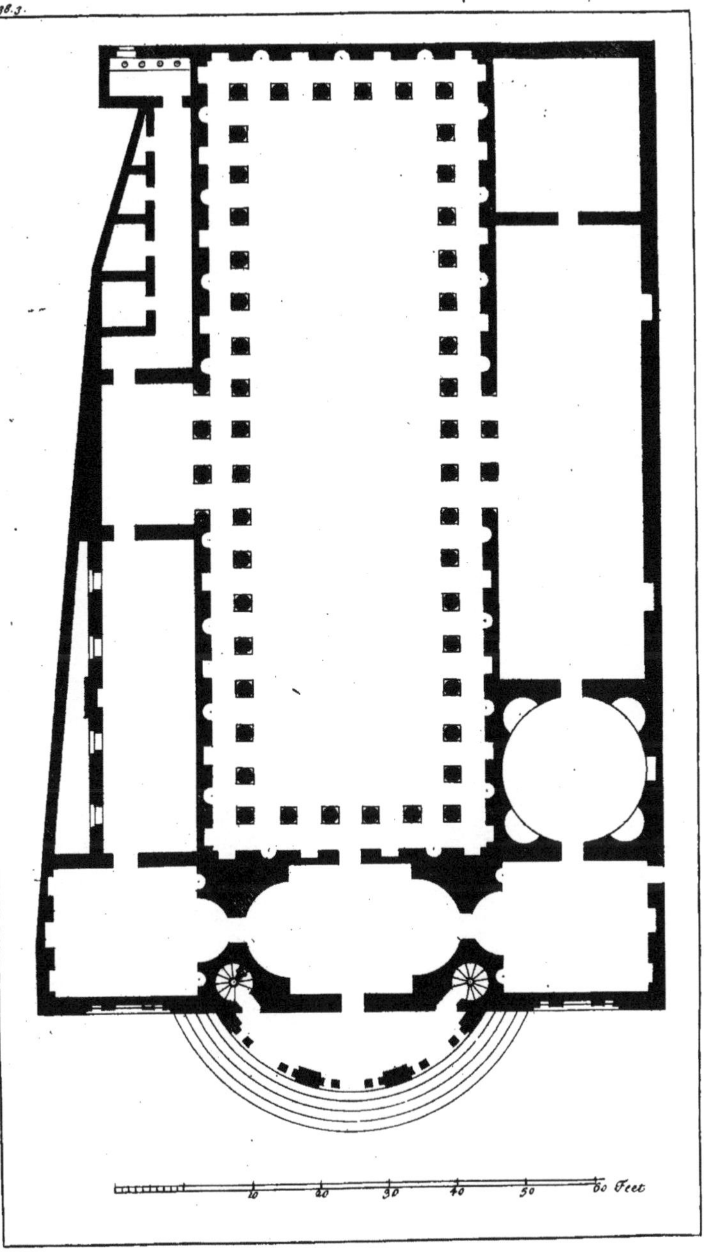

body to this earth, untill the blessed day of his resurrection, where body and soul united shall enjoy the crown purchased for them that look and watch for the suddein glorious coming of our anointed Saviour. BOOTHAM WARD.

All his dayes in this exile were about forty six years. Come lord Jesus *hasten to and tarry not, even soe.* Amen.

Here lyeth Jane *wife to* John Waterhouse *of* Shibden *in the county of* Yorke *esquier, who dyed the first day of* May 1592. Waterhouse 1592.

Here lyeth the body of Richard Calam *draper, mayor of this cittye in the yere of our Lord God* 1596; *who departed forthe of this transitory lyfe to the mercy of almighty God the 26th day of* February anno Dom. 1580: *And lady* Jane *his wyfe, who departed forthe of this transitorie lyfe to the mercy of God the 20th day of* November 1581. Calam 1580.

Dominus Deus adjutor meus.

Sub hoc marmore requiescunt Georgius Evers *scriba registrarius dum vixit almae curiae* Ebor. Beatrix *uxor ejusdem una cum filiis eorundem. Qui quidem* Georgius *obiit* XXI. *die mensis* Octobris, *anno Domini* MCCCCCXX. Evers 1520.

Here lyeth Francis Cooke, *late of the cittye of* York, *gentleman, one of the attorneys of the common pleas at* Westminster, *who departed this lyfe to the mercy of God the 26th day of* May anno Dom. 1583. Cooke 1583.

Hic jacet sepultum cadaver pii probique viri Willielmi Fothergill *notarii publici, nuper almae curiae consistorialis* Eboracensis *procuratorum generalium unius. Qui obiit* xvii° *die mensis* Martii *anno a nativitate* Christi *secundum computat. eccl. Ang.* M DCX. Fothergill 1610.

Ursula Fothergill *late wife of* William Fothergill, *is here buried, who deceased* April 20, 1614. *Idem* 1614.

Here lyeth Barbara *late wyef of* Anthony Teyll *gentleman, who dyed the 26th day* . . . . anno Dom. 1600. Teyle 1600.

Here under this stone lyeth John Johnson **merchant, and his two wifes** Katherine **and** Elizabeth, **of whose soules God have mercy,** December 9, 1483. Johnson 1483.

Here lyeth the dead corps of master Percivall Crawfourth, *sometyme major of this cittye of* Yorke, *who departed out of this miserable and sinfull worlde unto the mercy of almighty God* May 12, *in the yere of our Lord God* 1570. Crawforth 1570.

Hic jacet corpus Elizabethae Atkinson *dudum conjugis benignissimae* Johannis Atkinson *hujus civitatis* Ebor. *notarii publici, quae ut sobrie honesteque vixit ita piissime decessit* 19 August. *anno Dom.* 1594. *aet.* 36. Atkinson 1594.

Here lyeth the body of Thomas Fale, *sometyme common clerk of this cittye of* Yorke, *who departed fourth of this transitorie lyef to the mercy of allmighty God* March 13, 1570. Fale 1570.

John Killingbeck, *a devout, charitable, and most patient man, unwilling to hurt or offend any by word or deed, a rare example in these days, whose good lief, a comfort and pattern to his posterity, ended when he had lived above eighty three yeres, the 18th day of* March 1591. 34 Eliz. Killingbeck 1591.

Of your charity pray for the soules of Richard Craforth, Beatrix his wief and their two children. Craforth.

✠ **Orate pro anima magistri Gilberti Pynchbeck et Margarette uxoris sue.** Pynchbeck.

✠ **Hic jacet Thomas de Bolym quondam civis Ebor. et . . . . uxor ejus, quorum animabus propitietur Deus. Amen. qui obiit A. . . . .** Bolym.

✠ **Jesu Christi et matris ejus gloriosissime orate pro anima fratris Willielmi Cokerburn, qui obiit xiv die mensis August. A. Dom. MCCCC octavo, cujus anime propitietur Deus.** Cokerburn 1408.

✠ **Hic jacet Agnes Buller, cujus anime propitietur Deus.** Buller.

INSCRIPTIONS *and* ARMS *which were formerly in the windows of this church from Mr.* Dodsworth's *Manuscript.*

In three windows on the north side of the church:

ARMS. *Azure,* three Suns *or,* two and one. Archbishop *Zouch.*

✠ **Of your charity pray for the soule of Mr. Christopher Ceel, chanter of the churche of Yorke, and sometyme clerk of St. Peter's works; of whose devotion this window was glased in the yere of our Lord God MCCCCCXXXVII.** Ceel 1537.

✠ **Orate pro anima Magistri Hugonis de Ashton quondam canonici ressidentiarii eccl. cathedralis Ebor. cujus devotione hec fenestra vitreata fuit, A. Dom. Millesimo quingentesimo . . . .** Ashton.

ARMS

BOOTHAM WARD. ARMS quarterly. 1. *Argent*, three bars *sable*, a border ingrayled *sable*. 2. *Argent*, a chevron entre three rose chaplets *gules*. 3. as 2. 4. as 1.

Soza. **Of your charitie pray for the soules of Martin Soza, he was sometyme sheriff of Yorke, and goldsmyth, born in Spayne, and Ellen his wief, who caused this window to be made of his costes and chardges in the yere of our Lord God . . . .**

In the south east window.

Of your charity pray for the soules of William Tonson and . . . .

In the windows on the south side.

Elwald. **Of your charity pray for the soules of Mr. John Elwald, sometyme major of this cittye, and Dame Agnes his wief, and for the soules of Mr. Robert Elwald, sometyme sheriffe and alderman of the same cittye and Ellen his wief, who caused this window to be made at his proper costs and chardges in the yere of our Lord God 15 . . .**

Listar 1535. **Pray for the soules of Mr. John Listar sometyme sheriffe of Yorke and his three wifes, which . . . . A. Dom. M.CCCCC.XXXV.**

Marsar 1535. **Of your charity pray for the soule of Mr. Thomas Marsar, sometyme clerk of St. Peters workes, in whose tyme this church was newly erect and builded, and of his devotion caused this window to be glased with his own costs and chardges, A. Dom. Millesimo quingentesimo XXXV.**

Coltman. **Of your charity pray for the soule of Mr. John Coltman, late subthesaurer of the church of Yorke, and clerk of St. Peters workes . . . . of the first stone towards the building this church; it was the yere of our Lord MCCCCCXXV.**

Beckwith 1530. **Of your charity pray for the soules of William Beckwith and Jane his wief . . . . Beckwith and Ann his wief, which causyd this window to be glasyd A. Dom. M.CCCCC.XXX . . .**

The INSCRIPTIONS, &c. that follow are from Mr. *Torre*'s Manuscript, and what are to be seen in the church at present.
Under the table of benefactions.

Cooke. *Here lyeth the body of* Edward Cooke, *allied and long tyme brought up at the foot of that famous and worthy learned man of his tyme sir* Edward Coke, *knight, lord cheef justice of* England, *and one of his majesties most honourable privy counsell.*

ARMS in brass. A chevron chequé entre three cinque foils; a crescent difference.

Blackbeard 1671. *Here lyeth the body of that worthy and useful gentleman Mr.* Nicholas Blackbeard, *who after he had been town-clerk of this city twenty five years, and with great prudence and faithfulness served his generation, sweetly sleepeth in the Lord* May 27, 1671. aet. 59.

Vixit post funera virtus.

Sarcophago contenta jacet, sed marmore digna.

Medley 1691. (b) *Hic inhumatum corpus optimae foeminae* Dorotheae, *nuperrimae conjugis* Roberti Medley *curiae* Ebor. *advocati, ortu tam paterno quam et materno generis illustris, utpotè natae* Gulielmi Grimstone *de* Grimestone-garth *armigeri, ex secundis nuptiis, scil. a . . . . . filia domini* Roberti Strickland *de* Thornton-briggs, *mil. Quae, dum in vivis extiterit, virum ejus amore et foecunditate, liberos maternâ indulgentia, et amicos nativa sua affabilitate beavit. Ante obitum, multa quidem et aspera christianâ potius quam virili patientiâ, diu summisse tulit. Tandem mundanis omnibus relictis, et familiaribus valedictis, pacem suam cum Deo conciliavit; et sic e vita placide emigravit 17 die mensis* Augusti *anno Dom.* 1691.

Ellys 1626. *Here lyeth the body of sir* George Ellys, *one of the most honourable councel established in the north, who departed this life* May 22, 1626. aet. 59.

ARMS quarterly. First and last, *or on a cross sable*, five crescents of the first. *Ellys.* Second and third, a fess entre three mullets.

Marwood 168 . *Here lyeth interred the body of sir* George Marwood *of* Little-Busbye *in the county of* York, *baronet, who married* Frances *one of the daughters of sir* Walter Bethell *of* Alne, *knight, by whom he had seven sons and seven daughters. He dyed* Feb. 19, 168 . . *being then upwards of eighty four years of age.*

ARMS impaled, 1. *Gules*, a chevron *ermine* entre three goats heads erased *arg. Marwood.* 2. *Argent*, a chevron inter three boars heads trunked *sable*, langued *gules*. *Bethell.*

Yarborough 1653. John Yarborough, *youngest son to* Edmond Yarborough *and* Sarah *his wife was here buried the* 3d *day of* February 1653, *aged twenty four years.*

(b) Mr. *Torre* has given this epitaph for the lady with this further encomium, *that she deserved a memorial in brass and marble better than is here devised for her*. But it does not appear that it was ever put up for her in the church.

ARMS.

ARMS. Party per pale *argent* and *azure*, on a chevron inter three chaplets counter-changed, a martlett. BOOTHAM WARD.

Here lyeth the body of William St. Nicholas, *second son to* Thomas St. Nicholas *of* Ashe *near* Sandwich *in the county of* Kent, *esquire, by* Susannah *his wife daughter of* William Copley *of* Wadworth *in this county, esquire, deceased* November 20, 1648, *in the eighth year of his age.* St. Nicholas 1648.

Here lyeth Margaret *and* Elizabeth Topham, *daughters both to* Francis Topham *of* Agglethorp *esquire, and* Mary *his wife, which* Margaret *and* Elizabeth *both died in* January 1643. Topham 1643.

Here lyeth the body of Thomas Dawney *late of* Selby *esquire, son of* Thomas Dawney *of* Sutton-Manor *in* Coldfield *in* Warwickshire *esquire, who departed this life the* 27*th day of* December 1683, *aged forty four years.* Dawney 1683.
ARMS. *Sable*, three annuletts inter two cottises *argent*.

Here lyeth the body of Thomasin *wife to* William Farrer *of* Ewode, *within the vicarage of* Halifax, *and county of* York, *esquire, daughter of* Richard James *of* Portsmouth *esquire, who departed this life* Jan. 10, 1660. Farrer 1660.

Here lyeth the body of Mrs. Jane Adams *daughter of sir* William Adams *late of* Owston *knight, who departed this life the* 29*th day of* January 1684. Adams 1684.

Here lyeth also interred the body of Thomas Adams *esquire, recorder of the city of* York, *son of the above sir* William Adams, *who died* April 7, 1722, *aged sixty six years.* Adams 1722.

Here lyeth the body of Mrs. Mary Adams, *daughter of the abovenamed sir* William Adams *who departed this life* July 15, 1730. Adams 1730.

Here lyeth the bodies of John Thorne *of the city of* Yorke *gent. who deceased* Jan. 15, 1619. aet. 68. *And* William Thorne *his son, batchelor of arts, who deceased* June 10, 1617. Thorne 1619.

Here resteth the body of Thomas Masterman, *late of this city of* York, *doctor of physick, buried* December 1, anno Dom. 1656. Masterman 1656.

Here lyeth the body of John Gill, *late son of* Thomas Gill *of* Barton *in the county of* York *gent. who departed this life* Nov. 25, 1686, *aged nineteen years.* Gill 1686.

Here lyeth the body of Mr. John Pepper, *who died* October 4, anno Dom. 1633. Pepper 1633.

Here lyeth the body of James Montaign *of* Weston *esquire, in the east riding of the county of* York, ob. Nov. 2, 1697, *who married* Margaret *the daughter of* William St. Quintin *of* Hayton *esquire, and had by her one only daughter the last of that name.* Vivit post funera virtus. Montaign 1697.

Here lyeth the body of Thomas Wakefield *the son of* William Wakefield *of* Huby, *esquire, who departed the first of* April 1717. Wakefield 1717.

Hunc juvenem tantum moestis ostendit amicis,
Tunc migrare jubet magnus ad astra Deus.

Here lyeth also Dorothy *wife of the above* William Wakefield, *and mother to* Thomas, *who departed this life* March 25, 1722. *(c)* Wakefield 1722.
ARMS on the stone quarterly. First and third, a chevron inter three water budgets, second and last, three bars on a chief three martlets.

Here lyes the body of Thomas Wanless, *gent, who departed this life* Feb. 2, 1711. Wanless 1711.

Here lyes the body of Mary Wanless, *the wife of* Tho. Wanless, *gent. one of the daughters of* Henry Harrison *late of* Holtby *in the county of* York, *esquire, who deceased* December 27, 1710. Wanless 1710.

Here lyes the daughter of Rob. Stouteville, *esquire; also Mr.* John Close *of* Richmond *died* March 22, 1722. Stoutevile, Close 1722.

Here lyeth the body of Thomas Preston, *gent. late of this parish, who married* Elizabeth *daughter of* Darcy Conyers, *esquire, with whom he had six children, three sons and three daughters; he died the last day of* March 1691, *aged forty nine.* Preston 1691.

Here lyeth also the body of Elizabeth *the wife of the said* Thomas Preston, *formerly wife of* Henry Harrison *of* Holtby, *esquire, who departed the last of* May 1709, *aged sixty nine.* Preston 1709.

Here lyeth the body of Francis Wyvil, *esquire, who died* October 22, 1717. *in the* 71*st year of his age. He was second son of sir* Christopher Wyvill, *baronet, of* Burton *in the north-riding of the county of* York. Wyvil 1717.

(c) Here lyes also, as yet without any memorial, that worthy gentleman *William Wakefield* esquire, whose great skill in architecture will always be commended, as long as the houses of *Duncombe park* and *Gilling-castle* shall stand.

BOOTHAM WARD.

Wyvil 1718. *Here lyeth also the body of* Ann *his wife, who died* Feb. 4, 1718. *in the seventy first year of her age. She was daughter of sir* William Cayley, *baronet, of* Brompton *in the north-riding of the county of* York.

Thurcrofs 1644 *Bonae famae clarissimae* . . . . Elizabetha . . . . *quae superstes emicuit propria pietate et virtute nunc cupit splendere radiis mariti* D. Timothei Thurcrofs; *exuvias mortalitatis hic deposuit an. ultimae patientiae sanctorum* 1644. circa difficillimum illud tempus obsidionis et redditionis hujus urbis.

Quam qui non praecesserit sequetur.

Tildesley 1635. *Hic requiescit angeli tubam expectans vir clarissimus* Thomas Tildesley *miles nuper de consilio domini nostri regis in partibus* Angliae *borealibus praehonorabilis in ordinario; qui cum satis naturae ac famae, amicis autem et pauperibus non satis, vixisset, placida morte animam Deo reddidit* XVI *die* Aprilis *anno salutis humanae* MDCXXXV. *aet. suae* LXXVIII. *et fidelis servitii in eodem consilio* XIX. *Mortuo non deniges grav.* . . . .

Walker 1687. *Piae memoriae desideratissimae conjugis* Annae, *cujus corpus prope hic repositum jacet, filiae* Johannis Pierson *nuper de* Lowthorpe *in agro* Ebor. *arm.* Gulielmus Walker, *LL. B. hoc, quasi ultimum conjugale debitum, moestissime solvit ac posuit. Ob.* 19 Maii 1687. *aet. suae* 25.

Parvula pumilio Χαρίτων μία *tota merum sal.*

Parker 1692. *Conditur in hoc coemeterio* Franciscus Parker *notarius, dum vixit, publicus, procur. cur. consistor.* Ebor. *et regist. arch.* Clevelandiae. *Obiit* 17 Maii *an. sal.* 1692. *aet. suae* 80.

Sugar 1711. *Hic jacet* Nicholas Sugar *olim reg. gen. rever. archp.* Ebor. *qui post* 70 *an. nat. arthritide lassat. ab hac luce, non invite, migravit* 28 Martis *an. dom.* 1711.

Philips 1721. *Hic jacent reliquiae* Mariae Philips, *virginis ornatissimae. Posuit mater moerens, et quasi ad momentum plorans. Obiit* 2 Jun. 1721.

Forcer 1728. *Here lyes deposited the body of Mrs.* Eliz. Forcer, *a most vertuous and accomplished young gentlewoman, of noble family more noble in piety. She died* Aug. 21, 1728.

Seminatur in ignobilitate, surget in gloria.
It is laid down in obscurity, will rise in glory.

This was placed by her most affectionate sister Mary Forcer, *still weeping and with love and grief almost consumed; for they were always one heart and one soul.*

A monument of white marble with two effigies at full length, a man and woman, under them this inscription:

Squire 1707. *This monument is sacred to the memory of* Robert Squire *of the city of* York, *esquire, and* Priscilla *his wife; a man whose good nature, good sense and generosity rendered him most perfect in all the relative duties of life; and a wife worthy such a husband. He was the fifth son of* William Squire *of* Uskelf *in the west riding of* Yorkshire, *esquire, remarkable in our unhappy civil wars for his unwearied loyalty and courage, by* Ann *his second wife, daughter of* William Savile *of* Copley *in the same county, esquire; noted also for his loyalty, by* Jane *his wife, only sister and heiress to* John *lord* Darcy *of* Aston *in the said west-riding of the county of* York. Robert Squire *was born at* Uskelf-Manor *in the year* 1648, *and died at* York, Oct. 8, 1707, *where as proctor he practised the civil law, till being elected to serve his countrey in parliament he represented the borough of* Scarborough. *He was married the* 13*th day of* December 1684. *to* Priscilla *only child of* Edward Bower *of* Bridlington-key *in the east riding of* Yorkshire, *merchant, who was only son of* William Bower *of* Clenton *in the north riding of the same county, gent. She was born* Jan. 19, 1660, *and died the* 30*th of the same month* 1711. *They had one son and two daughters, the son named* Robert *died an infant, and is buried near this place. The daughters* Priscilla *and* Jane *survive them; and* Priscilla *is since married to* Bryan Cook, *esquire, eldest son to sir* George Cook *of* Wheatley, *baronet.*

ARMS impaling, 1. *Sable*, three swans necks *argent*. *Squire*. 2. *Argent*, on a chevron inter three heads erased *sable*, three mullets *or*. *Bower*. An escutcheon of pretence of the second.

White 1715. *Near this place is interred the body of Mr.* John White, *printer for the city of* York, *and the five northern counties, who departed* Jan. 10, 1715, *aged eighty.*

Αχθος Ανθρωπος.

Vavasour.

How vain a thing is man,
When God thinks meet
Oftimes with swadling clothes
To join the winding sheet?
A web of forty weeks
Spun forth in pain,

To

BOOTHAM WARD.

To his dear parents grief
Soon ravelled out again.
This babe, intombed,
Upon the world did peep,
Dislik'd it clos'd its eyes
Fell fast asleep.
Flens moerensque scripsit
VAVASOUR.

Near this place was interred Michael Fawkes, *esquire, great-grandfather to this child.*

Maii 18, 1728.

Drake 1728.

Positae juxta hanc columnam sunt exuviae
MARIAE
Francisci Drake, *inclytae huic civitati et perantiquae*
Chirurgi,
Uxoris dilectissimae;
Georgii Woodyeare *de* Crook-hill *prope* DUNI-FLUMINIS-CASTRUM *arm.*
Filiae.

Si virginem, si conjugem, si matrem spectes,
Castam, innocuam, amantem, amabilem,
Suorumque mirum in modum studiosam;
diceres.
Filiorum quinque parens, tres tantum reliquit
Superstites,
Anno aetatis tricesimo quinto.
Foeminae maritus desideratissimae
Memorem hanc moerens statuit
Tabellam.

ARMS over this last copartment:
Impaled, First, quarterly, 1. *Argent*, a wivern *gules*, a martlet difference. *Drake.* 2. *Gules*, a cross charged with five ogresses between four eagles displayed *or. Dickson.* Third as second, last as first. Second, *Sable*, inter nine flowers de luces *or*, three leopards heads proper. *Woodyeare.*

ARMS which were in the windows of this church in Mr. *Torre*'s time:
London see. *York* see. St. *William.*
Gules, a tower *or. Castile.* *Argent*, a lyon purpure. *Leon.*
York city.

This church is also adorned with many banners, escutcheons and atchievements of arms, belonging to divers very good families, whose ancestors have been buried here. But I have been already too prolix in the epitaphs, and therefore cannot insert them. I shall take leave of my parish church with observing that Mr. *Dodsworth* takes notice only of one chantry which was formerly in it, called the chantry of sir *Rauffe Bullmer*, knight, founded *anno* 1472. to pray, *&c.* at the altar of our lady in the said church, whose yearly value was 49*s.*

Stone-gate, antiently **Stayne-gate**, fronts the great minster gates. It had this name given, as is said, from the vast quantity of *stone* lead through this street for the building the cathedral. The old houses here being of wood, and most of them held by lease from the church, which is the reason that this street, though one of the most publick in the city, is but meanly built *(d)*. At the bottom of it is a small square formed at the meeting of many streets called *Cuckolds-corner*; but why it merited that opprobrious name I know not. Here is a court of some good houses, which has lately, from the owner of them, obtained the name of *Breary-court*. STONEGATE. CUCKOLD'S CORNER. BREARY COURT.

The parish church of St. *Helen*, or *Elene*, the fourth of that name which once stood in the city, or suburbs, is in *Stone-gate*. It was at first a rectory belonging to the nunnery of *Molseby*, whereunto it was appropriated. And *temp. Hen.* V. a vicaridge was therein ordained. *St.* HELEN'S *church.*

When the statute was made for uniting of churches within the city, first of *Edward* VI. this church of St. *Elens* was suppressed and defaced, because it seemed much to deform the city; being a great hindrance to some streets meeting and turning at it. The church-yard is so at this day, standing very inconvenient for the passing of coaches or carriages into *Blake-street*. However the parishioners procured an act the first of queen *Mary*, to make it lawful for them to re-edify both the church and church yard; which was done accordingly. But now there is a design revived to take off a piece of the latter, in order to render the passage for coaches to the assembly rooms in *Blake-street* more commodious.

First fruits	—	—	—	—	—	04 05 05
Tenths	—	—	—	—	—	00 08 06

(d) In this street stood anciently **Mulberry-hall**, as is proved by several ancient deeds, but where I cannot exactly tell; though I presume it stood up the little passage next Mr. *Hildyard's* the bookseller. See the *appendix*.

A C I-

A CATALOGUE of the RECTORS of St. ELENS.

Temp. instit. Anno.	*Rectores eccl.*	*Patroni.*	*Vacat.*
1232	. . . . *cler.*	*Priorissa et mon. de* Molesby.	
1250	Ric. de Lilling, *cler.*	*Eadem.*	
1273	Will. de Blyda.	*Eadem.*	
1287	Joh. Boneface, *diac.*	*Eadem.*	
1307	Ric. de Foston, *paup. cler.*	*Archiepiscopus per lapf.*	
1311	Joh. Brown, *acolitus.*	*Priorissa, &c.*	
1312	Gilber. de Ebor. *acolitus.*	*Eadem.*	
1314	Adam *filius* Rob. de Heton, *cap.*	*Eadem.*	
1326	Rob. de Huselbech.	*Eadem.*	*per resig.*
1343	Will. de Skipwith, *cap.*	*Eadem.*	*per mort.*
1349	Tho. de Langtofts, *cap.*	*Eadem.*	*per mort.*
1360	Ric. de Esewra, *cap.*	*Eadem.*	
	Will. Gysburn, *cap.*	*Eadem.*	*per mort.*
1403	Will. Sledmore, *presb.*	*Eadem.*	

A CATALOGUE of the VICARS ibidem.

Temp. instit. Anno.	*Vicarii eccl.*	*Patroni.*	*Vacat.*
	Will. de Sledmore.	*Priorissa et mon. de* Molesbey.	*per resig.*
1418	Joh. Clyveland, *presb.*	*Eadem.*	*per resig.*
1426	Hen. Money, *cler.*	*Eadem.*	*per resig.*
1446	Will. Marshall, *cap.*	*Eadem.*	*per mort.*
1475	Joh. Wynehill, *cap.*	*Eadem.*	*per resig.*
1480	Joh. Edwyn, *cap.*	*Eadem.*	
	Tho. Swyne, *presb.*	*Eadem.*	*per mort.*
1494	Joh. Rayner, *presb.*	*Eadem.*	*per resig.*
1516	Rob. Swynburn, *presb.*	*Eadem.*	*per mort.*
1517	Henry Burton, *presb.*	*Eadem.*	*per mort.*
1531	Tho. Hillary, *cap.*	*Eadem.*	*per mort.*
1533	Rob. Hardyng, *presb.*	*Eadem.*	
1632	Joh. Dugdale, *cler.*	Rex Car. I.	

Grantham's *chantry.*

(*e*) There were three chantries antiently in this church; the first founded, *anno* 1371, by *William de Grantham* merchant, who settled four messuages of one hundred pound yearly value, to find one priest to celebrate, *&c.* at the altar of St. *Mary the virgin*, situate on the south side of the said church; in which place the body of the said *William de Grantham* lies buried. Confirmed by *John* archbishop of *York*, who further ordained, that they should distribute six shillings and eight pence on the 16th of *May*, being the day of the *obit* of the said *William de Grantham*, yearly for the good of his soul. *l. s. d.*

Yearly value at the suppression ——— ——— —— 01 19 01

Hornby's *chantry.* Maii 8°. 1373.

Joan widow of *Ralph de Hornby* merchant of *York*, and *Tho. de Garton*, cap. executors to his will, having obtained the king's licence to authorize, did settle and grant according to his will, to a certain chaplain celebrating in this church at the altar of St. *Michael the archangel*, &c. and to his successors for ever, certain rents in *York*, viz.

Twenty shillings issuing out of certain tenements and a dove cote in **Walm-gate.**

Fifteen shillings out of a tenement in **Gotheram-gate.**

Twenty shillings out of one messuage in **Walm-gate**, and six shillings out of another messuage there.

Four marks *per annum* out of all his messuages in **Pickle-gate.**

Thirteen shillings and four pence out of two other messuages, and five shillings rent out of three messuages in **Stayne-gate.**

Confirmed *Aug.* 12, 1379, by *Alex.* archbishop of *York*; who further ordained an *obit* for the said *Hornby* and *Joan* his wife, annually on St. *Luke*'s day; and half a mark to be given for celebration of it. *l. s. d.*

At the suppression this chantry was rated at ——— ——— 02 06 08

Nassington's *chantry.*

There was another chantry founded in this church at the altar of St. *Mary the virgin*, by *John de Nassington.* Value, *&c.* unknown.

(*e*) Ex MS. Torre.

Monumental INSCRIPTIONS.

Exuvias hic deposuit Margareta Elmerhirste, *ux.* Ricardi Elmerhirste, *ex honesta familia* Mickletlwanorum *oriunda*; *foemina modestae et illibatae vitae, cujus virtutes ultra tumulum sunt loquaces.* Elmehurst.

Enegramma.
G . . . . . . baeret terra tales fatoque refracta
Hocque minuta latet stella corusca vide;
Quas natura polit gemmas secat, astraque reddunt
Parva galaxiam, quae reditura cadunt.

Hic situs est Tobias Conyers Conyers 1686
Apud Ebor. *canon. quondam:*
Ob. 23 Martii 1686. *Aetat.* 58.

Here lyeth the body of the worshipful John Bears *late alderman of this city, who dyed the* 54 *year of his age, upon the* 24*th of* December, 1671. *And did bequeath to the poor of this city one hundred pound, and for an anniversary sermon three pound twelve shillings* per ann. *for ever.* Bears 1671.
The righteous shall be had in everlasting remembrance.

Also here lyeth interred the lady Ann *his wife, who dyed* October 5, 1669. *Idem* 1669.

Here lyeth the body of Edward *son of* Edward Shillitoe *of this parish, who departed* Sept. 2, 1674; *being about* 20 *years of age, and gave to the poor of this parish ten pound* per ann. *and ten shillings for an anniversary sermon.* Shillitoe 1674

Here lyeth the body of William Theresby. Theresby.

Here lyeth the body of Ruth *the wife of* Edward Cooke . . . *who dyed* 1685. Cooke 1685.

This stone belongs to Mrs. Bridget Baskervile *and her children, daughter to* Humphrey Baskervile *of* Pontroybus *in the county of* Hereford *esquire*; *first wife to Mr.* Luke Thurgood, *son of Mr.* Thurgood *of* Roundy *in* Bedfordshire; *next wife to Mr.* Phineas Hodgson *son of alderman* Hodgson, *sometime lord-mayor of this city, by whome she had four sons and two daughters.* Baskervile.
If moral vertues have power souls to save,
Or natural endowments; here we have.

Hic jacet corpus Elizabethae *dilectae nuper conjugis* Richardi Achlam *de* Wiseton *in com.* Nott. *arm. et* Johannis Stanhope *de* Alta-Malwood, *infra insulam* Axholmiae *com.* Lincoln. *arm. filiae piae et cohaeredis, quae infantem mortuam enixa ob.* 7° *die* Martii *anno Dom.* 1722. *et aet.* 25. Acklam 1722
In charissimam ejus memoriam monumentum infra cancellariam eccl. paroch. de Claworth *com.* Nott. *maritus vere moestus erexit.*

Orate pro anima magist. Philippi Strangewese al. . . . . cujus anime propitietur Deus. Strangewese.

H. L. S. E. Clinch 1729.
MARTHA
Uxor Gul. Clinch *M. D.*
Viri admodum reverendi
Thomae Wagstaff Warwicensis
Filia.
Egregiis animi corporisque virtutibus
A prima etiam aetate conspicua.
Decora specie,
Pectore candido,
Praesenti ingenio
Puella.
Indolem vero
Quam praeclaram prodidit veteres
Fovit adultior.
Dotesque a natura insitas
Erudiit, auxit, expolivit.
Sermo illi castus et simul dulcis,
Actio idonea pariter et venusta,
Modestia hilaritate condita,

BOOTHAM WARD.

Innocentiae juncta urbanitas,
Sapuit
Non quam par est altius,
Non quam decuit demissius,
Alienae dignitati cedere,
Proprie consulere
Probe novit.
Animo
Sine fastu magno,
Sine sorde humili
Praedita.
Rem privatam,
Oeconomicarum rationum
Sagax arbitra,
Obiit naviter, prudentissime administravit:
Id sibi maxime agendum rata,
Ut dum frugalitati studeret
Non deesset elegantiae;
Dumque in alios propensior,
Haud iniqua in suos
Videretur.
Valetudine minus commoda diu multumque usa,
Ferre maturius patique didicit.
Utrique fortunae par,
Non otio torpuit sana,
Non dolori aegra succubuit,
Incolumi corpore mens vegeta, vivax, festiva;
Laborante placida, patiens, composita.
Obiit xiii *die mensis* April. *A. D.* M DCCXXIX. *aet.* XXXVIII.
Filiorum quos peperit Thomae *et* Gulielmi *unico superstite*
Gulielmo.
Hanc tabellam
Dulcissimae conjugis
Memoriae sacram
Moerens posuit maritus;
In eodem et ipso tumulo aliquando componendus.

Gordon 1724. *Near this place is interred the body of Mr.* David Gordon, *late mathematical teacher in this city; who died* December 21, 1724, *in a very advanced age, much lamented by all his acquaintance.*

He was a man of rare abilities both natural and acquired, an exquisite mathematician, and a great master of all useful and polite learning.

Providence placed and continued him in this town long in obscurity, where his admirable qualifications were of great service to many.

His conversation was a constant lesson of instruction, and the desire of all that knew him.

When 'ere he spoke who did not wish to hear.

ARMS which were in the windows of this church *anno* 1684.

Azure, three cheveronels brased in base and a chief *or.* *Fitzhugh.*

Gules, a fess between six cross crosslets *or.* *Beauchamp.*

Quarterly first and fourth *or,* a lion rampant *azure,* second and third *gules,* three lucies or pikefish hauriant *argent.* *Percy* and *Lucy.*

Quarterly *gules* and *azure,* in the first and fourth a leopard's head *or,* in the second and third a cup covered inter two buckles of the last. *Goldsmiths company.*

Argent, a cross of six battons *sable.* *Skirlaw.*

SWINEGATE. *Swine-gate,* old and new goes off from *Stone-gate,* in the former of which is a place called *Bennet's rents,* where a church stood dedicated to St. *Benedict.*

COFFEE-YARD. From Patrick-pol or *Swine-gate,* before mentioned, at the west end, goes a thoroughfare into *Stone-gate* called *Coffee-yard.* This name can be of no very old date, that berry having not been yet a century known in *England.* I suppose then the first *coffee-house* in *York* stood here. GRAPE-LANE. *Grape-lane* goes from the same corner into *Peter-gate;* whose name tending not a little to obscenity, as it is wrote very plain in some antient writings, I shall not pretend to etymologize. We well know our ancestors used to call a *spade a spade;* but custom has prevailed upon their descendants to be more modest in expression, whatever they are in action. However that the plainness and simplicity of our predecessors may have all due regard paid to it, I have given some authorities for the antient name of this lane in the

the *appendix*. It is very probable that this place was of old a *licenced brothel*; though so near the cathedral church as to be exactly opposite to the great gates of the *deanery*. Many of these places have been formerly so licenced, in other citys, *&c.* of *England*; particularly the bishop of *Winchester*'s stews in *Southwark*; which were kept open on that occasion till the time of *Henry* VIII; who, *abhorring such lewdness*, got an act of parliament to put them down. But that there were such open practices allowed formerly in this city, is evident from several orders about *common whores*, that I have met with in the city's registers; some of which I have given, and others will fall in the *appendix*. BOOTHAM WARD.

In *Petergate*, I end my general survey of the city and suburbs, a long and tedious march. I am very sensible how dull and tiresome it must be for the reader to follow me quite through this peregrination; but he must therefore reflect what a task it has been to the first wanderer to find his way in such a labyrinth of imperfect mazes and obscurities; and make our city appear, not only as it is at present, but as it stood in a much more flourishing condition some ages since.

CHAP.

The Arms of the several Earls and Dukes of York.

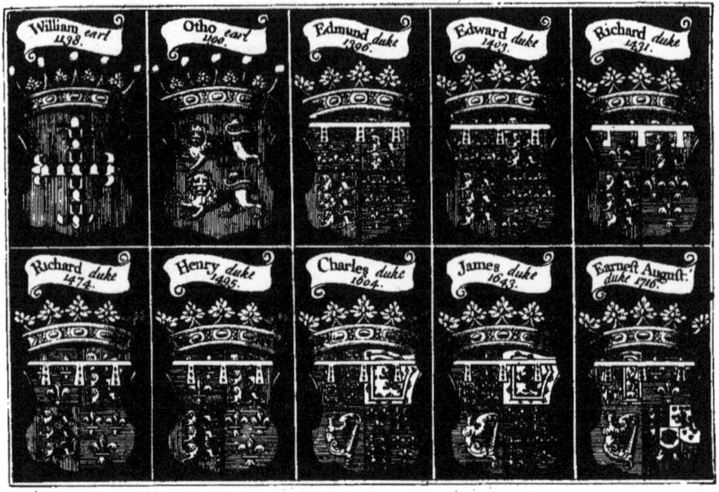

CHAP. VIII.

An historical account of the earls *and* dukes *of* York. *An exact list of all the* high sheriffs *of the county. The city's* representatives *in parliament. A catalogue of the* mayors *and* bayliffs, lord-mayors *and* sheriffs *from* anno 1274, *and upwards, to this time. The* lords presidents *of the* North, *with the learned council that attended that court at* York; *from its erection to the voting of it down by parliament. With a short account of the lives of some great and famous men, to whom this city has had the honour to give birth.*

THE reader may observe, in the annals of this work, that, before the conquest, the *comites* or earls of *Northumberland* were also governours of the city of *York*. Which, as it had been, during the *Heptarchy*, the capital and chief residence of the *Northumbrian* kings, so it continued to be the seat of the earls of that place. These presided over the county and city of *York*, as well as over the county of *Northumberland*, &c. till the confessor, as I have before taken notice, in the year 1056, after the death of *Siward*, gave the earldom of *Northumberland* to *Tosty* brother to earl *Harold*, and son to *Goodwin* earl of *Kent (a)*. I have mentioned *Morchar* to be the last earl of *Northumberland*, before the conquest, and who remained so till the fifth of the conquerour; *(b)* when after his revolt, and seizing the isle of *Ely*, *William* in the year 1069, gave this earldom to *Robert Comins (c)*, and he being slain, the conqueror then bestowed it on *Cospatric (d)*;

(*a*) *Comitatum* Eboracae Tostio *fratri comitis* Haraldi, &c. *Vide* Ingulfum *edit. antiq. f.* 510. *n.* 40.

(*b*) *Vide* H. Huntingdon *f.* 369. *n.* 30.

(*c*) *Consulatum* Northumbriae Roberti Comyns. *Vide* Hunting. *l.* 7 *f.* 211. *b.* Ordericum Vital. *f.* 512. *b.* Sim. Dunelm. *col.* 38. 198.

(*d*) *Comitatum* Northumbrorum Cospatrico. Hoveden, *parte priore f.* 159.

who

who being deprived of it in the year 1072 *(e)*; he lastly gave the earldom of *Northumberland* to *Waltheof*, the son of *Siward* *(f)*, so much taken notice of in the annals. Whether the city and county of *York* were included in this grant is disputable; it seems to me rather that it was only the present county of *Northumberland* and the bishoprick of *Durham*, over which he presided. For we read that *Waltheof* sat as judge, in temporal affairs, with *Walcher* bishop of *Durham*, in their county courts, and readily assisted that prelate with his secular authority *(g)*. The succession of the subsequent earls of *Northumberland* will be, therefore, foreign to my province, because *Yorkshire*, as I take it, was from this *aera* wholly discharged from the government of those earls, and under the jurisdiction of the *vicecomites*, *high sheriffs* of the county of *York*; under whose authority as governours of the castle of *York*, no doubt but the city was then included. These *vicecomites* were antiently substitutes to the earls, and removeable at their pleasure; but afterwards came to be annually nominated by the kings; for excepting *(h) William Mallet*, *(i) Robert Fitz-Richard*, and one or two *Estoteviles*, all of *Norman* extraction, which some would pretend were hereditary viscounts here, we read of no earl of *York* or *Yorkshire*, till a long time after the conquest.

The first mention that I find any where in history of a titular earl of this county is *(k)* *William le-Gros*, of the house of *Campaigne*, and earl of *Albermarle*, a great commander; who was by king *Stephen* after the victory over the *Scots*, at the famous battle of the Standard, in the year 1138, made earl of *Yorkshire*; or, according to some, of *York*. The arms our heralds have given this earl are, *gules*, a cross patonce vairy *(l)*. WILLIAM *first earl*, 1138.

Otho, duke of *Saxony*, son of *Henry Leon* duke of *Bavaria* by *Maud* the daughter of *Henry* II. king of *England*, in the year 1190, was created by his uncle *Richard* I. earl of *York* *(m)*. Whereupon some performed homage and fealty to him, but others refusing, the king gave him, as an exchange, the county of *Poictiers*. This prince was afterwards saluted emperor by the name of *Otho* IV; and, in the year 1200, sent ambassadors to his uncle king *John* to request the restoring the counties of *York* and *Poictiers*; which that king, by reason of the oath made by him to the king of *France* not to aid *Otho*, refused *(n)*. He bore the same arms with the first kings of *England*, which were of *Norman* descent, *viz.* on a field *gules*, two leopards or lions passant gardant *or* *(o)*. OTHO 1190.

For many years after this our city bestowed no title on any person; until *Richard* II. *anno* 1396, having called a parliament at *Westminster* in the ninth year of his *(p)* reign, amongst several other creations, *Edmund* of *Langley*, fifth son to *Edward* III. was made the first duke of *York*. This prince died and left issue by one of the daughters of *Peter*, king of *Castile* and *Leon*, two sons. EDMUND, *first duke*, 1396.

Edward Plantagenet the eldest, was first made earl of *Rutland*, then duke of *Albermarle*; and, after the death of his father, succeeded to the dukedom of *York*. He lost his life valiantly fighting, amongst the very few of the *English* that were slain, at the famous battle of *Agincourt*, on *October* 25, 1415, 3 *Henry* V, in *France*, and left no issue. His body was brought over into *England* by *Henry* V; and buried in the collegiate church of *Fotheringhay* in *Northamptonshire* with great *(q)* solemnity. *Richard* the other son was created earl of *Cambridge* at a parliament held at *Leicester*, the second of *Henry* V. He married *Anne* sister of *Edmund Mortimer*, earl of *March*; whose grandmother was the only daughter and heir of *Lionel* duke of *Clarence*, third son of king *Edward* III. This earl *Richard* attempting to set the crown upon the head of his wife's brother *Edmund* was detected, and beheaded, at *Southampton*, by the command of *Henry* V; upon the charge of being hired by the *French* to destroy him. EDWARD, 1403.

Richard his son, sixteen years after his father's death, by the great, but unwary, generosity of *Henry* VI, says my authority, was fully restored to the dukedom of *York*; as son of the last mentioned *Richard*, the brother of *Edward* duke of *York*, and cousin germain to *Edmund* earl of *March* *(r)*. Besides being duke of *York* he was earl of *March* and *Ulster*, lord of *Wigmore*, *Clare*, *Trim* and *Connaught*. This was the prince who first advanced the claim of the house of *York* to the crown of *England*; in opposition to the line of *Lancaster* then in possession of it. The duke raised some commotions against the government in order to try the affections of the people, and finding his party strong enough he at length laid claim to the crown in full parliament *(s)*. He alledged that he was son and heir to *Ann Mortimer*, sister and heir to *Edmund* earl of *March*, descended in a right line from *Philippa* the daughter and sole heir of *Lionel* duke of *Clarence*, third son of king *Edward* III; and therefore in all justice to be preferred in the succession to the crown be- RICHARD 1431.

(e) *Idem pars* 1. 454. *n.* 33.
(f) *Idem pars* 1. *f.* 260. *n.* 10.
(g) *Idem pars* 1. *f.* 260. *n.* 40.
(h) Sim. Dunelm. *col.* 198.
(i) Ordericus Vitalis *scribit quod* Robertus Richardi *filius* Eboracensis *praesidii custos cum multis peremptus est*, *anno* 1068. *f.* 512. *c.* Malet, *eadem pagina*, *vocatus est* praeses castrensis, that may be governour of *York-castle*.
(k) *Richard Hagulstad.*
(l) *Heylin.*
(m) *Hoveden's* words are that the king gave him *comitatum Eboraci*.
(n) *Idem pars* 2. *f.* 802.
(o) *Heylin.*
(p) *Parl.* 9 Ric. II. *n.* 24. *Cart.* 9 Ric. II. *n.* 26. *Pat.* 9 Ric. II. *p.* 1. *n*, 10. on the 6th of *August*.
(q) *Walsingh.* p. 393. n. 40.
(r) *Rot. parliam.* 10 Hen. VI. *Camden's* Brit.
(s) *Rot. parliam.* 39 Hen. VI. *n.* 10, *&c.*

a

fore the children of *John* of *Gaunt* the fourth son of the said *Edward*. It was among other things answered him, that the barons of the kingdom had swore allegiance to the king then reigning; that the kingdom by act of parliament was conferred and entailed upon *Hen.* IV. and his heirs; that this duke deriving his title from the duke of *Clarence* never took the arms of the said duke, and that *Henry* IV. was possessed of the crown by the right he had from *Henry* III. To this the duke of *York* replied, that the oath sworn to the king, being barely of human constitution, must not bind, because it was inconsistent with truth and justice, which are of divine appointment; that there had been no need of an act of parliament to settle the kingdom in the line of *Lancaster*, neither would they have desired it, if they could have relied upon any just title; and as for the arms of the duke of *Clarence*, which in right belonged to him, he had in prudence declined the using them as he had declined the challenging the kingdom till that moment; and that the title derived from *Henry* III, was a ridiculous pretext to cloak the injustice of the action, and was exploded by every body. These allegations, says *Camden*, pleaded strongly for the duke of *York*, and shewed his title to be clear and evident; yet by a wise foresight to prevent the dangers that might ensue upon it, the matter was so adjusted, that *Henry* VI. should possess and enjoy the kingdom for life, and that *Richard* duke of *York* should be appointed his heir and successor in it, and he and his heirs to succeed after him; with this proviso, that neither of them should contrive any thing to the prejudice of the other. But the duke, too ambitious to wait these dilatory methods, raised forces and set on foot the cruel war betwixt the *white* and *red rose* parties, in which the issue was unfortunate to himself, being slain at *Wakefield*, and his head set upon one of the gates at *York*. But it was soon after taken down by his victorious son, and buried with the body at *Fotheringhay* with the utmost solemnities.

Richard 1474. The next duke of *York* was *Richard*, called of *Shrewsbury*, second son to *Edward* IV, king of *England*, so created very young by his father, on *May* 28, 1474, 14 *Edward* IV. This unhappy prince is supposed to have been murthered with his elder brother, in the tower of *London*, by his barbarous and inhuman uncle *Richard* duke of *Glocester*.

Henry 1495. The next was *Henry*, the second son of *Henry* VII. king of *England*; who was afterwards king himself by the well known name of *Henry* VIII. From his investiture into the duchy of *York*, the kings of *England* have always used to confer that honour on the second son of the royal family.

Charles 1604. *Charles*, the second son of *James* I, king of *Great Britain*, who in *Scotland* had been made duke of *Albany*, marquiss of *Ormond*, earl of *Ross*, and baron *Ardmanoch*, was, when a child, not full four years old, created duke of *York*. By girding him with a sword, to use the words of the form, putting a cap and coronet of gold upon his head, and by delivering him a verge of gold; after the king his father, according to the usual manner, had created him, with eleven others of noble families, knights of the *Bath*. He was afterwards king of *Great Britain*.

James 1643. *James*, the second son of king *Charles*, was declared duke of *York* at his birth by his royal father; and so intituled, but not so created, till *Jan.* 27, 1643, by letters patents, bearing date at *Oxford*. For a further augmentation of his titles he had the earldom of *Ulster*, in the kingdom of *Ireland*, conferred upon him by his brother *Charles* II. *anno reg.* 10. afterwards he was king of *Great Britain*.

Ernest August. 1716. After the accession of king *George* I. to the throne, he was pleased on the 5th of *July* in the second year of his reign, 1716, to create his brother *Ernest August*, duke of *Brunswick* and *Lunenburgh*, bishop of *Osnaburgh*, earl of *Ulster* in *Ireland*, duke of *York* and *Albany* in *Great Britain* to him and the heirs males of his body, who died without issue.

A LIST of the NAMES of the VISCOUNTS or HIGH SHERIFFS of the county of YORK, *from the time of* William I. *to the present year* (*t*).

A.D.	*A. Reg.*	
	Wil. I.	
1069	3	Gulielmus Mallet (*u*).
		Robert Fitz Richard (*x*).
		Radulph Paganel (*y*).
		Hugo *vicecomes* (*z*).
	Wil. I.	
		Galf. de Estotevile.
	Hen. I.	
1118	18	Guliel. Punctell (*a*).
		Osbertus *vel* Osbertius de Archis.

(*t*) There is a list of the high sheriffs of the county of *York* printed in *Fuller*'s worthies, but very incorrect and imperfect. The present catalogue is taken from antient historians, *Doomsday book*, but chiefly from the *Pipe rolls* for the two first centuries from the conquest. The reader may observe, by comparing this list with *Fuller*'s, that it is not only much augmented, but the names of many of them corrected from that author's mistakes. The peerage of *England*, in the account of the lord *Gower*'s family, mentions one sir *Allen Gower* of *Stitnam* to be high sheriff of this county the year the conqueror came in. But as there is no authority produced for it, I take it as a compliment to that truly antient family which needs no such vain assertions to support its antiquity.

(*u*) Rog. Hoveden. &c. *Vide annal. sub hoc anno.*

(*x*) Ordericus Vital. *f.* 512. *c.*

(*y*) Lelandi *coll.* Rog. Hoveden, &c.

(*z*) *E libro* Doomesday. *Vide append.* The rest are from antient charters and the *Pipe-rolls*.

(*a*) *William Punctell* is said by *Ord. Vital.* to surrender the castle of *York anno* 1118. p. 843. he was nephew to *Rad. de Gniot*, &c. p. 846.

A. D. A. Reg.
HEN. I.
1118 18 Robert de Oketon.
STEPH.
1140 5 Bertram de Bulmer.
HEN. II.
1154 1 Bertram. de Bulmer *pro novem annis.*
1164 10 Radulph de Glanvile.
1170 16 *Idem et* Robert de Stutevile.
1171 17 Rob. de Stutevile *pro quinque an.*
1177 23 Radulph. de Glanvile *ad term. regni* Hen. II.
RIC. I.
1189 1 Radulphus de Glanvile.
1190 2 Johan. Mareschallus.
Osbertus de Longocampo.
1191 3 Osbert. de Longocampo.
1192 4 Hugo Bardulf.
Hugo de Boebi.
1193 5 *Iidem.*
1194 6 *Iidem.*
1195 7 { Galfrid. *archiep.* Ebor. *et* Rog. de Batuent (*b*) *pro quin. an.*
JOH.
1199 1 { Galfrid. *filius* Petri *et* Jacob. de Paterne.
1201 2 *Iidem.*
1202 3 { Will. de Stutevile *et* Will. Breto.
1203 4 *Iidem.*
1204 5 { Galfrid. *filius* Petri, Will. de Percy *et* Radolph. de Normanvile.
1205 6 { Galfrid. *fil.* Peter *et* Rad. de Normanvile.
1206 7 { Rob. de Lacy Const. Cestrien. *et* Robert. Walensis *pro quinque an.*
1211 12 { Galfrid. *filius* Renfredi *et* Henricus Rademan, *sive* Radenor, *pro quatuor an.*
1215 16 { Robert de Percy *et* Hen. de Midleton.
1216 17 { Petrus *filius* Herberti *et* Ric. de Husseburn.
HEN. III.
1217 1 { Galfrid. de Nevile *et* Simon de Hale.
1218 2 *Iidem.*
1219 3 *Iidem.*
1220 4 Galfrid. de Nevile.
1221 5 *Idem et* Simon de Hales.
1222 6 *Iidem.*
1223 7 *Iidem.*
1224 8 Simon de Hales.
1225 9 Eustachius de Ludham.
1226 10 *Idem et* Rob. de Cokefeld.
1227 11 Rob. de Cokefeld.
1228 12 *Idem.*
1229 13 *Idem.*
1230 14 { Will. de Stutevile *et* Phil. de Ascelles.
1231 15 *Iidem.*
1232 16 *Iidem.*

A. D. A. Reg.
HEN. III.
1233 17 Petrus de Rivall.
1234 18 Brianus de Insula.
1235 19 Johan. *filius* Galfridi
1236 20 *Idem.*
1237 21 { Brianus *filius* Alani *et* Roger de Stapleton.
1238 22 *Iidem.*
1239 23 { Brianus *fil.* Alani. Nicholas de Molis *et* Will. de Midelton.
1240 24 Nicholas de Molis.
1241 25 *Idem et* Will. de Midelton.
1242 26 { Nich. de Molis, Hen. de Bath *et* Remery de Cerve.
1243 27 Hen. de Bada *pro quat. ann.*
1247 31 Hen. de Bathon *pro duo an.*
1249 33 Will. Dacre.
1250 34 *Idem et* Rob. de Creppings.
1251 35 Rob. de Creppings.
1252 36 Will. Dacre.
1253 37 Rob. de Creppings.
1254 38 Will. de Horsenden.
1255 39 Will. le Latimer.
1256 40 { Will. le Latimer *et* Joh. de Oketon *pro quinque an.*
1261 45 Petrus de Percy.
1262 46 *Idem.*
1263 47 *Idem.*
1264 48 *Idem et* Rob. de Nevile.
1265 49 Will. de Basale.
1266 50 *Idem et* Johan. de Oketon.
1267 51 *Idem.*
1268 52 Will. le Latimer.
1269 53 *Idem.*
1270 54 *Idem.*
1271 55 { Roger. Extraneus *et* Hen. de Kirkby.
1272 56 *Iidem.*
ED. I.
1273 1 Roger. le Estraneus.
1274 2 *Idem.*
1275 3 Alex. de Kyrketon *pro quat. an.*
1279 7 Ranul. de Dacre.
1280 8 *Idem et* Joh. de Lythgrenes.
1281 9 Joh. de Lythgrenes *pro quin. an.*
1286 14 Gervasius de Clifton *pro sex an.*
1292 20 Joh. de Meaux.
1293 21 *Idem.*
1294 22 Joh. de Byrun *pro sex an.*
1300 28 Rob. Oughtred.
1301 29 Simon de Kyme *pro quat. an.*
1305 33 Will. de Houkes *pro tres an.*
ED. II.
1307 1 Joh. de Cripling.
1308 2 *Idem.*
1309 3 { Johan. de Guas *et* Johan. de Eure.
1310 4 { Gerard. de Salwayne *et* Joh. de Eure.
1311 5 *Iidem.*
1312 6 Gerard. de Salvayne.
1313 7 *Idem.*

(*b*) *Geofrey* archbishop of *York* gave three thousand marks, and one hundred marks increase of yearly rent, for having the office of the shrievalty of this county conferred upon him. Which argues it a place of great profit in those days, 10 *Ric.* I. *Maddox's* exchequer, p. 317.

1314

A. D.	*A. Reg.*	
ED. II.		
1314	8	Joh. Malebys *et* Nich. Meynel.
1315	9	Symon Warde.
1316	10	Nich. de Gray *et* Symon Warde.
1317	11	*Iidem.*
1318	12	*Iidem.*
1319	13	Symon Warde.
1320	14	*Idem (c).*
1321	15	*Idem.*
1322	16	Roger. de Somervile *pro quin. an*
ED. III.		
1327	1	Roger. de Somervile.
1328	2	Joh. Darcy.
1329	3	Hen. Falconberg.
1330	4	*Idem.*
1331	5	Rad. Bulmer.
1332	6	Petrus de Salfo Marifco. *Saltmarsh*
1333	7	*Idem.*
1334	8	Petrus de Middleton.
1335	9	*Idem.*
1336	10	Petrus de Salfo Marifco.
1337	11	Rad. de Haftinges *et* Tho. de Rokeby.
1338	12	Rad. de Haftinges.
1339	13	*Idem.*
1340	14	*Idem.*
1341	15	Joh. de Eland.
1342	16	Joh. Falconberg.
1343	17	Tho. de Rokeby *pro feptem. an.*
1350	24	Gerard. Salvayne.
1351	25	Will. de Plompton.
1352	26	Pet. de Nuttelle.
1353	27	Milo Stapleton (*d*).
1354	28	Petrus de Nuttelle.
1355	29	Milo Stapleton *mil. pro quin. an.*
1360	34	Tho. de Mufgrave.
1361	35	Marm. de Conftable.
1362	36	*Idem.*
1363	37	Tho. le Mufgrave.
1364	38	*Idem.*
1365	39	*Idem.*
1366	40	Marm. Conftable.
1367	41	*Idem.*
1368	42	Joh. Chamont *vel de calvo monte et* Will. Acton.
1369	43	*Iidem.*
1370	44	*Iidem.*
1371	45	Joh. Bygod.
1372	46	Rob. de Roos.
1373	47	Will. Acton.
1374	48	Joh. Bygod de Setterington.
1375	49	Will. Perciehay.
1376	50	Will. de Melton.
1377	51	Rad. de Haftinges.
RIC. II.		
1378	1	Joh. Conftable de Halefham.
1379	2	Rob. Nevill de Hornby.
1380	3	Joh. Savyle.
1381	4	Rad. Haftinges, *miles.*

A. D.	*A. Reg.*	
RIC. II.		
1382	5	Will. de Ergham.
1383	6	Joh. Savyle.
1384	7	Gerard. Usfleet.
1385	8	Rob. Conftable.
1386	9	*Idem.*
1387	10	Rob. de Hylton.
1388	11	Joh. Savile.
1389	12	Joh. Godard.
1390	13	Jac. Pykeryng.
1391	14	Will. de Melton.
1392	15	Rad. de Eure.
1393	16	Joh. Upeeden, *miles.*
1394	17	Jac. Pykeryng, *miles.*
1395	18	Rad. Conftable.
1396	19	Rad. de Eure.
1397	20	Rob. de Nevile.
1398	21	Jac. Pykeryng.
1399	22	Joh. Upeeden.
HEN. IV.		
1400	1	Joh. Conftable, *miles.*
1401	2	Tho. Bromflete *miles et* Will. Dronsfield *miles.*
1402	3	Joh. Savile.
1403	4	Ric. Redman.
1404	5	*Idem.*
1405	6	Will. Dronsfield, *miles.*
1406	7	Joh. de Etton, *miles.*
1407	8	Tho. Rokeby, *miles (e).*
1408	9	Will. Harrington, *miles.*
1409	10	Edward Haftings, *miles.*
1410	11	Edward. Sandford, *miles.*
1411	12	Tho. Rokeby, *miles.*
HEN. V.		
1413	1	Will. Harrington, *miles.*
1414	2	Tho. Bromflete, *miles.*
1415	3	Ric. Redman, *miles.*
1416	4	Edward. Haftings, *miles.*
1417	5	Rob. Hylton, *miles.*
1418	6	Joh. Bygod, *miles.*
1419	7	Tho. Bromflete, *miles.*
1420	8	Halnatheus Maleverer, *miles, de* Allerton.
1421	9	Will. Harrington, *miles.*
1422	10	Haln. Maleverer, *miles.*
HEN. VI.		
1423	1	Will. Harrington, *miles.*
1424	2	Rob. Hylton, *miles.*
1425	3	Joh. Langton, *miles.*
1426	4	Ric. Haftings, *miles.*
1427	5	Will. Ryther, *miles.*
1428	6	Rob. Hylton, *miles.*
1429	7	Will. Harrington, *miles.*
1430	1	John Clarevaulx.
1431	9	Will. Ryther, *miles.*
1432	10	Ric. Pykering, *miles.*
1433	11	Hen. Bromflete, *miles.*
1434	12	Ric. Haftings, *miles.*
1435	13	Will. Ryther, *miles.*
1436	14	Will. Tyrwhit, *miles.*
1437	15	Joh. Conftable de Halfham, *m.*

(*c*) **Simon Warde** gained a great victory over the barons at **Burrough-bridge**, where the earl of *Lancafter* was taken prifoner. The male line of this antient family expired in fir *Chrif. Warde* ftandard bearer to king *Henry* VIII. at *Boulogn.* Three daughters married to *Strickland*, *Mufgrave*, and *Ofborn*. *Fuller's* worthies.

(*d*) *Miles Stapleton*, one of the firft knights of the garter.

(*e*) *Tho. Rokeby* gained the victory, by the fole affiftance of his county, over the earl of *Northumberland* at *Bramham-moor*.

1438

A.D.	*A.Reg.*	
	HEN. VI.	
1438	16	Rob. Conftable, *miles.*
1439	17	Will. Ryther, *miles.*
1440	18	Joh. Tempeft, *miles.*
1441	19	Rob. Waterton, *miles.*
1442	20	Will. Gafcoign *de* Gauthorp, *miles.*
1443	21	Tho. Metham, *miles.*
1444	22	Edward Talbot *de* Bafhall, *m.*
1445	23	Will. Eure, *miles.*
1446	24	Jac. Strangeways *de* Ormfby, *miles.*
1447	25	Rob. Oughtrede, *miles.*
1448	26	Will. Plumpton *de* Plumpton, *miles.*
1449	27	Joh. Conyers, *miles.*
1450	28	Jac. Pykering, *miles.*
1451	29	Rob. Oughtrede, *miles.*
1452	30	Rad. Bygod, *miles.*
1453	31	Jac. Strangeways, *miles.*
1454	32	Joh. Melton, *jun. miles.*
1455	33	Joh. Savile, *miles.*
1456	34	Tho. Harrington, *miles.*
1457	35	Joh. Hotham, *miles.*
1458	36	Rad. Bygod, *miles.*
1459	37	Joh. Tempeft, *miles.*
1460	38	Tho. Metham, *miles.*
	ED. IV.	
1461	1	Joh. Savile, *miles.*
1462	2	Rob. Conftable, *miles.*
1463	3	*Idem.*
1464	4	Joh. Conftable, *miles.*
1465	5	Ed. Haftings, *miles.*
1466	6	Ric. Fitz-williams, *miles.*
1467	7	Jac. Harrington, *miles.*
1468	8	Joh. Conyers, *miles.*
1469	9	Jac. Strangeways, *miles.*
1470	10	Hen. Vavafour, *miles.*
1471	11	Ed. Haftings, *miles.*
1472	12	Rad. Afhton, *miles.*
1473	13	*Idem.*
1474	14	Walt. Griffith, *miles.*
1475	15	Joh. Conyers, *miles.*
1476	16	Joh. Harrington, *miles.*
1477	17	Ed. Haftings, *miles.*
1478	18	Will. Ryther, *miles.*
1479	19	Rob. Conftable.
1480	20	Hugo Haftings, *miles.*
1481	21	Marm. Conftable, *miles.*
1482	22	Rad. Bygod, *miles.*
	RIC. III.	
1483	1	Will. Eure, *miles.*
1484	2	Ed. Haftings, *miles.*
1485	3	Tho. Markenfield, *miles.*
	HEN. VII.	
1486	1	Joh. Savile, *miles.*
1487	2	Rob. Ryther, *miles.*
1488	3	Joh. Nevile, *miles.*
1489	4	Marm. Conftable.
1490	5	Hen. Wentworth *de* Woodhoufe, *miles.*
1491	6	Tho. Wortley, *miles.*
1492	7	Henry Wentworth, *miles.*
1493	8	Jac. Strangeways, *miles.*
1494	9	Marm. Conftable, *miles.*

A.D.	*A.Reg.*	
	HEN. VII.	
1495	10	Joh. Nevill, *miles.*
1496	11	Will. Gafcoign, *miles.*
1497	12	Joh. Melton, *miles.*
1498	13	Joh. Conyers, *miles.*
1499	14	Joh. Hotham, *miles.*
1500	15	*Idem.*
1501	16	Walterus Griffith, *miles.*
1502	17	Tho. Wortley, *miles.*
1503	18	Will. Conyers, *miles.*
1504	19	Rad. Ryther, *miles.*
1505	20	Joh. Cutts, *miles.*
1506	21	Rad. Eure, *miles.*
1507	22	Joh. Norton, *miles.*
1508	23	*Idem.*
	H. VIII.	
1509	1	Marm. Conftable *de* Flambo-borough, *miles.*
1510	2	(*g*) Rad. Eure, *miles.*
1511	3	Joh. Conftable, *miles.*
1512	4	Joh. Everingham, *miles*, *de* Wadfley.
1513	5	Will. Percy, *miles.*
1514	6	Joh. Norton, *miles.*
1515	7	John Carre, *miles.*
1516	8	Rad. Tempeft, *miles.*
1517	9	Will. Bulmer, *miles.*
1518	10	Joh. Nevile, *miles.*
1519	11	Pet. Vavafour, *miles.*
1520	12	Tho. Strangeways, *miles.*
1521	13	Will. Maleverer, *miles.*
1522	14	Hen. Clifford, *miles.*
1523	15	Joh. Nevill, *miles.*
1524	16	Joh. Conftable *de* Conftable-Burton, *miles.*
1525	17	Jac. Metcalf, *arm.*
1526	18	Will. Middleton, *miles.*
1527	19	Joh. Nevill, *miles.*
1528	20	Joh. Conftable, *miles.*
1529	21	Rad. Ellerker *fen. miles*, *de* Ellerker.
1530	22	Joh. Strangeways, *miles.*
1531	23	Nich. Fairfax, *miles.*
1532	24	Marm. Conftable, *miles.*
1533	25	Joh. Conftable, *miles.*
1534	26	Will. Fairfax, *miles.*
1535	27	George Darcy, *miles.*
1536	28	Bryan Haftings, *miles.*
1537	29	Hen. Savile, *miles.*
1538	30	Jac. Strangeways, *miles.*
1539	31	Will. Fairfax, *miles.*
1540	32	Rob. Nevill, *miles.*
1541	33	Hen. Savile, *miles.*
1542	34	Tho. Tempeft, *miles.*
1543	35	Tho. Dawney *de* Cowicke, *mil.*
1544	36	Nich. Fairfax, *miles.*
1545	37	Chrift. Danby, *miles.*
1546	38	Joh. Tempeft, *miles.*
	ED. VI.	
1547	1	Ric. Cholmley *de* Whitby, *m.*
1548	2	Will. Vavafour, *miles.*
1549	3	Walt. Calverley *de* Calverley, *m.*
1550	4	Leon. Beckwith *de* Aketon, *m.*
1551	5	Tho. Grefham, *miles.*
1552	6	Tho. Maleverer, *miles.*

(*g*) *Rad. Eure*, vel *Evers*, created baron by *Henry* VIII, the family had *Malton* caftle.

A.D.	*A. Reg.*	
	P. *et* M.	
1553	1	Tho. Waterton, *miles.*
1554	2	Ingram Clifford, *miles.*
1555	3	Chrift. Metcalfe, *miles.*
1556	4	Rich. Cholmley, *miles.*
1557	5	Rob. Conftable, *miles.*
1558	6	Rad. Ellerker, *miles.*
	Eliz.	
1559	1	Joh. Vaughan *de* Sutton, *arm.*
1560	2	Joh. Nevill, *miles.*
1561	3	Nich. Fairfax, *miles.*
1562	4	(*h*) Geo. Bowes *de* Stratham, *m.*
1563	5	Will. Vavafour, *miles.*
1564	6	Will. Ingleby *de* Ripley, *miles.*
1565	7	Tho. Gargrave *de* Nofthall, *m.*
1566	8	Joh. Conftable, *miles.*
1567	9	Hen. Savile, *miles.*
1568	10	Ric. Norton, *arm.*
1569	11	Tho. Gargrave, *miles.*
1570	12	Chrift. Hildyard, *miles.*
1571	13	Tho. Fairfax, *miles.*
1572	14	Joh. Dawney *de* Cowick, *arm.*
1573	15	Marm. Conftable, *miles.*
1574	16	Joh. Bellafis *de* Newborough, *m.*
1575	17	Tho. Danby, *miles.*
1576	18	Tho. Boynton *de* Barmfton, *ar.*
1577	19	Will. Fairfax, *arm.*
1578	20	Chrift. Wandsford *de* Kirklington, *miles.*
1579	21	Ric. Goodrick *de* Ribfton, *arm.*
1580	22	Rad. Bourchier, *arm.*
1581	23	(*i*) Rob. Stapleton, *miles.*
1582	24	Tho. Wentworth, *arm.*
1583	25	Cotton Gargrave, *miles.*
1584	26	Joh. Hotham *de* Scarbro' *arm.*
1585	27	Brian Stapleton, *miles.*
1586	28	Hen. Conftable *de* Conftable-Burton, *arm.*
1587	29	Rob. Afke, *arm.*
1588	30	Ric. Maleverer, *arm.*
1589	31	Joh. Dawney, *miles.*
1590	32	Phil. Conftable, *arm.*
1591	33	Ric. Goodrick, *arm.*
1592	34	Will. Mallery, *miles.*
1593	35	Rad. Eure primogen. D. Eure.
1594	36	Fran. Vaughan, *arm.*
1595	37	Chrift. Hildyard, *arm.*
1596	38	Fran. Boynton, *miles.*
1597	39	Tho. Lafcells, *arm.*
1598	40	Marm. Grimfton *de* Grimfton-garth, *arm.*
1599	41	Rob. Swyft *de* Doncafter, *arm.*
1600	42	(*k*) Fran. Clifford *de* Londefbro' *arm.*
1601	43	Will. Wentworth, *arm.*
1602	44	Tho. Strickland, *arm.*
1603	45	Hen. Bellafis, *miles.*
	Jac. I.	
	1	(*l*) Hen. Bellafis, *miles.*

A.D.	*A. Reg.*	
	Jac. I.	
1604	2	Ric. Gargrave, *miles.*
1605	3	Will. Banburgh *de* Howfam, *m.*
1606	4	Hen. Griffith *de* Agnes Burton, *miles.*
1607	5	Tim. Hutton *de* Mafk, *miles.*
1608	6	Hugh Bethell *de* Alne, *miles.*
1609	7	Fran. Hildefley, *miles.*
1610	8	Tho. Dawney, *miles.*
1611	9	Hen. Slingfby *de* Scriven, *mil.*
1612	10	Chrift. Hildyard, *miles.*
1613	11	Georg. Savile, *miles et bar.*
1614	12	Joh. Armitage *de* Kirklees, *ar.*
1615	13	Ed. Stanhope, *miles.*
1616	14	Mich. Warton *de* Beverley, *m.*
1617	15	Rob. Swyft *de* Doncafter, *mil.*
1618	16	Will. Alford *de* Bilton, *miles.*
1619	17	Arth. Ingram, *de civit.* Ebor. *m.*
1620	18	Tho. Gower *de* Stitenham, *miles et bar.*
1621	19	Ric. Tempeft, *miles.*
1622	20	Guido Palmes *de* Lindley, *m.*
1623	21	Hen. Jenkins *de* Grimfton *juxta* Ebor. *miles.*
1624	21	Ric. Cholmley, *miles.*
	Car. I.	
1625	1	(*m*) Tho. Wentworth, *mil. et bar.*
1626	2	Tho. Norcliffe *de* Manythorp, *m.*
1627	3	Tho. Fairfax, *miles.*
1628	4	Matthew Boynton, *mil. et bar.*
1629	5	Arthur Ingram, *jun.*
1630	6	Joh. Gibfon, *miles.*
1631	7	Tho. Layton *de* Layton, *miles.*
1632	8	Arthur Robinfon *de* Newby, *m.*
1633	9	Marm. Wyvil *de* Conftable-Burton, *miles et bar.*
1634	10	Joh. Hotham, *miles et bar.*
1635	11	Will. Pennyman *de* Mafke, *bar.*
1636	12	Joh. Ramfden, *miles.*
1637	13	Tho. Danby, *miles.*
1638	14	Will. Robinfon, *miles.*
1639	15	(*n*) Marm. Langdale *de* Dalton, *miles.*
1640	16	Joh. Buck *de* Filey, *miles.*
1641	17	Tho. Gower *jun. de* Stitnam, *miles.*
1642	18	Ric. Hutton *de* Goldfbro', *m.*
1643	19	Matthew Bointon *de* Barmfton, *miles et bar.*
1644	20	*Idem.*
1645	21	Joh. Bourchier, *miles.*
1646	22	Rob. Darley *de* Buttercrumb, *m.*
1647	23	Joh. Savile *de* Medley, *miles.*
1648	24	Will. S. Quintin *de* Harpham, *bar.*
	Car. II.	
1649	1	Joh. Savile *of* Lupfit, *miles.*
1650	2	Ed. Roads, *miles.*
1651	3	Geo. Marwood, *arm.*

(*h*) *Vid an fub an.* 1569.

(*i*) *Rob. Stapleton*, a lineal defcendant from fir *Miles*, married one of the coheirs of fir *Henry Sherrington*, by whom he had a numerous iffue.

(*k*) *Fran. Clifford*, he afterwards fucceeded his brother *George* in his honours and earldom of *Cumberland*, he was father to *Henry* the fifth and laft earl of that family, whofe fole daughter was married to the earl of *Cork*.

(*l*) *Hen. Bellafis*, created by *Car.* I. baron *Falconbridge* of *Yarum*.

(*m*) Afterwards earl of *Strafford*.

(*n*) Created by *Car.* II for his extraordinary loyalty baron *Langdale* in *April* 1658, two years before the *Restoration*.

Car. II.

A. D.	A. Reg.	
	CAR. II.	
1652	4	Hugh Bethell *jun. de* Rise.
1653	5	Will. Constable *de* Flambro', *miles et bar.*
1654	6	*Col.* Joh. Bright *of* Badsworth.
1655	7	John Bright.
1656	8	Thomas Harrison, *esq*;
1657	9	*The same.*
1658	10	Barrington Bourchier, *esq*;
1659	11	Robert Waters, *esq*;
1660	12	*Sir* Thomas Slingsby, *bart.*
1661	13	*Sir* Thomas Osborne, *bart.*
1662	14	*Sir* Thomas Gower *of* Stitnam, *knight and baronet.*
1663	15	*Sir* Roger Langley *of* Sheriff-Hoton, *bart.*
1664	16	*Sir* Francis Cobb, *knt.*
1665	17	*The same.*
1666	18	*Sir* John Reresby, *bart.*
1667	19	*Sir* Rich. Mauleverer, *knight and baronet.*
1668	20	*Sir* John Armitage, *bart.*
1669	21	*Sir* Philip Monckton, *knt.*
1670	22	*Sir* Solomon Swale, *bart.*
1671	23	*Sir* Will. Wentworth, *knt.*
1672	24	John Ramsden, *esq*;
1673	25	*Sir* Tho. Yarborough, *knt.*
1674	26	Henry Marwood, *esq*;
1675	27	*Sir* Edw. Jennings, *knt.*
1676	28	*Sir* Godfrey Copley, *bart.*
1677	29	*The same.*
1678	30	Rich. Shuttleworth, *esq*;
1679	31	*Sir* Thomas Daniel, *knt.*
1680	32	*Sir* Rich. Grahme *of* Norton-Coniers, *bart.*
1681	33	Will. Lowther, *esq*;
1682	34	Ambrose Pudsey, *esq*;
1683	35	*Sir* Brian Stapylton, *bart.*
1684	36	Christ. Tancred, *esq*;
	JAM. II.	
1685	1	Christ. Tancred, *esq*;
1686	2	Thomas Rookeby, *esq*;
1687	3	*The same.*
1688	4	*Sir* Rich. Grahme, *displaced, and in* April 1689.
	G. III. M.	
1689	1	William Robinson, *esq*;
1690	2	*Sir* Jonathan Jennings, *knt.*
1691	3	Henry Fairfax, *esq*;
1692	4	John Gill, *esq*;

A. D.	A. Reg.	
	G. III. M.	
1693	5	Ambrose Pudsey, *esq*;
1694	6	Charles Tancred, *esq*;
1695	7	Ingleby Daniel, *esq*;
1696	8	John Bradshaw, *esq*;
1697	9	Thomas Pulleine, *esq*;
1698	10	Will. Lowther, *esq*;
1699	11	John Lambert, *esq*;
1700	12	Fairfax Norcliff, *esq*;
1701	13	Robert Constable, *esq*;
	ANNÆ.	
1702	1	Robert Mitford, *esq*;
1703	2	*Sir* Tho. Pennyman, *bart.*
1704	3	Tho. Pulleine, *esq*;
1705	4	Godfrey Bosville, *esq*;
1706	5	*Sir* Mathew Pierson, *knt.*
1707	6	*Sir* Roger Beckwith, *bart.*
1708	7	Henry Iveson, *esq*;
1709	8	Will. Ellis, *esq*;
1710	9	Will. Turbutt, *esq*;
1711	10	Will. Neville, *esq*;
1712	11	Will. Vavasour, *esq*;
1713	13	Richard Beaumont, *esq*;
1714	13	Thomas Wrightson, *esq*;
	GEOR. I.	
1715	1	Fairfax Norcliffe, *esq*;
1716	2	Charles Wilkinson, *esq*;
1717	3	*Sir* Will. Hustler, *knt.*
1718	4	*Sir* Henry Goodrich, *bart.*
1719	5	Daniel Lascelles, *esq*;
1720	6	John Bourchier, *esq*;
1721	7	*Sir* Walter Hawkesworth, *bart.*
1722	8	*Sir* Ralph Milbank, *bart.*
1723	9	*Sir* Will. Wentworth, *bart.*
1724	10	Hugh Cholmley, *esq*;
1725	11	Cholmley Turner, *esq*;
1726	12	Tho. Ramsden, *esq*;
1727	13	Charles Bathurst, *esq*;
	GEO. II.	
1728	1	Thomas Duncombe *of* Duncombe-park, *esq*;
1729	2	William Harvey, *esq*;
1730	3	*Sir* Will. S. Quintin, *bart.*
1731	4	Bielby Thompson, *esq*;
1732	5	*Sir* Rowland Wynne, *bart.*
1733	6	Thomas Condon, *esq*;
1734	7	Hugh Bethell, *esq*;
1735	8	Francis Barlow, *esq*;

A CATALOGUE of the REPRESENTATIVES *in* PARLIAMENT *for the city of* YORK, *from the first summons and returns, beginning* anno regni EDWARD I. 23. *(o)*

West.	23 Ed. I.	Nicholas de Seleby. Roger Basy.
York,	26 Ed. I.	Joh. Le espicer. Nic. Clarevaux.
York.	28 Ed. I.	John de Sezevaux *(p)*. Gilbert de Arnald.
Lincoln.	28 Ed. I.	Joh. de Askam. And. de Bolingbroke.
Westm.	33 Ed. I.	Thomas le Anguiler. John de Sezevaux.
Westm,	34 Ed. I.	John de Graham. Roger de Roston.

(o) Mr. *Willis*, from whose papers I corrected and much enlarged this list, remarks that *Prynn* says citizens were elected and returned *anno* 49 *Hen.* III. but he adds, that their names are not to be met with in any of our records.

(p) De Sezevaux, or *de sexdecem vallibus*, is the town on the *Wolds*, now called *Thixendale*; corruptly, no doubt, from *sixteen dales*; which the place is remarkable for.

Carlisle,

Carlisle,	35 Ed. I.	John de Askam.
		John de Sezevaux.
Northᵒ.	1 Ed. II.	Joh. de Askam.
		Joh. de Ebor.
Westm.	2 Ed. II.	Tho. de Norfolke.
		Nic. Grantbridge.
Westm.	4 Ed. II.	Joh. de Graa.
		Tho. Aguiler.
Lond.	5 Ed. II.	Tho. de Alwerthorpe.
		Joh. Segge.
Westm.	6 Ed. II.	Tho. de Redness.
		Nic. Sezevaux.
Westm.	7 Ed. II.	Nic. Sezevaux.
		Joh. de Appelton.
Westm.	8 Ed. II.	Joh. de Appelton.
		Rog. Ughtred.
Westm.	12 Ed. II.	Joh. de Sexdecim vallibus.
York, iidem.		Hen. Calvert.
York,	15 Ed. II.	Hen. Calvert,
		Tho. de Rednefs.
Westm.	19 Ed. II.	Joh. de Askam.
		Symon de Kingston.
Westm.	20 Ed. II.	Will. de Rednefs.
		Hen. de Bolton.
York,	1 Ed. III.	Tho. de Rednefs.
		Nic. Sezevaux.
Lincoln,	———	Ric. Tannock.
		Tho. de Montefort.
Winch.	2 Ed. III.	Will. Fox.
		Will. de Baronia.
Northᵒ.	———	Tho. de Pontefracto.
		Joh. de Burton.
N. Sarum,	3 E. III.	Tho. de Gargrave.
		Joh. de Kyrkeby.
Northᵒ.	4 Ed. III.	Will. Fox.
		Tho. Middlestone.
York,	6 Ed. III.	*Cedula deest.*
York,	———	Will. Fox.
		Galf. Aldwark.
Westm.	7 Ed. III.	Tho. de Pontefracto.
		Joh. de Ryppon.
Westm.		Nic. de Scoreby.
York.		Ric. de Brickinhale.
Westm.	9 Ed. III.	Joh. de Bristow.
		Nic. de Appleby.
York.		Steph. de Setherington.
		Nic. de Scoreby.
Nott.	10 Ed. III.	Ric. de Briggenhale.
		Hen. Goldbeter.
Westm.	11 Ed. III.	Ric. de Briggenhale.
		Alex. Goldbeter.
Westm.		Nic. de Scoreby.
		Hamo de Hessay.
Westm.	12 Ed. III.	Joh. de Sezevaux.
		Hen. Calvert.
Westm.		Joh. de Womme.
		Rob. Sprottle.
Westm.		Joh. de Womme.
		Ric. de Saugerry.
Westm.	13 Ed. III.	Hamo de Hessay.
		Gilb. Picklington.
Westm.	14 Ed. III.	Walt. de Keldsterne.
		Hen. Goldbeter.
Westm.		Tho. *fil.* Ricardi.
		Joh. Ichon.
Westm.	15 Ed. III.	Hen. Goldbeter.
		Walt. de Keldstern.
Westm.	17 Ed. III.	Tho. de Rednefs.
		Joh. de Heton.
Westm.	20 Ed. III.	Joh. de Sherburne.
		Ric. de Setterington.
Westm.	21 Ed. III.	Will. Graa.
		Walt. Keldsterne.
Westm.	22 Ed. III.	Will. Graa.
		Will. Skipwith.
Westm.	24 Ed. III.	Rog. Noringwill.
		Walt. Kelleterne.
York,	26 Ed. III.	Hugo de Miton.
		Joh. de Creyke.
Westm.		(p) Hamo de Hessay.
Westm.	27 Ed. III.	Will. Graa.
		Hamo de Hessay.
Westm.	29 Ed. III.	Rog. de Normanville.
		Will. Graa.
Westm.	30 Ed. III.	Will. Graa.
		Rog. Henningham.
	33 Ed. III.	Tho. Auguber.
		Joh. de Sexdecim vallibus.
		Rog. de Henningham.
Westm.	34 Ed. III.	Joh. de Gisburn.
Westm.		Will. Graa.
Westm.	36 Ed. III.	Joh. de Allerton.
		Rog. de Selby.
Westm.	38 Ed. III.	Will. Graa.
		Rob. Hawton.
Westm.	39 Ed. III.	Will. Graa.
		Joh. de Acastre.
Westm.	43 Ed. III.	Will. Graa.
		Joh. de Acastre.
Win.	45 Ed. III.	Will. Graa.
Westm.	46 Ed. III.	Will. Graa.
		Rob. Hawton.
Westm.	47 Ed. III.	Joh. de Gisburn.
		Joh. de Astre *vel* Acastre.
Westm.	50 Ed. III.	Tho. Graa.
		Joh. Eshton.
Glouc.	2 Ric. II.	Joh. de Acastre.
		Tho. Graa.
Westm.	3 Ric. II.	Tho. Graa.
		Rog. de Moreton.
Westm.	6 Ric. II.	Will. Savage.
		Will. Selby.
N. Sarum,	7 Ric. II.	Tho. Graa.
		Will. Selby.
Westm.	8 Ric. II.	Tho. Quixley.
		Joh. de Hoveden.
Westm.	9 Ric. II.	Tho. Graa.
		Tho. de Hoveden.
Westm.	10 Ric. II.	Tho. Graa.
		Rob. Savage.
Westm.	11 Ric. II.	Tho. Holkore.
		Joh. de Hoveden.
Cambr.	12 Ric. II.	Joh. de Hoveden.
		Joh. de Ryppon.
Westm.	13 Ric. II.	Will. de Selby.
		Joh. de Hoveden.

(p) *Hamo*, or *Hamond, de Hessay* was sent up singly to assist at a council at *Westminster*. To these councils were seldom returned above one member, it was chiefly called together to consult about trade and traffick. So *anno* 34 *Ed.* III. *Will. Graa* was returned singly for the same reason. Again *anno* 45 *Ed.* III.

Westm

Westm. 18 Ric. II.	Tho. Graa. Will. Selby.
Westm. 20 Ric. II.	Tho. Graa. Will. Selby.
Warw. 1 Hen. IV.	Will. Frost. John Bolton.
Warw. 3 Hen. IV.	Rob. Token. Rob. Warde.
Glouc. 8 Hen. IV.	Rob. Tolken. Joh. de Bolton.
Warw. 12 Hen. IV.	Will. Ickham. Will. Rose.
Westm. 1 Hen. V.	Tho. Santon. Will. Alvey.
Westm. 2 Hen. V.	Rog. Howam. Joh. Northeby.
Westm. 3 Hen. V.	Will. Alvey. Will. Bowes.
Westm. 5 Hen. V.	Tho. Santon. Joh. Blackburn.
Westm. 7 Hen. V.	John Northeby. *(r)* Thomas Gare.
Westm. 8 Hen. V.	Joh. Penreth. Hen. Preston.
Westm. 9 Hen. V.	John Gave. Will. Ormshevell.
Westm. 1 Hen. VI.	Will. Bowes. Ric. Russell.
Westm. 2 Hen. VI.	Joh. Northby. Peter Buksby.
Westm. 3 Hen. VI.	Ric. Russell. Joh. Auldstanmore.
Leic. 4 Hen. VI.	Will. Bowes. Will. Ormsheved.
Westm. 6 Hen. VI.	Joh. Bolton. Tho. Snawden.
Westm. 7 Hen. VI.	Joh. Auldstanmoor. Joh. Bolton.
Westm. 9 Hen. VI.	Will. Bowes. Will. Ormsheved.
Westm. 11 Hen. VI.	Joh. Louth. Tho. Kirkham.
Westm. 13 Hen. VI.	Ric. Wartyr. Will. Bedale.
Camb. 13 Hen. VI.	Will. Bowes, *jun.* Ric. Louth.
Lond. 20 Hen. VI.	Tho. Ridley. Will. Girlington.
Camb. 25 Hen. VI.	Tho. Crathorn. Will. Stockton.
Westm. 27 Hen. VI.	Joh. Karr. Joh. Thresk.
Westm. 28 Hen. VI.	Tho. Barton. Joh. Catherick.
Westm. 29 Hen. VI.	Joh. Thresk. Will. Hauke.
Reading, 31 H. VI.	Tho. Dantry. Tho. Nelesort.
Westm. 38 Hen. VI.	Nic. Holgate. Joh. Marton.
Westm. 39 Hen. VI.	*The same.*
7 Ed. IV.	*(s)* . . . .
Westm. 12 Ed. IV.	Rich. Yorke. Tho. Wrangwish.
Westm. 17 Ed. IV.	Miles Metcalfe. Rob. Amyas. *Many returns wanting.*
Westm. 14 H. VIII.	Thomas Button. John Norman.
Westm. 33 H. VIII.	John Hogeston, *gent.* George Gayle, *ald.*
Westm. 1 Ed. VI.	Tho. Gargrave, *esq;* Will. Holme.
Westm. 6 Ed. VI.	*Schedula deest.*
Warw. 1 Mary.	John North, *gent.* Robert Hall, *gent.*
Oxford, 1 Mary.	John Beyne. Rich. White.
1, 2. P. M.	*The return lost.*
Westm. 2, 3.	Will. Holme, *ald.* Reginald Beesly, *gent.*
Westm. 3, 4.	Will. Holme, *gent.* Rob. Peycock, *gent.*
Eliz. 1	William Watson. Rob. Goldthorp, *ald.*
5.	William Watson, *gent.* Ralf Hall, *gent.*
13.	Ralf Hall, *gent.* Hugh Graves, *gent.*
14.	George Pocock, *ald.* Hugh Graves, *ald.*
27.	Will. Robinson, *ald.* Robert Brooke, *ald.*
28.	Will. Hilliard, *esq;* Rob. Brooke, *ald.*
31.	Rob. Askwith, *ald.* Will. Robinson, *ald.*
35.	Andrew Trew, *ald.* Jacob Birkby, *ald.*
39.	Jacob Birkby, Tho. Mosely, *ald.*
43.	John Bennet, *LL. D.* Henry Hall, *ald.*
1 James I.	Robert Askwith, *ald.* Christopher Brook, *esq;*
12	*This return wanting.*
18	*Sir* Robert Askwith, *knt.* Chrift. Brook, *esq;*
21	*Sir* Arthur Ingram, *knt.* Chrift. Brook, *esq;*
1 Charles I.	*Sir* Arthur Ingram, *knt.* Chrift. Brook, *esq;*
1	*The same.*
3	*Sir* Arthur Ingram, *knt.* *Sir* Thomas Savile, *knt.*
15	*Sir* Edward Osborn, *bart.* Henry Vane, *esq;*
16	*Sir* Will. Allenson, *knt.* Thomas Hoyle, *ald.*

(r) This return is not taken notice on by Mr. *Willis*; I had it from our own records. They are styled *cives et mercatores Ebor.* The same 14 *Hen.* VIII.

(s) Ult. die Sept. *an.* 2 Ed. *quarti* it was ordained and agreed by the assent of the council of the city, yet for als mykel as nowe late some aldermen being at the parliaments in time passed have gone to borde, wheras yai have at all times tofore holden house for the worship of the cite, yet fro hencefurth what alderman soever shall go to parliament and will hold house, shall have for his costs daily iiii *s.* and if he go to borde he shall have but ii *s.* upon the day and no more fro nowe forth. *E registro in cam. sup. pont.* Usae.

Rump Parliaments.

Westm.	1648	Sir *William Allenson*, knt.
		Thomas Hoyle.
	1654	Sir *Tho. Widdrington*, knt.
		Thomas Dickenson, ald.
	1656	The same.
	1658	Sir *Thomas Dickenson*, knt.
		Christopher Topham, esq;
	12 Char. II.	*Sir* Tho. Widdrington, *knt.*
		Metcalf Robinson, *esq;*
	13	(*t*) *Sir* Tho. Osborne, *bart.*
		Sir Henry Tomson, *knt.*
		Sir Metcalf Robinson, *bar.*
	29	*Sir* John Hewley, *knt.*
		Sir Hen. Thompson, *knt.*
	30	*The same.*
Oxf.	31	*The same.*
Westm.	1 James II.	*Sir* John Reresby, *bart.*
		Sir Metcalf Robinson, *bar.*
	1 W. *et* M.	*Hon.* Peregrine *Viscount* Dunblane.
		Edward Thompson, *esq;*
		Robert Waller, *ald.*
		Henry Thompson, *esq;*
	2 W. *et* M.	Robert Waller, *ald.*
		Edward Thompson, *esq;*
	7 Will. III.	Edward Thompson, *esq;*
		Tobias Jenkins, *jun. esq;*
	10	*Sir* Will. Robinson, *knt.*
		Tobias Jenkins, *jun. esq;*
	12	*Sir* Will. Robinson, *bart.*
		Tobias Jenkins, *jun. esq;*
	13	Tobias Jenkins, *mayor.*
		Sir Will. Robinson, *bart.*
	1 Anne.	*Sir* Will. Robinson, *bart.*
		Tobias Jenkins, *esq;*
	4	*Sir* Will. Robinson, *bart.*
		Robert Benson, *esq;*
	7	*Sir* Will. Robinson, *bart.*
		Robert Benson, *esq;*
	9	*The same.*
	12	*Sir* Will. Robinson, *bart.*
		Robert Fairfax, *esq;*
	1 George I.	*Sir* Will. Robinson, *bart.*
		Tobias Jenkins, *esq;*
	8	*Sir* William Milner, *bart.*
		Edward Thompson, *esq;*
	1 Geor. II.	*Sir* Will. Milner, *bart.*
		Edward Thompson, *esq;*
	8	*Sir* John Lister Kaye, *bar.*
		Edward Thompson, *esq;*

The election of members of parliament for this city is now very popular and tumultuous, but anciently it was otherways. For instead of every freeman of the city, resident or non-resident in it, having a vote in these elections, which is the case at present, I find in the old register-books that two citizens were formerly nominated to represent the city in parliament by the bench alone, and after by the bench and commons. An instance of the latter as low as the 26th of queen *Elizabeth* I give from the register as follows:

28th *Oct.* 26 *Eliz.*

" Assembled in the councell chamber upon *Ouze-bridge* the day and year abovesaid, when and where the queen's majesty's writ of election for two burgesses of this city was read in this court: And also these commoners, *viz. William Gilmyn, William Allen, James Stocke, John Stephenson, Robert Pearson, John Metcalf*, sen. *John Bilbowe, George Middleton, Oswald Dent, Robert Myers, William Beckwith*, draper, *Richard Huton, Parcyvall Levet, William Gibson, Edward Exilby, Thomas Waller, Christopher Turner, John Pinder, William Scott*, mercer, *William Young, Nicholas Haxup, Thomas Wilson, John Carter, Francis Newby, Lancelot Cowpland, Rowland Fawcet, John Clithero, Thomas Elwodd, George Tirry, George Kitching, Richard Whittington, William Maskewe, Simond Butterfield, George Clivicke, Henry Preston, Henry Wilkinson*, free-holders of this city, did now personally appear in this court, and were present at the reading of the said writ: And then afterwards went into the chequer court, and then and there having with them a clerk, did privately give their voices, as appeareth by a paper of their said voices hereunto annexed, and by their most voices they did chouse Mr. *Robert Asquith*, Mr. *William Robinson*, Mr. *Robert Brooke*, and Mr. *Christopher Maltby*, aldermen, as four elects for the said burgesses, and brought the same before this assembly, who one after another did give their private voices to the election of two of the said aldermen to be burgesses: And so Mr. recorder with a clerk taking their voices, by the most voices of these presents, the said Mr. *William Robinson* and *Robert Brooke* are now nominated to be burgesses for this city. And it is now further agreed by these presents, that on *Monday* the ninth of *November* next, the said Mr. *Robinson* and Mr. *Brooke* shall be published and nominated burgesses for the said city in the county court there; and all the said persons who was at the said election to be commanded to be then present at the said county: And that a letter of attorney shall be made to the said burgesses under the common seal as hath been accustomed.

9 *Nov.* 26 *Eliz.*

" Assembled at the councel chamber upon *Owse-bridge* the day and year abovesaid, and then the said lord-mayor and this assembly went into the sheriff's court, and then the queen's majestie's writt for choosing of two Burgesses was read openly, and then the

(*t*) Made a peer this parliament. Earl of *Danby*. Afterwards created duke of *Leeds*. Sir *Metcalf Robinson* returned in his room.

" said

" said lord-mayor, aldermen, and freeholders which were present at the nomination of the " said burgesses the 28th of *October*, did fully consent, chuse, and elect *William Robinson* and " *Robert Brook* aldermen to be burgesses, and then one pair of indentures were presently sealed " by my lord-mayor and twenty four, in the names of all the rest of freeholders of the one " part, and the sheriffs of the other part."

An ACCOUNT *of the* POLL *for the city of* YORK, *in the three last contested elections.*

Candidates, anno 1713.	*Sir* William Robinson, *bart.*	1368.
	Robert Fairfax, *esq*; — —	835.
	Tobias Jenkins, *esq*; — —	802.
(*u*) *Candidates* anno 1714.	*Sir* William Robinson, *bart.* —	1388.
	Tobias Jenkins, *esq*; — —	1225.
	Robert Fairfax, *esq*; — —	844.
Candidates, anno 1722.	*Sir* William Milner, *bart.* —	1421.
	Edward Thompson, *esq*; —	1399.
	Tancred Robinson, *esq*; —	1076.
Candidates, anno 1734.	*Sir* John Lister Kaye, *bart.*	
	Sir William Milner, *bart.*	
	Edward Thompson, *esq*;	

Three days before the election sir *William* gave up his pretensions; so that the other two were chosen without opposition. And to the eternal honour of the citizens of *York*, the first named worthy gentleman was sent for by them and elected without the least expence to him, but that of purchasing his freedom and paying the necessary fines to the city.

A CATALOGUE *of the* MAYORS *and* BAYLIFFS, LORD-MAYORS *and* SHERIFFS *of the city of* YORK *from* anno 1273, 1 EDWARD I, *and upwards, to the present year.*

Circa an. 1140 Nigell *was mayor of* York *in the time of* Stephen (*x*).
Circa an. 1195 Drugo Berentine *in the reign of* Richard I.
Took Flower, *father of St.* Robert *of* Knaresborough, *was twice mayor of* York *in the same reign* (*y*).
An. 1219 Thomas Palmer *mayor* (*y*).
Circa An. 1225 Henry de Sexdecim Vallibus, *or* Sezevaux, *mayor in the time of* Henry III (*y*).
An. 1230 Hugo de Seleby *mayor* (*z*).

A. D.	*A. Reg.* HEN. III.			
1249	33	Nicholas Orgar *mayor* (*z*).	Will. Fairfax,	*Bayliffs* (*z*).
1252	36	John de Seleby *was mayor* (*z*).	John de Warthill,	
1257	41	Gacius de Calvo Monte, *mayor* *, *or* Chamont.	Hen. de Sezevaux,	
			Martin de Norfoulk,	
1259	43	Hugo de Cressy *mayor* (*z*).	Will. de Brinkelan,	
1260	44	*The same* (*z*).		
1263	47	John de Seleby *mayor*.	Ivo de Usegate, Simon le Graunt, John de Conynton,	*Bayliffs* (*z*).
1271	56	Walter de Stokes, *mayor* (*z*). Adam de Cerf, *mayor* (*b*).	William de Holteby, John Spery, Ivo de Usegate,	*Bayliffs*.

A.D.	*A. Reg.* ED. II.	MAYORS (*c*).	BAYLIFFS.
1273	1	John le Espeeer *sen. aut* (*d*) Apotecarius.	Gilb. de Luda *or* Luye, Hen. de Holtby, Joh. de Conyngton.
1274	2	Rob. de Bromholme.	Hen. de Holtby, Joh. de Sutton, Joh. de Conyngton.

(*u*) In this contest, as appears by the numbers compared with the former, about four hundred freemen were made to serve a turn, at the expence of one of the candidates. The introduction of so many poor people into the city, is sensibly felt by it now, and will be so hereafter.

(*x*) *Stowe*'s chron. *Leland*. coll. *&c*.

(*y*) Sir *T. W.* from publick records.

(*z*) The leigerbook of *Fountain's abbey*, as witnesses, See the *appendix*.

(*a*) This name occurs in *Maddox's* exchequer, when he says, that the city was taken into the king's hands for disobedience in not paying their ferm, p. 645.

(*b*) From an old record in the *Fairfax* family as witnesses.

(*c*) This list from *anno* 1273, is taken chiefly from lawyer *Hildyard*'s, printed *anno* 1664; except, where upon good authority, as antient charters, publick records, *&c.* I have found reason to alter it.

(*d*) *John le Espicer* is called *Johannes Apotecarius*, as a witness to an old grant to *Fountain*'s. *Le espicer* is an old *French* term for what we now call a druggist. In *Italian* an apothecary is called, so at this day.

A. D.	*A. Reg.*	Mayors.	Bayliffs.
	Ed. II.		
1275	3	John de Bromholme 1.	Rob. Blunde, Rob. del Moore, And. de Bullingbroke.
1276	4	John de Bromholme 2.	Nic. de Selby, Pet. de Santon, Will. Sleight.
1277	5	John de Bromeholme 3.	Nic. le Espicer, Nic. de Selby, Roger Basy.
1278	6	Walter de Stokes.	John le Espicer, John de Conyngston, Joh. de Sutton.
1279	7	Walter de Stokes.	Steph. le Tughler, Rog. de Bonevill, John de Conynston.
1280	8	*These three years the city was in the king's hands, and* Richard de Rummundeby *was* custos *of it.*	
1281	9		
1282	10		
1283	11	*Sir* John Sampson 1.	John del Lissington, Will. Sleghte, Rob. Worall.
1284	12	*Sir* Gilb. de Luda *or* Luye.	Rog. de Carlton, Clem Pontefract, Hugh de Sutton.
1285	13	*Sir* John Sampson 2.	Nich. de Langton, Joh. Hawyse, Nich. de Selby.
1286	14	Nich. de Selby 1. 2. 3.	Peter de Appleby, Remeris Spery, Nic. le Blund.
1287	15		
1288	16		
1289	17	*In the king's hands.*	Peter de Santon, Adam Warthill, Ralph Wyles.
1290	18	Roger Basy 1.	*The same.*
1291	19	John le Espicer 1.	Will. Lyngtayle, Steph. le Caldronne, Rob. de Hessay.
1292	20	*These five years the government of the city was in the king's hands,* anno 1292, Roger de Esingwald, *and after sir* John de Melsa, *or* Maux, *knights were governours of it.*	
1293	21		
1294	22		
1295	23		
1295	24		
1297	25	Nich de Langton 1.	Simon Sichman, John Boni, John de Schupton.
1298	26	James le Fleming 1.	Laur. le Fleming, Will. Langley, Rob. Meeke.
1299	27	John Sampson, *knt.* 3.	Tho. de Appleby, Ralp. de Jayrum, Laur. Flower.
1300	28	John Sampson, *knt.* 4.	Will. de Ouseney, Nich. de Pocklinton, Will. Operye
1301	29	John le Espycer 1. *son of the former* John.	Gilb. Arnald, Ral. de Lincolne, Tho. de Selby.
1302	30	John le Espicer 2.	Rob. de Walton, And. Bullingbroke, Will. Durant.
1303	31	John le Espicer 3.	Will. de Useburn, Barth. de Newcastle, Vinc. Verdenell.
1304	32	John le Espicer 4.	Tho. Borovit, Walt. Whitem, Rob. de Lyndsey.
1305	33	And. de Bolingbroke 1.	Joh. de Appleby, Walt. Gower, Walt. Fleming.
1306	34	Nic. de Langton 2.	*The same.*
	Ed. II.		
1307	1	John de Askam 1.	Rog. de Allerton, Rog. de Roston, Ad. Stockfield.
1308	2	John de Askam 2.	Ad. de Pocklington, Giles Brabance, Ad. Stockfield.
1309	3	And. de Bullingbroke 2.	Will. de Rednefs, Ric. de Catton, Adam Stockfield.
1310	4	Rob. le Meeke 1.	Will. de Rednefs, Will. Gromsley, Ric. de Bilbrough
1311	5	Nich. le Fleming 1.	Tho. Agviler, Rob. de Wistow, Will. de Grantham.
1312	6	Nich. le Fleming 2.	Walt. de Scourby, Joh. de Lecestre, Will. de Useburn
1313	7	Nich. le Fleming 3.	Allan de Appleby, Joh. de Beverley, Nich. de Catton
1314	8	Nich. le Fleming 4.	John de Eseby, Allan Sleight, Joh. le Fysche.
1315	9	Nich. le Fleming 5.	Walt. de Scotton, Ric. de Duffeld, Will. de Abbay.
1316	10	Nich. le Fleming 6.	Tho. de Alverthorpe, Nic. de Colonia, Ric. le Toller
1317	11	Rob. le Meeke 2.	Adam de Kingston, Jordan Savage, Thomas Davy.
1318	13	Tho. de Rednesse.	Will. Fox, Will. de Dureme, Rob. de Selby.
1319	13	Nich. le Fleming 7.	John Raine, John Bachelsay, John Orback.
1320	14	Rob. le Meeke 3.	Henry Calvehird, Rich. Tinmack, John Scoreby.
1321	15	Rob. le Meeke 4.	Nich. Saxter, John de Selby, Will. de Fryston.
1322	16	Nich. Langton 1. *eldest son to the former* Nich.	Nich. Foulks, Rob. de Molsby, Rob. del Wald.
1323	17	Nich. de Langton 2.	Joh. de Colne, Nigel. le Potter, Rich. de Balne.
1324	18	Nich. de Langton 3.	Joh. Housum, Tho. Bilham, And. Bossale.
1325	19	Nich. de Langton 4.	Simon Gower, Will. Icon, Ric. de Tickhill.
	Ed. III.		
1326	1	Nich. Langton 5.	*The same.*
1327	2	Nich. Langton 6.	John Wome, Nich. Scoreby, Will. Hockam.
1328	3	Nich. Langton 7.	Will. Rednefs, Will. Selby, John Pichard.
1329	4	Nich. Langton 8.	Hen. de Belton, Tho. Askam, Will. Batnell.
1330	5	Nich. Langton 9.	Steph. Setterington, Ric. Brigenhall, Tho. Marefchal.
1331	6	Nich. Langton 10.	Will. de Bourgbrigg, Joh. de Catton, Joh. de Moreby
1332	7	Nich. Langton 11.	Hen. le Colbeter, Will. Fyske, Will. Estrington.
1333	8	Nich. Langton 12.	Will. Grantham, Ric. Lecestre, Will. Region.
1334	9	Hen. de Belton 1.	Rich. de Lecestre, Miles de Grafton, Will. le Spuryer.

A. D.	*A. Reg.* Ed. III.	Mayors.	Bayliffs.
1335	10	Hen. de Belton 2.	Will. de Sherburn, John de Bristol, Will. Caperon.
1336	11	Hen. de Belton 3.	John de Shurburn, Ric. de Sezay, Ric. Kelsterne.
1337	12	Hen. de Belton 4.	John Dorant, John Danby, Abel Hessell.
1338	13	Nich. Langton.	Will. de Holme, Rad. de Staynegrene, Joh. de Sourbye.
1339	14	Hen. de Belton 5.	Hugh de Miton, Rob. Skalton, Rob. Askeby.
1340	15	Nich. Langton 15.	John Redman, John Hansard, Will. de Grantham.
1341	16	Nich. Langton 16.	John de Acom, John de Rypon, John Cooke.
1342	17	Nich. Langton 17.	Rob. Walsh, Ric. Farome, Will. Fox.
1343	18	Nich. Foukes.	Will. de Sutton, Tho. de Estrington, Joh. de Eshton.
1344	19	John de Shereburn 1.	Simon Kingston, John Tuck, John de Coupenthorpe.
1345	20	John de Shereburn 2.	Will. de Akastre, Rob. de Selby, Will. de Hovingham
1346	21	John de Shereburn 3.	Will. Grai, Will. Pearcy, Tho. Yorke.
1347	22	Hen. le Goldbeter.	John Langton, Tho. Myton, Rob. Lydyate.
1348	23	Hen. Scorby 1.	Will. Skelton, Tho. Duffield, Will. Hatchington.
1349	24	Hen. Scorby 2.	Rob. de Lindeshay, Hen. de Manfield, Tho. Menningthorpe.
1350	25	Hen. Scorby 3.	Tho. Sigston, Will. Bell. Rob. Lindeshay,
1351	26	Hen. Scorby 4.	John de Clervaux, Nich. Santon, Will. Swetmouth.
1352	27	Hen. Scorby 5.	Hugh Myton, Roger Osbaldwyke, Ric. Amcoats.
1353	28	John Langton 1.	Will. de Swanland, Hen. Godburne, John Firebose.
1354	29	John Langton 2.	John de Alverton, Will. de Beverley, Rob. de Howme
1355	30	John Langton 3.	Will. Burton, Ric. Seaton, Rob. Faceby.
1356	31	John Langton 4.	Will. Savage, Hen. Kelfeld, Rob. de Skelton.
1357	32	John Langton 5.	John de Scoreby, John de Waldby, John de Rypon.
1358	33	John Langton 6.	Will. Farriner, John de Acastre, Tho. de Strensal.
1359	34	John Langton 7.	Rog. de Selby, Rob. de Crayke, Rog. Strickhill.
1360	35	John Langton 8.	Ralph de Hornby, Will. Frankes, Rob. de Ampleford.
1361	36	John Langton 9.	John de Sancton, John de Knapton, Rich de Barnby.
1362	37	John de Acaster 1.	Rich. Parrat, John de Knapton, John de Crome.
1363	38	John Langton 10.	Joh. de Twyselton, Rich. de Thoresby, Rob. de Pothowe.
1364	39	John de Acaster 2.	Rob. de Pothowe, Rob. del Gare, Simon Couke.
1365	40	Rich. Waldeby.	John Senehowe, Geo. Coupmanthorpe, Rob. Sutton.
1366	41	Rog. de Hovingham.	Rog. de Morton, Rob. Barry, Joh Barrester.
1367	42	Will. Graie.	John Youle, Tho. Holme, John Welande.
1368	43	Rob. de Holme.	Rog. de Morton, John Lasynby, John Clayton.
1369	44	Will. Savage *ob. in officio.*	Will. Burton, Will. Couper, Hugo de Haukswell.
1370	45	Roger de Selby.	Hen. de Ribston, Ric. de Waghen, Will. Gyry.
1371	46	John de Gyseburn 1. *merc.*	Rob. de Harome, Pet. Toulthorp, Ric. Acaster.
1372	47	John de Gyseburn 2.	Will. Tendew, Will. Hovingham. John Swerd.
1373	48	Rog. de Moreton.	John Bowden, John de Beverley, John de Poynton.
1374	49	Tho. de Howome.	Will. de Selby, John de Paythorn, Ric. de Cawthorn.
1375	50	Ralph de Hornby.	Sim. de Quixley, Will. de Helmsley, Rob. de Duffield.
1376	51	Tho. Graa . . .	Rob. Savage, John de Braithwait, John de Howden.
	R. II.		
1377	1	John de Sancton.	Tho. de Stanley, John de Darington, Tho. de Morton.
1378	2	John de Berden.	Tho. Smith, Hugh Dymock, John Wrayby.
1379	3	John de Acaster.	John de Sheffield, Elias Litester, Will. Tickill.
1380	4	John de Gysburn 3.	Rob. Ward, Rob. de Talkan, Rich. de Alne.
1381	5	Simon de Quyxley 1.	Will. Agland, Will. Golding, Will. de Pountfrayt.
1382	6	Simon de Quyxley 2.	Simon Clapham, Simon de Alne, Hen. de Bolton.
1383	7	Simon de Quyxley 3.	John de Whixley, Will. Fysshe, Will. de Bridsell.
1384	8	Simon de Quyxley 4.	Const. del Dam, Rich. de Santon, Tho. de Kelfield.
1385	9	Rob. Savage 1. *merch.*	Will. Dereham, Will. Yereby, John Thornton.
1386	10	Will. de Selby 1.	Hen. de Yarum, Will. Yereby, Rob. Wreach.
1387	11	John de Howeden.	Adam del Bank, John de Bolton, John Sesay.
1388	12	Will. de Selby 2.	Hen. Wyman, John de Stillington, Will. Lindsey.
		Lord-Mayors.	
1389	12	Will. de Selby 3. *first sword.*	John de Askam, Rob. Louth, John Lindsley.
1390	13	Tho. Smith 1.	John Todde, Kear Bakyrsaxther, John de Topcliffe,

A. D.	A. Reg.	Lord-Mayors.	Bayliffs.
	H. IV.		
1391	14	Tho. Smith 2.	Tho. de Doncaster, Will. Bickhead, Will. Haunby.
1392	15	Rob. Savage 2.	John Craven, Will. Hessay, Joh. Perith.
1393	16	Rob. Savage 3. *first mace.*	John Booth, Tho. Hornby, Rog. de Roston.
1394	17	Tho. de Stayvelay 1.	Nich. Warthill, Adam Delstok, Hugh Charter.
1395	18	Will. Helmsley.	John Raghton, Tho. del Gare, Rob. Bothe.
1396	19	Tho. Stavyelay 2.	Will. Redhead, Tho. Ruston, Will. Alne.
			Sheriffs.
1397	20	*Sir* Will. Frost, *knt.*	John Moreton, Tho. Howden.
1398	21	Tho. Gare.	Will. Selby, John Hewyke.
1399	22	Rob. Talken.	Rob. Howome, Will. Scawsby.
	H. IV.		
1400	1	*Sir* Will. Frost, *knt.* 2.	Tho. Doncaster, John Barnacastle.
1401	2	*Sir* Will. Frost, *knt.* 3.	John Wranby, Edward Cottsbrook.
1402	3	*Sir* Will. Frost, *knt.* 4.	Will. Bowes, Will. de Lee.
1403	4	*Sir* Will. Frost, *knt.* 5.	Adam Bridge, Thomas Santon.
1404	5	*Sir* Will. Frost, *knt.* 6.	Rich. Howe, Henry Preston.
1405	6	John del Bank.	John de Bedale, Joh. Wythen.
1406	7	*Sir* Will. Frost, *knt.* 7.	Rob. Kirkby, John Useburn.
1407	8	Hen. Wyman 1.	Tho. Hasle, Will. Marston.
1408	9	Hen. Wyman 2.	John Moreton, Rob. Gare.
1409	10	Hen. Wyman 3.	John Northby, Rob. del Gare.
1410	11	John Bolton.	Tho. del More, Rob. Lokton.
1411	12	John Craven.	Peter Buckcy, Tho. Esingwald.
	H. V.		
1412	1	Rob. Howom 1. *merch.*	Ric. Russell, John Pettyclerk.
1413	2	Nich. Blackburn 1. *merc.*	*No sheriffs.*
1414	3	Tho. de Santon.	Will. Winkburn, Godfrey Savage.
1415	4	Will. Alne, *merch.*	Will. Ormsheved, Ric. Spencer.
1416	5	John Northby *merch.*	Tho. Bracebridge, Ric. Burton.
1417	6	Will. Bowes 1. *merch.*	John Vaughan, Ric. Snawden.
1418	7	John de Moreton.	Rob. Yarum, John Lofthouse.
1419	8	John de Bedale.	Rob. Middleton, John Bainbrigg.
1420	9	Tho. del Gare.	John Bolton, Tho. Davy.
1421	10	Rich. Russel 1. *merch.*	John Lilling, Joh. Gascoign.
1422	11	Hen. Preston.	John Aldestonmar, Tho. Aton.
	H. VI.		
1423	1	Tho. Esingwald, *merch.*	Will. Craven, Tho. Kirkham.
1424	2	Tho. Bracebrigg, *merch.*	John Warde, John South.
1425	3	Will. Ormsheved, *merch.*	Will. Bedale, Will. Gateshed.
1426	4	Peter Buckcy.	Ric. Louth, John Dodyngton.
1427	5	John Aldestanmoor, *mer.*	Tho. Bromflete, Will. Girlington.
1428	6	Will. Bowes 2.	Nich. Blackburn, Tho. del Carre.
1429	7	Nich. Blackburne 2. *sen.*	Tho. Gare, John Raughton.
1430	8	Rich. Russel 2.	John Ratcliff, Tho. Catterick.
1431	9	John Bolton, *merch.*	Ric. Wartyr, Will. Bellford.
1432	10	Tho. Snawden, *pewterer.*	Will. Bowes, John Esingwald,
1433	11	Will. Ormeshed 2.	Tho. Kirk, Tho. Rotheram *ob.* Tho. Rokesby *elect.*
1434	12	Tho. Gayer.	Nich. Wyspyngton, Nich. Usflete.
1435	13	Tho. Kirkham.	Tho. Rydeley, Rob. Ebchester.
1436	14	Ric. Wartyr 1. *merch.*	John Thrusk, Ric. Bugden.
1437	15	Will. Bedale, *merch.*	Rich. Shorewood, Will. Burton.
1438	16	Nich. Usflete, *merch.*	Nich. Blackburn, Rob. Gray *ob.* Will. Stockton *elect.*
1439	17	Tho. Ridley.	Will. Northby, John Crosier.
1440	18	Will. Girlington, *draper.*	Will. Holbeck, Will. Dauby.
1441	19	Tho. Kirke, *mercer.*	Tho. Delgare, Will. Aberford.
1442	20	John Thruske 1. *merch. mayor of the staple.*	Tho. Craythorne, John Turpin.
1443	21	Will. Bowes.	Hern. Market, Tho. Burton.
1444	22	Ric. Buckden, *merch.*	Tho. Catterick, John Goodall.
1445	23	Tho. Crathorne.	Will. Cliffe, Ric. Claybroke.
1446	24	Will. Stockton.	Rob. Collinson, Will. Staines.
1447	25	John Crosyer.	Tho. Scausby, Ric. Thornton.
1448	26	John Carpe.	Ric. Lematon, Tho. Nelson.
1449	27	Will. Holbeck, *merchant of the staple.*	Nich. Holbeck, Rob. Pert.
1450	28	Tho. Burton, *grocer,*	John Morton, Tho. Curtoise.

A.D.	A.Reg.	LORD-MAYORS.	SHERIFFS.
		H. VI.	
1451	29	Rich. Wartyr 2.	Tho. Beverley, William Barlow.
1452	30	Tho. Dauby, *merchant.*	John Strenfal, Tho. Dangel.
1453	31	John Catterick.	John Gylliot, John Boure.
1454	32	Tho. Nelfon 1. *merchant.*	John Glafyn, Will. Wright.
1455	33	Rich. Lematon.	Will. Bracebrigg, Will. Sherewood.
1456	34	John Carre.	John Ince, Will. Cleveland.
1457	35	Rob. Collinfon, *merchant.*	Tho. Helmfley, Will. Sheffield.
1458	36	Will. Holbeck 1.	Tho. Bromflete, John Marfhal.
1459	37	Nich. Holgate.	John Copeland, Will. Bradley.
1460	38	Tho. Beverley, 1. *mer. of the ftaple*	Chrift. Booth, John Marfhall.
		ED. IV.	
1461	1	John Stockton.	John Kent, Rich. Claybrook.
1462	2	John Thrufke.	Will. Skynner, Chrift. Marfhal.
1463	3	Tho. Scawfby.	Will. Thorp, John Semper.
1464	4	John Gilliot, *knight of the* Bath.	Will. Crofby, John Coates.
1465	5	Tho. Nelfon 2.	John Brearton. Will. Snawfdale.
1466	6	John Kent, *merchant.*	Rich. Yorke, Tho. Catoure.
1467	7	John Marfhall 1. *merchant.*	Tho. Strangeways, John Towthorpe.
1468	8	Will. Snawfdell.	Will. Welles, John Leathley.
1469	9	Rich. Yorke, *knt.* 1. *merchant of the ftaple.*	Will. Lambe, John Tonge.
1470	10	Will. Holbeck 2.	Rob. Amias, Tho. Glafyn.
1471	11	Tho. Beverley 2.	John Lightlampe, Tho. Allen.
1472	12	Will. Holbeck 3.	Hen. Stockton, Rob. Harwood.
1473	13	Chrift. Marfhall.	John Ferriby, Will. Knowles.
1474	14	*Sir* John Gylliot, *knt.* 2.	Hen. Williamfon, Tho. Marriot.
1475	15	Will. Lamb.	John Newton, Will. Chimney.
1476	16	Tho. Wrangwifh 1.	Allen Wilberfofs, Tho. Stockton.
1477	17	John Tonge.	Will. Todde, Nich. Pierfon.
1478	18	John Ferriby 1. *merchant.*	Rob. Hancock, Will. Spencer.
1479	19	William Welles.	Rob. Gill, Will. Tayte.
1480	20	John Marfhall 2.	John Hagge, Mich. White.
1481	21	Rob. Amyas.	John Harper, Will. White.
1482	22	Rich. Yorke, *knt.* 1. *mayor of the ftaple.*	Tho. Peirfon, Miles Greenbanke.
		RIC. III.	
1483	1	John Newton, *dyer.*	Rich. Hardfong, Will. Barker.
1484	2	Tho. Wrangwifh, 2. *merchant.*	John Gilliot, Tho. Finch.
		HEN. VII.	
1485	1	Nich. Lancafter 1. *LL. D.*	John Beverley, Roger Appleby.
1486	2	Will. Chimney, *draper.*	John Beafley, John Shaw.
1487	3	Will. Todd, *knt. merchant.*	George Kirke, Rob. Johnfon.
1488	4	Rob. Hancock, *grocer.*	Tho. Falneby, Tho. Gray.
1489	5	John Harper, *merchant.*	Will. Barker, Alex. Dawfon.
1490	6	John Gilliot 1. *merchant.*	John Elwood, John Norman.
1491	7	John Ferriby *ob. in offi.* Will. White *elect.*	John Stockdale, John Hutton.
1492	8	Tho. Scotton, *merchant.*	Peter Cooke, Edward Forfter.
1493	9	Nich. Lancafter, 2. *LL. D. mer.*	Tho. Darby, John Cuftance.
1494	10	Michael White 1. *dyer.*	John Metcalf, John Petty.
1495	11	George Kirk 1. *merchant.*	Will. Nelfon, Rich. Thornton.
1496	12	Rob. Johnfon, *grocer.*	Miles Arwayn, Bertram Dawfon.
1497	13	Tho. Gray *goldfmith.*	Tho. Jamefon, John Dodfon.
1498	14	John Metcalf, *merchant.*	John Birkhead, Rich. Winder.
1499	15	John Elwald, *merchant.*	Allan Stavely, Rob. Petty.
1500	16	William Nelfon, *merchant.*	George Effex. Tho. Bankhoufe.
1501	17	John Stockdale, *merchant.*	Will. Skipton, Tho. Freeman.
1502	18	Rich. Thornton, *grocer.*	John Lincolne, Tho. Parker.
1503	19	*Sir* John Gilliot 2. *merchant.*	John Ellis, Tho. Braikes.
1504	20	Tho. Jamefon, *merchant.*	John Hall, Oliver Middleton, *ob.* Rob. Simpfon *elect.*
1505	21	Michael White 2.	Will. Willfon, Thomas Drawfword.
1506	22	Allan Staveley 1. *merchant.*	Roger Sawyer, Rich. Tew.
1507	23	John Birkhead, *merchant.*	John Beifby, Will. Huby.
1508	24	*Sir* John Petty, *knt. glafier, ob. in officio.*	John Thornton, John Bateman.

1509

A.D.	*A. Reg.*	LORD-MAYORS.	SHERIFFS.
	H.VIII.		
1509	1	George Essex, *apothecary.*	John Langton, John Greggs.
1510	2	John Shawe 1. *merchant.*	Will. Garnet, John White.
1511	3	Bertram Dawson, *merchant.*	Will. Wright, Will. Cary.
1512	4	George Kirk 2.	John Chapman, Chrift. Horner.
1513	5	Will. Willson, *goldsmith.*	Simon Viccars, Rich. North.
1514	6	John Thornton, *merchant.*	Paul Gillour, John Norman.
1515	7	Tho. Drawsword 1.	John Rasin, John Geldart.
1516	8	John Hall, *tanner.*	John Wetherell, Will. Barker.
1517	9	John Dodgson.	Tho. Dawson, John Gillbank.
1518	10	Will. Wright 1.	Tho. Burton, Tho. Mason.
1519	11	Allan Stavely 2.	Rob. Whitfield, Henry Holme.
1520	12	Tho. Parker.	Peter Jackson, Rob. Wilde.
1521	13	Tho. Bankhouse *ob in offi. draper* Simon Vickars *elect.*	Rob. Fowes, Tho. Gregge.
1522	14	Paul Gillour *ob. in offi. merchant,* Tho. Burton *elect.*	John Marshall, Tho. Bayley.
1523	15	Tho. Drawsworde 2.	James Blaides, Rich. Hutchenson.
1524	16	John Norman.	Hen. Dawson, John Rogers.
1525	17	Will. Barker 1.	Hugh Hawley, Rob. Cornot.
1526	18	Peter Jackson.	Ralph Pullein, John Smith, John Lister.
1527	19	Rob. Wylde, *merchant.*	John Hodgson, John Richardson.
1528	20	Tho. Mason.	John Shaw, John Collier.
1529	21	Rob. Whitfield.	John North, Rich. Simpson.
1530	22	George Lawson, *knt.*	George Gaile, Hen. Bielby.
1531	23	Henry Dawson.	Will. Harrington, Laur. Mouslome.
1532	24	Will. Barker 2.	Rob. Elwald, Will. Dodshon.
1533	25	John Hodgson.	Rob. Hall, John Plowman.
1534	26	George Gaile, *goldsmith.*	John Shadlock, Rob. Cooke.
1535	27	Will. Wright 2.	Rob. Heckleton, Will. Holme.
1536	28	Will. Harrington.	John Edwyn, Will. Swann.
1537	29	Ralph Pullein, *goldsmith.*	John Lewis, Peter Liddal.
1538	30	John Shawe 2. *ob. in officio,* John North *elect.*	Peter Robinson, John Beane.
1539	31	Rob. Elwald, *merchant.*	Tho. Thornton, Rich. Tomlinson.
1540	32	Will. Dodgson, *merchant.*	Rob. Peacock, Ric. Savage.
1541	33	Rob. Hall, *merchant.*	Will. Watson, Will. Harper.
1542	34	John Shadlock.	Tho. Appleyard, John Dobson.
1543	35	Rob. Heckleton, *fishmonger.*	Will. Beckwith, Will. Coupland.
1544	36	Peter Robinson, *merchant.*	Rich. White, Mich. Binkes.
1545	37	John Beane 1. *inholder.*	Ralph Elwick *ob. in officio,* Martin Soza, Rich. Foxgill.
1546	38	Will. Holmes.	Rob. Broddys, Peter Eshe.
	Ed. VI.		
1547	1	Will. Watson, *merchant.*	Tho. Standeven, James Simpson.
1548	2	Rob. Peacock 1. *merchant.*	Will. Batchelor, Tho. Goodyear.
1549	3	George Gaile 2.	James Harrington, George Hutchenson.
1550	4	John Lewis, *draper.*	Percival Crawforth, Edmund Greenbury.
1551	5	Tho. Appleyard.	Rich. Goldthorp, John Shillitoe.
1552	6	Rich. White, *draper.*	Tho. Lawson, Tho. Willson.
	P. *et* M.		
1553	1	Will. Coupland.	Ralph Hall, Will. Hargill.
1554	2	John North 2.	Rob. Cripling, Will. Grisdale.
1555	3	Will. Beckwith 1. *merchant.*	Rich. Breary, Rob. Hogge.
1556	4	Rich. Gouldthorpe.	Adam Binkes, Rich. Drew.
1557	5	Rob. Hall 2.	Chrift. Hall, Chrift. Liddal.
	Eliz.		
1558	1	Ralph Hall, *merchant.*	John Hall, Will. Brogden.
1559	2	Tho. Standeven.	Hugh Greaves, Tho. Harper.
1560	3	James Harrington.	Rich. Calome, Edward Willcocks.
1561	4	Parcival Crawforth.	Martin Straker, John Robinson.
1562	5	Tho. Lawson.	Will. Harrison, Tho. Harrison *ob.* Leon. Temple *elect.*
1563	6	Tho. Appleyard 2.	Rob. Maskew, John Weddel.
1564	7	Jacob Simpson, *tanner.*	Tho. Middleton, Will. Thompson.
1565	8	John Beane 2.	Edmond Richardson, John Smith.
1566	9	Will. Watson 2.	Gregory Peacock, Rich. Allen.

A.D.	A. Reg.	LORD-MAYORS.	SHERIFFS.
	Eliz.		
1567	10	Rob. Peacock, *merchant.*	Christ. Herbert, John Dincly.
1568	11	Will. Coupland.	Will. Robinson, And. Treve.
1569	12	Will. Beckwith 2.	Peter Hudless, John Wilkinson.
1570	13	Rich. Calom, *draper.*	Hen. Maye, Tho. Middleton.
1571	14	Gregory Peacock, *merchant.*	Jacob Birkby, Edward Turner.
1572	15	Will. Allen, *mercer.*	Ralph Micklethwait, Rob. Askwith.
1573	16	Christ. Herbert, *merchant.*	John Stephenson, Tho. Temple.
1574	17	Rob. Maskewe, *grocer.*	Rob. Brook, Tho. Jackson.
1575	18	Tho. Harrison 1. *inn-holder,*	Tho. Appleyard, Christ. Moltby.
1576	19	Ed. Richardson *ob. in off. pewt.* Ralph. Hall, *merchant. elect.*	Edmund Sands, Walter Mudd,
1577	20	John Dynely, *draper.*	Ralph Richardson, George Faucett.
1578	21	Hugh Graves, *merchant.*	Laur. Robinson, Edward Vavasour.
1579	22	Rob. Cripling.	Fran. Mapples, Edward Faucett.
1580	23	Rob. Askwith 1. *draper.*	Rob. Maude, Leon. Belt.
1581	24	Will. Robinson 1. *merchant.*	Christ. Beckwith, Rich. Morton.
1582	25	Rob. Brooke 1. *merchant.*	Christ. Concett, John Standeven.
1583	26	Christ. Maltby, *draper.*	Percival Brooke, Tho. Moseley.
1584	27	Thomas Appleyard.	Fran. Baine, Rob. Watter.
1585	28	Andrew Trene, *merchant.*	Rowland Faucett, Will. Gibson.
1586	29	Henry Maye, *innholder.*	Rob. Peacock, Henry Hall.
1587	30	Ralph Richardson, *merchant.*	Leon. Beckwith, John Weddel.
1588	31	James Birkby, *council attorney.*	Will. Peacock, James Mudd.
1589	32	Tho. Jackson, *council attorney.*	Marm. Sotheby, Will. Allen.
1590	33	Tho. Moseley 1. *merchant.*	Will. Calome, John Yewdale.
1591	34	Rob. Watter 1. *haberdasher.*	Tho. Herbert, Christ. Turner.
1592	35	Tho. Harrison 2.	Rob. Dawson, Tho. Askwith.
1593	36	Rob. Askwith 2.	Will. Wood, John Harrison.
1594	37	Will. Robinson 2.	Rob. Myers, Will. Greenbury.
1595	38	Robert Brooke 2.	George Watson, George Elwyke.
1596	39	Jacob Birkby.	George Watkinson, George Hall.
1597	40	Christ. Beckwith.	George Rosse, Percival Levett.
1598	41	Edward Faucett, *not. pub.*	Laur. Wade, Will. Breary.
1599	42	Christ. Concett 1. *apothecary.*	Rob. Askwith, Tho. Willson.
1600	43	Hen. Hall, *merchant.*	Laur. Edwards, John Busfield.
1601	44	Rob. Peacock.	Rob. Harrison, Henry Thompson.
1602	45	Tho. Moseley 2.	John Robinson, George Bucke.
	Jac. I.		
1603	1	*Sir* Rob. Watter, *knt.* 2.	Mich. Hartford, Rich. Binkes.
1604	2	Tho. Herbert, *merchant.*	Will. Sunley, Leon. Besson.
1605	3	Will. Greenbury, *draper.*	Elias Micklethwaite, George Aislaby.
1606	4	Rob. Askwith 1. *draper.*	John Wadsworth, Will. Maskew.
1607	5	Rob. Harrison, *merchant.*	Will. Robinson, Tho. Marshall.
1608	6	Rob. Miers 1. *mercer.*	Christ. Dickenson, John Standeven.
1609	7	Christ. Concett 2. *apothecary.*	Edward Cross, James Godson.
1610	8	Hen. Hall, 2.	Will. Morton, George Watson.
1611	9	Will. Breary 1. *merchant.*	Mich. Scarr, Edward Calvert.
1612	10	John Harrison, *merchant.*	Will. Watter, Tho. Agar.
1613	11	Tho. Marshall, *mercer.*	Mat. Topham, Tho. Kay.
1614	12	Leonard Besson 1. *sadler.*	Rob. Belt, Fran. Waide.
1615	13	Elias Micklewait, *merchant.*	George Faucett, Tho. Rawden.
1616	14	Will. Greenbury 2.	Fran. Wharton, Tho. Lawne.
1617	15	*Sir* Rob. Askwith, *knt.* 2.	John Hutchenson, Rob. Weddall.
1618	16	Tho. Agar, *tanner.*	Christ. Croft, Peter Middleton.
1619	17	Will. Robinson, *merchant.*	Abraham Hemmingway, Christ. Waid.
1620	18	Will. Watter, *sadler.*	Edmund Cooper, Rob. Hemsworth.
1621	19	Christ. Dickenson, *merchant.*	Tho. Hoyle, John Vaux.
1622	20	Rob. Myers 2.	Leon. Weddel, Will. Allenson.
1623	21	Will. Breary 2.	Christ. Topham, Rich. Hertford.
1624	21	Mathew Topham, *merchant.*	James Hutchenson, Leon. Jackson.
	Car. I.		
1625	1	Tho. Lawne.	Will. Scott, Will. Todde.
1626	2	Leon. Besson 2.	Tho. Hodgson, Will. Wharton.
1627	3	Elias Micklethwaite 2.	Hen. Thompson, Tho. Atkinson.
1628	4	Robert Belt, *merchant.*	Tho. Dawson, Roger Jaques.
1629	5	Christopher Croft 1. *mercer.*	Tho. Peigher, John Miers.

A. D.	*A. Reg.*	LORD-MAYORS.	SHERIFFS.
	CAR. I.		
1630	6	Edmund Cooper 1. *merchant.*	John Pepper, John Bradley.
1631	7	Robert Hemſworth, *draper.*	James Brooke, Tho. Hewley.
1632	8	Thomas Hoyle 1. *merchant.*	Phil. Herbert, John Geldart.
1633	9	*Sir* Will. Allenſon, *knt.* 1. *draper.*	Tho. Herbert, Will. Willſon.
1634	10	James Hutchenſon, *merchant.*	Steph. Watſon, Geo. Pullin.
1635	11	Thomas Hodgſon, *mercer.*	John Maſon, Tho. Maſterman.
1636	12	Henry Thomſon 1. *merchant.*	Rob. Horner, John Beake.
1637	13	John Vaulx, *prothonotary.*	Will. Ramſden, Will. Fairweather.
1638	14	Will. Scott, *merchant.*	Chriſt. Breary, Marm. Croft.
1639	15	*Sir* Roger Jaques, *knt. merchant.*	Leon. Thompſon, Simon Coulton.
1640	16	*Sir* Robert Belt, *knt.* 2.	Tho. Dickenſon, Paul Beale.
1641	17	*Sir* Chriſtopher Croft, *knt.* 2.	Tho. Caley, John Calvert.
1642	18	*Sir* Edmund Cooper, *knt.* 2.	Sam. Breary, Jonas Spacy.
1643	19	*Sir* Edmund Cooper, *knt.* 3.	John Kilvington, James Breary.
1644	20	*Sir* Edmund Cooper, *knt.* 4. *Diſplaced.* Tho. Hoyle *put in.*	Will. Taylor, Tho. Naylor.
1645	21	John Geldart, *merchant.*	Rob. Scott, Tho. Driffield.
1646	22	Stephen Watſon, *grocer.*	John Peighen, Edw. Gray.
1647	23	Thomas Dickenſon 1. *merchant.*	Chriſt. Topham, Barth. Watman.
	CAR. II.		
1648	1	Robert Horner 1. *merchant.*	Rich. Pagett, Tho. Maſon.
1649	2	Leonard Thompſon 1. *merchant.*	Hen. Tyreman, Peter Man.
1650	3	William Taylor, *merchant.*	Creſſy Burnet, Geo. Peacock.
1651	4	James Brooke 1. *merchant.*	Bryan Dawſon, Fran. Eubank.
1652	5	William Metcalf, *draper.*	Will. Siddal, *obiit.* Tho. White, *elect.* Ric. Newton.
1653	6	Henry Thompſon 2.	Ralph Chayter, George Mancklin.
1654	7	John Geldart 2.	Chriſt. Hewley, Will. Waſſe.
1655	8	*Sir* William Allenſon 2.	Rich. Hewit, Rich. Booth.
1656	9	Stephen Watſon.	Nich. Towers, *ob.* Henry Shaw, *elect.* Fran. Mawburn.
1657	10	Thomas Dickenſon 2. *knighted by* Oliver.	George Scott, York Horner.
1658	11	Robert Horner 2.	William Barwick, Will. Richardſon.
1659	12	Leonard Thompſon 2.	Will. Wilkinſon, Tho. Reynolds.
1660	13	Chriſtopher Topham, *merchant.*	Will. Pannet, John Peacock, *ob.* William Kitchinman.
1661	14	James Brooke 2. *by the king's mandate.*	Fran. Wheelwright, Rich. Shaw.
1662	15	George Lamplugh, *merchant.*	Tho. Williamſon, Joh. Beares.
1663	16	Henry Thompſon, *merchant.*	Tim. Squire, Geo. Gleadſtone.
1664	17	Edward Elwick, *apothecary.*	Phil. Herbert, Rich. Tenant.
1665	18	Richard Hewit, *merchant.*	Edw. Gaile, Abraham Faber.
1666	19	George Mancklin, *ſkinner.*	Rich. Metcalf, Joh. Morley.
1667	20	Creſſy Burnet, *merchant.*	Rich. Kilvington, Chriſt. Simpſon.
1668	21	Henry Tyreman, *draper.*	Chriſt. Cooke, Tho. Cooke.
1669	22	Chriſtopher Breary, *merchant.*	Will. Ramſden, Will. Bell.
1670	23	Thomas Bawtry, *merchant.*	And. Perrot, John Becket.
1671	24	William Richardſon, *draper.*	Tho. Niſbet, Fra. Calvert.
1672	25	*Sir* Hen. Thompſon, *knt. merch.*	Tho. Waynd, Rob. Horsfield.
1673	26	Thomas Williamſon, *merchant.*	John Pecket, George Ramſden.
1674	27	Richard Metcalfe, *merchant.*	Rob. Waller, Fran. Elwick.
1675	28	William Ramſden, *merchant.*	Tho. Carter, John Foſter.
1676	29	York Horner, *merchant.*	John Mowld, Joh. Blackburn.
1677	30	Francis Elcock, *grocer.*	Will. Baron, Will. Watſon.
1678	31	Philip Herbert, *merchant.*	Hen. Pawſon, Rog. Wilberfoſs.
1679	32	Richard Shawe, *butcher.*	Tho. Moſely, George Stockton.
1680	33	John Conſtable 1. *grocer.*	Tho. Thorndike, Geo. Bracebridge.
1681	34	John Carter, *merchant.*	Will. Heather, Will. Pickering.
1682	35	John Wood.	Will. Charlton, Rog. Shackleton.
1683	36	Edward Thompſon, *merchant.*	Francis Duckworth, Tho. Cooke.
1684	37	Robert Waller, *attorney.*	Joh. Pemberton, Tho. Sutton.
	JAM. II.		
1685	1	John Thompſon, *goldſmith.*	Fran. Taylor, Leon. Robinſon.
1686	2	Leonard Wilberfoſs.	Will. Appleton, Tho. Watſon.
1687	3	Thomas Moſely, *apothecary.*	John Bell, Pet. Richardſon.

A.D.	A. Reg.	LORD-MAYORS.	SHERIFFS.
	JAM. II.		
1688	4	Thomas Reyne, Robert Waller, *attornies.*	Matt. Bayock. Marm. Butler. Tho. Fothergill, Chrift. Hutton.
	W. *et* M.		
1689	1	John Fofter, *haberdafher.*	John Thorpe, Tho. Barftow,
1690	2	Samuel Dawfon, *merchant.*	Tho. Bradley, Rob. Clarke.
1691	3	George Stockton, *filk-weaver.*	Geo. Pickering, Rob. Fofter.
1692	4	Jofhua Earnfhaw, *merchant.*	Eman. Juftice, Mark Gill.
1693	5	Andrew Perrot, *merchant.*	Peter Dawfon, Geo. Fothergill.
1694	6	Robert Davy, *hofier.*	Charles Rhoads, Walt. Baines.
1695	7	*Sir* Gilb. Metcalf, *knt. merchant.*	John Peckit, Rob. Radftone, *obiit.* Fran. Tomlinfon.
1696	8	John Conftable 2.	Ric. Wood, Sam. Buxton.
1697	9	Mark Gill, *goldfmith.*	John Welburn, Tho. Agar.
1698	10	Roger Shackleton.	Will. Radley, John Smith.
1699	11	Henry Thompfon, *efq;*	John Thompfon, Barth. Geldart.
1700	12	*Sir* William Robinfon, *bart.*	Will. Redman, Will. Cornwall.
1701	13	Tobias Jenkins, *efq;*	Tho. Mafon, Geo. Jackfon.
	ANNE.		
1702	1	John Peckit, *merchant*, 1.	Joel Savile, *ob.* Hen. Baines, Rowl. Mofely.
1703	2	Thomas Dawfon, *merchant.*	Jofeph Leech, Ed. Seller.
1704	3	Elias Pawfon, *merchant.*	Mat. Ingram, Rob. Perrot.
1705	4	Charles Redman, *toyman.*	John Stainforth, Percy Winterfkelf.
1706	5	Emanuel Juftice, *merchant.*	James Scourfield, Leon. Thompfon.
1707	6	Robert Benfon, *efq; lord* Bingley.	Tho. Pickering, Fran. Hewett.
1708	7	Richard Thompfon, *merchant.*	Tho. Bradley, Rob. Hotham.
1709	8	William Pickering.	John Alderfon, Drury Peake.
1710	9	Charles Perrot, *merchant.*	Will. Lifter, Will. Weightman.
1711	10	Thomas Pickering, *attorney.*	John Dixon, Matt. Lindley.
1712	11	William Cornwall, *brewer.*	Matt. Bigg, Will. Jackfon.
1713	12	Chrift. Hutton, *glover.*	Will. Dobfon, Sam. Clark.
	GEOR. I.		
1714	1	William Redman, *pinner.*	Alex. Lifter, John Williamfon.
1715	2	Robert Fairfax, *efq;*	Tancred Robinfon, Rich. Denton.
1716	3	Richard Townes, *mercer.*	Edw. Jefferfon, James Barftow.
1717	4	Henry Baines, *toyman.*	John Whitehead, Eleazer Lowcock.
1718	5	Tancred Robinfon, *efq;*	Sam. Dawfon, Hen. Greenwood.
1719	6	John Reed, *toyman.*	John Raper, Rich. Cordukes.
1720	7	Tobias Jenkins, *efq;* 2.	John Bowes, John Owram.
1721	8	Richard Thompfon 2.	Will. Hotham. Jonathan Benfon.
1722	9	Charles Redman 2.	George Barnatt, William Cooper.
1723	10	Charles Perrot 2.	Henry Pawfon, Sam. Smith.
1724	11	Thomas Agar, *woollen-draper.*	Fran. Newark, Will. Hutchinfon.
1725	12	Will. Cornwell 2.	Rich. Chambers, Fran. Buckle.
1726	13	Sam. Clarke, *haberdafher.*	Chrift. Jackfon, George Atkinfon.
	GEO. II.		
1727	1	Rich. Baine, *grocer.*	John Ambler, Fran. Bolton.
1728	2	Peter Whitton, *grocer.*	John Haughton. Ifaac Mansfield.
1729	3	Will. Dobfon, *apothecary.*	James Dodfworth, Will. Lambert, *mort.* Benj. Barftow, *elect.*
1730	4	John Stainforth, *efq; receiver of the land-tax.*	John Suttell, Jof. Buckle.
1731	5	Jonas Thompfon, *attorney.*	Sam. Waud, Ed. Seller.
1732	6	Henry Baines 2.	John Richardfon, Ed. Wilfon.
1733	7	James Dodfworth, *apothecary and grocer.*	Will. Stephenfon. George Efkrick.
1734	8	Will. Whitehead, *attorney at law.*	—— Scolfield, John White.
1735	9	James Barnard, *mercer.*	

RECORDERS

RECORDERS of YORK *(e)*.

1417 5 Hen. V. William Wandesforde.
1427 4 Hen. VI. Guy Rowcliff.
1476 16 Ed. IV. *Sir* Guy Fairfax, *knight. judge of the king's bench.*
1477 17 Ed. IV. Miles Metcalfe, *justice of assize at* Lancaster.
1486 2 Hen. VII. *Sir* John Vavasour, *knt. judge of the common pleas.*
1489 5 Hen. VII. *Sir* William Fairfax, *serjeant at law, judge of the common pleas.*
1496 18 Hen. VII. Bryan Palmes, *serjeant at law.*
1509 1 Hen. VIII. Richard Tancred, *esq*;
1519 10 Hen. VIII. *Sir* Rich. Rokeby, *knt.*
1523 14 Hen. VIII. *Sir* Will. Gascoign, *knt.*
1527 18 Hen. VIII. Richard Page, *esq*;
1533 27 Hen. VIII. John Pullein, *esq*;
1537 31 Hen. VIII. Will. Tancred, *esq*;
1573 15 Eliz. Will. Birnand, *esq*;
1581 23 Eliz. *Sir* Will. Hildyard, *knt.*
1608 6 James. *Sir* Richard Hutton, *knt. judge of the court of common pleas.*
1617 11 James. Bernard Ellis, *esq*;
1625 1 Char. I. *Sir* William Belt, *knt.*
1638 13 Char. I. *Sir* Thomas Witherington, *knt.*
1661 13 Char. II. John Turner, *esq*;
1685 1 Jac. II. Rich. *earl of* Burlington.
1688 3 Jac. II. George Pricket, *esq*;
1700 Marmaduke Pricket, *esq*;
1713 Thomas Adams, *esq*;
1722 *April* 27. Thomas Place, *esq*;

LORD PRESIDENTS of the NORTH.

(f) Upon the suppression of the lesser monasteries in the 27th of *Hen.* VIII. there arose many insurrections in the northern parts; especially one under the lord *Hussy* in *Lincolnshire*, and that under sir *Robert Ask* in *Yorkshire*. All which rebellions fell out between the 28th and 30th of *Henry* the eighth. The king intending also the suppression of the greater monasteries, which he effected in the 31st of his reign, for the preventing of future dangers, and keeping those northern counties in quiet, he raised a president and council at *York*, and gave them two several powers and authorities, under one great seal, of *oyer* and *terminer*, *&c.* within the counties of *York*, *Durham*, *Northumberland*, *Westmoreland*, &c.
The officers of the court consisting of

1. Lord president.
2. The vice president.
3. Four or more learned council.
4. The secretary.
5. The king's attorney.
6. Two examiners.
7. One register.
8. Fourteen attorneys.
9. One clerk of the attachments.
10. Two clerks of the seal.
11. One clerk of the tickets.
12. One serjeant at arms.
13. One pursuivant.
14. Ten collectors of fines.
15. Two tip-staves.

A CATALOGUE of the LORD PRESIDENTS, &c.

28 *Hen.* VIII. 1537. *April* 23.

Thomas Howard *duke of* Norfolk, *lord president.*
Sir Marmaduke Constable, *knt. vice-president.*
Sir William Babthorpe, *knt. councellour.*

29 *Hen.* VIII. 1538. *Oct.* 18.

Cuthbert Tunstall *bishop of* Durham, *lord president.*
Learned council.
Sir Marm. Constable, *knt.*
Sir Thomas Tempest, *knt.*
Sir Ralph Ellerker, *knt.*
Sir William Babthorpe, *knt.*
Thomas Fairfax, *serjeant at law.*
Richard Bellasis, *esq*;
Robert Bowes, *esq*;
Robert Challoner, *esq*;

30 *Hen.* VIII. *Sept.* 30. 1539.

Robert Holgate *bishop of* Landaff, *afterwards of* York, *lord president.*
Learned council.
Sir Marm. Constable, *knt.*
Sir Thomas Tempest, *knt.*
Sir Ralph Ellerker, *knt.*
Sir Robert Bowes, *knt.*
Sir Henry Saville, *knt.*
Sir Nich. Fairfax, *knt.*
Thomas Fairfax, *serjeant at law.*
Rich. Bellasis, *esq*;
Rich. Norton, *esq*;
Rob. Challoner, *esq*;
Tho. Gargrave, *esq*;
Tho. Rokeby, *LL. D.*
John Eastdall, *secretary.*

(e) Sir *T. W.* has given a very imperfect list of his predecessors, beginning as this does: occasioned as he says by the ancient court books being lost or mislaid; for which reason I have not been able much to enlarge it.

(f) Ex MS. Torre *in cust. filii sui* Nich. Torre, *arm.*

4 Ed. VI.

4 *Ed.* VI. *Feb.* 24, 1556.

Francis Talbot *earl of* Salop, *lord president.*

Learned council.

Sir Robert Bowes, *knt.*
Sir Tho. Gargrave, *knt.*
Sir Arthur Nevil, *knt.*
Sir Leon. Beckwith, *knt.*
Sir George Conyers, *knt.*
Sir Will. Vavasour, *knt.*
Rob. Mennel, } *serjeants at law.*
Rob. Rokeby, }
Rich. Bellasis, *esq;*
Rich. Norton, *esq;*
Rob. Challoner, *esq;*
Hen. Savile, *esq;*
Fran. Forbysher, *esq;*
George Brown, *esq;*
Christ. Eastoft, *esq;*
John Browne, *LL.D.*
Tho. Ennys, *secretary.*

3 *Eliz.* I. *Feb.* 24, 1561.

Henry Manners *earl of* Rutland *lord president.*

Learned council.

Sir Nich. Fairfax, *knt.*
Sir George Conyers, *knt.*
Sir Will. Vavasour, *knt.*
Sir Henry Gates, *knt.*
Rob. Mennel, *serjeant at law.*
Anth. Bellasis, *cl.*
Henry Savile, *esq;*
George Brown, *esq;*
Fran. Forbisher, *esq;*
Christ. Eastoft, *esq;*
Rich. Corbett, *esq;*
John Brown, *LL.D.*
Tho. Ennys, *secretary.*

6 *Eliz.* *Junii* 20, 1564.

Thomas Younge, *archbishop of* York, *lord president.*

Learned council.

Sir Nath. Fairfax, *knt.*
Sir Henry Gates, *knt.*
Sir Thomas Gargrave, *knt.*
Sir John Foster, *knt.*
Anthony Bellasis, *cl.*
John Vaughan, *esq;*
Henry Savile, *esq;*
George Brown, *esq;*
Christ. Eastoft, *esq;*
Rich. Corbett, *esq;*
Will. Tancred, *esq;*
Allen Bellingham, *esq;*
Laur. Meeres, *esq;*
John Rookby, *LL.D.*
Tho. Ennys, *secretary.*

15 *Eliz.* *Dec.* 1, 1572.

Henry Hastings *earl of* Huntington, *lord president.*

Learned council.

Sir Thomas Gargrave, *knt.*
Sir Henry Gates, *knt.*
Sir Will. Fairfax, *knt.*
Sir George Bowes, *knt.*
Sir Tho. Fairfax, *knt.*
Sir Christ. Hildyard, *knt.*
Fran. Wortley, *esq;*
Laur. Meeres, *esq;*
John Rokeby, *esq;*
Br. Bridges, *esq;*
Humph. Purefoy, *esq;*
Laur. Bramston, *esq;*
Ralph Huddleston, *esq;*
Ed. Stanhope, *esq;*
George Gibson, *LL.D.*
Will. Cardinal, *esq;*
Charles Hales, *esq;*
John Rookeby, *LL.D.*
John Bennet, *LL.D.*
Thomas Ennys, *esq;* }
George Blyth, *esq;* }
Henry Cheeke, *esq;* } *Secretaries.*
Rad. Rookby, *esq;* }
John Fearne, *esq;* }

41 *Eliz.* *Dec.* 9, 1599.

Thomas Cecil *lord* Burleigh, *lord president.*

Learned council.

Sir Will. Bowes, *knt.*
Sir Rich. Maleverer, *knt.*
Sir Thomas Fairfax *de* Denton, *jun. knt.*
Sir Tho. Posthumus Hobby, *knt.*
Sir Tho. Reresby, *knt.*
Sir Thomas Lascelles, *knt.*
Sir Henry Slingsby, *knt.*
Sir Edw. Stanhope, *knt.*
Sir John Mallory, *knt.*
Sir Tho. Fairfax *de* Gilling, *knt.*
Sir Christ. Hildyard *de* Winsted, *knt.*
Sir Henry Griffith, *knt.*
Sir Henry Bellasis, *knt.*
Sir Rich. Wortley, *knt.*
Thomas Hesketh, *esq;*
Rich. Hutton, *serjeant at law.*
Charles Hales, *esq;*
Sam. Bevercote, *esq;*
George Gibson, *LL.D.*
John Bennet, *LL.D.*
John Fearne, *secretary.*

1 *Jam.* *Sept.* 19, 1602.

Edmund *lord* Sheffield, *earl of* Moulgrave, *lord president.*

Learned council.

Sir John Savile, *baro scac. knt.*
Sir Thomas Strickland, *knt.*
Sir William Bowes, *knt.*
Sir Tho. Fairfax *de* Denton, *knt.*
Sir Tho. Posthumus Hobby, *knt.*
Sir John Savile, *knt.*
Sir Thom. Reresby, *knt.*
Sir Tho. Lascelles, *knt.*
Sir Henry Slingsby, *knt.*
Sir John Mallory, *knt.*
Sir Tho. Fairfax *de* Gilling, *knt.*
Sir Phil. Constable, *knt.*
Sir Christ. Hildyard, *knt.*
Sir Henry Griffith, *knt.*
Sir Henry Bellasis, *knt.*
Sir Robert Swyft, *knt.*
Sir Fran. Boynton, *knt.*
Sir Marm. Grimston, *knt.*
Sir Tho. Hesketh, *knt. LL.D.*

Sir John Gibſon, *knt.* *LL. D.*
Sir John Bennett, *knt.* *LD. D.*
Sir Chriſt. Hales, *knt.*
Sir Cuthbert Pepper, *knt.*
Rich. Williamſon, } *ſerjeants at law.*
Rich. Hutton, }
Sir John Fearne, *knt.* }
Sir Will. Gee, *knt.* } *ſecretaries.*
Sir Arthur Ingram, *knt.* }

17 *Jam. Sept.* 1619.

Emanuel *lord* Scrope, *lord preſident.*

Learned council.

Sir William Ellys, *knt.*
Sir Geo. Ellys, *knt.*
Sir John Lowther, *knt.*
Sir Rich. Dyer, *knt.*
Sir Arthur Ingram, *knt.*
Sir William Ingram, *knt.* *LL. D.*

5 *Char.* I. 1629.

Thomas *lord viſcount* Wentworth, *lord preſident.*
Sir Edward Oſborne, *vice-preſident.*

Learned council.

Sir William Ellys, *knt.*
Sir Thomas Tildeſley, *knt.*
Sir John Lowther, *knt.*
Sir Rich. Dyer, *knt.*
Sir William Dalton, *knt.*
Sir William Wentworth, *knt.*
Edward Witherington.
Edward Manwaring, *LL. D.*
Phineas Hodſon, *D. D.*
Sir Arthur Ingram, *knt.* } *ſecretaries.*
Sir John Melton, *knt.* }

17 *Char.* I. 1641.

Thomas *viſcount* Savile, *baron of* Pontefract *and* Caſtle-bar, *lord preſident (g).*

PERSONS famous in Hiſtory, or otherways remarkable, born in the city of YORK.

CONSTANTINE THE GREAT, the firſt *chriſtian* emperor. The birth of this prince having been largely treated on in a former part of this work, I ſhall omit any farther diſquiſition on it here.

Circa an. 720. FLACCVS ALBINVS, or ALCVINVS, was born in *York*, and is ſaid by *Camden* to be *Eboraci gloria prima ſui.* This man imbibed his firſt rudiments of learning under venerable *Bede*; which he afterwards compleated under *Egbert* archbiſhop of *York.* He was conſtituted librarian to that noble prelate; but, travelling abroad, his extraordinary parts and learning were ſoon diſtinguiſhed, and, what *Ariſtotle* was to *Alexander*, our *Alcuine* was to *Charles* the firſt emperor. Who took the name of *great*, not from his conqueſts, but for being made *great*, in all arts and learning, by his tutor's inſtructions *(h)*.

(i) After the death of *Bede*, he is ſaid by *Bayle* to have taught the liberal ſciences at *Cambridge*, then at *York*; where, probably, *Egbert* archbiſhop had founded an *univerſity*; the wonderful library he placed there intimating no leſs. It is averred however, that our *Alcuin* laid the firſt foundation of the *univerſity* of *Paris*; ſo that, ſays *Fuller*, howſoever the *French* brag to the contrary, and ſlight our nation, their learning was *lumen a lumine noſtro, a taper lighted at our torch.*

If this ludicrous writer's aſſertion be diſputed by the *French*, they will however lend an ear and give credit to a very ingenious author of their own, who has treated this matter with great ſpirit and integrity *(k)*. He acknowledges, with ſurpriſe, that the ſtate of learning in *France* was at *Alcuin*'s coming over from *Britain* in ſuch a poor and wretched condition, that they were glad of any foreign teacher to inſtruct them. *Alcuin*, and one *Clement* his countryman, a *Northumbrian* alſo, went over to *Paris*, and theſe two cried about the ſtreets there *learning to be ſold.* The emperor ſoon diſtinguiſhed them, and joining to them two others of great knowledge, which he had drawn from *Italy*, ſet about erecting a little kind of an univerſity in his palace. Amongſt all theſe our author calls *Alcuin* the emperor's firſt maſter; and in his letters to the popes *Adrian* and *Leo* he ſtyles him himſelf *delicioſus noſter*, his dearly beloved maſter. *Charles* thought it no debaſement to the honour and grandeur of ſo great a conqueror to make himſelf familiar with learned men; and therefore as he had called himſelf *David*, he gave the name of *Flaccus* to *Alcuin*, to *Engilbert* that of *Homer*, to another *Damaetas*, and another he called *Virgil.* Nor did they want other marks of his eſteem as well as friendſhip, for he gave them the choiceſt of eccleſiaſtical preferments; amongſt which the rich abby of St. *Martin*'s in *Tours* fell to *Alcuin*'s ſhare.

Engilbert, or *Eginhard*, who wrote the life of *Charles the great*, and was contemporary with *Alcuin*, ſtyles him *vir undiquaque doctiſſimus.* The monk of St. *Gall*, *in omni latitudine ſcripturarum ſuper caeteros modernorum temporum exercitatus.* And another old author *(l)*

(g) This nobleman was created lord preſident by king *Charles* I. After the death of the earl of *Strafford.* The original inſtrument under the king's hand, with his inſtructions, engroſſed on four ſkins of parchment, was in Mr. *Thoreſby*'s *Muſaeum* at *Leeds.*

The bill for re-eſtabliſhing this court at *York*, *temp.* *Car.* II. may be ſeen in the appendix.

(h) *Fuller*'s worthies.

(i) *Baleus de Script. Brit num.* 17. *cent.* 1.

(k) Archon *de la chapelle des roys de* France; *ex* Egin. *in vita* Caroli *magni*, *Annal.* Metens, *et ex vita ejus per monachum S* Galli.

(l) Amalarius Fortunatus *de ordine* Antiphon, *c.* 18.

doctiſ-

doctiſſimus magiſter totius regionis noſtrae. Our country-man *William*, the learned librarian of *Malmſbury*, gives him this character, *erat enim omnium* Anglorum, *quos quidem legerim doctiſſimus; multiſque libris ingenii periculum fecit.* It is certain that numerous authors have handed this man down as a prodigy of his age; ſingularly well ſkilled in all the learned languages and in the liberal Sciences. A great divine, a good poet and an excellent orator; which are endowments rarely concurring in one perſon. Sir *T. W.* writes, that *Alcuin* gained much honour by his oppoſition to the canons of the *Nicene* council, wherein the ſuperſtitious adoration of images are enjoined; but from whom he quotes I know not.

The birth of this great man, like many others, has been contended for by ſeveral writers. *Buchanan*, the moſt partial one to his country that ever did write, proves him a *Scotch-man* from his name. *Albinus* being with him ſynonymous to *Scotus (m).* So pope *Innocent* was a *Scotchman*, becauſe he calls himſelf *Albanus*; *Albania* being ſuppoſed to be the proper *latin* name for *Scotland*; when moſt writers agree that this *Innocent* was born at *Long Alba* near *Rome*.

Some authors have brought him into the world near *London*. But *(n) Harpsfield*, in his eccleſiaſtical hiſtory, ſays, more juſtly, that he was a *Northumbrian*; *Eboraci nutritus et educatus. Northumberland* was then all the country on the north of *Humber*. But what gives the cleareſt proof that he was born at *York*, and early inſtructed by the fathers of that church, are his own words in a letter to them from *France*, which I render thus: *(o) You did cheriſh with maternal affection my tendereſt years of infancy; and the follies of my youth did bear with patience; with fatherly correction you brought me up to man's eſtate, and ſtrengthned me with the doctrine of ſacred writers.* Either this ſentence muſt expreſly argue his being born at *York*, or that he was brought to it in ſwadling clothes.

Alcuin was firſt made abbot of St. *Auguſtine*'s in *Canterbury*, and afterwards of St. *Martin*'s in the city of *Tours* in *France*; where dying, *anno* 710, he was buried in a ſmall convent appendant to his monaſtery.

He wrote many pious and learned books, reckoned by *Bale* above thirty in number; one of which is entituled *ad Anglorum eccleſiam.* Many are the quotations from his ſeveral letters, collected by *Leland* and publiſhed in his *collectanea.* Some of which will fall in their places in the eccleſiaſtical part of this work. Theſe letters have been collected and publiſhed in *France*, along with his other works, by the care of *Andrew Du Cheſne (p).* One memorable piece of our great man was retrieved in the laſt age, being an hiſtorical account of the archbiſhops of *York*, in *latin* verſe, down to his patron *Egbert*. This is publiſhed, *inter* xv *ſcript.* by that moſt induſtrious antiquary dean *Gale*; who tells you, in his preface, that the manuſcript was ſent him by father *Mabillon*. This piece I have before taken ſome quotations from; and what the learned dean ſays plainly hints, that *York* was the place of *Alcuin*'s nativity are theſe lines in the poem,

> ——— Patriae *quoniam mens dicere laudes*
> *Et veteres cunas properat proferre parumper*
> Euboricae *gratis praeclarae verſibus urbis.*

I ſhall conclude my account of this extraordinary perſon, with a quotation from one of his letters directed to the community of the church of *York*, declaring his diſintereſtedneſs in his purſuit of religious affairs, and beg leave to give it in his own words, and leave it to the eccleſiaſticks of this or any future ages to copy after: *Non enim* AURI AVARITIA, *teſtis eſt conditor cordis mei*, Franciam *veni, nec remanſi in ea, ſed eccleſiaſticae cauſa neceſſitatis, et ad confirmandam catholicae fidei rationem, quae a multis, heu! modo maculari nititur, et deſuper textam* Chriſti *tunicam, quam milites juxta* Chriſti *crucem ſcindere non auſi ſunt, in varias rumpere partes praeſumunt.*

(q) WALTHEOF earl of *Northumberland*, ſon to the valiant *Siward*, was born in this city; A.D. 1055.
for he was in the cradle when his father died in it. The life of this brave, but unfortunate, nobleman is ſo interwoven in the annals of this work, that 'tis needleſs to repeat it here. It ſuffices therefore to ſay of him, that he fell a ſacrifice to the *conqueror*'s policy, and was the firſt man of quality beheaded in *England*.

(r) ROBERT FLOUR, ſon of one *Took Flour*, who was twice mayor of *York*, about the lat- A.D. 1190.
ter end of the twelfth century, was born in this city. This man, running into the ſanctity of that age, laid the foundation of a priory which ſtood beneath *March-bridge* near *Knareſborough*. It was of the order of fryars ſtyled *de redemptione captivorum, alias ſanctae trinitatis (s).*

(m) Buchan. l. 5. p. 157.

(n) Harpsfield, p. 177.

(o) Ex epiſt. Albini *ad fratres* Ebor. *eccl. Vos fragiles infantiae meae annos materno foviſtis affectu, et laſciviam pueritiae meae pia ſuſtinuiſtis patientia; et paternae caſtigationis diſciplinis ad perfectam viri educaſtis aetatem, et ſacrarum literarum eruditione roboraſtis.* Lelandi *coll.* tom. I. p. 400.

*(p) Les lettres ſont imprimeés avec tous ſes autres oeuvres par le ſoin d'*André Du Cheſne, *in folio*, Pariſiis 1617. Matthaei Weiſſ. Lycaeum Benedictum, *ſive de* Alcuino *aliiſque bonarum artium ex ordine* S. Benedicti *profeſſoribus hiſtoria. En douze*, Pariſiis, Leonard, 1661. *Bibliotheque hiſtorique de la* France, &c. *par* Jaques le Long, *p.* 221. *num.* 4809.

(q) Polychron. Rog. Hoveden, &c.

(r) Leland's itin.

(s) Eodem anno, 1238, *claruit fama ſancti* Roberti

The

The life of this zealot, called St. *Robert* of *Knaresbrough*, is still kept in his cell, but it is imperfect. In an ancient manuscript I met with the following copy of it, and is as odd a legendary story as any can be found in the whole catalogue of *Romish* saints.

"St. *Robert* was born in the city of *York*, his father's name was *Tocklese Floure* (t), and "his mother's *Smimeria*. Who being of the best rank of citizens, and following a most christian rule of good life, had a son whom they named *Robert*, and brought him up in all "vertuous education; and as he grew in years of discretion, so they trained him up in learning and vertuous exercises. This holy man even from his infancy had a continual recourse "to godly prayer, never once stooping to the love of pleasures, but still increasing in holiness was at length made sub-deacon.

"Not long after this *Robert* went into the north parts of the country, and betook himself to a certain house called the *new monastery* of the *Cistertian* order, where he had a brother of that order; there he remained some four months, giving them a true pattern of "sobriety and good life, and then he returned to his father's house. After a few days this "servant of God privately fled from his parents to *Knaresbrough*, as God had inspired him "to an hermit there, leading a strict life amongst the rocks, who seemed at first glad of "such an associate as *Robert*, but afterwards being overcome by the temptation of our common enemy the devil, he returned again to his wife and children, and left *Robert* alone, "who with wonderful abstinence afflicted himself.

"After this *Robert* went to a certain matron, not far from his cell to ask an alms, who "gave him as much ground, with the chapel of St. *Hilda*, as he thought good to dig and "till. This alms *Robert* accepted of, and remained there almost a year chastising his flesh "with austere mortifications, and applying himself wholly to the service of God. A little "before he departed thence thieves broke into his cell and took all his provision away, and "upon that he determined to leave the place and went to *Spofford*, where he stayed for a "while attending only to prayer, and other services of God almighty. The fame of his "sanctity and holy conversation caused most of the country to come flocking to him; but "for avoiding of applause, the holy man, always rejecting vain-glory, secretly departed "and changed his abode.

"No sooner had the monks of *Adley* heard of *Robert's* retiring from *Spofford*, but they "were earnest with him to come and live amongst them; which the good man did, and "became a poor brother of their house, and submitted himself to their spiritual rules and "discipline. As for his garment it was only one, and that of white colour, which served "rather to cover his nakedness than to keep him warm. His bread was three parts barley "meal, his broth was made of unsavoury herbs, or a few beans served with a little salt; "save once a week he had a little meal put into it. His austerity of life was not suitable to "the looser sort in that monastery, who were emulous of his vertues, and impatient of rebuke, which the man of God perceiving, he returned again to the chapel of St. *Hilda*, "where he was joyfully accepted of the matron. She presently set on workmen to build a "place for the laying in of his corn, and for other necessary uses.

"This man of God spent whole nights in watching and prayer, and when he slept, "which was more for necessity than otherwise, he made the ground his bed. He had four "servants, two whereof he employed about tillage, the third he kept for divers uses, and "the fourth he commonly retained about himself, to send abroad into the country to collect "the people's alms for those poor brethren which he had taken into his company.

"One day it chanced as St. *Robert* slept on the grass being much wearied with his continual austereness, his mother, being lately dead, appeared unto him very sad, pale and "deformed, telling him that for usury and divers other transgressions she was judged to "most grievous pains unless he relieved her by his prayers; which St. *Robert* promised to "perform. Being greatly troubled for the discomfort of his mother, he went unto prayer, "and not long after his mother appeared to him again with a chearful aspect, giving thanks "to her son, and departed and praised God eternally.

"Not long after this (u) *William Stouteville*, lord of the forest, passing by his cell, demanded of his servants who lived there? They answered one *Robert* an holy hermit; no, answered *Stouteville*, rather a receiver of thieves, and in a distempered manner commanded his "followers to level it with the ground; which was done accordingly. Then *Robert* removed to a place near the town of *Knaresbrough*, where he had before remained; contriving "no better a dwelling than only a small receptacle by the chapel of St. *Gyles* made up with "the boughs of trees. The holy man still increasing in vertue and goodness, made the enemy of man more desirous of his overthrow, and thought once again by his former means "to disquiet his virtuous endeavours. *Stouteville*, a fit instrument for such a purpose, com-

heremitae apud Knaresburg; *cujus tumba oleum medicinale fertur abundanter emisisse.* M. Paris.

(t) The family of *Floure* continued in this city for some centuries after this, as appears by an epitaph in the minster, mid. quire, *num.* 11. See also *Trinity* church, *Muckle-gate*.

(u) *Anno* 1174. one *Robert de Stouteville* was high-sheriff of this county. See catalogue. St. *Robert's* cell is still shewn at *Knaresbro'*; being a room about three or four yards square, made out of a solid rock, with an altar, cells for images, and other decorations all out of the same rock. The site of this priory was sold to the earl of *Shrewsbury* amongst several other lands, &c. thereabouts, the 5th of *Ed.* VI. *Rolls* chapel.

"ing that way, by the instigation of the devil, took notice of a smoke that ascended from *Robert*'s cell, and demanded who lived there? Answer was made by his servants, *Robert* the hermit. Is it *Robert*, quoth he, whose house I overthrew, and expelled my forest? Answer was made, the same; whereat enraged, he swore, by the eyes of God, to raze it to the ground, and expel *Robert* the next day from his mansion house for ever. But in the night, in his sleep, there appeared unto him in a vision three men, terrible and fearful to behold, whereof two carried a burning engine of iron beset with sharp and fiery teeth; the third of a gyant-like stature holding two iron clubs in his hands, came furiously towards his bed, saying, cruel prince and instrument of the devil, rise quickly and make choice of one of these to defend thy self, for the injuries thou intendest against the man of God, for whom I am sent hither to fight with thee.

"Hereupon *Stoteville* cried out, and with remorse of conscience, cried to God for mercy, with protestations of amendment; whereat the fearful vision vanished. *Stoteville* coming to himself, presently construed that this revelation was sent from God, for the violence done and intended against *Robert* his servant. Wherefore the next day he conferred all the lands betwixt his cell and *Grimbald-cragg-stone* for a perpetual alms. And that the ground should not lie untilled, he gave him two oxen, two horses, and two kine. Not long after *Robert* took into his company a *Jew*, whom he employed as overseer of the poor and distributer of their alms. One day the *Jew*, being overcome by the devil, fled away from the holy man, and in his flight fell and broke his leg; which the holy man understanding, by revelation, made haste to him, and chiding him for his fault, which the *Jew* acknowledged and desired pardon, forthwith *Robert* blessing his leg, all embrued in blood, with his holy hand, restored him to his former state, and brought him back to his cell.

"*Robert*'s care of the poor was great, and, that he might the better relieve their wants, he desired his patron *Stoteville* to bestow a cow on him, which was granted; but withal such a cow, so wild and fierce, that none durst come near her. The man of God making haste to the forest found her, and, embracing her about the neck, brought her home, as meek as a lamb, to the great admiration of the spectators. One of *Stoteville*'s servants told his master of this thing, and withal said he would devise a way how to get the cow again from *Robert*. But his master did not approve of the motion; nevertheless the fellow with counterfeit looks and gestures, framing himself lame both of hands and feet, encountered *Robert* and desired some relief for his wife and children, who were miserably oppressed with hunger and want; unto whom *Robert* gave his cow, saying unto him, *God gave and God shall have, but so thou shalt be, as thou makest thyself to be*; and when this deceiver thought to depart with his cow, he was not able to stir but was lame indeed. Perceiving this to be the just judgment of God for deluding his servant, he cried out *Robert* true servant of God pardon my trespass, and the injury I have done unto you, which the indulgent and good old father instantly did, restoring him to his former ability, and returned unto his cell, where he was received with joy.

"A company of deer from the forest haunted his ground, and spoiled his corn, doing him much harm, whereof he complained to his patron, requiring some order to be taken therein. To whom his patron thus replied, *Robert, I give thee free leave to impound these deer, and to detain them till thou art satisfied.* Whereupon the holy man went into the fields, and with a little rod drove the deer out of the corn like lambes, and shut them up in his barn. Which done *Robert* went back to his patron acquainting him therewith, desiring withal to loose the said deer. His patron answered, that *Robert had leave freely to use the deer so impounded in the plough, or in any other service of husbandry*; for which *Robert* returned him many thanks, and went back to his cell. And taking the deer out of the barn he put them under the yoke to plough, and made them every day to plough his ground like oxen; which was daily seen and admired by all.

"King *John* coming that way and hearing such renown of *Robert*'s sanctity, was pleased to visit him at his poor cell; and conferred upon that place as much of his wast wood, next adjoining as he could convert to tillage with one plough or team. This servant of God told lord *Bryon* that came for his benediction, and to know what good or evil success he should have in a voyage he was to take upon the king's service? that he should effect his business and bring his occasions to a good period; but withal that he should never return.

"Not long after he foretold that presently after his death the monks of *Fountain's abby* would with force strive to take his body with them. He willed those of his house to resist, if need were with secular power; willing that his body should there rest, where he gave up his last breath. Which was done and effected accordingly. The holy man, perceiving himself to draw towards his end, commanded the blessed sacrament to be brought unto him; preparing to die with an holy and humble heart.

"At which time the monks of *Fountains*, hearing of his near approaching end, made haste to come unto him, bringing their habit; wherein his body was to be vested and interred. To whom he told, his own ordinary garment was enough, neither desired he any other.

" As he lay at the point of death, the *Jew* with his fellows came weeping before him " and desired his last blessing, which he willingly gave them; and in that exercise yielded " up the ghost. His body was with due reverence made ready for the grave, and the bruit " being divulged abroad, the monks of *Fountains* came and gave him their habit, which " he refused whilst he lived, endeavouring to carry away his body by force; but a com- " pany of armed men from the castle resisted them, who returned home sad for so great " a loss.

" In conclusion he was buried in the chapel of *Holy-cross* in a new tomb. There came " to honour his obsequies great multitudes of all sorts of people; kissing the coffin where- " in his body was inclosed.

John Romane, born at *York*, afterwards archbishop, where see for him,

(*x*) John Waldby, was born in this city, of honest parents, says *Fuller*, and in the catalogue of our magistrates, preceeding, there is one *John de Waldby*, who was one of the bayliffs of it, *anno* 1357, and was, probably, father to this *John*, and his brother *Robert* ensuing (*y*). *John* was bred up an *Augustinian*, and came to be provincial of his order, and doctor of divinity in *Oxford*. A man of ready wit and eloquent tongue, by which he so well pleased the *rabbins* at *York*, that, upon the death of *Alexander Nevill*, they elected him archbishop; but he was never confirmed. This observation is from *Pitz*, but *Goodwin* taking no notice of it, the matter is suspicious. The former writer makes him archbishop of *Dublin*; yet *Bale* who was an *Irish* bishop, and had the advantage of an exacter intelligence, says no such thing; from whence we may conclude this also a mistake. This *John* is allowed by all to have died in the place of his nativity, *anno* 1393. *Bale* adds that our priest was present at the council of *Stamford*, wherein the doctrine of the *Wichliffites* was condemned; but though he had been violent against them formerly, he seemed not to be well pleased with the proceedings at that convention. The author of the additional volume to the *Monasticon* contradicts this; in him may be found a catalogue of his writings (*z*).

Robert Waldby, brother to *John*, was also born in *York*, and was afterwards archbishop of this see. Whose life may be met with amongst our prelates.

John Erghom, a native of this city, was, also, a fryer **Eremite** of the order of St. *Augustine* at *York*; doctor and professor of divinity at *Oxford*. He was a great proficient in the study of the holy scriptures, and a great artist in expounding them. He followed the typical method in his sermons, which crowded his church with auditors, and, says *Fuller*, much pleased their fancies, though it little curbed their corruptions. Having with incredible industry perused all the *Greek* and *Latin* interpreters, in that figurative way, made choice collections from them, and added much of his own, of the whole he composed a vast work under this title, *Compilations of prophecies*; which he dedicated to the earl of *Hereford*. His other works were sermons on the *predictions of* John de Bridlington. *Of* John *the canon's poems. Astrological calculations*, &c. *Bale* tells us, that in his discourses he would sometimes utter *strange and unheard off things*, (*a*) and no wonder, if his head was so full of prophetical types of scripture. He died and was buried at *York* about the year 1490.

(*b*) John Bat, or Bate, was born at *York*; a *Carmelite* frier there, and in process of time prior of the monastery, and doctor of divinity at *Oxford*. His works, which *Leland* and others mention, are these, *Encomium of divinity*; *for the introduction of the sentences. Ordinary acts. Resolutions. Replications of arguments. Of the assumption of the blessed virgin. Sermons throughout the year. Synodal collations. To the* Oxford *clergy. Compendium of logick. On* Porphyrius's *universals. On* Aristotle's *predicaments. On* Porritanus *his six principles. Questions concerning the soul. Of the construction of the parts of speech*, &c. He died and was buried at *York* in 1429.

Sir Martin Bowes knight, lord-mayor of *London*, *anno* 1545, queen *Elizabeth*'s jeweller, was born in *York*, and deserves a mention in this catalogue, not only for his great wealth and charity, but for his particular munificence to his native place. He was the son of *Thomas Bowes*, who, though I do not find mentioned in the list of our senators, yet his ancestors were lord-mayors of *York*; one as high as the year 1417. He died *August* 4, 1565 (*c*).

(*x*) Bale *de script. Fuller's* worthies.
(*y*) So *Richard Waldeby* was mayor *anno* 1365, another of this family.
(*z*) V. 2. p. 220.
(*a*) *Nova et inandita*. Bale *n.* 40.
(*b*) *Steven's* mon. v. 2.
(*c*) *Stowe's* survey of *London*.

Valentine

VALENTINE FREES, and his wife were both born in this city, and are both made remarkable by *Fox* and *Fuller* for dying together for religion at a stake in it. The latter writer says, that it was in the year 1531, and, probably, by order of that cruel archbishop *Edward Lee*. He adds that he cannot call to mind a man and his wife thus *married* together in *martyrdom*; and is pretty confident this couple was the first and last of that kind (*d*).

(*e*) EDWARD FREES, brother to the aforesaid *Valentine*, was born in *York*, says *Fox*, and was there an apprentice to a painter. He was afterwards a novice monk, but leaving his convent he came to *Colchester* in *Essex*. Here his heretical inclinations, as then accounted, discovered itself in some pieces of scripture, which he painted on the borders of cloths. For which he was brought before *John Stoaksley* bishop of *London*, from whom he found such cruel usage, says *Fuller*, as is beyond belief. *Fox* seems here, indeed, to have far overshot himself in the account of this man's sufferings; for he says he was fed with *manchet* made of *sawdust*; and kept so long in prison menacled by the wrists, till the flesh had overgrown his *irons*; and not being able to comb his head became so distracted, that, being brought before the bishop, he could say nothing but *my lord is a good man*.

Fuller, in his usual style, says he confesses that distraction is not mentioned in the list of losses, reckoned up by our saviour, *he that left his house, or brethren, or sisters, or father or mother, or wife, or children, or lands, for my sake*, &c. But seeing, adds he, that a man's wit is dearer to him then his wealth, and what is so lost may be said to be left; no doubt this poor man's distraction may be said to be accepted of God; and his enemies severely punished.

GEORGE TANKERFEILD, born at *York*, is put down by sir *T. W.* as another martyr. That writer says he was a cook in *London*, and was by bishop *Bonner*, *antichrist's great cook*, roasted and burned to death. He adds that this man was of such note for answering *Bonner* readily and punctually, that the bishop called him Mr. *Speaker*. As he did one *Smith* examined at the same time Mr. *Comptroller*; because, says my authority, he rebuked *Bonner* for *swearing* (*f*).

THOMAS MORETON, was born *anno* 1564, in the city of *York* (*g*). His father *Richard Moreton*, allied, says *Fuller*, to cardinal *Moreton* archbishop of *Canterbury*, was a mercer in that city, and lived in the *Pavement*. From school he was sent to St. *John's* college *Cambridge*, of which college he was chosen fellow, out of eight competitors, purely by his merit. He was afterward rector of *Long-Marston* near *York*; then dean of *Glocester*, *Winchester*, bishop of *Chester*, *Litchfield* and *Coventry*, and lastly bishop of *Durham*. The life of this eminent prelate is written at large by Dr. *John Barwick* dean of *Durham*; the compass of my design will allow but few hints of it. He was a person of great learning and knowledge, and the best disputant of his time. *Fuller* relates, that commencing doctor of divinity, he made his position on his second question, which, though unusual, was arbitrary and in his own power; this, adds he, much defeated the expectation of Dr. *Playfere*; who replied upon him with some warmth *commovisti mihi stomachum*; to whom *Moreton* returned *gratulor tibi, reverende professor, de bono tuo stomacho*; *coenabis apud me hac nocte*.

When he was rector of *Marston* the plague was rife in *York*; and a number of infected persons were sent out of the city to *Hob-moor*, where tents were erected for them. Our pious clergyman visited these miserable objects every day; and brought what provisions he could along with him. Yet for the security of his own family, he had a door struck through the wall to his lodging, that he might come in and out without seeing them (*h*). A piece of *christian* charity and fortitude rarely imitated.

He paid great regard to his native place, and did intend, as he expressed himself in a letter to sir *T. W.* *when he was some body* to do great matters for it (*i*). In the year 1639, he purposed to have erected a cross, or cover for market-people in bad weather, in the *Pavement*; and intended to lay out four hundred pound to that end. But this his good design was frustrated by the obstinacy of a person, who owned the house which was to be pulled down, and would not dispose of it. He was zealous for the honour of our city, and defended that assertion that *Constantine the great* was born in it, against a bishop who argued that he was not born in *Britain*, but in *Bithynia*. He was so sure of the affirmative, that he told sir *T. W.* that he intended to erect a statue of that emperor in the minster as a constant memorial of it (*k*).

But whatever good intentions he had towards the city, they were all frustrated by the wickedness of the times; for falling under the displeasure of the house of commons, in that horrid long parliament, he was sequestered of all; but by an especial favour a pension of

(*d*) Fox's martyrs, p. 1017. *Fuller's* worthies.
(*e*) *Iidem.*
(*f*) *Ex MS.* D. T. W.
(*g*) *Anno* 1581. *Richard Moreton* sheriff of *York*.
(*h*) *E vita ejus per* Barwick.
(*i*) *Ex MS.* D. T. W.
(*k*) Some say that the old image, shewn for the emperor *Severus* in the minster was given to the church by bishop *Moreton* as the statue of *Constantine the great*.

eight

2

eight hundred pound *per annum* was settled on him; which, says *Fuller*, was a trumpet, however, that gave an uncertain sound, not assigning by whom or whence the money should be paid. The crimes that were alledged against him were his subscribing the bishops protestation for their votes in parliament, refusing to resign the seal of his bishoprick, and his baptizing a daughter of *John* earl of *Rutland* with the sign of the cross; an unpardonable offence in those hypocritical times. He got however one thousand pound out of *Goldsmiths-hall*, which was his chief support in his old age (*l*).

Many of the nobility honoured and respected him, particularly *John* earl of *Rutland*; to whose kinsman *Roger* earl of *Rutland* he had formerly been chaplain. Sir *George Savile* civilly paid him his purchased annuity of two hundred pound, with all advantages. And sir *Henry Yelverton* was, also, exceeding kind to him. It was at this last named gentleman's house, at *East-mauduit* in *Northamtonshire*, that our worthy prelate departed this life, *anno* 1659, in the ninety fifth year of his age. It was somewhat unfortunate that he should live to the brink of the happy restoration and not see it. His peculiar merits must have rendered him a fit object of the king's gratitude, though his extream old age would incapacitate him from enjoying the bounties, which would necessarily have been conferred upon him.

Sir *T. W.* and Dr. *Fuller* were both his contemporaries and acquaintance, the former had finished his work before the bishop died, but gives this testimony of his worth; which from a man, very different in principles, is the more remarkable. "I am the more sparing, " says sir *T.* in giving those praises which are justly due to him, because I understand that " he is yet living, though of the age of ninety years and upwards. The people that " would have commended *Dorcas*, being dead, shewed those fine and curious pieces of " work which she made when she was living. I shall only mention his learned works which " will outlive the author, aud may speak for him now he is living, as they will undoubted-" ly do to future ages after his death.

A catholick appeal for protestants. *London* 1610.

Of the institution of the blessed sacrament of the body and blood of *Christ*. *London* 1631.

Causa regia sive de authoritate et dignitate principum dissertatio. Lond. 1620.

Totius doctrinalis controversiae de eucharistica decisio. Cantabrigiae 1640.

Anecdotum contra merita. Cantab. 1637.

The grand imposture of the new church of *Rome*. *London* 1628.

A preamble to an encounter with *P. R.* the author of the deceitful treatise of mitigation. *London* 1608.

The encounter against Mr. *Parsons* by a review of his last sober reasoning. *London*.

Replicatio, seu adversus confutationem C. R.

Adversus apologiam cathol. brevis luctatio. Cant. 1638.

Apologia catholica, lib. 2. Lond. 1606.

Ezekiel's *wheels*, a treatise concerning divine providence. *London* 1653.

" These are some of many which he hath learnedly written, and I am informed, adds " sir *T.* that in his great age he is yet writing (*m*).

(*n*) Sir Robert Carr was born in this city, says *Fuller*, on this occasion, *Thomas Carr* his father, laird of *Furnihurst*, a man of great estate and power in the south of *Scotland*, was very active for *Mary* queen of *Scots*. On this account he was forced to fly his country and came to *York*. Notwithstanding this *Thomas* had been a great inroader into *England*, yet, for some reasons of state, he was permitted to live undisturbed at *York*; during which time his son *Robert* was born. This was the reason why the said *Robert* refused to be naturalized by an act of our parliament, because he was born in *England*.

It is said that the first time he was known to king *James* was by an accident of breaking his leg at a tilting in *London*. The king took great notice of one whose father had suffered so much on his mother's account; and he being of an amiable personage, a great recommendation to that prince, was taken into court; and in a small time almost crowded with honours. Being made a baron, viscount, earl of *Somerset*, knight of the garter, warden of the cinque ports, &c.

This great favourite is said to be a good natured man, and when in full power used it with more harm to himself than any other person. Barring one foul fact, into which he was seduced by his love to a beautiful, though wicked, lady, his conduct in the ministry stands without a blot, and his character runs clear to posterity. For this fact, so notoriously known that I need not mention it, he was banished the court; and lived and died very privately about the year of our lord 1638.

(*l*) *Fuller*'s worthies.

(*m*) The writer of this prelate's life says that he was school-fellow with *Guy Faulx*, or *Vaulx*, the famous popish incendiary, in this city. Who is also said to have been born here; but I can come to no further memoirs of his life. *John Vaulx*, probably of this family, was lord-mayor *anno* 1637.

(*n*) *Fuller*'s worthies.

p377

S.r John Swinburne *of* Capheaton *in the County of* Northumberland *Bar.t in regard of the name, family, and personal qualifications of this once eminent civilian, presents this plate of his monument to this work.*

1736.

(*o*) JOHN LEPTON of *York* esquire, servant to king *James*, has made himself remarkable for performing a piece of exercise so violent in its kind, as not to be equalled before or since. For a considerable wager, he undertook to ride six days together betwixt *York* and *London*, being one hundred and fifty computed miles, and performed it accordingly. He first set out from *Aldersgate May* 20, 1606; and accomplished his journey every day, before it was dark; to the greater praise, says *Fuller*, of his strength in acting, than his discretion in undertaking it. We have had one instance since, of a person's riding for his life, on one mare, from a place near *London*, where he had committed a robbery about sunrise in the morning, and reaching *York* that night before sunset. This person, whom king *Charles* II. called for his wonderful expedition *swift Nick*, was known to the people that he robbed, and, probably, pursued. He was taken some time after, and tried for the fact; but though the witnesses swore positively to the man, yet he proving himself at *York*, upon the *bowling-green*, within twelve hours of the time they said the robbery was committed, neither judge nor jury would believe them. I mention this, not as a parallel case with the other, which was a voluntary act of horsemanship; and I give it for the jockies of this or any future age to copy after.

(*p*) HENRY SWINBURNE was born in the city of *York*, and educated, in grammar learning, in the free school there. His father *Thomas Swinburne*, then living in *York*, sent this his son to *Oxford*, at sixteen years of age, and entered him a commoner at *Hart-hall*; where he for some time followed his studies. From whence he translated himself to *Broadgate-hall*, now *Pembroke-college*, where he took his degree of batchelor of the civil law.

Before he left the *university* he married *Helena* daughter of *Bartholomew Lant* of that city; which state of life being inconsistent with local fellowships, he retired with his wife to his native place; and for some time after he practised in the ecclesiastical courts there as *proctor*.

Having taken a degree in the *university* he thought it more expedient to practise in an higher station, to that end he commenced *doctor of the civil law*. As his contemporary and country-man *Gilpin* was called the *apostle of the north*, so our *Swinburne* was styled the *northern advocate*; the one being famous for his learning in divinity; and the other in the civil law. Having practised as an advocate for some years, he was advanced to be *commissary* of the *exchequer*, and *judge* of the *prerogative courts* of the archbishop of *York*; in which office he continued to his death. Feb. 10, 1612.

The publisher of the last edition of his wills and testaments allows our *civilian's* education to be very generous, and says we have very few or no instances, since his time, of a *proctor's* taking a degree of *batchelor of law* in any *university*, and afterwards pleading as an *advocate*; or of being *judge* of the prerogative court in either province. For all which employments, he adds, he was very well qualified.

There is no record, or memorial, extant giving an account what year this commissary was born in *York*; nor when he died, says the aforesaid editor, the epitaph on his monument mentioning neither. It would seem somewhat derogatory to the credit of our civilian, who wrote so learnedly on wills and testaments, to neglect his own. But Mr. *Torre* has found it from whom I take this abstract, by which it appears that he was twice married, and his second wife's name was *Wentworth*.

"*Henry Swinburn* of *York*, doctor of the civil law, made his last will dated *May* 30, " 1623, and proved *June* 12, 1624. whereby he commended his soul to God almighty his " creator, redeemer and comforter, *&c.* and his body to be buried near his former wife, " and constituted *Margaret* his then wife executrix. And by a codicil thereunto annexed, " dated *July* 15, 1623, he gave to his son *Toby* his dwelling house in *York*, to hold to him " and the heirs of his body, with remainder to his son's uncle *John Wentworth* and to his " heirs for ever; paying yearly to the lord-mayor of *York* for the time being the sum of " four or five pound, to be yearly distributed for ever amongst the poor of the city of *York* " as he directs.

He hath written,

A brief treatise of testaments and last wills, in seven parts; which has bore several impressions, *viz. anno* 1590, 1611, 1635, 1640, 1677, and 1728.

Treatise of spousals or matrimonial contracts, &c. *Lond.* 1686.

In both which books, says the *Oxford antiquary*, the author shews himself an able civilian, and excellently well read in the authors of his faculty. His monument in the north isle of the choir in the cathedral at *York* is represented in the annexed print.

(*q*) Sir THOMAS HERBERT was the son of *Christopher Herbert*, son of *Thomas Herbert* merchant and alderman of *York*. He was born in this city, and, probably, there educated till he was admitted commoner of *Jesus college*, *Oxon*; which was in the year 1621. under

(*o*) *Fuller's* worthies. *Sanderson's* life of king *James* I.

(*p*) *Wood's Ath. Oxon.* v. I. p. 455. Preface to the last edition of wills and test. The publisher of this last edition has committed a blunder in saying that the *Oxford antiquary* has put down the first edit. to be printed 1520, when it is really in *Wood* 1590, as he himself makes it.

(*q*) *Wood's Ath. Oxon.* v. II. 690.

the tuition of Mr. *Jenkin Lloyd* his kinsman. From hence he went to wait upon *William* earl of *Pembroke*; who, owning him for his relation, and purposing his advancement, sent him to travel, in the year 1626, with a sufficient allowance for his charges. After spending some years in travelling through *Africa* and *Asia the great*, he on his return, did wait on the said noble earl, who invited him to dine with him the next day at *Baynard's castle* in *London*. But the earl dying suddenly that very night, his expectation of preferment from him was frustrated, and he left *England* a second time in order to visit several parts of *Europe*. Upon finishing his travels he married, and settled in his native country; where says the antiquary, he delighted himself more with the converse of the muses, than in the rude and brutish pleasures which most gentlemen, now, follow.

In the time of the rebellion he adhered to the cause of the parliament; and, by the perswasions of *Philip* earl of *Pembroke* he became not only one of the commissioners to treat with those on the king's side for the surrender of *Oxford* garrison; but also one of those who resided in the army under sir *Thomas Fairfax*. He continued in this station till at the treaty at *Holdenby anno* 1646, he was put upon the king as one of his menial servants amongst others, in the room of several of his own whom the king was forced to part with to oblige the parliament's commissioners. Being thus settled in that honourable office, and having a nearer view, as it were, of his majesty, he soon discerned the real goodness of the king, dispelled of all those clouds of aspersions his party had endeavoured to blacken him with. From this moment he became a convert to the royal cause, and continued with the king, when all the rest of the chamber were removed, till his majesty was, to the horror of all the world, brought to the block.

In consideration of the faithful service to his father in the two last years of his life, king *Charles* II, immediately upon his restoration, by letters patent bearing date *July* 3, 1660, created him a baronet; by the name of sir *Thomas Herbert* of *Tintern* in *Monmouthshire*. Where he had an estate the seat of *Thomas Herbert* before mentioned.

He has written a relation of some years travels into *Africa* and the greater *Asia*; especially the territories of the *Persian* monarchy, and some part of the oriental *Indies*, and isles adjacent. *London* 1634, 1638, *&c.* 1677, which is the fourth impression, wherein many things are added which were not in the former. *Folio*, and adorned with cuts.

He also at the proposal of *John de Laet*, his familiar friend, living at *Leyden*, did translate some books of his *India Occidentalis*; but certain business interposing the perfecting of them was hindred.

He left behind him at his death an historical account of the two last years of the life of king *Charles* I. the martyr; which he entituled *Threnodia Carolina*; written by him *anno* 1678.

Ant. Wood is very copious in the account of this gentleman's life, to whom, for brevity's sake, I refer the reader. That author has published, from several letters he had from sir *Thomas*, an account of the last days of king *Charles* I, which, he says, is the substance of his *Threnodia*, and which the author desired him to make known to the world; giving for reasons, first, because there were many things in it that have not yet been divulged; secondly, that he was grown old and not in a capacity to publish it himself; thirdly, that if he should leave it to his relations to do it, they out of ignorance or partiality, might spoil it. The antiquary has done him justice; and, truly, it is so moving a representation of the insults and indignities put upon that good king, some time before his death; so pathetick an account of his more than human patience in suffering those affronts; that, whoever can read it and refrain tears, must have a heart almost as hard as the villains that sentenced, or the executioner that destroyed him.

At length this worthy person sir *Thomas Herbert*, who was his whole life a great observer of men and things, died at his house in *York*, *March* 1, 1681, in the seventy sixth year of his age; and was buried in the church of St. *Crux*, or holy cross, in *Foss-gate*, where a monumental inscription is put over him (*r*).

Christopher Cartwright was born in *York*. Sir *T. W.* calls him his *coetanean* in *Cambridge*, of whom, being living, he says, he shall only tell what Mr. *Leigh* a learned gentleman saith of him in a book lately printed (*s*). "*Christopher Cartwright* a learned pious "divine of *Peter-house* in *Cambridge*; not only well skilled in the learned languages, as *Hebrew*, *Greek* and *Latin*, but also well versed in the *Hebrew rabbins*; for which he is honourably mentioned by *Vorstius* in the last edition of his *bibliotheca*." His annotations on *Genesis* and *Exodus* are well liked by the learned in general. Mr. *Pocock* stiles him *vir eruditissimus* (*t*). The account of this man is taken wholly from sir *T. W.* for, as the learned world is not yet made happy with a history of the *Cambridge* writers, though it is much expected from the labours of that great antiquary Mr. *Baker* of St. *John's*, I am not able to give any further intelligence concerning Mr. *Cartwright's* life and writings.

(*r*) See his epitaph in that church.

(*s*) *Leigh's* treatise of religion and of religious and learned men, f. 155.

(*t*) *In notis misc.* c. 4.

(*u*) JOHN EARLE received his first being in the city of *York*, says *Ant. Wood*; he was admitted probationer fellow of *Merton* college in *Oxford*, *anno* 1620, at nineteen years old; and proceeded in arts four years after. His younger years were adorned with oratory, poetry, and witty fancies; and his elder with quaint preaching and subtle disputes. In 1631. he was one of the proctors of the *university*, and about that time chaplain to *Philip* earl of *Pembroke*, who, for his service and merits, bestowed on him the rectory of *Bishopston* in *Wilts*. Afterwards he was constituted chaplain and tutor to *Charles* prince of *Wales*, when Dr. *Duppa* was made bishop of *Salisbury*. He was created doctor of divinity in 1642, elected one of the *assembly of divines* in the year following, but refused to sit amongst them; and the latter end of the same year 1643, was chancellor of the cathedral church of *Salisbury* in the room of *William Chillingworth* deceased. He was afterwards deprived of all he had for adhering to his majesty king *Charles* I, and suffered in exile with his son *Charles* II; whom, after his defeat at *Worcester*, he saluted at *Roan*, upon his arrival in *Normandy*, and thereupon was made his chaplain and clerk of the closet. Upon the king's return he was made dean of *Westminster*; keeping his clerkship still, was consecrated bishop of *Worcester*, after the death of Dr. *Gauden*, *ult. Nov.* 1662; and at last, on the remove of Dr. *Humph. Henchman* to *London*, he was translated to the see of *Salisbury*, *Sept.* 28, 1663.

This Dr. *Earle* was a very genteel man, a contemner of the world, religious, and most worthy the office of a bishop. *Cressy* (*x*), a man of a different perswasion, gives him this character: "He was a person of the sweetest and most obliging nature that lived in our age; "and since Mr. *Richard Hooker* died, none have lived whom God had blest with more inno-"cent wisdom, more sanctified learning, or a more pious, peaceable, and primitive tem-"per than he." He hath written,

An elegy on Mr. *Francis Beaumont* the poet. —— Afterwards printed at the end of *Beaumont's poems*, *London* 1640, 4*to*.

Microcosmography, or, a piece of the world characterised in essays and characters, *London*, 1628, 12*o*. Published under the name of *Edward Blount*.

He also translated out of *English* into *Latin* Εικων Βασιλικη, which he intituled *Imago regis* Caroli *primi in aerumnis et solitudine*. *Hag. Com.* 1649. 12*o*.

A translation of the *laws of ecclesiastical polity*, written by *Richard Hooker* in eight books. This is in manuscript and not yet printed.

Dr. *Earle* being esteemed a witty man, says *Wood*, whilst he continued in the university, several copies of his ingenuity and poetry were greedily gathered up, some of which he had seen; particularly the *Latin* poem styled *Hortus Mertonensis*; the beginning of which is *Hortus deliciae domûs politae*, &c. He had also a hand, adds this author, in some of the *figures*, of which about ten were published, but which figure or figures claim him he knew not.

At length this worthy bishop retiring to *Oxon*, when the king, queen, and their respective courts settled there for a time, to avoid the plague then raging in *London* and *Westminster*, took up his quarters in *University* college, where dying on the 17th of *November* 1665, he was buried near the high altar in *Merton* college church. Being accompanied to his grave, from the publick schools, by an herald at arms, and the principal persons of the court and university.

MARMADUKE FOTHERGILL was born in the city of *York* in the year 1652; in the great house anciently called *Percy's inn*, in the parish of St. *Dyonis Walm-gate*; his father, an able citizen, having acquired a very considerable fortune there by trade. The family is very ancient in this county, and, if we believe the traditional story, given in a former part of this work, the name has been no stranger to the city for some ages. But howsoever that, *Thomas Fothergill*, his brother, and *George Fothergill*, were sheriffs of the city in the years 1688 and 1693; his father having fined for that and other offices some years before.

Marmaduke, the eldest son, had his first rudiments of learning in *York*, which he afterwards perfected in *Magdalene* college in *Cambridge*. Before the *Revolution*, he was possessed of the living of *Shipwith*, in the county of *York*, which at that grand *criterion* he quitted; as well as his pretensions to the rectory of the town of *Lancaster*; of which he had a promise for the next presentation, from the then patron of it —— *Tolson*, esquire, of *Shipwith* aforesaid. After that time he never took any oath to any king or queen, but lived upon the income of his own small estate with great content and chearfulness. Being a great admirer of learning and learned men, he frequently visited his mother, the university, always travelling on foot; and when he became of proper standing there, he performed all the exercises, and gave the usual treat for the degree of doctor in divinity; but by his not complying with the government oaths, as the statute directs, he never assumed the title, though, perhaps, no divine of this age was better qualified for it. His learning and piety were remarkable; and, in ecclesiastical antiquity, especially in the liturgies of the *Christian* church, no man had more skill or knowledge. He had made great collections of manuscripts, &c. in this way, and had a design of publishing somewhat on this head, as he himself has in-

(*u*) *Athen. Oxon.* vol. II. p. 363.

(*x*) In his *Epist. apologet.* 46, 47. Life of Mr. *Hooker*, &c.

formed me, but, I believe, his great modesty forbad it. By which means the learned world is prevented from seeing as extraordinary a performance on that divine subject, as perhaps ever was exhibited to publick view. The marginal notes which he has left on all his missals, rituals, and liturgies, shewing plainly that he was a master of it.

The middle part of his life he usually spent at one gentleman's house in the country or at another's; where his learning and parts gained him admittance and a welcome entertainment in their families; but the place of his own home he made for several years at *Pontfrete* in this county. Here it was, that, when he was a good way passed the meridian of life, he thought fit to take to wife *Dorothy* the daughter of Mr. *John Dickson*, an honest and an eminent practitioner of the law in that town. And being now entered into a new scene of life, his great oeconomy in it enabled him to be a chearful alms-giver; for he set apart a tenth of his small annual income for charity; and disposed of it as he received it to the most worthy objects. But his greatest donation of that kind was to the town of *Pontfrete*, where he resided some years after his marriage, in a quiet and submissive manner to the times; until he was driven from thence, to seek a sanctuary in *Westminster*, by a furious persecution raised against him, by a hot-headed, neighbouring justice of the peace. Before this happened, he had settled on the town of *Pontfrete* fifty pounds a year, arising from a fine piece of ground contiguous to it, and clear of all taxes and deductions, for the maintenance of a *catechist* in that parish. This donation he some time after confirmed, notwithstanding the unexpected births of two children, which his wife afterwards bore him, might reasonably have prevented it; and the bequest will actually take place on the death of his widow.

At last this venerable old man, being arrived at great maturity in years, died at his house in *Massam-street*, *Westminster*, *Sept.* 7, 1731, and was buried, according to his own direction, in a corner of the church yard belonging to the parish of St. *John the evangelist* in that city. By his last will he left a fine collection of books, as a standing library to the parish of *Shipwith*, of which he had been minister; but the parishioners being enjoined to build a proper room for them, at their own cost, the bequest is not accepted of. Therefore his widow is willing to bestow the books on the library of the cathedral of *York*, and a bill in chancery is preparing, by the dean and chapter, to reverse that part of the will for that purpose, and to have this handsome donation confirmed to them. The epitaph on his tombstone being concise, according to his own desire, and no ways answerable to so diffusive a character, as may be observed by the transcript of it below, I beg leave to give the following description of his person, and to subjoin a short, but handsome and real account of his manner of living and dying; said to be done by a neighbouring clergyman in *Westminster*, and published in the news-papers of that time. In stature he was of a middle size, somewhat corpulent, but of so robust a constitution that no cold could affect. Having used himself so much to harden it that in the depth of winter he has frequently jumped out of bed and rolled in the snow without danger. His deportment was grave and majestick, his hair as white as wool, with a clear sanguine complexion and manlike features, had altogether the air and reverence of a *primitive father*. "Though he had no church, he read the com-" mon-prayer daily and constantly at home to his own family only, and his life was a conti-" nual sermon to all who enjoyed the happiness of his conversation. His death was suita-" ble to such a life; remarkably easy, resigned and chearful, and supported by a firm hope" of a glorious immortality."

To conclude; I cannot avoid taking notice, that this good man's charities, patience and sufferings, through a course of so many years, seems, by providence to be particularly rewarded in the person of his only son; who is now in possession of a fine estate, left him since his father's death, by a somewhat distant relation, the late *Thomas Fothergill*, esq; of *York*.

The ARMS and EPITAPH on his tomb-stone are these:

Impaling, 1. A stag's head erased. *Fothergill.* 2. A cross charged with five ogresses between four eagles displayed. *Dickson.*

H. S. E.
MARMADUCUS FOTHERGILL,
S. T. P.
Qui obiit 7 die Septembris *anno Dom.* 1731. *aetatis* 78.

CHAP.

p. 380

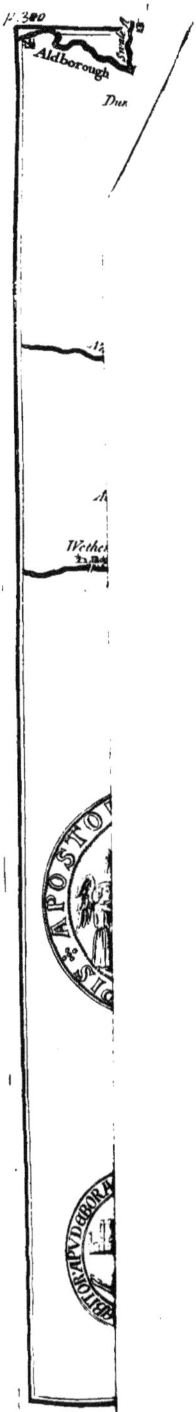

THE ASTOR LIBRARY NY

CHAP. IX.

A survey of the AINSTY, *or county of the city of* YORK; *wherein the ancient and present lords of manors within that district are taken notice of. A genealogical account of some ancient families therein. The churches and remarkable epitaphs, with the boundaries, bridges, highways,* &c.

AINSTY, is now a district on the west side *York* under the jurisdiction of the lord-mayor, aldermen and sheriffs of the city; to which it was annexed the 27th of *Hen.* VI; though before it was a hundred, or **weapontack**, of the *west-riding* in this county. And it has ever since then been called the county of the city of *York*.

The name of *Ainsty* is an odd appellation, which Mr. *Camden (a)* says some derive from the word **ancienty**, to denote its antiquity; but he is of opinion it comes rather from the *German* word **anstossen**, implying a bound or limit. There is little reason for this conjecture, for it is certain this district was called the *Ainsty* long before it was joined to the city. In some old writings that I have copied and given in the juridical part of this work, it is constantly called **Ainsty**; by which name, it was, probably, known when it was a weapontake of the county at large; and styled so from the old northern word **Anent**, yet well known amongst us to signify *a hundred contiguous, opposite,* or *near*, the city itself.

The whole district, or **weapontack**, of the **Ainsti** was anciently a *forest*; but disforested by the charters of king *Richard* I. and king *John*. For the first of which grants I find the inhabitants paid *(b)* nineteen pounds and eleven pence; and for the latter, that the men of this **weapontack**, and their heirs, as the charter expresses it, should be for ever free from **forest laws**, account was made to the king of the sum of the hundred and twenty marks and three palfrys *(c)*. Sir *T. W.* writes that the city of *York* has very anciently laid claim to this jurisdiction, by a charter from king *John*; as appears by the pleas before king *Edw.* I. *an. reg.* 8. when the mayor of this city did produce a charter of king *John*, by which he claimed the hundred of the *Ainsty*; which charter, upon inspection, was found rased in the date in the word *quarto*. Upon the search of the rolls in the exchequer *(d)* it was found, that king *John*, in the fifteenth year of his reign, did grant to the citizens of *York* the town of *York*, in fee-farm for the rent of one hundred and sixty pounds; and because the hundred aforesaid was not specified in the charter of *anno quarto*, and also because that charter was rased, judgment was given against the mayor and citizens, the charter quashed, and the mayor committed to prison; but shortly after bailed. The fourth of *Edward* I. the mayor and bailiffs were also summoned to answer the king, *quo warranto (e)*, they held the *weapontack* of the *Ainsty*; and says sir *T. W.* from whom I have taken this paragraph, it may be doubted whether they had any good warrant saving for the **leet**, and some other liberties, till the 27th of *Henry* VI, by whose charter or patent it was annexed to the city *(f)*; since which it has had the sanction of an act of parliament to confirm it *(g)*.

	Miles.
The boundary of the **Ainsty**, or weapontack of the city of *York*, is thus computed, from the confluence or meeting of the rivers *Ouse* and *Nid* and *Nun-Monkton*, on the north of the city to the confluence of the rivers *Wharf* and *Ouse* on the south, which is in computation — — — —	12
From the meeting of the rivers *Wharf* and *Ouse*, on the south, to the town of *Thorp-arch* on the west, is by computation — —	11
On the west it is bounded by the county of *York* from the town of *Thorp-arch* to the town of *Wilstropp* upon *Nidd*, by the out-range of the parishes of *Thorp-arch*, *Bickerton*, *Cattle-bridge* and *Wilstropp*; by computation — —	6
On the north it is bounded with the river *Nidd* from the town of *Wilstropp* to the confluence of the river *Ouse* at *Nun-monkton*; which is — —	3
In all	32

John Leland says, **that the fraunchises and libertys of** YORK **streatch far about the city, especially by the enclosynge of dyvers rivers; and one way it cometh to the very bridge of**

(a) Camden's Brit.

(b) Mag. rot. 5 Ric. *I. rot.* 5. *a.* **Evertwicscire.** *Maddox's* exchequer, *p.* 274. *lit. a.*

(c) Mag. rot. 10 Joh. *rot.* 18. *a.* Maddox 282. *(d) Wapontack de* **Ainsti** *r. c. de* c. *lib. pro habend. quiet. forest per cartam dom. regis et quod non fuit amplius in foresta.* Rot. Pipe. 2 Ric. I.

(d) In the receipt of the exchequer, in *rotulo majore*; also.

(e) In parvo record. rot. 8.

(f) De annex. hundred. de Kynsty *com. civ.* Ebor. *pat.* 27. Hen. VI. *p.* 1, *m.* 14.

(g) Pasch. 23 Car. I. *Regist.* B. *f.* 352.

AINSTY. TADCASTER upon WHARF. The citizens have asserted their right to this district several times, by their sheriffs meeting and attending the kings of *England* in their progresses, on the midst of *Tadcaster-bridge*. These have happened, as may be seen at large in the *annals*, and appears in the registers of the city, to be in 18 *Hen.* VII. 7 *Hen.* VIII. 17 *Jam.* I. and in the ninth, fifteenth, and sixteenth years of king *Charles* the first.

Anno 1661, a petition was drawn up by the city and presented to *Edward* earl of *Clarendon*, then lord chancellor of *England*, setting forth, that by the charter of 27 *Hen.* VI. "the weapontack of the *Ancitty* was annexed to the city, and thereby granted that the "mayor and aldermen of the said city should be justices of peace within the said weapontack as well as within the city. That these liberties and privileges had been confirmed to "them by divers kings, particularly *Charles* I; and that they and their predecessors, for "the space of two hundred years, have holden their general quarter sessions of the peace "within the city for the said district, the remotest part of which is not above eight miles "from it.

"That nevertheless some gentlemen, as sir *Thomas Slingsby*, sir *Miles Stapleton*, *James* "*Moyser* and *Richard Roundell*, who were not free of the city, had by his lordship's warrant been put in commission of peace within the said weapontack.

"The petitioners therefore humbly beseeched his lordship not to take away their ancient "rights and privileges, but to supersede the said commission.

The chancellor answered, that he would not by any act or order of his infringe or violate the city's privileges; but he had been informed the matter was otherways than they represented it, before the beginning of the late troubles; however he would hear both sides, and appointed a day accordingly. Upon hearing the commissions were superseded.

The city of *York*, together with the *Ancitty*, is accounted the eighth Part of the *west riding*, and the twentieth part of the whole county at large. In all assessments by act of parliament, the city is taxed at three fifths; the *Ancitty* two fifths. It is very particular, that the inhabitants of this district are not represented at all in parliament; their being annexed to the city did not make them capable of voting at any election of members in it, and their being cut off from the county deprives them from being free-holders of it at large. The inhabitants, however, vote for the members of the county, but are always taken with a *quere* against their names; that if the matter should come to be contested in the house, they might be admitted, or rejected, as the house was in an humour to allow it.

Within the whole liberty of the *Ancitty* are thirty five towns, or hamlets; thirty two of which are constableries. The names of them are as follows:

1. *Acombe.*	13. *Coulton.*	25. *Nether Poppleton.*
2. *Askam Richard.*	14. *Coppen thorpe.*	26. *Oxton.*
3. *Askam Bryan.*	15. *Catterton.*	27. *Rufforth.*
4. *Appleton.*	16. *Dring houses.*	28. *Steeton.*
5. *Acaster Malbis.*	17. *Hutton Wansley.*	29. *Thorp arch.*
6. *Acaster Selby.*	18. *Holgate.*	30. *Tockwith.*
7. *Angram.*	19. *Hessay.*	31. *Tadcaster,*
8. *Bickerton.*	20. *Helaugh.*	32. *Upper Poppleton.*
9. *Bolton Percy.*	21. *Knapton.*	33. *Walton.*
10. *Bilbrough.*	22. *Moore Monkton.*	34. *Wighill.*
11. *Bishopthorpe.*	23. *Marston.*	34. *Willstropp*, or *thorp.*
12. *Bilton.*	24. *Middlethorp.*	

There is a little rivulet called *Foss*, which waters a great part of the *Ainsty*. It begins about *Wetherby* woods, runneth through *Walton* park, *Wighill* park, *Helagh* park, by *Catterton*, over *Tadcaster* moor, by *Seaton*, *Paddocktborp*, and into the *Wharf* at *Bolton-Percy*.

I now begin my general description of the *Ainsty* at *Skelder-gate* postern; and the reader may observe, that the names of several small hamlets or seats will occur in it which are not townships, and consequently not put down in the preceding list.

MIDDLETHORPE comes first in my way, but being in the parish of St. *Mary's Bishophill* the elder, *York*, it may be said to lye in the suburbs of the city. By an ancient list of the lords of the several manors in the *Ainsty*, *temp. Ed.* II. (*b*) *Middlethorpe* is put down as then belonging to the abbot and convent of *Byland*; but I find no mention in the *Monast.* when or how they got it. It is at present part of the possessions of *Francis Barlow*, esq; whose father built a fine house here. But the manor is in dispute whether it belongs to him or the reverend Dr. *Breary*.

(*i*) BISHOPTHORPE, anciently St. **Andrew's-thorp**, alias **Thorpe super Use.** In this town *Robert Bustard* held two carucats of land of the king, *in capite*, at the rent of four marks *per annum*.

The archbishop of *York* held therein ten oxgang of land of the fee of *Lutterell*.

(*b*) Dated at *Clifton*, *teste rege*, *March* 5, *anno reg.* 9. 1316.

(*i*) *Ex MS.* sir *T. W.* *Torre.* 325.

Also

Alſo *Robert Holdebert* held ſix oxgangs of *Richard de Malbys* of the honour of *Eye*, at the rent of ſix pence. AINSTY.

Likewiſe the prior of St. *Andrew's York* held ſeventeen oxgangs of land in the ſame town.

Walter Grey, archbiſhop of *York* purchaſed the manor of **Thorpe St. Andrew**, of divers feefors, to himſelf, his heirs, and aſſigns for ever.

(*k*) The ſaid archbiſhop, to promote the good of him and his ſucceſſors, gave and granted the ſame manſion-houſes thereunto pertaining to the chapter of *York*; upon condition that they might grant it to his ſucceſſors, archbiſhops of *York*, whilſt they continue ſo, for the annual rent of twenty marks ſterling, to be paid at *Martinmas* to the treaſurer of the church of *York*; for the maintenance of his chantry. Whereupon the ſaid dean and chapter have ever ſince deviſed the ſaid manor, *&c.* to the ſucceeding archbiſhops for the term of their lives. And during the vacancy of the ſee the ſame does revert to themſelves, and remains in their ſeiſin till a new archbiſhop be placed.

The rectory of St. *Andrew* at *Thorpe* was by *Walter Giffard* archbiſhop, after the deceaſe of *Arnold de Berkeley* then rector, granted to the prioreſs and nuns of St. *Clement* without the walls of *York*, to be poſſeſſed to their own proper uſe for ever. The deed was dated *November* 1; *anno* 1269; it was alſo by the aforeſaid archbiſhop converted into a vicaridge, the vicar whereof was preſentable by the ſaid prioreſs and nuns. Who was to have for the portion of his vicaridge that whole manſion, with its gardens and virgult, which lies between the houſe of *Ralph Halidays*, &c. Together with two *ſelions* of land on the outſide of the ſaid garden ſouthward, and abutting to the ſaid virgult. He ſhall alſo receive the whole profits of the alterage of the church, and two marks *per annum* out of the chamber of the priory quarterly; and on every lord's day have one refectory in their houſe. The ſaid prioreſs and nuns ſhall pay all archiepiſcopal and archidiaconal dues; find books and ornaments of the church; and bear all other burthens thereof at their own coſts. Only the vicar ſhall repair the chancel when need requires; but at the new building thereof ſhall bear only his proportion (*l*).

At the diſſolution the gift of this vicaridge came to the crown, who conſtantly preſented to it, till the preſent archbiſhop got a change for the living of *Helperby*; by which means it came again to the ſee, after an alienation of near five hundred years. This ſmall vicaridge had likewiſe an augmentation by the late queen *Anne's* bounty; procured by the ſaid archbiſhop.

Gray's *chantry*.

Walter Gray, when he ſettled the manor of *Thorpe* upon his chapter, reſerved out of it twenty marks ſterling to be paid into the hands of the treaſurer, for the time being of the cathedral church, for him to diſtribute ſix pound yearly at *Pentecoſt* and *Martinmaſs*, for the maintenance of one chaplain, preſentable by the dean and chapter, or by the chapter if there be no dean, for ever.

Who ſhall celebrate in his chapel of *Thorpe* St. *Andrew* for the ſouls of *John* late king of *England*, and of him the ſaid archbiſhop, and of all faithful deceaſed (*m*).

The palace of *Biſhopthorpe* was built by the aforeſaid *Walter Grey*, in which is the neat chapel, ſtill ſtanding, where his chantry was founded. The houſe has had ſeveral reparations by the ſucceeding archbiſhops, which will be particularly taken notice of in the account of their lives. It is ſufficient here to ſay, that the preſent beautiful gardens were, almoſt, wholly laid out at the charge of archbiſhop *Sharp*; and the houſe received great alterations in the hall, dining rooms, *&c.* at the expence of the late archbiſhop *Dawes*.

At the ſale of the biſhop's lands, by our late bleſſed reformers, this palace and manor of *Biſhopthorpe* was ſold to *Walter White* eſq; *March* 10, 1647, for five hundred and twenty five pound ſeven ſhillings and ſix pence, who made it his ſeat till the *Reſtoration*.

The vicaridge at *Biſhopthorpe* is thus valued in the king's books.	*l.*	*s.*	*d.*
First fruits	04	00	00
Tenths	00	08	00

Monumental INSCRIPTIONS in the church of Biſhopthorpe.

Here lyeth he whoſe flower of youth in ſin was ſpent, Brighous 1579
But, through grace of the deity,
In age earneſtly he did repent.
And truſted in Chriſte from God being ſent.
Expecting now with ſaints alone
The longid for comynge of Jeſus to dome.
Robertus Brighous qui . . . .
. . . vita mutata . . . . ob. xxx die Aug.
A. D. 1579.

(*k*) Dated 11 kal. *April*, *anno* 1241.

(*l*) *Ex MS.* Torre, 325.

(*m*) *Idem f.* 328. A cottage in *Biſhopthorpe*, called **Chauntry-house**, one garden, a meadow and a croft adjoining, *&c.* was ſold to *Walter Wolflete*, *July* 25, 5 *Ed.* VI. amongſt many other chantry la ds. *Rolls* chap.

Depoſi-

Ainsty
Brthwayt
1675.

Depositum Richardi Brathwayt *filii*
Edwardi Brathwayt *et* Annae *uxoris ejus*,
qui obiit 22 *die Sept.* 1673.

The lord archbishop of *York* still lord of the manor of *Bishopthorpe*.

Acaster Malbys, or *Alcaster* bears a *Roman* sound in its name, antiently contained four carucats of land held by the family of *Malbys*; who had free warren in their lands in *Acaster*. The *Malbys*, from whom the town takes its name, flourished here for some centuries after the conquest; till at length a daughter and heiress of this family was married to *Fairfax* of *Walton*, created viscount *Emley*, whose descendants are still in possession of this estate (*n*).

The church of *Acaster* was given, by *Richard Malbys*, to the abbey of *Newbo*, *com. Lincoln*; *anno* 1348; till which time the *Malbys* were patrons of this rectory.

Jan. 15, 1348, this church was appropriated to the said abbot and convent of *Newbo*, by *John* archbishop of *York*, who ordained therein, that there be a perpetual vicar, *viz.* one of the canons regular of that monastery, in priests orders, and presentable by the said abbot and convent. The portion of whose vicaridge should consist in all the houses within the lower close of the rectory, for his mansion and habitation, with a curtelage adjoining, built and repaired the first time at the charge of the said abbot and convent. Also in name of the portion of his vicaridge shall receive of them twelve pound *per annum*, payable at *Martinmass* intirely. For which the vicar shall find bread and wine, vestments, and other ornaments of the altar, and shall be at the charge of washing them. And all other burdens ordinary and extraordinary which are incumbent on the church, the said abbot and convent shall wholly bear for ever.

At the dissolution the presentation fell to sir *Nicholas Fairfax*; which family have ever since presented except one turn of queen *Elizabeth*. I find this rectory was sold to *Robert Fairfax*, the tenth of *Elizabeth*, for twenty pound (*o*). The honourable *Charles Fairfax* of *Gilling* the present lord of this manor.

Monumental INSCRIPTIONS in this church.

Northfolk.

(*p*) ✠ **Orate pro animabus dom. Nicholas Northfolk de . . . . qui obiit . . mense Novembris, anno Dom. M.CCC . . . et Elene ux. ejus . . . . . . quorum animabus propitietur Deus. Amen.**

Under the south wall is a stone whereon is raised the solid portraiture of one of the *Malbys*, in armour, crosslegged; on his shield a chevron inter three hinds heads erased.

Acaster Selby, or *Over Acaster*, was so called from being part of the possessions of the abbot of *Selby*. It is now part of that great estate which belongs to the right honourable the lady *Petre*; but the manor is in sir *Lyonel Pilkington* bart.

Nun Appleton, took its name from a priory of nuns founded here, by a lady called *Adeliza de sancto Quintino*, *temp. reg. Steph.* with the consent of *Robert* her son and heir, and dedicated to God, St. *Mary*, St. *John the apostle*; which was confirmed by *Thomas* archbishop of *Canterbury*. The charter of the foundation of this nunnery grants in pure and perpetual alms to Fr. *Richard* and the nuns here serving God, all that place which *Juliana* held near **Appleton**, with the land about it, partly essarted and part not, on each bank of the river **Wharfe**, unto the bounds placed by *Hugh*, *Siward* and *William*. Also two oxgangs of land in **Appleton**, and one oxgang in **Thorpe** free from all earthly service, *&c.* The witnesses to this deed are *Osbert* archdeacon, *Henry* and *Godfrey* monks of *Pontefract*, *Gilbert* the son of *Fulk*, *Gilbert de* **Archis**, *Walter de* **Ristre**, *Agnes* daughter to the said lady St. *Quintine*, &c. (*q*).

The several donations made by the founders and other benefactors to the nunnery were confirmed by king *John* in the sixth year of his reign (*r*). Amongst the injunctions prescribed to the nuns of this house, *anno* 1489, there are these, *that the cloister doors be shut up in winter at seven, and in summer at eight at night; and the keys delivered to the prioress. That the prioress and all the sisters lodge nightly in the Dorter, unless sick or diseased. That none of the sisters use the ale-house, nor the waterside, where course of strangers daily resort. That none of the sisters have their service of meat and drink to their chambers, but keep the frater and the hall, unless sick. That no sister bring in any man, religious or secular, into their chamber or any secret place, day or night, &c. That the prioress licence no sister to go a pilgrimage or visit their friends, without great cause, and then to have a companion. That the convent grant no corrodies or liveries of bread, or ale, or other victual, to any person without special licence. That they take in no perhendinauncers or sojourners, unless children, or old persons*, &c.

Besides the donations mentioned in the *monast.* I have met with some original grants to

(*n*) Ex MS. D. T. W. *et* Torre, 319.
(*o*) Rolls chapel.
(*p*) See *Norfolk's* chantry St. *Mary Castlegate*.
(*q*) *Mon. Ang.* v. 1. 908, 909, *&c.*
(*r*) *Turre* Lond. *anno* 6 Joh. *cart.* 52.

this nunnery, which I ſhall give in the *appendix.* Mr. *Torre* (*s*) has the names of the following prioreſſes, but it cannot be called a cloſe catalogue. AINSTY.

PRIORESSES of APPLETON.

Anno.		
1303	*Domna*	Johanna de Normanvill.
1320	*Domna*	Iſabella de Normanvill, *common. domus.*
1392	*Domna*	Hawiſia.
	Domna	Eliz. de Holbeck, *commonialis domus.*
	Domna	Lucia de Gainſbury.
1367	*Domna*	Agnes de Egmonton, *common. domus.*
	Domna	Idonea Danyell.
1426	*Domna*	Eliz. Fitz Richard, *common. domus.*
14 .	*Domna*	Agnes de Ryther (*t*).
14 .	*Domna*	Johan. de Ryther.
1419	*Domna*	Matilda Tayleboice.
1506	*Domna*	Anna Langton, *commonialis domus.*

Chantry.

There was a chantry founded in the conventual church of this nunnery at the altar of St. *John Baptiſt*; of which the convent had the patronage.

December 5, 31 *Henry* VIII the ſurrender of this nunnery was inrolled. And the revenue was at the diſſolution valued at ſeventy three pound nine ſhillings and ten pence. *Dug.*

Lord *Thomas Fairfax*, whoſe anceſtors had a grant of the ſite and eſtate of this nunnery from the diſſolution, or near it, built a handſome houſe here; which has been ſince purchaſed, from that family, by Mr. *Milner* merchant in *Leeds*, whoſe ſon ſir *William Milner* bart. now enjoys it.

The town of APPLETON antiently contained twelve carucats of land, whereof *Walter de Falconberg*, *Henry Sampſon*, and others held three carucats of the abbot of St. *Mary's York.* The reſidue, *viz.* nine carucates, were held of the heirs of *Brus*, who held them of the barons *Moubray*, and they of the king in *capite* at the rent of eighteen pence *ob. q.*

The manor of **Southwood**, in **Appleton**, was ſometime the land of *Richard Falconberg*, and was given by him to ſir *John Sampſon* of *York* knight, and *Mary* his wife, their heirs and aſſigns.

Appleton is now in ſeveral hands; of which *John Moyſer* eſq; ſir *Henry Slingſby* bart. ſir *William Milner* bart. are the chief owners.

BOLTON PERCY, which has been ſometimes called **Brodleton**, ſays ſir *T. W.* antiently contained in its townſhip eight carucates of land; held by *Robert de Percy* of the heirs of *Henry de Percy*, baron of **Topcliffe**, who held it of the king *in capite*, at the rent of four ſhillings *per annum.*

King *Edward* I. granted licence to *Robert de Percy* to embattle his manſion houſe at **Bolton.**

In the book of *Doomſday* the lands of *William Percy* are ſaid to lie in the weſtriding in the weapontack of the *Ainſty*; and amongſt other things it is taken notice of that he had a wood at *Bolton*, a mile long and half a mile broad. A great part of this wood was afterwards given by a *Percy* to the building of the cathedral church at *York.*

This manor afterwards came to the lords *Beaumont*, who in the eleventh of *Edward* III. obtained a charter for free warren in all all his demeſn lands here. They had a manor houſe by the church, and their arms are in ſeveral places in the windows of it.

(*u*) The church of *Bolton* was given by *Picote de Percy* to the priory of **Noſtall.** But *anno* 1150, the prior and convent of *Noſtall* transferred the patronage thereof to the archbiſhops of *York*, and their ſucceſſors for ever.

January 10, 1323, pope *John* XXIII. appropriated it to the table of the archbiſhop, during the life of *William de Melton* then archbiſhop; granting to him power, when he ſhould ceaſe or deceaſe, to reduce the church to its priſtine ſtate. Whereupon the ſaid archbiſhop, according to the form of theſe apoſtolick letters collated *dom. Rob. de Byngham preſb.* to ſerve as vicar thereof during the ſaid union for the term of his life, aſſigning him a competent portion for a maintenance (*x*).

The rectory of *Bolton Percy* was thus valued in the kings books, *viz.*	*l.*	*s.*	*d.*
Firſt fruits 40*l.* now	39	15	02 ½
Tenths	03	17	04
Procurations	00	07	06

The preſent lord of this manor is ſir *William Milner* bart.

(*s*) *Torre* 143.
(*t*) See her epitaph in *Bolton* church.
(*u*) *Torre* p. 135.
(*x*) *Idem.*

AINSTY.

(y) *A CATALOGUE of the RECTORS of* Bolton Percy.

Temp. instit. Anno	*Rectores.*	*Patroni.*	*Vacat.*
1250	Radul. Briton.	*Collat. archiepis.*	
	Dom. Rog. d'Oyley.		*per mort.*
1309	Baldwin. de St. Albano *cler.*	*Idem.*	*per resig.*
1323	Rob. de Byngham *presb.*	*Idem.*	
1527	Nich. de Duffeld *presb.*	*Idem.*	
1340	Joh. de Pulkore *cap.*	*Rex* Ed. III. *sede vacant.*	*per resig.*
1345	Will. de Shireburn *presb.*	*Archiepisc.* Ebor.	*per mort.*
1349	Tho. de Halwell *cler.*	*Idem.*	*per resig.*
1351	Joh. de Aylestone *cap.*	*Idem.*	*per resig.*
1353	Joh. de Irford *presb.*	*Idem.*	
1365	Adam de Hedley *vel* Clareburgh.	*Idem.*	*per resig.*
1370	Tho. de Halwell . . .	*Idem.*	*per mort.*
1372	Hen. de Barton *presb.*	*Idem.*	
	Rich. Digell *presb.*	*Idem.*	*per resig.*
1407	Will. Crosse *presb.*	*Rex sede vac.*	*per resig.*
1411	Tho. Parker *presb.*	*Archiepiscopus* Ebor.	*per mort.*
1423	Joh. Sellowe *presb. decret. B.*	*Idem.*	*per mort.*
1438	Tho. Kempe.	*Idem.*	
1449	Joh. Berningham.	*Idem.*	*per resig.*
1450	Ric. Tene *decret. D.*	*Idem.*	*per mort.*
1463	Joh. Sendale *LL. D.*	*Idem.*	*per mort.*
1466	Tho. Pierson *decret. D.*	*Idem.*	*per mort.*
1490	Rob. Wellington *presb. sepult. apud* Gilling.	*Idem.*	
	Hen. Trafforde *decret. doct.*	*Idem.*	*per mort.*
1537	Arthur Cole *cler.*	*Idem.*	*per mort.*
1557	Rob. Johnson *cler. L. B.*	*Idem.*	
	Tho. Lakyn *S. T. P.*	*Idem.*	*per mort.*
1575	Edmund Bunny *S. T. B.*	*Idem.*	*per resig.*
1603	Rog. Akeroyde *S. T. P.*	*Idem.*	*per mort.*
1617	Hen. Wickam *cler.*	*Idem.*	
1660	Tobias Wickam *cler.*		

The present church at *Bolton Percy* was built by *Thomas Parker*, who died rector of it *anno* 1423; his epitaph, which was in the church on the south side the altar expressing it. The fabrick is one of the neatest in the country, but the builder did not live to see it consecrated, for we find that a commission issued out, dated *July* 8, 1424, to the bishop of *Dromore* to dedicate this parish church of *Bolton Percy*, and the church-yard; also the high altar of the church, newly erected and built (z).

Monumental INSCRIPTIONS which are or were in this church anno 1641.

On a grave stone.

Hic jacet Tho. Brocket et Dionisia uxor ejus, qui quidem Tho. obiit xiii die Aprilis anno Dom. M.CCCC.XXXV. Predictaque Dionisia ob. xiv Ap. anno M.CCCC.XXXVII.

Orate pro Thoma Parker quondam rectore hujus eccl. ac ejusdem fabricatore.

On a grave stone,

Hic recubat clausus sub marmore jam Gulielmus,
Grammatices quondam grammata qui docuit.
Quisquis eris puer aut juvenis qui carmina legis
Mason perpaucas funde refunde preces.

(a) Ryther. ✠ **Orate pro anima Agnetis de Ryther quondam priorisse hujus monasterii . . . xxxiii que obiit primo die mensis Martii M.CCCC . . . . cujus anime propitietur Deus. Amen.**

ARMS on this stone,

Impaling dext. three crescents *Ryther*, finist. blank. Semy of quarter foils, probably the arms or signet of the nunnery.

(y) *Torre*, 135.

(z) *Ibid.*

(a) This stone does not originally belong to this church, but was taken out of the nunnery chapel, and for many years served to stop water at a mill; till very lately my worthy friend the reverend Mr. *T. Lamplugh* the present rector, redeemed it and placed it in his church.

In a

In memory of the honourable, vertuous and religious lady Eleonora Selbie, *secunde daughter of the right honourable* Fardinando *lord* Fairfax, *baron of* Cameron, *and wife of sir* William Selbie *knt. of* Twistle *in* Northumberland. *Sir* William Forster *knt. and bart. of* Balmbrough-castle *there, and husband of their sole daughter and heire, caused this marble to be here placed.* AINSTY. Selbie 1670.

Which honourable lady having lived in strictest widowhood twenty one years, seen the sole pledge of her marriage worthly matcht, and blessed with much hopeful issue; having performed the several offices of wife, mother, sister, mistress, friend and neighbour, with all imaginable exactness, at last in great ease and composedness of mind, with entire and absolute resignation gave up her soule into the hands of her gratiouse and ever blessed redeemer, the 17th day of March *in the year of our lord* 1670; *of her age* —— *and lyeth here interred.*

M. S. Fairfax 1647.

Amplissimi desideratissimique Ferdinandi *dom.* Fairfax *baron. de* Cameron, *quem in* Britanniam *et fidei theatrum ager* Ebor.
Edidit.
Majorum splendore clarum,
Curatorem pacis studiosissimum,
Irarum (si quas peperit vicinia) sequestrum,
Aequi bonique tenacissimum.
Quippe summa domi forisque auctoritate,
Parique apud omnes ordines gratia,
Publicae quietis amans,
Sed bello insuperabilis,
Dextra gladium, sinistra stateram tenens
Utriusque laudis trophaea retulit;
Religionis cultor,
Literarum patronus,
Humanitatis repumicator,
Nobilissimae prolis numero et pietate felix,
Quem virum Maria Edmundi *com.* Mulgrave *filia,*
Novies beavit.
Quid igitur novi? si (quas singularis amor tamdiu
Tamque multiplici pignore sociavit)
Mors ipsa non dirimet.
Ob. anno { *Aet. suae* 64. / *Sal. humanae* 1647.

ARMS quarterly,
1. *Argent*, three bars gemels *gules*, over all a lion rampant *sable*, crowned *or*. *Fairfax*. 2. *Argent*, a cheveron entre three hinds heads couped *gules*. 3. *Argent*, four bars *gules*. 4. *Or*, a cross *sable*. 5. *Or*, a bend *sable*. 6. *Or*, a bend *azure* 7. *Argent*, a chevron entre three crows proper. 8. *Argent*, a fess *sable*, charged with three pomets *or*, entre three flowers de lices *gules*.

Here lyeth the bodyes of Henry Fairfax *late rector of this church, and of* Mary *his wife. He dyed* April 6, 1665, *aged* 77. *She dyed* December 24. 1649, *aged* 56. Fairfax 1665.

Arms on the stone, *Fairfax* impaling *Cholmdley*.

M. S. Fairfax 1649.
Mariae Fairfax.
Quam longum gloria sexus et generis certabat
Honos.
Cernis ut insolescit splendetque marmor
Ingentis depositi conscium.
Nihil tamen habet praeter involucrum gemmae
Quam Hen. Cholmeley *de* Roxby *ordinis equestris*
Ex Margareta Gulielmi de Babthorp *milit. filia*
Succussit in virtutum conceptaculum.
Unde forma, moribus, ingenio, fide clara
Scrivenum *ad* Knaresburgh *natalibus,*
Eboracum *geniali toro,*
Quadruplici prole virum,
Innocentia vitae gentem,
Et ferali pompa Bolton Percicum *honestavit.*
Ubi pleuritide correpta ad plures abiit
8 *calend.* Jan. 1649. *aet. suae* 56.
Hen. Fairfax, *altera sui parte spoliatus*
Praestantissimae conjugi
Pietatis et amoris ergo
Lugens posuit.

acted

Ainsty.

Sacred to the memory of mother and daughter.

Bladen 1692. *Near this place lies interred the body of* Isabella *the wife of* Nathanael Bladen *of* Hemsworth *esq; daughter of sir* William Fairfax *of* Steeton *knt. and dame* Frances *his wife, she departed this life* Oct. 25, 1691, *leaving six children* Isabella, Catherina, William, Francis, Elizabeth *and* Martin. *She was a most obedient child, a tender mother, and a faithful friend.*

And likewise of dame Frances *her mother, relict of sir* William Fairfax *aforesaid (daughter of sir* Thomas Chaloner *of* Gisburgh, *who was governour and chamberlain to prince* Henry;) *of their ten children four only lived,* viz. William, Thomas, Catherine *and* Isabella *named above.*

She lived mistress of Steeton *above 60 years, an eminent example of piety and charity. Born* February 1610, *died* January 1692.

Charae memoriae
Almae conjugis ejusque matris
Nathanael Bladen
Superstes hunc titulum posuit.
Vixi, et quem dederat cursum Jehova *peregi.*

Under, six escutcheons of arms.

1. Impaling *gules*, three cheverons *argent*, charged with three pellets of the same. Sinist. *Fairfax.*
2. Quarterly the same as the first.
3. *Azure*, a chevron entre three garbs *or.*
4. *Argent*, six pellets or bezants *sable*, three, two and one.
5. *Or*, a lion rampant *azure*, armed and langued *gules.*
6. *Azure*, a chevron entre three cherubims heads *or. Chaloner.*

Fairfax 1694. *Near this place lyes interred the body of* William Fairfax *of* Steeton *esq; who departed this life the 3d day of* July, 1694. *In memory of whom his brother* Robert Fairfax *esq; caused this small funeral stone to be erected.*

Fairfax 1669. *Here lyeth the body of* Thomas Fairfax *son of* William Fairfax *of* Steeton *esq; buried* Ap. 6, 1669, *near the tenth year of his age.*
Whom death made heir and no heir.

The windows in this church have been miserably defaced and broken; the arms and painted glass near destroyed, for I find by a book of drawings in the herald's office taken by sir *W. Dugdale*, 1641, that there were thirty three different coats of arms then in the windows. By the care of the present rector they are repaired with such materials of that kind as he could pick up from other places. For which reason there are several coats in the windows at present which did not originally belong to them; what are really old are these,

Quarterly *or*, a lion rampant *azure*. 2. *Azure*, three lucies or pikefish hauriant *argent. Percy* and *Lucy. Gules*, a lion rampant *argent. Beaumont. York* see, the pall, impaling *vert*, three bucks trippant *argent.* Archbishop *Rotheram.*

The site of the ancient manor-house of these two families is yet apparent, which is now in the possession of sir *William Milner* bart. And I must not forget that the rector's house was almost entirely rebuilt by the late worthy incumbent Dr. *Pierson*, chancellor of the diocese, who laid out above eight hundred pound in the work; the out buildings have received several considerable additions and reparations by the present rector the reverend Mr. *Thomas Lamplugh*, canon residentiary of *York.*

In this parish stood *Brochett-hall*, antiently the seat of the *Brochetts* of this county. Also,

(b) Steeton-hall, alias **Styveton**, which for some ages has been the seat of that truly antient family of *Fairfax*, was by the conqueror's survey in the possession of *Osbern de Archis.* Sir *John Chamont* knt. was owner of the greatest part of the lands of **Styveton** forty eighth *Edward* III, and had issue two daughters, *Joan* who was a nun, and *Margaret* married to *William* lord *Mowbray.* In this manor was antiently five carucates and half of land whereof *Richard de Styveton* held four and a half of *Walter de Falconberg*, who held the same of the heirs of *Brus*, and they of the barons *Mowbray*, who held them of the king, *in capite*, at the annual rent of seven pence halfpenny. Another carucate was of the fee of *Percy* as of his barony of **Spofford**; whereof the abbot of St. *Mary York* held half a carucate, and the prioress of *Appleton* the other.

This *Steeton* was the seat of sir *Guy Fairfax* knight, one of the judges of the king's bench, in the times of *Edward* IV, and *Henry* VII, and it has ever since continued in a younger branch of his family. *Thomas Fairfax* of *Newton* esq; the present possessor.

Colton, in the twentieth of *Edward* I. *Garo Chamont* or *de Calvo Monte*, was seised of the manor of *Colton*; and it has sometimes been called *Colton Chamont.*

(b) MS. Torre & sir T. W.

In

2

In the twenty second year of king *Hen.* VII. *Henry Oughtred* of *Kexby*, esq; in consideration of the right good counsel to him given by *William Fairfax*, esq; serjeant at law, did for the pleasure of the said *William* grant to him and his heirs free liberty and licence to hunt and hawk in the manor and town of *Colton*, in the shire of the city of *York*, with licence to fish and fowl therein; rendring one *red rose* at *Midsummer* only *(c)*. AINSTY.

Temp. Jac. prim. Colton was in the possession of sir *George Ratcliff*, knt. This manor is now the property of sir *John Bourn*, bart. which he had by marriage of the daughter and heiress of sir *Francis Leicester*, bart.

(d) COPMANTHORP, alias *Coppenthorp*, alias *Temple-Coppenthorp*, was anciently the lands of *Trusbutt*. *Robert* of that name divided his inheritance amongst his three sisters, *Rose*, *Hilaria* and *Agatha*; **Copmanthorp** among other things, was allotted to *Hilaria*, in the reign of king *John*. It was afterwards the lands of *Fairfax (e)* and sold to the *Vavasours*. I find by an office, says sir *T. W.* taken in the first year of queen *Elizabeth*, after the death of *Thomas Vavasor*, esq; that he died seised of the manor of **Temple-Copmanthorp**. In the reigns of king *James* and *Charles* I. sir *Thomas Vavasour*, knight marshal, and sir *William Vavasor* were owners. Now *William Boynton*, *John Wood* and —— *Adams*, esqs;

HORNINGTON, 9 *Edw.* II. did belong to the lady *Vescy*; it was afterwards part of the possessions of sir *William Ryther*, knt. who had free warren there. *Henry Topham* esq; of *York*, a reader of *Gray's-Inn*, a man sir *T. W.* calls famous in his time for wit and learning, was lord of this manor *temp. Jac.* I.

OXTON, or *Hoxton*, the greatest part of which belonged formerly to the abbot and convent of *Sawley*. The manor was 9 *Edw.* I. in the possession of *Simon de Kyme*, from thence it came to the *Percies*, and is now in the duke of *Somerset*.

Padecklthorp, was once the possession of *Gilbert Umfrevile* earl of *Angus*.

WOLSINGTON, alias *Wolston*, alias *Ouston*, alias *Weston*, was in the reign of *Edw.* III. the property of sir *Bernard Brocas*, knt. which my author thinks he had by the marriage of the daughter and heir of sir *Mauger Vavasor*; which sir *Mauger* was owner thereof by the grant of *Robert Aiou*, who by the deed of purchase held it by an annual rent to the king of twelve pence, called *alba-firma*, or **blanch-farm**; and to appear at the **Weapontack** held at **Ainsty-cross**.

TADCASTER, at the midst of the bridge from *York*, is the out-bounds of the *Ainsty*, and may be said to be the very out-port or gate of the city of *York* on that side. The lordship of this town was many ages in the truly great family of *Percy*, earls of *Northumberland*, *William de Percy* by the conqueror's survey being found lord thereof. But as the church, scite of the castle, and greatest part of the town are in the county at large, they are out of my district to treat on. And as to its claim to a *Roman* station, that has been largely discoursed on in another place. The present noble bridge, one of the best in a county remarkable for stone bridges, was built about forty years ago, by a general tax of 3 *d. per* pound, laid by act of parliament on all lands, *&c.* in the city, *Ainsty*, and county at large. The distich which *Camden* quotes on the river and bridge in his time is much better known than the occasion of it. It seems Dr. *Eades*, afterwards dean of *Worcester*, being a great admirer of the famous *Toby Matthews*, upon the latter's removal from *Christ-church*, *Oxford*, to the see of *Durham*, the doctor intending to go but one days journey with him, was enticed on, by the sweetness of the bishop's conversation, to *Durham* itself. Here it was that he wrote their whole journey in *latin* verse, and in his description of *Tadcaster*, happening to come over the bridge in a very dry summer, he applyed this distich:

> *Nil* Tadcaster *habet musis vel carmine dignum,*
> *Praeter magnificè structum sine flumine pontem.*
>
> The muse in *Tadcaster* can find no theam,
> But a most noble bridge without a stream.

But the doctor returning that way in the winter altered his opinion, and left the following memorial of it:

> *Quae* Tadcaster *erat sine flumine pulvere plena,*
> *Nunc habet immensum fluvium, et pro pulvere lutum.*
>
> The verse before on *Tadcaster* was just,
> But now great floods we see, and dirt for dust.

The present lord of this town is his grace the duke of *Somerset* from a marriage of the heiress of *Percy*.

HELAGH, in the town of *Helagh*, or *Helay*, were seven carucats of land, held by the barons *de Mowbray* who held them of the king, *in capite*, by no rent *(f)*.

(c) Sir *T. W.* dated at *York*, *Sept.* 2, 22 *Hen.* VII.
(d) MS. sir *T. W.*
(e) It came to the *Fairfax's* by the marriage with the heiress of *Malbis*. For 9 *Edw.* II. *Willielmus de Malbis* was lord of the manor of *Copmanthorpe*. City records.
(f) *Ex MS.* Torre, *p.* 83.

AINSTY. The priory at *Helagh* was founded by *Bertram Haget*, who granted to *Gilbert*, a monk of *maj. Monasterium* in *France*, and his successors in **Frank-Almoign**, the land of the hermitage, which was in his wood of *Helagh*, towards the east, as the water runs from **Lair-brigg**, to the passage of **Hangwat.** Also all his new essarted land without the ditch of **Heor-debrest** *(g)*.

Temp. reg. Johan.

Temp. Hen. III. *Jordan de S. Maria* and *Alice Haget* his wife, confirmed the said donation to *William* the prior and canons of the church of St. *John* the Evangelist *de Parco Helagh*, together with all the wood called **Horse-park**, *&c.*

Walter archbishop of *York* confirmed to these canons the church of St. *John* the evangelist, and the place in which their monastery was founded. And all the lands, woods and pastures in the park of **Helagh**, and in **Wychale**; where they had two oxgangs of land given by *Ralph Haget* *(h)*.

Besides the donations made these monks, which are mentioned in the *monast.* I have perused several original grants of lands and tenements given them in **Wyhale, Thorpe-arch, Walton, Esedyke, Hagundby, Plompton, Marston, Aykton, Bilton, Fetsayn, York, Kildale, Crathorn, Askham, Egburge, Bretteby, Heton, Pole, Katherton, Thresk,** and **Wombwell.** All which are in St. *Mary*'s chest at *York*.

William de Percy lord of **Kildale** gave to the canons of St. *John* the evangelist of **Helagh-Park**, the chapel of St. *Hilda* at **Kildale,** with diverse lands; for which the said canons were to find two of their own house, or two secular priests to celebrate the divine offices in the said chapel for ever *(i)*.

This priory of *Helagh-park* at its dissolution was valued at seventy two pounds ten shillings and seven pence, *Dugdale.* And it has ever since, till very lately, been part of the possessions of the lords *Wharton*, and was the seat of *Philip* lord *Wharton*, *temp. Car.* I. *(k)* *Stamp Fenton*, esq; the present lord of *Helagh*.

A close CATALOGUE *of the* PRIORS *of* HELAGH *(l)*.

Temp. instit. Anno	*Priores loci.*	*Vacat.*
1218	*Frater* Willielmus de Hameleis *stetit in prioratu* 18 *an.* ½ *ob. die S.* Praxydis *anno* 1233.	*per mort.*
1233	*Fra.* Elyas, *stetit* 23. *an.* 3. *mens. obiit die S.* Math. *ap.* 1256.	*per mort.*
1257	*Fr.* Johan. Necus, *stetit* 4. *an.* 3. *mens. ob.* 4. *id.* Jan. 1260.	*per mort.*
1260	*Fr.* Hamo de Eboraco, *stetit* 3 *an. et* 1. *mens. ob.* 13. *kal.* Jun. 1264.	
1264	*Fr.* Hen. de Quetelay, *stetit* 16. *an. exc.* 5. *diebus et mortuus est.*	*per mort.*
1281	*Fr.* Adam de Blyda, *fecit cessionem in manibus archiepiscopi* 13. *kal.* Nov. 1300.	*per cess.*
1300	*Fr.* Will. de Grymeston, *cellarius domus fecit cess.* 5. *id.* Ap. 1320.	*per cess.*
1320	*Fr.* Rob. de Spofford, *cellarius domus, stetit* 13. *an.*	*per mort.*
1333	*Fr.* Steph. de Levyngton, *canon. domus.*	*per cess.*
1352	*Fr.* Ric. de Levington, *canon. domus.*	*per cess.*
1357	*Fr.* Thomas de Yarum, *canon. domus.*	
1370	*Fr.* Steph. Clarell, *ob. ult.* Jan. 1423.	*per mort.*
1423	*Fr.* Johannes Byrkin, *canon. domus, stet.* 6. *an. et resig.*	*per cess.*
1429	*Fr.* Thomas York, *canon. dom. stet.* 6. *an. et postea depositus.*	*per depos.*
1435	*Fr.* Ric. Areton, *stetit* 1. *an. et* 3. *menses, et translat. erat ad* Gysburn.	*per cess.*
1437	*Fr.* Thomas Batson, *per* 2. *an. et trans. ad* Bolton.	*per cess.*
1440	*Fr.* Thom. Colyngham, *stetit* 21. *an. et resig.*	*per resig.*
1460	*Fr.* Christ. Lofthouse, *can. domus, stet.* 11. *an.*	
1471	*Fr.* Will. Berwyck.	*per mort.*
1475	*Fr.* Will. Bramham, *alias* Bolton, *reg.* 5. *an.*	*per resig.*
1580	*Fr.* Will. Elyngton, *can. dom. reg.* 18. *an.*	*per resig.*
1499	*Fr.* Peter Kendale.	
1520	*Fr.* Ric. Roundale.	

I shall take leave of *Helagh* with observing what *Leland*, in his itinerary, says of it; "From *Tadcaster* to *Helagh* pryory is about two mile, by inclosed ground. One *Geffrey* "*Haget*, a nobleman, was first founder of it. In this priory were buried sum of the *Depe-*"*dales* and *Stapleton*'s, gentlemen; of whom one sir *Bryan Stapleton*, a valiant knight, is "is much spoken of. *Geffry Haget* was owner of *Helagh* lordship, and besides a great ow-"ner in the *Ainsty*. From *Helagh* priory scant a mile to *Helagh* village I saw great ruins of

(g) *Mon. Ang.* vol. II. p. 287, *&c.*
(h) *Ex originali.*
(i) *Mon. Ang.* p. 291.
(k) The scite of this priory I find was granted, along with the rectory and advowson of vicarage, to one *Jacob Gage*, the thirty first of *Hen.* VIII. *Chapel of the Rolls.*
(l) *Mon. Ang.* vol. II. p. 289. MS. *Torre*, p. 84.

"An

" an ancient manor of stone, with a fair wooded park therby, that belongid to the earl of " *Northumberland*. It was as far as I can percieve sumtyme the *Haget's* land (*m*). AINSTY.

BILBROUGH, or **Beilburgh**, was in the hands of *Roger Bascy*, 9 *Edw*. III. and he, or his father, had free warren given him in all his demesne lands in *Bilbrough* and *Sandwith*; 32 *Edw*. I. the township anciently contained seven carucats and a half of land of the fee of *Paynel*, who held them of the king, *in capite*, paying no rent (*n*).

The town standeth upon a rising ground, or small hill to look at, yet, a plump of trees upon it may be seen at forty miles distance; and, one way, if I am rightly informed, was before the old trees was cut down, the *land-mark* for the entrance of ships into the *Humber*. The manor has long been in the possession of the *Fairfax* family; and was the birth-place of sir *Thomas Fairfax*, knight, the first lord *Fairfax* of the family of *Denton*. The house was afterwards pulled down upon an unhappy contention betwixt two brothers of that family, and never rebuilt (*o*). *Tho. Fairfax* of *Newton* esquire, the present lord.

There is a church or chapel in this town of *Bilbrough* which hath right of sepulture; but as it is a *donative*, no particular account can be given of it.

In it was a chantry founded in the chapel of St. *Saviour*, at the south end of the **Kyrke**, by *John Norton*, lord of the town *anno* 1492, who ordained and disposed towards the maintenance of sir *William Dryver*, chantry priest and his successors, 4*l*. 6*s*. 8*d*. in land and inclosure, that he and they should sing and occupy the service of God for the souls of the said *John Norton* and *Margaret* his wife, and *Richard*, *Thomas* and *Margaret* their children, &c. (*p*) Norton's *chantry*.

John Norton of *Bilbrough*, esq; made his will, proved *Dec*. 20, 1493, whereby he gave his soul to God almighty, and his body to be buried in the parish church of *Bilbrough*, in the vault between the church and the chapel newly built.

Thomas lord *Fairfax* baron of *Camerone* made his will *Nov*. 8, *anno* 1667, proved . . . . giving his soul to *God* almighty; hoping to be saved through *Jesus Christ*, and his body to be buried in the parish church of *Bilbrough* near the body of his wife (*q*).

Accordingly the remains of this great warrior lye interred in this church; over which is a mean tomb and this inscription:

Here lyes the bodies of the right honourable Thomas *lord* Fairfax *of* Denton, *baron of* Camerone; *who died* Nov. 12, 1671. *in the sixtieth year of his age: And of* Anne *his wife, daughter and coheir of* Horatio *lord* Vere, *baron of* Tilbury. *They had issue* Mary *duchess of* Buckingham *and* Elizabeth. Fairfax 16[illegible]

The memory of the just is blessed.

ASKAM BRYAN, 9 *Edw*. 2. *Gilbert de Stapleton* and *John Grey* were lords of it; sir *T. W.* writes, that *Askam-Bryan*, *Colton*, *Hessay*, *Styveton* were part of the possessions of sir *John Depedale*, who gave them in marriage to *William Mowbray* the son and heir of sir *John Mowbray*. This *Askam*, he adds, came afterwards to sir *Miles Stapleton* by the marriage of the daughter and heir of *Mowbray*.

This town contained eight carucats of land held of the fee of *Mowbray*. And what its distinguishing name is from, is, that *Bryan-Fitz-Alain* held the said town of the honour of *Richmond*, rendering 5 *s. per an.* to the warden of the castle of *Richmond* (*r*). All the tythes of this town and parish were granted to *Morgan Nutchent* the ninth of *Elizabeth* (*s*).

Temp. Car. I. *John Geldart*, an alderman of *York*, was owner of this manor, and, as sir *T. W.* writes, built a fine house here. It is at present in the possession of Mr. *Garforth* merchant of *York*; who has much enlarged and beautified the house and gardens.

(*t*) ASKAM RICHARD, alias *West-Askam*, had antiently six carucats and a half of land in its district; which were held of the heirs of *Bruse*, who held them of the barons *Mowbray*, by two shillings rent *per ann*. The ninth of *Edward* II. the priory of *Burlington* was possessed of this manor. *Samuel Clark*, esq; the present possessor.

(*u*) The church of *Askam Richard* was given by *William de Archis* and *Ivetta* his wife to the nunnery of *Monketon*, who from thence had the patronage of it.

And 8. *Id. Martii anno* 1329. the church of *Ascham-Richard* was appropriated to the prioress and nuns of *Monketon* by *Henry* archbishop of *York*; who apppointed a perpetual vicarage therein. It continued in the presentation of the nunnery till the dissolution, when it fell into the hands of *Henry Vavasour*, esq; whose executor presented three times. But *an*. 1625, and 1669, *John Swale*, gent. had the gift of this vicarage (*x*).

The vicarage of *Askam-Richard*, *Askam-Bryan*, and *Bilbrough*, was thus valued in the king's books.

	l.	*s.*	*d.*
First fruits — — — —	4	13	4
Tenths — — — — — — — —	0	4	4
Procuration — — — — — — — —	0	7	6

(*m*) *Lelandi itin*. vol. VIII.
(*n*) *Ex MSS*. Torre *et dom*. T. W.
(*o*) Sir *T. W.*
(*p*) *Torre*, p. 336, &c.
(*q*) This *Thomas* lord *Fairfax* gave the tythes of *Bilbrough* to the church there. *Thoresby* duc. *Leod*.
(*r*) *Torre*, 336.
(*s*) Chapel of the *Rolls*.
(*t*) *Torre*, 331.
(*u*) *Mon. Ang*. vol. I. p. 476.
(*x*) *Torre*, 331.

AINSTY. (*y*) Wighal, in the town of *Wighall* and *Esdyke* are five carucats of land, which town was held by *Reginald de Albo Monasterio* of *Roger de Mowbray*, who held it of the king *in capite*. Also one carucat of land therein was held by the prior *de Parco* of the lord of *Helagh*, who held the same of the barons *Mowbray* at the rent of two shillings.

Rand. de Bleminstre was the ninth of *Edw.* II, lord of **Whichale, Casewicke** and **Hamlake**; after him we find one sir *John Bleminstre*; but *Nicholas Stapleton* was owner of it *an.* 1343, as appears by the *Esch.* the seventeenth of *Edw.* III. This *Nicholas* had issue sir *Miles Stapleton*, who was made *knight* of the *garter* at the first institution of the order. It appears also by the fines of the forty ninth and fiftieth of *Edw.* III. that sir *Bryan Stapleton* and *Alice* his wife were owners of **Wighall** (*z*), &c.

The family of *Stapleton*, or *Stapylton*, have long been, and are still, in possession of this estate, on which is a noble old house. There have been a succession of many worthy knights of this family, and two of them knights of the *garter*. Sir *Rob. Stapilton*, who lived to the beginning of the reign of *James* I, was not inferior to any of his ancestors. Sir *John Harrington*, in his book of bishops addressed to prince *Henry*, gives him this great character, "Sir *Robert Stapilton* a knight of *Yorkshire*, whom your highness hath often seen, was a man "well spoken, properly seen in languages, a comely and goodly personage, and had scant "an equal, and, exept sir *Philip Sidney*, no superior in *England* (*a*)."

The church of **Wighale** was given to the priory of **Helagh-park**; and to the same was appropriated, and a vicarage ordained, which was endowed with the tythes of **Esdyke** and **Folifayt**, *&c.* At the dissolution of monasteries, the presentation of this Vicarage came to sir *Robert Stapilton*, whose descendants have ever since presented to it (*b*).

		l.	*s.*	*d.*
The vicarage of *Wighale* is valued in the king's books.	First fruits —	5	3	11½
	Tenths —	0	10	4¼
	Procurations —	0	7	6

Philip Stapylton, esq; is the present lord of this manor.

Monumental INSCRIPTIONS in the church at Wighill.

Burton 1498. ✠ **Hic jacet Dom. Will. Burton quondam vicarius istius eccle. qui obiit xxi. die mensis Martii an. Dom. 1498. cujus anime propitietur Deus. Amen.**

Stapylton 1503. ✠ **Orate pro anima dom. Willielmi Stapilton, milit. et pro anima dom^e. Margarete uxoris sue, qui quidem Willielmus obiit xvi. die mensis Decem. an. Dom. M.D. tertio, cujus anime propitietur Deus.**

Stapilton 1521. ✠ **Orate pro anima Alicie Stapilton quondam ux. dom. Briani Stapilton militis, que obiit xvi die mensis Novembris an. Dom. M.CCCCC.XXI. cujus, &c.**

Stapilton 1518. ✠ **Orate pro anima Henrici Stapilton, milit. filii et heredis Willielmi Stapilton milit. qui obiit xiii. die mensis Septem. an. Dom. Millesimo CCCCC.XVIII. cujus anime propitietur Deus. Amen.**

Stapilton 1542. ✠ **Orate pro anima domine Johanne Stapilton quondam uxoris domini Henrici Stapylton militis que obiit quinto die mensis Januarii an. Dom. M.CCCCC.XLII.**

Stapilton 1673. *Hic situs* Henricus Stapilton *dom. de* Wighall . . . . . *ex antiqua* Stapiltonorum *oriundus* . . . . . *vir justitia insignis* . . . . *mundum et vicit et deseruit. An. aetatis suae* 42. *annoque Dom.* 1673.

ARMS on a monument, *Stapilton* impaling *Fairfax.*

P. M. S.

Stapilton 1634. *Corpus* Roberti Stapilton *arm. olim domini de* Wighill *in agro* Ebor. . . . .
longa majorum serie nobilis . . . . *hic jacet, &c.*
Ob. Londini xi. Martii *aetat. suae* 33. *salut.* 1634.

In mandatis moriturus dedit ut viri cum patribus in eodem tumulo dormiat cinis. Catherina *filia illust. domini vicecomitis* Fairfax, *ut pietatem optimo manifestet conjugi, hoc monumentum posuit.*

Wilesthorpe was anciently the lands of *de Wilesthorpe* in the Time of king *John*; but *temp. Ed.* I. sir *Robert de Pontefract* was lord of this manor; as was his son *Thomas de Pontefract* the ninth of *Edw.* II. (*c*)

The king gave respite to *Rob. Wivelsthorpe* not to be made a knight from *Easter* next to come till a year. And it was commanded to the sheriff that he should not distrain him in that time.

(*y*) *Torre*, 277.
(*z*) MS. sir *T. W.*
(*a*) The pedigre of this ancient family is printed in *Thoresby's ducat. Leod.* drawn down to the late sir *John Stapylton* of *Myton*, bart. who left issue the present sir *Miles*, now knight of the shire for the county of *York*, *Bryan*, *Francis* since dead, *Henry*, *Christopher*, and three daughters.
(*b*) *Torre.*
(*c*) Sir *T. W.* City records.

Wilstrop

Wilstrop the feat of fir *Ofwald Wilstrop*, which was an ancient family in this tract. The right honourable the lord or lady *P tre* the prefent poffeffor.

BILTON, this was anciently the lands of *Waleys*. In the feventh of *Edw.* I. *John Vavafor* did hold in the name of *Alice* his wife, together with one *Stephen Waleys* his partner, the manors of **Helagh**, **Thorpe** and **Bilton**; in which they claimed to have free warren. In the ninth of *Edw.* II. *Bilton* belonged to *Richard Waleys* and *Nicholas Vavafor* (d).

Bilton came afterwards to *Snaufell* by the marriage of *Alice* the daughter and heir of *William Danyel*, lord of *Bilton*. Which family continued owners of it, till of late years it was purchafed by Mr. *Iveſon* alderman of *Leeds*. *John Iveſon*, efq; the prefent lord of this manor.

(e) MARSTON *cum* HOTON-WANDESLEY, in the town of *Marfton* are twelve carucats of land, whereof *William Fitz-Thomas* held fix carucats of *Moubray*. The refidue of thofe carucats were held by divers of the heirs of *Brus*, who held them, *ut fupra*. Alfo the prior of St. *Andrew* in *York* held one carucat and two oxgangs of land by the rent of thirteen pence.

In the town of *Hoton* were fix carucats of land which rendered *per ann.* eighteen pence. And *John de Crepping* held the faid town of the heirs of *Richard de Wyvelefthorpe*, who held it of the heirs of *Brus*, and they of the barons *Mowbray*.

John de Beckthorpe and the abbot of *Fountains* were owners of *Marfton* the ninth of *Edw.* II. which was afterwards the lands of *Ingleby*, and then of the *Thwaites*'s. From whom, I fuppofe, fir *Henry Thompfon*, knight, alderman of *York* bought it, and it is now the chief feat of his grandfon *Edward Thompfon*, efq;

(f) *Hoton* or *Hutton cum Angram*, was alfo the lands of *Ingleby*, but late of *Richard Roundele*, efq; who left three daughters, the eldeft of whom was married to fir *Darcy Dawes*, bart. fon of the late archbifhop *Dawes*. The eftate at *Hutton* as yet, I fuppofe, is undivided amongft them.

The church of *Marfton* is an ancient rectory belonging to the patronage of the *Wyvelethorps*, then of the *Crepings*, and from them to the *Middeltons*, then the *Nefsfields*, then the *Inglebys*. Since whom it has been in feveral hands till purchafed by the *Roundeles*.

Anno 1400. a commiffion was granted to the parifhioners of this town of *Marfton*, becaufe their old church was far diftant from their habitations, and then alfo ruinous and neceffary to be rebuilt, to tranflate the fame, together with the ftone thereof, from that place unto another chapel, fituate in the fame parifh, and there to build themfelves a new parifh church. Provided that they keep up inclofed the cemetery, where their old church ftood (g).

The rectory of *Marfton* is thus valued in the king's books.	*l.*	*s.*	*d.*
Firft fruits	24	3	9
Tenths	2	8	4½
Procurations	0	8	6
Subfidies	2	2	0

(h) RUFFORD, or *Rughford*, was the lands of *Geoffry Rughford*, and afterwards came by marriage of the daughter of *Fulk Rufford* to *Alain Breton*. Here are four carucats of land which were held by the faid *Alain* of the heirs of *Brus*; who held them of the barons *Mowbray*, and they of the king, *in capite*, at the rent of 2 *s. per annum*. *Alain* the tenth of *Edward* I. had free warren granted him in all his demefnes there. In the ninth of *Edward* II. *Alice*, widow to *William Bugthorp*, was owner of thefe lands; and about that time *Nicholas Stapleton*, the fon of *Miles Stapleton*, fued *John Maleverer*, that he fhould reftore unto him *William Bugthorp* to his cuftody, whofe father *William* held of him the manor of *Rufford* by half a knights fee, and fuit of court of the faid *Nicholas* at *Thorparches* from three weeks to three weeks, *&c.*

Moft of thefe lands were afterwards given to St. *Leonard*'s hofpital, york. The prefent lord is *Henry Juftice*, efq;

SCAKLETHORP, the ninth of *Edw.* II. was the lands of *William Rofs*; but *Thomas Ughtred* was owner thereof in the eighth year of *Edward* III, and had licence from the king to impark his woods of **Hesay**, **Popilton** upon the moor, and **Scakelthorpe**. (i)

In the book of *Doomefday* it is recorded, that in the **Scakelthorpe**, and in the two **Poppletons** are fix carucats of land and a half, of the land of *Ernum Catenas*; which *Ofborn de Archis* holds, as it is witneffed, to the ufe of *William Mallet*.

THORP-ARCH, in the town of *Thorp-arch*, were four carucats of land held by *John de Bella Aqua*, or *Belleu*, of the fee of *Roger de Mowbray*, who held the fame of the king, *in capite*, by the rent of two fhillings and eleven pence half-penny *per annum* (k).

This town feems to derive the latter part of its name from the family of *D'Archis*, who came in with the conqueror, and had great poffeffions in thefe parts. It has fometimes been

(d) Sir T.W. City records.
(e) *Torre*, p. 281. Sir T.W. &c.
(f) *Idem*.
(g) *Torre*, 281.
(h) Sir T.W. *Torre*, &c.
(i) Sir T.W.
(k) *Torre*, 339.

AINSTY. called *Ivettborpe*, from *Ivetta*, the mother of the first *Peter Brus*, who gave some lands in this place to the nuns of **Monkton**, with the wood as it was inclosed betwixt the aforesaid place and the town of **Werby**, now *Wetherby*. She was wife to *William de Archis (l)*.

(m) In the ninth of *Edw.* II. *Nicholas de Stapleton* is put down as lord of the manor of **Thorp-arch** at that time. Here was a park formerly, but, as it seems, not very well stocked with game; as appears by the following verses made by some that came to hunt here from *York*,

> *(n) Hinc parvum saltum petimus,* Thorpe *nomine dicunt.*
> *Longum iter, et frustra factum, nam fallimus illic*
> *Spemque diemque simul, rara est ut nulla voluptas,*
> *Non puto tam damis quam dumis esse repletum.*

(o) The church of **Thorp-Arch** was given by *Adam de Brus* and *Ivetta de Archis* his wife, to the chapel of St. *Mary* and *holy Angels*, then founded by archbishop *Roger* in *York-minster*.

Anno 1258. archbishop *Sewall* ordained a vicarage in this church of *Thorp-Arch*. And that the vicar should have the whole altaridge of the said church, and the mansion thereof; saving to the sacrist of the said chapel the easement of going and returning from his grange there, and to lay up his corn therein. Likewise the vicar shall have the tythes of the tythes belonging to the sacrist, or two marks out of his purse. And other two marks shall be yearly distributed by the said sacrist to the poor of the parish, *&c.*

The presentation of this vicarage at the dissolution of the chapel in *York* minster fell to the crown; but has since been in several hands. *Anno* 1672. *Arthur Savile*, esq; presented. It was thus taxed in the king's books:

	l.	*s.*	*d.*
First fruits	3	15	5
Tenths	0	7	0½
Procurations	0	6	8

The vicarage of *Thorp-Arch* was of late years only twenty four pounds *per annum*; but received an addition of two hundred pounds from the reverend Mr. *Robinson* of *Leeds*; by which donation it claimed two hundred pounds more of queen *Anne's* ever-memorable bounty-money. The present vicar the reverend Mr. *Weatherhead*, proposed a second augmentation in order to purchase the tythes, then in the possession of *William Wrightson* of *Cushworth*, esq; and valued at one thousand two hundred and fifty five pounds; which sum was raised in this manner, Mr. *Robinson* two hundred pounds, the government two hundred pounds, Mr. *Wheatherhead* two hundred pounds, the government two hundred pounds, in all eight hundred pounds. The great deficiency, being four hundred and fifty five pounds, was given by the lady *Elizabeth Hastings*, who also purchased the perpetual advowson of the living from the aforesaid Mr. *Wrightson*. The many benefactions, of this kind, which this lady has done to the church in general, deserves a nobler *encomium* than my pen can bestow. She is at present lady of the manor.

WALTON has long been in the possession of the family of *Fairfax*, and anciently contained three carucats of land held by the heirs of *Roger de Brus*, and divers others, who held the same of the barons *Mowbray*, but paid nothing certain to the king. *Peter de Brus* granted to *William Fairfax* and his heirs, nine oxgangs one acre and three perches of land with tofts and crofts in *Walton* of the fee of *Mowbray*, by a deed without date, *Henry de Sexdecim Vallibus* and thirty six other being witnesses; he was mayor of *York* in the time of *Hen.* III. and *Thomas Fairfax*, the son of this *William*, married the daughter and heiress of *Henry de Sexdecim Vallibus*, or *Sezevaux*.

Through this tract of ground, as *John Leland* first observed, run the great *Watling-street*, or *Roman* road, from the south to the wall now called **Rodgate**. It crossed the *Wharf* at a place called St. *Helen's-ford*; near *Walton*, where was a chapel in *Leland's* time, dedicated to St. *Helen* the mother of *Constantine*, but now gone. But of this I have said enough in another place.

Here is a chapel at *Walton* which by a composition made by *John de Waltham* sacrist of the chapel of St. *Mary* and holy angels, *York*, rector of the church of *Thorpe-arch*, appropriated to the said chapel, on one part, and the prioress and convent of *Monkton* on the other, for right of christnings and burials in the said chapel, *&c.* All which agreement was confirmed by *Walter* archbishop of *York*, *anno* 1226 *(p)*.

The pedigree of *Fairfax* of *Walton*, since created viscount *Emley* of the kingdom of *Ireland*, whose seat is now at *Gilling-castle* in *Rhidale*, sir *T. W.* has given in this manner:

(l) Mon. Ang. vol. I. 476.
(m) City records.
(n) Sir *T. W.*
(o) Torre, 339.
(p) Sir *T. W.* *Torre*, 343. In this chapel at *Walton* several of the *Fairfax* family have been buried, but only this epitaph now visible:

> *Here lyes the body of* Thomas *lord viscount* Fairfax, *who dyed* Sept. 24, 1641. *And of* Alethea *his wife, who dyed the* 2[d] *of the same month* 1677.
> *Those who read this pray for their souls.*

Temp.

AINSTY.

Temp. Hen. III. WILLIAM FAIRFAX of *Walton* had *Walton* from *Peter Brus.*

THOMAS FAIRFAX = ANN daughter and heir of *Henry de Sexdecem Vallibus*, or *Sezevaux*. Whose arms were chequè *or* and *azure*, on a canton of the second, a star of six points, *argent*.

WILLIAM son of *Thomas* and *Anne*.

JOHN son of *William*

THOMAS son of *John*

WILLIAM son of *Thomas*

THOMAS son of *William* = *Elizabeth Etton* (*q*); by which marriage *Fairfax*, though long after, got possession of *Gilling Castle*.

WILLIAM = CONSTANCE daughter to *Peter Mauley*, or *de Malolacu*, the seventh baron of that name.

THOMAS

RICHARD

WILLIAM

THOMAS knight of the *Bath* 10 *Hen.* VII. — Sir NICHOLAS FAIRFAX knight of *Rhodes.* — GUY.

THOMAS son of *Thomas* died 12 *Hen.* VIII.

Sir NICHOLAS FAIRFAX, twice high-sheriff, died 13 *Eliz.*

Sir THOMAS FAIRFAX, created viscount *Emley*, high-sheriff 3 *Car.* I. died 1636.

THOMAS viscount *Emley* died 1641.

WILLIAM viscount *Emley* died 1648.

CHARLES viscount *Emley*.

From GUY FAIRFAX, son of *Richard*, who was one of the justices of the *King's-bench*, *temp. Edw.* IV. came

WILLIAM FAIRFAX, knight.

THOMAS FAIRFAX of *Denton*, knight.

THOMAS FAIRFAX, knight, lord *Fairfax*.

FERDINANDO FAIRFAX, knight, lord *Fairfax*.

THOMAS FAIRFAX, knight, lord *Fairfax*.

The honourable CHARLES FAIRFAX of *Gilling*, a lineal descendant of this branch, is the present possessor of *Walton*.

SYNNYNGTHWAYTE, the nunnery of *Synnynthwayte* was founded by *Bertram Haget* who gave thereunto the place where their monastery stood, which was confirmed by *Roger de Moubray* his lord.

Besides the grants of lands belonging to this nunnery, mentioned in the *Monasticon*, I have seen the originals of several donations to it in lands lying and tenements being in **Bilton, Wombwell, Thorpe, Witinton, Elnwick, Lofthouse, Alwaldeley, Bedell, Newton, Cockwith, Farnham, Hoton, Usburn**, and **Hessington**; all in St. *Mary's* chest at *York*.

About the year 1200, *Geoffry*, archbishop of *York*, took these nuns into his protection, and denounced a malediction against those who should dare to wrong them, and a blessing to their benefactors.

(*q*) Barry of six *argent* and *gules* on a canton *sable*, a croslet *or*, *Etton*, The claim to the castle and estate at *Gilling*, &c. was made by petition to the king in chancery from *Thomas Fairfax* as heir to *Etton* 7 *Hen.* VII. and a commission was issued out to enquire into his right, and was given for him. The whole proceeding is in sir *T. W's* manuscript.

AINSTY

A CATALOGUE of the PRIORESSES of SINYNGTHWAITE.

A. D.	*Priorissae.*	*Vacat.*
1312	*Dom*^{na} Margareta . . . . *jam senilis et cepit.*	*per mort.*
	Dom^{na} Margareta Hewyck.	
1428	Agnes Sheffield *common. dom.*	
	Dom^{na} . . . . de Etton.	
1444	*Dom*^{na} Aliva	
	Dom^{na} Margaret. Banke.	*per mort.*
1482	*Dom*^{na} Alitia Etton.	*per mort.*
1489	*Dom*^{na} Eliz. Squier.	
1529	*Dom*^{na} Anna Goldesburg *com. dom.*	*per resig.*
1534	*Dom*^{na} Katherina Forster *monialis ibid.*	

This monastery which was of the *Cistertian* order had Esholt for a cell to it, founded by *Galfrid* the son of *Bertram Haget*.

At the dissolution the nunnery of *Sinningthwaite* was valued at 60*l.* 9*s.* 2*d.*

Esholt, which came into the *Shereburn* family, at 15*l.* 3*s.* 4*d.* *Dug.*

SCUKIRK, or rather *Scokirk*, was a cell to the prior and convent of St. *Oswald* at *Nostell.* King *Richard* II. granted to them free warren in all their demesn lands there.

Scuekirk was of later years the seat of sir *Thomas Harrison* knt.

TOCKWITH, alias *Todwick*, was in the possession of *William de Ross* and *Andrew de Kirkbie*, the ninth of *Edward* II. It was also the lands of *Rob. Trusbut* which was divided between his three sisters, *Rose*, *Hilaria*, and *Agatha*. The priory of *Sinningthwait* had divers lands here. And there was a chapel in the wood at Tockwith, which was given to the church of *All-saints* at Sockirk. This was sometime the land of *Brian Danyel* of *Bilton* esq; and went from him to *Snawsel.* The lady *Petre* the present possessor.

MONKTON, commonly called *More-Monkton* to distinguish it from the other, had six carucates of land, held of the fee of *Pagnel*, of which *John de Waleys* held three carucates at the rent of six pence; and the abbot of St. *Mary York*, held one carucate of the gift of *Philip Fitz Ranulph de* Monkton *(r)*.

The manor of Monkton sur le More did antiently belong to the family of the *Ughtreds*, for the twenty eighth of *Edward* I. *Robert Ughtred* obtained a charter for free warren in all his demesn lands there. The ninth of *Edward* II. *Thomas de Ughtred* was lord of it.

The church of More-Monkton has been an antient rectory of the patronage of the *Ughtreds*; from whom it came to the earls of *Salisbury*, and from them to the crown. The king has presented ever since *Henry* VII.

The rectory of *More-Monkton* is valued in the king's books.	*l.*	*s.*	*d.*
First fruits — — — — —	16	19	02
Tenths — — — — —	01	13	11
Procurations — — — —	00	07	06
Subsidies — — — —	01	10	00

Sir *Henry Slingsby* bart. is now lord of the manor of *More-Monkton.*

REDHOUSE belongs to the family of *Slingsby*; sir *T. W.* has been so particular in his description of this place and name, that I shall beg leave to give it in his own words.

" *Redhouse* hath been of late a seat of the *Slingsbys*, sir *Henry Slingsby* the elder, that " last was, having built a fair house here. But *Scriven* near *Knaresburgh* is a much " more antient seat of this family; for *William de Slingsby* their ancestor, married the daugh- " ter and heir of *Thomas de Scriven*, by which marriage he had *Scriven* and many other " good possessions. He had also the office of forester of the forests and parks of *Knares-* " *burgh*; in which family of *Scriven* that office had antiently been, as appears by an inqui- " sition which I have seen taken at *Knaresburgh* the second year of king *Edward*, the son " of king *Edward*. *Slingsby* by this marriage became heir to *Thomas de Walkingham*, whose " daughter and heir *Scriven* had formerly married. One of the ancestors of *Slingsby* did " also marry a daughter and heir of *William de Nesfield*, by which he had accession also of " the manors of *Scotton*, *Brereton* and *Thorp*; touching which I find a controversy between " *John* king of *Castile* and *Leon* duke of *Lancaster*, commonly called *John* of *Gaunt*, on the " one part, and *William de Gargrave* and *Hykedon de Slingsby*, who had married the two daugh- " ters and heirs of *William de Nesfield* on the other part. The duke claimed by purchase " from *Nesfield*, and the two heirs by an entail. This controversy is in an indenture writ- " ten in *French*, dated *July* 26, *anno* 1287, a copy of which was shewn me by *Henry* " *Slingsby* of *Kippax* esq; the son and heir of sir *William Slingsby*, who was a younger son " of this family. The controversy is by that indenture referred to twelve of the best knights " and esquires of the county of *York* near *Scotton.*

Thus far sir *T.* and I have no more to add, but that *Redhouse* has continued to be one of the seats of the antient and honourable family of *Slingsby* to this time. Sir *Henry*

(r) Torre 369.

Slingsby bart. member for *Knaresborough*, in several parliaments, being the present possessor of it. AINSTY

POPLETON, both *land* and *water Poppleton* as they are distinguished, or upper and lower, were formerly the lands of the abbot of St. *Mary York*; given by *Osbern de Archis* to this abbey, almost, at its first institution (*s*).

(*t*) In *South Poppleton* were lands belonging to the common of the church of *York*, for we find an agreement made betwixt *Thurstan* archbishop of *York* and *Godfrid* abbot of St. *Mary's*, touching a division of their lands in **Popylton** in this manner, that the abbey hath all that town of **Popylton** which contained four carucates of land, and which is situate upon the river **Ouse**. Also two carucates and half of land in the other **Popylton**, situate on the south of the other town. And the church or prebend of *York* hath in **South Popylton** seven carucates and half of land.

Sir *T. W.* writes that there was a mayor of *York* killed at *Popylton* in the reign of king *Richard* II, as he conjectures in some controversy betwixt the abby and citizens, mention being made of this fact amongst the records of the tower in *rotulo Romano*; but I could not upon search find the record here mentioned.

Popleton was the seat of *Thomas Hutton* esq; a descendant from archbishop *Hutton*, by whom, I suppose, it came from the church to that family. The last *Thomas Hutton* esq; dying unmarried, this estate was left amongst his relations, of whom the *Dawsons*, of *York*, are the chief.

CATHERTON was formerly the lands of *William de Catherton*, which he held of *William Kyme* lord of **Newton Kyme**. Sir *William Catherton*, gave some part of it to the monastery of **Furness**, in the year 1256, fortieth of *Henry* III, says sir *T. W.* but I find no mention of it in the *Monasticon*, the prior of **Helagh park** with *Henry de Cruce* were lords of **Cathorthorne**, the ninth of *Edward* II. (*u*) *Samuel Brookshank* esq; the present lord.

HAGENBY, this was antiently the lands of *Hugh Lelay*, and he gave the same to the monastery of **Helagh-park** (*x*).

(*y*) BICKERTON was formerly the lands of *Alain Walkingham*, which he held of sir *Rowland Quakin* knt. and he had free warren here.

The ninth of *Edward* II. it was in the possession of *Thomas Gramarye*, and afterwards I find one *Andrew le Gramarye* was owner of it. *John Brough* esq; of *Caltborpe*, ratified the estate and possession of *Bryan Rocliff*, one of the barons of the exchequer, son of *Joan* wife of *Guy Rocliff*, sister of the aforesaid *John Brough*, in the manor of *Caltborpe*, with the advowson of the church there, and lands in *Bickerton*. Colonel *Sidney* the present lord of this mano

(*z*) HESSAY was given to the abbey of St. *Mary York* by *Osbern de Archis*, and continued in their possession till the dissolution. Now in several hands.

KNAPTON, was the lands of *Alain Breton* the tenth of *Edward* I. and afterwards of sir *John Mowbray* knight of *Kirklington*. In the list of the lords of the *Ainsty* taken the ninth of *Edward* II. I found *Episcopus Cestrien.* put down as owner of this manor. This surprised me as well knowing that the bishoprick of *Chester* was founded long after by *Henry* VIII. But upon better information I find the bishops of *Litchfield* and *Coventry* were antiently stiled *episcopi Cestrienses*; as several of our monkish historians do testify. Yet this manor of *Knapton* did not belong to that see; but was the private property of *Walter de Langton* (*a*) then bishop. A family of great antiquity in *York*.

Peter Johnson esquire of *York* and others the present possessors.

ACOMBE, or rather ACHAM, antiently part of the possessions of the cathedral church of *York*, and was annexed to the treasurership. On the subversion of that office this manor came by exchange from the crown to the archbishop; and is at present held by lease from the see. The vicaridge is a *peculiar*, and consequently not taken notice of in Mr. *Torre's* diocesan manuscripts, though that industrious collector has left a particular manuscript of *peculiars*, at present in the possession of the dean and chapter, which I have not had an opportunity to inspect.

(*b*) DRING-HOUSES, one may conjecture, says sir *T. W.* that this place took its name from the tenure by which the lands were held. In the book of *Domesday* there is mention made of *Drenches* or *Dranches*, which are conceived to be the free tenure of a manor; and the tenure by *Dringage* or *Drainage*, adds that writer, was a frequent tenure of lands. The ninth of *Edward* II, *John Grey* was lord of this place; afterwards it was found to be part of the lands of *Alice de Aincourt* in the time of king *Henry* IV. The site of the capital mes-

(*s*) *Ex originali. M. A.*
(*t*) *Torre. York. S. M. p.* 821. *ex registro S.* Mariae. Ebor.
(*u*) City records.
(*x*) *Ex carta originali.*
(*y*) Sir *T. W.* city records.
(*z*) *Ex originali.*
(*a*) Thomas de Burgh escheator dom. regis ultra Trentam *r. c. de exit. manerii de* Knapton *quod fuit* Walteri de Langeton *nuper* Covent. *et* Litchfeld. *episc. et quod tenuit de* Galfrid. Lutterel *servicio unius militis. Rot.* Pipe *an.* 16 Ed. II. *Buttercrambe*, and *Baynton* manors belonged also to him. *Pipe* 17 *Ed.* II.

(*b*) In the *monast.* mention is made of two carucates of land given to the priory of St. *Trinity Ebor.* in this place; which is there spelt **Drengeshireles**, but whether corruptly or not I know not. *M. A.* 1, 564. The **Thanes** and **Drenges** of *Northumberland* were tallaged, *&c. Maddox's* ex. p. 483. See *Cowel's* law dictionary.

suage, or manor-house, called **Dreng-house-hall**, was sold to *Richard Vavasor* the tenth of *Elizabeth* from the crown. *Francis Barlow* esquire the present lord. I find in Mr. *Thoresby*'s ducat *Leod.* this place is said to be in the possession of *Robert Grey* the twenty third of *Edward* I, and is there called **Dreng-holme**; it came to this family of *Grey* from *Walter Grey* archbishop. Here was an house of *Lepers. Domus quam leprosi inhabitant* (c).

At *Dringhouses* I end my general survey of the *Ainsty*, and excepting *Holgate*, an inconsiderable village near the city, I know no town nor seat that I have omitted. What else remains to compleat this chapter are the high-ways, bridges, &c. the former of which will be best understood by the map of this district. *Tadcaster* bridge I have mentioned to be over the *Wharfe*, which has likewise two ferries upon it at *Uskelf* and *Nunappleton* before it enters the *Ouse*. Over the river *Nid* is first the ferry at *Nun-Monkton*, then *Skipbridge*, consisting of three spatious arches, with a noble cause-way on the west side of it lately made at the expence of the *West-riding*. The like work is now begun and near finished on the east side which renders the passage over this, sometimes, dangerous river, perfectly secure at all seasons. The cause-way from the bridge to the end of *Hessay-moor*, is three *Yorkshire* miles long, and *John Leland* in his itinerary gives the following description of it; "the causeway "by *Skyp-bridge* towards *Yorke* hath nineteen small bridges in it, for avoiding and over-"passinge carres cumming out of the mores therby. One *Blackburn* who was twys mair of "*Yorke* made this cawsey; and another without the suburb of *Yorke* (d). Over the *Nid* is also *Hamerton-bridge* and *Cattal-bridge*.

In the midst of the high road, betwixt *Dringhouses* and the city, stands the fatal tripple tree, being the gallows for the execution of criminals in the county at large. This being in the liberties of the city, must have been granted from them to the county, as a place very proper, from its situation in the most publick high road about us, for executions, *in terrorem*; before, as I am informed, the high sheriff caused this tragical affair to be performed within the precincts of the castle of *York*.

Near this is a piece of ground belonging to the city called **Hob-moor**. How long it has born that appellation I know not, but the pasture-masters of *Mickle-gate ward* have lately had a mind to perpetuate it, by placing an old statue on a pedestal, and putting under this inscription,

This statue long Hob's *name has bore,*
Who was a knight in days of yore,
And gave this common to the poor.

The figure is no more than that of a knight templar of the family of *Ross*, as appears by his shield; and it was very probably dragged out of the ruins of some of our demolished monasteries; and from a supine has had the honour to be placed in an erect posture, with the above mentioned memorable inscription under it.

On the other side *Tyburn* is a large common of pasture which has been of old called **Knavesmire**, now *Knaesmire*. Some have fancied it has got this name from its neighbourhood to the gallows, which is a mire that knaves frequently stick fast in. But antiently this word did not bear that opprobrious signification. *Knave*, from the *Anglo-Saxon* cnapa, *Belgick* **knape**, and the *Teut.* **knab**, meant formerly a menial servant, or very poor householder. *Mire* is a low watery piece of ground. So that this common of pasture had its name from what it was originally designed for, and is still intended, *viz.* for the benefit of the poor freemen of the city as a stray for what cattle they can put upon it. This common has been claimed by the inhabitants of *Middlethorpe*, a village near it; but I find an agreement betwixt the city and them about the bounds of **Knavesmire**, made *April* 23, 1567, the ninth of *Elizabeth*, wherein it is stipulated, *that the husbandholders of* Middlethorpe *shall have three cows a piece, and every cottager two cows and no more; nor any other cattle, and not to come upon the pasture before the city cattle be brought by the common herd, and they to fetch them off with their herd at the time the city brings off theirs. And that the new casten ditch made betwixt the city and* Middlethorp *shall be holden and kept for a knowledge of both their boundaries.*

One part of this agreement lay in the council-chamber *Ouse-bridge* in the chest with the common seal. This piece of ground, besides being a common to the city, is at present made use of for an *annual horse course*. And though the ground be a dead flat, and in many places very moist, yet by building arches, and drainage where it was proper, the course is made as convenient for this diversion as is requisite. The form of the race being like a horse shoe, the company in the midst, and on the scaffolds, can never lose sight of the horses; for all which reasons this piece of ground has acquired the reputation of being one of the best horsecourses in *England*.

(c) *Thoresby*'s duc. *Leod.* p. 130.

(d) Leland. *itin* v. 8.

BOOK the Second;

CONTAINS THE

HISTORY

OF THE

CATHEDRAL CHURCH of *YORK*:

WITH THE

LIVES of the ARCHBISHOPS of that SEE, &c.

ALSO, THE

History of the ABBEY *of St.* MARY *in that City*,

From the Foundation to its Dissolution, &c.

WITH THE

APPENDIX and *INDEX* to both VOLUMES.

By *FRANCIS DRAKE*, F.R.S.

MDCCXXXVI.

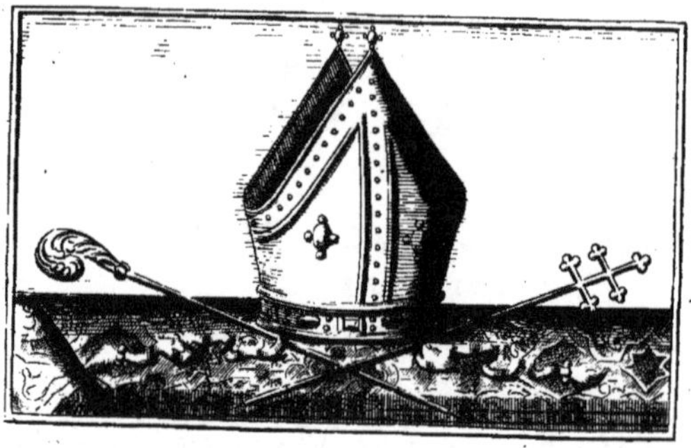

THE HISTORY AND ANTIQUITIES OF THE CHURCH of *YORK*.

BOOK II.

CHAP. I.

The history of the metropolitical church of YORK *from the first introduction of* Christianity *into the northern parts of this island; with the lives of the* ARCHBISHOPS *of that see, from the year* DCXXV. *to the present.*

SO many learned authors have employed their pens to transmit to posterity the miraculous tracts, whereby the light of the gospel first illuminated this isle, that it would be vain and frivolous in me to attempt it; neither shall I attempt any description of the religion of the antient *Britons*; but leave the doctrines of their *Druids* to be discussed by the doctors of the *christian* church. Amongst whom the inimitable *Usher* hath shewn us, as far as possible, the religion and rites of the primary inhabitants of this island, in their naked simplicity and dress. *Milton*, with others of his stamp, hath taken great pains to deduce *priest-craft*, as they are pleased to term it, from this high original (*a*). By quoting authorities, as they pretend, to prove that the *Druids*, or *British* priests, never communicated any thing to writing, but instructed their pupils and young novices in the mysteries of their religion by word of mouth; with the strictest injunction never to disclose them but in the same manner, for fear the bigotted populace should detect the cheat, and pay less regard to their spiritual directors. It is certain the *pagan* priests of all denominations had no better way to prevent the people from prying into and exploding their pretended oracles and illusions; but the poor illiterate *Britons* may be said to have been obliged to it, if they were, as I verily believe they were, intire strangers to letters till the

(*a*) Introduction to *Eng.* hist.

coming

coming of the *Romans* amongſt them. Nothing certain either by tradition, hiſtory or antient fame, can be gathered to the contrary; for thoſe, ſuppoſed, *Britiſh* coins, in the collections of the curious, are as diſputable as any other marks of their knowledge.

In this profound ſtate of ignorance did *Caeſar* find the nations inhabiting *Britain*; expert in nothing but their art of war, which their own homebred diviſions had ſufficiently taught them. As uncommon to the *Romans* as the *Romans* to them. The entire conqueſt which the ſucceeding emperors gained over the natives may be ſaid to have paved the way for the *chriſtian* religion to follow; which laſt found the eaſier paſſage when the *Roman* laws and manners had in ſome meaſure civilized the native fierceneſs of theſe, before, untamed iſlanders.

A. LVI. The learned churchmen *Uſher*, *Stillingfleet*, &c. have not wholly rejected the hiſtory of the firſt *chriſtian* king *Lucius*, and of his ſending over ambaſſadors to pope *Eleutherius* the fourteenth biſhop of *Rome*, including *Peter*, deſiring ſome miſſionaries to inſtruct him in the *chriſtian* religion. That the *Romans* ſuffered the *Britons* to enjoy a ſucceſſion of their own kings may be proved by claſſical authority; *reges in* Britannia *inſtrumenta ſervitutis*, ſays *Tacitus*, kings in *Britain* as means to keep the people ſlaves; and themſelves, indeed, were were little better. So *Cogidunus*, *Venutius*, *Praſutagus*, &c. are named by *Roman* authors on the ſame account; yet, ſuppoſe this *Lucius*, his embaſſy, and the return of two miſſionaries to inſtruct him true, we are not further to imagine his territories ſo large, or his power ſo great, under his *pagan* maſters, as to conſtitute biſhops and epiſcopal ſees; eſpecially, ſays an author, at York, *the then imperial city of* Britain (c).

However this, it is plain that the *chriſtian* religion had footing in *Britain*, long before the days of *Conſtantine the great*, and in the ſpace of little above a century, take it from the time that authors ſuppoſe this *Lucius* lived, to *Diocleſian*'s perſecution, had gained conſiderable ground in this iſland. *Tertullian*, *Origen*, *Gildas* and *Bede* ſufficiently atteſt the truth of this; but what puts the matter out of all doubt is the multitude of *Britiſh* martyrs that ſuffered in the dreadful perſecution under *Diocleſian* and *Maximian* his collegue.

During this interval the church could not be without teachers and preachers of the word, and even higher orders of prieſthood, as biſhops, &c. But who they were, in thoſe dangerous times, that durſt undertake the governance of a religion, invironed with ſo many mortal enemies, was, no doubt, then a great ſecret, but muſt be a far greater now. It was then the *nolo epiſcopari* took its riſe, and continued for ſome ages to be the *true anſwer* to the queſtion put to him that was thought proper to defend the church, in its infancy, againſt the ſtrongeſt opponents; and even to die for it upon occaſion. The *Romans* had in *Britain*, ſay our (d) *Britiſh* hiſtorians, twenty eight *flamins*, and three *archflamins*. Where there were flamins, add they, biſhops were placed, and upon the archflamins, archbiſhops. The ſees of the latter are ſaid to be placed at *London*, *York*, and *Carleon* upon *Uſk* in *Wales*. Allow the truth of this, and it is no ſmall honour to our own, for the firſt has changed its place, the laſt is long ſince quite extinct, *York* only, of the three, continues, as to title, in its primitive ſtate.

A. CCCXIV. Whatever was the caſe of the ſees, we muſt not look for the names of any *Britiſh* biſhops till *Conſtantine the great* ſwayed the imperial ſcepter. This emperor, according as he himſelf (e) writes to *Chreſtus* biſhop of *Syracuſe*, ſummoned a great many biſhops, from almoſt infinite places, to hear the cauſe of the *Donatiſts*. The council publiſhed at *Paris*, by *Jacobus Sirmondus*, and ſubſcribed by all or moſt of the prelates preſent, carries the names of theſe three from *Britain*.

Eborius *epiſcopus de civitate* Eboracenſi, *provincia* Brit.
Reſtitutus *epiſcopus de civitate* Londinenſi, *provincia ſuperſcripta.*
Adelfius *epiſcopus de civit. col.* Londinenſium.

The diſpute lay what part of *Britain* the laſt biſhop repreſented? but the learned Dr. *Stillingfleet* has expounded it thus, "the two firſt were miſſionaries from that diviſion "of the iſland, mentioned to be made by *Conſtantine the great*, viz. *Maxima Caeſarienſis*, the "capital Eboracum; *Britannia prima*, the capital Londinium; and *Britannia ſecunda*, "*civitas Legionis ad Iſcam:* whence ignorant tranſcribers have wrote *civitas coloniae Londinenſ.* for what muſt have been *ex civitate col. leg.* II. being the known ſtation of that "legion." But to proceed,

(f) This *Eborius*, ſays *Burton*, may be called the firſt biſhop of *Eboracum*, though neither mentioned by *Stubbs* in his chronicle of the biſhops of *York*, nor *Goodwin*. The laſt, however, has given us one *Taurinus*, placed here, as he ſays by *Conſtantius* the father of *Conſtantine*. But he is deceived by *Harriſon* in his deſcription of *Britain*, and both from reading a corrupt copy of *Vincentius Bellucenſis*; where you have *Eboracenſis* miſprinted for *Ebroicenſis* in *Gallia*. Theſe two ſees have been frequently miſtaken for one another by ſeveral authors.

In the ſubſcriptions to this council there are ſome things to be obſerved. Firſt, that *York* was no archbiſhoprick in thoſe days; though moſt certainly then primate of all *Britain.*

(c) *Burton*'s Ant. itin.
(d) *Gildas, Nennius, Galf. Mon.* See *Stillingfleet*'s *orig.* ſ.r on this head, p. 77.
(e) Euſebii *hiſt.*
(f) *Burton*'s itin.

tain. Nor, as our protestant writers assert, was then *Rome* itself; since when, notwithstanding, all dignities and titles have flowed. Our *Malmsbury* confesses it was not known where the archbishoprick was in those times. *Sylvester* the pope in the subsciptions above, allowing no mistake, is styled but *episcopus.* And long after this when *Gregory* the pope writes to *Augustine (g),* who *Bede* says was consecrated archbishop of the *English* nation by *Etherius* archbishop of *Arles,* he styles him no more than plain bishop. No not when he bestowed the *pall* upon him, and gave him precedency over all the bishops in *England.*

In the next place we must take notice that *Eborius* bishop of *York* precedes *Restitutus* of *London* in the subscription; where the primacy remained till *Austin* translated it to *Canterbury.* " For, says my author, (*h*) though *London* be at this day, and hath been for ma-" ny ages the chiefest city in *Britain,* and was near one thousand three hundred years ago " *vetus oppidum,* an old town, and commended long before by *Tacitus as a place of great* " *fame and renown for the concourse of merchants and provisions of all things necessary;* yet " *Philip Berterius* an excellent scholar, and a writer of late years, proves *York* to be the " antienter *metropolis* of the diocese of *Britain;* not only because it was a *Roman* colony " which *London* was not, but also the emperors palace and *praetorium,* tribunal or chief " seat of justice was there; whence it was called, by way of priority, or eminence, CI-" VITAS by *Roman* historians.

(*i*) Dr. *Stillingfleet* has taken no small pains to contradict the former assertion; and prove that *London* was always the metropolis of the *Roman* government in *Britain,* as well as the head of the *British* church. But with humble submission to that supereminent writer, who stands single in this opinion, nothing is so easy as to contradict the arguments he brings; which, if he had been dean of *York* instead of *Paul's,* would, I am persuaded, never have been thought on.

He begins with telling us that the superiority of one *metropolis* over another depended on the residence of the *Roman* governour, the *vicarius Britanniarum;* who, being a civil officer, wherever he resided the rest were summoned to attend upon extraordinary occasions at his *conventus;* which made that place the metropolis of the whole province of *Britain.* I take it that the *Dux Britanniarum* as the emperor's immediate representative was the chief officer in the province; but allow the former, and the doctor does not tell us, by any authority, that the vicar-general resided at *London.* He says indeed that *its admirable situation for trade and commerce made it remarkable in those days;* but does this prove it the capital of *Britain,* when it never was so much as called a city by the *Roman* historians? By the situation of *York* it must be allowed to be the properest residence for the emperor's immediate representative; since we well know that they themselves chose it when in the island. And tho' the doctor says this was because that they might be nearer the *Picts* and *Scots* in case of an irruption, or to send orders from in time of war, yet *York* being placed near the centre of the island, in a country newly conquered, and very hardly brooking *Roman* slavery, must be allowed the most commodious for observing every part; that they might send timely succour to stop each revolt at its first appearance. We have *Roman* authority for *civitas, palatium imperatoris, praetorium,* &c. the doctor's whole stress lies upon the title *Augusta* called so by one single author, which might allude to the pride which towns of such great trade and commerce by an affluence of riches and vanities from abroad are but too subject to import along with them. After all, where should a successor of the great *Papinian* sit to give judgment, but in the same *Praetorium* that he did?

For *London's* being sole metropolitan of the *British* church it is as impossible as the former. In the division of the empire by *Constantine,* the largest share of this island, by far, had *York* for its capital. Whence this district was called in the superlative degree *Maxima Caesariensis.* It was for this reason, no doubt, that the bishop whom that emperor summoned to attend the council at *Arles* from *York,* by way of supereminency signed first. A man that knows this and yet asserts to the contrary, as the doctor does, must have stronger reasons than he has given to support his opinion; in the mean time I shall discuss it no farther but proceed.

Dr. *Heylin,* in his catalogue of the archbishops of *York,* mentions *Sampson,* by others *Sanxo,* to be placed here by king *Lucius,* as first archbishop. Whether there ever was such a man is very uncertain, however our ancestors thought fit to consecrate a church to him in *York,* which I believe is the only one in *England* of that name. He who held out last in those tempestuous times was called *Tadiocus.* We have a *constat,* adds the doctor, only of two more, *viz. Taurinus* and *Pyrannus,* of all the rest no name nor mention is to be met with amongst all writers whatsoever (*k*).

It is certain the bishops of those days were not such considerable men as to deserve being taken notice of. At the council above they were provided for at the emperor's cost; and at home their stipends were perhaps little better than those *Irish* bishops whom *Adam Bremensis* says he saw in *Germany,* at their return out of *Italy;* which was no more than *three milch cows; and in case any one of them became dry, their parishioners were obliged to find them*

(*g*) *Epist. ad Aug. in hist.* Bedae.
(*h*) *Burton.*
(*i*) *Stillingfleet's orig. sacr.*
(*k*) *Heylin's* church history.

another. *Ammianus Marcel.* an heathen historian, gives this account of the poor country bishops in *Italy* in his time, (*l*) *whose spare diet and most abstemious drinking, their eyes cast on the ground, the meanness of their apparel, ever seeking God and his true adorers, are respected as good and meek men.* Whether any in these days would take this venerable character and pastoral care under such severe, but primitive, restrictions is foreign to these my enquiries.

From what is said before may be easily conjectured that christianity was not only planted, but in a thriving condition in this island, before the departure of the *Romans*, and it is very probable that the antient *British* religion was entirely abolished before the arrival of the *Saxons*. But here a dreadful change ensued. *Gildas* and *Bede* ascribe the calamities that befel the nation at this juncture to the profligate lives of both clergy and laity, who, say they, strove to out do one another in all manner of wickedness and vice. After the *Britons* had been most miserably harrassed by the *Picts* and *Scots*, the *Saxons* were called in to their assistance, who of friends became their deepest and cruellest enemies. And, as is shewn in another place, never left till they had utterly deprived the poor *Britons* of all their possessions in the island, *Wales* and *Cornwall* excepted. *Bede*, who was himself a *Saxon*, and therefore cannot be supposed to exaggerate the cruelties of his countrymen, expresses himself thus, *by the hands of the* SAXONS *a fire was lighted up in* BRITAIN, *that served to put in execution the just vengeance of God against the wicked* BRITONS, *as he had formerly burned* Jerusalem *by the* Chaldeans. *The island was so ravaged by the conquerors, or rather by the hand of God, making use of them as instruments, that there seemed to be a continued flame from sea to sea, which burned up the cities and covered the face of the whole isle. Publick and private devotions fell in one common ruin. The priests were murdered on the altars; the bishop with his flock perished by fire and sword, without any distinction; no one daring to give their scattered corps an honourable burial.* This terrible catastrophe may serve to shut up the same account I have given of the *British* church and *British* bishops to this period of time.

A. DCXX. The *Saxons* being now entire lords and masters over *England*, and the island divided into an *Heptarchy*, the christian religion was every where torn up and abolished by these *pagan* invaders; and their own idols and way of worship established. *Edwin*, surnamed *the great*, was king of *Northumberland*, whose chief residence was at *York*. Christianity had again just raised its head in the southern parts, for *Ethelbert* king of *Kent* was converted by *Austin*. But the occasion of this father's mission from *Gregory* bishop of *Rome* to convert the *English* nation was by an accident affecting our northern parts; and, though often told, yet must be inserted to introduce the sequel.

(*m*) *It happened at some time, as it often doth,* says the *Saxon* homily, *that some* English *merchants brought their merchandizes to* Rome, *and* Gregory *passing along the street taking a view of the* Englishmen's *goods, he there beheld, amongst their merchandizes, slaves set out to sale. They were white complexioned, and of pleasing countenance, having noble heads of hair.* Gregory, *when he saw the beauty of the young men, enquired from what country they were brought, and the men said from* England, *and that all the men in that country were as beautiful. Then* Gregory *asked whether the men of that land were christians or heathens, and the men said unto him they were heathens.* Gregory *then fetching a long sigh from the bottom of his heart said, alas! alas! that men of so fair a complexion should be subject to the prince of darkness. After that* Gregory *enquired how they called the nation from whence they came, to which he was answered that they were called* Angli, (*which is* English) *then said he, rightly they are called* Angli, *because they have the beauty of angels, and therefore it is very fit that they should be the companions of angels in heaven. Yet still* Gregory *enquired what the shire was named from which the young men were brought, and it was told him that the men of that shire were called* Deiri. Gregory *said well they are called* Deiri, *because they are delivered from the wrath of God,* de ira Dei, *and called to the mercy of* Christ. *Yet again he enquired what was the name of the king of that province, he was answered that the king's name was* Alla, *wherefore* Gregory, *playing upon the words in allusion to the name, said, it is fit that* Hallelujah *be sung in that land to the praise of the almighty creator.*

I have chose to give the reader the celebrated Mrs. *Elstob*'s literal translation of the antient *Saxon* homily, that he might have this odd story as near as possible in its genuine dress. And it is certain that the *Northumbrians* had at that time a custom, which continued some ages after, of selling their children for a small value into foreign lands. What followed was that *Gregory* immediately applied to *Palagius* II. the then pope to be sent a missionary in order to convert these islanders to the christian faith. The pope consented, but the inhabitants of *Rome* would not suffer so learned a doctor to leave them and undertake so dangerous an affair. Whilst this was in agitation the pope dies, and *Gregory* was unanimously elected into the chair. Who having still the conversion of the *Saxons* at heart, engaged six learned priests to undertake the mission. Their names were *Augustinus*, *Mellitus*, *Laurentius*, *Petrus*, *Johannes* and *Justus*. But the story of *Austin*'s converting *Ethelbert* king of *Kent*, and the success the rest met with is foreign to my subject; and I have barely mentioned it only as introductory to what follows.

(*l*) *Quos tenuitas edendi potandique parcissime, vilitas etiam indumentorum, et supercilia humum spectantia perpetuo numini verisque ejus cultoribus, et puros commendabant et verecundos.* Ammian. Mar.

(*m*) Mrs. *Elstob*'s *Saxon* homily.

Austin

Austin having sent an account of his success to *Gregory* he immediately orders him, in a *(n)* letter to that purpose, to erect episcopal sees in several places; and particularly mentions *York*, where was to be a metropolitan with twelve suffragans. And to do the same by *London*. The reason of this preference in regard to *York*, says a modern *(o)* author, was, because it had formerly, even under the *Romans*, been an archbishoprick as well as *London* and *Caerleon*; which last place being in the hands of the banished *Britons* who denied *Austin*'s authority, *Gregory*'s intent was to restore things, as far as possible, to their former state. Here it was the church of *York* lost the precedency over all the *British* churches; for *Austin* perceiving he could not have the superiority over *York*, whilst the other archbishoprick continued at *London*, got it removed to *Canterbury*, the metropolis of the *Kentish* kingdom. And had granted to him by the special favour of the pope, not only to have the jurisdiction over *York* and *London*, but over all the rest of the bishops in *Britain*. This however was but for his life; yet the *Northumbrians* not receiving the gospel as soon as that pope expected, and again deserting the faith after *Paulinus* was driven out, the continual troubles they were in hindred the first bishops of this see from taking advantage of *Gregory*'s farther regulation. *(p)* Which was that *Canterbury* and *York* should be both archbishop's sees, and that the eldest consecrated should always preside. But continuing unexecuted *Theodore* archbishop of *Canterbury* took advantage of the remission, and became possessed of all the authority, as well, over the northern, as southern churches. Thus, his successors, making him their precedent, lay claim to the primacy of *all England*, exclusive of the archbishop of *York*; which, however, as the reader will find in the sequel, they have not had indisputable possession of.

PAULINUS, *first archbishop*.

At this time *Edwin the great* swayed the *English* scepter, as sole monarch of *Englishmen*; A. DCXXV. the rest of the kings being tributary to him and little regarded. But to strengthen himself the better he sought to take to wife *Ethelburga* sister to *Ebald* king of *Kent*, the mightiest monarch next himself, in the island. This lady, as well as her brother were zealous *Christians*; and she would not consent to marry, even so great a monarch, without she might have the free exercise of her religion. This, though thought hard by her lover, was consented to; the many accomplishments that lady is said to be possessed of were attractions too strong to be resisted. Matters being settled betwixt all parties, *Ethelburga* set forwards from her brother's court towards *Northumberland*, with a magnificent retinue; amongst whom were some churchmen, particularly *Paulinus*, who had been consecrated archbishop of *York*, or *Northumberland*, by *Justus* archbishop of *Canterbury* *(q)*.

The scoffers and deriders of the *Christian* religion will here say that there could not be a more taking embassy invented, than to send a fine lady and a subtle priest on the errand to catch a young and amourous king. But the task was harder than was imagined. *Edwin*, though uxorious to the last degree, could not be prevailed upon, by any endearments, to forsake the religion and worship of his ancestors. And though *Paulinus* had, according to articles, free liberty to preach, yet in the space of a year little or no progress was made; but he continued bishop without a flock in his diocese.

(r) But an accident and a miracle coming close together, staggered the king's resolutions, and at length converted him. The accident has been recited in the annals of this work, of *Edwin*'s being assaulted by a villain at his country seat near *York*, and narrowly escaping assassination. *Paulinus* being at court, ran immediately at the first alarm this accident made, and finding the king in a great rage against the king of *Wessex*, for sending the ruffian to destroy him, told him that God to whom such wretches were an abomination would not fail to punish so horrid a villany. *Edwin*, breathing nothing but revenge, promised at the same time to renounce idolatry, if the God of the christians would avenge him of his enemy. In this very instant news was brought him that the queen, after a difficult labour, was delivered of a princess; for which *Edwin* returned thanks to his gods. But *Paulinus* was in extasy, for having been in no small fears for the queen's life, on which all his hopes depended, he fell down on his knees, and with great ardour thanked God for her safe deliverance. The prelate's zeal, no way feigned, was so pleasing to the king and begot in him so favourable opinion of the christian religion, that he immediately consented *Paulinus* should baptize the new-born infant. The new born princess was named *Ansleda*,

(n) Greg *epist*. Bede *l*. 1. *c*. 29.

(o) *Rapin*.

(p) *Sit vero inter* Londoniae *et* Eboracae *civitatis episcopos in posterum honoris ista distinctio, ut ipse prius habeatur qui prius fuerat ordinatus*, &c. *Epist* Greg. Bede. The bull of pope *Alexander* long after this confirms it in these words, *Alexander papa*. *Antequam* Eboracensis *ecclesiae dignitatem integram conservari auctore domini capientes, et praedecessorum nostrorum felicis memoriae* Calixti, Honorii, Innocentii, Eugenii, Romanorum *pontificum vestigiis inhaerentes, auctoritate apostolica prohibemus, ne aut* Cantuariensis *archiepiscopus ab* Eboracensi *professionem quamlibet exigat, aut* Eboracensis Cantuariensi *exhibeat, neque, quod penitus a beato* Gregorio *prohibitum est, ullo modo* Eboracensis Cantuariensis *ditioni subjaceat, sed juxta ejusdem patris constitutionem, ista inter eos honoris distinctio conservetur, ut prior habeatur qui prius fuerit ordinatus*. Rad. de Diceto.

(q) Norðhymbrum to bisceope, *hoc anno* Justus *archiepiscopus consecravit* Paulinum *in archiepiscopum* Northymbrorum Saxon. *annal*.

(r) *Bede*.

and

2

A. DCXXVI. and was the first that received baptism in the *Northumbrian* kingdom; though eleven of the queen's female servants were at the same time christned with her *(s)*.

After this, *Edwin* let not his resentment sleep, but raising an army overthrew the king of *Westsex*, forced him to sue for and accept of peace on his own terms, and returned victorious to his queen at *York*. But *Edwin*, no ways mindful of the vow he had made, continued an idolater, notwithstanding the queen and bishop took all opportunities to remind him of his solemn promise, and urged home the consequence of breaking it. Staggered, but not convinced, he remained doubtful some time; till one day as he sat musing alone, says *Bede*, of these things in his study, the bishop entered, and laying his right-hand on his head, asked if he knew that token? *Edwin* fell down at his feet, acknowledged the sign, said he was fully satisfied and ready to receive the christian faith. The ceremony of baptism was performed by *Paulinus* in the city of *York*, on *Easter-day*, *April* 12, 626; the whole court with a multitude of the commons attending.

The story of the sign is copied from venerable *(t) Bede* by most authors that have treated on this subject, and therefore unnecessary here. But I find before any open declaration came from the king about changing his religion, he had taken care to sound his own high-priest on that head. Who wisely guessing at the king's intentions by his arguments, jumped in with him and struck the first stroke at idolism himself. For *(u)* immediately he rode to the famous pagan temple at *Godmondham*, threw a spear at the chief idol, and burned it with the rest and the temple to the ground *(x)*.

Thus fell *paganism* in the north of *England*. *Paulinus* was now solemnly installed by the king in the archiepiscopal chair; and upon that news pope *Honorius* sent him the long designed *pall*, with letters of congratulation and advice to *Edwin*. Confirming *Gregory*'s design about the two metropolitan sees; which was that when either of the archbishops died, the survivor should consecrate a successor, that they might not have the trouble or danger of going to *Rome* for it.

Regis ad exemplum totus componitur orbis.

A. DCXXVII The *Northumbrians*, following the example of their monarch, came in by thousands at a time; and found the archbishop work enough to baptize and instruct the new converts. In every river that he travailed by multitudes had the sacred laver from his hands. In one day he is said to have baptized ten thousand in the *(y)* river *Swale* in this county. *Gervasius in act. pont. Cant.* makes St. *Austin* the baptizer of this multitude; from whom several others have copied; but the error is refuted by Mr. *Smith*, in his notes on *Bede*. That father having been dead some years before this time. For six years together did our holy prelate continue his spiritual function with vast fatigue; when a new and unforeseen accident spoiled all his harvest, overthrowed his plantations, and made the painful husbandman to desert his flock and seek shelter in another country.

Edwin, under whose protection and encouragement the *christian* religion mightily flourished, had many enemies who maligned his greatness. Amongst whom *Cadwallo* the *Welsh*
A. DCXXXIII. king, and *Penda* king of the *Mercians*, conjoining, came upon his territories, and at *Hatfield* overthrew *Edwin*'s army, slew himself, and afterwards laid his whole kingdom in ashes. Our pious bishop had just time enough to embark in a ship, from off the eastern coast, with the queen and her children, and sailed into *Kent*; where they were all joyfully received by her brother king *Ebald*, and *Honorius* archbishop of that country.

During these calamities neither priest nor deacon had the courage to preach the gospel in *Northumberland*. *James* the deacon, whom *Paulinus* had left at *York*, was by no means able to stop the general revolt. *Paulinus* continued in *Kent*, where the church of *Rochester* wanting a pastor, he was prevailed upon by the pope and king to undertake it. Here
A. DCXLIV. he continued for several years, dying *October* 10, 644; and was buried at *Rochester*.

Bede writes that *Paulinus* preached the word of God in the province of *Lincoln*, on the south side of the *Humber*. He converted the governour of *Lincoln* city, with all his house to the faith; and built a church of stone of admirable workmanship in the same. Whose covering, adds he, being by long neglect, or on purpose, thrown down, the walls of it continue to this day. The same author gives this description of the person of our prelate, that *he was a man of a tall stature, a little stooping, his nose thin and hooked, lean faced and black haired, of a countenance terrible enough, but very reverend*. If the reader would see more of the life of this our primitive prelate he may find it at large *en les vies des saintes par*

(s) Cum undecem aliis foeminis de familia reginae. Bede.

(t) Bede Stubbs act. pont. Ebor.

(u) Coisy *autem pontifex accepto a rege equo emissario, cum pontifici idolorum non liceret nisi super equam equitare, correptoque gladio et lancea, quod etiam non licebat*; aras quas ipse sacraverat *succendit cunctis videntibus et destruxit. Ostenditur autem locus idolorum non longe ab* Eboraco *ad orientem ultra amnem de* Derwent, *et vocatus hodie* Godmundingham, *i. e. idolorum domus.* Bede.

(x) Aras quas ipse sacraverat, so *Bede* in another place has *caeco carpitur igni*, this shews that the monks were not unacquainted with the *classicks* in those days. *Godmundingaham*, now *Godmundham*, a village near *Weighton*, signifies a house of gods.

(y) Tradition tells us that this ceremony was performed in the river *Swale* nigh *Helperby*'s which town's name is said to bear some allusion to it. *Paulinus* preaching here to the multitude, was asked by them what way they should attain to that salvation he spoke of? he answered, there is Help-hard-by, meaning the river where he immediately conducted them. This story, however ridiculous it may sound to some, is fresh in the mouths of the county people thereabouts at this day.

monsieur

monsieur Baillet. *October* 10. was the day assigned, in the *English* calendar, for the annual festival of this saint.

CEDDA, *second archbishop.* A. DCLXVI.

After the departure of *Paulinus* the church of *York* continued without a pastor for twenty; some say thirty years. The continual wars and troubles in the north and severe pagan persecution impeding it. Till at length *Egfrid*, a christian, being king of *Northumberland*, appointed one *Wilfrid* to the see of *York*, and sent him to *Agelbert* bishop of *Paris*, some time of *Winchester*, for consecration. *Wilfrid* stayed so long in *France* that the king, out of all patience, forced *Cedda* abbot of *Lestingham*, a man of devout life to accept of it, and thrust him into the chair due to *Wilfrid*. Having carefully attended his charge about three years, he was admonished by *Theodore* archbishop of *Canterbury* that he was not rightly and lawfully called to that see. Whereupon the good man presently relinquished it, and retired to his monastery. From whence he was soon after, by means of the said *Theodore*, made bishop of *Litchfield*, *anno* 669. *Bede* says he was a very godly and modest man, and died *March* 2, 672. Buried at *Litchfield*.

WILFRIDUS, *third archbishop.* A. DCLXIX.

(z) *Wilfrid* was born in the north of mean parentage, the time of his childhood he lost in his father's house, being uninstructed in any part of literature till he was fourteen years of age. At which time, not brooking the frowardness of his step-mother, he left his home in order to wander about the world. At his first setting out he met accidentally with certain courtiers, whom his father had some way or other obliged; and by them was presented to the queen as a lad of parts and beauty not unfit for her service. The queen, whose name was *Eansled*, questioning the youth, found his inclinations were for learning, and being desirous to have him a scholar she sent him to one *Cudda*, who from being councellor and chamberlain to the king was become a monk of *Lindisfarn*, or *Holy-island*. Under whom being diligently instructed, and having excellent natural parts, he wonderfully improved.

About the time that our *Wilfrid* was twenty years old there happened a great contention in the church about the celebration of *Easter*. The youth undertook to go to *Rome* that he might be well instructed in the controversy. By means of the queen, his patroness, and *Ercombert* king of *Kent*, he was equipped with all things necessary for his voyage, and sent along with one or two companions. In travelling through *France* he became acquainted with (a) *Dalsynus* archbishop of *Lyons*, who greatly caressed him, and retained *Wilfrid* some time in his family, to the great increase of his knowledge. This bishop was so fond of our youth that he offered to adopt him for his son, to settle a large territory on him in *France*, and to give him his neice, a beautiful young lady to wife, if he would constantly reside with him. But *Wilfrid*'s thirst after knowledge and travail made him reject this offer, and all the prelate could prevail upon him to do was to make him promise he would call upon him at his return. When he was arrived at *Rome* he was presented to pope *Boniface* V, who understanding the reason of his coming, took care to instruct him in all points of the controversy, and after many caresses blessed him and dismissed him for his own country.

At his return to *Lyons* the bishop renewed his endearments to him, and in all probability had engaged *Wilfrid* to accept of his generous offers, and never more to return into *England*; had not the reverend prelate been snatched from him by a persecution raised by a furious pagan queen, whom *Bede* calls *Brunchyld*. For amongst ten bishops that fell a sacrifice to her cruelty this *Dalsinus* was one. And thus our *Wilfrid* was at liberty to pursue his journey.

On his return home king *Egfrid* gave him a house and a maintenance, and many noblemen, admiring much his learning and eloquence, bestowed divers rich gifts upon him. Soon after he engaged *Colman*, with the *Scotch* and *Irish* bishops, on the subject of *Easter*, at a great council called for that purpose at the abby of **Streynshall** (b); the king, queen and all the nobility being present. Here though he could not convince *Colman* and the rest of their obstinacy, yet he was allowed by all to have much the better of the argument, insomuch that with one consent and general applause he was upon the spot chose bishop of this province (c).

But the difficulty lay in the consecration, for he refused it at the hands of the *Scotch* bishops; looking on them to be little better than schismaticks, as not agreeing with the church of *Rome* in the article of *Easter*. So he desired to be sent into *France*; which was accordingly done, and at *Paris* he was consecrated by the bishop thereof with great solemnity. No less than eleven other bishops being present at the ceremony.

(z) *E vita S.* Wilfridi *inter* xx *scriptores.*

(a) *Goodwin* calls him *Wulsinus*; but *Bede*, and also *Severtius* who wrote the history of *Lyons* from their own records, and lived upon the place stile him *Dalsinus.*

(b) *Streanshale*, *Sinus Phari*, *Prestby*, now *Whitby*, a monastery founded by St. *Hilda* sister to *Edwin* the great.

(c) *Eddius Stephanus*, who wrote the life of this prelate, as early as the year 720, stiles him no other than *episcopus Eboracensis*, bishop of *York*; throughout his work, But the titles of bishop and archbishop were indifferently used in those days. The *pope* himself had then no other title than bishop of *Rome*; but in the *Saxon* annals, to a charter there recited of king *Ethelred*, this *Wilfrid* subscribes himself *archbishop* of *York*. Chron. *Saxon*. 43.

In *France* he stayed beyond the time allowed him, being too much taken up with the company of many learned men of that country. And when he purposed to have returned he was by stress of weather driven into foreign countries, and long retarded in his voyage.

Coming home at length and finding another man in his place, he betook himself for a time to a private life. From which place he was often invited by *Wulphere* king of *Mercia* to the bishoprick of *Litchfield*. But in the end *Cedda* being removed, as is said before, he took possession of the archiepiscopal chair at *York*, and *Cedda* was placed in *Litchfield*. During his administration he was so well beloved by all sorts of people for his gentleness, affability and liberality, that many whilst alive, but more at their deaths, put their children and all their effects into his hands. In a very short time he became exceeding rich, having a numerous retinue of servants to attend him; great quantities of plate, with other rich and sumptuous furniture. *Theodore* archbishop of *Canterbury* hearing of this, liked not the rivalship; and it put him upon endeavouring to constitute two or three more bishopricks under *Wilfrid*, the country he found being well able to sustain them. Which when *Wilfrid* refused and the other strenuously insisted on, he appealed to the pope, and purposed to do it in person. Some insinuate, though *Goodwin* thinks not justly, that *Wilfrid* had endeavoured to perswade the queen to forsake her husband, and to retire into a monastery. And that the king, being greatly displeased therewith, first thought to diminish his authority by making more bishops; and afterwards made several loud complaints against him to the pope in order to have him deprived.

However this, he set sail for *Italy*, and meeting with a dreadful storm at sea he was driven in *Friezland*. Where he staid all winter preaching to and converting the king and the natives of that country. The pope was at the council of *Constance* when he reached him, from whom *Wilfrid* obtained an order that the state of his bishoprick of *York* should not be altered without his consent. But king *Egfride* so favoured *Theodore*'s scheme, that *Wilfrid* saw plainly at his return that he must either submit to it, or leave the country. The prelate chose banishment and went in great poverty into *Sussex*, where the inhabitants together with their king were as yet all pagans, and whom by degrees he brought over to the faith. He had assigned him an habitation in **Seolsey**, being a *peninsula* and contained eighty seven families, here he built a monastery and established an episcopal see.

Amongst all the miracles recorded of *Wilfrid* by the author of his life, this, if true, was very extraordinary, and would go far to convert the most obdurate pagan. It is said that at this time God so blessed the holy man's endeavours towards the propagation of the faith, that, on a solemn day set for baptizing some thousands of the people of *Sussex*, the ceremony was no sooner ended but the heavens distilled such plentiful showers of rain, that the country was by it relieved from the most prodigious famine ever heard of. So great was the drought and provision so scarce, that in the extremity of hunger fifty at a time would join hand in hand and fling themselves into the sea, in order to avoid dying by famine at land. But thus by *Wilfrid*'s means their bodies and souls were both preserved.

After he had staid five years in this country, the tenth of his banishment king *Edfrid* (*d*) died, and *Alfred* succeeding him sent for our prelate to return to his pastoral care at *York*. Which he did, but continued not above five years more in it, when this king also taking a disgust against him he was forced to go to *Rome* to purge himself by oath of several accusations laid to his charge. He obtained from thence the pope's letters in his behalf, and returning was, by the intercession of his friends, with much ado reinstated in his chair. Here at last he continued in peace to the end of his days, which was four years after; and then concluded the course of a various life *Oct.* 12, *anno* 711. in the seventy sixth year of his age, and forty five years after his first consecration. He was buried in the monastery of *Ripon* which he himself had founded; but the church there falling down for want of reparation, *Odo* archbishop of *Canterbury* removed our prelate's bones to *Canterbury*, *an.* 940.

The life of this prelate is wrote at large by *Eddius Stephanus*, printed in the xx. *script. ed. Gale.* There are also many things to be met with about him in venerable *Bede*, too copious for this design (*e*). His epitaph, preserved by the last named author, runs thus:

> Wilfridus *hic magnus requiescit corpore praesul,*
> *Hanc domino qui aulam, ductus pietatis amore*
> *Fecit, et eximio sacravit nomine* Petri;
> *Cui claves coeli* Christus *dedit arbiter orbis*;
> *Atque auro et* Tyrio *devotus vestiit ostro.*
> *Quin etiam sublime crucis radiante metallo*
> *Hic posuit trophaeum*; *nec non quatuor auro*
> *Scribi Evangelii praecepit in ordine libros,*
> *Ac thecam e rutilo his condignam condidit auro.*
> *Paschali qui etiam solemnia tempora cursus*

(*d*) This *Edfrid* or *Ecfrid*, whatever he was to *York*, was a great benefactor to the church of *Durham* even in this city; for I find this note in *Leland. in vet. libros monast.* Dunelm. *scribitur rex* Edtridus *in civitate* Ebor, *dedit totam terram a muro eccles.* S. Petri *usque ad magnam portam versus occidentem, et a muro ipsius ecclesiae usque ad murum civitatis versus austrum.* Coll. tom. I. 369. But I cannot make out where these lands lay.

(*e*) See *Nicholson*'s historical library. *Et vitam* Wilfridi *en vies de saints per* Baillet; *sub* xii. Oct.

Catho-

Catholici et justum correxit dogma canonis,
Quem statuere patres, dubioque errore remoto,
Certa suae genti ostendit moderamina ritus,
Inque locis istis monachorum examina crebra
Colligit, ac monitis cavit quae regula patrum,
Sedulus instituit; multisque, domique, forisque,
Jactatus nimium per tempora longa periclis,
Quin decies ternos postquam egit episcopus annos,
Transiit, et gaudens coelestia regna petivit.
Dona, Jesu, *grex ut pastoris calle sequatur.*

BOSA, *fourth archbishop.* A. DCLXXVII.

After the first departure of *Wilfrid* from his see to appeal to the pope, *Theodore*, proceeding in his intended alteration, divided the diocese into four parts; and planted *Eata* first at *Hagulstad*, then removed him to *Lindisfarn* whom *Tumbert* succeeded at *Hagulstad*, *Trumwyn* in the province of the *Picts*, and *Bosa* here at *York*. But, upon the return of *Wilfrid*, *Bosa* was obliged to resign. Yet upon his second exile he was restored again, and died in possession of the see. He was esteemed a very meek and devout man. He lived ten years after his first consecration, and was the first archbishop buried in the cathedral at *York*, *anno* 687 *(f)*.

JOHANNES, *fifth archbishop.* A. DCLXXXVII.

John, commonly called St. *John* of *Beverley* succeeded *Bosa* in *Wilfrid*'s exile, and upon his last restoration was continued by him therein. Whilst *Wilfrid* for a time contented himself with *Hagulstad*, *John* was a gentleman, born of a very good *Saxon* family at *Harpham*, says *Goodwin*, but at *Beverley* according to *Stubbs*; which is more probable. He was brought up first under St. *Hilda* the famous abbess of *Whitby*, then under *Theodore* the fifth archbishop of *Canterbury*, who preferred him to the bishoprick of *Hexam* or *Hagulstad*. He is said to have been sometime a student in the university of *Oxford*. Venerable *Bede* is copious in reciting many miracles done by this holy man, as the curing diverse people desperately sick by prayer, making a dumb man speak, *&c.* All which the historian says he had of his own knowledge, or else from such as were eye witnesses of the same; for he not only lived in his diocese, but also received the order of priesthood at his hands. But were the venerable old man to return and report the miracles, *viva voce*, they scarce would, in this unbelieving age, find credit. For which reason I shall forbear a farther recital. *John* was archbishop of this province above thirty three years, filling the chair with great honour and piety. At length, grown aged and infirm, he with the consent of his clergy resigned his bishoprick, and procured that his chaplain, whose name was *Wilfride* should be consecrated in his stead. After which he retired to *Beverley (g)*, where he lived privately in a college of priests of his own foundation for four years, and, where we suppose he first drew breath, he died *May* 7, *anno* 721. And was buried in the church porch belonging to that college. Many miracles were also reported to be done at his tomb after his death, and several privileges were granted by divers kings to the church at *Beverley* for his sake *(h)*. Amongst which that of king *Athelstane*'s is the most remarkable. In a convocation held at *London*, *anno* 1416, the aforesaid day of his death was appointed annually to be kept holy as a perpetual memorial of the sanctity and goodness of this prelate. And also the feast of his translation on the twenty fifth of *October* on account of the victory at *Agincourt* gained on that day, as was believed by the merits of this saint *(i)*.

(k) Bishop *Nicholson* says, that the life of St. *John* of *Beverly* was first wrote at the request of *Aldred* archbishop of *York* by *Folcard* a *Benedictine* monk, about the year 1066. Which was enlarged by *William Asketel*, or *Chattel*, clerk of *Beverley*, *anno* 1320. Another draught of him was taken by *Alfred*, canon of that church and treasurer in the beginning of the twelfth century. And a third or fourth by an anonymous writer about 1373.

(l) Bale has ascribed these writings to St. *John* of *Beverley*,
Pro Luca exponendo lib. I. *ad Bedam.*
Saepe quidem tuae sancte frater ———
Homilias Evangeliorum. lib. I.

(f) St. *Cuthbert* bishop of *Durham* lived at this time; of whom I find this note in *Leland*'s coll. worth inserting, *Rex* Ecbertus *cum* Trumwino *epis. navigant ad* Farn. *i. e.* Holy Island, *et* Cuthbertum *nolentem volentem a solitari vita ad curam pastor. abducunt. Nec multo post* Eata, *exactis in episcopatu* Lindisfarn. 14. *annis, reductus est ad sedem* Hagustuldensem, *et* Cuthbertus *fit epis.* Lindisfarn. *Consecratusque est* Eboraci *a* Theodoro *archiep.* Cant. *praesente rege* Ecberto *et* 7 *episcopis anno* 685, *et rege* Ecfridi 12. *Cui rex* Ecfrid *villam de* Crek, *vel* Creac, *nunc* Creyke *et* 3 *in circuitu milliaria ei dedit, ut haberet* Ebor. *iens vel inde rediens mansionem ubi requiescere posset. Vide Chron.* Sax. *hoc anno. Creyk*, about nine miles from *York*. is still in the county and diocese of *Durham*.

(g) Deirwold *locus memorosus, i. e. Silva* Deirorum, *postea* Beverlac, *quasi locus vel lacus castrorum, dictus a castoribus quibus* Hulla *aqua vicina abundabit. Ex vita S.* Johannis *epis.*

(h) See more of St. *John*, and the privileges granted to this church for his sake in sir *T. Herbert*'s account of *Beverley* in the appendix. *Et vita ejus en vies de saints par* Baillet Maii 7.

(i) Linwood's Provinciale, p. 104. See the annals of this work.

(k) Hist. library.

(l) Baleus *de script.* Brit.

Ad

I

Ad Hildam abbatissam epis. plures.
Ad Herebaldum discip. ep. 1. *Ad Andoenum et Bertinum ep.* 1.

A. DCCXVIII. WILFRID II. *sixth archbishop.*

Wilfrid, chaplain to his predecessor succeeded, but has very little said of him. He sat in the archiepiscopal chair, some say eleven, others fifteen years, and died *anno* 731, without any thing memorable; except that this *Wilfride* began the grand dispute betwixt the two metropolitan sees about priority, which continued to disturb the whole *English* church some ages (*m*). The *Saxon* annals relates the cession of *John* and the succession of this *Wilfrid*, in the *Latin* version, after this manner, *postea capessit* Johannes Eboracensem *episcopatum, quippe* Bosa *episcopus decesserat. Deinde* Wilferthus *ejus presbyter consecratus est in* Eboracensem *episcopatum, et* Johannes *se recepit ad monasterium suum de* Derawude. I mention this because the see of *York* is here twice called only Eaꞅꞇꞃe-Biꞅcopꝺome (*n*).

A. DCCXXXI. EGBERTUS, *seventh archbishop.*

Egbert brother to *Eadbert* king of *Northumberland*, was preferred to this see; who by his own wisdom and the authority of the king greatly amended the state of the church in these parts. This prince and prelate bear a wonderful character in history for learning, piety and beneficence. He procured the archiepiscopal pall to be restored to the church of *York*; which had been withheld from it ever since the days of *Paulinus*, by the machinations of the archbishops of *Canterbury*. Whence some (*o*) take the liberty to call this *Egbert* the first archbishop of this see. He founded a famous library in his cathedral church, which I shall mention in the sequel. This prelate was not only a favourer and encourager of learning in others, but was himself a great proficient in arts and sciences.

Bale has preserved the titles of several tracts wrote by our archbishop as follows:

Poenitentiale quoddam, lib. 1.
Constitutiones ecclesiae, lib. 1.
Eruditiones discipulorum, lib. 1.
Homilias et lectiones, lib. 1.
Ad ecclesiarum pastores, lib. 1.
Ad Zachariam *pro pallio, epis.* 1.
Ad Eadbertum *fratrem regem, epis.* 1.
Ad Alcuinum *diaconum epis. plures.*

Egbert, after he had filled the chair thirty six Years with much honour, died *November* 19, 766, and was buried in the porch of his cathedral church near his brother. Chron. *Saxon.*

It will not be improper in this place to give some description of the *pall*, which *Egbert* procured from *Rome* to the church of *York*; and which cost his successors some trouble, but more money to obtain. The ancient *pall*, from the *Latin pallium*, was an entire and magnificent habit, designed, says my authority (*p*), to put the bishop in mind that his life should answer up to the dignity of his appearance. But the chief thing, or symbol of sovereignty, was a white piece of woolen cloth, about the breadth of a border, made round and thrown over the shoulders. Upon this are two others of the same matter and form, one of which falls down on the breast, and the other on the back with each of them a red cross. Several crosses of the same colour being likewise on the upper part of it round the shoulders. This pall is laid upon St. *Peter*'s tomb by the pope, and then sent away to the respective metropolitans. Which till they have received from the see of *Rome* they cannot call a council, bless the chrism, consecrate churches, or a bishop, ordain a priest, &c. At the delivery of it they were to swear fealty to the pope. By virtue of this pall, and the extent of their jurisdictions, the archiepiscopal power was very great in those days. *William* of *Malmsbury* says, that the archbishop of *York* had formerly all the bishops on the north of the *Humber* subject to his authority. As at this time were the bishops of *Ripon*, *Hagulstad*, or *Hexam*, *Lindisfarn*, or *Holy Island*, the bishop of *Whitehaven*, and all the bishops of *Scotland* and the *Orcades*. This last power continued long in the see of *York*, till the wars during the reigns of the three *Edwards* of *England* made the *Scotch* throw off their subjection to it. Sir *Henry Spelman* has preserved some ecclesiastical constitutions made and published by this archbishop *Egbert*, which he has given us in his councils under this title: *Excerptiones D.* Egberti *archiep.* Ebor. *a dictis et canonibus sanctorum patrum concinnatae et ecclesiasticae politiae institutionem conducentes* (*q*).

A. DCCLXVII. ALBERTUS, ADELBERTUS *vel* AETHELBERHTUS, *eighth archbishop.*

To *Egbert* succeeded *Albert*, called by *Florence* of *Worcester Caena*, he was consecrated *Apr.* 24, *anno* 767; and received the pall from pope *Paul* I. He sat fourteen years, and died at *Chester*, says *Goodwin*, *an.* 781, without any other memorial that I can learn of him. Our author here is mistaken by taking Eaꞅꞇeꞃ for *Chester*, when it is *York*, and is so translated in the *Latin* version of the *Saxon* annals, *anno* 780.

(*m*) Gul. Malmf.
(*n*) *Saxon* ann. p 46. *Gibson.*
(*o*) *Inett's* church history.
(*p*) *Petrus de Marca.*
(*q*) Spelman. *concilia*, p. 258, &c.

EANBALDUS.

EANBALDUS, *ninth archbishop.* A. DCCLXXX.

Caena yet living, but whether he resigned or took him for a coadjutor is uncertain, says *Goodwin*; *Eanbald* being an old man was consecrated archbishop, and lived after his consecration seventeen years. When he is said to die in the monastery of *Arleet*, or *Atleet*, and was buried very honourably in his own cathedral (*q*). This prelate was a disciple of our famous *Alcuin*, who in an epistle to him from *France* writes thus, *laus et gloria Deo, in prosperitate bona conservavit, ut in exaltatione filii mei charissimi gauderem, qui laboraret vice mea in ecclesia*, ubi ego nutritus et eruditus fueram (*r*).

EANBALDUS II. *tenth archbishop.*

Another *Eanbald* succeeded; who *Hoveden* says was a priest of the church of *York*, and was consecrated in the monastery of *Socaburg* (*s*), *Nov.* 19, 797. Before the end of his first year *Stubs* writes, that he called a synod or convocation of his clergy at *Pinchambalch* (*t*), in which he caused divers things amiss to be reformed. What time he died, or how long he sate I cannot find. A. DCCXCVII.

WULSIUS, *eleventh archbishop.* A. DCCCXII.

Wulsius occurs next in the catalogue, who came in *anno* 812. and enjoyed his honour nineteen years; he died *anno* 831.

WIMUNDUS, *twelfth archbishop.*

Wulsius was succeeded by *Wimundus*, who governed the church about twenty years; and died, as *Mat. Westminster* informs us, *anno* 854. A. DCCCXXXI.

WILFERUS, *thirteenth archbishop.* A. DCCCLIV

Wilfere is next, who was archbishop of this diocese, as some write, forty six years in a most terrible and turbulent time; for now the *Danes* made their first invasion, and drove all before them with fire and sword. *York*, the chief city of the province, felt their fury in a more especial manner, having burned and wasted all round it for many miles. The two kings *Osbright* and *Ella* were slain in the city itself; but the archbishop escaped the slaughter, and fled to *Addyngham* where he was kindly received by *Burrhed* king of *Mercia*. In the year following the *Danish* king *Ricsius*, being converted to christianity, recalled the archbishop and placed him on his throne. But their ravages had so spoiled the profits of the archbishoprick, that it was then and some time after augmented with the commendam of *Worcester*. He died about the year 900, or according to *Mat. Westminster*, whose computation is very uncertain, 895 (*u*).

ETHELBALDUS (*x*), *fourteenth archbishop* A. DCCCC.

REDWARDUS, *fifteenth archbishop.* Called by *Stubbs*, *Leodwardus.* A. DCCCCXXI.

WULSTANUS, *sixteenth archbishop.* A. DCCCCXLI.

By the favour of king *Athelstane*, *Wulstan* was made archbishop, and that king likewise augmented the revenues of the church by the donation of all **Agmonderness** to it; which he had bought of the *Danes*. But the prelate repayed this high generosity with great ingratitude, for not long after he was convict of a very heinous offence, unbecoming his office, his allegiance and his country. For he sided with the *Danes* against his own countrymen the *Saxons*, assisted the *Pagans* against the *Christians*, and was in arms against his own natural prince *Edred*, brother to his benefactor *Athelstane*. For which fact he was committed close prisoner by *Edred*, but the year after was released and restored to his episcopal dignity at *Dorchester* (*y*). *Mat. Westminster* tells us, that the occasion of his imprisonment was, that he had caused to be slain several citizens of *Thetford*, in revenge of the death of one *Adelm* an abbot, whom they had murdered without cause. But the former is more likely from the account I have given of *Edred* in the annals, and what *Simeon* of *Durham* relates, which the reader may please to observe under this note (*z*). He lived two years after his release, and then died on St. *Stephen*'s day, *an.* 955, and was buried at *Oundle* in *Northamptonshire*. Mr. *Willis* (*a*) says this archbishop obtained to his see *Beverley*, *Ripon*, *Bishop-Wilton*, *Otley*, *Cawood* and the barony of *Shireburn*.

(*q*) *Stubbes vit. pont.* Ebor. But I find no mention of any such monastery either in the *Monast.* or elsewhere.
(*r*) Gul. Malmſ. *de pont.* Ebor.
(*s*) *Hodie* Socburn *in agro* Dunelm.
(*t*) *Hodie* Finkley *in eodem com. Vide chron.* Saxon. *in nom. locorum.*
(*u*) *Obiit* 892. *pont. sui* 39. Sim. Dunelm.
(*x*) *Ordinatur archiep. an.* 900. Sim. Dunelm.
(*y*) Rog. Hoveden. Gul. Malmſ.
(*z*) *Anno Dom.* 949. Wulstanus Ebor. *archiepiscopus, proceresque* Northumbrenses, *omnes in villa quae dicitur* Taddenesscylf *egregio regi* Anglorum Edredo *fidelitatem juravere sed non diu tenuerunt. Adscriptum erat in margine per* Lelandum, Taddenes scylf *tunc erat villa regia quae nunc vocatur* Romanè Pontfract; *Anglice* Kirkeby. Lel. *coll. tom.* II. *p.* 359.
(*a*) *Willis* on cath. churches.

The laws of the *Northumbrian* priests are supposed to have been first made at *York anno* 950, under this *Wulstan*, or *Oskytel* archbishop, *Anlaff* then being king of *Northumberland*. These are taken notice on both by sir *Henry Spelman* and *Somner*; and have lately had an *English* version from the *Saxon* by a reverend divine (*a*). They are a curious body of laws; the last of which is somewhat remarkable; which recites, "let landlord's rightful gift be "firmly maintained; and especially one christianity, and one monarchy in the nation for "ever." But whether this respects the kingdom in general, or only that of *Northumberland*, which had just then suffered by having two kings, I shall not determine.

Oskitellus, *seventeenth archbishop*.

A. DCCCCLV. *Oskitell* succeeded, a man of very good life and well learned; he is said to govern the see wisely sixteen years, and died in 971. *Willis* writes that this bishop procured to his see, the manor of *Southwell*. I find by the *Saxon* chronicle that he was buried at *Bedford*.

Athelwoldus, *eighteenth archbishop*.

A. DCCCCLXXI. Next followed *Athelwold*, but he not affecting greatness resigned his bishoprick, and made choice of a retired obscurity.

Oswaldus, *nineteenth archbishop*.

A. DCCCCLXXI In the space of one year the see of *York* had three archbishops, *Oskitell* lately deceased, *Athelwold* who abdicated, and this *Oswald*. Who was near kinsman to *Oskitell* his predecessor, but much nearer to *Odo* archbishop of *Canterbury*, being his own nephew, called by *Bayle Oswaldus Odonius*. By his uncle's means he was first made canon of *Winchester*, and after dean of the same. For at that time the cathedral church of *Winchester* had no monks, but maintained a number of secular priests. But the monks beginning now to gain great esteem by their regular lives and great temperance, compared to the other clergy, *Oswald* was advised by his uncle to leave his place at *Winchester* and travel to the monastery of *Floriack* in *France*; which he did, and entered himself a monk of that society. He continued this situation five or six years, during which time the archbishop growing very old and infirm, wrote often to him to return, but could never prevail till he sent him word of his last sickness, whereof soon after he died. *Oswald* now made haste to see his uncle but came too late, so *Oskitell* archbishop of *York* entertained him, as another kinsman, till by the means of *Dunstan*, *Odo*'s successor, he was in the year 960 preferred to the bishoprick of *Worcester*. Here he built the church dedicated to St. *Mary*, and placed monks therein, which was just by the church of St. *Peter* in that city.

About this time the see of *York* becoming void, king *Edgar* studious to prefer a fit person to the care of these northern parts, which were then very rude and barbarous, offered it to *Oswald*, who seemed to decline the acceptance as loth to forsake *Worcester*; wherefore the king was content that he should hold both. He reigned archbishop of this province twenty one years, and died suddenly at *Worcester*, having washed the feet of certain poor men, as was his daily custom; after which kneeling down to pray without any precedent sickness he gave up the ghost, *February* 27, 992. *Malmsbury*, who reports this of him, says also that the day before his death he told several of his friends that he should die the next day.

He was one of the principal founders of the abby of *Ramsey* in the isle of *Ely*; and was a very liberal benefactor to the monastery of *Floriack*, where he had lived. For the integrity of his life he was much valued in his time. *Goodwin* speaks well of him, and says he was a very learned and good man, and that he had but one fault, which was his great vehemence in opposing the marriage of the clergy. But *Bayle* has a terrble fling at him upon that account, and in a most outragious manner insults the memory of our dead prelate for joining with *Dunstan* in prohibiting the marriage of the clergy, or excluding them the church; *ut deinceps sub religioso coelibatus titulo sodomitice viverent*.

Divers miracles, however, were said to be done at his tomb after his death, and his successor took care to build a very costly shrine over it, which was in the church of his own foundation at *Worcester* (*c*). He is also honoured with a solemn day in the *English* calendar, appointed in commemoration of him (*d*). His life is wrote at length by *Eadmer* a monk of *Canterbury*; which is printed in *Wharton's Anglia sacra p.* 2. wherein he has a much better character than the protestant bishop of *Ossory* will allow him; who calls him the *Archflamen* of *York*; and his writings the *dregs of a depraved genius*. They are these,

Ad Abbonem monachum, epist. 1. *Praescientia Dei monachus* Oswald.

Ad sanctos dum esset Floriaci, *lib.* 1. Oswaldus *simplex monachus. Statuta synodalia lib.* 1.

(*b*) *John Johnson* M. A. see his preface to the laws.

(*c*) *Hujus insula purpurea auro et gemmis ornata, et prisca fulgitudine fulgida*, Beverlacensi *adhuc reservatur ecclesia.* Stubbii *act. pont.* Ebor.

(*d*) *Oct.* x. *Vita ejus en les vies des saints par* Baillet.

Abul-

ADULFUS *vel* ALDULFUS, *twentieth archbishop.* A. Dccccxcii.

Adulf abbot of *Peterborough* succeeded *Oswald* in both his sees of *York* and *Worcester*, a holy and reverend man, says *Malmsbury*, and one who strove to outdo his predecessor in his liberality to the monastery of *Floriack*. In any thing else history is silent, so he died *May* 6, *anno* 1002, and lies buried in St. *Mary's* church in *Worcester (e)*.

WULSTANUS II, *twenty first archbishop.*

Another *Wulstan* by the favour of king *Knute* held both the sees as formerly, for the A. MII.
which *Malmsbury* blames him *quod contra regulas canonum duas sedes tenuerit*. He died *May* 28, 1023, and was buried in the monastery at *Ely*. Where, Mr. *Willis* says, is yet a painted representation of him against the wall in the north transept of the choir under the lanthorn.

ALFRICUS PUTTOC, *twenty second archbishop.*

Alfric Puttoc provost of *Winchester* was made archbishop of *York*. Some ill things are A. MXXII.
reported by *Malmsbury*, &c. of this prelate, as that because he missed the holding the bishoprick of *Worcester in commendam* as three of his predecessors had done upon a slight pretence, he urged king *Hardiknute*, with whom he was a great favourite, to set the city on fire. Which was done to the no small damage of the citizens. As also that he caused the dead body of *Harold*, the king's brother to be dug up, decapitated and cast into the *Thames*, for what reason I know not. This seems to be an idle story, but it is not to be wondered, that old *William* and his brother monks bore hard upon this archbishop, who gave so much to churches in the possession of secular clergy, and nothing to them. He was very liberal to the church and college of *Beverley*; he first built a most magnificent and costly shrine over the tomb of their saint. Also a hall and a dormitory in their beddern, and turned it into a house for their provost. He constituted three offices in that church, a sacrist, a chancellor and a precentor. He likewise obtained from king *Edward the confessor*, that three annual fairs should be held in *Beverley*. And instituted a custom, that the principal inhabitants of that town and the neighbouring gentlemen should thrice every year follow the reliques of St. *John* in and about the town fasting and barefoot *(f)*.

Alfric purchased lands at *Midleton*, *Holm*, and *Frydaythorp*, which he settled on his church at *York*. He was also a great benefactor to that at *Southwell*. At which last place he died *Jan*. 22, *anno* 1050, and was buried at *Peterborough*. Neither did this church want a taste of his generosity, for many ornaments of gold and silver, and several rich copes he gave to it *(g)*.

KINSIUS, *twenty third archbishop.*

Kinsius, or rather *Kinsine*, chaplain to *Edward the confessor*, succeeded. He is said to A. ML.
have been a man of great austerity of life, and would walk barefoot in his parochial visitations. He was another special benefactor to the church at *Beverley*, where he built a high tower and placed two great bells in it. Two of the same mould he likewise gave to *Southwell*; and two more to the church at *Stow*. He also gave many books and ornaments to *Skyreston*, and other churches in his diocese. To *Peterborough* he gave ornaments to the value of three hundred pound, but queen *Edgit* afterwards took them away from thence *(h)*.

Of this bishop it was the common opinion, says *Stubbs*, that he was not born, but came into the world by the *Caesarian* section. He died at *York*, *December* 22, 1060, and was buried at *Peterborough*; where he had formerly been a monk.

The tombs of these two last prelates are yet to be seen behind the altar in the church at *Peterborough*; on which some much later person has put the two following inscriptions,

HIC SEPULTA SUNT OSSA ELFRICI ARCHIEPISCOPI EBOR.
A. M L.

HIC SEPULTA SUNT OSSA KYNSII ARCHIEPISCOPI EBOR.
A. M LXI.

ALDREDUS, *twenty fourth archbishop.*

The see of *York* falling void by the death of *Kinsius*, *Aldred*, who was first a monk of A. MLXI.
Winchester, then abbot of *Tavistock*, afterwards bishop of *Worcester*, making his way by money and bribes, says *Malmsbury*, which he liberally bestowed on the courtiers, got hold of the arbishoprick of this province. The prelate had no sooner possession of it, but he prevailed upon king *Edward* to let him hold *Worcester in commendam*, also, as four of his predecessors had done. Having gained so far on holy *Edward*'s goodness, he set out nobly attended to fetch his pall from *Rome*. Along with *Aldred* went *Tosty* the furious earl of

(e) I have seen a curious original deed in the possession of *James West* of the *Temple*, esq; being a charter of king *Etheldred*'s, dated *anno* 998, to which this prelate subscribes himself *Ego* Aldulfus Eboracensis *basil. prim. hoc eulogium agie crucis taumate confirmavi* ✠.

(f) *E vita S*. Johan. Bever. *in coll*. Lelandi.

(g) *Ex libro* Hugonis *mon*. Peterbur. *coll*. Lelan.

(h) *Ex eodem.*

Northum-

Northumberland, already ſpoken of, brother to the queen, *Giſo* biſhop of *Wells*, and *Walter* biſhop of *Hereford*. At his arrival in *Rome* the pope, *Nicholas* II, who had been informed of his *ſimoniacal* contrivances, not only refuſed to confirm him in the archbiſhoprick, but alſo deprived him of that he had before. The other two biſhops were received and entertained with great honour.

They all ſet out together to return to *England*, but with very different affections; *Giſo* and *Walter* much elated with the honour lately done them, but *Toſti* and *Aldred* chagrined to the laſt degree. Travelling from *Rome* over the *Alps* they were met by a band of robbers, who took from them all they had, except their cloaths; ſo that they were obliged to go back to *Rome* to get a farther ſupply for their journey.

Now it was that *Toſti* let looſe his fiery diſpoſition, and really played the bully for his friend. For he ſtuck not with open mouth to rail againſt the perſon of the pope; declaring how unreaſonable it was for them to be obliged to come ſo far, at ſo vaſt an expence and trouble as ſuch a voyage muſt neceſſarily coſt, and then to be without ſecurity or protection for their return. Then when the king of *England* ſhould hear of this uſage, *Nicholas* might depend upon it he would withdraw the tribute due to the holy chair. The thunder of theſe threats, ſays (*i*) *Malmſbury*, frightned the pope, and at laſt his deſire was granted, and the pall delivered to *Aldred*, on condition that he ſhould quit *Worceſter*; which at his return he accordingly did.

Being ſeated quietly in his chair at *York* he began to do ſome good things, for he built an hall for the canons to dine together in; and another at *Southwell*. At *Beverley* the hall begun by his predeceſſor, but left imperfect he finiſhed. The preſbytery there he raiſed from the very foundbtion, and alſo rebuilt the new cathedral church at *Glouceſter* deſtroyed by the *Danes*. Another of his meritorious actions was his obliging the clergy of his province to wear an uniform and decent ſort of habit; whereas before the laity and they were indiſtinguiſhable. In the year 1050, when he was biſhop of *Worceſter*, he undertook a pilgrimage to *Jeruſalem* through *Hungary*; a thing which no biſhop of this realm ever attempted before him. Theſe are all or moſt of the vertues which his panegyriſt *Stubbs* aſcribes to his ſanctity; who ſeems fond of his memory becauſe he was the laſt archbiſhop of the *Saxon* race.

But view this prelate in a political light, and he greatly belies the character *Stubbs* beſtows on him, and appears what he really was, a meer worldling and an odious timeſerver. No ſooner was *Edward*, his patron, dead, but *Harold*, earl *Goodwin*'s ſon, reached at the crown without the leaſt title to it, and by means of our pious archbiſhop obtained it. He ſolemnly crowned him with his own hands and ſwore allegiance to him. After this, when the conqueror had waded through a ſea of blood, and laid as juſt a title to the crown as his predeceſſor, (*k*) our prelate had made a firm compact with the *Londoners*, that if *Harold* ſhould be worſted they ſhould immediately proclaim *Edgar Atheling* king. Yet, when *Stigand* archbiſhop of *Canterbury* refuſed to crown *William* (*l*), our good archprelate run in with the ſtream, and performed the ceremony; only exacting a fooliſh oath from the *Norman*, that he would love and protect the *Engliſh*, equal with his own natural ſubjects. This when he found, after poſſeſſion, that *William* little regarded, why then, truly, he thundered out an excommunication againſt him; which the conqueror ſome ſmall time after, for a round ſome of money, I ſuppoſe, bought off. But when the *Daniſh* invaſion came on, and the citizens of *York* with the *Northumbrians*, &c. had declared for prince *Edgar*'s title, the prelate ſickened at the news, and, either (*m*) through fear, or remorſe, or both, gave up the ghoſt *September* 10, 1069, juſt before the *Danes* landed, and was buried, according to our writers, in his church at *York*; though Mr. *Willis* ſuppoſes, I know for what reaſon, that he lies in his own church at *Glouceſter*.

I cannot take leave of this prelate without giving the reader a taſte of his ſpiritual pride, which *Stubbs* is pleaſed to call conſtancy, in a ſtory recorded of him by that author. It ſeems a great quantity of proviſions was bringing towards the biſhop's offices at *York* when the high ſheriff of the county met them on the road, ſtopped the carts and horſes and aſked them who they belonged to? The men that conducted them anſwered, they were ſervants to the archbiſhop, and were carrying thoſe proviſions for his uſe. But the high ſheriff, deſpiſing both the prelate and his ſervants, ordered the officers who attended him to ſeize upon the carriages, *&c.* and convey them to the caſtle of *York*, and place them in the king's granary. The archbiſhop when he heard of this ſent ſeveral of his clergy and citizens to demand reſtitution from the high ſheriff, and threatned that if he did not make ſatisfaction to St. *Peter* and his vicar, he ſhould act in another manner towards him. The ſheriff ſet at nought his threats, and returned him word that he might do his worſt. The prelate

(*i*) *Haec rex* Anglorum *audiens*, *ait* Tofty, *tributum* S Petri *merito* Nicholao *ſubtraheret*. *Hoc minarum fulmine* Romani *territi papam flexerunt*. Gul. Meldun.

(*k*) *Fabian*'s chron.

(*l*) *Et quia* Stigandus *tunc* Cantuarienſis *archiepiſ*. *viro tam cruento et* alieni juris invaſori *manus imponere recuſavit*, *ab* Aldredo *tunc* Ebor. *archiepiſ*. *magnifice coronatus regni diadema ſuſcepit*. *Chron*. T. Wykes *inter* v. *ſcript*. *hiſt*. Ang.

(*m*) *De quorum omnium adventu* Ebor. *arch*. Aldredus, *valde triſtis affectus*, *in magnam decidit infirmitatem*, *et decimo anno ſui epiſcop*. *vitam finivit*; *et in eccleſia S*. Petri *ſepult*. *eſt*. Simeon Dunel.

upon

upon this answer hastens up to *London*; where, when arrived and habited *in pontificalibus*, attended with a numerous suit of bishops and other ecclesiasticks in town, he went directly to *Westminster* where the king then was in council. The monarch no sooner cast eyes upon the prelate, than he arose up to salute him as usual; which the latter put by with his crosier, and taking no notice of the king's standing, nor of all his croud of courtiers, he addressed himself to him in these words, *Hear me*, William, says he, *since thou art an alien, and God has permitted thee for our sins and through much blood to reign over us; I anointed thee king and placed the crown upon thy head with a blessing, but now because thou deservest it not, I shall change that blessing into a curse, as a persecutor and oppressor of God and his ministers, and a breaker and contemner of oaths and promises which thou sworest to me before the altar of S.* Peter. The king astonished at these menaces threw himself at the archbishop's feet, and humbly begged to know wherein he had offended him to deserve so severe a sentence? The noblemen in the presence were irritated to a high degree at the prelate's arrogance, to suffer so great a king to lie at his feet and not raise him. But he, modestly said to them *let him alone, gentlemen, let him lie; he does not fall down at my feet, but at the feet of St.* Peter. And after some time thought fit to raise him and told him his errand. The king was too much frightned to deny his request. He rewarded the prelate with rich gifts, sent him honourably away, and at the same time dispatched an express to the high sheriff with a mandate for the restitution of the goods. Which were punctually restored, says my author, even to the value of a sackstring (*n*).

Another story out of *Malmsbury* shall concude the account of this prelate.

Ursus, earl of *Worcester*, had built a castle to the prejudice of a neighbouring monastery; for the ditch of the said castle took off part of the churchyard belonging to the monks. *Aldred* had often admonished the earl by letters to do justice to the monks. But finding that course would not answer, he went to him in person, and asked *Ursus* whether it was by his appoinment that this encroachment was made? The earl not denying the fact, the prelate said (*o*) **Hightest thou Urse? have thou God's curse**; *and know assuredly that thy posterity shall not inherit the patrimony of St.* Mary. This curse, says my author, seemed to take effect, for *Ursus* died soon after; and *Roger* his son enjoyed his father's honour but a very small time; for, having slain an officer of the king's, he was forced to fly his country. Who would not value a bishop's blessing, when their curses are so fatal?

(*p*) *Fulchard*, a monk of *Durham*, at the instigation of *Aldred*, wrote the life of St. *John* of *Beverley*, and dedicated it to him.

THOMAS, *twenty fifth archbishop.*

The see vacant the conqueror appointed one *Thomas*, his chaplain, a *Norman* and canon of *Bayeux*, to fill the chair. *Thomas*, though but a canon, was very rich, and assisted the duke in his enterprise against *England* with all his fortune. For which he promised him a bishoprick, if he succeeded, and payed him with *York*. *Goodwin* writes that he was the son of a married priest. *Thomas* was educated in the schools of the *Saxons* in *France*, says *Goodwin*, but what schools they were I know not, and spent some time in *Spain* and *Germany* in order to finish his studies. A. MLXX.

This prelate bears an excellent character in history, for not only being a very learned man, but of a mild and gentle disposition, both in words and behaviour. He had a sweet and amiable countenance and a goodly personage (*q*). In his youth he was beautiful, in his age florid; and his hair as white as snow. Add to these, that through the whole conduct of his life he was of an unblemished character as to *chastity*.

At his first entrance to the see he refused profession of obedience to *Lanfranc* archbishop of *Canterbury*. On which a contest began, which continued with equal warmth in their successors for some ages. *Goodwin* quotes an anonymous author for saying, that before the conquest the two metropolitans of *England*, were not only equal in authority, dignity and office, but also in number of *suffragan* bishops. But at this time the *Cantuarians* persuaded the king that *York* ought to be subject to their see; and that it was for the good and safety of the whole kingdom that the church should be obedient principally unto one; lest one of them might set the crown on one man's head, and the other do as much for some body else. This advice did not displease *William*, and *Thomas* though overborn by the king's and *Lanfranc*'s authority, however appealed to the pope. To *Rome* the two archbishops travelled; where *Lanfranc* alledged prescription for his right, and offered to make proof of the same. *Thomas* was as ready, as he, to plead his own cause; but the pope unwilling to concern himself in this nice affair, remitted the hearing thereof back again to the king, who, partially enough, in the year 1070, gave it for *Canterbury* (*r*).

(*n*) *Ad ligamen facci.*

(*o*) *Hightest thou* Urse, in old *English*, means art thou called *Urse*?

(*p*) Baleus *de script*. Brit.

(*q*) *Elegantia personatus, spectabilis, desiderio videntibus erat; juvenis vigore et aequalitate membrorum commodus, senex vividus faciei et capillis cygneus.* Malmf.

(*r*) *Causa de primatu inter archiepiscopos ventilata est coram rege in civitate* Wynton; *postea determinata est apud* Wyndesor ✠ *sig.* Willielmi *regis* ✠ *sig.* Mathildis *reginae, ex autographo in archivo eccles.* Cantuar. *Vide* Malmf. *lib.* 3. *p.* 117.

(*s*) *Thomas* had a more difficult affair to manage than his opponent, ſays *Eadmer*, becauſe moſt of the ancient charters and privileges, granted to the ſee of *York*, were deſtroyed by fire a little before his coming to it. The ſeparate titles for primacy, as drawn up by *Fuller* in his church hiſtory, may not be unacceptable to the reader. But the whole controverſy about the bones of St. *Wilfrid* ſaid to be removed by *Odo* archbiſhop of *Canterbury*, and which may properly be ſaid to have been *bones of contention*; as alſo the affair at length relating to the diſpute about primacy, from the firſt to the final determination under *Edward* III, may be ſeen in *Wharton*'s *Ang. ſac. t.* 1.

Canterbury.

1. No catholick perſon will deny but that the pope is the fountain of ſpiritual honour, to place and diſplace at pleaſure. He firſt gave the primacy to *Canterbury*, and wherefore as the proper place of the archbiſhop of *Canterbury* in a general council, was next the biſhop of St. *Ruffinus*; *Anſelm* and his ſucceſſors were advanced by pope *Urban* to ſit at the pope's right foot; as *alterius orbis papa*.

2. The *Engliſh* kings have ever allowed the priority to *Canterbury*; for a *duarchy* in the church, *viz.* two archbiſhops, equal in power, being inconſiſtent with a monarchy in ſtate, they have ever countenanced the ſuperiority of *Canterbury*, that the church government might be uniform with the commonwealth.

3. Cuſtom has been accounted a king in all places; which, time out of mind, hath decided the precedency to *Canterbury*.

York.

1. When *Gregory the great*, made *York* and *Canterbury* archbiſhops ſees, he affixed precedency to neither, but that they ſhould take place acccording to the ſeniority of their conſecrations. Untill *Lanfranc* chaplain to king *William* thinking it but reaſon that he ſhould domineer over all the clergy, as his maſter did over the laity of *England*, uſurped the ſuperiority over the ſee of *York*.

2. If antiquity be to be reſpected, long before *Gregory*'s time *York* was the ſee of an archbiſhop, whilſt as yet *pagan Canterbury* was never dreamed of for that purpoſe. *Lucius* the firſt chriſtian *Britiſh* king founding a cathedral therein, and placing *Samſon* as archbiſhop of the ſame, who had *Taurinus*, *Pyrannus* and *Tadiacus* for his ſucceſſors.

3. If the extent of the juriſdiction be meaſured, *York*, though the leſſer in *England*, is the larger in *Britain*. As having the entire kingdom of *Scotland* ſubject to it. Beſides, if the three biſhopricks, *viz. Worceſter*, *Litchfield* and *Lincoln*, formerly injuriouſly taken from *York*, were reſtored unto it; it would vye, even *Engliſh* latitude, with *Canterbury* itſelf.

After the king had given ſentence againſt him, *Thomas* repaired to his ſee at *York*, where he found the whole ſtate of his dioceſe, the city and cathedral church eſpecially, in a forlorn and miſerable condition. The fire that had happened at the taking of the caſtles of *York* by the *Danes*, had conſumed the church, and, well nigh, laid the whole city in aſhes. And *William*'s barbarity coming on the neck of this had done as much for the country round it. Seven poor hunger-ſtarved canons were all that were left, the reſt were either dead, or through fear and want gone into a voluntary exile. However the prelate ſet himſelf heartily to reſtore all again. The church he rebuilt, called back the canons, as many as he could find, to their ſtalls, or placed others in their rooms. Then he took order for a competent proviſion for them. He built them a hall and a dortoir; and appointed one of them to be the provoſt or governour of the reſt. Certain manors and lands of his own he ſettled on them; and took care to get reſtored what had been unjuſtly, in the late troubles, taken from them. And at length finding it inconvenient for them to live together on the common charges of the church, at one table, like the fellows of houſes in our univerſities, he thought fit to divide the lands belonging to his cathedral church into independent prebends. To allot a particular portion for the ſubſiſtence of each eccleſiaſtick, that they might better improve the lands which were waſted, by every perſon's building upon and cultivating his own ſhare.

The ſeveral offices of dean, treaſurer, precentor, and chancellor were now appointed. He likewiſe conſtituted archdeacons, and ſent them through his dioceſe to ſee that good induſtrious prieſts were every where encouraged. To the church newly built by him he added a library, and furniſhed it with good and uſeful books; with a ſchoolmaſter to teach and inſtruct the youth in languages. The church he repleniſhed with all kinds of neceſſary habits and ornaments; but his more eſpecial care was that it ſhould be filled with learned, honeſt and ſound divines. Which he alſo took care to ſee planted through his whole dioceſe.

Thus did this truly provident paſtor attend his flock and ſpent his time amongſt them; ſometimes converſing with one of his prieſts and then with another, partly for his own

(*s*) *Qui eo quidem magis in iſto laboravit, quod antiqua ipſius eccleſiae privilegia in ea conflagratione quae eandem eccl. conſumpſit, pene omnia perierant.* Eadmeri *hiſt.*

amuſe-

amusement, and partly to know their worth, that he might place each man according to his merit. He was himself a great proficient in arts and sciences; he wrote several things, and is said to have been, by *Hoveden*, an excellent musician, and could not only play well upon the organ, but did compose and set many pieces of church musick *(t)*. *Bale* has injudiciously given this faculty to his successor *Thomas* II; who, he says, composed for the use of the church of *York*

Cantus ecclesiasticos lib. 1.
Officiorum ejusdem ecc. lib. 1.

but it is a mistake in that author, for it was this *Thomas* that had that turn to musick; a faculty very rare in those days.

Thirty years did this worthy prelate fill the archiepiscopal chair at *York*; none before or since, even down to the present, with more honour and credit to it. At length after he had lived to crown king *Henry* I. on the 5th of *August* 1100, the 18th of *November* following he finished the course of a virtuous and painful life at *Ripon*; and was buried in his own cathedral, which he lived to finish, next unto *Aldred* his immediate predecessor. The epitaph following is ascribed by some to his successor *Thomas* II; but by several things in it as the date of his death, description of his person, *&c.* it ought to belong to this *Thomas*. And here accordingly I place it.

Orba pio, viduata bono, pastore, patrono,
Urbs Eboraca *dolet, non habitura parem.*
Qualia vix uni, persona, scientia, vita,
Contigerat Thomae, *nobilis, alta, bona.*
Canities, hilaris facies, statura venusta,
Angelici vultus splendor et instar erat,
Hic numero atque modo doctrinae seu probitatis
Clericus omnis erat vel magis omnis homo.
Haec domus et clerus sub tanto praesule felix,
Paene quod est et habet muneris omne sui est;
Octavis igitur Martini *transit ille*
Qui pietate Deo sit comes in requie.

GERARDUS, *twenty sixth archbishop.*

After the death of *Thomas*, *Gerard* nephew to *Walkling* bishop of *Winchester*, and chancellour of *England*, *temp. William* I. and *William Rufus*, having been some small time bishop of *Hereford* was elected to *York*. He, like his predecessor, denied to pay obedience to *Canterbury*, for which reason he was not consecrated of a long time, till being commanded to it by letters from the pope, he at length submitted. This prelate also was a great benefactor to the church at *York*, for he obtained from the king the grant and impropriation of the church of *Laughton*, which he gave to the chapter, and it was annexed to the chancellorship. He got into his hands likewise the churches of *Driffield*, *Killam*, *Pocklington*, *Pickering* and *Burgh*, which he bestowed in like manner upon that church, *Snaith* also he had the possession of, but this he gave to the abbey of *Selby*. A. MC.

These were his benefactions, but *William* of *Newborough* accuses him for living an unsteady life, and spunging by very indirect methods the purses of his clergy and subjects. He allows him, however, to be a sensible and learned man. He sat archbishop seven years and almost six months, and died suddenly in his *(u)* garden at *Southwell*, at a time when nobody was present, *May* 21, 1108. For which reason he was not suffered to be buried in his church at *York*, but only in the church-yard. But *Thomas* his successor caused his body to be removed, and placed behind the high altar; under a stone which had an inscription on it, as *Leland* informs us; but what he says not. *Stubbs* writes that he was a man of great learning, and for eloquence admirable. But *Goodwin* is offended at him, as he was before with St. *Oswald* his predecessor, for his acerbity to the married priests. *Bayle* has a worse fling at him, for the same reason, and sticks not to lay sorcery and conjuration to his charge; because the bishop happened to have a volume of *Firmicus*, on astrology, found under his pillow *(x)*.

THOMAS II, *twenty seventh archbishop.*

Thomas the second of that name and chaplain to king *Henry* I. succeeded. He was nephew to the former *Thomas*, son unto *Sampson* bishop of *Worcester*, and brother to *Richard* bishop of *Bayeux*. He is said to have been a very corpulent man, and but young in years A. MCVIII

(t) Of what antiquity organs and church musick are, see the reverend Mr. *Johnson's* collections of ecclesiasticall laws, *&c. sub anno* 1305; who has made a learned remark upon this subject. *London* 1720. two vol. 8°.

(u) *Apud* Southwellum *cum pransus in horto juxta cubiculum clericis prope spatiantibus super cervical sub dio quiesceret letali sopore diriguit. Corpus raro agmine* Ebor. *delatum extra ecclesiam sine honore sepultum, neque clericis nec civibus cum pompa exequiali ex more occurrentibus, sed pueris, ut dicebatur, sandapilam lapidantibus sine honore sepulturae traditum.* Gul. Newburg.

(x) This book of conjuration may be seen in manuscript, intituled *Julius Firmicus de astrologia. In catal.* Kenelmi Digby. Wanley, 1813, 212.

when

when he was elected bishop. Yet he was of such good parts and proficiency in learning, that he was called from the provostship of *Beverley* to the see of *London*, then vacant by the death of *Mauritius*; and had just accepted of it, when *York* falling too he was translated to that see; and consecrated *June* 26, *an.* 1109. Like his predecessors he was very unwilling to bow the knee to *Canterbury*, though often summoned by archbishop *Anselm* to that purpose, which he as often excused. *Anselm* at length falling sick, and perceiving his end to draw nigh, wrote unto all the bishops in *England* commanding them not to consecrate *Thomas* before he had made his profession, on pain of excommunication and the censures of the church. The curse of father *Anselm*, on this occasion, is so remarkable that I have transcribed great part of it from *Eadmer*; and the reader will find it under this note (*y*). *Anselm* dying, the king commanded the bishop of *Worcester*, whose son our elect was, to consecrate him, but the bishop refused it and said, he would not do a thing whereby he might incur father *Anselm*'s curse for any worldly profit or preferment. But in the end *Thomas* being perswaded to yield, (*z*) as others had done before him, he had consecration *June* 27, 1108. by the then bishop of *London*; making his profession with this clause, saving his obedience to the pope and king, and the right of his church of *York*.

This prelate constituted two new prebends in his church; of which *Weighton* is supposed to be one. He placed canons at *Hexam*; he gave several parcels of land to the college of *Southwell*, and purchased from the king the like privileges and liberties for them, which the prebendaries of *York*, *Beverley* and *Ripon* enjoyed. He sat but a little above five years, for he died *February* 16, *anno* 1114, and was buried in his cathedral church at *York* next to his uncle.

I must not omit to mention what several historians have thought fit to record of this archbishop, that he was a most eminent example of an unspotted chastity; for, falling into very bad state of health, he was told by his physicians, I suppose on account of his gross habit of body, that if he would use *the company of woman*, he need not doubt of his recovery; otherways nothing was to be looked for but inevitable death. The prelate rejected the prescript, and chose rather to die than to pollute his high and sacred calling with so foul and heinous an offence (*a*).

Whether so easy a remedy would be rejected * * * * * * * * * * * * * * * * * * *
1735. * * * * * * * * * after this manner die a kind of a *martyr to celibacy, and shew such an uncommon contempt for carnal affection?*

THURSTANUS, *twenty eighth archbishop.*

A. MCXIV. *Thomas* dying, as is before related, *Thurstan* a canon of St. *Paul*'s, and chaplain to king *Henry* I. succeeded (*b*). This man after his election made a stronger push to obviate the profession claimed by *Canterbury* than any of his predecessors. For when by no means he could gain consecration from *Ralph* the archbishop without it; he renounced and forsook the benefit of his election. But remembring himself at last, he travelled to *Rome* to plead his cause, and the cause of the see, before the pope; and him he satisfied so well in the justice of it, that *Thurstan* returned with letters both to the king and archbishop of *Canterbury* in his favour. But these letters not prevailing, that prelate being resolute to oppose him, and *Thurstan* as resolved to deny subjection, the see remained void a long time.

At last it happened that a general council was summoned to be held at *Rheims*, *Thurstan* asked leave of the king to attend it; but could not obtain that favour before he had promised that he would not receive consecration at it. This promise, however, he little minded, but plied his own business so well that before any of the *English* bishops came over, he was a bishop ready consecrate as well as they; and had that dignity conferred on him by the hands of the pope himself. Thus *Thurstan* of all the archbishops of *York*, since the conquest, was the only man who never made profession of subjection to the see of *Canterbury*. This bishop *Goodwin* asserts; but it must be a mistake, in part, for the council at *Rheims* was not held till 1148, some years after our prelate's death.

The king hearing of this affair of *Thurstan*'s was highly displeased at him, and forbad his return into the realm of *England*. Neither could the pope, meeting with the king

(*y*) Anselmus *minister ecclesiae* Cant. Thomae *elect. archiep.* Ebor. *Tibi* Thomae *in conspectu omnipotentis Dei Ego* Anselmus *archiep.* Cant. *et totius* Britanniae *primas loquor. Loquens ex parte ipsius Dei, sacerdotale officium, quod meo jussu in parochia mea per suffraganeum meum suscepisti, tibi interdico atque praecipio ne te de aliqua cura pastorali ullo modo praesumas intromittere, donec a rebellione quam contra ecclesiam* Cant. *incepisti, discedes, et ei subjectionem quam antecessores tui*, Thomas *videlicet et* Gerardus *archiep. ex antiqua antecessorum consuetudine professi sunt, profitearis; quod si in iis quae coepisti magis perseverare quam eis desistere delegeris, omnibus episcopis totius* Britanniae *sub perpetuo anathemate interdico, ne tibi ullus eorum manus ad promotionem pontificatus imponat, vel si in externis promotus fueris, pro episcopo vel in aliqua christiana communitate te suscipiat. Tibi quoque*, Thoma, *sub eodem anathemate ex parte Dei interdico, ut nunquam benedictionem episcopatus* Ebor. *suscipias nisi prius professionem, quam antecessores tui* Thomas *et* Gerardus *ecclesiae* Cant. *fecerunt, facies, &c.* Eadmeri *hist.*

(*z*) *Cessit ille non rationi sed potentiae, factaque professione suscepit a ministro* Richardo *scil.* Lond. *epis. quod detrectaverat a magistro*, as *Malmsbury* in a pretty turn expresses it.

(*a*) *Verba* Thomae Ebor. *arch. morituri quia recusabat concubitum mulieris*, Propter salutem carnis tandem moriturae immortale pudicitiae decus non omittam. *Gul. Newbrig.*

(*b*) *Eligitur die assumptionis S.* Mariae *an.* 1114. Hoveden. 271. *n.* 3. Sim. Dun. *c.* 236.

at *Gisors*, so pacify his displeasure that he would recall him. Five years he continued in banishment, and might have done so to the end of his days, had not the holy father raised the apostolical thunderbolt in his favour, which he threatned to throw both against the king and the archbishop of *Canterbury* if they refused him any longer admission to his see and charge. This method prevailed, *Thurstan* was recalled, and soon after entirely reconciled to the king.

This prelate is much praised by historians for his learning, great wisdom and discretion. As also for his industry, diligence, his care and painfulness in well executing his episcopal charge. He was very kind to his canons, unto whom, amongst other things, he granted this privilege that the yearly profit of their prebends being divided into three parts, it should be lawful for any canon to bequeath two parts of the year next ensuing his death to his heirs; allotting the remaining part to the fabrick; that is, to the reparation of the church. This order he fixed not only at *York* but at *Beverley*, *Southwell* and *Ripon*, which were colleges founded by archbishops of *York*, and likewise in the free chapel of St. *Oswald*'s in *Gloucester*, which was under the sole Jurisdiction of the archbishop of *York*, being originally granted by the king in consideration of the archbishop's consent to the removal of the episcopol see from *Dorchester* to *Lincoln*. But if our prelate was thus kind to the regular clegy, he was much more beneficent to the seculars, for he is said to have either founded or renewed and repaired no less than eight monasteries. Amongst which the abbey of *Fountains*, near *Ripon*, valued at the dissolution at one thousand one hundred and seventy three pounds and seven pence half-penny *per annum*, was very considerable.

It was the custom in his time and after, for the kings of *England* to be solemnly crowned at the three great festivals every year; and *Henry* I. having summoned all the prelates and nobility of the realm to *Windsor* on that occasion, our archbishop appeared, and would there have crowned the king equally with the archbishop of *Canterbury*, but he was rebuffed, and the bearer of his cross, together with the cross itself, was thrown out of the king's chapel. For it was alledged that no metropolitan out of his own province could have any cross born before him.

Grown old and very infirm having sat in the chair twenty six years, that is from his first election to it, he determined to forsake the world and become a monk in a monastery dedicated to St. *John*, of the *Cluniack* order, in *Pontfrete*. And accordingly he resigned his bishoprick, *Jan.* 15, 1143; but his cowle was scarce warm on his back, says *Goodwin*, when death altered his condition, on the fifth of *February* following; and he was buried in the church belonging to that monastery at *Pontfrete*. I made a search for his grave, near a place in the wall on the south side of the choir of this church, which is now in ruin; but instead of the prelate, we found vast numbers of human sculls and bones, all regularly piled up, and laid in admirable order. A pious action of the monks, and which has been met with in the ruins of several other monasteries in this kingdom. The life of this prelate was also wrote by two monks of this priory, the manuscript copy of it is in the *Cotton* library, but somewhat damaged by the fire *(c)*.

HENRICUS MURDAC, *twenty ninth archbishop*. A. MCXLIV.

King *Stephen* had a nephew called *William* son unto *Emma* his sister by earl *Herbert*; being a man, says *Stubbs*, no less noble in mind and virtue than stock and lineage. From being treasurer of *York*, he was elected archbishop, and having also obtained consecration he sent to *Rome*, according to custom, for his pall. But his suit there was retarded by reason of some adversaries who made several objections against him; and at length a process came out from the *Vatican* to warn him to come thither and answer in person to the things laid to his charge. At his arrival in *Rome* he found his adversaries more in number and more powerful than he expected; amongst whom St. *Bernard* was none of the least. *Eugenius*, the then pope, had been brought up in the abby of *Clareval*, under this abbot *Bernard*; together with *(d) Henry Murdac*, afterwards abbot of *Fountains*, whom *William*'s opponents had set up against him. And notwithstanding all he could do, or say, this *Henry* was consecrated archbishop of *York* by the pope himself; and sent into *England* with his pall.

King *Stephen* hearing of this was much troubled at the disgrace his nephew had met with MCXLVII.
at *Rome*; and therefore stood upon terms with the new prelate, requiring him to swear fealty to him in an extraordinary manner. Which being refused the king took hold of that occasion to quarrel with him. In this interval our prelate remained at *Hexam*; and when he would have made his entrance into *York*; he was not only opposed by the canons of the cathedral church, but the *(e)* citizens siding with the king shut him out of the city. Upon which he retired to *Beverley*. It is said that in this tumult an archdeacon, a friend to archbishop *Murdac*, was taken and beheaded in the city. From *Beverley* he thundered out his anathema's against them all, and not only suspended the canons of the church, but laid the whole city under an interdict. *Eustace* son of king *Stephen* was then at *York*, and endea-

(c) *Vita S* Thurstani *arch.* Ebor. *partim oratione soluta, partim ligata per* Hugonem de Pontefracto *monachum, et* Galfrid. de Nottingham. Titus, A. xix. 13.

(d) *Chron* Gervasii *monach.* Cant. Hen. de Murdac *abbas de* Fontibus *electus et consecratus arch.* Ebor. *per papam oct. S.* Andr. *anno* 1147. Chron. de Mailros.

(e) *Cont. Hist.* Simeon. Dunelm.

voured to perſwade the prelate to remit his ſentence; but when he could not prevail with him to take off the interdict, of his own power and authority he cauſed proclamation to be made in the city, that all divine offices ſhould be performed as uſual.

Theſe contentions laſted two or three years, and much miſchief enſued upon them, till at laſt the king was in ſome meaſure reconciled to him, ſo that he continued archbiſhop peaceably the reſt of his life; but never entered the city to the day of his interment. He ſat according to *Stubbs*, ſeven years, by others ten, and dyed at *Beverley (f) Oct.* 14, 1153, and was buried in the cathedral at *York*.

MCLIII. Gulielmus *ſanctus, thirtieth archbiſhop.*

(g) William, immediately after his deprivation at *Rome*, being greatly moved with the falſe calumnies caſt upon him by his enemies, retired into *England*, and betook himſelf with much patience and reſignation to the monaſtery at *Wincheſter*. Where he ſpent moſt of his time with his uncle *Henry*, the biſhop of that ſee, who firſt conſecrated him. It chanced, a little before *Henry Murdac* died, that pope *Eugenius* his old acquaintance, as alſo St. *Bernard*, preceptor to them both, departed this life. *William*, upon this turn, was much encouraged by his friends to make complaint unto *Anaſtaſius* the new pope, of the wrong done him by his predeceſſor. With much importuning he was prevailed upon to undertake the journey, but had ſcarce begun to ſtate his caſe, when he had certain information of the death of his rival and adverſary *Murdac*. Following the advice of one *Gregory* a cardinal, as it is ſaid, with little trouble he was reſtored unto all his honours; and had the pall alſo delivered to him.

Returning into *England* before *Eaſter*, he kept that feſtival with his unkle of *Wincheſter*, and then ſet out for his dioceſe. On the road he was met by *Robert de Gaunt* dean of *York*, and *Oſbert* archdeacon of the ſame, who poſitively forbad him entrance into their church. For what reaſon I know not, but the prelate, taking no notice of them, continued his journey, and was met on the confines of his province by all the reſt of his clergy, with commonality innumerable. *Polydore Virgil* writes, that *William* paſſing the river at *Ferry-bridge*, near *Pontfrete*, ſo great a crowd of people preſſed after him that the bridge, then made of wood, gave way and fell into the river with all the company upon it. The pious biſhop beholding this diſaſter, though ſafe himſelf from it, yet greatly commiſerating the caſe of ſo many poor mortals who came to do him honour, inſtantly fell on his knees and implored the divine goodneſs to preſerve their lives, which, adds my authority, was granted, for not one of the whole multitude periſhed, but all got ſafe to ſhoar.

Our *Italian* author, an excellent miracle writer, has catched this ſtory upon the rebound, and given it a new ſanction from the name of *Pontefract*, a town as he ſays truly not far from *Ferry-bridge*. But *Pontefract*, or rather the *Norman Pontfrete*, took its name from a different occaſion, as I could ſhew, were it to my purpoſe in this place to do it. *Brompton*, who writes this ſtory at large, ſeems to make *York* the place where this miracle happened; *cum autem* civitatem Eboracenſem *intraret, et pontem poſt patrem effrenata multitudo filiorum populorum tranſire vellet, &c.* Now *civitas Eboracenſis*, in this place, moſt certainly ſignifies the city itſelf; there is no room to ſuſpect the old monk for imitating *Caeſar* and *Tacitus* in their ſignification of *civitas*; and he would undoubtedly have mentioned what river or bridge, if it was in the county at large. But *Stubbs* puts the matter out of all diſpute, and expreſsly mentions the city of *York*, and the river *Ouſe*, over which this wooden bridge then ſtood. Beſides, as I have elſewhere hinted, a chapel was built on *Ouſe-bridge* and dedicated to this ſaint; which ſtood till the reformation, and in all probability was firſt erected in memory of the accident. I am perſwaded a *true blue proteſtant* will not believe this miracle at all; but that ſhall not hinder me from doing juſtice to the prelate I am writing of, and therefore the reader may find the ſtory as recorded by *Brompton* and *Stubbs* under this note *(g)*.

Having been received with great honour in his metropolitical city, our prelate began a mild and gentle government, ſuitable to the ſweetneſs of his natural diſpoſition. Nor did he ſhew any token or the leaſt appearance of gall or malice againſt his moſt inveterate enemies. He is reported to have laid ſchemes for doing many good works in his dioceſe, but was ſnatched away by death before any of them was finiſhed. He fell ſick ſoon after *Whit-*

(f) *Stubbs* ſays *Shireburn*; but *John* the prior of *Hexam*, contemporary, makes him die at *Beverley*.

(g) *Sim. Dunelm*, 276, 279. *Mon. Ang.* vol. I. p. 749.

(h) *Cum autem* civitatem Eboracenſem *intraret, et pontem poſt patrem effrenata filiorum multitudo populorum tranſire vellet, ponderoſitate rupta eſt lignei pontis compago, itaque, quod horrendum eſt viſu, et ſtupendum relatu, multitudines virorum, mulierum, et praecipuè infantium, catervatim inter rabida fluvii fluena ceciderunt. Ubi profunda fluminis habebatur altitudo, mixtis hominibus equis phaleratis. Converſus vir dei ad populum inſanis undis undique involutum ſalutifero ſigno crucis eos inſignivit, et reſolutus in fletum orationes Deo obtulit ne profunda obſorberet eos aqua. Quod et factum eſt ita quod nec anima una periclitavit.* Brompton *inter* x. *ſcript.*

Venit autem Eboracum *die dominica prox. ante feſt. aſcenſionis domini 7. id.* Maii 1154, *et maxima cum devotione cleri et populi ſibi occurrentis ſuſcepeus in civitatem perductus eſt. Cum autem ultra pontem* Uſae, *tunc ligneum, comitante plebe tranſiret, dirupta prae populi ponderoſitate lignei pontis ſtructura, magna virorum et mulierum et praecipuè infantium multitudo in profundo fluminis ex alto corruens inter rabida fluvii fluenta periclitando volutabat. Quod cum audiſſet ſanctiſſimus pater* Willielmus, *fuſa cum lachrymis ad dominum oratione, ne pro eo Deum laudantes profundum abſorberet, ſubmerſo ſigno crucis ſignavit, et mox orationis ſuae virtute, univerſos a periculo mortis ſuccurrente divina pietate libravit.* Stubbs *act. pont.* Ebor. *in vita S.* Willielmi.

ſunt ide

ſuntide of a kind of an ague, as ſome write, and within a day or two after departed this life *June* 8, 1154.

The ſuddenneſs of his death occaſioned a report to go that he was poiſoned in the chalice at maſs. *Hoveden* writes, that the poyſon was conveyed into the water in which he waſhed his hands before conſecration *(i)*. But *Newburgenſis* denies both. However it is certain, ſays *Stubbs*, that ſeveral ſymptoms the biſhop had before he died rendered it ſuſpicious. Inſomuch that his chaplain adviſed him to take ſome antidote againſt poyſon, which ſome ſay he did; others that he would not *antidotum humanum adjicere divino*, alluding to the ſacrament that he had taken it in. His teeth and nails turned black before he died. Authors accuſe no perſons by name for this fact; but, allowing it true, the dean and archdeacon before mentioned may be greatly ſuſpected for it. Part of the anthem appointed to be ſung at his feſtival, after our archbiſhop was canonized, infers as much. Biſhop *Goodwin* gives it thus:

> Eboracum *praeſul redit,*
> *Pontis caſus nullum laedit,*
> *De tot turbae millibus.*
> *In octavis* Pentecoſtes
> *Quidem malignantes hoſtes,*
> *In eum pacificum,*
> *Et ut ipſum priveni vita,*
> *Celebrantes aconita,*
> *Propinant in calice.*
> *Toxicatur a profanis*
> *Ille potus, ille panis,*
> *Per quem perit toxicatum, &c.*

William's death happening on the eighth of *June* 1154, as has been obſerved, his body was buried in his cathedral; and his exemplary piety having gained him a great character in his life-time, his tomb could not fail being viſited, according to the cuſtom of that age, after his death. It was not long before ſeveral miracles were atteſted to have been done at his grave; from whoſe body, ſays *Stubbs (k)*, diſtilled a moſt ſalutiferous oil, which God, for his merits, ſuffered to perform many wonderful cures on ſeveral infirm perſons. The credit of this gained him the honour of a red letter in the calendar; for about one hundred and fifty years after his death, pope *Nicholas*, at the earneſt requeſt of *Stephen Mauley* then archdeacon of *Cleveland*, canonized our archbiſhop, and appointed the aforeſaid eighth of *June* for the annual celebration of his feſtival. The ſaid pope alſo granted an indulgence of a year and forty days relaxation of ſins to all ſuch who ſhould devoutly viſit his tomb, eight days after his feſtival, and pray to him in theſe words:

> O Willielme, *paſtor bone,*
> *Cleri pater, et patrone*
> *Mundi, nobis in agone*
> *Confer opem, et depone*
> *Vitae ſordes, et coronae*
> *Celeſtis da gaudia, &c.*

The table of the miracles, aſcribed to this ſaint, which are thirty ſix in number, with the indulgenee of pope *Nicholas*, are yet to be ſeen in our veſtry. But time, and of late years no care, has ſo obliterated them that a perfect tranſcript cannot be had of them. Inſtead of which I think proper to give part of the anthem ſung at the feaſt of his tranſlation, which was ſolemnized annually on *January* 7; and which, if true, proves our ſaint to be as good a miracle worker as any in the calendar.

> *(l) Claudi recti redeunt, furor effagatur,*
> *Epilepſis paſſio ſanitati datur.*
> *Purgantur ydropici, laudes fantur muti,*
> *Dat paralyticis ſuis membris uti.*
> *Lepra tergit maculas, membra dat caſtratis,*
> *Lumen dat pluribus ſine luce natis.*
> *Pii patris hodie corpus eſt tranſlatum,*

(i) *Eodem anno, ſcil.* 1154. Willielmus *arch.* Ebor. *in ſedem ſuam honorifice ſuſceptus eſt; ſed non multo poſt, proditione clericorum ſuorum, poſt perceptionem euchariſtiae infra ablutiones liquore lethali infectus, extinctus eſt.* R. Hoveden.

In ſacra ſolempnitate Pentecoſtes *inter miſſarum ſolempnia veneno infectus eſt; et poſt paucos dies migravit ad Dominum.* Chron. Gervaſii *ſub rege* Hen. II.

Vide epiſt. 122. Joh. Sariſburienſis, *ubi de accuſatione clerici ſuper crimine veneficii.*

(k) *Quo in loco effluente de ſacro corpore ejus oleo ſalutifero, Deus maximus pro ejus meritis plurima infirmis operatus eſt miracula.* Stubbs *act. pont.* Ebor. *in vita S.* Willielmi.

(l) *Ex breviario in uſum inſignis metrop. eccl.* Ebor. *&c. pro temp. hyemali. Imp.* Pariſ. *an.* 1526. *N.B.* This book was lately given to the church library, and it is remarkable the prayers, *&c.* for the feſtivals of St. *Thomas*, martyr, St. *William*, St *Cuthbert*, and St. *Wilfrid*, are all of them blotted out of the book.

Quod in imo jacuit in alto eſt locatum.
Quondam theſaurarius, jam theſaurus
Cleri,
Dedit opus medici non dat opem veri, &c.

At *William*'s canonization his bones were taken up from the place where they were firſt laid, and depoſited in the nave of the cathedral by *William Wickwane*, then archbiſhop of this ſee, the king, (*Edw.* I.) the queen, eleven other biſhops, with the whole court attending the ſolemnity. Over theſe bones the ſaid archbiſhop built a moſt coſtly ſhrine, which was afterward enriched with plate and jewels, as appears by the inventory, to a very great value. At the *Reformation* the ſhrine was demoliſhed, and no remembrance left of the place, but a tradition that this ſaint laid under a long marble ſtone ſpotted, in the nave of the church. *May* 27, 1732, at the laying the new pavement in the cathedral, I got leave to ſearch under this ſtone; the reverend the dean and ſome other gentlemen being preſent. At the raiſing of it we found that the ſtone had been inverted, and by the moldings round the edge it appeared to have been an altar-ſtone. Upon digging about a yard deep, the workmen came to a ſtone coffin ſix foot ſix inches long, the lid arched, on which was a croſs the length of the coffin. When the lid was turned aſide, there appeared a ſquare leaden box, three quarters of a yard long, about eight inches diameter at the top, and gradually decreaſing to the bottom. In this box the bones were depoſited, it had been cloſely ſoddered up, but was decayed in many places, and was eaſily opened with the fingers. The ſmaller bones, and thoſe of the ſkull, which were broken, were wrapt in a piece of ſarcenet double, which had acquired the colour of the bones it contained. Some of which ſarcenet for curioſity ſake we took out. The larger bones were put down to the bottom of the box; and by the menſuration of a thigh bone, entire, our prelate appears to have been about five foot ſix inches high. On the middle of the box was a ſmall plain croſs made of two pieces of lead of equal bigneſs; and at the end was laid a piece of ſtuff which mouldered upon touching. There was nothing like an inſcription either within or without the box, or upon the altar-ſtone, that I could find, to denote that it was the ſaint we looked for; but the circumſtances put together, the matter to me ſeems indiſputable. The remains of this once famous prelate were carefully repoſited in the coffin, that cloſed, and the grave filled up. But that the curious may be farther ſatisfied about it, I have cauſed the repreſentation of the coffin and box to be engraven; and the place where they lye to be marked in the plate of the ichnography of the cathedral.

S^t. Williams Coffin.

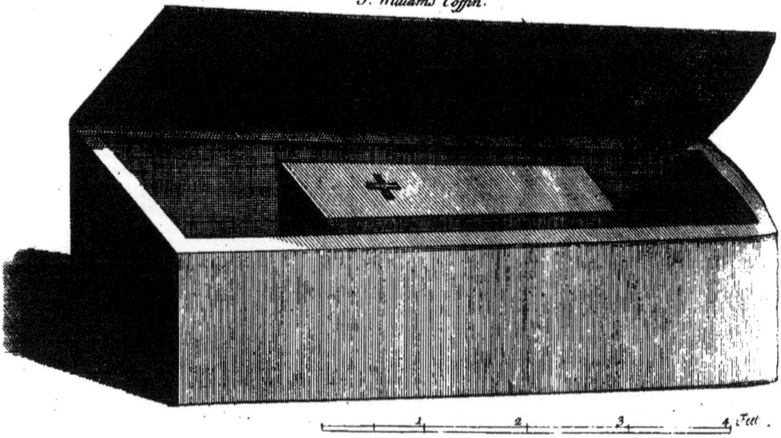

Rogerus,

ROGERUS, *thirty first archbishop.* A. MCLIV.

Roger, commonly called of *Bishop-bridge*, the place I suppose where he was born, archdeacon of *Canterbury*, and chaplain to king *Henry* II. was by means of *Robert* the dean of *York*, and *Osbert* the archdeacon, who ruled all now in the chapter, elected into the chair. He was consecrated by *Theobald* archbishop of *Canterbury* at *Westminster (m)*, *Oct.* 10, 1154, but made no profession to that see. The character of this prelate is variously related by the monks and seculars; the latter praising him so high as to give him the surname of *Bonus*, whilst the former charge him with avarice, hatred to monks, clipping of their privileges; and that he minded the shearing more than the feeding the sheep committed to his care *(n)*. The amassing of riches seems, indeed, to have been his chief goust; I find in the *Scotch* chronicle that in the days of their king *Malcolm* this *Roger* was constituted the pope's legate, but was not suffered to enter that kingdom, by reason he was a man, say they, much defamed for covetous practices, and would enrich himself by any unlawful means. The legate however was even with them for this piece of presumption, for he excommunicated their king, and laid the whole kingdom under an interdict *(o)*.

A remarkable instance of the pride of this prelate is recorded in our own chronicles, which carried him far beyond the rules of decency and good manners. A great convocation of clergy being called to *Westminster*, where the pope's legate was present, the archbishop of *Canterbury* took place at the legate's right hand, which when our archbishop perceived, disdaining to take the left, he came in a rude manner and clapped his bum betwixt the legate and his brother; who not readily giving way to him, he sat him down upon *Canterbury*'s knee. This when seen by the rest of the bishops and clergy of that province, scandalized to the last degree at the affront offered to their metropolitan, they came and pulled off *Roger*, and threw him on the ground, and, not content with that, laid on him with fists and sticks unmercifully; insomuch that *Canterbury* was fain to interpose, and protect his brother from further violence. *Roger* got up, and with his cope and habit half torn off, ran streight to the king, and made a grievous complaint against his male-treaters, which the king at first took gravely; but, upon a rehearing of the whole matter, our prelate got nothing for his pains, but to be well laughed at into the bargain. This story is given by most historians of those times.

Roger was violently suspected to have a hand in the murder of *Thomas a Becket*, and was for some time suspended, by the pope for it; but upon his taking a solemn oath that he neither by word, writing, nor deed, was the least concerned in that matter he was restored to his possessions. Yet it appears that at this time there was no small suspicion of it, for when he was mobbed, as above, for his ill manners to the archbishop of *Canterbury* he was upbraided with these words, *vade, vade, traditor sancti* Thomae, Begone, begone, thou traytor to St. *Thomas (p)*.

Roger sate twenty seven years in this archbishoprick; when being very aged he fell into his last sickness at *Louth* in *Lincolnshire*; and sent for many abbots, priors and other religious, to help to make his will, and advise him, in the best manner how to dispose of the vast fund of wealth which he had accumulated. It was first ordered by him that great sums of money should be distributed to the poor, and other good purposes. That the archbishops of *Canterbury*, *Rheims* and *Roan* should have each of them five hundred pounds given to them to that purpose; and to almost every bishop in *England* and *Normandy* he gave a proportionable sum for the same use. After this he removed to *York*, *Hoveden* says to *Shireburn*, and there died on *Sunday Nov.* 22, 1181; and was buried, by *Hugh* bishop of *Durham*; near the door of St. *Sepulchre*'s chapel, in the cathedral, which himself had founded. After his demise the king immediately seized on all his great riches and effects, which are said by *M. Paris (q)* to be eleven thousand pound in silver and three hundred in gold, besides an infinite deal of plate and sumptuous houshold-stuff, and converted them all to his own use. It seems *Roger* had procured from pope *Alexander* this privilege, that if any clergyman died in his province, and delivered not his goods away by hand before his death, that the archbishop should have the disposal of them. The king made use of this pretence to lay claim to *Roger*'s effects, and said *it was unreasonable his will should stand good, who had disannulled the testaments of so many others (r)*. This prelate's buildings, endowments, *&c.* respecting the particular history of the fabrick, may be found in that chapter. His tomb, being the oldest in the church, is represented in the plate. The coffin of lead, seems to have been laid in the wall, for it may be knocked against with a stick through the openings of the fret-work. This kind of sepulture in the wall,

(m) In festo S. Paulini. R. de Diceto.

(n) Gul. Neuburgen. *Is vitam autem magis tondendis intendit ovibus quam pascendis.* Brompton *inter* x. *script.*

(o) Stubs *in vita* Rogeri.

(p) M. Parker, *de arch.* Cant. *ed.* Drake, *in vita* Richardi *arch.* Cant. *Rapin* says, that he told the king that as long as *Becket* lived it was impossible for *England* to be at peace. *Hoveden* remarks, that *Roger* bore an ancient hatred to him.

(q) Quorum summa undecim millia librarum argenti *et* auri tricenta, *cuppa aurea et argenteae septem, cyphi argentei novem, tria salsaria argentea, tres cuppae myrtinae, cochlearia quadraginta, octo scutellae argenteae, pelvis argenteus, et discus magnus argenteus.* M. Paris. It is to be noted that a pound of silver in those days was a pound weight, which is equal to three pounds of our money. So a pound of gold in proportion.

(r) Brompton.

may be one reaſon why his bones have lain quiet ſo long; for they cannot be diſturbed without endangering that part of the fabrick of the church. The ſeal which this archbiſhop made uſe of I have ſeen appendant to an ancient deed of his in the dutchy office, from whence I have cauſed it to be drawn; and the reader will find it in the plate of the collections of ſeals and arms belonging to the archbiſhops of this province, at the end of this account. The ſtrange miſtake in the reverſe or counterſeal of *Roger*'s, by taking three antique heads cut on a *Roman* gem for a repreſentation of the *Trinity*, I ſhall diſcuſs amongſt ſome other ſuch proofs of the ignorance and ſuperſtition of theſe dark ages in the *addenda* to this work.

Archbishop Roger.

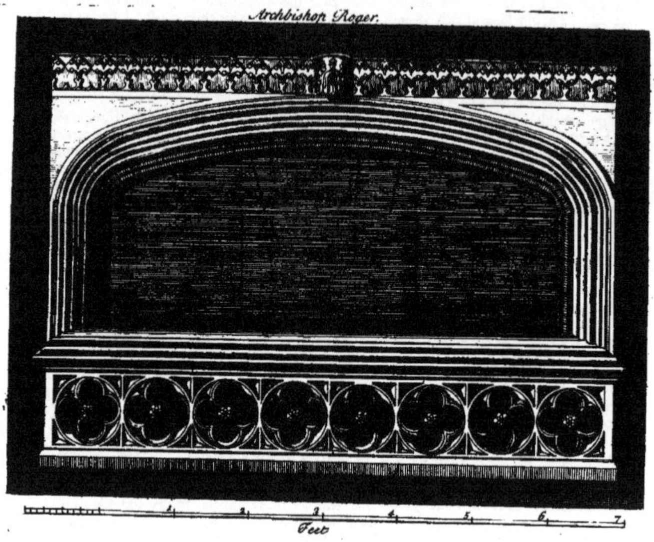

A. MCXC. GEOFFRY PLANTAGENET, *thirty ſecond archbiſhop.*

Henry the ſecond, having ſeized the temporalities of the ſee of *York*, kept them in his hands, during the remainder of his reign, and no biſhop was elected till under king *Richard* I. his ſucceſſor; who underſtanding that the people murmured at this long vacancy, which was no leſs than ten years, thought fit to kill two birds with one ſtone; that is, to fill up the vacant chair; and at the ſame time to provide a good benefice for *Geoffry*, his natural brother.

(*s*) *Geoffry* was baſe ſon to *Henry* II. by the celebrated *Roſamond*. The warmeſt love betwixt two ſuch extraordinary perſonages, could not produce an ordinary offspring. And our *Geoffry*, being a ſprightly youth, was well taken care on by his father in his education. Being arrived at man's eſtate, though very young ſtill, he was firſt made archdeacon of *Lincoln*, and afterwards elected to that biſhoprick, by the power of his father, whilſt a layman. *Geoffry* made no haſte to be conſecrated to it, but contented himſelf with the revenues of that rich ſee, which he enjoyed after this manner, for ſeven years. At the end of which time the king, his father, finding no inclination in him to be conſecrated, he called him to court, and after a reſignation of his intereſt in *Lincoln*, gave him the ſeals and conſtituted him lord chancellor of *England*. Which great office he held eight years, that is, to his father's death, which happened *anno* 1181.

(*s*) *Natus eſt* 5 Hen. II. *factus eſt miles* 25 Hen. II. *elect. in epiſcop.* Lincoln. 28 Hen. II. *ſed non conſecratus, et* 2 Ric. I. *elect. eſt in archiep.* Ebor. *Chron. de* Kirkſtall, Domitian A. 12. *De appellatione contra ejus elect. propter abſentiam decani, et quia homicida et* natus in adulterio, *vide* Brompton 1169.

Richard

Richard his brother succeeding to the crown he removed *Geoffry* from the chancellorship; but, to make him amends, got him, though with some difficulty, elected archbishop by the chapter of *York*. He was first ordained priest by *John* the suffragan bishop of *Whithern*, or *candida casa (t)*, at *Southwell*. And was consecrated *Aug.* 18, 1191. at *Tours* by the archbishop of that see; for which slight put upon the metropolitan, *Baldwin*, the archbishop of *Canterbury*, appealed to *Rome*. Immediately after his consecration he came over into *England*, contrary to a solemn oath he had made the king at his going to the holy war. For *Richard* had been told that if *Geoffry* came into *England* in his absence he would sooner bring a sword than an olive branch along with him *(u)*. At his landing at *Dover* he was clapped up close prisoner in that castle; by command of the bishop of *Ely*, then lord chancellor and regent. But being soon after released he came down to his diocese and was solemnly installed in his own cathedral with great splendour.

He proved a better bishop, says *Stubbs*, than was expected; governing his province very commendably and well. He praises him much for his temperance, sobriety and gravity, both of countenance and behaviour. But that author has made saints of every prelate he writes on. It is plain that his canons had not the same good opinion of him, for they exhibited numberless complaints against *Geoffry* both to the pope and king; which must make him very uneasy in his station, of all which *Roger Hoveden* is very particular in the recital. The origine of these squabbles and dissensions betwixt the prelate and his chapter was about the election of a dean. It seems *Geoffry* had a brother of the same blood as himself, called *Peter*; him he proposed for that office, but was opposed in it by his canons, who chose one *Simon* their dean in despight to the archbishop and all he could do or say in it. This produced appeals from both sides to *Rome*, excommunications, and interdicts; but a further account of these ecclesiastical heats and animosities, *tantaene animis coelestibus irae*, will fall apter in the historical remarks on the deans of this church.

As *Geoffry* was sufficiently embroiled in these church disputes, so was he no less unfortunate in being embarrassed in state affairs. For king *Richard*, at his return from the *Holy-land*, took from him all his lay possessions *(x)*, and being at that time under a suspension from the pope, his spiritualities were also seized into the king's hands *(y)*. For the former of which he was fain to compound and pay down the sum of three thousand pound sterling as a fine to the king; the suspension he found means to get released from some time after. *John*, the succeeding king, had also a very bad opinion of him; and his resentment ran so high against him, that in the second year of his reign he commanded the high sheriff of *Yorkshire* to sieze upon all the goods and lands of our archbishop, and to return the profit into the exchequer, which was done accordingly. The archbishop excommunicated *James de Poterne* the high-sheriff, and all his officers concerned in this business, by bell, book, and candle, with all those who had advised the king in this affair; which only served to raise the king's anger more against him. The reasons *John* had to use him thus, are said to be many *(z)*; that the archbishop throughout his province hindred the sheriff from collecting a tax of three shillings on each ploughed land, which the king had laid on all the lands in *England*. That he refused to go over with the king into *Normandy*, in order to settle a marriage betwixt the *French* king's son and his niece. And *lastly*, the excommunication of his officer and his laying the whole province of *York* under an interdict, made the king almost implacable to him *(a)*. Notwithstanding all this the archbishop found means, at the king's return out of *Normandy*, to be in some measure reconciled to him; and upon the

(t) Brompton. M. Paris.

(u) Hoveden.

(x) The temporal estate which was given him by his father consisted of these, *viz. Villa de* Wicumbe, *cum pertinentiis, in* Anglia; *et in* Normannia *comitatum* Gisfardi, *et in* Andigavia *honorem de* Blangery. R. *Hov.*

(y) It may not be unacceptable to the reader to give him the value of the rents of the whole archbishoprick at this time; as *William de Stontevile, &c.* accounted for it to the king for one year, whilst it remained in the king's hands; extracted from the *Pipe-rolls* as follows:

Willielmus de Stuteville, Jordanus Clericus *et* Philippus Escrop *red computum de uno anno archiepiscopatus* Eboraci.

De nundinis Beverlaci ——	xl *s.*
De firma de Burton ——	xii *l. et de* vii *l.* vii *s.*
Redd. de Schetebi ——	x *l.*
De firma de Wetwang ——	xii *l.* xvii. *s.* i *d.*
Firma de Wilton ——	v *l.* vii *s.* v *d.*
Firma de Chalde ——	vii *l.* i *s.* iii *d.*
Firma terrarum juxta civit. Ebor.	ii *l.* viii *s.* vi *d.*
Firma de Ripun *infra burgum dim. anni* ——	xxxvi *l.* xiii *s.* iii *d.*

Et firma terrar. archiepisc. juxta burgum xiiii *l.* xii *s.* ix *d.*

Et de iiii *l. et* xii *d. de passuagio praedictarum terrarum.*

Et de xx *mar. de decima lane q.* Will. de Bolonia *asportavit per breve* H. Cant. *archiepiscopi.*

Id. red. comp. ut custos de xlviii *l. et* xiiii *s. et* x *d. de firma de* Beverlaco *et de terris ad eam pertinentibus.*

De telonio ejusdem ville xii *l.*

Idem red. com. de xxx *l. et* v *s. et* x *d. de firma de* Paterington.

Idem red. comp. de xxiii *l. de firma de* Elegeton.

Idem red. comp. de xviii *l. et* xii *s. et* iiii *d. de nundinis et firmis domorum archiepiscopi infra civitatem.*

Idem red. comp. de xliii *l. et* xiiii *s. et* iiii *d. de firma de* Extoldesham *cum pertinentiis.*

Idem red. comp de xxviii *l. et* viii *s. de denariis* S. Petri.

Idem. red. comp. de xx *l.* iiii *s. et* vii *d. de placitis de herbariis et perquisitionibus predictar. terrarum.*

Idem red. comp. de c *et qt. r.* xx *l. et* x *s. et* iii *d. de instauramentis archiepiscopi venditis.* Rot. Pipe 6 Ric. I.

(z) Causa multiplex erat. Paris.

(a) A letter from the king to the Dean and Chapter of *York* on this occasion Mr. *Maddox* has given us in these words:

Rex S. [Simon de Apulia] *decano et capitulo* Ebor. *Sciatis quod pro debitis quae* Eboracensis *archiepiscopis et pro defaltis et aliis causis rationabilibus cepimus in manum nost.* Baroniam *et regalia quae archiep.* Ebor. *de nobis tenet. Et hoc fecimus* per judicium curiae nostrae. *Nos autem contra eundem archiep. ad dominum* papam *appellavimus pro nobis et nostris et pro statu regni nostri. Teste* G. Filio Petri *com.* Essex. *apud* Cunesburgum v. *die* Martii. Charta 2 *Joh.* m. ii. dorso. *Maddox* exchequer, *p.* 696. *(p)*

payment

payment of one thousand sterling had his temporalities restored, after they had been detained from him a whole year. But his moveable goods he never saw again; nor was the king's anger so far lessened as he did not still watch all opportunities to be farther revenged of him.

However, he sate still and quiet at *York* for six or seven years more, when a fresh accident happened to disturb him. *John* being much straitned for a supply towards carrying on the *French* war, called a council of the estates, and demanded a subsidy of the thirteenth shilling out of all the moveable goods, both of clergy and laity, in *England*. This was openly opposed by none, though many inwardly murmured at the exorbitancy of it, but our archbishop; who not only refused his consent to it, but forbad his clergy, on the severest penalties, to pay it. An opposition like this provoked *John* to the last degree, and the prelate finding that this kingdom would soon be too hot for him, withdrew privately into *Normandy*. Excommunicating, before he went, such of his jurisdiction who had either paid, or were any ways instrumental in gathering this tax. He lived in exile seven years, says *Paris*, and died at *Grosmont* at *Normandy anno* 1212; having been somewhat more than twenty one years archbishop of this see.

This prince and prelate's life is wrote at length by *Giraldus Cambrensis* (*b*), who gives a different character of him than what is gone before. Being descended from a king, and a daughter of the illustrious family of Clifford, the blood which ran in his veins might make him a little too headstrong; but his positiveness seems to be wholly on the side of his country. (*c*) *Polidore Virgil* says, that he only reprehended his brother *John* for his shameless exactions on the people; when he took such a revenge on him for it. And adds, that after having suffered a seven years banishment from his country, for exerting himself in the liberties of the church and the execution of justice, he ended his days with honour (*d*).

It must not here be omitted, that in this archbishop *Geoffry*'s time, and probably whilst he laid under suspension from the pope, *Hubert Walter*, who had been dean of *York*, and was then archbishop of *Canterbury*, thought fit to hold a general *council* for the whole kingdom at *York*; but, particularly, it was said to reform the manners of that church. This was the first and last instance of any archbishop of *Canterbury* sitting in council at *York*; and had it not been for *Geoffry*'s disgrace, I am perswaded it would never have been suffered. *Hoveden* relates the fact in this manner:

" *Hubert* had been constituted by the pope his legate *à latere*, and was at the same time " chief justice of *England*; a man represented to be very magnificent and generous in his ex- " pences and works, but withal had an immoderate affectation of secular power and gran- " deur. By the authority he had from the pope he sent out his letters mandatory to the " dean and chapter of *York* to convene themselves and the whole province together, and to " receive him at his coming with the honours due to an apostolical legate. They an- " swered they would receive him as such, but not as archbishop of *Canterbury*, or their " primate. *Hubert* accordingly came to *York* on the feast of St. *Barnabas*, being *Sunday*, in " the year 1195, and the seventh of king *Richard* the first; and was received by the clergy " in solemn procession, and introduced into the cathedral church. On *Monday* he caused " assizes *de noveil disseisin*; and *de mort d'ancestre*, and of all pleas of the crown to be holden " by his officers; but he and his officials held pleas of *Christianity* (*e*). On *Tuesday* he pro- " ceeded to visit as a legate the abby of St. *Mary*'s *York*, and was received also by the " monks in solemn procession. Then he went into the chapter-house of the abbey, and " upon the monk's complaint that *Robert* their abbot, by reason of his weakness and bodily " infirmities, was capable of doing no good to their house, he deposed him from his care " and administration of the house; who made great outcries and appealed to his lord the " pope. On the following *Wednesday* and *Thursday* having assembled together in the church " of St. *Peter* at *York*, *Simon* dean of the said church, *Hamo* precentor, *William Testard* and " *Geoffry de Muschamp*, archdeacons of *Nottingham* and *Cleveland*, *John* the chancellor, and " *Robert* provost of *Beverley*, with some canons of the same church; almost all the abbots, " priors, officials, deans and parsons of churches in the diocese of *York*; the said legate him- " self, sitting in a chair aloft, celebrated a most famous council, in which he ordained the " underwritten decrees to be kept."

The decrees themselves are too long to insert, but the reader may find them in *R. Hoveden, pars posterior, p.* 430. called *Decreta* Eboracensis *concilii*. Sir *H. Spelman*'s councils, vol. II. p. 121. or in a late book published by *J. Johnson* vicar of *Cranbroke*; where the articles are translated into *English*, being nineteen in number (*f*).

In the year 1201, and during the hierarchy of *Geoffry Plantagenet*, happened another extraordinary thing of this nature at *York*; though acted by a person of much less authority

(*b*) *Wharton*'s *Anglia sacra*, tom. I.

(*c*) *In qua re cum a* Gaufrido *fratre antistite* Ebor. *reprehenderetur, tantum abfuit ut eum spoliaris, ab seque ablegarit; nec ullo obsequio placari, leniri, mitigari deinde potuerit, ut ante duodecim menses in gratiam reciperet.* Pol. Virg.

(*d*) *Postquam per septennium pro libertate ecclesiae et executione justitiae exilium passus est, diem clausit extremum. Idem et* M. Paris.

(*e*) The jurisdiction of prelates, together with all their privileges often passes under the name of *Christianity:* and the ecclesiastical court was frequently called the *Court-christian*.

(*f*) A collection of eccl. laws, *London* 1720, 2 vol. 8vo.

than

2

than the former (*g*). One *Eustace*, abbot of *Flay*, came into *England*, and took upon him to terrify men into a cessation from labour from three o' clock on *Saturday* till sun-rising on *Monday*. He shewed a letter written from *Christ* and found on the altar of St. *Simon* at *Golgotha*, containing severe objurgations against *Christians* for their negligence in observing the Lord's-day and feasts of the church. Charged with this extraordinary embassy he came to *York*, as *Hoveden* writes, and was received by *Geoffry* archbishop, the clergy and people with great honour. Here he shewed his credentials and preached to the people on the subject; he gave absolution and enjoined penance to those who confessed their guilt in this respect. He enjoined his penitents to give a farthing out of every five shillings of their personal estate for buying lights to the church and for burying the poor; had a box placed in every parish church for the collecting of it, and an alms dish for the tables of the richer sort, in which a share of victuals was to be put for their poor neighbours; and he forbad buying and selling and pleadings in churches and church porches. But as the devil, the enemy of mankind, adds *Hoveden*, would have it, these pious precepts were little regarded; and those who undertook to interrupt men in transacting their business on the Lord's-day, were called to an account for it by the civil power. But *Roger* has taken care to record several miracles, which, if true, must be evident tokens of the divine mission of abbot *Eustace*. A carpenter of *Beverlay* having presumed to work after three o'clock on *Saturday* was struck with a dead palsy. A woman weaving after the same hour was taken in like manner. At *Nafferton*, a village belonging to *Roger Arundel*, says *Hoveden*, a certain man made a cake, baked, and eat part of it at the same time as the former; which when he broke the remainder the next day blood flowed from it. Who saw this, adds he, bore testimony of it, and his testimony is true. At *Wakefield*, when a certain miller would grind his corn after three o' clock on *Saturday*, the corn was turned into blood, insomuch as to fill a large vessel, and the wheel of the mill stood immoveable against the force of the waters. A woman put her paste into the heated oven at this time, and when she thought it baked found it paste still. Another woman, by the advice of her husband kept her paste till *Monday* morning, wrapt up in a linnen cloth, and they found it ready baked. Thus the old monk runs on with his miracles; which I should not have troubled myself about, did I not find a near allusion in them to the *pious frauds* of our *true blue protestants* of the last age; invented on the very same occasion.

WALTER GREY, *thirty third archbishop*.

A. MCCXVI.

The see of *York* continued void, after the last prelate's death, four years. But in that space *Simon de Langton*, brother to *Stephen Langton* archbishop of *Canterbury* had found means to get himself elected by the chapter. King *John*, who was then in good terms with the pope, set aside this election. Alledging how dangerous it would be to the state to have the whole church of *England*, that in the south, and this in the north, governed by two brothers. Whether it was by reason of the king's old grudge to *Stephen Langton*, or his desire to have his chief councellor *Walter Gray*, bishop of *Worcester* removed to this see; but the canons of *York* when they declared their election of *Simon* to the pope, found him strongly prepossessed against it. Not only disannulling their election, but threatning if they did not immediately nominate another, he himself would do it for them. Upon which, knowing it was the king's desire, *Walter Grey* was pitched upon for the man; and when presented to the pope for his approbation, the orator, who recommended him for his other good qualities, thought fit to mention his extraordinary *chastity*, *having never known woman from his cradle*. *By* St. Peter, says the pope, *chastity is a very great virtue, and therefore you shall have him*.

Walter was bishop of *Litchfield anno* 1210; from thence he was translated to *Worcester*, *anno* 1214; and, in the year 1216, was consecrated archbishop of *York* (*h*). The conditions which the pope made him agree to for his exaltation to this dignity were very extraordinary. *M. Paris* affirms that he was obliged to pay ten thousand pound sterling for his *pall*. An excessive sum in those days; and which straightned his circumstances so much to raise, that he was long after obliged to live in the most penurious manner in order to retrieve it. This gained him the infamous character, especially for a bishop, of being a covetous worldling, a griper and oppressor of the poor; and the same author gives an odd story, invented perhaps by the country people, of a singular judgment on his oppressions. In the year 1234, says *Paris*, was a great dearth and scarcity of corn throughout the whole kingdom; but more especially in the northern parts of it. For three years after a great mortality raged; multitudes died as well of pestilence as famine; the great men of that time taking no care to relieve them. Our archbishop had then, in granaries,

(*g*) Rog. Hoveden *pars post*. *p*. 467. Sir *H. Spelman*, vol. II p. 128.

This *Eustace*, abbot of *Flay* in *Normandy*, had been in *England*, with another story the year before, about blessing of springs, &c. Here *Roger* reports a miracle of his so monstrously absurd and beyond credit, as to outdo the best monkish miracle writer that ever undertook to deceive mankind by such inventions. *Vide* R. H. *p post*. *pag*. 457.

(*h*) *Anni pontificat. sui super ecclesiam* Ebor. *numerantur a* 10, *vel* 11, *die* Novem. 1215; *ut patet ex rotulo suo majori in ecclesia* Ebor. *reservato*.

and elsewhere, a stock of corn, which, if delivered out, would have supplied the whole country for five years. But whether they did not offer him price enough, or for some other reason he would not part with a grain of it. At length being told that the corn-stacks and great ricks would suffer for want of threshing, being apt to be consumed by mice and other vermine, he ordered it should be delivered to the husbandmen, who dwelt in his manors, upon condition they should pay as much new corn for it after harvest. Accordingly some of his officers went to *Ripon*, where his largest stores were reposited, and coming to a great stack to take it down, they saw the heads of many *(i)* snakes, adders, toads and other venomous creatures peeping out at the end of the sheaves. This being told to the archbishop he sent his steward, and others of good credit, to enquire into the truth of it; who finding it true, would nevertheless force some of the countrymen to mount to the top with ladders and throw down the sheaves. They had no sooner ascended but a thick black smoke seemed to arise from the midst of the corn, which made such an intolerable stench that it soon obliged the husbandmen to come down again; declaring they never smelt any thing like it before. As they descended they heard a voice say, *(k) let the corn alone, for the archbishop and all that belongs to him is the devil's due.* In fine they were obliged to build a wall about the stack, and then set it on fire lest such a number of venemous creatures should get out and infest the whole country. This is the honest monk of St. *Alban*'s story, which, without any paraphrase, I shall leave to the reader's judgment.

However this archbishop is not without his commendations, *Mat. Westminster* instances his great wisdom and government; and his steady loyalty to his prince shewn on several publick occasions. When queen *Eleanor*, wife to *Henry* III, was entrusted by her husband with the government of the realm during his stay in *France*, our prelate was also left as her principal councellor. And when she went thither to the king, to confer with him about some extraordinary matters, he was with much perswasion prevailed upon to undertake the sole regency; being then both old and very infirm. This occurred *anno* 1253; but I find by *Paris* that he had been intrusted in that high office *anno* 1241. And this writer himself, who has so handsomely given him to the devil in the foregoing story, gives quite a different character of our prelate in the grand entertainment he made the whole court, at the nuptials of *Henry*'s daughter to the king of *Scotland* at *York*. The archbishop, says he, like a northern prince, bestowed the greatest hospitality on his royal guests. At the first course of one dinner was served up the carcases of sixty fat oxen. The whole of this and his other entertainments cost him four thousand marks; which, adds he, was sown on a barren soil, and never rose to his profit; except that by this magnificence he added to his *usual character*, and stopped the mouths of all invidious slanderers.

Near forty years *Walter* governed this see and did many things for the good of his church and diocese. He founded the subdeanery and succentorship, with the prebends of *Wistow* and *Fenton*. He purchased the manor of *Thorp* with the church of the same, which he gave to this see in effect; but, *verbo tenus*, to the dean and chapter; taking assurance of them that they should always grant it over to the archbishop for the time being. This course he took to the end that if the temporalities of the archbishoprick should be seized into the king's hands, either *sede plena*, which sometimes happened, or *sede vacante*, which was then constantly practised, with this manor the king's officers should have no right to meddle. To this wise precaution his successors owe their present, and, now, only archiepiscopal palace; which in all probability would have been stripped from them had it been held under any other tenure. This prelate erected many chantries in divers places; he gave to the cathedral at *York* thirty two rich and sumptuous copes. He bequeathed to his successors a large stock of cattle, procuring the king to confirm the gift, and to take care that every succeeding archbishop should leave as many on the several manors of the see. It was this prelate who purchased the house, now called *White-hall*, of the *friars-preachers* in *Westminster*, which *Hubert de Burg* built and gave them. From hence it was called *York-place*, and was always the palace where the archbishop of *York* resided, when in *London*; till by cardinal *Wolsey*'s disgrace, it fell into the hands of *Henry* VIII, who obliged *Wolsey* to give it him. It then became a royal palace; and continued to be the principal seat of the kings of *England*, till of late years it was casually consumed by fire.

Nor was our prelate unmindful of his family, as well as his church, for during his long prelacy here, he had acquired a vast temporal estate, which he procured to be settled on his brother sir *Richard Gray*, with remainder to his nephew sir *Walter Gray*, the son of the former, by a charter of king *Henry* III. This charter of confirmation, by *inspeximus*, I have copied from the record in the *Tower*; and though very long, yet, it being very particular in the recital of all these estates in the neighbourhood of *York*, I have thought fit to place a copy of it in the *appendix*.

Our archbishop, at last grown very aged, took his death-bed sickness at *York-place*, *Westminster*; and removing to *Fulham* for the benefit of the air, was attended on with great care by the bishop of *London*. But three days after his arrival, and on *May* 1, 1255, he died. His body, being *(l)* embalmed, was brought down to his own cathedral

(i) *Capita vermium, serpentium, scilicet, colubrorum, bufonum terribilium, &c.* M. Paris.

(k) *Vocem autem audierunt sibi dicentem ne ad bladum manus apponerent, quia archiepiscopus et omnia quae habebat diaboli possessio erat.* M. Paris.

(l) *Anatomia facta*, says *Paris*.

dral, and there with all due honours was interred before the altar of St. *Michael*, in the south end of the crofs ifle which he himfelf had erected. His tomb, as appears by the annexed plate, is a curious *Gothick* performance, of grey, but what others call factitious, marble. And tradition has conftantly averred that his body was depofited in the canopy over the pillars, as dying under fentence of excommunication from the pope, and therefore not fuffered burial in holy ground. I am forry to be the occafion of overthrowing this fine ftory, which has fo long been a great embellifhment to the defcription our vergers give of the church and monuments; but in reality the whole is falfe. Indeed *M. Paris* fays, that the pope was much offended at our prelate, for refufing to admit foreigners into his benefices at his requeft; and took away his crofs, which was ufually carried before him by the chief clergyman of his church; but the pope's refentment did not run to an excommunication againft him. And further, being defirous to know whether the body was laid in that *depofitum* or not, I got leave of the prefent dean to open it at the end of the window; when I faw the workman pierce near a yard into it, and it was all folid. The tomb has no manner of epitaph, wherefore Mr. *Willis* fays he found, in the *Cotton* library, a manufcript which had this jingle inftead of one;

Ille fuis fumptibus villam adoptavit
Thorp, *et fucceſſoribus fuis aſſignavit.*
Obiit catholicus preful et fidelis,
Ad altare ponitur fancti Michaelis.

In the year 1250, this *Walter Grey*, archbifhop of *York*, publifhed fome conftitutions, which are ftiled *provincial*, as being clearly intended to be obferved by the whole province of *York*, though publifhed by the fole authority of the archbifhop before named. There are other inftances befides this of archbifhops making conftitutions without confent of fynods. I the rather place it, fays Mr. *Johnfon*, amongft the provincials, becaufe it will appear, that fome conftitutions of the greater province of *Canterbury* were copied from thofe of archbifhop *Grey*. The preamble runs thus,

The decree of the lord *Walter Grey*, formerly archbifhop of *York*, legate of the apoftolical fee, publifhed at *York*, at the time of his vifitation, to the honour of God, and the prefant information of the church of *York*, and to the memory of all that are to come.

Whereas, &c. (m)

0 1 2 3 4 5 Feet.

(m) See *Johnfon*'s [illegible] laws, &c. fir *H. S.* vol. 2. p. 390.

SEWAL

Sewal de Bovil (*l*) *twenty fourth archbishop.*

A.MCCLVI. During the long reign of *Henry* III, all the bishopricks in *England* had at one time or other become void; from whence he had reaped no small profit to his treasury. *Walter Grey*'s longevity kept him out of *York*, till, at length, the death of this prelate also happening, the king was in no haste to supply the vacancy; but kept the temporalities in his own hands for at least three years and three months (*n*). *Sewall* dean of *York* was in this time elected by the chapter, but they could not procure the king's consent to it, he still alledging that *Sewal* was a bastard, which was very true, and therefore incapable by the canons to enjoy the dignity. *Sewal* upon this was obliged to have a dispensation from *Rome*, and at last by the (*o*) pope's power he had consecration in his own church, says *Goodwin*, by the suffragan bishops of his province, *July* 23, *anno* 1256.

Sewal was educated in the university of *Oxford*, and was a diligent hearer of *Edmund de Abingdon*, afterwards archbishop of *Canterbury* and canonized, at the time he read divinity lectures in that university. This learned man used often to say that his scholar *Sewal* would be a great proficient, but without dispute would die a martyr. During his short government of this see he underwent much trouble and affliction for opposing the preferment of forreigners, especially of one *Jordan*, whom the pope had constituted dean of *York*, and who by a wile had also got himself installed to it. The archbishop stoutly withstood this innovation of the pope's, even to a sentence of excommunication, which was thundered out against him. The prelate still stood the shock, and would not consent that an *Italian*, and one who was found to be altogether illiterate, should have the second place to him in his church. *M. Paris*, who is very particular in this affair, says that the *Italians* had then in *England* seventy thousand marks *per annum* in ecclesiastical revenues; that they held all the best livings in the kingdom, kept no hospitality, and were most, or all, of them, boys or blockheads.

This sentence by bell, book, and candle, (*p*) as *Paris* stiles it, laid heav yon our archbishop, which notwithstanding he bore with great patience and resignation. And being strengthned, adds my author, by the example of the blessed *Thomas the martyr*, by that also and the doctrine which he had learned from his preceptor St. *Edmund*, and likewise by the example of the blessed *Robert Grosthed* bishop of *Lincoln*, he withstood this (*q*) *papal tyranny* to the last. *Stubbs*, a more partial writer to the see of *Rome*, affirms, that our prelate began to squeak, at last, and called out loudly for absolution on his death bed. But *Paris*, who was contemporary with him, and must undoubtedly have known this whole affair, gives us his last, remarkable, words in this manner. And now, says he, our holy prelate, when he saw death inevitably approaching, raising himself up in bed, joining his hands, and casting up his weeping eyes towards heaven, said, "O Lord *Jesus Christ*, the "justest of judges, thy infallible discernment must know that the pope, whom thou hast "permitted to be the head of thy church, has much harrassed my innocence; for that, "which God knows, and the world is not ignorant of, I would not admit unworthy and "ignorant persons to the rule of those churches which thou hast committed to my care. "Nevertheless, lest by my contempt of this papal decree, this unjust sentence should be "thought just upon me, I humbly beg to be loosed and absolved from these bonds. But "before the most high and incorruptible judge of all men I call the pope, that both "heaven and earth may be witnesses how much he has injured me, and many times pro"voked and offended me, *&c.*"

Sewal, during his short reign, corrected and reformed many abuses in his church and diocese. He erected several vicaridges in impropriate churches, which, till that time were very ill served. He caused likewise the stipends of the priests of St. *Sepulchres* chapel to be increased, and appointed them to be called canons. He did many other things worthy of notice, and would have done more had not death deprived his church of its best friend on *Ascension day*, *anno* 1258. He was buried in the cathedral, on the right hand his predecessor, where a plain tomb remains still over him, in the form the plate represents it; but without any inscription.

His sepulcher was much frequented after his death by the common people, who had him in high veneration for his sanctity and sufferings, and reported many miracles to be done at it. *Paris* says, that he performed a miracle of turning water into wine in his life time, which may be as easily credited as those after his death. Many disputes have arose about the conduct of this archbishop betwixt the popish and protestant clergy; the former blaming him for his obstinacy, and the latter praising him for his constancy (*r*). *Bayle* commends

(*m*) Chron. *T. Wykes*, *Sewal de Bainill.*

(*n*) *Ait enim rex: nunquam illum archiepiscopatum antea in manu tenui, ideo cavendum est ne nimis cito illabatur.* M. Paris.

(*o*) *Sir, nolente volente rege, obtinuit et pontificatum et pallium.* Stubbs.

(*p*) *Accensis candelis et pulsatis libris et campanis.* M. Paris.

(*q*) *Omnem papalem tyrannidem patienter sustinendo.* *Idem.*

(*r*) *Tenuit autem adhuc* genu flectere Baal, *et indignis barbaris opima beneficia ecclesiae suae, quasi margaritas porcis, imo spurcis distribuere.* M. Paris 964.

him

him highly; and *Goodwin* says he deserved canonizing much more than any of his predecessors, because he couragiously and resolutely withstood the power of the pope, scorning to condescend to his command, or be terrified by his fulminations. A special plea at *Rome* to gain the honour of a red letter in their calendar.

The writings which *Bayle* and *Pitts* ascribe to this prelate are these,

Breviloquium ad Alexandrum *papam lib.* 1.
Statuta synodalia lib. 1.
Ad suos sacerdotes lib. 1.
Sermones et epistolae lib. 1.

Archbishop Sewal.

GODFREY DE LUDHAM, *aias* KIMETON, *thirty fifth archbishop.*

The Pope and conclave at *Rome*, being vexed at the obstinacy of *Sewal*, had made an ordinance, a little before his death, that every elect bishop of *England* should, before his confecration, appear there in person, and take the pope's approbation from thence. The first who obeyed this mandate was *Godfrey de Kimeton*, alias *Ludham*, dean of *York*, whom the chapter had elected archbishop on the death of *Sewal*. *Godfrey* travelled to *Rome*, at great cost and expences, and there received consecration (*s*) *September* 23, 1258. At his return to *England* he came to *London*, where the court then was, and had his cross born before him quite through the city to the king; of whom, being honourably received, he took leave and set out for his diocese. A. MCCLVIII.

In the year 1260, at the beginning of *Lent*, says *Stubbs*, this prelate laid the whole city of *York* under an interdict; which continued till the third of *May* following. But for what reason I am ignorant. He appropriated *Mexborough* to his church, which is now annexed to the archdeaconry of *York*; and dying *January* 12, 1264, was buried in the cathedral. The place of his interment is unknown. He governed this see six years, three months and sixteen days.

(*s*) *Circa nativitatem consecratur.* M. Paris.

Walter Giffard, *thirty sixth archbishop.*

A. MCCLXV After the death of *Godfrey*, *William de Langton*, dean of the church, was elected by the chapter to succeed him *(t)*. But the pope rejected him, and gave it to one *Bonaventure*, who resigned it again to his holiness; who then thought fit to translate *Walter Giffard*, formerly his own chaplain, after canon of *Wells*, then treasurer and chancellor of *England*, from the bishoprick of *Bath* and *Wells* to *York*. He was elected to the former *May* 15, 1254, and translated hither *October* 15, 1265. He died *April* 25, 1279, and lies buried, says *Goodwin*, in the cathedral near the east window. *Leland* mentions this inscription legible on his grave-stone in his days, *(u)*.

Walter Gisfart obiit vii kal. Maii mcclxxix.

William Wickwane, *thirty seventh archbishop.*

MCLXXIX. The dean and chapter of *York*, soon after the death of the last *Walter*, elected *William Wickwane*, chancellour of the church for his successor, and he had confirmation accordingly *(x)*. Of this prelate little is recorded, but that in the first year of his government he removed the bones of his predecessor St. *William* and placed them in a costly shrine, as I have before related, with great solemnity. He likewise provided, with the consent of his chapter, that thirty two oxen, fifty four plough horses, and a thousand sheep should be assigned of his goods to his successors. He got the royal assent to this, and that his successors should be obliged to keep the same stock upon the manors belonging to the see *in perpetuum*.

Having sat about six years and half, this prelate thought fit to resign his charge *(y)*, and retiring beyond sea he fell sick of a desperate disease at *Pontiniac* in *Normandy*, departed this life *April* 27, 1285, and was there buried in the abbey. The people of that country, says *Stubbs*, report many miracles to have been done at his tomb; for which, that author has dignified him with the appellation of *sanctus*.

John le Romaine, *(z) thirty eighth archbishop.*

A. MCCLXXXV. On the 29th of *October* following the demise of the last, *John Romaine* chanter of the church of *Lincoln*, and not *York*, as many write, was elected archbishop; and shortly after had his consecration at *Rome*. His father was sometime treasurer of this church, and being a *Roman* born, his son took the appellation, surnames coming now much in use, of *John le Romane*. The father being an ecclesiastick, the son could not be born in wedlock; and indeed *Knighton* has proved him a bastard, and says he was begot of a servant maid *(a)*. Our treasurer not having the gift of continency, so peculiar to the clergy in those days.

John is reported to be a wise, stout, and a very learned man; and went beyond any of his predecessors, says *Stubbs*, in keeping up the dignity of his office by the numerous retinue of knights, gentlemen, *&c.* which he kept in his service. He was a great benefactor to the fabrick of his church, and to St. *Peter*'s, or St. *Leonard*'s hospital in this city; of which see more under those titles. He sat ten years and died at his manor of *Burton* near *Beverley March* 15, 1295, and was buried in his cathedral church near *Walter Giffard* his predecessor. The cause of his death, says *Goodwin*, some attribute to the grief he took for being obliged to pay four thousand marks to regain the king's favour; whom he had highly incensed by presuming to excommunicate *Anthony Beck*, bishop of *Durham*, one of the king's council, and abroad in his service *(b)*. This affair is upon record as I have given

(t) Gulielmus de Ruderfeld, *alias* Langton, *elect. in archiep.* 4 *id.* Maii, 1264. *Sed cassata electione* Willielmi *decani* Ebor. *Papa contulit archiepiscopatum cuidam fratri de ordine Minorum dicto* Bonaventurae *qui timens pelli suae, &c. resignavit. Chron.* T. Wykes, *anno* 1265.

(u) Walterus Giffard *elect.* Ebor. *scribit priori et convent.* Bathon.——*Vobis denunciamus die beati* Thomae *Apost. nos cessisse et curam* Ebor. *eccl. recepisse, ut de elect. futuri pont. cogitetis.* C. Bathon. *in biblioth. hospitii* Lincoln. *p.* 96.

(x) Temporalia restituta Oct. 28. 1279 *pat.* 7 Ed. I. *m.* 9. *Rex adhibuit assensum election. magist.* Willielmi *cancellarii* Ebor. *in archiep. et hoc significat. est papae quod suum est in hac parte exequatur.* 4 Julii *pat.* 7 Ed. I. *m.* 14.

(y) Vacat Sept. 15 Ed. I. *m.* 14.

(z) Johannes Romanus *canon. ecclesiae electus et habet regis assensum* 15 Nov. *pat.* 13 Ed. I. *m.* 3. *Temporalia restituta* Ap. 12. *p.* 14 Ed. I. *m.*

(a) A Johanne Romano, *quondam* Eboracensi *thesaurario, et quadam* pedissequa *procreatus.* H. Knighton.

(b) The whole proceeding of a parliamentary inquiry into this matter (*anno reg.* Ed. I 21.) is published in *Ryley's placita parliamentaria*, p. 135. The archbishop was cast, and entered into this bond to the king for the payment of his fine. See also p. 172.

Noverint universi quod nos Johannes *providentia divina* Ebor. *arch.* Ang. *prim. tenemur serenissimo principi domino nostro domino* Ed. *Dei gratia regi* Ang. *dom.* Hibern. *et duci* Aquitan. *in quatuor millibus marcarum de quibus coram ipso domino rege ad placita sua in rotulis suis ibidem et etiam in scaccario ipsius domini regis fit mentio solvendarum eidem pro suae beneplacito voluntatis. Ad quarum solutionem faciend. obligamus nos et omnia bona nostra per quae distringamur prout domino regi placuerit ad eandem. Ad quod faciendum hos fidejussores invenimus, viz. venerabilem fratrem nostrum* J. Karl. Epm. Henricum *decanum* Ebor. Willielmum *archidiaconum* Ebor. Johan. *archidiac.* Estrithing *et* Willielmum *archid.* Not. *In cujus rei testimonium sigillum nostrum una cum sigillis praed. fidejussorum*

given it from the authority below. There is likewise another complaint against him exhibited by the prior and convent of *Bridlington*, the same parliament as the former, for concealing the effects of an exiled *Jew* of *York*, and defrauding the king of them. Of this also he was found guilty and put upon the king's mercy. These matters occurred *an.* 1293, and they seem to confirm *Knighton*'s character of this prelate; who represents him as a covetous worldling, and to carry on his extortions to a degree of madness (*a*). He adds, that he died, by the just judgment of God, suddenly, without having time to make a will, whereby his ill-got goods became the king's property; no one daring to give an *halfpenny*, or a *morsel of bread* out of it, for the relief of his soul at his funeral (*b*). This character seems to be somewhat injurious to the memory of our prelate, and entirely inconsistent with his many publick benefactions.

HENRY DE NEWARK, *thirty ninth archbishop.*

Henry de Newark, dean of *York*, was chosen archbishop on the seventh of *May* following (*c*). But because of a war in *Europe* at that time he did not go to *Rome*, so had confirmation by bull, as also to be consecrated in his own church by *Anthony Beck* bishop of *Durham*, which was done accordingly *June* 24, 1298; two years after his election. He sat not above one year after this and then died *August* 15, 1299, and was buried near his predecessor. A. MCCXCVIII

THOMAS DE CORBRIDGE, *fortieth archbishop.*

After him succeeded a great and learned divine, says *Goodwin*, *Thomas de Corbridge*, canon of *York*, (*d*) and *custos*, or sacrist, of the chapel of St. *Sepulchre's* contiguous to that cathedral. He was elected *November* 12, and consecrated at *Rome February* 28, following (*e*). The pope bestowed the place of sacrist, vacant on this promotion, on a kinsman of his own, who soon after dying, the archbishop placed in his room *Gilbert Segrave*, afterwards bishop of *London*. Notwithstanding the king's express letters to the archbishop in behalf of *John Busk* his secretary. This contumely provoked the king so much, that he took from the bishoprick three manors, there called baronies, which of old belonged to the see, and detained them as long as this prelate lived. Which indeed was not long, for he died at *Lanham, com. Nottingham, September* 2, 1303; and was buried at *Southwell*, under a plain altar stone in the choir, which had his effigies, at full length, in brass upon it; but long ago torn off and defaced. A. MCCXCIX.

WILLIAM DE GRENEFELD *forty first archbishop.*

The chapter of *York* then elected *William*, called by *Stubbs*, *de Grenesfeld*, canon of *York*, and chancellor of *England* to succeed; who after his election travelled to *Rome* for approbation (*f*). Here he was obliged to dance attendance two years; and it cost him nine thousand five hundred marks, in presents only, before the pope, *Clement* V, thought fit to confirm him; which was at last performed *January* 30, 1305. This extraordinary expence made him very bare at his coming to his see; insomuch that he was obliged to raise two collections amongst his clergy in one year. The first he called a *benevolence*, the second an *aid*; though the revenues of the archbishoprick are said then to amount to three thousand one hundred and forty five pound thirteen shillings and five pence, *sterling*, yearly. A. MCCCV.

This prelate favoured the *knights templars* very much; whom the pope and the *French* king thought every where to extirpate; alledging for it their exorbitant and scandalous lives, when in truth it was rather their being over rich than wicked, that occasioned their fall. It seems our prelate had the same opinion of them; for when those of his province were entirely dispossessed of all their estates and goods, he took care to place them in several monasteries; that they might not starve for want of necessary subsistence (*g*).

He was present at the grand council of *Vienna*, and had place assigned him next to the archbishop of *Triers*. He was so jealous of the privileges of the archiepiscopal see of *York*,

nostrorum praesentibus est appensum. Dat. apud Westm. *die* Merc. *prox. ante festum* Pentecost. *anno gr.* M. CC. *nonagesimo tertio*, &c.

(*a*) *Homo valde literatus, sed non tamen multas literas, sed avaritia maxima eum fecit quasi insanire.* H. Knighton.

(*b*) *Non enim panis vel obolus pro anima ipsius dabatur.* H. Knighton.

(*c*) Hen. de Newark *decanus* Ebor. *habet regis assensum* Junii 5. *pat.* 24 Ed. I. *temporalia restituta prima pars p.* 25 Ed. I.

(*d*) Prebendary of *Stillington*, Mr. *Torre.*

(*e*) Tho. de Corbridge *canon.* Ebor. *habet regis assensum ad archiepiscopatum* Nov. 16. *pat.* 27 Ed. I. *temporalia restituta* Ap. 30, *pat.* 28 Ed. I.

(*f*) *Magister* Willielmus do Grenefeld *canonicus in ecclesia beati* Petri Ebor. *habet regis assensum ad electionem suam* Dec. 24. *p.* 33. Ed. I. *p.* 1. *Temporalia restituta, litera regis ad papam commendand.* Willielmum de Grenefeld *elect.* Ebor. Julii 6. 33 Ed. I. *registrum* Cant. Martii 31. *p.* 34 Ed. I.

(*g*) *Arch.* Will. *pietate motus super statu* Templariorum *suae dioecesis, omni auxilio destitutorum, eos in diversa suae dioecesis instituit monasteria, eisque sua perpetuae vitae necessaria ministrari praecepit.* M. A. 2. 564. *de Temp. ord. destructione.*

in

in regard to that of *Canterbury*, that on a time being invited by the abbot of the monastery of St. *Austin* in that city, he would not wave the bearing of his cross before him even in that place *(b)*. He died *December* 6, 1315, at *Cawood*; having sat nine years eleven months and two days; and was buried before the altar of St. *Nicholas* in his own cathedral *(i)*. His tomb is represented in this plate.

WILLIAM DE MELTON, *forty second archbishop*.

A.MCCCXV. Soon after the foregoing archbishop's death, *William de Melton (k)* provost of *Beverley*, and canon of *York*, at the earnest request of king *Edward* II, was elected. The election was made *January* 21, 1315, but he did not receive consecration till two years after; in which the court of *Rome* was very dilatory, notwithstanding the repeated sollicitations of the king in his favour *(l)*. The dignity was at length conferred on him *September* 25, 1317, at *Avignon*.

Goodwin writes, that this prelate ruled his see very worthily; attending diligently, not only to the business of his church, but kept a strict guard on his own private actions. He adds, that he endeavoured by fasting, prayer, chastity, alms-deeds, hospitality and vertuous behaviour, like a good pastor, not only to teach and instruct by preaching and doctrine, but also by example of life. He visited his diocese constantly twice a year; was very kind to his tenants, but careful to preserve, and rather to increase, than any way diminish, the rents and revenues of his church. Yet was he not forgetful of preferring as occasion served, his kindred or servants to very good places, both in church and state. Amongst the rest he purchased, for his nephew, the manors of *Kingskiln*, *Kingsclere* and *Wentworth*; at that time part of the revenue belonging to the private patrimony of the

(b) *Chron*. W. Thorn. *de archiep*. Cant.

(i) Thomas de S. Albano *canon. de* Suthwell, *et* Will. *fil.* Roberti de Grenefeld *testamenti executores archiep*. 3 Ed. III. *m*. 7.

(k) There are several *Meltons* in this county, but it is probable *Melton* in *Holderness* was the place of this prelate's nativity.

(l) There are no less than twelve letters wrote by the king to the pope, his nephew and cardinals, extant in the *Fœd. Ang*. tom. III. to expedite the confirmation of this archbishop. *Et cum papa* W. de Melton *in archiepiscopum praefecit rex restituit temporalia* Oct. 8. 1, par 11 Ed. II.

then

2

archbishop of *Roan*. From this nephew descended several men of worth, who served their country, as high sheriffs of this county, at several times, for some ages after.

This prelate bestowed great cost in finishing the west end of the cathedral; and laid out twenty pound in renewing the shrine of St. *William*. He compounded a long and tedious controversy which had been betwixt the archbishops, his predecessors, and the dean and chapter of the church; procuring the order made by him to be confirmed by the pope (*l*). He held the offices of being successively chancellor and treasurer of *England*, and dying, at *Cawood*, *April* 22, 1340; was buried near the font, in the west end of the cathedral.

On the laying the new pavement of the church, the stone which covered the grave of this prelate was taken up. It was of blew marble, very large, but quarterly cloven, and had been plated with brass on the borders, and all over the middle part of it. Upon trial for a vault the workmen came, at about two yards depth, to six large unhewn stones which laid cross and cross, as a drain is covered. Upon removing two or three of them we discovered a curious walled grave of ashler stone, in which the archbishop was laid. He had been put in a lead coffin, and afterwards in a mighty strong oaken one; but both were so decayed that it was easy to get to his bones. On the top of the uppermost coffin, near his breast, stood a silver chalice and paten which had been gilt. On the foot of the chalice was stampt a crucifix, of no mean workmanship, and on the inside the paten a hand giving the *benediction*. We could not find that he had been buried in his robes, his pastoral staff laid on his left side, but no ring could be met with. His bones as they laid together measured six foot, which argues him to have been a very tall man. His grey hairs were pretty fresh; after we had taken a short survey of the *exuviae* of this once famous man, the grave was closed up in the manner it was before; but the chalice and paten were carried to the vestry.

WILLIAM DE LA ZOUCH, *forty third archbishop.*

Upon the death of the former, *William de la Souche*, or *Zouch*, succeeded; but had a great struggle for the chair with one *William Killesby*. The day of election was made *May* 2, 1340, when *Zouch* had thirteen voices in chapter against five; notwithstanding which majority, *Killesby* would not give it up, but followed *Zouch* to the pope; and it was full two years before he could get his election confirmed. But at last he was consecrated by pope *Clement* VI. at *Avignon*, *July* 7, 1342; and was inthronized in his own church at *York*, *December* 9. following. A. 1396.

King *Edward* III. persuing his wars in *France* left our prelate warden of the north parts of *England*. And *anno* 1346, the *Scots* taking advantage of the king's absence, made an invasion with a powerful army; and were met by the archbishop and his forces at a place called *Bewre-park*, near *Durham*. A sharp fight ensued, in which our church general was so fortunate as to give the *Scots* a total overthrow; slew two earls, twenty one knights and an infinite number of common men; taking also many prisoners, amongst which was *David Bruse* their king. And thus revenged his predecessor's loss at the battle of *Myton*, as mentioned in the annals of this work. I find there were great dissensions betwixt this archbishop and the dean and chapter; insomuch that he put the church under an *interdict*; which caused the king to summon them all before the next parliament (*m*).

This prelate began a chapel on the south side of the cathedral, in which he intended to have been buried; but lived not long enough to see it finished. Mr. *Torre* has given us a short abstract of his will, which is still extant in the office, dated at *Ripon*, *June* 28, 1349, and proved *July* 27, 1352; whereby he commends his soul to God almighty, St. *Mary* and *All-saints*, and appointed his sepulture in the cathedral church of *York*, bequeathing five hundred pound sterling to erect one perpetual chantry of two priests to celebrate for the good estate of his soul (*n*), &c.

This building is now the vestry, of which more in its proper place; for our prelate being taken off, as I said before, upon *July* 19, 1352, he was laid before the altar of St. *Edmund* king and confessor in his cathedral. His tomb, says *Stubbs*, lay a long time after covered with a stone pavement, to denote the greatness of his stock and lineage; and in regard to those, to whom in his life time he had proved an extraordinary benefactor. I own I do not thoroughly understand this passage in *Stubbs*, but the course of my work will not suffer me further to descant about it, so I give it in the author's words (*o*) below; I shall only say, that his family was noble; the *Zouches*, says *Camden*, derived from a stump or stock of a tree, deduced their genealogy from the earls of *Britany*; and were at this time possessed of two baronies, *viz.* *Zouch* of *Ashby*, whence *Ashby de la Zouch*, and *Zouch* baron of *Haringworth* (*p*).

(*l*) *Vide Fœd Ang. tom.* IV. *p.* 327.

(*m*) *Clauf.* 2 Ed. III. *m.* 5. *dorso. et de dissensione inter archiepiscopum et ep* Dunelm. *super aliquibus tangentibus ecclesias suas. Clauf.* 3 Ed. III. *m.* 5. *dorso.*

(*n*) P. 461.

(*o*) *Sepulchrum ejus diu postea* pavimento lapideo *jacuit coopertum, in argumentum magnitudinis parentum suorum, et aliorum quibus eximius dum vixit exstiterat benefactor* Stubbs *in vita ejus. x. script.*

(*p*) *Dugdale*'s baronage, vol. I.

William le Zouche, archbishop of *York*, published a series of constitutions, in the year 1347, made in a provincial synod held at *Thorp*, near the city of *York*; *John Thoresby*, his immediate successor, gave them a new sanction, and from his constitutions, only, we have them. Beginning, *William*, by divine providence, *&c.* (q)

JOHN THORESBY *vel* THURSBY, *forty fourth archbishop.*

A. 1352. If we may give credit to the genealogy of this prelate, given by our late antiquary *Ralph Thoresby* of *Leeds*, esq; this family is of a much more ancient *British* stock than the former, being derived from *Aykfith*, a noble baron, lord of *Dent*, *Sedbergh*, *&c.* in the time of king *Knute* the *Dane* (r). But however that, the pedigree seems to make it appear that this *John Thoresby* was second son of *Hugh Thoresby*, son of sir *Hugh Thoresby* of *Thoresby* knt. by *Isabel* the daughter of sir *Tho. le Grose* of *Suffolk*, knt. He was probably born at *Thoresby*, near *Midleham* in this county, which, according to the foregoing authority, continued long after this to be the seat of the family.

John Thoresby had his chief education in the university of *Oxford*; where he was much esteemed for his learning, being a very great divine and a good canonist. Being soon after distinguished at court, king *Edward* III. made him keeper of the great seal *July* 2, 1347, and *Sept.* 23, following, he was consecrated bishop of St. *David*'s. From hence our prelate was translated to *Worcester*, and, in *Oct.* 1352, was elected to *York*. Having sued out his pall from the pope, he came to visit his flock, and on the nativity of our lady *anno* 1354, arrived at *York*; where he was met, and honourably received, by a vast concourse of his clergy and people, and enthronized the same day, in great pomp, in the archiepiscopal chair; and had the temporalities restored to him *Feb.* 8. following.

Being lord chancellor of *England*, at the time of his election, our prelate resigned that most honourable office; and laying aside all secular affairs he set himself to visit his flock, and to compose differences; in which last article he was more than ordinary remarkable. Shewing himself, as he is truly characterised to be, *contentionum et litium hostis, et pacis et concordiae amicus.*

King *Edward* III, says the author of the controversies betwixt (s) the two archiepiscopal sees, considering the danger which both bodies and souls were subject to, by the long contentions betwixt them; and greatly affecting the quiet and satisfaction of his subjects, invited the two archbishops to a meeting, in parliament, at *Westminster*. Here, the matter being talked over, our prelate (t), without the consent of his chapter, made a firm compact with his brother of *Canterbury* for bearing his cross in that province. It was now near two hundred years since *Roger* archbishop of *York* had assumed an equality with him of *Canterbury*, and claimed the same privilege of having his cross born up before him when he was in the province of *Canterbury*, which the other claimed and used in the province of *York*. These contentions about this vain piece of ceremony, frequently rose so high, betwixt the two metropolitans, as to obstruct all business at the meetings of parliaments. And if one had got before the other into an assembly of that nature, the latter would have a door broke open on purpose for him to enter at; that he might not be said to follow his brother. The two present archbishops, *Simon Islip* and *John Thoresby* put an amicable end to this dispute, by the mediation, as is said, of the king, without the interposition of the pope. The sum of the *concordat* may be met with in a later part of this work. This agreement was however afterwards ratified and confirmed by pope *Innocent* VI, by his Bull bearing date *Feb.* 22, 1354, at *Avignon* (u). In the confirmation the pope, seeking to please both parties, about precedency, invented that nice distinction of *primate of England*, and *all England*; which last was given to *Canterbury*. Thus when two children, says *Fuller*, in his ludicrous style, cry for the same apple, the indulgent father divides it betwixt them; yet not so, but that he giveth the larger and better half to the child that is his darling (x).

Our prelate had likewise the honour to put a final determination to a long controverted dispute, in chancery, betwixt the abbot of St. *Mary*'s, and the mayor and commonality of the city of *York*, about the liberties of *Bootham*. He brought them to sign an indenture by which the boundaries of each are assigned; and which agreement was so firm, that there never were any more disputes betwixt them. A copy of this indenture is extant in another part of this work.

Anno 1361. he began the new foundation of the quire of his cathedral church, towards the charge of which work he instantly laid down one hundred pound; and promised to contribute 200 *l. per ann.* to it till it was finished, which he faithfully performed as long as he lived. But of this more in another place. He bestowed great cost in beautifying and painting our lady's chapel with images and pictures of excellent workmanship. And removing the bodies of diverse of his predecessors that lay buried in several places about the quire, he entombed them anew, at his own expence, before the entrance into this chapel, reserving a

(q) See *Johnson*'s collections of ecclesiastical laws, *&c.* Sir *H S.* p. 603.

(r) Thoresby's *Ducat.* Leod. p. 69. *Idem Vicaria* Leod. p. 186.

(s) *Wharton*'s *Anglia sacra*, vol. I.

(t) *Ex MS.* Torre.

(u) Printed at length in *Anglia sacra*

(x) *Fuller*'s church history.

place

place in the midst of them for himself. He took possession of his tomb soon after, for dying at *Bishopsthorp Nov.* 6, 1373, he was, on the vigil of St. *Martyn* following, most solemnly interred in the place he had directed *(y)*. *Leland* has given us a broken inscription, which he says was on a grave-stone in his time, *viz.*

Johannes de Thoresby quondam Menevensis, postquam Wigorniensis, et Ebor. archiepiscopus, qui fabricam —— Obiit vi. die Novembris A. D. MCCCLXXIII. *(z)*

Bale, in his centuries of *British* writers, has constituted our prelate a cardinal; and says he was made one by pope *Urban* V. at *St. Savine.* Mr. *Torre* confirms this, and gives us his title *St. Peter ad vincula.* As appears by the inscription on the circumference of his seal, which seal, adds he, I have seen, *viz.* **S. Johannis Sancti Petri ad Vincula Presbiteri Cardinalis.** But since this prelate is not mentioned by *Ciaconius* in his lives of the cardinals, nor by any of the *Italian* writers on that subject, I presume that they are both mistaken. Mr. *Torre* does not give us any abstract of the deed, or writing, to which this seal is affixed, to shew that it actually was the seal of *John Thoresby.* And since in all his publick acts, even in his last will he never assumed the title of cardinal, there is great reason to believe the seal that Mr. *Torre* saw belonged to some other person. One thing which made our prelate very remarkable, and must not be omitted, is his publishing an exposition on the ten commandments, in the *English tongue*, requiring all the clergy in his diocese to read it diligently to their parishioners. This work, *Goodwin* says he had by him, and comments much upon it, as a monument worthy to be esteemed. The publick service under *Antichrist*, adds that author, being *Latin* in the temples, so that people understood nothing of it. Our late diligent antiquary, and kinsman to this archbishop, Mr. *Thoresby*, says he long sought for this curiosity in vain; till at length he found it amongst the records in the archbishop's register office at *York*. From whence he transcribed it, and the reader may find it printed in the *appendix* to his *Vicaria Leodensis (a)*. About the year 1363, says Mr. *Johnson*, archbishop *Thoresby* published his constitutions; which begin *John* by divine providence archbishop of *York*, primate of *England*, and legate of the apostolick see, *&c.* In these, his predecessor's constitutions are transcribed and ratified *(b)*. The writings which *Bale* further ascribes to our prelate are,

Processum quendam, lib. I. *Pridem sanctissimus in Christo pater.*
Pro docendis laicis, lib. I. *Attendite populus meus legem meam.*
Ad ecclesiarum pastores, lib. I.

ALEXANDER NEVILL, *forty-fifth archbishop.*

Alexander Nevill, prebendary of *Bole* in this church, was appointed next unto this see, by the pope's provisionary bull; dated 16 *kal. Maii an. pont.* 4°. which was received and read in the chapter on *May* 30, 1374. And on *June* 4. following he was consecrated in *Westminster-abby* by the hands of *Thomas* bishop of *Durham*; *Thomas* bishop of *Ely*, and *William* bishop of *Winchester (c)*. A. 1374.

This prelate was highly in favour with king *Richard* II, which proved his ruin. For many of the malecontent nobility and gentry, rebelliously taking arms against their sovereign, forced most of his friends, and those he favoured, to answer certain articles alledged against them in parliament. Some of whom they condemned to death and others imprisoned; amongst the rest our archbishop was accused and sentenced to perpetual imprisonment in *Rochester* castle. The crime they laid to his charge, says *Goodwin*, was endeavouring to abuse the king's youth, and to exasperate him against the nobility. But *Knighton*, his contemporary, gives a better reason, which was straining the king's prerogative too high, by advising him to set aside and disannul an act of parliament with his own authority *(d)*. King *Richard* being now in disgrace, his friends could expect small favour, and our prelate seeing the storm look black upon him, withdrew himself privately from his palace at *Cawood*, in a poor priest's habit, and got beyond sea. Leaving all his goods, *&c.* as a prey to his enemies; which, by a writ of outlawry, at the meeting of the parliament, were all forfeited to the king.

It is most certain our prelate's case would have been very bad if he had fallen into his enemy's hands; but as it was he was deplorable enough. He lived in exile some time in great want, till pope *Urban* V. took pity of him, and upon his resignation of *York*, translated him to St. *Andrews* in *Scotland (e)*. But alas! his evil fate still attended him. The *Scots*, it

(y) See the church account of these grave-stones, chapel, *&c.*

(z) Lelandi *Itin.*

(a) This prelate's will is extant in the prerogative office, and begins, *I* John de Thoresby, *by the grace of God, archbishop of* York, *primate of* England, *and legate of the apostolick see, &c.* Dated *apud* Thorpe *juxta* Ebor. *Sept.* 12, 1373 proved *Nov.* 17, 1373. *Torre*, 461.

(b) See *Johnson*'s collections, *&c.* Sir *H. S.* vol. II. p. 602.

(c) *Habet regis assensum Jan.* 1. 2 *Pat.* 47 *Ed.* III. *m.* 4.

(d) H. Knighton *inter* x. *script.*

(e) *Cum summus pontifex* Alexandrum *nuper archiep.* Eborum *a vinculo quo dictae eccl. tenebatur absolverit, et ipsum ad eccles. S.* Andrae *transtulerit, &c. Pat* 12. *Ric* II. *m.* 22.

seems,

4

ſeems, refuſed to acknowledge *Urban* as pope, and ſided with his adverſary the anti-pope; wherefore they rejected his nomination of *Nevill* to St. *Andrews*. Deprived thus of both ſees, he was conſtrained, through mere neceſſity, to become a pariſh prieſt and teach ſchool at *Lovain*; in which poor ſituation he lived three years, then died and was buried in the church of the fryars *Carmelites* in that town, about the end of *May* 1392. After he had been five years in exile, and fourteen years primate of this ſee.

This prelate is ſaid to have beſtowed much coſt on his caſtle of *Cawood*; building divers towers and other edifices about it. *Knighton*, who is plainly no friend to him, accuſes him of being at diſcord and variance with his canons of *York* and *Beverley*; the latter of which he deprived *ab officiis et beneficiis*, keeping the perquiſites in his own Hands. The citizens of *York* alſo fell much under his diſpleaſure, which king *Richard*, at his coming to the city, made up to their content; but refuſed to meddle at all with his quarrels in the church.

Thomas Arundel, *forty-ſixth archbiſhop.*

A. 1388. *Alexander* being outlawed and baniſhed the realm, and having likewiſe ſurrendered up his ſee, on the hopes of enjoying that in *Scotland*, as has been ſaid, *Thomas Arundel*, ſon to the earl of *Arundel*, though by ſome circumſtances in his arms he is ſuſpected to be only a baſtard of the family, firſt archdeacon of *Taunton*, then biſhop of *Ely*, and lord chancellor, was tranſlated hither by papal proviſion. The bull bearing date *April* 3, 1388 *(f)*.

At *York*, whilſt he ſtaid here, he was a great benefactor to the church and manors of the ſee, beſtowing much in buildings and reparations of divers archiepiſcopal houſes. To the church, beſides many rich ornaments, he gave a great quantity of maſſy plate; the particulars of which may be ſeen in the church's inventory. Being then lord chancellor, and preſuming to quell the pride and arrogance of the *Londoners*, who had highly offended their king, he removed his ſeals, and got all the king's courts adjourned from *London* to *York*; where they ſtaid ſix months, to the great advantage of the city *(g)*.

Having ſat ſix years he was by the pope's proviſionary bulls tranſlated to *Canterbury* *Jan.* 18, 1396; where I ſhall leave him; being the firſt inſtance of a tranſlation from *York* to that ſee; and none but *Kempe* and *Grindall* after him.

Robert Waldby, *forty-ſeventh archbiſhop.*

A. 1396. *Robert Waldby* was born in *York*, and was brother to *John Waldby*, whom I have mentioned before. He was firſt a fryar *Eremite* of St. *Auſtin* in the monaſtery of that order in this city; having been educated at *Oxford*. But leaving his monaſtick life he followed *Edward* the heroick black prince into *France*, where he continued long a ſtudent in the univerſity of *Thoulouſe*. With the learning he acquired at both theſe famous places, he became the greateſt proficient of his age in all kinds of literature. He is ſaid to have been a good linguiſt, very well read in philoſophy, both natural and moral; in phyſick and in the canon law eſteemed very eminent; and was looked upon as ſo profound a divine that he was made profeſſor of divinity in the univerſity of *Tholouſe*. Theſe ſhining qualifications gained him the eſteem of prince *Edward*; who never failed to encourage and patronize men of learning and morals; and he beſtowed upon him the biſhoprick of *Ayre* in *Aquitain* *(h)*. From this firſt preferment he was afterwards tranſlated to the archbiſhoprick of *Dublin*, *anno* 1387, from thence to *Chicheſter* 1395; and the year following to *York*. The bull of whoſe tranſlation being read and notified to the chapter of *York*, *March* 20, 1396. he had the temporalities reſtored to him *June* 14, 1397 *(i)*.

He lived not a year after this, but died *Jan.* 6, 1397, and was buried in St. *Edmund's* chapel in *Weſtminſter-abby*. Where a fair marble is laid over him, on which is his effigies and epitaph as repreſented in the enſuing plate. The writings which *Bale* aſcribes to this prelate are,

Lecturam ſententiarum, lib. IV.
Quaeſtiones ordinarias, lib. I.
Quodlibeta varia, lib. I.
Contra Wicklivistas, lib. I.
Sermones per annum, lib. I.
Et alia plura.

(*f*) *Literae Papae ſuper tranſlatione* Al. Nevill *ab* Eboracenſi *ad eccleſiam S.* Andreae; *et pro* Eboracenſi *eccleſia proviſione. Dat.* Romae, Apr. 3, 1388. Foed. Ang. *tom.* VII. *p.* 573.

(*g*) *Remotio curiarum de* Londinis *ad* Eboracum, *Mar.* 30. 1392. *Id. tom.* VII. *p.* 713.

(*h*) *Bale* calls it *Adurenſis in Vaſconia. Goodwin* corrects this, and ſays he was biſhop of the *Iſle of Man*, *praeſul Adurenſis* for *Sodorenſis* in his epitaph; but the miſtake is on his ſide, for it was *Ayre* in *Aquitain*. *Stevens's* monaſt.

(*i*) *De temporalibus arch.* Ebor. *commiſſ. Junii* 14, *an.* 1597. *Foed. Ang. tom.* VII. *p.* 849.

Hic fuit expertus in quovis jure Robertus
De Waldby *dictus, nunc est sub marmore strictus.*
Sacrae scripturae doctor fuit et geniturae;
Ingenuus medicus et plebis semper amicus.
Praesul Adurensis, *post haec archas* Dublinensis,
Hinc Cicestrensis, *tandem primas* Eborensis
Quarto kalend Junij *migravit cursibus anni*
Milleni ter centum septem nonies quoque decem.
Vos precor orate quod sint sibi dona beata
Cum sanctis vitae requiescat, et hic sine lite.

Richard Scrope, *forty eighth archbishop.*

A. 1398. *Richard le Scrope*, brother to *William le Scrope* earl of *Wiltshire* and treasurer of *England*, after the death of *Waldby*, was promoted to this see; to which he attained, says *Walsingham*, not so much by favour, as by his own personal merit. They were both the sons of sir *Richard Scrope*, knt. lord chancellor of *England*, *temp. Ric.* II. who was preferred to that high station, says the aforesaid author, as one that had not his equal in the kingdom for wisdom and unbiass'd justice. This great man took care to give his sons suitable education, and to sow those seeds of religion and loyalty in their hearts, which, when sprung up, kept their verdure all their lives, and blossomed even at their deaths.

Richard, our prelate, after he had been instructed in the inferior schools, was sent to *Cambridge*, says *Bale*, but *Matt. Westminster*, who should know better, says to *Oxford*, where he proceeded first master of arts, and then took the degree of doctor both of the civil and canon law. Being thus qualified he went abroad, travelled through *France* into *Italy*, and came to *Rome*; where he continued some time in the employment of an advocate in the pope's courts; in which station he is said to have particularly applied himself to the defence of the poor. Returning home with great reputation, he was soon after made lord chancellor of *England* by king *Richard* II. in the room of his father. He continued not above one year in that place, when entering into holy orders, he was soon after consecrated bishop of *Litchfield* and *Coventry*, and lastly translated to the archiepiscopal see of *York*. The bull of whose translation bears date *apud S.* Petrum *tertio kal.* Martii *anno pont. papae* Bonifacii *nono.* And *July* 10. the same year he was installed archbishop by *William de Kexby* then precentor of the church.

The character of this prelate runs in so high a strain in most authors that it would seem partiality in any writer to copy them. His very enemies cannot sully his shining qualities, the cause he laid down his life for being the only crime attributed to him. He adorned the high station he was in as well by his noble and venerable mien and amiable deportment, as by his excellent behaviour and singular integrity. In point of learning very few came near him; and yet so far was he from being elated with his knowledge, that he was to all a pattern of courtesy and humility (*k*). He was affable to the meanest persons, and yet at the same time of such a composed and decent behaviour, as struck an awe and gained the respect of all that had occasion to approach him. The whole course of his life was religious; for he thought it not sufficient to perform the usual duty of saying mass and the divine office every day, but, notwithstanding the great business he must necessarily be engaged in, preached frequently, and devoted several hours to private prayer; fasting much and practising many other acts of mortification. No vice ever drew the least reproach upon him; so that even those who took away his life, and would have stained his reputation, could not find the least handle to lay hold on against him.

The worst that can be alledged against this truly vertuous man, and must be esteemed a blemish to his general character, is his submission to king *Henry* the fourth, whom he looked upon as an usurper (*l*). And yet in this point he is in some measure excusable. He saw the generality of the people run headlong into this change of government, and it was altogether out of his power to stem the impetuous torrent. He therefore chose to retire to his diocese till a fit opportunity should offer, the first of which he readily laid hold on. The method and ill success of this enterprise has been recited in the annals of this work. Our prelate had too much sincerity for a politician, and too much religion for a soldier. The first made him suppose the man he treated withal as honest as himself, the last urged him to lay hold on any occasion to stop the effusion of *christian* blood.

Tricked out of his life, by the subtlety of the earl of *Westmorland*, he was carried to the king at *Pontefract*, who had him conveyed to his own house at *Bishoptborp*. There *Henry* commanded *William Gascoign*, esq; at that time chief justice of *England*, to pronounce sentence against the archbishop, as a traytor to his king and country. But that upright and memorable judge, as my author styles him (*m*), answered the king in this manner; *neither you my lord the king, nor any liegeman of yours in your name, can legally, according to the rights of the kingdom, adjudge any bishop to death.* For which reason he absolutely refused to try the archbishop, *whose memory* (adds my author) *be blessed for ever and ever. Henry*, greatly incensed at *Gascoign*, for this bold denial of his orders, commanded sir *William Fultborpe*, a lawyer, but no judge, to pronounce sentence of death against our prelate. This man servilely obeyed the orders, and being mounted on a high stage erected in the hall of the palace, the archbishop standing bareheaded before him, he did it in these words: *We*

(*k*) *Quem cunctis commendabant, et aetatis gravitas et vitae praecedentis sanctitas, et incomparabilis literaturae scientia —— et cunctis amabilis ipsa persona.* T. Walsingham

(*l*) *Thomas Arundel*, then archbishop of *Canterbury*, ran as much on the other side, for he preached a sermon before this king at his accession on *Samuel's* words, *vir dominabitur populo*; wherein he shewed himself, says *Fuller*, a satyrist in the first part of the discourse, a parasite in the latter, and a traytor in both. *Fuller's* church history. *Fabian* in his chronicle has this sermon or speech at length.

(*m*) Clemens Maydestone *de martyrio* Ricardi Scrope. *Ang. Sacra, pars* II.

be

adjudge thee Richard, *traytor to the king to death; and by the king's command do order thee to be beheaded.* Upon hearing of this ſentence the archbiſhop replyed, *the juſt and true God knows that I never deſigned any ill againſt the perſon of the king, now* Henry *the fourth*; and turning about to the by-ſtanders he ſaid ſeveral times, *pray that God may not avenge my death on the king or his.* Which words, adds my author, he often repeated like St. *Stephen*, who prayed for thoſe that ſtoned him *(n)*. As our prelate's tryal and ſentence were brief, his execution immediately followed. He was ſet on a ſorry horſe of the value of forty pence, without a ſaddle, and with his face to the tail, and was led in this manner to the place of execution; ſaying as he went along, that *he never rid upon a horſe that he liked better than this in all his life.* He was habited in a ſky coloured looſe garment with the ſleeves of the ſame, for it was not permitted him to wear his own and a purple, or ſuch like coloured hood, hanging on his ſhoulders. Being come to the place of execution, he ſaid, *Almighty God, I offer up my ſelf and the cauſe for which I ſuffer; and beg pardon and forgiveneſs of thee for all I have committed or omitted.* Then he laid his hood and tunick on the ground, and turning to the executioner ſaid, *My ſon, God forgive thee my death, I forgive thee; but I beg this that thou wilt with thy ſword give me five wounds in my neck, which I deſire to bear for the love of my lord* Jeſus Chriſt, *who being for us obedient to his father until death, bore five principal wounds in his body.* He then kiſſed the executioner three times, and kneeling down prayed, *into thy hands moſt ſweet* Jeſus *I commend my ſpirit*, with his hands joined and his eyes lift up to heaven. Then ſtretching out his hands and croſſing his breaſt, the executioner, at five ſtrokes, ſeparated his head from his body. It is remarkable that this prodigious fortitude ſhewed in the prelate was in alluſion to his *banner*, which was painted with the five wounds of our ſaviour *(o)*.

The execution was done in a field betwixt *Biſhopſthorpe* and *York* on *Monday June* 8, *anno* 1405; after which he was buried betwixt two pillars in the eaſt end of his cathedral; where his plain monument, as repreſented in the plate, is to be ſeen at this day. I have chiefly followed *Clement Maidſtone*'s account of the martyrdom, as he terms it, of this prelate; but ſhall not follow him in the miracles he aſcribes to his martyr's vertues after his death; which were ſaid to be done both at his grave and in the field where he was beheaded *(p)*. It is certain this prelate was in high veneration by the populace whilſt he lived; and his manner of dying would not abate their opinion of him. No wonder then if his tomb was viſited, according to the cuſtom of that age, by great numbers of people; but *Henry* being informed of it, he ſtrictly forbad it, and ordered great logs of wood to be laid upon the grave, to prevent an adoration very impolitick in him to ſuffer.

Thus fell our worthy primate, a ſacrifice for loyalty and fidelity to his patron king *Richard*. He was the firſt biſhop in *England* that ſuffered death by any form of law; and which the pope no ſooner heard of, but he excommunicated the king and all that were the authors and abettors of this *execrable murder*. *Henry* found means, not long after, upon his ſubmiſſion and repentance, to obtain a bull of pardon from the holy ſee. This abſolution is recorded in our regiſter's office; and is of ſo ſingular a nature being indorſed, **Gratis**, for fear the age ſhould ſuppoſe a pardon of that kind could be purchaſed for money from the apoſtolick chamber, that I have thought fit to place an exact copy of it in the *appendix*. *Bale* aſcribes theſe writings to archbiſhop *Scrope*:

Super epiſtolas quotidianas, lib. 1.
Invecturarum in regem Henricum, *lib.* 1.
Feneſtrum facies in archa haec.
Coram domino Deo noſtro Jeſu.

It is remarkable that there is yet in *York* an inſtance of this prelate's popularity; for in the ſhoemaker's company is kept a bowl, called a *(q)* **Mazeur bowl**, edged about with ſilver, double gilt, with three ſilver feet, cherub's heads, to it. Round the rim on one ſide is this inſcription, **Recharde arche beſchope Scrope grant unto all tho that drinkis of this cope xl[ti] dayes to pardon.** On the other is, **Robert Gobſon beſchope meſm grant in ſame forme aforeſaide xl[ti] dayis to pardon. Robert Strenſall.** I take theſe laſt to have been the ſuffragan biſhops of the ſee. Every feaſt day, after dinner, the company have this bowl filled with ſpiced ale, and, according to ancient cuſtom, the bowl is drank round amongſt them. It has ſince had an additional lining of ſilver and the company's arms put upon it *anno* 1669.

(n) The prophecy of a dying canon of *Burlington*, relating to this prelate's fate, is ſomewhat remarkable; who foretold it darkly enough in theſe words:

Pacem tractabunt, ſed fraudem ſubter arabunt,
Pro nulla marca ſalvabitur ille HIERARCHA [archiep.]
Tho. Walſingham.

(o) *Thomas Walſingham.*

(p) This author ſays, that *Henry* was ſtruck with a leproſy the night after the execution. Enumerates ſeveral miracles, and concludes with a ſeeming authentick account that *Henry*'s body was never buried at *Canterbury*, but being ſent down by water was thrown over board in a ſtorm, and a coffin filled with ſtone buried in his ſtead. *Vide Ang. Sac.* vol. II.

(q) *Mazer*, a Belg. **Maſer**, **Meeſer**, *tuber ligni aceris ex qua materia praecipue haec pocula confici ſolebant.* Skinner. *Acer* is ſuppoſed to be our *Maple*.

Archbishop Scrope.

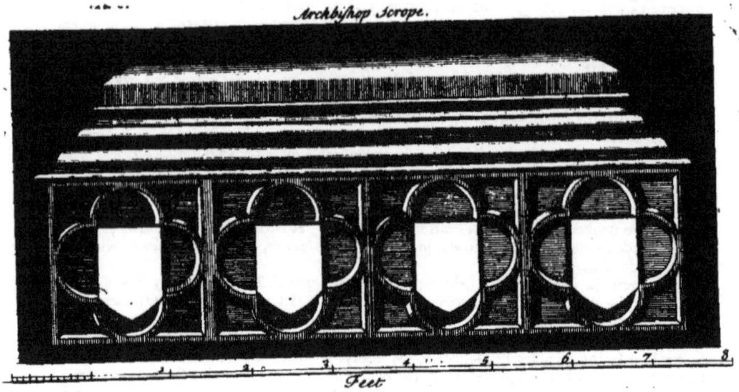

HENRY BOWET, *forty ninth archbishop.*

A. 1407. The see of *York* remained void for the space of two years and half; during which time there were two nominations to it, but neither of them were confirmed. The first was of *Thomas Longley*, dean of the church, who obtained the king's assent to his election by the chapter; but, for what reason I am ignorant, was set aside from this, and, sometime after, was constituted bishop of *Durham*. The pope thought fit to appoint *Robert Halom*, then chancellor of the university of *Oxford*, to this see, which the king understanding, was much displeased at it; whereupon his holiness consecrated him bishop of *Salisbury*. At length all parties concurred in the nomination of *Henry Bowett* bishop of *Bath* and *Wells*; he had the temporalities restored to him *December* 1, 1407 *(r)*; and on the ninth of the same month was installed in person in his cathedral church, near the altar of our lady, by the hands of *William Kexby* precentor; the dean being then in remote parts *(s)*.

This prelate was first archdeacon and prebendary of *Lincoln*; then made canon of *Wells*; afterwards he travelled for some time in *France* and *Italy* and at his return home *anno* 1402, was made bishop of *Bath* and lord treasurer of *England*. There is nothing memorable recorded of him in history relating to *York*, save that in the year 1417. the *Scots* invading *England*, as it was usually their custom when our kings were warring in *France*, so whilst *Henry* V. was carrying on a successful war against the *French*, the wardens of the north parts of *England* assembled their forces to stop the progress of the *Scotch* who had already besieged *Berwick* and *Roxborough*. Our prelate, though old, and so infirm that he could neither walk nor ride, yet would needs go in this expedition, and was therefore carried in a chair. Which action so animated the *English* army, that they fell upon the *Scots* and drove them back, with great slaughter, into their own country *(t)*.

This archbishop is also much commended for his great hospitality, even above any of his predecessors *(u)*. And, truly, if the consumption of fourscore tun of *claret*, which is said to have been yearly spent in his several palaces, can make us guess at lesser matters, it must argue *beef* and *ale* in abundance. To this purpose, I suppose, he built the great hall

(r) 1 *Pat.* 9 Hen. IV, *m.* 15.

(s) Fœd. *Ang.* tom. VIII. p. 503. MS. *Torre*, p. 465. *John Prophete* then dean.

(t) *Thomas Walsingham.*

(u) *Goodwin.*

in

in the castle of *Cawood* and the kitchens in his manor house at *Ottley*. He died at the first named place *Oct*. 20, 1423, and was buried in the east part of the cathedral, near the altar of all saints, which he had built and adorned very sumptuously. His tomb, exactly opposite to that of his unfortunate predecessor's, is a curious piece of *Gothick* architecture. The stone which covered the grave, being thought proper to be removed and sawn for the use of the new pavement, the remains appeared; among which was found nothing remarkable, but his archiepiscopal ring, which is gold, and has an odd kind of stone set in it. On the inner verge is engraven, as a poesy, these words **Honneur et Joye**.

This *Henry*, by divine providence archbishop of *York*, primate of *England*, and legate of the apostolick see, made his will, dated at *Thorpe juxta Ebor. September* 9, *anno* 1421; and proved before the chapter of *York*, *October* 26, 1423. By which he gave his soul to God almighty his creator, and his body to be interred as above. He gave for the expences of his funeral one hundred pound; and twenty pound more to have a thousand Masses, after the manner of St. *Gregory*'s trental, celebrated for his soul, and those of his parents, &c. within a month after his death (*x*).

Archbishop Bowet

JOHN KEMP, *fiftieth archbishop*.

After the demise of *Henry Bowet*, the pope preferred *Richard Fleming*, bishop of *Lincoln*, to this see; but the king, with the dean and chapter, taking advantage, says *Goodwin*, of the law lately made against the usurpations of *Rome*, so stoutly opposed him, that the pope was glad to draw in his horns, and to return *Fleming* to *Lincoln*. However, not to lose his papal authority, in this matter, he sent out a mandate directed to the citizens and populace of the diocese of *York*, directing them, in very odd terms, to acknowledge *Kempe* as their archbishop (*y*). And accordingly he was translated hither, and had the temporalities restored to him, *April* 8, 1426. A. 1426.

(*x*) *Torre*, p. 237.

(*y*) *Ex registro in camera supra pont*. Usae. *Vide* Append.

This *John Kempe* was doctor of laws, dean of the arches, and vicar general, and at the same time archdeacon of *Durham*. He was afterwards, *anno* 1418, consecrated bishop of *Rochester*, from thence to *Chichester*, *anno* 1422, the same year was translated to *London*; and, as before, to *York*. He came afterwards to be in great favour at *Rome*; being made cardinal-priest by the title of St. *Balbine anno* 1439 *(z)*. And *anno* 1450, he was made lord high chancellor of *England (a)*.

(b) John Leland writes, that this *Kempe* was a poor husbandman's son of *Wye* in *Kent*; whereupon for to pray for the souls of those who put him to school, and those that otherways preferred him, he converted the parish church of *Wye* into a college, in the twenty-third year of his archbishoprick of *York*. In this he placed secular priests, to attend divine service, and teach the youth of the parish; the governour thereof was to be a prebendary.

There are several letters, papers, *&c.* in the *Foedera*, relating to the State Negotiations this prelate was concerned in, which the compass of my design will not suffer me to search into. There is particularly one which constitutes him embassador to the general council then held at *Basil*, *anno* 1432, and several years after *(c)*.

After he had continued at *York* almost twenty eight years, and in a very old age, he was translated to *Canterbury*, by the bull of pope *Nicholas* V; which also constituted him a second time cardinal, by the title of cardinal-bishop of St. *Ruffine*. All these preferments are briefly expressed in this verse

(d) Bis primas, *ter* praesul, *erat bis* cardine *functus*.

Whilst *John Kempe* remained archbishop of *York*, and in the year 1444, in a provincial synod then held in his metropolical church, he constituted several decrees, which were afterwards registred by archbishop *George Nevile* at the end of his own constitutions, in the year 1466. The preamble which *Nevile* gives to them is this:

" Upon examining the registries of *John* late priest cardinal of the church of *Rome*, by
" the title of St. *Balbine*, and our predecessor of worthy memory, we remember that the
" underwritten constitutions, were duly and lawfully made by him, yet not inserted or in-
" corporated into the book of statutes. We will therefore that they be published, and in-
" corporated amongst the other constitutions, and firmly observed by all the subjects of our
" province *(e)*.

He continued not at *Canterbury* above a year and a half before he died, and was buried in a handsome monument, on the south-side of the presbytery in that cathedral *(f)*. We have no memorial of him in this see of *York* but what he left himself, which is the gate-house to the palace of *Cawood*, yet standing; adorned, both inside and out, with his arms and ensigns of a cardinal. There are likewise several such testimonials in the wood-work of this now desolate palace, which denotes that this prelate built and repaired much of it. And lest time should utterly deface, even, the ruins of this once magnificent structure, I chuse here to subjoin the following draughts of it; as it appears at this day. The gate-house of which is another monument sacred to the memory of cardinal *Kempe*; whose effects in this diocese I find were sequestred, after his death, to carry on the work of repairing this palace *(g)*.

(z) Goodwin. Spell. Gloss.
(a) Dugd. Chan.
(b) Leland's Itin vol. VI. *N. B.* His arms bear some allusion to his parentage *Vide Mon. Ang.* p. 191.
(c) Tom. X. p. 525, *&c.* This council at *Basil* was held in fifty four articles against pope *Eugenius*; deposes him, and chuses *Felix* V. Declares a general council to be above the pope; the virgin's conception to be immaculate, and for the oriental tongues. *Talent's* tables.
(d) Leland's Itin.
(e) See *Johnson, sub. anno* 1444.
(f) Vide M. Parker *in vita* Kempe, *ed.* Drake.
(g) Deputatio administrator. bonorum, quae fuerant Joh. Kempe *nuper archiep infra dioc.* Ebor. *sequest. ad reparationem novi operis in Palatio de* Cawode. *Reg.* W. Bothe *archiep.* p. 171. Aug. 2, 1454.

WILLIAM

Jno Haines delin. I. Basire excud.

The outside and inside views of the Gatehouse to the archiepiscopal palace at Cawood, *built by Cardinal* Kempe.

William Bothe, *fifty first archbishop.*

A. 1452. The person that succeeded, upon *Kempe*'s removal, was *William Bothe*, bishop of *Litchfield* and *Coventry*; who by bull of pope *Nicholas* V. was translated hither. On the 14th of *September*, 1452, he received the pall by the hands of *Thomas* bishop of *London* in his lordship's chapel at *Fulham*. And on the 26th of the same month, the bull was published and openly declared in the metropolitical church of *York*. Where *September* 4, the next year, he was solemnly inthronized by the treasurer of the church in the dean's absence; and had the temporalities restored *October* 26. following *(g)*.

William was first a student of the common law at *Gray*'s *inn*, but, suddenly, forsaking that course, he became chancellor of the cathedral church of St. *Paul* in *London*, *Anno* 1457, he was constituted bishop of *Coventry*, and five years after translated to *York*.

This prelate sat about twelve years, and dying at *Southwell September* 12, 1464, was interred in St. *John Baptist*'s chapel, on the south side of that church; where his tomb, being only a plain altar stone, still remains.

William Bothe, by divine providence, archbishop of *York*, primate of *England*, and legate of the apostolick see, made his will, *dat. apud Southwell, August* 6, 1464, proved *November* 24. following. Whereby he commended his soul to God almighty, his body to be buried as above; and, amongst several rich legacies to his relations, he bequeathed to his *spouse the cathedral church of* York, one miter with a pastoral staff *(h)*.

He is said to have bestowed much cost in repairing his palaces of *Southwell* and *York*.

George Nevile, *fifty second archbishop.*

A. 1464. *Richard Nevill*, the great earl of *Warwick*, that setter up and puller down of kings, called by our historians *make king*, took care to raise his brother *George*, by swift degrees, to high places and preferments. He was first a student in *Baliol* college in *Oxford*, and for some time was chancellor of that university. In the year 1446, he was collated to the prebend of *Massam*, in the cathedral church of *York*; and *anno* 1454, he was also collated to the prebend of *Thorpe* in the church of *Ripon*, and was master of St. *Leonard*'s hospital in *York*, 1458. But in the year 1459, by the earl's means when not fully twenty years of age *(i)*, he was by the pope's provision nominated to the bishoprick of *Exeter*; and the year following made lord high chancellor of *England*; which office he held eight years.

Anno 1464, this prelate was translated from *Exeter* to *York*; the bull of whose translation was published in our cathedral *June* 4, in the year following. *June* 17, he had the temporalities restored to him; and on the 6th of *September*, the same year, his pall was delivered to him in *Cawood* castle, by the hands of *John* bishop of *Lincoln*, the pope's especial commissioner for investing him; all which was done in the presence of his brothers, *Richard* earl of *Warwick*, and *John* earl of *Northumberland (k)*.

On the feast of St. *Maurice*, *January* 15, *anno* 1466, he was inthronized, in person, in his archiepiscopal seat. And the same day had his installation feast; the greatest entertainment that ever subject made; whether we respect the quantity of provisions, or the number and quality of the guests. Insomuch that the *Spanish* ambassador's remark, which he is said to have made on taking a view of the markets and people in *London*, may well be applied to this entertainment. In short, the bill of fare is incredible; for since the feast was in winter, else four thousand woodcocks would have been rarities indeed, how to reconcile them with the summer birds, which were also present at this feast; and bucks and does which are seldom in season together in our days, I shall not determine. An account of all this monstrous quantity of edibles which was taken care should not stick in their throats for want of drink, with the order of each service, and the placing of the guests is given by *Goodwin*. But that industrious antiquary Mr. *Hearn*, from an old paper roll he met with, is much more exact in the description of this entertainment, *&c.* printed in his additions to *Leland*'s *collectanea*. It was since copied from him and published in the two volumes of *Stevens*'s *monasticon*; for all which reasons I have no further occasion to take notice of it.

The whole time this archbishop sat in this chair it was little less to him than a series of troubles. The earl of *Warwick*'s desertion from the interest of the house of *York*, made king *Edward* look on the whole family of them with a jealous eye. And though the earl could never get the archbishop, nor his brother the marquiss, to join heartily with him in his aversion to *Edward*, yet it was reason enough for the king to suspect them. The earl of *Warwick*'s

(g) *Prim. pat.* 31. Hen. VI. *m.* 21.

(h) *Ex MS* Torre, *p.* 467. See the inventary where these gifts are described.

(i) Mr. *Torre* has proved that upon the then archbishop's collation this *George Nevill* clerk, as he is there called, son to the most noble and potent lord *Rich*, earl of *Sarum* was admitted to this prebend of *Massam* *March* 9, 1446. If so, and that he was under twenty years of age when he became bishop of *Exeter*, which is also attested by several; he was a prebendary at seven or eight years old. *MS* Torre *p.* 1135.

(k) The marquiss of *Montacute* was made so by king *Edward* IV, but not confirmed.

affairs

a

affairs profpering beyond expectation, he had the good fortune to furprize *Edward*, unawares, at *Oundle* in *Northamptonfhire*, and took him prifoner (*l*). The earl committed the cuftody of this valuable prize to his brother the archbifhop, who had him conveyed to a caftle, then belonging to their family, at *Midleham* in this county. But here inftead of the ufage and ftrict reftraint the king might have expected from the brother of his, now, mortal enemy, he met with all the courtefie imaginable. His kind keeper fuffering him to walk abroad, and even to hunt at his pleafure, with what number he pleafed to attend him. *Edward* eafily found means to break through fo flight a durance, and efcaped to *London*; where he foon after had the fortune in his turn to furprize king *Henry* and our archbifhop in his palace at *London*, and fent them both prifoners to the *Tower*. The latter had a pardon granted him, and was fet at liberty foon after; but the king was fo material a prifoner that nothing but death could releafe him.

After this our prelate being, as he thought, in good favour with *Edward*, though his two brothers were both flain at the battle of *Barnet* in direct oppofition to him, he took an occafion whilft he was hunting with the king, on a time, to mention an extraordinary kind of game he had about a feat of his called *Moor-park*, which he had juft built in *Hartfordfhire* (*m*). He invited the king to come to his houfe and partake of the diverfion, which *Edward*, who long had watched an opportunity to enfnare the prelate, and get rid of this laft ftem of a now detefted family, readily confented to, and promifed to come at fuch a day. The archbifhop upon this haftened home to make fuitable provifion for fuch a gueft, and omitted nothing that might do the king honour in his preparations. Skillful in fumptuous entertainments, he made his provifion accordingly, and to grace it with proper decorations fent for all the plate he had in the world; moft of which he had hid at the time of *Tewfkbury* and *Barnet* fields, and borrowed alfo much of his friends. The deer which the king hunted being thus brought into the toyle; the day before the appointed time he fent for the archbifhop, commanding him, all manner excufes fet apart, to come immediately to him at *Windfor*. At his coming, he was prefently arrefted of high treafon; all his plate money, furniture, and other moveable goods, to the value of twenty thoufand pound, confifcated to the king's ufe; and himfelf firft fent prifoner to *Calais*, and after to the caftle of *Guifnes*. Amongft other things taken from him he had a mitre of very great value fet with many jewels and pretious ftones; which the king thought fit break to pieces and make a crown thereof for himfelf.

This calamity happened to our prelate in the year 1472; and though by interceffion and the earneft intreaty of his friends, he with much a-do obtained his liberty, after he had been four years a prifoner, he enjoyed it but a little while. For coming from *Calais* he arrived in the *Downs December* 19, 1416, and went from thence to his fee. But with anguifh of heart to think of his former condition, compared to the prefent, having notwithftanding his liberty little left to fupport himfelf on, the king having received the profits of his temporalities during his confinement, he died at *Blithlaw*, as he was coming from *York*, *June* 8, 1476, and was buried in his own cathedral. He died inteftate, and adminiftration of his goods was granted, fays Mr. *Torre*, *Auguft* 26, 1476, to *John Harbiry* and *Richard Wartyr* clerks (*n*).

The meannefs of circumftances this unfortunate prelate was in at his death, or the fear of difobliging the king by it, is the reafon, I prefume, that no tomb, or fo much as a graveftone, was ever laid over him. But about five years ago in digging the foundation for filling up the arch in the dean's veftry, a grave was difcovered, where a body had been laid in a habit; a filver chalice gilt was on its right fide, and a pontifical ring, which I have feen, was faid to be found in the fame grave. If this laft circumftance be true, thefe probably might be the remains of *George Nevill*, for there was no particular ftone to mark that there was a grave of that confequence in the place. The chalice is now in the veftry; and the ring, at prefent, in the poffeffion of Mr. *Smith* in *Grape-lane*. But *Leland* mentions archbifhop *Nevill* and *Rotheram* to lie together in the north fide of our lady's chapel in the choir, fo that the matter is very difputable, as the reader will find in the fequel.

This *George Nevil* archbifhop held a provincial fynod in his metropolitical church at *York*, on the 26th day of *April*, in the year of our Lord 1466. In which fome new conftitutions were made, and feveral old ones eftablifhed. The preamble runs thus, "*George* "by divine permiffion archbifhop of *York*, primate of *England* and legate of the apoftolick "fee, to all and fingular abbots, priors, minifters, rectors, vicars, and other prelates of "the churches, and to all clerks and laymen of our diocefe and province of *York*, eternal "health in the Lord, &c." Thefe ordinancies are eleven in number (befides *Kemps*) and are dated in the metropolitan church of *York* as above (*o*).

LAURENCE BOTHE, *fifty third archbifhop*.

Lawrence Bothe, half brother to *William Bothe*, bifhop of *Durham*, was on *Nevill's* death tranflated to this fee. *September* 8, 1476, he was with great folemnity inftalled in the ca- A. 1476.

(*l*) *Hollingfhead*, *Stow*.
(*m*) The fame.

(*n*) Ex MS Torre p. 468.
(*o*) See *Johnfon fub anno* 1466

thedral

thedral of *York*; the patent reſtoring the temporalities to him bears date *October* 8. following (*p*).

(*q*) The preferments this man had gone through before he reached this dignity, was firſt maſter of *Pembroke-hall* in *Cambridge*, and rector of *Cottingham* in that county. He was after made dean of St. *Paul's London*; archdeacon of *Richmond* and *Stow*, and was beſides prebendary of *York*, *London* and *Litchfield*. He was conſtituted biſhop of *Durham*, *September* 15, 1457, and near twenty years after was tranſlated to *York*. Two years before this he had been made lord high chancellor of *England*, but held not that office above twelve months (*r*).

This prelate proved a good benefactor to his ſee, even in the ſhort time he enjoyed it; for he purchaſed the manor of *Batterſea*, *com. Surry*, of one *Nicholas Stanley*; and, after building an houſe upon it, ſettled it upon the church of *York*. Appointing his ſucceſſors to pay ſtipends to two chantry prieſts to celebrate for his and brother's ſouls in the church at *Southwell*. Which ſtipends, ſays Mr. *Willis*, are now given to the free ſchool at *Guilford* (*s*).

(*t*) This *Lawrence Bothe*, by divine providence archbiſhop of *York*, primate of *England*, and legate of the apoſtolick ſee, made his will dated *September* 28, 1479, and proved *July* 11, 1480, wherein he commended his ſoul to God almighty, St. *Mary*, St. *Peter*, and St. *Paul*, the apoſtles, St. *William*, St. *John*, St. *Wilfrid*, and all ſaints. And appointed his body to be buried in St. *John Baptiſt* chapel in the collegiate church of *Southwell*, on the ſouth ſide of the wall. On *Friday May* 19, 1480, he died at *Southwell*, after he had ſat here three years and nine months, and was there interred beſide his brother.

A. 1480. THOMAS SCOT, *alias de* ROTHERAM, *fifty fourth archbiſhop.*

On *Bothe's* death *Thomas Scot*, born at *Rotheram* in this county, from whence, according to the cuſtom of religious perſons in that age, he choſe his ſurname, was, by bull of pope *Calixtus* IV, bearing date at St. *Peter's July* 7, 1480, and publiſhed in the cathedral church *December* 12. following, tranſlated to this ſee. The king's patent reſtoring the temporalities bears date *September* 9, 1480 (*u*).

He firſt took ſuch education as the country where he was born, afforded him; and being ripe for the univerſity he was ſent by his friends to *Cambridge*. Here he was choſen fellow of *King's* college, and afterwards maſter of *Pembroke-hall*; and, being chaplain to king *Edward* IV, he was made prebendary of *Sarum* and *Beverley*, and keeper of the privy ſeal; then biſhop of *Rocheſter*, *anno* 1467, from thence he was removed to *Lincoln*, *anno* 1471, and having ſat nine years in that ſee, being alſo lord chancellor of *England*, he was removed to *York*.

(*x*) He was made chancellor *anno* 1475, in which office he continued all king *Edward's* days; but upon his death was committed to the *Tower*, by the protector, for delivering up the ſeals to the queen. In this place our prelate was kept cloſe priſoner under the cuſtody of Sir *James Tyrrel* for ſome time; till, upon the death of *Richard's* queen, he was releaſed in order to perſwade the queen dowager to give conſent that her daughter *Elizabeth* ſhould marry her uncle (*y*). In all probability this match would have taken place if *Richard's* death had not prevented it; but, whether the dowager was perſwaded by our prelate's rhetorick, or the fear that her daughter might ſhare the ſame fate with her ſons, if ſhe refuſed, is uncertain.

The publick benefactions that are aſcribed to this prelate are, that whan he was biſhop of *Lincoln*, he beſtowed a round ſum in building the gate of the ſchools at *Cambridge*, laying out the walks on each ſide thereof, and erecting the library which is, or was, on the eaſt of that building. All this was done at his own charge, ſays *Goodwin*, whilſt he was chancellor, with ſome ſmall contribution from the univerſity. The work was begun in 1470, and finiſhed in ſix years (*z*).

After he was tranſlated to *York*, he founded a college at *Rotheram*, the place of his nativity, by the name of *Jeſus college*, for a provoſt, five prieſts, ſix choriſters and three ſchoolmaſters; one for grammar, one for ſinging, and the laſt for writing. This college was valued, at the ſuppreſſion, at the yearly rent of fifty eight pound five ſhillings and nine pence half-penny, *Speed*. He finiſhed *Lincoln* college in *Oxford*, left very imperfect by *Robert Fleming* the firſt founder; and added five fellowſhips to it. In ſeveral of the palaces belonging to the ſee of *York* he built much. At *Whitehall* he erected the great kitchen; at *Southwell* the pantry, bakehouſe, and new chambers adjoining to the river. And at *Biſhopthorpe* the pantry, bakehouſe and chambers on the northſide towards, what was then called, the **woods** (*a*). He gave to the church of *York* a wonderfull rich mitre, with ſeveral other valuable jewels and ornaments, as the inventary teſtifies. He is ſaid

(*p*) Goodwin. *Foed.* Ang. *tom.* XII. *p.* 34. *Pat.* 16 Ed. IV. *m.* 17.
(*q*) *Goodwin*, *Torre*, p. 468.
(*r*) *Dugd.* chan.
(*s*) *Willis* on cathedral churches.
(*t*) *Ex MS* Torre, *p.* 468. *ex officio prerog.* Ebor.
(*u*) *Foed.* Ang. *tom.* XII. *p.* 136. Goodwin, Torre, &c. 1. *pat.* 20 Ed. IV. *m.* 3.
(*x*) *Spelm.* gloſſ. *Dugd.* chan.
(*y*) *Polidor. Virgil.*
(*z*) Goodwin *de praeſul.*
(*a*) *Stowe's* chron.

to
a

to have been very sollicitous in advancing those who either for good service or kindred could lay claim to his favours. Some by marriage, others by offices, temporal livings, or spiritual endowments (*b*).

(*c*) On the feast of St. *John*'s translation, *viz. August* 6, 1498, this *Thomas Rotheram*, archbishop of *York*, by his own decree and his clergy's assent, made his will, proved *November* 1502, whereby he commended his soul to almighty God, his creator and redeemer, to St. *Mary*, St. *Michael*, St. *Gabriel*, and divers of the apostles and saints; giving his body to be interred in the north arch, or arm, in the chapel of St. *Mary* in his church of *York* where he himself had erected a tomb. And having been born at *Rotheram*, and baptized in that church, he willed the foundation of a college there, and settled lands and revenues upon it very largely. Besides he gave to sir *Thomas Rotheram*, and his brother's eldest son, the manors of *Somerasse*, *Luton*, *Houghton*, *Fenells*, *Dobington*, *Aspley* and *Stopesley*, in the counties of *Bedford*, *Hartford* and *Bucks*.

He died of the plague at *Cawood*, *May* 29, 1500; in the seventy sixth year of his age; having governed this see nineteen years, nine months and some odd days. He was interred in the cathedral, on the north side the lady's chapel, according to his will; where his tomb is still standing, as represented in the plate; but robbed of the inscription, decorations in brass, and other *insignia*. On removing the pavement this last year a vault was discovered to run under this tomb, it was easily got to, in which the bones were laid, but nothing remarkable about them, save that a wooden head was found in it, exactly resembling a barber's block, and had a stick thrust into the neck to carry it on. This head is a piece of extraordinary sculpture for that age, but whether it be a representation of his own, or that of some titular saint I cannot determine. It seems most probable that it was a resemblance of his own, for dying of the plague, his body being buried immediately, an image, was substituted instead of it, for a more solemn and grand interment, of which this served for the head. A representation of it may be seen in the print of the furniture of the vestry, page 480.

Archbishop Rotheram.

(*b*) Goodwin.

(*c*) Ex MS. Torre, p. 229. ex officio prærog.

THOMAS

THOMAS SAVAGE, *fifty fifth archbishop.*

The next prelate was *Thomas Savage*, of a knightly family, as *Goodwin* relates from information. He was doctor of laws in *Cambridge*, though of a moderate character for learning; his genius leading more to a court life. Notwithstanding the deficiency in that point, he was by *Henry* VII, a prince well read in mankind, first made bishop of *Rochester*, then of *London*, and lastly translated to *York*. The bull of his translation being published in a solemn manner *February* 12, *anno* 1501.

Goodwin writes that this prelate was not elected to the see of *York*, after the antient custom; but nominated by the king, and confirmed by the pope. As he was singular in this instance so he was in another; for he was not installed in person, but stole it in a secret manner by a deputy. By which means he broke the antient custom of making a sumptuous feast at his installation; which had hitherto been always practised by his predecessors.

Our prelate is said to have been too much employed in temporal affairs, when at court, and in the country in hunting, a diversion he was passionately fond of, to mind the business of his see. He affected much grandeur, having, according to old *Stowe*, many tall yeomen for his guard. However he laid out much on his palaces of *Cawood* and *Scrooby*, which, it seems, were his peculiar hunting seats.

Having been seven years in this archbishoprick, he died at *Cawood September* 2, *anno* 1507, and was buried in our cathedral, where an handsome monument is still over him; in the top of which was a wooden closet, for a chantry, erected; and on the stone work above is inscribed **Doctor ✠ Savage ✠ London ✠ Yorke ✠ Rochester ✠ Thomas Dalby**, the name of an archdeacon of *Richmond*, who lies near him, formerly the archbishop's chaplain, who took care to erect this monument to his memory. *Goodwin* says, that he ordered his heart to be taken out of him and buried at *Macclesfield*, in *Cheshire*, where he was born; and intended to have founded a college, after the manner that his predecessor, had done at *Rotheram*.

Archbishop Savage.

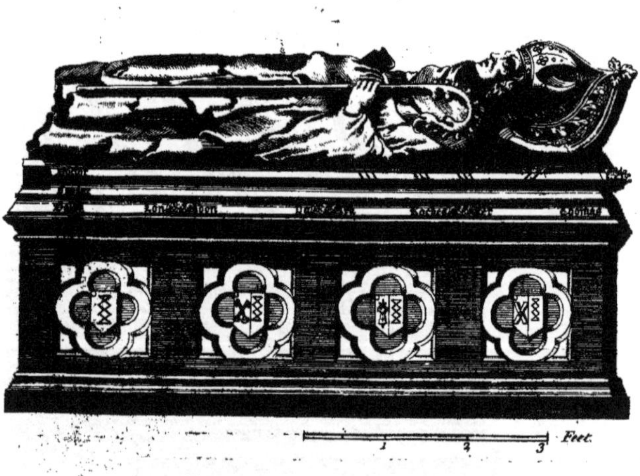

CHRISTOPHER BAYNBRIDGE, *fifty sixth archbishop.*

A. 1388. To him succeeded in this see *Christopher Bainbridge*, born, of an antient family, at *Hilton (d)*, near *Apleby* in *Westmorland*. He was brought up at *Queen's college Oxford*, commenced doctor of both laws in that university; was afterwards master of the *Rolls*, then made dean of *York*; on *November* 15, 1505, he was constituted lord chancellor of *England*,

(*d*) *Wood's* Athen. Oxon.

and 1507, consecrated bishop of *Durham*; from whence he was translated to *York*. The bull of whose translation, granted by pope *Julian* II, bore date at *Rome*, 12 *kal. Oct. anno* 1508; which was published before the chapter and a great appearance of clergy and people in the cathedral; and he had the temporalities restored *December* 12. following (*e*).

After he was invested with this last dignity, in the next year he was sent ambassador, or the king's (*f*) proctor, to the court of *Rome*, by *Henry* VIII, in order to settle a great difference betwixt the holy father and *Lewis* XII. king of *France*. Our prelate perswaded his king to take the pope's part in the quarrel; for which, says (*g*) *Ciaconius*, he was made a cardinal by the title of St. *Praxides*. Whether he staid so long at *Rome* or made a second journey to it I know not, but it is certain, that there our prelate met his fate, in an *Italian* dress, being poisoned by one *Rinaldo de Modena*, a priest, whom he had made his steward. It seems this *Italian* was disgusted at his master for giving him a blow, for which he played him that dogtrick, as the murderer himself confessed, according to *Paulus Jovius*, at his execution. But *Ciaconius* writes, that our prelate was a man of most insolent and violent passions; of great sourness of temper, both to his domesticks and others. And amongst those that he had beat and abused, it happened this *Modenese* his servant was one, who resented it so high as to poison his master. For which, being put into prison, to avoid a more shameful death, he took a dose of poison himself. His body was afterwards, adds he, cut in two, and placed upon the city gates.

The archbishop was buried in the hospital of St. *Thomas the martyr*, in *Rome*, in the second year of pope *Leo* X, with this epitaph,

Christophoro *archiepiscopo* Eboracensi *S.* Praxidis *presbytero cardinali* Angliae, *a* Julio II, *pontifice maximo ob egregiam operam* S. R: *ecclesiae praestitam, dum sui regni legatus esset, assumpto, quam mox domi, et foris, castris pontificiis praefectus, tutatus est.*

Obiit pridie idus Junii M DXIV.

THOMAS WOLSEY, *fifty seventh archbishop*.

The death of the last prelate made way for *Thomas Wolsey* to ascend yet higher than he A. 1514. had got, and to be preferred to this see. The life and death of this famous cardinal has been treated on by all our historians of, and since, his time; but most copiously and amply by the reverend Dr. *Fiddes*, in a particular treatise on that great subject. Here his original, rise, progress, exaltation and fall are set down in so large and just a manner, that I shall have little to do but run cursorily through the series of his wonderful life; that he may not be wholly neglected in this catalogue.

First then, he is said to have been the son of a poor man, a butcher, at *Ipswich*; from thence being sent very young to the university of *Oxford*, he was settled in *Magdalene* college; proceeded master of arts at fifteen years of age (*h*), and at that time was preferred to be master of the grammar school adjoining to that college. By the marquiss of *Dorset*, to whose son he was tutor, he was removed to a benefice in *Somersetshire* called *Limington* (*i*). At this place it was, that sir *Amias Pawlet* knight, a gentleman in his neighbourhood, did him some disgrace, undeservedly as it is said, but if we may give credit to sir *John Harrington*, an anteprelatical writer, whom I shall have often occasion to quote in the sequel, it was because, that *Wolsey* being concerned in a drunken fray, the knight set him in the stocks (*k*). Let this affront be what it would, *Wolsey* never forgave it; for when he was lord chancellor, and sir *Amias* having a suit to come before him, he made the knight dance attendance seven years 'ere the cause was suffered to pass through his hands. The marquiss of *Dorset* dying, *Wolsey* saw himself out of all likelihood of further preferment that way; and being made uneasy in his benefice, by that knight, he determined to forsake it, and boldly venture into the world to try his fortune. Soon after, it was his luck to meet with an old knight, one sir *John Naphent*; who had been long a courtier, and was then settled in an office of importance at *Calais*. *Wolsey* was his chaplain, but growing weary of it, his boundless spirit not brooking so narrow a confinement, he begged leave to resign; which his patron not only consented to, but, mindful of *Wolsey*'s services, whilst with him, he got him preferred to be one of the king's chaplains.

On this stage it was that *Wolsey*'s great genius had room to exert itself; he soon insinuated himself into the good graces of *Fox* bishop of *Winchester*, at that time chief councellor to *Henry* VII. By this prelate's means our chaplain was dispatched on some affairs of great moment to the emperor; which with incredible celerity he accomplished, and was back in four days, at court again, having ordered every thing to the king's content. From

(*e*) *Foed.* Ang. *tom.* XIII. *p.* 235. *Torre* says he was made dean of *York December* 18, 1503. p. 566.

(*f*) *Charta de arch.* Ebor. *procuratore in curia* Romana *constituto. dat.* Septem. 24, 1509. *Foed. tom.* XIII. *p.* 264.

(*g*) Alfrod. Ciaconius *hist. pont.* Rom. *et* S. R. E. *card.*

(*h*) *Athen.* Oxon. *Wood.*

(*i*) *Fuit rector eccles. de* Limington, Oct. 4, 1500. *Reg.* King *episc.* Bath *et* Wells.

(*k*) Sir *John Harrington*'s address to prince *Henry* on this prediction,

Henry the eighth pulled down monks, and their cells;
Henry the ninth shall pull down bishops and their bells. *London* 1653.

this time being looked upon by that wise monarch as a man fit for business and dispatch, he immediately bestowed upon him the deanry of *Lincoln*; and, soon after, made him his *almoner*.

Henry VIII. coming to the crown, *Wolsey* made it his whole business to gain the affections of the young king; and won so far upon him as to be appointed one of the privy council. Here he had an opportunity to dive deeper into that monarch's inclinations, which he soon found were not so wholly set upon business, but that pleasure had the greatest share in his heart. He complied with this humour of the king's as much as possible; diverting him from the toil of treaties and negotiations, that he might be more at leisure to mind his amours and gallantries. By this he gained his point; for the king, soon finding that he could do nothing without him, took *Wolsey* along with him to *Tournay*; where the bishop of that diocese being banished for siding with the *French*, the revenues thereof were bestowed on *Wolsey*. Soon after this, the see of *Lincoln* fell void, which was given to him *anno* 1514; and immediately after he was preferred to *York*; the bull of whose translation bore date at *Rome*, *October* 1, 1514, in the pontificate of *Leo* X; on the third of *December* following it was published to the chapter, clergy and people of *York*, and the same day he was installed, by proxy, in the cathedral.

Being now in the full stream of his good fortune, he procured the pope to constitute him his legate, *a latere*; and *September* 7, 1515, he was made a cardinal by the title of St. *Cicilia trans Tiberim*. The next year he got the archbishop of *Canterbury* displaced from being chancellor, and had it conferred upon himself. Thus great he still grew greater, and by exchanging of bishopricks when he had all at his devotion, he held, besides his other benefices which were innumerable, the bishoprick of *Winchester* and the abbey of St. *Albans in commendam*.

We see our prelate now like a meteor, at his height and the fullness of his lustre; which he no sooner arrived at but he more suddenly fell. For soon after his acceptance of the rich bishoprick of *Winchester*, the king's favour forsook him. He was first discharged from his chancellorship, then had all his goods and effects seized to his majesty's use; and himself ready to be attainted in parliament, had not his faithful servant *Thomas Cromwell* stood the shock, and warded off the blow. When that succeeded not, he was charged with exercising his legatine power without the king's licence; but this almost every body knew to be false; however, at length he was deprived of his preferments, and lived, for about half a year in great penury, one while at *Esher*, near *London*, and sometimes at *Richmond*, having all that time scarce a cup to drink in or a bed to lie on, but what was lent him by others; the king having taken all his goods and moveables of, almost, an inestimable value to his own use. Soon after this he was sent down to his diocese, where he lived at his palace of *Cawood*, a whole summer and some part of the winter, in a reasonable good sort; but as he was preparing for a publick installation at *York*, he was arrested of high treason by the earl of *Northumberland*; who had orders to bring him up to *London* to his trial. In the road, however, he slipped from all his enemies, dying at *Leicester*, of a flux attended with a continual fever, as is said, but no doubt the king's unkindness was the main occasion of it. After eight days illness, he resigned his last breath in the abbey of *Leicester*, *November* 29, 1530, and was buried in the body of the abbey church before the choir door. This prelate never was at *York*, though he came so near it as *Cawood*; which makes good a prophecy of mother *Shipton*, esteemed an *old witch* in those days, who foretold, he should see *York*, but never come at it. I should not have mentioned this idle story, but that it is fresh in the mouths of our country people at this day; but whether it was a real prediction, or raised after the event, I shall not take upon me to determine. It is more than probable, like all the rest of these kind of tales, the accident gave occasion to the story.

Thus ended the life of this great man; whose natural endowments, policies, apothegms, and learned speeches, port and grandeur, buildings, and publick benefactions may be found, in that incomparable piece of the life of *Henry* VIII, by the lord *Herbert* of *Cherbury*; *Stowe*'s annals; *Alph. Ciaconius* in his lives of the cardinals, *Wood*'s *Athenae Oxonienses*, or altogether in Dr. *Fiddes*'s history of this cardinal; the clearest and liveliest performance in *biography* this age has produced.

After all, our prelate is a sad example to the present and future ages, how uncertain the dependance is on a monarch's favour. The words he spoke in the bitterness of his soul, in his last agonies, ought to be inscribed in large characters in every apartment of a *chief minister's* house, as a special *memento* to him.

If I had served my GOD with half the zeal that I have served my KING, he would not, in my grey hairs, have thus forsaken me (*l*).

(*l*) This man's greatness is the shortest exemplified in the collection of letters and negotiations, pensions from foreign princes, he had and was engaged in, from his acceptance of this archbishoprick to his fall. They are to be seen in *Rymer*'s publick acts under these titles.

Edward

EDWARD LEE, *fifty eighth archbishop.*

The see having been void, by the death of cardinal *Wolsey*, almost a year, the king thought fit to prefer unto it his almoner *Edward Lee, S. T. P*; brought up for a time in *Magdalene* college in *Oxford*, where he proceeded batchelor of arts; but, removing from thence to *Cambridge*, he took his other degrees in that university. He had been archdeacon of *Colchester*, prebendary of *York* and *Salisbury*, was sent abroad on several important embassies, particularly to the pope at *Bononia* on the intricate affair of queen *Catherine*'s marriage. Soon after his return from this last embassy, he was by bull of pope *Clement* VII, dated *October* 30, 1531, promoted to the see of *York*. He was consecrated *December* 10, next following, was inthroned by proxy the seventeenth of the same month; and *April* 1, 1534, was installed in proper person *(m)*. A. 1531.

Being much employed by the king, as a statesman, he had not leisure to visit his diocese till some years after his first installment; as appears by the last mentioned dates. In the year 1536, the rebellion called the *pilgrimage of grace* began; when our prelate with the lord *Darcy* were seized upon, by the rebels, and carried prisoners to *Pontfrett* castle. They obliged them both to take an oath to be true to their party, *&c.* for which the lord *Darcy*, afterwards lost his head, but the archbishop was pardoned *(n)*.

In this man's time the *Reformation* had made a great progress, though I do not find him concerned at all in it. It was now, also, that alienations from this see first began; for by indenture dated *November* 12, 1542, the manors of *Beverley*, *Southwell*, *Skidby*, and *Bishop-Burton*, were exchanged with the crown for the dissolved priory of *Marton cum Membris*, in this county; and other manors formerly belonging to religious houses; such as *Kilburn*, *Sutton* under *Whitsoncliff*, &c. *(o)* But this was no very ill bargain, the church

T. XIII. *p.* 412. *Pro episcopo* Lincolnien. *electo* Eboracensi. *dat.* Aug. 5. 1514.
439. *Litera regis* Francorum *electo* Ebor. T. Wolsey. *dat.* Sept. 2, 1514.
507. *De custodia mag. sigill. commissa arch.* Ebor. *dat.* Maii 15, 1515.
525. *Promissio secretarii ducis* Mediolani *pro* 10000 *ducat. solvend. sing. annis card.* Ebor. *dat.* Oct. 19, 1515.
529. *De liberatione magni sigill. card.* Ebor. *et ejusdem juramento, dat.* Decem. 22, 1515.
530. *Pro card.* Ebor. *archiep. de custodia commissa*, Jan. 29, 1516.
573. *Pro card.* Ebor. *super lite in curia* Romana *pendente de potestatibus dat.* Decem. 22, 1516.
591. *De pensione pro card.* Ebor. *per regem* Castellae, *dat.* Jun. 8, 1517.
584. *Charta pro card.* Ebor. *de administratione episcop.* Turnacensis *in spiritual. et temporalibus concessa, dat.* Ap. 15, 1517.
598. *Pro card.* Ebor. *bulla decimarum, dat.* Aug. 24, 1517.
605. *De potestatibus card.* Ebor. *exemplificatio*, Maii 6, 1518.
609. *Super privatione* Adriani *cardinalis bulla pro card.* Ebor. Jul. 30, 1518.
691. *De potestatibus commissio regis* Francorum *pro card.* Ebor. Jan. 10, 1519.
703. *Pro domino card.* Ebor. Oct. 24, 1519.
714. *Pro card.* Ebor. *pensio imperatoris*, Mar. 29, 1520.
718. *Pensio ducis* Venet. *card.* Ebor. Maii 5, 1520.
725. *Bulla de pensione card.* Ebor. Jul 7, 1520.
742. *Bulla pro card.* Ebor. *de potestatibus super lectione librorum* Martini Lutheri, Ap. 17, 1521.
749. *Pro card.* Ebor. *commissio ad tractand. cum rege* Francorum, Jul. 29, 1521.
786. Anthonius Grimanus Venetiarum *dux ad card.* Ebor. Mar. 9, 1523.
788. *Pro card.* Ebor. Thom. *archiep.* Ap. 24, 1523.
795. *Prorogatio legationis per papam* Adrianum *pro card.* Ebor. Jun. 12, 1523.
T. XIV. *p.* 96. Andreas Gritti *dux* Venetiarum *ad card.* Ebor. Oct. 1, 1525.
100. *De pensione per regentem* Franciae *per card.* Ebor. Novem. 18, 1525.
T. XIV. *p.* 121. Franciscus Sforza *dux* Mediolani *ad card.* Ebor. Feb. 7, 1526.
128. *Ducis* Mediolani *literae card.* Ebor. Mar. 12, 1526.
155. *De monasteriis suppressis et collegio card.* Ebor. *concessis* Maii 1, 1526.
174. *Pro domino card.* Ebor. *licentia impropriandi* Maii 10, 1526.
179. *Dux* Venetiarum *ad card.* Ebor. *pro collegio card.* Ebor. Jul. 23, 1526.
180. *Pro collegio card.* Ebor. *in* Oxonia, Jul. 24, 1526.
196. *Rex* Poloniae *ad card.* Ebor. Maii 7, 1527.
202. *Commissio card.* Ebor. *ad carceratos deliberandos*, Jul. 14, 1527.
212. *Tractatus regis* Francorum *in propria persona cum card.* Ebor. *de generali concilio non indicendo confirmatio, dat.* Aug. 18, 1527.
217. *Instrumentum juramentorum regis* Francisci *et card.* Ebor. *dat. ut supra.*
230. *Acquietatio mercatorum de* Luca *ad instantiam card.* Ebor. Sept. 25, 1527.
239. *Pro card.* Ebor. *facultas ad degradand. clericos* Maii 28, 1528.
268. *Pro card.* Ebor. *de custodia temporalium* Winton. *concess.* Oct. 20, 1528.
287. *Pro card.* Ebor. *cura de* Winton. *ecclesiae et provisione papali* Feb. 1529.
289. *Papa ad vassales* Wintonienses *pro card.* Ebor.
299. *De commissariis ad audiend. causas in cancellaria ad relevamen card.* Ebor. Jun. 11, 1529.
350. *De attornatis card.* Ebor. *constitutis.*
350. *Pro domino rege ad recuperationem contra card.* Ebor. *dat.* Feb. 7, 1530.
371. *Indentura inter regem et dom. card.* Ebor. Feb. 17, 1530.
402. *Super possessionibus card.* Ebor. *de inquirendo*, Jul. 15, 1530.
408. *Super extinctione card.* Ebor. *de concessionibus*, Decem. 5, 1530.

N. B. The cardinal died *November* 29, 1530, of what illness is easy to be guessed by the course and nature of these last instruments.

(*m*) *Goodwin*, *Torre*, p. 472.

(*n*) *Stowe*'s annals, *Hollingshead*'s chron, *&c.*

(*o*) Chapel of the *Rolls*.

suffered

ſuffered little by the exchange; eſpecially when compared with the great devaſtation made in the time of his immediate ſucceſſor.

Edward ſat archbiſhop of this ſee thirteen years, and died *September* 13, 1544; he was buried in his own church, in the ſouth choir, where a large blew marble ſtone was laid over him; with the effigies of a biſhop in braſs to the waiſt, and four eſcutcheons of arms, as Mr. *Dodſworth* writes, but they were long ſince torn off. Upon removal of this ſtone for the new pavement his remains appeared, laid in a walled grave, but nothing remarkable was found, beſides his epiſcopal ring, which is now in the dean's cuſtody. I ſhall conclude my account of this prelate with a character given him by his contemporary *Polidore Virgil*, which may ſerve as an addition to his epitaph; which epitaph, as preſerved by Mr. *Dodſworth* is as follows,

Edwardus Leeus archiepiſcopus Eboracenſis theologus eximius, atque in omnium bonarum literarum longe eruditiſſimus, ſapientie et vite ſanctitate clarus, evangelice doctrine ſyncerum preconem ſemper agens, pauperibus beneficus, omnibus ordinibus juxta clarus, magno de ſe apud omnes deſiderio relicto hic ſepultus jacet. Sedit archiepiſcopus annis paulo minus xiii, obiit ſexto Septembris etatis anno LXII, anno Christi M.DXLIIII.

Edwardus Leeus, *vir natura frugi*, *ſanctus*, *religioſus*, Latinis *pariter atque* Graecis, Hebraicis *literis eruditus*, *ac ſumma in noſtra theologia probatus* (p).

ROBERT HOLGATE, *fifty ninth archbiſhop.*

A. 1544. Before the end of the ſame year *Robert Holgate* D. D. born, ſays *Willis*, at *Hemſworth*, near *Pontfrete*, in this county, found means with the king to be tranſlated from the biſhoprick of *Landaff* to this ſee. This man was bred up amongſt the *Gilbertine* monks at *Sempringham* in *Lincolnſhire*, and was afterwards prior of *Watton* in this county. On ſurrendring up his priory he had firſt a benefice in *Lincolnſhire*; but ſir *Francis Aſkue*, a gentleman in his neighbourhood, proving very troubleſome, by commencing a vexatious lawſuit againſt him, he quitted the living and came to *London*. He found means ſoon after to be made one of the king's chaplains; and *Henry* finding him a very fit man for his purpoſe, being a buſy ſtickler in the *Reformation*, firſt promoted him to the ſee of *Landaff*, and next tranſlated him hither, *January* 10, 1544.

Within a month after his tranſlation it was eaſy to ſee what was *Henry*'s deſign in it, for our prelate paſſed away to the king, as it is ſaid in one morning, thirteen manors in *Northumberland*, forty in *Yorkſhire*, ſix in *Notinghamſhire*, and eight in *Gloceſterſhire*; all belonging to this ſee. In lieu of which he obtained thirty three impropriations and advowſons, which came to the crown by the diſſolution of ſome monaſteries in the north parts; a further account of which will be given in the next chapter. By theſe, and other ſuch unworthy meaſures, he greatly impoveriſhed his ſee, but amaſſed great riches to himſelf, beyond what any other biſhop in *England* was then maſter of; how long this ill gotten wealth continued with him will appear in the ſequel.

Our prelate, now grown to a fullneſs of riches and power, and forgetting his vow of *celibacy*, thought fit to take unto himſelf a wife. I find in a ritual of one *Robert Perkins*, a prieſt in the nunnery of *Hampole* in this county, that banns of marriage were publiſhed at *Biſhopthorp*, and at *Aithwick in the ſtreet*, near *Doncaſter*, betwixt *Barbara Wentworth*, daughter of *Roger Wentworth*, eſq; and *Robert* archbiſhop of *York*. They were married, ſays my authority (q) who was contemporary, and lived in the neighbourhood of *Aithwick*, publickly *January* 15, 1549; but, adds he, one Dr. *Tonge* ſaid in court that he had married them privately ſome time before. It ſeems this lady had been betrothed and was actually married, in her childhood, to a young gentleman called *Anthony Norman*; which her parents thought fit to ſet aſide, and our prelate made no ſcruple to break through the engagement. *Norman*, we find, was not paſſive in this affair, (r) but in the reign of *Edward* VI. actually petitioned the king and council to have his wife reſtored him. The matter occaſioned a great conteſt betwixt the two huſbands; but our prelate held faſt by the *apron-ſtrings*, till the beginning of the reign of queen *Mary*, when he was not only diſpoſſeſſed of his wife, but all his great riches ſeized on, and himſelf ſent priſoner to the *Tower*. This ſtroke was made at him, not ſo much for being a married biſhop, as *Goodwin* himſelf writes, but for oppoſing that princeſs's title to the crown. Though he, as well as ſome more biſhops, were hardlier dealt with, by reaſon, that being brought up in religious houſes, they had taken vows of celibacy.

When *Robert* had lain priſoner a year and half in the *Tower*, he was, by procurement of king *Philip*, releaſed from his confinement. After this he retired to *Hemſworth* his native place; where he died, and was ſo obſcurely buried that though I ſearched the church of

(p) There are ſeveral books, writings, letters, &c. ſaid to be compoſed and written by this prelate; a catalogue of which is extant in *Wood's Athen. Oxon.* vol I.

(q) Manuſcript at preſent, in the cuſtody of ſir *Brian Cook* bart. of *Wheatly*. A curious piece on ſeveral accounts.

(r) *Goodwin*, *Burnet*'s hiſt. reform.

that

I

that place, and enquired of tradition for it I cou'd learn no account of his grave. What time he died is alſo uncertain; but Mr. *Willis* has given us a ſhort abſtract of his will, which he ſays was proved *December* 4, 1556. (*s*).

There are however ſome acts of piety recorded of this archbiſhop; and, which is more remarkable, are ſtill ſubſiſting. He founded and endowed three free ſchools, *viz.* at *York*, *Old-Melton* and at *Hemſworth*; the original foundation deed is now amongſt our city records; an account of which, in regard to the ſchool at *York*, I ſhall give in its proper place. There is a remarkable ſtory alſo told of him, which, if true, ſhews him a perſon of a more forgiving temper than his predeceſſor *Wolſey*; in a caſe ſomewhat parallel. This archbiſhop, being lord preſident of the north, ſir *Francis Aſkue*, the knight aforementioned, happened to have a ſuit depending in that court. Doubting much of hard meaſure from the preſident, whoſe adverſary he had been, he gave up his cauſe for loſt. When, contrary to his expectation, he found the archbiſhop, according to juſtice, to ſtand up in favour of him, by which means he gained his cauſe. The prelate ſaying merrily to ſome of his friends, that he was more obliged to ſir *Francis* than any man in *England*; for had it not been for his puſhing him to *London*, he had lived a poor prieſt all his days (*t*).

NICHOLAS HEATH, *ſixtieth archbiſhop.*

Nicholas Heath, a *Londoner* born, was doctor of divinity in *Cambridge*, and afterwards almoner to king *Henry* VIII. His next preferment was that, *anno* 1539, he was conſecrated biſhop of *Landaff*, and the ſame year was removed to *Rocheſter*; where he did not ſit above four years till he was tranſlated to *Worceſter*. In the time of *Edward* VI, he was deprived of the biſhoprick of *Worceſter*, for refuſing to take the oath of ſupremacy, but queen *Mary* reſtored him again in the beginning of her reign, and alſo made him lord preſident of *Wales*. He was ſoon after tranſlated to *York*, the bull of pope Paul IV, which confirmed his election thereto, and is the laſt inſtrument of that kind acknowledged in this ſee, bears date 11 *kal. Julii*, *anno* 1555. On the third of *October* following, the pall was ſent him for the plenary adminiſtration of his office, and on the twenty ſecond of *January* the ſame year, he was ſolemnly inſtalled and inthroned in perſon (*u*). A. 1555.

Whilſt he ſat here, as archbiſhop, he made it his buſineſs to retrieve what was loſt from the ſee by his predeceſſors; and by his intereſt in queen *Mary* he obtained *Suffolk-houſe* in *Southwark*, in recompence for *White-hall*. But this being at too great a diſtance from court he procured inſtead thereof *York-place* in the *Strand*; which himſelf and ſucceſſors enjoyed, till king *James* I, to pleaſe the duke of *Buckingham*, exchanged it with archbiſhop *Mathews* for lands elſewhere. Our prelate alſo prevailed upon the queen to reſtore *Ripon* lordſhip, with ſeven other manors, members thereof, alienated by *Holgate*; *Southwell* he alſo got reverted, and five more manors in *Nottinghamſhire*. Inſomuch, that it may be truly ſaid, that the ſee of *York* owes to queen *Mary*, and this archbiſhop, more than a third part of its preſent revenues (*x*).

Upon *Stephen Gardiner*'s death, *Nicholas* being then archbiſhop of *York*, was conſtituted lord chancellor of *England*; which place he held all the reign of queen *Mary*. Upon the death of this princeſs, he, by his authority, called together the nobility and commons in parliament then lately aſſembled, but diſſolved by her demiſe, and gave order for proclaiming of *Elizabeth* (*y*). A circumſtance the more remarkable, in that immediately upon her acceſſion to the crown, our prelate was deprived; though not ſo much for want of loyalty to her perſon, and right of ſucceſſion, as for his religion; in which he always kept ſteady to the church of *Rome* (*z*). The queen however paid ſuch regard to his merit, that ſhe ſuffered him to retire to a ſmall eſtate he had at *Cobham* in *Surrey*. Here it was that he ſpent the remainder of his days, unmoleſted, in a ſtudious and religious manner, and free from harbouring any thoughts of faction or revenge. He died in this place *anno* 1566, and was buried in the chancel of the church there, under a blue ſtone, as our writers inform us, and the inhabitants have ſtill a tradition (*a*).

The author of the lives of the lords chancellors gives this prelate the character of being " a very wiſe and learned man; of deep policy, yet greater integrity. More devout to " purſue the dictates of his own conſcience, than cruel to perſecute others. In ſhort he " was ſo moderate and free from violent extreams, that in the diſputations betwixt the pa- " piſts and proteſtants, in the firſt year of queen *Elizabeth*, he was choſen one of the mo- " derators; ſir *Nicholas Bacon* being the other.

(*s*) *Dodſworth*'s collections vol. 118. p. 80. *V. Librum* Kitchin *in curia prerogat.* Cant.

(*t*) Sir *John Harrington.*

(*u*) *Goodwin*, *Torre*, 473.

(*x*) *Iidem et* Willis.

(*y*) An inſtrument in the *Foedera* bears this title, *Pro archiepiſcopo* Eborum *cancellario* Angliae *de exoneratione dat.* Feb. 8, 1556. *tom.* XV. *p.* 429.

(*z*) *MS.* ſir *T. W.*

(*a*) *Harrington. Willis.*

THOMAS YOUNG, *sixty first archbishop.*

A. 1560. Upon the deprivation of the former in the year 1560, *Henry Maye*, LL. D. dean of St. *Paul*'s, was certified to the queen, by the dean and chapter of *York*, to be elected to this archbishoprick. But this man dying before consecration, *Thomas Young*, LL. D. bishop of St. *Davids*, was translated to this see; to which he was elected, according to the queen's *conge de elire* (c), *Feb.* 3, 1560; and about the same time was constituted lord president of the north.

This man being the first protestant archbishop of this see, I could have wished that he had deserved a better character than sir *John Harington*, Mr. *Le Neve* or Mr. *Willis* have given him. Mr. *Le Neve* has published the lives, *&c.* of the protestant archbishops of both sees (d); the book is so lately printed, and almost in every body's hands, that I shall have little occasion to swell this volume with any thing else than a bare recital of the promotions, deaths, burials, *&c.* of our protestant prelates from this period.

Young, was indeed a very remarkable one; for his chief care, whilst he sat archbishop, was providing for himself and family; by settling the estates of the best prebends upon them. In his elderly years he married a lady, by whom he had a son, afterwards sir *George Young*, knight. To get an estate for this son, the father took the most unjustifiable means possible, and actually pulled down the great hall in the old and magnificent archiepiscopal palace at *York*. This was for the lucre of the lead upon it, *plumbi sacra fames*, says *Harrington*, which made him destroy a building erected near five hundred years before, by *Thomas* the elder, his predecessor. Sir *John* is very severe upon him for this deed, and wishes some of the lead had been melted and poured down his throat for it; however, he adds, that it did him not much good, being tricked out of a ship-load sent up to *London* for sale; by the subtlety of a courtier, to whom the archbishop had made great protestations of his extream poverty (e).

Having ruled this see seven years and six months he died at *Sheffield-Manor*, a seat of the then earl of *Shrewsbury*'s, *June* 26, 1568, and was buried in the north side the quire, in a vault, over which a blue marble was laid, which once bore an epitaph and escutcheons of arms upon it, but they are all now gone. He was the first protestant, *English*, bishop that died in queen *Elizabeth*'s days; though she survived many of those whom she had promoted. His epitaph Mr. *Dodsworth* has preserved and given us as follows:

Thomas Youngus nuper Eboracensis archiepiscopus civilis juris doctor peritissimus, quem propter gravitatem, summum ingenium, excellentemque rerum politicarum scientiam illustrissima regina Eliz. **septentrionalibus hujus regni partibus praesidem constituit, quo magistratu quinque annos perfunctus est. Sedit archiepiscopus annos septem et sex menses, obiit vicesimo die mensis Junii anno Domini millesimo quingentesimo sexagesimo octavo.**

EDMOND GRINDAL, *sixty second archbishop.*

A. 1570. Upon the deprivation and imprisonment of *Edmund Bonner* bishop of *London*, *Edmund Grindal* was placed in that see; his preferments before were first fellow, then master of *Pembroke-hall* in *Cambridge*. After a vacancy of near two years from the death of *Young*, *Grindal* was translated to *York*; and had the temporalities restored to him *June* 1, 1570 (f). Here he sat till *Feb.* 15, 1575, when he was translated to *Canterbury*.

EDWIN SANDYS, *sixty third archbishop.*

A. 1576. *Edwin Sandys* was doctor of divinity, and master of *Catherine-hall* in *Cambridge*, he was vice-chancellor of that university at the time when the lady *Jane Grey* was proclaimed queen there. He preached a sermon, by the order of the duke of *Northumberland*, in defence of lady *Jane*'s title; for which he was thrown into prison by queen *Mary*. He continued a prisoner near a year, and being at length discharged he fled into *Germany*, where he lived all the days of queen *Mary*. Returning then to *England*, he was soon distinguished by her successor; and was appointed one of the eight divines who were to hold a disputation against the *Romanists*, before the two houses of parliament at *Westminster*. *Anno* 1559. he was consecrated bishop of *Worcester*, and 1570. removed thence to *London*; where having sat six years he was at last translated to *York*. He was enthronized, by proxy, *March* 13, 1576, and had the temporalities restored *March* 16. following (g).

The life of this prelate is given at length in *Le Neve*'s account of the protestant bishops of this see; to which Mr. *Willis* has added some remarks. It would be needless in me to

(c) *Licentia eligendi* Eborum. *Dat.* Jul. 25, 1560. *Goodwin. Foed. tom.* XV. *p.* 599.

(d) *London* 1720.

(e) See the story at large in *Harrington*'s addition to

(f) *Foed. Ang. tom.* XV. *p.* 682.

(g) *Foed. Ang. tom.* XV. *p.* 771.

repeat

repeat what has been already publiſhed of him by thoſe authors; or to give the reader ſir *John Harington*'s ſtory of this prelate and the hoſteſs of *Doncaſter*. The quarel betwixt ſir *Robert Stapylton* and the archbiſhop, about this laſt named affair, fell heavy on the knight; who underwent a grievous cenſure and fine in the ſtar-chamber for it. But to ſee how a revolution of ſomewhat more than an age eraſes all diſcords in families, the late ſir *John Stapylton* of *Myton*, bart. a lineal deſcendant from ſir *Robert*, married an heireſs of this archbiſhop's houſe, without either of them knowing any thing of the inveterate hatred that had been betwixt their progenitors. Give me leave, ſince I have mentioned ſir *John Stapylton*, to bewail the untimely and unfortunate loſs of that moſt worthy gentleman; which would have been greater, did he not ſeem yet to live in the perſon of his eldeſt ſon and ſucceſſor. From the aforeſaid marriage proceded a numerous progeny, and may they, as they ſeem to promiſe, increaſe, flouriſh and deſcend, endowed with all the virtues of their parents and anceſtors to the lateſt ages.

Our prelate continued in this ſee near eleven years, and died at *Southwell July* 10, 1588, and was interred in that collegiate church; where he lyes in the north corner of the choir under a monument, which bears the form and inſcription repreſented in the plate. Mr. *Torre* has given us the preamble to his will from our prerogative office, dated *Aug.* 1, 1587. in this manner, "This *Edwyn Sandys*, miniſter of God's word and ſacraments, made his "will, proved *Nov.* 16, 1588, whereby he commends his ſoul into the hands of God al-"mighty, his creator, hoping to be ſaved through the merits of *Jeſus Chriſt*; and beque-"thed his body decently to be buried, *&c.*

"Then gave all his plate, of which he had great ſtore, amongſt his children and bre-"thren, and conſtituted *Cecily* his wife ſole executrix *(i)*. E. EBOR.

But in the preamble to this prelate's will there is a more remarkable paragraph than what Mr. *Torre* has extracted from it; which, as it contains the ſubſtance of his faith, at a time when the *Reformation* was very young in the *Engliſh* church, I ſhall beg leave to tranſcribe *verbatim.*

"*Thirdly*, Becauſe I have lived an old man in the miſterie of *Chriſt*, a faithful diſpoſer "of the miſteries of God, and to my power, an earneſt labourer in the vineyard of "the lord, I teſtifie before God and his angels and men of this world I reſt reſolute "and yield up my ſpirit in that doctrine which I have privately ſtudied and publickly "preached, and which is this day maintained in the church of *England*, both taking "the ſame to be the whole councill of God, the word and bread of eternal life, the foun-"tain of living water, the power of God unto ſalvation unto all them that believe, and be-"ſeeching the lord beſides ſoe to turn us unto him that we may be turned; leſt, if we repent "not, the candleſtick be moved out of its place, and the goſpel of the kingdom for our un-"thankfullneſs be taken from us and given to a nation that ſhall bring forth the fruites "thereof. And further proteſting in an upright conſcience of mine owne, and in the "knowledge of his majeſty before whom I ſtand, that in the preaching of the truth of "*Chriſt* I have not laboured to pleaſe man, but ſtudied to ſerve my maſter, who ſent me not "to flatter either prince or people, but by the law to tell all ſorts of their ſinns, by the "ſpirit to rebuke the world of ſinne, of righteouſneſs and judgment, by the goſpell "to teſtify of that faith which is in *Jeſus Chriſt* and him crucifyed. *Fourthly*, concerning "rights and ceremonies by political conſtitutions authoriſed amongſt us, as I am and have "been perſuaded that ſuch as are now ſett downe by publick authority in this church of "*England*, are no way either ungodly or unlawful, but may with good conſcience, for or-"der and obedience ſake, be uſed of a good chriſtian; for the private baptiſme to be mi-"niſtered by women, I take neither to be preſcribed nor permitted, ſo have I ever been "and preſently am perſuaded, that ſome of them be not ſoe expedient in this church now, "but that in the church reformed, and in all this time of the goſpell wherein the ſeed of "ſcripture hath ſo long been ſown, they may better be diſuſed by little and little, than "more and more urged; howbeit as I doe eaſily acknowledge our eccleſiaſticall pollite "in ſome points may be bettered, ſoe doe I utterly miſlike even in my conſcience "all ſuch rude and indigeſted platformes as have been more lately and boldly then "either learnedly or wiſely preferred, tending not to the reformation, but to the "deſtruction of the church of *England*, particularities of both ſorts reſerved to the "diſcretion of the godly wiſe; of the latter I only ſay this, that the ſtate of a ſmall "private church, and the forme of a learned chriſtian kingdome, neither would long "like nor can at all brooke one and the ſame eccleſiaſtical government. Thus much "I thought good to teſtify concerning theſe eccleſiaſtical matters to clear me from all "ſuſpicion of double and indirect dealing in the houſe of God, wherein as touching mine "office I have not halted but walked ſincerely according to that ſkill and ability which I "received at God's mercyful hands. Lord, as a great ſinner by reaſon of my fraile fleſh

(h) I have ſeen a volume of ſermons, publiſhed *anno* 1583. 4to, wrote by this archbiſhop; the ſtyle and manner far exceeds any thing I have yet met with amongſt the *Engliſh* writers of that age. The book was in the poſſeſſion of the late lady *Stapylton*. A copy of this archbiſhop's letter to queen *Eliz.* publiſhed in *Le Neve*, was alſo communicated to that author, from that lady, though ſent him by ſir *Brian Stapylton* her huſband's father.

(i) *MS.* Torre, 476.

"and

"and manifold infirmities. I flee unto thee for mercy, Lord forgive me my sins, for I acknowledge my sinns; lord performe thy promise, and doe away all my iniquities, haste the comeing of thy *Christ*, and deliver me from this body of sin, *veni cito domine Jesu*, cloth me with immortality, and give me that promised crown of glory, so be it."

I shall add *Fuller*'s character of this prelate, to conclude my account of him. "He was, says he, an excellent and painful preacher, of a pious and godly life, which increased in his old age; so that by a great and good stride, whilst he had one foot in the grave he had the other in heaven. He was buried in *Southwell*, it is hard to say whether he was more eminent in his own vertues, or more happy in his flourishing posterity *(k)*." The epitaph which was on his tomb ran thus:

Edwinus Sandes sacre theologie doctor, postquam Wigorniensem episcopat. xi. annos, totidemque tribus demptis, Londinensem gessisset; Eboracensis sui archiepiscopatus anno xv. vite autem lxix. obiit Julii x. anno Dom. 1588.

Cujus hic conditum cadaver jacet, genere non humilis, vixit dignitate locoque magnus; exemplo major, duplici functus episcopatu, archiepiscopali tandem amplitudine etiam illustris: Honores hosce mercatus grandi pretio, meritis virtutibusque. Homo hominum a malitia et vindicta innocentissimus, magnanimus, apertus, et tantum nescius adulari; summe liberalis atque misericors, hospitalissimus, optimus, facilis, & in sola vitia superbus: Scilicet haud minora quam loquutus est; vixit, & fuit. In Evangelii praedicandi laboribus ad extremum usque halitum mirabiliter assiduus. A sermonibus ejus nunquam non melior discederes. Facundus volebat esse, et videbatur: Ignavos, sedulitatis suae conscius, oderat. Bonas literas auxit pro facultatibus: Ecclesiae patrimonium, velut rem Deo Sacratam decuit, intactum defendit. Gratia qua floruit apud illustrissimam mortalium Elizabetham *effecit, ne hanc in qua jaces ecclesiam tu jacentem cerneres, venerande praesul. Utriusque memorandum fortunae exemplar, qui tanta cum gesseris, multo his majora animo ad omnia semper impavido perpessus est. Carceres, exilia, amplissimarum facultatum amissiones, quodque omnium difficillimum, innocens perferre animus consuevit immanes calumnias; et hac re una votis tuis minor, quod* Christo *testimonium etiam sanguine non praebueris. Attamen qui in prosperis tantos fluctus, & post agonum tot adversa, tandem quietis sempiternae portum, fessus mundi, deique sitiens reperisti. Aeternum laetare, vice sanguinis sunt sudores tui. Abi, lector, nec ista scias tantum ut sciveris, sed ut imitere, Verbum Domini manet in aeternum.*

JOHN PIERS, *sixty fourth archbishop.*

A. 1588. *John Piers*, was born of plebejan parents, says *Wood*, at *South-Henxsey* near *Abingdon* in *Bucks*. He had his academical education in *Magdalene* college, *Oxford*; commenced doctor of divinity, and was dean of *Christ-church* in that university. He was afterwards made bishop of *Rochester* and the queen's almoner; from thence he was removed to *Salisbury*, where having sat eleven years he was translated to *York*. And on the 27*th* of *February* 1588. was installed, by proxy, in our cathedral.

He is said to be a man that was master of all kinds of learning, and beloved by every one for his humanity, excellent behaviour and generosity. The last of which vertues he exercised to such a degree that he scarce left at his death sufficient, as is said, to erect a monument to his memory. The small one set up in the church for him having been placed there, as the inscription intimates, by Dr. *Bennett* one of his grateful chaplains and testimentary heir to what he left behind him. In his younger years, when he resided on a small living in *Oxfordshire*, he fell into an excess of drinking and keeping mean company; but upon being admonished of it by a grave divine he quite forsook that course, and followed his studies so hard that he deservedly attained to great honours and preferments. He was was in great favour with queen *Elizabeth*, who, as I said, made him her almoner; and he must be a wise and good man whom that thrifty princess, says *Fuller*, would trust with the distribution of her monies. He lived and died with the character of one of the most grave and reverend prelates of his age; and, after his reduced life, was so abstemious, that, in his advanced years, when his constitution required such a support, his physician could not persuade him to drink any wine. So habituated he was then to sobriety, and bore such a detestation to his former excess.

This primitive bishop lived in a state of celibacy all his days; and died at *Bishopthorp*, *Sept.* 28, 1594, having leased nothing from the church, nor hurt its revenues. He was buried in the third chapel, called *All-saints* chapel, at the east of the cathedral, under the window. Where his monument, as it is here exhibited, was placed, till it was removed to make way for the fine tomb of the honourable *Thomas Wentworth*. It is now put over a door in the corner, and bears this inscription:

Joannes Piers *sacrae theologiae doctor coelebs, postquam decanatu* Cestriae, *ecclesiae* Christi *in academia* Oxon. *et* Sarisburiae *functus esset, ac postquam episcopatus* Roffensem *viginti menses*, Sarisburiensem *undecim plus minus annos gessisset*, Eboracensis *sui episcopatus anno sexto, vitae autem septuagesimo primo, obiit* 28 Septembris, *anno Dom.* 1594; *cujus hic repositum est cadaver.*

(k) Fuller's church history.

Archbishop Sandes.

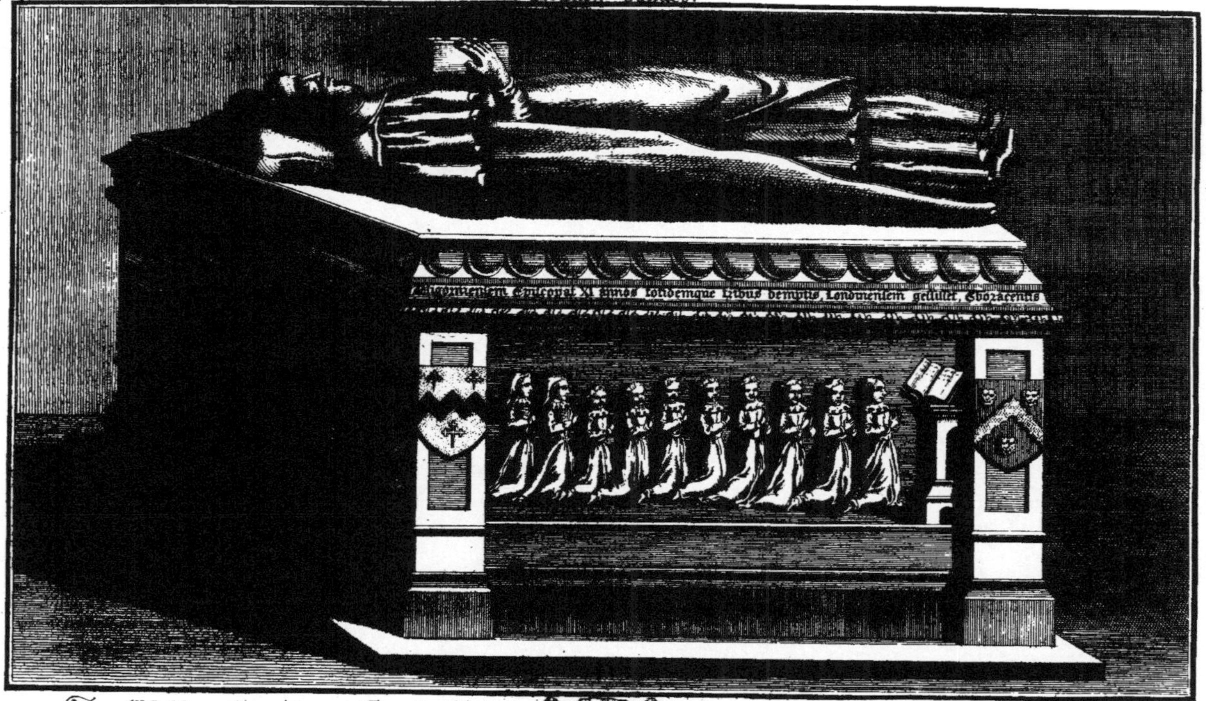

To Sr Miles Stapylton *Bar.^t, Knight of the Shire for the County of* York *the author of this work inscribes this plate*. 1736.

ver. Genere non magnus fuit (nec tamen humilis) dignitate locoque major, exemplo maximus: Homo si quisquam mortalium a malitia et vindicta planè innocens, summè liberalis in omnes; pauperibus ita beneficus, ut non suam modo, sed et principis sui munificentiam eleemosynarius regius, larga manu, per multos annos, erogarit. Hospitalis adeo ut expensae reditus aequarint, nonnunquam superarint; contemptor mundi, optimus, facilis, et in sola vitia superbus; scilicet non minus factis quam sermonibus syncerum verbi praeconem egit, et fuit in Evangelio *praedicando, tam in* aula *et* Academia *quam in* Ecclesia, *ut semper, valde nervosus, ita ad extremum usque halitum mirabiliter assiduus. Veram et germanam* Christi *religionem modis omnibus propagavit, falsam et adulterinam totis viribus oppugnavit. Bonas literas pro facultatibus auxit; ignavos, sedulitatis suae conscius, ferre non potuit; manus nemini temere imposuit.* Ecclesiae patrimonium, veluti rem deo sacratam intactum defendit. *Summatim semper apud illustrissimam mortalium* Elizabetham *gratia floruit; ineffabili apud Deum immortalem gloria aeternum florebit. Vivit in coelis anima ejus, vivant in terris memoria,* utinam et vivum exemplar in omnibus episcopis ecclesiaeque pastoribus cerneretur *.

Joannes Benett, *legum doctor, haeres in testamento scriptus, memoriae tanti praesulis, talisque patroni sui, cui omnibus officii ac observantiae nominibus se deditissimum profitetur, hoc pii gratique animi, non tantae haereditatis monumentum, suis sumptibus posuit.* Archbishop Piers.

MATTHEW HUTTON, *sixty fifth archbishop.*

In the beginning of *March* following *Matthew Hutton* bishop of *Durham* was translated to this see; and on the last day of that month was inthroned by proxy in the cathedral. A. 1595.

The great preferments this prelate attained to are more surprising when we consider his lowness of birth. He was born of poor parents, nay some do not stick to say, that he was a foundling child, at a place called *Warton* in *Lancashire* (*l*). In this village is still a tradi-

* Most of this epitaph is the same as his predecessor *Sandys*'s; but being put up in different churches the writer did not imagine they would ever come together.

(*l*) He founded an hospital at this town, and endowed it with thirty five pounds *per annum*. *Le Neve. Willis.* See a further account of this alms-house and prelate in *Thoresby*'s *Vicaria* Leodensis.

tional account of the manner of his education, which being too extraordinary I think proper to omit. He was brought up in *Trinity-hall* in *Cambridge*, of which he became fellow; was afterwards master of *Pembroke*, and one of the divinity professors of that university. In 1567. he was made dean of *York*, being then rector of *Boxworth* in the county of *Cambridge*, prebendary of *Ely*, of *Westminster*, and of St. *Paul's* in *London*. In the year 1589. he was consecrated bishop of *Durham*, by the hands of the archbishop of *York*; the bishops of *Carlisle* and *Chester* assisting; from whence he was translated to this see, as above (*m*).

This prelate was a man of great learning, and was accounted the most able preacher of the age he lived in; but much dipped in worldly affairs in his younger years, says an author (*n*), having married no less than three wives before he got a bishoprick. He sat here eleven years and died at *Bishopthorp Jan.* 15, 1605, leaving a fine estate to sir *Timothy Hutton* his eldest son, who two years after his father's death was high-sheriff of this county. The estate of *Marsk* still continues in the family. He was buried in the south quire of the cathedral where a handsome monument is erected to his memory; on which is this inscription:

Epitaphium Matthaei Huttoni *celeberrimi archiepiscopi* Eboracensis *memoriae sacrum.*

Cujus expressam corporis effigiem cernis, lector, si mentis quoque imaginem videre cupis, Ambrosium *vel etiam* Augustinum *cogita; alterius quippe ingenium argutum, alterius limatum judicium hoc praesule vivente viguit. Qui in academia* Cantabrigiensi *olim sacrae theologiae professor publicus, et literarum columen claruit; postea erat ad decanatum* Eboracensem, *hinc ad episcopatum* Dunelmensem, *illinc ad archi-praesulatum* Eboracensem, *providentia divina, serenissimae reginae* Elizabethae *auspiciis, propter admirabilem eruditionis, integritatis, et prudentiae laudem provectus; decurso tandem aetatis suae annorum* LXXX *curriculo, corpus* Adae, *animam* Christi *gremio commendavit. Ecquid vis amplius, lector? Nosce teipsum. Obiit* 16. *die mensis* Januarii *anno Dom.* MDCV.

TOBIAS MATTHEW, *sixty sixth archbishop.*

A. 1606. *Toby Matthew* was born in the city of *Bristol*, brought up in *Christ-church*, *Oxford*, and, being doctor of divinity, he rose by many steps of preferment, first to the archdeaconry of *Wells*; the presidentship of St. *John's* college, *Oxford*; canon and dean of *Christ-church*, dean of *Durham*; bishop of *Durham*, and lastly translated thence to the archbishoprick of *York*, where he was enthronized, by proxy, *Sept.* 11, 1606.

This prelate is praised through the whole course of his life for his great learning, eloquence, sweet conversation, bounty; but above all, by sir *John Harrington* and Mr. *Fuller*, both infected with the same kind of wit, for what they term a *chearful Sharpness* in discourse. Which, says sir *John*, so sauced all his words and behaviour, that well was he, in the university, that could be in the company of *Toby Matthew*. *Fuller* adds, that none could condemn him for his chearful spirit, though often he would condemn himself for the levity of it; yet he was so habited therein that he could as well not be, as not be merry. Pun and quibble was then in high vogue, and a man was to expect no preferment in that age, either in church or state, who was not a proficient in that kind of wit. Our archbishop is reported to have said at his leaving *Durham*, for a benefice of less income, that it was for *lack of grace*. The before quoted authors have thought fit to record two or three remarkable stories, which I shall beg leave to subjoin for the reader's better notion of our prelate's readiness in this way.

"Being vice-chancellor of *Oxford*, and some slight matters and men coming before him, "one man was very importunate to have the court stay for his council. Who is your council? says the vice-chancellor, Mr. *Leasteed*, answers the man; alas, replies the vice-chancellor, no man can stand you in *less stead*. No remedy, adds the other, necessity has no law; indeed, quoth he, no more I think has your councellor.

"Another man was to be bound in a bond, very like to be forfeited, and came in great haste to offer it, saying he would be bound if he might be taken in: Yes, says the judge, I think you will be taken in, what is your name? *Cox*, says the party, and so press'd, as the manner is, to come into court. Make him room there, said the vice-chancellor, let *Cox-come* in.

These two, out of two or three hundred, nay, as many as would fill a large volume, says sir *John*, are sufficient to shew his aptness. I hope I shall not incur the reader's displeasure for inserting them, since I take them as curiosities of their kind; nor do I remember that I ever met with them in those volumes of puns and apothegms ascribed to the wits of each university.

After he had arrived at his greatness, he made one journey into the west, to visit his two mothers, says *Fuller*, she that bare him at *Bristol*, and her that bred him in learning, the university of *Oxford*. Coming near to the latter, attended with a train suitable to his condition

(*m*) MS. *Torre*.

(*n*) *Willis* on cathedral churches.

Mr. John Dawson of York,  descended by the Mothers side
from Archbishop Hutton, gives and inscribes this plate
of his monument to his memory.

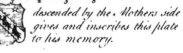

NY

p. 459.

0 1 2 3 4 5 Feet.

Archbishop Matthews.

dition, he was met, adds my author, with an equal number, or more, which came out of *Oxford* to give him entertainment. Thus augmented with another troop, and remembring he had p[illegible]ed over a small water, a poor scholar, when he first came to the university, he kneeled down and took up the expression of *Jacob*, *with my staff passed I over this* Jordan, *and now am I become two bands*. I am credibly informed, says my author, that, *mutatis mutandis*, the same thing was done by his predecessor archbishop *Hutton* at *Sophisters hills* near *Cambridge* (o).

Our prelate was in great favour with those two monarchs of *England*, queen *Elizabeth* and king *James*, and was so remarkable a preacher that *Campian* the *Jesuit* allows him *dominari in concionibus*. If he was an able preacher, he must also be allowed to be an indefatigable one, for he kept an account of all his sermons, by which it appears that he preached, whilst dean of *Durham*, 721; whilst bishop of *Durham* 550; and whilst archbishop of *York* 721; in all 1992 sermons; and amongst them several *extempore* (p). Whilst he sate here, if he had not alienated from the see, to please the duke of *Buckingham*, *York-Place* in the *Strand*, which was no *jest*, he might have preached and punned on to the end of his days, leaving a much better memorial. He died at *Cawood*, *March* 29, 1628, after he had sat twenty two years, and was buried in the south quire of the cathedral; where a neat monument is erected over him, which bears this inscription:

TOBIAS MATTHAEUS

Illustri MATTHAEORUM *familia apud* CAMBROS *oriundus*; BRISTOLIAM *natalibus*, OXONIAM *studiis ornavit. Cum omni politiori doctrinae theologiam conjunxerat, statim in concionibus dominari coepit. In aula, academia, urbe, rure juxta celebris. Neque* CHRYSOSTOMUM GRAECIA *quam* TOBIAM *suum* ANGLIA *jactantius olim profitebitur. Innotuit simul ac summa apud reginam* ELIZABETHAM *gratia invaluit. Neminem illa libentius audivit, aut praedicantem susius praedicabat. Anno aetatis* 28. *collegio* D. JOHAN. BAPTISTAE OXONIENSIS *praeficiebatur, archidiaconus una in ecclesia* WELLENSI, *ac in aedibus* CHRISTI *canonicus; mox iisdem aedibus decanus praefuit. Omnibus tandem qui academicos beare solent honoribus perfunctus ad* DUNELMENSEM *decanatum provectus est. Post aliquot annos major decanatu succrevit viri fama, ac prono in eum reginae favore* DUNELMENSIS *episcopus ecclesiae constituitur. Cui cum praefuerat annos circiter* XII. *serenissimi regis* JACOBI *auspiciis ad archiepiscopatum* EBORACEN. *translatus est. Non potuit enim tanta indoles, quocunque vergeret, infra summum se sistere. Hisce gradibus ad tantum culmen evasit, virtutes quibus illud ornavit non capit marmor; historicum quaerunt, non sculptorem. Inter caetera, hospitalitatis laus pene illius propria fuit;* TOBIAE *aedes et divitum aula et pauperum* XENODOCHIUM *indies fuere. Cathedram hanc tenuit ann.* 22, *rara felicitate; cum sexagenarius eandem occupaverat, vix ad extremam senectutem exaruit dives illa concionandi vena; cum erat septuagenario major, nemo in concionibus frequentior, nemo felicior, nemo quem in aeternum magis audire velis. Deficientibus ad pulpita viribus coepit ipse statim languescere; quasi sola illa vitalis aura quam concionando hauserit, nec studio nec labori superesse voluerit. Beatissimus senex impleto aetatis anno* 82. *placide emigravit* 29. Martii 1628. *Corporis exuviae summo cum omnium moerore huc illatae,* CHRISTI *adventum expectant et animam reducem. Noli illum putare, viator, ab hoc angusto marmore quicquam nominis mutuari; quovis augustissimo mausoleo augustius est quod hic conditur.* TOBIAE *nomen et tibi, marmor, et huic sacratissimo templo, monumenti instar quovis aere perennioris.*

GEORGE MONTEIGN, *sixty seventh archbishop*.

(p) *George Monteign*, S. T. P. was also bishop of *Durham*, and translated hither like his two predecessors. He was elected to this see *June* 6, and enthroned in the same *Oct*. 24, 1628. Scarce warm in his church 'ere cold in his coffin, says *Fuller*, dying *Nov*. 6. the same year, and was buried at *Cawood*, the place of his nativity. A. 1628.

Mr. *Torre* mentions a nuncupative will made by this prelate whilst he was bishop of *London*, whereby he gave to the poor of *Cawood*, where he was born, one hundred pound; and constituted his brother *Isaac Monteign* his sole executor. This last person, as the epitaph testifies, erected a monument for him in the parish church of *Cawood*, which is now much decayed, and the inscription scarce legible. But a draught of it was taken in the year 1641. from which drawing, now in the office of arms, the annexed print was engraven. The inhabitants of *Cawood*, by tradition, shew you the house where he was born; and it is somewhat extraordinary that he should go a poor boy from that town, being only a farmer's son, and return to it archbishop of *York*, dye and be buried in the place where he first drew breath. His other preferments, besides what I have mentioned, are expressed in his epitaph; which was made by the noted *Hugh Holland*, a poet of that age; and is as follows:

(o) See *Thoresby*'s Vic. *Leod*.

(p) *Idem*. From this archbishop's original diary then in Mr. *Thoresby*'s *Musaeum*.

(q) Another punster if we give credit to the old story of removing a *mountain* and casting it into the *see*.

Quater

Quater antistes qui praefuit urbibus, arce
Hac satus est infans, hac situs arce senex.
Nec mera provexit geminorum gratia regum,
Sed meritum, summis par ubicunque locis.
Sic juvenis, sic pene puer septem imbibit artes,
Granta *ubi* Castaliis *praedominatur aquis.*
Moribus haud tetricis, nec pectore turpis avaro,
Non etenim nimias pone reliquit opes.

Hugo Hollandus *flevit.*

GEORGIO MOUNTAIGNEO

Honestis hoc in oppido penatibus oriundo, per cunctos disciplinarum gradus Cantab. *provecto, et academiae procuratori, sub initio* D. Jacobi *hospitio quod* Sabaudiam *vocant, et ecclesiae* Westmonasteriensi *praefecto, ab eodem R. ad praesulatum* Lincolniensem, *ac inde post aliqua temporum spiramenta* Londiniensem *promoto, a* Carolo *divi F. ad* Dunelmensem *honestiss. senii et valetudinis secessum translato; moxque, H. E. infra spatium trimestre, ad archiepiscopatum* Eboracensem *benigniter sublevato. Viro venerabili, aspectu gravi, moribus non injucundis, ad beneficia non ingrato, injuriarum non ultori unquam, nec (quantum natura humana patitur) memori, amborum principum Domini suoque semper eleemosinario.*

Isaacus Montaignus *testamenti curator fratri*
B. M. P. Vixit A. 59, *M.* 6. *D.* 2.

Samuel

SAMUEL HARSNET, *sixty eighth archbishop.*

Samuel Harsnet, D. D. bishop of *Norwich* was elected to this see, and was installed by proxy *April* 23, 1629. He was born at *Colchester*, brought up at *Cambridge*, was first fellow, then master of *Pembroke-hall*. His other preferments were a prebendary of St. *Paul's*, rector of *Shanfield*, vicar of *Chigwell* and *Hutton*, &c. He was afterwards consecrated bishop of *Chichester*, and with it held his mastership of *Pembroke*, till, says Mr. *Willis*, he was ejected out of the latter for several scandalous practices exhibited against him in fifty seven articles. All which, adds he, were so flagrant, that he was glad to quit his mastership to prevent a further enquiry (*x*). A. 1629.

(*y*) *February* 13, *anno* 1630, this *Samuel Harsnet* made his will, proved *June* 28, *anno* 1631, whereby he commended his soul to God, hoping to be saved through the merits of *Jesus Christ* his redeemer; professing to die in the antient faith of the true catholick and apostolick church, called the primitive church, *i. e. in that faith that was professed by the holy fathers next after the blessed apostles. Renouncing from his heart as well all modern* POPISH SUPERSTITIONS, *as all novelties of* GENEVA.

And appointed his body to be buried in the parish church of *Chigwell*, at the feet of *Thomasine* his beloved wife. Ordering only a marble stone to be laid over his grave, with a brass plate moulten into the same an inch thick, whereon is to be stamped the effigies of a bishop with his mitre and crosier staff. And the said brass to be so rivetted and fastned clear through the stone, as sacrilegious hands may not rend off the one without breaking the other. And further willed that this inscription should be engraven on the brass,

Hic jacet SAMUEL HARSNET *quondam vicarius hujus ecclesiae, primo indignus episcopus* CICESTRIENSIS, *dein indignior* NORWICENSIS, *demum indignissimus archiepiscopus* EBORACENSIS.

Which was performed accordingly with these additional words,

Qui obiit 25 *die Maii A. D.* 1631, *quod ipsissimum epitaphium ex abundanti humilitate sibi poni curavit, testamento reverendissimus praesul* (*z*).

RICHARD NEILE, *sixty ninth archbishop.*

After about nine months consideration, who was the fittest person to succeed to this see, it pleased his majesty king *Charles* to pitch upon *Richard Neile* bishop of *Winchester*; who was translated hither *March* 19, and on *April* 16, 1632, he was inthroned, by proxy, in the cathedral. A. 1632.

This man, by his merit alone, says *Eachard*, passed through all the degrees and orders of the church of *England*. Having been schoolmaster, curate, vicar, parson, chaplain, master of the *Savoy*, dean of *Westminster*, clerk of the closet to two kings, bishop of *Rochester*, *Lincoln*, *Durham*, *Winchester*, and lastly translated to the archbishoprick of *York* (*a*).

His episcopal character, and steady attachment to the true interest of the church and monarchy, gained him many enemies amongst the *puritans*; who were now grown up to be a powerful faction in this kingdom. *Cromwell* himself, in a committee of the house of commons, complained of him, whilst bishop of *Winchester*, for countenancing some divines that preached *flat popery* as he called it. No doubt his case would have been as bad as archbishop *Laud's* had he lived long enough; but he was happily called away before the flame broke out; dying at *York*, in the *Minster-yard*, in the house belonging to the prebend of *Stillington*, *October* 51, 1640.

" (*b*) This *Richard*, by God's providence, archbishop of *York*, primate of *England* and " metropolitan, one of his majesty's most honourable privy council, made his will, proved " *ult. Oct.* 1640, whereby he commended his soul to God Almighty his creator and re-" deemer; giving him hearty thanks, for that he was born in the year 1562, in which the " articles of religion and faith of the church of *England*, were established and published. " In the profession of which faith he was bred, lived and yielded up his soul.

" He bequeathed to his son sir *Paul Neile*, his executor, his ring of nine diamonds which " the king of *Denmark* gave him; charging him to preserve the same to his children, as " an honourable monument of the donor; and of his nearness in service, as having been " clerk of the closet to king *James*, &c."

His body was buried in *All-saints* chapel in the cathedral; but his son sir *Paul*, though he left him a good estate, run it out so fast, that he could not afford his father a monu-

(*x*) *Le Neve* says, these articles are still extant; but though he knows where they are, he could not prevail upon the present possessors to part with a copy of them.

(*y*) *MS.* Torre, *p.* 478.

(*z*) The epitaph remains to this day, says *Willis*, but it is not worth the trouble of engraving.

(*a*) *Eachard's* history of *England*.

(*b*) *MS.* Torre 479.

ment; nor is there a ftone of any kind to denote where he was buried. For want of an epitaph take Mr. *Eachard's* character of him.

" He died full of years, yet was he as full of honours. A faithful fubject to his prince, " an indulgent father to his clergy, a bountiful patron to his chaplains, and a true friend " to all that relied upon him.

John Williams, *feventieth archbifhop.*

A. 1641. To *Richard Neile* fucceeded *John Williams*, who was elected hither *December* 4, 1641; and on the 27th of *June*, 1642, was enthroned, in perfon, in the cathedral. The king and his loyal nobility, *&c.* being then at *York*.

This man was born at *Aber-Conway* in *Wales*, and had *Welfh* blood enough in him to ftyle him a gentleman; he was educated in St. *John's* college in *Cambridge*, where he was fellow, and *anno* 1612, was proctor of that univerfity. Whilft he was in this office the *Spanifh* ambaffador came to *Cambridge*, accompanied with the lord chancellor *Egerton*; where with the gracefulnefs of his prefence, ingenuity of his difcourfe, and the nice conduct of thofe exercifes, whereof he was moderator, he fo charmed the chancellor, that when he took his leave of the univerfity, he faid publickly to *Williams*, that he had behaved himfelf fo well in his treatment of the ambaffador, that he was fit to ferve a king; and that he would fee him as much welcomed at court as they were in the univerfity (*c*).

At his coming to *London*, he became chaplain to the lord chancellor *Egerton*; which great ftatefman, taking a fancy for him, let him into feveral mifteries of ftate. Here it was that our prelate firft commenced politician and courtier; firm to retain and apt to improve from the precepts of his mafter. So dear was the chaplain to his patron, that the latter, lying on his death-bed, afked *Williams* to chufe what moft acceptable legacy he fhould leave him. The doctor flighting money, only requefted four books, being that noble lord's own collections on thefe heads,

1. The prerogative royal.
2. The privileges of parliaments.
3. The proceedings in chancery.
4. The power of the ftar-chamber.

This legacy was bequeathed him, and the doctor, fays *Fuller*, made fuch ufe of it, that he tranfcribed thefe four books into his own brains. Books, adds he, that were the four elements of our *Englifh* ftate; and he made himfelf abfolute mafter of all the materials and paffages therein.

Full fraught with this kind of knowledge he got to court, and by favour of the duke of *Buckingham* was introduced to king *James*, to whom he prefented his four books. The king regarding him as an able man to ferve himfelf, firft made him dean of *Weftminfter*, then bifhop of *Lincoln*, and keeper of the great feal; which place he enjoyed all the days of king *James*.

This is fufficient to give a notion of our prelate's rife, for whilft he was bifhop of *Lincoln* he is out of my province to treat on (*d*). Our hiftories are full enough of the ufes he made of his former politick inftructions; but fo ill they throve with him that, in the firft year of king *Charles*, he had the feals taken from him, and was fent prifoner to the tower.

Here he continued for fome time; till that parliament met, fays *Fuller*, *which many feared would never begin and afterwards had the fame fears it would never have an end.* The bifhop of *Lincoln* being looked upon as the propereft advocate to defend the epifcopal caufe, in the cafe of the bifhop's votes in the houfe, which the king knew would be ftruck at; he was releafed out of prifon, and to make him amends and hearty in the caufe, the archbifhoprick of *York*, juft then vacant, was conferred upon him.

How he behaved in this affair may be feen at large in my lord *Clarendon*'s and Mr. *Eachard*'s hiftories, and therefore needlefs to be repeated here. When the bifhops were excluded from all, our prelate retired to an eftate which he had purchafed in *Wales*. Here he lived, at firft in perfect duty and loyalty to his fovereign, and fpared neither money nor trouble to advantage the royal caufe; but at laft by an unaccountable turn of politicks he forfook his royal mafter's intereft; and joined fo heartily with the rebels that he changed his lawn for buff, and commanded at the fiege of the town and caftle of *Aber-conway*; both which he reduced to the obedience of the parliament. This bold ftep, fays my author, acting fo directly contrary to his epifcopal character, gained him few new friends at *London*, but quite loft him all his old ones at *Oxford*. It is true he faved by it a compofition in *Goldfmith's-hall* for his eftate; but his memory, adds *Fuller*, is ftill to *compound* before a tolerable report can be given of it. It is of this prelate *Hudibrafs* fpeaks,

More plainly than that reverend writer
Who to our churches vail'd his mitre, &c.

He was very modeft in his converfation, whatfoever a namelefs author fays to the contrary;

(*c*) *Lloyd's* memoirs.

(*d*) The life of this prelate at large is wrote and publifhed by Dr. *Hatchett*. *London*.

trary; but whether this was any virtue or no, I leave to the sequel; when, says my author, I am certainly informed, from such who knew the privacies and casualties of his infancy, that our prelate was but one degree removed from a *mysogynist*. Yet to palliate his infirmities, pursues he, to females, he was a very polite addresser to the other sex.

He lived some time in great obscurity, neglected by the rebels he had obliged, and despised by the royalists whom he had basely deserted, till the year 1650, at which time, on *March* 25, he died, and was buried in *Llandegay* church, about two miles from *Bangor*. Mr. *Eachard* says, that he certainly died a firm protestant of the church of *England*; for wanting a regular priest to do the last offices for him, he purposely ordained an old honest servant of his own to administer the sacrament, &c. to him on his death-bed. Mr. *Willis* has seen his monument, which, he says, is a copartment of white marble, fixed to the wall of the church, and contains his effigies kneeling, with the arms of the sees of *Lincoln*, and *York*, and deanery of *Westminster*, severally impaled with his own, and has on a tablet this inscription.

Hospes lege, relege. Quod in hoc sacello, paucis noto, haud expectares,
Hic situs est Johannes Wilhelmus, *omnium praesulum celeberrimus,*
A paternis natalibus e familia Wilhelmorum *de* Cogwhillin *ortus,*
A maternis de Griffithis *de* Pentrin.
Cujus summum ingenium, et in omni genere litterarum praestantia
Meruit, ut regis Jacobi *gratia ad decanatum* Sarum,
Post Westmonasterii *eveheretur :*
Ut simul atque uno munere tanto regi esset a consiliis secretis et delitiis;
Magni sigilli custos et sedis Lincolniensis *episcopus :*
Quem Carolus *primus insula episcopat.* Eborac. *decoraret.*
Omnes scientias valde edoctus, novem linguarum thesaurus,
Theologiae purae et illibatae medulla; prudentiae politicae cortina,
Sacrae, canonicae, civilis, municipalis sapientiae apex et ornamentum,
Dulciloquii cymbalum, memoriae tenacissimae, plusquam humanae,
Historiarum omnis generis myrothecium,
Magnorum operum, usque ad sumptum viginti mille librarum, structor:
Munificentiae, liberalitatis, hospitalitatis, lautitiae,
Misericordiae erga pauperes insigne exemplar;
Postquam inter tempora luctuosissima,
Satur esset omnium quae audiret et videret,
Nec regi aut patriae, per rabiem perduellium, amplius servire potuit;
Anno aetat. 68, *expleto* Martii 25, *qui fuit ei natalis,*
Summa fide in Christo, *inconcussa erga regem fidelitate,*
Animam, angina extinctus, piissime Deo reddidit.
Nec refert quod tantillum monumentum, in occulto angulo positum,
Tanti viri memoriam servat,
Cujus virtutes omnium aetatum tempora celebrabunt.
Abi, viator, sat tuis occulis debes.

ACCEPTED FREWEN, *seventy first archbishop.*

After the death of *Williams* the see of *York*, during the times of *anarchy* and *confusion*, continued vacant ten years; till upon the happy restoration of *church* and *monarchy*, *Accepted Frewen*, D. D. bishop of *Litchfield*, was nominated to this see, and installed in person *October* 11, 1660. A. 1660.

He was the eldest son of *John Frewen*, the puritanical rector of *Northiam* in *Sussex*, says *Wood*, and indeed his very name carries a symbol of his father's sanctity (*e*). He was born in *Kent*, educated in the free-school in *Canterbury*, became a student, and afterwards a demy of *Magdalene* college in *Oxford*; where, making great proficiency in learning, he was elected fellow *anno* 1612, being then master of arts. When he entered into holy orders, he became a frequent preacher, having puritanical inclinations from his father. But, notwithstanding that, he had interest enough at court to get to attend prince *Charles* in his expedition to *Spain*; by reason, says *Eachard*, of his great parts and abilities. In the year 1625, he was made chaplain to the king; and the next year was elected president of his own college, and was four times vicechancellor of the university. He was a prebendary of *Canterbury*, and dean of *Glocester*, afterwards of *Wells*, and in 1643, was consecrated bishop of *Litchfield* and *Coventry*. This last preferment was little better than titular, the hierarchy being about that time silenced; however he had ample amends at the restoration, by his promotion to the see of *York*; and having the liberty to renew leases in both bishopricks, which must raise a vast sum.

(*e*) His next brother was called *Thankful*. *Wood*.

This

This prelate was a single man, and so strictly nice in his character that way, that he would not, as I have been told, suffer a woman servant in his family. Living in this state, and the great opportunities he had of amassing wealth, yet I do not find any of it laid out on the church, or in charities. It is said indeed, by Mr. *le Neve*, that the sum of fifteen thousand pounds was expended somewhere, in his time, and of his treasure, but where I am not able to find. The only thing of this kind that is publickly known, is the new building and repairing of the dining room and chambers over it at *Bishopthorp*; which might probably have gone much to decay during the usurpation. The time he sat here, indeed, was short, for he died, at the above mentioned palace, *March* 28, 1664; and, on the third of *May* following, was buried in our lady's chapel, at the east end of the cathedral; where a neat monument is erected over him.

(*f*) "On the 22d of *May*, 1663, this *Accepted Frewen*, by divine providence archbishop "of *York*, made his will, proved *July* 23, 1664, whereby he commended his soul to Al-" mighty God, hoping, through the merits of *Jesus Christ* to be saved, *&c.* and appoint-" ed his body to be buried in the parish church of *Northiam* in *Sussex*, &c. He bequeathed " five hundred pounds to *Magdalene* college, *Oxon*, where he was bred; and to every bishop " of the kingdom a ring with this inscription:

NEQUE MELIOR SUM QUAM PATRES MEI.
RE. 19. A. F.

His epitaph runs thus,

Hic requiescit in spe novissimam praestolans tubam
ACCEPTUS FREWEN,
Johannis Frewen *rectoris ecclesiae* Nordiamensis
In comitatu Suffexiae *filius, natu maximus,*
Sac. Theol. professor,
Collegii B. Mariae Magdalene Oxonii;
Annos plus minus undeviginti praeses,
Academiae ibidem quater vice-cancellarius,
Decanus Glouceftriae,
Postea factus episcop. Covent. *et* Litchf.
Deinde archiepiscopus Eborac.
Qui inter vivos esse desiit Mar. 28, *an. Dom.* 1664.
Aetat. suae 76, *pene exacto.*

RICHARD STERN, *seventy second archbishop.*

A. 1664. *Richard Stern*, was born at *Mansfield* in *Nottinghamshire* of honest parents, as his epitaph expresses; he was educated in *Corpus Christi* college in *Cambridge*, and afterwards made master of *Jesus* in that university. Whilst he was in this situation he became very instrumental in sending the university plate to the king to supply his necessities. For which, he with vice-chancellor *Holdsworth*, and two other masters of colleges, were sent for up to *London*, and imprisoned in the *Tower* (*g*). In the year 1643, he was put out of his college for refusing to take the covenant; stripped of all he had and used with great barbarity besides. At this time doctor *Stern* was chaplain to archbishop *Laud*; and, when his master suffered for his loyalty, he stood on the fatal scaffold with him. During the usurpation he betook himself to the country, where he taught school for his livelihood, and lived in great obscurity and want till the happy restauration. These glorious sufferings recommended him primarily to the gratitude and care of his royal master king *Charles* II, who immediately, upon his return, bestowed on him the bishoprick of *Carlisle*. From whence he was translated hither *April* 28, 1664; and on the tenth of *June* following inthroned in the cathedral.

The epitaphs of our archbishops, about this time, and before, are so full of the steps of their preferments, lives and characters, that there needs little else be said of them. Yet Dr. *Stern*, says Mr. *Willis*, would have deserved a larger encomium than most of them, had he not demised *Heugrave* in *Nottinghamshire*, to his son and his son's wife, from this see (*h*). For whilst he sat here, says an historian, his whole behaviour was worthy of the high station he bore; and his learning is best seen by his accurate book of *logick*; and the hand he had in composing the *polyglot bible*. He is also much suspected for, being the author of that most excellent divine and moral treatise called the *whole duty of man*. This worthy prelate built the new buildings at the end of the stables at *Bishopthorp*; and died at that palace *June* 18, 1683; and lies interred under a noble monument, in St. *Stephen*'s chapel, at the east end of the cathedral; on which is the following inscription,

(*f*) *Torre* p. 230.
(*g*) *Fuller*'s church history.

(*h*) *Thoroton*'s *Nottinghamshire*. *Willis* on cathedral churches.

Hic

p. 464.

Thomas Frewen *of* Brickwall *in* *the County of* Suffex *Esq*.^r *in regard to the name & family of* *this Prelate, contributes this plate.* 1736.

Fra.^o Haynes delin.^t

Richard Sterne *of* Elvington *Esqr great Grandson to this once most eminent Prelate dedicates this Plate of his Monument to his Memory.* 1736

Hic spe futurae gloriae situs est
RICHARDUS STERNE, MANSFELDIAE *honestis parentibus ortus:*
Tria apud CANTABRIGIENSES *collegia certatim*
Ipsum cum superbia arripiunt, et jactant suum,
SANCTAE *et* INDIVIDUAE TRINITATIS *scholarem,*
CORPORIS CHRISTI *socium,* JESU *tandem praefectum meritissimum:*
GULIELMO CANTUARIENSI *martyri a sacris in fatali pegmate astitit;*
Ausus et ipse inter pessimos esse bonus, et vel cum illo commori,
Postea honesto consilio nobili formandae juventuti operam dedit,
Ne deessent qui Deo et regi, cum licuerit, rite servirent:
Quo tandem reduce (etiam cum apologia et prece) rogatur
Ut CARLEOLENSIS *esse episcopus non dedignaretur.*
At non illi, magis quam soli, diu latere licuit:
In humili illa provincia satis constitit se summam meruisse,
Ad primatum igitur EBORACENSEM, *ut plenis splenderet gloria, evectus est.*
In utroque ita se gessit, ut Deo prius quam sibi prospiceret;
Ecclesias spoliatas olim de suo vel dotavit, vel ditavit amplius.
Non antiquis ecclesiae patribus impar fuisset, si coaevus;
Omnis in illo enituit, quae antistitem deceat, et ornet, virtus,
Gravitas, sanctitas, charitas, rerum omnium scientia,
In utraque fortuna par animi firmitas, et constantia,
Aequissimus ubique vitae tenor, regiminis justitia, et moderatio;
In sexto supra octogesimum anno corpus erectum,
Oris dignitas, oculorum vigor auriumque, animi praesentia,
Nec ulla in senectute faex, sed adhuc flos prudentiae
Satis probarunt quid mensa possit et vita sobria.
Obiit Jun. 18, *anno* { *Salutis* 1683. / *Aetatis suae* 87. }

JOHN DOLBEN, *seventy third archbishop.*

John Dolben, son of *William Dolben*, D. D. of a very antient family at *Segrayd* in the county of *Denbigh*, was born at *Stanwich* in *Northamptonshire*; of which parish his father was rector. He was educated in *Westminster* school, and at fifteen years of age was elected scholar in *Christ-Church Oxon*. The civil wars commencing betwixt king and parliament, he took arms for the royal cause; and served as ensign at the siege of *York*, and battle of *Marston-moor*; where he was dangerously wounded in the shoulder with a musket-ball. He had afterwards his thigh bone broke, in another battle, by the like accident. Upon the surrender of *Oxford*, and the decline of the king's affairs, he went to his college again; and staid there till he was ejected from his student's place by the visitors appointed by parliament. He then married and lived privately in *Oxford*, till the king's *restauration*. Where with Dr. *Fell*, and some others of his friends, he kept up a congregation, in which the *common-prayer* was read, and all other usages of the church of *England* constantly solemnized. When his royal master was restored, for whose cause, and his father's, he had so often ventured his life, he was first installed canon of *Christ-church*; afterwards, by means of his wife's relation the then bishop of *London*, Dr. *Sheldon*, he was, deservedly, made archdeacon of *London*; clerk of the closet, and dean of *Westminster*. In the year 1666, he was consecrated bishop of *Rochester*, and made the king's almoner; when, says my author, *(h)* that place was managed, to the great benefit of the poor, with great justice and integrity. On the 26th of *July*, 1683, he was, by the king's *conge d' elire*, elected archbishop of this diocese, and enthronized in person *August* 23. following. A. 1683.

This prelate was a man, says *Ant. Wood*, of a free generous and noble disposition, and withal of a natural, bold and happy eloquence. And, adds our *Oxford* antiquary, by a sort of hereditary right, he succeeded his uncle *Williams* in his honours; both in his deanry of *Westminster* and archbishoprick of *York*. He died at *Bishopthorpe* of the small pox, at a very advanced age for the attack of that distemper, *April* 11, 1686, aged sixty three years. He lies interred in the south choir of the *Minster*, where a noble tomb is erected to his memory; to the inscription on which I refer the reader for a further account of this worthy prelate.

Hic situs est
JOHANNES DOLBEN, *filius* GULIELMI *S. Th. professoris,*
Ex antiqua familia in CAMBRIA *septentrionali oriundus,*
Natus STANVICI *in agro* NORTHAMPTONIENSI Martii 20, *A. D.* 1624.
Anno aetatis 12. *Regiam scholam* WESTMONAST. *auspicato ingressus*
Singulari istius loci genio plenus 15. *exivit,*
In numerum alumnorum aedis CHRISTI OXON. *electus.*

(i) Wood's *Ath.Oxon.* ed. prim.

Exardente bello civili
Partes regias secutus est, in pugna Marstonensi *vexillarius;*
In defensione Eboraci *graviter vulneratus,*
Effuso sanguine consecravit locum,
Olim morti suae destinatum.
A. D. 1656, *a rev. episcop.* Cicestrensi *sacris ordinibus initiatus,*
Instaurata monarchia factus est aedis Christi *canonicus,*
Deinde decanus Westmonasteriensis;
Mox Carolo II. *regi optimo ab oratorio clericus,*
Episcopus postea Roffensis,
Et post novennium regis eleemosynarius;
Anno denique 1683, *metropolitae* Eboracensis *honore cumulatus est.*
Hanc provinciam ingenti animo et pari industria administravit,
Gregi et pastoribus exemplo.
Intra 30 *circiter menses, seculi laboribus exhaustis,*
Coelo tandem maturus,
Lethargia et variolis per quatriduum lecto affixus,
A. D. 1686, *aet.* 62, *potentissimi principis* Jacobi II. *altero, die dominico,*
(Eodem die quo praeeunte anno sacras synaxes
In ecclesia sua cathedrali septimanatim celebrandas instituerat)
Coelo fruebatur.
Moestissima conjux magni Gilberti Cantuar. *archiep. neptis,*
Ex qua tres liberos suscepit Gilbertum, Catharin. *et* Johan.
Monumentum hoc posuit
Desideratissimo marito.
In aede Christi *sub illius auspiciis partim extructa,*
Bromleiensi *palatio reparato, coenobio* Westmonas. *conservato;*
In senatu et ecclesiis eloquentiae gloria, in dioecesibus suis
Episcopali diligentia;
In omnium piorum animis, justa veneratione semper victuro.

Thomas Lamplugh, *seventy fourth archbishop.*

A. 1688. The see of *York* was kept vacant by king *James* II, two years after archbishop *Dolben*'s death, for reasons not to be approved of. Upon the landing of the prince of *Orange*, and his advancing towards *Exeter*, Dr. *Thomas Lamplugh*, bishop of that see, in a speech, advised the clergy and gentry of that city and country, to stand firm to king *James*; but finding the tide run too strong for him, he left the place, came to *London*, and presented himself to the king at *Whitehall*. In a time of, almost, universal defection from the king's interest, this act of loyalty of the bishop's was taken so kindly, that his majesty immediately translated him to *York*; where he was enthronized, by proxy, *December* 19, 1688, when he was almost seventy four years of age.

This prelate was descended from a very antient family in *Cumberland*; where it had flourished many centuries under several knightly honours. *Christopher Lamplugh*, of *Reston*, in the county of *York*, his father, was a younger branch of the family of *Lamplugh*, of *Lamplugh* in *Cumberland*. Our prelate was born at *Thwing* in this county, but educated at St. *Bege*'s school in *Cumberland*, and from thence sent to *Oxford*; and, when master of arts, was chosen fellow of *Queen's* college in that university. His other preferments were the rectory of *Binfield* in *Berkshire*, and afterwards of *Carlton* in *Ottmore*, com. *Oxon*; principal of *Alban-hall*, archdeacon of *London*, prebendary of *Worcester*, vicar of St. *Martin's in the fields*, *Westminster*, dean of *Rochester*, bishop of *Exeter*, and lastly archbishop of *York*.

In the spurious edition of *Wood*'s *Athenae Oxon.* printed 1721, are many things highly injurious to the character of this worthy prelate. I call it spurious, because it is impossible that author should leave such notes of persons actions behind him which were transacted after his own death; and of such there are many instances in this later edition. The editors of it, therefore, are highly to blame to trump upon the world such things under the name of *Anthony Wood*, as *Anthony* himself, notwithstanding all his bitterness, would have been ashamed of. In short, some of these Articles contain direct falsities; as I could shew were it to my purpose to do it; but, as such, they are not worth my further notice. Our archbishop is also handsomely vindicated from great part of this charge, by the author of the preface to Dr. *Allestree*'s sermons; who takes notice that "when that great Divine undertook one of the lectureships of the city of *Oxford*, in order to instil principles of loyalty there, in opposition to the contrary infusions of rebel teachers, whose doctrine had been for many years the gospel of that place; and discountenanced by none of the parochial ministers besides Mr. *Lamplugh*." *Who*, adds he, *had the courage and loyalty to own the doctrine of the church of* England *there in the worst of times*. And I have to add, from very good authority, that when he was a curate at *Southampton*, in the height of fanaticism, he got by heart almost the whole *Liturgy* of the church of *England*, which he

Jos. Haynes Delin. | J. Basire sculp.

The reverend Sir John Dolben Bar.t D.D. and Prebendary of Durham grandson to this once pious, valiant and loyal prelate dedicates this plate of his monument to his memory. 1736.

1 2 3 4 5 6 Feet

Jn. Haynes Delin. — J. Basire sculp.

The reverend **Thomas Lamplugh** *A.M. Rector of* **Bolton Percy** *and Canon-residentiary of the Church of* **York** *in memory of his grand fathers great worth and Virtue bestows this plate of his monument on this Work. 1736*

used to speak off book to his hearers, in imitation of the zealots of those times. Especially the burial-service, with which the people were so taken, that the relations and friends of such as were buried frequently made him presents; and desired, when they died to be buried in the same manner; but he acquainted them that it was not his own composition, but the words in the *Liturgy* so much then set at nought and despised.

This prelate died at *Bishopthorp May* 5, 1691, and was interred in the cathedral, to which church, considering his short reign, he had been an eminent benefactor. An account of which benefactions the reader may find in the sequel. By his will he left his private communion plate for the use of the archbishops, his successors, in *Bishopthorp* chapel; and appointing the dean and chapter to be keepers of it in a vacancy of the see. The epitaph on his monument runs in these words,

Hic
In spe resurgendi depositum jacet
Quod mortale fuit
Reverendissimi in CHRISTO *patris* THOMAE LAMPLUGH,
Archiepiscopi EBORACENSIS, *S. T. P.*
Ex antiqua et generosa LAMPLUGHORUM *de* LAMPLUGH,
In agro CUMBRIENSI *familia oriundi.*
Qui OXONIAE *in collegio reginae alumnus et socius,*
(Ubi literas humaniores et sacras hausit)
Aulae S. ALBANI *in eadem academia principalis.*
Ecclesiae S. MARTINI *juxta* WESTMONASTERIUM *vicarius,*
Decanus ROFFENSIS, *et anno* 1676, *episcopus* EXONIENSIS *consecratus:*
Tandem (licet dignitatem multum deprecatus)
In sedem hanc metropoliticam evectus est anno 1688, *mense* Novembri.
Vir (si quis alius) per varios vitae honorumque gradus spectabilis,
Ob vitae innocentiam, morum probitatem,
Verbi divini praedicationem, charitatem in patriam,
Et zelum erga domum Dei ecclesiam ANGLICANAM
In memoria aeterna cum justis futurus.
Obdormivit in Dom. 5 Maii *an. salutis* 1691, *aetat.* 76.
Uxorem habuit CATHERINAM *filiam* EDWARDI
DAVENANT *S. T. P. neptem* JOHANNIS
Davenant episcopi SARISBURIENSIS,
E qua tulit liberos quinque;
THOMAS *liberorum superstes,*
Hoc monumentum
P. M. P.

JOHN SHARP, *seventy fifth archbishop.*

John Sharp, D. D. was consecrated archbishop of this see, *July* 5, 1691; and on the fixteenth of the same month was enthronized by proxy, in the cathedral. The epitaph on the tomb of this great divine, wrote by bishop *Smallridge*, his contemporary and intimate acquaintance, is so full, in every particular, as to his promotions and personal merits, that it would look like aiming at a translation of that correct and noble inscription, in which the *Latin* tongue shines with classical lustre, and debasing it into barbarous incoherent sentences of our own language, to attempt his character from it. I am told, however, that the life of this most excellent prelate, from his cradle to his grave, is drawn up by his son Dr. *Sharp*, now archdeacon of *Northumberland*. Every one that is acquainted with the eminent qualifications of the son, must know that he is capable of doing justice to his father's memory. I shall therefore add no more of him, than that he died at *Bath*, *Feb.* 16, 1713, as much lamented as a man in his station could be, and was interred in his own cathedral with great solemnity. Over him is put a noble monument, on the two tables of which, above and below the figure, is the following inscription, A. 1691.

M. S.
Reverendissimi in CHRISTO *patris*
JOHANNIS SHARP *archiepiscopi* EBORACENSIS,
Qui
Honestis parentibus in hoc comitatu prognatus,
CANTABRIGIAE *optimarum artium studiis innutritus,*
Tum soli, unde ortus,
Tum loci, ubi institutus est, famam
Sui nominis celebritate adauxit.
Ab academia in domum illustrissimi dom. HENEAGII FINCH,
Tunc temporis attornati generalis,

Summi

Summi postea Angliae *cancellarii,*
Virtutum omnium altricem fautricemque evocatus,
Et facellani ministerium diligenter absolvit,
Et sacerdotis dignitatem una sustinuit.
Talis tantique viri patrocinio adjutus,
Et natura pariter ac doctrinae dotibus plurimum commendatus;
Peracto rite munerum ecclesiasticorum cursu,
Cum parochi, archidiaconi, decani officia
Summa cum laude praestitisset,
Ob eximia erga ecclesiam Anglicanam *merita*
Quam iniquissimis temporibus, magno suo periculo
Contra apertam pontificiorum rabiem
Argumentis invictissimis
Asseruerat, propugnaverat, stabiliverat;
Apostolicae simul veritatis praeco, ac fortitudinis aemulus,
Faventibus Gulielmo *et* Maria *regibus,*
Plaudentibus bonis omnibus,
Ad archiepiscopalis dignitatis fastigium tandem evectus est.
Nec hujusce tantum provinciae negotia satis ardua feliciter expediit,
Sed et Annae *principum optimae tum a consiliis, tum ab*
Eleemosynis, fuit;
Quas utcunque amplas, utcunque diffluentes,
Ne quem forte inopum a se tristem dimitteret
De suis saepenumero facultatibus supplevit.

Below.

Erat in sermone apertus, comis, affabilis;
In concionibus profluens, ardens, nervosus;
In explicandis theologiae casuisticae nodis
Dilucidus, argutus, promptus;
In eximendis dubitantium scrupulis,
Utcunque naturae bonitate ad leniores partes aliquanto propensior,
Aequi tamen rectique custos semper fidissimus.
Primaeva morum simplicitate,
Inculpabili vitae tenore,
Propensa in calamitosos benignitate,
Diffusa in universos benevolentia,
Studio in amicos perpetuo ac singulari
Inter deterioris saeculi tenebras emicuit,
Purioris aevi lumina aequavit.
Tam acri rerum coelestium desiderio flagrabat,
Ut his solis inhians, harum unice avarus,
Terrenas omnes neglexerit, spreverit, conculcarit.
Eo erat erga Deum pietatis ardore,
Ut illum totus adamaverit, spiraverit,
Illum ubique praesentem,
Illum semper intuentem,
Animo suo ac ipsis fere oculis observaverit.
Publicas hasce virtutes domesticis uberrime cumulavit,
Maritus et pater amantissimus,
Et a conjuge, liberisque impense dilectus,
Qui, ne deesset etiam mortuo pietatis suae testimonium,
Hoc marmor ei moerentes posuerunt,

Promotus	Natus
Ad archidiaconatum Bercheriensem 20 Feb. 1672.	Bradfordiae *in hoc comitatu* 16 Feb. 1644.
Canonicatum Norvicensem 26 Mart. 1675.	*In academiam cooptatus* 16 Apr. 1660.
Rectoriam S. Bartholomaei 22 Apr. 1675.	*Gradus suscepit*
Sancti Egidii in campis 3 Jan. 1675.	*Artium baccalaurei* 26 Dec. 1663.
Decanatum Norvicensem 8 Julii 1681.	*Artium magistri* 9 Julii 1667.
Cantuariensem 25 Nov. 1689.	*Sanctae theologiae professoris* 8 Julii 1679.
Archiepiscopatum Eboracensem 5 Julii 1691.	Bathoniae *mortuus aetat. suae* 69, 2 Feb. 1713.
	Sepultus eodem quo natus est die Feb. 16, 1713.

Sir

2

The revd. Thomas Sharp, *D.D. Rector of* Rothbury, *Archdeacon of* Northumberland, *&c; presents this plate of his pious fathers monument to this Work and to Posterity. 1736*

1 2 3 4 5 6 Feet

Sir WILLIAM DAWES, *bart. seventy sixth archbishop.*

Queen *Ann*, upon the death of the former worthy and most reverend prelate, immediately translated sir *William Dawes*, bart. from the bishoprick of *Chester* to this see. The quick nomination of this gentleman proceeded, as is verily believed, from his predecessor's recommendation of him to her majesty, as a person every way qualified to succeed him. He was elected ten days after the former died; and was inthroned, by proxy, *March* 24. following. A. 1713.

Sir *William Dawes* was born at *Lyons* near *Braintree*, in *Essex*, *anno* 1671, of an honourable and once very opulent family; sir *Abraham Dawes*, our prelate's great grandfather, being esteemed one of the richest commoners of his time. By following the fortunes of the *royal martyr*, they in a great measure lost their own; and his son, unable to recompence them in their estate, bestowed a title upon the family; sir *John Dawes*, father to the archbishop, being created baronet the fourteenth of *Charles* II.

Our prelate had his first rudiments at *Merchant-Taylor's* school in *London*; from whence *anno* 1687, he was sent to St. *John's* college in *Oxford*; of which, in two years time he was made fellow. He was the youngest of three sons his father had; and the two eldest dying so close together that one post brought him the news of both their deaths, the title and estate of the family descended to him. After this he removed himself to *Catherine-hall* in *Cambridge*, as a fellow commoner; and commenced master of arts, at a proper standing, in that university. His original design of entering into holy orders was not diverted by the acquisition of his title and fortune; and the college of which he was a member, having a desire to chuse him their master, he was made doctor in divinity, in order to it, by royal mandate, at twenty seven years of age; and was the next year vice-chancellor of the university. His other preferments, besides the mastership of *Catharine-hall*, was the deanry of *Bocking* in *Kent*, prebendary of   and one of the queen's chaplains. *Anno* 1708, the bishoprick of *Chester* becoming void; her majesty gave it to sir *William*, as to a person every way deserving such a dignity in the church. And from thence he was translated, as I said before, to the archbishoprick of *York*.

This *gentleman*, and such indeed he was, as well as *christian bishop*, was a very great ornament to the high station he enjoyed. Being of a noble and majestick personage, and a sweet engaging behaviour, kind and respectful to his clergy, and human to all the world; no wonder the loss of such a governor is so long, and so sensibly, felt in this diocese. The mildness and indulgence that this prelate, and his excellent predecessor, shewed to their clergy, and to every one else that they had any authority over, will ever be remembered by them. They were sent, and they actually executed that *christian office*, not to *sheer* and *fleece*, but to defend, protect, and cherish the flock committed to their care. No cries of widows or orphans pursued them for scandalous extortions in renewing their leases; nor was the church's patrimony raked into, and plundered to the detriment of it and their successors. In fine, he was snatched away from us by the angry hand of providence, much too immaturely; for his age, health, constitution and remarkable temperance seemed to prognosticate length of days to himself, and of consequence, a longer happiness to his diocese. He died of a feaver, attended with a *diarrhoea*, at his house in *Suffolk-street*, *London*, *April* 30, 1724, aged fifty three years, and was buried in the chapel belonging to his college in *Cambridge*, near his lady. There is no monument as yet put up over this worthy prelate, which makes me more copious in the recital of his preferments and character; and if the reader desires to see a larger account of his family, of himself, or of his pious writings, he may find it in the preface to the last edition of his sermons.

LANCELOT BLACKBURN, *seventy seventh archbishop.* A. 1724.

A CATALOGUE of the Succession of the ARCHBISHOPS *of* YORK, *with their contemporary* POPES *and* KINGS.

Bishops or popes of Rome.	*Anno Dom.*	*Archbishops of* York.	*Kings of* Northumberland, *&c.*	*Anno Reg.*
Honorius I.	625.	1. Paulinus.	Edwin.	9.
Vitalianus.	663.	2. Cedda.	Oswyn.	
	666.	3. S. Wilfrid.		
Donus	677.	4. Bosa.	Egfrid.	9.
Agatho.	692.	5. St. John *of* Beverley.		
Gregory II.	718.	6. Wilfrid II.	Osric II.	2.
Gregory III.	731.	7. Egbert.	Ceolwulph.	5.
Sede vacante.	767.	8. Coena, *or* Adelbert.	Ethelwald.	
Adrian I.	780.	9. Eanbald.	Edelred.	2.
Leo III.	797.	10. Eanbald II.	Alred.	
	812.	11. Wulsius.		
Gregory IV.	832.	12. Wymond.	*Danish kings or gouvernours.*	
Leo IV.	854.	13. Wilferus.		
Benedict IV.	900.	14. Adelbald.	Edward, *sen.*	1.
John XI.	921.	15. Lodeward.	Edward, *sen.*	21.
Stephen VII.	930.	16. Wulstan I.	Eadmund.	
Agapetus II.	955.	17. Oskitel.	Edred.	9.
John XIV.	971.	18. Athelwald.	Edgar.	12.
	971.	19. St. Oswald.		
John XVI.	992.	20. Adulph.	Ethelred.	16.
Silvester II.	1002.	21. Wolstan II.		25.
Benedict VIII.	1025.	22. Alfric Puttoc.	Canute.	7.
Leo IX.	1051.	23. Kinsius.	Edward the Confessor.	9.
Nicholas II.	1060.	24. Aldred.		20.
Alexander II.	1070.	25. Thomas, *sen.*	William the Conqueror.	5.
Paschal II.	1100.	26. Gerard.	Henry I.	1.
	1107.	27. Thomas *jun.*		10.
	1114.	28. Thurstan.		15.
Innocent II.	1140.	29. Henry Murdac.	Stephen.	5.
Anastasius IV.	1153.	30. St. William.		18.
	1154.	31. Roger.	Henry II.	1.
Celestine III.	1190.	32. Geofry Plantagenet.	Richard I.	1.
Innocent III.	1216.	33. Walter Grey.	John.	18.
Alexander IV.	1256.	34. Sewal de Bovil.	Henry III.	41.
	1258.	35. Godfrey de Ludham.		43.
Clement IV.	1265.	36. Walter Giffard		51.
Nicholas III.	1279.	37. William Wickwane	Edward I.	7.
Honorius IV.	1285.	38. John le Romane.		13.
Boniface VIII.	1296.	39. Henry de Newarke.		26.
	1299.	40. Tho. Corbridge.		27.
Clement V.	1305.	41. Will. de Grenefelde.		34.
John XXIII.	1315.	42. William de Melton.	Edward II.	11.
Benedict XII.	1340.	43. William le Zouch.	Edward III.	16.
Innocent VI.	1352.	44. John Thoresby.		28.
Gregory XI.	1374.	45. Alexander de Nevill.		48.
Urban VI.	1388.	46. Thomas Arundel.	Richard II.	12.
Boniface IX.	1397.	47. Robert Waldby.		20.
	1398.	48. Richard le Scrope		22.
Innocent VII.	1406.	49. Henry Bowet.	Henry IV.	9.
Martyn V.	1426.	50. John Kempe.	Henry VI.	4.
Nicholas V.	1452.	51. William Bothe.		31.
Paul II.	1464.	52. George Nevill.	Edward IV.	3.
Sixtus IV.	1477.	53. Laurence Bothe.		16.
	1480.	54. Tho. de Rotheram.		20.
Alexander VI.	1501.	55. Thomas Savage.	Henry VII.	16.
Julius II.	1508.	56. Christ. Baynbridge.		24.
Leo X.	1514.	57. Thomas Wolsey.	Henry VIII.	6.
Clement VII.	1531.	58. Edward Lee		23.
Paul III.	1544.	59. Robert Holgate.		36.

ASTOR LIBRARY
NY

The particular devices, or family Arms, belonging to several Archbishops of York.

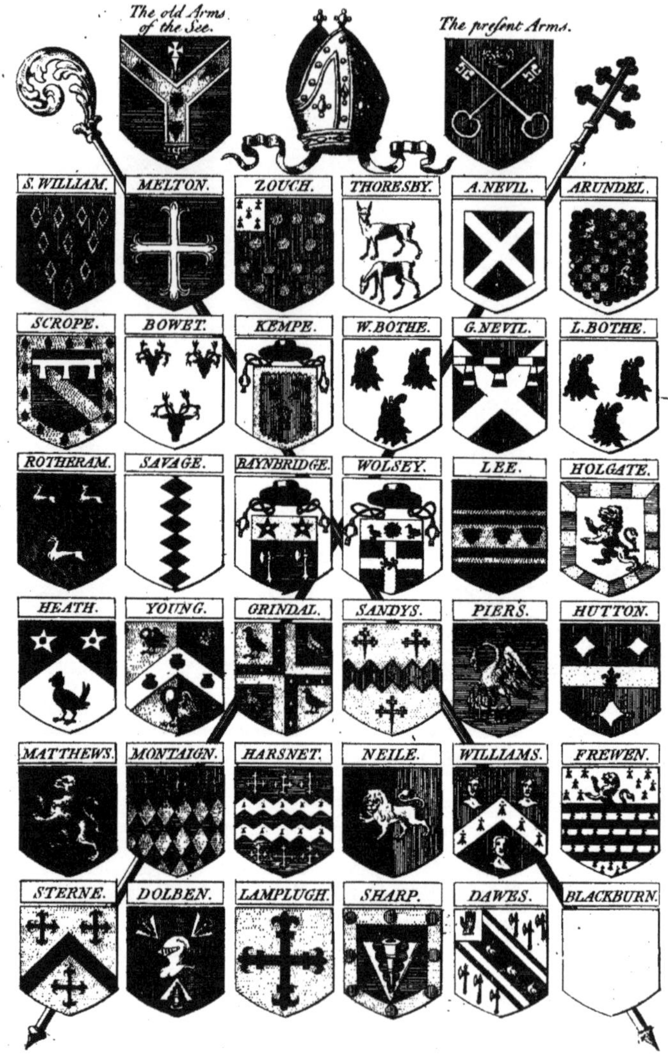

	Anno Dom.	*Archbishops of* York.	*Kings of* Northumberland, *&c.*	*Anno Reg.*
	1555.	60. Nicholas Heath.	Philip *and* Mary.	1 *and* 2.
The pope's authority ceases in England.	1561.	61. Thomas Younge.	Elizabeth.	2.
	1570.	62. Edmond Grindale.		12.
	1576.	63. Edwyn Sandys.		18.
	1588.	64. John Piers.		30.
	1594.	65. Mat. Hutton.		36.
	1606.	66. Tobias Matthews.	James I.	3.
	1628.	67. George Mountain.	Charles I.	3.
	1629.	68. Samuel Harfnet.		4.
	1631.	69. Richard Neile.		6.
	1641.	70. John Williams.		16.
	1660.	71. Accepted Frewen.	Charles II.	12.
	1664.	72. Richard Sterne.		16.
	1683.	73. John Dolben.		35.
	1688.	74. Thomas Lamplugh.	James II.	4.
	1691.	75. John Sharp.	William III.	3.
	1713.	76. *Sir* William Dawes.	Ann.	12.
	1724.	77. Lancelot Blackburne	George I.	10.

CHAP.

CHAP. II.

The particular hiſtory of the fabrick of the cathedral church of York; *from its firſt foundation to the preſent condition of that noble ſtructure. With the ſcite of the tombs, monuments, reſpective epitaphs,* &c.

SO much has been ſaid in the preceding chapter, on the converſion of the *Saxons* to the *chriſtian* faith, that there needs no repetition of it here. What is properly introductory to this ſubject is the baptiſm of *Edwin* the *Saxon* king; whom when *Paulinus* the biſhop had influenced to receive the ſacred laver from his hands; and a day was appointed to perform the ceremony; the whole city of *York* was at that time reduced to ſo low an ebb, by the late devaſtations, that it could not afford a temple big though for the occaſion. Whether the *Roman* ſtructures were then quite eraſed in the city, as well as the *Britiſh* churches, which *Monmouth* tells us *Aurelius* firſt, and afterwards king *Arthur*, took ſuch care to rebuild and reſtore to their former glory, I ſhall not take upon me to determine. But it is certain, by venerable *Bede*'s account, that no place was then found in the city, or at leaſt was thought proper by the prelate, for initiating ſo great a king into the myſteries of our moſt holy religion. A little oratory of wood was therefore occaſionally thrown up, in the very place where the great church now ſtands, and dedicated to St. *Peter*. In which, on *Eaſter-day*, being *April* 12, 627, one hundred and eight years after the coming of the *Saxons* into *Britain*, the king and his two ſons *Oſfrid* and *Edfrid*, whom he had by a former wife, with many more of the nobility, were ſolemnly baptized.

A. DCXXVII The ceremony over, ſays *Bede*, the prelate took care to acquaint the king, that ſince he was become a *Chriſtian*, he ought to build an houſe of prayer more ſuitable to the divinity he now adored; and adequate to the power and grandeur of ſo mighty a monarch as himſelf. By the biſhop's directions he began to build a magnificent fabrick of *ſtone, ipſo in loco* (a), where the other ſtood, and in the midſt of which encloſed the oratory already erected. For, as the carrying on a work of this nature muſt alſo be a work of time, the oratory aforeſaid was to ſerve for the ſolemnizing the divine offices till the other was finiſhed. The building went on very faſt, but ſcarcely were the walls erected, that is ſo far as to come to roofing, when the royal founder was ſlain, the prelate forced to fly the country, and the fabrick left in the naked condition it was juſt arrived to.

A. DCXXXII In this manner the church lay neglected ſome time, untill *Oſwald*, a ſucceſſor of *Edwin*'s, about the year 632, undertook to finiſh what was ſo worthily begun, and lived to compleat it. But ſcarcely was it brought to this perfection, when *Oſwald* was likewiſe ſlain in battle by *Penda* the pagan king of *Mercia*; and his new erected ſtructure well nigh demoliſhed.

Bede tells us, that this firſt temple of ſtone was a (b) ſquare building, and that it was alſo dedicated to St. *Peter*; the feaſt of which dedication was very anciently inſtituted, and long held in this church, with great ſolemnity, annually, on the firſt day of *October* and ſeven days following. The order for making this a double feſtival, ſays *Torre*, was renewed *anno* 1462.

In the ruinous condition deſcribed above did *Wilfrid* find it, on his being made archbiſhop of this province, in the year 669. The prelate much troubled, ſays *Bede*, at the uſage the
A. DCLXIX. church had undergone, being then ſo deſolate as to be fit only for birds to build their neſts in, ſet about with the utmoſt vigour to repair and reſtore it to its former grandeur. The walls he repaired, fixed on the roof, took care to cover all with lead, and glazed the windows, to preſerve it from the injuries of the weather, and prevent the birds from defiling of it (c). *Eddius*, who wrote the life of *Wilfrid*, and who is ſaid to have flouriſhed about the year 720, gives this account of the cathedral's firſt reparation. It is plain by both his teſtimony, and that of venerable *Bede*, contemporary, that maſonry and glazing were uſed here long before *Benedict* the monk, who is put down as the firſt introducer of theſe arts into *England*.

And now, by the hand of providence, the church ſtood and flouriſhed, under the ſucceſſive beneficence of its ſpiritual governors, for near four hundred years. In which time ſeveral additions and reparations muſt have been made to it by them; but, what or how,
A. DCCLX. hiſtory is ſilent in. Except the library beſtowed upon it by archbiſhop *Egbert*; and this ex-

(a) *In quo poſtmodum loco* per quadrum *aedificata baſilica doctori ſuo* Paulino *ſedem epiſcopatus dedit*. Bede. Gervaſ. *act. pont.* Cant. Ðær ſe cining ſealde Pauline biſcop-ſetl, ⁊ þær he het eft timbrian of ſtane. Chron *Saxon*. p. 28.

(b) *Templum per quadrum aedific.* Bede.

(c) *Culmina corrupta tecti renovans, artificiosè plumbo puro tegens, per feneſtras introitum avium et imbrium* vitro *prohibuit, per quod tamen intra lumen radiabat. Vita* S. Wilfridi Eddio Stephano, *Inter ſcript*. xv. *ed*. Gale.

traordinary

traordinary donation, which our *Alcuin* gives so high an *encomium* of, became the rich furniture of our church about the year 740; of which I shall be more particular in its proper place. CATHEDRAL CHURCH.

During the *Danish* invasions, which were carried on with fire and sword quite through the kingdom, our city, and consequently the cathedral, must have shared the same fate; though no account appears of the latter's misfortunes till the year 1069. And then the A. 1069.
Northumbrians, aided by the *Danes*, seeking to throw off the *conqueror's* tyrannical yoke, the garisons in the castles, as has been more largely treated on in the annals of this work, fearing least the houses in the suburbs should serve the enemy to fill up the motes and ditches, set fire to them; which spreading by an accidental wind farther than it was designed, burned down great part of the city, and with it our cathedral fell, in, almost, one common ruin.

The ancient fabrick thus destroyed and laid in ashes, the canons of the church were expulsed from their stalls, and the revenues of it siezed into the conqueror's hands. But after some time having made *Thomas* his chaplain and treasurer, archbishop of this province, the temporalities were restored to him. And this prelate took possession of his church A. 1070.
and diocese, at a time when both were made desolate, and near totally destroyed.

Thomas, however, set himself heartily to work to restore them to their former splendor. The church he rebuilt, much larger and nobler than it was before, recalled the banished ecclesiasticks, filled vacancies, and in short established, in every particular, the fabrick, in as good, or better, condition than ever *(d)*.

Once more raised to grandeur, the church continued in great prosperity till the year 1137; A. 1137.
when *June* 4, a casual fire began in the city, which burned down the cathedral again; and along with it St. *Mary*'s abby, and thirty nine parish churches. This accident happened in the episcopacy of archbishop *Thurstan*; and we find an indulgence granted soon after, by *Jocline* bishop of *Sarum*; setting forth, that "whereas the metropolitical church of *York* "was consumed by a new fire, and almost subverted, destroyed, and miserably spoiled of "its ornaments, therefore to such as bountifully contributed towards the re-edification of it, "he released to them forty days of penance injoyned *(e)*.

Notwithstanding this, our church lay in ashes all the time of archbishop *Henry Murdac*, and St. *William*, *Thurstan*'s immediate successors; until *Roger* archbishop, *anno* 1171, be- A. 1171.
gan to rebuild the quire, with its vaults, and lived to perfect them. Afterwards in the reign of *Henry* III. *Walter Grey*, *Roger's* successor, added the south part of the cross isle of A. 1227.
the church; for we find that *anno* 1227, another indulgence was published, by the said *Walter*, of forty days relaxation, *&c.* to those benefactors who liberally contributed towards the work of the fabrick thereof *(f)*.

About the beginning of the reign of king *Edward* I, *John le Romain*, then trea- A. 1260.
surer of the church, father to the archbishop of the same name, began and finished the north transept, as also a handsome steeple in the midst *(g)*. His son proved yet a greater benefactor, for history informs us that *Apr.* 7, 1291, the foundation of the nave of this great
church of St. *Peter* was laid from the west end eastward; there being then present *John le* A. 1291.
Romain archbishop, *Henry de Newark* dean, and *Peter de Ross* precentor of the church; the rest of the canons in their richest copes attending. Before whom the said archbishop, invocating the grace of the holy ghost, in great devotion laid the first stone with his own hands *(h)*. This is agreeable to the account the table bears which still hangs up in the vestry, containing these words.

An. Dom. MCCXCI.
Inceptum est novum opus corporis eccl. Ebor. per Johannem Romanum archiep^m ejusdem et infra xl annos quasi completum per Willielmum de Melton archiepiscopum.

William de Melton, archbishop, was the next founder; who getting together good work- A. 1320.
men, says *Stubbs*, carried on the building his predecessor had begun, and finished the west end with the steeples as it remains at this day. In this work the prelate is said to expend seven hundred pounds of his own money; but he must have had large contributions from the nobility, gentry and religious devotees of that age, to enable him to go through with this noble performance. Accordingly our records furnish us with this evidence how some of the money was raised.

Dat. kal. Feb. anno 1320.

William de Melton, archbishop, granted an indulgence of forty days relaxion to all such well disposed people, as pleased to extend their charitable contributions, towards the building of this late prostrate fabrick; whereby he might be the better enabled to finish so noble a structure then newly begun *(i)*. And again,

(d) Th. Stubbs *act. pont.* Ebor. *in vita* Thomae I.
(e) *Ex MS.* Torre, *p.* 2. *ex registro magno albo in custodia decani cap.* Ebor.
(f) *Ex eodem. A rot. major.* W. Grey.
(g) Th. Stubbs *act. pont.* Ebor.
(h) Th. Stubbs.
(i) *Ex MS.* Torre, *p.* 3.

On the first of *March* 1352, a brief issued out by the archbishop's authority (*John Thoresby*) directed to all abbots, barons, colleges, archdeacons, officials, rural-deans, parsons, vicars, *&c.* within the city, diocese and province of *York*; requiring and exhorting them, in the name of the lord, to ask and demand the alms and charitable benevolence of the people, and cause the same to be duly collected for the use and consummation of this fabrick begun, of so noble a stone work and so laudable a structure. And,

According to the indulgences already granted, letters mandatory issued out, from the chapter of *York*; directed to all rectors, vicars, and parochial chaplains, within the respective prebends, dignities and community of the church, enjoining them by virtue of their canonical obedience, and under pain of the greater excommunication, to suffer their collectors in their parishes and chapelries to ask and gather the charitable alms of the people for the use of the fabrick of this church. This act of chapter was dated *Festo S. Mich. anno* 1355 (*k*).

These briefs and letters mandatory were circulated through the province, in order to raise a sum sufficient for *John Thoresby*, archbishop, to begin and carry on a noble design he had formed of building a new quire. The old one, built by *Roger*, being like the old nave in its ancient pravity and deformity; and no ways answerable to the west end of the church lately erected. Accordingly,

On the twentieth of *July* 1361. *John Thoresby* archbishop, together with the chapter, taking into consideration that this cathedral church ought in all respects to be of the same uniformity and proportion: And that the quire, a place peculiarly assigned for offering expiatory sacrifices, and exercising other divine offices, more especially, ought to be adorned with the neatest structure. And that in this church of *York*, there was no place suitable where our lady's mass, the glorious mother of God, could decently be celebrated. Therefore they unanimously agreed and consented to begin the new work of the quire, which then if compared with the new erected nave was very rude and disorderly, and so resolved that the old quire should be wholly taken down and re-edified. And that the old hall and chambers of the archbishop's manor of **Shireburn**, being then ruinous and unnecessary, should be demolished, and the stone and other materials thereof be applied to the work of the new quire which was then with all expedition to be carried on (*l*).

A. 1361. Whereupon, on the twenty ninth of *July* 1361, this *John Thoresby*, archbishop, laid the first stone of the new quire; and the same table in the vestry bears this testimony of it:

An. Dom. M.CCCLXI. Inceptum est novum opus chori eccl. Ebor. per Johannem de Thursby archiepiscopum.

I shall next beg leave to subjoin an account of what this pious archbishop bestowed out of his own private purse to carry on his new design; which must be allowed extraordinary, considering the value of money then and now. The wages of workmen about this time, according to bishop *Fleetwood*'s *chronicon pretiosum*, was three pence a day to a master mason, or carpenter, and three half pence to their **knaves** or servants. A pound of silver at that time was a pound weight, which is equal to three pounds of our present money; so that one hundred pounds of silver in those days, would buy as much provision, or pay for as much work done, to speak within compass, as fifteen hundred will do now; which makes our prelate's generosity very considerable. Nor was the court of *Rome* unmindful of furthering this pious design, but, in their way, granted a number of plenary indulgences which must also raise a large sum. And indeed whoever surveys this part of the building with circumspection, must imagine that it could not be carried on and finished under a greater contribution than I believe any protestant country could now raise on the like occasion. But to proceed,

	l.	*m.*
(*m*) *Aug.* 1, 1361. archbishop *Thoresby* directed his letters to *William de Wicklesworth*, ordering him to pay into the hands of *John de Codyngham*, then *custos* of the fabrick, the sum of one hundred marks which he had before given to the new foundation of the quire ——	—	100
Oct. 3, 1361. he gave to the fabrick more	50	—
Apr. 5, 1362. he ordered his receiver to pay uuto *Robert Ryther*, lord of *Ryther*, twenty pound sterling, being the price of twenty four oaks bought of him for the use of the fabrick of this church —— ——	20	—
Aug. 16, 1362. the said archbishop paid into the hands of the *custos* of the new work of the quire for the use thereof —— ——	100	—
Feb. 11, 1362. he gave more for the same use —— ——	100	—
Apr. 18, 1363. he gave —— —— —— ——	100	—
July 3, 1363. he gave more —— —— ——	100	—
Carried over	470	100

(*k*) *Ex MS.* Torre, *p.* 3.
(*l*) *Ex MS.* Torre *ab act. capit. orig.*

(*m*) *Ex MS.* Torre *extract. a registro* Thoresby, *p.* 5.

Nov. 3,

CATHEDRAL CHURCH.

	l.	m.
Brought over — —	470	100
November 3, 1363, he commanded his receiver to pay unto *John de Sandale* and *John de Feriby*, keepers of the fabrick, one hundred pound, which he had given towards this new work of the choir.	100	—
July, 13, 1365, he contributed more — —	100	—
Aug. 20, 1366, the archbishop issued out his precept to his receiver to pay unto *Adam de Heredlay*, all and singular the portions of that subsidy, formerly granted by the clergy of the diocese of *York*, for the use of the *minster*; and at the same time added of his own donation	100	—
November 5, 1366, he gave to the use of the said work another	100	—
July 7, 1367, he bestowed another — — —	100	—
April 2, 1368, he gave to the same use — —	100	—
November 14, 1368, another — —	100	—
January 18, 1369, he likewise contributed another — —	100	—
July 28, 1370, another — — —	100	—
November 15, 1370, he gave more — — —	100	—
May 10, 1371, he ordered to be paid to the *custos* —		40
July 15, 1371, and *November* 1, 1371, he bestowed on the fabrick	200	—
In all	1670	140

Anno 1361, archbishop *Thoresby* granted an indulgence of forty days relaxation to the benefactors of the fabrick to this new choir.

Likewise pope *Innocent* VI. ganted another indulgence of two years and two quarters relaxation to the liberal contributors to this new work.

On the 13th of *February*, 1361, the chapter of *York* laid an imposition, or subsidy, of the twentieth part of all ecclesiastical benefices, *viz.* of dignities, prebends, administrations, and offices belonging to the church, for the necessary repairs and re-edification of the quire, steeples, and defects of other places, *&c.* To continue for the term of three years ensuing, and payable at the feasts of the purification of St. *Mary*, her nativity, and St. *John Baptist*, by equal portions.

In the year 1366, pope *Urban* V. granted one years indulgence to the charitable benefactors of the fabrick of this new choir.

And pope *Urban* VI, by his apostolical bull, dated *kal. Aug. anno* 1379, in the second year of his pontificate, granted licence to the dean and chapter to receive the fruits of the church of *Misterton*, then rated at thirty five marks sterling *per annum*, during the space of ten years, to be applied to the use of the fabrick of this new choir (*n*).

By these, and other like, methods of raising money, a vast sum must have been collected; which not only enabled the undertakers to build up the choir, but made them cast their eyes on the lanthorn steeple built by *John Romain*; which now seemed too mean for the rest of the fabrick. Encouraged by a large donation made them by *Walter Skirlaw*, prebendary of *Fenton*, archdeacon of the east riding; and afterwards made bishop of the two sees of *Litchfield* and *Durham*, the old steeple was taken down and a new one erected. The work was begun *anno* 1370; and was seven or eight years in building. I purposely omit giving the abstracts, which Mr. *Torre* has taken, from the original indentures, betwixt the several workmen concerned in the building and the master of the fabrick about their wages. I shall only take notice here that *John le Plommer* of *Blake-street* covenanted to undertake the whole plummer's work of the church, and to perform it with his own hands; and was to have for his wages two shillings and six pence *per* week. The articles of agreement in relation to the glazing the windows, especially the noble east light, will fall better in another place.

And we now see our church erected in the manner it stands in at this day. If we compute the time it was in building from the first beginning of the south cross, by *Walter Grey*, which was about the year 1227, it will appear to be near two hundred years in compleating the whole. For though the work went on briskly in archbishop *Thoresby's* time, yet it was not near finished, as appears by the arms of several of his successors on the stone work and windows of the church; particularly *Scrope* and *Bowett*; the latter of which entered upon his dignity *anno* 1405. And further, our records inform us that the dean and chapter granted out of their spiritual revenues a full tenth to the use of the fabrick then *newly built*. Which grant was dated *April* 11, 1426 (*o*).

In all which time of different erections great care was taken in the joining and uniting of one building to another, by which it seems to be one entire edifice at this day; though composed of five several tastes of *Gothick* architecture. Yet they could not be so nice in this, but that an apparent irregularity shews itself to a discerning eye, which will be taken notice of in the sequel. However that, posterity ought to revere the memory of the kings,

(*n*) *Ex MS.* Torre.

(*o*) *Torre* p. 7. where he recites, that *anno* 1432, they granted to the fabrick another tenth out of their benefices.

 princes,

CATHEDRAL CHURCH. princes, prelates, nobility and gentry of those days, who were contributors, at several times, to the carrying on this noble and magnificent building; as their arms in divers parts of the walls and windows do sufficiently testify. Particularly the prelates, who, with a liberality, not common to the order in our days, bestowed great part of the revenues of their see in furthering on this commendable work. I shall conclude this historical account of the erection of our present cathedral, with an encomium an old poet has bestowed on its principal founders, wherein the honesty of the thought must excuse the metre.

> (p) Grey, Romain, Melton, Thursby, Skirlaw, *who*
> York's *greatest good and splendour added to:*
> *Five generous souls have wrought that good, which now*
> *A nation's, ah, faint zeal, can scarce allow.*
> *May fame triumphant bear them from the grave,*
> *And grant a longer life than nature gave.*
> *And may the church still florish, still be strong,*
> *From all its governours receive no wrong,*
> *But by their cares still look for ever young.*

Having now built up our church, it will be necessary, in the next place, to take an exact survey of it both inside and outside; to mention the several out-buildings, chapels, chantries, oratories, benefactions and particular reparations which have since been added, before I enter upon the tombs and epitaphs. To begin with the dimensions, the whole pile is in the form of a cross extending from east to west,

	Feet.
The whole length besides the buttresses is	524 ½
Breadth of the east end	105
Breadth of the west end	109
Length of the cross isle from north to south	222
Height of the lanthorn steeple to the vault	188
Height of it to the top of the leads	213
Height of the body of the church	99

Chapter-house. To begin with the out-buildings, I must first enter upon a description of the chapter-house; which disdains to allow an equal, in *Gothick* architecture, in the universe. There is some difficulty to ascertain the time of erecting this magnificent structure, the remaining records of the church bearing no account thereof. *Stubbs*, who is particular enough in his memoirs of the rest of the buildings, entirely omits this; for which reasons we are much at a loss to know to whose memory to ascribe the praises due for this excellent performance. By the style of architecture it is composed on, it looks to be as antient as any part of the church; and exactly corresponds, in taste, to that part of the fabrick begun and finished by *Walter Grey*. And, indeed, if we may be allowed to guess at the founder, that eminent prelate stands the fairest of any in the succession for it. The pillars which surround the dome are of the same kind of marble of those which support his tomb. But what seems to put the matter out of dispute, is the picture of an archbishop, betwixt, those of a king and queen over the entrance; which by having a serpent under his feet, into the mouth of which his crosier enters, exactly corresponds with the like representation of *Walter Grey* on his monument. If this conjecture be allowed, as it is surely very probable, the world is indebted, for the hint, to the sagacious *Roger Gale* esq; who taking a view with me, some time since, of this room, made the observation.

The whole pile of this building is an octagon, of sixty three feet diameter, the height of it to the middle knot of the roof is sixty seven feet ten inches, unsupported by any pillar, and entirely dependant upon one pin, or plug, geometrically placed in the centre. The outside, however, is strongly supported by eight buttresses. The whole roof has been richly painted with the effigies of kings, bishops, *&c.* and large silver knots of carved wood at the uniting of the timbers; all which are now much defaced and sullied by time. Over this is a spire of timberwork, covered with lead, so excellent in its kind, that I have thought fit, for the honour of the carpenter's art, to give a representation of it in the draught.

The entrance from the church to this noble room is in the form of a mason's square. Against the pillar, betwixt the two doors, stands an image of stone of the virgin, with our saviour in her arms, trampling on the serpent. The image, with the drapery, is somewhat elegant, and has been all richly gilt; but it bears a mark of those times which made even stone statues feel their malice. At your entrance into the house, the first thing you observe are the canons seats, placed quite round the dome, which are all arched over; every arch being supported by small marble pillars which are set at due distance round, and separate the stalls. Over these arches, which are built like canopies, runs a gallery about the house, but so exquisitely carved, and has been so richly gilt and painted as to be above descrip-

(p) *Ex MS.* Gale. *Goodwin* writes, that *anno* 1464, the minster of *York* was burned down, but it is certainly a mistake. *Goodwin de præsul.*

tion.

An internal perspective view of the Chapter house at York.

J. Haynes delin. *The reverend* John Drake *B.D. Rector of* Kirk Smeaton, *Vicar of* Pontefract, *and Prebendary of ye Metropolitical Church of* York, *lest Time, or other accident should either destroy or deface this magnificent structure, presents this View of it to Posterity.* 1736. Harris sculp

ASTOR LIBRARY
NY

tion. The chapiters or capitals of the aforesaid small pillars have such a variety of carved fancies upon them, alluding in some places to the ridicule the regular clergy were always fond of expressing against the seculars; in others to history, with strange conceits of the over witty workmen of that age, that it is impossible to which stall to give the preference. Here you have antick postures both of men and beasts in abundance, over one is a man cut out half way, as if he was thrusting and striving to get through a window or some narrow passage. On others are faces with different aspects, some crying, some laughing, some distorted and grinning; but above all and what is never omitted shewing to strangers, by those living registers of the church, the vergers, is the figure of an old bald-pated friar, hugging and kissing a young nun, very amorously in a corner; and, round the capitals of the adjoining pillars, are several faces of other nuns, as well old as young, peeping, laughing, and sneering at the wanton dalliance of the old letcher. In other places you have a friar shooing a goose, greasing a fat sow in the ——; which are all testimonies of the sorry opinion that the regular clergy had of a monastick life in those days.

CATHEDRAL CHURCH.

The eight squares of the *octagon* have each a noble light window in them, adorned with coats of arms, pennances, and other devices. Except one square, which is joined to the other building over the entrance, and this has been painted with the representations of saints, kings, bishops, &c. the three figures in the midst, I take to be archbishop *Walter Grey*, standing betwixt *Henry* III, and his queen. At the base of this square was placed the images of the twelve apostles with that of the virgin, and child *Jesus*, in the midst of them. Tradition assures us, that these images were all of solid silver double gilt; the apostles were about a foot high, but that of the virgin must have been near two foot, as appears by the marks where they stood. These were morsels too pretious to miss swallowing at the first depredations made into churches; and since they are not put in the catalogue, printed in the *monasticon*, of the riches of this church, which was taken in *Edward* the sixth's time, we may readily suppose his father *Henry* had the honour of this piece of plunder. Or else that archbishop *Holgate* made him a present of them, along with the manors that prelate thought fit to give him from this see.

To enter upon a description of the imagery, in painted glass, which is still preserved in the windows of this place, and the rest of the church would be endless; and swell my volume to an enormous size indeed. Yet the indefatigable Mr. *Torre* has gone through it all, nor is there a single square in any window of the whole building that he has not described. But the arms of the nobility and gentry of *England*, who were contributors, originally to the charge of erecting this and other parts of the church are worth preserving. Especially since glass is of so frail a substance that it is almost a miracle so many coats are up in the windows at this day. In the year 1641, some curious person, and in all probability it was the industrious Mr. *Dodsworth*, took pains along with the monuments, to take drawings of all the coats armorial and bearings on the stone-work and windows of this church, chapterhouse, &c. A copy was obtained from the original, then in the possession of the lord *Fairfax*, by sir *William Dugdale* knt. and given by him to the college of arms *London*; as the title of the book does evidently shew. What relates to my purpose is from thence extracted; and I have taken out all the different bearings in the several parts of the church and chapterhouse, to shew the original benefactors to it. Their names, by some gentlemen well skilled in *heraldry*, being put over each coat. It is remarkable, that there are two coats in the windows of the chapterhouse, which go further to clear up the time of the building of it, and these are first cheque *or* and *azure*, a canton *ermine*, which arms *Heylin* gives to *Peter de Dreux*, duke of *Britain*; and *or*, a cross *gules*, *Hubert de Burgh*, earl of *Kent*; both contemporaries with *Walter Grey*; nor are there any descendants from them that I know of.

The title of the chapterhouse informs us of its use; namely; for the dean, prebendaries, and other dignitaries of the church to assemble in. It is also the place where the convocation for the clergy of the province of *York* used to meet; but, of late years, it has not been much frequented on that occasion.

I cannot take leave of this beautiful structure without observing, from *Camden*, the character *Aeneas Silvius*, afterwards pope *Pius* II, gives our church, and this place in particular, "It is, says he, famous for its magnificence and workmanship all the world over; "*but especially for a fine lightsome chapel, with shining walls, and small thin wasted pillars quite round.*" Neither must I omit an encomium bestowed upon it by a great traveller, as is said, in an old *monkish* verse, and is inscribed on the wall in *Saxon* letters as follows;

UT ROSA FLOS FLORUM SIC EST DOMUS ISTA DOMORUM.

"*The chief of houses as the rose of flowers.*"

CATHEDRAL CHURCH.

After all, this noble ſtructure had like to have met its fate, in the late days of rapine and ſacrilege; for we have a tradition very much credited, that a certain perſon in this city had obtained a grant, from the pious legiſlature, of thoſe days to pull down the chapter-houſe as an uſeleſs part of the church. We are further told, that the man had certainly effected it, and had deſigned to have built ſtables out of the materials, had not death ſurpriſed him a week before the intended execution of his wicked project.

In the ſquare paſſage to the chapter-houſe from the church, remarkable for its beautiful windows of painted glaſs, have been alſo many coats of arms delineated on the wall in their proper colours; particularly over the entrance. But time has ſo defaced them, that very few of them can be now made out. Here have been ſeveral ſepultures, but the grave ſtones are all robbed of their inſcriptions on braſs, and only one in ſtone remaining; which is this,

Mercifull Jhesu son of heven, for thi holi name, and thi bitter passion do thi grete mercy to the soule of Annes Huet, the whilk decesid the vii day of November in the yere of our Lord MCCCCLXXI.

St Sepulchre's chapel.

On the north ſide of the church, alſo, and near the archiepiſcopal palace, ſtood formerly the chapel of St. *Sepulchre*; which had a door ſtill remaining, opening into the north iſle of the nave. The foundation of this chapel being very antient and extraordinary, I ſhall tranſcribe from Mr. *Torre* as follows,

" *Roger* archbiſhop of *York* having built againſt the great church a chapel, he dedicated it to the name of the bleſſed and immaculate virgin *Mary* and holy angels; for the celebration of divine ſervices, to the eternal honour of God, glory of his ſucceſſors, and remiſſion of his own ſins. He ordained the ſame to be a perpetual habitation, for thirteen clerks of different orders, *viz.*

" Four prieſts.
" Four deacons.
" Four ſubdeacons.
" One ſacriſt.

" All theſe to be ſubſervient to the will of the archbiſhop, eſpecially the ſacriſt, who ſhall be conſtituted procurator of the rents and revenues belonging to it. Paying to each of the prieſts ten marks *per annum*; to each of the deacons one hundred ſhillings; to each of the ſubdeacons ſix marks. And he himſelf ſhall receive ten marks *per annum* for his own ſalary, beſides the reſidue of the rents that remain over, and beſides what will compleat the ſum of all the portions of the prieſts, deacons and ſubdeacons.

" Alſo he willed that the ſaid ſacriſt of his own coſt expend ten ſhillings on *Maunday*, as well in veiles, wine, ale, veſſels and water for waſhing the feet of the canons, and of other poor clerks, to the uſe of thoſe poor clerks. And alſo to contribute ſixteen ſhillings to the diet of the ſaid poor clerks; that in all things the fraternity and unity of the church may be preſerved.

" And for their neceſſary ſuſtentation he of his own bounty gave them

" The churches of
- **Everton**,
- **Sutton** with **Scroby** chapel,
- **Payton**,
- **Berdesey**,
- **Otteley** one mediety.

" And procured of the liberality of theſe other faithful perſons,

" The church of **Calverley**, *ex dono* Willielmi de Scoty.
" The church of **Hoton**, *ex dono* Willielmi Paganel.
" The church of **Harwode**, *ex dono* Avicie de Ruminilly.
" The church of **Thorpe**, *ex dono* Ade de Bruys *et* Ievtte de Arches *uxoris ſuae*.

" To this chapel alſo did belong the

" Churches of
- **Colingham**.
- **Clareburg**.
- **Retford**.

" *Roger* provided alſo that the churches which were not of his donation ſhould be free from ſynodals and all other things due to the archbiſhops, his ſucceſſors, and their officials. And ordered that they ſhould as quietly and freely hold and enjoy thoſe churches which are of his donation as others have done before them. Laſtly, he ordained, for the more diligent ſerving of the chapel, that none of the ſaid clerks ſhould dwell out of the city, which if they preſumed to do, they ſhould be diſplaced, by the archbiſhop, and another of the ſame order be by him collated.

Sewal

Sewal, archbishop, perceiving the revenues of these churches to be very much increased, appointed vicars to be established in them presentable by the *sacristan*; and made divers orders for the better government of the ministers, whom from thenceforth he caused to be called canons. These orders are at large in Mr. *Torre*'s, and printed in the first volume of *Stevens*'s *monasticon*; both extracted and translated from *Dugdale*. It would be needless here to insert them, as well as Mr. *Torre*'s catalogues of the names, and times of collation, of the *sacrists*, and all the sacerdotal prebendaries of this chapel, from its first original foundation to its dissolution. We may believe it underwent the last change very early in the work of the *Reformation*; for it was certified into the court of augmentations held in the thirty seventh year of the reign of *Henry* VIII. to be of the yearly value of one hundred and ninety two pounds sixteen shillings and six pence. But it was standing here much later, for I find that the tithes belonging to this chapel and the chapel itself, was sold to one *Webster* the fourth of *Elizabeth* (r). CATHEDRAL CHURCH.

The next out-building I shall mention is the vestry which joins to the church on the south side of it; it has a council room and treasury contiguous to it. In this last was kept all the rents, revenues, grants and charters with the common seal belonging to the church; and had a particular officer to inspect and take care of them. In the large inventary of the riches belonging to this cathedral, taken in *Edward* the sixth's time, is an account of the money then in St. *Peter*'s chest; which was all soon after seized upon and the treasurer's office dissolved. For a very good reason, says Mr. *Willis*, *nam*; Vestry.

Abrepto omni thesauro, desiit thesaurarii munus.

The council room, or inner vestry, where his grace of *York* robes himself, when he comes to his cathedral, is a convenient place, rendered warm and commodious for the clergy to adjourn to from the chapter-house in cold weather. In it is a large press, where are kept those acts and registers of the church which they want more immediately to consult on these occasions.

The vestry is a room forty four foot by twenty two; in the south corner of which, in the very wall is a well, of excellent water, called St. *Peter*'s *well*. Opposite is a great chest, of a triangular figure, strongly bound about with iron barrs, which by its shape must have once served to lay up the copes and priests vestments in. Along the north side are several large cupboards, in the wall, in which formerly were locked up the churches plate and other valuable things; but at present they are only enriched with the following curiosities. A canopy of state of gold tissue and two small coronets of silver gilt; which were given by the city for the honour of king *James* I. at his coming out of *Scotland* to this place in his progress to *London*. Two silver chalices found in the graves of two archbishops; some other of lead found elsewhere, with other curiosities taken out of several graves in laying the new pavement. The head of archbishop *Rotheram*. A cope of plain white sattin, the only one left us out of the large inventory of this churche's ornaments. And lastly the famous horn, if I may so call it, made of an elephant's tooth, which is indeed the greatest piece of antiquity the church can exhibit.

(r) *Capella, vocat* St. Sepulchre's chapel, *prope ecclesiam cath.* Eborum *cum decimis ejusdem* W. Webster Apr. 4. *ab.* 4° Elis. Rolls chap.

This

Curiositys in the Vestry.

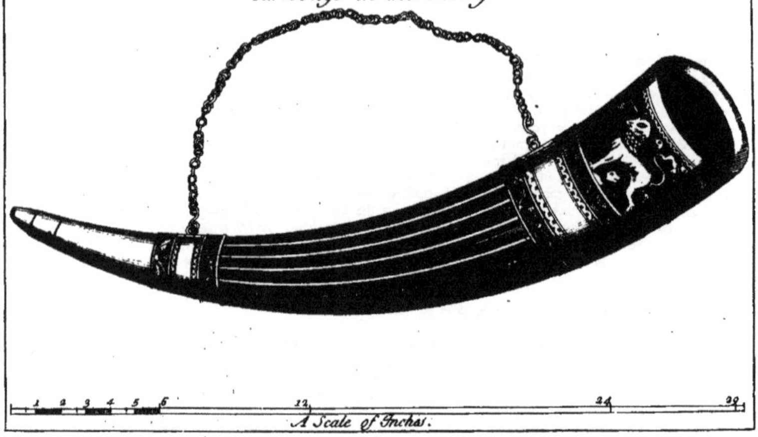

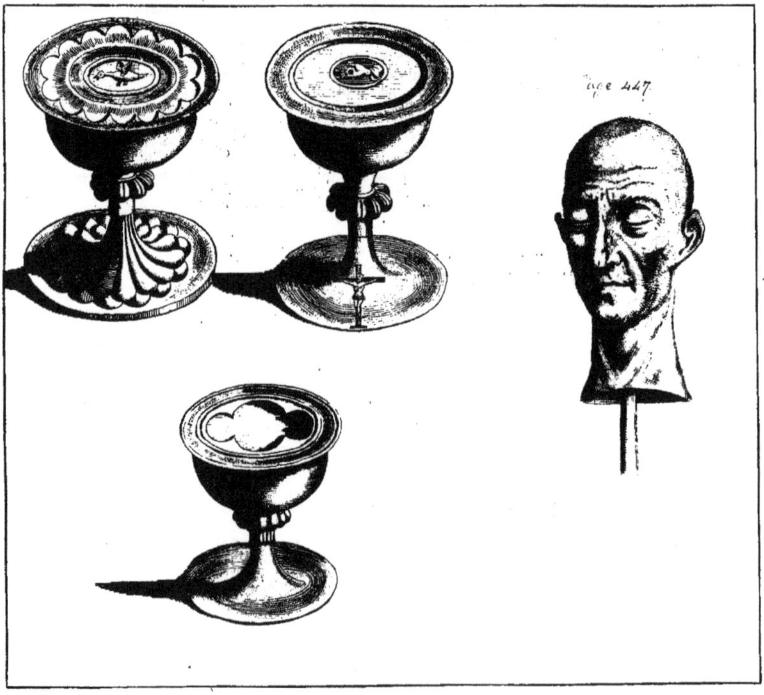

CATHEDRAL CHURCH.

This horn Mr. *Camden* particularly mentions as a mark of a strange way of endowment formerly used; and from an old book, as he terms it, gives us this quotation about it. " *Ulphus* the son of *Toraldus* governed in the west parts of *Deira*, and by reason of a diffe- " rence like to happen betwixt his eldest son and his youngest, about his lordships, when " he was dead, presently took this course to make them equal. Without delay he went to " *York*, and taking the horn wherein he was wont to drink with him, he filled it with wine, " and, kneeling upon his knees before the altar, bestowed upon God and the blessed St. *Pe-* " *ter* all his lands, tenements *(r)*, &c.

In ancient times there are several instances of estates that were passed without any writings at all; by the lord's delivery of such pledges as these, a sword, a helmet, a horn, a cup, a bow or arrow; *nudo verbo, absque scripto vel chartæ, tantum cum domini gladio, vel galea, vel cornu*, are the express words of *Ingulphus*. But I shall say less about this venerable piece of antiquity, because my ingenious friend Mr. *Sam. Gale* has wrote a dissertation upon that particular subject; which, I am given to hope, will see light in the *appendix* to this work.

The church of *York* ought to pay a high veneration to this horn, several lands belonging to it are still called *de terra Ulphi*; and before the *Reformation* it was handsomely adorned with gold, and was pendant in a chain of the same metal. These ornaments were the occasion of its being taken away at that time; for it is plain by Mr. *Camden*'s words that the horn was not there in his days. " I was informed, says he, that this great curiosity was kept " in the church till the last age." We are not therefore to blame the civil wars for this piece of pillage; for a principal actor in them, *Thomas* lord *Fairfax*, was the occasion of its being preserved and restored to the church. Where it had lain, or where he got it, is uncertain; but, stript of its golden ornaments, it was returned by *Henry* lord *Fairfax* his successor. The chapter thought fit to decorate it anew, and to bestow the following inscription to the memory of the restorer upon it:

CORNV HOC, VLPHVS, IN OCCIDENTALI PARTE
DEIRAE PRINCEPS, VNA CVM OMNIBVS TERRIS
ET REDDITIBVS SVIS OLIM DONAVIT.
AMISSVM VEL ABREPTVM
HENRICVS DOM. FAIRFAX DEMVM RESTITVIT.
DEC. ET CAPIT. DE NOVO ORNAVIT
A. D. M.DC.LXXV.

On the south side of the vestry hang up, against the wall, two ancient tables, which are little taken notice of, and yet must not be omitted in this survey. The one contains a catalogue of the miracles ascribed to the virtues of our S. *William*, twenty three years after his death, and are thirty nine in number. The other is a copy of an indulgence granted by pope *Nicholas*, mentioned in the life of that prelate, with other abstracts from history relating to this church. These tables, I take it, are the only rags of popery we have left us; and I am persuaded had they been worth carrying away, our eyes would never have seen them.

Here is also an antique chair in which several kings of *England* have been crowned; and which the archbishop also makes use of, within the rails of the altar, at ordinations, &c. On the furniture cloths of the vestry are the arms of *Scrope* lord *Masham*, *Booth*, archbishop, and *Kemp*. To conclude this account of the vestry I should give the inventory of the plate, jewels, vestments, &c. which were reposited in the treasury here, or adorned the several shrines and altars in the church. But since this is printed at large in *Stevens*'s *Monasticon*, translated from *Dugdale*'s, and is, indeed, too copious for this design, I shall refer thither. And only beg leave to give a much shorter account, as I find it in another epitome of the *monasticon* in these words *(s)*:

" To this cathedral church did belong abundance of jewels, vessels of gold and silver, and " other ornaments, rich vestments and books, amongst which were ten mitres of great va- " lue; and one small mitre set with stones, *pro episcopo puerorum*, for the bishop of the boys, " or children *(t)*. One silver and gilt pastoral staff, many pastoral rings, amongst which one " for the bishop of the boys. Chalices, viols, pots, basons, candlesticks, thuribules, holy- " water-pots, crosses of silver, one of which weighed eight pounds six ounces, Images of " silver and gold, relicts in cases extreamly rich, great bowls of silver, an unicorn's horn, " a table of silver and gilt, with the image of the virgin enamelled thereon, weighing nine " pounds eight ounces and a half. Several gospellaries and epistolaries richly adorned " with silver, gold and precious stones. Jewels affix'd to shrines and tombs of, almost, " an inestimable value. Altar-cloths and hangings very rich; copes of tissue, damask " and velvet, white, red, blue, green, black and purple; with other vestments of the " same colours. Besides this there was a great treasure, deposited in the common chest, in " gold chains, collars of SS, &c. with large sums of old gold and silver.

(r) *Camden*'s *Britannia*. See *York*.
(s) Fol. printed at *London* 1693.

(t) In these articles, the *episcopus puerorum*, or the barne bushop, was the chorister's boy-bishop. Mr. *Gre-*

I have

CATHEDRAL CHURCH.

I have nothing to add to the churches being plundered of all these immense riches, but a small robbery, in comparison of the former, done in the Night of *Feb.* 5, 1676; when the church was broke open, as well as the cupboards in the vestry, and most of the plate, they then were possessed of, stole from thence. But the actors of this sacrilegious fact were never yet known. *Sic parvis componere, &c.*

Zouch's chapel.

The place which is now called the vestry was not anciently such, but a chapel begun by archbishop *Zouch*; who we are told laid the foundation of a chapel, about the year 1350, in which he intended to have been buried, but dying before it was finished, he was interred elsewhere (u). This chapel is said to have been erected on the south-side of the church, and Mr. *Torre* brings several testimonies from the records, to prove that this was the place (x). At the new erection of the choir it was taken down, but rebuilt at the charge of archbishop *Zouche*'s executors, and it continued a chantry chapel, to pray for the good of that prelate's soul, to the dissolution.

Library.

The library is a building adjoining to the church, on the south side, being a chamber of oblong square over another room now made use of for the singing school. In the midst is a long gallery, or walk, running from east to west, which divides it into two parts, wherein are set up frames or classes for the convenient standing of the books. Most of the volumes were the gift of Mrs. *Mathews* the relict of *Toby Mathews* archbishop, whose son sir *Toby* having been disinherited by his father, was probably the reason that the mother bestowed her husband's books, to the number of three thousand volumes, on the church. Upon a table, now broken, is an inscription in memory of this bequest in these words:

Nomina virorum illustrium, aliorumque bonarum artium fautorum, qui post immensam variamque rei literariae supellectilem, musaeo reverendissimi in Christo patris Tobiae Matthaei *archiepiscopi* Eborum *aeternae memoriae viri post obitum illius huc translatb per munificentiam insignis foeminae*

FRANCISCAE MATTHEW;

Bibliothecam hujus ecclesiae cathedralis et metropoliticae suis impensis ac liberalitate ornarunt auxeruntque.

Dux foemina facti.

But great was the loss to the learned world when the library, placed in this church by archbishop *Egbert*, *anno* 740, was burnt with the whole fabrick about three hundred years after. So choice was this collection that *William*, the librarian of *Malmsbury*, calls it the *noblest repository and cabinet of arts and sciences then in the whole world.* (y) *Alcuinus Eboracensis*, the preceptor of the emperour *Charles* the great, at his return into *Britain* wrote his royal pupil a letter; in which the highest encomiums are bestowed on this library. I cannot do better than to give the reader them in his own words and phrase (z).

—— *Sed ex parte detis mihi servulo vestro exquisitiores scholasticae eruditionis libellos, quos habui in patria per bonam et devotiss. magistri mei, scil.* Egberti, *industriam, vel etiam mei ipsius qualemcunque sudorem. Ideo haec vestrae excellentiae dico, ne forte vestro placeat totius sapientiae desiderantiss. consilio; ut aliquos ex pueris nostris remittam, qui excipiant nobis inde necessaria quaeque, et revehant in* Franciam flores Britanniae. *Ut non sit tantummodo in* Euborica *civitate hortus conclusus, sed in* Turonica *emissiones paradysi cum pomorum fructibus, ut veniens auster perflare [possit] hortos, Ligeri, fluminis, et fluant auromata illius, &c.*

The same ancient writer in his elegant poem *de pontificibus et sanctis ecclesiae Ebor.* printed in Dr. *Gale*'s xv. *scriptores* has left this description of the volumes contained in this library. Which manuscripts, were they now in being, would be almost of inestimable value.

Illic invenies veterum vestigia patrum,
Quicquid habet pro se Latio Romanus *in orbe,*
Graecia *vel quidquid transmisit clara* Latinis;
Hebraicus *vel quod populus bibit imbre superno,*
Africa *lucisluo vel quidquid lumine sparsit.*
Quod pater Hyeronymus, *quod sensit* Hilarius, *atque*
Ambrosius *praesul, simul* Augustinus, *& ipse*
Sanctus Athanasius, *quod* Orosius *edit acutus*;
Quidquid Gregorius *summus docet, et* Leo *papa*;
Basilius *quidquid,* Fulgentius *atque coruscans,*
Cassiodorus *item,* Chrysostomus *atque* Johannes.
Quidquid et Althelmus *docuit, quid* Beda *magister,*
Quae Victorinus *scripsere,* Boetius; *atque*

gorie has wrote a curious treatise concerning the *episcopus puerorum in die innocentium*; upon the discovery of a grave-stone in the cathedral of *Salisbury*, whereon was the effigies of a boy bishop with his mitre and crosier. *Gregorii posthuma*, p. 114.

(u) Stubbs *in vita* Gul. Zouch.

(x) *MS.* p. 112.

(y) *Gul. Meld. in vita* Egberti *arch.* Ebor.

(z) Lelandi *coll. tom.* I. *p.* 399. *ex epistola* Alcuini *ad* Carolum *regem.*

Historici

Historici veteres Pompeius, Plinius, *ipse*
Acer Aristoteles, *rhetor quoque* Tullius *ingens.*
Quid quoque Sedulius, *vel quid canit ipse* Juvencus,
Alcuinus, Clemens, Prosper, Paulinus, Arator,
Quid Fortunatus *vel quid* Lactantius *edunt.*
Quae Maro Virgilius, Statius, Lucanus, *et auctor*
Artis grammaticae, vel quid scripsere magistri;
Quid Probus *atque* Phocas, Donatus, Priscianusve,
Servius, Euticius, Pompeius, Comminianus.
Invenies alios perplures, lector, ibidem
Egregios studiis, arte et sermone magistros,
Plurima qui claro scripsere volumina sensu;
Nomina sed quorum praesenti in carmine scribi
Longius est visum, quam plectri postulet usus.

J. Leland laments the loss of this wonderful collection, when he was sent by *Henry* VIII. with commission to search every library in the kingdom. His words are these, *In bibliotheca S.* Petri *quam* Flaccus Albinus, *alias* Alcuinus, *subinde miris laudibus extollit propter insignem copiam librorum, tam* Latinorum *quam* Graecorum, *jam fere bonorum librorum nihil est. Exhausit enim hos thesauros, ut pluraque alia, et* Danica *immanitas, et* Gulielmi Nothi *violentia.*

Thomas, the first archbishop of this see of that name, amongst his other great benefactions to his church, is said to replenish the library, just then destroyed, with good and useful books. But these also underwent the same fate with the fabrick being both consumed in the fire which happened in the city, *anno* 1137, in the reign of king *Stephen.*

I cannot find after this, that our church was remarkable for a collection of books, but continued in the same state in which *Leland* says he found it, till the great gift of Mrs. *Mathews* once more gave it the face of a library. The books are methodically digested into classes, according to the various learning they treat on, and a faithful catalogue made of them. This was done by the care of Dr. *Comber*, then precentor of the church. They have since been augmented, at different times; and lately, by the bequest of dean *Finch*, have received the addition of the *Foedera Anglicana* in seventeen tomes, &c. The books are chiefly remarkable for several valuable tracts in divinity and history; some manuscripts amongst which is a *Tully de inventione, ad Herennium*, very perfect, and in a most neat character, bibles and psalters, the original register of St. *Mary*'s abbey at *York*, &c. But the manuscripts that are almost inestimable, to this library especially, are Mr. *Torre*'s painful collections from the original records, of all the ecclesiastical affairs relating to this church and diocese. And when the fine collection of the late reverend Mr. *Marmaduke Fothergill* comes likewise to be added to this library, as I have taken notice in his life is so designed by his widow, it then may contain a body of manuscripts, especially in the *English* ritual and liturgical way, equal to most libraries in the kingdom.

The arms that are, or were in the windows of this room in Mr. *Torre*'s time, and probably belonged to some ancient benefactors to the library, are first *England*, then *Mowbray*, *Percy* and *Lucy*, *Nevill*, *Ross*, *Clifford*, *Fitzhugh*, *Vavasour*, *Bowett*, archbishops, *Langley*, *Skirlaw*, *Dacres*, *Haxey*, *Scrope* of *Massam*, and *Fenton*.

Having now described all the out-buildings, belonging more immediately to the church; I shall next take an external view of the whole fabrick. The cathedral church of *York* is commonly called **York Minster**; which word in the *Anglo-Saxon* is **Mynster**, in the old *Franco-Gaulick*, *Monstier*, but all from the *Latin Monasterium*. A cathedral church and monastery being formerly synonymous terms. The whole building shews more window than solid in it; and the different taste of architecture, as well as the different age of each part, is easily discernable. I shall begin with the west end.

The

CATHEDRAL CHURCH.

West end. The front, or west end, contains two uniform steeples, running up to the setting on of their square tops, in ten several contractions, all cloistered for imagery. Indeed this part of the church has lost much of its beauty, by being robbed of a vast number of curious statues, which once adorned it; the pedestals and niches of which look bare without them. But still it carries a grandeur inexpressible. On the top of the great doors sits the figure of archbishop *William de Melton*, the principal founder of this part of the church; but the image is much abused. Below, and on each side of the double doors, are the statues of a *Vavasour* and a *Percy* as their shields of arms do testify.

Vavasour. It appears by a deed that *Robert le Vavasour* granted to God, St. *Peter* and the church of *York*, for the health of his own soul, and the souls of his wife *Julian* and his ancestors, full and free use of his quarry at Tadcaster in Thevesdale. With liberty to take and carry thence a sufficient quantity of stone for the fabrick of this church, as oft as they had need to repair, re-edify, or enlarge the same (*a*).

Percy. (*b*) Likewise *Robert de Percy*, lord of *Boulton*, granted to *John* archbishop of *York*, free liberty for the mariners, or carters, to carry the fabrick stone from Tadcaster, either by land or water, through his grounds lying along the river Wherfe; or up that river to *York*. As also his wood at Boulton for roofing the new building.

In memory of these two extraordinary benefactions the church thought fit to erect two statues; one represented with a piece of rough unhewn stone in his hands, the other with a similitude of a piece of wrought timber. These two families have many more memorials of their beneficence to the fabrick on the inside of the church.

In the arch over the door, in fine tracery work, is the story of *Adam* and *Eve* in paradise, with their expulsion thence. These double doors are seldom opened but at funerals; or the reception of an archbishop, in solemn procession, for installation. At the basis of each of these towers are two more doors dayly open, by a wicket, for entrance into the church at this end of the fabrick. I shall be less particular in describing this and the rest of the church, because the draughts will give the reader a much better idea of the building than words can possibly express.

(*a*) *Mon. Ang.* vol. III. p. 162. MS. *Torre*, p. 2. (*b*) The same.

Decem. 8,

Decem. 8, 1660, a great wind blew down the whole battlement of the south steeple, with two pinacles of the same; the top of one of the spires of the other steeple fell likewise by the same wind, which did great damage to the rest of the church. The steeples have not yet been repaired. The north steeple is called St. *Mary's*, or our lady's, steeple, probably for being nearest the chapel of that name already described. In it did hang once four bells, but *an.* 1655, they were removed into the other steeple, the charge of which was born by a collection through the city *(c)*. CATHEDRAL CHURCH.

In the south tower hangs a ring of twelve bells, the largest tenor of which is fifty nine hundred weight, the diameter five feet nine inches and a half. This great bell was cast *an.* 1628; it is usually tolled at funerals; *Toby Matthews* archbishop was the first it went for on that occasion. One of the bells, which probably came out of the other steeple bears this inscription, Bell.

Vocata dum voco pulsata mundo Maria.

In the year 1466, there was then delivered into the hands of *Thomas Innocent* bell-founder, by *John Knapton* under-treasurer, for the founding of four bells, certain metals, all particularly named in the record; which also shews the weight of each bell *(d)*. In the year 16[illegible], the eleventh, or the largest bell but one was broke and new cast; the fourth bell being likewise untuneable, was broke and melted down, and to add metal to these the biggest bell of three belonging to the demolished church of St. *Nicholas, extra Walmgate*, was given. Towards the charge of this, and to make the chimes go on all the bells the lord-mayor and commonality gave one hundred and thirty pounds from the chamber. So close, says a manuscript by me, were the then spiritual governours of the church; although, adds the author, they had all the revenues of it in their own hands at that time. *Dickenson*, lord-mayor that year, and one of *Oliver*'s knights, has his name remembred in the inscription on the eleventh bell, *viz.* Thoma Dickenson *milite majore civit.* Eboraci *vice ada. sumptus procurante.*

About two years ago, *viz. anno* 1733, the frames of all these bells were renewed, and they rehung in a manner much more commodious for ringing than before. Towards the expence of which a set of publick spirited citizens, great admirers of this kind of musick and exercise, contributed twenty pounds. They also, at their own expence, built a new floor, twenty one feet higher than the old one, for a greater convenience in ringing the bells. This diversion has been long in great vogue in *England*, though it is remarkable that it is not practised out of our King's dominions, any where else in the world. This society of ringers in *York*, gave also two trebles to the church of St. *Martin* in *Conyn-street*, which makes the peal there now run on eight, at the expence of fifty nine pounds ten shillings. These kinds of publick benefactions, in an age little addicted that way, are not below an historian's observation.

The principal benefactor to the rebuilding this south steeple has his name on the stone work in large letters on the west side thus,

BIR·MIN·HAM.

John Birmingham was treasurer of this church about the year 1432, and was no doubt a great promoter of the work; besides by his will proved *May* 28, 1457, he left amongst other legacies fifty pounds to the further reparation of the fabrick *(d)*.

(*c*) *MS. penes me.*
(*e*) *MS.* Torre, 172.
(*d*) *MS.* Torre *et ex altero penes me.*

CATHEDRAL

South-ſide. In taking a view of the ſouth ſide of the church we firſt obſerve ſix tall pinnacles; which have been raiſed, as well for buttreſſes to the upper building of the nave, as ornaments. Though now all the arches which joined them are taken away; I ſuppoſe, not being thought of any ſervice. Towards the top of each of theſe pinnacles is a cell for an image, which by great luck are yet ſtanding in them. The four to the weſt, I take to be the repreſentations of the four evangeliſts; the next *Chriſt* with the paſchal lamb; the laſt an archbiſhop, probably, from his juvenile look, our peculiar ſaint, St. *William.*

The ſouth entrance is aſcended to by ſeveral courſes of ſteps; and tradition aſſures us that there was once as great an aſcent to the weſt door. If ſo, the ground has been much raiſed at that end, the ſoil being now level with the pavement of the church. However this might happen from the vaſt quantity of chippings of ſtone, which not only ſerved to level this part, but alſo was uſed to raiſe the foundations of all the houſes on that ſide; as the ground when dug into does ſufficiently teſtify. It being near two yards deep before you can come to the natural ſoil. Over this entrance hung formerly the bell for calling to prayers, but in the late dean's time it was removed to the top of the lanthorn ſteeple. A little ſpiral turret, called the fidler's turret, from an image of a fidler on the top of it, was taken ſome few years ago from another part of the building, and placed on the ſummit of this end, which has added much to its decoration. In it the clock bell hangs. Over the doors, by the care of the ſame dean, was alſo placed a handſome dial, both horary and ſolar; on each ſide of which two images beat the quarters on two ſmall bells. After the reformation ſome avaritious dean leaſed out the ground for ſome ſpace on each ſide the ſteps for building houſes and ſhops on. Theſe were ſtanding, juſt as they are repreſented in *Hollar's* draught of this part of the church in the *monaſticon*, and were of great diſcredit as well as annoyance to the fabrick, till the worthy dean *Gale*, amongſt other particular benefactions, ſuffered the leaſes to run out, pulled down the houſes and cleaned this part of the church from the ſcurf it had contracted by the ſmoke proceeding from theſe dwellings.

Choir-end. Eaſtward you take a view of archbiſhop *Thoreſby*'s fine additional building, being all the choir end of the cathedral. It is eaſily diſcernible, by the out-ſide, that this part is much newer, as well as of a nobler *Gothick* taſte than the weſt end. To the eaſt, over the fineſt window in the world, ſits the ſaid archbiſhop, mitred and robed, in his epiſcopal chair, having in his left hand the repreſentation of a church, and ſeeming to point to this window with his right. At the baſis of this noble light are thirteen heads, placed on a row in the wall, from angle to angle. They are designed to represent the heads of our saviour and his twelve apostles himself in the midst of them. At the south corner is the head of a king crowned; designed, no doubt, for that magnanimous prince *Edw.* III, in whose time this structure was erected. And at the north a mitred bishop projects, which can represent none likelier than the founder. On each side of this end of the church stands also the statues of *Percy* and *Vavasour* armed; their shields of arms hanging by them. I observe that *Percy* takes the right hand here, as *Vavasour* does at the west end; but for what reason I know not. CATHEDRAL CHURCH.

On the north-side is nothing remarkable to be viewed more than what is already described. Unless I take notice of a brick wall and gate, cop'd with stone, which the late dean *Finch* caused to be built to prevent night walkers, and other disorderly persons from nesting and intriguing in the obscure corners of the walls and buttresses. *North-side.*

The grand tower, or *lantborn-steeple*, so called, I presume, from its resemblance to that luminary, is the next we must raise our eyes to. It is a square building supported on the inside by four large and massy pillars of stone, which make four arches. This tower is very lofty, yet tradition assures it was meant to be carried much higher, by a spire of wood covered with lead on the top of it. But the foundation was thought too weak for such a superstructure. On the south west angle is now placed a cupola for the prayer bell to hang in, which structure is really a deformity, being of a different order from the rest of the church, and only taking up one corner of the square. However by the advantage of this situation the silver sound of this small bell may be heard some miles off the city; the motto upon it alludes to its ringing early in the morning for six o'clock prayers in this distich, *Lanthorn-steeple.*

Surge cito, propera, cunctos citat, excitat hora;
Cur dormis? Vigila, me resonante leva.

In the year 1666, by order of the duke of *Buckingham*, a turret of wood was erected, covered with lead and glazed, on the top of this steeple. This was to put lights into upon occasion to serve as a beacon to alarm the country in case the *Hollanders*, or *French*, with both which powers we were then at war, should attempt to land on our coasts.

Thus I have given a short description of the external parts of this great fabrick; which will only serve to let a stranger into a juster notion of the plates, which for better information I have caused to be placed in the order they appear in. I have but to add, on this subject, that by the care and management of the two late governors, the fabrick money has been so well applied to its proper use, the one taking care to preserve the roof, new leading of it where there was occasion, &c. the other setting workmen on to stop up all cracks, flaws and perishing of the stones, with excellent cement and mortar, that at present the whole structure has almost regained its primitive lustre. Were but its lost spires and pinnacles restored, it would altogether appear so; and this fabrick might yet bid defiance to time and weather for many succeeding generations.

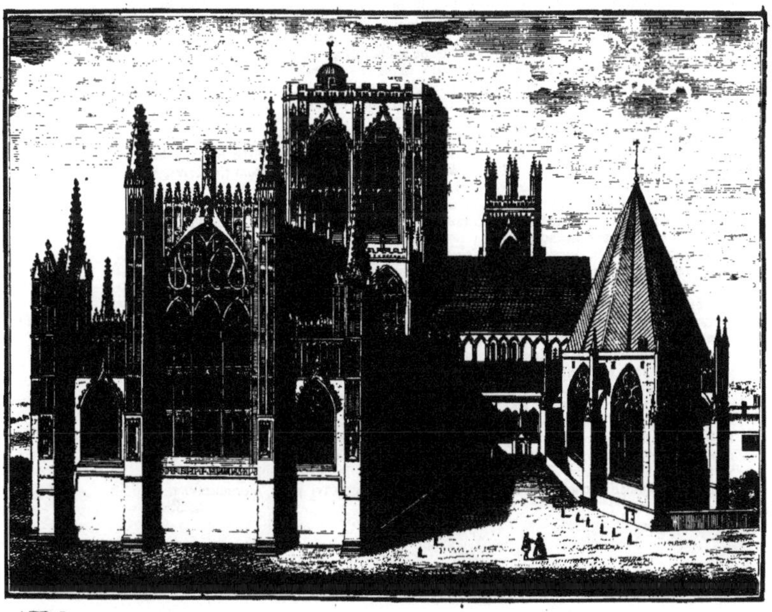

CATHEDRAL CHURCH. At my entrance into the church, before I look upwards and dazzle my eyes with the loftiness and spatiousness of the building, it will be necessary to cast them on the ground. Here, in the old pavement of this church, were, almost, an innumerable quantity of grave-stones; many of which formerly shone like embroidery; being enriched with the images, *&c.* in brass, of bishops, and other ecclesiasticks, represented in their proper habits. Of which the grave-stone of archdeacon *Dalby*, as the draught of it expresses in the sequel, though the original is long since torn off, is a shining instance. These stones had also monumental inscriptions upon them, in order to carry down the names and qualities of the venerable dead to the latest posterity. But to see how all sublunary things are subject to change or decay, what was thought the most durable, by our fore-fathers, for this purpose, by an unaccountable turn of fate proved the very occasion of destruction by their sons. Let no man henceforth say *exegi monumentum aere perennius*, in the strict sense of the words; I have given one instance of the loss of a fine palace for the lucre of the lead upon it, and now this *aeris sacra fames* has robbed us of most of the ancient monumental inscriptions that were in the church. At the *Reformation*, this hair-brained zeal began to shew itself against painted glass, stone statues and grave-stones; many of which were defaced, and utterly destroyed, along with other more valuable monuments of the church, till queen *Elizabeth* put a stop to these most scandalous doings by an express act of parliament. In our late civil wars, and during the usurpation, our zealots began again these depredations on grave-stones; and stripped and pillaged them to the minutest piece of metal. I know it is urged that their hatred to popery was so great, that they could not endure to see an *orate pro anima*, or even a cross on a monument without defacing of it. But it is plain that it was more the poor lucre of the brass, than zeal, which tempted these miscreants to this act; for there was no grave stone, which had an inscription cut on itself, that was defaced by any thing but age throughout this whole church.

The present noble pavement, which is put in place of the ragged and shattered old one, has quite taken away the few inscriptions that were left us, which, indeed, were by no means significant enough to hinder the design. And had it not been for the care of the famous *Roger Dodsworth* who luckily collected the epitaphs, before the times of plunder and rapine in the civil wars; the names of most of these venerable dead, some of which are remarkable on several occasions, would for ever have been lost in silence. This man seems now to be sent by providence before the face of a devouring fire, to collect and save what was valuable from sure destruction by the approaching flames. To instance in this, a manuscript fell lately into my hands, which carries only this preface, but needs no other recommendation, *Epitaphs out of the metropolitical church and all the other, parochial, churches within the most famous and ancient cittie of* Yorke; *most faithfully collected by me* Roger Dodsworthe *the* xii^th^ *of* February *an. dom.* 1618. This manuscript Mr. *Torre* has seen, as, I think, nothing escaped him, and out of it he has filled up what would otherways have been a great chasm in his monumental account of the church. From both these authorities I shall be able, in some measure, to restore every person his own epitaph; and by a plan of the old pavement, as near as possible, give the reader an idea where the grave-stone was placed that once bore the inscription. It will not be amiss, before I proceed to those particulars, to speak something of epitaphs in general; to make a comparison betwixt ancient and modern ones; and lastly to take notice of some great personages who have been buried in this cathedral, without having any monumental inscription over them at all; at least, that can now be restored.

To observe of epitaphs in general, we ought to consider, first, the original design of them, next, the nature and manner of the inscriptions, and, lastly, how the last age has swelled them to a size enormous. The etymology of the word *epitaph*, from the *Greek*, is obvious and signifies no more than *superscribere*, to write upon any thing; but it is by custom confined to this kind of memorial of the dead. The *Greeks* and *Romans* made use of inscriptions in stones, *&c.* to transmit to posterity the names and qualities, as to offices, of their heroes, commanders and relations; but we meet with few encomiums on their personal virtues in *Gruter*'s, *Spon*'s, or *Montfaucon*'s collections. *A D. M.* or *diis manibus*, was all the recommendations the *pagan* funeral monuments bestowed, and our *Christian* ancestors were as modest in their *orate pro anima*, or *cujus animae propitietur Deus*. We are not to suppose but that there were men of as much probity, honour and honesty, in this country, in former ages as in later. Yet they strove to build monuments for themselves in their life-time, in or about the church. And certainly, to have a bare coat of arms, fixed on the walls, as a contributor to the building, or repairing, of this magnificent fabrick, is a much greater glory than to be represented in a fulsom panegyrical epitaph, though under a statue carved by another *Praxiteles*.

A good man deserves praise, and the speaking often of such is of great use in promoting virtue: But then to represent ill men as good, and to raise them up to heaven, in an epitaph, as sure as they are laid in the earth beneath it, is one effectual way to encourage wickedness. And yet this is now a-days, but too frequently, practised. The *French* have a severe proverb on this head, *il mentoit comme une epitaph*, he lies like an epitaph; in allusion to the elogies usually contained therein, which are not always over just. Our ancestors, no question,

question. had their defects as well as vertues, but then they were not guilty of such extravagancies in their praises of the dead. For instance in our own church, CATHEDRAL CHURCH.

Who can bear to read a long dull *encomium* on a child of six years old, where the author, some trencher scholar to the family no doubt, shamefully dresses it up in the garb and gravity of a man of threescore. Or, *risum teneatis* if you can, when you are told, by an old doating doctor of divinity, that his wife, who he says died of her twenty fourth child, stood death like a soldier, and looked as lovely in her coffin as a young blooming virgin. This puts me in mind of one still carried higher in *Westminster-abbey*, where a tender husband bewails the loss of his plaything bitterly; and tells us he was so struck with the accident, that he was incapable, for a time, to do the common offices of nature; and, having a good place at court, forsook it to retire and weep himself into a *Niobe* in the country *(f)*.

These absurdities, I say, are what the antients were strangers to, and would have been ashamed of; but are not so to us. And yet I do not deny but that there were many worthy prelates, clergy, gentry, *&c.* who are deservedly praised; having been men, some of them in our own age, of known worth and integrity. A fond husband also may be allowed to launch out a little in praises of an excellent wife. But yet I could wish; that even the best of these persons had no further recommendation to posterity, over them, than Mr. *Addison*'s noble thought this way; which he modestly says was wrote by another person for his own tomb-stone, *viz.*

Hic jacet R. C. *in expectatione diei supremi;*
Qualis erat iste dies indicabit.

I hope this digression will be pardonable, I mean not to abstract from any character in our church epitaphs; I only speak the sense of the last named author, in general, and what I have learned from very good judges of this affair in particular. I shall now just mention the names of some eminent persons which history informs us were buried in this cathedral without any other memorial. The tombs, without epitaphs, that are assigned to such prelates, as either had them not at first, or have been robbed of them, I have given draughts of at the end of their lives. And shall refer the reader to the site and distinct places of those, and the rest which have monumental inscriptions on them to the two plans of the church.

To begin with the burials, from the first, I shall not look for the sepulcher of king *Ebrank*; nor of the rest of the *British* kings and princes which *Geofry Monmouth* assures us died and were buried at *York*. But, to descend to greater certainties and better authorities, I shall begin with Venerable *Bede*, who writes that the head of our famous king *Edwin*, was interred in the cathedral at *York*, of his own founding; and his body was Edwin.
buried at *Whitby (g)*. As also *Ethelm* and *Etheldrida*, a son and a daughter of this king. Ethelm. Etheldrida.
These two last, says *Bede*, died so soon after baptism, that they had not put off the white A. DCLXXX.
rayment, then worn, for some time, by such proselytes as received the sacred laver.

Bosa archbishop of this province died and was buried in his cathedral *(h)*. Bosa DCLXXXVI.

Eadbert king of *Northumberland* died and was interred in the porch of St. *Peter*'s church Eadbert.
in *York*. Two years after, *Egbert* his brother, archbishop of this province, died and was buried besides him *(i)*. Egbert DCCLXVII.

Eanbald successor to the last named king was here also interred *(k)*. Eanbald DCCXCVII.

For many years after this, during the *Danish* wars, the archbishops of this province died and were buried none knows where. Nor is there any notice taken in history of any considerable person's being interred at *York*; except we mention St. *Everilda*, an abbatess, whom the *Danes* slew with all her convent; and she is said to have been buried at *York (k)*. St. Everilda.

In the year 1014, says *Simeon* of *Durham*, *Sweyne* the pagan *Danish* king, a man represented to be horribly cruel, was slain, by a miracle at *Gainsborough*, in the midst of his conquests, and buried at *York*. The miracle is too extraordinary to insert. Sweyne 1014.

Tosty, the furious earl of *Northumberland*, killed at the battle of *Stainford bridge*, was brought to *York* and there interred *(l)*. Tosty 1066.

Aldred archbishop, next occurs to be laid in his cathedral, just before the destruction of it by *William* the conqueror. Aldred 1069.

Thomas his successor, who rebuilt the church, died here and was buried in it. So was Gerard, archbishop, *anno* 1108. Thomas 1108

(f) *Monument.* West. Keep.

(g) *Adlatum est autem caput* Edwini *regis* EBURACUM, *et inlatum postea in ecclesia beati apostoli* Petri, *quam ipse cepit*, &c. *Bede.* The heads also of *Oswin* and *Oswald*, kings and martyrs, are said to be buried at *York*.

(h) *Ex eodem.*

(i) Stubbs *act. pontif.* Ebor.

(k) *Ex vita sanctor. in eccle.* Ebor *sepult.*

(l) See the annals of this work, and the accounts of these prelates lives for the rest.

CATHEDRAL CHURCH. Thomas II. 1114.

Thomas the second was here also interred, though now no memorial is in being of either of them.

Henry Murdac 1153.

Henry Murdac, archbishop lies buried in this cathedral; but without any monument that I know of.

William 1154.

The first prelate that we can fix a place of sepulture to, in this cathedral, is *William*; commonly called St. *William*. It is true his bones were removed from the place of their first interment, and were laid in the nave of the church, under a long narrow marble altar table; of the same kind of stone the font is made on. What appeared upon taking up this altar stone I have described in the account of this prelate's life. His shrine which was exceedingly adorned with gold, jewels, *&c.* was built over his bones; a description of which the reader will meet with in the sequel.

Roger 1181.

Archbishop *Roger* comes next in this list, who lies in an antique tomb in the nort h isle of the nave, as is already taken notice of.

Walter Grey 1255.

Walter Grey's tomb bears, also, no inscription. Here was a chantry.

Sewal 1258.

His immediate successor *Sewal de Bovil* has also a monument in this church without any inscription.

Godfrey 1264.

Archbishop *Godfrey de Kinton* is said, by *Stubbs*, to be buried in his cathedral; but the place of his interment is unknown, unless we suppose the tomb on the right hand *Walter Grey*'s to be his.

Langton 1279.

The tomb of *William Langton*, dean of *York*, which once stood near the clock case, is the first that bore any inscription. An account of which, with an accurate draught taken before it was demolished, may be found in the description of that part of the church where it stood. The fragments of it lye now upon archbishop *Bowet*'s tomb; it is plain this fine monument was torn in pieces by the *Puritans* in the usurpation, for it was standing intire *anno* 1641, when the draught of it was taken.

Walter Giffard 1279.

Walter Giffard, archbishop, was buried in this cathedral, as *Leland* writes in the choir end of the church; with this modest inscription on his grave-stone, WALTER GISFART OBIIT VII KAL. MAII MCCLXXIX. I observe he is the first that is taken notice of to be interred in the choir, but the place now not known.

Romain, Newark 1295, 1299.

John Romain, and *Henry Newark*, successors to the former, are said, by *Stubbs*, to be both laid in the cathedral; but now without any more memorial of them.

Greenfield 1315.

William de Greenfield comes next. *Stubbs* has laid him in *porticu S.* Nicholai, St. *Nicholas*'s porch in this church; where his monument, as is represented, still remains. The portraiture of that saint is in the window, but the tomb has no inscription.

Melton 1340.

William de Melton, archbishop, founder of the west end of the church, died *anno* 1340, and was buried near the font, *ad fontem*, says *Stubbs*, where his grave was found; which was covered with a large blew marble, quaterly cloven; this had been plated with brass on the borders, and all over in the middle, but all quite erased. This mischief must have been done at or near the *Reformation*, since *Dodsworth* is silent as to any epitaph on this grave-stone in his time.

William de Hatfield 1344.

In the year 1344, our historians take notice that *William de Hatfield* second son to king *Edward* III, died and was buried in our cathedral *(n)*. The place where is now uncertain; but there is an image of a young prince in alabaster, prostrate with a ducal coronet on his head, and a lion couchant at his feet, which in all probability was designed for him, this prince dying in his childhood. Our judicious antiquaries the vergers have long told a fine story of the emperor *Severus* and his son, buried at *Acombe-hills*, where they say this image and that of an old man was found, brought hither and deposited in this church. The other statue I am more at a loss to account for; I have read in a manuscript that bishop *Moreton* gave it to the church as the image of *Constantine the great*; but where he got it is not taken notice of. It has been painted, and certainly represents a christian by the cross on the breast, what further I shall leave to the reader's conjecture by the drawings.

(n) This prince was born at *Hatfield*, near *Doncaster*, from whence he took his surname, and not at *Hatfield* in *Hartfordshire* as several historians mistake. The queen *Philippa*, his mother, on this occasion, gave five marks *per annum* to the neighbouring abbey of *Roch*, and five nobles to the monks there; which sum, when he died, were transferred to the church of *York*, where the prince was buried, to pray for his soul; and are to this day paid to the dean and chapter, out of the impropriation of the rectory of *Hatfield*, as appears by the rolls.

William

William de la Zouch archbiſhop died *anno* 1352, and was interred according to *Stubbs*; Zouch 1352.
againſt the altar of St. *Edward* king and confeſſor. But where that altar ſtood in the church is now unknown.

John Thoreſby, the laſt prelate which *Stubbs* mentions, was buried in this church; and Thoreſby
laid, as that author writes, before the altar of the bleſſed virgin *Mary* in his new work 1353.
of the choir. This altar was under the great eaſt window, but no ſtone or monument does now mark the place of his interment; yet, as long as this part of the fabrick ſtands, he cannot want a memorial.

The next prelate that occurs to be buried in this church is *Richard Scrope*, beheaded Scrope 1405.
anno 1405. His tomb, at the eaſt end, is ſtill remaining, but robbed of its inſcription in braſs which run round the verge. To this monument did belong a large quantity of veſtments, jewels, &c. as appears by *Dugdale's* inventary, that were offered to the ſhrine of this loyal martyr. At the ſame time with the archbiſhop were buried the bodies of *Thomas Mowbray* duke of *Norfolk* and ſir *John Laneplugh*, beheaded for the ſame crime, Mowbray. Laneplugh.
but without any memorial.

Henry Bowett, archbiſhop, lies oppoſite to *Scrope*, as they were ſo in principles, but Bowett 1423.
without any epitaph. His fine tomb is repreſented at the end of his life.

George Nevill, an unfortunate prelate, died after his return from baniſhment, and was Nevill 1476.
interred in the cathedral; *Leland* writes that he and his ſucceſſor *Rotheram* lie together in the north ſide of our lady's chapel in the choir.

The tomb of *Thomas de Rotheram* is repreſented at the end of his life, but it is robb'd Rotheram
of the inſcription. 1500.

Savage, *Lee*, and *Young* are all taken notice of, and the rest of the monuments will now follow in their proper places.

I observe first that in the choir end of the church in fifty two epitaphs which Mr. *Dodsworth* gives us, near thirty of them were remaining entire and legible before the pavement was lately altered. These seem to have been preserved by the choir doors, which, being kept for the most part shut, did secure them from plunder. But what has escaped, within that enclosure, bears no proportion to those which are stripped without; for in the body of the church in one hundred and thirteen epitaphs, not twenty of them were left, and half of those were cut on stone. Which plainly proves, as I hinted before, that the poor lucre of the brass was the greatest motive to the defacing these venerable remains of antiquity.

Again, I take notice that there are but two in the whole catalogue of inscriptions that rise higher in date then the thirteenth century. Nor are there any, commonly to be met with, in *England*, that I know of. The tomb of dean *Langton* claims seniority to any in his church, for an epitaph; being dated *anno* 1279, as is visible upon the remains of it at this day. This tomb Mr. *Dodsworth* says stood within an iron-grate near the clock, on the right; he calls it a brass tomb, and supposes that the dean was slain by an armed man at mass, because the image had a representation of a wound in its head; and the story was depicted in the adjoining window. I take this to have been some allusion to the murder of St. *Thomas a Becket*, for we are not to suppose, that the brother of *Stephen Langton*, then archbishop of *Canterbury*, could be slain in so publick a manner and no notice taken of it in history. The monument fared no better for its covering with brass, for the plunderers in the stripping broke the stone to pieces; which were lately found buried in the ground, probably by some considerate person of those times, in digging dean *Finche*'s grave. I shall begin my description of the gravestones, monuments, &c. from the south entrance of the cross isle, and then this remarkable tomb of *Langton*'s takes place according to its seniority.

Monumental

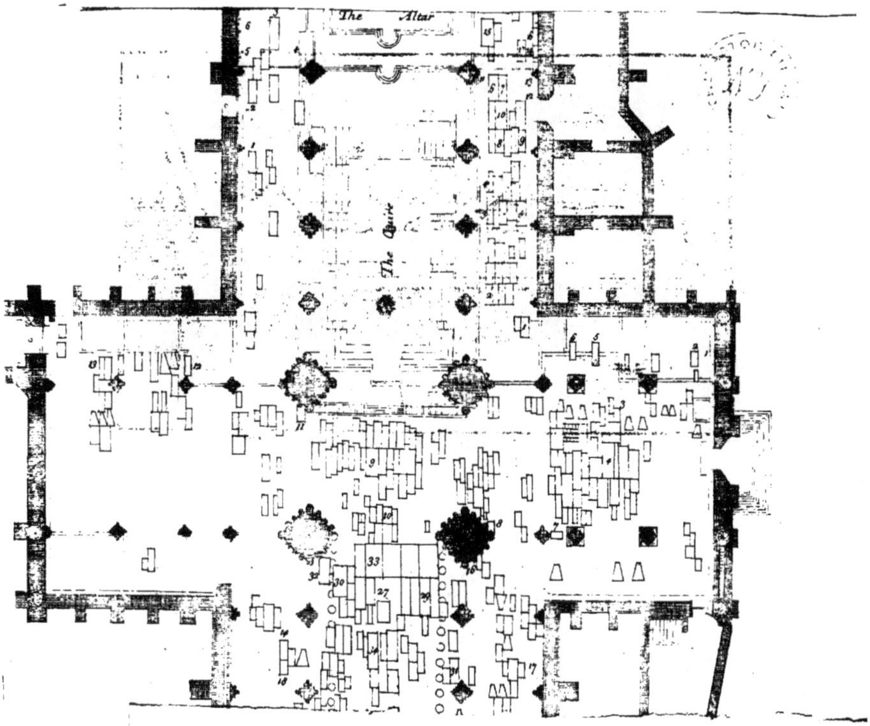
The Altar
The Quire

Monumental INSCRIPTIONS *from Mr.* Dodsworth's *manuscript.*

South Cross-Isle.

N. B. Those marked *L* in the margin, were legible before the old pavement was taken up; *S* where the inscription was cut on stone, and the figures refer to the site of the grave-stones in the old ichnography.

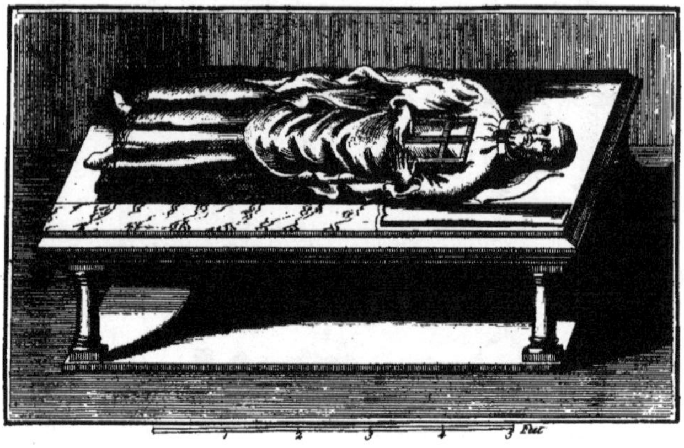

1. Langton 1279. ✠ HIC REQUIESCIT CORPUS WILIELMI DE LANGUETON A QUONDAM DECANI EBORACI, QUI OBIIT DIE SCI. SWITHINI ANNO DOM. MCCLXXIX. CUJUS ANIMA SIT CUM DEO.

2. Archbishop *Sewal de Bosvil*; see his life for the print.

3. Soza 1560. *L. S.* ✠ **Of your charitie pray for the soulis of Martin Soza goldsmith, born in Saphire in Spayne, and Elyne his wieff, whose soules God pardon. Of this cytte he was sheriffe, who was buried in this place, and dyed the 17th day of October in the year of our Lord God** 1560.

In the window by the clock.

Edlington. ✠ **Orate pro anima Dom. Johannis Edlington quondam rectoris ecclesie de Ravenswath.**

Richardson 1609. ✠ *Hic jacet* Johannes Richardson, *clericus succentor quondam ecclesie metropol.* Ebor. *qui obiit* 9 Julii 1609.

Shelford 1409 ✠ **Orate pro anima magistri Johannis de Shelford, quondam curie Ebor. examinatoris et persone altaris S. Willielmi in ecclesia cath. Ebor. qui obiit xiii die mensis Julii anno Dom,** 1409. **cujus anime propitietur Deus.**

Esenwald 1446. ✠ **Hic jacet magister Robertus Esenwald quondam curie Ebor. procurator generalis, qui obiit xxv die mensis Decembris anno Dom.** 1466, **cujus anime propitietur Deus. Amen.**

Style 1485. ✠ **Orate pro anima dom. Thome Style quondam vicarii hujus ecclesie, qui obiit vii die mensis Septembris anno Dom.** 1485. **cujus &c. Amen.**

te

✠ Orate pro anima dom. Thome Robinson quondam vicar. istius ecclesie, qui obiit x. die mensis Maii an. Dom. 1543. Cujus anime, &c. Amen. CATHEDRAL CHURCH. *Cross-Isle.* Robinson 1543

✠ Hic jacet Georgius Sheffield arm. quondam frater Willielmi Sheffield decani, qui obiit xv. die Apr. an. Dom. 1497. Sheffield 1497.

Jesu miserere mei.

Miserere mei, domine Deus, secundum magnam misericordiam tuam.

✠ Sepultura Willielmi Sheffield decani 8. die Decem. an. Dom. 1497. Sheffield 1497.

Hic jacet dom. Johannes Fitz-herbert quondam vicarius istius ecclesie, qui obiit xviii. die mensis . . . . an. Dom. 1406. Fitzherbert 1406.

O mercyfull Jesu, of thy blessed pitie
Have mercy of the soul of Isbell Kerby. Kerby.

Archbishop *Walter Grey.* See his life. 5.

Supposed archbishop *Godfrey de Kinton* in the print above. 6.

Hic jacet egregius cantor Kirkbieus in urna, Kirkby.
Organa qui scite tangeret unus erat.
Edidit insignes cantus modulamine dulci,
Hujus erat templi gloria, splendor, honor.
Magna hujus fuerat probitas, sapientia, virtus,
Consilio enituit, moribus, ingenio.

✠ Hic jacet Radulphus Coltonus sacre theologie baccalaurius, Clivelandie archidiaconus, Eboracensis ecclesie prebendarius, et ejusdem residens, qui obdormivit 8. Maii, aetat. vero 55, 1582. Colton 1582.

✠ Of your charity pray for the soul of Margarett Tesh wife unto Mr. Tristram Tesh, of the cittye of Yorke notarie, and principal register of the archbishoprick of Yorke, which Margarett departed unto the mercy of allmighty God the viii. day of December, an. Dom. 1537. Tesh.

✠ Hic jacet dom. Johannes Herberi, quondam vicarius istius ecclesie, qui obiit 1478. Herbery 1478.

✠ Orate pro anima magistri Willielmi Lambron in utroque jure baccalaure et in capella beate Marie et sanct. Angelorum canonici, et reverendissimorum pat. dominorum Georgii Laurentii et Thome archiepiscoporum Eborum registrarii. Qui obiit xxvi. die mensis Octob. an. Dom. 1481. Cujus anime propitietur Deus. Amen. Lambron 1481.

✠ Hic jacet Milo Metcalf quondam recordator istius civitatis ac etiam unus justiciarius dom. regis apud Lancastre, qui obiit xxv. die mensis Februarii an. Dom. 1495. Cujus anime propitietur Deus. Amen. Metcalf 1495.

✠ Orate pro anima magistri Alain de Newark curie Eborum quondam advocati, qui obiit xiii. die mensis Junii an. Dom. 1412. viam universe carnis est ingressus. Cujus anime, &c. Newark 1412.

✠ Orate pro anima dom. Johannis Burn quondam parsone ecclesie cath. Ebor. celebrant. ad altare S. Christoferi, qui obiit xvii. die mensis Feb. an. Dom. 1479. Cujus anime propitietur Deus. Burn 1479.

✠ Orate pro anima Thome Eston quondam cap. cantarie ad altare S. Christoferi, qui obiit v. die mensis Augusti an. Dom. 1494. Eston 1494.

Soli Deo honor et gloria, Bothe 1487.
Ingenio, virtute, fide dare vir locus iste
Vulgi voce parem noverat ante diem.
✠ Robertus Bothe decanus 1487.

Here lyeth the body of William Wooler late of the cittye of Yorke merchant, who died the xxi. day of December 1597, and did give liberal legacys to the poore of this cittye, to prisoners, and to the erection of a free school in Bingley where he was borne. Wooler 1597.

✠ Pray for the soul of Thomas Nelson, late comissary of the Consistory-court within this church, an. 1553. Nelson 1553.

✠ Hic jacet Willielmus Chaumbre generosus qui obiit xxii. die mensis Novembris an. 1478. cujus anime propitietur Deus. Amen. Chaumber 1478.

✠ Orate pro animabus magistri Gilberti Pynchbeck quondam magistri scholarum gramaticalium S. Petri Ebor. qui obiit penultimo die mensis Januarii A. D. 1457. Et Agnetis uxoris sue, que obiit . . . die mensis Octobris A. D. 1431. quorum animabus propitietur Deus. Amen. Pinchbeck 1457.

✠ Hic

CATHEDRAL CHURCH. *Croſs-iſle.* ✠ Hic jacet Dom. Philippus Lewes quondam parſona altaris S. Willielmi, qui obiit vi. die menſis Maii A. D. 1476. cujus, &c.

Lewes 1476.
Kirkby. Hic Kirkby ſtrictus jacet hoc ſub marmore pictus;
Reddat ei munus, qui regnat trinus et unus.

Vavaſour 1523. ✠ Hic jacet Henricus Vavaſour generoſus nuper filius Johannis Vavaſour de Newton, qui obiit viceſimo primo die Octobris An. Dom. 1523. cujus anime propitietur Deus. Amen.

Harpham 1414. ✠ Hic jacet Dom. Williemus Harpham quondam parſona altaris S. Michaelis, qui obiit v. die Apr. An. Dom. 1414. cujus anime propitietur Deus. Amen.

Roch. Roch jacet hic Will'mus mortis devictus in urna,
Et ſua ſe conjux volvitur Agnes humo.
Horum cuncti-potens animabus ſit miſerator,
Ut valeant placide ſcandere regna poli.

Bell. O merciful Jeſu, that brought man's ſoule from Hell,
Have mercy of the ſoule of Jane Bell.

Wyrnal. Muſicus et logicus Wyrnal hic jacet ecce Johannes,
Organa namque quaſi fecerat ille loqui (*o*).

Wandesford 1487. Hic duo caute ſiti infantes uterini Thoma patre ſati Wandesford, nomine ſunt his Willielmus Wandesford et Johannes frater ejus, obierunt viceſ. die menſis Oct. A. Dom. 1487.

Marſar 1546. ✠ Orate pro anima magiſtri Thome Marſar quondam canon. reſiden. hujus alme ecc. metrop. Ebor. et prebend. de Langtoft ac rectoris de Eſcrick, qui obiit viii. die Jan. an. Dom. 1546.
Qui dapibus multos pavit, nunc paſcitur ipſe,
Expoſcit precibus nil petit ipſe magis.

Simpſon 1491. ✠ Orate pro anima Dom. Thomae Simpſon quondam parſone ad altare S. Chriſtopher. in eccl. cath. Ebor, qui obiit xvi. die Apr. An. Dom. 1491. cujus anime propitietur Deus. Amen.

Tanfield 1442. ✠ Orate pro anima dom. Johannis Tanfeld, quondam vicarii hujus eccleſie, qui obiit ult. die menſis Apr. an. Dom. 1442.

Againſt the wall.

7. Higden, *dean*, 1539. ✠ Of your charitie pray for the ſoule of maſter Bryan Higden, ſometime dean of this metropolitical church, and reſidentiary of the ſame by the ſpace of xxiii. yeares, which departed to the mercy of almighty God the fifth of June in the yere of our Lord God 1539.

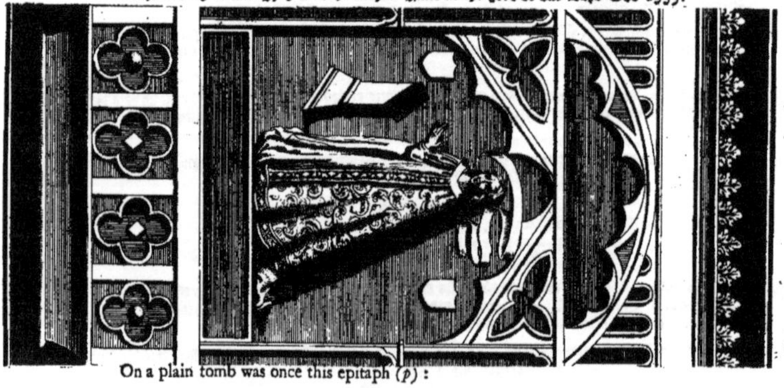

On a plain tomb was once this epitaph (*p*):

8 Eymes. 1578. ✠ Here lyeth the body of Thomas Eymes eſquier, one of her majeſties counſell eſtabliſhed in the north parts, and ſecretary and keeper of her highneſs ſignett appointed for the ſaid counſell, who married Elizabeth one of the daughters of ſir Edward Nevill knight, and departed out of this life to the mercy of God the ſixth day of Auguſt an. Dom. 1578.

(*o*) Who made the organ to ſpeak, as it were. *Spectator.*

(*p*) This tomb was removed for the laying the new pavement.

On

On a copper plate in the wall over this tomb is the effigies of a woman, in her hand a book with this inscription: CATHEDRAL CHURCH. *Cross-isle.*

I have chosen the way of thy truth, and thy judgments have I laid before me. Thy statutes have been my songs in the house of my pilgrimage.

Underneath,

Here lyeth the body of Elizabeth Eymes widow, late wife of Thomas Eymes esquier deceased, one of the gentlewomen of queen Elizabeth her privy chamber, and daughter of Sir Edward Nevill knight, one of the privy chamber to king Henry the eighth, who departed this life to the mercy of God the third day of February Anno Dom. 1583. Eymes 1583.

Hic Egremond Will'mus Dromorensis episcopus olim 9. Egremond, *Bishop suffragan.*
Marmore pro nitidis tectus utrinque mitris.
Pavit oves ethiso qui sub bis presule bino,
Atque lupi rabiem movit ab ede trucem.
Unguine quot sanxit pueros, quot presbyterosque,
Astra nisi sciret, credere nemo valet.
Ante prophanus erat locus hic quem dextra beavit
Ejus, et hinc pro se dicite quisquis ave.

Here lyeth George Gayle esquier who was twys mayor of thys cittye, and of the kings mynt he was also tresurare; with whome lyethe hereby lady Marye his wyffe, and Thomas his sone, whose soulles God pardon. All thoys that redythe this or see, of your charyty say on pater noster and on ave for thyer soules and Xten souls. A. 1557. 10. Gayle 1557.

. . . . . 11. *L. S.*

IHU.
Marcy Marcy Marcy
LADY
Helpe Helpe Helpe
And all the saints of heaven
pray for us.

Archbishop *William de Grenefeld.* See his life. 12.

✠ Hic jacet Thomas Danby nuper . . . . . in com. banco comitatus Ebor. Civitatis Ebor. et villa de Kingston supra Hull. Et Agnes uxor ejus ac Johannes unicus filius eorundem, qui quidem . . . . obierunt A. Dom. 1477. Quorum animabus, &c. Danby 1477.

✠ Orate pro anima Dom. Johannis Dovanby quondam vicar. istius ecclesie qui obiit xxv. die mensis Jan an. Dom. 1481. cujus, &c. Amen. Dovanby 1481.

✠ Orate pro anima dom. Roberti Gyllow quondam vicarii hujus ecclesie, qui obiit xvii. die Martii an. Dom. 1402. Gyllow, 1402.

✠ Orate pro anima Johannis Dove quondam capellani cantarie de sancta Anna, qui obiit vi. die mensis Feb. an. Dom. 1485. cujus, &c. Amen. Dove, 1485.

✠ HIC IACET DOM. HUGO DE LUBBESDORPE QUONDAM VICARIUS CHORI ISTIUS ECCLESIE CUIUS ANIME PROPITIETUR DEUS . . . . QUI OBIIT . . . . A. DOM. MCCCLXI. 13. *L. S.* Lubbesthorpe, 1361.

Monumental INSCRIPTIONS *which were in the* North Isle *of the* NAVE *or* BODY.

✠ Hic jacet magister Thomas Appilby quondam curie Ebor. procurator generalis, qui obiit septimo die mensis Oct. An. Dom. 1400. tricesimo tertio, cujus anime propitietur Deus. Amen. 14. Appilby, 1433. *L. S.*

✠ Hic jacet corpus magistri Johannis Harewod quondam curie Ebor. advocatus, qui obiit xiii. die mensis Septembris A. Dom. 1406. cujus anime propitietur Deus. Amen. 15. Harewood, 1406. *L. S.*

✠ Orate pro anima Johannis Kai vicarii istius ecclesie A. Dom. 1475. Kai, 1475.

✠ Orate pro anima dom. Thome Eston quondam vicarii hujus ecclesie. Cujus anime propitietur Deus. Eston.

A Hoope by birth a Harmyt's wight Hoope, 1608.
A hopeless Gibson's wief,
Here buried lyeth her body aright
Assured her hopefull lief.

6 L In

CATHEDRAL CHURCH.

In hope she lived, in hope she died
Through faithe to lyve for aye,
Lyke lief and death him may betide
When hence he parts away.
Obiit 21. April 1608.

South-Isle. South-Isle *of the* Body.

16. *Mauley (q).*

On a brass plate in the wall, under an image is this inscription:

17 Cotterel, 1595. Jacobo Cotrel Dublino *primaria* Hiberniae *civitate oriundo, postmodum vero civi* Eboracensi *armigero; cujus corpus sub saxo insigniis ejus notato astantium pedibus urgetur, qui annis plus minus viginti sereniss. dom. reg.* Elizabethae, *ejusque in his partibus borealibus senatui (quod concilium dicimus) testes examinando fideliter et gnaviter inservivit, viro certè prudenti, gravi, erudito, misericordi, benefico, in se tamen abjectissimo, Deumque imprimis timenti; quique hic sedentibus vivus curavit (e multis minimum) ut inoffensa valetudine liberius sederent; sedentes, stantes hoc benevolentiae vicissim tribuite, ut una cum illo vivo, vivi ipsi dominum* Jesum *concelebretis; et licet adhuc in terris agatis, coelestia tamen sedulo cogitetis. Obiit* 5. *Cal.* Sept. *anno Dom.* 1595. Eliz. 37.

Bradley, 1505. Sepultura Willielmi Bradley armigeri et latomi quondam magistri cementariorum hujus ecclesie metropolit. Ebor. qui obiit in festo omnium sanctorum anno Domini 1505. Cujus anime propitietur Deus.

Barton 1400. ✠ Hic jacet Willielmus Barton pelliparius Ebor qui obiit xx. die mensis . . . . . an. Dom. 1400. et Margarete uxor ejus, que obiit xxx. die mensis Novembris an. Dom. 1430. quorum animabus propitietur Deus. Amen.

18. Barton, 1487. *L.* ✠ Hic jacet Rogerus Barton quondam parsona ecclesie cath. Ebor. ad altare sancti Christofori, qui obiit 2. die mensis Oct. an. 1487. cujus anime propitietur Deus. Amen.

Mare. ✠ Sepultura parentum Willielmi Mare capellani.

Sharparrow, 1411. ✠ Orate pro anima dom. Johannis Sharparrowe, quondam parsone in ecclesia cath. Ebor. ad altare sancti Christofori, qui obiit xxv. die Oct. an. 1411.
Jesu have mercy.

Warde, 1495.
Perpetua pace Warde hic requiesce Willelmi,
Pro te dicat ave, qui legit ista; vale.
Obiit primo die mensis Augusti an. Dom. 1495.

Brigg, 1404. ✠ Hic jacet Adam de Brigg quondam civis Ebor. qui obiit xvii. die mensis Junii an. Dom. 1404.

Dighton, 1456. ✠ Hic jacet Willielmus de Dighton nuper vintarius civitatis Eboraci, & Johanna uxor ejus, qui obiit xix. die Septembris an. Dom. 1456.

Pelleson, 1434. ✠ Orate pro anima magistri Willielmi Pelleson quondam archideaconi Cleveland, &c. qui obiit 28. die Augusti an. Dom. 1434.
ARMS. A fess entre three pellicans wings erected.

Middle-isle. Middle-isle, *from the west door.*

19. Newsome, 1678, *L.S.* *Here lyeth the body of* John Newsome *verger of this church eight years, aged thirty years, died* Jan. 22, 1678.

20. Grave, 1666, *L.S.* *Here lyeth the body of* Robert Grave, *jun. who was verger of this church thirty eighty years, and died aged eighty five years* A. D. 1666.

Albain. ✠ Hic jacet Johannes Albain pictor et Alicia uxor ejus, pro quibus concessi sunt octoginta dies venie. Tu quilibet dicito pro eis pater et ave.

21. Parke, *L.S.* ✠ Orate pro anima Ricardi Parke.

22 Kumpton, *L.S.* ✠ Hic jacet Johannes Kumpton quondam sacrista hujus ecclesie, cujus anime propitietur Deus.

Spilasby. 1472. ✠ Hic jacet magister Robertus Spilesby quondam magister cementariorum hujus ecclesie, qui obiit anno Dom. 1472. Cujus anime, &c.

Delamare 1461. ✠ Hic jacet magister Willielmus Delamare quondam canonicus hujus ecclesie, qui obiit xxvi. die Novembris an. Dom. 1461. cujus anime propitietur Deus. Amen.

(q) An image removed into the north isle of the choir, where see the figure.

✠ Orate

CATHEDRAL CHURCH. *Middle-iſle.*

✠ Hic jacet magiſter Thomas Kerby quondam cancellarius hujus eccleſie et doctor in theo- CHURCH.
logia, qui obiit xxx. die menſis Maii an. Dom. 1452. cujus anime propitietur Deus. Amen. Kexby 1452.

✠ Hic jacet magiſter Johannes de Shireburne doctor in theologia, quondam cancellarius Shireburn.
iſtius eccleſie. Cujus anime propitietur Deus. Amen.

✠ Orate pro anima dom. Johannis Edlinton, quondam rectoris eccleſie de Ravenſwath, qui Edlinton.
obiit xvi. die menſis Martii . . . . . Cujus anime, &c. Amen.

On a ſtone where the figure of a prieſt in braſs is taken off, are theſe words in divers places of it:

Jeſu fili Dei miſerere tui Ranulphi, Ranulph.
Dignatus es naſci, miſerere tui Ranulphi (r).

✠ Orate pro anima magiſtri Ricardi Arnall, quondam ſubdecani et canonici iſtius eccleſie Arnall 1441.
cath. ac curie Ebor. officialis qui obiit ix. die menſis Junii an. Dom. 1441.
Coeli ſolamen ſibi det Chriſtus precor, amen.
Repoſita eſt hec ſpes mea in ſinu,
Auxilium meum a Domino.

✠ Hic jacet dom. Willielmus de Feriby, quondam archideaconus Clevelandie et iſtius ec- Feriby 1479.
cleſie canonicus, qui obiit in feſto ſancti Mathei apoſtoli an. Dom. 1479.

✠ Hic jacet dom. Johannes Caſtell miſer et indignus ſacerdos. 23. Caſtell, *L. S.*

✠ Orate pro anima magiſtri Johannis Caſtell miſeri et indigni ſacerdotis.

✠ Miſerere mei, Deus, ſecundum magnam miſericordiam tuam.

✠ Sanctiſſima Maria, mater miſericordie, ora pro me.

✠ Miſerere mei, Chriſte, quoniam in te confidit anima mea.

Archbiſhop *William de Melton*; ſee his life. 24.

✠ Hic jacet Johannes Chapell cocus. Cujus anime propitietur Deus. Chappell.

✠ Orate pro anima dom. Johannis Howe, qui obiit xxix. die menſis Decembris an. Dom. Howe 1508.
1508. Cujus anime propitietur Deus.

✠ Hic jacet magiſter Johannes Nottingham theſaurarius eccleſie cath. Ebor. dum vixit, qui Nottingham,
obiit xi. die menſis Decembris an. Dom. 1418. Cujus anime propitietur Deus. 1418.
Amen.

✠ Orate pro anima magiſtri Lanceloti Colinſon, quondam theſaurarii ac reſidentiarii hujus Colinſon,
eccleſie qui obiit viii. die menſis Aprilis A. Dom. 1538. Cujus anime propitietur Deus. 1538.
Amen.

✠ Hic jacet Willielmus Dent clericus, defunctus xiii. die menſis Junii an. Dom. 1446. Dent, 1446.
Cujus, &c.

✠ Orate pro anima magiſtri Johannis Pakengham hujus eccleſie theſaurarii ac eccleſ. col- Pakengham,
leg. Rippon. canonici reſidentiarii, qui obiit ſecundo die menſis Oct. an. Dom. 1477. 1477.
Cujus anime propitietur Deus. Amen.

✠ Orate pro anima dom. Johannis Birmyngham theſaurarii iſtius eccleſie ac prepoſitus ec- Birmingham,
cleſ. beati Johannis Beverlaci, qui obiit xxiii. die menſis Maii A. Dom. 1458. Cujus 1458.
anime propitietur Deus. Amen.

✠ All good men pray for charitie for the ſoule of Mr. Edward Kellet doctar, chantor of this Kellet, 1539.
churche, and commiſſary and receiver general of the exchequer, who deceaſed the fifth of
September anno 1539.

✠ Hic jacet Thomas Pereſon hujus eccleſie cathedralis ſubdecanus, qui obiit xxviii. die men- Pereſon, 1490.
ſis Octobris an. Dom. 1490. Cujus anime propitietur Deus. Amen.

✠ Orate pro anima magiſtri Johannis Aleyne, quondam curie conſiſt. Ebor. commiſſarii Aleyne, 1488.
generalis, qui obiit iii. die Feb. A. D. 1488.

✠ Orate pro animabus Margarete Water vidue, que obiit xv. die menſis Septem. A. Dom. Water, 1410.
1410. Et Thome Water nuper Willielmi et Margarete predict. filii, notarii publici, 1439.
attornati ſcribe et regiſtrarii dominorum decani et capituli hujus eccleſie qui obiit primo
die menſis Januarii an. Dom. 1439. Quorum animabus propitietur Deus. Amen.
Orate pro mortuis quia morimini.
Et inchoantes attendite clamantes.

(r) Mr. *Torre* ſuppoſes this to be *Ralph Bird*, canon of this church, who died *an.* 1483.

Miſe-

CATHEDRAL CHURCH.

Middle isle.

Miseremini mei, miseremini mei
Vos amici mei, quia manus domini tetigit me.

Smert, 1489. ✠ Orate pro animabus magistri Johannis Smert prebendarii in capella beate Marie et sanctorum angelorum et Willielmi Smert fratris sui, qui quidem Johannes xxviii. die mensis Januarii an. Dom. 1489.

25. Belcby, 1553. *L S.* ✠ Here lyeth Christopher Belcby, sometime register to the chapter of this church, of his soule Jesu have mercy, he died the xxiv. day of November 1553.

Holmes, 1579. Here lyeth the corps of James Holmes gent. unfortunately murdered July 28, 1579.
ARMS. A gryffin *(s)*.

26 Huet, 1463 *L.* ✠ Orate pro animabus magistri Johannis Huet, quondam procuratoris curie Ebor. qui obiit an. Dom. 1463. et Margarete uxoris sue, quorum animabus propitietur Deus. Amen.

Kepwick, 1418. ✠ Orate pro Willielmo Kepwick, qui obiit in die sancte Cecilie virginis et martyris, an. Dom. 1418.

27. Girlington, 1584. *L.* Hic jacet magister Nicolaus Girlingtonius Hackfordiensis familie armiger preclarus, vera pietate insignis, et omni splendoris genere instructissimus, qui ex hac vita migravit decimo die Januarii an. Dom. 1584. etatis sue vero 76.

Thorne, 1573.

Here lyeth Thorne musitian most perfitt in art,
In logicks lore who did excell, all vice who set apart,
Whose lief and conversation did all mens love allure,
And now doth reign above the skyes in joyes most firm and pure.
Who dyed Decemb. 7, 1573.

Wilberfoss, 1492. ✠ Orate pro anima Alani Willberfoss generosi, qui obiit Augusti xxii. 1492.

Langton, 1496. ✠ Orate pro anima magistri Willielmi Langton sacre theologie professoris ac hujus ecclesie precentoris, qui obiit x. die Novem. an. Dom. 1496. Cujus anime propitietur Deus. Amen.

28. Goldthorp, *L.* Here lyeth the body of Richard Goldthorpe lord-mayor of this city of York, who dyed the tenth of March anno Dom. 1557, and left nine children begotten of the lady Jane his wife, videlicet, Thomas, Peter, Ann, Jane, Elizabeth, Elyne, Maud, Joan and Frances.

29. Westrope, 1606. *L.* *Here lyeth the body of* Ralph Westrope *esquier, serjeant at armes before queen* Elizabeth *queen of* England *in the counsell established in the north, and the first sworne for that attendance to our gratious sovereigne king* James *the first in his entrance into this kingdome of* Englande, *who departed the fifteenth day of* June, an. Dom. 1606.

Mansell, 1541. ✠ Orate pro anima magistri Willielmi Mansell armigeri, qui obiit xi. die Decembris an. Dom. 1541. Cujus, &c.

30. Underwood, 1615. *L.* ✠ Sub hoc lapide in spe sancta et fide christiana catholica eternae resurrectionis reponitur corpus magistri Johannis Underwode, olim in legibus baccalaurii consultissimi, qui in curia hac ecclesiast. annis plurimis nomen merebatur sapientis, pii ac justi advocati. Obiit vero xxiii. die mensis Julii an. Dom. 1515. Cujus anime propitietur Deus.

Hunsdale, 1526. ✠ Orate pro anima dom. Johannis Hunsdale, quondam vicarii chorialis in eccles. metrop. beati Petri Eborum, qui viam universe carnis ingressus est, sub spe promissionis Christi xxvi. die mensis Junii an. Dom. 1526. Cujus anime propitietur Deus. Amen.

Hert, 1495. ✠ Sepultura Johannis Hert, quondam hujus ecclesie precentoris ac prebendarii, prebend. de Driffield et residentiarii ejusdem, qui obiit octavo die Decem. an. Dom. 1495. Cuius, &c.

Cressacre, 1504. ✠ Orate pro anima magistri Edwardi Cressacre quondam istius ecclesie subdecani, qui obiit ult. die mensis Martii an. Dom. 1504. Cujus anime propitietur Deus.
ARMS. Three lyons saliant.

Thorp, 1384. *(t)* ✠ Ecce magister Adam de Thorpe jacet hic tumulatus . . . .
. . . . par quam resonabat
. . . . supra astra levatum
Justus veredicus munitus . . . .
. . . . non servitturus.

(s) This Mr. *Holmes* was slain in the streets of this city. *MS penes me.*

(t) These two last epitaphs were thus imperfect in Mr. *Dodsworth*'s time; but Mr. *Torre* remarks, that *Adam de Thorpe* canon of the church of *York* made his will, proved Oct. 15, 1384. whereby he gave his body to be buried in this cathedral. As also *Richard de Thoren*, *an.* 1391.

✠ Hic

✠ Hic jacet Ricardus de Thoren quondam canonicus residentiarius istius ecclesie . . . CATHEDRAL CHURCH.
. . . . qui obiit . . . . 1391. . . . . . *Middle isle.*
. . . . redemptor meus vivit et in Thoren, 1391.
novissimo die . . . . sum et in carne mea
videro Deum salvatorem . . . .
sum ego ipse et non alius et oculi mei conspecturi . . . . . .

Robert Broddys was buried in this place, draper, and sheriff of this city he was an. Dom. 1553. Broddys 1553.

✠ Jesu have mercy on master Son's soll. Amen. Sons.

✠ Hic jacet magister Thomas Wylton quondam doctor in medicinis, qui obiit tertio decimo die mensis Februarii an. Dom. 1447. Cujus anime propitietur Deus. Amen. 31. Wylton, 1447. *L.S.*

✠ Hunc benedic Christe quem claudit humo lapis iste Branktre, 1375.
Johan. Branktre (*u*) dictus jacet . . . . nis
Ille istius ecclesie fuit vir presto sophia
Scriba fuit regis senis in . . . .
Anglorum jura firmata, fuit sibi cura
Pauperibus favit inopes multos ope pavit.

✠ Hic jacet dom. Johannes de Clifford quondam thesaurarius istius ecclesie, qui obiit xiiii. die mensis Maii 1369. Finiente viam universe carnis es ingressus. Cujus anime propitietur Deus. Amen. Clifford 1396.

ARMS. Cheque on a fess, three leopards faces.

✠ Hic jacet. dom. Will'mus Fenton nuper rector de Nether-Wallop, qui obiit xxiii. die Novembris an. Dom. 1470. Cujus anime propitietur Deus. Fenton, 1470.

✠ Orate pro anima Ricardi Dawson, quondam parsone istius ecclesie, qui obiit penult. die mens. Julii, an. Dom. 1509. Cujus anime, &c. Dawson, 1509.

✠ Sub hoc lapide jacent Will'mus Clerke et Alicia uxor ejus, qui obierunt iv. die mensis Augusti an. Dom. 1509. Quorum animae in pace requiescant. Clerke, 1509.

✠ Hic jacet Johannes Harby, quondam thesaurarius istius ecclesie qui obiit 21. die mensis Januarii an. Dom. 1424. Cujus anime propitietur Deus. Amen. Haxby, 1424.

Haxby's tomb, removed now nearer the spiritual court. 32.

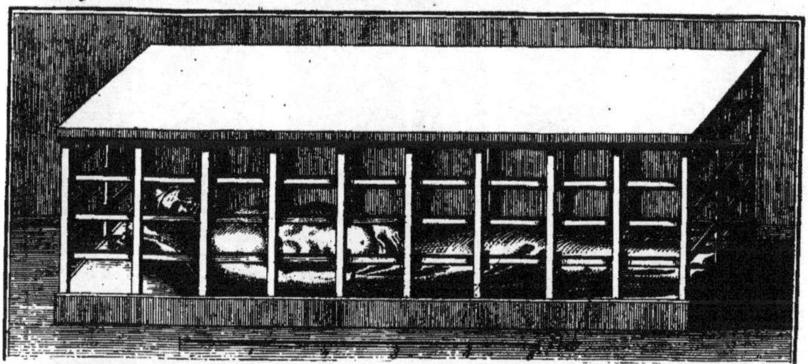

✠ Sub hoc lapide reconditum jacet corpus magistri Martini Colyns decr. doct^ris olim thesaurarii cath. Ebor. et ejusdem ecclesie canonicus residentiarius, qui quoque magistratum gessit primo commissarii deinde officialis dom. archiepiscopi in curia Ebor. usque ad diem ejus extremum, ob. fide catholica et spe beate future resurrectionis in novissimo die, obiit autem ab hoc seculo in dominica septuages. viz. quarto die mensis Feb. an. Dom. juxta computationem Anglicanam 1508. Cujus anime semper propitius sit Deus. Amen. 33. Colyns, 1508, *L.*

ARMS. On a bend three martlets.

St. *William*, archbishop. See his life. 34.

Monumental INSCRIPTIONS in the North Isle *of the* CHOIR. *Choir and North isle.*

✠ Orate pro anima Gerardi Haldynby quondam cognati magistri Thome Portington quondam thesaurarii istius ecclesie, qui obiit primo die mensis Februarii an. Dom. 1480. Cujus anime propitietur Deus. Amen. Haldyngby, 1480.

✠ Hic jacet dom. Robertus Helperby, quondam vicarius istius ecclesie, parentes ejus et Agnes soror ejusdem, qui obiit primo die mensis Februarii an. Dom. 1435. 1. Helperby, 1435, *L.*

✠ Hic jacet dom. Johannes Nigropontens episcopus Eborum suffraganeus, archidiaconus Nottinghamie et prebendarius prebende de Wskelfe, qui obiit xxv. die mensis Aprilis an. Dom. 1516. 2. Nigropontens, 1516, *L.*

(*u*) *Joh. Branktre*, treasorour of this church, had his will proved *Dec.* 29, 1375. *Torre.*

p. 502

The right honourable Sr. Thomas Belasyse of Newborough, Bart. Viscount Fauconberg of Henknowle Baron Fauconbridge of Yarum, in commemmoration of his Lordship's Ancestor who erected this Monument contributes this plate. 1736

BONNE ET BELLE ASSEZ

The right hon.ble the Lady Lechmere, *widow* of Nicholas *Lord* Lechmere, *eldest daughter to the right hon.ble* Charles Howard *Earl of* Carlisle *&c. (at present the wife of Sr* Thomas Robinson *of* Rookby-park *in the* North-riding *of the County of* York, *Bart. member in the last Parliament for the borough of* Morpeth *in* Northumberland, *and now, one of the hon.ble Commissioners of Excise) in true regard to the memory of so near a relation as the Lady who erected this monument, transmits this single instance of her many vertues to posterity.*

17 36.

✠ Orate pro anima magistri Thome Dalby decretorii doctoris et archidiaconi Richmond, prebendarii prebende de Stenellington ac canonici residentiarii in ecclesia metropoliticana Ebor. prepositi ac canonici residentiarii in ecclesia sancti Johannis Beverlaci ac thesaurarii hospitii Thome Savage, quondam Ebor. archiepiscopi, capellani et consiliarii illustrissimi regis Henrici VII. capellani et consiliarii serenissimi et prepotentissimi regis Henrici VIII. et decani capelle illustrissimi principis ducis Richmondie et Somersette, qui obiit xxvi. die mensis Januarii an. Dom. 1525. Cujus anime propitietur Deus. Amen. CATHEDRAL CHURCH. *Choir end; North isle.* 3. Dalby, 1525.

Misereminі mei my friends all
This world hath informed me to fall.
Here may I no longer endure, pray for
My soul for this world is transitorie
And terrestriall. Redde quod debes.

Archbishop *Savage*. See his life. 4. Savage.

✠ Hic jacet Richardus Ucchilt quondam persona altaris S. Will'mi, qui obiit viii. die mensis Septembris an. Dom. 1466. Cujus anime propitietur Deus. Amen. 9. Ucchilt, 1466.

Margareta Byng Londinensis, *ter vidua, pia, honesta, proba, filium ex primo marite unicum, quem unice dilexit, in hac ecclesia residentem invisens diuturno confectum morbo corpus in hac quasi peregrina terra humandum reliquit. Animam vero animarum anchorae Christo Jesu innixam in vera, nativa et coelesti patria glorificandam divinae misericordiae tradidit; et placatè placideque in Domino obdormivit,* Byng, 1600.

Maii 11. *an. Dom.* 1600.

Henricus Belassis, *miles et baronettus, filius* Gulielmi Belassis *militis ex* Margareta *filia primogenita* Nicholas Fairfax *de* Gilling *militis, mortalitatis memor hunc tumulum sibi et* Ursulae *conjugi charissimae filiae primogenitae* Thomae Fairfax *de* Denton *militis posuit. Sub quo simul requiescunt et gloriosum* Christi *redemptoris adventum expectant.* 5. Belassis.

Mors certa est, incerta dies; nec certa sequentum
Cura, sibi tumulum qui parat, ille sapit.
Frequens mortis et novissimi judicii recordatio à peccato revocat.

Swinburn, a plate. See his life. 6 Swinburn.

On one column of a monument,

Near this place lyes interred Charles Howard, *earl of* Carlisle, *viscount* Morpeth, *baron* Dacres *of* Gilsland, *lord lieutenant of* Cumberland *and* Westmorland, *vice-admiral of the coasts of* Northumberland, Cumberland, *bishoprick of* Durham, *town and county of* Newcastle *and maritime parts adjacent; governour of* Jamaica, *privy councellour to king* CHARLES *the second, and his embassador extraordinary to the* CZAR *of* Muscovy, *and the kings of* Sweden *and* Denmark *in the years* 1663 *and* 1664; *whose effigies is placed at the top of this monument. He was not more distinguished by the nobility and antiquity of his family, than he was by the sweetness and affability of a natural charming temper, which, being improved by the peculiar ornaments of solid greatness, courage, justice, generosity, and a publick spirit, made him a great blessing to the age and nation wherein he lived. In business, he was sagacious and diligent; in war circumspect, steady and intrepid; in council wise and penetrating; and though this may secure him a place in the annals of fame, yet the filial piety of a daughter may be allowed to dedicate this monumental pillar to his memory.* Obiit 24. Feb. 1684. aetatis 56. 7. Carlisle.

On another column of the same,

This monumental pillar is erected and dedicated by the right honourable the lady Mary Fenwicke, *eldest daughter to* Charles Howard *earl of* Carlisle, *as a testimony of respect to the memory of sir* John Fenwicke, *baronet, of* Fenwicke-castle *in the county of* Northumberland, *her deceased husband; by whom she had four children one daughter and three sons:* Jane, *her eldest, died very young, and was buried in a vault in the parish church of St.* Nicholas *in* Newcastle upon Tyne. Charles *having attained the age of fifteen years died of the small pox:* William *was six years old, and* Howard *a year and a half, when they departed this life. These three sons do all lie with their father in the parish church of St.* Martin in the Fields, London; *near the altar, where he was interred* January 28, 1696, *aged* 52.

In the midst of the same monument,

Here lyeth the body of the right honourable the lady Mary Fenwicke, *relict of sir* John Fenwicke, *baronet, of* Northumberland, *and daughter of* Charles Howard *earl of* Carlisle. *She died on the* 27th *of* October 1708, *in the fiftieth year of her age. Her life was a patrimony to the poor and friendless; and her many vertues make her memory precious.*

Over

4

CATHEDRAL CHURCH. *Chair end. North iſle.* Over the vault,

Here lyeth the body of Charles Howard *earl of* Carliſle, *who died the fourth of* February 1684. aetat. ſuae 56.

Spinke, 1685. *Here lyeth the body of* William Spinke *gent. late of* Dalby *in the north-riding of* Yorkſhire, *who departed this life, being aged ſixty four years,* March 6, 1685.

8. Three ancient images. See the plate page 491.

Cattell, 1403. ✠ Hic jacet dom. Thomas de Cattell vicarius hujus ecclesie, qui obiit iiii. non. Julii an. Dom. 1403. Cujus anime, &c.

Hatton, 1533. ✠ Orate pro anima Georgii Hatton, qui obiit 28. Decem. an. Dom. 1533.

Langton. 1470. ✠ Orate pro anima magistri Ricardi Langton, quondam rectoris ecclesiae parochialis de obiit 10. die mensis Mart. an. Dom. 1470.

Hardwick, 1592. Sepultura perlustri, candide viator, venerabilis viri Thome Hardwick, qui pietate, religione, liberalitate, omnibus denique generositatis virtutibus tam splendide ornabatur ut Dei amorem, bonorumque gratiam sibi facile comparaverit. Mortem tandem vir tamen vicerit, maturis in annis anima sydera petiit; corpus hic sepelitur 3. mensis Martii 1592, aet. 48.

10. Carnaby, 1665. *L.* *Here lyeth the body of ſir* Thomas Carnaby *knight and colonel, who ſerved his king and country in the time of king* Charles I. *and king* Charles II. *valiantly and faithfully. He died at the age of* 46, Sept. 20, an. Dom. 1665. Veni, Domine Deus.

On a table,

11. Chapman, 1530, *L.*

Pray for the soule of Mr. John Chapman.

Johanni Chapman Eborum civi honestissimo, quem ob singularem et in rebus agendis insignem industriam, reverendissimi patres D. Thomas Savage, Christopherus Baynebridge, Thomas Wulseius hujus sedis archiepiscopi, ab actis sibi primarium esse voluerunt; heredes officii et pietatis non immemores bene merenti sepulchrum posuerunt. Hic vita coelibi functus et de patria ob gymnasium suo sumptu erectum bene meritus ix. Martii commigravit ad superos anno aetat. 63. Christi vero 1530.

12. Beverley, 1493, *L.*

✠ Gulielmus dura jacet hac sub rupe Beverley,
Qui precentoris fulsit honore nimis.
Canonicus residens fuit hic heu tempore pauco
Per decies ternas non magis ebdomades.
Iste decanus erat Middelham venerabilis olim,
Spiritus eternam nunceat in requiem.
Qui obiit quarto die mensis Januarii, an. Dom. 1493.

13. Scrope, 1463, *L.* ✠ Hic jacet magister Will'mus le Scrope archidiaconus Dunelmie et residentiarius in ecclesiis collegiatis S. Johannis Beverlaci, et beati Wilfridi Rippon, qui obiit xxii die Maii an. Dom. 1463. Cujus anime propitietur Deus. Amen.

14. Scrope, 1452, *L.* ✠ Hic jacet Johannes le Scrope, qui obiit octo decima die Septembris an. Dom. 1452. Cujus anime, &c.

Giſbrugh 1481. ✠ Hic jacet dom. Johannis Gisbrugh, quondam precentor hujus ecclesie ac canonicus residentiarius ac prebendarius prebende de Bugthorpe in eadem, et rector ecclesiarum parochialium de Spafforth et Brompton in Pykeryng-lythe, qui obiit vii. die mensis Novem. an. Dom. 1481. Cujus anime propitietur Deus. Amen.
Je u mercy. Lady helpe.

15. Sorſby, 1683, *L.* *Hic jacet* Robertus Sorſby, *S. T. B. Precentor hujus ecclesie cathedralis, natus* Sheffield *educatus* Cantabrigiae *collegii* Emanuelis, *qui obiit* 15. *die menſis* Aug. *A. D.* 1683. *aet. ſuae* 74.

16. Fall, 1711. *L.* *Hic dormit in* Chriſto *quod mortale fuit venerabilis et primaevae pietatis viri* Jacobi Fall, *S. T. P. olim regiae majeſtati apud* Scotos *ab hiſtoriis et academiae* Glaſcuenſis *principalis plurimum colendi: quem hierarcha apoſtolica e* Scotia *ſua exulante oſtraciſmo ſimul inſignitum haec eccleſia metropol. in praecentorem, archideaconum* Clevelandiae, *et canon. reſident. cooptaſſe ſummo in honore et lucro poſuit; ubi per* 19, *et quod excurrit, annos confratribus conjunctiſſimus. Pauperibus, peregrinis, omnibus bonis charus vixit, flebilis obiit pridie idus* Junii *anno ſalutis* 1711. *aetatis ſuae* 64.

17 Field, 1680. *Hic jacet* Robertus Field, *S. T. P. archidiaconus de* Cleveland, *nec non hujus eccleſiae ſubdecanus et prebendarius, qui obiit* Sept. 9, 1680. *aet. ſuae* 42.

18. Pearſon.
19. Terrick.
20 Gibſon.

Sterne,

Copartments
Pearson, Terrick *and* Gibson.

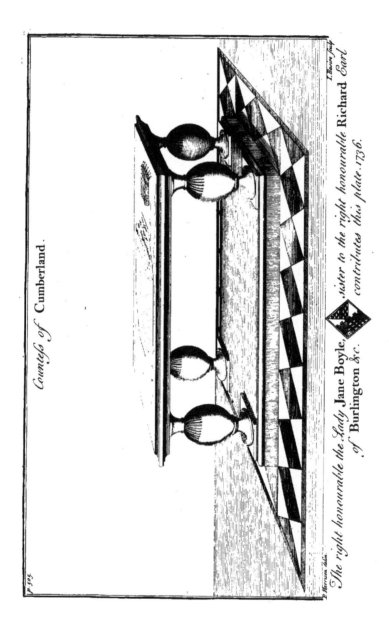

Countess of Cumberland.

P. Harrison delin. I. Basire sculp.

The right honourable the Lady Jane Boyle, sister to the right honourable Richard Earl of Burlington &c. contributes this plate. 1736.

CATHEDRAL CHURCH. *Choir end. North-iſle.*

Sterne, archbiſhop. See his life. . . . . 21. Sterne.

Anna Sterne *filia* Ricardi *archiepiſcopi* Ebor.
Ad coetum virginum abiit
Martii xxiv. *an. Dom.* MDCLXVIII. 22. Sterne, 1668, *L.*
Aetatis ſuae xviii.

Here lyeth in reſt the body of the right honourable FRANCES CECIL, *counteſs of* Cumberland, *daughter of the right honourable* Robert *earl of* Saliſbury, *(lord high-treaſurer of* England, *and knight of the moſt noble order of the* Garter, *and maſter of the court of wards and liveries) ſhe married the right honourable* Henry *lord* Clifford, Bromfleet, Vetrepont *and* Veſſey, *earl of* Cumberland, *and lord lieutenant of the county of* York *under king* CHARLES *the firſt, the laſt earl of that ancient and moſt noble family of* CLIFFORD; *by whom the ſaid lady had iſſue the right honourable the lady* Elizabeth Clifford, *(married to the right honourable* Richard *lord* Boyle, *baron* Clifford *and earl of* Burlington *in* England, *earl of* Cork *and lord high-treaſurer of* Ireland;) *alſo three ſons,* viz. Francis, Charles *and* Henry, *and one daughter more, the lady* Frances Clifford *who all died young. This noble lady being of the age of forty nine years and eleven months, departed this mortal life at* York, *on the fourth day of* February *in the year of our Lord* 1643. 23. Clifford, 1643.

Scrope, archbiſhop. See his life. 24. Scrope.

In St. *Stephen*'s chapel, which was at the eaſt end of this iſle, were interred many of the noble family of *Scrope*. Beſides what I have mentioned, which laid before the door of it, *Leland* ſays, that in his time were theſe broken inſcriptions: Scrope.

. . . . . . **Thomas de Maſham dominus le Scrope vir nobilis obiit** . . . . 1406.
. . . . . . **f.** . . . . **in ſacello S.** . . . . **duas cantarias.**

. . . . **Henricus primogenitus Johannis dom. le Scrope** 1418.
. . . .

. . . . **Philipa uxor Henrici domini le Scrope de Maſham filia Guidonis domini de Brien. Ob. ixx. die Novem. an.** 1406.

. . . . **Stephanus le Scrope arch. Richmondis** . . . . .
. . . . **obiit** . . . . **an. Dom.** 1418.

Monumental INSCRIPTIONS in the South-iſle *of the* CHOIR.

✠ **Hic jacet dom. Johannes Halton quondam parſona ad altare S. Willielmi in eccleſ. metrop. Ebor. qui viam univerſe carnis ingreſſus eſt viii. die Junii an. Dom.** 1516. **Cujus, &c.** 1. Halton, 1516. *L.*

✠ **Orate pro anima dom. Johannis Redneſs, quondam parſone in iſta eccleſia, qui obiit xi. die Oct. an. Dom.** 1428. **Cujus anime propitietur Deus.** 2. Redneſs, 1428, *L.*

✠ **Hic jacet magiſter Will'mus Cawode canonicus et reſidentiarius iſtius eccleſie, qui obiit xix. die menſis Martii an. Dom.** 1439. **Cujus anime propitietur Deus. Amen.** 3. Cawode, 1439, *L.*

✠ **Hic jacet magiſter Thomas Greenwode, legum doctor, canonicus reſidentiarius iſtius eccleſie qui obiit xi. die menſis Maii an. Dom.** 1421. **Cujus anima in pace requieſcat. Amen.** 4. Greenwode, 1421, *L.*

Hic ſitus eſt Richardus Whittington, rector eccleſie de Wheldrake, vir pius et providus, Dei eximius praeco qui quod verbo docuit facto confirmavit, omnes quippe facultates ad redimendas decimas in uſum eccleſie allocavit, ejuſque ſumptibus rectoriam de Holme in Spaldingmoor ſe liberatam et reducem eccleſiae gaudet, foelix ſcil. oeconomus haeres iſte Dei et coheres cum Chriſto, Chriſtum ſibi haeredem inſtituit. 5 Whittington, 1628, *L.*

Ob. Sept. die Aprilis 1628.

Orate pro mortuis quia moriemini.

✠ **Orate pro anima magiſtri Thome Forne, ſubtheſaurarii hujus eccleſia Ebor. canonicique capelle beate Marie et ſanctorum angelorum atque parſona ad altare ſancte Agathe in eadem eccleſia, qui obiit xv. die Julii an.** 1533. **Cujus anime propitietur Deus.** Forne, 1533.

CATHEDRAL CHURCH.

6. Newton, 1416, *L.* ✠ Hic jacet dom. Johannes de Newton capellanus, qui obiit xiiii. die mensis Julii an. Dom. 1416. Cujus anime propitietur Deus.

7. Wath, 1424, *L.* ✠ Orate pro anima dom. Will'mi Wath quondam vicarii istius ecclesie, qui obiit xii. die mensis Januarii an. Dom. 1426. Cujus, &c. Amen.

Beale. ✠ Orate pro anima domini Roberti Beale.

8. Beleby, 1447, *S, L.* ✠ Hic jacet Thomas Beleby quondam parsona ecclesie cath. Ebor. clericus fabrice ejusdem, qui obiit xxviii. die mensis Februarii an. Dom. 1443. Cujus anime propitietur Deus. Amen.

Knapton, 1471. ✠ Orate pro anima Johannis Knapton olim subthesaurarii hujus eccles. qui obiit iii. die mens. Novem. an. 1471. Cujus anime propitietur Deus.

Awham. ✠ Orate pro anima Johannis Awham quondam magistri carpentariorum istius ecclesie cath. Eborum.

9 Godson, 1416, *L.* ✠ Hic jacet dom. Ricardus Godsonus quondam parsona ac subthesaurarius istius ecclesie, qui obiit xx. die mensis Maii an. Dom. 1416. Cujus anime propitietur Deus. Amen.

Garton, 1419. ✠ Orate pro anima Thome Garton quondam subthesaurarii istius ecclesie, qui obiit xiiii. die mensis Novem. an. Dom. 1419. Cujus anime propitietur Deus. Amen.

10. Garland, 1408, *L.* ✠ Orate pro anima dom. Will'mi Garland quondam vicarii istius eccles. qui quarto die mensis April. an. Dom. 1408. viam universe carnis ingressus est. Cujus anime propitietur Deus. Amen.

Marshal, 1549. Here lieth the body of Cuthbert Marshall, doctor of divinity, late archdeacon of Nottingham, prebendary of Ulstwayte, canon residentiary of this metropolitan church of York, of whose soule God have mercy, the burial of whom was the xxvth day of January in the yeare of our Lord God 1549.

CATHEDRAL CHURCH. Choir end. South isle.

11 Wanton. *Hic jacet* NICHOLAUS WANTON *arm. filius aetate minimus et haeres* THOMAE WANTON *de civitate* Londini *arm. et* Joh. *uxoris ejus unicae filiae et haeredis* JOHAN. LAXTON, *fratris et haeredis* GULIELMI LAXTON *militis aurati, qui dum vivus fuerat immaculata morum probitate, religionis sanctitate, corporis castitate, et pacis denique tranquillitate, erga omnes justum, sanctum, purum et quietum se praebuit, et quod sanum solummodo animum virtutis studio applicaret, ab immundis mundi illecebris et conjugii curis securus vixit, adeo vitam degit contemplativam qua melius ad finem pergeret summa cum consolatione placidam et obtineat consolationem sine fine sempiternam. Obiit secundo die mensis* Martii *anno Dom.* 1617.

Me juxta fratrem quicunque videt tumulatum,
Mortis venturae sit memor illa suae.

Prope hunc tumulum sepultus est GULIELMUS WANTON, *filius secundus* THOMAE WANTON *praedicti et fratris dicti* NICHOLAI *qui obiit* 23. *die mensis* Septembris *anno* 1577. JOHANNES LAYIR *arm. haeres et nepos* NICH. WANTON, *propter amoris sui comprobationem, et avunculi defuncti famae conservationem, hunc struxit tumulum.*

12. Palmer. GULIELMUS PALMER, CANTABR. *aul.* PEMBR. *quondam socius; in terris peregrinatus est annos* 66; *sacrosancto ecclesiastici pastoris munere functus* 45; *cancellarius hujus ecclesiae* 34; *obiit anno gratiae* 1605, Octobris 23. *Cujus doctrinam, hospitalitatem, vigilantiam, mores, rostra publica, aedes privatae, ecclesiae fabrica, civium eulogia resonant.* ANNAM *conjugem,* ROWLANDI TALERI *L. V. doctoris et martyris filiam et ex ea* 7 *liberos superstites reliquit, tribus praemissis. Sub hoc marmore* Christi *adventum expectans obdormit.*

13. Hodson. *Selectissimae conjugis virtuti hoc qualicunque elogio parentavit, afflictui indulsit vir si quis alius moestissimus.* JANA HODSON, *uxor* PHINEAE HODSON *S. theologiae professoris, et hujus ecclesiae cancellarii, foemina in exemplum nata et super omnem adulationem absoluta, sexus sui praeclarum specimen et totius etiam urbis insigne ornamentum. Hinc merito delitiae et letitiae viri, suis dilecta, omnibus gratiosa, pietatem, modestiam, beneficentiam, obnixe coluit. Familiae norma, hospes benigna, pauperum altrix munifica, quibus erogando providus, et foelix oeconomia facultates auxit, propinquos cupide extraneos humanissime excepit. Conjux fidelis, mater foecunda et quae non minore sollicitudine liberos educavit quos peperit. Postquam numerosa utriusque sexus sobole maritum suum adauxisset, in vicesimo quarto tandem partu, doloris acerbitate, tanquam miles in statione summa animi constantia succubuit, et integris adhuc aetate et forma adeo ut virginem diceres quae toties mater erat. Turbato naturae ordine provectiorem jam virum reliquit ardentissimo ipsius desiderio quotidie canescentem. Dulcissimam interim conjugem non exaudientem vocat desertissimus maritus P. H. Obiit aetatis suae* 38. *et circiter* 8. *menses* 2. Sept. 1636.

On a monument,

14. Gee. *In humanis magnus, in divinis multus.*

On one side,

Non opus est tumulo, victrix cui fama superstes,
Lucrum cui mors est non opus est lachrymis;
Solamen vivi, venturis utile seclis,
Virtutis calcar, sed pia facta patrum;
Quod super est relegas, pietate imitare, viator,
Hac praesens causa construitur tumulus.

On the other,

Quid monumenta paro, nostro cui pectore nullo
Interitura die stent monumenta tibi?
His ego non celanda tuae praeconia laudis
Celavi, et summis aemula facta viris.
Mi satis: at nostrum cunctis testemur amorem
Hunc quoque virtuti do, cumulo, tumulum.

Underneath,

ANNO DOM. 1611.

In aeternam primaevae labis memoriam.

Stay gentle Passenger, and read
A sentence sent thee from the dead.
If wisdom, wealth, honour or honesty,
Chastity, zeal, faith, hope or charity;
If universal learning, language, law,
Pure piety, religion's reverend awe,
Firm friends, fair issue; if a virtuous wife,
A quiet conscience, a contented life,
The clergy's prayers, or the poor man's tears;
Could have lent length to man's determin'd years;
Sure as the fate which for our fault we fear,
Proud death had ne'er advanc'd his trophy here;

In a

p. 508

Thomas Gee *of* Bishop Burton *Esq; a lineal descendant from* S^r. William Gee, *presents this plate of his ancestors monument to this work. 1736.*

In it behold thy doom, thy tomb provide, CATHEDRAL CHURCH.
Sir WILLIAM GEE *had all these pleas, yet dy'd.* *Choir and South-isle.*

GULIELMUS GEE, *nuper de* B. Burton *in com.* Eborum. *equ. aurat.* JACOBO Mag. Brit. *monarch. primo a consiliis simul et secretis. Vir pietate, religione et munificentia, (praecipue in ministros verbi) prae ceteris insignis. Linguarum* Latinae, Graecae, Hebraicae, *cultiorum fere omnium (addo et literarum scientia) spectabilis, utriusque juris prudentia, et sacrae quod supremum, theologiae non minus practicae quam theoricae ad miraculum celebris. Postquam uxores primo* THOMASINAM *reverendiss. in* CHRISTO *patris D. D.* HUTTON *archiepisc.* Eborac. *filiam, ac deinde* MARIAM *ex generoso* CROMPTONORUM *stirpe oriundam, virgines duxisset, et ex utrisque satis pulchra et liberali utriusque sexus prole auct. ad virtutibus aeque ac speciei propag. intendisset, annos in hac lachrymabili valle natus circiter quinquag. retardari sustineret, inconcussa in* CHRISTUM *fide, inviolata erga proximos charitate, suaviter obdormiens in Domino, animam Deo patri, exuvias terrae matri, resumpturus olim cum foenore placide resignavit.*

Cui dom. MARIA GEE, *(consors dum convixerunt) felicitates et prae sexus modulo, (virtut. futura etiam ubi fata volunt) et sepulchri exiguum hoc eximii tamen amoris et fidei conjugalis monumentum pro voto dedicant certe aeternum post tot annos vidua posuit.* Nec mors mihi finis amoris.

Lee, archbishop, a grave-stone. See his life. 15. Lee.

Hutton, archbishop, a monument. See his life. 16. Hutton.

✠ Hic jacet Huttoni conjux pia fida Beatrix,
Terra tegit terram, mens loca summa tenet.
Felix illa fuit tum viris prole viroque,
Junctior at Christo morte beata magis.
Obdormivit quinto die Maii 1582.

✠ Hic sepelitur Will'mus Savage decret. baccalaur. quondam subthesaurarius hujus eccles. metropol. qui obiit xxv. die mensis Julii an. Dom. 1508. Cujus anime propitietur Deus. Amen. 17. Savage, 1508, L.

✠ Orate pro anima dom. Will'mi Evers nuper unius personarum hujus alme eccles. et rectoris eccles. omnium sanctorum in marisco civit. Ebor. qui obiit xviii. die mensis Maii an. Dom. 1419. Evers, 1419.

✠ Orate pro anima dom. Caroli Fatro nuper persone in ista ecclesia ad altare sancte Marie Magdalene in scriptis ac custod. fabricas ejusdem eccles. qui obiit xxiv. die Sept. 1414. 18. Fatro, 1414, L.

Penelope *the daughter of sir* Gervase Cuttler *of* Stainborough *knt. departed this life* Dec. 21, an. Dom. 1686. 19. Cutler, 1686, L.

Against the wall,

JOANNES BROOKE *sac. theol. professor, collegii universitatis* Oxon. *olim socius*, Emliensis *primum, tum* Silkstoniae, *denique* Baintoniae *ecclesiae rector dignissimus; hujus ecclesiae metropoliticae praecentor, et canonicus residentiarius. Vir prudens et providus, in concionibus frequens et doctus, vixit ad annum aetatis suae* 40, *obdormivit Domino* 23 Martii *A. D.* 1616. *et positus est juxta hoc monumentum, expectans noviss. sanctorum resurrectionem.* 20. Brook.

Pastor eras plebi dilectus, pabula vitae,
Saepe tuae, et docta doctor in urbe dabas,
Officium gregis hic tu praecentoris obibas,
Tempora sed vitae sunt nimis arcta tuae;
Quae te dilexit moeret tua funera conjux;
Accipe suprema haec funera moesta tibi.

Under a painted board with his effigies, &c.

Haec senis EDMUNDI BUNNE *est quem cernis imago,* 21. Bunny.
A quo Bunnaei *villula nomen habet.*
Clarus erat; tanti tumuit neque sanguinis aestu;
Haeres patris erat, profuit esse nihil.
Demsit aetatem gravitas, resolutio mentem,
Zelum scripta, aciem pulpita, facta fidem.
Vasa sacra librosque dedit post funera templo,
Et bona pauperibus; caetera seque Deo.

EDMUNDI BUNNEY *ex nobili* Bunniorum *familia oriundus, sacrae theologiae bach. collegii* Mertonensis *in* Oxon. *olim socius, parochiae* Bolton-Per. *pastor, ecclesiarum* B. Pauli Lond. B. Petri Eborum. B. Mariae Carliol. *prebendarius dignissimus. Concionator frequentissimus, vicatim et oppidatim, praedicando multos annos consumpsit. Cum ob amorem* Christi *hereditatem paternam fratri* RICHARDO *juniori reliquisset, obiit* 6. *die mensis* Februarii 1617.

Lamplugh, archbishop, a monument. See his life. 22. Lamplugh.

Dolben, archbishop, a monument. See his life. 23. Dolben.

✠ Hic jacet dom. Symon Browne quondam persona in ecclesia cath. Eborum ac prepositus collegii sancti Willielmi, qui obiit viii. die mensis Februarii an. Dom. 1470. Cujus anime propitietur Deus. Amen. Browne, 1470.

✠ Hic jacet dom. Will'mus Horneby, quondam persona altaris sanctorum innocentium, qui obiit vi. die mensis Novembris an. Dom. 1436. Cujus anime propitietur Deus. Amen. Horneby, 1436.

CATHEDRAL CHURCH. *South isle Choir* Clerke, 1506. ✠ **Hic jacet dom. Robertus Clerke, quondam parsona ad altare . . . . in eccl. cath. Ebor. qui obiit xx. die mensis Julii an. Dom.** 1506.

24. Carver, 1665, *L.* *Lector, si pietatis amator, si doctrinae aestimator, si scias quantus sub hoc lapide thesaurarius situs est,*

MARMADUCUS CARVER,

Ecclesiae Hartilliensis *quondam rector, sed erat chronologiae et geographiae callentissimus, linguarum peritus, concionando praepotens, hic scilicet qui cum scriptis ad invidiam usque doctis verum terrestris paradisi locum orbi monstrasset, ad coelestem quem praedicando auditoribus commendaverat, cujus adeundi ingenti desiderio teneremur monendo petiit, translatus est. . . . die* Aug. 1665.

25. Meriton, 1624, *L.* *Here lyeth the body of* George Meriton, *D. D. late dean of this church, who departed this life* Dec. 23, A. D. 1624.

26. Younge. *Young*, archbishop, a grave-stone. See his life.

27. Younge, 1614, *L.* *Here lyeth the body of* Jane Younge *widow, late wyfe of* Thomas Young *late archbishop of* Yorke, *and lord president of the councell established in the northe partes, who after his decease remained a widow forty four years, and departed this life in the eighty fourth year of her age,* an. Dom. 1614.

28. Younge, 1620, *L.* *Here lyeth the body of sir* George Younge *knight, son of the said* Thomas Younge *late archbishop of* Yorke, *and* Jane *his wife, who in the reigne of the late queen* Elizabeth *was captain under the right honourable* Robert *earl of* Essex *in the* Irish *war, who married the daughter of* Jasper Cholmley *of* Highgate *in the county of* Middlesex, *by whom he had issue five children, viz.* Thomas, Margaret, Catherine, Frances *and* Faith, *and departed this life in the fifty third year of his age,* July 10, A. D. 1620.

29. Younge, 1622, *L.* *Here lyeth the body of Mrs.* Faith Younge *daughter to sir* George Younge *knight, who died* March 7, 1622. *aged twenty four years.*

30. Younge, 1628, *L.* *Here lyeth the body of* Thomas Younge *esquire, son of sir* George Young *knight, who married the daughter of* Philippe Adams *of* Auston *esquire, and had issue by her* Thomas *and* Frances *and departed this life the thirtieth year of his age,* May 26, 1628.

31. Younge, 1629, *L.* *Here lyeth the body of lady* Mary Younge, *late wife of sir* George Younge *knight, who lived nine years a widow after his decease, and departed this life* Decemb. 6, 1629. *and in the year of her age* 57.

Mrs Bennet.

1 2 *Feet.*

p. 511

WILLIAM WENTWORTH Earl of STRAFFORD,
Viscount WENTWORTH, Baron WENTWORTH of
WENTWORTH WOODHOUSE, NEWMARSH, OVERSLY &
RABY, & Knight of ye most Noble Order of ye GARTER &c.
Feet

The right honourable Sr Thomas Watson Wentworth, *Knight of the most hon.^ble Order of the* Bath, *Baron of* Malton, *of* Wath, *Viscount* Higham Ferrers *and Earl of* Malton, *Lord Lieutenant & Custos Rotulorum of ye* West riding *of ye County of* York, *in memory of a Noble Person to whom his Lordship's family owes ye greatest obligation, bestows this plate.* 1736.

EN DIEU EST TOUT

John Haynes. del. *G. Du Bosc. sculp.*

The Right Honourable THOMAS EARL *of* MALTON,
as a further testimony of his regard for such a Parent, contributes this Plate. 1736.

ANNAE BENETTAE filiae CHRISTOPHERI WEEKES de SARUM in com. WILTS. arm. foeminae integrae famae, pietatis eximiae ac pudicitiae singularis, uxori optimae et obsequentissimae JO. BENNET, L. D. moestiss. maritus hoc amoris conjugalis monumentum posuit. CATHEDRAL CHURCH. 32. Bennet.

Suscepit ex marito plures liberos, sex ea decedente superstites quatuor filios et duas filias, &c.

Obiit nono die Februarii, anno Dom. 1601.

WILLIAM WENTWORTH, earl of Strafford, viscount Wentworth, baron Wentworth of Wentworth-Woodhouse, Newmarsh, Overfley, and Raby, and knight of the most noble order of the Garter, was the son of the right honourable THOMAS earl of STRAFFORD, by ARABELLA second daughter of the right honourable JOHN earl of Clare. 33. Strafford 1687.

The 27th of February, 1654, he married HENRIETTA MARY STANLEY, second daughter of the right honourable JAMES earl of Derby, (who the 15th of October, 1651, was beheaded at Bolton in Lancashire for his loyalty to king CHARLES the second) by the lady CHARLOTTE DE TREMOILLE, countess of Derby, daughter to CLAUDE duke of Tremoille and CHARLOTTE BRABANTINE DE NASSAU, second daughter to WILLIAM prince of Orange by CHARLOTTE DE BOURBON princess of Orange. His second wife was the lady HENRIETTA DE ROY DE LA ROCHEFAUCAULD daughter of FREDERICK CHARLES DE ROY DE LA ROCHEFAUCAULD, earl of Roy and Roucy, knight of the most illustrious and most noble order of the elephant, and generalissimo of the armies of the king of Denmark, son of FRANCIS DE ROY de la Rochefaucauld, earl of Rouci and Roy, by JULIANA CATHERINA de la tour de Auvergne, born princess of Bouillon and Sedan.

The mother of this lady HENRIETTA was ISABELLA de Durfort, countess of Roy and Rouci, daughter of GUI ALPHONSO de Durfort, marquis of Duras, by ELIZABETH CHARLOTTE de la tour de Auvergne, born princess of Bouillon and Sedan.

He having no issue made the honourable THOMAS WATSON third son of the right honourable EDWARD lord Rockingham, by ANNE, eldest daughter of THOMAS earl of Strafford, heir of his estates in England and Ireland, and required him to take upon him the name of WENTWORTH. He was born the 8th of June, 1626, and died the 16th of October, 1695; as full of good deeds as of days.

On a stone, under, is inscribed,

The earl of Strafford's vault appointed to be made by William earl of Strafford, anno Dom. 1687.

The honourable
THOMAS WATSON WENTWORTH, 34. Wentworth.
Third son of Edward lord Rockingham,
By Anne eldest daughter of Thomas earl of Strafford
Lord Lieutenant of Ireland.
He succeeded to the antient estate of the Wentworth family:
By the last will of his uncle William earl of Strafford;
He married Alice the only daughter of sir Thomas Proby
Of Etton in Huntingtonshire;
By whom he had one son Thomas lord Malton
And two daughters who died in their infancy;
He departed this life at Harrowden in Northamptonshire
October 6, 1723. Aetat. 58.
His virtues were equal to his descent:
By abilities he was formed for publick,
By inclination determined to private life:
If that life can be called private, which was dayly imployed
In successive acts of beneficence to the publick.
He was in religion exemplary, in senate impartial,
In friendship sincere, in domestick relation
The best husband, the most indulgent father.
His justly afflicted relict and son
Thomas lord Malton,
To transmit the memory of so great worth to future times,
Erected this monument.

Piers, archbishop, a copartment. See his life. 35. Piers.

Bowett, archbishop, a monument, see his life. 36. Bowet.

In the Middle Choir, or Lady's Chapel. Middle Choir.

Archbishop Sharp, a monument, see his life. 1. Sharp.

Archbishop Matthews, a monument, see his life. 2. Matthews.

A mo-

CATHEDRAL CHURCH. *Middle-choir.*

A monument.

3. Matthew. FRANCES MATTHEW, *first married to* Matthew Parker, *son to* Matthew Parker, *archbishop of* Canterbury; *afterwards to* Tobie Matthew, *that famous archbishop of this see: she was a woman of exemplary wisdom, gravity, piety, bounty, and indeed in other vertues not only above her sex, but the times. One excellent act of her, first derived upon this church, and through it flowing upon the country, deserves to live as long as the church itself. The library of the deceased archbishop, consisting of above three thousand books, she gave it entirely to the publick use of this church. A rare example that so great care to advance learning should lodge in a woman's breast! but it was the less wonder in her because she was kin to so much learning. She was daughter of* William Barlow, *bishop of* Chichester, *and in king* HENRY *the eighth's time ambassador into* Scotland, *of that antient family of the* Barlows *in* Wales. *She had four sisters married to four bishops, one to* William Wickham, *bishop of* Winchester, *another to* Overton *bishop of* Coventry *and* Litchfield, *a third to* Westphaling *bishop of* Hereford, *a fourth to* Day *that succeeded* Wickham *in* Winchester, *so that a bishop was her father, an archbishop her father-in-law; she had four bishops her brethren and an archbishop her husband. When she had lived seventy eight years, the 8th of* May, *she changed this life as full of honour as of years,* anno Dom. 1629.

4. Frewen. Archbishop *Frewen*, a monument. See his life.

5. Rotheram. Archbishop *Rotheram*, a monument. See his life.

Uirtus vite laus.

6. Hurleston 1587. *L. S. on the wall.* **The body of Raulph Hurleston esquire, one of the honourable counsell in these north parts, lyeth here in hope of joyfull resurrection; who adorned with great giftes of learning, gravity, wisdom, joined with rare godlinesse, was alwayes carefull for the advancing of the sincere doctrine of Christ, and of that equity which every where ought to be observed, never ceasing his faithful labours to profit this church and commonwealth. Untill it pleased our gracious God, mercifully and in a very short moment, without any or the least dolours of death to end all the labours of his faithfull servant, and to translate his soul into eternal rest, April 13, anno Christi incarnati 1587.**

All the days of his peregrination were 62 years, for whose godly life the anointed Saviour be praysed for ever. Amen.

ARMS to this, quarterly, first and last *argent*, a cross of four quevées *azure*, second and third *azure*, three garbs *argent*; and a border plateé.

On the ground under archbishop *Frewen*'s monument,

Hic prope sita est,

7. Frewen 1666. *L.* Judetha *nuper uxor* Thomae Frewen *armigeri filia, et haeres unica* Johannis Wolverstone *de* Fulham *in comitatu* Middlesex *generosi, quae post quintum partum* Sept. 29. *aet. suae* 27 *nuptiarum* 11. *A. D.* 1666, *duos filios totidem filias superstites relinquens ad coelum migravit.*

On a table, ARMS, impaled, 1. *Frewen*, 2. *Or*, a fess wavy *inter* three griffins heads erased *gules*.

M. S.

8. Laton 1675. *L.* Carolus Laton *arm.* Thomae Laton *de* Laton *in com.* Ebor. *militis et* Brigittae *uxoris ejus filius unicus. Obiit* x *die* Augusti *anno salutis* 75, *aetatis* 37.

Brigitta *soror ejus et nuper uxor* Thomae Frewen *in memoriam charissimi fratris hoc poni curavit.*

ARMS on a stone, a fess *inter* six crosslets.

9. Jenkins 1596. **Hic jacet Johannes Jenkins arm. qui pie in Christo vixit; ex uxore sua Margaretta septem filios Henricum, Mattheum, Radulfum, Gulielmum, Georgium et Johannem, et duas filias, Mariam et Margarettam in mundo reliquit 2 die Oct. A. D. 1596.**

Terrea terrenis, mundo mundana relinquo;
Reddo animam Domino, reddoque corpus humo;
Spiritus O Jesu meus . . . . . . suscipiatur,
Spes mea tu, Jesu, gratia, non opera.

ARMS impaled, 1. *Or*, a lion rampant regardant *sable*. 2. On a fess *inter* three griffins heads erased, as many crosses patée fitchée.

Wyvell 1565. **Here lyeth Elizabeth Wyvell daughter of Christopher Wyvell, esq; and Margarete his wyfe, whyche dyed the xiii day of April, in the yere of our Lord God 1565.**

10. Dalton 1682. *L.* Michael *the youngest son of sir* William Dalton *of* Hawkeswell *knt. lieth here interred, who departed this life the 5th day of* November 1682, *in the eleventh year of his age.*

11. Floure 1452. *L.* ✠ **Hic jacet Jacobus Floure, quondam nobilis armiger Johannis domini Scrope, qui obiit 14 die mensis Maii anno Dom. 1452. Cujus anime propitietur Deus. Amen.**

ARMS

Mrs. Matthews.

p512

The honourable Mrs. **Fox** *of*

Bramham-park, *daughter and heir to the right honourable* **Robert** *Lord* **Bingley**, *descended from a Sister of this Lady presents this plate. 1736.*

The honourable and reverend **Edward Finch** *A.M. Canonresidentiary of the Church of* **York**, *in great regard to the memory of his deceased brother, erected this monument and gave this plate of it to this Work. 1736*

1 2 3 4 5 6 Feet

ARMS at each corner, *ermine*, a cinque foil. CATHEDRAL CHURCH. *Middle-choir.*

✠ Hic jacet Ricardus Fournabi quondam armiger domini nostri regis, qui obiit vicesimo sexto die mensis Septembris anno Dom. 1407. Cujus anime propicietur Deus. Fournabi 1407

Here lieth the body of Ann Stanhope *daughter of Dr.* Stanhope *and* Susan *his wife, who died the 27th day of* October, 1939, *being of the age of eighteen years.* 12. Stanhope 1639.

Here lyeth the body of Henry Cheek, *esq; one of her majesties counsell established in the north partes, and her graces secretary,* &c. 13 Cheek 1586. *L.*

Here lyeth Matthew Pollard esquire, son and heir of sir Richard Pollard knight, who departed this present life June 30, 1589. 14. Pollard 1589. *L.*

Anne Sandie Sandys.
Virtuti sacrum.
Hunc tibi, sed moerens, supremum sacrat honorem
Conjuge te foelix conjux tuus, illicet ipsa
Foemina foeminee virtusque decusque cohortis;
Mistus amore pudor, certans multa indole virtus,
Exuperans annos pietas mens ardua sapiens:
Hic tibi pulcher honos, justusque, ergo aurea mundi
Regia, sanctam animam, quae jam nunc debita coelo
Et matura Deo primisque excepta sub annis
Numen et astra sitit, Stellanti sede recepit.
Sic, O sic vivas, vivesque eterna tryumphis,
Felici in divum templo felicior ipsa.

On a gravestone,

Here lyes the body of the honourable Mr. Finch, *dean of this church, who died at* Bath. 1[illegible] Finch 1728.

On the monument.

HENRICUS FINCH, *A. M.*
Hujus ecclesiae decanus
Obiit 8 Sept. *anno Dom.* 1728.
Vir vere nobilis,
Nobilis natu et amplitudine majorum;
Sed non peritura virtutum
Qua ornatus erat corona
Longe nobilior.
Vultu, majestas et decor et alacritas,
Sanae mentis indicia,
Effulgebant.
Dictis non indecore facetus erat,
Et cum suavitate severus.
Omnibus se praebuit facilem et aequum;
Omnibus, praesertim vero fidelibus;
Quam maxime benignum.
Justi tenacem
Nec spes sordida nec metus servilis
A semita recta consiliisque honestis
Unquam potuit detorquere.
Pietate simulationis nescia
Et ab omni fuco abhorrente.
(Quippe qui religionis Christianae mysteriis
Fidem habuit firmam)
Meritos Deo solvebat honores:
Quaecunque pura, honesta, decora, laudanda sunt,
(Ut summatim omnia) excoluit ipse;
Eademque ut alii excolerent,
Quantum in ipso erat, curavit.
Ecclesiae Anglicanae *decus fuit et ornamentum,*
Ecclesiae cui praeerat Eboracensi
Cum munimentum tum deliciae;
Eheu! vix ullum inveniet parem,
Meliorem nedum sperare fas est.

CATHEDRAL CHURCH. *Middle choir.*

Beatae apud superos vitae permaturum
E seculo male merenti
Deus accersivit.

16. Dryden 1702. *L.* *Hic jacet* Jonathan Dryden *A. M. prebendarius de* Frydaythorp *et hujus ecclesiae canonicus residentiarius. Obiit* xxx *die* Augusti *anno aerae Christianae* 1702, *aet. suae* 63.

17. Beckwith 1585. *L.* **Here lyeth the body of dame Elizabeth Beckwith widow, daughter and coheir of sir Roger Cholmley, knt. deceased and late wife of sir Leonard Beckwith, knt. by whom she had two sons Roger and Frauncis, both dyed without issue, and two daughters Elizabeth married to William Vavasour of Weston in the countie of Yorke esquire, and Fraunces married to George Hervey of Merks in the countie of Esser Esquier, by whom they have issue. She dyed on Sunday being** 24 **of November,** 1563.

Felter 1451. ✠ **Orate pro anima magistri Willielmi Felter decretorum doctoris quondam decani et canonici residentiarii istius ecclesie cath. ac prebendarii de Driffeld in eadem qui obiit** 10 **die mensis Aprilis anno Dom.** 1451.

Constable 1607.

Memoriae sacrum.

Mark well this stone, it hides a pretious treasure,
A pearle wherein both heaven and earth took pleasure;
A gentleman sage, grave, chast and full of grace,
Well born, yet meek below his birth and place,
Modest of cheer, yet sweetly cheerfull still,
Holy of life, and free from taynt of ill,
Zealous, devout on earth, a saynt above,
In brief, here lyes embalm'd with teares of love

Marmaduke Constable *of* Wassand *in* Holdernesse *esquier, husband of* Elizabeth Shirley, *having by her three sons and one daughter* Philip, Edmund, William *and* Susannah; *who deceased* Oct. 12, *anno* 1607, *et aetatis suae* XLII.

18 Moore 1597. *L.* *Hic jacet inhumatum cadaver* Johannis Moor *armigeri causidici docti, viri vere pii, probi, prudentis, morum non minus suavitate quam integritate insignis, qui et opem et opes pauperibus lubens semper impertit, causas minus justas nunquam nimis pertinaciter defendit, omnis avaritiae, injuriae, invidiae suspicione, invidia judice, caruit. . . . . Hoc fretus bonae conscientiae testimonio, plena in solum Christum fiducia, quam multis quum morientem viderunt testatissimum fecit; anno aetatis suae sexagesimo primo, placide et quiete naturae spiritum, animam Deo reddidit,* Decem. 21, *anno Dom.* 1597.

18. Moore 1634. *L.* *Here lyeth the body of Mrs.* Katherine Moore *wife of* John Moore *esquier, late of the citie of* York *deceased, who lived a widow thirty six years, and departed this life* June 8, 1634, *in the year of her age* 90.

19. Aislaby 1674. *L.* *Hic jacet* Georgius (*x*) Aislaby *de civitate* Ebor. *arm. principalis archiepiscopat. registrarius, qui obiit decimo die* Januarii *A. D.* 1674.

20. Aislaby 1682. *L.* *Hic jacet* Maria *filia dom.* Johannis Mallory *nuper de* Studley *militis defuncti, ac nuper uxor* Georgii Aislaby *de civitate* Ebor. *arm. principalis archiepiscop.* Ebor. *registrarii et jam defuncti, quae obiit decimo nono die* Januarii *anno Domini* 1682.

21. Gale 1702 *L.*

Æ. M. S.
Thomae Gale, *S. T. P. decani* Ebor.
Viri, si quis alius,
Ob multifariam eruditionem
Apud suos exterosque celeberrimi.
Quale nomen sibi conquisivit
Apud Cantabrigienses
Collegium S. Trinitatis; *et*
Graecae *linguae professoris regii, cathedra:*
Apud Londinates
Viri literatissimi ad rem publicam
Et patriae commodum
Ex gymnasio Paulino *emissi*;
Apud Eboracenses
Hujus res ecclesiae,
Heu vix quinquennio,
At dum per mortem licuit
Sedulo et fideliter administratas,

(*x*) Slain in a duel by sir *Edward Jennings*.

Et,

2

CATHEDRAL CHURCH *Middle-choir.*

Et, ubicunque agebat, donata luce
Veneranda linguae Graecae
Et historiae Anglicanae
Monumenta,
Marmore loquaciora;
Perenniora
Testantur.
Obiit April. VIII *A. S. H.* M DCCII. *aetat. suae* LXVIII.

Here lyeth the body of Tobias Wickham, *esq; barrister at law, son to the reverend* Tobias Wickam, *D. D. dean of this metropolitan church. He married* Amy *daughter of sir* Stephen Thompson *of* York, *knt. and departed this life* July 30, 22. Wickham 1691. L.

Anno { *Salutis* 1691.
Aetatis suae 28.

In memoriam Marmaduci Cooke, *S. T. P. canonici et prebendarii prebendae de* Riccal, *moestissima conjux* Elizabetha Cooke, *cui triste sui desiderium reliquit, marmor hoc poni curavit.* *Obiit 7 cal.* Januarii *aerae christianae* 1684, *aetatis suae* 60. 23. Cooke 1684. L.

A copartment.

Intra septem ulnas hujus tabulae jacet MARIA RAYNES *armigeri uxor,* Roberti Conyers *de* Boulby *in comitatu* Eborum *armigeri filia; virtutibus vixit clara et inter ineffabiles* Gangraenae *cruciatus patientia mira efflavit animam* 20 *die* Decembris, 1689. 24. Raines.

Mrs Raynes.

A co-

CATHEDRAL CHURCH. *Middle-choir.*

A copartment.

15. Ingram. LYONELLUS INGRAM, *filius* Arthuri Ingram *militis ex matre* Maria, *a nobilissima* Grevillorum *familia oriunda, cum propter eximias corporis et animi, in tenera aetate, dotes, patris esset spes et oblectamentum; matris cura, negotium, deliciae et solatium unicum; fratrum ludus, idemque aemulus; domus et familiae decus et ornamentum singulare; omnium quotquot puerum viderint amor et admiratio; qui nondum sexennis aulicus audiebat, et certe videbatur; qui post exactum biennium aliquoties visus lachrymare, vix unquam auditus obstrepere; qui moribus vir obsequio parentibus eo usque processerat, ut absens etiam in iis quae maxime vellet, nec prece nec pretio adduci poterat ut fidem falleret quam praesens matri dederat; qui denique pro ratione annorum literis satis excultus, religione et pietate insignis vel ad miraculum extiterit, (violento enim et fatali morbo correptus, eo tamen grassante et vires ejus depascente, orare preces astantium, ultro flagitare coelum, sibi auspicari beatus puerulus non desierat) postquam sex annos et tres circiter menses foelix sidus orbi affulserat, subduxit se et placide in Domino requievit. Ipse in coelo tripudiant; nos moestos, ac sui, heu nimium, memores reliquit.*

A monument.

16. Ingram. *Dom.* GULIEL. INGRAM *e nobiliore* Ingramiorum *ortus prosapia, eques auratus a* JACOBO *rege insignitus inter illius ordinis* Eboracenses, *aetate maximus, charitate et vero eccles.* Anglicanae *cultu ditissimus. Obiit kal.* Sept. *regnante* CAROLO *secundo. Abiit in locum hunc* 6 *kal. ejus et mensis, anno Dom.* 1670.

In obitum ornatissimi viri GULIELMI INGRAM *equitis aurati, legum doctoris, e conciliis regiae majestati in partibus borealibus, almae curiae cancellariae dict. dom. regis magistrorum unius et socii, et curiae prerogativae archiepiscopatus* Ebor. *commissarii unice deputati, qui obiit* 24 *die* Julii *anno Dom.* 1625.

EPITA-

CATHEDRAL CHURCH. *Middle-choir.*

EPITAPHIUM.

Hic testatorum judex in judice Christo,
Testatore novi foederis occubuit.
Haec legata dedit: Domino se, gaudia coelo,
Orbi gesta, suis parta, cadaver humo:
En formam at melius sculptam dat pectus amici;
Cernere facta tamen si petis, astra pete.

CATHEDRAL CHURCH.
27. Wickham. 1625.

A copartment.

28, 29, &c. The large blue stones under which archbishop *Thoresby* deposited his brethren, and was laid himself in the midst of them. Their stone coffins were discovered on the removal of these stones for the new pavement; but nothing else remarkable about them.

Before

p. 219.

The ichnography

Tombs and Monuments.

1. *Archbishop* Sewal.
2. *Archbp.* Walter Grey.
3. *Sr.* William Gee.
4. *Archbp.* Hutton.
5. *Archbp.* Lamplugh.
6. *The Earl of* Strafford.
7. *Archbp.* Piers.
8. *The hon.ble* Tho. Wentworth *Esqr.*
9. *Archbp.* Bowett.
10. *Archbp.* Sharp.
11. *Archbp.* Matthews.
12. *Mrs.* Matthews.
13. *Archbp.* Rotheram.
14. *Archbp.* Frewen.
15. *Archbp.* Scrope.
16. *Countess of* Cumberland.
17. *Archbp.* Sterne.
18. *Lady Mary* Fenwick.
19. *Commissary* Swinburn.
20. *Sr. Henry* Bellassis.
21. *Table of Benefactions.*
22. *Archbp.* Savage.
23. *Dean* Finch.

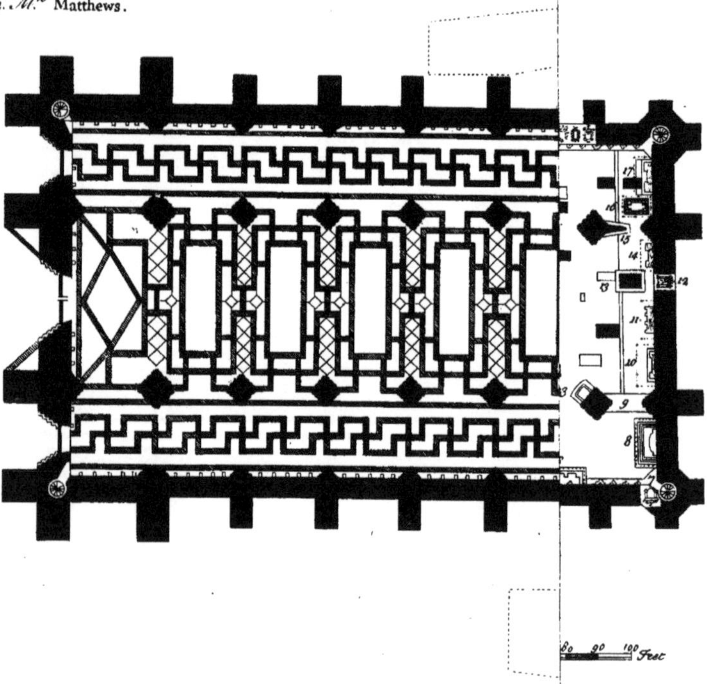

Before I leave the ground, I muſt take notice, that in the old pavement of the church, were a number of circles, which ranged from the weſt end, up the middle iſle, on each ſide and in the center. They were about forty four on a ſide, about two foot diſtance from one another, and as much in diameter. Thoſe in the midſt were fewer in number, larger, and exactly fronted the entrance of the great weſt door. That circle neareſt the entrance in this row being the largeſt of all. I take all theſe to have been drawn out for the eccleſiaſticks and dignitaries of the church to ſtand in, habited according to their proper diſtinctions, to receive an archbiſhop for inſtallation, or on any other ſolemn occaſion. The dean, and the other great dignitaries, I preſume, poſſeſſed the middle ſpace; whilſt the prebendaries, vicars, ſacriſts, prieſts at altars, *&c.* belonging to the church, ranged on each ſide. And altogether, when clad in their proper copes and veſtments, muſt have made a glorious appearance. From whence, I take it, this iſle was called the **Proceſſional iſle.** CATHEDRAL CHURCH. *Proceſſional-iſle.*

Whilſt I am writing this, is now a carrying on a new pavement for the body of the church; which noble deſign was begun by ſubſcription, from the clergy and others. Set on foot and brought to perfection by the care and management of the preſent governour. The plan was drawn by that eminent painter and architect Mr. *Kent*, under the direction of the lord *Burlington*. It is a kind of *moſaick* work, thought propereſt for a *Gothick* building, in which all the old marble grave-ſtones of the church are wrought up. The ſtone was given, from his quarry at *Huddleſtone*, by ſir *Edward Gaſcoign* of *Parlington*, bart. by which generous act the antient name of *Gaſcoign* ſhould, in the liſt of benefactions, follow thoſe of *Percy* and *Vavaſour*. The whole pavement is a brick floor, laid hollow, to prevent the damp from affecting of it. To give the reader a juſt idea of the new and old pavements of the church, I refer to the plans; the old draught was taken by Mr. *Torre* from whom I cauſed it to be copied. The figures, letters, *&c.* refer to the moſt remarkable grave-ſtones which were in the church; and this plate muſt be allowed to be a great curioſity, ſince the whole, except in the choir end, is now quite taken up and eraſed. *New pavement.*

The chantries and altars dedicated to particular ſaints, which were diſperſed in ſeveral places of this church come next to be conſidered. It is difficult, at this day, to aſſign any of their reſpective ſituations; and as impoſſible in a great many of them, as it is now to find out the lands the chantries were originally endowed with. It appears by a catalogue of all the chantries within this cathedral, as they were certified into the court of augmentations, *anno* 37 *Henry* VIII, that there were above forty altars erected in different parts of it. What regard ought to be paid to the piety of the founders of them, I ſhall not ſay; but it is certain they muſt have been a great disfigurement to the beauty of the church, whilſt they were up; yet when taken down, it is pity the lands, *&c.* aſſigned for the maintenance of the chantry prieſts, the rents of which would now amount to a very conſiderable value, was not given to the ſupport of the fabrick. But they were too good morſels to eſcape ſwallowing in that age. In Mr. *Dodſworth*'s collections, printed in *Steven*'s additional volumes to the *monaſticon*, is a catalogue of theſe chantries, and their ſeveral founders, with their yearly value. But this is not near ſo particular an account of them as may be met with in Mr. *Torre*'s manuſcripts; who has extracted from the regiſters all their original endowments; and at the ſame has given cloſe liſts of the parſons attending at each altar. The whole would make a volume of itſelf, and is therefore too copious for my deſign. I ſhall therefore only give the reader a catalogue of the names and yearly valuations of them, from Mr. *Dodſworth*, as follows (*y*); *Chantries.*

	l.	*s.*	*d.*
1. The chantry at the altar of *holy innocents*, *per annum*	05	13	04
2. Ditto of a different foundation ——	05	13	04
3. Another at the ſame altar —— ——	03	06	08
4. A chantry at the altar of S. *Saviour* in the loft, on the ſouth ſide the church	16	16	10
5. The chantry of St. *Friſwith* on the ſame ſide ——	17	00	00
6. The chantry at the altar of St. *Cuthbert* ——	12	00	00
7. 8. Two chantries at the altar of *Allhallows* ——	36	08	00
9. The chantry of St. *Mary Magdalene* ——	03	01	00
10. The chantry of St. *Saviour* and St. *Anne* ——	10	07	04
11. The chantry of St. *John the evangeliſt* ——	06	13	04
12. The chantry of St. *Agatha*, *Scolace* and *Lucia* ——	08	00	00
13. The chantry of St. *Anne* and St. *Anthony* ——	06	13	04
14. The chantry of St. *Laurence* ——	03	01	04
15. The chantry of St. *William* —— ——	08	07	06

(*y*) Confirmations of all or moſt of theſe chantries may be ſeen amongſt the records of the *Tower* of *London*.

16. The

CATHEDRAL CHURCH.

		l.	s.	d.
16.	The chantry of St. *Nicholas*	02	13	04
17.	The chantry of St. *Thomas* the apostle	02	04	00
18.	The chantry of St. *Michael*	10	13	04
19.	The chantry of St. *Christopher (z)*	02	02	00
20.	The chantry of our lady	08	19	00
21.	Ditto	05	08	00
22.	The chantry of St. *Andrew*	04	13	04
23.	The chantry of St. *Wilfrid*	06	13	04
24.	The chantry of *Jesus* and our lady	06	13	04
25. 26.	Two chantries at the altar of St. *Stephen*	13	06	00
27. 28.	Two chantries at the altar of *holy cross*	06	13	04
29. 30.	Two chantries at the altar of St. *Agatha Scolace*	04	08	02
31.	One more chantry at the altar of St. *Laurence*	03	06	08
32.	The chantry at the altar of St. *James minor*	03	06	08
33.	The chantry at the altar of St. *Pauline* and *Cedda*	03	06	08
34.	The chantry of St. *Gregory*	03	06	08
35.	The chantry of St. *Edmund* king and martyr	03	06	08
36.	The chantry at the altar of St. *John* the evangelist	04	13	00
37.	The chantry at the altar of St. *John* of *Beverley*	03	06	08
38.	One more chantry at the altar of *Innocents*	03	06	08
39.	Another chantry at the altar of St. *Nicholas*	03	13	00
40.	The chantry at the altar of St. *Blaise*	03	18	04
41.	One more there of another foundation	03	06	08
42.	The chantry at the altar of *holy Trinity* and *cross*	05	13	04
43.	A second chantry at the altar of St. *Gregory*	03	06	08
44.	A chantry at the altar of St. *Thomas a Becket*	04	02	08

These are all the chantries which Mr. *Dodsworth* gives, from the authority abovesaid; but Mr. *Torre* accounts for more than threescore; besides forty six *obits*; though probably some of their stipends had failed before the dissolution. By a statute which was ordained in the year 1291, by the dean and chapter of *York*, these regulations were made *(a)*.

That those who are called *Parsons* within the church, who at least have an altar, or others that hold altars do present their letters obligatory, which binds them to perform the offices of the dead, to the dean and chapter to be registred in a book, *in perpetuam rei memoriam*.

That on *Martinmas-day* every year they do, though not required, offer themselves to make oath, that to the best of their abilities they have fulfilled the will of the dead, for whom they were deputed to celebrate, according to the contents of their writings. And in case they have failed, in any respect, faithfully to discharge their duties, within the compass of that time, that they then make their humble confessions to the dean and chapter; from whom they are to receive their pennances according to their defaults.

That all who celebrate at any altar within the church shall be present at mattins, masses and other hours; on the feast of nine lections and other grand festivals.

That the altars whereat they do honestly serve be duly provided with vestments, ornaments, lights and other appurtenances.

Ornaments belonging to altars were,

One missale.
One chalice of silver.
Two silver phyals.
One vestment for double festivals of sattin embroidered.
One vestment for *Sundays* and other lesser festivals of *Indian* camake.
One or two vestments of a stuff called *Bordealisandre* for week days.
Six *pallas* for the altar.
Three *corporals* of cloath.
Three cases of silk for the corporals.
Three *frontals* for the altar.
One *towel* to wipe the priests hands.
One *Flanders* chest to put the vestments in.
One *aruareolum* of wood *(b)*.
One box for the bread.

I shall conclude this head with a short account concerning the masses that were celebrated at these altars, as it is expressed in one of their endowments, *viz.*

"That amongst other suffrages of mankind's salvation and restauration, the celebra-
"tion of masses, in which God the son offered himself a victim to God the father for

(z) There was a gild, or fraternity, erected in the cathedral, in honour of St. *Christopher*, founded *anno* 19 of *Rich.* II. *pat.* 19 *Ric.* II. *p.* 2. *m.* 6. *Pro tenementis in eadem civitate pat.* 2. Hen. IV. *p.* 2. *m.* 11. & *pat.* 1 Hen. V. *p.* 1. *m.* 36.

(a) *MS.* Torre *f.* 1381.

(b) *Arula* is rendred by our dict. a vessel to put fire in before the altar; but what this word means I know not.

"the

a

" the health of the living and the quiet of the dead. And before other things, on the CATHEDRAL CHURCH.
" day of attonement, they counted it moſt meritorious chiefly to proſecute thoſe things,
" with reſpect to the multiplicity of maſſes, and the increaſe of divine worſhip.

Moſt of the chantries before mentioned were placed in chapels in divers parts of the *Chapels.* church; ſeveral of which ranged from the chapter-houſe door to the north iſle of the choir, and from the ſouth iſle to the clock. About the wood work of the former Mr. *Dodſworth*, in his time, read the following inſcription,

✠ **Orate pro anima magiſtri Johannis Rainald nuper archidiaconi ac prebendarii prebende de Stillington in eccle. cath. Eborum, qui obiit in vigilia natalis anno Dom. milleſimo quingenteſimo ſexto. cujus ſumptibus et expenſis et de ejus voluntate et mandato hoc opus factum eſt anno Dom. Milleſimo quingenteſimo ſeptimo, et anno regni regis Henrici ſeptimi viceſimo tertio.**

And near the clock-houſe was this engraven in wood,

✠ **Orate pro anima magiſtri Johannis Rainald . . . . archiepiſcopi capellani et cancellarii canonici in hac alma eccleſia metropol. et prebendarii prebende de Stillington in eadem eccleſia, archidiaconi Clevelandie. qui . . . . in etate ſeptuageſima quatuor annorum in vigilia natalis Dom. noſtri Jeſu Chriſti circiter horam quintam poſt meridiem anno Dom. Milleſimo quingenteſimo ſexto, et regni regis illuſtriſſimi Henrici ſeptimi viceſimo tertio, cujus bonis, &c. ejus executores Johannes Chapman et Georgius Evers notarii publici et Willielmus Eure hoc opus ligneum ad quatuor altarea public. fabric.** *caetera deſunt.*

The moſt remarkable of theſe chapels were three at the eaſt end of the church. That *St. Stephen's,* of St. *Stephen*'s to the north, *Allſaints* to the ſouth, and betwixt them was the famous cha- *All-ſaints,* pel of St. *Mary*, made by archbiſhop *Thoreſby*. Which laſt, ſays *Stubbs*, that prelate, *St. Mary's.* *as a true reſpecter of the virgin mother of God, adorned with wonderful ſculpture and painting* (d). At the reformation this chapel, without any regard to the founder of this part of the cathedral, was torn in pieces and deſtroyed. Our northern antiquary, the late Mr. *Thoreſby*, got a large piece of the carved work, which, he ſays, was preſerved by ſomebody in a neighbouring houſe to the church, being encloſed betwixt two walls. This had a place in his *muſaeum* as a great curioſity; both in regard of the excellency of the ſculpture and the reſpect he paid to the memory of the archbiſhop his anceſtor. His regret for the deſtruction of this curious chapel makes him break out in the words of the *Pſalmiſt*, *A man was famous according as he had lifted up axes upon the thick tree; but now they break down the carved work thereof with axes and hammers* (e).

The wood work about all theſe chapels in the choir is now taken down, by order of the two laſt governours of the church. By which this end of the choir is now laid quite open. But the chapels in the croſs-iſle are moſt of them made uſe of for veſtries for the dean and reſidentiaries. That next the clock has, in memory of man, been uſed for ſix o'clock prayers.

The *ſervice-choir*, or that part of the church which, only, ſerves for divine worſhip, at *Service choir.* preſent, is ſeparated from the reſt of the church by a thick partition wall. The front whereof is adorned with various mouldings of curious workmanſhip in ſtone. Amongſt *Stone Screen.* which is a row of our kings from the conqueſt to king *Henry* VI. The image of this laſt monarch was certainly taken down in compliment to his enemy and ſucceſſor *Ed.* IV. by the archbiſhop's orders then in being. The policy of this was juſt; for the common people bore ſo high a veneration for the memory of this ſanctified king that they began to pay adoration to his ſtatue. The cell remained empty till the reign of king *James* I, at whoſe firſt coming to this city the dean and chapter thought fit to fill up the vacancy with his figure. It is obſervable that his name is put underneath **Jacobus primus rex Ang.** I ſuppoſe in diſtinction to the ſixth of *Scotland*. For it was improper for them to ſtyle him firſt of *England*, otherwiſe.

In the midſt of this ſcreen is placed the door into the choir; which, together with the paſſage is curiouſly wrought with pretty mouldings and carvings. On the centre of the ſtone roof is a very neat piece of imagery of the virgin; with her arms a-croſs her breaſt and adored by three little angels. The door itſelf was formerly wood-work; but of late years a handſome iron one was given, painted and gilt. The donor Mrs. *Mary Wandesford*. The two ſide iſles have now each of them a handſome door of iron work. Theſe were placed here by the care, or at the ſole charge of the late dean *Finch*, as his creſt upon them teſtifies.

The organ is now placed over the choir door, where it antiently ſtood, but was removed *Organ.* thence by order of king *Charles* I, and placed oppoſite to the biſhop's throne. His majeſty giving for reaſon, that it ſpoiled the proſpect of the fine eaſt window from the body

(d) *Ut verus amator virginis Dei genitricis mirabili artis ſculptura atque notabili pictura peregit.* Stubb's *act. pont.* Ebor.

(e) Pſalm lxxiv. 6, 7. *Thoreſby*'s *ducat. Leod.*

CATHEDRAL CHURCH.

of the church: which it certainly does. It was brought back in the year 1688. archbishop *Lamplugh* and the then earl of *Strafford* contributed to the charge of it; as appears by their arms on the woodwork.

Since I have mentioned the reason of the first removal of the organ, it will not be improper to add, from Mr. *Torre* (*f*), what the king bestowed upon the church towards the charge of it, and purchasing a new instrument, *&c.* by which, and other beneficences to the fabrick, that excellent monarch has justly a place in the table of benefactions.

It appears upon our records that on the 26th of *July*, 1632, in his majesty's high commission court, before his ecclesiastical commissioners within the province of *York*, there was imposed a fine of one thousand pound upon *Edward Paylor*, esq; of *Thoraldby*, for the crime of incest by him committed with *Elizabeth Bulmer* wife of *Francis Bulmer*, the said *Edward Paylor*'s sister's daughter, to be paid by him to the king's use.

Therefore king *Charles* I, by his order dated at *Westminster Novem.* 28, 8 *reg.* and directed to the treasurer, chancellor and barons of the exchequer, signifies that he had granted the same fine of one thousand pound to the dean and residentiaries of the cathedral church of *York*,

1. For repairing the ruins of their church.
2. For setting up a new organ.
3. For furnishing and ordering the altar.
4. For enabling them to maintain a library keeper.

And on *March* 22, 1632. articles of agreement were made between dean *Scott* and other canons residentiary of the church on the one part, and *Robert Dillum* blacksmith of *London*, on the other, touching the making a great organ for the church for two hundred and ninety seven pound, *&c.*

Anno 1634, *John Rawson*, chamberlain of the church, accounted for the laying out the said fine of one thousand pound, about the organ, and other disbursments, *&c.* It is pity the money would not reach to the settling the last article of the king's bequest.

The service-choir is still adorned with its antient wood-work, carved and set up with clusters of knotted pinnacles of different heights. In which are a great number of small cells which have had images of wood in them for greater decoration. Under these are the stalls for the canons, *&c.* beginning with the dean's stall on the right and the precentor's on the left hand. Each stall being assigned to a particular dignitary by a written label over it. The four seats next the pulpit are now possessed by the four archdeacons of the diocese; though formerly the lord-mayor and aldermen sat on that side. Some years ago there arose a dispute betwixt the church and city about the right of these seats. But it was finally determined by judge *Jeffrys*, *anno* 1684, that the archdeacons should possess them. Whereupon his lordship and his brethren have ever since sat on the opposite side. Over the stall of the preaching dignitary for the day is always a moveable table with this title, *Ordo perpetuus pro concionibus*, &c. The order for preachers in this church was first begun by archbishop *Grindall*, and constantly observed till the year 1685; when archbishop *Dolben* made a new regulation, which was ratified by the dean and chapter. The rest of the seats for vicars, choristers, *&c.* are as usual in other cathedrals. The present dean has lately caused doors to be put to the passages of the uppermost stalls. In order to keep those seats, which used to be crowded with mob, for the dignitaries, gentlemen, and better sort of citizens, which attend divine service.

Ordo perpetuus pro concionibus in ecclesia S. Petri Ebor.

Adventus Dom.
Prima Dom. post Adv. Cancellarius.
Secunda —— *Archidiac.* Ebor.
Tertia —— *Archidiac.* Notingham.
Quarta —— *Archidiac.* Eastrid.
Natalis Dom. Decanus.
S. Stephani Archcleavland.
S. Johannis Wetwang.
Innocent. Strensall.
Dom. inter Innoc. et Eph. succentor canonicorum.
Circumcisio Praecentor.
Epiph. Wistow.
Prima Dom. post Epiph. Subdecanus.
Secunda —— Stillington.
Tertia —— Fenton.
Quarta —— Apesthorp.
Quinta —— Givendale.
Sexta —— Tockrington.
Septuagesima Cancellarius.
Sexagesima Husthwait.
Quinquagesima Riccall.
Prima Dom. post Quadrag. Wighton.
Secunda —— Knaresbrough.
Tertia —— Ulleskelfe.
Quarta —— Bugthorpe.
Quinta —— Langtoffe.
Sexta —— Northnewbald.
Good Friday, Dom. Archiep. Ebor.
Dom. Paschae, Decanus.
Die Lunae post Pascham, Subdecan.
Die Martis —— *Praecentor.*
Prima Dom. post Pasch. Grindall.
Secunda —— Bole *alias* Bolum.
Tertia —— Ampleford.
Quarta —— Warthill.
Quinta —— Frydaythorpe.
Ascentionis, Archidiac. Ebor.
Dom. post Ascen. Dunnington.

(*f*) Ex MS. Torre, *f.* 109.

Dom.

p. 522.

J. Haynes delin. Harris fecit.

An internal perspective view of the Choir-end of the Cathedral church of York.

TOR LIB
N.Y

CATHEDRAL CHURCH.

Dom. Pentecost. Decanus.
Die Lunae post Pent. Archidiac. Eastrid.
Die Martis post Pent. Archdiac. Notting.
Dom. Trinitatis, Wistow.
Prima —— Southnewball.
Secunda —— Barnby.
Tertia —— Bilton.
Quarta —— Osbaldwick.
Quinta —— Holm *archiepiscopi.*
Sexta —— *Archd.* Cleaveland.
Septima —— *Praecentor.*
Octava —— Langtoff.
Nona —— Wetwang.
Decima —— Strensall.
Undecima —— Fenton.
Duodecima —— Stillington.
Decima Tertia —— Husthwait.
Decima quarta —— Riccall
Decima quinta —— Ulleskelfe.
Decima sexta —— Knaresbrough.
Decima septima —— Bugthorpe.
Decima octava —— Wighton.
Decima nona —— Northnewbald.
Vicesima Dom. post Trinitatem, Frydaythorp.
Vicesima prima —— Southnewbald.
Vicesima secunda —— Bilton.
Vicesima tertia —— Ampleford.
Vicesima quarta —— Tockrington.
Vicesima quinta —— Apesthorp.
Vicesima sexta —— Givendale.

Festa.

S. Andreae, Dunnington.
S. Thomae, Bole *alias* Bolum.
Fest. purificationis, Decanus.
S. Matthiae, *Archd.* Ebor.
Fest. Annuntiationis, Archd. Eastrid.
S. Marci, Wetwang.
S. Phil. *et* Jacobi, Strensall.
S. Johannis Bapt. *Cancellarius.*
S. Petri, *Subdecan.*
S. Jacobi, *Archidiac.* Notting.
S. Barthol. Wistow.
S. Matthaei, Langtoff.
S. Michaelis, Botivant.
S. Lucae, Fenton.
S. Simonis *et* Judae, *Archd.* Cleaveland.
Fest. omnium sanctorum, Decanus.

The eagle of brass from which the lessons are read bears this inscription,

THO. CRACROFT, *S. T. P.*
Aquilam hanc, ex aere conflatam,
In usum et ornatum
CATHEDRALIS TEMPLI EBOR.
Divo PETRO *sacri*
Contulit
M DCLXXXVI.

The *cathedra,* or throne for the archbishop, is situated at the end of the prebendal stalls on the south side. It is a plain piece of oak wainscot, no ways suitable to the dignity of the primate. Archbishop *Lamplugh* intended, if he had lived, to have erected a new one; a draught of a then noble design being taken for it. *Throne.*

The pulpit used to be brought, on preaching days, to the first ascent betwixt the ladies pews; but it being judged by the late dean, that the preacher's voice, for want of repercussion of sound, was lost in the vaults of the church; he ordered the old pulpit, which had been long disused, but more suitable to the rest of the wood-work, to be placed where it now stands. *Pulpit.*

The ascent from the body of the church, through the choir to the altar is by a gradation of sixteen steps. The altar has lately received a considerable improvement, as to its situation, and the whole church in its beauty, by taking away a large wooden screen, which almost obstructed the view of the east window. This screen was handsomely painted and gilt. It had a door at each end, which opened into a place, behind the altar, where antiently the archbishops used to robe themselves at the time of their inthronizations, and thence proceeded to the high altar, where they were invested with the *pall.* On the top of this screen was a gallery for musick; as is usual in *popish* churches, for the celebration of high mass. At the taking away of this the altar was carried back one arch, to a stone screen behind it of an excellent *Gothick* architecture; which now, not only, shews a beauty in itself which was hid before; but also opens a view of one of the noblest lights in the world. This work was done by order of the late dean *Finch*; and it is pity some design of an altar-piece is not pitched upon to answer the building; that the tapestry might be taken away and placed on each side. Many designs have been drawn for it, but they are all of the regular orders which will by no means suit a *Gothick* cathedral. And for my part I think the fine altar at *Beverley,* to be rather a blemish, than an embellishment to that church. *Altar.*

Antiently there were two altars one on each side the high altar; that on the north side dedicated to St. *Stephen,* the opposite to the blessed virgin. Concerning the great or high altar we find the following account relating to the celebration of it (*g*).

(*g*) *Torre* f. 110.

In

2

CATHEDRAL CHURCH.

In the year 1159, pope *Alexander* III, sent his letters mandatory to *Roger* then archbishop of *York*, commanding him that he, together with the chapter of his church, get it by decree established that none do presume to celebrate mass at the high altar of the cathedral church, except he be a bishop or some canon of the same. And that none do read the gospel or epistle at time of celebration of mass at this high altar, unless he be a canon of the church. For before every priest was admitted to celebrate mass thereat, whereby the dignity of the church was in some respect diminished and grown vile.

The numerous ornaments belonging to this altar may be seen in the catalogue of the church's vestment, *&c.* taken in *Henry* the eighth's time. There is likewise a particular account, in our own records, of such plate, copes, vestments and other things belonging to the choir, as they were given in charge to be kept by *William Ambler* clerk of the vestry, *anno* 1633. By which it appears that our second reformers cleared off with what the first had left.

Lest the altar should again be robbed of its present ornaments, plate, *&c.* I think proper to give an account of what it is now enriched with; as likewise the donors of them.

King *Charles* I. bestowed upon the church a large quantity of communion plate. When there was scarce as much left, out of their long inventory of riches, as to perform the office with decency; also a common prayer-book and bible, large folio, bound in crimson velvet.

Archbishop *Stern* gave plate to the weight of two hundred and eighteen ounces.

Archbishop *Dolben* gave one hundred and ninety five ounces.

The lord *Beaumont* gave two silver candlesticks weighing fifty three ounces.

Archbishop *Lamplugh* gave the covering or *antependium* of the table of crimson velvet, richly adorned with a deep embroidery of gold and fringe, with the velvet for the back of the altar. He gave also three pieces of fine tapestry for the same use. He, likewise, erected the innermost rails, and paved the space with black and white marble. And And lastly he gave three large common prayer-books and a bible for the use of the altar.

Vaults.

Under the altar are the vaults, which are entered into at north and south by two iron-grated doors. Those vaults make an equilateral square of fourteen yards over, and are divided into four isles by nine short middle pillars of stone, which support the arched roof. According to the number of these four isles, these vaults had in them as many altars and chantries. One of which chantries was remarkable, called the chantry at the altar of St. *Mary in cryptis*, where her mass was daily celebrated with note and organ (*g*). On the west side is a draw-well, with a stone cistern.

Lights.

In winter, from *All-saints* to *Candlemass*, the choir is illuminated, at evening service, by seven large branches. Besides a small wax candle fixed at every other stall. Three of these branches were the gift of sir *Arthur Ingram*, *anno* 1638; as appears by an inscription on each. Who also settled four pound *per annum* on the church for finding them with lights. Two more were given by *Ralph Lowther* of *Ackworth*, esq; the last unknown. These, with two large tapers for the altar, are all the lights commonly made use of. But on the vigils of particular holy days the four grand dignatories of the church have each a branch of seven candles placed before them at their stalls.

There is nothing else to be described in the service-choir but what is common to other cathedrals. And I shall be less particular in my description of the other parts of the church. The perspective views of the building will give the reader a much better

(*g*) *Torre* f. 1647.

idea

P.525.

J. Haynes delin. T. Harris fecit

An internal perspective

CATHEDRAL CHURCH. *Nave.*

idea of it than words can pretend to. From the great weſt entrance we count ſeven pillars of a ſide to the *lantborn*; which form eight arches. The two firſt ſerve as a baſis to the higheſt, lighteſt and moſt extenſive arch in the world, which ſupports great part of the weight of two ſteeples. Over the other arches are placed, in ſtone, the arms of the principal benefactors to the fabrick; one of each ſide. On the top of theſe arches runs an open gallery on both ſides the nave. Exactly over the joining of each arch ſtood, formerly, an image, in ſtone, of the tutelar ſaints or patrons of the ſeveral nations in *Europe*. But our zealots depoſed them all, except St. *George*, whom they left for a reaſon not worth mentioning. Being an idle ſtory of his oppoſite a dragon's head. Over theſe are the windows of this middle iſle adorned with imagery and divers coats of arms. One of theſe arches as is here repreſented, expreſſes the reſt.

The roof of the nave is wood; the ribs or groins of which compoſe a moſt curious and admired tracery; adorned with large carved knots, which have been gilt, and are in the nature of key-ſtones to ſupport the work. Each of theſe knots repreſents ſome part of ſacred hiſtory. The reſt of the wood-work has been formerly painted a ſky colour, but the preſent dean cauſed it to be all waſhed over white.

The great window at the weſt end of the church is a very noble light, though not near ſo fine as its oppoſite. In it is depicted, in full proportion, the figures of the eight firſt archbiſhops and eight ſaints of the church. Under this, on each ſide of the great doors, are placed the arms of *England*, probably of *Edward* II, in whoſe time this part of the fabrick was perfected, and thoſe aſſigned to *Ulphus* the *Saxon* prince; as two principal benefactors to this church. The whole has been filled up with imagery, the pedeſtals of which do now only remain. For the reſt I refer to the draught.

Cathedral Church.

The west window.

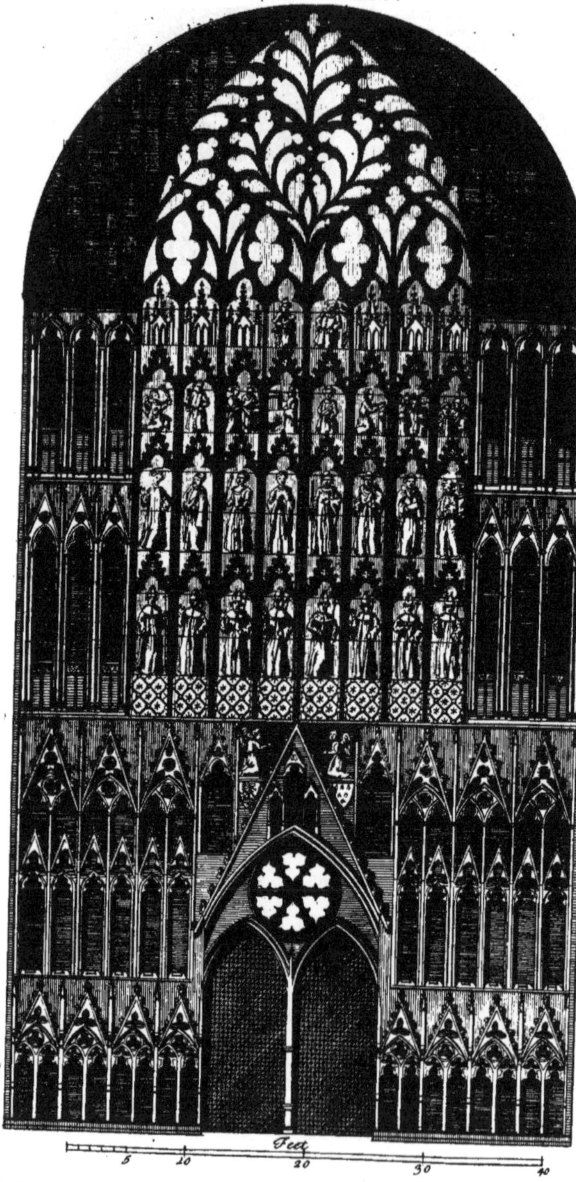

P. 57.

The window armorial.

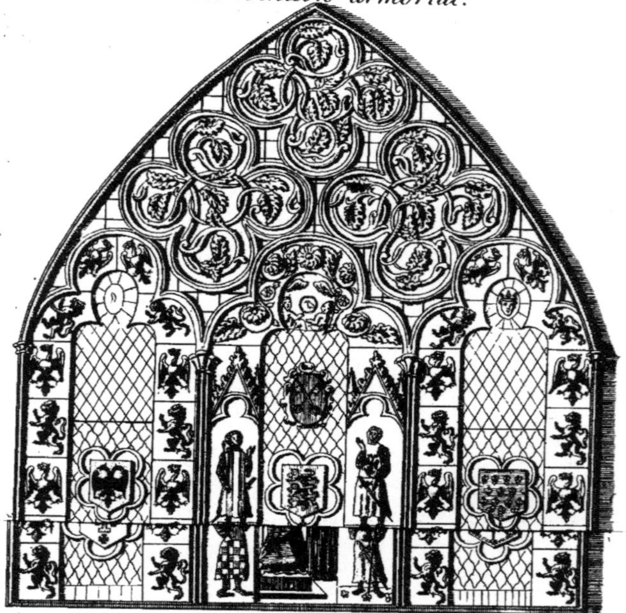

To John Anstis *sen.*r *Esq.*r *Arms, this plate is most obliged humble servant*

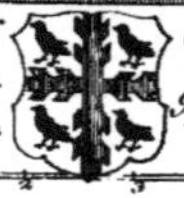

Garter *principal King at gratefully inscribed by his* Francis Drake. *1736*.

Feet.

P. 527.

The east window.

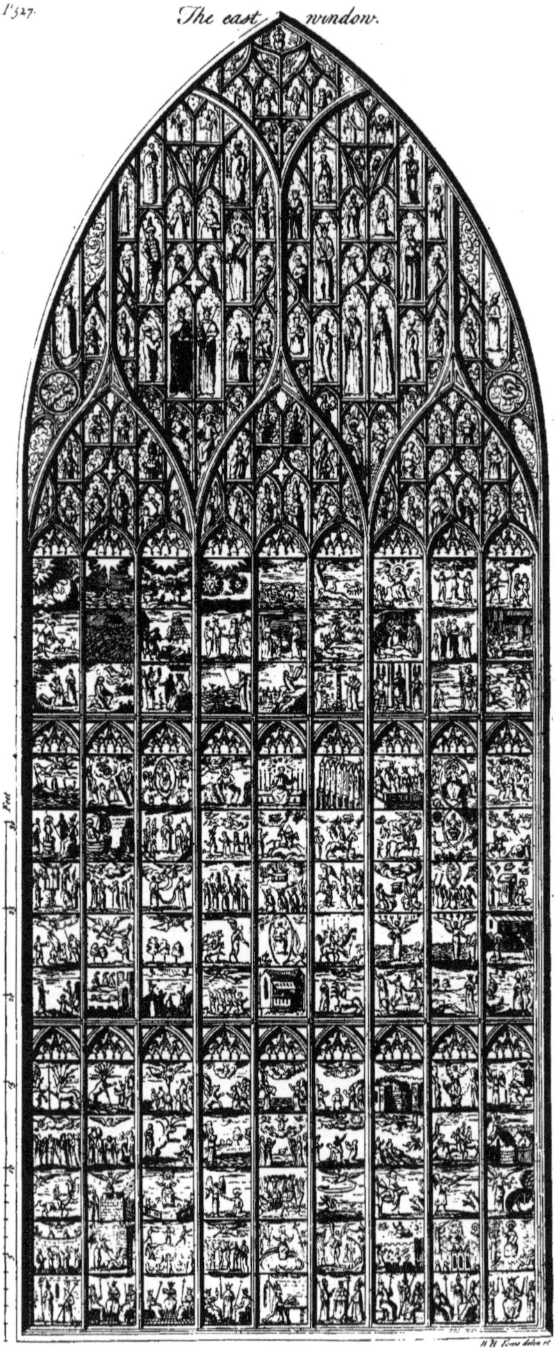

The side isles are arched with stone, the spondils, as the workmen call them, being stone plaistered over. The knots at the angles have been curiously carved and painted. These roofs have also been lately washed over beautified and repaired. Over each of the entrances into these isles are representations of hunting and killing of wild beasts in a sort of *basso relievo*; as also *Sampson* tearing the lion, *&c.* The sixteen windows which give light to these isles are all, except two, of the old painted glass, and in very good order. The arms and bearings I have picked out of them, but their several histories I shall not take upon me to read. The uppermost window in the north isle was taken *anno* 1641, by some careful hand, as a most curious portrait of royal and noble bearings; which window I give the reader as a specimen of the rest. The shields of arms upon it are from the top, first, St. *Peter*, then, the imperial, *England*, old *France*, *Arragon*, king of the *Romans*, *Castile* and *Leon*, *Jerusalem* and *Navarre*. The figures in coats armorial are first the emperor, king of *Arragon*, old *England*, old *France*, twice over, *Beauchamp*, *Clare*, *Warren*, *Beauchamp* again, *Ross*, *Mowbray*, *Clifford* and *Percy*. CATHEDRAL CHURCH.

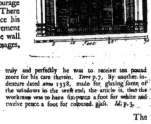

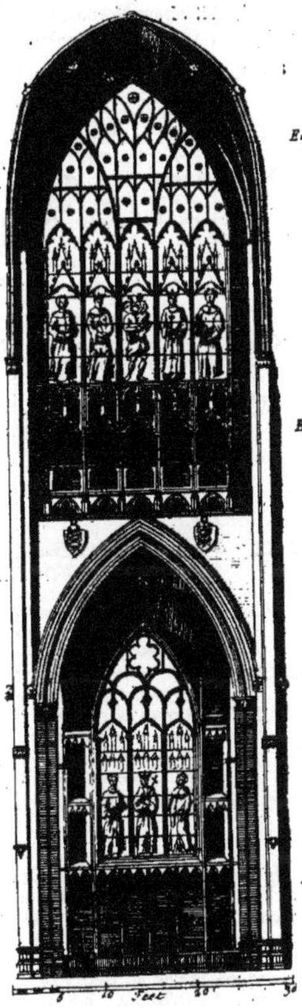

The east end of the church has nine arches, with arms, galleries, windows, and a wooden roof over it as before. In the uppermost windows are the figures of those kings, bishops and noblemen, who were benefactors to this part of the building; with their arms underneath. And all in their robes in most glorious colours *(b)*. The side isles of the choir are arched with stone, the windows of them wonderfully preserved; those especially which are in the transept or cross of the choir cannot be too much admired. They reach almost to the roof of the church, are divided into one hundred and eight partitions; each of which represents a piece of sacred story: But, *East end.*

What may justly be called the wonder of the world, both for masonry and glasing, is the noble east window. It is very near the breadth and height of the middle choir. The upper part is a piece of admirable tracery; below which are one hundred and seventeen partitions representing so much of holy writ that it almost takes in the whole history of the bible. This window was begun to be glazed, at the charge of the dean and chapter, *anno* 1405; who then contracted with *John Thornton* of *Coventry* glazier to execute it. He was to receive for his own work four shillings a week, and to finish the whole in less than three years *(i)*. We may suppose this man to have been the best artist in his time, for this kind of work, by their sending so far for him. And indeed the window shews it. I hope my drawer and engraver have done justice to his memory. *East window.*

On the wall in the north isle of the choir, dean *Gale*, who had the interest of the fabrick much at heart, caused a large table to be erected; with the names and dates of the several founders and benefactors to this church. In order to preserve the memory of them to posterity, and to encourage other publick spirited persons to do the same. There has been no addition to the catalogue since his time. But the contributors to the new pavement deserve a memorial in it. Below this, in the wall near the doors, are several large cells for images, which have been finely painted.

(b) The arms of archbishop *Scrope* and *Bowett* in several places of these windows shew they were special benefactors to the church.

(i) The indenture witnesses that he was to have four shillings *per* week, and one hundred shillings sterling every of the three years, and if he did his work truly and perfectly he was to receive ten pound more for his care therein. *Torre* p. 7. By another indenture dated *anno* 1338, made for glazing some of the windows in the west end, the article is, that the workman was to have six-pence a foot for white and twelve pence a foot for coloured glass. *Id.* p. 3.

The

The Table *of the* Founders, *&c. in the* North Side-Isle *of the* Choir.

ANNO DOM. MDCXCIX.

Ecclesiae Eboracensis *gratitudo.*

Anno Dom.	*Fundatores.*	*Anno Dom.*	*Benefactores.*
DCXXVII.	Edwynus Northumbrorum *rex primus fundator.*		*Decanus et capitulum variis temporibus.*
DCXXXII.	Oswaldus Northumbrorum *rex secundus fundator.*	*Incertis temporibus.*	Robertus Vavasor *miles.* Will. de Perci *miles.* Will. de Aguillon. Will. Fitz Alice. Richardus de Dalton.
DCLXVI.	Wilfridus Ebor. *archiep. tertius fundator.*	MDCXXIX.	Francisca Matthews *uxor* T. Matthews *archiep.* Ebor.
DCCLXII.	Albertus Ebor. *archiep. quartus fundator, primus bibliothecam condidit.*	MDCXXXIII.	Carolus I. *rex* Angliae.
		MDCXXXVIII.	Arthurus Ingram *baronettus.*
MLXVIII.	Thomas Ebor. *archiep. quintus fundator.*	MDCLXXIII.	Maria *domina* Beaumont
	Reparatores.	MDCLXXXIII.	Ricardus Sterne *archiep.* Ebor.
MCLXXI.	Rogerus Ebor. *archiep. chorum novum aedificavit.*	MDCLXXXVI.	Thomas Cracroft *S.T.P.*
		MDCLXXXVI.	Johannes Dolben *archie.* Ebor.
MCCXXVII.	Walterus Gray Ebor. *archiep. multum promovit fabricam.*	MDCXCI.	Thomas Lamplugh *archiep.* Ebor.
		MDCXCV.	Thomas *comes* Fauconberg.
MCCL.	Johannes Romanus *partem chori borealis et Campanile in medio aedificavit.*	MDCXCV.	Williel. *comes* Strafford *mille libras legavit.*
MCCXCI.	Johan. Romanus Ebor. *archiep. navem ecclesiae inchoavit.*		
MCCCXXX.	Will. de Melton Ebor. *archiep. navem ecclesiae consummavit.*		
MCCCLXII.	Johan. Thursby *inchoavit novum opus chori.*		
MCCCLXX.	Walterus Skirlaw *praebendarius de* Fenton *in hac ecclesia postea episcopus* Dunelm. *campanile aedificavit.*		

South cross-isle. The south part of the cross-isle was built by *Walter Grey*; and is the oldest part of the whole fabrick. The architecture of both ends of this isle differs from any of the rest. It is raised upon round stone and marble pillars, alternately running up by clusters to their flowered chapiters, whereon are turned the arches of the little side isles. In washing the church over lately these pillars are now made undistinguishable; the smaller of them are of marble, and there being no quarry of the sort in all this country some people have imagined them to be factitious. But upon better information they appear to be taken from a quarry near *Petworth* in *Sussex*; for upon comparing a polished specimen sent me by the reverend Dr. *Langwith*, rector of that place, with these pillars, no sensible difference can be observed betwixt them. The doctor's memory suggested to him that the marble which composed these pillars, as well as the pillars in the chapter-house, and these of *Walter Grey*'s tomb were got out of that quarry; and the distance from thence to *York* being no objection, *Petworth* being within twelve miles of the sea, and within five or six of a navigable river, it altogether has a very probable appearance. The doctor farther observes

observes, that this marble has been used in some other old cathedrals at a greater distance from the quarry than *York*; and therefore it can be no wonder to find it in so expensive and stately a building as *York-minster*. From the capitals of these pillars are turned the arches of the wooden roof; part of which bears testimony that it is of a later date than the stone work, by an escutcheon of arms of king *Edward* III, being carved on a centre knot on the north side of the lanthorn. *(k)* The roof of this part of the building is so low, that it obstructs some part of the upper windows at both ends. This can proceed from nothing, but what I have before hinted in the description of the out side of the west-end of the church, that it had a stone roof once upon it. And being judged too heavy, this was built under it, and the upper roof taken away; which occasions it to be so much lower than it ought to be. CATHEDRAL CHURCH

The south-end of the church is enlightned by six windows, that at the top being the most remarkable. It is a fine piece of masonry in form of a wheel, or as Mr. *Torre* writes a marygold; from whence it is called the *marygold window*. Its coloured glass representing an image of that flower. The first window over the clock-house is adorned with a large image of St. *William* habited *in pontificalibus* with his shield of arms under his feet *(l)*. The second window consists of two lights, and hath at the top of both a small image of an old king sitting in azure robes with a globe in his hand, placed in triangle to the sun and moon on each side below. Without doubt this figure was designed to represent God the father; many instances of the like nature in the churches abroad in painting, &c. shew that the *catholicks* have frequently aimed at a representation of that immense and inscrutable deity. On one side is a large image of St. *Peter*, on the other that of St. *Paul*; with their *insignia* underneath them *(m)*. In the last is the figure of St. *Wilfrid* in robes as before, and under him is placed an escutcheon of arms which Mr. *Torre* says is ascribed to that prelate *(n)*.

In one of the windows under the former is depicted a magistrate in his gown, kneeling at a desk; below it is this imperfect inscription,

✠ **Orate pro anima Johannis Pety Glasiarii et majoris . . . . Ebor. qui obiit 12 Novem. 1508.**

This window was glazed by sir John Pety *knight, sometime time lordmayor of the citie of* Yorke. *who died* 8 *of* November anno Dom. 1408.

The present dean has a design to pull down the old clock-case, which greatly disfigures this end of the church, and place the dial-plate directly over the south entrance within, as it is without, for which reason I have omitted it in the draught.

(k) Quarterly semi de lyz of *France*, three lions of *England*.

(l) Or, seven mascles *gules*, three, three and one. These arms was the bearing of *Sayar de Quincy* earl of *Winchester* of which family our St. *William* was.

(m) *Gules*, two keys in saltire *argent* and *or*, and *gules* two swords in saltire *argent*, hilted and pommelled *or*.

(n) *Azure*, three estoiles *argent*.

The

CATHEDRAL CHURCH.

South cross end.

North cross end.

CATHEDRAL CHURCH.
North transept.

The north part of the transept, though of a later date, is of the same *Gothick* taste as the former, for which reason this representation of one arch will give the reader an idea of all. It is here to be noted that the arches in both these ends of the church are bolder, and nearer segments of a circle, than what was built in succeeding times. In the *Anglo-Norman* age, all their arches made use of in churches, were nearer to the *Roman* taste, than the acuter oxey arch, which came afterwards into fashion. Several antient seals of churches which I have seen and are finely drawn in a manuscript lent me by the celebrated *John Anstis*, esquire, garter king, do witness the truth of this. For here the representations of their oldest churches are made use of for seals, after the newer were rebuilt by the ecclesiasticks of succeeding ages. The end of this building is beautified with five noble lights which constitute one large window; and reach almost from top to bottom of this north end. This window has been called the *Jewish* window, but for what reason I know not. There is also a tradition that five maiden sisters were at the expence of these lights; the painted glass in them representing a kind of embroidery or needle-work, might perhaps give occasion for this story. These windows are of a very uncommon make, and are about fifty feet high and five feet broad a piece. In the year 1715, they were much set off in their beauty, by a small border of clear glass, which runs round the painted, and illustrates it wonderfully. The archbishop's consistorial court is in one of the side isles to this part of the building. As also the dean and chapter's near the chapter-house doors. In the windows of these small side isles are, or were, the following bearings, lord *Latimer*, over the entrance, a *Saxon* king, *Scrope* archbishop, St. *Paul*, *azure* a chevron ingrailed inter three hinds heads erased *or*. *Malbyss*. On the other side was, in Mr. *Torre's* time, the antient arms of the see, impaled with *vert*, three roebucks trippant *argent*, attired *or*. Archbishop *Rotheram*.

We

An internal perspective view of the Cathedral at York *from the South cross.*

J. Haynes del.

The reverend Thomas Lamplugh *M.A. Rector of* Bolton Percy, *Canon-residentiary of this Cathedral, transmits this idea of it to posterity. 1736.*

CATHEDRAL CHURCH. *Nave. Lanthorn steeple.*

We come last to describe the great tower or *lanthorn-steeple*, as it is commonly called, I suppose, from bearing a resemblance to that luminary. It is founded on four great pillars; each composed of clusters of round columns gradually less as they conjoin the body of it. Over the four great arches these pillars make are placed eight coats of arms, two and two of a side. On the west the arms of *England*, the flowers de liz distinguished; with the arms of *Edward the confessor*. On the east the *pallium* or antient bearing of the see of *York* and St. *Wilfrid*. To the north the arms assigned to two *Saxon* kings, *Edwin* and *Edmund* the martyr. And on the south the peculiar arms of the church and those of *Walter Skirlaw* the great benefactor to this part of the building. The arms of *England* shew that this steeple was not finished till the reigns of *Henry* V, or VI; who, as I have elsewhere noted, were the first that altered the old *French* bearing. Over these arms are several flowers, cherubims and cloistered cells for images, till you come to a handsome stone balcony or terras which is embattled and goes quite round the squares of the tower. The windows are eight in number, two on a side. The roof is adorned with tracery, archwise, with wooden beams gilt and knotted. The center knot, which is the largest, is carved, and represents the two images of St. *Peter* and St. *Paul*, with a church betwixt them.

In the joining the old work to this new steeple there is somewhat remarkable to be taken notice of. Upon a view may be observed, that from each end of the cross and on each side proceed two arches of a large sweep, and a third is begun of the same dimensions. But by the interposition of the north and south isles, of the nave and choir, they are intersected, and let drop into four such narrow arches, that one of them was thought fit antiently to be filled up, and the rest have lately been the same; as judging them no support to the fabrick without it. By this we may learn how difficult it was to join the new building to the old, and yet preserve regularity. What I have omitted in my description of this part of the church may be supplied from the draught I have caused to be taken of the cross view of it.

To conclude this low account of our magnificent fabrick, but which indeed no words can illustrate as it ought to be, I shall only say, that it is a building of that magnitude and extent, that, even in those ages which affected the erecting of religious structures, it took near two centuries to compleat. Since which it has stood above three more, and hitherto escaped the teeth of corroding time by wind and weather; or, what is much more de-

CATHEDRAL ſtructive than either of them, *party zeal.* Let it be then the prayers of all good men, that
CHURCH. this glorious building, the great monument of our forefathers piety, may never want a
governour, leſs devoted to its preſervation, than the two laſt actually were or the preſent
ſeems to be. That this fabrick may ſtand firm and tranſmit to late poſterity the vertues
of its founders; and continue, what it has long been, not only a ſingular ornament to the
city and theſe northern parts, but to the whole kingdom.

Fabrick rents. The particular rents aſſigned for the ſupport of the fabrick amounts, according to
Mr. *Torre's* calculation, but to one hundred and ſeventy one pound two ſhillings and eight
pence *per annum*; beſides St. *Peter's* part as a reſidentiary *(a)*. There has ſince been an
addition made to theſe rents by a legacy left the church of one thouſand pound, by *William*
earl of *Strafford*; which purchaſed lands in *Barrowby* and *Little-Leek* to the value of forty
eight pound *per annum.* Theſe annual ſums, and what accrues ſometimes upon the renewal of leaſes, are all that is now left to keep and maintain this vaſt building in repair.
But, ſmall as they are, the ſectaries, under their adminiſtration, would needs have in-
volved them in the common ſale of the dean and chapter's revenues. By which means
this noble fabrick muſt long e'er this have been a heap of ruins. Our magiſtracy was
ſomewhat alarmed at it, and wrote a ſpecial letter to their then worthy repreſentatives
in parliament, in order to put a ſtop to this moſt ſcandalous affair. The original letter
was communicated to me by our preſent dean; a copy of which I here ſubjoin, taken *literatim,* with which I ſhall conclude this chapter.

LORD-MAYOR's letter for fabrick rents.

Gentlemen,

*W*E *underſtand that the ſurveyors of the deane and chapters landes intend to retorne parte
of the fabrick landes by this poſt, and other part thereof by the next, diſtinctly by themſelves. You know what an ornament and of what publique uſe the minſter is to this cittie; we
have therefore writt to Mr.* Bowles *to get a petition drawn for continuance of thoſe rents to the
uſe for which they were given, and doe earneſtly deſire your care and aſſiſtance herein, and upon Mr.* Bowles *retorne hither, that you will direct captaine* Wood *what you think fit, and
we are aſſured he will be carefull to obſerve your directions. See in the aſſurance of your care
herein, we remayne*

Your aſſured frinds,

York *the* 22*d of* Leon. Thompſon *major.*
January 1649. He. Thomſon,
 Rob. Horner.

To the right worſhipful William Allanſon, *knt. and* Thomas Hoyle, *eſq; members of parliament at* Weſtminſter.

Sealed with the city's ſeal.

(a) See the ſeveral demiſes of the fabrick lands by the dean and chapter in Mr. *Torre's* manuſcript, from
p. 6. to *p.* 18.

CHAP.

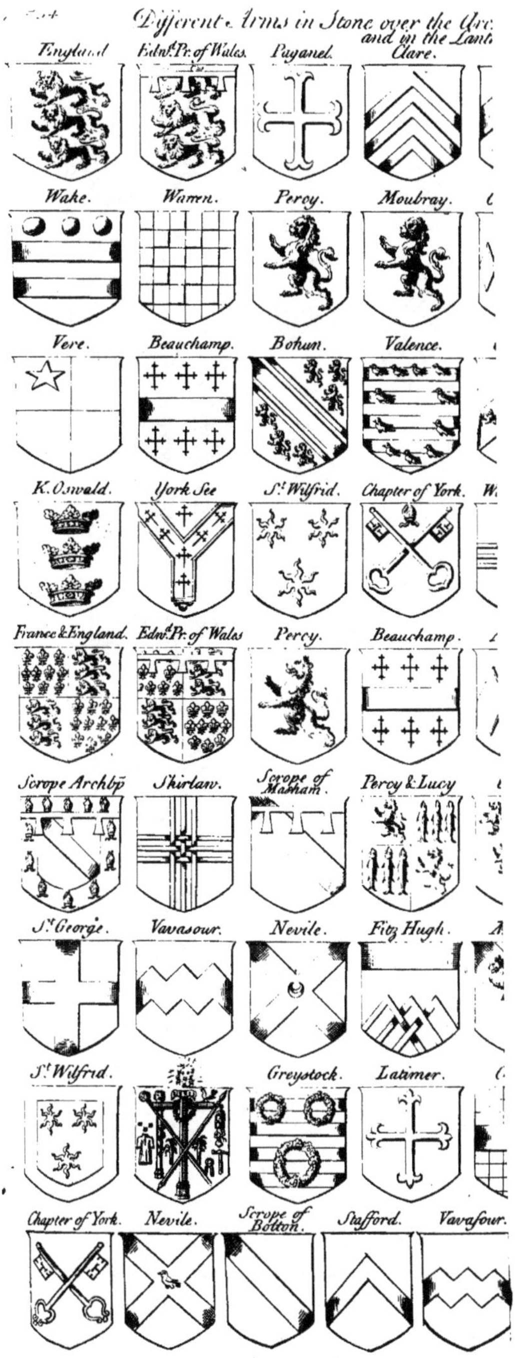

Archiepiscopal
te.

Antiquity.

. DCXXVII.

ll.
. DCXXXIV.

Edmund of Woodstock. John of Eltham. Lacy Earl of Lincoln.

Bohun. Clare Earl of Gloucester. Vavasour. Moubray.

Warren. Roos. Clare. Hubert de Burgh Earl of Kent.

Hainault. Baliol. Old Percy. Vesey.

Clare. England Mauley Mauley

Tempest. Lascells. Vernon. Sr. Walter Faulconberg, temp. E.1

Vere. Constable. Roos. Holland.

Haxby Treasurer. Walworth, Mayor of London, 1381 Arundel

Gascoign Moubray. Percy & Lucy. Nevile.

CHAP. III.

The archiepiſcopal ſee of YORK, *its antiquity, juriſdiction,* &c. *The dean and chapter, their charters and liberties, privileges and immunities granted to them by diverſe kings. The principal dignitaries of the cathedral. The cloſe of* YORK *and the* Bederne.

IN treating on this head I ſhall exactly follow Mr. *Torre*'s method, who has divided the ſubject in the following manner,

1. The archiepiſcopal ſee.
2. The dean and chapter.
3. The dean ſole.
4. The dignitaries.
5. The canons or prebends.
6. The vicars choral.
7. The parſons or chantry prieſts.
8. Other inferior officers, *&c.*

The archiepiſcopal ſee may be conſidered *Archiepiſcopal ſee.*

In its
1. Antiquity,
2. Dignity,
3. Juriſdiction,
4. Revenues,
5. Primates.

The firſt and laſt of theſe heads have been already ſufficiently treated on; but in order to begin methodically it will be neceſſary to recapitulate ſomewhat relating to the antiquity of this ſee. I ſhall paſs by the hiſtory of the *Britiſh* church, and proceed to what is much more authentick, the primary inſtitution of it under the *Saxon* government in *Britain*. *Antiquity.*

The archiepiſcopal ſee of *York* was in form inſtituted ſome time before the days of *Paulinus*, though not in ſubſtance. It appears by the letters of pope *Gregory the great*, which bore date x. *kal. Julii imperante domino noſtro* Mauritio *piiſſimo auguſto anno* xix. *poſt conſulat ejuſdem domini* xviii. *indictione quart.* which was about the year of *Chriſt* 602, that he commanded *Auguſtine*, to whom he had then ſent the pall by which he deſigned him archbiſhop of *London*, to appoint a biſhop at the city of *York*, ſuch a perſon as he himſelf ſhould think fit to ordain. Which biſhop, as ſoon as this city and northern parts of the realm were converted to chriſtianity, ſhould enjoy the honour of a metropolitan, and exerciſe the right of ordaining twelve ſuffragan biſhops under him. He was alſo to have the dignity of the *pall* conferred upon him, and to be made equal in privilege with the other province *(a)*.

But it was not until the year of *Chriſt* 627, that this archiepiſcopal ſee was erected in ſubſtance, as I have before related; for then what was only deſigned by pope *Gregory*, was accompliſhed in the primacy of *Paulinus*. Pope *Honorius*, in the year 634, ſent this prelate the *pall*, and directed his decretal letters to king *Edwyn*, recounting the parity which St. *Gregory* had appointed between the two metropolitans of *England*. Expreſsly granting them mutual power of ordaining each other; that, in time of a vacancy of either ſee, the ſurviving archbiſhop ſhould be qualified to ordain another in his place, and not be forced to undergo ſuch tedious and long journeys to *Rome*, on every ordination *(b)*. A. DCXXVII. *Pall.* A. DCXXXIV.

This privilege as ſoon as it was granted was put in practice; for the ſame year *Honorius* the fifth archbiſhop of *Canterbury* was conſecrated at *Lincoln* by *Paulinus* then archbiſhop of *York*. And afterwards *Boza* the fourth primate of this ſee was ordained by *Theodore* archbiſhop of *Canterbury (c)*.

The pall, that great ſymbol of eccleſiaſtical ſovereignty was omitted from the time of *Paulinus* to the reign of *Egbert*; which prelate, at his coming to the ſee, again procured it from *Rome*, and reſtored it to his church. And after him all his ſucceſſors to the *Reformation*, received the archiepiſcopal pall at their confirmations. It was firſt taken off the tomb of St. *Peter*, and ſent as an emblem of archiepiſcopal plenitude, in token of humility, vigilancy, *&c.* to be uſed or worn by the archbiſhop in his church, at the celebration of maſs on the following principal days *(d)*.

(a) Bedae *hiſt.* Gul. Meldun. *in pontificibus* Ebor. T. Stubbs *in iiſdem.*

(b) Tho. Stubbs. Brad. *hiſt.*

(c) Stubbs. Goodwin *de praeſul.*

(d) Pope *Honorius* II. gave a pall to *Thurſtan* then archbiſhop of *York* and his ſucceſſors, which grant mentions the former made by pope *Gregory*. *Regiſtro* Greenfield, *f.* 44. In an original charter which was in St *Mary*'s tower, *York*, the title of which was *Pallium conceſſum archiepiſcopo* Ebor *per* Alexandrum *papam*, a pall was

1. *Chriſt-*

SEE *of* YORK. *Juriſdiction.*

1. *Chriſtmaſs* day.
2. St. *Stephen*'s day.
3. *Epiphany.*
4. *Ypopanton.*
5. *Coena Domini.*
6. *Eaſter-day.*
7. *Aſcenſion-day,*
8. *Pentecoſt.*
9. The feaſts of St. *Mary's* { *Nativity. Annuntiation. Aſſumption.* }
10. The nativity of St. *John Baptiſt.*
11. The feſtivals of all the holy apoſtles.
12. On the commemorations of all the ſaints, martyrs, or confeſſors, that lye in the ſame church.
13. At conſecrations of biſhops, prieſts, deacons or churches.
14. On the anniverſary day of the a: biſhop's own conſecration.

There was an ancient cuſtom between the two metropolitans of *England*, that the ſurviving ſhould exerciſe all archiepiſcopal juriſdiction within the province of the defunct, *viz.* to conſecrate biſhops, to crown the king, to ſing high maſs before the king at *Chriſtmaſs*, *Eaſter* and *Pentecoſt*. According to this uſage, in the year 684, St. *Cuthbert* was conſecrated biſhop of *Lindisfarn* at *York*, the ſee being then vacant, by *Theodore* archbiſhop of *Canterbury*. Alſo, on the other ſide *Thomas* archbiſhop of *York* ordained theſe biſhops of the province of *Canterbury*, *viz.* (*e*)

Hervey, *Ralf*, *Hervey*, } biſhop of { *Norwich. Chicheſter. Bangor.*

But when *Lanfranc*, abbot of *Caen* in *Normandy*, was made archbiſhop of *Canterbury* by *William* I. and afterwards going to *Rome* for his pall, *Thomas* archbiſhop of *York*, whom he had conſecrated, went with him. *Thomas* propounded to pope *Alexander* II. the controverſy betwixt them, about the primacy and ſubjection of the ſee of *York* to *Canterbury*; and claimed the biſhopricks of *Lincoln*, *Worceſter* and *Litchfield*, as ſubject to this ſee. The pope decreed that the cauſe ought to be heard in *England*, and decided by the teſtimony and judgment of all the biſhops and abbots of the whole realm. After two diſcuſſions of this matter, one at *Wincheſter*, in the king's chapel within that caſtle, during the ſolemnity
A. 1071. of *Eaſter*, and the other at *Windſor* in the feaſt of *Pentecoſt*, it was finally determined in the preſence of the king, biſhops, abbots, *Hubert* legate of the *Roman* church, and many other orders of men there aſſembled, upon proof made by old authorities and writings,

1. That the church of *York* ought to be ſubject to that of *Canterbury*, and the archbiſhop of *York* to obey the archbiſhop of *Canterbury* in all things pertaining to chriſtian religion, as the primate of all *Britain*.

2. That if the archbiſhop of *Canterbury* called a council, whereſoever he pleaſed, the archbiſhop of *York* with his ſuffragans, ought there to be preſent, and give obedience to what ſhould be determined.

3. That the archbiſhop of *York* ought to receive epiſcopal benediction from him, and under oath to make unto him canonical obedience.

To theſe conditions the king, archbiſhops, biſhops, abbots and all there preſent agreed (*f*).

Theſe hard articles againſt the ſee of *York*, were obtained againſt *Thomas* archbiſhop, partly by the king's partiality to *Lanfranc*, and partly by the loſs of all the records belonging to the church; which were burnt in the great conflagration which happened in the city a few years before. But it was not long after that the ſee of *York* again raiſed her head to be, at leaſt, equal with *Canterbury*; and all her former privileges were reſtored.

A. 1128. Pope *Honorius* II. granted his bull of exemption to *Thurſtan* archbiſhop of *York*, and his ſucceſſors; thereby confirming to that ſee its ancient dignity over his own ſuffragan biſhops, together with all the right parochial, epiſcopal or metropolitical, which in any reſpect did ever appertain to his church. And by authority of the ſee apoſtolick prohibited as well the archbiſhop of *Canterbury* from exerciſing any profeſſion, or oath of Subjection, over the ſee of *York*; or *York* from requiring the like from *Canterbury*. Alſo whatever pope *Gregory* had before granted ſhould now ſtand good, *viz.* that *York* ſhould in no reſpect yield any ſubjection to *Canterbury*, but be directed according to the conſtitution of that holy father, which ordained that this diſtinction of honour ſhould perpetually be obſerved betwixt them,

1. That he ſhould be accounted the firſt primate who was firſt ordained.

2. That if the archbiſhop of *Canterbury* would not *gratis*, and without exacting ſubjection, conſecrate the elect archbiſhop of *York*; that then the ſaid elect ſhould either be conſecrated by his own ſuffragan biſhops, or elſe by the hands of his holyneſs himſelf (*g*).

(*h*) The ſame pope *Honorius* did, by his letters mandatory, bearing date at the *Lateran*, v *id. Dec.* and directed to king *Henry* I, *William* archbiſhop of *Canterbury* and others, command them to permit *Thomas*, ſecond archbiſhop, of *York*, to have his croſs carried before him, in any part of *England*, according to the ancient cuſtom and prerogative of the church

granted to the archbiſhop of *York*, wherein he appoints upon what days and occaſions he ſhall uſe it. Sir *T. W.*

(*e*) T. Stubbs, Goodwin, &c.

(*f*) *Eadmeri* hiſt. Gul. Meldun. &c.

(*g*) *Mon. Ang.* vol. III. p. 132. *Torre*, p. 341.

(*h*) *Mon. Ang.* vol. III. p. 147. *Torre*, ditto.

of *York*. As also to crown the king after the usual manner. In the time of king *Stephen* this privilege was again confirmed to *Roger* archbishop of *York*, by the authority of pope *Alexander* II. SEE of YORK. *Jurisdiction.*

In much later times, *viz.* in the year 1538, there was an award made between these two metropolitans touching probats of wills, administration of goods, *&c.* that if any person died in either province, having goods in both, then the will ought to be proved, and administration taken in both provinces for the goods within the same (*i*).

The suffragan bishops subject to the primate of *York* were these,

1. *Lindisferne* or *Durham*, } in *England*.
2. *Caerlisle*,
3. *Chester*,
4. *St. Andrews*, } in *Scotland*.
5. *Glasgow*,
6. *Candida casa*,
7. *Orcades*,
8. The *islands*.
9. *Sodor*, in the *Isle of Man*.

The see of *Durham* from all antiquity was subject to the primacy of *York*. And, in the fifth of *William* I. it was determined by all the bishops, abbots, *&c.* of the realm, in those constitutions made at *Winchester* and *Windsor*, that the bishoprick of *Durham*, and all the counties from the bounds of the bishoprick of *Litchfield*, and from the great river *Humber* to the farthest part of *Scotland*, should be in the province, and under the jurisdiction of the see of *York* (*k*). Durham.

Pope *Innocent* IV, in his confirmation of the possessions and liberties of this primate, ratified to *Walter* archbishop of *York*, and his successors, the subjection of the see of *Durham*; as his metropolitical right (*l*).

In the year 1080. *William de Kairilipho*, abbot of St. *Viveants*, being elected bishop of *Durham*, received his consecration from the hands of *Thomas* archbishop of *York* (*m*).

Anno 1099, *Ranulf Flamberd* was consecrated bishop of *Durham* by the said archbishop *Thomas*, and signed the instrument of his profession unto him (*n*).

Anno 1129, *Geffry Rufus* was consecrated bishop of that see by *Thurstan* archbishop of *York*; into whose hands he delivered the instrument of his canonical oath (*o*).

Anno 1143, pope *Celestine* II. acquaints *Geffry* elect of *York*, by his apostolical letters, that he had commanded *Hugh* bishop of *Durham* to assist him as well before as after consecration; and to yield to him due obedience as his primate; to whom both he and his church of *Durham* are and ought to be subject (*p*).

(*q*) According to an ancient custom the bishop of *Durham*, after his consecration, is bound to offer at *York*, one very rich cope. And, when he comes to do it, is to be received at the church door with procession.

It likewise appears, by divers records, that sundry precedents of subjection have been made to the primacy of *York*, by the see of *Durham* in these following respects:

I. When the see of *Durham* is full,

1. The archbishop of *York* makes metropolitical visitations in that *Palatinate*.
2. He summons their bishops to provincial synods or convocations.
3. Proves wills in his prerogative court of persons deceasing within his diocese, or having goods within the province.
4. All appeals from *Durham* are made to the archbishop of *York* as metropolitan.

II. In the vacancy of the see of *Durham*;

1. The archbishop of *York* assumes into his hands all ecclesiastical jurisdiction thereof; and so doing he constitutes his own ecclesiastical judges over the same.
2. Grants institutions to benefices therein.
3. Makes diocesan visitations there.
4. Confirms the elections of their bishops, and consecrates them. At which time such bishops take the oath of obedience and subjection to the archbishop in the same manner as the rest of the bishops of the province do at their confirmation and consecration (*r*).

The bishoprick of *Carlisle* is also subject and suffragan to the primacy of *York*; and that from the time of its first erection. For, in the year 1133, when *Adelwald* the first bishop thereof was consecrated by *Thurstan* archbishop of *York*, he both took his canonical oath of subjection, and the deliverance of the instrument thereof signed with his own hand (*s*). Carlisle.

(*i*) Torre *ut supra*.
(*k*) *Brad.* hist.
(*l*) *Mon. Ang.* vol. III. p 143.
(*m*) *Goodwin*, p. 641.
(*n*) *Stubbs*, 1709.
(*o*) *Idem*, 1720.
(*p*) *Mon. Ang.* vol. III. p. 148.
(*q*) *Mon. Ang.* vol. III. p. 164.
(*r*) Torre, *f* 343. *Processus controversiae inter episcop.* Dunelm. *et archiep.* Ebor. *de visitatione, regist.* W. Wickwain, *p.* 25. *Vide etiam regist.* Corbridge, *p.* 107. Melton, *p.* 470. Joh. Romani, *p.* 69, 101, 102, 103, 104.
(*s*) *Stubbs*, p. 1720. *Goodwin*, p. 675.

See *of* York. *Jurisdiction.* In the reign of *Henry* III. pope *Innocent* IV. confirmed to *Walter* archbishop of *York*, and his successors the subjection of the bishoprick of *Carlisle* to him and his church by metropolitical right *(t)*.

Chester. The bishoprick of *Chester*, erected by king *Henry* VIII. was also added to the province of *York*; and thenceforth have all its succeeding bishops ever answered the archbishops of *York* their metropolitical rights and privileges *(u)*.

Scottish bishops. Anciently all the bishops of *Scotland* were subject to the see of *York*. For it appears by the letter of pope *Calixtus*, bearing date at *Tarentum* xviii. *kal. Feb.* and directed to *Alexander* king of *Scots*, that his holiness earnestly exhorts the *Scottish* nobility, and enjoins the king by no means to suffer his bishops to consecrate one another; without first obtaining licence from their metropolitan. That, as oft as need required, they should with all reverence repair to the elect archbishop of *York*, their metropolitan, and from him receive their particular consecrations; either from his own hands, or, in case of necessity by his licence first obtained, from one another. Further, the said pope, by his apostolical authority, strictly enjoins both them and him humbly to obey the said archbishop as their father and master *(x)*.

S. Andrews. But to examine their particular subjections apart we shall begin with that of St. *Andrews*;

Fodewith bishop of St. *Andrews*, by the council and command of *Malcolm* king of *Scots*, came into *England* in the reign of *William* I. to make acknowledgment of his fault for having been ordained by the bishops of *Scotland*; whereas by right he ought to have been ordained by his metropolitan of *York*. He then made his humble profession to *Thomas* archbishop of *York* and his successors; delivering the instruments with his own hands, after he had read the form thereof, to the primate *(y)*.

Not long after this, in the reign of *Henry* I. *Thurstan*, prior of *Durham*, received his consecration to the bishoprick of St. *Andrews*, at the hands of *Thomas* archbishop of *York*; who took likewise his canonical oath of subjection and the instrument thereof by him subscribed *(z)*.

Hence the bishops of St. *Andrews* were successively within the province of *York*; until pope *Calixtus* IV. made the bishop of St. *Andrews* primate of all *Scotland*, and appointed twelve bishops under him *(a)*. This happened in the reign of *Edward* IV. and the primacy of *George Nevill*.

Glasgow. The bishops of *Glascow* also paid obedience to this archiepiscopal see of *York*; as is evident by these following examples,

Kinsius the twenty third archbishop ordained *Magsuen* bishop of *Glasgow*, and after that consecrated *John* his successor, and took the charter of his profession; which was burnt with other evidences of the church of *York*, in that deplorable conflagration of this city by the *Norman* soldiers *(b)*.

In the reign of *Henry* I. archbishop *Thomas* consecrated *Michael* bishop of *Glasgow*, who made his publick profession of obedience to him, and his successors, and then delivered the instrument into his hands.

About the same time pope *Calixtus* wrote to *John* the next bishop of *Glasgow*, who having been formerly consecrated by pope *Paschall* his predecessor, was grown so elated by that favour as he refused to yield due obedience to his metropolitan of *York*. And had so far withdrawn his subjection from him that he regarded not this pope's mandate, which required him to do it within thirty days, but contemptuously persevered in his fault. This so highly provoked his holiness that he sent another mandatory bull, dated at *Tarentum*, requiring him to repair to the church of *York*, in which chapter as a suffragan he had been elected, and acknowledge her for his mother, making his profession to *Thomas* then archbishop, his metropolitan. Otherways the sentence, which the archbishop should canonically pronounce against him, the pope would by his own authority ratify and confirm *(c)*.

Candida Casa or Galloway. This bishoprick was also subject to the see of *York*; as is manifest by the submission of *Gilla-Aldan* elect bishop of *Candida Casa*; who being consecrated by *Thurstan* archbishop of *York* made his recognition according to the tenour of these words:

"That whereas he understood, both by the authentick writings of the fathers, and by the "undeniable testimonies of ancient men, that the bishop of *Candida Casa* ought anciently to "respect the metropolitical church of *York* as its mother; and in all spiritual matters truly "to obey her. Whereupon he, the said bishop thereof, promised thenceforth to the church "of *York*, and to archbishop *Thurstan* and his successors all due subjection and canonical obe-"dience, as was instituted by the holy fathers of old *(d)*.

(t) *Mon. Ang.* vol. III. p. 143.
(u) *Goodwin*, p. 685.
(x) *Mon. Ang.* vol. III. p. 146.
(y) T. *Stubbs*, p. 1709.
(z) *Idem.* p. 1713.
(a) *Goodwin*, p. 611.
(b) *Stubbs*, p. 1700.
(c) *Mon. Ang.* vol. III. p. 147.
(d) *Mon. Ang.* vol. III. p. 148. *T. Stubbs*, p. 1720.

Thomas

Thomas the second archbishop of *York* consecrated and ordained *Ralph* bishop of the *Orca-* SEE *of* YORK.
dian islands; and took his profession in writing under his hand touching his subjection to his *Jurisdiction.*
archiepiscopal see *(e)*. Orcades.

Pope *Calixtus* II. sends his exhortatory letters to *Aistan* and *Seward* kings of *Norway*, to receive the said bishop of *Orcades*, who was canonically elected and consecrated in his metropolitical church of *York*; and to protect him in the quiet exercise of his function *(f)*.

Olave king of *the isles* writes to *Thomas* archbishop of *York*, desiring him to confer the The isles.
episcopal order on the abbot of *Fourness*; whom he had for that purpose sent unto him *(g)*.

Hence one *Wymunde* (the said abbot I suppose) was ordained and consecrated bishop of *the islands* by the said archbishop; he making his open profession of subjection, and delivering the instrument of it into the archbishop's hands *(h)*.

Pope *Celestine* II. by his bull, dated at St. *Peter's June* 11, 1458. made the cathedral Sodor.
church of *Sodor*, in the isle of *Man*, subject to the archbishoprick of *York* *(i)*.

Notwithstanding the plainness of the evidence in regard of the jurisdiction the see of *York* had anciently over all *Scotland*, yet it is stiffly denied by their historians. It is true this subjection has been often contested, but that does not prove their exemption from it. In a council at *Northampton*, held *anno* 1175, where were present *Henry* II. king of *England*, *William* I. of *Scotland*, the two archbishops, and all the bishops and clergy of both kingdoms, this affair was warmly contested by both parties. Here it was that one *Gilbert*, a young *Scotch* priest, stood up and made an elegant oration on the subject. He endeavours to prove that the *kirk of Scotland* was more ancient than that of *York*, that she was *York*'s mother church, and first instructed the *Northumbrian* kings and princes in the principles of *Christianity*. That she ordained the bishops and priests of *Northumberland* at first for more than thirty years; and had the primacy of the churches north of *Humber*. For all which he appeals to the testimony of venerable *Bede*. And concludes with an appeal to the pope, to whose precepts alone he adds the church of *Scotland* is subject.

This bold harangue was of no service to the argument, and seems to have been despised by *Roger* then archbishop of *York*; for at the breaking up of the assembly the prelate took occasion to lay his hand on the orator's head, and, with a smiling countenance, said, *Well shot sir* Gilbert; *but these arrows come not out of your own quiver.*

It would be endless to mention all the struggles about this precedency over *Scotland*; sufficient it is to say that the records of this matter are still preserved with us; and may be seen in a very ancient book in the register's office, styled *Registrum magnum album*. A book of that antiquity that it was lent to *Polydore Vergil* to peruse, by *Edward Lee* then archbishop of *York*, as the greatest rarity of that kind in the church *(k)*.

This precedency was certainly very inconvenient in the exercise by reason of the constant wars between the two nations. And at last *James* III. of *Scotland* wrote a letter to pope *Sixtus* IV. requiring him to constitute the bishop of St. *Andrews* primate of all *Scotland*. This request was granted, and though *George Nevill*, then archbishop of *York*, withstood it with all his might; yet the pope over-ruled him; alledging, *that it was unfit that an enemy should be metropolitan of* Scotland. *Polydore Vergil* writes, that his contemporary *Edward Lee*, archbishop, had intentions to have revived his claim in the reign of *Henry* VIII. if the fate of those times hrd permitted a *general council*. But now we may presume to say that the precedency the see of *York* once had over all *Scotland* is irrecoverably lost.

Besides the former there were other kinds of suffragan bishops in the diocese; the names *Bishop's suffra-*
of several of which we meet with in our registers. And I wonder so exact a man as Mr. *gans.*
Torre omitted taking a catalogue of them. That the reader may better understand what kind of dignitaries these were, I shall beg leave to subjoin an abstract of a letter from the reverend Dr. *Brett*, relating to this peculiar order of ecclesiasticks.

"*(l)* The bishop's suffragan, though they had foreign titles were all *Englishmen*; the original of them I take to have proceeded from hence. Most of the great abbies procured Bulls from *Rome* to exempt them from episcopal jurisdiction; and to be immediately subject to the pope only. But having occasion for episcopal offices to be performed in their monasteries to consecrate altars, chalices, vestments, and other ecclesiastical ornaments, and to confirm novices taken into their houses, they found, if on such occasions they should apply to any diocesan bishop, it would be taken as a submission to his jurisdiction; and therefore they got one of their own monks to be consecrated a bishop with some foreign title (most commonly a title in *Greece* or some part of the *Greek* church) who could therefore challenge no jurisdiction in any part of *England*; though with the consent of those who had jurisdiction here, he might exercise any part of the episcopal

(e) T. *Stubbs*, p. 1713.
(f) *Mon. Ang.* vol. III. p. 144, 5.
(g) *Idem.* p. 145.
(h) T. *Stubbs*, p. 1713.
(i) *Torre ex registro* Willielmi Booth *archiepiscopi* f. 369.

(k) *Ex MS.* sir *T.W.*
(l) This letter was wrote on occasion of an enquiry made by this gentleman about archbishop *Kemp*'s suffragans, from his register; in order to illustrate the life of that prelate now in writing by the reverend Mr. *Peg* of *Gamonham* in *Kent*.

" function.

4

SEE *of* YORK. *Jurisdiction.* " function. And the archbishops and other bishops who had large dioceses, or who were " employed in secular affairs, being made lord chancellors, as *Kemp* was, or lord treasurers, " or the like, made these titular bishops their suffragans, to perform episcopal functions " for them, which they could not perform themselves by reason of their secular employ- " ments; or sometimes by reason of age or infirmities, or the largeness of the diocese. That " these suffragans, though their titles were foreign, were all *Englishmen*, you may be satis- " fied from their names, and their education in our universities, for *Wood* in his *Athenae* " gives us an account of several such bishops educated at *Oxford*, as *Thomas Woulf episcopus* " *Lacedaemonensis*; of whom he speaks, *vol.* I. *col.* 555. *(m) John Hatton* bishop of *Nigro-* " *pont*, *col.* 560. *Richard Wilson*, who had after *Hatton*'s death the same title, *col.* 561. *John* " *Young* bishop of *Callipolis*, *col.* 567, and several others: I could give you a catalogue of be- " tween thirty and forty such suffragans all *English* men with foreign titles whose names I have " met with in *Wood* and other authors. But tho' our archbishops and bishops made such use " of these suffragans, Mr. *Wharton*, in his letter printed at the end of *Strype*'s memorials of " archbishop *Cranmer*, tells us that they treated them with contempt enough; and generally " made them dine at their steward's table, seldom admitting them to their own. And yet " these suffragans were called lords, as I find by some letters I have now by me in manu- " script. At the reformation there was an act made, 26 *Henry* VIII. appointing towns in " *England* for the titles of bishops suffragan, as *Dover*, *Nottingham*, *Hull*, *Colchester*, *Thet-* " *ford*, *Ipswich*, &c. to the number of twenty six. And there have been several suffragans " since the reformation to these *English* titles. Thus in the year 1536. *Thomas Mannyng* " was consecrated bishop of *Ipswich*, *John Salisbury* bishop of *Thetford*, *Thomas Spark* bishop " of *Berwick*; and divers others in the reign of *Henry* VIII. And in 1552. in the reign of " *Edward* VI. *Robert Purseglove* was consecrated bishop of *Hull*; and in 1557, the begin- " ning of queen *Elizabeth*'s reign *Richard Barnes* was consecrated bishop of *Nottingham*, " and 1592. *John Sterne* was consecrated bishop of *Colchester*. Since which time I have not " met with a consecration of a bishop suffragan. There never was any settled maintenance " provided for these suffragans; which is the reason, I suppose, why they have been dropped, " though any bishop may have one that desires it. And if a bishop desires a suffragan, he, " according to the act of *Henry* VIII. is to present two persons to the king, who chuses " one of them, gives him the title of one of the towns mentioned in the act, and orders the " consecration. I find several of these suffragan bishops have been raised to be diocesan, " and some of them whilst they have continued suffragans have joined in the consecration of " diocesans. *John Hodgeskin*, who was suffragan with the title of *Bedford*, was one of the " consecrators of archbishop *Parker* and of no less than fourteen other bishops in several " reigns, yet was never more than a suffragan himself."

Courts. The archbishop of *York*'s consistorial and prerogative courts with their power and authority are too well known to be here treated on.

Cross bearing. Many contests happened betwixt the two metropolitans of *England* about bearing their crosses in each others provinces. Insomuch that our archbishop many times directed his letters to the dean and chapter to inhibit the archbishop of *Canterbury* from having his cross born before him in the diocese or province of *York*. Whereby he did incline the people, by his benedictions and other ways, contrary to right. The royal authority used frequently to interpose in this debate, as the copies of several charters published in the *Foedera Ang.* do testify *(n)*.

On the *20th* of *April* 1353, a composition was made, by the king, between the lord *Symon* archbishop of *Canterbury*, and lord *John* archbishop of *York*; about bearing their crosses. Whereby the archbishop of *York* for peaceable bearing his cross within the city, diocese or province of *Canterbury*, was bound in two month's space from the time of his first entrance into that province to send a special messenger, who must be either his official, chancellor, auditor of causes, or a doctor of laws, or a knight, to the church of *Canterbury*, with a golden image to the value of forty pounds sterling; engraven with the similitude of an archbishop bearing a cross in his hand. Or else some other remarkable jewel of the same value; which was to be offered at the shrine of St. *Thomas* the martyr; to the honour and reverence of God and of him the said martyr. And upon the said messenger's entrance into the minster-yard at *Canterbury*, he was to be met by the prior, sub-prior, or at least by the monk who is *custos* of the said shrine, by whom he is to be conducted effectually to make his said publick offering *(o)*.

In parliaments and other councils of the king, when these two archbishops are present, the archbishop of *Canterbury* shall sit on the king's right, and the archbishop of *York* on his

(m) Probably the same that lies buried in the north isle of the choir, No. 2. Besides this there are many more in the registers with foreign titles as *Dromorensis*, *Pharatensis*, *Phillopotensis*, *&c.*

(n) Pro archiepiscopo Cant. *super bajul crucis infra provinciam* Ebor. *teste rege apud* Ebor. 4. *die* Novembris 1322. Foed. Ang. *tom.* III. *p.* 979, *&c.*

(o) I find a protestation entered in *Bowett*'s register relating to this offering in these words, *Non virtute alicujus ordinationis seu compositionis praetensae inter aliquos praedecessores suos* Ebor. *archiepiscopos et* Cant. *archiep. factae, seu supra aliqua oblatione imaginis vel jocal. valor.* 40 l. Bowett *extra dioc.* p. 13.

One hundred years after this *concordat William Bothe* archbishop of *York* did send such an oblation by the hands of a knight. *Ang. Sac.* vol. I. p. 74, 75.

left

left hand. And the cross of the former shall be laid on the right side of the king's seat, and the cross of the other on the left; if *Canterbury* be then present. SEE *of* YORK. *Privileges.*

Moreover in councils, conventions, and other places, in which these archbishops happen to meet, the archbishop of *Canterbury* shall have the chief place and more eminent seat, and the archbishop of *York* the next. The cross bearers of these two archbishops, in any broad way when the crosses can be born together, ought to go together with their crosses before their respective archbishops. But in the entrance of any door, or any strait place, the cross of the lord archbishop of *Canterbury* shall precede; and the cross of the archbishop of *York* follow after (*p*).

The archbishop of *York* claims by the grant of king *Athelstan*, and the confirmation of other kings, **soc, sac, toll, theam,** a market every *Thursday*, assize of bread and ale, and of weights and measures. The amendalls of the pillory, tumbrill, theef, wherever he be taken, **infangtheof** and **outfangtheof,** judgment of iron and water, gallows, gibbet, prison, goal-delivery, his own coroners, goods and chattels of felons and fugitives, chattels owned by fugitives, wreck, waife, estray, merchett, bloodwitt, his own court, cognizance of false judgment, and of all manner of pleas wheresoever moved by his burgesses and tenants. To act in all processes as the justices of the king; and to make execution by his bailiffs; to have pleas of fresh force; to make inquisitions of felonies and robberies and terminations of sheriffs; and to do all that belongs to a sheriff by his bayliffs. That the archbishop and the tenants of his fee, wherever they reside, be free and quiet from suits of assize, county, wapontack, trithing, geld, and from performances to the king; and from tollage, portage, passage, pannage, throughout all the king's dominions. That he hath his fair twice in the year. He claims to plead in his courts by his own justices, in the presence of one or two of the justices of the king, all pleas of the crown, as well as others which arise within his liberty (*q*).

King *Henry* II. did grant and confirm that neither his steward, nor marshal of his house, nor his clerk of the market, nor his deputy should enter within the bounds of the liberty of the archbishop (*r*).

He had view of Frank-pledge, pleas of *Withernam*, return of writs (*s*), quittance for sheriff's turns, and from presentments at the hundreds of hue and cry, levied in his manors of *Southwell*, *Latham*, *Scrooby*, *Sutton*, *Askam*, and in the members of those which are in his barony of *Shireburn* (*t*).

He had *jura regalia* within the liberty of **Hextoldesham,** or **Hexham,** and the levying of tenths and fifteenths there by his own ministers (*u*). *Hexbam*, which *Bede* calls *Haugustald*, was the *Roman* VXELODVNVM, and was given by king *Egfrid*, in the year 675, to St. *Wilfrid*, in order to erect an episcopal see therein. This see continued for seven successive bishops, till the *Danish* wars put an end to that hierarchy. But this manor, or regality as it is called, continued in the possession of the archbishops of *York* for many ages after. There is a proviso made in the statute, 27 *Hen.* VIII. *cap.* 24. that *Edward* archbishop of *York* and his successors, and their temporal chancellors of the shire and liberty of *Hexham*, alias **Hextoldesham,** for the time being, and every of them shall be thenceforth justices of peace within the shire and liberty of *Hexham*. But by the statute of 14 *Eliz. cap.* 13. *Hexham* and *Hexbamshire* are made and declared part of the county of *Northumberland* (*x*). This was esteemed a temporal barony of the archbishop of *York* (*y*). Hexham.

The archbishop of *York* had a market and a fair at his manor of *Otley*, and a market and a fair at *Shireburn*. A market and a fair at his manor of *Pattrington*, in the county of *York*. A fair at *Southwell* in the county of *Nottingham*, and another at *Hexham*, now in *Northumberland* (*z*). *Fairs and markets.*

He had his prisons and justices in the towns of *Ripon* and *Beverley*, with other great liberties there (*a*).

He claimed a passage over the river of *Hull* where there used to be a bridge (*b*). He used to have his port and prizage of wines in the said river, and of all merchandizes coming thither as the king had elsewhere (*c*). Hull.

Amongst the pleas of *Quo Warranto* held at *York* before *John de Mettingham* and his companions, 8 *Edw*. I. a *Quo Warranto* was brought against *William* archbishop of *York* to know by what warrant he claimed to have gallows, return of writs, estreats, pleas of **Withernam,** and his proper coroners within the city of *York* and without; and to have coroners on each side of *Hull*, and to take prizes in that river; to have the assize of bread and beer, and Beverley. Ripon, &c.

(*p*) *Vid. regist*. Laur. Bothe, *f*. 77.

(*q*) *Mon. Ang*. vol. III. p. 132, 133, *&c*. MS. sir *T. W.*

(*r*) *Mon. Ang*. vol. III. p. 135.

(*s*) *Concess*. Edwardo (Lee) *archiep*. Ebor. *et successor. quod habeant return. brevium, &c. nec non omnimod. summon. de Scaccario*, 2 *pars pat*. 26 Hen. VIII.

(*t*) *Pat*. 52 Hen. III. *m*. 7. *et in schedula pro libertatibus confirmandis pat*. 52 Hen. III. *m*. 32.

(*u*) *Clause anno* 13 Ed. III. *p*. 2. *m*. 34.

(*x*) *Ex MS*. sir *T. W.*

(*y*) See *Rob. Holgate's* seal. *Recognitio servitii prioris de* Hexham *domino archiepiscopo* Ebor. *regist*. de la Zouch, p. 300.

(*z*) *Clause anno* 11 Hen. III. *m*. 10.

(*a*) *Pat*. 7. Ed. IV. *p*. 1. *m*. 13.

(*b*) *Fin. anno* 17 Ed. II. *m*. 25.

(*c*) *Chart. pro archiepiscopo* Ebor. *de prisis vinorum ad portum* Kyngston *supra* Hull. Foed. Ang. *tom*. IV. *p*. 297. *pat*. 19 Ed. II. *p*. 2. *m*. 13. *anno* 4 Ed. III. *n*. 41. *Petitio in parliament. apud* West. *pro hac libertate. Et clause anno* 1 Ed. III. *p*. 1. *m*. 11. *et pars* 2. *m*. 18. *in turre* London.

 broken wreck of the sea and waif at *Patrington*, to have free warren, and his land quit from suit, in *Wilton*, *Beverley* and *Burton* and elsewhere in his lands in that county; to have a park and free warren, and to have his lands quit from suit at *Beverley*, *Burton*, *Wilton*, *Ripon*, *Otley*, *Schireburne*, and *Thorp*, and to have a park and free warren at *Cawood*. To which the archbishop answered, that, as to the gallows, he claimed them, without *York*, in his baronies of *Schireburne*, *Wilton*, *Patrington*, *Otley*, *Beverley*, and *Ripon*, by this warrant that king *Athelstane* gave the said manors to the archbishop of *York* and his successors before the conquest; from which time all the archbishops of *York* had enjoyed the said liberties. That afterwards king *Henry* I. the son of the conqueror, did, amongst divers other liberties, grant to the archbishop **infangtheof** in the aforesaid lands, by his charter, which he produced in court. He said further that he claimed return of writs and pleas of **Withernam** in *Beverley* and *Ripon* with their members; and the taking of estreats by the hands of the sheriffs for the levying of the king's debts upon those persons who had nothing without his liberties; and this they have used time out of mind. As to coroners within the city of *York* he said he claimed none.

Mints. The same *Quo Warranto* (*e*) urged him to shew cause why he claimed to have two mints for coining of money within the city of *York* without the king's licence. To which the archbishop pleaded that he and his predecessors had been in seisin of these two mints time out of mind. And further said that in the time of king *Henry*, son to the conqueror, one *Odo*, sheriff of *Yorkshire*, did hinder *Gerard* then archbishop of *York* from holding pleas and giving judgment in his court *de Monetariis*. The bishop complained to the king, and shewed his seisin and the right of the church of St. *Peter*; whereupon the king did send his letters patents to the sheriff, the effect of which was to will and command him that *Gerard* archbishop, in the lands of his archbishoprick should have pleas in his court *de monetariis suis*, of thiefs, and of all others, as *Thomas* archbishop had in the time of his father or brother. And that he should execute the kings new statutes of judgments or pleas of thieves and false coiners, and that he may do this at his own proper instance, in his own court; and that neither he, nor the church, shall lose any thing by our new statutes, but let him do in his own courts by his own instance according to our statutes. *Teste R. Cestrien. episcopo apud Winton.* And the bishop said, that he and his predecessors had always had the same mints as he claimed them. Upon this issue was joined, and the jury found for the bishop, and judgment given that the bishop should be without day. But of this more in another place.

In the reign of king *Henry* V. *Henry*, then archbishop of *York* made a petition to the king, who with consent of parliament confirmed to him all the liberties of his church with this clause, *licet*; and further grants and confirms to him that he and his officers may hold the sheriff's turn within the towns of *Beverley* and *Ripon*; and there hear and determine and punish all manner of felonies, as justices of the peace, notwithstanding any liberties granted to the town of *Beverley* to the contrary; all which are therein repealed (*d*).

Queen-hall, Oxon. The archbishop of *York* did exercise jurisdiction, as a visitor, in the college called *Queen-hall* in *Oxon*, as several testimonies both in the *Foedera* and the registers do witness. *Pat.* 12 *Hen.* IV. *m.* 19.

In fine he had a most ample charter and confirmation of all his charters, liberties, privileges and gifts; as appears *pat. an.* 20 *Hen.* VI. *p.* 4. *m.* 11. but they are too large for any further disquisition.

Palaces. There were several palaces anciently belonging to the see of *York*, of which only that at *Bishopthorp* is now standing; habitable, or in their possession. In the close of the cathedral at *York* stood once a very magnificent palace built by *Thomas* the first archbishop of that name. Five hundred years after, the great hall of this palace was scandalously stripped of its leaden covering by another prelate, and the remains and ruins of the whole are now leased out from the see. There was anciently a palace at *Schireburn*, in *Elmet*, belonging to the archbishop of *York*; no manner of remains do now appear of it, nor any traditional account there; except a piece of ground on the east side the church which is now called **Hall-garth**. I suppose this was deserted on their building a palace in a place of greater security, though in a much worse situation, at *Cawood*. This palace continued to be the residence of our archbishops until the time of the civil wars when it was demolished and has ever since laid in ruins. The site of which ruins I give the following draught of, in order to perpetuate the memory of the several founders and repairers of this once great mansion of hospitality. They had likewise a palace at *Ripon* and *Beverley*, another at *Otley*, in this county; at *Southwell* in *Nottinghamshire*, *White-hall*, and *York-Place* in *London*, and at *Battersea* in the county of *Surry*, a place there now called also **York-Place**, still denoting its site; all which are now demolished, and alienated from the see.

(*d*) *Rot. parliament. anno* 3 Hen. V. *n.* 48. *Turre* London.

(*e*) The affair of this *Quo Warranto* is copied from sir *T. W.* who had it from an *Inspeximus* 3 Hen. V. *n.* 15. in which he says many other liberties of the church of *York* are mentioned. But, he adds, that the original record of the eighth of *Edw.* I. is in the custody of the chamberlains of the exchequer, marked thus, *J. de vallibus placita de juratis et assizis, &c. Quo Warranto J. de Vallibus, rot.* 9.

These are many grants and charters relating to the archbishop's mints in this city in the *Foedera*, some of which the reader may find in these pages, *tom.* V. *p.* 755. *tom.* VII. *p.* 47, 178. And regist. *Wickwain*, *p.* 41.

A perspective view of the ruins of Cawood-Castle.

SEE *of* YORK. Revenues.

In the account relating to the revenues, belonging to the see of *York*, the compass of my design will not allow me to be as particular as Mr. *Torre* has been. Who has traced them through all the donations, he could find, to the church; as well as demises and leases from it. I shall therefore run succinctly through the whole, and refer the more curious to the manuscript itself for further enquiry. *Terra archiepiscopi, in libro* **Doomsday**, may be seen in the *addenda*.

In the time of the *Heptarchy*, when the *Northumbrian* princes were converted to the *christian* faith, they bestowed very considerable revenues on this church of *York*. Amongst which none remains now upon record more famous than *Ulphus* the son of *Toraldus*, a *Saxon* prince, who is said to have lived in the west part of *Deira* (*f*). This prince finding dissensions to arise amongst his sons about the division of his lands, resolved to make them all equal. And coming to *York* he kneeled down before the altar of God and St. *Peter*, and by the ceremony of drinking wine out of his horn, thereby made over to the church all his lands and signiories (*g*).

This horn, as well as the donor, has been held in high veneration by the successive dignitaries of the church; as appears by the figure of it cut in stone in two several places of the fabrick. And by the arms put up in honour of the prince, which, in a window, are thus blazoned, *vert*, six lions rampant *or*.

It appears by several antient surveys taken of the church lands and mentioned in the *monasticon* and our records, that a great deal of the possessions gained by this donation lay in the city and suburbs of *York*. Which are styled **de terra Ulphi**. In the escheat rolls of 13 *Edward* I. remaining in the exchequer, the lands in these townships following are put down as held of the fee of *Ulphus*.

Kekolthorp. **Kekolthorp**, three carucates of land, since held by the knights templars of the church of St. *Peter*.

Newbald. **Newbald**, twenty eight carucates of land, now a prebend.

Goodmundham. **Goodmundham**, four carucates of land now belonging to the prebend of *Fridaythorp*.

Barneby. Pocklington. **Barneby**, the whole town intirely, with the fourth part of the parish of **Pokelington**, the first belonging to the prebend thereof; and the latter to the dean and chapter.

Millington Beneldale. **Millington** and **Beneldale**, three carucates of land, now belonging to the prebend of *Givendale*.

Alvesthorpe. **Alvesthorpe**, two bowates of land, with the heir of **Robert Stiveton**, held of the fee of *Ulphus* (*h*).

The next very antient and considerable benefactor to the church of *York* was *Athelstan*, king of *England*; who granted to it the following large possessions,

Bishop Wilton. **Bishop Wilton**, the manor of which was given by the said king, with three carucates of land there, to the archbishop of *York* and his successors. Part of which belongs now to the prebend of *Wilton*, as part did to the treasury of *York*. Yet the archbishop hath still in this lordship of *Wilton*, two sheep pastures which *Edward* archbishop of *York* demised unto *Geoffrey Lee*, esq; his brother and one *Creyke* for the term of forty years, at the rent of seventeen pound fifteen shillings (*i*).

Agmondernefs. **Agemundernesse**, *in com. Lanc.* was given by king *Athelstan* to God, St. *Peter*, and the church of *York* in the prelacy of archbishop *Wolstan*. This place was held in the conqueror's time by *Roger de Poictiers*, and given to *Theobald Walter* by *Richard* II. ancestor to the *Butlers* of *Ireland* (*k*).

Shireburne. The manor of **Shireburne**, *in com. Ebor.* was also given by king *Athelstan* to the archbishop of *York* and his successors; who made it one of their principal seats in after times.

Edward archbishop of *York*, thirtieth *Henry* VIII. demised this manor unto *Anthony Hammond* of *Scardingwell* for the term of thirty years at twenty five pound *per annum* rent (*l*).

Beverley. King *Athelstane* gave likewise to the archbishop of *York* and his successors the manor of **Beverlac**, *com. Ebor.* where they sometimes resided. This was held by them until

Edward Lee, the thirty fifth of *Henry* VIII. granted it to the king, his heirs and successors, excepting the advowson of provostship and prebendaries thereof. But these were likewise given up to that king some time after in exchange for some lands of the crown.

Ripon. The manor of **Rippon** was also by the said king *Athelstan* given to the see of *York* for ever. But

In the time of *Henry* VIII. and his immediate successors, this manor was demised and parcelled out to divers persons, by the archbishops of those times; the particulars whereof may be seen at large in Mr. *Torre*'s manuscripts (*m*).

Southwell. In the year of our lord 958, the lordship of **Suthwell**, *in com. Not.* was given by *Edwy*, king of *Egland*, to *Oscbitell* then archbishop of *York*, and his successors for ever.

It continued in the possession of this see untill the thirty fifth of *Henry* VIII. when *Edward* archbishop granted his capital mansion or messuage in *Southwell*, and also his

(*f*) By the estates below he must have lived very near *York*; and probably at *Aldby*.
(*g*) *Camb. Brit.*
(*h*) *Torre* f. 3 9.
(*i*) *Ibid.* p. 350. 29, 30 *Hen.* VIII.
(*k*) *Mon. Ang.* vol. III. p. 129. *Cam. Brit.* 752.
(*l*) *Torre* p. *ut supra.*
(*m*) *Idem* p. 351, *ad* 355.

lordship

lordship and manor thereof unto king *Henry* VIII, his heirs and successors for ever. Some part of this manor was given back to the see by queen *Mary*, which was again demised by several succeeding archbishops, though still a reserved annual rent is paid out of it to the see (*n*). **See of York. Revenues.**

In the year 1033, king *Knute* gave to *Alfric*, archbishop of this see, for the redemption of his soul, forty three cassates of land in **Patrington**, to hold the same in perpetual inheritance. *Edward*, archbishop of *York*, the thirty fourth of *Henry* VIII. demised unto *Edward Nevill* of *Patrington*, gent. for the term of forty years, the lands therein specified at the rent of seven pound three shillings and eight pence *per annum* (*o*). **Patrington**

These are some of the most antient possessions belonging to the see of *York*; there were several others bestowed on it, by the *Conqueror* and his successors, all specified in Mr. *Torre*, with their particular demises from it. It would be too tedious to copy that indefatigable author exactly, and ask a volume sooner than a chapter. The following tables will present the reader at one view, with a list of the manors that were granted from the see to king *Henry* VIII. in lieu of divers impropriations, &c. which were then fallen into his hands from the dissolved monasteries in these parts: and to conclude this head I shall also subjoin a rental of the possessions, or reserved rents, from the several leases demised or granted out at different times since the *Reformation*, taken from the aforesaid authority.

(*p*) *A CATALOGUE of those* Manors, &c. *which were granted to king* Henry VIII. *his heirs and successors for ever, by the archbishop of* York, &c. *as by indenture bearing date* February 6, 36 Hen. VIII. *and confirmed by act of parliament*, 37 Hen. VIII. *chap.* 16. *doth plainly appear.*

MANORS.	COUNTIES.	MANORS.	COUNTIES.
Ascenby.		*Newby.*	
Askam,	*Nottingham.*	*Northby.*	
Ayton.		*Newland.*	
Atome.		*Northsoke,*	*Nottinghamshire.*
Bishopside.		*Ninibinross.*	
Bishop-places.		*Norton.*	
Colesakeshill.		*Odington.*	
Castledike.		*Penicroste.*	
Catton.		*Patrington,*	*Ebor.*
Crakhall.		*Rippon.*	
Cercleton.		*Ripponholm.*	
Cadden.		*Renton.*	
Churchdowne,	*Gloucestershire.*	*Ravensfield.*	
Cerney.		*Sharrow* juxta *Ripon.*	
Compton.		*Stanley* juxta *Ripon.*	—
Dalton.		*Sherburn* in *Elmet.*	——
Difford.		*Skipton.*	——
Erington.		*Scroby,*	*Nottinghamshire.*
Esclawant.		*Sutton,*	*Ebor.*
Fismake.		*Sherdington.*	—
Gryngton,	— *Northumberland.*	*Thorpe* prope *Ripon.*	——
Gloughton.	——	*Thornton.*	——
Griscthwayte.		*Thurethorpe.*	
Gloucester.	——	*Topclyffe.*	
Halgarth.	——	*Threske.*	
Hexam,	*Northumberland.*	*Upleatholme.*	——
Halidon.	——	*Whitclyffe.*	
Huckilcote.		*Wawane.*	
Kepwicke.	——	*Wilton.*	
Kenelaga.		*Wilton* episcop.	----
Milford.	——	*Waplowe.*	
Maske.		*Wall,*	*Lincolnshire.*
Monketon prope *Ripon.*		*Wescalland.*	------
Netherdale.		*Widecombe.*	

(*n*) *Vide* Torre p. 355, &c.

(*o*) *Idem* p. 358. *Mon. Ang.* vol. III. p. 130.

(*p*) *Torre* 394. This instrument of a monstrous length being contained in no less than fifteen membranes of parchment, is inrolled in the chapel of the *Rolls*, and has this remarkable preamble, This indenture made the syxthe day of February in the syxe and thyrtye yere of the reyne of the most excellent and vyctoryous prince our natural soveraign liege lord Henry the eyght by the grace of God king of England, and of France and Irland, defendour of the faith, and of the churche of England and of Irland, in erth the supreme hedde between the same our soveraign lorde of thone partie, and the reverend father in God Robert archebusshoppe of York, on t'other partie witnesseth, that the said archbusshoppe hath bargayned and sold, and by these present indentures for hym and his successors doth fully and clerely give, grant, bargayne and sell all those his lordships and manors of Hexham, Gryngton, &c. sealed interchangeably by the king and the archbishop; who on the 2d of *April* came before the king in chancery at *Westminster* and confirmed the same. The same day ratified by the dean and chapter of *York*. *Claus.* 36 Hen. VIII. *pars* 5. *n.* 38.

SEE of YORK. Revenues.

A LIST of the several impropriations, *&c. settled on the see of* York, *by the charter of king* Henry VIII. *bearing date at* Westminster, anno regni 38, *in exchange for other antient lands of that see.*

The churches of
- *Gisburn.*
- *Ormesby.*
- *Eston.*
- *Marton.*
- *Kirk-Levington.*
- *Stainton.*
- *Shereffe Hoton.*
- *Hoton* supra *Derwent.*
- *Hoton* juxta *Gysburn.*
- *Threske.*
- *Brafferton.*
- *Thurkilby.*
- *Haxey* and *Ouston* } in the isle.
- *Rowston.*
- *Felkirk.*
- *Yarum.*

The churches of
- *Suton in Galtres.*
- *Darrington.*
- *Doncaster.*
- *N. Popleton.*
- *Agnes Burton.*
- *Whitby.*
- *Malton.*
- *Wistow.*
- *Cramborne.*
- *Hinderskelf.*
- *Nafferton.*
- *Skypse.*
- *Esington.*
- *N. Feriby.*
- *Lyeth.*
- *Molesby.*
- *Knapton.*
- *Kayngham.*

Lands in *Lastingham.*

The patronage of these following benefices were also granted to the archbishop of *York* by way of the aforesaid exchange.

The parsonages of
- *Ackworth.*
- *Rowley.*
- *Beeford.*
- *Stokesley.*
- *Skrayngham.*

The parsonages of
- *Eton.*
- *Kirkby* in *Cleveland.*
- *Barton* in fabis and *Leek.* } *com. Not.*

The vicaridges of
- *Leeds.*
- *Hemesley.*
- *Doncaster.*

The chantry of *Topcliff.*

(p) *A summary of all the rents belonging to the archbishoprick of* York.

	l.	s.	d.		l.	d.	d.
Bishop Wilton ——	17	15	00	*Whenby* ——	16	13	04
Rippon ——	143	04	08	*Bishoptborp*	03	17	00
Suthwell ——	40	06	07 ½	*Bishop Lathes*	13	06	08
Patrington ——	07	03	08	*York*, for *Nunnfields*	14	18	10 ½
Cawood ——	70	13	04	*London* rents			
Kynatton ——	12	00	00	*Angram grange*	13	06	08
Lanum ——	17	16	08	*Felkirk* ——	78	17	08
Scroby ——	32	14	08	*Lastingham* ——	14	06	08
Plumtree ——	12	12	00	*Yarum* ——	12	13	04
Everton ——	04	06	08	*Gisburn* ——	30	00	00
Askham ——	12	06	08	*Skelton* ——	18	00	00
Ottrington ——	16	13	04	*Ormesby* and *Eston*	26	13	04
Sutton upon *Lound*	22	00	00	*Kirklevington* ——	19	06	08
Thorpe in *le Willoughs*	17	13	04	*Marton* in *Clyveland*	08	00	00
Bishop Burton	20	10	00	*Marton* priory ——	50	00	00
Ottley ——	34	17	11	*Sutton* in *Galtres*	30	15	04
Cerney	05	13	04	*Stayneton* ——	50	00	00
The *Marrays* ——	59	06	08	*Sheriff Hutton*	49	13	04
Battersey ——	29	04	11	*Hutton* sup. *Derwent*	09	16	00
Kingston sup. *Hull*	10	00	00	*Hutton* juxta *Gysburn*	04	13	04
Halydyn	07	13	04	*Threske* ——	20	00	00
Hexgrave ——	06	13	04	*Brafferton* ——	15	08	00
Hasselford-Ferry	01	10	04	*Thurkilby* ——	06	13	04
Kilburn ——	18	10	00	*Rowston* ——	47	16	08
Wetwang ——	10	00	00	*Darrington* ——	10	00	00
Whitclyffe ——	11	06	08	*Doncaster* ——	36	13	04

(p) *Torre* p. 430. For an antient account of the rents and reburstments of this see, whilst it remained in the king's hands, see *Maddox's* excheq. p. 211. bi

Nether

SEE *of* YORK. *Revenues.*

	l.	*s.*	*d.*		*l.*	*s.*	*d.*
Nether Poppleton	08	00	00	*Easington*	43	10	08
Burton Agnes	30	00	00	*Lyeth*	59	00	00
Whitby	50	00	00	*Molseby Pr.*	12	15	00
Malton	16	00	00	*Knapton*	02	00	00
Wistowe	13	16	10	*Kayingham*	14	15	04
Crambe	08	01	02	*Marsom*	01	06	08
Hinderskelf	01	13	04	*N. Feriby*			

Haxey and *Oweston* rent corn.
Nafferton, rent corn
Skypse, rent corn.

The archbishop of *York* has used to pay to the *pope* ten thousand ducats for his confirmation.

Besides for the pall fifty thousand ducats *(r)*.

Peter pence of the whole diocese was 10*l.* 10*s.* *(s)*.

The scutage of the archbishoprick of *York* was various, I find this imposition for the redemption of king *Richard* I. for the archbishop's knights fees was twenty pounds. *(t)* By another scutage that his knights might be excused from attendance on the king into *Ireland*, the archbishop made account to the king's treasury of the like sum *(u)*. In another scutage for his barony of Chertwickshire, as it is there termed, to excuse going into *Wales* he paid also twenty pounds *(x)*. But for the first scutage, assessed at two marks, after the first coronation of king *John*, the archbishop of *York* paid for his share forty marks, *et quietus est (y)*. *Scutage.*

The valuation of this archbishoprick in the king's books is now 1610*l.*

The arms of the see of *York* were antiently, *azure*, a staff in pale *or*, surmounted by a pall *argent*, fringed as the second, charged with five crosses pattee fitched *sable*, in chief another such a cross *or*.

These arms, the same with the see of *Canterbury*, are impaled with the arms of *Bowett*, *Rotheram* and *Savage* in the windows of the cathedral; but it has since been changed for this bearing; *Gules*, two keys in saltire *argent*, in chief a *crown imperial or (z)*, and sometimes a mitre.

The ecclesiastical estate of this church, besides the archbishop, consisted also of a certain number of canons secular, over whom he presided. These were a body politick by prescription, had a common refectory and dormitory, like canons regular in other places, and lived upon the profits and revenues of the church; enjoyed by them in common. DEAN *and* CHAPTER, *Canons.*

They were antiently but seven in number, and performed the divine offices of the church and altar; for which respect they had peculiar privileges and revenues conferred upon them, in the name of the church, and of the canons therein serving God. The most antient charters of pious donations to them usually run in these words, *Deo et eccles. S.* Petri Ebor. *et canonicis in eadem Deo servientibus (a)*.

In the time of the *Danish* wars, and at the *Norman* conquest, which made great devastations in these northern parts, these canons were fellow sufferers in that great calamity, and were most of them dispersed into foreign parts. Insomuch that there were but three of them left when *Thomas* the first was preferred to this see. This prelate recalled the banished canons, and added others to their number; rebuilt them the hall which his predecessor archbishop *Aldred*, had founded for their refectory, as also a dortor for them to lodge in; and besides constituted one of them a provost to govern the rest.

In this state the church of *York* continued some time, till at last the same prelate thought good to divide the lands of St. *Peter* into *prebends*, by allotting unto each canon a particular portion. From whence they ceased to live in common, upon the joint revenues of the church, at one table. At the same time, for the better governing of the church he instituted a dean, treasurer and chanter to preside and rule over it *(b)*. *Prebends.*

King *Henry* I. granted the first charter to the church of *York*; I speak since the *Norman* conquest, for all charters both to the city and church, before that period, were burnt in the general conflagration which happened at that time. This charter of *Henry* I. is not extant, at least it is not to be met with, nor doth it appear but by an *inspeximus* of later times *(c)*. *Privileges.*

King *Henry* II. grants and confirms all their former liberties and privileges granted unto them by several antient kings and archbishops; and particularly mentions those by king *Edward* the confessor and archbishop *Alfred*.

(r) Goodwin *de praesulibus p.* 626.
(s) Torre *ex reg.* Laur. Bothe *archp. p.* 5.
(t) Rot. Pipe 6 Ric. I. *Mad.* excheq. p. 411.
(u) *Idem* p. 438.
(x) *Idem* p. 441. 38 *Hen.* II.
(y) Rot. Pipe 1 *Joh.*
(z) The crown was given to it as being once an imperial city. *Maximilian* II. honoured the arms of the city of *Roterdam* with the same crown. The kings of *Spain* have also given one to the arms of the cities of *Madrid*, *Toledo*, *Burgos*, &c.
(a) *Torre* p. 487.
(b) See the life of archbishop *Thomas* I.
(c) Sir *T. W.* perhaps this charter might be destroyed in the second dreadful fire which happened in this city. *temp. reg.* Steph.

The

Dean and Chapter. Charter.

The extract of this extraordinary charter of liberties is as follows,

First, that if any criminal or person convict be apprehended or arrested within the church porch (*d*), the person that takes him shall make amends by the universal judgment of the hundred, who shall give damage for the same. But if he take him within the church, then he shall be judged by twelve hundredors. If within the city of *York*, then by eighteen of the hundred who shall cause amends to be made accordingly.

Arrests.

But if any be so desperately wicked and audacious, as to presume to take any person from the sanctuary called **Fridstoll**, that is the stone chair of peace and quietness placed against the altar; for that heinous sacrilege there shall no jury pass, nor pecuniary mulct be laid upon him, but he shall be accounted **Boteles**, that is without capacity of making amends or reparation. The damages or amerciaments thus imposed shall all accrue to the canons solely, and none of them to the archbishop.

Offences.

2. If any person commit an offence to another in the church, church-yard, in the canons houses, or upon their lands; or if the canons amongst themselves injure one another, or any other person, or another person wrong them, for such a fault no forfeiture shall be made to the archbishop, but to the canons only.

3. These canons shall be called the **canons of St. Peter in Hird**, that is, of his domestick family; and the lands of the canons shall be called the **lands of St. Peter's own table.**

Collations.

4. The archbishop shall exercise no other jurisdiction over the canons than this, that upon the death of a canon he shall collate another to his benefice.

Not to contribute to the archbishop when fined.

5. If the archbishop happen to commit any offence against the see apostolick, or the king, which requires a pecuniary mulct or reparation, in such a case the canons shall not be liable to contribute any thing towards it, but what they please to do out of their own good wills.

Liberties in their lands.

6. The canons shall enjoy all their houses and lands with the privileges of **Sac, Soc, Toll** and **Theam, Intoll, Out-toll** and **Infangentheof.** Also all those honours and customary liberties which belong to them as well as those the king doth which he hath in his hands, or which the archbishop, holding of God and the king, hath in his.

Their tenants where tried.

7. No tenant holding land of the canons of St. *Peter* shall do suit or be impleaded in the courts of the **Weapontach, Tridingmot**, or **Schiresmot**; but the plaintiff and defendant shall be tried and justified before the door of St. *Peter*'s monastery.

Pleadings.

8. If any canon be pleading in court in his own cause upon a signal given, or the toll of the bell, he may leave off, and at canonical hours return to his devotions. Which is more than the archbishop himself can do, because he may proceed in the cause by his stewards, knights and officers.

Lands afterwards obtained.

9. If any person do hereafter give or sell land to St. *Peter*, none shall thenceforth claim therein the privilege of **Sac, Toll** and **Theam**. But the canons themselves shall have therein the same privileges as in the other lands of St. *Peter*.

To find one soldier in the king's wars.

10. When the king shall raise an army, the canons shall for their lands set forth one man, who shall carry the banner of St. *Peter*; and be captain and ensign to the burgesses of the city, if they go to war; but in case they do not, then the canons man shall be excused.

Exempt from free quarter.

11. No person belonging to the king's courts or his armies shall have free lodging or quarters in the canons houses, whether they be within the city or elsewhere.

Duels.

12. If any fight a combat in *York*, the parties shall make their oath upon the text, or relicts of St. *Peter*'s church; and when the same is over, the victor shall offer the arms of the vanquished in the said church; returning thanks to God and St. *Peter* for his victory obtained.

Criminal causes

13. If any of the canons or their tenants be tried in pleas of the crown, their cause shall be heard before any others, and also be determined as far as it can, saving the churche's dignity (*e*).

Privileges confirmed to the dean and chapter by the pope. Free from archiepiscopal sentences.

18. *kal.* Julii 1194. Pope *Celestine* III. confirmed to the church of *York* their antient privileges and possessions. And by virtue of his apostolical authority prohibited the archbishop, for the time being, from denouncing any sentences of excommunication, interdicts, suspensions or expulsions against the dean or any of their canons or their ministers, whether clerks or laicks; or against the immunity of their predecessors which they had hitherto enjoyed, without assent of the dean and chapter first obtained.

Ordination of canons.

He also decreed that the ordination of canons or parsons should be free, as was usually heretofore observed from the very foundation of the place, *viz.*

Prebends collation. Admission. Investures. Oath.

That an honest and fit person, whom the archbishop shall please to nominate, shall be collated to every dignity or prebend in the church; and so be presented to the dean and chapter, and be by them admitted into their canonship or dignity by the tradition of a book and bread, and be invested by the hands of the dean in the chapter-house, and then be received by a kiss of the brethren. And when that is done to administer the usual oath

(*d*) *Infra atrium ecclesiae.*

(*e*) *Monast. Ang.* vol. III. 135. Torre *ex registro albo p.* 6. *Decan. et cap.* Ebor. *confirm. ampla cart. et privileg. pat.* 3 Ed. IV. *p.* 3. *m.* 3.

consisting

consisting of fealty to the church, defending its liberties and legal customs, and not re- *DEAN and*
vealing the secrets of the chapter. After that he is to be installed by the hands of the *CHAPTER.*
chantor by a mandate from the dean and chapter, and take the second oath to them in *Installation.*
all things lawful and canonical.

Lastly this pope ratified to the dean and chapter of *York* the privilege which the *Late-* *Right of colla-*
ran council gave them, *viz.* of conferring any prebend or parsonage to the church be- *tion in case of*
longing, which by lapse of the archbishop continues vacant beyond the limitted time of *lapse, &c.*
his collating. This grant also confirms to the dean and chapter the possession of several
of their estates *(f)*.

The church of *York* had likewise these following privileges granted and confirmed by king *Henry* III. dated *July* 5, *anno* 1223.

1. That they should have the goods and chattels of any of their men, if they be out- *Forfeits.*
lawed, attaint, or fugitives. And also such cattle as are waifed upon their own lands.

2. That the said dean and chapter, each canon and their successors, and all their tenants *Toll free, &c.*
and men *(g)*, in city, town, markets, fairs, bridges and sea-ports, within the realms of *England*, *Ireland* and *Wales*, be free from payment of **toll, tallage, passage, pedage, lastage, stallage, ludage, wardage**; also from works and aids belonging to *castles*, *walls*, *bridges*, *parks*, *banks*, *ditches*, *vivaries*; or from the buildings at the king's *navy* or *houses royal*; likewise from **castle guard, carriage** and **summage.** Neither shall their *wains*, *carriages* or *horses* be taken for any service whatsoever.

3. To be quit of all gelds, **danegelds, fengelds, hangelds, forgelds, penygelds, tything-** *Free from gelds.*
peny, hundred-peny, thuskemung, chevage, cheanage, and **herbage**; and of other **vectigals** and tributes of the army and horsemanship.

4. That they be free and quit of all suits at **counties, hundreds, wappontaks, tythyngs,** and of *murder*, *larceny*, *escape* and *concealments*; also of **hansoline, gribruch, blodewite, fitwite, forstall, leirwite, hengwite, ward-peny,** and **harward-peny.**

5. Of all aids of *sherriffs* and ther ministers; of *scutages*, *assizes*, *recognitions*, *inquisitions* *Aids.*
and *summons*; except it be for the liberty and affairs of the church.

6. That they the said dean and chapter have their own court and proper justices, *Their court.*
with **soc** and **sac**, **toll**, and **theam**, **infangentheof**, and **utfangentheof, flementfyth, ordeal,** and **orester** as well within time as without. And if they, their canons, or their men have any plea against others or amongst themselves, or others against them, the said pleas shall be no where else heard but at the church door of St. *Peter's*; saving pleas of the crown, which shall be held in some one of the canon's houses, or in the church yard, as the dean and chapter have hitherto used. And when the said pleas are ended, the dean and chapter shall have the estreats out of the king's justices rolls, who hold those pleas touching the amerciaments of any of their men.

7. No sheriff or his bayliff, or minister shall enter the lands of the dean and chapter, *No distresses.*
or their liberties, without leave given to make any distress and seize any of their goods.
But they shall for ever have return of the king's writs, in all things relating to themselves, *Return of writs.*
their men, or their lands.

8. All the king's sheriffs, bayliffs or other ministers, are hereby prohibited, within the *No arrests.*
lands of the dean and chapter, or their church, from arresting, binding, beating or killing any man; also from bloodshed, committing rapine, or any other violence. Likewise from molesting them, or their men, in their concerns out of pretence of any custom, service or exaction, or upon any cause whatever *(h)*.

Feb. 20. *anno* 51 *Hen.* III.

The same king *Henry* furthermore granted to *Walter* archbishop, and the dean and chap- *Coroners.*
ter of *York*, the liberty of having coroners of their own men and tenants within the city; who shall answer to the king's in all things to the coroner office appertaining. Whereupon he prohibited, upon forfeiture of ten pound, either the sheriff, his bayliff, or any other coroner from intermeddling in any thing belonging to the office of a coroner without the licence or assent of the said dean and chapter and their successors. *(i)*

The jurisdiction of the archbishoprick when vacant, wholly belongs to the dean and *Liberties sede*
chapter. *vacante.*

Item, the institutions of all clerks presentative.

Item, the examinations, confirmations and informations of all elections of bishops, abbots, priors and other persons whatever.

Item, the corrections of all excesses of the ministers of the choir. *Corrections, &c*

Item, to them belongs the placing of vicars in the stalls of such canons as are absent and out of the realm.

Item, the placing of auditors over their own clergy, the placing of their own steward, subtreasurer, and the master of St. *Laurence's* hospital *(k)*.

(f) Torre *ex reg. albo p.* 54.

(g) *Homines suos.* King *Edward* III. by charter dated *West. Jun.* 19. *anno reg.* 10. declares that these words shall extend to freemen, as well as to natives of the dean and chapter. *Decan. et cap.* Ebor. *placit. coram justiciar. itinerant anno* 3 Ed III. *de libertat. et privileg. olim concess. et usurpat. per cartas regum.* Record. 5 *Ric.* II. *n.* 107. *Turre* London.

(h) Torre *p.* 489. *ex reg albo.*

(i) *Ex eodem.*

(k) Torre *p. eadem.*

7 A King

4

DEAN and CHAPTER.

(*l*) King *Richard* II. by his charter under his broad-seal dated *July* 24, 7 *reg.* grants and confirms, that the lord-mayor, *&c.* should not enter within the *Minster yard* or *Beddern*, or any houses of canons, *&c.* within or without to exercise any jurisdiction, *&c.*

A tedious controversy between the dean and chapter of *York* about the archbishop's visitation of them was by *William de Melton* compounded. And the order set down by himself he procured to be confirmed by pope *John* XXIII; his apostolick letters bearing date at *Avignion* 6 *id. Mar. anno pontif.* 12. *id est anno Dom.* 1328, who commissioned *William* bishop of *Norwich* and master *Hugh de Engolisme* archdeacon of *Canterbury* his procurators to compound the same, which they did accordingly. But the articles of this agreement are too long for my purpose (*m*).

Last charter.

The dean and chapter of *York* at present enjoy the following privileges; which were granted them, on their humble petition, by the charter of king *Edward* VI. bearing date *April* 20, 1547. *anno reg.* 1.

Whereby the said king confirmed unto them, or rather *commissioned them to exercise under him*, all spiritual jurisdiction in these matters.

1. To have probats of wills and testaments of all his subjects within those parishes, towns and places which they or their predecessors formerly used. Also to grant administrations of the goods and chattels of such persons as shall die inteftate; so that they exceed not the sum of five pound of debtless goods.

2. The collations to ecclesiastical benefices within their respective jurisdictions. Also institutions and inductions to such as are presented to them.

3. Visitations of the clergy and people in their respective parishes, vicaridges and ecclesiastical places. And to make enquiry, either by themselves or delegates, of the defects, excesses, crimes, and defaults whatsoever belonging to the ecclesiastical court within their jurisdiction; and the same to reform and punish according to that law.

4. To receive due and accustomary procurations, in their visitations, and proceed against the contumacious according to the king's ecclesiastical law.

5. To hear and determine such causes and suits, which were then depending before them, or their commissioners, or any other which may hereafter belong to the spiritual court of which they shall have cognizance (*n*).

It is observable that this commission was granted only *durante bene placito regis*, from whom and his crown all ecclesiastical and secular power, authority, judicature and jurisdiction is derived; as being then declared the supream head of the church of *England*, and of all magisterial government within this realm.

The dean and chapter of *York* have jurisdiction, in some respect, over the parishes and towns within the several dignitaries and prebends of the church. And over the prebendal places themselves. Also in these towns following,

Abberford	*Fenton* preb.
Acclam	Chanc.
Accome	Treas.
Aldburgh	*Massam* preb.
Aldwark	Treas.
Alne	Treas.
St. *Anston*	*Laughton* preb.
Barthorpe	Canc.
Belthorpe *Bolton*	} *Fenton* preb.
Bishop lathes	*Osbaldwyke* preb.
Biggins	*Fenton* preb.
Brakehouse	*Laughton* preb.
Brewby	*Salton* preb.
Bromflete	*Cave* preb.
Burne	*Massam* preb.
N. Cave	{ Part *Hustwait* preb. Part N. *Newbald* preb. Part *Osbaldwyke* preb.
Carrhouse	*Laughton* preb.
Carlton	{ *Hustwaite* preb. *Wistow* preb.
Cawood	*Fenton*
Clifton	{ Part *Strensal* preb. Part Treas.
Cotton	*Langtoft* preb.
Colton	*Stillington* preb.
Dringhouses	{ *Osbaldwyke* preb and Treas.
Ellington *Ellingthorpe*	} *Massam* preb.
Elloughton	*Wetwang* preb.
Ereewyke	*Strensal* preb.
Fetherby	*Massam* preb.
Finnimore	*Wetwang* preb.
Firbeck	*Laughton* preb.
Flaxton	*Salton* preb.
Flawith in *Alne* par.	Treas.
Foxflete	*S. Cave* preb.
Fryton	*Wistow* preb.
Walter Fulford	*Ampleford* preb.
Godmondham	*Frydaythorpe* preb.
Gilldenwells	*Laughton* preb.
Givingdale	*Salton.*
Golthorpe	*Bishop Wilton* parish.
Grafton	*Grendall* preb.
Grimston and	*Dunnington* preb.
Grimston	*Langtoft* preb.
N. Hayton	*Laughton* preb.
Hamelton	*Wistow* preb.
Hansworth	*Laughton* preb.
Haxby	*Strensall* preb.
Headen	Subdecan.
Gate Helmisley	*Osbaldwyke* preb.

(*l*) P. 533. *ex charta penes dom.* Rob. Squire.
(*m*) *Vide* Torre *p.* 491.
(*n*) *Idem ex reg. mag. alb.* 37.

Heslington

Heslington	*Ampleford* preb. and *Driffield*	*Roucliffe*	*Strensal* preb.
Hewyke	*Donnington* preb.	*Shereburn*	*Fenton* / *Newthorpe* prebends.
Ilton	*Massam* preb.	*Shipton*	*Wighton* preb.
Kirkby-malesart	*Massam* preb.	*Skelton*	Treas.
Kirkby-wharfe	*Wetwang* preb.	*Slade-Hutton*	*Laughton* preb.
Leavning in *Acclam* parish	*Cave.*	*Stainford-brig*	*Osbaldwyke* preb.
Letwell	*Laughton* preb.	*Stockton*	*Bugthorpe* preb.
N. Liverton	*Ampleford* preb.	*Suardby*	*Bugthorpe* preb.
Malton part	*Donnington* preb.	*Sutton*	*Massam* preb.
Mapleton	A. D. East riding.	*Tollerton* and *Thoresthorpe*	Treasurer.
Marton near *Burlington*	*Bugthorp* preb.	*Towthorpe*	*Strensal* preb.
Marton in *Burghshire*	*Donnington* preb.	*Tunstall*	Succ. canon.
Mexburgh	A. D. *Ebor.*	*Usburn parva*	Precentor.
Mickleburg	*Salton* preb.	*Wedworth*	*S. Cave* preb.
Millington	*Givingdale.*	*Waghen*	Canc.
Newton Staingrave parish	*Salton* preb.	*Wales* / *Wallenwells*	*Laughton* preb.
Newthorp	Treas.	*Wardesmark*	*Massam* preb.
Oxmerdyke	*S. Cave* preb.	*Wigginton*	Treasurer.
Pocklington	*Barmby* preb.	*Wimbleton*	*Stillington* preb.
Preston-Hold	Subdecan.	*Wodsetts*	*Laughton* preb.
		Yaltborp	*Bishop Wilton* preb.

(o) *Parishes and Towns wherein the dean and chapter have all manner of spiritual jurisdiction.*

Aldborough, near *Burroughbridge*, the church, the vicaridge house and seven tenements.
Askham, in *Nottinghamshire*, chapel and town of the parish of *East-Drayton.*
Brotherton, church and town.
Bubwith, sixteen tenements.
Byrome, a town in the parish of *Brotherton.*
Burton-pydsey, all the parish.
Burton-Leonard, the church, the vicaridge, three tenements, and *Humberton* manor-house.
Copmanthorp, chapel and town of the parish of *St. Mary's* upon *Bishop-hill.*
Dalton, upon *Tease*, town.
East Drayton, in *Nottinghamshire*, the parish.
East Lutton, chapelry of the parish of *Wevertborpe.*
Helpthorpe, parish.
Helperby, town.
Horncby, the church and parsonage, vicaridge houses, and five other tenements there; with the chapel of *Hackford* and one tenement there, and two tenements in *Hunton.*
Kirby-irelyth, in *Lancashire*, the church and six tenements.
Laneham, in *Nottinghamshire*, the church and parish.
Misterton, church and parish.
Over-popleton, of the parish of St. *Mary's Bishop-hill.*
Poole, a town in the parish of *Brotherton.*
Stokam, in *Nottinghamshire*, chapelry in the parish of *East Drayton.*
Sutton, a town in the parish of *Brotherton.*
Topliff, twelve tenements.
Weaverthorpe, parish.
West Lutton, chapelry of the parish of *Weaverthorpe.*
Wharram, in the street, parish.

Churches in the city of York *which are, or were, in the gift, and of the jurisdiction of the dean and chapter.*

St. *Michael's de Berefrido.*
St. *Martin's* in *Conystreet.*
St. *Mary's*, *Bishophill* jun.
St. *John's*, *Ouse-bridge* end.
St. *Laurence*, extra *Walmgate.*
St. *Andrews.*
St. *John de le pique.*
St. *Ellen's* near the Walls.
St. *John's* in *Hungate.*
St. *Mary's* in *Laythorpe.*
St. *Sampson's.*

(o) This and the following is taken from a manuscript of R. *Dodsworth, penes me.*

DEAN *and* CHAPTER.

Houses in the city and suburbs of York *of the jurisdiction of the dean and chapter.*

Minster-yard, all houses whatsoever within the close.

Beddern, all houses within the *Beddern*.

Petergate, all houses from the north side *Bootham-bar* to the back gates of the deanery.

On the south side seventeen houses.

All the houses on the south side from the *Minster-gates* to *Grapelane-end*.

Stonegate, fourteen houses.

Jubbergate, four houses.

St. *Andrewgate*, five houses.

Salve-rent, three houses.

Shambles, seventeen houses.

Aldwarke, sixteen houses.

Loblain, one house.

Goodramgate, thirty three houses.

Coppergate, one house.

Water-lane, one house.

Bennet-rents, seven houses.

Pavement, two houses.

Ousegate, one house.

Walmgate, one house.

St. *Laurence* church yard, two houses.

Fossgate, one house.

Davygate, one house.

Highmangergate, two houses.

Colliergate, one house.

Micklegate, three houses.

St. *Martin's-lane*, five houses.

Patrick-pool, two houses.

Hornpot-lane, two houses.

Cham-hall-garth, one house.

St. *Martin's* church-yard *Conyng-street*, two houses.

Monkgate, five houses.

Laythorpe, two houses.

Barker-hill, one house.

Thursday-market, one house.

(p) Grape-lane, all that side of *Grape-lane* towards *Stonegate*.

Revenues.

The revenues of the dean and chapter were also very considerable, but have been much diminished by long leasing of their tithes, lands, *&c.* since the reformation. I shall not enter into these particulars for reasons before mentioned, and shall only give Mr. *Torre's* account of the whole rents as they occurred to him from the leases themselves.

The particular rents of the dean and chapter of *York* are to be thus reckoned,

	l.	*s.*	*d.*		*l.*	*s.*	*d.*
Aldborough —	72	13	10	*Langwith* —	08	00	00
Askam and *Drayton*	25	00	00	*Heworth* —	01	13	04
Brotherton —	43	06	08	*Sturton in the clay*	30	00	00
Bubwith —	15	06	08	*Stillingflete* —	33	13	04
Burton-pydsey —	23	00	00	*Worleby* —	05	00	00
Burton-Leonard —	11	00	00	*London* —	05	03	04
Bishop Burton —	37	00	00	*Holgate* —	10	00	00
Broddesworth —	13	06	08	*Popleton* —	10	00	00
S. Cave —	03	06	08	*Bishop-fields* —	02	13	04
Cotum —	09	15	02	*Copmanthorp* —	16	00	04
Wevertborp —	26	00	00	St. *Laurence* church	09	13	04
Dalton super *Tease*	18	13	04	*Laythorp* —	02	18	09
Lanum —	17	00	00	Pensions —	153	08	02
Horneby —	29	06	08	Several houses in *York*.			
Kirkby-Irelith —	29	06	08				

The houses and ground rent belonging to the dean and chapter of *York* in *Fleetstreet*, *London*, commonly called *Serjeant's-Inn*, came originally to the church by the will of one *Dalby*; who did devise four hundred pound to the dean and chapter to find a *chantry* in their church perpetually, and an *obit* for the soul of *Dalby*; and that the chantry priest should have forty eight marks yearly, *&c.* King *Henry* IV. granted licence to them to purchase the house now called **Sergeants-Inn** in *Fleetstreet*, and some houses and shops thereunto adjoining, with some other lands at *York*, *ad onera et opera pietatis*, according to *Dalby's* will *(q)*. Thereupon they purchased these houses and lands, and made ordinances how the priest should be maintained; and agreed with the executors of *Dalby* for finding him perpetually. They after received the four hundred pound, and obliged themselves *ac omnia bona sua ad performandum*, &c. The dean and chapter employed eight pound yearly for the maintenance of a priest, and other sums for the *obit*. These lands, says sir *T. W.* from whose manuscript I have extracted this account, were in the first year of *Edward* VI. certified to be employed for a chantry, and the king had it as chantry land, and gave it to sir *Edward Montague*. All this appeared upon a special verdict in the court of common pleas, where it was adjudged contrary to the opinions of *Daniel* and *Warburton*, there being five judges then present, that these lands were not given to the king by the statute of the first of *Edward* VI. because there were no lands given by *Dalby*; and his intent could not make a chantry; and the dean and chapter did not make any chantry or appoint any land thereto, but obliged their goods for the payment of an annual sum to

(p) Mr. *Torre* writes this word, from the old church records, **Grappecuntlane** p. 527.

(q) *Pat.* 10 Hen. IV. *p.* 2. *m.* 3. *Unum messuag. et quinque* **Shoppe** *cum solariis super aedific. in parochia* **St. Dunstant West** *in* **Fleet-street** *in suburbio* **London**, *&c.*

the

the priest, and the sum paid was not out of this land only, but out of all their possessions (r).

Thus this morsel escaped being swallowed up by those times; and the church of *York*, I mean the dean and residentiaries, are now the lessors of this ground and houses. Which, however, has been several time disputed with them by the judges, who were then tenants in the *Inn*. The church has at last gained a total victory, by law, over those executors of it; and the ground being leased out into other hands, several fine new buildings are now erecting upon it.

The first fruits of the chapter of *York* are valued in the king's books at 439 2 6
The arms of the dean and chapter are, *gules*, two keys in saltire *or*.

Before I conclude this head I shall present the reader with an abstract from sir *T. Widderington's* manuscript, relating to some differences arising betwixt the dean and chapter and the city; in a note upon which that author writes; that he loves the city but the truth better; and therefore he shall not conceal the particulars. Though perhaps then, adds he, the table of St. *Peter* had more respect than the sword of the lord-mayor in the disquisition of them. In another place, he tells you, that the large possessions of the church of *York*, spangled and embroidered with so many royal favours, did blow up this spiritual body into a tumour or tympany, and it became a much greater body than the city of *York*; as the gates of *Mindus* were greater than the city of *Mindus*. What sir *Thomas* has given us on these controversies is taken from the *regist. mag. alb.* now in the custody of the dean and chapter; a book of great authority and antiquity.

(s) *Anno* 1275. *an. reg.* Ed. *fil.* Henrici xv. *cal.* Aprilis *coram* Roberto de Nevile, Alexandro de Kirkton, Johanne de Reygate, Ricardo de Chaccum, *et* Willielmo de Northbrough, *et postea crast. quindene purificationis beate* Marie *apud* Eborum, between the mayor and citizens and dean and chapter, an inquest was taken by twenty four knights, all therein named, who was charged to enquire of the following articles. The verdict was given up at **Scarthbourg** before the king and council.

The articles on the behalf of the mayor and bailiffs against the dean and chapter were these,

1. Whether *Ralph de Curteis*, a citizen of *York*, was excommunicated by the dean and chapter for his fidelity which they required from him, as the mayor and citizens say; or was he excommunicated for his contumacy, because he did not appear before the judges of causes in the church of St. *Peter*, to render an account touching the will of one *Roger Samond* whose executor he is.

2. If the dean and chapter did excommunicate *John de Conington* a citizen of *York* for a debt which was not testamentary or matrimonial, or for his contumacy in not appearing before the judges of causes, &c. *pro lesione fidei*, because he did not observe his days of payment of a debt to the dean and chapter, which he was bound upon his faith to pay.

3. If the tenants of the dean and chapter, within the city, ought to receive their measures from the bailiffs of the city, signed with the seal of the city, as heretofore they have been accustomed; or if the dean and chapter have a standard of their own, and all that belongs to a standard, sealed with the seal of St. *Peter*.

4. If the dean and chapter do appropriate to themselves the pleas of the king's tenants, or only the pleas of their own men and tenants; or whether they hold pleas by writ or without writ as in court-barons.

5. If the mayor and bailiffs do distrain the men of the dean and chapter, as well within the liberties of St. *Peter* as without, as the mayor and citizens say, or otherwise; and if they did, if it were not *per* **eskekum**, in time of war or peace. Or if the mayor used to enter into the lands of St. *Peter* to levy the king's debts, as well after these charters made to the church as before, or whether the dean and chapter have return of writs, and may levy the king's debts.

6. If the men of the dean and chapter have used to be tallaged with the citizens, at what time soever the king should think fit to tallage the city; or if these tenants ought to be free as tenants to the dean and chapter, who are of the table of St. *Peter*, after the making of these charters; and if they have been tallaged at any time if it were not *per* **eskekum**, and in the time of war or peace.

7. If the mayor and bailiffs may enter into the lands of St. *Peter* in the city and suburbs; and take felons or malefactors there only; or that they ought not to be taken by the bailiffs of the dean and chapter.

8. If the dean and chapter have excommunicated any by name for such takings and arrests by the mayor and bailiffs; or if they have not excommunicated any by name but only in general, twice a year, all the intruders into the liberty of holy church; as it has been used always in the catholick church.

(r) Mich. 2 Jac. C. B. Holloway *versus* Watkins. 1. Cr. 51.
(s) *Ex registro magno albo*. There is mention also made of this *inter annales Monast.* B. MARIAE Ebor. *in biblioth.* Bodleian. Oxon. NERO A. 3. 20.

9. If none of the men of the dean and chapter ought to be free of toll within the city, but only the tenants of twenty four carucates of land of *Ulphus* the son of *Thorald*; and if the servants of these tenants ought to render yearly to the mayor and citizens for ever the carucate of land paid for acquittance for that toll upon St. *James*'s day, as the mayor and citizens say; or that all the tenants of the dean and chapter ought to be free by the aforesaid charter.

10. If the dean and chapter did excommunicate *John Matherb* and *Hugh Payte*, the bayliffs of the city, because they did arrest a labourer or reaper of *Akum* in the high street, being a tenant of the treasurer of the church; or if the dean and chapter did excommunicate them because they arrested him in the church-yard of St. *Mary*'s, which is near the church of St. *Peter*, and not in the high street.

11. If the men of the dean and chapter did hinder the bayliffs of the city to arrest a felon, who killed his companion in the hospital of St. *Leonard*.

Articles propounded by the dean and chapter against the mayor and citizens.

1. If all the men of the dean and chapter ought to be, and used to be free of toll, tallage, pavage, stallage, and murage, by the charters of kings, except the tenants of the twenty four carucates of land of *Ulphus*, or not?

2. If the tenants of the dean and chapter ought not to use and have not used their court with *sac*, *soc*, *toll* and *theam*, *infangtheof* and *outfangtheof* within the time of pleading, and without their tenants of St. *Peter*; so that none of their tenants ought to be impleaded but in their own court.

3. If all pleas of land within the city and suburbs may be tried before the mayor; and if the mayor and bayliffs did not make a publick proclamation, throughout the whole city, that no person upon pain of imprisonment should come before the dean and chapter to answer, unless it be in case of marriage or testament.

4. If any sheriff, bailiff or minister of the king ought to enter into the lands and tenements of the dean and chapter to take any distress or pledge, or to levy any of the king's debts; or that the dean and chapter ought not to have, and have wont to do, these things themselves; or that the mayor and bailiffs have return of writs, levied the king's debts, and answered them in the exchequer, as the mayor and citizens say.

5. If no vicar or clerk of the church of St. *Peter* hath hitherto used to answer for any personal trespass, before the mayor and citizens by the charters of the king's predecessors, and not before the mayor in the court of the city.

6. If the dean and chapter have a standard for measures and ells by the delivery of king *Henry*, the father of the present king, to be sealed with the seal of St. *Peter*. Or that in the third year of this king, the mayor and bailiffs did not come into the house of the treasurer of *York*, would have tried the measures, and would have sealed them with the king's mark, and have delivered a standard unto them as the king's marshals have used to do; and the mayor and bayliffs did hinder them in the performance of their office, or that none ought to have a standard within the city, but by the delivery of the mayor and citizens.

There were some other articles of complaint on both sides.

The jurors as to the articles of the mayor and citizens against the dean and chapter give this verdict and judgment.

1. That the dean and chapter have not usurped any pleas of layfees, or of debts or chatels, which are not of testament or marriage, or breach of faith, or violent laying on of hands upon priests or clerks, which pleas belong to the liberty of the church; and judgment was given, that the dean and chapter shall be without day, and the mayor and citizens *in misericordia pro falso clamore*.

2. The dean and chapter and every canon of St. *Peter*'s having land within the city and suburbs, hath his court of his tenants, and ought to have the pleas of his tenants by the king's writ directed to them; and shall hear and determine all plaints of their tenants in their own courts by the king's writ to them directed; and this they have used, *sicut magnates et liberi de regno faciunt per Angliam*, from the time of the confirmation of king *Henry* III.

And the judgment, that the dean and chapter and canons shall have and hold their courts of all their tenants within the city and suburbs, when the king's writs are directed to them in that behalf; and shall hear and determine the complaints of their tenants in their courts for ever; as other great men of the kingdom do.

3. That the said *Ralph Curteis* was not excommunicated for his fidelity required by the dean and chapter, but for his contumacy in not appearing before them of the causes of the chapter to give an account of the testament of *Roger de Samond*, whose executor he was; and the said *John de Couingston* was excommunicated by the said judge for breach of faith, because he did not observe the days of payment of a debt which he owed the dean.

Therefore

Therefore judgment was given that the dean and chapter as to this article ſhould be *ſine die*, and the mayor and citizens in mercy for their falſe clamour.

4. That the dean and chapter do not appropriate to themſelves any men but their own men, and that only when the king's writs are directed unto them, and they hear and determine the plaints of their tenants in their own courts, as other great men of the kingdom do.

And the judgment was that the dean and chapter ſhould be without day, and the mayor and citizens in mercy for their falſe clamour.

5. That the mayor and citizens of *York*, after the confirmation of king *Henry* III. made to the dean and chapter of their liberties, did take no pledge or diſtreſs in the land of the dean and chapter, nor of any other within the fee of St. *Peter*; for any debts of the citizens unleſs it were *per* **eſkekum**, or in time of war, and that they ought to take no ſuch pledge or diſtreſs within thoſe liberties.

And the judgment was that the mayor and citizens thenceforth ſhould take no pledge nor diſtreſs in the fee of St. *Peter*, within the city or ſuburbs for any debts of the citizens, or of any other; and the mayor in mercy for his falſe clamour.

6. That none of the men or tenants of the dean and chapter of the fee of St. *Peter*, ought nor uſed to be tallaged, unleſs by reaſon of their merchandiſe if they ſhall uſe any within the city of *York* out of the land and fee of St. *Peter*; and by reaſon of their merchandiſe ſuch men and tenants of St. *Peter* being within the city ought to be tallaged when the king will tallage the city aforeſaid, according to the quantity of merchandiſe which they uſe as aforeſaid.

The judgment was, that all the men and tenants of the dean and chapter, and alſo of the fee of St. *Peter* within the city and ſuburbs, ſhall be quit from tallage for ever; unleſs the merchandiſe they uſe be within the city and ſuburbs without the land or fee of St. *Peter*; and the mayor and citizens in mercy.

7. That all men and tenants of the dean and chapter ought to be free from paying toll in the city and ſuburbs, and have been free from it by the charters of the kings of *England*, and by the confirmation of king *Henry* III. and they ſay that the forinſical tenants of the dean and chapter of the lands of *Ulpbus* do yearly pay to the mayor and citizens half a mark of ancient cuſtom, which they have uſed to pay to this day; but they know not whether this was paid for an acquitttance of their toll or no.

Therefore the judgment was that all the forinſical tenants of the dean and chapter of the lands of *Ulpbut*, do pay to the mayor and citizens half a mark yearly for ever as they have uſed to pay; and the mayor and citizens in mercy.

8. That the dean and chapter ought by their bailiffs to receive and arreſt thieves and malefactors within the liberties of St. *Peter* in the city and ſuburbs of *York*, and to detain them in priſon till they be delivered by the law of the land; and this they have uſed fully and conſtantly from the time of the confirmation made to the dean and chapter by king *Henry* III. and if the mayor and bailiffs have at any time taken and arreſted ſuch malefactors within the liberties of St. *Peter*, it hath been *per* **eſkekum** in the time of war.

Therefore judgment in this was given for the dean and chapter, and the mayor and citizens in mercy.

9. The dean and chapter have not excommunicated any of the citizens by name, by reaſon of any arreſt made by them in the liberty of St. *Peter* within the city and ſuburbs of *York*, but have only twice a year excommunicated all treſpaſſers upon the rights and liberties of the church, as is uſed in every church in the kingdom.

For this alſo judgment was given for the dean and chapter.

That the dean and chapter did not reſcue the felon who killed his fellow in the hoſpital of St. *Leonard*, but ſay that the felon was mad and killed his fellow, and taken and put in bonds by the men of the hoſpital, and he died in that heat of infirmity.

In this alſo judgment was given for the dean and chapter.

For the articles of the dean and chapter againſt the mayor and citizens they find,

That the men of the dean and chapter and their tenants ought to be free of toll, murage and ſtallage, both by the charters of the kings of *England*, and by the confirmation of *Henry* III.

For paving, they ſay that the dean and every canon, and every tenant of St. *Peter* ought to pave before their doors when the city is to be paved.

And judgment was given in both theſe, and that the dean and canons and their men hereafter ſhould make the paving aforeſaid in form aforeſaid; and the mayor and citizens were as to this *ſine die*, and the dean and chapter in mercy.

That the dean and chapter ought to have their free court, with *toll* and **theam, ſac, ſoc ingfangtheff and outfangtheff** within the time of pleading and without, of all the tenants of St. *Peter*, ſo that out of that court they ought not to be impleaded unleſs they will ſubmit to it *gratis*.

And judgment was given accordingly.

That the mayor and bayliffs did not make any publick proclamation under the pain of impriſonment that none of the city or ſuburbs ſhould anſwer before the dean and chapter of any

any pleas as the dean and chapter have alledged. But they gave warning that none of the city or ſuburbs ſhould go to anſwer before them for any thing but plea teſtamentary or matrimonial.

Therefore judgment was given that the mayor and citizens be *ſine die*, and the dean and chapter in mercy.

That no vicar or clerk of the church of St. *Peter* ſhall anſwer to any matter of the court of the city, but only of ſuch things and poſſeſſions as concern the liberty of the city, and of perſonal treſpaſſes within the city done without the fee of St. *Peter*; and if any be attached to anſwer before the mayor and bailiffs in the court of the city, if the dean and chapter or any on their behalf ſhall come into the court of the city and demand their court of ſuch vicars and clerks they ought to have it.

Judgment was given accordingly.

They ſay that the mayor and citizens, *die Martii* xxi. *prex. ante Paſch. floridum* laſt paſt, came into the lands of St. *Peter* in the ſuburbs of the city, and there did take up the meaſures, gallons, and ells or yards and carried them away by force; but they broke no doors, nor took away any other goods.

Judgment was that the mayor ſhould be in mercy for the treſpaſs, and the dean and chapter in mercy as to the complaint of breaking the doors and taking away other goods.

For the article by which the dean and chapter claim the ſtandard, they ſay that the dean and chapter have anciently received meaſures in their own lands from the mayor and bayliffs until king *Henry* III. did by his marſhal deliver a ſtandard unto the dean and chapter, and all things belonging to a ſtandard, becauſe that in the charters of ancient kings it was contained that the lands of the canons is the proper table of St. *Peter*, and that the canons of the church ſhould in their houſes and lands have all liberties, honours and cuſtoms as the kings had in their lands. And they ſay that in the time of the king that now is, the marſhals of the king came to *York*, and would have delivered the ſtandard to the dean and chapter but the mayor and citizens would not permit them; and ſo by this impediment they are not in ſeiſin of the ſtandard, although they were in ſeiſin thereof in the time of king *Henry* III. and long before.

Therefore this article was reſpited to another day, and in the mean time to ſpeak with the king.

For the article whereby the dean and chapter claim return of writs, they ſay they have ſuch return, and to levy the king's debts in their lands. And if the mayor and bailiffs have entered their lands to levy theſe debts, it was by force and **eſkeknm** and in time of war. But in regard it is not contained in any of their charters, nor in the confirmation of king *Henry* III. that they may by their own hands levy the king's debts, nor anſwer for them to the exchequer, but only that they ſhall have return of writs.

Therefore this article was alſo reſpited.

For the article of excommunicating *John Maleherb* and *Hugh Payte* by the dean and chapter for taking of a reaper at *Acombe*, they ſay they were excommunicated for that caption. But it does not appear to them whether the reaper was taken within the church-yard or without.

Therefore it was reſpited for a further enquiry.

It was enquired of theſe jurors, that if the liberties granted to the dean and chapter and to the abbot of St. *Mary*'s ſhould all be allowed, if the citizens would be able to pay their fee-farm rent to the king?

The anſwer was, they were able and did know that when they took the farm.

I have mentioned theſe things, ſays ſir *Thomas*, that ye may ſee the vogue and humour of thoſe times; their blind devotion to the church, and their blindneſs in juſtice. The ſword of the city muſt be lodged under the table of St. *Peter*, adds he, and that poor ſword was afterwards prohibited to be carried with the point upwards in St. *Peter*'s church. This laſt ſtroke with the ſword is aimed at king *Charles* the firſt, who by his letters mandatory to the lord-mayor, *&c.* firſt prohibited the bearing of the enſigns of authority, at all, in the church (*t*). And when they were allowed to enter, it was with the point of the ſword debaſed, and the mace unſhouldered.

But that **Holy Church** may not aſſume to itſelf unlimited favours in former days, I here give a tranſlation from a record in the tower of *London*, of a ſevere mandate ſent to the dean and chapter of *York* from king *Henry* III. in relation to their meddling too much in temporals in thoſe days; and making uſe of the churches thunder (excommunications) to ſerve their own purpoſes. The mandate is the moſt extraordinary of any thing I ever met with of that kind; the original *Latin* of it may be found in the *addenda* (*u*).

(*t*) A copy of this mandate, or order, which I had by [illegible]vour of the preſent dean may be ſeen in the *appendix*.

(*u*) *Clauſ.* 39 *Hen.* III. *m.* 17. *dorſo. intitul. De querela civium* Ebor. *verſus archiep.* Ebor. *errore pro verſus decan. et cap.* Ebor.

" The

5

"The king to the dean and chapter of St. *Peter's* of *York*, greeting; from the complaints of the mayor and citizens of our city of *York* we frequently understand, that you usurp to yourselves pleas of layick fees and of chattels and debts, which are not of testament or matrimony, and other rights and liberties in the said city, to our mayor and bayliffs of the said city belonging; neither do you permit the keepers of our measures in the said city, to try measures in the grounds which you say be yours, nor them with our seal to sign, but with a counterfeit seal you cause them to be signed; likewise you do not permit the said citizens to take the (*x*) distresses of your men for their debts, according to the tenure of our charter, which thereupon they have, whereby neither your men nor others are excepted; likewise you appropriate to yourselves our men, and all their pleas you hold in your court by force of excommunication by reason of their lands wherein they reside; neither do you permit our bailiffs of the said city to enter the lands which you say be yours, although they are not, our debts to levy, nor thieves nor malefactors to take and arrest, but if your lands without your licence they enter, and endeavour to preserve themselves through our right from the said grievances, forthwith you cause sentence of excommunication, without our assent of amends to be made, to be proclaimed against them; nor the same, upon any of our commands, you take care to discharge, unless oath be made for obeying the ecclesiastical rights. *Seeing therefore*, that the premisses happen now to be no little prejudice to our rights, and the great injuring of our royal dignity, and that you have been often required by our letters that you should desist from the like exactions and usurpations; we admonish, exhort and command you again, to the end that the mayor and bayliffs and citizens aforesaid, we permitting them peaceably to enjoy the rights and liberties before used in the said city, from henceforth you attempt nothing which may happen to the prejudice of our rights; and the sentence of excommunication, if any of you have caused to be proclaimed through the occasion aforesaid against the bailiffs and citizens aforesaid, you forthwith without delay cause to be recalled; any longer to forbear we shall not, as indeed we ought not, but of so great excess and injuries to us offerred, which not only redounds to our disinheritance, but also to our most grievous disgrace and reproach, a heavy revenge, as we ought, we shall surely take. DEAN *and* CHAPTER.

"We also enjoin the mayor and bailiffs aforesaid, that our rights and liberties uninjured they preserve, and firmly on our side and behalf cause to be inhibited that not any one of the said city appear before you in your court, to answer for any matters belonging to our crown and dignity.

Witness the KING.

At Westminster, 19 die Febr.

"In like manner the abbot of St. *Mary's* of *York*, and the prior of the *Holy Trinity* of *York*, and the master of the hospital of St. *Leonard* of *York* were commanded; excepting that in these letters there be no mention of the sentence of excommunication brought upon the mayor, citizens and bailiffs of the said city; nor that the said abbot, prior and master shall be otherwise required by the king's letters to desist from the like exactions.

Witness as above.

The deanery of *York* was first instituted by *Thomas*, the first of that name, archbishop of this see. He is the chiefest officer in the church, next the archbishop, and in the chapter the greatest of all. In the archbishop's absence he ought to have the middle place in all processionals of the church. And purely, by virtue of his joint authority, makes his chapter to gain or lose in matters of law; which otherways, if it had not his proper concurrence, would be invalid. DEAN *of* YORK.

The dean is elected by the chapter, invested by a gold ring, and installed by the precentor of the church. According to which, in the year 1194, pope *Celestine* III. ended that controversy which arose betwixt *Geofry* archbishop and his chapter, about the right of appointing a new dean. It seems the chapter having then elected one, the archbishop refused to confirm him; and nominated another to the place. Alledging that the deanry belonged to his donation. The chapter hereupon appealed to the pope; and sent their proxies to negotiate the affair; where, after a full hearing before the holy father and his college of cardinals the archbishop's collation was cassated and made void. And, upon the new dean's resignation of that dignity into his hands, he by his apostolical authority, regranted him the said deanry; confirming to the canons, or chapter of *York*, for the future their right of electing their dean and his investiture by a gold ring.

It belongs to the office of the dean, by the chapter's consent, to make convocations; to admit persons presented to dignities or prebends; to invest them by the book and bread; and to command the precentor to install them. *The dean's office.*

(*x*) The *latin* word made use of here is *namia*; which comes from the *Saxon* Næme, *captio*, *captura*, a taking or siezing on, whence our nimming, which is now stealing. See *Somner's Sax.* dict. *Spelman's* glossary.

Dean *of* York. *In the choir anciently.*

In the choir it was his office anciently, if present, to say the confession at the *prime* and *completorie*; with *fidelium* at the end. So likewise in the chapter. On solemn and principal days, he, having first received the accustomary benediction, ought in his own stall to read the *nine lections* at *mattins*. Also to celebrate mass, having three deacons and as many subdeacons to administer to him. At vespers and mattins, his own proper vicar, habited in a silk cope, shall bring him his cope to his stall; who shall be ushered in by two torch bearers while the fifth psalm is singing. And then the dean shall read his chapter and his prayers. The dean shall begin the *antiphony super P*, the *magnificat* and *benedictus*; which being sung, the clerk of the vestry, accompanied by the torch and censer-bearers, with their censers full of hot coals, shall carry and lay the incense on the coals before the dean, and say the benediction. Then the rector of the choir shall begin to intonize, and the dean, ushered up by the torch and censer-bearers, shall advance, through the midst of the choir, to the altar; where he shall perform the sanctuary. The rector of the choir, together with all the majors and minors thereof, shall rise up from their seats and turn their faces towards the dean, both at his going to the altar and coming back. But on grand solemnities he is bound to begin the last *antiphony* at the great *procession*.

To the dean's office did also belong the hallowing the candles on the feast of *Purification*, sprinkle the ashes on *Ash-wednesday*, and give the absolution, if present. Also on *Palm-sunday* he did hallow the palms, and begin the *ave rex noster* before the cross. And on that day, either by himself or some other, did preach a sermon to the people. Likewise on *Die caenae*, or *Maunday-thursday*, he used to receive the penitents; and after dinner, by the assistance of other canons, did wash the feet of the poor, and then make the distribution of alms amongst them; which was always used to be done at the charge of the sacrist of the chapel. And when that was ended, the dean with two of the majors of the church did go and wash the altars. But in one of the four grand days, if the archbishop, was present, he was obliged to perform the said service.

An ancient custom.

By an ancient custom of this church, the dean of it was obliged for ever to feed or relieve, at his deanry, ten poor people daily. This was for the soul of good queen *Maud*; and for which cause he had the churches of *Killum*, *Pickering* and *Pocklington* annexed to his deanry (y).

Revenues.

The ancient revenues of the deanry amounted, according to Mr. *Torre*, to the yearly rent of 373*l.* 6*s.* 8*d.* I shall not particularize the several demises from it, which I find was first begun by *Bryan Higden* dean, 23 *Hen.* VIII; the aforesaid writer has summed up the rents of the deanry as follows:

	l.	*s.*	*d.*
Killum, ——	51	12	00
Pickering, ——	100	00	00
Pocklington, &c.	119	00	09
Kilnwyck, —	6	00	00
	276	12	09

Besides the dean's part of the residentiary money.

The valuation of the deanry of *York* in the king's books is ——	308	10	7½
Tenths ——	30	17	0¾
Procurations ——	5	00	0
Subsidies ——	27	08	0

Anno 1265, 49 *Hen.* III. the dean of *York* had a summons to parliament by writ, as the bishops, abbots and barons had; but I do not find any more of them so called. (z).

A CATALOGUE of the DEANS of York.

Year of creation.	*DEANS.*	*VACATIONS.*
	Mr. *Hugo*	
	Will. de Sancta Barbara	For the bishoprick of *Durham*.
1142	*Rob. de Gant*	By death.
11..	*Rob. de Botevillin*	
1186	*Hubert Walker*, cl.	For the bishoprick of *Sarum*.
1189	*Henry Marshal*	For the bishoprick of *Exeter*.
1191	Mr. *Symon de Apulia*	For the bishoprick of *Exeter*.
1206	Mr. *Hamo*	
12..	*Roger de Insula*	
12..	*Galf. de Norwico*	

(y) This account is all taken from Mr. *Torre*, *p.* 535. who has collected it from the *Monast. Reg. mag. alb.* and other records.

(z) *Selden*'s titles of honour, *p.* 783. *Anno reg. regis* Johan. 2. *Capella de* Barnaby *concess. decano* Ebor. *Cart. num.* 60. *Rectoria de* Stillingfleet *concess. decano* Ebor. &c. 19 Jac. I. *pars* 2. *num.* 20.

Year

DEANS *of* YORK.

Year of creation.	*DEANS.*	*VACATIONS.*
12..	*Fulco Baſſett*	For the biſhoprick of *London.*
1244	Mr. *Willielmus*	
124.	*Walter de Kyrkham*	
12..	*Sewall de Bovile*	For the archbiſhoprick of *York.*
1256	*Godfrey de Ludham*	For the ſame.
1258	*Roger de Holderneſs*	
1264	*Will. de Langton* . .	By death.
1279	*Rob. de Scardeburgh*	By death.
1290	*Hen. de Newark*	Archbiſhop.
1298	*Will. de Hamelton*	
1309	*Reginald de la Goth*, cardinalis	By death.
1310	*Will. de Pykering*	By death.
1312	*Rob. de Pykering*	By death.
1332	*Will. de Colby*	By death.
1333	*Will. de la Zouch*	Archbiſhop.
1347	*Phil. de Weſton*	
	Dom. *Tailerand*, ep. *Alban.*	By death.
1366	Dom. *Joh. Anglicus*, cardinalis	Deprived.
1381	Dom. *Adam (a) Eaſton*, cardinalis	Deprived.
1385	Mr. *Edm. de Strafford*, LL. D.	
	Roger Walden	For the archbiſhoprick of *Canterbury.*
1392	*Rich. Clyfford*, L. B.	For the biſhoprick of *Worceſter.*
1401	*Tho. Langley*, preſb.	For the biſhoprick of *Durham.*
1407	*John Prophete*	By death.
1416	*Tho. Polton*, L. B.	
1421	*Will. Grey*, L. D.	Biſhoprick of *London.*
1426	*Rob. Gilbert*, S. T. P.	Biſhoprick of *London.*
1437	*Will. Felter*, Dec. Dr.	By death.
1454	*Rich. Andrews*, LL. D.	By death.
1477	*Rob. Bothe*, LL. D.	By death.
1488	*Chriſt. Urſwyke*, Dec. Dr.	Reſigned.
1494	*Will. Sheffield*, Dec. Dr.	By death.
1496	*Geffry Blythe*, S. T. B.	Biſhoprick of *Coventry.*
1503	*Chriſt. Baynbrigge*, LL. D.	Archbiſhoprick of *York.*
1507	*James Harrington*, preſb.	By death.
1512	*Thomas Wolſie*, S. T. D.	For the biſhoprick of *Lincoln.*
1514	*John Younge*, Leg. D.	By death.
1516	*Brian Higden*, Leg. D.	By death.
1539	*Rich. Layton*, Leg. D.	By death.
1544	*Nich. Wotton*, L. D.	By death.
1567	*Math. Hutton*, S. T. B.	Biſhoprick of *Durham.*
1589	*John Thornburgh*, S. T. P.	Biſhoprick of *Worceſter.*
1617	*George Meriton*, S. T. P.	By death.
1624	*John Scott*, S. T. P.	
1660	*Rich. Marſh*	By death.
1663	*Will. Sancroft*, S. T. P.	Reſigned.
1664	*Rob. Hitch*, S. T. P.	By death.
1676	*Tobias Wickam*, S. T. P.	By death.
	Thomas Gale, S. T. P.	By death.
1702	*Henry Finch*, A. M.	By death.
1728	*Rich. Oſbaldeſton*, S. T. P.	

I have copied exactly Mr. *Torre*'s catalogue of our deans, becauſe his authorities are unqueſtionable. But Mr. *Willis (b)* has added to the number, and introduces *Aldred*, and another *Hugh*, betwixt the firſt and *William de St. Barbara*. He alſo mentions one *William* archdeacon of *Nottingham*, and *Maugerius* whom *Leland* ſays was made biſhop of *Worceſter* from this dignity; theſe he places betwixt *Simon de Apulia* and *Hamo*, about the latter end of the eleventh century. Our church records not riſing ſo high, we cannot contradict this, and indeed there are nothing but old hiſtorians and ancient charters, to whoſe grants theſe principal dignitaries were uſually witneſſes, to collect from in thoſe times. I myſelf have met with the name of one *Thomas* dean of *York*, as a witneſs to a grant of ſome tenements

(a) Mr. *Torre* calls this man only *Adam* card. but I find in the *Fœd. Ang. tom.* VII. p. that his name was *Adam* *Eaſton*.

(b) Survey of cathedrals. *London* 1727.

in

4

Dean of York. in *York*, to the abby of *Fountains*; but where to place him I know not, the deed bearing no date, though 'tis unquestionably of great antiquity (*c*).

These are all the names of the deans of *York*, from the first institution down to the present, that are to be met with in Mr. *Torre*'s, *le Neve*'s, or Mr. *Willis*'s catalogues. I shall next subjoin a short account of these dignitaries, many of whom have been men of great rank in their time, and have rose from this preferment to some of the first places in church and state.

Hugh. In the year 1090. *Hugo* or *Hugh*, was consecrated first dean of *York*. This man was one of those who was present at the consecration of *Anselm* into the see of *Canterbury* by *Thomas* archbishop of *York*; which solemnity happened *December* 4, 1093. And in the year 1108. when king *Henry* I. had thoughts only to prefer *Thomas* II. unto the see of *London*; yet, at the request of this dean *Hugh*, he promoted the said *Thomas* unto the archbishoprick of *York*. And afterwards *Hugh* was so great a stickler in that archbishop's affairs, that being by him employed to the king in *Normandy*, he procured his royal letters to the pope, on his said master's behalf; whereby he obtained for him the pall, with a commission from his holiness to consecrate *Thomas* in the church of St. *Paul London*; in order to elude the subjection to *Canterbury* (*d*).

In the reign of this *Henry*, when *Thurstan*, successor to *Thomas*, founded the nunnery of St. *Clements York*, this dean *Hugo* was primary witness to the foundation charter (*e*).

In his latter days he quitted his deanry and retired to *Fountains* abbey, then newly erected, where he sickned and died. Being a very wealthy man, the riches he brought along with him contributed very much to relieve the necessities of that house then in great want and distress (*f*).

William de St. Barbara. *William de S. Barbara* was elected next, says Mr. *Torre*, to this deanry of *York*. In the year 1138. when *Thurstan* archbishop of *York* was old and infirm, he directed this his dean *William* to interdict and establish ecclesiastical laws as occasion should require (*g*).

In the year 1143. this *William de S. Barbara* was for his learning, gravity, prudence and honesty, consecrated bishop of *Durham*; which see he governed nine years and died *November* 15, 1153 (*h*).

Robert de Gant. *Robert de Gant* succeeded next to this deanry; he was king *Stephen*'s chancellor, and was made dean of *York* in the year 1144. This dean with *Hugh* the treasurer, and *Osbert* the archdeacon, although they had been preferred to their dignities by *William* archbishop, since called St. *William*, yet when he was removed from his archiepiscopal function, in the year 1148; they consented to the election of one *Hillary* the pope's clerk to the chair; though on the other side the greatest part of the chapter had elected *Henry Murdac* thereunto. This *Robert*, with his partners, are not a little suspected by historians, to have a hand in poisoning their prelate in the sacramental cup.

Robert II. *Robert* II. or *de Boutvellein*, was the next in succession to this deanry. This man, in the presence of archbishop *Roger*, obtained the king's letters testimonial, dated at *Roan*, to be owned for his chaplain, although he had neither before made his fealty to his mother *Maud* the empress nor to himself; and that he did not now require it at his hands, and should permit none to injure him either in his body or goods (*i*).

This dean obtained from *Robert de Percy* the grant of the church of *Kilnwyck* to be appropriated to him and his chapter for ever (*k*). In the year 1186. this *Robert de Boutvillin* dean of *York* died and was succeeded by (*l*)

HubertWalter. *Hubert Walter*, who had it by the king's gift. In the year 1189. this dean opposed the election of *Geoffry* archbishop to this see of *York*, and appealed to *Rome* against it. Whereupon the ecclesiastical jurisdiction of this see returned into the hands of himself, being dean, and the chapter of *York* (*m*).

Hubertus, *vocat.* Eboracensis *eccl. decanus*, founded the abbey of *West-Dereham* in *Norfolk*; where he was born (*n*). In the year 1189. he was consecrated bishop of *Sarum*; and attended *Richard* I. in his famous expedition to the holy land (*o*). Afterwards archbishop of *Canterbury*.

Henry Marshal. *Henry Marshall*, brother to *William* earl *Marshall*, archdeacon of *Stafford*, was by the king preferred to the deanry of the church of *York*; then vacant by the promotion of *Hubert Walter*, last dean, to the bishoprick of *Sarum*. But when he came to his church he found none to install him into his new dignity, the clergy alledging that none but the archbishop himself could put him into the dean's stall. However *Hamo*, then precentor

(*c*) In the original register of *Fountains*. See the *appendix*. In a charter made to *Ranulf de Glanvile* by *Henry* II. but without date, *T. H. decano Eboracensi* is a witness to it. *Maddox*'s exchequer p. 35. y.

(*d*) T. Stubbs *inter x script.*

(*e*) *Monast. Ang.* 1. 510.

(*f*) *Idem* 742.

(*g*) *Sim. Dunelm.*

(*h*) Rog. Hoveden. Rich. Hagulst. Sim. Dunelm. *historiæ istius ecclesiæ, nolentemque et maxime reluctantem ad klerum traxerunt. Edit.* Bedford *p.* 274.

(*i*) Torre *ex reg. albo* 84.

(*k*) *Monast. Ang.* vol. III. *p.* 150.

(*l*) R. *Hoveden.*

(*m*) *Idem.*

(*n*) *Monast. Ang.* vol. II. *p.* 624.

(*o*) R. *Hoveden, Ralph de Diceto, Goodwin*'s bishops.

of

of the church, sent him to the stall of the prebend which the king had also given him. Deans *of* In *October* following when *Geffry* elect archbishop of *York* came to his church, and was York. received with great procession, he denied to install him also, till such time as his own election was confirmed by the pope. This and some other affairs brought on the king's displeasure against the archbishop, as may be seen in his life; and *Henry* the dean joined with others of the church, in an appeal to *Rome*, against the election of the said *Geffry* to the see. But some time after, the prelate being reconciled to the king, the dean, and those who sided with him, released their appeals against him; and then the archbishop confirmed him in his deanry, and promised to put his archiepiscopal seal to it after his consecration *(o)*.

But on the vigil of *epiphany*, after, a greater difference arose betwixt them; for when the said *Geffry* elect, was coming to church to hear vespers, in a solemn manner, this dean *Henry* with *Buchard* the treasurer would not tarry for him, but began the same before he got into the choir, being attended by the precentor and the canons. The elect being come into the church he was angry at them and commanded them to be silent; but they, in contradiction to him, bad their choir go on, which at the command of the elect and precentor was silent. Then the elect began again the vespers, and the treasurer ordered all the candles to be put out, which being done accordingly, and the vespers at an end, the elect complained to God, the clergy and people of this injury done him; and suspended them and their church from celebration of divine offices till they made him satisfaction.

The next day, being the feast of *Epiphany*, all the citizens came to the cathedral to hear divine service, as usual; and the elect himself and the said dean and treasurer were in the choir, together with the canons of the church to make peace between them. But the dean and treasurer would make the elect no satisfaction for their transgression, but spoke high words against him. Whereupon the people were so provoked, that they would have faln upon them, but the elect would not permit it. But they were both so frightned that they fled for it, the one to St. *William*'s tomb, for sanctuary, and the other to his deanry. The elect excommunicated them both and divine service ceased in the cathedral *(p)*.

In the year 1191, this dean *Henry* was, by the king's gift, elected and consecrated bishop of *Exeter*; where having sat twelve years he died and was buried in that church *(q)*.

Peter brother to the archbishop by fair *Rosamond* his mother, had this deanry then given him by the king, which was vacant by the promotion of *Henry Marshall* last dean to the bishoprick of *Exeter*. But because that the said *Peter* was then at *Paris*, the king desired the archbishop to confer the said deanry on *John* provost of *Doway*, but the prelate, through the advice of his friends, to quit himself of the king's request conferred the deanry on his clerk *Simon de Apulia*.

Afterwards the archbishop would have contradicted his act, telling *Simon* that he had Simon de not given it to him, but in custody to the use of *Peter* his brother; yet the canons of Apulia. *York*, expresly against the mind of the archbishop, unanimously elected the said *Simon* to the deanry. The prelate on the other hand bestowed the dignity on one sir *Philip* the king's clerk and his familiar friend; from whence arose great discords betwixt the metropolitan and his canons.

Another accident aggravated this matter; it seems the archbishop had requested them to give the fourth part of their revenues towards the king's redemption, then prisoner in *Germany*. But they refusing and alledging the same to be a subversion of the liberties of the church, the archbishop hereupon declared the deanry vacant, and said the donation thereof belonged to him as archbishop, the chapter affirming the election thereunto was their right, the prelate appealed to the pope and the king for justice. Notwithstanding this the chapter proceeded in their election of *Simon* to the deanry, who immediately after set out to find the king in *Germany*. The archbishop was not backward in the affair but sent his advocates over to the pope to prosecute his appeal; who were to make *Germany* their way and first acquaint the king with the business. *Richard*, having heard the matter, inhibited both parties from going to *Rome* at all; proposing to make peace betwixt them himself as soon as possible. In the interim the canons of *York*, suspended their church from celebration of divine offices and ringing of bells, making bare their altars, and set a lock upon the archbishop's stall in the choir; and also another in the passage door of his palace to the church *(r)*.

In *Christmas*, 1194, the archbishop came to *York*, and finding the church empty, he appointed ministers in it, who should solemnly serve therein, as they ought to do; till such time as the canons and their chaplains might be restored by lay-power and force. But the four majors of the church, who had been excommunicated by the archbishop, went over to the king, then set at liberty, and, having obtained his liberty passed on to *Rome*, where they begged the pope to determine their cause, *viz.* whether the donation of the deanry belonged to the archbishop, or the election to the chapter? And, saving the right

(o) *John Brompton*, R. *Hoveden.* (q) R. *Hoveden*, *Goodwin.*
(p) R. *Hoveden.* ——— *tantae ne animis celestibus irae.* (r) R. *Hoveden.*

of

Deans of York.

of the archbishop and the chapter collated and confirmed the said *Simon* and invested him with a gold ring.

During this the canons of *York* complained of their archbishop to the archbishop of *Canterbury*, then the king's justiciary; who sent sir *Roger Bygod* and other commissioners to hear and determine the controversy. Who caused the canons to be placed into their stalls again out of which the archbishop had put them.

A little before *Michaelmas* that year, the four principal masters of the church, whereof this dean *Simon* was one, arrived from *Rome*. And brought with them letters of absolution, as well from their excommunication as interdict; which were read and denounced by the bishop of *Durham* in the great church at *York*, on *Michaelmas* day, with celebration of mass. At their approaching the city, there went out to meet them the clergy and citizens, in great numbers, and when the new dean came to his mother church, he was received, by the canons, with solemn procession.

In the year 1196, the king sent for the dean and canons of *York* to come to him into *Normandy*, that he might reconcile them to the archbishop, who was then with him. But the prelate thought fit to depart from thence and was gone to *Rome* before they arrived. Nor could he get the dean and chapter to stand to any award. However in the next reign, and the first year of it, both the archbishop, dean, &c. promised before *Peter de Capua* cardinal, the pope's legate to stand to the award of *Hugh* bishop, and *Roger* dean of *Lincoln*. But not long after they all appeared at *Westminster* before *Herbert* bishop of *Sarum* and *Alain* abbot of *Teukesbury*, the pope's delegates on this account, who agreed them so far, that they should all amongst themselves make satisfaction for all controversies to the chapter of *York* (r).

In the year 1202, this dean *Simon* obtained for his church, from the prior and canons of St. *Andrew* in *Fishergate*, a piece of ground at the west end of the cathedral.

Some time after he was consecrated bishop of *Exeter*, where having sat eighteen years he died and was buried in that church (s).

Hamo.

Hamo . . . . . was next preferred to this deanry then vacant by the promotion of the last. All we can find of him is, that he was a witness to a charter made by the abbot of *Fountains* to *Walter* archbishop of *York*, of the church of *Kyrkeby-Useburne*, *dat. kal. Martii* 1217 (t).

Roger de Insula.

Roger de Insula, or *L'isle*, was next elected to this deanry of *York*.

In the year 1221, he, by the consent of his chapter, made the old statutes of residentiaries in the church (u).

And, *anno* 1226, this dean *Roger* was one of the chief witnesses to *William de Percy*'s charter, granting the church of *Topcliffe* to the use of the fabrick of the cathedral (x).

Geffry de Norwich.

In the year 1235, *Geffry de Norwich*, precentor of this church, was elected and confirmed into the deanry of *York*. All we can meet with about him is that he, being dean, settled lands for the maintenance of a chantry, ordained for himself, at the altar of St. *Mary Magdalene* in the vaults of the *Minster* (y).

Fulk Basset.

Fulco Basset, second son to *Alain* lord *Basset* of *Wycombe*, was next elected to this deanry of *York anno* 1240.

In the same year, he, being then dean, together with his chapter, consented to the ordination of the vicaridges of *Shereburn* and *Fenton* (z).

Anno 1241, he was primary witness to archbishop *Grey*'s charter of settlement of the manor of *Bishop-thorp* (a).

Anno 1244, he was consecrated bishop of *London*; and the year after he became heir of his house, his elder brother dying without issue. And in 1258. he died at *London* of the plague, and was interred in St. *Paul*'s cathedral (b).

William.

In the year 1244, one *William* . . . . succeeded to this deanry. Our records mention no more of him than this, that in the same year this *William*, with his chapter granted institution to the vicaridge of *Wagben* (c).

Walter de Kyrkham.

Walter de Kyrkham occurs next as dean of *York*. Of whom there is this notice, that *Walter de Kyrkham*, *dec. Ebor.* consented to the donation of the church of *Bothelston* to the archdeaconry of *Richmond* (d).

Sewal de Bovile.

Sewal de Bovile was next elected. And in the year 1252, he, being then dean, obtained the archbishop's ordinations of the vicaridges of his deanry, *Pocklington*, *Pickering* and *Kilum* (e).

(r) All this affair is translated from *Hoveden*, but he is much more particular in it. *Vide* Hoveden *p.* 416. *&c.*

(s) *Wharton*'s annal. *Wigorn.*

(t) Torre *ex reg. albo.*

(u) *Monast. Ang.* vol. III. p. 165.

(x) Torre *p.* 532. *ex reg. albo Mon. Ang.* vol. I. p. 151.

(y) Torre *p. eadem.*

(z) *Idem ex reg. albo.*

(a) *Monast Ang.* vol. III. 157.

(b) *Dug. Bar. Goodwin.*

(c) *Torre* p. 533.

(d) *Idem.*

(e) *Idem.*

Four

Four years after he succeeded *Walter Grey* in the archbishoprick of *York*. Where see more of him. DEANS *of* YORK.

Godfrey de Ludham, alias *Keinton*, was elected in the year 1256. to this deanry, then vacant by the promotion of *Sewal* to the see. The pope, however, put in a bar to this man's claim, and bestowed the dignity on one *Jordan* an *Italian*; who clandestinely took possession of the dean's stall. But at length this stranger, being made very uneasy in his place by the archbishop, resigned it, and accepted of a pension of one hundred marks a year *(f)*. After two years enjoyment of his office *Godfrey*, upon the death of *Sewal*, was promoted to the archbishoprick and so succeeded him in both. Godfrey de Ludham.

Roger de Holderness, vel *Skeffings*, clerk of St. *Albans* occurs next by the authority of *M. Paris*, in the year 1258. But we have no other testimony of it. Roger de Holderness.

William de Langton was elected to this deanry *anno* 1263, says Mr. *Torre*, who finds him a witness that year and subscribing first, as dean, to the ordination of a chantry in the cathedral. The next year he was elected archbishop, but had his election cassated by the pope. He continued dean till the year 1279, when he died and was buried in the cathedral near the clock-house. His tomb, finely inlayed with brass, and gilt with gold, stood entire till the rebellion; when sacrilegious hands defaced and broke it to pieces. The miserable remains are yet to be seen in the choir, and his epitaph, the oldest in the church, very legible. See the plate. William de Langton.

On *Langton*'s death *Robert de Scardeburgh* archdeacon of the east riding was elected and admitted dean; for on *Monday* after the feast of *All-saints*, *anno* 1279, he had his election, says Mr. *Torre*, confirmed to him. He died in the year 1290, as the same author writes, for administration of his goods was then granted to his executors *(g)*. Robert de Scardeburg.

Henry Newark, archdeacon of *Richmond*, was next elected, confirmed and installed into this deanry, on the feast of St. *Barnabas* in the year 1290. Six years after he was elected into this archiepiscopal see; where you may find more of him. Henry de Newark.

After a vacancy of four years *William de Hamelton*, archdeacon of *York*, was elected dean. It seems the pope had bestowed it on an *Italian* cardinal; but he, at last, resigning this *William* was confirmed. *September* 3, 1300. William de Hamelton.

This man being parson of the church of *Brayton* appropriated the same to his own archdeaconry of *York*. He also *anno* 1302, gave certain lands for the maintenance of his new founded chantry in the church of *Brayton*, for him and his successors, deans of *York*. As likewise the church of *Broddesworth* for the same use *(h)*.

January 16, 1305. 32 *Edward* I. This *William de Hamelton* had the great seal delivered to him as lord chancellor of *England* *(i)*.

He continued dean of this church till the year 1314, when he dyed, as Mr. *Torre* writes, in the king's debt. The royal precept about it was directed to the dean and chapter and bears date *May* 6, 1314. *an. reg. Ed.* II. 7.

Anno 1300. *Reginald de Gote*, Mr. *Willis* calls him *Reymond de la Goth*, *cardinalis diaconus*, was next promoted to this deanry of *York* by the pope's authority I suppose; but he did not enjoy it long, for the next year he died and was succeeded by Regidald de Gote.

William Pickering, archdeacon of *Nottingham*, he lived but two years in his dignity when he died, and William Pickering.

Robert Pickering, his brother, professor of the civil law, was elected and installed into it. This dean founded the hospital of St. *Mary* in *Bootham*, and gave the patronage thereof to his successors for ever. He lived to the year 1332, when Robert Pickering.

William de Colby succeeded by the pope's provisional bull, and he was inducted accordingly. On *Friday* after the feast of St. *Leonard*, *anno* 1333, this *William de Colby* made his will, gave his soul to God Almighty, St. *Mary* and *All-saints*, and his body to be buried in the church of St. *Peter Ebor.* William de Colby.

The same year, 1333, *William de la Zouch* succeeded to the deanry. In the year 1340, he was elected by the canons archbishop. Where see more of him. William de la Zouch.

Here is a gap of a considerable space, for no successor to the last occurs till the year 1347, when *Philip de Weston*, Mr. *Torre* writes, exhibited, by his proxy, the king's letters on his behalf to be elected to this deanry of *York*. And *August* 24. that year he was admitted dean both by the king's and archbishop's letters. What year he died we know not, but the next that occurs is Philip de Weston.

Talyrandos de Petagoricis cardinal, whom Mr. *Willis* says, the pope thrust into this deanry, and outed *Weston*. The same author adds, that he enjoyed it till he died, which happened in the year 1366, and then Talyrand de Patagoricis.

Johannes Anglicus sanct. Roman. ecc. presb. cardinalis, by virtue of the pope's letters, was by proxy admitted to this deanry. He was on *May* 1, 1381. deprived by the pope, and Johannes Anglicus.

(f) Goodwin *de praesul.*
(g) *Torre* p. 555.
(h) *Idem.*
(i) To save the reader and my self any more trouble in notes, I shall tell him at once that the next accounts are taken wholly from Mr. *Torre*'s and Mr. *Willis*'s authorities.

Adam,

DEANS of YORK. Adam Easton. *Adam*, called in the *Foed. Ang. Easton*, S. *Ceciliae presb. card.* was admitted in his place. He was likewise deprived, which made way for

Edmund de Strafford. *Edmond de Strafford*, doctor of laws and canon of *Lincoln* to be elected and confirmed to this deanry. *Anno* 1395, he was made bishop of *Exeter*.

Roger Walden *Roger Walden*, treasurer of *Callais*, was next preferred to this deanry, *anno* 1395, says *Willis*; he is said to have rose from a very low degree to be made secretary to king *Richard* II, and in the year 1396. was constituted lord treasurer of *England*. He was afterwards, *viz. anno* 1398, by the pope advanced to the archbishoprick of *Canterbury*.

Richard Clifford. After him came *Richard Clifford* batchelor of laws, he was keeper of the king's privy seal, and by his donation, who at that time had the temporalities of the see in his hands, confirmed dean of *York*. And *June* 20, 1398. he was admitted in proper person by the customary tradition of a book, bread, &c. In the year 1401. he was consecrated bishop of *Worcester*.

Thomas Longley. *Thomas Longley* presb. canon of *York*, having been elected, was by proxy, *January* 25, *anno* 1401. admitted to this deanry; and was invested in proper person *August* 8, 1403. This was a person whom *John* duke of *Lancaster* so much confided in, that he nominated him in his will one of his eighteen executors. He was also one of the executors to the will of *Walter Skirlaw* bishop of *Durham*. In the year 1405, he was constituted lord high chancellor of *England*, and the year after consecrated bishop of *Durham*.

John Prophete *John Prophete*, canon of *York*, on the pope's collation was by proxy *April* 1, 1407, admitted to this deanry, and *March* 23, 1408, he was admitted in proper person.

London, *April* 8, 1416, this *John Prophete* dean of *York*, made his will, proved *May* 4, following, whereby he gave his soul to God, and his body to be buried in the church of *Leighton Buzard*, or in his church of *Ringwood*, if he chanced to die within the province of *Canterbury*; or, if he died in the north, then either to be buried in the cathedral of *York*, or his parochial church of *Pocklington*. In his will also he bequeathed one hundred shillings a piece to his nieces *Elizabeth Deigncourt* and *Margery Edolf* to pray for his soul, and to Mr. *Bryan Fairfax* a silver cup with a cover.

Thomas Polton. *Thomas Polton* presb. succeeds next, *anno* 1416, Mr. *Willis* says, that he was, *anno* 1420, promoted to the see of *Hereford*.

William Grey. *William Grey* LL. D. was next elected and confirmed dean on the last of *May* 1421. In the year 1426. he was made bishop of *London*.

Robert Gilbert. *Robert Gilbert* presb. S. T. P. occurs next in the catalogue. He was warden of *Merton* college *Oxon*, and was elected by the chapter, and confirmed to this deanry *September* 15, 1426. In the year 1436, he was advanced to the bishoprick of *London*; and succeeded by

William Felter. *William Felter*, doctor of decretals, who was admitted dean *March* 4, 1437. He died dean of this place *April* 18, 1451, as appears by his epitaph; which see amongst the, now, lost inscriptions in the middle choir of the cathedral.

Richard Andrew. *Richard Andrew*, doctor of laws, was by the chapter elected, and in his proper person admitted dean *June* .. 1454. On the 6th of *May* 1477, he resigned his deanry and died soon after, and was buried in the south cross of the cathedral, but his epitaph is lost. Mr. *Torre* has given us an abstract of his will proved *November* 5, 1477.

Rob. Bothe. *Robert Bothe*, doctor of laws, succeeded *Andrews* in this deanry. He died in this office *anno* 1487, as appears by his epitaph which was on his grave stone in the south cross of the *Minster*, which see. Mr. *Torre* has also abstracted his will.

Christopher Urstwyk. *Christopher Urstwyk*, doctor of decretals came in upon the death of the former; admitted *May* 25, 1488. This man was employed in many affairs of state, and enjoyed a number of ecclesiastical preferments, which *Newcourt* particularizes. He resigned his deanry of *York*, and was succeeded by

William Sheffield. *William Sheffield*, who was elected and confirmed dean *penult. Maii* 1494; he sat but two years in his office, died and was buried in the south cross of the cathedral. His tomb was laid open, on the removal of the old pavement, where his body had been lain in a stone coffin arrayed in a silken habit, wrought about the borders with texts of scripture in gold letters, and adorned with fringe. Part of the habit, with the soles of his shoes, were taken out and laid in the vestry. This place of his sepulture is marked in the old ichnography of the church, and his epitaph may be seen amongst those in that part of it.

Geoffry Blythe *Geoffry Blythe*, S. T. B. comes next, for he was elected and confirmed dean *March* 22, 1496. In the year 1503, he was made bishop of *Litchfield*.

Christopher Bainbrigg. *Christopher Bainbridge*, doctor of laws had his election next confirmed to the deanry of *York* in the year 1503. But four years after he was promoted to the see of *Durham*, and next to the archbishoprick of *York*.

James Harrington. *James Harrington* presb. was elected and installed to this deanry, *Jan.* 29, 1507, then vacant. He died in *Decem.* 1512. intestate; for administration of his goods were granted by the chapter to

Thomas

DEANS of YORK. **Tho. Wolsey.** *Thomas Wolsey* his successor, who was elected *Feb.* 19. the same year. *Anno* 1514, he was made, from hence, bishop of *Lincoln.*

John Young. *John Young*, LL. D. succeeded, being admitted *May* 15, 1514. He died and was buried in the *Rolls-chapel*, *London*, under a handsome monument bearing this inscription,

Dominus firmamentum meum. Joh. Young, **LL. doctori sacrorum scriniorum, ac hujus domus custodi, decano olim** Ebor. **vita defuncta Ap.** 26, 1516, **sui fideles executores hoc posuerunt.**

Brian Higden. *Brian Higden*, LL. D. occurs next as dean, being admitted *June* 21, 1516. He governed the church several years, and lies buried in the south cross of the cathedral; the place is marked in the old ichnography; the monument is defaced, but a draught of it was preserved with the epitaph; and I refer the reader to the plate of it.

Richard Layton. *Richard Layton*, doctor of laws, was admitted dean on the death of the former, and was admitted in proper person *June* 25, 1539. This man was one of the five persons whom *Cromwell* made general visitor of the monasteries in this kingdom, before their dissolution. This induced him, says Mr. *Willis*, to pawn the jewels of his church, which were redeemed after his death by order of the chapter. He died beyond sea *anno* 1544, where he was employed on some state affairs.

Nicholas Wootton. *Nicholas Wootton*, doctor of laws, dean of *Canterbury*, and the king's ambassador to the emperor, was next admitted to this deanry *August* 7, 1544. For his good services done to the crown, he was so much respected by king *Henry* VIII. that he made him one of the executors to his will; and left him a legacy of three hundred pound. He died in the year 1567, and was buried at *Canterbury*. Having been, at the same time dean of both cathedrals, and doctor of both laws, and privy councellor to king *Henry* VIII. *Edward* VI. queen *Mary* and queen *Elizabeth.*

Matthew Hutton. *Matthew Hutton*, S. T. P. succeeded, and was installed into the office *May* 11, 1567. In the year 1589, he was promoted to the see of *Durham*; and afterwards to *York.*

John Thornborough. *John Thornborough*, S. T. P. comes next, and was admitted *November* 7, 1589. He was afterwards made bishop of *Limerick* in *Ireland*; from thence translated to *Bristol* with liberty to hold this deanry *in commendam*; which he held till his translation to *Worcester*. And then upon his resignation

George Meriton. *George Meriton*, doctor of divinity, succeeded *March* 27, 1617. He died *December* 23, 1624, and lies buried in the south choir of the cathedral, with a plain epitaph on his grave-stone; which see.

John Scot. *John Scot*, S. T. P. was next elected, confirmed and installed to this deanry *Feb.* 3, 1624. How he got this dignity is intimated in *Hatchet*'s life of archbishop *Williams*, who tells us that he died in the *Fleet-prison London*, *anno* 1644. On his death

Richard Marsh. *Richard Marsh*, S. T. P. was, as our writers intimate, nominated, but not regularly presented, to it, till *July* 25, 1660. He was installed *August* 20, following. And dying *October* 23, 1663, he was buried in the south choir of the cathedral, without any monument.

William Sancroft. *William Sancroft*, S. T. P. afterwards archbishop of *Canterbury*, was nominated *June* 23, and installed 26, 1663. He quitted this deanry for that of St. *Paul*'s in *London*, and was succeeded by

Robert Hitch. *Robert Hitch*, who was installed into it *March* 8, 1664. He died *February* 13, 1676, at *Guiseley*, in this county, and was buried in that church. Mr. *Torre* says, this dean left a personal estate of twenty four thousand pound.

Tho. Wickham. *Tobias Wickam*, S. T. P. admitted *March* 1, 1676, and installed the 31*st* of the same month. He died *April* 27, 1697, and was buried in the cathedral behind the high altar, without any monument.

Thomas Gale. *Thomas Gale*, S. T. P. was admitted dean of this church *September* 16, 1697. Of whom and his many learned and useful books see an account in *Collier*'s dictionary. He was a great ornament to this particular church whilst he lived, and was an universal loss to the learned world when he died. The compass of my design will not allow me to run into any further encomiums of this truly great man; whose loss would have been irreparable, did not the father's genius still subsist in the son. When I mention *Roger Gale* esq; the world must know that it is greatly indebted to him for some curious and useful books of his own publishing, and for several notable discoveries in *Roman* antiquities, *&c.* which adorn the works of others. The dean died *April* 8, 1702, and was buried in the cathedral, middle choir, with an epitaph on his grave-stone; which see.

Henry Finch. *Henry Finch*, A. M. brother to the then earl of *Nottingham*, succeeded. He was admitted *May* 22, and installed *June* 13, 1702. He governed the church, very honourably, somewhat more than twenty six years, and died *September* 8, 1728. His further character I leave to the epitaph on his monument.

Richard Osbaldeston. *Richard Osbaldeston*, S. T. P. the present dean, was admitted *November* 8, 1728.

The PRECENTOR.

The dignity of the precentor, or chantor, was founded in this church by archbishop *Thomas* I. in the reign of the conquerour. To his office does belong first,

Office. The installment of every person, who by the dean and chapter is invested into any dignity, canonship, parsonage or office in the church.

2. The government of the choir in such matters as relate to the singing, or musical part of it.

3. On double festivals to order the antiphonies upon the psalms, also in vespers and mattins both on grand or lesser days.

4. To present to the archbishop when he celebrates mass the antiphony, psalms, magnificat, benedicts and gaudies.

5. To officiate in a silken cope on the left hand of the archbishop when he goes to the altar to offer incense, as the dean is to serve on the right.

6. To confer on singing men their places in the schools; and to hear and determine their causes, leaving the execution thereof to the dean and chapter.

Oath. By the precentor's oath he is bound to observe all the statutes, ordinances and customs of the church. To obey all the lawful and canonical mandats of the dean and chapter, or their ministers. To observe the ordination and decree made by archbishop *Thomas*, about the union or annexation of the prebend of *Driffield* to the precentorship.

Revenue. The particular rents belonging to this dignity are thus enumerated by Mr. *Torre* (k).

	l.	s.	d.
Kirky Useburn	21	00	06
Waddington	05	05	04
Gowle	00	10	06
Heslington	02	02	00
Tadcaster	01	16	08
	30	14	00

The prebend of *Driffield* was, *anno* 1485, annexed to the precentorship by archbishop *Rotheram*, whose old valuation was } 62 00 00

For non-residence he shall lose the profits of *Driffield*.

Valuation in the king's books,

The first fruits with the aforesaid.

	l.	s.	d.
Prebend	89	10	10
Tenths	08	19	06
Subsidies	08	00	00

A CATALOGUE of the PRECENTORS of York.

Anno	
	Gilbert.
11..	*William de Augo.*
118.	*Hamo*
12..	*Reginald Arundel.*
12..	*Galfrid de Norwich.*
123.	*Walter.*
124,	*Simon de Evesham.*
	William de Passemere.
125.	*Robert de Winton.*
	Hugh de Cantelupe.
126.	*John Romane.*
1283	*William de Corneys.*
1289	*Peter de Ross.*
1312	*Thomas Cobham.*
1317	*Robert de Valoignes.*
1320	*Thomas de Berton.*
1321	*William de Alburwyke.*
1332	*Robert de Nassington.*
1335	*Rob. de Patrington* alias *Thurgatts.*
1349	*Simon de Bekynham.*
1351	*Hugo de Wymondeswold.*
1364	*Nicholas de Cave.*
1365	*Adam de Ebor.*
1370	*Henry de Barton.*
1371	*Hugh de Wymondeswold* again.
1379	*Roger de Ripon.*
1379	*William de Kexby.*
1410	*John Burrel.*
1410	*Bryan Fairfax.*
1436	*John Selow.*
1439	*Robert Dobbes.*
1447	*John Castell.*
1460	*John Gisburgh.*
1481	*William de Eure.*
1493	*William de Beverley.*
1494	*Hugh Frotter.*
1495	*John Hert.*
1496	*William Langton.*
1503	*Martin Collyns.*
1519	*John Perrotte.*
1519	*Thomas Linacre.*
1522	*Richard Wyatt.*
1534	*William Holgill.*
1538	*William Clyffe.*
1539	*Edward Kellett.*
1545	*Nicholas Everard.*
1574	*John Rokeby.*
1613	*John Gibson*, knt.
1613	*Henry Banks.*
1615	*John Brook.*

(k) Pag. 576.

ANNO		ANNO	
1616	*John Favour.*	1661	*Robert Soresby.*
1623	*Henry Hooke.*	1685	*Thomas Comber.*
1624	*Rich. Palmer.*	169.	*James Fall.*
1631	*George Stanhope.*	1711	*John Richardson.*
1660	*Toby Wickham.*	1735	*Jaques Sterne.*
1660	*Thomas Harwood.*		

The CHANCELLOR *of the* CHURCH.

The chancellorship of this cathedral church was founded by *Thomas* I. a little before the dean and prebends were by him appointed. This office is the next in dignity to the precentorship.

The chancellor, anciently termed *master of the schools* (l), ought to be master also in divinity; and an actual reader according to the custom of the church. He hath the collation of all the grammar schools; and ought to preach on the first *Sunday in Advent*, on *Septuagesima Sunday*, and at the clergy's synods. He also should assign days for others to preach in during that season. To him belongs the custody of the seal of citations; also the making up chronologies concerning all remarkable occurrences which relate to the church. To him, and the sub-chantor, belongs the licencing of readers, entring their names in the tables, and hearing them read at the vestry-door. Also to assign what lections the readers are to read on double festivals. *Office.*

The rents peculiar to this office are thus set down:

	l.	s.	d.	
The church of *Acclam, cum membris*	13	06	08	*Revenues.*
The church of *Wagben*	20	00	08	
	33	07	04	

Which sum was the old valuation of the chancellorship by it self considered; but *anno* 1484, the prebend of *Laghton en la Morthing* was appropriated to this dignity by archbishop *Rotheram*. The valuation uncertain. For non-residence he shall lose the profits of *Laghton*.

The valuation of the chancellorship in the king's books.		l.	s.	d.
	First-fruits	85	06	08
	Tenths	8	10	08
	Subsidies	7	12	00

A CATALOGUE *of the* CHANCELLORS *of this church.*

ANNO		ANNO	
	Symon de Apulia.	1452	*Thomas Gascoigne.*
12..	*John de Saint Laurence.*	1451	*William Morton.*
12..	*Rich. de Cornwall.*	1466	*Tho. Chandler.*
124.	*John Blund.*	1490	*Will. Langton.*
1270	*William Wickwane.*	1495	*Will. de Melton.*
1279	*Thomas Corbett.*	1528	*Henry Trafford.*
1290	*Symon.*	1537	*Galfrid Downes.*
1290	*Thomas de Wakefield.*	1561	*Richard Barnes.*
1297	*Rob. de Riplingham.*	1571	*Will. Palmer.*
1332	*William de Alburwyk.*	1605	*Will. Goodwin.*
1349	*Symon de Bekyngham.*	1616	*Phineas Hodgson.*
1369	*Tho. de Farnelaye.*	1660	*Tho. Clutterbuck.*
1379	*John de Shireburne.*	1660	*Christ. Stones.*
1410	*John de Rykynghale.*	1687	*John Covel.*
1426	*John Estcourt.*	1722	*Dan. Waterland.*
1427	*John Kexby.*		

The TREASURER.

The treasurership in this cathedral church is the last of the four great dignitaries, but was equal in value with the first. This office had likewise its foundation by the aforesaid prelate of this see, *Thomas* the first.

To the office of the treasurer did belong the custody of the church, and cognizance to hear and determine all excesses committed therein. Except they be done in the choir, and then their corrections belong to the dean and chapter. This officer ought to find lights and candles to burn in the choir at the great altar, and on our lady's altar, on special anniversary days. With other lights of daily use in the church elsewhere. He ought to find coals, and salt for the holy water. To repair the copes and vestments belonging to the church, and to provide new ones as need shall require. To provide hangings for the choir and pulpit, *Office.*

(l) *Magister scholarum.* See *Newport's repertorium.*

and

and other ornaments of the church. To find bread and wine for all masses celebrated in the church, and at other communions at *Easter*. To find bell-ropes and other necessaries about the bells, as works of brass, iron, wood, *&c.* Excepting the new founding of the bells, and other new work about them, which appertains to the chapter in common.

Oath. The ancient oath of the treasurer was faithfully to keep and observe the lawful customs of the church. Defend its liberties to the utmost of his power. To keep inviolably the secrets of the chapter; and to conserve and support all burdens of the church according to the quality of the benefice which he either hath or shall have in the same; when it shall be, by the chapter required.

Revenues. The particular lands and other rents belonging to the treasurership are thus accounted for by Mr. *Torre*, though the certain sums of most of them are now unknown,

	l. s. d.	
Alne, *cum membris*, —	23 06 08	Laundesburg.
Broughton, *cum membris*,	13 06 08	Clerc.
Acombe, *cum membris.*		Staynton.
Newthorpe *preb. cum membris.*	30 13 04	Wigginton.
Wilton *preb. cum membris.*		Skelton.
Rypon.		York *city*.
Wyverthorp.		Cliffton, *juxta* Ebor.

		l. s. d.
The ancient valuation of this treasuryship was accounted at	—	233 06 08
In the king's books.	First fruits — —	220 00 00
	Tenths — — —	23 06 08

A LIST of the TREASURERS of York.

Anno		Anno	
11..	*Radulphus.*	1335	*Francis de Filiis Ursi.*
11..	*William Fitzherbert.*	1352	*John de Wynewycks.*
1141	*Hugh Pudsey.*	1360	*Henry de Barton.*
	John.	1360	*John de Branktree.*
1186	*Bucardus de Puteaco.*	1374	*John de Clyfford.*
1196	*Eustachius.*	1375	*Rob. Cardinalis.*
12..	*Hamo.*	1380	*John Clyfford.*
12..	*William.*	1393	*John de Newton.*
1239	*William de Rutherfield.*	1414	*Richard Pitts.*
1241	*Robert Hagett.*	1415	*John de Nottyngham.*
125.	*John Mancel.*	1418	*Thomas Haxey.*
126.	*Henry.*	1425	*Robert Gilbert.*
126.	*John le Romane.*	1426	*Robert Wolveden.*
1265	*Edmund Mortimer.*	1432	*John Bermyngham.*
127.	*Nicholas de Well.*	1457	*John Bothe.*
127.	*Bego Fairfax* vel *de Clare.*	1459	*John Pakengam.*
1281	*John Columna.*	1477	*Thomas Portington.*
1297	*Theobald de Barr.*	1485	*William Sheffield.*
1303	*Francis de Millan.*	1494	*Hugh Trotter.*
1306	*Walter de Bedewynde.*	1503	*Martyn Collyns.*
1328	*William de la Mare.*	1509	*Robert Langton.*
1329	*Walter de Yarwell.*	1514	*Lancelot Collynson.*
1330	*William de la Mare.*	1538	*William Clyffe.*

Dissolution. *May* 26, 1547, the last named *William Clyffe* resigned this dignity to king *Edw.* 6. with all its demesnes, manors, rights, members and appurtenances, with the advowsons of all its churches, vicarages, chapelries, *&c.* A caption whereof was taken and recognized *June* 1. following, by the said Dr. *Cliff*, before sir *Edward North* chancellor, afterwards ratified by archbishop *Holgate*, and lastly confirmed by Dr. *Wotton* dean, and the chapter of *York*, *July* 8, 1547.

Subtreasurer. The office of sub-treasurership fell with the former; whose duty it was to provide sacrists and other officers to do the servile offices of the church, as opening the doors, ringing of bells and cleaning it, blowing the organs, *&c.* For which the treasurer usually paid him a salary of fifty marks.

Both these offices became early extinct in this church, and the reason given for dissolving them is an unanswerable one, *viz.*

Abrepto omni thesauro, desiit thesaurarii munus.

Having given some account of the four principal dignitaries of this cathedral, I should next proceed to the rest of the ecclesiastical officers, as sub-deans, sub-chantors or succentors, archdeacons, canons or prebends, vicars choral, parsons or chantry-priests; which are drawn

drawn out by Mr. *Torre*, whose prodigious industry has carried him through all the inferior offices which are now, or have been, in the church. But this would ask a large volume of itself; and since the archdeacons and prebendaries of our cathedral have been lately published by Mr. *Willis* (m), I have less occasion to take notice of them here. It will be necessary, however, to give a short account of the residentiaries, now and formerly, belonging to the church; which, with a description of the close of *York*, or *Minster-yard*, and the *Bedern*, or college of vicars-choral, I shall conclude this chapter.

The custom of the ancient residency in the cathedral church of *York* was thus, that the dean, chantor, chancellor and treasurer, shall be accounted continual residents; not because they were always to reside, but only for the greatest part of the year. It was then also the usual custom for all the canons of the church, resident, to convene on the vigil of *All-saints*, before nine o' clock in the morning, in the church, and then they were to invite such as they thought good to dine with them during all the double festivals which should happen in that year's summer's residency. The winter's residency begun on the feast of St. *Martyn*. These invitations were always made in the morning, because it was held a disgrace for any canon to go into the city after dinner. *Residentiaries.*

The grand residency used to be performed after this manner; he that had a prebend, and was not litigious, and designed to make his residency was first to go to the dean, if he was within twenty miles of the city, and if without that distance then he shall appear before the major of the chapter, and make his protestation that on such a day he designs to begin his residency. Then the dean or the major shall say to him, on such a day you shall appear before us, in the habit of the choir, in the chapter-house, and there protest to make your residency after the custom thereof. Then the chamberlain shall set down the day in his calendar. The first residency shall contain twenty six weeks, in which the canon shall be present at all canonical hours, except he be infirm, &c. he shall then also have at his table double the number of vicars and ministers. And during which time shall not lye out of the city any night, but be within his residentiary house before **Corfew-bell**, at furthest; otherways his residency shall be accounted for none. If he chance to be absent any day, during this great residency, he shall keep up his hospitality for the ministers of the church and others in the same manner as if he were present. And not till this grand residency be over shall receive any thing of the common with the rest of the canons residentiary.

When a canon makes his lesser residency, which is to be kept twenty four weeks, he shall not be obliged to continue the same throughout, but keep it by months, weeks or days, so that he be present on greater festivals, if he possibly can.

The canons residentiary, in the time of their residencies, ought to be present in the service of the choir, especially at mattins, vespers and masses; unless otherways hindred.

In the year 1221 the dean and chapter, having first consulted the customs and usages of neighbouring churches, made the following ordination of residency in the cathedral church of *York*.

1. They ordained that the four persons, *viz.* dean, chantor, chancellor and treasurer shall reside as they were wont to do. And that the archdeacons, being canons, who are bound by their offices to visit their churches, and diligently discharge their trust about cure of souls committed to them, shall observe to make their residencies for three months. *Ordinations.*

2. Each single canon shall be bound to keep half a year's residency, either all together, or else a quarter in one half year and a quarter in another.

3. That they do see the faculties of the church, excepting the customary daily expences, equally divided among the residentiaries, without respect of persons. So as every day there be allowed to each residentiary six pence, in the feast of nine lections twelve pence, and on double festivals two shillings.

4. These canons residentiary, who are to be allowed these daily contributions, are to have their dwellings within the city of *York*; near the church which they are to serve. And at least ought to be present at mattins and other canonical hours, unless sickness, or any other reasonable cause, hinder them.

5. When the said daily distributions are made, what remains overplus shall be equally divided amongst the said residentiaries, either on the feast of *Pentecost*, or St. *Martin* in winter at the end of their term.

6. Those canons who study or read divinity, according to the tenor of pope *Honorius* his constitution, shall receive their full proportions (n).

These were some of the ancient regulations of the aforesaid offices in the cathedral. The hospitality was great that attended the execution of them; amounting, as some write, to one thousand marks *per ann.* for every residence. By a statute of *Hen.* VIII. dated *West.* *July* 30, *an. reg.* 33. their ancient customs and privileges were very much altered and confined. As this ordinance is printed at length in the *Monasticon* (o), and is too long for my purpose, I shall omit it.

(m) *Willis* on cathedral churches.

(n) *Torre*, p. 763. *ex charta in cust. clerici vestibul. cum litera* Z.

(o) *Mon. Ang.* 165, 166.

The Close *of* York.

The close of the cathedral church of *York*, commonly called the *Minster-yard*, or Minster-garth, is situated in the north east angle of the city; whose walls make one part of its enclosure; and anciently it had its own wall to fence it from the city. The circumference of this district is near three quarters of a mile; beginning from *Bootham-bar*, along *Peter-gate*, and ending again at the same gate by a large circuit of the city walls. The course of this enclosure will be better understood by the black line drawn of it in the general plan of the city, to which I refer. It has at this day four large gates to it. The principal gate which leads to the south entrance of the cathedral is in *Peter-gate*, facing *Stone-gate*; the next is in the same street, facing *Lop-lane*; a third is in *Gotheram-gate*, facing the *Bedern*, and a fourth in *Uggleforth*. Anciently these gates were closed in every night, but now they are constantly open.

Within the close, besides the parish church of St. *Michael le Belfrey* which stands upon the line of its wall, was formerly two more parish churches; the one called the church of St. *Mary ad Valvas*, the other St. *John del Pyke*.

Church of St. Mary ad Valvas.

The church of St. *Mary ad Valvas*, in the Minster-garth, was anciently a rectory belonging to the jurisdiction and patronage of the dean and chapter of *York*. But in the year 1365, to enlarge the walks about the minster, it was removed and united to the church of St. *John del Pyke*, and consolidated into one parish with it by the common consent of the chapter (*p*). I suppose this church took its name, *ad Valvas*, from standing somewhere near the great folding doors, that were in the old quire end of the church.

St. John del Pyke.

The parish church of St. *John Baptist del Pyke*, within the close of the *Minster*, was also an ancient rectory belonging to the jurisdiction of the dean and chapter of *York*; of which rectory Mr. *Torre* has given the names, *&c.* of some few incumbents. *January* 27, 1585, this church of St. *John del Pyke*, according to the statute, was united, together with its parish, to the church of the *Holy Trinity* in *Gotheram-gate*; excepting all and singular the mansion-houses within the close of the cathedral church, which, as to their parochial rights, were to remain in the same condition as before (*q*).

	l.	*s.*	*d.*
This church was valued in the king's books at —— ——	04	10	00

The site of this now demolished church is marked in the general plan of the city to be near the gate of the close which leads into *Uggle-forth*. The rectory house is in the angle on the other side of it; which the present incumbent of the united parishes, my worthy friend the reverend Mr. *Knight*, has at a considerable expence near rebuilt and beautified.

Holgate's *free-school.*

In this corner also of the close is a *Free-school*, erected and endowed by archbishop *Holgate*, who settled 12 *l. per annum* on the school-master, over and above all charges and reprises; and built an house and a school-room in the said close adjoining to the church of St. *John del Pyke*. He also constituted *Thomas Swan* as the first school master of it; and ordained that the said *Thomas Swan* his successors, *&c.* shall be a body corporate for ever; and the said master, his successors, *&c.* to be called master of the free-school of *Robert Holgate*; and by that name to sue and be sued, implead and be impleaded, *&c.* and to have a common seal for the affairs and matters of the said school. And further he ordaineth that the archbishops his successors shall be patrons of the said school for ever; *sede vacante* the dean and chapter; if they do not present within twenty days the lord-mayor and aldermen; and if they do not present in the same time the patronage is left to the archdeacon of *York*, and twelve of the most substantial house-keepers in the parish, to present as they please. The rest of the articles run upon the good behaviour of the master, usher and scholars (*r*).

Treasurer's house.

We find by our records that the treasurer of the church had one messuage within the close of the cathedral, which he continued possessed of till that office was dissolved. The site of this house is very large, and coming to the crown, the same was granted out again, but to whom or when I know not. It was rebuilt in the manner it stands in at present, about forty years ago, by *Robert Squire* esq; it is now possessed and occupied by the honourable and reverend Mr. *Finch* canon residentiary of the church in the north end; the other by my very good friend *Bacon Morrett* esq;

In a lane called anciently *Vicar's-lane* within the close, but now *Little-Alice-Lane*, from some diminutive old woman, as I have been told, who not many years ago kept an inn or ale-house in it, is the site of a college, formerly called St. *William's* college.

St. William's *college.*

It appears by records that king *Hen.* VI. granted his letters patents for erecting a college to the honour of St. *William*, archbishop of *York*, in the close of *York*, for the parsons and chantry priests of the cathedral to reside in; whereas before they lived promiscuously in houses of laymen and women, contrary to the honour and decency of the said church, as the patent expresses, and their spiritual orders, *&c.* (*s*) It does not appear that this grant was put in execution, probably the civil wars prevented it; but king *Edw.* IV. in the first year of his reign, granted other letters patents, of the same tenor, to *George Nevill*, then bishop

(*p*) Ex MS. Torre.

(*q*) *Ex eodem.*

(*r*) From the original deed kept amongst the city records, dated *anno Dom.* 1546, signed Robert Holgate. By this grant he erects another grammar-school at *Hemsworth*, in this county, and one at *Old-Malton*, with a Salary of twenty four pounds *per annum*; which are all still subsisting. See also 12 *pars paten.* 38 Hen. VIII. *Rolls* chapel.

(*s*) *Pat.* 33 *Hen.* VI. *p.* 1. *m.* 1.

bishop of *Exeter*, and to his brother *Richard Nevill*, then earl of *Warwick*, and their heirs to found and sustain this college, without reciting any thing of the former grant, and to have the nomination of the provost of it for ever. The patent is very large and full, and contains all the rules and statutes to be observed by the members of it. Dated at *York May* 11. in the first year of his reign (*t*). In Mr. *Dodsworth*'s collections, *v.* 129. *f.* 140. are some extracts of the statutes belonging to this college; there were twenty three chantry priests or petty canons in it, over whom presided a provost. They had lands and tenements in common amongst them, towards their maintenance, reparations, *&c.* over and above the endowments of their several chantries to the yearly value, as it was certified, of 12 *l.* 12 *s.* 8 *d.* At the dissolution the house and site of this college, great part of which is yet standing, being a small quadrangle with the old gate and the image of St. *William* over the door, was sold to one *Michael Stanhope* (*u*), from whom, I suppose, it came to the ancient family of *Jenkins* in this county; sir *Henry Jenkins* knight, possessed it in the time of king *Charles* the first; for whilst that unfortunate prince staid at *York*, the king's printing press was erected in this house. Since which, it has of late years been part of the great estate of the right honourable *Robert Benson* lord *Bingley*; and, by marriage of his daughter and heir, it is at present in *George Fox* of *Bramham-park* esquire; a gentleman whose true publick spirit of patriotism, hospitality, and unbiassed integrity, renders him a singular ornament to this country.

In the book of **Doomesday**, one of the divisions of the city is termed *Schyra archiepiscopi*, the shire of the archbishop, and is said to have contained in the days of *Edward* the confessor two hundred eleven houses inhabited; but, at the time of the taking that survey there were only one hundred dwelling houses, great and small, besides the archbishop's palace and the houses of the canons (*x*). If this shire, or district, meant only the close of the cathedral it is plain there were more houses in it before the conquest than there are now, or indeed could well stand in the compass. But I take this to have been an account of all the houses the church was then possessed of in the city, as well as the close; and, as I have taken notice before, **Old Bail** was anciently the property of the archbishop, and under his immediate jurisdiction. I take it that, of old, none but the principal dignitaries of the church, canons and other ecclesiasticks belonging to it, had houses within the close, and except the treasurer's and St. *William*'s college already described, all houses whatsoever are held by lease from the church within this district. There are also the sites of several prebendal houses which were without the pale; as in *Stone-gate*, *Peter-gate*, particularly *Massam-house* there, which prebend was constantly annexed to the treasurership and so fell together; and in *Lop-lane*, all which are specified at length in Mr. *Torre*'s manuscript. I shall only observe, that there is not one house either within or without the close at present that is inhabited by any dignitary, or prebendary, to whom it of right belongs, except the deanery.

The palace belonging to the archbishops of *York*, in the *Minster-yard*, has long been leased out from the church. And that house in which the primate of *England* used of old to inhabit and keep up the greatest hospitality, is now, such is the mutability of times and fashions, converted into a dancing-school at one end, and a play-house at the other. Some other of its ancient apartments were of late years honoured with a weekly assembly of ladies and gentlemen; until the new rooms in *Blake-street* were erected for that purpose. *Archiepiscopal palace.*

The deanry, as I said, is the only house inhabited within the close by its proper owner, in right of the church to which it belongs. It is a spacious and convenient old building, with large gardens beyond it; and has a gate of its own leading into *Peter-gate*, which was also, upon the line of the wall of the close. *Deanry.*

The archbishop's *register* and *prerogative-office* is kept in an old stone building at the east end of *Belfray*'s church. In it is a noble repository of the archiepiscopal registers, beginning from an older date than, perhaps, any other ecclesiastical registers in the kingdom. Those in the archives at *Lambeth*, belonging to the see of *Canterbury*, go no higher than archbishop *Rayner*, about the year 1307; whereas these begin with the rolls of *Walter Grey*, who entered upon his dignity in the year 1216, near one hundred years before them. I should be glad I could say that the registers since the *Reformation* are kept with that care and exactness as they were before it. In the former may be found a vast fund of ecclesiastical and other history, which it is hoped some able hand will, some time or other, sift from them and preserve. The dean and chapter's registry office is also kept here, or in the cathedral, in which are all the archives, now in being, particularly belonging to the church. Some account of which may be met with in the *addenda*, and amongst them is the *registrum magnum album* the oldest record the church can now boast of. *Register office.*

The *area* the church stands in is much too strait for its circumference; for were it set off, only in the manner that St. *Paul*'s is, it would have a much grander appearance. And yet this thought has been little regarded by the lessors of the ground within the close; who have choaked up the only grand entrance to the church by a row of paltry houses and shops on each

(*t*) *Pat.* 1 Ed. IV. *p.* 2. *m.* 17. Rolls chapel.

(*u*) *Domus et scitus collegii S. Willielmi in clauso metropol.* Ebor. Michael Stanhope Apr. 2. 1 *pars* 3 Ed. VI.

(*x*) See the copy from this record in the *addenda*.

each side of it. Nay the avarice of some went still much further, when they leased out the ground on each side the steps to the south entrance to build on. Which houses were standing until dean *Gale* let the leases run out, and pulled down those great nusances to the church, and cleaned it from the filth contracted from them.

The best houses which are now standing in the *Minster-yard* and are held by church leases, to begin from the north-east corner, is first Mrs. *Lowther's* of *Ackworth*, built by Dr. *Pearson* late chancellor of the diocese. Next the house at present inhabited by the reverend Mr. *Bradley*, canon residentiary of the church; Dr. *Ward's*, commissary of the diocese; two houses contiguous, at the east end of the church, built by Mr. *Jubb*, deputy register to the archbishop, &c. The house, anciently known by the name of *Wartbill-house*, contiguous to the deanery, at present belonging to the honourable *Thomas Willoughby* of *Birdsal* esquire; a gentleman of uncommon merit, to whose acquaintance and friendship the author of this work has the honour to be particularly related. This house came to Mr. *Willoughby*, along with other great possessions in this county, by the marriage of the daughter and heir of *Thomas Southeby* esq; of *Birdsal* aforesaid. In a lane, called *Precentor's-lane*, are also some good houses; but none of note save two or three at the bottom; amongst which that to the east, at present possessed and inhabited by my much respected friend the reverend Mr. *Lamplugh*, canon residentiary, is the most considerable. Here is a little postern gate, or passage, into *Peter-gate*, but whether long used or not to me is uncertain.

Bedern. The *Bedern*, or college of vicars choral belonging to the cathedral, is in *Guthramgate*, and extends itself, with the gardens, &c. to *Aldwark* and St. *Andrew-gate*. Concerning the etymology of the word *Bedern*, there have been various conjectures. I have taken notice, in the *Roman* account of this city, that *Constantine the great* was said to be born *in* Peterna *civitatis Eboraci*; from which some historians, and particularly archbishop *Usher* have supposed that the regal palace, which stood here, was anciently called Pertenna; now corruptly Bedherna. A very easy mistake, saith the primate, if we consider that the *Britains* usually pronounced *P* for *B*, and *T* like *D*. Tradition, amongst us, has spun the etymology of *Bedern* somewhat finer; and would have it come from *Baderan*, which word is said to bear some allusion to the baths, or bathing places, of the imperial palace; to *Bade* and to bath being, at present, synonimous in our common north country dialect. Besides, the same authority assures us that some tessalated pavements were anciently discovered in digging in this very place, which probably were the floors of the baths aforesaid.

But, indeed, we need look no further back than our *Saxon* ancestors for the etymology of this word, which is plainly deduced from the *Anglo-Saxon* Beade, *oratio*, and that from the *Maeso-Gothick* verb Bedian, *precari*, *rogare*. *Hern*, or *Herm*, is a cell or hermitage, as *Potbern*, *Whitbern*, so that it signifies no more than a cloisture built and set apart for a number of religious to dwell in. Besides there are places so called near the cathedral churches of *Ripon* and *Beverley*; which must have served for the same purpose as ours, and can have no allusion to a *Roman* etymology.

Vicars-choral. For many ages last past this place has been assigned for the habitation of the vicars choral, of old probably called Beadsmen; which were formerly thirty six, according to the number of the prebendal stalls in the cathedral. Their duty was, besides attending the daily office in the choir, to perform the offices of the dead, at certain hours day and night, in the several chapels and oratories erected for that purpose. Each canon was to have his own peculiar vicar, in priest's orders, to attend and officiate for him. Which said canon, after he shall receive the profits of his prebend, was to pay his vicar 40 *s. per ann.* at the two usual terms of the year. And when a canon died, his vicar was to have his choral habit according to ancient custom.

In the year 1275, 4 *Edw.* I. it was found by inquisition then taken, that the Bederne was given to *God*, St. *Peter*, and the vicars serving God, in pure and perpetual alms, by one *William de Lanum* canon of the church. But the major part thereof was of the common of the land of *Ulphus*. With another certain part of the fee of the archbishop, and by him eleemosynated to them (*y*).

Walter Grey archbishop, with the consent of the dean and chapter, first ordained the college of the vicars-choral; this was in the year 1252. Afterwards king *Henry* III. confirmed the ordinances by his royal charter, bearing date 15 *id. Oct. A. D.* 1269. Both these evidences are still preserved amongst their own records. By them it appears that these thirty six vicars, and their successors, shall be thenceforth named *the college of the vicars of every of the canons, by the dean and chapter of* York *placed and congregated in a certain place called* le Bederne, &c. One of the body is appointed *custos* by the rest; which said *custos* is to preside over them, and together with the other vicars shall have a common seal, and retain to themselves all their lands, rents and possessions to be held of the king in free burgage.

According to the ancient oath of the vicars they were obliged to continue in commons, and live with the rest of their brethren at meat and drink, in their common hall. That they do their utmost endeavour to get by heart, within the first year, the psalms and all other things which are in the church, to be sung without book. That they do diligently keep

(*y*) *Mon. Ang.* vol. III. p. 155. *ex registro albo.*

and

and observe the statutes of the church, and do nothing fraudulently that the church may be deprived of its due obedience. BEDERN.

The ancient statute-book of this college is yet in being; wherein are many ordinancies and regulations in regard to their bursars, stewards, hours of dining and supping, quantity of drink allowed at meals, *&c.* And in the year 1353, the chapter of *York* made this ordination, *viz.* that no vicar-choral from thenceforth shall keep any *woman* to serve him within the *Bederne*. And the sub-chantor do acquaint the vicars that they warn all their women servants to depart their service, on the penalty of twenty shillings payable to the fabrick of the church for every one not observing this ordinance *(z)*.

I find that in the second year of the reign of king *Edward* the sixth, this whole college and site of the *Bederne* was actually sold to one *Thomas Goulding* and others *(a)* for the sum of 1924*l.* 10*s.* 1*d.* But upon the earnest solicitations of the dean and chapter to the king and council, this bargain was some time after disannulled; for in the sixth of *Edward* VI. it was ordained and decreed by the chancellor and surveyor-general of the court of augmentations, by and with the advice of the king's judges, that the dean and chapter of *York*, for themselves and for the sub-chantor and vicars-choral, shall from thenceforth have and enjoy the said house called the *Bederne*, and all the possessions belonging to it, except the chantries and obits to them anciently assured, without any interruption or molestation of the said court, *&c.* so it was adjudged that this their college was appendant to the cathedral church, and not within the statute of dissolved free colleges, chantries, *&c.*

By escaping that blow the *Bederne* is still in the possession of the vicars-choral. But the chantries and obits being dissolved, their chiefest support, the number of them strangely is lessened, and from thirty six they are now dwindled to four, of which number the sub-chantor, or *Succentor vicariorum*, is one. The *Bederne* is usually their habitation still, but they are not at present confined to it, but may let their houses and live elsewhere in the city. In Mr. *Torre's* time the old collegiate hall, where the vicars usually dined in common, was standing; but it is now pulled down.

The chapel in the *Bederne* was founded, *anno* 1348, by *Thomas de Otteley* and *William de Cotingham*. It was consecrated the same year, by order of *William de la Zouch*, then archbishop, by *Hugh*, entituled archbishop of *Damesten*, and dedicated to the holy trinity, the virgin *Mary*, and St. *Katherine*. It still remains in good repair and its painted glass windows are pretty entire. Divine service is sometimes said in it; and christnings performed, for which purpose there is on the left hand of the door an old font. There is, likewise, a holy water pot; and a handsome marble altar table. Here was also a chantry of five marks *per annum*. Chapel.

The revenues of the vicars-choral are very much impaired, and would not be sufficient to maintain the small number of them at present, did not the dean and chapter assist in bestowing upon them some of their parochial churches in *York*. And early in the reformation several tenements were also bestowed upon them by the dean and chapter, in consideration of their poverty, as the charter expresses it, which bears date in the thirty eighth year of *Henry* VIII. *(b)* Besides their houses in the *Bederne*, and some other houses in the city, with their peculiar parish church of St. *Sampson's*, I find that king *Richard* II. notwithstanding the statute of *Mortmain*, granted licence to the *custos* of this college, *&c.* for ever, to enjoy the advowson of the parish church of *Cotingham (c)*. Sir *Henry le Vavasour*, in the year 1332, bestowed upon them the church of *Fryston*; which was then appropriated to their college. They were possessed also of the churches of *Huntington, juxta Ebor.* and of *Nether-Wallop* in *Hampshire*; the rectory of which last was leased out to queen *Elizabeth*, by the then sub-chantor and vicars, in the twenty-fifth year of her reign. These possessions, besides 40*s.* *per annum* paid to them by each prebendary, as settled by act of chapter *anno* 1563, and 5*l.* sterling of every canon residentiary at his first entrance into his office, and the yearly sum of 6*l.* 13*s.* 4*d.* paid them by each residentiary for their disclaiming the right they had to his table, as provided by the new statute of residency granted by *Henry* VIII. are all that I can find belonging to this community. Revenues.

The valuation of the vicars-choral in the king's books are,

		l.	*s.*	*d.*
First-fruits	—	136	05	05

(z) Mr. *Torre* from a book indorsed *Acta correctionum clericorum*, has collected a great number of criminal conversations with women, committed by the clergy in those days. The vicars-choral have by far the greatest share in them, *p.* 1851.

(a) *Totum situm et capital. messuag. nuper collegii* S. Petri Ebor. *vocat.* le Bederne, *alias dict.* le Vicarscoralls *infra civit. pred. collegio pred. spect. tenend. in burgagio* Thom. Goulding *et aliis pro* 1924*l.* 10*s.* 1*d.* 3. *pat.* 2 Edw. VI. *Rolls chapel.*

(b) Amongst their own records, which are kept in a chest with three locks, a catalogue of which records the reader may meet with in the *appendix*.

(c) *Torre*, p. 1231. There are several confirmations, by different kings, of divers grants made to the *vicars choral* of *York*, in the tower of *London*, which are too many to give in particular.

CHAP. IV.

St. Mary's Abbey, *from its foundation to its dissolution; with the present state of the* King's-manor, *as it is now called, at* York.

St. Mary's Abbey. *Situation.*

THIS noble and magnificent monastery, antiently one of the glories of the city of *York*, was situated under the walls without, and on the north side of the town. There is no place, in or about the city, which could boast of a more agreeable site; being on a rising ground, the aspect south west, declining every where to the river *Ouse*, which forms a grand canal at the bottom of it. *J. Leland* informs us from an ancient manuscript, that where now the abbey of St. *Mary* stands, was, before the conqueror's time, a place the citizens made use of to lay the sweepings of their streets and other kinds of filth in; and where their malefactors were executed (*a*). But be that as it may, it is a noble spot of ground, almost square, and is inclosed, on the north and east side, with a fair and stately wall, built with many orderly and large towers embattled; on the west with the river *Ouse*, and on the south with the rampire and walls of the city. The whole circumference, by an exact mensuration, is one thousand two hundred and eighty yards, or about three quarters of a mile. (*b*) In the abbey wall were only two principal gates; the one on the east side, opening into *Bootham*, near the gate of the city; the other on the north side, which, as I take it, has been the main entrance into the abbey, and opens into a street called St. *Mary gate*.

Almry-garth.

North of this street, is a spacious piece of rich ground, yet called *Almry-garth*. Which name it takes from the *French aumonier*, *Latin eleemosynarius*; and was formerly the place where the convent kept their cattle which were ready for killing; and also put in what was charitably bestowed upon them. The ground has been all walled in, except on the side next the river. In it were the abbot's fishponds; the traces of which appear at this day. I shall chuse to begin my account of this monastery not from its erection but from its fall.

The Manor.

At the dissolution of monasteries by *Henry* VIII. the site of this noble and rich abbey with all its revenues fell to the crown. And here it was that prince ordered a palace to be built, out of its ruins, which was to be the residence of the lord presidents of the north, for the time being, and called the *King's-manor*. That the very name and memory of the abbey might be lost for ever. It continued in that state to the reign of *James* I. who, at his first coming to *York*, gave orders to have it repaired and converted into a regal palace; intending to make use of it as such at his going to and returning from *Scotland*. Many testimonials are of this prince's design in arms and other decorations about the several portals of the building. However this palace continued to be the seat of the lords presidents to the last; and we may believe had some reparations at the charge of that truly great, but unfortunate, nobleman *Thomas* earl *of Strafford*; for over an entrance in one of the inner courts is placed the arms and different quarterings, in stone work, of that noble and antient family. This circumstance, trivial as it is, ought to have its memorial, since it was made use of by his cruel and most inveterate enemies, as one of the articles against him; *that he had the arrogance to put up his own arms in one of the king's palaces.*

After this it continued in the crown to the *Revolution*; and when king *Charles* II. took some displeasure at the city, and appointed a governour over it, this house again became the residence of that officer. I find that the lord *Fretchvile* baron of *Stavely* was then appointed; and after his death, sir *John Reresby*, bart. representative in parliament for this city, was made governour of it by king *James* II. and lived in the king's house, till displaced by a stronger power.

In the unfortunate reign of king *James* II. a large room in the *Manor* was fitted up and made use of as a *popish* chapel; where one bishop *Smith*, as he was called, celebrated mass openly. But it was not long before the enraged populace pulled it to pieces; and this consecrated room has since had the fate, in our days, to be converted into an *assembly-room* for the meeting together of the nobility, gentry and ladies at the *races*. As also to be the common entertaining room for the high sheriffs of the county at the different assizes.

After the revolution *Robert Waller*, esq; sometime lord-mayor, and representative in parliament for this city, found means to procure a lease of this abbey or manor for thirty one years from the crown. Which when run out was obtained again for *Tancred Robinson*, esq; second son to sir *William Robinson*, bart. who is the present lessee. The former lease, being somewhat remarkable, I have thought fit to give a copy of it at the end of this chapter.

St. Mary's *goal.* *Court.*

Adjoining to the north-gate of the abbey was the prison for debtors in the liberties of St. *Mary*, which the reader will find in the sequel were very extensive. The court for the liberties of St. *Mary*'s was also here kept by the steward of the same, for the time being;

(*a*) *Ubi nunc est coenobium S.* Mariae *temp.* Gulielmi *Nothi locus ejiciendis sordibus destinatus; et in quo solebant de sontibus supplicium sumere. Coll.* iv. 36.

(*b*) From *Bootham-bar* to St. *Marygate* tower one hundred and ninety four yards. From St. *Mary-gate tower* to the *West-tower*, abutting upon the river *Ouse*, four hundred and twenty yards. From the said *West tower* to the *Water-house tower*, on the south, two hundred and forty six yards. From the *Water-house tower* by the rampire of the city to *Bootham-bar* four hundred and twenty yards.

who

p. Abby, York.

'y eradicate and destroy all traces of

Esq.r contributes this plate. 1736.

who by charters from both king *James* and *Charles* I. (*c*) and their successors, had all those judicial privileges granted him which were ever given to the abbot of this convent by the former kings of *England*. At the death of *Thomas Adams*, esq; the last steward of this court, two gentlemen of the law in *York* made interest for the patent, to be executed betwixt them. But a more prevailing interest prevented it. Since which this stewardship has been vacant, the goal neglected, and the chamber where the court was kept, by a late accident, well nigh demolished. *St. Mary's Abbey.*

Anno 1696, and 97, the old hammered money, with the clipt and counterfeit, being every where called in, in this kingdom, a mint for coinage was erected in the manor at *York*; where the sum of three hundred and twelve thousand five hundred and twenty pounds and six pence was coined (*d*). This money, for distinction sake, bears a Y under the king's head on the coin. *Mint.*

The wall of the abbey quite round has been very strong, on the inside of which towards *Bootham*, has run a wooden gallery for the better defence of it. The continual bickerings between the citizens and monks of this abbey, was the occasion of the building this wall; which is more singular, in that I believe it is the only religious house that was thus fortified in the kingdom. *Anno* 1262, an attempt was made by the citizens, we are told, to destroy the abbey, and much plundering and slaughter ensued. For which reason, and to prevent the like for the future, *Simon* then abbot got leave of the king to build a wall. This wall is said to reach from the church of St. *Olave* to *Bootham-bar*, and was perfected *anno* 1266. (*e*). *Walls.*

On the north east corner of these walls is a tower, called St. *Mary*'s *tower*, in which all the records taken out of the religious houses, at their dissolutions, on the north side *Trent*, were reposited. It seems this tower had been originally built by some abbot of this monastery, and probably it was the *Simon* above, for the preservation of their own records from fire, in a place not likely for them to suffer by that element. And here, as I said, were the other monastical records brought under the care of the lord president, and kept in their several chests within this tower, until an unforeseen accident, for ever, dispersed and separated the greatest part of them. I find this repository had antiently, also, been made use of as a place of security for some of our royal records of chancery, by a particular grant of king *Edward* III. to one *John de S. Paul* as keeper of them (*f*). Yet no foresight could preserve the sacred magazine, then deposited in this tower, from such an unexpected accident; and our painful countryman Mr. *Dodsworth*, had but just finished his transcripts of these valuable remains, when the originals, with the tower were blown up, in the siege of *York*, *anno* 1644. and mixed with common dust. These are the transcripts that make great part of that numerous collection of manuscripts preserved from the rancour of the times, and afterwards presented to the *Bodleian* library at *Oxford* by *Thomas* lord *Fairfax*. And is the substance of what the learned and painfull collector calls his (*g*) *Monasticon Boreale* in the manuscripts. However the records themselves were not all destroyed; for we are told by Mr. *Wanley*, in his extracts from *Dodsworth*, that a careful hand had searched the rubbish for them, not without imminent danger of his own life (*h*), and carried a great part to the archbishop's archives at *York*. These were afterwards in custody of *Charles Fairfax* of *Menston*, esq; where, Mr. *Dodsworth* says, he again saw them, and took notes out of them; six weeks after they were blown up by gunpowder in the siege. From the *Fairfax* family I suppose they were once more restored to the custody of the steward of St. *Mary*'s after the *Restoration*, and deposited in the chamber where St. *Mary*'s court was usually kept. For it was here they were seen by the late industrious Mr. *Torre*, who set himself about to separate the legible ones from the other that were defaced. To collect them into different rolls, or bundles; each grant, as well as the bundle, numerically marked. And then to make a register, or catalogue, of the whole; so that the religious houses, and towns that belonged to them, being alphabetically disposed, any of the originals may be found in an instant. This curious collection of antient deeds, &c. since the disuse of St. *Mary*'s court, and by the death of *Thomas Adams*, esq; the last steward, is fallen into the hands of a gentleman in *York*, whose name I am not allowed to mention. But yet I am not out of hopes to get them deposited in the *Minster library*; the present possessor having shewn himself a person of a publick spirit on all occasions. I am the more happy in meeting with this noble magazine of antiquity since none of them, as I can find, were ever before printed, either in the *Monasticon*, or in those additional volumes published under the name of captain *Stevens*. *St. Mary's tower.*

(*c*) *Confirmatio abbat*. S. Mariae Ebor. *diversar. libertat. Primo an*. Jac. *f*. 13. b. *et pars* 20. *pat*. 2. Car. *n*. 10. Rolls chap.

(*d*) *Thoresby*'s *ducat. Leod.*

(*e*) Lelandi *collect. tom*. I. *p*. 28. *inceptus est a* Simone *abbate petrinus murus circuiens abbatiam, incipiens ab ecclesia* S. Olavi, *et tendens versus portam civitatis ejusdem quae vocatur* Galmanhith; *nunc* Botham-bar.

(*f*) *Rex concessit dom*. Joh. de S. Paulo *clerico custod. rotulor. &c. in locis diversis; et particulariter quidam alii clavi cujusdam alterius cistae apud* Eborum, *in abbathia beat*. Mariae Ebor. *existentis, in qua quaedam rotuli et brevia ejusdem cancellariae similiter includuntur, Claus*. ii. *l*. 3. *pars* 1. *m*. 23.

(*g*) See *Wanley*'s manuscripts in *England*, &c. 4149. from vol. VII. VIII. and IX. of the manuscripts and vol. XCII. f. 81. vol. XCV. n. 2.

(*h*) Thomas Tomson, *homo integerrimus, maximam eorum partem ad archiva publica archiepis*. Ebor. *extremo mortis periculo, adduxisset*. Junii 16, 1644.

The

St. Mary's Abbey.

The ichnography of the conventual Church of St. Mary in York.

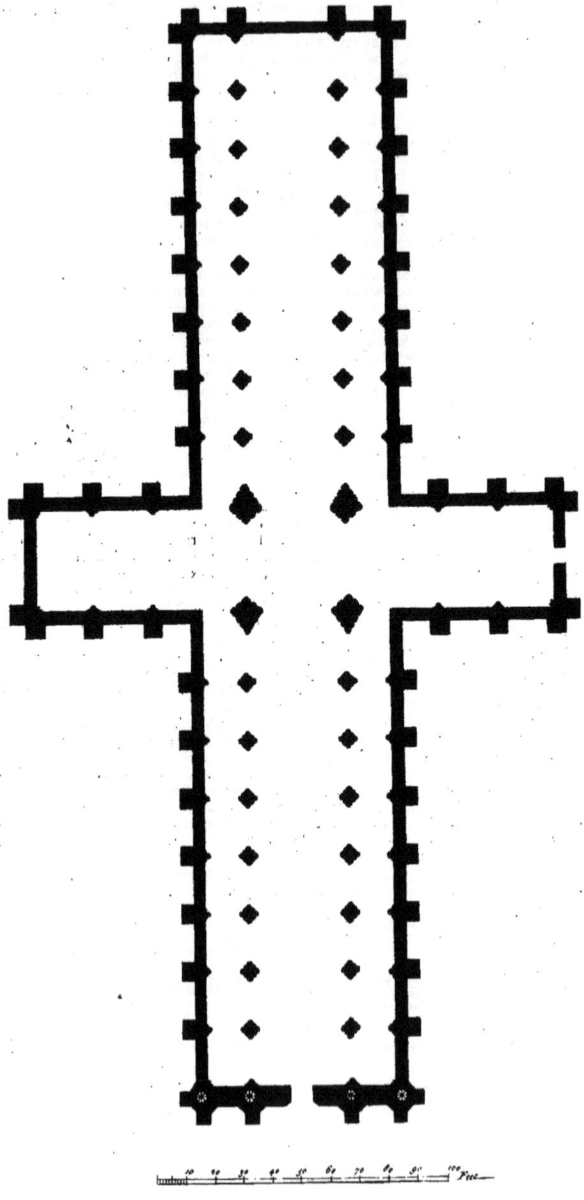

The present condition of this once magnificent pile of *Gothick* architecture, is very deplorable; there being now only so much left of the cloisters, *&c.* as is represented in the larger plate. But yet we may say with the poet that it ST. MARY'S ABBEY.

——— *looks great in ruin, noble in decay.*

The late ingenious Mr. *Place*, who lived in the *Manor*, took pains to trace and measure out the dimensions of the abbey-church, or cloisters, from the ruins, and has given it us at three hundred and seventy one feet in length, and sixty in breadth. This agrees very near with the annexed plan of it, which, for the greater curiosity I have caused to be taken by careful hands; that, though the superstructure be now near totally consumed, this plan may convey some idea of its pristine grandeur to posterity. What has contributed much to the almost total destruction of it was some grants from the crown, for the pulling down and carrying away its stone for the reparation of other buildings. *Anno* 1701, king *William*, at the petition of the knights, citizens and burgesses serving in parliament for the city and county of *York*, and others the justices of the peace for the said county, under his sign manual, gave licence for them, or such as they should nominate, to pull down and carry away so many of the stones belonging to the *Manor*, or abbey of *York*, as should be set out and approved of by sir *William Robinson*, bart. and *Robert Byerley*, esq; towards the rebuilding of the county goal of *York*. Accordingly a large and spatious stable was pulled down, and with other stone of the abbey, the present noble structure of the castle of *York* was chiefly built. *Anno* 1705, queen *Anne* granted off some more stone from this abbey, towards the reparation of the parish church of St. *Olave*, then become ruinous, and the parishioners unable to repair the same. Lastly, *anno* 1717, his late majesty king *George*, at the petition of sir *Charles Hotham* and sir *Michael Wharton* burgesses, and of the mayor and aldermen of *Beverley*, granted licence to them, for the space of three years ensuing, to pull down and carry away stone from the dissolved monastery of St. *Mary York*, towards the reparation of the church of St. *John* of *Beverley*; commonly called *Beverley minster*; then in great ruin and decay. Accordingly a great quantity of stone was taken and carried by water to *Beverley*. The foundations of the wall which faced and ran parallel with the river, were of late years dug up, which I my self saw run very deep in the ground, and all ashler stone. The stone was carried to build the *Staith*, or *Key*, on, which is now at *Lendal-ferry*. The kitchens and other offices of the abbey have been built near this wall; some vestiges of them do yet appear. They had formerly a staith or landing place opposite to a spring now made use of for a cold bath. The walk by the river side might be made very agreeable were it well planted and laid out; as indeed the site of the whole is capable of making one of the finest things of that nature in *England*. In the lords presidents times a large bowling green was used near the ruins of the church; where the *Scots* had that memorable defeat after blowing up and entering St. *Mary*'s tower. I must not forget the noble stone vaults which are still in being and may be compared to any thing of that kind in *Britain*. To conclude this account of its present state, the greatest part of this large enclosure is now a pasture; through which a foot way, by sufferance, runs from the great gate of St. *Mary*'s to *Lendal-ferry*, and enters the city there without gate or postern. The rest of the ground is chiefly disposed and let off by the lessee into gardens. The house was fitted up and is inhabited by the present possessor; and there are several tenants, besides, who occupy the rest of the palace that is now tenantable.

I must here begin to look back and give the reader an account of the first foundation of this great abbey, with the grants and beneficences of several kings to it; the large revenues which were bestowed upon it by the nobility and others, who seemed to vye with one another in their extraordinary liberality to the monks of this convent. The abbot had the honour to be mitred, and had a seat in parliament, whence he was always stiled *lord abbot*; nor were there any but this and the abbot of *Selby*, in the north of *England*, which had that privilege. Whenever he went abroad, either by water or land, his retinue was numerous and grand; and it was little inferior to that of the archbishop of the province. He had several country houses to retire to upon occasion; of which those at *Deighton* and *Overton* were the chief. These houses were situated at about three miles distance from the city, north and south of it. *Overton*, was the chief, and stood upon the most agreeable site of any in this country. The old house was standing here of late years, in the parlour of which, in the year 1661, Dr. *Hutton* read the following inscription on the wood-work (*i*),

Post tenebras lucem

Anno Dom. M.CCCCC. VI. et regni regis Henrici septimi vicesimo primo Robertus Wanop abbas Eborum edificari fecit hoc opus novum, cui mercedem det Deus almus, post tenebras sperans lucem.

(*i*) *Ex MS.* D. Hutton *in biblioth.* Harley.

4

St. Mary's Abbey.

There were ſeveral other broken inſcriptions and coats of armories then in the windows, but none wholly legible or to be made out. They had a fine park, well ſtocked with game, at *Beningburg*, near this houſe; a confirmation of the grant of king *John* to them for making this park may be ſeen in the ſequel *(k)*. The houſe called *Overton-hall* continued in the crown till the fifth of *Elizabeth* when it was ſold to one *John Herbert*; and again, the thirteenth of the ſame queen, to *Elizabeth Herbert*, for ſeventy five pound *(l)*. But the ſite of the houſe, with the park at *Beningburg*, &c. is now part of the poſſeſſions of *John Bourchier*, eſq; In ſhort, the riches of this monaſtery were very great, and their poſſeſſions in land, *&c.* very extenſive, as will be ſhewn in the ſequel. At the diſſolution its yearly revenues were computed to amount to one thouſand five hundred and fifty pound ſeven ſhillings and nine pence by *Dugdale*; but two thouſand and eighty five pound one ſhilling and five pence three farthings *Speed*. Which, conſidering that theſe computations were then uſually made by thoſe that had a mind to be purchaſers, and the difference of money then and now, the bare rents of the lands would amount to an inconceivable value at this day.

Antiquity.

There is great reaſon to believe that there was a monaſtery ſtanding, at, or near the ſite of this abbey, in the time of the *Saxons* and *Danes*. There is great authority to believe that it was built by *Siward*, the valiant earl of *Northumberland*, and the founder was buried in it *(m)*. The monaſtery was then dedicated to St. *Olave*; *Sanctus Olavus* the *Daniſh* king and martyr; which name it retained, even after the conquerour had refounded it, till, by by *William Rufus*, it was changed to that of St. *Mary*. But what order the monks of this older monaſtery were of is not known, the pariſh church, adjoining to the abbey, ſtill retains the antient name of its firſt patron St. *Olave*.

The origine of the abbey of St. *Mary* will be beſt underſtood by a tranſlation, from *J. Leland*'s collections, of an abſtract that induſtrious antiquary made from a little book wrote by *Stephen* the firſt abbot, concerning the riſe and foundation of the ſaid monaſtery. The *Monaſticon* begins the account of this famous place with the hiſtory of its origine done by *Simon Warwick*, who was abbot about *anno* 1270; wherein he has copied what was wrote by his predeceſſor *Stephen*, and brought the hiſtory of it to his own time *(n)*. From both theſe authentick accounts we ſhall be able to make out a tolerable one concerning the foundation, *&c.* of our monaſtery. *Leland*'s abſtract will run in *Engliſh* as follows,

Hiſtory of its foundation.

Anno Dom. 1078, *and twelfth of the reign of* William *the great king of* England, *I took upon me the habit of a monk at* Whitby.

For there were in that place certain brethren, who led an heremetical life, to whom I aſſociated myſelf; the chief of whom was one Remfridus.

This man had dwelt ſome time at Gerua *in* Northumberland, *where ſeeking divine contemplation, he became an hermit; to whom many brethren aſſociated.*

The place, viz. Gerua, *at his coming to it was only inhabited by birds of prey and wild beaſts, but had formerly been a fruitful ſpot of ground to the ſervants of God that dwelt in it.*

But Remfrid, *for the the ſake of leading a more ſolitary life, took leave of his brethren, who were very ſorrowful to part with him, and came to* Whitby. *But there alſo the fame of his ſanctity brought many unto him.*

At which place I being joined unto them, took the habit of a monk upon me.

Remfrid, *with the conſent of the whole fraternity placed me as chief ſuperintendant of the monaſtery; ſo that I was, as it were, abbot elect.*

A certain baron of the king's called William de Percy, *who had given the place unto us, obſerving, that from a perfect deſert, we had much improved the ground; repented him of the good he had done us, and ſtrove as much as poſſible to miſchief us, both by himſelf and followers, in order to make us fly from it.*

And late one night, having collected together a company of thieves and pirates, he came upon us and forced us to abandon our dwelling, took every thing away we had; and ſuch as fell into his hands he tranſported into unknown countries.

There was a place, not far from Whitby, *called* Leſtingham, *which belonged to the king, then uninhabited; but of old it had been famous for a ſociety of monks and religious men.*

At Leſtingham, *having nothing to fear, that place being ſolely under the king's power, I was conſecrated abbot of the ſame.*

But William de Percy, *bearing us an immortal hatred, was not to content take from us very iniuſtly* Whitby, *but finding us ſettled at* Leſtingham, *and deſirous to abide there, he got the king to diſplace us.*

(k) See charter the laſt in this chapter.

(l) Rolls chapel.

(m) *An Dom.* 1056 *ſtrenuus comes* Siwardus *obiit et ſepultus eſt in clauſtro monaſterii ſanctae* Mariae, *extra muros ejuſdem urbis, quod ipſe conſtruxerat.* Ingulphus, p 510. *In monaſterio,* Galmanho. *Vide etiam chron.* Saxon. *ſub hoc anno.* R. Hoveden. *Seward* was a *Dane*, and dedicated his monaſtery to a king of that country canoniſed for his martyrdom to the *chriſtian* religion.

(n) *Ex libello* Stephani, *primi abbatis coenobii. coll. tom.* III. 365. *Biblioth.* Bodleian. *NE. A.* 3. 20.

It

It was now that we were in a terrible state exposed on every side to drunkards and robbers, who frequently took from us our provision, and afflicted us with fear and famine. St. MARY's ABBEY.

About this time I became intimately acquainted with a certain earl called Alan, *of a most noble family, being the son of* Eudo *earl of* Britain; *who commiserating our condition, gave us a church near the city of* York, *dedicated to St.* Olave, *with four acres of land adjoining to build offices on. And, having obtained licence from the king, he kindly perswaded us to come thither and make it the seat of our abbey.*

But Thomas *archbishop of* York *claimed the ground given us by* Alan *to belong of right to him.*

However, when the king came to York, William Rufus, *he came to visit us in our new monastery; and seeing that the building was too strait and narrow for us, he projected a larger and with his own hand first opened the ground for laying the foundation of the church of the monastery. Several lands which are not here necessary to mention, the king also gave towards the maintenance of the monks, free from all regal exaction for ever. Earl* Alan *gave us a town which is in the suburbs of the city, near the church, upon the same conditions. This happened* anno 1088, *and not long after our good friend* Alan *dying, the king, for the sake of his soul, gave us the towns of* Clifton *and* Oureton, *which were of his demesne.*

Thus far *Leland*'s abstract which I have endeavoured to translate *verbatim*, in order to do justice to an author of that great antiquity as our abbot *Stephen* is. But this account being too short I shall enlarge it from that of abbot *Simon*'s printed in the *Monasticon*; the original of which is still preserved in the *Bodleian* library at *Oxford (o)*.

It seems the contest about the four acres of land which earl *Alan* had given to those monks, and the archbishop claimed, was very considerable. The prelate sued them for the same and the earl defended them; but the matter could not be determined. Whereupon king *William* I. to compose the difference, promised the archbishop other lands in lieu thereof, and so the business ceased for that time.

But *anno* 1088, 2 *Will*. II. that king came in person attended with a great number of nobility to *York*; and visiting this monastery of St. *Olave*'s, he found the same to be too little for such a convent to inhabit, and therefore enlarged their ground for the foundation of a new church. For it appears by his charter that he added thereunto the church itself and the site of the abbey, which extended from Galmun, a place so called in the charter to the banks of the river *Ouse*; together with the *Mindam*.

He gave other lands and revenues towards the sustaining these monks; *Alan* their friend and first founder bestowed on them that borough, without the city walls, some time called Earlsburgh; and to strengthen the abbey with the defence of the regal authority the earl granted the advowson thereof into the king's hands.

Anno 1089, the first foundation of this abbey was laid in the presence of the king, who layed the first stone, and many of his principal courtiers, as well lords spiritual as temporal. The king then changed the dedication of the church from St. *Olave* to St. *Mary*.

After this, when *Thomas* archbishop of *York* perceived that this religious house daily increased, he, through the perswasion of some that envied it, renued his suit again for the said four acres of land. *Stephen* the abbot thereupon consulted the king, and he in a great council of the realm held at *Gloucester*, at the feast of our Lord's nativity, granted to the said archbishop, on condition that he waved his suit, the church of St. *Stephen (p)* in *York*, in exchange for the said four acres of land. Besides, abbot *Stephen* himself, that he might be perfectly reconciled to the archbishop, added of his own free will to the revenues of his see, one carucate of land in *Clifton* and another in *Heslington (q)*.

In a general conflagration which burnt down the whole city, *temp. regis Steph.* this former fabrick was destroyed. And *anno* 1270. it was begun to be rebuilt under the direction of *Simon de Warwick* then abbot; who sitting in his chair, with mortar in his hand, the whole convent standing about him, after he had given benediction to it, &c. laid the first stone of the new church; which, in twenty two years he lived to see finished *(r)*. This was the very fabrick whose noble remains we see at this day. *Rebuilding.*

To this abbey of St. *Mary*'s *York* did formerly belong these six following cells *(s)*. *Distant cells.*

St. *Beez*, or St. *Bega* in *Cumberland*. St. *Bega* was a vailed nun, born in *Ireland*, she built a small monastery in Coupland, on the borders, not far from *Carlisle*. This monastery was, *temp Hen*. I. given to the abbey of St. *Mary*'s *York*, by *William Meschines*, son of *Ranulf* lord of *Coupland*, for a cell to their abbey; together with several lands and tythes. They were to send here a prior, and, at least six monks to be constantly resident. One *Robert* is said to have been the first prior of this cell *(t)*. Valued at 143*l*. 17*s*. 2*d*. $\frac{1}{2}$ *per annum*. *St Beez.*

(*o*) Called *annales monast. beatae* Mariae Eborum. *Monast*. Ang. *v*. I. *p* 383. The same book in the *Bodleian* library as the former.

(*p*) Where this church stood is now unknown.

(*q*) *Mon*. Ang. *v*. I. *p*. 386.

(*r*) *Idem*, *et* Lelandi *coll*.

(*s*) *Mon*. Ang *v*. I. *p*. 395. *et paginis subsequentibus*.

(*t*) Lelandi *coll*. A monastery called *Neddrum*, in the county of *Downe* in *Ireland*, was also given to this cell, and to St. *Mary*'s abbey at *York*, by *John de Courcy*, in honour, I suppose of the *Irish* patroness St. *Beez*. *Mon*. Aug. *v* II. *p*. 1022.

Wetherhal,

4

S. Mary's Abbey. Wetherhall. *Wetherhal*, or *Wederhall*, in *Cumberland*, at the time of the foundation of the abbey was given to it by *Radulph Meſchines* earl of *Cumberland*. Here was a church dedicated to St *Conſtantine* to which ſeveral benefactors are mentioned; amongſt them *David* king of *Scotland*, and his ſon prince *Henry* are the chief. *Richard de Reme* was the firſt prior. Valued at 117*l.* 11*s.* 10*d.* ¼.

St. Martin. St. *Martin*'s at *Richmond*, or near it, was a cell given to this abbey by *Wymar*, ſewer to the earl of *Richmond*, with ſeveral lands. Confirmed to it, *anno* 1146, by pope *Eugenius*. The ſeveral rents and revenues of this houſe may be ſeen in the *Monaſticon*. *John de Poppylton* firſt prior. Valued at 43*l.* 16*s.* 8*d.*

Romburch. *Romburch*, in *Cambridgeſhire*, was given as a cell to the abbey of St. *Mary York*, by *Alan*, ſome ſay *Steven*, earl of *Britain* and *Richmond*. Confirmed to it by *Theobald* archbiſhop of *Canterbury*, *Gaufrid* biſhop of *Ely*, and *Everard* biſhop of *Norwich*. And that the abbot and convent might place and diſplace the prior and monks at their pleaſure. *Humphrey de Wouchum* firſt prior. No valuation.

Sandtoft *and* Henes. *Sandtoft* and *Henes*, in *Lincolnſhire*. *Roger Moubray* gave the iſle called *Sandtoft* and large poſſeſſions with it for a cell to the church of St. *Mary*'s *York*. And *William* earl of *Warren* gave *Henes* to the ſaid monaſtery. *Thomas Plunketh* firſt prior of *Sandtoft* and *Henes*. No valuation.

St. Magdalene. The cell of St. *Magdalene*, near the city of *Lincoln*, is put down in a catalogue of the cells belonging to our monaſtery; of which one *Robert de Rothwelle* is ſaid to be the firſt prior. But this is only mentioned in the *collectanea*; though the reader will find other proofs of it in the ſequel.

I now come to the immunities and privileges granted to this monaſtery by *William Rufus*, and his ſucceſſors kings of *England*; which were very great, and equalled if not exceeded moſt of the abbies in the kingdom. By the charter of *Rufus* was granted to them the following immunities *(u)*,

Immunities. William II. 1. That their lands be exempt from all regal exactions.

2. That they be quit of all pleas and quarrels for murder, larceny, ſcutage, gelds, and danegelds, hidages; works done at caſtles, bridges, and parks, and of ferdwite. He alſo granted to it breach of peace.

3. Fightings within their houſe, invaſions of their houſe; and all aſſaults upon their men. With **ſoc, ſac, tol, tem, infangthef,** and **utfangthef.**

4. And further granted them that the men of St. *Mary*'s ſhall not be compelled to attend or do ſuit and ſervice at county courts, **trythyngs, wapontaks** or **hundreds**. That if the ſheriff or his miniſterial officers have any cauſe of quarrel againſt the men of St. *Mary*'s, they ſhall firſt acquaint the abbot therewith; and at an appointed time ſhall come to the gates of the abbey and there receive juſtice and right.

5. This king likewiſe granted them the power of electing their abbot from amongſt their own congregation.

Henry II. King *Henry* II. by his charter ratified all the before ſpecified privileges, and further granted to abbot *Severius* and his ſucceſſors, &c. to enjoy the ſame laws, liberties, dignities and cuſtoms which either the church of St. *Peter* in *York* or that of St. *John* of *Beverley* had ever enjoyed. Whereof this eſpecially was one, that when *Yorkſhire* was ſummoned to ſerve the king in his army, then the abbot hereof ſhall find one man to bear the ſtandard of St. *Mary* in the ſaid hoſt; as the ſaid churches were wont to ſend theirs.

Henry III. King *Henry* III. confirmed, by *inſpeximus*, to the ſaid abbot and convent of St. *Mary*'s all their antient liberties, &c. which his predeceſſors had granted to them. And they were likewiſe confirmed to them by the kings of *England* his ſucceſſors, moſt of which confirmations may be ſeen amongſt the records of the tower of *London*, as by *Edward* I. *Edward* II. *Edward* III. *Richard* II. *Henry* IV. *Henry* V. *Henry* VI. *Henry* VII. and even by *Henry* VIII. who by a large charter of *inſpeximus* confirmed all thoſe liberties to them at firſt, which he afterwards took from them *(x)*.

Viſitation. The archbiſhop of *York*, for the time being, had power once a year to viſit this abbey of St. *Mary*'s, to correct and reform the ſame by the council of the ſaid religious and by five or ſix of his canons of the beſt note. Whence it was that in the year 1343, *William* archbiſhop of *York*, in his viſitation, queſtioning by what right and title the abbot and convent here did claim and receive the tithes, portions and penſions from ſeveral places there mentioned, amounting to a very great number; they produced the bulls of ſeveral popes, and grants of his predeceſſors, archbiſhops of *York*. Whereupon they were by the ſaid prelate allowed, and their title declared good and ſufficient *(y)*.

Order. The religious of this houſe were black monks of the order of St. *Benedict*; which order and habit is too well known to want an explanation here. There is one thing in their

(u) *Mon.* Ang. *v* I. *p* 387 *ad* 390.

(x) A copy of this laſt charter is in my poſſeſſion; but, by reaſon it repeats all that was granted before, it is too long to inſert. The renewing of theſe charters of liberties was not always *gratis* from the throne; for I find that the abbot paid one hundred pound for it in the firſt of king *John*; a great ſum in thoſe days. *Maddox* excheq. p. 560. *Pro cartis renovandis et habend. confirm. regis pro decima venationis Mag. rot.* Joh. *anno primo rot.* 8. b *p.* 276.

(y) *M. A. ibidem.*

worſhip

worship remarkable however, that as several cathedral churches had their liturgies *secundum usum sacrum*, as *York*, *Sarum*, &c. so this monastery had a psalter or office compiled for their devotion; which was agreed upon and published *May* 30, 1390, and styled *consuetudinarium beatae* Mariae Eborum; which book is now in the library of St. *John's* college *Cambridge*. St. Mary's Abbey.

I have before hinted that great animosities and divisions were carried on betwixt the mayor and citizens of one side, and the abbot and convent of St. *Mary's* on the other, about their separate jurisdictions and privileges. And, by what I can gather, were not the monks well supported by the civil power, their sanctity would scarce have protected them from the resentment of the citizens; who seemed to watch all opportunities to destroy them. The annals of the convent before quoted, mention a violent fray betwixt them, *anno* 1262, wherein the citizens slew several of their men, and burned a number of their houses out of *Bootham-bar*. *Simon* the abbot bought his peace at the price of an hundred pounds; but terrified to the last degree at this extraordinary insult, he thought fit to leave the convent for a year or more; for he did not return to it till *Christmass* 1264. *Anno* 1266, upon the instance of divers persons, the citizens of *York* were reconciled to the abbot and convent, and did voluntarily give several releases each to the other, with a saving of the liberties of each party, and of those which belonged to the crown. *Disputes betwixt the monks and citizens.*

This peace did not continue long, for, *anno* 1301, pleas were held of the liberties of St. *Mary's* within the gate of the said abbey; and there sat on the *quinden* of the purification of the *virgin*, *Benedict* being then abbot, the king's justices sir *Ralph de Mettingham*, *William de Bereforth*, *William de Hauward*, *Peter Maleuerer*, *E. de Bermingham*, and *Lambert de Trickingham* in the thirtieth year of the reign of king *Edward* I. in the presence of the lord *Edward* prince of *Wales*.

Anno 1308. there was a charter obtained for the liberties of St. *Mary's*, and confirmed by king *Edward* II. in the first year of his reign, that there should be a fair and market in *Bootham*. This was proclaimed throughout the whole county of *York*, and was inrolled in chancery; but upon the earnest sollicitations of the citizens setting forth the great damage it would do to them and the king's revenue, the same was some time after revoked and a penalty laid thereon.

In the year 1315, on *Martinmass* day, says the annals, the citizens of *York* came with a strong hand and did fill up the ditches joining upon the walls of the abbey, which were made by *Alan* the abbot against the enemies of *England*, *scil.* the *Scots*. This they did, adds my authority, at the instigation of *Nicholas Flemming* then mayor, and others of the citizens, amongst whom one *Sezevaus* (z) was a principal, against divine law and regal justice.

Anno 1316. the mayor and citizens of *York* came to the said abbey, and pulled down an earthen wall made there; but by the just judgment of God, says our annalist, five of the workmen were killed by the fall of it. In the same year the mayor and citizens made a great ditch between S. *Leonard's* hospital and the abbey. And thus they continued to vex one another till archbishop *Thoresby*, scandalized at their proceedings, brought them with much ado to an agreement, and indentures were interchangeably sealed and delivered betwixt them. The original indenture from the abbot is yet amongst the city records, it is in *French*, and dated *January* 16, 1343; and because I take it to be somewhat curious in describing the distinct boundaries, &c. of each jurisdiction, I have thought fit to give a translation of it in the sequel.

An odd case or two relating to the church of St. *Olave's*, and adjudged for the convent in the consistorial court of *York*, may not be improper in this place;

" Master *Nicholas de Easingwald* procurator for the abbot and convent of St. *Mary's*
" *York* shews, that though the abbey hath long had that chapel of St. *Olave's* in their pro-
" per use, yet they did permit the parishioners to meet and offer oblations, &c. Yet hearing
" that the said parishioners intend to make it parochial to the prejudice of the abbey,
" he did, in the name of his said masters, appeal against them in the cathedral church of
" *York*, *Feb.* 4, 1390. *pontificat*, Bonifacii *noni secundo*.

" And afterwards the same procurator, *viz.* *July* 15, 1398, exhibited articles against
" three women, *viz.* *Johan Park*, *Agnes Chandler* and *Maud Bell*, for that they did bury
" one *John* an inhabitant of *Fulford* in the chapel yard at *Fulford*, and not in the
" chapel yard of St. *Olave's*, where such inhabitants ought to be buried; the same being
" done without consent of the said abbot and convent of St. *Mary*, and without due so-
" lemnity or priestly function. Now, lest the inhabitants of *Fulford* aforesaid, by this
" execrable example, should be drawn to commit the like offence, the court enjoyned them
" for pennance that the said *Johan*, *Agnes* and *Maud* should, within three days then next
" following, dig up the body of the said *John*, and carry it to the church yard of St. *Olave's*
" there to be buried with due solemnity. And further, that the said *Johan*, *Agnes* and
" *Maud* should go in procession six *Sundays* in the cathedral church of *York*; six *Sundays*

(z) Sixth and seventh of *Ed.* II. *Nich. Sezevaus*, was representative in Parliament for the city. See the list 1313, 1314.

before

St. Mary's Abbey.

" before the procession of the said abbot and convent in the church of St. *Mary's*; six " *Sundays* about the chapel of St. *Olave's* aforesaid, and six *Sundays* about the chapel of " St. *Oswald* at *Fulford*, bareheaded and barefoot, after the manner of penitents, each of " them holding a wax candle in their hands each of the said *Sundays*. And that hereafter " they do not commit the like offence, and shall submit to this pennance under pain of " the greater excommunication; and to this they were made to swear upon the gospel. " *In quorum omnium testimon. atque fidem presentes literas nostras ex inde fieri fecimus testimo-* " *niales, per magistrum* Rogerum de Cathrick *clericum, publicum apostolica auctoritate notarium,* " *dicteque curie scribam et registratorem. dat. &c. pontificatus* Bonifacii *noni nono* (a).

I come now to give an account of the large possessions and revenues which were bestowed upon this abbey, at several times, by the piously disposed persons of those days; amongst whom were several kings and princes, with the nobility, gentry and others of the realm. The industrious Mr. *Torre* has taken pains to dispose the catalogue of these revenues into an alphabetical order; in relation to the names of the towns where their estates laid. I cannot copy a more exact writer, and shall therefore follow him; observing, first, that before he enters upon a list of the towns, he begins with the site of the abbey, and their possessions in and about the city of *York*. The reader must further take notice that M. A. stands for *Monast. Ang.* R. M. is *Registrum Mariae*; which book, though ill preserved, is now in the library of our cathedral. B. 1. 2. or more, is put for *bundle the first, second*, &c. N°. 1. 2. and the like; refers to the original grants yet in being. I shall take the liberty to transcribe, at length, as many of these valuable remains belonging to the abbey, as have not been before printed. Several of the grants, *&c.* in the register, or leiger book of the abbey, are published, though incorrectly, in the second volume of the additions to the *Monasticon*. And now since the first volume of the *Monasticon* in which the account of our abbey is contained, is allowed to be authentick; and further that the register, with the original grants, are yet to be come at; I believe I may venture to say that no religious house in *England* can produce so many authorities, at this day, of such undeniable evidence.

REVENUES (b).

Abbey site. St. Olave's church.

Alan Rufus earl of *Britain*, the first founder, granted to this abbey the church of St. *Olave*, in which the head of the abbey consists; and also the **burgh**, wherein the church is situate, from **Galmon**, towards **Clifton**. M. A. 390. v. I.

St. Marygate.

Richard de Beverlac and his wife granted to this abbey all their land with the edifices which they had in St. *Marygate*, in the suburbs of *York*. R. M. 61.

Walter son of *Robert Brun* sold unto the said abbey one toft in St. *Marygate*. R. M. 61.

Alice daughter of *Richard Shupton* granted to *Simon* abbot hereof one messuage in St. *Marygate* in *Bootham*. R. M. 61.

Christiana de Karl, wife of *Gilbert* the baker, granted to this abbey all the land which she had in *Bootham* in St. *Marygate*. R. M. 63.

William Brun of *York* granted thereunto all his land in St. *Marygate*. R. M. 64.

Thomas de Wilton granted to it one messuage in St. *Marygate*. R. M. 64.

Robert son of *Ralph de Bakerthorp* granted to it all his land in St. *Marygate*. R. M. 65.

John Rabott clerk, son of *Roger Rabott*, granted thereunto one toft in St. *Marygate* in *Bouthum*. R. M. 67. 81.

John de Cottingham, parson of *N. Cave*, granted to it all his lands and tenements in St. *Marygate* in *Bouthum*; from the king's street to the abbey on one side, to the abbot's garden on the other. R. M. 113.

Roger Rabot of *Hovingham* granted to the abbot and convent hereof one messuage in the burgh of *Bouthum*. R. M. 69.

Boutham.

William de Pontefract granted to this abby one toft in *Butbum*. B. 20. N°. 4. R. M. 72.

William de Nesse rector of *Kirkby* in **Hundesdale**, granted and released thereto one place with its buildings in *Bouthum*. R. M. 70.

John Bothill, vicar of *Kirkby Stephen*, granted to it one toft in the town of *Boutham*. R. M. 71.

Stephen, surnamed *le Messenger* of *Boutham*, granted to it all his capital messuages with their edifices in the *King's-street* of *Boutham*, as far as the head of a garden with a croft adjoining. R. M. 71.

(a) From sir *T. W*'s manuscript, who says the original transcript from the record was, in his time, in the possession of Mr. *Bellwood* vicar of St *Olave's*.

(b) To give the reader an idea of the yearly revenues of this abbey as early as the 19 *Hen.* II. *anno* 1173, I shall give the following account of some payments out of them whilst it remained in the king's hands; *Abbatia de* **Everwick** Godefridus de Lucy *reddit computum de* **so much whereof paid** *in camera curie* LXX *marcas per breve regis, et item in camera curie* XX *l. per breve regis, et elemosina constituta* IV *l. et* VII. *s. ad pannos prebendariorum hoc anno, et in operatione eccl.* IV *l. et* VII *s. hoc anno; et precentori eccl.* XXXI. *s* IV. *d. ad faciendos libros ecclesie; et sacriste ejusdem ecclesf.* XX *l.* XI. *s.* VIII *d. ad luminaria et vestimenta et alia ornamenta eccl. hoc anno; et camerario eccl.* XXXVI *l. et* XVII. *s et* II. *d. ad vestimenta monachorum hoc anno, et ad procurationem monachor.* C *et* LVII *l. et* XVII *s. et* II *d. hoc anno; et celerario ecclesf. ad potum monachorum* XIII *l. et* VII *s. et* IX *d. hoc anno; monachis ejusdem ecclesie* C *et* V *s. et* VIII *d. veteris monete ad faciend. calicem vel textum in obsequio ecclesf. per breve regis. Mag. rot.* 19 Hen. II. 31. *Madox*'s excheq. p. 211. g.

Reginald

Reginald, son of *Thomas de Clifton*, granted to it one toft in *Boutham*. R. M. 72. St. MARY'S
Cecily, late wife of *Thomas de Carleol* of *Boutham*, granted thereunto all her messuages ABBEY.
which she had within the liberty of St. *Mary* of *Boutham*. R. M. 74.

Richard Russel citizen of *York*, granted to it all his land in the street of *Boutham*, which lies westward towards the city ditch. R. M.

Hanco le Grant citizen of *York*, granted to *Simon* abbot thereof a certain piece of land in *Boutham*. R. M. 76.

Adam, son of *Alan Romand*, granted to *Robert de Bello Campo* abbot, *&c.* all his land in *Boutham* on the east side. R. M. 76.

Roger, son of *Hugh*, granted to this abbey all his land in *Boutham-street*, lying west of the port *de* **Galmanlith**. R. M. 77.

Osbert, porter of St. *Mary*'s, granted thereunto, especially to the *infirmary* of the said abbey, all his land in *Boutham*. R. M. 79.

Paulinus, clerk, son of *Stephen de Shupton*, granted to the same infirmary one toft and half in *Boutham*. R. M. 79.

John de Gilling, parson of *Smythton*, &c. demised and released to it eleven messuages and ten acres of land in *Boutham*. And twelve acres of land and one of meadow in a place called **Hurtebuke**. R. M. 115.

Anno 1286. *William Mauger*, being upon a pilgrimage to *Rome*, made his will and be- Petergate.
queathed in perpetual alms to this abbey of St. *Mary* the reversion of all his land in *Peter-gate*. R. M. 54.

William a goldsmith, son of *Godwin*, granted to the abbey of St. *Mary* one land in Haymanger-gate.
Haymangergate.

Walter, a goldsmith of *York*, granted to this abbey, towards the sustentation of the *infir-* Gotheramgate
mary (*c*), a certain land against the church-yard of St. *Trinity* in *Gotheromgate*. R. M. 59. B. 24. N° 23.

Robert Kikelot and *Margery* his wife granted to *Simon* abbot hereof all his land with a Fishergate.
messuage in *Fishergate*.

Lambert Talliator in *York* granted to this abbey all his land in *Usegate*, which extended Ousegate.
in length and breadth between *Usegate* and *Coppergate*. R. M. 57. And one *Wigot* gave thereunto all the land that he had in *Usegate*. M. A. 588.

Emma, daughter of *William de Tikehill* of *York*, granted unto it two messuages in *Walm-* Walmgate.
gate in the parish of St. *Mary*. R. M. 58.

Emma, daughter of *William de Tikehill*, granted thereunto all her land in *Micklegate*. And Micklegate.
three messuages in the same street which are situate on the west side of St. *Martin*'s church yard. R. M. 58.

Mainerus, son of *Richard* artificer of *Durham*, granted to it one messuage in *Sceldergate* Skeldergate.
against the church of St. *John*. R. M. 58.

Roger, son of *Bernulf*, granted to it his land whereon he dwelt in *Monkgate*. R. M. 86. Monkgate.

Alice, daughter of *Richard Grascy*, late wife of *Hamo le Graunt*, granted thereunto all her land in *Monkgate*. R. M. 86.

King *William* the conqueror gave to this abbey one carucate of land at **Munkebrigge**. M. A. 387.

Osbert de Arches gave to this abbey two mansures of land in *York*. M. A. 390.

And one *Groceline* gave four other mansures of land in *York*. M. A. 388.

Richard, son of *Fin*, granted to this abbey the church of St. *Wilfrid* in *York*, with all St. Wilfrid's
the lands appertaining. R. M. 55. *church*.

Lambertus the chaplain granted to it the church of St. *Andrew* with all its purtenancies St. Andrew's.
whereon it is founded, being of his patrimony. R. M. 57.

King *William* the conqueror gave thereunto the churches of St. *Saviour* and St. *Michael* St. Saviour.
at *Ousebridge-end*. M. A. 394. St. Michael.

Nigell Fossard granted to the same the church of St. *Crux* in *York*. St. Crux.

Elyas Flour, son of *William de Merkington*, granted to it all his land in the suburbs of Newbigging.
York in **Newbigging**. R. M. 82.

Reginald Carayser and *Maud* his wife granted thereunto all his land in *Newbigging*. B. 19. N°. 42. R. M. 83.

Thomas Fitz-Thomas Fitz-Gerard gave to it all his land which he had in the suburbs of *York* between the abbey-grange, *&c.* R. M. 83.

Michael de Roumangour and *Gundreda* his wife gave thereunto two tofts in *Newbigging-street*. R. M. 85.

William the conqueror gave to this abbey four carucates of land in *Apelton*. M. A. I. Apelton.
387. 390.

(*c*) Every religious house had an infirmary belonging to it both for the care of their own sick and other charitable uses. The brass mortar made use of to pound their drugs or spices here, is yet in being. I saw it at Mr. *Smith*'s bell-founder in *Micklegate*, but is since sold to Mr. *Addington* perfumer in the *Minster-yard*. Round the verge is this inscription, MORTARIUM. SCI. JOHIS. EWANGEL. DE. JEFIRMARIA. BE. MARIE. EBOR. FR WILLS. DE. TOVTHORP. ME. FECIT. A. D. MCCC.VIII.

Osbert

2

St. Mary's Abbey. *Osbert de Arches* gave thereunto three carucates of land and half in *Apelton* and the miln-dam. B. 2. N°. 42.

Robert de Brus gave to it the manor of *Apelton*. M. A. I. 388.

Robert, son of *Walter de Skegnesse*, granted thereunto half a carucate of land in *Apelton*, which he held of *Simon de Kyme*. B. 4. N°. 7. B. 19. N°. 66. B. 2. N°. 29.

William de Doncaster released to it one toft and twenty acres of land in the town of *Apelton*. B. 4. N°. 12.

John, son of *Alexander de Burdevile*, granted to it three oxgangs of land in *Apelton supra Wyske*, and also certain annual rents. B. 4. N°. 23.

Anno 1367, *Adam de Thornton* clerk, granted to it three messuages and three oxgangs of land and pasturage in *Apelton supra Wyske*. B. 9. N°. 53. R. M. 386.

Anno 1263, sir *Philip de Fauconberge*, knt. granted thereunto two cultures of land in the territory of *Apelton*. B. 2. N°. 18. B. 19. N°. 48.

Also three places of meadow in *Apelton* westings. B. 14. N°. 7.

Sir *John de Reygate*, knt. granted to it all his land in *Apelton*. B. 14. N. 12.

Sir *Philip de Fauconberge*, knt. granted to it four acres of wood with the soil in west-wood at *Apelton*. B. 19. N°. 48. 77.

Anno 1272, *Walter*, son of sir *Philip de Fauconberge*, passed by fine unto *Simon* abbot of St. *Mary's*, *&c.* one miln, two hundred acres of land and ten acres of meadow, and thirteen shillings and eight pence rent at *Apelton* in the *Aynsti*. R. M. 270. 283. 284. 262.

John de Gillings, dwelling in *Apelton juxta Spaunton*, granted to this abbey one messuage and nine acres of arable land in *Apelton*. R. M. 191.

Robert Page of *Apelton juxta Spaunton*, granted thereunto all his land which he had in the town and territory of *Apelton*. R. M. 194.

William, son of *Severic de Apelton*, granted to it three acres of land in *Apelton*. R. M. 197. And also by another charter one oxgang of land there. R. M. 198.

Ralph de Clerc, by the assent of *Mabilla* his wife, granted thereunto the wood called *Calangia*. R. M. 266.

John Harrald and *Simon de Wodapelton* granted to this abbey one messuage called a toft and croft, together with one oxgang of land in *Wodapelton*. R. M. 369.

Abicton. *Stephen*, earl of *Britain*, granted to this abbey his tithes of *Abicton*, in *Cambridgeshire*; so likewise did *Maud* the wife of *Walter Deyncourt*. M. A. I. 387. 389.

Acaster. *Stephen*, earl of *Albermarle*, granted thereunto five oxgangs of land in *Acaster*. M. A. I. 387.

John Malebysse granted thereunto half a carucate of land in *Utter-Acaster*. B. 5. N°. 16. R. M. 375.

Richard Malebysse granted to it two oxgangs of land in *Utter-Acaster*. B. 7. N°. 34.

Thomas, parson of *Acaster*, granted to it his third of twelve acres of land in *Acaster*. R. M. 375. 374.

Alwardthorp. *Stephen*, earl of *Albermarle*, granted to this house of St. *Mary* one carucate of land in *Alward-thorp*. M. A. I. 387.

St. Andrew. *Adam Fitz-Swain* gave to this abbey the hermitage of St. *Andrew*. M. A. I. 389.

Amorsett. *Maud*, wife to *Godard* the sewer, granted to it the town of *Amersett*. M. A. I. 389.

Anloneby. *Walter de Renningwood* granted to this abbey twenty two oxgangs of land in *Anloneby*. M. A. I. 390.

Aynderby. *Asketell de Furneis* granted thereunto two parts of the tithes of his demesnes in *Aynderby*.

Aliton. (*d*) *Robert de Mainill* granted to the same the town of *Alitone*. B. 13. N°. 24.

Aclom. *William de Scuris* granted two oxgangs of land in *Aclom*. B. 19. N°. 36.

Boston. *Alan Rufus*, earl of *Britain*, granted to this abbey the church of St. *Botolph* in *Boston*, *com. Linc.* with one carucate of land, and the miln-dam. *Stephen* earl of *Britain* confirmed it. M. A. I. 390. 387.

Bek. *Berenger de Todeni* granted thereunto one carucate of land in Lindethag in Bek. M. A. 390.

Binbroke. *Berenger de Todeni* granted to the same the church of *Binbroke* with eighty acres of land in *com. Linc.* M. A. I. 390.

William Ascbetill granted it the miln against *Bunebroc*. M. A. I. 389.

Banham. *Walter de Estois* granted thereunto the church and one carucate of land in *Banham*. M. A. I. 387. 390.

Bramham. *Hugh*, son of *Robert German* of *Bramham*, granted to it three acres of land in *Bramham*. B. 23. N°. 12.

Brinston. *Ribaldus* of *Middleham* granted to this house four carucates of land in *Brinston*. M. A. I. 394.

Stephen, earl of *Britain*, granted to it the church of *Bringstune*. M. A. 387.

Bolton. *Stephen*, earl of *Britain*, gave thereunto the church of *Boelton*. M. A. I. 390.

(*d*) This is a mistake in Mr. *Torre*, in the original grant it is *Mitone*, and not *Alitone*.

Hemerius,

a

Hernerius, son of *Arckill*, granted two oxgangs of land in *Bolton*. R. M. 274. St. Mary's
Richard de Rullos granted to this abbey the church of *Bolton super Swale*, and two ox- Abbey.
gangs of land there. R. M. 274.

Acarius de Tunstal granted unto it a certain land in *Bolton* called **Waltheofs laund**, containing two acres. R. M. 275.

Thomas, son of *Elias de Bellerby*, released to *Simon* abbot thereof, &c. all the right which he had in four messuages and half a carucate of land which he had in *Bolton supra Swale*, together with its church; which is a chapel to the mother church of *Catterick*. R. M. 275.

Stephen, earl of *Britain*, granted to it the church of *Patrick Brunton*, and one carucate Brunton.
of land. M. A. 390. 378.

Bardolf granted the same. M. A. 388.

Robert de Musters granted to this abbey four carucates of land and the church at *Brunaton*. M. A. 388.

Stephen, earl of *Britain*, granted to it his tithes of *Basingburg*, in *Cambridgshire*. M. A. Basingburg.
387. 390.

Bernard de Baillol granted to it the church of *Bernard-castle*. M. A. 393. Bernard-castle.

Nigel Fossard granted thereunto the church of *Baynton*, and one carucate of land with his Baynton.
tithes there. M. A. 399.

Stephen, earl of *Albemarle*, granted to it three carucates of land in *Bulford*. M. A. Bulford.
387.

Robert de Stutevile granted to this house the tithes of his demesnes in *Buttercram*, and one Buttercram.
oxgang of land there. M. A. 388.

Gosfred Bainard granted to the same the church of *Burton* and the tithes thereof. M. A. Burton.
388. R. M. 356.

Ivo Talboys granted to this abbey the church of *Burton* in *Kendale*, and one carucate of land. M. A. 389.

Maud, wife of *Walter D'eyncourt*, granted thereunto the land **Northunda** *juxta Burton* in *Lincolnshire*. M. A. 389.

William de Rusmar granted to the same the church of *Burton* in *Holderness*. R. M. 354.

Alan de Spineto and *Adam de Burton* granted to it two oxgangs of land in *Burton*. R. M. 354.

Walter de Spineto granted to it twenty acres of land and pasture in *Burton* which lay near *Hornsey-meer* on the south. R. M. 354.

Goisfrid Bainard granted to this house the land in *Butterwick*, as belonging to the church Butterwyk.
of *Burton*. M. A. 388.

Robert, son of *Durand de Butterwyk*, granted to it the advowson of the church at *Butterwyk*. R. M. 356.

Richard, son of *Richard de Butterwyk*, gave thereunto two oxgangs of land in *Butter-* Rydale.
wyk in *Rydale*. R. M. 219.

Emma, daughter of *Walter de Butterwyk*, granted also one oxgang of land with two tofts and crofts in *Butterwyk*. R. M. 220.

Bertram de Verdun, granted to this abbey the church and two hides of land in *Bosward*. Bosward.
M. A. 388.

Robert de Bridsale granted the church of *Bridsale*. M. A. I. 389. Bridsale.

Alan, the son of *Waldave*, granted the miln in *Bridsale*. M. A. I. 389.

Everard de Breddale granted to this abbey half a carucate of land in the territory of Breddale.
Breddale. R. M. 312.

Robert, son of *Nicholas de Breddale*, granted to it half a carucate of land with the capital messuage in the town and territory of *Breddale*. R. M. 372.

Henry Waleys also granted half a carucate of land in *Breddale*. R. M. 372.

Ivo Talboys granted thereunto the church of *Bethum*, and the land called **Haterbek**. Bethum.
M. A. I. 389.

William Aschetill granted to it two milns in *Belton*. M. A. 389. Belton.

Walter Deyncourt gave to it the church with three carucates and half of land with two milns in the same town. M. A. 389.

Walter D'eyncourt granted to it his tithes in *Blankennai*. M. A. 389. Blankney.

Ascatill Swale granted to it two carucates of land in *Bramtone*. M. A. 387. Bramton.

Waltheof, son of *Gospatrick*, granted to it the church of *Brounfeld* with the corps of his Brounfeld.
manor. M. A. 389.

Godard the sewer granted to it the church of *Botle*. M. A. 389. Botle.

William de Grymestone granted two acres and one rood of meadow in *Bradeleingham*. Bradlingham.
B. 19. N°. 22.

Maud, late wife of *John Nuvell*, granted to this abbey two oxgangs of land in *Bening-* Beningburg.
burg. B. 21. N°. 58.

John, son of *Walter de Marisco*, granted to it six oxgangs of land in *Beningburg*. R. M. 131.

St. Mary's Abbey. And alſo all Grizeriding, and that aſſart called Pate-crofts, and Hugh-riding; and five ſelions of land upon Langlands, together with one oxgang of meadow. R. M. 131.

Walter Fitz-Walter de Beningburg granted thereunto one oxgang of land in *Beningburg*. R. M. 131.

Robert de Beningburg granted to it all his land in *Beningburg* lying between the new garden of *Richard de Malbyſſe* and the eaſt-end of the town. R. M. 131.

Peter de Bruſe granted to this abbey ſix oxgang of land in *Beningburg* which he had of the gift of *John Nuvell*, and three other oxgangs there. R. M. I. 132.

Walter Fitz-William de Beningburg granted thereunto three oxgangs of land in *Beningburg*. R. M. 133.

Robert de Uſegate, rector of St. *Crux* church *York*, granted to it three acres of land and three roods of meadow in *Beningburg*. R. M. I. 135.

Bilburgh. Sir *Robert de Sbegneſs* knight, granted to this abbey all his land in the territory of *Billeburg*; as well in demeſnes as ſervice. R. M. I. 378.

Maud de Mortimer granted to it twenty acres of land in the territory of *Bilburg*. R. M. I. 379.

St. Bees. *William Meſchines* ſon of *Ranulph* granted to this abbey of St. *Mary*'s the cell of St. *Bees* in *Cumberland*. M. A. I. 395.

Bugthorp. *Odo Baliſtarius* granted to it his tythes in *Bugthorpe*. M. A. I. 387, 390.

Barton. *William*, ſon of *William de Barton* granted to it ſix oxgangs of land and two tofts in the town of *Barton*. R. M. II. 170.

Clifton. King *William Rufus* granted to this abbey the town of *Clifton*. M. A. I. 387.

Alan Rufus, earl of *Britain*, granted to it nine carucates and a half towards the water-ſide in *Clifton*. M. A. I. 390.

Caterick. *Alan Rufus*, earl of *Britain*, granted to it the church of *Caterick*; which *Stephen*, earl of *Britain*, confirmed. M. A. I. 390.

Croft. *Stephen*, earl of *Britain*, granted thereunto the church of *Croft*; and the fourth part of the town. M. A. I. 390, 394.

Eniſant Murdake, or *Muſard*, granted the ſame. R. M. II. 272.

Curtune. *Stephen*, earl of *Britain*, gave to it the chapel of *Curtune*. M. A. 390, 397.

Cottingwith. *Nigell Foſſard* granted to this abbey two carucates of land in *Cottingwith*. M. A. 394.

Carthorp. *Nigell Foſſard* granted alſo to it four carucats of land in *Carthorpe*, M. A. 394.

Cokwald. *Robert de Stutevile* granted the tythes of his demeſne lands and two oxgangs of land in *Cukewald*, M. A. 388.

Chevermont. *Berenger de Todenai* granted to the ſame half a carucat of land againſt *Chevermont*, M. A. 388.

Claxton. *Ivo Talleboys* granted to it three carucats of land in *Claxtone*, M. A. 389.

Clapham. *Ivo Talleboys* granted thereunto the church of *Clapham*; with one carucate of land. M. A. III. 9. I. 389.

Colgrim. *William Aſcbetill* granted to it two carucats and a half of land in *Colegrim*, M. A. I. 389.

Crown. *Alan de Crown* granted thereunto half a carucate of land in *Crown*. M. A. 389.

Corby. *Walter D'eyncourt* granted to it all his tythes in *Coreby*. M. A. 389.

And *Maud* his wife granted one carucate of land in *Corby*, with the wood belonging. M. A. 389.

Cotes. *Walter D'eyncourt* gave alſo to it his tythes in *Cotes*.

Cartune. And in *Cartune*. M. A. 389.

Crogeline. *Adam Fitz-Swane* granted to the ſame three parts of *Crogeline* with its church.

Cunquintun. And half a carucate of land in *Cunquintune*. M. A. 389.

Colby. *Eniſant Fitz-Walter* granted one carucate of land in *Colby*. M. A. 389.

Cokermouth. *Alan* ſon of *Waldeve* granted to it fourteen ſalmons yearly out of his piſcary in *Cokermouth*. M. A. 389.

Colton. *William* ſon of *Symon de Colton* granted to this abbey one oxgang of his land in *Colton*. R. M. II. 381.

Dalby. *Berenger de Todenai* granted to this abbey three carucats of land in *Dalby*. M. A. 390.

Elyas de Flamvill releaſed to *Symon*, abbot thereof, all his land in the town of *Daleby*; together with his miln and ſuit to the ſame; and alſo the advowſon of the church. B. 14. N°. 42.

Imania, late wife of *Alan de Flaumvill*, releaſed to the ſaid abbot *Symon* all the right which ſhe had, by reaſon of dower, in the wood of *Dalby*; called *Dalby-Buxtby*. B. 15. N°. 3.

Danby. *Stephen*, earl of *Britain*, granted to it the wood of *Danby-parva*. M. A. I. 387, 390.

William de la Mara granted thereunto one carucate of land in *Danby*. R. M. 25.

Herman and *Brian Brito* granted to it twelve acres of land and certain houſes in *Parva-Danby*. R. M. II. 252.

Richard de Bretevilla granted to it ſixteen acres of land called West-crofts, and three tofts in *Parva-Danby*. R. M. 254.

Nigell

Nigell Fossard granted to this abbey the church of *Doncaster (e)*, and sixteen mansures of land in the same. M. A. I. 394. St. MARY's ABBEY. Doncaster.

Ostrede de Mideltone granted to it one carucate of land in *Dibe*. M. A. 388. Dibe.

Berenger de Todenai granted his tythe in *Dalton*. M. A. 388. Dalton.

Aschatill Swale granted to this abby one carucate and a half of land in *Dunsford*. M. A. 389. Dunsford.

King *Henry* I. confirmed to this abbey all their land from the river *Dun* as far as the water of *Sivena*; as they formerly used to enjoy it before it was afforrested, &c. B. 9. N°. 3. Dun, fl.

Robert, son of *Stephen de West-Cottingwic*, granted to this abbey all the right which he had *in applicatione navium, et in carcatione in aqua de Derwent*; to the bank of **Crossum**. B. 2. N°. 31. Derwent, fl.

Sir *Thomas Baudewin* knight, granted to it one toft and croft, and two oxgangs of land in a culture called **Pykehel**, and another culture called **Knyghthwaytes**, in the town and territory of *Dighton*, R. M. I. 344. Dighton.

Nicholas, son of *William de Holteby*, released unto *Simon* abbot of St. *Mary*'s all his right in five acres of land lying against the **Southgate**, and in one assart towards *Escrick* containing thirty seven acres and a half and two tofts in *Dighton*. R. M. I. 349.

Geffry the chaplain, son of *John de Fulford*, granted to it twenty acres of land in the township of *Deighton* against *Escrick*. R. M. 351.

Anno 1273, sir *Hugh de Nevill* knight, granted to it the manor of *Deighton*. R. M. I. 347, 348.

Ivo Tailboys granted to this abby the church of *Eversham*. M. A. I. 389. Eversham.

King *William Rufus* granted to the same the town of *Elmeswell*. M. A. 387. Elmeswell.

Ribald of *Midleham* granted to it three oxgang of land in *Esby* near *Richmond*. M. A. 386. Esby.

Stephen, earl of *Britain*, granted thereunto the church of *Erghum*. M. A. 387. Erghum.

John, son of *Nicholas de Erghum* granted to it all his culture in *Erghum* lying between the church yard and the river *Teese*; *viz*. four acres of land and a half, and two acres of meadow in the fields of *Erghum*. B. 8. N°. 20. B. 21. N° 61. R. M. 260.

Anno 1187. 33 *Hen*. II. *Philip de Erghum* by fine then levied acknowledged the advowson of the church at *Erghum* to be the right of *Robert* abbot of St. *Mary*'s. R. M. II. 260.

Clemens de Edelingthorp granted to this abby two oxgang of land with a toft and croft in *Edelingthorpe juxta Myton* in *Swaledale*, R. M. II. 236. Edelingthorp.

And by another charter granted in a meadow in *Swaledale* as much as belongs to one carucate of land. R. M. 237.

Stephen de Ponteburg, now *Burrough bridge*, granted to the said abby for the repairs of *Myton-bridge* certain roods of land in **Swaledale**. R. M. 238.

John Rabotts de Hovingham granted to it one messuage and all his land in the town and territory of *Edelingthorp*. R. M. 241.

Roger de Sutton, vicar of *Midelton*, granted to the same one oxgang and fourteen acres of land and a half in *Edelingthorp*. R. M. 241.

Robert Chauncellor granted to it six acres of arable land and a certain meadow in *Edelingthorpe*.

Robert de Stutevile granted one carucate of land in *Edelingthorp*. M. A. I. 388.

Adam, son of *William de Richmond*, granted to this abbey seven acres of land, and one toft and croft in *Erethorp*. R. M. 255. Erethorp.

Adam, son of *Swain*, granted two oxgangs of land in *Elston*. M. A. 389. Elston.

Odo Balistarius granted to this abbey ten oxgangs of land in *Feriby*. M. A. 387, 390. Feriby.

Robert de Vescy granted to it two oxgangs of land in *South-Feriby*. M. A. 388.

Stephen, earl of *Britain*, gave to this abbey the town of *Fulford*, with the whole soke, free from all terrene service. M. A. 387. Fulford.

Stephen, earl of *Albemarle*, granted to it eleven oxgangs of land in the other *Fulford*. M. A. 387.

John Skelton, burgess and dyer of *Northampton* granted thereunto one messuage and two acres of land in *Over-Fulford*. R. M. I. 185.

Bryan, bishop of *Worcester*, granted to it eight messuages and gardens, one dove-coat, thirty acres of land, with four of meadow and four of pasture in *Over-Fulford*; which he had from *William Baxter* clerk. R. M. I. 228.

Jeremiah de Bretegrave granted to it one carucate of land, with its tofts and crofts in *Fulford-magna*. R. M. I. 324.

William de Fulford clerk, and *Thomas de Fulford*, granted seven acres and a half of land arable in *Fulford*; lying in **Newridyngs**. R. M. I. 331.

Nicholas, son of *Richard de Fulford*, granted five acres of land in *Fulford*; lying in a new essart abutting on **Tillemyre**. R. M. I. 381, 343.

Stephen, earl of *Britain*, granted the church of *Forsete*. M. A. 387. Forsete.

Stephen, earl of *Albemarle*, gave one carucate of land in *Fingale*. M. A. 387. Fingale.

(e) *Confirm. eccl. de* Doncaster *abbatiae*. p. 14. Ed. II. p. m. 9. *Turre Lond*.

Odo,

St. Mary's Abbey. Fletham. *Odo*, chamberlain to the earl of *Richmond*, granted to it two parts of the tythes of his demesnes in *Fletham*. M. A. 394. And four carucates of land in *Fingale*. 394.

Foston. *Stephen*, earl of *Albemarle*, granted the town of *Foston*. M. A. 387.

Richard de Morland granted two oxgangs of land in *Foston*. R. M. II. 168.

John Harrald chaplain, granted to it one messuage three cottages and fourteen oxgangs of land in *Foston juxta Kirkham*. R. M. 347.

Flete. One *Harvey* gave to this abbey the town of *Flet*. M. A. 388.

Finmere. *Berenger de Todenai* granted to it nine carucats and a half of land in *Finmere*. M. A. 388.

John, son of *John de Ridlington*, gave to it two carucates of land in *Finimere*. R. M. I. 366. Dated 34 *Hen*. II.

Alice, late wife of *Robert de Braddale*, granted to it two oxgangs of land with two tofts and crofts in *Fynemer*. R. M. I. 370.

John, son of *William le Taylior* of *Fynemer*, gave thereunto two oxgangs of land in *Fynemer*. R. M. 370.

William, son of *Gyles* and *Agnes* his wife, passed by fine unto the abbot of St. *Mary's*, &c. five oxgangs of land, and four shillings and six pence rent in *Fynmere*. R. M. 371. Dated 42 *Hen*. III.

Flaxton. *Stephen*, earl of *Albemarle*, granted to this abbey eleven oxgangs of land in *Flaxton*. M. A. 387.

Herbert de Etton gave to it two carucates of land in *Flaxton*. R. M. I. 370.

Fulkwarethorp. One *Gilbert* gave to it two carucates of land in *Fulkwarethorpe*. M. A. 388.

Foxholes. *Gosfrid Bainard* granted thereunto the church of *Foxholes*. M. A. 388. R. M. I. 356.

Frydaythorpe. *Hugh Burd* granted to it four oxgangs of land in *Frydaythorpe*. R. M. I. 365.

Grimeston. King *William Rufus* granted to this abbey four carucates and a half of land in *Grimeston*. M. A. 390.

Odo Balistarius granted the same quantity. M. A. 387, 390.

King *John* granted to it free warren in *Grimeston*. R. M. I. 186.

Robert de Musters granted to it the church of *Grimeston*, and four carucates of land there. R. M. 229.

Ribald de Midelham granted unto *Stephen* abbot of St. *Mary's*, &c. four oxgangs of land in *Grimeston*. R. M. I. 229.

Jolland de Nevill released unto the abbot of St. *Mary's*, all his right which he had in a piece of pasture in *Grimeston*, lying at *Nesse*. R. M. I. 231.

Gilling in Richmondsh. *Alan Rufus*, earl of *Britain*, granted to it the church of *Gilling*. M. A. I. 390.

Stephen, earl of *Britain*, confirmed it with one carucate of land.

Gilling in Rydale. *Ivo de Vescy* granted thereunto two carucates of land in *Gilling* in *Rydale*. M. A. 388.

Eustace Fitz-John granted to it four carucates of land in *Gilling* in *Rydale*, and the church of the same town. R. M. II. 215.

Gerford. *Ilbert de Lacy* granted to this abbey the church and part of five carucates and a half of land in *Gerford*. M. A. 387, 390.

Gamesthorp. *Maud*, wife of *William D'eyncourt* granted to it the tythes of *Gamesthorp*. M. A. 389.

Garton. *Roger Hovechel* granted to it half a carucate of land and ten acres of his tythes in *Gartune*. M. A. 388.

Graneby. *William D'eyncourt* granted his tythes in *Graneby*. M. A. 389.

Gainford. *Bernard de Baillol* granted to it the church of *Gainford*. M. A. 393.

Guido de Baillol ratified the same donation, and granted to it two oxgangs of land, and the tythes of his manor of *Gaynesford*. R. M. II. 327.

Gofford. *Alan*, son of *Waldeve*, granted to the same two oxgangs of land in *Goleford*. M. A. 389.

Gilmanby. *William de Stokes* granted one oxgang of land with one toft in *Gilmanby*. R. M. II. 278.

Richard de Gilmanby gave all his lands as well in demesne as services, which he had in the town of *Gilmanby*. R. M. II. 278.

Hunkelby. King *William* the conqueror granted to this abbey all that he had in *Hunkelby*. M. A. 390.

Berenger de Todenai gave four carucates of land in *Hunkelby*. M. A. 388.

Huntington. King *William* the conqueror gave to it one carucate of land in *Huntington*. M. A. 387, 390.

Hoton. *Hugh Fitz-Baldric* granted to it eight carucates of land in *Hoton*. M. A. 390, 393.

Nigell Fossard gave to it the church of *Hoton* and one carucate of land there. M. A. 394.

Hoton croft. *Ivo Tallboys* gave to it the town of *Hoton-croft*. M. A. 389.

Sheriff-hoton. *Emma de Humai* granted to it twenty marks of silver annually to be received out of the church of *Sheriff-hoton* from the parson thereof. R. M. II. 155.

Hoton sub Hegh. *Lambert*, son of *Richard de* . . . . granted to the same abbey two oxgangs of land in *Hoton*. R. M. II. 172.

Simeon, son of *Walter Sykelings* of *Hoton sub Hegh*, granted to it his capital messuage, and four oxgangs of land in *Hoton sub Hegh*. R. M. II. 174.

Hugh, son of *Henry* son of *Roger de Hoton*, granted to it two oxgangs of land, with one toft and croft in the town of *Hoton under Hegh*. M. A. 174.

Walter de Percehay released to this abbey all his land under *Houthwit*, called **le Ridings**, against *Hoton subtus le Hegh*. R. M. II. 175.

Roger de Moubray granted to it the town of *Hoton in Rydale*. R. M. 177.

Osbert

ST. MARY's ABBEY.

Osbert de Arches granted thereunto two carucates and a half of land in *Hesei.* M. A. 387, 390. B. 2. N°. 42. Hessey.

Robertus Andegavensis granted to it his tythe and two oxgangs of land in *Hesell.* M. A. 388. Hesell.

Stephen, earl of *Britain*, gave to it the church of *Housewell* and one carucate of land. M. A. 387, 390. Housewell.

Ulfus Fornesan granted to the same one carucate of land in *Hawkeswell.* M. A. 388. Hawkeswell.

Stephen, earl of *Britain*, gave to it the church of *Hornabi* and one carucate of land. M. A. 387, 388, 394. Likewise one *Wigot* gave the same. *Wigan Fitz-Landric* gave the church of *Hornby.* Hornby.

Anno 1367. *John Danby* vicar of *Grymeston* gave to it one messuage and two oxgangs of land in *Horneby juxta Smithton*, which he had of the feoffment of *William de Horneby.* B. 19. N°. 29.

King *Henry* I. gave thereunto all that he had in *Haldenby.* M. A. 387. Haldenby.

Stephen, earl of *Britain*, gave to it two hides of land in *Heselingfield*, in *Cambridgeshire.* And *Segfride* gave nine acres there. M. A. 387, 388. Heselingfeld.

Robert Scales and *Alice* his wife granted to it three acres of land in *Heselingfeld.* B. 23. N°. 44. R. M. 407.

Thomas Fitz-Aldred granted five roods of land in *Heselingfeld.* R. M. I. 407.

Roger de Sumery gave to it the church and tythe and half a hide of land in *Heselingfeld.* M. A. 388.

William de Waren gave this abbey the isle of *Henes*, and piscaries thereunto belonging. This became a cell to St. *Mary's.* Henes.

Roald Fitz-Galfrid de Coleburn granted to the fabrick of this abbey two acres of land in *Hippeswell.* B. 11. N°. 51. Hippeswell.

Gosfrid Bainard gave to it the church of *Harpham.* M. A 388. R. M. 346. Harpham.

Geffry Fitz-Richard of *Harpham* granted to the same three oxgangs of land in the territory of *Harpham.* B. 21. N°. 35.

William Fraunceis of *Harpham* gave one oxgang of land in *Harpham.* R. M. I. 348.

Odo, earl of *Champaign*, and *Stephen* his son, gave thereunto the manor and church of *Horeshay.* M. A. I. 387. Horsey.

Robert de Stutevile gave twelve carucates of land in *Hartune.* Harton.

Ralph Paynell gave thereunto the church and tythes of *Hugeth.* M. A. I. 388. Hugeth.

And also six oxgangs of land in *Howald.* *Id.* 388. Howald.

Gilbert Tyson gave to it two oxgangs of land in *Helmelei.* *Id.* 388. Helmley.

One *Goceline* gave four carucates and a half of land in *Huldelvesdale.* *Id.* Huldelvesdale.

Ivo Tallboys gave the land called *Haverbek.* *Id.* 389. Haverbek.

Walter D'eyncourt gave to it his tythes in *Hanworth.* Hanworth.

And also his tythes of *Hikeling.* *Id.* 389. Hikeling.

Maud, wife of *Walter D'eyncourt*, gave the tythe of *Hevingthorp.* *Id.* 389. Hevingthorp.

Hugh Fitz-Hugh granted to it all his lands that belonged to two oxgangs in *Harneshaw*, and all his meadow upon *Derwent.* R. M. I. 225. Harneshaw.

Gerragot Fitz-Hugh gave also his land and meadow adjoining extending as far as *Hylam-bridge.* R. M. I. 228. Hylam.

John de Huddreswell granted to this abbey one toft and croft and two oxgangs of land in the town and territory of *Huddreswell.* R. M. I. 249. Huddreswell.

Roger Fitz-Gilbert gave to it two oxgangs of land in *Hellingham.* M. A. I. 389. Hellingham.

King *William* the conqueror granted to this abbey of St. *Mary's* all that he had in *Kirkeby.* M. A. 390. Kirkeby.

Berenger de Todenai gave to it eight carucates of land in *Misperton-Kirkby.* *Id.* 390. Kirkeby-Misperton.

Hugh Fitz-Baldric gave four carucates of land in *Kirkby-Misperton.* *Id.* 390, 393.

Patrick de Gaures gave half a carucate of land in *Kirkby-Misperton.* *Id.* 389.

Ralph Fitz-Gerald granted to it the church of *Kirkeby-Misperton*, with all its tythe and two carucates of land. The advowson whereof *John* abbot of St. *Mary's* granted to *William* lord *Ros* of *Hamlake.* R. M. 210, 213.

Robert de Stutevill gave thereunto the tythes of his demesnes in *Kirkeby.* M. A. 388. Kirkeby.

Hernegrine the monk gave to it the church of *Kirkeby* in *Hundelfsdale.* *Id.* 388. Kirkeby-Hundelfsdale.

Gamel de Grymston gave ten oxgangs of land in *Kirkeby.* *Id.* 388. Kirkeby.

Ivo Tallboys gave to the same the church of *Kirkeby-Stephen*, with three carucates of land, his tythes, and half of his demesnes there. *Id.* 389. Kirkeby-Stephen.

Ivo Tallboys gave also the church and tythes of *Kirkeby* in *Kendall.* Kirkeby-Kendall.

Ivo Tallboys gave to this abbey the church and tythe of *Kirkby-Lonesdale.* M. A. I. 389. Kirkeby-Lonesdale.

Nigell Fossard granted to this abbey one carucate of land in *Kymondsall*, and five oxgangs of land on the moors. *Id.* 394. Kymondsal.

One *Orleman* gave to it two carucates of land in *Knapton.* *Id.* 388. Knapton.

William lord *D'eyncourt* gave the tythes of *Knapthorp.* *Id.* 389. Knapthorp.

John de Nesse, rector of St. *Saviour's York*, granted thereunto one messuage and one acre of land in *Kelkfeld.* R. M. 241. Kelfield.

St. Mary's Abbey. Kneton.

Richard, son of *Thomas de Midelton*, granted two oxgangs of land with a toft and croft in the town of *Kneton*. R. M. II. 283.

Lestingham.

King *William* the conqueror gave to this abbey three carucates of land in *Lestingham*. M. A. I. 387, 390.

Berenger de Todenai gave one carucate of land in *Lestingham*. *Id.* 390.

Langthorn.

Stephen, earl of *Britain*, gave four carucates of land in *Langthorn*. *Id.* 387.

Odo, chamberlain to the earl of *Richmond*, gave also four carucates of land in *Langthorne*. *Id.* 394.

Note this belonged to the priory of St. *Martin juxta Richmond* a cell of St. *Mary*. R. M. II. 258.

Lintone.

Stephen, earl of *Britain*, granted to it his tythes of *Lintone*, *com. Cantab.* and one carucate of land there. M. A. 387.

Lynn.

The same earl gave also the tythes of *Lynn*. *Id.* 390.

Maud, wife of *Walter D'eyncourt* gave to the same the tythes of her demesnes in *Lynn*. *Id.* 389.

Langton.

Robert de Stutevill granted thereunto the tythes of his demesnes in *Langeton*, and one oxgang of land there. *Id.* 388.

East-Laton.

Geffry de Forsette granted to it two oxgangs of land in *East-Laton*, in *Richmondshire*. R. M. II. 268.

Lincoln.

One *Goscelina* gave to this abbey eight mansures in the city of *Lincoln*. M. A. 388.

Picote de Lincoln gave the church of St. *Peter*'s in *Lincoln*. *Id.* 388.

One *Norman* gave one culture of land, *juxta Lincoln*. *Id.* 388.

Osbert Goldrun gave thereunto one mansure with certain lands and tythes within and without the walls of *Lincoln*. *Id.* 389.

Picote, son of *Colfuanus*, gave two mansures of land in *Lincoln*, and four acres in the fields, with **le Hevedlande.** *Id.* 389.

One *Romphere* gave all the lands he had in *Lincoln* fields, and the meadow called **Ingland.** *Id.* 389.

Ascbetil Swale gave also one mansure of land in *Lincoln*. *Id.* 389.

Roger, dean and chapter of *Lincoln*, granted to this abbey a burying-place for their monks without their oratory of St. *Mary Magdalene* on the east-side of *Lincoln*. B. 16. N°. 28.

Lovewater.

Alan Fitz-Waldeve gave to it the church of *Lovenefwater*. M. A. I. 389.

London.

Peter de Walins gave thereunto one mansure of land in *Lundune*. *Id.* 390.

Lofthus.

William, son of *Ralph de Lofthus*, gave to it three acres and one rood of land in *Lofthus*. B. 22. N°. 28.

Layburn.

Michael Fitz-Robert gave thereunto two parts of the tythes of his demesnes in *Layburne*. R. M. II. 254.

Midleton-Tyas.

Stephen, earl of *Britain*, granted to this abbey the church of *Mideltone*. M. A. III. 387.

Bernard de Baillol granted to it the church of *Mideltone*, and two oxgangs of land with a toft and croft therein. M. A. I. 393.

Utrect, the son of *Ulph*, gave to it the church of *Mideltone* in *Richmondshire*. *Id.* 390.

Aliva de Midelton granted thereunto all the land in *Midelton* which her son *Patrick* held of her. R. M. II. 282.

Millington.

Ralph Paynel granted to this abbey six carucates and one oxgang of land in *Millington*. M. A. I. 388.

Morton.

Alan Fitz-Waldeve gave three carucates of land in *Moretone*. *Id.* 389.

Myton.

Nicholas le Jovene de Myton granted to it four acres and a half of arable, and four acres and a half of meadow, in the fields of *Myton*. Also eleven acres more of land and two of meadow. B. 12. N°. 66. R. M. II. 144.

Anno 1367. *Thomas*, vicar of *Myton*, granted to it two oxgangs of land in *Myton*, which he had of the feoffment of *John de Fletham* and *Elizabeth* his wife. B. 8. N°. 58.

Robert de Manul, or *Maisnil*, granted to it the town of *Myton*. R. M. 138. M. A. 388. B. 13. N°. 24.

Stephen de Maisnil, his son, confirmed it. R. M. 138.

Richard Molendarius de Myton gave six acres of land and one acre of meadow in *Myton*. R. M. II. 142.

William de Brompton clerk, granted two messuages and sixty acres of land in *Myton*. R. M. II. 148.

John de Hellebek gave to it three tofts and four oxgangs of land in *Myton*. R. M. II. 149.

Stephen, the son of *Ralph de Myton*, gave three acres of land in the fields of *Myton*. And by another charter two acres in the same. R. M. 148.

Roger de Mowbray, in his charter of liberties granted to this abbey, gave leave that they should have a miln and a dam, with a fishery at *Myton*. And because he had demolished their bridge there, he gave them a ferry-boat to make use of till the bridge was repaired *(f)*. R. M. 148. B. 19. N°. 71.

(f) Licentia pro ponte apud Miton *super aquam de* Swale *pro abbate St.* Mariae Ebor. *aut battellum facere aut pontem maintenand' pro libero hominum transitu.* Esch. 31 Ed. III. num. 45.

Odo,

2

Odo, earl of *Champaign*, granted to them the manor of *Marram*, with its piscary. St. MARY's ABBEY.
M. A. 387.

One *Hervey* gave the town of *Mersk*. Marram. Mersk.

Jordan Turchet de Monkton granted to it one oxgang of land and half a toft in *Monketon*. Monkton.
R. M. 388. And sold to it for fifteen marks two other oxgangs with tofts and crofts in the
same town. R. M. 389.

Roger de Clere granted to this abbey six oxgangs and thirty acres of land, five tofts and Marton.
five acres of meadow in *Marton*. R. M. 222. Also seven acres of land more.

Emma de Benefeld granted half an oxgang of land in *Marton*, which the abbey had of the
gift of *Nicholas de Alneto*. And also one oxgang of land which it had of the lord *Robert
D'arcy*. R. M. 222, 229.

Robert Bateman of *Marton* granted to it six oxgangs of land in *Marton*, which it had of
the gift of *Nicholas de Alneto*. Also five acres of meadow which it had of the gift of *Matthew de Marton*. *Id.* 223.

Davide de Morthum passed by fine to this abbey the advowson of the chapel of *Morthum* Morthum.
belonging to the church at *Gilling*. R. M. 268. dat. 10 *Ric.* I.

Ketel Fitz-Elred gave the church of *Mayland* with three carucates of land there. M. A. Moyland.
I. 389.

King *William* the conqueror gave to this abbey three carucates of land in *Northmanbi*. Normanby.

Hugh Fitz-Baldric granted the same. *Id.* 387, 390, 393.

Turgesius de Roderham granted to it two carucates of land in *Nunnington*. *Id.* 390. Nunnington.

King *William Rufus* granted to this abbey the town of *Overton*. *Id.* 387. Overton.

One *Rompharus* gave to it eight oxgangs of land in *Osgadby*. *Id.* 388. Osgodby.

Osbert de Arches gave to this abbey four carucates of land in *Popilton*. M. A. 387, 390. Popilton.
B. 2. N°. 42. R. M. 411. *vide*.

Ketel Fitz-Elred gave the town of *Preston* with the wood. M. A. 389. Preston.

Stephen, earl of *Britain*, granted to it the chapel in the castle of *Richmond*, being a cell Richmond.
of St. *Martyn*. M. A. I. 387, 401.

Also the tythes of his demesne lands and of his men belonging to his castellarie of *Richmond*. *Id.* 387.

Stephen, earl of *Britain*, gave thereunto the church of *Rafenswald*, with one carucate of Refwelitz.
land there. *Id.* 387.

Stephen, earl of *Britain*, gave to it half a carucate of land in *Ryswick*. *Id.* 387. And Rysewick.
one *Dunwald* gave the same. *Id.* 388.

Alan, earl of *Richmond* gave to it the cell of *Romburgh* in *Cambridgeshire*. M. A. I. 404. Romburgh.

Odo, earl of *Champaign*, gave to it three carucates of land in *Runthorpe*. *Id.* 387. Runthorp.

One (g) *Bardolf* gave to this abbey the church of *Ravenswath*, with one carucate of land Ravenswath.
there. *Id.* 388.

Walter Peverell granted to it eight carucates of land with the advowson of the church in Rudston.
Rudstan. M. A. I. 388. R. M. 359.

Stephen de Champenes in *Erydaythorp*, and *Katherine* his wife, granted to it half an oxgang
of land, with the whole part of their wood in the town and territory of *Rudstan*. B. 11.
N°. 34. R. M. 362.

Robert de Canteburg, and *Alice* his wife, granted to *Simon*, abbot, half an oxgang of land
with his whole part of three tofts in the town and territory of *Rudstan*. B. 25. N°. 46.

Cecily de Walkington released the same. B. 22. N°. 47.

Walter Fitz-Geffry de Hugate, and *Beatrix* his wife, released unto *Robert* the abbot all the
right they had in the advowson of the church of *Rudstane*. R. M. 359.

Maud, late wife of *Walter de Garton*, granted to it one toft and half an oxgang of land
in *Rudstan*. *Id.* 360.

Juliana, late wife of *John de Cornwall*, granted thereunto half an oxgang of land with the
whole part of three tofts in *Ruddestan*. *Id.* 361.

Hugh Fitz-Hugh granted to it one toft in *Roston*, and all his land appertaining to two ox- Roston.
gangs of land in [illegible]. R. M. II. 225.

William, bishop of *Durham*, granted to it one carucate of land in *Roudeclive*. M. A. 388. Rocliffe.

William Fitz-Thomas de Roucliffe granted one toft and two oxgangs of land in *Roucliffe*.
R. M. 321.

Reyner, the sewer, gave two oxgangs of land in *Rolingtune*. M. A. 389. Rolington.

Ralph Fitz-Robert de Rednesse granted to it a place within his court in the town of *Rednes* Rednes.
to build a granary on. B. 10. N°. 46.

William, son of *Ranulph Rure of Rednesse*, granted to it six acres of land in *Rednes*.
B. 18. N°. 13. R. M. 393.

John de Burringham of *Rednesse* granted to it two tofts and crofts in *Rednes*. B. 18.
N°. 49.

William, son of *Emma de Rednes*, gave a piece of land in the field of *Rednes* in a place
called le places with the site of a wind-miln. B. 19. N°. 49.

(g) Ancestor to the lords *Fitzhugh*, says Mr. *Torre*.

William

St. Mary's Abbey. *William Fitz-Ralph de Redness* granted thereunto two selions of land containing three acres in the territory of *Rednesse*. B. 20. N°. 37.

Richard Aunger de Redness granted to it six acres and half of land in the territory of *Redness*. R. M. 392.

Stephen Lawys of *Whitgist* granted to it two selions of land in *Redness*; one whereof is called **Neubrek**, and the other **Rysfeld**. *Id.* 393.

Spaunton. King *William* the conqueror gave to this abbey two carucates of land in *Spanton*. M. A. 387, 390.

Berenger de Todenai gave thereunto six carucates of land in *Spanton*. *Id.* 390. 393.

John, son of *Peter de Spaunton*, granted to it one messuage, one toft, and two oxgangs of land in the town of *Spaunton*. B. 9. N°. 19. R. M. 179.

John Shalcoks de *Hoton underhegh* granted to it a culture of land called **Ryddinges** against **Pyperthwaites** in the town of *Spaunton*. R. M. 179.

Sutton in Holland. *Alan Rufus*, earl of *Britain*, granted to this abbey the town of *Sutton* in *Hoiland*. M. A. 390.

Robert de Maisnil granted twelve oxgangs of land in *Sutton*. *Id.* 388.

Geffry Murdac gave to it twelve oxgangs of land in the same town. M. A. 388.

Sutton. *Patrick de Gaurges* granted to it two carucates and half an oxgang of land in *Sutton*, against *Norton-bridge*. *Id.* 389.

Sutton in Galtres. *Ranulph de Nevil*, sold to *Simon* the abbot, all the wood, timber and underwood growing being and standing in the **Lunds** of *Sutton* in **Galtres**, dated *anno* 1294. R. M. 137.

Stakelden. *Berenger de Todenai* granted to it six oxgangs of land in *Stakelden*. M. A. 390.

Skirtembeck. *Odo Balistarius* gave thereunto his tythes in *Skirpenbek*. *Id.* 387. 390.

Stephen, earl of *Britain*, gave to it one carucate of land with the *Milndam* in *Scirebek*. *Id.* 387.

Ulfus Fornesan gave to it one carucate of land in *Skirtonbeck*. *Id.* 388.

Stretton. *Ilbert de Lacy* gave thereunto part of five carucates and half of land in *Stretton*. *Id.* 387. 390.

Sezay. *Astinus de Pykering* gave half a carucate of land in *Sezevall*.

Marmaduke de Arell granted thereunto the church of *Sezai*. B. 10. N°. 7. R. M. 317.

Suthorp. *Richard Fitz-Richard de Spineto* released unto this abbey three oxgangs of land in *Suthorpe*, which stands against *Hornsey-meer*. B. 10. N°. 25.

Ralph, son of *Beatrix de Uvegate*, granted to it one oxgang of land in *Suthorp*. B. 20. N°. 56. R. M. 355.

Reginald, son of *William le Paumer de Suthorpe* granted to it one oxgang of land in *Suthorp-field*. R. M. 354.

Smithton. *Hardwine des Escalliers* gave thereunto the church of *Smitheton* and four carucates of land. M. A. 388.

One *Bernald* granted one carucate of land more in the same town. *Id.*

Reginald, called the son of the lady of *Smitheton*, in *Richmondshire*, granted unto *Simon* abbot, one messuage and a croft, four oxgangs, and six acres of land in *Smitheton*. B. 2. N°. 11.

Walter de Killingholm granted to it his miln in *Great Smitheton*, situate on the river *Tees* against **Pilcetworth**. R. M. 285.

Geffry Fitz-Ranulf of *Great Smithton* granted thereunto six oxgangs of lands in the town and territory of *Smytheton*, with four crofts and tofts and half a carucate of land appertaining. Also five other crofts with tofts adjoining and two acres of land. R. M. 287.

Stainburn. *Waltheof*, the son of *Gospatrick*, gave the town of *Stainburn*. M. A. 389.

John, son of *Adam de Whitegist*, granted to it five tofts and four oxgangs of land in *Stainburn*, which was of the fee of the abbey. B. 19. N°. 73.

Stiviton. *Stephen*, earl of *Britain*, gave thereunto five carucates of land and the church of *Stivetune*. M. A. 387.

Sir *Robert*, son of *Walter de Skegness*, knt. granted to it all his land which he had in the town of *Stivetune*, as well in demesn as services. R. M. 381.

Scotton. *Stephen*, earl of *Britain*, gave to it four carucates of land in *Scottane*. M. A. 387.

Stephen, earl of *Britain*, gave two carucates of land in *Skelton*, *Cambridgeshire*. *Id.* 387.

Santoft. *Godfrey de le Wyrch*, gave thereunto the isle of *Santoft* for a cell. *Id.* 389. 405.

Semere. *Bareth*, son of *Corby*, gave one carucate of land in *Semere*. *Id.* 388.

Straingham. *Robert de Stutevile* gave to it the tithes of his demesnes in *Straingham*. *Id.* 388.

Scainston. One *Hugh* gave thereunto twelve oxgangs of land in *Scamston*. And *Robert de Insula* gave twelve oxgangs more in the same place. *Id.* 388.

Robert de Insula gave one carucate and half of land in *Scamston*. R. M. 363.

Astine de Pykerings granted to it two oxgangs of land in *Scamston*. *Id.* 363.

Sproxton. *Waldingius* gave thereunto one carucate of land in *Sproxton*. M. A. 388.

Stokeley. *Wido de Baillol* gave to it one carucate of land and the church of *Stokely*. M. A. 388. R. M. 302.

Wido

Wido de Baillol gave allo the church and two oxgangs of land in *Stayneton*, with the tithe of his demesnes. *Iidem*. St. MARY'S ABBEY. Stayneton.

Robert de Brus gave thereunto two carucates of land and one miln in *Sunderlandwick*. M. A. 388. Sunderlandwick.

Robert de Bridesale gave two carucates of land in *Steresby*. *Id.* 389. Steresby.

Ured, son of *Ligolf*, gave to it the miln at *Stotby*. *Id.* Stotby.

Ured, son of *Ligolf*, gave also the tithe of his demesn in *Saurby*. *Id.* Saurby.

Waltheof, son of *Gospatrick*, gave thereunto the tithes of his demesnes in *Salchild* in Coupland. *Id.* 389. Salkeld.

Gospatrick, gave to it the town of *Saltergh*. M. A. 389. Saltergh.

William, son of *Gilbert*, gave to it all his lands in *Snachevel*. *Id.* 389. Snachevel.

Adam de Thornton, rector of *Patrick-Brunton*, granted to it three messuages, one wind-miln, four oxgangs and two acres of land in *Sixendale*. R. M. 249. dated 7 *Rich.* II. Sixendale.

Ralph de Camera granted to it two acres of land in *Shupton*, and three acres more there in the moor called Sevilands. *Id.* 113. Shipton (*h*).

Ralph, son of *Richard de Camera*, released to it also two oxgangs of land in *Shupton*, out of sixteen oxgangs which he there held of the said abbey. *Id.* 112.

Richard, son of *Ralph de Camera*, released to *Simon* abbot thereof his capital messuage with the edifices in the town of *Shupton*, and six oxgangs of land with the demesne of the third part of the town; with certain annual rents, with the homages and services of three freeholders, of four oxgangs of land and eight acres. *Id.* 119.

David de Longocampo granted unto *Simon* abbot all his land with his messuage in *Shupton* in Galtres, as well in demesne as services. *Id.* 120.

Stephen de Shupton released to it all his right in two carucates of land in *Schupton*. And granted also two other carucates, with five tofts and crofts in the same town. *Id.* 120. 121.

Roger de Thornton gave to *Simon* the abbot one toft and croft and one oxgang of land in *Shupton* in Galtres. *Id.* 124.

Margery, late wife of *Roger Ungton*, granted to it two oxgangs of land four shillings rent in the town of *Shupton* in Galtres. *Id.* 127.

Maud, wife of *Walter D'eyncourt* gave to this abbey the tythes of her dominion in *Tudesham*. M. A. 389. Tudesham.

King *William* the conqueror gave to this abbey six mansures of land in *Paines Thorp*. *Id.* 390. Thorp.

Odo, earl of *Champaign*, gave to it the town of *Thorpe juxta Marram*. *Id.* 387.

Stephen, earl of *Britain*, gave the church of *Torenton*, and one carucate of land. *Id.* 387. Torenton.

Nigel Fossard gave three carucates of land in *Thornton*. *Id.* 394. Thornton.

Stephen, earl of *Albemarle*, gave two carucates of land in *Thornton*. *Id.* 387.

Geffry de Thornton granted to it three oxgangs of land in *Thornton*, held of the abbey in *demesne*. R. M. 162.

Roger, son of *Hulco de Foston*, granted to it all his meadow in the field of *Thornton* called Pilverdale. *Id.* 165.

Adam de Butterwick granted to it two oxgangs of land with a toft and croft in *Thornton*. *Id.* 165.

John Danby chaplain gave to it one toft and croft and two oxgangs of land in *Thornton juxta Foston*. *Id.* 336.

Walter D'eyncourt gave thereunto his tythes of *Thurgeston*. M. A. 389. Thurgeston.

Roger de Lascells granted to it the third part of the tythes of his demesne in *Thirntofts*. R.M. 261. Thirntofts.

King *Henry* I. gave to this abbey the town of *Usefleet*, and whatsoever to it belongs lying between *Usflet* and *Ayremyn*. M. A. 387. Usefleet.

John de Graunt released to to this abbey all his common of pasture which he had in forty acres of land in *Usflete*, and which *John de Usflete* had given to these monks. B. 24. N°. 28.

One *Gosceline* gave to it one carucate of land in *Wassand*. M. A. 388. Wassand.

Stephen, son of *Walter de Haytefeld*, released to this abbey all the right and claim that he had of fishing in the meres of *Wassand*, *Seton*, *Hornsey*, and *Agnesburton*, &c. B. 8. N°. 38.

William de Escois gave to it the church of *Wyllweby* and his demesne tythes there. M. A. 387. 390. Willoughby.

William de Evereus by fine acknowledged the advowson of the church of *Wyleby juxta Castell-Bukenham* to be the right of *Simon* abbot of St. *Mary's*, &c. R. M. 410. dated 14 *Edward* I.

Stephen, earl of *Britain*, gave to it his tythes and one oxgang of land in *Witrene* in *Cambridgeshire*. M. A. 387. Witrene.

Nigell Fossard gave thereunto one carucate of land in *Wormesworth*. *Id.* 394. Wormesworth

(*h*) *Confirmat. diversarum terr. et ten. in* Schupton. *pat.* 14 Ed. II. *p.* 1. *m.* 9. *Turre Lond.*

St. Mary's Abbey. Wederhall. Watton. Wintrington. Winton. Wreth. Werkinton.

King *William* the conqueror gave to it the cell of *Wederhall*, in *Cumberland*. *Id.* 397.

One *Humphry* gave a carucate of land in *Watton*. *Id.* 388.

Alvoredus gave four oxgangs of land in *Wintrington*. *Id.* 388.

Ivo Tallboys gave to it two oxgangs of land in *Winton*, with his tythe there. *Id.* 389.

Gosfrid de Stutevile gave the isle of *Wreth* and the piscaries. *Id.* 389.

Retel Fitz-Elred gave the church of *Wirchintune* with two carucates of land with the miln there. *Id.* 389.

Whitingham. *Rainer* the sewer gave the church of *Whitingham*. *Id.* 389.

Yorkshire. King *William Rufus* granted to this abbey the tythes of his demesne throughout his whole castellary in *Yorkshire*. M. A. 390.

King *Henry* I. gave to it the tythes of all his venison, both in flesh and skins, in *Yorkshire*. R.M. 178.

Besides these revenues several churches paid tythes, portions and annual pensions to this abbey, all specified in a visitation by *William* archbishop of *York*; made *anno* 1344. M. A. 392.

Inrolment. *November* 29, 30 of *Henry* VIII. the surrender of this abbey of St. *Mary York* was inrolled (*i*).

A CATALOGUE of the ABBOTS of St. Mary's.

When instituted.	Abbots *names.*	*When vacated.*	*Authorities.*
Anno Dom. 1088	Stephen de Whitby, soon after the foundation, was appointed first abbot of this place. He is said to have governed with great prudence twenty four years.	By death *Anno Dom.* 1112.	Leland. *coll. t.* I. *p.* 22. *t.* II. *p.* 199 *M. A.* I. *p.* 395.
1112	Richard succeeded; he governed eighteen years and five months.	1131. *prid. cal.* Jan.	The same.
1131	Godfrid reigned one year and six months.	1132. 16 *cal.* Aug.	Leland. *coll. t.* II: *p.* 199. *M. A.* I. *p.* 395.
1132	Savaricus, or Saverinus, was abbot; he governed thirty years.	1161. 3 *nones* Ap.	The same.
1161	Clement succeeded, who is said to have ruled the convent, very ill, for twenty three years.	1184. 15 *cal.* Sept.	x *script. p.* 503. *M. A.* as before. R. Hoved. 355.
1184	Robert de Harpham reigned five years.	1189. 13 *cal.* Maii.	*M. A.* as before.
1189.	Robert de Longocampo, prior of *Ely*, *B. Willis* says, was elected abbot this year and died *anno* 1239, a fifty years reign, which is scarce possible. *R. de Diceto* mentions one *Robert* to have been chose abbot of this monastery, *anno* 1197, and calls him prior of *Ely*.	Deposed 1195.	x *script.* 523. *M. A.* I. 395. R. Hoved. 429.
1239.	William Roundele was abbot and reigned five years.	1244. 3 *cal.* Dec.	*M. A.* 395.
1244.	Thomas de Warterhille, governed fourteen years.	1258. 16 *cal.* Junii.	The same.
1258. *In fest. nat. S.* Johan. *bapt.*	Simon de Warwick, a great and learned man, and an excellent governour and benefactor to the fabrick. He ruled the monastery thirty eight or thirty nine years (*k*).	1296. 3 *non.* Jul.	*Ibidem.* Lelandi *coll. t.* I. *p.* 23.
1299. *Pridie fest.* S. Jacob *ap.*	Benedict de Malton, called in the *monasticon* erroneously Menton. He ruled seven years, and then resigned his charge.	By resignation. 1303. 7 *kal.* Aug.	*Pat.* 24 Ed. III. *M. A.* I. 395.
1303. *Id.* Aug.	John de Gillings, first a monk of this abbey, afterwards prior of *Wetherhale*, was elected. He sat ten years.	By death, 1313. 9 *cal.* Julii.	*M.A.* 395. *Torre* 827. from the church records.
1313. 4 *non.* Jul.	Alan de Nesse a monk of this house succeeded.	1331.	*M. A.* 395. Torre.
1331. 7 *kal.* Jul.	Thomas de Malton another monk of this convent was elected.	1359.	*Pat.* 6 Ed. III. Torre.

(*i*) The inrolment of the surrender of this abbey, in the usual form, is in *claus. an.* 31 Hen. VIII. *pars quarta n.* 19. with this title, *De scripto abbatis et conventus S.* Marie *juxta civitatem* Ebor. *Dat. in domo sua capitulari et recog. apud* Seynt Maryes *vicesimo nono die mensis* Novembris *anno regni reg.* Hen. VIII. *tricesimo primo*, 1540. Rolls chap.

(*k*) *Anno* 1296. 3 *non* Julii *obiit*. Simon de Warwick *abbas monasterii S.* Mariae Eboraci, *cui praefuit ann.* 39. *Sepultus fuit coram mag. altari eccle. S.* Mariae *quam infra* 24 *an. de novo aedificabit. Col.* Lelandi.

When

When instituted.	ABBOTS *names.*	*When vacated.*	*Authorities.*
1359. 16 Maii.	WILLIAM DE MAREYS a brother of this monastery came in.	1382.	*Pat.* 34 Ed. III. Torre.
1382. 7 Sept.	WILLIAM DE BRIDFORD a monk was elected.	1389.	
	THOMAS STAYNEGRAVE.	Died 1398.	Wood. *Ath. Ox. t.* I. *coll.* 553.
1398. Maii 24.	THOMAS PIGOTT was confirmed abbot of this monastery.	1405.	*Idem.*
1405. Jun. 21.	(*l*) THOMAS SPOFFORD, he was afterwards bishop of *Hereford*.	By resignation 1422.	Goodw. *de praes. p.* 580.
1422.	WILLIAM DALTON who died the year following. And	1423.	*Pat.* 10 Hen. V.
1423.	WILLIAM WELLS was elected abbot. He was made bishop of *Rochester*.	Resigned 1437.	*Pat.* 1 Hen. VI. Goodwin *p.* 580.
1437. *ult.* Maii.	ROGER KIRKEBY was elected. He died the same year and was succeeded by	1437.	
1438. Nov. 6.	JOHN COTTINGHAM the prior of this monastery.	1464.	Torre *p.* 827.
1464. Oct. 4.	THOMAS BOTHE, I do not find when he died, but *Anthony Wood* tells us he was succeeded by		*Ath. Ox. t.* I. *col.* 553.
	WILLIAM SEVER, *alias* SEVEYER. *An.* 1495, he was elected bishop of *Carlisle*; and by a special indulgence from the pope held this abbey *in commendam*. But being afterwards preferred to *Durham* it became vacant, and he was succeeded by	1502, by translation to *Durham*.	Goodw. *de praes.* 152. *A.* 9. 165.
1502. Dec. 20.	ROBERT WANHOP a brother of this house; after whom came	By death 1507.	Wood. *Ath. Ox. t.* I. *coll.* 553.
1507. Maii 6.	EDMUND THORNTON, who dying was succeeded by	1507.	Torre 827.
1521. Mart. 13.	EDMUND WHALLEY, after whom came		*Idem.*
1530. Feb. 23.	WILLIAM THORNTON, or *William de Dent*, who was abbot at the time of the dissolution, and, surrendering up his abbey to the king, obtained a very large pension of four hundred marks *per an.* for his life (*m*).	1540, surrendered.	*Torre.* *Willis* on the mitred abbies.

(*n*) *ARTICLES of agreement betwixt the abbot and convent of St.* Mary *and the mayor and commonality of the city of* York.

THIS indenture witnesseth, that whereas great debates, dangerous and perilous, have long been between the abbot and convent of our lady of *York* of the one party, and the mayor and commonality of the city of *York* on the other part, about the jurisdiction of *Bootham*; which the said abbot and convent claim as their free burgh, and the mayor and commonality claim to be the suburbs of the said city. Be it known, to eschew the evils and perils that may come of the said debate, it is agreed that agreement shall be made betwixt the parties aforesaid, by the mediation of the archbishop of *York*, in manner that followeth. That is to say, that *Bootham* intirely, with the curtilagies, tofts and all other appurtenances, except one street which is called St. *Marygate*, with other tenements underneath specified to the jurisdiction of the said abbot and convent reserved, shall become peaceably for ever within the jurisdiction of the said mayor and commonality, their heirs

(*l*) King *Henry* IV's mandate to his escheator in the county of *York* to deliver up the temporalities of this abbey to *Thomas de Spofforth*, in his election to be abbot, bears date at *Duresme June* 1, 1405. *Foed. Ang. t.* VII. *p.* 386.

(*m*) The abbots that died here in all probability were buried in the monastery, but no remains of any of their tombs appear in the ruins of the abbey church at this day; except one without any inscription, *Leland* has this remark, Gul. Senows *electus epis.* Dunelm. *anno* 1502, *obiit* 1505, *sepult. est* Ebor. *in monasterio S.* Mariae *ubi antea monachus fuerat. Coll.* Lelandi.

(*n*) The original of this, in *French*, is amongst the records on *Ousebridge*, drawer 3. I have met with a translation of it in a manuscript lent me, but very incorrect.

and successors, as suburbs of the same city, and within the franchise of the same, without challenge of the said abbey and convent and their successors. And the said street of St. *Marygate*, and all the tenements within the same, with all the gardens and curtilagies to the said tenements appertaining, from the *new round tower* unto the water of *Ouse* and the place called *l' Aumonerie-garth* inclosed with a wall and a hedge against the *north* to the fields of *Clifton*; and from thence against the *west* by a ditch to the water of *Ouse* be wholly in the jurisdiction of the said abbey and convent and their successors for ever. And that the said mayor and commonality, nor none of their heirs and successors, shall have any jurisdiction in any of the said places for ever. And moreover it is agreed that it shall be lawful for the said abbot and convent and their successors to cleanse a *ditch* which extendeth from the said *round tower*, butting on St. *Marygate*, to the gate of the said city which is called *Bootham-bar*; which ditch is within the suburbs aforesaid, as oft as it shall please them for the safeguard of the walls, by which the abbey is inclosed against the great street of *Bootham*; and also that at what hour that need shall require to repair the walls of the said abbey. That the said abbot and convent and their successors have power in the *high street*, from thence for the said tower and walls which descend from St. *Marygate* to *Bootham-bar* before, as the wall of the abbey extends itself, to re-edify, make new or repair every time that need requires at their pleasures. Also to have power in the place which descendeth from *Bootham-bar* to the water of *Ouse*, between the walls of the said abbey and the ditch of the said city, for the said walls, there to make new, re-edify and repair, every time that need shall be, at their pleasure. Also it is agreed that the said mayor and commonality, and their heirs or successors shall not build in the place where the said ditch is, which extends from St. *Marygate* to *Bootham-bar*; and if it shall happen that the said place or parcel there where the said wall stands, between the said *round tower* to *Bootham-bar*, shall be builded upon by the said abbot and convent, or their successors, with houses or dwelling opening against the said street of *Bootham*, that then the said place so builded from that time to come shall be within the franchises and jurisdiction of the said mayor and commonality, and their heirs and successors as parcel of the suburbs of the said city; and otherways not.

It is also agreed that the said abbot and the monks of the said house, which for the time shall be, shall not be arrested or attached by their body in any part of *Bootham* by the said mayor and commonality, or their heirs or successors in any part of the same, except it be for felony, trespass, or by the commandment of the king, or of the justices, stewards or marshals of the king's house; and that the victuals, cattle, goods and chattles of the said abbey and convent, and their successors, shall not be taken or arrested in any part of *Bootham*, by the said mayor and commonality, their successors, nor their ministers for any cause. And that none who carry the said victuals, beasts, goods or chattels towards the said abbey, or any of them, by *Bootham*, be there for any cause arrested and hindred from bringing thither the said victuals, goods, and chattels. And the said mayor and commonality, of their courtesy and liberality, grant for them and their successors, that those who shall make any arrest shall give warning, for the continuance of friendship between the city and the abbey, to the porter, or him that shall be found at the gate of the said abbey, to search the said victuals, beasts, goods and chattels, so as they shall not perish, be lost or purloined. Also for that it is not reason that the tenants of the said abbey and convent and their successors, which be or shall be within the jurisdiction of the said mayor and commonality, be twice charged; that is to say towards those of the city, and also towards those of the geldable, in charges or quotas that shall be granted; it is agreed that the said mayor and commonality, their heirs and successors, to whom they are or shall be contributary, shall aid them by all the ways they can, that they may not be chargeable with those of the geldable. And that they shall give them all the assistance they well can, that those who are and shall be in the jurisdiction of the said abbey and convent, and their successors, in St. *Marygate* shall not be charged extravagantly with those of the geldable, but shall pay according as they have been wont to pay, and this clause to be put in another indenture if needful. Moreover the abbot and monks aforesaid, and their successors, as other men of trade, shall have the same privilege, and be of the same condition in the water of *Ouse*, from the ditch which runneth on the back side of **l' Amoury-garth**, between the meadow and the abbey which is called the *Little-ing*, and the meadows of *Clifton* on the one side, and the ditch which runneth between the abbey and the wall of the said city on the other; so that from thence the said mayor and commonality and their successors have the jurisdiction as before this time they have had. And that the abbot, nor any of his monks, nor their successors, be not from thenceforth arrested, except for trespass or felony, or by commandment of the king, his justices, stewards or marshals of his house; and the victuals, meats, beasts, wares, goods or chattels of the said abbot and monks, or their successors, from henceforth shall not be arrested or taken by the said mayor and commonality, their successors or ministers, for any cause (saving the said matter) on the water within the said bounds. But deodands, chattels of fugitives, and of felons, and other franchises royal, shall be to the said mayor and commonality, their heirs and successors; and that it shall be lawful for the said abbot and convent freely to act

act their will upon the ſaid water in like manner as it is begun. Moreover the abbot and convent ſhall not be arreſted for any manner of debt within the manors of Painlaythes and Siwardhow with the appurtenances; nor ſhall be arreſted for debt in the ſtreet of St. *Gilli-gate*, by no goods, chattels, beaſts, victuals or carriages which ſhall come or be ſent within the manors aforeſaid; except it be for debt or damages recovered within the ſaid city, by judgment againſt the ſaid abbot or his ſucceſſors, and that ſhall be paid ten days after the judgment given, within which time no execution from thence, if it be not that the goods and chattels within the ſaid manors by fraud be ſold, given or purloined for to hinder the ſaid execution; ſo that immediately after judgment given in the ſaid city againſt the ſaid abbot or his ſucceſſors, and in every other place within the juriſdiction of the ſaid city, as well by land as by water, except the places before excepted, let the execution go, and every other manner of arreſt, againſt the ſaid abbot and his ſucceſſors, notwithſtanding any privilege or franchiſe granted to the ſaid abbot and convent to the contrary before this time hath been uſed; ſaving to the ſaid mayor and commonality and their ſucceſſors in thoſe manors and places aforeſaid with the appurtenances, all other juriſdictions at all times, ſo that the ſaid abbot and monks, their goods and chattels from henceforth be not taxed or tallaged with thoſe of the city by reaſon of the manors aforeſaid. ST. MARY'S ABBEY.

For this accord and for peace the ſaid mayor and commonality, at their proper coſts, ſhall procure licence to the ſaid abbot and convent from our ſovereign lord the king, and alſo the appropriation of the ſaid honourable father, and confirmation of the chapter of *York* of the church of *Rudſtayne*, taxed to forty marks, which church is of the advowſon of the ſaid abbot and convent; and the ſaid mayor and commonality ſhall bear all the charges and coſts which ſhall be made between the licence and appropriation thereof againſt the perſons hereafter to be diſturbed, if any ſhall be. And laſtly, theſe things ſhall be affirmed and ingroſſed, as well by the counſel of one party as of the other, in as good ſpeed as may well be, ſo always that the matter be not changed in any point.

In witneſs of which agreement as well the ſaid abbot as the ſaid mayor have interchangeably to theſe put their ſeals.

Given at *York* the xvi day of the month of *January* in the year of our lord M CCC LIII.

Thomas de Multon, then abbot, his private ſeal appendant to this deed is, on white wax, a chevron entre three lions rampant.

(p) The ORDER *and* AWARD *made betwixt the mayor and commonality of the one part, and the abbot and convent of St.* Mary's *nigh the city of* York *on the other part, concerning the bounds and common of paſture in* Clifton *and* Foulford, *made by commiſſioners* Aug. 19. *anno* 1484; *et regis* Ric. III. 2.

FIRST, the bounds of the franchiſe of the city of *York*, towards *Cliſton*, to begin at the eaſt end of the dyke that cloſeth the *Almery-garth*, at the end of *Bootham*, on the weſt ſide of the king's high way leading from *York* to *Cliſton*. And ſo by the weſt part of the ſame way, north, to againſt the ſouth end of *Maudlen-chapel*. And overthwart the way eaſt, by the ſouth end of the ſaid chapel, into a way leading to a *wind-miln*, ſometime called *John* of *Roucliff's* miln, unto the next *head-land* on the ſouth ſide of the ſame way, and ſo down by the ſaid *head-land* unto a *ſtyle*, and ſo forth overthwart the lands, and overthwart the *outgange* called a way that goeth toward *Sutton*, to a *moor* that goes into a way that goes towards *Huntington*; and from the eaſt end of the ſaid *moor* on by the ſaid way unto the *ſtone-croſs* that is written upon, that ſtands above *Aſtyl-brigg*; and from the croſs even to the water of *Foſs*, and forth by the weſt ſide of the water of *Foſs*, toward *York*, and the weſt part of the water-milns of the ſaid abbot and convent, and the *ſtanke* of the ſaid milns, and then over the water of *Foſs* beneath the ſaid milns. Clifton.

Item, the bounds of the franchiſe betwixt the ſaid city and *Foulford*, ſhall begin at the ſouth-weſt end of the *Green-Dykes*, beſides St. *Nicholas*; and from thence by a dyke that lies betwixt the ſouth end of the arable lands of a field called *Seward Howfield*, and a paſture called the *Ox-paſture* to the ſouth end of a moor that goes from *Seward-How-milne* to the ſaid *Ox-paſture*; and from thenceforth by the ſaid *dyke* towards the weſt to a *headland* of the ſaid abbot and convent, and by the north ſide of the *headland* unto a *high-way* that goes from *York* to *Foulford*, and there a croſs to be ſet and called the *Franchiſe-croſs* of the ſaid city; and ſo overthwart the ſaid way north, towards *York*, by the eaſt ſide of the ſaid way to a little ſtone-bridge, upon a cauſeway, leading from *Foulford* aforeſaid into *Fiſhergate*, butting upon the *King's-dyke* on the eaſt and weſt part of the ſaid bridge, and ſo by the ſaid *King's-dyke* to the water of *Ouſe*. Foulford.

Item, the mayor and commonality of the ſaid city, and their ſucceſſors, for their hackneys, key, whyes *(q)* and beaſts that they hold and occupy, couching and riſing, within the

(p) I copied this from an old manuſcript, which ſays, *the antient record of this matter remaineth in the cuſtodie of Mr.* Belt *common clerk of* Yorke, but I confeſs I never met with the original. I ſuppoſe this a tranſlation.

(q) Cows and heifers.

St. MARY's ABBEY. *Common of* Clifton.

said city, shall have common in avaridge time, under Pittesbalse, in all the fields and meadows on the east side of the town of *Clifton*, betwixt the outgang that goes from *Clifton* into the forrest of *Galtress* and *York* unto the water of *Foss*, when they lye unsown, except that a close of the said abbot and convent called Paynelathecrofts, otherwise called Turpyn-croft, alias Paynlathes, and also divers other closes and garthings, to the same closes annexed, be keeped several at all times. And that the said mayor and commonality and their successors have common of pasture in the fields betwixt *York* and *Foulford*, for

Common of Foulford.

the said cattle within the said bounds of the franchise of the said city every time there after the corn and hay be had away called averidge time, when they lye unsowen, until *Candlemass* next following. Foreseen always that winter corn in the said fields in the said time then alway to be keeped and saved. And that it be lawful to the said abbot and convent and their successors, servants and their tenants of *Foulford*, in all the fields, meadows and pastures of the said town of *Foulford*, out of the said boundes and franchise of the said city, to cast up dykes at their pleasure, to keep and defend the cattle of the said city from the said meadows and pastures. And if the cattle of the said mayor and commonality enter, or come by escape in any ways into any other of the fields then not sown,

Escape of cattle in Foulford *and* Clifton.

meadows and pastures of the said common of *Foulford* and *Clifton*, where they have no common, out of the said boundes of the franchise limits of the said city in avaridge time, after all the corn and the hay be had away, the said abbot and convent and their successors,

Not pindable.

officers and their servants shall not pind or empark them, but drive them out in godly wise; so that the said cattle escape not voluntarily, or by evil will, or by cause of negligent keeping. And the said mayor and commonality and their successors shall not vex or trouble the said abbot and convent or their successors, servants, officers or tenants, nor none of them for driving out the said cattle out of the said fields, meadows and pastures in the form aforesaid. And that it shall be lawful for the mayor and commonality and their successors to have use and occupy their ways and their moors and pastures as they

Watering of cattle.

have used towards *Fulford*, between the *Green-dykes* on the east side of *Seward-bow-fields*, and the *Green-dykes* to *Heslington*; and on towards *Clifton* by one outgange that goes from *Clifton* into the forest of *Galtress*, and by the outgange that goes from *York* by the *Horse-fair* towards *Sutton*; and in the summer season from the foresaid forest by the said outgange of *Clifton* to the water of *Ouse*, for watering their cattle, at times necessary, as it has been aforetime used, and from the moors of *Foulford* and *Heslington* by a highway that goes from *Heslington* to the water of *Ouse*, betwixt the *miln-syke* and the *Brekks* to the said water, for watering the said beasts time necessary as it has been aforetime used without interruption or disturbance of the said abbot and convent, their successors, officers or tenants to be done or demanded; so that the said cattle tarry not in the fields of *Fulford*

What cattle shall have pasture. *Tethering of cattle.*

and *Clifton*, except within the bounds and time after rehearsed. Alway foreseeing that no man of the said city shall have no other cattle pasturing within the said lordships of *Foulford* and *Clifton*, but *hackneys*, *key*, and *whyes*, couching and rising within the said city in the manner and form aforesaid. Nor that they, nor any other man of the said city, shall tether or fasten horse nor cattle in the said fields sowne, or meadows within the boundes aforesaid, but in avaridge time after the corn and hay be led away. Also forseeing that this award be no prejudice nor hurt to no man of the said city of his common within the lordships of *Foulford* and *Clifton*, that they have by reason of their holding as tenants with-

Enclosures.

in the said lordships. And in case the said abbot and convent, or their successors, or their tenants enclose any fields, or parcel of field pertaining to the lordships of *Foulford* and *Clifton*, being or lying within the boundes aforesaid, that the said abbot and convent, or

Gaps.

their successors, servants or tenants shall every year, in avaridge time, after corn and hay be had away make reasonable gaps for all manner of cattle for them that have any right of common to enter into the said fields or parcel of fields so enclosed, within six days after having away of corn and hay. And if the said abbot and convent, and their successors and and servants will not make reasonable gaps within the time aforesaid, that then it be lawful to any man or person that have any common right within the said bounds to make reasonable gaps in the said fields contained within the said bounds, or any parcel thereof so enclosed.

Reparations of highways, &c.

Item, That neither the said mayor, sheriffs nor commonality, nor no officer, nor no minister of theirs shall raise or make to be raised issues, fines, amerciaments, nor pains, set or to be set, upon the said abbot and convent, their successors, and tenants by reason of any lands or tenements that they hold of the said abbot and convent for making, or mending, or repairilling, or unmaking, unmending, or unrepairilling of any ways, or bridges, sewers, or cawseys, within the said bounds of the franchises of the said city. And that the said mayor and commonality and their successors shall acquit and discharge the said abbot and convent, their successors, and their tenants for the land they hold of them for evermore, against the king his heirs and successors, of all such amerciaments of pains for making, amending or reparilling and for none amending, making and reparilling of the said bridges, ways, sewers and cawseys within the said bounds of the franchise of the city. Foreseeing alway that within the said city and suburbs of the same, the said abbot and convent and their successors for their tenements edified within the said city shall make to be amended and reparilled in tim.

of need the bridges, highways and causeways before the tenements within the said city to the midst of the said highways and causeways, after the use and custom of the said city. ST. MARY's ABBEY.

Item, That within the fields, arable and meadows, pertaining to the lordships of *Foulford* and *Clifton* being and lying betwixt the said city and the said towns, nor in the ways within the boundes and metes aforesaid without the said city and suburbs of the same, except in the *Paynelathcrofts*, *Boothamlez*, the *Horse-fair* and the closes in *Fisher-gate*, shall neither the said abbot nor convent, nor their successors, their servants nor tenants, nor none of them, nor none of their goods, nor cattle be arrested nor disturbed by the said mayor nor sheriffs, nor their successors, nor their ministers, nor none of them within the said arable lands, fields and meadows or highways, occupying, coming and going to and fro, for no cause nor quarrel, but if it be for treason or lawful warrant by process to be made of felons out of foreign courts and counties, directed to the officers of the said city, for the time being, or in any wrestling time in the presence of their officers; saving always to the said mayor, sheriffs and commonality all manner of executions of law against the said tenants and their servants of *Foulford* and *Clifton*, within the said highways, within the boundes abovesaid, not being occupied, coming and going about, to nor fro, their husbandry, and against all other persons or person, except before excepted, throughout all the fields, meadows and ways within the aforesaid boundes, and also against the said abbot and convent, and their successors, their tenants and their servants in other places within the said city and suburbs of the same, reserving to the said abbot and convent and their successors all such liberties in *Bootham* as is comprehended in an old accord betwixt the said parties afore-time made. *Arrests.* *Bootham.*

The form of an exemption from several duties granted to the inhabitants within the liberties of St. Mary *by the steward of the court. Taken from an original.*

TO all christian people to whom these presents shall come, greeting. *Whereas* our late sovereign lord king *Charles* the first, of ever blessed memory, by his letters patents under the great seal of *England*, was graciously pleased to ratify and confirm unto all his tenants inhabitants and resiants within the view and leete of his majesty's high court of St. *Mary's* nigh the walls of the city of *York*, and within the precincts and liberties thereof divers ancient liberties, privileges and immunities which heretofore have been enjoyed by virtue of former royal charters and grants, as namely by *William Rufus* son to *William* the conqueror, as also confirmed and enlarged by *Henry* II, *Henry* III, *Edward* I, *Edward* II, *Edward* III, *Richard* II, *Henry* IV, *Henry* VI, *Henry* VII, and *Henry* VIII, all kings of *England*, his majesty's royal progenitors, in as large and ample manner as when these possessions were in the lord abbot of *York* his hands, that is to say, amongst many other privileges and immunities thereby formerly granted of and from payment of all manner of tolls, tallage, passage, pedage, pontage, stallage, wardage, carriage, and chiminage throughout all the kingdoms of *England* and *Ireland*, and dominion of *Wales*; and also of and from suit and service within the county or hundred courts, and from all attendance at assizes and sessions for the county, (excepting only their service to the courts of St. *Mary's* of *York* aforesaid, or within the jurisdiction thereof, where they are properly to attend and do their service,) *now* know ye that I *Christopher Hildyard*, chief steward under his now majestie of the courts and liberties of St. *Mary's* of *York* aforesaid, at the request and instance of *John Wressell* of *Rednes* in the county of *York* yeoman, as also for the preventing and avoiding all suits and controversies that might happen and arise for want of true knowledge of the premisses, do hereby advertise and certify, that the said *John Wressell* is an inhabitant and resiant within the manor of *Whitgift* and *Ayrmine* in the said county of *York*, which is parcel and a member of the manor and liberties of St. *Mary's* of *York* aforesaid, whom ye are to permit and suffer to enjoy the benefit of all the privileges and immunities aforesaid, without hindrance or molestation of him the said *John Wressell*, his goods or waires, servants or messengers which shall come or go, by land or by water, about his or their lawful occasions.

Given under my hand and seal of my office the fifth day of *May* in the twenty-ninth year of the reign of king *Charles* the second, and in the year of our Lord God 1677.

Seal the virgin Mary, *with our saviour in her arms, on black wax; the inscription about it illegible.*

CHRISTOPHER HILDYARD,
Senasch.

Alderman Waller's *lease of the site of the abbey*, &c. *from the crown.*

" GUlielmus et *Maria*, Dei gratia *Angliae*, *Scotiae*, *Franciae* et *Hiberniae*, rex et regina, fidei defensores, &c. omnibus ad quos presentes literae nostrae pervenerint, salutem.
" Sciatis quod nos tam pro et in consideratione reddituum et conventionum inferius reservat.
" et expressf. ex parte dilecti subditi nostri *Roberti Waller* armigeri, vel assignatorum suorum
" reddend. et performand. ac etiam pro diversis aliis bonis causis et considerationibus nos ad
" presentes movend. per advisamentum perdilectorum et perquam fidelium *Sidney Godolphin*
" consiliarii nostri, *Johannis Lowther* de *Lowther* baronetti consiliar. nostri et vice-camerarii
" hospitii

St. Mary's Abbey.

“ hoſpitii noſtri, *Ricardi Hampden* armigeri conſil. noſtri et cancellarii et ſub-theſaur. curiae
“ ſcaccarii noſtri, *Stephani Fox* militis, et *Thomae Pelham* arm. commiſſion. theſaurarii noſtri,
“ tradimus conceſſimus et ad firmam dimiſimus ac per preſentes pro nobis heredibus et ſuc-
“ ceſſoribus noſtris tradimus conceſſimus et ad firmam dimiſimus prefato *Roberto Waller* to-
“ tum illum ſcitum nuper monaſterii beatae *Mariae* ſcituat. in ſuburbio civit. *Eboraci*, cum
“ columbariis, hortis, gardinis, pomariis, ſtagnis et aliis commoditatibus eidem ſcitui dicti
“ monaſterii pertinent. infra precinctos ejuſdem ſcitus; ſcilicet, totum illum palatium ſive
“ domus manſionalis ſcituat. extra muros civit. *Ebor.* una cum omnibus extra domibus, ſta-
“ bulis, hortis, areis, gardinis, pomariis, et ſolo eidem palatio ſive dom. manſion. ſpectan-
“ tibus aut cum eodem occupat. ſive uſitat. continend. in toto per eſtimationem treſdecim
“ acras, ſive plus ſive minus, modo vel nuper in tenura vel occupatione *Johannis Fareſby*
“ gubernatoris civit. *Ebor.* ſive cuſtodis dict. dom. manſion. Quae premiſſa nuper fuerunt
“ parcell. nuper diſſolut. monaſterii beatae *Mariae* ſcituat. in ſuburb. civ. *Ebor*. predict. et in
“ diſpoſitione domini nuper regis *Henrici* octavi viceſimo nono die *Novembris* anno regni ſui
“ triceſimo primo per *Willielmum Dent* tunc abbatem dicti monaſterii et ejuſdem loci con-
“ vent. ſive ſui reddit. ſive libere reſignat. fuerat. Exceptis tamen ſemper et omnimodo re-
“ ſervat. nobis heredibus et ſucceſſoribus noſtris uſu et beneficio omnium talium romearium,
“ camerarum, et locorum qual. modo vel nuper uſitat. per *Seneſhal.* noſtrum manerii noſtri
“ de *Sancta Maria* ibidem ad conſervand. curias et letas ibidem ad manerium illud ſpectan.
“ ſive pertinen. Ac etiam except. omnibus miner. invent. ſive inveniend. infra ſcitum pre-
“ miſſorum predict. aut alicujus inde parcel. ſic per literas paten. Dom. nuper regis *Jacobi*
“ ſecundi geren. dat. viceſimo quarto die *Novembris* anno regni ſui tertio, dimiſ. et conceſſ.
“ *Henrico Lawſon* arm. filio et herede *Johannis Lawſon* de *Brough* in com. predict. baron. exe-
“ cutoribus adminiſt. et aſſig. ſuis pro termino trigint. et unius annorum a confectione dicta-
“ rum literarum patent. reddend. inde annuatim ad feſta *Annuntiationis beatae Mariae* et
“ *Sancti Michaelis Archang*. per equal. portion. ſummam decem ſolidorum. Habend. et te-
“ nend. omnia et ſingul. premiſſ. ſuperius per preſentes dimiſſ. ſeu dimitti mentionat. cum
“ eorum pertinent. univerſis (except. preexcept.) prefato *Roberto Waller* executoribus, ad-
“ miniſtratoribus, et aſſignis ſuis a confectione harum lit. noſt. paten. uſque ad finem termini
“ et pro termino trigint. et unius annor. extunc prox. ſequen. et plenarum complend. et fi-
“ niend. reddendo inde annuatim nobis heredibus et ſucceſſoribus noſtris annual. reddit. ſive
“ ſummam decem ſolidorum legal. monet. *Ang.* ad recept. ſcaccarii noſt. heredum et ſucceſ-
“ ſorum noſt. apud *Weſtmon.* ſeu ad manus receptoris noſt. pro pred. com. *Ebor.* pro temp.
“ exiſtend. ad feſta *Annuntiationis beat. Mariae* virg. et *Sancti Michaelis Archangeli* per
“ equal. portiones ſolvend. durante termino per preſentes conceſſ. *Proviſo* ſemper quod
“ ſi contigerit predict. annual. reddit. decem ſolidorum ſuperius per preſent. reſervat. a
“ retro fore vel inſolut. in parte vel in toto per ſpatium quadragint. dierum prox. poſt ali-
“ quod feſtum feſtor. predict. quibus ut prefertur ſolvi debet, quod tunc et deinceps bene
“ liceat et licebit nobis heredibus et ſucceſſoribus noſtris per miniſtros et officiarios noſt.
“ in premiſſa predict. ſup. iis dimiſſ. et aliquem inde parcel. intrare eademque rehabere
“ et repoſſidere et has literas patent. ceſſare et omnimodo cauſa revacari. *Et predictus*
“ *Robertus Waller* per ſe heredibus execut. adminiſt. et aſſig. ſuis convenit et conce-
“ dit nobis heredibus execut. adminiſt. et aſſig. ſuis per preſent. quod ipſe predict.
“ *Robertus Waller* executor. vel aſſig. ſui de tempore in tempus durant. termino predict.
“ exonerabunt et indempnes conſervabunt nos heredes et ſucceſſores noſt. de et a ſolutione feod.
“ decem mercar. ad cuſtod. dom. manſion. pred. uſualiter ſolut. et debit ſeu
“ clamat. *Et predict. Robertus Waller* execut. vel aſſign. ſui durante termin. pred. per has
“ literas noſt. conceſſ. ſinent et permittent *Seneſchallum* noſt. manerii noſt. de S. *Maria* ibidem
“ pro temp. exiſtent. libere et quiete poſſidere uti et gaudere omnes et ſing. romeas cameras
“ et al. locos quoſcunque quae ſeneſchall. noſt. ibidem ad aliquod temp. ante dat. harum lit.
“ noſt. patent. ad conſervand. et tenend. curias ſive letas uti vel poſſidere conſuet. fuit aliquo
“ in preſentibus in contrar. inde non obſtante. *Et inſuper pred. Robertus Waller* per ſe hered.
“ execut. adminiſt. et aſſign. ſuis ulterius convenit et concedit ad et cum nobis hered. et ſuc-
“ ceſſor. noſt. per preſent, quod ipſe pred. *Robertus Waller* execut. vel aſſig. ſui dom. man-
“ ſion. pred. et omnia alia edificia horrea ſtabul. ſtruct. et muros cum pertin. ad eundem
“ dom. ſpect. ad ſua propria onera et cuſtag. bene et ſufficient. in omnibus et per omnia re-
“ parari indilate cauſabunt. *Ac etiam* dict. dom. manſion. ac omnia edificia ſepes foſſat. li-
“ tera ripas et muros maritt. nec non omnia alia neceſſaria reparat. premiſſ. in omnibus et per
“ omn. de tempore in temp. toties quoties neceſſe et opportun. fuit ſumptibus ſuis prop. et
“ expenſis bene et ſufficient. reparabunt ſupportabunt ſuſtinebunt eſcurabunt purgabunt et
“ manu tenebunt durante term. pred. ac premiſſ. ſic ſufficienter reparat. et manutent. in fine
“ termini pred. demittent et relinquent. *Et denique* quod ipſe *Robertus Waller* execut. vel
“ aſſig. ſui infra ſpatium unius anni prox. ſequen. dat. harum liter. noſt. pat. et ſic deinceps
“ quolibet ſeptimo anno durant. term. pred. facient et deliberabunt ſeu fieri et deliberari cau-
“ ſabunt *auditori* noſt. premiſſ. perfect. terrar. ſive particular. premiſſ. inde diſtincta oſten-
“ dend. et demonſtrand. veras quantitat. ſive reputatat. quantitat. premiſſorum ac numerum
“ acrar eorundem premiſſ. ac metas et bundas eorundem, *Ang. the buttals and boundaries*
“ *thereof*, de recordo remanſur. pro futuro beneficio et commodo coronae noſt. *Proviſo*
“ etiam

"etiam semper quod supradict. *Robertus Waller* execut. vel affig. fui irrotulabunt seu irrotul. caufabunt has liter. nost. paten. coram auditore nost. com. *Ebor.* pred. vel deputato suo sufficient. pro temp. exist. infra spatium sex mensium prox. sequent. post dat. earundem quod nunc et deinceps haec praesens dimissio et concessio nost. vacua sit et nullius vigor. in lege aliquo in praesent. in contrarium inde non obstante. ST. MARY'S ABBEY.

"*In cujus* rei testimon. has literas nost. fieri fecimus patent. predict. predictis person. fidel. commission. thesaur. nost. apud *Westmon.* 16. die *Martii* anno regni nost. quarto.

RUSSEL.

Per Ward. *commiss. thesaur. ac cancel. scaccarii.*

Exam. p. W. Whitaker *dep. cl.* Pipe.

Indorf.

Irrotulatur in officio auditor. com. Ebor.
14. *die* Maii 1692. *per*

ROBERT HEWITT, Auditor.

COPIES, from the originals, of several ancient charters and grants made to the abbey of St. MARY'S YORK; *none of them ever before printed.*

Charta Rogeri de Smitchton.

"OMnibus Christi fidelibus ad quos presens scriptum pervenerit *Rogerus* dictus filius *Anne de Smitchton* in *Richmondeschyr*, salutem in Domino. Noveritis me dedisse remisisse reddidisse et hac presenti charta mea confirmasse *Symoni* abbati et conventui *Sancte Marie Eboraci* totam terram meam quam habui in villa et territorio de *Smitchton*, videlicet, unum messuagium cum crofto, quatuor bovatas et sex acras terre quas de eisdem abbati et conventui tenui in eadem, cum omnibus et omnimodis pertinentibus suis sine aliquo retenemento, tenend. et habend. eisdem abbati et conventui et eorundem successoribus universis in liberam puram et perpetuam eleemosinam, libere quiete et integre, cum omnibus modis pertinentibus suis infra villam et extra, ita quod nec ego *Rogerus* nec aliquis heredum meorum aliquod jus vel clamium in predicto tenemento vel in aliquo dictorum tenementorum tangere —— exigere vel vendicare poterimus. Et ego *Rogerus* et heredes mei vel assignati warrantizabimus adquietabimus et defendemus totum predictum tenementum cum omnibus et omnimodis pertinentibus suis in liberam puram et perpetuam eleemosinam predictis abbati et conventui et eorum successoribus universis contra omnes homines tam *Judeos* quam *Christianos* in perpetuum. Et ut hec mea donatio redditio et confirmatio rata et stabilis permaneat in perpetuum presenti carte sigillum meum apposui. B. 2. N°. 11. Smitchton.

"Hiis testibus, Dominis *Johanne de Oketon*, *Johanne de Raygate*, *Roberto de Lasseles* militibus, *Johanne de Caneby*, *Johanne Abundevill*, *Willielmo de Abundevill*, *Henrico* filio *Roberti de Apelton*, *Thoma Weder de Smitchton*, *Rogero de Wretteby* de eadem, *Thoma de Langeton* de eadem, et multis aliis.

Charta Philippi de Faukenberg, *mil.*

"OMnibus (q) Christi fidelibus hoc scriptum visuris vel audituris *Philippus de Faukenberg* miles, eternam in Domino salutem. Noveritis universitas vestra me dedisse concessisse et hac presenti charta me confirmasse *Symoni* abbati et conventui sancte *Marie Eboraci* duas culturas meas in territorio de *Apilton* quarum una jacet in **Middelgethille** inter terram *Ydonie* filie mee et terram *Willielmi de Hornington*, et abuttat in occidentali capite super **Elyckerdike**, et in orientali capite super **Littelthaurth**. Et altera cultura notata **Schortebuttes** et jacet inter terram *Walteri* filii mei et terram *Ade de Cerf*; et abuttat in occidentali capite super **Ryckeffy**, et in orientali capite super **Littelthaurth**. Tenendum et habendum predictum tenementum cum omnibus pertinentibus, libertatibus asyamentis suis in campis de *Apilton*, ubi liberi homines communicant, predictis abbati et conventui et eorum successoribus, in liberam puram et perpetuam elemosinam, libere quiete pacifice et integre, in perpetuum, sine omni terreno servitio seculari exactione et demand. Et ego *Philippus* et heredes mei warantizabimus, defendemus et adquietabimus predictum tenementum cum omnibus pertinentibus, libertatibus et asyamentis suis, sicut predictum est, predictis abbati et conventui et eorum successoribus in liberam puram et perpetuam eleemosinam contra omnes gentes in perpetuum. B. 2 N°. 18. Apilton.

"In cujus rei testimonium presenti scripto sigillum meum apposui.

"Hiis testibus, domino *Johanne de Oketona* tunc vicecom. *Ebor.* domino *Johanne de Raygate* militibus, *Johanne de Merston*, *Waltero de Ask*, *Hugone de Acaster*, *Richardo de Colton*, *Wydone de Apilton*, *Nicholo de Camera de Popilton*, *Thoma* de eadem clerico et aliis.

"Dat. die annuntiationis beate *Marie* anno gratie M.CC.LX. primo.

(q) This, as well as many of the rest, is in so beautiful a character as deserves engraving.

St. Mary's Abbey.

Charta Roberti de Skegenesse *mil.*

B. 2. N°. 29. Apilton.

"OMnibus Christi fidelibus ad quorum notitiam hoc presens scriptum pervenerit *Robertus* "filius *Walteri de Skegenesse*, salutem eternam in Domino. Sciatis me dedisse concessisse "et hac presenti mea carta confirmasse Deo et abbatie sancte *Marie Eboraci* et monachis ibi-"dem Deo servientibus, ubi corpus meum legavi sepeliendum, totam illam placeam terre "que jacet inter Wandhagh et *Apilton* et decem et octo acras terre per perticam viginti pe-"dum in *Apilton* cum pertinentiis, que jacent juxta essarton meum quod notatum est Wand-"hagh, et abuttant versus occidentem super tresdecim acris terre mee que jacent inter fossam "et Wandhagh juxta *Wilkes*, et extendit se versus orientem et versus *Tyndhayt*, inter "fossam et *Telkes*, et octo pedes in latitudine circum circa prenotatam placeam et preno-"tatas acras, et quatuor perticas terre propinquiores fosse ex occidentali parte et aquilonali, "quacumque terra mea se extendit inter *Heebrige* et *Farebrige*, et totam fossam quacunque "terra mea se extendit ibidem ex alia parte de fossa; et duodecim acras terre cum perti-"nentibus in *Apilton* inter *Wilvelyt* et *Telks*, scilicet totam terram que vocatur Wandhagh, "et quatuor acras terre cum pertinentibus in *Apilton*, et omnes perticulas prenotatas que "clauduntur infra fossatum meum quod est circa Wandhagh, sicut plenius continetur in car-"tis quas habeo de domino *Philippo de Faukenberge*. *Habend. et tenend.* predictis abbatie et "monachis in liberam puram et perpet. eleemosinam. Et ego *Robertus* et heredes mei totam "predictam terram, sicut predictum est, predictis abbatie et monachis contra omnes gentes "warrantizabimus adquietabimus et defendemus in perpetuum. Et ut hoc scriptum hujusce "donationis et concessionis perpetue firmitatis robur obtineat, presenti scripto sigillum meum "apposui.

"Hiis testibus, magistro *Johanne de Hamerton*, domino *Willielmo de Longa-villa*, *Waltero* "*de Gaugy*, *Herberto de Duffend* clericis, *David de Popelton*, *Thoma* ejusdem ville, "*Mich. Janitore*, *Waltero de Ask*, *Willielmo Savarici* filio, *Willielmo de Popelton*, "*Mich. Henrici* . . . .

Charta Roberti de West-Cotingwick.

B. 2. N°. 31. *Fluvium de* Derwent.

"OMnibus *Christi* fidelibus ad quos presens scriptum pervenerit *Robertus* filius *Stephani* de "*West-cottingwic* salutem in Domino. Noveritis me pro salute anime mee et om-"nium parentum meorum concessisse dedisse et hac presenti carta mea confirmasse Deo et "eccl. beate *Marie Ebor.* et monachis ibidem Deo servientibus in puram et perpetuam "eleemosinam quicquid juris habui et habere potui in applicatione navium et in carcatione in "aqua de *Derewent* ad ripam de *Crossum*. Ita quod licite possint de cetero ad predictam ri-"pam applicare et carcare quotienscunque et quandocunque volunt per se et per homines "suos; nec licebit michi vel alieni heredum meorum vel alicui clamando ratione juris mei ad "predictam ripam navem vel bacellum carucare vel applicare sine assensu et voluntate pre-"dictorum abbatis et monachorum sanct. *Marie Ebor.* Et ego et heredes mei dictam appli-"cationem et carcationem quicunque in vel meo tenemento solebat dictis abbati et mona-"chis et ecclesie sue contra omnes homines in perpetuum warrantizabimus adquietabimus et "defendemus.

"In cujus rei testimonium presenti scripto sigillum meum apposui.

"Hiis testibus, *Waltero de Egkeschwe* milite tunc ballivo de *Rychemund*, *Johanne de Ho-*"*tton* tunc seenescall. sanct. *Marie Ebor. Roberto de Sutton*, *Regero de Wedyrhall* cleri-"cis; *Waltero de Ask*, *Nicholao de Camera*, *Waltero de Wyllwetoft*, *Roberto Le Barn de* "*West-Cottingwic*, *Willielmo Chaumpeney de Crossum*, et multis aliis.

Charta Osberni de Archis.

B. 2. N°. 42. Popilton, Apilton. Hessey. York.

"*OSbernus* (r) *de Archis* omnibus legentibus vel audientibus literas has salutem. Sciatis me "dedisse et hac presenti carta mea confirmasse Deo et sancte *Marie Eboraci* et mona-"chis ibidem Deo servientibus, in puram et perpetuam eleemosinam et ab omni terreno "servitio vel exactione liberas, videlicet, in *Popiltona* quatuor carrucatas terre et dimidiam, "in *Apiltona* tres carucatas et sedem molendini, in *Hesseye* duas carucatas et dimidiam cum "omnibus pertinentiis suis et asiamentis infra predictas villas et extra; et in *Eboraco* duas "mansuras terre in vico sancti *Salvatoris*. Pro anima domini mei regis *Willielmi*, et pro ani-"ma patris mei et matris mee et omnium parentum meorum, nec non pro animabus omni-"um fidelium defunctorum.

"Hiis testibus *Roberto de Brus*, *Guihomaro dapifero*, *Odone camerario*, *Conano capellano*, "*Radulpho Ribaldi* filio, *Rogero* filio *Pigoti*, *Alano de Munbi*, *Ymfredo de Turp*, *Alano* "*pincerna*, *Adam de Brus*, *Petro de Threst*, *Hanano* sancti *Michaelis* monacho, et mul-"tis aliis.

(r) This very ancient deed is wrote in a very large fair-hand somewhat resembling the old black print. It seems to be older than the use of seals, and I take it to be near six hundred years date. *Osbertus* or *Osbernus* was high sheriff of this county 1 *Hen.* I.

Concessio

St. MARY's ABBEY.

Concessio Cantuariae *in monasterio* S. Mariae Eboraci.

" NOverint universi quod nos *Alanus* permissione divina abbas monasterii beate *Marie* " *Eboraci* et ejusdem loci conventus, tenemur et obligamur et per presentes literas " fac. . . . . gari pro nobis et successoribus nostris *Johanni de Hellebek* et " heredibus suis quibus . . . . eidem *Johanni* perpetuo unum capellanum " celebraturum pro anima dicti *Johannis* . . . . . et omnium fidelium defunctorum " in capella beate *Marie* virginis ad portam monasterii nostri pro quibusdam terris et tene- " mentis nobis per eundem *Johannem* donatis et concessis, viz. pro quinque toftis et quatuor " bovatis terre cum suis pertinentiis que et quas idem *Johannes* habuit in villa de *Myton* et " de nobis ut de capitalibus dominis tenuit. Ad quam cap. . . . . perpetuo fideliter " . . . . inveniendam obligamus nos monasterium nostrum et . . . " successores nost. . . . . predictam terram et tenementa ad cujuscunque manus do- " naverit. Et si quocunque . . . . . . Cantuariam . . . . . . quod absit " defecerimus, volumus et concedimus pro nobis et successoribus nostris quod heres predicti " *Johannis* quicunque fuerit predictam terram et tenementa . . . . atur et " ea sibi habeat et retineat sine impedimento nostro et . . . . vel succes- " cessorum nostrorum.

B. 3. N°. 25. Myton.

" In cujus rei testimonium sigillum nostrum com. . . . . consensu nostro " presentibus apposuimus.

" Dat. in capitulo nostro *Ebor.* die sabbati in vigilia S. *Matthei* apostoli et evangeliste an- " no dom. millesimo trecentesimo vicesimo . . . . regis *Edwardi* " quarto decimo.

" Hiis testibus domino *Thoma de* . . . . . *Thoma* . . . . . *Willielmo de* " *Thornton*, *Johanne de Thorneton*, *Simone de* . . . . et aliis.

Charta Alexandri de Bundevile.

OMnibus hoc scriptum visuris vel auditituris *Johannes* filius *Alexandri de Bundevill*, salu- " tem. Noveritis me dedisse concessisse reddidisse et hac presenti charta me confir- " masse *Symoni* abbati et conventui S. *Marie Ebor.* unum messuagium et tres bovatas terre " cum pertinentiis in *Apelton* super *Wisk*, et annualem redditum triginta denariorum cum ho- " magio et servitio heredum *Johannis de Sinington* de tribus bovatis terre cum pertinentiis in " eadem villa. Et annualem redditum decem denariorum et oboli cum homagio et servitio " *Henrici* filii *Roberti de Apelton* et heredum suorum de una bovata terre cum pertinentiis in " eadem villa. Et annualem redditum viginti denariorum cum homagio et servitio *Wil-* " *lielmi de Amundevill*, *Alitie* uxoris ejus, et heredum suorum de duabus bovatis terre cum " pertinentiis in eadem villa. Et annualem redditum viginti denariorum cum homagio et " servitio *Galfridi de Piketon* de duabus bovatis terre in eadem villa. Quas quidem tres bova- " tas terre cum messuagio redditibus homagiis et servitiis liberorum predictorum tam in do- " minio quam in servitio de eisdem abbati et conventui tenui. Habend. et tenend. eisdem " abbati et conventui et eorum successoribus universis totum predictum tenementum cum " messuagio redditibus homagiis wardis releviis et omnibus aliis servitiis et escheattis in libe- " beram puram et perpetuam eleemosinam quiete de me et heredibus meis in perpetuum. " Ita quod nec ego nec heredes mei vel aliquis ex parte nostra aliquod jus vel clamium in " predictis tribus bovatis cum messuagio et aliis pertinentiis esset in redditibus homagiis war- " dis releviis escheattis vel aliquibus aliis servitiis dicta libere tenentes vel eorum tenemen- " mentorum tangentibus de cetero aliquo casu contingente exigere vel vendicare poteri- " mus.

B. 4. N°. 23. Apelton super Wisk.

" In cujus rei testimonium presenti charte sigillum meum apposui.

" Hiis testibus, dominis *Rogero de Rascall*, *Roberto de Rascall* militibus, *Johanne de Horne-* " *by*, *Johanne de Daneby*, *Roberto* filio *Henrici de Apelton*, *Stephano de Schupton*, *Richar-* " *do de Camera* clerico, et aliis.

Charta Roberti de Skegenesse *mil.*

" OMnibus Christi fidelibus ad quorum notitiam hoc presens scriptum pervenerit *Rober-* " *tus* filius *Walteri de Skegenesse* miles, salutem eternam in domino. Noveritis me " dedisse concepisse et hac presenti carta mea confirmasse Deo et abbatie S. *Marie Eboraci* et " monachis ibidem Deo servientibus, ubi corpus meum legavi sepeliend. dimidiam carru- " catam terre quam tenui de feodo *Symonis de Kyme* in *Apelton*, et *Thome de Thorp* cum tota " sequela sua et cum omnibus cattallis suis, et omnes alias terras meas cum omnibus perti- " nentiis in eadem villa tam in essartis quam in aliis locis sine ullo retenemento, et per illud " essartum quod tenui de feodo *Johannis de Roucestre* in eadem villa. Habend. et tenend. " dictis abbatie et monachis in liberam puram et perpetuam eleemosinam faciendo inde illud

B. 4. N°. 7. Apelton.

" servitium

"servitium quod ego solebam facere dictis feodis tenere carcar. quos habeo de dominis "qui me feodaverunt. Et ego *Robertus* et heredes mei totam predictam terram cum omni- "bus pertinentiis, sicut predictum est, predictis abbatie et monachis contra omnes homines "warrantisabimus adquietabimus et defendemus in perpetuum.

"In cujus rei testimonium presenti scripto sigillum meum apposui.

"Hiis testibus, magistro *Johanne de Hanton*, domino *Willielmo de Longa villa*, *Waltero de* "*Gaugy*, *Herberto de Duffend* clericis, *Michaele Janitore*, *Willielmo de Lilling*, *Waltero* "*de Ask*, *Willielmo* filio *Savarici*, *Hamo de Popelton*, *Thoma* ejusdem ville clericis, *Jo-* "*hanne de Merston*, *Michaele*, *Henrico* et *Rogero* et aliis.

Charta Willielmi de Doncester.

B. 4. N. 12. Apelton. "OMnibus hoc scriptum visuris vel audituris *Willielmus de Doncester* salutem in Domino. "Noveritis me dedisse confirmasse et omnino quiet. clamasse de me et heredibus meis "Deo et beate *Marie* et *Simoni* abbati et conventui sancte *Marie Eboraci* pro salute anime "mee et animarum antecessorum et successorum meorum unum tostum et viginti acras terre "cum pertinentiis in villa et territorio de *Apelton* que habuerunt de dono domini *Johannis* "*de Raygate*, et quendam annualem redditum duorum denariorum de eodem tenemento in "debito super très acras terre cum pertinentiis in predicto territorio que habuerunt de dono "*Henrici le Garden* et *Cicilie* uxoris ejus . . . dedisse quondam annualem reddit. viii. de- "nariorum in debitum de eodem tenemento. Habend. et tenend. predictis abbati et conven- "tui et eorum successoribus in liberam puram et perpetuam eleemosinam in perpetuum. "Claudendi et commodum sunt in omnibus prenotatis sicuti melius viderint expedire facien- "di sine impedimento mei vel heredum meorum. Et ego vero *Willielmus* et heredes mei "predict. abbati et conventui et eorum successoribus warrantizabimus adquietabimus et de- "fendemus in perpetuum contra omnes gentes . . . . *Johannes* pater meus die quo "feoffavit *Willielmum Dekest* feoffatorem domini *Johannis de Raygate*.

"In cujus rei testimonium huic presenti scripto sigillum meum apposui.

"Hiis testibus domino *Johanne de Raygate*, domino *Willielmo de Sancto Quintino* militibus, "*Willielmo de Buterwyk*, *Ricardo de Buterwyk*, *Wydone de Apelton*, *Hugone de Acaster*, "*Mich. de Merston* et aliis.

Charta regis Henrici *tertii*.

B. 4. N°. 35. "*HEnricus* Dei gratia rex *Anglie*, dominus *Hibernie*, dux *Aquitanie*, archiepiscopis, epis- "copis, abbatibus, prioribus, comitibus, baronibus, justitiariis, vicecomitibus, "prepositis, ministris et omnibus ballivis et fidelibus nostris, salutem. *Inspeximus* cartam "quam inclite recordationis *Henricus* quondam rex *Anglie* avus noster fecit abbati et mona- "chis St. *Marie Eboraci* in hec verba, *Henricus* Dei gratia rex *Anglie*, dux *Normannie* et "*Aquitanie* comes *Andegavie* archiep. episcop. abbat. et omnibus comit. baron. et justit. et "vicecom. et ministris suis et omnibus fidel. suis *Francis* et *Anglis* per *Angliam*, salutem. "*Sciatis* nos concessisse et dedisse in puram et perpetuam eleemosinam pro salute anime mee "et pro salute animarum avi nostri regis *Henrici* et matris nostre et omnium antecessorum "nostrorum, nec non pro statu regni nostri, *Roberto* abbati et successoribus suis et abbatie "sancte *Marie Ebor.* et monachis ibidem Deo servientibus terras, ecclesias, cellas, maneria "decimas, silvas, stagna, plana, molendina et alias possessiones suas possidendas, libere et "quiete, ab omni terreno servitio in perpetuam possessionem, sicut unquam melius tempori- "bus antecessorum nost. tenuerunt, cum eisdem legibus et libertatibus et dignitatibus et con- "suetudinibus quas habet ecclesia sancti *Petri Eboraci*, et ecclesia S. *Johannis Beverlaci*. Et "ne homines S. *Marie* eant ad comitatus vel schiras, vel tridings, vel wepentag. vel hun- "drez, nec etiam pro vicecomit. vel minist. eorum, sed si vicecom. vel ministri eorum ha- "bent querelam contra homines sancte *Marie* dicant abbati *Ebor.* et statuto die venient in "curiam S. *Marie* et ibi habeant rectum de capitali placito suo, et St. *Maria* habeat quic- "quid pertinet ad curiam suam, et sicut aliqua ecclesia in tota *Anglia* magis est libera sic et "hec libera et omnes terre ad eam pertinentes quas nunc habet vel quas rationabiliter ad- "quirere poterit; et maneria et celle et qualibet alie possessiones sint quiete de *placitis* et "*querelis*, et *murdro*, et *latrocinio*, et *scutagio*, et *geld*, et *Dane-geld*, et *hidagiis*, et *assisis*, et "de *operationibus castellorum* et *pontium*, et *parcorum*, et de **ferdwita** et **hangwyta**, et **Fle-** "**menes-franch**, et de **wardpeny**, et de **averpeny**, et de **blodwyta**, et de **furwyta**, et de **hun-** "**dredpeny**, et de **thethyngpeny**, et de **leirwyta**, et de *thelonio*, et de *passagio*, et *pontagio*, et "*lestagio*. Concessimus insuper eidem abbatie *pacis fracturam*, et *pugnam* in domo factam, "et *domus invasionem*, et omnes *assultus hominum* suorum, et **forestall**, et **grithbreke** et **ham-** "**soke**, et **soc**, et **sac**, et **tol** et **theam**, et **infangenethef**, et **outfangenetheft**. Post obitum "vero abbatis ejusdem ecclesie ex eadem congregatione eligatur abbas alter qui dignus sit; "aliunde vero nullus, nisi ibi invenire nequiverit qui dignus sit tali fungi officio: quod si "evenit de alio noto et familiari loco potestatem liberam habeant eligendi abbatem ido- "neum.

" neum. Testibus hiis *Gaufry Helyensi* episc. *Hugone Dunelm.* episc. *Willielmo* comite de *Maunderyll*, *Ranulfo Glanvile*, *Hugone Bardulfo*, apud *Wudestoke*. Nos autem predictas concessionem et donationem habentes ratas et gratas, eas quantum in nobis est pro nobis et heredibus nostris in perpetuum concedimus et confirmamus sicut carta predict. rationabiliter testatur, volentes insuper predictis abbati et monach. pro salute nostra et animarum antecessorum et heredum nost. gratiam facere uberiorem ut quietantie et libertates predict. sibi et successoribus suis integre et inconcusse remaneant in futurum, precipimus et concedimus pro nobis et heredibus nost. quod predicti abbas et eorum successores universis et singul. libertatum et quietantiarum articulis supra dict. libere et sine occasione et impedimento nostri et hered. nost. justiciar. et omnium ballivorum nost. uti valeant de cetero quandocunque voluerint, et ubicunque sibi viderint expedire quamquam predict. libertatibus vel quietantiis in aliquo articulo minus plene usi fuerint prout fecisse poterant et debeant secundum continentiam carte predict. temporibus retroactis. Et prohibemus super forisfacturam nost. ne quis prefatus abbatem et monachos contra predict. concessionem et quietantiam in aliquo vexare inquietare vel molestare presumat. St. MARY's ABBEY.

" Hiis testibus, venerabili patre *Waltero Bathon.* et *Wellens.* episc. *Henrico* filio regis *Alemann.* nepote nostro *Rogero de Leyburn*. *Johanne de Verdun*, *Willielmo de Grey*, *Roberto Auyllum*, *Willielmo de Aette*, *Nicholao de Leukenor*, *Galfrido de Percy*, *Radulpho de . . . Keffaz*, *Petro Squydemor*, *Barth. le Bygod* et aliis.

" Datum per manum nost. apud *Kenillewurth* octavo die Septem. anno regni nostri quinquagesimo.

Charta Johannis Malebysse.

" OMnibus has literas visuris vel audituris *Johannes Malebysse* salutem. Sciatis me pro salute anime mee et patris et matris mee concessisse dedisse, et presenti carta mea confirmasse in puram liberam et perpetuam elemosinam Deo et eccle. beate *Marie Ebor.* et monachis ibidem Deo servientibus dimidiam karucatam terre in *Utter-Acastre* cum omnibus pertinentiis suis quam *Rich. Malebysse* filius *Roberti Malebysse* remitt. de patre meo et de me in dominico et servitiis; illam scilicet dimidiam karucatam terre quam *Emma de* . . . . avia mea tenuit; cum *Roberto* filio *Arkilli* et sequela sua cum omnibus libertatibus et aisiamentis infra villam et extra ad predictam terram pertinentibus et in omnibus. Hanc predictam terram in omnibus, sicut predict. est, Ego *Johannes* et heredes mei predict. eccles. et predict. monachis pacifice integre et quiete in perpetuum tenendam et habendam contra omnes homines et feminas warrantizabimus defendemus et adquietabimus in perpetuum ab omnibus secularibus servitiis et exactionibus. Et ut hec mea donatio firma et stabilis in perpetuum permaneat, huic scripto sigillum meum apposui. B. 5. N. 16. Acaster.

Hiis testibus, *Johanne de Byrkyn*, *Briano* fil. *Alani*, *Willielmo de Tamton*, *Roberto de Kent*, *Roberto de Medville*, *Rogero de Estures*, *Henrico de Scilton*, *Richardo Maunsel*, *Roberto de Skegnesse*, *Waltero de Torp*, *G. de sancto Audoeno*, *Will. 'cuo*, *Roberto Suppe*, *Richardo de Camera*, *Rogero Coco*, *Radulpho Cokes*, *Willielmo de Lilling*, *Thom. Janitore*, *Johanne de Selely* et aliis.

Charta Richardi Soudan.

" OMnibus Christi fidelibus ad quos presens scriptum pervenerit *Ricardus* filius *Ricardi Soudan* salutem. Sciatis me dedisse concessisse et hac presenti carta mea confirmasse Deo et eccl. S. *Marie Ebor.* et prioratui S. *Martini juxta Richemunde*, et monachis ibidem Deo servientibus in liberam puram et perpetuam elemosinam sex acras terre cum pertinentiis in territorio de *Apelton*; scilicet unam acram et tres rodas super *forlandes*, juxta terram *Thome* filii *Hermeri*, et unam acram ad *Crakehou* juxta terram *Thome* fil. *Ingrid.*; et totam terram meam in *Trespleges* que jacet inter terram *Henrici* clerici et terram *Alicie* matris mee; et duas acras et dimidiam rodam exceptis quatuor perticatis in *Threpleges* que jacent inter regiam viam et terram *Thome* fil. *Ingrid.* habend et tenend. dictis prioratui et monachis libere et quiete et honorifice integre et pacifice in liberam puram et perpetuam elemosinam cum communa ville et cum omnibus pertinentiis suis et aisiamentis et libertatibus et liberis consuetudinibus infra villam et extra, in omnibus locis integris absque aliquo retenemento ad eandam terram pertinentibus in perpetuum. Et ego *Ricardus* et heredes mei totam predict. terram cum communa ville et cum omnibus pertinentiis suis et aisiamentis et libertatibus et liberis consuetudinibus infra villam vel extra et in omnibus locis integris absque aliquo retenemento dictis eccles. S. *Marie Ebor.* et prioratui S. *Martini* juxta *Richemunde* et monachis ibidem Deo servientibus warrantizabimus adquietabimus et defendemus contra omnes gentes in perpetuum. B. 6. N. 35. Apelton.

" Hiis testibus *Hugone de Magneby*, *Thoma de Laceles*, *Petro de Crachale*, *Alano de Crachale*, *Roberto de Haindeby*, *Willielmo Lunghespee*, *Thoma de Burgo*, *Alano* fil. *Willielmi de Apelton*, *Helia de Dunn*, *Johanne de Walebury*, et **aliis**.

7 P Charta

St. Mary's Abbey.

Charta Richardi Malebysse.

B. 7. N. 33. Acaster. "SCiant omnes hoc scriptum visuri vel audituri quod ego *Ricardus Malebysse*, filius "*Roberti Malebysse*, pro salute anime mee concessi et dedi et presenti carta mea "confirmavi cum corpore meo Deo et ecclesie sancte *Marie Ebor.* et monachis ibi-"dem Deo servientibus ubi sepulturam elegi, duas bovatas terre et dimidiam in *Utter-*"*Acastre* cum hominibus et servitiis ad terram illam pertinentibus. Et preterea totum "servitium unius bovate terre et dimid. quam *Raebgnild* quondam uxor *Roberti Tuel* tenet "de me pro quatuor solid. et sex denariis et dimidia libra cimini michi inde annuatim "reddend. scil. medietatem ad *Pentecosten* et medietatem in festo S. *Martini*, cum omnibus "pertinentiis. Et dicti monach. predict. duas bovatas terre et dimidiam cum toto servi-"tio predict. bovate terre et dimid. et cum pertinentiis et aisiamentis infra villam et ex-"tra tenebunt et habebunt in puram et perpet. elemosinam, libere integre et quiete. Red-"dendo inde annuatim domino *Johanni Malebisse* et heredibus suis quatuor denarios pro "omni servitio et exactione mediet. ad *Pentecosten* et mediet. in festo S. *Martini*. Excepta "tamen *Warda de Eya* quantum pertinet ad dimidiam karucat. terre cujus quindecim "karucate terre faciunt feodum unius militis. Et ut hoc scriptum perpetuum obtineat "firmitatem illud sigilli mei appositione corroboravi.

Hiis testibus, domino *Roberto de Skegnesse* tunc seneschall. abbatie S. *Marie Ebor.* ma-"gistris *Eustachio de Kyma*, *Johanne de Merleberg*, *Roberto de Grimiston*, *Radulpho de* "*Wilebech*, *Willielmo de Walecote*, *Rogero Coco*, *Thoma Janitore*, *Willielmo de Lilling*, "*Willielmo Cervo*, et pluribus aliis.

Charta Stephani de Haytefeld.

B. 8. N. 38. Waffand, Seton, Hornesey et Burtonmeres. "OMnibus Christi fidelibus ad quos presens scriptum pervenerit *Stephanus* filius *Walteri* "*de Haytefeld* salutem in dom. eternam. Noveritis me remisisse et quietum clamasse "de me et heredibus meis in perpetuum Deo et eccl. S. *Marie Ebor.* et *Thome* abbati et "monachis ibidem Deo servientibus et eorum successoribus totum jus et clamium quod ha-"bui vel habere potui in maris de *Waffand*, *Seton*, *Hornese* et *Anese-Burton*, ita quod nec "ego nec heredes mei nec aliquis ex parte mea vel heredum meorum de cetero in predictis "maris aliquo modo piscare poterimus per batellum vel sine batello, vel per rete, vel aliquo "alio modo piscandi sine voluntate et assensu dictorum abbatis et monachorum vel suc-"cessorum eorum. Nec ego nec heredes mei nec aliquis ex parte nost. de cetero impe-"diemus predictos abbatem vel monachos vel eorum successores piscare in predict. maris "quandocunque et ubicunque voluerint. Et ut hec mea remissio et quieta clamatio rate "et stabiles maneant in posterum, hoc presens scriptum sigilli mei munimine roboravi.

"Hiis testibus domino *Johanne de Oketon* tunc seneschallo S. *Marie Ebor.* *Johanne de* "*Danthorp* mil. *Galfrido Agelun* mil. *Ricardo de Anlatheby*, *Johanne de Monteaus*, "*Roberto de Waffand*, et aliis (*s*).

Charta Thomae *vicar. de* Myton.

B. 8. N. 58. Myton. "SCiant presentes et futuri quod ego *Thomas* vicarius eccl. de *Myton* dedi et concessi et "hac presenti carta mea confirmavi religiosis viris abbati et conventui monast. beate "*Marie Ebor.* duo messugia et duas bovatas terre cum omnibus aliis pertinentiis in villa "et territorio de *Myton* que habui de dono et feoffamento *Johannis de Fletham* et *Eliza-*"*bethe* uxoris sue in villa de *Myton* supradicta. Habend. et tenend. omn. predict. terras "et tenementa cum omnibus libertatibus et aisiamentis prefatis abbati et conventui et suc-"cessoribus suis in liberam puram et perpetuam elemosinam libere et quiete ab omnibus "secularibus exactionibus et demandis.

"In cujus rei testimonium huic presenti carte sigillum meum apposui.

"Datum apud *Myton* die festi annuntiationis beate *Marie* virginis anno Domini mille-"simo trecentesimo sexagesimo septimo.

"Hiis testibus, *Ricardo Bernardi* filio, *Willielmo de Estrington de Myton*, *Willielmo Ven-*"*do*, *Thoma Lovell*, *Ricardo de Pykeryng*, *Willielmo de Berneby* et aliis.

(*s*) Seal now appendant to this deed is a flower de liz on green wax; inscription; S. STEPHANI DE HAITFELD.

Charta

St. MARY's ABBEY.

Charta regis Henrici I.

B. 9. N. 3. Dune *and* Sivena.

" HEN. (t) rex *Anglor Osb.* vicec. et omnibus baronibus suis. *Francis* et *Anglis* de " " *Eborascira* sal. Precipio quod abbas et monachi de *Eborat.* teneant bene et in " pace et honorifice totum boscum suum et totam terram suam ab aqua *Dune* usq. ad " aquam que appellatur *Sivena*, sicut unquam melius tenuerunt antequam foresta fuit. Et " defendo forestariis meis ne se intromittant. Concedo etiam ipsius abbati et successoribus " ejus totam forestariam in. Et faciat custodire ad opus meum tam cervum cervam por- " cum et aneipitrem . . . . test. *Lud. Dapif.* ap. *Westmonast.* in *festo Domini*.

Charta Johannis de Spaunton.

" OMnibus hoc scriptum visuris vel audituris *Johannes* filius *Petri de Spaunton* salutem " in Domino sempiternam. Noveritis me dedisse concessisse et hac presenti scripto " meo confirmasse S. abbati sancte *Marie Ebor.* et ejusdem loci conventui et eorum successo- " ribus universis unum messuagium et unum toftum cum duabus bovatis terre in villa de " *Spaunton*, habend. et tenend. dict. abbati et conventui et eorum successoribus universis in " liberam puram et perpetuam elemosinam in perpetuum. Et ego *Johannes* et heredes mei " predict. messuagium et toftum cum predict. bovatis terre contra omnes homines warran- " tizabimus, acquietabimus et defendemus in perpetuum. B. 9. N. 19. Spaunton.

" In cujus rei testimon. huic presenti scripto sigillum meum apposui.

" Hiis testibus, Domino *Willielmo de Sancto Quintino* milite, *Waltero de Romeyn*, *Rogero de* " *Wrelington*, *Thoma le Lardiner*, *Richardo Bullok* de Kirkeby ..., *Johanne de* " *Sarcrino de Wodde-Apilton* et *Simone* filio *Matilde* de eadem et aliis.

Charta Adam de Thornton.

" SCiant presentes et futuri quod ego *Adam de Thornton* cler. dedi concessi et hac pre- " senti carta mea confirmavi religiosis viris abbati et conventui monasterii beate " *Marie Ebor.* tria messuagia et tres bovatas terre cum pratis et pasturis et omnibus aliis " pertinentiis in *Apilton* supra *Wyske* que habui de dono et feoffamento *Johannis* fil. *Ricardi* " *de Irby* de *Apilton* super *Wysk*; habend. et tenend. omnia predictas terras et tenementa " cum omnibus pertinentiis suis libertatibus et aisiamentis prefatis abbati et conventui et " eorum successoribus in liberam puram et perpetuam elemosinam in perpetuum, libere et " quiete ab omnibus servitiis secularibus exactionibus et demandis. B. 9. N. 53. Apilton *sup.* Wisk.

" In cujus rei testimonium sigillum meum huic presenti carte apposui.

" Hiis testibus, *Ricardo de Richmonde*, *Henrico de Bellerby*, ... , *Thoma* " *del Hill de Smitheton*, *Willielmo* filio *Rogeri de Horneby*, *Thoma* . . . . et aliis.

" Dat. apud *Apilton* super *Wysk* die dominica prox. post fest. annuntiationis beate *Marie* " virginis anno Dom. Millesimo trecentesimo sexagesimo septimb.

Charta Richardi de Galeby.

" NOverint per presentes quod ego *Ricardus de Galeby* manens in *Aynderby* dedi con- " cessi et presenti carta mea confirmavi Deo et abbatie sancte *Marie Ebor.* et prio- " ratui sancti *Martini* juxta *Richmund* et monachis ibidem Deo servientibus unam placeam " terre cum tota grangia mea in *Aynderby* et cum . . . . . . que jacet inter toftum *Roberti* " *Cunning* ex una parte et toftum *Alitie de Galeby* ex altera, que continet in longitudine " . . . . . perticatas et quindecim pedes terre, et in latitudine quinquaginta et quinque pe- " des terre. Tenend. et habend. dictis abatie prioratui et monachis cum libero introitu et " exitu versus orientem et occidentem cum . . gis et plaustris ad blada sua capienda et ad " omnimoda alia necessaria facienda quandocunque et quotiescunque ibi . . placuerint de " capitali dominio feodi illius in perpetuum, cum omnimodis aisiamentis dicte placee infra " villam de *Aynderby* et extra pertinentibus sicut ego *Ricardus* vel antecessores mei illam " placeam unquam liberius vel quiet. tenuerunt. Et ego *Ricardus de Galeby* et heredes mei " et assignati mei in quibuscunque manibus capitale messuagium meum et terra . . . de *An-* " *derby* devenit predict. abbatie et prioratui monachis et eorum successoribus universis to- B. 9. N. 63. Ainderby.

(t) This very antient grant from king *Henry* I. is a little imperfect. It is indorsed *Cart.* Henrici *prim.* *de* Farndale *cum* Spanniton. Probably this *Osbert*, who was highsheriff at this time, was *Osber. de Archis* mentioned before. A copy of this very grant is taken out of the register of St. *Mary*, and printed in the appendix to the additional volume of the monast. p. 86. n. 69. But how incorrect the reader may see if he pleases.

" tam

4

" tam placeam predict. cum omnibus suis pertinentiis, sicut predict. est, contra omnes " homines warrantizabimus adquietabimus et in perpetuum defendemus.

" In cujus rei testimonium presenti scripto sigillum meum apposui.

" Hiis testibus, *Johanne de Hellerbeco, Rogero* . . . . . . , *Willielmo Puring, Johanne* " *Lungtayne, Roberto de Anderby, Johanne de le Lyche* et multis aliis.

Charta Willielmi de Arel.

B. 10. N. 7. *Ecclesia de Sezay.*

" SCiant (u) omnes qui viderint vel audierint litteras has quod ego *Willielmus de Arel* vo- " luntate et assensu uxoris mee et heredum meorum, et pro salute anime mee et pa- " tris et matris mee et omnium antecessorum meorum concessi et hac presenti carta mea " confirmavi Deo et beate *Marie Ebor.* et monachis ibidem deo servientibus ecclesiam de " *Sezeie* cum omnibus pertinentiis suis in puram et perpetuam elemosinam sicut carta pa- " tris mei *Marmeduci* quam in manibus habent testatur. Et ut ista concessio et confir- " matio rata et inconcussa in posterum a me et heredibus meis permaneat, presens scrip- " tum sigilli mei appositione roboravi.

" Hiis testibus, *Willielmo de Perci, Waltero de Boigte.* magistro *Waltero de Dribend.* magis- " *Michaele de Clavill, Ricardo de Camera, Osberto Janitore, Roberto Bachel. Rob. Lup-* " *Rad. de Longa villa, Willielmo Pincerna, Johanne de Ha'm't, Johanne Coco,* et mul- " tis aliis.

Charta Johannis de Erghum.

B. 10. N. 20. Erghum.

" SCiant omnes tam presentes quam futuri quod ego *Johannes* filius *Nicholai de Erghum* " pro salute anime mee et omnium parentum meorum concessi dedi et hac presenti " carta confirmavi Deo et ecclesie S. *Marie Ebor.* et monachis ibidem Deo servientibus to- " tam illam culturam meam que jacet in territorio de *Erghum* inter cemiterium et aquam " que vocatur *These* cum fossato extra illam culturam proximo jacente, scil. quatuor acras " et dimid. de terra arabili et unam rodam terre super **Humbelonkeberg** que jacet inter cul- " turam quondam domini *Rogeri* filii *Ricardi* et terram *Radulfi de Smitheton*, et duas acras " prati in campo de *Erghum*, scil. in *Hales*, propinquiores prato *Simonis* filii *Walteri de* " *Chillington* versus austrum. Habendas et possidendas cum omnibus aisiamentis perti- " nent. ad eandem terram infra villlam et extra in puram liberam et perpetuam elemo- " sinam.

" Hiis testibus, *Roberto Arundel, Willielmo de Lilling, Thoma* fil. *Lamberti, Thoma* clerico " de infirmaria, *Gilberto* socio suo et **multis aliis.**

Charta Richardi de Spineto.

B. 10. N. 25. Sutthop.

" OMnibus hanc cartam visuris vel audituris ego *Ricardus* filius *Ricardi de Spyneto* salu- " tem. Noverit universitas vestra me remisisse et quietum clamasse de me et he- " redibus meis in perpetuum Deo et ecclesie beate *Marie Ebor.* et monachis ibidem Deo " servientibus tres bovatas terre in *Sutthorp* que stant juxta maram de *Hornese*, cum omni- " bus pertinentiis suis infra villam et extra et in omnibus locis absque ullo retenemento, " scil. servitium de duabus bovatis terre que *Nich.* fil *Walteri* clerici quondam tenuit, et " alteram bovatam tenendam in dominico cum omnibus suis pertinentiis dictis abbati et " monach. in liberam puram et perpetuam elemosinam in perpetuum, absque aliquo rete- " nemento. Et ego *Ricardus* et heredes mei predict. omnia servitia et tenementa cum om- " nibus suis pertinentiis dict. eccl. et monach. in liberam puram et perpetuam elemosinam " warrantizabimus defendemus et adquietabimus contra omnes gentes in perpetuum, ita " . . . . . . dicti monachi tenebuntur exhibere in me vel heredibus meis cartam *Willielmi* " militis . . . . et cartam *Willielmi de Friboys* eisdem monachis reddidi in predicta " remissione et quieta clamatione quam habui de eodem tenemento, si ego vel heredes mei " in placiten. de predicto tenemento.

" In cujus rei testimonium huic scripto sigillum meum apposui.

" Hiis testibus, *Waltero de Pikeryng, Roberto de Coushel, Waltero de Spineto, Yvone Soc-* " *vayn, Reginaldo* filio *Reginaldi de Suttborp, Ade Clerico* tunc ballivo de *Hornese,* " *Willielmo Grayneport, Ricardo* filio *Martini de Hornese Burton,* et multis aliis.

(u) The church of *Sezay* was given to this abbey by by *Marmaduke de Arell* and confirmed by this and other grants. See additional volume to the *Mon.* appen. p. 93. n. 85, &c.

Charta

Charta Richardi Soudan.

Literatim ut antea in charta filii sui *Richardi* B. 6. N°. 35. cum testibus iisdem. B. 10. N. 29. Apelton.

Charta Richardi Collan.

" OMnibus sancte matris ecclesie filiis ad quos presens scriptum pervenerit, *Th.* filius B. 10. N. 36. Horwayt.
" *Ricardi Collan* de *Egremunde* salutem in Domino. Noveritis me dedisse concessisse
" et hac presenti carta mea confirmasse Deo et beate *Marie Ebor.* et sancte *Bege* in *Coup-*
" *lande* et monachis ibidem Deo servientibus unam viam per mediam terram meam, con-
" tinentem in latitudine viginti pedes et longitudine de *Horwayt* usque ad moram de *Hen-* Hensing. via.
" *singh* cum libero introitu et exitu ad voluntates dictorum monachorum. Tenend. et ha-
" bend. dict. monachis in liberam puram et perpetuam eleemosinam libere quiete integre
" et honorifice sicut aliqua terra eleemosinata liberius poterint dari vel concedi. Ego dict.
" *Th.* et heredes mei dictam terram sicut predict. est dict. monachis warrantizabimus
" adquietabimus et defendemus in perpetuum. Et si contigit quod animalia dict. mona-
" chorum tam magnum dampnum in blado meo causa dicte vie fecerint, bene licebit mihi
" et heredibus meis ex utraque parte dict. vie tensare vel fossare ita tum quod dict. mo-
" nachi medietatem cust. habere fosse adquietabunt. Preterea sciendum est quod qualiscun-
" que dicta via sic fossata vel tensata longitudo et latitudo dict. viginti pedum integra et li-
" bera dict. via semper remanebit.

" In cujus rei testimonium presenti scripto sigillum meum apposui.

" Hiis testibus, dominis *Ricardo de Clec'*, *Roberto de Langplogh*, *Nicholao de Meurby*,
" *Elya* tunc ballivo, *Michaele de Huvington*, *Roberto de Wilton*, *Johanne de Hale*, *Ri-*
" *cardo Fleming*, *Benedict. de Cotington* et aliis.

Charta Rand. de Rednes.

" OMnibus hanc cartam visuris vel audituris *Randulfus* filius *Roberti de Rednes* salut. in B. 10. N. 46. Rednes.
" Domino. Noverit universitas vestra me dedisse concessisse et hac presenti carta
" mea confirmasse Deo et ecclesie S. *Marie Ebor.* et monachis ibidem Deo servientibus unam
" placeam in curia mea in villa de *Rednes*, continentem in longitudine quadraginta pedes
" et triginta in latitudine, ad construendum quoddam granarium ad opus eleemosinarii cum
" cum libero introitu et exitu usque ad regiam viam et cum omnibus aliis pertinentiis di-
" ctam placeam contingentibus. Tenend. et habend. dictis ecclesie et monachis in liberam
" puram et perpetuam elemosinam in perpetuum. Et sciendum est quod licebit dict. mo-
" nachis dict. placeam includere quocunque modo voluerint vel sibi viderint expedire.
" Et ego *Randulfus* et heredes mei dictam placeam cum libero introitu et exitu et cum om-
" nibus aliis pertinentiis absque aliquo impedimento mei vel heredum meorum dict. ecclesie
" et monachis in liberam puram et perpetuam eleemosinam warrantizabimus defendemus ad-
" quietabimus contra omnes gentes in perpetuum.

" In cujus rei testimonium presenti scripto sigillum meum apposui.

" Hiis testibus, *Roberto de Skegnesse* tunc seneschal. S. *Marie Ebor.* *Willielmo de Kirton*,
" *Johanne de Huc*, *Johanne de Griglingston*, *Roberto* filio *Ang'i*. *Willielmo* filio *Roberti*,
" *Ricardo de Withington*, ... *Waltero de Ase*, *Johanne de* . . . .
" *Alano do Ecclesia*, *Adam de Eleemosinaria*, *Roberto de Fenton*, *Roberto de Aregi* et mul-
" tis aliis.

Charta Roaldi de Colebrunne.

" OMnibus has literas visuris vel audituris *Roaldus* filius *Galfridi de Colebrunne* salutem. B. 11. N. 31. Hippeswell.
" Sciatis me pro salute anime mee concessisse et dedisse et presenti carta mea con-
" firmasse cum corpore meo Deo et ecclesie sancte *Marie Ebor.* et monachis ibidem Deo
" servientibus ubi sepulturam elegi ad fabricam ejusdem ecclesie duas acras terre in terri-
" torio de *Hypplesswell* que jacent super *Arenberg* propinquiores terre prioratus sancti *Mar-*
" *tini* juxta *Richmund* cum libero introitu et exitu et cum omnibus pertinentiis suis, tenen-
" das et habendas in perpetuum in puram liberam et perpetuam eleemosinam pacifice, in-
" tegre, libere et quiete, ab omni seculari servitio et exactione. Et ego et heredes mei
" predictas duas acras terre cum pertinentiis predicte ecclesie et predictis monachis warran-
" tizabimus defendemus et adquietabimus in perpetuum contra omnes homines et feminas.
" Et ut hoc scriptum perpetuam obtineat firmitatem illud sigilli mei appositione ro-
" boravi.

" Hiis testibus, *Henrico* filio *Roaldi*, *Johanne de Mersc* clerico, *Henrico le Buteiler*, *Jo-*
" *hanne* fratre ejus, *Cunano de Appelby*, *Johanne de Seleby* et AL. . IIS.

St. Mary's Abbey.

Charta Stephani Shampenes.

B. 11. N. 54. Rudstane. " SCiant presentes et futuri quod ego *Stephanus Shampenes* in *Fridaythorp* et *Katherina* uxor " mea dedimus, concessimus et presenti carta confirmamus *Simoni* abbati beate *Marie* " *Eboraci* et ejusdem loci conventui ad spirituales eorundem augmentandas dimidium bo- " vate terre cum tota parte suorum boscorum in villa et territorio de *Ruddestan* nos con- " tingente jure hereditario per mortem *Henrici de Etton* fratris predicte *Katherine*. Habend. " et tenend. dict. *Simoni* abbati et ejusdem loci conventui in perpetuum; ita tam quod nec " ego *Stephanus* nec ego *Katherina*, nec aliquis heredum nostrorum, nec aliquis ex parte " nostra aliquod jus vel clamium in dicta dimidia bovata terre cum parte suorum boscorum " in posterum poterimus apponere vel vendicare. Nos *Stephanus* et *Katherina* uxor mea et " heredes et assigni nost. dictam dimid bovatam terre cum tota parte suorum boscorum " dictis *Simoni* abbati et conventui et eorum successoribus universis contra omnes homines " warrantizabimus.

" In cujus rei testimonium huic scripto sigilla nostra apposuimus.

" Hiis testibus dom. *Willielmo de Sancto Quintino*, *Ada de Garton*, *Thoma de Orderne*, " *Thoma de Plumsted*, *Johanne Welard*, *Simone* . . . . . *boys* in *Ruddestan* et " aliis.

B. 12. N. 47. *Cecilia de Walkington* quondam uxor . . . . . . de *Rydal* confirmat *Simoni* abbati et con- " ventui dim. bovat. terre cum tota parte sua trium boscorum in villa et territorio de " *Rudestan*, que se continget habere jure hereditario per mortem *Henrici de Etton*, &c.

" Testibus domino *Willielmo de Sancto Quintino* tunc senefchallo abbatis et conventus sancte " *Marie Ebor.* &c.

Charta Nicholai le Joevene.

B. 12. N. 66. Miton. " OMnibus hoc scriptum visuris vel audituris *Nicholaus le Joevene* de *Miton* salutem in " Domino sempiternam. Noverit universitas vestra me dedisse concessisse reddidisse " et presenti scripto confirmasse *Johanni* abbati monasterii sancte *Marie Ebor.* et ejusdem " loci conventui et eorum successoribus universis quatuor acras et dimidiam terre arabilis, " et quatuor acras et dimidiam prati in territorio et campo de *Miton* quas de prior. ab- " bate et conven. aliquando tenui in eadem villa, quarum due acre terre jacent . . . . *othedike*, " una acra ad gardinum *Batemani*, dimidia acra ad *Barcarium* domini abbatis, dimidia " acra ad *Gategynela* . . ., dimid. acra ad *Guwylandes*. Pratum jacet in locis subscriptis " videlicet una acra in *Banco* et *Fenerdale* . . - . . . *Raveneffyk*, una acra et dimid. ad " *longas rodas*, et una acra ad *Hendikedale*. Tenend. et habend. predict. abbati et conven- " tui et eorum successoribus universis in liberam puram et perpetuam eleemosinam cum " omnibus libertatibus pertinentiis et asiamentis infra villam de *Miton* et extra predict. acris " et predicto prato pertinentibus in perpetuum. Et ego *Nicholaus* et heredes mei predict. " terram predictis abbati et conventui et eorum successoribus univer. sicut predict. est con- " tra omnes homines warrantizabimus acquietabimus et defendemus in perpetuum.

" In cujus rei testimonium presenti scripto sigillum meum apposui.

" Hiis testibus, dom. *Willielmo de Ros de Bolton* milite, *Simone de Stutevile*, *Symone de* " *Leycestre* vicario de *Gilling*, ... *Barne* de *Miton*, *Johanne* fil. *Willielmi* de eadem, " *Willielmo de Walton* clerico, *Johanne de Edelingthorp*, et aliis.

(*x*) *Charta* Roberti de Mainil.

B. 13. N. 24. Miton. " ✠ NOtum sit omnibus tam futuris quam presentibus quod ego *Robertus de Mainil* " dedi ecclesie sancte *Marie Eboracensis* abbatie villam que vocatur *Mitone* in " eleemosinam liberam ab omni re que ad me vel ad heredes meos pertinet, ita ut nichil " amplius ex illa exigere debeam, et meam donationem super altare prescripte ecclesie po- " nens sic liberam concessi sicut aliquis rem a se possessam liberius donare potest.

" Coram hiis testibus, Stephano primo abbate dicte ecclesie, *Laurentio Grammatico*, " *Willielmo de Verli*, ejus fratre *Hugone*, *Hamone Camerario*, *Malgero de Rodestein*, *Ge-* " *rardo Cementario*, *Daniele*, *Rogero Portario*, *Reinero*, *Torgero Gernano*, hii sunt testes " qui cum multis aliis fuerunt in ecclesia cum monachis quando predictus *Robertus* " donum hoc super altare posuit, pro qua eleemosina ipse et uxor sua *Gertreda* et fi- " lius ejus *Stephanus* in eleemosinis et orationibus, et omnibus aliis beneficiis ab omni " conventu monachorum recepti fuerunt.

(*x*) This very antient grant, which must be upwards of six hundred years old, is copied from the register and printed in the appendix to the additional volumes of the *Monast.* n. LXIV, but the original being in this collection I thought fit to give this copy of it. The antient family of *Mainel* is yet in this county.

Charta

Charta Philippi de Faukenberg *mil.*

" OMnibus *Christi* fidelibus hoc scriptum visuris vel audituris *Philippus de Faukenberg* B 14. N°. 7. Apelton.
" miles eternam in Domino salutem. Noverit universitas vestra me dedisse concessisse et hac presenti carta mea confirmasse *Symoni* abbati et conventui sancte *Marie Ebor.* tres placeas prati in prato de *Appelton* quod vocatur *Westhengs*, quarum una placea notatur *Pitdale* et jacet inter pratum *Willielmi de Horwington* et pratum quod *Henricus Burghaad* tunc tenuit, et abuttat in occidentale capite super aquam de *Werf* et extendit se versus orientem usque ad *Lepitte*; et alia placea notatur *Hyldale* et jacet inter pratum predicti *Willielmi* et pratum quod *Adam Carpentarias* tunc tenuit, et abuttat in uno capite super aquam de *Werf*, et sic se extendit in longitudine usque ad *Tungedai*; et tertia placea vocatur *Tungedale* et jacet inter pratum predicti *Willielmi* et pratum quod vocatur *Waddales*, et abuttat in imo capite super *Suthwod* et sic se extendit in longitudine versus *Mickeldales*. Tenendas et habendas predict. tres placeas prati cum omnibus pertinentiis suis et cum libero introitu et exitu predict. abbati et conventui et eorum successoribus in liberam puram et perpetuam eleemosinam in perpetuum, sine omni servitio seculari consuetudine vel demanda. Et ego *Philippus* et heredes mei warrantizabimus defendemus et adquietabimus predictas tres placeas prati cum omnibus pertinentiis suis et cum libero introitu et exitu predict. abbati et conventui et eorum successoribus in liberam puram et perpetuam eleemosinam contra omnes gentes in perpetuum.

" In cujus rei testimonium presenti scripto sigillum meum apposui.

" Hiis testibus dominis *Johanne de Oketon* tunc senescallo sancte *Marie Ebor. Johanne de Raygate* et *Symone de Lilling* militibus, *Johanne de Merston*, *Ricardo de Colton*, *Hugone de Acaster*, *Henrico de Cave*, *Wydone de Appelton*, *Nicholao de Camera* et aliis.

" Dat. vigilia sancti *Andree* apostoli anno gratie millesimo . . . . ducentesimo " . . . . sexagesimo . . . PRIMO.

Charta Johannis de Reygate *mil.*

" OMnibus *Christi* fidelibus visuris vel audituris *Johannes de Reygate* miles salutem in Do- B. 14. N°. 12. Apelton.
" mino sempiternam. Noverit universitas vestra me dedisse concessisse et hac presenti carta mea confirmasse pro salute anime mee et animarum antecessorum et successorum meorum Deo et beate *Marie* et *Simoni* abbati beate *Marie Ebor.* et monachis ibidem Deo et beate *Marie* servientibus et eorum successoribus totam terram meam in *Apilton*, cum omnibus pertinentiis suis sine aliquo retenemento, una cum dote cum acciderit in perpetuum. Habend. et tenend. de me et heredibus meis predicto *Simoni* abbati beate *Marie Ebor.* et monachis ibidem Deo et beate *Marie* servientibus et eorum successoribus libere, quiete, bene, integre et in pace, in liberam et perpetuam eleemosinam in perpetuum, faciendo inde . . . capitali domino debitum et consuetudinem. Et ego *Johannes* et heredes mei predictam terram predict. *Simoni* abbati beate *Marie* et monachis Deo ibidem et beate *Marie* servientibus et eorum successoribus in forma predicta contra omnes gentes warrantizabimus defendemus et adquietabimus.

" In cujus rei testimonium presentem cartam sigillo meo signavi.

" Hiis testibus domino *Willielmo de Rye*, *Willielmo de Doncestre*, *Ricardo Malebice*, *Willielmo de Burgewiks* clerico, *Totto de Apilto*, *Stephano de Schupton*, *Johanne de Picling*, " *Thoma de* . . . et aliis.

" Dat. mense *Octobris* anno regni regis *Edvardi* fil. regis *Henrici*, secundo.

Charta Roberti de Skegenesse.

Eadem cum *B.* 2. *N.* 29. B. 14. N°. 32. Apelton.

Charta Elyas de Flaunville *mil.*

" UNiversis *Christi* fidelibus hoc scriptum visuris vel audituris *Elyas de Flaunville* miles B. 14. N°. 42. Dalby.
" eternam in Domino salutem. Noveritis me dedisse concessisse et hac presenti carta mea confirmasse et de me et heredibus meis remisisse et omnimodo quietum clamasse *Simoni* abbati sancte *Marie Ebor.* et ejusdem loci conventui et eorum successoribus in perpetuum, pro salute anime mee et animarum antecessorum meorum totam terram in villa de *Daleby*, una cum dote matris mee et cum villanis meis et eorum sequelis, molendino meo cum secta, et cum advocatione et jure patronatus ecclesie ejusdem ville cum omnibus pertinentiis suis infra villam et extra, ut in boscis, moris, terris arabilibus, pratis, pascuis, et pasturis, et omnibus aliis aisiamentis et juribus que ratione dicti tenementi sive tenentium me vel heredibus meis competere posset vel descendere sine aliquo retenemento in perpetuum. Tenend. et habend. eisdem abbati et conventui et eorum successoribus libere, quiete, pacifice,

St. MARY's ABBEY. " integre in liberam puram et perpetuam eleemosinam quietam ab omni terreno servitio seculari, exactione et demanda in perpetuum. Et ego *Elyas* et heredes mei omnia supradicta " cum pertinentiis sicut predictum est predictis abbati et conventui et eorum successoribus in " liberam puram et perpetuam eleemosinam contra omnes gentes warrantizabimus, adquietabimus, et in omnibus defendemus in perpetuum.

" In cujus rei testimonium presenti scripto sigillum meum apposui.

" Hiis testibus domino *Johanne de Oketon* tunc vicecomite *Ebor.* Domino *Johanne de Raygate*, domino *Simone de Lilling*, domino *Roberto de Kyrkeby* militibus, *Ricardo de Camera*, *Roberto de Breddale*, *Simone de Sartia*, *Stephano* fil. *Clementis de Schupton*, *Johanne de Merston*, *Waltero de Ask*, *Nicholao de Camera*, et aliis.

Charta Ymanyae de Flaumville.

B. 15. N°. 3. Dalby. " OMnibus hoc scriptum visuris vel audituris *Ymanya* quondam uxor *Alani de Flaumville* " salutem in Domino. Noverit universitas vestra me in propria viduitate et potestate mea reddidisse relaxasse et omni modo de in perpetuum quietum clamasse domino *Simoni* abbati sancte *Marie Ebor.* et ejusdem loci conventui totum jus et clamium quod habui vel " aliquo modo. . . . . in bosco de *Dalby*, qui vocatur *Dalby-Buxby* ratione dotis mee " in contingen . . . . . . tenemento predicti *Alani* viri mei in eadem, quod nec ego " nec aliquis per me aliquod jus vel clamium in predicto bosco aliqua ratione vel casu contingente de cetero poterimus vendicare.

" In cujus rei testimonium huic presenti scripto sigillum meum apposui.

" Hiis testibus domino *Johanne de Oketon*, *Simone de Lilling* militibus, *Ricardo de Camera*, *Nicholao de Camera*, *Thoma de Routbecline*, *Waltero de Colton*, *Reginaldo de Thorneton* forestario et aliis (z).

Charta Huberti de Newton.

B. 15. N°. 36. Newton. " SCiant omnes tam presentes quam futuri quod ego *Hubertus de Neutona* dedi concessi et " hac presenti carta mea confirmavi Deo et beate *Marie Eboraci* et beate *Bege* et monachis ibidem Deo servientibus septem acras terre in territorio de *Neuton* et totum jus quod " habui vel unquam habere potui in predictas septem acras cum omnibus suis pertinentiis, &c.

" Hiis testibus dominis *Johanne de Langelene*, *Roberto de Laneplogh*, *Nicholao de Morneby*, " *Elya* tunc seneschallo de *Egremonte*, *Johanne de Hale*, *Johanne de Goseford*, *Benedicto* " *de Rodinton*, aliis.

Charta Philippi de Faukenberg.

B. 15. N°. 48. Appleton. " UNiversis *Christi* fidelibus hoc scriptum visuris vel audituris eternam in Domino salutem. Noverit universitas vestra me dedisse concessisse et hac presenti carta mea " confirmasse S. abbati et conventui sancte *Marie Ebor.* septemdecim acras terre cum pertinentiis suis in territorio de *Apilton*, de quibus septemdecim acris terre duodecim sunt bosci, " et jacent inter boscum meum et boscum qui quondam fuit *Roberti de Munecell*, et abuttant " in orientali capite super viam que it usque ad *Coupemanthorp*, et occidentali capite super " boscum de *Colton*. Et quinque acre de predictis septemdecim acris terre sunt terra arabilis " et jacent in quadam cultura que vocatur *Wyndmilnestake* inter terram *Ydonie* filie mee et " terram *Willielmi de Hornington*, et totum pratum quod pertinet ad predictam culturam que " vocatur *Wyndmilnestake* sicut jacet in longitudine et latitudine sine aliqua diminutione. " Preterea dedi et concessi predictis abbati et conventui totum pratum quod pertinebat ad " culturam quam *Gage* tenet et vocatur *Tungedal* in *Brumberiker*. Preterea dedi et concessi iisdem abbati et conventui *molendinum ad ventum*, quod situm est in predicto " territorio de *Apilton* in quadam cultura que vocatur *Stubbe* cum latitudine quadraginta pedum undique circa predictum molendinum, et cum libero introitu et exitu " ad predictum molendinum. Tenend. et habend. omnia predicta tenementa cum omnibus " libertatibus et aisiamentis infra villam et extra eisdem tenementis pertinentibus, et cum libero introitu et exitu ad omnia singula loca supradicta predictis abbati et conventui et eorum successoribus in liberam puram et perpetuam eleemosinam libere quiete integre et in " perpetuum absque omni servitio seculari exactione et demanda. Et sciendum est quod " bene licebit predictis abbati et conventui includere et imparcare predictas duodecim acras " terre que sunt bosci secundum quod ipsis et eorum successoribus melius videbitur expedire, " sine aliqua contradictione mei vel heredum meorum vel aliquo aliorum ex parte nostra. " Et ego *Philippus* et heredes mei warrantizabimus, defendemus et adquietabimus omnia " predicta tenementa cum omnibus pertinentiis suis sicut predictum est predictis abbati et

(z) Seal on white wax a *Fleur de lys*, the inscription gone.

" conventui

St. Mary's Abbey.

" conventui et eorum successoribus in liberam puram et perpetuam eleemosinam contra omnes gentes in perpetuum.

" In cujus rei testimonium presenti scripto sigillum meum apposui.

" His testibus, dominis *Johanne de Oketon*, *Johanne de Raygate* militibus, *Stephano de Schupeton*, *Johanne de Merstona*, *Ricardo fil. Willielmi de Coltone*, *Hugone* fil. *Willielmi de Acaster*, *Wydone de Apilton*, *Nicholao de Camera*, *Ricardo de Minting*, et aliis.

Charta Rogeri *decani et capit.* Lincoln.

B. 16. No. 28. *Cemeterium conceff. cellae* S Marie Mag. *juxta* Lincoln.

" OMnibus sancte matris ecclesie filiis ad quos presens scriptum pervenerit *Rogerus* decanus et capitulum *Lincoln.* ecclesie eternam in Domino salutem. Noverit universitas vestra nos de assensu et voluntate domini *Willielmi Lincolniensis* episcopi ad instantiam etiam et petitionem venerabilium amicorum nostrorum domini *Roberti* abbatis et conventus monasterii sancte *Marie* de *Ebor.* concessisse eisdem abbati et conventui cemeterium habendum apud oratorium suum sancte *Marie Magdalene*, juxta civit. *Lincoln.* ex parte scilicet orientali ejusdem civitatis ad sepulturas monachorum suorum qui de prefato monasterio suo sancte *Marie* de *Ebor.* illuc advenerint, vel qui apud prefatum oratorium in sua incolumitate habitum monachalem susceperint, sive ibi exerceant munera monachorum sive non. Predicti vero abbas et conventus firmiter nobis permiserunt quod alium neminem ibidem ad sepulturam admittent sine assensu capit. *Lincolnie.* Et ut hoc ratum sit et stabile et ut tam juri episcopali quam *Lincoln.* ecclesie indempnati similiter . . . . ecclesie quieti ac tranquillitati plenius prospiciatur sepedicti abbas et conventus insuper in verbo veritatis nobis promiserunt, sicut in literis suis patentibus continetur, quod contra hoc nullo futuris temporibus privilegio vel alio beneficio impetrato vel impetrando utentur, quod si secus actum fuerit dominus episcop. *Lincoln.* qui pro tempore fuerit id remoto appellationis obstaclo et mediatione qualibet cessante adhibita competenti cohibitione justitia mediante faciet observari. Et ut hec concessio perpetue firmitatis robur optineat eam presentem et sigilli nostri munimine roboravimus.

Charta Johannis de Danby.

B. 17. No. 29. Hornby.

" SCiant presentes et futuri quod ego *Johannes de Danby* vicarius ecclesie de *Grimstone* nuper vicarius ecclesie de *Crewyks* dedi concessi et hac presenti carta mea confirmavi religiosis viris abbati et conventui monasterii beate *Marie Ebor.* unum messuagium et duas bovatas terre cum pratis pasturis et omnibus aliis pertinentiis in *Horneby* juxta *Smethton* que habui ex dono et feoffamento *Willielmi* filii *Rogeri de Horneby* in villa de *Horneby* supradict. Habend. et tenend. omnes predictas terras et tenementa cum omnibus pertinentiis suis libertatibus et aisiamentis prefatis abbati et conventui et eorum successoribus in liberam puram et perpetuam eleemosinam in perpetuum libere et quiete ab omnibus serviciis secularibus exactionibus et demandis.

" In cujus rei testimonium huic presenti carte sigillum meum apposui.

" Hiis testibus, *Ricardo de Richmund*, *Henrico de Bellerby*, *Milone de Aldbury de Richmund*, *Rogero de Donyngton*, *Thoma del Hill de Smethton*, *Willielmo* filio *Rogeri de Hornby*, *Thoma Coleman de Appilton*, *Willielmo de Middelton* et aliis.

" Dat. apud *Hornby* die dom. prox. post festum annuntiationis beate *Marie* virginis, anno dom. millesimo trescentesimo sexagesimo septimo (a).

Charta Richardi de East-Houkeswelle.

B. 18. No. 4. Easthoukswell

" NOtum sit omnibus videntibus vel audientibus literas has, quod ego *Ricardus* filius *Willielmi de Estboukeswelle*, cum concilio et assensu *Constantie* matris mee, et heredum meorum dedi et concessi et hac presenti karta mea confirmavi Deo et abbatie beate *Marie Ebor.* et monachis ibidem Deo servientibus et prioratui sancti *Martini* juxta *Richmund* pro salute anime mee et antecessorum meorum in puram et perpetuam eleemosinam unum thoftum et croftum in *Estboukeswelle*, et duas acras terre de dimidia karukata terre quam habeo in dominio in territorio ejusdem ville de *Estboukeswell*, scil. thoftum et croftum propinquiorem me que tendit versus *Huntun* in parte aquilonali ejusdem et unam acram terre et dimidiam acram duodecim perkatis super *Larchild* cum prato quod pertinet ad eandem culturam, et dimidiam acram terre, quatuor pertikatas terre super *Kirkeby*, et ad duas acras terre perficiendas dedi predicte abbatie totam partem terre mee que descendit versus *Westlageland* versus aquilonem. Hanc terram dedi prefate abbatie in puram et perpetuam eleemosinam possidendam in perpetuum libere et quiete ab omni terreno servi-

(a) Seal, in white wax, whereon is the image of the virgin, sitting with her book in her lap, and another kneeling before her. The inscription illegible.

St. Mary's Abbey. " tio et consuetudine et exactione seculari sicut eleemosinam cum omnibus pertinentiis et om-
" nibus aisiamentis in villa et extra villam absque omni retenemento.

" Testibus hiis, *Roaldo Constabulario Richmund*, *Nicolao de Gerrestun*, *Gileberto de Huntun*, *Hamone de Stodhat*, *Alano de Fol* . . . . , *Richardo filio Radulfi*, *Alexandro de Houkeswelle*, *Ricardo Staalwardi*, *Laurentio* filio ejus, *Batawino de Houkeswelle*, *Ricardo* fil. *Ricardi* et aliis.

Charta Willielmi Pore.

B. 18. N°. 13. Rednefs. " OMnibus *Christi* fidelibus ad quos presens scriptum pervenerit *Willielmus* filius *Ranulphi Pore de Rednesse* eternam in Domino salutem. Noverit universitas vestra me dedisse concessisse et hac presenti carta mea confirmasse religiosis S. abbati et conventui sancte *Marie Ebor.* sex acras terre cum pertinentiis in territorio de *Rednesse*, quarum tres acre jacent in campo orientali, et due acre in *Barfeld*, et una acra jacet in *Underwude*. Habend. et tenend. predict. abbati et conventui et eorum successoribus in liberam puram et perpetuam eleemosinam in perpetuum. Et ego *Willielmus* et heredes mei warrantizabimus defendemus et adquietabimus predictas sex acras terre cum pertinentiis predict. abbati et conventui et eorum successoribus in liberam puram et perpetuam eleemosynam contra omnes gentes in perpetuum.

" In cujus rei testimonium presenti scripto sigillum meum apposui.

" Hiis testibus, domino *Johanne de Oketona* tunc seneschallo abbatis, dominis *Johanne de Ussflet* et *Simone de Lilling* militibus, *Ricardo de Camera*, *Roberto Bredale*, *Stephano de Schapton*, *Waltero de Ask*, *Johanne de Brettevill*, *Rogero de Wederhale* clerico, et aliis.

Charta Johannis de Burringham.

B. 18. N°. 49. Rednefs. " JOhannes de Burringham de Rednefs concessit abbati et conventui beate *Marie Ebor.* unum toftum et croftum in *Rednefs*.

" Testibus dominis *Gerardo de Usflete*, *Thoma de Metham*, *Willielmo de Rednesse* militibus, *Petro de Thorneton-house*, *Johanne de Wynton*, *Willielmo de Gatorest*, et aliis.

" Dat. die sabbati prox. post fest. nativ. beate *Marie* an. Dom. millesimo trecentesimo quadragesimo quarto.

Charta Willielmi de Grimeston.

B. 19. N°. 22. Bradingham. " OMnibus hanc cartam visuris vel audituris *Willielmus de Grimeston* salutem. Noverit universitas vestra me omni pietatis intuitu dedisse et concessisse et hac presenti carta mea confirmasse Deo et ecclesie beate *Marie Ebor.* et monachis ibidem Deo servientibus duas acras prati et unam rodam in *Bradebeingham* cum omnibus pertinentiis suis. Tenend. et habend. predict. ecclesie et monachis in puram et perpetuam eleemosinam in perpetuum, libere, quiete, pacifice, integre, honorifice, absque omni seculari servitio et exactione. Et ego *Willielmus* et heredes mei predict. duas acras et predict. rodam prati prefatis ecclesie et monachis warrantizabimus defendemus et adquietabimus contra omnes gentes in perpetuum.

" In cujus rei testimonium huic scripto sigillum meum apposui.

" Hiis testibus domino *Willielmo de Skegenesse*, *Germano* tunc serviente de *Grimeston*, magistro *Waltero de Kyrkeby*, *Johanne* fratre ejus, *Willielmo de Lilling*, *Willielmo Coco*, *Johanne Lupe*, *Ric. de Kamera*, *Johanne Mort* clerico, et aliis.

Charta Willielmi de Rednesse.

B. 19. N°. 29. Rednefs. " OMnibus hoc scriptum visuris vel audituris *Willielmus* filius *Emme de Rednefs*, salutem. Noveritis me dedisse concessisse et hac presenti carta mea confirmasse *Simoni* abbati ecclesie beate *Marie Ebor.* et eodem loci conventui unam placeam terre in campo de *Rednefs* vocat. *les Plotes* jacentem in latitudine inter terram *Walteri Aunger* ex parte orientali et terram . . . *ari le Forayst* in occidentali, et in longitudine a regia via usque ad *Middelsandykes*, cum suo molendino ad ventum. Habend. et tenend. eisdem abbati et conventui et eorum successoribus universis cum omnibus modis pertinentiis suis tam in situ molendini quam in omnibus aliis appropriamentis suis sine aliquo retenemento in liberam puram et perpetuam eleemosinam in perpetuum. Et ego *Willielmus* et heredes mei vel assignati warrantizabimus, &c. Et ut hec mea donatio firma et stabilis permaneat huic scripto sigillum meum apposui.

" Hiis testibus domino *Christ. de Huby*, *Willielmo de Rednesse* militibus, *Aime de Rednesse*, *Waltero* . . . . *Rogero de Usflete*, *Christo. de Balliolo in Rednesse*, *Waltero Garerest*, *Petro Piccatore de* . . . . *Ricardo* filio *Rad. de Swineflete*, et aliis.

Charta

Charta Reginaldi Corvaysor.

" OMnibus hanc cartam visuris vel audituris *Reginaldus Corvaser* et *Matilda* uxor ejus " salutem. Noveritis nos dedisse concessisse et presenti carta nostra confirmasse Deo " et ecclesie sancte *Marie Ebor.* et monachis ibidem Deo servientibus totam terram nostram " quam habuimus in *Neubingings*, tenendam et habendam in puram et perpetuam eleemo- " sinam in perpetuum libere integre et quiete cum omnibus libertatibus et aisiamentis et " cum omnibus pertinentiis infra villam et extra et in omnibus locis, absque aliquo retene- " mento. Et totam predict. terram cum pertinentiis dicte ecclesie et dictis monachis in " liberam puram et perpetuam eleemosinam contra omnes gentes warrantizabimus defen- " demus et adquietabimus in perpetuum. B. 19. N°. 42 Newbigging.

" Hiis testibus, *Roberto de Skegenesse* tunc senescallo abbatie beate *Marie Ebor. Johanne* " *de Warthille*, *Petro de Barneby*, *Nicholao Orger*, *Laurentio Buchar*, *Willielmo de Lil-* " *ling*, *Ella Flur*, *Roberto de Thornethon*, *Galfrido de Cruce*, *Galfrido de Aula*, *Ri-* " *cardo de Porta*, *Willielmo de Sartrina*.

Charta Philippi de Faukenberg, *mil.*

" OMnibus Christi fidelibus hoc scriptum visuris vel audituris *Phillippus de Faukenberg* " miles eternam in Domino salutem. Noverit universitas vestra me dedisse con- " cessisse et presenti carta mea confirmasse *Symoni* abbati et conventui sancte *Marie Ebor.* " quatuor acras bosci cum solio in *Apilton*, qui quidem boscus est in *Westwod*, inter " boscum meum et boscum predictorum abbatis et conventus, et abuttat in occidentali ca- " pite super boscum de *Coltona*, et extendit se in longitudine versus orientem usque ad " exitum quo itur apud *Coupemanthorp*. Tenendum et habendum predict. boscum cum " solio et cum libero introitu et exitu per communem stratam qua itur de *Apilton* usque " ad *Coupemanthorp*, predict. abbati et conventui et eorum successoribus in liberam puram " et perpetuam eleemosinam in perpetuum. Et sciendum est quod bene licebit predict. " abbati et conventui includere imparcare et appruare predict. boscum cum solio prout me- " lius sibi et successoribus suis viderint expedire. Et ego *Philippus*, &c. B. 19. N°. 48. Apilton.

" Hiis testibus, Domino *Johanne de Oketona* tunc vicecom. *Ebor.* Dom. *Johanne de* " *Raygate*, *Hugone de Acaster*, *Johanne de Merstona*, *Nicholao de Gamero de Popilton*, " *Thoma* de eadem clerico, *Ricardo de Coltona*, *Henrico de Gave de Apilton*, *Wydone de* " *Apilton* et aliis.

Charta Roberti de Skegeness, *mil.*

Eadem cum charta B. 4. N. 7. ut prius, nisi quod *ubi corpus meum legavi sepeliendum* omittitur. B. 19. N°. 66. Apilton.

Charta Rogeri de Mulbrai.

" UNiversis (*b*) ecclesie filiis *Regerus de Mulbrai* salutem. Quoniam tam per me quam " per meos multa dampna multotiens abbatie *Eboracensi* illata fuerunt in recom- " pensationem et satisfactionem eorum firmam et perpetuam pacem futuris temporibus a " me et heredibus meis et omnibus qui ad me pertinent predicte ecclesie concessi et pre- " senti cartula confirmavi; videlicet ut ipsa ecclesia deinceps libera et quieta sit ab omni " exactione mei et meorum tam de operibus castrorum quam de tensariis qui violenter et " injuste a castrensibus erigi solent. Concessi etiam prefate ecclesie ut habeant apud *Mi-* " *tonam* villam suam molendinum et stagnum et piscariam suum sicut unquam melius pre- " teritis temporibus habuerunt. Quoniam vero pontem ejusdem ville destruxi ad propri- " um transitum suum et suorum, et omnium, salva pace et indempnitate castra mea tran- " sire volentium, et ad deferenda sive referenda quecunque eis necessaria sunt, navem eis " concessi donec eis pontem suum quem in tempore patris mei et meo habuerunt reparare " licuerit. Contentionem quoque illam que diu habita fuit inter *Beninburg* et duas villas " eorum *Overtonam*, scilicet, et *Shipetonam* de terra interjacente in bosco et plano per ju- " ramentum duodecim legitimorum virorum quos abbas predicte ecclesie supposuit, pre- " sente *Augustino* priore de *Novo-Burgo*, et hominibus *Willielmi de Arches* ad cujus feudum " predicta villa de *Beningburg* pertinet, *Wydone*, scilicet, *de Wroelesthorp*, *Alberico de Mer-* " *stona*, *Fulcone de Hamertona*, qui ex precepto meo ad diem statutum interfuerunt, prorsus " pacificando removi, ita, videlicet, ut terram illam ab omni calumpnia deinceps quietam " et liberam futuris temporibus possideant. Terram etiam de *Usafleth* in prato et in terra B. 19. N°. 71. Myton, &c.

(*b*) This very curious and particular grant is printed in the additional volume to the *Monast.* n. LXVI., but how incorrectly taken from the register may be judged by this copy from the original.

" culta

4

St. Mary's Abbey. "culta quam *Normannus* et *Willielmus* filii *Mazelme* ob patrocinium et tuicionem meam "mihi dederant, prefate ecclesie libere et quiete reddidi. Hanc conventionem et pacem in- "violabiliter tenendam propria manu affidavi, et *Robertus de Daivilla* et *Hugo Mala Bissa* "similiter affidaverunt.

Charta Johannis de Wytegift.

B. 19. N°. 75. Stainburn. "SCiant omnes tam presentes quam futuri quod ego *Johannes* filius *Ade de Wytegift* dedi "concessi reddidi et hoc presenti scripto meo confirmavi religiosis viris dominis meis "*Johanni de Gillings* abbati monasterii beate *Marie Ebor.* et ejusdem loci conventui quin- "que tofta et quatuor bovatas terre cum omnibus suis pertinentiis in villa de *Staynburn* que "sunt de feodo dict. abbatis et conventus dominorum meorum sine ullo retenemento michi "et heredibus meis. Habend. et tenend. eisdem abbati et conventui et successoribus suis "in perpetuum libere quiete bene et integre cum communi pastura et cum omnibus liber- "tatibus et aisiamentis ad predicta tofta et quatuor bovatas terre infra villam de *Stayneburn* "et extra qualitercumque pertinentibus ab omni servitio seculari exactione et demanda michi "et heredibus meis pertinente. Et ego vero *Johannes* filius *Ade* et heredes mei predict. "quinque tofta et quatuor bovatas terre infra villam de *Stayneburn* cum omnibus suis per- "tinent. ut predict. est predict. dom. meis abbati et conventui et successoribus suis contra "omnes gentes warrantizabimus, &c.

"In cujus rei test. &c.

"Hiis testibus, dominis *Gilberto de Colewen*, *Johanne de Haveryngton*, *Ricardo de Clet* "militibus, *Roberto de Bampton*, *Johanne de Eglesfield*, *Roberto de Harrays*, *Waltero* "*de Plumland*, *Thoma de . . ouchir* et aliis.

Charta Philippi de Faukenberg. *mil.*

B. 19. N°. 77. Literatim cum charta B. 19. N. 48. et testibus iisdem.

Charta Willielmi de Pontefracto.

B. 20. N°. 4. Bootham. "OMnibus sancte matris ecclesie filiis ad quos presens scriptum pervenerit *Willielmus de* "*Pontefracto* salutem in Domino. Sciatis me concessisse dedisse et hac presenti carta "mea confirmasse Deo et ecclesie beate *Marie Ebor.* et monachis ibidem Deo servientibus "pro salute anime mee et omnium antecessorum meorum unum toftum cum pertinentiis "in *Buthum*, illud scilicet quod jacet inter toftum quod fuit *Samson. Speciar* et toftum "quod fuit *Reginaldi de Clifton.* Tenend. et habend. in puram liberam et perpetuam "eleemosinam reddendo inde annuatim *Roberto de Musters* et heredibus suis tantum sexdecim "denarios, pro omni servitio et exactione, ad duos terminos, octo denarios ad *Pentecosten*, "et octo den. ad festum sancti *Martini* in hyeme. Et ego *Willielmus de Pontefracto* et he- "redes mei predict. toftum cum pertinentiis predict. ecclesie et monachis ibidem Deo ser- "vientibus in puram liberam et perpetuam eleemosinam warrantizabimus in perpetuum "contra omnes gentes.

"In cujus rei testimonium sigillum meum huic scripto apposui.

"Hiis testibus, *Roberto de Skegenesse* tunc temporis seneschallo abbatie, *Waltero de Kar-* "*leol*, *Johanne de Roto* magistro, *Roberto Lupe*, *Willielmo de Lilling*, *Rogero Coco*, *Ri-* "*cardo de Camera*, *Johanne le Barn*, *Johanne de Seleby* clerico, et aliis.

Charta Willielmi de Rednesse.

B. 20. N°. 37. Rednesse. "OMnibus Christi fidelibus hoc scriptum visuris vel audituris *Willielmus* filius *Radnulfi* "*de Radenesse* eternam in Dom. salut. Noverit universitas vestra me dedisse con- "cessisse et hac presenti carta mea confirmasse *Simoni* abbati monasterii S. *Marie Ebor.* et "ejusdem loci conventui et eorum successoribus universis duas selliones in territorio de *Rede-* "*ness* continentis in se tres acras terre, quarum una jacet in *Langfeld* inter terram *Roberti* "filii *Met. de Redenesse* ex una parte, et terram quam *Adam de Maynil* tenet de predicto "abbate ex altera, cum tota latitudine et longitudine sicut se extendit inter fossata; et "altera jacet in *Morefeld* inter terram *Johannis de Bayleul* ex una parte, et terram *Pagani* "*de Witegift* ex altera, cum tota latitudine et longitudine pertendente de . . . . . . ver- "sus austrum usque ad fossatam ex . . . . . . Tenend. et habend. &c. Et ego *Williel-* "*mus* et heredes mei dictas selliones cum pertinentiis, &c.

"In cujus rei testimonium, &c.

"Hiis testibus, *Ricardo de Multon* tunc seneschallo domini abbatis S. *Marie Ebor.* *Wil-* "*lielmo* filio *Willielmi de Redenes*, *Radulfo* fratre ejusdem, *Waltero* filio *Galfridi* de ea- "dem, *Ricardo le Cerf*, *Petro* procuratore, *James de Saudoy*, *Angero* et *Ricardo* fratri- "bus et aliis.

Charta

Charta Radulfi de Oveortomuttum.

" OMnibus Christi fidelibus hanc cartam visuris vel audituris *Radulfus* filius *Beatricis* " *de Oveortomutium* eternam in dom. sal. Noveritis me dedisse et presenti carta " confirmasse Deo et abbatie sancte *Marie Ebor.* et monachis ibidem Deo servientibus unam " bovatam terre cum pertinentiis in *Sutborp*, illam videlicet quam tenui de *Reginaldo* filio " *Willielmi le Painuet de Sutborp.* Habendam et tenendam libere et quiete de me et here- " dibus meis in perpetuum, ab omni terreno servitio, excepto quod ipsi monachi reddent " annuatim predicto *Reginaldo* et heredibus suis triginta denarios . . . . et heredibus meis " in perpetuum, medietatem ad fest. S. *Martini* in hyeme et aliam med. ad *Pentecosten.* " Ego vero &c. B. 23. N°. 56. Suthorp.

" In cujus &c.

" Hiis testibus, magistro *Simone de Catelkarroc* tunc parsona de *Hornbesse*, *Baldwino* " presbitero, *Galfrido de Cruce*, *Thurstano* clerico comitis *Albemarlie*, *Roberto de Fit-* " *ling*, *Roberto de Fentona*, *Jurdeno Scoto*, et aliis.

Charta Adam de Sesevaus.

" ADAM *de Sesevaus* concessit Deo et sancte *Marie Ebor.* et *Roberto* abbati et conventui " ejusdem dimid. carucatam terre in *Sescevaus.* Carta cum nominibus test. pene " obliterat. B. 20 N°. 86. Sessay.

Charta Johannis de Erghum.

" SCiant omnes tam presentes quam futuri quod ego *Johannes* filius *Nicholai de Ergbum* " pro salute anime mee et omnium parentum meorum concessi et dedi et hac " presenti carta confirmavi Deo et ecclesie sancte *Marie Ebor.* et monachis ibidem Deo " servientibus totam illam culturam meam que jacet in territorio de *Ergbum* inter cemi- " terium et aquam que vocatur *These*, cum fossato et illam culturam proximo jacente, sci- " licet quatuor acras et dimid. de terra arabili et unam rodam terre super *Humbelouke-* " *berg*, que jacet inter culturam quondam domini *Rogeri* filii *Ricardi* et terram *Radulfi de* " *Smytheton*, et duas acras prati in campo de *Ergbum* in *Hales* propinquiores prato *Simo-* " *nis* filio *Simonis de Chillington* versus austrum. Habendas et possidendas cum omnibus ai- " siamentis et pertinentiis ad eandem terram infra villam et extra pertinentibus in puram " liberam et perpetuam elemosinam. B. 21. N°. 61. Erghum.

" Hiis testibus, *Roberto Arundell*, *Willielmo de Lilling*, *Thoma* fil. *Lamberti*, *Thoma* cle- " rico de infirmario, *Gilberto* socio suo et multis aliis.

Charta Galfridi de Harpham.

" OMnibus has literas visuris vel audituris *Galfridus* filius *Ricardi de Harpham* salutem. " Sciatis me *vendidisse Roberto* abbati S. *Marie Ebor.* et monachis ejusdem loci pro " *certa pecunia sua* quam michi dederunt unam bovatam terre cum pertinentiis in territo- " rio de *Harpham*, scilicet illam bovatam terre quam tenui de *Johanne de Harpham* que " jacet inter terras meas et terras *Willelmi* filii *Gilberti*, et tres rodas terre ad eandem bo- " vatam terre pertinentes in eodem territorio loco tofti, scilicet unam rodam que jacet ad " caput de *Bydayl* versus boream, et unam rodam que jacet ad *Accremilne* versus orientem, " et unam rodam que jacet ad *Outtlanges* inter terram meam et terram dicti *Willielmi* fil. " *Gilberti.* Tenend. et habend. &c. Reddendo inde annuatim dicto G. et heredibus suis " tantum sexdecem denarios pro omni servitio et exactione, &c. B. 21. N°. 35. Harpham.

" Hiis testibus, *Roberto de Skegeness* tunc temporis senescallo S. *Marie Ebor. Willielmo de* " *Lilling*, *Thoma* janitore, *Nicholao de Burton*, *Rogero Coco*, *Roberto de Karleton*, *Ri-* " *cardo de Camera*, *Johanne de Seleby* clerico et aliis.

Charta Matildis Nuvel.

" MAtildis quondam uxor *Johannis Nuvel* concessit domino abbati et conventui S. *Marie* " *Ebor.* duas bovatas terre cum pertinentiis et tres acras terre et . . . . rodas " in *Beningburg*, et totam partem capitalis messuagii et totam partem redditus liberorum " hominum qui tenebant de dict. *Johanne Nuvel* in eadem villa &c. Charta ista pene obli- " terata. B. 21. N°. 58. Beningburg.

" Hiis testibus, domino *Rob. de Skegeness* tunc seneschallo abbatie, *Willielmo de Wyrton*, " *Willielmo de Lilling*, *Galfrido de Cruce*, *Waltero de Asc*, *Roberto de Fenton*, *Nicholao* " *de Camera*, *Nicholao* et *Rogero Chassator.* cum aliis.

Charta Willielmi de Lofthuses.

B. 22. N°. 28. Lofthouse. " OMnibus Christi fidelibus ad quos presens scriptum pervenerit, *Willielmus* filius *Radulfi* " *de Lofthuses* salutem in Domino. Noverit universitas vestra me pro salute ani- " me mee et omnium antecessorum meorum dedisse concessisse et hac presenti carta mea " confirmasse Deo et ecclesie St. *Marie Ebor.* et monachis ibidem Deo servientibus in libe- " ram puram et perpetuam eleemosinam tres acras terre et unam rodam cum pertinentiis " et unum tostum &c.

" Hiis testibus, domino *Roberto de Skegeness* tunc senescallo abbatie, *Willielmo de Lil-* " *ling*, *Johanne Puero*, *Roberto Supe*, *Johanne de Overton*, *Henrico de Foubebusses*, *Ro-* " *gero de Henhale*, *Henrico de Gauketborp*, *Jordano de Lofthuses*, et multis aliis.

Charta Gaufridi de Colebrun.

B. 22. N°. 58. Hippswell. " UNiversis S. matris ecclesie filiis *Gaufridus* filius *Habraeham de Colebrun* salutem. " Sciatis me dedisse concessisse et hac presenti carta mea confirmasse Deo et abba- " tie St. *Marie Ebor.* et monachis ibidem Deo servientibus et prioratui S. *Martini* juxta " *Richmundiam* pro salute anime mee et antecessorum meorum in puram et perpetuam elee- " mosinam unam culturam terre que vocatur *Norflatt* in territorio de *Hippeswell*, que se " extendit super terram monachorum de S. *Martino* versus occidentem, scilicet illam cultu- " ram que fuit quondam *Astini* de *Hippeswell*. Et insuper dedi predictis monachis unam " acram terre in cultura illa que vocatur *Schefacer* versus aquilonem, que se extendit super " terram que fuit quondam *Roberti Fornecorn*, quam acram dedi eis in excambium pro " quadam acra quam *Alanus* frater ejus aliquando de illis tenuit in territorio de *Colebrun*. " Ego vero *Gaufridus*, &c.

" Hiis testibus, *Roaldo* constabulario *Richmundie*, *Philippo* filio *Johannis de Colebrun*, *Gau-* " *frido de Huddeswell*, *Petro* capellano de *Richmundia*, *Radulfo* capellano de *Hudde-* " *swell*, *Roberto* capellano de sancto *Nicholao*, *Willielmo* tinctore de *Richmundia*, *Gau-* " *frido* diacono de sancto *Martino* et multis aliis.

Charta T. Ebor. *archiep.*

B. 23. N°. 6. *Ecclesia de* Snaith. " T. Dei gratia *Eboracensis* archiepiscopus *Willielmo* decano et capitulo S. *Petri Ebo-* " *raci* et ceteris fidelibus ecclesie salutem et benedictionem. Scire volo fraterni- " tatem vestram me concessisse, et, presentis cartule testimonio, confirmasse conventionem " inter monachos sancte *Marie Eboraci* abbatie, et monachos sancti *Germani* de *Salebi*, de " ecclesia quam *Eboracenses* monachi fecerunt infra parochiam de *Snaith*, et cemeterio ibi- " dem facto, cum ceteris concessis sicut in carta utriusque abbatie continetur. Salva con- " suetudine mea, scilicet, duobus solidis dandis per annum ab *Eboracensibus* pro supra- " dicta ecclesia et cemeterio. Vos quoque ut hujus rei testes in perpetuum sitis exoro. " Vale.

Charta Roberti Gernum.

B. 23. N°. 12. Brambam. " OMnibus hanc cartam visuris vel audituris *Hugo* filius *Roberti Gernum* de *Brambam* sa- " lutem in Domino. Sciatis me dedisse concessisse et hac presenti carta mea con- " firmasse Deo et ecclesie S. *Marie Eboraci* et monachis ibidem Deo servientibus tres acras " terre cum pertinentiis in *Brambam*, scilicet, duas acras et unam rodam cum pertinentiis " in cultura que vocatur *Rodes*, et tres rodas cum pertinentiis que jacent inter terras dic- " torum monachorum juxta *Savevillemille* et se extendunt versus orientem. Habend. et " tenend. &c. Et ego *Hugo* et heredes mei &c.

" In cujus rei test. &c.

" Hiis testibus, domino *Roberto de Skegeness*, *Thoma de Eboraco*, *Hugone* filio *Henrici*, " *Roberto de Langthwayt*, *Willielmo* filio *Alexandri*, *Ricardo de Camera*, *Willielmo Cervo*, " *Nicholao de Alverton*, *Johanne Malet* clerico et aliis.

Charta Ricardi Soudan.

B. 23. N°. 29. Apelton Mag. " OMnibus Christi fidelibus ad quos presens scriptum pervenerit *Richardus* filius *Ri-* " *cardi Soudan* salut. Sciatis me dedisse et hac presenti carta mea confirmasse Deo " et ecclesie S. *Marie Ebor.* et prioratui S. *Martini* juxta *Richemund* et monachis ibidem " Deo servientibus in liberam puram et perpetuam eleemosinam duo tofta et crofta et

(*d*) This *T.* was *Thurstan* archbishop. *William de S. Barbara* was dean of *York anno* 1138, a year or two before *Thurstan* resigned and died. This is also a very curious antient charter and very perfect.

" tres

" tres acras terre et dimidiam perticatam cum pertinentiis in territorio de *Magna Apel-* St. MARY'S
" *tona.* Scilicet unum toftum et croftum de dimidia acra quod *Henricus Halleman* aliquan- ABBEY.
" do tenuit, et quod jacet juxta toftum *Rogeri* filii *Ricardi* versus orientem, et unum tof-
" tum et croftum quod jacet inter toftum meum et toftum *Roberti* filii *Galfridi de Hake-*
" *ford*, et duas rodas terre et dimid. super *Fornlandes* que jacent juxta terram *Thome* filii
" *Hermeri* versus occidentem, et unam rodam terre et dimid. super *Gnatbou* juxta terram
" abbatis de *Gervaus*, et duas acras terre et dimid. perticatam *Hallebodine* versus orientem.
" Habend. et tenend. &c.

" Hiis testibus, *Thoma de Laceles*, *Alano de Hartfortd*, *Petro de Crachale*, *Alano* fratre
" ejus, *Michaele de Hakefortd*, *Roberto* filio ejus, *Willielmo Lungbespee*, *Thoma* filio
" *Hermeri*, *Alano* filio *Willielmi* et aliis.

Charta Astini de Pickering.

" OMnibus hanc cartam visuris vel audituris *Astinus de Pykeryng* salut. in Domino. B. 23. N°. 38.
" Noveritis me pro salute anime mee *Emme* uxoris mee et omnium parentum Sezevaux.
" meorum concessisse dedisse et hac presenti carta mea confirmasse Deo et ecclesie sancte
" *Marie Ebor.* et monachis ibidem Deo servientibus dimidiam carucatam terre in *Sezewaus*
" cum pertinentiis quam habui de *Henrico* filio *Radulfi de Sezewaus*, et duas bovatas terre
" in *Scameston* cum pertinentiis quas habui de *Laurentio* de *Scameston*, et annualem redditum
" undecim solidorum de sex bovatis terre in *Kyrkeby-raveneswat* quas *Alanus* clericus filius
" *Alani* et *Willielmus* filius *Rogeri* tenent ibidem de feodo S. *Marie Ebor.* Tenendum et
" habendum dictis ecclesie et monachis in perpetuum &c. Ita scilicet quod terra de *Sezewaus*
" cedat in usus monachorum ad species emendas in perpetuum. Et redditus terre de
" *Scameston* sit ad — meum faciendum in perpetuum. Et redditus de *Kyrkebyraveneswat* cel-
" lario assignetur. Et ego *Astinus*, &c. Et ut hec mea concessio et donatio perpetue fir-
" mitatis robur obtineat presenti scripto sigillum meum apposui.

" Hiis testibus, *Roberto de Skegeness* tunc seneschallo abbatis, magist. *Johanne de Hamerton*,
" *Roberto de Saam*, *Rogero Pepin*, *Waltero de Gaugy*, *Willielmo de Lilling*, *Ricardo de*
" *Camera*, *Nicholao Portario*, *Rogero Coco*, *Johanne Puero*, et multis aliis.

Charta Roberti de Scales.

" OMnibus hoc scriptum visuris vel audituris *Robertus de Scales* et *Alicia* uxor ejus salu- B. 23. N°. 44.
" tem in Domino. Ad universitatis vestre notitiam volumus pervenire nos divini Haselingfeld.
" amoris intuitu et pro animabus nostris et antecessorum nostrorum dedisse concessisse et
" hac presenti carta nostra confirmasse *Willielmo* abbati et conventui S. *Marie Eboracen.* in
" liberam puram et perpetuam elemosinam sine aliquo retenemento et exactione seculari
" tres acras terre cum pertinentibus in *Haselingfeld*, scilicet duas acras que jacent juxta ter-
" ram *Rogeri de Meleford* et abuttant super *Shutmeoduc*, et unam acram in *Develand* juxta
" terram priorisse de *Stratford*. Ita quod si aliquo tempore per nos vel heredes nostros
" dicte acre fuerint revocate vel easdem revocare nisi fuerimus, licebit dictis abbati et
" conventui subtrahere nobis et heredibus nostris celebrationem divinorum in oratorio ma-
" nerii nostri de *Haselingfeld* nobis ab eisdem concessam sine aliquo impedimento a nobis vel
" heredibus nostris prestando. Et hoc pro nobis et heredibus nostris tactis sacrosanctis
" evangeliis juravimus, renuntiando pro nobis et heredibus nostris privilegio fori civilis et
" specialiter brevi regie prohibitionis de laico tenemento.

" In cujus rei testimonium presenti scripto sigillum nostrum apposui.

" Hiis testibus, magistris *Johanne de Hamerton*, *Rogero Pepin*, *Gill. de Lincoln*. *Johanne*
" *de Popeltun*, *Johanne Malet*, *Galfrido de Cruce*, *Roberto de Futeling*, *Waltero de Ask*,
" *Roberto Sope* clerico, *Nicholao* janitore, *Willielmo de Lilling*, *Johanne* vicario de *Hase-*
" *lingfeld*, *Rogero de Melford*, *Thoma* filio *Alberici*, *Willielmo Bole* et aliis.

Charta Johannis le Grant.

" OMnibus has litteras visuris vel audituris *Johannes le Grant* salutem. Noverit uni- B. 24. N°. 18.
" versitas vestra me dedisse concessisse et quietum clamasse in perpetuum de me Ousleet.
" et heredibus meis Deo et ecclesie beate *Marie Ebor.* et monachis ibidem Deo servienti-
" bus totam communam pasture quam habui in quadraginta acris terre in *Usflet*, quas
" *Johannes de Usflet* dedit Deo et ecclesie beate *Marie Ebor.* et monachis ibidem Deo
" servientibus. Habendam et tenendam in puram et perpetuam elemosinam in perpetuum
" quietam ab omni seculari servitio et exactione.

" Et in hujus rei testimon. huic presenti scripto sigillum meum apposui.

" Hiis testibus, *Ricardo de Wilestorp*, magistris *Johanne de Hamerton*, *Eustachio de Kime*,
" *Rogero de Lecestre*, *Willielmo Pointel*, *Roberto de Skegenesse* tunc senescallo abbatie
" *Ebor.* *Roberto de Apelton*, *Waltero* parsona de *Smitton*, *Petro de Knapeton*, *Willielmo*
" de Mara, *Galfrido de Sancto Andoeno* et multis aliis.

Charta

St. Mary's Abbey.

Charta Walteri Aurifabris.

B. 24. N°. 23. York.

" OMnibus ſancte matris eccleſie filiis *Walterus Aurifaber* de *Eboraco* ſalutem. Noverit " univerſitas veſtra me conſenſu uxoris mee caritatis intuitu dediſſe et hac preſenti " carta mea confirmaſſe Deo et eccleſie beate *Marie Ebor.* et monachis ibidem Deo ſervien- " tibus, ad ſuſtentationem fratrum infirmorum ejuſdem domus, terram quandam in *Eboraco* " juxta cemeterium ſancte *Trinitatis* in *Gutburumgate*, illam ſcilicet terram quam emi de " *Everardo de Marſton* et redditum ſex denariorum in eadem villa de terra in **Iſpingayt** quam " *Eudo* carnifex tenet. Habend. et tenend. eiſdem monachis et ſucceſſoribus ſuis in liberam " puram et perpetuam eleemoſinam. Et, ut hec mea donatio perpetue firmitatis robur ob- " tineat, eam ſigilli mei munimine roboravi.

" Hiis teſtibus, *Roberto de Mubray*, *Philippo* filio *Johannis*, *Rogero de Mubray* clerico, " *Thoma de Wilton*, *Roberto Ebor.* *Radulfo Nuvell*, magiſtro *Job de Hamerton*, *Sanſone* " clerico et multis aliis.

Indentura inter Simon. *abb. et* Johannem Bowes.

Hec charta innotata.

" OMnibus ſancte matris eccleſie filiis preſens ſcriptum inſpecturis *Fr. Simon* Dei gratia " abbas monaſterii beate *Marie Ebor.* et ejuſdem loci conventus ſal. in Domino. " Noveritis nos remiſiſſe pro nobis et ſucceſſoribus noſtris *Johanni de Bowes* preſbytero et " aſſignatis ſuis in perpetuum tres ſolidos annuos quos *Pape* ſolvebamus de terra ſua jacente " ex oppoſito orientalis gabuli eccle. S. *Trinitatis* in *Gutberumgate* ad infirmitorium noſtrum " per annum pro tribus ſolidis annuis quos emit per conſilium noſt. in feodo noſtro in vil- " la de *Munketon* de terra et tenemento *Philippi* filii *Roberti* filii *Willielmi* de *Munketon* et " quos ad predict. infirmarium noſtrum in perpetuum aſſignavit loco predict. trium ſolid. " annuorum. Ita quod nec nos nec ſucceſſores noſtri aliquod jus vel clamium in prefata " terra de *Gutberumgate* de cetero exigere poterimus aut aliquatenus vendicare.

" In cujus rei teſt. uni parti preſentis ſcripti cyrographaci ſigillum capituli noſtri ap- " poſuimus, altera parte penes nos reſidente ſigillo prefati *Johannis* ſignata.

" Dat. *Ebor.* menſe Februarii anno Dom. M CC LX.

Charta Richardi Soudan.

B. 24. N°. 53. AppeltonMag.

" UNiverſis ſancte matris eccleſ. filiis, *Ricardus* filius *Henrici Soudan* de *Apeltona* ſal. " Sciatis me cum conſilio et aſſenſu heredum meorum dediſſe et conceſſiſſe et hac " preſenti carta mea confirmaſſe Deo et abbatie ſancte *Marie Ebor.* et monachis ibidem " Deo ſervientibus et prioratui S. *Martini* juxta *Richmundiam* pro ſalute anime mee et an- " teceſſ. meorum in puram et perpetuam eleemoſinam totam terram meam quam habui ſu- " per *Laytric* in territorio majoris *Appeltone*, que jacet inter terram *Willielmi Lungeſpei* de " *Appeltona* et terram que fuit *Hugonis de Scottona*, cum communi paſtura ejuſdem ville et " cum omnibus aliis aiſiamentis ad eandem terram pertinentibus infra villam et extra. Ego " vero *Ricardus* &c.

" Hiis teſtibus, *Philippo* filio *Johannis de Colebrun*, *Gaufrido* filio *Habranke de Colebrun*, " *Nicholao de Gertheſtona*, *Ricardo de Laibrun*, *Thoma de Herneby*, *Helia de Dunnay*, " *Willielmo Lungeſpei*, *Toma* filio *Roberti*, *Richardo de Holteby*, *Nicolao de Knetona*, " *Alano* filio *Willielmi de Apeltona*, et multis aliis.

Charta Roberti de Parlyngton.

B. 24. N°. 80. Gerford.

" OMnibus ſancte matris eccl. filiis ad quos preſens ſcriptum pervenerit, *Robertus* filius " *Ade de Parlyngton* manens in *Weſt-Gerford* ſal. in Dom. ſempiternam. Noveritis " me dediſſe conceſſiſſe et hac preſenti carta mea confirmaſſe *Simoni* abbati et conventui " monaſt. beate *Marie Ebor.* quatuor acras terre jacentes in campo de *Gerford* per diviſas " ſubſcriptas, ſcilicet, unam acram que abuttat ſuper regiam viam de **Wottelyngeſtrete**, " et jacet inter terram *Roberti* filii *Cuſtantie* ex parte boreali et terram *Ade* filii *Johannis* " ex parte meridionali. Et unam acram jacentem ſuper *le toftes* verſus domum *Matildis* " *de Preſton*. Et tres rodas terre jacentes ad le *Colepittes* inter terram *Roberti* filii *Cuſtancie* " ex parte occidentali et terram *Ade* filii *Ade de Morehuſes* ex parte orientali. Et unam " rodam jacentem ſub prato *Aule* inter terram predictorum *Roberti* et *Ade*. Et tres rodas " jacentes in cultura que abuttat ſuper le *Fryth* inter terram *Roberti* et *Ade* predict. Et " unam rodam jacentem ſuper le *Horethorne* inter terram *Martini* ex parte occidentali et " terram *Ade* filii *Ade de Morehuſes* ſepedict. Tenend. et habend. &c.

" Hiis teſt. *Hugone de Swyllyngton* milite, *Simone de Rupe* clerico, *Roberto* filio *Cuſtancie*, " *Radulfo de Aula de Gerford*, *Adam de Morehuſes* clerico, *Ricardo* fil. *Jordani* et aliis.

Charta

Charta Walteri de Smythton.

" OMnibus hanc cartam visuris vel audituris *Walterus* parsona *de Smythton* sal. in Dom. B. 25. N°. 6. Smithton.
" Noveritis me pro salute anime mee et omnium parentum meorum concessisse
" dedisse et hac presenti carta mea confirmasse Deo et eccl. S. *Marie Ebor.* et monachis
" ibidem Deo servientibus duas bovatas terre cum pertinentiis in territorio de *Smythton*,
" unam, videlicet, quam emi de *Galfrido* filio *Ranulfi* de *Smythton*, et aliam quam emi
" de *Turstino de Apelton.* Habend. et tenend. dict. ecclesie et monachis in liberam puram
" et perpetuam eleemosinam &c. Et ut hec mea donatio perpetue firmitatis robur obtine-
" at eam sigilli me impressione roboravi.

" Hiis test. *Roberto de Skegenesse* tunc seneschallo abbatis, magist. *Johanne de Hamerton*,
" *Roberto de Saham*, *Willielmo de Lelinge*, *Willielmo* clerico de *Smytheton*, *Henrico* filio
" *Simonis de Horneby*, *Henrico* clerico de *Horneby*, *Giked del Hil*, *Gilberto* filio *Symonis*,
" *Waltero* filio *Galfridi*, *Luca de Horneby* et aliis.

Charta Thome de Burg.

" UNiversis sancte matris ecc. filiis *Thomas* filius *Thome de Burg*. salutem. Sciatis me B. 25. N°. 28. AppeltonMag.
" pro salute anime mee et omnium antecessorum meorum concessisse et hac pre-
" senti carta mea confirmasse in puram et perpetuam eleemosinam Deo et abbatie S. *Marie*
" *Ebor.* et monachis ibidem Deo servientibus et prioratui S. *Martini* juxta *Richmundiam*
" duas bovatas terre in *Magna Apeltona*, cum omnibus pertinentiis suis infra villam et ex-
" tra sine ullo retenemento, illas, scilicet, duas bovatas terre quas *Rogerus* filius *Acaris de*
" *Tunstal* dedit prenotatis monachis in puram et perpetuam eleemosinam in predicta villa
" de *Apeltona*, sicuti carta ipsius *Rogeri* testatur. Et ego *Thomas* &c.
" Testibus hiis, *Roaldo* constabulario, *Philippo* filio *Johannis de Colebrun*, *Gaufrido* filio
" *Habraham de Colebrun*, *Nicolao de Gerthstona*, *Nicolao de Stapeltona*, *Gaufrido* filio
" *Gaufridi de Hudeswelle*, *Willielmo* clerico de *Richmundia*, *Alano de Magnebi*, *Thoma*
" *de Ruebi*, *Ricardo Soudan* de *Appelton*, *Hugone de Magnebi*, *Ricardo de Danebi*, *Hen-*
" *rico de Holtbi* et multis aliis.

Charta Gilberti de Hothwayt.

" SCiant omnes tam presentes quam futuri quod ego *Gilbertus* filius *Roberti de Hothwayt* B. 25. N°. 32. Hothwayt.
" et *Christiana* sponsa mea cum consilio amicorum nostrorum dedimus, concessimus,
" quietum clamavimus et hec presenti carta nostra confirmavimus Deo et beate *Marie*
" *Ebor.* et S. *Bege* in *Coupland* et monachis ibidem Deo servientibus totam terram meam in
" campo de *Hothwayt* cum omnibus pertinentiis suis sine aliquo retenemento, per has di-
" visas scilicet per domum quod fuit *Ade* fil. *Halkyl*, et cum thofto et crofto in quo con-
" tinetur una acra terre et dimid. que jacet ex parte australi spine, et quatuor acre
" terre et dimid. jacentes juxta terram *Henrici de Hothwayt* fratris mei. Tenend. et ha-
" bend. &c.

" Hiis testibus, domino *Richardo de Clet*, domino *Johanne de Langplogh*, domino *Elya*
" tunc ballivo de *Egremond*, *Alexandro de Puntuby*, *Roberto de Brainthwayte*, *Nicholao*
" *de Moriceby*, *Benedicto de Rotingthon* et aliis.

Charta Roberti de Canteburg.

" SCiant presentes et futuri quod ego *Robertus de Canteburg* et *Alicia* uxor mea dedimus B. 25. N°. 46. Audestan.
" concessimus et hac presenti carta nostra confirmamus *Simoni* abbati beate *Marie*
" *Ebor.* et ejusdem loci coventui, ad species eorundem augmentandas, dimidiam bovatam
" terre cum tota parte trium toftorum in villa et territorio de *Auddestan* nos contingente
" jure hereditario per mortem *Henrici de Etton* fratris predicte *Alicie* uxoris mee. Habend.
" et tenend. dicto *Simoni* abbati &c.

" Hiis testibus, domino *Willielmo de Sancto Quintino*, *Radulfo de Gartona*, *Thoma de*
" *Orderne*, *Thoma de* . . . . *Johanne Werlard*, *Simone de Freboys* in *Auddestan*
" et aliis.

Charta Henrici de Sezevaus.

" OMnibus hanc cartam visuris vel audituris *Henricus* filius *Radulfi de Sezevaus* sal. B. 25. N°. 51. Sezevaus.
" Noveritis me pro salute anime mee et omnium parentum meorum dedisse con-
" cessisse et presenti carta mea confirmasse Deo et ecclesie beate *Marie Ebor.* et monachis
" ibidem Deo servientibus dimidiam carucatam terre cum toftis et croftis et omnibus aliis

ST. MARY'S ABBEY.

“ pertinentiis in *Sezevaus (d)*, scilicet, illam quam de eis tenui et quam *Amabilis* avia mea
“ aliquando tenuit. Habend. et tenend. &c.

“ Hiis testibus, *Roberto de Skegeness* tunc seneschallo abbatie beate *Marie Ebor.* magistris
“ *Eustachio de Kime*, *Ricardo de Kirkeby*, *Willielmo* filio *Hugonis de Grimeston*, *Johanne*
“ *de Kirkeby*, *Willielmo de Restorp* clerico, *Galfrido de Cruce*, *Ricardo de Camera*, *Johannne*
“ filio *Turgis*, *Stephano Haget* et multis aliis.

Indentura inter Abbatem et Dom. Phil. de Fauconberg.

B. 25. N°. 60. Appleton.

“ ANno Dom. millesimo ducentesimo quinquagesimo septimo in crastino S. *Barnabe* ita
“ convenit inter dominum *Thomam* abbatem S. *Marie Ebor.* et ejusdem loci conven-
“ tum ex una parte, et dominum *Philippum de Faucunberg* ex altera, videlicet quod dicti
“ abbas et conventus concesserunt et quietum clamaverunt dicto *Philippo* et heredibus suis
“ vel suis assignatis totum jus et clamium quod habuerunt vel habere potuerunt in stagno
“ suo de *Appelton*, sicut se extendit in longitudine et latitudine de veteri molendino usque
“ ad tostum *Durandi* cum omnibus fossatis predictum stagnum concurrentibus, et fossa-
“ tam ab angulo gardini usque ad viam que est ad *Wandhang*, extra parcum predicti *Phi-*
“ *lippi* in longitudine, ita scilicet quod bene licebit dicto *Philippo* et heredibus suis vel suis
“ assignatis totum predictum stagnum et dicta fossata exaltare, levare, appruare quocun-
“ que modo voluerit sine aliqua contradictione dictorum abbatis et conventus. Pro hac
“ autem concessione et quietum clamatione dedit dictus *Philippus* dictis abbati et conventui
“ et eorum successoribus in puram et perpetuam eleemosinam septem acras terre in *Appel-*
“ *tona* in *Nortgasberch*, illas scilicet septem acras terre que jacent inter terram *Ada le Cerf*
“ et terram *Walteri de Faucunberg* filii dicti *Philippi*. Tenendas et habendas dictis abbati
“ et conventui et eorum successoribus cum libero introitu et cum omnibus aliis aisiamen-
“ tis dictis septem acris terre pertinentibus. Concessit idem *Philippus* pro se et heredibus
“ suis dictis abbati et conventui et eorum successoribus, et eorum hominibus in *Apeltona*
“ una cum hominibus dicti *Philippi* unum chiminum ultra dictum stagnum suum usque ad
“ terram arabilem de latitudine quadraginta pedum sine aliqua contradictione dicti *Philippi*
“ et heredum suorum vel ejus assignatorum, salvo cursu aque ad molendinum. Et si ita
“ contingat quod animalia dictorum abbatis et conventus vel hominum suorum intrent
“ predictum stagnum pro defectu sepis vel fossati benigne et sine dampno vel peccamento
“ predicti *Philippi* et heredum suorum vel ejus assignatorum amoveantur. Predictus vero
“ *Philippus* et heredes sui dictas septem acras terre cum pertinentiis dictis abbati et con-
“ ventui et eorum successoribus contra omnes gentes in perpetuum warrantizabunt, defen-
“ dent et adquietabunt.

“ In cujus rei testimonium presenti scripto in modum chirographi confecto partes hinc inde
“ sigilla sua apposuerunt.

“ Hiis testibus, domino *Johanne de Oketon* tunc seneschallo sancte *Marie Ebor.* *Johanne*
“ *de Marston*, *Hugone de Acaster*, *Gilberto Tait de Eskeric*, *Wyot de Apeltona*, *Rogero* fo-
“ restario de *Apeltona*, *Benedicto de Hewirth* et aliis.

Charta indenturae inter Abbatem et Will. Roundel.

“ IN nomine Patris et Filii et Spiritus Sancti, Amen. Carta dudum inter religiosos viros abbatem et conventum S. *Marie Ebor.* ex parte una, et *Willielmum Roundel* vica-
“ rium ecclesie de *Gaynesford* ex altera, super taxationem et moderationem . . . . . ejus-
“ dem ecclesie anno bone memorie *W.* quondam *Dunelm.* episcopi immoderate et contra
“ justitiam ac sedis . . . . privilegium . . . . ut iidem religiosi dicebant coram nobis ma-
“ gistro *R. de Horteburne R.* Dei gratia *Dunelm.* epis. officio . . . . . . commissario . . . .
“ negotio memorato materie questionis ex parte dictorum religiosorum fuit propositum
“ coram . . . . autoritate apostolica usque ad summam quadraginta marcarum an-
“ nuarum tum modo fuisse taxatam et . . . . bone memorie *W.* quondam *Dunelm.* episcopi
“ usque ad summam quatuor viginti marcarum annuarum et amplius videbit taxatam.
“ Tandem mediantibus nobis et magistro *Rogero de Laycestre* clerico et aliis amicis commu-
“ nibus in forma amicabili inferius contenta acquiescunt, videlicet quod idem vicarius pro
“ se et successoribus suis nomine dicte vicarie concessit et in manibus dicti abbatis de no-
“ stris applicatione et consensu pure et absolute resignavit omnes decimas garbarum de *Su-*
“ *merbuses* et unum toftum et croftum cum tota terra et prato que habuit et tenuit idem
“ vicarius in villa de *Querington* et omnes decimas feni de tribus villis in dicta parochia
“ percipiendas, videlicet de *Querington*, *Ledwyc* et *Westwyt*, ac mansum sibi assignatum
“ in villa de *Gastro Bernardi*. Ita quod decime predicte, terra et pratum, mansus ac om-

(*d*) I take this to be the town now corruptly called *Thixendale*, on the *Wolds*, for *Sixtendale*; in *Latin Sex-decem vallibus*, in old *French Sezevaus*.

“ nia

" nia alia supradicta remaneant et accrescant excant religiosis supradictis ratione dicte eccle- *St.* MARY's ABBEY.
" sie sue de *Gaynesford* quam in usus proprios obtinent in perpetuum. Dicti vero religiosi
" nomine monasterii sui voluerunt et concesserunt eidem vicario et successoribus suis, qui
" pro tempore fuerint, omnes et singulas alias minutas decimas, oblationes et obventiones,
" cum domibus suis apud *Gaynesford* et terra de *Staynton*, in quarum possessione vel qui idem
" vicarius tempore hujus compositionis existebat. Ita tamen quod dictus vicarius et uni-
" versi successores sui omnia onera episcopalia et archidiaconalia tam matris ecclesie de
" *Gaynesford* quam omnium capellarum suarum sustinebunt, una cum capellanis et clericis,
" uneis et oneribus librorum, vestimentorum, reparationis cancellorum, et aliorum omni-
" um ornamentorum in dicta ecclesia et suis capellis . . . Nos autem dictam compositio-
" nem puram et gratam . . . ipsam auctoritate nobis in hac parte commissa confirmamus
" et presentis scripti patrocinio . . . . Omnem alteram ordinationem et taxationem
" auctoritate dicti domini *W.* supradicto vicario factam cassamus, cruamus et viribus ca-
" rere determinamus.

" In cujus rei testimonium presentibus litteris chyrographicis sigillum nostrum est ap-
" pensum.

" Act. apud *Dunelm.* XII. kal. *Julii* anno Dom. MCCX. in presentia subscriptorum ma-
" gistrorum *Roberti de Sancta Agatha* tunc archidiaconi *Dunelm. Rogeri de Seyton,*
" *Ranulfi de Huckelby* procuratoris de officio prefati archidiac. *Ricardi de Malteby. W.*
" tunc scholarum magistri, *Ricardi* tunc vicarii de *Midetham, Gilberto de Rokeby; Jo-*
" *hannis de Thorp*, et aliorum.

Ebor. *abbatia beate* Mariae *ibidem pro bosco ipsorum de* Overton *includend. et parcum inde fact. per metas et bundas. Pat.* 18 Ric. II. *p.* 1. *m.* 24. *Confirm. anno* 22 Hen. VI. *p.* 2. *m.* 3. *Turre* Lond.

" REX omnibus ad quos salutem. Inspeximus cartam dom. *Johannis* quondam re-
" gis *Anglie* progenitoris nost. factam in hec verba. *Johannes* Dei gratia rex *An-*
" *glie*, dom. *Hybernie*, dux *Normannie* et *Aquitan.* comes *Andeg.* archiep. epis. abbat. comit.
" baron. justi. vicecom. prepolit. et omnibus ballivis et fidelibus suis per *Ang.* constitutis
" salutem. Sciatis nos pro salute anime nost. et predecess. nost. dedisse licentiam abbati
" et conventui S. *Marie Ebor*, includendi boscum suum de Overton et faciendi in liberum
" parcum sicut antique divise jacent inter predict. boscum et villam de Beninburg et sicut
" antique divise jacent inter villam de Wapetun et villam de Overton et sicut divise an-
" tique jacent inter Schipton et Overton usque ad ripam de Use. Quare volumus et fir-
" miter precipimus quod idem abbas et conventus et eorum successores habeant et teneant
" in perpetuum predict. parcum suum infra clausum illud secundum divisas prenotatas bene
" et libere et quiete cum bosco tam viridi quam sicco et cum bestiis et cum omnibus aliis
" pertinentiis suis ad faciend. inde commodum suum et voluntatem.

" Test. hiis, dom. *H. Cant.* archiepiscopo, *Galfrid.* filio *Petri*, *Willielmo Marest*, *Ro-*
" *berto* filio *Rogeri*, *Hugone de Nevill*, *Petro de Stok*, *Willielmo de Cantelou*, *Roberto de*
" *Repelee.*

" Dat. per manum dom. *D. Cicestren.* electi apud *Winton* xiii *April.* anno regni quinto.
" Nos autem cartam predict. et omnia et singula in eadem carta contenta rata habemus,
" et grata ea pro nob. et hered. nost. quantum in nob. est acceptamus approbamus
" et dilect. nob. in Christo nunc abbati et conventui loci predict. et eorum succes-
" soribus tenore presentium concedimus et confirmamus sicut carta predict. rationab.
" testatur.

" In cujus, &c.

" Teste rege apud *Gloucestre* xxii die *Aug.*

" *per dimid. marce solut. in Hanappio.*

(e) *Breve tempore vac. abbatis monasterii beate* Mariae Ebor.

" RICARDUS Dei gratia rex *Angliae* et *Franciae* et dominus *Hiberniae* majori civita-
" tis suae *Ebor.* et eschaetori nostro in eadem civitate salutem. Cum per certam ma-
" nucaptionem pro octoginta libris quas dilecti nobis in Christo prior et conventus
" abbiae beatae *Marie Ebor.* nobis solvend. concesserimus eis custodiam abbiae praedictae
" per mortem bonae memoriae *Thomae Stayngreve* ultimi abbatis loci illius vacantis et in
" manu nostra existentis habend. cum omnibus ad abbiam praedictam spectantibus quae
" ad nos pertinere possent, sicut ea in manu nostra retinerentur a tempore mortis praedicti
" *Thomae* usque ad finem duorum mensium proxime sequentium plenarie completorum, ita
" quod nullus eschaetor aut alius ballivus seu minister noster vel haeredum nostrorum se
" de custodia praedicta vel de aliquibus ad abbiam predictam spectantibus durantibus duo-

(e) *Ex regist. antique civitatis in cam. supra pont. Use f.* 51.

" bus

St. Mary's Abbey.

" bus mensibus praedictis intromittat, nec ipsos priorem et conventum super hoc aliqualiter " impediat; quominus ipsi per se et ministros suos per predictos duos menses habeant ple- " nam et liberam administrationem omnium possessionum proventuum et redditaum ad " abbiam illam si per tantum tempus vacaverit spectantium, necnon omnium exituum " proventuum et proficuorum inde provenientium salvis nobis et haeredibus nostris feodis " militum advocationibus ecclesiarum *Wardis Maritagiis* et releviis ad abbiam praedictam " pertinentibus quae tempore praesentis vacationis accedere contigerit; et si contingat vaca- " tionem abbiae praedictae ultra dictos duos menses perdurare, tunc praedicti prior et con- " ventus habeant custodiam abbiae praedictae cum omnibus ad eam pertinentibus in forma " praedicta durante ulterius vacatione ejusdem, et pro quolibet mense quo vacatio illa du- " raverit ultra dictos duos menses, solvant nobis quadraginta libras, et si vacatio illa ultra " dictos duos menses per minus tempus duraverit quam per mensem tunc pro rata tempo- " ris illius de dictis quadraginta libris minus nobis solvant prout in literis nostris patentibus " inde confectis plenius continetur vobis praecipimus, Quod ipsos priorem et conventum " custodiam abbiae praedictae cum omnibus ad abbiam illam spectantibus in balliva vestra " una cum exitibus unde a tempore mortis praedicti *Thomae* perceptis habere permittatis " juxta tenorem literarum nostrarum predictarum vos inde ratione praesentis vacationis contra " tenorem earundem literarum in aliquo nullatenus intromittentes, volumus enim vos in- " de a tempore praedicto, erga nos exonerari feodis advocationibus wardis maritagiis et " releviis praedictis nobis et heredibus nostris ut praemittitur semper salvis.

" Teste me ipso apud *Salop.* vicesimo nono die *Januarii*, anno regni nostri vicesimo primo.

(*f*) *The names of all the Towns and Villages in her majesty's liberty and court of records of the late dissolved monastery of St.* Mary's *near the walls of the city of* York, *holden before* Thomas Adams *esq; steward of the said court, by virtue of several charters from the kings of this realm, and confirmed by several acts of parliament; digested under the several weapentacks and hundreds in the county of* York;

N. B. If there be but one house in a village or town, the chief bailiff by the process of the court can justify the arresting or distraining in the highway or common thereunto belonging, by the custom of the court, and the queen's royal prerogative being lady paramount; and note, the towns marked with the letter [r.] the records remain in the abbey; and the towns marked with the letter [f.] pay a fee farm rent, belonging to the abbey; and the towns marked with [Mon.] are taken out of the *Monasticum Anglicanum*, being allowed as an authority since the late wars, that the round tower in which the records were lodged of all the monasteries of this side *Trent* was burnt.

Agbrigo and Morley in the *West-riding*.
Allertonshire in the *North-riding*.
Winton, r.
Ainsty in the *West-riding*.
Apelton-nun cum Coulton, r. f.
Acaster and *Acaster Selby*, r. f.
Acombe, r.
Askam Bryan, Mon. f.
Bilton, r. f.
Bilbrough, r. f.
Hessay, r. f.
Knapton, r. f.
Moor-munckton, r. f.
Marston, Mo.
Nun-munckton, Mon. f.
Poppletons ambo, r. f.
Redhouses, Mon.
Rufforth, Mon.
Walton, Mon.
Barkston Ash in the *West-riding*.
Brambam and *Brambam-moor*, r.
Birdforth in the *North-riding*.
Birdforth, r.
Coxwould, r. f.
Cessa, r. f.
Coulby, Mon.
Osgodby, Mon.
Sessay, r. f.
Sowerby, r.
Thursk, f.
Yapham, Mon.
Buckrose in the *East-riding*.
Burdsall, r. f.
Burdall, r.
Bugthorp, Mon. r. f.
Barthorp, Mon.
Eddlethorp, Mon.
Finmer, r. f.
Fridaythorpe, r. f.
Grimston cum membris, r. f.
Grimston, *North-riding*.
Hunckleby, r. f.
Howould, r.
Kirby-under-dale, r. f.
Kennythorp, r.
Langton, Mon. f.
Paintborp, r. f.
Raisthorp, Mon. f.
Skirtenbeck, r. f.
Skirringham, Mon.
Scampston, r.
Sutton near *Malton*, r.
Thixtondale, r. f.
Wintringham, r.
Wellam, Mon.
Bulmer in the *North-riding*.
Alne, r.
Bootham cum *Mary-gate*, r. f.
Bennibrough, r.
Buttercrambe, r. f.
Barton in the Willows, r. f.
Boswell, Mon. f.
Clifton, r. f.
Claxton, r.
Cromb, r.
Dalby, r. f.
Eastlilling, Mon. f.
Foston, r.
Flaxton, r. f.
Flouwith, r. f.
Forest of Galtress, r.
Gate-helmsly, Mon.
Gowthorpe, Mon. f.
Huntington to *Munck-bridge* on both sides of the way, r. f.
Hutton-sheriff, r. f.
Harton, Mon.
Helmsly-gate, r.
Heworth and *Heworth-moor*, r. f.

(*f*) From a paper printed at *York*, by order of the steward of St. *Mary's*, anno 1703.

Hutton upon Derwent, Mon.
Lylling East, Mon. f.
Myton, r. f.
Munckbridge, r.
Marton, r.
Moor between *Tholthorpe* and *Myton*, r.
Newton upon Ouse, r.
Newparke, Mon.
Overton, r. f.
Owzegatte Sutton, Mon. f.
Roclive, r. f.
Roynes in Galtress, Mon.
Sutton in Galtress, r. f.
Steresby, r. f.
Scackelden, Mon.
Skipton, r. f.
Stilnam, r.
Skelton, Mon. f.
Sheriff-Hutton, r. f.
Terrington alias *Torrington*, Mon.
Thornton Lilling, r.
York manor and *Queen's palace*, *Horse-fair*, *Goose-lane*, *Gilly-gate*, *Munck-bridge*, and *Grange-house*.
CLARO in the *West-riding*.
Aldbrough, Mon.
Burrow-bridge, r. f.
Branton-green, Mon. f.
Dunsford ambo.
Denton-hall,
Ellingthorp, r.
Grafton, r.
Minskipp.
Rowcliff.
Stocalia.
Staineburne, r.
DICKERING in the *East-riding*.
Arpam alias *Harpham* cum *Quinton*, r. f.
Butterwick, r.
Bridlingham alias *Burlington*, r.
Burton-north, r. f.
Brunton, r.
Burton Agnes, Mon. f.
Bempton, r. f.
Foxholds, r. f.
Foston, Mon.
Garton, r. f.
Ruston, r. f.
Rudston, r. f.
Willerby, Mon.
EUECROSSE in the *West-riding*.
Clapham, r. f.
GILLING-EAST in the *North-riding*.
Appelton, r. f.
Boulton upon Swale, r.
Brugh, r. f.
Barton, r. f.
Croft, r. f.
Couton-long, Mon. f.
Danby-parva, r. f.
Dalton upon Tease, r. f.
Danby upon Wisk, Mon. f.
Ergam nigh *Tease*, r.
Ellerton juxta *Swale*, r. f.
Ereholm, Mon. f.
Gerreford, r.
Garford, r. f.
Gainford, r. f.
Kneeton, r.
Kirby-Wisk, r. f.
Middleton-Tys, r. f.
Moultons ambo, r. f.
Morton cum *Fingall*, Mon.
Redmire, Mon.
Smeaton, r. f.
Scorton, Mon.
Stapleton, Mon.
Stainebow, Mon. f.
Sedbury, Mon. f.
Uckerby, r. f.
GILLINGWEST in the *North-riding*.
Appleton, r. f.
Ask, Mon.
Askgrig, Mon.
Barforth, r. f.
Brignal, r. f.
Cella Sancti Martini prope *Richmond*, r. f.
Cleasby, r.
Easby prope *Richmund*, r. f.
East-laton, r. f.
Epleby cum *Carlton*, Mon. f.
Forsett, r. f.
Gillingwest, r. f.
Gillmonby, r. f.
Hindertbwait, Mon.
Kirby-hill, r. f.
Kirby-Ravensworth, r. f.
Kirkham in *Ask*, Mon.
Langtons ambo, r. f.
Lanytons ambo, r. f.
Maske, r.
Neusam, Mon.
Newton-Morall, r. f.
Ovington, Mon. f.
Richmond-chapel and *French-gate*, r.
Ravensworth, r. f.
Rombold-kirk, Mon.
Thorp, r.
Wicliffe, r.
HARTHILL in the *East-riding*.
Baynton, r.
Brugh, r.
Burnby, r.
Brantinham, Mon.
Burnholme, Mon. f.
Brumfleet, r. f.
Cottingwith-east, r. f.
Dalton-north, r. f.
Driffield magna, Mon. f.
Elmswell, r. f.
Everthorp, r.
Eastburne, r.
Ellerton, Mon. f.
Foggerthorp, r. f.
Fulsutton, r. f.
Goodmadam, Mon. f.
Huggitt, r. f.
Hesse, r.
Hermitage, r.
Kirkburne, Mon. f.
Latham, r. f.
Lund, Mon.
Millington, r. f.
North Dalton, r. f.
Sunderland-wick, r.
Thorpesield parva, r. f.
Thornton, Mon.
Wasland alias *Wawland*, r.
Willerby, Mon.
Watton, Mon.
Yapham, Mon.
HOLDERNESS in the *East-riding*.
Beeforth, r. f.
Coniston, r. f.
Constable-burton, or *Hornsey-burton*.
Eske, Mon.
Hornsey-burton, f.
Hornsey and *Hornsey-beckhold*, r. f.
Long-preston, r.
Long-ruston, r.
Sutton and *Norton-bridge*, r.
Tunsdale, r.
Wassand, r.
HULLSHIRE in the *East-riding*.
Anlaby alias *Onlonby*, r.
Ferreby.
HALLEKELD in the *North-riding*.
Ainderby-whernhow, r.
Burniston, r. f.
Baldersby, r.
Brugh, r. f.
Carthorp, r. f.
Exelby, Mon. f.
Gatenby, Mon. f.
Holme, r. f.
Kirklington, Mon.
Langthorne cum *Twinghall*, r. f.
Leeming and *Leeming-lane*, Mon. f.
Middleton in *Teasdale*, r.
Milby, r.
Middleton, r.
Melmerby, Mon.
Marton upon the Moor, Mon.
Pickall, Mon. f.
Snape cum *Wells*, Mon.
Theaxton, r. f.
Tanfields ambo, Mon. f.
Wath, Mon.
HANGEAST in the *North-riding*.
Appleton magna in *Catterick* parish, r. f.
Aldburgh or *Audbrough*, r.
Askrigg, Mon.
Appleton East and *West*, r.

St. Mary's Abbey.

Brunton-patterick, r. f.
Catterick, r. f.
Crakehall ambo, Mon. f.
Coleburne, Mon. f.
Cowpland, Mon.
Fleta alias *Fletham*, r. f.
Fearby, Mon.
Firby, Mon.
Horneby near *Smeaton*, r.
Hipswell, r. f.
Kirby-Fleatham, Mon.
Morton, Mon.
Pattrickbrunton, Mon.
Richmond-chapel and *Frenchgate*, r.
Riswick, r. f.
Scuton, r.
Stainton nigh *Ellerton*, r.
Scotton parva, r. f.
Thorntonwatlas, r.
Tunsdale, r. f.
Wells, Mon. f.
HANGWEST in the *North-riding*.
Bellerby, Mon.
Coram, r.
Carleton cum *Coverdale*, Mon. f.
Coveram, Mon. f.
Dunham, r. f.
East-Witton, Mon. f.
Fingall, r.
Hawkswell ambo, r. f.
Hudswell, r. f.
Layburne, r.
Morton, Mon.
Melmerby, Mon. f.
Middleham, Mon.
Redmire, Mon.
Scruton, r.
Spennythorne, r.
Skitby, Mon.
Sandbeck, Mon.
Thornton-Steward, r.
Thoroby, r.
Witton-east, Mon. f.
HOWDENSHIRE in the *East-riding*.
Aislaby, Mon. r.
LANGBAURGH in the *North-riding*.
Eston, Mon.
Easeby, Mon. f.
Exilby, r.
Hutton juxta *Rudby*, r. f.
Liverton, Mon. f.
Lofthouse ambo.
Porto, Mon. f.
Stoxley, r.
Stainton, r.
Scotherskelfe, r.
Wasall, r.
Whorleton, f.
Yarm, r.

OSGODCROSSE in the *West-riding*.
Adlingfleet-part, Mon. f.
Armin, Mon. r.
Eastoft, Mon.
Gould, Mon. f.
Haudenby, r.
Hemsworth, Mon.
Hooke, r.
Holdenby, r.
Marshland all of it, Mon. r. f.
Rednesse, r. f.
Swinfleet, Mon. f.
Usfleet, r. f.
Whitgift, r. f.
OUSE and DARVENT in the *East-riding*.
Cottingwith-west, r. f.
Derwent water to *Ouse*, r. f.
Deighton, r. f.
Escrigg, r. f.
Fulforths ambo, r. f.
Kellfeild, r. f.
Thorgonby, r. f.
Wheldrake, Mon. f.
PICKERINGLYTH in the *North-riding*.
Hutton-bushell, Mon.
Kirby-misperton, r. f.
Middleton, r. f.
Murton, r.
Osgoodby, r.
Ruston, r.
Seamer, r. f.
Thornton, r.
Wickham alias *Wikeham*, r. f.
RYDALE in the *North-riding*.
Appleton-wood, r. f.
Barton in the street, r. f.
Butterwick, r. f.
Colton, r.
Calongia-wood so called, nigh *Wood-appleton*, r.
Dowthwaite-dale, r. f.
Edston, Mon. r.
Farndale, r. f.
Forrest of *Spawnton*, r.
Gilling, r. f.
Hutton in the hole, r. f.
Holvingham, r. f.
Holme-south, r.
Kirkby moor side, r. f.
Keldam, r.
Lestingham, r. f.
Malton, r. f.
The moor between *Normandby* and *Spawnton* called *Sinynton-moor*, r.
Normandby, r. f.
Nunnington, Mon. f.
Rosdale, r. f.
Spaunton, r. f.
Sproxton, r.

Terrington alias *Torrington*, Mon.
STAINECROSS in the *West-riding*.
Skyracke in the *West-riding*.
Bramham and *Bramham-moor*, r.
Bingley, Mon.
STRAFFORD in the *West-riding*.
Doncaster church and sixteen houses, r.
Warmeswick, r.
STAINECLIFFE and *Cliffordsfee* in the *West riding*.
Clapham, r. f.
Eastby, r.
Stretton, r.
TICKHILL in the *West-riding*.
WHITBY-STRAND in the *North-riding*.

The names of several places within the liberty which are not placed in the weapontacks or hundreds before mentioned.

St. *Andrew-hermitage*, r.
Allerthorpe-hall, r. f.
Agotha, r.
Amersett, r.
Baynham, r.
Baynham, r.
Brumfield, r. f.
Besward, r.
Baldersby-hall, r.
Bingholme, r.
Birker, r.
Barnby, r.
Corbow, r.
Coates, r.
Elston, r.
East-kirk, r.
Eversham, r.
Greenby, r.
Garford, Mon.
Hempfield, r.
Hickling, r.
Hylom, r.
Kirkland, Mon.
Kirby and *Sandwith*, Mon.
Marrow the manor, r.
Murton, r.
Mogsikes, r.
Morthum, r.
Newton i' th Willows.
Syron-flu.
Summerhouse, r.
Thoralthorpe, r.
Tilehouse, r.
Thurntoft, r.
Wicke, Mon. r.

The

The CLERKS *Fees in the court of St.* MARY's.

	s. d.		s. d.
For every plaint and action entring	00 02	For copy of every record	06 08
For every diſt. cap. or ſecond warrant	00 08	For copy of every plaint	00 04
For warrant of attorney in actions of caſe	00 04	For every ſearch	00 04
For warrant of attorney in debt	00 02	For every eſſoine upon a plaint	00 04
For copy of every declaration	01 00	For every eſſoine at the court leet	00 02
If contracts, for every contract after the firſt	00 04	For every certificate out of the charter	02 06
If ſheets, for every ſheet after the firſt	00 04	For allowing of a writ of error	12 05
For every order in ejectment	01 00	For *certiorari* or *habeas corpus cum cauſa*	04 10
For every rule	00 04	For every *veſa*, and *hato jur.*	01 00
For entring an order	00 04	For every *et hato jur.*	00 08
For copy thereof	00 04	For *war. ad teſtificand*	01 00
For every default by *non ſum cogn.* or the like	00 04	For *ſuperſedeas* to an execution	62 04
For copy of every ſpecial pleading	01 00	For *ſuperperſed.* to an ordinary proceſs	00 04
For every general iſſue	00 04	For every protection or the privilege	00 08
For every judgment	00 08	For every liberate	01 00
For every proceſs after judgment *a caſa, fi, fa, ſciſa,*	01 00	For every replevin	63 04
For copy of a plea in arreſt of judgment	01 00	For dividing every plaint	00 08
For drawing up ſpecial verdict and copy	00 08	For every non-ſuit or non-proceſs	00 04
		For renewing any judicial proceſs	00 08
		For every *venditione exponaſ.*	00 08
		For every ſpecial imparlance	01 00
		For entry of every *concordantur* or *retraxit.*	00 04

In Dr. *Tanner*'s *notitia Monaſt.* are theſe chartularys, regiſters, *&c.* put down for this abbey.

Regiſtrum, in bibliotheca Deuviſiana. 1646.

Regiſt. penes decanum et capit. Ebor.

Collectanea MS. Rogeri Dodſworth, *biblioth.* Bodley. *v.* 7. 9.

Stephan. Witebienſenſem *de fundatione monaſterii S.* Mariae Ebor. *et hiſtoria ejuſdem mon. una cunc figuris abbatum ſciagraphice depictis, &c.*

Biblioth. Bodl. NERO. *A.* 3. 20.

This book brings down the hiſtory of the abbey to the year 1290, or 1300. The drawings are with a pen, rudely done, yet ſome things in it are not unworthy of an antiquary's conſideration. There is a rude draught, alſo, of ſome part of the abbey, **ecclesia nova**, is put upon it, a ſpire, *&c.* The heads of perſons ſeem to be done *ad libitum ſcriptoris*, but they are very ſmall, as is the ſize of the book.

Reyner. *apoſt.* Benedict. *in* Ang. *Tr.* 2. *p.* 145.

From other authorities.

Conſuetudinarium, in bib. coll. S. Johan. Cant. *d.* 27.

Libertates eccleſiae S. Mariae Ebor. *conceſſ. per regem* Henricum *primum, irrotulat. in itinere* 40 Hen. III. *in curia recept. ſcaccarii.*

Libertates chart. fundationis et indotationis prioratus de Wedderhall, *et cellae* Conſtantini, *prope* Carliolum.

Chartae quaedam abbat. beat. Mariae Ebor.

Miſcellanea, terras et poſſeſſiones prioratus de Wedderhall *ſpectantia*, 4. *antiquo et nitido charactere*;

In biblioth. eccl. cath. apud. Carliol. Wanley, *n.* 603.

Regiſtrum abbatiae S. Marie Ebor. *quarto*, Harley. 36. *c.* 19.

This book contains the charters of king *William Rufus, Henry* I. *Henry* III. *Edward* I. and *Edward* III. granted to the abbey of St. *Mary*'s *York.*

Compoſitions and tythes of ſeveral churches belonging to the abbey.

Grants relating to divers manors.

Charters of the abbey granted to ſeveral freeholders in *Richmondſhire, Myton,* and *Appleton ſup. Wyſk.*

Grants relating to their manor of *Huddeſwell.*

Charters of the churches of *Kirkby-Loneſdale, Kendal* and *Kirkby Stephen, ultra moras.*

Pleadings before the juſtices of the king's bench, term. St. *Mich. an. reg. Ed.* III. about the church of *Bannum, com. Norfolk.*

An inquiſition taken at *Wyſett* about the vacancy of the priory of *Romburgh*, &c.

APPNEDIX.

References, additions and emendations.

AT the end of so long and tedious a work I have neither leisure nor inclination to begin again, and recapitulate the matter thoroughly. Yet, as I have a desire that it should see the light in as exact a dress as possible, I shall subjoin the animadversions of two gentlemen, of known taste in literature, who have done me the honour to give me their thoughts on some passages in the first chapters of it since the sheets were printed; for which reasons their corrections, *&c.* have hitherto escaped the press. When I mention the reverend doctor *Langwith*, rector of *Petworth* in *Sussex*, and *John Anstis* sen. esq; *garter* principal king at arms, I need say no more in regard to the characters of those gentlemen. His cotemporaries in the university of *Cambridge*, are thoroughly sensible of the great abilities of the former gentleman; and the latter has given the world so many proofs of his elegant taste in polite literature, and of his extensive knowledge in the history and laws of his own country, that I am not a little proud to stand corrected in many places of this work by two such judicious observers. Their marginal notes therefore, without any further apology, shall begin this chapter of references; *&c.* and I must beg that the reader would correct the smaller *errata* of the press with his pen; which I believe will be found to be as few as have been published in a work of this extensive matter and composition.

The first chapter, except the etymologies, being wholly taken from *Geofry Monmouth's* legendary account of *Britain*, I have been somewhat blamed by the reverend doctor for paying such a deference to it. The reader may please to observe that though I have made some quotations from that, singular, historian, yet they are not given for *gospel*; and, I think, I could do no less than pass cursorily over what *Geofry* has delivered, in relation to the history and antiquity of this city, since abler historians have done it for other cities; and since his testimony, though denied by many, can never be thorougly confuted; I shall therefore pass on to the animadversions of the next chapter, in which some errors are more plainly pointed out in the manner as follows.

P. 7. for, from its derivative *opes*, read, primitive.

P. 7. *Urbs, civitas, & oppidum*, &c. on this whole paragraph this learned criticism is made by Dr. *Langwith.*

" 1. You say that *oppidum* respects the buildings only and never includes the people: if " this be so I dont know what to make of some of the epithets which *Tully* bestows upon " *oppida*; for instance, he calls *Latina, oppidum locuples honestum copiosum, lib.* 4. *in Verrem* " In another place he has *oppidum miserrimum*, which, with some of the former, cannot I " think relate to any thing but the people. *Oppida metu continere*, in *Livy*, is as hard " to be accounted for as the former, for it is impossible that buildings should be affected " by fear, so that the people must here also be necessarily included.

" 2. You say that *oppidum* chiefly regarded a mercantile situation. I know not how " this is to be proved; for the derivation from *opes* is to me no proof at all, since I had " rather, with some of the antients, derive it from *opem dare*, and then it will imply a " place of help, aid, security, *&c.* without any regard to its wealth. Besides, I am very " much mistaken if I don't quickly shew that many towns were called *oppida* which were " far enough from having a mercantile situation.

" 3. You say that it is always *oppidum Londini*. I do not deny the truth of this obser- " vation; and yet I do not doubt but if *London* had been frequently mentioned in the " classick writers we should have met with it by the name of *urbs*, as well as *oppidum*. " This you may think is talking by guess, but I think I can offer a pretty good reason " for my opinion: it is taken from the name *Augusta*, by which *London* was called, as " appears from *Ammianus Marcellinus, lib.* 27. *cap.* 18. Now, as *London* was no *colonia*, " I think *Augusta* cannot belong to any thing so properly as *urbs*: I am sure it can have " no relation to *oppidum*.

" 4. You say that *Athens* and even *Constantinople* by classical authority claim but the " title of *oppida*; but I think I can prove that each of them, by that authority, claims " the title of *urbs*, as well as *oppidum*. First as to *Athens*, *Tully* speaking of *Athens* calls " it

" it *urbs*; *propter summam et doctoris autoritatem et* urbis. *De officiis lib.* 1. *s.* 1. And again
" of the same place, *consolarenturque nos non tam philosophi qui* Athenis *fuerunt — quam*
" *clarissimi viri qui illa* urbe *pulsi carere ingrata civitate quam manere in improba maluerunt.*
" I shall not trouble you with any more quotations because I think these sufficient for the
" purpose.

" Next as to *Constantinople.*

" This, as you know, was antiently called *Byzantium*: now if it shall appear that *Byzantium* had the title of *urbs*, it is not to be imagined that after having been so much
" enlarged and adorned by *Constantine*, it should be degraded into a mere *oppidum*. And
" that *Byzantium* was called *urbs*, *Justin* shall be my voucher, *Byzantium nobilis et maritima urbs*. Just. *hist. lib.* 9. *s.* 1. When *Byzantium* became *Constantinopolis*, it was so far
" from sinking in its titles that it was made equal in them to old *Rome* it self, both by
" the *Greek* and *Latin* writers. See *Spanheim de Numism. tom.* II. *p.* 401, and *p.* 443. I
" think what has been said is sufficient to prove that *Athens* and *Constantinople* were called
" *urbes* as well as *oppida*. I shall add that this is no more than what holds in many
" other instances, and there is a remarkable place in *Cicero*, where a town is called both *urbs*
" and *oppidum* in the same sentence, Pherae — *urbs erat* in Thessalia — *in quo oppido*, &c.
" Cic. *de divin. lib.* 1.

" That great critick and reviver of learning *Laurentius Valla* carries this matter so far
" as to affirm that all *urbes* whatever, *Rome* only excepted, were called *oppida — oppidum*
" *omnis urbs est praeter* Romam, *quae peculiari nomine urbs vocari coepta fecit ut caeterae urbes oppida vocarentur, quia ipsa oppidum amplius non est.* If all *urbes* except *Rome* were
" called *oppida*, I think it plain that many *oppida* had not mercantile situations."

P. 9. Sect. 5. " *Severus* in the thirteenth year of his reign undertook an expedition into
" *Britain*."

I hope, you dont mean that he set out upon this expedition in the thirteenth year of his reign; for if you do, I dont see how it can possibly be reconciled with *Dio Cassius* [in *Xiphilin*] who is the most particular of all the antients as to the time of these events, and indeed, upon many accounts, the most worthy of credit. Now he tells us that *Severus* died in the third year after his arrival into *Britain*, after having reigned seventeen years nine months and twenty five days: it is plain therefore that his arrrival here could not be till the fifteenth year of his reign at the soonest.

Ibid. " *Severus* arrived in *Britain* with his two sons, *&c.* in the year 207, say some
" chronologers, *&c.*"

I believe it may easily be made appear that *Severus*'s arrival here could not possibly have happened sooner than the year 208, and I wish that your numbers upon the margin had been CCVIII *vel* CCIX instead of CCVII *vel* CCVIII.

Mediobarbus, who had the assistance of cardinal *Noris*, and who by his great acquaintance with the antient coins was himself very well qualified for adjusting of times, is for CCVIII. *Musgrave*, who took a good deal of pains about the *domus Severiana*, as he calls it, is for CCIX. See *Mediobarbus* upon *Occo*, p. 279. and *Musgrave*'s synchron. Dom. *Sev.* p. 126.

P. 9. *Sect.* 6. " *Severus* was sixty years of age when he undertook this expedition."

Xiphilin from *Dio Cassius* informs us, that *Severus* lived sixty five years, nine months and twenty five days, and since he also acquaints us that he died in the third year after his arrival in *Britain*, it is evident that when he came hither he was above sixty two years old. See *Xiphilin* of *H. Stephen*'s edit. in 1592. p. 339, 344. Dr. *Langwith.*

P. 10. *Sect.* 1. " *Severus* chose to build a *stone-wall*, &c. in the place where *Hadrian*
" had thrown up his rampart of earth."

I should rather say that *Severus made a wall*, &c. *near* the place where, *&c.* For it does not appear that *Severus*'s wall was of *stone*, nor was it in the place where *Hadrian* had thrown up, *&c.* but only *near* it. The stone-wall was not built by *Severus*, but, long after his time, by the provincial *Britains*, with the assistance of the *Romans*. See *Camden* and *Gordon*.

P. 10. Sect. 3. " *Severus* lived more than three years in the praetorian palace in this
" city."

If *Dio*'s testimony is to be allowed of, this is impossible. See above.

Ibid. " *Herodian* writes that some years after his first coming to *York* he and his son *Caracalla*, sat in the *praetorium*, and gave judgment, *&c.*"

I cannot find any thing of this either in *Herodian* or any other antient writer.

Ibid. " Common cases as that of *Sicilia*, &c."

Read *Caecilia.* See *Musgrave*'s *Geta Britannicus*, p. 105. Caeciliae *rescriptum est.* Dr. *Langwith.*

I submit to you whether you should not alter this word of *Sicilia* (lest it might be mistaken to relate to that island) into that of one *Caecilia*, who might probably be a *British* lady and then resident at *York*. I take it, this is the only law of *Severus* that expresses the place where it was made. Mr. *Anstis.*

5

P. 10. *Sect.* 6. "The date [of the rescript] runs from the third of the nones of *May*, "*Faustinus* and *Rufus* being consuls."

This very date, together with the affinity between the names *Rufus* and *Rufinus* or *Rufinianus*, has occasioned great disputes among the chronologers about the names of the consuls in the two last years of *Severus*; but I believe all may be set right by an easy emendation. I imagine that the date of the rescript originally ran thus,

P. P. III NON. MAII. EBORACI
FAVSTINO ET RVF°. COSS.

This RVF°. (I suppose by the mistake of the copyers) afterwards became RVFO, whereas it ought to have been *Rufino* or *Rufiniano*. Upon this supposition all will be made easy; the date of the rescript reconciled with the *fasti*, and the chronologers with one another.

The consuls according to the *fasti*, as they are published in *Collier*'s appendix, were in the year 210. *M. Acilius* FAVSTINVS, *C. Caesonius Macer*.

According to *Mediobarbus*, p. 278. they were *Man. Acilius* FAVSTIN *C. Caeson. Macer* RVFINIANUS.

You see there is no difference between the rescript, the *fasti* and *Mediobarbus* as to *Faustinus*; and there will be no more as to the other *Caius Caesonius Macer*, if my emendation be admitted of, and *Rufo* be by a mistake put down for *Rufino* or *Rufiniano*.

The consuls for the next year 211, were according to the *fasti* *Q. E. Rufus*, *Pomponius Bassus*.

According to those eminent chronologers *C. Noris* and *F. Pagi*, *Gentianus*, *Bassus*.

Here again is no difference as to *Bassus*; nor will there be as to the other *Q. E. Rufus* if his *Agnomen* GENTIANUS be added to his other names; for according to *Mediobarbus* the consuls for this year were *Q. Elpidius Rufus* GENTIANVS, POMPONIVS BASSVS. See *Mediobarbus* p. 278, 279.

You may think me very bold in daring to alter an imperial rescript, but I know no other method of setting things upon a right footing, unless one could imagine that *Rufus* was consul two years running. Dr. *Langwith*.

P. 10. *Sect.* 6. "*Severus* is said to have died *A. D.* 212."

This is contrary to the best chronologers that I have by me; for *Helvicus*, *Petavius*, *Mediobarbus*, &c. all agree that he died *A. D.* 211.

You will pardon my adding a word or two more with regard to the rescript. *Musgrave* wonders that no notice was taken of *Geta* in it, since he was at this time dignified with the title of *Augustus*; but for my part I rather believe that no notice was taken of *Bassianus*, but that *Geta* himself is the *Antoninus* of the rescript.

You know, from *J. Capitolinus*, &c. that *Severus* gave *Geta* the name of *Antoninus*, and delighted to have him called so, and that he left him to administer justice at *York*, &c. while he took his brother along with him in his northern expedition; now it appears from good authority, that *Severus* upon his return from the north left *Bassianus* there to command the army and finish the wall: at this time I imagine the rescript was signed at *York* by *Severus* and *Geta*, or the younger *Antonine*, without any notice taken of the elder who was absent. This may perhaps appear a bold conjecture; but I shall be willing to give it up if it do not prove, at least, no improbable one.

N. B. I don't think that *Antonine* staid long in the north after *Severus* had left the army; for he chose rather to patch up a scandalous peace than bring the war to such a conclusion as his brave old father could have wished.

Ibid. "third of the *nones* of *May*, or *May* 4."

Since *May* has six *nones* the third of the nones of *May* is not *May* 4, but *May* 5.

Ibid. "*Feb.* 5."

February has four nones, and therefore *pridie non. Februarii* is *Feb.* 4.

Ibid. For "must have lived in *Britain* near two or three," read, lived in *Britain* two or three years.

P. 14. *Sect.* 7. "deposited in the *capitol*."

I cannot tell what to make of this passage unless there be an error of the press, and that it should be *capital* [*i. e.* capital city] instead of *capitol*; for the monument, in which the ashes of *Severus* were deposited was not in the *capitol*, but at a considerable distance from it, between the *mons Palatinus* and *mons Caelius*, to the north of the *Septizonium*. See *Georgii Fabricii Roma c.* 20. The consequence from hence is, that the monuments of the *Antonines* was not in the *capitol*, but elsewhere. See *Spartian*'s *lives of Severus*, *Caracalla* and and *Geta*; or, at least, those that go under his name with the annotations of *Causabon*. Dr. *Langwith*.

P. 14. *Sect.* *Severus*'s *hills*.

To give the reader a better notion of the size and magnitude of these hills than the perspective view of them, taken at such a distance, can possibly shew, I have had them measured. Their exact mensuration as to diameter, altitude, &c. the annexed draught exhibits.

P. 15.

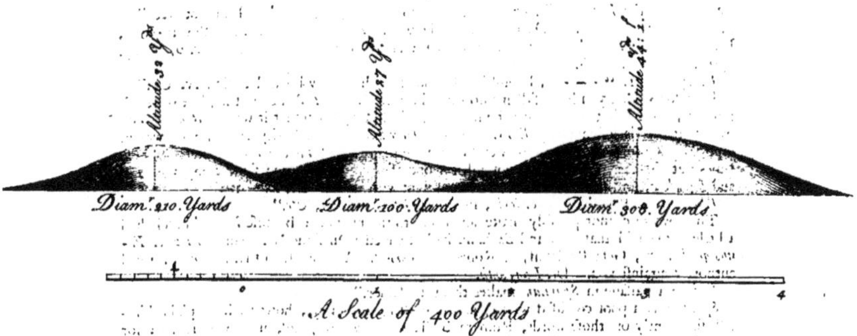

P. 15. *Sect.* 3. " *Dion Cassius* the consular historian who lived a few years after *Se-* " *verus.*"

I wonder at your expressing your self in this manner; it is true indeed that *Dio* lived and was made *consul*, the second time, some years after the death of *Severus*; but his testimony would have more weight with your readers if they had been told that he was a senator and had been *consul* before the reign of *Severus*. Dr. *Langwith.*

P. 16. *Sect.* 2. " *Caracalla*, from the short coats he gave to his soldiers."

They were not short coats but long which he gave, not only to the soldiers, but to the people. The *caracalla*, was a *Gaulish* garment made with a hood or cowl, and was originally short till he lengthened it to the ancles, and was so fond of it as to give it the name of *Antoniniana.* See *Spartian* in *Caracalla* with *Salmasius*'s notes, as also *Aurelius Victor* in *Caracalla.* You will find a strange derivation of the word *Caracalla* in Dr. *Littleton*'s dictionary taken from *Greek* and *Latin*; whereas I make no question but the word was *Gaulish*, and perhaps is still preserved in the old *Irish*, in which *caran* signifies the top of the head and *calla* a veil or covering. Dr. *Langwith.*

P. 16. *Sect.* 4. " that he was not eight and thirty, *&c.*"

The inscription for *Papinian. Aemilio Paulo Papiniano praef. praetor J. C. qui vix. anni* XXXVI. *mens.* III. *dies* X. *Papinianus Hostilius et Eugenia gracilis turbato ordine in senio bon parentes fecerunt filio opt.* So that your making him not above thirty eight should be ascertained, according to this inscription which you will find in *Gruter f.* CCCLVIII. and said by him to remain in the palace of the cardinal of *Genoa* at *Rome*; so that if this most famous lawyer was beheaded at *York*, this was only in the nature of a *cenotaphium* or honorary remembrance, unless the urn with his ashes was removed to *Rome*, which might probably be done, notwithstanding his execution by an axe, (which as I remember hath given some authors, whom I have not time to consult to mention the method by the sword) for the custom of disposing the bodies of those who suffered for state or other crimes by the emperors or monarchs did not, as I could easily prove, obtain till several ages afterwards. Though you have cited the authorities of the greatest character given to *Papinian* by some of the *Roman* writers, and by the most competent judge in later time *Cujacius*, yet if you think it any honour to your city I will send you the civil lawyers who were his contemporaries or soon succeeded him, that give him the most honourable epithets, and I doubt not but you will be enabled to add, if you can get *Fischard de vitis jurisconsultorum*, which I have not. It is astonishing that in so early years, he should obtain that knowledge in equity, which stands the test of all ages, and ever will do so, save in our narrow chanceries. I take it for granted that there are so many characterists in this inscription that it must certainly belong to your lawyer; and at present I have not time to inspect the usual forms in other inscriptions to discover whether the words *turbato ordine* have been used by other parents in memorials of their children, the usual expression being *C. V.* that is *contra votum*, so it may be intended so commemorate likewise the manner of his unhappy death, as well as his death before them. Mr. *Anstis.*

Ibid. " Nor was *Papinian* alone in the *praetorium*, *&c.*"

I am certain that I have somewhere met with a citation that *Ulpian*, (who you know was a *Syrian* rhetor at first, and at length scholar to *Papinian* whilst *praefectus praetorio*, of whom *Lampridius*, speaking of *Alexander Severus*, writes, *ideo summum imperatorem fuisse, idque multa adhuc sua juventa quia* Ulpiani *potissimum consilia auscultarat*) did, whilst he was in *Britain* write to *Terentius Modestinus*, then in *Dalmatia*, as I take it, it is his opinion which we have in the *Pandects lib.* 47. *tit.* 2. *de furtis lege* 52. *sect.* 20. but I cannot recollect the authority. *Selden* and *Duck* conjecture he was at *York*, but mention not this passage, I have not *Cujacius*, but probably he cites it; and it may be in *lib.* 13. *observ.* 6, & 27. *observ.* 26. Mr. *Anstis.*

P. 17. *Sect.* 1. " —— yet I must be of opinion with a very learned antiquary, &c."

I am sorry that you have fallen into this odd notion of *Burton*'s about the place of *Geta*'s murder; for I think nothing can be more clear in history than that it was at *Rome*. You own that this is affirmed by *Dio Cassius* and *Herodian*, the authority of either of which, especially the former, is of more weight with me than that of all the *Latin* writers of those times put together. But this is not all, for one of them affirms the same thing with *Dio* and *Herodian*, and none of the rest are inconsistent with them. Dr. *Langwith.*

Ibid. Sect. 2. " —— *quae victoria*, meaning *Geta*'s murder, &c."

These words cannot possibly make any thing to the purpose; because *Victor* himself had a little above said that *Geta* and *Bassianus* had attended their father's remains to *Rome. Funus quod liberi*, Geta Bassianusque, Romam *detulerunt*. You see then that *Victor* is a third authority against you. Dr. *Langwith.*

Ibid. " a passage in *Spartian* makes this yet plainer."

Spartian is a poor confused writer, and so of little authority; however he explains himself sufficiently on those words, Romam Bassianus *redire non potuit*, if they were his; for he tells us, that after the death of *Geta*, he went to the camp at *Alba*, where the soldiers were so inraged at him that they shut the gates against him; but that he softned them partly by the complaints against *Geta* and partly by the prodigious allowances that he was obliged to make them before he returned to *Rome*. See *Spartian* in *Caracalla* with *Casaubon*'s notes. Dr. *Langwith.*

Ibid. " *Eutropius* writes, &c."

It is no wonder that *Eutropius*, who huddles up every thing in so short manner, should make such quick work with *Geta*; for it is agreed on all hands that his wicked brother did not suffer him to survive his father for any considerable time. —— The testimony of *Ignatius* is not worth consuting. Dr. *Langwith.*

P. 17. *Sect.* 3. " except *Rome* or *Constantinople*."

Have you added any honour to your city at the time of *Severus* by taking it to be next after *Rome* and *Constantinople*, which later name was not then in being, and I could see what was the state of *Bizantium* at that time, which I think *Severus* himself took? Mr. *Anstis.*

P. 21. *Sect.* 4. " the goddess NEHALENNIA."

I wish the dean, for whose memory I have a very great honour, had been a more particular on this occasion; for I cannot find that *Nehalennia* was the patroness of chalk-workers, in particular, but of all people in general, that trafficked by sea; as those of *Zealand* did. See *Reinesius p.* 192. You will find there also an attempt at a learned derivation of the name; but I think that of *Baxter* is more natural, who deduces it from *Ne* and *Halen* [of the salt or sea] so that *Deae Nehalenniae* is *Divae salis vel maris*. This is consistent enough with the opinion of a *German* author, who holds that *Nehalennia* is the new moon; I have not seen the book, but the notion is mentioned by Dr. *Gale* with some degree of approbation. Dr. *Langwith.*

P. 23. *Sect.* 2. " — the distance at sixteen *Italian* miles."

The distance betwixt *York* and *Aldburg* might be better adjusted to the numbers of the *itinerary*, without having recourse to *French* leagues, *viz.* if the distance of these two places be twelve *Yorkshire* miles, it is at least fifteen statute miles, and by consequence above sixteen *Roman* miles; for since the *Roman* mile is to the statute mile very near as 11 to 12, or 15 to $16\frac{4}{11}$, it is evident that 15 statute miles will be nearly equal to $16\frac{4}{11}$ *Roman* miles. You see I have in this computation reckoned twelve *Yorkshire* miles only fifteen statute miles, whereas they are certainly somewhat more in that part of the country; so that instead of $16\frac{4}{11}$ *Roman* miles, we may very well say 17, which is exactly the number in the *itinerary*. Dr. *Langwith.*

Ibid. Sect. 3. " *Burgh*, then, was a common appellation for such a sanctuary."

I do not doubt but *Burgus* frequently signified a walled town; but I suppose you will find by inspecting *Du Fresne*'s glossary, *Cluver*'s geography and many other authors, that have commented upon the laws of the northern nations, that this term was likewise attributed to places not fortresses, or secured by walls. — As to your notion of *civitas*, there can be no dispute that it signified not only the place, but the whole district or territory; and, if my memory doth not fail me, you may meet with several proofs in Dr. *Maurices* diocesan episcopacy, in *England*; at the time of the conquest, the terms *villa*, *villata*, *burgus*, and *civitas* were indiscriminately used for the same places, of which I could furnish you with proofs out of *Doomsday-book*. Mr. *Anstis.*

P. 25. at the end of the note (*b*) add, and one kind of it *vermiculatum*, the reason of which name appears on first sight of two of your pavements. Dr. *Langwith.*

P. 25. *Sect.* 2. " *Suetonius* tells us that a very noble one was built for *Domitian*."

Suetonius says no more than *stadium excitavit*; it is from other authors we learn that it was

was a very noble one. The words which you quote in the margin are not in *Domitian*, but *Julius Caesar*, *c.* 39. § 9. and imply no more than that it was a work designed only to serve a present occasion, and so probably run up in haste, without much magnificence. Dr. *Langwith.*

P. 26. *Sect.* 1. " —I am persuaded the poor *Britons* were not only destitute of tools."

What tools the poor *Britons* had we cannot tell; but that they were able to do works of surprising curiosity and ingenuity is most certain; witness their arrow heads and other weapons made of flints, and other the hardest stones, their *Druidical* magic glasses, adders-beads, *&c.* specimens of all which I have by me so curiously done that it would puzzle our best artists to imitate them. I mention these things only to shew that they were an ingenious people, and that as they were able to do these little works, though we cannot tell how, so they might be able to do great works, which require more labour but not more ingenuity. Besides these obelisks, and even *Stone-henge* itself, are mere trifles in comparison to the works which the *Spaniards* found amongst the *Americans*, at their first arrival there; though they were not acquainted with any of our tools, nor even with iron, which it is certain the *Britons* were; and I cannot see why we should not allow as much ingenuity to them as to the *Americans*. Upon the whole I have seen both these obelisks and *Stone-henge*, and take them to be far too rude for *Roman* works; and since there are arguments enough to prove they were neither *Saxon* nor *Danish*, I cannot but conclude they were *British*.

N. B. I have viewed *Stone-henge*, with a great deal of care, and cannot but think that *Inigo Jones* has imposed upon the world in his account of it, for I can no way reconcile what is now left of it with his plan and description. He has made a fine thing of it, such as would have been worthy of the *Romans*, or such an architect as himself; but it is such a thing as never stood upon *Salisbury* plain. I shall only add that one of the most entire works of this kind is still remaining in *Lewis*, one of the western islands of *Scotland*, which cannot possibly be imagined to have been made by the *Romans*, or any but the ancient inhabitants of those isles. See an account and draught of this in *Martin*'s description of the western isles of *Scotland p.* 9. I am told that Dr. *Stukely* has by him, a great many observations on works of this nature; I wish he would oblige the world with them, for I do not doubt but they are very curious. Dr. *Langwith.*

P. 28. in the note (*n*) correct Mr. *Morris* for Mr. *Gale.*

P. 29. *Sect.* 1. " also *Caracticus* and *Alectus*."

I am sorry for the sake of my good old friend that you suffered this part of his letter to be printed; for there was no *Roman* emperor of the name of *Caracticus* nor any thing like it; *Carausius* comes the nearest, but he was mentioned before. I fancy the good old gentleman meant *Caratacus*, and had forgot that he was not a *Roman* emperor, but a *British* king. However I should chuse to correct this place by leaving out the words, *with* Carausius, in the seventh line, and by changing *Caracticus* and *Alectus* into *Carausius* and *Alectus* in the eight line. Dr. *Langwith.*

P. 43. *Sect.* 6. " with this difference only, that at *Rome* an ivory image was substituted " of *Severus*, but at *York* it was done on the real body of *Constantius*."

There was not that difference made, for it was the *Roman* custom to bury the true body with a sumptuous funeral, but to perform the solemnity of consecration upon an image done to the life. This image was not of ivory but of wax. Dr. *Langwith.*

Ibid. Sect. 7. " image of the dead emperor being exquisitely carved — was laid on an " ivory bedstead."

The image being of wax might therefore be said to be made, cast or molded, but not carved. ——— It should not be bedstead but bed. For all these particulars see *Herodian* in the original, for there is a blunder in the translation, which runs thus, *viz. Certam imaginem defuncto quam simillimam fingunt*, whereas it should be *ceream*, for the original is κηρῷ. Dr. *Langwith.*

P. 44. *Sect.* 1. " Whilst others represented great kings and princes in their chariots."

Rather represented those amongst the *Romans* who had commanded armies; or governed the empire with the greatest glory. Dr. *Langwith.*

Ibid. Sect. 2. " This was the last ceremony of its kind, *&c.*"

When you wrote this, I believe, you were not aware that the *Apotheosis* was not discontinued till considerably above one hundred years after that of *Constantius*; for not only his son *Constantine* was consecrated, but several others, quite down to the times of *Placidus Valerianus.* See *Gutherius de jure manium*, *lib.* 2. *c.* 5. It is probable they omitted some parts of the old ceremony; but what, I will not pretend to inform you. *Constantine*'s consecration medals might have done very well for any of the *Pagan* emperors. Dr. *Langwith.*

P. 48. *Sect.* 4. " He not only deserted *York* and *Britain* but even *Europe*."

He did not desert *Europe* by this; for *Byzantium*, or *Constantinople*, is in *Europe.* Dr. *Langwith.*

P. 55. *Sect.* 7. " The *Sextumvir* of the *Roman* colony at *York*."

As he was a magistrate of a colony, I should be for translating it one of the six judges of, *&c.* or else for not translating it at all. Dr. *Langwith.*

Ibid. " A native or citizen of *Bourdeaux* in *France.*"

The people of *Bourdeaux* were not called *Bituriges Cubi*, but *Bituriges Ubisci*; the *Bituriges Cubi* were the people of *Berri*. See *Hardouin*'s notes on *Pliny*, *lib.* 4. *c.* 19. *p.* 226.

P. 58. *Sect.* 1. For *necteric* read *nesteric*.

Ibid. Sect. 5. " GENIO LOCI FELICITER [*regnanti*]"

I cannot approve of *regnanti*, or any such word; because I think the inscription may be better explained without them. FELICITER was one of the *verba solennia*, and was often used alone, to wish prosperity and good success upon any remarkable occasion, either publick or private; and then amounts to the same as *quod felix faustumque sit*, or any other of the like *formulae*. In the present case it is a short wish, or prayer, for a happy issue of the dedication of this votive tablet to the *genius* of the place. The party concerned had some reason to doubt of this; for as the deity was *British* and he a *Roman*, he could not tell whether his present would be acceptable or no; or however might justly think that a *British* deity would rather be propitious to the *Britains* than the *Romans* their conquerors. I own that *Feliciter* seems sometimes to be used as a word of compliment or approbation, but I do not take that to be the meaning of it here. I shall however give you a few instances, from good authors, where it is used simply, and leave you to judge for your self. The first shall be from *Juvenal*, upon the execrable marriage of *Gracchus* to one of his own sex —— *signatae tabulae: dictum* FELICITER. *Sat. lib.* 1. *Sat.* 2. *v.* 119. The next from *Suetonius in vita Claudii cap.* 7. *acclamante populo* FELICITER, *partim patruo imperatoris, partim* Germanici *fratri.* Again, in *Domitian, domino et dominae* FELICITER. I could give more proofs, but I shall only add one from *Seneca*, FELICITER, *quod agis, epist.* 67. *Lipsius*, upon this place would have it to be only a *formula approbandi et in re laeta gratandi:* this might admit of some dispute; but I think the sense of the other will not admit of any; especially if we compare them with *Plutarch* in *Galba*, καί ποτε θέας ἄγης, καὶ τῶν χιλιάρχων καὶ λοχαγῶν, τὸ Ῥωμαίοις συνῆθες, εὐτυχίαν ἐπιβοωμένων τῷ αὐτοκράτορι Γάλβᾳ. *Cum ederetur aliquando spectaculum, tribunique militum ac turmarum ductores solenne illud* Romanorum FELICITER [*felicitatem*] Galbae *imperatori precarentur, &c.* Dr. *Langwith.*

Ibid. Sect. 7. " **Barguest** of *York.*"

I have been so often frightned with stories of this **Barguest**, when I was a child, that I cannot help throwing away an etymology upon it. I suppose it comes from the A. S. burh, a town, and gast, a ghost, and so signifies a *town-sprite*. *N. B.* That gast is in the *Belgic* and *Teut.* softned into **Gheest** and **Geyst**. Dr. *Langwith.*

P. 60. *Sect.* 4. On *Roman* coins found at *York*. " Whatever has been discovered in " *York* of these curiosities, both of late years and anciently, are now so dispersed that it is " not possible to give any particular account of them."

Since the printing of this sheet the reverend Dr. *Langwith* has sent me a catalogue of *Roman* coins, from *Augustus* down to *Gratianus*, but not successively, found at *York*, and all in his own possession. Upon my enquiring, how he could assert the truth of this? He answered, that they were all collected at *York*, partly by himself and partly by his friends, but especially by his father; who was a studious inquisitive person, though not bred a regular scholar. His way was, the doctor adds, when he met with any thing curious at *York* to secure it for his son, if possible; such as medals, urns, *&c.* and send them to *Cambridge*. Thus his collection of *York* rarities was increasing from the year 1700, in which he went to *Cambridge*, to the year 1723, in which his father died. He adds, that as his father and his other friends lived altogether at *York*, it is a probable argument that what medals they sent were found there; but could not be positive either for the time when, or place where they were first found. And concludes on this head with saying, that where he was doubtful whether a coin came out of *York*, or no, he omitted it in the catalogue; and that he had a great many more brass coins of the lower empire, which were so wretched that he did not set them down, though found at the same place. Thus far the doctor; and I shall only add, that as his father lived at the time when the ground for gardens round about the city was first opened, as also when the fields out of *Bootham-bar* were first searched into and dug for clay to make brick, such an inquisitive and diligent collector might amass together a great number of *Roman* coin; then every day discovered. The celebrated *Museum* of our late *Leeds* antiquary, was, amongst many other curiosities, greatly enriched with a number of *Roman* medals, also, found here. For at that time there were few or none, besides Mr. *Thoresby* and the doctor's father, who made collections of any such curiosities in the county. The catalogue therefore, boldly, claims a place in these *addenda*; and, notwithstanding there are not many of the *rarissimi*, or even *rariores*, in it, yet I may venture to say that there is not such a collection of *Roman* coin, found in one city except *Rome*, and all in one man's hands, in the universe.

AUGUSTUS.

Ar. 1. Augustus Divi F.
Rev. C. Caesar Augus. F.
Figura equestris cum tribus signis mil.

1

AGRIPPA.

AE. 2. Agrippa L. F. Cos. III.
Rev. S. C.
Neptunus stans, dextra delphinum, sinistra tridentem.

TIBE-

TIBERIUS.

Ar. 3. Ti. Caesar Divi Aug. F.
Rev. Pontif. Maxim.
Figura sedens, dextra bastam, sinistra ramum tenens.

GERMANICUS.

AE. 4. Germanicus Caesar Ti. Augus. F. Divi Aug. N.
Rev. SC. C. Caesar Aug. Germanicus Pon. M. Tr. Pot.

CALIGULA.

AE. 5. C. Caesar Aug. Germanicus Pont. M. Tr. P.
Rev. Vesta S. C.
Vesta sedens, dextrâ pateram.

CLAUDIUS.

AE. 6. Ti. Claudius Caesar Aug. P. M. Tr. P. Imp.
Rev. Spes Augusta.
Spei Typus.

NERO.

Ar. 7. Nero Caesar Aug.
Rev. Juppiter Custos.
Jupiter sedens, dextrâ fulmen, sinistrâ bastam.

AE. 8. Nero Claud. Caesar Aug. Germanicus.
Rev. Certã. Quinq. Romae Cons. S. C.
Mensa in qua Corolla et Olla.

OTHO.

Ar. 9. Imp. M. Otho Caesar Aug. Tr. P.
Rev. Pax Orbis Terrarum.
Figura stans, dextra ramum, sinistra caduceum.

VITELLIUS.

Ar. 10. A. Vitellius Germ. Imp. Aug. Tr. P.
Rev. Libertas Restituta.
Figura stolata, dextra pileum, sinistra bastam.

VESPASIANUS.

Ar. 11. Imp. Caesar Vesp. Aug.
Rev. Cos. V. inter duas laurus.

Ar. 12. Imp. Caes. Vesp. Aug. P. M. Cos. IIII. Cens.
Rev. Fides Publ.
Duae dextrae junctae, cum caduceo, papaveribus et spicis duabus.

Ar. 13. Imp. Caes. Vesp. Cens.
Rev. Salus Aug.
Figura sedens, dextrâ pateram tenens.

Ar. 14. Imp. Caesar Vespasianus Aug. Tr. P.
Rev. Titus et Domitian. Caesares Prin. Juvent.
Duae figurae togatae sedentes, dextris ramos lauri.

Ar. 15. Divus Augustus Vespasianus.
Rev. Ex. S. C.
Duo lauri: In medio columna cum clypeo in quo S. C.

AE. 16. Imp. Caesar Vespasianus Cos. III.
Rev. Provident. S. C.
Ara.

TITUS.

Ar. 17. T. Caesar Imp. Vespasianus.
Rev. Jovis Custos.
Figura stans, dextram supra aram protendens, sinistrâ bastam tenens.

18. T. Caesar Imp. Vespasianus.
Rev. Cos. VI.
Bos et Vacca cum Aratro.

19. T. Caesar Imp. Vespasianus.
Rev. Tr. Pot. VIII. Cos. VII.
Quadriga triumphalis e quâ flos erumpit.

DOMITIANUS.

Ar. 20. Imp. Caes. Domit. Aug. Germ. P. M. TR. P. V.
Rev. Imp. XIII. Cos. XI. Cens. P. P. P.
Pallas, dextrâ fulmen, sinistrâ clypeum.

Ar. 21. .... Pallas cum noctuâ.

AE. 22. Imp. Caes. Domit. Aug. Germ. Cos. XII. Cens. Perp. P. P.
Rev. Fortuna Augusti S. C.
Fortuna stans, dextra temonem navis, sinistra Cornucopiae.

AE. 23. Imp. Caes. Domit. Aug. Germ. Cos. XIIII. Cens. Perp. P. P.
Rev. Virtuti Augusti.
Figura galeata stans, dextra bastam, sinistra Parazonium, sinistro pede globum calcans.

TRAJANUS.

Ar. 24. Imp. Caes Nerva Trajan. Aug. Germ.
Rev. P. M. TR. P. Cos. IIII. P. P.
Victoria stans, dextra sertum, sinistra Palmam.

25. Imp. Trajano Aug. P. M. TR. P.
Rev. Cos. V. P. P. S. P. Q. R. optimo Principi.
Victoria, dextra sertum, sinistra bastam.

26. .... It. *Figura stans, dextra bilancem, sinistra cornucopiae.*

27. Imp. Caes. Ner. Trajano optimo Aug. Ger. Dac.
Rev. P. M. Tr. P. Cos. VI. PP. S. P. Q. R. Fort. Red.
Figura sedens, dextra temonem navis, sinistra cornucopiae.

28. Imp. Caes. Nervae Trajano Aug. Ger. Dac. Parth.
Rev. Cos. VI...... MO Prin.
Figura stans, dextra ramum, sinistra parazonium, ad pedes struthio.

HADRIANUS.

Ar. 29. Hadrianus Augustus P. P.
Rev. Cos. III.
Figura stans, dextra bilancem, sinistra cornucopiae.

30. Hadrianus Augus.
Rev. Cos. III.
Figura militaris stans, dextra victoriolam, sinistra bastam.

SABINA Hadriani uxor.

31. Sabina Augusta Hadriani Aug. PP.
Rev. Pudicitia.
Pudicitiae stantis typus.

ANTONINUS PIUS.

Ar. 32. Antoninus Augustus P. P. Tr. P. Cos. III.
Rev. Aequitas Aug.
Figura stans, dextra bilancem, sinistra bastam.

AE. An-

AE. Antoninus Aug. Pius.
Rev. Britanniae . . . . .
33. Britannia *rupibus insidens, dextra signum militare, sinistra* . . . .

FAUSTINA.

Ar. 34. Diva Faustina.
Rev. *Figura stans, dextra pomum ferens, sinistra velum levans circa caput.*
35. . . . . *Rev.* Augusta.
Figura stans, dextra hastam.

M. AURELIUS.

Ar. 36. Aurelius Caesar. Anton. Aug. Pii F.
Rev. Tr. P. XI. Cos. II.
Figura militaris dextra hastam, sinistra parazonium.
37. M. Antoninus Aug. Tr. P. XXIX. Cos. III.
Figura sedens, dextra pateram, sinistra cornucopiae.

COMMODUS.

Ar. 38. M. Comm. Ant. P. Fel. Aug. Brit.
Rev. P. M. Tr. P. XIII. Imp. VIII. Cos. V. P.P.
Figura nuda stans, dextra pateram, sinistra spicas.
Ar. 39. M. Comm. Ant. P. Fel. Aug. Brit. P. P.
Rev. Min. Aug. P. M. Tr. P. XVI. Cos. VI.
MINERVA.

SEVERUS.

Ar. 40. Severus Pius Aug.
Rev. Fundator Pacis.
Imperator sac. cultu capite velato, olivae ramum dextra,
Ar. 41. L. Sep. Sev. Pert. Aug. Imp. IX.
Rev. Providentia Aug.
Figura stolata dextram protendens supra globum, sinistra hastam gerens.

JULIA DOMNA Severi uxor.

Ar. 42. Julia Augusta.
Rev. Diana Lucifera.
Ar. 43. . . . . *Rev.* *Figura stans, dextra pateram, sinistra hastam puram,*

CARACALLA.

Ar. 44. Imp. Antoninus Pius Aug.
Rev. Securitas saeculi.
Figura sedens dextram capiti admovens, sinistra sceptrum gerens.
45. Antoninus Aug. Brit.
Rev. P.M. Tr. P. XVI. Cos. IIII. P. P.
Hercules nudus, dextra ramum, sinistra spolia leonis cum clava.

GETA.

Ar. 46. P. Sept. Geta Pont.
Rev. Princ. Juventutis.
Caesar paludatus stans, dextra ramum, sinistra hastam, cum tropaeo a tergo.
47. . . . . . *Figura stans, dextra ramum, sinistra hastam.*

ELAGABALUS.

Ar. 48. Imp. Antoninus Pius Aug.
Rev. P. M. Tr. P. IIII. Cos. III. P.P.
Solis typus, cum stella.

JULIA MAESA avia Elagab.

Ar. 49. Julia Maesa Aug.
Rev. Saeculi Felicitas.
Figura stolata stans, dextra pateram, sinistra hastam cum caduceo. A tergo stella.

JULIA PAULA Elagabali uxor.

Ar. 50. Julia Paula Aug.
Rev. Concordia.
Figura sedens, dextra pateram. A fronte stella.

JULIA AQUILIA SEVERA altera Elagabali uxor.

Ar. 51. Julia Aquilia Severa.
Rev. Provid. Deorum.
Providentiae typus.

JULIA SOAEMIAS Elagabali mater.

Ar. 52. Julia Soaemias Aug.
Rev. Venus coelestis.
Venus sedens, dextra pomum, sinistra hastam puram. A tergo stella.

M. AURELIUS SEVERUS ALEXANDER.

Ar. 53. Imp. C. M. Sev. Alexand. Aug.
R. Libertas Aug.
Foemina stolata, dextra pileum, sinistra hastam puram.
It.
54. *Rev.* P. M. Tr. P. II. Cos. P. P.
Figura stans, dextra ramum, sinistra hastam puram.
It.
55. *Rev.* P. M. Tr. P. VI. Cos. II. P. P.
It.
56. *Rev.* Salus Publica.
Salus sedens, dextra pateram serpenti porrigens.

JULIA MAMMAEA Alexandri mater.

Ar. 57. Julia Mammaea Aug.
Rev. Vesta.
Figura velata stans, dextra palladium, sinistra hastam puram.

SAL. BARBIA ORBIANA Alexandri uxor.

Ar. 58. Sall. Barbia Orbiana Aug.
Rev. Felicitas Publica.
Figura stans, dextra caduceum gerens, sinistra nixa columnae.

MAXIMINUS.

Ar. 59. Maximinus Pius Aug. Germ.
Rev. Fides Militum.
Figura stans, utraque manu tenens signum militare.

GORDIANUS III.

Ar. 60. Imp. Gordianus Pius Fel. Aug.
Rev. Virtuti Augusti.
Hercules cum leonis exuviis et clava.
61. It.
Rev. Laetitia Aug. N.
Figura muliebris stans, dextra sertum, sinistra anchoram.

MARCUS JULIUS PHILIPPUS ARABS.

Ar. 62. Imp. Philippus Aug.
Rev. Securitas Perp. . . . .

OTACILIA SEVERA Philippi uxor.

Ar. 63. Marcia Otacil. Severa Aug.
Rev. Concordia Aug. g. S. C.

Figura sedens, dextra pateram, sinistra cornucopiae.

TRAJANUS DECIUS.

Ar. 64. Imp. Trajanus Decius Aug.
Rev. Dacia.
Figura stans, dextra baculum cum capite equino.

TREBONIANUS GALLUS.

Ar. 65. Imp. Cae. C. Vib. Treb. Gallus.
Rev. Apoll. Salutari.
Apollo, dextra ramum lauri, sinistra citharam.

VOLUSIANUS.

Rev. Concordia Augg.

VALERIANUS.

66. Imp. C. P. Lic. Valerianus Aug.
Rev. Apollini Conserva.
Apollo stans, dextra ramum, sinistra citharam.

GALLIENUS.

AE. 67. Gallienus Aug.
Rev. Pax publica.
68. .... *Rev.* Provid. Aug.
69. .... *Rev.* Virtus Aug.
70. .... *Rev.* Dianae. Conf.
Diana cum venabulo et arcu, ad pedes animal cervini generis.
71. .... *Rev.* Soli Conf. Aug.
Pegasus.
72. .... *Rev.* Apollini Conf. Aug.
Centaurus, dextra globum.
73. .... *Rev.* Neptuno Conf. Aug.
Hippopotamus, al. *Hippocampus.*
74. .... Jovi Conf. Capra.

SALONINA.

AE. 75. Salonina Aug.
Rev. Juno Conservat.
76. .... Venus victrix.
Venus, dextra galeam, sinistra hastam cum clypeo.

POSTUMUS SEN. GALLIAE TYRANNUS.

77. Imp. C. Postumus Pius F. Aug.
Rev. Victoria Aug.

VICTORINUS.

AE. 77. Imp. C. Victorinus.
Rev. Providentia Aug.
78. .... *Rev.* Pax Augusti.
79. .... *Rev.* Invictus.
Solis typus.
80. .... *Rev.* Pietas Aug.
81. .... *Rev.* Hilaritas Aug.
82. .... *Rev.* Victoria Aug.

TETRICUS.

AE. 83. Imp. C. Tetricus P. F. Aug.
Rev. Spes publica.
84. .... *Rev.* Laetitia Aug. n.
Laetitia, dextra sertum. sinistra anchoram.
85. ... Salus Augg.
Salutis typus.

TETRICUS, jun.

AE. 86. C. P. E. Tetricus Caes.
Rev. Pietas Augg.
Vasa pontificalia.
87. .... Spes.

C. PIVESU TETRICUS.

88. *Rev.* Spes Augg.

CLAUDIUS GOTHICUS.

AE. 89. Imp. C. Claudius Aug.
.... *Rev.* Aequitas Aug.
.... *Rev.* Felicitas Aug.

QUINTILLUS.

AE. 90. Imp. C. M. Aur. Cl. Quintillus Aug.
Rev. Pax Augusti.

CARINUS.

AE. 91. Imp. Carinus P. F. Aug.
Rev. Felicit. Publica.

DIOCLETIANUS.

Imp. C. C. Val. Diocletianus P. F. Aug.
92. *Rev.* Jovi Conser. Augg.

TYRANNI *sub* DIOCLETIANO.

1. AELIANUS.

AE. 93. C. L. Aelianus P. F. Aug.
Rev. Victoria Aug.
Victoriae typus.

2. CARAUSIUS.

AE. 94. Imp. Carausius P. F. Aug.
Rev. Pax Aug.

3. ALLECTUS.

AE. 95. Imp. Cae. Allectus P. F. Aug.
Rev. Laetitia Aug.
96. .... Providentia Aug.

CONSTANTIUS.

AE. 97. Constantius Nobil. Caesar.
Rev. Genio Populi Romani.

FLAVIA HELENA.

AE. 98. .... Helena Augusta.
Rev. Securitas Reipublicae.

FLAVIA THEODORA.

AE. 99. Theodora Aug.
Rev. Pietas Romana.
Mulier stans cum puerulo lactente.

MAXIMIANUS.

AE. 100. Imp. Maximianus P. F. Aug.
Rev. Genio Populi Romani.

MAXIMINUS.

AE. 101. Imp. Maximinus Aug.
Rev. Genio Pop. Rom.
Genius stans, dextra pateram, sinistra cornucopiae, a tergo stella P. L. N.

LICINIUS.

AE. 102. Imp. Licinius P. F. Aug.
Rev. Genio Pop. Rom.

CONSTANTINUS M.

AE. 103. Constantinus P. F. Aug.
Rev. Comiti Augg. N. N. P. L. N.
Sol gradiens.
104. .... Soli invicto Comiti. P. T. R.
Sol.
105. Constantinus Aug.
Rev. D. N. Constantini Max. Aug. S. T.*
Sertum in quo vot. XX.
106. .... Sarmatia devicta.
Victoria gradiens ad cujus pedes captivus.
107. Divo Constantino ...
Rev. .... Pietas.
Figura militaris stans, dextra hastam sinistra globum.
108. .... *Rev.* .... Quadrigae.

CONSTANTINUS jun.

AE. 109. J. Constantinus jun. Nob. C.
Rev. Caesarum Nostrorum Vot. X. T. R.
110. ... Dominor. nostror. Caes. Vot. X.
111. ... Providentiae Caess. P. Lon.
Arx, vel forte horrea publica.

CONSTANS.

AE. 112. D. N. Constans P. F. Aug.
Fel. Temp. Reparatio.
Figura militaris stans in navi, dextra victoriolam, sinistra labarum. Victoria navem gubernat.
113. .... *Rev.* Eadem epigraphe.
Phoenix radiatus monti vel fortasse rogo insistens.
113. It. *Phoenix globo insistens.*
114. It. *Imp. manu globum gerens.*
115. It. *Figura militaris, sinistra hastam tenens, dextra parvulum ex antro, vel pergula ducens.*

CONSTANTIUS.

116. D. N. Constantius P. F. Aug.
Rev. Fel. Temp. Reparatio.
Figura militaris in navi, dextra globum cum Phoenice, sinistra labarum in quo ☧, ad pedes victoria navim gubernans.

MAGNENTIUS.

AE. 117. D. N. Magnentius P. F. Aug.
Rev. Salus D. D. N. N. et Caes.
A ☧ ω.
118. .... Victoria D. D. N. N. Augg. et Caess.
Duae victoriae clypeum tenentes in in quo Vot. V. *mult.* X.

JULIANUS.

Ar. 119. D. N. Fl. Cl. Julianus P. F. Aug.
Rev. Vot. X. Mult. XX. P. Const.
AE. .... *Rev.* Votis X. mult. XX. Heracl. a.

VALENTINIANUS.

AE. 120. Valentinianus P. F. Aug.
Rev. Gloria Romanorum.
Figura mil. dextra captivum crinibus trahens, sinistra labarum tenens.
121. D. N. Valentinianus P. F. Aug.
Rev. Securitas Reipublicae. S--SIS.

VALENS.

AE. 122. D. N. Valens P. F. Aug.
Rev. Securitas Reipublicae OF. I.
Victoria gradiens, dextra sertum, sinistra palmam.
123. ..... *Rev.* Gloria Romanorum OF. II.
Miles sinistra labarum tenens, dextra captivum prosternens.

GRATIANUS.

AE. 124. D. N. Gratianus Augg. Aug.
Gloria Novi Saeculi OF. III. Con.
Figura militaris stans, dextra labarum cum Monogrammate ☧, *sinistra clypeum.*

P. 60. *Sect.* 4. " a gold *Chrispus.*" Dele (*b*).

P. 61. *Sect.* 5. " It is a *Beryl* on which is engraven, as I think, a *Pallas.*"

This curiosity, the last time I had the honour to shew it to the antiquarian society, when I presented it to their collection, was judged by Mr. *Bowman* to be a representation of MINERVA MEDICA. That gentleman being a great *connoisseur* in these matters I sent his opinion of it to the reverend Dr. *Langwith*, for his approbation; whose reasons for differing from him in it I shall subjoin in his own words as follows, *viz.*

" *Good Sir,*

" WHEN I wrote to you last I told you that a sudden thought had shot in my head " which I committed to paper that minute, and sent away by the post: it was, " that the figure upon your antique stone represents *Bellona*. I cannot help saying that I was " pleased with the thought, as the stone was found so very near the place where you ima- " gine *Bellona*'s temple to have stood; and I own I am loth to give it up without good " reasons for so doing. You tell me that an eminent member of the society of antiquaries " imagines the figure to be *Minerva Medica*. The great character you give this gentle- " man is enough to make me diffident of my own opinion, but not enough to make me " fall in with his: for the air of this figure seems to me to be so violent and mannish, and " the garment so raised and indecent that I cannot think it proper to represent *Minerva* in " her medical capacity, or indeed as concerned in any thing but what relates to war. *Mi-* " *nerva* considered in this last view is, indeed *generally* represented in violent action; as " marching like *Mars*, or lifting up her arm as if she were going to dart the javelin or " perhaps the thunderbolt; but when she is considered as *Minerva Medica*, her garments " come down to her feet, and her posture is grave and steady; for she is *commonly* sitting, " or else standing without any action, except perhaps that of sacrificing, or of reaching " out something to a snake which you very well know is the grand symbol of health. The " ancients seem to have intimated by these fixt postures that their supplications were for " such a state of health as would be steady and lasting. If I guess right, the main reason " that determined this learned gentleman to think this figure to be *Minerva Medica* must be " taken from the serpent on this stone; but, with submission, this does not seem to me " to be sufficient. Indeed if *Minerva* had held it in her hand, or had been offering any " thing to it, the case would not have admitted of any dispute; but since the serpent on- " ly exerts itself from the shield, it may be well imagined that it was placed there for no- " thing but a mark of distinction; to shew that the shield is the *aegis*, and she by whom " it stands is the goddess *Minerva*. If you say that her *aegis* had many serpents upon it;

" I own

" I own it is true; but the signet was too small to express them, and so the engraver chose " to represent them by one; just as a whole army is in some small antiques exhibited by " two or three figures. What is said of this signet holds also in coins, in some of which " there is only a single snake upon *Minerva*'s shield, even when she is represented in such " a manner that she cannot easily be taken for *Minerva medica*.

" Perhaps you may think by this time that I am arguing against my self, and proving " that the figure is, not *Bellona*, but *Minerva*: I must therefore explain my self by ac- " quainting you that I take the *Minerva Bellica* and the goddess *Bellona* to be the same, " and that I am not alone in this opinion. For *Bellona* may be taken either for the god- " dess of war, or the fury of war: in the former case, she is armed like *Minerva* with " the helmet, shield and spear, as I can prove from good authority; in short I know of " no marks of distinction: but when she is considered as the fury of war, she makes a " quite different figure: her hair then instead of being confined under the helmet, is dishe- " velled, and besmeared with blood: she carries in her hands swords, scithes, burning " torches and bloody scourges, all terrible emblems of havock and desolation, and is in all " respects more like a fiend from hell than a goddess. *Bellona* in this view is as different " from *Minerva* as madness and barbarity are from wisdom and magnanimity.

" I think I could have given you very plain proofs for the truth of every thing that I have " advanced, had I not been afraid of being tedious: however I shall send them at any " time if you desire it. I shall only take notice that if your notions about the site of *Bel- " lona*'s temple, and mine about the goddess her self are right; your intaglio may, for " ought you know, have been used as a signet by a priest of *Bellona* as well as a monk " of St. *Mary*'s. Let this pass a fancy, for I designed it for nothing else.

" *N. B.* There seems to be a disagreement amongst authors about the *aegis*, for some " will have it to be her shield, others the *lorica*, which also had the gorgon's head upon it; " but matters are easily set right, for it is plain enough that both the *shield* and *lorica* were " called by the name of *aegis*.

Petworth, *Feb.* 29, 1735-6.

" P. S. I hope it will not be thought foreign to the subject if I take notice, that as " *Minerva* was the tutelar goddess of health by the name of *Medica* among the *Romans*, she " was the same among the *Greeks* by the name of Ὑγίεια. I the rather take notice of this, " because from their customs we may conjecture what that round thing is, which we see often " offered to the snake; for when it is hollow we may fairly conclude it to be the *poculum* " *salutis*, when flat it is a kind of *placenta* made of flower, oil and wine, both which, as " well as the goddess, went amongst the *Greeks* by the name of Ὑγίεια."

P. 61. *Sect.* 6. " and by calling it *secretum*, or private seal he seemed to place greater " confidence in this than his publick one."

Being ignorant of the nature of these antient seals I used this expression. But since the printing of this sheet, I have been favoured with the loan of a most curious manuscript, wrote by the celebrated Mr. *Anstis* on the antiquity, form, and use of seals. Whereby I find that this practice of making use of *Roman* gems, for more modern seals, was very common, amongst our ecclesiasticks and laicks, in the later ages. And when inscribed *secretum*, &c. was used as the counterseal to the deed; to prevent any possibility of imitating both sides of the seal. It was, also, very frequent for the religious in those days to mistake a *Roman* deity, lady, or emperor, for some *Christian* representation. The seal of an abbot of *Selby* is an unaccountable proof of their ignorance in these matters; which has for its reverse the impression of the head of *Honorius* the *Roman* emperor, with this very inscription round it, D. HONORIUS AUG. and yet his ignorance and superstition suffered him to mistake it for the head of *Christ*; and there is actually a rim put round it, on which he caused to be inscribed, in very bad *Latin*, also, CAPUD DOC CRISTUS EST. But the counter seal of *Roger* archbishop of *York* betrays the profound ignorance of those times beyond belief, that a person of his eminence, in church and state, should know no better than to mistake three heads, cut on a *Roman* gem, one young, another middle aged, and the other bald, which as the learned author of the manuscript observes, were probably designed for the bust of *Minerva*, which sometimes was represented with the heads of *Socrates* and *Plato*,* for the holy *Trinity*. This is evident by the inscription the piety of the prelate caused to be put round the verge, CAPUT NOSTR. TRINITAS EST. These two original impressions are in the duchy of *Lancaster*'s office amongst many more of the like kind, in that great magazine of antient deeds deposited in it. I shall only observe further what the same learned gentleman has told me, that all, or most of these seals, or counter-seals, with *Roman* gems that he has yet seen were of *York*, or the neighbourhood of it; where he supposes the greatest number of these antique curiosities were then found.

P. 62. *Sect.* 2. " I was led into the story and reading of this seal by that excellent an- " tiquary *Roger Gale*, esq;"

I am mightily pleased with the sagacity and ingenuity which Mr. *Gale* has shewn on

* See the seal at ~~the end of this appendix~~. The heads are judged to be of a *chimera*.

this

this explanation of your seal; however I shall venture to make an observation or two upon it: the legs are said to be *satyr's* legs, methinks then the feet should be so too, which they are not, for they have claws upon them. That which is called a flaming torch seems to me to be rather a branch of myrtle, the tree sacred to *Venus*. As to the F. C. I should read it *fascinum consecrat.*; for I think it will agree better with the representation which is designed to be as obscene and satyrical as possible. Dr. *Langwith.*

Ibid. Sect. 14.

The author of this work observes that the same *intaglio* is also represented in *Gorlaeus*, cut on an *onyx*. That author calls it *Bellerophon* and *Chimaera*; and adds that the story is thus represented on several *Corinthian* coins. *Abrahami Gorlaei dactyliothecae pars* 2. *n.* 2.

P. 63. *Sect.* 5. "The plate represents both."

In an additional plate of *Roman* analects found at *York* and *Aldburgh*, drawings of which have been sent me since the engraving of the former, and which I chuse to place here, are the prints of two more *intaglios* from Dr. *Langwith's* collection, marked 1 and 2 in the plate. They are cut on *Cornelians*, but by a very indifferent artist: the first represents a military figure hanging up a trophy on a laurel; the second a disarmed soldier or *gladiator* reposing himself upon the stump of a tree and seems to be in a posture of resigning his very helmet, which he holds in his left hand.

P. 66. *Sect.* 4. "*Et querimur*, &c."

Here has been a strange slip of the press, or my pen; the lines should run thus,

Et querimur, genus infelix, humana labare
Membra aevo, cum regna palam moriantur et urbes.

References to the additional plate.

Found at *York*, now in the *Ashmolean Museum.*

3. A *Roman* enamel chequered, found with certain urns.
4. A *Roman* lamp.
5. The leg of a *Tripos*, brass.
6. A *Roman* ring of jet found in digging clay for bricks, with urns.

In Dr. *Langwith's* collection.

7. A *Roman patera*, the same size with the original.
8. A curious *Roman* urn, the original eight inches high, the colour of the clay a yellowish brown. I have the fragments of another urn at *York*, entirely this shape and size, but the colour a blewish grey.
9. The flew of an *Hypocaustum*. This is exactly a *Roman* foot in height, the other parts in proportion. The doctor observes that the *Hypocaustum*, which this was designed for, must have been such a one as that described in the *Phil. trans. n.* 306.

10, 11. Two other draughts of urns; the doctor adds, that he has other urns of different shapes, sizes, and materials found in the *Roman* burying place at *York*, but these being the most curious he sent these draughts. He strongly suspects that there was a *Roman* pottery as well as a burying-place at or near where these urns, &c. are, and wishes it was carefully observed with that view.

In the doctor's *Museum* is likewise a round stone ball, which Mr. *Thoresby* calls an *harpastum p.* 563. a name which can by no means agree with it, for it is fitter to knock a man's brains out than to play withal. Also,

A brass ring found in the place above. It is big enough for an ordinary man's wrist, and was perhaps formerly put about that of a slave.

A *Roman* bead found in the same place. It is of a reddish colour and looks as if it were made of baked earth; but it is enamelled with yellow and green which looks like glass; the size of it is much the same with *n.* 24. in your plate of antiquities. Mr. *Thoresby* fancies these kinds of beads to be like the *adder's beads*; but I have several of these in my collection, and cannot see any resemblance. I cannot help taking notice that one of my *adder's-beads* has a juster title to that name than any that I ever saw or read of; and I should send you an account of it with pleasure, if it had been found any where about *York*; but as it was lately sent me from the north of *Scotland* by my brother, and so is foreign to your purpose, I shall say no more of it. Dr. *Langwith.*

Roman *curiosities found at* Aldburgh, *which there was not room to insert in the former plate, or have been discovered since.*

12, 13. Two bases of columns of the regular orders found on *Burrough-hill.*

14. A flew of an *hypocaustum* of the same size of the former found at *York.*

15. Another part of the *Roman* pavement on the hill.

16, 17. Two drawings backwards and forwards, of a most curious pensile *Roman* lamp of brass found about a year ago. It is drawn to the size; and is not to be matched with any in *Licetus* or * *Monfaucon's* large collection of them. The posture seems to be that of a young slave asleep, sitting on a *modius*, or bushel. To the rings about the shoulders was fastned the several chains, by which, when conjoined, it hung in *equilibrio*. To the seat betwixt the legs

* Licetus, *de lucernis antiquorum.*

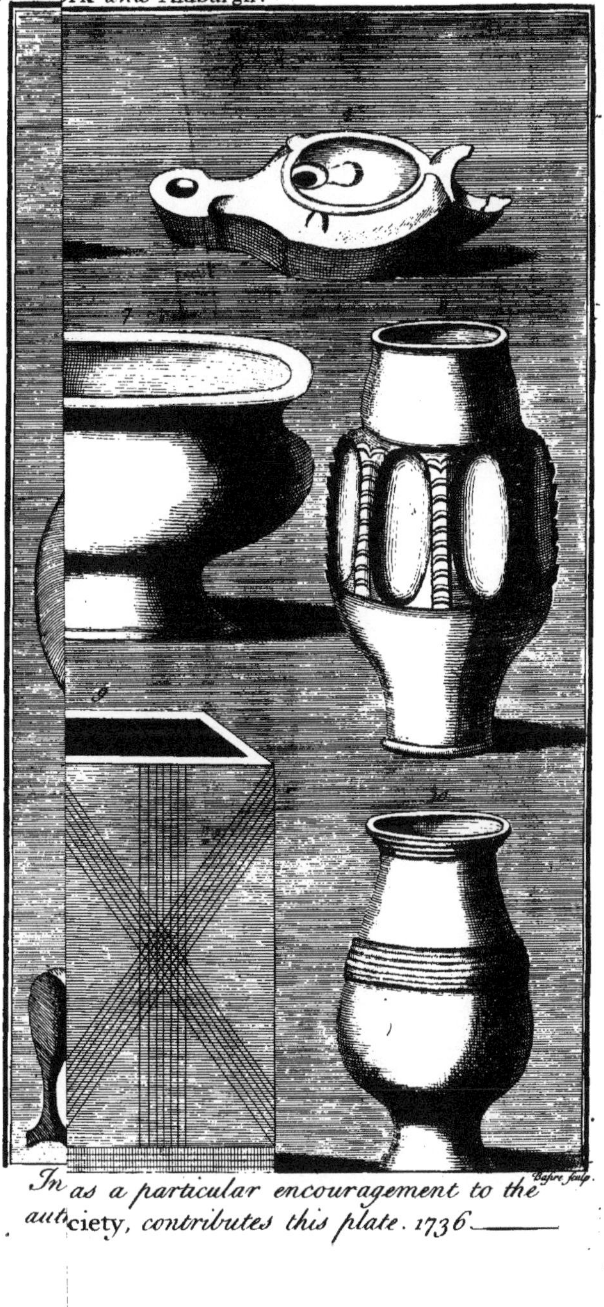

In as a particular encouragement to the aut ciety, contributes this plate. 1736

legs was alſo faſtened a proper inſtrument for trimming the lamp. This curioſity is, at preſent, in the poſſeſſion of *Andrew Wilkinſon* of *Burroughbridge* eſq;

P. 65. *Sect.* 7. "and put on the habit of a *jeſter*."

If the word in the original be *joculator*, often contracted to *juglator*, it ſignifies a player upon a cimbal; and ſtill termed in *France* **jougleurs**. The tranſlation of *Langtoft* of *Arthur*'s coronation, **Jogeleurs were there inouh**, &c. In *Doomeſday* in *Glouceſterſhire* is *joculator regis*. *Chaucer*'s tranſlation of the *Romance of the roſe*, **Flatours, minſtrels, and eke joglours**; and in his houſe of fame, 168, **Jogelours, magitiens and tragetours.** Mr. *Anſtis*.

P. 77. *Sect.* 4. and the note (*q*).

Lothbroch's, or rather *Lodbrog*'s, name, does not ſeem to me to have been leather-breech but rough-breeches; from the *Run. Dan.* **loden**, rough, and **brog**, breeches. I know you have pretty good authorities on your ſide, and ſo inſtead of entring into a diſpute upon the ſubject which would be a very merry one, I ſhall endeavour to compromiſe the matter, by ſuppoſing that the breeches were of leather, but with the hair, furr, or rough ſide, turned outwards. After all, ſince our northern anceſtors were pleaſed to give merry names, I don't ſee why we their poſterity ſhould not laugh at them.

I am ſorry you have taken ſo little notice of our towns-man *K. Guthram*, who ſeems to me to have been the king-paramont of *Denmark* when the application was made by *Beorn*, and is by *Verſtegan* called *Godern*: his quality muſt have been very conſiderable, or elſe *Alfred* would never have allotted him ſuch large dominions as thoſe of *Northumberland* and the *Eaſt-Angles*. Dr. *Langwith*.

P. 84. *Sect.* 3. "except a piece of ground called **Battle-flats** to this day."

Hear what an hiſtorian, near contemporary with theſe times, ſays of this field of battle, *Locus etiam belli pertranſeuntibus evidenter patet, ubi magna congeries oſſium mortuorum* uſque hodie jacet; *et indicium ruinae multiplicis utriuſque gentis exhibet.* Order. vitalis p. 500. A.

P. 85. *Sect.* 1. "for excepting our countryman *R. Hoveden* who was a layman."

A miſtake, *Roger Hoveden* was a ſecular prieſt and chaplain to *Henry* II. See *Benedictus abbas, p.* 93, 108. Mr. *Anſtis*.

P. 90. *Sect.* 2. "*—excepit et ingemuit*; *adde*

Quapropter multis ruinis quaſſata, ultima peſte, &c.

P. 91. *Sect.* 3. "or trouble the reader with any more proofs to make good my aſſer-"tion."

Since the printing off this ſheet Mr. *Anſtis* ſhewed me a very antient church hiſtorian, who flouriſhed about the year 1100; *Ordericus Vitalis Uticenſis*, a monk of St. *Euroles* in *Normandy*, as biſhop *Nicholſon* calls him. This man being near contemporary with this accident cannot excuſe his countryman *William* for his inhuman barbarity executed on this occaſion. What he ſays of it take in his own words,

Spatia centum milliarum caſtra ejus diffunduntur. Pleroſque gladio vindice ferit, aliorum latebras evertit, terras devaſtat, et domos cum rebus omnibus concremat. Nuſquam tanta crudelitate uſus eſt Gulielmus, *hic turpiter vitio ſuccubuit, dum iram ſuam regere contempſit, et reos innocuoſque pari animadverſione peremit. Juſſit enim, ira ſtimulante, ſegetibus et pecoribus cum vaſis et omni genere alimentorum repleri, et igne injecto penitus omnia ſimul comburi; et ſic omnem alimoniam per totam regionem trans* Humbram *pariter devaſtari. Unde ſequenti tempore tam gravis in* Anglia *late ſaevit penuria, et inermem et ſimplicem populum tanta famis involvit miſeria, ut* Chriſtianae *gentis utriuſque ſexus et omnis aetatis homines perirent pluſquam centum millia. In multis* Gulielmum *noſtra libenter extulit relatio; ſed in hoc, quod una juſtum et injuſtum tabidae famis lancea aeque transfixit, laudare non audeo. Nam, dum innocuos, infantes, juveneſque, vernantes, et floridos canicie ſenes fame periclitari video, miſericordia motus miſerabilis populi moeroribus et anxietatibus magis condoleo, quam frivolis adulationibus inutiliter ſtudeo. Praeterea indubitanter aſſero, quod impune non remittitur tam fatalis occiſio; ſummos enim et imos intuetur omnipotens judex, ac aeque omnium facta diſcutiet ac puniet diſtrictiſſimus vindex, et palam omnibus enodat Dei perpetua lex. lib.* 4. *p.* 514. *D. A.*

P. 95. *Sect.* 1. "— the houſe of *Jocenus*; which though ſtrongly fortified with conſider-"able towers."

Newburgh's words are — *domum* Jocei, *conſtructionis magnitudine et firmitate, arces non ignobiles aemulantem.* Gul. Neub. *c.* ix. *p.* 363. *ed.* Hearne.

P. 96. *Sect.* 4. "And after having taken a hundred hoſtages of the city, *&c.*"

Theſe hoſtages I find were kept at *Northampton*, and the citizens made account of ten marks to the king for their redemption. *Rot. Pipe* 5 *Ric.* I. 1194. So that they laid four years in cuſtody.

Ibid. not (*x*). add, and that he, *Richard Malbyſſe*, and *Walter de Carlton* with *Richard de Rukeney*, his eſquires, ſhould enjoy the king's peace to the king's return. *Rot. Pipe* 4 *Ric.* I.

P. 97. *Sect.* 2. "that the *Jews* at *York* carried on their old trade of uſury there is evi-"dent, *&c.*"

The grant to *William Latimer* here mentioned is loſt; but in a leiger-book, antiently belonging to *Fountain's-abbey*, are ſome of their mortgages on lands, in our neighbourhood, with the relaxations, which I here give.

Ex registro criginali de Fontibus *hoc tempore penes me. p.* 465. **Grenehamerton.**

" OMnibus hoc scriptum visuris vel audituris *Alanus* filius *Alexandri de Hamerton* salutem. " Noveritis quod ego vendidi monachis de *Fontibus* duas bovatas terre in territorio " de *Hamerton* cum tostis et croftis infra villam et extra; illas, scilicet, quas prius habu- " erunt de me ad terminum, pro decem marcis argenti quas pacaverunt pro me **Ursello** " **Judeo Ebor.** cui obligatus eram. Ita quod si ego, vel heredes mei, aut aliquis alius, cla- " mium vel calumpniam, gravamen vel molestiam, versus predictos monachos de predicta " terra cum pertinentiis unquam . . . . . licebit eisdem monachis cartam meam cum talliis " de predicta pecunia, quas habent penes se, prefato **Judeo** vel heredibus suis reddere; li- " cebit etiam eidem **Judeo** vel heredibus suis, sine aliqua contradictione, prefatam terram in " manu sua saisire, donec de tanta pecunia eisdem monachis fuerit satisfact.

" In cujus rei testimonium presenti scripto sigillum meum apposui.

" *Willielmo de Hamerton, Alano de Kyrkeby, Roberto de Muncketon, Christianis,* **Leone epis-** " **copo, Aaron et Jocein Judeis Ebor.** et multis aliis.

" OMnibus ad quos presens scriptum pervenerit **Ursellus** filius **Samsonis Judeus Ebor.** " salutem. Noveritis quod *Alanus* filius *Alexandri de Hamerton* et heredes sui sunt " quieti de omnibus debitis et demandis in quibus idem *Alanus* unquam michi tenebatur " ab initio seculi usque ad festum sancti *Michaelis* anno gratie **M.CC.** tricesimo octavo, " 1238.

" In cujus rei testimonium presens scriptum littera mea **Hebraica** consignavi.

" OMnibus ad quos presens scriptum pervenerit **Ursellus** filius **Samsonis Judeus Ebor.** ' salutem. Noveritis me quietum clamasse de me et heredibus meis in perpetuum " monachis de *Fontibus*, duas bovatas terre cum pertinentiis in territorio de *Hamerton*, " quas *Alanus* filius *Alex.* de *Hamerton* eis vendidit. Ita quod ego vel heredes mei versus " predictas duas bovatas nichil exigere possumus aliquo tempore occasione alicujus debiti " quod predictus *Alanus* unquam nobis debuit ab initio seculi usque ad finem seculi.

" In cujus rei testimonium presens scriptum littera mea **Ebrayca** consignavi.

The *Jews* made use of no seals where the figure was prominent or convex on the wax, as forbid by their laws; so I suppose this man, as well as others, signed his own name, or some other word, in *Hebrew*, as a testimony, instead of a seal. But Mr. *Anstis*, in his excellent manuscript treatise of antient seals, observes that they sometimes used signatures which made a concave impression, and brings this quotation out of *Maimonides* to prove it, *Annulum cujus signum est hominis figura, si ea sit gibbosa induere interdicitur,* obsignare *tamen eo licet; seu figura sit depressa licebit induere,* obsignare *eo non item; quippe sigillo impresso figura fiet gibbosa.* Maimonides *de idolat. c.* 3. *n.* 13.

P. 97. "*Anno* 1201. After *Christmas* that year, *viz. Jan.* 9. a great earthquake was " felt at *York* and parts adjacent. *R. Hoveden.*"

P. 101. *Sect.* 1. " lord *William Airmine.*"

William Airmine under *Ed.* II. was a clergyman, and chaplain to the king. *Rot. Pipe* 14 *Ed.* II. afterwards made bishop of ———

Ibid. Sect. 4. " was sentenced to be beheaded."

This judgment is enrolled in the king's bench in *Hillary-term*, 18 *Edward* II. *rot.* 34. Mr. *Anstis.*

Ibid. Sect. 5. " made prince of *Wales* and duke of *Aquitain.*"

Mistake, whereof see *Vincent* against *Brook p.* 110, 111.

Ibid. Sect. 6. " amongst whom was *John* earl of *Richmond.*"

This earl of *Richmond* was *John de Dreux*, duke of *Britain*; thus taken prisoner on the second of the ides of *October*; and kept by the *Scotch* for three years. Mr. *Anstis.*

P. 104. *Sect.* 4. This story of the penetrating bishop and given by a *grave divine.*"

I hope the *manes* of this industrious antiquary will not be disturbed for calling him so; all must own he had gravity and learning enough for a divine, though, as I have since been informed he was never initiated to that spiritual function.

P. 105. *Sect.* 4. It appears in *Cotton's* collections, published by *Prynn*, that in the reigns of *Edward* II. and *Edward* III. there were no less than twelve parliaments held at *York*, under these years 3, 8, 12, 12, 13, 15 of *Edward* II. and 1, 2, 6, 7, 9, 10 of *Edward* III.

P. 107. *Sect.* 2. " For he being of a deeper reach in politicks."

The earl marshal was too young for having then a great reach in politicks; it appears by *rot. parl.* 3 H. *m.* 4. that he was under age at his execution. Mr. *Anstis.*

Ibid. Sect. 3. " But his head, fixed upon a stake, stood long on the walls of the city."

It was placed on the bridge; for the writ in the *tower* for removing it has these words, *quod*

quod custodes civitatis Eborum *caput* Thomae *nuper* Mareschalli, *super pontem positum, latori praesentium liberent. Claus.* 6 Hen. IV. *m.* 2. *dat.* Aug. 6. Mr. *Anstis.*

P. 108. *Sect.* 8. "to sieze and confiscate the estate and effects of *Thomas* lord *Scrope* of *Massam.*"

The proceedings in this matter taken in the city follow in these words, from their registers,

"Die Mercurii viz. ultima die mensis *Julii* anno Domini millesimo quadringentesimo decimo quinto et regni regis *Henrici* quinti post conquestum *Angliae* anno tertio. Dominus *Richardus d' York* comes *Cantabrigiae* frater honorabilis ducis domini *Edwardi* ducis *Ebor.* necnon dominus *Henricus* dominus *Lestrop de Masham*, quem dictus dominus rex plus aliis diligebat, et cui contra quam plures sibi emulos gratitudinis maxime insignia exhibebat, et dominus *Thomas Gray de Heton* arrestati fuerunt apud castrum de *Portbestre* juxta *Southampton*, pro quibusdam proditionibus contra ligeantiam suam in destructionem personae dicti domini nostri regis nequiter praeexcogitatis, et per ipsos sponte voluntarie et sine vi publice confessatis, et post modum die Lunae, viz. quinto die mensis *Augusti* annis domini et regis praedictis, iidem domini *Richardus Henricus* et *Thomas* apud *Southampton*, causante proditione eorum fuerunt adjudicati morti et postea decollati, et caput dicti domini *Henrici Lestrop* positum super portam de **Mickellyth** *Ebor.* post cujus mortem, *Willielmus Alne* tunc major et escaetor infra civitatem et suburbia ac procinctum civitatis *Ebor.* quam plura bona ejusdem domini *Lestrop* in thesaurario ecclesiae cathedralis *Ebor.* existentia, ad usum domini nostri regis praedicti confiscari nitebatur et illuc veniens ibidem invenit *Johannem Waterton* armigerum et *Petrum de la Hay*, escaetores domini regis in comitatu *Ebor.* de bonis praedictis se intromittentes, et hoc comperto, dictus *Willielmus Alne* major et escaetor praedictus in presentia nonnullorum civium dictae civitatis eis inhibuit, ne quidquam attemptare praesumerent. Quod libertatem ejusdem civitatis cum ex concessione nonnullorum regum et confirmationum praefati domini nostri regis *Angliae* officium escaetoris in quibuscunque locis dictae civitatis suburbiisque et procinctu ejusdem, ubilibet ad majorem dictae civitatis qui pro tempore fuerit, pertinuit et debet pertinere. Et memoratus *Johannes Waterton* asseruit quod non erat intentionis suae libertatibus ipsius civitatis praejudicare in aliquo: imo hoc quod in hoc casu facere videbatur id fecit virtute quarundam literarum domini nostri regis sibi specialiter directarum quas ostendit ibidem et earum tenor sequitur et est talis: *Henricus* Dei gratia rex *Angliae* et *Franciae*, et dominus *Hiberniae* dilecto sibi *Johanni Waterton* armigero salutem. Sciatis quod quibusdam certis de causis nos ad praesens specialiter moventibus assignavimus vos ad omnia et singula bona et cattalla quae fuerunt *Henrici Lescrop* qui erga nos et ligeantiam nostram forisfecit, et quae occasione illa nobis pertinent et pertinere debent, ubicunque fuerint inventa, sine dilatione arrestandum, et ea sub hujusmodi arresto quousque aliud inde duxerimus demandandum salvo et secure custodiendum seu custodiri faciendum. Et ideo vobis praecipimus quod circa praemissa diligenter intendatis et ea faciatis et exequamini in forma praedicta. Damus autem universis et singulis viris majoribus ballivis constabulariis ministris ac aliis fidelibus et subditis nostris tam infra libertates quam extra tenore praesentium firmiter in mandatis quod vobis in executione praemissorum intendentes sint, consulentes et auxiliantes, prout decet. In cujus rei testimonium has literas nostras fieri fecimus patentes teste meipso apud *Southampton* sexto die *Augusti* anno regni nostri tertio. Subsequente vicesimo die dicti mensis *Augusti* annis Domini et regis supradictis dictus *Willielmus Alne* major et escaetor ad hospitale sancti *Leonardi* in civitate *Ebor.* accessit, et in praesentia domini *Galfridi Lescrop* militis necnon fratris *Johannis Danyell Gardiani* ejusdem hospitalis et aliorum fratrum, quandam longam cistam in infirmario ipsius hospitalis stantem, vinculis ferreis undique fortissime ligatam, cum nonnullis cartis et scripturis terras et tenementa dicti domini *Henrici Lescrop* in diversis *Angliae* partibus, in ipsa cista repositis, arrestant et ipsam cistam versus utrumque finem super foramina feraturarum sigillo officii majoratus dictae civitatis in cera rubra sigillant quadam sera pendente in medio ipsius cistae appensa. Sigillata signeto *Rogeri de Burton* clerici communis de mandato dicti majoris et escaetoris. Et contigit vicesimo tertio die dicti mensis *Augusti* annis Domini et regis supradictis, quod quaedam navis carcata cum nonnullis bonis praetensis dicti domini *Henrici Lescrop* apud **Seint Leonard Lendyngs** in aqua de *Use* arrestata fuit tanquam forisfactura domino regi debita, et facta inquisitione diligenti, tandem compertum erat, per dictum *Willielmum Alne* majorem *Thomam Santon Johannem Moreton* et alios aldermanos civitatis praedictae, quod omnia et singula bona quae fuerunt in ipsa navi fuerint liberata *Johannae* ducissae *Eboraci*, relictae dicti domini *Henrici Lescrop*, per *Johannem Waterton* supradictum, per quandam indenturam inter eos inde confectam: cujus tenor sequitur in haec verba. Teste endente facte a *Everwyk* le 23. d' *August* l'an du regne le roy *Henry* quint, puys le conquest d'*Angleterre* tierce, peutre *John de Warterton* esquier et par nostre treredoubte par le roy d'une parte et *Johanne* duchesse *Deverwyk* d'autre parte, temoigne que le dit *John* ad livere au dicte doure *Johanne* par garder, les parcelles suys escriptz à la voluntée du roy, en primes quatre pottes d'argent auntiens chescun contenant dymy galon. Item un petit hanap d'or, round chasée a le manier d'un gobelet. Item sept ha-

" naps d'argent aunciens, platt' ouesque deu covertes de mesme, la suyt. Item 24. disces " d'argent aunciens, nomès potageers de diverses formes. Item 12 salsar d'argent aunciens, " de diverses formes. Item 3 basyns d'argent, aunciens, de diverses formes. Item 3 ewers " d'argent, aunciens, des queux un saunz coverter. Item un entier lice, aunciens, de dymy " worsted de rouge noir, et blaunks, ouesque 3 curtyns et 3 costiers de mesme la suyt. " Item 2 quysshyns de sylk, aunciens. Item 6 quysshyns de dymy worsted de diverses co- " lors. Item 2 materas aunciens. Item 7 pair de Fustians Blanketts, 2 carpes, 2 pair de " hucheux. Item une ymage de nostre dame d'or coronnée, ouesque perillez. Item 2 pe- " titz hanaps d'argent, d'orrez, gravez, ouesque wrethes d'une suyte. Item une hanap " d'argent, dorrè, grave, ouesque une wrethe de tresoillez. Item une hanap d'argent " ouesque lez armes de sire *Lescrop*. Item une hanap d'argent d'orre, chased, en mannier " d'une estoile. Item 2 petitz ewers d'argent, d'orrez, l'une chased et l'autre pounched. " Item un payr basyns d'argent, d'orrez, pounched en la fountz lez armes *Lescrop*. Item " 6 chargeors d'argent, novell, oue lez armes *Lescrop*. Item 12 esquellez d'argent novelles, " oue mesmes lez armes. Item 12 pottageours et 12 salsers d'argent, novelles de mesme la " suyte, et armes. Item une hanap d'or, grave, en mannier de losenge en le pomell, un " petit perell. Item 1 petit ewer d'or par mesme, la hanap pounched, oue une wreth de di- " vers foilez, oue une knop de perell. En tesmoignance de quele chose, lez partiez superdictes " aycestes endenteurs ont myslors sealz, donne a *Euerwick* le an et jour suisdites et subsequente " decimo die *Octobris* anno praedicto, dictus *Willielmus Alne* major, de voluntate et praecepto " domini *Johannis* ducis *Bedford*, custodis *Angliae* sigillum officii sui supra foramina dictae cistae " ut praefertur, positum et dictam seram pendentem amovit et abstulit in praesentia magi- " strorum *Roberti Fitz Hugh*, magistri dicti hospitalis, *Willielmi Cawood* canonici *Ebor.* do- " mini *Galfridi Lescrop* cler', *Johannes Neusom* armigeri, *Richardi Beverlay*, jurisperiti, " *Rogeri Burton* praedicti notarii publici et aliorum."

P. 112. *Sect.* 1. " in the former was found the royal cap called **Abacot**,"

Spelman cites only the chronicle of this year for this word, which he says signifieth a royal cap ensigned with two crowns, which doubtless were those of *England* and *France*. I know not the etymology of this word. Mr. *Anstis*.

P. 112. *Sect.* 2. " The whole record is so singular that it must find a place in the " *appendix*."

The record is in these words,

Pro majore et civibus civitatis Ebor. *rex*. Ed. IV.

" REX omnibus ad quos, &c. salutem. Sciatis quod nos nedum decasuram et ruinam " civitatis nost. *Ebor*. ac grandia expensa deperdita et onera que dilecti nobis cives " ejusdem civitat. occasione guerrarum litium et discensionum in partibus borealibus hic nu- " per sustinuerunt quo pretextu ipsi in extremam paupertatis abissum penitus sunt ejecti, verum " etiam excessivam feodi firmam quam iidem cives pro civitate *predict.* ac si esset in statu " pristine felicitatis sue, nobis annuatim reddere tenentur, considerantes de gratia nost. speciali " ac in ipsor. civium paupertatis et indigentie relevamen nec non dictor. gravium onerum " suorum supportationem dedimus et concedimus ac per presentes damus et concedimus dile- " ctis nobis majori et civibus civitatis nost. predict. quadraginta libras percipiend. annuatim " eisdem majori et civibus durante termino duodecim annor. de subsidio trium solidor. de " dolio et duodecim denariorum de libra in portu de villa nost. de *Kingeston super Hull* per- " venient. et crescent. per manus custumariorum sive collectorum ejusdem subsidii pro temp. " existent. ad festa S. *Michael.* et *Pasche* per equales portiones, aliquo statuto actu ordinatione " permissione seu restrictione in contrarium fact. et ordinat. seu provis. aut aliqua alia re cau- " sa vel materia quacunque in aliquo non obstante.

" In cujus, &c.

" Teste rege apud *Ebor.* x. die Junii.

Per ipsum regem et de data predict. &c.

" Et mandatum est customariis sive collectoribus subsidii trium solid. de dolio et duode- " cim denarior. de libra in portu ville nost. de *Kingeston super Hull* qui nunc sunt et qui pro " tempore erunt quod eisdem majori et civibus dilectis quadraginta libras durante termino pre- " dict. ad festa predicta de subsidio predict. in portu predict. pervenient. de tempore in tem- " pus solvant juxta tenorem litt. nost. predict. recipientes a prefatis majore et civibus litte- " ras suas acquietientie que pro nobis sufficientes fuerint in hac parte (*a*).

Teste ut supra.

P. 122. *Sect.* 1. In this proclamation *Thomas* earl of *Surrey* is said to be slain in the battle of *Bosworth*; but it is evidently a mistake, as even appears by *p.* 126. hereafter. Mr. *Anstis*.

(*a*) 1464. *Pat.* 4. Ed. IV. *p.* 3. *m.* 9.

P. 127. *Sect.* 1. "And so departed on her journey."

The ceremonial of attending this lady in her progress and her reception into the city of *York*, is better recorded by a, then, officer at arms; from whose original record of it Mr. *Anstis* favoured me with the following transcript;

"The fifteenth day of the said monneth departed the quene fro *Pountfret* in faire company, "as others times before, the mayr, aldermen, bourges, and habitanns in the conveying of "her and from thens she want to dynner to *Dadcaster*.

"And att the partyng after dynner cam to hyr my lord *Latymer* and my lady his wiffe "vary well appoynted, companyed of many gentylmen, and gentylwomen to the nombre "of L. horses hys folke arayed liveray.

"And out of the said *Dadcaster* cam the two shriffs of the city of *Yorke*, wellcommyng "the quene in ther fraunchyses in company of many officers of the towne and oth bourges "and habitanns well honestly apoynted and horst to the nombre of iiii^{xx} horsys. And two "mille fro *Dadcaster* cam to her the lord *Scroupp* of *Bolton*, and the lord *Scroopp* of *Upsall* "his sone, in company of many gentylmen well appoyntyd, and ther folke in suchwise to "the nombre of xx. horsys of ther liverays, and well horsys.

"And fore mille from the sayd towne met the sayd quene the lady *Conyars* nobly drest, "and in hyr company many gentyllwomen, and others honnestly appoynted to the nombre "of 60. horsys.

"At two mille fro the sayd cite cam toward the said quene my lord the earle of *Northumberland* well horst opon a fayr corser, with a forr cloth to the grounde of cramsyn velvett "all borded of orsavery; his armes vary rich in many places, uppon his saddle and harnays, "his sterrops gylt.

"Hymselfe arayd of a gowne of the said cramsyn; the opnyngs of the slyves and the "collar of grett bordeux of stones, hys boutts of velvett black, his spours gylt and in many "places maid gambads plaisants for to see; ny to him two fotemen ther jackets of that sam as "before to hys devyses. And before hee him had 3 hunsmen mounted upon fayr horsys there "short jackets of orsavery and harnays of the said horsys of that same rychly drest and "after them rode the maister of hys horse arayd of hys liveray of velvyt monted upon a gentyl horse, and campanes of silver and gylt, and held in his haund annother fayr corser of "all thyngs, his harnays apoynted as before is sayd.

"Wyth hym in hys company was many noble knyghts, that is to weytt, sur *John Haystyngs*, sur *John Penyntbon*, sur *Lancelot Thirlekeld*, sur *Thomas Curwen*, sur *John Normanville*, "sur *Robert* of *Aske*, all knyghts arayd of hys sayd liveray of velvet with some goldsmyth "warke; grett chaynnes and war well mounted, some of ther horse harnes full of campanes, sum of gold and silver, and the others of sylver.

"Also ther was hys officer of armes, named *Northumberland-Herault*, aray'd of his sayd "liveray of velvet berring hys cotte sens the mettyng tyll to hys departyng thorough all "the entryng and yssue of good towns and citez.

"Also others gentylmen in such wys aray'd of hys said liveray, sum in velvet, others in "damaske and chamlett, the others of cloth, well monted to the nombre of three hundreth "horsys.

"And a mylle owte of the said cite the said quene apoynted hyr in hyr horse letere rychly "besene, hyr ladys and gentelwomen right freshly aray'd.

"Also all the nobles, lordes, knyghts and gentylmen and others of her company apoynted "in so good manere and so ryche that a goodly sight it was for to beholde.

"And at the entryng of the soubarbes was the iiii. orders mendiens in processyon before "hyr.

"And in the stat as before in fayr order she entred in the sayd cyte, trompetts, mynstrells, sakebowtts and high wods retentysynge that was fayr for here cotts of armes open, ryches masses in haund, horsys of desyr, and noble herts delibered.

"And within the sayd cite ny to the gatt was my lord the mayr syr *John Guillot* knyght "compenyd of the aldermen all on horseback and honnestly arayed in gownys of scarlatte, "the sayd mayr of sattin cramsyn, goods channes on ther necks, and resayved the said quene "varey mykely, and after they rod before hyr to the mother church the sayd mayr beryng hys masse.

"And ny to them wer within the streytts on fowte and in good order the honnests bourges and habitanns of the sayd cite honnestly besene in ther best aray, all the wyndowes so "full of nobles ladyes gentylwomen damsells bourgesys and others in so grett multitude "that it was a fayr sight for to see.

"Thus contynued the space of too houres, or she wer conveyed to the mother church, "wher was the reverends fathers in God my lord the archbyschop of *Yorke*, the byschop "of *Durbam*, the abbot saunt *Marie* and the sonsfringham in pontificall, with the college togeder revested of riches coppes. And ny to the founte was notably appynted the place "wher the crosse was, the wich shee kissed, and after to the hert of the church she wente "to make hyr offrynge.

"And that doon she was conveyd thorough the said company to the pallays, wher she "was lodged, and so every men hym owtdrew to hys lodgyngs them to rasresh; bot it was "grett melodie for to here the bells rynge thorough the cite.

"And the next day that was the *Sonday* the xvi[th] day of the said monneth remayn'd "the said quene in the said towne of *Yorke*, and at ten of the clock she was convey'd to the "church with the said archbyschop, byschops of *Durham*, *Morrey* and *Norwysche* the pre-"lats before and others honorable folks of the churche, my lord of *Surrey*, the lord hyr "chammerlayn, and others nobles knyghts, squires, gentylmen the said mayre, aldermen, and "scheryffs to the nomber of two hundreth and more. With hyr wer ladys and gentylwomen "of hyr company, and straungers to the nombre of xl, and so was she convey'd to the "church, it was a fair syght for to see the company so rychly apoynted.

"Thus noble she was convey'd into her travers, wher befor her was an auter drest of "many ryches and noble jewels, and an hygh awter in likewyse. And hard masse in "meane time that the said archbyschop maid hymselse redy.

"After the said masse begonne the processyon generall varey fayr, wher was fyrst the cros-"sys and the colleges vested of varey rych copys, and after them came the souffringham "subdyacon, the abbot of saunte *Marye* dyacon, the crosse borne before the archbyschop, "with hym the byschop of *Durham*, all in pontificall.

"After them cam the lords that followeth rychly apoynted, the lord *Willeby*, lord *Scroupp*, "and hys son the lord *Latimer*, the lord *Hastyngs*, therle of *Kent*, and hys son the lord *Straunge*, "therle of *Northumberland*, the byschop of *Morrey*, and of *Norwyche*, the lord maire, therle "of *Surrey*, the lord chamberlain, the officers of armes and the sergents.

"And after cam the quene rychly aray'd in a gowne of cloth of gold, a rych coller of "precyouses stones and a gyrdle wrought of fin gold hauntyng doo to the gerth, and the "countesse of *Surry* bare her trayne, a gentleman huyscher helping after hyr the ladys and "gentylwomen as before varey rychly drest in goodly gownys, gretts collers, gretts chaynnes, "gyrdles of gold and others richesses.

"And after hyr followed the nobles, knyghts, gentylmen and squires in fayr aray, honnestly "apoynted, having grett chaynnes upon them, and the said church was so full of honneste per-"sonnes, ladyes and gentylwomen of the said towne and many other people in so grett nom-"ber, that impossible schould be for to be nombred; but so good ordre there was, that none "cry ne noise was maid.

"The erle of *Northumberland* was arayed in a varey ryche gowne of cloth of gold, hys "thre gentylmen of honor drest with longs jackets full of orsavery, varey rychly wrought "with his devyses, like wys hys folks.

"After the processyon doon begonne the hygh masse by the said archbyschop, the which "was stalled as the custome is to do in company of hym the said abbot and souffringhan "with others honnorable personnes of the churche, and sange the servyce of the said masse, "the chappelle of my said lord of *Northumberland* much solempnelly.

"And at the hour of the offertory was the said quene brought to the offrynge in the pre-"sence of the said prelats, lords, and others knyghts, squyers and gentylmen, &c. whome "sche offred she retourned ageyn, eidy man went ageyn in hys place as before, and to hyr "gaffe hyr offryng the said erle of *Surrey*.

"The masse doon the quene was by the said company precedente in fayr aray and or-"dre brought agayn to the pallays, and within the grett chammer was presented before hyr "my lady the countesse of *Northumberland*, well accompany'd of many knyghts and gen-"tylmen and ladyes and gentylwomen, the quene kissing hyr in the welcommynge, and "as soon as sche was com in hyr chammer she begonne to dynne, trompetts and other instrue-"ments rang to the auncyenne manere lastyng the said dynner.

"The said archbyschop holdyng open hows in makyng good cher to all commyng toge-"der; my lord the mayre the scheryffs so, as raporte to me them that was ther persons.

"The xvii[th] day of the said monneth the said quene departed frō the said cite of *York* in "varey fayr company and ordre rychly apoynted, the said archbishop and byschops before-"said, the lord the mayr, scheryffs and the aldermen, the streytts, and the wyndows so full "of people that it was a fair thynge for to see.

"And without the said cite the said lord mayre and his company take licence, and fur-"thermore dyd the lords the byschop of *Norwych* of *Kent* of *Straunge Hastyngs* and *Willeby* "and many others mor knyghts gentylmen went with them ageyn.

"And after this doon, she took hyr way to *Newbrough* the priore, to the which place she "was receyved by the said prior and religyous honnestly revested with the crosse at the gatt "of the church.

Ibid. Sect. 6. "Sir *Stephen Hamilton* read sir *Stephen Hamerton*.

P. 137. *Sect.* 3. "in another purse thirty nine single pennys being just the age of the king" The number of his own years being thirty nine; which was the custom in some later centuries. Mr. *Anstis*.

P. 140. *Sect.* 10. "that hated the lord *Strafford* and even the king himself, as their fu-"ture conduct sufficiently attested."

I ask

I ask pardon of the memory of some of these noblemen for this unwary assertion, which page one hundred and fifty of this very book contradicts. The earl of *Hertford*, not *Hereford*, as in the note *(f)*, created marquis *June* 3, 1641, came over heartily to the *royal cause*. As did also the earl of *Salisbury*, the lords *Pawlet*, *Savile*, *Dunsmore* and *Leigh*, who were of the number of these commissioners; for when they saw what bent the puritans were then taking, they forsook their cause, and some of them with their own blood sealed their determined loyalty to their injured sovereign.

P. 140. *Sect.* 15. " From the 24th of *September* to the 18th of *October* following, did the " king, *&c.*"

In this month of *October* the king held a chapter of the garter at *York*, wherein the earl of *Strafford* was elected a companion. The entry of this is in the register of the *garter*, wherein the tragical reason for that unfortunate nobleman's being never installed, is put down in such strong terms, that I chuse to give it *verbatim* from the copy sent me by Mr. *Anstis*.

Out of the REGISTER of the GARTER.

Anno MDCXL. *cum rebelles Scoti Angliæ finibus incubarent, beatissimae memoriae princeps* Carolus *primus, convocato* Eboraci *magno procerum concilio, mense* Octobris *virum illustrissimum* Thomam *comitem* Straffordiae, *vicecomitem* Wentworthiae, *et* Hiberniae *pro-regem, nobilissimi ordinis comitem elegit, nunquam vero inaugurabatur, quippe qui paulo post a parliamento tanquam majestatis pro tribunali postulatus, et quanquam magna animi praesentia inimicorum articulos et criminationes quam facillime dilueret, ipse rex sese interponeret, et innocentiam ejus (quantum ad summa articulorum capita) judiciorum poena liberare conaretur, perduellionis nihilominus damnatus, et apud turris* Londinensis *collem* Maii 12° 1641. *capite plexus est. Sic cecidit prudentissimus rei civilis administrator; regiaeque causae, ecclesiastici ordinis, patriaeque libertatis, veluti victima occubuit, illud vero sanguinis profluvium, quod ex illius venis incisis effluebat, permultos exinde annos sistere non potuerunt.*

P. 144. *Sect.* 3. " where the day following the king kept the festival of St. *George* in " great state."

The register of the *Garter* saith *April* 20, 1642. when the companions present at the election were the prince of *Wales*, the elector *Palatine* and the earl of *Lindsey*; at which said chapter prince *Rupert* was likewise elected. I send a copy of the entry. Mr. *Anstis*.

From the REGISTER of the GARTER.

Sub finem anni 1641. *rex factiosis civium* Londinensium *tumultibus, a curia albae basilicae pulsus, gradatim versus* Eboracum *tendit ubi* Aprilis 20, 1642. *capitulum celebravit supremus praesentibus bonoratissimis DD. illustrissimo* Walliae *principe, electore* Palatino *duce* Richmondio, *et comite* Lindseio *in boc capitulo supremus, commilitonum numero requisito ad capitulum complendum insuper babito filium suum secundum illustrissimum principem* Jacobum *ducem* Eboracensem *et nepotem principem* Rupertum *electorem ad* Rhenum *nobilissimi ordinis commilitones elegit, iisque sic in ordinem cooptatis indulsit, ut titulo, bonore et superioritate pro electionis tempore fruerentur, quamvis pro solenni more inaugurari non possint, quum* Windesora *bisce solennitatibus peragendis sacrata, sub rebellium ditione teneretur, cum bac tamen exceptionis clausula, ut quam primum per tumultus liceret, ambo* Windesorae *inaugurarentur.*

The inscription on the plate for *James* duke of *York* in the second stall of the chapel at *Windsor* is thus, after his titles,

——— *eleu à* YORK, *le vingtiesme jour d'*Avril 1642; *et à cause de la rebellion suivante ne fut pas installé au chateau de* Windesore *jusq'au quinziesme jour d'*Avril 1661.

P. 179. *Sect.* 2. " *Papinian*, the judge advocate."

Rather, supream judge of all the *Roman* empire.

P. 180. *Sect.* 1. " was held first *by* the bishop"

For *by*, read *before*; and so in the next line.

P. 180. *Sect.* 6. " Copies of all such grants, *&c.* may be seen in the *appendix.*"

Ex registro originali Fontinensis *abbatiae olim contingenti.* Eborum, *p.* 201.

1. " Sciant omnes tam presentes quam futuri quod ego *Walterus* parsona de *Hedbelingflet* " dedi et concessi et hac presenti carta mea confirmavi *Gerardo Saunter* civi *Ebor.* totam ter- " ram meam in *Eboraco* que jacet inter *molendinum de Castello* et inter terram monachorum de " *fontibus* in parochia sancte *Marie de Castello.* Habendam et tenendam, &c.

" Hiis testibus *Rad. Nuvel*, *Willielmo Fairfaix*, *Nicholao de Buggbethorp*, *Willielmo Otewi*, " *Reginaldo de Wardbil*, *Phil.* filio *Baldew*, *Waltero* filio *Widonis*, *Waltero de Beluaco*, " *Matheo Taillur*, *Rogero de Alwarthorp*, *Thoma Albo*, *Willielmo de Elethost*, et multis " aliis.

2. " Sciant omnes presentes et futuri, quod ego *Willielmus Gerold* dedi et concessi et hac " carta mea presenti confirmavi *Waltero* filio *Tankardi* illas duas terras in Fishergate quas " pater suus tenuit, scilicet unam terram juxta Fosse et juxta ecclesiam sancti Stephani et " aliam

" aliam terram propinquiorem terre *Roberti Baſſet* in eodem vico ſibi et heredibus ſuis.
" Tenend. *&c.*

" Hii ſunt teſtes *Will. de Stutevill*, *Rog. Baduent*, *Rob. Foreſt*, *Henricus de Knareſburg*, " *Rad. de Boſco*, *Johannes de Hameleſt*, *Rob. de Apeltun*, *Thomas Palmer*, *Nicol.* frater " ejus, *Rad. Damaiſele*, *Johannes* filius *Gunneware*, *Steph. Tinctor*, *Arnaldus Tinctor*, " *Will. Harald*, *Will. Frainſer*, *Johannes Ruffus*, *Rob. Fab. Thom. le Wairt.* et plures.

4. " Univerſis ſancte eccleſie filiis preſentibus et futuris *Franco de Beluaco* ſalut. Sciatis " me dediſſe et hac mea carta confirmaſſe Deo et monachis eccleſie ſancte *Marie de Font.* totam " terram meam in *Neſſegate* quam tenui de *Roberto Lepuber* ſolutam, quietam, *&c.*

" Hii ſunt teſtes qui preſentes fuerunt, quam eccleſiam *de Font.* de terra illa ſaiſiam, ſcilicet, " *Thomas* decanus *Ebor. Helias* preſbyter, *Thomas* parſona eccl. S. *Michaelis Ebor. Rog.* " *Diaconus*, *Rob. de Camare*, *Guillielmus de bona villa*, *Alexand. de Lund*, *Ranul. de Ca-* " *ſtello*, et *Mainard* filius ejus, *Guillielmus Pya*, *Gualt.* fil. *Yſaac*, *Rog. de Morbi*, *Sym.* " *Dorna*, *Paulinus Hubbarat*, *Durand Andenel*, *Sym. Owein*, *Philippus Warinerus*, *Sym.* " *Cocus*, *Ulkil* et *Orm.*

5. " Hii preſentes et teſtes fuerunt, ubi *Rob. Puber* vendidit monachis de *Font.* terram ſuam " de *Neſſegata* quam Franco habuit in vadium, **Thomas decanus** qui plegius fuit eandem " terram warrantizare per unum annum et diem, *Stephanus* et *Hugo* clerici **Conſtabular.** " **Ebor.** *Will. de Bonevill*, &c.

8. " Sciant preſentes &c. Quod ego *Awreda* que fui uxor *Walteri de Acum* ex aſſenſu et " conſenſu *Rob.* filii *Symeonis* et **cuſtodum pontis de Uſa** dedi conceſſi &c. totam terram meam " in **Parva Bretegate** &c.

11. " Omnibus ſancte eccleſie filiis preſentibus et futuris *Agnes* quondam filia *Nigelli le* " *Huſer* de *Ebor.* ſalutem. Sciatis me in mea viduitate et ligia poteſtate mea dediſſe con- " ceſſiſſe et preſenti carta mea confirmaſſe Deo et monachis ſancte *Marie de Fontibus* totam " terram meam cum pertin. in parva **Bretegata,** quam *Nigell.* pater meus emit de *Awere-* " *da* que fuit uxor *Walt. de Acum.* Tenend. &c.

" Hiis teſtibus *Gileberto* rectore eccl. *Omn. Sanctor.* in **Huſegate,** *Hugone de Selebi* tunc ma- " jore, *Johanne Warthill*, *Henr. de Sexdecim vallibus*, *Rob. de Claravall*, *Thoma le Grant*, " *Reinero Sciſſore*, *Helia Flur*, *Rogero de Seſcevaus* civibus *Ebor.* et aliis.

13. " Ad aliam cartam de eadem terra et domo in **Parva Bretegate** dat. anno gratie " **MCC,** quinquageſimo primo, hii ſunt teſtes,

" **Johannes tunc major Eboraci,** *Andreas* frater ſuus, *Paulinus le mercer*, *Ricardus* ad " pontem, *Robertus de Clyſton* et alii. 1251.

14. " Memorand. Quod cum nuper abbas de *Fontibus* tuliſſet breve domini regis, deceſ- " ſavit per brevium coram *J. Stonor* et ſoc. ſuis juſtic. dom. regis de *Banco* apud *Weſtm.* ter- " mino Hillar. anno r. r. *Ed.* tertii poſt conqueſt. *Angl.* xxii°. verſus *Willielmum de Schireburn* " et petiit verſus eum unum meſſ. cum pertin. in *Eboraco*, videlicet, unum in **Joubret-** " **gate**, &c.

16. " Sciant preſentes et futuri quod hoc eſt conventio facta inter abbatem et conventum de " *Fontibus* ex una parte et *Ricardum Springald* de *Ebor.* ex altera, ſcilicet, quod idem abbas " et conventus dederunt et preſenti ſcripto conceſſerunt predicto *Ricardo* et heredibus ſuis " domum noſt. in *Eboraco*, que vocatur **Salthuſes,** juxta terram *Johannis de Birkin* in parochia " ſancte *Marie* ad portam *Caſtri.* Tenend. &c.

" Hiis teſt. **Hugone de Seleby tunc majore civit. Ebor.** *Johanne de Warthill*, *Adam Flur.* " *Paul. de Mubray*, *Nich. Winemer*, *Thoma le Grant*, *Yberto le ſaint*, et aliis.

17. " Hec carta chirographata teſtatur quod *Johannes Blundus* capellanus *Ebor.* dedit mo- " nachis de *Fontibus* terram ſuam **Hannaldam** in **Patric pol** que jacet inter terram *Henrici* " ſervientis domino archiepiſcop. et terram que fuit *Thome de Languath*, ſub hac forma, &c.

" Hiis teſtibus, *G.* decano, *R.* precentore, *J.* cancellario, *J.* ſubdecano, *Bernardo de* " *Sancto Odomaro*, canonicis *Ebor.* **Hugone de Seleby tunc majore Ebor.** *Thoma le* " *Graunt* **preposito** ejuſdem ville, *Henrico et Rogero de Sexdecim vallibus*, et aliis pluri- " bus.

N. B. Galf. de Norwich decanus *Ebor.* erat *an.* 1235. *Robertus* precentor. *Johannes Blund* cancellarius, *Johannes Romanus* ſubdecanus eodem tempore. Vide catal. decanorum, &c.

19. " Omnibus Chriſti fidelibus ad quos preſens ſcriptum pervenerit, *Alex.* abbas de *Fon-* " *tibus* et ejuſdem loci conventus ſalutem in Domino ſempiternam. Noverit univerſi- " tas veſtra nos conceſſiſſe dediſſe et preſenti carta noſt. confirmaſſe *Johanni le Kaudruner* " et hered. ſuis meſſuagium &c. in vico de *Petergate*, &c.

" His teſt. **Johanni de Seleby tunc maiore Ebor. Ivone de Uſegate, Simone le Graunte,** " **Johanne de Cunningeſton tunc ballivis Ebor.** *Henr. Clutepot*, *Ricardo Hornepot*, *Wil-* " *lielmo de Beverlay*, *Alex. le Waunter*, *Rob. de Craven*, *Willielmo de Haukeſwell*, et aliis.

" Dat. apud *Fontes* die *Martis* prox. poſt feſt. ſancti *Wilfridi* anno domini **MCC.** ſexag. " quarto. 1264.

24. Con-

24. Conventio inter *Stephanum* abbatem et conventum de *Fontibus* ex una parte et *Ricar-*
“ *dum Moserne*, burgensem *Eboraci* ex altera, de quadam terra in *Ebor.* in vico illo qui vocat.
“ *Staingate*, illam scilicet terram que jacet inter feodum *Rogeri de Mubray* ex una parte et
“ feodum *Ricardi de Percy* ex altera. Tenend. &c.

“ Hiis test. **Nicholao Orger tunc majore Eborum,** *Henrico* de sexdecim vallibus, *Thom.*
“ fil. *Jol.* *Johanne de Seleby*, *Andrea* fratre suo, *Willielmo* fratre ejusdem *Andreae*,
“ et aliis.

29. “ Omnibus hoc script. visuris &c. *Hugo*, filius *Ymberti le Saynter*, salutem. Dedit &c.
“ Deo et monachis ecclesie sancte *Marie* de *Fontibus* totam terram cum edificiis in ea con-
“ structis que jacet inter ecclesiam sancti *Martini* de *Eborato* et domum **Aaron Judei**, &c.
“ Hanc autem resignationem et quietam clamationem feci predict. monachis coram do-
“ mino **Hugone de Seleby** tunc **majore**, et aliis civibus et **prepositis** *Ebor.*

“ Hiis test. *Hugone de Seleby* tunc majore *Eboraci*, *Johanne de Wardbil*, *Henrico* de sexde-
“ cim vallibus, *Alexandro del Hil*, *Martino de Nortfolke*, *Willielmo Orger*, *Paulino de*
“ *Mubray*, *Nich. Wynemer*, *Thoma le Graunt* et multis aliis.

35. Charta *Walteri Bustard* concess. monast. de *Fontibus* de terra et tenementis, &c. in
“ vico de *Mickelgate* et de *Scheldergate*, que jacet inter *domum lapideam* que fuit *Rogeri* de
“ *Knaresburg* et terram *Roberti Copin*, &c.

“ Hiis testibus **Hugone de Seleby** tunc **majore** *Ebor.* **Willielmo Fairfax, Johanne de**
“ **Warthill, Henrico de sexdecim vallibus, Martino de Norfouke, Willielmo de Brin-**
“ **kelan** tunc **ballivis** *Ebor.* *Thoma* fil. *Alani*, *Alano capellano de Bouton*, *Johanne Albo*,
“ capellano, *Rad. de Wysebeck*, et multis aliis.

38. “ *Rog. de Molbray* vic. et omnibus civibus *Eboraci* *Francis* et *Anglis* clericis et laicis
“ salutem. Sciatis quod quando *Galfridus de Rotomago* viam sancti *Jacobi* incepit, ego dedi
“ et concessi *Adelitie Caren* uxori sue et heredibus suis totam domum suam et terram in
“ feodo et hereditate. Tenend. de me heredibus meis et eodem servitio quo ipse *Gaufridus*
“ tenuit, scilicet, xii. *d.* reddendo per annum, quare deprecor omnes amicos meos quod
“ ipsum pro amore meo adjuvent et manu teneant ad hanc domum et terram tenendam,
“ quia non erit michi amicus qui ei inde contumeliam fecerit.

“ Test. *Nigel.* fil. meo, *Olivar. de Buc'*, *Bertram Hagett*, *Rog. de Flamevill*, *Rog. de*
“ *Cund.* *Rad. Bel'.* *Rog. de Cun.* et *Baldwino* fratre suo.

45. “ Ad hanc chartam hii testes appositi sunt, domino *Waltero de Stokes* tunc majore
“ *Ebor.* *Johanne* filio *Johannis le Especer*, *Johanne de Sutton*, *Johanne de Coningston*, tunc ba-
“ livis *Ebor.* &c.

50. “ Ad alteram chartam hii sunt testes, **Johanne apotecario tunc majore Ebor. civita-**
“ **tis**, *Radulfo de Jarum*, *Willielmo Sleght*, *Alano* filio ejus, *Johanne de Schupton*, *Johanne*
“ *de Seszevaus* clerico, *Johanne de Thornton* clerico, et aliis.

“ Dat. *Ebor.* in crast. nativitatis sancti *Johannis Baptiste* anno regni regis *Edwardi*, filii re-
“ gis *Henrici*, vicesimo nono, 1301.

51. “ Ad proximam chartam ejusdem tenoris et datae, testes iidem sunt appositi; nisi quod
“ **Johannes Apotecarius** supra dictus, illic vocatus est **Johannes le Spicer**, tunc major ci-
“ vitatis *Ebor.* *Vide p.* 359, *et notam* (d) *in eadem pagina.*

Ex registro antiquo penes Brian. Fairfax *armig. familiae suae perantiquae contingenti. p.* 99. *dorso.*

“ Omnibus Christi fidelibus presens scriptum visuris inspecturis vel audituris *Thomas Ro-*
“ *mundus* de *Ebor.* clericus salutem in Domino. Noveritis me concessisse remisisse et pre-
“ senti scripto chirographato de me et heredibus meis in perpetuum quietum clamasse
“ *Thome de Overton* auri fabro et civi *Ebor* et heredibus suis, pro sex marcis sterlingorum,
“ quas michi dedit per manus, totum jus et clamium quod habui vel habere potui in
“ illa terra in vico sancti *Andree* que quondam fuit gardinum *Hugonis Pusetb'* et *Henrici* fi-
“ lii sui avunculi mei, que jacet in latitudine inter terram ejusdem *Hugonis Pusetb'* ex una
“ parte et terram *Serlon' Molendinar.* ex altera, et in longitudine a vico sancti *Andree* usque
“ ad terram dicti *Thom. de Overton* quam emit de *Roberto Wlsy.* Habend. et tenend. &c.

“ Hiis testibus *Johanne de Seleby*, *Andrea de Seleby* fratre ejus, *Richardo de Grusty*, *Roberto*
“ *de Longocampo* tunc rectore eccl. de *Foston*, *Roberto Verdenell de Marisco*, *Roberto*
“ *Spery*, **Adam de Cerf tunc majore Ebor. Willielmo de Holteby, Johanne Spery,**
“ **Phone de Usegate tunc ballivis ejusdem,** *Alano Romund'*, *Johanne de Malton*, ca-
“ pellano, et aliis.

P. 181. *Sect.* 2. "Which sword, by the express words of the charter, or any other sword "they pleased was to be born before them with the *point erected*, except in the king's pre-"sence within the precincts of their liberties *in perpetuum*."

When that great officer, the lord president of the north, resided and kept his court at *York*, he insisted upon an abatement of this ensign of authority in his presence. The lord-mayor refused and the cause was tried in the earl marshals court, when the following judgment was given upon it and entered,

"WHEREAS the lord *Sheffield* president of his majesty's councel established in the "north, being his majesty's lieutenant of his highness county of *York* and city "of *York*, hath challenged and demanded as a thing of right and duty appertaining to "his lieutenancy, that the sword carried before the lord-mayor of the city of *York* for the "time being should be delivered up to him by the lord-mayor at his coming into the said "city, and should not be carried with the *point upwards but abased* at all times and in all "places in his presence, whereupon difference and controversy arising, a petition by con-"sent of both parties was preferred by the lord-mayor, aldermen, sheriffs and commona-"lity of the said city unto his majesty, for the hearing and determining of the same, which "by his highness was referred for the ending thereof unto us the lords commissioners for "causes determinable by the earle marshal court. And whereas we the said commissioners "by virtue of his majesty's said reference about the beginning of *July* last past having "caused to come before us in the counsel chamber at *White-hall*, both the said lord *Sheffield* "himself and those that followed the cause on the part and behalfe of the said city, en-"tred into the hearing of the said cause and heard at large the allegations on both sides, "amongst which there were read unto us by those which followed the matter for the city "certain words of a charter granted unto them by king *Richard* the second, as followeth, "*Et insuper concessimus et hac carta nostra confirmavimus nobis et hered. nostris prefatis* "*civibus et eorum hered. et successoribus, imprimis quod major dict. civitatis et successores sui qui* "*pro tempore fuerint gladium suum eis per nos datum aut alium gladium qualem eis placuerit* "*extra presentiam nostram et hered. nostrorum habeant portatum, et portari facere possint coram* "*eis punctu erecto in presentia tam aliorum magnatum et dominorum regni nostri* Anglie *qui nos* "*linea consanguinitatis attingunt et quorumcunque aliorum quam alio modo quocumque, et quod* "*servientes clavarum majoris et vicecomitum civitatis predicte et successorum suorum qui pro tem-*"*pore fuerint clavas suas auratas vel argenteas aut argentatas et signo armorum nostrorum et he-*"*red. nostrorum ornatas tam in presentia nostra et heredum nostrorum quam in presentia consor-*"*tis nostre future aut matrum heredum nostrorum predictorum infra dictam civitatem et suburbia* "*ejusdem et eorum precinctum prout proprii servientes nostri ad arma pro libito deferre valeant licite* "*impune absque occasione vel impetitione nostri vel hered. nostrorum in futurum*, which words "they for the city urged against the challenges of the said lord *Sheffield*, unto which at the "time answer was given, that the said lord *Sheffield* being his highness's lieutenant within "the said city was not restrained or barred by the said words, by reason of which pre-"tences of right on either side some scruple and doubt in law arising upon the words of that "said antient clause, and the letters patents of lieutenancy of the said lord *Sheffield*, we "could not determine the said controversy ourselves, nor make relation of the state of the "said cause to the satisfaction of his majesty, until that doubt in point of law were other-"wise cleared unto us, whereupon our resolutions at that time were to make stay of fur-"ther proceeding untill we had conferred with some of the judges, and received their opi-"nions therein; and afterwards having been sundry times petitioned by those that solli-"cited the cause for the said city to enter into some further consideration and hearing there-"of, we directed our letters unto sir *Edward Coke*, knt. lord chief justice of the common "pleas and sir *Lawrence Tanfield*, knt. lord chief baron of his highness's court of exche-"quer, intreating their lordships by our said letters to consider both of the words of the "charter granted unto the said city, and likewise of the right claimed by the said lord "*Sheffield*, by virtue of his patent of lieutenancy, and thereof to certify their opinions as "by our said letters bearing date the 15*th* day of *December*, 1608. it doth and may more "at large and more plainly appear. Upon receipt of which our letters the said reverend "and learned judges met and perused the clauses of the said antient charter made to the "said city, and of the patent of lieutenancy granted to the said lord *Sheffield*, and touch-"ing the question in law and right thereof, certified their opinions by their letters, *viz.* "that the mayor of *York* ought not to deliver up the sword of justice which he holdeth "by charter, nor to abase and bear down the same (especially in time of peace) in the "presence of the lord *Sheffield* his majesty's lieutenant there; and the said judges princi-"pally grounded their reasons upon the charter of king *Richard* the second made to the "said city, in the words aforesaid, as by the said letters bearing date the 18*th* day of *Fe-*"*bruary*, 1608. it doth and may more at large appear. We therefore the said commis-"missioners being resolved of the said ambiguity and doubt in law, and having before "that time with advice and mature deliberation duly pondered and considered the said "challenges and the reasons thereof, and all other allegations on both sides, as well in "matter of precedent and practice as otherwise, and finding no reason in any thing to

" dissent

'different from the opinion of the said two reverend judges, did after due consideration acquaint his majesty with the state of the said cause and controversy aforesaid, and with the whole passage and proceeding therein: and thereupon his majesty was pleased to deliver his royal opinion and censure to this effect, that for his own part he had been of the same mind ever since his first reading of the petition, though it pleased him for his own better satisfaction to require the judgment of the lords commissioners for the office of earl marshal, which do commonly examine matters of this nature with great judgment and equity, wherefore finding how that upon further consideration the laws of honour do so fitly suite and concur with the laws of the land, and the judges of the court of chivalry in their opinion with the judges of the point in law, his majesty doth likewise declare himself to agree resolutely with both their opinions. We therefore his said majesty's commissioners for causes determinable by the earle marshal's court according unto his highness's reference unto us for ending of the said controversy, finding no great difficulty in the same, and being warranted both by the the opinion of the said reverend judges, and by his majesty's most wise and royal censure for the avoiding of all future and further differences, do order and determine that from henceforth the said lord-mayor, aldermen, sheriffs and commonality of the said city of *York* for the time being, shall quietly and peaceably enjoy the liberty and priviledge of the said charter of king *Richard* the second unto them granted, according to the words of the said charter, and the true intent and meaning of the same, plainly expounded by the lords of the commission and those two grave and learned judges of the law, and confirmed by his royal majesty, and may have the sword carried before the said lord-mayor for the time being with the point erect upward and not abased, in the presence of the said lord lieutenant for the time being, without any delivery up of the same at all, the aforesaid challenge or claime of the said lord *Sheffield* as lieutenant of the said county and city of *York*, or any like challenge and claime of any other lieutenant for the time to come, or any other pretence or former precedent to the contrary in any wise notwithstanding. For confirmation and publick testimony whereof we have hereunto set our hands and fixed our several seals of arms, the twelfth day of *May* in the years of the reign of our soveraign lord *James*, by the grace of God king of *England, Scotland, France* and *Ireland* defender of the faith, *&c.* that is to say, of *England, France* and *Ireland* the seventh, and of *Scotland* the two and fortieth.

H. NOTHAMPTON, LENOX,
NOTINGHAM, T. SUFFOLKE.
S. F. WORCESTER.

" *Irrotulat. et examinat. per me* Johannem Givillim *registrum officii curie* Mariscal.

P. 184. *Sect.* 1. " should have the precedence of the merchant."

Since we are here upon precedence I shall chuse to subjoin a decree for precedency of place between the citizens of *York* and the dignitaries, ecclesiasticks, and men of the spiritual court, belonging to the church of *York*, made by cardinal *Wolsey*. Also a case betwixt two aldermen of *York* answered by sir *William Dugdale*, knt. relating to the like affair of precedency betwixt them.

A decree for predecency of place between the citizens of York, *and them of the spiritual court.*

" IN *Dei nomine, Amen.* By this present publique instrument it may evidently appear to all men, and be known that in the year of our Lord God 1526, the *14th induction*, the third year of the prelacy of the most holy father in Christ and our Lord the lord *Clement* by the divine providence pope the seventh of that name, the *11th* day of the moneth of *June* within the metropolitical church of St. *Peter* in *York*, in the consistory of the most reverend father in Christ and Lord, lord *Thomas* by divine mercy of the tytle of St. *Cicily* priest, *Tho. Wolsey* cardinal of the most holy *Roman* church archbishop of *York*, primate of *England*, chancellor and legate of the apostolical see, and of the *laterane*, before the venerable man Mr. *William Clifton* doctor of the decrees official and general commissary of the sacred church of *York*, *Reginald Bassey*, notary publique of the sacred apostolical authority, and one of the general proctors of the said court of *York*, being thereunto personally appointed, presented and exhibited to the aforesaid Mr. *Commissary*, a certain publique instrument made, subscribed and signed as thereby (*prima facie*) may appear by Mr. *Peter* of *Winton*, clerk of the diocese of *Carlisle*, notary publique by the apostolical authority under the year, day and place in the said instrument contained, not corrupted, not cancelled, not rased, not worne out, nor in any part thereof suspected, but altogether without blemish, clear of all suspicion. The tenor whereof doth follow in these words,

" IN *Dei nomine, Amen.* By this present publick instrument it may manifestly appear to all men, that in the year of our Lord God 1411, in the first year of the bishoprick of the most holy father in Christ and Lord, lord *John* by the divine providence pope of that name the three and twentieth, the fourth induction, and the *11th* " day

"day of the moneth of *August*, the most reverend father in God and Lord lord *Henry* by the divine mercy archbishop of *York*, primate of *England* and legate of the apostolical see, sitting publickly in his cathedral church of *York*, calling before him the honourable man *Nicholas Blackburne*, the same year lord major of the city of *York*, with two aldermen of the said city hereafter named, for making of an order for ever hereafter faithfully to be observed between the worthy men, the advocates and proctors and the rest of the ministers of their court of *York* of the one partie, the citizens of the city of *York* by their express assent and also by the consent of the major and aldermen hereafter named, for them and their successors, the commonalitye and all and singular the citizens of the same city on the other partie, for certain reasonable causes them thereunto moveing, and especially for avoiding of strife and contention between the aforesaid parties, did ordaine, determine and decree in and by all things as hereafter is contained; first, the said most reverend father the forenamed lord archbishop hath ordained, determined and decreed that the advocates of the court of *York*, which are prebendaries in his cathedral church of *York*, shall give place and preheminence to the major of the city of *York* for the time being, but of the rest of the citizens, yea aldermen which have been majors of the said city, they shall take place and precedencye: also he hath ordained, determined and agreed that the advocates of the said courts of *York*, being doctors of the one or the other law and not prebendarys, shall equally associate themselves with the aldermen which have been majors; that the elder doctor shall associate himself with the elder aldermen which have been majors in this manner, that when many advocates being doctors shall meet with many aldermen which have been majors, the elder doctor shall associate himself with the elder aldermen, and the younger doctor with the younger aldermen: also he hath ordained, determined and decreed that the advocates of the said court, not being prebendaries nor doctors, shall give place to the aldermen which have been majors, but to the other aldermen which do expect the majoralty they shall associate together and if many meet with many, the elder with the elder and the younger with the younger shall associate together in the manner as aforesaid; but such advocates shall take place of all other citizens, yea the sheriff of *York* for the time being: also he hath ordained, determined and decreed that the proctors of his said court which are scribes or registers of the said most reverend father in God or of the dean and chapter of *York*, as the registry of his consistory court of *York*, chancery, exchequer, or clerk of the chapter of *York*, shall give place to the sheriffs of *York* for the time being, but shall go before all other citizens, yea such as have passed that office: also he hath ordained, determined and decreed that all proctors of his said court, which do not enjoy the said offices, shall give place to the sheriffes for the time being, the clerks of the mayor, sheriffes or commonality of the said city, the keeper or master of the fraternity, or guild of St. *Christopher* and St. *George* for the time being: also he hath ordained, determined and decreed that the general apparitor of his said court of *York*, and subnotaries of the said court, shall give place to the chamberlains of the city of *York*, and also to the mayor and sheriffs or commonalities clerks, and to the keeper or master of the fraternity or guild aforesaid, but shall keep place of all other citizens of the said city; and hereupon the aforenamed lord-mayor with the aldermen within named, in their names and of all the city for them and their successors, openly, publickly, plainly and expresly did give their consent, that all and singular in these present ordinancies, determinations and decrees contained and comprehended by the said most reverend father lord *Henry* archbishop aforesaid made, decreed and ordained; and moreover the said most reverend father in God the lord *Henry* archbishop aforesaid, by his ordinary and pastoral power hath decreed all and singular the premisses contained in the statutes aforementioned between the parties. These written subscribed, recited and delivered in the year abovesaid, being the day of the moneth aforesaid, the most honourable man *Nicholas Blackburne* then lord-mayor of the city of *York*, *John Craven* and *Richard Holme* aldermen of the city of *York*, and *Richard Buryke* and *Richard Arnell* advocates to the court of *York*, being doctors of the law, with many other citizens called to be witnesses, and I *Peter* of *Winton*, clerk of the diocese of *Carlisle*, publick notary by apostolical authority under the most reverend father in God *Henry* archbishop of *York* as aforesaid, and in the year of pontifical induction aforesaid.

"Subscribed by the hands and seals of both parties and the witnesses aforesaid, I do proclame this to be a true and perfect decree.

"Recorded in the exchequer amongst the rolls, registred in the book of cardinal *Wolsey* where in the latter part thereof this ordination is registered.

The

The case between two aldermen of York *answered by* William Dugdale, *Norroy king of arms* Aug. 12, 1669, *as to the question of precedency in a corporation by the youngest alderman who hath obtained the dignity of knighthood, before a more antient alderman who is no knight.* Ex MS.

" THAT these aldermen are in that corporation to take place according to their se-
" niority, as aldermen, notwithstanding the dignity of knighthood conferred upon
" either of them; that title and dignity giving him no precedency there.

" I do remember that, not long since, there was some such question proposed upon the
" like case, concerning some of the aldermen of *Bristol*, and resolved accordingly; but till
" I come to *London* I cannot give a punctual answer to the names of the persons nor to
" the direct time when it happened.

" In the society of the lawyers at *Lincoln*'s-*inn* there was a special order, as appears by
" the register, made in the eighteenth year of king *James*, upon advice and considera-
" tion had of the practice held in other inns of court and publick places of corporations,
" where additions give no precedency of their antients, (as are the words of that order)
" that no bencher being knighted and made master of chancery in ordinary shall take
" place within the house; but in the course of antiquity and not otherways.

" The same rule is held amongst the heralds at arms, (who are a body corporate) *viz.*
" that a younger herald though a knight doth not preceed his senior in time though no
" knight; as it was in the case of sir *Henry St. George* knight, who was *Richmond* in the
" late king's time. And is now the case of sir *Thomas St. George*, who is *Somerset* he-
" rald at this present, all his seniors preceding him since he was knighted, as they did
" before.

P. 185. *Sect.* 3. On the election of a mayor. " But more antiently it was otherwise; and
" being chosen then by the whole body of the citizens, without any form, day or order,
" the elections were usually tumultuous and attended with dangerous consequences."

I shall here add copies from two records relating to these dissensions; the latter of which was little less than an absolute rebellion against the civil power, and a fine of a thousand marks was laid upon the citizens before they could obtain a pardon for it.

De eligendo majorem in civitate Ebor. *Claus.* 45 Ed. III. *m.* 1.

" REX ballivis et probis hominibus civitatis nostrae *Ebor.* salutem. Cum, ut accepi-
" mus, contentio inter *Johannem de Langeton* et *Johannem de Gisebourne* cives ejusdem
" civitatis, videlicet quis eorum pro anno praesenti major dictae civitatis fieret, habeatur,
" per quod quamplures cives nostri dictae civitatis uni et alteri parti adherentes inter se
" graviter certant et contendunt in terrorem populi nostri dictae civitatis ac pacis nostrae
" ibidem lesionem et perturbationem manifestam, unde quamplurimum conturbamur: nos
" volentes periculo in hac parte imminenti prout convenit obviare et pro bono regimine ejus-
" dem civitatis ordinare, vobis mandamus firmiter injungentes quod statim visis praesen-
" tibus de communi assensu vestro unum civem idoneum dictae civitatis pro regimine ejus-
" dem civitatis utilem et fidelem pro anno presenti in majorem ibidem eligi et ordinari
" faciatis. Dum tamen neuter praedictorum *Johannis* et *Johannis* major. ibidem aliqualiter
" existat nec se de electione ejusdem majoris in aliquo intromittat. Vobis etiam districtius
" qua poterimus inhibemus, ne debata contumelias aut conventicula aliqua in civitate prae-
" dicta per quod pax nostra ledi aut populus noster ibidem terreri valeant, qualitercunque
" fieri permittatis.

" Teste rege apud *West.* 26 die *Januarii.*

Per ipsum regem et concilium.

Rot. parl. 4. *Ric.* II. n. 50. *translated from the original* French.

" *ANNO* 4 *Ric.* II. a complaint was made in parliament of a horrible affair, as it is
" there called, then acted in the city of *York* by divers evil disposed persons of the
" same city, nearly touching the royal power by a false confederacy amongst themselves.
" It seems that *John de Gisburgh* had been duly elected mayor at the usual day, and had
" held the office peaceably till the *Monday* after the feast of St. *Catherine* [*November* 27.]
" following. When the same evil minded persons assembled themselves and drove the
" said mayor out of the city. Then these people with axes and other instruments broke
" open the doors and windows of the *Gild-hall*, entered and made one *Simon de Quixley*
" swear to be their mayor against his inclinations and those of the principal inhabitants of
" the said city, whom notwithstanding they also made swear, for fear of death, to their
" new mayor. After this they made a new ordinance, that when the clocks upon the bridge
" should strike aukeward as well by day as by night, that then the commons of the said
" city should rise and make proclamation of several other new ordinances by them made,

" contrary to the good cuſtoms of the city heretofore made. That the ſaid people con-
" tinued and abounded in theſe and ſeveral other horrible facts from day to day almoſt to
" the utter undoing of the ſaid city, and ſome peril to the whole realm, unleſs a ſpeedy
" chaſtiſement be ordered ſuch as it ſhall pleaſe the lords and other wiſe men of the king-
" dom to order, that other miſcreants of the kingdom may take warning by the puniſh-
" ment of theſe.

" The king would that by the conſent of the lords and commons in parliament, that a
" commiſſion ſhould be ſent in all haſte to the earl of *Northumberland* and ſome other lords,
" knights and eſquires of the countrey, to enquire of theſe malefactors by the help of ſome
" honeſt people near the city, *viis et modis*, and in every other manner that to them ſeems
" proper, in order to come at the truth of this affair, and take the names of the moſt
" guilty, and certify them to the king and council without delay; in order to inflict ſuch a
" puniſhment on them as ſhould be an example to all other rioters in the kingdom. Briefs
" were made and ſent to *York* by two ſerjeants at arms to ſeize and bring up to the king
" and council twenty four of the moſt notorious offenders, councellors and abettors of the
" ſaid riot; of which twenty four, their names ſhould be brought to the chancellor of *En-*
" *gland*, and themſelves put into ſafe cuſtody without bail or mainprize, until the ſaid earl
" and his companions juſtices in the ſame commiſſion had certified what they had found
" out relating to the affair.

" A writ was alſo ſent to *Simon de Quixley* the mayor only of the confederacy not to med-
" dle at all with the office of mayor, nor take to himſelf royal power contrary to the king's
" crown and dignity; and that he ſhould appear at a certain day before the king and
" council to anſwer to the fact, *&c.*

" Alſo another brief was ſent to *John de Giſburgh* the real mayor of the ſaid city, com-
" manding him to execute his office of mayoralty during his year, according to the cuſtoms
" and uſages of the ſaid city.

" One other brief was ſent to the bailiffs and honeſt citizens and all the commonality
" of the ſaid city, commanding them to acknowledge the ſaid *John* as their mayor, as one
" that repreſented the eſtate of our lord the king, on pain of forfeiting every thing that
" could be forfeited to the king; and the king commanded that proclamation ſhould be
" made of theſe matters throughout the city, that none might plead ignorance of them.

P. 187. *Sect.* 6. " they unanimouſly joined in a petition to a *parliament*, &c."

The petition with the king's aſſent to it is as follows,

Ex rotulo parliamenti anno 29. Hen. VI. *n.* 21.

Beſechen mekely the maire and citezens of the citie of Yorke, that where grete inconveniencies and hurt hath fallen of late in the ſaide cite, and moo in time comyng been likely to fall withoute proviſion therin be hadde by that that dyvers and erteyn perſones citezeins of the ſaid citee have purchaſed and goten of oure ſoverayne loꝛd the king, ſeveral letters patentes, they thereby to be exempte of the offices and occupations of mairalty, ſhirref-wyke, chaumberleynſhip, collectoꝛ of dymes and xvmes and citezen of the ſaid citee to come to parliaments of our ſaid ſoverayn loꝛd the kyng and his heirs within the ſaid citee. That it pleaſe you to pꝛay oure ſoverayne loꝛd the king to eſtabliſh and enacte by this pꝛeſent parlement by thaſſent of his loꝛds ſpiritualx and temporalx in this preſent parlement aſſembled and by thauthoꝛitie of the ſame, that all ſuch letters pattentes to any perſone or perſonnes now citezens of the ſaid citee, oꝛ that in tyme comyng ſhall be made, graunted, oꝛ to be made oꝛ graunted, be voide and of noon effectr. And over that yf any citezeyn of the ſaid citee now beyng, oꝛ that in tyme comyng ſhall be purchaſe, admitte, take oꝛ gete any ſuch letters patentes therby to be exempted of any of the officies oꝛ occupations afoꝛeſaid within the ſame citee foꝛfeit foꝛty pounds, the oon half to oure ſovereign loꝛd the king, and the other half to the maire and citezeins of the ſaid citee and their ſucceſſours. And that the maire foꝛ the tyme being and his ſucceſſours may have aud maynten actions of dette, to demaunde the ſaid foꝛty pound agaynes every of the ſaid perſone oꝛ perſones, ſuch letters patentes of exemption, purchaſing, admytting, takyng oꝛ gettyng the oon halfe of the ſaid foꝛty pound ſoo recovered to be to the uſe of oure ſaid ſoverayne the loꝛd the king and his heires, and the other half of the ſaid forty pound to be to the uſe of the maire of the ſaid citee foꝛ the tyme beyng, and of the citezeins of the ſame citee and their ſucceſſours; and that in ſuch actions of dette hereafter to be ſued the parties defendauntes ne the partie defendaunt in noo wiſe be admitted to their lawe.

R°. le roy le voet.

This is a true copy of the record, *George Holmes* deputy keeper of the records in the tower of *London*.

P. 201 and 202. On paying toll at *Burrough-bridge*.

The following entry is made in the city's oldeſt regiſter, now remaining in the common hall, *fol.* 315. of a *bill of complaint*, exhibited to the court and council of *John* duke of *Lancaſter*, then lord of the *honour* of *Knareſburgh* relating to a capture of tolls from the citizens of *York* at *Burrough-bridge*. Which, with the dukes mandate and inquiſition taken there-

thereupon, as alſo a copy of the inrolment in the court at *Knareſburgh*, ſhall be given in the original language,

" A tſſage conſeil court ſgracioufe ſeign. le roy de *Chaſtill* et *Leon* duc de *Lancaſtre*
" ſuppliont lez citezeins de la citee noſtre ſur le roy *Deverwyk* que come ils ont eſtee devant
" ces heures quites de touz maner de tolnuz et cuſtumes a *Burghbrigg* ſanz aſcune deſtour-
" bance come il eſt bien conuz par tote la pais environ et ore de novelle les ditz citezeins ſont
" deſtreintz par les miniſtres lour ditz ſeign. a ditz ville de *Burghbrigg* pur paier tolnuz en-
" contre les uſages avant ces heures a grant damage des ditz citee et citezeins, quil pleſe
" comander les ditz miniſtres de ceſſer des cieux deſtreſſes et demandes et qils ſeoffrent les
" ditz citezeins eſtre quytes de touz maner de tolnuz come ils ount avant ces heures eiantz
" regarde ſi vous pleſe que lourditz gracious ſeign. lour prometta qil ne voleit lever des
" ditz citezeins novelles cuſtomes.

" Et ſur ceo le ditz ſeign. manda ces lettres en maner que enſuytz.

" *Johan* par la grace de Dieu roi de *Caſtill* et de *Leon* duc de *Lancaſtre*, a noſtre chier
" et bien ameez *William de Neſſefeld* noſtre chief ſeneſhal deins l'onor de *Knareſeburgh* ſaluz.
" Nos vos envoi omes cloſe deins ceſtes une bille qele eſtoit baillier a noſtre conſaill par
" les citeins du citee de *Everwick* mandantz que vieio et entenduz la dite bille et l'endorce-
" ment duycelle et liew ſur les articles contenuz en y celles bone et diligent information
" ſi bien par inquiſition eut affair par bones et loialx gentz de noſtre ſeignier celles parties
" come en autre maner et de ceo que vous troverez par meſmes les inquiſition et informa-
" tion certifiez a noſtre ditz conſeil a *Loundre* entre cy et la lendemayne de la purification
" noſtre dame prochaine avenir ſouz veſtre ſeal et les ſealz des ceaux par quex meſme la
" inquiſition ſerra fait diſtinctement et apartement remandantz a noſtre ditz conſeill adon-
" ques ceſtes noz lettres oveſque la dite bille. Donne a noſtre manoir de la *Savvoie* le
" tiercz jour de *Decemb.* l'anne du regne noſtre tres reſdoute ſeign. et peer et le roi de *En-*
" *gleterre* 47 et de *Fraunce* 34.

" Par vertu de qele lettre le dit *William* priſt enqueſt en maner que enſuyte, inquiſitio
" capt apud *Knareſburgh* 10. die *Januar.* anno regni regis *Edwardi* tertii poſt conqueſtum
" quadrageſimo ſeptimo coram *Willielmo de Neſſefeld* capital. ſeneſcall. ibidem virtute li-
" tere domini regis *Caſtill.* et *Legion.* duc *Lanc.* eidem *Willielmo* direct. ad inquirend. de
" certis articulis in quadam billa infra literam predictam clauſa content. ad perſecutionem
" civium civit. *Ebor.* per ſacrament. *Ricardi de Pykering Roberti de Normandy Ad. de Kygbeley*
" *Johannis Ward Hug. Tankard Johannis Guddale Roberti Percy Johannis Ward de Skot-*
" *ton Roberti Kay*, *Johannis de Newton Ad. de Kendale*, *Johannis Sturgys* et *Johannis de Brune*
" *de Rouclyf* jur. qui dicunt ſuper ſacrament. ſuum quod predicti cives civit. predicte de toto
" tempore quo non extat memoria quieti fuerunt de tolneto infra villam et dominium de
" *Burghbrigg* prout iidem cives civitat. predicte per billam ſuam predictam in predicta litera
" annex. ſupponunt et ſicut per diverſas cartas regum *Anglie* progenitor. domini regis nunc
" *Angl.* de omni tolneto predictis civibus factas et conceſſ. rationabilit. teſtant. quouſque mi-
" niſtri predicte ultime regine *Angl.* pro tolneto predicto cives predictos diſtr. que quidem
" diſtrictiones poſtea deliberat. fuerunt per breve domini regis virtute cartarum progenito-
" rum domini regis nunc *Angl.* predictarum, et ſic quieti fuerunt ab illo tempore quouſque
" miniſtri dicti domini regis *Caſtelle* et *Legion.* nunc de novo ſuper eiſdem civibus civitat.
" predicte pro tolneto predicto ceperunt vadia et diſtrictiones contra libertat. ſuas pre-
" dictas antiquitus, et de jure conceſſ. et uſitat. In cujus rei teſtimon. pred. jur. huic in-
" quiſ. ſigilla ſua appoſuer. dat. loco die et anno ſuperdictis.

" Quedam irrotulatio facta in cur. de *Knareſburgh* tent. ibidem die *Mercurii* 18 die *Ja-*
" *nuarii* anno regni regis *Edwardi* tertii poſt conqueſtum 47. de quadam inquiſitione capt
" ibidem die *Martis* 17 die *Januar.* anno ſuperdicto coram *Willielmo de Neſſefeld* capital.
" ſeneſcall. domini *Johannis* reg. *Caſtell.* et *Legion.* et duc. *Lancaſtre* et de honore de *Kna-*
" *reſburgh* virtute cujuſdam litere ipſius regis *Caſtell.* et *Legion.* &c. eidem *Willielmo* directe
" ad inquirend. de certis articulis in litera predicta content. ad proſecutionem *Rogeri de*
" *Moreton* tunc major. civit. *Eborum* et aliorum civium civitat. predicte in hec verba.
" *Johan.* par la grace de Dieu roi de *Caſtill.* &c. ut patet ex altera parte folii &c. Et vir-
" tute bille predicte infra dictam literam clauſe in hec verba, a tſſage conſeil &c. et ut patet
" ex altera parte folii &c. l'endocement du dite bille in hec verba, les dits citeins ount jour
" tanqe lendemayne de la chaundeleur. Et pur ceo ſoit la petition mande encloſe les let-
" tres monſtre mande a *William de Neſſefeld* ſen. illequos pur diligentement enquere com-
" ment les ditz citeins ount paiez tolnuz avant ces heures et en qele maner et de totes
" les circumſtances et pur certifier iſſuit qe droit poit eſtre fait videlicet per ſacrament *Ri-*
" *cardi de Pikeryng*, *Roberti de Normandeby Ade de Kygblay Johannis Ward Hugonis Tankard*
" *Johannis Gudeale Roberti Percy Johannis Warde de Skotton Roberti Kay Johannis de New-*
" *ton*, *Johannis Browne* et *Johannis Sturgys* jur. qui dicunt ſuper ſacrament ſuum quod pre-
" dicti cives civit. predicte de toto tempore quo non extat memoria quieti fuerunt de tol-
" neto infra villam et dominium de *Burghbrigg* prout iidem cives civitat. predicte per bil-
" lam ſuam predictam in predicta litera clauſ. ſupponunt. Et ſicut per diverſas cartas
" regnum *Angl.* progenitor. domini regis nunc *Angl.* de omni tolneto predictis civi-
" bus factas et conceſſas rationabilit teſtant. quouſque miniſtri predicte ultime regine

" *Angl.*

" *Angl.* pro tolncto predicto cives predictos distrinxerunt, que quidem districtiones postea
" deliberat. fuerunt per breve domini regis virtute cartarum progenitorum domini regis
" nunc *Angl.* predictarum et sic quieti fuerunt ab illo tempore quousque ministri dicti domi-
" ni regis *Castell.* et *Legion.* nunc de novo super eisdem civib. civitat. predicte pro tolneto
" predicto ceperunt vadia et districtiones contra libertates suas predictas antiquitus et de jure
" concess. et usitat.

" In cujus rei testimon. predicti jurator. sigilla sua apposuerunt dat. loco die et anno
"" supradictis.

P. 204. In the charter of *Henry* III. for *nos autem predicti concessiones*, read, *predictas concessiones.*

P. 222. in swords and maces, " the largest was the gift of the emperor *Sigismund*."

It seems that *Sigismund* offered this sword at the altar of St. *George* in the chapel of *Windsor*, when he was made knight of the *garter* the eighth of *Henry* V. It was afterwards given to this city by *Henry Hanshap*, canon of *Windsor*, born at or near *York*, *anno* 1438, *Thomas Ridley* then lord-mayor. From a loose note in sir *T. W.* MS.

P. 223. *Sect. penult.* " **Corpus-Christi-play.**"

This piece of religious solemnity I have extracted and translated as follows,

The feast and pageantry of the play of Corpus Christi, *anciently annually exhibited in* York, *translated from an entry in an old register belonging to the city. fol.* 269.

" *IN the name of God, Amen.* Whereas for a long course of time the artificers and " tradesmen of the city of *York* have, at their own expence, acted plays; and particularly a certain sumptuous play, exhibited in several pageants, wherein the history of " the old and new testament in divers places of the said city, in the feast of *Corporis* " *Christi*, by a solemn procession, is represented, in reverence to the sacrament of the " body of Christ. Beginning first at the great gates of the priory of the holy *Trinity* in " *York*, and so going in procession to and into the cathedral church of the same; and afterwards to the hospital of St. *Leonard* in *York*, leaving the aforesaid sacrament in that " place. Preceded by a vast number of lighted torches, and a great multitude of priests " in their proper habits, and followed by the mayor and citizens with a prodigious croud " of the populace attending. And whereas, upon this, a certain very religious father, " *William Melton*, of the order of the *friars minors*, professor of holy pageantry, and a " most famous preacher of the word of God, coming to this city, in several sermons recommended the aforesaid play to the people; affirming that it was good in it self and " very commendable so to do. Yet also said that the citizens of the said city, and other " foreigners coming to the said feast, had greatly disgraced the play by revellings, drunkenness, shouts, songs and other insolencies, little regarding the divine offices of the said " day. And what is to be lamented they loose, for that reason, the indulgences, by the " holy father pope *Urban* IV, in this part gratiously conceded. Those, *viz.* faithful in " *Christ*, who attended at morning service at the said feast in the church where it was " celebrated, an hundred days; those at the mass the same; those also, who came to the " first vespers of the said feast, the like an hundred days; the same in the second; to " those also, who were at the first, third, sixth and ninth completory offices, for every " hour of those forty days; to those also, who attended service on the octaves of the said " feast, at mattins or vespers, mass or the aforesaid hours, an hundred days for every day " of the said octaves; as in the holy canons, for this end made, is more fully contained; " and therefore, as it seemed most wholsome to the said father *William*, the people of the " city were inclined that the play should be played on one day and the procession on another, so that people might attend divine service at the churches on the said feast for the " indulgences aforesaid. Wherefore *Peter Buckcy*, mayor of this city of *York*, *Richard* " *Russel*, late mayor of the staple of *Calais*, *John Northeby*, *William Bowes*, sen. *John* " *Moreton*, *Thomas Gare*, sen. *Henry Preston*, *Thomas Esyngwald*, *Thomas Bracebrigge*, *William Ormesheved*, *John Aldestanemore*, aldermen; *Richard Louth*, *John Dodyngton*, sheriffs; " *John Hewich*, *Thomas Doncaster*, *John Usburn*, *Thomas More*, *Robert Yarum*, *Robert Mydelton*, *Geoffry Savage*, *Thomas Snawdon*, *John Lofthouse*, *John Bolton*, *John Lyllyng*, *John* " *Gascoigne*, *William Craven*, *Thomas Acton*, *Thomas Davy*, *John Baynbrig*, *Thomas Kyrkham*, *William Bedale*, *William Gaytesheved*, *John Louth*, and *John Ward* of the number " of the twenty four, were met in the council chamber of the said city the *6th* day of " *June*, in the year of grace 1426, and of the reign of king *Henry* VI. after the conquest " of *England*, the fourth, and by the said wholsome exhortations and admonitions of the " said father *William* being incited, that it is no crime, nor can it offend God *if good be* " *converted into better.* Therefore, having diligently considered of the premisses, they " gave their express and unanimous consent that the cause aforesaid should be published to " the whole city in the common-hall of the same, and having their consent that the premisses should be better reformed. Upon which the aforesaid mayor convened the citizens together in the said hall the tenth day of the month aforesaid and the same year,

" and

"and made proclamation in a solemn manner, where it was ordained by the common as-
"sent that this solemn play of *Corpus Christi*, should be played every year on the vigil of
"the said feast, and that the procession should be made constantly on the day of the said
"feast; so that all people then being in the said city might have leisure to attend devout-
"ly the mattins, vespers, and the other hours of the said feast, and be made partakers of
"the indulgences, in that part, by the said *Roman* pope *Urban* the fourth most graciously
"granted and confirmed.

BURTON.

The order for the pageants of the play of Corpus Christi, *in the time of the mayoralty of* William Alne, *in the third year of the reign of king* Henry V. anno 1415. *compiled by* Roger Burton *town clerk.*

Tanners.	*God* the father almighty, creating and forming the heavens, angels, and archangels; *Lucifer* and the angels that fell with him into *hell*.
Plaisterers.	*God* the father, in his own substance, creating the earth, and all which is therein, in the space of five days.
Cardmakers.	*God* the father creating *Adam* of the slime of the earth, and making *Eve* of the rib, and inspiring them with the spirit of life.
Fullers.	*God* prohibiting *Adam* and *Eve* from eating of the tree of life.
Coupers.	*Adam* and *Eve* with a tree betwixt them; the serpent deceiving them with apples, *God* speaking to them and cursing the serpent, and an angel with a sword driving them out of *paradise*.
Armourers.	*Adam* and *Eve*, an angel with a spade and a distaff assigning them labour.
Gaunters.	*Abel* and *Cain* killing sacrifices.
Shipwrights.	*God* foretelling *Noah* to make an ark of light wood.
Fyshmongers, Pessyners, Mariners.	*Noah* in the ark with his wife and three children and divers animals.
Parchmyners, Bukbynders.	*Abraham* sacrificing his son *Isaac*; a ram, bush and angel.
Hosyers.	*Moyses* exalting the serpent in the wilderness, king *Pharao*, eight *Jews*, admiring and expecting.
Spicers.	*Mary* and a doctor declaring the sayings of the prophets about the future birth of *Christ*; an angel saluting her. *Mary* saluting *Elizabeth*.
Peuterers, Founders.	*Mary*, *Joseph* willing to put her away, an angel speaking to them that they should go to *Bedlem*.
Tylers.	*Mary*, *Joseph*, a midwife, the child born lying in a manger betwixt an ox and an ass, and the angel speaking to the shepherds.
Chaundelers.	The shepherds speaking by turns; the star in the east, an angel giving joy to the shepherds that a child was born.
Gold-smithes, Orfevers.	The three kings coming from the east, *Herod* asking them about the child *Christ*; with the son of *Herod*, two councellors and a messengers.
Gold-beters, Mone-makers.	*Mary* with the child and the star above and the three kings offering gifts.
Masons.	*Mary* with the child, *Joseph*, *Anna*, and a nurse with young pigeons, *Symeon* receiving the child in his arms, and two sons of *Symeon*.
Marshals.	*Mary* with the child and *Joseph* flying into *Egypt* by an angel's telling them.
Girdellers, Naylers, Sawters.	*Herod* commanding the children to be slain; four soldiers with lances, two councellors of the king, and four women lamenting the slaughter of them.
Sporiers. Lorymers.	The doctors, the child *Jesus* sitting in the temple in the midst of them, hearing them and asking them questions. Four *Jews*, *Mary*, and *Joseph* seeking him and finding him in the temple.
Barbers.	*Jesus*, *John the baptist* baptizing him, and two angels helping them.
Vyntners.	*Jesus*, *Mary*, bridegroom and bride, master of the houshold with his family with six water-pots, where water is turned into wine.
Smythes, Febers.	*Jesus* upon the pinnacle of the temple; *Satan* tempting with stones; two angels administring, &c.
C	*Peter*, *James* and *John*, *Jesus* ascending into the mountain and transfiguring himself before them. *Moyses* and *Elyas* appearing, and a voice speaking from a cloud.
Cennagers.	*Simon* the leper asking *Jesus* if he would eat with him. Two disciples, *Mary Magdalene* washing the feet of *Jesus*, and wiping them with her hair.

8 F. Plummers,

5

Plummers, Patten-makers.	*Jesus*, two apostles, the woman taken in adultery, four *Jews* accusing her.
Pouch-makers, Botillers, Cap-makers.	*Lazarus* in the sepulchre, *Mary Magdalene*, *Martha*, and two *Jews* admiring.
Vestment-makers, Skynners.	*Jesus* upon an ass with its foal; twelve apostles following *Jesus*, six rich and six poor men, with eight boys with branches of palm-trees, constantly saying *blessed*, *&c.* and *Zacheus* ascending into a *sycamore-tree*.
Cuttellers, Blade-smythes, Shethers, Scalers, Bukle-makers. Horners.	*Pylat*, *Cayphas*, two soldiers, three *Jews*, *Judas* selling *Jesus*.
Bakers, Waterleders.	The supper of the Lord and paschal lamb, twelve apostles; *Jesus* tied about with a linen towel, washing their feet. The institution of the sacrament of the body of *Christ* in the new law and communion of the apostles.
Cordwaners.	*Pylat*, *Cayphas*, *Annas*, forty armed soldiers, *Malchas*, *Peter*, *James*, *John*, *Jesus*, and *Judas* kissing and betraying him.
Bowers, Fletchers.	*Jesus*, *Annas*, *Cayphas* and four *Jews*, striking and bastinadoing *Christ*. *Peter*, the woman accusing him, and *Malchas*.
Tapisers, Couchers.	*Jesus*, *Pylat*, *Annas*, *Cayphas*, two councellors and four *Jews* accusing *Christ*.
Littesters.	*Herod*, two councellors, four soldiers, *Jesus* and three *Jews*.
Cukes, Waterleders.	*Pylat*, *Annas*, *Cayphas*, two *Jews* and *Judas* carrying from them thirty pieces of silver.
Sauce-makers.	*Judas* hanging himself.
Milners, Tiel-makers, Ropers, Cevers, Turners, Hayresters, Bollers.	*Jesus*, *Pilat*, *Cayphas*, *Annas*, six soldiers, carrying spears and ensigns, and other four leading *Jesus* from *Herod*, desiring *Barabas* to be released and *Jesus* to be crucified, and then binding and scourging him, putting a crown of thorns upon his head; three soldiers casting lots for the vesture of *Jesus*.
Shermen.	*Jesus* covered with blood bearing his cross towards mount *Calvery*, *Simon Sereneus*, &c.
Pynners, Lateners, Payntors.	The cross, *Jesus* extended upon it on the earth, four *Jews* scourging him with whips, and afterwards erecting the cross with *Jesus* upon it on mount *Calvery*.
Bouchers, Pulterers.	The cross, two thieves crucified and *Jesus* suspended betwixt them; *Mary* the mother of *Jesus*, *John*, *Mary*, *James* and *Salome*; a soldier with a lance, and a servant with a spunge. *Pilat*, *Annas*, *Cayphas*, a centurion, *Joseph* of *Arimathea* and *Nichodemus* taking him down and laying him in the sepulchre.
Satellers, Sellers, Glasiers.	*Jesus* destroying *hell*, twelve good and twelve evil spirits.
Carpenters, Joyners.	The centurion declaring to *Pylat*, *Cayphas* and *Annas*, with other *Jews* the signs appearing on the death of *Jesus*.
Cartwrights, Carvers, Sawyers.	*Jesus* rising from the sepulcher, four soldiers armed and three *Marys* lamenting; *Pilat*, *Cayphas* and *Annas*; a young man clothed in white, sitting in the sepulchre and talking to the women.
Wyndrawers.	*Jesus*, *Mary*, *Mary Magdalene* with spices.
Broggers, Wool-pakkers, Wadmen.	*Jesus*, *Luke* and *Cleophas* in the form of travellors.
Escriveners, Lumners, Questors, Dubbors.	*Jesus*, *Peter*, *John*, *James*, *Philip* and other apostles; *Thomas* feeling the wounds of *Jesus*.
Taillyoures.	*Mary*, *John* the evangelist, two angels, and eleven apostles; *Jesus* ascending before them and four angels bearing a cloud.
Potters.	*Mary*, two angels, eleven apostles, the holy ghost descending upon them and four *Jews* admiring.
Drapers.	*Jesus*, *Mary*, *Gabriel* with two angels, two virgins and three *Jews* of the kindred of *Mary*; eight apostles and two devils.

Lynwevers.

Lynwevers. Four apoſtles bearing the ſhrine of *Mary*, *Fergus* hanging upon it with two other *Jews* and one angel.

Wevers of wollen. *Mary* aſcending with a multitude of angels; eight apoſtles with *Thomas* preaching in the deſert.

Hostilers. *Mary*, and *Jeſus* crowning of her with a great number of angels.

Mercers. *Jeſus*, *Mary*, twelve apoſtles, four angels with trumpets, and four with a lance with two ſcourges, four good and four bad ſpirits and ſix devils.

Porters eight **torches.**
Coblers four **torches.**
Cordwaners fourteen **torches.**
Cotellers two **torches.**
Wevers **torches.**
Carpenters ſix **torches.**
Chaloners four **torches.**
Fullers four **torches.**
Girdellers **torches.**
Taillers **torches.**

And fifty eight citizens had torches alike on the day of **Corpus Christi.**

It is ordained that the **porters** and **coblers** ſhould go firſt, then of the right the **wevers** and **cordwaners**, on the left the **fullers, cutlers, girdellers, chaloners, carpenters** and **taillours**; then the better ſort of citizens and after the twenty four, the twelve, the mayor and four **torches** of Mr. **Thomas Buckton.**

A proclamation for the play of **Corpus Christi** *made in the vigil of the feaſt.*

OYEZ, &c. We comand of ye kynges behalve and ye major and ye shirefs of yis citee yat no man go armed in yis citee with swerdes ne with carlikkaxes, ne none othir defences in distorbaunce of ye kynges pees and ye play or hynderyng of the procession of Corpore Christi, and yat yai leve yaire wapens in yare ines knyghtes and sqwyers of wirship yat awe have swerdes born eftir yame of payne of forfature of yaire wapen and imprisonment of yaire bodys. And yat men yat brynges furth pagentz yat yai play at the places yat is assigned yerfore and nowere elles of ye payne of the forfatture to be raysed yat is ordayned. yerfore yatys to say xl s. And yat men of craftes and all othir men yat fyndes torches yat yai come furth in array and in ye manners as it has been used and custumed before yis time, haveyng wapen saveyin keepers of ye pagentz, end officers yat ar keepers of ye pees of payne of forfatture of yaire fraunchis and yaire bodyes to prison: and all manner of craftmen yat bringeth furthe ther pageantez in order and course by good players well arrayed and openly spekyng upon payn of lesyng of C s. to be payde to the chambre without any pardon. And that every player yat shall play be redy in his pagiaunt at convenyant tyme, that is to say, at the betwixt iv and v of the cloke in the mornynge, and then all oyer pageantz fast folowyng ilken after oyer as your course is without tarieng. Sub pena for. camere vi. viii. d.

Extract out of an order for the regulation of the play of Corpus Chriſti; *dated the 7th day of* June 1417. William Bowes, *major. E regiſt. f.* 167. 170.

" IT is ordained that for the convenience of the citeizens and of all ſtrangers coming to " the ſaid feaſt, that all the pageants of the play called **Corpus Christi play** ſhould " be brought forth in order by the artificers of the ſaid city, and to begin to play firſt at " the gates of the pryory of the *holy trinity* in **Mikel-gate**, next at the door of *Robert* " *Harpham*, next at the door of the late *John Gyſeburn*, next at **Skeldergate-hend** and " **North-strete-hend**, next at the end of **Conyng-strete** towards **Castel-gate**, next at the " end of **Jubir-gate**, next at the door of *Henry Wyman*, deceaſed, in **Conyng-strete**, then " at the *common-hall* at the end of **Conyng-strete**, then at the door of *Adam del Brygs*, de- " ceaſed in **Stayne-gate**, then at the end of **Stayn-gate** at the *Minſter-gates*, then at the " end of **Girdler gate** in **Peter-gate**, and laſtly upon the *Pavement*, *&c.*

" Be it remembered alſo that the abovesaid father *William de Melton* willing to deſtroy " ſin, and a great lover of virtue, by preaching exhorted the populace, that they would " cauſe to be removed all publick concubines in fornication or adultery and whores out of " the city. Wherefore the mayor by conſent of the community ordained, that the anci- " ent conſtitution of the city about whores be put in practice, and that they ſhould depart " the city within eight days on pain of impriſonment, unleſs any of theſe whores ſhould " come before the mayor and find good ſecurity that ſhe would not for the future admit " any perſon to cohabit with her either in fornication or adultery.

BURTON.

P. 224. *Sect.* 4. For charters and liberties granted to the *weavers* of *York*, ſee *Hen.* VII. *pars* 4. *f.* 54. *pat.* 3 *Hen.* VIII. *pars* 2. *et anno* 3 *Eliz. pars* i. *Rolls chapel.*

P. 228. *Sect.* 4. " who only confirms to the *gild of merchants*."

Gilda mercatoria, or **gild-merchant** is a certain liberty or privilege belonging to merchants to enable them to hold certain pleas within their own precincts. The word **geldes** or **gelhalda** *Teutonicorum*, is uſed for the fraternity of *Eaſterling* merchants in *London*, called now the *Stillyard*.

Ibid.

5

Ibid. " and that they [*Jews*] had houses in *York* more like princes palaces then subjects " dwellings."

Newburgh's words are these, — *aedificaverunt autem in medio civitatis, profusissimis sumptibus, domos amplissimas regalibus conferendas palatiis.* Gul. Neuburg. *c.* ix. *p.* 363. *edit.* Hearne.

Ibid. Sect. ult. " the **tallage** of the whole city sometimes amounted to cccc marks."

Many have been the particular taxes laid on this city by different kings. c *et* XLII *l.* VII *s. et* VIII *d. de dono civitatis* Ebor. 3 Ric. I. *in tallagio. cives* Ebor. *quorum nomina et debita annotantur in rotulo, quem predict. liberaverunt in thesauro, r.* c *de quater* XX *et* VII*l. de predicto tallagio in thesauro* LXXVII *l. et* XVIII *s. et debent* IX *l.* XVIII *s. et* VI *d. mag. rot.* 9 Ric. I. *rot.* 4. (b) Maddox's *excheq. p.* 483. *Cives de* **Everwick** *r.* c. *de* ccc *marcis de dono ad auxilium redemptionis domini regis. Rot. Pipe* 7 Ric. I. *Cives* Ebor. *r.* c *de* cc *marcis pro gaudio adventus dom. regis ab* Almania *Rot. Pipe* 6 Ric. I. *De tallagio assiso per* Johan. Kirkeby, *cives* Ebor. *r.* c *de* ccc *mar. de eodem in thesaur. et q. e. Mag. rot.* 14 Hen. III. *tit. residuum* Ebor. Maddox's *exch. p.* 489. Amongst a levy of money granted to the king by way of loan the city of *York* was charged with 100 *l. Rot. parl.* 32 Hen. VI. *n.* 48.

P. 229. *Sect.* 6. " *Anno reg.* 27 Ed. III. **Staple of wool**, before kept at *Bruges* in *Flanders*, by act of parliament was fixed *York*, &c."

The city had a seal given by the same king to the same purpose; and is now in the custody of the lord-mayor, and called the seal of **statute merchant**. It has the impress of that king's head with a lion on his breast, on each side two representations of the antient church of *York*, one of which is loose, and the impression thereof was to be made by the party. The inscription, *Sigillum* Edwardi *regis* Anglie *ad recognitionem debitorum apud* Eboracum *. The **staple of wool** being long since removed from *York*, the use of this seal has also been remitted. But, that our present citizens may have some notion how much this trade flourished antiently in this city, under the statute aforesaid and the influence of our kings, I shall give an extract from a printed book, relating to a parcel of wools, belonging to the staple at *York*, and seized on by a foreign lord, amounting, in value, to the sum of one thousand nine hundred pound. Which sum, considering the distance of time, in regard to its present value, and that a pound sterling was then a pound weight, which is equal to three of ours, I believe I shall not be far out in my calculation if I say that this sum may be put in balance with twenty thousand pound of our present money.

Cotton's collections, by *Prynne*, p. 137. 50 *Ed.* III. " The citizens of *York* desire, that " whereas the lord of *Arde* and *Cockham* in *Holland* hath stayed six and thirty surples of their " wools, to the value of one thousand nine hundred pound, supposing that the king oweth " him money for his service in *France*; and will neither for the king's letters, nor other " means, deliver their wools; that therefore they may have licence to stay the ships of the " same lord at *Calais*, or in *England*, till they be paid and answered to the value.

" Let it be declared to the grand council, and they shall have remedy according to " reason."

Since we are now upon seals, I shall here chuse to give an explanation of the rest of them belonging to the city which I have caused to be engraven in the plate of the *Ainsty*, &c. The first, marked 1. is most certainly of great antiquity, and if not equal, near coeval, with the *conquest*. The shape of the letters, SIGILLVM CIVIUM EBORACI, with the reverse S. B̄T̄I PETRI PRINCIPIS APOSTOLOR' come very near up to the beauty and exactness of the *Roman* characters; which were used by the *Saxons* and *Normans*, until the crook backed *High Dutch* black letter cut them out. For instance, the inscription round the two next seals, though the letters seem older, yet they are indisputably of a much later date. But what confirms this, beyond contradiction, is the representation of the antient church of St. *Peter* in *York*, probably that built by archbishop *Thomas* the first; and pulled down for the re-erecting the present structure. In Mr. *Anstis*'s collection of antient seals I have seen the old churches of *Canterbury*, *Ely* and *Norwich*, represented in like manner. And indeed so well performed as shews them no very mean artists at drawing in those ages. In those seals of *Canterbury* and *Norwich* is also one thing to be remarked, very particular; that there runs an inscription round the verge, in the manner of our present milled crowns; and which is not easy to conceive how they did it. But to return to our own seal; in this representation of the old church of St. *Peter* at *York*, which seems to exhibit the grand entrance to it, the arches in the doors are to be particularly observed; which if they do not exactly correspond with the *Roman* arch, yet must be allowed to approach very near to it. All judges of antiquity and antient architecture acknowledge, that the *Saxons*, as well as the *Normans*, copied the old *Roman* taste, in their buildings, but more especially in their arches. The different tastes of *Gothick* architecture which may be seen in our present cathedral evidently demonstrate this. For in the arches which compose the south and north cross ends may be observed a sweep or turn, approaching nearer to a segment of a circle, than in the arches of the west and east ends, which are of a much more modern date; the acuter, oxeyed, arch coming then into fashion. So the representation of the arches in the seal, as well as the letters, are very evident tokens of the great antiquity of it.

* See the seal marked n°. 2. in the plate of the map of the *Ainsty*, &c p. 381.

The

The *matrix* of this ſeal is kept in a cupboard in the council chamber on *Ouſe-bridge* under two locks; one key is in the town-clerk's poſſeſſion, and the other is in the foreman of the commons. It is at preſent uſed to all leaſes, grants, *&c.* from the city.

The ſeal marked N°. 3. with the inſcription SIGILLUM OFFICII MAIORATUS CIVIT. EBORACI is uſed to be put to ſuch deeds as are acknowledged before the mayor by any *feme covert*, when ſhe and her huſband ſell their eſtate in the city; and by the wife's making ſuch acknowledgment, her huſband and ſhe by the cuſtom of the city, are enabled to diſpoſe of their eſtate in the like manner as if the wife had been ſole and unmarried. This ſeal is alſo put to certificates of the execution of deeds which are ſent beyond-ſea. The ſeal it ſelf repreſents the arms of the city on a flowered field, the old way, ſurmounted by a coronet; and on each ſide a feather; the emblems of the dukedom of *York*.

The ſeal, inſcribed SIGNACVLVM EBORACENSIVM, N°. 4. is modern, and daily uſed in the office for ſealing certificats of people's being freemen, and therefore exempted from paying toll, *&c.* juſtice of peace warrants ſigned by the mayor, *&c.* all ſeſſions proceſſes, *&c.*

5. The ſeal inſcribed EBORACVS, with the repreſentation of St. *Peter* with the church on his right hand and key in his left, as alſo the three ſeals, like creſts, which are ſet on the verge of a ring; and which I take to have been counter-ſeals, are all now out of uſe. The ſeal of the office of mayoralty, as alſo the two ſeals for warrants and paſſports, are delivered by the old to the new mayor on the ſwearing day *Feb.* 3. The plate, houſhold-goods and other utenſils belonging to the city, are delivered to the mayor-elect on St. *Paul's* day, as alſo poſſeſſion of the lord mayor's houſe.

P. 231. *Sect.* 5. Since the printing of this paragraph, a copy of the original drawing of this grand deſign has been ſent me from the city. By which it appears that it was projected *anno* 1616; when an exact ſurvey was taken of the ground, through which the cut was to be made, and the different nature of the ſoil marked, by colours, in the map. This alſo, I have added to the plate of the *Ainſty*, *&c.* with the preſent courſe of the river *Ouſe*, from the *Humber* to the city. In which is deſcribed the propoſed cuts for ſhorning the courſe of the river, as mentioned at *Sect.* 4. of the enſuing page. By the date of the drawing of the grand cut or canal, from *Bromfleet* to *Water-Foulford*, it appears that the project of it was on foot in the reign of king *James* I. long before the duke of *Bolton* was in being. So whether the ſtory of his offering to perform it or no is true is uncertain. It is more probable that the ſurvey was taken by order of king *James* the firſt, to make good his promiſe which he made to the city *to have their river amended and made more navigable.* But whether the monarch or his ſubjects, the citizens of *York*, were to blame in not having the deſign executed I know not. If the latter, the memory of them ought to be branded with want of care and duty to the city by all poſterity.

P. 234. *Sect.* 8. The extract from Doomeſday-book, relating to the city of *York* and ſome of the adjacent villages, is in theſe words,

CIVITAS EBORUM.

" IN *Eboraco* civitate tempore regis *E.* preter ſcyram archiepiſcopi fuerunt vi. ſcyre una ex
" his eſt vaſtata in caſtellis. In v. ſcyris fuerunt M. et quadringente et xviii. manſio-
" nes hoſpitate. De i. harum ſcyrarum habet archiepiſcopus adhuc iii. partem. In his ne-
" mo alius habebat conſuetudinem niſi ut burgenſis preter *Merleſuaim* in 1. domo que eſt infra
" caſtellum et preter canonicos ubicumque manſiſſent et preter iiii. judices quibus rex dabat
" hoc donum per ſuum breve et quamdiu vivebant.

" Archiepiſcopus autem de ſua ſcyra habebat plenam conſuetudinem.

" De ſupradictis omnibus manſionibus ſunt modo hoſpitate, in manu regis reddentes con-
" ſuetudinem, quadringente ix. minus, inter magnas et parvas et cccc. manſiones non ho-
" ſpitate que reddunt, melior 1. denarium et alie minus et quingente et xl. manſiones ita vacue;
" quod nil omnino reddunt, et cxlv. manſiones tenent *Francigene.* Sanctus *Cutbertus* habet i. do-
" mum quam ſemper habuit (ut plures dicunt) quietam ab omni conſuetudine, ſet burgenſes
" dicunt non eam fuiſſe quietam tempore regis *E.* niſi ſicut i. burgenſium niſi tantum quod
" propter ea habeat tholoneum ſuum et canonicorum. Preter hanc habet epiſcopus *Dunelmi*
" de dono regis eccleſiam *Omnium Sanctorum*, et que ad eam pertinent. et totam terram
" *Uctred*, et terram *Ernuin* quam *Hugo* vicecomes deliberabat *Walchero* epiſcopo per breve
" regis. Et burgenſes qui in ea manent dicunt quod eam ſub rege tenent.

§ " Comes *Moritonienſis* habet ibi xiiii. manſiones et ii. bancos in macello et eccleſiam *Sancte*
" *Crucis* has recepit *Oſb.* filius *Baſonis* et quicquid ad eas pertinet. He manſiones fuerunt ho-
" rum hominum *Conulf.* i. preſbiteri i. *Morulfi* i. *Sterri.* i. *Eſnarri.* i. *Gamel.* i. cum iiii.
" drinighis. *Archil.* v. *Leningi* preſbiteri ii. *Turfin.* i. *Ligulfi* i.

§ " *Nigellus de Monnevile* habet i. manſionem cujuſdam monetarii.

" *Nigellus Foſſart* habet ii. manſiones *Modene* et tenet de rege.

" *Waldinus* intercepit ii. manſiones *Retel* preſbiteri pro i. manſione *Sterre.*

" *Hamelinus* habet i. manſionem in foſſato urbis et *Waldi* i. manſionem *Einulfi* et i. man-
" ſionem *Alwini.*

8 F *Ricardus*

" *Ricardus de Surdetal* ii. manſiones *Turchil.* et *Ranechil.*

" *Nigellus Foſſart* intercepit ii. manſiones, ſet dixit ſe eas reddidiſſe epiſcopo *Conſtantienſi.*

" *Willielmus de Perci* habet xiiii. manſiones horum hominum *Bernulfi. Gamelbar. Sort. Eg-*
" *bert. Selecolf. Algrim. Norman. Dunſtan. Odulfi. Weleret. Ulchel. Goddent. Sonnete. Oiberti.*
" et eccleſiam ſancte *Marie.*

" De *Hugone* comite habet idem *Willielmus* ii. manſiones duorum prepoſitorum *Haroldi* co-
" mitis, ſet burgenſes dicunt i. ex eis non fuiſſe comitis. Alteram verò ſibi fuiſſe forisfactam.
" Eccleſiam etiam ſancti *Cutberti* advocat idem *Willielmus de Hug.* comite et vii. minutas
" manſiones continentes l. pedes lati. preterea de i. manſione *Uctred* cujuſdam dicunt bur-
" genſes *W. de Perci* aſportaſſe ſibi in caſtellum poſtquam de *Scocia* rediit. Ipſe verò *Wil-*
" *lielmus* terram ejuſdem *Uctred* negat ſe habuiſſe, ſet per *Hugonem* vicecomitem dominum
" ipſius dicit ſe in caſtellum tuliſſe primo anno poſt deſtructionem caſtellorum. *Hugo* filius
" *Baldvici* habet iiii. manſiones *Adulfi. Hedned. Turchil.* et *Goſpatric.* et xxix. minuta hoſpicia
" et eccleſiam ſancti *Andree* quam emit. *Rob. Malet* habet ix. manſiones horum hominum,
" *Tumme. Grim. Grinchetel. Ernni. Elfi.* et alterius *Ernni. Glunier. Halden. Ravenchel.*
" *Erners de Burmi* habet iiii. manſiones, *Grim. Aluuini. Goſpatric.* et *Goſpatric.* et eccleſiam
" ſancti *Martini.* Due ex eis manſionibus reddunt xiiii. ſolidos. *Giſlebertus Maminot* habet
" iii. manſiones. *Meurdoch. Berengarius de Todenai* habet manſ. *Gamelcarle* et *Aluuini,* et viii.
" manſiones ad hoſpicia. De his medietas eſt in foſſato urbis. *Oſbertus de Archis* habet ii.
" manſiones. *Brun* preſbyteri et matris ejus, et xii. manſiones in hoſpicia et li. manſiones de
" epiſcopo *Conſtantienſi.* *Odo Baliſtarius* habet ii. manſiones, *Forne* et *Orme.* et i. hoſpitium
" *Elaf.* et i. eccleſiam. *Ricardus* filius *Erfaſt.* iii. manſiones, *Alchemont.* et *Goſpatric.* et *Ber-*
" *nulf.* et eccleſiam ſancte *Trinitatis.* *Hubertus de Montcaniſi* i. manſ. *Bundi.* *Landricus*
" *Carpentarius* habet x. manſ. et dimidiam quas ei preſtitit. vicecomes tempore regis *Edwar-*
" *di.* Valebat civitas regi liiii. libras modo c. libras ad penſum.

§ " In ſcyra archiepiſcopi fuerunt tempore regis *Eduuardi* hoſpitate ducente manſiones xi.
" minus. Modò ſunt c. hoſpitate, inter magnas et parvas, preter curiam archiepiſcopi et
" domos canonicorum. In hac ſcyra habet archiepiſcopus quantum rex habet in ſuis ſcyris.
" In geldo civitatis ſunt xxiiii. et iiii. carucate terre et unaqueque geldabat quantum i.
" domus civitatis et in tribus operibus regis cum civibus erant. De his habet archiepiſcopus
" vi. carucatas, quas poſſunt arare iii. caruce, he ſunt ad firmam aule ſue, hec non fuit hoſpi-
" tata tempore regis *Eduuardi,* ſed per loca culta a burgenſibus, nunc eſt ſimiliter. De hac
" terra necavit ſtagn. reg. ii. molendinos novos valentes xx. ſolidos, et de arabili terra et pra-
" tis et hortis plene i. carucata tempore regis *Eduuardi* valebat xv. ſolidos modò iii. ſolidos.

" In *Oſboldervis* terra canonicorum de vi. carucatis ubi poſſunt eſſe iii. caruce. Ibi habent
" modò canonici ii. car. et dimidiam et vi. villanos et iii. bordarios habentes ii. car. et dimi-
" diam. Item in *Mortun* habent canonici iiii. carucatas ubi ii. caruce poſſunt eſſe, ſed waſta
" eſt. He due ville habent i. leucam lati. et i. longi. In *Icolthun* ſunt vi. car. ubi poſſunt
" eſſe car. waſte ſunt de his ſunt tres canonicorum et iii. comitis *Alain* habent dimidiam leu-
" cam longi et dimidiam lati. In his nec pratum nec ſilva. In *Sambura* ſunt iii. carucate
" ubi poteſt eſſe i. caruca et dimidia, waſta eſt. *Radulphus Pagenel* tenet. canonici dicunt ſe
" eam habuiſſe tempore regis *Eduuardi.* In *Hewarde* habebat *Orm* unum manerium de vi. ca-
" catis terre quam iii. caruce poſſunt arare, modo habet *Hugo* filius *Baldvici* i. hominem et i.
" car. tempore regis *Eduuardi* valebat x. ſolidos modo v. ſolidos. In eadem villa habet *Wal-*
" *tef.* i. manerium de iii. carucatis terre, modò habet *Ricardus de Com. Moriton,* tempore
" regis *Edwardi* valebat x. ſolidos modò x. ſolidos et viii *d.* Hec villa 1. leuca longi et dimi-
" dia lati. In *Fuleford* habebat *Morcarius* i. manerium de x. carucatis, modò habet *Alanus*
" comes ibi poſſunt eſſe v. caruce. In dominio ſunt modò ii. carucate, et vi. villani habent,
" ibi ii. car. habet in longo i. leugatam et dimidiam leugatam lati. Tempore regis *Eduuardi*
" valebat xx. ſolidos, modò xvi. ſolidos. In circuitu civitatis habuit *Torfinus* i. carucatam
" terre, et *Turchillus* ii. carucatas terre, he poſſunt arare ii. car. In *Cliftone* ſunt xviii. caru-
" cate terre geldantes, he poſſunt ix. car. arare, modò eſt waſta. Tempore regis *Eduuardi*
" valuit xx. ſolidos. De his habuit *Morcarius* ix. carucatas terre et dimidiam ad geldum,
" quas poſſunt v. car. arare. Modò habet ibi comes *Alanus* ii. carucatas et ii. villanos et iiii.
" bordarios cum i. car. In ea ſunt l. acre prati. Ex his xxix. ſancti *Petri,* et alie ſunt co-
" mitis. Preter has habet archiepiſcopus ibi viii. acras prati. Hoc manerium i. leugata et
" alia lati. Tempore regis *Eduuardi* valuit ix. ſolidos, modò ſimiliter. Canonici habent
" viii. carucatas et dimidiam, waſte ſunt. In *Roudclif* ſunt iii. carucate terre ad geldum
" quas poſſunt arare ii. car. De his habuit *Saxfordus* diaconus ii. carucatas cum aula, modò
" ſanctus *Petrus,* et valuerunt x. ſolidos. Et *Turber* habuit i. carucatam cum aula, modo
" rex et valuit v. ſolidos, modo waſta eſt utrumque, ibi ſunt iii. acre prati. Inter totum di-
" midia leugata longi et tantundem lati. In *Overtun* ſunt ad geldum v. carucate quas poſ-
" ſunt arare ii. car. et dimidia. Ibi habuit *Morcarius* hallam modò habet ibi *Alanus* comes
" i. carucatam et v. villanos et iii. bordarios cum iiii. car. et xxx. acr. prati et ſilva paſcualis
" i. leugate longi et ii. quarteriorum lati. Inter totum i. leugata longi et ii. leugate et
" duorum quarteriorum lati tempore regis *Eduuardi* et modo xx. ſolidos. In *Sceltun* ſunt
" ad geldum ix. carucate terre quas poſſunt arare iiii. car. De ſancto *Petro* habuit et habet
" iii. car. Tempore regis *Eduuardi* valuit vi. ſolidos, modò eſt waſta. De hac terra tenuit

" *Turber*

" *Turber* ii. carucatas cum halla et vi. bovatas. Nunc habet sub rege unus censorius et sunt " ibi ii. carucate et vi. villani. Tempore regis *Eduuardi* vi. solidos modò viii. de eadem ter" ra pertinent ad *Overtun* ii. carucate et vi bovate. Ibi habet *Alanus* comes i. hominem " cum i. caruca. Inter totum dimidia leugata longi et dimidia lati. In *Mortun* sunt ad gel" dum iii. carucate terre quas potest una caruca arare. Hanc terram tenuit *Archillus* et va" let x. solidos, modò wasta est. In *Wibitun* est ad geldum i. carucata quam potest i. caru" ca arare, hoc tenuit *Saxfordus* diaconus, modo habet sanctus *Petrus*, wasta fuit et est, ibi " est silva minuta. Inter totum dimidia leugata longi et dimidia lati.

" Hi habuerunt socam et sacam. et tol et thaim. et omnes consuetudines. Tempore regis " *Eduuardi Haroldus* comes *Merlesven*. *Visenisc*. *Turgodlag*. *Tochi*. filius *Outi Eduinus* et *Mor*" *carius* super terra *Ingold*. tant. *Gamelinus* filius *Osberti* super *Cotingeham* tant. *Copsi* super " *Cutmalt* tant. et *Cnut*. Ex his qui forisfecit nemini emendavit nisi regi et comiti. In domi" nicis maneriis nihil omnino comes habuit, neque rex in maneriis comitis, preter quod per" tinet ad christianitatem que ad archiepiscopum pertinet.

" In omni terra sancti *Petri* de *Eboraco*, et sancti *Johannis*, et sancti *Wilfridi*, et sancti *Cut*" *barti*, et sancte *Trinitatis* similiter rex ibi non habuit nec comes nec aliquis alius aliquam " consuetudinem.

" Rex habet tres vias per terram et iiii^or per aquam. In his omne forisfactum est regis et " comitis ubicunque vadant vie vel per terram regis vel archiepiscopi vel comitis.

" Pax data manu regis vel sigillo ejus, si fuerit infracta, regi solummodo emendatur per " xii. hundreda, unumquodque hundredum viii. libr.

" Pax a comite data et infracta à quolibet, ipsi comiti per vi. hundreda emendatur, unum" quodque viii. libr.

" Si quis secundum legem exulatus fuerit, nullus nisi rex ei pacem dabit. Si vero comes " vel vicecomes aliquem de regione foras miserit, ipsi eum revocare et pacem ei dare possunt " si voluerint.

§ " Relevationem terrarum dant solummodo regi illi *Taini* qui plusquam vi. maneria ha" buerint, relevatio est viii. libr. Si verò sex tantum maneria vel minus habuerit, viceco" comiti pro relevatione dat iiii. marcas argenti. Burgenses autem *Eborace* civitatis non " dant relevationem."

P. 233. *Sect*. 1. This very sessions of parliament, *anno* 1735-6, a bill was ordered to be brought in, and was brought in accordingly, to most of the purpose this paragraph speaks to. But the undertaker having clogged the bill with some cuts to be made in the river *Dun*, and being besides suspected to have views of his own in it, not consistent with the interest of the city, it was opposed by them, and the scheme let drop; to be revived, I hope, by the city themselves, on some better footing, at a more convenient opportunity.

P. 238. *Sect*. 1. There was a bill, however, brought into parliament for establishing again this court at *York*, but why dropped I know not. The copy of the printed bill is as follows;

The BILL *is for the establishing of a court at* YORK.

THE inducement is, that *Hen*. VIII. in the thirty-first year of his reign, did erect a court there, extending through the county of *York*, the county and city of *York*, the town " and county of *Kingston* upon *Hull*, the bishoprick of *Durham*, county of *Northumberland*; " the town and county of *Newcastle upon Tyne*, the city of *Carlile*, the town of *Berwick upon* " *Tweed* and liberties there, counties of *Cumberland* and *Westmerland*, which being found " commodious for the people of those parts, was confirmed and continued by *Edw*. VI. " queen *Mary*, queen *Elizabeth*, king *James*, and king *Charles* I. until by by the troubles in " this nation, it was discontinued. And in respect of the distance from *Westminster*, the sub" jects of those parts, cannot without great charge and expence repair thither, but must ei" ther quit their interests, or else redeem them at excessive loss and charge. Therefore the " bill desires, it may be enacted, that it shall be in his majesty's power, by his commission " under the great seal of *England*, to erect a court there, and to nominate such person for " judicial and ministerial charges, to act according to such powers, as by such certain an" nexed Instructions are declared.

The INSTRUCTIONS *are*,

1. " The court to consist of officers, to be distinguished by his majesty and such judges " learned in the laws, not exceeding the number of   and of his majesty's fee in " ordinary, and such of the nobility and gentry of those parts (as assistants to the court) as " his majesty shall think fit: The fees and salaries left to his majesty.

2. " A seal or signet to attend the court, with such inscriptions as his majesty shall think " fit.

3. " Four general sittings or sessions in the year, in the city of *York*, *viz*.
"   But with power to adjourn upon contagion, or any dangerous Sick" ness.

" 4. To

4. " To have power to examine, search out, and suppress treasons, misprisions of trea-
" sons, petty treasons, and felonies, and to apprehend and commit the offenders, till dis-
" charged by Law. And any three of the Judges shall hear and determine all other crimi-
" nal matters, either at common-law or statute.

5. To be a court of equity, and by any three judges to determine matters in equity, as
" is done in chancery; to stay suits at law, establish possessions, as at the time of the bill
" exhibited, or greatest part of three years before. And the decree to be penal, unless ei-
" ther party within fourteen days appeal to the chancery; before which appeal, the appel-
" lant shall give security to prosecute his appeal, and to pay the other side costs, (to be as-
" certained by the affidavit of the party, his attorney or sollicitor) and to perform the decree,
" if confirmed in chancery.

6. " No decree is to be reversed for want of form only, but for matter of substance ap-
" pearing in the body of the decree.

7. " Because the experience of more than one hundred years has shewed, that tryal of
" personal actions by *English* bill to be a great ease and advantage to the country, and (mat-
" ters being commonly of small value) that the same may be continued, where the title of
" land, or chattel-real, shall not come in question.

8. " By *English* bill, to decree all debts for rents, under one hundred pound.

9. " Power to assess and tax costs, as well to plaintiff as defendant, and to execute their
" decrees by such ways as is done in chancery; and if any against whom a decree, either in
" equity or personal action is had, shall fly out of the jurisdiction, a commission of rebelli-
" on may issue into any part of *England*, and after a serjeant at arms.

10. " All decrees shall pass by majority of voices; but when the voices are equal, the
" first senior judge's voice shall carry it.

11. " First, process to be a letter-missive to be granted by warrant under the hand of one
" of the judges, not having the custody of the seal. Upon default and oath of service of
" the letter, an attachment to issue; and such other process as in chancery. And
" if the person to be served with the letter, be a dweller within the jurisdiction; and, be-
" fore the service of it, depart out of it, the service at his dwelling, and oath thereof, shall
" be as sufficient, as if it had been an actual service: The same rule touching all absconding
" persons.

12. " Keeper of the seal, or his deputy, not to seal any process, without the privity of
" one of the judges; nor to be absent without urgent occasion, in which case the seal shall
" rest with the first or senior judge for the time being.

13. " Power to direct precepts to all sheriffs within their jurisdiction, for return of juries
" in criminal causes, and all persons to be assisting and obedient to the precepts of the
" court.

14. " Any judge may take bonds, recognizances of the peace and good behaviour; and
" for appearance and performance of the orders of the court. The judges and keeper of the
" seal to be masters of the chancery extraordinary.

15. " All decrees and judgments to be in open court, and so touching interlocutory or-
" ders and rules, except such as concern the practice of the court, or the attorneys on both
" sides consent to rules before a judge for expedition-sake. Nor shall any order be reversed
" or altered in substance after its entry, but a hearing both sides in open court, or consent,
" as aforesaid. But if notice in writing be given by one party to the other of any motion to
" reverse or alter an order, and of the points to be moved on; and the party makes no de-
" fence, or affidavit of such notice, the court may alter the said order, giving day to shew
" cause to the other side.

16. " No orders to be made in vacation, except for the redress of pressing misdemeanors;
" forcible entries, riots, and sudden spoils, which may be done by any two of the judges;
" as also assignment of counsel and attorney to persons in *forma pauperis*.

17. " Any three judges may set fines according to law; and mitigate and compound re-
" cognizances forfeited to his majesty, and such fines to be registred and accounted to his
" majesty.

18. No indictment or information to be removed, but by writ of error; and none impri-
" soned before judgment to be removed by *habeas corpus*, or *corpus cum causa*; but that it
" shall be a good return to the *habeas corpus*, that the party is imprisoned for a matter where-
" in judgment is not given; if the return be false, the party imprisoned to have his ordinary
" remedy at law for such false return.

19. " If after a prohibition a *procedendo* be awarded, any two judges may tax costs for the
" causeless vexation; but if (hanging the prohibition) the party shall endeavour to escape out
" of the jurisdiction, or convey his estate out of it, the lord may attach such till recogni-
" zance given for the performance of the decree. Proviso, if any be imprisoned falsly, he
" may bring his action of false imprisonment in any county of *England*, and recover double
" damages and costs. And to avoid error in such attachments, the register of the court, be-
" fore it issue, shall cause the party suggesting such attachment, to enter his name and abode;
" if he be not of value for answering the damages, the register shall refuse the attachment
" till some of value avow the suggestion. This article not to extend to the judges or mini-
" sters of the court.

20. " A

i

"20. A table of fees, such as were taken during the late court, to be hanged up in some "publick place; and he that shall take more, shall be punished as an extortioner.

"21. All suitors or witnesses to be priviledged, *eundo, morando, redeundo,* except for "treason, felony, or execution after judgment; and accordingly a *supersedeas* of priviledge "to issue.

"22. All proceedings in this court to be good evidence in any his majesty's courts, and "the keeper of the seal to make entry of all rules, orders, and decrees, without fee, other "than shall be appointed in the table of fees.

"23. Judges to take the oath of allegiance and supremacy; and another oath for the "discharge of their places; before they sit, and to administer the same to other.

P. 245. *Sect.* 1, 2. The boundaries of the city to the east, *&c.* are described in the map of the *Ainsty*; as well as the compass of the scale of that map would admit of. And since the antient forest of **Galtres** is so much concerned with the city as to come up to the very walls of it one way, I have likewise attempted a sketch of its boundaries from an antient perambulation, which I met with amongst the records in the *Tower*, and which I subjoin here in its own words as follows,

Perambulatio forest. de Galtres *juxta* Ebor.

"INquisitio capta apud *Ebor.* in majori eccl. beati *Petri* die Lune in festo inventionis an. "S.*Crucis* reg. regis *Ed.* nono per *Robertum de Umframvyle*, com. de *Angous*, custodem "forester. dom. regis ultra *Trentam* secund. tenorem brevis huic inquisitioni consueti tam "super sacrament. omnium ministror. foreste predict. quam per sacramentum *Willielmi* "*Wysburn*, *Roberti Cademan*, *Steph. Sampson*, *Hugo. de Clifford*, *Tho. le Harpour*, *Thome* "*de Wandsford*, *Rich. Paytevyn*, *Johan. de Hoby*, *Johan.* filii *Hugonis*, *Willielmi* filii *Simonis*, "*Walteri Brogh*, *Roberti Brown*; qui jurati dicunt quod ultima perambulatio facta fuit in "foresta de *Galtres* per dominum *Johan. de Lytbegraynes* et socios suos incipiendo ad pe- "dem muri civitatis *Ebor.* apud pontem de *Layrthorpe* sequendo murum ascendendo usque "ad portas ejusdem civit. de *Boutham* et sic sequendo murum usque ad aquam de *Use* us- "que *Benyngburgh* et usque pontem de *Newton*, et sic per rivulum aque de *Lynton* per "medium stagni de *Lynton* sequendo sub villa de *Thollerton* ex parte occidentali us- "que *Carnebrig* et de ponte de *Caren* sequendo dict. rivulum aque per medium stagni de "*Alne* et sic sequendo aquam de *Kyle* per medium *Mikelkar* usque ad pontem de *Raskelf* et "sic ascendendo usque ad molendina de *Waneless* et sic per rivulum aque de *Wyteker* inter "dominicos dom. regis et boscum de *Thornton* usque ad parcum de *Crayk* ascendendo et se- "quendo haias ejusdem parci usque ad aquam de *Foss* usque ad molendinum de *Stiveling-* "*ton* et per eandem aquam usque ad priorat. de *Melsenby* et sic usque le *Brendmilne* de "*Ferlington* et sic per dict. aquam usque ad molend. de *Bulford* et sic usque *Strensale* et sic "usque *Huntingdon* per eandem aquam usque ad pedem muri pontis de *Layrethorpe* ubi in- "cipiunt. Et dicunt quod in predict. perambulatione fuerunt posite extra forestam in bal- "liva de *Kyle* villa de *Lynton*, *Aldwark*, *Thoraldthorpe*, *Brafferton*, *Helperby*, *Flauthworth*, "*Miton*, *Faldington*, *Thornotby*, *Cessey*, *Raskelf*, et *Toulton* cum earum boscis et campis; "et in balliva de *Esingwald* ville de *Baxby*, *Husthwait*, *Thorneton* et *Elleston* cum earum bos- "cis et campis; et in balliva de *Myrescough* ville de *Brandesby*, *Queneby*, *Marton*, *Farling-* "*ton*, *Cornburgh*, *Hoton*, *West Lilling*, *East Lilling*, *Sticlen*, *Thornton*, *Foston*, *Barton*, *Flax-* "*ton*, *Claxton*, *Harton*, *Bossale*, *Barneby*, *Buttercramb*, *Sutton ourgarth*, *Pons* belli pro parte, "*Gate Helmesley*, *Over Helmesley*, *Sandy Hoton*, *Holteby*, *Warthill*, *Stokton*, *Strenshale*, *Tow-* "*thorp*, *Earswick*, *Huntington*, *Morton*, *Osbalwick*, *Heworth* et *Tonge*, cum boscis et cam- "pis earum, et dicunt quod omnes ville predict. cum boscis et campis predict. fuerunt in "foresta ut intendunt in aliquo tempore ante afforestationem factam per bone memorie "*Hen.* avum dom. *Hen.* regis avi dom. nost. regis nunc. Item fuerunt posite extra fo- "restam in predict. perambul. le *Brounemor* et bosce de *Myrscogh* et bosce de *Sandy Ho-* "*ton* et mora de *Sandyburne* in balliva de *Myrescough* et que fuerunt et adhuc sunt de do- "miniis dom. regis, et predicts villa de *Raskelf* cum toto dominio ejusdem que posita fuit "extra forestam aliquo tempore fuit escheat. progenit. dom. regis et data fuit integraliter "antecessoribus dom. *Ranulphi de Nevyle.* Et dicunt quod non habetur in forest. predict. "forestarius de feodo set *Johan. Hayword* est forestarius et tenet balliam suam ad terminum "vite sue de dono dom. regis *Ed.* patris dom. regis *Ed.* nunc, et habet attornatum suum "*Willielmum de Wulley* in partibus illis, et qui premunitus est secund. tenor. brevis et qui "se bene et fideliter gerit pro statu dict. *Johan.* dom. sui, et predict. premiss. consilio dom. "regis super sacrament. suum predict. testificant esse vera.

Bundel. Forest. n. 3. 9. Ed. II.

There are a great number of grants, *&c.* relating to this forest amongst the records of the *Tower*; as to the forest keepers timber, underwoods, venison, *&c.* the tithes of this last was given to the abbey of St. *Mary's York. Claus.* 9 *Ed.* II. *m.* 16.

P. 248. *Sect.* 13. Nunnery of *Clementhorp*, "all these grants were confirmed to it."

The first confirmation made to this religious house was from king *John*; who in the first year of his reign, when at *York*, gave them the following charter.

Confirmatio monialibus S. Clementis Ebor.

"JOHANNES Dei gratia, &c. sciatis nos concessisse et hac carta nostra confirmasse "in puram et perpetuam eleemosynam Deo et sancto *Clementi* et monialibus ibi-"dem Deo servientibus terram quam *Rogerus Ebor.* archiep. emit de proprio de *Hugone* "filio *Sichling* et quod predictis Deo sancto *Clementi* et monialibus dedit et carta sua con-"firmavit cujus scilicet portionem terre predicte moniales coemerant a prefato *Hugone*. "Quare volumus et firmiter precipimus quod ipse moniales habeant et teneant predictam "terram bene et in pace libere et quiete et integre sicut carta predicti archiep. in hunc ra-"tionabiliter testatur.

"*T. G.* filio *Petri* com. *Essex*, *Willielmo de Stutevile*, *Hugone de Bard*.

"Dat. per manus S. *Wellens.* archidiac. et *Johannis de Gray* apud *Eborac.* xxvi die *Martis* "an. reg. nost. primo.

P. 249. *Sect.* 7. "These milns were granted from the crown but when I know not."

Since the printing of this I have found amongst the records in the *rolls* that these milns called **Castell-mylls**, under the castle of *York*, were sold by queen *Elizabeth* to one *Francis Guilpyn* for xii *l. anno reg.* 13.

Ibid. Sect. 8. St. *Andrew*'s priory.

Some extracts of grants to this priory, from the records in the *Tower*, run in these words,

Monast. St. Andree Ebor.

(*a*) "Rex omnibus, &c. Remissionem et quietam-clamantiam quam *Thomas de Chaun-*"*cy* nuper dom. de *Skirpenbeck* per scriptum suum pro se et hered. suis dilectis nobis in "Christo priori et convent S. *Andree Ebor.* de tota communa pasture quam idem *Thomas* "habuit in omnibus terris et dictorum prioris et conventus in *Thoraldby* in com. *Ebor.* ra-"tas habentes et gratas eas pro nobis et hered. nost. quant. in nob. est per finem quem "dict. prior fecit nobiscum concedimus et confirmamus sicut scriptum predict. rationab. "testatur.

"In cujus, &c.

"T. R. apud *Grove* xii die *Jan.*

Per breve de privato sigillo. duplicat.

(*b*) "Rex omnibus, &c. salutem. Sciatis quod cum nuper per litteras nost. patent. "concesserimus et licentiam dederimus pro nobis et heredibus nost. quantum in nob. fuerit "dilectis nob. in Christo priori et conventui sancti *Andree* in *Ebor.* quod ipsi terras tene-"ment. et redditus cum pertinent. ad valorem decem marcarum per ann. juxta verum va-"lorem eorundem tam de feodo suo proprio quam alieno, exceptis terris tenem. et redditi-"bus que de nobis tenentur in capite, adquirere possent habend. et tenend. sibi et success. "suis in perpetuum. Sciatis de terris et tenem. ad manum mort. non ponend. edito non "obstante prout in litt. nost. predict. plenius continetur. Nos volumus concessionem no-"stram predict. effectam mancipari ac pro duabus marcis quas predict. prior nob. solvit "concessimus et licentiam dedimus pro nob. et hered. nost. quantum in nob. est *Johanni de* "*Buttercrambe* capellano et *Roberto* filio *Alani* armiger. capellano quod ipsi tresdecem tofta "quatuor decem bovatas terre et dimid. et sex solidatas unam denaratam et unam obolatam "redditus in *Ebor.* et *Flaxton* unde quatuor solid. reddit cum pertin. in *Ebor.* de nobis in "*Burgagio* ut parcella civit. *Ebor.* tenent. et residua tofta terra et due solid. una denar. et una "obolat. redditus de nobis non tenent. et quidem tofta et terra servitia inde debita valent per "ann. in omnibus exitibus juxta verum valorem eorund. centum solidos sicut per inquisi-"tionem inde per dilect. nob. *Willielmum de Nessefeld* escheat. nost. in com. *Ebor.* de man-"dato nost. factam et in cancellario nost. retornat. et compert. dare possint et assignare "prefatis priori et convent. Habend. et tenend. sibi et successor. suis in plenam satisfactio-"nem decem marcarum terrar. tenem. et reddit. predict. in perpetuum, &c.

"In cujus, &c,

"T. R. apud *Westm.* xii die *Maii.*

"Rex omnibus, &c. Licet, &c. de gratia nost. speciali et pro quatuor marcis quas "dilectus nob. *Thomas Thurkill* nob. solvit in hanap. nost. concessimus et licentiam dedimus "pro nobis et hered. nost. quantum in nob. est, quod ipse duo messuagia et duodecim acras "terre et dimid. cum pertinent. in *Overfulford* et *Waterfulford* que de nob. non tenentur, "dare possit et assignare dilect. nob. in Christo priori et conventui sancti *Andree* in sub-

(*a*) *Pat.* 3 Ed. II. *m.* 24.
(*b*) *Pat.* 34 Ed. III. *p.* 1. *m.* 14.
(*c*) *Pat.* 19 Ric. II *p.* 1. *m.* 31.

"urbio

" urbio *Ebor.* habend. et tenend. eidem priori et conventui et successor. suis in auxilium
" sustentationis sue in perpetuum. Et eisdem priori et convent. quod ipsi mess. et terram
" predict. a prefato *Thoma* recipere possint et tenere sibi et successoribus suis in auxilium
" sustent. sue ut predict. est in perpetuum, statuto de manu. mort non obstante, &c.
" In cujus, &c.
" T. R. apud *Westm.* primo die *Julii.*
P. 250. *Sect. ult.* St. *Nicholas* hospital.

Ebor. Leprosi *ibidem pro terris in suburb. ejusdem per* Matildam *reginam* Angliae, *aut imperatricem, dat. hosp. S.* Nicholai *ibidem.*
Hosp. S. Nicholai *extra* Walm-gate.

(*d*) " INquisitio facta inter dominum regem ex una parte et magistrum et fratres hospitalis S. *Nicholai Ebor.* per *Walterum de Grimston Ebor. Will. de Melton* de eadem, " *Alex. Cissore* de eadem, *Will. Longum* de eadem, *Thomam de Nafferton* de eadem, *Will. de* " *Roston* de eadem, *Robertum* filium *Benedicti de Hewrde*, *Thomam de Hoton* de eadem, *Michaelem de Hewrde*, *Johannem Neulode* de eadem, *Petrum de Dieton* de eadem, *Will. de Wynestawe*, " jurati per sacramentum dicunt quod *Matilda* bona regina *Anglie* dedit predictis magistro " et fratribus dicti hospitalis unam carucatam terre et unam acram prati et dimid. in campo " suburbii civitatis *Ebor.* confirmatam per regem *Stephanum* ad pascendum omnes leprosos " de comitatu *Ebor.* ibidem de consuetudine venientes in vigilia apostolorum *Petri* et *Pauli*, " pro animabus omnium antecessorum et successorum eorum et fuerint in saisina predicti " prati a tempore predicte bone regine *Matilde* usque ad secundum tempus quo *Robertus* " *de Creppyngs* fuit vicecomes *Ebor.* qui eos de predicto prato desessiavit et tenuit ad opus " equorum suorum, et sic aliter vicecomes post alium illud pratum detenuerunt et valuit " illud pratum dimidium marce et spatium dicte disseisine continuavit viginti annos et plus.

P. 295. *Sect.* 10. Free school in *Bootham.*

The whole grant of *Philip* and *Mary*, relating the foundation of this school being too long to insert I shall only give the preamble, as follows,

From a manuscript entitled, *viz. Omnium instrumentorum et monumentorum exemplaria liberam scholam gramaticalem apud le* Horse-faire Ebor. *conservantiam, in hoc volumine conscripta ordine sequuntur.*

Concess. decano et capitul. Ebor.

Licentia dominor. regis et regine concessa magistro hospitalie de Bowthom *ad donandum dicto hospitale ecclesie cathedral.* Ebor. *et decano et capitulo ibidem, ad illud recipiend. et ad usum libere schole convertendum,*

" *Philippus* et *Maria* Dei gratia rex et regina &c. omnibus ad quos salutem. Cum hospital. sancte *Marie* extra *Bothome-barre* civitatis *Ebor.* vulgarit. nuncupat. the *Horse-faire* " jam olim terris decimis spiritualibus ac aliis bonis et rebus competend. ad certum capellanorum et pauperum numerum in ead. exhibend. uti asseritur antiquitus fuerit fundatum " et dotatum, et a multis jam exactis annis, partim temporum malitia partim hominum " negligentia seu verius inexhausta cupiditate prima ipsius hospitalis fundatione neglecta, " quasi vacuum diu remansit, adeo quod hospitalis nomine solum retento omne hospitalitatis et pii loci meritum amiserit, nullaque in eo hospitalitatis, nullus ibi pauper sustentatur, nullus denique Domini cultus aut decorum in eo foveatur, sed omnes ejusdem hospitalis juventus in unius magistri et duorum capellanorum extra dictum hospitale continuo " degentium ac alibi forsan beneficatorum usuum et comoditatem indebite convertuntur, capellaque ibidem, uti vestigia demonstrant, decenter constructa et ministrorum numero sufficienti, ut apparuit, deputata in suis muris fabrica et tectura adeo lacerata existit " et ruinosa quod per magistrum et socios ejusdem ad pristinum statum suum de facili neque " at reparari et restitui in fundatorum ipsius hospitalis injuriam et abutentium hujusmodi " animarum grave periculum: Cumque ut accipimus decanus et capitulum ecclesie cathedralis sancti *Petri Ebor.* quandam scholam grammaticalem et certi numeri scolarium " educatione et eruditione ac ludimagistri et aliorum ministrorum in eadem alimentatione " et perpetua exhibitione apud ecclesiam cathedralem predictam erigere fundare et stabilire " proponant et intendant, quo in ecclesia cathedrali predicta et alibi ministrorum jam diu decrescentium numerus uberiorum existat et divinus cultus hoc exacto pernitiosi scismatis tempore prope labefactatus decentius exornetur, quod sine magnis eorum decani et capituli sumptibus et expenso perfici nequeat et per impleri; cumque etiam dilectus nobis in Christo *Robert. Johnson* in decret. baccalaurius ipsius hospitalis nunc magister et socii ejusdem de et cum " consensu, assensu et ratificatione per dilecti nostri *Willielmi* domini de *Eure* ac dilecti nobis " *Tho. Eglesfield* de *Barton in le willows* in com. nostro *Ebor.* generosi et *Ric. Marshall* de " *Butterwicke* in com. predicto gen. dicti hospital. verorum et indubitatorum procuratorum " nostrorum hujusmodi tam pium opus quantum in illis prout promover. et ad effectum " perducere charitatis intuitu studiose cupientes dictum hospital. cum singulis suis terris tenementis et aliis pervenient. et hereditament. quibuscunque eidem pertinen. dictis decano " et capitulo et eorum successor. in sustentationem dicte schole in forma predicta erigend.

(*d*) *Esch.* 3 Ed. I. *n.* 76.

" et

4

" ſtabiliend. ac in ſupportationem onerum ejuſdem dare concedere et confirmare, quantum " in illis eſt licentia noſtra regali ad hoc obtinend. decreverunt ut informamur. Sciatis " igitur quod nos hujuſmodi tam pium propoſitum et intentionem tam decani et ca- " pituli predict. quam eorundem magiſtri et ſociorum dicti hoſpital. leto animo juvare " cupientes conſiderantesque nihil ad Chriſtianam religionem fovendam conducibilius " quam ut doctorum virorum turba in eccleſia Dei perpetuis futuris temporibus vigeat et " floreat id quod facilius fieri ſperamus ſi pubes noſtra *Anglicana* literis et doctrina imbiben- " dis apta rebus neceſſariis et competentibus ſufficient. aliementetur et ſuſtentetur, de gratia " noſtra ſpeciali ac ex certa ſcientia et mero motu noſtris nec non pro conſiderationibus, pre- " dictis conceſſimus et licentiam dedimus ac per preſentes pro nobis hered. et ſucceſſor. no- " ſtris prefata regina quantum in nobis eſt concedimus et licentiam damus prefat. *Roberto* " *Johnſon*, &c.

" Teſte R. et R. apud *Greenwich* decimo quarto die *Martii* annis regnorum regis et re- " gine *Philippi* et *Marie* tertio et quarto.

Per breve de privato ſigillo &c.

P. 256. *Sect.* 1. *Gilly-gate.*

The caſe of Gilly-gate *ſtated.*

" 1. *Gilly-gate* formerly was all abbot lands. And the abbot being lord thereof and owner " of the houſes and grounds adjoining on both ſides the ſtreet, did maintain and pave the " king's highway there lyeing through the ſaide ſtreet, and a mile further, *viz.* unto the " foreſt and through part of the foreſt of *Galtres*, he being alſo lord thereof; the lord ab- " bot upon the requeſt of the major and guildable of the citty of *Yorke*, did give unto " them a ſummer ſtray upon the foreſt of *Galtres* aforeſaide, and a winter ſtray over his " grounds and demains lyeing and being without *Bowdam* and *Monk-barrs*, and likewiſe " three faires for cattle being yearly holden without *Gilly gate end*, (in a place there " called the *Horſe-faire)* the ſaide lord abbot gave the toles of two of the ſaide faires to the " citizens aforeſaid, and the tole of the third fair is reſerved to the lord biſhop, other " toles likewiſe of corne, &c. the lord abbot gave unto them; in lieu whereof and for " the conſiderations aforeſaide, the ſaide mayor and guildable was to maintaine and pave, " as often as need required the king's highways in *Bowdam*, *Gillilate*, unto the foreſt, part " upon the foreſt and *Monck-gate*, and the ſaide highwayes, not to be any wayes charge- " able unto the ſaide lord abbot or his tenants, the conſiderations aforeſaid far ſurmount- " ing the charges thereof.

" 2. The ſheriffs of *Yorke* upon the two faire dayes aforeſaide ride down a lane called " *Chapel-lane* adjoining upon *Cliſton*, leading unto the one end of the ſaide faire, and " comes back through *Gilly-gate*, on the other end of the faire, which they do not do " through pretending any titles to the ſaide lands or lanes, but as principal highwayes " leading to the ſaide faire as all other paſſingers do, for upon their fixt and ſett day of " rideing about nine dayes after *Martinmaſs*, whereupon their bounds and claims lie, they " do not, or ever did ride down *Gilly-gate* or came therein.

" 3. The lord biſhop's ſteward and officers rideing the ſaide faire, rides downe the ſaide " lane and comes back likewiſe through *Gilly-gate*, and ſetts ſervants in the ſaide lane " and ſtreet to take tole therein, which the ſheriffs does not, or ever did.

" 4. In *Gilly-gate* ſome few perſons pave before their houſes for their own convenien- " ces (by reaſon that the workmen or pavers imployed by the lord-major, make the " cauſy which is the king's highway narrower then it has been formerly, ſo certainly ſuch " perſons as pave ought not to be puniſhed for their well doing, but the others for " leſſening and diminiſhing the king's highway in breadth ought to be preſented.

" 5. If the lord-major have any power to conſtraine ſome perſons to pave, why does " he not compel all perſons to pave (all along by the king's cauſy) which pave not at all, " three parts of the ſtreet of *Gilly-gate* and *Bowdam* lyeing unpaved, ſaveing the king's " high way paved at the lord-major's charges for the conſiderations aforeſaide.

" 6. Theſe bargains and agreements betwixt the lord abbot and major altered not the " property or liberty of the lands adjoining upon the ſaide high ways; nor the ſaid high " ways, nor the lands over which he gave the ſtray, but at the diſſolution of the abby " was layd or annexed to the crowne, and ſold from thence by queen *Elizabeth*, &c. with " the ſame libertyes and freedoms which the abbot enjoyed, or ever did enjoy; and by " the king's prerogative (which ought not to be infringed) thoſe lands and houſes ought " to do ſuite and ſervice to the king's court holden for the liberty of St. *Mary's*, and " not to the citty.

" 7. Treſpaſſes are locall actions, and by the ſtatute of *anno* 1 and 2 of *Phillip* and " *Mary chap.* 12. all cattle treſpaſſing ought to be impounded within the county or ju- " riſdiction where the treſpaſs is done, ſo that a replevy may be had (if neceſſary) within " the ſaide juriſdiction, otherways the perſon impounding the cattel contrary to the ſaid " ſtatute, forfeits for every beaſt ſo by them impounded one hundred ſhilling, and treble " damage to the perſon grieved. *Vide the ſtatute.*

" 8. By

"By this the pinfold in *Gilly-gate*, which was permitted by the lord abbot to be sett "within the liberty of the stray, stands in the liberty of St. *Mary*'s and in the county; "and not in the jurisdiction of the citty, for all the cattle therein impounded are taken "from of the lands formerly belonging to the lord abbot being within the liberty and "county aforesaid; so if the said pindfold stands in the citty jurisdiction (as they erroniously "affirme) then does the pasture masters and other persons impounding cattle there bring "themselves within the penalty of the saide statute.

"The pinfold belonging to the citty for waves, strayers, and trespasses done in the "citty jurisdiction stands in a place called *Toft-green* within the walls of the saide citty.

"10. Lastly in the time of rebellion, the houses without *Bowdam-barr* being burnt "down; the most of them being rebuilt by freemen of the citty, the owners and occupiers "thereof, by reason of their freedoms oath, and by the threats of the lord-majors and al-"dermen in those bad times of being fined or imprisoned, one of the constables of "St. *Olave*'s, or St, *Mary*'s was compelled to be sworne at the citty court leets; yet not-"withstanding being a constablery not within their antient books of rates, or antient *no-"mina villarum*, never payd any quarter payes to the city, *viz.* bridg-money, house of "correction mony, lame soldiers money, &c. but the other constable of St. *Mary*'s or "St. *Olave*'s pays the whole proportion for both constableryes to the weapontake of *Bul-"mer*, and in lieu thereof keepes the poor mony to their own constablery, which should "be destributed throughout both constableryes, they being both one parish and con-"stablery.

P. 258. *Sect. ult.* St. *Olave*'s church.

Olave, or *Olaf*, king of *Norway*, was a very pious innocent prince, but so zealous against wizzards and witches that he banished some and put others to death. The few remaining magicians, together with the relations of those that had suffered, were so enraged at this, that they combined together and took an opportunity of killing the king; who for the innocence of his life and the suffering for the cause of God, according at least to the judgment of those times, was reckoned afterwards a saint and martyr.

This is the common account of him; but some writers charge *Canutus* with his death, and say that he spirited up his subjects to this wicked act in order to make himself master of his kingdom; which he actually did immediately after the good king's death. You may find the whole story in *Cressy*'s church history of *Britain*, *lib.* xxxiv. *c.* 9. *p.* 942. He is an author of no great credit, but here he brings his proper vouchers, and therefore deserves the more regard.

I fancy the *English* had a greater value than ordinary for this saint out of hatred to the *Danes*; for there are so many churches dedicated to him in *England* as can hardly be accounted for any other way. I need not tell you that his name is often very odly corrupted into '*Tooley*, as St. *Anne* into '*Tan*, St. *Andrew* into '*Tandrew*, St. *Alcuin* in '*Tawkin*, &c. Dr. *Langwith*.

P. 260. *Sect.* 17.

I find that the rectory of *Clifton*, alias St. *Olave*'s, was sold to *Thomas Eymis* for vii *l.* vii *s.* 15 *Eliz. Rolls chap.*

P. 261. *Sect. ult. et. P.* 262. *Sect.* 1.

Toll, &c. granted for the reparations of the city walls.

De villa Ebor. *claudenda.*

"REX (e) majori et probis hominibus *Ebor.* salutem. Sciatis quod concessimus vobis "in auxilium ville *Ebor. ad securitatem et tuitionem ejusdem ville*, simul et partium "adjacentium, quod capiatis a die *Pentecostes* anno regni nostri x. usque ad festum S. *Mi-"chaelis* anno regni nostri xi. de qualibet caretta sive carro comitatus *Ebor.* ferente res ve-"nales in eandem villam ibidem vendendas unum obulum; et de qualibet caretta sive carro "alterius comitatus ferente res venales in eandem villam ibidem vendendas unum denarium; "et de quolibet summagio rerum venalium ibidem vendendarum, preterque de summagio "*Busch.* unum quadrantem; et de quolibet equo et equa et bove et vacca venali illuc "ductis ad vendendum unum obolum; et de decem ovibus vel capris vel porcis venalibus, "illuc ductis ad vendendum unum denarium; et de quinque ovibus vel porcis vel capris "unum obulum; et de qualibet nave veniente in villam *Ebor.* carcata rebus venalibus ibi-"dem vendendis quatuor denarios. Ita cum quod occasione istius concessionis nostre de "hujusmodi carettis carris summagiis equis equabus bobus vaccis ovibus capris vel por-"cis vel nave veniente in villa carcata rebus venalibus nihil capiatur post predictum ter-"minum completum, sed statim completo termino illo cadet consuetudo illa et penitus abo-"letur. Et ideo vobis mandamus quod in auxilium ville predicte *claudende* consuetudi-"dinem predictam capiatis usque ad predictum terminum completum sicut predictum est.

"T. R. apud *Westm.* xiii. die *Maii* anno reg. x. coram justiciariis; mandatum viceco-"miti *Ebor.* quod hanc consuetudinem predictam per totam ballivam suam clamari "faciat et firmiter observari, sicut predictum est, T. rege apud *Westm.* ut supra.

(e) *Pat.* 10. Hen. III. *m.* 5.

Ad decanum et cap. pro eadem causa.

" REX *(f)* decano et capitulo *Ebor.* salutem. Rogamus vos quod in consuetudinem " quam capi concessimus in civitate *Ebor.* ad eandem civitatem claudendam, ad " tuitionem et defensionem ejusdem civitatis, et partium illarum, et ad indempnitatem ve- " stram et communem utilitatem omnium de partibus illis, ab hominibus vestris capi per- " mittatis ad presens usque ad terminum quem ad hoc per litteras nostras concessimus; sic " uti quod nolumus quod hujusmodi consuetudo predicta terminum illum illapsum non ce- " vobis in prejudicium vel trahetur in consuetudinem.

" In cujus rei testimonium has litteras patentes vobis mittimus.

" Teste et data ut supra.

Ebor. de tallagio ibidem super reddit. et catall. pro muris fossatis &c, reparandis.

Ad decanum Ebor. *super eandem causam.*

" REX *(g)* dilecto clerico suo magistro *Roberto Pykerynge* decano eccle. beati *Petri Ebor.* " salutem. Cum ut intelleximus major ballivi et cives civitatis nostre *Ebor.* quod- " dam tallagium super redditibus et catallis suis in eadem civitate pro muris et fossatis ac " aliis fortaliciis dicte civitatis reparand. et corroborand. pro salvatione et defensione civi- " tat. illius, ex unanimo consensu suo apposuerunt per constabularios wardarium dicte ci- " vitatis levand. Vos levationem hujusmodi tallagii per predict. majorem ballivos et ci- " ves ex unanimo consensu eorundem ex causa predicta sunt assessi, impedire nitentes pre- " dictos constabularios quo minus tallagium illud sic assessum de aliquibus tenent. que de " nob. tenentur in capite in predict. civitate levare possint per censuras ecclesiasticas im- " peditis, in maximum periculum civitatis predicte, ac hominum in eadem civitate com- " morantium et nost. prejudicium manifestum; unde plurimum admiramur, nos securitati " dicte civitatis et indempnitatis hominum in eadem commorantium modis et viis, quibus " bono modo poterimus providere volentes, vobis mandamus firmiter injungentes quod, si " ita est, tunc constabularios predictos hujusmodi tallagium per predictos majorem ballivos " et cives ex unanimo consensu eorundem ut promittetur appositum juxta ipsorum ordina- " tionem factam levare absque impedimento aliquo permittatis. Taliter vos habentes in " hac parte quod ex defectu vestro in premissis per nos redargui non debeatis quovis " modo.

" Teste R. apud *Marlebergh* primo die *Januarii.*

P. 263. *Sect.* 1. " Priory of the *Holy Trinity York.*

Pro priore ecclesie Sancte Trinitatis Ebor. *de confirmatione.*

" REX *(h)* omnibus ad quos, &c. salutem. Inspeximus cartam quam celebris memorie " dom. *Hen.* rex *Anglie* progenitor nost. fecit in hec verba: *Hen.* rex *Anglie* ar- " chiepis. epis. just. vicecomit. baronibus et omnibus fidelibus suis *Francis* et *Angiis* salu- " tem. Sciatis quod ego concedo Deo et ecclesie S. *Trinitatis* de *Eboraco* et monachis in " ea Deo servientibus omnes tenuras suas in eleemosynis in ecclesiis et terris et decimis et ho- " minibus et omnibus aliis beneficiis que *Radulphus Paganellus* illis dedit et concessit, sicut " in carta sua continetur, ipsam scilicet ecclesiam *Sancte Trinitatis* et terras suas extra por- " tam de *Micklelith* que jacent ad occidentalem partem ipsius civitatis, cum omnibus perti- " nentiis et cum omnibus libertatibus suis et liberis consuetudinibus suis eidem ecclesie per- " tinentibus, cum soca et sacca et tol et them et infangentheft liberas et quietas ab omnibus " secular. servitiis in eadem civitate ecclesiam S. *Helene* et quecunque ad eandem pertinen- " tia ante eandem ecclesiam, toftum unius diaconi in *Lincolniensi scira*, ecclesiam de *Irnam* et " quicquid ad eam pertinet et duas partes decimarum de dominico ejusdem ville et duas " partes omnium decimarum de dominicis de *Scallebia* et de *Ashcelenade* feodo *Odonis Tus- " tbe*, et duas partes omnium decimarum de dominico de *Tanclesbia* et molendinum ejus- " dem ville de feudo *Rad. de Bolliaco*, ecclesiam de *Rasa* et quicquid ad illam pertinet et " decimas aule, ecclesiam de *Berthona* et que ad eam pertinent, et duas partes omnium de- " cimarum de dominico ejusdem ville, ecclesiam de *Rokesbeia* et quicquid ad eam pertinet, et " duas partes omnium decimarum ejusdem ville dom°. In *Eboracensi scira* in villa que " vocatur *Dracx* piscatoriam unam et decimam ceterarum piscatur. et unam carrucatam " terre in *Bardelbeia*, ecclesiam de *Newtona* et quicquid ad eam pertin. et decimas de do- " minio ejusdem ville, ecclesiam de *Monketona* et quicquid ad eam pertinet et unam carru- " cat. terre et dimid. in eadem villa et quatuordecim bovat. terre in *Heselsay*, ecclesiam " de *Ledes* et quicquid ad eam pertinet, et decimas de dominio et dimid. carucat. terre in " eadem villa, totam etiam villam de *Strettona* cum omnib. pertin. suis et duas partes decim.

(f) Pat 10 Hen. III. m. 3.
(g) Claus. 14 Ed. III. m. 12. dorso.
(h) Pat. 30 Ed. III. p. 1. m. 14.

de

" de dominio, ecclesiam de *Hotona* et quicquid ad eam pertinet, et duas partes omnium decim. " de dominio ejusd. ville, ecclesiam S. *Helene* de *Tirnescogh* et quicquid ad eam pertinet, ec- " clesiam S. *Johan.* de *Adela* et quicquid ad eam pertinet et unam carrucatam terre in eadem " villa et decimas de *Ardingtona* et omnium villarum que eidem adjacent, et decim. de do- " minio, dimid. ecclesiam de *Cramburn* et quicquid ad illam pertin. ecclesiam de *Borthona* in " *Ridala* et quicquid ad eam pertinet et duas partes omnium decim. de dominio ejusd. ville, " decimas etiam de *Fademora* ex dono *Jordani Painel* filii ipsius *Radulphi*, villam de *Kunyngef-* " *thorp* totam et integram cum omnib. pertinen. suis sicut carta ipsius testatur, duas partes " omnium decim. de dom. de *Newtona* super *Wald*. Et volo et concedo et firmiter precipio " quod honorifice et bene et pace et libere et quiete omnia super nominata habeant et tene- " ant non disturbent, et ubicunque terras habent volo ut sint quieti et liberi ab omni servitute " et consuetudine de hundredo et wapontack. Test. *Nigello de Albini*, *Roberto de Brus*, *Si-* " *mone Dapifero*, *Rad. de Bolliaco*, *Alano Flealdi filio*, *Ranulpho Thesaurario* nost. apud *Ebora-* " *cum*. Inspeximus etiam quandam aliam cartam ejusdem progenit. nost. in hec verba. *Hen.* " Dei gratia rex *Ang.* dux *Norman. Aquit.* et comes *Andeg.* archiepiscopis episcopis abb. comit. " baron. justic. vicecom. balliv. et omnibus minist. et fidel. suis totius *Ang.* et *Norman.* salu- " tem. Sciatis me concessisse et hac presenti carta mea confirmasse Deo et ecc. S. *Trin. Ebor.* " et monachis de *Majori monasterio* ibidem Deo servient. ecclef. S. *Johan.* de *Adela* cum " omnib. pertin. suis et unam carucat. terre in eadem villa de donat. *Rad. Paganelli* et con- " firm. filior. ejus sicut carte eorum testant. Et ideo volo et firmiter precipio quod predict. " monachi pred. ecc. habeant et teneant bene et in pace quiete et honorifice cum omnib. " libert. ad eandem ecclef. pertin. *T. Stephano* de *Turon.* senescaldo *Andegavie*, *Ranulpho de* " *Glanvillis*, apud *Turon.* Nos autem cartas predict. et omnia et singula in eis contenta ra- " ta habentes et grata ea pro nob. et hered. nost. dilecto nob. in Christo *Johannis de Chesiaco* " nunc priori loci predict. ac monach. ibidem Deo servient. eorum success. ratificamus con- " ced. et confirm. prout carte predict. rationab. testantur.

" In cujus, &c.

" T. R. apud *Westm.* xxv. die *Novembris.*

" *Pro dimid. marca solut. in hanappio.*

P. 264. *Sect.* 8. " It is now called *Trinity-gardens, &c.*"

The scite of the priory of the *Holy-Trinity* in *York* was sold to *Leonard Beckwith*, with the demesne lands there, 34 *Hen.* VIII. *Rolls Chapel.*

P. 265. *Sect. penult.* " *Old Baile.*"

Ebor. *archiep. de memorand. irrotulat. de custod. et defens. cujusdam partis civitatis voc.* **Ballium** *tempore guerrae, viz. cum ad prefat. archiep. aut ad cives ib. de jure pertineat* (*i*).

" MEmorand. quod die *Mercurii* proximo ante festum S. *Petri* ad vincula anno regni re- " gis *Eduardi* tertii post conquestum primo coram concilio dom. regis in palatio " venerabilis patris *W.* archiep. *Ebor. Anglie* primatis, ubi domina *Isabella* regina *Anglie* ho- " spitata fuit in presentia ejusdem archiep. ac venerabilium patrum *J. Elienf.* cancellar. et " *H. Lincoln.* thesaur. ipsius regis et *J. Wynton.* episcoporum, *Galfrid. Lescrope* ac aliorum " de concilio dom. regis, *Nicholaus de Langton* major civitatis *Ebor.* et *Nicholaus de Sexdecim* " *vallibus* clericus ejusdem civitatis personaliter constituti petierunt a prefato archiep. quod " ipse suis sumptibus custodire faciet locum suum vocatum **Vetus Ballium** contra *Scotorum* " aggressus prout ipsi muros ejusdem civitatis faciunt custodiri, asserentes quod ipse et prede- " cessores sui locum illum temporibus retroactis tempore guerre custodire et munire consue- " verunt, et idem archiep. asseruit quod major et communitas *Ebor.* tenent eandem civita- " tem de domino rege ad firmam perpetuam sine periculo custodiend. tam tempore guerre " quam pacis, nullo loco infra eandem civitatem excepto, videlicet nec **Ballio** predicto nec " alio quocunque, et quod **Ballium** predict. est parcella civitatis predicte et infra fossata ejus- " dem civitatis, quousque locum custodire non tenet nec predecessores sui eundem locum " custodire consueverunt, sed quod alia vice propter maximum periculum quod eidem civi- " tati tunc imminebat dari fecit locum illum et quosdam homines pro munitione ejusdem " durante periculo predicto posuit, et super hoc facta fuit indentura inter prefatum archie- " piscopum et majorem et ballivos et communitatem civitatis predicte, quod idem archiepisco- " pus sic fecit imminente dicto periculo de sua liberalitate et gratia, non cederet sibi aut suc- " cessoribus suis prejudicium nec traheretur in consequentiam in futuro. Et predicti major " et clericus non dedixerunt indenturam predictam, sed dixerunt quod predictus locus non est " parcella civitatis predicte, nec infra fossata ejusdem civitatis, sed quod fossata circa locum " illum sunt propria fossata ipsius archiepiscopi, nec major et communitas civitatis illius se de " loco illo habeant in aliquo intromittere, et quod idem archiepiscopus et successores sui lo- " cum illum suo periculo custodire debent et illum custodire consueverunt totis temporibus " retroactis. Et postmodum idem archiep. pro eo quod premissa discuti et terminari tunc " non potuerunt, dixit quod contemplatione dicte domine regine ac filii et filiarum suarum

(*i*) *Claus.* 1 Ed. III. *p.* 2. *m.* 17. *dorso.* 1327.

" infra

5

" infra eandem civitatem tum commorantium ponere voluit de hominibus suis ad custodien-
" dum locum predict. ista vice, ita tamen quod si periculum per ipsorum *Scotorum* aggressus
" loco illi quod absit immineat, idem major et cives civitatis illius ordinent pro defensione
" loci illius cum hominibus dicti archiepiscopi sicuti de aliis locis civitatis predict. prout
" melius viderint expedire, ita etiam quod illud quod sit factum de gratia sua ex
" causa predict. sibi seu successoribus suis non cedat in prejudicium temporibus futuris. Et
" predicti major et clericus concesserunt quod ipsi ordinabunt de custodia loci predict. cum
" hominibus predict. archiep. si magnum periculum ibidem immineat precipue pro securitate
" dicte civitatis melius fore viderint faciend. et quod illud quod sit factum non cedat eidem
" archiepiscopo aut ecclesie sue seu successoribus suis in prejudicium in futuro. Salva tamen
" prefatis majori et civibus calumpnia sua si quam habeant in hac parte cum voluerint inde
" loqui.

P. 274. *Sect.* 3. " The monastery of the *Fryars-preachers.*"

Ebor. *fratres predic. ibidem de capella beate* Marie *ibidem concess. cum quadam placea terrae vocat.* **Kingestoftes.** *(k)*

" HEnricus Dei gratia rex *Anglie* &c. Ballivis *Ebor.* salut. Sciatis nos dedisse et carta " nostra confirmasse fratribus *ordinis Predicatorum* commorantibus in civitate nost. " *Ebor.* capellam nost. S. *Marie Magdalene* in *Ebor.* que sita est in placea que vocat. " **Kingestoftes** et partem quandam ejusdem placee ad edificandum et habitandum ibidem sic- " ut plenius continetur in carta nost. eis inde facta, et ideo vobis mandamus quod eisdem " fratribus de predict. capella et de predict. parte predict. placee secundum metas contentas " in predict. carta nost. sine dilatione plenam saisinam habere faciatis.

" Teste me apud *Westm.* viii. die *Martii* an. reg. xii.

" REX majori et ballivis *Ebor.* salut. Sciatis quod intuitu Dei dedimus et concessimus " fratribus *ordinis Predicatorum* de placea nost. qua vocat. **Kingestoftes** partem il- " lam quam incluserunt quodam fossato versus occidentalem usque ad dunam fossati civitatis " *Ebor.* versus borealem partem quandam ubi plana terra se extendit. Ita quod nihil habeant " de fossato civitatis predict. et sic versum partem orientalem usque ad curtilagium *Roberti* " filii *Baldewni*, et ideo vobis mandamus quod. de predict. placea per metas predict. clau- " denda plenam saisinam eis libere faciatis, ita quod habeant liberum exitum usque ad a- " quam de *Use* per fossatum civitatis predicte.

" Teste rege apud *Pontemfractum* xxx. die *Decem.* 1228.

Ebor. *confirmatio cartar. et donat. fratribus predicator. ibidem concess.*

" REX omnibus ad quos litt. &c. salutem. Inspeximus literas patentes dom. *R.* nuper " regis *Anglie* fact. in hec verba. *Richardus* Dei gratia rex *Anglie* et *Francie* et dom. " *Hibernie* omnibus ad quos presentes litt. pervenir. salutem. Inspeximus cartam dom. *H.* " quondam regis *Anglie* progenitoris nost. in hec verba. *Henricus* Dei gratia rex *Ang.* dom. " *Hiber.* dux *Norman.* et *Aquitain.* comes *Andeg.* archiepiscopis episcop. abbat. priorib. comi- " tib. baronib. justiciar. vicecomit. prepositis minist. et omnibus ballivis et fidelibus suis, sa- " lutem. Sciatis nos intuitu Dei et pro salute anime nostre et animar. antecessor. nost. dedisse " concessisse et hac carta nostra confirmasse fratribus ordinis predicatorum in civitate *Ebor.* " commorantibus capellam nost. S. *Marie Magdalene* in *Eboraco* que sita est in placea nost. " que vocat. **Kingestoftes**, et partem quandam ejusdem placee ad edificand. ibidem, cujus lon- " gitudo est a fossato quod *Willielmus Moulsoures* levavit ex occidentali parte ejusdem capelle " per dunam fossati predict. civitatis usque ad cortillagium *Roberti* filii *Baldwini* in oriente, " latitudo autem ejusdem partis quam eis dedimus est ex occidentali parte predict. capelle et " predict. duna fossati predict. civitat. per memoratum fossatum quod predict. *Willielmus* le- " vavit usque ad magnam stratam que est contigua ipsius capelle ex parte australi, et ita di- " recte versus orientem ad predict. curtilagium predict. *Roberti* filii *Baldewini.* Tenend. et " habend. de nobis et hered. nost. eisdem fratrib. et successoribus suis bene et in pace libere " quiete integre in liberam puram et perpetuam eleemosinam. Quare volumus et firmiter " precipimus quod predict. fratres et eorum successores habeant et teneant predict. capellam " et partem predict. placee predict. cum omnibus libertatibus et liberis consuetudin. ad eas " pertinent. per metas predict. sicut predict. est. Hiis testibus *J. Bathon.* et *W. Carliol.* epis- " copis *H. de Burgo* comite *Kantie* justiciario *Anglie*, *Willielmo Marescillo* comite *Pembrochie* " *Philippo de Albemarlo*, *Radulpho* filio *Nicholai Godofrido de Craucombe*, *Richardo de Molys* " *Galfrido* dispensario et aliis. Data per manum venerabilis patris *R. Cicestrensis* epis. cancel- " larii nost. apud *Westm.* octavo die *Martii* anno regni nost. duodecimo. Inspeximus etiam " litt. patent. ejusdem dom. *H.* in haec verba, *Henricus* Dei gratia rex *Anglie* dom. *Hibern.* " et dux *Aquitan.* omnibus ad quos present. litt. perven. salutem. Quia accepimus per in- " quisitionem quam per majorem et ballivos nost. *Ebor.* fieri fecimus quod non est ad dam-

(k) Claus. 12 Hen. III. *m.* 2. *in schedula et in m.* 14. *ejusdem.*

" num

" num noſt. nec nocumentum civitat. prediċt. ſi concedamus fratribus *Predicator.* quod quan-
" dam portionem terre noſt. ſitui domus ſue contiguam latitudine decem et octo pedum que in
" longitudine ab alia via ſe extendit uſque ad murum diċt. civit. includere poſſint et eam te-
" nere incluſam ad ampliationem ſitus ſui prediċt. in perpetuum. Dum tamen pro quodam
" puteo infra diċtam portionem terre exiſtent. quendam alium puteum fieri faciant in alio
" loco competenti, nos intuitu caritatis concedimus pro nob. et hered. noſt. fratrib. ante-
" diċtis portionem terre prediċt. ad ampliationem diċti ſitus ſibi includant et incluſam teneant
" in perpetuum dum tamen pro puteo infra portionem illam exiſtente quendam puteum fieri
" faciant alibi in loco competenti ſicut prediċt. eſt. In cujus, &c. Teſte me ipſo apud
" *Ebor.* viceſimo tertio die *Sept.* anno reg. noſt. quinquageſimo ſecundo. Inſpeximus inſu-
" per litt. patent. dom. *E.* quondam regis *Anglie* progenitoris noſt. in hac verba, *Edwardus*
" Dei gra. rex *Ang.* dom. *Hybern.* et dux *Aquit.* omnibus &c. ſalutem. Licet de conſilio
" regni noſt. ſtatuimus quod non liceat viris religioſis ſeu aliis ingredi feodum alicujus ita
" quod ad manum mortuam deveniat ſine licentia noſt. et capitalis domini de quo res illa im-
" mediate tenetur; volentes tamen *Hamoni Gruſay* gratiam facere ſpecialem dedimus ei li-
" centiam quantum in nob. eſt, quod ipſa tria tofta cum pertin. in civit. noſt. *Ebor.* que de no-
" bis tenentur per ſervitium duorum denariorum per an. per *buſegable* dare poſſit et aſſignare
" dileċt. nob. in Chriſto priori et fratrib. ordin. *Predicat.* ejuſdem civitatis habend. et tenend.
" eiſdem priori et fratrib. et ſucceſſor. ſuis in perpetuum ad elargationem placee ſue ibidem et
" eiſdem priori et fratribus quod ipſi prediċt. toſta cum pertinent. a prefato *Hamone* ſic recipere
" poſſint tenore preſent. Similiter licentiam dedimus ſpecialem, ſalvo nobis et hered. noſt. pre-
" diċt. ſervitio duorum denar. annuorum percipiend. prout illud ſemper prius percipere conſue-
" vimus et ſalvo jure cujuſlibet. Nolentes quod prediċt. *Hamo* et heredes ſui aut prediċt. prior
" et fratres ſeu ſucceſſ. ſui ratione ſtatuti prediċt. per nos vel hered. noſt. inde occaſionentur
" moleſtentur in aliquo ſeu graventur. In cujus &c. Teſte *Edwardo* filio noſt. apud
" *Langelee* xviii. die *Feb.* an. reg. noſt. viceſ. ſexto. Inſpeximus etiam quaſdam alias litt.
" patent. ejuſdem dom. *E.* in hec verba, *Edwardus* Dei gratia rex *Anglie* &c. Quia acce-
" pimus per inquiſitionem quam per vicecomit. noſt. *Ebor.* fieri fecimus quod non eſt ad
" dampnum noſt. vel prejudicium noſt. aut aliorum ſi concedimus dileċt. nobis in Chriſto
" priori et fratrib. ord. *Predic.* de *Ebor.* quandam placeam noſt. vacuam de *Ebor.* aree ſue
" verſus aquam de *Uſe* contiguam habend. et tenend. eiſdem priori et fratrib. et ſucceſſ. ſuis
" ad elargationem aree ſue prediċt. in perpetuum. Nos eiſdem priori et fratribus volentes
" in hac parte gratiam facere ſpecialem dedimus et conceſſimus eis pro nobis et hered. noſt.
" placeam prediċt. habend. et tenend. eiſdem priori et fratribus et ſucceſſ. ſuis in perpetuum
" ad elargationem aree ſue prediċt. ſicut prediċt. eſt. Salvo jure cujuſlibet. In cujus, &c.
" Teſte me ipſo apud *Stamford* primo die *Maii* an. reg. noſt. viceſ. octavo. Inſpeximus
" inſuper litt. patent. dom. *E.* nuper regis *Anglie* progenitoris noſt. in hec verba, *Edwardus*
" Dei gratia rex *Anglie* dom. *Hibernie* et dux *Aquitan.* omnibus ad quos &c. ſalutem. Scia-
" tis quod pro ſalut. anime noſtre et animarum anteceſſorum et hered. noſt. conceſſimus pro
" nobis et hered. noſt. quantum in nob. eſt quod dileċti nobis in Chriſto fratres ord. *Predicat.*
" in civit. noſt. *Ebor.* commorantes duas perticatas terre et dimidiam ſitui ſuo contiguas, per
" perticatam noſtram viginti pedum in latitudine, et quindecim perticatas terre per eandem
" perticatam in longitudine de illa vacua placea noſt. que vocat. *Kingeſtoſtes* infra civit. pre-
" diċt. includere et eas ſic incluſas ſalvo jure cujuſlibet in perpetuum habere et tenere, ac
" quendam fontem infra locum illum exiſtent. obſtruere poſſint, ita quod alium fontem loco
" ejuſdem fontis ubi commodius in placea prediċt. extra prediċt. terram includend. fieri po-
" terint ſumptibus ſuis propriis adeo bonum et utilem ſicut eſt fons qui nunc eſt in placea
" prediċt. faciant pro communi utilitate homin. civit. prediċte. In cujus &c. Teſte me ipſo
" apud *Weſtm.* xv. die *Novem.* an. reg. noſt. octavo. Nos autem donationem conceſſiones et
" confirmationes prediċtas ratas habentes et gratas eas pro nob. et hered. noſt. quantum in
" nobis eſt, dileċt. nob. in Chriſto nunc priori et fratrib. loci prediċti et ſucceſſ. ſuis ratifica-
" mus et approbamus et tenore preſentium concedimus et confirmamus, ſicut carta et litere
" prediċt. rationabiliter teſtantur, conceſſimus; inſuper et licentiam dedimus pro nobis et he-
" red. noſt. quantum in nob. eſt eiſdem priori et fratrib. quod ipſi placeas prediċt. quarum
" clauſura nuper abſque debito proceſſu confraċta extitit et proſtrata per metas et bundas in
" carta et literis prediċt. contentas et expreſſas reincludere et eas ſic reincluſas tenere poſſint
" ſibi et ſucceſſoribus ſuis in perpetuum, prout ipſi et predeceſſores ſui eas a tempore dona-
" tionis conceſſionum et confirmationum placearum illar. rationabiliter tenuerunt. In cujus
" rei teſt. has lit. noſt. fieri fecim. paten. Teſte me ipſo apud *Weſtm.* viceſ. quarto die
" *Novem.* an. reg. noſt. quinto. Nos autem lit. prediċtas ac omnia et ſingula contenta in
" eiſdem rata habentes et grata, ea pro nobis et hered. noſt. quantum in nobis eſt acceptamus
" et approbamus ac dileċt. nob. in Chriſto nunc priori et fratribus loci prediċt. et eorum
" ſucceſſoribus ratificamus et confirmamus, prout litere prediċt. rationabiliter teſtant.
" In cujus &c. Teſte rege apud *Ebor.* xxi. die *Junii* (*l*).

Per ipſum regem et de data prediċt. autoritate.

(*l*) Pat. 4 Ed.IV. p. 1. m. 9. 1464.

P. 274. *Sect.* 3. *Brian Godson*, pryor, or guardian, of the *Fryars-Preachers*, otherways called **les tofts**, within the city of *York*, gave up his monastery to the king. The instrument bears date in their chapter-house *Nov.* 27. *anno reg. Hen.* VIII. 30. *Claus.* 30. *Hen.* VIII. *pars* 5. *num.* 61.

P. 282. *Sect.* 9. Monastery of *Fryars-minors*.

Ebor. Fratres minor. *ibidem de quodam fossato de dominico regis contiguo aree dict. fratrum ex parte orient. inter eandem aream et* **Pontem Ballii** *concess. per regem ad aream suam elargand.* (c)

" REX omnibus, &c. Quia accepimus per inquisitionem factam per majorem et ballivos nost. *Ebor.* sciri fecimus quod non est ad damnum nostrum nec non civitat. nost. *Ebor.* concedere dilectis nobis in Christo *Fratribus Minoribus* ejusdem civitat. quoddam fossatum quod est in dominico nostro, contiguum aree dictorum fratrum, ex parte orientali, inter eandem aream et **Pontem Ballii**; nos, pro salute anime nost. et hered. nost. dedimus concessimus eisdem fratribus fossatum predictum ad ampliationem aree sue predicte, ita quod fossatum illud muro terreo includant, et exaltent in altitudine usque ad duodecim pedes, ad predicationes factas in eodem loco tenendas, prout ingredientibus ad predicationes illas audiendas, et egredientibus locum illum magis viderint expedire, et fossatum illud sic inclusum tenere possint in perpetuum. Ita etiam quod, si per turbulationem et guerram vel alio modo necesse fuerit, fossatum illud evacuari ad defensionem castri *Ebor.* nos et heredes nost. fossatum illud evacuari faciamus, prout melius ad opus nost. novimus fore faciend.

" In cujus, &c.

Pro Fratribus Minor. Ebor. *de quadam venella includenda* (d).

" REX omnibus ad quos, &c. salutem. Quia accepimus per inquisitionem quam per vicecomitem nost. *Ebor.* et dilectos fideles nost. *Johannem de Lithegregnes* et *Nicholaum de Seleby* majorem civit. nost. *Ebor.* fieri fecimus, quod non est ad dampnum seu prejudicium nost. seu alior. si concedamus dilectis nob. in Christo fratribus de ord. *Minor.* ejusdem civitat. quod ipsi quandam venellam que contigua est muro suo ibidem et que se extendit in longitudine et latitudine a via regia usque ad venellam que se ducit versus molendina juxta castrum nost. *Ebor.* includere et eam sic inclusam tenere possint sibi et successoribus suis in perpetuum. Ita tamen quod quandam aliam venellam ejusdem longitudinis et latitudinis eidem venelle contiguam in solo suo proprio faciant. Nos eisdem fratribus gratiam facere volentes in hac parte concessimus eis pro nob. et hered. nost. quantum in nobis est, quod ipsi predict. venellam includere et eam inclusam tenere possint sibi et successoribus suis in perpetuum. Ita tamen quod quandam aliam venellam ejusdem longitudinis et latitudinis eidem venelle contiguam in solo suo proprio faciant sicut predict. est.

" In cujus, &c.

" Test. rege apud. *Westm.* xxvii. die *Jan.* 1290.

Ebor. *de ordine* Fratrum Minor. *ibidem de situat. domus sue, &c.* (e)

" REX omnibus ad quos, &c. salutem. Sciatis quod ad requisitionem *Isabelle* regine *Anglie* consortis nost. carissime concessimus et licentiam dedimus pro nob. et heredibus nost. quantum in nob. est priori et fratribus de ordine *Minor. Ebor.* quod ipsi omnes domus et placeas a media porta ipsorum fratrum juxta caput cancelli eccles. sue ibidem ex transverso usque in venellam que vocatur *Hertorgate* et sic descendendo usque ad aquam de *Ouse* versus occidentem aree sue ibidem contiguas adquirere possint et tenere sibi et successoribus suis ad elargationem aree sue predicte in perpetuum, statuto de terris et tenementis ad manum mort. non ponend. edito non obstante. Cum tamen per inquisitiones inde in forma debita faciendas et in cancellaria nostra et heredum nost. retornandas compertum est sic quod id fieri poterint absque dampno vel prejudicio nost. vel hered. nost. et alterius cujuscunque.

" Teste rege apud *Ebor.* secundo die *Aug.*

Per breve de privato sigillo.

Privilegia Fratrum Minorum *civitatis* Ebor. (f)

" EDwardus Dei gratia rex *Angliae* et *Franciae* et dominus *Hiberniae* vic. *Ebor.* ac majori et ballivis civitatis ejusdem qui nunc sunt vel qui pro tempore fuerint, necnon omnibus aliis ballivis et fidelibus nostris ad quos presentes literae pervenerint, salutem. Ex querelosa insinuatione dilectorum nobis in Christo *Gardiani* et fratrum de ordine *Minorum* civitatis praedictae concepimus qualiter quibusdam felonibus nostris et aliis ad hospitium

(c) *Pat.* 3 Hen. III. *m.* 4. 1269.
(d) *Pat.* 18 Ed. I. *m.* 42.
(e) *Pat* 8 Ed. II *p.* 1. *m.* 27.
(f) *Ex registro antiq.* Ebor. *folio* 142.

" et

"et ecclesiam ipsorum fratrum metu mortis sibi inferendae pro immunitate ecclesiastica ob-
"tinenda saepius ante haec tempora fugientibus vos vel saltem quidam vestrum caeterique
"quamplures vestra authoritate vel mandato seu saltem velamine vestro vel instinctu insidi-
"as et tam diurnas quam nocturnas vigilias infra fratrum septa perperam fecistis et quan-
"doque nepharie dicta septa intrantes et in hujus facientes ausu sacrilego irruentes et manus
"et plagas imponentes ipsos extra dicta septa expulistis et extraxistis ipsos fratres et liberta-
"tem ecclesiasticam temere contemnendo domos suas et muros enormiter frangend. et gar-
"dina sua calcand. et alia quamplurima illicita et inhonesta impetuoso animo attemptando
"per quae dicta libertas violatur, divinorum celebrationes perturbantur, pax et quies popu-
"laris laeduntur, ac dicti gardianus et fratres ibidem Deo servituri non modicum turbantur;
"adeoque perterriti redduntur quod saepius clausam suam egredi non sunt ausi; nos dicta
"gravamina et nepharia corditer abhorrentes honorem et reverentiam sanctae matris eccle-
"siae quos delectabiliter amplectimur et libertates ecclesiasticas in suis juribus teneri volu-
"mus pro viribus et fovere ad quietem dictorum gardiani et fratrum suscepimus ipsos et eo-
"rum hospitium ecclesiam et omnia infra septa habitationis suae ipsaque septa in pro-
"tectionem et defensionem nostram specialem, et ideo vobis omnibus et singulis sub gravi fo-
"risfactura nostra inhibemus firmiter injungentes ne dicta septa manu violenta seu teme-
"raria ingredi de cetero praesumatis clam vel palam, nec muros aut gardina sua seu domos
"suas frangere vel calcare vel alia quaecunque, quominus ipsi gardianus et fratres circa di-
"vina celebrand. et alia quae ad ipsos ratione ordinis et regulae suorum pertinent faciend.
"in quiete vacare valeant attemptare seu fugientes ad dictum hospitium pro tuitione inde
"consequenda postquam septa habitationis ingressi fuerint insequi vel in ipsos manum vio-
"lentam et sacrilegam vincere aut imponere aut vigilias super eos de die vel de nocte seu
"insidias apertas vel occultas infra dicta septa facere de cetero aut fieri procurare aut ipsis
"gardiano aut fratribus aut familiaribus seu servientibus suis quibuscunque in personis vel
"rebus suis dampnum injuriam molestiam impetitionem violentiam aliquod seu gravamen
"inferre seu ab aliis inferri colore aliquo procurare aut ipsos ratione ministrationum victu-
"alium hujus fugientibus caritative faciend. impetire aut causare praesumatis sub poena
"antedicta, et si quid contrarium, quod absit, actum vel gestum fuerit id sine dilatione de-
"bite reformari et plene corrigi faciatis.

"In cujus rei testimonium has literas nostras fieri fecimus patentes.

"Teste me ipso apud *Westmonasterium* vicesimo octavo die *Julii* anno regni nostri *An-*
"*gliae* tricesimo tertio, regni vero nostri *Franciae* vicesimo.

Ebor. *ne intestina et alie sordes per lamos, &c. ibidem projiciantur prope domum* Fratrum Minor. *ibidem in quo dom. rex solebat hospitari.*

"REX (*f*) omnibus ad quos &c. salutem. Monstratum est nobis ex parte dilector. nob.
"in *Christo* gard. et conventus domus ordinis *Fratrum Minor.* de civitat. nost.
"*Ebor.* qualiter ipsi per carnifices et alios de civitat. nost. predict. sunt et diu extiterunt
"pergravati ex causa quod iidem carnifices et alii fimos et alias feditates ac exitus et in-
"testina bestiarum ibidem occisar. prope ecclesiam et mansionem gard. et convent. pre-
"dictor. ponunt, quod tam pre fetore et horribilitate dictar. feditatum quam pre muscis et
"alia vermina de eisdem feditatibus provenient. predict. gard. et convent. in domo
"sua predict. absque maxima poena et inquietudine morari seu divinum obsequium de die
"vel de nocte ut deberent ad exorand. pro animabus progenitorum nost. aut alior. bene-
"factorum suorum et omnium Christianorum ibidem facere seu secundum quod eorum or-
"do et religio exigunt ibidem ministrare non possunt; unde nob. supplicarunt de remedio
"opportuno sibi providendo, nos ad premissa, et quomodo dicta domus per progenitores
"nost. est fundata et quod nos in casu quo ad civitatem nost. predict. veniremus in domo
"ante dicta essemus hospitati, prout dom. *Ed.* nuper rex *Anglie* anno tempore suo extitit,
"condignam habentem considerationem, concessimus pro nobis et hered. nost. quantum in
"nobis est prefatis gard. et conventui et eorum successoribus quod exuant in futurum ali-
"qua fimi feditates exitus vel intestina bestiarum aut alia sordida quecunque per carnifices
"vel aliquas alias personas non ponantur laventur seu projiciantur in aqua de *Ouse* vel in
"venellis aut aliis locis infra civitatem predictam vel extra prope domum supradict. in no-
"cumentum dictor. gard. et conventus vel aliquorum aliorum habitantium sive conflu-
"entium apud dictam domum seu omnimode fimi feditates exitus et intestina bestiarum et
"alia sordida quecunque provenientia tam de carnificio quam de aliis locis infra dictam ci-
"vitatem et suburbia ejusdem ponantur laventur et projiciantur in aliis placeis vel alia
"placea per ordinationem majoris et ballivorum ejusdem in tantum distantibus vel distante
"de predict. domo quod prefati gard. et convent. et successores sui in perpetuum; et
"omnes alii ad confluentes eandem domum inhabitare valeant et morari continue in ipsa
"domo absque fetore aut alio gravamine inquietudine vel nocumento fimorum feditatum

(*f*) *Pat.* 4 Ric. II. *p.* 1. *m.* 39.

"exituum

" exituum inteſtinorum et ſordidorum prediƈt. Inhibentes diſtriƈtius et precipientes majori
" et ballivis et probis hominibus diƈte civitatis noſt. quod ipſi quicquam non faciant vel
" fieri permittant per aliquem habitantium vel confluentium in prediƈt. civitatem contra
" conceſſionem noſt. ſuper diƈt. ſub pena incarcerationis corporum delinquentium in hac
" parte vel alia pena graviori delinquentibus hujuſmodi imponend. ad voluntatem noſt. et
" hered. noſt. prediƈt.

" In cujus, &c.

" Teſte rege apud *Weſt.* xxiii die *Junii.*

Per breve de privato ſigillo.

De ſcripto prioris Fratrum Minor. civitate Ebor.

" Omnibus *(g)* Chriſti fidelibus ad quos preſens ſcriptum pervenerit *Willielmus Vava-*
" *ſour* ſacre theologie ˈprofeſſor prior ſive gardianus *Fratrum Minorum* infra muros
" civitatis *Ebor.* et ejuſdem loci conventus ſalutem in Domino ſempiternam et fidem indu-
" biam preſentibus adhibere. Noveritis nos prefatos priorem ſive gardianum et conven-
" tum unanimi aſſenſu et conſenſu noſtris, animis deliberatis, certa ſcientia et mero motu'
" noſtris ex quibuſdam cauſis juſtis et rationabilibus animas et conſcientias noſtras ſpeciali-
" ter monentibus, ultro et ſponte, dediſſe et conceſſiſſe ac per preſentes dare et concedere
" reddere deliberare et confitmare illuſtriſſimo in Chriſto principi et domino noſt. *Henrico*
" octavo Dei gratia *Anglie* et *Francie* regi fidei defenſori domino *Hibernie,* et in terris ſupre-
" mo eccleſie *Anglicane* ſub Chriſto capiti, totum diƈtum prioratum ſive domum conventua-
" lem noſt. prediƈtam ac totum ſcitum fundum circuitum et precinƈtum ejuſdem domus no-
" ſtre, nec non omnia et ſingula maneria dom. meſſuagia gardina curtilagia toſta terras et
" tenementa noſtra, prata paſcua paſturas boſcos redditus reverſiones molendina paſſagia
" communias libertates aquas piſcarias penſiones portiones annuitates oblationes ac omnia
" et ſingula emolumenta proficua poſſeſſiones hereditamenta et jura noſtra ſpiritualia et
" temporalia quaecunque, tam infra regnum *Anglie* et marchiarum ejuſdem quam alibi ubi-
" cunque prefate domui noſtre quoquo modo pertinentes ſpeƈtantes appendentes ſive in-
" cumbentes et omnimodas cartas evidentias ſcripta munimenta noſt. diƈte domui noſtre
" maneriis terris et tenementis ejuſdem ac ceteris premiſſis cum pertinentiis ſive alicujus in-
" de parcelle quoquo modo pertinentibus et ſpeƈtantibus, habend. et tenend. et gaudend.
" diƈte domui ſive prioratui noſt. ſcitum fundum circuitum et precinƈtum ejuſdem, nec
" non omnia et ſingula prediƈta maneria dominia meſſuagia gardina terras et tenementa
" ac cetera premiſſa cum omnibus et ſingulis ſuis pertinentiis prefato inviƈtiſſimo principi
" et domino noſtro regi heredibus et aſſignatis ſuis in perpetuum, cui in hac parte ad om-
" nem juris effeƈtum qui exinde ſequi poterit aut poteſt nos et domum noſtram prediƈt. ac
" omnia jura nobis qualitercunque acquiſita, ut decet, ſubjecimus et ſubmittimus ; dantes et
" concedentes eidem regie majeſtati omnem et omnimodam plenam et liberam facultatem
" autoritatem et poteſtatem nos et domum noſtram prediƈtam, una cum omnibus et ſingulis
" maneriis terris tenementis redditibus reverſionibus ac ceteris premiſſis cum ſuis juribus
" et pertinentiis univerſis diſponend. ac pro ſue libere voluntatis regie libito ad quoſcun-
" que uſus majeſtati ſue placentes alienand. donand. convertend. et transferend. hujuſmodi
" diſpoſitiones alienationes donationes converſiones et translationes per diƈtam majeſtatem
" ſuam quoviſmodo fiend. ex nunc ratificantes rataſque et gratas ac perpetuo firmas habi-
" turos promittimus per preſentes. Et ut premiſſa omnia et ſingula ſuum debitum ſortiri
" valeant effeƈtum, eleƈtionibus nobis et ſucceſſoribus noſtris, nec non omnibus querelis pro-
" vocationibus appellationibus accuſationibus litibus et inſtanciis aliiſque quibuſcunque juris
" et faƈti remediis ac beneficiis nobis forſan ac ſucceſſoribus noſtris in ea parte pretextu diſ-
" poſitionis alienationis tranſlationis et converſionis pred. et ceterorum premiſſorum quali-
" tercunque competentium ; et competitur omnibus doli metus erroris ignorancie vel alterius
" materie ſive diſpoſitionibus exceptionibus objeƈtionibus et allegationibus prorſus ſemotis
" et depoſitis palam public et expreſſe ex certa ſcientia noſtra animeſque deliberatis et ſpon-
" taneis renunciavimus et ceſſimus, prout per preſentes renunciamus et cedimus ac ab eiſdem
" recedimus in hiis ſcriptis. Et nos prediƈt. prior ſive gardianus et conventus et ſucceſſores
" noſtri diƈtam domum ſive prioratum noſtrum precinƈtum ſcitum manſionem et eccleſiam
" noſt. prediƈtam ac premiſſa omnia et ſingula cum ſuis juribus et pertinentiis univerſis pre-
" fato domino noſt. regi heredibus et aſſignatis ſuis contra omnes gentes warrantizabimus
" et defendemus per preſentes.

" In quorum teſtimonium atque fidem nos prefati prior ſive gardianus et conventus ſigil-
" lum noſt. commune preſentibus apponi fecimus.

" Dat. in domo noſtra capitulari viceſimo ſeptimo die menſis *Novembris* anno regni regis
" *Henrici* octavi triceſimo.

P. 284. *Seƈt.* 1. Monaſtery of St. *Auguſtine York.*

(g) Clauſ. 30 Hen. VIII. pars 5.
x

Ebor.

Ebor. *prior. S.* Auguſtini *ibidem de reddit. de* xx *s. provenient. de tenement. in* Rotſey, *&c.*

" REX *(r)* omnibus ad quos &c. ſalutem. Sciatis quod de gratia noſt. ſpeciali conceſ-" ſimus et licentiam dedimus pro nobis et hered. noſt. quantum in nob. eſt, *Thome* " *de Thwenge* clerico, quod ipſe et heredes ſui viginti ſolidatas ann. reddit. provenientes de " terris et tenement. ſuis cum pertinent. in *Rotſe* in com. *Ebor.* dare poſſint et aſſignare di-" lectis nobis in Chriſto priori et conventui ordinis S. *Auguſtini* de *Ebor.* Tenend. et ha-" bend. ſibi et ſucceſſoribus ſuis in perpetuum in auxilium inveniendi panem et vinum pro " divinis ibidem celebrandis, &c.

" In cujus rei, &c.

" Teſte rege apud Caleſium xii die *Auguſti.*

Ebor. *fratres S.* Auguſtini *ibidem pro manſo elargard.*

" REX *(s)* omnibus, &c. ſalut. Licet, &c. tamen de gratia noſt. ſpeciali et pro " quatuor marcis quas dilect. nob. in Chriſto prior ordinis S. *Auguſtini* in *Ebor.* no-" bis ſolvit conceſſimus et licentiam dedimus pro nobis et heredibus noſtris, quantum in " nobis eſt, dilect. nob. *Willielmo de Hakthorp* clerico *Willielmo de Hedon* clerico, quod ipſi " unum meſſuagium cum pertinentiis in *Ebor.* manſo predicti prioris et fratrum ordinis pre-" dicti in eadem civitate contiguum, quod quidem meſſuag. de nobis tenetur in burgagi-" um per ſervitium reddendi nobis et hered. noſtris per annum ad huſgabulum per ma-" nus ballivorum ejuſdem civitatis duos denarios ad feſtum S. *Jacobi* apoſt. pro omni " ſervitio, dare poſſit et aſſignare prefatis priori et fratribus habend. et tenend. ſibi et " ſucceſſoribus ſuis in elargationem manſi ſui predicti in perpetuum. Et eiſdem priori et " fratribus, quod ipſi meſſuag. predict. cum pertinent. a prefatis *Willielmo* et *Willielmo* reci-" pere poſſit et tenere ſibi et ſucceſſoribus ſuis in perpetuum, ſicut predict. eſt tenore pre-" ſentium: ſimiliter licentiam dedimus ſpecialem ſtatuto predict. non obſtante, nolentes quod " predict. *Willielmus* et *Willielmus* vel heredes ſui aut prefati prior et fratres ſeu ſucceſſo-" res ſui ratione premiſſorum aut ſtatuti predict. ſeu pro eo quod predict. meſſuagium de " nobis tenetur ut predicitur per nos vel heredes noſt. juſticiario, eſch. vic. aut alios bal-" livos ſeu miniſtros noſt. quoſcunque occaſionentur moleſtentur in aliquo ſeu graventur. " Salvis tamen nobis et heredibus noſt. ſervitiis inde debitis et conſuetis.

" In cujus, &c.

" Teſte R. apud *Weſtm.* xxii die *Octob.*

Et dicte quatuor marce ſolut. ſunt in hanappio.

The ſite of the priory of S. *Auguſtine* in *York* was granted to *Thomas Lawſon* and *Chriſtian* his wife, fifth and ſixth of *Philip* and *Mary. Rolls chap.*

P. 289. *Clifford*'s tower.

Clifford'*s* Tower *in the city of* York, *from a MS. of ſir* Tho. Widdrington'*s.*
Which was built by William *the conquerour.*

" THE round tower near the caſtle is called *Clifford*'s tower, probably it hath de-" rived the name, becauſe the lord *Clifford* was caſteleyn, wardein and keeper of " it, as *Walter Strickland* of *Boynton* a good antiquary was of opinion.

" The lord *Clifford* hath alſo antiently claimed to carry the ſword of the city before " the king in this city, at ſuch time as the king came there, and I find ſome memo-" rials of this in the books of the city; the firſt was upon the coming of the late king " *James* in the year 1603, out of *Scotland*, which is mentioned in the city book in this " manner, the 26*th* of *April*, 1603. one Mr. *Liſter* came from the right noble lord *George* " earl of *Cumberland* lord *Clifford*, knight of the moſt honourable order of the garter, " to acquaint the lord-mayor and aldermen how that the ſaid earl, according to his right, " expected to bear the ſword before the king in this city, in ſuch ſort as his anceſtors have " been accuſtomed to do; to whom this anſwer was made, *that for as much as it doth not* " *appear by any of the antient preſidents of the city, that either the earl or any of his anceſtors* " *have before this time born the ſaid ſword before any of the king's progenitors, nor hath the ſaid* " *earl ſhewed any writing in that behalf, but claims this by preſcription*; therefore they or-" dered that Mr. *Recorder* and Mr. *Robert Aſkwith* alderman ſhould wait upon the " earl, and anſwer him, *that the lord-mayor will deliver the ſword to the king himſelf, and* " *leave it to his pleaſure who ſhall bear the ſame, whether the lord-mayor, earl, or any* " *other.* And the ſame 26*th* day of *April*, before the king came to the city, ſir *Tho-*" *mas Chaloner* came to the lord-mayor, recorder and aldermen to know from them

(*r*) *Pat.* 27 Ed. III. *p.* 2. *m.* 3. 1353.

(*s*) *Pat.* 29 Ed. III. *m.* 9.

" who had formerly born the sword before the king within the city, because he heard " that the earl of *Cumberland* did claime to carry the same within the city, as his in- " heritance, and that the lord *Burleigh* pretended to carry the same as lord president of " the councel established in the north parts. And sir *Thomas Challoner* affirmed that the " king's special care was, that such persons as had right should carry the same. Hereunto " the lord-mayor with the advice of Mr. *Recorder* and of the aldermen made this answer, " *that the earle of* Cumberland *had oftentimes affirmed in the time of queen* Elizabeth, *that he* " *ought and had right to carry the sword before the queen, if she came to the city of* York, *and* " *that his ancestors had born the same before other her progenitors kings of* England *within this* " *city, and that it was his inheritance; and since the death of the late queen he hath claimed the* " *same, and the common and general report of the antient citizens is, and of long time hath* " *been that it belonged to the said earle, and by report of ancient men the last time that king* " Henry VIII. *was at this city, the then lord* Clifford *father of this earle, the then earle of* " Cumberland *father to the said lord* Clifford, *being employed in the special affaires of the said* " *king in the north parts, offered to carry the sword before the said king* Henry VIII. *within the city* " *which was then opposed by some honourable persons then in favour with the king; and the lord* Clif- " ford *then made the earle his father's right and title thereto so clear and apparent, that the op-* " *posers could not gainsay the same; but to prevent the lord* Clifford's *desire for the present,* " *did alledge, that howbeit the earl of* Cumberland *had such right, yet his son the lord* Clif- " ford *could have no title thereunto in the life of his father; and they also objected that the lord* " Clifford *rode on a gelding furnished on the* northern fashion, *which was not comely for that place.* " To the first the lord *Clifford* answered, that *the earl his father being employed in the king's affairs* " *he trusted that his absence should not be made use of to the prejudice of his inheritance, and for* " *the supply of the defects of his horse and furniture, sir* Francis Knolls *a pensioner alighted from* " *his horse, and gave him to the lord* Clifford, *and king* Henry VIII. *perceiving the earl's right* " *dispensed with his absence, and delivered the sword to the lord* Clifford *his son, who carried* " *it before the king within the city.*

" In the year 1617, the late king *James* in his progress towards *Scotland* came to this ci- " ty; but before the king's entry into the city, the king being then in the *Ainsty* the coun- " ty of the city, the earl of *Pembroke* then lord chamberlain asked for sir *Francis Clifford* " lord *Clifford* then earl of *Cumberland* for to carry the king's sword before the king, which " the said earl refused, answering that *his ancestors had always used to carry the city's sword* " *before the king and his noble progenitors within the city.* The lord *Sheffield* then lord presi- " dent of the north hearing this, said, *if he will not carry it give me it to carry*; the lord " chamberlaine replied, *shall the king ride in state and have no sword carried before him?* " thereupon the lord chamberlaine and the earl of *Cumberland* went to the king to know " his pleasure, which he signified to be, that the earl of *Cumberland* should carry his sword " till he came within the gates of the city, and then should take the city's sword, which " the earl did accordingly; and when the king came within the bar of the city *Robert* " *Askwith* lord-mayor delivered the keys, sword and mace to the king, and the king de- " livered the sword of the city to the earl of *Cumberland*, which he carried before the king " in the city.

" The 30*th* of *March* 1639, when the late king *Charles* came to *York*, in his progress " towards *Berwick*, I find an entry made in the book of the city to this effect, annent " this matter, the sword of the city was born before the king by *Thomas* earl of *Arundel* " and *Surrey*, earl marshal of *England*, for that the lord *Clifford*, who was chief captain " of this city, was then absent and in the king's service at the city of *Carlisle*, who of " right should otherwise have born the same as at other times his father and others of his " ancestors had done; and the lord-mayor bore the city's mace, and afterwards during the " king's abode in the city (which was for the space of one month) the sword of the city " was born before the king by divers of the lords in their courses, severally and not always " by one and the same person, till the lord *Clifford* came to the city, and then he bore " the sword before the king as of right due to his father the earl of *Cumberland*, who was " then infirm and not able to attend the service.

P. 309. *Sect.* 3. Monastery of the fryars *Carmelites.*

Carta confirm. priorat. de monte Carmeli *in* Ebor.

" REX (*k*) archiep. &c. salutem. Inspeximus cartam quam *Willielmus de Vescy* fecit priori " et fratribus ordinis beate *Marie* de monte *Carmeli* de *Ebor.* in hec verba. Sciant " presentes et futuri quod ego *Willielmus de Vescy* dedi concessi et hac presenti carta mea " confirmavi pro salute anime mee et animar. antecessor. meorum in augmentum cultus di- " vini priori et fratribus ordinis beate *Marie* de monte *Carmeli* de *Ebor.* totum illud mes- " suagium ac tenementum cum pertinentiis quod habui in vico vocat. le *Stainbogh* in civi- " tat. dom. regis predicta, viz. quicquid ibidem adquisivi in fundo vel edificiis messuagio

(*k*) Cart. 28 Ed. I. n. 20.

" seu

" ſeu tenemento, prout ſe extendit in longitudine et latitudine a predicto vico verſus aquam
" de *Foſſe* ad partem auſtralem, et a vico qui vocatur le *Merſk* verſus viam regiam que vo-
" catur *Foſſgate* ad partem occidentalem, cum omnibus redditibus et aliis libertatibus qui et
" que ad me ratione predicti meſſuagii ſeu tenementi ſolebant aliqualiter pertinere. Tenend.
" et habend. eiſdem priori et fratribus et ſucceſſoribus ſuis in perpetuum, ſalvis tamen
" capitalibus domin. feodi ſervitiis inde debitis et conſuetis. Et ego *Willielmus* et heredes
" mei vel aſſignati mei omnia predicta cum pertinentiis eiſdem priori et fratribus et ſuc-
" ceſſ. ſuis contra omnes mortales warrantizabimus acquietabimus et in perpetuum defen-
" demus.

" In cujus rei teſtimonium preſenti carte ſigillum meum appoſui.

" Hiis teſtibus, domino *Willielmo de Barneby*, dom. *Thoma de Benſum*, capellanis *Johanne*
" *de Wyreſdale*, *Richardo Moryn*, *Galfrido de Gippeſmer* clerico et aliis.

" Nos autem donationem et conceſſionem predict. ratas habentes et gratas, pro nobis et
" hered. noſt. quantum in nobis eſt predict. priori et fratribus et ſucceſſ. ſuis concedimus
" et confirmamus, ſicut carta predict. rationabiliter teſtat.

" Hiis teſtibus, venerab. patre. *W. Covent.* et *Lychfield.* epiſcopo theſaur. noſt. *Rogero*
" *de Bigod* comite *Norfolk.* et mareſcallo *Anglie*, *Johanne de Britannia* juniore, *Ottone de*
" *Grandeſone*, *Johan. de Metingham*, *Waltero de Bellocampo* ſeneſchallo hoſpitii noſt.
" *Petro de Tatindon*, *Johan. de Merks*, *Thoma de Bikenore* et aliis.

" Dat. per manum noſtram apud *Ebor.* tertio decimo die *Junii*.

Per ipſum regem.

Fratres de monte Carmeli *in* Ebor. *quod ipſi in proprio ſolo ſuo infra manſum ſuum ſuper ripam vivarii regis de* Foſſe *quandam* **kaiam** *conſtruere poſſint.*

" REX *(l)* omnibus ad quos, &c. ſalut. Sciatis quod ad devotionem et affectionem
" quas erga dilectos nobis in Chriſto priorem et fratres ordinis beate *Marie* de
" monte *Carmeli* apud *Ebor.* commorantes, gerimus et habemus, conceſſimus eis et licen-
" tiam dedimus pro nobis et hered. noſt. quod ipſi in proprio ſolo ſuo infra manſum ſuum
" in civitat. predict. ſuper *ripam* vivarii noſt. de *Foſſe* quandam **kayam** conſtruere et eam
" conſtructam tenere poſſint ſibi et ſucceſſoribus ſuis in perpetuum, et inſuper quod ipſi et
" ſucceſſores ſui predictam in perpetuum habeant, cum batello in vivario predicto ad pe-
" tram buſca et aliis neceſſariis ſuis tam ſubtus pontem de *Foſſe* quam alibi in vivario
" predicto uſque manſum ſuum predict. ducendis.

" In cujus &c.

" Teſte rege apud *Ebor.* tertio die *Oct.*

Per ipſum regem.

Fratres de monte Carmeli Ebor. *de meſſ. et placea in vico de* Merſke *que rex habuit ex dono* Galfrid. de Sancto Quintino *conceſſ. per regem pro manſo elargand.*

" REX *(m)* omnibus &c. ſalutem. Sciatis quod ob devotionem et affectionem quos erga
" dilectos nobis in Chriſto fratres ordinis beate *Marie* de monte *Carmeli* gerimus et
" habemus, dedimus et conceſſimus et hac carta noſtra confirmavimus priori et fratribus or-
" dinis predicti apud *Ebor.* commorantibus illud meſſuagium et placeas cum pertinentiis in
" *Ebor.* in vico de **Merske** manſo predict. prioris et fratrum contigua, que nuper habuimus
" de dono et conceſſione dilecti et fidelis noſtri *Galfridi de Sancto Quintino*, habend. et te-
" nend. eiſdem priori et fratribus et ſucceſſoribus ſuis de nobis et heredibus noſt. in liberam
" quietam et perpetuam eleemoſinam ad elargationem manſi ſui predict. in perpetuum.

" In cujus rei teſt. &c.

" Teſte rege apud *Ebor.* ſecundo die *Octobris.*

" COnceſſio regis *Ed.* II. fratribus de monte *Carmeli Ebor.* terrae cum omnibus edificiis
" et pertinent. ſuis in civitate predict. quam habuit ex dono *Thome* filii *Willielmi le*
" *Aguiller* de *Ebor.* et *Cicilie* ux. ejus, ſicut ſe extendit in longitudine et latitudine per bun-
" das in cart. predict. *Thom.* et *Cicilie* contentas &c. *(n)*

" Teſte rege apud *Lincoln.* primo die *Sept.*

(l) Pat. 8 Ed. II. p. 1. m. 17.
(m) Pat. 8 Ed. II. p. 1. m. 19.
(n) Pat. 9 Ed. p. 1. m. 23. 1316.

Fratres

2

Fratres de monte Carmeli *de terris et edificiis in* Fosſgate *conceſſis, &c.*

" REX (*o*) omnibus &c. ſalut. Sciatis quod ob devotionem quam ad glorioſam virginem
" *Mariam,* nec non ob affectionem quam ad fratres ordinis beate *Marie* de monte
" *Carmeli* gerimus et habemus volentes dilectis nobis in Chriſto priori et fratribus ejuſdem
" ordinis apud *Ebor.* commorantibus ; per gratiam noſt. ſpecialem dedimus et conceſſimus
" eiſdem priori et fratribus totam illam terram cum edificiis et pertinentiis ſuis in **Foſſe-**
" **gate** in civitate noſtra *Ebor.* quam *Thomas* filius *Willielmi le Aguiller* de *Ebor.* et *Cicilia*
" uxor. ejus per ſcriptum ſuum, nec non totam terram illam cum pertinentiis in eadem ci-
" vitate quam *Abel de Rikbale* de *Ebor.* per ſcriptum ſuum nobis et heredibus noſt. dede-
" rint et conceſſerint ſicut terre ille ſe extendunt in longitudine et latitudine per bundas
" in dictis ſcriptis contentas. Habend. et tenend. eiſdem priori et fratribus et ſucceſſoribus
" ſuis de nobis et hered. noſt. in puram eleemoſinam ad elargationem manſi eorundem
" fratrum ibidem in perpetuum, ſalvo jure cujuſlibet.

" Teſte rege apud *Ebor.* xxiiii *Sept.*

Per ipſum regem.

Ebor. prior. de monte Carmeli *ibidem pro quadam pecia terrae ibidem conceſſ. pro manſo ipſor.*
elargand.

" REX (*p*) omnibus ad quos &c. ſalutem. Licet &c. de gratia noſtra ſpeciali pro du-
" abus marcis nobis ſolut. in hannapio noſtro conceſſimus et licentiam dedimus pro
" nobis et hered. noſtris quantum in nob. eſt *Johanni Berden* et *Johanni Braythwayt,* quod
" ipſi concedere poſſint quod centum pedes terre in longitudine et centum pedes terre in
" latitudine eccleſie prioris et fratrum ordinis beate *Marie* de monte *Carmeli Ebor.* ex parte
" occidentali contigue ; que quidem terra de nobis in burgagio tenetur et quam *Matilda* que
" fuit uxor *Henrici de Ryhſtane* tenet ad vitam ſuam et que poſt mortem predicte *Matilde*
" ad prefatos *Johannem* et *Johan.* reverti debet poſt mortem eorund. *Johannis* et *Jo-*
" *bannis* remaneat prefatis priori et fratribus tenend. ſibi et ſucceſſoribus ſuis in elargatio-
" nem manſi ſui in perpetuum, et eiſdem priori et fratrib. quod ipſi predict. terram cum
" pertinentiis poſt mortem prefate *Matilde* ingredi poſſint et tenere ſibi et ſucceſſoribus ſuis
" predict. in forma predict. in perpetuum ſicut predict. eſt tenore preſentium : ſimiliter li-
" centiam dedimus ſpecialem ſtatuto predict. ſeu eo quod predict. terra de nobis in burga-
" gio tenetur non obſtante nolentes quod predicti *Johannes* et *Johan.* vel heredes ſui aut
" prefati prior et fratres ſeu ſucceſſores ſui ratione premiſſor. per nos vel heredes noſt.
" juſticiar. eſchaet. vicecomit. aut alios ballivos ſeu miniſtros noſt. vel heredum noſt. quoſ-
" cunque inde occaſionent. moleſtent. in aliquo ſeu graventur. Salvis tamen nob, et he-
" red. noſt. ſervitiis inde debitis et conſuetis.

" In cujus &c.

" Teſte rege apud *Ebor.* xx die *Novembris.*

" IDEM rex (*q*) *Ric.* II. licentiam dat *Henrico de Percy,* domino de *Spafford* et *Johan. de*
" *Acom.* nuper parſone eccl. de *Catton,* quod ipſi concedere poſſint ſexagint. pedes
" terre in longitudine et ſexagint. pedes in latitud. eccl. prioris et fratrum ordinis beate *Ma-*
" rie de monte *Carmeli Ebor.* ex parte occidental. contig. in eiſdem verbis ut ſupra.

" Teſte rege apud *Oxon. Sept.* xxvii.

P. 316. Sect. 1. On the charity ſchools at *York.*

The following is a catalogue of the original and preſent benefactors to the ſchools,
printed yearly, and given away every *Good-Friday* ; on which day a charity ſermon is annually preached, in *Bellfray's* church, for the benefit of the ſchools. The collections, on
this occaſion, have ſome years amounted to near one hundred pounds ; but of late this charity is grown much colder ; and by ſeveral of its chiefeſt ſupporters being dead, and others
withdrawing their ſubſcriptions, the whole is likely to ſink ſoon, as the laſt paragraph of
their paper intimates, unleſs a ſuperior providence ſupports this, piouſly deſigned, undertaking.

The BENEFACTORS *to the* CHARITY-SCHOOLS *at* YORK, *for the*
year 1736.

To the boys *per Annum.*						
	l.	*s.*	*d.*	*l.*	*s.*	*d.*

	l.	*s.*	*d.*		*l.*	*s.*	*d.*
THE reverend Dr. *Oſbal-deſton,* dean of *York*	05	00	00	The honourable and reverend Mr. *Finch*	06	00	60
				Dr. *Audley* chancellor ———	02	00	00

(*o*) Pat. 10 Ed. II. p. 1. m. 14. (*q*) Eadem m. 28.
(*p*) Pat. 16 Ric. II. p. 2. m. 21.

Dr. *Wa-*

	l.	s.	d.
Dr. *Waterland*, chancellor of the church of *York*	02	00	00
Mr. *Lamplugh*, residentiary	02	00	00
Mr. *Bradley*, residentiary	02	00	00
Mr. *Buck* of *Marston* —	01	00	00
Mr. *Harrison* —	01	01	00
Mr. *Knight* —	01	00	00
Mr. *Fuller* —	01	00	00
Mr. *Warneford* —	01	00	00
Mr. *Allat* —	00	10	00
Mr. *Foster* —	00	10	00
Mr. *Bourn* —	00	10	00
Mr. *John Foster* —	00	10	00
Mr. *Nicholas Moseley*	00	10	00
Mr. *Richard Molesey*	00	10	00
Mr. *Dodsworth* —	00	10	06
Mr. *Sheppeard* —	00	10	00
Mr. *Blake* —	00	10	00
Mr. *Dryden* —	00	10	00
Mr. *Reynolds* —	00	10	00
Mr. *Beckett* —	00	05	00
A.			
Mr. *John Ambler* —	00	05	00
Mr. *John Allan* —	00	05	00
Mr. *Samuel Ascough* —	00	05	00
Mr. *Joseph Addington* —	00	02	06
B.			
Mr. *Francis Bolton* —	00	05	00
Dr. *Barnard* —	02	00	00
Lady *Baynes* —	01	00	00
George Barnatt, esq; alderman	01	00	00
James Barnard, esq; alderman	01	00	00
Mr. *John Browne* —	00	10	00
Mr. *Robert Bower* —	00	05	00
Mr. *John Beverley* —	00	05	00
Mr. *Benjamin Barstow* —	00	05	00
Mr. *Beckwith* —	00	05	00
Mr. *William Barstow* —	00	05	00
Mr. *Brennand* —	00	05	00
C.			
The right honourable *Samuel Clarke*, esq; lord-mayor	01	00	00
Mr. *Richard Cordukes*	00	10	00
Dr. *Clinch* —	01	01	00
Mr. *Carr* — —	00	02	06
Mr. *William Coates* —	00	02	06
Mrs. *Colton* in *Coppergate*	00	05	00
Mr. *Richard Corney* —	00	02	06
Mr. *Jacob Custobodie* —	00	10	06
Mr. *John Chippendale* —	00	05	00
Mr. *Francis Cordukes* —	00	02	06
Mr. *Richard Chambers*	00	10	00
D.			
William Dawson, esq;	01	01	00
Dr. *Dawes* —	01	01	00
Mr. *Joseph Deighton* —	00	02	06
E.			
Richard Elcock, esq; —	01	01	00
George Escrick, esq; alderman	01	00	00
F.			
Mr. *John Fothergill* —	00	10	00
Thomas Fairfax, esq; —	01	01	00

	l.	s.	d.
G.			
Mrs. *Gowland*, widow	00	05	00
Mr. *Henry Grey* —	00	10	00
William Garforth, esq;	02	00	00
Thomas Gee, esq; —	01	01	00
Mrs. *Sarah Grayson*, widow	00	05	00
Mr. *Thomas Gent* —	00	05	00
H.			
Mr. *William Hotham* —	00	05	00
Mr. *William Hutchinson*	00	10	00
Mr. *John Haughton* —	00	10	06
Mr. *John Harrison* —	00	02	06
Mr. *Timothy Hudson* —	00	05	00
Mr. *Thomas Hammond* —	00	10	00
Mr. *John Hildyard* —	00	10	06
I.			
Dr. *Johnson* —	01	01	00
Mr. *Edward Jefferson*	00	05	00
Mr. *Thomas Jubb* —	02	00	00
Peter Johnson, esq; —	01	01	00
Mr. *James Jenkinson* —	00	05	00
Mr. *Francis Ingram* —	00	05	00
K.			
Mr. *Kenyon* —	00	05	00
L.			
Mr. *Lancaster* —	00	02	06
Mr. *Edmund Lee* —	00	05	00
M.			
Bacon Morrit, esq; —	01	01	00
Mr. *William Mudd* —	00	05	00
Mr. *William Musgrave*	00	02	06
Mr. *Richard Mancklin*	00	10	00
N.			
Mr. *Joseph Netherwood*	00	05	00
Mr. *Thomas Norfolk* —	00	05	00
P.			
Mr. *Darcy Preston* —	01	01	00
Mr. *Christopher Peake*	00	05	00
Mr. *Plant* —	00	05	00
Mr. *Jaques Priestly* —	00	05	00
R.			
Mr. *Benjamin Rhodes* —	00	02	06
John Read, esq; alderman	01	01	00
William Redman, esq;	02	00	00
Mr. *Henry Richmond* —	00	10	00
S.			
Richard Sterne, esq; —	02	02	00
Mr. *William Stevenson*	00	10	00
Mr. *John Shaw* —	01	01	00
Mr. *Nicholas Sugar* —	00	10	00
Mr. *Jacob Simpson* of *Leeds*	00	10	00
Mr. *Roger Shackleton* —	00	10	00
Mr. *Edward Seller* —	00	10	00
Mr. *William Shaw* —	00	05	00
Mr. *Richard Stockton* —	01	01	00
Mr. *Henry Stainton* —	00	05	00
Mr. *David Sanders* —	00	10	00
Mr. *Low. Slater* —	00	05	00
T.			
Edward Thompson esq; —	05	00	00
Jonas Thompson, esq; —	00	10	00

	l.	s.	d.
Mrs. *Todd*, Widow	00	02	06
Mr. *John Thomlinson*	00	05	00
Mr. *Leonard Terry*	00	02	06
V			
Mr. *Vougler*	00	10	00
W			
Mr. *Richard Wilson*	00	10	00
Mr. *Edward Wilson*	00	05	00
Mr. *Henry Waite*	00	10	00
Mr. *Jonathan White*	00	05	00
Mr. *William White*	00	05	00
Mr. *John Walker*	00	05	00
William Whitehead esq; alderman	00	10	00
James Winlow esq;	00	10	00
Dr. *Wintringham*	01	01	00
Mr. *John Wilmer*	00	10	00
Mr. *Samuel Waud*	00	10	00
Mr. *Wilcock*	00	02	06
Mr. *Richard Wright*	00	05	00
John Wood esq;	01	01	00
Mr. *James Whytehead*	00	10	06
Mrs. *Mary Wood*	00	10	06
Mr. *Wakefield*	00	05	00
Y			
Mrs. *Yates*, widow	00	02	06
Mr. *Richard Yoward*	00	05	00

Commoners *in* Micklegate-Ward.

	l.	s.	d.
Mr. *Richard Reynolds*	00	15	00
Mr. *James Robinson*	00	05	00
Mr. *John Telford*	00	07	06
Mr. *Jonathan Perrit*	00	05	00
Mr. *John Benington*	00	05	00
Mr. *Matthew Rayson*	00	00	00
Mr. *Barnard Dickinson*	00	05	00
Mr. *Robrt Stainton*	00	05	00
Mr. *George Burton*	00	05	00
Mr. *Marmaduke Misburn*	00	05	00
Mr. *Christopher Rawden*	00	05	00
Mr. *James Disney*	00	05	00
Mr. *Samuel Smith*	00	05	00
Mr. *John Richardson*	00	05	00
Mr. *Charles Charnock*	00	05	00
Mr. *Francis Proctor*	00	05	00
Mr. *Thomas Mason*	00	05	00
Mr. *John Greenup*	00	05	00

Walmgate-Ward.

	l.	s.	d.
Mr. *Emanuel Stabler*	00	10	00
Mr. *Robert Waite*	00	00	00
Mr. *John Hunter*	00	05	00
Mr. *Michael Benington*	00	05	00
Mr. *John Ethrington*	00	07	06
Mr. *Thomas Siddall*	00	07	06
Mr. *Arthur Brooke*	00	00	00
Mr. *Francis Jefferson*	00	07	06
Mr. *Thomas Spooner*	00	07	06
Mr. *George Skelton*	00	07	06
Mr. *Henry Myres*	00	07	06
Mr. *Charles Wightman*	00	07	06
Mr. *Stephen Beverley*	00	07	06
Mr. *William Thompson*	00	05	00
Mr. *Thomas Clifton*	00	07	06
Mr. *John Lowcock*	00	07	06
Mr. *Peter Cass*	00	07	06
Mr. *Thomas Kellington*	00	07	06

Bootham-Ward.

	l.	s.	d.
Mr. *Henry Scott*	00	05	00
Mr. *William Roberts*	00	05	00
Mr. *Thomas Agar*	00	07	06
Mr. *John Raper*	00	07	06
Mr. *John Marsden*	00	07	06
Mr. *Thomas Hardwick*	00	07	06
Mr. *Henry Tireman*	00	07	06
Mr. *David Wood*	00	05	00
Mr. *Henry Bower*	00	07	06
Mr. *Thomas Reed*	00	07	06
Mr. *James Boreham*	00	05	00
Mr. *John Busfield*	00	07	06
Mr. *John Hilileigh*	00	07	06
Mr. *Thomas Matthews*	00	07	06
Mr. *John Mayer*	00	07	06
Mr. *Richard Lawson*	00	10	06
Mr. *Draper Wood*	00	07	06
Mr. *Henry Grice*	00	07	06

Monk-Ward.

	l.	s.	d.
Mr. *John Askham*	00	05	00
Mr. *William Thompson*	00	05	00
Mr. *William Dunn*	00	05	00
Mr. *John Fawkingham*	00	05	00
Mr. *John Clark*	00	00	00
Mr. *Richard Agar*	00	05	00
Mr. *John Preston*	00	05	00
Mr. *Thomas Rodwell*	00	05	00
Mr. *Isaac Robinson*	00	05	00
Mr. *James Rowe*	00	05	00
Mr. *Joseph Sowray*	00	05	00
Mr. *George Atkinson*	00	05	00
Mr. *Matthew Owram*	00	05	00
Mr. *Robert Wilton*	00	05	00
Mr. *Thomas Woodhouse*	00	05	00
Mr. *Martin Croft*	00	05	00
Mr. *Thomas Wilson*	00	05	00
Mr. *Winwood*	00	05	00

An Account of all the Money-Legacies and Gifts to the Boys *since the first setting up of the* Charity-School *in the Year* 1705, *to the Year* 1735. *inclusive.*

	l.	s.	d.
Lord-mayor and commonalty of *York*	100	00	00
Thomas Hesletine, esq;	10	00	00
Sir *William Robinson*, bart.	100	00	00
Lord viscount *Down*	10	15	00
Lady *Hewly*	200	00	00
Mr. *Samuel Moxon*	05	00	00
Mr. *John Webster*	20	00	00
Mr. *Francis Hildyard*	20	00	00
Charles Perrot, esq;	20	00	00

	l.	s.	d.
Marmaduke Pricket, esq;	40	00	00
Dr. *William Stainforth*	40	00	00
Mr. *Thomas Thompson*	40	00	00
William Headlam, esq;	40	00	00
Mr. *Harrison*, Mint-yard	20	00	00
Michael Fothergill, esq, alderman	10	00	00
Mrs. *Squires*	100	00	00
Mrs. *Ann Dealtry*	10	00	00
Mr. *Thomas Empson*	20	00	00
Mr. *John Bolling*	20	00	00
John Headlam, esq;	40	00	00
Mr. *John Dealtry*	100	00	00
Robert Fairfax, esq; alderman	110	00	00
John Wood, esq;	20	00	00
Mr. *Thomas Sugden*	50	00	00
Richard Roundel, esq;	100	00	00
Dr. *Fall*	10	00	00
Dr. *Dering*, dean of *Ripon*	20	00	00
William Dobson, esq; alderman	20	00	00
Ladies of the *Thursday* assembly	40	00	00
The rev. Mr. *Terrick*	20	00	00
Mr. *Charles Mann*	10	00	00
Mr. *George Wright*	50	00	00
Mr. *Edward Wilkinson*	8	00	00
Mrs. *Elizabeth Harland*	50	00	00
The hon. and rev. Mr. *Finch*, late dean of *York*	100	00	00
Mrs. *Ann Lowther*	20	00	00
Mr. *John Foster*	50	00	00
Mrs. *Elizabeth Woodyear*	50	00	00
Mr. *Zachary Scott*	100	00	00
Mr. *William Gossip*	05	00	00
John Atkins, esquire	05	00	00
Anonymous	12	00	00

BENEFACTORS *to the* BOYS *by Annuities.*

Lord-mayor and commonalty of *York*	10	00	00
Mr. *Nathaniel Wilson*	01	00	00
Mr. *Ellis* of *Rawmarsh*	05	00	00
Mrs. *Ramsden* paid by the city	10	00	00
Christopher Hutton, esq;	04	00	00
St. *Anthony*'s charity, being an house in the shambles	02	10	00
Mrs. *Prince* paid by the city	02	00	00
Richard Sterne, esq; paid by the city	05	00	00
Mr. *Thomas Harrison*, jun. deceased, paid by Mr. *Joseph Harrison* of *Selby*	2	00	00

An Account of all the Money-Legacies and Gifts to the GIRLS *since 1705.*

	l.	s.	d.
Lady *Hewley*	100	00	00
Mrs. *Squires*	100	00	00
John Headlam, esq;	20	00	00
Alderm. *Fairfax*'s Lady	40	00	00
Mrs. *Anne Garnett*	100	00	00
Lady *Perrot*	20	00	00
Mr. *Charles Mann*	10	00	00
Mrs. *Barker*	40	00	00
Mrs. *Sarah Pawson*	40	00	00
Mrs. *Roundel*	50	00	00
Mary the wife of Mr. *John Forster*.	10	00	00
Anne widow of *Will. Headlam*, esq;	10	00	00
Mrs. *Anne Dealtry*	10	00	00
Mrs. *Ann Hodgson*	10	00	00
Mrs. *Fothergill*	10	00	00
Mrs. *Margaret Weddal*	100	00	00
Lady *Redman*	50	00	00

BENEFACTORS *to the* GIRLS, *per annum.*

Mrs. *Finch*	10	00	00
Mrs. *Gee*'s tickets in the lottery	07	00	00
Richard Sterne, esq;	05	00	00
Mrs. *Pawson*	01	00	00
Lady *Dawes*	02	02	00
Mrs. *Ramsden* paid by the city	04	00	00
Mrs. *Prince* paid by the city	02	00	00
Mrs. *Barker* paid by the city	02	00	00
Mrs. *Thornhill* paid by the city	05	00	00
The hon. Mrs. *Graham*	01	01	00
Lady *Dodsworth*	00	10	06
Mrs. *Lamplugh*	01	01	00
Mrs. *Weddal*	01	01	00
Mrs. *Mann*	00	10	06
Mrs. *Horsfield*	00	10	06
Mrs. *Redman*	01	01	00
Mrs. *Preston*	01	01	00

The Girls have one third of the charity collected on *Good-Friday*.

Five Boys put out Apprentices in 1735.

All the Boys put out since the first setting up of the CHARITY-SCHOOL, are one hundred and ninety three.

N. B. All boys in this school hereafter are intended to be put out to sea, or husbandry; or bound servants into private families, if they can be disposed of that way.

No boy to be taken in under ten years of age; and none to be put out under sixteen.

N. B. The amount of the subscriptions for the year 1734. was fifty pounds less than of 1733, and of those for the year 1735. twenty pounds under the preceding year. The declining state of the school's revenue, giving great concern to those, by whose assistance and oeconomy this publick and useful charity is regulated, they think it incumbent on them to acquaint the world with the present necessity of both the schools. They have already reduced the number of girls, and must soon be obliged to use the same method with the boys too, unless prevented by the timely and generous assistance of those who wish well to an undertaking, so truly charitable, and so beneficial to the publick, in training up many in the principles of the protestant religion, honesty and industry, who (very probably) would otherwise be a burthen to their country.

Dr. *Johnson*, Physician, *William Dobson*, esq; alderman, apothecary, Mr. *Francis Drake*, surgeon, to the SCHOOLS, *gratis*.

P. 330.

P. 330. *Sect. penult.* " The imperial crown shews that it [the statue] was erected in honour of some of our kings since *Hen.* VI."

I find this entry in the city's books relating to this statue, " on *Jan.* 15, and the 17th of " *Henry* VII, the image of *Ebranke*, which stood at the west end of St. *Saviour-gate*, was " taken down, new made and transposed from thence, and set up at the east end of the " chapel at the common-hall." So that it appears that this statue, now taken down again and laid in the common-hall, was a representation of king *Ebranke* under the figure of the king then reigning, *Henry* the seventh. See *page* 310.

P. 338. *Sect.* 1. " The new assembly rooms."

Indentures, leases, releases, relating to the purchase of the ground, &c.

3 *June* 1730. 3 Geo. II. " INdenture of bargain and sale quinquepartite inrolled, made " between *Ellen Bayock* of the city of *York*, late widow and " relict of *Matthew Bayock* deceased, but formerly widow and relict, and also devisee of the " last will and testament of *Christopher Beers* gent. deceased of the first part; *Hannah Wakefield* and *Bridget Wakefield* spinsters, daughters of *William Wakefield* and *Dorothy* his wife " deceased, of the second part; *Thomas Grimston* of the city of *York* esq; of the third part; " *Richard Thomson* of *Cursitor's-Alley, London*, gent. and *Christopher Goulton* of *Staples-Inn*, " *London*, gent. of the fourth part; and sir *William Wentworth* of *Britton* in the county of " *York* aforesaid baronet, sir *Walter Hawksworth* of *Hawksworth* in the same county baronet, *Henry Thompson*, *Thomas Fothergill*, *Michael Barston*, *George Neltbrope* and *Bacon* " *Morritt* of the city of *York* esquires of the fifth part. *Hannah Wakefield* in consideration " of seven hundred pounds, and *Ellen Bayock*, *Bridget Wakefield* and *Thomas Grimston* of " five shillings, grant, bargain and sell to sir *William Wentworth*, &c. all that messuage or " tenement, with a stable, kiln and garden thereto belonging in *Blake-street*, within the city aforesaid, which said messuage is now divided into several tenements, and now is or " late was in the possession of *Francis Drake* gent. *James Carpenter*, *Thomas Matthews*, *Robert Jackson*, *Alexander Lawson*, and *Ann Young*, or some of them, their under-tenants or " assigns; and all other the messuages, houses or buildings late the estate of *Christ. Beers* " gent. deceased, or of *William Wakefield* aforesaid deceased, or to which they the said *Ellen* " *Bayock*, *Hannah Wakefield*, *Brid. Wakefield* and *Thomas Grimston*, or the said *William Wakefield* or any of them, are or were any ways intitled or have any estate or interest, situate, " lying, and being on the west-side of *Blake-street* aforesaid, with all out-houses, yards, " gardens, orchards, ways, &c. to hold to sir *William Wentworth*, &c. In trust neverthe" less for all and every the persons who now are or hereafter shall be subscribers to the mu" sick assembly or assembly rooms within the city of *York*, pursuant to the proposals now " settled, bearing date the first day of *March* last, for raising the sum of three thousand " pounds for building assembly rooms within the city of *York*, in such manner as in and by " one indenture intended to bear date on or about the month of *June* instant, shall be decla" red and settled.

Inrolled in Chancery 15 June, 4 Geo. II.

Fine levied / *Recovery suffered* } *Trinity-Term*, 3 and 4 *Geo.* II.

29 & 30 *June*, 4 Geo. II. 1730. " LEase and release between *George Gibson* of the city of *York* " innholder, of the one part; and sir *William Wentworth* " of *Britton* in the county of *York* bart. sir *Walter Hawkesworth* " of *Hawksworth* in the same county, baronet, *Henry Thompson*, *Thomas Fothergill*, *Michael* " *Barston*, *George Neltborp* and *Bacon Morritt* of the city of *York* esquires, of the other part. " *Gibson* in consideration of ninety pounds sells them all that part of a messuage or tenement " in or near *Lendal-street*, thentofore in the occupation of *Mary Lund* widow, lying between " the entry or passage in the said house on the west, and on the house wherein Mrs. *Turner* " widow lately dwelt on the east; and also all that stable or out-house behind the same now " belonging to the *Black-horse* alehouse, the same containing in the front to the street eigh" teen feet, and in the back sixteen feet three inches, and sixty feet in length from the front " in the street aforesaid to the back extent thereof.

" BY indenture of lease and release dated the 17th and 18th of *November* 9 *Geo.* II, 1735. " the release being tripartite, and made between sir *William Wentworth* baronet, " *Henry Thompson*, *Michael Barstow*, *George Neltborp* and *Bacon Morritt* esqs; (trustees to " stand seized of the passage or parcel of ground hereafter mentioned, to be by them con" veyed for the benefit of the subscribers to the assembly rooms in *York*,) of the first part; " *George Gibson*, inn-holder, of the second part; and *Francis Barlow* esq; and *Darcy Preston* gent. of the third part. Reciting, that *George Gibson* had thentofore sold and con" veyed to, and to the use of the said trustees, together with sir *Walter Hawkesworth* baro" net, and *Thomas Fothergill* esq; deceased, and their heirs, as trustees as aforesaid, all that

" passage

" passage or parcel of ground containing sixty two feet or thereabouts in depth from the " street called *Finkill-street* backwards to the assembly rooms towards the south or southerly, " and eighteen feet or thereabouts in breadth towards the front of the said street called *Finkill-* " *street* west or westerly, and sixteen feet ten inches in breadth at the other end of the said " passage or parcel of ground next the said assembly rooms: And that *George Gibson* since " purchased to him and his heirs two houses or tenements which stood on the east or easter- " ly side of the said passage, one of which he hath caused to be pulled down; and that the " directors appointed for the direction and management of the affairs relating to the said " assembly rooms, being minded, with the consent of the said subscribers, to enlarge the " street before the said assembly rooms for the more commodious coming to and going from " the same, with coaches, chairs and otherwise, treated with the said *George Gibson* for the " purchase of the ground whereon the said purchased house pulled down stood, and the said " other purchased house stands; and the said *George Gibson* agreed with the directors who " met on the 4th of *June* last, to sell the ground whereon the said house so by him pulled " down stood, and the ground whereon the said other house stands, to the said directors for " two hundred and thirty pounds, he taking the materials of the said house standing at sixty " pound in part of payment, and clearing the ground of all the rubbish, so as he might " have and enjoy to him and his heirs for ever, all such building as should be by him or " them built upon a wall or pillars or both as should be erected at each end, and on the east " or easterly side of the said passage or parcel of ground, at the expence of the proprietors " or directors of the said assembly rooms, the said wall or pillars and front above the same, " to be in such manner as should be approved on by the right honourable the earl of *Burling-* " *ton*; and that *George Gibson* also agreed to covenant not to stop up any lights belonging " to the said assembly rooms, to which agreement the directors then present consented, pro- " vided the same should be approved of at a general court of the said subscribers to be held " on the 27th day of the same month of *June*: And that at such general court on *Friday* " the said 27th of *June* it was resolved, that the said agreement made with the said *George* " *Gibson* should be confirmed. In consideration and performance of the said agreement, on " the part of the said trustees, directors and subscribers, the said trustees conveyed all the " said passage or parcel of ground, containing sixty two feet or thereabouts in depth, and " eighteen feet or thereabouts in front to *Finkill-street*, and so to be continued by a strait line " to sixteen feet and ten inches at the other end adjoining upon the north east end of the " house of the said *George Gibson*, and upon the said *Finkill-street* north west and the other " end on the said assembly rooms, with the appurtenances to the said passage or parcel of " ground belonging unto the said *Francis Barlow* and *Darcy Preston* and their heirs, to the " uses, intents and purposes following, *viz.* As to so much of the said passage or parcel of " ground as measures to the height of the bottom of the floor up one pair of stairs in the said " house of the said *George Gibson*, to the use of the said sir *William Wenworth*, *Hen. Thomp-* " *son*, *M. Barstow*, *G. Neltborp* and *B. Morritt*, their heirs and assigns for ever, upon the " like trusts as they before stood seized of the said passage or parcel of ground; and as for " and concerning all the residue of the said passage upwards, to the use of the said *George* " *Gibson* his heirs and assigns for ever, with liberty for the said *George Gibson*, his heirs " and assigns, at his and their expence, to build such walls and fire places, and to " lay such floors, and make such room or rooms and lights as he and they shall think fit " upon and in the walls or pillars, or both, as shall be so erected at each end, and on the " east or easterly side of the said passage or parcel of ground; the same walls or pillars at " the bottom, and to the said height of the bottom of the said floor up one pair of stairs in " the said *George Gibson*'s house, to be built substantially, sufficient, and proper to bear such " fire-places and walls above the same, and for ever after to be kept in good and sufficient " repair at the expence of the proprietors or directors of the said assembly rooms; and all " the said walls or pillars, and also the walls and fire-places above the same to be built in " such manner as shall be approved by the said earl, or in default of such approbation, to " be well firmly and substantially erected and built with brick or stone, or both, and to be " so continued, and the timber and chambers to be laid thereon, and the roof thereof, to be " covered with slate or tile, and from time to time to be kept in good and sufficient repair " therewith by the said *George Gibson*, his heirs and assigns, but so as no part of the said " building so, or at any time hereafter, to be made, shall over-hang the walls or pillars so " to be built, or project in any part thereof beyond the same, save only usual and proper " offsets and cornishes over the windows and at the top.

" There is an agreement therein, that *Gibson* his heirs and assigns, shall not by building " upon any part of his ground adjoining to the said assembly rooms at any time hereafter " darken or stop any light belonging to or of the said assembly rooms; and that the said tru- " stees or directors, their heirs or assigns, or any of them, shall not darken, stop or obstruct " any light or lights which the said *George Gibson* shall make to the rooms, or any of them, " intended to be by him made over the said passage.

"BY indentures of leafe and releafe dated 17th and 18th *November*, 9 *Geo.* II, 1735, made between *George Gibfon*, innholder, of the one part; and fir *William Wentworth* baronet, *Henry Thompfon*, *Mich. Barftow*, *George Neltborp* and *Bacon Morritt* efqs; of the other part; reciting, that it has been agreed, that the faid *George Gibfon* fhould convey unto the faid fir *William Wentworth*, &c. and their heirs, all that parcel of ground whereon is now ftanding a meffuage or tenement in *Blake-ftreet* in the faid city of *York* wherein *Eleanor Waud* widow lately dwelt (but now uninhabited,) being the corner houfe there over-againft the mint-yard, and near oppofite the houfe belonging to the mayor and commonalty of the city of *York*, which is now in the poffeffion of fir *William Robinfon* baronet; and alfo all that parcel of void ground at the fouth or foutherly end of the faid houfe wherein the faid Mrs. *Waud* lived, and betwixt the paffage leading from the new affembly rooms to *Finkill-ftreet*, to wit, from the faid paffage to *Blake-ftreet*, and on which ground did lately ftand an houfe formerly in the occupation of *John Wilkinfon*, fhoemaker, and late in the occupation of *William Huntley*; and in confideration thereof the faid fir *William Wentworth* &c. have agreed to pay the faid *George Gibfon* one hundred and feventy pounds, and it is agreed *George Gibfon*, at his own expence, fhall within fourteen weeks pull down the faid meffuage now ftanding on the faid intended to be purchafed ground, and difpofe of the materials to his own ufe, and remove within the faid time all the rubbifh thereof; and that the faid *George Gibfon* fhall be at liberty to build fire-places and roomsupon a wall or pillars, or both, to be erected to inclofe the paffage now leading from the faid affembly rooms to *Finkel ftreet*, to the level of the faid *George Gibfon*'s firft floor, which pillars or wall are to be built well and fubftantially at the expence of the proprietors of the faid affembly rooms, in fuch manner as between them has been agreed, and as the earl of *Burlington* fhall approve of, and by them from time to time for ever repaired and kept in repair; and that the faid *George Gibfon* fhall not ftop up, obftruct or darken any lights now placed in the faid affembly rooms. In completion of the faid agreement, and in confideration of one hundred and feventy pounds, the faid *George Gibfon* conveys to, and to the ufe of the faid fir *William Wentworth*, *Henry Thompfon*, *Mich. Barftow*, *George Neltborp* and *Bacon Morritt*, and their heirs, the above defcribed parcel of ground whereon now ftands the houfe wherein *Eleanor Waud* widow lately dwelt; and alfo all that other parcel of void ground from the paffage leading from the new affembly rooms to *Finkell-ftreet* aforefaid, as is above defcribed, with all yards, backfides, ways, paffages, walls, fences, drains, eafements, advantages and appurtenances.

"There is a covenant that *George Gibfon* fhall not darken, obftruct or ftop up any the lights which are now in any part of the faid affembly rooms; but that the faid fir *William Wentworth*, &c. may quietly enjoy, and have the benefit of the faid lights in the fame manner that they are now placed.

"13 *Sept.* 1734. It was ordered at an houfe, if the fubfcribers to the affembly rooms think proper, and do buy the two houfes adjoining to the new affembly rooms, now belonging to Mr. *George Gibfon*, that fifty pounds be contributed and paid towards purchafing the fame out of the common chamber of this city, provided it be expreffed in fome article, that the ground whereon they now or lately did ftand be not built upon, but fhall lay open to the ftreet.

"The two houfes are both pulled down but no erection made, though a plan of it is got from lord *Burlington* for that purpofe. The city have not been yet called upon by the directors for their fifty pounds, *anno* 1736.

A general LIST of the SUBSCRIBERS to the new ASSEMBLY-ROOMS *in* YORK.

	l.
John Aiflabie, efq; ——	25
Sir *Edmund Anderfon*, bart.	25
The hon. *Richard Arundel*, efq;	25
The rev. Mr. *Bryon Allot* —	25
The rev. Mr. *Leonard Afh* —	25
Charles Allen, gent. — —	25
John Agar, efq; — —	25
The right hon. earl of *Burlington*	50
The right hon. lady *Burlington*	50
The right hon. lady dowager *Burlington*	50
The right hon. lord *Bruce* —	25
The right hon. lady *Bruce* —	25
Lady *Dorothea Boyle* ——	50
Lady *Charlotte Boyle* ——	50
Sir *Francis Boynton*, bart. —	25
Bryan Benfon, efq; ——	25
Francis Barlow, efq; — —	50
Ramfden Barnard, efq; — —	25
Michael Barftow, efq; — —	25
William Barftow, efq; — —	25
Charles Bathurft, efq; — —	50
Francis Beft, efq; — —	25
Hugh Bethel of *Rice*, efq;	25
Hugh Bethel of *Swinden*, efq;	25
Walter Blackett, efq; —	25
John Bourchier, efq; —	25
William Bourchier, efq; —	25
George Bows, efq; — —	25
Mrs. *Ellen Bows* — —	25
Ellerker Bradfhaw, efq; —	25
Samuel Braithwait, efq; —	25

Samuel

	l.
Samuel Breary, S. T. P.	25
Thomas Brown, esq;	25
Robert Buck, esq;	25
Philip Byerley, esq;	25
The right hon. earl of Carlisle	25
Sir Marmaduke Constable, bart.	25
Sir George Caley, bart.	25
Doctor Clinch	25
Marmaduke Constable, esq;	25
Doctor Cook	25
Stephen Croft, esq;	25
George Crowle, esq;	25
Haworth Currer, esq;	25
Jacob Custobady, gent.	25
Cuthbert Constable, esq;	25
William Chaloner, esq;	25
The right hon. lord Darcy	25
Sir Darcy Dawes, bart.	25
Abstrupus Danby, esq;	25
Samuel Dawson, esq;	25
John Dawson, esq;	25
Fitz. Dawes, gent.	25
James Deleuze, esq;	25
William Dobson, esq;	25
John Dodgson, esq;	25
Francis Drake, gent.	25
Daniel Draper, esq;	25
Richard Darley, esq;	25
Lewis Elstob, esq;	25
The right hon. lord visc. Falconberg	25
Sir Thomas Frankland, bart.	25
The hon. Charles Fairfax, esq;	25
Thomas Fairfax, esq;	25
Bryan Fairfax, esq;	25
Thomas Fothergill, esq;	50
George Fox, esq;	25
Housley Freeman, esq;	25
His grace the duke of Grafton	25
The right hon. lord Galloway	25
Sir Reginald Graham, bart.	25
Sir Edward Gascoign, bart.	25
Richard Gee, esq;	25
John Goodrick, esq;	25
William Gee, esq;	25
William Gossip, esq;	25
The hon. Mrs. Mary Graham	25
Thomas Grimston, esq;	25
Henry Greenwood, gent.	25
Sir Charles Hotham, bart.	25
Sir Robert Hildyard, bart.	25
Sir Walter Hawksworth, bart.	50
Sir William Hustler, knt.	25
William Harvey, esq;	25
Thomas Hassel, esq;	25
Francis Hildyard, gent.	25
Henry Hitch, esq;	25
The hon. colonel Howard	25
Jeremiah Horsfield, esq;	25
James Hustler, esq;	25
John Hutton, esq;	25
Mrs. Ellen Hutton	25
The right hon. lord visc. Irwyn.	25
The right hon. lady Irwyn.	25
James Ibbotson, esq;	25
John Ingleby, esq;	25
Doctor Johnson, jun.	25
Ralph Jenison, esq;	25
Sir John Kay, bart.	25
Mark Kirkby, esq;	25
Lord Langdale	25
The right hon. lord visc. Londsdale	25
The right hon. lady Lechmere	25
Sir Thomas Legard, bart.	25
Sir William Lowther, bart.	25
Richard Langley, esq;	25
Thomas Lister, esq;	25
Richard Lawson, gent.	25
The right hon. lord Malton	25
The hon. colonel Mordant	25
The hon. Mrs. Midleton	25
Sir Ralph Milbank, bart.	25
Sir William Milner, bart.	25
Henry Maisters, esq;	25
Henry Medley, esq;	25
William Metcalf, esq;	25
William Milner, esq;	25
Thomas Moor, esq;	25
Bacon Morrit, esq;	25
John Moyser, esq;	25
Richard Mancklin, gent.	25
John Marsden, gent.	25
The musick assembly	25
Ladies of the Monday assembly	50
Hugh Montgomery, esq;	25
Mr. Thomas Moon	25
Sir Michael Newton	25
George Nelthorpe, esq;	25
Thomas Norcliff, esq;	25
Duke of Norfolk	25
William Osbaldiston, esq;	25
Right hon. lady Preston	25
Sir Joseph Pennington, bart.	25
Sir Lyon Pilkington, bart.	50
Henry Pawson, esq;	25
Nathaniel Payler, esq;	25
Henry Pearce, esq;	25
Thomas Place, esq;	25
Michael Procter, esq;	25
Thomas Pulleyn, esq;	25
Darcy Preston, esq;	25
His grace the duke of Rutland	25
Sir Thomas Robinson, bart.	25
Gregory Rhodes, esq;	25
Nicholas Robinson, esq;	25
Mrs. Roundell	25
John Robinson, esq;	25
William Redman, esq;	25
The right hon. earl of Scarborough	25
The right hon. earl of Strafford	25
Sir William St. Quintin, bart.	25
Sir William Strickland, bart.	25
Sir George Saville, bart.	50
The lady Saville	50
Sir Thomas Sanderson, bart.	25
Sir Henry Slingsby, bart.	25
Lady St. Quintin	25
Thomas Scawen, esq;	25
Thomas Selby, esq;	25
Matthew St. Quintin, esq;	25
William Stainforth, esq;	25
John Shaw, gent.	25
Mrs. Smith	25
Miles Stapleton, esq;	25
William Spencer, esq;	25

	l.		l.
Stephen Tempest, esq; — —	25	*Godfrey Wentworth*, esq; —	25
Henry Thompson, esq; — —	25	*William Wharton*, esq; —	25
Richard Thompson, esq; — —	25	*Wharton Wharton*, esq; —	25
Leonard Thompson, esq; — —	50	*Peter Whitton*, esq; — —	25
Jonas Thompson, esq; —	25	*William Wickham*, esq; — —	25
Stephen Thompson, esq; —	25	The hon. *Tho. Willoughby*, esq;	25
Edward Thompson, esq; —	25	*Thomas Worsley*, esq; —	25
Cholmley Turner, esq; —	50	*Richard White*, esq; —	25
Marwood Turner, esq; —	25	*Richard Witton*, esq; —	50
William Turner, esq; —	25	*John Wood*, esq; — —	25
John Twisleton, esq; —	25	*John Wilmer*, gent. — —	25
Benjamin Tilden, esq; —	25	*John Wilkinson*, esq; —	25
Mr. *Henry Tireman* —	25	The city of *York* —	50
The right hon. sir *Rob. Walpole*	25		
Sir *William Wentworth*, bart. —	50		
Lady *Wentworth* —	25		
Sir *Rowland Wynne*, bart. —	25		
Doctor *Ward* — —	25		
William Wakefield, esq; —	25		

N. B. There are several gentlemen subscribers who have not yet paid in their first subscriptions; but, as I apprehend they may do it, I do not care to distinguish them.

" 1 *May* 1730. At a meeting of the subscribers in the *Monday* assembly-rooms the fol-
" lowing gentlemen were by ballotting elected first directors or stewards to these buildings.

Sir *William Wentworth*,
Sir *Walter Hawksworth*,
Sir *Edmund Anderson*,
Sir *Darcy Dawes*, } baronets.

Michael Barstow,
George Neltharp,
Henry Thomson,
Bacon Morritt,
Thomas Fothergill,
John Twisleton,
Stephen Tempest,
William Gossip. } esquires.

That it may be better understood what advantage the pulling down these houses has been to the opening the street and the area before the assembly, this plan has been taken; by which the angle the old streets made is delineated.

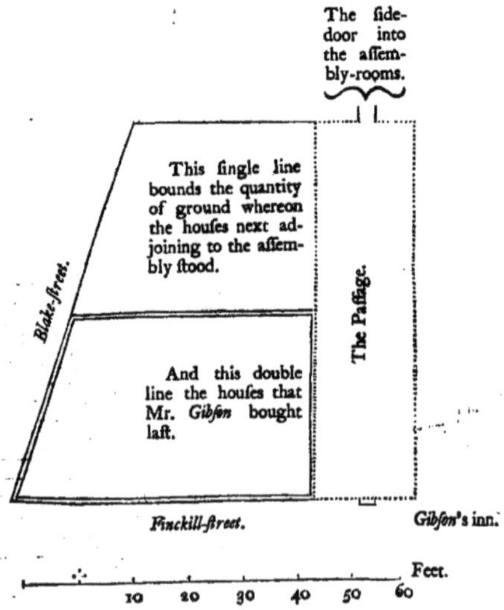

P. 346.

P. 346. *Sect. ult. Grapelane.*

Spurbury-hall *in* York. *(t)*

" OMnibus hoc scriptum cirographat. visur. vel audit. *Robertus de Wykford* canonicus ec-
" clesie *Ebor.* et prebendarius prebend. de *North-Newbald* in eadem eccl. salutem
" in auctore salutis. Noveritis me concessisse demisisse et hoc presenti scripto cirograph.
" confirmasse *Willielmo de Hovyngham* civi *Ebor.* et aurifabro *Ebor.* totum illud messuag.
" meum vocat. Spurbury-hall in vico de *Stayne-gate* in civit. *Ebor.* pertinens ad prebendam
" predict. cum omnibus domibus superedificatis et aliis suis pertinentiis, prout jacet in lati-
" tudine inter terram prioris S. *Oswaldi* ex parte una et terram que fuit *Richardi de Seleby*
" nuper civis *Ebor.* ex parte altera, et in longitudine a regia strata de *Stayne-gate* ante us-
" que ad quoddam gardinum in fine dicti messuagii versus Grapecuntlane retro, &c.

" OMnibus Christi fidelibus presens scriptum visur. vel auditur. *Johannes* filii *Thomae de*
" *Strensale* de *Ebor.* salutem *(u)*. Noverit universitas vestra me concessisse et presenti
" scripto meo pro me et heredibus meis confirmasse domino *Johanni de Ellerker* juniori,
" quod totum illud mesuagium in Grapcuntlane in civitate *Ebor.* quod *Hen. de Coupman-*
" *thorp* et *Matill. de Stransale* uxor ejus mater mea tenent ad terminum vitae ipsius matris
" meae de hereditate mea, et quod post mortem ejusdem matris meae ad me et heredes
" meos reverti deberet, post mortem praefatae *Matill.* matris meae dicto domino *Johanni*
" remaneat; habend. et tenend. sibi heredibus et assignatis suis una cum shopis selariis so-
" lariis et aliis quibuscunque dicto mesuagio circumquaque et ubicunque adjacentibus de ca-
" pitalibus dominis feodi illius per servitia inde debita et consueta imperpetuum. Praete-
" rea remisi relaxavi et omnino de me et heredibus meis imperpeuum quietum clamavi pre-
" fato domino *Johanni de Ellerker* totum jus et clameum quae habeo seu quovismodo ha-
" bere potui in illis duobus mesuagiis cum pertin. in *carnificio* in *Curia domini regis* in civi-
" tate *Ebor.* quae nuper idem dominus *Johannes* habuit ibidem de dono meo. Ita quod
" ego nec aliquis nomine meo in dictis duobus mesuagiis cum pertin. seu parte eorundem
" quicquam exigere vel vendicare poterimus quoquo modo, set inde sumus exclusi ab acti-
" one qualibet imperpetuum per presentes. Et ego predictus *Johannes de Stransale* et
" heredes mei omnia predicta mesuagia cum omnibus pertinentiis suis supradictis pre-
" fato domino *Johanni* heredibus et assignatis suis warrentizabimus imperpetuum contra
" omnes.

" In cujus rei testimonium presenti scripto sigillum meum apposui.

" Hiis testibus dominis *Johanne de Stonere*, *Simon de Drayton* et *Johanne de Hotbum* mi-
" litibus, *Elia de Assheburn* et *Will. Gylour* et aliis.

" Dat. apud *London.* xii die mensis *Martii* anno domini millesimo trescentesimo vicesimo
" octavo, regni vero regis *Edwardi* tertii post conquestum tertio.

P. 381. *Sect.* 3. Survey of the *Ainsty.* " Since which it has had the sanction of an act
" of parliament to confirm it."

Some of my papers being mislaid, I am at present ignorant what led me into this mistake, and the note of reference *(g)* belonging to it; but since the printing of this sheet, an affair has happened, whereby the city's right to this district has been particularly fought into, and by it the patent of *Henry* VI. is found to be the only grant or confirmation of it. It is plain, however, that the city has much more antiently laid claim to this wapontack; for besides the pleas which sir *T. W.* writes were held about it, eight of *Edward* I. I find a grant of the same king to the city, for restitution of their mayoralty and liberties then seized into the king's hands, either for non-payment of their ferm, or for failure in their proof of the claim, wherein the *Ainsty* is particularly mentioned. A copy of which dated the ninth of *Edward* I. follows in these words,

De libertatibus restitut. civibus Ebor. *(x).*

" REX dilecto suo *Johanni de Lithegraynes* vicecom. *Ebor.* et custodi civitatis sue
" *Ebor.* salutem. Sciatis quod de gratia nostra speciali reddidimus civibus nostris
" *Ebor.* majoratem ejusdem ville cum villa et libertate ejusdem, cum pertinentiis que nu-
" per capte fuerint in manum nostram per considerationem curie nostre tanquam forisfacte,
" habend. et tenend. eisdem civibus eodem modo et cum eisdem libertatibus et pertinen-
" tiis, quo eas habuerunt ante predictam captionem earundem in manum nost. ita quod
" de firma debita et aliis que ad nos pertinent ibidem de cetero respondeant per annum, sic-
" ut prius fieri consuevit. Commisimus etiam eisdem civibus Wapontack de Aynesty cum
" pertinentiis, quod clamant pertinere ad civitatem predict. tenend. usque ad festum ascen-

(t) *Pat.* 50 Ed. III. *p.* 1. *m.* 24.
(u) *Claus.* 3 Ed. III. *m.* 23. *d.*
(x) *Pat.* 9 Ed. I *m.* 16.

" sionis Domini proxime futurum, et tunc eis inde scire faciamus voluntatem nostram. Et " ideo vobis mandamus quod eisdem civibus predictas majoratem villam et libertatem te- " nend. in forma predicta. Et eis predictum **Wapontack** tenend. sicut predict. est una " cum omnibus de predictis villa et *Wapontack*, a festo S. *Michaelis* proxime preterito per- " ceptis.

" In cujus rei, &c.

" T. R. apud *Roth.* xx. die *Novem.*

P. 382. *Sect.* 5. " It is very particular that the inhabitants of this district are not re- " presented at all in parliament, *&c.*"

Since this sheet passed the press, as I said before, the contest on the petition relating to the last election, for knights of the shire for the county of *York*, has occasioned this matter to be debated before the house of *commons*. And a copy of the record of the patent of annexation of the district of *Aynsty* to the city of *York* by king *Henry* VI, being produced and read, which has a strong saving clause at the end of it; a resolution of allowing the votes of freeholders of this wapontack to be good was agreed unto by the house without a division. The author of this work had the honour to carry in the copy of the record and vouch it in the house; which saved a debate of some hours, and perfectly settled the right of these freeholders for the future voting at the county election. The proceedings in this matter claim a place in these additions; but the patent itself having been printed at length in *Maddox's firma Burgi* p. 293. and 294. *(g)*; except some particular specifications of tolls, it is needless to insert it here. The original enrolment may be found *pat.* 27 *Hen.* VI. *p.* 1. *m.* 14. *Turre London.*

VOTES *of the* HOUSE OF COMMONS.

" *Martis* 9. *die Martii* 1735. *p.* 185.

" THE house proceeded (according to order) to the further hearing the matters of the " several petitions, complaining of an undue election for the county of *York*.

" And the counsel were called in.

" And the counsel for the petitioner sir *Rowland Winn* bart. and the other petitioners, " whose petition complains of an undue election and return of sir *Miles Stapylton* bart. for " the said county, having proposed to disqualify *William Stolbard*, who voted for the said " sitting member, at the said election, in right of a freehold at *Acomb* in the hundred or " wapentake of AYNSTY, within the county of the city of *York*; and having examined " a witness in order to prove that *Acomb* is within the said hundred or wapontake, and " that the said hundred or wapontake is within the county of the said city; and having exa- " mined the said witness concerning the usage of voting for freeholds, lying in the said hun- " dred or wapontake, at the election of knights of the shire for the county of *York*; and ha- " ving proposed to disqualify several other persons, who voted for the sitting member, in " right of such freeholds

" The counsel for the said sitting member were heard in answer to the evidence of that " disqualification.

" And a copy of the record of the letters patent granted by king *Henry* VI. the 11*th* " day of *February* in the twenty seventh year of his reign to the mayor and citizens of the " city of *York* was produced and read; reciting that the said city, the suburbs or precincts " thereof, was then a county by itself, divided and separated from the county of *York*, " and called the county of the city of *York*; and that the mayor and citizens of the said city " were bayliffs of and in the hundred or wapontake of *Aynsty*; and granting to them and " their successors, that the said hundred or wapontake with the appurtenances, should be " annexed and united to the county of the said city, and be parcel thereof; and that the " said city, suburbs and precinct, hundred or wapontake, and each of them, with their " appurtenances, and every thing in them and each of them contained, except the castle " of *York*, the towers, fosses, and ditches to the said castle belonging, be the county of the " said city, separated and divided from the county of *York*; *saving always* to the church " and the archbishop, dean and chapter thereof, and every other community temporal and " spiritual, and all and singular other persons, all kinds of franchises, privileges, rights, " commodities and customs to them or any of them of right belonging.

" And the counsel for the said petitioners being heard by way of reply,

" The counsel were directed to withdraw.

" *Resolved*,

" That the persons whose freeholds lye within that part of the county of the city of " *York*, which is commonly called the *Ainsty*, have a right to vote for knights of the shire " for the county of *York*.

P. 426.

P. 426. *Sect.* 4. Archbiſhop *Walter Grey*'s temporal poſſeſſions.

Chart. Hen. III. Walter. Grey *archiep.* Ebor. *de diverſis terris et aliis reddit. conceſſ. dom.* Roberto de Grey *fratri ejus* (y).

" *HEN.* Dei gratia rex *Anglie*, &c. archiepiſcopis epiſcopis abbatibus prioribus comiti-
" bus baronibus juſtic. vic. prepoſitis miniſtris et fidelibus ſuis ſalutem. Inſpexi-
" mus cartam quam venerabilis pater *Walterus Ebor.* archiep. *Anglie* primas fecit *Roberto de*
" *Grey* fratri ſuo in hec verba, Omnibus Chriſti fidelibus viſuris vel audituris *Walterus*
" Dei gratia *Ebor.* archiep. *Angliae* primas ſalutem in Domino. Noveritis me dediſſe con-
" ceſſiſſe et preſenti carta confirmaſſe *Roberto de Grey* fratri meo pro homagio et ſervitio
" ſuo totum manerium de *Upton* cum pertinentiis quod habui de dono *Galfridi de R*[illegible],
" et totam terram redditum molendinum et pratum cum pertinentiis in *Stivelingflet* quam habui
" de dono *Normanni de Haſelerton*, et totum boſcum cum pertinent. in eadem villa quem ha-
" bui de dono *Willielmi de Albiniaco* et *Agatha* uxore ejus, et totum boſcum cum pert. quem
" habui de dono *Roberti Truſſebut* in eadem villa, et totum boſcum cum pertin. quem habui
" de dono *Willielmi de Ros*, et unam bovatam terre cum pertin. in eadem villa quam habui
" de dono *Radulphi de Thorp*, et unam bovatam terre cum pertin. in eadem villa quam ha-
" bui de *Philippo* vicario eccleſ. de *Stivelingflet*, et totam terram cum pertin. in *Morby*
" quam habui de dono *Agnetis* de *Morevill*, et homagium et ſervitium *Willielmi* filii *Thome*
" *de Belkertorp* de toto tenemento quod tenet in altera *Morby* que habui de dono ipſius *Ag-*
" *netis*, et totum pratum cum pertinen. in *Naburn* quod habui de dono *Willielmi de Pau-*
" *mes*, et totam terram et pratum in eadem villa quod habui de dono *Ricardi de Maunſel*,
" et terram cum pertinent. in *Drenghuſes* quam habui de priore et conventu *S. Trinitatis*
" *Ebor.* et totam terram cum pertinentiis quam habui de dono *Willielmi de Gygleſwyk*, et
" totam terram redditum pratum et gardinum cum pertinent. in *Boyſtardthorp* que habui de
" dono *Petri de Knapeton*, et totum pratum cum pertin. in eadem villa quod habui de prio-
" re et conventu S. *Andreae Ebor.* et totum pratum cum pertin. in eadem villa quod habui
" de dono *Henrici de Karleton*, et totum pratum cum pertin. in *Thorpmalteby* quod habui de
" priore hoſpitalis *Jereſolumitan.* in *Anglia*, et totam terram cum pertin. in *Thorp* S. *Andreae*
" quam habui de dono *Galfridi de Thorney* cum molendino ad ventum ſuper eandem terram
" ſito, et totam terram cum pertin. quam habui de abbate et conventu de *Kirkeſtall* in vil-
" lis de *Thorp* S. *Andree* et *Thorpmalteby*, excepto vivario ad opus meum reſervato et mo-
" lendino aquario ſuper idem ſito, et excepta tota terra verſus auſtrum in campo de
" *Thorp* S. *Andree* de cujuſcunque dono fuit ſicut *Kaldekoteſiks* deſcendit de boſco ejuſdem
" *Thorp* per bercariam meam uſque ad predict. vivarium, et totam terram cum pertinentiis
" quam habui de dono abbatis et conventus de *Maleby* in *Greneruding* in villa de *Stiveling-*
" *flet*, et duas acras et dimid. de waſto in eadem villa in quibus domus ipſius *Roberti* ſite
" ſunt quas habui de conceſſione *Willielmi de Stutevill* et aliis dominis ejuſdem ville, et unam
" bovatam terre cum pertin. et unam acram prati quas habui de dono *Nicholai* filii *Hu-*
" *gonis Palmeri* in villa de *Morby*, et totum pratum quod habui de *Willielmo Fayrfax* cum
" pertin. in territorio de *Stivelingflet* et *Morby*, et totum pratum quod habui de dono *Hen-*
" *rici Neve* in villa de *Acaſter*, et unum molendinum ad ventum quod habui de dono *Hu-*
" *gonis* filii *Serlonis* de *Northſtrete* capellani in *Drenghuſes*, et totam terram cum pertinent.
" que habui de *Henrico Boyſtard* in *Boyſtardthory* et in *Dringhuſes*. Habenda omnia et te-
" nenda eidem *Roberto* et heredibus ſuis de capitalibus dominicis ſingulorum feodorum ſu-
" pradict. libere quiete et integre jure hereditario in perpetuum. Faciendo capital. domi-
" nis qui pro tempore fuerint pro manerio de *Upton* ſervitium feodi dimidii militis, et pro
" terre redditu molendino et prato in *Stivelingflet* que habui de dono *Normanni de Heſeler-*
" *ton* ſervitium feodi dimidii militis pro omni ſervitio, et reddendo ad luminare eccleſ.
" beate *Marie* de *Stivelingflet* unum denarium annuatim pro predicta bovata terre quam ha-
" bui de dono predict. *Philippi* vicarii de *Stivelingflet*, et faciendo forinſecum ſervitium
" quantum pertinet ad duas carucatas terre de quibus duodecim carucate terre faciunt feo-
" dum unius militis pro predict. terra homagio et ſervitio *Willielmi* filii *Thome de Belker-*
" *thorp* que habui de dono ſupradicte *Agnetis de Morvil* in duabus *Morbyes* ſupradictis, et
" reddendo unam libram incenſi vel duos denarios eccl. *S. Trinitatis Ebor.* in die *S. Trini-*
" *tatis* pro predicta terra cum pertin. quam habui de dono *Willielmi de Gygleſwyk*, et red-
" dendo duodecim denar. ſupradicto *Petro de Knapeton* ad duos terminos annuat. viz. ad
" *Pentecoſten* ſex denar. et ad feſtum S. *Martini* in hyeme ſex denar. pro predictis terre red-
" ditu prato et gardino que habui de dono ipſius *Petri de Knapeton* et reddendo unum de-
" nar. et unum par chirothec. in die *Paſche* Domino de *Acaſter Malebiſſe* pro predict.
" terra cum pertinentiis quam habui de *Galfrido de Thorenny* in *Thorp* S. *Andree* pro omni-
" bus conſuetudin. exaction. demandis et rebus aliis. Omnia vero predictas terras tenemen-
" ta prata molendina boſcos redditus et gardina cum omnibus pertinent. ſepedict. capitales
" domini et heredes ſui, prout in cartis particularibus eorum quas mihi fecerunt de war-

(y) *Rot.* 36 *Hen.* III. *m.* 13.

" ranti-

" rantizatione mihi et heredibus meis et assignatis meis facienda continetur, sepedicto *Ro-*
" *berto de Grey* et hered. suis contra omnes et singulos homines et feminas warrantizabunt.
" Et ut hec mea donatio concessio et confirmatio perpetuum robur obtineant, presentem car-
" tam sigilli mei munimine duxi roborare. Hiis test. dom. *Fulcone Basseth* decano *Ebor.*
" magistris *Laurentio de Lincoln.* et *Roberto Hageth* archidiacon. *Ebor.* et *Richmund* magistris
" *Sewallo de Bovill.* canon. *Ebor.* et *Willielmo de Senedon*, dominis *Galfrido de Booland* et *Ala-*
" *no de Wassand*, domino *Willielmo de Wydinton*, *Willielmo de Bradeleys*, *Petro de Kayvill*,
" *Falcone de Wakfeld*, *Michaele de Hek*, *Galfrido de Basing* et aliis. Inspeximus etiam aliam
" cartam quam idem archiep. fecit predict. *Roberto de Grey* fratri suo in hec verba: Omni-
" bus Christi fidelibus ad quos presens scriptum pervenerit *Walterus de Gray* Dei gratia
" *Ebor.* archiep. *Anglie* primas salut. in Domino. Noveritis me concessisse dediss. et presenti
" carta nost. confirmasse dilecto fratri nost. dom. *Roberto de Grey* unam carucat. terre cum
" omnibus pertinentiis in villa de *Couthorp* quam habuimus de dono *Alexandri* filii *Williel-*
" *mi* parsone de *Fangefosse* quietam a solutione redditus viginti solidorum quos idem *Alexander*
" solvere consuevit *Juliane de Newtona*, quem quidem redditum viginti solidorum dicta
" *Juliana* nobis concessit et quietum clamavit. Homagium, &c. *Gilberti de Hopertona* et
" *Amabilis* uxor. sue cum ipsorum et heredum suorum servitio, videlicet quinque solidor.
" per annum quorum homagium et servitium habuimus de dono dicte domine *Juliane de*
" *Newtona*. Preterea unum toftum in *Couthorp* quod *Robertus Lanoc* quondam tenuit et
" duas acras terre cum pertinentiis in eadem villa, quam terram cum tofto habuimus de
" dono *Erneburge* de *Fangefosse*, similiter unam bovatam terre et dimid. cum prato in *Cou-*
" *thorp* quam habuimus de dono *Nicholai de Hugate* et *Aceline* uxoris sue. Insuper unam
" bovatam terre cum pertinentiis suis in *Yolthorp*, quam habuimus de dono et concessione
" *Ade* filii *Alani* et *Alicie* filie et heredis *Willielmi de Ergum*, secundum quod in cartis om-
" nium predict. super hoc nobis confectis plenius continetur. Et preterea omnes terras
" quas in eisdem villis de *Yoltorp* et *Coutorp* de emptione habuimus vel adquisitione cum
" omnibus pertin. suis. Habendas et tenendas eidem domino *Roberto de Grey* et hered. suis
" libere quiete integre et pacifice cum omnibus libertat. et consuetudin. ad predict. terras
" pertinent. faciendo inde forinsecum servitium capitalibus dominicis quantum pertinet ad
" terras predictas pro omni servitio. Et ut hec nost. concessio donatio et confirmatio per-
" petuum robur obtineant presenti scripto sigillum nost. duximus apponend. Test. magi-
" stris *Roberto Hageth* canon. *Ebor.* et *Willielmo de Wysebeth* canon. *Beverlac. Johan. del*
" *Ecbbrec* canon. *Ebor. Willielmo de Vescy* canon. *Ripon*, magistro *Ricardo de Watlinton* et
" *Ricardo de Lethebroc* canon. *Beverlac. Willielmo de Martel*, *Willielmo de Wydinden*, *Rogero*
" *de Oseberton*, *Roberto de Boelton*, *Thoma de Stanford* et *Reginaldo de Stowa* clericis et aliis.
" Dat. apud *Suwell* quinto decimo kal. *Octob.* anno Dom. millesimo ducentes. tricess. quinto.
" Inspeximus etiam aliam cartam quam predict. archiep. fecit predict. *Roberto de Grey* fra-
" tri suo in hec verba, Omnibus Christi fidel. ad quos &c. *Walterus de Grey* Dei gratia
" *Ebor.* archiep. &c. Noveritis nos concessisse dedisse et presenti carta nost. confirm. di-
" lecto frat. nost. dom. *R. de Grey* pro homagio et servitio suo totam terram quam *Williel-*
" *mus de Boelton* nob. concess. et quiet. clamav. in *Boelton* et *Japum* cum homagiis et servi-
" tiis et reddit. et villenagiis et omnibus pertin. suis sine aliquo retenimento. Similiter et
" duas bovat. et octo acras terre cum pertin. quas *Thomas de Bubwyth* et *Agnes* soror. pred.
" *Willielmi de Boelton* nob. concesserunt et quietum clamaverunt, et decem bovatas terre cum
" mansa et tofto et omnibus pertinent. suis in *Japum* quas *Petrus de Wyverthorp*, nobis dimisit
" et concessit et quiet. clamavit prout in cartis predict. *Willielmi de Boelton*, *Thome de Bubwith*
" et *Agnetis* sororis ipsius *Willielmi Petri de Wyvertorp*, *Stephani de Baugi* et *Rog. de Baugi*
" nob. super hoc confectis quas quidem eidem *Rob. de Grey* reddidimus plenius continetur.
" Tenend. et habend. de nobis et successoribus nost. etiam et heredibus suis cum omnib.
" pertin. suis libere integre et quiete ab omni servitio et exact. faciendo inde servitium an-
" nuatim nobis et successoribus nost. et aliis predict. terrarum dominis quod predicti *Wil-*
" *lielmus Thomas* et *Agnes Petrus Stephanus* et *Rogerus* nobis et predecess. nost. et aliis
" dict. terrarum dominis facere consueverint pro omni servitio. Et ut hec nost. concess.
" donat et carte nost. confirm. perpetuum robur obtineant presenti scripto sigillum nostrum
" duximus apponend. Testib. magistris *Laurentio de Lincoln.* canon. *Ebor.* et *Roberto Ha-*
" *geth* canon. *Hertforden. Galfrid. de Becland* canon. *Beverlac. Willielmo de Vescy*, *Odone de*
" *Richmund*, *Willielmo de Wyndendon*, *Ada de Stavel*, *Henrico Walens*, *Rog. de Oseberton* et
" *Reginaldo de Stowa* cleric. et aliis. Dat. apud *Scroby* sept. kal *Maii* pontif. nost. anno de-
" cimo octavo. Nos autem donationes et concessiones predict. ratas habentes et gratas
" eas pro nob. et heredibus nost. *Waltero de Grey* filio et heredi predict. *Roberti de Grey*
" concedimus et confirmamus, sicut carte predicti archiep. quas idem *Walterus* filius et heres
" predict. *Roberti* inde habet rationaliter testantur.

" Hiis test. venerab. patre *Waltero Wygorn.* episcopo *Ricardo de Clare* comite *Gloucestre*
" et *Hereford*, *Simone de Monteforti*, comite *Leycestre*, *Rogero de Quency* com. *Wynton.*
" *Guydone de Laziman* fratre nost. *Petro de Sabaud. Johanne Mansell* preposito *Bever-*
" *lac.* magistro *Willielmo de Kilkenny* archidiacono *Coventrien. Bertramo de Crioll*, *Ri-*
" *cardo*

" *cardo de Grey, Johan. de Grey, Gilberto de Segrave,* magistro *Simone de Wanton, Egi-*
" *dio de Erdington, Roberto le Noreys* et aliis.

" Data per manum nost. apud *Westm.* vicef. nono die *April.* anno regni nost. tricesimo
" sexto.

P. 431. *Sect.* 3. *Thomas de Corbridge* archbishop.
There was a severe judgment given against this archbishop in a cause betwixt the king and him relating to the prebendary of *Stillington*; which take as follows,

Inter diversa judicia in episcopos ob contempt. &c. E collect. J. Anstis *arm.* (*x*)

" SEde vacante archiepiscopatus *Ebor.* dom. rex contulit magistro *Johanni Benbill* clerico re-
" gis prebend. de *Styvelington* in ecclesia beati *Petri Ebor.* vacan. et ad regis dona-
" tionem, &c. Quem *Thomas* archiep. admittere recusavit in regis contemptum decem
" mill. librarum. Et predict. *Thomas* venit et defendit, &c. Et bene cognoscit quod ipse
" predicta mandata regia admisit, et quod ipse paratus est et erit et semper fuit man-
" datis regiis parere in quantum potuit et sibi incumbit, &c. Sed dicit quod predict. cle-
" ricum domini regis ad predict. prebendam et capellam ad presens admittere non potuit;
" et quod dominus papa ratione vacationis que alias se fecit, in curia *Romana* de eisdem
" prebenda et capella per consecrationem ipsius episcopi ibidem qui easdem prius tenuit,
" ipsas easdem ex collatione sua dedit clericis, &c. De quibus eadem prebenda et capella
" nunc plenae sunt, unde dicit quod ipse ratione sacramenti sui et obedientiae suae quae do-
" mino papae fecit, &c. factum ipsius domini, &c. papae superioris sui infirmare non potest
" nec pred. clericus, &c. Inde privare, &c. Et petit quod dominus rex ipsum in isto casu
" excusatum habere velit, &c. Et quaesitum est a prefato archiepiscopo si aliquid aliud ad
" pred. mandatum domini regis liceat respondere, &c. Qui dicit, ut prius, quod non po-
" test, &c. Et quia causa pred. quam idem archiepiscopus de impedimento seu non posse
" suo in curia hic pro se assignat, pro nulla habetur, eo quod factum domini papae supe-
" rioris sui in curia *Romana* factum in curia hac deduci non potest, nec terminari, immo
" ad inobedientiam ipsius archiepiscopi expresse reputat et tenet, eo quod pred. clericum, &c.
" ad mandat. domini regis pred. admittere recusavit; consideratum est quod temporalitas
" quae archiepiscopus de domino rege tenet &c. capiat in manu domini regis quousque cle-
" ricum pred. ad mandatum domini regis admiserit, et ipsi domino regi de contemptu
" et in obedientia pred. satisfecerit. Et super hoc publice in plena curia hic inhibitum est
" ex parte domini regis prefato archiepiscopo et omnibus aliis de regno et de potestate re-
" gis tam laicis quam clericis, &c. sub forisfactura omnium quae forisfacere poterunt, ne
" aliquis eorum aliquid sequatur vel qui faciat erga *cur. Romanam nec alibi* contra jus co-
" ronae et dignitatis regis, &c. in ista causa vel aliis quibuscunque, nec aliquas appella-
" tiones provocationes seu instrumenta quaecunque faciant nec auxilium consilians seu assen-
" sum ad hoc prebeant quoquo modo per quod dissentio aliqua vel discordia inter cur. *Ro-*
" *manam* et cur. regis poterunt evenire vel pax inter easdem aliqualiter (quod absit) infir-
" mari, &c.

P. 441. *Sect. ult.* The pope's bull of translation of *J. Kempe*, bishop of *London*, to the archbishoprick of *York*.

Litera papalis de admissione et receptione Johannis Kempe *nuper* London. *episcopi in archiepiscopum* Ebor. (*y*)

" MARTINUS episcopus servus servorum Dei dilectis filiis populo civitatis et dioece-
" sios *Eboracen.* salutem et apostolicam benedictionem. *Romani* pontificis, quem pa-
" stor ille coelestis et episcopus animarum potestatis sibi plenitudine tradita ecclesiis praetu-
" lit universis, plena vigiliis solicitudo requirit, ut ipse cum statum cujuslibet orbis ecclesiae
" sic vigilanter excogitet sicque prospiciat diligenter, quod per ejus providentiam circum-
" spectam, nunc per simplicis provisionis officium nunc per ministerium translationis ac-
" commodae, prout personarum locorum et temporum qualitas exigit et ecclesiarum utilitas
" persuadet, ecclesiis singulis pastor accedat idoneus et rector providus deputetur qui po-
" pulum sibi commissum salubriter dirigat et informet ac ecclesiis votivae prosperitatis ef-
" ferat incrementa. Sane ecclesia *Eboracensis* eo pastoris solatio destituta quod nos ho-
" die venerabilem nostrum *Ricardum* episcopum *Lincolnien.* tunc *Eboracen.* archiepiscopum
" licet absentem, a vinculo quo eidem *Eboracensi* ecclesiae cui tunc praeerat tenebatur de
" fratrum nostrorum consilio et apostolicae potestatis plenitudine absolventes ipsum, ad ec-
" clesiam *Lincolniensem* tunc vacantem duximus authoritate apostolica transferendum, praefi-
" ciendo eum ipsi *Lincolniensi* ecclesiae in episcopum et pastorem, nos ad provisionem ipsius
" *Eboracensis* ecclesiae celere et feliciter, ne ecclesia ipsa longae vacationis permaneret incom-

(*x*) *Trin.* 32 Ed. I. *rot.* 75. *coram rege.*

(*y*) *Ex regist. ant. in camera super pontem* Usae *f.* 268.

4

" modo, paternis et follicitis ftudiis intendentes poft deliberationem quam de praeficiendo " eidem *Eboracenfi* ecclefiae perfonam utilem et etiam fructuofam cum dictis fratribus " tractatum habuimus diligentem, demum ad venerabilem fratrum noftrum *Johannem* epif-" copum *London.* confideratis grandium virtutum meritis quibus perfona fua prout fide " dignorum teftimoniis accepimus divina gratia infignivit, et quod ipfe *Johannes* qui re-" gimini dictae *Londonen.* ecclefiae hactenus laudabiliter prefuit dictam *Eboracenfem* eccle-" fiam fciet et poterit, auctore Domino, utiliter regere et feliciter gubernare, convertimus ocu-" los noftrae mentis. Intendentes igitur tam dictae *Eboracenfi* ecclefiae quam ejus gregi do-" minico falubriter providere, praefatum *Johannem*, a vinculo quo eidem *Londonen.* ecclefiae " cui tunc praeerat tenebatur, de ipforum fratrum confilio et ejufdem poteftatis plenitudine " abfolventes eum, ad dictam ecclefiam *Eboracenfem* authoritate apoftolica tranftulimus ip-" fumque illi praefecimus in archiepifcopum et paftorem curam et adminiftrationem ip-" fius *Eboracenfis* ecclefiae fibi in fpiritualibus et temporalibus plenarie committendo, libe-" ramque ei dando licentiam ad ipfam *Eboracenfem* ecclefiam tranfeundi, firma fpe fiducia-" que conceptis quod, dirigente Domino, actus fuos praefata *Eboracenfis* ecclefia per ipfius *Jo-*" *hannis* induftriae et circumfpectionis ftudium fructuofum regetur utiliter et profpere di-" rigetur ac grata in eifdem fpirituabibus et temporalibus fufcipiet incrementa; quocirca u-" niverfitatem veftram rogamus et hortamur attente per apoftolica vobis fcripta mandan-" tes quatenus eundem archiepifcopum, tanquam patrem et paftorem animarum veftrarum " grato admittentes honore, exhibeatis eidem obedientiam et reverentiam debitam et devo-" tam, ita quod ipfe in vobis devotionis filios et vos in eo pro confequend. patrem inveniffe " benevolum gaudeatis.

" Dat. *Romae* apud fanctos apoftolos decimo tertio kalendarum *Augufti* pontificatus no-" ftri anno octavo.

P. 490. *Sect.* 7. *and P.* 493. " unlefs we fuppofe the tomb on the right hand *Walter* " *Grey*'s to be his."

Supposed the Tomb of Godfrey de Kimeton Archbishop.

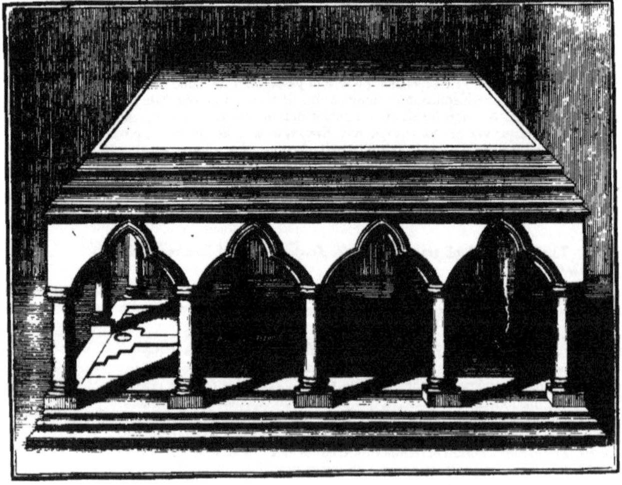

P. 497. *Sect.* 4. *Egremond.*

P. 528. *Sect. ult.* P. 529. *Sect. prim.*

On ſome of the pillars in the *Minſter* Dr. *Langwith* further expreſſes himſelf in this manner,

"Since I wrote to you about the pillars in *York Minſter*, I find by Dr. *Woodward*'s ca-
"talogues, that the ſmall ſhafts of the pillars in *Weſtminſter-abbey* and the *Temple church*
"are of our marble, as alſo ſome of thoſe in *Saliſbury cathedral*, and indeed in moſt of
"the larger *Gothick* buildings in *England*. I find alſo upon further inquiry, that the ri-
"ver is navigable for boats to within four or five miles of the place where this marble was
"found in the greateſt plenty and perfection, and might probably have been ſo, ſtill nearer
"before the mills, &c. were built upon it. I hope after this, that the diſtance between
"this pariſh and *York* will not be made uſe of as an objection to my conjecture; for the
"carriage from hence to *York* being in a manner all by water the expence muſt have
"been a meer trifle in compariſon to that of conveying it to many other places at a di-
"ſtance, where more land carriage would be required. It is pretty remarkable that in
"moſt places where theſe pillars are to be met with the common people have a notion
"that they are of an artificial marble and caſt in molds." But upon the whole a piece of marble, broke off from *Walter Grey*'s tomb, and a piece of the marble at *Petworth* have been compared by an experienced workman; who at firſt was of the common opinion that the former only conſiſted of bits of marble wrought in plaiſter, but a little rubbing and poliſhing ſoon ſhewed him his miſtake, and he was convinced that they were one and the ſame kind of ſtone. It is further to be noted, that though there are ſeveral quarries, in the north of *England* which produce ſtone and marble, in which large quantities of foſſile ſhells are found petrified, as in this, and in the marble out of which the old *font* in the cathedral is cut, which is the ſame ſort with the old altar-table, once laid over our St. *William*'s remains, and is now ſawn into ſlips to compoſe part of the moſaick work in the new pavement under the *lanthorn-ſteeple*, yet no ſort in our country bears any compariſon

riſon to the marble of the pillars aforeſaid. The ſhell which abounds moſt in this marble Dr. *Langwith* ſuppoſes to be the *cochlea faſciata vivipara fluviatilis*. He adds that he takes theſe kinds of petrifactions to be the nobleſt of antiquities, as being divine monuments of of that dreadful confuſion and deſtruction which was brought upon the earth by the deluge.

P. 546. and 547. The rents and revenues of the archbiſhoprick of *York*, in the county of the ſame, from **Doomsday-book**.

EVREPIRSCIRE.

Terra archiepiſcopi Eboracenſis.

" In *Patrictone* cum iiii. berewitis. *Wiſtede*, *Halſam*, *Torp*, *Torveleſtorp* ſunt xxxv. carucate et dimidia et ii. bovate et ii. particate, i. bovata ad geldum. Hoc manerium fuit et eſt archiepiſcopi *Eboracenſis*. De terra hujus manerii habent ii. milites, vi. carucatas, et duo clerici ii. carucatas et iii. bovatas et iii. particatas unius bovate.

" In *Swine* cum iiii. berewitis ſunt x. carucate et ii. bovate ad geldum. In *Bruneby* iiii. carucate ad geldum. Nunc habet *Goisfridus* homo archiepiſcopi in dominio.

" In *Coletun* villa regis habet archiepiſcopus dimidiam carucatam terre de qua pertinet ſoca ad *Almelai* manerium regis.

" In *Scireburne* cum berewitis ſuis ſunt ad geldum regis quater viginti et xvi. carucate, in quibus poſſunt eſſe lx. caruce. De iſta terra habent milites archiepiſcopi liii. carucatas. De ipſa terra habet unus tainus v. carucatas et i. bovatam. De ipſa habent ii. clerici vi. carucatas. De eadem terra habet abbas de Salebi vii. carucatas. Hoc manerium eſt in *Barcheſtone* wapentachio.

" Archiepiſcopus habet juxta civitatem xv. carucatas ad geldum. In *Eglendon* et in *Walbi* ſunt ad geldum xvii. carucate. De ipſa habet unus miles ii. In *Walchinton* ſunt ad geldum viii. carucate et i. bovata. Canonici habent ſub archiepiſcopo. In *Cave* eſt ad geldum una carucata et vi. bovate. Canonici tenent et eſt waſta. In *Newebolt* ſunt xxviii. carucate et ii. bovate ad geldum. Canonici tenent. In *Richal*. ſunt ad geldum ii. carucate. Canonici tenent. In *Doninton* ſunt iiii. carucate ad geldum. Canonici tenent. In *Euringham* cum berewitis ſuis *Londeneſburg*, *Toletorp*, *Gudmundham* ſunt ad geldum xvii. carucate. Nunc ſub *Thoma* archiepiſcopo habent terram duo clerici et unus miles. In *Weſtwangham* ſunt ad geldum xviii. carucate et dimidia, nunc habet archiepiſcopus *Thomas* et waſta eſt. In *Wiltone* cum berewitis ſuis *Bodelton*, *Ghevetorp*, *Aucltorp*, *Grenewic*, *Fridarſtorp* ſunt ad geldum xxx. carucate et vi. bovate. In *Fridarſtorp* eſt ad geldum i. carucata et dimidia, de qua pertinet ſoca ad *Wiliton*, waſta eſt. In *Grenedale* ſunt ad geldum iiii. carucate, nunc waſta eſt. In *Barnebi* et *Milleton* ſunt ad geldum x. carucate et ii. bovate. In *Ach*. ad geldum vi. bovate et dimidia. In *Caretorp* ſunt ad geldum iiii. carucate. In *Langeton* ſunt ad geldum ix. carucate, nunc habet ſanctus *Petrus* et waſta eſt. In *Coltun* ſunt ad geldum ix. carucate, nunc habet ſanctus *Petrus* et waſta eſt. In *Wifretorp* xviii. carucate cum berewicis his. *Meletorp* v. carucate. In *Scireburne* ſunt ad geldum xxvi. carucate. Ad hoc manerium pertinet *Elpetorp*, ubi ſunt ad geldum xii. carucate, vi. ſub ſoca, et vi. cum ſaca et ſoca, waſta eſt. Ad eundem manerium pertinet ſoca harum terrarum. *Grimſtone* iii. carucate et dimidia. *Sudtone* dimidia carucata. *Briteſhale* ii. carucate et dimidia. *Croum* iii. carucate. *Turyileby* i. carucata. *Ludton* viii. carucate. *Ulchitorp* i. carucata. *Walkelinus* miles habet ſub archiepiſcopo *Grimſtone*. *Eccleſia de Colnun* eſt archiepiſcopi *Thome* cum dimidia carucata. In *Buſhetorp* ſunt ad geldum iiii. carucate et dimidia.

NORT TREDING.

" In *Wichum* eſt ad geldum dimidia carucata, S. *Petrus* habet et waſta eſt. In *Salttun* ſunt ad geldum ix. carucate. In *Brayebi* ſunt ad geldum vi. carucate, waſta eſt. In *Berg* et alia *Berg* ſunt ad geldum iii. carucate et dimidia et waſta eſt. In *Nementon* ſunt ad geldum iiii. carucate. Gamel dedit ſancto *Petro* tempore regis *Edwardi*, modo waſta eſt. In *Nagbelten* ſunt ad geldum iiii. carucate, waſta eſt. In *Maltun* ad geldum i. carucata. In *Wilbeton* eſt ad geldum i. carucata. In *Pochelaf* ad geldum i. carucata. In *Ambeforde* ad geldum iii. carucate. In *Flaxtun* ad geldum vi. bovate. In *Mortun* ad geldum ii. carucate et dimidia. In *Bachegbi* ad geldum vi. carucate et i. bovata. In *Carletun* ad geldum iiii. carucate et dimidia, ſanctus *Petrus* habet, waſta ſunt, preter quod iiii. villani habentes ii. carucatas. In *Staneyvif* habet *Ulf* vi. bovatas. Idem dedit ſancto *Petro*. In *Balgetorp* ſunt ad geldum iiii. carucate. In *Hamelſey* ad geldum iiii. carucate et ii. bovate. In *Wardille* ad geldum iii. carucate. In *Careltone* ad geldum iii. carucate. Inter omnes xiiii. carucate. Sanctus *Petrus* habet, et ſunt in eis viii. villani habentes v. carucatas. Reliqua waſta ſunt. In *Marton* ad geldum iii. carucate. Sanctus *Petrus* habuit et habet cum ſaca et ſoca. In *Stivelinctun* ad geldum x. carucate. In *Axebi* ad geldum vi. carucate et i. bovata. In *Tolnetun* ad geldum viii. caracate. In *Alne* ad geldum viii. carucate. In *Hilperbi* ad geldum v. carucate. Ad hanc villam pertinet ſoca harum terrarum. *Loletone*, *Turulveſtorp* et *Wipeſtone*, *Mitune*. Inter omnes ad geldum xi. carucate et ii. bovate. In eodem *Hilperbi* habet ſanctus *Petrus* iii. carucatas, waſta eſt. In *Strenſhale* v. carucate ad geldum, waſta. In *Tovetorp* iii. carucate ad geldum, waſta eſt. In *Edeſwic* iii. carucate ad geldum, waſta. In *Coteborne* iii. carucate. Omnia hec waſta ſunt.

VEST

VEST TREDING.

"In *Warnesfeld* ad geldum ix. carucate. Sanctus *Petrus* habuit et habet. *Ilbertus* tenet, "ad *Osbaldewir* pertinet, set tamen manerium fuit. In *Popletune* ad geldum viii. carucate, "archiepiscopus tenet. In *Acbum* ad geldum xiiii. carucate et dimidia. Sanctus *Petrus* "habet. In *Notbelai* cum berewicis his, *Stube*, *Middeltone*, *Dentune*, *Cliftun*, *Bikertun*, "*Fernelai*, *Timbe*, *Estone*, *Povelie*, *Gigele*, *Henokesworde* alia *Henokesworde*, *Beldone*, *Mar-* "*fintone*, *Burghel.i*, *Illeclive*. Inter omnes sunt ad geldum lx. carucate et vi. bovate. Archi-"episcopus habet in dominio. In *Graftone* ad geldum iii. carucate. Hec pertinent ad vi-"ctum canonicorum, set wasta est. In *Olestec* cum berewicis suis sunt ad geldum xiii. caru-"cate, una bovata minus. *Willielmus de Verli* habet de archiepiscopo.

"In *Ripum* leuga sancti *Wilfridi* possunt esse x. carucate, hoc manerium tenet archiepisco-"pus. De hac terra habent canonici xiiii. bovatas, totum circa ecclesiam i. leuga. Adja-"cent huic manerio he berewite. *Torp*, *Estvinc*, *Westvic*, *Munecheton*, *Niz*, *Kilingala*, *Toren-* "*tune*, *Sallaia*, *Evestone*, *Wisleshale*, *Kenaresforde*, *Grentelaia*, *Erleshols*, *Merchintone*, simul "ad geldum sunt xliii carucate. Omnis hec terra wasta est preter quod in *Merchintone* "est in dominio i. carucata et ii. villani, et iii. bordarii cum i. carucata et ii. villanis, et iii. "bordariis cum i. carucata, et i. socha cum i. carucata. In *Monechetun* i. tainus habet iiii. ca-"rucatas. In *Erleshoit* ii. carucatas. In *Aldefelt* ad geldum ii. bovate. In *Ripum* jacet et "wasta est. Ad *Ripum* pertinet soca harum terrarum *Estanlai* et *Sudton*, alia *Estollaia*.

"In *Ordstanlia*, *Scleneforde*, *Sutbeunic*, inter omnes ad geldum xxi. carucate et dimidia. "In *Nonnewich* ad geldum, in land. iiii. carucate et dimidia, et dimidia carucata in soca; *Ri-* "*pum* *Rainaldus* tenet. In *Hawinc* ad geldum iii. carucate. In *Gherindale* ad geldum xi. "carucate. Et in *Sceldone* berewita ad geldum viii. carucate. In *Hegram* ii. carucate. In "*Holtone* ii. bovate. In *Hasbundebi* ii. carucate. In *Merchintone* et *Stanlai* i. carucata. Hec "terra sancti *Petri* est libera a geldo regis, wasta est.

"In *Beureli* fuit semper carucata sancti *Johannis* libera à geldo regis. Huic manerio adja-"cent he berewice, *Schitebi*, *Burtone*. In his sunt ad geldum xxxi. carucate.

"In *Deltone* ad geldum xii. carucate, sanctus *Johannes* habet. In *Alotemanebi* habent cle-"rici de *Beureli* i. bovatam. In *Rigbi* ad geldum vi. carucate. In *Locheton* ii. carucate "et dimidia ad geldum. In *Ettone* ad geldum viii. carucate. Hoc fuit et est manerium "sancti *Johannis*. In *Rageneltorp* ad geldum iii. carucate, sanctus *Johannes* habet. In *Bur-* "*tone* xii. carucate et vi. bovate. In *Molescroft* iii. carucate ad geldum. Medietas est ar-"chiepiscopi et alia sancti *Johannis*. In *Calgetorp* habet sanctus *Johannes* ii. bovatas ad gel-"dum. In *Climbicote* ad geldum ii. carucate et dimidia, sanctus *Johannes* habet, wasta est. "*Chetel* tenet in *Middeltun* ad geldum v. carucatas et vi. bovatas, sanctus *Johannes* habet in "dominio. In *Lacbinfeld* habet sanctus *Johannes* ii. bovatas. In *Chelche* cum berewicis his, "*Ghemelinge*, *Ristone* sunt ad geldum xiii. carucate. In *Gartone* ad geldum ix. carucate, "sanctus *Johannes* habet. In *Langetorp* cum berewicis *Roveston*, *Ascheltorp* sunt ad geldum "xii. carucate et dimidia, wasta est.

"In *Benedlage* ad geldum ii. carucate, wasta est. Berewite in *Beureli* et *Holdornesse* per-"tinentes ad archiepiscopum.

"In *Wagene* ii. carucate et ii. bovate ad geldum. In *Wale* ii. carucate ad geldum. In "*Tichetun* xii. bovate ad geldum. In *Asch.* ii. carucate ad geldum. Hoc non est in *Holdernesse*.

"In *Estroch* i. carucata ad geldum. He berewite sunt sancti *Johannis*, et sunt in *Holder-* "*nesse*, *Uth* hundret.

"In *Welwic* iiii. carucate ad geldum, et in *Wdeton* ii. carucate, et v. bovate ad geldum. "In *Grimestone* ii. carucate ad geldum, wasta est. In *Monewic* ii. carucate ad geldum. In "*Oiringebam* vi. carucate et dimidia, *Mith-hundret*.

"*Billetone* iii. carucate ad geldum. In *Santriburtone* v. carucate ad geldum.

"In *Neutone* iii. carucate ad geldum. In *Flintone* vi. bovate ad geldum. In *Danetorp* i. "carucata ad geldum. In *Witfornewinc* i. carucata ad geldum. In *Rutha* xv. bovate ad gel-"dum. In eadem villa aufert drogo sancto *Johanni* ii. carucatas, que et wasta est. In *Sud-* "*tone* ix. bovate ad geldum. In *Sotecote* i. carucata ad geldum. In *Dritpol* iii. bovate, et "soca super v. bovatis, hec wasta est.

NORD HUNDRET.

"In *Coledun* ix. carucate ad geldum. In *Rigon* dimidia carucata ad geldum, wasta est. "In *Siglestorne* viii. carucate ad geldum. In *Catingewic* i. carucata ad geldum. In *Brantis-* "*burtone* l. carucate ad geldum. In *Levene* vi. carucate ad geldum."

P. 552. "After the houses, *&c.* in the jurisdiction of the dean and chapter,"

The dean and chapter's court and prison is kept on the north-side, and contiguous to the great gate of the close, opposite to *Lop-lane*. Here all criminal and judicial causes are tryed by the dean and the justices of peace for the liberty of St. *Peter*. A table of fees relating to this court, is fallen into my hands, made in the time of *William Battbersby*, clerk of the court, admitted so by the king's letters patents, *Nov.* 21, 1677. and may not be improper here to insert.

Fees to the ſteward and clerk in St. Peter's *court.*

	l.	*s.*	*d.*
EVery plaint and action entering, and writ thereon, or without writ	00	00	10
For every diſtreſs and every caption	00	00	08
For writ attorn' in actions of caſe	00	00	04
For writ attorn' in debt	00	00	02
For copy of every declaration	00	01	00
If contract, for every contract after the firſt	00	00	04
If ſheets, for every ſheet	00	00	04
For every order in ejectment	00	01	00
Fer every rule to declare or plead	00	00	04
For entering an order	00	00	04
For copy thereof	00	00	04
For every default by non-ſummons, cognizance, or the like	00	00	04
For copy of every ſpecial pleading	00	01	00
For every general iſſue	00	00	04
For every judgment	00	02	08
For every proceſs after judgment, as *caſa*, *fifa*, *ſcifa*,	00	00	08
For allowing a plea in arreſt of judgment	00	01	00
For copy thereof	00	01	00
For drawing up ſpecial verdict and copy	00	00	08
For copy of every record	00	06	08
For copy of every plaint	00	00	04
For every ſearch	00	00	04
For every eſſoign upon a plaint	00	00	02
For every eſſoign at the court-leet	00	00	04
For every certificate out of the charter	00	02	06
For allowing a writ of error	00	12	05
For *certiorari* or *habeas corpus cum cauſa*	00	04	10
For every *veſa*, *et habito jur.*	00	01	04
For every *al. habito jur.*	00	00	08
For every warrant for witneſſes	00	00	08
For *ſuperſedeas* to an execution	00	02	04
For *ſuperſedeas* to an ordinary proceſs	00	00	04
For every protection or privilege	00	00	08
For every *liberate*	00	00	04
For every *replevin*	00	03	04
For dividing every action	00	00	08
For every nonſuit	00	00	04
For renewing any judicial proceſs	00	00	08
For copy of any judical proceſs	00	00	08
For every *venditioni exponas.*	00	00	08
For every ſpecial imparlance	00	02	00

Bailiff's fees in St. Peter's.

Chief bailiff. For every defendant in ſummons	00	00	08
For every arreſt	00	01	08
For every gaol fee	00	07	00
For every tryal upon the firſt appointment	00	05	00
If a cauſe be appointed though not tryed	00	04	00
For every *al. habito jur.*	00	02	00

Deputies fees in St. Peter's.

Of the plaintiff in ſummons or arreſt, every name	00	00	04
Out of 2 *s.* 4 *d.* taken for arreſt, the chief bailiff allows his deputy	00	00	08
For warning every jury	00	01	00
For keeping a jury	00	00	04
Fee from the plaintiff upon a judicial proceſs	00	01	00

The like in St. Mary's, *except*

For the return of *venire facias* and *habito*	00	04	00
For every *al. habito jur.*	00	02	00

To the deputy bailiff.

Of the plaintiff every name in ſummons	00	00	08
Warning every jury	00	00	04

P. 555.

P. 555. Sect. penult. "prohibited the bearing the ensigns of authority in the church."

The king's letter that the lord-mayor shall not bear his ensigns in the church, and for receiving the communion, &c. (z)

CHARLES, R.

"Right trustie and well-beloved and trustie and well-beloved, we greet you well.
"Whereas for the preservation of the solemnity of divine service in some of our cathedral
"churches, and for the good of the inhabitants of those cities, we have required the mayor,
"aldermen, and their companies, to frequent those holy places upon *Sundays* and holidays
"with all due reverence; and that they be there at the beginning of divine service, and at
"their going out and coming in, and whilst they are there, carry themselves so as becom-
"eth them in obedience to the canons of the church and the customs of those cathedrals; re-
"quiring also the mayors of those cities, that they shall not use the ensigns of their autho-
"rity within our said cathedral churches; that hereafter the distinct liberties and privileges
"granted by our royal progenitors to those several bodies be inviolably kept. We there-
"fore casting the same gracious eye upon our cathedral and metropolitical church of St. *Pe-*
"*ter* in our citie of *York*, to have it regulated in like manner, do hereby require you accor-
"ding to your several duties, to take care for the due performance of all the said orders in
"that church. And further, that as well you the lord-mayor, and also the recorder and al-
"dermen, at some solemn times every year, shall receive the holy communion in the said
"cathedral church of *York*, to manifest your conformitie to the orders established in the said
"church.

"Given under our signet at our court at *Greenwich* the second day of *July*, in the thir-
"teenth year of our reign, 1637.

"*To our right trustie and well-beloved the lord-mayor*
"*of our citie of* York, *and to our trustie and well-*
"*beloved the recorder and aldermen of the said citie.*"

Ibid. Sect. ult. "But that holy church, *&c.*"

The mandate, in its original *Latin*, runs in these words:

De querela civium Ebor. *versus decanum et capitulum* Ebor. *(a)*

"REX decano et capit. S. *Petri Ebor.* salutem. Ex querelis majoris et civium nost.
"*Ebor.* frequenter intelleximus, quod usurpastis vobis placita de laicis feodis et de
"catallis et debitis que non sunt de testamento vel matrimonio, et alia jura et libertates in
"predicta civitate ad majorem et ballivos nostros ejusdem civitatis spectantes, nec permiseri-
"tis custodes mensurarum nost. in eadem civitate probare mensuras in terris quas dicitis esse
"vestras nec eas signo nostro signare, sed signo adulterino eas facitis signari; etiam non per-
"mittitis eosdem cives capere namia hominum vest. pro debitis suis secundum tenorem carte
"nostre quam inde habent, in qua nec homines vest. nec alii excipiuntur. Etiam appropria-
"stis vobis homines nost. et omnia placita eorum tenetis in curia vestra vi excommunicationis
"ratione terrarum in quibus manent, nec permittitis ballivos nost. predict. civitatis ingredi ter-
"ras quas dicitis esse vestras, licet non sint, ad debita nost. levanda nec ad latrones seu male-
"factores capiend. et arrestandos. Set si terras vest. ad hoc sine licentia vestra ingrediantur et
"gravaminibus predictis pro jure nost. salvand. se apposuerint, statim in eos, assensu nostro
"irrequisito de emendis faciendis, sententiam excommunicationis promulgari facitis, nec eam
"pro aliquo mandato nost. relaxare curatis, nisi prestito sacramento de reparando juri ecclesia-
"stico. Cum igitur premissa in jurium nost. prejudicium non modicum et dignitatis regis
"maximam cedat lesionem, et per literas nost. frequenter requisiti fueritis quod ab hujusmodi
"exactionibus et usurpationibus desistatis, vos iterato monendos duximus exhortandos, man-
"dantes quatenus majorem et ballivos et cives predict. immo nos juribus et libertatibus prius
"usitatis in civitate predict. gaudere pacifice permittentes, de cetero nihil attemptetis quod in
"jurium nost. cedat prejudicium, sententiam excommunicationis si quam in ballivos et cives
"predict. occasione predict. promulgari redditis sine dilatatione revocantes, securi indubitanter
"quod nisi feceritis diutius non sustinere non poterimus, sicut nec debemus, quin de tantis exces-
"sibus et injuriis nobis illatis que non solum in exheredationem nost. set etiam in dedecus nost.
"et opprobrium redundant, gravissimam vindictum qualem debemus capiemus. Injunximus
"etiam majori et ballivis predict. jura et libertates nost. illesas pro posse suo conservent et firmi-
"ter ex parte nost. inhiberi facitis ne aliqui de civitate predict. coram vobis compareant in cu-
"ria vestra ad respondend. de aliquibus pertinentibus ad coronam et dignitatem nostram.

"Teste rege apud *Westm.* xix. die *Feb.*

"Eodem modo mandatum est abbati beate *Marie Ebor.* et priori S. *Trinitatis Ebor.* et ma-
"gistro hospital. S. *Leonardi Ebor.* eo excepto quod literis istis nihil fit mentio de sententia
"excommunicationis lata in majorem cives et ballivos ejusdem civitatis, nec quod predict.
"abbas prior et magister alias requisiti fuerint per literas regis quod ab hujusmodi exactio-
"nibus desistant.

"Teste ut supra.

(z) Regist. of leases begin. 1624. *f.* 135, 6.

(a) *Claus.* 39 Hen. III. *m.* 17. *dorso.* 1255

P. 572. *Sect.* 7. "*Walter Gray*, archbishop of *York*, with the consent of the dean and "chapter first ordained the college of vicars choral, *&c.*"

The original instrument, still preserved amongst the archives of this body, I have procured a copy of; which I think worthy a place, for the sake of antiquity, in these *addenda*. *Walter Gray*'s seal appendant is also drawn, with the seal then used by the chapter of *York*, and the reader may find them in the plate of seals at the end of this *appendix*.

"Omnibus ad quos presens scriptum pervenerit *W.* miseratione divina *Eborum* archiepis-"copus *Anglie* primas, decanus et capitulum *Eborum* salutem in domino sempiternam. Nove-"ritis nos concessisse et ad petitionem omnium vicariorum nostrorum in ecclesia nostra de-"gentium ordinasse quod *Alanus Salvator* vice succentoris in dicta ecclesia nostra gerens et "pro tempore in illo officio succedentes custodiam et liberam habeant administrationem de om-"nibus terris possessionibus tenementis redditibus et bonis immobilibus ipsis vicariis concessis "concedendis et quomodolibet deputatis vel etiam deputandis; ita quod ipse *Alanus* et "successores sui rite constituti agant defendant et respondeant in quibuscunque curiis pro ter-"ris possessionibus tenementis redditibus et bonis predictis sicut custos eorum perpetuus. Et "ut premissa perpetue firmitatis robur optineant sigilla nostra apposuimus huic scripto."

P. 573. *Sect. ult. adue.* In the earl of *Oxford*'s library is a MS. *folio*, on vellom, 93. *D.* 4. *p.* 46. in which are contained copies of the most ancient charters, *&c.* belonging to the church of *York*. As, also, some pieces of history collected from old authors, *&c.* There is, besides, a brief historical account of this church, in monkish *Latin* verse, from *Geoffry Monmouth*'s and other histories to archbishop *Thomas* the first. The heads of all these as they stand in the manuscript are as follows. *N. B.* There is a rude representation of the city inclosed, with the river running through it, the bridge, some churches, bishops, *&c.* drawn opposite to the first page and coloured; but the draught is so miserably performed as to be worth no further notice.

In the *Cotton* library, are also many things worthy the notice of an historian, who shall hereafter attempt a more particular history of this church than I am able to give. An account of the manuscripts may be seen in the catalogue of the manuscripts in *England* (*b*). And, as many of them as are saved from the fire, are given in a book lately published by Mr. *Casley*, the deputy librarian, in *quarto*.

The heads in my lord *Oxford*'s manuscript are these:

De origine et prima fundatione ecc. cath. Ebor. Gul. Mon.
Ven. Bed. *de gest.* Angl. *et* H. Hunt.
W. Malmsf. *de regibus.*
Alfrid. Beverlac. *thesaur.*
Bulla beati Gregorii *pap.*
Bulla Honor. *pap.*
Bulla Calixt. *pap. continens sent. pro libert. ecc.* Ebor.
Privilegium deferendi crucem et regem coronandi.
Super eodem Honor. *papa.*

In VERSIBUS.

Prologus de or. et statu Ebor. *eccl.*
Per quem et quando civitas Ebor. *cond. est.*
De erectione templi Metr. *et creatione arch. flam.*
De prim. fund. eccl. Ebor. *et consecrat. arch.*
Nota quod eccl. Ebor. *prim. fund. fuit de beat. virg.* Maria.
De causa et temp. prim. advent. Angl. *in* Brit.
De secunda reparatione eccl. per regem Aurel. *et* S. Sampson *arch.*
De tertia reparatione per regem. Arthurum *et* Pyram. *arch.*
Causa amissionis regni Brit. *et de* Tadiaco *arch.*
De occasione commissionis Anglor. *per beat.* Gregor.
De occasione Northanhumb. *&c. per* Paulin. *et* Edwin. *regem.*
De defensione sedis et eccl. per mag. Wilfrid. *arch.*
De recuperatione Pallii *per* Egbert. *archiep.*
De libertat. et possess. dat. per regem Athelst. *et alios.*
De Will. *bast. duce* Norman.
De reformatione ecclesiae dig. et prebend. per Thom. *arch.*
De sentent. libert ecclesiae obtent. per S. Thurst. *arch.*
De rege W. *conquest.*
De suffragan. in provincia eccl. Ebor.
De advent. Scotor. *in* Brit.
Nomina quorund. suffragan. professor.
Conclusio invectiva.

Bulla Innocent. *pap. epis.* Scotiae *in genere directa.*
Bull. pap. Adrian. *direct. omn. epis.* Scotiae *in specie et nominatim.*
Episcop. Scotiae *quod. obediant metrop. suae* Ebor. *arch.*
Regi Scotiae *quod ipse et epis. pareant* Eborac. *suo archiepiscopo.*

(*b*) *Catalogi Libror. MSS. in* Anglia, *&c.* 2 *vol. fol.* Oxon. 1697

Recognitio

Recognitio reg. Scot. *super subject. epis.* Scotiae Ebor. *eccl. debita.*
Recog. clavi regis Mannie *et insularum.*
Supplicatio regis Orcadum *decano et cap.* Ebor.
Recog. comitis Orchad.
Carta regis Athelstani.
Carta regis Edwii.
Carta Edgari *regis.*
Carta Knuti *regis.*
Carta S. Ed. *conf. regis.*

In Mr. *Torre*'s most painful collections relating to this church, at the beginning of one of the manuscript volumes is placed an exact list or catalogue of all the registers, *&c.* belonging to it, from whence he has extracted his memoirs, and to which his notes of books and pages refer. The following is an abstract, from the same records, made by Dr. *Comber*, then precentor of this church, but afterwards dean of *Durham*. A copy of this, taken from the original by himself, was communicated to me by my very ingenious friend, and brother antiquary, Mr. *Samuel Gale*; amongst many more papers of great notice already made use of in this work. This also, may be of service to any future historian who shall attempt to write on the affairs of the church or diocese of *York*.

Collections out of the registers belonging to the archbishops of York *in the office of the register of the archbishop* anno 1699. Ex chartis *T. Comber precentor.*

Registr. WALT. GREY, 1224.

The archbishop makes statutes for residence at *Southwell.*
Indulgences towards the building a new bridge at *York.* ——— *Ouse-bridge.*
Fulco Basset provost of *Beverley*, 1225.
Indulgences for building the cathedral.
A contest about the patronage of *Thornton*, *p.* 42.
Durham see void, the archbishop presents to *Elleden.*
Robert Ross grants *Ribston* to the templars.
Jo. Romanus can. Ebor. founds the subdeanery, and endows it with *Preston* 1228. *p.* 126.
Archd. of *Richmond* patron of St. *Sampson*'s in *York*, 46.
Napleton and other churches annex'd to the dignitarians, 220. *Rotul. minor.* 40 ———
William de Ebor. provost of *Beverley*, 1241.

Registr. W. DE GIFFARD.

A cane measure is eleven foot long.
Michelburgh annexed to the archdeacon of *Ebor.*

Several pensions secured out of this diocese to cardinals and others at Rome. — *Out of several Registers.*

1272. The archbishop had then fifty two knights fees and two parts of one, besides his oxgangs and carucates in *Kesteven*, *Westrid* and *Northumberland*, *p.* 7, 8.
The archbishop payeth one thousand marks *annuatim* towards the debts of his church.
1275. Articles of the archbishop's visitation of his prov. dioces.

Registr. DE WICKWAINE.

1279. The Bishop of *Durham* swears obedience to the archbishop, the prior and cov. protest against it.
A strife betwixt the archbishops about carrying up the cross in the diocese of *Canterbury*, 1280. *& etiam fol.* 38.
Archbishop excommunicates the prior of *Durham*, complains of the disobedience of the bishop of *Durham.*
The archbishop visits the chapter, but declares he will not prejudice their liberties, which he had engaged to defend, *fol.* 33.
1281. An order made formerly by *Thurstan* archbishop, that the profits of a prebend should for one year go to pay the debts of the deceased prebendary.
An enquiry after papers to prove the archbishop's jurisdiction over *Durham.*
The church ornaments let out to women in child-bed.
Durham void, the archbishop confirms *A. B.* prioress of *Halyston.*
1283. The archbishop gives five hundred and two oxen, *&c.* to the successor, and of the king *sede vacante.*
Whenby appropriated to the nuns of *Moseby.*
Articles of complaint by the clergy exhibited in parliament, and the king's answer, *fol.* 54.
A bayliff by the king's command beheadeth several clerks taken in a robbery, the archbishop excommunicates the bayliff.

The minister of *Simpringham* swears obedience to the archbishop for his churches. *See* 1294.

A Recital of appropriations —— half of *Michelsburg* to the archd. of *York*, *Wivertborp* to the com. *temp. W. Grey*.

Registr. Jo. Romani.

1286. A composition betwixt the archbishop and prior of *Durham sede vacante*, about the jurisdiction.

Henry bishop of *Whitbern* swears obedience.

William Rotherfield dean of *York*.

Several Provisors.

The vicar of *Th.* instituted in the vacancy; instituted *de novo*.

Welton near *Otly*, granted to *York*, *in augmentum luminationum*, a record.

Dalston settled — a third part of it for twelve poor scholars.

The archbishop expostulates with the bishop of *Durham* for several injuries, and designs to excommunicate him. *V. A. Beck*.

1289. The archbishop inhibits P. *de Th.* to sue in his diocese for goods recovered on an appeal to *Canterbury*.

The *Jews* ordered by the king to depart the realm.

The sacristy of the chapel of our lady and the angel to be given to one that would reside.

The archbishop degrades certain clerks by pulling off their surplices — *exauctorizamus te ab ordine psalmistatus*, *fol.* 80.

1293. A new taxation of benefices for the king's going to the holy war.

J. Roman, treasurer of *York*, the archbishop was his executor.

The archbishop and dean in person, the chapter by one proxy, the clergy by two, summoned to *Westminster*. See such *summons*.

The king of *Scots* desires the archbishop not to consecrate the bishop of *Whitbern* or *Kirkenbright*.

Q. *Elenor* died in *Clifton* parish, and a chantry there instituted for her soul.

The preb. of *Bilton* founded, but not to partake of the *Communia*, till he or his successors had given twenty pounds *per annum* to the *Commune*, 1294. *See* 1295.

Registr. Henrici de Newerck.

1297. A convoc. for a subsidy for a confirmation of *Magna Charta* and *de Foresta*, granted in the prov. of *Canterbury*, denied in the prov. of *York*.

The chapter elect *William de Hambleton* dean, upon the archbishop's promotion, protesting that they did not intend to hinder the pope's provisor of *Fr.* card. of *C.*

William Hambleton, dean, institutes a priest to the chapel of St. *Mary's*, in the church-yard of St. *Columbus* at *Topcliff*. The chapel was founded by *Roger* dean of *York*, 1222.

Registrum de Greenfeld *et* Melton.

William de Gr. Abp. appropriates *Brodsworth* to the *Commune*.

Robert the dean, &c.

Robert de Pykering, dean, founded the hospital of St. *Mary's* in *Bootham*.

1337. *Sim. de Beck*, precentor, and *A. de K.* settle a composition about *Useburn*.

The preb. of *H.* let his house in *Uggleforth*.

Registr. de la Zouch *et* Thoresby.

1342. The profits of the deanry vacant, *viz.* 235*l.* 13*s.* 4*d.* paid to the chapter.

1343. The archbishop visits according to the composition made with archbishop *Melton*. See *Thoresby*, 1356, 1362, 1375, 1409, 1534.

All the prebends of *York* then declared sacerdotal.

The precentor shall examine choiristers, and chuse the choiristers, &c.

The archbishop gives to the nine canon residentiaries to each of them two oaks in his wood of *Langwath*, together with the faggots of the said oaks felled.

— *Libera novem residentiariis canonicis in ecclesia nostra* Ebor. *cuilibet eorum duas quercus in bosco nostro de* Langwath, *una cum fagottis earundem quercuum prostrat. quas pro liberata sua hac via de nostra gratia dedimus speciali* 15 Junii 1343. Dr. *Hutton*'s collect.

1346. A great dearth.

The *Inspeximus* entred at large in the first book, *p.* 31.

Several chantries, by whom founded.

Licence granted to the archbishop to found a chapel on the south-side of the cathedral.

Archbishop *Zouch* died *July* 19.

The treasurer and others sent to beg leave of the king to chuse, *anno* 1373.

The treasurer and *H. de Ingleby (decanus in remotis)* diocesan proxies for parliament.

Hugo Peregrine, vic. gen. to *Taillerand* the dean — *quere*.

The sub-dean and succentor presented for non-residence, 1356, 1362.

The

The vicars presented for coming in after *Gloria Patri*.
Proxies for parl. 1357, 1360, 1369, 1370, 1375, 6, 7, 8.
A convocation for the repair of the fabrick.
A twentieth part of all prebends taxed to the repair of the fabrick.
The new choir begun, the archbishop gave his old palace at *Sherburn* towards it.
1364. The chapter's table augmented.
The chapter visits the priests and vicars.
Four hundred and sixty pounds for the deanry and preb. of *Strensal* paid to the pope's recetors.
1368. Each residentiary to have off *Langwith* two oaks, five hundred faggots *per annum*.
A list of all the benefices belonging to the church of *York* sent to the king.
A proxy for convocation.
1373. *Thoresby* deceased, leave begged of the king to chuse, in the king's breve none named, *Decemb.* 12. *Nevil* chosen and sent to the king.
Grimoald de Grisant, card. dean.
(*Nevil*, *Bowet*, *Kemp*, *Rotheram*.)
1380. The houses near the archbishop's palace were given by *Roger Pepyn*.
Misterton annexed to the fabrick.
1381. The deanry under sequestration to the king for five years.
Tho. de Eaton card. S. *Cecil* admitted D. of *York*, 1381.
The pope demands the profits of the deanry.
1385. Dr. *Stafford* dean.

Archbishop ARUNDEL'*s Regist. v. infra.*

The precentor, treasurer and three residentiaries present at archbishop *Bowet*'s visitation.
The chapter visit the church, all dignities and prebends called, absents noted.
The sub-dean, penitentiary of the church and city, presented for non-residency.
1410. The library.
1416. The deanry void *Jo. Prophet* deceased. *Tho. Bolton* succeeded 1416.
1421. The archbishop being sick chuses coadjutors.
W. Grey dean.
The vacant livings to be disposed of by the dean and chapter in their turns. See the book of 1427, *postea*.
The cross delivered to the new archbishop *Kemp*.
1437. *Felter* the dean admonisheth the vicars, and they swear obedience to him.
St. *William*'s cross demanded of archbishop *Kemp*, now removed to *Cant.*
1454. The chapter swear canonical obedience to the dean after his confirmation.
Procurators to a convocation summoned by archbishop *Nevil*. See 1486.
1474. A vicar suspended three weeks for absence without leave.
Rich. Andrews dean, resigns, *Rob. Booth* chosen.
1479. The precedence of the residentiaries stated by an act of chapter.
1488. The vicars not under the archbishop, but under the chapter.
Ursick dean 1488.
1493. *William Beverley* died, his residence allow'd, though he had kept in two days of the sweating-sicknefs.
Dean *Sheffield* orders the clerks of the vestry and the sacrists, to divide herse-cloths amongst them.
James Harrington, dean, resigns the subdeanry to the chapter, they name *Knols* subdean.
Dignitaries to keep residence, not in the stalls of their prebend, but in the stalls of their dignitaries.
The dean sick in his major residence, dispensed with from coming to church.
1511. Leave given to Dr. *Langton*, though in residence, to travel three years.

Out of the registers.

1512. Convocation and proxies.
Dean *Harrington* deceased, *Machel* made *custos decanatus*.
1514. The deanry void the precentor alone orders a new election.
A commission from the residentiary to visit the *Bedhern*.
Card. *Bambridge* names *B. Higden* dean, the chapter refuse him because not of their body and chapter; so made preb. of *Ulfskelf*, then admitted.
Dean *Higden* dispensed with for not sitting in his preb. stall in his residence.
The archbishoprick void, the king presents prebends.
Edward Lee archbishop, the chapter protests against his undue and new way of giving prebends.
Dr. *Colet*, Dr. *Stubs*, &c. proxies of convocation.
1538. The king's visitation on the chapter by *Tho. Leigh*.

King

King *Henry* the eighth's letter to allow Dr. *Layton* the profits of residence before he came down.

The chapter (after) demurs upon the doctor's residence. — Dr. *Layton* vacates the old oaths, takes new ones.

The new statutes of *Henry* VIII. published.

Dr. *Layton* warns a convocation at *Martms*.

Chanteries in the minster, thirty seven in number.

Registrum imperfectum. Act-Book, Nov. 11, 1565, *as afore.*

1544. The form of electing a new dean.

Archbishop *Holgate* visits by authority of the king's great seal.

The archbishop declares a visitation according to the composition.

1547. A commission from king *Edward* VI. to confirm the dean and chapter's jurisdiction.

The king's commissioners to visit the church of *York*.

Edward VI's injunctions to the dean and chapter.

Divers prebends excluded, others presented by queen *Mary, jure coronae.*

Registrum imperfectum, temp. N. Heath, *ab anno* 1544. *ad* 1565.

V. p. 126. *(The Act-Book beginning* 1565.)

1567. The form of chusing the subchantor.

1568. Archbishop *Young* dies, the jurisdiction assumed.

1571. Archbishop *Grindall*'s inhibition in order to visit.

1572. The table for preachers courses.

The precentor's grant of the next turn of *Odington* to *M.* confirmed by the chapter.

1580. The prebends enjoined to keep all in good repair.

Archbishop *Sands* visiteth.

1587. The dean and chapter visit their jurisdiction.

1588. *York* and *Durham* both void, the dean and chapter grant a commission to *T. M.* to exercise jurisdiction there.

1589. Archbishop *Piers*.

1591. A pew ordered for the wives of the lord-mayor.

1595. Archbishop *Hutton*'s visitation.

1604. The grand chapter *(Nov.* 11.) held at *Eskrig*, because of the plague in *York*. Archbishop *Hutton* deceaseth.

A decree to keep a resid. place for *And. Byng* imployed then in translating the bible.

Archbishop *Matthews* visits the dean and chapter.

1612. A long contest about Dr. *Bank*'s keeping resid. composed *Oct.* 3, 1614.

1617. A seat in the cathedral decreed for the archbishop.

1622. The archdeacons seated.

The dean and chapter visit their jurisdiction.

Archbishop *Matthews* deceased.

Harsenet archbishop.

Neal archbishop.

The archdeacon of *York* removeth to the seat of the archdeacon of the *East-riding* when the mayor is at church, but the mayor first renounceth all claim of right to the seat, *Jan.* 25, 1633.

Ex libro grandi qui inscribitur et notatur WAGGEN et SUTTON ab anno CIↃCCCCXXIX.

Totus fere completur tractatione unius causae de jure sepulturae Waghen *et* Sutton. Waghen *annexa et incorporata cancellariae eccl.* Ebor. *Ordinatio ejusdem capellae de* Waghen.

Archiep. ARUNDEL, registr. ab anno 1388.

1394. *Convocatio, variae dilationes, procuratoria, certificatorium*; the same are in the register of *Durham*.

Ex libro actorum incipiente ab anno 1427, et definente ad an. 1504.

P. 1. *Inthronizatio archiepiscopi* Joannis.

2. *M.* Wil. Petison *residentiarius capitulum faciens.*

6. *Protestatio cum juramento de regressu ad praeb. depositam, si praebenda nunc acceptanda per pont.* Rom *fuerit jam alteri collata.*

7. *Capitul. levet subsidium omnibus dignitates beneficia parsonatus, vel aliqua ecclesiastica obtinentibus, impositum in plena convocat. confr. et concanonicorum, ad novam fabricam et tabulam principalem summi altaris faciendam.*

8. Johannes Haxy *cancellarius citat, capitulo jubente,* Joannem Cicestrensem *episcopum nuper cancell.* Ebor. *pro dilapidationibus. Haec citatio dirigitur ad archiep.* Cant. *rogando eum, &c.*

9. Tho-

9. Thomas Haxy *nuper thesaurarius cantariam fundarat.*
10. *Ecclesia S.* Trinit. *in curia regis, ibidem altare* P. *et* Pauli *fundatum per* Ric. Bar.
Capitulum dispensat cum canonico residen. Londinum *profecturo pro necessit. ecclesiae, ubi quilibet canonicus residentiarius tenetur per vigint. quat.* Sept. *annuatim residere in ecclesia ut jura et emol. residentia integre percipiat exceptis archidiaconis.*
Capitulum ei 30. *dies concedit ita ut camerarius ei solvat integram istius termini sc. Pentecostes proximae, de proventibus ecclesiae (quotidianis distributionibus exceptis) proportionem pro istis diebus, ac si residisset per eosdem in dies* 30.
Clerici de vestibulo et sacristae habeantur tam in eccles. quam in domibus canonicorum ut valetti et in statu valettorum reputentur cui libris computationum et solution. dicuntur saxtons.
19. J. Berningham *eligitur in thesaurarium.*
33. *Postea incipit residentiam non nominat. suam prebendam (sed se pacifice praebendatum dicit) et petit stallum ad residentiam assignari, protestaturque se nec suo ne successorum juri prejudicaturum: assignatur stallum de* Wilton *(v. ord.* Walt. Grey *in fine libri statutorum Thes.*Berningham) *nullam habuit, prebendam praeter* Wilton *annexum thesaurariae, cum autem jam nemo nisi canonicus praebendatus admitteretur ad res. vide quae nunc difficultates sequuntur ob defectum stalli praebendalis, nam* Wilton *fuit incorporata thesaurariae.*
37. Gysclay, Ward *patronus* Sherburn *rector.*
38. *Decanus postulat a vicariis &c. obedient. canonicalem sibi praestari, prout decanis praedecessorib. suis praestari consuevit.*
Capitulum respondet se velle praestari ipsi obedient. et capitulo conjunctim prout statuta et consuetudines ecclesiae exigunt, &c.
N. hic capitulum vult sibi ipsi jurare quod est atopon, alibi in alio libro juratur decano in primo ingressus et capitulo seorsim.
38. *Officium camerarii conceditur* R. *St. vicario chorali, sub juramento.*
34. W. Felter *admittitur dec. sine praebenda exigit canonicalem obedientiam ab omnibus prout praestari consuevit praedecessoribus suis; admittitur ad praeb. de* Apestorp *eodem tempore protestatur de majori residentia anno* 1441. *Protestatur ut canonicus non ut decanus.*
56. Berningham *solus capitulum facit.*
64. *Capitulum injungit vicariis chori ne verba minacia contra ministros ecclesiae mittant sub poena amissionis habitas.*
72. *Residentiam intendo incipere hoc die et ipsam realiter incipio, sic saepe.*
W. Felter *dec. resignat.* Apesthorp *et admittitur ad* Driffeild, *sic* W. *dec. & capitul. honoratis. viro* W. Felter *de cujus mentis plenam fiduciam obtinemus &c. admittimus et pro recipientes* —— *ita.*
82. Rich. Andrews *praeb. de* N. Newbald *fit decanus; obedientiam postulat, conceditur dec. et capitulo conjunctim facienda. Protestat. ut canonicus.*
90. *Senior canonicus residentiarius est praesidens capituli* 95. *in actib. capituli.*
125. *Procuratorium pro dec. et capitulo ad comparend. in convocatione archi.*
Certificatorium super summonitione facta.
137. *Canonicus res. ad mensam sedens post manus lotas tenebatur convivantibus cerevisiam per vicarium suum benedictam semel bibere.*
140. *Vicarius suspenditur ab habitu eo quod sine licentia petita et obtenta se per* 3. *septim. absentaverat a choro in grave periculum animae.*
159. R. Andrew *resignat. decanatum archiepiscopus dat auctoritatem* D. Polman *admittendi resignationem extra capitulum;* Polman *pronunciat. resign. et capitulo notificat. statuit capitulum quod decanus futurus solvet capitulo pro vacatione decanatus ex provent. dec. marcas* l. Robert. Bowthe *pr. de* Wetwang *succedit obedientia ei praestatur per capitulum.*
160. *Inthroniz.* D. Laur. *archiepiscopi.*
Decanus ore tenus suam potestatem in omnibus in capitulo agendis committit tribus residentiariis.
R. Bowthe *protestatur ut canonicus de* Westwang. R. B. *nominat ad ratione decanatus primo hic nominat. (ut alibi.)*
Succentoris collatio, rat. vac. sedis archiepiscopalis ad capitulum spectantis.
Tunstal *eidem suc. annectitur ab. dim.*
170. *Publicatio Bullarum de transl.* T. Rother. *episcopi* Linc. *ad archiepiscopatum* Ebor. *in praesentia alderm. civit.* Ebor. *et aliorum.*
172. *Collatio, &c. per decanum ratione majoris suae residentiae.*
Mentio prima (in hoc libro) decreti T. Rother. *annectentis pr. de* Driffeild *praecentoriae* Ebor. *anno* 1485. *v.* 201. B.
191. *Procuratorium dec. et cap. ad comparendum in convocatione archiepiscopi.*
198. *Approbatio resid.* W. Sheffield *et post exam. vicariorum et ministror. &c.*
Canonici res. prae aliis dignitates habentibus decano excepto celebrabunt.
204. *Vicarii — et vicarii dominorum residentiariorum [plane hic distinguuntur quemadmodum distinguuntur in statut.* Sarum] *an hi vicarii chorales, illi dominorum residentiariorum.*
209. William Sheffield *decanus. Obed. conjunctim.*
Urstwic *decanus ulterius citatur per capitulum de dilapidationibus.*

8 R 213. Will.

213. Will. Langton *admittitur in praecentorem; hic nulla mentio* Driffeild *nec decreti ut prius mox, commissio fit vicariis de* Ufburn *et* Driffeild *ad inducendum.* Mart. Collyns *(mortuo* Langton*) admittitur ad praec. et pr.* Driffeild *eidem annexam, non seorsim sed ut prius ibid. p.* 225. *aliter p.* 226.
Feoda in installatione decani vicar. et sacerd. debita vid. xl. *solidi.*
218. Galf. Blyth *deca. non habet nunc praeb.*
227. Galf. Blyth *dicitur praeb. de* Strenfal, *fit episcopus* Litchfeild.
230. *Parsonae et quidam vicarii de habitu.*
231. *Dignitas subdecanatus vacans dimittitur ad firmam [archiepiscopus solebat conferre] et post haac confertur.*
233. *Procuratorium (et publicatio ejusdem) pro convocatione archiepiscopi.*
Liber iste praelectus plurimas habet admissiones et pauca alia.

Many things relating to the estate of the college of the *Bedern* are registered in a thin folio paper book, in the registry of the dean and chapter.
Many things relating to St. *William*'s college are registred, *ibid.*
All the chantries dissolved belonging to St. *Peter* or the dean and chapter, *ibid.*
A book of survey of all the chantries within St. *Peter*'s *York* (whose pensions were paid by the vicars of the *Bedberne*) made unto the late king *Henry* VIII. — A note or catalogue of them out of that book here.

Liber actorum cap. et miscellanea ab 1343. *ad* 1368.

Visitatio per *Zouch* archiepiscopum, capitulum corrigit quaedam.

Art. I. *Decanus tenetur personaliter residere et pascere* 50. *pauperes quotidie; aedificia et maneria sustentare et reparare.*
Subdecanus tenetur personaliter residere, quod non faciet; cancellarius tenetur personaliter residere.
Tot sunt residentiarii in ecclesia quod expedit augmentatio communiarum (x. *sic.*)
Vicarii chori multoties se absentant a choro.
Magist. scholarum grammaticalium debet interesse divinis officiis.
Succentor vicariorum tenetur per juram. interesse choro.

Mensuratio terrae, p. 110.

Quando acra terrae continet x. *particas in longitudine, tunc continebit in latitudine* xv. *particas. Quando* xi. *tunc* xiiii. *et dimidiam et unum pedem. Quand.* xiii. *tunc* xiii. *et* v. *pedes et* i. *pollicem. Quando* xiiii. *tunc* xii. vii. *pedes et* i. *pollicem. Qu.* xv. *tunc* x. *et dim. et duos pedes. Qu.* xvi. *tunc* x. *particas. Qu.* xvii. *tunc* ix. *et* iii. *pedes et pollices et dim. Qu.* xviii. *tunc* viii. *et dim. et* v. *pedes et dim. et* v. *pollices. Qu.* xix. *tunc* viii. *et* vi. *pedes et* iiii. *pollices et dim. Qu.* xx. *tunc* viii. *particas. Qu.* xxi. *tunc* vii. *et dim. et* ii. *pedes et* i. *pollicem. Qu.* xxii. *tunc* vii. *et unum quartum et* iiii. *pollices et dim. Qu.* xxiii. *tunc* vi. *et dim. et* iii. *pedes. et* v. *poll. et dim. Qu.* xxiiii. *tunc* vi. *et dim. et* ii. *pedes et dim. et* iii. *pollices. Qu.* xxv. *tunc* vi. *et* i. *quartam* ii. *pedes et dim. pollic. Qu.* xxvi. *tunc* vi. *et* ii. *pedes et dim. pollicis. Qu.* xxvii. *tunc* v. *et dim. et* iii. *ped. Qu.* xxviii. *tunc* v. *et* vii. *ped. et dim. Qu.* xxviiii. *tunc* v—vi *ped. et dim. Qu.* xxx. *tunc* v. *et* vi. *ped. Qu.* xxxi. *tunc* v — ii. *ped. et dim. Qu.* xxxii. *tunc quinque particas. Qu.* xxxiii. *tunc* iiii. *et dim. et* i. *quartam et* i. *ped. et dim. poll. Qu.* xxxiiii. *tunc* iiii. *et dim. quarti* iiii. *pedes et* iiii. *pollic. Qu.* xxxv. *tunc* iiii. *et dim.* i. *ped.* ii. *poll. et dim. Qu.* xxxvi. *tunc* iiii. *et unam quartam* iii. *pedes* i. *pollicem et dim. Qu.* xxxvii. *tunc t.* iiii. *et dim. quarti,* iii. *ped. et dim. Qu.* xxxviii. *tunc* iiii. *et* iiii. *ped. et dim. Qu.* xxxix. *tnnc* iiii. *et* iiii. *pedes et dim. Qu.* xl. *tunc* iiii. *particas. Qu.* xli. *t.* iii. *et dim. et* i. *quart. et* i. *pedem. Qu.* xlii. *et* iii. *et* i. *quartum et* i. *pedum. Qu.* xliii. *t.* iii. — iii. *ped. et dim. Qu.* xliiii. *tunc* ii. *et dim.* iiii. *pedes. Quando* xlv. *tunc* ii. *particas.*

Taxatio dignitatum ecclesia *Ebor*. ibid. p. 64.

		l.	*s.*	*d.*
Decanus	—— —— —— ——	ccclxxiii	6	5
Praebendarum, &c.				
Vicariorum, &c.				

Ecclesiae et maneria ad communiam spectantia.

Burton *aestimatio praeter vicariam* lx. *marcar. et habeat vicarius ejusdem ecclesiae oblationes, mortuaria et personales decimas parochianorum. Item decimas hortorum virgultorum et nutrimenti animalum exceptis decimis lanae et agn. et faciet ecclesiae suis sumptibus honeste, et honorifice in omnibus deserviri. Residuum totum habeat canonicus ad firmam* xlviii. *marcis terminis subscriptis capitulo solvendis sub poena praetaxata.*
Bubbwith *aestimatio preter vicar. est* lx. *mar. quae de novo taxatur ad quadraginta mar. vicarius ejusdem habeat &c. et faciet &c. Residuum totum habeat canonic. pro* xlviii. *mar.*

Lanii

Lanii, *aestimatio preter vic.* lx. *mar. habeat oblationes, &c, residuum canonit. pro* xlii. *marc.* v. *solid. et* iv. *denar.*

Askeham, *cum* Drayton *et* Gipismeri, *aestimatio praeter vic.* lv. *marc. vicarius, &c. Residuum habeat canonic. pro* lv. *marcis, cum* Gipismeri, *sed donec vacat* Drayton *solvat tantum viginti marc.*

Brotherton, *aestimatio preter vic.* lx. *mar. vic. habeat, &c. Resid. totum preter molend. aquatic. habeat canonicus pro* xl. *octo marc.*

Copenthorpe *et* St. Marie Bishopthorpe, *aestimatio preter vic.* lx. *mar. vic. habeat, &c. & reddat canonico nomine capituli annuatim vigint. solid. Residuum totum habeat canonic. pro* xl. *octo marcis.*

Sti. Laurentii *cum* Farburn, *aestimatio praeter vicariam* xxx. *mar. vic. habeat, &c. Residuum canonic. pro vigint.* iiii. *marcis.*

Ecclesia de Burgh *cum* Burton, *aestimatio preter vicarias nom. viginti mar. vic. de* Burgh *habeat oblationes, &c. et faciet ecclesiae matrici deserviri & capellis de* Dunford *et* Pyteburgh *honeste ut supra.*

Burton-Leonardo. *Vic. de* B. L. *habeat, &c. totum alteragium, & si non sufficiat ad cent. solid. suppleatur a canonicis firmam habentibus. Residuum totum habeant duo canonici pro cent. libr.*

Horneby, *aestimatio preter vic. octogint. marc. vic. hab. &c. si excedantur refundat capitulo vel canonico annuat. quod superent in pecunia, si non sit tanti valoris, quod deest supplebitur per capitulum, vel canonic. Residuum bab. canonic. &c.*

Kirkeby-Irelyth, *aestimatio octogint. marc. et canonic. residuum totum pro* lxiiii. *marcis.*

Wiverthorpe *aestimatio totalis* cxl. *mar. habeat vic.* xxiv. *marc. in certis rebus alteragii, &c. habeat etiam de ecclesie predicta canonicus presbyterve prebendae* vi. *marc.* xxx. *marc. annuatim secundum ordinem, domini archiepisc. supradict. vic. et trigint. marcas confectam. Residuum vero canonicus habeat pro* xxiv. *marcis.*

Dalton, *aestimatio vigint. quinque marc. et habeat, canonico pro vigint. marc. solvend.*

Lyffington, *aestimatio vigint. marc. totum habeat canonicus cum* Lexington *decem libris.*

Sti. Johannis *ad pontem* Ebor. *totum habeat vic. solvendo duodecim marc. annuatim capitulo.*

Lairthorpe *vic. totum. hab. solvendo annuatim capitulo* xl. *solidos, &c.*

Sti. Andreae, *vic. totum hab. pro duobus solid. capitulo solvendis.*

Sancti Stephani *vic. hab. totum pro* ii. *solid. &c.*

Sancti Johannis *in marisco vic. totum hab. solvend. an. capitulo* vi *s.* viii *d.*

Sancti Michaelis *vic. totum habeat solvend.* x. *marcas.*

Sancti Martini, *vic. totum hab. solvendo capitulo decem marcas annuatim.*

Ordinatio haec supradicta facta est per Henricum *decanum et cap. consilio et consensu domini* Sewalli *archiepiscopi* Ebor. *anno* 1291.

Carta *Reginaldi* filii *Petri* de ecclesia de *Wyvertborp*, p. 46.

Omnibus Christi *fidelibus, &c. noveritis me dedisse concessisse et hac praesenti charta mea confirmasse dec. et cap. sancti* Petri Ebor. *pro salute animae meae, &c. advocationem ecclesiae de* Wyverthorpe *habendam et tenend. in puram et perpet. eleemosynam, &c.*

In cujus rei test. prius scriptum sigillo meo roboravi.

Iis testibus dom. Rob. de Roos, *dom.* Petro de Roos, *dom.* Will. de Roos, *dom.* Rob. de Twenge, *dom.* Johanne de Oketon, *dom.* Willielmo de Winebe, *dom.* Rob. de Weyley, *dom.* Gilb. de Brideshall, *et aliis.*

Carta *Galfridi* filii *Petri* comitis *Essex* super jure suo, quod habuit in capella de *Drayton.*

Omnibus Sancte matris ecclesiae, &c. Noverit universitas vestra quod intuitu Dei et pro salute animae et antecessorum nostrorum concessimus et quietum clamavimus de nobis et heredibus nostris in perpetuum Deo et B. Mariae *et B.* Petro *apostolo ecclesiae* Ebor. *et canonicis ibidem servientibus totum jus nostrum quod habuimus in capella sancti* Petri *de* Drayton. *Et ut haec concessio rata et firma in posterum permaneat eam presenti scripto et sigilli impressione confirmamus.*

His testibus Tho. de Muleton, Gilb. de Benyngward, Jacobo de Calte, Walt. de Preston, Walt. de Tradleg, Hug. de Hedon, Rand. de Novoforo, Ricardo *filio* Roberti, *cum multis aliis.*

Omnibus Christi *fidelibus ad quos presens scriptum pervenerit* Thomas de Bellaque *miles, salutem in Domino. Noveritis me redidisse et quietum clamasse de me et heredibus meis domino decano et capitulo B.* Petri Ebor. *omnes terras cum pert. suis in* Gippesinere, Sunwell *et* Morton *quas de eisdem tenui. Ita quod ego nec haeredes mei nec aliquis alius nomine meo jus vel clamium poterimus in eisdem de caetero vindicare, &c. Haec autem quieta clamatio facta fuit in predicto capitulo* ii. *idus* Junii *an. gra.* MCCLV. *In manu domini* Sewalli *decani presentibus* J. *de* W. Ebor. *et aliis.*

Miscellanea.

Formam protestationis pro residentia majori facienda secundum tenorem novi statuti per H. VIII. *Vide in libro actorum capit. ab. an.* 1504.

Anno

1

Anno dom. 1519. *menſe* Octobr. Johanne Colet *moritur cui in prebenda de* Botevaunt *ſuccedit* Cuthbertus Tunſtall. *Lib. actorum ab anno* 1504. *f.* 102.

Altare SS. Petri *et* Pauli *in eccleſia S.* Trin. *in curia regis* [an. in Gutheram-gate] Gutheram, Gwurth curia, *ut in* Hengwarth, *vetus curia*, Beddernis, Gwurth-Gwurther-ham-gate.

Henry VIII. alloweth all penſions and arrearages ſince the diſſolution of abbeys due to St. *Peter Ebor.* to be paid to St. *P.* *(enumeratio Penſionum.)*

Liberae Scholae in *Le-Horſe-Fair* donatio.

Dec. et cap. nominans ludimagiſtrum qui durante eorundem beneplacito et non aliter neque alio modo percipiet. feoda, vadia, commoditates, &c. eidem ſcholae ſpectant. pro dicto officio ludimag. Lib. act. ab 1565. *fol.* 127.

Multa habet. Dr. Tod *de* Bederna. *Can.* Carleol. *Lib. act. ab anno* 1543. *ad* 1558.

Injunctions of Edw. VI. *to the dean and chapter of* York. *See the archbiſhop's regiſter.*

They ſhall not take of any prebendary entring his reſidence above 20*l.* that he may be able to diſpend above 40*l.* yearly, and hath a convenient manſion houſe to keep reſidence in.

The dean for his prebend and dignity ſhall preach or cauſe to be preached two ſermons yearly at *Chriſtmas* and *Eaſter-day.* *(Tokerington.)*

A decree in favour of the dean and chapter, concerning the *Bedderne*, in which *fol.* 61.

That the vicars choral had their living aſſigned them by the dean and chapter out of the poſſeſſions of the church of *York*, and is ſtill part of the poſſeſſion of that church.

Henry V. erected the houſe of the *Bedderne* depending wholly on the principal college and under the juriſdiction of the ſaid dean and chapter for ever.

That the vicars are preſentable, and put into the ſtalls of the canons of the church by the canons of the church, and admitted by the dean and chapter.

That they were reſtrained from all unlawful alienations and charge of the ſaid poſſeſſions without the authority of the ſaid dean and chapter. (See archbiſhop *Frewen*'s viſit.)

That they are under the order and government of the dean and chapter as by the letters patents of *Hen.* V. may appear. *Vide libros MSS. D.* Tod *in catalogo* Oxon. *& nunc apud* R. Squire, *fol.* 68.

Free ſchool of *Old Malton* founded by archbiſhop *Holgate*, if the archbiſhop named not a ſucceſſor (the place being vacant) within twenty days, the dean and chapter ſhall name a maſter for life, *ſi tamen diligenter officio functus fuerit, juxta verba fundationis, &c.*

Lib. act. ab. 1543. *ad* 1558.

To the archbiſhop and prebends of York.

Hen. *R.*

—— We have nominated Dr. *Nic. Wooton* to be dean, and whereas you have ſtatutes and cuſtoms of ſuch as be elected deans, ought to have been prebendars and of the corps of your church; it is our pleaſure notwithſtanding ſuch orders and ſtatutes, ye with all celerity elect the ſaid doctor. Furthermore we deſire the ſaid archbiſhop to provide the ſaid Dr. *Nic.* of a prebend ſo ſoon as, *&c.*

Dr. *Wooton* was then dean of *Canterbury.*

Gulielmus *Rex,*

Cum nuper, ut accepimus, ex humili petitione decani et reſidentiariorum eccleſiae noſtrae Sancti Petri Ebor. *quidam dictae eccleſiae canonici multum dubitarint an decanus predictus inter reſidentiarios ejus eccleſiae poſſit admitti, eo quod ſtatuta olim ea de re condita minus nunc clara et plana exiſtant: nos paci et tranquillitati predictae eccleſiae conſulentes, declaramus ſtatuimus et ordinamus quod decanus qui nunc eſt poteſt eſſe reſidentiarius ratione decanatus ſui, ſicut quilibet canonicus ejuſdem eccleſiae reſidentiarius eſſe poteſt ratione ſui canonicatus; idemque decanus percipiet omnia proficua et emolumenta quae ad reſidentiam ſpectant. Si reſidentiam proteſtatus fuerit et tenuerit ſecundum ſtatuta et ordinationes conſuetudines ejuſdem eccleſiae. Quo detiam ad alios decani praedicti ſucceſſores extendi volumus.*

Porro quoniam numerus reſidentiariorum in eadem eccleſia per ſtatuta hactenus proviſa incertus ſit et indefinitus, nos reſpectu habito ad patrimonium et facultates ejuſdem eccleſiae quas ſatis tenues eſſe comperimus, volumus et ordinamus et ſtatuimus ut eſſe poſſint in dicta eccleſia quinque reſidentiarii et non plures, quorum ſinguli quantum percipient propter reſidentiam tantundem, et theſaurarius Sancti Petri *percipiet juxta tenorem ſtatutorum dictae eccleſiae.*

Declarationes has et limitationes ſive ordinationes inter ſtatuta eccleſiae noſtrae ſancti Petri Eborum *recipi et regiſtrari et ab omnibus obſervari volumus et firmiter ſancimus.*

Kingſingtoniae *A. D.* 169¾.

Lib. act. ab 1409 *ad* 1424.

Fraternitas inter eccleſiam B. Petri Ebor. *et* Rothomagenſem.

Willielmus Gray *decanus admittitur an.* 1521. Apr. 4.

Thomas Haxy *theſaurarius.*

Lib.

1

Lib. act. ab anno 1290

Literae regis de subjectione Scotiae, Galliae *ad perpetuam rei memoriam inregistratae. fol.* 3.
25. Boscus de Broth *vendatur, pecunia cedat in usus capituli, mox cedat in usus residentium prox.*
28. *Archiepiscopi* Joannis de L. S. *litera decano et cap. viz. singulis canonicis residentibus cuilibet eorum residentium duas quercus &c.*
Decano et canonic. residentibus duntaxat unum damam et unam damam.

Liber *Doomsday Ebor.*

Privilegia et consuetudines &c. Ebor. *fol.* 1.
Privil. Coelestini *papae de juribus. vid.* Mon. Anglic. 3.
Bulla Coelestin. *de modo elegendi dec. &c.* 3.
Confirmatio Innocentii *ut electiones liberae fiant, &c. petita regis licentia temp.* Joh. *regis, cujus literae ibi recitantur.*
Bulla Alex. *contra infractores libertatum ecclesiae et in specie* Ebor. *pro qua major et cives* Ebor. *excommunicantur, ubi de jure seneschalli eccl. St.* Petri 5.
Charta Ed. III. *de libertatibus* 5.
Chartae aliquot Ed. III. 8.
Ed. homines capituli quasdam libertates 8.
Charta Hen. III. *pro coronatore habendo &c.* 9.
Charta Hen. III. *quam concessit a primo regni apud* Bristol, *de libertat.* Angliae 11.
Alia cum quibusdam additis ad praecedent. chartam sine data.
Charta de foresta Hen. III. *itidem sub sigillis cardinalis et com.* Pembrochiae, 13.
Querelae coram justiciariis regiis inter cives et capitulum; hae querel. habentur alio libro actorum, 16.
Axminster, *de preb. de* Warthil *et* Grendal, *charta regis, placita, &c.* 25.
Curia tenta per seneschallum capituli contra pejeratos, 27.
De manerio de Thorpe, Haya de Langwath *et* Kynalton, 28.
Assisa apud Ebor. *pro libertatibus S.* Petri, 30.
Quo warranto super libertatibus eccl. Ebor. 31.
Charta Hen. *regis quod capitulum liberum sit ab auxiliis murorum, pontium infra civit.* Ebor. *libertates ejusdem,* 125.
Compositio inter capitulum Ebor. *et* Dunelm. *sede utraque vacante de juribus,* 41.
Composit. inter archiepiscopum et cap. Ebor. *et abbatem S.* Albani *de non comparendo in synodo* Ebor. *pro ecclesia de* Appleton *in* Rydale *ita ut vicar. compar.* 44.
Curia tenta coram seneschallo de nova desesina infra libertates S. Petri, 47.
Pensiones de Pontfract, Melsa, Watton *pro* Cranswick-Hoton; *B.* Mariae Ebor. 100.

In repertorio.

Extenta 21 *prebendarum, ibid.*
Ordinatio praeb. de Bilton *ita quod praebendarius ejusdem non percipiat quotidianas distributiones vel communas priusquam* 21 *librae sterling annui redditus provisae fuerint eidem communiae per ipsum preb. vel successores,* 121.
Litera papalis pro constituend. certos episcopos et priores conservatores jurium eccl. Ebor. *et hi alios deputant subconservatores,* 122.
Augmentatio choristarum ad N. 12. *per* Th. Dalby, 127.
Annui redditus de S. Barthol. Smithfield. *de majore et civ.* Ebor.
Placita de Sneris *apud* Howden, *unde dec. et cap. quietati fuerunt,* 146.
Feoda S. Petri *apud* Southcave, 152.
Concessio x *marcarum de* Ledham, *ibid.*
Ordinatio Cantariae W. Bruyse *in eccl. de* Pykering, *ibid.*
Placita de quo warranto coram W. de Harle *et sociis &c. quo warranto clamant quod nullus de familia domini regis, vel de exercitu, in propriis domibus canonicorum, &c. quere in lib.* 4. *evang. qui servatur in registro dec. et cap.* Ebor. *anno* 1700.

Ex repertorio.

Nulla appellatio a decano et capitulo nisi ad dominum regem.

Emendationes per T. G. *ad cartas eccle.* Ebor. *ex* Dugdale. *M. v.* 3.

Carta regis *Edgari* de xx cassatis in *Shireburne.* *Ex cod. MS. vocato magno registro albo penes dec. et cap. Eborum f.* 56.
In nomine, &c.
Pag. 129. *lin.* 5. *pro* Minister, *l. tantum* M⁷ M⁷.
Ibid. l. 66. *pro* nobili sumire, *l. Guimere.*
Ibid. l. 16. *pro* dipsinapaland semaera, &c. *l.* thissin ya l s'emera to.
Collatio terrae non modicae in *Eborscira* B. *Petro* concessa per regem *Athelstanum* tempore domini S. *Wulstani Eborum* archiepiscopi.

4

Ibid. l. 35. *pro*, feceris, *l.*
Ibid. l. 44. *pro*, *Agemunderness*, *l. Abemundesness.*
P. 130. *l.* 11. *pro*, gaminulis, *l.* gramulis.
Ibid. l. 12. *lege*, sed prius decurrant termini hiisque decursis.
Ibid. l. 14. *lege*, primitus autem a mari sursum in locur usque ad fontem illius fluminis.
Ibid. l. 40. *pro*, Sculc, *l.* Scule dux, *et pro* minister, *l.* M7 sic.
Ibid. l. 47. *expunge*, et plures alii milites, *&c.*
P. 132. *l.* 12. *et* 13. *lege*, ecclesiam sancti *Petri* et tu, *Gaufride*, libera eam sine mora.
P. 133. *l.* 49. *pro*, P. vicecomiti, *l.* G. vicecom.
Ibid. l. 14. *lege*, *Waltero* et *Euremaro.*
Ibid. l. 27. *pro*, Carta ejusdem regis, *&c. l.* Carta *Thurstani* archiepiscopi super eodem confirmatoria.
Ibid. l. 30. *lege*, *Eboracensis* ecclesiae, interventu *Girardi* archiepiscopi donavit, et *Stephanus.*
Adde ad p. 133. *post l.* 63. *col.* 1. Alia charta *H. R.* de decanatu ecclae. *Ebor.* in qua istae terrae conceduntur S. *Petro* et *Girardo* archiepiscopo et ecclesiae *Ebor.* cod. *Cott.* Claud. B. 3. Alia charta pro *Hugone* decano de eisdem, carta *H. R. Angl.* de decanatu *Ebor.* eccle. *H. R. G.* vic. et om. &c. cod. *Cott.* Vitel. A. 2.
Adde post l. 25. *col.* 2. Aliae chartae pro *Pykering. Cott.* ut supra.
Adde post l. 53. Carta ista *Thurstani* extat. integra inr. *Cott.* Vitel. A. 2.
P. 135. *post*, Carta ejusdem regis super libertatibus, *&c. adde*, Quo warranto contra archiepiscopum allato archiepiscopus respondit, rex confirmat.
Ibid. post, apud *Winton* in *Pascha*, *adde*, *Hen.* V. confirmavit archiepiscopo *Bowet* cum aliis franchesiis.
P. 136. *post*, S. filio *Sigulfi* apud *Wynton*, *adde*, Charta *Hen.* III. declarans et amplians istam chart. in cod. *Cot.* Claud. B. 3.
P. 143. *adde post*, *Pelagium Alban.* episc. &c. Amen, &c. Littera (seu bulla) *Urbani* ad *Eboracensem* contra professionem.
Ibid. col. 2. *post*, *ibid. fol.* 48. *in margine additur*, *Charta* Pelagii de eodem.
Ibid. col. 2. *adde, post*, nec tibi obedientiam debet; hic sequitur litera *Gelasii* ad *Ebor.* electum *Turst.*
P. 135. *l.* 6. *pro*, filio *Geronis*, *l. Gozo.*
Ibid. l. 17. *lege*, exequatur, et format.
Ibid. l. 20. *pro*, si ea, *l.* sed. *l.* faciat.
Ibid. l. 21. *lege*, propriam justiciam secundum statuta mea.
Ibid. l. 48. *lege*, *Eborum Thomae* II. capellano.
Ex albo registro &c. *P.* 143. *l.* 6. Innocentius episcopus, &c.
Dies in quibus *Ibid. l.* 35. *Epiphania*, *Hypapante:* dominica in ramis *Palmarum.*
pallio uti potest. *Ibid. l.* 6. *lege*, fratri *Rodulpho Cantuar.* archiepis.
Ibid. l. 23. *pro*, proscriptam, *l.* praescriptam.
Ibid. l. 31. *pro*, et si cum, *l.* et si eum prioris locum optineas. *q.* si non esset optineat.
P. 144. *l.* 22. *lege*, jam per gratiam Dei, pace inter Dominum meum.
Ibid. l. 37. *lege*, data *Anayn.*
Ibid. l. 50. *l. Radulphum* in *Orcheneia* episcopum consecravit.
P. 147. *l.* 34. *pro*, conservetur, *forte*, consequetur.
P. 151. *l.* 5. *post*, *Joh. Romano* et aliis, *adde haec verba*, *Hen. de Aquileya* claimed the church of *Topcliffe*, and was cast. Charta antiqua in a box plated with iron in the treasury.
P. 151. *l.* 41. *pro*, *Rob. de Fekeby*, *l. Robert de Fereby*,
P. 154. *l.* 26. *lege.* Inquisitio capta de terris *&c.* infra libertatem S. *Petri.*
P. 158. *l.* 46. *pro*, commune, *l.* communiae.

Monasticon vol. III. 154. b. *De terris, &c. infra libertatem S.* Petri.

P. 154. *lin.* 2. *for*, suburbiis, *r.* suburbio.
Ibid. l. 13. *after*, milites, *add*, iidem jur. dicunt.
Ibid. l. 14. *for*, celdam, *r.* cellam, *and for Apothecarii*, *r. Ypothecarii.*
P. 155. b. *l.* 15. *for*, *Mulberin*, *r. Mulberi.*
Ibid. l. 18. *for*, devenerint, *r.* devenit.
Ibid. l. 24. *for*, *Swinegalle*, *r. Swinegatte.*
Ibid. l. 30. *for*, quem, *r.* quam.
Ibid. l. 33. *for*, non sunt, *r.* nec dant.
Ibid. l. 35. *Ypothecar.*
P. 155. b. *l.* 6. *the* et *left out.*
Ibid. 15. *after Wyphale these words are wanting*, tenuit et terra quondam *Willielmi de Horleeus* quam *Rogerus de Wyton* tenet, sunt de libertate B. *Petri* et domus *Johannis de Wyphale.*
Ibid. l. 18. et terra.
Ibid. l. 29. data fuit.
Ibid. l. 56. *for*, ante, *r.* inter.
Ibid. l. 57. *for*, quam, *r.* in qua.
Ibid. l. 65. *for*, Gavells, *r.* Gavell.
P. 155. b. *l.* 18. *for*, *Weighton*, *r. Wixton.*
Ibib. l. 22. *for*, *Merks*, *r. Merk.*
Ibid. l. 37, 38. *for*, *Christiane*, *r. Chripian.*
Ibid. l. 50. *for*, sunt, *r.* dant.
Ibid. l. 65. prius capit.
P. 156. *l.* 9. *for*, vicarius, *r.* vicarii.
Ibid. l. 30. *after*, strata, *add*, ante.
Ibid. l. 31. *for*, cymiteriam, *r.* cymeterium.

The

ANALECTA EBORACENSIA: *or, Some remains of the antient city of* YORK, *Collected by a Citizen of* YORK.

Note that this is the first draught out of his own papers.

A second my lord *Fairfax* has by his delivery, with this note in the front, *viz.* that in the last and perfect copy he has expunged divers things in both the former, and made some small additions as were defective in both.

Sic quod fuit ante relictum est. Ovid. Met. *lib.* 5.

York'*s not so great as old* York *was of yore,*
Yet York *it is though wasted to the core:*
It's not that York *which* Ebrank *built of old;*
Nor yet that York *which was of* Roman *mould;*
York *was the third time burnt and what you see,*
Are York'*s small ashes of antiquity* (*a*).

(*b*) This is a more imperfect copy than that which sir *Thomas Widderington* delivered to my lord *Fairfax*, for it evidently appears that my lord's book was copyed out of this.

And yet without question this is much more compleat then the last, because in the last he has expunged (it is his own word, but very improper for so learned a work) divers things in the former.

To the honourable the lord-mayor of the city of York, *and to the aldermen, sheriffs, common-councel and citizens of the same city.*

" *My lord-mayor and gentlemen,*

" I Shall not tell you what time I have spent in gathering these fragments, but assure " you I spent no time at all to consider to what persons I should direct them, most " of the things concern you and the rights of the city, with the government whereof you " are trusted : the dedication hereof is as proper to you as *Tully*'s book *de Senectute* was to " an old man, no persons so fit for this frontispiece as your selves, for whose cause they " were collected, and the rather also because, if any thing be mistaken, wanting or omitted, " you are best able to correct or supply it.

" I will acknowledge now in the beginning that, which is usually set at the end of im- " perfect pieces, *multa desunt*; and really I have not taken in all to this which I have met " withal, for I have done with those materials which I have found as the poet *Virgil* did " with the verses of *Ennius*, *pauca ex multis et optima ex illis paucis eligendo*, taking few out " of many, and the best (as my judgment would serve me) out of those few; nor have I " found out all, yet I was not discouraged by that from doing what I have done. He " that cannot see so far nor so clearly as *Lynceus*, did must be contented with that eye sight " which he hath.

" I thought fit to put it into an *English* habit, considering the persons for whom I chiefly " intended it, lest it might be said of it, as *Aristotle* said of his *Acroasis*, *it is published and* " *not published to the advantage of those for whom I design it.*

" The dial of this city hath a long time gone backward, and many special pieces of an- " tiquities are already mouldred to dust, and I was doubtful that the small scattered remains " of it might also in time vanish, cities as well as persons being subject to mortality, which " gave an edge to my desires and endeavours to preserve the memory of those things from " the injury of time in such a way as this poor confused pamphlet can afford ; it is not un- " profitable for us to know the passages of former ages, nor can it be any regret unto us " to hear that our predecessors were rich and great, though we ourselves be little and poor. " But it is rather a shame and reproach unto us to be ignorant of the antient rights of the " city. An *Egyptian* priest told *Solon* that the most antient *Greeks* of his time were but " babes and children, because they could tell nothing beyond their own and their father's " memory. It was a foul shame to the men of *Syracuse*, a city of *Sicily*, that they could " not tell *Cicero* the place of the sepulchre and monument of their famous *Archimedes*, " though it were amongst them, which he being a stranger could do; as it hath been my " care in this to recount things, privileges and persons which conduce to the honour of " this antient city, so I have not concealed the misfortunes and miscarriages of our pre- " decessors, the memory of these obliquities is peradventure as useful though not so plea- " sant as that of the former.

" Herein, as also in those matters which relate to the possessions or rights of other per- " sons within the body of this city, I have dealt clearly and impartially, I cannot nor will " not do the city right by doing wrong to others, my love to the city set me upon this

(*a*) *York* was burnt, 1. by the *Saxons*, 2. by the *Danes*, 3 by the *Normans*.

(*b*) Note that this has all that is in my lord *Fairfax*'s book, but not so well ordered as to the *Ainsty* of *York*.

work

"work, but it cannot carry me beyond or besides the bounds of truth so far as the "light or the glimmerings thereof have appeared to me. I have touched little in this up-"on the present government of the city or things lately acted; things fresh in your memo-"ries need not a remembrancer, though we cannot but see poverty rushing in upon us as "an armed man, or this city, if you please, in a deep consumption, there being a decay in "their vital parts of trade, commerce and confluence; yet I may say thus much without "adulation or ostentation, that the present government of the city is very commendable, "unanimous in itself, and retains also a good harmony with their spiritual guides, there "is no strife between *Moses* and *Aaron*. *Themistocles* boasted that he could make of a lit-"tle city a great one: if I were master of that art *York* should be as great as ever it was. "You will see by the following discourse what I can do, which is no more then what a li-"tle bee doth that sucks from several flowers that honey which she afterwards brings into "one hive. What I have learned out of histories, records, year books, acts of parliament "and your own records and books remaining in the city, and from the relations of other "persons, or by my own observation in the course of my service to the city, they are "all digested into this little model; which is but a nosegay of some flowers of the city "which lay confusedly scattered before.

"*Julius Caesar* did by his will give a legacy in silver to each citizen of *Rome*. Though "I have a large affection for the city of *York*, yet my purse is not wide enough for such "a distribution, this rude collection is what I have to bestow upon all my fellow citizens "of *York*; not a gift to each citizen, but one poor contracted legacy to them all; which "I do heartily offer unto you as that which may remain as a lasting testimony of the truth "and sincerity of my affections to the city and citizens of *York*.

"*SIR*,

"YOU have told us by the former discourse what this city was, and what our prede-"cessors have been, we know not what this may have of honour in it, sure we are, "it hath but little of comfort. The shoes of our predecessors are too big for our feet, and "the ornaments which they had will not serve now to cover our nakedness, nor will their "wealth feed us who are not able to tell you what we are, unless it be this, that we are "poor and miserable. Our predecessors if they could see us would either disclaim us or "be ashamed of us. You have told us that this city was sometime the metropolis of the "*Britains*, the royal court of the *Roman* emperors, and a seat of justice antiently, and "also in latter times; how is it now become unlike itself? the inhabitants have many of "them forsaken it, and those who have not, she cannot maintain; whilst some other cities "are become so big with buildings and numerous with inhabitants as they can be hardly "fed or governed. *York* is left alone situate in a country plentiful for provisions and stored "if the people had money to buy them. Trade is decayed, the river become unnavigable "by reason of shelves, *Leeds* is nearer the manufactures, and *Hull* more commodious for "the vending of them, so *York* is in each respect furthest from the profit. The body of "*York* is so dismembred, that no person cares for being the head of it; the suburbs which "were the legs of the city are cut off; the late court of justice which indeed was built upon "the sand only is sunk, and with it many considerable persons are swallowed up; you "cannot now see any confluence of suitors or people: he that looks upon the city may see "her paps dry, and her eyes bedewed with tears, refusing to be comforted, because all "these are gone. Now sir for the *Britains* whom you mention, we can neither derive pe-"digree nor wealth from them; nor can we hear of any of their descendants, unless in "*Wales* or *Cornwall*, or upon some mountain or hill in *Cumberland*; and when we have "found them we fear that they will not own us for their kindred or relations; we have "have lost our genealogy, and forgot the *British* dialect: they tell us that our blood is "not *British*, but *Roman*, *Saxon* or *Norman*, which, or some of which did expell those "ancient *Britains*, and we might expect the same reception from the *Roman*, *Norman*, "or *Saxon*, if we should appeal to any of them; and we find by experience, that it is "not a long series or beadrol of ancestors or predecessors, but wealth and estate which set "a value upon men and places. As for our wealth it is reduced to a narrow scantling; "if we look upon the fabrick and materials of the city, we have lost the suburbs which "were our skirts, our whole body is in great weakness and distemper, our merchandi-"zes and trade, our nerves and sinews are weakned and become very mean and incon-"siderable: for the earls, dukes, arch-bishops, deans, prebends and abbots of *York*, they "were no homogeneal parts of our body, but only garnishments, embroideries and orna-"ments, and sometimes pricks and goades; our present misery is, that we can hardly "keep together our homogeneal and essential members, some of them using us as *Absalom's* "mule did him, either leaving of us or refusing to act as magistrates amongst us, when "our very government seems to hang by a weak or upon some slender twig.

"Now for all the monuments of our former state and glory we find no warmth or "comfort from them; but it seems to add to our unhappiness that our predecessors were "so happy.

"1. To

"Give us leave for conclusion to tell you, that a good purse is more useful to us than
"a long story which might enable us,
"1. To make our river more navigable.
"2. To re-edify the decayed parts of the city.
"3. To raise a stock to set up some manufacture in the city.
"4. To relieve our poor, into which number we may all of us fall if some timely course be
"not taken, by which through God's blessing this tottering and wasted city may be upheld.

The Bidding *of* Prayer *according to the use of the church of* York, *copied out of a manuscript of the late reverend* Marmaduke Fothergill.

Explicit manuale secundum usum Ebor.

Deprecatio pro pace ecclesie et regni in diebus dominicis.

"*DEpretemur Deum Patrem omnipotentem pro statu et stabilitate sancte matris ecclesie, et pro* "*pace regis et regni.* We sall make a speciall prayer unto God allmyghty, and to "the glorious virgin his moder, ouer lady sante *Mary*, and to al the fare felichyp of he- "ven. For all the state and the stabilite of all haly kirke, specially for our haly fader the "pope of *Rome* and for all hys trewe cardenals; for the patriark of *Ierusalem*; and spe- "cially for the haly crose that God was done upon, that God for hys mercy bringe itt "oute of hethen men handes unto cristen menes kepyng. Also we sall pray specially for "our haly fader the archbyschop of this cee, and for all other archbischopes and by- "schopes, ande for all maner of men and women of relygion, that God gyfe thame grace "perseverance in onest and clene relygion kepinge.

"We sall pray specially for the person or for the vikar of this kirke that hase your "saules for to kepe, and for all thaes that cure has tane of cristenmen saules, that God gyf "thame grace so well for to teche thare sugettis ilke curet in his degre, ande the sugettes "so weill to wyrke eftir heylfull teching, that bothe the techers and the sugettes may com "the blys that aye sall last. We sall pray specially for all prestes and clerkes that redis "or synges in this kirke or in any other, and for all other thurgh whame Goddes servys es "mayntened or uphalden.

"We sall pray specially for oure kynge and the queyn and all the kynges childer, and "for the peris and the lordes and the gode communers of the lande, and specially for all "thas that hafes the gude counsale of the lande for to kepe; that God gif thame grase swilk "counsell to take and orden, and for to do thare efter that itt may be louyng to God allmygh- "ty, profet and weilfare to the rein, and shame and senchyp to ouer enmyse, gaynstan "dyng and restrenyng of thare power and thare males.

"We sall pray specially for the meer, the twelve, the schirrives, and the twenty four, and "for all gode communers of this cite, and for thame that has this cite for to govern, that "God gife thame grace so weil to rewle itt that may be to God louyng, and savyng to the "cite, and profet and help to the communers.

"We sall pray specialy for all our gode parechens wharesoever thai be, on land or on wa- "ter, that God almyghty save thame fra all maner of parels, and bring tham whare thai "walde be in quart and heill both of body and of saule.

"We sall pray specialy for all thase that lely and trewly pays thare tendes and thare of- "ferandes to God and to haly kirke, that God do thame meid in the blise of heven, and "thai that dose noght so, that God brynge thame sone till amendment.

"We sall pray also for all trewe pilgrams and palmers wharesoever thai be on lande or on "water, that God of his gudenes graunt thame parte of our gode prayers and us of thare "gode gates.

"Also we sall pray specially for all lande tyllande, that God for his godenes and his "he grace, and thurgh our gude prayers maynteyn thame so that thai may be upstandand. "And for all the see farand that God allmyghtry save thame fra all maner of parels, and "bringe thame and their gudes in quart whare thaie walde be.

"We sall pray specially for all thais that er bun in dett or in dedely syn, that God "for hys mercy bryng tham sone out therof; and for all thase that er in gode lyfe that God "maynten thame tharein, and gif tham gode perseverance in thair gudenes, and that this "prayer may be harde and sped the titter thurgh your praier, ilk a man and woman that "here is helpes hartly with a *Pater Noster* and a *Ave*.

"*Deus misereatur nostri*, et cetera cum *Gloria Patri. Kyrieleeson, Christeleeson, Kyrie-* "*leeson. Pater noster.* Sacerdos sn. no. *Et ne nos sacerdotes tui. Domine salvum fac re-* "*gem. Salvum fac populum tuum Domine. Domine fiat pax. Exurge Domine. Domine Deus* "*virtutis. Domine exta. Dominus nobiscum. Oremus.*

"Oratio: *Ecclesiae tuae quaesumus, Domine, preces placatus admitte, ut destructis adversi-* "*tatibus et erroribus universis secura tibi serviat libertate.*

"Oratio: *Deus, a quo sancta desideria.*

"Oratio: *Deus, qui caritatis.*

" We sall make a speciall prayer to our lady saynt *Mary*, and to all the feir falychyp that " is in heven, for all the brether and sistirs of our moder kirke saynt *Petyr* house of *York*, " saynt *John* house of *Beverlay*, saynt *Wilfride* of *Rypon*, and saynt *Mary* of *Suthwell*; and " specially for all thaes that are seik in this parych or in any other, that God of his god-" hede relese thame of thare panes and seknes, and turne thame to that way that is maste " to Goddes louynge and heill of thare saules.

" We sal pray specialy for all thaes that wirchips this kirke owther with buke or bell, vest-" ment or chales, awterclath or towel, or any other anourment thurgh qwhilke haly kirk is " or may be more honorde or wirchipt.

" We sall pray also specialy for all thase that gifes or sendes, or in testment wyles any gode " in mayntenyng of this kirk or kirk warke: And for all thase that fyndes any lyght in this " kirk, as torche, serge, or lampe in wirchyping of God or any of his halouse.

" We sall pray also for all women that er bun with childer in this parichin or in any other, " that God comforth thame and delyver thame with joy, and send thare childer cristendom, " and the moders puryfying of haly kirk, and relese of payn in thare travelyng.

" We sall also pray for thame that this day gafe brede to this kirk, haly brede to be " made of, for thame it first began and langest haldes opon. For thame and for us, and for " all other that neid has of prayer in wirchyp of our lady saynt *Mary*, ilk man and woman " hayls oure lady with five *aves*. A. *Ave regina celorum, ave domina angelorum*. 5. *Post* " *partum*. Oratio: *Famulorum tuorum*. Tempore paschali a. *Regina celi*. 5. *Post partum*. " Oratio: *Gratiam tuam*.

" We sal make a speciall prayer for oure faders saules, moder sauls, oure godfader saules, " godmoder saules, brether saules, sisters saules, and all oure evenkyn saules, and for all " our gude frend saules, and for all the saules whas banes er berryd in this kirke, or in this " kirk-yerd, or in any other, and specialy for all the saules that abydes the mercy of God " in the paynes of purgatory, that God for his mykil mercy relese thame of thare payns if " it be his will, and that our prayers myght sumwhat stand thame in steide, ilk man and " woman helpes hertly with a *Pater Noster* and a *Ave*.

" *De profundis. Kyrieleeson, Christeleeson, Kyrieleeson. Pater noster. Et ne nos ind. Requiem* " *eternam. Credo videre. A porta inferi. Dominus noster.* Oratio: *Fidelium Deus omnium,* " *requiescant in pace fidelium anime per m.*

The first foundation of the collegiate church of blessed JOHN *of* Beverley. Ex MS. dom. *T. Herbert* *.

Regist. mag. Beverlac.

THE collegiate church of blessed *John* of *Beverley* was anciently founded in the county of *York*, in a certain country called *Deyira*, to wit, in the wood of the *Deyirians* in the time of *Lucius*, the most illustrious king of (*England* then called) *Brittany*, the first king of the same, the son of *Coil* a pagan king, anointed by pope *Eleutherius* the thirteenth after *Peter*, in the year of our lord *Jesus Christ*, the son of God the father almighty, creator of heaven and earth, together with the Holy Ghost, according to the computation of the church of *England* 126.

Afterwards it was destroyed by the pagans *Orse* and *Hengist*; and is again renewed and founded by the aforesaid blessed *John* archbishop of *York*; is ordained a monastery of black monks, of religious nuns virgins, seven secular priests for the service of God, and divers other ministers, to wit, in the year of our Lord 704.

And also again it is destroyed by the pagans *Hubba* and *Hungar Danes*, the sons of *Swayn* king of the *Danes*.

After that it is refounded and augmented by the most illustrious king of *England Athelstane*, who endowed the said church with divers priviledges, gifts and benefices, and so it remained honourably endowed under the government of seven canons, until the coming of *William* called *the bastard, the conqueror* and *king*, and so until the year of our Lord 1082.

And then by the consent of *William* called *Rufus* of *England*, *Thomas* archbishop, called the elder, by the assent of the canons and others whom it concerned, *Thomas* the nephew of the said lord archbishop, a priest, was ordained and called the first provost, to whom succeeded *Thurstan* of blessed memory, to whom *Thomas* called *the Norman*, to whom *Robert*, to whom *Thomas Becket*, archbishop of *Canterbury*, to whom another *Robert*, to whom *Galfrid*, to whom *Symon*, to whom *Fulco Basset*, to whom *John Chesull*, to whom *William* of *York*, to whom *John Mauncell*, to whom *Alane*, to whom *Morgan* the provost, to whom the venerable father and lord, lord *Peter* of *Chester*, who purchased many tenements, revenues and services to the said provostship and provost thereof, and left implements of divers goods and chattels in all the manors of the said provostship both quick and dead; to whom *Hamo*, to whom Mr. *Robert* of *Alburwick*, to whom Mr. *William* of *Melton*, to whom Mr. *Nicholas* of *Hugate*, to whom Mr. *William de la Mare*, to whom Mr. *Richard* of *Ravens*, to whom Mr. *Adam* of *Lynbergsh*, to whom the venerable circumspect man Mr. *John* of *Thoresby*, to whom the noble and venerable father and circumspect man Mr. *Robert Manseley*, provost, prebendary of the prebend of St. *James*, president of the chapter, canon residentiary of the said church, prebendary of the prebend of *Husthwait* of the cathedral church

* These collections are all of them printed in *English* and *Latin* in *Leland's Collectanea*, published by Mr. *Hearne*.

church of *York*, prebendary of the prebend of *Brannefwood* of the church of St. *Paul* in *London*, prebendary of the prebend of *Cressall* in the church of St. *Martin the great* in *London*, parson of the church of *Hacneyes*, and master of the free chapel in *Malden* in whose time the said treatise was compiled by *Symon Russel*, in the year of our Lord 1416, in the month of *January*.

ARCHBISHOPS *of* YORK.

A. C.

622. 1. St. *Paulinus* died 644.
Vacat annos 20.
666. 2. *Cedda*.
3. *Wilfridus*.
4. St. *Boza*.
687. 5. St. *John* of *Beverley*, he was bishop thirty three years three months and thirteen days, after which he lived privately at *Beverley* in the college there, built and founded by himself, &c. and dying the 7th of *May* in the year 721, was buried in the porch of the church belonging to the college.

The better to illustrate the antiquity and history of this church, and to supply the defect of the provosts, from the above cited register, I shall here add the translation of an antient manuscript, *De vita S.* Johannis *archiepiscopi* Eboracen. *sive de antiquitate* Beverlacensi *liber authoris incerti*, which he divides in three parts. Ex Lelandi collect. vol. III. In biblioth. Westmonast.

In *Bernicia*, is *Hexam*, *Richmond*, *Carlisle* and *Copland*.

In *Deira* is *York* and *Beverley*, and many other.

Anciently, that country alone, which was situated between the eastern ocean the rivers *Darwent* and *Humber*, was called *Deira*, but now *East-riding*.

Deirwent, i. e. or the ford of *Deira*, or *Deirians*.

Low Deira, in respect of the higher between the sea and *Humber*, becaufe it extends itself like a nose, the syllable *ness* is added by the inhabitants, and is commonly called *Holderness*.

Coifi, the last archflamen of the pagan worship at *York*.

Godmundigham, a place of idols, not far from *York* eastwards, on the other side *Darwent*.

Paulinus baptized in the river *Trent* near *Southwell*.

Saint *John* archbishop of *York* was born, as is commonly believed, in the village of *Harpham*.

Folchardus of *Canterbury* writ the life of St. *John* archbishop of *York*.

St. *John* was the first doctor of divinity in *Oxford*.

The Venerable *Bede* was the scholar of St. *John*.

St. *John* was the scholar of *Theodore* archbishop of *Canterbury*.

St. *John* was a hermit at *Harnesleigh*, i. e. in the mountain of the eagle, upon the bank of the river *Tyne* near *Hexam*.

King *Alfrid* a favourer of St. *John*.

St. *John* succeeded *Eata* bishop of *Hagustald*.

St. *John* frequented the oratory of St. *Michael* near *Hexam*.

St. *John* was made archbishop of *York*.

Herebaldus the disciple of St. *John* and his inseparable companion.

Brithunus the disciple of St. *John*, afterwards abbot of *Beverly*.

St. *Sigga*, St. *John*'s deacon.

Wilfrid the less, afterwards archbishop of *York*, the disciple of St. *John*.

Hereburgis abbess of *Wetandun*.

Quenburgis a nun of *Wetandun*, cured by St. *John*.

Deirewald a woody place, *i. e.* the wood of the *Deirians*, afterwards *Beverlac*, or the *Lake of Bevers*, so named from the bevers with which the neighbouring river *Hull* abounded.

St. *John* founded in *Beverley* a parish church dedicated to St. *John the evangelist*, and having obtained the site and title of this place, he converted the aforesaid holy church into a monastery, and assigned it to monks. He there built anew the presbytery or choir of the church, the prior of St. *John*'s having a place in the nave of the church. He built to the south of the said church the oratory of St. *Martin*, where he afterwards placed nuns.

He added to those monasteries seven presbyters and as many clerks in the nave of the church of St. *John*.

St. *John* procured to his monasteries the manor of *Ridinge*, and then built the church of St. *Nicholas* in the land of his lordship.

Earl *Puca* having a manor at *South Burton* two miles from *Beverley*, *Yelfrida* the daughter of earl *Puca* was made nun at *Beverley*, whose mother St. *John* had delivered from a fit of sickness. *Puca* gave with his daughter the manor of *Walkington*. *Yelfrida* died on the 3d of the ides of *March* in the year of our Lord 742. whose bones are buried at *Beverley*.

Earl *Addi* of *North Burton*, gave *North Burton* with the advowson of the same to the church of *Beverley* in the time of St. *John* the archbishop. After those chapels were built in *Lekingfeild* and *Scorburgh*, which were in the parish of *Burton*, and in process of time made parish churches.

(*a*) Lelandi *col. tom.* II. *ed.* Hearne. (*b*) *In fundo Domini sui.*

Here-

Herebaldus the disciple of St. *John*, abbot of *Tinmouth*

King *Osred* for his love of St. *John* gave *Dalton* to the church of *York*, in which village at that time was a manor of the king's.

St. *John* having left his bishoprick passed four years in *Beverley*.

St. *John* purchased to the church of *Beverley* lands in *Middleton*, *Welwick*, *Bilton* and *Patrington*.

Britbunus, the first abbot of *Beverley*, died on the ides of *May*, *A. D.* 733. and was buried near St. *John*.

Winwaldus a monk of the same place, the second abbot, died *A. D.* 751.

Wulfeth, third abbot of *Beverley*, died *A. D.* 773.

The names of the rest of the abbots are unknown.

In the year 146. from St. *John's* death the monastery of *Beverley* was destroyed by the *Danes*, with the books and all the ornaments.

The monastery of *Beverley* remained three years desolate.

Part II. Afterwards the presbyters and clerks returned to *Beverley* and repaired the place.

Beverley, a village situated in the hundred of *Succolfros*.

King *Athelstane* came to *Beverley*, and having conquered the *Scots*, built there a new college of secular canons.

St. John's town in *Scotland*, so called by king *Athelstan*, for the love which he had to the church of St. *John* of *Beverley*.

Adelstan gave lands to the church of *Beverley* in *Brandesburton* and *Lokington*. King *Athelstan* his right of *horstraffa*, i. e. *of the feeding of horses*, of the forage of horses which was paid to him yearly in the *East-riding*. (Havers and thraves.)

St. *John's* standard carried by king *Athelstan* when he vanquished the *Scots*. King *Athelstan* seeking a sign by which he might know the *Scots* subject by right to the *English*, deeply wounded a rock with his sword at *Dunbar*.

Deira which is incompassed on one side with the river *Darwent*, on the other with the *Humber*, and on the third with the northern or eastern ocean.

The charter of the same king *Athelstan* of the immunity, liberty and sanctuary of the lands of St. *John*. Writ in *Saxon*.

The cross on the farther side *Molescroft* valley one of the bounds of peace, and the place of refuge or sanctuary of St. *John*; king *Athelstan* ordained, that *Beverley* should be the head of all *East-riding*.

Athelstan confirmed these priviledges *A. D.* 938, and from the death of St. *John* 217. From this time the town of *Beverley* became larger, and great was the concourse of people. In these times the people resorting in great numbers, by the consent of the canons of *Beverley*, two chapels are built at *York*, one in honour of the blessed virgin, the other of St. *Thomas* the apostle; saving the right of the mother church.

Alfric the seventeenth archbishop of *York*, translated the bones of St. *John*. A ring, with the fragments of a book of the gospels was found in St. *John's* sepulchre. This translation was made in the year from the death of *John* 316, *A. D.* 1037, the 8th of the kalends of *November*, in the time of *Edward*, before he had obtained the dignity of the kingdom. This writing was afterwards found in the case of relicks of St. *John*.

Anno Dom. 1188, *Sept.* 6, St. *John's* church was burnt in the night after the feast of St. *Mathew* the apostle. At the same time were translated the bones of St. *Britbunus* abbot of *Beverley*. This *Alfred* bishop of *York* ordained there officiaries in the church of *Beverley*, a sexton, a chancellor, and a precentor, who should wear a canonical habit. This *Alfrid* bought of one *Fortius* a rich man, land at *Middleton*, *Holme* and *Fridaythorp*, to these also *Alfrid* obtained from king *Edward*, that there should be three annual fairs, at *Beverley*. He also made a custom, that the more noble of those who dwelt nigh, should thrice in the year follow the relicks of St. *John* within and without the town both fasting and barefooted. He also designed to have built the refectory and dormitory at *Beverley*, but was prevented by death. (Sacristam.)

Kinsius archbishop of *York*, built a high tower in the church of *Beverley*.

Aldred archbishop of *York*, finished the refectory and dormitory, in the *Bedhern* at *York* (c).

Dominium. King *Edward*, at the instance of *Aldred*, gave to the church of *Beverley* a lordship in *Leven*. He first made the seven canons prebendaries. He also assigned certain places to the prebendaries, and appointed vicars for them. This *Aldred* adorned the old church with a new choir. He also added an eigth canon prebendary. He also decorated the whole church from the choir to the tower, with painting, which he called heaven. He also adorned the pulpit over the entrance of the choir with brass, silver and gold with wonderful *Teutonic* work. (Opere Teutonico)

Part III. *Alveredus* the historian, sacrist and treasurer of *Beverley*, writ the history of the *English* affairs.

King *William* the first had fixed his tents seven miles from *Beverley*, *Thurstinus* a knight

(c) A mistake for *Beverley*.

I of

of *William* I. purſued a *Veteran* in the church of *Beverley* with his drawn ſword, and was there miſerably ſtruck with a diſeaſe.

William I. gave *Sigleſthorn* to the church of *Beverley*, and commanded that his army ſhould not hurt the church of *Beverley*.

William I. to earl *Marchar*, and *Gamalael* the ſon of *Oſbern*. *Deeſt in Monaſt.*

Thomas the elder, archbiſhop of *York*, gave to *Thomas the younger* his nephew, a new dignity by reaſon the diſcord of the canons, *i. e.* the provoſtſhip of *Beverley*, yet ſo as that he ſhould neither have a vote in the chapter, or a ſtall in the choir. This place which was anciently called *Bedern* is now the provoſt's houſe, and the new *Bedern* is joined to his houſe, where are now the vicars of the prebendaries, to whom the provoſt pays their ſtipends. *Ex libello adjuncto de praepoſ. Beverl.*

1. *Thomas* junior.
2. *Thurſtan*, afterwards archbiſhop of *York*. He was the firſt archbiſhop, &c. who had a prebend in *Beverley*, and this honour the archbiſhops his ſucceſſors retained.
3. *Thomas* the *Norman*.
4. *Robert*.
5. *Thomas Becket*.
6. *Robert*.
7. *Geoffry*, in the time of *Henry* II.
8. *Simon*.
9. *Fulco Baſſet*.
10. *John Cheſhul*.
11. *William* of *York* in the time of *Henry* III. he was biſhop of *Saliſbury*.
12. *John Maunſell* treaſurer of *York*.
13. *Alan*.
14. *Morgan*.
15. *Peter* of *Cheſter*.
16. *Haymo de Charto*, a foreigner, he was deprived of the provoſtſhip, and afterwards made biſhop of *G*. *Epiſcopus* Gibenenſis.
17. *Robert de Alburwick*.
18. Maſter *Walter*.
19. *William de Melton*.
20. *Nicholas Hugate*.
21. *William de la Mar* in the time of *Edward* III.
22. *Richard de Ravenſar* who improved the provoſtſhip.
23. *Adam Limbergh*.
24. Mr. *John Thoreſby*.
25. Mr. *Robert Manſeild*.
26. *William Kinwolmarſech* afterwards treaſurer of *England*.
27. *Robert Nevelle*. He built the tower of *Bedhern* in the time of *Henry* VI.
28. *Robert Rolleſton*.
29. *John Gerningham* treaſurer of *York*.
30. *Laurence Bouth*, afterwards biſhop of *Durham*, and archbiſhop of *York*.
31. Mr. *John Bouth*, afterwards biſhop of *Exon*.
32. *Henry Webber*.
33. *Peter Taſtar* a foreigner.
34. *William Potman*.
35. *Hugh Trotter*.
36. . . . .
37. *Thomas Dalby*.
38. *Thomas Winter*.

Godmundham is a mile from *Wighton* by eaſt.

Harpham in the *Woolde* not very far from *Driffeild*.

The church of St. *Nicholas* in *Beverley* commonly called *Holme* church, where there is a cut for ſmall veſſels, the cut out of *Hull* river to the bridge at *Holme*, on the cut about half a mile.

South Burton, alias *Biſhops Burton*, two miles from *Beverley* in the way to *York*. *Walkington* two miles by weſt from *Beverley*. *North-Burton* half a mile ſouth weſt from *Lekinfeild*. *Scorburgh* a mile north eaſt from *Lekingfeild*. *Dalton* four miles north weſt from *Beverley*, the provoſt has a pretty houſe there.

Moleſcroft croſs, a limit of the ſanctuary, hard by entering *Lekingfeild* park from *Beverley*.

There was another towards *North-Burton* a mile out of *Beverley*.

There was another towards *Kinwalgreves* a mile out of *Beverley*.

There was another croſs by ſouth toward *Humber*, all thoſe were marks of ſanctuary, each a mile out of *Beverley*.

Sigleſthorn in *Holderneſs*.

The inscription.

Haec sedes lapidea ab Anglis *dicebatur* Fridstolidt, *i. e. pacis cathedra ad quam reus fugiendo perveniens omnimodam pacis securitatem habebat.*

Ex vita D. Joannis A. Ebor. *auctore* Folchardo Durovernensi.

Hereburgas abbess of the monastery of *Wetandune.*

John dedicated the church of *South-Burton.*

Herebald, afterwards a monk of *Tinmouth*, a servant of *John* the bishop.

John came to the synod appointed by king *Osred.*

Brithun abbot of *Beverley.*

Herebald the clerk of *John*, afterward abbot of *Tinmouth.*

John remained in the bishoprick thirty three years. Resigned it to his chaplain *Wilfrid*, and died in *Beverley* on the nones of *May A. D.* 721.

Ex libro Gulielm. *clerici* Beverlac. *ad* Thomam *praeposit. de mirac* Joannis *archiepiscopi* Ebor.

Trustin a noble captain together with the *Normans* came to *Beverley* to plunder the town, but perished.

William the bastard, king of *England*, was very bountiful to the people of *Beverley.*

Robert de Stutevill, lord of the castle of *Cottingham.*

The charter of privileges given to king Athelstan *by St.* John *of* Beverley, anno Dom. DCCCCXXV (*d*).

Anno ab incarnatione Domini millesimo centesimo octogesimo octavo combusta fuit haec ecclesia in mense Septembri *in sequenti nocte post festum sancti* Matthaei *apostoli: et in anno millesimo centesimo nonagesimo septimo, sexto iduum* Martii *facta fuit inquisitio reliquiarum beati* Johannis *in hoc loco, et inventa sunt haec ossa in orientali parte sepulchri et hic recondita, et pulvis caemento mixtus ibidem inventus est et reconditus.*

Collected by sir *Tho. Herbert*, bart.

The CHURCH *of* RIPON.

MS. written by sir Tho. Herbert.

THE collegiate church of *Rippon* was first founded by St. *Wilfrid* (who after *Paulinus*, was the third archbishop of *York* in succession) buried in the said church or monastery in the year of our Lord 710. and there rested until about two hundred and twenty years after, his embalmed corps were removed to the monastery of *Christ* church in *Canterbury*, by *Odo* surnamed *Severus*, archbishop thereof, who, as Mr. *Camden* observes, was in those days a great master of ceremonial mysteries; his epitaph is recorded by *Bede lib.* 5. *cap.* 20. During many sharp contests that after happened betwixt the *Saxon* and *Dane* for supremacy, this church at *Ripon* had its equal share in the misery of other places, being, by the enraged *Dane*, who, as histories report, at that time feared neither God nor man, in a sort thrown down and made even with the ground, the town being also utterly wasted and destroyed, so as for some years the place was uninhabited, until, through the royal bounty of that victorious prince king *Athelstan* and liberal contribution of the archbishop and several other worthy persons lay and clergy, the town was rebuilt and peopled, and the church in short time recovered fresh lustre; yea for further encouragement endowed with sundry privileges and immunities, by making it a sanctuary or place of refuge, as by the copy of the charter then granted may appear, *viz.*

" IN nomine sanctae et individuae trinitatis *Athelstanus* Dei gratia rex *Angliae* omnibus hominibus suis de *Eborascira* et per totam *Angliam* salutem. Sciatis quod ego confirmo ecclesiae et capitulo *Ripon* pacem suam et omnes libertates et consuetudines suas, et concedo eis curiam suam de omnibus querelis et in omnibus curiis de hominibus S. *Wilfridi* pro ipsis et hominibus suis, vel contra ipsos, vel inter se adinvicem, vel quae fieri possunt, et judicium suum pro *Freedmortell*, et quod homines sui sint credendi per suum *Ya* et per suum *Na*, et omnes terras habitas et habendas et homines suos ita liberos, quod nec rex *Angliae*, nec ministri ejus nec archiepiscopus *Eborum*, nec ministri ejus aliquid faciant vel habeant, quod est ad terras suas, vel ad *Sok* capituli.

" Testibus *T.* archiepiscopo *Eborum* et *P.* praeposito *Beverlaci.*

Alia charta regis Adelstani.

Witen all yat is and is gane
Yat ich king Adelstane
Has yeaven as freelich as ich may
To kirk and capital of St. Wilfray
Of my free devotion
Tair pees at Ripon
On ilk side that kirk a mile
For all ill deeds and ilk a guile
And within the kirken yate
And at the stane that grithstool hate

Within the kirk door and the quaire
They have theire pees for less and mare
Ilken of theire steeds
Sall have pees of freed-mortell and ill deeds
Yat withouten it done is toll, thame
Sok, sac, with yrne and with water deme
And do wrack and at land at St. Wilfray
Of ilken guiid frea sall been ay
Yat ine have nane that langs me to
In thair harshape schat have at so

(*d*) *Vide Monast. vol.* I. *p.* 171.

And

And for ich wald yat yai been save
Ich will yat yai ilken freedeem have
And in all things be as free
As heart may think or eigh may see
At the power of a kinge.
Yat mast make free any thinge
And my seile have ich sett yarto
For I will yat na man this gift undo.

By virtue of which charters and the publick peace that ensued, this monastery continued in prosperity for many years, even until the *Norman* conquest, which happened in the year of our Lord 1066.

A revolution that at first was mixed with much vigour and some broiles wherein this place ran an equal fate with *York*, and several other parts of that county which were subjected to the merciless cruelty of fire and spoil, the usual concomitants of war. Nevertheless as the publick affairs settled, this church and town recovered fresh breath, and through the conqueror's royal favour, and benevolence of succeeding princes received fresh confirmation of liberties, as by the respective charters at this day extant are acknowledged, that granted by the conqueror's youngest son king *Henry* I. for the benefit of the town being as followeth.

" HENRICUS rex *Angliae* vicecomitibus et ministris et omnibus baronibus *Francis* " et *Anglis* de *Eboracifcira* et *Northumberlandia* salutem. Sciatis me concessisse S. *Wilfrido* de *Ripun* et *Thomae* archiepiscopo *Eboracensi* habere feriam per quatuor dies ad festum S. *Wilfridi* de *Aprili* duobus diebus ante festum et die festi et in crastino; et praecipio quod omnes illuc euntes et inde redeuntes cum omnibus mercatis suis habeant meam firmam pacem ne eis injuria vel contumelia fiat, neque disturbentur, super decem librarum forisfacturam.

" Testes *Nigellus de Albineo* et *Gaufridus* filius *Pagani*, et *Gaufridus de Clynton* apud *Woodstokam*.

Confirmatio regis Stephani *de libertatibus infra* Leucam.

" STephanus rex *Angliae* archiepiscopis episcopis, abbatibus, baronibus, vicecomitibus et " omnibus ministris suis fidelibus *Francis* et *Anglis* totius *Angliae* salutem. Praesentis " chartae testimonio confirm. ecclesiae S. *Wilfridi de Ripun* pacem suam infra leucam suam " et ejusdem pacis violatae emendationem sicut est ab aliquo praedecessorum meorum melius ipsi ecclesiae collata, et a me cum eisdem regibus confirmata. Privilegia quoque " et donationes quae a regibus *Edwardo* scilicet et avo meo *Willielmo* consecuta est; et libertates omnes et dignitates et consuetudines et rectitudines suas, tam in aquis quam in " terris, et in omnibus possessionibus suis in *Saca* et *Socca* et in his quae ad illam ubique " pertinent. Ferias etiam suas quinque diebus omnibus illuc venientibus et illinc redeuntibus, cum omnibus rebus suis cum mea pace concedo et volo et firmiter praecipio, quod " ipsa ecclesia ita teneat bene et in pace et honorifice in omnibus rebus in bosco et plano, " in pratis et pasturis in terris et aquis, in navibus et portubus, et in omnibus aliis rebus " sicut ipsa unquam melius et plenius et honorabilius tenuit tempore regis *Edwardi* et tempore *Willielmi* avi mei et tempore avunculorum meorum, *Willielmi* regis et *Henrici* regis, " et sicut chartae praedecessorum meorum testificantur.

" Testibus *Alexandro* episcopo *Lincolniensi*, et *Nigello* episcopo *Elensi*, et . . . . . . " episcopo *Eboracensi*, et *Adelpho* episcopo *Carliensi*, et *Roberto de Vere* apud *Eborum*.

So as this church of S. *Wilfrid* by the influence of those and other royal favours held up in a flourishing condition until the year of our Lord 1318, about which gloomy time in the unhappy reign of king *Edward* II. this town and collegiate church, that had escaped the miseries several other places had suffered during the barons wars, were forced to redeem themselves from plunder and destruction, by payment of a thousand marks in money to the invading *Scots*, who whilst the *English* were besieging *Berwick*, had by *Carlile* made an unexpected inroad into *Yorkshire*, harrassing those parts with fire and sword, returning the same way they came with so considerable a booty and so little opposition, as encouraged them to enter *England* the next year with a running army, spoiling the country where they came, and at *Ripon* making the like demand, which the impoverished inhabitants denying (being indeed unable to pay) the town and church were forthwith fired, and several of the people put to the sword, insomuch as for some years both of them in a manner remained desolate, until king *Edward* the third's reign, who in the pursuit of his just claim to the crown of *France*, and vindication of his honour, and subjects sufferings by the *Scot*, marched both ways with his victorious army, witness the battle at *Halydon* hills in *Scotland*, and *Poictiers* in *France*; and through his princely munificence, together with the care and charge of the archbishops, together with the liberal contribution of several worthy benefactors, whose names in the windows and other parts of the church are a memorial, the town was in a manner new built, and the *Minster* raised well nigh from the foundation, and the three steeples and spires erected with more beauty and magnificence than formerly. In which flourishing estate it stood undefaced even during all that sharp dispute about

5

about the crown, which for one hundred and forty years had continued betwixt the puiſſant and illuſtrious houſes of *Lancaſter* and *York*, yea until the thirty ſixth year of king *Henry* VIII. when ſo many monaſteries, colleges, hoſpitals, chanteries, and free chapels were thrown down by the boiſterous ſtorm that then happened, and by which deſolation (amongſt which that of *Fountains* in its neighbourhood) the revenues thereof were converted to temporal uſes, ſo as the collegiate church muſt needs tremble under ſo dreadful a tempeſt. Albeit at that time it was a pariſh church, having an incorporation therein of ſeven prebendaries, having ſix vicars inducted under them, which for their living had the tythes, oblations, and other profits apertaining to thoſe ſeven cures. Six of theſe prebendaries having ſix vicars inducted under them in that church called *Vicars choral*, which ſix vicars were bound to diſcharge the prebendaries of all cures and ſervice in the ſaid church; each of thoſe vicars having from thoſe prebendaries an annual ſtipend of ſix pound. The ſeventh prebendary is made of the parſonage of *Stainwich*, who is called the chanter of the ſaid church, and at *Stainwich* hath a vicar endowed under him to diſcharge him of all cures and ſervices in that church. The neceſſity was to maintain God's worſhip in the ſaid church, the keeping of hoſpitality, of ſix prebendaries, for the relief of the poor, two prebendaries being conſtantly reſident, the other five abſent.

There were alſo nine chantries founded in the ſaid churches by divers perſons, as by their particular foundations may appear. The incumbents being obliged to be perſonally preſent in the choir of the *Minſter* at all the ſervice, and as occaſion ſerved, to aſſiſt the vicars in adminiſtring the ſacraments to the pariſhioners, eſteemed in number nine thouſand, and were then named petty canons. The chantries were as followeth, *viz.*

1. The chantry of our lady in the *Minſter* or collegiate church.
2. The chantry of our lady in the manor of *Ripon*.
3. The chantry of *Holy Trinity*, beneath the choir in the *Minſter*.
4. The chantry of St. *Thomas the martyr*.
5. The chantry of St. *Andrew* in the *Minſter*.
6. The chantry of St. *Wilfrid* in the *Minſter*.
7. The chantry of St. *John the evangeliſt*, and St. *John the baptiſt* in the *Minſter*.
8. The chantry of St. *James* in the *Minſter*.
9. The chantry of the *Holy Trinity* above the choir in the *Minſter*.

The other chantries in the ſame pariſh of *Ripon* were, *viz.*

1. The chantry of the chapel of *Hutton Conyers*.
2. The chantry of the chapel of *Cletherom*.
3. The chantry of the two prieſts in the hoſpital of *Mary Magdalene*.
4. The chantry of the hoſpital of St. *John baptiſt*.

Belonging likewiſe to the ſaid collegiate church were three deacons, three ſubdeacons, ſix treblers, an organiſt and grammar ſchool-maſter. The three deacons had for their yearly ſtipend five pound ten ſhillings. The three ſubdeacons for their yearly ſalary four pound ten ſhillings. The ſix choriſters for their yearly ſtipend three pound eight ſhillings. The ſix treblers for their yearly ſtipend two pound twelve ſhillings and ſix pence. To the ſix choriſters for the liveries one pound four ſhillings. To the organ player fourteen ſhillings and four pence, and to the ſchool-maſter two pound. All which ſtipends be paid yearly forth of the common of the church.

In the ſaid church were alſo certain lands belonging as well for the maintenance of ſundry chantries therein, as certain yearly obits obſerved in memory of the donors of thoſe lands, and likewiſe for the reparations to be from time to time made in and upon the ſaid church, as alſo upon ſeveral tenements and cottages appertaining thereunto, which lands are called the common of the church.

And in further favour thereof, in the thirty ſixth year of the reign of king *Henry* VIII. a commiſſion iſſued under the great ſeal impowering the archbiſhop for the time being to diſpoſe of the government of the hoſpitals of St. *John baptiſt* and *Mary Magdalene* in and near the town of *Ripon*, as alſo of all and ſingular the prebends and canons of the ſaid collegiate church, as they ſhould from time to time become void, and to viſit and reform what ſhould be found amiſs, as by the tenor of ſuch part thereof as relates thereto, may appear as followeth,

" Sciatis etiam quod, cum archiepiſcopi *Eboracenſes*, in quorum provincia haec eccleſia " fundata et ſtabilita eſt, ſummi fautores et adjutores iſtius operis fuerunt et in poſterum " futuri ſunt, maxime in perpetua donatione et collatione in uſum praedictae eccleſiae ma- " giſterii ſive cuſtodis hoſpitalii *Mariae Magdalenae* ac magiſterii ſive cuſtodis hoſpitalii " S. *Joannis baptiſtae* in et juxta *Ripon* in praedicto comitatu *Eborum*, Nos pro nobis hae- " redibus et ſucceſſoribus noſtris, has eorum donationes et collationes factas et faciendas, " per noſtras has literas confirmamus et regia authoritate corroboramus; ac ratione publicae " eorundem archiepiſcoporum beneficentiae in hanc eccleſiam continuandae, nos pro no- " bis haeredibus et ſucceſſoribus noſtris ex gratia noſtra ſpeciali et ex certa ſcientia et me- " ro motu per praeſentes damus et concedimus archiepiſcopo *Eborum* et ſucceſſoribus ſuis, " advocationem, donationem, liberam diſpoſitionem et jus patronatus omnium et ſingulo- " rum praebendarum et canonicatuum ſive praebendarum in eadem eccleſia quos vacare con-

" tigerit

" tigerit; ad ejusmodi canonicatus, sive praebendarum aliquam illarum e tribus illis quae per " praedictum decanum et paternitati nominati seu commendati fuerint, conferre, eidemque " litteras collationis ad hoc sufficienter et jure validas facere sigillare et tradere, ut per- " sonam hujusmodi in canonicae sive praebendae illius possessionem facere et exequi, facien- " dum et exequendum: Habendum dictam advocationem, donationem, liberam dispositio- " nem et jus patronatus, et caetera praemissa eidem archiepiscopo per praesentes praeconcessa " eidem archiepiscopo et successoribus suis in perpetuum; Tenendum de nobis et haeredi- " bus nostris in pura et perpetua eleemosyna.

" Et sciatis ulterius, quod nos de meliore gubernatione et regimine ejusdem ecclesiae col- " legiatae de *Ripon*, de gratia nostra speciali ac ex certa scientia et mero motu nostro; vo- " lumus et concedimus quod idem archiepiscopus *Eborum* et successores sui pro tempore " existentes, visitatores ecclesiae collegiatae de *Ripon* praedicta exstiterint; eidemque archie- " piscopo et successoribus suis, licentiam, potestatem et authoritatem damus per praesentes, " quoties et quandocunque praedicto archiepiscopo vel successoribus suis viderit necessarium, " visitare reformare corrigere et emendare omnes et omnimodos errores, excessus, abu- " sus, delicta, negligentias et contemptus eorum decani et capituli aliorum in eadem eccle- " sia existentium, et omnia alia agere et exequi in et circa ecclesiam colleg. praedictam, " quae visitatores alicujus collegii in academia *Oxoniae* aut *Cantabrigiae* agere aut exequi va- " leant, aut de jure debeant, &c.

Enjoying not only that but all other its antient endowments and immunities until the reign of king *Edward* IV. in whose minority was that law enacted in parliament concerning chantries and colleges by force, whereof this church (with several other collegiate churches which at that time depended upon the archiepiscopal see of *York*) was dissolved, and in that sad condition lay gaping, until through the pious commiseration of king *James* of glorious memory, it got some respiration, such as with all due thankfulness it now holds and acknowledges, albeit much short of those primitive rights it formerly enjoyed.

This collegiate church of *Ripon* hath belonging to it,

					l.	*s.*	*d.*
A dean.				Four singing men, two assistants	60	00	00
A sub-dean.				Six choristers	40	00	00
Seven prebends	*Thorpe*, *Stainwick*, *Givendale*, *Nunwick*, *Sharrow*, *Studley*, *Munckton*,	*l.* 6 24		One organist	20	00	00
				One verger	05	00	00
				One clerk	05	00	00
				One auditor	05	00	00
				One register	05	00	00
				One library keeper	05	00	00
				Clock keeper	02	03	04
Two vicars choral		120 00 00		Keeper of the organs	02	00	00

Redditus ecclesiae.

Olim duo stipendiarii	40	00	00	*Decimae molendinorum*	03	00	00
Fines quadragesimales	20	00	00	*Pro fabrica ecclesiae redditus*	09	00	00
Decimae de Ripon	80	00	00	*Risaw* wood	20	00	00
Decimae Thesaurarii	40	00	00	Reduced prebends *post mortem*			
Redditus cantariorum	60	00	00	Prebends and free rents	198	13	02
Pately Brigs	20	00	00	*Aismonderby* rents	28	12	02
Decimae de Nyd	10	00	00	Communities	179	04	04
Decimae de Grantley	02	00	00	Several chantries	52	14	02
Mortuaria	04	00	00	Obits	10	08	08
Liberi redditus	03	00	00	Fabrick rents	19	00	00
Alii redditus	02	00	00				

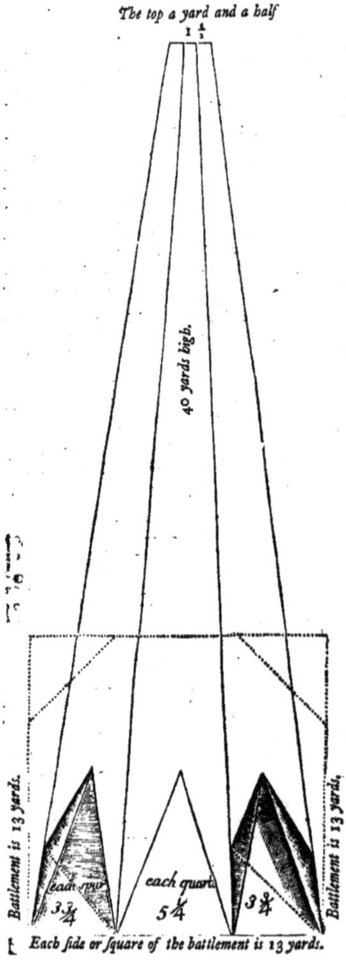

St. Wilfrid's *steeple.*

Height 40 yards.
The top 1 yard ½.
Eight squares, the base of each 5 yds. ¼.
Four spurs, the height 7 yards.
The base of the spur 4 yards.
Each square is 100 yards, in all 800.
Each spur is 9 yards, in all 36.
Four battlements, each containing 13 yards, in all 52.
So that all the lead upon St. *Wilfrid's* steeple is 888 yards square.
And every five yards square, containing 25 yards, will take a fother of lead, which at 8 *l.* a fother is 284 *l.* 3 *s.* 5 *d.*
To be abated out of the 244 for 4 yards ½ of the top which was wasted by fire— about
And for much lead wanting in some decayed places of the steeple about

The common seal antiently used by the chapter was the holy lamb standing upon a table, and holding a banner crusaded; the inscription *Sigillum* S. Wilfridi Riponensis *ecclesiae.* The reverse is *Sigillum capituli circumscribed.*

Thus far sir *Thomas Herbert*, who also writ the history of the three other churches, *York*, *Beverley* and *Southwell.*

OMIS-

OMISSIONS in the APPENDIX, &c.

IN the *Roman* account of the city, P. 57. of the book, the reader will find Dr. *Lister's* observations on the multangular tower at *York*. I have to add, that Dr. *Langwith* remarks that this manner of building with brick and stone was, originally, *African*; upon no less authority than that of *Vitruvius*. If so, in all probability it was brought hither by the emperor *Severus*, who was an *African* born. Dr. *Lister* in his journey to *Paris*, takes notice of this, see p. 55. where he describes the ruins of a *Roman* building of the same kind with the multangular tower at *York*.

P. 230. *Sect.* 3. In sir *T. W*'s manuscript history, which I have seen a copy, or the original, of in *London*, is the case betwixt *York* and *Hull* drawn up by himself; this I chuse to give in his own Words. It is the only thing that I can find omitted, of any consequence, in the city's copy at *York*.

York and Kingston upon Hull.

"THE relation betweene this citty and the towne of *Kingston* upon *Hull* in trade and "commerce hath occasioned this chapter: they are two sister townes in this respect, and yet differences (as some tyme betweene sisters) have heretofore fallen betweene them. "But I find they were all settled by an agreement made the 28*th* of *June ann. Dom.* 1578. "in the twentieth yeare of the late queene *Elizabeth*, by certeyne articles agreed upon be- "tween *Hugh Graves* then lord-major of the citty of *Yorke*, and the citizens of the said "city of the one party, and *John Thornton* major of *Kingston upon Hull*, and the burgesses "of the same of the other party, by the mediation and before the right honourable *Henry* "earle of *Huntington*, &c. lord president of the then queenes majesties counsell established "in the north parts for quietness, and a fynall end and order then after to be had be- "tween them.

"I forbeare the mention of the particular articles which are long, and they are not soe "fit for this discourse. They are concluded with this agreement, that if any doubt or "difference do arise upon any of the articles agreed upon, that the lord president then be- "ing, during his tyme shall expound and order the same, and after that, the said lord- "major of *Yorke*, for the tyme being, and the major of *Hull*, with the advice of their re- "corders, shall compound all doubts and differences arising between them the said par- "ties; and if they cannot agree, the said lord-major of the city of *Yorke* and the major "of *Kingston upon Hull* to make choice of some one person, or more, as they shall thinke "fit to order and determine the same. I wysh this peace and unity may long continue be- "teen them, for they are sisters as I have sayd before, and *Yorke* the elder sister.

"The towne of *Hull* being situate with more conveniency for foreigne trade,

"I hope it may not weary the reader nor offend the towne of *Hull*, if in few words I "tell you the story of *Hull*, even from the beginning. It is no disparagement to great- "ness to have been little, which is the case of *Hull*.

"But somewhat miserable for a place to be little that hath been great, which is the case "of the citty of *Yorke*.

"*Hull* if we may believe *John Leland* in his Itinerary, was but a mean fysher towne in "the dayes of king *Edward* III. and a member of the village of *Hasell*: the first groweth "of it was trading for fish into islands, from whence this towne had the trade of stocke "fysh. In the tyme of king *Richard* II. it waxed very rich, and *Michael de la Pole* mer- "chant of *Hull*, and prentice (as the same *Leland* reports, by what warrant I knowe not) "to one *Rotten Hearing* of that town, became in soe great favour with the former king, "*Edward* III. and the present king, that he was first (as sir *Roger Owen* in this parti- "cular reports) made chiefe baron of the exchequer, and afterwards lord treasurer of "*England*. This great man being then in high esteeme and honour, with his promises "procured many grants and priviledges from the kinge to this towne, (for what shall not "be done to the towne which the king's favourite did favour) and the towne hath since "that tyme continued in good repute, and is very considerable for trade at this day; *Le- "land* writes of *Heddon* an ancient port not far from *Hull*; that as *Hull* increases, so *Hed- "don* decreased. I wysh the like might not be applied to *Yorke*. I mention not these "things out of any disaffection to *Hull*: I really affect it and desire it may still grow "and flourish.

At *P.* 439. *Sect.* 3. of the book, the reader is promised a bull of pardon, from the then pope, for all the accomplices in the tryal and beheading of archbishop *Scrope*. This inſtrument was miſlaid from my papers, and before I could recover it again, the preſs had gone over that part of the work. For which reaſon it can only find a place here; but is of ſo ſingular a nature as muſt not be omitted; no hiſtorian, that I know of, having ſo much as hinted at this circumſtance, except *Godwin*, who has met with ſome traces of it by this expreſſion in his life of *Scrope*, "*Necis pontificiae authores papa excommunicavit, ſed ut brevi tempore abſolveret; facile exoratus eſt.*"

This put me upon inſpecting the inſtruments in the *Foedera Ang.* of theſe times to ſee if any notice was taken there of the excommunication or abſolution; but all is huſh and ſilent as to this matter. The traces that I could make out from thence are theſe,

First, I obſerve that the inſtrument for conſtituting a deputy for executing the office of conſtable and marſhal was dated at Biſhops-thorpe, *juxta Eborum*, *June* 6, 1405. two days before the archbiſhop and earl marſhal was beheaded; at which time *Henry* was endeavouring to make out ſome law proceſs againſt the prelate, to juſtify, in ſome meaſure, the intended execution of him. *Foed Aug. tom.* VIII. *p.* 399.

Next, it is ſomewhat ſtrange that *Henry*, in his notification of the vacancy of the archbiſhoprick, and of the chapter's electing of *Thomas Longley* their dean into the chair, ſhould make uſe of this expreſſion, *vacante nuper archiepiſcopatu* Ebor. *per mortem* bonae memoriae Richardi *ultimi archiep. loci illius*. This inſtrument was dated at the caſtle of Pountefreyt, *Aug.* 8. the ſame year. *Tom.* VIII. *p.* 407, 408.

In the inſtrument for conſtituting ſir *John Cheyne*, knt. and Mr. *Henry Chichly*, doctor of laws, the king's proctors or envoys, to the court of *Rome*, is this hint, *de et ſuper certis negotiis nos et ſtatum regni noſtri* intime concernentibus. This inſtrument was dated at the caſtle of *Hertford July* 18, 1405. (*a*) by which it appears that *Henry* was ſomewhat afraid of the thunder from the *Vatican*, and theſe legates were ſent in all haſte in order to divert the blow. *Innocent* VII. was then pope, and, notwithſtanding this precaution of *Henry*'s, no doubt iſſued out ſome ſevere decrees againſt him, but of theſe no notice is taken at all in the *Foedera*. *Innocent* VII. died *anno* 1406, and *Gregory* XII. ſucceeding, I find that *Henry* again ſent the ſame ambaſſadors to *Rome*, by an inſtrument of the ſame tenour with the former, but dated at *Weſtminſter*, *Auguſt* 18, 1407. The bull of pardon bears date *April* 12, 1408, ſo that it was ſome time before *Henry*'s envoys, by the perſuaſive arguments of princes, could bring matters to bear in that court. It ſeems *Gregory*'s reign proved milder than his predeceſſors; and he not only conſented to the filling up the ſee, which had been vacant above two years and a half, by *Bowett*, but iſſued out, alſo, this pardon. It is true, that neither the king nor any one elſe is mentioned by name in the bull; but Cujuscunque Status was certainly inſerted to include within the pardon *Henry* as well as the reſt. Gratis, in a natural ſenſe, is a word of great mildneſs and lenity; but whether the court of *Rome* did ever grant ſuch favours to monarchs, on ſuch terms, I leave to the reader's judgment. There is another inſtrument in the *Foedera* of the reſtitution of the temporalities to *Bowet*, in which the excommunication is plainly hinted at; and by which it appears that *Bowet*, whilſt biſhop of *Bath* and *Wells*, had publiſhed ſome of the pope's decrees againſt *Henry*, which he in this inſtrument diſclaims. The tenour of it is this, *Rex*, &c.——— *nos pro eo quod idem archiepiſcopus omnibus et ſingulis verbis nobis et coronae noſtrae praejudicialibus in litteris bullatis ipſius domini ſummi pontificis (ſibi inde ut dicitur confectis) contentis, coram nobis palam et expreſſe renunciavit, et gratiae noſtrae humiliter ſe ſubmiſit, volentes cum eo in hac parte agere gratioſe,*—*cepimus fidelitatem ipſius archiepiſ.* &c. *Dat. apud* Gloucest. i. *die* Decemb. 1407. *Foed. Ang. tom.* VIII. *p.* 503. 504.

Theſe are all the hints that I can meet with amongſt the publick acts of thoſe times, relating to this affair; which no doubt was induſtriouſly kept ſecret then, and all traces of ſuch a ſcandalous excommunication kept out of the publick records. Thus much I thought fit to premiſe before I gave the inſtrument; which might ſtill have lain in oblivion, had not my brother the reverend Dr. *Drake* met with it in a ſearch he was then making into the regiſters at *York*, towards compleating his deſign of publiſhing his fine edition of *Matthew Parker de antiquitate eccleſiae Anglicanae.*—I take notice that in a ſearch for this inſtrument it could not poſſibly have been found; for it is ſtrangely miſplaced, having got into *Alexander Nevyl*'s regiſter, *Scrope*'s predeceſſor, amongſt ſome other acts out of courſe; when one would certainly have looked for it in the regiſter of his ſucceſſor *Bowett*.

Bulla papalis, pro pardonatione malefactorum in decapitatione Richardi Scrope *archiepiſcopi* Ebor. Regiſt. *Alex. Nevyl.* pars ſecunda p. 30.

"GREGORIUS epiſcopus, ſervus ſervorum Dei, venerabilibus fratribus *Thomae Du-* "*nelm.* et *Philippo Lincoln.* epiſ. ſalutem et apoſt. bened. *Romanus* pontifex beati *Petri* "coeleſtis regni clavigeri ſucceſſor, collatis ſibi coelitus ſolvendi atque ligandi clavibus ex "injuncti officii debito ſalutem quaerens ſingulorum, perinde diſponit, ut collapſis ad

(*a*) *Foed. Ang. tom.* VIII. *p.* 446.

"gremium

gremium ecclesiae cum humilitate redeuntibus ipsam clementia aperiat januam pietatis. Cum itaque, sicut accepimus, dudum suadente humani generis hoste in regno *Angliae* diversa intestina bella seditiones et proditiones contra charissimum in Christo filium nostrum *Henricum* regem *Angliae* illustrem, praeter ipsius regis culpam, per quosdam subditos ejusdem suscitata fuissent; ac etiam *Ricardus* quondam archiep. *Ebor.* quem ipse rex speciali honore et reverentia prosequebatur, et de quo nullam suspicionem prorsus habebat, quod contra se aut statum suum aliquid sinistrum machinari aut attemptare vellet, contra praefatum regem ejusque status et honoris enervationem concepisset, ac nonnullos potentes et proceres dicti regni, ac etiam alios inferioris status; necnon viros ecclesiasticos saeculares ac regulares sibi attraxisset; et tandem illa quae conceperat satagens ad effectum perducere, ipse archiep. armatus et stipatus potentia saeculari, cum octo millibus armatorum, vel circa, ad campum progrediens una cum suis complicibus conatus fuit, quantum potuit, ad exterminium dicti regis effectualiter devenire. Quae quantum a quibusdam aliis nobilibus dicti regni, necnon etiam inferioris conditionis fidelibus dicti regis, cognita fuissent, ipsi fideliter et constanter in ejusdem regis auxilium et regni praefati liberationem, ipso rege tamen tunc absente ET HOC IGNORANTE, similiter armati contra praefatum archiep. ejusque complices processerunt, perpetratoque hinc inde proelio cum archiepiscopus et complices sui in campo superati fuissent, ipse archiepiscopus et aliqui secum in ipso campo per hujusmodi victores capti subito ad praesentiam dicti regis adducti fuerunt, clamantibus ipsis victoribus et supervenientibus populis in multitudine copiosa, quod rex praefatus juxta leges et consuetudines dicti regni, quae dictant quod seditiosi et proditores morte moriantur; et quae leges jurisjurandi religione ejusdem regis, dum ad culmen regni assumeretur, vallatae fuerunt, de hujusmodi captivis justitiam faceret ministrari: alioquin, si super tantis proditionibus regni sui justitiam facere negligeret, ipsum regem solum in manibus aliorum, inimicorum suorum, qui hujusmodi novitatis conscii non longe ab ipso manu armata distabant, in campo dimitterent, et ipsum et se de praefato archiepiscopo vindicarent. Quibus clamoribus continuè accrescentibus ipse rex timens verisimiliter, quod, si hujusmodi rumoribus et importunis tam numerosae multitudinis instantiis qualitercunque resisteret, personam suam et regnum in grandi periculo poneret; et quod populo procedente ad vindictam multa ac varia pericula sequi possent, et quod absque delectu personarum talia judicia de cetero in casibus similibus per ipsam multitudinem usurparentur; ad evitandum majus scandalum, pro sui ac regni praefati liberatione, permisit, quod hujusmodi captivi juxta easdem leges et consuetudines judicari deberent. Propter quod etiam deventum fuit ad hoc, quod idem archiepiscopus et aliqui secum capti ex supradictis causis judicium capitale subirent; quod proculdubio gravis et improbandi exempli fuisse constat; cum, licet archiepiscopus praefatus deliquerit, correctio et punitio tamen secundum canonica instituta ecclesiastico judici fuerit relinquenda: cum tamen, ut audivimus, multi de hiis, qui in eadem multitudine praesentes fuerunt, de captivitate dicti archiepiscopi et morte subsecuta, doleant ab intimis: NOS attendentes, quod ecclesia gremium se recognoscere volentibus nunquam claudere consuevit, et simul considerantes, quod ista pro evitando majori periculo regni ac personarum fuerant perpetrata; et volentes, pro salute ipsius regni et fidelium quiete, rigorem justitiae temperare, fraternitati vestrae, de qua in hiis et aliis specialem in Domino fiduciam obtinemus, per apostolica scripta commisimus et mandamus, quatenus omnes et singulas personas, quae in praemissis praesentes fuerint, et ad hoc faciendum opem vel operam qualitercunque, verbo aut nutu, consilio vel facto, dederint, et in illis culpabiles se recognoscant, CUJUSCUNQUE STATUS, praeeminentiae, dignitatis, aut conditionis existant, si hoc humiliter a vobis petierint, ab excommunicationis et aliis censuris et poenis, quas propter praemissa qualitercunque incurrerint, autoritate nostra absolvere in forma ecclesiae consueta, injunctis eorum singulis pro modo culpae poena salutari, et aliis quae de jure fuerint injungenda; et nihilominus interdictum ecclesiasticum, quod propterea a jure vel ab homine in civitatibus, castris, villis, terris et locis extitit promulgatum, eadem autoritate tollere et relaxare; necnon omnes et singulos processus de mandato sanctissimi *Innocentii* papae VII. praedecessoris nostri factos contra ipsos qui circa praemissa quomodolibet excesserunt, ac omnia exinde vel ob id secuta, quae omnia haberi volumus pro sufficient. dep. abolere curetis. Nos enim vobis absolvendi personas praefatas et interdictum, quod propterea promulgatum fuerit, tollendi et relaxandi .... processus hujus ac omnia inde secuta abolend. ac omnia et singula, quae in praemissis quomodolibet opportuna fuerint et expedire conspexeritis, faciendi plenam et liberam autoritate apostolica tenore praesentium concedimus facultatem: Ita tamen, quod hujusmodi facultas vobis concessa ad absolutionem clericorum nullatenus se extendat. Volumus autem, quod postquam personaliter ad invicem convenientes super hac materia, quae agenda sunt, disposueritis, alter alteri vestrum executionem committere possit; quodque si, quod absit, aliquis vestrum ante conventionem et dispositionem hujus ex hac vita migrare contigerit, ille, qui superstes fuerit, alium praelatum laudabilis vitae sibi collegam eligere debeat; super cujus electione ejusdem superstitis conscientiam oneramus:

" quibus ad invicem convenientibus post dispositionem hujus, alter alteri, eodem modo, ut " supradictum est, valeat in hujus materiae processu executioni mandare.

" Dat. (b) *Lucae*, 2 id. *Apr.* (c) pontificatus nostri anno secundo.

" Gratis, de mandato dom. nostr. papae.

The next thing I shall give is an omission in the *appendix* of an insertion which should have followed the list of the subscribers to the new *assembly-rooms*, but by accident was mislaid. I give it now, and ask pardon of the worthy gentleman, who occasioned the paragraph, for it. An abstract, also, of a letter from Dr. *Langwith*, which came too late to be inserted in its right place, containing his thoughts on the *Roman* lamp as I take it, mentioned p. xiii. of this *appendix*, and referred to in the additional plate of *Roman* curiosities at N°. 16, 17.

At a grand meeting of the subscribers to these rooms, in *August* 1732, a motion was made that thanks ought to be given to the earl of *Burlington*, for his noble plan and great care in the execution of and contribution to it; sir *Thomas Robinson*, of *Rockby-park*, in the north riding of this county, bart. then in the chair, was deputed for that purpose. Lord *Burlington*, being at that time in *York*, at the *races*, sir *Thomas* waited upon his lordship, attended by several other gentlemen subscribers, and gave his lordship the sincere thanks of the society, in a speech suitable to the occasion.

" *Good Sir*,

" I Have been a little tardy in my answer to your last, as not thinking that any thing " I should say would come soon enough for the press: for the same reason I shall now " be very short, only giving you my opinion in general, instead of troubling you with a " long detail of reasonings about it. As to the *Roman* lamp, 1. I think that neither the " dress, nor the proportion, will allow us to think it *Roman*, and if it be not *Roman*, I don't " know what it should be but *British*, considering where it was found. I believe you will " be inclined to favour this conjecture if you please to cast your eye upon *La religion des* " *Gaulois*, where you will find several figures whose habits and proportions resemble these, " and yet were unquestionably druidical. 2. I cannot take it to have been a lamp, be- " cause the make of it seems to be by no means proper for that purpose: in particular, I " cannot see why the hole in the head should be made so much too large for any wick. " You will ask me then what I take it to be? In answer to this I shall say, that I take it " to have been either barely a vessel to burn incense in, in which case a large hole was ne- " cessary for putting in the fire: or perhaps it had a still higher use, and was one of the " *British Lares* made in imitation of those of *Egypt*.

" For that the old *Celtae* borrowed many of their customs from the *Egyptians*, or at " least had them in common with them, I think is pretty certain, and it is equally cer- " tain, that the *Egyptians* used to make holes in the heads of their gods in order to burn " incense in them; and thus, as Dr. *Lister* has it, made their heads serve for perfuming " pots for themselves. See *Lister*'s journey to *Paris* p. 44.

" *Licetus* and *Monfaucon* may, for ought I know, have been deceived in taking such " vessels for lamps.

In *P.* 125, in the beginning of chapter V. mention is made of a descent from *Ireland*, headed by the earl of *Lincoln* and lord *Lovel*, in support of *Lambert Symnel*, whom they caused to be proclaimed by the style of king *Edward* VI. against *Henry* VII. A copy of the letter sent by this sham monarch to the city of *York*, soon after his landing, has been very lately sent to me; which, with the Resolutions of the magistracy upon it, at this juncture, were entered in one of their registers, and is as follows.

Copy of a letter directed to the mayor, &c. *from the lords of* Lincoln, Lovel, *et al. late landed in* Froneys, *in the name of their king, calling himself* king Edward the sixth. Will. Todd *mayor* 2 Hen. VII.

" TO our trusty and well beloved the mayor, his brethren and commonalty of our city " of *York*; trusty and well beloved, we greet you well. And for so much as we " been comen within this our realme, not only by God's grace to attain our Right of the " same, but also for the reliefe and weal of our said realm; you and all other our true " subjects, which hath been gretely injured and oppressed in default of nowne ministration " of good rules and justice, desire therefore, and in our right herty wise pray you, that in " this behalfe ye woll shew unto us your good aides and favours; and where we and such " power as we have brought with us by meane of travayle of the see, and upon the land, " beene gretely weryed and laboured, it woll like you, that we may have reliefe, and ease " of logeing and vitaills within our citie there, and soe to depart, and truly pay for that as

(b) *Lucca*.

(c) *Ap.* 12, 1408.

" we

"we shall take; and in your so doing, ye shall doe thing unto us of right acceptable plea-
"sure; and for the same find us your good and soveraign lord at all times hereafter, and
"of your dispositions herein to ascertain us by this bringer.

"Yeven undre our signet at *Masham* the viii day of *June*.

"The which Letter was immediately sent to the earl of *Northumberland* for to see. And "a copy of the same was sent to sir *Richard Tunstall*, and another delivered to master *Payne* "to shew it to the king's grace. And further what the mayor, aldermen, sheriffs and "common counsel of the city of *York*, assembled in the counsel chamber within the *Guild-hall*, departed from the counsel, and commanded and was agreed, that every warden "should be in harness and raise his ward, and keep due watch, that no person should have "entry into the said city, but such as be true leige-men unto our soveraign lord the king, "*Henry* the seventh. And the said mayor incontinently, by the advice of his brethren, "aldermen, sheriffs and common-council aforesaid, sent in message unto the said lords of "*Lincoln* and *Lovel*, three of the chamberlains, giving them in commandment to shew un-"to the said lords, that my lord the mayor, my masters his brethren, aldermen, the she-"riffs, common-council, with the whole commonality of the city of *York* be finally deter-"mined, that he, whom the said lords called their king, they, nor none of their retinue "or company intending to approach this city, should have any entry into the same, but "to withstand them with their bodies and goods, if they would atteyne so to do."

This lord *Lovel* had some affinity to the city of *York*, having an estate in the liberties of it. Of which, relating to his manor-house at *Dring-houses*, and the right of common of pasture belonging to it, in *Knaesmire*, are the following entries in the city's registers.

(*d*) "Lord *Lovel*, chamberlain to the king, claimed to have, by reason of his chief "place in Dringhouses, common of pasture for twenty kine and a bull in the pasture of "Knaysmyr, of the which common the said lord and his ancestors have been possessed and "seized, as he said, without the time of mind. And it being proved, that the said lord "*Lovel*'s tenants of his chief place in Dringhouses had the said common, till of late in the "time of *Richard Carbett* his tenant, who was indicted for misusing the said pasture; it was "agreed, that it should be this day answered unto the council of my said lord *Lovel*, that "my said lord-mayor and his brethren will not be against the right of my said lord *Lo-vel*, but will be agreeable, that he shall have his right, so as no other of Dringhouses "have common in the said pasture, but only the tenant of my said lord *Lovel* of his chief "place, there to the number of twenty kine and a bull; so that the said tenant take no "other mens beasts to assist, but occupy the common with his own proper beasts. And "that his beasts have a mark, that they may be known from others.

(*e*) "Lord *Lovel* came personally and claimed as above; and *Miles Metcalf* the recorder, "in the name of the city, answered, *that neither the said lord, nor any of his tenants of right* "*had nor ought to have pasture there, except the citizens of the city of* York; whereupon the "said lord *Lovel* prayed time that he by his counsel might search his evidences.

An explanation of the plate of ANCIENT SEALS, *&c.*

N°. I. Is a representation of the seal and counterseal of *Roger* archbishop of *York*, so consecrated *anno* 1154. This seal is mentioned p. 422. of the book; and explained, p. xii. of the *appendix*. What is further proper to say of it here, is, that the impression on red wax, from whence this was drawn, is appendant to a deed, without date, from the said archbishop to the abbot of *Furnese*, *com. Lanc.* of certain lands; and is in the duchy of *Lancaster*'s office; box 35.

II. The seal and counterseal of *Walter Grey*, archbishop of *York*, appendant to a deed, without date, in the said office, from *Robert de Lascy*, constable of *Chester* to the said *Walter Grey* of the town of *Upton*, *com. Ebor.* &c. The reading, *sigillum* Walteri Eboracensis *archiepiscopi*; the reverse, the heads of St. *Peter* and St. *Paul*, *Orate pro nobis sancti Dei apostoli*; box 10.

III. An impression of another seal of the said archbishop, appendant to his charter constituting the vicars choral of the cathedral church of *York*, a body corporate; mentioned p. 572. of the book, and given at length p. lxxiii. of the *appendix*. The reverse, by the fineness of what is visible on it seems to have been made by an antique gem, and is part of a bull. Circumscription, *Sigillum* Walteri *archiepiscopi* Eborac. Amongst the records, at present, in the custody of *Vicars-choral* of *York*.

IV. Is a very fine seal appendant to a writing of *Walter Giffard*, archbishop of this province, in the nature of a letter of attorney, constituting and ordaining *John de Nevill*, constable of the *tower* of *London*, and others therein named, his proctors or receivers of a sum of money, XL *l. sterling*, to be paid him by *Peter de Malo Lacu apud novum templum London*, &c. Dated *London*, 3[d] of the ides of *April*, in the year of grace 1272.

(*d*) 15 *Sept.* 1 *Ric.* III. *John Newton* mayor. (*e*) 14 *Aug.* 19 *Ed.* IV. *William Wellis* mayor.

The

The inscription almost obliterated. This antient deed and seal was given to me; and I presented it to the society of antiquaries *London*.

V. Represents an impression from the *matrix* of a seal now, or lately, in the possession of Mr. *Taylor*, innholder in *Durham*, a collector of antiquities, of *Robert Holgate* archbishop of *York*, so constituted *anno* 1544. This seal is hinted at p. 543. of this book; and was probably used, only, in the *barony* of *Hexam*, then a temporal *barony* appertaining to the see of *York*. The seal is the pall, the ancient bearing of this see, impaled with his own arms: circumscribed, *Sigillum* Roberti Eboracensis *archiepiscopi* Angliae *primatis, et domini de* Hextildelham. Reverse is the same inscription though somewhat differently put in. This impression was likewise given to the antiquarian society by the author of this work.

VI. Is an ancient seal made use of by the chapter of *York*, which was in the possession of Mr. *Thoresby* of *Leeds*, *anno* 1719; and engraven by the society of antiquaries; from whose print this was taken. The circumscription, *Sigillum* capituli *ecclesiae beati* Petri Eborac. *ad causas et negotia*.

VII. An antient and very rude seal, belonging to the abbey of St. *Mary*'s in *York*. In all probability this seal was as old as the abbey, or as the use of seals; and continued to be their common seal to the dissolution. The deed to which this is appendant is dated 18 of *Edward* IV. [*anno* 1478.] and is of an uncommon length for one of that age. The instrument recites an agreement made betwixt *Thomas* [*Bothe*] the abbot and convent of St. *Mary*'s, *York*, and *Thomas*, cardinal, archbishop of *Canterbury*, *Richard*, bishop of *Salisbury* and several other bishops, lords, knights, &c. there named, about the manor of *Whitgift*, and certain lands and tenements in *Rednes*, *Hook*, *Swinfleet*, &c. A counter part to this deed I have seen in the duchy office; but this falling into my hands by chance, I gave it, as above, to the collection of the society. The inscription is illegible, and must have been worn out of the *matrix* before this impression was made. The counter seal is stamped in four different places on the back of it; I apprehend it to be a gem; but it is so faint that I can make nothing of it, nor of its circumscription.

VIII. The arms of the abbey of St. *Mary* in *York*, from an ancient folio velum book of arms in the herald's office. This is different from what bishop *Tanner* has given us in his *Notitia Mon.* The king, in the center, I suppose was given to denote the royal foundation of this abbey.

IX. A draught, exactly taken from a rude drawing in a manuscript book in the *Bodleyan* library; to shew the excellence of the draughts-men of that age. See a description of the book p. 627. The inscription, as far as I can read it, is this, *De installatione et electione et prim. domini* Symonis *abbatis monasterii beatae* Marie Ebor. Over the church *ecclesia nova*; probably a coarse representation of the church this abbot *Simon* built in the monastery.

P. 332, &c. X. The broken remains of the ancient seal of the famous hospital of St. *Peter*, after of St. *Leonard*, in *York*. This is appendant to a deed amongst the records of the city on *Ouse-bridge*, as are the eleven following impressions to N°. XXI. but they did not send me up to what deeds these seals are fixed, or the purport of them. I could not meet with any other, or better, impressions of these seals in the *Augmentation office*, nor the other offices where I might have expected to have found them.

P. 263. XI. The seal of the priory of the *Holy Trinity* in *York*; the inscription partly illegible, but the deed styles him *Prior domus sive prioratus sanctae* Trinitatis Ebor. *ordinis sancti* Benedicti, *et ejusdem loci conventus*.

P. 284. XII, XIII. Two seals, antiently belonging to the monastery of St. *Augustine* in *York*. The titles are, *Sigillum commune conventus fratrum* Heremitarum *in civitate* Ebor. *et sigillum patris sui provincialis*.

XIV. Another seal belonging to the prior of the same monastery; the title of the deed stiles him, *Prior fratrum* Heremitarum *ordinis sancti* Augustini *in civitate* Ebor.

P. 309. XV. The seal of the monastery of the friars *Carmelites* in *York*. The deed has it, *Prior et conventus fratrum ordinis beatae* Mariae *de monte* Carmeli *in civitate* Ebor.

P. 282. XVI. The seal of the monastery of the *Fryars-minors* in *York*. The reading, *Sigillum gardiani* Fratrum-minorum Eboraci.

P. 274. XVII. The seal of the monastery of the *Fryars-preachers* in *York*. The title in the deed, *Prior et conventus ordinis* Fratrum-predicatorum *de* **Kingis Toftis** *in civitate* Ebor. There are two of these, one of them was the priors, and the lesser the common seal of the convent.

XVIII. The seal of the father provincial of this monastery. His title in the deed is, *Prior provincialis* Fratrum-predicatorum *in* Anglia.

P. 246. XIX. The seal of the hospital of St. *Thomas York*. The title in *English*. The seal of **the hospital of St. Thomas without Mikellith-barr in the suburbs of the citee of Yorke.**

P. 301. XX. The antient seal of the hospital of the *Holy Trinity*, belonging to the company of merchant adventurers in *York*. The title from the deed, *Commune sigillum hospitalis sanctae* Trinitatis *in* **Fosse-gate** *in civitate* Ebor.

XXI.

See p. 246.

P. 247.

P. 213.

ci

V.

V:

V:

V

I)

P. 332, &c. X

P. 263. X

P. 284. X

X

P. 309. X

P. 282. X

P. 274. X

X

P. 246. X

P. 301. X

XXI. The common seal of the Gild of *Corpus Christi* in *York* bears this inscription, *Sigillum* *fraternitatis* Corporis Christi *in* Eboraco *fundat.* See p. 246.

XXII. Is an antient seal which did belong to the nunnery of St. *Clement* in the suburbs of *York*. This seal is appendant to a grant in the *Ducby-office*, from the prioress and convent of it, of some lands, &c. in *Horton* in *Riblesdale*. Dated in their chapter-house *anno regn. reg.* Ed. III. 30. [1356.] Circumscription, *Sigillum conventus sancti* Clementis *papae in* Eboraco. P. 247.

XXIII. This very curious and very antient seal is appendant to a deed, as curious, which the reader may find printed at length p. 313. It was the city's seal; and if I may be allowed to guess at the time, by the fineness of the hand writing, it is above six hundred years since this seal was put to the deed. The first side which is put last in the plate, is a bad representation of the ancient cathedral church of *York*. It is not unlike the old seal the city uses at present, as may be seen by a preceding plate, where all their seals are engraven. See p. 381. But my drawer has made sad work with the inscription, and I was not able to get it rectified without a journey to *York* on purpose. The instruments being amongst the city records, from which I took the copy myself; but had a draught of the seal sent me since from thence. P. 213.

XXIV, XXV. Are the seals of the church of *Ripon* and the town of *Beverley*; but whether they are used in either place now I know not. The latter of them is in metal, and has been gilt; it has a hole for its appendance to some grant from the township. The figure represents St. *John* of *Beverley* sitting on the chair, or Freed-stole; with a *Bever* at his feet, from which animal the town is supposed to have taken its name. This seal seems to be of no older date than archbishop *Savage*'s time; because, as I take it, it is that prelate's arms which are impaled with the old arms of the see of *York* in one of the sheilds. The circumscription, *Sigillum communitatis burgensium* Beverlaci. The other, *Sigillum sancti* Wilfridi Riponensis *ecclesiae*. What the KOLAMVRE on the counterseal means I am ignorant of. This is from a drawing which came into my hands with the copy of sir *Thomas Herbert*'s short account of this church communicated to me by Mr. *Samuel Gale*. The *Beverley* seal was given me by a collector of coins who met with it by chance, and I have since presented it, with other impressions of antient seals, to the antiquarian society.

XXVI. An inscription round the outer verge of a large and massy gold ring. This ring was found about two years ago on *Bramham-moor*, or near it; but where I cannot justly learn for fear of a resumption by way of treasure-trove. It is quite plain with square edges; the letters are cut, raised, and the interstices filled up with lead, or a kind of enamel, which makes it smooth and even. The inscription is certainly *Runic*, but to all the *Connoisseurs* in those old and obsolete characters, who have seen it hitherto, unintelligible. The reverend Mr. *Serenius*, a *Swedish* minister, and well skilled in the northern languages, took great pains to come at an explanation of this mistick ring. But in vain, being not able to make out any thing more than one word of the inscription; which he reads GLASTA-PONTO. This makes the learned divine conjecture, that it had some reference to the abbey of *Glastenbury*; and might have been the wedding ring of some abbot to that monastery; or, on his translation from thence, to the church of *York*. Upon looking backward into the account of our prelates, I can find none of them that came from *Glastenbury*; nor upon search into the catalogue of abbots there can I find any of them who were *Danes*, or sent as missionaries into *Norway*. No doubt, but this ring must have been transported hither by some *Dane* or *Norwegian*; the characters it bears giving proof of the now, almost, lost language of those antient northern nations. This is all the interpretation I can learn, or all the conjecture I can make relating to this very antient curiosity; which is, at present, in the hands of Mr. *T. Gill* of *York*, who just preserved it from the crucible, and weighs, within a trifle, five guineas, or one ounce six penny weights.

An account of the Saxon *and* Danish *coins struck at* York, *with some account, also, of the money minted from the* Norman *conquest, to the last mint erected in that city.*

IN the second chapter of this work I have hinted the great probability, that the *Romans*, when their emperors were resident at *Eboracum*, had a mint attending them; as well as the *propraetors* in their absence. But, as this was only a supposition, and since no diagnosticks on their coin do evidence the truth of it, except the coin which *Goltzius* and *Camden* ascribe to the sixth legion at *York*, I shall not discuss that point any further. Nor shall I waste any time in an enquiry after *British* coins struck here, either after the *Romans* left the island, or before it. Especially, when we are informed by their natural historian, *Gildas*, that the *Britons* had none of their own; but that all the gold, silver, and brass coins, which they had, were stamped with the image of *Caesar*.

x Page 61.

But, under the *Saxon* government in *Britain*, we have undoubted testimony of a mint at *York*; both, in their *heptarchical* division of this kingdom, and under their *universal* monarchy. Nor were the *Danish* kings amongst us so long, without leaving us several such evidences as the former. In the *Heptarchy*, though I have great reason to ascribe every coin the *Northumbrian* kings struck to be done at *York*; yet I have been so cautious as to take and engrave none, but what have the name of the city evidently upon them.

The first which I think proper to mention, though it stands at N°. 29. in the plate, is the coin of *Edwin* the great. This curious piece is represented in sir *Andrew Fountain*'s tables at the end of Dr. *Hickes*'s *Thesaurus linguarum*, &c. TAB. VIII. and in the last edition of *Camden*, TAB. IV. N°. 38. It is an *unic* of very great rarity and worth; being the antientest coin of the *Saxon* money, known to the *Connoisseurs* in this way. It is probable this coin was struck at *York* after *Edwin* became universal monarch; the inscription EDƿIN REX A. or *Edwin rex Anglorum*, implying no less. *Bede* informing us, that he was the first *Saxon* monarch who stiled himself king of *English-men*. On the reverse of this very fair coin is read SEEVEL ON. EOFERwic, or *Seevel*, [the mint-master] at *York*. I shall not follow my countryman, honest Mr. *Thoresby*'s notion, in ascribing the great antiquity of the name and family of *Savile* in *Yorkshire*, to this mint-master; that antient family needing no such strained efforts to denote its antiquity. I shall only take notice, how early the *Saxons* began to corrupt the *Roman* name EBORACUM, and barbarize it into their own dialect. This name however stuck to the city, with little variation quite thorough the *Saxon* government in this island. But to begin with the plate.

N. B. That these coins are all taken from sir *Andrew Fountain*'s tables; except a few from the curious collection of the gentleman who does me the honour to give the plate.

FIG. 1. ÆÐELRED REX ANGLOrum; on the reverse, STEORGER MOneta, vel MOnetarius, de EOFeRwic. York. TAB. I. i. 3.

2. ÆÐELRED REX ANGLOrum; on the reverse, ODA MOneta, vel MOnetarius, de EOFeRƿIC, York. *Eadem tab.* N°. 19, 20.

3. Another reverse of the same king's coin, ƿINT----ED MOneta, vel MOnetarius, de EOFerwic, York. *Eadem* N°. 21.

4. Another reverse to the same, SYMERLEÐI MOneta, vel MOnetarius, de EOferwic, York. *Ead.* N°. 28.

The first coin is put down for *Ethered*, or *Ethelred*, the third son of *Ethelwulph*; and the latter were struck for *Ethelred*, the son of *Eadgar*. They were both universal monarchs; and reigned, one of them about the year 866, and the other began his long reign *anno* 978. From whom prince *Edgar Atheling* was descended.

5. EÐELSTAN REX; reverse, ROTBERT MOneta, vel MOnetarius, de EOFerwic, York. TAB. XI. N°. 9.

6. EÐelSTAN REX; reverse, ABERTEE MOneta, vel MOnetarius, de EOferwic, York. *Ead.* N°. 11.

The reverse of this coin was omitted, through mistake, and was obliged to be put in the last of all.

These two coins were struck for *Athelstan the great*, the son of *Edward the Elder*, who began his reign in the year 925. An universal king.

7. ÆÐELSTAN REX; reverse, ƿVLSIG, the name of some nobleman, or the mint-master. *Ead.* N°. 12.

8. REGNALD MOnetarius. *Ead.* N°. 13.

In this reverse about the building is read EBORACA, from whence it appears to be struck at York. And very probably, adds the *Tabulist*, these two coins were designed to represent the cathedral church there; as well as the artists of that age could express it.

9. EÐELSTANREX TOtius BRITanniae; on the reverse, REGNALD MOneta, vel MOnetarius, de EFORƿIC, York.

This coin is also ascribed to the same monarch as the former; and is singular on account of the *totius* BRITANNIAE on the head side. Our country-man Mr. *Thoresby* has the honour to be the first who hit on that reading; having been plainly mistook before by Mr. *Obadiah Walker*, and others. *Athelstan*, says our (*d*) antiquary, was the first *Saxon* monarch who assumed that title, as *Simeon* of *Durham* hints, Athelstan *primusque regum* TOTIUS BRITANNIAE *adeptus est imperium* (*e*). This coin was taken from one in the collection of *James West*, esq; *Class.* 2. 2. 4.

10. The same reading as the former, both round the head and reverse, but is struck from a different die, as may easily be observed. *Eforwic* for *Eoferwic* is also the same in both coins.

(*d*) Ducat. Leod. 345. (*e*) Inter x scriptores, p. 14.

Saxon *and* Danish *Coins struck at* York.

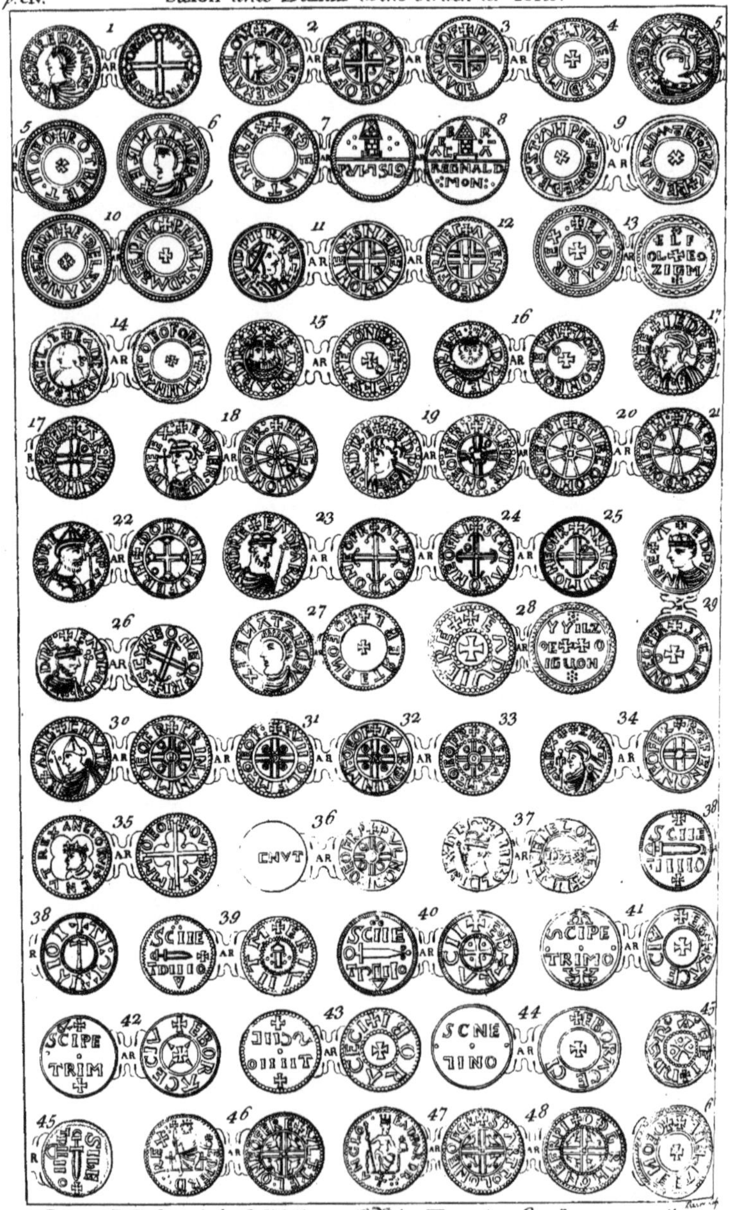

James West *of the* Middle-Temple *Esq.r a great collector of Antiquities, and encourager of Antiquarian Studys, contributes this plate. 1736.*

11. EADPARD REX; reverse, SNEBENRI ON, de EOforwic, York.

12. ALEN ON, de, EOFeRPIEC, York. TAB. VII. N°. 35, 36.
These were the coins of *Edward the confessor*.

13. EADGAR REX; reverse, ÆLFSIG Monetarius, OL. EO.
This coin is allowed by the *Tabulist* to have been struck at York; and was designed for *Edgar*, the brother of *Edwy*, who began his reign *anno* 957. TAB. V. N°. 5. 12.

14. EADGAR REX ANGLOR; reverse, PANNON ON EOFORPIC, York.
Another coin of the same king in the collection of *James West*, esq; *Class.* 2. 5. 3.

15. EDPARD REX; reverse, VCESTEL ON EOferwic, York.

16. EDPAERD REX; reverse, ÐORR ON EOFERPIc, York.

17. IEDPERD REEX; reverse, ARNERIM ON EOFERwic, York.

18. EDRERD REEX; reverse, ERNGRIM ON EOFERwic, York.

19. EDPARD REX; reverse, ELFPINE ON EOFERPIC, York.

20. STIRCOL ON EOFERPic, York.

21. LEOFENOÐ ON EOFHerwic, York.

22. EDPARD REX; reverse, ÐORR ON EOFERHwic, York.
All these different stamps of coins were struck for *Edward the confessor* at *York*; and are in TAB. VI. N°. 4, 5, 8, 9, 11, 14, 16, 18.

23. EADPARD RD REX; reverse, ALFPOLD ON EOFeRwic, York.

24. SCVIAE ON EOFeRPic, York.

25. ARNGRIM ON EOFeRwic, York.
ÐORR ON EOFRPICE, York. Another reverse in the tables, but not engraven.
These are also *Edward the confessor's* coins, and are in TAB. VII. N°. 25, 28, 29, 30, 33.

26. Another coin of this king. EADPARD REX; reverse, SCYINE ON EOFeRwIc, York. In the custody of Mr. *West*. Class. 3, 6.

27. XER NATZLEGEA; reverse, AEERTEE. M. ON. EOferwic. York.
The king's head and inscription is reversed on this coin; but for all that it is a very curious one, and was struck for *Guthrum the Dane*; who upon his conversion to *Christianity*, had the name of *Athelstan* given him at the font, by *Alfred the great*, his godfather. This coin is in sir *Andrew Fountain*'s tables; and is engraven at N°. 6. in this plate. It is there given to *Athelstan the great*; but in the last edition of *Camden* TAB. IV. N°. 18. and in *Thoresby*'s *Ducat. Leod.* p. 344. N°. 71. it is agreed to belong to this converted *Dane*.

This *Danish* general has a near reference to *York*; a street in the city still bearing his name. For which reason I subjoin here an account of the various names and variation of them which historians have given this ruler: who, I must take notice, is the only *Northumbrian* king, except *Edwin*, who put the initial letters EO for *Eoferwic York*, on his coin; at least that I have met with. The account I had from the reverend Dr. *Langwith* is as follows,

"I mention *Guthrum*, as an odd instance of the great variety of names given by our "*Teutonic* ancestors to the same person, and of the confusion in history that must have "been occasioned thereby. This prince seems to have had three names, first, *Gutram*, with "its variations, his proper name; secondly, *Gormund*, &c. which I take to have been "his nick-name: I could shew you by many instances how fond, not only the *Teutonic* na-"tions, but others more polite, were of giving nick-names to their princes. His third "name was *Aethelstan*, &c. which was his baptismal name given him by king *Alfred*.

"These three names, either by variety of dialects, or an affectation of *Latin* termina-"tions, or downright negligence in writing, became at least five times as many. His "first name *Gutram* may be derived from *Gut Bonus* and *Ram* or *Rhum Fama*, and so an-"swers *Agathocles*. The first part of this name, *Gut*, or, with an aspirate *Guth*, is in "other dialects of the old northern language Gud or God. Hence we have,

"1. *Gutram*. *Kilian*.
"2. *Gudrum*. *Thoresby* in *Camden*, cc.
"3. *Guthrum*. *Camden* from *Malmsbury* and *J. Picus* 443. 504.
"4. *Godrun*, by changing *m*, into *n*. Bishop *Gibson* in *Camden*. 1.
"5. *Godern*. Corrupted from the former. *Verstegan*.
"6. *Gurtbrun*. Another corruption.
"7. *Godrus*, by giving a *Latin* termination, *Camden* from *Asserius*. 72.
"8. *Gytro*, which is worst of all. *Mat. Westmon.* 320.

"His nick-name seems to have been *Gormund*, from the *Teut.* word Goor, *dirt, filth*, "&c. [in the *A. S.* Gor, *fimus, lutum, sanguis, tabum*] and mund, *a mouth*, q. d. *foul-mouthed.* "It may have been given him, either from his ravenous filthy way of eating, or from "his insolent and vain glorious boasting, &c. The variations of this name are,

x "9. Gor-

" 9. *Gormond*. *Camden* from *J. Picus*.
" 10. *Gourmound*, a corruption from the former. *Speed* 374.
" 11. *Gormon*, in the name of *Gormanchester*.
" 12. *Gormo*, by giving a *Latin* termination. *Camden* from *Malmsbury* 443.
" The variations of his third or baptismal name *Aethelstan*, most noble, are chiefly in " the way of writing it, *&c*.
" 13. *Athelstan*. *Camden* from *J. Picus*.
" 14. *Aethelstan*. *Mat. West*, &c.
" 15. *Ethelstan*.
" I think it pretty odd, that *Guthrum-gate* and *Gormondchester* should take their deno- " minations, one from the name, the other from the nick-name of this prince.
" *Qu*. Whether the name of *Gormund* did not afterwards become proverbial, and give " rise to the *French* word *gourmand*, whence comes *gourmander*, to play the glutton, or the " hector, *gurmandise*, gluttony, and our word *gormandize*.

28. EADVIG REX; reverse, WILSIG MONeta, vel MONetarius, de EOferwic, **York**.
This coin was struck for *Edwy*, an universal monarch, the successor to *Edred*, and son to his brother *Edmund*; who began to reign *anno* 955. TAB. VIII. N°. 1. 4.

29. The curious coin of *Edwin the great*, struck at *York*, already described.

30. CNVT REX ANGlorum; reverse, CRINAN MOneta, vel MOnetarius, de EOFeRwic, **York**.

31. SVNOLF MOnetarius de EOFerwic, **York**.

32. FARÐEIN MOnetarius de EOFeRwic, **York**.

33. ELFNAN MOnetarius de EOFeRwic, **York**.

34. CNVT REX; reverse, RÆFEN ON EOFERwic, **York**.

35. CNVT REX ANGLORVM; reverse, OVÐGRIM MOneta, vel MOnetarius de EOFerwic, **York**.

36. CNVT; reverse, ƿVLNOÐ MOneta, vel MOnetarius, ON EOFeRƿic, **York**.
All these are different coins of king *Canute the great*, struck at **York**, about the year 1020. TAB. IV. N°. 1, 3, 4, 5, 9, 12, 19, 21.

37. HAROLD REX ANGlorum; reverse, VRCETEL ON EOferwic, **York**; on the cross PAX.
This coin was struck for *Harold* the son and successor of *Canute the great*; who began his reign *anno* 1036. It is in the collection of *James West*, esq; class. 3, 3, 8.

38. SCI. (sancti) PETRI MOneta; reverse unintelligible.

39. SCI. PETRI MOneta; reverse, ERIVIITM, these letters are also acknowledged unintelligible by the *Tabulist*.

40. SCI. PETRI MOneta; reverse, EBORAcensis CIVitas.

41. SCI. PETRI MOneta; reverse, EBORACEnsis CIVitas.

42. SCI. PETRI Moneta, reverse, EBORACEnsis CIVitas.

43. SCI. PETRI MOneta; reverse, EBORACEnsis CIvitas.

44. SCI. PETRI MOneta; reverse, EBORACEnsis civitas.

45. Is a different coin of this kind from any of the former. The letters on the first side cannot be made out, but the reverse is *Sancti* Petri *moneta*, as plain as any of the foregoing. It is in Mr. *West*'s collection, class. 3. 3.

The coins here exhibited have occasioned some disputes amongst the *Connoisseurs* in these kinds of antiquities. The question is whether they were coined on purpose for the tax payable to the court at *Rome*, called **Peter-pence**, or **Romescot**; or were peculiar to the church of St. *Peter*, in *York*; and struck by the archbishops of that see, before the *conquest*? In my opinion this will bear no manner of dispute at all. That the archbishops of *York* enjoyed this royal privilege by immemorial custom, as well as *Canterbury*, is certain. And, as the annotator on the *tables* remarks, if this had been paid to *Rome* as **Peter-pence**, in all probability, some of these coins would have been found at this day in the pope's collections, which they are not. Though these coins have near, all the same legends, yet it is plain they were all struck from different dies. Coin 39, seems to have the name of some mint-master upon it; and, as the *Tabulist* observes, coin 44. is of the same kind as the former, though *Walker* reads it St. *Neglino*, for S. *Petri moneta*. After the conquest, this favour, granted to the prelates of the two metropolitical sees, and a few of the rest, was in some measure curtailed. They certainly continued to coin money, but then it bore the same stamp as the king's own coin. *Roger Hoveden* observes, that in the turbulent time of king *Stephen*, the weak title he had to the crown allowing of ſuch an innovation, that all the nobility, as well biſhops, as earls and barons, coined their own money *(f)*. But *Henry* II. coming to the crown, remedied this uſurpation of the baronage; and made a new money which was ſolely received and paid through the kingdom *(g)*. It is true, ſays ſir *Matthew Hales*, *(h)* that by certain antient privileges, derived by charter and uſage from the crown, divers, eſpecially of the eminent clergy had their mints or coinage of money. As the abbot of St. *Edmondſbury*, *clauſ.* 32 *Hen.* III. *m.* 15. *dorſo*; and the archbiſhop of *York*, *clauſ.* 5 *Ed.* III. *p. m.* 10. 19. *dorſo*; and ſome others. But although they had the profit of the coinage, adds that author, yet they had neither the denomination, ſtamp, nor allay. For upon every change of the coin, by the king's proclamation, there iſſued out a mandate to the treaſurer and barons to deliver a ſtamp over to theſe private mints, to be uſed by the ſeveral proprietors of them. That eminent lawyer ſtill adds, that the liberty of coinage in private lords, has been long ſince diſuſed, and in a great meaſure, if not altogether reſtrained by the ſtatute of 7 *Hen.* VII. *c.* 6. I ſuppoſe he means lay-lords, for we have undoubted teſtimony, that the archbiſhops of *York* continued to uſe this ancient privilege long after the date of the ſtatute above; even down to the reign of queen *Elizabeth*, and that from the coins themſelves. Thus much I thought proper to ſay relating to this coinage; ſeveral inſtruments are given in the *publick acts* to this purpoſe, and in p.547. of this book, the reader will find ſome further teſtimonies about it. I ſhall only add, that in reference to the *Sancti* Petri *moneta*, above, authorities tell us, that the archbiſhop's coinage at *York* was of old called *Peter-pence*; as may be ſeen in *Maddox*, in two or three inſtances *(i)*. I ſhall alſo beg leave to add a copy of a ſhort charter granted from *Henry* III. as early as the ſecond of his reign to *Walter Grey* then archbiſhop of this province, wherein the antient cuſtom of their coining money is ſpecified, and a new power is delegated to them *(k)*.

Cuneus *archiep.* Ebor.

"REX vicecom. *Ebor.* ſalutem. Mandamus tibi firmiter praecipientes quod facias venerabilem patrem noſtrum dominum *W. Ebor.* archiep. bene et libere habere cuneos ſuos monete noſt. in civitate noſt. *Ebor.* ſicut predeceſſores ſui archiepiſcopi *Ebor.* eos melius et liberius habuerunt. Salvo nobis jure noſtro quod ad nos inde pertinet.

"Teſte dom. *P. Winton.* epiſcopo apud *Weſtm.*

Eodem modo ſcribitur majori Ebor. *Clauſ.* 2 Hen. III. *m.* 6.

45. Is a different coin of *Edward the confeſſor* from any of the former. The legend EDƿARD REX; reverſe, VLFKEL ON EOFERwic, 𝔜𝔬𝔯𝔨.

46, 47. Two more different coins of the ſame king. Legend, EADƿARD REX ANGLOrum; reverſe, SƿARTCOL ON EOFERwic, 𝔜𝔬𝔯𝔨.

The next ODGRIM ON EOFERwic, 𝔜𝔬𝔯𝔨.

In theſe the king is repreſented ſitting, half naked, with his globe, ſcepter and crown; The globe was anciently peculiar to the *Saxon* kings of this iſland; and is ſaid to have been handed down to them from the time of *Conſtantine the great*; who firſt accepted of this emblem from the *Britiſh* ſoldiery, at his inauguration at *York*, as lord of the iſland of *Britain*. See *p.* 45. of this book. On the reverſe of all theſe coins are the martlets repreſented; the peculiar device of this monarch.

Fig. 6. and laſt, is put in here, but it belongs to the ſame figure above, and is the reverſe of that coin omitted by miſtake.

I have now gone through all the different *Saxon* and *Daniſh* coins, ſtruck at *York*, which are exhibited in ſir *Andrew Fountain*'s tables, thoſe in the new edition of *Camden*, or what Mr. *Weſt* has collected. I hinted before, that we have a ſtrong claim to all the coins, that any of the *Northumbrian* kings coined; but as none of their reverſes have the name of the city particularly upon them, except thoſe two remarkables of *Edwin* and *Guthrum*; I have purpoſely omitted them. I now proceed to a ſhort diſſertation on the coinage at *York* from the *Norman* conqueſt to the laſt mint erected in that city. I think it needleſs to engrave theſe coins, ſince they are moſt of them common enough; and are to be met with in the cabinets of the collectors.

The curious in this way, are much indebted to a diſcovery made ſome years ago, at *York*, of a large quantity of the conqueror's and his ſucceſſor's coins. By which means the ſtamp of thoſe kings, before ſcarce, are made pretty common. The accident happened in this manner: A dreadful fire having burnt down many houſes in *Upper-Ouſegate*, *York*, *April* 3, 1694, upon the digging the foundation of one of the houſes for erecting a new one, the workmen dug to a conſiderable depth, and diſcovered another foundation, very

(f) —— *omnes potentes, tam epiſcopi quam comites et barones ſuam faciebant monetam*. R. H. parte prior. *p* 281. ſub anno 1149.

(g) Idem p. 282.

(h) Sir *Matthew Hales*'s ſheriff's accounts.

(i) Geof. Plantaginet, *archiep* Ebor. *r. c.* [*redd comp*] *de* xxiv *l.* viii *s. de denariis S.* Petri. *Maddox*'s excheq. p. 493. See alſo p. 211. (c) (r)

(k) See biſhop *Nicholſon*'s *Engliſh* hiſtorical library, for ſome more account of this privilege, p 263, 264. folio *London* 1714.

probably, unknown to the builders of the later house. This lower foundation was very well supported, at several angles, with good oak-piles. Some of which were so firm and found, that they served again for the same purpose. Besides these piles there were laid several great timber trees, a-cross, in order to make the stronger foundation. These lower foundations very well answer the accounts of the timber buildings in those days. Betwixt the heads of two piles, in this lower foundation, the workmen discovered a little decayed oak box; wherein had been hoarded about two hundred or two hundred and fifty pieces of the *Norman* coin. But age and the moisture of the place had so defaced them, that not above a hundred of them could be preserved. Mr. *Thoresby*, from whose account of this discovery to the *Royal Society* I have taken this extract, (*k*) had the perusal of about half that number; which proved, as he says, the noblest stock that ever he saw, or indeed heard of, of *William the conqueror's* coin. Not above two or three in the whole cargo being of any other prince; and these, though later in times, are more rare in value than many of the *Roman* or *Saxon* coins.

Amongst these coins were several minted at different places. But what I shall take notice of are those which our antiquary has given in his catalogue of antiquities (*l*) then reposited in his *Museum* at *Leeds*.

111. William I. ƿILLEMV. REX; reverse, ÐORR ON EOFERwic, **York.**

112. ƿILLEMV REX ⸝ (for A) reverse, ƿINÐ BEORN ON EOferwic, **York.** The king's head with full face, labels at each ear, hanging down from a diadem of pearls, with one large or rather two small arches over the head.

126. William II. ƿILEMV. REX. The king's half face and scepter, the diadem of pearls and the helm; reverse ORÐNORIN ON EOFeRwic, **York.** This last is of *William Rufus*, and two former *William the conqueror*.

132. EVTACIVS. *Eustachius*, son and heir apparent to king *Stephen*, but died before him. The figure of the said prince with a large sword in his hand, a pellet in each quarter of the cross surrounded with a rose; reverse, EBORACI. E. D. T. S. In all probability, this coin was struck at *York*, for the prince, when his father had sent him down a sort of a governour here of these parts (*m*).

135. Henry II. HENRICVS REX; reverse, NICOLE ON EVErwic, **York.** Mr. *Thoresby* observes, that is the only piece that hath six points, and a line in the middle part, on which is placed the cross. I take notice also, that this was the last coin with the *Saxon* name of *York* on it; though somewhat altered; **Everwic** for **Eoferwic.** This coin is of king *Henry* the second.

Edward I. EDW. REX ANG. DNS. HYB. Edwardus *rex* Angliae *dominus* Hyberniae; reverse, CIVITAS EBORACI. A penny of king *Edward* I. in the great collection of *Brown Willis*, esq; Mr. *Thoresby*, also exhibits another of the same king, with the
160. inscription *Civitas Eborac.* on the reverse. And a half penny, found in a grave at *Sez-*
174. *zay* with the reverse, *Civi. Eboraci.*

Edward III. EDWARD DEI G. REX ANL. Z. FRANC. D. HYB. Edwardus *Dei gratia*
198. *rex* Angliae *et* Franciae, *dominus* Hyberniae; reverse, CIVITAS EBORACI. A groat
201. of *Edward* the third's coin, very fair, the mint-mark a bell. Mr. *Willis* has a half groat and a penny of the same king coined at *York*.

208. Richard II. RICARDVS REX ANGIE; reverse, CIVITAS EBORACI. A very fair *York* penny of king *Richard* the second. One of the same in Mr. *Willis*'s collection.

Henry IV. Henry V. A groat of *Henry* the fourth, or *Henry* the fifth, with E on the king's breast, and CIVITAS EBORACI on the reverse. A penny with the same reverse. Mr. *Willis*.

220. Henry VI. HENRIC. DI. GRA. REX ANG. Z. FRANC. By the key on either side the king's head this half groat appears to have been struck in the archbishop's mint at *York*. Mr. *Willis* has another half groat of this king's coin with the arched crown; on the re-
225. verse, CIVITAS EBORACI. Mr. *Thoresby* exhibits a penny, also, of this king. H. D. G. ROSA SIE. SPA. Henricus *Dei gratia rosa sine spina*; reverse CIVITAS EBORACI. Three pellets in each quarter of the cross.

230. Edward IV. EDWARD. DI. GRA. REX ANGL. Z. FRANC. reverse, *Posui Deum*, &c. CIVITAS EBORACI. A very fair groat of king *Edward* the fourth with an E, for *Ebor.* also on the king's breast. This coin is given in Mr. *Thoresby*'s plate, as are
238. several of the former. He had also a duplicate of the same coin. Mr. *Willis* has a penny of this king, with *Civitas Eboraci* on the reverse.

247. Henry VII. HENRIC. DI. GRA. REX ANG. reverse, CIVITAS EBORACI. A penny of *Henry* the seventh. The two keys denote it of the archbishop's coinage. Mr. *Willis*

(*k*) Abr. *Philosoph.* transf. vol. V. p. 30. edit. *Jones.* See also *Ducat. Leoden.* p. 349.

(*l*) *Ducat. Leod.* p. 350, 351.

(*m*) See p. 417, 418. of this book.

has

has another of this stamp. There is a half groat also of *Henry* the seventh, the two keys under the arms, in Dr. *Langwith*'s collection.

HENRIC. VIII. D. G. REX. AGL. Z. FRA'C. reverse, CIVITAS EBORA- 250.
CI. This coin has T. W. on each side the arms, and a cardinal's cap below, for *Tho-* Henry VIII.
mas Wolsey, cardinal, and archbishop of *York*. A very fair groat of Mr. *Thoresby*'s. Mr. *Holms* of the *Tower* has this coin with the king's head, half faced, the same Inscription and emblems as the former. Mr. *Willis* also has one of them, and a half groat inscribed as above. These coins are to be met with in, almost, all the cabinets of the curious. This king had also a mint to himself at *York*; Dr. *Langwith* has a groat of his coinage; reverse, CIVITAS EBORACI. Mr. *Thoresby* mentions a penny of pure, and another of base metal of this king in his collection; on the reverse of which is *Civitas Eboraci*. Mr. *Willis* has a half penny, also, coined by *Edward Lee* archbishop of *York*, having on the face side E. L. and on the reverse, CIVITAS EBORACI. It seems by this that what was esteemed a high crime and misdeameanour in *Wolsey*, and made one of the articles of impeachment against him, was none in his immediate successor; who stamped the same presumptive letters on the king's coin; and would have put the cardinal's cap there, no doubt, if he had been honoured with the title.

Mr. *Willis* has, in his collection, a crown and half crown of *Edward* the sixth's coin, re- Edward VI.
presenting him on horseback, struck at *York*; as the Y in the legend declares, dated
1551. Mr. *Thoresby* had the same. The former gentleman has, also, his half-faced shil- 280, 283.
ling of base metal, and full-faced shilling of the purer silver; which have likewise a Y upon the face side to shew them minted at *York*. Dr. *Langwith* has a very fair shilling of this king's coin, with a Y for *York*, on both the sides. Mr. *Willis* has a six pence of the same king, side faced, with a Y for *York*. But I have seen a six-pence in Mr. *Gill*'s collection at *York*, side faced, on the reverse of which is CIVITAS EBORACI. Mr. *Willis* has a three-pence, of this sort, and with the same legend.

Mr. *Thoresby* had a shilling of queen *Elizabeth*'s coin, which he says was struck in the arch- Elizabeth.
bishop of *York*'s mint, as appears by the key before the legend. The arms garnished. I take this to be the last stamp the prelates of *York* were permitted to use in their old privilege of coinage. For I never could hear of any other. Mr. *Willis* has a three halfpenny piece of this queen; which has a rose instead of the queen's head, on the face side; and, on the reverse, round the arms, CIVITAS EBORACI. This coin, he observes, is the only one of that denomination ever coined.

The half crowns of king *Charles* the first, minted at *York*, have the king on horseback Charles I.
with a sword advanced, and under the horse EBOR. A lion passant gardant for the 362.
mint-mark. CAROLVS D. G. MAG. BRIT. FRAN. ET HIB. REX; reverse, the arms in an oval crowned, the usual legend, but the stamp curious. Four dif- 369, &c.
ferent shillings of this king, coined at *York*, were, also, in Mr. *Thoresby*'s *Museum*. Two
of which stamps Mr. *Willis* has in his collection. He has also a three-pence with EBOR. 393.
on the king's arms; the same with Mr. *Thoresby*'s. Mr. *Willis* rightly observes, that, no doubt, other moneys, as six-pences, groats, two-pences, and pennies were coined at *York*, when this unfortunate prince set up the royal mint in that city, but they are not in his collection. The mint-mark on all these coins is a lion passant gardant, part of the arms of the city of *York*, as well as the king's arms.

In the reign of king *William* the third, when all the clipped and diminished money was William III.
called in, a mint for a new coinage was erected at *York* from the years 1695, to 1697. At this mint, as Mr. *Thoresby* writes, from the information of major *Wyvil* the master of the mint, there were coined *three hundred and twelve thousand five hundred and twenty pounds and sixpence*. But in a manuscript collection of *James West*, esq; from the papers of *Benjamin Woodnot*, esq; then comptroller of the coins, the mint at *York* is put down thus,

Silver, 67,000 ℔. 423 ℥.
Tale 20,9011 *l.* 6 *s.*

At this coinage was minted at *York* half-crowns, shillings and six-pences. Those of 96, have a Y under the king's head; those of 97, Y. This mint worked at the *Manor*, and is the last mint which has been erected in the city of *York*.

There is no dispute to be made, but the coinage for gold, as well as silver, was kept up in the mints at *York*, from the time of *Edward* III. who first struck that metal, to much later reigns. I have seen, and took pains to copy out a mandate, from the records in the *Tower*, of this king's to the high-sheriff of *Yorkshire*, for erecting a mint for coining *gold and silver* money in the *castle* of *York*. Which I would have printed, but I think it needless here, because several of that sort are published in the *Foedera Ang*. though of later reigns. The reason that I have few or none to exhibit in this list, of gold coins, is because they seldom, or never had any particular mark or legend on them, in that metal, to denote where the coins were struck. There are but two exceptions that I have met with, and they of the same king, against this general rule. One of them a soveraign of *Edward* VI. repre-

representing him sitting on his throne, with a Y for a mint-mark after his titles; which letter is also struck on the reverse, over the arms. This piece is in Mr. *Willis*'s noble collection of *English* gold coins, esteemed the finest in *England*; and weighs as he informs me to the value of twenty seven shillings.

A very fair half sovereign of the same king; the king's bust crowned, with a sword in his right hand, and a globe and a cross in his left. EDWARD VI. D. G. AGL. FRA. Z. HIB. REX. with Y for *York*; the reverse as usual, IESVS AVTEM, *&c.* This coin was in Mr. *Thoresby*'s collection, and is further described p. 364. N°. 284. of his *Ducat. Leod.*

In Mr. *Willis*'s extracts from the indentures in the *Tower* are noted some mint-master's names, appointed for the coinage at *York*; which that gentleman has communicated to me as follows,

Anno 1 of *Henry* VI. *Bartholomew Goldbeter*, master and worker of the king's mints, was to make at the *Tower* of *London*, cities of *York* and *Bristol*, *nobles*, *half* and *quarter-nobles* gold; and in silver at the said places or mints, *groats*, *half-groats*, *pennies*, *half-pennies* and *farthings*. Dated *July* 16.

Anno 12 of *Henry* VI. *John Paddesley*, master aud worker, had the same licence.

Anno 9 of *Edward* IV. *William* lord *Hastings* had licence of coinage of all sorts of the king's money, at the mints of the *Tower* of *London*, and at *York*, *Coventry*, *Norwich* and *Bristol* mints.

Anno 2 of *Edward* VI. 1548. *George Gale* was constituted master and worker of the king's mints at *York*.

I have to add, that *Goldbeter*, mentioned in the first indenture, must have been mint-master at the time when the counties of *York*, *Northumberland*, and other eight northern counties petitioned the king in parliament to send down a mint-master to *York*, as usual, to coin gold and silver for the ease and advantage of the said counties, *&c.* The petition I have thought proper to extract from the parliament rolls, and I shall give it in its original language.

" *La petition des communes de countees* D'Everwyk, *&c. pour avoir le coignè à* **Everwyk.**
Rot. parl. 2 *Hen.* VI. N°. 12.

" AU roy nostre soveraigne seigneur et as autres tres graciouses seigneurs espirituelx et temporalx assemblez en cet present parlement supplient humblement toure le lieges du roy nostre soveraigne seigneur des countees d'**Everwyke, Northumbre'. Westmerl'. Cumbre'. Lancastre'. Cestre, Nichol, Nottingh'. Derb'. Levesque de Duresm**, et toutes les parties de North, que come nadgaires en le parlement de vostre pier, que dieu assoille, tenuz a **Westmonstre** lan de son regne noefisme, ordeignè feust et establè que de la viell de **Noell** adonques prochein avenir en avant nul liege du roy receveroyt aucune monoye dor **Englois** en paiement, si non par le poys du roy sur ce ordeignè, et per apres a votre darraine parlement fuiste ordeignè al pursuyt des ditz supplyantz pur le proufit de vous et aise de tout le pays la envyron, que le maytre et overour des monoies le roy denes le **Tour** de **Loundres** deust venir a **Everwyk** pur illoeques coigner lor et largent du dite pays, que ne feust de droit poys per commandment de votre counseil pur y demeurer tanque a vostre plesir, par vertue du quell ordenance le dit mestre a este au dite citee d'**Everwyke**, et mis sus illoeques le dit mynt a graunt proufit du roy et aise de les ditz countees, mais ores est, le dit mestre et les overours retournez dilloeques per ont les lieges du roy en les ditz parties pur lour singular avauntage payent resceivent communement leur or que est defectif per rates et abatements countre lordenounce de lestatut avant dit en contempt du roy et damage de luy et son people.

" Que plese a vostre hautesse par autorite de cest present parlement ordeigner que le dit maistre soit charge de retourner a vostre dit citee et illocques coigner, come ill fist per devaunt et demourer, ou lesser illoeques un son suffisaunt deputee pour qui ill veult repoundre tanque come vous plerra.

" Et en oultre ordeigner per estatut que tout lor des ditx parties, que default droit poys soit appert a le **Chastell d'Everwyk** et illoeques coigne devant le feste de S. **Michell** prochien avenir, et que nul or que ne soit de joust poys ne courge de lors enavant en payment ne ait cours dedeigns les countees avauntditz naillours deigns vostre roialme, et que sur ce soit fait proclamation per mye le vostre roialme.

" *A la quelle petition devaunt les seigneurs du dit parlement leux et entenduz per mesmes les seigneurs de lassent des communes avant ditz du royalme en ycell parlement fuist responduz en la fourme persuite.*

" **La petition est graunt sicome il est desire par icell.**

I have

I have now passed through a sort of a series of our *Saxon*, *Norman* and *English* coins struck at *York*, from the time of *Edwin the great* to the year 1697, a course of a thousand years and upwards. I am persuaded this series might be made a great deal more compleat from other collections in this kingdom; but I own I have neither time nor inclination to do it. Sufficient it is for my design, to shew, that there have been mints at *York* from the reign aforesaid to the last mentioned period, under, almost, every different king. And I only give this as a specimen for some person of this kind of taste, of more leisure and less avocation from it, to enlarge and fill up.

The last thing I think proper to mention and exhibit a draught of, on the head of the coinage at *York*, are the *tradesmens half-pennies* struck there, which the plate gives to the number of fifty different stamps.

This privilege was first obtained under the *Usurpation* (*a*); but it was not restrained till the 24 of *Charles* II. or *anno* 1672; when the king's copper half-pence and farthings took place in their stead. There are of the years 1670, and 71. in this collection; which I take to be singular, both on the account of the large number, and their being all in one person's possession at *York*; Mr. *Samuel Smith* baker in *Grape-lane*. I think it not amiss to transmit these trifling coins to posterity, since there never were before such things struck in the kingdom, and, in all probability, never will be again (*b*).

(*a*) One of this sort of coins in Mr. *West's* collection is as early as the year 1649. Which shews that the *patriots* of those days gave this as one proof of a release from the *royal prerogative*.

(*b*) See a further account of this kind of coinage at *York*, and other places in *Thoresby's Ducat. Leod.* 381.

E X E G I.

York *half-pennys.*

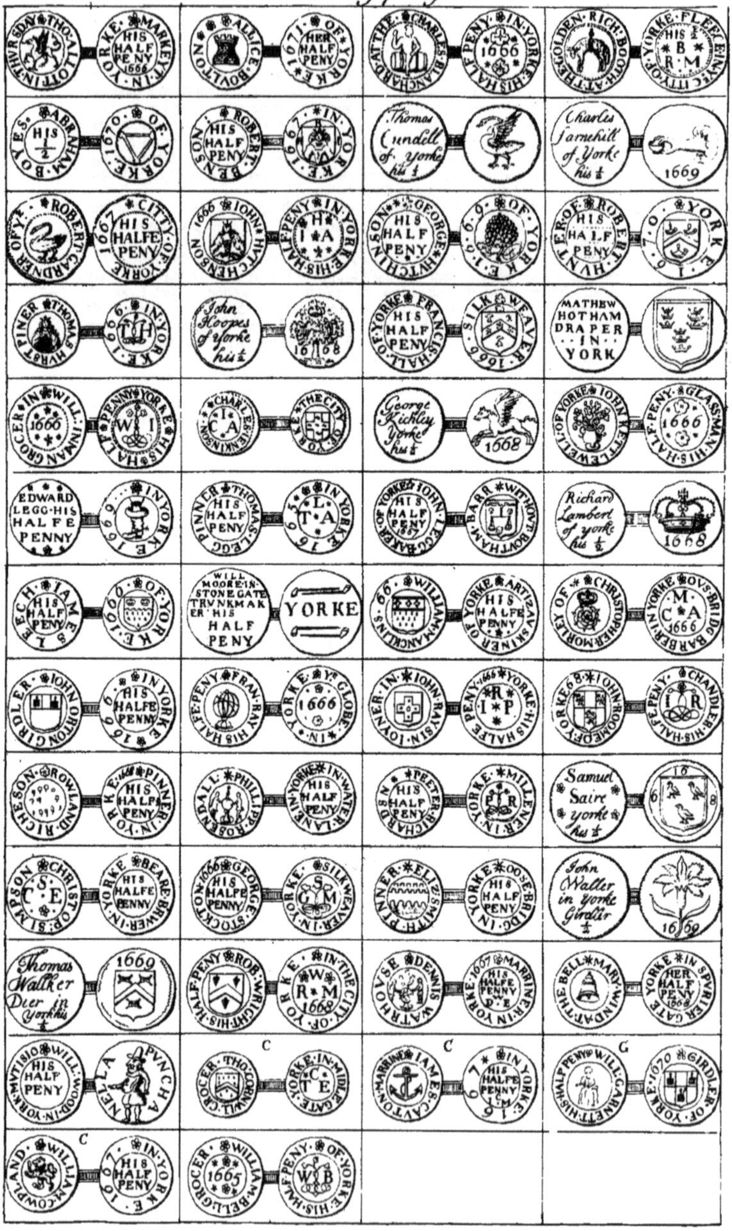

AN

INDEX

OF

PLACES and PERSONS.

A.

INDEX.

1 3

St. Augustine,

INDEX.

I N D E X.

Borow,

INDEX.

Buckay,

INDEX.

C.

Cartune,

INDEX.

INDEX.

INDEX.

INDEX.

F.

INDEX.

H.

Hammerton,

I N D E X.

F 9 Herodian,

INDEX.

Kawode,

4

L.

INDEX.

INDEX.

2

N. Na-

INDEX.

N.

O.

INDEX.

Q. Qua

INDEX.

Q.

R.

S.

INDEX.

Su'picia,

INDEX.

5

Tintern,

INDEX.

V, U.

Ulfby,

W.

I N D E X.

F I N I S.

LEATHER —
NEUMANN —

Lightning Source UK Ltd.
Milton Keynes UK
UKHW02n1529200218
318193UK00003B/209/P

9 781297 845666